Property Law

Property Law

Rules, Policies, and Practices
Fourth Edition

JOSEPH WILLIAM SINGER
Professor of Law, Harvard University

PUBLISHERS

76 Ninth Avenue, New York, NY 10011
http://lawschool.aspenpublishers.com

Printed in the United States of America.

1 2 3 4 5 6 7 8 9 0

ISBN 0-7355-5547-8

Library of Congress Cataloging-in-Publication Data

Singer, Joseph William, 1954-
    Property law : rules, policies, and practices / Joseph William Singer.— 4th ed.
      p. cm.
    Includes bibliographical references and index.
  1. Property—United States—Cases. I. Title.

  KF560.S56 2005
  346.7304—dc22

2005029888

About Aspen Publishers

Aspen Publishers, headquartered in New York City, is a leading information provider for attorneys, business professionals, and law students. Written by preeminent authorities, our products consist of analytical and practical information covering both U.S. and international topics. We publish in the full range of formats, including updated manuals, books, periodicals, CDs, and online products.

Our proprietary content is complemented by 2,500 legal databases, containing over 11 million documents, available through our Loislaw division. Aspen Publishers also offers a wide range of topical legal and business databases linked to Loislaw's primary material. Our mission is to provide accurate, timely, and authoritative content in easily accessible formats, supported by unmatched customer care.

To order any Aspen Publishers title, go to *http://lawschool.aspenpublishers.com* or call 1-800-638-8437.

To reinstate your manual update service, call 1-800-638-8437.

For more information on Loislaw products, go to *www.loislaw.com* or call 1-800-364-2512.

For Customer Care issues, e-mail *CustomerCare@aspenpublishers.com*; call 1-800-234-1660; or fax 1-800-901-9075.

Aspen Publishers
a Wolters Kluwer business

For Martha Minow
who has made all the difference

In memory of
Mary Joe Frug

Property rights serve human values.
They are recognized to that end,
and are limited by it.

Chief Justice Joseph Weintraub
Supreme Court of New Jersey, 1971

Summary of Contents

Contents   xv
Preface   xxxvii
A Guide to the Book   xxxix
How to Brief a Case and Prepare for Class   li
Acknowledgments   lvii

1

Access to Property   *1*

1. Competing Claims to Original Acquisition of Property   3
2. Trespass and Public Rights of Access to Property   103

II

Relations Among Neighbors   **177**

3. Adverse Possession   179
4. Nuisance: Rules Governing Relations Among Neighbors
   in the Absence of Agreement   227
5. Servitudes: Public Regulation of Private Agreements
   Restricting Land Use   317

III
Common Ownership of Property   491

6. Present Estates and Future Interests   493
7. Concurrent Ownership and Family Property   569

IV
Regulation of the Market for Shelter   637

8. Leaseholds   639
9. Real Estate Transactions   743
10. Fair Housing Law   817
11. Zoning: Governmental Land Use Planning   911

V
Property and Sovereignty   951

12. Regulatory Takings Law   953
13. American Indian Nations   1069

VI
Beyond Real Property   1085

14. Intellectual Property   1087
15. Property in People   1143

Table of Cases   1173
Table of Statutes   1189
Index   1197

Contents

Preface   xxxvii
A Guide to the Book   xxxix
How to Brief a Case and Prepare for Class   li
Acknowledgments   lvii

I

Access to Property

1

1

Competing Claims to Original Acquisition of Property

3

§1.1   Conquest   3
       §1.1.1   Property Rights Derived from Competing Sovereigns   3
                Johnson v. M'Intosh   4
                Notes and Questions   13
       §1.1.2   Forced Seizures of Property from American Indian
                Nations   14
                Tee-Hit-Ton Indians v. United States   14
                Notes and Questions   19
       §1.1.3   Current Indian Land Claims   20
                Problem   22
§1.2   Government Grant   24
       §1.2.1   Homestead Acts and Land Grants   24
       §1.2.2   Squatters   25
                James Willard Hurst, Law and the
                  Conditions of Freedom in the
                  Nineteenth-Century United States   25
       §1.2.3   Freed Slaves   26
                Leon Litwack, Been in the Storm So Long:
                  The Aftermath of Slavery   26

		Harriet A. Jacobs, Incidents in the Life of a Slave Girl: Written by Herself	29
		Notes and Questions	29
		Problem	30
	§1.2.4	The Right of Families to Stay Together and Basic Needs Fulfillment	30
§1.3	Labor and Investment		32
	§1.3.1	News and the Law of Unfair Competition	32
		International News Service v. Associated Press	32
		Notes and Questions	41
		Problems	44
	§1.3.2	Patents in Human Genes	45
		Moore v. Regents of the University of California	45
		Notes and Questions	52
		Problem	53
	§1.3.3	Work and Family	53
		Upton v. JWP Businessland	53
		Notes and Questions	55
	§1.3.4	Who Owns the Corporation? Shareholders & Stakeholders	55
		Local 1330, United Steel Workers of America v. United States Steel Corporation	55
		Notes and Questions	60
		Problem	62
§1.4	Family		63
	§1.4.1	Wills and Inheritance	63
		Babbitt v. Youpee	64
		Notes and Questions	68
		Problems	69
	§1.4.2	Marriage	69
		Montana Equitable Distribution Statute	70
		In re Marriage of King	71
		Notes and Questions	73
		Problem	74
	§1.4.3	Gifts	75
		Problems	75
§1.5	Possession		76
	§1.5.1	Wild Animals	76
		Pierson v. Post	76
		Popov v. Hayashi	79
		Notes and Questions	82
		Problem	83
	§1.5.2	Oil and Gas	83
		Elliff v. Texon Drilling Co.	83
		Kenneth Vandevelde, The New Property of the Nineteenth Century: The Development of the Modern Concept of Property	87
		Problem	89

§1.5.3   Water   89
    §1.5.3.1   Groundwater   90
    §1.5.3.2   Streams   91
            Problems   91
§1.5.4   Finders   92
        Charrier v. Bell   92
        Notes and Questions   95
        Problems   96
§1.6   Transfer: Relativity of Title   97
    §1.6.1   Real Property   97
        Tapscott v. Lessee of Cobbs   97
        Notes and Questions   100
        Problem   100
    §1.6.2   Personal Property   101
        Problem   102

2

Trespass and Public Rights of Access to Property   103

§2.1   Trespass   103
    §2.1.1   Public Policy Limits on the Right to Exclude   103
        State v. Shack   104
        Desnick v. American Broadcasting Companies, Inc.   108
        Notes and Questions   112
        Problems   115
    §2.1.2   Right of Reasonable Access to Property Open
             to the Public   116
        Uston v. Resorts International Hotel, Inc.   116
        Patricia J. Williams, Spirit-Murdering the
             Messenger: The Discourse of Fingerpointing as
             the Law's Response to Racism   118
        Walter E. Williams, The Intelligent Bayesian   120
        Notes and Questions   120
        Problems   122
§2.2   Public Accommodations Statutes and Antidiscrimination Policy 124
    §2.2.1   Race, Sex, and Sexual Orientation Discrimination   124
        §2.2.1.1   Federal Law   124
            Civil Rights Act of 1964, Title II   124
            Civil Rights Act of 1866   125
            Notes and Questions   126
            Karl Llewellyn, The Common Law Tradition:
                 Deciding Appeals   130
            Problems   131
        §2.2.1.2   State Laws   132
            New Jersey Law Against Discrimination   132
            Dale v. Boy Scouts of America   133
            Boy Scouts of America v. Dale   140

		Notes and Questions	142
		Problems	143
	§2.2.2	Discrimination Against Persons with Disabilities	144
		Americans with Disabilities Act of 1990,	
		Title III	145
		Problems	149
§2.3		Free Speech Rights of Access to Private Property	153
	§2.3.1	United States Constitution: The First Amendment	153
		Lloyd Corp., Ltd. v. Tanner	153
		Hudgens v. NLRB	158
	§2.3.2	State Constitutions: The Right to Speak Freely	158
		NJ Coalition Against War in the Middle East v.	
		J.M.B. Realty Corp.	158
		United Food and Commercial Workers Union,	
		Local 919, AFL-CIO v. Crystal Mall Assocs.	160
		Notes and Questions	161
		Problems	163
§2.4		Beach Access and the Public Trust	164
		Matthews v. Bay Head Improvement Association	164
		Notes and Questions	170
		Problems	172
§2.5		The Right to Be Somewhere and the Problem	
		of Homelessness	173

II

Relations Among Neighbors

177

3

Adverse Possession

179

			179
§3.1		Title versus Possession	179
	§3.1.1	Border Disputes	179
		Brown v. Gobble	179
	§3.1.2	Color of Title	185
		Romero v. Garcia	185
	§3.1.3	Squatters	187
		Nome 2000 v. Fagerstrom	187
		Notes and Questions	191
§3.2		Hohfeldian Terminology	198
		Arthur Corbin, Jural Relations and	
		Their Classification	198
		Joseph William Singer, The Legal Rights Debate	
		in Analytical Jurisprudence from Bentham	
		to Hohfeld	199
		Notes and Questions	200

§3.3	Justifications for Adverse Possession: "Roots Which We Should Not Disturb" or "Land Piracy"?	202
	Problems	207
§3.4	Prescriptive Easements	207
	Community Feed Store, Inc. v. Northeastern Culvert Corp.	*207*
	Notes and Questions	210
	Problems	214
§3.5	Other Informal Ways to Transfer Title to Real Property	215
	§3.5.1 The Improving Trespasser	215
	§3.5.1.1 Removal of Encroaching Structure: Relative Hardship	215
	§3.5.1.2 Unjust Enrichment versus Forced Sale	218
	Somerville v. Jacobs	*218*
	Notes and Questions	221
	Problem	222
	§3.5.2 Boundary Settlement	223
	§3.5.2.1 Oral Agreement	223
	§3.5.2.2 Acquiescence	223
	§3.5.2.3 Estoppel	224
	§3.5.3 Dedication	224
	§3.5.4 Riparian Owners: Accretion and Avulsion	225
§3.6	Adverse Possession of Personal Property	225
	Problem	226

4

Nuisance: Rules Governing Relations Among Neighbors in the Absence of Agreement

227

§4.1	Land Use Conflicts Among Neighbors	227
	§4.1.1 Trespassory and Nontrespassory Invasions	227
	§4.1.2 Basic Solutions to Land Use Conflicts Between Neighbors	228
	§4.1.2.1 Entitlements	228
	§4.1.2.2 Remedies	229
	§4.1.3 The Reciprocal Nature of the Problem	230
	Ronald Coase, The Problem of Social Cost	230
	Notes and Questions	231
§4.2	Water Rights	232
	§4.2.1 Diffuse Surface Water: Flooding Problems	232
	§4.2.1.1 Legal Doctrines	232
	Armstrong v. Francis Corp.	*232*
	Notes and Questions	235

§4.2.1.2   Policy Arguments   237
            Rights: Freedom of Action versus Security   238
            Social Utility: Competition versus Secure
              Investment   239
            Formal Realizability or Administrability: Rigid
              Rules versus Flexible Standards   240
            Problem   242
§4.2.2   Water as a Commercial Resource   242
§4.3   Support Easements   242
§4.3.1   Lateral Support   243
§4.3.1.1   Common Law   243
            Noone v. Price   243
            Notes and Questions   247
§4.3.1.2   Building Codes and Private Rights of Action   249
            Massachusetts General Laws   250
            Massachusetts Building Code   250
            Notes and Questions   251
            Problem   251
§4.3.2   Subjacent Support   251
§4.3.2.1   Right to Dig versus Right to Support   251
            Friendswood Development Co. v. Smith-Southwest
              Industries, Inc.   251
            Notes and Questions   258
            Problem   260
§4.3.2.2   Precedent   261
            Karl Llewellyn, The Bramble Bush   261
§4.3.2.3   Judicial Role   265
            David Shapiro, Courts, Legislatures and
              Paternalism   265
            Joseph William Singer, Catcher in the Rye
              Jurisprudence   269
§4.4   Nuisance   271
§4.4.1   Protection of Use and Enjoyment of Land   271
§4.4.2   Radiation: Defining Unreasonable Land Use   273
            Page County Appliance Center, Inc. v.
              Honeywell, Inc.   273
            Notes and Questions   276
            Problems   282
§4.4.3   Light and Air   284
§4.4.3.1   Rejection of Nuisance Doctrine: No Easement
              for Light and Air   284
            Fontainebleau Hotel Corp. v. Forty-Five
              Twenty-Five, Inc.   284
            Law and Economics   286
§4.4.3.2   Nuisance Doctrine Applied to Light   302
            Prah v. Maretti   302
            Notes and Questions   307
            Arguments and Counterarguments   309

5

---

*Servitudes: Public Regulation of Private
Agreements Restricting Land Use* 317

---

§5.1   Servitudes   317
§5.2   Licenses   319
§5.3   Easements   320
       §5.3.1   Creation by Implication   320
                §5.3.1.1   Easements by Estoppel (Irrevocable Licenses) 320
                           Holbrook v. Taylor   321
                §5.3.1.2   Constructive Trusts   323
                           Rase v. Castle Mountain Ranch, Inc.   323
                           Notes and Questions   328
                           Problem   332
                §5.3.1.3   Prescriptive Easements   332
                §5.3.1.4   Easements Implied from Prior Use   332
                           *Granite Properties Limited Partnership v.
                           Manns*   333
                §5.3.1.5   Easements by Necessity   339
                           Finn v. Williams   339
                           Notes and Questions   340
                           Problems   344
       §5.3.2   Creation by Express Agreement   344
                §5.3.2.1   Historical Background   344
                §5.3.2.2   Formal Requirements to Create   345
                           (a) Writing   345
                           (b) Rule Against Reserving an Easement in a
                                Third Party   345
                §5.3.2.3   Validity: Substantive Limitations on the Kinds of Easements
                           That Can Be Created   346
                           (a) Limits on Negative Easements   346
                           (b) No Affirmative Easements to Act on One's
                                Own Land   347
                §5.3.2.4   Running with the Land   348
                           (a) Requirements for the Burden to Run with the Land 348
                           (b) Requirements for the Benefit to Run with the Land
                                (Appurtenant versus In Gross)   349
                           Green v. Lupo   350
                           Notes and Questions   352
       §5.3.3   Interpretation of Ambiguous Easements: Scope and
                Apportionment   353
                §5.3.3.1   Appurtenant Easements   353
                           Cox v. Glenbrook Company   353
                §5.3.3.2   Easements in Gross   358
                           *Henley v. Continental Cablevision of St. Louis
                           County, Inc.*   358

		Notes and Questions	361
		Problems	364
	§5.3.4	Modifying and Terminating Easements	364
§5.4	Covenants		365
	§5.4.1	Historical Background	365
	§5.4.2	Creation of Covenants	367
	§5.4.2.1	Express Agreement	367
		Davidson Bros., Inc. v. D. Katz & Sons, Inc.	*367*
		Whitinsville Plaza v. Kotseas	*376*
		Notes and Questions	377
		Problem	393
	§5.4.2.2	Implied Reciprocal Negative Servitudes in Residential Subdivisions	394
		Evans v. Pollock	*395*
		Sanborn v. McLean	*399*
		Riley v. Bear Creek Planning Committee	*399*
		Notes and Questions	400
		Problems	404
	§5.4.3	Interpretation of Ambiguous Covenants	406
		Blevins v. Barry-Lawrence County Association for Retarded Citizens	*406*
		Notes and Questions	408
		Problems	411
	§5.4.4	Modifying and Terminating Covenants	411
	§5.4.4.1	Changed Conditions	411
		El Di, Inc. v. Town of Bethany Beach	*411*
		Notes and Questions	415
	§5.4.4.2	Relative Hardship	416
	§5.4.4.3	Other Equitable Defenses	417
		Problems	418
	§5.4.4.4	Statutes	419
		Massachusetts General Laws	419
		Blakeley v. Gorin	*420*
		Notes and Questions	424
		Problems	424
§5.5	Regulation of Covenants and Homeowners Associations		425
	§5.5.1	Common Interest Communities	425
	§5.5.1.1	Homeowners Associations and Condominiums	425
	§5.5.1.2	Cooperatives	427
	§5.5.1.3	Community Land Trusts and Limited Equity Coops	427
	§5.5.1.4	Private Governments and Gated Communities	429
	§5.5.2	Relations Between Unit Owners and Developers	429
		Appel v. Presley Companies	*429*
		Notes and Questions	432
	§5.5.3	Racially Discriminatory Covenants	433
		Shelley v. Kraemer	*433*
		Evans v. Abney	*439*
		Notes and Questions	446
		Problems	449

§5.5.4 Restraints on Alienation 450
 §5.5.4.1 Direct Restraints on Alienation 451
  Horse Pond Fish & Game Club, Inc. v. Cormier 451
 §5.5.4.2 Consent to Sell Provisions 453
  (a) Grantor Consent Clauses 453
   Northwest Real Estate Co. v. Serio 453
   Riste v. Eastern Washington Bible Camp, Inc. 454
  (b) Consent of the Association 455
   Aquarian Foundation, Inc. v. Sholom House, Inc. 455
 §5.5.4.3 Rights of First Refusal or Preemptive Rights 458
  Wolinsky v. Kadison 458
  Notes and Questions 460
  Problem 465
 §5.5.4.4 Restrictions on Leasing 466
  Woodside Village Condominium Association,
   Inc. V. Jahren 466
  Notes and Questions 471
§5.5.5 Anticompetitive Covenants 472
 Problem 473
§5.5.6 Public Policy Limitations and Review for Reasonableness 474
 §5.5.6.1 Covenants 474
  Davidson Brothers, Inc. v. D. Katz & Sons, Inc. 474
  Notes and Questions 479
  Problems 481
 §5.5.6.2 Rules and ByLaws 483
  O'Buck v. Cottonwood Village Condominium
   Association, Inc. 483
  Neuman v. Grandview at Emerald Hills, Inc. 485
  Notes and Questions 488
  Problems 489

III

Common Ownership of Property *491*

6

Present Estates and Future Interests *493*

§6.1 Division of Ownership Over Time 493
§6.2 Historical Background: From Feudalism to the Market 496
 §6.2.1 A Modern Analogy 496
 §6.2.2 The Feudal Hierarchy 496
 §6.2.3 Free Tenures 497
  §6.2.3.1 Tenures and Services 497
  §6.2.3.2 Feudal Incidents 498

§6.2.4   Unfree Tenures   499
§6.2.5   Growth of the Fee Simple   499
     §6.2.5.1   Inheritability   499
     §6.2.5.2   Alienability   499
§6.2.6   Avoiding Feudal Incidents   500
§6.2.7   The Perpetual Conflict Between the Generations:
          Dead Hand Control and Alienability   501
§6.2.8   Historical Categories of Current Significance   503
     §6.2.8.1   Freehold and Nonfreehold Interests   503
     §6.2.8.2   Legal and Equitable Interests: Executory Interests
                 and the Development of Trusts   503
§6.3   The Estates System   505
     §6.3.1   Fee Simple Interests   505
          §6.3.1.1   Fee Simple Absolute   505
          §6.3.1.2   Defeasible Fees   506
               (a) When the future interest belongs to the grantor   506
               (b) When the future interest belongs to a third party   508
     §6.3.2   Life Estates   508
          §6.3.2.1   Reversions and Remainders   508
          §6.3.2.2   Contingent and Vested Remainders   509
          §6.3.2.3   Destructibility of Contingent Remainders   511
          §6.3.2.4   Doctrine of Worthier Title   511
          §6.3.2.5   Rule in *Shelley's Case*   512
     §6.3.3   Fee Tail   513
     §6.3.4   Regulation of Future Interests   513
     §6.3.5   Trusts   514
     §6.3.6   Summary   514
               Estates System: Chart of Freehold Interests   515
§6.4   Interpretation of Ambiguous Conveyances   515
     §6.4.1   Presumption Against Forfeitures and the Grantor's Intent   515
          §6.4.1.1   Fee Simple versus Defeasible Fee   516
                     *Wood v. Board of County Commissioners of
                     Fremont County*   516
                     *Cathedral of the Incarnation in the Diocese of
                     Long Island, Inc. v. Garden City Company*   518
          §6.4.1.2   Fee Simple versus Life Estate   521
                     Edwards v. Bradley   521
                     Notes and Questions   523
     §6.4.2   Trusts and the *Cy Pres* Doctrine   526
§6.5   Regulatory Rules   527
     §6.5.1   Rule Against Creation of New Estates   528
                     Johnson v. Whiton   528
     §6.5.2   Rule Against Unreasonable Restraints on Alienation   529
     §6.5.3   Rule Against Perpetuities   529
          §6.5.3.1   Traditional Rule   529
          §6.5.3.2   Modern Modifications   534
               (a) Wait and See, or Second Look   534
               (b) Equitable Reformation or *Cy Pres*   535

§6.5.3.3 Statutory Limits on Future Interests 535
    (a) Statutory Cut-offs for Possibilities of Reverter
      and Rights of Entry 535
    (b) Marketable Title Acts 536
    (c) Uniform Statutory Rule Against Perpetuities 536
    (d) Abolition of the Rule 537
§6.5.3.4 Examples and Explanations 537
§6.5.3.5 Options to Purchase 541
    Central Delaware County Authority v.
      Greyhound Corp. 541
    Texaco Refining and Marketing,
      Inc. v. Samowitz 545
§6.5.3.6 Preemptive Rights 546
    Cambridge Co. v. East Slope Investment Corp. 546
    Notes and Questions 549
    Problem 553
§6.5.4 Waste 553
    Moore v. Phillips 553
    Notes and Questions 556
§6.5.5 Racial Conditions 557
    Problem 559
§6.5.6 Rule Against Unreasonable Restraints on Marriage 561
    Lewis v. Searles 561
    Mary Joe Frug, Re-Reading Contracts: A Feminist
      Analysis of a Contracts Casebook 564
    Notes and Questions 565

7

Concurrent Ownership and Family Property 569

§7.1 Varieties of Common Ownership 569
§7.2 Rights and Obligations of Co-Owners 570
    §7.2.1 Tenancy in Common and Joint Tenancy 571
    §7.2.2 Tenancy by the Entirety 575
§7.3 Conflicts over Rent and Possession 576
    Olivas v. Olivas 576
    Notes and Questions 578
    Problems 579
§7.4 Conflicts over Transfers by One Co-Owner 579
    §7.4.1 Tenancy in Common and Joint Tenancy 580
      §7.4.1.1 Family Conflicts over Use of Common Property 580
      Carr v. Deking 580
      §7.4.1.2 Death 581
      Tenhet v. Boswell 581
      §7.4.1.3 Divorce 584
      Kresha v. Kresha 584
      Notes and Questions 585
      Problem 587

§7.4.2	Tenancy by the Entirety	587
	Sawada v. Endo	587
	Notes and Questions	591
	Problem	592
§7.5	Marital Property	593
§7.5.1	Historical Background	593
§7.5.1.1	Coverture, Dower, and Curtesy	593
§7.5.1.2	Married Women's Property Acts	594
§7.5.2	Community Property and Separate Property	595
§7.5.2.1	Separate Property	595
	During Marriage	595
	On Divorce	595
	On Death	596
§7.5.2.2	Community Property	596
	During Marriage	597
	On Divorce	597
	On Death	597
§7.5.2.3	Premarital Agreements	597
§7.5.2.4	Homestead Laws	598
§7.5.3	Marital Breakup	599
§7.5.3.1	Equitable Distribution of "Property" Acquired During Marriage	599
	O'Brien v. O'Brien	599
	Notes and Questions	604
	Problem	607
§7.5.3.2	Rights in the Family Home	607
§7.6	Unmarried Partners	608
§7.6.1	Male-Female Couples	608
	Watts v. Watts	608
	Clare Dalton, An Essay in the Deconstruction of Contract Doctrine	612
	Notes and Questions	614
	Problem	619
§7.6.2	Same-Sex Partners	620
§7.6.2.1	Marriage	620
§7.6.2.2	Property Division on Breaking Up or Death	621
	Problems	622
§7.7	Children's Claims on Family Assets	624
§7.7.1	Child Support	624
	Bayliss v. Bayliss	624
	Notes and Questions	627
§7.7.2	The Family's Right to Live Together	628
§7.7.3	Wills and Inheritance	628
§7.8	Forfeiture	628
§7.8.1	Domestic Violence and Protective Orders	628
	Wisconsin Domestic Abuse Restraining Order Statute	628
	Cote v. Cote	631
	Problem	632
§7.8.2	Forfeiture for a Family Member's Illegal Conduct	632

```
┌─────────────────────────┐
│           IV            │
│  ────────────────────   │
│ Regulation of Market    │
│      for Shelter        │
└─────────────────────────┘
```
                                                                    637

```
┌─────────────────────────┐
│            8            │
│  ────────────────────   │
│       Leaseholds        │
└─────────────────────────┘
```
                                                                    639

§8.1   Leasehold Estates   639
       §8.1.1   Types of Tenancies   639
                §8.1.1.1   Commercial and Residential Tenancies   639
                §8.1.1.2   Categories of Tenancies   640
                §8.1.1.3   Statute of Frauds   641
                §8.1.1.4   Regulation of Landlord-Tenant Relationships   641
       §8.1.2   Identifying Landlord-Tenant Relationships: Self-Help
                versus Judicial Process   642
                     New Jersey Anti-Eviction Act   *642*
                     Vásquez v. Glassboro Service Association, Inc.   *644*
                     Alan Schwartz, Justice and the Law of
                        Contracts: A Case for the Traditional
                        Approach   650
                     Robert Hale, Bargaining, Duress, and
                        Economic Liberty   651
                     Notes and Questions   656
                     Problems   658
§8.2   Conflicts About Rent   658
       §8.2.1   Landlord's Right to Receive Rent   658
                §8.2.1.1   Landlord's Remedies When Tenant Breaches
                           and Refuses to Leave: Summary Process   659
                §8.2.1.2   Landlord's Remedies When Tenant Breaches
                           and Leaves   661
                   (a) Landlord's Duty to Mitigate Damages   661
                        Sommer v. Kridel   *663*
                        Notes and Questions   667
                        Problem   669
                   (b) Regulation of Security Deposits   669
       §8.2.2   Rent Control   670
                §8.2.2.1   Statutory Interpretation: Who Is Protected?   670
                        Braschi v. Stahl Associates   *670*
                        Notes and Questions   673
                        Problems   675
                §8.2.2.2   The Economics of Rent Control   675
                        The Argument Against Rent Control   676
                        The Argument for Rent Control   677

§8.3   Conflicts About Occupancy   679
        §8.3.1   Landlord's Duty to Deliver Possession   679
        §8.3.2   Tenant's Right to Leave and Transfer the Leasehold
                 versus Landlord's Right to Control Occupancy   680
                 §8.3.2.1   Transfer of the Landlord's Reversion   680
                 §8.3.2.2   Tenant's Right to Assign or Sublet   680
                 (a)   When the Lease Is Silent   681
                 (b)   When the Lease Requires the Landlord's Consent   682
                       Kendall v. Ernest Pestana, Inc.   683
                       Slavin v. Rent Control Board of Brookline   688
                       Notes and Questions   690
                       Problems   692
                 §8.3.2.3   Tenant's Good Faith Duty to Operate   692
                       The College Block v. Atlantic Richfield Co.   692
                       Notes and Questions   694
                       Problem   696
        §8.3.3   Tenant's Right to Stay versus Landlord's Right to
                 Recover Possession   697
                 §8.3.3.1   Just Cause Eviction   697
                 (a)   Private Housing Market   697
                       New Jersey Anti-Eviction Act   698
                       Problem   699
                 (b)   Publicly Subsidized Housing   699
                 §8.3.3.2   Regulation of Condominium Conversion   700
§8.4   Tenant's Rights to Habitable Premises   701
        §8.4.1   The Covenant of Quiet Enjoyment and Constructive
                 Eviction   701
                       Minjak Co. v. Randolph   701
                       Blackett v. Olanoff   703
                       Notes and Questions   705
                       Problem   708
        §8.4.2   Implied Warranty of Habitability   708
                 §8.4.2.1   Doctrinal Development   708
                       Javins v. First National Realty Corp.   709
                       Notes and Questions   714
                       Problems   718
                 §8.4.2.2   Arguments and Counterarguments on Compulsory
                            Contract Terms   720
        §8.4.3   Retaliatory Eviction   726
                       Hillview Associates v. Bloomquist   726
                       Imperial Colliery Co. v. Fout   730
                       Notes and Questions   733
                       Problems   736
        §8.4.4   Landlord's Liability to Tenants   737
                 §8.4.4.1   Consumer Protection Legislation   737
                       Problem   738
                 §8.4.4.2   Landlord's Tort Liability to Tenants   738
                       Problems   741

9

Real Estate Transactions

743

§9.1	Structure of the Transaction	743
	§9.1.1 Attorney's Role	743
	§9.1.2 Brokers	744
	§9.1.3 Sales Contract	748
	§9.1.4 Executory Period	749
	§9.1.5 Closing	750
	§9.1.6 After the Closing	751
	Sample Offer to Purchase Real Estate	752
	Sample Purchase and Sale Agreement	753
	Sample Deed	757
§9.2	Sales Contract	758
	§9.2.1 Formalities: Statute of Frauds versus Part Performance and Estoppel	758
	Burns v. McCormick	758
	Hickey v. Green	760
	Gardner v. Gardner	762
	Notes and Questions	763
	§9.2.2 What Constitutes a Breach of the Contract	767
	§9.2.2.1 Misrepresentation and Fraudulent Nondisclosure	767
	Johnson v. Davis	767
	Notes and Questions	770
	Problem	775
	§9.2.2.2 Seller's Failure to Provide Marketable Title	776
	§9.2.2.3 Seller's Breach of Warranty of Habitability	776
	§9.2.2.4 Buyer's Failure to Make Good Faith Efforts to Obtain Financing	777
	§9.2.3 Remedies for Breach of the Purchase and Sale Agreement	777
	§9.2.3.1 Buyer's Remedies	777
	§9.2.3.2 Seller's Remedies	778
	§9.2.4 Risk of Loss During the Executory Period: Equitable Conversion	778
§9.3	Deeds and Title Protection	779
	§9.3.1 Formalities	779
	§9.3.1.1 Essential Terms	779
	§9.3.1.2 Delivery	780
	§9.3.2 Title Covenants	781
	§9.3.2.1 Warranties of Title	781
	§9.3.2.2 Remedies for Breach of Warranty of Title	783
	§9.3.3 Recording Acts	783
	§9.3.3.1 The Recording System	783

§9.3.3.2	How to Conduct a Title Search	785
§9.3.3.3	Types of Recording Acts	786
§9.3.3.4	Chain of Title Problems	787
	Sabo v. Horvath	*787*
	Notes and Questions	789
	Problems	792
§9.3.3.5	Fraud and Forgery	793
	Zurstrassen v. Stonier	*793*
	McCoy v. Love	*796*
	Notes and Questions	797
§9.3.4	Marketable Title Acts	798
§9.3.5	Title Insurance	798
§9.3.6	Title Registration	799
§9.4	Real Estate Finance	799
§9.4.1	Mortgages	799
§9.4.1.1	Debtor Protection Legislation	799
§9.4.1.2	Regulating the Foreclosure Process	803
	Central Financial Services, Inc. v. Spears	*803*
	Problems	805
§9.4.2	Installment Land Contracts	806
§9.4.2.1	Forfeiture	806
	Stonebraker v. Zinn	*806*
§9.4.2.2	Making Mortgage Protection Nondisclaimable	808
	Sebastian v. Floyd	*808*
	Notes and Questions	809
§9.4.3	Equitable Mortgages	812
	Koenig v. Van Reken	*812*
	Notes and Questions	813
	Problem	814

10

Fair Housing Law   *817*

§10.1	Intentional Discrimination or Discriminatory Treatment	817
§10.1.1	Race Discrimination	817
§10.1.1.1	Fair Housing Act	817
	Fair Housing Act, 42 U.S.C. §§3601-3631	*817*
§10.1.1.2	Discrimination by Housing Providers	822
	Ashbury v. Broughman	*822*
	United States v. Starrett City Associates	*826*
	Notes and Questions	830
	Problems	834
§10.1.1.3	*Civil Rights Act of 1866*	*835*
	City of Memphis v. Greene	*836*
	Problem	837

§10.1.2   Sex Discrimination: Sexual Harassment 837
          Edouard v. Kozubal 837
          Notes and Questions 841
          Problems 843
§10.1.3   Discrimination Based on Family Status 844
    §10.1.3.1   Familial Status: Families with Children 844
                Human Rights Commission v. LaBrie, Inc. 844
                Problems 848
    §10.1.3.2   Marital Status: Unmarried Couples 849
                McCready v. Hoffius 849
                Notes and Questions 855
                Problems 858
§10.1.4   Discrimination Based on Sexual Orientation 858
          State ex rel. Sprague v. City of Madison 858
          Notes and Questions 860
          Problems 861
§10.1.5   Discrimination Against Persons with Disabilities 863
    §10.1.5.1   Persons with AIDS 863
                Poff v. Caro 863
                Notes and Questions 864
    §10.1.5.2   Reasonable Accommodation of Persons with Disabilites .. 865
                Problems 867
§10.1.6   Economic Discrimination 867
    §10.1.6.1   Welfare Recipients 867
                Attorney General v. Brown 867
    §10.1.6.2   Discrimination Based on Income 869
§10.2 Disparate Impact Claims 871
    §10.2.1   Racially Discriminatory Zoning Practices 871
              Huntington Branch, NAACP v. Town of Huntington 871
              Notes and Questions 877
              Problem 880
    §10.2.2   Sex Discrimination: Shelters for Battered Women 881
              Doe v. City of Butler 881
              Problems 882
    §10.2.3   Nontraditional Families 883
        §10.2.3.1   Restrictive Covenants 883
        §10.2.3.2   Exclusionary Zoning 883
            (a)   Federal Constitution 883
                  Village of Belle Terre v. Boraas 883
            (b)   State Constitutions 886
                  Charter Township of Delta v. Dinolfo 886
                  Notes and Questions 888
            (c)   Fair Housing Act 890
                  Problem 890
    §10.2.4   Group Homes for Persons with Disabilities 890
        §10.2.4.1   AIDS Hospices 890
                    *Association of Relatives and Friends of AIDS Patients
                    (AFAPS) v. Regulations and Permits Administration,
                    or Administración de Reglamentos y Permisos (ARPE)* .. 890

§10.2.4.2   Group Homes for Persons with Mental Illness   892
            Familystyle of St. Paul, Inc. v. City of St. Paul   892
            Notes and Questions   893
            Problems   897
§10.2.5   Sexual Orientation   897
          Problem   897
§10.2.6   Religion   897
          Problems   898
§10.2.7   National Origin Discrimination   899
          Problem   899
§10.2.8   Land Use Regulation and Low-Income Families   899
          §10.2.8.1   Exclusionary Zoning   899
                      Southern Burlington County, NAACP v.
                      Township of Mount Laurel   899
                      Notes and Questions   907
          §10.2.8.2   Homelessness   910

11

Zoning: Governmental Land Use Planning   911

§11.1   The Planning Process   911
        §11.1.1   Legislative Process: Enacting the Zoning Ordinance   911
                  §11.1.1.1   Zoning Enabling Acts   911
                  §11.1.1.2   The Comprehensive Plan and Zoning Ordinance   912
                  §11.1.1.3   Planned Unit Developments   913
                  §11.1.1.4   Conditional or Contract Zoning   913
        §11.1.2   Administrative Procedures: The Zoning Board
                  of Adjustment   914
§11.2   Zoning: Police Power and Property Rights   915
        §11.2.1   Historical Background   915
                  Mugler v. Kansas   915
                  Powell v. Pennsylvania   916
                  Hadacheck v. Sebastian   916
                  Buchanan v. Warley   916
                  Pennsylvania Coal Co. v. Mahon   916
                  Village of Euclid v. Ambler Realty Co.   919
                  Nectow v. City of Cambridge   920
        §11.2.2   Limits to Zoning Laws Designed to Protect
                  Preexisting Property Rights   922
                  §11.2.2.1   Prior Nonconforming Uses   922
                              Town of Belleville v. Parrillo's, Inc.   922
                  §11.2.2.2   Variances   925
                              Cochran v. Fairfax County Board of
                              Zoning Appeals   925
                              Notes and Questions   930
                  §11.2.2.3   Vested Rights   931
                              Stone v. City of Wilton   931

		Notes and Questions	935
		Problems	935
	§11.2.3	Limits on Preferential Zoning	937
	§11.2.3.1	Special Exceptions	937
	§11.2.3.2	Spot Zoning	937
	§11.2.4	Exclusionary Zoning	938
	§11.2.5	Equal Protection, Substantive Due Process, & Free Speech	938
		Village of Willowbrook v. Olech	*938*
		Notes and Questions	939
		Problem	941
§11.3	Ethical Issues in Real Estate Development: SLAPP Suits		941
		Problem	943
§11.4	Environmental Regulations: Liability of Property Owners for Cleanup of Hazardous Waste		944
		Acme Laundry Co. v. Secretary of Environmental Affairs	*945*

V

Property and Sovereignty

951

12

Regulatory Takings Law

953

§12.1	Property as a Mediator Between Citizens and the State		953
	§12.1.1	Defining versus Defending Property Rights	953
	§12.1.2	Historical Background	955
	§12.1.3	*Per Se* Takings and the *Ad Hoc* Test	955
§12.2	*Ad Hoc* Test: Fairness and Justice		957
		Miller v. Schoene	*957*
		Penn Central Transportation Co. v. New York City	*959*
		Keystone Bituminous Coal Association v. DeBenedictis	*965*
		Notes and Questions	966
		Problems	975
§12.3	*Per Se* Takings		976
	§12.3.1	Physical Invasions	976
		PruneYard Shopping Center v. Robins	*976*
		Loretto v. Teleprompter Manhattan CATV Corp.	*979*
		Notes and Questions	984
		Problems	990

§12.3.2   Deprivation of Economically Viable Use   991
            Lucas v. South Carolina Coastal Council   *991*
            Palazzolo v. Rhode Island   1004
            Tahoe-Sierra Preservation Council, Inc. v. Tahoe
                Regional Planning Agency   *1006*
            Notes and Questions   1008
            Problems   1011
§12.4   Special Cases   1012
    §12.4.1   Deprivation of Core Property Rights   1012
            Babbitt v. Youpee   *1013*
            Notes and Questions   1013
            Problems   1016
    §12.4.2   Vested Rights   1017
        §12.4.2.1   Established Investments   1017
        §12.4.2.2   Forfeiture and the Innocent Owner   1020
            Bennis v. Michigan   *1020*
            Notes and Questions   1024
            Problems   1024
    §12.4.3   Exactions and Linkage Requirements   1026
            Dolan v. City of Tigard   *1026*
            Notes and Questions   1036
            Problems   1039
§12.5   Just Compensation   1042
            Almota Farmers Elevator & Warehouse v.
                United States   *1042*
            United States v. 564.54 Acres of Land,
                More or Less   *1046*
            Notes and Questions   1048
§12.6   Public Use   1051
    §12.6.1   Federal Constitution   1051
            Kelo v. City of New London   *1051*
    §12.6.2   State Constitutions   1065
            Problem   1066

13

American Indian Nations

1069

§13.1   History of Federal Indian Law   1069
§13.2   Original Indian Title   1072
    §13.2.1   "Title of Occupancy"   1072
    §13.2.2   Takings Doctrine   1072
§13.3   Recognized Title   1072
    §13.3.1   Treaty Abrogation   1072
            Treaty with the Cherokees (February 14, 1883)   1072
            Lyman Abbott, Statement to the Lake Mohonk
                Conference Supporting the Dawes Act (1885)   1073
            Francis Paul Prucha, The Great Father: The

United States Government and the American
Indians   1073
§13.3.2   Takings Doctrine   1074
United States v. Sioux Nation of Indians   *1074*
Notes and Questions   1082
§13.3.3   Current Indian Land Claims   1083
§13.4   Restricted Trust Allotments   1083

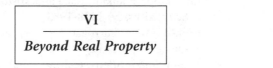

VI

Beyond Real Property   *1085*

14

Intellectual Property   *1087*

§14.1   Intangible Property   1087
§14.2   Unfair Competition and Misappropriation   1088
§14.3   Trademark Law   1088
Qualitex Co. v. Jacobson Products Co.   *1089*
Notes and Questions   1092
Problem   1093
§14.4   Copyright Law   1093
14.4.1   Original Works of Authorship   1093
Copyright Act of 1976   *1094*
*Feist Publications, Inc. v. Rural Telephone
Service Co., Inc.*   *1095*
14.4.2   Contributory Infringement   1099
*Metro-Goldwyn-Mayer Studios Inc. v.
Grokster Ltd.,*   *1100*
14.4.3   Fair Use   1117
Suntrust Bank v. Houghton Mifflin Co.,   *1117*
Problems   1128
§14.5   Patent Law   1128
§14.5.1   Property in Genetic Information   1128
§14.5.2   Business Methods   1129
§14.6   Publicity Rights   1129
*Martin Luther King, Jr. Center for Social
Change v. American Heritage Products*   *1129*
Notes and Questions   1137
Problems   1140
§14.7   Moral Rights   1140

15

Property in People   *1143*

§15.1   Property Rights in Human Beings   1143
§15.2   Slavery   1143
            Dred Scott v. Sandford   *1143*
            John Hope Franklin, Race and History:
                Selected Essays 1938-1988   1147
            Anita L. Allen, Surrogacy, Slavery, and the
                Ownership of Life   1148
            Aviam Soifer, Status, Contract, and Promises
                Unkept   1149
            The Antelope   *1152*
            Notes and Questions   1152
§15.3   Children   1154
            In the Matter of Baby M   *1154*
            Notes and Questions   1159
§15.4   Frozen Embryos   1162
§15.5   Body Parts and Human Genes   1166
§15.6   American Indian Human Remains   1166
            *Wana the Bear v. Community
                Construction, Inc.*   *1166*
            Tony Hillerman, Talking God   1167
            Notes and Questions   1169
            Problems   1170

Table of Cases   *1173*
Table of Statutes   *1189*
Index   *1197*

Preface to the Fourth Edition

It is surprising how fast the law is changing in an area one might have thought settled in a mature, free market economy. When the first edition of this book was published in 1993, a majority of states still adhered to the old rule that protected landlords from the duty to mitigate damages; almost all states have now changed their law to include such a duty (with the exception of a few notable states such as New York). The Uniform Statutory Rule Against Perpetuities is now the law in more than half the states and more than a few states have abolished the rule against perpetuities altogether, at least as applied to income from trusts of personal property. The *Restatement (Third) of Property (Servitudes)* just adopted in 2000 is beginning to influence the law of property; at the same time, some proposed changes in the law have seen only sporadic acceptance. Several proposed rules in the *Restatement* — such as the right of the servient estate owner to move an easement without the consent of the easement owner — have been accepted by some states and emphatically rejected by others. Several states have adopted laws guaranteeing the right to fly the American flag, regardless of any condominium rules or covenants to the contrary. Massachusetts, as well some foreign nations, have recognized same-sex marriages, creating new issues in family law when those couples travel, divorce, and die. Oregon has adopted a law called Measure 37 that prohibits any changes in land use regulation laws that decrease the value of property unless those harms are compensated; it thereby may have the effect of freezing current regulatory laws in place. And since 2001, the Supreme Court has issued an astonishing series of cases in the area of regulatory takings that literally forced me to completely reorganize and rewrite my chapter on that subject.

This edition, like the previous editions, seeks to present a contemporary introduction to the law of property, focusing on pressing issues of current concern as well as the basic rules governing the property system. As before, I have attempted to ensure that students and professors can get a clear and accurate picture of the current law, as well as understanding the many disagreements among the states on the applicable rules in force. Some of the rules governing property are arcane and complex and students should be able to learn them without reading a treatise on the side. At the same time, many of the cases have dissents and almost all have policy discussion justifying the approach taken by the court. Where no dissents are present and the states disagree about the law, I have made this clear in the note material. I have also presented problems that place students in real lawyering roles so that they can use the materials in the book (principal cases, subsidiary cases, textual explanation of the doctrine and policy concerns) to make arguments on both sides of hard cases and to learn both to justify their judgments and to criticize the results reached by the courts and legislatures.

Joseph William Singer
Cambridge, Massachusetts
5766/2006

A Guide to the Book

What Is Property?

Property rights concern relations among people regarding control of valued resources. Property law gives owners the power to control things, and it does this by placing duties on non-owners. For example, owners have the right to exclude non-owners from their property; this right imposes a duty on others not to enter property without the owner's consent. Property rights are relational; ownership is not just power over things but entails relations among people. This is true not only of the right to exclude but of the privilege to use property. An owner who operates a business on a particular parcel may benefit the community by creating jobs and providing needed services, and she may harm the community by increasing traffic or causing pollution. Development of a subdivision may affect drainage patterns and cause flooding on neighboring land. Property use makes others vulnerable to the effects of that use, for better or for worse. Power over things is actually power over people.

Property rights are *not absolute*. The recognition and exercise of a property right in one person often affects and may even conflict with the personal or property rights of others. To give one person an absolute legal entitlement would mean that others could not exercise similar entitlements. Property rights are therefore limited to ensure that property use and ownership do not unreasonably harm the legitimate, legally protected personal or property interests of others. The duty to exercise property rights in a manner compatible with the legal rights of others means that *owners have obligations as well as rights*.

Owners of property generally possess a *bundle of entitlements*. The most important are the privilege to use the property, the right to exclude others, the power to transfer title to the property, and immunity from having the property taken or damaged without your consent. These entitlements may be disaggregated—an owner can give up some of the sticks in the bundle while keeping others. Landlords, for example, grant tenants the right to possess their property in exchange for periodic rental payments while retaining the right to regain possession at the end of the leasehold. Because property rights are limited to protect the legitimate interests of others and because owners have the power to disaggregate property rights, entitlements in a particular piece of property are more often shared than unitary. It is almost always the case that more than one person will have something to say about the use of a particular piece of property. Property law therefore cannot be reduced to the rules that determine ownership; rather, it comprises rules that allocate particular entitlements and define their scope.

Property is owned in a *variety of forms*. An infinite number of bundles of rights can be created from the sticks in the bundle that comprise full ownership. However, some bundles are widely used and they comprise the basic forms or models of ownership. Some forms are used by individuals while others are used by couples (married or unmarried) or families. Other forms are used by groups of unrelated owners. Differences exist between forms that give owners management powers and those that separate ownership from management. Further distinctions exist between residential and commercial property and between nonprofit organizations and for-profit businesses. Within each of these categories are multiple subcategories, such as the distinction between partnerships and corporations or between male-female couples and same-sex couples. Particular models of property ownership have been created for different social contexts and types of property. Each model has a different way of bundling and dispersing the rights and obligations of ownership among various persons. Understanding property requires knowledge both of the individual sticks in the bundle of property rights and the characteristic bundles that characterize particular ownership forms.

Property is a *system* as well as an *entitlement*. A property right is a legal entitlement granted to an individual or entity but the extent of the legal right is partly determined by rules designed to ensure that the property system functions effectively and fairly. Many property law rules are geared not to protecting individual entitlements, but to ensuring that the environment in which those rights are exercised is one that maximizes the benefits of property ownership for everyone and is compatible with the norms underlying a free and democratic society. Some rules promote efficiency, such as the rules that promote the smooth operation of the real estate market. Other rules promote fairness or distributive justice, such the fair housing laws that prohibit owners from denying access to property on the basis of race, sex, religion or disability.

Tensions Within the Property System

In 1990, roughly a year after his nation was freed from Soviet domination, the foreign minister of Czechoslovakia, Jiri Dienstbier, commented that "[i]t was easier to make a revolution than to write 600 to 800 laws to create a market economy."[1] If anything, he understated the case. Each of the basic property entitlements is limited to ensure that the exercise of a property right by one person is compatible with the property and personal rights of others. The construction of a property system requires property law to adjudicate characteristic core tensions in the system.

Right to exclude versus right of access. It is often said that the most fundamental right associated with property ownership is the right to exclude non-owners from the property. If the right to exclude were unlimited, owners could exclude non-owners based on race or religion. Although at one time owners were empowered (and in some states required) to do this, current law prohibits discrimination on the basis of race, sex, national origin, religion or disability in public accommodations, housing and employment. Although individuals are free to choose whom to invite to their homes for dinner, market actors are regulated to ensure that access to property is available without regard to invidious discrimination. Property therefore entails a tension between privacy and free association norms on one side and equality norms on the other. Sometimes the right of access will take precedence over the right to exclude. The tension between these claims is one that property law must resolve.

Privilege to use versus security from harm. Owners are generally free to use their property as they wish, but they are not free to harm their neighbors' property substantially and unreasonably. A factory that emits pollutants into the air may be regulated to prevent

---

[1] William Echikson, *Euphoria Dies Down in Czechoslovakia*, Wall St. J., Sept. 18, 1990, at A26, 1990 WL-WSJ 56114.

the use of its property in ways that will destroy the individual property rights of others and common resources in air and water. Many uses of property impose "externalities" or spillover effects on other owners and on the community as a whole. Because owners are legally entitled to have their own property protected from pollutants dispatched to their property by others, owners' freedom to use their property is limited to ensure that their property use does not cause such unreasonable negative externalities.

Power to transfer versus powers of ownership. Owners are generally free to transfer their property to whomever they wish, on whatever terms they want. Freedom of disposition gives them the power to sell it, give it away, or write a will identifying who will get it when they die. They are also free to contract with others to transfer particular sticks in the bundle of sticks comprising full ownership to others while keeping the rest for themselves. Owners may even place conditions on the use of property when they sell it, limiting what future owners may do with it. They may, for example, limit the property to residential purposes by including a restriction in the deed limiting the property to such uses.

Although owners are free to disaggregate property rights in various ways, and to impose particular restrictions on the use and ownership of land, that freedom is not unlimited. Owners are not allowed to impose conditions that violate public policy or that unduly infringe on the liberty interests of future owners. For example, an owner could not impose an enforceable condition that all future owners agree to vote for the Democratic candidate for president; this condition infringes on the liberty of future owners and wrongfully attempts to tie ownership of the land to membership in a particular political party. Nor are owners allowed to limit the sale of the property to persons of a particular race. Similarly, restrictions limiting the transfer of property will ordinarily not be enforced, both to protect the freedom of owners to move and to promote the efficient transfer of property in the marketplace. The freedom of an owner to restrict the future use or disposition of property must be curtailed to protect the freedom of future owners to use their property as they wish. The law limits freedom of contract and freedom of disposition to ensure that owners have sufficient powers over the property they own.

Immunity from loss versus power to acquire. Property owners have the right not to have their property taken or damaged by others against their will. However, it is often lawful to interfere with the property interests of others. For example, an owner who builds a house on a vacant lot may block a view enjoyed by the neighbor for many years. A new company may put a prior company out of business or reduce its profits through competition. Property rights must be limited to ensure that others can exercise similar rights in acquiring and using property. In addition, immunity from forced seizure or loss of property rights is not absolute when the needs of the community take precedence. To construct a new public highway or municipal building, for example, the government may exercise its eminent power to take private property for public uses with just compensation.

Recurring Themes

A number of important themes will recur throughout this book. They include the following:

Social context. Social context matters in defining property rights. We have different typical models of property depending on whether it is owned individually or jointly, among family members or non-family members, by a private or a governmental entity, devoted to profitable or charitable purposes, for residential or commercial purposes, open to public use or limited to private use.

Formal versus informal sources of rights. Property rights generally have their source in some formal grant, such as a deed, a will, a lease, a contract, or a government grant. However, property rights also arise informally, by an oral promise, a course of conduct, actual possession, a family relationship, an oral gift, longstanding reliance, and social customs and norms. Many of the basic rules of property law concern contests between formal and informal sources of property rights. While the law usually insists on formality to create property rights, it often protects informally created expectations over formally created ones. Determining when expectations based on informal arrangements should prevail over formal ones is a central issue in property law.

The alienability dilemma. It is a fundamental tenet of the property law system that property should be "alienable," meaning that it should be transferable from one person to another. Transferability allows a market to function and enables efficient transactions and property use to occur. It also promotes individual autonomy by allowing owners to sell or give away property when they please on terms they have chosen. This suggests that the law should allow owners to disaggregate property rights as they please. However, if owners are allowed to disaggregate property rights at will, it may be difficult to reconsolidate those rights. If property is burdened by obsolete restrictions, it may be expensive or impossible to get rid of them. Similarly, if property is disaggregated among too many owners, transaction costs may block agreements to reconsolidate the interests and make the property useable for current needs. The property may therefore be rendered inalienable.

Many rules of property law limit contractual freedom to ensure that particular bundles of property rights are consolidated in the same person — the "owner." Consolidating power in an "owner" ensures that resources can be used for current purposes and current needs and allows property to be freely transferred in the marketplace. We therefore face a tension between promoting alienability by consolidating rights in owners and promoting alienability by allowing owners to disaggregate their rights into unique bundles constructed by them.

Contractual freedom and minimum standards. Individuals want to be free to develop human relationships without having government dictate the terms of their association with others. Having the ability to rearrange property rights to create desirable packages of entitlements will help enable various relationships to flourish. However, there are also bounds to what is acceptable; this is why the law imposes certain minimum standards on contractual relationships. For example, although landlords are entitled to evict residential tenants who do not pay rent, the law in almost every state requires landlords to use court eviction proceedings to dispossess defaulting tenants. These proceedings give tenants a chance to contest the landlord's possessory claim and to have time to find a new place to live, rather than having their belongings tossed on the street and being dispossessed over night. These limitations on free contract protect basic norms of fair dealing and promote the justified expectations of individuals who enter market transactions.

Social welfare. Granting owners power over property ensures that they can obtain resources to satisfy human needs. It also promotes social welfare by encouraging productive activity and by granting security to those who invest in economic projects. Clear property rights facilitate exchange and lower the costs of transactions by clarifying who owns what. At the same time, owners may use their property in socially harmful ways, and clear property rights may promote harmful, as well as beneficial, actions. Property rights must be limited to ensure that conflicting uses are accommodated to minimize the costs of desirable development on other owners and on the community. Moreover, rigid property rights may inhibit bargaining rather than facilitate it by granting owners the power to act unreasonably, thereby encouraging litigation to clarify the limits on the owner's entitlements. Reasonableness requirements, while less predictable than clear rules, may promote efficient bargaining by encouraging competing claimants to compromise in ways that minimize the costs of property use on others. We need to design rules of ownership and transfer that promote efficiency and social welfare by decreasing the costs of using and obtaining property while maximizing its benefits both to individual owners and to society as a whole.

Justified expectations. In a famous phrase, Jeremy Bentham wrote that "[p]roperty is nothing but a basis of expectation; the expectation of deriving certain advantages from a thing which we are said to possess, in consequence of the relation in which we stand towards it."[2] Owners justifiably expect to use their own property for their own purposes and to transfer it on terms chosen by them. However, because the property use often affects others, it must be limited to protect the expectations of others. Property law protects justified expectations. A central function of property law is to determine what the parties' actual expectations are and when they are, and are not, justified.

Distributive justice. Property rights are the legal form of wealth. Wealth takes many forms, including the right to control tangible assets, such as land and buildings, and intangible assets, such as stocks that give the holder the right to control and derive profit from a business enterprise. In fact, any legal entitlement that benefits the right holder may be viewed as a species of property. The rules of property law, like the rules of contract, family, and tax law, play an enormous role in determining the distribution of both wealth and income.

How well is property dispersed in the United States? One expert has noted that "[b]y several measurements, the United States in the late twentieth century led all other major industrial countries in the gap dividing the upper fifth of the population from the lower — in the disparity between top and bottom."[3]

One indicator of the distribution of property is income. Since 1967, income distribution has become increasingly unequal in the United States. In 1999, the Census Bureau reported that the share of total income going to the top fifth of American households increased from 43.8% in 1967 to 49.4% in 1999.[4] The share of the top 5% climbed from 17.5% in 1967 to 21.5% in 1999. In contrast, the lowest 20% of the population dropped from 4% of income in 1967 to 3.6% in 1999. The second lowest fifth from the bottom received 8.9% of total income in 1999, while the third (middle) fifth received 14.9% and the fourth fifth 23.2%. Together the top two/fifths received 72.6% of total income in 1999.

---

[2] Jeremy Bentham, 1 *Theory of Legislation* 137 (Boston: Weeks, Jordan & Co., R. Hildreth trans. 1840).

[3] Kevin Phillips, *The Politics of Rich and Poor: Wealth and American Electorate in the Reagan Aftermath* 8 (1990).

[4] U.S. Census Bureau, Current Population Reports, P60-209, *Money Income in the United States: 1999* (Sept. 2000) (http://www.census.gov).

It is telling that the share of income going to the bottom fifth of the population fell between 1967 and 1999 while the share going to the top fifth increased. However, it is as important to know that within the top fifth of the population, the bulk of this increase was obtained by those at the very top. A Congressional Budget Office study showed that "between 1979 and 1997, the after-tax incomes of the top 1 percent of families rose 157 percent, compared with only a 10 percent gain for families near the middle of the income distribution."[5] The growth in executive pay has also been nothing short of astounding in the last thirty years. Writing in 2002, Paul Krugman explained:

> Is it news that C.E.O.'s of large American corporations make a lot of money? Actually, it is. They were always well paid compared with the average worker, but there is simply no comparison between what executives got a generation ago and what they are paid today.
>
> Over the past 30 years most people have seen only modest salary increases: the average annual salary in America, expressed in 1998 dollars (that is, adjusted for inflation), rose from $32,522 in 1970 to $35,864 in 1999. That's about a 10 percent increase over 29 years — progress, but not much. Over the same period, however, according to Fortune magazine, the average real annual compensation of the top 100 C.E.O.'s went from $1.3 million — 39 times the pay of an average worker — to $37.5 million, more than 1,000 times the pay of ordinary workers.[6]

The distribution of income also varies according to race, gender and age. The median income of households in the United States was $40,816 in 1999; half of all households received more and half less than that amount. However, differences are substantial along racial lines. While the median income of white, non-Hispanic families was $44,366 in 1999, the median income for African American households was only $27,910. The median income for Latino households was $30,735 while that of American Indians and Native Alaskan households was $30,784.[7] Although per capita income for all races was $21,181 in 1999, the figure for white, non-Hispanic individuals was $24,109, while that for African Americans was only $14,397 and that for Latinos $11,621.

Poverty is similarly unequally distributed by race. While 11.8% of all persons were poor by federal standards in 1999, only 7.7% of non-Hispanic whites were poor; by comparison, 23.6% of African Americans and 22.8% of Latinos fell below the poverty line. Data averaged from 1997 to 1999 show that 25.9% of American Indians and Native Alaskans were poor by official standards.[8] In 2003, the poverty rate had risen to 12.5%, which included 35.9 million people. However, in 2003, the poverty rate for non-Hispanic whites was 8.2%, while the poverty rate for African Americans was 24.4%, for Latinos 22.5%, and for American Indians, 23.2%.[9]

Although the gap in incomes between men and women has narrowed over the last quarter century, men still earn more than women on average. In 1999, men who worked full time earned an average of $36,476 while women who worked full time earned only $26,324, or 72% of male earnings.

---

[5] Paul Krugman, *For Richer*, N.Y. Times Magazine, Oct. 20, 2002, at 62.

[6] *Id.*

[7] This figure masks huge differences within the Indian and Native Alaskan population. Incomes of those living on reservations is much lower than that of off-reservation Indians. Moreover, differences among tribes are large. Although some tribes are wealthy, others are among the poorest groups in the United States.

[8] Joseph Dalaker & Bernadette D. Procter, U.S. Census Bureau, Current Population Reports, P60-210, *Poverty in the United States: 1999* (Sept. 2000)(http://www.census.gov).

[9] U.S. Census Bureau, *Income, Poverty, and Health Insurance Coverage in the United States: 2003*, at http://www.census.gov/hhes/www/income.html

Children are disproportionately poor in the United States. Although children made up 26% of the total population in 1999, they make up 38% of the poor. Although 11.8% of the population fell below the poverty line, 16.9% of children did so. That figure rose to 17.6% in 2003. In 1999, 37% of African American children were living in poverty. These figures differ greatly for married couples and unmarried female-headed households. Children who live in households without an adult male are extremely likely to be poor.

While only 5.8% of children in families of married couples were poor in 1999, 30.4% of children living in female-headed households were poor. Moreover, half of all children under six living in female-headed households (50.3%) were poor. Although 19.8% of children in white, non-Hispanic female-headed households were poor, 41% of children of African American female-headed households were poor. While the median income of all households in 1999 was $49,940, the median income of married couples with children was $56,827 while the median income of female-headed households was only $26,164 and the median income of male-headed households was $41,838.

Inequalities of both income and wealth are somewhat alleviated by transfer payments in the form of public assistance. Until the 1970s, elderly persons were more likely to be poor than the non-elderly. By 1990, however, the poverty rate for persons over 65 was less than that for the rest of the population, with the result that, during the 1980s, very few elderly persons were among the homeless and extremely poor. This change in the position of the elderly was the result of public spending in the form of Social Security pensions, Medicare, and housing subsidies.[10] In 1999, the poverty rate for those 65 and older was at an all-time low of 9.7%, rising to 10.2% in 2003.[11]

Wealth data show even greater inequality than that existing for income. In 1986, the top one-half of 1% of U.S. households — the top 420,000 households in the country — owned 26.9% of U.S. family net wealth. The same year, the top 10% of households owned about 68% of the nation's total wealth.[12] The richest 1% of U.S. households increased their share of net worth from 31% of the total in 1983 to 37% in 1989.[13] And in 1995, the share of total household wealth (net worth) belonging to the top 1% went up to 38.5%. The next 4% owned 21.8% of household wealth and the next 5% owned an additional 11.5%. This means that, in 1995, the top 10% of all households owned 71.8% of all household wealth. The top 20% owned 83.9% of all household wealth.[14]

Normative Approaches

How should the courts and the legislatures adjudicate conflicting property claims? Various approaches can be used to conceptualize property rights and to adjudicate conflicts among property claimants.[15] Here is a brief description of the most common approaches.[16]

---

[10] Peter H. Rossi, *Down and Out in America: The Origins of Homelessness* 193 (1989).

[11] U.S. Census Bureau, *Income, Poverty, and Health Insurance Coverage in the United States: 2003,* at http://www.census.gov/hhes/www/income.html.

[12] Kevin Phillips, *The Politics of Rich and Poor: Wealth and the American Electorate in the Reagan Aftermath* 1-13 (1990).

[13] Joel I. Nelson, *Post-Industrial Capitalism* 9(1995).

[14] Lisa A. Keister, *Wealth in America* 64 (2000).

[15] For collections of scholary approaches to poverty, *see, Perspectives on Property Law* (Robert C. Ellickson, Carol M. Rose & Bruce A. Ackerman, 2d ed. 1995; *A Property Anthology* (Richard H. Chused, 2d ed. 1997).

[16] Many, if not most, scholars combine various approaches. *See, e.g.,* Stephen R. Munzer, *A Theory of Property* (1990) (adopting a pluralist perspective including justice and equality, desert based on labor, and utility and efficiency); Carol M. Rose, *Property & Persuasion: Essays on*

Traditional American Indian conceptions of property. The original possessors of land in the United States were American Indian nations. With more than 550 federally recognized tribes and scores of unrecognized tribes, it is difficult to generalize about American Indian land use systems, either in the past or the present. Nonetheless, several characteristics of traditional Indian property systems stand out and remain important to this day.

First, land was traditionally regarded as spiritual: All parts of the material universe have a direct relationship with the spirit world or with the Creator. Specific areas are connected to specific tribes by history and spiritual linkages. For example, certain areas are believed to be the place where members of the tribe first came to earth from the spirit world. Given this spiritual bonding, American Indians traditionally believed it was not possible to "own" the land in the sense used by non-Indians. Robert Jim, the Chairman of the Yakima Nation, said, "This high country is our religion. When our souls die, this is where they come. That is why this mountain is sacred to my people."[17] A policy statement issued by the National Indian Youth Council in 1961 explained: "The land is our spiritual mother whom we can no easier sell than our physical mother. We will resist, to the death if necessary, any more of our mother being sold into slavery."[18]

Second, many American Indian nations developed property systems that were far more oriented to sharing than are non-Indian property systems. Property was conceptualized less in terms of ownership than of limited use rights. Individual tribes would have fairly clearly understood borders to their property, much like borders between sovereign nations. The tribe itself would have mechanisms for assigning specific pieces of land to individuals or families, and if needs changed, the tribal government might reallocate assignments. Thus, property was not generally sold in a way that gave as full powers to owners as exist in non-Indian systems. Moreover, property rights were not exclusive; rather, uses of property would overlap. While a particular family might use a piece of land to plant crops, this would not preclude other tribal members from entering to gather nonagricultural food on such lands. Nor did most tribes have any conception of deriving rent from land.[19]

Positivism and legal realism. Positivist theories identify law with the "commands of the sovereign" or the rules promulgated by authoritative government officials for reasons of public policy.[20] Those rules may be intended to protect individual rights, promote the general welfare, increase social wealth, or maximize social utility. Judges are therefore directed to apply the law, as promulgated by authoritative government lawmakers, and to exercise discretion where there are gaps, conflicts, or ambiguities in the law while respecting the need for consistency with the letter and spirit of preexisting laws. Jeremy Bentham wrote that the "idea of property consists in an established expectation . . . of being able to draw . . . an advantage from the thing possessed."[21] He believed that "this expectation, this persuasion, can only be the work of law. It is only through the

---

the History, Theory, and Rhetoric of Ownership (1994)(combining economic analysis, justice-based arguments, and feminist legal theory); Joseph William Singer, *Entitlement: The Paradoxes of Property* (2000)(using both justice and utilitarian considerations, as well as narrative theory, feminism, critical race theory, and critical legal studies).

[17] Sharon O' Brien, *American Indian Tribal Governments* 217 (1989).

[18] *Id.* at 86.

[19] William Cronon, *Changes in the Land* (1983).

[20] John Austin, *Lectures of Jurisprudence* (1861-1863); H. L. A. Hart, *The Concept of Law (1961)*.

[21] Jeremy Bentham, *The Theory of Legislation* 138 (Boston: Weeks, Jordan & Co., R. Hildreth trans. 1840).

protection of law that I am able to inclose a field, and to give myself up to its cultivation with the sure though distant hope of harvest...."[22] Property exists to the extent the law will protect it. "Property and law are born together, and die together. Before laws were made there was no property; take away laws, and property ceases."[23]

Positivists separate law and morals; they emphasize that, although moral judgments may underlie rules of law, they are not fully or consistently enforced by legal sanctions. Positivism was adopted by Progressive-era judges and scholars such as Oliver Wendell Holmes, who suggested analyzing legal rules in the way a "bad man" would. Such a person would not be interested in the moral content of the law but would simply want to predict what legal sanctions would be imposed on him if he engaged in prohibited conduct.[24] This approach was adopted by legal realist scholars of the 1920s and 1930s such as Karl Llewellyn, who argued that the law is what officials will do in resolving disputes.[25]

All lawyers are positivists in some sense because the job of advising clients necessarily entails identifying the rules of law that have been explicitly or implicitly adopted by authoritative lawmakers and predicting how those rules will be applied to the client's situation. Judges may also see their jobs as the enforcement of existing law and leave the job of amending law to legislatures. On the other hand, determining whether an existing rule was intended to apply to a particular situation requires judgment, as well as techniques of *statutory interpretation* and analysis of *precedent*, and a conception about the proper role of courts in the lawmaking process.

Justice and fairness. Positivism has been criticized by scholars who argue that ambiguities in existing laws must be filled in by judges, and that judges should not exercise untrammeled discretion in doing so. Rather, they should interpret gaps, conflicts and ambiguities in the law in a manner that protects individual rights, promotes fairness, or ensures justice.

Rights theorists attempt to identify individual interests that are so important from a moral point of view that they not only deserve legal protection but may count as "trumps" that override more general considerations of public policy by which competing interests are balanced against each other. Such individual rights cannot legitimately be sacrificed for the good of the community.[26] Some *natural rights* theorists argue that rights have roots in the nature of human beings or that they are natural in the sense that people who think about human relationships from a rational and moral point of view are bound to understand particular individual interests as fundamental.[27] Other scholars, building on Immanuel Kant, ask whether a claim that an interest should be protected could be *universalized* such that every person in similar circumstances would be entitled to similar protection. Still others build on the *social contract* tradition begun by John Locke and Thomas Hobbes and ask whether individuals would choose to protect certain interests if they had to come to agreement in a suitably defined decision making context. John Rawls, for example, asks what principles of justice would be

---

[22] *Id.*

[23] *Id.* at 139

[24] *See* Oliver Wendell Holmes, *The Path of the Law*, 8 Harv. L. Rev. 1 (1894).

[25] Karl Llewellyn, *The Bramble Bush* (1930).

[26] Ronald Dworkin, *Law's Empire* (1986); Ronald Dworkin, *Taking Rights Seriously* (1978), Charles Fried, *Right and Wrong* (1978); Allan Gewirth, *The Community of Rights* (1996); Jeremy Waldron, *The Right to Private Property* (1998).

[27] *See* Robert Nozick, *Anarchy, State and Utopia* (1974); Judith Jarvis Thompson, *The Realm of Rights* (1990).

adopted by individuals who did not know morally irrelevant facts about themselves, such as their race or sex.[28]

Some theorists focus on *desert*. John Locke argued that labor is the foundation of property. "Whatsoever then he removes out of the state that nature has provided and left it in, he has mixed his labor with, and joined to it something that is his own, and thereby makes it his property."[29] Other theorists focus on the role that property rights play in developing individual *autonomy*.[30] Hegel believed that property was a way that human beings constituted themselves as people by extending their will to manipulate the objects of the external world.[31] Professor Margaret Jane Radin, for example, has argued that "to be a *person* ... an individual needs some control over resources in the external environment."[32] She distinguishes between forms of property that are important for the meaning they have to individuals (personal property such as a wedding ring) and property that is important solely because it can be used in exchange (fungible property such as money and investments).[33]

Other scholars focus on satisfying *human needs* or ensuring *distributive justice*. Nancy Fraser has argued that an important way to think about property rights is to focus on the ways we define people's needs and the ways in which the legal system does or does not meet those needs.[34] Frank Michelman has similarly argued that a system of private property requires, by its very nature, that property be widely dispersed. If all property were owned by one person, that person would be a dictator. Private property implies wide availability. It therefore entails a compromise between the principle of protecting possession and promoting widespread distribution.[35]

Utilitarianism, social welfare and efficiency. Utilitarians focus on the *consequences* of alternative legal rules. They compare the costs and benefits of alternative property rules or institutions with the goal of adopting rules that will maximize *social utility* or *welfare*. Some scholars in the law and economics school of thought measure social utility by the concept of economic *efficiency*. Efficiency theorists measure costs and benefits by reference to what people are willing and able to pay for entitlements, given their resources.[36]

Individual property rights are thought to increase efficiency by encouraging productive activity and by granting security to those who invest in economic projects. Clear property rights also facilitate exchange by clarifying who owns what. They therefore create incentives to use resources efficiently.[37] On the other hand, Carol Rose has argued

---

[28] John Rawls, *A Theory of Justice* (1971). *See also* Thomas M. Scanlon, *What We Owe Each Other* (1998).

[29] John Locke, *Second Treatise of Government* 17-18 (Bobbs-Merrill ed. 1952)(originally published in 1960).

[30] Richard A. Epstein, *Simple Rules for a Complex World* 53-70 (1995).

[31] Georg Wilhelm Friedrich Hegel, *Philosophy of Right* 40-41 (T. Knox trans. 1942).

[32] Margaret Jane Radin, *Property and Personhood*, 34 Stan. L. Rev. 957 (1982).

[33] Margaret Jane Radin, *Market-Inalienability*, 100 Harv. L. Rev. 1849 (1987). *See also* Margaret Jane Radin, *Contested Commodities: The Trouble with Trade in Sex, Children, Body Parts, and Other Things (1996)*; Margaret Jane Radin, Reinterpreting Property (1993).

[34] Nancy Fraser, *Unruly Practices, Power, Discourse, and Gender in Contemporary Social Theory* (1989).

[35] Frank Michelman, *Possession and Distribution in the Constitutional Idea of Property*, 72 Iowa. L. Rev. 1319 (1987). *See also* Jeremy Waldron, *The Right to Private Property* (1988).

[36] *Economic Foundations of Property Law* (Bruce Ackerman ed. 1975); Richard A. Posner, *Economic Analysis and Law* 35-99 (5th ed. 1998).

[37] Richard Posner, *Economic Analysis of Law* §3.1, at 36 (5th ed. 1998). *See also* Garrett Hardin, *The Tragedy of the Commons*, reprinted in *Economic Foundations of Property Law* 4

that clear definitions of property rights may be overly rigid, upsetting settled expectations and reliance interests.[38] This is why property rights are often defined by flexible standards, such as a reasonableness requirement, that adjust the relations of the parties to achieve a fair and efficient result. Rose has also argued that common ownership is sometimes the most efficient way to manage property.[39] Michelman and Duncan Kennedy have also argued that efficiency requires a mixture of private property, sharing, and deregulation.[40] Cass Sunstein has noted that preferences are partially shaped by law and that cognitive biases may affect individuals' perceptions of their preferences.[41]

Social relations. Social relations approaches analyze property rights as relations among persons regarding control of valued resources. Legal rights are correlative; every legal entitlement in an individual implies a correlative vulnerability in someone else, and every entitlement is limited by the competing rights of others.[42] This analysis was developed by pragmatic legal scholars — called "legal realists" — from the 1920s through the 1930s. Property rights are interpreted as delegations of sovereign power to individuals by the state; these rights should therefore be defined to accommodate the conflicting interests of social actors.[43] Current social relations theorists have broadened the scope of this analysis by examining the role property rights play in structuring social relations and the ways in which social relations shape access to property.[44] These approaches include feminist legal theory, critical race theory, critical legal studies, communitarianism, law and society, deconstruction and cultural studies.

Feminists such as Martha Minow argue that our identities, values and needs are developed in relation to and in connection with others. The legal system relies on implicit conceptions of social relations and often implicitly treats certain groups or individuals as the norm and others as the exception. She argues that we must become conscious of the ways those underlying assumptions function in both social relations and the legal system.[45] Elizabeth V. Spelman similarly analyzes the implicit assumptions underlying conceptions of human relations. In particular, she focuses on the role that race, class and gender play in shaping the concepts with which we understand human relations.[46]

These new insights have permeated recent discussions of property law. Property has traditionally been associated with the idea of autonomy within boundaries; for example, we

---

(B. Ackerman ed. 1975); Harold Demsetz, *Toward a Theory of Property Rights,* 57 Am. Econ, Rev. 347 (1967).

[38] Carol Rose, *Crystals and Mud in Property Law,* 40 Stan. L. Rev. 577 (1988).

[39] Carol Rose, *The Comedy of the Commons: Customs, Commerce, and Inheretently Public Property,* 53 U. Chi. L. Rev. 711 (1986). *See also* Frank Michelman, *Ethics, Economics, and the Law of Property,* 24 Nomos: Ethics, Economics, and the Law 3 (1982) (arguing that the institution of property, by its nature, requires a large amount of cooperative activity).

[40] Duncan Kennedy and Frank Michelman, *Are Property and Contract Efficient?,* 8 Hofstra L. Rev. 711 (1980).

[41] Cass R. Sunstein, *Free Markets and Social Justice* (1997).

[42] Wesley Honfield, *Some Fundamental Legal Conception as Applied in Judicial Reasoning,* 28 Yale L.J. 16 (1913).

[43] Walter Wheeler Cook, *Privileges of Labor Unions in the Struggle for Life,* 27 Yale L. J. 779 (1918); Robert Hale, *Bargaining, Duress, and Economic Liberty,* 43 Colum. L. Rev. 603 (1943); Morris Cohen, *Property and Sovereignty,* 13 Cornell L. Q. 8 (1927).

[44] Gregory Alexander, *Community & Property: Competing Visions of Property in American Legal Thought, 1776-1970;* C. Edwin Baker, *Property and Its Relation to Constitutionally Protected Liberty,* 134 U. Pa. L. Rev. 741(1986).

[45] Martha Minow, *Making All the Difference: Inclusion, Exclusion, and American Law (1990).*

[46] Elizabeth V. Spelman, *Inessential Woman: Problems of Exclusion in Feminist Thought* (1989).

assume that people are generally free to do what they like within the borders of their land. Yet Jennifer Nedelsky has argued that "[w]hat makes human autonomy possible is not isolation but relationship" with others.[47] She proposes that we replace the idea of *boundary* as the central metaphor for property rights with the idea of *relationships*.[48] Social relations approaches assume that people are situated in a complicated network of relationships with others, from relations among strangers, to relations among neighbors, to continuing relations in the market, to intimate relations in the family. Moreover, many of the legal developments of the twentieth century can be described as recognition of obligations that emerge over time out of relationships of interdependence.[49] The relational approach shifts our attention from asking who the owner is to the question of what relationships have been established.[50]

Feminists[51] and critical race theorists have explored the relationship between race, sex and property.[52] Patricia Williams has written eloquently about the social meaning of race and gender and their relation to power and to property law.[53] Keith Aoki has described the thinking that led to the alien land laws that denied property ownership to Japanese immigrants and provided the precursor to internment during World War II.[54] Alice Kessler-Harris and many other scholars have explored the social factors that determine the unequal wages paid to women and men as well as the relation between those factors and the distribution of property and power based on gender.[55]

Critical legal theorists have explored tensions or contradictions within property theory and law and used marginalized doctrines to argue for reform of property rules and institutions.[56] Communitarians and environmentalists emphasize the importance of community life as well as individual rights and argue that individuals have obligations as well as rights.[57] Law and society theorists investigate the "law in practice" rather than the "law on the books" to determine what norms actually govern behavior in the real world with respect to property.[58] Other scholars have used deconstruction, poststructuralism, or cultural theory to explore the unconscious assumptions underlying property law.[59]

---

[47] Jennifer Nedelsky, *Law, Boundaries, and the Bounded Self*, 30 Representations 162, 169 (1990).

[48] *Id.* at 171-184. *See also* Jennifer Nedelsky, *Reconceiving Rights as Relationships*, 1 Rev.Const. Studies/Revue d'études Constitutionelles 1(1993); Joseph William Singer, *Entitlement: The Paradoxes of Property* (2000).

[49] Roberto Mangabeira Unger, *The Critical Legal Studies Movement* 83-84 (1983).

[50] Joseph William Singer, *The Reliance Interest in Property*, 40 Stan L. Rev. 611, 657 (1988).

[51] Martha Albertson Fineman, *The Illusion of Equality: The Rhetoric and Reality of Divorce Reform* (1991); Vicki Schultz, *Life's Work*, 100 Colum. L. Rev. 1881 (2000); Reva B. Siegel, *The Modernization of Marital Status Law: Adjudicating Wives' Rights to Earnings, (1860-1930)*, 82 Geo. L. J. 2127 (1994); Reva B. Siegel, *Home as Work: The First Women's Rights Claim Concerning Wives' Household Labor, 1850-1880*, 103 Yale L. J. 1073, 1077 (1994). Joan Williams, *Unbending Gender: Why Family and Work Conflict and What to Do About It* (2000).

[52] *Critical Race Theory: The Cutting Edge* (Richard Delgado ed. 1995).

[53] Patricia Williams, *Fetal Fictions: An Exploration of Property Archetypes in Racial and Gendered Contexts*, 42 Fla. L. Rev. 81 (1990).

[54] Keith Aoki, *No Right to Own? The Early Twentieth-Century "Alien Land Laws" as a Prelude to Internment*, 40 B.C. L. Rev. 37 (1998).

[55] Alice Kessler-Harris, *A Woman's Wage* (1990).

[56] Joseph William Singer, *Entitlement: The Paradoxes of Property* (2000).

[57] Mary Ann Glendon, *Rights Talk* (1991); Avishai Margalit, *The Decent Society* (1998); Jedediah Purdy, *For Common Things: Irony, Trust, and Commitment in America Today* (1999).

[58] Robert C. Ellickson, *Order without Law: How Neighbors Settle Disputes* (1991).

[59] Jeanne Lorraine Schroeder, *The Vestal and The Fasces: Hegel, Lacan, Property, and the Feminine* (1998).

Sources of Law

Legal rules are promulgated by a wide variety of government bodies in a hierarchical scheme. The major sources of law in that system include the following:

1. *United States Constitution.* The federal Constitution is the fundamental law of the land. It was adopted by state constitutional conventions, whose members were elected by (a small subset of) the people.* Constitutional amendments are generally passed by Congress and ratified by state legislatures. The Constitution determines the structure of the federal government, including the relations among the executive, legislative and judicial branches of the federal government, and the relations between the federal government and the state governments. It also defines the powers of the federal government and limits the powers of both the federal government and the states to protect individual rights, including property rights and other rights such as freedom of speech, freedom from unreasonable searches and seizures, equal protection of the laws, and due process.

2. *Federal statutes.* Legislation is passed by the Congress of the United States and ratified by the president, or passed over the president's veto. Federal statutes address a wide variety of matters relating to property law; examples include the *Fair Housing Act of 1968*, the *Civil Rights Act of 1964*, the Internal Revenue Code, the *Sherman Antitrust Act*, and the *Worker Adjustment and Retraining Notification Act of 1988*.

3. *Administrative regulations.* Congress may pass legislation creating administrative agencies, such as the Environmental Protection Agency, the Equal Employment Opportunity Commission, the Federal Trade Commission, or the Internal Revenue Service; these agencies may have the power to promulgate regulations in a particular field (environmental protection, employment discrimination, or tax law).

4. *State constitutions.* Each state has its own constitution defining the structure of state government and defining certain fundamental individual rights against the state. In some instances, state constitutions grant greater protection to individual rights than does the federal Constitution. For example, a search by the police that is allowed under the fourth amendment to the U.S. Constitution may be prohibited under the New Jersey constitution. Although state constitutions may not grant citizens less protection than provided by the federal Constitution, they may grant their citizens more protection by going further than the U.S. Constitution in limiting the power of state officials.

5. *State statutes.* State statutes are passed by state legislatures with the consent of the governor (or by a supermajority vote over the governor's veto). Many state statutes deal

---

* It is important to note that when the United States Constitution was adopted in 1789, the voting population in the 13 states excluded women, African American men, American Indians, and white men who owned less than a certain amount of property.

with property law matters such as landlord-tenant legislation, recording acts, civil rights statutes, and regulation of family property on divorce.

6. *State administrative regulations.* State legislatures, like the federal Congress, may create administrative agencies that have the power to promulgate regulations in limited fields of law. The Massachusetts legislature, for example, has created a Building Code Commission endowed with the power to promulgate and enforce regulations on building construction and materials to protect the public from unsafe structures.

7. *Common law.* In the absence of any controlling statute or regulation, state courts adjudicate civil disputes by promulgating rules of law. Judicial opinions explain and justify the rules adopted by judges to adjudicate civil disputes. During the first year of law school, most courses focus on common law rules and the process of common law decision making by judges.

8. *City ordinances and town by-laws.* State legislatures delegate to cities and towns the power to promulgate ordinances or by-laws in limited areas of law, including zoning, rent control, schools, traffic, and parking.

Lawyers' Skills

In reading case materials and in preparing for class, you should keep in mind three basic tasks that lawyers perform.

1. *Counseling.* In advising clients, lawyers perform a variety of roles. First, they answer clients' questions about their legal rights. They do so by looking up the law in statutes, regulations and judicial opinions. In so doing, they may or may not find legal rules that specifically address the question they need to answer. In either case, lawyers must predict how the courts would rule on the question if they had the opportunity to do so. This requires lawyers to make educated judgments about how prior case law will be applied to new fact situations. Second, lawyers counsel clients on how to conform their conduct to the dictates of the law and how to achieve their goals in a lawful manner. Third, lawyers draft legal documents for clients, including leases, deeds, purchase and sale agreements, bond documents, and employment contracts. They may also draft statutes for clients that intend to submit them to legislatures for possible consideration. Fourth, lawyers negotiate with other parties or their attorneys to settle disputes or to make deals.

2. *Advocacy.* If a dispute cannot be resolved amicably, one of the parties — called the "plaintiff" — may bring a lawsuit against the other party — called the "defendant" — claiming that the defendant engaged in wrongful conduct that violated the plaintiff's legal rights. To prevail in such a lawsuit, the plaintiff must be able to (a) prove in court by testimony, documentation, or other admissible evidence that the defendant engaged in the wrongful conduct and that the conduct caused the plaintiff's harm, and (b) demonstrate that the defendant's conduct violates a legally protected interest guaranteed to the plaintiff in a way that violates the plaintiff's legal rights. The parties will normally hire attorneys to conduct the lawsuit. Lawyers argue before judges about what the legal rules are governing the dispute. Sometimes the rules in force are clear. Often, however, the rule governing a particular situation is not clear. The rules contain numerous gaps, conflicts and ambiguities, and lawyers are experts in using the open texture of the law to develop plausible competing arguments about alternative possible rules of law to govern the situation.

The attorneys for each side engage in advocacy of alternative possible rules of law, both in written arguments called "briefs" and in oral arguments before judges. In these settings, lawyers attempt to persuade judges to interpret existing rules or to create new legal rules in ways that favor their clients' interests. Lawyers must therefore learn the kinds of arguments judges find persuasive in interpreting and in modernizing the rules in force. Lawyers may also represent clients before legislative committees considering the passage of legislation.

3. *Decision making.* Finally, it is important to remember that the judges who decide cases are also lawyers. Their role is to adjudicate the cases before them by choosing the applicable legal rules to govern the dispute and others like it in the future. Similarly, legislatures promulgate statutes regulating conduct and resolving conflicts among competing interests. It is also important for you as a participant in the legal system to develop your own views about the wisdom and justice of our legal institutions and rules. Legal education teaches us to consider both sides of important contested questions of law before reaching a judgment about the proper outcome of the dispute. This does not mean we should be indifferent to what those outcomes are or that we should not criticize the rules in force. Your ability to argue for and against a position does not mean that you cannot make up your mind or present persuasive arguments to justify the result you reach; it means simply that your judgment about right and wrong should be true to the complexity of your own moral beliefs and that it is important to recognize what is lost, as well as what is gained, by any choice.

Reading Cases

Rules of law. In researching the law, attorneys might (1) find a rule of law that clearly defines the parties' respective rights; (2) find no rule of law directly on point (a gap in the law); (3) find a rule of law that does not clearly answer the question (an ambiguity in an existing rule); or (4) find two or more rules of law that arguably govern the dispute (a conflict among possibly applicable rules). Moreover, attorneys might find rules of law applying to situations that are arguably analogous to the case at hand. Lawyers find and exploit the gaps, conflicts and ambiguities in the law to attempt to define the law in ways that benefit their clients.

In preparing for class, you should try to identify the rule of law — the general principle — each side in the case would like the court to promulgate. Ask yourself: What rule of law did the plaintiff urge the court to adopt? What rule of law did the defendant urge the court to adopt?

This is harder than it seems. Sometimes the parties' proposed rules of law are described in the judicial opinion, sometimes not. In either event, you must ask whether it would be wise to argue for a broad rule of law or a narrow one. For example, one might argue for a broad, rather vague, rule of law: "Non-owners are privileged to enter property when their activity will further a significant public policy." Or one might argue for a narrow rule of law, tied very closely to the facts of the case: "Lawyers and physicians working for agencies funded by the federal government may enter property to give professional assistance to migrant farmworkers." Similarly, an owner might argue for a broad rule of law granting owners the right to exclude non-owners under all circumstances, or she might argue for a narrower rule granting owners the right to exclude non-owners only if the owner can show just cause. It is up to you to identify the different ways each side might have framed its proposed rules of law.

Arguments

After identifying possible rules of law for each side, you should ask what arguments the parties might have given to justify adopting their proposed rules, as well as what arguments they could have given against the rule proposed by the other side. These arguments should include considerations about the fairness of the proposed rules to the parties: Which rule better protects individual rights? You should also consider the social consequences of the competing rules: Which rule better promotes the general welfare?

Briefing Cases

In preparing for class, at least at the beginning, you should brief your cases. This means writing an outline of the important elements of the decision. These elements include the following.

1. *Facts.* Who did what to whom? What is the relationship between the parties? What is the wrongful conduct the plaintiff claims the defendant engaged in, and how did it harm the plaintiff? What is the dispute between the parties about?

2. *Procedural history.* How did the courts below rule on the case? First, how did the trial court resolve the matter? Who won, and why? Did the party who lost in the trial court appeal an adverse ruling of law to an intermediate appellate court? If so, how did the appellate court rule, and why? Did one of the parties appeal the result in the appellate court to the state supreme court? What court issued the opinion you are reading — the state supreme court or some lower court? (Note that because cases in this and other casebooks have been edited, some portion of the procedural history may be omitted from the text reprinted in the book.)

3. *Relief sought and judgment.* What relief did the plaintiff seek? Did she ask for (a) a declaration of her rights (a declaratory judgment); (b) an injunction ordering the defendant to act or not to act in certain ways; or (c) damages to compensate the plaintiff for the harm?

What was the judgment of the court issuing the opinion you are reading? Did it grant a declaratory judgment, issue an injunction, or order the payment of damages? Did it remand the case to a lower court for further proceedings, such as a new trial?

4. *Legal question, or rule choice.* What is the legal question or questions the court resolved? To answer this, you should determine what rule of law the plaintiff favored and what rule of law the defendant favored. What different legal rules did the court consider? What rules should it have considered? What rule of law would you propose if you were the plaintiff's attorney? The defendant's attorney?

5. *Arguments and counterarguments.* Place yourself in the position of the plaintiff's lawyer. What arguments would you give to persuade the court to adopt the rule of law favored by your client, and what arguments can you give against the rule of law favored by the defendant? Next, place yourself in the position of the defendant's lawyer. What arguments would you give to persuade the court to adopt the rule of law favored by your client, and what arguments can you give against the rule of law favored by the plaintiff?

a. *Precedential arguments.* These arguments appeal to existing rules of law. You may argue that an ambiguous rule of law — such as a rule creating a reasonableness standard of conduct — entitles your client to win. You may also argue that one of two conflicting rules of law governs the fact situation in your case or that a rule of law applies by analogy. To do either of these things, you must argue that a prior case establishes a principle of law that governs a situation that is identical — or sufficiently similar — to the case at hand such that the policies or principles that underlie and justify the earlier decision are applicable to the current case. Under these circumstances, you can argue that the prior case establishes a precedent that applies to your case. The lawyer on the other side will argue that the case at hand is different in important ways from the prior case and that because of those differences, the policies and principles underlying the earlier case do not apply to the case at hand. When the rule of law in the prior case does not apply to the case at hand, we say the lawyer has distinguished the precedent. What rules have you learned that can be applied either directly or by analogy to govern this case?

b. *Statutory interpretation.* The rights of the parties may be governed by a federal or state statute that regulates their conduct. Judges must interpret ambiguities in those statutes by reference to (1) the language of the statute; and (2) the legislative intent behind the statute, which may be elucidated by reference to the policies and purposes the legislation was intended to serve. How can you persuade the judge that your proposed interpretation of the statutory language or purposes best accords with the intent of the legislature? What counterarguments will the attorney on the other side make to answer your claims?

c. *Policy arguments.* These arguments appeal to a variety of considerations, including (1) fairness, individual and group rights, and justice in social relationships; and (2) the social consequences of alternative rules such that the choice of rules promotes social utility, efficiency, or the general welfare. What reasons can you give to persuade the judge that your proposed rule promotes both justice and social welfare? What counterarguments will the attorney on the other side make to answer your claims?

6. *Holding.* What rule of law did the court adopt, and how did it apply to the case? In identifying the holding of the case, it is important to consider several possibilities. Try to describe the rule of law in as broad a fashion as possible by (a) identifying a general category or a broad range of situations to which the rule would apply, and/or (b) appealing to general principles such as foreseeability, reasonableness, or promotion of alienability. Then try to describe the rule of law in as narrow a fashion as possible so as to limit the application of the rule to a narrow range of circumstances by (a) identifying the specific facts of the case as necessary to application of the rule, and/or

(b) appealing to specific, rather than general, principles. For example, a possible broad holding of a case is that owners have an absolute right to exclude non-owners from their property unless the owner's act of exclusion violates public policy. An alternative narrow holding would be that owners of property open to the general public for business purposes have a right to exclude non-owners from their property unless those non-owners are engaging in expressive political activity that does not interfere with the operation of the business.

7. *Reasoning of the court and criticism of that reasoning.* What reasons did the court give for deciding the case the way it did? What problems can you find with the court's reasoning? Do you agree or disagree?

Acknowledgments

This book would not have been possible without the substantial help, suggestions, encouragement, and support of many people. I would like especially to thank Duncan Kennedy, whose imprint is evident throughout the book. He is responsible for some of the large structural components of the book, including the idea of organizing materials around the concept of consumer protection in the market for shelter, and many details, such as the inclusion of building code materials in the land use regulation section. He also developed the idea of systematizing legal arguments as a device for legal education. His personal, moral and intellectual support over the years has been invaluable to me.

Jeremy Paul contributed in fundamental ways to the ideas about property and law school teaching represented in this book. The takings materials especially are shaped by his perspective. I want to thank Jack Beermann for getting me to write this book. His encouragement and intellectual support over the years buoyed me tremendously. Elizabeth V. Spelman has been essential in teaching me to "think about thinking" and to explore gender, race, and class issues in social relations. I would like also to thank Williamson Chang and Robert A. Williams, Jr., for prompting my interest in the legal relations between the United States and American Indian nations and between the United States and native Alaskans and native Hawaiians. Their personal insights and scholarly contributions on the property rights of Native American peoples contributed significantly to my own intellectual development and to various aspects of this book.

Various colleagues and friends who have provided detailed suggestions include Kathy Abrams, Greg Alexander, Keith Aoki, David Barron, Jack Beermann, Robert Brauneis, Betsy Clark, Alan Feld, Tamar Frankel, James Holmes, Ian Haney López, Martha Mahoney, Allan Macurdy, Robert Merges, Ron Meyer, Frank Michelman, Nell Jessup Newton, Eduardo Peñalver, john powell, John Rattigan, Aviam Soifer, Debra Pogrund Stark, Nomi Stoltzenberg, Gerald Torres, Robert Tuttle, André van der Walt, Johan van der Walt, and Kelly Weisberg.

Though they may not know it, a number of colleagues have especially influenced my understanding of property, including, but not limited to, Adeno Addis, Bob Anderson, Derrick Bell, Bethany Berger, James Boyle, Victor Brudney, Clark Byse, William W. Fisher III, William Forbath, Jerry Frug, Mary Joe Frug, Mary Ann Glendon, Carole Goldberg, Robert Gordon, Neil Gotanda, Kent Greenfield, Morton Horwitz, Karl Klare, John LaVelle, Charles Lawrence, Mari Matsuda, Gary Minda, Martha Minow, Nell Newton, Frances Olsen, Jennifer Nedelsky, Margaret Jane Radin, Carol Rose, Judy Royster, Katherine Stone, Rennard Strickland, Cass Sunstein, Lucie White, and Patricia Williams. Any failings in this book cannot be attributed to anyone in this disparate group.

The library reference staffs at Boston University School of Law and Harvard Law School made my life wonderfully easy and contributed enormously to the research necessary to this project. Special thanks go to Daniel Freehling, Marlene Alderman, Kim Dulin, Cynthia Murphy, Kristin Cheney, Jon Fernald, Naomi Ronen, and Janet Katz.

William Kaleva, Carol Igoe, Holly Escott, and Patricia Fazzone provided cheerful and dedicated administrative assistance, at various times performing feats I would have thought impossible for human beings.

I would like to thank Deans Elena Kagan and Robert Clark of Harvard Law School and Dean Ronald Cass of the Boston University School of Law for financial support for research. Many aspects of the book would have been less developed were it not for a slew of research assistants who labored over the years, including David Bunis, Jeffrey Engelsman, Joel Freedman, Steven Gould, Margaret Guzman, Philander Huynh, Gregory Ikonen, Vikas Khanna, Laura Kershner, Garrett Moritz, Edward Tumavicus, Loren Washburn, David Wiseman, Ben Wizner, and Alithea Zymaris.

I would like also to thank the staff at Aspen for their invaluable help in preparing and editing this book. I am also grateful to the anonymous reviewers whose suggestions have been incorporated into the final product. I continue to be amazed by the wonders of WESTLAW and LEXIS. The availability of computer research techniques and the ability to download cases and statutes shortened by years the time needed to write this book.

Lila Singer has taught me about teaching and social action. Max Singer has inspired me with his work on low-income housing and hunger. I want to thank them for my education and for their example of how to live — my greatest inheritance. Robert Singer and Anne Rayman have both taught me about caretaking, and Adam and Rachel have shown me how to take care of those who take care of you. Gale Singer Adland and Peter Adland have taught me about making a home, and Ari, Jesse, and Naomi have shown me how to grow up.

Newton Minow has taught me to look at the real world and to figure out what works so that valuable resources are not wasted. Josephine Minow has taught me about attentiveness to others, involvement in causes, and how to get things done. Nell Minow and David Apatoff have taught me about the government of business and the business of government, and Benjamin and Rachel have shown me how to get totally and fanatically engrossed in something. Mary Minow and James Robenolt have taught me about getting information and how to use it once I have gotten it.

I would like also to thank the late Justice Morris Pashman (ז״ל) of the Supreme Court of New Jersey for teaching me about the art of judging. It is impossible to define exactly what good judgment entails, but it can be understood, at least partly, through example. Justice Pashman's sensitivity to the perspectives of each litigant epitomizes, for me, the preconditions for justice. When I try to imagine how a good judge would react to a particular problem, I turn to his example.

I wish I could show this book to Marcel Pallais Checa (ז״ל). Marcel taught me what it meant to be a committed intellectual and how to tie one's spiritual life to one's political commitments. He taught me that a philosopher could also be an economist. His assassination reminds me of both the value and the limits of the rule of law.

On May 31, 1992, Mira Judith Minow Singer made her astonishing entry into this world, voicing strong opinions, questioning authority, and generally sticking up for herself. She has increased my respect and admiration for parents generally and made me wonder how single parents manage. Her presence has reminded me that one out of every five children in the United States lives below the poverty line, and that almost half of all African-American children do so. I wonder how we could take good care of her if we did not have a home. Mira has caused me to ponder anew the fact that we reward only some kinds of work with property while other kinds are not so rewarded, despite their social value, and the resultant inequalities that go along with such distinctions.

Special Acknowledgments for the Fourth Edition

I would like to especially thank those who contributed to various aspects of this fourth edition through conversations, ideas, and suggestions, including David Barron, Louise Halper, Ian Haney López, Eduardo Peñalver, Debra Pogrund Stark, and Laura Underkuffler. Outstanding research assistance was provided by Philander Huynh, Vikas Khanna, and Alithea Zymaris. Patricia Fazzone provided administrative assistance and continues to remind me about the connections between professional and spiritual work.

Copyright Permissions

I would like to thank the following authors and publishers for kindly granting permission to reproduce excerpts of, or illustrations from, the following material.

First, I would like to thank Rutgers Law Review for allowing me to reprint an excerpt from Joseph William Singer, *Catcher in the Rye Jurisprudence*, 35 Rutgers L. Rev. 275 (1983). Excerpts also appear from articles previously published in the Wisconsin Law Review and the Stanford Law Review, Joseph William Singer, *The Legal Rights Debate in Analytical Jurisprudence from Bentham to Hohfeld*, 1982 Wis. L. Rev. 975.

Cases were downloaded from WESTLAW © West 2005 and LEXIS © LexisNexis 2005.

Allen, Anita, *Surrogacy, Slavery, and the Ownership of Life*, 13 Harv. J.L. & Pub. Pol'y 139 (1990). Reprinted with permission of the Harvard Journal of Law & Public Policy.

American Law Institute, Excerpts from *Restatement (Second) of Torts; Restatement (Second) of Property (Landlord and Tenant); Restatement (Third) of Property (Servitudes)*. Reprinted by permission of the American Law Institute.

Black Hills photograph, provided courtesy of Richard Erdoes.

Coase, R. H., *The Problem of Social Cost*, 3 J.L. & Econ. 1 (1960). Copyright © 1960 by The University of Chicago. All rights reserved. Reprinted with permission of R. H. Coase, The Journal of Law & Economics and The University of Chicago.

Dalton, Clare, *An Essay in the Deconstruction of Contract Doctrine*, 94 Yale L.J. 997 (1985). Reprinted by permission of The Yale Law Journal Company, and William S. Hein & Co., Inc.

Engler, Russell, and Craig S. Bloomgarden, *Summary Process Actions in the Boston Housing Court: An Empirical Study and Recommendations for Reform* (May 20, 1983). Reprinted by permission of Russell Engler and Craig S. Bloomgarden.

Franklin, John Hope, *Race and History: Selected Essays 1938-1988* (1989). First published in The University of Chicago Magazine. Copyright © 1975 by The University of Chicago Magazine. Reprinted by permission.

Frug, Mary Joe, *Re-Reading Contracts: A Feminist Analysis of a Contracts Casebook*, 34 Am. U. L. Rev. 1065 (1985). Reprinted by permission of Gerry Frug and The American University Law Review.

Greater Boston Real Estate Board, standard form for Offer to Purchase. Copyright © 2005 Greater Boston Real Estate Board. This form has been made available through the courtesy of the Greater Boston Real Estate Board and is protected by the copyright laws.

Greater Boston Real Estate Board, standard form for Purchase and Sale Agreement. Copyright © 2005 Greater Boston Real Estate Board. Same as above.

Hale, Robert, *Bargaining, Duress, and Economic Liberty*, 43 Colum. L. Rev. 603 (1943). Reprinted by permission.

Hillerman, Tony, *Talking God* 1-6 (1989). Copyright © 1989 by Tony Hillerman. Reprinted by permission of HarperCollins Publishers, Inc.

Hurst, J. Willard, *Law and the Conditions of Freedom in the Nineteenth-Century United States* (1956). Reprinted by permission of The University of Wisconsin Press.

Kelman, Mark, *Consumption Theory, Production Theory, and Ideology in the Coase Theorem*, 52 S. Cal. L. Rev. 669 (1979). Reprinted by permission of the Southern California Law Review.

Kennedy, Duncan, *Form and Substance in Private Law Adjudication*, 89 Harv. L. Rev. 1687 (1976). Reprinted by permission of Duncan Kennedy and Harvard Law Review.

Langbein, John, *The Twentieth-Century Revolution in Family Wealth Transmission*, 86 Mich. L. Rev. 722 (1988). Reprinted by permission of John Langbein and the Michigan Law Review.

Litwack, Leon, *Been in the Storm So Long: The Aftermath of Slavery* (1980). Copyright © 1979 by Leon S. Litwack. Reprinted by permission of Alfred A. Knopf, Inc., a division of Random House, Inc.

Llewellyn, Karl, *The Bramble Bush* (1960 ed.) (first published 1930). Reprinted by permission of Oceana Publications Inc.

Llewellyn, Karl, *The Common Law Tradition: Deciding Appeals* (1960). Reprinted by permission of Little, Brown and Company.

Millon, David, *Redefining Corporate Law*, 24 Ind. L. Rev. 223 (1991). Reprinted by permission of the Trustees of Indiana University.

Nash, Diane, photograph, provided courtesy of The Tennessean.

Olsen, Frances, *The Family and the Market: A Study of Ideology and Legal Reform*, 96 Harv. L. Rev. 1497 (1983). Reprinted by permission of Frances Olsen and Harvard Law Review.

Prucha, Francis Paul, *The Great Father: The United States Government and the American Indians*, vol. 2 (1984). Copyright © 1984 by the University of Nebraska Press. Reprinted by permission.

Schwartz, Alan, *Justice and the Law of Contracts: A Case for the Traditional Approach*, 9 Harv. J.L. & Pub. Pol'y 1 (1986). Reprinted by permission of the Harvard Journal of Law & Public Policy.

Shapiro, David, Courts, *Legislatures and Paternalism*, 74 Va. L. Rev. 519 (1988). Reprinted by permission of David Shapiro, the Virginia Law Review Association, and William S. Hein & Co., Inc.

Shelley family, photograph by George Harris, provided courtesy of Black Star Agency.

Simpson, A. W. B., A History of the Land Law (2d ed. 1986). Reprinted by permission of Oxford University Press.

Soifer, Aviam, *Status, Contract, and Promises Unkept*, 90 Yale L.J. 1916 (1987). Reprinted by permission of Aviam Soifer, The Yale Law Journal Company, and William S. Hein & Co., Inc.

Vandevelde, Kenneth, *The New Property of the Nineteenth Century: The Development of the Modern Concept of Property,* 29 Buff. L. Rev. 325 (1990). Reprinted by permission of Buffalo Law Review.

Waldron, Jeremy, *Homelessness and the Issue of Freedom,* 39 UCLA L. Rev. 295 (1991). Copyright © 1991 by The Regents of the University of California. All rights reserved. Reprinted by permission of Jeremy Waldron, UCLA Law Review, and William S. Hein & Co., Inc.

Williams, Patricia J., *Spirit-Murdering the Messenger: The Discourse of Fingerpointing as the Law's Response to Racism,* 42 U. Miami L. Rev. 127 (1987). Reprinted by permission of the University of Miami Law Review.

Williams, Walter E., *The Intelligent Bayesian,* in *Symposium, The Jeweler's Dilemma,* The New Republic, Nov. 10, 1986, at 18. Copyright © 1986 by The New Republic, Inc. Reprinted by permission.

Youngstown, Ohio, U.S. Steel Mill demolition photograph, courtesy of Bettman/CORBIS.

This book is doubly (in both senses of the word) dedicated to Martha Minow and Mary Joe Frug (ל״ז).

Mary Joe Frug's scholarship on gender issues in contracts casebooks heavily influenced both the content and the structure of this book. From her I learned about hidden messages — often unintended — and how to ask who was left out of a seemingly comprehensive treatment of a subject. Her work encouraged me to ask whether there were entitlements important to women that are not traditionally included in introductory property courses. Addressing this question prompted me to include materials in this casebook on public accommodations statutes applicable to "private" clubs that discriminate against women, child support, AFDC, domestic violence restraining-order statutes, unemployment benefits for women who leave work to take care of children or to be with a loved one, enforceability of restraints on marriage, statutes prohibiting discrimination on the basis of marital status, statutes prohibiting discrimination against families with children, the relationship between sex and race discrimination, statutes prohibiting discrimination on the basis of sexual orientation, equitable distribution, community property, property rights of unmarried couples, and nontraditional family relationships. Her work also encouraged me to look for cases that included women as central actors, including opinions written by female judges and cases involving women in a variety of roles, as both landlords and tenants, business executives and housekeepers, victims and villains.

Like dozens of other people, I had set up a date to talk with Mary Joe. I hoped to get further advice from her about this casebook. Our conversation setting up our date took place several days before her death. I have been playing out the conversation we might have had ever since. I hope that some of her appears in this book.

This book is dedicated also to Martha Minow. Martha has taught me about multiplicity — the properties of family and the families of property — and the way it all looks from the differing perspectives of different people in their different situations. She has taught me to ask what difference an argument or practice makes to real people in real relationships in the real world. In her hands, abstract concepts become relations among people; real estate is not a lifeless thing, but a *setting* in which people have families, engage in work and commerce, make a home. It is those relationships that matter.

Imagine a walled city bursting at its seams; with too many people, the constraints of the wall cause division among the inhabitants and the possibility of oppression — the powerful are inclined to exclude the weak. Where others see constraints, scarcity, and frustration, Martha thinks about how to break the wall down or how to create openings in it; if these things cannot be done — for now — she imagines how relationships among people in the city might be restructured so that this artificial constraint becomes understood as everyone's problem and not just the problem of minority groups. She embodies possibility; when everything seems hopeless, she opens doors to the land of change. In ways too many to count, to me and to many other people, she has made all the difference.

Joseph William Singer
Cambridge, Massachusetts
5766/2006

Property Law

I

Access to Property

1

Competing Claims to Original Acquisition of Property

§1.1 Conquest

§1.1.1 PROPERTY RIGHTS DERIVED FROM COMPETING SOVEREIGNS

In the mid-fifteenth century, an estimated 5 to 10 million native inhabitants occupied the land mass that is now the United States. By a process of cultural extermination and diseases such as measles and small pox, the population of American Indians shrank to about 200,000 by 1910. Louise Erdrich notes that this "is proportionately as if the population of the United States were to decrease from its present level to the population of Cleveland." Louise Erdrich, *Where I Ought to Be: A Writer's Sense of Place*, N.Y. Times Book Rev., July 28, 1985, at 1, 23. Milner Ball notes that the "reduction of the Native American population caused by the coming of Europeans has been more gradual than a nuclear holocaust but proportionately equivalent to one." Milner Ball, *Constitution, Court, Indian Tribes*, 1987 Am. B. Found. Res. J. 1, 3.

The invasion of North America by European nations began a long process of struggle over sovereignty and property rights, both among the European powers and between those powers and the numerous American Indian nations. The process by which property rights in land were obtained from native nations was complicated. Representatives of colonial powers often declared themselves to be the sovereign rulers of vast stretches of land inhabited by thousands of American Indians. The governments of France, Spain, and England then induced or forced Indian nations to transfer sovereignty over specific areas of land to them. The miscommunication and cultural misunderstanding in these transactions was enormous. What the colonists understood as a transfer of property and sovereignty was often understood by Indians as a set of temporary accommodations of land use. William Cronon, *Changes in the Land* (1983). In colonial theory, all land was supposed to devolve to the imperial government, which then determined how the land was to be distributed. In practice, colonial governments and individual groups of colonists made separate arrangements with individual tribes.

3

The course of events naturally brought intense conflicts over land rights, both between American Indian nations and settlers and among the settlers themselves.

The case of *Johnson v. M'Intosh*, 21 U.S. (8 Wheat.) 543 (1823), considered the process by which the property and sovereignty of American Indian nations was transferred, first to the colonial powers of England, France, and Spain, and then to the United States. After the lands of American Indian nations were obtained by the United States, the federal government distributed the public lands to individual claimants. Sometimes the federal government ratified deals made by individuals with Indian nations; sometimes it nullified them. In either case, ultimate title was thought to transfer from American Indian nations to the colonial powers whose rights were inherited by the United States upon independence. The United States then distributed the public lands to individual claimants. Individuals who derived their titles by transfer from the earlier colonial powers were protected in their possession. In this way, all land in the United States held by non-Indians theoretically can be traced to title ultimately derived from the United States government or a prior colonial power, which in turn obtained title by conquest, coercion, voluntary cession, or judicial fiat from an American Indian nation.[1]

Johnson v. M'Intosh involved a conflict between competing non-Indian claimants to land. The first group claimed to have obtained title directly from the Illinois and Piankeshaw Indians. The second group was later granted title by the U.S. government. In adjudicating this dispute, the Supreme Court had the unenviable task of justifying the process by which American Indian nations were robbed of their ancestral lands. At the same time, Chief Justice John Marshall's opinion provided the basis for substantial legal protection of Indian possessions. How well did the Chief Justice do in attempting to reconcile the demands of justice and power?

JOHNSON v. M'INTOSH
21 U.S. 543 (1823)

This was an action of ejectment for lands in the State and District of Illinois, claimed by the plaintiffs under a purchase and conveyance from the Piankeshaw Indians, and by the defendant, under a grant from the United States. . . . The case stated set out the following facts:

1st. That on the 23d of May, 1609, James I., King of England, by his letters patent of that date, under the great seal of England, did erect, form, and establish Robert, Earl of Salisbury, and others, his associates, . . . and their successors, into a body corporate and politic, by the name and style of "The Treasurer and Company of Adventurers and Planters of the City of London, for the first Colony in Virginia," with perpetual succession . . . and did give, grant, and confirm unto this company, and their successors, . . ." All the lands, countries, and territories, situate, lying, and being in that part of North America called Virginia, from the point of land called Cape or Point Comfort, all along the seacoast to the northward two hundred miles; and from the said Cape or Point Comfort, all along the seacoast to the southward, two hundred miles; and all that space and circuit of land lying from the seacoast of the precinct aforesaid, up into the land throughout from the sea, west and northwest; . . ."

---

1. For an excellent history of the relations between American Indian nations and the United States, *see* Francis Paul Prucha, *The Great Father* (1984).

3d. That at the time of granting these letters patent, and of the discovery of the continent of North America by the Europeans, and during the whole intermediate time, the whole of the territory, in the letters patent described, except a small district on James River, where a settlement of Europeans had previously been made, was held, occupied, and possessed, in full sovereignty, by various independent tribes or nations of Indians, who were the sovereigns of their respective portions of the territory, and the absolute owners and proprietors of the soil; and who neither acknowledged nor owed any allegiance or obedience to any European sovereign or state whatever: and that in making settlements within this territory, and in all the other parts of North America, where settlements were made, under the authority of the English government, or by its subjects, the right of soil was previously obtained by purchase or conquest, from the particular Indian tribe or nation by which the soil was claimed and held; or the consent of such tribe or nation was secured.

4th. That in the year 1624, this corporation was dissolved by due course of law, and all its powers, together with its rights of soil and jurisdiction, under the letters patent in question, were revested in the crown of England; whereupon the colony became a royal government, with the same territorial limits and extent which had been established by the letters patent, and so continued until it became a free and independent State; except so far as its limits and extent were altered and curtailed by the treaty of February 10th, 1763, between Great Britain and France, and by the letters patent granted by the King of England, for establishing the colonies of Carolina, Maryland, and Pennsylvania.

5th. That some time previous to the year 1756, the French government, laying a claim to the country west of the Allegheny or Appalachian mountains, on the Ohio and Mississippi rivers, and their branches, took possession of certain parts of it, with the consent of the several tribes or nations of Indians possessing and owning them; . . . and that the government of Great Britain, after complaining of these establishments as encroachments, and remonstrating against them, at length, in the year 1756, took up arms to resist and repel them; which produced a war between those two nations, . . . and that on the 10th of February, 1763, this war was terminated by a definitive treaty of peace between Great Britain and France, and their allies, by which it was stipulated and agreed, that the river Mississippi, from its source to the Iberville, should for ever after form the boundary between the dominions of Great Britain and those of France, in that part of North America, and between their respective allies there. . . .

10th. That on the 7th of October, 1763, the King of Great Britain made and published a proclamation, [reserving for the Indians] the countries ceded to Great Britain by that treaty, [and prohibiting all British subjects to purchase or settle on any of those lands]. . . .

12th. That on the 5th of July, 1773, certain chiefs of the Illinois Indians, then jointly representing, acting for, and being duly authorized by that tribe . . . did, by their deed poll, duly executed and delivered, . . . for and on behalf of the said Illinois nation of Indians, . . . for a good and valuable consideration in the said deed stated, grant, bargain, sell, alien, lease, enfeoff, and confirm, to . . . William Murray [and others], their heirs and assigns for ever, in severalty, or to George the Third, then King of Great Britain and Ireland, his heirs and successors, for the use, benefit, and behoof of the grantees, their heirs and assigns, in severalty, by whichever of those tenures they might most legally hold, all those two several tracts or parcels of land, situated, lying, and being within the limits of Virginia, on the east of the Mississippi, northwest of the Ohio, and west of the Great Miami. . . .

13th. That the consideration in this deed expressed, was of the value of 24,000 dollars, current money of the United States, and upwards, and was paid and delivered, at the time of the execution of the deed, by William Murray, one of the grantees, in behalf of himself and the other grantees, to the Illinois Indians, who freely accepted it, and divided it among themselves. . . .

15th. That on the 18th of October, 1775, Tabac, and certain other Indians, all being chiefs of the Piankeshaws, and jointly representing, acting for, and duly authorized by that nation, . . . did, by their deed poll, duly executed, . . . for good and valuable consideration . . . grant, bargain, sell, alien, enfeoff, release, ratify, and confirm to . . . Louis Viviat, and [others], their heirs and assigns, equally to be divided, or to George III, then king of Great Britain and Ireland, his heirs and successors, for the use, benefit, and behoof of all the above mentioned grantees, their heirs and assigns, in severalty, by which ever of those tenures they might most legally hold, all those two several tracts of land, in the deed particularly described, situate, lying, and being northwest of the Ohio, east of the Mississippi, and west of the Great Miami, within the limits of Virginia, and on both sides of the Ouabache, otherwise called the Wabash. . . .

16th. That the consideration in this deed expressed, was of the value of 31,000 dollars, current money of the United States, and upwards, and was paid and delivered at the time of the execution of the deed, by the grantee, Louis Viviat, in behalf of himself and the other grantees, to the Piankeshaw Indians, who freely accepted it, and divided it among themselves. . . .

17th. That on the 6th of May, 1776, the colony of Virginia threw off its dependence on the crown and government of Great Britain, and declared itself an independent State and government. . . .

18th. That on the 5th of October, 1778, the General Assembly of Virginia . . . did, by an act of Assembly of that date, entitled, "An act for establishing the county of Illinois, and for the more effectual protection and defence thereof," erect that country, with certain other portions of territory within the limits of the State, and northwest of the Ohio, into a county, by the name of the county of Illinois.

19th. That on the 20th of December, 1783, the State of Virginia, by an act of Assembly of that date, authorized their Delegates in the Congress of the United States, or such of them, to the number of three at least, as should be assembled in Congress, on behalf of the State, and by proper deeds or instruments in writing under their hands and seals, to convey, transfer, assign, and make over to the United States, in Congress assembled, for the benefit of the said States, all right, title, and claim, as well of soil as jurisdiction, which Virginia had to the territory or tract of country within her limits, as defined and prescribed by the letters patent of May 23d, 1609, and lying to the northwest of the Ohio; subject to certain limitations and conditions in the act prescribed and specified; and that on the 1st of March, 1784, Thomas Jefferson, Samuel Hardy, Arthur Lee, and James Monroe, then being four of the Delegates of Virginia to the Congress of the United States, did, by their deed poll, under their hands and seals, in pursuance and execution of the authority to them given by this act of Assembly, convey, transfer, assign, and make over to the United States, in Congress assembled, for the benefit of the said States, all right, title, and claim, as well of soil as jurisdiction, which that State had to the territory northwest of the Ohio, with the reservations, limitations, and conditions, in the act of Assembly prescribed; which cession the United States accepted.

20th. That on the twentieth day of July, in the year of our Lord one thousand eight hundred and eighteen, the United States, by their officers duly authorized for that purpose, did sell, grant, and convey to the defendant in this action, William M'Intosh, all those several tracts or parcels of land, containing 11,560 acres, and butted, bounded, and described, as will fully appear in and by the patent for the said lands, duly executed, which was set out at length.

21st. That the lands described and granted in and by this patent, are situated within the State of Illinois, and are contained within the lines of the last, or second of the two tracts, described and purporting to be granted and conveyed to Louis Viviat and others, by the deed of October 18th, 1775; and that William M'Intosh, the defendant, entered upon these lands under, and by virtue of his patent, and became possessed thereof before the institution of this suit.

22d. That Thomas Johnson, one of the grantees, in and under the deed of October 18th, 1775, departed this life on or about the 1st day of October, 1819, seised of all his undivided part or share of, and in the two several tracts of land, described and purporting to be granted and conveyed to him and others by that deed, having first duly made and published his last will and testament in writing, attested by three credible witnesses, which he left in full force, and by which he devised all his undivided share and part of those two tracts of land, to his son, Joshua Johnson, and his heirs, and his grandson, Thomas J. Graham, and his heirs, the lessors of the plaintiff in this action, as tenants in common.

23d. That Joshua Johnson, and Thomas J. Graham, the devisees, entered into the two tracts of land last above mentioned, under and by virtue of the will, and became thereof seised as the law requires. . . .

24th. And that neither William Murray, nor any other of the grantees under the deed of July the 5th, 1773, nor Louis Viviat, nor any other of the grantees under the deed of October the [18th,] 1775, nor any person for them, or any of them, ever obtained, or had the actual possession, under and by virtue of those deeds, or either of them, of any part of the lands in them, or either of them, described and purporting to be granted, but were prevented by the war of the American revolution, which soon after commenced, and by the disputes and troubles which preceded it, from obtaining such possession; and that since the termination of the war, and before it, they have repeatedly, and at various times, from the year 1781, till the year 1816, petitioned the Congress of the United States to acknowledge and confirm their title to those lands, under the purchases and deeds in question, but without success. . . .

On the part of the plaintiffs, it was contended,

1. That . . . the Piankeshaw Indians were the owners of the lands in dispute, at the time of executing the deed of October 10th, 1775, and had power to sell. But as the United States had [later] purchased the same lands of the same Indians, both parties claim from the same source. . . . [The Indian] title by occupancy is to be respected, as much as that of an individual, obtained by the same right, in a civilized state. The circumstance, that the members of the society held in common, did not affect the strength of their title by occupancy. . . . In short, all, or nearly all, the lands in the United States, is holden under purchases from the Indian nations; and the only question in this case must be, whether it be competent to individuals to make such purchases, or whether that be the exclusive prerogative of government.

2. That the British king's proclamation of October 7th, 1763, could not affect this right of the Indians to sell; because they were not British subjects, nor in any manner bound by the authority of the British government, legislative or executive. And, because, even admitting them to be British subjects, absolutely, or sub modo, they were still proprietors of the soil, and could not be devested of their rights of property,

or any of its incidents, by a mere act of the executive government, such as this proclamation.

3. That the proclamation of 1763 could not restrain the purchasers under these deeds from purchasing. . . . [T]he establishment of a government establishes a system of laws, and excludes the power of legislating by proclamation. The proclamation could not have the force of law within the chartered limits of Virginia. A proclamation, that no person should purchase land in England or Canada, would be clearly void.

4. That the act of Assembly of Virginia, passed in May, 1779, cannot affect the right of the plaintiffs, and others claiming under these deeds; because, on general principles, and by the constitution of Virginia, the legislature was not competent to take away private, vested rights, or appropriate private property to public use, under the circumstances of this case. . . .

On the part of the defendants, it was insisted, that the uniform understanding and practice of European nations, and the settled law, as laid down by the tribunals of civilized states, denied the right of the Indians to be considered as independent communities, having a permanent property in the soil, capable of alienation to private individuals. They remain in a state of nature, and have never been admitted into the general society of nations. . . . Even if it should be admitted that the Indians were originally an independent people, they have ceased to be so. A nation that has passed under the dominion of another, is no longer a sovereign state. The same treaties and negotiations, before referred to, show their dependent condition. Or, if it be admitted that they are now independent and foreign states, the title of the plaintiffs would still be invalid: as grantees from the Indians, they must take according to their laws of property, and as Indian subjects. The law of every dominion affects all persons and property situate within it; and the Indians never had any idea of individual property in lands. It cannot be said that the lands conveyed were disjoined from their dominion; because the grantees could not take the sovereignty and eminent domain to themselves.

. . . By the law of nature, [American Indians] had not acquired a fixed property capable of being transferred. The measure of property acquired by occupancy is determined, according to the law of nature, by the extent of men's wants, and their capacity of using it to supply them. It is a violation of the rights of others to exclude them from the use of what we do not want, and they have an occasion for. Upon this principle the North American Indians could have acquired no proprietary interest in the vast tracts of territory which they wandered over; and their right to the lands on which they hunted, could not be considered as superior to that which is acquired to the sea by fishing in it. The use in the one case, as well as the other, is not exclusive. According to every theory of property, the Indians had no individual rights to land; nor had they any collectively, or in their national capacity; for the lands occupied by each tribe were not used by them in such a manner as to prevent their being appropriated by a people of cultivators. All the proprietary rights of civilized nations on this continent are founded on this principle. . . .

Mr. Chief Justice JOHN MARSHALL delivered the opinion of the Court.

The plaintiffs in this cause claim the land, in their declaration mentioned, under two grants, purporting to be made, the first in 1773, and the last in 1775, by the chiefs of certain Indian tribes, constituting the Illinois and the Piankeshaw nations; and the question is, whether this title can be recognized in the Courts of the United States?

The facts, as stated in the case agreed, show the authority of the chiefs who executed this conveyance, so far as it could be given by their own people; and likewise show, that the particular tribes for whom these chiefs acted were in rightful possession of the land they sold. The inquiry, therefore, is, in a great measure, confined to the power of Indians to give, and of private individuals to receive, a title which can be sustained in the Courts of this country.

As the right of society, to prescribe those rules by which property may be acquired and preserved is not, and cannot be drawn into question; as the title to lands, especially, is and must be admitted to depend entirely on the law of the nation in which they lie; it will be necessary, in pursuing this inquiry, to examine, not singly those principles of abstract justice, which the Creator of all things has impressed on the mind of his creature man, and which are admitted to regulate, in a great degree, the rights of civilized nations, whose perfect independence is acknowledged; but those principles also which our own government has adopted in the particular case, and given us as the rule for our decision.

On the discovery of this immense continent, the great nations of Europe were eager to appropriate to themselves so much of it as they could respectively acquire. Its vast extent offered an ample field to the ambition and enterprise of all; and the character and religion of its inhabitants afforded an apology for considering them as a people over whom the superior genius of Europe might claim an ascendency. The potentates of the old world found no difficulty in convincing themselves that they made ample compensation to the inhabitants of the new, by bestowing on them civilization and Christianity, in exchange for unlimited independence. But, as they were all in pursuit of nearly the same object, it was necessary, in order to avoid conflicting settlements, and consequent war with each other, to establish a principle, which all should acknowledge as the law by which the right of acquisition, which they all asserted, should be regulated as between themselves. This principle was, that discovery gave title to the government by whose subjects, or by whose authority, it was made, against all other European governments, which title might be consummated by possession.

The exclusion of all other Europeans, necessarily gave to the nation making the discovery the sole right of acquiring the soil from the natives, and establishing settlements upon it. It was a right with which no Europeans could interfere. It was a right which all asserted for themselves, and to the assertion of which, by others, all assented.

Those relations which were to exist between the discoverer and the natives, were to be regulated by themselves. The rights thus acquired being exclusive, no other power could interpose between them.

In the establishment of these relations, the rights of the original inhabitants were, in no instance, entirely disregarded; but were necessarily, to a considerable extent, impaired. They were admitted to be the rightful occupants of the soil, with a legal as well as just claim to retain possession of it, and to use it according to their own discretion; but their rights to complete sovereignty, as independent nations, were necessarily diminished, and their power to dispose of the soil at their own will, to whomsoever they pleased, was denied by the original fundamental principle, that discovery gave exclusive title to those who made it.

While the different nations of Europe respected the right of the natives, as occupants, they asserted the ultimate dominion to be in themselves; and claimed and exercised, as a consequence of this ultimate dominion, a power to grant the soil, while yet in possession of the natives. These grants have been understood by all, to convey a title to the grantees, subject only to the Indian right of occupancy.

The history of America, from its discovery to the present day, proves, we think, the universal recognition of these principles. . . .

No one of the powers of Europe gave its full assent to this principle, more unequivocally than England. The documents upon this subject are ample and complete. So early as the year 1496, her monarch granted a commission to the Cabots, to discover countries then unknown to Christian people, and to take possession of them in the name of the king of England. Two years afterwards, Cabot proceeded on this voyage, and discovered the continent of North America, along which he sailed as far south as Virginia. To this discovery the English trace their title. . . .

[A]ll the nations of Europe, who have acquired territory on this continent, have asserted in themselves, and have recognized in others, the exclusive right of the discoverer to appropriate the lands occupied by the Indians. Have the American States rejected or adopted this principle?

By the treaty which concluded the war of our revolution, Great Britain relinquished all claim, not only to the government, but to the "propriety and territorial rights of the United States," whose boundaries were fixed in the second article. By this treaty, the powers of government, and the right to soil, which had previously been in Great Britain, passed definitively to these States. We had before taken possession of them, by declaring independence; but neither the declaration of independence, nor the treaty confirming it, could give us more than that which we before possessed, or to which Great Britain was before entitled. It has never been doubted, that either the United States, or the several States, had a clear title to all the lands within the boundary lines described in the treaty, subject only to the Indian right of occupancy, and that the exclusive power to extinguish that right, was vested in that government which might constitutionally exercise it. . . .

The States, having within their chartered limits different portions of territory covered by Indians, ceded that territory, generally, to the United States, on conditions expressed in their deeds of cession, which demonstrate the opinion, that they ceded the soil as well as jurisdiction, and that in doing so, they granted a productive fund to the government of the Union. The lands in controversy lay within the chartered limits of Virginia, and were ceded with the whole country northwest of the river Ohio. . . .

The ceded territory was occupied by numerous and warlike tribes of Indians; but the exclusive right of the United States to extinguish their title, and to grant the soil, has never, we believe, been doubted. . . .

The magnificent purchase of Louisiana, was the purchase from France of a country almost entirely occupied by numerous tribes of Indians, who are in fact independent. Yet, any attempt of others to intrude into that country, would be considered as an aggression which would justify war.

Our late acquisitions from Spain are of the same character; and the negotiations which preceded those acquisitions, recognize and elucidate the principle which has been received as the foundation of all European title in America.

The United States, then, have unequivocally acceded to that great and broad rule by which its civilized inhabitants now hold this country. They hold, and assert in themselves, the title by which it was acquired. They maintain, as all others have maintained, that discovery gave an exclusive right to extinguish the Indian title of occupancy, either by purchase or by conquest; and gave also a right to such a degree of sovereignty, as the circumstances of the people would allow them to exercise.

The power now possessed by the government of the United States to grant lands, resided, while we were colonies, in the crown, or its grantees. The validity of the titles given by either has never been questioned in our Courts. It has been exercised uniformly over territory in possession of the Indians. The existence of this power must negative the existence of any right which may conflict with, and control it. An absolute title to lands cannot exist, at the same time, in different persons, or in different governments. An absolute, must be an exclusive title, or at least a title which excludes all others not compatible with it. All our institutions recognise the absolute title of the crown, subject only to the Indian right of occupancy, and recognise the absolute title of the crown to extinguish that right. This is incompatible with an absolute and complete title in the Indians.

We will not enter into the controversy, whether agriculturists, merchants, and manufacturers, have a right, on abstract principles, to expel hunters from the territory they possess, or to contract their limits. Conquest gives a title which the Courts of the conqueror cannot deny, whatever the private and speculative opinions of individuals may be, respecting the original justice of the claim which has been successfully asserted. The British government, which was then our government, and whose rights have passed to the United States, asserted title to all the lands occupied by Indians, within the chartered limits of the British colonies. It asserted also a limited sovereignty over them, and the exclusive right of extinguishing the title which occupancy gave to them. These claims have been maintained and established as far west as the river Mississippi, by the sword. The title to a vast portion of the lands we now hold, originates in them. It is not for the Courts of this country to question the validity of this title, or to sustain one which is incompatible with it.

Although we do not mean to engage in the defence of those principles which Europeans have applied to Indian title, they may, we think, find some excuse, if not justification, in the character and habits of the people whose rights have been wrested from them.

The title by conquest is acquired and maintained by force. The conqueror pre-scribes its limits. Humanity, however, acting on public opinion, has established, as a general rule, that the conquered shall not be wantonly oppressed, and that their con-dition shall remain as eligible as is compatible with the objects of the conquest. Most usually, they are incorporated with the victorious nation, and become subjects or citizens of the government with which they are connected. The new and old members of the society mingle with each other; the distinction between them is gradually lost, and they make one people. Where this incorporation is practicable, humanity demands, and a wise policy requires, that the rights of the conquered to property should remain unimpaired; that the new subjects should be governed as equitably as the old, and that confidence in their security should gradually banish the painful sense of being separated from their ancient connexions, and united by force to strangers.

When the conquest is complete, and the conquered inhabitants can be blended with the conquerors, or safely governed as a distinct people, public opinion, which not even the conqueror can disregard, imposes these restraints upon him; and he cannot neglect them without injury to his fame, and hazard to his power.

But the tribes of Indians inhabiting this country were fierce savages, whose occupation was war, and whose subsistence was drawn chiefly from the forest. To leave them in possession of their country, was to leave the country a wilderness; to govern them as a distinct people, was impossible, because they were as brave and as high spirited as they were fierce, and were ready to repel by arms every attempt on their independence.

What was the inevitable consequence of this state of things? The Europeans were under the necessity either of abandoning the country, and relinquishing their pompous claims to it, or of enforcing those claims by the sword, and by the adoption of principles adapted to the condition of a people with whom it was impossible to mix, and who could not be governed as a distinct society, or of remaining in their neighbour-hood, and exposing themselves and their families to the perpetual hazard of being massacred.

Frequent and bloody wars, in which the whites were not always the aggressors, unavoidably ensued. European policy, numbers, and skill, prevailed. As the white population advanced, that of the Indians necessarily receded. The country in the immediate neighbourhood of agriculturists became unfit for them. The game fled into thicker and more unbroken forests, and the Indians followed. The soil, to which the crown originally claimed title, being no longer occupied by its ancient inhabitants, was parcelled out according to the will of the sovereign power, and taken possession of by persons who claimed immediately from the crown, or medi-ately, through its grantees or deputies.

That law which regulates, and ought to regulate in general, the relations between the conqueror and conquered, was incapable of application to a people under such circumstances. The resort to some new and different rule, better adapted to the actual state of things, was unavoidable. Every rule which can be suggested will be found to be attended with great difficulty.

However extravagant the pretension of converting the discovery of an inhabited country into conquest may appear; if the principle has been asserted in the first instance, and afterwards sustained; if a country has been acquired and held under it; if the property of the great mass of the community originates in it, it becomes the law of the land, and cannot be questioned. So, too, with respect to the concomitant principle, that the Indian inhabitants are to be considered merely as occupants, to be protected, indeed, while in peace, in the possession of their lands, but to be deemed incapable of transferring the absolute title to others. However this restriction may be opposed to natural right, and to the usages of civilized nations, yet, if it be indispen-sable to that system under which the country has been settled, and be adapted to the actual condition of the two people, it may, perhaps, be supported by reason, and certainly cannot be rejected by Courts of justice. . . .

. . . The absolute ultimate title has been considered as acquired by discovery, subject only to the Indian title of occupancy, which title the discoverers possessed the exclusive right of acquiring. Such a right is no more incompatible with a seisin in fee, than a lease for years, and might as effectually bar an ejectment.

Another view has been taken of this question, which deserves to be considered. The title of the crown, whatever it might be, could be acquired only by a conveyance from the crown. If an individual might extinguish the Indian title for his own benefit, or, in other words, might purchase it, still he could acquire only that title. Admitting their power to change their laws or usages, so far as to allow an individual to separate a portion of their lands from the common stock, and hold it in severalty, still it is a part of their territory, and is held under them, by a title dependent on their laws. The grant derives its efficacy from their will; and, if they choose to resume it, and make a different disposition of the land, the Courts of the United States cannot interpose for the protection of the title. The person who purchases lands from the Indians, within their territory, incorporates himself with them, so far as respects the property pur-chased; holds their title under their protection, and subject to their laws. If they annul the grant, we know of no tribunal which can revise and set aside the proceeding. We know of no principle which can distinguish this case from a grant made to a native Indian, authorizing him to hold a particular tract of land in severalty.

As such a grant could not separate the Indian from his nation, nor give a title which our Courts could distinguish from the title of his tribe, as it might still be conquered from, or ceded by his tribe, we can perceive no legal principle which will authorize a Court to say, that different consequences are attached to this purchase, because it was made by a stranger. By the treaties concluded between the United States and the Indian nations, whose title the plaintiffs claim, the country comprehending the lands in controversy has been ceded to the United States, without any reservation of their title. These nations had been at war with the United States, and had an unquestionable right to annul any grant they had made to American citizens. Their cession of the country, without a reservation of this land, affords a fair presumption, that they considered it as of no validity. They ceded to the United States this very property, after having used it in common with other lands, as their own, from the date of their deeds to the time of cession; and the attempt now made, is to set up their title against that of the United States. . . .

It has never been contended, that the Indian title amounted to nothing. Their right of possession has never been questioned. The claim of government extends to the complete ultimate title, charged with this right of possession, and to the exclusive power of acquiring that right. . . .

After bestowing on this subject a degree of attention which was more required by the magnitude of the interest in litigation, and the able and elaborate arguments of the bar, than by its intrinsic difficulty, the Court is decidedly of opinion, that the plaintiffs do not exhibit a title which can be sustained in the Courts of the United States. . . .

NOTES AND QUESTIONS

1. Chief Justice John Marshall described the property rights of American Indian nations to their traditional lands as "Indian title," "title of occupancy," and as a "right of occupancy." He described the rights of the United States government to the same lands as a "title," "ultimate dominion," "a power to grant the soil," "absolute title," "complete ultimate title," "fee title," a "seisin in fee," and as "the sole right of acquiring the soil." What interests were encompassed by the "title of occupancy" in Indian tribes, and what interests were encompassed by the "title" reserved to the United States? Can you tell from the opinion? What interpretations are possible?

2. In a famous sentence, Justice Marshall declared: "Conquest gives a title which the Courts of the conqueror cannot deny, whatever the private and speculative opinions of individuals may be, respecting the original justice of the claim which has been successfully asserted." What does this mean? Had the Piankeshaw and Illinois Indian nations been conquered? When did that happen?

3. In another famous sentence, Justice Marshall wrote: "[D]iscovery gave title to the government by whose subjects, or by whose authority, it was made, against all other European governments, which title might be consummated by possession." What property rights were acquired by "discovery"? Can they be justified? Recall that Marshall also wrote: "Those relations which were to exist between the discoverer and the natives, were to be regulated by themselves." What does this mean, and how does it relate to the doctrine of discovery?

4. In 1835, the Supreme Court stated that "it [is] a settled principle, that their right of occupancy is considered as sacred as the fee simple of the whites." *Mitchel v.*

United States, 34 U.S. 711, 746 (1835). Is this statement consistent with the ruling in *Johnson v. M'Intosh* or at odds with it?

5. In *United States v. Percheman*, 32 U.S. 51 (1833), the Supreme Court interpreted federal statutes and a treaty with Spain to validate titles to private citizens granted by Spain before the United States acquired Florida. Chief Justice Marshall's opinion explained, *id.* at 86-87:

> It may not be unworthy of remark, that it is very unusual, even in cases of conquest, for the conqueror to do more than to displace the sovereign and assume dominion over the country. The modern usage of nations, which has become law, would be violated; that sense of justice and of right which is acknowledged and felt by the whole civilized world would be outraged, if private property should be generally confiscated, and private rights annulled: The people change their allegiance; their relation to their ancient sovereign is dissolved: but their relations to each other, and their rights of property, remain undisturbed.

Did the Supreme Court adopt this principle in the case of the American Indian nations in whole or in part, or did it reject it? Is *Percheman* consistent with *Johnson*?

§1.1.2 FORCED SEIZURES OF PROPERTY FROM AMERICAN INDIAN NATIONS

TEE-HIT-TON INDIANS v. UNITED STATES
348 U.S. 272 (1955)

Mr. Justice STANLEY REED delivered the opinion of the Court.

This case rests upon a claim under the Fifth Amendment by petitioner, an identifiable group of American Indians of between 60 and 70 individuals residing in Alaska, for compensation for a taking by the United States of certain timber from Alaskan lands allegedly belonging to the group. The area claimed is said to contain over 350,000 acres of land and 150 square miles of water. The Tee-Hit-Tons, a clan of the Tlingit Tribe, brought this suit in the Court of Claims under 28 U.S.C. §1505. The compensation claimed does not arise from any statutory direction to pay. Payment, if it can be compelled, must be based upon a constitutional right of the Indians to recover. This is not a case that is connected with any phase of the policy of the Congress, continued throughout our history, to extinguish Indian title through negotiation rather than by force, and to grant payments from the public purse to needy descendants of exploited Indians. The legislation in support of that policy has received consistent interpretation from this Court in sympathy with its compassionate purpose.

... The Court of Claims ... held that petitioner was an identifiable group of American Indians residing in Alaska; that its interest in the lands prior to purchase of Alaska by the United States in 1867 was "original Indian title" or "Indian right of occupancy." It was further held that if such original Indian title survived the Treaty of 1867, 15 Stat. 539, Arts. III and VI, by which Russia conveyed Alaska to the United States, such title was not sufficient basis to maintain this suit as there had been no recognition by Congress of any legal rights in petitioner to the land in question. The court said that no rights inured to plaintiff by virtue of legislation by Congress. ... [W]e granted certiorari.

The Alaskan area in which petitioner claims a compensable interest is located near and within the exterior lines of the Tongass National Forest. By Joint Resolution of August 8, 1947, 61 Stat. 920, the Secretary of Agriculture was authorized to contract for the sale of national forest timber located within this National Forest "notwithstanding any claim of possessory rights." The Resolution defines "possessory rights"[7] and provides for all receipts from the sale of timber to be maintained in a special account in the Treasury until the timber and land rights are finally determined.

The Secretary of Agriculture, on August 20, 1951, pursuant to this authority contracted for sale to a private company of all merchantable timber in the area claimed by petitioner. This is the sale of timber which petitioner alleges constitutes a compensable taking by the United States of a portion of its proprietary interest in the land.

The problem presented is the nature of the petitioner's interest in the land, if any. Petitioner claims a "full proprietary ownership" of the land; or, in the alternative, at least a "recognized" right to unrestricted possession, occupation and use. Either ownership or recognized possession, petitioner asserts, is compensable. If it has a fee simple interest in the entire tract, it has an interest in the timber and its sale is a partial taking of its right to "possess, use and dispose of it." *United States v. General Motors*, 323 U.S. 373, 378 (1945). It is petitioner's contention that its tribal predecessors have continually claimed, occupied and used the land from time immemorial; that when Russia took Alaska, the Tlingits had a well-developed social order which included a concept of property ownership; that Russia while it possessed Alaska in no manner interfered with their claim to the land; that Congress has by subsequent acts confirmed and recognized petitioner's right to occupy the land permanently and therefore the sale of the timber off such lands constitutes a taking pro tanto of its asserted rights in the area.

The Government denies that petitioner has any compensable interest. It asserts that the Tee-Hit-Tons' property interest, if any, is merely that of the right to the use of the land at the Government's will; that Congress has never recognized any legal interest of petitioner in the land and therefore without such recognition no compensation is due the petitioner for any taking by the United States.

I. Recognition

The question of recognition may be disposed of shortly. Where the Congress by treaty or other agreement has declared that thereafter Indians were to hold the lands permanently, compensation must be paid for subsequent taking. The petitioner contends that Congress has sufficiently "recognized" its possessory rights in the land in question so as to make its interest compensable. Petitioner points specifically to two statutes to sustain this contention. . . .

We have carefully examined these statutes and the pertinent legislative history and find nothing to indicate any intention by Congress to grant to the Indians any permanent rights in the lands of Alaska occupied by them by permission of Congress. . . .

---

7. "That 'possessory rights' as used in this resolution shall mean all rights, if any should exist, which are based upon aboriginal occupancy or title, or upon section 8 of the Act of May 17, 1884 (23 Stat. 24), section 14 of the Act of March 3, 1891 (26 Stat. 1095), or section 27 of the Act of June 6, 1900 (31 Stat. 321), whether claimed by native tribes, native villages, native individuals, or other persons, and which have not been confirmed by patent or court decision or included within any reservation."

II. *Indian Title*

(a) The nature of aboriginal Indian interest in land and the various rights as between the Indians and the United States dependent on such interest are far from novel as concerns our Indian inhabitants. It is well settled that in all the States of the Union the tribes who inhabited the lands of the States held claim to such lands after the coming of the white man, under what is sometimes termed original Indian title or permission from the whites to occupy. That description means mere possession not specifically recognized as ownership by Congress. After conquest they were permitted to occupy portions of territory over which they had previously exercised "sovereignty," as we use that term. This is not a property right but amounts to a right of occupancy which the sovereign grants and protects against intrusion by third parties but which right of occupancy may be terminated and such lands fully disposed of by the sovereign itself without any legally enforceable obligation to compensate the Indians.

This position of the Indian has long been rationalized by the legal theory that discovery and conquest gave the conquerors sovereignty over and ownership of the lands thus obtained. The great case of *Johnson v. M'Intosh*, 21 U.S. (8 Wheat.) 543 (1823), denied the power of an Indian tribe to pass their right of occupancy to another. It confirmed the practice of two hundred years of American history "that discovery gave an exclusive right to extinguish the Indian title of occupancy, either by purchase or by conquest." 8 Wheat. at 587.

> . . . Conquest gives a title which the Courts of the conqueror cannot deny, whatever the private and speculative opinions of individuals may be, respecting the original justice of the claim which has been successfully asserted. . . . 8 Wheat. at 590-591.

In *Beecher v. Wetherby*, 95 U.S. 517 (1877), a tract of land which Indians were then expressly permitted by the United States to occupy was granted to Wisconsin. In a controversy over timber, this Court held the Wisconsin title good.

> The grantee, it is true, would take only the naked fee, and could not disturb the occupancy of the Indians: that occupancy could only be interfered with or determined by the United States. It is to be presumed that in this matter the United States would be governed by such considerations of justice as would control a Christian people in their treatment of an ignorant and dependent race. Be that as it may, the propriety or justice of their action towards the Indians with respect to their lands is a question of governmental policy, and is not a matter open to discussion in a controversy between third parties, neither of whom derives title from the Indians. The right of the United States to dispose of the fee of lands occupied by them has always been recognized by this court from the foundation of the government. 95 U.S. at 525.

In 1941 a unanimous Court wrote, concerning Indian title, the following:

> Extinguishment of Indian title based on aboriginal possession is of course a different matter. The power of Congress in that regard is supreme. The manner, method and time of such extinguishment raise political, not justiciable issues. *United States v. Santa Fe Pacific R. Co.*, 314 U.S. 339, 347 (1941).

No case in this Court has ever held that taking of Indian title or use by Congress required compensation. The American people have compassion for the descendants of those Indians who were deprived of their homes and hunting grounds by the drive of civilization. They seek to have the Indians share the benefits of our society as citizens of this Nation. Generous provision has been willingly made to allow tribes to recover for wrongs, as a matter of grace, not because of legal liability. . . .

This is true, not because an Indian or an Indian tribe has no standing to sue or because the United States has not consented to be sued for the taking of original Indian title, but because Indian occupation of land without government recognition of ownership creates no rights against taking or extinction by the United States protected by the Fifth Amendment or any other principle of law.

(c) What has been heretofore set out deals largely with the Indians of the Plains and east of the Mississippi. The Tee-Hit-Tons urge, however, that their stage of civilization and their concept of ownership of property takes them out of the rule applicable to the Indians of the States. They assert that Russia never took their lands in the sense that European nations seized the rest of America. The Court of Claims, however, saw no distinction between their use of the land and that of the Indians of the Eastern United States. That court had no evidence that the Russian handling of the Indian land problem differed from ours. The natives were left the use of the great part of their vast hunting and fishing territory but what Russia wanted for its use and that of its licensees, it took. The court's conclusion on this issue was based on strong evidence.

In considering the character of the Tee-Hit-Tons' use of the land, the Court of Claims had before it the testimony of a single witness who was offered by plaintiff. He stated that he was the chief of the Tee-Hit-Ton tribe. He qualified as an expert on the Tlingits, a group composed of numerous interconnected tribes including the Tee-Hit-Tons. His testimony showed that the Tee-Hit-Tons had become greatly reduced in numbers. Membership descends only through the female line. At the present time there are only a few women of childbearing age and a total membership of some 65.

The witness pointed out that their claim of ownership was based on possession and use. The use that was made of the controverted area was for the location in winter of villages in sheltered spots and in summer along fishing streams and/or bays. The ownership was not individual but tribal. As the witness stated, "Any member of the tribe may use any portion of the land that he wishes, and as long as he uses it that is his for his own enjoyment, and is not to be trespassed upon by anybody else, but the minute he stops using it then any other member of the tribe can come in and use that area."

When the Russians first came to the Tlingit territory, the most important of the chiefs moved the people to what is now the location of the town of Wrangell. Each tribe took a portion of Wrangell harbor and the chief gave permission to the Russians to build a house on the shore.

The witness learned the alleged boundaries of the Tee-Hit-Ton area from hunting and fishing with his uncle after his return from Carlisle Indian School about 1904. From the knowledge so obtained, he outlined in red on the map, which petitioner filed as an exhibit, the territory claimed by the Tee-Hit-Tons. Use by other tribal members is sketchily asserted. This is the same 350,000 acres claimed by the petition. On it he marked six places to show the Indians' use of the land: (1) his great uncle was buried here, (2) a town, (3) his uncle's house, (4) a town, (5) his mother's house, (6) smokehouse. He also pointed out the uses of this tract for fishing salmon and for hunting beaver, deer and mink.

The testimony further shows that while membership in the tribe and therefore ownership in the common property descended only through the female line, the various tribes of the Tlingits allowed one another to use their lands. Before power boats, the Indians would put their shelters for hunting and fishing away from villages. With the power boats, they used them as living quarters.

In addition to this verbal testimony, exhibits were introduced by both sides as to the land use. These exhibits are secondary authorities but they bear out the general proposition that land claims among the Tlingits, and likewise of their smaller group, the Tee-Hit-Tons, [were] wholly tribal. It was more a claim of sovereignty than of ownership. The articles presented to the Court of Claims by those who have studied and written of the tribal groups agree with the above testimony. There were scattered shelters and villages moved from place to place as game or fish became scarce. There was recognition of tribal rights to hunt and fish on certain general areas, with claims to that effect carved on totem poles. From all that was presented, the Court of Claims concluded, and we agree, that the Tee-Hit-Tons were in a hunting and fishing stage of civilization, with shelters fitted to their environment, and claims to rights to use identified territory for these activities as well as the gathering of wild products of the earth. We think this evidence introduced by both sides confirms the Court of Claims' conclusion that the petitioner's use of its lands was like the use of the nomadic tribes of the States Indians.

The line of cases adjudicating Indian rights on American soil leads to the conclusion that Indian occupancy, not specifically recognized as ownership by action authorized by Congress, may be extinguished by the Government without compensation. Every American schoolboy knows that the savage tribes of this continent were deprived of their ancestral ranges by force and that, even when the Indians ceded millions of acres by treaty in return for blankets, food and trinkets, it was not a sale but the conquerors' will that deprived them of their land. . . .

In the light of the history of Indian relations in this Nation, no other course would meet the problem of the growth of the United States except to make congressional contributions for Indian lands rather than to subject the Government to an obligation to pay the value when taken with interest to the date of payment. Our conclusion does not uphold harshness as against tenderness toward the Indians, but it leaves with Congress, where it belongs, the policy of Indian gratuities for the termination of Indian occupancy of Government-owned land rather than making compensation for its value a rigid constitutional principle. . . .

Mr. Justice WILLIAM O. DOUGLAS, with whom the CHIEF JUSTICE and Mr. Justice FELIX FRANKFURTER, concur, dissenting.

The first Organic Act for Alaska became a law on May 17, 1884, 23 Stat. 24. [Section 8 provides that] "the Indians or other persons in said district shall not be disturbed in the possession of any lands actually in their use or occupation or now claimed by them but the terms under which such persons may acquire title to such lands is reserved for future legislation by Congress. . . ." Respondent contends, and the Court apparently agrees, that this provision should be read, not as recognizing Indian title, but as reserving the question whether they have any rights in the land. . . .

[In the debates about the Act,] Senator Benjamin Harrison [said] it was the intention of the committee "to save from all possible invasion the rights of the Indian residents of Alaska . . . except in so far as it was necessary in order to establish title to mining claims in the Territory." . . . The conclusion seems clear that Congress in the 1884 Act recognized the claims of these Indians to their Alaskan lands. What those lands were was not known. Where they were located, what were their metes and bounds, were also unknown. . . . It must be remembered that the Congress was legislating about a Territory concerning which little was known. No report was available showing the nature and extent of any claims to the land. No Indian was present to point out his tribe's domain. Therefore, Congress did the humane thing of saving to the Indians all rights claimed; it let them keep what they had prior to the new Act. The future course of action was made clear — conflicting claims would be reconciled and the Indian lands would be put into reservations.

That purpose is wholly at war with the one now attributed to the Congress of reserving for some future day the question whether the Indians were to have any rights to the land. . . .

NOTES AND QUESTIONS

1. Did the Supreme Court in *Tee-Hit-Ton* correctly apply the principles laid out in *Johnson v. M'Intosh*? What happened to the Tee-Hit-Tons' "title of occupancy"? Recall the ruling in *Mitchel v. United States*, 34 U.S. 711, 746 (1835), which held that Indian title is "as sacred as the fee simple of the whites." Did the Court live up to that principle in *Tee-Hit-Ton*?

2. What reasons did the Court give for refusing to recognize property rights in the Tee-Hit-Tons over the lands they claimed? Are these reasons persuasive? Do they apply to non-Indian property holders?

3. Did Justice Reed use the term "conquest" in the same way that Chief Justice Marshall used it in *Johnson v. M'Intosh*? What did conquest mean to Justice Reed? When and how did it happen, exactly? Milner Ball has noted that the "peace-loving Tlingit have never been conquered. No one has made the attempt except the Supreme Court." Milner Ball, *Constitution, Courts, Indian Tribes*, 1987 Am. B. Found. Res. J. 1, 115. Nell Jessup Newton explains:

> Justice Reed's use of the term "conquest" is itself questionable. Both at the time of *Johnson* and today, conquest has been a narrow concept with clearly defined effects on the conquered people. For example, conquest generally requires some sort of physical possession by force of arms. Thus, the conclusion that all Indian land has been conquered was as illogical as it was unprecedented. . . . [T]he Alaska natives had never fought a skirmish with either Russia or the United States, but instead welcomed newcomers to Alaska with open arms. To say that the Alaska natives were subjugated by conquest stretches the imagination too far. The only sovereign act that can be said to have conquered the Alaska native was the *Tee-Hit-Ton* opinion itself.

Nell Jessup Newton, *At the Whim of the Sovereign: Aboriginal Title Reconsidered*, 31 Hastings L.J. 1215, 1243-1244 (1980).

4. *Claims statutes.* Although not constitutionally compelled to do so, Congress eventually passed a statute compensating native inhabitants of Alaska for the loss of their land in the amount of $962.5 million plus about 40 million acres of federal public lands. *Alaska Native Claims Settlement Act of 1971*, 43 U.S.C. §§1601 *et seq.*; *Felix S. Cohen's Handbook of Federal Indian Law* 746-749 (1982 ed.). The act extinguished land claims to 335 million acres. Lloyd Benton Miller, *Caught in a Crossfire: Conflict in the Courts, Alaska Tribes in the Balance*, 1989 Harv. Indian L. Symp. 135, 138 n.9 (1990).

Not mentioned in the *Tee-Hit-Ton* opinion is the fact that Congress had passed a statute in 1946 called the *Indian Claims Commission Act* (ICCA), 60 Stat. 1049, 25

U.S.C. §70 *et seq.*, which allowed Indian nations to bring claims against the United States for uncompensated (or poorly compensated) takings of their property. These claims were being heard by the Commission at the time *Tee-Hit-Ton* was decided. The practical effect of the *Tee-Hit-Ton* ruling was to require interest to be paid on takings of recognized title property (because those takings were accomplished without "just compensation" as the constitution required) but not to be paid on takings of original Indian title lands. Does this alter your understanding of the meaning of the last paragraph in the majority opinion? Should the passage of the ICCA have affected the Court's ruling in *Tee-Hit-Ton?* In what way? American Indian tribal property is further considered in Chapter 13.

5. American Indians are not the only group whose right to own property has received less than equal protection of the law. In addition to the obvious case of African Americans, who were themselves treated as property, western states passed "alien land laws" in the first half of the twentieth century that limited the right to own property to aliens eligible to naturalize, thereby effectively prohibiting foreign-born Asian residents from acquiring certain types of land. These laws were not struck down until 1947 in *Oyama v. California*, 332 U.S. 633 (1947). *See* Keith Aoki, *No Right to Own? The Early Twentieth-Century "Alien Land Laws" as a Prelude to Internment*, 40 B.C. L. Rev. 37 (1998).

§1.1.3   CURRENT INDIAN LAND CLAIMS

After the United States broke away from England in 1776, the states generally dealt with Indians on their own until the Articles of Confederation were adopted in 1781. The Articles gave the federal government most powers over Indian affairs while reserving some powers to the states. Because the Articles did not clearly allocate their respective powers, the states and the federal government engaged in a power struggle over who should be primary in Indian affairs. Land invasions by settlers during this period led to unrest on the frontier. One of the major reasons for adopting the Constitution in 1789 was to centralize power over Indian affairs in the federal government, which was given the sole power to "regulate Commerce . . . with the Indian Tribes," omitting whatever residual state powers had been protected under the Articles of Confederation. U.S. Const. art. I §8 cl. 3. Pursuant to this policy, Congress passed the first *Trade and Intercourse Act* in 1790 (often called the *Nonintercourse Act*), which prohibited non-Indians from settling in Indian country without the consent of the United States and prohibited sales of tribal land to anyone other than the United States. The statute provided that

> no sale of lands made by any Indians, or any nation or tribe of Indians within the United States, shall be valid to any person or persons, or to any state, whether having the right of pre-emption to such lands or not, unless the same shall be made and duly executed at some public treaty, held under the authority of the United States.

The act was amended several times and remains in effect to this day. 25 U.S.C. §177.

Despite the statute, several states, including New York, continued to enter into treaties with various Indian nations, arranging for cession of lands. These transfers violated the clear terms of the *Nonintercourse Act*. In the late 1960s, eastern tribes began to bring lawsuits claiming that these transfers of title were invalid and seeking remedies for the violation. One of these suits brought by the Oneida Indian Nation against Onedia County in New York reached the Supreme Court, which ruled in favor of the Oneidas' claim for damages for occupation of their land. The Court interpreted the *Nonintercourse Act* to contain an implied private right of action, granting the tribes a federal common law right to sue for violations of the act. *Oneida Indian Nation v. County of Oneida*, 414 U.S. 661 (1974) (*Oneida I*). When the case came to the Court a second time, it further held that state statutes of limitation cutting off tribal land claims are preempted by federal law. The Court found no federal statute of limitations applicable to the *Nonintercourse Act* and no explicit ratification of the treaties between the Oneida Indian Nation and the state of New York by the federal government either in the language of later statutes or in later treaties entered into between the Oneida Indian Nation and the United States. *County of Oneida v. Oneida Indian Nation*, 470 U.S. 226 (1985) (*Oneida II*). The Oneida Indian Nation therefore retained title to huge amounts of land in New York currently occupied by non-Indians.

Justice Lewis F. Powell, Jr. explained, "Absent explicit statutory language, this Court . . . has refused to find that Congress has abrogated Indian treaty rights." *Id.* at 247. The Court recognized "the potential consequences of affirmance," *id.* at 253, alluding to the fact that most of the land was currently occupied by non-Indians, but Justice Powell observed that Congress had the power to pass a statute extinguishing Indian title. "One would have thought that claims dating back for more than a century and a half would have been barred long ago," but no federal law expressly barred the Oneida property claim. *Id.* at 253. The remedy sought by the tribe against Oneida County was rental payment for one year on all the occupied land; the tribe had not sought to regain possession, nor had it not sought the right to eject the non-Indian occupants or charge them rent for occupying Oneida land.

Justices Stevens, White, and Rehnquist and Chief Justice Burger dissented. Justice Stevens argued that "there was no legal impediment to the maintenance of this cause of action at any time after 1795," *id.* at 266, and that the Oneida Indian Nation had "waited 175 years before bringing suit to avoid a 1795 conveyance that the Tribe freely made, for a valuable consideration," *id.* at 255. Justice Stevens noted that the lands had been improved and settled; the claim "arose when George Washington was the President of the United States" and was therefore "barred by the extraordinary passage of time." *Id.* at 256. The dissenters would have held that the claim was barred by the equitable doctrine of *laches* because unjustified delay worked to the prejudice of others. "The remedy for the ancient wrong established at trial should be provided by Congress, not by judges seeking to rewrite history at this late date." *Id.* at 270. The majority opinion did not reach the question of whether *laches* barred the claim but did note that, as an equitable defense, it might not apply to a claim at law for damages and that "this Court has indicated that extinguishment of Indian title requires a sovereign act" by the Congress—an act clearly missing in this case, *id.* at 245 n.16.

In a follow-up case, the Oneida Indian Nation bought back some of its own land from the non-Indian possessor. The parcels had been sold by a tribal member to a non-Indian in 1807 in violation of the *Nonintercourse Act* and were repurchased by the tribe in 1997 and 1998. The tribe began to operate a gas station, convenience store, and a textile facility on the disputed parcels. The tribe argued that, under the ruling in *Oneida II*, it had never lost title to the land and that Congress had never diminished the scope of the Oneida reservation; as tribal land it would therefore be classified as "Indian country" and exempt from state property taxation. The federal district court agreed with the tribe but the Supreme Court reversed on the ground that the long passage of time meant that it would be inequitable to grant the tribe the equitable remedy it sought. *Sherrill v. Oneida Indian Nation of New York*, — U.S. —, 2005 U.S. LEXIS 2927 (2005). The Court noted that the state had exercised sovereignty over the lost Oneida lands for almost 200 years and that the Oneidas had *acquiesced* in this state of affairs, unreasonably delaying in going to court to seek return of the land and protection of tribal sovereignty (*laches*). The Court also found that it would be disruptive and *impracticable* to alter the sovereignty arrangements by allowing the tribe to recover sovereignty over its land bit by bit as it bought back its own land; this would create checkerboard jurisdiction with some parcels governed by the tribe and others by the local municipal government. The Court therefore applied the doctrines of *laches*, acquiescence, and impracticability and barred the Oneida claim. *But See Oneida Indian Nation of New York v. Madison County*, 2005 U.S. Dist, LEXIS 22536 (N.D.N.Y. 2005) (holding that N.Y. cannot foreclose on Onedia land for failure to pay property taxes because the tribe has sovereign immunity and the *Nonintercourse Act* preempts state foreclosure law).

It should be noted that federal courts had no general jurisdiction over federal questions until 1875, and arguably no jurisdiction to hear claims brought by Indian nations as plaintiffs without the consent of the United States until 1966, when Congress passed a statute authorizing suits in federal courts by federally recognized Indian tribes, 28 U.S.C. §1362. Before 1966, the tribes approached Congress to obtain special jurisdictional acts allowing them to sue in federal court, or they asked the United States to sue on their behalf. Such bills raised political questions, and, although Congress passed more than a hundred such bills, they often limited the questions that could be pursued in court. Of course, the tribe could have sued in New York state court, but the claim would likely have been barred by sovereign immunity, *see Blatchford v. Native Village of Noatak*, 501 U.S. 775 (1991) (a state has sovereign immunity protecting it from any lawsuit brought by a federally recognized Indian nation unless the state voluntarily waives its sovereign immunity or Congress abrogates state sovereign immunity by explicit federal legislation), and perhaps one might forgive the tribe for thinking that state judges in New York were not about to nullify a land transfer effectuated by the state government. The curious result seems to be that the Oneida Indian Nation retains title to its land, because that title was never extinguished by Congress, but that it possesses no rights over the land; the non-Indian possessors, although they do not have title, appear to have vested property rights protected by a variety of equitable doctrines. *Cf. Banner v. United States*, 238 F.3d 1348 (Fed. Cir. 2001), *aff'g* 44 Fed. Cl. 568 (Fed. Cl. 1999) (Seneca Nation entitled to evict homeowners who built homes on land leased from the Seneca Nation for $1 per year when their 99-year leases were up and those owners refused to agree to pay market rents for the property).

PROBLEM

In a similar case involving the Cayuga Indian Nation, *Cayuga Indian Nation of New York v. Cuomo*, 1999 WL 509442 (N.D.N.Y. 1999), 2001 WL 1182395 (2001), the district court found that, although transfers of land from the Cayuga Nation to New York in 1795 and 1807 were void under the *Nonintercourse Act* and that title to those lands remained in the tribe, the tribe did not have the right to eject the non-Indian possessors. Judge McCurn noted that the tribal interest was a strong one. "[T]he loss of their homeland has had an immeasurable impact upon the Cayuga culture and Cayuga society as a whole." Because land is unique, damages are usually viewed as inadequate remedies for wrongful possession of land belonging to another. And although one might think that the Cayugas delayed unreasonably by waiting until 1980 to bring a claim based on conduct in 1795 and 1807, the court found that the delay was not unreasonable given the consistent efforts of the Cayugas over that time, other than court action, to recover their lands and the fact the governments that were supposed to protect their interests (especially the federal government) failed to do so; indeed, the "systems which theoretically should have assisted the Cayugas seemingly thwarted their efforts."

On the other hand, the court concluded that the long delay had the effect of creating substantial reliance interests in the non-Indian owners who did develop the land and that the "public interest" would not be served by granting the Cayugas the right to eject occupants of Cayuga land, partly because many occupants would refuse to comply with a court ejectment order. Balancing the "[i]ndisputably great hardships [that] have befallen the Cayugas as a result of the 1795 and 1807 cessions . . . , the court must balance those . . . hardships . . . against those which would result from ejectment." Ejectment would "potentially displace literally thousands of private landowners and several public landowners" and would "prove all too vividly the old axiom: 'Two wrongs don't make a right.'" In a later opinion, the court awarded the Cayuga Indian Nation approximately $247 million in damages for the lost rental value of their land (comprised of $1.9 million for the fair rental value of the claim area from 1795 to 2000, $35 million for the future loss of use and possession of the land, and $211 million in prejudgment interest). *Cayuga Indian Nation of New York v. Pataki*, 165 F. Supp. 2d 266 (N.D.N.Y. 2002).

1. Was Judge Burns correct to deny the Cayuga Indian Nation the right to eject those occupying Cayuga land? Remember that Congress has the power to extinguish tribal title by express legislation and has passed a number of land claims settlement acts that do so while recognizing the tribe's retained land and granting it both compensation and other lands in mitigation of the wrongful taking. Such acts have been passed, for example, involving the Penobscot, Passamaquoddy and Maliseet Tribes in Maine, the Narragansetts in Rhode Island, the Miccosukee Indian Tribe in Florida, and the Mashantucket Pequots in Connecticut, as well as Native Alaskans. *See, e.g., Maine Indian Claims Settlement Act*, 25 U.S.C. §§1721 *et seq.* Does this congressional role affect your view about what remedy the trial judge should have imposed in the *Cayuga* case? Congress has not extinguished the Cayuga title, but the Cayuga Indian Nation has no right to occupy its own land, to charge rent, or to regulate land use of current occupants. What ownership rights does the Cayuga Indian Nation have left?

2. On appeal, the Second Circuit applied the equitable doctrines of *laches*, acquiescence, and impossibility that had been used in *Sherrill* to deny the Cayuga Indian Nation protection from state property taxes to hold that even the claim for damages brought by the United States on behalf of the Cayuga Indian Nation of New York and the Seneca-Cayuga Tribe of Oklahoma against the state of New York was barred. *Cayuga Indian Nation of New York v. Pataki*, 2005 U.S. App. LEXIS 12764 (2005). Justice Cabranes explained that the United States had waited 200 years to bring the lawsuit on behalf of the tribes and that even though the court awarded a damages remedy, the claim had sought a declaration that the tribes had a legal right to possession of their land and hence a right to eject the non-Indian inhabitants. He noted that the trespass claim (with the associated remedy of damages) was also barred by *laches* because "we must recognize that the trespass claim, like all of plaintiffs' claims in this action, is predicated entirely

upon plaintiffs' possessory claim, for the simple reason that there can be no trespass unless the Cayugas possessed the land in question." *Id.* at *35. Recall (a) that the tribes could not sue the state on their own because the state was protected by sovereign immunity in state court; (b) the federal courts had no jurisdiction over federal questions until 1875; (c) tribes could not sue anyone in federal court without the consent of the United States until 1966; and (d) tribes could not hire their own lawyers without federal approval until 2000. Did the Second Circuit decide the case correctly?

§1.2   Government Grant

§1.2.1   HOMESTEAD ACTS AND LAND GRANTS

Once lands were taken from American Indian nations, they were held by the United States government as public lands. How were those lands distributed? The United States adopted a mixed strategy. Although the federal government retained a substantial amount, especially in the western states, it also sold or gave away millions of acres. "A whole continent was sold or given away — to veterans, settlers, squatters, railroads, states, colleges, speculators, and land companies." Lawrence M. Friedman, *A History of American Law* 231 (2d ed. 1985). The main reason for getting rid of the land was the promotion of the "basic postulate of American social structure. The ideal was a country of free citizens, small-holders living on their own bits of land." *Id.* at 232. Much of the land was granted as a gift under specific conditions rather than sold. A great deal of land was given to colleges and railroads, and other lands were granted to the state governments themselves. At least 130 million acres were granted to railroads. *Id.* at 415.

Beginning in 1796, land was sold in large tracts for relatively high prices. This policy provoked fears of land monopoly and seemed to favor speculators over farmers. Demands for cheaper, more available land prompted passage of an 1820 law reducing the price of land. Yet many settlers resisted federal policy, occupying federal lands before formally purchasing them. Bowing to settler demands, a series of laws was passed giving preferences (preemption rights) to actual settlers, including illegal settlers, culminating in a general law in 1841. That law gave the head of a family who had settled "in person" on land and "improved" it the first claim to buy the land, up to a maximum of 160 acres, at the minimum government price. *Id.* at 233-234.

After the Civil War, the *Morrill Act of 1862* gave away vast tracts of land to the states: 30,000 acres for each senator and representative the state was entitled to under the 1860 census. The land was to be used to establish "Colleges for the Benefit of Agriculture and Mechanic Arts." In addition, the *Homestead Act of 1861* granted most heads of families, persons over 21, and veterans (except those who had "borne arms against the United States or given aid and comfort to its enemies") the right to "enter one quarter section or a less quantity of unappropriated public lands" if they would certify that they wanted the land for their own "exclusive use and benefit" and "for the purpose of actual settlement." *Id.* at 416. After five years of settlement, the government would issue a patent for the land. An actual settler who qualified could, however, buy up the land at the minimum price (generally $1.25 an acre) before the end of the five-year period.

The land laws were, in Friedman's words, "hopelessly inconsistent." A variety of policies were followed. "Some land was free for settlers; other land was for sale. The government proposed to sell some land to the highest bidder; proposed using other land to induce private enterprise to build railroads; gave other land to the state to fund their colleges." *Id.* at 417. The "homestead principle" of "giving land free to the landless poor" was the "weakest of all, and the first to go. The government continued to sell land for cash; and the best land was 'snapped up' by speculators." *Id.*

§1.2.2 SQUATTERS

LAW AND THE CONDITIONS OF FREEDOM IN THE
NINETEENTH-CENTURY UNITED STATES
JAMES WILLARD HURST

3-5 (1956)

One day in February of 1836, in the scarce-born village of Pike Creek on the southeastern Wisconsin shore of Lake Michigan, Jason Lothrop — Baptist minister, schoolteacher, boarding house proprietor, and civic leader — set up on a stump a rude press of his own construction and with ink which he had made himself printed a handbill setting forth the record of the organizational meeting of "The Pike River Claimants Union . . . for the attainment and security of titles to claims on Government lands."

The settlers whose Union this was had begun to move into the lands around Pike Creek beginning in the summer of 1835. They were squatters; put less sympathetically, they were trespassers. They might not lawfully come upon the lands before the federal survey was made, and this was not completed in this area until about February 1, 1836; they might not make formal entry and buy until the president proclaimed a sale day, and Presidents Jackson and Van Buren withheld proclaiming these newly surveyed lands until 1839; they might not establish claims by preemption, for the existing preemption law expired by limitation in June, 1836, and was not immediately renewed because of objections to speculators' abuses. These were formidable legal obstacles. The settlers' reaction tells us some basic things about the working legal philosophy of our nineteenth-century ancestors.

Jason Lothrop recalled twenty years later:

> Much conflicting interest was manifest between the settlers, from the first, in making their claims. Some were greedy in securing at least one section of 640 acres for themselves, and some as much for all their friends whom they expected to settle in the country. Before the lands were surveyed, this often brought confusion and disputes with reference to boundary lines, and still greater confusion followed when the Government surveys were made in the winter of 1835-36. These contentions often led to bitter quarrels and even bloodshed.

The settlers met several times to discuss the need of a more orderly framework within which growth might go on. Finally their discussions produced a meeting at Bullen's store in Pike Creek on February 13, 1836, where they adopted the constitution of their Claimants Union. They created the office of Clerk and set the terms on which claims might be recorded with him, and they established a Board of Censors to adjudicate claims disputes. Through the turgid grandiloquence of their Constitution's preamble shows a pattern of attitudes and values that explains much about nineteenth-century law in the United States, reaching to concerns far greater than those of the tiny frontier village.

Whereas, a union and co-operation of all the inhabitants will be indispensably necessary, in case the pre-emption law should not pass, for the securing and protecting of our claims;

And whereas, we duly appreciate the benefit which may result from such an association, not only in regulating the manner of making and sustaining claims, and settling differences in regard to them, but in securing the same to the holders thereof against speculators at the land sale; and being well aware that consequences the most dangerous to the interests of settlers will follow, if such a union be not formed; and as Government has heretofore encouraged emigration by granting pre-emption to actual settlers, we are assured that our settling and cultivating the public lands is in accordance with the best wishes of Government; and knowing that in some instances our neighbors have been dealt with in an unfeeling manner, driven from their homes, their property destroyed, their persons attacked, and their lives jeopardized, to satisfy the malignant disposition of unprincipled and avaricious men; and looking upon such proceedings as unjust, calculated to produce anarchy, confusion and the like among us, destroy our fair prospects, subvert the good order of society, and render our homes the habitations of terror and distrust — those homes, to obtain which we left our friends, deprived ourselves of the many blessings and privileges of society, have borne the expenses, and encountered the hardships of a perilous journey, advancing into a space beyond the bounds of civilization, and having the many difficulties and obstructions of a state of nature to overcome, and on the peaceable possession of which our all is depending;

We, therefore, as well meaning inhabitants, having in view the promotion of the interest of our settlement, and knowing the many advantages derived from unity of feeling and action, do come forward this day, and solemnly pledge ourselves to render each other our mutual assistance, in the protection of our just rights....

. . . From the survey Ordinance of 1785 on, squatters settled large areas of the public lands in defiance of law, ahead of official survey, without color of title other than that created by the impact of a popular feeling that would not be denied. At government auctions, they assembled in force unlawfully to frighten off free outside bidding and prevent competition from forcing any of their company to pay the public land office more than the legal minimum to regularize his holdings. But, as at Pike Creek, while they waited for the public sale day, these settlers all over the central and mid-western states set up local governments in the form of "claims associations," elected officers with whom to record their land claims and from whom to obtain decisions of conflicts, and then generally abided among themselves by these records and decisions. Often unlawful in origin, settlement nevertheless quickly brought effective demand for law.

§1.2.3   FREED SLAVES

BEEN IN THE STORM SO LONG: THE AFTERMATH OF SLAVERY
LEON LITWACK

399-407 (1980)

Even as they toiled in the same fields, performed the familiar tasks, and returned at dusk to the same cabins, scores of freedmen refused to resign themselves to the permanent status of a landless agricultural working-class. Like most Americans, they aspired to something better and yearned for economic independence and self-employment. Without that independence, their freedom seemed incomplete, even precarious. . . . Although often expressed vaguely, as if to talk about it openly might be unwise, the expectation many ex-slaves shared in the aftermath of the war was that "something extraordinary" would soon intervene to reshape the course of their lives. In the Jubilee they envisioned, the government provided them with forty-acre lots and thereby emancipated them from dependency on their former masters. . . .

The only real question among some blacks was not whether the lands belonging to the former slaveholders would be divided and distributed, but when and how. Freedmen in South Carolina heard that the large plantations along the coast were to be distributed. Equally persistent reports suggested that the lands on which the ex-slaves were working would be divided among them. Few blacks in Mississippi, a Bureau officer reported in November 1865, expressed any interest in hiring themselves out for the next year. "Nearly all of them have heard, that at Christmas, Government is going to take the planters' lands and other property from *them*, and give it to the colored people, and that, in this way they are going to begin to farm on their own account." . . .

. . . When planters had fled, abandoning their properties, the freed slaves had in numerous instances seized control and they gave little indication after the war of yielding their authority to the returning owners. Along the Savannah River, blacks under the leadership of Abalod Shigg seized two major plantations on the assumption that they were entitled to "forty acres and a mule." Federal troops had to be called in to dislodge them. . . .

To apportion the large landed estates among those who worked them and who had already expended years of uncompensated toil made such eminent sense to the ex-slave that he could not easily dismiss this aspiration as but another "exaggerated" or "absurd" view of freedom. "My master has had me ever since I was seven years old, and never give me nothing," observed a twenty-one-year-old laborer in Richmond. "I worked for him twelve years, and I think something is due me." Expecting nothing from his old master, he now trusted the government to do "something for us." The day a South Carolina rice planter anticipated trouble was when one of his field hands told him that "the land ought to belong to the man who (alone) *could work it*," not to those who "sit in the house" and profit by the labor of others. . . . With the acquisition of land, the ex-slave viewed himself raising the crops with which to sustain himself and his family. . . .

. . . When the Yankees finally arrived, they reinforced the land fever by assuring the freed slaves of their right to forty acres and a mule. . . .

[P]lanters derived considerable comfort from the knowledge that Federal officials were prepared to confirm their property rights. Until the blacks acknowledged the futility of land expectations, the Freedmen's Bureau recognised how difficult it would be to stabilize agricultural operations. With that sense of priorities, the Bureau instructed its agents to do everything in their power to disabuse the ex-slaves of any lingering illusions about taking over their masters' lands. . . . If the blacks refused to believe their old masters, Bureau agents were quite prepared to visit the plantations in person and impart the necessary confirmation: "The government owns no lands in this State. It therefore can give away none. Freedmen can obtain farms with the money which they have earned by their labor. Every one, therefore, shall work diligently, and carefully save his wages, till he may be able to buy land and possess his own home." . . .

As an alternative to confiscation, Freedmen's Bureau officers and northern white missionaries and teachers advanced the classic mid-nineteenth-century self-help ideology and implored the newly freed slaves to heed its lessons. Rather than entertain notions of government bounties, they should cultivate habits of frugality, temperance, honesty, and hard work; if they did so, they might not only accumulate the savings to purchase land but would derive greater personal satisfaction from having earned it in this manner. Almost identical advice permeated the editorials of black newspapers, the speeches of black leaders, and the resolutions adopted by black meetings. "Let us go to work faithfully for whoever pays fairly, until we ourselves shall become employers and planters," the Black Republican, a New Orleans newspaper, editorialized in its first issue. With an even finer grasp of American values, a black Charlestonian thought economic success capable of overriding the remaining vestiges of racial slavery. "This is the panacea which will heal all the maladies of a Negro-phobia type. Let colored men simply do as anybody else in business does, be self-reliant, industrious, producers of the staples for market and merchandise, and he will have no more trouble on account of his complexion, than the white men have about the color of their hair or beards."

To provide proper models for their people, black newspapers featured examples of self-made freedmen who had managed to accumulate land and were forming the nucleus of a propertied and entrepreneurial class in the South. Actually, a number of blacks had done precisely that, some of them fortunate enough to have purchased tax lands and still others who had taken advantage of the *Homestead Act* or who had made enough money to purchase a plot in their old neighborhoods. But the number of propertied blacks remained small, and some of these found they had been defrauded by whites who had an equal appreciation of the self-help philosophy and made the most of it. Even the blacks who obtained legitimate title to lands soon discovered the elusive quality of economic success. The land often turned out to be of an inferior quality, the freedman usually lacked the capital and credit to develop it properly, and he might consequently find himself enmeshed in the very web of indebtedness and dependency he had sought to escape. By the acquisition of land, he hardly avoided the same problems plaguing so many white farmers.

. . . On May 29, 1865, President Andrew Johnson announced his Proclamation of Amnesty, whereby most former Confederates were to be pardoned and recover any of their lands which might have been confiscated or occupied. . . . In some communities, the news [of the Amnesty] coincided with a rumor, said to have been circulated by planters, that the President had revoked the Emancipation Proclamation. To many freedmen, contemplating what would happen to the lands they had worked and expected to own, that was no rumor at all. "Amnesty for the persons, no amnesty for the property," the New Orleans Tribune cried. "It is enough for the republic to spare the life of the rebels — without restoring to them their plantations and palaces." Under Johnson's magnanimous pardoning policy, any faint hope of a land division collapsed, along with the promising wartime precedents. Rather than confirm the settlers in possession of the land they had cultivated and on which they had erected their homes, the government now proposed to return the plantations to those for whom they had previously labored as slaves. Not satisfied with having their lands returned, some of the owners displayed their own brands of "insolence" and "ingratitude" by claiming damages for any alterations made by the black settlers and by suing them for "back rents" for the use of the land.

[General O. O. Howard] articulated the government's position [to black settlers on Edisto Island]. They should lay aside any bitter feelings they harbored for their former masters and contract to work for them. By working for wages or shares, he assured them, they would be achieving the same ends as possession of the soil would have given them. . . .

The hope Bureau officials held out for the freedmen was largely a cruel delusion. The same men who had been disabusing the minds of the ex-slaves of their land expectations now urged them to bind themselves to the white man's land. . . . What the freedmen on Edisto Island found most offensive in Howard's speech, apart from having to give up their claims to the land, was the suggestion that they should now work for their former masters. In the petition they addressed to the President, the Edisto blacks argued that no man who had only recently faced his master on the field of battle should now be expected to submit to him for the necessities of life. . . .

To inform the blacks that their land aspirations were all a delusion was difficult enough. But to remove them from the lands they had come to regard as their own often required more than verbal skills. In Norfolk County, Virginia, the freedmen who had settled on Taylor's farm refused to leave, ignoring court orders and ousting the sheriffs and Federal officers who tried to enforce them. After assembling together, the blacks refused offers of compromise, questioned the President's right to pardon the original owner, and resolved to defend their property. At this meeting, Richard Parker ("better known as 'Uncle Dick,'" said the Norfolk newspaper) explained to his fellow freedmen that the white man had secured this land only by forcibly expelling the Indians and he suggested that they now exercise the same prerogative. . . . After a pitched battle with county agents, the black settlers were finally driven off the land.

If blacks could not acquire land by government action, neither would they find it easy to obtain it by any other means, even if they adopted the self-help precepts and accumulated the necessary funds. Appreciating the threat black proprietorship posed to a dependent, stable, and contented work force, and the feelings of "impudence and independence" it might generate, many planters refused to sell or to rent any land to blacks. . . .

Within a year of the war's end, the planter class had virtually completed the recovery of its property. . . .

INCIDENTS IN THE LIFE OF A SLAVE GIRL: WRITTEN BY HERSELF
HARRIET A. JACOBS

201 (Harvard University Press 1987) (originally published in 1861)

I and my children are now free! We are as free from the power of slaveholders as are the white people of the north; and though that, according to my ideas, is not saying a great deal, it is a vast improvement in *my* condition. The dream of my life is not yet realized. I do not sit with my children in a home of my own. I still long for a hearth-stone of my own, however humble. I wish it for my children's sake far more than for my own.

NOTES AND QUESTIONS

Chief Justice John Marshall explains in *Johnson v. M'Intosh* how the United States expropriated vast amounts of land from American Indian nations. Lawrence Friedman reports that a great deal of land was given to the railroads for free. Dee Brown notes that in the middle of the nineteenth century, land grants to railroads encompassed 155 million acres, "or more than one fourth of the Louisiana purchase, one ninth of what was then the nation's entire land area." Dee Brown, *Hear That Lonesome Whistle Blow*

176-177 (1977). Some of this land was kept for railroad use, and some of it was sold off. Other land in the West was sold or distributed by the government at below market prices. Still other land was sold at fair market value; some of this land went to speculators who resold it. James Willard Hurst notes that squatters often defeated federal land policies by trespassing on public lands; many of their claims were later recognized by the federal government. Leon Litwack recounts how freed slaves were denied not only access to land but compensation for their years of unpaid labor and were often constrained by economic necessity to continue working that same land, sometimes for the same master. Harriet Jacobs reports to us what it would have meant to her to raise her children in her own home.

Together, these historical reports suggest an activist government taking and distributing land for a variety of purposes. They also suggest a fair amount of self-help and creation of law by communities of settlers who squatted on government land. What implications does such government policy have for us today?

PROBLEM

A group of homeless persons takes over abandoned property in a major city. The city has foreclosed on the property for failure to pay property taxes and has not yet resold it or begun looking for a buyer since the property is dilapidated. The squatters claim a right to take over the abandoned property and point to the experience of the American West, where squatters took over property and interfered with land sales to others. More often than not, those squatters' claims were later confirmed by legislation. The city objects to random occupations of its property and hopes to develop a rational plan for the future use of the property.

1. As attorney for the city, what advice would you give the mayor?

2. As attorney for the squatters, what arguments would you make to persuade the city to allow your clients to claim possessory rights in abandoned city property? As attorney for the city, how would you respond to these arguments?

§1.2.4   THE RIGHT OF FAMILIES TO STAY TOGETHER AND BASIC NEEDS FULFILLMENT

The constitutions of some countries, such as South Africa, contain a right to housing and basic welfare needs. *See, e.g.*, S. Afr. Const. ch. 2 §26 ("Everyone has the right to have access to adequate housing"); S. Afr. Const. ch. 2 §27(1) ("Everyone has the right to have access to a. health care services, including reproductive health care; b. sufficient food and water; and c. social security, including, if they are unable to support themselves and their dependants, appropriate social assistance"). The United States Constitution does not contain such a guarantee. In 1969, Professor Frank Michelman argued that the Constitution should be interpreted to require the states to provide minimum levels of government financial assistance sufficient to enable the poor to provide for their basic needs and to avoid severe deprivation. In effect, he suggested that individuals have a constitutional right to minimum protection to obtain access to the means necessary for human life. Frank Michelman, *In Pursuit of Constitutional Welfare Rights: One View of Rawls' Theory of Justice*, 121 U. Pa. L. Rev. 962 (1973); Frank Michelman, *Foreword: On Protecting the Poor Through the Fourteenth Amend-*

ment, 83 Harv. L. Rev. 7 (1969). No court in the United States has accepted this argument.

The New York Constitution requires provision of social welfare for the needy, but its enforcement is subject to legislative discretion. N.Y. Const. art. XVII, §1 ("The aid, care and support of the needy are public concerns and shall be provided by the state and by such of its subdivisions, and in such manner and by such means, as the legislature may from time to tine determine"); *Tucker v. Toia*, 371 N.E.2d 449, 451 (N.Y. 1977) (although the legislature has the discretion to determine the means and amount of aid to the needy, it prohibits the legislature from refusing to aid those it has classified as needy). Some courts have interpreted their state welfare statutes to impose obligations on the legislature to provide sufficient funding to enable families to live with their children and avoid placing their children in foster care. *See, e.g., Massachusetts Coalition for the Homeless v. Secretary of Human Services*, 511 N.E.2d 603 (Mass. 1987); *Jiggetts v. Grinker*, 553 N.E.2d 570 (N.Y. 1990); *Martin A. v. Gross*, 524 N.Y.S.2d 121 (Sup. Ct. 1987); *Hodge v. Ginsberg*, 303 S.E.2d 245 (W. Va. 1983). Such rulings are subject to legislative amendment; the Massachusetts legislature overruled the *Massachusetts Coalition* case by inserting the words "subject to appropriation" in the statute. *See, e.g.*, Mass. Gen. Laws ch. 18, §2. Most state courts have agreed with a New Jersey court that ruled that "the extent to which funds are to be made available to meet the standard of need under New Jersey statutes is a political question to be decided by the representatives of the people." *In re Petitions for Rulemaking*, 538 A.2d 1302 (N.J. Super. Ct. App. Div. 1988). *Accord, Tilden v. Hayward*, 1990 WL 131162 (Del. Ch. 1990).

At the time Professor Michelman wrote, federal welfare legislation guaranteed families with children an entitlement to a minimum level of government benefits. However, in 1996, Congress passed the *Personal Responsibility and Work Opportunity Act of 1996*, 42 U.S.C. §§601 to 619. This "welfare reform" bill abolished the old *Aid to Families with Dependent Children* (AFDC) program and replaced it with *Temporary Assistance to Needy Families* (TANF). The new law abolishes the welfare entitlement and replaces it with a more limited right to temporary assistance with a five-year lifetime limit on such government benefits and a requirement that recipients start working within two years in order to continue receiving benefits. States are empowered to apply even more stringent requirements, such as requiring recipients to go to work immediately, a policy that was originally adopted in Wisconsin. Wis. Stat. §49.141(2)(b) (repealed, 1999 Wis. Laws Act 9).

If a mother obtains a job paying the minimum wage, she is unlikely to be able to take care of herself and her children and pay for housing, clothing, adequate childcare, and transportation without additional funding from some other source. Kathryn Edin and Laura Lein, *Making Ends Meet: How Single Mothers Survive Welfare and Low-Wage Work* (1997). Should individuals be entitled to minimum levels of assistance? Should parents be entitled to sufficient resources to live with their children? Consider the following story from the New York Times.

> The [welfare mother] had signed an agreement with the state to go to college, which she believed offered her the best route to a job that paid enough to support her three children. She was put on a waiting list. Her caseworker told her she would have to get a job in the meantime. A few weeks after she began working for $5.50 an hour, her 5-year-old got sick. The boy was running a fever and could not go to the day-care center. The worker then told the mother that the only acceptable excuse for missing work was a doctor's note saying

that she herself was ill. So she left her son with a neighbor. When she came home, she found him alone and untended. She stayed home with him and was fired from her job. Her welfare benefits were then reduced because she had not done what her worker required. Unable to pay the rent, the family was evicted . . . and slept in a friend's car. Because of the family homelessness, one of the children's teachers reported them to child-protection services. The child-protection worker told the mother that her children would be placed in foster care if she could not provide for them.

Celia W. Dugger, *Iowa Plan Tries to Cut Off the Cash*, New York Times, Apr. 7, 1995, at A1, quoted in Joel F. Handler and Yeheskel Hasenfeld, *We the Poor People: Work, Poverty, and Welfare* 98 (New Haven: Yale Univ. Press, 1997).

   Assume the mother sues the state, claiming that she has a constitutional right not to be separated from her child and that, if government assistance is needed to ensure this right, that she is constitutionally entitled to it so that she can raise her child in her own home. How would you decide the case?

§1.3   Labor and Investment

§1.3.1   NEWS AND THE LAW OF UNFAIR COMPETITION

INTERNATIONAL NEWS SERVICE v. ASSOCIATED PRESS
248 U.S. 215 (1918)

Mr. Justice MAHLON PITNEY delivered the opinion of the Court.

The parties are competitors in the gathering and distribution of news and its publication for profit in newspapers throughout the United States. The Associated Press, which was complainant in the District Court, is a co-operative organization, incorporated under the *Membership Corporations Law* of the state of New York, its members being individuals who are either proprietors or representatives of about 950 daily newspapers published in all parts of the United States. . . . Complainant gathers in all parts of the world, by means of various instrumentalities of its own, by exchange with its members, and by other appropriate means, news and intelligence of current and recent events of interest to newspaper readers and distributes it daily to its members for publication in their newspapers. The cost of the service, amounting approximately to $3,500,000 per annum, is assessed upon the members and becomes a part of their costs of operation, to be recouped, presumably with profit, through the publication of their several newspapers. Under complainant's by-laws each member agrees upon assuming membership that news received through complainant's service is received exclusively for publication in a particular newspaper, language, and place specified in the certificate of membership, that no other use of it shall be permitted, and that no member shall furnish or permit any one in his employ or connected with his newspaper to furnish any of complainant's news in advance of publication to any person not a member. And each member is required to gather the local news of his district and supply it to the Associated Press and to no one else.

   Defendant [International News Service] is a corporation organized under the laws of the state of New Jersey, whose business is the gathering and selling of news to its customers and clients, consisting of newspapers published throughout the United States, under contracts by which they pay certain amounts at stated times for defendant's service. It has widespread news-gathering agencies; the cost of its operations amounts, it is said, to more than $2,000,000 per annum; and it serves about 400 newspapers located in the various cities of the United States and abroad, a few of which are represented, also, in the membership of the Associated Press.

The parties are in the keenest competition between themselves in the distribution of news throughout the United States; and so, as a rule, are the newspapers that they serve, in their several districts.

Complainant in its bill, defendant in its answer, have set forth in almost identical terms the rather obvious circumstances and conditions under which their business is conducted. The value of the service, and of the news furnished, depends upon the promptness of transmission, as well as upon the accuracy and impartiality of the news; it being essential that the news be transmitted to members or subscribers as early or earlier than similar information can be furnished to competing newspapers by other news services, and that the news furnished by each agency shall not be furnished to newspapers which do not contribute to the expense of gathering it. And further, to quote from the answer:

> Prompt knowledge and publication of worldwide news is essential to the conduct of a modern newspaper, and by reason of the enormous expense incident to the gathering and distribution of such news, the only practical way in which a proprietor of a newspaper can obtain the same is, either through co-operation with a considerable number of other newspaper proprietors in the work of collecting and distributing such news, and the equitable division with them of the expenses thereof, or by the purchase of such news from some existing agency engaged in that business.

The bill was filed to restrain the pirating of complainant's news by defendant in three ways: First, by bribing employes of newspapers published by complainant's members to furnish Associated Press news to defendant before publication, for transmission by telegraph and telephone to defendant's clients for publication by them; second, by inducing Associated Press members to violate its by-laws and permit defendant to obtain news before publication; and, third, by copying news from bulletin boards and from early editions of complainant's newspapers and selling this, either bodily or after rewriting it, to defendant's customers. . . .

The only matter that has been argued before us is whether defendant may lawfully be restrained from appropriating news taken from bulletins issued by complainant or any of its members, or from newspapers published by them, for the purpose of selling it to defendant's clients. Complainant asserts that defendant's admitted course of conduct in this regard both violates complainant's property right in the news and constitutes unfair competition in business. And notwithstanding [that] the case has proceeded only to the stage of a preliminary injunction, we have deemed it proper to consider the underlying questions, since they go to the very merits of the action and are presented upon facts that are not in dispute. As presented in argument, these questions are: (1) Whether there is any property in news; (2) Whether, if there be property in news collected for the purpose of being published, it survives the instant of its publication in the first newspaper to which it is communicated by the newsgatherer; and (3) Whether defendant's admitted course of conduct in appropriating for commercial use matter taken from bulletins or early editions of Associated Press publications constitutes unfair competition in trade.

. . . Complainant's news matter is not copyrighted. It is said that it could not, in practice, be copyrighted, because of the large number of dispatches that are sent daily;

and, according to complainant's contention, news is not within the operation of the copyright act. Defendant, while apparently conceding this, nevertheless invokes the analogies of the law of literary property and copyright, insisting as its principal contention that, assuming complainant has a right of property in its news, it can be maintained (unless the copyright act be complied with) only by being kept secret and confidential, and that upon the publication with complainant's consent of uncopyrighted news of any of complainant's members in a newspaper or upon a bulletin board, the right of property is lost, and the subsequent use of the news by the public or by defendant for any purpose whatever becomes lawful. . . .

In considering the general question of property in news matter, it is necessary to recognize its dual character, distinguishing between the substance of the information and the particular form or collocation of words in which the writer has communicated it.

No doubt news articles often possess a literary quality, and are the subject of literary property at the common law; nor do we question that such an article, as a literary production, is the subject of copyright by the terms of the act as it now stands. . . .

But the news element — the information respecting current events contained in the literary production — is not the creation of the writer, but is a report of matters that ordinarily are *publici juris*; it is the history of the day. It is not to be supposed that the framers of the Constitution, when they empowered Congress "to promote the progress of science and useful arts, by securing for limited times to authors and inventors the exclusive right to their respective writings and discoveries" (Const. art. 1, §8, par. 8), intended to confer upon one who might happen to be the first to report a historic event the exclusive right for any period to spread the knowledge of it.

We need spend no time, however, upon the general question of property in news matter at common law, or the application of the copyright act, since it seems to us the case must turn upon the question of unfair competition in business. And, in our opinion, this does not depend upon any general right of property analogous to the common-law right of the proprietor of an unpublished work to prevent its publication without his consent; nor is it foreclosed by showing that the benefits of the copyright act have been waived. We are dealing here not with restrictions upon publication but with the very facilities and processes of publication. The peculiar value of news is in the spreading of it while it is fresh; and it is evident that a valuable property interest in the news, as news, cannot be maintained by keeping it secret. Besides, except for matters improperly disclosed, or published in breach of trust or confidence, or in violation of law, none of which is involved in this branch of the case, the news of current events may be regarded as common property. What we are concerned with is the business of making it known to the world, in which both parties to the present suit are engaged. That business consists in maintaining a prompt, sure, steady, and reliable service designed to place the daily events of the world at the breakfast table of the millions at a price that, while of trifling moment to each reader, is sufficient in the aggregate to afford compensation for the cost of gathering and distributing it, with the added profit so necessary as an incentive to effective action in the commercial world. The service thus performed for newspaper readers is not only innocent but extremely useful in itself, and indubitably constitutes a legitimate business. The parties are competitors in this field; and, on fundamental principles, applicable here as elsewhere, when the rights or privileges of the one are liable to conflict with those of the other, each party is under a duty so to conduct its own business as not unnecessarily or unfairly to injure that of the other.

Obviously, the question of what is unfair competition in business must be determined with particular reference to the character and circumstances of the business. The question here is not so much the rights of either party as against the public but their rights as between themselves. And, although we may and do assume that neither party has any remaining property interest as against the public in uncopyrighted news matter after the moment of its first publication, it by no means follows that there is no remaining property interest in it as between themselves. For, to both of them alike, news matter, however little susceptible of ownership or dominion in the absolute sense, is stock in trade, to be gathered at the cost of enterprise, organization, skill, labor, and money, and to be distributed and sold to those who will pay money for it, as for any other merchandise. Regarding the news, therefore, as but the material out of which both parties are seeking to make profits at the same time and in the same field, we hardly can fail to recognize that for this purpose, and as between them, it must be regarded as *quasi* property, irrespective of the rights of either as against the public. . . .

Not only do the acquisition and transmission of news require elaborate organization and a large expenditure of money, skill, and effort; not only has [news] an exchange value to the gatherer, dependent chiefly upon its novelty and freshness, the regularity of the service, its reputed reliability and thoroughness, and its adaptability to the public needs; but also, as is evident, the news has an exchange value to one who can misappropriate it.

The peculiar features of the case arise from the fact that, while novelty and freshness form so important an element in the success of the business, the very processes of distribution and publication necessarily occupy a good deal of time. Complainant's service, as well as defendant's, is a daily service to daily newspapers; most of the foreign news reaches this country at the Atlantic seaboard, principally at the city of New York, and because of this, and of time differentials due to the earth's rotation, the distribution of news matter throughout the country is principally from east to west; and, since in speed the telegraph and telephone easily outstrip the rotation of the earth, it is a simple matter for defendant to take complainant's news from bulletins or early editions of complainant's members in the eastern cities and at the mere cost of telegraphic transmission cause it to be published in western papers issued at least as early as those served by complainant. Besides this, and irrespective of time differentials, irregularities in telegraphic transmission on different lines, and the normal consumption of time in printing and distributing the newspaper, result in permitting pirated news to be placed in the hands of defendant's readers sometimes simultaneously with the service of competing Associated Press papers, occasionally even earlier.

Defendant insists that when, with the sanction and approval of complainant, and as the result of the use of its news for the very purpose for which it is distributed, a portion of complainant's members communicate it to the general public by posting it upon bulletin boards so that all may read, or by issuing it to newspapers and distributing it indiscriminately, complainant no longer has the right to control the use to be made of it; that when it thus reaches the light of day it becomes the common possession of all to whom it is accessible; and that any purchaser of a newspaper has the right to communicate the intelligence which it contains to anybody and for any purpose, even for the purpose of selling it for profit to newspapers published for profit in competition with complainant's members.

The fault in the reasoning lies in applying as a test the right of the complainant as against the public, instead of considering the rights of complainant and defendant, competitors in business, as between themselves. The right of the purchaser of a single newspaper to spread knowledge of its contents gratuitously, for any legitimate purpose not unreasonably interfering with complainant's right to make merchandise of it, may be admitted; but to transmit that news for commercial use, in competition with complainant — which is what defendant has done and seeks to justify — is a very different matter. In doing this defendant, by its very act, admits that it is taking material that has been acquired by complainant as the result of organization and the expenditure of labor, skill, and money, and which is salable by complainant for money, and that defendant in appropriating it and selling it as its own is endeavoring to reap where it has not sown, and by disposing of it to newspapers that are competitors of complainant's members is appropriating to itself the harvest of those who have sown. Stripped of all disguises, the process amounts to an unauthorized interference with the normal operation of complainant's legitimate business precisely at the point where the profit is to be reaped, in order to divert a material portion of the profit from those who have earned it to those who have not; with special advantage to defendant in the competition because of the fact that it is not burdened with any part of the expense of gathering the news. The transaction speaks for itself and a court of equity ought not to hesitate long in characterizing it as unfair competition in business. . . .

The contention that the news is abandoned to the public for all purposes when published in the first newspaper is untenable. Abandonment is a question of intent, and the entire organization of the Associated Press negatives such a purpose. The cost of the service would be [prohibitive] if the reward were to be so limited. No single newspaper, no small group of newspapers, could sustain the expenditure. Indeed, it is one of the most obvious results of defendant's theory that, by permitting indiscriminate publication by anybody and everybody for purposes of profit in competition with the news-gatherer, it would render publication profitless, or so little profitable as in effect to cut off the service by rendering the cost prohibitive in comparison with the return. The practical needs and requirements of the business are reflected in complainant's by-laws which have been referred to. Their effect is that publication by each member must be deemed not by any means an abandonment of the news to the world for any and all purposes, but a publication for limited purposes; for the benefit of the readers of the bulletin or the newspaper as such; not for the purpose of making merchandise of it as news, with the result of depriving complainant's other members of their reasonable opportunity to obtain just returns for their expenditures.

It is to be observed that the view we adopt does not result in giving to complainant the right to monopolize either the gathering or the distribution of the news, or, without complying with the copyright act, to prevent the reproduction of its news articles, but only postpones participation by complainant's competitor in the processes of distribution and reproduction of news that it has not gathered, and only to the extent necessary to prevent that competitor from reaping the fruits of complainant's efforts and expenditure, to the partial exclusion of complainant, and in violation of the principle that underlies the maxim *sic utere tuo*, etc. . . .

Besides the misappropriation, there are elements of imitation, of false pretense, in defendant's practices. The device of rewriting complainant's news articles, frequently resorted to, carries its own comment. The habitual failure to give credit to complainant for that which is taken is significant. Indeed, the entire system of appropriating complainant's news and transmitting it as commercial product to defendant's clients and patrons amounts to a false representation to them and to their newspaper readers that the news transmitted is the result of defendant's own investigation in the field. But these elements, although accentuating the wrong, are not the essence of it. It is something more than the advantage of celebrity of which complainant is being deprived. . . .

Mr. Justice OLIVER WENDELL HOLMES, JR., dissenting.

When an uncopyrighted combination of words is published there is no general right to forbid other people repeating them — in other words there is no property in the combination or in the thoughts or facts that the words express. Property, a creation of law, does not arise from value, although exchangeable — a matter of fact. Many exchangeable values may be destroyed intentionally without compensation. Property depends upon exclusion by law from interference, and a person is not excluded from using any combination of words merely because some one has used it before, even if it took labor and genius to make it. If a given person is to be prohibited from making the use of words that his neighbors are free to make some other ground must be found. One such ground is vaguely expressed in the phrase unfair trade. This means that the words are repeated by a competitor in business in such a way as to convey a misrepresentation that materially injures the person who first used them, by appropriating credit of some kind which the first user has earned. The ordinary case is a representation by device, appearance, or other indirection that the defendant's goods come from the plaintiff. But the only reason why it is actionable to make such a representation is that it tends to give the defendant an advantage in his competition with the plaintiff and that it is thought undesirable that an advantage should be gained in that way. Apart from that the defendant may use such unpatented devices and uncopyrighted combinations of words as he likes. The ordinary case, I say, is palming off the defendant's product as the plaintiff's but the same evil may follow from the opposite falsehood — from saying whether in words or by implication that the plaintiff's product is the defendant's, and that, it seems to me, is what has happened here.

Fresh news is got only by enterprise and expense. To produce such news as it is produced by the defendant represents by implication that it has been acquired by the defendant's enterprise and at its expense. When it comes from one of the great news collecting agencies like the Associated Press, the source generally is indicated, plainly importing that credit; and that such a representation is implied may be inferred with some confidence from the unwillingness of the defendant to give the credit and tell the truth. If the plaintiff produces the news at the same time that the defendant does, the defendant's presentation impliedly denies to the plaintiff the credit of collecting the facts and assumes that credit to the defendant. If the plaintiff is later in Western cities it naturally will be supposed to have obtained its information from the defendant. The falsehood is a little more subtle, the injury, a little more indirect, than in ordinary cases of unfair trade, but I think that the principle that condemns the one condemns the other. It is a question of how strong an infusion of fraud is necessary to turn a flavor into a poison. The dose seems to me strong enough here to need a remedy from the law. But as, in my view, the only ground of complaint that can be recognized without legislation is the implied misstatement, it can be corrected by stating the truth; and a suitable acknowledgment of the source is all that the plaintiff can require. I think that within the limits recognized by the decision of the Court the defendant should be enjoined from publishing news obtained from the Associated Press for hours after publication by the plaintiff unless it gives express credit to the Associated Press; the number of hours and the form of acknowledgment to be settled by the District Court.

Mr. Justice LOUIS D. BRANDEIS, dissenting.

There are published in the United States about 2,500 daily papers. More than 800 of them are supplied with domestic and foreign news of general interest by the Associated Press — a corporation without capital stock which does not sell news or earn or seek to earn profits, but serves merely as an instrumentality by means of which these papers supply themselves at joint expense with such news. Papers not members of the Associated Press depend for their news of general interest largely upon agencies organized for profit. Among these agencies is the International News Service which supplies news to about 400 subscribing papers. It has, like the Associated Press, bureaus and correspondents in this and foreign countries; and its annual expenditures in gathering and distributing news is about $2,000,000. Ever since its organization in 1909, it has included among the sources from which it gathers news, copies (purchased in the open market) of early editions of some papers published by members of the Associated Press and the bulletins publicly posted by them. These items, which constitute but a small part of the news transmitted to its subscribers, are generally verified by the International News Service before transmission; but frequently items are transmitted without verification; and occasionally even without being re-written. In no case is the fact disclosed that such item was suggested by or taken from a paper or bulletin published by an Associated Press member.

No question of statutory copyright is involved. The sole question for our consideration is this: Was the International News Service properly enjoined from using, or causing to be used gainfully, news of which it acquired knowledge by lawful means (namely, by reading publicly posted bulletins or papers purchased by it in the open market) merely because the news had been originally gathered by the Associated Press and continued to be of value to some of its members, or because it did not reveal the source from which it was acquired? . . .

News is a report of recent occurrences. The business of the news agency is to gather systematically knowledge of such occurrences of interest and to distribute reports thereof. The Associated Press contended that knowledge so acquired is property, because it costs money and labor to produce and because it has value for which those who have it not are ready to pay; that it remains property and is entitled to protection as long as it has commercial value as news; and that to protect it effectively, the defendant must be enjoined from making, or causing to be made, any gainful use of it while it retains such value. An essential element of individual property is the legal right to exclude others from enjoying it. If the property is private, the right of exclusion may be absolute; if the property is affected with a public interest, the right of exclusion is qualified. But the fact that a product of the mind has cost its producer money and labor, and has a value for which others are willing to pay, is not sufficient to ensure to it this legal attribute of property. The general rule of law is, that the noblest of human productions — knowledge, truths ascertained, conceptions, and ideas — become, after voluntary communication to others, free as the air to common use. Upon these incorporeal productions the attribute of property is continued after such communication only in certain classes of cases where public policy has seemed to demand it. These exceptions are confined to productions which, in some degree, involve creation, invention, or discovery. But by no means all such are endowed with this attribute of property. The creations which are recognized as property by the common law are literary, dramatic, musical, and other artistic creations; and these have also protection under the copyright statutes. The inventions and discoveries upon which this attribute of property is conferred only by statute, are the few comprised within the patent law.

There are also many other cases in which courts interfere to prevent curtailment of plaintiff's enjoyment of incorporeal productions; and in which the right to relief is often called a property right, but is such only in a special sense. In those cases, the plaintiff has no absolute right to the protection of his production; he has merely the qualified right to be protected as against the defendant's acts, because of the special relation in which the latter stands or the wrongful method or means employed in acquiring the knowledge or the manner in which it is used. Protection of this character is afforded where the suit is based upon breach of contract or of trust or upon unfair competition.

The knowledge for which protection is sought in the case at bar is not of a kind upon which the law has heretofore conferred the attributes of property; nor is the manner of its acquisition or use nor the purpose to which it is applied, such as has heretofore been recognized as entitling a plaintiff to relief. . . .

Plaintiff . . . contended that defendant's practice constitutes unfair competition, because there is "appropriation without cost to itself of values created by" the plaintiff; and it is upon this ground that the decision of this court appears to be based. To appropriate and use for profit, knowledge and ideas produced by other men, without making compensation or even acknowledgment, may be inconsistent with a finer sense of propriety; but, with the exceptions indicated above, the law has heretofore sanctioned the practice. Thus it was held that one may ordinarily make and sell anything in any form, may copy with exactness that which another has produced, or may otherwise use his ideas without his consent and without the payment of compensation, and yet not inflict a legal injury; and that ordinarily one is at perfect liberty to find out, if he can by lawful means, trade secrets of another, however valuable, and then use the knowledge so acquired gainfully, although it cost the original owner much in effort and in money to collect or produce.

Such taking and gainful use of a product of another which, for reasons of public policy, the law has refused to endow with the attributes of property, does not become unlawful because the product happens to have been taken from a rival and is used in competition with him. The unfairness in competition which hitherto has been recognized by the law as a basis for relief, lay in the manner or means of conducting the business; and the manner or means held legally unfair, involves either fraud or force or the doing of acts otherwise prohibited by law. In the "passing off" cases (the typical and most common case of unfair competition), the wrong consists in fraudulently representing by word or act that defendant's goods are those of plaintiff. In the other cases, the diversion of trade was effected through physical or moral coercion, or by inducing breaches of contract or of trust or by enticing away employes. In some others, called cases of simulated competition, relief was granted because defendant's purpose was unlawful; namely, not competition but deliberate and wanton destruction of plaintiff's business.

That competition is not unfair in a legal sense, merely because the profits gained are unearned, even if made at the expense of a rival, is shown by many cases besides those referred to above. He who follows the pioneer into a new market, or who engages in the manufacture of an article newly introduced by another, seeks profits due largely to the labor and expense of the first adventurer; but the law sanctions, indeed encourages, the pursuit. He who makes a city known through his product, must submit to sharing the resultant trade with others who, perhaps for that reason, locate there later. He who has made his name a guaranty of quality, protests in vain when another with the same name engages, perhaps for that reason, in the same lines of business;

provided, precaution is taken to prevent the public from being deceived into the belief that what he is selling, was made by his competitor. One bearing a name made famous by another is permitted to enjoy the unearned benefit which necessarily flows from such use, even though the use proves harmful to him who gave the name value.

The means by which the International News Service obtains news gathered by the Associated Press is also clearly unobjectionable. It is taken from papers bought in the open market or from bulletins publicly posted. No breach of contract or of trust, and neither fraud nor force, is involved. The manner of use is likewise unobjectionable. No reference is made by word or by act to the Associated Press, either in transmitting the news to subscribers or by them in publishing it in their papers. Neither the International News Service nor its subscribers is gaining or seeking to gain in its business a benefit from the reputation of the Associated Press. They are merely using its product without making compensation. That they have a legal right to do, because the product is not property, and they do not stand in any relation to the Associated Press, either of contract or of trust, which otherwise precludes such use. The argument is not advanced by characterizing such taking and use a misappropriation.

It is also suggested that the fact that defendant does not refer to the Associated Press as the source of the news may furnish a basis for the relief. But the defendant and its subscribers, unlike members of the Associated Press, were under no contractual obligation to disclose the source of the news; and there is no rule of law requiring acknowledgment to be made where uncopyrighted matter is reproduced. The International News Service is said to mislead its subscribers into believing that the news transmitted was originally gathered by it and that they in turn mislead their readers. There is, in fact, no representation by either of any kind. Sources of information are sometimes given because required by contract; sometimes because naming the source gives authority to an otherwise incredible statement; and sometimes the source is named because the agency does not wish to take the responsibility itself of giving currency to the news. But no representation can properly be implied from omission to mention the source of information except that the International News Service is transmitting news which it believes to be credible. . . .

The great development of agencies now furnishing country-wide distribution of news, the vastness of our territory, and improvements in the means of transmitting intelligence, have made it possible for a news agency or newspapers to obtain, without paying compensation, the fruit of another's efforts and to use news so obtained gainfully in competition with the original collector. The injustice of such action is obvious. But to give relief against it would involve more than the application of existing rules of law to new facts. It would require the making of a new rule in analogy to existing ones. The unwritten law possesses capacity for growth; and has often satisfied new demands for justice by invoking analogies or by expanding a rule or principle. This process has been in the main wisely applied and should not be discontinued. Where the problem is relatively simple, as it is apt to be when private interests only are involved, it generally proves adequate. But with the increasing complexity of society, the public interest tends to become omnipresent; and the problems presented by new demands for justice cease to be simple. Then the creation or recognition by courts of a new private right may work serious injury to the general public, unless the boundaries of the right are definitely established and wisely guarded. In order to reconcile the new private right with the public interest, it may be necessary to prescribe limitations and rules for its enjoyment; and also to provide administrative machinery for enforcing the rules. It is largely for this reason that, in the effort to meet the many new demands for justice incident to a rapidly changing civilization, resort to legislation has latterly been had with increasing frequency.

The rule for which the plaintiff contends would effect an important extension of property rights and a corresponding curtailment of the free use of knowledge and of ideas; and the facts of this case admonish us of the danger involved in recognizing such a property right in news, without imposing upon news-gatherers corresponding obligations....

A Legislature, urged to enact a law by which one news agency or newspaper may prevent appropriation of the fruits of its labors by another, would consider such facts and possibilities and others which appropriate inquiry might disclose. Legislators might conclude that it was impossible to put an end to the obvious injustice involved in such appropriation of news, without opening the door to other evils, greater than that sought to be remedied....

Or legislators dealing with the subject might conclude, that the right to news values should be protected to the extent of permitting recovery of damages for any unauthorized use, but that protection by injunction should be denied.... If a Legislature concluded to recognize property in published news to the extent of permitting recovery at law, it might, with a view to making the remedy more certain and adequate, provide a fixed measure of damages, as in the case of copyright infringement.

Or again, a Legislature might conclude that it was unwise to recognize even so limited a property right in published news as that above indicated; but that a news agency should, on some conditions, be given full protection of its business; and to that end a remedy by injunction as well as one for damages should be granted, where news collected by it is gainfully used without permission. If a Legislature concluded that under certain circumstances news-gathering is a business affected with a public interest; it might declare that, in such cases, news should be protected against appropriation, only if the gatherer assumed the obligation of supplying it at reasonable rates and without discrimination, to all papers which applied therefor. If legislators reached that conclusion, they would probably go further, and prescribe the conditions under which and the extent to which the protection should be afforded; and they might also provide the administrative machinery necessary for insuring to the public, the press, and the news agencies, full enjoyment of the rights so conferred.

Courts are ill-equipped to make the investigations which should precede a determination of the limitations which should be set upon any property right in news or of the circumstances under which news gathered by a private agency should be deemed affected with a public interest. Courts would be powerless to prescribe the detailed regulations essential to full enjoyment of the rights conferred or to introduce the machinery required for enforcement of such regulations. Considerations such as these should lead us to decline to establish a new rule of law in the effort to redress a newly disclosed wrong, although the propriety of some remedy appears to be clear.

NOTES AND QUESTIONS

1. *Property in information versus freedom to compete.* The plaintiff in *INS v. AP* claimed that it had invested both labor and capital in gathering the news and developing a distribution system to sell the news it gathered. This labor and investment created something of value that should be recognized as its property. Defendant INS

noted that plaintiff AP had made the information public and that once it was public, it was no longer subject to private ownership or control; defendant had just as much right as anyone else to engage in free speech by sharing information in the public realm. Plaintiff responded to this argument by noting that defendant was not just any old member of the public but was a competitor in the news business and that it was not just sharing the information but selling it. Because defendant did not pay the cost of obtaining the information, it could sell it at a lower price than plaintiff, which needed to recoup the costs of obtaining the information in the first place. Defendant was thus reaping where it had not sowed and wrongfully appropriating the result of another's efforts; if lawful, this behavior might make the news business less profitable (or unprofitable) and discourage others from entering the newsgathering business, resulting in less news being gathered and disseminated. It was a form of unfair competition. Defendant could respond by noting that it was free to compete with plaintiff in the news business and that it should be free to use all publicly available sources of information in that endeavor. Ruling to the contrary would give plaintiff a monopoly in the distribution of particular information. Such a monopoly would inhibit competition and drive up the price of the news, as well as infringe on defendant's free speech rights.

2. *Relativity of title.* This debate partly revolves around the question of whether or not plaintiff has a property right in information it has gathered. On one hand, Justice Pitney agrees with plaintiff that its efforts should result in some form of legal protection because the "acquisition and transmission of news require elaborate organization and large expenditure of money, skill, and effort." Plaintiff AP's substantial investment in obtaining the news justifies protecting it from having the information so acquired appropriated and sold by a competitor. This both allows it to reap the rewards of its investment and provides an incentive to engage in the news business to benefit the public. On the other hand, Justice Pitney agrees with the defendant that information, once made public, is in the public domain; "the news of current events may be regarded as common property" and can be used or repeated by anyone. If the information, once revealed, is not plaintiff's private property but is owned by everyone, including defendant, why did the plaintiff win?

Pitney notes that property rights may extend against particular individuals rather than against the public at large. In a dispute between plaintiff and a member of the public who repeated the information to her friends, the plaintiff would lose, but in a dispute between plaintiff and a competitor in the news business, the plaintiff wins. Plaintiff does have a property right in the news it gathered, but it is a limited property right that extends only against competitors in the news business. Title to property is not absolute but relative. The question is not whether plaintiff would win against everyone in the world but only whether plaintiff's title is better than defendant's title. The relationship between the parties is significant; an owner may be protected against a competitor but not against a non-competitor.

3. *Exchange value as a function of the extent of legal protection of an interest.* Justice Pitney notes that news has "exchange value, dependent on its novelty and freshness." Because it is valuable, it should be protected as a property right with rules against misappropriation by a competitor. On the other hand, Justice Pitney states that the news will have no value unless it is legally protected; allowing INS to disseminate information collected by AP would render news collection "profitless, or so little profitable as in effect to cut off the service by rendering the cost prohibitive in comparison with the return." Is news valuable or isn't it?

News is valuable in the sense that many people benefit from its collection and distribution and are willing to pay for it. At the same time, its market value to news gatherers will vary depending on how much protection the legal system provides for it. Pitney suggests that the news should be protected because it has exchange value. But isn't this reasoning circular? If it has market value only if legally protected, the question is then *whether to create market value* for the news by extending legal protection for it. Economic value is not intrinsic; it may be created or increased by granting legal protection for specific interests.

Not all valuable interests are privately owned; many of the most valuable pieces of information, such as scientific truths or historical facts, are the common property of humankind. News does have value to many people. At the same time, its market value will vary depending on how much legal protection the courts grant for the news as against competitors. The greater the legal protection granted the plaintiff's interest, the more valuable the property interest to the plaintiff. Is there a way out of this circle?

4. *Unfair competition.* Because the property interest is held only against competitors, the rule in *INS v. AP* is a rule against unfair competition. Why was it unfair for a competitor to do what any member of the public could have done? In *Cheney Brothers v. Doris Silk Corp.*, 35 F.2d 279 (2d Cir. 1929), a silk manufacturer sued another company for copying the patterns on its fabric and undercutting its price, claiming that this took plaintiff's property rights in its designs and citing *INS v. AP*. The court rejected the argument, holding that, in the absence of a statute to the contrary, "a man's property is limited to the chattels which embody his invention. Others may imitate these at their pleasure." *Id.* at 280. Judge Learned Hand held that preventing a competitor from imitating a product would be "to set up a monopoly." *Id.* at 280. *Accord, Knitwaves, Inc. v. Lollytogs, Ltd.*, 71 F.3d 996 (2d Cir. 1995). Imitation of products is what creates and allows for needed competition. Unless a statute provides to the contrary, individuals are generally entitled to copy products made by others and sell them. Note that trademark and trade dress law limits the ability to copy designs if this will confuse customers about the origin or manufacture of the product. *Wal-Mart Stores, Inc. v. Samara Bros., Inc.*, 529 U.S. 205 (2000). *See infra* §15.3. Why did plaintiff win in *INS v. AP* but lose in *Cheney Brothers*? Are the cases distinguishable? If not, which case was correctly decided in your view?

5. *Copyright law.* Copyright law protects authors of original works such as books, music, and artwork. The federal copyright statute protects only original expressions of ideas and prohibits copying, distributing, and performing them without the author's consent. In *National Basketball Association v. Motorola, Inc.*, 105 F.3d 841 (2d Cir. 1997), a professional basketball league (NBA) sued the manufacturer of handheld pagers that provided "real-time" information about professional basketball games, including updated scores and statistics as the games were in process. The NBA claimed that Motorola's copying of this information violated its copyright in the broadcast and constituted commercial misappropriation under the ruling of *INS v. AP*. The Second Circuit rejected both claims. Although the NBA did have an exclusive copyright to distribute the broadcast of its games, it did not have a right to prevent others from repeating facts learned from those broadcasts. The act does not give anyone a monopoly on facts; they remain in the public domain and can be disseminated at will. The court also rejected the misappropriation claim, holding that the 1976 amendments to the *Copyright Act*, 17 U.S.C. §§101 *et seq.* had preempted state common law of misappropriation, as developed in *INS v. AP* and other cases, unless it met strict criteria

suggested in *INS v. AP* itself. Judge Winter explained, *id.* at 852, that a common law claim for misappropriation can be based on disseminating facts only where

> (i) a plaintiff generates or gathers information at a cost; (ii) the information is time-sensitive; (iii) a defendant's use of the information constitutes free riding on the plaintiff's efforts; (iv) the defendant is in direct competition with a product or service offered by the plaintiffs; and (v) the ability of other parties to free-ride on the efforts of the plaintiff or others would so reduce the incentive to produce the product or service that its existence or quality would be substantially threatened.

Motorola's conduct in making scores available on its pagers did not satisfy this test because it was not in direct competition with the NBA. It was engaged, not in the broadcast of a sporting event, but the "collection and retransmission of strictly factual material." *Id.* at 853. Nor was Motorola free-riding by rebroadcasting scores posted by someone else; rather, it collected the information itself from reporters who watched the games. For more on copyright law, *see* Chapter 14.

PROBLEMS

1. In *Feist Publications, Inc. v. Rural Telephone Service Co.*, 499 U.S. 340 (1991), defendant (Feist) copied the listings in the white pages of a telephone directory published by plaintiff telephone company (Rural Telephone) and published them in defendant's own, competing directory. Plaintiff had obtained the data from its subscribers who provided their names and addresses to obtain telephone service. Defendant published area-wide telephone directories that reduce the need to consult multiple directories. Thus, the information it copied from plaintiff's directory was only a fraction of the listings in its publication. Plaintiff claimed that it had a copyright on the listings it had gathered in its white pages and that defendant had no right to copy and distribute those listings without its consent. The Supreme Court rejected the plaintiff's claim on the ground that copyright law only protects "original works of authorship" and not facts. Compilations of facts may be original if they are organized in a distinctive, creative manner, but an alphabetical listing did not satisfy this requirement.[2] If plaintiff had based its claim on the tort of misappropriation as developed in *INS v. AP* instead of copyright law, would it have won? Does the case satisfy the test for misappropriation as stated in *NBA v. Motorola*?

2. In *eBay, Inc. v. Bidder's Edge, Inc.*, 100 F. Supp. 2d 1058 (N.D. Cal. 2000), an Internet auction site (eBay) sought an injunction against an auction aggregating site (Bidder's Edge) to stop it from accessing eBay's web site. Bidder's Edge provided links to all the Internet sites involving auctions. eBay is a web auction site with over 7 million registered users who can place items for auction and bid on items placed by others. Every minute, approximately 600 bids are placed on over 3 million items. eBay users are required to sign an agreement not to use a "software robot" to monitor or copy eBay web pages without eBay's consent. A software robot is a computer program that searches, copies, and retrieves information from the web sites of others. Such programs can execute thousands of instructions per minute and can consume the processing and storage resources of a system, slowing down the processing of the system and even

---

2. For more on *Feist, see infra* §15.4.

overloading it such that it can malfunction or "crash." Bidder's Edge admittedly accessed the eBay site 100,000 times a day, or roughly 1% or more of the number of requests received by eBay in late 1999. The court granted a preliminary injunction against Bidder's Edge on the ground that it was committing a continuing trespass to eBay's computer system, violating eBay's "fundamental property right to exclude others from its computer system. . . ." 100 F. Supp. 2d at 1067. Although trespass is a doctrine generally associated with real property, it may also apply to chattels or movable property, such as cars. The court found that the electronic signals sent by Bidder's Edge were "sufficiently tangible to support a trespass cause of action." *Id.* at 1069.

    a.   What is plaintiff's argument that Bidder's Edge is engaged in unfair competition under the doctrine of *INS v. AP* as limited by *NBA v. Motorola*?

    b.   What is defendant's argument that it is not engaged in unfair competition?

    c.   How would you decide the case?

§1.3.2   PATENTS IN HUMAN GENES

MOORE v. REGENTS OF THE UNIVERSITY OF CALIFORNIA
793 P.2d 479 (Cal. 1990)

EDWARD A. PANELLI, Justice. . . .

I.   Introduction

. . . The plaintiff is John Moore (Moore), who underwent treatment for hairy-cell leukemia at the Medical Center of the University of California at Los Angeles (UCLA Medical Center). The five defendants are: (1) Dr. David W. Golde (Golde), a physician who attended Moore at UCLA Medical Center; (2) the Regents of the University of California (Regents), who own and operate the university; (3) Shirley G. Quan [(Quan)], a researcher employed by the Regents; (4) Genetics Institute, Inc. (Genetics Institute); and (5) Sandoz Pharmaceuticals Corporation and related entities (collectively Sandoz).

Moore first visited UCLA Medical Center on October 5, 1976, shortly after he learned that he had hairy-cell leukemia. After hospitalizing Moore and "withdraw[ing] extensive amounts of blood, bone marrow aspirate, and other bodily substances," Golde confirmed that diagnosis. At this time all defendants, including Golde, were aware that "certain blood products and blood components were of great value in a number of commercial and scientific efforts" and that access to a patient whose blood contained these substances would provide "competitive, commercial, and scientific advantages."

On October 8, 1976, Golde recommended that Moore's spleen be removed. Golde informed Moore "that he had reason to fear for his life, and that the proposed splenectomy operation . . . was necessary to slow down the progress of his disease." Based upon Golde's representations, Moore signed a written consent form authorizing the splenectomy.

Before the operation, Golde and Quan "formed the intent and made arrangements to obtain portions of [Moore's] spleen following its removal" and to take them to a separate research unit. Golde gave written instructions to this effect on October 18 and 19, 1976. These research activities "were not intended to have . . . any relation to [Moore's] medical . . . care." However, neither Golde nor Quan informed Moore of their plans to conduct this research or requested his permission. Surgeons at UCLA Medical Center, whom the complaint does not name as defendants, removed Moore's spleen on October 20, 1976.

Moore returned to the UCLA Medical Center several times between November 1976 and September 1983. He did so at Golde's direction and based upon representations "that such visits were necessary and required for his health and well-being, and based upon the trust inherent in and by virtue of the physician-patient relationship. . . ." On each of these visits Golde withdrew additional samples of "blood, blood serum, skin, bone marrow aspirate, and sperm." On each occasion Moore travelled to the UCLA Medical Center from his home in Seattle because he had been told that the procedures were to be performed only there and only under Golde's direction.

[The court then quoted plaintiff's complaint:] "In fact, [however,] throughout the period of time that [Moore] was under [Golde's] care and treatment, . . . the defendants were actively involved in a number of activities which they concealed from [Moore]. . . ." Specifically, defendants were conducting research on Moore's cells and planned to "benefit financially and competitively . . . [by exploiting the cells] and [their] exclusive access to [the cells] by virtue of [Golde's] on-going physician-patient relationship. . . ."

Sometime before August 1979, Golde established a cell line from Moore's T-lymphocytes. On January 30, 1981, the Regents applied for a patent on the cell line, listing Golde and Quan as inventors. "[B]y virtue of an established policy . . . , [the] Regents, Golde, and Quan would share in any royalties or profits . . . arising out of [the] patent." The patent issued on March 20, 1984, naming Golde and Quan as the inventors of the cell line and the Regents as the assignee of the patent. (U.S. Patent No. 4,438,032 (Mar. 20, 1984).)

The Regents' patent also covers various methods for using the cell line to produce lymphokines. Moore admits in his complaint that "the true clinical potential of each of the lymphokines . . . [is] difficult to predict, [but] . . . competing commercial firms in these relevant fields have published reports in biotechnology industry periodicals predicting a potential market of approximately 3.01 Billion Dollars by the year 1990 for a whole range of [such lymphokines]. . . ."

With the Regents' assistance, Golde negotiated agreements for commercial development of the cell line and products to be derived from it. Under an agreement with Genetics Institute, Golde "became a paid consultant" and "acquired the rights to 75,000 shares of common stock." Genetics Institute also agreed to pay Golde and the Regents "at least $330,000 over three years, including a pro-rata share of [Golde's] salary and fringe benefits, in exchange for . . . exclusive access to the materials and research performed" on the cell line and products derived from it. On June 4, 1982, Sandoz "was added to the agreement," and compensation payable to Golde and the Regents was increased by $110,000. "[T]hroughout this period, . . . Quan spent as much as 70 [percent] of her time working for [the] Regents on research" related to the cell line. . . .

III.   Discussion

A.   BREACH OF FIDUCIARY DUTY AND LACK OF INFORMED CONSENT

Moore repeatedly alleges that Golde failed to disclose the extent of his research and economic interests in Moore's cells before obtaining consent to the medical procedures by which the cells were extracted. These allegations, in our view, state a cause of action against Golde for invading a legally protected interest of his patient. This cause of action can properly be characterized either as the breach of a fiduciary duty to disclose facts material to the patient's consent or, alternatively, as the performance of medical procedures without first having obtained the patient's informed consent....

B.   CONVERSION

Moore also attempts to characterize the invasion of his rights as a conversion—a tort that protects against interference with possessory and ownership interests in personal property. He theorizes that he continued to own his cells following their removal from his body, at least for the purpose of directing their use, and that he never consented to their use in potentially lucrative medical research. Thus, to complete Moore's argument, defendants' unauthorized use of his cells constitutes a conversion. As a result of the alleged conversion, Moore claims a proprietary interest in each of the products that any of the defendants might ever create from his cells or the patented cell line....

1.   Moore's Claim Under Existing Law

...Since Moore clearly did not expect to retain possession of his cells following their removal, to sue for their conversion he must have retained an ownership interest in them....

...Moore relies, as did the Court of Appeal, primarily on decisions addressing privacy rights. One line of cases involves unwanted publicity. These opinions hold that every person has a proprietary interest in his own likeness and that unauthorized, business use of a likeness is redressible as a tort....

...Moore...argues that "[i]f the courts have found a sufficient proprietary interest in one's persona, how could one not have a right in one's own genetic material, something far more profoundly the essence of one's human uniqueness than a name or a face?" However,...the goal and result of defendants' efforts has been to manufacture lymphokines. Lymphokines, unlike a name or a face, have the same molecular structure in every human being and the same, important functions in every human being's immune system. Moreover, the particular genetic material which is responsible for the natural production of lymphokines, and which defendants use to manufacture lymphokines in the laboratory, is also the same in every person; it is no more unique to Moore than the number of vertebrae in the spine or the chemical formula of hemoglobin.

[Moore also appeals to privacy cases holding that patients have the right to refuse medical treatment because each person has a right to determine what shall be done with his or her own body. However, we can protect privacy and personal dignity by requiring disclosure under fiduciary duty and informed consent doctrines, rather than] accepting the extremely problematic conclusion that interference with those interests amounts to a conversion of personal property....

The next consideration that makes Moore's claim of ownership problematic is California statutory law, which drastically limits a patient's control over excised cells [by regulating disposal of human tissues to protect public health and safety. *Cal. Health & Safety Code* §§7001, 7054.4].... By restricting how excised cells may be used and requiring their eventual destruction, the statute eliminates so many of the rights ordinarily attached to property that one cannot simply assume that what is left amounts to "property" or "ownership" for purposes of conversion law....

Finally, the subject matter of the Regents' patent — the patented cell line and the products derived from it — cannot be Moore's property. This is because the patented cell line is both factually and legally distinct from the cells taken from Moore's body. Federal law permits the patenting of organisms that represent the product of "human ingenuity," but not naturally occurring organisms. *Diamond v. Chakrabarty*, 447 U.S. 303, 309-310 (1980). Human cell lines are patentable because "[l]ong-term adaptation and growth of human tissues and cells in culture is difficult — often considered an art...," and the probability of success is low. It is this inventive effort that patent law rewards, not the discovery of naturally occurring raw materials. Thus, Moore's allegations that he owns the cell line and the products derived from it are inconsistent with the patent, which constitutes an authoritative determination that the cell line is the product of invention....

2. Should Conversion Liability Be Extended? . . .

Of the relevant policy considerations, two are of overriding importance. The first is protection of a competent patient's right to make autonomous medical decisions.... This policy weighs in favor of providing a remedy to patients when physicians act with undisclosed motives that may affect their professional judgment. The second important policy consideration is that we not threaten with disabling civil liability innocent parties who are engaged in socially useful activities, such as researchers who have no reason to believe that their use of a particular cell sample is, or may be, against a donor's wishes....

Research on human cells plays a critical role in medical research. This is so because researchers are increasingly able to isolate naturally occurring, medically useful biological substances and to produce useful quantities of such substances through genetic engineering. These efforts are beginning to bear fruit. Products developed through biotechnology that have already been approved for marketing in this country include treatments and tests for leukemia, cancer, diabetes, dwarfism, hepatitis-B, kidney transplant rejection, emphysema, osteoporosis, ulcers, anemia, infertility, and gynecological tumors, to name but a few.

The extension of conversion law into this area will hinder research by restricting access to the necessary raw materials. Thousands of human cell lines already exist in tissue repositories, such as the American Type Culture Collection and those operated by the National Institutes of Health and the American Cancer Society. These repositories respond to tens of thousands of requests for samples annually. Since the patent office requires the holders of patents on cell lines to make samples available to anyone, many patent holders place their cell lines in repositories to avoid the administrative burden of responding to requests. At present, human cell lines are routinely copied and distributed to other researchers for experimental purposes, usually free of charge. This exchange of scientific materials, which still is relatively free and efficient, will surely be compromised if each cell sample becomes the potential subject matter of a lawsuit.

To expand liability by extending conversion law into this area would have a broad impact. The House Committee on Science and Technology of the United States Congress found that "49 percent of the researchers at medical institutions surveyed used human tissues or cells in their research." Many receive grants from the National Institutes of Health for this work. In addition, "there are nearly 350 commercial biotechnology firms in the United States actively engaged in biotechnology research and commercial product development and approximately 25 to 30 percent appear to be engaged in research to develop a human therapeutic or diagnostic reagent. . . . Most, but not all, of the human therapeutic products are derived from human tissues and cells, or human cell lines or cloned genes." . . .

If the scientific users of human cells are to be held liable for failing to investigate the consensual pedigree of their raw materials, we believe the Legislature should make that decision. Complex policy choices affecting all society are involved, and "[l]egislatures, in making such policy decisions, have the ability to gather empirical evidence, solicit the advice of experts, and hold hearings at which all interested parties present evidence and express their views. . . ." *Foley v. Interactive Data Corp.*, 765 P.2d 373, 397 n.31 (Cal. 1988). . . .

For these reasons, we hold that the allegations of Moore's third amended complaint state a cause of action for breach of fiduciary duty or lack of informed consent, but not conversion.

ARMAND ARABIAN, Justice, concurring.

. . . Plaintiff has asked us to recognize and enforce a right to sell one's own body tissue for profit. He entreats us to regard the human vessel — the single most venerated and protected subject in any civilized society — as equal with the basest commercial commodity. He urges us to commingle the sacred with the profane. He asks much. . . .

I share Justice Mosk's sense of outrage [at defendants' conduct], but I cannot follow its path. His eloquent pacan to the human spirit illuminates the problem, not the solution. Does it uplift or degrade the "unique human persona" to treat human tissue as a fungible article of commerce? Would it advance or impede the human condition, spiritually or scientifically, by delivering the majestic force of the law behind plaintiff's claim? I do not know the answers to these troubling questions, nor am I willing — like Justice Mosk — to treat them simply as issues of "tort" law, susceptible of judicial resolution.

Where then shall a complete resolution be found? Clearly the Legislature, as the majority opinion suggests, is the proper deliberative forum. . . .

ALLEN BROUSSARD, Justice, concurring and dissenting.

. . . If defendants had informed plaintiff, prior to removal, of the possible uses to which his body part could be put and plaintiff had authorized one particular use, it is clear . . . that defendants would be liable for conversion if they disregarded plaintiff's decision and used the body part in an unauthorized manner for their own economic benefit. Although in this case defendants did not disregard a specific directive from plaintiff with regard to the future use of his body part, the complaint alleges that, before the body part was removed, defendants intentionally withheld material information that they were under an obligation to disclose to plaintiff and that was necessary for his exercise of control over the body part; the complaint also alleges that defendants withheld such information in order to appropriate the control over the future use of such body part for their own economic benefit. If these allegations are true, defendants clearly improperly interfered with plaintiff's right in his body part at a time when he had the authority to determine the future use of such part, thereby misappropriating plaintiff's right of control for their own advantage. Under these circumstances, the complaint fully satisfies the established requirements of a conversion cause of action. . . .

[T]he majority's fear that the availability of a conversion remedy will restrict access to existing cell lines is unrealistic. In the vast majority of instances the tissues and cells in existing repositories will not represent a potential source of liability because they will have come from patients who consented to their organ's use for scientific purposes under circumstances in which such consent was not tainted by a failure to disclose the known valuable nature of the cells. . . .

Furthermore, even in the rare instance — like the present case — in which a conversion action might be successfully pursued, the potential liability is not likely "to destroy the economic incentive to conduct important medical research," as the majority asserts. If, as the majority suggests, the great bulk of the value of a cell line patent and derivative products is attributable to the efforts of medical researchers and drug companies, rather than to the "raw materials" taken from a patient, the patient's damages will be correspondingly limited, and innocent medical researchers and drug manufacturers will retain the considerable economic benefits resulting from their own work. . . .

. . . Justice Arabian's concurring opinion suggests that the majority's conclusion is informed by the precept that it is immoral to sell human body parts for profit. But the majority's rejection of plaintiff's conversion cause of action does not mean that body parts may not be bought or sold for research or commercial purposes or that no private individual or entity may benefit economically from the fortuitous value of plaintiff's diseased cells. Far from elevating these biological materials above the marketplace, the majority's holding simply bars plaintiff, the source of the cells, from obtaining the benefit of the cells' value, but permits defendants, who allegedly obtained the cells from plaintiff by improper means, to retain and exploit the full economic value of their ill-gotten gains free of their ordinary common law liability for conversion. . . .

STANLEY MOSK, Justice, dissenting. . . .

[T]he concept of property is often said to refer to a "bundle of rights" that may be exercised with respect to that object — principally the rights to possess the property, to use the property, to exclude others from the property, and to dispose of the property by sale or by gift. . . . But the same bundle of rights does not attach to all forms of property. For a variety of policy reasons, the law limits or even forbids the exercise of certain rights over certain forms of property. For example, both law and contract may limit the right of an owner of real property to use his parcel as he sees fit. Owners of various forms of personal property may likewise be subject to restrictions on the time, place, and manner of their use. Limitations on the disposition of real property, while less common, may also be imposed. Finally, some types of personal property may be sold but not given away,[9] while others may be given away but not sold,[10] and still others may neither be given away nor sold.[11]

---

9. A person contemplating bankruptcy may sell his property at its "reasonably equivalent value," but he may not make a gift of the same property. (*See* 11 U.S.C. §548(a).)

10. A sportsman may give away wild fish or game that he has caught or killed pursuant to his license, but he may not sell it. (*Fish & Game Code*, §§3039, 7121.) The transfer of human organs and blood is a special case that I discuss below.

11. *E.g.*, a license to practice a profession, or a prescription drug in the hands of the person for whom it is prescribed.

In each of the foregoing instances, the limitation or prohibition diminishes the bundle of rights that would otherwise attach to the property, yet what remains is still deemed in law to be a protectible property interest. . . . [Moore] at least had the right to do with his own tissue whatever the defendants did with it: i.e., he could have contracted with researchers and pharmaceutical companies to develop and exploit the vast commercial potential of his tissue and its products. Defendants certainly believe that their right to do the foregoing is not barred by section 7054.4 and is a significant property right. . . . The Court of Appeal summed up the point by observing that "Defendants' position that plaintiff cannot own his tissue, but that they can, is fraught with irony." It is also legally untenable. . . .

[Nor does the patent on the cell line preclude plaintiff's property claim.] To be sure, the patent granted defendants the exclusive right to make, use, or sell the invention for a period of 17 years. But Moore does not assert any such right for himself. Rather, he seeks to show that he is entitled, in fairness and equity, to some share in the profits that defendants have made and will make from their commercial exploitation of the Mo cell line. I do not question that the cell line is primarily the product of defendants' inventive effort. Yet likewise no one can question Moore's crucial contribution to the invention — an invention named, ironically, after him: but for the cells of Moore's body taken by defendants, there would have been no Mo cell line. . . .

[E]very individual has a legally protectible property interest in his own body and its products. First, our society acknowledges a profound ethical imperative to respect the human body as the physical and temporal expression of the unique human persona. One manifestation of that respect is our prohibition against direct abuse of the body by torture or other forms of cruel or unusual punishment. Another is our prohibition against indirect abuse of the body by its economic exploitation for the sole benefit of another person. The most abhorrent form of such exploitation, of course, was the institution of slavery. Lesser forms, such as indentured servitude or even debtor's prison, have also disappeared. Yet their specter haunts the laboratories and boardrooms of today's biotechnological research-industrial complex. It arises wherever scientists or industrialists claim, as defendants claim here, the right to appropriate and exploit a patient's tissue for their sole economic benefit — the right, in other words, to freely mine or harvest valuable physical properties of the patient's body: ". . . Such research tends to treat the human body as a commodity — a means to a profitable end. The dignity and sanctity with which we regard the human whole, body as well as mind and soul, are absent when we allow researchers to further their own interests without the patient's participation by using a patient's cells as the basis for a marketable product." Danforth, *Cells, Sales, & Royalties: The Patient's Right to a Portion of the Profits*, 6 Yale L. & Pol'y Rev. 179, 190 (1988).

A second policy consideration adds notions of equity to those of ethics. Our society values fundamental fairness in dealings between its members, and condemns the unjust enrichment of any member at the expense of another. This is particularly true when, as here, the parties are not in equal bargaining positions. We are repeatedly told that the commercial products of the biotechnological revolution "hold the promise of tremendous profit." In the case at bar, for example, the complaint alleges that the market for the kinds of proteins produced by the Mo cell line was predicted to exceed $3 billion by 1990. These profits are currently shared exclusively between the biotechnology industry and the universities that support that industry. . . .

There is, however, a third party to the biotechnology enterprise — the patient who is the source of the blood or tissue from which all these profits are derived. While he may be a silent partner, his contribution to the venture is absolutely crucial: . . . but for the cells of Moore's body taken by defendants there would have been no Mo cell line at all. Yet defendants deny that Moore is entitled to any share whatever in the proceeds of this cell line. This is both inequitable and immoral. . . .

NOTES AND QUESTIONS

1. In *Brotherton v. Cleveland*, 923 F.2d 477 (6th Cir. 1991), plaintiff Deborah Brotherton alleged that defendants, in the course of performing an autopsy, removed her deceased husband's corneas for use as anatomical gifts without her consent. The court noted that "Ohio Rev. Code §2108.02(B), as part of the *Uniform Anatomical Gift Act* governing gifts of organs and tissues for research or transplants, granted her the right to control the disposal of Steven Brotherton's body." It held that "the aggregate of rights granted by the state of Ohio to Deborah Brotherton rises to the level of a 'legitimate claim of entitlement' in Steven Brotherton's body, including his corneas," and that this was sufficient to establish a property interest protected by the fourteenth amendment's prohibition on deprivations of property without due process of law. *See also Newman v. Sathyavaglswaran*, 287 F.3d 786 (9th Cir. 2002) (parents had property interest in deceased children's corneas removed by county workers without their consent); *Whaley v. County of Tuscola*, 58 F.3d 1111 (6th Cir. 1991) (recognizing a property interest in body parts and refusing to dismiss lawsuits by relatives of deceased persons whose eyeballs and corneas had been removed without permission by a pathology assistant at a county hospital).

Suppose these events had occurred in California. Would the California Supreme Court reach the same result as the Sixth Circuit?

2. Should it be lawful for people to sell their blood to blood banks? Should blood banks be able to offer money to induce people to donate blood?

3. Suppose that before the operation Golde had informed Moore of his intent to use Moore's cells to create a cell line. Would the case have come out the same way?

4. If Golde and Moore had signed a contract in which Golde agreed to pay Moore a percentage of the earnings from the cell line, would such a contract be enforceable under the majority's analysis in *Moore*? If Golde did not commit the tort of conversion (an unprivileged appropriation of Moore's property), is Moore free to treat his body parts or cells as property that he can sell for the use of another?

5. On one hand, Justice Panelli argues that granting Moore a property right in his spleen or in the genetic information derived from it would stifle development of biotechnology by crippling liability. Investment in and development of medically useful biological substances requires treating Moore's spleen as a "necessary raw material" that is part of the common property of the public at large and that can therefore be appropriated to develop human cell lines. On the other hand, Justice Panelli argues that the biotechnology industry is large and increasingly profitable partly because patent law protects a property interest in the cell lines developed from those "raw materials." Promotion of useful industry appears sometimes to require recognizing private property rights and sometimes failing to recognize them. How does the court reconcile these conflicting arguments? If property rights protect labor and inventiveness, then is possession not entitled to legal protection? Are naturally occurring raw materials such as oil, gas, and gold not subject to private

ownership? Do the principles of rewarding useful labor and protecting control of first possessors conflict? If so, how should they be reconciled?

PROBLEM

A man who is sick with cancer deposits his sperm in a sperm bank for the purpose of impregnating his fiancée through in vitro fertilization. He dies before they are married and before the procedure can be completed, having left a will bequeathing all his "personal property" to his two adult children. The children claim the sperm are their property and want them to be destroyed, while the fiancée wants to try to have a child using the sperm. What should the court do? *See Hecht v. Superior Court,* 59 Cal. Rptr. 2d 222, 226 (Ct. App. 1996) (wrestling with the question of whether sperm should be treated as "property" and deciding in the negative).

§1.3.3 Work and Family

Like society, courts sometimes reward labor with property and sometimes do not. In both *INS v. AP* and *Moore, supra,* the courts defined property interests in part to reward labor, and in part to encourage activities useful to society at large: news-gathering and biotechnology research. Raising children also requires considerable labor and is socially useful. In the following case, consider the court's reasoning with respect to these factors. Did the court take a different approach to encouraging socially useful labor than did the courts in *INS v. AP* and *Moore*? Should it have? Or is this case different? How?

UPTON v. JWP BUSINESSLAND
682 N.E.2d 1357 (Mass. 1997)

HERBERT WILKINS, C.J. The plaintiff, a former at-will employee of the defendant and a divorced single parent, appeals from the entry of summary judgment for the defendant. She asserts that the defendant discharged her when, because of the need to be with her young son, she was unwilling to work long hours. She argues that such a discharge is contrary to public policy and entitles her to damages. We granted the plaintiff's application for direct appellate review. We affirm the judgment.

. . . At the time of her discharge, the plaintiff was the mother of a young son whom she cared for herself and supported entirely from her earnings. She commuted from Cape Cod to work for the defendant in Canton. When she was hired in April, 1991, she was told that her hours of work would be 8:15 a.m. to 5:30 p.m., with the need to work late on one or two days each month. The plaintiff arranged child care accordingly. In fact, the requirements of her job kept her until 6:30 p.m. to 7 p.m. from the outset and even later as the job progressed. In late July, 1991, the plaintiff was told that she would have to work until 9 or 10 p.m. each evening and all day Saturday for at least several months. The plaintiff informed her employer that she would not be able to work such hours because of her responsibilities as a mother. She was discharged two weeks later.

The general rule is that an at-will employee may be terminated at any time for any reason or for no reason at all. Liability may be imposed on an employer, however, if an at-will employee is terminated for a reason that violates a clearly established public policy. The public policy exception makes redress available to employees who are terminated for asserting a legal right (*e.g.,* filing a workers' compensation claim), for doing what the law requires (*e.g.,* serving on a jury), or for refusing to disobey the law (*e.g.,* refusing to commit perjury). We have identified additional reasons for terminations which would directly contradict well-defined public policies of the Commonwealth. *See Flesner v. Technical Communications Corp.,* 575 N.E.2d 1107 (1991) (at-will employee cooperated with law enforcement agency investigation of his employer); *Hobson v. McLean Hosp. Corp.,* 522 N.E.2d 975 (1988) (at-will employee allegedly discharged for enforcing safety laws which were her responsibility to enforce). . . .

On the other hand, we have held that other reasons for termination do not warrant recovery by an at-will employee.

The plaintiff seeks to recover for a termination that was not, on its face, made because she did something that public policy strongly encourages (such as serving on a jury) or because she refused to engage in conduct that public policy strongly discourages (such as refusing to lie on behalf of her employer). There is no clearly established public policy which requires employers to refrain from demanding that their adult employees work long hours. Nor is any public policy directly served by an employee's refusal to work long hours. Because no public purpose is served by the conduct for which the plaintiff asserts she was discharged, this case is unlike those cases in which we have held that the employer may be liable for the discharge of an at-will employee.

To advance her claim that her termination violated public policy, the plaintiff relies on the Commonwealth's strong policy favoring the care and protection of children. Her theory is that an employer may not properly discharge an employee whose refusal to work long hours is based on her sense of obligation to be with her young child. She argues that meeting the defendant's demands regarding work hours would cause her to neglect her child in contravention of public policy. . . .

[No] court to our knowledge allowed recovery against an employer who terminated an at-will employee who refused to work newly imposed hours due to an irreconcilable conflict between her new work schedule and the obligations of parenting. There is no public policy which mandates that an employer must adjust its expectations, based on a case-by-case analysis of an at-will employee's domestic circumstances, or face liability for having discharged the employee. Construing the public policy exception to cover terminations of employees in the plaintiff's situation would tend to convert the general rule "into a rule that requires just cause to terminate an at-will employee." *Smith-Pfeffer v. Superintendent of the Walter E. Fernald State Sch.,* 533 N.E.2d 1368, 1371 (Mass. 1989). Liability to an at-will employee for a discharge in violation of public policy must be based on general principles, and not on the special domestic circumstances of any particular employee.

The plaintiff argues briefly that the defendant was estopped from firing her because she relied to her detriment on the defendant's representations regarding her expected hours of work. To avoid the entry of summary judgment against her, an at-will employee asserting estoppel would have to show that she reasonably relied on an unambiguous promise. The summary judgment record shows no such promise, only that the plaintiff asked about regular work hours and was so told. No promise in a contractual sense is shown.

We sympathize with the difficulties of persons in the position of the plaintiff who face the challenge of reconciling parental responsibilities with the demands of employment. However, employer liability under common-law principles is not an appropriate means of addressing the problem in the at-will employment context.

Judgment affirmed.

NOTES AND QUESTIONS

1. The work of taking care of children in the home traditionally was uncompensated. It is still the case that more women than men engage in this uncompensated labor. This affects the ability of women to enter the workforce full time and is a primary reason for the continued disparity in incomes between men and women. In 1999, men who worked full time earned an average of $36,476, while women who worked full time earned only $26,324, or 72% of male earnings. U.S. Census Bureau, Current Population Reports, P60-209, *Money Income in the United States: 1999* (Sept. 2000) (*http:// www.census.gov*).

Most women now work outside the home. The 1996 federal welfare reform statute, the *Personal Responsibility and Work Opportunity Act of 1996*, 42 U.S.C. §§601 to 619, requires most women with children to do so as a condition of receiving welfare benefits. Despite this fact, the organization of work remains hostile to parents and makes it difficult to meet the challenges of reconciling market work with care of one's children. Mary Joe Frug, *Securing Job Equality for Women: Labor Market Hostility to Working Mothers*, 59 B.U. L. Rev. 55 (1979).

2. Joanna Upton would have been subject to criminal penalties if she had failed to support and protect her child or had otherwise neglected him. *Commonwealth v. Twitchell*, 617 N.E.2d 609 (Mass. 1993). She also would have lost custody. *In re Adoption of Greta*, 729 N.E.2d 273 (Mass. 2000). Why then was the duty to care for her children not deemed a "clearly established public policy"?

3. The court opinion in *Upton* does not reveal whether JWP Businessland was paying Joanna Upton enough so that she could pay for child care for her child during times when she could not be with him. Nor does the court state how much, if anything, she was receiving in child support payments from her ex-husband. Suppose it turned out that she was not earning enough, in combination with child support, to afford to pay for child care for her child in the evenings or on Saturday. Should this fact have been relevant to the court's ruling?

§1.3.4   Who Owns the Corporation? Shareholders and Stakeholders

LOCAL 1330, UNITED STEEL WORKERS OF AMERICA v. UNITED STATES STEEL CORPORATION

631 F.2d 1264 (6th Cir. 1980)

GEORGE CLIFTON EDWARDS, JR., C.J.

This appeal represents a cry for help from steelworkers and townspeople in the City of Youngstown, Ohio who are distressed by the prospective impact upon their lives and their city of the closing of two large steel mills. These two mills were built and have been operated by the United States Steel Corporation since the turn of the century. The Ohio Works began producing in 1901; the McDonald Works in 1918. The District Court which heard this cause of action found that as of the notice of closing, the two plants employed 3,500 employees.

Demolition of four blast furnaces at the U.S. Steel Mill in Youngstown, Ohio (reprinted by permission of the Bettman Archive).

The leading plaintiffs are two labor organizations, Locals 1330 and 1307 of the United Steel Workers of America. This union has had a collective bargaining contract with the United States Steel Corporation for many years. These local unions represent production and maintenance employees at the Ohio and McDonald Works, respectively.

In the background of this litigation is the obsolescence of the two plants concerned, occasioned both by the age of the facilities and machinery involved and by the changes in technology and marketing in steelmaking in the years intervening since the early nineteen hundreds.

For all of the years United States Steel has been operating in Youngstown, it has been a dominant factor in the lives of its thousands of employees and their families, and in the life of the city itself. The contemplated abrupt departure of United States Steel from Youngstown will, of course, have direct impact on 3,500 workers and their families. It will doubtless mean a devastating blow to them, to the business community and to the City of Youngstown itself. While we cannot read the future of Youngstown from this record, what the record does indicate clearly is that we deal with an economic tragedy of major proportion to Youngstown and Ohio's Mahoning Valley....

In the face of this tragedy, the steel worker local unions, the Congressman from this district, and the Attorney General of Ohio have sued United States Steel Corporation, asking the federal courts to order the United States Steel Corporation to keep the two plants at issue in operation. Alternatively, if they could not legally prevail on that issue, they have sought intervention of the courts by injunction to require the United States Steel Corporation to sell the two plants to the plaintiffs under an as yet tentative plan of purchase and operation by a community corporation and to restrain the piecemeal sale or dismantling of the plants until such a proposal could be brought to fruition.

Defendant United States Steel Corporation answered plaintiffs' complaints, claiming that the plants were unprofitable and could not be made otherwise due to obsolescence and change in technology, markets, and transportation. The company also asserts an absolute right to make a business decision to discharge its former employees and abandon Youngstown. It states that there is no law in either the State of Ohio or the United States of America which provides either legal or equitable remedy for plaintiffs.

The District Judge, after originally restraining the corporation from ceasing operations as it had announced it would, and after advancing the case for prompt hearing, entered a formal opinion holding that the plants had become unprofitable and denying all relief. We believe the dispositive paragraphs of a lengthy opinion entered by the District Judge are the following:

> This Court has spent many hours searching for a way to cut to the heart of the economic reality that obsolescence and market forces demand the close of the Mahoning Valley plants, and yet the lives of 3500 workers and their families and the supporting Youngstown community cannot be dismissed as inconsequential. United States Steel should not be permitted to leave the Youngstown area devastated after drawing from the lifeblood of the community for so many years.
> Unfortunately, the mechanism to reach this ideal settlement, to recognize this new property right, is not now in existence in the code of laws of our nation....
> This Court is mindful of the efforts taken by the workers to increase productivity, and has applauded these efforts in the preceding paragraphs. In view of the fact, however, that this Court has found that no contract or enforceable promise was entered into by the company and that, additionally, there is clear evidence to support the company's decision that the plants were not profitable, the various acts of forbearance taken by the plaintiffs do not give them the basis for relief against defendant.

Plaintiffs-appellants claim that certain of the District Judge's findings of fact are clearly erroneous....

III.   The Community Property Claim

At a pretrial hearing of this case on February 28, 1980, the District Judge made a statement at some length about the relationship between the parties to this case and the public interest involved therein. He said:

> Everything that has happened in the Mahoning Valley has been happening for many years because of steel. Schools have been built, roads have been built. Expansion that has taken place is because of steel. And to accommodate that industry, lives and destinies of the inhabitants of that community were based and planned on the basis of that institution: Steel....
> We are talking about an institution, a large corporate institution that is virtually the reason for the existence of that segment of this nation [Youngstown]. Without it, that segment of this nation perhaps suffers, instantly and severely. Whether it becomes a ghost town or not, I don't know. I am not aware of its capability for adapting....
> But what has happened over the years between U.S. Steel, Youngstown and the inhabitants? Hasn't something come out of that relationship, something that out of

which—not reaching for a case on property law or a series of cases but looking at the law as a whole, the Constitution, the whole body of law, not only contract law, but tort, corporations, agency, negotiable instruments taking a look at the whole body of American law and then sitting back and reflecting on what it seeks to do, and that is to adjust human relationships in keeping with the whole spirit and foundation of the American system of law, to preserve property rights. . . .

It would seem to me that when we take a look at the whole body of American law and the principles we attempt to come out with—and although a legislature has not pronounced any laws with respect to such a property right, that is not to suggest that there will not be a need for such a law in the future dealing with similar situations— *it seems to me that a property right has arisen from this lengthy, long-established relationship between United States Steel, the steel industry as an institution, the community in Youngstown, the people in Mahoning County and the Mahoning Valley in having given and devoted their lives to this industry.* Perhaps not a property right to the extent that can be remedied by compelling U.S. Steel to remain in Youngstown. But *I think the law can recognize the property right to the extent that U.S. Steel cannot leave that Mahoning Valley and the Youngstown area in a state of waste, that it cannot completely abandon its obligation to that community, because certain vested rights have arisen out of this long relationship and institution.* [Emphasis supplied by court.]

Subsequently thereto, steelworkers' complaint was amended, realleging the first cause of action, paragraphs 1-49, claiming pendent jurisdiction over claims arising out of the laws of the State of Ohio and asserting as follows:

52. A property right has arisen from the long-established relation between the community of the 19th Congressional District and Plaintiffs, on the one hand, and Defendant on the other hand, which this Court can enforce.

53. This right, in the nature of an easement, requires that Defendant:

a. Assist in the preservation of the institution of steel in that community;

b. Figure into its cost of withdrawing and closing the Ohio and McDonald Works the cost of rehabilitating the community and the workers;

c. Be restrained from leaving the Mahoning Valley in a state of waste and from abandoning its obligation to that community.

This court has examined these allegations with care and with great sympathy for the community interest reflected therein. Our problem in dealing with plaintiffs' fourth cause of action is one of authority. Neither in brief nor oral argument have plaintiffs pointed to any constitutional provision contained in either the Constitution of the United States or the Constitution of the State of Ohio, nor any law enacted by the United States Congress or the Legislature of Ohio, nor any case decided by the courts of either of these jurisdictions which would convey authority to this court to require the United States Steel Corporation to continue operations in Youngstown which its officers and Board of Directors had decided to discontinue on the basis of unprofitability.

This court has in fact dealt with this specific issue in *Charland v. Norge Division, Borg-Warner Corp.*, 407 F.2d 1062 (6th Cir. 1969). The case was, as appellants point out, substantially different from the present complaint in that there was a single individual plaintiff involved. He was, however, one of many Norge employees who had been thrown out of work by the removal of the Norge Muskegon Heights plant to Fort Smith, Arkansas. As is true in this case, there was a union contractual agreement for very limited severance pay. The union at the Norge plant in Muskegon Heights had succeeded in negotiating some severance pay and "very limited removal rights to Fort Smith." Appellant Charland refused to accept the union-negotiated removal agreement. We recite his position as follows:

> Appellant does not by any means limit his petition for relief to §301 contract rights. He tells us, in effect, I worked 30 years for defendant Norge. At the end I am thrown out of a job unless I move hundreds of miles to another city and start as a new employee behind hundreds of local residents and without either accumulated seniority or pension rights. In the alternative if I sign a complete release of all rights arising out of my job, I get $1,500. This is fundamentally unfair. And it is a deprivation of my property rights in my job in violation of Article V of the United States Constitution. *Charland v. Norge Division, Borg-Warner Corp.*, 407 F.2d at 1064.

This court's response to Charland's claims bears repetition here:

> Article V of the Constitution, of course, makes no mention of employment. But it (and the Fourteenth Amendment) does prohibit deprivation of property without due process of law. Thus appellant's assumption submits the fundamental question of whether or not there is a legally recognizable property right in a job which has been held for something approaching a lifetime. The claim presented by this appellant brings sharply into focus such problems as unemployment crises, the mobility of capital, technological change and the right of an industrial owner to go out of business. Thus far federal law has sought to protect the human values to which appellant calls our attention by means of such legislation as unemployment compensation, and social security laws. These statutes afford limited financial protection to the individual worker, but they assume his loss of employment. Whatever the future may bring, neither by statute nor by court decision has appellant's claimed property right been recognized to date in this country. . . . *Id.* at 1065.

Appellants, however, cite and rely upon a decision of the Supreme Court of the United States, *Munn v. Illinois*, 94 U.S. 113 (1877), claiming "that a corporation affected by the public interest, which seeks to take action injurious to that interest, may be restrained from doing so by the equitable powers of a court of law." This case does represent a fundamental statement of the power of the legislative branch of government over private business and private property. It pertained to the question as to whether or not the General Assembly of Illinois could, within the federal commerce clause and the due process clause of the Federal Constitution, "Fix by law the maximum of charges for the storage of grain in warehouses at Chicago and other places in the State having not less than one hundred thousand inhabitants." Justice Waite held that no federal constitutional principle was violated by the state legislative enactment.

The case is undoubtedly important precedent establishing power on the part of state legislatures to regulate private property (particularly public utilities) in the public interest. It cannot, however, properly be cited for holding that federal courts have such legislative power in their own hands.

We recognize that plaintiffs rely upon one sentence: "So, too, in matters which do affect the public interest, and as to which legislative control may be exercised, if there are no statutory regulations upon the subject, the courts must determine what is reasonable. The controlling fact is the power to regulate at all. If that exists, the right to establish the maximum of charge, as one of the means of regulation, is implied." *Id.* at 134. This dictum was laid down in connection with an enterprise which the court treated as essentially a public utility. We find no ground to extend it to assert judicial power to order a steel manufacturing corporation to continue the operation of two plants which it (and a District Court on competent evidence) have found to be unprofitable.

The problem of plant closing and plant removal from one section of the country to another is by no means new in American history. The former mill towns of New England, with their empty textile factory buildings, are monuments to the migration of textile manufacturers to the South, without hindrance from the Congress of the United States, from the legislatures of the states concerned, or, for that matter, from the courts of the land.

In the view of this court, formulation of public policy on the great issues involved in plant closings and removals is clearly the responsibility of the legislatures of the states or of the Congress of the United States.

We find no legal basis for judicial relief as to appellants' fourth cause of action.

NOTES AND QUESTIONS

1. *Who owns the corporation?* A business corporation is established by obtaining a certificate of incorporation from a state. The corporation thus created is a legal entity separate from its shareholders who, in conventional wisdom, own the corporation. Corporations own property and have potentially perpetual existence; the income and assets of the corporation are used to pay off its liabilities, and shareholders are not personally liable for the debts of the corporation. Corporate law gives shareholders the power to elect the board of directors, which in turn picks the management, which in turn hires the workers. Corporate law imposes fiduciary obligations on the management to operate the corporation in the interests of the shareholders (rather than the personal interests of the managers); specifically, it requires the managers to attempt to maximize corporate profits for the benefit of the shareholders, while complying with all applicable regulatory laws and contractual obligations to its employees and creditors.

Shareholders have been treated as the owners of the corporation because they either establish the corporation or have purchased or inherited their interests (their "shares") from the founders of the corporation and because their contracts with the corporation give them the rights to the profits and the residual value of the corporate entity once its other obligations have been paid. Although they are generally treated as the "owners" of the corporation, the shareholders do not manage its daily affairs. They are entitled only to elect the board of directors which formulates general corporate policy and then delegates day-to-day management to subordinate managers and employees. Some countries, however, such as Germany, have sometimes allowed workers to place representatives on the board of directors of the corporation, giving them both access to information and a say in the formation of long-term corporate strategy. In the U.S., this is not the case; employees' and creditors' interests are protected only by the terms of their own contracts with the corporation.

The corporation itself can be understood as a nexus of contracts among shareholders, between shareholders and managers, and between the corporation as an entity and its employees and creditors. Both corporate law and contract law (including labor law) determine the obligations arising out of those consensual agreements. For this reason, some scholars have argued that "it is not particularly useful to think of corporations in terms of property rights." Jonathan R. Macey, *Externalities, Firm-Specific Capital Investments, and the Legal Treatment of Fundamental Corporate Changes,* 1989 Duke L.J. 173, 175 (1989). "To be sure, shareholders own their shares. But bondholders own their bonds, suppliers their inventory and workers their labor. They all contribute what they own to the corporate enterprise." Kent Greenfield, *The Place of Workers in Corporate Law,* 39 B.C. L.Rev. 283, 293 (1998). The question is what obligations arise out of these contractual arrangements.

2. *Stakeholder statutes.* Do corporations have any obligations to their employees or to the communities in which they operate? In other words, do they have any social responsibilities to anyone other than the shareholders? In one famous incident, when a textile factory burned down in Lawrence, Massachusetts just before Christmas, its owner Aaron Feuerstein promised to pay his workers' salaries for as long as he could and to rebuild the textile factory. He was lauded as a hero in the press and praised by both politicians and religious leaders. However, he owned the company personally and was thus able to moderate his pursuit of profit to protect the interests of the workers and the community in preserving jobs. In contrast, corporate law traditionally has required corporations to be managed so as to maximize shareholder profits. This means that the corporation has no general duties to its employees or the community unless it has made explicit promises to the contrary, as it routinely does in employment contracts and agreements with its creditors from whom it borrows money. But it means more than that; because the managers are legally obligated to maximize corporate profits, it is not at all clear that a corporation could have imitated Feuerstein in a similar situation even if the board of directors and the management wanted to do so. Joseph William Singer, *The Edges of the Field: Lessons on the Obligations of Ownership* (2000).

The public support for the actions taken by Feuerstein suggest that it is not uncontroversial to assume that shareholders are more interested in maximizing profits than in anything else, such as preserving the environment, paying a living wage, or treating workers fairly. *See* Daniel J.H. Greenwood, *Fictional Shareholders: For Whom Are Corporate Managers Trustees, Revisited,* 69 S. Cal. L. Rev. 1021 (1996) (arguing that actual shareholders hold much more nuanced goals than profit maximization). Partly for this reason, following a spate of corporate mergers in the 1980s that resulted in the loss of many jobs, more than half of the states amended their incorporation statutes to grant directors of corporations the discretion (but not the obligation) to consider the interests of persons other than shareholders, such as employees, customers, suppliers, creditors, and the communities in which the corporation does business. David Millon, *Redefining Corporate Law,* 24 Ind. L. Rev. 223, 241 (1991). In practice, however, the courts have continued to interpret corporate law to preserve the goal of profit maximization as the central purpose of the corporation.

These stakeholder statutes have been criticized on the ground that they grant management the power to act in their own interests rather than the interests of shareholders and then to justify their self-dealing by arguing that they are protecting the interests of other stakeholders. Robert A. G. Monks and Nell Minow, *Power and Accountability* 101, 117-121 (1991). If managers have divided loyalties and no clear standards to control their decisions, then they can do whatever they want and justify it as congruent with *some* stakeholder's long-term interests. Nell Minow, *Shareholders, Stakeholders, and Boards of Directors,* 21 Stetson L. Rev. 197, 234 (1991). Minow concludes that stakeholders are best protected if corporate managers are accountable to shareholders such as pension funds that have long-run interests in the economic well-being of the company. "Directors who fail to consider the interests of customers, employees, suppliers, and the community fail in their duty to shareholders; a company that neglects those interests will surely decline." *Id.* at 219.

In contrast, David Millon and Marleen A. O'Connor have argued that stakeholder accountability statutes are unlikely to help nonshareholder groups unless they have enforceable rights of action. Millon, *supra*; Marleen A. O'Connor, *Restructuring the Corporation's Nexus of Contracts: Recognizing a Fiduciary Duty to Protect Displaced Workers*, 69 N.C. L. Rev. 1189 (1991). Millon suggests that stakeholder statutes be interpreted to prohibit managers from promoting "short-term profits at the expense of management's discretion to pursue longer-term strategies from which both shareholders and nonshareholders might benefit . . . if frustration of legitimate nonshareholder expectations will result." Millon, *supra*, at 266. Although the long run interests of the company may require factories to close, "management should conduct such transitions in a manner that minimizes losses to the affected parties." *Id.* at 268.

3. *Contract and reliance.* The union in *Local 1330* asked the court to order the company to sell the factory to it for its fair market value. The court determined that the factory was owned by the corporation and the corporation had the power to determine whether, and to whom, to sell the factory. After winning the lawsuit, the U.S. Steel Corp. demolished the factory. If the union could have obtained the funds to buy the factory, should it have been entitled to do so?

On one hand, it can be argued that such a sale should be left to the bargaining of the parties. Professor Jonathan Macey has argued that regulation of plant closings, like most regulation of contractual relationships, will increase the costs of business and wind up hurting the very parties it is supposed to protect. The workers should be *free to contract* for protections but the corporation has no enforceable legal obligations to the workers in cases like this. Macey, *supra* at 174-175. On the other hand, it can be argued that corporations form long-term relationships with employees and communities involving substantial investments by all parties and that it is not unfair to require corporations to undertake obligations to minimize the disruptive social effects of large plant closings. In this case, the workers are not asking for a gift but merely the right to buy the factory for its fair market value; this would allow the company to take the money and invest it elsewhere while allowing the union to attempt to preserve jobs in the community in which they live. Joseph William Singer, *The Reliance Interest in Property*, 40 Stan. L. Rev. 611 (1988).

4. *WARN.* In 1988, Congress passed the *Worker Adjustment and Retraining Notification Act* (WARN), 29 U.S.C. §§2101-2102. The act requires employers with 100 or more employees to provide 60 days' notice of plant closings or mass layoffs. Exceptions exist for business circumstances that were not "reasonably foreseeable" at the time notice would have been required, §2102(b)(2)(A), and natural disasters such as floods or earthquakes, §2102(b)(2)(B). A third exception is allowed if the employer was seeking capital or business that might have avoided the shutdown and providing notice would have "precluded the employer from obtaining the needed capital or business" §2102(b)(1).

PROBLEM

Ohio now has a stakeholder statute, Ohio Rev. Code Ann. §1701.59, which provides in part:

(B) A director shall perform the director's duties as a director, including the duties as a member of any committee of the directors upon which the director may serve, in good faith, in a manner the director reasonably believes to be in or not opposed to the best interests of the corporation, and with the care that an ordinarily prudent person in a like position would use under similar circumstances. . . .

(E) [A] director, in determining what the director reasonably believes to be in the best interests of the corporation, shall consider the interests of the corporation's shareholders and, in the director's discretion, may consider any of the following:

(1) The interests of the corporation's employees, suppliers, creditors, and customers;

(2) The economy of the state and nation;

(3) Community and societal considerations;

(4) The long-term as well as short-term interests of the corporation and its shareholders, including the possibility that these interests may be best served by the continued independence of the corporation.

Suppose a case like *United Steel Workers* arises today in Ohio. The board of directors of the company (the "employer") determines that continued operation of the two plants is much less profitable than alternative investments. The union proposes to purchase the two factories for their fair market value and has been able to arrange for financing to accomplish this. The board agrees to the proposal, rejecting an alternative proposal by another company (the "outside buyer") to purchase the property for $1 million more than the price offered by the union because this outside buyer intends to destroy the factories and convert the property to another use and would be unlikely to hire the workers for the new business. The board concludes that the avoidance of harm to the community and the workers, in the form of long-term unemployment, and harm to the company, in the form of a damaged reputation as a good employer, together outweigh the higher price offered by the outside buyer.

A pension fund that owns substantial stock in the company brings a lawsuit against the board of directors for breach of the directors' duty of care. The complaint alleges that by taking the lower offer, the board failed to "consider the interests of the corporation's shareholders" as it was required to do by the statute.

1. What arguments could you make on behalf of the pension fund that (a) the board violated its obligations to shareholders under the statute and (b) that the shareholders are therefore entitled to injunctive relief against the corporation ordering it to sell the factories to the highest bidder?

2. As the lawyer for the board of directors, make the arguments (a) that the board complied with its statutory mandate to consider the long-run interests of shareholders; (b) that its actions were justified by the best interests of both the employees and the community; and (c) even if it breached its duties under the statute, those duties are not enforceable by shareholders in court.

§1.4 Family

§1.4.1 Wills and Inheritance

In the United States, individuals are generally free to write a will determining who will own their property when they die. Statutes require wills to be in writing and to be witnessed (generally by two persons). Individuals are free to sell or give away their property before death so as to leave nothing to their family members when they pass on. Family members have no right to inherit property. U.S. law generally allows parents to disinherit their children. Every state does provide some protection for surviving spouses, however. Most states allow a surviving spouse to reject the will and recover a set portion of the decedent's estate (*statutory forced share statutes*). Many states also protect the right of a surviving spouse to continue living in the marital *homestead*. Other states provide for joint ownership of property acquired during marriage and give the surviving spouse half the *community property* acquired during the marriage on the death of the spouse.[3] The property of those who die without a valid will is distributed to the decedent's *heirs* as specified in the state *intestacy statute*. Some intestacy laws divide the decedent's property between a surviving spouse and the children, while others leave everything to the surviving spouse. If the decedent leaves no spouse and no children, then other relatives are entitled to inherit, such as parents, uncles and aunts, and cousins. If the decedent leaves no heirs, the property will *escheat* to the state.

Could the state completely abolish the power to pass on one's property when one dies? Consider the following case.

BABBITT v. YOUPEE
519 U.S. 234 (1997)

Justice RUTH BADER GINSBURG delivered the opinion of the Court.

In this case, we consider for a second time the constitutionality of an escheat-to-tribe provision of the *Indian Land Consolidation Act* (ILCA). 96 Stat. 2519, *as amended*, 25 U.S.C. §2206. Specifically, we address §207 of the ILCA, as amended in 1984. Congress enacted the original provision in 1983 to ameliorate the extreme fractionation problem attending a century-old allotment policy that yielded multiple ownership of single parcels of Indian land. Amended §207 provides that certain small interests in Indian lands will transfer — or "escheat" — to the tribe upon the death of the owner of the interest. In *Hodel v. Irving*, 481 U.S. 704 (1987), this Court held that the original version of §207 of the ILCA effected a taking of private property without just compensation, in violation of the Fifth Amendment to the United States Constitution. We now hold that amended §207 does not cure the constitutional deficiency this Court identified in the original version of §207.

I

In the late Nineteenth Century, Congress initiated an Indian land program that authorized the division of communal Indian property. Pursuant to this allotment policy, some Indian land was parceled out to individual tribal members. Lands not allotted to individual Indians were opened to non-Indians for settlement. *See Indian General Allotment Act of 1887*, ch. 119, 24 Stat. 388. Allotted lands were held in trust by the United States or owned by the allottee subject to restrictions on alienation. On the death of the allottee, the land descended according to the laws of the State or Territory in which the land was located. In 1910, Congress also provided that allottees could devise their interests in allotted land.

The allotment policy "quickly proved disastrous for the Indians." *Irving*, 481 U.S. at 707. The program produced a dramatic decline in the amount of land in Indian

---

3. For more on family property, *see infra* Chapter 7.

hands. And as allottees passed their interests on to multiple heirs, ownership of allotments became increasingly fractionated, with some parcels held by dozens of owners. A number of factors augmented the problem: Because Indians often died without wills, many interests passed to multiple heirs; Congress' allotment Acts subjected trust lands to alienation restrictions that impeded holders of small interests from transferring those interests; Indian lands were not subject to state real estate taxes, which ordinarily serve as a strong disincentive to retaining small fractional interests in land. The fractionation problem proliferated with each succeeding generation as multiple heirs took undivided interests in allotments.

The administrative difficulties and economic inefficiencies associated with multiple undivided ownership in allotted lands gained official attention as early as 1928. *See* L. Meriam, *Institute for Government Research, The Problem of Indian Administration* 40-41 (1928). Governmental administration of these fractionated interests proved costly, and individual owners of small undivided interests could not make productive use of the land. Congress ended further allotment in 1934. *See Indian Reorganization Act*, 25 U.S.C. §§461 *et seq*. But that action left the legacy in place. As most owners had more than one heir, interests in lands already allotted continued to splinter with each generation. In the 1960's, congressional studies revealed that approximately half of all allotted trust lands were held in fractionated ownership; for over a quarter of allotted trust lands, individual allotments were held by more than six owners to a parcel.

In 1983, Congress adopted the ILCA in part to reduce fractionated ownership of allotted lands. Section 207 of the Act — the "escheat" provision — prohibited the descent or devise of small fractional interests in allotments. Instead of passing to heirs, such fractional interests would escheat to the tribe, thereby consolidating the ownership of Indian lands. Congress defined the targeted fractional interest as one that both constituted 2 percent or less of the total acreage in an allotted tract and had earned less than $100 in the preceding year. Section 207 made no provision for the payment of compensation to those who held such interests.

In *Hodel v. Irving*, this Court invalidated §207 on the ground that it effected a taking of property without just compensation, in violation of the Fifth Amendment. The appellees in *Irving* were, or represented, heirs or devisees of members of the Oglala Sioux Tribe. But for §207, the appellees would have received 41 fractional interests in allotments; under §207, those interests would escheat to the Tribe. This Court tested the legitimacy of §207 by considering its economic impact, its effect on investment-backed expectations, and the essential character of the measure. Turning first to the economic impact of §207, the Court in *Irving* observed that the provision's income-generation test might fail to capture the actual economic value of the land. The Court next indicated that §207 likely did not interfere with investment-backed expectations. Key to the decision in *Irving*, however, was the "extraordinary" character of the Government regulation. As this Court noted, §207 amounted to the "virtual abrogation of the right to pass on a certain type of property." Such a complete abrogation of the rights of descent and devise could not be upheld.

II

In 1984, while *Irving* was still pending in the Court of Appeals for the Eighth Circuit, Congress amended §207. Amended §207 differs from the original escheat provision in three relevant respects. First, an interest is considered fractional if it both constitutes 2 percent or less of the total acreage of the parcel and "is incapable of earning $100 in any one of the five years [following the] decedent's death" — as opposed to one year before the decedent's death in the original §207. 25 U.S.C. §2206(a). If the interest earned less than $100 in any one of five years prior to the decedent's death, "there shall be a rebuttable presumption that such interest is incapable of earning $100 in any one of the five years following the death of the decedent." *Id.* Second, in lieu of a total ban on devise and descent of fractional interests, amended §207 permits devise of an otherwise escheatable interest to "any other owner of an undivided fractional interest in such parcel or tract" of land. 25 U.S.C. §2206(b). Finally, tribes are authorized to override the provisions of amended §207 through the adoption of their own codes governing the disposition of fractional interests; these codes are subject to the approval of the Secretary of the Interior. 25 U.S.C. §2206(c). In *Irving*, "we express[ed] no opinion on the constitutionality of §207 as amended." 481 U.S. at 710, n.1.

Under amended §207, the interests in this case would escheat to tribal governments. The initiating plaintiffs, respondents here, are the children and potential heirs of William Youpee. An enrolled member of the Sioux and Assiniboine Tribes of the Fort Peck Reservation in Montana, William Youpee died testate in October 1990. His will devised to respondents, all of them enrolled tribal members, his several undivided interests in allotted trust lands on various reservations in Montana and North Dakota. These interests, as the Ninth Circuit reported, were valued together at $1,239. Each interest was devised to a single descendant. Youpee's will thus perpetuated existing fractionation, but it did not splinter ownership further by bequeathing any single fractional interest to multiple devisees. . . .

III

In determining whether the 1984 amendments to §207 render the provision constitutional, we are guided by *Irving*.[3] The United States maintains that the amendments, though enacted three years prior to the *Irving* decision, effectively anticipated the concerns expressed in the Court's opinion. As already noted, amended §207 differs from the original in three relevant respects: It looks back five years instead of one to determine the income produced from a small interest, and creates a rebuttable presumption that this income stream will continue; it permits devise of otherwise escheatable interests to persons who already own an interest in the same parcel; and it authorizes tribes to develop their own codes governing the disposition of fractional interests. These modifications, according to the United States, rescue amended §207 from the fate of its predecessor. The Government maintains that the revisions moderate the economic impact of the provision and temper the character of the Government's regulation; the latter factor weighed most heavily against the constitutionality of the original version of §207.

The narrow revisions Congress made to §207, without benefit of our ruling in *Irving*, do not warrant a disposition different from the one this Court announced and explained in *Irving*. Amended §207 permits a five-year window rather than a one-year

---

3. In *Irving* we relied on *Penn Central Transp. Co. v. New York City*, 438 U.S. 104 (1978). Because we find *Irving* dispositive, we do not reach respondents' argument that amended §207 effects a "categorical" taking, and is therefore subject to the more stringent analysis employed in *Lucas v. South Carolina Coastal Council*, 505 U.S. 1003 (1992).

window to assess the income-generating capacity of the interest. As the Ninth Circuit observed, however, argument that this change substantially mitigates the economic impact of §207 "misses the point." Amended §207 still trains on income generated from the land, not on the value of the parcel. The Court observed in *Irving* that "even if . . . the income generated by such parcels may be properly thought of as *de minimis*," the value of the land may not fit that description. The parcels at issue in *Irving* were valued by the Bureau of Indian Affairs at $2,700 and $1,816, amounts we found "not trivial." The value of the disputed parcels in this case is not of a different order; as the Ninth Circuit reported, the value of decedent Youpee's fractional interests was $1,239. In short, the economic impact of amended §207 might still be palpable.

Even if the economic impact of amended §207 is not significantly less than the impact of the original provision, the United States correctly comprehends that *Irving* rested primarily on the "extraordinary" character of the governmental regulation. *Irving* stressed that the original §207 "amount[ed] to virtually the abrogation of the right to pass on a certain type of property — the small undivided interest — to one's heirs." 481 U.S. at 716. The *Irving* Court further noted that the original §207 "effectively abolish[ed] both descent and devise [of fractional interests] even when the passing of the property to the heir might result in consolidation of property." 481 U.S. at 716. As the United States construes *Irving*, Congress cured the fatal infirmity in §207 when it revised the section to allow transmission of fractional interests to successors who already own an interest in the allotment.

Congress' creation of an ever-so-slight class of individuals equipped to receive fractional interests by devise does not suffice, under a fair reading of *Irving*, to rehabilitate the measure. Amended §207 severely restricts the right of an individual to direct the descent of his property. Allowing a decedent to leave an interest only to a current owner in the same parcel shrinks drastically the universe of possible successors. And, as the Ninth Circuit observed, the "very limited group [of permissible devisees] is unlikely to contain any lineal descendants." Moreover, amended §207 continues to restrict devise "even in circumstances when the governmental purpose sought to be advanced, consolidation of ownership of Indian lands, does not conflict with the further descent of the property." *Irving*, 481 U.S. at 718. William Youpee's will, the United States acknowledges, bequeathed each fractional interest to one heir. Giving effect to Youpee's directive, therefore, would not further fractionate Indian land holdings. . . .

The third alteration made in amended §207 also fails to bring the provision outside the reach of this Court's holding in *Irving*. Amended §207 permits tribes to establish their own codes to govern the disposition of fractional interests; if approved by the Secretary of the Interior, these codes would govern in lieu of amended §207. *See* 25 U.S.C. §2206(c). The United States does not rely on this new provision to defend the statute. Nor does it appear that the United States could do so at this time: Tribal codes governing disposition of escheatable interests have apparently not been developed. . . .

Justice JOHN PAUL STEVENS, dissenting.

Section 207 of the *Indian Land Consolidation Act*, 25 U.S.C. §2206, did not, in my view, effect an unconstitutional taking of William Youpee's right to make a testamentary disposition of his property. As I explained in *Hodel v. Irving*, 481 U.S. 704 (1987) (opinion concurring in judgment), the Federal Government, like a State, has a valid interest in removing legal impediments to the productive development of real estate. For this reason, the Court has repeatedly "upheld the power of the State to condition the retention of a property right upon the performance of an act within a limited period of time." *Texaco, Inc. v. Short,* 454 U.S. 516, 529 (1982). I remain convinced that "Congress has ample power to require the owners of fractional interests in allotted lands to consolidate their holdings during their lifetimes or to face the risk that their interests will be deemed to be abandoned." *Hodel,* 481 U.S. at 732 (Stevens, J., concurring in judgment). The federal interest in minimizing the fractionated ownership of Indian lands — and thereby paving the way to the productive development of their property — is strong enough to justify the legislative remedy created by §207, provided, of course, that affected owners have adequate notice of the requirements of the law and an adequate opportunity to adjust their affairs to protect against loss.

In my opinion, William Youpee did have such notice and opportunity.... More than six years passed from the time §207 was amended until Mr. Youpee died on October 19, 1990 (this period spans more than seven years if we count from the date §207 was originally enacted). During this time, Mr. Youpee could have realized the value of his fractional interests (approximately $1,239) in a variety of ways, including selling the property, giving it to his children as a gift, or putting it in trust for them. I assume that he failed to do so because he was not aware of the requirements of §207. This loss is unfortunate. But I believe Mr. Youpee's failure to pass on his property is the product of inadequate legal advice rather than an unconstitutional defect in the statute....

NOTES AND QUESTIONS

1. *Family as a source of property.* One of the major sources of property rights for most people is the property owned by their parents. Parents have legal obligations to care for their children until they reach the age of majority. Many parents continue to provide support after that age. At death, most parents leave the bulk of their property to a surviving spouse. If there is no surviving spouse, they tend overwhelmingly to leave their property to their children. Family relationships constitute a major source of property for most people. Wealthier families are not only more likely to be able to provide their children with a good education but are more likely to produce children who will themselves be well off.

2. *Is inherited wealth a problem?* On June 8, 2001, President George W. Bush signed into a law a bill that, if extended at the appropriate time, would eliminate the estate tax entirely, allowing individuals to leave all their property to their families or other designees free of taxes. Is inherited wealth a problem? *Babbitt v. Youpee* holds that legislatures may adopt substantial limits on inherited wealth but that they may not completely abolish the right to pass on real property owned at death.

One can argue that individuals have a moral and legal right to pass on their wealth to their children. Those who earn wealth have a right to do with it as they please. Children are, in a sense, an extension of oneself, and the wish to provide for them is very strong. Others have no right to complain when parents favor their children. Children rely on their families; it would seem to countenance an extreme individualism to preclude the ability of parents to support their children by passing on their wealth when they die.

On the other hand, it has been argued that inherited wealth is a problem. It arguably deprives children of incentives to go out and be productive themselves. Moreover, it helps perpetuate vast inequalities that violate basic norms of equality of opportunity. Mark Ascher has argued that inherited wealth should be drastically curtailed. Mark Ascher, *Curtailing Inherited Wealth,* 89 Mich. L. Rev. 69 (1990). He suggests that individuals do not necessarily deserve all the property they accumulate during their lives. "Wealth in the modern world does not come merely from individual effort; it results from a combination of individual effort and of the manifold uses to which the community puts that effort." *Id.* at 87. He notes that while we cannot control "differences in native ability" or "many forms of luck" resulting from the opportunities that arise in different families, he argues that "we can — and ought to — curb one form of luck. Children lucky enough to have been raised, acculturated, and educated by wealthy parents need not be allowed the additional good fortune of inheriting their parents' property." *Id.* at 74. Rather than eliminate the estate tax, he proposed to increase it, although not to 100 percent.

3. *Allotment.* The property interests at issue in *Babbitt* result from a complex history involving dispossession of Indian tribes. These issues are addressed below at §12.2.2.1 and §13.1.

PROBLEMS

1. Unlike some European countries, parents in the United States are entitled to completely disinherit their children, leaving them nothing when they die. Should parents be allowed to disinherit their children, or should children, like surviving spouses, be entitled to a portion of the decedent's property owned at death?

2. In *Eyerman v. Mercantile Trust Co.*, 524 S.W.2d 210 (Mo. Ct. App. 1975), Louise Woodruff Johnson left a will directing her executor to raze her attractive house in St. Louis, sell the land, and distribute the proceeds to stated beneficiaries. Although her beneficiaries appear not to have objected to the destruction of the house, the neighbors did object and sued to obtain injunctive relief preventing this from occurring. The court agreed, finding the will provision ordering the house to be destroyed both to be "eccentric" and to violate public policy. "Destruction of the house harms the neighbors, detrimentally affects the community, causes monetary loss in excess of $39,000.00 to the estate and is without benefit to the dead woman." *Id.* at 214. Do you agree? *See* Lior Jacob Strahilevitz, *The Right to Destroy*, 114 Yale L.J. 781 (2005) (arguing that good reasons exist to honor such will provisions). *But see* Joseph L. Sax, *Playing Darts with a Rembrandt: Public and Private Rights in Cultural Treasures* (1999) (arguing for restrictions on certain types of property to protect public interests in conservation of historic and artistic treasures).

§1.4.2   Marriage

Access to property differs by gender and age, as well as race. Women, on average, earn less than men. In 1999, men who worked full time earned an average of $36,476, while women who worked full time earned only $26,324, or 72% of male earnings. U.S. Census Bureau, Current Population Reports, P60-209, *Money Income in the United States: 1999* (Sept. 2000) (*http://www.census.gov*). The reasons for the disparities between women and men are complicated. It is clear, however, that a major factor is that women continue to undertake the bulk of the responsibility for raising children. This work not only is unpaid but interferes with women's ability to work full time. *See* Martha Albertson Fineman, *The Illusion of Equality: The Rhetoric and Reality of Divorce Reform* (1991); Victor Fuchs, *Women's Quest for Economic Equality* (1988); Vicki

Schultz, *Life's Work,* 100 Colum. L. Rev. 1881 (2000); Joan Williams, *Unbending Gender: Why Family and Work Conflict and What to Do About It* (2000).

Women also suffer disproportionately from divorce. After divorce, men's standard of living tends to go up by 10 percent, while women's standard of living declines by 27 percent. Richard R. Peterson, *A Re-Evaluation of the Economic Consequences of Divorce,* 61 Am. Soc. Rev. 528, 534 (1996); Lenore J. Weitzman, *The Economic Consequences of Divorce Are Still Unequal: Comment on Peterson,* 61 Am. Soc. Rev. 537, 538 (1996).

Children are more likely to be poor than adults, and some children are very likely to be poor. Although 11.8 percent of the population fell below the poverty line in 1999, 16.9 percent of children did so; moreover, 37 percent of African American children were living in poverty. Children who live in households without an adult male are extremely likely to be poor. While only 5.8 percent of children in families of married couples were poor in 1999, 30.4 percent of children living in female-headed households were poor. Half of all children under six living in female-headed households (50.3 percent) were poor. Although 19.8 percent of children in white, non-Hispanic female-headed households were poor, 41 percent of children of African American female-headed households were poor. While the median income of married couples with children was $56,827, the median income of female-headed households was only $26,164, and the median income of male-headed households was $41,838. Joseph Dalaker & Bernadette D. Proctor, U.S. Census Bureau, Current Population Reports, P60-210 *Poverty in the United States: 1999* (Sept. 2000) (*http://www.census.gov*).

Upon divorce, the property obtained during the marriage is distributed between the parties. Under the *community property* system followed in about ten states, most property acquired during the marriage is owned equally by husband and wife unless they have signed an enforceable premarital agreement to the contrary. The majority of states provide for *separate property,* meaning the property earned by each spouse is his or her separate property during marriage unless the couple agrees to the contrary. However, spouses have enforceable obligations to support each other during marriage, and, upon divorce, the property accumulated during the marriage will be *equitably distributed* between the parties according to such factors as duration of marriage, contribution of labor or resources, and need. Although a few community property jurisdictions grant each spouse one-half of the community property accumulated during the marriage, most adopt a version of the equitable distribution standard to divide up such property on divorce. These issues are further developed below in Chapter 14.

The following materials focus on who gets the family home upon divorce and whether the house should be sold. How should these determinations be made? Do children have a right to continue living in their home with the custodial parent? How do gender roles in the family and societal sex discrimination affect the distribution of property between men and women and between adults and children?

MONTANA EQUITABLE DISTRIBUTION STATUTE

Mont. Code Ann. §40-4-202

§40-4-202   *Division of Property*

(1) In a proceeding for dissolution of a marriage, legal separation, or division of property following a decree of dissolution of marriage or legal separation by a court

which lacked personal jurisdiction over the absent spouse or lacked jurisdiction to divide the property, the court, without regard to marital misconduct, shall, and in a proceeding for legal separation may, finally equitably apportion between the parties the property and assets belonging to either or both, however and whenever acquired and whether the title thereto is in the name of the husband or wife or both. In making apportionment, the court shall consider the duration of the marriage and prior marriage of either party; the age, health, station, occupation, amount and sources of income, vocational skills, employability, estate, liabilities, and needs of each of the parties; custodial provisions; whether the apportionment is in lieu of or in addition to maintenance; and the opportunity of each for future acquisition of capital assets and income. The court shall also consider the contribution or dissipation of value of the respective estates and the contribution of a spouse as a homemaker or to the family unit. In dividing property acquired prior to the marriage; property acquired by gift, bequest, devise, or descent; property acquired in exchange for property acquired before the marriage or in exchange for property acquired by gift, bequest, devise, or descent; the increased value of property acquired prior to marriage; and property acquired by a spouse after a decree of legal separation, the court shall consider those contributions of the other spouse to the marriage, including:

(a) the nonmonetary contribution of a homemaker;

(b) the extent to which such contributions have facilitated the maintenance of this property; and

(c) whether or not the property division serves as an alternative to maintenance arrangements.

(2) In a proceeding, the court may protect and promote the best interests of the children by setting aside a portion of the jointly and separately held estates of the parties in a separate fund or trust for the support, maintenance, education, and general welfare of any minor, dependent, or incompetent children of the parties. . . .

IN RE MARRIAGE OF KING

700 P.2d 591 (Mont. 1985)

WILLIAM HUNT, SR., Justice . . .

Jack and Pamela King married in March 1971, in Mexico. Thereafter, they resided in California, where their two children were born, in 1971 and 1973. In 1977, they moved to Montana. They separated in June 1980, and the District Court dissolved their marriage in June 1981, . . . [and on February 29, 1984, the court] awarded each party the personal property then in their possession, and awarded the family residence to Pamela.

Jack asserts several of the court's findings of fact are unsupported by substantial evidence. We will address them in order. In its finding no. 2, the court noted: "The distribution of the proceeds of the sale of the family home if it is ordered sold makes inadequate provision for the support of the minor children of the parties."

Finding no. 3: "A substantial hardship would be imposed upon the children of the parties if they would be required to vacate the family home if it is ordered sold."

Finding no. 4: "The expenses of sale, including realtors' commissions, attorneys' fees and potential capital gain tax liability would take a disproportionate amount of marital assets needed for child support."

And no. 5: "It would be in the best interests of the minor children of the parties to continue to reside in the family home."

Jack contends the division of property should be separate from and not contingent upon child support. However, a fair reading of Mont. Code Ann. §40-4-202, shows that the District Court, in a proceeding for dissolution of marriage, may take into account support considerations, and may protect and promote the best interests of the children by setting aside a portion of the jointly and separately held estate of the parties for the support of their children. In reaching such a result, the court shall equitably apportion between the parties, the property or assets belonging to either or both. The court is neither required to divide each asset 50-50, nor to sell all the parties' property and divide the proceeds 50-50. Equitable apportionment is the guideline under any or all of the many factors which apply. To order the sale of the family residence would subject the marital estate to realty fees, would lose a favorable interest rate, and would uproot the children from their home and possibly from their neighborhood. These findings are well supported in the record. . . .

Finally, Jack assails finding no. 10: "Awarding the Petitioner the Respondent's share of the equity in the family home is the only reasonable means to insure that the Respondent will contribute to the care and support of the minor children of the parties." Again, the District Court was in the best position to view the parties, the witnesses and the evidence, and to render a decision based on its view. Our role is not to examine other possible means of ensuring Jack will contribute to the care and support of his and Pamela's children, but to determine whether the means chosen has a lawful basis of support in the record. The income earned from Jack's chosen occupation as a professional gambler, is by its very nature, inadequate to ensure he will always or regularly or even predictably have that income. To accede to such speculation is a gamble that neither party nor the District Court is advised to undertake. We find substantial evidence supports the findings of the District Court.

The second issue Jack presents is whether the District Court erred in awarding the custodial spouse the family residence "in lieu of any child support obligation on the part of the [non-custodial spouse.]" He contends the award was erroneous because the issues of property and support are totally irrelevant to each other. Pamela, on the other hand, claims the award was proper because the issues of property, support, custody and visitation rights are "inextricably interwoven." The record does not support a conclusion favoring either of those extremes. Rather, the District Court considered all the factors, and made a decision based on the extent to which they were interrelated. . . .

We held in *Perkins v. Perkins*, 540 P.2d 957 (Mont. 1975), that where the husband was financially unable to contribute to the support of the minor children, it was not error to grant the wife a proportionally larger share of the marital property to offset her increased obligation. Similarly, in *Bailey v. Bailey*, 603 P.2d 259 (Mont. 1979), the trial court awarded the family residence to the wife, plus other property, for a total award of approximately 67% of the marital estate. After noting the District Court weighed all the applicable factors of Mont. Code Ann. §40-4-202, we held a division of the marital estate which favors one party over the other may be acceptable if there is reason for it. Here, the District Court stated its reasons — the best interests of the children are served by allowing them to remain in the family home; forced sale of the family home would divert and dissipate assets needed for support; and the only reasonable means to protect and promote the best interests of the children is to award the home to Pamela. That award was made in lieu of a support obligation.

No reasonable purpose would be served by ordering the residence sold. Jack would not reside there in any event, the children would be uprooted, and the marital estate would be lessened because of realty fees attendant to the sale. . . .

We believe the District Court did a thorough job of dividing the marital assets and resolving the respective support obligations of the parties. We hold there was no abuse of discretion. . . .

NOTES AND QUESTIONS

1. *Sale of the home or a refuge for the children?* Did the court in *In re King* base its decision on the children's right to stay in their home or on the fact that Jack King was a professional gambler with an uncertain source of income? Did a combination of these factors lead to the outcome?

When a married couple gets divorced, the courts face the task of dividing property acquired during the marriage. The marital home is ordinarily the most valuable asset of the parties. Spouses often attempt to work out a settlement, which may be reviewed by the court for fairness and legality. Many considerations influence the outcome. On one hand, requiring the house to be sold means that neither party can continue to live there. Having to move is especially disruptive to children. On the other hand, because both parties contribute to the joint enterprise of the marriage, they have a right to equitably share in the property acquired during the marriage. If the couple has invested in a home, it may be impossible to divide the monetary value of the home between the parties without selling it; the person to whom the home is given ordinarily does not have enough assets simply to pay off the other party. Moreover, the cost of maintaining the house may be greater than the cost of moving to more modest accommodations and may tax the limited resources of the couple, whose expenses may have risen since living separately. Finally, sale of the home may be the only way to obtain a significant source of funds to pay the added expenses of splitting up the household, allowing each of the parties to attain economic independence.

Perhaps because of these conflicting pressures, the court in *Ramsey v. Ramsey*, 546 N.E.2d 1280 (Ind. Ct. App. 1989), ordered the house sold over the objections of *both* the husband and wife, a couple who had been married for 20 years and who wished the wife to continue living in the marital home with the five children where the father could continue to visit the children daily. The ruling was upheld on appeal as within the trial judge's discretion but was accompanied by a vigorous dissent.

In *Behrens v. Behrens*, 532 N.Y.S.2d 893 (App. Div. 1988), the court ordered the family house sold on the grounds that neither party had sufficient resources to afford the maintenance costs of the home. The wife had objected to the sale on the grounds that it would force her and the children to leave their present community, where the family had established strong ties. A dissenting opinion argued that the imagined savings of moving were illusory since the lower rents in alternative housing would increase over time, while the mortgage payments on the current home would remain constant. Similarly, in *Stallworth v. Stallworth*, 237 Cal. Rptr. 829 (Ct. App. 1987), the court held that the adverse economic, emotional, and social impact on the minor child from being forced to move out of the family home would be minimal, even though the child was under psychiatric care and in a special education program at school. The court concluded that the adverse effect on the child was outweighed by the husband's economic interest in the sale of the home.

In a variation on this theme, the court in *Stolow v. Stolow*, 540 N.Y.S.2d 484 (App. Div. 1989), ordered the sale of the family "mini-mansion" on the grounds that it was extravagant and that the wife and children could use the proceeds of the sale to buy another "fine residence." The court ordered the sale so that the husband could obtain his share of the value of the house, despite the fact that the husband was wealthy enough to be able to afford the house payments and in the face of the "well settled principle of matrimonial law that exclusive possession of a marital residence is generally awarded to a custodial spouse with minor children." *Id.* at 486.

2. *The feminization of poverty.* Victor Fuchs notes that the weaker economic position of women is primarily caused by the fact that women assume the bulk of the responsibility for rearing children. This situation causes severe conflicts between career and family. Victor Fuchs, *Women's Quest for Economic Equality* 4, 94 (1988). Having children imposes costs that are disproportionately borne by women in the form of lower wages. Fuchs explains, *id.* at 60, 86:

> First, many women leave the labor market during pregnancy, at childbirth, or when their children are young. These child-related interruptions are damaging to subsequent earnings because three out of four births occur to women before the age of 30 — the same time that men are gaining the training and experience that lead to higher earnings later in life. Second, even when mothers stay in the labor force, responsibility for children frequently constrains their choice of job: they accept lower wages in exchange for shorter or more flexible hours, location near home, limited out-of-town travel, and the like. Third, women who devote a great deal of time and energy to childcare and associated housework are often less able to devote maximum effort to market work. For instance, when a young child is present, women are more likely than men to be absent from work, even at equal levels of education and wages. . . .
>
> Why is the percentage of adult poor who are women always over 50 percent . . . ? On average, men earn appreciably more money than women, but if all men and women lived in two-sex households, the proportion of poor who are women would always be approximately one-half. It is the presence of one-sex households and the lower income of women with respect to men in those types of households that determine the feminization of poverty.

3. *Child care.* Why is taking care of children in the home unpaid? What, if anything, should the government do to alleviate the plight of single mothers? Should the house automatically go to the divorced spouse who has primary custody of the children?

PROBLEM

In *Pascale v. Pascale*, 660 A.2d 485 (N.J. 1995), Debra and James Pascale divorced after a 13-year marriage. Although they were granted "joint legal custody" of the three children, Debra was the "primary caretaker" with "physical custody" of the children most of the time. James was ordered to pay 60 percent of the costs of supporting the children. He was granted visitation rights with the children at his home from 5:30 to 8:30 p.m. for dinner on Wednesday and Thursday evenings and would keep the children for a 24-hour period each weekend. During the summer the children would stay with him overnight on Wednesdays and Thursdays, and the couple was ordered to alternate major holidays with the children. At the time of the divorce, Debra had a gross annual income of $52,500, and James had an income of $72,500.

The court interpreted statutory child support requirements to guarantee "the right of children of divorce to be supported at least according to the standard of living to which they had grown accustomed prior to the separation of their parents." *Id.* at 489. The court determined that the parties could not maintain two large and equal houses. It was faced with a choice between ordering the house sold immediately, allowing each spouse to obtain a house of equal size and quality, or allowing the primary caretaker to stay in the larger family home until the children were older, thereby forcing the husband to live in a smaller home than he could afford if he could immediately obtain his 50 percent of the equity built up in the family home. The court compromised by awarding the family house to Debra on the understanding that she had agreed to sell it in five years when the oldest child was to begin high school.

    a.   What arguments would you make for James that the court should order the house to be sold immediately?

    b.   What arguments would you make for Debra that she should be given possession of the house until the youngest child reaches 18?

    c.   What should the court do, and why?

§1.4.3   GIFTS

A gift is a transfer of property from one person to another without payment. *Inter vivos* gifts are transfers from one living person to another, while *testamentary transfers* are those effectuated at death through a valid will or inheritance.

The law of gifts requires (1) *intent* to transfer title, (2) *delivery* of the property, and (3) *acceptance* by the donee. *Westleigh v. Conger*, 755 A.2d 518, 519, 2000 Me. 134 at ¶7 (Me. 2000). Delivery generally requires physical transfer of the object itself. However, constructive or symbolic delivery might be sufficient. For example, constructive delivery would be recognized if the owner of a locked box gave the only key to the donee. Some courts, however, recognize constructive delivery only if physical delivery is inconvenient or impossible. Today, the delivery requirement may be accomplished by a writing rather than physical delivery. Many states allow a gift to be made through a formal deed or even a more informal writing that indicates a present intent to relinquish possession and to transfer title to the donee.

To make a gift, the donor must have a *present intent* to transfer ownership rights in the object. However, this does not mean that actual possession of the gift must be transferred to the donee. For example, a mother could give her daughter a piano but retain the right to keep it in her house until her death. In effect, the mother has retained a life estate in the piano and presently transferred a vested remainder to the daughter. *Gruen v. Gruen*, 496 N.E.2d 869 (N.Y. 1986).

PROBLEMS

1. Two people get engaged and exchange rings; they break off the engagement. Must they return the rings? Traditionally, donors were not allowed to impose conditions on gifts. Delivery of a gift with intent to transfer title would be held to be irrevocable. *Albinger v. Harris*, 48 P.3d 711, 719, 2002 MT 118 ¶¶32-34 (Mont. 2002). However, some courts have begun to abandon this rule, and most will do so

in the context of gifts given in contemplation of marriage. Because a wedding ring is clearly given under the understanding that the parties would be married, most courts will require the ring to be returned if the engagement is called off. *Lipton v. Lipton*, 514 N.Y.S.2d 158 (N.Y. Sup. Ct. 1986); *Lindh v. Surman*, 742 A.2d 643 (Pa. 1999).

Should it matter whose fault it is that the marriage fell through? Some courts refuse to look into fault, *Vigil v. Haber*, 888 P.2d 455 (N.M. 1994); *Aronow v. Silver*, 538 A.2d 851 (N.J. Super. Ct. Ch. Div. 1987); *Cooper v. Smith*, 800 N.E.2d 372 (Ohio Ct. App. 2003), while others will not allow an individual to recover a ring if he broke off the engagement without justification, *Spinnell v. Quigley*, 785 P.2d 1149 (Wash. Ct. App. 1990) (fault relevant); *Heiman v. Parish*, 942 P.2d 631 (Kan. 1997) (fault should be a factor in extreme cases); *Curtis v. Anderson*, 106 S.W.3d 251, 256 (Tex. Ct. App. 2003)("absent a written agreement a donor is not entitled to the return of an engagement ring if he terminates the engagement"). Which approach is better?

2. Two parties open a joint bank account. Should they each be entitled to use all the money in the account, or do they have an obligation not to withdraw excessive amounts of the money to ensure that some is left for their co-owner? Do the circumstances under which the money was deposited matter?

§1.5   Possession

§1.5.1   WILD ANIMALS

Rights in land ultimately derive from the government and are then transferred to others. The government has often distributed property based on possession even when possessors were violating prior law. Sometimes, as in *Johnson v. M'Intosh*, the government ignored possessory claims and transferred property to others. Nonetheless, possession is a crucial concept in the law (recall the common expression "Possession is nine-tenths of the law"). Actual possession of a contested resource often creates a presumption of a right to possess that may be rebutted only by evidence of a superior claim. What happens when conflicts about possession arise? What kinds of labor or investment are sufficient to give rise to possessory rights? What kinds of economic activity constitute unfair competition amounting to infringement on property rights?

<hr>

PIERSON v. POST

3 Cai. R. 175, 2 Am. Dec. 264 (N.Y. 1805)

This was an action of trespass on the case commenced in a justice's court, by the present defendant against the now plaintiff.

The declaration stated that Post, being in possession of certain dogs and hounds under his command, did, "upon a certain wild and uninhabited, unpossessed and waste land, called the beach, find and start one of those noxious beasts called a fox," and whilst there hunting, chasing and pursuing the same with his dogs and hounds, and when in view thereof, Pierson, well knowing the fox was so hunted and pursued, did, in the sight of Post, to prevent his catching the same, kill and carry it off. A verdict having been rendered for the plaintiff below, the defendant there sued out a certiorari, and now assigned for error, that the declaration and the matters therein contained were not sufficient in law to maintain an action. . . .

DANIEL TOMPKINS, J., delivered the opinion of the court. . . .

The question submitted by the counsel in this cause for our determination is, whether Lodowick Post, by the pursuit with his hounds in the manner alleged in his declaration, acquired such a right to, or property in, the fox, as will sustain an action against Pierson for killing and taking him away.

The cause was argued with much ability by the counsel on both sides, and presents for our decision a novel and nice question. It is admitted that a fox is an animal *ferae naturae* and that property in such animals is acquired by occupancy only. These admissions narrow the discussion to the simple question of what acts amount to occupancy, applied to acquiring right to wild animals?

If we have recourse to the ancient writers upon general principles of law, the judgment below is obviously erroneous. Justinian's Institutes, lib. 2, tit. 1, s.13, and Fleta, lib. 3, c.2, p.175, adopt the principle, that pursuit alone vests no property or right in the huntsman; and that even pursuit, accompanied with wounding, is equally ineffectual for that purpose, unless the animal be actually taken. The same principle is recognised by Bracton, lib. 2, c.1, p.8.

Puffendorf, lib. 4, c.6, s.2 and 10, defines occupancy of beasts *ferae naturae*, to be the actual corporal possession of them, and Bynkershoek is cited as coinciding in this definition. It is indeed with hesitation that Puffendorf affirms that a wild beast mortally wounded, or greatly maimed, cannot be fairly intercepted by another, whilst the pursuit of the person inflicting the wound continues. The foregoing authorities are decisive to show that mere pursuit gave Post no legal right to the fox, but that he became the property of Pierson, who intercepted and killed him.

It therefore only remains to inquire whether there are any contrary principles, or authorities, to be found in other books, which ought to induce a different decision. . . .

Barbeyrac, in his notes on Puffendorf, does not accede to the definition of occupancy by the latter, but, on the contrary, affirms, that actual bodily seizure is not, in all cases, necessary to constitute possession of wild animals. He does not, however, *describe* the acts which, according to his ideas, will amount to an appropriation of such animals to private use, so as to exclude the claims of all other persons, by title of occupancy, to the same animals; and he is far from averring that pursuit alone is sufficient for that purpose. To a certain extent, and as far as Barbeyrac appears to me to go, his objections to Puffendorf's definition of occupancy are reasonable and correct. That is to say, that actual bodily seizure is not indispensable to acquire right to, or possession of, wild beasts; but that, on the contrary, the mortal wounding of such beasts, by one not abandoning his pursuit, may, with the utmost propriety, be deemed possession of him; since, thereby, the pursuer manifests an unequivocal intention of appropriating the animal to his individual use, has deprived him of his natural liberty, and brought him within his certain control. So also, encompassing and securing such animals with nets and toils, or otherwise intercepting them in such a manner as to deprive them of their natural liberty, and render escape impossible, may justly be deemed to give possession of them to those persons who, by their industry and labor, have used such means of apprehending them. Barbeyrac seems to have adopted, and had in view of his notes, the more accurate opinion of Grotius, with respect to occupancy. . . . The case now under consideration is one of mere pursuit, and presents no circumstances or acts which can bring it within the definition of occupancy by Puffendorf, or Grotius, or the ideas of Barbeyrac upon that subject.

The case cited . . . I think clearly distinguishable from the present; inasmuch as there the action was for maliciously hindering and disturbing the plaintiff in the exercise and enjoyment of a private franchise; and . . . that the ducks were in the plaintiff's decoy pond, and *so in his possession,* from which it is obvious that the court laid much stress in the opinion upon the plaintiff's possession of the ducks. . . .

We are the more readily inclined to confine possession or occupancy of beasts *ferae naturae,* within the limits prescribed by the learned authors above cited, for the sake of certainty, and preserving peace and order in society. If the first seeing, starting, or pursuing such animals, without having so wounded, circumvented or ensnared them, so as to deprive them of their natural liberty, and subject them to the control of their pursuer, should afford the basis of actions against others for intercepting and killing them, it would prove a fertile source of quarrels and litigation.

However uncourteous or unkind the conduct of Pierson towards Post, in this instance, may have been, yet his act was productive of no injury or damage for which a legal remedy can be applied. We are of opinion the judgment below was erroneous, and ought to be reversed.

BROCKHOLST LIVINGSTON, J. My opinion differs from that of the court. . . .

Whether a person who, with his own hounds, starts and hunts a fox on waste and uninhabited ground, and is on the point of seizing his prey, acquires such an interest in the animal, as to have a right of action against another, who in view of the huntsman and his dogs in full pursuit, and with knowledge of the chase, shall kill and carry him away?

This is a knotty point, and should have been submitted to the arbitration of sportsmen, without poring over Justinian, Fleta, Bracton, Puffendorf, Locke, Barbeyrac, or Blackstone, all of whom have been cited; they would have had no difficulty in coming to a prompt and correct conclusion. In a court thus constituted, the skin and carcass of poor *reynard* would have been properly disposed of, and a precedent set, interfering with no usage or custom which the experience of ages has sanctioned, and which must be so well known to every votary of Diana. But the parties have referred the question to our judgment, and we must dispose of it as well as we can, from the partial lights we possess, leaving to a higher tribunal, the correction of any mistake which we may be so unfortunate as to make. By the pleadings it is admitted that a fox is a "wild and noxious beast." Both parties have regarded him, as the law of nations does a pirate, *hostem humani generis,* and although *de mortuis nil nisi bonum,* be a maxim of our profession, the memory of the deceased has not been spared. His depredations on farmers and on barn yards have not been forgotten; and to put him to death wherever found, is allowed to be meritorious, and of public benefit. Hence it follows, that our decision should have in view the greatest possible encouragement to the destruction of an animal, so cunning and ruthless in his career. But who would keep a pack of hounds; or what gentleman, at the sound of the horn, and at peep of day, would mount his steed, and for hours together, *sub jove frigido,* or a vertical sun, pursue the windings of this wily quadruped, if, just as night came on, and his stratagems and strength were nearly exhausted, a saucy intruder, who had not shared in the honours or labours of the chase, were permitted to come in at the death, and bear away in triumph the object of pursuit? Whatever Justinian may have thought of the matter, it must be recollected that his code was compiled many hundred years ago, and it would be very hard indeed, at the distance of so many centuries, not to have a right to establish a rule for ourselves. In his day, we read of no order of men who made it a business, in the language of the declaration in this cause, "with hounds and dogs to find, start, pursue, hunt and chase," these animals, and that, too, without any other motive than the preservation of Roman poultry; if this diversion had been then in fashion, the lawyers who composed his institutes would have taken care not to pass it by, without suitable encouragement. If any thing, therefore, in the digests or pandects shall appear to militate against the defendant in error, who, on this occasion, was the foxhunter, we have only to say *tempora mutantur*, and if men themselves change with the times, why should not laws also undergo an alteration?

It may be expected, however, by the learned counsel, that more particular notice be taken of their authorities. I have examined them all, and feel great difficulty in determining, whether to acquire dominion over a thing, before in common, it be sufficient that we barely see it, or know where it is, or wish for it, or make a declaration of our will respecting it; or whether, in the case of wild beasts, setting a trap, or lying in wait, or starting, or pursuing, be enough; or if an actual wounding, or killing, or bodily tact and occupation be necessary. Writers on general law, who have favoured us with their speculations on these points, differ on them all; but, great as is the diversity of sentiment among them, some conclusion must be adopted on the question immediately before us. After mature deliberation, I embrace that of Barbeyrac, as the most rational, and least liable to objection. If at liberty, we might imitate the courtesy of a certain emperor, who, to avoid giving offence to the advocates of any of these different doctrines, adopted a middle course, and by ingenious distinctions, rendered it difficult to say (as often happens after a fierce and angry contest) to whom the palm of victory belonged. He ordained, that if a beast be followed with *large dogs and hounds*, he shall belong to the hunter, not to the chance occupant; and in like manner, if he be killed or wounded with a lance or sword; but if chased with *beagles only*, then he passed to the captor, not to the first pursuer. If slain with a dart, a sling, or a bow, he fell to the hunter, if still in chase, and not to him who might afterwards find and seize him.

Now, as we are without any municipal regulations of our own, and the pursuit here, for aught that appears on the case, being with dogs and hounds of *imperial stature*, we are at liberty to adopt one of the provisions just cited, which comports also with the learned conclusion of Barbeyrac, that property in animals *ferae naturae* may be acquired without bodily touch or manucaption, provided the pursuer be within reach, or have a *reasonable* prospect (which certainly existed here) of taking, what he has *thus* discovered an intention of converting to his own use.

When we reflect also that the interest of our husbandmen, the most useful of men in any community, will be advanced by the destruction of a beast so pernicious and incorrigible, we cannot greatly err, in saying, that a pursuit like the present, through waste and unoccupied lands, and which must inevitably and speedily have terminated in corporal possession, or bodily *seisin*, confers such a right to the object of it, as to make any one a wrongdoer, who shall interfere and shoulder the spoil. The justice's judgment ought, therefore, in my opinion, to be affirmed. . . .

Popov v. Hayashi, 2002 WL 31833731 (Cal. Super. Ct. 2002). Alex Popov caught the ball hit by Barry Bonds on October 7, 2001 that gave him his 73rd home run of the season, beating the world record previously held by Mark McGwire. However, Popov caught the ball in the upper portion of the webbing of a softball glove and "[w]hile the glove stopped the trajectory of the ball, it is not at all clear that the ball was secure. Popov had to reach for the ball and in doing so, may have lost his balance." As the ball was entering his glove, Popov was engulfed by a crowd that tackled him and threw him to the ground. At some point Popov lost the ball which was picked up by

Patrick Hayashi. When Hayashi refused to turn the ball over to Popov, Popov sued him for *conversion*, which is the wrongful possession of personal property rightfully owned or possessed by another.

Judge Patrick McCarthy explained that the ball had been originally "possessed and owned by Major League Baseball" but that "[a]t the time it was hit it became intentionally abandoned property. The first person who came in possession of the ball became its new owner." Quoting Professor Roger Bernhardt, Judge McCarthy explained that "[p]ossession requires both physical control over the item and an intent to control it or exclude others from it." Since Popov clearly "evidenced an intent to possess the baseball," the only question is whether Popov did enough to "reduce the ball to his exclusive dominion and control . . . sufficient to create a legally cognizable interest in the ball" before it was taken by Hayashi.

Hayashi argued that "possession does not occur until the fan has complete control of the ball" — a definition proposed by Professor Brian Gray. However, Popov cited *Pierson v. Post* for the proposition that possession occurs when an individual "intends to take control of a ball and manifests that intent by stopping the forward momentum of the ball whether or not complete control is achieved" — a definition proposed by Professors Bernhardt and Paul Finkelman. They argued that precedent established the proposition that possession exists when "the actor [is] actively and ably engaged in efforts to establish complete control [if those acts are] reasonably calculated to result in unequivocal dominion and control at some point in the near future." Judge McCarthy explained:

> This rule is applied in cases involving the hunting or fishing of wild animals or the salvage of sunken vessels. The hunting and fishing cases recognize that a mortally wounded animal may run for a distance before falling. The hunter acquires possession upon the act of wounding the animal not the eventual capture. Similarly, whalers acquire possession by landing a harpoon, not by subduing the animal. . . . In the salvage cases, an individual may take possession of a wreck by exerting as much control "as its nature and situation permit". . . .
>
> These rules are contextual in nature. The are crafted in response to the unique nature of the conduct they seek to regulate. Moreover, they are influenced by the custom and practice of each industry. The reason that absolute dominion and control is not required to establish possession in the cases cited by Mr. Popov is that such a rule would be unworkable and unreasonable. The "nature and situation" of the property at issue does not immediately lend itself to unequivocal dominion and control. It is impossible to wrap one's arms around a whale, a fleeing fox, or a sunken ship.
>
> The opposite is true of a baseball hit into the stands of a stadium. Not only is it physically possible for a person to acquire unequivocal dominion and control of an abandoned baseball, but fans generally expect a claimant to have accomplished as much. The custom and practice of the stands creates a reasonable expectation that a person will achieve full control of a ball before claiming possession. There is no reason for the legal rule to be inconsistent with that expectation. Therefore Gray's Rule is adopted as the definition of possession in this case.
>
> The central tenant of Gray's Rule is that the actor must retain control of the ball after incidental contact with people and things. Mr. Popov has not established by a preponderance of the evidence that he would have retained control of the ball after all momentum ceased and after any incidental contact with people or objects. Consequently, he did not achieve full possession.

This finding, however, did not resolve the case because Popov may have been prevented from obtaining control of the ball because "his efforts to establish possession were interrupted by the collective assault of a band of wrongdoers."

As a matter of fundamental fairness, Mr. Popov should have had the opportunity to try to complete his catch unimpeded by unlawful activity. To hold otherwise would be to allow the result in this case to be dictated by violence. That will not happen....

The legal question presented at this point is whether an action for conversion can proceed where the plaintiff has failed to establish possession or title. It can. An action for conversion may be brought where the plaintiff has title, possession or the right to possession.

Here Mr. Popov seeks, in effect, a declaratory judgment that he has either possession or the right to possession. In addition he seeks the remedies of injunctive relief and a constructive trust. These are all actions in equity. A court sitting in equity has the authority to fashion rules and remedies designed to achieve fundamental fairness.

Consistent with this principle, the court adopts the following rule. Where an actor undertakes significant but incomplete steps to achieve possession of a piece of abandoned personal property and the effort is interrupted by the unlawful acts of others, the actor has a legally cognizable pre-possessory interest in the property. That pre-possessory interest constitutes a qualified right to possession which can support a cause of action for conversion.

Possession can be likened to a journey down a path. Mr. Popov began his journey unimpeded. He was fast approaching a fork in the road. A turn in one direction would lead to possession of the ball — he would complete the catch. A turn in the other direction would result in a failure to achieve possession — he would drop the ball. Our problem is that before Mr. Popov got to the point where the road forked, he was set upon by a gang of bandits, who dislodged the ball from his grasp.

Recognition of a legally protected pre-possessory interest, vests Mr. Popov with a qualified right to possession and enables him to advance a legitimate claim to the baseball based on a conversion theory. Moreover it addresses the harm done by the unlawful actions of the crowd.

It does not, however, address the interests of Mr. Hayashi. The court is required to balance the interests of all parties.

Mr. Hayashi was not a wrongdoer. He was a victim of the same bandits that attacked Mr. Popov. The difference is that he was able to extract himself from their assault and move to the side of the road. It was there that he discovered the loose ball. When he picked up and put it in his pocket he attained unequivocal dominion and control.

If Mr. Popov had achieved complete possession before Mr. Hayashi got the ball, those actions would not have divested Mr. Popov of any rights, nor would they have created any rights to which Mr. Hayashi could lay claim. Mr. Popov, however, was able to establish only a qualified pre-possessory interest in the ball. That interest does not establish a full right to possession that is protected from a subsequent legitimate claim.

On the other hand, while Mr. Hayashi appears on the surface to have done everything necessary to claim full possession of the ball, the ball itself is encumbered by the qualified pre-possessory interest of Mr. Popov. At the time Mr. Hayashi came into possession of the ball, it had, in effect, a cloud on its title.

An award of the ball to Mr. Popov would be unfair to Mr. Hayashi. It would be premised on the assumption that Mr. Popov would have caught the ball. That assumption is not supported by the facts. An award of the ball to Mr. Hayashi would unfairly penalize Mr. Popov. It would be based on the assumption that Mr. Popov would have dropped the ball. That conclusion is also unsupported by the facts.

Both men have a superior claim to the ball as against all the world. Each man has a claim of equal dignity as to the other. We are, therefore, left with something of a dilemma.

Thankfully, there is a middle ground.

The concept of equitable division was fully explored in a law review article authored by Professor R.H. Helmholz in the December 1983 edition of the Fordham Law Review.[38] Professor Helmholz addressed the problems associated with rules governing finders of lost and mislaid property. For a variety of reasons not directly relevant to the issues raised in this case, Helmholz suggested employing the equitable remedy of division to resolve competing claims between finders of lost or mislaid property and the owners of land on which the property was found.

There is no reason, however, that the same remedy cannot be applied in a case such as this, where issues of property, tort and equity intersect. . . .

The principle at work here is that where more than one party has a valid claim to a single piece of property, the court will recognize an undivided interest in the property in proportion to the strength of the claim.

Here, the issue is . . . the legal quality of the claim. With respect to that, neither can present a superior argument as against the other.

Mr. Hayashi's claim is compromised by Mr. Popov's pre-possessory interest. Mr. Popov cannot demonstrate full control. Albeit for different reasons, they stand before the court in exactly the same legal position as did the five boys. Their legal claims are of equal quality and they are equally entitled to the ball.

The court therefore declares that both plaintiff and defendant have an equal and undivided interest in the ball. Plaintiff's cause of action for conversion is sustained only as to his equal and undivided interest. In order to effectuate this ruling, the ball must be sold and the proceeds divided equally between the parties. . . .

The ball was sold several years later for $450,000.

NOTES AND QUESTIONS

1. *Fairness and justice.* The court suggested that Pierson's conduct in seizing the fox at the last moment was "uncourteous or unkind" but not unlawful. Was Pierson's conduct unfair? And if so, why should it be lawful? If it was not fair, what was unfair about it? Do you need to know more about the social customs of hunters to answer this question? Or can it be answered without looking into social practice?

Who do you think had a right to take possession of the fox? Suppose Post had been hunting the fox for a week, and Pierson had been outside for a few minutes before coming upon it and seizing it. Does the principle of rewarding labor suggest giving property rights to Post — who worked for a week toward the goal of getting the fox? Or does it suggest that one who took a week was a poor hunter and deserved to lose the fox to Pierson?

2. *Social utility.* What rule of law would best encourage productive labor? Justice Livingston notes that wild foxes were "noxious beasts" who preyed on barnyards. He suggested that the rules of law should encourage people to hunt them. How could you argue that the rule of law promulgated by the court in Justice Tompkins' opinion achieved that end? What reasons did Justice Livingston give for believing that his

---

38. *Equitable Division and the Law of Finders,* (1983) Fordham Law Review, Professor R.H. Helmholz, University of Chicago School of Law. This article built on a student comment published in 1939. *Lost, Mislaid and Abandoned Property* (1939) 8 Fordham Law Review 222.

proposed rule would better serve this purpose? With current fears about extinction of species, how do we determine whether social welfare will be best advanced by promoting hunting of wild animals or by preserving them?

3. *Certainty.* What rule of law — Tompkins' or Livingston's — creates the most certainty about ownership rights? Is the rule that creates the most certainty also the most just? Consider Gray's Rule adopted in *Popov v. Hayashi.* Would that rule have worked better in *Pierson v. Post?* Was it the best resolution to determine ownership of the baseball in *Popov?* And did the certainty of the rule evaporate once the judge decided to equitably divide interests in the ball?

4. *Trespassing.* How would the case have been resolved if Pierson had been trespassing on Post's land? Should the rule of capture still apply? Would it make a difference if Pierson had begun hunting the fox on his own land and chased it onto Post's land to make the capture? Today, the result in a case like this is likely to depend on the intent of the owner of the land. One is not allowed to hunt on land owned by another without the owner's consent, and the terms of entry may decide who prevails in disputes among hunters.

PROBLEM

The ball that won the World Series for the Boston Red Sox in 2004 was caught by backup first baseman Doug Mientkiewicz. When he kept the ball, John Henry, the team's principal owner, asked him to give the ball to the Red Sox ball club. Who should own the ball?

§1.5.2   OIL AND GAS

ELLIFF v. TEXON DRILLING CO.
210 S.W.2d 558 (Tex. 1948)

A. J. FOLLEY, Justice.

This is a suit by the petitioners, Mrs. Mabel Elliff, Frank Elliff, and Charles C. Elliff, against the respondents, Texon Drilling Company, a Texas corporation, Texon Royalty Company, a Texas corporation, Texon Royalty Company, a Delaware corporation, and John L. Sullivan, for damages resulting from a "blowout" gas well drilled by respondents in the Agua Dulce Field in Nueces County.

The petitioners owned the surface and certain royalty interests in 3054.9 acres of land in Nueces County, upon which there was a producing well known as Elliff No. 1. They owned all the mineral estate underlying the west 1500 acres of the tract, and an undivided one-half interest in the mineral estate underlying the east 1554.9 acres. Both tracts were subject to oil and gas leases, and therefore their royalty interest in the west 1500 acres was one-eighth of the oil or gas, and in the east 1554.9 acres was one-sixteenth of the oil and gas.

It was alleged that these lands overlaid approximately fifty per cent of a huge reservoir of gas and distillate and that the remainder of the reservoir was under the lands owned by Mrs. Clara Driscoll, adjoining the lands of petitioners on the east. Prior to November 1936, respondents were engaged in the drilling of Driscoll-Sevier No. 2 as an offset well at a location 466 feet east of petitioners' east line. On the date stated, when respondents had reached a depth of approximately 6838 feet, the well blew out, caught fire and cratered. Attempts to control it were unsuccessful, and huge quantities of gas, distillate and some oil were blown into the air, dissipating large quantities from the reservoir into which the offset well was drilled. When the Driscoll-Sevier No. 2 well blew out, the fissure or opening in the ground around the well gradually increased until it enveloped and destroyed Elliff No. 1. The latter well also blew out, cratered, caught fire and burned for several years. Two water wells on petitioners' land became involved in the cratering and each of them blew out. Certain damages also resulted to the surface of petitioners' lands and to their cattle thereon. The cratering process and the eruption continued until large quantities of gas and distillate were drained from under petitioners' land and escaped into the air, all of which was alleged to be the direct and proximate result of the negligence of respondents in permitting their well to blow out. The extent of the emissions from the Driscoll-Sevier No. 2 and Elliff No. 1, and the two water wells on petitioners' lands, was shown at various times during the several years between the blowout in November 1936, and the time of the trial in June 1946. There was also expert testimony from petroleum engineers showing the extent of the losses from the underground reservoir, which computations extended from the date of the blowout only up to June 1938. It was indicated that it was not feasible to calculate the losses subsequent thereto, although lesser emissions of gas continued even up to the time of the trial. All the evidence with reference to the damages included all losses from the reservoir beneath petitioners' land without regard to whether they were wasted and dissipated from above the Driscoll land or from petitioners' land.

The jury found that respondents were negligent in failing to use drilling mud of sufficient weight in drilling their well, and that such negligence was the proximate cause of the well blowing out. . . .

On the findings of the jury the trial court rendered judgment for petitioners for $154,518.19, which included $148,548.19 for the gas and distillate, and $5970 for damages to the land and cattle. The Court of Civil Appeals reversed the judgment and remanded the cause.

The reversal by the Court of Civil Appeals rests [on the ground] that since substantially all of the gas and distillate which was drained from under petitioners' lands was lost through respondents' blowout well, petitioners could not recover because under the law of capture they had lost all property rights in the gas or distillate which had migrated from their lands. . . .

[T]he sole question [is] whether the law of capture absolves respondents of any liability for the negligent waste or destruction of petitioners' gas and distillate, though substantially all of such waste or destruction occurred after the minerals had been drained from beneath petitioners' lands.

We do not regard as authoritative the three decisions by the Supreme Court of Louisiana to the effect that an adjoining owner is without right of action for gas wasted from the common pool by his neighbor, because in that state only qualified ownership of oil and gas is recognized, no absolute ownership of minerals in place exists, and the unqualified rule is that under the law of capture the minerals belong exclusively to the one that produces them. Moreover, from an examination of those cases it will be seen that the decisions rested in part on the theory that "the loss complained of was, manifestly, more a matter of uncertainty and speculation than of fact or estimate." In the more recent trend of the decisions of our state, with the growth and development of scientific knowledge of oil and gas, it is now recognized "that when a[n] oil field has been fairly tested and developed, experts can determine approximately the amount of oil and gas in place in a common pool, and can also equitably determine the amount of oil and gas recoverable by the owner of each tract of land under certain operating conditions." *Brown v. Humble Oil & Refining Co.*, 83 S.W.2d 935, 940 (Tex. 1935).

In Texas, and in other jurisdictions, a different rule exists as to ownership. In our state the landowner is regarded as having absolute title in severalty to the oil and gas in place beneath his land. The only qualification of that rule of ownership is that it must be considered in connection with the law of capture and is subject to police regulations. The oil and gas beneath the soil are considered a part of the realty. Each owner of land owns separately, distinctly and exclusively all the oil and gas under his land and is accorded the usual remedies against trespassers who appropriate the minerals or destroy their market value.

The conflict in the decisions of the various states with reference to the character of ownership is traceable to some extent to the divergent views entertained by the courts, particularly in the earlier cases, as to the nature and migratory character of oil and gas in the soil. In the absence of common law precedent, and owing to the lack of scientific information as to the movement of these minerals, some of the courts have sought by analogy to compare oil and gas to other types of property such as wild animals, birds, subterranean waters and other migratory things, with reference to which the common law had established rules denying any character of ownership prior to capture. However, as was said by Professor A. W. Walker, Jr., of the School of Law of the University of Texas: "There is no oil or gas producing state today which follows the wild-animal analogy to its logical conclusion that the landowner has no property interest in the oil and gas in place." 16 Tex. L. Rev. 370, 371. In the light of modern scientific knowledge these early analogies have been disproven, and courts generally have come to recognize that oil and gas, as commonly found in underground reservoirs, are securely entrapped in a static condition in the original pool, and, ordinarily, so remain until disturbed by penetrations from the surface. It is further established, nevertheless, that these minerals will migrate across property lines towards any low pressure area created by production from the common pool. This migratory character of oil and gas has given rise to the so-called rule or law of capture. That rule simply is that the owner of a tract of land acquires title to the oil or gas which he produces from wells on his land, though part of the oil or gas may have migrated from adjoining lands. He may thus appropriate the oil and gas that have flowed from adjacent lands without the consent of the owner of those lands, and without incurring liability to him for drainage. The non-liability is based upon the theory that after the drainage the title or property interest of the former owner is gone. This rule, at first blush, would seem to conflict with the view of absolute ownership of the minerals in place, but it was otherwise decided in the early case of *Stephens County v. Mid-Kansas Oil & Gas Co.*, 254 S.W. 290 (Tex. 1923). Mr. Justice Greenwood there stated, 254 S.W. at 292: "The objection lacks substantial foundation that gas or oil in a certain tract of land cannot be owned in place, because subject to appropriation, without the consent of the owner of the tract, through drainage from wells on adjacent lands. If the owners of adjacent lands have the right to appropriate, without liability, the gas and oil underlying their neighbor's land, then their neighbor has the correlative right to appropriate, through like methods of drainage, the gas and oil underlying the tracts adjacent to his own."

Thus it is seen that, notwithstanding the fact that oil and gas beneath the surface are subject both to capture and administrative regulation, the fundamental rule of absolute ownership of the minerals in place is not affected in our state. In recognition of such ownership, our courts, in decisions involving well-spacing regulations of our Railroad Commission, have frequently announced the sound view that each landowner should be afforded the opportunity to produce his fair share of the recoverable oil and gas beneath his land, which is but another way of recognizing the existence of correlative rights between the various landowners over a common reservoir of oil or gas.

It must be conceded that under the law of capture there is no liability for reasonable and legitimate drainage from the common pool. The landowner is privileged to sink as many wells as he desires upon his tract of land and extract therefrom and appropriate all the oil and gas that he may produce, so long as he operates within the spirit and purpose of conservation statutes and orders of the Railroad Commission. These laws and regulations are designed to afford each owner a reasonable opportunity to produce his proportionate part of the oil and gas from the entire pool and to prevent operating practices injurious to the common reservoir. In this manner, if all operators exercise the same degree of skill and diligence, each owner will recover in most instances his fair share of the oil and gas. This reasonable opportunity to produce his fair share of the oil and gas is the landowner's common law right under our theory of absolute ownership of the minerals in place. But from the very nature of this theory the right of each land holder is qualified, and is limited to legitimate operations. Each owner whose land overlies the basin has a like interest, and each must of necessity exercise his right with some regard to the rights of others. No owner should be permitted to carry on his operations in reckless or lawless irresponsibility, but must submit to such limitations as are necessary to enable each to get his own.

While we are cognizant of the fact that there is a certain amount of reasonable and necessary waste incident to the production of oil and gas to which the non-liability rule must also apply, we do not think this immunity should be extended so as to include the negligent waste or destruction of the oil and gas. . . .

In 85 A.L.R. 1156, . . . the annotator states: ". . . The fact that the owner of the land has a right to take and to use gas and oil, even to the diminution or exhaustion of the supply under his neighbor's land, does not give him the right to waste the gas. His property in the gas underlying his land consists of the right to appropriate the same, and permitting the gas to escape into the air is not an appropriation thereof in the proper sense of the term."

In like manner, the negligent waste and destruction of petitioners' gas and distillate was neither a legitimate drainage of the minerals from beneath their lands nor a lawful or reasonable appropriation of them. Consequently, the petitioners did not lose their right, title and interest in them under the law of capture. At the time of their removal they belonged to petitioners, and their wrongful dissipation deprived these owners of the right and opportunity to produce them. That right is forever lost, the same cannot be restored, and petitioners are without an adequate legal remedy unless we allow a recovery under the same common law which governs other actions for damages and under which the property rights in oil and gas are vested. This remedy should not be denied.

In common with others who are familiar with the nature of oil and gas and the risks involved in their production, the respondents had knowledge that a failure to use due care in drilling their well might result in a blowout with the consequent waste and dissipation of the oil, gas and distillate from the common reservoir. In the conduct of one's business or in the use and exploitation of one's property, the law imposes upon all persons the duty to exercise ordinary care to avoid injury or damage to the property of others. Thus under the common law, and independent of the conservation statutes, the respondents were legally bound to use due care to avoid the negligent waste or destruction of the minerals imbedded in petitioners' oil and gas-bearing strata. This common-law duty the respondents failed to discharge. For that omission they should be required to respond in such damages as will reasonably compensate the injured parties for the loss sustained as the proximate result of the negligent conduct. The fact that the major portion of the gas and distillate escaped from the well on respondents' premises is immaterial. Irrespective of the opening from which the minerals escaped, they belonged to the petitioners and the loss was the same. They would not have been dissipated at any opening except for the wrongful conduct of the respondents. Being responsible for the loss they are in no position to deny liability because the gas and distillate did not escape through the surface of petitioners' lands.

We are therefore of the opinion the Court of Civil Appeals erred in holding that under the law of capture the petitioners cannot recover for the damages resulting from the wrongful drainage of the gas and distillate from beneath their lands. . . .

THE NEW PROPERTY OF THE NINETEENTH CENTURY: THE DEVELOPMENT OF THE MODERN CONCEPT OF PROPERTY
KENNETH VANDEVELDE

29 Buffalo L. Rev. 325, 354-357 (1980)

. . . The emergence of an oil and gas industry in the early nineteenth century thrust upon the courts the need to develop a theory of property in oil and gas law with little or no precedent to guide them. The earliest cases had little trouble finding property in oil and gas, perhaps because of the tangible nature of these minerals. The courts also applied the absolutist conception of property to these minerals. For example, in *Hail v. Reed*, 54 Ky. 383 (1854), the defendant took three barrels of oil from a well on the plaintiff's land and was sued for recovery of the oil. The plaintiff argued that the owner of land on which a well is situated "should be considered as having the exclusive property in all that well contains." The defendant replied that oil "is ever moving" and therefore should be analogized to animals *ferae naturae*, which become the property of the first person to reduce them to possession. Alternatively, the defendant argued that oil is analogous to a surface stream and claimed that no right to the oil existed until the oil had been appropriated. The court seized upon yet another analogy — that of a spring which arises on one's land — and held that the owner of the freehold on which the well was located was the exclusive owner of the oil.

The nature of oil, however, strained the concept of absolute rights in property because several landowners who had access to the same oil could raise competing claims. The Pennsylvania court in *Funk v. Haldeman*, 53 Pa. 229 (1866), considered such competing claims and struggled to preserve the absolutist conception of property in oil. The plaintiff paid the defendants, owners of a farm, $200 for the right to prospect for oil on a portion of the farm and for the exclusive use of one acre of land around each well; he also agreed to give the defendants one-third of all the oil he extracted from the land. After the plaintiff struck oil, the defendants sank their own wells and the plaintiff sued to enjoin the defendants' drilling. The plaintiff argued that the oil pool was indivisible and that the drilling of other wells diminished his exclusive right. As in *Hail*, the defendants proposed an analogy to streams, claiming that the plaintiff had a right only to such oil as he possessed. The court held that the plaintiff had the exclusive right to drill for oil on the portion of the farm on which he had the right to prospect. It observed that the plaintiff already had invested $800,000 in the development of the well, and then noted that although there was no express stipulation in the agreement that the plaintiff would have the exclusive right to drill for oil, that was the only fair inference. A contrary holding would have placed all the risks of exploration on the plaintiff, and then, when he struck oil, would have allowed the defendants to sink their own wells, rendering the plaintiff's investment essentially worthless. The court concluded that the defendants' right to drill for oil was restricted to the land on which the plaintiff had no right to prospect. The plaintiff's right to the oil was thus limited, but only because he had purchased drilling rights for merely a portion of the farm.

The total inapplicability of the absolutist conception of property to oil and gas soon became apparent to the courts. The *Funk* court had permitted the defendants to drill on portions of the farm where the plaintiff had no drilling rights, even though such drilling could ruin the plaintiff's investment as easily as the prohibited drilling. Similarly, the *Hail* court had never suggested that the plaintiff could prevent drilling into the same pool by others on adjoining land, despite the court's references to exclusive ownership.

The exclusive ownership issue was finally confronted directly in a series of cases involving landowners who had tapped into the same mineral reservoir. If the value of the investment of both parties was to be protected, some form of limited property rights was essential. The solution was to retreat to the analogy, rejected in *Hail*, of animals *ferae naturae*. A new rule was established in *Westmoreland & Cambria Natural Gas Co. v. Dewitt*, 18 A. 724 (Pa. 1889), that oil and gas were held to be minerals *ferae naturae* because they were not fixed to a particular piece of land. Like animals *ferae naturae*, oil and gas would be considered the property of the owner of the superadjacent land as long as they were in his possession. If another landowner acquired possession of the minerals, however, title would pass to him. Thus, every landowner was entitled to tap any oil or gas pool he had access to, regardless of whether others had already tapped it.

The new rule of minerals *ferae naturae* quickly became the majority rule in the United States. The theoretically absolute right to exclude others from tapping a pool had been limited to exclude only those whose land was not superadjacent to the mineral reservoir. The right to use the minerals, however, was still absolute. Any superadjacent landowner was legally entitled to take as much oil or gas as he could get by any available means. And what could the other landowners do to protect their interests in the minerals? As one court put it: "Nothing, only go and do likewise." Indeed, an Indiana court held that one could explode nitroglycerin in one's gas well in order to increase the gas flow, even though that might result in a more rapid depletion of the pool and diminish the quantity of gas a neighbor could draw before the well was exhausted.

The absolute right of usufruct was the next portion of the owner's property in oil and gas to come under attack. The minerals *ferae naturae* rule gave many people access to the same pool, but failed to limit the methods of extracting the minerals. Thus, it encouraged landowners to exhaust a pool as quickly as possible, before others did, even if such rapid exhaustion entailed enormous waste. By the turn of the century, the courts had begun to address the problem of waste. In *Manufacturers Gas & Oil Co. v. Indiana Natural Gas & Oil Co.*, 57 N.E. 912 (Ind. 1900), the plaintiff, who owned land over a pool of gas, sought to enjoin a superadjacent landowner from using pumps to force gas out of the ground at such a pressure that it sucked saltwater into the pool, destroying the value of the remaining gas. In granting the injunction, the court reasoned that, although a superadjacent landowner had a property right entitling him to mine the gas, he had no right to induce an unnatural flow into his own well or to take any action which might damage the common reservoir. In other words, the taking of gas from the pool had to be reasonable. A similar rule of reason imposed by statute had been approved by the U.S. Supreme Court the year before and other jurisdictions quickly adopted the rule, either by statute or by judicial decision. The adoption of a rule of reason was, however, an abandonment of the superadjacent landowner's absolute right of usufruct in oil and gas. The rule also precluded the application of any fixed or determinant set of rights in the owner of property in oil and gas. The rule stated that whether the owner of such property was entitled to mine the minerals in a particular way depended on what was reasonable under the circumstances, a matter for the court to decide based on the policy of preventing waste or other considerations. Once again, as with trademarks and trade secrets, the designation of oil and gas as objects of property did not permit the court to deduce logically the rights of the parties involved. Only considerations of public policy would decide cases.

PROBLEM

Although oil and gas production are subject to extensive regulation to prevent waste and protect the environment, the rule of capture generally remains the law. *Browning Oil Co., Inc. v. Luecke*, 38 S.W.3d 625 (Tex. Ct. App. 2000). The effect of the rule has been diminished by spacing regulations that limit, but do not completely prevent, the ability of owners to extract oil from beneath neighboring land. Is the rule fair? Does it promote or inhibit investment in producing oil and gas? Consider the following case.

Plaintiff Corporation invests $1 million in exploring for oil on its property. After it discovers oil and begins to extract it for sale, its neighboring landowner, Defendant Corporation, begins to do likewise. Because the oil is part of a common pool underlying the neighboring pieces of property, the defendant is able to extract oil from the same pool discovered by the plaintiff. Defendant's costs are much less than plaintiff's because it does not have to undergo the expense of searching for the oil. Because its costs are lower, defendant is able to sell the oil it extracts at a much lower market price than that charged by plaintiff. Plaintiff sues defendant, asking for an injunction ordering defendant to stop exploiting oil discovered by plaintiff's investment and labor. Defendant claims a right to extract oil from beneath its property.

1. As plaintiff's attorney, what rule of law would you advocate that the court adopt? How would you justify that rule in terms of both fairness and social utility?

2. As defendant's attorney, what rule of law would you advocate that the court adopt? How would you justify that rule in terms of both fairness and social utility?

3. As the judge deciding the case, what rule of law would you adopt, and why?

§1.5.3 WATER

Surface water is generally a nuisance; property owners are eager to get rid of it and to protect their land from flooding. *See infra* §4.2. In contrast, other kinds of water sources constitute valuable commercial resources. For example, owners may dig wells on their property to withdraw water collected in underground aquifers. Similarly, property owners may use rivers or streams bordering or crossing their property.

§1.5.3.1   Groundwater

Water collects under the surface of the earth in permeable rock, sand, and gravel in reservoirs known as "aquifers." Surface owners may use wells to extract this water, which is diffused through the soil beneath the surface. The water may be withdrawn for drinking purposes, irrigation, or power. Since aquifers underlie the lands of many persons, the withdrawal by one owner may have the effect of drawing off water under-lying a neighbor's property. To the extent the water in the aquifer is depleted, withdrawal by one owner may interfere with the ability of others to make like use of the water. Underground water diffused through the soil is called *groundwater* or *percolating water*.

In *Acton v. Blundell*, 152 Eng. Rep. 1223 (Exch. 1843), defendants excavated on their property to extract coal. The excavation resulted in drainage of groundwater underlying neighboring property belonging to plaintiff. Plaintiff had previously dug wells on its property to extract the groundwater for use in running its cotton mill. After defendant's excavations, however, the water supply was insufficient to run the mill. Plaintiff sued to recover damages for the loss of its groundwater. The court adopted the doctrine of *free use* or *absolute ownership*. Under this rule of law, each surface owner is free to withdraw as much water as he likes from beneath the surface of his property without liability, even if it has the effect of withdrawing water from underneath his neighbor's property. The court justified its decision in the following way:

> [I]f the man who sinks the well in his own land can acquire by that act an absolute and indefeasible right to the water that collects in it, he has the power of preventing his neighbour from making any use of the spring in his own soil which shall interfere with the enjoyment of the well. He has the power, still further, of debarring the owner of the land in which the spring is first found, or through which it is transmitted, from draining his land for the proper cultivation of the soil: and thus by an act which is voluntary on his part, and which may be entirely unsuspected by his neighbour, he may impose on such neighbour the necessity of bearing a heavy expense, if the latter has erected machinery for the purposes of mining, and discovers, when too late, that the appropriation of the water has already been made. Further, the advantage on one side, and the detriment to the other, may bear no proportion. The well may be sunk to supply a cottage, or a drinking-place for cattle; whilst the owner of the adjoining land may be prevented from winning metals and minerals of inestimable value.

Many states in the United States currently follow this approach, effectively grant-ing landowners the freedom to extract as much water as they can from their property, even if this means draining water from underneath neighboring property. *Sipriano v. Great Springs Waters of America, Inc.*, 1 S.W.3d 75 (Tex. 1999). One exception is that owners are not permitted to withdraw the water in a way that wastes it.

Other states reject the free use approach. Instead, they adopt rules of law that require underground water to be shared by placing limits on the ability of surface owners to deprive their neighbors of access to groundwater. Under the *reasonable use* test, each owner must accommodate the interests of neighboring owners; alternatively, courts may have to balance the interests of the parties. A second approach is a *corre-lative rights* test, allowing each owner to withdraw a specified portion of the ground-water, perhaps in proportion to what percentage of the aquifer underlies their property. Still other states adopt a *prior appropriation* test, effectively granting rights to the property owner that first invested in withdrawing the water. Finally, some states regulate water uses by a permit system administered by state or local agencies.

§1.5.3.2 Streams

Surface streams or lakes are often beneficial to property owners whose property borders on them (called "riparian owners"). This water may be used for a variety of purposes, including irrigation, power, drinking water, and recreation. Lawsuits arise when one owner's use interferes with the ability of other riparian owners to use the stream. For example, in *Evans v. Merriweather*, 4 Ill. 492 (1842), an upstream owner built a dam across a river on which he owned a mill to increase the amount of water available for use to create steam to run the mill. A downstream owner, who also owned a mill along the same river, was left with insufficient water power to run his mill and sued the upstream owner to obtain damages and an injunction against continued interference with the natural flow of the water.

The majority of states resolve disputes of this kind by applying a reasonable use test, which asks the decisionmaker to consider and balance such factors as the relative social value of each owner's use, the extent of the harm to the defendant, and the cost of preventing the harm relative to the benefit. Reasonable use might mean comparing the relative utility of the competing uses and choosing the one that is most valuable to society. Or it might mean apportioning the use so that all riparian owners have the right to some portion of the water.

A minority of states in the arid western part of the United States adopt the prior appropriation doctrine, which provides that the first user or developer prevails over a later user. This rule allows prior owners to prevail against later users whose riparian activity harms their interests in access to the water. Many states combine the prior appropriation doctrine with the reasonable use test. States that have adopted the prior appropriation system also have established state water management systems. These regulatory programs include statutes requiring water users to obtain permits for use of water from the relevant administrative agency or official.

PROBLEMS

1. A residential community depends on a reservoir for its water supply. A developer builds an industrial park for light manufacturing in the vicinity of the reservoir. The park relies partly on well water drawn from beneath its surface to supply its needs. This withdrawal of groundwater lowers the water level in the reservoir nearby to a point below that needed for the residential community. The municipal government responds by purchasing water from a reservoir in another town at much greater expense; as a result, taxes to pay for water rise in the town. The municipality sues the factory, claiming the factory's use of its property violates the reasonable use test by unreasonably interfering with the town's right of access to water in the reservoir. The factory argues that the free use test should apply and that it has the right to withdraw water from beneath its own property without having to foresee and account for any interference with water resources on other property.

    a.   Construct defendant's arguments in favor of the free use rule.
    b.   Construct plaintiff's arguments in favor of the reasonable use test.

2. Assume the facts of Problem 1, except that the industrial park was established first and claims that the prior appropriation doctrine should apply, while the town argues for the reasonable use test.

§1.5.4   Finders

The next case raises the question of who owns American Indian cultural objects that were buried long ago, often as part of funeral rites for a deceased tribal member. Do they belong to the descendants of the tribe or clan that lived in the area? What if the tribe no longer exists? Can related tribes located in the vicinity claim the objects? If the tribe does not own them, do the objects rightly belong to the landowner on whose property they were found or to the person who invested the time and effort to excavate them?

CHARRIER v. BELL

496 So. 2d 601 (La. Ct. App. 1986)

ELVEN PONDER, Judge, retired. . . .

Plaintiff is a former Corrections Officer at the Louisiana State Penitentiary in Angola, Louisiana, who describes himself as an "amateur archeologist." After researching colonial maps, records and texts, he concluded that Trudeau Plantation, near Angola, was the possible site of an ancient village of the Tunica Indians. He alleges that in 1967 he obtained the permission of Mr. Frank Hoshman, Sr., who he believed was the owner of Trudeau Plantation, to survey the property with a metal detector for possible burial locations. After locating and excavating approximately 30 to 40 burial plots lying in a circular pattern, plaintiff notified Mr. Hoshman that he had located the Tunica village. Although the evidence is contradictory, plaintiff contends that it was at that time that Mr. Hoshman first advised that he was the caretaker, not the owner, of the property.

Plaintiff continued to excavate the area for the next three years until he had located and excavated approximately 150 burial sites containing beads, European ceramics, stoneware, glass bottles; iron kettles, vessels and skillets; knives, muskets, gunflints, balls and shots; crucifixes, rings and bracelets; and native pottery. The excavated artifacts are estimated to weigh two to two and one-half tons.

In search of a buyer for the collection, plaintiff talked to Dr. Robert S. Neitzel of Louisiana State University, who, in turn, informed Dr. Jeffrey D. Brain of Harvard University. Dr. Brain, who was involved in a survey of archeology along the lower Mississippi River, viewed the artifacts and began discussions of their sale to the Peabody Museum of Harvard University. The discussions resulted in the lease of the artifacts to the Museum, where they were inventoried, catalogued and displayed.

Plaintiff initially informed Dr. Neitzel and Dr. Brain that he had found the artifacts in a cave in Mississippi, so as to conceal their source; later he did disclose the actual site of the find to Dr. Brain, who had expressed his concern over the title of the artifacts. Dr. Brain then obtained permission from the landowners to do further site testing and confirmed that it was the true source of the artifacts.

Confronted with the inability to sell the collection because he could not prove ownership, plaintiff filed suit against the six nonresident landowners of Trudeau Plantation, requesting declaratory relief confirming that he was the owner of the artifacts. Alternatively, plaintiff requested that he be awarded compensation under the theory of unjust enrichment for his time and expenses.

The State of Louisiana intervened in the proceeding on numerous grounds, including its duty to protect its citizens in the absence of the lawful heirs of the artifacts.

In 1978, the State purchased Trudeau Plantation and the artifacts from the six land-owners and agreed to defend, indemnify and hold the prior owners harmless from any and all actions.

In 1981 the Tunica and Biloxi Indians were recognized as an American Indian Tribe by the Bureau of Indian Affairs of the Department of the Interior....

The trial judge held that the Tunica-Biloxi Tribe is the lawful owner of the artifacts, finding that plaintiff was not entitled to the artifacts under La. Civ. Code art. 3423 as it read prior to amendment by Act No. 187 of 1982, which required discovery "by chance." The judge also found that plaintiff had no claim to the artifacts on the basis of abandonment under La. Civ. Code art. 3421, as it read prior to the amendment by Act No. 187 of 1982, because the legal concept of abandonment does not extend to burial goods.

The trial court also denied relief under the theory of unjust enrichment, finding that any impoverishment claimed by plaintiff was a result of his attempts "for his own gain" and that his presence and actions on the property of a third party placed him in a "precarious position, if not in legal bad faith."

The issues before this court are the adequacy of proof that the Tunica-Biloxi Indians are descendants of the inhabitants of Trudeau, the ownership of the artifacts, and the applicability of the theory of unjust enrichment.

Plaintiff first argues that the evidence that the members of the Tunica-Biloxi Indians of Louisiana, Inc., are legal descendants of the inhabitants of Trudeau Plantation was insufficient to entitle them to the artifacts....

The fact that members of other tribes are intermixed with the Tunicas does not negate or diminish the Tunicas' relationship to the historical tribe. Despite the fact that the Tunicas have not produced a perfect "chain of title" back to those buried at Trudeau Plantation, the tribe is an accumulation of the descendants of former Tunica Indians and has adequately satisfied the proof of descent....

Plaintiff next argues that the Indians abandoned the artifacts when they moved from Trudeau Plantation, and the artifacts became *res nullius* until found and reduced to possession by plaintiff who then became the owner.

Plaintiff contends that he has obtained ownership of the property through occupancy, which is a "mode of acquiring property by which a thing which belongs to nobody, becomes the property of the person who took possession of it, with the intention of acquiring a right of ownership upon it." La. Civ. Code art. 3412. [4]

One of the five methods of acquiring property by occupancy is "By finding (that is, by discovering precious stones on the sea shore, or things abandoned, or a treasure)." La. Civ. Code art. 3414. [5] Plaintiff contends that the artifacts were abandoned by the Tunicas and that by finding them he became the owner....

[T]he fact that the descendants or fellow tribesmen of the deceased Tunica Indians resolved, for some customary, religious or spiritual belief, to bury certain items along with the bodies of the deceased, does not result in a conclusion that the goods were abandoned. While the relinquishment of immediate possession may have been proved, an objective viewing of the circumstances and intent of the relinquishment does not result in a finding of abandonment. Objects may be buried with a

---

4. Amended by 1982 Acts 187, §1, La. Civ. Code art. 3412 now reads "Occupancy is the taking of possession of a corporeal movable that does not belong to anyone. The occupant acquires ownership the moment he takes possession." — ED.

5. This statute has been repealed as unnecessary. — ED.

decedent for any number of reasons. The relinquishment of possession normally serves some spiritual, moral, or religious purpose of the descendant/owner, but is not intended as a means of relinquishing ownership to a stranger. Plaintiff's argument carried to its logical conclusion would render a grave subject to despoliation either immediately after interment or definitely after removal of the descendants of the deceased from the neighborhood of the cemetery.

Although plaintiff has referred to the artifacts as *res nullius*, under French law, the source of Louisiana's occupancy law, that term refers specifically to such things as wild game and fish, which are originally without an owner. The term *res derelictae* refers to "things voluntarily abandoned by their owner with the intention to have them go to the first person taking possession." P. Esmein, Aubry & Rau, *Droit Civil Francais*, Vol. II, §168, at 46 (7th ed. 1966). Some examples of *res derelictae* given by Aubry and Rau include things left on public ways, in the cities or to be removed by garbage collectors.

The artifacts fall into the category of *res derelictae*, if subject to abandonment. The intent to abandon *res derelictae* must include the intent to let the first person who comes along acquire them. Obviously, such is not the case with burial goods.

French sources have generally held that human remains and burial goods located in cemeteries or burial grounds are not "treasure" under article 716 of the French Civil Code and thereby not subject to occupancy upon discovery. The reasoning has been that any contrary decision would lead to and promote commercial speculation and despoilment of burial grounds. The French commentator Demolombe noted the special treatment that should be given to burial goods, stating that such objects "have not been placed underground with the same intention which informs the deposit of what is called treasure, which in the latter case is, for a temporary period. . . . Rather, they are an emplacement for a perpetual residence therein. . . ." 13 C. Demolombe, *Cours de Code Napoleon* §37, at 45-46 (2d ed. 1862).

The same reasoning that the French have used to treat burial goods applies in determining if such items can be abandoned. The intent in interring objects with the deceased is that they will remain there perpetually, and not that they are available for someone to recover and possess as owner.

For these reasons, we do not uphold the transfer of ownership to some unrelated third party who uncovers burial goods. The trial court concluded that La. Civ. Code art. 3421[6] was not intended to require that objects buried with the dead were abandoned or that objects could be acquired by obtaining possession over the objections of the descendants. We agree with this conclusion. . . .

Plaintiff next argues that he is entitled to recover a sum of money to compensate his services and expenses on the basis of an *actio de in rem verso*.

The five criteria of such a claim *de in rem verso* are: (1) there must be an enrichment, (2) there must be an impoverishment, (3) there must be a connection between the enrichment and resulting impoverishment, (4) there must be an absence of justification or cause for the enrichment and impoverishment, and (5) there must be no other remedy at law available to plaintiff.

We first question whether there has been an enrichment. While the nonresident landowners were "enriched" by the sale of the property to the state, the ultimate owners of the artifacts presented substantial evidence that the excavation caused substantial upset over the ruin of "ancestrial burial grounds," rather than any enrichment.

---

6. Later reclassified as La. Civ. Code art. 3418. — ED.

Even if the Indians have been enriched, plaintiff has failed to prove that he has sustained the type [of] impoverishment for which *de in rem verso,* may be used. His alleged loss resulted from the hours he spent excavating the artifacts, the greater portion of which activity was done at a time when plaintiff knew he was on property without the consent of the landowner. While contradictory testimony was presented regarding whether plaintiff initially had permission to go on the property, and whether that permission was adequate, by his own admission, plaintiff was informed by Hoshman that he did not own the property before the cessation of the excavating. Plaintiff's knowledge is further evidenced by his attempts to keep the location of his work secret; he did not identify Trudeau Plantation as the location of the find for almost five years after his discovery and he failed to seek out the landowners of the property until it was required for sale negotiations, although he removed two and one half tons of artifacts from their property. Plaintiff further acknowledges that he knew that the Tunica Indians might object to his excavations.

... The impoverishment element in French law is met only when the factual circumstances show that it was not a result of the plaintiff's own fault or negligence or was not undertaken at his own risk. Obviously the intent is to avoid awarding one who has helped another through his own negligence or fault or through action taken at his own risk. Plaintiff was acting possibly out of his own negligence, but more probably knowingly and at his own risk. Under these circumstances, plaintiff has not proven the type of impoverishment necessary for a claim of unjust enrichment.

Additionally, plaintiff has failed to show that any enrichment was unjustified, entitling him to an action to recover from the enriched party. An enrichment will be unjustified "only if no legal justification for it exists." . . . Any enrichment received by the Tribe was justified. . . .

For these reasons the judgment of the trial court is affirmed at appellant's costs.

NOTES AND QUESTIONS

1. *Lost, mislaid, and abandoned property.* The courts have historically divided lost personal property into three categories. Property is *lost* when the owner accidentally misplaced it; it is *mislaid* when the owner intentionally left it somewhere — and then forgets where she put it; it is *abandoned* when the owner forms an intent to relinquish all rights in the property. Property that has been lost or mislaid may subsequently be *abandoned* if the owner intends to give up any claim to the property.

2. *Conflicts between the true (original) owner and the finder.* The finder of lost or mislaid property does not acquire title to that property against the true owner, contrary to the saying "Finders keepers, losers weepers." Rather, the true owner has a right to recover the lost property from the finder. On the other hand, the finder has the right to keep property that has been abandoned since the original owner relinquished her rights. Thus, whether the finder gets to be the "keeper" in a dispute with the true owner has traditionally depended on whether the owner intended to abandon the property or merely lost or mislaid it.

3. *Conflicts between the finder and third parties.* Even though the true owner has the right to recover lost or mislaid property from the finder, the finder generally has the right to prevail over everyone but the true owner. If the true owner does not know the whereabouts of the property and is unaware that it has been found and therefore does not claim it, the finder is entitled to keep the property as against third parties. *See*

Armory v. Delamirie, 93 Eng. Rep. 664 (K.B. 1722) (a chimney sweep who found a jewel had superior rights to it as against a jeweler to whom he had entrusted the jewel for appraisal). Property rights are *relative* rather than absolute; a finder is entitled to keep the property if challenged by a third party but must turn it over if challenged by the true owner.

4. *Conflicts between the finder and the owner of the premises where the property was found.* What happens if a person finds an abandoned, lost, or mislaid object on someone else's property? In a dispute between the landowner and the finder, the landowner will win if the finder was trespassing at the time she found the object. However, the cases are split when the dispute is between a trespassing finder and a subsequent possessor of the object; older cases grant the finder rights against subsequent possessors, while some modern cases deny possessory rights to those who obtained possession illegally. If the finder is on the property with the landowner's permission, the courts are wildly divided. If an object is found in a private home, it is ordinarily awarded to the homeowner, but if the object is found in a place open to the public, some courts grant ownership to the finder and others to the landowner. Some courts distinguish between lost and mislaid property, awarding lost property to the finder (perhaps to reward her) and mislaid property to the owner of the premises (perhaps because the true owner may remember where she mislaid the object and came back to claim it). *Terry v. Lock Hospitality, Inc.*, 37 S.W.3d 202 (Ark. 2001).

If personal property is found *embedded* in the soil, courts ordinarily award it to the landowner rather than the finder, in the absence of agreement or statute to the contrary, on the ground that it is, in effect, part of the real property. A possible exception to this principle applies to so-called *treasure trove* or gold, silver, or money intentionally buried in the earth for recovery later. In England, ownership of treasure trove was historically given to the Crown, while in the United States ownership was given to the finder rather than the owner of the land, as long as the finder was not trespassing at the time it was found.

5. *Finders statutes.* Many states have legislation concerning lost property. *See, e.g.,* Fla. Stat. §§705.102 to 705.104. These laws usually get rid of the distinction between lost, mislaid, and abandoned property. They generally require the finder to report the find to the police and generally award the property to the finder if it is not claimed after a reasonable period. Del. Code tit. 11, §8307(c) (lost money). *See* Del. Code tit. 11, §8307(a) (property other than money that comes to the police is sold after one year for police benefit).

6. *Native American Graves Protection and Repatriation Act of 1990.* This statute provides that Indian cultural objects found on tribal or federal lands belong to the tribe having the strongest connection with them. It does not apply to objects found on private property. It also regulates ownership of human remains and funerary and religious objects in the hands of museums that receive federal funds. *See infra* §16.6.

PROBLEMS

1. An archeologist obtains permission to dig on private property in Georgia. After two years of work, she finds some 300-year-old objects. After evaluating them, she determines that they were made by Cherokees before the Cherokee Nation was forcibly banished from Georgia to Indian Territory (what is now Oklahoma).

    (a)   What arguments could you make that the Cherokee Nation has a right to recover possession of the cultural objects?

    (b)   What arguments could you make that the archeologist has a right to keep the cultural objects?

    (c)   What arguments could you make that the owner of the land where the objects were found has the right to possess them?

2. In *Hendle v. Stevens*, 586 N.E.2d 826 (Ill. App. Ct. 1992), some children were playing in the wooded area of property belonging to a neighbor with the neighbor's permission. While digging on the property, they found a substantial amount of money that had clearly been placed in the soil by someone. The children reported the find to the police and handed over the money. Who should get the money: the landowner or the children?

3. Is property put out on the curb in trash bins abandoned property? Does the person who placed the trash have any privacy interests in preventing others from searching the trash? *See Long v. Dilling Mechanical Contractors, Inc.*, 705 N.E.2d 1022 (Ind. Ct. App. 1999) (trash placed in dumpster by employer was abandoned property that could be removed by union organizers to find names and addresses of employees).

§1.6 Transfer: Relativity of Title

§1.6.1 REAL PROPERTY

Because property rights involve relationships between people, it is crucial to determine which persons are disputing the right to control a certain resource and to ascertain their relationships to one another. Suppose A takes property wrongfully from the true owner, O. It is quite clear that O has a right to get the property back from A. But suppose A is dispossessed by B. As between A and B, neither of whom is the true owner, who wins? The rules in force generally award both real and personal property in this situation to the prior peaceable possessor, even though she does not have title to the property. This result illustrates the concept of the *relativity of title*— although A may prevail over B, O would prevail in a dispute with A. A's title is not absolute but relative; it may be good as against one person but not as against another who has a better claim. The question is, which of the competing claimants has the better claim?

TAPSCOTT v. LESSEE OF COBBS
52 Va. (11 Gratt.) 172 (1854)

This was an action of ejectment in the Circuit court of Buckingham county, brought in February 1846, by the lessee of Elizabeth A. Cobbs and others against William H. Tapscott. Upon the trial the defendant demurred to the evidence. It appears that Thomas Anderson died in 1800, having made a will, by which he appointed several persons his executors, of whom John Harris, Robert Rives and Nathaniel Anderson qualified as such. By his will his executors were authorized to sell his real estate.

At the time of Thomas Anderson's death the land in controversy had been surveyed for him, and in 1802 a patent was issued therefor to Harris, Rives and N. Anderson as executors. Some time between the years 1820 and 1825, the executors sold the land at public auction, when it was knocked off to Robert Rives; though it appears from a contract between Rives and Sarah Lewis, dated in September 1825, that the land had, prior to that date, been sold by the executors to Mrs. Lewis for three hundred and sixty-seven dollars and fifty cents. This contract was for the sale by Mrs. Lewis to Rives of her dower interest in another tract of land, for which Rives was to pay to the executors of Thomas Anderson the sum of two hundred and seventeen dollars and fifty cents in part of her purchase. In a short time after her purchase she moved upon the land, built upon and improved it, and continued in possession until 1835, when she died. In 1825 the executor Harris was dead, and Nathaniel Anderson died in 1831, leaving Rives surviving him. And it appears that in an account settled by a commissioner in a suit by the devisees and legatees of Thomas Anderson against the executors of Robert Rives, there was an item under date of the 28th of August 1826, charging Rives with the whole amount of the purchase money, in which it is said, "The whole not yet collected, but Robert Rives assumes the liability."

There is no evidence that the heirs of Mrs. Lewis [who include Elizabeth A. Cobbs] were in possession of the land after her death, except as it may be inferred from the fact that she had been living upon the land from the time of her purchase until her death, and that she died upon it.

The proof was that [Tapscott] took possession of the land about the year 1842, without, so far as appears, any pretense of title. He made an entry with the surveyor of the county in December 1844, with a view to obtain a patent for it.

The court gave a judgment upon the demurrer for the plaintiffs, and Tapscott thereupon applied to this court for a supersedeas, which was allowed.

WILLIAM DANIEL, J.

It is no doubt true, as a general rule, that the right of a plaintiff in ejectment to recover, rests on the strength of his own title, and is not established by the exhibition of defects in the title of the defendant, and that the defendant may maintain his defense by simply showing that the title is not in the plaintiff, but in someone else. And the rule is usually thus broadly stated by the authorities, without qualification. There are, however, exceptions to the rule as thus announced, as well established as the rule itself. As when the defendant has entered under the title of the plaintiff he cannot set up a title in a third person in contradiction to that under which he entered. Other instances might be cited in which it is equally as well settled that the defendant would be estopped from showing defects in the title of the plaintiff. In such cases, the plaintiff may, and often does recover, not by the exhibition of a title good in itself, but by showing that the relations between himself and the defendant are such that the latter cannot question it. The relation between the parties stands in the place of title; and though the title of the plaintiff is tainted with vices or defects that would prove fatal to his recovery in a controversy with any other defendant in peaceable possession, it is yet all sufficient in a litigation with one who entered into the possession under it, or otherwise stands so related to it that the law will not allow him to plead its defects in his defense.

Whether the case of an intrusion by a stranger without title, on a peaceable possession, is not one to meet the exigencies of which the courts will recognize a still further qualification or explanation of the rule requiring the plaintiff to recover only on the strength of his own title, is a question which, I believe, has not as yet been decided by this court. . . .

. . . I have found no case in which the question seems to have been more fully examined or maturely considered than in *Sowden, etc. v. McMillan's heirs*, 4 Dana's R. 456.

> [The better cases] establish unquestionably the right of the plaintiff to recover when it appears that he was in possession, and that the defendant entered upon and ousted his possession, without title or authority to enter; and prove that when the possession of the plaintiff and an entry upon it by the defendant are shown, the right of recovery cannot be resisted by showing that there is or may be an outstanding title in another; but only by showing that the defendant himself either has title or authority to enter under the title.
>
> It is a natural principle of justice, that he who is in possession has the right to maintain it, and if wrongfully expelled, to regain it by entry on the wrong-doer. When titles are acknowledged as separate and distinct from the possession, this right of maintaining and regaining the possession is, of course, subject to the exception that it cannot be exercised against the real owner, in competition with whose title it wholly fails. But surely it is not accordant with the principles of justice, that he who ousts a previous possession should be permitted to defend his wrongful possession against the claim of restitution merely by showing that a stranger, and not the previous possessor whom he has ousted, was entitled to the possession. The law protects a peaceable possession against all except him who has the actual right to the possession, and no other can rightfully disturb or intrude upon it. While the peaceable possession continues, it is protected against a claimant in the action of ejectment, by permitting the defendant to show that a third person and not the claimant has the right. But if the claimant, instead of resorting to his action, attempts to gain the possession by entering upon and ousting the existing peaceable possession, he does not thereby acquire a rightful or a peaceable possession. The law does not protect him against the prior possessor. Neither does it indulge any presumption in his favor, nor permit him to gain any advantage by his own wrongful act.

In this state of the law, untrammeled as we are by any decisions of our own courts, I feel free to adopt that rule which seems to me best calculated to attain the ends of justice. . . . I am disposed to follow those decisions which uphold a peaceable possession for the protection as well of a plaintiff as of a defendant in ejectment, rather than those which invite disorderly scrambles for the possession, and clothe a mere trespasser with the means of maintaining his wrong, by showing defects, however slight, in the title of him on whose peaceable possession he has intruded without shadow of authority or title.

The authorities in support of the maintenance of ejectment upon the force of a mere prior possession, however, hold it essential that the prior possession must have been removed by the entry or intrusion of the defendant; and that the entry under which the defendant holds the possession must have been a trespass upon the prior possession. And it is also said that constructive possession is not sufficient to maintain trespass to real property; that actual possession is required, and hence that where the injury is done to an heir or devisee by an abator, before he has entered, he cannot maintain trespass until his re-entry. An apparent difficulty, therefore, in the way of a recovery by the plaintiffs, arises from the absence of positive proof of their possession at the time of the defendant's entry. It is to be observed, however, that there is no proof to the contrary. Mrs. Lewis died in possession of the premises, and there is no proof that they were vacant at the time of the defendant's entry. . . . [A]s the heir has the right to the hereditaments descending, the law presumes that he has the possession also. The presumption may indeed, like all other presumptions, be rebutted: but if the possession be not shown to be in another, the law concludes it to be in the heir.

The presumption is but a fair and reasonable one; and does, I think, arise here; and as the only evidence tending to show that the defendant sets up any pretense of right to the land, is the certificate of the surveyor of Buckingham, of an entry by the defendant, for the same, in his office, in December 1844; and his possession of the land must, according to the evidence, have commenced at least as early as some time in the year 1842; it seems to me that he must be regarded as standing in the attitude of a mere intruder on the possession of the plaintiffs.

Whether we might not in this case presume the whole of the purchase money to be paid, and regard the plaintiffs as having a perfect equitable title to the premises, and in that view as entitled to recover by force of such title; or whether we might not resort to the still further presumption in their favor, of a conveyance of the legal title, are questions which I have not thought it necessary to consider; the view, which I have already taken of the case, being sufficient, in my opinion, to justify us in affirming the judgment. . . .

NOTES AND QUESTIONS

Cobbs's fictitious lessee and the remedy of ejectment. In 1854 it was well understood that when an owner brought an ejectment action in the name of her lessee, it was almost certainly the case that the lease was fictitious. Why would Elizabeth Cobbs bring a claim in the name of her lessee when she had never leased the property? The answer has to do with the vestiges of medieval land law procedure. Lessees were entitled to a remedy of *ejectment* by which one who was dispossessed from property could bring a relatively rapid lawsuit to eject a wrongful possessor. Owners of ordinary property interests other than leases were relegated to the more cumbersome procedure of *novel disseisin.* Some owners brought lawsuits in the name of fictitious tenants in order to obtain the remedy of ejectment, and the courts acquiesced in the fiction. Soon the remedy of ejectment was available to owners as well as tenants, and it was no longer necessary for plaintiffs to bring lawsuits in the name of fictitious tenants. Charles M. Haar and Lance Liebman, *Property and Law* 69-72 (2d ed. 1985). The result is that the judges understood that the land claimed by Cobbs may well have been vacant when Tapscott took possession in 1842. It is also important to note that there appears to have been no proof that Sarah Lewis, from whom Cobbs derived her title, ever paid the full purchase price for the land or that Lewis received a deed to the land that had not been lost and that Cobbs could have used to prove her ownership rights.

PROBLEM

Three law students rent an apartment under a one-year lease. The lease contains a "no subletting" clause preventing the tenants from granting possession of any part of the premises to another person during the lease term. Two months into the school year, one of the roommates has to return to her home in another state to take care of her sick mother. The two remaining roommates, *A* and *B*, cannot afford to pay the rent by themselves. They decide, therefore, to violate the terms of the lease by asking a new third roommate, *C*, to move in. *C* makes an oral contract with *A* and *B* to pay one-third of the rent for the rest of the year. *C* moves in but has unpleasant quarrels with both *A* and *B*. After a few weeks, *A* and *B* find a friend, *D*, to take *C*'s place. They tell *C* it is not working out and she will have to move out. *C* protests that she wants to stay. One day during school, *A* and *B* change the lock on the door of the apartment and carry *C*'s belongings to the basement of the building to a storage area. *D* moves in and takes *C*'s place. *C* is now homeless. *C* sues *A*, *B*, and *D* and asks the court to order *D* to vacate the premises and allow *C* to return. *A*, *B*, and *D* defend by claiming that *C* never had a legal right to be in the apartment to begin with. You are the judge charged with deciding the case. What would you do?

§1.6.2 PERSONAL PROPERTY

Suppose *O* leaves his car with *A* to be repaired, or perhaps *O* leases his car to *A*, and then *A* sells the property to *B*, an innocent party who does not know that *A* was not entitled to sell it, before *O* can sue to get it back. *A* then absconds to a foreign jurisdiction. *O* sues *B* to get his car back. Although *O* would have had the right to get the car back from *A*, does *O* have the right to get the car back from *B*? The law resolves this conflict between two innocent persons by sometimes vesting title in the original "true owner" and sometimes granting title to the innocent or "bona fide" purchaser. This result again illustrates the concept of the *relativity of title* — *O* may have title as against *A*, but not as against *B*.

You can convey to someone else only what you own. If someone does not own Radio City Music Hall but attempts to sell it to you by granting you a deed, you get exactly what your "grantor" had — nothing. Similarly, if I steal your personal property and then resell it to an innocent purchaser who has no knowledge that the property is stolen (a "bona fide purchaser"), the innocent buyer generally is out of luck. A thief ordinarily has no right to transfer title to a third party. In *Autocephalous Greek-Orthodox Church of Cyprus v. Goldberg & Feldman Fine Arts, Inc.*, 717 F. Supp. 1374 (S.D. Ind. 1989), some valuable Christian mosaics were stolen from a church on the island of Cyprus after it was invaded by Turkey. Years later, they wound up, through a series of transactions, in the hands of defendant art dealers. The court held that "a thief never obtains title to stolen items, and . . . one can pass no greater title than one has. Therefore, one who obtains stolen items from a thief never obtains title to or right to possession of the item." *Id.* at 1398. The thief "cannot pass any title to any subsequent transferees, including subsequent purchasers" even if they are bona fide purchasers who have no notice of the theft. *Id.*[7] *See also* Ray Andrews Brown, *The Law of Personal Property* §9.4, at 194 (3d ed. 1975).

When an owner voluntarily entrusts another with possession of her property, the law sometimes gives the grantee the power to transfer title to a bona fide purchaser. When a possessor has the power to transfer title in a bona fide purchaser, we say the possessor has "voidable title"; although the true owner has the right to recover property from someone to whom she entrusted the property, the law may give that possessor the power to divest the true owner of title by transferring title to a bona fide purchaser.

---

7. A nonowner *may* be able to obtain title by adverse possession. *See infra* §3.7.

For example, in *Carlsen v. Rivera*, 382 So. 2d 825 (Fla. Dist. Ct. App. 1980), Coradino Rivera, owner of a Canadian car rental agency, leased a car to James McEnroe, who forged a title to the car in the name of a business he owned and sold it to a third party who obtained a facially valid title certificate in Florida. The car was then sold again to a fourth party, who finally sold it to defendant Carlsen. Rivera sued Carlsen to get his car back. The court applied the Florida version of the *Uniform Commercial Code*, U.C.C. §2-403(2), which provides that a bona fide purchaser will prevail over the true owner when the true owner has entrusted the property to a merchant who regularly deals in such goods. Fla. Stat. §672.403. Similarly, if an owner is induced to sell his property by fraud or duress, the seller may recover the property from the buyer unless the buyer has subsequently transferred the property to a bona fide purchaser. U.C.C. §2-403(1). On the other hand, when a thief takes property away from an owner, such that the initial transfer of possession is involuntary, neither the thief nor subsequent purchasers are entitled to keep title as against the true owner from whom the property was stolen even if those later possessors are bona fide purchasers. *Candela v. Port Motors, Inc.*, 617 N.Y.S.2d 49 (App. Div. 1994).

What justifies a rule of law that prevents the true owner of stolen property from recovering it from a bona fide purchaser just because the thief who wrongfully arranged for the sale "deals in goods of that kind"?

PROBLEM

Plaintiff lent his car to a friend. The friend turns out not to be such a true friend, forges a title to the car, and sells it to a bona fide purchaser. Since the friend is not a merchant, the common law rule, rather than the *Uniform Commercial Code*, applies, enabling the plaintiff to recover the car from the bona fide purchaser on the grounds that a thief cannot transfer good title. Defendant argues that the common law should be changed to protect the rights of bona fide purchasers to obtain title to property even when the true owner did not entrust the property to a merchant.

1. What arguments can you make for the defendant's proposed rule of law? What can you say on the plaintiff's behalf? In answering these questions, consider whether it makes sense to distinguish merchants from other persons who wrongfully transfer title to stolen goods. How should the court rule?

2. Assume now that the car was stolen from the plaintiff's driveway rather than entrusted to a false friend. Does this make any difference in the analysis?

2

Trespass and Public Rights of Access to Property

§2.1 Trespass

§2.1.1 PUBLIC POLICY LIMITS ON THE RIGHT TO EXCLUDE

Many rights go along with ownership or possession of property. One of the most important is the right to *exclude* others from the property. Possessors of property may exercise this right, or they may waive it by allowing others to come onto the property. The right to exclude is not absolute: In a variety of circumstances, legal rules limit the possessor's right to exclude nonowners from the property. In such cases, nonowners may have a right of access to the property. These rights of access are created by different sources of law, including common law, federal and state public accommodations statutes and labor relations statutes, and federal and state constitutional guarantees of freedom of speech.

The cases in this chapter explore the contours of these competing rights in different contexts. In general, the more an owner has opened her property to the public, the more likely it is that the courts will find public rights of access to the property. In one class of cases, nonowners may have rights of access to the property of others even if the owner has excluded almost everyone from the property. For example, nonowners may enter an owner's property to save a human life. A second class of cases concerns situations in which owners have allowed nonowners to possess all or part of their property. These cases concern, for example, the right of tenants to receive visitors in their homes. A third class of cases concerns property that has been opened generally to the public, such as a shopping center, restaurant, or movie theater. Such public accommodations are generally prohibited from discriminating on illegitimate grounds, such as race or sex.

In reading the following material, you should ask yourself what factual context is presented in each case. What interests are asserted by the possessor in excluding the nonowner from the property? What interests are asserted by the nonowner to justify a right of access? What source of law is claimed as the basis for the right of access —

common law, statute, or constitution? How do the judges analyze the competing interests in the case, and what reasons do they give for the accommodation they reach?

STATE v. SHACK
—————————————————
277 A.2d 369 (N.J. 1971)

JOSEPH WEINTRAUB, C.J.

Defendants entered upon private property to aid migrant farmworkers employed and housed there. Having refused to depart upon the demand of the owner, defendants were charged with violating N.J. Stat. Ann. §2A:170-31[1] which provides that "[a]ny person who trespasses on any lands . . . after being forbidden so to trespass by the owner . . . is a disorderly person and shall be punished by a fine of not more than $50." Defendants were convicted in the Municipal Court of Deerfield Township. . . .

Complainant, Tedesco, a farmer, employs migrant workers for his seasonal needs. As part of their compensation, these workers are housed at a camp on his property.

Defendant Tejeras is a field worker for the Farm Workers Division of the Southwest Citizens Organization for Poverty Elimination, known by the acronym SCOPE, a nonprofit corporation funded by the Office of Economic Opportunity pursuant to an act of Congress, 42 U.S.C.A. §§2861-2864.[2] The role of SCOPE includes providing for the "health services of the migrant farm worker."

Defendant Shack is a staff attorney with the Farm Workers Division of Camden Regional Legal Services, Inc., known as "CRLS," also a nonprofit corporation funded by the Office of Economic Opportunity pursuant to an act of Congress, 42 U.S.C.A. §2809(a)(3). The mission of CRLS includes legal advice and representation for these workers.

Differences had developed between Tedesco and these defendants prior to the events which led to the trespass charges now before us. Hence when defendant Tejeras wanted to go upon Tedesco's farm to find a migrant worker who needed medical aid for the removal of 28 sutures, he called upon defendant Shack for his help with respect to the legalities involved. Shack, too, had a mission to perform on Tedesco's farm; he wanted to discuss a legal problem with another migrant worker there employed and housed. Defendants arranged to go to the farm together. Shack carried literature to inform the migrant farmworkers of the assistance available to them under federal statutes, but no mention seems to have been made of that literature when Shack was later confronted by Tedesco.

Defendants entered upon Tedesco's property and as they neared the camp site where the farmworkers were housed, they were confronted by Tedesco who inquired of their purpose. Tejeras and Shack stated their missions. In response, Tedesco offered to find the injured worker, and as to the worker who needed legal advice, Tedesco also offered to locate the man but insisted that the consultation would have to take place in Tedesco's office and in his presence. Defendants declined, saying they had the right to see the men in the privacy of their living quarters and without Tedesco's supervision.

—————————————————

1. This statute has been superseded by N.J. Stat. §2C:18-3. — ED.

2. This statute, as well as the subsequently referenced statute, 42 U.S.C.A. §2809(a)(3), have been repealed. *See* Pub. L. No. 95-568, §8(a)(2), Nov. 2, 1978, 92 Stat. 2428; Pub. L. No. 97-35, tit. VI, §683(a), Aug. 13, 1981, 95 Stat. 519. — ED.

Tedesco thereupon summoned a State Trooper who, however, refused to remove defendants except upon Tedesco's written complaint. Tedesco then executed the formal complaints charging violations of the trespass statute.

I

The constitutionality of the trespass statute, as applied here, is challenged on several scores.

It is urged that the First Amendment rights of the defendants and of the migrant farmworkers were thereby offended. Reliance is placed on *Marsh v. Alabama*, 326 U.S. 501 (1946), where it was held that free speech was assured by the First Amendment in a company-owned town which was open to the public generally and was indistinguishable from any other town except for the fact that the title to the property was vested in a private corporation. Hence a Jehovah's Witness who distributed literature on a sidewalk within the town could not be held as a trespasser. Later, on the strength of that case, it was held that there was a First Amendment right to picket peacefully in a privately owned shopping center which was found to be the functional equivalent of the business district of the company-owned town in *Marsh*. *Amalgamated Food Employees Union Local 590 v. Logan Valley Plaza, Inc.*, 391 U.S. 308 (1968). [*Logan Valley* rests] upon the fact that the property was in fact opened to the general public.[3] There may be some migrant camps with the attributes of the company town in *Marsh* and of course they would come within its holding. But there is nothing of that character in the case before us, and hence there would have to be an extension of *Marsh* to embrace the immediate situation.

Defendants also maintain that the application of the trespass statute to them is barred by the Supremacy Clause of the United States Constitution, Art. VI, cl. 2,[4] and this on the premise that the application of the trespass statute would defeat the purpose of the federal statutes, under which SCOPE and CRLS are funded, to reach and aid the migrant farmworker. The brief of the United States, amicus curiae, supports that approach. Here defendants rely upon cases construing the National Labor Relations Act, 29 U.S.C.A. §§151 *et seq.*, and holding that an employer may in some circumstances be guilty of an unfair labor practice in violation of that statute if the employer denies union organizers an opportunity to communicate with his employees at some suitable place upon the employer's premises. . . .

These constitutional claims are not established by any definitive holding. We think it unnecessary to explore their validity. The reason is that we are satisfied that under our State law the ownership of real property does not include the right to bar access to governmental services available to migrant workers and hence there was no trespass within the meaning of the penal statute. The policy considerations which underlie that conclusion may be much the same as those which would be weighed

---

3. *Logan Valley* was substantially limited in application by the Supreme Court in *Lloyd Corp., Ltd. v. Tanner*, 407 U.S. 551 (1972) and substantially overruled in *Hudgens v. National Labor Relations Board*, 424 U.S. 507 (1976). *See infra* §2.3. — ED.

4. That clause states: "This Constitution, and the Laws of the United States which shall be made in Pursuance thereof; and all Treaties made, or which shall be made, under the Authority of the United States, shall be the supreme Law of the Land; and the Judges in every State shall be bound thereby, any Thing in the Constitution or laws of any State to the Contrary notwithstanding." — ED.

with respect to one or more of the constitutional challenges, but a decision in non-constitutional terms is more satisfactory, because the interests of migrant workers are more expansively served in that way than they would be if they had no more freedom than these constitutional concepts could be found to mandate if indeed they apply at all.

II

Property rights serve human values. They are recognized to that end, and are limited by it. Title to real property cannot include dominion over the destiny of persons the owner permits to come upon the premises. Their well-being must remain the paramount concern of a system of law. Indeed the needs of the occupants may be so imperative and their strength so weak, that the law will deny the occupants the power to contract away what is deemed essential to their health, welfare, or dignity.

Here we are concerned with a highly disadvantaged segment of our society. We are told that every year farmworkers and their families numbering more than one million leave their home areas to fill the seasonal demand for farm labor in the United States. The migrant farmworkers come to New Jersey in substantial numbers....

The migrant farmworkers are a community within but apart from the local scene. They are rootless and isolated. Although the need for their labors is evident, they are unorganized and without economic or political power. It is their plight alone that summoned government to their aid. In response, Congress provided under Title III-B of the *Economic Opportunity Act of 1964* (42 U.S.C.A. §§2701 *et seq.*) for "assistance for migrant and other seasonally employed farmworkers and their families." Section 2861 states "the purpose of this part is to assist migrant and seasonal farmworkers and their families to improve their living conditions and develop skills necessary for a productive and self-sufficient life in an increasingly complex and technological society." Section 2862(b)(1) provides for funding of programs "to meet the immediate needs of migrant and seasonal farmworkers and their families, such as day care for children, education, health services, improved housing and sanitation (including the provision and maintenance of emergency and temporary housing and sanitation facilities), legal advice and representation, and consumer training and counseling." As we have said, SCOPE is engaged in a program funded under this section, and CRLS also pursues the objectives of this section although, we gather, it is funded under §2809(a)(3), which is not limited in its concern to the migrant and other seasonally employed farmworkers and seeks "to further the cause of justice among persons living in poverty by mobilizing the assistance of lawyers and legal institutions and by providing legal advice, legal representation, counseling, education, and other appropriate services."

These ends would not be gained if the intended beneficiaries could be insulated from efforts to reach them. It is in this framework that we must decide whether the camp operator's rights in his lands may stand between the migrant workers and those who would aid them. The key to that aid is communication. Since the migrant workers are outside the mainstream of the communities in which they are housed and are unaware of their rights and opportunities and of the services available to them, they can be reached only by positive efforts tailored to that end. The *Report of the Governor's Task Force on Migrant Farm Labor* (1968) noted that "One of the major problems related to seasonal farm labor is the lack of adequate direct information with regard to the availability of public services," and that "there is a dire need to provide the workers with basic educational and informational material in a language and style that can be readily understood by the migrant." The report stressed the problem of access and deplored the notion that property rights may stand as a barrier, saying "In our judgment, 'no trespass' signs represent the last dying remnants of paternalistic behavior."

A man's right in his real property of course is not absolute. It was a maxim of the common law that one should so use his property as not to injure the rights of others. [*Sic utere tuo ut alienum non laedas.*] Although hardly a precise solvent of actual controversies, the maxim does express the inevitable proposition that rights are relative and there must be an accommodation when they meet. Hence it has long been true that necessity, private or public, may justify entry upon the lands of another....

The subject is not static. As pointed out in 5 Powell, *Real Property* §745, at 493-494 (Rohan 1970), while society will protect the owner in his permissible interests in land, yet

> ... [S]uch an owner must expect to find the absoluteness of his property rights curtailed by the organs of society, for the promotion of the best interests of others for whom these organs also operate as protective agencies. The necessity for such curtailments is greater in a modern industrialized and urbanized society than it was in the relatively simple American society of fifty, 100, or 200 years ago. The current balance between individualism and dominance of the social interest depends not only upon political and social ideologies, but also upon the physical and social facts of the time and place under discussion.

Professor Powell added in §746, at 494-496:

> As one looks back along the historic road traversed by the law of land in England and in America, one sees a change from the viewpoint that he who owns may do as he pleases with what he owns, to a position which hesitatingly embodies an ingredient of stewardship; which grudgingly, but steadily, broadens the recognized scope of social interests in the utilization of things....
>
> To one seeing history through the glasses of religion, these changes may seem to evidence increasing embodiments of the golden rule. To one thinking in terms of political and economic ideologies, they are likely to be labeled evidences of "social enlightenment" or of "creeping socialism" or even of "communistic infiltration," according to the individual's assumed definitions and retained or acquired prejudices. With slight attention to words or labels, time marches on toward new adjustments between individualism and the social interests.

This process involves not only the accommodation between the right of the owner and the interests of the general public in his use of his property, but involves also an accommodation between the right of the owner and the right of individuals who are parties with him in consensual transactions relating to the use of the property. Accordingly substantial alterations have been made as between a landlord and his tenant.

The argument in this case understandably included the question whether the migrant worker should be deemed to be a tenant and thus entitled to the tenant's right to receive visitors, *Williams v. Lubbering,* 63 A. 90 (N.J. Sup. Ct. 1906), or whether his residence on the employer's property should be deemed to be merely incidental and in aid of his employment, and hence to involve no possessory interest in the realty. *See Scottish Rite Co. v. Salkowitz,* 197 A. 43 (N.J. 1938). These cases did not reach employment situations at all comparable with the one before us. Nor did they involve the question whether an employee who is not a tenant may have visitors notwithstanding the employer's prohibition. Rather they were concerned with whether notice must be given to end the employee's right to remain upon the premises, with whether the employer may remove the discharged employee without court order, and with the availability of a particular judicial remedy to achieve his removal by process. We of course are not concerned here with the right of a migrant worker to remain on the employer's property after the employment is ended.

We see no profit in trying to decide upon a conventional category and then forcing the present subject into it. That approach would be artificial and distorting. The quest is for a fair adjustment of the competing needs of the parties, in the light of the realities of the relationship between the migrant worker and the operator of the housing facility.

Thus approaching the case, we find it unthinkable that the farmer-employer can assert a right to isolate the migrant worker in any respect significant for the worker's well-being. The farmer, of course, is entitled to pursue his farming activities without interference, and this defendants readily concede. But we see no legitimate need for a right in the farmer to deny the worker the opportunity for aid available from federal, State, or local services, or from recognized charitable groups seeking to assist him. Hence representatives of these agencies and organizations may enter upon the premises to seek out the worker at his living quarters. So, too, the migrant worker must be allowed to receive visitors there of his own choice, so long as there is no behavior hurtful to others, and members of the press may not be denied reasonable access to workers who do not object to seeing them.

It is not our purpose to open the employer's premises to the general public if in fact the employer himself has not done so. We do not say, for example, that solicitors or peddlers of all kinds may enter on their own; we may assume for the present that the employer may regulate their entry or bar them, at least if the employer's purpose is not to gain a commercial advantage for himself or if the regulation does not deprive the migrant worker of practical access to things he needs.

And we are mindful of the employer's interest in his own and in his employees' security. Hence he may reasonably require a visitor to identify himself, and also to state his general purpose if the migrant worker has not already informed him that the visitor is expected. But the employer may not deny the worker his privacy or interfere with his opportunity to live with dignity and to enjoy associations customary among our citizens. These rights are too fundamental to be denied on the basis of an interest in real property and too fragile to be left to the unequal bargaining strength of the parties.

It follows that defendants here invaded no possessory right of the farmer-employer. Their conduct was therefore beyond the reach of the trespass statute. The judgments are accordingly reversed and the matters remanded to the County Court with directions to enter judgments of acquittal.

DESNICK v. AMERICAN BROADCASTING COMPANIES, INC.

44 F.3d 1345 (7th Cir. 1995)

Opinion by RICHARD POSNER, Chief Judge.

The plaintiffs — an ophthalmic clinic known as the "Desnick Eye Center" after its owner, Dr. Desnick, and two ophthalmic surgeons employed by the clinic, Glazer and

Simon — appeal from the dismissal of their suit against the ABC television network, a producer of the ABC program *PrimeTime Live* named Entine, and the program's star reporter, Donaldson. The suit is for trespass, defamation, and other torts arising out of the production and broadcast of a program segment of *PrimeTime Live* that was highly critical of the Desnick Eye Center. . . .

In March of 1993 Entine telephoned Dr. Desnick and told him that *PrimeTime Live* wanted to do a broadcast segment on large cataract practices. The Desnick Eye Center has 25 offices in four midwestern states and performs more than 10,000 cataract operations a year, mostly on elderly persons whose cataract surgery is paid for by Medicare. The complaint alleges — and in the posture of the case we must take the allegations to be true, though of course they may not be — that Entine told Desnick that the segment would not be about just one cataract practice, that it would not involve "ambush" interviews or "undercover" surveillance, and that it would be "fair and balanced." Thus reassured, Desnick permitted an ABC crew to videotape the Desnick Eye Center's main premises in Chicago, to film a cataract operation "live," and to interview doctors, technicians, and patients. Desnick also gave Entine a video- tape explaining the Desnick Eye Center's services.

Unbeknownst to Desnick, Entine had dispatched persons equipped with con- cealed cameras to offices of the Desnick Eye Center in Wisconsin and Indiana. Posing as patients, these persons — seven in all — requested eye examinations. Plaintiffs Gla- zer and Simon are among the employees of the Desnick Eye Center who were secretly videotaped examining these "test patients."

The program aired on June 10. Donaldson introduces the segment by saying, "We begin tonight with the story of a so-called 'big cutter,' Dr. James Desnick. . . . In our undercover investigation of the big cutter you'll meet tonight, we turned up evidence that he may also be a big charger, doing unnecessary cataract surgery for the money." Brief interviews with four patients of the Desnick Eye Center follow. One of the patients is satisfied ("I was blessed"); the other three are not — one of them says, "If you got three eyes, he'll get three eyes." Donaldson then reports on the experiences of the seven test patients. The two who were under 65 and thus not eligible for Medicare reimbursement were told they didn't need cataract surgery. Four of the other five were told they did. Glazer and Simon are shown recommending cataract surgery to them. Donaldson tells the viewer that *PrimeTime Live* has hired a professor of ophthalmology to examine the test patients who had been told they needed cataract surgery, and the professor tells the viewer that they didn't need it — with regard to one he says, "I think it would be near malpractice to do surgery on him." Later in the segment he denies that this could just be an honest difference of opinion between professionals.

An ophthalmic surgeon is interviewed who had turned down a job at the Desnick Eye Center because he would not have been "able to screen who I was going to operate on." He claims to have been told by one of the doctors at the Center (not Glazer or Simon) that "as soon as I reject them [*i.e.*, turn down a patient for cataract surgery], they're going in the next room to get surgery." A former marketing executive for the Center says Desnick took advantage of "people who had Alzheimer's, people who did not know what planet they were on, people whose quality of life wouldn't change one iota by having cataract surgery done." Two patients are interviewed who report miserable experiences with the Center — one claiming that the doctors there had failed to spot an easily visible melanoma, another that as a result of unnecessary cataract surgery her "eye ruptured," producing "running pus." A former employee tells the viewer that Dr. Desnick alters patients' medical records to show they need cataract surgery — for example, changing the record of one patient's vision test from 20/30 to 20/80 — and that he instructs all members of his staff to use pens of the same color in order to facilitate the alteration of patients' records.

One symptom of cataracts is that lights of normal brightness produce glare. Glazer is shown telling a patient, "You know, you're getting glare. I would say we could do significantly better [with an operation]." And Simon is shown asking two patients, "Do you ever notice any glare or blurriness when you're driving, or difficulty with the signs?" Both say no, and immediately Donaldson tells the viewer that "the Desnick Center uses a very interesting machine, called an auto-refractor, to determine whether there are glare problems." Donaldson demonstrates the machine, then says that "Paddy Kalish is an optometrist who says that when he worked at the Desnick clinic from 1987 to 1990, the machine was regularly rigged. He says he watched a technician tamper with the machine, this way" — and then Kalish gives a demonstration, adding, "This happened routinely for all the older patients that came in for the eye exams." Donaldson reveals that Dr. Desnick has obtained a judgment against Kalish for defamation, but adds that "Kalish is not the only one to tell us the machine may have been rigged. PrimeTime talked to four other former Desnick employees who say almost everyone failed the glare test." . . .

[Plaintiff claims] that the defendants committed a trespass in insinuating the test patients into the Wisconsin and Indiana offices of the Desnick Eye Center, that they invaded the right of privacy of the Center and its doctors at those offices (specifically Glazer and Simon), that they violated federal and state statutes regulating electronic surveillance, and that they committed fraud by gaining access to the Chicago office by means of a false promise that they would present a "fair and balanced" picture of the Center's operations and would not use "ambush" interviews or undercover surveillance.

To enter upon another's land without consent is a trespass. The force of this rule has, it is true, been diluted somewhat by concepts of privilege and of implied consent. But there is no journalists' privilege to trespass. And there can be no implied consent in any nonfictitious sense of the term when express consent is procured by a misrepresentation or a misleading omission. The Desnick Eye Center would not have agreed to the entry of the test patients into its offices had it known they wanted eye examinations only in order to gather material for a television expose of the Center and that they were going to make secret videotapes of the examinations. Yet some cases deem consent effective even though it was procured by fraud. There must be *something* to this surprising result. Without it a restaurant critic could not conceal his identity when he ordered a meal, or a browser pretend to be interested in merchandise that he could not afford to buy. Dinner guests would be trespassers if they were false friends who never would have been invited had the host known their true character, and a consumer who in an effort to bargain down an automobile dealer falsely claimed to be able to buy the same car elsewhere at a lower price would be a trespasser in the dealer's showroom. Some of these might be classified as privileged trespasses, designed to promote competition. Others might be thought justified by some kind of implied consent — the restaurant critic for example might point by way of analogy to the use of the "fair use" defense by book reviewers charged with copyright infringement and argue that the restaurant industry as a whole would be injured if restaurants could exclude critics. But most such efforts at rationalization would be little better than evasions. The fact is that consent to an entry is often given legal effect even though the entrant has intentions that if known to the owner of the property would cause him for perfectly understandable and generally ethical or at least lawful reasons to revoke his consent.

The law's willingness to give effect to consent procured by fraud is not limited to the tort of trespass. The *Restatement* gives the example of a man who obtains consent to sexual intercourse by promising a woman $100, yet (unbeknownst to her, of course) he pays her with a counterfeit bill and intended to do so from the start. The man is not guilty of battery, even though unconsented-to sexual intercourse is a battery. *Restatement (Second) of Torts* §892B, illustration 9, pp. 373-374 (1979). Yet we know that to conceal the fact that one has a venereal disease transforms "consensual" intercourse into battery. *Crowell v. Crowell,* 105 S.E. 206 (N.C. 1920). Seduction, standardly effected by false promises of love, is not rape; intercourse under the pretense of rendering medical or psychiatric treatment is, at least in most states. It certainly is battery. Trespass presents close parallels. If a homeowner opens his door to a purported meter reader who is in fact nothing of the sort — just a busybody curious about the interior of the home — the homeowner's consent to his entry is not a defense to a suit for trespass. *See State v. Donahue,* 762 P.2d 1022, 1025 (Or. Ct. App. 1988); *Bouillon v. Laclede Gaslight Co.,* 129 S.W. 401, 402 (Mo. Ct. App. 1910). And likewise if a competitor gained entry to a business firm's premises posing as a customer but in fact hoping to steal the firm's trade secrets. *Rockwell Graphic Systems, Inc. v. DEV Industries, Inc.,* 925 F.2d 174, 178 (7th Cir. 1991); *E.I. duPont deNemours & Co. v. Christopher,* 431 F.2d 1012, 1014 (5th Cir. 1970).

How to distinguish the two classes of case — the seducer from the medical impersonator, the restaurant critic from the meter-reader impersonator? The answer can have nothing to do with fraud; there is fraud in all the cases. It has to do with the interest that the torts in question, battery and trespass, protect. The one protects the inviolability of the person, the other the inviolability of the person's property. The woman who is seduced wants to have sex with her seducer, and the restaurant owner wants to have customers. The woman who is victimized by the medical impersonator has no desire to have sex with her doctor; she wants medical treatment. And the homeowner victimized by the phony meter reader does not want strangers in his house unless they have authorized service functions. The dealer's objection to the customer who claims falsely to have a lower price from a competing dealer is not to the physical presence of the customer, but to the fraud that he is trying to perpetuate. The lines are not bright — they are not even inevitable. They are the traces of the old forms of action, which have resulted in a multitude of artificial distinctions in modern law. But that is nothing new.

There was no invasion in the present case of any of the specific interests that the tort of trespass seeks to protect. The test patients entered offices that were open to anyone expressing a desire for ophthalmic services and videotaped physicians engaged in professional, not personal, communications with strangers (the testers themselves). The activities of the offices were not disrupted. . . . Nor was there any "inva[sion of] a person's private space," as in our hypothetical meter-reader case, as in the famous case of *De May v. Roberts,* 9 N.W. 146 (Mich. 1881) (where a doctor, called to the plaintiff's home to deliver her baby, brought along with him a friend who was curious to see a birth but was not a medical doctor, and represented the friend to be his medical assistant), as in *Dietemann v. Time, Inc.,* 449 F.2d 245 (9th Cir. 1971), on which the plaintiffs in our case rely. *Dietemann* involved a home. True, the portion invaded was an office, where the plaintiff performed quack healing of nonexistent ailments. The parallel to this case is plain enough, but there is a difference. Dietemann was not in business, and did not advertise his services or charge for them. His quackery was private.

No embarrassingly intimate details of anybody's life were publicized in the present case. There was no eavesdropping on a private conversation; the testers recorded their own conversations with the Desnick Eye Center's physicians. There was no violation of the doctor-patient privilege. There was no theft, or intent to steal, trade secrets; no disruption of decorum, of peace and quiet; no noisy or distracting demonstrations. Had the testers been undercover FBI agents, there would have been no violation of the Fourth Amendment, because there would have been no invasion of a legally protected interest in property or privacy. *United States v. White*, 401 U.S. 745 (1971); *Northside Realty Associates, Inc. v. United States*, 605 F.2d 1348, 1355 (5th Cir. 1979). "Testers" who pose as prospective home buyers in order to gather evidence of housing discrimination are not trespassers even if they are private persons not acting under color of law. The situation of the defendants' "testers" is analogous. Like testers seeking evidence of violation of antidiscrimination laws, the defendants' test patients gained entry into the plaintiffs' premises by misrepresenting their purposes (more precisely by a misleading omission to disclose those purposes). But the entry was not invasive in the sense of infringing the kind of interest of the plaintiffs that the law of trespass protects; it was not an interference with the ownership or possession of land. We need not consider what if any difference it would make if the plaintiffs had festooned the premises with signs forbidding the entry of testers or other snoops. Perhaps none, but that is an issue for another day....

NOTES AND QUESTIONS

1. A trespass is an *unprivileged intentional intrusion on property possessed by another*. The *intent* requirement is met if the defendant engaged in a voluntary act, such as walking onto the property. It is not necessary to show that the trespasser intended to violate the owner's legal rights; thus, mistaken entry on the land of another does not relieve the trespasser of liability. The intent requirement is not met if the trespasser is carried onto the property against her will by others. The *intrusion* occurs the moment the nonowner enters the property. "The gist of an action of trespass is infringement on the right of possession." *Walker Drug Co., Inc. v. La Sal Oil Co.*, 972 P.2d 1238 (Utah 1998). An intrusion may occur upon physical entry by a person, an agent such as an employee, or an object such as a building that extends over the boundary onto a neighbor's property. A trespass may occur both above or below the surface. For example, a well dug on one's property that slants to an area underneath the neighbor's property constitutes a trespass. Similarly, a second-story porch that overhangs the neighbor's property also qualifies as a trespass.

A trespass is *privileged*, and thus not wrongful, if (1) the entry is done with the *consent* of the owner;[4] (2) the entry is justified by the *necessity* to prevent a more serious harm to persons or property; or (3) the entry is otherwise encouraged by *public policy*. Entry on property of another may be privileged, for example, if one is doing so to stop a crime or to help someone out of a burning house. Individuals may also have rights of

---

4. One who enters property with the permission of the owner or possessor is called a *licensee* and has a property interest called a *license*. If the owner revokes the license, the nonowner must leave the land within a reasonable time; failure to do so will constitute a trespass.

access to cemeteries to visit the graves of their loved ones even if those graves are located on private property that has been sold to a subsequent owner. *Common Wealth of Kentucky Dept. of Fish and Wildlife Resources v. Garner*, 896 S.W. 2d 10 (Ky. 1995) (cemetery on public land has duty to give a key to the locked gate to an individual for his use and that of his heirs to visit the graves of their family members); *David v. May*, 135 S.W. 2d 747 (Tex. Ct. App. 2003) (plaintiff has the right of access to land to visit the graves of her grandparents).

2. *Trespass remedies.* Civil litigants generally may request three kinds of relief. First, they may ask for *damages* payable to the injured party by the wrongdoer. A possessor may always recover *nominal damages* for trespass even if no other harm has occurred. The possessor may recover *compensatory damages* if the trespasser has caused other harm to the property. The amount of compensatory damages is measured either by the cost of restoring the property to its previous condition or by the diminution in its market value. The cost of the lawsuit might exceed the amount of damages recovered. However, a possessor might sue even for nominal damages as a way to establish that he has the right to possess the property — to have the court declare that the owner has the right to exclude others from the property in question. A trespasser may also be liable for *punitive damages* to punish and deter outrageous or malicious behavior.

Second, the plaintiff may ask the court to issue an *injunction* ordering the wrongdoer to cease her wrongful conduct or remedy any harm to the property caused by the trespass. Failure to obey such an injunction is punishable by contempt proceedings, and the recalcitrant party may be fined or imprisoned. If the entry by the trespasser has occupied the property, the plaintiff may bring a lawsuit for *ejectment* to remove the trespasser from the land.

Third, the plaintiff may ask the court for a *declaratory judgment* stating his legal rights against the other party. For example, Shack and Tejeras might sue Tedesco, claiming they have legal right to enter Tedesco's property to visit the farmworkers and asking the court to issue both a declaratory judgment confirming that right and an injunction ordering Tedesco not to interfere with the exercise of their legal rights.

3. *Criminal trespass.* Shack and Tejeras were charged with *criminal trespass* as defined by the New Jersey statute, N.J. Stat. §2A:170-31.[5] Tedesco invoked the criminal system by calling the police and filing a criminal complaint against Shack and Tejeras. Criminal proceedings are generally initiated by federal, state, or local government officials rather than by private citizens, and their purpose is to deter wrongful activities and to punish those who engage in them. These proceedings may include arrest, criminal complaint or indictment by the prosecutor, arraignment (bringing formal charges against the accused in court), plea bargaining, and trial. Punishment may include imposition of a fine payable to the state, probation (continued supervision), incarceration, and, in some states, the death penalty. How did the criminal charge of criminal trespass differ from the common law definition of trespass?

4. *Legal basis for decision.* Did the court in *Shack* rest its ruling on the U.S. Constitution, a federal statute, a state statute, or the state common law? If the court

---

5. This law has been superseded by N.J. Stat. §2C:18-3, which provides, at §2C:18-3(b), that a "person commits a petty disorderly persons offense if, knowing that he is not licensed or privileged to do so, he enters or remains in any place as to which notice against trespass is given by: (1) Actual communication to the actor; or (2) Posting in a manner prescribed by law or reasonably likely to come to the attention of intruders; or (3) Fencing or other enclosure manifestly designed to exclude intruders."

rested its opinion on only one of these sources of law, what role did the others play in determining the outcome of the case?

5. *Investigative journalism.* In a case somewhat similar to *Desnick, Food Lion, Inc. v. Capital Cities/ABC, Inc.,* 194 F.3d 505 (4th Cir. 1999), *aff'g in part and rev'g in part* 887 F. Supp. 811 (M.D.N.C. 1995), *PrimeTime Live* sent two ABC television reporters to use false resumes to get jobs at Food Lion supermarkets. While working there, they secretly videotaped "what appeared to be unwholesome food handling practices" for later broadcast on television. Food Lion sued ABC, claiming, among other things, that ABC had committed the tort of fraud, that it had violated the duty of loyalty owed by employees to employers, and that its intrusion onto Food Lion's property constituted a trespass. The trial court held that ABC had committed a trespass when its reporters had entered the property because defendants had engaged in "wrongful conduct which could negate any consent to enter given by Food Lion." 887 F. Supp. at 820. Finding ABC liable for both fraud and trespass, the jury awarded Food Lion $1.00 nominal damages for trespass and $1.00 for violation of the duty of loyalty. It imposed $1,400 damages for the tort of fraud and a whopping $5,545,750 in punitive damages to punish and deter ABC from engaging in this kind of fraudulent deception in the future. The trial judge reduced the punitive damages to $315,000. *Accord, Medical Laboratory Management Consultants v. ABC, Inc.,* 30 F. Supp. 2d 1182 (D. Ariz. 1998); *Shiffman v. Empire Blue Cross and Blue Shield,* 681 N.Y.S.2d 511, 512 (App. Div. 1998) (reporters who gained entry to medical offices by posing as a potential patients could not assert consent as defense to trespass claim "since consent obtained by misrepresentation or fraud is invalid"); *Restatement (Second) of Torts,* §892B(2) (1965) ("if the person consenting to the conduct of another . . . is induced [to consent] by the other's misrepresentation, the consent is not effective for the unexpected invasion or harm"). *But see American Transmission, Inc. v. Channel 7 of Detroit, Inc.,* 609 N.W.2d 607 (Mich. Ct. App. 2000) (agreeing with *Desnick* and holding that despite the existence of fraudulent misrepresentations by employees of television station investigating dishonest practices in transmission repair shops, the shop owners had validly consented to the investigators' presence on their premises and that no specific interests relating to the peaceable possession of land were invaded).

The Fourth Circuit reversed in part, agreeing with *Desnick* that the initial entry was consensual despite having been obtained by fraud so no trespass occurred when the reporters initially entered the property. However, the court found that a trespass had occurred *after* the initial entry when the reporters secretly videotaped the meat packing process because this action exceeded the scope of the initial invitation. However, the Fourth Circuit threw out the fraud claim. Although the fraud had caused Food Lion to hire the employees, it could not demonstrate any harm resulting from the hirings themselves. As at-will employees, they could leave at any time, and had made no promises to work for any particular length of time. Thus Food Lion could not complain that they only stayed for two weeks. Any harm to Food Lion was caused by the broadcast and not by the fraud. The First Amendment generally protects the right to publish truthful information, allowing remedies only for defamation — false statements that injure reputation — and even then only in restricted circumstances. Because the punitive damages judgment had been premised on the fraud, and the fraud claim had now been thrown out, the Fourth Circuit also threw out the punitive damages judgment, leaving defendants with a nominal damages judgment of two dollars.

6. *Trespass to computer systems.* Trespass is usually a doctrine that concerns intrusions to real property. A version of the doctrine, called *trespass to chattels,* applies

to personal property. The tort of trespass to chattels allows owners of personal property to recover damages for intentional interferences with the possession of personal property. The owner is entitled to injunctive relief stopping any such interference with the chattel. Mere touching of the object is not sufficient to constitute trespass; the plaintiff must either allege some injury to the property or show either dispossession or intentional "using or intermeddling" with it. Restatement (*Second*) *of Torts* §218 (1965).

In *Intel Corp. v. Hamidi*, 71 P.3d 296 (Cal. 2003), a former employee named Kourosh Kenneth Hamidi sent numerous e-mails to his former co-employees criticizing the employer. The e-mails breached no security barriers nor disrupted the employer's e-mail system. The lower courts held that the former employee had committed trespass to chattels on the ground that the former employee was "disrupting [the employer's] business by using its property." *Id.* at 302. However, the California Supreme Court reversed, holding that no trespass could be shown in the absence of dispossession unless the communication damaged the recipient's computer system or impaired its functioning. *Accord, CompuServe v. Cyber Promotions, Inc.*, 962 F.Supp. 1015, 1022 (S.D. Ohio 1997). *Cf. eBay, Inc. v. Bidder's Edge, Inc.*, 100 F.Supp. 2d 1058, 1071 (N.D. Cal. 2000) (damage found when defendant Bidder's Edge's Internet-based auction aggregation site accessed plaintiff eBay's Internet-based auction trading site through an automated program that sent 80,000 to 100,000 information requests per day to plaintiff's site by "diminish[ing] the quality or value of eBay's computer systems [by consuming] at least a portion of [eBay's] bandwidth and server capacity").

PROBLEMS

1. Suppose one of the farmworkers in *Shack* has a sister who comes to stay with her temporarily at the camp on Tedesco's farm while she goes out to look for work. The sister cannot afford to stay at a hotel and cannot obtain her own apartment until she finds a job. As soon as she finds a job, she intends to move into her own apartment. Tedesco asks the sister to leave because she is not working for him and therefore has no right to stay at the camp. When she refuses to leave, Tedesco brings eviction proceedings against her. She defends the suit by arguing that her sister has a right to have visitors at her residence. Should the rule in *State v. Shack* be interpreted to allow Tedesco to evict the sister or to allow her to stay until she finds work and her own apartment? What arguments can you make on both sides? How should the court rule?

2. A tenant in a three-unit apartment building allows his girlfriend to move into the apartment with him. The landlord, who occupies one of the three apartments, objects that she rented to him alone and not to his girlfriend and asks him to have the girlfriend leave. After he refuses, the landlord sues to evict him. He argues that, like all other tenants, he has the right to receive visitors and that this right encompasses the right to choose to have family members or intimate associates stay with him at his home. What arguments can you make on both sides of this question? What rule of law would you promulgate if you were the judge?

3. Were *Desnick* and *Food Lion* decided correctly?

    a. *Consent.* Should fraudulently obtained consent be a defense to a trespass claim as *Desnick* held or should such consent be ineffective as a defense to a trespass claim as *Shiffman* held? Was the Fourth Circuit in *Food Lion* correct to find a trespass when the reporters exceeded the scope of the invitation by secretly videotaping or was *Desnick* correct to find no trespass based on the secret videotaping?

   b. *Public policy.* Should trespasses by investigative journalists be privileged because they further a strong public policy of protecting consumers from harmful products and services?

   c. *Punitive damages.* If a trespass can be shown either because entry is obtained by fraud or because secret videotaping exceeds the scope of the permission to enter, should punitive damages be available for trespass to deter investigative journalists from entering property on false pretenses and thus obtaining embarrassing information they can broadcast to the world? Consider that in *Jacque v. Steenberg Homes, Inc.,* 563 N.W.2d 154 (Wis. 1997), the court approved $100,000 in punitive damages awarded on top of $1 in nominal damages for an intentional trespass that occurred when defendant moved a mobile home across plaintiffs' property knowing it did not have their permission to do so. The court explained that "a right is hollow if the legal system provides insufficient means to protect it," *id.* at 160, and that the $1 in nominal damages and a $30 fine were certainly insufficient to "restrain [the defendant] from similar conduct in the future." Punitive damages are generally to punish and deter "outrageous" or "egregious" conduct, including conduct that displays willful or reckless disregard of the rights of others. *Olds v. Appleby,* 537 N.W.2d 147 (Wis. Ct. App. 1995). Does intentional trespass rise to that level? Did the conduct in *Desnick* and *Food Lion* rise to that level? If the actual damages are only $1, is a $100,000 punitive award excessive in relation to the harm?

4. Ryan Parry, a reporter for the Daily Mirror, obtained a job as a footman to the royal family in Great Britain. He used his own name but a fake résumé. Parry worked in Buckingham Palace for about eight weeks and then published stories about the day-to-day lives of the members of the royal family. The newspaper justified the intrusion by invoking national security (what if Parry had been a terrorist?), and Buckingham Palace did order an in-depth review of its security arrangements. After the incident, Queen Elizabeth II sued the Daily Mirror, which then agreed to stop publishing further articles about Parry's experiences. *See Lizette Alvarez, Palace Snoop Reveals All, Down to (Gasp!) Tupperware,* N.Y. Times, Nov. 27, 2003, at A4. Did Parry or the Daily Mirror commit a trespass?

§2.1.2 RIGHT of REASONABLE ACCESS to PROPERTY OPEN to the PUBLIC

USTON v. RESORTS INTERNATIONAL HOTEL, INC.
445 A.2d 370 (N.J. 1982)

MORRIS PASHMAN, J.

Since January 30, 1979, appellant Resorts International Hotel, Inc. (Resorts) has excluded respondent, Kenneth Uston, from the blackjack tables in its casino because Uston's strategy increases his chances of winning money. Uston concedes that his strategy of card counting can tilt the odds in his favor under the current blackjack rules promulgated by the Casino Control Commission (Commission). However, Uston contends that Resorts has no common law or statutory right to exclude him because of his strategy for playing blackjack. . . .

Kenneth Uston is a renowned teacher and practitioner of a complex strategy for playing blackjack known as card counting. Card counters keep track of the playing cards as they are dealt and adjust their betting patterns when the odds are in their favor. When used over a period of time, this method allegedly ensures a profitable encounter with the casino. . . .

The right of an amusement place owner to exclude unwanted patrons and the patron's competing right of reasonable access both have deep roots in the common law. In this century, however, courts have disregarded the right of reasonable access in the common law of some jurisdictions at the time the *Civil War Amendments* and *Civil Rights Act of 1866* were passed.

As Justice Goldberg noted in his concurrence in *Bell v. Maryland,* 378 U.S. 226 (1964):

> Underlying the congressional discussions and at the heart of the Fourteenth Amendment's guarantee of equal protection, was the assumption that the State by statute or by "the good old common law" was obligated to guarantee all citizens access to places of public accommodation. [378 U.S. at 296, Goldberg, J., concurring.]

See, e.g., Ferguson v. Gies, 46 N.W. 718 (Mich. 1890) (after passage of the Fourteenth Amendment, both the civil rights statutes and the common law provided grounds for a non-white plaintiff to recover damages from a restaurant owner's refusal to serve him, because the common law as it existed before passage of the civil rights laws "gave to the white man a remedy against any unjust discrimination to the citizen in all public places"); *Donnell v. State,* 48 Miss. 661 (1873) (state's common law includes a right of reasonable access to all public places).

The current majority American rule has for many years disregarded the right of reasonable access,[4] granting to proprietors of amusement places an absolute right arbitrarily to eject or exclude any person consistent with state and federal civil rights laws.

At one time, an absolute right of exclusion prevailed in this state, though more for reasons of deference to the noted English precedent of *Wood v. Leadbitter,* 153 Eng. Rep. 351 (Ex. 1845), than for reasons of policy. In *Shubert v. Nixon Amusement Co.,* 83 A. 369 (N.J. Sup. Ct. 1912), the former Supreme Court dismissed a suit for damages resulting from plaintiff's ejection from defendants' theater. Noting that plaintiff made no allegation of exclusion on the basis of race, color or previous condition of servitude, the Court concluded:

> In view of the substantially uniform approval of, and reliance on, the decision in *Wood v. Leadbitter* in our state adjudications, it must fairly be considered to be adopted as part of our jurisprudence, and whatever views may be entertained as to the natural justice or injustice of ejecting a theater patron without reason after he has paid for his ticket and taken his seat, we feel constrained to follow that decision as the settled law. 83 A. at 371.

It hardly bears mention that our common law has evolved in the intervening 70 years. In fact, *Leadbitter* itself was disapproved three years after the *Shubert* decision by *Hurst v. Picture Theatres Limited,* 1 K.B. 1 (1914). Of far greater importance, the decisions of this Court have recognized that "the more private property is devoted to public

---

4. One who enters property with the permission of the owner or possessor is called a *licensee* and has a property interest called a *license*. If the owner revokes the license, the non-owner must leave the land within a reasonable time; failure to do so will constitute a trespass.

use, the more it must accommodate the rights which inhere in individual members of the general public who use that property." *State v. Schmid,* 423 A.2d 615, 629 (N.J. 1980).

State v. Schmid involved the constitutional right to distribute literature on a private university campus. The Court's approach in that case balanced individual rights against property rights. It is therefore analogous to a description of the common law right of exclusion. Balancing the university's interest in controlling its property against plaintiff's interest in access to that property to express his views, the Court clearly refused to protect unreasonable exclusions. Justice Handler noted that

> Regulations . . . devoid of reasonable standards designed to protect both the legitimate interests of the University as an institution of higher education and the individual exercise of expressional freedom cannot constitutionally be invoked to prohibit the otherwise noninjurious and reasonable exercise of [First Amendment] freedoms. *Id.* at 632.

In *State v. Shack,* 277 A.2d 369 (N.J. 1971), the Court held that although an employer of migrant farmworkers "may reasonably require" those visiting his employees to identify themselves, "the employer may not deny the worker his privacy or interfere with his opportunity to live with dignity and to enjoy associations customary among our citizens." The Court reversed the trespass convictions of an attorney and a social services worker who had entered the property to assist farmworkers there.

Schmid recognizes implicitly that when property owners open their premises to the general public in the pursuit of their own property interests, they have no right to exclude people unreasonably. On the contrary, they have a duty not to act in an arbitrary or discriminatory manner toward persons who come on their premises. That duty applies not only to common carriers, innkeepers, owners of gasoline service stations, or to private hospitals, but to all property owners who open their premises to the public. Property owners have no legitimate interest in unreasonably excluding particular members of the public when they open their premises for public use.

No party in this appeal questions the right of property owners to exclude from their premises those whose actions "disrupt the regular and essential operations of the [premises]," or threaten the security of the premises and its occupants. In some circumstances, proprietors have a duty to remove disorderly or otherwise dangerous persons from the premises. These common law principles enable the casino to bar from its entire facility, for instance, the disorderly, the intoxicated, and the repetitive petty offender.

Whether a decision to exclude is reasonable must be determined from the facts of each case. Respondent Uston does not threaten the security of any casino occupant. Nor has he disrupted the functioning of any casino operations. Absent a valid contrary rule by the Commission, Uston possesses the usual right of reasonable access to Resorts International's blackjack tables.

SPIRIT-MURDERING THE MESSENGER: THE DISCOURSE OF FINGERPOINTING AS THE LAW'S RESPONSE TO RACISM
PATRICIA J. WILLIAMS

42 U. Miami L. Rev. 127, 127-129 (1987)

Buzzers are big in New York City. Favored particularly by smaller stores and boutiques, merchants throughout the city have installed them as screening devices to reduce the incidence of robbery. When the buzzer sounds, if the face at the door looks "desirable," the door is unlocked. If the face is that of an "undesirable," the door stays locked. Predictably, the issue of undesirability has revealed itself to be primarily a racial determination. Although the buzzer system was controversial at first, even civil rights organizations have backed down in the face of arguments that the system is a "necessary evil," that it is a "mere inconvenience" compared to the risks of being murdered, that discrimination is not as bad as assault, and that in any event, it is not *all* blacks who are barred, just "17-year-old black males wearing running shoes and hooded sweatshirts."

Two Saturdays before Christmas, I saw a sweater that I wanted to purchase for my mother. I pressed my brown face to the store window and my finger to the buzzer, seeking admittance. A narrow-eyed white youth who looked barely seventeen, wearing tennis sneakers and feasting on bubble gum, glared at me, evaluating me for signs that would pit me against the limits of his social understanding. After about five seconds, he mouthed, "We're closed," and blew pink rubber at me. It was one o'clock in the afternoon. There were several white people in the store who appeared to be shopping for things for *their* mothers.

I was enraged. At that moment I literally wanted to break all of the windows in the store and *take* lots of sweaters for my mother. In the flicker of his judgmental grey eyes, that saleschild had reduced my brightly sentimental, joy-to-the-world, pre-Christmas spree to a shambles. He had snuffed my sense of humanitarian catholicity, and there was nothing I could do to snuff his, without simply making a spectacle of myself.

I am still struck by the structure of power that drove me into such a blizzard of rage. There was almost nothing I could do, short of physically intruding upon him, that would humiliate him the way he humiliated me. No words, no gestures, no prejudices of my own would make a bit of difference to him. His refusal to let me into the store was an outward manifestation of his never having let someone like me into the realm of his reality. He had no connection, no compassion, no remorse, no reference to me, and no desire to acknowledge me even at the estranged level of arm's length transactor. He saw me only as one who would take his money and therefore could not conceive that I was there to give him money.

In this weird ontological imbalance, I realized that buying something in that store was like bestowing a gift: the gift of my commerce. In the wake of my outrage, I wanted to take back the gift of my appreciation, which my peering into the window must have appeared to be. I wanted to take it back in the form of unappreciation, disrespect, and defilement. I wanted to work so hard at wishing he could feel what I felt that he would never again mistake my *hatred* for some sort of plaintive wish to be included. I was quite willing to disenfranchise myself in the heat of my need to revoke the flattery of my purchasing power. I was willing to boycott this particular store, random white-owned businesses, and anyone who blew bubble gum in my face again.

My rage was admittedly diffuse, even self-destructive, but it was symmetrical. The perhaps loose-ended but utter propriety of that rage is no doubt lost not just to the young man who barred me, but to those who appreciate my being barred only as an abstract precaution, and who approve of those who would bar, even as they deny that *they* would bar *me*.

The violence of my desire to have burst into that store is probably quite apparent to the reader. I wonder if the violence and the exclusionary hatred are equally apparent in the repeated public urging that blacks put themselves in the shoes of white store owners, and that, in effect, blacks look into the mirror of frightened white faces to the reality of their undesirability; and that then blacks would "just as surely conclude that [they] would not let [themselves] in under similar circumstances."

THE INTELLIGENT BAYESIAN
WALTER E. WILLIAMS
The New Republic, Nov. 10, 1986, at 18

...Men are not gods. Therefore, men face challenges gods would not have to endure—ignorance and uncertainty. To make decisions, we need to have information about the world around us. The information we gather is not only imperfect, it is costly as well. So we learn to economize by guessing, prejudging, and using stereotypes.

Imagine you are challenged to a basketball game and must select five out of 20 people who appear to be equal in every respect except race and sex. There are five black and five white females, five black and five white males. You have no information about their basketball proficiency. There is a million-dollar prize for the contest. How would you choose a team? If you thought basketball skills were randomly distributed by race and sex, you would randomly select. Most people would perceive a strong associative relationship between basketball skills on the one hand, and race and sex on the other. Most would confine their choice to males, and their choice would be dominated by black males.

Can we say such a person is a sexist/racist? An alternative answer is that he is behaving like an intelligent Bayesian (Sir Thomas Bayes, the father of statistics). Inexpensively obtained information about race and sex is a proxy for information that costs more to obtain, namely, basketball proficiency.

There is a large class of human behavior that generally falls into the same testing procedures. Doctors can predict the probability of hypertension by knowing race, and osteoporosis by knowing sex. A white jeweler who does not open his door to young black males cannot be labeled a racist any more than a black taxi driver who refuses to pick up young black males at night. Black females and white females and white males commit holdups, but in this world of imperfect information cab drivers and jewelers play the odds. To ask them to behave differently is to disarm them.

NOTES AND QUESTIONS

1. Five years before *Uston v. Resorts International,* Kenneth Uston had filed an earlier case much like it against a casino in Las Vegas, Nevada. The Ninth Circuit Court of Appeals, applying Nevada law, upheld the casino's right to exclude him, arguing that "the relationship [between the casino and Uston] was not one of innkeeper and patron, but rather one of casino owner and prospective gambler. The policies upon which the innkeeper's special common law duties rested are not present in such a relationship." *Uston v. Airport Casino, Inc.,* 564 F.2d 1216, 1217 (9th Cir. 1977).

2. The traditional common law rule imposes a duty on innkeepers and common carriers (planes, trains, buses) to serve members of the public without discrimination unless they have a good reason not to provide services to a particular individual. This obligation grants the public a right of reasonable access to these businesses. *Uston* changed the common law rule by extending that right of reasonable access to all

businesses open to the public. Most states, however, retain the traditional absolute right to exclude without cause and limit the duty to serve the public (the right of reasonable access) to innkeepers and common carriers.

The leading case promulgating the absolute right to exclude is *Madden v. Queens County Jockey Club, Inc.*, 72 N.E.2d 697 (N.Y. 1947). In that case, the defendant barred the plaintiff "Coley" Madden from attending races at its racetrack on the mistaken belief that he was "Owney" Madden, a well-known bookmaker. Plaintiff sued the race-track, claiming that he had a right "as a citizen and a taxpayer—upon paying the required admission price—to enter the race course and patronize the pari-mutuel betting there conducted." *Id.* at 698. Rather than admit that it made a mistake and allow him to patronize the racetrack, the defendant sought to establish an "unlimited power of exclusion" for any reason or even no reason. The court concluded that the common law right of reasonable access applied only to innkeepers and common carriers, not to places of amusement and resort, which enjoyed "an absolute power to serve whom they pleased." *Id.* That right to exclude remained, the court argued, until changed by the legislature. The only statutory limits on the right to exclude enacted by the New York legislature were found in the state *Civil Rights Law* prohibiting discrimination on account of race, creed, color, or national origin. Because Coley Madden was not excluded for any of these reasons—indeed, he seems to have been excluded simply to make a point about the racetrack's prerogatives—then he had no right of access, and the defendant need not explain why it excluded him.

3. The New Jersey Supreme Court in *Uston* gave a series of policy arguments for extending the right of access to all businesses open to the public rather than limiting this obligation to innkeepers and common carriers. What policies could justify the majority rule, imposing a duty to serve the public on innkeepers and common carriers but granting most businesses a broad right to exclude? *Garafine v. Monmouth Park Jockey Club*, 148 A.2d 1, 2-3 (N.J. 1959), the case overruled by *Uston*, noted that "[t]here was a time in English history when the common law recognized in many callings the duty to serve the public without discrimination. . . . With the passing of time and the changing of conditions, the common law confined this duty to exceptional callings where the needs of the public urgently called for its continuance."

Three justifications have traditionally been offered for the special obligations on innkeepers and common carriers. First, inns and common carriers were more likely to be monopolies than other businesses so denial of service was tantamount to denying the ability to travel or to find a place to sleep away from home. Second, these businesses provided necessities whose denial would place individuals in risk from the elements or bandits on the highway. Third, innkeepers and common carriers hold themselves out as ready to serve the public and the public relies on this representation. Joseph William Singer, *No Right to Exclude: Public Accommodations and Private Property*, 90 Nw. U. L. Rev. 1283, 1305-1331 (1996). Do these rationales distinguish innkeepers and common carriers from other businesses, such as retail stores?

In deciding to keep the traditional rule granting owners of most businesses the absolute right to exclude, the Arizona Court of Appeals argued in *Nation v. Apache Greyhound Park, Inc.*, 579 P.2d 580, 582 (Ariz. Ct. App. 1978), that "[t]he race track proprietor must be able to control admission to its facilities without risk of a lawsuit and the necessity of proving that every person excluded would actually engage in some unlawful activity." In *Brooks v. Chicago Downs Association, Inc.*, 791 F.2d 512, 517, 518-519 (7th Cir. 1986), the Seventh Circuit Court of Appeals explained the basis for the doctrine as follows:

[P]roprietors of amusement facilities, whose very survival depends on bringing the public into their place of amusement, are reasonable people who usually do not exclude their customers unless they have a reason to do so. What the proprietor of a race track does not want to have to do is *prove* or *explain* that his reason for exclusion is a *just* reason. He doesn't want to be liable to [an excluded patron] solely because he mistakenly believed he was a mobster. The proprietor wants to be able to keep someone off his private property even if they only *look like* a mobster. As long as the proprietor is not excluding the mobster look-alike because of his national origin (or because of race, color, creed, or sex), then the common law, and the law of Illinois, allows him to do just that.

. . . As a policy matter, it is arguably unfair to allow a place of amusement to exclude for any reason or no reason, and to be free of accountability, except in cases of obvious discrimination. In this case, the general public is not only invited but, through advertising, is encouraged to come to the race track and wager on the races' outcome. But the common law allows the race track to exclude patrons, no matter if they come from near or far, or in reasonable reliance on representations of accessibility. We may ultimately believe that market forces would preclude any outrageous excesses — such as excluding anyone who has blond hair, or (like the plaintiffs) who is from Pennsylvania, or (even more outrageous) who has $250,000 to spend in one day of betting. But the premise of the consumer protection laws that the New Jersey Supreme Court alluded to in *Uston* and *Marzocca* [*v. Ferone,* 461 A.2d 1133 (N.J. 1983)] recognizes that the reality of an imperfect market allows numerous consumer depredations. Excluding a patron simply because he is named Adam Smith arguably offends the very precepts of equality and fair dealing expressed in everything from the antitrust statutes to the Illinois Consumer Fraud and Deceptive Business Practices Act. . . .

But the market here is not so demonstrably imperfect that there is a monopoly or any allegation of consumer fraud. Consequently, there is no such explicit legislative directive in the context of patrons attending horse races in Illinois — so the common law rule, relic though it may be[1] still controls.

Does this argument distinguish innkeepers and common carriers from other businesses? If not, can you imagine a better distinction? If there is no reasonable distinction between those businesses with a duty to serve the public and those that have no such duty, what should the rule be? Should businesses have a duty to serve the public without unjust discrimination or should they have an absolute right to exclude?

PROBLEMS

1. *Homeless persons.* A large department store is located in downtown Boston. It is connected to the subway and thus forms a path road for visitors going from home to work. During the winter months, a dozen homeless persons begin spending time inside the store. The store has eight floors and can accommodate hundreds of customers. The homeless persons enter the store to escape the bitter cold, snow, and ice on the streets of the city. Some customers complain to the management that they are uncomfortable entering the store to shop because of the presence of the homeless people. The cus-

---

1. As the New Jersey Supreme Court noted in *Uston*, the rise of the American common law right to exclude without cause alarmingly corresponds to the fall of the old segregation laws. . . .

tomers' discomfort comes from the disheveled appearance of the homeless persons and the worry that some of them are afflicted with mental illness. No customers have been accosted or even approached by a homeless person while at the store. Nonetheless, the store manager believes that the presence of homeless people in the store has caused some potential customers to avoid shopping there. To remedy this problem, the management develops a policy that any person who appears to be homeless will be asked to leave the store. One such excluded person sues the store, arguing that it has a duty to serve the public and can exclude homeless persons only for good cause.

a. *Right of access.* Assume that the common law in Massachusetts imposes obligations on innkeepers and common carriers to serve the public without discrimination, but has not extended that obligation to all businesses open to the public. Plaintiffs argue that the Massachusetts court should adopt the rule of law promulgated by the Supreme Court of New Jersey in *Uston v. Resorts International,* and extend the right of reasonable access to all businesses open to the public. What is plaintiffs' argument to create a right of reasonable access to all property open to the public? What is defendant store's argument to retain the absolute right to exclude? Which rule of law should the court adopt?

b. *Reasonableness of exclusion.* Plaintiffs further argue that they have engaged in no activity that would justify their exclusion from the store. If Massachusetts decides to adopt the rule of law in *Uston* granting plaintiffs a right of reasonable access, was defendant's exclusion of plaintiffs reasonable? How should the case be resolved? Do you need more facts to answer this question? What test should be adopted to define what constitutes a "reasonable" exclusion?

2. *Teenagers.* A suburban mall has turned into a hangout for teenagers. The customers begin to complain because some of the teenagers congregate near eating areas, video arcades, and music stores, occasionally blocking passage through the mall. Many dress in unusual ways and wear what other customers see as bizarre haircuts. Several times, certain teenagers blocked the entrance to shops and acted in a manner the customers considered obnoxious. Complaining that they are scared by the teenagers, some customers are avoiding the shopping mall or certain areas within it. The mall manager institutes an antiloitering policy, asking teenagers to leave if they are not in the mall to shop. One of the teenagers brings a lawsuit against the owner of the mall for a declaratory judgment that the owner has no right to exclude teenagers without a showing that they are disruptive, and that dressing in punk outfits and haircuts is not a sufficient reason to exclude them, regardless of the reaction of other patrons.

Should the mall owner have the right to exclude the teenagers? What arguments can you make for the mall owner? For the teenagers? What rule of law should the court promulgate?

3. A retail clothing store routinely has its employees follow African American customers around the store. One such customer is stopped and loudly accused of stealing the shirt he is wearing. He had purchased the shirt in the store several days earlier and, by some miracle, even has the receipt in his pocket to prove it. He sues the store, claiming that he was subjected to discriminatory surveillance because of his race and that the store's practice of giving greater scrutiny to African American customers than to other customers denies his right of reasonable access to a place of public

accommodation. The store defends the claim by noting that it is not a public accommodation, because it is neither a common carrier nor an innkeeper, and that even if it is a common carrier, it did not deny him reasonable access to the store.

    a. Are retail stores places of public accommodation with the duty to serve the public?

    b. If they are subject to this duty, is racially discriminatory surveillance a violation of the right of reasonable access under the common law of property?

§2.2 Public Accommodations Statutes and Antidiscrimination Policy

§2.2.1 RACE, SEX, AND SEXUAL ORIENTATION DISCRIMINATION

§2.2.1.1 Federal Law

CIVIL RIGHTS ACT OF 1964, TITLE II

42 U.S.C. §§2000a to 2000a-6

§2000a. Prohibition Against Discrimination or Segregation in Places of Public Accommodation

    (a) *Equal access.* All persons shall be entitled to the full and equal enjoyment of the goods, services, facilities, privileges, advantages, and accommodations of any place of public accommodation, as defined in this section, without discrimination or segregation on the ground of race, color, religion, or national origin.

    (b) . . . Each of the following establishments which serves the public is a place of public accommodation within the meaning of this subchapter if its operations affect commerce, or if discrimination or segregation by it is supported by State action:

    (1) any inn, hotel, motel, or other establishment which provides lodging to transient guests, other than an establishment located within a building which contains not more than five rooms for rent or hire and which is actually occupied by the proprietor of such establishment as his residence;

    (2) any restaurant, cafeteria, lunchroom, lunch counter, soda fountain, or other facility principally engaged in selling food for consumption on the premises, including, but not limited to, any such facility located on the premises of any retail establishment; or any gasoline station;

    (3) any motion picture house, theater, concert hall, sports arena, stadium or other place of exhibition or entertainment; and

    (4) any establishment (A)(i) which is physically located within the premises of any establishment otherwise covered by this subsection, or (ii) within the premises of which is physically located any such covered establishment, and (B) which holds itself out as serving patrons of such covered establishments. . . .

    (e) *Private establishments.* The provisions of this subchapter shall not apply to a private club or other establishment not in fact open to the public, except to the extent that the facilities of such establishment are made available to the customers or patrons of an establishment within the scope of subsection (b) of this section.

Diane Nash (second from left), a leader of the movement to desegrate the lunch counters of Nashville's department stores, sits at an integrated lunch counter. (Reprinted by permission of the Tennessean.)

§2000a-6.   [A]SSERTION of RIGHTS BASED on OTHER FEDERAL or STATE LAWS and PURSUIT of REMEDIES for ENFORCEMENT of SUCH RIGHTS

(b) . . . [N]othing in this subchapter shall preclude any individual or any State or local agency from asserting any right based on any other Federal or State law not inconsistent with this subchapter, including any statute or ordinance requiring non-discrimination in public establishments or accommodations, or from pursuing any remedy, civil or criminal, which may be available for the vindication or enforcement of such right.

CIVIL RIGHTS ACT OF 1866

42 U.S.C. §§1981-1982

§1981.   *Equal Rights Under the Law*

(a) *Statement of Equal Rights*

All persons within the jurisdiction of the United States shall have the same right in every State and Territory to make and enforce contracts, to sue, be parties, give evidence, and to the full and equal benefit of all laws and proceedings for the security of persons and property as is enjoyed by white citizens, and shall be subject to like punishment, pains, penalties, taxes, licenses, and exactions of every kind, and to no other.

(b) *"Make and Enforce Contracts" Defined*

For purposes of this section, the term "make and enforce contracts" includes the making, performance, modification, and termination of contracts, and the enjoyment of all benefits, privileges, terms, and conditions of the contractual relationship.

(c) *Protection Against Impairment*

The rights protected by this section are protected against impairment by nongovernmental discrimination and impairment under color of State law.

§1982. Property Rights of Citizens

All citizens of the United States shall have the same right, in every State and Territory, as is enjoyed by white citizens thereof to inherit, purchase, lease, sell, hold, and convey real and personal property.

NOTES AND QUESTIONS

1. *Common carriers.* Common carriers engaged in interstate commerce are regulated by the *Interstate Commerce Act* and are prohibited from all forms of unreasonable discrimination, not just discrimination based on race, religion, and national origin. 49 U.S.C. §§10741(b), 11101(a).

2. *The Civil Rights Act of 1964.* The public accommodations provisions of title II of the *Civil Rights Act of 1964*, 42 U.S.C. §§2000a to 2000a-6, directly addressed the problem of racial discrimination in motels, restaurants, lunch counters in department stores, gas stations, and theaters. It was intended to rectify some aspects of the enormous problem of racial segregation in the United States and was passed after a long period of struggle that included sit-ins, demonstrations, and litigation. Passage of the act was followed by widespread resistance, including refusals by some public officials to enforce the law. Note that the statute only regulates discrimination on the basis of race, color, religion, and national origin. It does not prohibit discrimination on the basis of sex. Nor does any other general federal statute prohibit sex discrimination in public accommodations.

Section 2000a-3(c) requires plaintiffs to refer their complaint to a state agency for resolution before proceeding in federal court. The state must have a chance to resolve the dispute if it has a law on the subject. If a claim is later brought in federal court under the act, the plaintiff is entitled only to declaratory and injunctive relief. There is no provision for damages. An injured party may seek a court order requiring the defendant to stop discriminating in access to public accommodations covered by the act but may not seek damages. 42 U.S.C. §2000a-3(a). The plaintiff may be able to recover attorney's fees from the defendant if the plaintiff prevails. §2000a-3(b).

3. *The Civil Rights Act of 1866.* Unlike the 1964 act, the *Civil Rights Act of 1866*, 42 U.S.C. §§1981 & 1982, regulates race discrimination only. Also, unlike the 1964 public accommodations law, damages are available for violations of the *Civil Right Act of 1866*. Although §1981 was already in effect at the time the *Civil Rights Act of 1964* was passed, it had not yet been interpreted by the courts to regulate private conduct, such as the refusal by a restaurant owner to serve a patron. Rather, it was thought in 1964 that §1981 merely prohibited state legislatures from passing statutes that deprived black citizens of the capacity to enter binding contracts. In important opinions in 1968 and 1976, the Supreme Court held that the *Civil Rights Act of 1866* applied to private conduct as well

as to legislation passed by state legislatures. *Jones v. Alfred Mayer Co.*, 392 U.S. 409 (1968) (holding that §1982 prohibits discrimination in the market for selling or leasing real property); *Runyon v. McCrary*, 427 U.S. 160 (1976) (holding that §1981 prohibits commercially operated, nonreligious schools from excluding qualified children solely on the basis of race). *See also Patterson v. McLean Credit Union*, 491 U.S. 164 (1989) (reaffirming the applicability of the *Civil Rights Act of 1866* to private conduct). The *Civil Rights Act of 1991*, Pub. L. No. 102-166, Title I, §101, Nov. 21, 1991, 105 Stat. 1071, amended §1981 to affirm both that it reaches private conduct and that it regulates the terms and conditions of contracts and not just the "right to make and enforce" contracts. No such amendment was approved for §1982.

4. *Retail stores.* Is the list of covered establishments in the 1964 public accommodations law exclusive or merely illustrative? Compare *Sellers v. Philip's Barber Shop*, 217 A.2d 121 (N.J. 1966) (interpreting a state public accommodations statute providing that public accommodations "shall include" a long list of business establishments as covering barber shops even though they were not listed) with *Rhone v. Loomis*, 77 N.W. 31 (Minn. 1898) (holding that a statute prohibiting discrimination in inns, taverns, restaurants, and places of "refreshment" did not prohibit a "saloon" from excluding an African American customer).

Some courts have recently held that the *Civil Rights Act of 1866* regulates establishments that are not listed in the 1964 act such as retail stores and service establishments and that such stores may be liable for damages if they deny the right to contract under §1981 or the right to purchase property under §1982. *See Washington v. Duty Free Shoppers, Ltd.*, 710 F. Supp. 1288 (N.D. Cal. 1988) (§1981 prohibits retail store from refusing to serve customers because of race); *Perry v. Command Performance*, 913 F.2d 99 (3d Cir. 1990) (§1981 may have been violated when a salon refused to cut the hair of an African American woman); *Watson v. Fraternal Order of Eagles*, 915 F.2d 235, 240 (6th Cir. 1990) (noting that a "department store . . . is not directly covered by Title II but would be amenable to suit under §1981").

The Supreme Court has never addressed the question of whether the *Civil Rights Act of 1866* regulates the conduct of public accommodations such as restaurants, innkeepers, or retail stores. Although the refusal to serve a patron because of that person's race arguably comes within the language of both §1981 and §1982, it is important to know that a public accommodations law, much like the 1964 act, was passed in 1875. After doubts were expressed about the constitutionality of the *Civil Rights Act of 1866*, it was re-passed in 1870 after passage of the fourteenth amendment in 1868 with its prohibition against state deprivations of "equal protection of the laws." U.S. Const. art. XIV. Five years later, Congress passed the *Public Accommodations Act of 1875*, 18 Stat. 335, ch. 114 (1875). That law was struck down as unconstitutional by the Supreme Court in 1883 in *The Civil Rights Cases*, 109 U.S. 3 (1883), on the ground that the fourteenth amendment authorized Congress to regulate state action but not private action by owners of private property, such as inns and restaurants. If the *Civil Rights Act of 1866* regulates the conduct of public accommodations, wouldn't this have made the 1875 statute superfluous and unnecessary? If §1981 or §1982 regulate public accommodations, why did Congress pass the 1875 statute?

To get around the holding of *The Civil Rights Cases* that the fourteenth amendment authorizes regulation of state action but not private action, Congress passed the *Civil Rights Act of 1964* pursuant to the commerce clause, which authorizes Congress to regulate "interstate commerce." *Heart of Atlanta Motel*, 379 U.S. 241 (1964) and *Katzenbach v. McClung*, 379 U.S. 294 (1964) (both upholding the act as a valid exercise of Congress's power to regulate interstate commerce). Remember that the *Civil Rights Act of 1866* was not interpreted to apply to private conduct until 1968. But *what* private conduct is regulated by §§1981 and 1982? Can you think of a reason §§1981 and 1982 should be interpreted to regulate public accommodations when Congress passed a more specific statute regulating them in 1964 — a statute that clearly omits any provision for damages?

5. *Racially discriminatory surveillance.* The courts appear to agree that the "right to make contracts" under §1981 includes the right to enter a store or other service provider. *Causey v. Sewell Cadillac-Chevrolet, Inc.,* 394 F.3d 285 (5th Cir. 2004); *Christian v. Wal-Mart Stores, Inc.,* 252 F.3d 862 (6th Cir. 2001); *Ackaa v. Tommy Hilfiger,* 1998 WL 136522 (E.D. Pa. 1998). Can you think of a way to interpret the language or purpose of §1981 in a way that would not view it as creating an obligation to allow individuals to enter retail stores to purchase goods or services? Assuming §1981 does require stores to allow individuals to enter without regard to race, does §1981 prohibit stores from discriminatorily following African American, Latino, or American Indian patrons around the store, searching them, and subjecting them to insults?

A minority of courts hold that such conduct violates the right to contract under §1981 and/or the right to purchase personal property under §1982. *Chapman v. Higbee,* 319 F.3d 825 (6th Cir. 2003) (equal benefits clause in §1981 gives right to equal treatment in seeking contract); *Phillip v. University of Rochester,* 316 F.3d 291 (2d Cir. 2003) (equal benefits clause of §1981 applies to private university whose security guards detained African American students but not their white friends in library lobby, calling police who arrested them and kept them detained overnight); *McCaleb v. Pizza Hut of America, Inc.,* 28 F. Supp. 2d 1043 (N.D. Ill. 1998) (family denied "full benefits" of the contract when denied utensils and harassed and threatened while at restaurant); *Nwakpuda v. Falley's, Inc.,* 14 F. Supp. 2d 1213 (D. Kan. 1998) (§1981 claim for store patron who was wrongfully detained because he was thought to be individual who had previously robbed the store); *Turner v. Wong,* 832 A.2d 340 (N.J. Super. Ct. App. Div. 2003). However, most courts have interpreted the "right to make contracts" extremely narrowly, holding that this right is denied *only* when a patron is "actually prevented, and not merely deterred, from making a purchase or receiving service after attempting to do so." *Ackerman v. Food-4-Less,* 1998 WL 316084 at *2 (E.D. Pa. 1988). *Accord, Hampton v. Dillard Dept. Stores, Inc.,* 247 F.3d 1091 (10th Cir. 2001). These courts have denied relief when a patron was treated disrespectfully or refused assistance, *Arguello v. Conoco, Inc.,* 330 F.3d 355 (5th Cir. 2003)(no §1981 claim when clerk shouted obscenities and made racially derogatory remarks at Latino customer after she completed her purchase); *Wesley v. Don Stein Buick, Inc.,* 42 F.Supp. 2d 1192 (D. Kan. 1999); subjected to discriminatory surveillance, searches or detention, *Morris v. Office Max, Inc.,* 89 F.3d 411 (7th Cir. 1996); removed from a store for discriminatory reasons after making a purchase, *Flowers v. TJX Cos.,* 1994 WL 382515 (N.D.N.Y. 1994), or put under surveillance and accused of shoplifting after purchasing items and leaving the store, *Garrett v. Tandy Corp.,* 295 F.3d 94 (1st Cir. 2002). Which interpretation of §1981 is correct?

6. *Private clubs.* In *Watson v. Fraternal Order of Eagles,* 915 F.2d 235 (6th Cir. 1990), a private club was held to have violated §1981 when it refused to serve drinks to African American guests at a party held at the club. Because defendant was clearly a private club under 42 U.S.C. §2000a(e), its actions were not covered by the 1964 act. Nonetheless, Judge Merritt held that, although the defendant was immune from liability under that act, the plaintiff could bring an independent claim for relief under §1981. He noted that later, more specific statutes generally limit the interpretation of earlier, more general

ones. Nonetheless, the earlier, broader statute continues in force if the legislature that passed the later act intended the general act to retain independent force.

However, in *Cornelius v. Benevolent Protective Order of the Elks*, 382 F. Supp. 1182 (D. Conn. 1974), Judge Blumenfeld held that an irrevocable conflict between a statute that authorizes conduct and one that prohibits it must be adjudicated by applying the later act. Thus §1981 could not be applied to a private club. Judge Blumenfeld argued that "the provisions of one statute which specifically focus on a particular problem will always, in the absence of express contrary legislative intent, be held to prevail over provisions of a different statute more general in its coverage." *Id.* at 1201. Moreover, when Congress passed the 1964 act, it believed it was enacting the first federal legislation prohibiting private discrimination in public accommodations. "Prior to *Jones v. Mayer*, 392 U.S. 409 (1968), sections 1981 and 1982 were thought to apply only to 'state action.' . . . Thus, the absence of express language in the 1964 Act limiting the 1866 Act is hardly evidence of an intention not to have that effect. . . ." *Id. Accord, Durham v. Red Lake Fishing and Hunting Club, Inc.*, 666 F. Supp. 954 (W.D. Tex. 1987).

7. *Interpreting statutes.* In interpreting a state public accommodations law, Chief Justice Ellen Peters of the Connecticut Supreme Court noted that the language of a statute is determinative if it is "plain and unambiguous" because it "expresses the intention of the legislature." *Quinnipiac Council, Boy Scouts of America, Inc. v. Commission on Human Rights and Opportunities*, 528 A.2d 352, 356-357 (Conn. 1987). However, "[w]hen we are faced with ambiguity in a statute . . . we turn for interpretive guidance to its legislative history, the circumstances surrounding its enactment, and the purpose the statute is to serve." *Id.*

In interpreting the meaning of statutes, several basic rules are followed:

a.   Start with the *language* of the statute. Lawyers argue about the meaning of statutes by focusing on the specific words of the statute.

b.   Get guidance from the *legislative history.* One clearly relevant type of legislative history is the record of prior versions of the bill that was passed into law. If particular words in prior versions of a bill were omitted from enacted legislation, this may mean that the legislature meant to exclude coverage for the omitted terms. On the other hand, it may mean that the language was deemed to be redundant. A second type of legislative history is committee reports issued in conjunction with the legislation that may explain the purpose of the statute or its intended scope. Similarly, debate on the floor of the legislature may be reported and may reveal the intent of the legislature. Legislative history in state legislatures is often sparse to nonexistent, while it may be voluminous (although often contradictory) in federal legislation. Although Justice Scalia has argued against using legislative history to interpret statutes, limiting his attention to the statutory language and structure, many judges find such information relevant and helpful.

c.   Determine the *intent of the legislature* both by reference to the language used in the statute and by reference to the *policies* underlying the statute and the *purposes* the legislation was intended to achieve. Language in the statute itself or in the legislative history can help determine the legislative purpose. Sometimes, however, legislative intent can be discerned only by conjecture.

d.   Use *canons of statutory interpretation.* Courts use a variety of principles to construe the meaning of ambiguous statutes. For example, courts often state that remedial statutes should be liberally construed to effectuate their purposes. On the other hand, they also note that unambiguous language must be given effect even if it appears to conflict with the purpose of the law. Note that canons of statutory interpretation are often contradictory; there is almost always a canon to which each side in the dispute can appeal. The following reading is a famous illustration of this fact by the legal realist Karl Llewellyn.

THE COMMON LAW TRADITION: DECIDING APPEALS
KARL LLEWELLYN
521-535 (1960)

When it comes to presenting a proposed statutory construction in court, there is an accepted conventional vocabulary. As in argument over points of case-law, the accepted convention still, unhappily, requires discussion as if only one single correct meaning could exist. Hence there are two opposing canons on almost every point. An arranged selection is appended. Every lawyer must be familiar with them all: they are still needed tools of argument. At least as early as Fortescue the general picture was clear, on this, to any eye which would see.

Plainly, to make any canon take hold in a particular instance, the construction contended for must be sold, essentially, by means other than the use of the canon: The good sense of the situation and a *simple* construction of the available language to achieve that sense, *by tenable means, out of the statutory language.*

CANONS OF CONSTRUCTION

THRUST	BUT	PARRY
1. A statute cannot go beyond its text.		1. To effect its purpose a statute may be implemented beyond its text.
2. Statutes in derogation of the common law will not be extended by construction.		2. Such acts will be liberally construed if their nature is remedial.
3. Statutes are to be read in the light of the common law and a statute affirming a common law rule is to be construed in accordance with the common law.		3. The common law gives way to a statute which is inconsistent with it and when a statute is designed as a re-vision of a whole body of law applicable to a given subject it supersedes the common law....
11. Titles do not control meaning; preambles do not expand scope; section headings do not change language.		11. The title may be consulted as a guide when there is doubt or obscurity in the body; preambles may be consulted to determine rationale, and thus the true construction of terms; section headings may be looked upon as part of the statute itself.
12. If language is plain and unambiguous it must be given effect.		12. Not when literal interpretation would lead to absurd or mischievous consequences or thwart manifest purpose....
15. Words are to be taken in their ordinary meaning unless they		15. Popular words may bear a technical meaning and technical words may

are technical terms or words of art.	have a popular signification and they should be so construed as to agree with evident intention or to make the statute operative.
16. Every word and clause must be given effect.	16. If inadvertently inserted or if repugnant to the rest of the statute, they may be rejected as surplusage....
19. Exceptions not made cannot be read in.	19. The letter is only the "bark." Whatever is within the reason of the law is within the law itself.
20. Expression of one thing excludes another.	20. The language may fairly comprehend many different cases where some only are expressly mentioned by way of example....

PROBLEMS

1. Professor Williams describes the recent practice of locking stores and installing buzzers in New York City. The ostensible goal is to protect the store from armed robbery and other forms of theft and assault. Store owners and managers use the buzzer system to exclude selected members of the public from access to their stores. If a store installs a lock-and-buzzer system and allows entry only to patrons that the management or employees consider "safe," does the store come within the definition of a "place of public accommodation" under §2000a(b), or is it a "private establishment not in fact open to the public" under §2000a(e)?

    a. Are retail stores "places of public accommodation" as defined in §2000a(b)?

    b. If retail stores are generally covered by §2000a(b), do they "serve the public" if they install a buzzer and serve selected customers who show up on their doorsteps or are they "not in fact open to the public" and thus exempt from the statute under §2000a(e)?

    c. Was Professor Williams excluded "on the ground of race"? How could you prove this in court?

In developing arguments for both sides on each question, you should focus on (1) the language or words in the statute to which each side would appeal; (2) the purposes or policies each side would attribute to Congress and how each side's interpretation would further those purposes; and (3) the canons of statutory construction each side could suggest to bolster its case.

2. Assume that the 1964 act is held not to cover retail stores.

    a. Are retail stores exempt from regulation or can an excluded patron obtain relief under §1981 or §1982 of the 1866 act?

    b. If a retail store has its personnel follow African American patrons around the store and does not subject white patrons to the same treatment, does this violate either §1981 or §1982?

3. The 1964 statute exempts private clubs, while the 1866 act says nothing that distinguishes public accommodations from private clubs. Was the 1964 act

intended to immunize private clubs from the duty to serve the public, or did it simply not regulate those clubs, leaving them subject to regulation under the 1866 act? If the 1866 act regulates the behavior of private clubs, is it "inconsistent" with §2000a (the 1964 act)?

§2.2.1.2 State Laws

NEW JERSEY LAW AGAINST DISCRIMINATION

N.J. Stat. §§10:5-1 to 10:5-49

§10:5-3. *Findings, Declarations*

The Legislature finds and declares that practices of discrimination against any of its inhabitants, because of race, creed, color, national origin, ancestry, age, sex, affectional or sexual orientation, marital status, familial status, liability for service in the Armed Forces of the United States, or nationality, are matters of concern to the government of the State, and that such discrimination threatens not only the rights and proper privileges of the inhabitants of the State but menaces the institutions and foundation of a free democratic State. . . .

The Legislature further declares its opposition to such practices of discrimination when directed against any person by reason of the race, creed, color, national origin, ancestry, age, sex, affectional or sexual orientation, marital status, liability for service in the Armed Forces of the United States, or nationality of that person or that person's spouse, partners, members, stockholders, directors, officers, managers, superintendents, agents, employees, business associates, suppliers, or customers, in order that the economic prosperity and general welfare of the inhabitants of the State may be protected and ensured. . . .

. . . The Legislature intends that . . . this act shall be liberally construed in combination with other protections available under the laws of this State.

§10:5-4. *Obtaining Employment, Accommodations and Privileges without Discrimination; Civil Right*

All persons shall have the opportunity to obtain employment, and to obtain all the accommodations, advantages, facilities, and privileges of any place of public accommodation, publicly assisted housing accommodation, and other real property without discrimination because of race, creed, color, national origin, ancestry, age, marital status, affectional or sexual orientation, familial status, or sex, subject only to conditions and limitations applicable alike to all persons. This opportunity is recognized as and declared to be a civil right.

§10:5-5. *Definitions Relative to Discrimination . . .*

l. "A place of public accommodation" shall include[, but not be limited to:][6] any tavern, roadhouse, hotel, motel, trailer camp, summer camp, day camp, or resort

---

6. The bracketed phrase was added in 1966. 1966 N.J. Laws ch. 17 — ED.

camp, whether for entertainment of transient guests or accommodation of those seeking health, recreation or rest; any producer, manufacturer, wholesaler, distributor, retail shop, store, establishment, or concession dealing with goods or services of any kind; any restaurant, eating house, or place where food is sold for consumption on the premises; any place maintained for the sale of ice cream, ice and fruit preparations or their derivatives, soda water or confections, or where any beverages of any kind are retailed for consumption on the premises; any garage, any public conveyance operated on land or water, or in the air, any stations and terminals thereof; any bathhouse, boardwalk, or seashore accommodation; any auditorium, meeting place, or hall; any theatre, motion-picture house, music hall, roof garden, skating rink, swimming pool, amusement and recreation park, fair, bowling alley, gymnasium, shooting gallery, billiard and pool parlor, or other place of amusement; any comfort station; any dispensary, clinic or hospital; any public library; any kindergarten, primary and secondary school, trade or business school, high school, academy, college and university, or any educational institution under the supervision of the State Board of Education, or the Commissioner of Education of the State of New Jersey. Nothing herein contained shall be construed to include or to apply to any institution, bona fide club, or place of accommodation, which is in its nature distinctly private; nor shall anything herein contained apply to any educational facility operated or maintained by a bona fide religious or sectarian institution, and the right of a natural parent or one in loco parentis to direct the education and upbringing of a child under his control is hereby affirmed; nor shall anything herein contained be construed to bar any private secondary or post secondary school from using in good faith criteria other than race, creed, color, national origin, ancestry or affectional or sexual orientation in the admission of students.

DALE v. BOY SCOUTS OF AMERICA
734 A.2d 1196 (N.J. 1999), *rev'd sub nom.*
Boy Scouts of America v. Dale, 530 U.S. 640 (2000)

The opinion of the court was delivered by DEBORAH T. PORITZ, C.J.

In 1991, the New Jersey Legislature amended the *Law Against Discrimination* (LAD), N.J. Stat. §§10:5-1 to -49, to include protections based on "affectional or sexual orientation." This case requires us to decide whether that law prohibits Boy Scouts of America (BSA) from expelling a member solely because he is an avowed homosexual. . . .

I. Facts

BSA, a federally chartered corporation, 36 U.S.C.A. §30901, operates four scout membership programs: Cub Scouts (for boys eight to eleven-and-a-half), Boy Scouts (for boys and young men eleven to seventeen), Varsity Scouts (for young men fourteen to seventeen), and Explorers (for young men and women fourteen to twenty). . . .

BSA membership is an American tradition. Since the program's inception in 1910 through the beginning of this decade, over eighty-seven million youths and adults have joined BSA. As of December 1992, over four million youths and over one million adults were active BSA members. . . .

According to BSA's federal charter, BSA seeks "to promote, through organization, and cooperation with other agencies, the ability of boys to do things for themselves and others, to train them in Scoutcraft, and to teach them patriotism, courage, self-reliance, and kindred virtues." BSA's Mission Statement also describes BSA's purpose: "It is the mission of the Boy Scouts of America to serve others by helping to instill values in young people and, in other ways, to prepare them to make ethical choices over their lifetime in achieving their full potential." The Scout Oath and Scout Law set forth the guiding principles of BSA:

Scout Oath
On my honor I will do my best
To do my duty to God and my country and to obey the Scout Law;
To help other people at all times;
To keep myself physically strong, mentally awake, and morally straight.

Scout Law
A Scout is TRUSTWORTHY. A Scout tells the truth. He keeps his promises. Honesty is a part of his code of conduct. People can always depend on him.
A Scout is LOYAL. A Scout is true to his family, friends, Scout leaders, school, nation, and world community.
A Scout is HELPFUL. A Scout is concerned about other people. He willingly volunteers to help others without expecting payment or reward.
A Scout is FRIENDLY. A Scout is a friend to all. He is a brother to other Scouts. He seeks to understand others. He respects those with ideas and customs that are different from his own.
A Scout is COURTEOUS. A Scout is polite to everyone regardless of age or position. He knows that good manners make it easier for people to get along together.
A Scout is KIND. A Scout understands there is strength in being gentle. He treats others as he wants to be treated. He does not harm or kill anything without reason.
A Scout is OBEDIENT. A Scout follows the rules of his family, school, and troop. He obeys the laws of his community and country. If he thinks these rules and laws are unfair, he tries to have them changed in an orderly manner rather than disobey them.
A Scout is CHEERFUL. A Scout looks for the bright side of life. He cheerfully does tasks that come his way. He tries to make others happy.
A Scout is THRIFTY. A Scout works to pay his way and to help others. He saves for the future. He protects and conserves natural resources. He carefully uses time and property.
A Scout is BRAVE. A Scout can face danger even if he is afraid. He has the courage to stand for what he thinks is right even if others laugh at him or threaten him.
A Scout is CLEAN. A Scout keeps his body and mind fit and clean. He goes around with those who believe in living by these same ideals. He helps keep his home and community clean.
A Scout is REVERENT. A Scout is reverent toward God. He is faithful in his religious duties. He respects the beliefs of others.

In its briefs below and to this Court, Boy Scouts claims that the language "morally straight" and "clean" in the Oath and Law, respectively, constitutes a rejection of homosexuality. The Boy Scout Handbook, at 551, defines "morally straight" as follows:

> To be a person of strong character, guide your life with honesty, purity, and justice. Respect and defend the rights of all people.

Your relationships with others should be honest and open. Be clean in your speech and actions, and faithful in your religious beliefs. The values you follow as a Scout will help you become virtuous and self-reliant.

Although one of BSA's stated purposes is to encourage members' ethical development, BSA does not endorse any specific set of moral beliefs. Instead, "moral fitness" is deemed an individual choice. . . .

BSA also does not espouse any one religion, explaining in the Scoutmaster Handbook that "there is a close association between the Boy Scouts of America and virtually all religious bodies and denominations in the United States." Consistent with its nonsectarian nature, BSA Bylaws require "respect [for] the convictions of others in matters of custom and religion." Boy Scouts "encourages no particular affiliation, [and does not] assume [the] functions of religious bodies"; indeed, in a training manual entitled Scoutmaster Fundamentals prepared "for Scoutmasters, Assistant Scoutmasters, Troop Committee members, and parents," BSA categorically states: "Religious instruction is the responsibility of the home and church." . . .

. . . BSA . . . encourages its leaders to refrain from talking about sexual topics. Although the Boy Scout Handbook, at 528, contains a subchapter entitled "Sexual Responsibility" which states that "for the followers of most religions, sex should take place only between married couples," sexual topics are not formally discussed during Boy Scout activities. Rather, BSA "believes that boys should learn about sex and family life from their parents, consistent with their spiritual beliefs."

In 1992, of the five million members of BSA, approximately one million youths and 420,000 adults were involved in the Boy Scout division. Those members belonged to over 44,000 Boy Scout troops throughout the country. [Boy Scouts are required to repeat the Pledge of Allegiance and "understand and agree to live by the Scout Oath, the Scout Law, the Scout motto, the Scout slogan, and the Outdoor Code." The BSA's Declaration of Religious Principle states: The Boy Scouts of America maintains that no member can grow into the best kind of citizen without recognizing an obligation to God. . . . No matter what the religious faith of the members may be, this fundamental need of good citizenship should be kept before them.]

James Dale first became a BSA member in 1978 when, at the age of eight, he joined Monmouth Council's Cub Scout Pack 142. He remained a Cub Scout until 1981, when he became a member of Boy Scout Troop 220, also in Monmouth Council. He joined Monmouth Council's Boy Scout Troop 128 in 1983, and Troop 73 in 1985. Until his eighteenth birthday in 1988, he remained a youth member of Troop 73.

Dale was an exemplary scout. Over the ten years of his membership, he earned more than twenty-five merit badges. In 1983, he was admitted into Boy Scouts' Order of the Arrow, the organization's honor camping society, and achieved the status of Virgil Honor. The pinnacle of Dale's career as a youth member came in 1988, when BSA awarded him an Eagle Scout Badge, an honor achieved by only the top three percent of all scouts.

Dale's participation in Boy Scout leadership began at an early age. Throughout his years as a member, Dale was an assistant patrol leader, patrol leader, and bugler, and from 1985 to 1988, Dale served as a Junior Assistant Scoutmaster for Troop 73. He was also invited to speak at organized Boy Scout functions, such as the Joshua Huddy Distinguished Citizenship Award Dinner, and attended national events, including the National Boy Scout Jamboree. On March 21, 1989, Dale sought adult membership in Boy Scouts. Monmouth Council and BSA accepted and approved his application for the position of Assistant Scoutmaster of Troop 73 where he served for approximately sixteen months.

At about the same time that Dale applied for adult membership, he left home to attend Rutgers University. While at college, Dale first acknowledged to himself, and to his family and friends, that he was gay. Shortly thereafter, he became involved with, and eventually became the co-president of the Rutgers University Lesbian/Gay Alliance. Then, in July 1990, Dale attended a seminar that addressed the psychological and health needs of lesbian and gay teenagers. The Star-Ledger interviewed Dale and published an article on July 8, 1990 that discussed the seminar. The article included Dale's photograph and a caption identifying him as "co-president of the Rutgers University Lesbian/Gay Alliance."

Later that month, Dale received a letter from Monmouth Council Executive James W. Kay, revoking his BSA membership. The letter asked Dale to "sever any relations [he] may have with the Boy Scouts of America." . . . He was later informed that "the Boy Scouts does not admit avowed homosexuals to membership in the organization. . . ."

III. State Law Claims

A. The LAW AGAINST DISCRIMINATION (LAD)

We first consider whether Boy Scouts is subject to the LAD, which provides that "all persons shall have the opportunity . . . to obtain all the accommodations, advantages, facilities, and privileges of any place of public accommodation, . . . without discrimination because of . . . affectional or sexual orientation." N.J. Stat. §10:5-4. . . .

1. Place of Public Accommodation

"The overarching goal of the [LAD] is nothing less than the eradication 'of the cancer of discrimination.'" *Fuchilla v. Layman*, 537 A.2d 652, 660 (N.J. 1988). "Discrimination threatens not only the rights and proper privileges of the inhabitants of [New Jersey,] but menaces the institutions and foundation of a free democratic State." N.J. Stat. §10:5-3. In furtherance of its purpose to root out discrimination, the Legislature has directed that the LAD "shall be liberally construed." *Id.* . . .

a. *Place.* In 1965, the Court held that places of public accommodation were not limited to those enumerated in the statute. *Fraser v. Robin Dee Day Camp*, 210 A.2d 208 (N.J. 1965). At that time, the statutory definition used the word "include" to preface a list of specific "places" of public accommodation. We reasoned that the Legislature's choice of the word "include" indicated that the "places" expressly mentioned were "merely illustrative of the accommodations the Legislature intended to be within the scope of the statute. Other accommodations, similar in nature to those enumerated, were also intended to be covered." Less than a year later, the Legislature amended the LAD to expressly state that " 'a place of public accommodation' shall include, *but not be limited to*" the various examples identified, 1966 N.J. Laws ch. 17 [codified at N.J. Stat. §10:5-5*l*] (emphasis added), thereby reaffirming our broad construction of the statutory language.

Later, the word "place" became a further source of legal dispute. In *National Organization of Women v. Little League Baseball, Inc.*, 338 A.2d 198 (N.J. 1974), we affirmed the decision of the Appellate Division holding that: "the statutory noun 'place' . . . is a term of convenience, not of limitation[,] . . . employed to reflect the fact that public accommodations are commonly provided at fixed 'places.'" The defendant in *Little League* was a chartered baseball league that excluded girls between the ages of eight and twelve years from participation in its programs. The league contended that it did not come "within the meaning of the statute, primarily because it [was] a membership organization which does not operate from any fixed parcel of real estate in New Jersey of which it had exclusive possession by ownership or lease." The court rejected that narrow view of "place":

> The "place" of public accommodation in the case of Little League is obviously the ball field at which tryouts are arranged, instructions given, practices held and games played. The statutory "accommodations, advantages, facilities and privileges" at the place of public accommodation is the entire agglomeration of the arrangements which Little League and its local chartered leagues make and the facilities they provide for the playing of baseball by the children.

As Boy Scouts correctly observes, other jurisdictions interpreting their antidiscrimination laws have found "place" to be a limiting factor encompassing only a fixed location. *See, e.g., Welsh v. Boy Scouts of America,* 993 F.2d 1267, 1269 (7th Cir. 1993) (holding that Boy Scouts is not [a] "place of public accommodation" under *Title II of Civil Rights Act of 1964* because "Congress when enacting §2000a(b) never intended to include membership organizations that do not maintain a close connection to a structural facility within the meaning of 'place of public accommodation'"); *United States Jaycees v. Richardet,* 666 P.2d 1008, 1011 (Alaska 1983) (stating that "the word 'place'...would not encompass a service organization lacking a fixed geographical situs"); *United States Jaycees v. Bloomfield,* 434 A.2d 1379, 1381 (D.C. 1981) (disagreeing with lower court's conclusion that "it is not necessary that there be a building...in order to categorize an existing entity as a place of public accommodation"); *United States Jaycees v. Iowa Civil Rights Comm'n,* 427 N.W.2d 450, 454 (Iowa 1988) (stating that "United States Jaycees is not a 'place' within our definition of 'public accommodation'"); *United States Jaycees v. Massachusetts Comm'n Against Discrimination,* 463 N.E.2d 1151, 1156 (Mass. 1984) (finding that Massachusetts antidiscrimination law "does not apply to [a] membership organization, since such an organization does not fall within the commonly accepted definition of 'place'").

We observe that not all jurisdictions have interpreted "place" so narrowly. The New York Court of Appeals has held that a "place of public accommodation need not be a fixed location, it is the place where petitioners do what they do," including "the place where petitioners' meetings and activities occur." *United States Power Squadrons v. State Human Rights Appeal Bd.,* 452 N.E.2d 1199, 1204 (N.Y. 1983). The Supreme Court of Minnesota has also approved a flexible construction of the term "place." In *United States Jaycees v. McClure,* 305 N.W.2d 764, 773 (Minn. 1981), the Minnesota court agreed with the Little League premise that a "'place of public accommodation'...is less a matter of whether the organization operates on a permanent site, and more a matter of whether the organization engages in activities in places to which an unselected public is given an open invitation."

Despite numerous additions and modifications to the LAD in the twenty-four years since *Little League* was decided, the New Jersey Legislature has not enacted a limiting definition of place. We decline now to construe "place" so as to include only membership associations that are connected to a particular geographic location or facility. As the Appellate Division has so aptly pointed out, "to have the LAD's reach turn on the definition of 'place' is irrational because 'places do not discriminate; people who own and operate places do.'" 706 A.2d at 279 (quoting *Welsh,* 993 F.2d at 1282 (Cummings, J., dissenting)). A membership association, like Boy Scouts, may be a "place" of public accommodation even if the accommodation is provided at "a moving situs." In this case it is readily apparent that the various locations where Boy Scout troops meet fulfill the LAD "place" requirement.

b. *Public accommodation.* Our case law identifies various factors that are helpful in determining whether Boy Scouts is a "public accommodation." We ask, generally, whether the entity before us engages in broad public solicitation, whether it maintains close relationships with the government or other public accommodations, or whether it is similar to enumerated or other previously recognized public accommodations.

Broad public solicitation has consistently been a principal characteristic of public accommodations. Our courts have repeatedly held that when an entity invites the public to join, attend, or participate in some way, that entity is a public accommodation within the meaning of the LAD.

BSA engages in broad public solicitation through various media. In 1989, for example, BSA spent more than $1 million on a national television advertising campaign. . . . BSA has also advertised in widely distributed magazines, such as Sports Afield and Redbook. Local Boy Scout councils engage in substantial public solicitation. . . .

Boy Scout troops also take part in perhaps the most powerful invitation of all, albeit an implied one: the symbolic invitation extended by a Boy Scout each time he wears his uniform in public. A boy in a uniform may well be Boy Scouts' strongest recruiting tool. . . .

Boy Scouts is a "public accommodation," not simply because of its solicitation activities, but also because it maintains close relationships with federal and state governmental bodies and with other recognized public accommodations. Our cases have held that certain organizations that benefit from relationships with the government and other public accommodations are themselves places of public accommodation within the meaning of the LAD. In *Little League,* for example, the court concluded that Little League was "public in the added sense that local governmental bodies characteristically make the playing areas available to the local leagues, ordinarily without charge." 318 A.2d at 38. More recently, in *Frank v. Ivy Club,* 576 A.2d 241 (1990), a female student sought membership in the all-male eating clubs at Princeton University. Although they did not publicly solicit new members, we held that the clubs' close relationship to the University, a place of public accommodation, rendered them subject to the LAD.

It is clear that Boy Scouts benefits from a close relationship with the federal government. Indeed, BSA was chartered by Congress in 1916, 36 U.S.C.A. §30901, and has been the recipient of equipment, supplies, and services from the federal government, also by act of Congress, 10 U.S.C.A. §2544. . . .

One of the causes contributing to the success of the Boy Scouts of America has been the thoughtful, wholehearted way in which each President of the United States since William Howard Taft in 1910 has taken an active part in the work of the movement. Each served as Honorary President during his term in office. . . . Another fact sheet states that 78 percent of the members of the 100th Congress participated in scouting. . . .

Moreover, [p]ublic schools not only aid Boy Scouts by allowing the organization to use their facilities after school, but also during the school day. . . . In 1992, close to 700,000 students throughout the nation were taught the Boy Scouts' Learning for Life curriculum during the school day.

Given Boy Scouts' public solicitation activities, and considering its close relationship with governmental entities, it is not surprising that Boy Scouts resembles many of the recognized and enumerated places of public accommodation. . . . Boy Scouts' educational and recreational nature . . . further supports our conclusion that Boy Scouts is a "place of public accommodation" under the LAD.

2. LAD Exceptions

Boy Scouts claims that even if it is a place of public accommodation, it is nonetheless exempt from the LAD under . . . the "distinctly private" exception. . . . The LAD provides that "nothing herein contained shall be construed to include or to apply to any institution, bona fide club, or place of accommodation, which is in its nature distinctly private." N.J. Stat. 10:5-5*l*. . . .

Thirty-three years ago, in *Clover Hill Swimming Club v. Goldsboro*, 219 A.2d 161 (1966), we said that "not every establishment using the 'club' label can be considered 'distinctly private.' Self-serving declarations by . . . an accommodation are not determinative of its character." Although the swimming club had represented to the public that "all applications [for membership] would be subject to approval by club officials," it appeared that Clover Hill was only selective when black families applied. The Court refused to accept bogus representations concerning the "private" nature of the club when it was quite clear that membership was generally open and had to do with a family's interest in recreation and not much else. *Little League* primarily relied on the baseball league's "open [invitation] to children in the community at large, with no restriction (other than sex) whatever" as a basis for the court's finding that the league was a "public accommodation." The lack of any membership selectivity — except for the prohibition against the admission of girls — weighed in the public accommodation calculus; it also bears upon the "distinctly private" exception.

Kiwanis Int'l v. Ridgewood Kiwanis Club, 806 F.2d 468 (3d Cir. 1986), is the only case to hold a club exempt under the "distinctly private" exception. The Third Circuit . . . found that the local club was selective based on its membership practices [which engaged in large-scale solicitations but which also limited membership to fewer than 30 persons, required new members to be sponsored by a current member, and required members to pray at meetings]. Unlike Kiwanis Ridgewood, . . . Boy Scouts does not require new members "to be sponsored by a current member." . . .

Boy Scouts' large membership further undercuts its claim to selective membership. Nationally, over four million boys and one million adults were Boy Scout members in 1992. Since its inception, over 87 million people have joined Boy Scouts. In 1991, Monmouth Council alone had over 8400 youths and over 2700 adult members. The New York Court of Appeals, construing "distinctly private" in *United States Power Squadrons, supra*, has suggested that an organization's failure to limit its maximum membership, in and of itself, demonstrates that the club is not private. . . . We note only that the size of the Boy Scout organization certainly implies an open membership policy.

Boy Scouts argues, however, that it is "distinctly private" because its Scout Oath and Scout Law constitute genuine selectivity criteria. . . . We acknowledge that Boy Scouts' membership application requires members to comply with the Scout Oath and Law. We do not find, however, that the Oath and Law operate as genuine selectivity criteria. To the contrary, the record discloses few instances in which the Oath and Law have been used to exclude a prospective member; in practice, they present no real impediment to joining Boy Scouts. Joining requirements are insufficient to establish selectivity where they do not function as true limits on the admission of members. Here, there is no evidence that Boy Scouts does anything but accept at face value a scout's affirmation of the Oath and Law.

Most important, it is clear that Boy Scouts does not limit its membership to individuals who belong to a particular religion or subscribe to a specific set of moral beliefs. Boy Scouts asserts that "there is a close association between the Boy Scouts of America and virtually all religious bodies and denominations in the United States," and that each member's concept of "moral fitness" should be determined by his "courage to do what his head and heart tell him is right." Moreover, Boy Scouts encourages its members to "respect and defend the rights of others whose beliefs may differ." Scoutmaster Handbook, at 561. By its own teachings then, Boy Scouts is inclusive, not selective, in its membership practices....

We hold that Boy Scouts is a "place of public accommodation" and is not exempt from the LAD under any of the statute's exceptions.

3. Have Boy Scouts Violated the LAD?

N.J. Stat. §10:5–4 states that "all persons shall have the opportunity to obtain all the accommodations, advantages, facilities, and privileges of any place of public accommodation." Because we hold that an assistant scoutmaster position is a "privilege" and an "advantage" of Boy Scout membership, and because Boy Scouts has "revoked" Dale's registration based on his "avowed" homosexuality, a prohibited form of discrimination under the statute, we conclude that Boy Scouts has violated the LAD....

Boy Scouts of America v. Dale, 530 U.S. 640 (2000), rev'g Dale v. Boy Scouts of America, 734 A.2d 1196 (N.J. 1999). *Dale* was reversed by the Supreme Court in a 5-4 vote on the ground that a state public accommodations law that prohibited the Boy Scouts from excluding gay Scouts violated the First Amendment's protections for freedom of association. This constitutional right includes both a right of intimate association (such as the right to marry) and a right of "expressive association" or the "right to associate with others in pursuit of a wide variety of political, social, economic, educational, religious, and cultural ends." 530 U.S. at 647.

Chief Justice Rehnquist noted for himself and Justices Kennedy, O'Connor, Scalia, and Thomas, that the Boy Scouts "engaged in instilling its system of values in young people" and "that homosexual conduct is inconsistent with the values it seeks to instill." *Id.* at 643. "It seems indisputable," Justice Rehnquist noted, "that an association that seeks to transmit such a system of values engages in expressive activity." *Id.* at 650. The Scout Oath requires Scouts to agree to be "morally straight" and "clean" and the Boy Scouts hold that "homosexual conduct is not morally straight." *Id.* at 651. It would significantly burden its associational rights to be forced to accept for membership Scouts and Scoutmasters who are openly gay. "The forced inclusion of an unwanted person in a group infringes the group's freedom of expressive association if the presence of that person affects in a significant way the group's ability to advocate public or private viewpoints." *Id.* at 648. Disagreeing with the Supreme Court of New Jersey that "the Boy Scouts' ability to disseminate its message . . . [would not be] significantly affected by the forced inclusion of Dale," the Court ruled that "Dale's presence as an assistant scoutmaster would significantly burden the Boy Scouts' desire to not 'promote homosexual conduct as a legitimate form of behavior.'" *Id.* at 654, 653.

Limits on associational rights are constitutional if they "serve compelling state interests, unrelated to the suppression of ideas, that cannot be achieved through means significantly less restrictive of associational freedoms." *Id.* at 648. Although the Supreme Court of New Jersey had concluded that "New Jersey has a compelling interest in eliminating 'the destructive consequences of discrimination from our society,'" the Supreme Court found that the "state interests embodied in New Jersey's public accommodations law do not justify such a severe intrusion on the Boy Scouts' rights to freedom of expressive association." *Id.* at 647, 659.

The Court distinguished earlier cases involving private clubs, such as the Jaycees and the Rotary Club, that had held that it was not a violation of free association rights to require them to admit women. *New York State Club Association, Inc. v. City of New York,* 487 U.S. 1 (1988); *Board of Directors of Rotary International v. Rotary Club of Duarte,* 481 U.S. 537 (1987); *Roberts v. United States Jaycees,* 468 U.S. 609 (1984). In contrast to the Boy Scouts, those clubs had not shown that admitting women would affect any message they intended to communicate; they had therefore not alleged any effect on their freedom of expressive association.

Justices Breyer, Ginsburg, Souter, and Stevens dissented. They disagreed that the Boy Scouts had a well-publicized position on homosexuality. Justice Stevens noted that nothing in the Scout Oath or Law "says the slightest thing about homosexuality" and Scoutmasters are directed "not [to] undertake to instruct Scouts, in any formalized manner, in the subject of sex and family life. The reasons are that it is not construed to be Scouting's proper area, and that you are probably not well qualified to do this." *Id.* at 669. Although the Boy Scouts issued policy statements on the question, nothing on homosexuality was placed in the Boy Scout or Scoutmaster Handbook. "[N]o lessons were imparted to Scouts; no change was made to BSA's policy on limiting discussion of sexual matters; and no effort was made to restrict acceptable religious affiliations to those that condemn homosexuality. In short, there is no evidence that this view was part of any collective effort to foster beliefs about homosexuality." *Id.* at 675. Moreover, the Boy Scouts declares itself to be "absolutely nonsectarian" on religious matters and "a number of religious groups do not view homosexuality as immoral or wrong and reject discrimination against homosexuals." *Id.* at 670.

Justice Stevens further noted that the Supreme Court had never before "found a claimed right to associate in the selection of members to prevail in the face of a State's antidiscrimination law." *Id.* at 679. "The evidence before this Court makes it exceptionally clear that BSA has, at most, simply adopted an exclusionary membership policy and has no shared goal of disapproving of homosexuality." *Id.* at 684. "In short, Boy Scouts of America is simply silent on homosexuality. There is no shared goal or collective effort to foster a belief about homosexuality at all — let alone one that is significantly burdened by admitting homosexuals." *Id.* He criticized the majority for giving deference to the Boy Scouts' assertions regarding the nature of its expression. "To prevail in asserting a right of expressive association as a defense to a charge of violating an antidiscrimination law, the organization must at least show it has adopted and advocated an unequivocal position inconsistent with a position advocated or epitomized by the person whom the organization seeks to exclude." *Id.* at 687.

Justice Stevens also rejected the majority's view that "Dale's mere presence among the Boy Scouts will itself force the group to convey a message about homosexuality — even if Dale has no intention of doing so." *Id.* at 692. He distinguished a prior case that reversed a Massachusetts Supreme Judicial Court decision that had interpreted the state public accommodations laws to require a privately operated St.

Patrick's Day parade to allow a gay, lesbian, and bisexual organization to march because marching in a parade with a banner for the purpose of expressing views about one's own sexual orientation is "an inherently expressive undertaking." *Id.* at 693. Dale, in contrast, "did not carry a banner or a sign; he did not distribute any fact sheet; and he expressed no intent to send any message. If there is any kind of message being sent, then, it is by the mere act of joining the Boy Scouts. Such an act does not constitute an instance of symbolic speech under the First Amendment." *Id.* at 694–695.

Justice Souter agreed in a separate dissenting opinion that "no group can claim a right of expressive association without identifying a clear position to be advocated over time in an unequivocal way." *Id.* at 701.

NOTES AND QUESTIONS

1. *Federal versus state statutes.* The federal public accommodations law was passed in 1964 as Title II of the *Civil Rights Act.* The statute applies across the country and, under the supremacy clause of the Constitution, will prevail over any contrary state law.[7] Most states have also adopted public accommodations laws that apply only within their borders. State statutes that are *inconsistent* with federal statutes are "preempted" by federal law and are unenforceable; state statutes not inconsistent with federal law are enforceable. State statutes and constitutional provisions may go *further* than federal law in protecting individual rights.

For example, many state statutes prohibit discrimination in places of public accommodation on account of sex; the federal statute, in contrast, does not prohibit sex discrimination in access to public places. State statutes may also be worded differently from the federal statute; they may therefore apply to more kinds of property or to more types of discriminatory acts than does federal law. Even when the wording in state and federal statutes is identical, the state statute may be interpreted by a state court to grant *more* protection against discrimination than does federal law. Because statutory interpretation involves interpreting the intent of the legislature, a state court could conclude from the context surrounding passage of the state law that the legislature intended to grant greater protection than did Congress when it passed the federal statute.

2. *What is a "place" of public accommodation?* Like New Jersey, the supreme courts of Minnesota and Connecticut have interpreted their state public accommodations statutes to apply to membership organizations that do not have a fixed place of operations. *See, e.g., Quinnipiac Council, Boy Scouts of America, Inc. v. Commission on Human Rights and Opportunities,* 528 A.2d 352 (Conn. 1987) (holding that the Boy Scouts is a public accommodation as defined in the Connecticut statute); *United States Jaycees v. McClure,* 305 N.W.2d 764 (Minn. 1981), *aff'd sub nom. Roberts v. United States Jaycees,* 468 U.S. 609 (1984) (Jaycees held to be a "public accommodation"). *But see Welsh v. Boy Scouts of America,* 993 F.2d 1267 (7th Cir. 1993) (holding that a membership organization such as the Boy Scouts is not a "place" of public accommodation under Title II of the *Civil Rights Act of 1964*).

---

7. Article VI of the Constitution provides that the "Constitution, and the Laws of the United States which shall be made in Pursuance thereof . . . shall be the supreme Law of the Land; and the Judges in every State shall be bound thereby, any Thing in the Constitution or Laws of any State to the Contrary notwithstanding."

In contrast, the Massachusetts Supreme Judicial Court held that the state public accommodations law did not apply to the United States Jaycees because it only applied to "places" of public accommodation. *United States Jaycees v. Massachusetts Commission Against Discrimination*, 463 N.E.2d 1151 (Mass. 1984). *Cf. Noah v. AOL Time Warner Inc.*, 2004 U.S. App. LEXIS 5495 (4th Cir. 2004), *aff'g*, 261 F.Supp.2d 532 (D.Va. 2003) (Internet chat rooms are not places of public accommodation under Title II of the *Civil Rights Act of 1964* because they are not "actual, physical places [or] structures"). The court gave the word "place" its *ordinary meaning*, arguing that the language in the statute should generally be interpreted in the way a layperson — a nonlawyer — would interpret it. In contrast, when it determined that the Jaycees were a "place of public accommodation," the Minnesota Supreme Court rejected the idea of "substitut[ing] a literal, ordinary definition of 'place of public accommodation' for the one enacted by the legislature." *United States Jaycees v. McClure*, 305 N.W.2d at 772. Words in statutes are often given *technical meanings* different from their ordinary meaning; thus, to effectuate legislative intent, the courts should focus on the technical, rather than the ordinary, meaning of the language in the statute. In a similar vein, Chief Justice Poritz argued in *Dale* that the statutory term "place" was a "term of convenience, not of limitation" and that any ambiguities should be decided in favor of broad application because the statute itself provided that it should be "liberally construed."

3. *Private clubs.* What is the difference between a public accommodation and a private club? Courts generally look to see whether the organization is *selective* in its membership and has *limits* on the number of persons who can join. If the selection criteria track a statutory category, it is unlikely the group will be held to be a private club. A group that is limited to men, but has no other selection criteria and is unlimited is size, is likely to be held to be a public accommodation that is violating the law rather than a selective private club. Does it matter whether the organization is engaged in the sale of goods or services? Could a restaurant call itself the Segregation Society, grant memberships to all white persons who enter for a fee of 25 cents, and thereby exclude African American patrons? Could it do so if its fee was $1,000 a year?

PROBLEMS

1. A divorce lawyer in New Jersey refuses to act as an attorney for a man in a divorce proceeding. The man sues her, claiming she has violated the *New Jersey Law Against Discrimination*. She claims a professional right as an attorney to choose her clients; she is not obligated to take every client who walks in the door but has the right to exercise professional and ethical judgment in choosing which causes and kinds of clients to help. *See* Mark A. Cohen, *Can Attorneys Reject Any Potential Client?* 24 Mass. Law. Wkly. 1213 (Feb. 26, 1996) (discussing a similar case). She argues that attorneys should be able to specialize in representing only employers, for example, in labor or employment discrimination cases, or representing only tenants in landlord-tenant disputes. Women have unique problems in divorce situations because they are more likely to interrupt their careers to care for their children and because their economic situation usually deteriorates after divorce, while men generally do better after divorce. Has the attorney violated the state public accommodations statute?

2. A state law prohibits sex discrimination in places of public accommodation. A health club for women refuses to admit a man for membership. Has it violated the act? Compare *LivingWell (North) Inc. v. Pennyslvania Human Relations Commission*,

606 A.2d 1287 (Pa. Commw. Ct. 1992) (no) with *Foster v. Back Bay Spas, Inc.*, 1997 WL 634354 (Mass. Super. Ct. 1997) (yes).

3. In *Harjo v. Pro-Football, Inc.*, 50 U.S.P.Q.2d 1705, 1999 TTAB LEXIS 181 (Trademark & Trial & App. Bd. 1999), *rev'd sub nom. Pro-Football, Inc. v. Harjo*, 284 F.Supp.2d 96 (D.D.C. 2003), *rev'd and remanded on other grounds*, 2005 U.S. App. LEXIS 14312 (D.C.Cir. 2005), the Patent and Trademark Office removed federal trademark registration for the Redskins football organization on the ground the name was "immoral, deceptive, or scandalous," 15 U.S.C. §1052(a), and that it "consists of or comprises matter which may disparage persons, living or dead, institutions, beliefs, or national symbols, or bring them into contempt or disrepute" 15 U.S.C. §1064. That decision was reversed by the D.C. District court on the ground that plaintiffs had not carried their burden of proof in showing that the term "redskin" would have been viewed as disparaging by a substantial majority of American Indians when the mark was registered in 1967. Plaintiffs claimed that the term "redskins" is a "pejorative, derogatory, denigrating, offensive, scandalous, contemptuous, disreputable, disparaging and racist designation for a Native American person" and is as offensive to most American Indians as the worst epithets ever targeted at African Americans, Jews, or other groups that have been victims of racist hatred. Defendant claimed that the name was intended to honor American Indians, that it was intended to be complimentary, and that it had a first amendment right to use the name even if American Indians found it offensive.

a.   Would it violate the federal public accommodations law, 42 U.S.C. §2000a, to call a sports stadium the Redskins Stadium? *See Note: A Public Accommodations Challenge to the Use of Indian Team Names and Mascots in Professional Sports*, 112 Harv. L. Rev. 904 (1999) (arguing that it would).

b.   If it would violate the statute, does the first amendment's guarantee of "free speech" override the statute? Should the court hold that a statute that prohibits an owner from using the name "Redskins" is unconstitutional? *Compare Urban League of Rhode Island v. Sambo's of Rhode Island, Inc.*, File Nos. 79 PRA 074-06/06, 79 ERA 073-06/06, EEOC No. 011790461 (R.I. Commission for Human Rights 1981) (restaurant violated state public accommodations law by using racially offensive name) *with Sambo's Restaurants, Inc. v. City of Ann Arbor*, 663 F.2d 686 (6th Cir. 1981) (holding that the first amendment's free speech clause protected the right to use the name "Sambo's").

§2.2.2   DISCRIMINATION AGAINST PERSONS with DISABILITIES

The *Americans with Disabilities Act* (ADA), passed in 1990, is one of the most important pieces of civil rights legislation approved by Congress since the *Civil Rights Act of 1964*. It prohibits discrimination on the basis of disability in both employment and public accommodations.[8] Title III requires *new construction* of covered dwellings built after January 26, 1993, to be designed to be accessible to persons with disabilities, 42 U.S.C. §12183, 28 C.F.R. §§36.301 to 36.406. It also prohibits discrimination on the basis of disability in *existing businesses* open to the public and imposes obligations on

---

8. The Justice Department has promulgated regulations implementing the statute and clarifying the scope of the obligations imposed on businesses, including modification of physical premises, policies and practices. *See* 28 C.F.R. §§36.301 to 36.311.

them to make reasonable accommodations to ensure accessibility. *See* 28 C.F.R. §§36.101 to 36.608.[9]

AMERICANS WITH DISABILITIES ACT OF 1990,
TITLE III — PUBLIC ACCOMMODATIONS
AND SERVICES OPERATED BY PRIVATE ENTITIES

42 U.S.C. §§12101 to 12213

§12102. Definitions

As used in this chapter:
... (2) *Disability.* — The term "disability" means, with respect to an individual —

(A) a physical or mental impairment that substantially limits one or more of the major life activities of such individual;

(B) a record of such an impairment; or

(C) being regarded as having such an impairment. ...

§12181. Definitions

... (7) *Public accommodation.* — The following private entities are considered public accommodations for purposes of this title, if the operations of such entities affect commerce —

(A) an inn, hotel, motel, or other place of lodging, except for an establishment located within a building that contains not more than five rooms for rent or hire and that is actually occupied by the proprietor of such establishment as the residence of such proprietor;

(B) a restaurant, bar, or other establishment serving food or drink;

(C) a motion picture house, theater, concert hall, stadium, or other place of exhibition or entertainment;

(D) an auditorium, convention center, lecture hall, or other place of public gathering;

(E) a bakery, grocery store, clothing store, hardware store, shopping center, or other sales or rental establishment;

(F) a laundromat, dry-cleaner, bank, barber shop, beauty shop, travel service, shoe repair service, funeral parlor, gas station, office of an accountant or lawyer, pharmacy, insurance office, professional office of a health care provider, hospital or other service establishment;

(G) a terminal, depot, or other station used for specified public transportation;

(H) a museum, library, gallery, or other place of public display or collection;

(I) a park, zoo, amusement park, or other place of recreation;

---

9. In 1988, two years before passage of the ADA, Congress amended *Fair Housing Act of 1968*, 42 U.S.C. §§3601-3631, to prohibit discrimination on the basis of disability in the sale or rental of dwellings. *See* Chapter 10 *infra*.

(J) a nursery, elementary, secondary, undergraduate, or postgraduate private school, or other place of education;

(K) a day care center, senior citizen center, homeless shelter, food bank, adoption agency, or other social service center establishment; and

(L) a gymnasium, health spa, bowling alley, golf course, or other place of exercise or recreation. . . .

(9) *Readily achievable.* — The term "readily achievable" means easily accomplishable and able to be carried out without much difficulty or expense. In determining whether an action is readily achievable, factors to be considered include —

(A) the nature and cost of the action needed under this chapter;

(B) the overall financial resources of the facility or facilities involved in the action; the number of persons employed at such facility; the effect on expenses and resources, or the impact otherwise of such action upon the operation of the facility;

(C) the overall financial resources of the covered entity; the overall size of the business of a covered entity with respect to the number of its employees; the number, type, and location of its facilities; and

(D) the type of operation or operations of the covered entity, including the composition, structure, and functions of the workforce of such entity; the geographic separateness, administrative or fiscal relationship of the facility or facilities in question to the covered entity.

§12182. Prohibition of Discrimination by Public Accommodations

(a) *General rule.* — No individual shall be discriminated against on the basis of disability in the full and equal enjoyment of the goods, services, facilities, privileges, advantages, or accommodations of any place of public accommodation by any person who owns, leases (or leases to), or operates a place of public accommodation. . . .

(b) *Construction*

(1) *General prohibition*

(A) *Activities*

(i) *Denial of participation*

It shall be discriminatory to subject an individual or class of individuals on the basis of a disability or disabilities of such individual or class, directly, or through contractual, licensing, or other arrangements, to a denial of the opportunity of the individual or class to participate in or benefit from the goods, services, facilities, privileges, advantages, or accommodations of an entity.

(ii) *Participation in unequal benefit*

It shall be discriminatory to afford an individual or class of individuals, on the basis of a disability or disabilities of such individual or class, directly, or through contractual, licensing, or other arrangements with the opportunity to participate in or benefit from a good, service, facility, privilege, advantage, or accommodation that is not equal to that afforded to other individuals.

(iii) *Separate benefit*

It shall be discriminatory to provide an individual or class of individuals, on the basis of a disability or disabilities of such individual or class, directly, or through contractual, licensing, or other arrangements with a good, service, facility, privilege, advantage, or accommodation that is different or separate from that provided to other individuals, unless such action is necessary to provide the individual or class of individuals with a good, service, facility, privilege, advantage, or accommodation, or other opportunity that is as effective as that provided to others.

(iv) *Individual or class of individuals*

For purposes of clauses (i) through (iii) of this subparagraph, the term "individual or class of individuals" refers to the clients or customers of the covered public accommodation that enters into the contractual, licensing or other arrangement.

(B) *Integrated settings*

Goods, services, facilities, privileges, advantages, and accommodations shall be afforded to an individual with a disability in the most integrated setting appropriate to the needs of the individual.

(C) *Opportunity to participate*

Notwithstanding the existence of separate or different programs or activities provided in accordance with this section, an individual with a disability shall not be denied the opportunity to participate in such programs or activities that are not separate or different.

(D) *Administrative methods*

An individual or entity shall not, directly or through contractual or other arrangements, utilize standards or criteria or methods of administration—

(i) that have the effect of discriminating on the basis of disability; or

(ii) that perpetuate the discrimination of others who are subject to common administrative control.

(E) *Association*

It shall be discriminatory to exclude or otherwise deny equal goods, services, facilities, privileges, advantages, accommodations, or other opportunities to an individual or entity because of the known disability of an individual with whom the individual or entity is known to have a relationship or association.

(2) *Specific prohibitions*

(A) *Discrimination.*—For purposes of subsection (a) of this section, discrimination includes—

(i) the imposition or application of eligibility criteria that screen out or tend to screen out an individual with a disability or any class of individuals with disabilities from fully and equally enjoying any goods, services, facilities, privileges, advantages, or accommodations, unless such criteria can be shown to be necessary for the provision of the goods, services, facilities, privileges, advantages, or accommodations being offered;

(ii) a failure to make reasonable modifications in policies, practices, or procedures, when such modifications are necessary to afford such goods, services, facilities, privileges, advantages, or accommodations to individuals with disabilities, unless the entity can demonstrate that making such modifications would fundamentally alter the nature of such goods, services, facilities, privileges, advantages, or accommodations;

(iii) a failure to take such steps as may be necessary to ensure that no individual with a disability is excluded, denied services, segregated or otherwise treated differently than other individuals because of the absence of auxiliary aids and services, unless the entity can demonstrate that taking such steps would fundamentally alter the nature of the good, service, facility, privilege, advantage, or accommodation being offered or would result in an undue burden;

(iv) a failure to remove architectural barriers, and communication barriers that are structural in nature, in existing facilities, and transportation barriers in existing vehicles and rail passenger cars used by an establishment for transporting individuals (not including barriers that can only be removed through the retrofitting of vehicles or rail passenger cars by the installation of a hydraulic or other lift), where such removal is readily achiev-able; and

(v) where an entity can demonstrate that the removal of a barrier under clause (iv) is not readily achievable, a failure to make such goods, services, facilities, privileges, advantages, or accommodations available through alternative methods if such methods are readily achievable. . . .

(3) *Specific construction*

Nothing in this subchapter shall require an entity to permit an individual to participate in or benefit from the goods, services, facilities, privileges, advantages and accommodations of such entity where such individual poses a direct threat to the health or safety of others. The term "direct threat" means a significant risk to the health or safety of others that cannot be eliminated by a modification of policies, practices, or procedures or by the provision of auxiliary aids or services.

§12183. New Construction and Alterations in Public Accommodations and Commercial Facilities

(a) *Application of term*

Except as provided in subsection (b) of this section, as applied to public accommodations and commercial facilities, discrimination for purposes of section 12182(a) of this title includes —

(1) a failure to design and construct facilities for first occupancy later than 30 months after July 26, 1990, that are readily accessible to and usable by individuals with disabilities, except where an entity can demonstrate that it is structurally impracticable to meet the requirements of such subsection in accordance with standards set forth or incorporated by reference in regulations issued under this subchapter; and

(2) with respect to a facility or part thereof that is altered by, on behalf of, or for the use of an establishment in a manner that affects or could affect the usability of the facility or part thereof, a failure to make alterations in such a manner that, to the maximum extent feasible, the altered portions of the facility are readily accessible to and usable by individuals with disabilities, including individuals who use wheelchairs. Where the entity is undertaking an alteration that affects or could affect usability of or access to an area of the facility containing a primary function, the entity shall also make the alterations in such a manner that, to the maximum extent feasible, the path of travel to the altered area and the bathrooms, telephones, and drinking fountains serving the altered area, are readily accessible to and usable by individuals with disabilities where such alterations to the path of travel or the bathrooms, telephones, and drinking fountains serving the altered area are not disproportionate to the overall alterations in terms of cost and scope (as determined under criteria established by the Attorney General).

(b) *Elevator*

Subsection (a) of this section shall not be construed to require the installation of an elevator for facilities that are less than three stories or have less than 3,000 square feet per story unless the building is a shopping center, a shopping mall, or the professional office of a health care provider or unless the Attorney General determines that a particular category of such facilities requires the installation of elevators based on the usage of such facilities.

§12187. Exemptions for Private Clubs and Religious Organizations

The provisions of this subchapter shall not apply to private clubs or establishments exempted from coverage under title II of the *Civil Rights Act of 1964* (42 U.S.C. 2000-a(e)) [42 U.S.C.A. §§2000a *et seq.*] or to religious organizations or entities controlled by religious organizations, including places of worship.

§12201. Construction . . .

(b) *Relationship to other laws.* . . . Nothing in this chapter shall be construed to preclude the prohibition of, or the imposition of restrictions on, smoking [in] . . . places of public accommodation covered by . . . this chapter. . . .

§12210. Illegal Use of Drugs

(a) *In general.* For purposes of this chapter, the term "individual with a disability" does not include an individual who is currently engaging in the illegal use of drugs, when the covered entity acts on the basis of such use.

(b) *Rules of construction.* Nothing in subsection (a) of this section shall be construed to exclude as an individual with a disability an individual who— . . .

(3) is erroneously regarded as engaging in such use, but is not engaging in such use. . . .

§12211. Definitions

(a) *Homosexuality and bisexuality.* — For purposes of the definition of "disability" in section 3(2) [§12102(2)], homosexuality and bisexuality are not impairments and as such are not disabilities under this chapter.

PROBLEMS

1. A man whose legs and arms are substantially paralyzed but who has some movement in his hands and lower arms, and in his neck and part of his upper torso, is admitted to law school. His wheelchair is motor-operated, and he can use his hands to move himself around in the wheelchair. He applies for and obtains a room in the law school dormitory that he can share with his trained full-time attendant. He needs to be constantly attended because he is on a respirator to enable him to breathe and may require immediate attention if something goes wrong with the breathing

mechanism. The law school notifies him that he will have to pay rent (the dormitory fee) both for himself and his attendant, effectively doubling the rent he must pay, because the attendant takes a space that would otherwise go to another paying law student. Has the law school violated the public accommodations provisions of the ADA?

2. A law school library is being renovated. Right now the only access to the library is through an underground tunnel through the elevator, with the entrance to the library on the fourth floor. The library stacks are not accessible by wheelchair. The $20 million renovation project will move the library entrance to the first floor and create two wheelchair-accessible entrances on the south side of the building. Although these south entrances visually appear to be the "back doors" to the library, in fact 90 percent of the students enter the library through these south entrances. The north entrance has a grand staircase and is architecturally the main entrance to the building from a design standpoint, although only about 10 percent of the users enter the building this way. Installing a lift or a ramp at this northern entrance would cost $80,000 to $150,000. Is the school required by §12183 to make the north entrance accessible by wheelchair?

3. In *Staron v. McDonald's Corp.*, 51 F.3d 353 (2d Cir. 1995), smoke-sensitive individuals, including children with asthma and a woman with lupus, sued a McDonald's and a Burger King restaurant, asking the court to order the restaurants to ban smoking entirely in their business establishments. Defendants argued that a complete ban on smoking could not constitute a "reasonable" modification of policies as required by §12182(b)(2)(A)(ii). The court held that such a policy might indeed be reasonable if it did not impose an undue financial burden on the restaurants and if it did not "fundamentally alter the nature of such goods [and] services" provided by the defendants. However, the court in *Emery v. Caravan of Dreams, Inc.*, 879 F. Supp. 640 (N.D. Tex. 1995), *aff'd sub. nom Emery v. Dreams Spirits, Inc.*, 85 F.3d 622 (5th Cir. 1996), ruled that a musical entertainment facility had no obligation to exclude smokers even though failure to do so meant that plaintiffs suffering from cystic fibrosis, allergies, and asthma could not attend concerts there. Which case was correctly decided?

4. In *Bragdon v. Abbott*, 524 U.S. 624 (1998), a dentist refused to treat a patient with HIV infection in his office, instead offering to treat her in the hospital. She sued for violation of the ADA. The Supreme Court held that HIV infection is a "disability" under the ADA, even when the infection has not yet progressed to the so-called symptomatic phase (AIDS), because it is a physical impairment that substantially limits the major life activity of reproduction, given the possibility that the infection can be transmitted from mother to child in the womb. The Court remanded for consideration of whether it would constitute a "direct threat" to the dentist's health to treat such a patient. On remand, the First Circuit held that filling a patient's cavity would not constitute a "significant risk to the health or safety of others." *Abbott v. Bragdon*, 163 F.3d 87 (1st Cir. 1998). *Accord, D.B. v. Bloom*, 896 F. Supp. 166, 170 n.6 (D.N.J. 1995) (no medically justified reason existed for defendant's refusal to treat HIV-infected plaintiff); *United States v. Morvant*, 898 F. Supp. 1157, 1166-1167 (E.D. La. 1995) (similar).

    a.   A man with HIV infection but who has not yet developed full-blown AIDS and has no observable symptoms has no intention of ever having children. Does he have a "disability" under the ADA?

    b.   Dr. Bragdon introduced evidence of 42 documented cases of occupational transmission of HIV from patients to health-care workers (none of whom were dental workers). On remand from the Supreme Court, the First Circuit found that if a dentist followed the American Dental Association's guidelines for treating patients that the risk of transmission of AIDS from patient to doctor was "insignificant." The court rejected the doctor's evidence as insufficient because he did not show that the risks to dentists and other health-care workers were comparable. *Abbott v. Bragdon,* 163 F.3d at 90. Assume the case is appealed to the Supreme Court. How should the Court rule? What legal standard should it apply to determine whether treatment "poses a significant risk to the health or safety of others that cannot be eliminated by a modification of policies, practices, or procedures..." under 42 U.S.C. §12182(b)(3)?

5. A new movie theater has stadium-style seating at a sharp incline on steep stairs and provides spaces for wheelchairs only down on the lowest level in the front row just in front of the screen in a sloped area. These seats are always the last to fill up because individuals must crane their necks back to see the film and the picture is somewhat distorted at that angle. However, those seats are used by the general public when the theater is full. A Justice Department regulation under the ADA requires movie theaters and stadiums to provide "wheelchair areas" that are "an integral part of any fixed seating plan" and to ensure that they possess "lines of sight comparable to those for members of the general public." *ADA Accessibility Guidelines,* 28 C.F.R. pt. 36, App. A, §4.33.3.

a. Has the theater violated the ADA? *Compare Lara v. Cinemark USA, Inc.,* 207 F.3d 783 (5th Cir. 2000) (no violation) *with Oregon Paralyzed Veterans of America v. Regal Cinemas, Inc.,* 339 F.3d 1126 (9th Cir. 2003)(violation). *Cf. United States v. Hoyts Cinemas Corp.,* 380 F.3d 558 (1st Cir. 2004)(rejecting the holdings of both *Lara* and *Oregon Paralyzed Veterans* and remanding for factual findings on the angles of view and visual distortion in seat placements in the sloped area). *See* Felicia H. Ellsworth, *The Worst Seats in the House: Stadium-Style Movie Theaters and the Americans with Disabilities Act,* 71 U. Chi. L. Rev. 1109 (2004).

b. Must the theater reserve seats next to spots reserved for wheelchair users for companions who accompany them so that they can sit together, thereby requiring individuals who have taken those seats to move to other available seats in the theater? In *Fortyune v. American Multi-Cinema, Inc.,* 364 F.3d 1075 (9th Cir. 2004), the court held that a quadriplegic had the right to have his wife sit next to him because his condition made it necessary to have someone with him at all times, making a modification of the theater's policy both "necessary" for him to enjoy the services and a "reasonable modification" of the theater's policy which would not "fundamentally alter" the nature of the services being offered. It held that theaters must reserve companion seats near wheelchair spots until ten minutes before show time. Would the case come out the same way if the plaintiff were not a quadriplegic? If you were the attorney for the theater, what policy would you advise them to adopt to ensure compliance with the ADA?

6. The ADA requirements for alteration of existing facilities do not apply to buildings that have been designated historic landmarks under federal or state law if

the alterations will "threaten or destroy the historic significance" of the building. 42 U.S.C. §12204(a); 28 C.F.R. §36.405. A building that is now listed as a historical landmark under the *National Historic Preservation Act*, 16 U.S.C. §§470 *et seq.*, has been in continuous use as a law school classroom building since 1880. The ceilings are very high and the acoustics in the classrooms are terrible. Students have great difficulty hearing each other when they speak. The law school wants either to drop the ceilings, float panels hung from the ceiling in the rooms, or install microphones at every seat to rectify the situation. The local historic preservation board refuses to grant the school permission to do any of these things on the ground that they would impair the historical and architectural integrity of the building. How should a court reconcile the requirements of the ADA with the historic preservation laws that prohibit alterations of historic buildings that would impair their historic significance?

7. In *PGA Tour, Inc. v. Martin*, 531 U.S. 1049 (U.S. 2001), the Supreme Court ruled that the Professional Golf Association (PGA) violated the ADA when it refused to allow golfer Casey Martin to use a cart to travel between holes in a professional golf tournament. Martin has a degenerative circulatory disorder that causes pain when he walks too far, and he sought a "reasonable modification" of the policy prohibiting the use of golf carts in its competitions under §12182(b)(2)(A)(ii). The PGA claimed that this would "fundamentally alter the nature" of the game because walking induced fatigue and was an essential part of the game at the high level of competition the PGA represented. The Court found to the contrary, concluding that waiving the rule would neither give Martin a competitive advantage nor alter the "essential character of the game of golf," which had always been shot-making. Justice Stevens noted that the trial court had found that the fatigue from walking during the tournament was not significant, thereby finding the defendant's justification insubstantial. Justices Scalia and Thomas dissented. Justice Scalia argued that the ADA gives individuals a right to participate in whatever services a public accommodation offers, not to change the nature of those services.

A law school professor gives an eight-hour take-home exam to be picked up at 8:30 A.M. and returned at 4:30 P.M. A student with dyslexia asks to be allowed to add 24 hours to the exam, picking it up at 8:30 A.M. one day and returning it at 4:30 P.M. the next day. Is the school obligated to comply?

8. Does the ADA apply to businesses that do not operate at specific physical location but offer services over the phone, by mail, or through the Internet? *Compare Carparts Distribution Center, Inc. v. Automotive Wholesalers Ass'n of New England*, 37 F.3d 12, 26 (1st Cir. 1994) (ADA applies to goods and services "sold over the telephone or by mail with customers never physically entering the premises of a commercial entity to purchase the goods or services") *with Parker v. Metropolitan Life Ins. Co.*, 121 F.3d 1006 (6th Cir. 1997) (public accommodations provisions of ADA only require access to physical places). Does it require that Internet chat rooms be accessible by blind persons? *See* Tara E. Thompson, *Locating Discrimination: Interactive Web Sites as Public Accommodations under Title II of the Civil Rights Act*, 2002 U.Chi. Leg. F. 409. Does it require health insurance companies to offer coverage for mental illness as well as physical illness? *See MacNeil v. Time Ins. Co.*, 205 F.3d 179, 186 (5th Cir. 2000)(insurance company does not violate ADA when it caps benefits for patients with AIDS because the ADA does not "regulate the content of goods and services that are offered"); *Ford v. Schering-Plough Corp.*, 145 F.3d 601 (3d Cir. 1998)(no ADA violation when insurance company capped benefits for mental but not physical disabilities).

§2.3   Free Speech Rights of Access to Private Property

§2.3.1   UNITED STATES CONSTITUTION: The FIRST AMENDMENT

LLOYD CORP., LTD. v. TANNER
407 U.S. 551 (1972)

Mr. Justice LEWIS F. POWELL delivered the opinion of the Court.

This case presents the question reserved by the Court in *Amalgamated Food Employees Union v. Logan Valley Plaza*, 391 U.S. 308 (1968), as to the right of a privately owned shopping center to prohibit the distribution of handbills on its property when the handbilling is unrelated to the shopping center's operations. Relying primarily on *Marsh v. Alabama*, 326 U.S. 501 (1946), and *Logan Valley*, the United States District Court for the District of Oregon sustained an asserted First Amendment right to distribute handbills in petitioner's shopping center, and issued a permanent injunction restraining petitioner from interfering with such right. The Court of Appeals for the Ninth Circuit affirmed. We granted certiorari to consider petitioner's contention that the decision below violates rights of private property protected by the Fifth and Fourteenth Amendments.

Lloyd Corp., Ltd. (Lloyd), owns a large, modern retail shopping center in Portland, Oregon. Lloyd Center embraces altogether about 50 acres, including some 20 acres of open and covered parking facilities which accommodate more than 1,000 automobiles. It has a perimeter of almost one and one-half miles, bounded by four public streets. It is crossed in varying degrees by several other public streets, all of which have adjacent public sidewalks. Lloyd owns all land and buildings within the Center, except these public streets and sidewalks. There are some 60 commercial tenants, including small shops and department stores.

The Center embodies a relatively new concept in shopping center design. The stores are all located within a single large, multi-level building complex sometimes referred to as the "Mall." Within this complex, in addition to the stores, there are parking facilities, malls, private sidewalks, stairways, escalators, gardens, an auditorium, and a skating rink. Some of the stores open directly on the outside public sidewalks, but most open on the interior privately owned malls. Some stores open on both. There are no public streets or public sidewalks within the building complex, which is enclosed and entirely covered except for the landscaped portions of some of the interior malls.

The distribution of the handbills occurred in the malls. . . .

The Center is open generally to the public, with a considerable effort being made to attract shoppers and prospective shoppers, and to create "customer motivation" as well as customer goodwill in the community. In this respect the Center pursues policies comparable to those of major stores and shopping centers across the country, although the Center affords superior facilities for these purposes. Groups and organizations are permitted, by invitation and advance arrangement, to use the auditorium and other facilities. Rent is charged for use of the auditorium except with respect to certain civic and charitable organizations, such as the Cancer Society and Boy and Girl Scouts. The Center also allows limited use of the malls by the American Legion to sell poppies for disabled veterans, and by the Salvation Army and Volunteers of America to solicit Christmas contributions. It has denied similar use to other civic and charitable organizations. Political use is also forbidden, except that presidential candidates of both parties have been allowed to speak in the auditorium. . . .

On November 14, 1968, the respondents in this case distributed within the Center handbill invitations to a meeting of the "Resistance Community" to protest the draft and the Vietnam war. The distribution, made in several different places on the mall walkways by five young people, was quiet and orderly, and there was no littering. There was a complaint from one customer. Security guards informed the respondents that they were trespassing and would be arrested unless they stopped distributing the handbills within the Center. The guards suggested that respondents distribute their literature on the public streets and sidewalks adjacent to but outside of the Center complex. Respondents left the premises as requested "to avoid arrest" and continued the handbilling outside. Subsequently this suit was instituted in the District Court, seeking declaratory and injunctive relief.

I

The District Court, emphasizing that the Center "is open to the general public," found that it is "the functional equivalent of a public business district." That court then held that Lloyd's "rule prohibiting the distribution of handbills within the Mall violates . . . First Amendment rights." In a *per curiam* opinion, the Court of Appeals held that it was bound by the "factual determination" as to the character of the Center, and concluded that the decisions of this Court in *Marsh v. Alabama*, 326 U.S. 501 (1946), and *Amalgamated Food Employees Union v. Logan Valley Plaza*, 391 U.S. 308 (1968), compelled affirmance.

Marsh involved Chickasaw, Alabama, a company town wholly owned by the Gulf Shipbuilding Corp. The opinion of the Court, by Mr. Justice Black, described Chickasaw as follows:

> Except for [ownership by a private corporation] it has all the characteristics of any other American town. The property consists of residential buildings, streets, a system of sewers, a sewage disposal plant and a "business block" on which business places are situated. A deputy of the Mobile County Sheriff, paid by the company, serves as the town's policeman. Merchants and service establishments have rented the stores and business places on the business block and the United States uses one of the places as a post office from which six carriers deliver mail to the people of Chickasaw and the adjacent area. The town and the surrounding neighborhood, which cannot be distinguished from the Gulf property by anyone not familiar with the property lines, are thickly settled, and according to all indications the residents use the business block as their regular shopping center. To do so, they now, as they have for many years, make use of a company-owned paved street and sidewalk located alongside the store fronts in order to enter and leave the stores and the post office. Intersecting company-owned roads at each end of the business block lead into a four-lane public highway which runs parallel to the business block at a distance of thirty feet. There is nothing to stop highway traffic from coming onto the business block and upon arrival a traveler may make free use of the facilities available there. In short the town and its shopping district are accessible to and freely used by the public in general and there is nothing to distinguish them from any other town and shopping center except the fact that the title to the property belongs to a private corporation. 326 U.S., at 502-503.

A Jehovah's Witness undertook to distribute religious literature on a sidewalk near the post office and was arrested on a trespassing charge. In holding that First and

Fourteenth Amendment rights were infringed, the Court emphasized that the business district was within a company-owned town, an anachronism long prevalent in some southern States and now rarely found. . . .

II

The courts below considered the critical inquiry to be whether Lloyd Center was "the functional equivalent of a public business district." This phrase was first used in *Logan Valley*, but its genesis was in *Marsh*. It is well to consider what *Marsh* actually decided. As noted above, it involved an economic anomaly of the past, "the company town." One must have seen such towns to understand that "functionally" they were no different from municipalities of comparable size. They developed primarily in the Deep South to meet economic conditions, especially those which existed following the Civil War. Impoverished States, and especially backward areas thereof, needed an influx of industry and capital. Corporations attracted to the area by natural resources and abundant labor were willing to assume the role of local government. Quite literally, towns were built and operated by private capital with all of the customary services and utilities normally afforded by a municipal or state government: there were streets, sidewalks, sewers, public lighting, police and fire protection, business and residential areas, churches, postal facilities, and sometimes schools. In short, as Mr. Justice Black said, Chickasaw, Alabama, had "all the characteristics of any other American town." The Court simply held that where private interests were substituting for and performing the customary functions of government, First Amendment freedoms could not be denied where exercised in the customary manner on the town's sidewalks and streets. Indeed, as title to the entire town was held privately, there were no publicly owned streets, sidewalks, or parks where such rights could be exercised. . . .

Logan Valley extended *Marsh* to a shopping center situation in a different context from the company town setting, but it did so only in a context where the First Amendment activity was related to the shopping center's operations. There is some language in *Logan Valley*, unnecessary to the decision, suggesting that the key focus of *Marsh* was upon the "business district," and that whenever a privately owned business district serves the public generally its sidewalks and streets become the functional equivalents of similar public facilities. . . .

The holding in *Logan Valley* was not dependent upon the suggestion that the privately owned streets and sidewalks of a business district or a shopping center are the equivalent, for First Amendment purposes, of municipally owned streets and sidewalks. No such expansive reading of the opinion of the Court is necessary or appropriate. The opinion was carefully phrased to limit its holding to the picketing involved, where the picketing was "directly related in its purpose to the use to which the shopping center property was being put," and where the store was located in the center of a large private enclave with the consequence that no other reasonable opportunities for the pickets to convey their message to their intended audience were available.

III

The basic issue in this case is whether respondents, in the exercise of asserted First Amendment rights, may distribute handbills on Lloyd's private property contrary to its wishes and contrary to a policy enforced against *all* handbilling. In addressing this issue, it must be remembered that the First and Fourteenth Amendments safeguard the rights of free speech and assembly by limitations on *state* action, not on action by the owner of private property used nondiscriminatorily for private purposes only. The Due Process Clauses of the Fifth and Fourteenth Amendments are also relevant to this case. They provide that "[n]o person shall . . . be deprived of life, liberty, or property, without due process of law." There is the further proscription in the Fifth Amendment against the taking of "private property . . . for public use, without just compensation."

Although accommodations between the values protected by these three Amendments are sometimes necessary, and the courts properly have shown a special solicitude for the guarantees of the First Amendment, this Court has never held that a trespasser or an uninvited guest may exercise general rights of free speech on property privately owned and used nondiscriminatorily for private purposes only. . . .

Respondents contend, however, that the property of a large shopping center is "open to the public," serves the same purposes as a "business district" of a municipality, and therefore has been dedicated to certain types of public use. The argument is that such a center has sidewalks, streets, and parking areas which are fundamentally similar to facilities customarily provided by municipalities. It is then asserted that all members of the public, whether invited as customers or not, have the same right of free speech as they would have on the similar public facilities in the streets of a city or town.

The argument reaches too far. The Constitution by no means requires such an attenuated doctrine of dedication of private property to public use. The closest decision in theory, *Marsh v. Alabama, supra,* involved the assumption by a private enterprise of all of the attributes of a state-created municipality and the exercise by that enterprise of semi-official municipal functions as a delegate of the State. In effect, the owner of the company town was performing the full spectrum of municipal powers and stood in the shoes of the State. In the instant case there is no comparable assumption or exercise of municipal functions or power.

Nor does property lose its private character merely because the public is generally invited to use it for designated purposes. Few would argue that a free-standing store, with abutting parking space for customers, assumes significant public attributes merely because the public is invited to shop there. Nor is size alone the controlling factor. The essentially private character of a store and its privately owned abutting property does not change by virtue of being large or clustered with other stores in a modern shopping center. This is not to say that no differences may exist with respect to government regulation or rights of citizens arising by virtue of the size and diversity of activities carried on within a privately owned facility serving the public. There will be, for example, problems with respect to public health and safety which vary in degree and in the appropriate government response, depending upon the size and character of a shopping center, an office building, a sports arena, or other large facility serving the public for commercial purposes. We do say that the Fifth and Fourteenth Amendment rights of private property owners, as well as the First Amendment rights of all citizens, must be respected and protected. The Framers of the Constitution certainly did not think these fundamental rights of a free society are incompatible with each other. There may be situations where accommodations between them, and the drawing of lines to assure due protection of both, are not easy. But on the facts presented in this case, the answer is clear.

We hold that there has been no such dedication of Lloyd's privately owned and operated shopping center to public use as to entitle respondents to exercise therein the asserted First Amendment rights. Accordingly, we reverse the judgment and remand the case to the Court of Appeals with directions to vacate the injunction.

Mr. Justice THURGOOD MARSHALL, with whom Mr. Justice DOUGLAS, Mr. Justice BRENNAN, and Mr. Justice STEWART join, dissenting. . . .

This Court held in *Marsh v. Alabama, supra,* that even though property is privately owned, under some circumstances it may be treated as though it were publicly held, at least for purposes of the First Amendment. . . . The Court reasoned that "[t]he more an owner, for his advantage, opens up his property for use by the public in general, the more do his rights become circumscribed by the statutory and constitutional rights of those who use it." Noting that the stifling effect produced by any ban on free expression in a community's central business district was the same whether the ban was imposed by public or private owners, the Court concluded that:

> When we balance the Constitutional rights of owners of property against those of the people to enjoy freedom of press and religion, as we must here, we remain mindful of the fact that the latter occupy a preferred position. As we have stated before, the right to exercise the liberties safeguarded by the First Amendment "lies at the foundation of free government by free men" and we must in all cases "weigh the circumstances and . . . appraise the . . . reasons . . . in support of the regulation . . . of the rights." . . . In our view the circumstance that the property rights to the premises where the deprivation of liberty, here involved, took place, were held by others than the public, is not sufficient to justify the State's permitting a corporation to govern a community of citizens so as to restrict their fundamental liberties and the enforcement of such restraint by the application of a state statute. *Id.,* at 509.

. . . We must remember that it is a balance that we are striking—a balance between the freedom to speak, a freedom that is given a preferred place in our hierarchy of values, and the freedom of a private property owner to control his property. When the competing interests are fairly weighed, the balance can only be struck in favor of speech.

Members of the Portland community are able to see doctors, dentists, lawyers, bankers, travel agents, and persons offering countless other services in Lloyd Center. They can buy almost anything that they want or need there. For many Portland citizens, Lloyd Center will so completely satisfy their wants that they will have no reason to go elsewhere for goods or services. If speech is to reach these people, it must reach them in Lloyd Center. The Center itself recognizes this. For example, in 1964 its director of public relations offered candidates for President and Vice President the use of the center for political speeches, boasting "that our convenient location and setting would provide the largest audience [the candidates] could attract in Oregon."

For many persons who do not have easy access to television, radio, the major newspapers, and the other forms of mass media, the only way they can express themselves to a broad range of citizens on issues of general public concern is to picket, or to handbill, or to utilize other free or relatively inexpensive means of communication. The only hope that these people have to be able to communicate effectively is to be permitted to speak in those areas in which most of their fellow citizens can be found. One such area is the business district of a city or town or its functional equivalent. And this is why respondents have a tremendous need to express themselves within Lloyd Center.

Petitioner's interests, on the other hand, pale in comparison. For example, petitioner urges that respondents' First Amendment activity would disturb the Center's customers. It is undisputed that some patrons will be disturbed by any First Amendment activity that goes on, regardless of its object. . . .

We noted in *Logan Valley* that the large-scale movement of this country's population from the cities to the suburbs has been accompanied by the growth of suburban shopping centers. In response to this phenomenon, cities like Portland are providing for large-scale shopping areas within the city. It is obvious that privately owned shopping areas could prove to be greatly advantageous to cities. They are totally self-sufficient, needing no financial support from local government; and if, as here, they truly are the functional equivalent of a public business area, the city reaps the advantages of having such an area without paying for them. Some of the advantages are an increased tax base, a drawing attraction for residents, and a stimulus to further growth.

It would not be surprising in the future to see cities rely more and more on private businesses to perform functions once performed by governmental agencies. The advantage of reduced expenses and an increased tax base cannot be overstated. As governments rely on private enterprise, public property decreases in favor of privately owned property. It becomes harder and harder for citizens to find means to communicate with other citizens. Only the wealthy may find effective communication possible unless we adhere to *Marsh v. Alabama* and continue to hold that "[t]he more an owner, for his advantage, opens up his property for use by the public in general, the more do his rights become circumscribed by the statutory and constitutional rights of those who use it," 326 U.S. at 506.

When there are no effective means of communication, free speech is a mere shibboleth. I believe that the First Amendment requires it to be a reality. Accordingly, I would affirm the decision of the Court of Appeals.

Hudgens v. NLRB, 424 U.S. 507 (1976). Four years after *Lloyd*, the Supreme Court heard a case similar to *Logan Valley* involving labor picketing in a shopping center. It concluded that the "the reasoning of the Court's opinion in Lloyd cannot be squared with the reasoning of the Court's opinion in *Logan Valley*." *Id.* at 518. Because the two cases could not be distinguished, the Court formally overruled *Logan Valley*. The Court held that the constitutional guarantee of free speech is a guarantee only against abridgement by federal or state government and does not give individuals the right to speak on private property. That view was reaffirmed in *PruneYard Shopping Center v. Robins*, 447 U.S. 74, 81 (1980). This meant that the only first amendment rights that are left on private property are those recognized in the context of the company town in *Marsh* where the company was effectively exercising all municipal functions.

§2.3.2 STATE CONSTITUTIONS: The RIGHT to SPEAK FREELY

New Jersey Coalition Against War in the Middle East v. J.M.B. Realty Corp., 650 A.2d 757 (N.J. 1994). In the fall of 1990 when the nation was debating whether to go to war with Iraq, a coalition of groups opposed to war began a major leafleting campaign. When members were excluded from many shopping centers in New Jersey, they sued, claiming that the free speech guarantees of the New Jersey Constitution protected their right to hand out leaflets in the "public" areas of shopping centers. The Supreme Court of New Jersey had previously held that, unlike the federal constitution, the state constitution's free speech guarantee extended to some private property. *State v. Schmid*, 423 A.2d 615 (N.J. 1980) (granting a right to leaflet on the private university campus of Princeton University). It reaffirmed that ruling and extended it to large regional shopping centers, thereby siding with the dissenters in *Lloyd Corp. v. Tanner* and the reasoning of the majority in *Logal Valley Plaza. See also Green Party of New Jersey v. Hartz Mountain Industries, Inc.*, 752 A.2d 315 (N.J. 2000) (extending free speech leafleting rights to smaller community shopping centers).

Chief Justice Robert Wilentz noted that the free speech clause in the state constitution was worded more expansively than that in the federal constitution, providing that "[e]very person may freely speak, write and publish his sentiments on all subjects . . ." N.J. Const. art. I, ¶6. He also emphasized that, while states may not grant fewer constitutional rights than the minimum conferred by the federal constitution, they may grant *greater* rights. *Schmid* had held that the free speech rights must be balanced against property rights and had cited *Marsh* for the proposition that "[t]he more an owner, for his advantage, opens up his property for use by the public in general, the more do his rights become circumscribed by the statutory and constitutional rights of those who use it." *Marsh v. Alabama*, 326 U.S. 501, 506 (1946).

Leafleting must be allowed in shopping centers, Chief Justice Wilentz explained, because expressional interests were very strong and leafleting would not interfere with the normal uses of the property. Moreover, shopping centers have become the functional equivalent of downtown areas, and in some towns had completely replaced them as places of public gathering. "[M]alls are where people can be found today." *Id.* at 767. Mall owners extend an open invitation to the public to shop, browse, walk, sit down, and talk. "The activities and uses, the design of the property, the open spaces, the non-retail activities, the expressive uses, all are designed to make the centers attractive to everyone, for all purposes, to make them a magnet for all people, not just shoppers. The hope is that once there they will spend. . . ." *Id.* at 773. Nor was there any evidence the leafleting had or would have any financial impact on the center owners. In addition, they could minimize any possible disruption by time, place, and manner regulations for leafleting. The Court found the balance of interests to favor speech rights, *id.* at 776, 778:

> There is no doubt about the outcome of this balance. On one side, the weight of the private property owners' interest in controlling and limiting activities on their property has greatly diminished in view of the uses permitted and invited on that property. The private property owners in this case, the operators of regional and community malls, have intentionally transformed their property into a public square or market, a public gathering place, a downtown business district, a community; they have told this public in every way possible that the property is theirs, to come to, to visit, to do what they please, and hopefully to shop and spend; they have done so in many ways, but mostly through the practically unlimited permitted public uses found and encouraged on their property. The sliding scale cannot slide any farther in the direction of public use and diminished private property interests.
>
> On the other side of the balance, the weight of plaintiff's free speech interest is the most substantial in our constitutional scheme. Those interests involve speech that is central to the purpose of our right of free speech. At these centers, free speech, such as leafletting, can be exercised without discernible interference with the owners' profits or the shoppers' and non-shoppers' enjoyment. The weight of the free speech interest is thus composed of a constant and a variable: the constant is the quality of free speech, here free speech that is the most important to society; the variable is its potential interference with this diminished private property interest of the owner. Given the limited free speech right sought, leafletting accompanied only by that speech normally associated with and necessary for leafletting, and subject to the owners' broad power to regulate, that interference, if any, will be negligible. . . .

Furthermore, television is not available as a practical matter to these issue-oriented groups. In the fourth quarter of 1993 the average cost of a national thirty-second television commercial ranged from $23,000 during daytime hours to $155,000 during prime-time hours. . . .

. . . For these small groups, indeed for the country itself, television falls short in serving the core value of free speech — the belief that the unpopular views of a minority, if heard, can in time become the majority view. We are a poorer nation when these small groups are silenced. The effect of the dominance of television has been to increase the need of these issue-oriented groups to reach the public through other means, and their only other practicable means is the leafletting they seek here. . . .

If constitutional provisions of this magnitude should be interpreted in light of a changed society, and we believe they should, the most important change is the emergence of these centers as the competitors of the downtown business district and to a great extent as the successors to the downtown business district. The significance of the historical path of free speech is unmistakable and compelling: the parks, the squares, and the streets, traditionally the home of free speech, were succeeded by the downtown business districts, often including those areas, the downtown business districts where that free speech followed. Those districts have now been substantially displaced by these centers. If our State constitutional right of free speech has any substance, it must continue to follow that historic path. . . .

Justice Marie Garibaldi dissented on the ground that shopping centers "are in business for business sake," are "not yet instruments of the state" and that leafleting was beyond the scope of the invitation extended by those centers. *Id.* at 791. Moreover, free speech by fringe or unpopular groups can cause disruption and even violence. "Should the Ku Klux Klan in their flowing white robes or the Black Separatists in their paramilitary gear be permitted on the mall's property? These groups would offend even the most tolerant of shoppers." *Id.* at 792.

United Food and Commercial Workers Union, Local 919, AFL-CIO v. Crystal Mall Associates, L.P., 852 A.2d 659 (Conn. 2004). Plaintiff union sought to enter a privately owned shopping mall to distribute literature and speak to patrons about the rights of the center's employees. The Connecticut Supreme Court affirmed its earlier ruling in *Cologne v. Westfarms Associates,* 469 A.2d 1201 (Conn. 1984), which interpreted the state constitutional free speech guarantee only to apply to public actors and facilities. Justice Joette Katz noted that almost all states have agreed, and that only five jurisdictions, (California, Colorado, Massachusetts, New Jersey, and Washington) interpret their state constitutions to allow some petitioning activity in private shopping centers, *id.* at 673:

Under *Cologne,* as in the overwhelming majority of our sister jurisdictions, the size of the mall, the number of patrons it serves, and the fact that the general public is invited to enter the mall free of charge do not, even when considered together, advance the plaintiff's cause in converting private action into government action. "Property [does not] lose its private character merely because the public is generally invited to use it for designated purposes. . . . The essentially private character of a store and its privately owned abutting property does not change by virtue of being large or clustered with other stores in a modern shopping center. . . . If the furnishing of building permits, police protection and public transportation were deemed to constitute sufficient government involvement to transform the actions of the defendants in refusing the plaintiffs' requests into those of public officials . . . almost every improved property would be subject to the same burden the plaintiffs seek to impose upon the mall." *Cologne, supra,* at 1210.

NOTES AND QUESTIONS

1. *Statutory versus constitutional law.* Judicial decisions construing constitutional provisions have consequences different from those that interpret statutes such as the public accommodations laws. Statutes may be repealed or amended by the legislatures that passed them. In contrast, constitutions are much harder to amend since amendment generally requires a vote by the people rather than merely by the legislature.

Constitutions limit state power to act in ways that interfere with individual rights. Constitutions also may require government officials to act affirmatively in certain ways. Any state statute or common law rule that contravenes constitutional requirements will be held unconstitutional by courts and will be unenforceable. If a court misinterprets a statute, the legislature is free to correct the mistake by amending the statute or passing a new law. However, an interpretation of the constitution cannot be overridden by passage of new legislation; recognition of a constitutional right against the state means that any legislation infringing on the right is unenforceable. The only way to overrule the court decision is to amend the constitution by popular vote.

2. *Federal versus state constitutional law.* Both the U.S. Constitution and the various state constitutions have clauses that protect free speech. These constitutional provisions limit the power of state and federal governments to interfere with the ability of citizens to speak freely. The state constitutions are not entitled to provide *less* protection for free speech than that mandated by the federal constitution; the supremacy clause invalidates any state laws, including constitutional provisions, that conflict with federal law. However, the states are entitled to provide *more* protection for free speech rights than that mandated by the federal constitution. Thus, as Chief Justice Wilentz notes, almost all state courts have agreed with the Supreme Court's decision in *Lloyd Corp.* not to provide free speech rights to private shopping centers. *See, e.g., City of West Des Moines v. Engler,* 641 N.W.2d 803 (Iowa 2002) (no free speech access rights to shopping centers). *Logan Valley* was formally overruled by *Hudgens v. NLRB,* 424 U.S. 507 (1976), leaving only *Marsh v. Alabama* in force.

However, a few state courts have interpreted their state constitutions to provide free speech access to shopping centers either for general purposes, such as handing out leaflets, *see Robins v. PruneYard Shopping Center,* 592 P.2d 341 (Cal. 1979), *aff'd sub nom. PruneYard Shopping Center v. Robins,* 447 U.S. 74 (1980), or for specific purposes, such as seeking signatures to place someone's name on the ballot to run for office or to get an initiative or referendum question placed on the ballot, *Batchelder v. Allied Stores International, Inc.,* 445 N.E.2d 590 (Mass. 1983); *Alderwood Associates v. Washington Environmental Council,* 635 P.2d 108 (Wash. 1981). *See also Wood v. State,* 2003 WL 1955433 (Fla. Cir. Ct. 2003)(state constitution prohibits a private owner of a "quasi-public" place from using state trespass laws to exclude peaceful political activity).

3. *Conflicting free speech claims.* Note that one of the issues raised by these cases is the conflict between rights asserted by the parties. Those claiming a right of access to shopping centers to speak argue that the Constitution prohibits the state from enforcing its trespass laws against them when they exercise their right to speak. Shopping center owners claim in response that they similarly have free speech rights. They argue that it would infringe on their rights to require them to allow speech on their property with which they may disagree; moreover, they argue that the state cannot force anyone to devote their property to speech against their will. Indeed, choosing what opinions may be expressed on one's own land may itself be a protected form of speech.

4. *Free speech versus property rights.* Shopping center owners have also claimed that allowing rights of access for free speech purposes interferes with their property rights — specifically, the right to exclude. Property rights, as well as free speech rights, are protected by the Constitution. Some mall owners have claimed that the state's failure to enforce its trespass laws against unwanted persons distributing leaflets violates the owner's rights under the fifth and fourteenth amendments not to have their property taken for public use without just compensation. The Supreme Court held, in *PruneYard Shopping Center v. Robins*, 447 U.S. 74 (1980), that no constitutionally protected property rights were violated by the California state constitutional provision that granted rights of access for free speech purposes to shopping centers. This question is dealt with in depth in Chapter 12.

It is important to understand that the federal constitutional protection of property rights is distinct from property rights defined by state statutory or common law. Federal constitutional law defines a *minimum* level of protection for property rights that the states may not infringe. So long as the states do not deprive citizens of core property interests protected by the federal Constitution, they are free to define and restrict property rights as they see fit.

There were three possible outcomes of the free speech/property claims involved in *Lloyd Corp.* and *PruneYard.* One possibility would have been to hold that the first amendment to the U.S. Constitution granted citizens a right of access to public shopping centers for free speech purposes. The Supreme Court rejected this approach in *Lloyd Corp.* A second possible holding would have been that not only is no right of access created by the federal constitution but any right of access created *by state law* would represent a taking of property without just compensation and thus violate the owners' property rights protected by the fifth and fourteenth amendments. The Supreme Court rejected this approach in *PruneYard.* A third possibility would have been to hold that free speech access is *neither required* by the first amendment (the holding in *Lloyd*) nor prohibited by the fourteenth amendment (the holding in *Prune-Yard*); rather, the states are *free to choose* between protecting the right of shopping center owners to exclude nonowners and protecting the right of access for free speech purposes to property otherwise open to the public. Either result is consistent with core protections of free speech and property rights protected by the U.S. Constitution. This was the Supreme Court's approach in *PruneYard.*

5. *Labor picketing.* Although there is no federal constitutional right of access to property open to the public for free speech purposes under the first amendment, the *National Labor Relations Act* (NLRA), a federal statute governing employment relations between employees and employers, does provide for some rights of access for labor organizations. Sections 7 and 8 of the NLRA prohibit employers from engaging in certain enumerated "unfair labor practices" that interfere with the rights of employees to form unions and engage in collective bargaining and other types of concerted activities for "mutual aid or protection," including striking and picketing. 29 U.S.C. §§157, 158. The Supreme Court has held that, under some circumstances, it may constitute an unfair labor practice under the NLRA for an employer to deny a right of access to certain areas of her property for purposes of picketing that property owner herself or an employer who is a lessee of a portion of that property. *Hudgens v. National Labor Relations Board*, 424 U.S. 507 (1976). Employees who are on strike or involved in a labor dispute with their employer may want access to the employer's property to picket, communicating to the employer and the public their side in the controversy. Nonemployees may want access to the parking lot or cafeteria of a workplace to

distribute information designed to encourage the employees to form or join a union. In determining whether a right of access should be provided, the courts must balance the employer's property rights against the employees' rights under §7 to be free of unfair labor practices. *See Lechmere v. NLRB,* 502 U.S. 527 (1992) (holding that union organizers had no right to enter the parking lot of a shopping center to put leaflets on the windshields of cars when there were reasonably effective alternative means of communicating with the employees); *Seattle-First National Bank v. NLRB,* 651 F.2d 1272 (9th Cir. 1980) (unfair labor practice for the owner of an office building to refuse to allow striking restaurant employees to picket in the foyer outside a restaurant on the forty-sixth floor of the building); *Scott Hudgens,* 230 N.L.R.B. 414 (1977) (striking employees of a business located in a shopping mall had a right to enter the mall to picket in front of their employer's place of business).

PROBLEMS

1. A shopping mall allows members of the Republican Party to hand out leaflets urging customers to vote for Republican candidates for Congress and for the president but refuses to allow members of the Democratic Party to hand out leaflets. Assume you are in a state that has not interpreted its constitution to require owners of private property open to the public to grant rights of access for free speech purposes. A Democrat who is excluded from handing out leaflets sues the shopping center owner and claims that even though the owner has no duty to allow all members of the public to pass out leaflets, once the owner allows *some* members of the public to do this, it must allow others to do so on a nondiscriminatory basis. Argue both sides.

2. A large shopping mall in New Jersey is owned by a survivor of the Nazi concentration camps. The Ku Klux Klan begins peaceably handing out literature in the shopping center, praising the Nazi party and urging shoppers to vote for a member of the KKK who is running for public office and who has stated that the United States should adopt Nazi methods to deal with African Americans, Latinos, Asian Americans, and American Jews. The owner ejects the KKK members from the mall. They subsequently sue and claim that the owner is violating their free speech rights under the state constitution, as defined in *New Jersey Coalition.* The owner defends by arguing that she has the right to prevent her property from being used as a base from which to hand out literature that preaches hatred against particular ethnic groups. What should the court do?

3. A major Internet search engine begins refusing to list web pages that criticize the third-world labor practices of the conglomerate that owns the search engine. The group that maintains the pages complains that this violates their rights to free speech; they argue that since nearly all Internet users locate web pages using a few major search engines, these engines are the equivalent of a public square or a modern shopping mall. The group is also worried that if the search engine is allowed to exclude anything it chooses from its database, their group may have difficulty getting its message to the public. The search engine company responds that a search engine is private property: the company can choose to make accessible whatever information it wants, and it must have this right if it is to exclude pages containing pornography from its database. The company also argues that storing information is expensive, and it must be able to exclude at will to prevent its database from growing too large. The Electronic Frontier Foundation, a nonprofit organization that promotes free speech on the Internet, proposes legislation prohibiting search engines from refusing to include any web

page in their database if the pages' owner requests inclusion. If you were a member of the legislature, how would you vote and why?

4. A couple of weeks before the United States invaded Iraq in March 2003, a father and son were ousted from a mall in New York State for wearing T-shirts that protested the decision to go to war. The father's T-shirt said "Give Peace a Chance," while his son's shirt read "No War with Iraq" on one side and "Let Inspections Work" on the other. Winnie Hu, *A Message of Peace on 2 Shirts Touches Off Hostilities at a Mall,* N.Y. Times, Mar. 6, 2003, at B-1. As the father and son were eating lunch, security guards asked them to remove the shirts or to leave the premises. Although the son complied by removing his shirt, the father did not. It appears that he also refused to leave the premises. He was arrested and charged with criminal trespass. New York has not adopted the *PruneYard* rule, and no other New York law apparently limited the owner's decision to exclude under these circumstances. The director of operations of the mall explained that the father and son were interfering with other shoppers and that "[t]heir behavior, coupled with their clothing, to express to others their personal views on world affairs were disruptive of customers." *Id.* On the other hand, the legal director of the New York Civil Liberties Union asked whether the mall was going to start excluding customers who wore political buttons. "The ultimate point is that we are a diverse society in which individuals hold diverse views." *Id.* Should the law protect the owner's right to exclude in a case like this, or should the courts recognize a right based on either the common law or the state constitution that would prohibit exclusion under these circumstances?

§2.4   Beach Access and the Public Trust

MATTHEWS v. BAY HEAD IMPROVEMENT ASSOCIATION
471 A.2d 355 (N.J. 1984)

SIDNEY M. SCHREIBER, J.

The public trust doctrine acknowledges that the ownership, dominion and sovereignty over land flowed by tidal waters, which extend to the mean high water mark, is vested in the State in trust for the people. The public's right to use the tidal lands and water encompasses navigation, fishing and recreational uses, including bathing, swimming and other shore activities. *Borough of Neptune City v. Borough of Avon-by-the-Sea,* 294 A.2d 47 (N.J. 1972). In *Avon* we held that the public trust applied to the municipally-owned dry sand beach immediately landward of the high water mark.[1] The major issue in this case is whether, ancillary to the public's right to enjoy the tidal lands, the public has a right to gain access through and to use the dry sand area not owned by a municipality but by a quasi-public body. . . .

I.   Facts

The Borough of Bay Head (Bay Head) borders the Atlantic Ocean. Adjacent to it on the north is the Borough of Point Pleasant Beach, on the south the Borough of Mantolok-

---

1. As the New Jersey Supreme Court noted in *Uston,* the rise of the American common law right to exclude without cause alarmingly corresponds to the fall of the old segregation laws. . . .

ing, and on the west Barnegat Bay. Bay Head consists of a fairly narrow strip of land, 6,667 feet long (about 1 1/4 miles). A beach runs along its entire length adjacent to the Atlantic Ocean. There are 76 separate parcels of land that border the beach. All except six are owned by private individuals. Title to those six is vested in the [Bay Head Improvement] Association [(the Association)].

The Association was founded in 1910 and incorporated as a nonprofit corporation in 1932. Its certificate of incorporation states that its purposes are the improving and beautifying of the Borough of Bay Head, New Jersey, cleaning, policing and otherwise making attractive and safe the bathing beaches in said Borough, and the doing of any act which may be found necessary or desirable for the greater convenience, comfort and enjoyment of the residents. Its constitution delineates the Association's object to promote the best interests of the Borough and "in so doing to own property, operate bathing beaches, hire life guards, beach cleaners and policemen. . . ."

Nine streets in the Borough, which are perpendicular to the beach, end at the dry sand. The Association owns the land commencing at the end of seven of these streets for the width of each street and extending through the upper dry sand to the mean high water line, the beginning of the wet sand area or foreshore. In addition, the Association owns the fee in six shore front properties, three of which are contiguous and have a frontage aggregating 310 feet. Many owners of beachfront property executed and delivered to the Association leases of the upper dry sand area. These leases are revocable by either party to the lease on thirty days' notice. Some owners have not executed such leases and have not permitted the Association to use their beaches. Some also have acquired riparian grants from the State extending approximately 1000 feet east of the high water line.

The Association controls and supervises its beach property between the third week in June and Labor Day. It engages about 40 employees who serve as lifeguards, beach police and beach cleaners. Lifeguards, stationed at five operating beaches, indicate by use of flags whether the ocean condition is dangerous (red), requires caution (yellow), or is satisfactory (green). In addition to observing and, if need be, assisting those in the water, when called upon lifeguards render first aid. Beach cleaners are engaged to rake and keep the beach clean of debris. Beach police are stationed at the entrances to the beaches where the public streets lead into the beach to ensure that only Association members or their guests enter. Some beach police patrol the beaches to enforce its membership rules.

Membership is generally limited to residents of Bay Head. Class A members are property owners. Class B are non-owners. Large families (six or more) pay $90 per year and small families pay $60 per year. Upon application residents are routinely accepted. Membership is evidenced by badges that signify permission to use the beaches. Members, which include local hotels, motels and inns, can also acquire badges for guests. The charge for each guest badge is $12. Members of the Bay Head Fire Company, Bay Head Borough employees, and teachers in the municipality's school system have been issued beach badges irrespective of residency.

Except for fishermen, who are permitted to walk through the upper dry sand area to the foreshore, only the membership may use the beach between 10:00 A.M. and 5:30 P.M. during the summer season. The public is permitted to use the Association's beach from 5:30 P.M. to 10:00 A.M. during the summer and, with no hourly restrictions, between Labor Day and mid-June.

No attempt has ever been made to stop anyone from occupying the terrain east of the high water mark. During certain parts of the day, when the tide is low, the foreshore could consist of about 50 feet of sand not being flowed by the water. The public could gain access to the foreshore by coming from the Borough of Point Pleasant Beach on the north or from the Borough of Mantoloking on the south.

Association membership totals between 4,800 to 5,000. The Association President testified during depositions that its restrictive policy, in existence since 1932, was due to limited parking facilities and to the overcrowding of the beaches. The Association's avowed purpose was to provide the beach for the residents of Bay Head.

There is also a public boardwalk, about one-third of a mile long, parallel to the ocean on the westerly side of the dry sand area. The boardwalk is owned and maintained by the municipality. . . .

II. The Public Trust

In *Borough of Neptune City v. Borough of Avon-by-the-Sea,* 294 A.2d 47, 51 (N.J. 1972), Justice Hall alluded to the ancient principle "that land covered by tidal waters belonged to the sovereign, but for the common use of all the people." . . . This underlying concept was applied in New Jersey in *Arnold v. Mundy,* 6 N.J.L. 1 (Sup. Ct. 1821).

The defendant in *Arnold* tested the plaintiff's claim of an exclusive right to harvest oysters by taking some oysters that the plaintiff had planted in beds in the Raritan River adjacent to his farm in Perth Amboy. The oyster beds extended about 150 feet below the ordinary low water mark. The tide ebbed and flowed over it. . . .

Chief Justice Kirkpatrick . . . concluded that all navigable rivers in which the tide ebbs and flows and the coasts of the sea, including the water and land under the water, are "common to all the citizens, and that each [citizen] has a right to use them according to his necessities, subject only to the laws which regulate that use. . . ." *Id.* at 93. . . . Later in *Illinois Central R.R. v. Illinois,* 146 U.S. 387, 453 (1892), the Supreme Court, in referring to the common property, stated that "[t]he State can no more abdicate its trust over property in which the whole people are interested . . . than it can abdicate its police powers. . . ."

In *Avon,* Justice Hall reaffirmed the public's right to use the waterfront as announced in *Arnold v. Mundy.* He observed that the public has a right to use the land below the mean average high water mark where the tide ebbs and flows. These uses have historically included navigation and fishing. In *Avon* the public's rights were extended "to recreational uses, including bathing, swimming and other shore activities." 294 A.2d at 54. The Florida Supreme Court has held:

> The constant enjoyment of this privilege [bathing in salt waters] of thus using the ocean and its fore-shore for ages without dispute should prove sufficient to establish it as an American common law right, similar to that of fishing in the sea, even if this right had not come down to us as a part of the English common law, which it undoubtedly has. It has been said that "[h]ealth, recreation and sports are encompassed in and intimately related to the general welfare of a well-balanced state." Extension of the public trust doctrine to include bathing, swimming and other shore activities is consonant with and furthers the general welfare. The public's right to enjoy these privileges must be respected. *White v. Hughes,* 190 So. 446, 449 (Fla. 1939).

In order to exercise these rights guaranteed by the public trust doctrine, the public must have access to municipally-owned dry sand areas as well as the foreshore. The extension of the public trust doctrine to include municipally-owned dry sand areas was necessitated by our conclusion that enjoyment of rights in the foreshore is inseparable from use of dry sand beaches. In *Avon* we struck down a municipal ordinance that required nonresidents to pay a higher fee than residents for the use of the beach. We held that where a municipal beach is dedicated to public use, the public trust doctrine "dictates that the beach and the ocean waters must be open to all on equal terms and without preference and that any contrary state or municipal action is impermissible." 294 A.2d at 54. . . .

III.   Public Rights in Privately-Owned Dry Sand Beaches

In *Avon* . . . our finding of public rights in dry sand areas was specifically and appropriately limited to those beaches owned by a municipality. We now address the extent of the public's interest in privately-owned dry sand beaches. This interest may take one of two forms. First, the public may have a right to cross privately owned dry sand beaches in order to gain access to the foreshore. Second, this interest may be of the sort enjoyed by the public in municipal beaches under *Avon* . . . , namely, the right to sunbathe and generally enjoy recreational activities.

Beaches are a unique resource and are irreplaceable. The public demand for beaches has increased with the growth of population and improvement of transportation facilities. Furthermore the projected demand for salt water swimming will not be met "unless the existing swimming capacities of the four coastal counties are expanded." Department of Environmental Protection, Statewide Comprehensive Outdoor Recreation Plan 200 (1977). The DEP estimates that, compared to 1976, the State's salt water swimming areas "must accommodate 764,812 more persons by 1985 and 1,021,112 persons by 1995." . . .

Exercise of the public's right to swim and bathe below the mean high water mark may depend upon a right to pass across the upland beach. Without some means of access the public right to use the foreshore would be meaningless. To say that the public trust doctrine entitles the public to swim in the ocean and to use the foreshore in connection therewith without assuring the public of a feasible access route would seriously impinge on, if not effectively eliminate, the rights of the public trust doctrine. This does not mean the public has an unrestricted right to cross at will over any and all property bordering on the common property. The public interest is satisfied so long as there is reasonable access to the sea. . . .

[T]he particular circumstances must be considered and examined before arriving at a solution that will accommodate the public's right and the private interests involved. Thus an undeveloped segment of the shore may have been available and used for access so as to establish a public right-of-way to the wet sand. Or there may be publicly-owned property, such as in *Avon*, which is suitable. Or, as in this case, the public streets and adjacent upland sand area might serve as a proper means of entry. The test is whether those means are reasonably satisfactory so that the public's right to use the beachfront can be satisfied.

The bather's right in the upland sands is not limited to passage. Reasonable enjoyment of the foreshore and the sea cannot be realized unless some enjoyment of the dry sand area is also allowed. The complete pleasure of swimming must be accompanied by intermittent periods of rest and relaxation beyond the water's edge. The unavailability of the physical situs for such rest and relaxation would seriously curtail and in many situations eliminate the right to the recreational use of the ocean. This was a principal reason why in *Avon* and [*Van Ness v. Borough of Deal*, 393

A.2d 571 (N.J. 1978),] we held that municipally-owned dry sand beaches "must be open to all on equal terms. . . ." *Avon*, 294 A.2d at 54. We see no reason why rights under the public trust doctrine to use of the upland dry sand area should be limited to municipally-owned property. It is true that the private owner's interest in the upland dry sand area is not identical to that of a municipality. Nonetheless, where use of dry sand is essential or reasonably necessary for enjoyment of the ocean, the doctrine warrants the public's use of the upland dry sand area subject to an accommodation of the interests of the owner.

We perceive no need to attempt to apply notions of prescription, *City of Daytona Beach v. Tona-Rama, Inc.*, 294 So. 2d 73 (Fla. 1974), dedication, *Gion v. City of Santa Cruz*, 465 P.2d 50 (Cal. 1970), or custom, *State ex rel. Thornton v. Hay*, 462 P.2d 671 (Or. 1969), as an alternative to application of the public trust doctrine. Archaic judicial responses are not an answer to a modern social problem. Rather, we perceive the public trust doctrine not to be "fixed or static," but one to "be molded and extended to meet changing conditions and needs of the public it was created to benefit." *Avon*, 294 A.2d at 54.

Precisely what privately-owned upland sand area will be available and required to satisfy the public's rights under the public trust doctrine will depend on the circumstances. Location of the dry sand area in relation to the foreshore, extent and availability of publicly-owned upland sand area, nature and extent of the public demand, and usage of the upland sand land by the owner are all factors to be weighed and considered in fixing the contours of the usage of the upper sand.

Today, recognizing the increasing demand for our State's beaches and the dynamic nature of the public trust doctrine, we find that the public must be given both access to and use of privately-owned dry sand areas as reasonably necessary. While the public's rights in private beaches are not co-extensive with the rights enjoyed in municipal beaches, private landowners may not in all instances prevent the public from exercising its rights under the public trust doctrine. The public must be afforded reasonable access to the foreshore as well as a suitable area for recreation on the dry sand. . . .

V. The Beaches of Bay Head

The Bay Head Improvement Association, which services the needs of all residents of the Borough for swimming and bathing in the public trust property, owns the street-wide strip of dry sand area at the foot of seven public streets that extends to the mean high water line. It also owns the fee in six other upland sand properties connected or adjacent to the tracts it owns at the end of two streets. In addition, it holds leases to approximately 42 tracts of upland sand area. The question that we must address is whether the dry sand area that the Association owns or leases should be open to the public to satisfy the public's rights under the public trust doctrine. Our analysis turns upon whether the Association may restrict its membership to Bay Head residents and thereby preclude public use of the dry sand area.

The general rule is that courts will not compel admission to a voluntary association. Ordinarily, a society or association may set its own membership qualifications and restrictions. However, that is not an inexorable rule. Where an organization is quasi-public, its power to exclude must be reasonably and lawfully exercised in furtherance of the public welfare related to its public characteristics.

[A] nonprofit association that is authorized and endeavors to carry out a purpose serving the general welfare of the community and is a quasi-public institution holds in trust its powers of exclusive control in the areas of vital public concern. When a nonprofit association rejects a membership application for reasons unrelated to its purposes and contrary to the general welfare, courts have "broad judicial authority to insure that exclusionary policies are lawful and are not applied arbitrarily or [discriminatorily]." *Greisman v. Newcomb Hospital*, 192 A.2d 817, 820 (1963). That is the situation here.

Bay Head Improvement Association is a non-profit corporation whose primary purpose as stated in its certificate of incorporation is the "cleaning, policing and otherwise making attractive and safe the bathing beaches" in the Borough of Bay Head "and the doing of any act which may be found necessary or desirable for the greater convenience, comfort and enjoyment of the residents." . . .

The Association's activities paralleled those of a municipality in its operation of the beachfront. The size of the beach was so great that it stationed lifeguards at five separate locations. The beach serviced about 5,000 members. The lifeguards performed the functions characteristic of those on a public beach. . . . When viewed in its totality — its purposes, relationship with the municipality, communal characteristic, activities, and virtual monopoly over the Bay Head beachfront — the quasi-public nature of the Association is apparent. The Association makes available to the Bay Head public access to the common tidal property for swimming and bathing and to the upland dry sand area for use incidental thereto, preserving the residents' interests in a fashion similar to *Avon*. . . .

There is no public beach in the Borough of Bay Head. If the residents of every municipality bordering the Jersey shore were to adopt the Bay Head policy, the public would be prevented from exercising its right to enjoy the foreshore. The Bay Head residents may not frustrate the public's right in this manner. By limiting membership only to residents and foreclosing the public, the Association is acting in conflict with the public good and contrary to the strong public policy "in favor of encouraging and expanding public access to and use of shoreline areas." *Gion v. City of Santa Cruz*, 465 P.2d 50, 59 (Cal. 1970). Indeed, the Association is frustrating the public's right under the public trust doctrine. It should not be permitted to do so.

Accordingly, membership in the Association must be open to the public at large. . . .

The Public Advocate has urged that all the privately-owned beachfront property likewise must be opened to the public. Nothing has been developed on this record to justify that conclusion. We have decided that the Association's membership and thereby its beach must be open to the public. That area might reasonably satisfy the public need at this time. [I]f the Association were to sell all or part of its property, it may necessitate further adjudication of the public's claims in favor of the public trust on part or all of these or other privately-owned upland dry sand lands depending upon the circumstances. However, we see no necessity to have those issues resolved judicially at this time since the beach under the Association's control will be open to the public and may be adequate to satisfy the public trust interests. . . .

The record in this case makes it clear that a right of access to the beach is available over the quasi-public lands owned by the Association, as well as the right to use the Association's upland dry sand. It is not necessary for us to determine under what circumstances and to what extent there will be a need to use the dry sand of private owners who either now or in the future may have no leases with the Association.

Resolution of the competing interests, private ownership and the public trust, may in some cases be simple, but in many it may be most complex. In any event, resolution would depend upon the specific facts in controversy.

We realize that considerable uncertainty will continue to surround the question of the public's right to cross private land and to use a portion of the dry sand as discussed above. Where the parties are unable to agree as to the application of the principles enunciated herein, the claim of the private owner shall be honored until the contrary is established. . . .

NOTES AND QUESTIONS

1. *Public trust.* In *Illinois Central Railroad Co. v. Illinois,* 146 U.S. 387, 435 (1892), the Supreme Court held as follows:

> It is the settled law of this country that the ownership of and dominion and sovereignty over lands covered by tide waters, within the limits of the several states, belong to the respective states within which they are found, with the consequent right to use or dispose of any portion thereof, when that can be done without substantial impairment of the interest of the public in the waters, and subject always to the paramount right of Congress to control their navigation so far as may be necessary for the regulation of commerce with foreign nations and among the states.

However, some courts have held that the state may extinguish public rights of access under the public trust doctrine by conveying property to private owners free of such rights. *See, e.g., Greater Providence Chamber of Commerce v. State of Rhode Island,* 657 A.2d 1038 (R.I. 1995). Other courts, however, have held that the rights encompassed by the public trust doctrine are inalienable and lands subject to those rights cannot be reduced to private property free from public trust obligations. *See, e.g., Glass v. Goeckel,* 2005 Mich. LEXIS 1314 (Mich. 2005).

2. *Uses encompassed by the public trust doctrine.* The New Jersey Supreme Court notes its earlier holding that the public trust doctrine included the right to enjoy the lands over which the tides flowed (tidal lands) for a broad variety of purposes, including navigation, fishing, and recreation such as swimming. It further extended the doctrine to encompass public rights of access to the dry sand area adjacent to the tidal lands, inland from the tidal lands to the line where vegetation started on lands owned by the municipalities. *See also Raleigh Avenue Beach Ass'n. v. Atlantis Beach Club, Inc.,* 2005 N.J. LEXIS 932 (N.J. 2005) (private club that holds title to the only beach in the township could not exclude members of the public from access to the dry sand area of the beach beyond the high tide line and could not charge high fees designed to limit access). In the earlier case of *Borough of Neptune City v. Borough of Avon-by-the-Sea,* 294 A.2d 47, 54 (N.J. 1972), Justice Hall explained the extension of the public trust doctrine to recreational uses in the following way:

> We have no difficulty in finding that, in this latter half of the twentieth century, the public rights in tidal lands are not limited to the ancient prerogatives of navigation and fishing, but extend as well to recreational uses, including bathing, swimming and other shore activities. The public trust doctrine, like all common law principles, should not be considered fixed or static, but should be molded and extended to meet changing conditions and needs of the public it was created to benefit.

Cf. Leydon v. Town of Greenwich, 750 A.2d 1122 (Conn. Ct. App. 2000), *aff'd on other grounds by* 777 A.2d 552 (Conn. 2001) (public trust doctrine prohibits town from limiting access to town beach to town residents).

In contrast, the Supreme Judicial Court of Massachusetts has limited public access under the public trust doctrine to tidal lands (defined as the lands seaward of the mean high water line) rather than the dry sand area. The court also limited public use rights to navigation and fishing purposes, specifically excluding recreational uses such as walking along the beachfront or bathing. *Opinion of the Justices,* 313 N.E.2d 561 (Mass. 1974). The court rejected the idea adopted by the New Jersey Supreme Court in *Avon* that the uses encompassed by the public trust doctrine could change or expand over time as social values and conditions changed. Rather, the Massachusetts court held that a statute redefining the public trust doctrine to allow a right of way for the public to walk along the beach on tidal lands constituted a physical invasion of the property rights of beachfront owners and could not be constitutionally required without paying just compensation to those owners for the loss of their property rights. To allow an expansion of public access would infringe on the property owners' right to exclude. *Accord, Bell v. Town of Wells,* 557 A.2d 168 (Me. 1989).

Should it make a difference whether the public has customarily used the beachfront adjoining private property for recreational purposes? Does long-standing customary use justify recognizing rights of access in the public?

If there is no long-standing public use, should the courts interpret the scope of the public trust doctrine to be rigidly limited to those uses customarily enjoyed in colonial times? Or should the doctrine be interpreted to authorize uses needed by the public and considered legitimate under evolving community standards? If the common law changes over time, as we have seen in *State v. Shack* and *Uston v. Resorts International,* why should the public trust doctrine be frozen in its colonial form? Was the New Jersey Supreme Court wrong to change the law in *Shack* and *Uston* to adjust the balance between the right to exclude and the right of access?

3. *Dedication, prescription, and custom.* Justice Schreiber notes that state courts have relied on three common law doctrines, besides public trust, to grant rights of access to beaches by the general public. The doctrines are dedication, prescription, and custom.

Dedication involves a gift of real property from a private owner to the public at large. It requires an offer by the owner and acceptance by the public. Such an offer generally must be made by some unequivocal act by the property owner giving clear evidence of an intent to dedicate the land to public use. Long-standing acquiescence in use of beachfront property by the public may be interpreted as an implied dedication by the property owner and acceptance by the public. *Gion v. City of Santa Cruz,* 465 P.2d 50 (Cal. 1970). However, *Gion* was effectively overturned by the California legislature, which prohibited acquisition of public rights by implied dedication, although allowing public rights of access to arise by prescription. Cal. Civ. Code §1009.

Some states grant public rights of access to tidelands or the dry sand area of beaches under the doctrine of *prescription.* If the public has used property possessed by another for a particular purpose for a long time (measured by the relevant state statute of limitations), the public can acquire such rights permanently even if they never had them originally or if they had previously been reduced to private ownership. The permanent right to do something on another's land is called an *easement.* Such rights are generally created by agreement. However, if the owner fails to exclude trespassers from her property, she may lose her right to sue them under the relevant statute of limitations. The public acquires what is called a *prescriptive easement* to continue using the property for this purpose. *City of Daytona Beach v. Tona-Rama, Inc.*, 294 So. 2d 73 (Fla. 1974); *Concerned Citizens of Brunswick County Taxpayers Association v. Rhodes*, 404 S.E.2d 677 (N.C. 1991).

Most courts traditionally refused to allow the public to obtain an easement by prescription. Today, most courts will recognize such easements. Jon Bruce and James W. Ely, Jr., *The Law of Easements and Licenses in Land* ¶5.09[1] (rev. ed. 1995). They did so partly because (a) it was difficult to show continuous use by the public at large; (b) prescription might apply only to the particular tract of land at issue in the case, necessitating cumbersome and expensive litigation about every disputed parcel along the oceanfront; and (c) when private land is used by the public, courts may imply that the use was permissive, thereby defeating an element needed for prescriptive rights to vest.

Perhaps to avoid these problems, the Oregon Supreme Court has relied on the doctrine of *custom*, rather than prescription, to hold that long-standing, uninterrupted, peaceable, reasonable, uniform use of the beachfront by the public for recreational purposes conferred continuing rights of access.

> The dry-sand area in Oregon has been enjoyed by the general public as a recreational adjunct of the wet-sand or foreshore area since the beginning of the state's political history. The first European settlers on these shores found the aboriginal inhabitants using the foreshore for clam-digging and the dry-sand area for their cooking fires. The newcomers continued these customs after statehood. Thus, from the time of the earliest settlement to the present day, the general public has assumed that the dry-sand area was a part of the public beach, and the public has used the dry-sand area for picnics, gathering wood, building warming fires, and generally as a headquarters from which to supervise children or to range out over the foreshore as the tides advance and recede.

State ex rel. Thornton v. Hay, 462 P.2d 671, 674 (Or. 1969). Applying the doctrine, the court prevented beachfront owners from enclosing the dry-sand area of their property in an attempt to limit access to members of a private beach club. *But see McDonald v. Halvorson*, 780 P.2d 714 (Or. 1989) (holding that the doctrine of custom applied only to those beaches for which proof could be shown of actual public use). *See also Ka Pa'akai O Ka'aina v. Land Use Commission, State of Hawaii*, 7 P.3d 1068 (Haw. 2000) and *Public Access Shoreline Hawaii (PASH) v. Hawaii County Planning Commission*, 903 P.2d 1246 (Haw. 1995) (recognizing customary gathering rights of native Hawaiians along the shoreline); *In re Banning*, 832 P.2d 724 (Hawai'i 1992) *and Akau v. Olohana Corp.*, 652 P.2d 1130 (Hawai'i 1982) (public rights of access to beaches in Hawai'i)(both recognizing public rights to use beaches and considering issues relating to means of access to those beaches); *Matcha v. Mattox*, 711 S.W.2d 95 (Tex. Ct. App. 1986) (adopting the doctrine of custom).

PROBLEMS

Matthews involved beachfront property owned by a nonprofit charitable organization.

1. In *Raleigh Avenue Beach Ass'n. v. Atlantis Beach Club, Inc.*, 2005 N.J. LEXIS 932 (N.J. 2005), the Supreme Court of New Jersey extended the *Matthews* ruling to require the owner of a beach club to allow anyone to become a member and prohibited the club

from charging exorbitant fees designed to limit membership. The private owner had previously allowed the public to use the beach and had only recently converted it to a private beach club accessible only by members upon payment of fees higher than necessary to pay for costs of operation. The Court applied the *Matthews* factors and found that the public interests in access outweighed the private interests in exclusion when there were no publicly owned beaches in the township and demand for beach access was very high. Two judges dissented on the ground that a nearby hotel allowed the public to use its beach. Did the court reach the correct result?

2. Now suppose members of the public begin using the dry-sand area between the mean high water mark and the vegetation line in an area next to a private home. The owner puts up a fence and signs warning against trespassing on the beach. A member of the public sues the beachfront owner and asks for declaratory and injunctive relief preventing the owner from interfering with the public's right of access to the dry-sand area along the beach.

a. What arguments could you make for the plaintiff that the principle underlying the rule of *Matthews* applies to this case? What arguments could you make for the defendant that this case is distinguishable from *Matthews* and that the plaintiff has no right of access to the beach adjoining a private home?

b. If you were the judge deciding this case, what rule of law would you promulgate and how would you justify it?

§2.5   The Right to Be Somewhere and the Problem of Homelessness

The American Civil Liberties Union brought a lawsuit in Miami, Florida, challenging the city's sweep of homeless people from city parks before the 1988 Orange Bowl parade. *Pottinger v. City of Miami*, 810 F. Supp. 1551 (S.D. Fla. 1992). Miami had many more homeless people than it could handle in shelters. On November 16, 1992, District Judge C. Clyde Atkins ordered the police to stop arresting homeless persons for "innocent, harmless, and inoffensive acts" such as sleeping, eating, bathing, and sitting down in public and ordered the city to establish two " 'safe zones' where homeless people who have no alternative shelter can remain without being arrested for harmless conduct such as sleeping or eating." *Id.* at 1584. The case presented a conflict between the "need of homeless individuals to perform essential, life-sustaining acts in public and the responsibility of the government to maintain orderly, aesthetically pleasing public parks and streets." *Id.* at 1554. Judge Atkins explained his ruling this way:

> As a number of expert witnesses testified, people rarely choose to be homeless. Rather, homelessness is due to various economic, physical or psychological factors that are beyond the homeless individual's control.
>
> Professor Wright testified that one common characteristic of homeless individuals is that they are socially isolated; they are part of no community and have no family or friends who can take them in. Professor Wright also testified that homelessness is both a consequence and a cause of physical or mental illness. Many people become homeless after losing their jobs, and ultimately their homes, as a result of an illness. Many have no home of their own in the first place, but end up on the street after their families or friends are unable to care for or shelter them. Dr. Greer testified that once a person is on the street, illnesses can worsen or occur more frequently due to a variety of factors such as the difficulty or impossibility of obtaining adequate health care, exposure to the elements,

insect and rodent bites, and the absence of sanitary facilities for sleeping, bathing, or cooking. Both Professor Wright and Dr. Greer testified that, except in rare cases, people do not choose to live under these conditions.

According to Professor Wright's testimony, joblessness, like physical and mental illness, becomes more of a problem once a person becomes homeless. This is so because of the barriers homeless individuals face in searching for a job. For example, they have no legal address or telephone. Also, they must spend an inordinate amount of time waiting in line or searching for seemingly basic things like food, a space in a shelter bed or a place to bathe.

In addition to the problems of social isolation, illness, and unemployment, homelessness is exacerbated by the unavailability of many forms of government assistance. Gail Lucy, an expert in the area of government benefits available to homeless people, testified that many homeless individuals are ineligible for most government assistance programs. For example, Supplemental Security Income is available only to people who are sixty-five years of age or more, who are blind or disabled, and who are without other resources. Social Security Disability Insurance is available only to workers who have paid into the Social Security fund for five of the past ten years prior to the onset of the disability. Aid to Families with Dependent Children is available only to low-income families with physical custody of children under the age of eighteen. The only benefit that is widely available to the homeless is food stamps.

Another notable form of assistance that is unavailable to a substantial number of homeless individuals is shelter space. Lucy testified that there are approximately 700 beds available in local shelters. However, approximately 200 of these are "program beds," for which one must qualify. In addition, some of these beds are set aside for families. Given the estimated 6,000 individuals who were homeless at the time of trial and the untold number of people left homeless by Hurricane Andrew, the lack of adequate housing alternatives cannot be overstated. The plaintiffs truly have no place to go.

In sum, class members rarely choose to be homeless. They become homeless due to a variety of factors that are beyond their control. In addition, plaintiffs do not have the choice, much less the luxury, of being in the privacy of their own homes. Because of the unavailability of low-income housing or alternative shelter, plaintiffs have no choice but to conduct involuntary, life-sustaining activities in public places. The harmless conduct for which they are arrested is inseparable from their involuntary condition of being homeless. Consequently, arresting homeless people for harmless acts they are forced to perform in public effectively punishes them for being homeless. . . . [A]rresting the homeless for harmless, involuntary, life-sustaining acts such as sleeping, sitting or eating in public is cruel and unusual [punishment.]

The City suggests, apparently in reference to the aftermath of Hurricane Andrew, that even if homelessness is an involuntary condition in that most persons would not consciously choose to live on the streets, "it is not involuntary in the sense of a situation over which the individual has absolutely no control such as a natural disaster which results in the destruction of one's place of residence so as to render that person homeless." The court cannot accept this distinction. An individual who loses his home as a result of economic hard times or physical or mental illness exercises no more control over these events than he would over a natural disaster. Furthermore, as was established at trial, the City does not have enough shelter to house Miami's homeless residents. Consequently, the City cannot argue persuasively that the homeless have made a deliberate choice to live in public places or that their decision to sleep in the park as opposed to some other exposed place is a volitional act. As Professor Wright testified, the lack of reasonable alternatives should not be mistaken for choice.

Id. at 1564-1565. *Accord, Johnson v. City of Dallas,* 860 F. Supp. 344 (N.D. Tex. 1994). Consider the following argument by Jeremy Waldron.

Everything that is done has to be done somewhere. No one is free to perform an action unless there is somewhere he is free to perform it. . . .

One of the functions of property rules, particularly as far as land is concerned, is to provide a basis for determining who is allowed to be where. . . .

A person who is homeless is, obviously enough, a person who has no home. One way of describing the plight of a homeless individual might be to say that there is no place governed by a private property rule where he is allowed to be. . . .

Our society saves the homeless from this catastrophe only by virtue of the fact that some of its territory is held as collective property and made available for common use. The homeless are allowed to be — provided they are on the streets, in the parks, or under the bridges. Some of them are allowed to crowd together into publicly provided "shelters" after dark (though these are dangerous places and there are not nearly enough shelters for all of them). But in the daytime and, for many of them, all through the night, wandering in public places is their only option.

[There] is . . . increasing regulation of the streets, subways, parks, and other public places to restrict the activities that can be performed there. What is emerging — and it is not just a matter of fantasy–is a state of affairs in which a million or more citizens have no place to perform elementary human activities like urinating, washing, sleeping, cooking, eating, and standing around. . . .

For a person who has no home, and has no expectation of being allowed into something like a private office building or a restaurant, prohibitions on things like sleeping that apply particularly to public places pose a special problem. For although there is no general prohibition on acts of these types, still they are effectively ruled out altogether for anyone who is homeless and who has no shelter to go to. The prohibition is comprehensive in effect because of the cumulation, in the case of the homeless, of a number of different bans, differently imposed. The rules of property prohibit the homeless person from doing any of these acts in private, since there is no private place that he has a right to be. And the rules governing public places prohibit him from doing any of these acts in public, since that is how we have decided to regulate the use of public places. So what is the result? Since private places and public places between them exhaust all the places that there are, there is nowhere that these actions may be performed by the homeless person. And since freedom to perform a concrete action requires freedom to perform it at some place, it follows that the homeless person does not have the freedom to perform them. If sleeping is prohibited in public places, then sleeping is comprehensively prohibited to the homeless. If urinating is prohibited in public places (and if there are no public lavatories) then the homeless are simply unfree to urinate. These are not altogether comfortable conclusions, and they are certainly not comfortable for those who have to live with them

Jeremy Waldron, *Homelessness and the Issue of Freedom*, 39 UCLA L. Rev. 295 (1991).

In contrast to the ruling in *Pottinger*, the California Supreme Court upheld a municipal ordinance that banned camping and storage of personal property in public areas despite evidence that the number of available shelter beds was 2,500 less than the need. *Tobe v. City of Santa Ana*, 892 P.2d 1145 (Cal. 1995). At the same time, the court merely sustained the ordinance from a facial challenge, finding that it did not inevitably conflict with constitutional prohibitions; the court, however, did not rule on the question whether, as applied to the particular facts of the case, the ordinance had the effect of infringing on constitutionally protected rights. In finding that the ordinance did not infringe on the right to travel, the court noted that "Santa Ana has no constitutional obligation to make accommodations on or in public property available to the transient homeless to facilitate their exercise of the right to travel." *Id.* at 1166. The court also rejected the notion that the ordinance punished individuals for the "involuntary status of being homeless" because the ordinance regulated conduct, not merely status.

Id. Disagreeing with the analysis in *Pottinger*, the court concluded that "[a]ssuming arguendo the accuracy of the declarants' descriptions of the circumstances in which they were cited under the ordinance, it is far from clear that none had alternatives to either the condition of being homeless or the conduct that led to homelessness and to the citations." *Id.* at 1167. At the same time, concurring Justice Kennard emphasized that the ruling merely upheld the ordinance on its face and did not reject on the merits the claim accepted in *Pottinger* that "a homeless person may not constitutionally be punished for publicly engaging in harmless activities necessary to life, such as sleeping." *Id. Accord, Davison v. City of Tucson,* 924 F. Supp. 989 (D. Ariz. 1996).

Do you agree with the *Pottinger* ruling?

II

Relations Among Neighbors

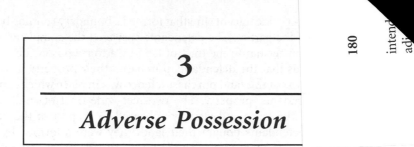

3

Adverse Possession

§3.1   Title versus Possession

An unprivileged entry on property possessed by another is a *trespass*.[1] When, however, one possesses another's property in a manner that is exclusive, visible ("open and notorious"), continuous, and without the owner's permission ("adverse or hostile") for a period defined by state statute, the rules in force transfer title from the title holder (the "true" or "record" owner) to the adverse possessor. If possession lasts for more than the period defined by the relevant statute of limitations, the owner is barred from bringing an action in ejectment against the possessor. Adverse possession doctrine magically transforms trespassers into owners. The following materials address the circumstances under which this occurs and the justifications for it.

§3.1.1   BORDER DISPUTES

BROWN v. GOBBLE

474 S.E.2d 489 (W. Va. 1996)

FRANKLIN D. CLECKLEY, Justice:
  This case involves the doctrines of adverse possession and tacking. David L. Gobble and Sue Ann Gobble, appellants/defendants below, appeal from a final order of the Circuit Court of Mercer County. At the conclusion of a bench trial the circuit court granted judgment for a strip of land to Gary S. Brown and Mitzi Brown, appellees/plaintiffs below....

I.   Factual and Procedural Background

The plaintiffs instituted this action by filing a complaint on August 25, 1994. The complaint sought to have the defendants enjoined from interfering with the plaintiffs'

---

1. *See supra* Chapter 2 for further discussion of trespass law.

ed use of a two-feet-wide tract of land that formed a boundary running between the oining properties of the parties. The defendants answered the complaint and filed a counterclaim alleging ownership to the tract of land by adverse possession.

The record reveals that the defendants purchased their property by deed dated April 24, 1985. At the time of this land purchase a fence was in place which ran along the rear boundary of defendants' property. The two-feet-wide tract of land in question here, was enclosed by the fence and visually appeared to be part of the defendants' property. When the defendants bought their land, they were informed by their real estate agent that their property ran up to and included the fence. The call references in their deed "read" as though the two-feet-wide tract of land was part of the conveyance.[4] The defendants believed the two-feet-wide tract of land was part of their property, and utilized it consistent with ownership rights up until the filing of this law suit.

The plaintiffs purchased their property by deed dated April 28, 1989. Shortly before making this purchase, the plaintiffs had a survey of the property done. The survey revealed that the fenced-in two-feet-wide tract of land was part of plaintiffs' property. Although the plaintiffs were aware at the time of the purchase of their property that the two-feet-wide tract of land was, in fact, theirs, they did nothing to show ownership to the tract until around August, 1994. It was in August of 1994, that the plaintiffs decided to build a road along the two-feet-wide tract of land. To do this meant cutting down several trees that were along the tract. The defendants apparently attempted to prevent the plaintiffs from building the road by asserting that they owned the tract of land. The plaintiffs thereafter instituted the present suit. The trial of this matter was held by the circuit court, sitting as factfinder, on December 13, 1994. The trial court made findings of fact and conclusions of law, wherein it held that "the defendants have failed to show by clear and convincing evidence their ownership by way of adverse possession[.]"

II. Discussion . . .

A. STANDARD OF PROOF FOR ADVERSE POSSESSION CLAIMS

The first argument raised by the defendants is that the circuit court committed error by requiring them to prove adverse possession by clear and convincing evidence. . . .

There is a minority view that a preponderance of the evidence is sufficient to establish adverse possession. There is little reason given for adopting this standard other than it is the usual rule in civil cases.

On the other hand, the view adopted by a majority of jurisdictions is that adverse possession must be shown by clear and convincing evidence.

It is appropriate, in our opinion, that adverse possession be proved by a more stringent standard than a mere preponderance of the evidence. . . .

---

4. The pertinent call references of defendants' deed provide:

> thence leaving the said Willowbrook Road N 71 degrees 28' E 184.80 feet *to a fence post* in the line of said private driveway, thence S 32 degrees 33' E 133.80 feet to a fence post in the line of said driveway, thence S 17 degrees 04' W 13 feet to a fence post in the line of said private driveway[.] [Emphasis added.]

[O]n policy grounds there is sound and reasonable justification for the majority view. The function of a standard of proof is to "instruct the factfinder concerning the degree of confidence our society thinks he [or she] should have in the correctness of a factual conclusion for a particular kind of adjudication." *In re Winship*, 397 U.S. 358, 370 (1970) (Harlan, J., concurring). "The standard [of proof] serves to allocate the risk of error between the litigants and to indicate the relative importance attached to the ultimate decision." *Addington v. Texas*, 441 U.S. 418, 423 (1979).

While the preponderance standard applies across the board in civil cases, a higher standard is needed where fairness and equity require more persuasive proof. Although the standard clear and convincing is less commonly used, it nonetheless is no stranger to West Virginia civil cases. In *Wheeling Dollar Sav. & Trust Co. v. Singer*, 250 S.E.2d 369, 374 (W. Va. 1978), this Court stated that "clear and convincing" is the measure or degree of proof that will produce in the mind of the factfinder a firm belief or conviction as to the allegations sought to be established. It should be the highest possible standard of civil proof. The interest at stake in an adverse possession claim is not the mere loss of money as is the case in the normal civil proceedings. Rather, it often involves the loss of a homestead, a family farm or other property associated with traditional family and societal values. To this extent, most courts have used the clear and convincing standard to protect these important property interests. Adopting the clear and convincing standard of proof is more than a mere academic exercise. At a minimum, it reflects the value society places on the rights and interests being asserted.

The bottom line is that the function of the legal process is to minimize the risk of erroneous decisions. The law should not allow the land of one to be taken by another, without a conveyance or consideration, merely upon slight presumption or probabilities. The relevant evidence in an adverse action must necessarily expand over a ten year period. A preponderance standard, in our judgment, would create the risk of increasing the number of cases whereby land is erroneously taken from the title owner under spurious adverse possession claims. This heightened standard of clear and convincing is one way to impress the factfinder with the importance of the decision, and thereby reduce the chances that spurious claims of adverse possession will be successful. Having concluded that the preponderance standard falls short of meeting the demands of fairness and accuracy in the factfinding process in the adjudication of adverse possession claims, we hold that the burden is upon the party who claims title by adverse possession to prove by clear and convincing evidence all elements essential to such title. . . .

B. THE SUFFICIENCY OF THE EVIDENCE

The next argument raised by the defendants is that their evidence was sufficient to establish adverse possession under either a preponderance of the evidence standard or, on the other hand, under the clear and convincing evidence standard. . . .

Regarding the doctrine of adverse possession, we stated in *Naab v. Nolan*, 327 S.E.2d 151, 153-154 (W. Va. 1985), the following: The doctrine of adverse possession is firmly established in our property law and accompanies W. Va. Code §55-2-1 in settling land disputes equitably and efficiently. This doctrine enables one who has been in possession of a piece of real property for more than ten years to bring an action asserting that he is now the owner of that piece of property even when title rests in another. In Syllabus Point 3 of

Somon v. Murphy Fabrication and Erection Co., 232 S.E.2d 524 (W. Va. 1977) this Court stated:

> One who seeks to assert title to a tract of land under the doctrine of adverse possession must prove each of the following elements for the requisite statutory period: (1) That he has held the tract adversely or hostilely; (2) That the possession has been actual; (3) That it has been open and notorious (sometimes stated in the cases as visible and notorious); (4) That possession has been exclusive; (5) That possession has been continuous; (6) That possession has been under claim of title or color of title.

We also held in Syllabus Point 4 of *Somon,* that: "Where one by mistake occupies land up to a line beyond his actual boundary, believing it to be the true line, such belief will not defeat his right to claim that he holds such land adversely or hostilely under the doctrine of adverse possession."[9] In addition to recognizing the common law doctrine of adverse possession, we have long recognized the principle of "tacking." In Syllabus Point 3 of *Jarrett v. Stevens,* 15 S.E. 177 (W. Va. 1892), we stated that, "[t]o tack different adverse possessions to make up the period of bar the persons holding such possessions must be connected by privity of title or claim." . . .

With the above principles of law in view, we now turn to the evidence presented below. . . .

The defendants do not contend that they are the lawful owners of the two-feet-wide tract of boundary land as a result of call references in their deed. That is, they do not claim possession under color of title. They have alleged ownership through claim of title or right. The defendants also do not contend that they have personally possessed the two-feet-wide tract for the requisite ten-year period. Instead, they contend that they have established adverse possession by tacking on the time periods that their predecessors in title claimed the two-feet-wide tract. We have held that "tacking" permits adding together the time period that successive adverse possessors claim property, and that should this period of time added together be more than ten years, adverse possession may be allowed.

To establish the element of "tacking" the defendants presented evidence that Edward and Virgie Blevins (the "Blevins") were the original owners of the property they purchased in 1985. The Blevins owned the property as far back as 1937, and during the entire time of their ownership they believed the two-feet-wide tract was part of their land, and they exercised dominion and control over the tract consistent with ownership rights. The Blevins sold their property on October 30, 1978, to Norman and Martha Fletcher (the "Fletchers"), believing that they were also conveying the two-feet-wide tract. Mr. Fletcher testified that when they bought the property they believed that they had purchased the two-feet-wide tract, and possessed it consistent with ownership rights. The defendants testified that they bought their property from the Fletchers in 1985, and believed their land purchase included the two-feet-wide tract of boundary

---

9. Thus, the law in West Virginia is that where a person, acting under a mistake as to the true boundary lines between his or her land and that of another, takes possession of land believing it to be his or her own, up to the mistaken line, claims a prescriptive right to it and so holds, the holding is adverse, and, if continued for the requisite period may ripen into adverse possession. The fact that the one who takes possession under these circumstances had no intention of taking what did not belong to him or her, does not affect the operation of this rule. In all cases, the intention and not the mistake is the test by which the character of the possession is determined.

land, and that they possessed it consistent with ownership rights, up until the filing of this law suit. Based upon this tacking evidence, the defendants contend that they are entitled as a matter of law to add the period 1937-1985, to their nine-and-a-half year claim to the two-feet-wide tract, which would give them far in excess of ten years adverse possession of the tract.[11]

To establish the element of "hostile" or "adverse" possession by tacking, the defendants called several witnesses who testified that the two-feet-wide tract was fenced off as far back as 1937, that the Blevins placed the fence along the tract, and that the Blevins claimed the tract as theirs.[12] Evidence was presented to show that the Fletchers maintained the fence along the two-feet-wide tract, and that the fence remained in place throughout their ownership of the property. The defendants testified that they purchased their property from the Fletchers in 1985, and that they claimed ownership of the two-feet-wide tract, and that it remained fenced off up until the start of the instant law suit.

To establish the element of "actual" possession by tacking, the defendants called several witnesses who testified that the Blevins periodically repaired the fence surrounding the two-feet-wide tract, that they routinely planted a garden along the tract, and that the Blevins constructed and maintained a shed along a portion of the tract. Mr. Fletcher testified that he regularly planted a garden along the tract, that he routinely removed weeds from along the tract and fence, and that he picked blackberries from the area and walnuts from trees that had grown along the tract.[13] The defendants testified that they planted gardens along the tract, that they built a treehouse in one of the trees that had grown along the tract, and that they regularly mowed the grass and weeds in the area.

To establish the element of "open and notorious" possession by tacking, the defendants called several witnesses who testified that during the period that the Blevins owned the defendants' property, the reputation of the two-feet-wide tract in the community was that it belonged to the Blevins.[14] Mr. Fletcher testified that the reputation

---

11. Based upon the evidence the defendants presented regarding the Belvins and Fletchers, the defendants actually misunderstand the import of their evidence. The evidence seems to suggest that the Blevins may very well have established adverse possession to the two-feet-wide tract, because they maintained the tract for over ten years. The Blevins conveyed their adversely possessed property to the Fletchers, and the Fletchers in turn conveyed the same to the defendants. Therefore the tacking involved here does not require analysis of the defendants' period of ownership, unless it is established that the Blevins did not in fact acquire adverse possession. If it is determined that the Blevins acquired adverse possession of the two-feet-wide tract, the issue then merely becomes whether the Blevins intended to convey the two-feet-wide tract to the Fletchers, and whether the Fletchers intended to convey the two-feet-wide tract to the defendants. The period of ownership by the defendants becomes irrelevant under this scenario. It is only if a determination is made that the Blevins did not establish adverse possession that the defendants' period of ownership becomes relevant for tacking on the time period of the Fletchers.

12. We have held that to establish "hostile" or "adverse" possession, evidence must be presented which shows that possession of disputed property was against the right of the true owner and is inconsistent with the title of the true owner for the entire requisite ten-year period.

13. We have held that to establish "actual" possession, evidence must be presented which shows that possession of disputed property was used for enjoyment, cultivation, residence or improvements for the entire requisite ten-year period.

14. We have held that to establish "open and notorious" possession, evidence must be presented which shows that possession of disputed property was in such a manner as to give notice to the true owner that the property is being claimed by another for the entire requisite ten-year period.

in the community was that the two-feet-wide tract was part of his property. The defendants testified that the reputation in the community was that the two-feet-wide tract was part of their property.

To establish the element of "exclusive" possession by tacking, the defendants presented testimony by two of the original owners of plaintiffs' property.[15] These two witnesses testified that neither the Blevins' nor the Fletchers' claim to the two-feet-wide tract was ever objected to by them or those who owned the property with them. The defendants also presented evidence to show that only the Blevins and Fletchers respectively had control and dominion over the two-feet-wide tract. The defendants also testified that they had exclusive control and dominion over the two-feet-wide tract up until the time of this law suit.

To establish the element of "continuous" possession the defendants presented testimony that the Blevins enclosed, maintained, cultivated and claimed ownership of the two-feet-wide tract up until they sold their property to the Fletchers. Mr. Fletcher testified that he maintained, cultivated and claimed ownership of the two-feet-wide tract up until he sold the property to the defendants. The defendants testified that they maintained, cultivated and claimed ownership of the two-feet-wide tract up until the instant law suit.

To establish the element of "claim of title" the defendants presented evidence to show that neither the Blevins, Fletchers nor the defendants had actual title to the two-feet-wide tract, yet each claimed ownership of it pursuant to all of the above conduct, during their entire respective occupancy.

Based upon the above evidence of tacking and adverse possession, the defendants contend that they established adverse possession under the clear and convincing evidence standard. The trial court found that this evidence did not establish tacking or adverse possession by clear and convincing evidence. The trial court made this finding notwithstanding the fact that none of the defendants' tacking or adverse possession evidence was challenged or rebutted by the plaintiffs. . . .

. . . The findings made by the trial court are inadequate to allow this Court to find that all relevant factors were considered. Though helpful, the findings are not all-encompassing. Indeed, the findings of the circuit court ignored the central thrust of the defendants' evidence.

The circuit court either misunderstood or misapplied the theory of the defendants. The defendants do not claim that their actual possession of the property in question is sufficient to establish adverse possession. Rather, they contend that their predecessors in interest met all the necessary prerequisites of adverse possession and under the doctrine of tacking, the predecessors' interest was passed onto the defendants. The circuit court's findings never addressed this aspect of the defendants' case. . . .

The upshot is that the circuit court failed to make any findings that would dispose of the defendants' tacking claim. . . . [Accordingly, the judgment of the Circuit Court of Mercer County is reversed and remanded.]

---

15. We have held that to establish "exclusive" possession, evidence must be presented which shows that possession of disputed property was used only by the occupant and others were not permitted to use it or claim ownership during the entire requisite ten-year period.

§3.1.2 COLOR OF TITLE

ROMERO v. GARCIA
546 P.2d 66 (N.M. 1976)

DAN SOSA, JR., J.

Plaintiff-appellee Ida Romero, formerly Garcia, filed suit to quiet title against defendants-appellants Mr. and Mrs. Antonio Garcia, who are her former father-in-law and mother-in-law. The suit to quiet title was based upon adverse possession for more than ten years under color of title and payment of taxes. From judgment for the plaintiff, defendants appeal. We affirm the trial court.

The facts are the following: In 1947 plaintiff Ida Garcia Romero and her deceased husband Octaviano Garcia, son of the defendants, purchased the 13 acres in dispute for $290 from Octaviano's father, Antonio Garcia. Mrs. Antonio Garcia failed to join in the conveyance. The 13 acres were carved out of 165 acres Antonio Garcia had purchased in 1923. The plaintiff and her deceased husband entered into possession in 1947 and built a home on the land with the help of both defendants. The deed was recorded in May, 1950. Ida and Octaviano lived in their home until 1962, when he died, whereupon she moved to Colorado and subsequently remarried.

The main thrust of the appellants' argument concerns the deed. Appellants argue that (1) the void deed was inadequate for color of title and (2) the deed's description was inadequate for adverse possession because it failed to describe a specific piece of property. The first argument is clearly erroneous. A deed is sufficient for the purpose of color of title even though it is void because it lacks the signature of a member of the community.

We move to the question of whether the deed was insufficient for adverse possession because it failed to describe adequately a parcel of land which can be ascertained on the ground. Since the deed in question was in Spanish, the court and the parties relied on the following English translation of the description:

> A piece of land containing 13 acres more or less, within the following description: NE 1/4 SE 1/4, S 1/2 SE 1/4 NE 1/4, Section 32, NW 1/4 SW 1/4, S 1/2 SW 1/4 NW 1/4, Section 33, Township 32 N. Range 7E N.M.P.M., said 13 acres are bounded as follows: East and South bounded by property of Antonio Garcia; on the North by the National Forest and on the West by property of Alfonso Marquez. The said 13 acres are in the NW corner of the ranch above described.

Not translated but part of the deed to the appellee's husband are the following words in Spanish: "Con derecho de agua del Sublet del Rio de Los Pinos," which translated mean "with water rights assigned from the Sublet [creek] of the Los Pinos river."

The description in the deed specified that the land is bounded on the north by the National Forest and on the west by Alfonso Marquez and on the south and east by the grantor. The deed also specified that there shall be water rights to the land from the Los Pinos River. The Los Pinos River is generally to the south of this property and at one point only some twenty feet from the alleged southern boundary. In *Richardson v. Duggar*, 525 P.2d 854, 857 (N.M. 1974) we held that the deed is not void for want of proper description if, with the deed and with extrinsic evidence on the ground, a surveyor can ascertain the boundaries....

In the case at bar we had testimony from the grantor that the fence line along the entire northern boundary had been there for over fifty years, and the fence line on the western boundary of the property which he conveyed to his son had also been there for more than fifty years. We therefore see that the northwest corner was adequately established as being the intersection of these two fence lines. The surveyor testified that the plaintiff showed him generally where the land was and pointed to the house that was built by the plaintiff and the defendants. The surveyor walked down the western boundary line and found a pipe in position; he established that pipe as the southwest corner. He shot an angle parallel to the northern boundary line and found a pile of rocks which he established as the southeastern corner. He then closed the parallelogram by shooting a line to the northern boundary parallel to the western fence. This parallelogram measured 12.95 acres; the deed granted "13 acres more or less." Thus, the land is in the shape of a parallelogram and is bounded by the National Forest on the north, by Alfonso Marquez (now lands of Mr. L. C. White) on the west, and on the south and east by the grantor. This parallelogram is also in close proximity to the river from which water could be used in accordance with the assignment of the water rights.

Mrs. Romero consistently identified this land as the property she and her deceased husband had purchased and which she thereafter possessed and from which she sold the hay for several years. Defendant failed to object to this testimony. . . .

The trial court made the following findings of fact:

> 15. The land described in the complaint of the plaintiff herein, by virtue of the description of the said deed itself and the actions and understandings of the parties as to the boundaries of said land, is capable of determination as to the exact location of the boundaries of said land conveyed to Plaintiff's deceased husband.
>
> 16. The Northwest corner of the land conveyed is established by the intersection of a fence line extending along the entire northern boundary of said property from east to west, and the point where an existing fence line along the westerly boundary of said property intersected; the Southwest corner of said lands of the Plaintiff was marked by an iron pipe found in place by a surveyor, and the Southeast corner of said property conveyed was marked by a pile of rocks, and the Northeast corner of said tract was marked by an existing fence extending from East to West along the entire northerly boundary of said tract of land.

The court feels that when the evidence, with all reasonable inferences deducible therefrom, is viewed in the light most favorable in support of the findings, there was substantial evidence to support these findings of fact and others relevant to this issue. . . .

The court in *Garcia v. Garcia*, 525 P.2d 863, 865 (N.M. 1974) stated that ". . . an indefinite and uncertain description may be clarified by subsequent acts of the parties," and found that:

> The evidence here is clear that subsequent acts of the parties in going upon and generally pointing out the boundaries of the lands to the surveyor, aided by other extrinsic evidence, enabled the surveyor to prepare the plat relied upon by all the parties. In fact, if it were not for the extrinsic evidence by which the surveyor was able to locate the lands, the 1968 deed from Nazario to plaintiffs would fail for lack of means by which to identify any lands.

In the case at bar the subsequent acts of the parties in erecting a house and pointing to the land were sufficient to ascertain the boundaries.

Finally, appellants argue that appellee failed to pay the tax continuously, for appellee had been in arrears several times, ranging from 1 1/2 to almost 4 years. However, appellee did pay the taxes in each case before a tax deed was issued to the state. Thus, we hold that appellee complied substantially with the continuous payment of taxes requirement of adverse possession under N.M. Stat. Ann. §23-1-22.

The judgment of the trial court will be affirmed.

§3.1.3 SQUATTERS

NOME 2000 v. FAGERSTROM
799 P.2d 304 (Alaska 1990)

WARREN MATTHEWS, JR., Chief Justice.

This appeal involves a dispute over a tract of land measuring approximately seven and one-half acres, overlooking the Nome River (hereinafter the disputed parcel). Record title to a tract of land known as mineral survey 1161, which includes the disputed parcel, is held by Nome 2000.

On July 24, 1987, Nome 2000 filed suit to eject Charles and Peggy Fagerstrom from the disputed parcel. The Fagerstroms counterclaimed that through their use of the parcel they had acquired title by adverse possession. . . .

The disputed parcel is located in a rural area known as Osborn. During the warmer seasons, property in Osborn is suitable for homesites and subsistence and recreational activities. During the colder seasons, little or no use is made of Osborn property.

Charles Fagerstrom's earliest recollection of the disputed parcel is his family's use of it around 1944 or 1945. At that time, he and his family used an abandoned boy scout cabin present on the parcel as a subsistence base camp during summer months. Around 1947 or 1948, they moved their summer campsite to an area south of the disputed parcel. However, Charles and his family continued to make seasonal use of the disputed parcel for subsistence and recreation.

In 1963, Charles and Peggy Fagerstrom were married and, in 1966, they brought a small quantity of building materials to the north end of the disputed parcel. They intended to build a cabin.

In 1970 or 1971, the Fagerstroms used four cornerposts to stake off a twelve acre, rectangular parcel for purposes of a Native Allotment application.[3] The northeast and southeast stakes were located on or very near mineral survey 1161. The northwest and southwest stakes were located well to the west of mineral survey 1161. The overlap constitutes the disputed parcel. The southeast stake disappeared at an unknown time.

Also around 1970, the Fagerstroms built a picnic area on the north end of the disputed parcel. The area included a gravel pit, beachwood blocks as chairs, firewood and a 50-gallon barrel for use as a stove.

---

3. Federal law authorizes the Secretary of the Interior to allot certain non-mineral lands to Native Alaskans. . . . As a result of her application, Peggy was awarded two lots (lots 3 and 12) which border the disputed parcel along its western boundary.

About mid-July 1974, the Fagerstroms placed a camper trailer on the north end of the disputed parcel. The trailer was leveled on blocks and remained in place through late September. Thereafter, until 1978, the Fagerstroms parked their camper trailer on the north end of the disputed parcel from early June through September. The camper was equipped with food, bedding, a stove and other household items.

About the same time that the Fagerstroms began parking the trailer on the disputed parcel, they built an outhouse and a fish rack on the north end of the parcel. Both fixtures remained through the time of trial in their original locations. The Fagerstroms also planted some spruce trees, not indigenous to the Osborn area, in 1975-76.

During the summer of 1977, the Fagerstroms built a reindeer shelter on the north end of the disputed parcel. The shelter was about 8 x 8 feet wide, and tall enough for Charles Fagerstrom to stand in. Around the shelter, the Fagerstroms constructed a pen which was 75 feet in diameter and 5 feet high. The shelter and pen housed a reindeer for about six weeks and the pen remained in place until the summer of 1978.

During their testimony, the Fagerstroms estimated that they were personally present on the disputed parcel from 1974 through 1978, "every other weekend or so" and "[a] couple times during the week . . . if the weather was good." When present they used the north end of the parcel as a base camp while using the entire parcel for subsistence and recreational purposes. Their activities included gathering berries, catching and drying fish and picnicking. Their children played on the parcel. The Fagerstroms also kept the property clean, picking up litter left by others.

While so using the disputed parcel, the Fagerstroms walked along various paths which traverse the entire parcel. The paths were present prior to the Fagerstroms' use of the parcel and, according to Peggy Fagerstrom, were free for use by others in connection with picking berries and fishing. On one occasion, however, Charles Fagerstrom excluded campers from the land. They were burning the Fagerstroms' firewood.

Nome 2000 placed into evidence the deposition testimony of Dr. Steven McNabb, an expert in anthropology, who stated that the Fagerstroms' use of the disputed parcel was consistent with the traditional Native Alaskan system of land use. According to McNabb, unlike the non-Native system, the traditional Native system does not recognize exclusive ownership of land. Instead, customary use of land, such as the Fagerstroms' use of the disputed parcel, establishes only a first priority claim to the land's resources. The claim is not exclusive and is not a matter of ownership, but is more in the nature of a stewardship. That is, other members of the claimant's social group may share in the resources of the land without obtaining permission, so long as the resources are not abused or destroyed. McNabb explained that Charles' exclusion of the campers from the land was a response to the campers' use of the Fagerstroms' personal property (their firewood), not a response to an invasion of a perceived real property interest.

Nevertheless, several persons from the community testified that the Fagerstroms' use of the property from 1974 through 1977 was consistent with that of an owner of the property. For example, one Nome resident testified that since 1974 "[the Fagerstroms] cared for [the disputed parcel] as if they owned it. They made improvements on it as if they owned it. It was my belief that they did own it."

During the summer of 1978, the Fagerstroms put a cabin on the north end of the disputed parcel. Nome 2000 admits that from the time that the cabin was so placed until the time that Nome 2000 filed this suit, the Fagerstroms adversely possessed the north end of the disputed parcel. Nome 2000 filed its complaint on July 24, 1987. . . .

The Fagerstroms' claim of title by adverse possession is governed by Alaska Stat. §09.10.030, which provides for a ten-year limitations period for actions to recover real property.[6] Thus, if the Fagerstroms adversely possessed the disputed parcel, or any portion thereof, for ten consecutive years, then they have acquired title to that property. Because the Fagerstroms' use of the parcel increased over the years, and because Nome 2000 filed its complaint on July 24, 1987, the relevant period is July 24, 1977 through July 24, 1987.

We recently described the elements of adverse possession as follows: "In order to acquire title by adverse possession, the claimant must prove, by clear and convincing evidence, . . . that for the statutory period 'his use of the land was continuous, open and notorious, exclusive and hostile to the true owner.'" *Smith v. Krebs,* 768 P.2d 124, 125 (Alaska 1989). The first three conditions — continuity, notoriety and exclusivity — describe the physical requirements of the doctrine. The fourth condition, hostility, is often imprecisely described as the "intent" requirement.

. . . Nome 2000 argues that as a matter of law the physical requirements are not met absent "significant physical improvements" or "substantial activity" on the land. Thus, according to Nome 2000, only when the Fagerstroms placed a cabin on the disputed parcel in the summer of 1978 did their possession become adverse. For the prior year, so the argument goes, the Fagerstroms' physical use of the property was insufficient because they did not construct "significant structure[s]" and their use was only seasonal. Nome 2000 also argues that the Fagerstroms' use of the disputed parcel was not exclusive because "[o]thers were free to pick the berries, use the paths and fish in the area." We reject these arguments.

Whether a claimant's physical acts upon the land are sufficiently continuous, notorious and exclusive does not necessarily depend on the existence of significant improvements, substantial activity or absolute exclusivity. Indeed, this area of law is not susceptible to fixed standards because the quality and quantity of acts required for adverse possession depend on the character of the land in question. Thus, the conditions of continuity and exclusivity require only that the land be used for the statutory period as an average owner of similar property would use it. Where, as in the present case, the land is rural, a lesser exercise of dominion and control may be reasonable.

The character of the land in question is also relevant to the notoriety requirement. Use consistent with ownership which gives visible evidence of the claimant's possession, such that the reasonably diligent owner "could see that a hostile flag was being flown over his property," is sufficient. *Shilts v. Young,* 567 P.2d 769, 776 (Alaska 1977). Where physical visibility is established, community repute is also relevant evidence that the true owner was put on notice.[7]

Applying the foregoing principles to this case, we hold that the jury could reasonably conclude that the Fagerstroms established, by clear and convincing evidence, continuous, notorious and exclusive possession for ten years prior to the date Nome 2000 filed suit. We point out that we are concerned only with the first year, the summer of 1977 through the summer of 1978, as Nome 2000 admits that the

---

6. A seven-year period is provided for by Alaska Stat. §09.25.050 when possession is under "color and claim of title." The Fagerstroms do not maintain that their possession was under color of title.

7. The function of the notoriety requirement is to afford the true owner an opportunity for notice. However, actual notice is not required; the true owner is charged with knowing what a reasonably diligent owner would have known.

requirements of adverse possession were met from the summer of 1978 through the summer of 1987.

The disputed parcel is located in a rural area suitable as a seasonal homesite for subsistence and recreational activities. This is exactly how the Fagerstroms used it during the year in question. On the premises throughout the entire year were an out-house, a fish rack, a large reindeer pen (which, for six weeks, housed a reindeer), a picnic area, a small quantity of building materials and some trees not indigenous to the area. During the warmer season, for about 13 weeks, the Fagerstroms also placed a camper trailer on blocks on the disputed parcel. The Fagerstroms and their children visited the property several times during the warmer season to fish, gather berries, clean the pre-mises, and play. In total, their conduct and improvements went well beyond "mere casual and occasional trespasses" and instead "evince[d] a purpose to exercise exclusive dominion over the property." *See Peters v. Juneau-Douglas Girl Scout Council,* 519 P.2d 826, 830 (Alaska 1974). That others were free to pick berries and fish is consistent with the conduct of a hospitable landowner, and undermines neither the continuity nor exclu-sivity of their possession. *See id.* at 831 (claimant "merely acting as any other hospitable landowner might" in allowing strangers to come on land to dig clams).

With respect to the notoriety requirement, a quick investigation of the premises, especially during the season which it was best suited for use, would have been sufficient to place a reasonably diligent landowner on notice that someone may have been exercising dominion and control over at least the northern portion of the property. Upon such notice, further inquiry would indicate that members of the community regarded the Fagerstroms as the owners. Continuous, exclusive, and notorious posses-sion were thus established.

Nome 2000 also argues that the Fagerstroms did not establish hostility. It claims that "the Fagerstroms were required to prove that they intended to claim the property as their own." According to Nome 2000, this intent was lacking as the Fagerstroms thought of themselves not as owners but as stewards pursuant to the traditional system of Native Alaskan land usage. We reject this argument and hold that all of the elements of adverse possession were met.

What the Fagerstroms believed or intended has nothing to do with the question whether their possession was hostile. Hostility is instead determined by application of an objective test which simply asks whether the possessor "acted toward the land as if he owned it," without the permission of one with legal authority to give possession. *Hubbard v. Curtis,* 684 P.2d 842, 848 (Alaska 1984). As indicated, the Fagerstroms' actions toward the property were consistent with ownership of it, and Nome 2000 offers no proof that the Fagerstroms so acted with anyone's permission. That the Fagerstroms' objective manifestations of ownership may have been accompanied by what was described as a traditional Native Alaskan mind-set is irrelevant. To hold otherwise would be inconsistent with precedent and patently unfair.

Having concluded that the Fagerstroms established the elements of adverse pos-session, we turn to the question whether they were entitled to the entire disputed parcel. Specifically, the question presented is whether the jury could reasonably conclude that the Fagerstroms adversely possessed the southerly portion of the disputed parcel.

Absent color of title,[10] only property actually possessed may be acquired by adverse possession. Here, from the summer of 1977 through the summer of 1978,

---

10. "Color of title exists only by virtue of a written instrument which purports to pass title to the claimant, but which is ineffective because of a defect in the means of conveyance or

the Fagerstroms' only activity on the southerly portion of the land included use of the pre-existing trails in connection with subsistence and recreational activities, and picking up litter. They claim that these activities, together with their placement of the cornerposts, constituted actual possession of the southerly portion of the parcel. Nome 2000 argues that this activity did not constitute actual possession and, at most, entitled the Fagerstroms to an easement by prescription across the southerly portion of the disputed parcel.

Nome 2000 is correct. The Fagerstroms' use of the trails and picking up of litter, although perhaps indicative of adverse use, would not provide the reasonably diligent owner with visible evidence of another's exercise of dominion and control. To this, the cornerposts add virtually nothing. Two of the four posts are located well to the west of the disputed parcel. Of the two that were allegedly placed on the parcel in 1970, the one located on the southerly portion of the parcel disappeared at an unknown time. The Fagerstroms maintain that because the disappearing stake was securely in place in 1970, we should infer that it remained for a "significant period." Even if we draw this inference, we fail to see how two posts on a rectangular parcel of property can, as the Fagerstroms put it, constitute "[t]he objective act of taking physical possession" of the parcel. The two posts simply do not serve to mark off the boundaries of the disputed parcel and, therefore, do not evince an exercise of dominion and control over the entire parcel. Thus, we conclude that the superior court erred in its denial of Nome 2000's motion for a directed verdict as to the southerly portion. This case is remanded to the trial court, with instructions to determine the extent of the Fagerstroms' acquisition in a manner consistent with this opinion. . . .

NOTES AND QUESTIONS

1. *Adverse possession claims generate substantial litigation.* Each of the elements of adverse possession has caused problems of interpretation and application. Moreover, a significant number of states either add other elements to the standard list or identify multiple ways to acquire property by adverse possession. It is therefore crucial to examine carefully the version of the doctrine that has been adopted in your jurisdiction.

Adverse possession doctrine allows a non-owner to acquire full ownership rights in real property if the non-owner "actually possesses" property without permission by the "true" owner (meaning the formal title holder) in a visible manner for a period of time established by statute. The basic elements of the claim include (1) actual possession that is (2) open and notorious, (3) exclusive, (4) continuous, and (5) adverse or hostile (6) for the statutory period. Most states agree on this list of elements. However, significant differences exist as to how each element is interpreted and applied. Some states have enacted different statutes of limitation depending on whether the possessor has acted under (7) "color of title" or has (8) paid property taxes on the land. Some courts have formally required a showing that the occupation (9) was in "good faith"

---

because the grantor did not actually own the land he sought to convey." *Hubbard,* 684 P.2d at 847. As noted above, the Fagerstroms do not claim the disputed parcel by virtue of a written instrument.

(meaning that the possessor did not know she was trespassing on land formally owned by another), and some states suggest that the possessor must act (10) "under a claim of right"—an element susceptible of widely varying interpretations. These last factors (good faith and claim of right) are really particular variations on the "adversity" requirement and embody significant substantive disagreements about the meaning of the requirement.

Although adverse possession doctrine is intended to settle land claims in long-term possessors, it often generates litigation because it is not always clear under a given set of facts whether the elements have been satisfied. For this reason, a court judgment establishing ownership or the correct boundary may be required to make the property marketable.

Adverse possession claims may be brought by the adverse possessor herself in a lawsuit against the record owner to "quiet title." This kind of claim asks the court to grant a declaratory judgment that the adverse possessor has become the owner of the disputed property through adverse possession. Adverse possession claims may also arise as *defenses* to trespass or ejectment claims by record owners. In ejectment lawsuits, the record owner claims that the adverse possessor is wrongfully occupying her property and seeks a court order ejecting the adverse possessor from the property; the adverse possessor defends by asserting that she has acquired title by adverse possession and that plaintiff therefore has no right to eject her. In trespass cases, the plaintiff alleges an intentional intrusion on her property, while the adverse possessor defends by alleging that she is not trespassing because she has acquired ownership of the property by adverse possession.

2. *Actual possession.* The adverse possessor must physically occupy the property in some manner. Some states have statutes that state what types of actions are required to establish "actual" possession. Cal. Code Civ. Proc. §323; Fla. Stat. §95.16; N.Y. Real Prop. Acts §522. In the absence of a statute, "[a]ctual occupancy means the ordinary use to which the land is capable and such as an owner would make of it." *Smith v. Hayden,* 772 P.2d 47, 55 (Colo. 1989). This may be shown by enclosing the property by a fence and treating it as one's own. *Krosmico v. Pettit,* 968 P.2d 345 (Okla. 1998). *But see Hovendick v. Ruby,* 10 P.3d 1119 (Wyo. 2000) ("fence of convenience" designed to contain or keep out animals gives rise to a presumption of permissive use while a boundary fence gives rise to a presumption of adverse possession). In the absence of a fence, one must demonstrate actual possession by engaging in significant activities on the land, such as building on the land and/or living or conducting a business there. Other actions that are often sufficient to show actual possession are farming, clearing the land, and planting shrubs. *Harris v. Lynch,* 940 S.W.2d 42 (Mo. Ct. App. 1997). The touchstone is proof the possessor treated the land as an "average owner" would. *Jarvis v. Gillespie,* 587 A.2d 981, 985 (Vt. 1991).

An adverse possessor who has a deed that purports to transfer the land in question but is ineffective to transfer title because of a defect in the deed (such as lack of a signature) or a defect in the process by which the deed was issued (lack of notice to the owner when the property is sold for failure to pay property taxes, for example) has "color of title" to the property. In that case, occupation of any portion of the land described in the defective title is generally deemed to be actual possession of the whole lot described in the void deed.

If the scope of the non-owner's actions is *limited* rather than general, she may be granted a *prescriptive easement* rather than adverse possession. Easements are limited rights to use the property of another. For example, the right to cross neighboring property—known as a "right of way"—is an *affirmative* easement, that is, a right to do something specific on the land of another. In contrast, negative easements are rights to limit or control the use of neighboring property. For example, to prevent a neighbor from adding an extra story onto her building, one can purchase from that neighbor the right to prevent any construction above the existing building.

Affirmative easements, unlike negative easements, may be acquired by prescription. The elements for prescriptive easements are substantially the same as the elements for adverse possession, except that the "actual possession" element is replaced by "actual use," and most courts will drop the requirement that the use be "exclusive." Thus someone who drives across another's land without permission for a sufficiently long time will obtain a right to continue doing that, as long as the use was nonpermissive and visible. Possessory claims demonstrate an intent to treat the property as one's own in a general sense, while use claims are limited in scope. Use for a limited purpose, such as using a neighbor's road, is likely to result in a prescriptive easement rather than ownership of the road. In contrast, the adverse possessors in *Brown v. Gobble* occupied property enclosed by a fence and treated it generally as part of their land and were therefore eligible for adverse possession.

Cases involving mistaken boundaries may generate claims of either adverse possession or prescriptive easement. For example, if a property owner builds a driveway on what he believes is the edge of his property but is really on his neighbor's side of the line, he may claim adverse possession of the strip or he may claim merely an easement to use the strip for driveway purposes. If granted only an easement, he cannot use the strip for any other purpose; if granted adverse possession of the strip, then he can change the use by, for example, taking out the driveway and putting in grass or shrubs or building a structure on it. The result will depend on the extent of his use of the strip and whether his actions could reasonably have been interpreted as asserting general powers over the strip of land. Deciding this issue requires difficult factual and interpretive judgments. It also requires a policy judgment about which owner's interests are more deserving of legal protection.

3. *Open and notorious.* Courts generally agree that the possessory acts must be sufficiently visible and obvious to put a reasonable owner on notice that her property is being occupied by a non-owner. *Lawrence v. Town of Concord,* 788 N.E.2d 546, 551-552 (Mass. 2003); *Grappo v. Blanks,* 400 S.E.2d 168 (Va. 1991). The adverse possessor need not demonstrate that the "true owner" (the formal title holder) observed or knew about the adverse possessor's use of the property; rather, the true owner is "charged with seeing what reasonable inspection would disclose." William B. Stoebuck & Dale A. Whitman, *The Law of Property* §11.7, at 856 (3d ed. 2000). *Accord, Lawrence v. Town of Concord,* 788 N.E.2d at 552 (adverse possession available even when record owner did not know it owned the property in question).

A great deal of litigation has been generated over what acts are sufficient to put owners on notice. Enclosing land by a fence or a wall, as in *Brown v. Gobble,* is universally recognized as sufficiently open and notorious. *Smith v. Tippett,* 569 A.2d 1186 (D.C. 1990). Other acts deemed sufficient include building a structure, *Smith v. Hayden, supra* (garage located on neighboring property); clearing the land, laying down a driveway, mowing grass, and using the strip for parking, storage, garbage removal, and picnicking, *Chaplin v. Sanders,* 676 P.2d 431 (Wash. 1984); and planting and harvesting crops, *Cheek v. Wainwright,* 269 S.E.2d 443 (Ga. 1980) (timber). *Cf. Rhodes v. Cahill,* 802 S.W.2d 643 (Tex. 1990) (holding that isolated and selective clearing of trees for timber or grazing purposes and grazing cattle and goats without enclosing the land are insufficient to show adverse possession over a ten-year period).

4. *Exclusive.* The exclusivity requirement does not mean that no one but the owner used the property for the statutory period. Owners routinely allow others to enter their property for various purposes. *Exclusivity* generally means that the use "is of a type that would be expected of a true owner of the land in question" and that "the adverse claimant's possession cannot be shared with the true owner." *Smith v. Tippett,* 569 A.2d at 1190. Proving that possession was not shared with the true owner may require a showing that "the record owner has been effectively excluded," *Smith v. Hayden,* 772 P.2d at 52, although occasional entry by the true owner may not defeat the claim. *Id.* at 53. Two adverse possessors who possess property jointly may acquire joint ownership rights as co-owners.[2]

5. *Continuous (tacking doctrine).* The requirement that the adverse possessor's use be continuous does not mean that she must be on the property 24 hours a day. Nor does it mean that the owner may never leave the property for extended periods of time. Depending on the type of property in question, even extended absences may not defeat the claim. In *Howard v. Kunto,* 477 P.2d 210 (Wash. Ct. App. 1970), for example, adverse possession was established over a parcel of land used seasonally as a summer cabin. The court held the continuity requirement to mean that the adverse possessor must exercise control over the property in the ways customarily pursued by owners of that type of property. "[T]he requisite possession requires such possession and dominion 'as ordinarily marks the conduct of owners in general in holding, managing, and caring for property of like nature and condition." *Id.* at 213-214.

What happens if someone adversely possesses property for less than the time period required by the relevant statute and sells the property — or, more precisely, *purports* to sell it — to another owner? The general rule is that the succeeding periods of possession by different persons may be added together; this is called *tacking.* Successors can add the original adverse possessor's holding period only if they are in *privity* with one another, meaning that the original adverse possessor purported to transfer title to the property to the successor. *Shelton v. Strickland,* 21 P.3d 1179, 1184 (Wash. Ct. App. 2001). If, however, the successor dispossessed the prior adverse possessor, the tacking doctrine does not apply.

6. *Adverse or hostile.* Of all the elements of adverse possession, the adverseness requirement has given rise to the most confused and varied treatment. The courts agree that the adverseness requirement means that the use be nonpermissive. A showing that the true owner has permitted the use will defeat the claim. Beyond this basic premise, however, much disagreement ensues. It is important to distinguish the requirements for the state of mind of the true owner from the requirements for the state of mind of the adverse possessor.

7. *True owner's state of mind.* If someone is occupying another's land with the owner's permission, they cannot acquire it by adverse possession. The court's question, therefore, is whether the true owner *permitted* the use; if so, this defeats an adverse possession claim. Although it is counterintuitive, the adverse possessor must show that her use was *nonpermissive* to obtain ownership by adverse possession. What evidence is sufficient to prove that possession is nonpermissive? This is generally not a problem if the owner has expressly granted permission (through granting a license or lease, for example) or has expressly denied permission (by posting "No Trespassing" signs, for

---

2. They will own the property as tenants in common. *See infra* §7.2.

example). In many cases, however, the owner has said nothing either way. In such cases, the courts almost always hold that there is a *presumption* that possession of another's property is *nonpermissive. Robarge v. Willett,* 636 N.Y.S.2d 938 (App. Div. 1996). This means that adverse possession can be established by long-standing, visible, continuous possession of another's land. No proof need be given on the question of adverseness; lack of permission is presumed. If all the elements are met, adverse possession can be claimed unless the true owner produces evidence to show that the use was permissive.

Co-owners of property, such as two sisters who own a house jointly or two roommates who share an apartment, are each legally entitled to possess the whole property. They work out actual usage informally between or among themselves. Use of the whole property by one of two co-owners is as of right because each is acting within her legal rights if she occupies the whole property. No permission is needed to possess the whole property so no trespass has occurred if an owner possesses the whole. To acquire adverse possession against a co-owner, one must make an explicit statement of intent to take possession of the entire property by adverse possession; this is called an "ouster."[3]

Similarly, possession that begins as permissive will stay that way unless the owner explicitly revokes permission or the adverse possessor announces that she is ousting the true owner and claiming the property as her own. However, if the owner allows another to possess her property for a very long time and the possessor reasonably relies on that permission to invest in the land, she may be granted possessory rights on the ground that the owner is estopped from denying continued permission.[4]

8. *Adverse possessor's state of mind.* Four approaches exist. They include (1) an *objective test* based on possession (the rule in most states); and subjective tests based on (2) a *claim of right;* (3) *intentional dispossession;* and (4) *good faith.* An objective test makes the adverse possessor's state of mind irrelevant, while a subjective test requires the adverse possessor to prove a particular attitude on her part *in addition* to showing that the true owner did not permit the possession.

   a. *Lack of permission.* The first approach is an *objective* test, meaning that the adverse possessor's state of mind is irrelevant. All that matters is that the possessor *lacked permission* from the true owner. This is the law in the overwhelming majority of states.

   b. *Claim of right.* Some courts state that the adverse possessor must allege a "claim of right." This looks like a subjective test because it means "a possessor's intention to appropriate and use the land as his own to the exclusion of all others." *Grappo v. Blanks,* 400 S.E.2d at 171. However, in most states, this second test is actually a variant on the first. States that require a "claim of right" generally do not require proof of what the adverse possessor was thinking; all they require is that the adverse possessor act toward the land as an average owner would act. "That intention need not be expressed but may be implied by a claimant's conduct. Actual occupation, use, and improvement of the property by the claimant, as if he were in fact the owner, is conduct that can prove a claim of right." *Id.* This collapses the claim of right test into the "actual possession" test, automatically satisfying the claim of right if actual possession has been shown.

---

3. For rules about joint owners and the definition of ouster, *see infra* §7.2.
4. *See infra* §5.3.1.1.

Some states, however, that require a showing of a "claim of right" will allow the presumption that actual possession is under a claim of right to be defeated if the evidence shows that the adverse possessor knew where the boundary was and never intended to claim property outside her borders as her own. *Mid-Valley Resources, Inc. v. Engelson,* 13 P.3d 118 (Or. Ct. App. 2000); *Petsch v. Widger,* 335 N.W.2d 254, 260 (Neb. 1983). Other courts will even deny adverse possession when the adverse possessor was unsure of where the boundary lay but testifies that she never intended to take over ownership of property that was not hers. *Ellis v. Jansing,* 620 S.W.2d 569 (Tex. 1981). In these states, the claim of right requirement is identical to the intentional dispossession test, discussed next.

c. *Intentional dispossession.* Some states require a showing of *intentional dispossession* in certain cases. Under this test, the adverse possessor must be aware that she is occupying property owned by someone else and must intend to oust or dispossess the true owner. In these states, mistaken occupation of land cannot give rise to adverse possession if the adverse possessor has no intention of taking over property she does not own. As explained above, this test may be phrased as a "claim of right." The courts that adopt this test ordinarily limit it to boundary disputes. *See, e.g., Ellis v. Jansing,* 620 S.W.2d 569 (Tex. 1981) (holding that adverse possession could not be established where the adverse possessor "never claimed or intended to claim any property other than that described in his deed . . . and he never intended to claim any property owned by the abutting property owner"). *Accord, McQueen v. Black,* 425 N.W.2d 203 (Mich. Ct. App. 1988); *Perry v. Heirs at Law and Distributees of Gadsden,* 449 S.E.2d 250 (S.C. 1994).

The vast majority of scholars and courts reject this test on the grounds that it rewards wrongdoers (intentional trespassers) and fails to protect innocent persons who have mistakenly occupied land belonging to another. There is something perverse denying protection to good faith possessors while granting repose to those who intended to invade and steal neighboring land. "To limit the doctrine of adverse possession to the latter type places a premium on intentional wrongdoing, contrary to fundamental justice and policy." *Smith v. Tippett,* 569 A.2d at 1191.

d. *Good faith.* Some states require the exact opposite of an intent to oust the true owner: instead, they require *good faith* occupation to prevail. In these jurisdictions, *only innocent* possessors — those who *mistakenly* occupy property owned by someone else — can acquire ownership by adverse possession. N.M. Stat. §37-1-22; Ga. Code §§44-5-161 to -162; *Halpern v. Lacy Investment Corp.,* 379 S.E.2d 519 (Ga. 1989) (holding that those who knowingly occupy land of others are "trespassers" or "squatters" and cannot obtain title by adverse possession because they have not entered the land with a good faith claim of right); *Carpenter v. Ruperto,* 315 N.W.2d 782 (Iowa 1982) (no adverse possession because "claim of right" is essential element and it cannot be established if the adverse possessor knew she was possessing land she did not own).

Some states provide a shorter statute of limitations if the possession was in good faith. *Compare* La. Civ. Code arts. 3473 and 3475 with art. 3486 (10-year period for prescription if possession was in good faith and 30-year period if possession was in bad faith). Professor Richard Helmholz has argued that even though most states reject a good faith test, they *in fact* grant adverse possession only to good faith possessors. They do this, he claims, by manipulating the other elements of the test, such as the open and notorious, exclusivity, or continuity requirements. Richard Helmholz, *Adverse Possession and Subjective Intent*, 61 Wash. U. L.Q. 331 (1983); Richard Helmholz, *More on Subjective Intent: A Response to Professor Cunningham*, 64 Wash. U. L.Q. 65 (1986). Professor Roger Cunningham has rejected Helmholz's claim, arguing instead that the courts do not in fact require good faith to prevail. Roger Cunningham, *Adverse Possession and Subjective Intent: A Reply to Professor Helmholz*, 64 Wash. U. L.Q. 1 (1986). Whoever is correct in this debate, it is clear that most courts have so far rejected the idea of adopting a good faith test as a formal element in adverse possession doctrine. *Chaplin v. Sanders*, 676 P.2d 431 (Wash. 1984).

9. *For the statutory period.* The statutory period varies widely from state to state. As of 1998, the periods include 5 years (3 states), 7 years (4 states), 10 years (16 states), 15 years (9 states), 18 years (1 state), 20 years (12 states), 21 years (2 states), 30 years (2 states), and 40 years (1 state). *See Thompson on Real Property, Thomas Edition* §87.01 (David A. Thomas ed. 1998). Some define different periods, depending on whether the adverse possessor has paid property taxes on the property in question or whether the adverse possessor had color of title.

Many states will *toll* the statute of limitations if the true owner is under a *disability* such as infancy, insanity, or incompetence (wardship), either providing that the statute begin running only after the disability ends, shortening the limitations period once the disability is removed, or providing a maximum period longer than the standard statute of limitations even if the disability has not terminated. Other categories may include imprisonment and absence from the state.

10. *Color of title.* Some states lower the number of years required to obtain adverse possession when the owner has "color of title." *Compare* Tex. Code §16.026 (10 years if no color of title) *with* Tex. Code §16.025 (5 years if cultivated, paid taxes, with registered deed) *and* Tex. Code §16.024 (3 years if under color of title). "An individual acquires color of title when a written conveyance appears to pass title but does not do so, either from want of title in the person making it, or the defective mode of conveyance." *Glaser v. Bayliff*, 1999 WL 34709 at *4 (Ohio Ct. App. 1999). The defective title may be void because it lacks a signature, *Romero v. Garcia*, 546 P.2d 66 (N.M. 1976), because it contains mistaken or ambiguous descriptions of the land to be conveyed, *Quarles v. Arcega*, 841 P.2d 550 (N.M. Ct. App. 1992), or because it was procured through a faulty procedure, such as a deed granted at a tax sale when the sheriff failed to follow statutorily mandated procedures, *Green v. Dixon*, 727 So. 2d 781 (Ala. 1998) (color of title established by tax deed that was void because of lack of notice to the owner).

In all states, when color of title exists, courts generally use the land area described in the title as conclusive evidence of the property that is being adversely possessed. Actual possession of any portion of that land constitutes adverse possession of the whole. In such a case, color of title functions as fences do to help the court determine the boundaries of the land being claimed by adverse possession.

11. *Claims against the government.* Courts generally hold that adverse possession claims cannot prevail against government property. Thus, those who possess or use public property can never acquire prescriptive rights in that property. The fact that

the true owner is a government entity constitutes an absolute defense to an adverse possession claim. *Stickney v. City of Saco*, 770 A.2d 592, 603, 2001 ME 69, ¶25 (Me. 2001). However, a significant number of states have passed statutes limiting or abolishing governmental immunity from adverse possession. Paula R. Latovick, *Adverse Possession Against the States: The Hornbooks Have It Wrong*, 29 U. Mich. J.L. Reform 939 (1996). *See* Ky. Rev. Stat. §413.150; N.C. Gen. Stat. §1-35; N.D. Cent. Code §28-01-01; Wis. Stat. §893.29. Other states have limited the rule by common law, thereby allowing adverse possession claims against government owners if the property is not held for public use or is dedicated to commercial purposes or is otherwise not open to the public. *American Trading Real Estate Properties, Inc. v. Town of Trumbull*, 574 A.2d 796, 800 (Conn. 1990); *Devins v. Borough of Bogota*, 592 A.2d 199 (N.J. 1991). A federal statute allows adverse possession of federal lands in certain instances if a claimant has occupied the property for 20 years in good faith reliance on a claim or color of title and has either cultivated the land or constructed improvements. 43 U.S.C. §1068.

12. *Effect on preexisting nonpossessory interests.* Adverse possessors generally obtain ownership rights subject to preexisting liens, easements, restrictive covenants, and mineral interests. Unless the adverse possessor has acted in a manner inconsistent with those interests, they have been held to persist.

13. *Protecting the "true owner."* Once a record owner discovers that a neighbor has encroached on its land, what can that owner do to protect its interests?

14. *Native land claims.* The "true owner" in *Nome 2000* claimed that the Fagerstroms had not acquired the property by adverse possession because they were Native Alaskans and their use did not establish sufficient "possessory" control as to constitute a claim of ownership protectable by adverse possession law. The court rejects this argument. Why? If you were the attorney for the true owner, what better argument could you have presented to support your client's position?

§3.2　Hohfeldian Terminology

JURAL RELATIONS AND
THEIR CLASSIFICATION
ARTHUR CORBIN

30 Yale L.J. 226, 226-229 (1921)

In determining what is the law in any given case, we are invariably interested in finding the answer to one question: what will our organized society, acting through its appointed agents, do? . . .

[T]here is no law and there can be no legal relations of any sort where there is no organized society. The fact that is essential is the existence of societal force; and the question that is of supreme interest is as to when and how that force will be applied. What will the community of citizens cause their agents to do? It is this multitude of busy little fellow citizens who constitute "society" or "the state," and it is their cumulative strength that constitutes the personified giant whose arm may be so powerful to aid or to destroy. In law, the ultimate question is, what will this giant do?

Now with respect to the little individual, who will be called *A*, in whose fortunes we may be interested, this giant either will or he will not act; there is no third possibility (although a wide variety is possible in the kind of act that he may do). And the little individual, *A*, himself, either can or he cannot do something that will stimulate the giant to act or not to act. The giant sleeps; can I wake him? He wakens; can I soothe him to inaction? From this it appears that we have four interesting possibilities: The giant will act so as to affect *A*, or he will not so act; *A* can influence the giant's conduct, or he cannot influence his conduct. Introduce a second little individual, *B*, and you at once double these interesting possibilities. The giant will act for *A* as against *B*, or he will not; he will act for *B* as against *A*, or he will not. *A* can influence the giant's action with respect to *B*, or he cannot; *B* can influence the giant's action with respect to *A*, or he cannot. Of course we are deeply interested in the particular sort of act the giant will do, and in the various ways in which *A* and *B* are able to affect the giant's conduct.... [However,] underneath [all legal relations] we have eight fundamental conceptions with respect to any two little individuals, *A* and *B*. The giant will aid *A* against *B*, or he will not; he will aid *B* against *A*, or he will not. *A* can stimulate the giant's conduct with respect to himself and *B*, or he cannot; *B* can so stimulate the giant's conduct, or he cannot....

[Wesley Hohfeld chose words used in judicial reasoning to express these legal relations.] The concept that the giant will aid *A* by forcibly controlling *B*'s conduct we express by saying that *A* has a RIGHT. If the giant will not so aid *A*, he has NO RIGHT. If the giant will aid *B* by using force to control *A*'s conduct, *A* has a DUTY. If he will not so aid *B*, and *A* is free from such constraint, this fact is expressed by saying that *A* has a PRIVILEGE. If *A* can, by his voluntary act, influence the giant's conduct with respect to *B*, whether to act or not to act, and whether presently or contingently, *A* has a POWER. If *A* cannot do this, he has a DISABILITY. If *B* can, by his voluntary act, influence the giant's conduct with respect to *A*, *A* has a LIABILITY. If *B* cannot do this, *A* has an IMMUNITY....

THE LEGAL RIGHTS DEBATE IN ANALYTICAL JURISPRUDENCE FROM BENTHAM TO HOHFELD
JOSEPH WILLIAM SINGER

1982 Wis. L. Rev. 975, 986-987

Hohfeld identifies eight basic legal rights: four primary legal entitlements (rights, privileges, powers and immunities) and their opposites (no-rights, duties, disabilities and liabilities). "Rights" are claims, enforceable by state power, that others act in a certain manner in relation to the rightholder. "Privileges" are permissions to act in a certain manner without being liable for damages to others and without others being able to summon state power to prevent those acts. "Powers" are state-enforced abilities to change legal entitlements held by oneself or others, and "immunities" are security from having one's own entitlements changed by others.

The four negations or opposites of the primary legal entitlements refer to the absence of such entitlements. One has "no-right" if one does not have the power to summon the aid of the state to alter or control the behavior of others. "Duties" refer to the absence of permission to act in a certain manner. "Disabilities" are the absence of power to alter legal entitlements and "liabilities" refer to the absence of immunity from having one's own entitlements changed by others.

The eight terms are arranged in two tables of "correlatives" and "opposites" that structure the internal relationships among the different fundamental legal rights.

JURAL OPPOSITES

right	privilege	power	immunity
no-right	duty	disability	liability

JURAL CORRELATIVES

right	privilege	power	immunity
duty	no-right	liability	disability

Hohfeld's concept of "opposites" conveys the message that one must have one or the other but not both of the two opposites. For example, with regard to any class of acts one must either have a right that others act in a certain manner or no right. Similarly, one must have either a privilege to do certain acts or a duty not to do them.

The concept of "correlatives" is harder to grasp. Legal rights, according to Hohfeld, are not merely advantages conferred by the state on individuals. Any time the state confers an advantage on some citizen, it necessarily simultaneously creates a vulnerability on the part of others. Legal rights are not simply entitlements, but jural relations. Correlatives express a single legal relation from the point of view of the two parties. "[I]f *X* has a right against *Y* that he shall stay off the former's land, the correlative (and equivalent) is that *Y* is under a duty toward *X* to stay off the place." If *A* has a duty toward *B*, then *B* has a right against *A*. The expressions are equivalent. Similarly, privileges are the correlatives of no-rights. "[W]hereas *X* has a *right* or *claim* that *Y*, the other man, should stay off the land, he himself has the *privilege* of entering on the land; or in equivalent words, *X* does not have a duty to stay off." If *A* has no duty toward *B*, *A* has a privilege to act and *B* has no right against *A*. Thus, if *A* has the privilege to do certain acts or to refrain from doing those acts, *B* is vulnerable to the effects of *A*'s actions. *B* cannot summon the aid of the state to prevent *A* from acting in such a manner no matter how *A*'s actions affect *B*'s interests.

NOTES AND QUESTIONS

1. *Hohfeldian terminology.* The concepts identified and systematized by Wesley Hohfeld[5] are extremely useful in legal analysis for two reasons. First, they serve as a reminder that all legal rights entail relations among persons. *A*'s right not to be harmed in a certain way implies duties on others not to harm *A* in that way. *A*'s privilege to act implies that others have no right to prevent *A* from acting and therefore may be vulnerable to negative effects of *A*'s actions, so long as *A* keeps her conduct within the scope of her privilege. In thinking about legal rights, it is important to identify (a) who has the entitlement, (b) against which specific individuals does the entitlement run, and (c) what specific acts are encompassed by the entitlement.

Second, Hohfeld's concepts help disentangle bundles of rights into their constituent parts. For example, the owner of a restaurant has the *privilege* of entering the

---

5. *See* Wesley Hohfeld, *Some Fundamental Legal Conceptions as Applied in Judicial Reasoning*, 23 Yale L.J. 16 (1913).

property; non-owners have no right to prevent the owner from so doing. Does the owner's privilege to enter also mean that the owner has the right to exclude non-owners from the property? Yes and no. While the owner has the right to exclude patrons who are "rowdy," federal civil rights statutes provide that the owner has no right to exclude patrons on account of their race; on the contrary, such persons have a privilege to enter the restaurant and be served. The owner's privilege to enter does not necessarily mean that others have a duty not to enter. Both the owner and the patron have a privilege to enter the restaurant — the owner to run the place and the patron to obtain service.

The distinction between privileges and rights can be illustrated by another example. Suppose my wallet drops out of my pocket while I am walking on the street. I notice it is missing, turn around and see it on the sidewalk, and walk back toward it to pick it up. I have a privilege to do so; if I pick up my wallet, I will not be violating anyone else's rights. A bystander sees the wallet, reaches it before me, and picks it up. Since the wallet was not abandoned, I have a right to have that person hand the wallet over to me; she has a duty to hand it over. Her duty means that she has no privilege to keep it. Her failure to hand over the wallet will violate my property rights and could constitute theft. Therefore, along with my privileges to pick up my own wallet and to keep it, I also have a right to have the bystander hand the wallet over to me.

Suppose, however, I am walking down the street and see an abandoned dollar bill on the sidewalk. I walk toward it to pick it up. A bystander also sees it and begins to walk toward it to pick it up. In this case, because the property is abandoned, each of us has a privilege to pick up the dollar bill and keep it. Whoever picks it up first becomes the owner and then acquires a right not to have the other person take it away. Until it is picked up, however, *each* of us has a privilege to possess it and neither of us has a legal right that imposes a duty on the other not to possess it.

In the first example, I had a privilege to recover my wallet; doing so would violate no rights of others. But I also had a right to recover my wallet — a right that imposed a duty on the bystander to return the wallet to me. In the second case, however, my privilege to pick up the dollar bill does not carry with it a right to prevent others from appropriating it. Rather, each of us has a privilege to appropriate the dollar bill but neither of us has a right to the dollar bill. Those privileges conflict in the sense that ownership will be determined by whoever reaches the dollar bill first. After one of us picks up the dollar bill, however, that person acquires a right to the dollar bill as well as a privilege to keep it.

2. *Hohfeldian terminology and adverse possession.* Adverse possession is often explained as an application of the statute of limitations. An adverse possessor is trespassing on someone else's property. If a trespass is continuing and amounts to an occupation of the property, the record owner may sue for ejectment and obtain an injunction ordering the trespasser to leave the land. The statute of limitations limits the time one can wait to sue for ejectment. After that period has passed, the record owner can no longer remove the trespasser from the land.

Nor can anyone else exclude the possessor. Possession is "nine-tenths of the law." Peaceable possessors of property have a right to exclude everyone from the property *except the true owner. Tapscott v. Lessee of Cobbs*, 52 Va. (11 Gratt.) 172 (1854) (although a wrongful possessor may not exclude the true owner from the land, the current possessor may exclude others even if there is a defect in the possessor's title that would allow the true owner to eject the current possessor). Because an actual possessor has the right to exclude everyone but the true owner, and the true owner's right to exclude the adverse possessor has now been lost, no one has a legal right to exclude the adverse possessor from the property.

However, adverse possession does more than this. If we stopped here, then both the true owner and the adverse possessor would have a privilege to enter the property. Adverse possession doctrine not only makes the adverse possessor's use privileged but also *makes the true owner's use unprivileged.* After the statute of limitations has run, the true owner has a duty to stay off the premises. We say that *title* to the property has shifted from the true owner to the adverse possessor. Because the adverse possessor has effectively excluded the true owner from the premises for the statutory period, the true owner loses the privilege to enter the property. Moreover, the true owner loses all other rights associated with the property, including the right to transfer it, devise it, and mortgage it. This means not only that the true owner would lose an ejectment suit against the adverse possessor, but that the adverse possessor would win a suit to quiet title.

"'Adverse possession' functions as a method of transferring interests in land without the consent of the prior owner, and even in spite of the dissent of such owner." *Powell on Real Property* §91.01[2] (Michael Allan Wolf ed. 2000). What could possibly justify this extraordinary result?

§3.3 Justifications for Adverse Possession: "Roots Which We Should Not Disturb" or "Land Piracy"?

The traditional policy justifications for adverse possession include (1) providing a degree of certainty of ownership to possessors of land by eliminating the possibility of stale claims to land title, and (2) encouraging maximum utilization of land. *Powell on Real Property* §91.01[2] (Michael Allan Wolf ed. 2000); John G. Sprankling, *Understanding Property Law* §27.06, at 449-451 (2000).

Robert Cooter and Thomas Ulen translate the two traditional policy justifications for adverse possession into economic language. First they argue that by quieting title and closing off stale claims, adverse possession "lowers the administrative costs of establishing rightful ownership claims in the event of a delayed dispute about rightful ownership." Robert Cooter and Thomas Ulen, *Law and Economics* 155 (1988). Uncertainty inhibits transactions, or it raises their costs, thereby lowering their profitability. This is because people can sell only what they own; if it is unclear what people own, they will be inhibited from entering transactions because of the risk that they will not in fact be buying or selling what they are purporting to buy or sell. By defining who is the lawful owner in the case of boundary disputes, adverse possession doctrine both settles the dispute and allows further transactions to take place. *Id.* Richard Epstein similarly argues that adverse possession "spares the rightful owner the costs of litigation that might otherwise be needed to establish title." Richard Epstein, *Past and Future: The Temporal Dimension in the Law of Property,* 64 Wash. U. L.Q. 667, 678 (1986).

This explanation is superficially appealing but is probably wrong in practice. It may be true that adverse possession settled boundary disputes before a recording system was in place; with both a recording system and the ability to use scientific surveying methods to fix the boundaries of property, however, it is almost always more efficient and economical to rely on the boundaries fixed in the record title to identify the record owner than it is to conduct a lawsuit to determine whether the complicated and confusing elements of adverse possession have been met. Even in cases of conflicting deeds — where two deeds purport to grant ownership to the same parcel or strip to different persons — it would be less expensive simply to rely on a rule that ownership vests in the person whose deed was recorded first.

Epstein provides another explanation of how adverse possession lowers the costs of determining the title holder. He argues that it "shorten[s] the period during which prospective purchasers and lenders (both noted for their squeamishness) need examine the state of the title." *Id.* at 678. Of course, in the case of a record owner whose deed properly describes the land in question and an adverse possessor whose deed does *not* cover that land, this explanation is wanting. Rather than fixing the owner in a certain fashion, the rule tends to generate litigation. In this type of dispute, it would almost certainly be more predictable simply to fix title in the record owner. And in the case of conflicting deeds (two deeds whose land descriptions both cover the strip of property in question), it would almost certainly be less expensive simply to limit the time period (to 50 years or so) within which one must search the title records and then fix ownership in the person whose deed was recorded first. In fact, many states have "marketable title" acts that do just that.

The second explanation Cooter and Ulen advance for adverse possession "is that it tends to prevent valuable resources from being left idle for long periods of time by specifying procedures for a productive user to take title from an unproductive user." Cooter and Ulen, *supra*, at 156. Those who do not use their property run the risk of losing that property to an adverse possessor. Cooter and Ulen do note, however, that using property is not always beneficial to society. Moreover, if the adverse possessor really values the property more than the true owner, why not require the adverse possessor to find out who the true owner is and offer to buy the property from him?

A completely different explanation was offered by Justice Oliver Wendell Holmes in a letter to William James, in which he explained adverse possession as based on the desire to protect the expectations of the adverse possessor who has come to "shape his roots to his surroundings, and when the roots have grown to a certain size, cannot be displaced without cutting at his life." *Tioga Coal Co. v. Supermarkets General Corp.*, 546 A.2d 1, 5 (Pa. 1988) (quoting Holmes). This explanation rests on the desire to protect the settled expectations of the adverse possessor as against the true owner, who would regard recovery of the land as an unexpected windfall — like winning the lottery.

Judge Richard Posner of the Seventh Circuit Court of Appeals adopts Holmes's explanation but translates it into economic language. Posner argues:

> Over time, a person becomes attached to property that he regards as his own, and the deprivation of the property would be wrenching. Over the same time, a person loses attachment to property that he regards as no longer his own, and the restoration of the property would cause only moderate pleasure. This is a point about diminishing marginal utility of income. The adverse possessor would experience the deprivation of the property as a diminution in his wealth; the original owner would experience the restoration of the property as an increase in his wealth. If they have the same wealth, then probably their combined utility will be greater if the adverse possessor is allowed to keep the property.

Richard Posner, *Economic Analysis of Law* §3.11, at 89-90 (5th ed. 1998). Stewart Sterk has similarly presented an economic defense of prescriptive rights. Like Posner and Cooter and Ulen, Sterk asserts that the adverse possessor is likely to value the property more than the true owner. Stewart Sterk, *Neighbors in American*

Land Law, 87 Colum. L. Rev. 55 (1987). He explains that the true owner has "demonstrated virtually no concern with the possessor's occupation." *Id.* at 80. Because the encroaching adverse possessor has shown by her actions that she values the strip more, it is therefore wealth-maximizing to transfer ownership to her. If this is so, why not rely on private bargaining to do this? If the adverse possessor really values the strip more than the true owner, why shouldn't she *have* to offer the true owner enough money to induce the true owner to sell? After all, requiring a transaction will *test* the proposition that the adverse possessor is the most valued user.

Sterk answers that the costs of strategic bargaining may discourage such a wealth-maximizing transaction. In a two-person bargaining situation, each party must guess what the other party's bottom line is — how much time she has to bargain and what price she is willing to pay or accept — and what bargaining strategy the other side will adopt. "If the costs of transmitting offers and counter-offers are high, the bargainer may find that his best strategy is to eschew bargaining altogether." *Id.* at 72. If the adverse possessor usually values the strip more, and the costs of bargaining prohibit a transfer from the true owner to the adverse possessor, then adverse possession doctrine promotes efficiency by vesting ownership in the adverse possessor.

As Sterk and others have noted, however, it is not a foregone conclusion that the adverse possessor places a higher value on the property than the true owner. "[T]he adverse possessor's offer price is likely to be lower, and may be much lower, than her asking price. The adverse possessor may not be able to come up with $10,000 in cash, or be willing to borrow $10,000 to buy the strip, but may be very willing to keep the strip rather than sell it to the true owner for the same price." Jack Beermann and Joseph William Singer, *Baseline Questions in Legal Reasoning: The Example of Property in Jobs*, 23 Ga. L. Rev. 911, 964-965 (1989). Determining who values the strip more may differ according to which side is required to buy the strip from the other. "Because of the difference between offer and asking prices, the result may differ depending on which party is declared the owner of the disputed strip." *Id.* Under these circumstances, efficiency analysis is indeterminate. The most valued user varies depending on which baseline is chosen. In cases like this, other criteria are needed. Sterk, for example, argues that efficiency analysis must be supplemented by social norms about the proper relationships among neighbors. Sterk, *supra*, at 86-104. The question then focuses on what social norms should be chosen.

Professor Margaret Jane Radin provides a possible answer to this question. She adopts Holmes's explanation for adverse possession but uses the language of justice and fairness rather than economics. Her approach centers on the significant distinction between personal and fungible property: An object is "fungible" if "it is perfectly replaceable with money"; it is "personal" if it "has become bound up with the personhood of the holder and is no longer commensurate with money." Radin argues that the adverse possessor's interest is "initially fungible" but "becomes more and more personal as time passes." Margaret Jane Radin, *Time, Possession, and Alienation*, 64 Wash. U. L.Q. 739, 748 n.26 (1986). "At the same time, the titleholder's interest fades from personal to fungible and finally to nothingness. At what point is the titleholder detached enough and the adverse possessor attached enough to make the switch? This [requires] a moral judgment." *Id.* at 748-749. One problem with this explanation, as Radin concedes, is that the personality theory does not always apply to corporations. *Id.* at 749.

Another moral basis for adverse possession lies in "the reliance interests that the possessor may have developed through longstanding possession of the property."

Thomas Merrill, *Property Rules, Liability Rules, and Adverse Possession,* 79 Nw. U. L. Rev. 1122, 1131 (1984-1985). Thus, adverse possession may be justified by the moral principle of protecting reliance on relationships. The adverse possessor and the true owner develop a kind of relationship based on the true owner's acquiescence in having her property occupied by the adverse possessor. "The possessor comes to expect and may have come to rely on the fact that the true owner will not interfere with the possessor's use of the property . . . and the true owner has fed those expectations by her actions (or her failure to act)." Joseph William Singer, *The Reliance Interest in Property,* 40 Stan. L. Rev. 611, 666-667 (1988). The true owner has failed to interfere with the adverse possessor's use, thereby generating expectations of continued access on the part of the adverse possessor. For that reason, "[i]t is morally wrong for the true owner to allow a relationship of dependence to be established and then to cut off the dependent party." *Id.*

Notice, however, that this argument does not distinguish permissive from nonpermissive use, while adverse possession doctrine grants property rights to long-term users only when their use has been nonpermissive. This may mean either that an additional justification is required to distinguish permissive from nonpermissive use or that the reliance principle would be better protected by abolishing the adverseness requirement, granting adverse possession whenever one owner has acquiesced in another's occupation of a portion of his property for a substantial period of time.

Is there any way to justify morally the extension of adverse possession doctrine to the knowing trespasser — the land pirate who intentionally trespasses and occupies neighboring land, knowing that the neighbor is ignorant of the actual border? It seems perverse to reward such a person. Under this view, the law of adverse possession should include a good faith standard, either as an element of the claim that must be proved by the adverse possessor or as a defense that can rebut an adverse possession claim, allowing the true owner to defeat a claim if the true owner can show the presence of bad faith.

Three arguments might justify granting protection to the land pirate. First, one purpose of the adverse possession doctrine is to create security by encouraging owners to rely on existing practical arrangements that have persisted for a long time. Thus, the right of all owners generally to rely on actual use and occupation rather than formal title creates more security and predictability for all property owners. Resting title on something as difficult to prove as good faith (how can we easily determine someone's state of mind?) will make property rights too unpredictable and generate even more litigation, making ownership less stable, certain, and predictable than it now is. Second, the failure of the true owner to object might be understood as effective abandonment of the owner's rights. Finders generally become owners of abandoned goods. If an owner abandons her rights, it is not accurate to call the intentional trespasser a pirate or thief. After all, the doctrine requires the occupation to be open and notorious; a true owner who does not object to such an occupation may indicate a lack of complaint about the encroachment. Third, even if we view the land pirate as an immoral thief, one policy behind the statute of limitations is to give victims incentives to bring lawsuits within a reasonable time; when this is done, everyone has repose, knowing that she is not subject to lawsuits for actions undertaken long ago. The interest in repose is a strong one. Moreover, it is wrong for the victim to wait too long to vindicate her rights. After a long time, the failure of the victim to come forward creates expectations in the intentional encroacher that ripen into legitimate interests.[6] One can argue about the amount of time that is appropriate, but at some point expectations become fixed. Consider that failing to allow time to create secure possessory rights in current possessors might have the result of authorizing ejectment actions by American Indian tribes ousting the current possessors of land that was illegally taken from them in the eighteenth and nineteenth centuries. Long-standing occupation creates property rights in current possessors that have strong claims to protection, whatever their origin.[7]

Because adverse possession doctrine is a relatively flexible standard, it allows substantial room for manipulation by decisionmakers and, in certain cases, significant uncertainty for property owners. To avoid such uncertainty, more rigid rules could be adopted to settle boundary disputes. For example, ownership rights could be fixed in the record owner (and, in cases of conflicts among record owners, in the owner whose deed was recorded first). Yet adverse possession is one of the oldest rules of property law, and some version of it already exists in every jurisdiction. Lawmakers continue to think that it both promotes justice and fulfills important social and individual needs.

Professor Rose has noted that property doctrine sometimes allocates property rights through rigid rules and sometimes through flexible standards. Rigid rules carry two advantages. First, they clarify who has the power to control a particular resource, thus quickly settling disputes. Second, they promote transactions by identifying who owns a particular set of rights in land, thereby clarifying who has the power to sell it. Without such clear rules, negotiations will be more drawn out and costly; before the exchange can take place, the parties will spend time fighting about who really owns the entitlements about which they are supposed to be bargaining. Carol Rose, *Crystals and Mud in Property Law*, 40 Stan. L. Rev. 577 (1988).

To legislatures and courts, rigid rules often look good at the planning stage. "We call for crystals [rigid rules] when we are in what Mel Eisenberg has called our 'rule-making' mode, that is, when private parties make contracts with strangers or when legislatures make prospective law for an unknown future." *Id.* at 603. It is comforting to think that lawmakers can establish with certainty the rules that will govern future conduct and transactions.

When a dispute arises, however, rigid rules often bring unanticipated, and substantial, injustice. Time and again, courts have shown themselves to be unwilling to live with such unfairness. "We call for mud and exceptions [flexible standards] only later, after things have gone awry, but at that point we stand before judges." *Id.* Judges often respond to the perceived unjust effects of rigid rules by adopting exceptions that take the form of standards. Thus, courts can adjust relationships in ways that more closely approach the judges' intuitions about the just results in particular cases.[8] At some

---

6. Jewish law requires the wrongdoer to correct a mistake by undoing the wrongful act or by compensation and by asking forgiveness from the victim. If the victim does not forgive, the wrongdoer is to go back a second and third time with witnesses to seek forgiveness. The victim is obligated to forgive the wrongdoer who repents and compensates for the harm; if, after the third time, the victim does not forgive, the victim has become the sinner, and the original wrongdoer must forgive *him.* Abraham Cohen, *Everyman"s Talmud: The Major Teachings of the Rabbinic Sages* 228-230 (1995).

7. This does not mean that no remedies should be available for wrongful seizures of land by the state. In fact, the *Indian Claims Commission Act,* passed in 1945, provided millions of dollars in compensation to Indian nations for wrongful seizures of territory. Recent Indian Claims Settlement Acts have resulted in compensation and some land for tribes in Maine, Rhode Island, and Alaska.

8. When this happens, private parties sometimes try to bargain around the new standards adopted by judges; in so doing, the parties may try to re-create the effects of rigid rules by

point, however, these exceptions can make the rules so "muddy" that "as rulemakers we will start over with new boundaries, followed by new muddiness, and so on." *Id.* at 604.

PROBLEMS

1. *Good faith.* Should an adverse possessor gain title to property if she knows she is occupying property belonging to another, as the Fagerstroms did? Would your opinion of the proper result in *Brown v. Gobble* change if you knew that the adverse possessors intentionally and knowingly built the fence in a manner that encroached several feet onto their neighbor's property? What are the arguments for and against adopting a good faith requirement?

2. *Rural land.* When land is possessed in a rural area, as in *Nome 2000,* on land that is wooded and/or unimproved, some courts adopt different standards.

a. *Actual possession.* Some courts hold that actual possession can be established by lesser acts than would be required in an urban area. This is because the law requires the adverse possessor to use the land as an average owner would use it and if land in the area is not used intensively, then actual possession may be shown with fewer acts on the land. However, other courts focus on the fact that the use must be "open and notorious" and that greater acts should be required in rural areas to ensure that a reasonable owner would be on notice of the occupation of her land. Most courts refuse to adopt a special rule for rural, wooded, or unimproved land. Which of these three approaches is best?

b. *Adverse.* Should the courts presume that possession of rural land is permissive rather than nonpermissive? The owner in *Nome 2000,* for example, may have had no objection to the Fagerstroms' use of the land because it did not, for the moment, interfere with any of the owner's interests. Should the presumption that land use is nonpermissive be reversed for unimproved land in areas that are wooded, remote and unimproved?

3. Should possession be presumed to be permissive when the adverse possessor and record title holder are in the same family or otherwise related to each other? *Compare Petch v. Widger,* 335 N.W.2d 254 (Neb. 1983) (yes) *with Totman v. Malloy,* 725 N.E.2d 1045 (Mass. 2000) (no).

§3.4 *Prescriptive Easements*

COMMUNITY FEED STORE, INC. v. NORTHEASTERN CULVERT CORP.
559 A.2d 1068 (Vt. 1989)

ERNEST W. GIBSON III, Justice.

Plaintiff brought an action claiming a prescriptive easement over a portion of defendant's land. The trial court rejected the claim and, instead, entered judgment for defendant on its counterclaim for ejectment, from which plaintiff appeals. We reverse. . . .

Plaintiff operates a small wholesale and retail animal feed business in Westminster Station, Vermont. Defendant is a neighboring business which owns the land adjacent to that upon which plaintiff's buildings stand. At issue is a parcel of land to the north of plaintiff's principal building (the "mill"), which testimony showed to be a rectangular area measuring approximately 60 × 90 feet, covered with gravel but not otherwise improved. Plaintiff owns that part of the gravel area extending approximately twenty-eight feet to the north of the mill; the remainder belongs to defendant.

The mill has loading areas on both the north and south sides: the north loading dock is used mostly by trucks delivering bag feed and by customers coming to pick up feed, while the southern area is where plaintiff receives shipments of feed in bulk. Testimony showed that vehicles using either loading area would use the gravel lot for turning and backing. Evidence tended to show that the suppliers' trucks as well as the customers' smaller vehicles used the gravel lot for this purpose.

Although defendant bought its land in 1956, it was not until a new survey was made in 1984 that it was conclusively established that the bulk of the gravel area used by plaintiff's vehicles actually belonged to defendant. Defendant then erected a barrier at approximately the location of the survey line to prevent cars and trucks from using its portion of the gravel area, precipitating plaintiff's lawsuit for declaration of a prescriptive easement.

The court, after making findings of fact, concluded that plaintiff's claim of a prescriptive easement failed for two reasons: first, plaintiff failed to prove with sufficient particularity the width and length of the easement; and second, any use of the area in question by plaintiff or its customers was made with the permission of the fee owner. Plaintiff claims that the court erred in these conclusions and in the findings of fact supporting them, and that the record as a whole supports the conclusion that a prescriptive easement exists. . . .

Findings of fact will not be overturned on appeal unless they are clearly erroneous. The evidence must be viewed in the light most favorable to the prevailing party, and the findings will be upheld if supported by reasonable or credible evidence, even if contrary evidence exists. Despite this strict standard, a thorough review of the record leads us to the conclusion that plaintiff is correct in its claims that the court erred in making two findings of fact. . . .

In Finding 18, the court held that although "all types of vehicles have turned and backed up to plaintiff's building for loading and unloading since the early 1920s," plaintiff had "failed to prove by the requisite measure of proof as to what portion, if any, of defendant's land" was used by plaintiff's vehicles. This finding, which entails both an issue of law (the measure of proof necessary to establish an easement) and an issue of fact, served as the basis for the court's first conclusion of law denying the claim for a prescriptive easement.

The elements necessary to establish a prescriptive easement and adverse possession are essentially the same under Vermont law: an adverse use or possession which is open, notorious, hostile and continuous for a period of fifteen years, and acquiescence in the use or possession by the person against whom the claim is asserted. The difference lies in the interest claimed. The term "prescription" applies to the acquisition of nonfee interests, while "adverse possession" indicates that the interest claimed is in fee.

Adverse possession may be asserted either under claim of title (where claimant took possession under a deed which is for some reason defective), or under a claim of right which arises from the open, notorious and hostile possession of the land at issue. Where there is color of title, it is relatively simple to ascertain the extent of the possession claimed, since "actual and exclusive occupation of any part of the deeded premises carr[ies] with it constructive possession of the whole. . . ." In the absence of color of title, however, and where a lot has no definite boundary marks, adverse possession can only extend as far as claimant has actually occupied and possessed the land in dispute.

Where prescriptive use is claimed, our law requires proof similar to that needed to establish adverse possession under claim of right. In *Morse v. Ranno*, 32 Vt. 600, 607 (1860), this Court held that where a claim of prescriptive easement for a public highway over private land was made,

> the extent of the acquisition, the width of the road, must be determined by the extent of the actual occupation and use. There can be no constructive possession beyond the limits which are defined by the user upon the land, or by other marks or boundaries marking the extent of the claim.

See also Gore v. Blanchard, 118 A. 888, 894 (Vt. 1922) (width of highway acquired by user is determined by the extent of the actual use and occupation or by other marks and boundaries indicating the extent of the claim). . . .

This approach to defining the extent of a prescriptive easement is reflected in the position taken by the drafters of the *Restatement of Property*, which states that "[t]he extent of an easement created by prescription is fixed by the use through which it was created." *Restatement of Property* §477 (1944).

> No use can be justified under a prescriptive easement unless it can fairly be regarded as within the range of the privileges asserted by the adverse user and acquiesced in by the owner of the servient tenement. Yet, no use can ever be exactly duplicated. If any practically useful easement is ever to arise by prescription, the use permitted under it must vary in some degree from the use by which it was created. Hence, the use under which a prescriptive easement arises determines the *general outlines* rather than the minute details of the interest. *Id.*, comment b (emphasis added).

In California, case law requires claimants to show prescriptive easements by "a definite and certain line of travel" for the statutory period. *Warsaw v. Chicago Metallic Ceilings, Inc.*, 676 P.2d 584, 587 (Cal. 1984). Despite the apparently restrictive nature of that standard, however, the *Warsaw* court, on facts almost identical to ours, found that an easement existed for the purpose of trucks turning around and positioning themselves at loading docks attached to plaintiff's building, stating that "[s]light deviations from the accustomed route will not defeat an easement, [only] substantial changes which break the continuity of the course of travel. . . ." *Id.*

From the case law cited above, it is clear that when a prescriptive easement is claimed, the extent of the user must be proved not with absolute precision, but only as to the general outlines consistent with the pattern of use throughout the prescriptive period. We hold that where a claimant adduces enough evidence to prove those general outlines with reasonable certainty, it has met its burden on that issue.

In this case, the trial court had before it extensive evidence as to the nature and scope of the user claimed. Testimony showed that the gravel area at issue was approximately 60 by 90 feet long, extending from the northern end of the mill approximately to where a railroad call box (attached to what resembles a telephone pole) is located.

Surveys were introduced showing the exact northern boundary of plaintiff's land, falling approximately twenty-eight feet to the north of the mill and, therefore, twenty-eight feet into the gravel area. Photographs were also admitted into evidence clearly showing the gravel area and the northern loading dock. In addition, plaintiff's president drew a diagram showing the use of the gravel area by trucks and cars, indicating the railroad call box as the north limit.

Under the standard discussed above, we conclude that plaintiff met its burden by establishing the general outlines of the easement with reasonable certainty....

The second — and in its own view, more important — basis upon which the court denied plaintiff's claim was its conclusion that any use made by plaintiff was with the fee owner's permission....

[T]he elements necessary to prove a prescriptive easement [are] open, notorious, hostile and continuous use over a fifteen-year period in which the fee owner has acquiesced. In its findings, the trial court found as fact that the area in dispute had been used by vehicles of all descriptions in a manner consistent with the claimed use since the 1920s. The record showed that this use continued uninterrupted, and in a manner substantially unchanged since then but for the modernization of the vehicles using the area, until the barrier was erected in 1984. On the facts as found by the court, this comprises "open, notorious and continuous" use of defendant's property.

The general rule is that open and notorious use will be presumed to be adverse. The trial court noted in its order (without further comment), and the defendant argues, that not this presumption but the presumption that public use of private property is by permission should apply. This case does not, however, involve... generalized public use....[2]

In order to prove the final element of its claim, the passing of the fifteen-year period set forth at Vt. Stat. Ann. tit. 12, §501, plaintiff proved the chain of title of its property from plaintiff's predecessors in interest from 1929 through the present, and showed through uncontradicted testimony that those predecessors had also made use of the gravel area now claimed by plaintiff as an easement by prescription. Under the doctrine of "tacking," plaintiff may add those previous periods of use to its own upon a showing that it has "assume[d] the use of the easement directly from his predecessor as a part of his receipt of the dominant estate." The record supports the conclusion that adverse use began no later than 1929, with the result that the prescriptive period expired in 1944....

The record supports a conclusion that the claimed use was made in an open, notorious, continuous and adverse manner from 1929 until at least 1956....

NOTES AND QUESTIONS

1. *Elements.* The elements for establishing a prescriptive easement are the same as those for adverse possession except that the claimant must show adverse "use" rather

---

2. Defendant's reliance on *Plimpton v. Converse,* 44 Vt. 158 (1871), is misplaced. That case, which also enunciated the "public use" exception to the general presumption of adversity, involved one shopholder's claim of prescriptive easement as to passage, both for himself and his customers, over a neighboring shopholder's land. There, the Court found that because the second shopholder had already opened his land to general passage by his own customers, there was a presumption of permission to all public users, including the first shopholder and his customers. Those facts are distinguishable from the instant case, in which no showing was made that defendant had "thrown open" its land to general passage.

than adverse "possession." "The party claiming the [prescriptive] easement must establish open, notorious, exclusive, adverse, continuous and uninterrupted use of the claimed easement for the statutory . . . period." *Han Farms, Inc. v. Molitor,* 760 P.3d 1238, 1240, 2003 MT 153 ¶12 (Mont. 2003). Most courts drop the exclusivity requirement, although some retain it. *See Hoffman v. United Iron and Metal Co.,* 671 A.2d 55, 64 (Md. Ct. Spec. App. 1996); *Rogers v. Marlin,* 754 So. 2d 1267, at 1272 (Miss. Ct. App. 1999). A few states require that the use be under a "claim of right" or "ownership." *Wood v. Hoglund,* 963 P.2d 383, 386-387 (Idaho 1998); *Rogers v. Marlin, supra.* Many courts add the requirement that the true owner "acquiesce" in the adverse use. These elements are discussed below.

Occasional or sporadic use is likely to violate the continuity requirement. *Barchowsky v. Silver Farms, Inc.,* 659 A.2d 347, 354 (Md. Ct. Spec. App. 1995). However, in *United States ex rel. Zuni Tribe of N.M. v. Platt,* 730 F. Supp. 318 (D. Ariz. 1990), the court recognized a prescriptive easement of passage in the Zuni Tribe which had traversed a 110-mile path located on private lands every four years on a pilgrimage to a sacred site and probably had been doing so since 1540).

As with adverse possession, many courts require proof of adverse use by clear and convincing evidence, *McDonald v. Harris,* 978 P.2d 81 (Alaska 1999), while some require only that the claimant prove the elements by a preponderance of the evidence. *Stiefel v. Lindemann,* 638 A.2d 642, 649 n.8 (Conn. Ct. App. 1994).

Adverse possession claims result in a transfer of title to the adverse possessor while prescriptive easement claims result in the right to continue the kind and amount of use that persisted during the statutory period. *Han Farms, supra,* at 1241, ¶24.

2. *Claim of right.* Those courts that require proof of a "claim of right" generally mean that the use is not permissive but is engaged in by the prescriptive easement claimant regardless of the wishes of the owner of the land. *Warnack v. Coneen Family Trust,* 923 P.2d 1087, 1089-1090 (Mont. 1996) ("[t]he use of the primary route was in fact exercised under a claim of right and not as a mere privilege or license revocable at the pleasure of the owners of the land"). This element is therefore generally duplicative of the requirement that use be nonpermissive. However, some courts may interpret this element to impose a state of mind requirement on the part of the adverse user, defeating the prescriptive easement claim if it can be shown that the user of the land did not intend to trespass but believed she had the permission of the land owner. As noted in the adverse possession materials, some courts will not find adverse possession in boundary dispute cases if the adverse possessor testifies that she did not intend to encroach on property that did not belong to her. Courts that adopt that rule may adopt a similar approach to prescriptive easements by disallowing the easement if the user believed she had the owner's permission and thus was not subordinate to the owner's powers while granting a prescriptive easement if the user's entry was independent of the true owner's permission and was based on her own "claim of right."

3. *Acquiescence.* As *Community Feed Store* demonstrates, a significant number of states require the prescriptive easement claimant to prove *acquiescence* by the true owner as one of the elements of the claim. This is a confusing term. How can the true owner both "acquiesce" in the use and "not permit" it?

The acquiescence requirement may have its origin in the theory that prescriptive easements are based, not on adverse or nonpermissive use, but on a "lost grant." Because statutes of limitation usually applied only to possessory claims in England, English law protected long-standing use on the premise that the use had a lawful origin. The device of choice was the fiction of a "lost grant." Jon W. Bruce and James W. Ely,

Jr., *The Law of Easements and Licenses in Land* ¶5.08, at 5-43 (rev. ed. 1995). This theory presumes initial permissive use and therefore contradicts the requirement of proving that use was "adverse" or nonpermissive.

For some courts today, acquiescence merely means that the owner did not assert her right to exclude by bringing a trespass action; this interpretation renders the requirement duplicative and unnecessary. For some courts, however, it does have independent significance; it means that the land owner must have *known* about the use and passively allowed it to continue without formally granting permission. *Sparling v. Fon du Lac Township,* 745 N.E.2d 660 (Ill. App. Ct. 2001). Alternatively, it could mean that a reasonable owner would or *should* have known of the use; this meaning duplicates the requirement that the use be open and notorious because use is only open and notorious if it is sufficiently visible to put a reasonable owner on notice of it. *Hodgins v. Sales,* 76 P.3d 969, 973 (Idaho 2003); *Jones v. Cullen,* 1998 WL 811558, at *5 (Minn. Ct. App. 1998); *Lingvall v. Bartmess,* 982 P.2d 690, 694 (Wash. Ct. App. 1999).

4. *Presumptions as to permission.* Most states presume that use by a non-owner of one's land is nonpermissive, as they do with adverse possession. *See, e.g., Harambasic v. Owens,* 920 P.2d 39, 40-41 (Ariz. Ct. App. 1996). However, a fair minority of courts presume that use, unlike possession, is presumptively permissive rather than adverse. *Johnson v. Coshatt,* 591 So. 2d 483, 485 (Ala. 1991); *McGill v. Wahl,* 839 P.2d 393, 397-398 (Alaska 1992). They do so because owners often do allow their neighbors to cross over their land as a "neighborly gesture," *Jones v. Cullen,* 1998 WL 811558, at *5 (Minn. Ct. App. 1998), and there may therefore be more warrant for assuming that limited uses are permissive than there is for presuming that occupation is permissive. *Johnson v. Stanley,* 384 S.E.2d 577, 579 (N.C. Ct. App. 1989). Some courts adopt a presumption that use is permissive only if it can be shown that there was a community custom to allow such uses on the land of others. *Warnack v. Coneen Family Trust,* 879 P.2d 715 (Mont. 1994). Finally, some states protect owners from prescriptive easements over large bodies of unenclosed land under a "neighborhood accommodation exception" where the owners could not reasonably know of passings over the land. *See Algermissen v. Sutin,* 61 P.3d 176, 182, 2003 NMSC 1, ¶¶15-17 (N.M. 2002) (describing but not applying this exception).

5. *The good faith problem.* In *Community Feed Store,* one person mistakenly used his neighbor's property. In contrast, in *Warsaw v. Chicago Metallic Ceilings, Inc.,* 676 P.2d 584 (Cal. 1984), cited by the Vermont court in *Community Feed Store,* the adverse user clearly knew that it was trespassing on neighboring property. In *Warsaw,* plaintiffs arranged for the construction of a large commercial building on their property but unfortunately left insufficient space between the edge of the building and their property line. The 40-foot driveway was "inadequate since the large trucks which carried material to and from plaintiffs' loading dock could not turn and position themselves at these docks without traveling onto the defendant's property," *id.* at 586, which they proceeded to do for the next seven years. When defendant developed plans to build on the portion of its property that had been used by plaintiffs to back up its delivery trucks, plaintiffs sued to establish a prescriptive easement over the 25-foot strip on the edge of defendant's property. Defendant unwisely continued construction over the disputed strip while litigation proceeded. Plaintiffs ultimately prevailed, obtaining a prescriptive easement since the relevant statute of limitations allowed a relatively short six-year period to establish such an easement.

The result in *Warsaw* is discomfiting because it appears to reward a party who knowingly trespassed on neighboring property, thereby taking property rights from an innocent owner and transferring them to a wrongdoer. Moreover, the wrongdoer's predicament is wholly the result of its own negligence in constructing its building too near the property line. The result appears not only unfair, because it rewards a knowing trespasser, but unwise as a matter of social policy, because it decreases incentives to plan correctly. For these reasons, some commentators have argued that the courts should differentiate good faith and bad faith trespassers and award prescriptive rights only to good faith trespassers — those who are mistaken about the boundary lines and are not knowingly infringing on their neighbor's property.

6. *No negative prescriptive easements.* It is important to note that *negative* easements cannot be acquired by prescription in the United States. For example, in *Fontainebleau Hotel v. Forty-Five Twenty-Five, Inc.*, 114 So. 2d 357 (Fla. Dist. Ct. App. 1959),[9] two neighboring hotels quarreled about the defendant's plan to build an addition to its structure that would cast a shadow over the plaintiff hotel's swimming pool. Plaintiff claimed that because it had enjoyed unobstructed access to light and air for a long time, it had acquired an easement by prescription. The court held that the mere fact that one has enjoyed light and air on one's property for many years will not create an easement for light and air that prevents one's neighbor from building on her property.

This result is justified on several grounds. First, if the basis of prescriptive rights is the statute of limitations, the owner claiming prescription must be trespassing on the true owner's property or otherwise interfering with the true owner's rights so as to give the true owner a legal claim for trespass. In the case of a negative easement, the owner claiming prescriptive rights has in no way violated her neighbor's property rights. Building a hotel on one's own property and enjoying the light and air in no way intrudes on the neighbor's protected property interests; therefore, there is no claim that could be barred by the statute of limitations. Second, lawful use of one's own property does not place the true owner on notice that she must bring a lawsuit to protect herself from losing her property rights. Finally, allowing negative easements to be acquired by prescription is thought to interfere too much with the free development of land.

7. *Implicit agreement or redistribution?* Does adverse possession and prescriptive easement doctrine rest on the notion that long-standing patterns of land use should be recognized as implicitly consensual? After all, the true owner's long-standing acquiescence of adverse use could be interpreted as abandonment of her property rights and the adverse possessor's long-standing use as an exercise of possession of unowned property. Or perhaps the true owner's long-standing acquiescence constitutes an implied offer to transfer the property to the adverse user, which the adverse user accepts by adverse possession or use — in other words, a unilateral contract. Does it make sense to think of these doctrines as protecting the will of the parties and therefore the transfer of property rights as consensual? Or does it make more sense to think of the doctrines as rules that redistribute property rights from one person to another for reasons of public policy?

8. *Acquisition by the public.* Many older cases and some modern cases hold that the public could not acquire an easement by prescription. *Mihalczo v. Borough of Woodmont*, 400 A.2d 270, 272 (Conn. 1978); *Forest Hills Gardens Corp. v. Baroth*, 555 N.Y.S.2d 1000, 1002 (Sup. Ct. 1990). This rule is based partly on the difficulty of proving continuity of use (how does one define the public?), partly on the difficulty of excluding the general public from certain areas, and partly on the presumption that public use of private property is permissive rather than adverse.

---

9. This case is covered in more depth in §4.4.3, *infra*.

However, the strong trend of modern cases is to recognize that the public may acquire prescriptive easements, while often presuming that public access to private land is permissive in the absence of clear evidence to the contrary, thereby defeating the claim for prescription. *Id. Weidner v. State*, 860 P.2d 1205, 1209 (Alaska 1993) (holding that the state could acquire an easement by prescription); *Limestone Development Corp. v. Village of Lemont*, 672 N.E.2d 763, 768 (Ill. App. Ct. 1996); *Fears v. YJ Land Corp.*, 539 N.W.2d 306, 308 (N.D. 1995). This is the approach adopted by the *Restatement (Third) of Property (Servitudes)*. *Restatement (Third) of Property (Servitudes)* §2.18 (2000). Some states have statutes providing that use by the public of a road for a certain amount of time creates a public highway. Idaho Code §40-202. A few states have used this doctrine to recognize prescriptive rights in the public to use beaches for recreational purposes. *City of Daytona Beach v. Tona-Rama, Inc.*, 294 So. 2d 73, 75 (Fla. 1974); *Villa Nova Resort, Inc. v. State*, 711 S.W.2d 120, 127 (Tex. Ct. Civ. App. 1986).

PROBLEMS

1. *Permissive use.* What arguments could you make for the plaintiff in *Community Feed Store* that use of another's property is presumptively nonpermissive? What arguments could you make for the defendant true owner that use of a neighbor's property in the context of the case should be held presumptively permissive (with the owner's implied consent) and thus not subject to prescription? Which presumption do you think the court should adopt?

2. *Good faith.* Assume the facts in *Warsaw v. Chicago Metallic Ceilings, supra*, in which the neighbor knew its trucks were trespassing on neighboring land. In each of the following questions, construct the strongest arguments on both sides, then determine what the rule of law should be and justify it.

   a. *Should there be a good faith requirement?* The adverse user clearly knew that it was using someone else's property. To obtain an easement by prescription, should the adverse user be required to have good faith, that is, not to know that it is trespassing on someone else's property?

   b. *Should the adverse user lose when the problem is the result of its own negligence?* Plaintiff adverse users in *Warsaw* negligently built their building too close to the property line. Plaintiff's need to trespass on defendant true owner's property for the purpose of backing up its trucks is therefore the result of its own bad planning. Should the court adopt an exception to the prescriptive easement rules to deny the plaintiff a remedy when the plaintiff's trespassory activity is necessitated by the plaintiff's own negligent planning?

   c. *Should there be compensation for the prescriptive easement when the adverse user acted in bad faith?* Adverse possessors and prescriptive easement claimants obtain property rights by prescription without obligation to compensate the true owner for the property rights lost by the true owner. In *Warsaw*, however, Justice Reynoso dissented, on the grounds that it was unfair to award a prescriptive easement to a bad faith trespasser — one who knew that she was trespassing on neighboring property — without requiring her to compensate the true owner for the property rights lost. What arguments can you make for and against this proposal? What rule of law should the court adopt?

3. *Trees.* A great deal of litigation has ensued between neighbors over encroaching trees. Owners are entitled to use self-help to cut branches of their neighbors' trees that encroach over their land. *Lane v. W.J. Curry & Sons*, 92 S.W.3d 355, 360 (Tenn. 2002). Can a tree owner obtain a prescriptive easement allowing the tree's branches to remain over neighboring land? Almost all courts hold no, creating an important exception to the prescriptive easement doctrine. *Koresko v. Farley*, 844 A.2d 607 (Pa. Commw. Ct. 2004); *Pierce v. Casady*, 711 P.2d 766 (Kan. Ct. App. 1985). However, some courts may allow such rights to ripen into easements. *Garcia v. Sanchez*, 772 P.2d 1311 (N.M. Ct. App. 1989); *Jones v. Wagner*, 624 A.2d 166, 171 n.3 (Pa. Super. Ct. 1993). What do you think?

§3.5 Other Informal Ways to Transfer Title to Real Property

The Statute of Frauds generally requires a formal writing to transfer interests in real property. As the adverse possession rules demonstrate, however, there are significant exceptions to this general principle. In boundary disputes, a variety of doctrines may result in transfers of ownership without the formalities that usually accompany property transfers. Unlike the case of adverse possession, these rules apply even when non-owners have occupied the property in question with the true owner's permission.

§3.5.1 THE IMPROVING TRESPASSER

What happens when someone mistakenly invests a lot of money in building a structure that encroaches on a neighbor's property? If the structure *decreases* the value of the neighboring property, the owner ordinarily wishes it to be removed. Owners normally have the right to end a continuing trespass. But should the result be any different when the structure costs a substantial amount to build and causes only a negligible amount of harm to the property interests of the landowner? Should it matter that the owner of the land on which the encroachment was placed failed to object or intervene while the construction was occurring?

The converse problem occurs when the structure *improves* the value of the neighboring property. In this case, the landowner may wish to keep the structure; because it is on her property, the courts generally hold that she has a right to do so. But does the builder have a right to be compensated for the amount spent in the construction to avoid unjust enrichment to the landowner, or would this unjustly force the landowner to pay for something she never wanted or bargained for? If the structure merely encroaches on the neighboring land, should the builder have a right to purchase the land over which it sits, even if the landowner objects?

§3.5.1.1 Removal of Encroaching Structure: Relative Hardship

The first situation involves construction of a structure that encroaches on neighboring property. The landowner may want the structure removed either because it decreases the value of the land or because it invades the landowner's possessory interest in the land — her right not to have a neighbor expropriate a portion of her property, no matter how small. The builder may want the structure to stay, perhaps upon payment of compensation to the landowner or a forced purchase of the land on which the building encroaches.

Many courts, especially in older cases, hold that the property owner has an absolute right to an injunction ordering an encroaching structure removed, no matter what the cost involved or the relative value of the properties or the extent of the encroachment. This is often done in the case of a fence or wall, driveway, or overhanging porch or fire escape, but some courts go so far as to order the removal of an encroaching building. For example, in *Bishop v. Reinhold*, 311 S.E.2d 298 (N.C. Ct. App. 1984), defendants partially erected their house on the adjoining, unimproved lot of the plaintiffs. The court held that the plaintiffs had an absolute right to have the part of the house that encroached on plaintiffs' property removed. A similar result was reached in *Geragosian v. Union Realty Co.*, 193 N.E. 726, 728 (Mass. 1935), where the court explained:

> The facts that the aggrieved owner suffers little or no damage from the trespass, that the wrongdoer acted in good faith and would be put to disproportionate expense by removal of the trespassing structures, and that neighborly conduct as well as business judgment would require acceptance of compensation in money for the land appropriated, are ordinarily no reasons for denying an injunction. Rights in real property cannot ordinarily be taken from the owner at a valuation, except under the power of eminent domain. Only when there is some estoppel or laches on the part of the plaintiff, or a refusal on his part to consent to acts necessary to the removal or abatement which he demands, will an injunction ordinarily be refused. . . . The general rule is that the owner of land is entitled to an injunction for the removal of trespassing structures.

The majority of states, however, now reject this approach and instead adopt the *relative hardship* doctrine. *Urban Site Venture II Limited Partnership v. Levering Associates Limited Partnership*, 665 A.2d 1062 (Md. 1995); *Restatement of Property* §563 (1944). If the encroachment is innocent (the result of a mistake), the harm minimal, the interference in the true owner's property interests small, and the costs of removal substantial, the courts often refuse to grant an injunction ordering removal of the structure. Instead, they will either order the encroaching party to pay damages to the landowner to compensate for the decrease in market value of the owner's land or order a forced sale of the property from the landowner to the owner of the encroaching structure with damages equal to the value of the land taken and possibly a premium to compensate for the involuntary nature of the transfer in ownership. If, however, the cost of removal is not substantial or the interference with the neighbor's ability to use its property is substantial, removal may well be ordered. The North Carolina Court of Appeals explained the doctrine in *Williams v. South & South Rentals, Inc.*, 346 S.E.2d 665, 669 (N.C. Ct. App. 1986):

> Where the encroachment is minimal and the cost of removing the encroachment is most likely substantial, two competing factors must be considered in fashioning a remedy. On the one hand, without court intervention, a defendant may well be forced to buy plaintiff's land at a price many times its worth rather than destroy the building that encroaches. On the other hand, without the threat of a mandatory injunction, builders may view the legal remedy as a license to engage in private eminent domain. The process of balancing the hardships and the equities is designed to eliminate either extreme. Factors to be considered are whether the owner acted in good faith or intentionally built on the adjacent land and whether the hardship incurred in removing the structure

is disproportionate to the harm caused by the encroachment. Mere inconvenience and expense are not sufficient to withhold injunctive relief. The relative hardship must be disproportionate.

Removal of the encroaching structure is ordinarily ordered if the builder *knowingly* built on neighboring property. For example, in *Warsaw v. Chicago Metallic Ceilings, Inc.*, 676 P.2d 584 (Cal. 1984), the defendant proceeded to build a structure that infringed on its neighbor's property, even though the defendant knew that plaintiff claimed that the structure would infringe on the plaintiff's property. The court ordered the structure removed. Although removal will not be ordered in cases of "innocent mistake or oversight" where the encroachment is slight and the "the damage to the owner of the buildings by their removal would be greatly disproportionate to the injury," removal will be ordered without regard to relative hardship "where it appears that the defendant acted with a full knowledge of the complainant's rights. . . ." *Id.* at 588. Because construction began while a lawsuit was pending regarding the parties' property rights, the court held that defendant "gambled on the outcome of the action and lost." *Id. Accord, Goulding v. Cook*, 661 N.E.2d 1322 (Mass. 1996) (ordering removal of septic tank built when builder knew land ownership was in dispute).

When the encroachment is innocent, the result depends both on the circumstances and on the views of the judge about the relative equities. Removal was ordered in *Leffingwell v. Glendenning*, 238 S.W.2d 942 (Ark. 1951), where a stone-and-cement wall encroached from three to four inches onto neighboring property. The court ordered removal of the encroachment on the ground that "the cost to appellees of removal is not disproportionate to the value appellant appears to place on the land." *Id.* at 944. Similarly, in *Storey v. Patterson*, 437 So. 2d 491 (Ala. 1983), the court ordered defendant to remove the portion of her concrete driveway that encroached 12 feet onto neighboring land on the grounds that "it reduced what already was a small residential lot to a lot not suitable for residential purposes, and that the encroachment thus permanently impaired the [plaintiffs'] use and enjoyment of their property." *Id.* at 495.

On the other hand, many courts refuse to order encroaching structures removed, relegating the plaintiff to compensation for the loss of her property rights. In *Yeakel v. Driscoll*, 467 A.2d 1342 (Pa. Super. Ct. 1983), the court refused to order defendant to remove a recently constructed fire wall that encroached two inches onto plaintiff's porch. The court invoked the maxim *de minimus non curat lex*, meaning "that the law will not concern itself with trifles. More specifically it means that a court will not grant equitable relief to a plaintiff who seeks a decree which will do him no good but which will work a hardship on another." *Id.* at 1344. *See Gilpin v. Jacob Ellis Realties*, 135 A.2d 204 (N.J. Super. Ct. App. Div. 1957) (denying an injunction removing an encroachment when the cost of removal was $11,500 and the damage to neighboring property was only $1,000); *Generalow v. Steinberger*, 517 N.Y.S.2d 22 (App. Div. 1987) (refusing to order removal of a driveway and wall that encroached 8.4 inches onto neighboring property and relegating plaintiff to damages); *Knuth v. Vogels*, 61 N.W.2d 301 (Wis. 1953) (refusing to order removal of a garage that encroached one to two feet onto plaintiff's property and giving the defendant trespasser the option of removing the structure or paying damages). When the trespasser is allowed to continue the encroachment, the courts will generally award damages to compensate the landowner for the permanent encroachment, effectively granting the encroacher an easement over the land, or order a forced sale of the land to the encroacher for fair market value with damages for any injury suffered because of the loss of the land.

§3.5.1.2   Unjust Enrichment versus Forced Sale

What happens when an *entire structure* is built on land belonging to another? Ordinarily, courts hold that the structure belongs to the owner of the land on which it sits. *Banner v. United States,* 238 F.3d 1348 (Fed. Cir. 2001). Does this result in unjust enrichment to the landowner? Or is it an appropriate result in light of the builder's negligence in building on someone else's land? If both parties were negligent in allowing the construction to happen, what should the court do? Should it order the landowner to pay for the building so that the landowner is not unjustly enriched? Or should the landowner be forced to sell the land to the builder? The following case deals with these questions.

SOMERVILLE v. JACOBS
170 S.E.2d 805 (W. Va. 1969)

FRANK C. HAYMOND, President:
The plaintiffs, W. J. Somerville and Hazel M. Somerville, . . . the owners of Lots 44, 45 and 46 in the Homeland Addition to the city of Parkersburg, in Wood County, believing that they were erecting a warehouse building on Lot 46 which they owned, [and in reliance on a surveyor's report and plat,] mistakenly constructed the building on Lot 47 owned by the defendants, William L. Jacobs and Marjorie S. Jacobs. . . . Construction of the building was completed in January 1967 and by deed dated January 14, 1967 the Somervilles conveyed Lots 44, 45 and 46 to the plaintiffs Fred C. Engle and Jimmy C. Pappas who subsequently leased the building to the Parkersburg Coca-Cola Bottling Company, a corporation. Soon after the building was completed but not until then, the defendants learned that the building was on their property and claimed ownership of the building and its fixtures on the theory of annexation. The plaintiffs then instituted this proceeding for equitable relief in the Circuit Court of Wood County and in their complaint prayed, among other things, for judgment in favor of the Somervilles for $20,500.00 as the value of the improvements made on Lot 47, or, in the alternative, that the defendants be ordered to convey their interest in Lot 47 to the Somervilles for a fair consideration. The Farmers Building and Loan Association, a corporation, the holder of a deed of trust lien upon the land of the defendants, was on motion permitted to intervene and be made a defendant in this proceeding. . . .

The controlling question for decision is whether a court of equity can award compensation to an improver for improvements which he has placed upon land not owned by him, which, because of mistake, he had reason to believe he owned, which improvements were not known to the owner until after their completion and were not induced or permitted by such owner, who is not guilty of any fraud or inequitable conduct, and require the owner to pay the fair value of such improvements or, in the alternative, to convey the land so improved to the improver upon his payment to the owner of the fair value of the land less the value of the improvements.

Though there are numerous decisions by this Court relating to improvements to land, the precise question here involved is one of first impression in this jurisdiction. . . .

[T]he question has been considered by appellate courts in other jurisdictions and though the cases are conflicting the decisions in some jurisdictions, upon particular facts, recognize and sustain the jurisdiction of a court of equity to award compensation to the improver to prevent unjust enrichment to the owner and in the alternative to require the owner to convey the land to the improver upon his payment to the owner of the fair value of the land less the improvements. . . .

In Section 625, Chapter 11, Volume 2, *Tiffany Real Property,* Third Edition, the text contains this language:

> Since the rule that erections or additions made by one who has no rights to land are fixtures, and therefore not removable by him, even though he made them in the belief that he was the owner of the land, is calculated to cause hardship to an innocent occupant of another's land, by giving the benefit of his labor and expenditures to the landowner, the courts of this country, without either imputing fraud or requiring proof of it, hold it inequitable to allow one to be enriched under such circumstances by the labor and expenditures of another who acted in good faith and in ignorance of any adverse claim or title. Applying this doctrine of "unjust enrichment," a court of equity will, on the principle that he who seeks equity must do equity, refuse its assistance to the rightful owner of land as against an occupant thereof unless he makes compensation for permanent and beneficial improvements, made by the latter without notice of the defect in his title. . . .

From the foregoing authorities it is manifest that equity has jurisdiction to, and will, grant relief to one who, through a reasonable mistake of fact and in good faith, places permanent improvements upon land of another, with reason to believe that the land so improved is that of the one who makes the improvements, and that the plaintiffs are entitled to the relief which they seek in this proceeding.

The undisputed facts, set forth in the agreed statement of counsel representing all parties, is that the plaintiff W. J. Somerville in placing the warehouse building upon Lot 47 entertained a reasonable belief based on the report of the surveyor that it was Lot 46, which he owned, and that the building was constructed by him because of a reasonable mistake of fact and in the good faith belief that he was constructing a building on his own property and he did not discover his mistake until after the building was completed. It is equally clear that the defendants who spent little if any time in the neighborhood were unaware of the construction of the building until after it was completed and were not at any time or in any way guilty of any fraud or inequitable conduct or of any act that would constitute an estoppel. In short, the narrow issue here is between two innocent parties and the solution of the question requires the application of principles of equity and fair dealing between them.

It is clear that the defendants claim the ownership of the building. Under the common law doctrine of annexation, the improvements passed to them as part of the land. This is conceded by the plaintiffs but they assert that the defendants can not keep and retain it without compensating them for the value of the improvements, and it is clear from the testimony of the defendant William L. Jacobs in his deposition that the defendants intend to keep and retain the improvements and refuse to compensate the plaintiffs for their value. The record does not disclose any express request by the plaintiffs for permission to remove the building from the premises if that could be done without its destruction, which is extremely doubtful as the building was constructed of solid concrete blocks on a concrete slab, and it is reasonably clear, from the claim of the defendants of their ownership of the building and their insistence that certain fixtures which have been removed from the building be replaced, that the defendants will not consent to the removal of the building even if that could be done.

In that situation if the defendants retain the building and refuse to pay any sum as compensation to the plaintiff W. J. Somerville they will be unjustly enriched in the amount of $17,500.00, the agreed value of the building, which is more than eight and one-half times the agreed $2,000.00 value of the lot of the defendants on which it is located, and by the retention of the building by the defendants the plaintiff W. J. Somerville will suffer a total loss of the amount of the value of the building. If, however, the defendants are unable or unwilling to pay for the building which they intend to keep but, in the alternative, would convey the lot upon which the building is constructed to the plaintiff W. J. Somerville upon payment of the sum of $2,000.00, the agreed value of the lot without the improvements, the plaintiffs would not lose the building and the defendants would suffer no financial loss because they would obtain payment for the agreed full value of the lot and the only hardship imposed upon the defendants, if this were required, would be to order them to do something which they are unwilling to do voluntarily. To compel the performance of such an act by litigants is not uncommon in litigation in which the rights of the parties are involved and are subject to determination by equitable principles. And the right to require the defendants to convey the lot to the plaintiff W. J. Somerville is recognized and sustained by numerous cases cited earlier in this opinion. Under the facts and circumstances of this case, if the defendants refuse and are not required to exercise their option either to pay W. J. Somerville the value of the improvements or to convey to him the lot on which they are located upon his payment of the agreed value, the defendants will be unduly and unjustly enriched at the expense of the plaintiff W. J. Somerville who will suffer the complete loss of the warehouse building which by bona fide mistake of fact he constructed upon the land of the defendants. Here, in that situation, to use the language of the Supreme Court of Michigan in *Hardy v. Burroughs,* 232 N.W. 200, "It is not equitable . . . that defendants profit by plaintiffs' innocent mistake, that defendants take all and plaintiffs nothing."

To prevent such unjust enrichment of the defendants, and to do equity between the parties, this Court holds that an improver of land owned by another, who through a reasonable mistake of fact and in good faith erects a building entirely upon the land of the owner, with reasonable belief that such land was owned by the improver, is entitled to recover the value of the improvements from the landowner and to a lien upon such property which may be sold to enforce the payment of such lien, or, in the alternative, to purchase the land so improved upon payment to the landowner of the value of the land less the improvements and such landowner, even though free from any inequitable conduct in connection with the construction of the building upon his land, who, however, retains but refuses to pay for the improvements, must, within a reasonable time, either pay the improver the amount by which the value of his land has been improved or convey such land to the improver upon the payment by the improver to the landowner of the value of the land without the improvements. . . .

FRED CAPLAN, Judge, dissenting:

Respectfully, but firmly, I dissent from the decision of the majority in this case. Although the majority expresses a view which it says would result in equitable treatment for both parties, I am of the opinion that such view is clearly contrary to law and to the principles of equity and that such holding, if carried into effect, will establish a dangerous precedent. . . .

I am aware of the apparent alarmist posture of my statements asserting that the adoption of the majority view will establish a dangerous precedent. Nonetheless, I believe just that and feel that my apprehension is justified. On the basis of unjust enrichment and equity, the majority has decided that the errant party who, without improper design, has encroached upon an innocent owner's property is entitled to equitable treatment. That is, that he should be made whole. How is this accomplished? It is accomplished by requiring the owner of the property to buy the building erroneously constructed on his property or by forcing (by court edict) such owner to sell his property for an amount to be determined by the court.

What of the property owner's right? The solution offered by the majority is designed to favor the plaintiff, the only party who had a duty to determine which lot was the proper one and who made a mistake. The defendants in this case, the owners of the property, had no duty to perform and were not parties to the mistake. Does equity protect only the errant and ignore the faultless? Certainly not.

It is not unusual for a property owner to have long range plans for his property. He should be permitted to feel secure in the ownership of such property by virtue of placing his deed therefor on record. He should be permitted to feel secure in his future plans for such property. However, if the decision expressed in the majority opinion is effectuated then security of ownership in property becomes a fleeting thing. It is very likely that a property owner in the circumstances of the instant case either cannot readily afford the building mistakenly built on his land or that such building does not suit his purpose. Having been entirely without fault, he should not be forced to purchase the building.

In my opinion for the court to permit the plaintiff to force the defendants to sell their property contrary to their wishes is unthinkable and unpardonable. This is nothing less than condemnation of private property by private parties for private use. Condemnation of property (eminent domain) is reserved for government or such entities as may be designated by the legislature. Under no theory of law or equity should an individual be permitted to acquire property by condemnation. The majority would allow just that.

I am aware of the doctrine that equity frowns on unjust enrichment. However, contrary to the view expressed by the majority, I am of the opinion that the circumstances of this case do not warrant the application of such doctrine. It clearly is the accepted law that as between two parties in the circumstances of this case he who made the mistake must suffer the hardship rather than he who was without fault.

I would . . . remand the case to [the circuit] court with directions that the trial court give the defendant, Jacobs, the party without fault, the election of purchasing the building, of selling the property, or of requiring the plaintiff to remove the building from defendant's property.[10]

NOTES AND QUESTIONS

1. *Mistake.* When a builder mistakenly constructs an entire structure on land belonging to another, the courts generally rule that the landowner becomes the owner of the structure built on her land by another. Does this rule make sense, given the fact that the landowner stood by and allowed the construction to occur without

---

10. The West Virginia Supreme Court recently acknowledged a change in the law measuring restitution damages, stating that the "measure of damages in an unjust enrichment claim is the greater of the enhanced market value of the property or the cost of the improvements to the property." *Real mark! Developments, Inc. v. Ranson,* 588 S.E. 2d 150 (W.Va. 2003). — ED.

intervening? Does the owner have any obligation to look out for her own rights? Does the landowner have to compensate the builder? The builder claims that failure to compensate will leave the landowner unjustly enriched by the builder's investment; moreover, both parties made a mistake — the builder by encroaching on neighboring property and the landowner by not noticing that someone was building on her own land and not taking action to prevent it. Which property claim should prevail?

Like the court in *Somerville v. Jacobs,* some courts hold that an innocent trespasser who improves property in the good faith belief that it was her own property has a right to compensation for the value of the improvements made when those improvements increase the value of the property. Most courts, however, hold that "trespassers cannot have the advantage of any benefits they have made to the property. Such improvements belong to the landowner, without compensation to trespassers for labor or materials." *Powell on Real Property* §64A.05[5] (Michael Allan Wolf ed. 2000). Do you agree with the majority or the dissenting opinions in *Somerville?*

2. *Bad faith.* Courts seem to agree that a *bad faith* improver — one who deliberately builds on someone else's property — will not be granted a right to compensation and will ordinarily be required to remove the encroaching structure if the landowner so wishes. *Goulding v. Cook,* 661 N.E.2d 1322 (Mass. 1996) (owners who built on property they thought was theirs but which they knew was also claimed by their neighbors were ordered to remove a septic tank built on the neighbor's land).

3. *Betterment statutes.* Some states have *betterment statutes* that allow owners to choose between paying the builder the value of improvements built on their land or selling the land on which the improvement sits to the builder. They generally allow compensation only when the builder had color of title and believed in good faith that the land was hers. *See, e.g.,* Ark. Code §18-60-213; N.C. §§1-340 to 1-351. In effect, these statutes force owners to pay for unwanted improvements or give up land they otherwise would have owned to the builder. Should the burden be on the builder to make sure she is building on her own land or should the landowner have an obligation to determine if someone else is building on her own land and act to stop the trespass?

PROBLEM

In *Banner v. United States,* 238 F.3d 1348 (Fed. Cir. 2001), *aff'g* 44 Fed. Cl. 568 (Fed. Cl. 1999), title to most of the town of Salamanca, New York, was held by the Seneca Nation of Indians. In the 1870s, non-Indians began to settle on Seneca land pursuant to leases granted them by the Seneca Nation. However, under federal Indian law,[11] those leases were not valid under federal law without the consent of the United States. An 1875 federal statute validated the leases and extended them for a number of years. Several statutes followed until Congress unilaterally extended those leases in an 1890 federal statute for 99 years. With no choice but to extend the leases, the Seneca Nation itself renewed the leases at nominal rents of $1 to $10 a year. Those rents were not raised over the entire period of the leases until they expired February 1, 1991.

At that point the City of Salamanca created a public authority to negotiate a new arrangement with the Seneca Nation. That agreement provided that "(1) the United States and the state of New York would pay a combined $60 million to the Seneca Nation to remedy the severe value inequities of the 99 year leases, (2) the Seneca Nation

---

11. For more on tribal title and federal Indian law, *see infra* Chapter 13.

would offer new leases to the then-existing lessees with a term of forty years, renewable for another forty years at fair market value. . . ." *Id.* The agreement left for the future the question of who would own the improvements on the land at the end of the leases if they ever expired and were not renewed. That agreement was ratified by Congress in legislation passed in 1990.

Because some individuals refused to accept the lease renewals, the United States brought suit against them on behalf of the Seneca Nation to eject them from Seneca lands. The court ruled that the tribe was not obligated to renew the leases and that ejectment was a proper remedy. The court also ruled that the Seneca Nation owned the improvements placed on the land. The ejected owners then brought a claim against the United States arguing that, by failing to provide compensation for the lost value of their dwellings, the United States had taken their property without just compensation. The Federal Circuit Court affirmed the ruling of the Court of Federal Claims that no such taking had occurred because the common law granted ownership of buildings built on land belonging to another to the owner of the land.

Were the courts correct to hold that the Seneca Nation owned the improvements built on their land? Does it matter that, in the past, the United States had consistently sided with the settlers and protected their interests when they conflicted with the interests of the Seneca Nation? Does it matter that Congress had several times passed statutes ratifying and extending the leases without regard to whether the Seneca Nation wanted the leases to be extended? Would it matter if the United States had, in the past, verbally assured the settlers that, at some point, the land would be transferred from the Seneca Nation to the non-Indian settlers?

What are the arguments for and against requiring the Seneca Nation to compensate the builders for the improvements placed on Seneca land? What are the arguments for a forced sale of the land from the Seneca Nation to the home builders who had lived on the land for more than 100 years?

§3.5.2 BOUNDARY SETTLEMENT

§3.5.2.1 Oral Agreement

Courts may uphold oral agreements between neighbors that set the boundary between their property if (1) both parties are uncertain where the true boundary lay or a genuine dispute exists over the location of the boundary, (2) the parties can prove the existence of an agreement setting the boundary, and (3) the parties take (and/or relinquish) possession to the agreed line. *Fogerty v. State,* 231 Cal. Rptr. 810 (Ct. App. 1986); *Shultz v. Johnson,* 654 So. 2d 567 (Fla. Dist. Ct. App. 1995); *Morrissey v. Haley,* 865 P.2d 961 (Idaho 1993); Lawrence Berger, *Unification of the Doctrines of Adverse Possession and Practical Location in the Establishment of Boundaries,* 78 Neb. L. Rev. 1, 7-11 (1999).

§3.5.2.2 Acquiescence

Even without an oral agreement, the courts may nonetheless recognize long-standing acquiescence by both neighbors in a common boundary. William B. Stoebuck & Dale A. Whitman, *The Law of Property* §11.8, at 864 (3d ed. 2000). "(1) [A]djoining owners (2) who occupy their respective tracts up to a clear and certain line (such as a fence), (3) which they mutually recognize and accept as the dividing line between their properties (4) for a long period of time, cannot thereafter claim that the boundary thus recognized is not the true boundary." *Tresemer v. Albuquerque Public School District*, 619 P.2d 819, 820 (N.M. 1980); *RHN Corp. v. Veibell*, 96 P.3d 935 (Utah 2004). *Accord, Jedlicka v. Clemmer*, 677 A.2d 1232 (Pa. Super. Ct. 1996); *Mason v. Loveless*, 24 P.3d 997, 1004 (Utah Ct. App. 2001).

§3.5.2.3 Estoppel

A boundary may be established by estoppel when one owner "erroneously represents to the other that the boundary between them is located along a certain line [and] the second, in reliance on the representations, builds improvements which encroach on the true boundary or takes other detrimental actions." William B. Stoebuck & Dale A. Whitman, *The Law of Property* §11.8, at 866 (3d ed. 2000). The party who made the representations is then "estopped to deny them, and the boundary is in effect shifted accordingly." *Id.* Some states may find estoppel even when no explicit representation is made; they may infer a representation "from an owner's silence in the face of knowledge that his neighbor is building an encroaching structure." *Id.* §11.8, at 867.

§3.5.3 DEDICATION

A dedication is a transfer of real property from a private owner to a government entity such as a city. A valid dedication requires an *offer* by the owner of the property and an *acceptance* by the public. The offer consists of words or conduct on the part of the owner that demonstrate an intent to turn the property over to the public. The offer may be made by a written or oral statement from the owner. The courts may also find an implied offer by one who invites or merely permits the public to use her land for a long period of time. The acceptance may be made formally by passing a city council resolution or informally by taking over maintenance of the area or ceasing to collect property taxes on the parcel. Finally, just as an offer may be implied from the owner's long-standing acquiescence in public use, an acceptance may be implied from long and substantial public use, even absent governmental action. William B. Stoebuck & Dale A. Whitman, *The Law of Property* §11.6, at 846-850 (3d ed. 2000).

Most courts take seriously the idea that the owner must express an intent to make a gift of the property to the public, whether this is expressed through an oral statement or by conduct evidencing an intent to make a gift. *See, e.g., General Auto Service Station v. Maniatis*, 765 N.E.2d 1176 (Ill. App. Ct. 2002)(evidence insufficient to show either dedication or acceptance despite long public usage). Some courts, however, have found dedication when the owner has objected to public use but has made no serious effort to stop that use. In *Gion v. City of Santa Cruz*, 465 P.2d 50 (Cal. 1970), for example, the California Supreme Court found that the owners of a private beach had "dedicated" their property to the public by acquiescing in long-standing public use; the owners' efforts to stop the use were "half-hearted and ineffectual." William B. Stoebuck & Dale A. Whitman, *The Law of Property* §11.6, at 848 (3d ed. 2000). This opinion proved controversial, however, and was effectively overturned by a subsequent California statute. *See* Cal. Civ. Code §§813, 1009.

§3.5.4   RIPARIAN OWNERS: ACCRETION AND AVULSION

Special rules have developed to govern changes in borders of "riparian property" located on a river or other body of water. Slow changes in build up of land caused by slow deposit of silt or sand on the border of the land (*accretion*) belong to the owner of the land whose borders are thus enlarged; gradual losses of land caused by *erosion* shrink the owner's land rights. However, very sudden changes caused by events such as earthquakes and floods (referred to as *avulsion*) are generally held not to change the borders of property. *City of Long Branch v. Liu,* 833 A.2d 106 (N.J. Super. Ct. Law Div. 2003)(avulsion found from government infusion of new sand); John G. Sprankling, *Understanding Property Law* §31.05[B], at 503-504 (2000).

§3.6   *Adverse Possession of Personal Property*

Like real property, personal property can be acquired by adverse possession. At least three different rules have developed in this context: (1) *conversion* rule, (2) the *discovery* rule, and (3) the *demand* rule.

The *conversion* rule starts the running of the statute of limitations when the property is wrongfully taken (converted) and the owner dispossessed of the property. *Songbyrd, Inc. v. Estate of Albert B. Grossman,* 23 F.Supp.2d 219 (N.D.N.Y. 1998) (adverse possession of music recordings); *Vigilant Ins. Co. of America v. Housing Authority of the City of El Paso,* 660 N.E.2d 1121 (N.Y. 1995)(bonds).

The leading case establishing the *discovery* rule is *O'Keeffe v. Snyder,* 416 A.2d 862 (N.J. 1980). In *O'Keeffe,* the painter Georgia O'Keeffe sued a New York gallery owned by Barry Snyder to recover three paintings stolen from her and purchased for $35,000 by Snyder from a third party, Ulrich A. Frank, who had inherited them from his father. Snyder claimed that he had acquired title to the paintings by adverse possession under New Jersey's six-year statute of limitations. Snyder claimed that the six-year period started to run when the paintings were stolen. In contrast, O'Keeffe argued that she had not known where the paintings were after they were stolen and thus could not reasonably have made a demand to have the paintings returned. Since she had sued the possessor within six years of discovering where the paintings were, her claim should not be barred. The court agreed, noting that a thief can never acquire good title and that no one can acquire good title from a thief; even a bona fide purchaser who is unaware that property was stolen will not ordinarily be able to retain ownership in a contest with the true owner. An exception to this principle is contained in the *Uniform Commercial Code,* which provides that entrusting possession of goods to a merchant who deals in that kind of goods gives the merchant the power to transfer all the rights of the entruster to a buyer in the ordinary course of business, thereby vesting good title in the buyer as against the original owner. *See* U.C.C. §2-403(2). The court held that if that section of the UCC did not apply, the statute of limitations for adverse possession (in someone other than the true owner) would start to run only when the true owner discovers, or reasonably should have discovered, where the stolen personal property is located. The question, therefore, was whether O'Keeffe had used due diligence to recover the paintings and whether the paintings had been concealed from her. *Accord, Charash v. Oberlin College,* 14 F.3d 291, 299 (6th Cir. 1994).

In contrast to the discovery rule for adverse possession of personal property, the New York Court of Appeals has promulgated a *demand* rule — one that is rather more protective of the interests of the true owner, at least when the artwork has been sold to a bona fide purchaser who was unaware of the theft. In *Solomon R. Guggenheim Foundation v. Lubell,* 569 N.E.2d 426 (N.Y. 1991), a Chagall gouache was stolen from the storeroom of the Guggenheim Museum in the late 1960s. However, the museum neither notified the police nor publicly announced the theft. The current possessor argued that the failure to attempt to recover the artwork meant that the museum's rights were barred by the three-year statute of limitations. The museum responded that this was a tactical decision "based upon its belief that to publicize the theft would succeed only in driving the gouache further underground and greatly diminishing the possibility that it would ever be recovered." The court rejected the discovery rule on the grounds that it was wrong to place a general obligation of due diligence on the true owner. Rather, the court held that "a cause of action for replevin against the good faith purchaser of a stolen chattel accrues when the true owner makes demand for return of the chattel and the person in possession of the chattel refuses to return it. Until demand is made and refused, possession of the stolen property by the good faith purchaser for value is not considered wrongful." The court explained, *id.* at 431:

> [O]ur decision today is in part influenced by our recognition that New York enjoys a worldwide reputation as a preeminent cultural center. To place the burden of locating stolen artwork on the true owner and to foreclose the rights of that owner to recover its property if the burden is not met would, we believe, encourage illicit trafficking in stolen art. Three years after the theft, any purchaser, good faith or not, would be able to hold onto stolen art work unless the true owner was able to establish that it had undertaken a reasonable search for the missing art. This shifting of the burden onto the wronged owner is inappropriate. In our opinion, the better rule gives the owner relatively greater protection and places the burden of investigating the provenance of a work of art on the potential purchaser.

Which rule is better? *See also Autocephalous Greek-Orthodox Church of Cyprus v. Goldberg & Feldman Fine Arts, Inc.,* 717 F. Supp. 1374 (S.D. Ind. 1989) (theft and sale of Christian mosaics from Cyprus and application of the discovery rule).

PROBLEM

Recently, attention has focused on artworks confiscated by the Nazis from Jewish families during World War II. *See, e.g.,* Howard J. Trienens, *Landscape with Smokestacks: The Case of the Allegedly Plundered Degas* (2000). Some of these works were subsequently sold and purchased by good faith buyers. Others were donated to museums. In either case, disputes have arisen between current possessors and the heirs of the original owners over ownership of the works.

Assume a painting was taken from a Jewish family by the Nazi regime pursuant to its racially motivated policy of extermination. The painting winds up in the hands of a private family and is later sold to a museum in the United States in 1960. The painting is displayed for 40 years. The granddaughter of the couple that owned the painting discovers in January 2001 that it belonged to her grandparents and sues to obtain ownership of the painting. The statute of limitations for adverse possession is 30 years.

1. What is the plaintiff's argument for adopting the discovery rule?
2. What is the defendant's argument for the demand rule?
3. What should the court do?

4

Nuisance: Rules Governing Relations Among Neighbors in the Absence of Agreement

§4.1 Land Use Conflicts Among Neighbors

§4.1.1 Trespassory and Nontrespassory Invasions

We do not live alone, and the use of one's own property can affect the property and personal interests of others even if we do not commit a trespass by physically intruding onto their land. Nontrespassory interferences with the property rights of others can occur when the use of *one's own property* harms the property interests of one's neighbors. Such conflicts may arise in a wide variety of situations, including excavation undermining lateral support of neighboring land, flooding, pollution, noise, odors, criminal activity, and access to light and air.

Because use of land often affects other landowners, the privilege to use one's property is limited by the legal rights of other owners to be protected from uses that unreasonably harm their use or enjoyment of their own property. At the same time, the right to be secure from conduct that interferes with one's use or enjoyment of property is not absolute. Because interests in free use often clash with interests in security, we cannot provide absolute protection for either. As the *Restatement (Second) of Torts* notes, "[i]t is an obvious truth that each individual in a community must put up with a certain amount of annoyance, inconvenience and interference and must take a certain amount of risk in order that all may get on together." *Restatement (Second) of Torts* §822, cmt. g (1977), *quoted in San Diego Gas & Electric Co. v. Superior Court*, 920 P.2d 669, 696 (Cal. 1996). However, free use rights must be limited when "the harm or risk to one is greater than he ought to be required to bear under the circumstances, at least without compensation." *Id.*

Courts and legislatures have developed special rules to govern support obligations, water rights, and access to light and air. *Nuisance* law regulates other kinds of land use conflicts. Nuisance doctrine provides remedies for conduct that causes *unreasonably harm to the use and enjoyment of land.*

§4.1.2   Basic Solutions to Land Use Conflicts Between Neighbors

§4.1.2.1   Entitlements

In the absence of regulatory legislation such as environmental protection statutes or local zoning ordinances, courts resolve land use conflicts in four basic ways. In reading the cases that follow, you should note which solution each of the parties favored and which the court adopted.[1]

1. *Defendant's privilege; freedom to act despite the harm (damnum absque injuria).*

     In some cases, courts hold that the defendant is at liberty to engage in an activity on her property even though it harms the property interests of the plaintiff. When courts rule that the defendant is privileged to engage in such activity, they may say that the plaintiff has "failed to state a claim upon which relief can be granted." In Hohfeldian terms, the defendant has a *privilege* to act without liability and plaintiff has *no right* to stop her or obtain a remedy for any harm caused by defendant's conduct; that is, the conduct of which plaintiff complains does not violate any legal duties owed by the defendant to the plaintiff. The phrase *damnum absque injuria* means "damage without legal redress"; the plaintiff has no legal right to protection from the defendant's harmful activity. Thus, the defendant is free to inflict this particular kind of injury, and the plaintiff can neither recover damages to compensate for the injury nor obtain an injunction to stop the harmful activity. If the plaintiff wants to stop the defendant's activity, she will have to persuade the defendant to stop — perhaps by paying the defendant to desist or by buying defendant's land.

2. *Plaintiff's security; strict liability or absolute right to be free from the harm (veto rights).*

     Under this solution, the plaintiff has an absolute right not to suffer a particular sort of harm caused by the defendant's activity. If the plaintiff can prove that defendant engaged in the prohibited conduct and that the conduct caused damage to the plaintiff's property interests, the plaintiff is entitled to damages to compensate for the harm and possibly an injunction ordering the defendant to refrain from engaging in the wrongful activity or taking other steps to mitigate its harmful effects. Under this solution to the conflict, defendant is not legally entitled to engage in the activity without liability unless he can get the plaintiff to agree to let him do so, perhaps by paying the plaintiff for permission. The plaintiff effectively has the power to veto the defendant's harmful activity.

3. *Reasonableness test.*

     The first two solutions are all-or-nothing rules; either the defendant is free to engage in the activity without liability or the plaintiff has the right to be secure from that particular sort of harm. In contrast, a reasonableness test represents a middle position; it authorizes the defendant to engage in the

---

1. These four basic ways to resolve land use disputes were identified by Professor Duncan Kennedy.

harmful activity if it is deemed to be reasonable but not if the conduct and/or the harm caused by it is deemed unreasonable.

Rather than applying a rigid rule defining the activity as lawful or unlawful, this test requires the decision maker to make a moral or policy judgment about the legitimacy of the conduct in the context of specific cases. This judgment may focus on the fairness or justice of stopping or allowing the activity. Alternatively, it may be based on an assessment of the social consequences of regulating or not regulating the conduct. This assessment may require comparing the costs and benefits of the competing activities with the goal of promoting social utility or economic efficiency. Whether basing a decision on fairness or utility, the decision maker may consider a variety of factors, such as (a) the extent of the harm to the plaintiff and the social utility of the plaintiff's activity; (b) the social benefits of the defendant's activity, measured by what society would lose by preventing the defendant from freely engaging in the harmful activity; (c) the overall relative social costs and benefits of the conflicting land uses of the plaintiff and defendant; (d) the availability of alternative means to mitigate or avoid the harm, and which owner can do so at the lowest cost; (e) the defendant's motive (profit may constitute a legitimate motive while spite or malice — committing the act for the sole purpose of hurting the plaintiff — may not); and (f) which use was established first (with greater protection sometimes given to prior uses).

4. **Prior use: prior appropriation or prescription.**

Sometimes legal entitlements are awarded to the person who established the first use. *Prior appropriation* grants a right to commit the harmful activity to the person who first established her use. *Right to farm* statutes grant farmers the right to operate without liability for nuisance if their farms were established before surrounding homes were built. Prescription or *adverse possession* grants the right only after the use has continued for a substantial period of time, which is determined by statute.

§4.1.2.2 Remedies

These four solutions — privilege, strict liability, reasonableness, and prior use — define different ways of drawing a line between the defendant's freedom to engage in the harmful activity and the plaintiff's right to be secure from harm. These legal rights mean very little, however, unless the injured party can secure redress from the legal system either to compensate for prior injury or to prevent future injury. In the absence of a legal remedy directed at the defendant, the defendant may have no incentive to stop engaging in the harmful activity. Four remedies have been adopted by the courts.

1. **Dismissal of the complaint.**

The defendant may respond to the plaintiff's complaint by making a motion to dismiss the complaint for failure to state a claim upon which relief can be granted. If the solution to the land use conflict is *privilege* or *damnum absque injuria*, the court will grant the motion, dismissing the complaint. This constitutes a ruling for the defendant, effectively granting the defendant the legal entitlement to engage in the harmful activity without liability. The defendant may also fend off a lawsuit by the plaintiff by bringing it herself; in that case, that defendant asks the court to issue a declaratory judgment establishing that the defendant has the privilege to engage in the harmful activity without liability to her neighbor.

2. **Damages.**

The plaintiff injured by her neighbor's land use may ask the court for damages to compensate for the harm already done; the measure of damages may vary from state to state and according to the factual and legal context. The most common measures are the *cost of restoration* — the cost of repairing the damage and bringing the property back to its prior condition — and the *diminution in the market value* of the property.

3. **Injuction.**

The plaintiff may ask for an injunction; this is an order to the defendant to do or not do certain specified acts. The plaintiff must determine what she wants the court to order the defendant to do. For example, the plaintiff may want the court to order the defendant to stop the harmful conduct altogether; or the plaintiff may want the court to order the defendant to conduct the activity so as to commit no further damage in the future — for example, by installing safety or pollution control devices. The plaintiff may want the court to order the defendant to remedy the harm already done by fixing the damage.

4. **Purchased injunction.**

In some cases, courts are inclined to issue an injunction stopping the defendant's harmful activity on the ground that its social benefits are substantially outweighed by its social costs; however, it may be unfair to place the financial burden of stopping the activity on the defendant. This may occur, for example, if the defendant's activity was established first and the plaintiff settled near the defendant's land, knowing what the defendant was doing. In such cases, the court may issue a conditional injunction, ordering the activity stopped on the condition that the plaintiff reimburse the defendant for the opportunity loss occasioned by ceasing the activity.

§4.1.3   THE RECIPROCAL NATURE OF THE PROBLEM

THE PROBLEM OF SOCIAL COST
RONALD COASE

3 J.L. & Econ. 1, 2 (1960)

The question is commonly thought of as one in which *A* inflicts harm on *B* and what has to be decided is: how should we restrain *A*? But this is wrong. We are dealing with a problem of a reciprocal nature. To avoid the harm to *B* would inflict harm on *A*. The real question that has to be decided is: should *A* be allowed to harm *B* or should *B* be allowed to harm *A*? The problem is to avoid the more serious harm. I instanced in my previous article the case of a confectioner the noise and vibrations from whose machinery disturbed a doctor in his work. To avoid harming the doctor would inflict harm on the confectioner. The problem posed by this case was essentially whether it was worth while, as a result of restricting the methods of production which could be used by the confectioner, to secure more doctoring at the cost of a reduced supply of confectionery products. Another example is afforded by the problem of straying cattle which destroy crops on neighbouring land. If it is inevitable that some cattle will stray, an increase in the supply of meat can only be obtained at the expense of a decrease in the supply of crops. The nature of the choice is clear: meat or crops. What answer should be given is, of course, not clear unless we know the value of what is obtained as well as the value of what is sacrificed to obtain it. To give another example, Professor George J. Stigler instances the contamination of a stream. If we assume that the harmful effect of the pollution is that it kills the fish, the question to be decided is: is the value of the fish lost greater or less than the value of the product which the contamination of the stream makes possible.

NOTES AND QUESTIONS

Ronald Coase correctly emphasizes that regulations that prevent the defendant from harming the plaintiff protect the plaintiff's interests by limiting the defendant's liberty — and thus harming the defendant. In the context of land use disputes, one owner is seeking to be secure from harms caused by another owner's land use; the question is whether to protect the plaintiff's interest in security from harm or the defendant's interest in freedom of action. It is important to understand that regulating an activity harms those who wish to engage in it either by banning it or by making it more expensive. Of course, it is also crucial to recognize that failing to regulate an activity also has harmful consequences: It authorizes one owner to interfere with or even destroy the property interests of others. Deciding not to protect property interests by failing to prohibit harmful use of land is as much a regulatory choice as choosing to prohibit or limit such uses.

Like most economists, Coase eschews moral judgment and appears studiously neutral as between the conflicting activities. The only question is which activity causes more harm. This suggests that the central question is the *magnitude* of the harms on both sides and not their *character*. This assumption seems innocuous when the two activities are equally legitimate, such as the conflict between the factory and the doctor or between the cattle rancher and the farmer. But is this assumption always warranted? Take the pollution example. It is true that regulation of the polluting activity may reduce the amount of the product created by that activity, and we would like to know what this cost is before we choose to regulate the conduct to avoid the pollution. This does not necessarily mean that we are — or should be — indifferent as between an economic activity that causes pollution and one that does not cause pollution. After all, other things being equal, we may prefer to live in a less-polluted environment. We need to consider the external effects of land use conflicts on society as a whole (externalities).

In determining how "serious" those external effects are, as Coase asks us to do, we should be interested not only in the dollar value of production or income but the full range of values we care about — some of which are hard to put a dollar value on. We care about the distribution of costs and benefits; it is wrong to make some people bear a disproportionate share of the burdens necessary to promote social welfare. In addition, some values are more fundamental than others are. For example, the law deems an unprivileged intrusion on property to be a trespass whether or not the benefits of entry outweigh the costs. Protection of individual interests in possession are granted a privileged status. How do we determine which interests are deemed fundamental? At the same time, economists are correct that we assign implicit numbers to non-material values when we decide that we are not willing to pay the cost necessary to reduce harms to zero. Although human life is priceless, we have not banned the automobile, even though it causes avoidable deaths. A central question is how we should evaluate costs and benefits that are hard to describe in monetary terms. Should we assign numbers explicitly to account for the magnitude of such costs and benefits or should we evaluate those considerations in another way?

§4.2   Water Rights

§4.2.1   Diffuse Surface Water: Flooding Problems

§4.2.1.1   Legal Doctrines

ARMSTRONG v. FRANCIS CORP.
120 A.2d 4 (N.J. 1956)

WILLIAM J. BRENNAN JR., J. . . .
A small natural stream rose in Francis [Corporation's] 42-acre tract, which lies immediately south of Lake Avenue in Rahway. The stream flowed in a northerly direction 1200 feet across the Francis lands through a seven-foot box culvert under Lake Avenue and emptied into Milton Lake, 900 feet north of the avenue. It was the natural drainway for the larger 85-acre area south of Lake Avenue which includes the Francis tract.

Francis stripped its tract and erected 186 small homes thereon in a development known as Duke Estates, Section 2. It also built some 14 houses on an adjacent small tract known as Duke Estates, Section 1, lying in another drainage area. It constructed a drainage system of streets, pavements, gutters, ditches, culverts and catch basins to serve both developments. The system emptied into a corrugated iron pipe laid by Francis below the level of the natural stream bed on its lands. The pipe followed the course of the stream bed to the box culvert under Lake Avenue, although deviating from the course at some places. The pipe was covered with fill on Francis' tract and all evidence of the natural stream there has disappeared.

The drainage of the original 85 acres was thus augmented not only by the drainage of some 2½ acres of the Duke Estates, Section 1, but also by waters percolating into the joints of the pipe where it lay below the level of the water table of the Francis tract. The pipe joints were expressly designed to receive such percolating waters, and, to the extent that the percolation lowered the level of the water table, the result was to provide a drier terrain more suitable to housing development.

Where the stream passes north of Lake Avenue en route to Milton Lake after leaving the box culvert it remains largely in its natural state and forms the boundary line between the residential tracts of the plaintiffs Armstrong and the defendants Klemp. The Klemps were made parties defendant by Francis' cross-claim but prevailed thereon and were allowed the same relief as the Armstrongs. The stream passes through a 36-inch culvert under the Klemp driveway and thence, across lands of the Union County Park Commission, to the Lake. The Francis improvement resulted in consequences for the

Armstrongs and the Klemps fully described by Judge Sullivan in his oral opinion as follows:

> Now the stream as it emerges from the underground pipe goes under Lake Avenue and then flows past and through the Armstrong and Klemp properties is no longer the "babbling brook" that Mr. Klemp described. Now there is a constant and materially increased flow in it. The stream is never dry. The water is now discolored and evil smelling and no longer has any fish in it. A heavy deposit of silt or muck up to eighteen inches in depth now covers the bottom of the stream. After a heavy rainstorm the stream undergoes a remarkable change for several hours. All of the upstream rain water that used to be absorbed or held back is now channeled in undiminished volume and at great speed into this stream. This causes a flash rise or crest in the stream, with a tremendous volume of water rushing through at an accelerated speed. As a result, the stream has flooded on several occasions within the last year, although this was unheard of previously. More distressing, however, is the fact that during these flash situations the body of water moving at the speed it does tears into the banks of the brook particularly where the bed may turn or twist. At a point even with the plaintiff's [Armstrong's] house the stream makes a sharp bend. Here the effect of the increased flow of water is most apparent since the bank on plaintiff's side of the stream has been eaten away to the extent of about ten feet. This erosion is now within fifteen feet of the Armstrong septic tank system. It is difficult to say where it will stop, where the erosion will stop. The silting has, of course, raised the bed of the stream up to eighteen inches in places and the raising of the stream results in water action against different areas of the bank so that the erosion problem while unpredictable is ominous. The eating away of the banks in several places has loosened rocks or boulders which have been rolled downstream by the force of the water. Those stones, however, as they rolled through the Klemp culvert cracked and broke the sides and bottom of the culvert and the water is now threatening to undermine the entire masonry. There is no doubt but that the defendant's activities have caused all of the condition just related.
>
> A matter of some concern is that defendant's housing development occupies only about one-half of the area which drains into this brook. At the present time there is a forty acre undeveloped section to the south of the defendant and it is reasonable to assume that it, too, will be improved and built upon at some future time. Defendant's underground trunk sewer was built to accommodate any possible runoff from this tract. If and when that section is developed, Armstrong and Klemp will have that much more erosion, silting and flooding to deal with.

Judge Sullivan concluded that the Armstrongs and the Klemps were plainly entitled to relief in these circumstances and "that the only sensible and permanent solution to the problem is to pipe the rest of the brook," that is, from the culvert outlet at Lake Avenue the entire distance to Milton Lake. A plan for that purpose had been prepared by Francis' engineer and approved by the Armstrongs and the Klemps at a time when efforts were being made to compromise the dispute before the trial. The final judgment orders Francis, at its expense, forthwith to proceed with and complete within 60 days the work detailed on that plan. The Union County Park Commission has given its formal consent to the doing of the work called for by the plan on its lands.

The important legal question raised by the appeal is whether the damage suffered by the Armstrongs and the Klemps is *damnum absque injuria*, namely, merely the non-actionable consequences of the privileged expulsion by Francis of waters from its tract as an incident to the improvement thereof....

The casting of surface waters from one's own land upon the land of another, in circumstances where the resultant material harm to the other was foreseen or foreseeable, would appear on the face of it to be tortious conduct, as actionable where the consequences of an unreasonable use of the possessor's land, as in the case of the abstraction or diversion of water from a stream which unreasonably interferes with the use of the stream below, and as in the case of the unreasonable use of percolating or subterranean waters, and as in the case of artificial construction on one's land which unreasonably speeds the waters of a stream past one's property onto that of an owner below, causing harm. Yet only the courts of the states of New Hampshire and Minnesota have expressly classified the possessor's liability, where imposed, for harm by the expulsion of surface waters to be a tort liability. Those courts have evolved the "reasonable use" rule laying down the test that each possessor is legally privileged to make a reasonable use of his land, even though the flow of surface waters is altered thereby and causes some harm to others, but incurs liability when his harmful interference with the flow of surface waters is unreasonable. *Franklin v. Durgee,* 51 A. 911 (N.H. 1901); *Sheehan v. Flynn,* 61 N.W. 462 (Minn. 1894).

All other states have treated the legal relations of the parties as a branch of property law — that is, have done so, if we emphasize only the language of the decisions and ignore the actual results reached. Two rules have been evolved which, in their statement, are directly opposed, for under one the possessor would not be liable in any case and under the other he would be liable in every case. But an analysis of the results reached under both rules shows that neither is anywhere strictly applied. The first rule, purportedly applicable in our own State, stems from the view that surface waters are the common enemy. The "common enemy" rule emphasizes the possessor's privilege to rid his lands of surface waters as he will. That rule "is, in substance, that a possessor of land has an unlimited and unrestricted legal privilege to deal with the surface water on his land as he pleases, regardless of the harm which he may thereby cause others." The other rule, borrowed from the civil law of foreign nations and called the "civil law" rule, emphasizes not the privileges of the possessor but the duties of the possessor to other landowners who are affected by his expulsion of surface waters from his lands. That rule is to the effect that "a person who interferes with the natural flow of surface waters so as to cause an invasion of another's interests in the use and enjoyment of his land is subject to liability to the other."

[T]he courts here and elsewhere, in terms of results, have actually come out at the "reasonable use" doctrine. Professor Kinyon and Mr. McClure have summarized the course of the decisions as follows:

> From the rationale of the common enemy rule, it would seem that a possessor of land has an unlimited privilege to rid his land of the surface water upon it or to alter its course by whatever means he wishes, irrespective of the manner of doing it or the harm thereby caused to others. However, in substantially all of the jurisdictions purportedly committed to that rule, the courts have refused to go that far. Most of these courts have developed a qualifying rule which is, in substance, that a possessor of land is not privileged to discharge upon adjoining land, by artificial means, large quantities of surface water in a concentrated flow otherwise than through natural drainways, regardless of the means by which the surface water is collected and discharged. The scope of this qualifying rule varies from jurisdiction to jurisdiction, but it has been adopted in one form or another. . . .
>
> In jurisdictions purportedly committed to the civil law rule, one would expect from the rationale of that rule to find that a possessor has no privilege, under any circumstances, to interfere with the surface water on his land so as to cause it to flow upon adjoining land in a manner or quantity substantially different from its natural flow. An examination of the cases in these jurisdictions, however, reveals that the courts have

refused to follow the rationale of the rule to that extent. In most of these jurisdictions the courts have recognized that a possessor must have a privilege, under certain circumstances, to make minor alterations in the natural flow of surface water where necessary to the normal use and improvement of his land, even though such alterations cause the surface water to flow upon adjoining land in a somewhat unnatural manner. This is especially true where the possessor disposes of the surface water by depositing it in existing natural drainways. Consequently, the courts . . . , with variations from state to state, have held that a possessor has a limited privilege to discharge surface water on other lands, by artificial means in a non-natural manner. . . . Kinyon & McClure, *Interferences with Surface Waters*, 24 Minn. L. Rev. 899, 916, 920, 913 (1940).

The authors conclude:

[Thus] even though the broad principle of reasonable use has not made much headway as an articulate basis of decision, substantially all of the jurisdictions which purport to follow the civil law or common enemy rules have engrafted upon them numerous qualifications and exceptions which, in actual result, produce decisions which are not as conflicting as would be expected, and which would generally be reached under the reasonable use rule.

We therefore think it appropriate that this court declare, as we now do, our adherence in terms to the reasonable use rule and thus accord our expressions in cases of this character to the actual practice of our courts. [I]t is significant of the true state of the law that the *Restatement* [(Second)] *of Torts*, §833, has adopted the reasonable use test as the rule actually prevailing.

The rule of reasonableness has the particular virtue of flexibility. The issue of reasonableness or unreasonableness becomes a question of fact to be determined in each case upon a consideration of all the relevant circumstances, including such factors as the amount of harm caused, the foreseeability of the harm which results, the purpose or motive with which the possessor acted, and all other relevant matter. It is, of course, true that society has a great interest that land shall be developed for the greater good. It is therefore properly a consideration in these cases whether the utility of the possessor's use of his land outweighs the gravity of the harm which results from his alteration of the flow of surface waters. But while today's mass home building projects, of which the Francis development is typical, are assuredly in the social good, no reason suggests itself why, in justice, the economic costs incident to the expulsion of surface waters in the transformation of the rural or semi-rural areas of our State into urban or suburban communities should be borne in every case by adjoining landowners rather than by those who engage in such projects for profit. Social progress and the common well-being are in actuality better served by a just and right balancing of the competing interests according to the general principles of fairness and common sense which attend the application of the rule of reason. . . .

NOTES AND QUESTIONS

1. *Diffuse surface water.* Diffuse surface water is "drainage water from rain, melting snow, and springs that runs over the surface of the earth . . . but does not amount to a stream." William B. Stoebuck & Dale A. Whitman, *The Law of Property* §7.6, at 430 (3d ed. 2000). Such water may coalesce into a pool or marsh but is not stable enough to

constitute a lake or stream. Surface water is generally considered a nuisance and property owners are anxious to get rid of it.

The power to withdraw surface water is subject to substantial regulation even if no other owners are harmed through flooding or discharge of water onto their lands. Federal and state environmental laws regulate drainage of "wetlands" and the ability of owners to fill in such lands for development purposes. The federal *Clean Water Act*, 33 U.S.C. §1344, for example, has been interpreted to place limits on the ability of owners to drain and fill in wetlands for development purposes and many states regulate such development to protect the environment. *See, e.g., Massachusetts Water Management Act,* Mass. Gen. Laws ch. 21G, §§1 to 19.

Disputes arise when property owners attempt to drain surface water off their property through pipes and drainage systems that may cause flooding or other water damage to neighboring property. Damage may also occur because development of property naturally changes drainage patterns and may cause increased runoff of surface water even if no drainage system is installed. Lower property owners object to the intentional or unintentional flooding of their property by development elsewhere.

2. *Common enemy rule.* As Justice Brennan explains, state courts have followed three different rules. One rule, the *common enemy* doctrine, allows property owners the absolute freedom to develop their property without liability for any resulting damage to neighbors caused by increased runoff of surface water. This doctrine adopts the *damnum absque injuria* solution to land use conflicts: The defendant is privileged to develop its property and to expel unwanted surface water without liability for any resultant damage to the neighbors' property. This rule may be the law in about 17 states. William B. Stoebuck & Dale A. Whitman, *The Law of Property* §7.6, at 431 (3d ed. 2000). Most courts adopting this rule have substantially modified it. Some impose liability for negligence, allowing damages for harm caused by conduct that foreseeably causes unreasonable harm to neighbors. Many impose liability on the developing property owner if she installs pipes or drainage devices designed to collect and expel water in greater quantity or with greater force than would naturally occur or in a different direction than the natural drainage patterns of the land. *See Haith v. Atchison County,* 793 S.W.2d 151 (Mo. Ct. App. 1990); *Halverson v. Skagit County,* 983 P.2d 643 (Wash. 1999). *Cf. Lucas v. Rawl Family Ltd. Partn.,* 598 S.E.2d 712 (S.C. 2004)(common enemy rule unless defendant's actions constitute a nuisance *per se).*

3. *Natural flow rule.* At the other extreme is the *natural flow* or *civil law* doctrine, which grants the injured property owner absolute security against injury from flooding caused by a neighboring property owner's development of her property. Owners are entitled to discharge water through natural drainage pathways but any development that alters the amount, force of flow, or direction of the natural drainage will result in liability for any resulting harm to neighboring land. This doctrine adopts the *strict liability* or *veto rights* solution to land use conflicts; the injured plaintiff has the legal right to stop the defendant's activity and to recover damages for harm already inflicted. *See* S.D. Codified Laws §46A-10A-70; *Powers v. Judd,* 553 A.2d 139 (Vt. 1988).

Until recently, the natural flow rule was the law in roughly half the states. Today it persists in only a few states. The natural flow doctrine might inhibit land development, because most development will change drainage patterns. To encourage development, most states following this rule have adopted exceptions to allow minor increases in the natural flow of surface water. Other states limit application of the natural flow doctrine to rural land and apply the reasonable use test to urban land. *See First Lady, LLC. v. JMF Properties, LLC.*, 681 N.W.2d 94 (S.D. 2004) (natural flow applicable except in urban settings where reasonable use test applies); William B. Stoebuck & Dale A. Whitman, *The Law of Property* §7.6, at 432 (3d ed. 2000). Of course, development is possible even with strict liability on developers for harm caused by their development; they simply must compensate those property owners harmed by their development. If the development is profitable enough, the project may well go forward despite liability for resulting damage or for investment to prevent flooding.

4. *Reasonable use test.* The New Jersey Supreme Court in *Armstrong* adopted a middle position, the *reasonable use* test. This rule requires the decision maker to determine in specific cases whether the defendant's conduct caused unreasonable interference with the neighbors' use of their land. This determination involves balancing the social benefit derived from development of defendant's property, the availability of cost-effective means to avoid or mitigate the harm, and the gravity of the harm to plaintiff's property. Substantial harm to neighboring property is likely to be found to be unreasonable even if the value of defendant's conduct far outweighs the value of the plaintiff's property. It is a separate question whether the plaintiff will be limited to damages for the harm or may get an injunction stopping the harmful development from occurring. This test has rapidly gained adherents and is now the majority rule. *See, e.g., Locklin v. City of Lafayette*, 867 P.2d 724 (Cal. 1994); *Westland Skating Center v. Gus Machado Buick, Inc.*, 542 So. 2d 959 (Fla. 1989); *Heins Implement Co. v. Missouri Highway & Transportation Commission*, 859 S.W.2d 681 (Mo. 1993).

5. *Policy considerations.* What reasons did the court give in *Armstrong* for adopting the reasonable use test? Are you persuaded? What are the disadvantages of the reasonable use test? What arguments could you make that the common enemy rule is preferable? What arguments could you make that the natural flow rule is better than both of the other rules?

§4.2.1.2 Policy Arguments

In *Armstrong v. Francis*, Justice Brennan used a range of policy arguments to explain and justify the choice the court made among the legal rules that could govern the relationship between the parties. This section will introduce you to three kinds of arguments used by Justice Brennan and routinely used by lawyers in advocating alternative possible rules and by judges in adjudicating conflicts over the allocation and use of property. You will see variations of each of these arguments in the judicial opinions excerpted in this book — and in other courses as well.

One of the major purposes of the first year of law school is to learn how to use these arguments persuasively on a variety of legal issues. Another purpose is to enable you to become sophisticated in identifying the competing considerations relevant to adjudicating legal disputes and to confront the need to accommodate conflicting values. Each of the arguments is unpersuasive in its extreme form; you should consider what objections or counterarguments you could raise to respond to each of them. Defining and applying legal rules require decision makers to assess the persuasiveness of competing considerations in the context of particular social problems and particular cases. The arguments will be illustrated by quotations from opinions included in this chapter.

Rights: Freedom of Action versus Security

1. **Justice in social relationships.**

    Rights arguments appeal to fairness or justice in social relationships. Those relationships sometimes involve conflicting interests, and it is the job of both courts and legislatures to take those interests into account, accommodating them when possible and choosing between them when necessary. Justice Shirley Abrahamson of the Wisconsin Supreme Court explains that the "rights of neighboring landowners are relative; the uses of one must not unreasonably impair the uses or enjoyment of the other." *Prah v. Maretti,* 321 N.W.2d 182, 187 (Wis. 1982). Although landowners are free to use their property as they wish, they do "not have an absolute or unlimited right to use the land in a way that injures the rights of others." *Id.*

2. **Rights as freedom of action.**

    On one hand, landowners may claim the "right . . . to use their property as they wish[ ]," or the "right to develop [their] property . . . without regard to the effect of such development upon [others]." *Id.* at 189, 188. As Justice William Callow, also a member of the Wisconsin Supreme Court, stated: "I firmly believe that a landowner's right to use his property within the limits of ordinances, statutes, and restrictions of record where such use is necessary to serve his legitimate needs is a fundamental precept of a free society. . . ." *Id.* at 194. We can refer to the right to control the use of one's property as a right of *freedom of action.* For example, the defendant in *Armstrong* claimed a right to develop its property without having to take into account the possibility of increased surface flooding on neighboring property. To require the developer to foresee and prevent all damage from surface water drainage to other property or to compensate for any losses caused by development would arguably interfere too much with the developer's freedom to develop its own property.

3. **Rights as security.**

    The converse of the right to use one's property is the right to have one's property protected from harm. Justice Abrahamson explains that property holders have a right to be protected from land use by a neighbor who "unreasonably interferes with another's enjoyment of his or her property. . . ." *Id.* at 187. The freedom to use property is limited to the extent necessary to protect other property holders' *rights of security.* Similarly, Justice Brennan argues in *Armstrong* that while development is "in the social good, no reason suggests itself why, in justice, the economic costs incident [to development] should be borne in every case by adjoining landowners rather than by those who engage in such projects for profit." 120 A.2d at 10.

4. **Value judgments.**

    Each case in this chapter raises the question where to draw the line between one possessor's right to use his property freely and another possessor's right to security. The best solution may be one that protects the legitimate interests of both parties to some extent. The issue requires careful reflection on the social context in which the dispute arises and value judgments about the merits of the competing claims. These judgments include determining whether the interests asserted are legitimate, just claims and deciding which should prevail when conflict between legitimate claims cannot be avoided.

Social Utility: Competition versus Secure Investment

1. ***Promoting the general welfare by enacting appropriate incentives.***
Social utility arguments appeal to the goal of generating rules of law that promote socially desirable conduct and deter socially harmful conduct. Most conduct has both beneficial and harmful effects. When two legitimate activities conflict, it becomes necessary to choose which activity should prevail. Legal rules may authorize or even encourage particular kinds of land use by declaring that use privileged, freeing the possessor to engage in the activity without fear of liability to others. The rules in force also may discourage or prohibit other kinds of land use by granting those injured by the activity the right to obtain damages or an injunction to limit or even terminate the activity.
Social utility arguments have two components. First, they assert that particular legal rules create specified *incentives* that encourage or discourage certain kinds of behavior. Second, they evaluate that behavior by asserting that a particular rule is better than the alternatives either because it promotes socially desirable conduct — behavior that has greater social benefits than social costs — or because it discourages socially harmful conduct — an activity whose costs outweigh its benefits.

2. ***Promoting competition.***
Lawyers often argue that social welfare is maximized when the government deregulates economic activity by freeing property holders to develop their property as they see fit. Justice William Callow argues that "society has a significant interest in not restricting land development." 321 N.W.2d at 194. Rules governing land use should be chosen in a way that promotes "land improvement and development" by protecting landowners from ruinous liability. *Id.* at 195. Shielding property holders from liability encourages investment in socially beneficial economic activities. Every use of land has potential effects on neighbors and the community as a whole, some positive and some negative. For example, building a house or factory may increase traffic and congestion in an area or block a beautiful view; requiring the developer to compensate those who suffer these negative effects may stifle desirable economic development.

3. ***Protecting the security of investment.***
The converse argument is that no one will invest to develop property if the investment is not secure. The basis of the institution of property is to provide security for justified expectations. Why take the risk of building a house if your neighbor is free to flood your property and destroy the value of your investment? Providing this kind of security requires legal rules that give developers incentives to use their property in ways that minimize the harm to other property owners. Development generally should be encouraged, but not to the extent that its harmful effects outweigh its benefits. As Justice Abrahamson notes, "unrestricted development of land" may cause more harm than good, *id.* at 190. The goal should be to promote only "reasonable"

development (whose social benefits outweigh its social costs) and to discourage "unreasonable" development. *Id.* at 191.

Land development benefits society, but it also may negatively affect neighboring property. If the developer does not have to pay for these negative effects, a divergence arises between the *private* costs of the project (the costs of building the homes) and the total *social* costs of the project (the costs to the developer of building the homes *plus* the external harmful effects on neighbors). Here the private benefits of the project will outweigh its private costs, even though the total *social* costs of the project may be higher than its total social benefits. Requiring the developer to compensate those burdened by the development induces the developer to take the external costs into account or to *internalize* them. By bringing private costs in line with social costs, the rules in force can encourage activity whose social benefits outweigh its social costs and discourage activity whose total social costs outweigh its social benefits.[2]

4. ***Balancing interests.***

Assessing social utility arguments requires a judgment about how people will actually respond to alternative legal rules; it also involves predicting and evaluating the relative costs and benefits of alternative legal rules. This is often expressed in judicial opinions by stating that it is necessary to "balance the interests" of the parties to determine which rule of law should be adopted.

Formal Realizability or Administrability: Rigid Rules *versus* Flexible Standards

1. ***Predictability versus justice in the individual case.***

While rights and social utility considerations appeal to the substantive justice or wisdom of legal rules, formal considerations concern the manner in which rules are expressed and implemented.

2. ***Rules.***

Legal rules are sometimes defined in a way that allows mechanical application. For example, the rigid rule allowing 18-year-olds to vote cleanly answers the question whether a 17-year-old may vote — the answer is no. No need for interpretation or judgment arises. Duncan Kennedy notes that "the two great social virtues of formally realizable rules, as opposed to standards or principles, are the restraint of official arbitrariness and certainty." Duncan Kennedy, *Form and Substance in Private Law Adjudication,* 89 Harv. L. Rev. 1687, 1688 (1976). Rules offer certainty or predictability because each citizen knows her rights and obligations. The rules also control arbitrary judicial discretion, with the propitious result that like cases are treated alike and

---

2. Note that property development has *external benefits* as well as *external costs*: It may create jobs, expand the tax base, or provide needed housing. Requiring the developer to pay the internal and external costs of the project may not result in the best result from the standpoint of society as a whole if the total social benefits of the project substantially exceed the private profits to the developer.

judges are prevented from deciding cases by reference to impermissible and perhaps unconscious biases.

> [I]f private actors can know in advance the incidence of official intervention, they will adjust their activities in advance to take account of them. From the point of view of the state, this increases the likelihood that private activity will follow a desired pattern. From the point of view of the citizenry, it removes the inhibiting effect on action that occurs when one's gains are subject to sporadic legal catastrophe.

Id. at 1688-1689.

Rigid rules, do, however, have distinct disadvantages. By definition, they require particular results, even if those results seem unfair under the circumstances. An 18-year-old-vote rule is both over- and underinclusive. Some persons younger than 18 are mature enough to vote but are not allowed to do so; some persons older than 18 are not mature enough to vote but are allowed to do so.

> From the point of view of the purpose of the rules, this combined over- and underinclusiveness amounts not just to licensing but to requiring official arbitrariness. If we adopt the rule, it is because of a judgment that this kind of arbitrariness is less serious than the arbitrariness and uncertainty that would result from empowering the official to apply [a standard] directly to the facts of each case.

Id. at 1689.

3. **Standards.**

In contrast to rigid rules, legal doctrines are sometimes flexible. Such doctrines take the form of *standards* or *principles*. Sometimes standards "refer directly to one of the substantive objectives of the legal order, such as good faith, due care, fairness, unconscionability, unjust enrichment, and reasonableness." *Id.* at 1688. Other times, standards take the form of lists of "factors" that are to be considered in adjudicating a case.

Flexible standards have the benefit of obtaining justice in the individual case by allowing the decision maker to take account of all relevant circumstances. Because they cannot be mechanically applied, however, they may offer less predictability to citizens or guidance to judges and juries in adjudicating cases.

4. **Formal realizability and social utility.**

Kennedy notes that the choice between rules and standards is affected by the substantive goal of developing rules that have desirable social effects.

> The use of rules, as opposed to standards, to deter immoral or antisocial conduct means that sometimes perfectly innocent behavior will be punished, and that sometimes plainly guilty behavior will escape sanction. These costs of mechanical over- and underinclusion are the price of avoiding the potential arbitrariness and uncertainty of a standard.
>
> As between the mechanical arbitrariness of rules and the biased arbitrariness of standards, there is an argument that bias is preferable, because it will "chill" behavior on the borderline of substantive obnoxiousness. For example, a measure of uncertainty about when a judge will find a representation, or a failure to disclose, to be fraudulent may encourage openness and honesty. Rules, on the other hand, allow the proverbial "bad man" to "walk the

line," that is, to take conscious advantage of underinclusion to perpetuate fraud with impunity.

There are three familiar counterarguments in favor of rules. First, a standard will deter desirable as well as undesirable conduct. Second, *in terrorem* general standards are likely to be paper tigers in practice. Uncertainty about whether the sanction will in fact materialize may lead to a lower level of actual social control than would occur if there were a well defined area within which there was a high probability of even a mild punishment. Death is likely to be an ineffective penalty for theft.

Third, where the substantively undesirable conduct can be deterred effectively by *private* vigilance, rules alert, or should alert the potential victims to the danger. For example, a formally realizable general rule of *caveat emptor* should stimulate buyers to take all kinds of precautions against the uncommunicative seller. It is true that the rule will also allow many successful frauds. But these may be *less* numerous in the end than those that would occur if buyers knew that there was the possibility, however uncertain, of a legal remedy to save them from their sloppiness in inspecting the goods. Likewise, the rigid rule that twenty-one-year-olds are adults for purposes of contractual capacity makes their change of status more conspicuous; it puts them on notice in a way that a standard (e.g., undue influence) would not.

Id. at 1695-1696

PROBLEM

Assume that the defendant in *Armstrong* advocated the *common enemy* rule, while the plaintiff advocated the *reasonable use* test.

1. Construct defendant's arguments in favor of the common enemy rule based on (a) rights, (b) social utility, and (c) formal realizability.
2. Construct plaintiff's arguments in favor of the reasonable use test based on (a) rights, (b) social utility, and (c) formal realizability.

§4.2.2   WATER AS A COMMERCIAL RESOURCE

See *supra* §1.5.3, at pages 89-91.

§4.3   *Support Easements*

Landowners own both the surface and the earth beneath the surface unless they have sold the subsurface to others in the form of mineral rights.[3] The subsurface is needed to support both the surface of the land and structures built on it. Excavation or construction on a particular parcel may have the unwanted effect of undermining the support for neighboring land. For example, if an owner excavates all the way up to the property line, the neighboring land may be insufficiently strong to stand up by itself; some of it may fall into the hole created by the excavation. The excavation has undermined the *lateral support* for the neighboring land by taking away the land along the

---

3. Mineral rights include the right to extract minerals from beneath the surface of the land.

side of the neighbor's subsurface that held it up. Alternatively, an owner may excavate and dig a well to draw water from underneath his own land. Since groundwater beneath the surface is diffused throughout it, the withdrawal of water may draw some water from beneath neighboring property. If enough water is withdrawn, the neighbor's subsurface may collapse, undermining support for the surface from underneath and depriving the neighbor of *subjacent support*. The materials in this section address the rules governing conflicts between neighbors whose activities undermine support for land and structures on it.

§4.3.1 LATERAL SUPPORT

§4.3.1.1 Common Law

NOONE v. PRICE
_____
298 S.E.2d 218 (W. Va. 1982)

RICHARD NEELY, Justice.

In 1960 the plaintiffs below, and appellants in this Court, Mr. and Mrs. William H. Noone, bought a house located on the side of a mountain in Glen Ferris, West Virginia. This house had been constructed in 1928 or 1929 by Union Carbide, and in 1964, four years after plaintiffs purchased the house, plaintiffs became aware that the wall under their front porch was giving way and that the living room plaster had cracked.

The defendant below, appellee in this Court, Mrs. Marion T. Price, lived directly below the plaintiffs at the foot of the hill in a house that was built in 1912. Sometime between 1912 and 1919 a wall of stone and concrete was constructed along the side of the hill, ten to twelve feet behind the defendant's house. This wall was a hundred to a hundred and twenty-five feet long, approximately four feet high, and of varying degrees of thickness. The wall lay entirely on the defendant's property, and was approximately ten to twelve feet from the property line that divided the defendant's property from the plaintiffs' property. The defendant purchased her house in 1955 and lived there until 1972, when she sold the property. Before the defendant's purchase, the wall had fallen into disrepair.

When the plaintiffs discovered that their house was slipping down the hill, they complained to the defendant that their problem was the result of deterioration in the defendant's retaining wall. The defendant did nothing to repair the wall and the plaintiffs repaired the damage to their house at a cost of approximately $6,000.

The action before us now was filed in 1968 for damages of $50,000 for failure of the defendant to provide lateral support for the plaintiffs' land, and her negligent failure to provide lateral support for their house. Plaintiffs alleged that the wall was constructed to provide support to the slope upon which their house was built, and that the disrepair and collapse of the wall caused the slipping and eventual damage to their property.

The defendant denied that the wall on her property provided support to the slope, or that the condition of her wall caused the slipping and damage to the plaintiffs' property. In addition, the defendant asserted that the plaintiffs were negligent in failing to take reasonable precautions to protect their own property and were estopped from suing her because the wall on her property was erected by her predecessor in title and the plaintiffs had purchased their property with knowledge of the wall's deteriorating condition. . . .

I

This case provides an opportunity that we have not had for many years to address the obligations of adjoining landowners to provide lateral support to each other's land. Support is lateral when the supported and supporting lands are divided by a vertical plane. The withdrawal of lateral support may subject the landowner withdrawing the support to strict liability or to liability for negligence. We have recognized both forms of liability in *Walker v. Strosnider*, 67 S.E. 1087 (W. Va. 1910) and this case, remarkably enough, is still in harmony with the modern weight of authority as articulated in the *Restatement (Second) of Torts.*

As a general rule, "[a] landowner is entitled, *ex jure naturae*,[4] to lateral support in the adjacent land for his soil." Point 2, syllabus, *McCabe v. City of Parkersburg*, 79 S.E.2d 87 (W. Va. 1953).Therefore, as we said in syllabus point 2 of *Walker, supra*:

> An excavation, made by an adjacent owner, so as to take away the lateral support, afforded to his neighbor's ground, by the earth so removed, and cause it, of its own weight, to fall, slide or break away, makes the former liable for the injury, no matter how carefully he may have excavated. Such right of support is a property right and absolute.

An adjacent landowner is strictly liable for acts of commission and omission on his part that result in the withdrawal of lateral support to his neighbor's property. This strict liability, however, is limited to land in its natural state; there is no obligation to support the added weight of buildings or other structures that land cannot naturally support. However, the majority of American jurisdictions hold that if land in its natural state would be capable of supporting the weight of a building or other structure, and such building or other structure is damaged because of the subsidence of the land itself, then the owner of the land on which the building or structure is constructed can recover damages for both the injury to his land and the injury to his building or structure. The West Virginia cases are largely consistent with this position, although none has expressly so held.

The converse of the preceding rule is also the law: where an adjacent landowner provides sufficient support to sustain the weight of land in its natural state, but the land slips as a direct result of the additional weight of a building or other structure, then in the absence of negligence on the part of the adjoining landowner, there is no cause of action against such adjoining landowner for damage either to the land, the building, or other structure.

The issue in the case before us concerns the proper application of the strict liability rule. The circuit court improperly awarded summary judgment because the

---

4. *Ex jure naturae* means "by natural law." This term described rights that were thought to inhere in ownership of land and did not have to be obtained by a separate bargain and contract with one's neighbor. — ED.

plaintiffs should have been allowed to prove that their land was sufficiently strong in its natural state to support the weight of their house, and that their house was damaged as a result of a chain reaction that began when the land in its natural state, toward the bottom of the hill, slipped as a result of the withdrawal of lateral support occasioned by the deterioration of the retaining wall, causing, in turn, successive parts of the hillside to subside until the ripple effect reached the foundation of the plaintiffs' house.

The cases recognize that lateral support sufficient to hold land in its natural state may be insufficient to support the additional weight of a building or other structure. If, therefore, as a result of the additional weight of a building or other structure, so much strain is placed upon existing natural or artificial lateral support that the support will no longer hold, then in the absence of negligence, there is no liability whatsoever on the part of an adjoining landowner. In the case before us, this means that if the weight of the plaintiffs' house placed so much pressure on the soil that the house itself caused the subsidence, and the land would not have subsided without the weight of the house, then the plaintiffs cannot recover.

II

A theoretical problem that presents itself in all of these cases is the extent to which the obligation of support runs with the land. The weight of authority appears to be that where an actor, whether he be an owner, possessor, lessee, or third-party stranger, removes necessary support he is liable, and an owner cannot avoid this liability by transferring the land to another. Nevertheless, when an actor who removes natural lateral support substitutes artificial support to replace it, such as a retaining wall, the wall then becomes an incident to and a burden on the land upon which it is constructed, and subsequent owners and possessors have an obligation to maintain it.

In the case *sub judice*, the plaintiffs' land had no buildings erected on it at the time the defendant's predecessor in title built the retaining wall on his property; therefore, he needed only to erect a retaining wall sufficient to provide support for their soil. He was not required to furnish a wall sufficient to support any structure which they might erect upon their property. The defendant, as his successor, merely had the obligation to maintain the wall to support the plaintiffs' land in its natural condition. Defendant was not required to strengthen the wall to the extent that it would provide support for the weight of plaintiffs' buildings.

III

Since the pleadings in the case before us make reference to negligence, it is appropriate here to address the scope of a negligence theory. In general, it has been held that while an adjoining landowner has no obligation to support the buildings and other structures on his neighbor's land, nonetheless, if those structures are actually being supported, a neighbor who withdraws such support must do it in a non-negligent way. In an action predicated on strict liability for removing support for the land in its natural state, the kind of lateral support withdrawn is material, but the quality of the actor's conduct is immaterial; however, in a proceeding based upon negligence, the kind of lateral support withdrawn is immaterial, and the quality of the actor's conduct is material. Comment e, *Restatement (Second) of Torts* §819 succinctly explains the nature of liability for negligence.

> The owner of land may be unreasonable in withdrawing lateral support needed by his neighbor for artificial conditions on the neighbor's land in either of two respects. First, he may make an unnecessary excavation, believing correctly that it will cause his neighbor's land to subside because of the pressure of artificial structures on the neighbor's land. If his conduct is unreasonable either in the digging or in the intentional failure to warn his neighbor of it, he is subject to liability to the neighbor for the harm caused by it. The high regard that the law has by long tradition shown for the interest of the owner in the improvement and utilization of his land weighs heavily in his favor in determining what constitutes unreasonable conduct on his part in such a case. Normally the owner of the supporting land may withdraw lateral support that is not naturally necessary, for any purpose that he regards as useful provided that the manner in which it is done is reasonable. But all the factors that enter into the determination of the reasonableness or unreasonableness of the actor's conduct must be considered, and in a particular case the withdrawal itself may be unreasonable. Thus, if the actor's sole purpose in excavating his land is to harm his neighbor's structures, the excavation itself is unreasonable. Furthermore, although for the purpose of permanently leveling the land it may be reasonable to withdraw support that is not naturally necessary, it may be unreasonable to make an excavation for a building that will itself require a foundation, without providing for the safeguarding of the neighbor's structures during the progress of the work. Likewise it is normally unreasonable not to notify an adjacent landowner of excavations that certainly will harm his structures, unless the neighbor otherwise has notice.
>
> Secondly, the owner of land may be negligent in failing to provide against the risk of harm to his neighbor's structures. This negligence may occur either when the actor does not realize that any harm will occur to his neighbor's structures or when the actor realizes that there is a substantial risk to his neighbor's land and fails to take adequate provisions to prevent subsidence, either by himself taking precautions or by giving his neighbor an opportunity to take precautions. Although the law accords the owner of the supporting land great freedom in withdrawing from another's land support that is not naturally necessary in respect to the withdrawal itself, it does not excuse withdrawal in a manner that involves an unreasonable risk of harm to the land of another. The owner in making the excavation is therefore required to take reasonable precautions to minimize the risk of causing subsidence of his neighbor's land. In determining whether a particular precaution is reasonably required, the extent of the burden that the taking of it will impose upon the actor is a factor of great importance.

In the case of *Walker v. Strosnider, supra,* Judge Poffenbarger, speaking for a unanimous court, explained the law of West Virginia in a way completely in accord with the modern *Restatement.* He summarized the cause of action for negligence as follows:

> [An owner] may use his property, but he must use it in a lawful, that is, careful, manner. In other words, he must execute the work, as far as is reasonably practicable, and not unduly burdensome, with a view to the safety of the buildings on the adjacent property. But for this rule, he might go at any hour of the day or night, without having given notice to the adjoining owner, indicating when, how or to what extent he intended to alter the condition of his property, and make an excavation for a cellar along the entire wall of a heavy valuable building, knowing it would fall in consequence thereof, and yet intending to replace, the earth removed by a wall. He would be under no duty to vary the mode or manner of his work in the slightest degree, in respect to the time thereof or

otherwise, in the interests of the safety of the building. Having thus made the excavation, he could build his wall at his leisure and would be under no duty to prosecute the work diligently even though it should be apparent that delay in this part of the work would endanger the building. Such conduct would be reckless, careless and wanton, in view of the ease with which the mode of work could be varied, in respect to time and manner, and previous notice given of the intention to alter the condition of the property, the extent of the alteration, the manner in which it is to be done and the time, so as to afford the owner of the building an opportunity to take such measures for its protection, as he might see fit to adopt. . . . 67 S.E. at 1090. . . .

IV

It would appear that the case before us either stands or falls on a question of strict liability. It is admitted that the retaining wall on the defendant's property was constructed at least sixty years ago, before the construction of the plaintiffs' house, and that all parties to this action were aware of the condition of the wall. Furthermore, there is no allegation that the defendant did anything to cause the collapse of the wall, but rather only failed to keep it in repair. Therefore, if the plaintiffs can recover, they must do so by proving that the disrepair of the retaining wall would have led ineluctably to the subsidence of their land in its natural condition. If, on the other hand, the land would not have subsided but for the weight of the plaintiffs' house, then they can recover nothing. . . .

NOTES AND QUESTIONS

1. *Easements and servitudes.* An *easement* is a limited right to do something on, or to control the use of, someone else's property. An *affirmative easement* is a right to do something on *someone else's* property. The right to cross someone else's property, for example, is called a *right of way*. A *negative easement* is a right to prevent someone else from using her *own* property in a certain way. Modern terminology confines the term "easement" to affirmative easements and uses the word "servitude" to describe restrictions on land use, including negative easements. Most easements and servitudes are created by agreement among neighbors. Some like the *servitude for lateral support of land* are created by the common law. Each owner has an obligation to maintain lateral support for neighboring land; conversely, each owner has a right to prevent their neighbors from excavating on their property to remove lateral support for their land.

2. *Land versus structures.* Courts have often distinguished lateral support of land from lateral support of buildings or other structures built on the land. The common law grants each landowner a servitude for lateral support of land in its natural condition. Owners who withdraw lateral support for neighboring land are *strictly liable* for any resulting damage to the land. On the other hand, owners have no duty to support structures on their neighbors' land. They do have a duty not to excavate in a *negligent* manner; they have a duty to act as a reasonably prudent person would — they cannot use unreasonably dangerous engineering methods or create unnecessary risks to adjoining property. They are also obligated to provide temporary support for neighboring land during excavation and to notify the neighbors if their excavation poses a

risk to neighboring structures. *Spall v. Janota*, 406 N.E.2d 378 (Ind. Ct. App. 1980); *Klebs v. Yim*, 772 P.2d 523 (Wash. Ct. App. 1989) (both holding that there is an absolute right of lateral support for land but only a duty to refrain from negligent injury to adjoining structures). However, the obligation to avoid negligence does not mean that owners have a duty to avoid foreseeable harm to neighboring structures if the land in its natural condition, in combination with the underlying foundation of the structures, would not have been sufficient to support those structures.

What happens if the land in its natural condition is sufficient to support a structure on neighboring land and the removal of support for the land causes a chain reaction resulting in damage to the building? Older law, retained in some states, denied a remedy to the owner of the building. *Thurston v. Hancock*, 12 Mass. 220 (1815). However, the modern approach adopted in *Noone* imposes damages for harm both to the land and to the building if the harm to the building was caused by removal of lateral support for the land. The damages to the building are *consequential damages* resulting from breach of a legal duty to support the land. If, on the other hand, the neighboring building was built negligently with inadequate support so that it would have been damaged eventually even if the defendant did not withdraw lateral support for the land, then plaintiff can recover no damages for harm to the building resulting from the withdrawal of lateral support, under either the older or the modern approach.

Why is the standard of care different for land and structures? This distinction can be traced in United States law to an early Massachusetts case, *Thurston v. Hancock, supra*, later reaffirmed by *Gilmore v. Driscoll*, 122 Mass. 199 (1877). In *Gilmore*, the Massachusetts Supreme Judicial Court explained the result in *Thurston* in the following manner, 122 Mass. at 203–204:

> In *Thurston v. Hancock*, 12 Mass. 220 (1815), which . . . is the leading American case on this subject, the plaintiff in 1802 bought a parcel of land upon Beacon Hill in Boston, bounded on the west by land of the town of Boston; and in 1804 built a brick dwelling-house thereon, with its rear two feet from this boundary, and its foundation fifteen feet below the ancient surface of the land. The defendants in 1811 took a deed of the adjoining land from the town, and began to dig and remove the earth therefrom, and, though notified by the plaintiff that his house was endangered, continued to do so to the depth of forty-five feet, and within six feet of the rear of the plaintiff's house, and thereby caused part of the earth on the surface of the plaintiff's land to fall away and slide upon the defendant's land, and rendered the foundations of the plaintiff's house insecure, and the occupation thereof dangerous, so that he was obliged to abandon it.

The court, after advisement, and upon a review of the earlier English authorities, held that the plaintiff could recover for the loss of or injury to the soil merely, and not for the damage to the house; and Chief Justice Parker, in delivering judgment said: "It is a common principle of the civil and of the common law, that the proprietor of land, unless restrained by covenant or custom, has the entire dominion, not only of the soil, but of the space above and below the surface, to any extent he may choose to occupy it. The law, founded upon principles of reason and common utility, has admitted a qualification to this dominion, restricting the proprietor so to use his own, as not to injure the property or impair any actual existing rights of another. *Sic utere tuo ut alienum non laedas*." "But this subjection of the use of a man's own property to the convenience of his neighbor is founded upon a supposed preexisting right in his neighbor to have and enjoy the privilege which by such act is impaired." "A man, in digging upon his own land, is to have regard to the position of his neighbor's land, and the probable consequences to his neighbor, if he digs too near his line; and if he disturbs the natural state of the soil, he shall answer in damages; but he is answerable only for the natural and necessary consequences of his act, and not for the value of a house put upon or near the line by his neighbor." "The plaintiff built his house within two feet of the western line of the lot, knowing that the town, or those who should hold under it, had a right to build equally near to the line, or to dig down into the soil for any other lawful purpose. He knew also the shape and nature of the ground, and that it was impossible to dig there without causing excavations. He built at his peril; for it was not possible for him, merely by building upon his own ground, to deprive the other party of such use of his as he should deem most advantageous.... It is, in fact, *damnum absque injuria* [damage without legal redress]."

Does this explanation make sense?

3. *Retaining walls.* If a retaining wall was built on defendant's land for the purpose of maintaining lateral support for plaintiff's land, defendant has a strict obligation to keep the wall in good repair to avoid loss of lateral support for the plaintiff's land. This obligation "runs with the land" and is binding on subsequent owners of the property. *Salmon v. Peterson,* 311 N.W.2d 205, 206-207 (S.D. 1981). However, the obligation extends only to such support as is needed to support the neighbor's land in its natural condition. In the absence of statute, an owner of a retaining wall has no obligation to keep it strong enough also to support the added weight of the neighbor's building. *See Klebs v. Yim,* 772 P.2d 523 (Wash. Ct. App. 1989) (defendant had "a duty to maintain an existing retaining wall on [defendant's] property" and was liable for failure to maintain the wall but was not liable for damage to plaintiff's property attributable to the additional weight imposed by plaintiff's swimming pool). If a retaining wall on defendant's land is actually supporting the buildings on plaintiff's land, defendant does have a duty to act non-negligently in withdrawing that support, by notifying the plaintiff of any changes so that plaintiff can take steps to support her own structure.

4. *Natural conditions.* Do owners have obligations to take reasonable steps to prevent natural conditions on their land from harming neighboring owners? Some courts have held that an owner who reasonably should know that her property is subject to landslides should take reasonable steps to protect property downhill from her. *Sprecher v. Adamson,* 636 P.2d 1121 (Cal. 1981). However, other courts take the position that owners are not liable for harms caused by the natural condition of their land, although they may be liable for conditions caused by their development of their own land. *Price ex rel. Estate of Price v. City of Seattle,* 24 P.3d 1098 (Wash. Ct. App. 2001).

5. *Measurement of damages.* Courts have used a variety of approaches to measure damages for injury to lateral support. Those approaches include (a) the cost of restoration; (b) the diminution in value of the property; and (c) in the case of liability for damage to a building, the value of the lost use of the building plus an amount representing permanent depreciation in the building's value. *Powell on Real Property* ¶702[2] (Michael Allan Wolf ed. 2000).

§4.3.1.2 Building Codes and Private Rights of Action

In addition to common law rules regulating land use, every state has passed statutes regulating both land use and building construction. These statutes may alter the common law rules concerning support. For example, the Massachusetts legislature created, by statute, a state building code commission with the power to create, implement, and enforce a building code for the Commonwealth of Massachusetts. How does this set of rules change the rights and obligations of landowners?

MASSACHUSETTS GENERAL LAWS
Mass. Gen. Laws Ann. ch. 143, §§3, 3A, 57, 59, 93, 94

§3. The chief administrative officer of each city and town shall employ and designate a ... building commissioner ... to administer and enforce the state building code.... Any additional persons employed by a city or town to assist the building commissioner ... in the performance of his duties shall be called local inspectors....

§3A. [T]he local inspector shall enforce the state building code as to any building or structure within the city or town from which he is appointed....

§57. The ... superior court shall have jurisdiction in equity to enforce ... the state building code..., the enforcement of which ... is the responsibility of [the] local inspector.....

§59. The ... superior court may, upon the application of the ... local inspector, enforce by any suitable process or decree ... the state building code....

§93. There is hereby established ... a board to be known as the state board of building regulations and standards[, which] shall adopt and administer a state building code....

§94.... Whoever violates any provision of the state building code ... shall be punished by a fine of not more than one thousand dollars or by imprisonment for not more than one year, or both, for each such violation. Each day during which a violation exists shall constitute a separate offense....

MASSACHUSETTS STATE BUILDING CODE
780 Code Mass. Regs. §§101.4, 3308.1, 3309.1, 3310.2 (1999)

§101.4. [The State Building Code], 780 Code Mass. Regs.[,] shall be construed to secure its expressed intent, which is to insure public safety, health and welfare insofar as they are affected by building construction ... and, in general, to secure safety to life and property from all hazards incident to the design, construction, reconstruction, alteration, repair, demolition, removal, use or occupancy of buildings, structures or premises.

§3308.1 General. Adjoining property shall be completely protected from any damage caused by the construction of a structure when the owner of the adjoining property permits free access to the structure at all reasonable times to provide the necessary safeguards....

§3309.1 Protection. All adjoining public and private property shall be protected from damage caused by construction.

§3310.2 Protection of adjoining property. If afforded the necessary license to enter the adjoining lot, building or structure, the person causing the demolition or excavation to be made shall at all times and at his or her own expense preserve and protect the lot, building or structure from damage or injury....

NOTES AND QUESTIONS

The regulations promulgated by the Massachusetts state building code commission apparently require all landowners to protect neighboring structures. If an owner violates the building code by undermining lateral support for a neighboring building, is the violator financially liable to the injured property owner for any resulting damage?

Three questions must be considered. First, do the regulations create a *private right of action*, i.e., a right to sue the neighbor for damages? The right may be *express* or *implied*. It is express if the text of the laws clearly creates a right to sue and implied if the court infers such a right from the text by reference to the purposes the regulations were intended to achieve or the policies underlying the regulations. Second, if no such right was created, are the remedies included in the statute (criminal penalties including fines and imprisonment and civil claims by the local inspector) intended to be *exclusive* or *nonexclusive*? If those remedies are exclusive, a private owner cannot seek a remedy under the common law. If they are nonexclusive, we reach the third question. Should the common law be changed to promote the policies underlying the statute and regulations, or should the legislature's failure to alter the common law rule induce the court to retain it until changed by the legislature?

PROBLEM

A building in an urban downtown area is demolished to make way for a new structure. The demolition of the building and excavation of the land underneath it undermine lateral support for a neighboring structure, causing damage to the foundation of the neighboring building. It seems that the foundation of the demolished building had been providing needed support for the neighboring structure. The owner of the damaged building sues the neighbor for damages to recoup the cost of fixing her building.

1. What is plaintiff's argument that the state building code and/or supporting legislation entitles her to recover such damages, either expressly or implicitly? What is defendant's argument in response?

2. If the legislation and regulations do not provide a private right of action for non-negligent harm to buildings on neighboring land, what is plaintiff's argument that the common law should be changed to provide such a remedy? What is defendant's argument that the common law negligence standard should be retained?

§4.3.2   Subjacent Support

§4.3.2.1   Right to Dig versus Right to Support

FRIENDSWOOD DEVELOPMENT CO. v.
SMITH-SOUTHWEST INDUSTRIES, INC.

576 S.W.2d 21 (Tex. 1978)

Price Daniel, J.

The question in this case is whether landowners who withdrew percolating ground waters from wells located on their own land are liable for subsidence which resulted on lands of others in the same general area.

Smith-Southwest Industries and other landowners located in the Seabrook and Clear Lake area of Harris County brought this class action in 1973 against Friendswood Development Company and its corporate parent, Exxon Corporation, alleging that severe subsidence of their lands was caused by the defendants' past and continuing withdrawals of vast quantities of underground water from wells on defendants' nearby lands....

Allegations and Summary Judgment Proof

[Plaintiff landowners alleged that defendant Friendswood had pumped large amounts of subsurface waters from its own property for sale primarily to industrial users.] These wells were drilled from 1964 through 1971, even though previous engineering reports to defendants showed that production therefrom would result in a certain amount of land subsidence in the area. Plaintiffs alleged that the wells were negligently spaced too close together, too near the common boundary of lands owned by plaintiffs and defendants, and that excessive quantities were produced with knowledge that this would cause subsidence and flooding of plaintiffs' lands. Plaintiffs alleged that this extensive withdrawal of ground water proximately caused the sinking and loss of elevation above mean sea level of their property and the property of others similarly situated along the shores of Galveston Bay and Clear Lake, resulting in the erosion and flooding of their lands and damage to their residences, businesses and improvements. Plaintiffs further allege that the manner in which Friendswood Development Company continues to use its property for the withdrawal and sale of large amounts of fresh water to commercial users on other lands constitutes a continuing nuisance and permanent loss and damage to their property....

... Plaintiffs concede that subsidence in the area complained of was known to be a "potential problem" before defendants' operations began, but they allege that Friendswood and Exxon knew that the problem "would be severely aggravated" by the withdrawals which the companies contemplated. There was summary judgment proof of such knowledge and aggravation....

Nature of Plaintiffs' Action

Plaintiffs have alleged an action in tort based upon the general rule that a landowner has a duty not to use his property so as to injure others. *Sic utere tuo ut alienum non laedas.* [However, this court has held that this general rule does not apply to withdrawals of underground water. Rather, this court has] adopted the common law rule that such rights are not correlative, but are absolute, and thus are not subject to the conflicting "reasonable use" rule. *Houston & T. C. Ry. Co. v. East,* 81 S.W. 279 (Tex. 1904).

Plaintiffs [contend] that the "reasonable use" doctrine should apply to ground water the same as it does to other real property.

... In [*East,*] the railroad company, with full knowledge of the long existence of Mr. East's small shallow well on his homestead, dug a well twenty feet in diameter and 66 feet deep on its own adjacent property, from which it pumped 25,000 gallons of water per day. This resulted in lowering the water level on plaintiff's land and drying up his well. [The plaintiff argued for the "reasonable use" or "American rule," which held that the right of a landowner to draw underground water from his land was not absolute, but limited to the amount necessary for the reasonable use of his land, and that the rights of adjoining landowners are correlative and limited to reasonable use. The defendant argued for the contrary English doctrine laid down in *Acton v. Blundell,* 152 Eng. Rep. 1223 (Ex. 1843), that, "if a man digs a well on his own field and thereby drains his neighbor's, he may do so unless he does it maliciously."]

Adoption of the Common Law Rule of Absolute Ownership

Thus, on the appeal of the *East* case to this Court, the conflicting aspects of the "reasonable use" rule and the common law rule, later referred to as the "English rule" or "absolute ownership rule," were clearly presented. This Court discussed both rules and made a deliberate choice of the common law rule as announced in *Acton v. Blundell, supra.*[9] . . .

In holding that the owner may withdraw water from beneath his land without liability for lowering the water table and thus damaging his neighbor's well and land, the Court mentioned only waste and malice as possible limitations to the rule. Absent these, the Court clearly embraced the doctrine stated in *Acton v. Blundell, supra,* that this type of damage "falls within the description *damnum absque injuria,* which cannot become the ground of action." This legal maxim denotes a loss without injury in the legal sense, that is, without the invasion of a legal right or the violation of a legal duty. . . .

The English rule of so-called "absolute ownership" was applied by this Court in *Texas Co. v. Burkett,* 296 S.W. 273 (Tex. 1927), which held that a landowner has the absolute right to sell percolating ground water for industrial purposes off the land. At a time when the trend in other jurisdictions was away from the English rule and toward the "reasonable use" rule, the English rule was reaffirmed by this Court in *City of Corpus Christi v. City of Pleasanton,* 276 S.W.2d 798 (Tex. 1955). . . .

Subsidence Cases Under the Common Law Rule

Although the *East, Corpus Christi,* and *Williams** cases involved damages to wells and lands of the plaintiffs because the water tables beneath their lands were lowered by ground water withdrawals of the defendants, none of these nor any other Texas case has dealt specifically with land subsidence resulting from such pumping of underground waters. In other jurisdictions adhering to the English ground water rule, liability for neighboring land subsidence has been denied. . . .

On the basis of the earlier decisions cited above, the *Restatement of Torts* §818 (1939), adopted the following rule:

---

9. The public policy considerations were said to be (1) "because the existence, origin, movement and course of such waters, . . . are so secret, occult and concealed that an attempt to administer any set of legal rules in respect to them would be involved in hopeless uncertainty, and would, therefore, be practically impossible"; and (2) "because any such recognition of correlative rights would interfere, to the material detriment of the commonwealth, with drainage and agriculture, mining, . . ." etc. 81 S.W. 279, 281.

*Pecos County Water Control & Improvement District 1 v. Williams, 271 S.W.2d 503 (Tex. Ct. App. 1954). — ED.

§818. WITHDRAWING SUBTERRANEAN WATER

To the extent that a person is not liable for withdrawing subterranean waters from the land of another, he is not liable for a subsidence of the other's land which is caused by the withdrawal....

We have found nothing in our Constitution, laws, or decisions inconsistent with the common law rule....

Stare Decisis

We agree that some aspects of the English or common law rule as to underground waters are harsh and outmoded, and the rule has been severely criticized since its reaffirmation by this Court in 1955. Most of the critics, however, recognize that it has become an established rule of property law in this State, under which many citizens own land and water rights. The rule has been relied upon by thousands of farmers, industries, and municipalities in purchasing and developing vast tracts of land overlying aquifers of underground water. Approximately 50,000 wells are used to irrigate 2,800,000 acres in the thirteen county High Plains area of West Texas. As shown in the official reports cited earlier in this opinion, over 2,600 water wells have been drilled in Harris County alone while this rule of immunity from liability was in effect. The very wells which brought about this action were drilled after the English rule had been reaffirmed by this Court in 1955.

On this subject, we are not writing on a clean slate. Even though good reasons may exist for lifting the immunity from tort actions in cases of this nature, it would be unjust to do so retroactively. The doctrine of *stare decisis* has been and should be strictly followed by this Court in cases involving established rules of property rights. It is for this reason that, as to past actions complained of in this case, we follow the English rule and *Restatement of Torts* §818 (1939) in holding that defendants are not liable on plaintiff's allegations of nuisance and negligence....

As to Future Wells and Subsidence

[T]he Legislature has entered the field of regulation of ground water withdrawals and subsidence. This occurred after geologists, hydrologists, and engineers had developed more accurate knowledge concerning the location, source, and measurement of percolating underground waters, and after legislators became aware of the potential conflicts inherent in the unregulated use of ground water under the English rule of ownership. With a rule that recognizes ownership of underground water by each individual under his own land, but with no limitation on the manner and amount which another individual landowner might produce (absent willful waste and malicious malice [sic]), legislative action was essential in order to provide for conservation and protection of public interests.

The legislative policy contained in Chapter 52 of the Texas Water Code is designed to limit the exercise of that portion of the English rule which has been interpreted as giving each landowner the right to take all the water he pleases without regard to the effect on other lands in the same area. For instance, §52.117 of the Water Code, applicable to Underground Water Conservation Districts, provides:

§52.117.   *Regulation of Spacing and Production*[*]

In order to minimize as far as practicable the drawdown of the water table or the reduction of artesian pressure, to control subsidence, or to prevent waste, the district may provide for the spacing of water wells and may regulate the production of wells.[*]

Ten of these Underground Water Conservation Districts are active in an area embracing much of West Texas. The need for additional legislation for creation of districts to cover unregulated ground water reservoirs and to solve other conflicts which may arise in this area of water law and subsidence seems to be inevitable. Providing policy and regulatory procedures in this field is a legislative function. It is well that the Legislature has assumed its proper role, because our courts are not equipped to regulate ground water uses and subsidence on a suit-by-suit basis.

This case, however, gives the Court its first opportunity to recognize, and to encourage compliance with, the policy set forth by the Legislature and its regulatory agencies in an effort to curb excessive underground water withdrawals and resulting land subsidence. It also affords us the opportunity to discard an objectionable aspect of the court-made English rule as it relates to subsidence by stating a rule for the future which is more in harmony with expressed legislative policy. We refer to the past immunity from negligence which heretofore has been afforded ground water producers solely because of their "absolute" ownership of the water.

As far as we can determine, there is no other use of private real property which enjoys such an immunity from liability under the law of negligence. This ownership of underground water comes with ownership of the surface; it is part of the soil. Yet, the use of one's ground-level surface and other elements of the soil is without such insulation from tort liability. Our consideration of this case convinces us that there is no valid reason to continue this special immunity insofar as it relates to future subsidence proximately caused by negligence in the manner which wells are drilled or produced in the future. It appears that the ownership and rights of all landowners will be better protected against subsidence if each has the duty to produce water from his land in a manner that will not negligently damage or destroy the lands of others.

Therefore, if the landowner's manner of withdrawing ground water from his land is negligent, willfully wasteful, or for the purpose of malicious injury, and such conduct is a proximate cause of the subsidence of the land of others, he will be liable for the consequences of his conduct. The addition of negligence as a ground of recovery shall apply only to future subsidence proximately caused by future withdrawals of ground water from wells which are either produced or drilled in a negligent manner after the date this opinion becomes final.

While this addition of negligence as a ground of recovery in subsidence cases applies to future negligence in producing water from existing wells and those drilled or produced in a negligent manner in the future, it has been suggested that this new ground of recovery should be applied in the present cause of action. This is often done when a court writes or adds a new rule applicable to personal injury cases, but seldom when rules of property law are involved. This is because precedent is necessarily a highly important factor when problems regarding land or contracts are concerned. In deeds, property transactions, and land developments, the parties should be able to rely on the law which existed at the time of their actions. . . .

---

[*]This section was replaced by Tex. Water Code §36.116 in 1995. — ED.

JACK POPE, J., dissenting.

I respectfully dissent. The court has decided this cause upon the mistaken belief that the case is governed by the ownership of ground water. Plaintiffs assert no ownerships to the percolating waters pumped and extracted from the ground by defendants. They make no complaint that their own wells have been or will be pumped dry. They seek no damages for the defendants' sale of the water. Plaintiffs' action calls for no change in nor even a review of the English rule of "absolute ownership" of ground water, the American rule of "reasonable use" of ground water, nor the Texas rule of "nonwasteful" use of ground water. They claim no correlative rights in the water. The Texas law of percolating waters is not put in issue by this suit, and there is no occasion to overrule that law either now or prospectively. . . .

Plaintiffs' complaint is that defendants are causing subsidence of their land. They assert an absolute right to keep the surface of their land at its natural horizon. The landowners' right to the subjacent support for their land is the only right in suit, and this is a case of original impression. . . . It is no more logical to say that this is a case concerning the right to ground water than it would be correct in a case in which an adjoining landowner removed lateral support by a caterpillar to say that the case would be governed by the law of caterpillars. In making this decision about one's right to subjacent support, I would use as analogies other kinds of cases concerning support, such as the right to lateral support.

A landowner's right to lateral support for his land is an absolute right. The instrument employed in causing land to slough off, cave in or wash away is not the real subject of inquiry. The inquiry is whether the adjoining owner actually causes the loss of support. Whether the support is destroyed by excavation, ditching, the flowing of water, the pumping of water, unnatural pressure, unnatural suction, or explosives, the right to support is the same, and it is an absolute right. . . .

A second analogous rule which protects one's subsurface from damage by an operator on other lands is found in *Gregg v. Delhi-Taylor Oil Corp.,* 344 S.W.2d 411, 416 (Tex. 1961). Mr. Gregg, in the development of his mineral lease, was preparing to use a sand fracturing technique to open cracks and veins extending some distance from his lease and to alter the substructure of neighboring land. By use of hydraulic pressure the ruptures of the subsurface formations would free greater quantities of gas. The rupture beneath the Delhi-Taylor's lands would create only small veins about one-tenth of an inch in diameter. This court regarded the creation of fissures on another's land as an invasion of property rights. . . . This court denied one landowner the right to interfere with the subsurface of lands beyond his own lease boundaries. The same principle was applied in *Gregg v. Delhi-Taylor Oil Corp.,* 344 S.W.2d 411 (Tex. 1961), and in *Delhi-Taylor Oil Corp. v. Holmes,* 344 S.W.2d 420 (Tex. 1961).

In my judgment, the examples are indistinguishable from the present case. . . .

Elliff v. Texon Drilling Co., 210 S.W.2d 558 (Tex. 1948), was another example in which this court looked at the damage done [to] a neighbor's subsurface estate by an oil driller who had the right to capture oil through the wellbore on his own lease. This court expressly rejected holdings by the Louisiana Supreme Court which held that an adjoining owner has no action against one who negligently destroys a reservoir. This court also rejected the defense that one's right to capture the oil rendered him immune from damages for his negligence in wasting it.

We thus reach the end result. Under our prior holdings compared with today's, one who mines for oil may not destroy his neighbor's subjacent geology; but the right to pump water, we inconsistently say, is the right to destroy the subsurface geology, the subjacent support and even the surface of the land. Defendants may pump the plaintiffs' land to the bottom of Galveston Bay. . . .

The error of the majority is its narrow focus upon the right of the defendants to pump ground water. We should enlarge our vision so we can see what this lawsuit is about. I do not believe it is sound law that the right to pump water is the power to destroy the surface of surrounding landowners. If defendants argue that they have an absolute right to pump groundwater, plaintiffs reply that they too have an absolute right to the support of their natural surface. . . .

There is yet another legal principle that we should observe. Many things, though lawful, when done to excess, become remediable. Church bells may toll the knell of parting day or announce the time for solemn services, but when bells continuously clang without interruption for many days, the rights of others spring into being. What we do cannot be understood except in relation to those we touch. We have in this case the pleadings and showing that the defendants have abused their right to pump water to the point that property and the rights of others are ignored and destroyed. . . .

I dissent from the court's holding that this case is governed by the *stare decisis* of ground water cases. There has not previously been a case like this in Texas and there is no *stare decisis* applicable. . . . Because there is no *stare decisis*, I also dissent from the court's holding that plaintiffs can have no remedy except by a retroactive application of the law. The defendants, according to some of the summary judgment proofs, had knowledge from expert opinions that their course of action would cause subsidence. When the defendants, after warning, elect to take their risks in an area in which there are no precedents, I see no reason to apply our holding prospectively. . . .

Finally, and importantly, I dissent from the majority's holding that landowners in the future may prosecute a suit for damages for the destruction of their property if, and only if the action is one for negligence, willful waste, or malicious injury. I rather assume that pumpers of ground water will carefully do so, will not waste their water, and will bear no ill will toward those whose property they are destroying. . . .

I would hold that an owner of land may assert an action against one who destroys the lateral or subjacent support to his land in its natural state when: (1) he engages in conduct knowing that it will cause damages to another's land by loss or destruction of the subjacent support, or (2) the plaintiff proves negligence, or (3) the plaintiff proves a nuisance, and here a balancing will be a factor. Justice Williams, the author of *East* also wrote *Gulf, C. & S. F. Ry. Co. v. Oakes*, 58 S.W. 999 (Tex. 1900), and accepted this reasonable solution to the resolution of the conflict between two property rights:

> It is a general principle of the law that the owner of property may use it as he chooses in any lawful way; but another maxim, in general terms, requires him to so use it as not to injure another. . . . [An owner] may be required to forego a particular use when it is not essential to the substantial enjoyment of his property, and is fraught with unreasonable loss to his neighbor. On the other hand, the particular use may be so important to the owner, and the loss or inconvenience to his neighbor so slight compared to his, were he forbidden to so employ his property, that it would be unreasonable and unjust to impose such a restriction. In such cases, it is evident that all of the circumstances of the situation must be taken into consideration. The importance of the use to the owner, as well as the extent of the damage to be inflicted upon his neighbor, and the rights of the parties, are to be adjusted in a practical way; the question being whether or not the proposed use is a reasonable one, under all the circumstances. . . . As is said in some of the authorities, there must, in such inquiries where rights and interests seem to conflict, be a balancing of them. *Id.* at 100-101.

The balancing of lawful but competing property rights has been the rule previously approved by our Texas courts. . . .

I also dissent from the court's denial of rights to the plaintiffs, while acknowledging that future landowners may have an action at least in negligence. This court, in recent years, has recognized a number of new actions, and each time, the successful party was allowed the victory. . . . In my opinion, it is basically unfair to treat the plaintiffs in this case unequally by recognizing that they possess an action, but by denying them the remedy. . . .

NOTES AND QUESTIONS

1. *Standard of care.* A major issue in defining the scope of legal rights concerns what lawyers call the *standard of care.* The right of subjacent support implies that other property owners have legal duties not to infringe on that right. Determining the scope of the owner's legal right therefore requires specification of the duties imposed on the neighbor: What kind of behavior violates the neighbor's obligation?

One possibility is a *strict liability* standard: The defendant is liable to the plaintiff whenever the defendant has caused harm to the plaintiff's property interest, even if the harm could not have been avoided by acting more reasonably. A second possibility is a *reasonableness* test. Under this standard, the decision maker must review the facts and make a judgment about the reasonableness of the defendant's conduct and the resulting harm to the plaintiff. This judgment may focus on the legitimacy of the defendant's conduct and/or the character of the harm. Did defendant create an unreasonable risk of harm or engage in an illegitimate or illegal use of the land? Did plaintiff suffer an amount or type of harm that an owner should not have to bear for the good of society, at least in the absence of compensation? Alternatively, the court may focus on the interests of society, asking whether the social benefits of the harmful land use outweigh the gravity of the harm to the victim. In practice, most courts consider a variety of factors in determining whether a land use is reasonable. These factors may include balancing the interests of the parties, determining whether one of the parties acted wrongfully or engaged in a disfavored activity, assessing the relative social costs and benefits of the competing activities of the plaintiff and the defendant, and adopting appropriate incentives to encourage desirable land development and discourage undesirable or socially destructive land uses.

In real property cases, several variations on the reasonableness standard exist. Under a *negligence* standard, the courts will impose liability if the defendant engaged in conduct that created an unreasonably great risk of causing harm. Liability will be found under a negligence standard only when the harm to the plaintiff's property interests was *foreseeable* at the time the defendant acted. The focus is therefore on the reasonableness or unreasonableness of the defendant's *conduct.* W. Page Keeton, Dan B. Dobbs, Robert E. Keeton, & David G. Owen, *Prosser and Keeton on Torts* §31, at 169-173 (5th ed. 1984). Under a *nuisance* standard, in contrast, the court determines whether the defendant's activity is both unreasonable and causes substantial harm to the use and enjoyment of the plaintiff's property. Nuisance focuses on the *consequences* of the defendant's conduct rather than the conduct itself; nuisance requires consideration of whether the defendant's activity causes more harm than good, comparing the gravity of the harm with the social utility of the harmful conduct. *Id.* §§87, 88, at 619-630.

Some kinds of conduct may have effects that are impossible to foresee with any certainty. Under these circumstances, we may judge the conduct non-negligent because the defendant could not foresee that its conduct would cause significant harm. Once the actual effects of the conduct are known, of course, we may conclude that the conduct constitutes a nuisance if its substantial harmful effects outweigh its beneficial effects.

Ordinarily, one would suppose that withdrawal of water in a manner that foreseeably destroys the surface of neighboring land would be negligent conduct. However, if one conceptualizes the absolute right to withdraw water as a property right, then the courts might well interpret the negligence standard to require only that normal engineering methods be used to withdraw the water with no implication that one must moderate the withdrawal to protect the surface of neighboring land. Some courts have in fact so interpreted the negligence standard. *See, e.g., Finley v. Teeter Stone, Inc.,* 248 A.2d 106 (Md. 1968). In that is the case, the dissenting judge in *Friendswood* was correct in his suggestion that the negligence standard adopted by the majority would in fact allow the defendant to carefully "pump the plaintiffs' land to the bottom of Galveston Bay."

2. *Current law.* Some courts agree with the majority in *Friendswood*, imposing liability for undermining subjacent support only when negligence can be shown. Other courts extend the absolute duty to provide lateral support for land to the context of subjacent support, imposing strict liability for removal of subjacent support. *See Los Osos Valley Assocs. v. City of San Luis Obispo,* 36 Cal. Rptr. 2d 758, 763 (Ct. App. 1994); *Muskatell v. City of Seattle,* 116 P.2d 363 (Wash. 1941); *Restatement (Second) of Torts* §818 illus. 1 & 2 (1977) (adopting this approach).

3. *Separation of the surface from the mineral estate.* One exception to the rule that there is no duty to provide subjacent support in the absence of negligence occurs when ownership of the minerals beneath the surface is separated from ownership of the surface. In the absence of agreement to the contrary the owner of the surface has an *absolute right* not to have its subjacent support undermined by the owner of the mineral estate. In *Large v. Clinchfield Coal Co.,* 387 S.E.2d 783 (Va. 1990), the plaintiffs, George and Betty Large, sought to prevent the defendant, Clinchfield Coal Company, from engaging in "longwall mining," a practice that involves removing coal without leaving any supporting pillars of coal, resulting in subsidence of the land surface. The court held that any appreciable damage to the surface or a diminution in its usability by the owner of the mineral estate will be sufficient to sustain a finding of liability without a need for a showing of negligence or unreasonableness. *Accord, Platts v. Sacramento Northern Railway,* 253 Cal. Rptr. 269 (Ct. App. 1988) (holding that a surface estate owner has an absolute right to subjacent support from the owner of a subsurface estate but that the obligation did not run with the land; the mineral estate owner who took possession of the property after the act causing the removal of the surface support was not responsible for the damage).

4. *Retroactivity.* The majority opinion in *Friendswood* argues that it is wrong to apply a new rule of law retroactively. What exactly does this mean? Although the opinion is confusingly worded, the majority sought to apply the new negligence rule both to new wells drilled after the date the opinion in *Friendswood* was issued and to withdrawals of water from existing wells that were drilled before the opinion was issued. Doesn't application of the new rule to withdrawal of water from existing wells constitute a retroactive application of the new rule? After all, investments were arguably made in digging existing wells based on an expectation that the developer would be free from liability for any resulting harm.

What arguments does the court give to justify refusing to apply the new rule retroactively to withdrawals of water that occurred in the past? What arguments could you make on behalf of the plaintiffs for retroactive application of the new rule? How could you argue that even if the new rule is applied prospectively as to all other landowners, it should be applied retroactively to benefit the plaintiffs who brought this particular lawsuit? Was the court correct to apply its new rule to future withdrawal of water from existing wells?

5. *Precedent.* The judges in *Friendswood* addressed a variety of policy arguments concerning the wisdom and justice of the competing rules advocated by the parties. They also interpreted prior decisions to determine whether the question was answered, directly or indirectly, by prior law. The majority opinion concluded that the case was governed by the previously established rule that owners have the absolute right to withdraw groundwater from their property even if this has the effect of withdrawing groundwater from beneath other land. The court then chose to overrule the cases that established the existing rule and to apply the new rule prospectively. In contrast, the dissenting judge argued that the issue in *Friendswood* was not governed by the rule about withdrawal of groundwater at all; instead, the dissenting opinion distinguished the prior cases establishing that rule and argued that the case was one of first impression, meaning that the specific issue before the court had never been precisely addressed by a prior case. In addition, each of the opinions referred to prior cases that established a variety of rules of law by arguing that those cases are *analogous* to the case at hand and that, therefore, the principles established in those prior cases should extend to the situation before the court.

In applying precedent, the lawyers for each side look for precedents that help them. The plaintiff, for example, may argue that a prior case stands for a broad rule of law that applies to the current case as well. To do this, the attorney must describe the holding of the earlier case — the rule of law for which it stands — in a way that encompasses both cases. The attorneys for the other side attempt to *distinguish* the earlier case by arguing that the factual context in the earlier case is different in significant ways from the case at hand and that there are good reasons of policy or justice to adjudicate this case differently from the earlier case. Note that there are two steps in distinguishing a precedent: (a) identifying significant factual differences between the prior case and the case at hand, and (b) explaining why, as a matter of social policy, the cases should be handled differently. The opposing attorneys must counter this argument by explaining why the case at hand is indistinguishable from the earlier case. This requires arguing that (a) the factual differences between the two cases are not important, and (b) the policies justifying the result in the earlier case apply to the current case as well.

What precedents did the majority and dissenting opinions rely on to decide the case in *Friendswood*? Which rules of law did the opinions mention?

PROBLEM

You are in a jurisdiction that has no precedent on the question of whether an owner can excavate on her property and withdraw water in a way that undermines subjacent support for property located some distance away. At least two prior cases, however, are relevant. Your jurisdiction has adopted the *reasonable use* test to govern conflicts over flooding caused by diffuse surface water, as established in *Armstrong v. Francis:* Owners have a duty to act reasonably in developing their property to avoid causing unreasonable harm to neighboring owners that results from the runoff of diffuse surface water. Your jurisdiction has also adopted the *free use* or *absolute ownership* test to govern disputes over groundwater, as established in *Acton v. Blundell*, 152 Eng. Rep. 1223 (Exch. 1843), and *Houston & T. C. Railway Co. v. East*, 81 S.W. 279 (Tex. 1904). Landowners may withdraw as much groundwater as they wish, unless they waste the water, even if the effect is to withdraw groundwater from beneath the plaintiff's land. In addition, your jurisdiction has adopted the common law rule concerning lateral support of land: an absolute duty to support neighboring land in its natural condition but only a duty not to act negligently in withdrawing support from neighboring structures.

1. *Water rights rules as precedent.*
    a. Make the argument for the plaintiff that:
        i. the reasonable use test applicable to flooding applies directly or by analogy; and
        ii. the free use test applicable to withdrawal of groundwater is distinguishable.
    b. Make the argument for the defendant that:
        i. the free use test applicable to withdrawal of groundwater applies directly or by analogy; and
        ii. the reasonable use test applicable to flooding is distinguishable.
2. *Lateral support rules as precedent.*
    a. Make the argument for the plaintiff that:
        i. the absolute duty of lateral support land applies directly or by analogy to the issue of subjacent support; and
        ii. the issue of lateral support of buildings is distinguishable from the issue of subjacent support of buildings and thus the negligence rule applicable to lateral support should be replaced by a rule imposing an absolute duty to provide subjacent support for neighboring structures.
    b. Make the argument for the defendant that the issues of lateral and subjacent support are distinguishable, such that:
        i. the absolute duty to provide lateral support of land should be rejected in favor of a rule imposing no duty (absolute freedom to withdraw water and hence subjacent support without liability); and
        ii. the negligence rule applicable to lateral support of buildings should similarly be replaced by a no-duty rule.

In constructing these arguments, consider the following readings on precedent and the judicial role.

§4.3.2.2 Precedent

THE BRAMBLE BUSH
KARL LLEWELLYN
2-3, 48, 70, 71-76 (1960 ed.) (originally published 1930)

... We have discovered in our teaching of the law that general propositions are empty. We have discovered that students who come eager to learn the rules and who do learn them, *and who learn nothing more*, will take away the shell and not the substance. We have discovered that rules *alone*, mere forms of words, are worthless. We have learned that the concrete instance, the heaping up of concrete instances, the present, vital memory of a multitude of concrete instances, is necessary in order to make any general proposition, be it rule of law or any other, *mean* anything at all. Without the concrete instances the general proposition is baggage, impedimenta, stuff about the feet. It not only does not help. It hinders. . . .

What, then, is this law business about? It is about the fact that our society is honeycombed with disputes. Disputes actual and potential; disputes to be settled and disputes to be prevented; both appealing to law, both making up the business of the law. But obviously those which most violently call for attention are the actual disputes, and to these our first attention must be directed. Actual disputes call for somebody to do something about them. First, so that there may be peace, for the disputants; for other persons whose ears and toes disputants are disturbing. And secondly, so that the dispute may really be put at rest, which means, so that a solution may be achieved which, at least in the main, is bearable to the parties and not disgusting to the lookers-on. This doing of something about disputes, this doing of it reasonably, is the business of law. And the people who have the doing in charge, whether they be judges or sheriffs or clerks or jailers or lawyers, are officials of the law. *What these officials do about disputes is, to my mind, the law itself.* . . .

This brings us at last to the case system. For the truth of the matter is a truth so obvious and trite that it is somewhat regularly overlooked by students. *That no case can have a meaning by itself!* Standing alone it gives you no guidance. It can give you no guidance as to how far it carries, as to how much of its language will hold water later. What counts, what gives you leads, what gives you sureness, *that is the background of the other cases* in relation to which you must read the one. They color the language, the technical terms, used in the opinion. But above all they give you the wherewithal to find which of the facts are significant, and in what aspect they are significant, and how far the rules laid down are to be trusted. . . .

. . . [W]hat is precedent? In the large, disregarding for the moment peculiarities of our law and of legal doctrine — in the large, precedent consists in an official doing over again under similar circumstances substantially what has been done by him or his predecessor before. The foundation, then, of precedent is the official analogue of what, in society at large, we know as folkways, or as institutions, and of what, in the individual, we know as habit. And the things which make for precedent in this broad sense are the same which make for habit and for institutions. It takes time and effort to solve problems. Once you have solved one it seems foolish to reopen it. Indeed, you are likely to be quite impatient with the notion of reopening it. Both inertia and convenience speak for building further on what you have already built; for incorporating the decision once made, *the solution once worked out*, into your operating technique *without reexamination* of what *earlier went into* reaching your solution. . . .

At this point there enters into the picture an ethical element, the argument that courts (and other officials) not only do, but *should* continue what they have been doing. Here, again, the first analogue is in the folkway or the individual habit. I do not know why, nor do I know how, but I observe the fact that what one has been doing acquires in due course another flavor, another level of value than mere practice; a flavor on the level of policy, or ethics, or morality. What one has been doing becomes the "right" thing to do; not only the expected thing but the thing whose happening will be welcomed and whose failure to happen will be resented. This is true in individuals whose habits are interrupted; this is true in social intercourse when the expected event, when the expectation based upon the knowledge of other people's habits, materializes or fails to materialize. Indeed, in social matters in the large, there develops distinct group pressure to *force conformity* with the existing and expected social ways.

All of this, now, the lawyer brings to bear upon law itself. Here speaks the judicial conscience.

And apart from the unreasoned and unreasoning fact that oughtness attaches to practice, they are, particularly in the case of officials, and most particularly in the case of judges, reasons of policy to buttress this ethical element. To continue past practices is to provide a new official in his inexperience with the accumulated experience of his predecessors. If he is ignorant, he can learn from them and profit by the knowledge of those who have gone before him. If he is idle he can have their action brought to his attention and profit by their industry. If he is foolish he can profit by their wisdom. If he is biased or corrupt the existence of past practices to compare his action with gives a public check upon his biases and his corruption, limits the frame in which he can indulge them unchallenged. Finally, even though his predecessors may themselves, as they set up the practice, have been idle, ignorant, foolish and biased, yet the knowledge that he will continue what they have done gives a basis from which men may predict the action of the courts; a basis to which they can adjust their expectations and their affairs in advance. To know the law is helpful, even when the law is bad. Hence it is readily understandable that in our system there has grown up first the habit of following precedent, and then the legal norm that precedent is to be followed. The main form that this principle takes we have seen. It is essentially the canon that each case must be decided as one instance under a general rule. This much is common to almost all systems of law. The other canons are to be regarded rather as subsidiary canons that have been built to facilitate working with and reasoning from our past decisions.

But it will have occurred to you that despite all that I have said in favor of precedent, there are objections. It may be the ignorance or folly, or idleness, or bias of the predecessor which chains a new strong judge. It may be, too, that conditions have changed, and that the precedent, good when it was made, has since become outworn. The rule laid down the first time that a case came up may have been badly phrased, may have failed to foresee the types of dispute which later came to plague the court. Our society is changing, and law, if it is to fit society, must also change. Our society is stable, else it would not be a society, and law which is to fit it must stay fixed. Both truths are true at once. Perhaps some reconciliation lies along this line; that the stability is needed most greatly in large things, that the change is needed most in matters of detail. At any rate, it now becomes our task to inquire into how the system of precedent which we actually have works out in fact, accomplishing at once stability and change.

We turn first to what I may call the orthodox doctrine of precedent, with which, in its essence, you are already familiar. Every case lays down a rule, the rule of the case. The express *ratio decidendi* is prima facie the rule of the case, since it is the ground upon which the court chose to rest its decision. But a later court can reexamine the case and can invoke the canon that no judge has power to decide what is not before him, can, through examination of the facts or of the procedural issue, narrow the picture of what was actually before the court and can hold that the ruling made requires to be understood as thus restricted. In the extreme form this results in what is known as expressly "confining the case to its particular facts." This rule holds only of redheaded Walpoles in pale magenta Buick cars. And when you find this said of a past case you know that in effect it has been overruled. Only a convention, a somewhat absurd convention, prevents flat overruling in such instances. It seems to be felt as definitely improper to state that the court in a prior case was wrong, peculiarly so if that case was in the same court which is speaking now. It seems to be felt that this would undermine the dogma of the infallibility of courts. So lip service is done to that dogma, while the rule which the prior court laid down is disemboweled. The execution proceeds with due respect, with mandarin courtesy.

Now this orthodox view of the authority of precedent — which I shall call the *strict* view — is but *one of two views* which seem to me wholly contradictory to each other. It is in practice the dogma which is applied to *unwelcome* precedents. It is the recognized, legitimate, honorable technique for whittling precedents away, for making the lawyer, in his argument, and the court, in its decision, free of them. It is a surgeon's knife. . . .

[W]hen you turn to the actual operation of the courts, or, indeed, to the arguments of lawyers, you will find a totally different view of precedent at work beside this first one. That I shall call, to give it a name, the *loose view* of precedent. That is the view that a court has decided, and decided authoritatively, *any* points or all points on which it chose to rest a case, or on which to [choose], after due argument, to pass. No matter how broad the statement, no matter how unnecessary on the facts or the procedural issues, if that was the rule the court laid down, then that the court has held. Indeed, this view carries over often into dicta, and even into dicta which are grandly obiter. In its extreme form this results in thinking and arguing exclusively from *language* that is found in past opinions, and in citing and working with that language wholly without reference to the facts of the case which called the language forth.

Now it is obvious that this is a device not for cutting past opinions away from judges' feet, but for using them as a springboard when they are found convenient. This is a device for *capitalizing welcome precedents*. And both the lawyers and the judges use it so. And judged by the *practice* of the most respected courts, as of the courts of ordinary stature, this doctrine of precedent is like the other, recognized, legitimate, honorable.

What I wish to sink deep into your minds about the doctrine of precedent, therefore, is that it is two-headed. It is Janus-faced. That it is not one doctrine, nor one line of doctrine, but two, and two which, *applied at the same time to the same precedent, are contradictory of each other.* That there is one doctrine for getting rid of precedents deemed troublesome and one doctrine for making use of precedents that seem helpful. That these two doctrines exist side by side. That the same lawyer in the same brief, the same judge in the same opinion, may be using the one doctrine, the technically strict one, to cut down half the older cases that he deals with, and using the other doctrine, the loose one, for building with the other half. Until you realize this you do not see how it is possible for law to change and to develop, and yet to stand on the past. You do not see how it is possible to avoid the past mistakes of courts, and yet to make use of every happy insight for which a judge in writing may have found expression. Indeed it seems to me that here we may have part of the answer to the problem as to whether precedent is not as bad as good — supporting a weak judge with the labors of strong predecessors, but binding a strong judge by the errors of the weak. For look again at this matter of the *difficulty* of the doctrine. The strict view — that view that cuts the past away — is *hard* to use. An ignorant, an unskillful judge will find it hard to use: the past will bind him. But the skilful judge — he whom we would make free — is thus made free. He has the knife in hand; and he can free himself.

Nor, until you see this double aspect of the doctrine-in-action, do you appreciate how little, in detail, you can predict *out of the rules alone*; how much you must turn, for purposes of prediction, to the reactions of the judges to the facts and to the life around them. . . .

Applying this two-faced doctrine of precedent to your work in a case class you get, it seems to me, some such a result as this: You read each case from the angle of its *maximum* value as a precedent, at least from the angle of its maximum value as a precedent *of the first water*. You will recall that I recommended taking down the *ratio decidendi* in substantially the court's own words. You see now what I had in mind. Contrariwise, you will also read each case for its *minimum* value as a precedent, to set against the maximum. In doing this you have your eyes out for the narrow issue in the case, the narrower the better. The first question is, how much can this case fairly be made to stand for by a later court to whom the precedent is welcome? You may well add — though this will be slightly flawed authority — the *dicta* which appear to have been well considered. The second question is, how much is there in this case that cannot be got around, even by a later court that wishes to avoid it?

You have now the tools for arguing from that case as counsel on *either* side of a new case. You turn them to the problem of prediction. Which view will this same court, on a later case on slightly different facts, take: will it choose the narrow or the loose? Which use will be made of this case by one of the other courts whose opinions are before you? Here you will call to your aid the matter of attitude that I have been discussing. Here you will use all that you know of individual judges, or of the trends in specific courts, or, indeed, of the trend in the line of business, or in the situation, or in the times at large — in anything which you may expect to become apparent and important to the court in later cases. But always and always, you will bear in mind that each precedent has not one value, but two, and that the two are wide apart, and that whichever value a later court assigns to it, such assignment will be respectable, traditionally sound, dogmatically correct. Above all, as you turn this information to your own training you will, I hope, come to see that in most doubtful cases the precedents *must* speak ambiguously until the court has made up its mind whether each one of them is welcome or unwelcome. And that the job of persuasion which falls upon you will call, therefore, not only for providing a technical ladder to reach on authority the result that you contend for, but even more, if you are to have *your* use of the precedents made as *you* propose it, the job calls for you, on the facts, to persuade the court your case is sound.

People — and they are curiously many — who think that precedent produces or ever did produce a certainty that did not involve matters of judgment and of persuasion, or who think that what I have described involves improper equivocation by the courts or departure from the court-ways of some golden age — such people simply do not know our system of precedent in which they live.

§4.3.2.3　Judicial Role

COURTS, LEGISLATURES AND
PATERNALISM

DAVID SHAPIRO

74 Va. L. Rev. 519, 551-558 (1988)

[The] institutional differences between legislatures and courts . . . , I believe, are often more a matter of degree than of kind. It is possible for courts to do many of the things that legislatures do, and vice-versa. Yet there comes a point when the effort involves a considerable strain on the institution in question — when it is clear that one branch is doing something that is done far better, or with a good deal more legitimacy, by the other. Thus I am interested not only in Separation of Powers questions that raise constitutional issues, but in separation of powers questions that involve a wise allocation of functions. . . .

First, courts act on cases brought to them by litigants, and thus have a very limited control over their agenda. Appellate courts with discretionary review powers have somewhat more control over the issues on their dockets, but even they are limited to the cases brought before them in the order that litigants present them. And only a few litigants have sufficiently far-ranging institutional concerns to plan in any rational way the issues to submit for adjudication. Thus courts are counterpunchers, responding to the more or less random submissions of a vast array of litigants.

Legislatures, on the other hand, can control their agendas and set their priorities on a much broader scale. Tax reform may be scheduled before consideration of revenue increases, and both may be scheduled before considering proposals for increasing expenditures. A cut in farm price supports may be put forward in conjunction with alternative proposals for subsidies or assistance of other kinds. A highway improvement program may be accompanied by specific tax proposals for financing it.

Of course, no one is a completely free agent, and legislators are subject to myriad political and time pressures that play havoc with any rational agenda. The capacity is there, however, and at least at times legislatures have managed to fulfill the promise of rational planning. At other times, they have had the sense to turn over a problem to an administrative agency that is in a better position to plan as well as to administer.

Second, courts are limited in their ability to investigate issues on the periphery of those brought to them by the litigants, or even to explore the issues before them in any more detail than the parties wish to provide. Thus if the issue in a case is whether an applicant for a license or grant is constitutionally entitled to a hearing on that application, the court may find it difficult or impossible to obtain information on such issues as the costs of providing hearings, the extent to which the jurisdiction affords hearings in similar contexts as a matter of custom or law, or the experience of other jurisdictions. Nor could the court easily obtain the views of those most affected by the present practice and the proposed change.

These "legislative facts" are appropriately named; legislatures are better equipped to obtain them than are courts, both because of the scope of their investigative powers and because of the resources at their command. Confronted with a shortfall in the information they may want to have, courts are apt to speculate about what the information might reveal, or to conclude that the "rights" at stake do not turn on such earthly concerns.

Once again, these generalizations may not hold true in a particular case. A legislature may act on information that is far skimpier than it should be, although such action is unlikely when the matter is one of substantial controversy and the legislature is considering a course that runs counter to traditional values. A court may manage to be exceptionally well-informed through its own research or the diligence of law clerks, through evidence offered by the parties, or through the testimony of experts appointed by the judge. Yet the difference in capacities remains. . . .

Third, the remedies available to a court in resolving a dispute are limited both by prevailing doctrine and by the scope of judicial power. In a typical private dispute, such as a claim of trespass to land, a court can grant or deny damages, and grant or deny injunctive relief. The authority is of the on/off kind: either the defendant trespassed and must pay damages, or he did not and pays nothing; if, and only if, there is a threat of repeated trespass, he will be enjoined. More imaginative solutions — cooperative undertakings, the use of inducements in lieu of or in addition to sanctions, the restructuring of relationships — while not wholly beyond the court's capacity, and certainly not beyond the power of the parties to negotiate, are unlikely to be judicially imposed.

In a public dispute, the remedial powers of the courts remain limited, despite the dramatic expansion of these powers in recent decades. If the question is the adequacy (as a matter of constitutional, statutory, or common law) of the living conditions in a prison or other state institution, a court may order specific improvements, and may even set up an administrative regime to see that they are carried out. But it must ultimately depend on other branches for the necessary resources, and cannot establish a "permanent" agency to oversee the running of the institution indefinitely. Even the ability to monitor temporarily is limited by the number of such undertakings already in progress and by other demands of the calendar.

In addition to the limitations of time and resources, a judge is confronted by the significant constraints of doctrine and precedent. All judges — perhaps most particularly those who have managed to push the law in bold new directions — have been aware of and responsive to these constraints. That awareness is sharpened by the sobering effect of the nomination or election process (and in many jurisdictions of the reelection process) as well as by the continuing scrutiny of the world at large and of the legal community. A lower court judge who sees a new and promising approach must grapple with his own conscience — can he square the new approach with the rules and decisions that bind him? That battle won, the judge must face not only the criticism of the outside world but also the scrutiny of the appellate courts. And the innovative appellate judge must be able to persuade both his colleagues and (unless he sits at the top of the judicial system) his superiors on a still higher court....

Fourth, courts find it more difficult than do legislatures to experiment, to monitor the results, and to revise the experiment in the light of those results. When a court decides that as a matter of constitutional or statutory right someone is entitled to a hearing, it may in theory modify or overrule that decision if the result turns out to be a net loss — if the benefits of the added protection are plainly outweighed by the observable burdens to those who administer and to those who are affected by the program. But talk of rights — the language courts use to reach results — does not readily yield to this kind of oscillation. And judges understand that too quick a trigger finger will undermine public confidence in the judiciary. Overruling of recent, major precedents is still a rarity.

Even in a legislature, what is thought of as an experiment may soon turn into a tradition, with its own expectations and vested interests. Yet experimentation remains an integral part of the legislative process, and there is no built-in cause for embarrassment if a few years' experience with a particular way of doing things reveals that another way would be better. Indeed, legislatures often set up mechanisms to guarantee that a review will be required and to oversee the operation of the program in the meantime.

These points all seem to cut against judicial capacity and in favor of legislative authority. In fact, they reveal the institutional strengths of courts as well as their weaknesses, and tell us something about the broader implications of separation of powers concepts. Federal judges are not elected, and in the states, where election is more common, a variety of efforts have been made to reduce the susceptibility of judges to political pressures. Greater resistance to these pressures carries many benefits. It enhances the ability of judges to crack down on unlawful action by the other branches, and in more questionable situations, to foster dialogue within the government itself about what the lawful course is or should be. It also enhances their ability to protect the weak against abuse by the other branches — a judicial role whose importance is highlighted in our constitutional plan by the Bill of Rights and the fourteenth amendment. And it makes the judges perhaps the most reliable guardians of our fundamental values, especially against the short-term passions that particular crises can arouse.

Yet the fact that judges are protected in significant ways from the popular will does make it inappropriate for them to reach outcomes on the basis of their personal (and possibly idiosyncratic) values. Despite all the palaver that this is what judges really do, the truth is that they really do not. The institutional constraints I have already mentioned — combined with the requirement of reasoned decision and a moral obligation of candor — are checks that deter the imposition of judges' personal values and that confine the courts to "molecular motions." Massive doctrinal shifts are rare. When they do occur, they are usually a long time building, and if they touch sensitive moral nerves, are at least as long a time commanding the general acceptance needed to make them effective. . . .

The idea that judges should not simply decide on the basis of their personal values — that those values must be subordinated, or at least filtered through all the constraints surrounding the judicial function — has been expressed in a variety of ways (and of course, as variously criticized by the skeptics). Herbert Wechsler spoke of "neutral principles." Ronald Dworkin, in a more elaborate effort, argued that judicial actions should be based not on policy, but on principle — that they should be grounded in notions of individual or group rights rather than in the furtherance of some collective goal of the community. Harry Wellington, in a similarly elaborate and more satisfying effort, argued that judges stand on firmer ground when they act on the basis of principle (which he viewed as rooted in conventional morality) than on the basis of policy (which he defined as an instrumental justification for a rule). To justify a judicial rule on policy grounds, he urged, the policy should be "widely regarded as socially desirable" and should be "relatively neutral."

The problematic nature of all these efforts demonstrates to me not the futility of the task but rather its importance and difficulty. My own leaning toward Wellington's approach is influenced by its greater flexibility: Wellington recognizes that policy, as he defines it, is not out of bounds, but is simply a shakier basis than principle for a judge's action in view of the judge's distance from the people and his inability to consider a problem in all its aspects. But even Wellington, I think, failed to take sufficient account of the need for judges to fill vacuums that others have left — to deal with the inevitable gaps, conflicts, and ambiguities to which any system of law continually gives rise. When a dispute comes before a court, one side or the other will achieve its goals if the case is not compromised. Thus a refusal to adjudicate is in many ways as effective a decision for the defendant as is a judgment against the plaintiff on the merits, and judges may find themselves implementing policies even when they purport to rest a decision on a principle — especially when that principle is one of institutional restraint.

Judges are involved in a continual dialogue with the people and with the other branches. Laws enacted by legislatures must be understood and applied by courts in situations that the legislators never imagined. Common law doctrines are subject to continual legislative sallies of codification or outright rejection. Statutes are challenged under the Constitution. And constitutional decisions sometimes give rise to movements to amend the Constitution itself. But in this process judges are likely to fare better, to commit their resources and their prestige to what they do best, if they keep in mind both their relative remoteness from the popular will and the inherent limitations of an agency that acts only when disputes are brought before it.

CATCHER IN THE RYE
JURISPRUDENCE
JOSEPH WILLIAM SINGER
35 Rutgers L. Rev. 275, 275-280 (1983)

Judges make law. Yet many of them are afraid to admit it. They are afraid because they want their exercise of judicial power to appear uncontroversial. Lawmakers engage in politics, and politics is a nasty, controversial business. Judges therefore invent arguments to convince themselves and others that they do not exercise law-making power. They have had several hundred years of experience doing this, and they do it quite well. . . .

I would define judicial activism as the willingness to change legal rules in a way that alters the existing distribution of social, economic, or political power. In public law, judges determine both the distribution of powers between governmental entities and the legal relation between governmental powers and individual liberties. Activism in public law is the willingness to interfere in political life in a way that contravenes the apparent will of the legislature or executive. In private law, where judges determine the legal relations among individuals, activism is the willingness to change the current legal rules in ways that disturb existing patterns of economic and social advantage. Activism has no inherent political direction to the right or to the left.

By contrast, passivist judges seek to enforce the existing legal rules governing relations among individuals or to defer to the will of one of the other branches of government. The passivist position assumes that there is almost always an established rule, precedent, statute, regulation, principle, or doctrine which cleanly and definitively answers the legal question before the judge. The judge can therefore decide the case without having to make new law. Like activism, passivism has no inherent political direction. The existing legal rules may further either a left or a right wing political program.

The problem of the judicial role makes the argument for passivism seem quite attractive. Unelected judges fear being seen as tyrants if they change the legal rules in a way that appears to usurp the lawmaking function of those officials. This fear motivates them to deny the activist elements of their decisions. . . .

Despite its attraction, passivism gives only the illusion of solving the problem of the judicial role. This is because a *consistent* passivist position would not only be impossible but, as I shall explain below, would constitute a radical departure from conventionally accepted principles of both public and private law. . . .

Consider a situation in which the plaintiff claims that the defendant invaded her legal rights, and the defendant claims that she was legally entitled to act as she did. The judge must decide whether the defendant behaved within the bounds of her legal right, or whether the law imposes upon her a duty to the plaintiff either to refrain from the action or to provide redress for damages. For a variety of reasons, passivism cannot solve the problem of the judicial role in situations like this.

Despite the undemocratic origin of their power, judges have no choice but to exercise power when they decide cases. Legal decisions are choices between alternative rules, and as Holmes remarked, "[w]hatever decisions are made must be against the wishes and opinion of one party...." If the judge rules that the defendant had a legal liberty to do the act, the plaintiff will be unhappy. If the judge rules that the plaintiff had a right which restricts the freedom of action of others, the defendant will be unhappy. Thus the question is not whether the judge should exercise power or not exercise power, but in whose interest the power should be exercised.

The intelligent passivist will concede this point and simply argue that judges should enforce the existing rules: they should, as the saying goes, "apply" the law rather than "make" it. Yet the existing legal rules, whether derived from common law or statutory interpretation, were made by other judges in the past. As Jeremy Bentham wrote, "whatever *now* is established, *once* was innovation." Deferring to the will of previous judges is no more democratic than changing the rules which they promulgated. There may be other good reasons to follow precedent — e.g., because of an interest in stability or because the precedent is wise or fair — but the fact that judicial power is undemocratic cannot be one of them.

When judges decide cases, whether or not they enforce existing rules, they place the coercive force of the state at the disposal of one of the parties against the other. Although there may be good reasons for applying existing rules, there is nothing passive about enforcing them. The notion that judges do not exercise lawmaking power in these situations is simply false. Judges take sides in controversies, and by articulating a rule or principle to justify their position, they contribute to the law of the land, whether the decision upholds or challenges the status quo.

The passivist position not only hides the reality of judicial lawmaking, but contradicts one of the underlying principles of the common law as it has been practiced for hundreds of years. As every law student knows, two opposite and contradictory principles operate in the common law system. The first is that judges should follow precedent: it is the legislature's job to change the law. This is obviously consistent with the passivist position. The second principle of the common law, however, is that law protects rights: if any of the existing legal rules are unfair or bad policy, they should be overturned. According to this view, judges need not wait for legislative action to modernize judge-made law. This is the activist position, and it is as much a part of the common law tradition as passivism.

The institution of the common law is constituted by the theory that precedent should be followed only if it adequately protects legitimate rights. An absolute passivist position would mean that the decisions of prior judges must be enforced forever, until changed by the legislature, no matter how stupid or cruel they are. No jurist or judge in the history of American law has *ever* taken this position.

No one has been able to invent a non-contradictory theory which could tell us precisely when judges should follow precedent and when they should overturn it in the interest of fairness or progress. In the end, judges are vulnerable to charges of tyranny whatever they do. If they overturn precedent, they can be accused of overstepping their institutional bounds by usurping legislative power. Yet the legitimacy of our legal system would be severely undermined if individual judges did not have the courage to overturn archaic precedents which have become oppressive. If judges do not overturn precedents which have come to be seen as oppressive, they can be accused of a different sort of tyranny. Moreover, such actions are so crucial to the legitimacy of the legal system that they have been institutionalized as a central component of common law adjudication. Activist judges recognize that the second charge is as serious as the first.

I have argued that both judicial activism and passivism in private law can leave judges vulnerable to the accusation that they have abused their power. But the problem is even worse than this. Consistent passivism would not only contradict fundamental tenets of the private law system, but would be virtually impossible to carry out in practice.

The argument for passivism severely underestimates the extent to which the legal rules in force contain gaps, conflicts, and ambiguities. In these cases, the judge has no choice but to promulgate some rule or standard to justify the result. In other words, the judge has to make law....

§4.4 Nuisance

§4.4.1 PROTECTION OF USE AND ENJOYMENT OF LAND

A nuisance is a substantial and unreasonable interference with the use or enjoyment of land. *Schneider Natl. Carriers, Inc. v. Bates,* 147 S.W.3d 264, 269 (Tex. 2004); *San Diego Gas & Electric Co. v. Superior Court,* 920 P.2d 669, 696 (Cal. 1996); *Hanes v. Continental Grain Co.,* 2001 WL 118532 at *1 (Mo. Ct. App. 2001); *Bargmann v. Soll Oil Co.,* 574 N.W.2d 478, 486 (Neb. 1998). We have seen that special rules may apply to govern support rights and water rights. Nuisance law is used when no such special rules have been created by courts or legislatures. It is a flexible doctrine that has been applied in a variety of circumstances.

Typical nuisance cases involve activities that are "offensive, physically, to the senses and [which] by such offensiveness makes life uncomfortable [such as] noise, odor, smoke, dust, or even flies." *In re Chicago Flood Litigation,* 680 N.E.2d 265, 278 (Ill. 1997). Nuisances have been found in the case of vibration or blasting that damages a house, the emission of pollutants, such as smoke, dust, gas or chemicals, offensive odors, and noise. *See, e.g., Howard Opera House Ass'n v. Urban Outfitters, Inc.,* 322 F.3d 125 (2d Cir. 2003) (applying Vt. law) (loud music in retail store that violates local noise ordinance constitutes nuisance against neighboring tenants); *Shutes v. Platte Chemical Co.,* 564 So. 2d 1382 (Miss. 1990) (toxic waste spilled at chemical factory seeps through the ground, killing vegetation on nearby parcels of land and depreciating the value of the property constitutes a nuisance); *Padilla v. Lawrence,* 685 P.2d 964 (N.M. Ct. App. 1984) (homeowners recover from manure processing plant for damage to property interests resulting from odors, dust, noise, and flies); *Bradley v. American Smelting & Refining Co.,* 709 P.2d 782 (Wash. 1985) (homeowner entitled to bring a claim for nuisance against copper smelting factory that emitted microscopic airborne particles of heavy metals in the manufacturing process).

Nuisance must be distinguished from *trespass.* "[T]respass is any intentional invasion of the plaintiff's interest in the exclusive possession of his property, whereas nuisance is a substantial and unreasonable interference with the plaintiff's use and enjoyment of his property." *Silvester v. Spring Valley Country Club,* 543 S.E.2d 563, 567 (S.C. Ct. App. 2001). Trespass law concerns physical invasions of land. The interest being protected is the plaintiff's possessory interest in the land, and, at least in theory, this interest is granted absolute protection. Nuisance concerns use of one's own land that interferes with a neighbor's use and enjoyment of his property. The interest being protected is the right not to exclusive possession but to quiet enjoyment of the land; protection of this interest is not absolute because the harm must be substantial and the interference deemed unreasonable before a nuisance will be found.

Some harms that were traditionally not counted as trespasses clearly involve the physical invasion of land. For example, air pollution involves the physical invasion of land by smoke particles but has traditionally been characterized as a nuisance rather than a trespass. Some courts have tried to distinguish trespass from nuisance by arguing that a trespass must be "direct," such as a bullet fired across land, and that smoke particles carried by the wind constitute an "indirect" invasion and therefore do not qualify as an intentional invasion. Other courts have sometimes held that trespass requires invasion by physical objects that are larger than microscopic particles.

The trend is to recognize invasion by particles as both a trespass and a nuisance and to allow the plaintiff to proceed on both theories. *Stevenson v. E.F. Dupont de Nemours,* 327 F.3d 400 (5th Cr. 2003) (applying Texas law); *Gill v. LDI,* 19 F. Supp. 2d 1188 (W.D. Wash. 1998); *Hoery v. United States,* 64 P.3d 214 (Colo. 2003); *State of New York v. Fermenta ASC Corp.,* 630 N.Y.S.2d 884 (N.Y. Sup. Ct. 1995). For example, in *Bradley, supra,* the court allowed plaintiffs to proceed on both trespass and nuisance claims against a factory emitting arsenic and cadmium that fell on plaintiffs' land. However, the court in *Bradley* made two significant changes in trespass law as it applied to microscopic particles. It held, first, that a trespass could occur only if the particles fell to the ground and stayed there rather than dissipating through the air. Second, the court held that liability for trespass could be found only if plaintiffs could prove substantial damage. The court justified this change by arguing that a "reconciliation must be found between the interest of the many who are unaffected by the possible poisoning and the few who may be affected." 709 P.2d at 785. It further explained that "[n]o useful purpose would be served by sanctioning actions in trespass by every landowner within a hundred miles of a manufacturing plant. Manufacturers would be harassed and the litigious few would cause the escalation of costs to the detriment of the many." *Id.* at 791. *Accord, Public Service Co. of Colo. v. Van Wyck,* 27 P.3d 377, 390 (Colo. 2001) ("in Colorado, an intangible intrusion may give rise to claim for trespass, but only if an aggrieved party is able to prove physical damage to the property caused by such intangible intrusion"). Some other courts, however, resist this trend, holding that physical invasion by dust, noise, and vibration does not constitute a trespass, although it may well be a nuisance. *See, e.g., Adams v. Cleveland-Cliffs Iron Co.,* 602 N.W.2d 215 (Mich. Ct. App. 1999).

Nuisance must also be distinguished from *negligence.* Negligence law prohibits and provides remedies for unreasonable *conduct;* this implies a judgment that a reasonable person would have foreseen the harm and prevented it. Nuisance focuses on the *result* of the conduct rather than the conduct itself; the question is not whether the defendant's conduct was unreasonable but whether the *interference* is unreasonable. Such interference is unreasonable under nuisance law if it involves substantial harm that an owner should not have to bear for the good of society. Thus, conduct that is not negligent (such as conduct that the defendant could not reasonably have foreseen would harm her neighbor) may constitute a nuisance (because the conduct in fact results in harm to the neighbors' property interests that is not justified by the social utility of the conduct causing it).

Many courts distinguish between *temporary* and *permanent* nuisances. A permanent nuisance either irreparably injures the plaintiff's property or is of such a character that it is likely to continue indefinitely; in such a case, and the statute of limitations for bringing a claim begins at the time the nuisance begins. In contrast, a temporary nuisance can be alleviated by changes in the defendant's conduct and the claim "accrues anew up on each injury," or occurs intermittently, *Schneider, supra,* at 270, 272.

Some courts impose *strict liability* on landowners if they engage in "ultrahazardous activities" that cause harm to neighboring land. In such cases, nontrespassory conduct may result in liability without a need to prove either negligence or the unreasonableness and substantial harm requirements of nuisance doctrine. Some recent cases have imposed strict liability on land owners who have stored toxic waste on their property. *See, e.g., T & E Indus. v. Safety Light Corp.,* 587 A.2d 1249 (N.J. 1991); *State v. Ventron Corp.,* 468 A.2d 150 (N.J. 1983).

Although most nuisance cases involve physical harm to land or discomfort or danger to persons, the doctrine is broad enough to encompass any conduct that causes unreasonable and substantial harm to the use and enjoyment of land. Thus, in recent years, nuisance claims have been brought against owners who have allowed their property to be overrun by drug dealers, thereby interfering with the interests of landowners in the neighborhood. *Lew v. Superior Court,* 25 Cal. Rptr. 2d 42 (Ct. App. 1993). And in several cases, home owners have been enjoined from lavish displays of lights and loud Christmas music that drew an enormous influx of visitors to a residential neighborhood. *See, e.g., Osborne v. Power,* 908 S.W.2d 340 (Ark. 1995); *Rodrigue v. Copeland,* 475 So. 2d 1071 (La. 1985).

§4.4.2 RADIATION: DEFINING UNREASONABLE LAND USE

PAGE COUNTY APPLIANCE
CENTER, INC. v. HONEYWELL, INC.
347 N.W.2d 171 (Iowa 1984)

W. W. REYNOLDSON, Chief Justice.

Plaintiff Page County Appliance Center, Inc. (Appliance Center), sued Honeywell, Inc. (Honeywell), and ITT Electronic Travel Services, Inc. (ITT), for nuisance and tortious interference with business relations. Defendants appeal from judgment entered on jury verdicts awarding compensatory and punitive damages. Honeywell appeals from a judgment rendered against it on ITT's cross-claim for indemnification. We reverse and remand for new trial.

Appliance Center has owned and operated an appliance store in Shenandoah, Iowa, since 1953. . . . Before 1980, [the owner, John Pearson,] had no reception trouble with his display televisions. In early January 1980, how-ever, ITT placed one of its computers with Central Travel Service in Shenandoah as part of a nationwide plan to lease computers to retail travel agents. Central Travel was separated by only one other business from the Appliance Center. This ITT computer was manufactured, installed, and maintained by Honeywell.

Thereafter many of Pearson's customers told him his display television pictures were bad; on two of the three channels available in Shenandoah he had a difficult time "getting a picture that was fit to watch." After unsuccessfully attempting several remedial measures, in late January 1980, he finally traced the interference to the operations of Central Travel's computer. Both defendants concede Pearson's problems were caused by radiation leaking from the Honeywell computer. . . .

[After Pearson complained to Kay Crowell, owner of Central Travel,] Honeywell technicians made repeated trips to make various unsuccessful adjustments to the computer. They found the computer was operating properly; the interference-causing radiation was a design and not a service problem. . . .

The Honeywell engineers effected a 70 percent improvement in the television reception by certain modifications of the computer in the fall of 1980. Pearson, still dissatisfied, started this action in December. While the suit was pending, Honeywell further modified the computer, finally alleviating Pearson's problems in May 1982.

At trial a Honeywell senior staff engineer admitted the technology to manufacture a non-radiation-emitting computer was available long before it developed this computer, but opined it would have been neither cost nor consumer effective to utilize that technology. He testified Honeywell believed it had corrected Pearson's problems in the fall of 1980.

The Appliance Center's case against Honeywell and ITT finally was submitted to the jury on the theories of nuisance and tortious interference with prospective business relations. It asked for only injunctive relief against Kay Crowell, doing business as Central Travel Service. The latter's motion for summary judgment was sustained. The jury found for the Appliance Center against the remaining defendants on both theories, and further found the Appliance Center should recover $71,000 in compensatory damages and $150,000 in exemplary damages. . . . Trial court awarded ITT full indemnity against Honeywell, in the amount of $221,000, together with attorney fees and costs. Both defendants appeal from the judgment in favor of Appliance Center; Honeywell additionally appeals from the judgment awarding ITT indemnity. . . .

Our analysis of ITT's first contention must start with Iowa Code section 657.1, which in relevant part states:

> Whatever is . . . an obstruction to the free use of property, so as essentially to interfere with the . . . enjoyment of . . . property, is a nuisance, and a civil action by ordinary proceedings may be brought to enjoin and abate the same and to recover damages sustained on account thereof.

Narrowing our focus, we note the Appliance Center is alleging a "private nuisance," that is, an actionable interference with a person's interest in the private use and enjoyment of his or her property. It also is apparent that if Central Travel's computer emissions constitute a nuisance it is a "nuisance *per accidens*, or in fact"—a lawful activity conducted in such a manner as to be a nuisance.

Principles governing our consideration of nuisance claims are well established. One's use of property should not unreasonably interfere with or disturb a neighbor's comfortable and reasonable use and enjoyment of his or her estate. A fair test of whether the operation of a lawful trade or industry constitutes a nuisance is the reasonableness of conducting it in the manner, at the place, and under the circumstances shown by the evidence. Each case turns on its own facts and ordinarily the ultimate issue is one of fact, not law. The existence of a nuisance is not affected by the intention of its creator not to injure anyone. Priority of occupation and location—"who was there first"—is a circumstance of considerable weight.

When the alleged nuisance is claimed to be offensive to the person, courts apply the standard of "normal persons in a particular locality" to measure the existence of a nuisance. This normalcy standard also is applied where the use of property is claimed to be affected. "The plaintiff cannot, by devoting his own land to an unusually sensitive use, . . . make a nuisance out of conduct of the adjoining defendant which would otherwise be harmless." W. Prosser, *The Law of Torts* §87, at 579 (4th ed. 1971).

In the case before us, ITT asserts the Appliance Center's display televisions constituted a hypersensitive use of its premises as a matter of law, and equates this situation to cases involving light thrown on outdoor theater screens in which light-throwing defendants have carried the day. . . .

We cannot equate the rare outdoor theater screen with the ubiquitous television that exists, in various numbers, in almost every home. Clearly, the presence of televisions on any premises is not such an abnormal condition that we can say, as a matter of law, that the owner has engaged in a peculiarly sensitive use of the property. This consideration, as well as related considerations of unreasonableness, gravity of harm, utility of conduct, and priority of occupation, are factual determinations that should have been submitted to the jury in this case. We find no trial court error in refusing to direct a verdict on this ground.

ITT's second contention asserts trial court should have directed a verdict in its favor because it did not participate in the creation or maintenance of the alleged nuisance. We have noted ITT was engaged in a multimillion dollar, national program to lease computers to travel agencies. It owned this computer and leased it to Central Travel. It was to ITT that the agency first turned when the effect of the computer radiation became apparent. ITT continued to collect its lease payments; the computer did not operate for the benefit of Crowell alone. The jury could have found ITT evidenced some measure of its responsibility, as owner of the computer, in contacting Honeywell and making belated inquiries regarding Appliance Center's problems both to Pearson and Crowell. . . .

An action for damages for nuisance need not be predicated on negligence. Nuisance ordinarily is considered as a condition, and not as an act or failure to act on the part of the responsible party. A person responsible for a harmful condition found to be a nuisance may be liable even though that person has used the highest possible degree of care to prevent or minimize the effect.

Where there is reasonable doubt whether one of several persons is substantially participating in carrying on an activity, the question is for the trier of fact. We hold such reasonable doubt existed on the record made in this case, and trial court did not err in refusing to direct a verdict on this ground. . . .

. . . Honeywell asserts trial court should have granted its motion for directed verdict because, even though it manufactured the computer, Central Travel and ITT were in control of the instrument at all relevant times; thus Honeywell did not have the legal right to terminate its use. Honeywell devotes ten and one-half pages of its brief to this thesis without mentioning that it had an ongoing contract to service and maintain the computer.

Much of what we have written [above] applies here. Again, the issue is one of material participation. Honeywell's design permitted radiation to escape this computer, although technology was available to minimize this effect. Apparently factors of cost and ease of service access weighed more in the design decision. Honeywell was the only party with the technological know-how to control the radiation leakage. Its maintenance contract with ITT clearly absolved it of any liability if anyone else made any alterations or additions to the equipment, and reserved the right to terminate the agreement should that occur. As with ITT, we think Honeywell's material participation was an issue for the finder of fact. . . .

Trial court's instructions required Appliance Center to prove defendants "unreasonably" interfered with the Center's use and enjoyment of its property. Honeywell and ITT objected, in essence, that this permitted the jury to judge "unreasonableness" in a vacuum; that the instructions made no attempt to define the unreasonableness concept. Because reasonableness under our nuisance decisions ordinarily is a question for the jury, the court on retrial should provide more guidance for the jury.

In *Bates v. Quality Ready Mix Co.*, 154 N.W.2d 852, 857 (Iowa 1968), we noted that reasonableness is a function of the manner in which, and the place where, defendant's business is conducted, and the circumstances under which defendant operates. Additional factors . . . include priority of location, character of the neighborhood, and the nature of the alleged wrong. The "character and gravity of the resulting injury" is, in fact, "a major factor in determining reasonableness," *Montgomery v. Bremer County Board of Supervisors*, 299 N.W.2d 687, 697 (Iowa 1980). Balanced against the gravity of the wrong is the utility and meritoriousness of the defendant's conduct. . . .

Another instruction given in this case stated that "[o]ne who contributes to the creation or continuance of a nuisance may be liable." ITT objected that neither this instruction nor any other informed the jury that a defendant's conduct must be a "substantial factor" in bringing about the alleged harm. Upon retrial the instructions should incorporate this requirement. . . .

Both Honeywell and ITT objected because the court did not submit to the jury the issue whether Appliance Center was devoting its premises to an unusually sensitive use. The discussion in division I is relevant here. We hold defendants were entitled to have this question resolved by the jury.

We reverse and remand with instructions to set aside the judgment in favor of Appliance Center against Honeywell and ITT, and the judgment entered on ITT's cross-claim against Honeywell. Defendants shall be granted a new trial in conformance with this opinion.

NOTES AND QUESTIONS

1. *Unreasonable harm to the use and enjoyment of land.* How do the courts determine when an interference with the use and enjoyment of land is unreasonable? First, they must determine what *interests* are encompassed by the right to the "use and enjoyment of land." Those interests include freedom from pollution, noise, odors, and smoke. Second, how serious must the interference be for a nuisance to be present? Traditionally, the court required the harm to be *substantial* before it would be legally protected. Third, if defendant has substantially interfered in one's use and enjoyment of land, how do we determine whether that harm is *unreasonable*?

In answering this last question, one possibility is to focus on *rights* or *fairness*. One might conclude that the harm is a nuisance because the type or amount of harm is one that owners should not have to bear for the good of society, at least in the absence of compensation. A second possibility is to focus on *social utility* or *welfare* analysis, comparing the costs and benefits of providing a remedy. Under this approach, the court would find a nuisance when the gravity of the harm outweighs the social utility of the harmful conduct. *Rights* analysis focuses on the parties themselves, asking whether the plaintiff's right to security should prevail over the defendant's right to freedom of action. *Social welfare* analysis focuses on society as a whole, asking whether society in general is better off if the activity goes forward despite the harm.

2. *Rights considerations in nuisance law.* Nuisance law poses conflicts between the defendant's interest in free use of her land and the plaintiff's interest in being secure

from harm. In some cases, an activity will be deemed a nuisance because the defendant's conduct is disfavored. For example, many states will grant injunctions against so-called *spite fences* constructed for the sole purpose of blocking their neighbors' light and air. When such fences serve no purpose other than the builders' desire to hurt their neighbors, some states will grant an injunction ordering the fence torn down. *See Wilson v. Handley*, 119 Cal. Rptr.2d 263 (Cal. Ct. App. 2002) (applying Cal. Civ. Code §841.4); *DeCecco v. Beach*, 381 A.2d 543 (Conn. 1977) (*applying* Conn. Gen. Stat. §52-570). *But see Maioriello v. Arlotta*, 73 A.2d 374 (Pa. 1950) (refusing to enjoin a spite fence). In other cases, an activity will be deemed to be a nuisance because the type of harm involved is one that owners should not have to bear, at least without compensation. Some activities may be so disfavored that they will be held to constitute nuisances no matter where they take place—so-called nuisances *per se*. An example would be criminal activity such as property routinely used for illegal drug manufacture or sale. Other activities may constitute nuisances because they are "a right thing in a wrong place,—like a pig in the parlor instead of the barnyard."[5] An activity that is not customary to the area is likely to be deemed unreasonable. William B. Stoebuck & Dale A. Whitman, *The Law of Property* §7.2, at 415 (3d ed. 2000).

Some activities will be deemed not to be nuisances because regulating them will go too far in limiting freedom of action of property owners or because regulation will cause unfair surprise. For example, even serious harms may be privileged if the plaintiff is "*unusually sensitive*" and the court concludes that it would be wrong to regulate the defendant's generally inoffensive activity or impose damages for the plaintiff's harm. *Jenkins v. CSX Transportation, Inc.*, 906 S.W.2d 460 (Tenn. Ct. App. 1995) (no remedy for plaintiff who had an extremely rare allergy to fumes from railroad ties near his land).

In other cases, a harm will be deemed not to be a nuisance because the harmful activity was established first. When the plaintiff *comes to the nuisance*, one can argue that she created the problem herself. An owner who builds a house next to a pig farm should not be surprised at the resulting odors. For this reason, in all states, it will be harder for a plaintiff to prevail in a nuisance case if she came to the nuisance. At the same time, coming to the nuisance is not an absolute defense; it may be wrong to continue operating a polluting activity once it becomes surrounded by numerous other homes and businesses. Some statutes do make it an absolute defense in certain cases that the plaintiff came to the nuisance. Many states have passed *right to farm* statutes that protect farmers from liability for nuisance if their farms were established before surrounding residential property was constructed. However, one court has struck down one such law on the ground that it unconstitutionally took away the right to sue for nuisance. *Bormann v. Board of Supervisors in and for Kossuth County*, 584 N.W.2d 309 (Iowa 1998).

When owners come to the nuisance, the courts may enjoin the offending activity on condition that those who came to the nuisance compensate the prior developer for the costs associated with shutting down and/or relocating. In *Spur Industries v. Webb*, 494 P.2d 700 (Ariz. 1972), for example, a developer built a residential community near a cattle ranch. Ordinarily, it would be possible to convince a court that the smells generated by a cattle ranch constitute a substantial and unreasonable interference in the use and enjoyment of residential property. However, because the homeowners "came to the nuisance," they had a much harder time convincing the court that

---

5. *Village of Euclid v. Ambler Realty Co.*, 272 U.S. 365, 388(1962).

the cattle feedlot should be shut down than they would have had if the residential community had been established first. This is probably why the court in *Spur* granted the plaintiffs an injunction only on the condition that they compensate the defendant for the costs that relocation would impose on him.

3. *Social welfare considerations in nuisance law.* Nuisance law requires the decision maker to compare the costs and benefits of allowing versus prohibiting the activity. The *Restatement (Second) of Torts* §826(a) defines land use as "unreasonable" when the "gravity of the harm outweighs the utility of the actor's conduct." In evaluating the gravity of the harm, the courts are to look at (a) the *extent* and (b) *character* of the harm involved; (c) the "social value that the law attaches to the type of use or enjoyment invaded; (d) the suitability of the particular use or enjoyment invaded to the character of the locality; and (e) the burden on the person harmed of avoiding the harm." *Id.* §827. In evaluating the utility of the conduct, the courts are to analyze "(a) the social value that the law attaches to the primary purpose of the conduct; (b) the suitability of the conduct to the character of the locality; and (c) the impracticability of preventing or avoiding the invasion." *Id.* §828.

In evaluating these factors, the courts consider both fairness and welfare. On the fairness side, the courts will consider:

(1)   *The character of the harm.* Aesthetic harms will be viewed as less serious than health or safety concerns.

(2)   *Distributive considerations.* Is it fair to make an individual owner bear the costs of defendant's socially beneficial activity or should those costs be spread around to the owner causing the damage and its employees and customers?

(3)   *Fault.* Is one of the owners engaged in a disfavored activity? Is the conduct appropriate for the area? Did the plaintiff come to the nuisance?

On the welfare side, courts will consider:

(1)   *Costs and benefits.* The costs and benefits of allowing the harmful conduct must be compared with the costs and benefits of prohibiting it.

(2)   *Incentives.* What effects will liability or immunity have on incentives to engage in the respective activities? How will the distribution of the burdens and benefits of conflicting land uses affect incentives to invest in safety or to engage in desirable economic activities?

(3)   *Lowest cost avoider.* Which party can more cheaply avoid the cost? Should this party also bear the burden of paying that cost?

4. *Remedies.* There are two separate questions in all nuisance cases. The first question focuses on determining which party has the basic entitlement. Does the plaintiff have a right to be secure from this kind of harm, or does the defendant have the right to engage in the activity? The second question has to do with the remedy used to vindicate the entitlement. There are three basic kinds of remedies in the nuisance context: property rules, liability rules, and inalienability rules. Guido Calabresi and A. Douglas Melamed, *Property Rules, Liability Rules, and Inalienability: One View of the Cathedral*, 85 Harv. L. Rev. 1089 (1972).

Entitlements

Remedies	Plaintiff's entitlement	Defendant's entitlement
Property rule	π can get an injunction ordering Δ to stop the harmful conduct; if Δ wants to commit the harm, Δ must offer π enough money to induce π to agree to give up π's right to be free from harm *(injunction)*	Δ has legal liberty to commit the harm without liability; if π wants to prevent the harm, π must offer Δ enough money to induce Δ to agree to stop the harmful conduct *(dismiss the complaint)*
Liability rule	π can get damages from Δ for committing the harm, but no injunction; Δ is free to commit the harm if Δ is willing to pay a damage judgment *(damages)*	π can stop Δ's conduct if π is willing to pay damages as determined by a court to compensate Δ for Δ's loss of profits *(purchased injunction)*
Inalienability rule	Δ has no right to commit the harm; any agreement by π to allow Δ to commit the harm is unenforceable	Δ has the right to engage in the protected activity; any agreement whereby Δ gives up the right to engage in the conduct is unenforceable

Property rules fix an absolute entitlement either to engage in the conduct (*no liability*) or to be secure from the harm (*injunctive relief ordering defendant to stop committing the harm*). In either case, the parties can bargain to give up their rights to commit or be free from the harm. The price of the entitlement would therefore be fixed by private bargaining rather than by a court order.

Liability rules, in contrast, prohibit each party from interfering with the interests of the other unless the party is willing to pay damages determined by a court of law. If the plaintiff is entitled to be protected from the harm, then defendant's failure to prevent the harm subjects the defendant to *damages.* Conversely, if defendant is free to engage in the harmful activity, the plaintiffs will not be entitled to an injunction stopping that activity unless they compensate the defendant for the economic losses associated with stopping the activity; this later remedy is called a *purchased* or *conditional injunction.* Plaintiffs will be granted an injunction only if they pay damages to compensate defendant for its losses.[6]

Inalienability rules assign entitlements and prohibit those entitlements from being sold or exchanged. For example, an environmental statute might require mining companies that purchase mineral rights under someone else's land to excavate in a way

---

6. The usual version is the *option* where plaintiffs have the power to shut down the offending activity by obtaining an injunction if they choose to pay damages. They have the option to force a sale of the entitlement from the defendant to them. An alternative version is the *put* whereby defendant can force the plaintiffs to purchase the injunction whether or not they wish to do so. *See, e.g.,* Ian Ayres, *Protecting Property with Puts,* 32 Val. U. L. Rev. 793 (1988).

that leaves sufficient support for the surface so that the land and any structures on it are protected from loss of subjacent support. The statute may further provide that it supersedes any private agreements to the contrary. The effect is to make the right to be free from the harm inalienable. This might be justified because of the significant negative externalities of destroying a scarce resource. *See, e.g., Keystone Bituminous Coal Association v. DeBenedictis,* 480 U.S. 470 (1987).

5. *Nuisance in the courts.* Courts are often unclear about the standards for obtaining an injunction versus damages in nuisance cases. The definition of a nuisance is that the conduct is both unreasonable (causes more harm than good) and causes substantial harm. If conduct is both unreasonable and highly invasive, one would think it should be enjoined because it not only decreases social utility but violates the plaintiff's right to security. Yet in *Boomer v. Atlantic Cement Co.,* 257 N.E.2d 870 (N.Y. 1970), despite the court's finding that a cement factory constituted a nuisance when it spewed black smoke and ash on a residential neighborhood, the court failed to enjoin the nuisance; rather, it simply granted plaintiffs the right to receive damages. Although the pollution was deemed a nuisance, the court refused to grant an injunction shutting down the factory because the factory's benefits to society outweighed its costs. But if that was the case, why did the court order damages? If the activity caused more good than harm, why was it unreasonable? It was reasonable on the social level but unreasonable as between the parties. In other words, allowing the activity maximized social utility (because the total benefits of the activity outweighed its costs), but the activity violated the plaintiff's right to security; the harm was greater than any individual should be forced to bear for the good of society. Requiring damages but not awarding an injunction, therefore, was a determination that the activity was efficient — it increased social utility to allow it to go forward because its overall benefits outweighed its costs — but that the costs of the activity are unfairly distributed — the plaintiff's property interests were being unfairly sacrificed for the greater good. Damages may serve to recompense the wrong being perpetrated on the plaintiff while allowing the more socially valuable use to continue.

After the *Boomer* decision, this interpretation was adopted by the American Law Institute in a revision of the *Restatement (Second) of Torts.* Section 826(a) of the *Restatement (Second)* retains the traditional balancing test for nuisance that requires a comparison between the gravity of the harm and the utility of the conduct. Section 826(b) of the *Restatement (Second)* supplements the balancing test with one that provides for damages, if not injunctive relief, when "the harm caused by the conduct is serious and the financial burden of compensating for this and similar harm to others would not make the continuation of the conduct not feasible."

The following outline describes current nuisance law in the courts.

a. π may obtain an *injunction* against Δ's conduct when:
    Δ's conduct is unreasonable (causes more social harm than good) and causes substantial harm to π

b. π may obtain *damages* but no injunction if:
    Δ's conduct is reasonable (it causes more social good than harm and therefore should be allowed to go forward), *but* the harm to π is substantial so that it is unfair to burden Δ with the costs of Δ's socially useful conduct

c. π is entitled to *no remedy* if:

    (1)   the harm to π is not substantial; or

    (2)   Δ's conduct causes more social good than harm, and it is not unfair to impose the costs of Δ's activity on or

    (3)   the imposition of damages would put Δ out of business and avoiding this result (because of the social value of Δ's conduct) is more important than preventing the harm to π

   d.   π is entitled to a *purchased injunction* if:

       Δ's conduct causes more harm than good; *but* it is fair to impose the cost of shutting down π's activity on (for example, when comes to the nuisance)

    6. Who can be sued. Can a manufacturer of a hazardous substance be sued for damages for nuisance when it leaks through the ground and causes harm to neighboring land? *Page County* adopts the general rule that imposes liability on any actor who "materially participated" in causing the harm. *See also Parks Hiway Enterprises, LLC v. CEM Leasing, Inc.*, 995 P.2d 657, 667 (Alaska 2000) (question is whether defendant's conduct was a "substantial factor" in causing the harm). What factors led the court to determine that the evidence showed that Honeywell contributed to the harm? Would Honeywell have been liable if its only participation was the design and sale of the computer? *Compare Hall v. Phillips*, 436 N.W.2d 139 (Neb. 1989) (manufacturer and distributor of herbicide liable for nuisance); *State of New York v. Fermenta ASC Corp.*, 630 N.Y.S.2d 884 (N.Y. Sup. Ct. 1995) (holding the manufacturer and distributor of an herbicide liable for trespass when it broke down in the soil after usage by customers and a chemical by-product leached through the soil and invaded the public water supply) *with Parks Hiway Enterprises, supra* (gas producer not liable for nuisance merely because it produced the gas that bled into neighboring land).

    7. Public nuisances. A public nuisance is "an unreasonable interference with a right common to the general public." *Restatement (Second) of Torts* §821B(1) (1977). The traditional example is obstruction of public highways. As it originated in England, the public nuisance doctrine covered a host of minor criminal offenses. It was extended to allow common law actions involving such claims as

> interference with the public health, as in the case of keeping diseased animals or the maintenance of a pond breeding malarial mosquitoes; with the public safety, as in the case of the storage of explosives in the midst of a city or the shooting of fireworks in the public streets; with the public morals, as in the case of houses of prostitution or indecent exhibitions; with the public peace, as by loud and disturbing noises; with the public comfort, as in the case of widely disseminated bad odors, dust and smoke; with the public convenience, as by the obstruction of a public highway or a navigable stream.

Id. §821B. Traditionally, public nuisances could be enjoined only by public officials. Private landowners could obtain a remedy against a public nuisance only if they suffered some special damage different from that generally suffered by the public as a whole. The *Restatement (Second) of Torts*, however, provides that any member of the public affected by the activity should be able to bring a lawsuit, and this seems to represent the trend in the law. *Restatement (Second) of Torts* §821c (1979). Statutes may authorize individuals to bring claims to abate public nuisances. *See Kellner v. Capelini*, 516 N.Y.S.2d 827 (Civ. Ct. 1986) (applying an ordinance giving citizens the right to sue to shut down a public nuisance and granting an injunction ordering a landlord to evict tenants who used the property for illegal crack cocaine sales).

Recent years have seen an explosion of public nuisance litigation. It has been used to challenge liquor stores that sell liquor to minors, theaters, or stores showing or selling pornographic materials, and motels that are used for prostitution. *See, e.g., City of Miami v. Keshbro, Inc.*, 717 So. 2d 601 (Fla. Dist. Ct. App. 1998) (motel closed for prostitution and drug use); *Bosarge v. State ex rel. Price*, 666 So. 2d 485 (Miss. 1995) (club closed for selling liquor to minors); *State ex rel. Bowers v. Elida Road Video & Books, Inc.*, 696 N.E.2d 668 (Ohio Ct. App. 1997) (adult bookstore closed because of sexual activity).

8. *Statutory and administrative regulation of land use.* Although nuisance litigation retains significance, in recent years it has been eclipsed to a substantial extent by federal and state environmental protection legislation. Federal legislation includes the *Clean Air Act*, 42 U.S.C. §§7401-7642, the *Clean Water Act*, 33 U.S.C. §§1251-1376, the *Comprehensive Environmental Response, Compensation, and Liability Act* (the "Superfund Act," or CERCLA), 42 U.S.C. §§6901-9657, and the *Superfund Amendments and Reauthorization Act of 1986* (SARA), Pub. L. No. 99-499, 100 Stat. 1613 (1986). State environmental regulation may place more stringent limits on environmental pollution. In addition, local zoning law may regulate and separate incompatible neighboring land uses.

Environmental protection statutes ordinarily establish administrative agencies with powers to issue regulations having the force of law. Those agencies generally have enforcement powers, such as the power to impose fines on persons who violate the regulations or to obtain injunctive relief in court to compel compliance.

PROBLEMS

1. *Drug dealing.* A half-vacant apartment building is used by drug dealers and drug users. Some of the dealers are tenants in the building who sell crack cocaine in their apartments, while other dealers have entered the building without the owner's permission, using vacant apartments to conduct their business. The illegal activities have attracted a large number of drug buyers and users into the neighborhood, disrupting a formerly quiet neighborhood of brownstone homes and turning the area into a drug market. The landlord is a real estate company engaged in the business of renting housing. The landlord in no way encouraged or participated in the illegal activities, but it has failed to do anything to remedy the problem. Twenty neighbors bring a lawsuit against the landlord claiming the landlord's use of its property constitutes a nuisance. They ask for damages and for an injunction ordering the landlord to stop the illegal activity.

In *Lew v. Superior Court*, 25 Cal. Rptr. 2d 42 (Ct. App. 1994), the court enforced a state statute providing that landlords could be held liable for nuisance when the landlords' apartment complex had become a hub of drug activity and landlords did not act reasonably in dealing with the problem. The defendant argued that such liability for the criminal acts of third parties should not be imposed on the landlord in the absence of a state statute. Commentators have disagreed about the fairness of imposing such obligations on landlords. Compare David C. Anderson, *How to Rescue a Crack House*, N.Y. Times, Feb. 8, 1993, at A16 with Gideon Kanner, *California Makes Landlords Do the Police's Job*, Wall St. J., Jan. 27, 1993, at A19. *See City of Seattle v. McCoy*, 4 P.3d 159, 168 (Wash. Ct. App. 2000) (an innocent owner who does not cause and could not have reasonably prevented illegal drug use on the premises has not caused a nuisance).

Accord, Restatement (Second) of Torts §838 (1977) ("A possessor of land upon which a third party carries on an activity that causes a nuisance is subject to liability for the nuisance if . . . (a) the possessor knows or has reason to know [of the activity] and (b) he consents to the activity or fails to exercise reasonable care to prevent the nuisance").

    a.   What arguments could you make on behalf of the plaintiffs for both damages and injunctive relief?

    b.   What arguments could you make on behalf of the defendant landlord that it is not responsible for criminal actions committed by its tenants and that it is certainly not responsible for the actions of trespassers and therefore is not liable for either damages or injunctive relief to abate the nuisance?

    c.   What should the court do?

    2. *Proximity to toxic dump.* In *DeSario v. Industrial Excess Land Fill Inc.*, No. 89-570 (Ohio Ct. Common Pleas, 1994), a jury awarded the owners of noncontaminated property within two miles of a toxic waste dump $6.7 million in damages for the loss of their property value caused by the "stigma" of being near the dump. 17 Nat'l L.J. A13 (Jan. 16, 1995). *Accord, Scheg v. Agway, Inc.*, 645 N.Y.S.2d 687 (App. Div. 1996). Most courts deny such claims even if the loss of market value of the land is substantial. For example, in *Adams v. Star Enterprise*, 51 F.3d 417 (4th Cir. 1995), the court refused to allow owners of property adjacent to land contaminated by a leak at an oil distribution facility to recover damages for mere fear of future health effects or for diminution in the value of their property absent a showing of detectable, physical encroachment on their property. Which case was correctly decided?

    3. *Gun dealing.* A number of municipalities have brought claims against gun dealers claiming that the sale of guns constitutes a public nuisance. Most of these claims have been dismissed on the ground that the harm is caused by criminal use of the guns not the manufacture or sale of the guns themselves. *City of Chicago v. Beretta U.S.A. Corp.*, 821 N.E.2d 1099 (Ill. 2004); *Young v. Bryco Arms*, 821 N.E.2d 1078 (Ill. 2004). *Accord, District of Columbia v. Beretta, U.S.A., Corp.*, 872 A.2d 633 (D.C. 2005). However, several courts have allowed claims against gun manufacturers and/or dealers to proceed based on claims that they have designed guns specifically for criminal use, marketed those guns to criminals, or distributed them in a manner designed to facilitate their flow into the illegal market to persons not legally entitled to purchase them. *Ileto v. Glock, Inc.*, 349 F.3d 1191 (9th Cir. 2003) (applying Cal. law); *James v. Arms Technology, Inc.*, 820 A.2d 27 (N.J. Super. Ct. App. Div. 2003); *City of Gary v. Smith & Wesson Corp.*, 801 N.E.2d 1222 (Ind. 2003); *City of Cincinnati v. Beretta U.S.A. Corp.*, 768 N.E.2d 1136 (Ohio 2002). For example, the Supreme Court of Illinois reversed a lower court ruling that found that gun dealers outside the City of Chicago might have caused a public nuisance by selling handguns to residents of Chicago when Chicago city ordinances make it illegal to possess such weapons. *City of Chicago v. Beretta USA Corp., supra.* Do you agree with the lower court ruling allowing the claim to be made or the Supreme Court ruling protecting the gun dealers from suit?

    4. *Damage by encroaching trees.* In *Lane v. W.J. Curry & Sons*, 92 S.W.3d 355, 357 (Tenn. 2002), the encroaching branches of a tree extended over the plaintiff's house, shading it and preventing rainwater on it from evaporating, eventually rotting the roof. In addition, a branch fell off the tree and punched a hole in plaintiff's roof. Because owners are entitled to use self-help to cut encroaching branches, some courts deny any remedy to such a plaintiff on the ground that she could have avoided the damage by

cutting the branch. *Melnick v. CSX Corp.*, 540 A.2d 1133 (Md. 1988). In *Lane*, however, the plaintiff argued that she could not cut the branches herself and could not afford to hire someone to do so. The Tennessee Supreme Court held that, although trees and bushes are ordinarily not nuisances, they can become so if they cause damage or an imminent danger of danger to neighboring property. Should it matter whether the owner planted the tree or it grew naturally? *See Restatement (Second) of Torts* §839 (owner liable if the tree is artificial but not if it is natural). Which approach is better?

§4.4.3   LIGHT AND AIR

§4.4.3.1   Rejection of Nuisance Doctrine: No Easement for Light and Air

FONTAINEBLEAU HOTEL CORP. v.
FORTY-FIVE TWENTY-FIVE, INC.

114 So. 2d 357 (Fla. Dist. Ct. App. 1959)

PER CURIAM.

This is an interlocutory appeal from an order temporarily enjoining the appellants from continuing with the construction of a fourteen-story addition to the Fontaine-bleau Hotel, owned and operated by the appellants. Appellee, plaintiff below, owns the Eden Roc Hotel, which was constructed in 1955, about a year after the Fontainebleau, and adjoins the Fontainebleau on the north. Both are luxury hotels, facing the Atlantic Ocean. The proposed addition to the Fontainebleau is being constructed twenty feet from its north property line, 130 feet from the mean high water mark of the Atlantic Ocean, and 76 feet 8 inches from the ocean bulkhead line. The 14-story tower will extend 160 feet above grade in height and is 416 feet long from east to west. During the winter months, from around two o'clock in the afternoon for the remainder of the day, the shadow of the addition will extend over the cabana, swimming pool, and sunbathing areas of the Eden Roc, which are located in the southern portion of its property.

In this action, plaintiff-appellee sought to enjoin the defendants-appellants from proceeding with the construction of the addition to the Fontainebleau (it appears to have been roughly eight stories high at the time suit was filed), alleging that the construction would interfere with the light and air on the beach in front of the Eden Roc and cast a shadow of such size as to render the beach wholly unfitted for the use and enjoyment of its guests, to the irreparable injury of the plaintiff; further, that the construction of such addition on the north side of defendants' property, rather than the south side, was actuated by malice and ill will on the part of the defendants' president toward the plaintiff's president; and that the construction was in violation of a building ordinance requiring a 100-foot setback from the ocean. It was also alleged that the construction would interfere with the easements of light and air enjoyed by plaintiff and its predecessors in title for more than twenty years and "impliedly granted by virtue of the acts of the plaintiff's predecessors in title, as well as under the common law and the express recognition of such rights by virtue of Chapter 9837, Laws of Florida 1923. . . . " Some attempt was also made to allege an easement by implication in favor of the plaintiff's property, as the dominant, and against the defendants' property, as the servient, tenement.

The defendants' answer denied the material allegations of the complaint, pleaded laches and estoppel by judgment.

The chancellor heard considerable testimony on the issues made by the complaint and the answer and, as noted, entered a temporary injunction restraining the defendants from continuing with the construction of the addition. His reason for so doing was stated by him, in a memorandum opinion, as follows:

> [N]o one has a right to use his property to the injury of another. In this case it is clear from the evidence that the proposed use by the Fontainebleau will materially damage the Eden Roc. There is evidence indicating that the construction of the proposed annex by the Fontainebleau is malicious or deliberate for the purpose of injuring the Eden Roc, but it is scarcely sufficient, standing alone, to afford a basis for equitable relief.

This is indeed a novel application of the maxim *sic utere tuo ut alienum non laedas*. This maxim does not mean that one must never use his own property in such a way as to do any injury to his neighbor. It means only that one must use his property so as not to injure the lawful *rights* of another. In *Reaver v. Martin Theatres*, 52 So. 2d 682, 683 (Fla. 1951), under this maxim, it was stated that "it is well settled that a property owner may put his own property to any reasonable and lawful use, so long as he does not thereby deprive the adjoining landowner of any right of enjoyment of his property *which is recognized and protected by law, and so long as his use is not such a one as the law will pronounce a nuisance.*" [Emphasis supplied.]

No American decision has been cited, and independent research has revealed none, in which it has been held that — in the absence of some contractual or statutory obligation — a landowner has a legal right to the free flow of light and air across the adjoining land of his neighbor. Even at common law, the landowner had no legal right, in the absence of an easement or uninterrupted use and enjoyment for a period of 20 years, to unobstructed light and air from the adjoining land. And the English doctrine of "ancient lights" has been unanimously repudiated in this country.

There being, then, no legal right to the free flow of light and air from the adjoining land, it is universally held that where a structure serves a useful and beneficial purpose, it does not give rise to a cause of action, either for damages or for an injunction under the maxim *sic utere tuo ut alienum non laedas*, even though it causes injury to another by cutting off the light and air and interfering with the view that would otherwise be available over adjoining land in its natural state, regardless of the fact that the structure may have been erected partly for spite. . . .

We see no reason for departing from this universal rule. If, as contended on behalf of plaintiff, public policy demands that a landowner in the Miami Beach area refrain from constructing buildings on his premises that will cast a shadow on the adjoining premises, an amendment of its comprehensive planning and zoning ordinance, applicable to the public as a whole, is the means by which such purpose should be achieved. . . . But to change the universal rule — and the custom followed in this state since its inception — that adjoining landowners have an equal right under the law to build to the line of their respective tracts and to such a height as is desired by them (in the absence, of course, of building restrictions or regulations) amounts, in our opinion, to judicial legislation. . . .

Since it affirmatively appears that the plaintiff has not established a cause of action against the defendants by reason of the structure here in question, the order granting a temporary injunction should be and it is hereby reversed with directions to dismiss the complaint. . . .

Law and Economics

Economics analysis of law. "Law and economics" is a school of thought among legal academics and some judges that applies economic analysis to the study of law. Some scholars engage in *descriptive* analysis, explaining the existing pattern of legal doctrine as a set of rules that promote efficiency. Other scholars engage in *prescriptive* or *normative* analysis, using the criterion of economic efficiency to help determine what the legal rules should be. *See, e.g.,* Robert Cooter and Thomas Ulen, *Law and Economics* (1988); *Economic Foundations of Property Law* (Bruce Ackerman ed. 1975); Mitchell Polinsky, *An Introduction to Law and Economics* (1983); Richard Posner, *Economic Analysis of Law* (5th ed. 1998); Guido Calabresi and A. Douglas Melamed, *Property Rules, Liability Rules, and Inalienability: One View of the Cathedral,* 85 Harv. L. Rev. 1089 (1972).

Economic analysis of law is nothing more than fancy cost-benefit analysis. Economists have invented a particular way to measure costs and benefits — *market value* — that in turn is determined by how much individuals are willing and able to pay for entitlements. Given the scarcity of resources, economists assume that the value people place on an entitlement can be determined by asking either what they would pay to obtain it or how much they would have to be paid to release it. Economists thus assume that parties may engage in market transactions to buy and sell property rights or entitlements. These transactions occur when the owner of an entitlement is willing to sell it at a price that a buyer is willing and able to offer. Voluntary transactions are said to increase social wealth because both parties feel better off after the transaction than before; the seller valued the money offered more than the entitlement given up and the buyer valued the entitlement more than the money used to purchase it.

Economic analysis of law involves cost-benefit analysis of legal rules. The question is whether a change from one legal rule (the baseline) to another will increase or decrease social wealth. Market transactions give economists a way to measure costs and benefits. Transactions include three elements: (1) an initial distribution of property rights, (2) an offer price by a nonowner, and (3) an asking price by an owner. To define costs and benefits by reference to market transactions, it is essential to start with some distribution of entitlements. After all, people can exchange only what they own; it is therefore necessary to determine the initial distribution of wealth and the initial allocation of the entitlement in question.

We can apply economic analysis, for example, to the famous case of *Boomer v. Atlantic Cement,* 257 N.E.2d 870 (N.Y. 1970). In *Boomer* the neighbors complained that a cement factory near Albany, New York, was billowing black smoke and depositing soot on a nearby residential community. Plaintiff homeowners claimed that operation of the factory constituted a nuisance. To answer this question using economic analysis, we must assume both a particular distribution of wealth between the factory owner and the homeowners and an initial allocation of the entitlement in question. That entitlement is the right to pollute versus the right to be free from pollution. We can assume either that the company initially has the right to pollute or that the homeowners initially have the right to be free from pollution. If we assume that the factory owner has the right to pollute, we then compare the amount of money the neighbors would be willing and able to pay the factory owner to induce it to stop polluting with the amount of money the factory owner would ask before it agreed to shut down. If the homeowners' offer price exceeds the factory owner's asking price, then all parties will be better off in their own terms if the transaction takes places and the factory shuts down. This analysis measures the costs of the harmful activity by reference to the homeowners' *offer price*—the amount they are willing and able to pay to stop the harmful activity. It measures the benefits of the harmful activity by reference to the factory owner's *asking price*—the amount it would need to be offered before it would agree to give up the right to engage in the harmful activity.

If we assume that the homeowners initially have a right to be free from pollution, we ask what amount of money the factory owner would be willing and able to pay the homeowners to induce them to agree to allow the factory to continue to pollute—the factory owner's offer price. We compare that amount with the homeowners' asking price—the amount they would demand to give up their right to be free from pollution. This way of measuring costs and benefits differs from the earlier analysis. Costs are measured by the homeowners' asking price, and benefits are measured by the factory owner's offer price.

Definitions of efficiency. Economic analysis of law seeks to identify the more *efficient* rule of law among several alternatives. Just as economic analysis is simply a fancy way to do cost-benefit analysis, efficiency is one way to view the goal of increasing social utility or promoting the general welfare by satisfying human wants at the lowest possible cost. Several different definitions of efficiency have been used by lawyers and economists.

1. *Pareto superiority.* A change from one situation to another is *Pareto superior* if someone gains by the change and no one is injured or made worse off by it. Changes in allocations of entitlements most likely to be Pareto superior are voluntary exchanges. Both parties feel better off after the change than before; otherwise, they would have not agreed to the exchange. If no third parties are affected adversely by the exchange, it is Pareto superior.

2. *Pareto optimality.* A situation is *Pareto optimal* if no further exchanges can be made that are Pareto superior, that is, no other changes in allocation of resources can be made without harming others or making them worse off than before. Neither Pareto superiority nor Pareto optimality is used much in economic analysis of law, however, since almost all exchanges or changes in rules or allocations of entitlements make some people better off and others worse off. For this reason, most lawyers engaged in economic analysis of law use a third criterion—wealth maximization.

3. *Wealth maximization (or Kaldor-Hicks criterion, or potential Pareto superiority).* A change in allocation of resources or a change from one legal rule to another is *wealth maximizing* if the benefits of the change outweigh the costs. Another way to say this is that the winners from the change could fully compensate the losers and still be better off than before. This criterion does not in fact require the losers to be compensated. Thus, the change is said to be efficient even though some people may be significantly worse off after the change than before; the losses to the individuals who are worse off are less than the gains to those who are better off. This criterion is sometimes called "potential Pareto superiority" because the winners from the change *could* compensate the losers; if they did (assuming monetary compensation is fully adequate compensation for what the losers lost), the change would be Pareto superior since the winners would be better off (even though they have had to compensate the losers) and the losers would be no worse off (because their losses have been compensated).

The wealth maximization criterion is the one most often used in the economic analysis of law. The goal is to choose legal rules that increase efficiency in the sense that the benefits to society as a whole from the new rules are greater than the costs of moving to those new rules. This criterion does not require that the losers actually be compensated. A change may be efficient in the sense of being wealth maximizing even if a substantial number of people are much worse off after the change than before.

Traditional Externalities Analysis: Cost Internalization. Traditional analysis of efficiency in nuisance cases starts from the notion of *externalities*. Externalities are costs imposed on third parties by legal actors that are not taken into account in the actor's own revenue-cost determinations. For example, the factory owner in *Boomer* harms neighboring homeowners by causing pollution. This harm is a cost of the factory's economic activity; it is a loss that must be borne by society as a consequence of operation of the factory. Yet, unless the law intervenes, the factory will not have to take account of this cost in determining whether its operations are profitable.

The goal of efficiency analysis is to increase social wealth by choosing legal rules that give economic actors incentives to engage in activities whose benefits to society outweigh their costs to society. If the factory does not have to account for the harm its operation causes, its *private* cost-benefit calculation will not match the *social* cost-benefit calculation. If the harm the factory causes is substantial, it is possible that the social costs of operating the factory (losses to all individuals harmed by the factory) are greater than the social benefits (gains to all individuals benefited by operation of the factory). In this case, the efficient or wealth-maximizing result would be either to shut down the factory because it causes more harm than good or to install a cost-effective pollution control device (cost-effective in the sense that the costs of preventing the harm are outweighed by the benefits). Yet the factory's own profit calculations may be positive; its private costs may be less than the revenues it pulls in. So the factory may continue operating, without any pollution control devices, thereby decreasing social wealth. The efficient result (causing the factory to shut down or installing pollution controls) can be obtained by forcing the factory to pay for the external harms that its operation causes. This legal remedy would require the factory to *internalize its external costs.* By requiring the company to account to society for the harm it causes, the factory's private cost-benefit calculations will be made congruent with the social cost-benefit calculation; its decisions about the level and manner of operation will therefore promote social welfare.

Requiring the factory to pay for the harm it causes may help achieve the efficient result even if the costs and benefits of the different alternatives are uncertain. If the factory can pay damages to the homeowners and still operate profitably, and if the factory then chooses to remain in the same business (rather than moving into another business where it can make more money), then there is good evidence that the operation of the factory is efficient. The good it causes (measured by its profits) is greater than the harm it causes (measured by the damages it pays). If, however, the factory can afford neither to pay the damages to the homeowners nor to install the pollution control device and still remain in business, then its operations cause more harm than good; it is therefore inefficient and it *should* close down.[8]

---

8. Note that this argument ignores the possibility of *positive externalities* generated by the operation of the factory and the fact that transaction costs may prevent third parties benefited by operation of the factory from contracting with those harmed by it to induce them to agree to continued operation of the factory.

Justice Brennan used this analysis in *Armstrong*, arguing that *those who profit from an activity should bear its costs.* Justice Brennan noted that it is important to determine whether the "utility of the possessor's use of his land outweighs the gravity of the harm" the possessor causes. He argued that the "economic costs" incident to land development should be borne by "those who engage in such projects for profit" rather than by the adjoining landowners. This reasoning encompasses both a rights argument and a social utility argument. The rights argument is that those who benefit from an activity should not impose costs on others; property should be used so as not to harm unfairly the legitimate security interests of the neighbors (the *sic utere* doctrine). The social utility or efficiency argument is that economic actors should internalize their external costs to promote efficiency.

The Coase Theorem. The argument that property owners should internalize their external costs was criticized by Ronald Coase in a famous article, *The Problem of Social Cost,* 3 J.L. & Econ. 1 (1960).

1. *Joint costs.* Coase argued that, from an economic standpoint, it makes no sense to argue that the factory should internalize the costs it imposes on homeowners. Although pollution caused by operation of the factory obviously harms homeowners, their demand that the factory stop polluting interferes with the factory owner's ability to use its property as it sees fit. Granting the factory a right of freedom of action will impose external costs on the homeowners, but giving the homeowners the right to an unpolluted neighborhood will impose external costs on the factory (by requiring the factory either to shut down, to move to another location, or to install safety devices). To avoid the harm on the homeowners would inflict harm on the factory owner; to avoid the harm on the factory owner would inflict harm on the homeowners. The costs are reciprocal.

The problem arises because two conflicting activities are located near each other. If the factory were not located near the houses, there would be no problem. Thus, it is just as sensible to say that the cost of avoiding pollution is a cost of homeowning inflicted on the factory as it is to say that the cost of bearing the effects of pollution is the cost of factory operation inflicted on the homeowners. A better way to understand the situation is to consider the problem as involving *joint costs* that each activity imposes on the other. The problem is to avoid the more serious harm.

It is inappropriate to assume that efficiency will be achieved by requiring the factory to pay for the damage it causes. It could easily be said that the homeowners should internalize the external costs of homeowning by compensating the factory for the losses associated with moving or installing pollution control devices to accommodate the needs of the homeowners. Each activity imposes costs on the other, and preventing the costs of each activity will have the effect of imposing costs on the other activity.

2. *Subsequent bargains.* In addition to understanding nuisance cases as involving joint costs of conflicting activities, Coase argued that it was crucial to remember that the parties are free to bargain around any allocation of entitlements made by the courts. Even if the court rules that the factory operation is a nuisance and that the homeowners have the right to an injunction ordering the factory to stop operating (assuming no pollution control devices are economically feasible), the factory will not necessarily shut down. Rather, the factory may attempt to persuade the homeowners to give up their entitlement to shut down the factory by offering them a money payment (sometimes referred to as a "bribe") to induce them to sell their property right to prevent the

nuisance. In that case, the factory will have purchased from the homeowners the entitlement to commit a nuisance. If, however, the court rules that the factory operation is not a nuisance, the homeowners may attempt to bribe the factory owner to induce it not to exercise its right to operate the factory. The possibility that the parties will bargain around whatever allocation of entitlements is made by the courts is a crucial element of economic analysis of law because it means that the parties may bargain to achieve the efficient result notwithstanding the legal rule chosen by the court.

3. *No transaction costs.* The possibility that the parties will bargain around any allocation of entitlements by the court arises only when no significant impediments to bargaining are present. If the costs of transacting are zero, then the choice of legal rules or the allocation of the entitlement in question will arguably have no effect on allocative efficiency. Whoever values the entitlement more will either keep it — if they already own it — or will buy it from the other party. This is part I of the Coase Theorem: *If there are no transaction costs, it does not matter which legal rule is chosen because any legal rule will produce an efficient result.*

Take the case of *Fontainebleau Hotel Corp. v. Forty-Five Twenty-Five, Inc.* The legal issue is whether the Fontainebleau Hotel has a legal liberty to build an addition onto its hotel that would cast a shadow over the swimming pool of the Eden Roc. Either the Fontainebleau has an entitlement to build freely, without liability to its neighbor, or the Eden Roc has an entitlement to be free from wrongful interference with its light and air. Assume the Fontainebleau Hotel anticipates that its profits will rise if it builds the addition both because it can accommodate more people and because it will increase the demand for rooms at the Fontainebleau by decreasing the number of people willing to take rooms at the Eden Roc. This anticipated rise in profits translates into a $10 million increase in the market value of the Fontainebleau's property. At the same time, if the addition is built, the Eden Roc will suffer a decrease of $6 million in the market value of its property. Assuming that no third parties are affected by this decision (an unrealistic but simplifying assumption), social wealth will be increased by allowing the addition to be built. It will cause $10 million of benefit and only $6 million of harm, making society better off overall by $4 million.

If the transaction costs are zero, the Fontainebleau will go ahead and build the addition. If the court holds that the addition is a nuisance and that the Eden Roc has the right to an injunction stopping the addition, the parties will bargain around this result, since the Fontainebleau stands to gain $10 million if the addition is built while the Eden Roc will lose only $6 million. If the Fontainebleau offers the Eden Roc any amount over $6 million, it will be better off accepting the money and selling to the Fontainebleau the right to build without liability than insisting on preventing the addition from being built. A $6 million payment will fully compensate the Eden Roc for the losses associated with the addition; in theory, there should be no difference between not having the addition built and having the addition built with a $6 million payment. Any money offered over $6 million will leave the Eden Roc better off than before.

At the same time, so long as the Fontainebleau makes a payment under $10 million, it will be better off building the addition while paying a bribe to the Eden Roc to induce it to give up its nuisance claim than not going ahead with the project. The costs of paying off the Eden Roc will be less than the benefits of constructing the addition. Thus, in the absence of transaction costs, the parties will agree for some sum between $6 million and $10 million to allow the project to go forward.

If the court holds that the addition is not a nuisance, the project will similarly go forward. In this case, the Eden Roc would be willing to offer the Fontainebleau up to $6 million to prevent the building of the addition. Any amount over $6 million would be irrational; the Eden Roc would be worse off than if it paid nothing. It would make no sense to pay $7 million to avoid a $6 million harm. At the same time, the Fontainebleau would not accept any payment under $10 million to give up its right to build. Any payment under $10 million would leave it worse off than if it built the project.

Efficiency is achieved by giving the entitlement to the party who values it most, with value measured by willingness and ability to pay. Coase argued that, in the absence of transaction costs, it does not matter whether the court finds the construction of the addition to be a nuisance. Whoever values the entitlement more will either keep it (if the court assigns it to them) or buy it (if the court assigns it to the other party). In our hypothetical, the Fontainebleau values the entitlement to build more than the Eden Roc values the entitlement to be free from interference with its light and air. Thus, in the absence of transaction costs, the Fontainebleau will either bribe the Eden Roc to give up its right to stop the project or the Fontainebleau will keep its initial entitlement to build.

4. *Distributive issues.* It is important to note that even though the choice of legal rule has no effect on efficiency in the absence of transaction costs, it has an enormous effect on the *distribution of wealth* between the parties. If the court holds that interference with light and air is a nuisance and that the Eden Roc is entitled to an injunction stopping the project, then the Fontainebleau will have to purchase from the Eden Roc the right to build for some sum between $6 million and $10 million. In this case, both parties will be better off than before; they will share in the increased wealth created by the project. The distribution of the increased wealth between them will depend on their relative bargaining power or bargaining skills. If, however, the court holds that interference with light and air can never constitute a nuisance and that the Fontainebleau is free to build the project without liability, the Eden Roc will be worse off than before (by $6 million) while the Fontainebleau will be much better off (by $10 million).

Even though, from an efficiency standpoint, we may be indifferent to the choice of legal rules, we may prefer one entitlement over the other from the standpoint of *distributive justice.* The Eden Roc, for example, might argue that finding the project to be a nuisance is the fairest result because it does not sacrifice the property interests of the Eden Roc for the greater good of the community. The Fontainebleau might argue, in contrast, that the opposite result is fair because it rewards economic actors according to merit; those who triumph in the competitive struggle have the right to reap the full rewards of their risky activity, while those who lose deserve to lose because they contribute less to the common weal.

This example has assumed that the only possible outcomes of the lawsuit are an injunction against the defendant Fontainebleau or a ruling that the plaintiff has no remedy. Of course, two other solutions are possible: damages assessed against the Fontainebleau and a purchased injunction by which the Eden Roc compensates the Fontainebleau for giving up its right to build. It is important to note that efficiency analysis tells us whether the activity should go forward *but tells us nothing whatsoever about who should pay for this outcome.* In our example, we have assumed that the project is wealth maximizing because it creates benefits of $10 million and costs of only $6 million; we therefore conclude that the project is efficient and should go forward despite the losses it will inflict on the Eden Roc.[9] But efficiency analysis tells us nothing about who should bear the $6 million cost of obtaining this $10 million benefit. The court could choose to impose the cost either on the plaintiff Eden Roc, by denying the plaintiff any remedy, or on the Fontainebleau, by requiring it to pay damages of $6 million to the Eden Roc. Allowing the plaintiff to receive damages, but not an injunction, will achieve the efficient result because the project will go forward (the cost of the damages are less than the expected profits); at the same time, such a result will achieve the distributive goal of placing the burden on the party that profits from the activity.

Similarly, if the numbers were reversed, and the project were inefficient, the court could choose who should bear the economic costs of forgoing the project. Assume the benefits to the Fontainebleau are $6 million and the costs to the Eden Roc are $10 million. In this case, the losses outweigh the benefits and the project will decrease, rather than increase, social wealth; it should therefore be enjoined. Granting the plaintiff an injunction stopping the project will achieve the efficient result. Again, efficiency analysis tells us nothing about who should pay the costs associated with the injunction. The court could choose to impose the burden on the Fontainebleau by granting the plaintiffs a simple injunction, thereby denying the Fontainebleau the opportunity to make $6 million; this loss is called an *opportunity cost*. Or, the court could impose the cost on the plaintiff by granting the Eden Roc a purchased injunction, conditioning the injunction on the Eden Roc's compensating the Fontainebleau for the $6 million loss the injunction imposes on it. Only an analysis of distributive justice can tell us who should bear the cost.

5. *Transaction costs.* The argument that the choice of legal rules has no effect on allocative efficiency depends on the assumption that there are no transaction costs. This assumption is clearly false. If there are transaction costs, the legal rule chosen by the court may affect the outcome. If the court chooses the wealth-maximizing result, all well and good; but if the court chooses the inefficient result, transaction costs may be so high as to prevent the parties from correcting the mistake by a subsequent bargain. If transaction costs are present, courts may increase efficiency by assigning the entitlement to the party who would purchase it in the absence of transaction costs.

Suppose an agreement between the Fontainebleau and the Eden Roc costs $5 million to reach. This sum includes the cost of conducting the negotiations, hiring attorneys, getting financing to buy off the other party, and bringing into the talks third parties who might be benefited or harmed by construction of the project. The court's choice of entitlement will either increase social wealth or decrease it; it will have an effect on efficiency. If the court grants the Fontainebleau the right to build by holding that the project is not a nuisance, the Fontainebleau will go ahead and build, thereby achieving the efficient result. If, however, the court rules the project a nuisance, thereby assigning the entitlement to the Eden Roc, the project will not go forward: The Eden Roc will not accept less than $6 million to give up its rights to stop the project, and the cost of arranging such a deal is $5 million. The total cost of buying the right to build is therefore $6 million plus $5 million, or $11 million. But the Fontainebleau stands to gain only $10 million by building the addition. It will not pay $11 million to get a $10 million gain; it would be better off not building. This result is inefficient since the benefits to society of the project are greater than the costs. This, then, is part II of the Coase Theorem: *In the presence of transaction costs, the choice of entitlements by the courts may have an effect on*

---

9. The example assumes that the Fontainebleau cannot avoid the harm by relocating its construction project.

efficiency. The courts may increase efficiency by assigning entitlements to the parties who would purchase them in the absence of transaction costs.

6. *Kinds of transaction costs.* For our purposes, two kinds of transaction costs are important: *bargaining costs* and *information costs.*[10] Bargaining costs are incurred in finding and negotiating with others. They include the time spent in negotiating and reaching agreement, the cost of getting advice necessary to complete the agreement (such as legal and financial advice), and the costs of generating information necessary to determine whether to go ahead with the deal. They may also include the cost of litigation; as part of the bargaining process, one party may file suit as a way to pressure the other party into reaching an agreement.

Bargaining costs are even greater if the transaction involves more than two parties. So far, we have assumed that the Eden Roc and the Fontainebleau are the only legal actors affected by the decision to build the addition to the Fontainebleau. This is clearly a false assumption. Whichever way the decision goes, there are many people who will be affected by it, both positively and negatively. Those who will benefit by construction of the addition may include present and future employees and share-holders of the Fontainebleau, the city government (if the project has the effect of increasing tourism and therefore increasing the tax base of the city), other businesses in the city that will provide services to the Fontainebleau and its customers, and the families of all the persons benefited by the Fontainebleau's operations. Those who may be harmed by the project include the shareholders and employees of the Eden Roc (assuming none benefits from the Fontainebleau's renewed prosperity) and their families, the city government (if the net effect of the project is to decrease the market value of the Eden Roc more than the Fontainebleau's value increases, thereby nega-tively affecting tax revenues), and citizens who may lose access to part of the beach.

The cost of finding all the individuals affected by this dispute, getting them involved in negotiations on one side or the other, and reaching agreement are enor-mous. The costs are so great that it is implausible to believe that all persons affected by the decision could actually register their views by becoming involved.

As mentioned previously, the costs of bargaining include the cost of acquiring information. Each party to the dispute has limited information both about the other party and about the effects of the decision whether to build. Many individuals affected by the dispute may not even know about it. Those who do know may under- or overestimate its impact on their welfare. Moreover, parties who have imperfect infor-mation may enter a bargain that actually makes them worse off.

---

10. Three other kinds of transaction costs often discussed are (1) *administrative costs* (the costs of litigation or enforcement); (2) *agency costs* (the costs associated with hiring other people to carry out a task, including the possibility that they may not carry out the employer's purposes accurately and diligently); and (3) *strategic bargaining costs*, including *holdout* and *freeloader* problems. Strategic bargaining arises when each party attempts to get as much as possible out of the other party by stalling or waiting or otherwise trying to capture the most gains from the deal. Holdout problems arise when one party holds out for more money on the wrongful assumption that the other party is willing to pay more; imperfect information about the other party's desires may squelch a deal that would be to both parties' advantage. Freeloader problems arise when one party waits for others to take care of the problem; a party may not bring a nuisance suit because it wrongly assumes or hopes that others will bring the suit and pay the costs. Freeloader problems are common in fund-raising drives by public television and radio stations; many listeners may fail to make a donation because they assume others will do so, thereby enabling the freeloaders to get something for nothing.

The costs of bargaining and acquiring information may prevent the parties from making mutually beneficial exchanges. Because of the prevalence of these costs, the courts may be able to improve efficiency by paying attention to these, and like, impediments to bargaining. If the court can both identify relevant transaction costs and make fairly accurate judgments about which party would purchase the entitlement in the absence of these impediments to agreement, it can increase social wealth by assigning the entitlement to the party that would purchase it in the absence of these transaction costs.

7. *Lowest cost avoider.* Often the court itself lacks perfect information concerning the wants of the parties. Courts attempting to choose legal rules in a way that promotes efficiency therefore may resort to second-best solutions. A common solution is to place the burden either on the party that has the best access to the best information and the greatest incentives to make a general social cost-benefit analysis or on the party that can avoid the harm at the lowest cost. This is an imperfect solution because the lowest cost avoider (on whom the burden has been placed) may be the party that values the entitlement the most; transaction costs may prevent this party from purchasing the entitlement from the other party, thereby promoting an inefficient result.

Critiques of transaction cost analysis. Economic analysis of law has been subject to some scathing critiques. Below we will examine some of the most important objections to efficiency analysis.

1. *Efficiency is a function of the initial distribution of wealth.* As noted at the beginning of this discussion, the economic analysis of law provides a way to measure costs and benefits. Law and economics scholars define value by reference to willingness and ability to pay. This means, of course, that those who have more wealth have greater "votes"; their preferences count more in the analysis since their ability to pay is greater than those with less wealth. Efficiency is a function of the distribution of wealth. In legal terms, the distribution of wealth translates into the definition and assignment of property rights or entitlements. Concern with the distribution of wealth (or entitlements) poses a major challenge to the economic analysis of law. C. Edwin Baker, *The Ideology of the Economic Analysis of Law,* 5 Phil. & Pub. Aff. 3 (1975); C. Edwin Baker, *Starting Points in Economic Analysis of Law,* 8 Hofstra L. Rev. 939 (1980).

Judge Richard Posner, of the Seventh Circuit Court of Appeals, is one of the inventors, and most influential proponents, of the economic analysis of law. Although he justifies the use of wealth maximization as a measure of both social welfare and justice, *see* Richard Posner, *The Economics of Justice* (2d ed. 1983), he notes that reliance on "willingness to pay" as a criterion of value may sometimes conflict with achieving a result that maximizes social utility. He gives an example of a poor person desperately in need of an expensive medicine being outbid by a rich person who will benefit marginally from the medicine but who does not really need it. "In the sense of value used in this book, the pituitary extract is more valuable to the rich than to the poor family, because value is measured by willingness to pay; but the extract would confer greater happiness in the hands of the poor family than in the hands of the rich one." Posner, *Economic Analysis of Law* 13 (5th ed. 1998). Judge Posner notes that because value (as economic analysis defines it) is a function of ability to pay, efficiency "has limitations as an ethical criterion of social decisionmaking." *Id.*

Measuring social utility by reference to willingness and ability to pay gives greater weight to the interests of the wealthy. This has the effect of treating different individuals' interests differently; each individual's utility is not counted equally. For this reason, Ronald Dworkin, one of the most influential legal theorists now working in the rights tradition, has argued that wealth does not constitute a value in and of itself. Ronald Dworkin, *Is Wealth a Value?*, in *A Matter of Principle* 237 (1985). Dworkin contends that the use of market criteria to determine which allocation of entitlements maximizes social welfare is wholly arbitrary. He illustrates this in the following example about which of two people values a book more, *id.* at 245:

> Derek is poor and sick and miserable, and the book is one of his few comforts. He is willing to sell it for $2 only because he needs medicine. Amartya is rich and content. He is willing to spend $3 for the book, which is a very small part of his wealth, on the odd chance that he might someday read it, although he knows that he probably will not. If the [state transfers the book to Amartya with no compensation], total utility will sharply fall. But wealth, as specifically defined [by law and economics scholars], will improve. . . . I ask whether, if the [transfer is made], the situation will be in any way an improvement. I believe it will not. In such circumstances, the fact that goods are in the hands of those who would pay more to have them is as morally irrelevant as the book's being in the hands of the alphabetically prior party.

Since efficiency is a function of the distribution of wealth, it is incomplete as a criterion of justice without a defense of the existing distribution of wealth. Yet economic analysis cannot itself provide such a justification since it determines value by willingness and ability to pay, which in turn is determined by an initial distribution of wealth. To apply efficiency analysis, we must assume an initial distribution of property rights; we have to know who owns the entitlement in question *and* the initial distribution of wealth. This information is essential to understand both the object of the bargain and the resources each party has to back up its demands by a money payment. The definition of the efficient result is a function of the relative bargaining power of the parties; richer parties have more bargaining power than poorer ones since they have greater ability to translate their wants into a monetary offer. It is therefore circular to define property rights by reference to the bargains people would make in the absence of transaction costs because what bargains they are likely to make depends partly on the initial distribution of property rights between them. For this reason, the initial distribution of wealth or property rights must be justified on other grounds, such as a political theory of justice.

2. *Offer/asking problem.* Transaction cost analysis depends on the assumption that it is possible, in most cases, to generate a single answer to the question who values the entitlement more by asking who is likely to end up with it after a bargaining process in the absence of transaction costs. This analysis assumes that, in the absence of transaction costs, the same party will end up with the entitlement no matter who owned the entitlement at the start of the bargaining. Whoever values the entitlement more will either keep it (if she is the initial owner) or buy it (if she is initially the non-owner). This prediction depends on the assumption that offer and asking prices are unlikely to differ very much.

Some scholars have argued that this assumption is unwarranted. They suggest that, in many cases, the result of transaction cost analysis will depend on which party is given the entitlement initially. Duncan Kennedy, *Cost-Benefit Analysis of Entitlement Problems: A Critique*, 33 Stan. L. Rev. 387 (1981). This is true because, for a variety of reasons, offer prices are likely to be lower, and in some situations, much lower, than asking prices. For example, in *Boomer v. Atlantic Cement*, suppose the factory is given the right to pollute. To apply transaction cost analysis, we compare the factory's asking price (to give up its freedom of action) with the homeowners' offer price (to obtain security from infliction of the harm). The homeowners' offer price is limited by their wealth, including the amount of money and other assets they currently own and the amount they would be willing and able to borrow. This amount is likely to be low and may very well be less than the amount of lost profits the factory owner would demand to shut down the factory or install pollution control devices. Assume that 50 homeowners could offer the company $50,000 ($1,000 each), but the lowest cost method of avoiding the harm by installing pollution control devices would cost the factory $500,000. The cost of avoiding the harm ($500,000) is 10 times greater than the value of avoiding it ($50,000). If this is the case, the efficient solution is to let the factory operate freely.

On the other hand, suppose we initially grant the homeowners an entitlement to be free from pollution. We then compare the homeowners' asking price and the factory owner's offer price. For purposes of simplicity, assume the cost of avoiding the harm is still $500,000 and that the factory owner is willing and able to pay any amount less than this to avoid the $500,000 expense. Assume also that each of the homeowners equally opposes operation of the factory. The most the factory owner would offer each homeowner to avoid installing the pollution control devices is $500,000 divided by 50, or $10,000. Although each of the homeowners would not be able to offer the company more than $1,000 to induce it to stop polluting, $10,000 may not be acceptable as a payment for living with the grime and dirt and health problems produced by the pollution. Each homeowner's asking price, in other words, may be higher than $10,000. Why is this so?

The answer is that the asking price is not limited by wealth in the same way that the offer price is. The homeowners already *own* the entitlement to prevent the pollution; they do not need to purchase it. They are therefore richer than they were when the entitlements were reversed. Suppose the homeowners are avid environmentalists and are not willing to accept a $10,000 payment to live in a polluted neighborhood that may make them sick and may significantly lower their quality of life. The smallest amount they would accept to give up their right is in the order of $200,000 apiece, enough to enable them to sell their homes and move to a nearby, cleaner community. In this case, the asking price of the homeowners is 50 times $200,000, or $10 million, many times more than the factory owner's offer price of $500,000. In this case, the efficient result is for the factory to install the pollution control device, which is many times cheaper than paying the neighbors to agree to live with the pollution.

The homeowners' collective offer price was only $50,000, while their asking price was $10 million. This means that what we identify as the efficient result depends on which initial distribution of entitlements we choose. If we presume that the factory owner has the entitlement to pollute, then that result is efficient since it would not be corrected by a subsequent transaction. But if we presume that the homeowners have the entitlement to be free from pollution, then that result is efficient because that, too, will not be corrected by a subsequent transaction. We have arrived at conflicting definitions of the efficient result depending on which party is presumed to own the entitlement in question.

If asking prices are likely to be higher than offer prices, we may arrive at conflicting definitions of which allocation of entitlements is efficient or wealth maximizing. In cases like this, efficiency analysis is indeterminate. We need some other criterion to tell us which starting place is appropriate.

Why might asking prices be higher than offer prices? One answer is the wealth effect of assigning the entitlement to a particular party. Whoever is assigned the entitlement is richer than he would be without the entitlement; he no longer needs to shell out money to purchase it. Another answer is a psychological one. We may value what we have more than what we could have. This is true perhaps because spending money to buy an entitlement hurts more than "spending" it by giving up an opportunity that is offered to us.

Mark Kelman gives several examples:

> A fully rational individual, a professor at a business school, buys a bottle of imported wine for $5. After its value increases, a wine dealer with whom he regularly deals offers him $100 for the bottle of wine. Although he has never purchased a bottle of wine for $100, in fact, he has never paid more than $35 for one and would not do so now, the professor drinks the wine rather than sell it. [The professor's offer price is $35 while his asking price is greater than $100; he will not sell it for that amount.]
>
> ...A consumer buys a new color television and decides to keep his old black and white set for which he could realize $50 [if he sold it]. If that second television were destroyed, he would not pay $50 for a second television.... Again, the $50 of opportunity income is spent on preserving the status quo, keeping the television, [giving up the $50 he could get by selling the TV,] although $50 of received income would not be spent to get to the same substantive two-television state. [The consumer's offer price is zero — he would not pay anything for a second television — but his asking price is greater than $50; he will not sell it for that amount.]
>
> ...In a survey course of middle-aged male students in a business school cost-benefit course, the students were asked two questions. The first question was: Suppose you have been exposed to a disease that would kill you painlessly in one week. The probability that you have contracted it is .001. There is a vaccine, limited in supply, that will cure you if taken now. How much will you pay? [offer price] You will have thirty years to pay, so problems of raising large lump sums of income are eliminated. The second question was: How much would a person have to offer you to expose yourself to the same disease? There is a .001 chance you will contract it if exposed, and no cure will be available if you contract it. Again, if people behaved as they must to verify the Coase Theorem, the answers to both questions would be roughly the same, although there might be some small divergence insofar as the marginal utility of money declines. The answers, however, differed by orders of magnitude for many students; for example, the same student answered that he would pay only $200 for the vaccine, but would demand $50,000 to be exposed to the disease....
>
> ...In a similar classroom survey, a number of persons were asked two sets of questions: First, what would they pay to buy out of a madman's lottery where 1 in 100,000 persons would be shot? What would one have to pay them to enter such a lottery? Again, answers differed by orders of magnitude. Second, in an example quite close to the user-polluter paradigm case, people were asked what they would pay to be able to see a mountain view that had been blocked off for some time by factory smoke, and what one would have to pay them to block off the view if it were not currently blocked. Again, answers invariably followed the same pattern: People would pay out a lower order magnitude of money to clear an obstructed view than they would demand to allow the factory smoke to block it.

Mark Kelman, *Consumption Theory, Production Theory, and Ideology in the Coase Theorem*, 52 S. Cal. L. Rev. 669, 678-679, 681-682 (1979) (emphasis in original).

Because of the difference between offer and asking prices, it is possible to describe at least six different ways of measuring efficiency.

(a) *Fair market value.* We might choose rules or results that maximize the joint fair market value of the affected parcels. This measure ignores offer and asking prices of the parties and focuses instead on the amount the parcels would likely to be worth on the open market under alternative legal rules or assignments of the entitlement under discussion.

(b) *Auction.* We might assume the entitlement was not owned by anyone and ask which party or parties would pay the most to acquire it. This auction measure looks at the willingness and ability to pay of the parties and focuses on the amount they would *offer* to acquire the entitlement. In a case like *Boomer*, we would be likely to expect the profitable factory to outbid the homeowners, suggesting that denial of an injunction would promote efficiency.

(c) *Status quo.* We might assign the entitlement to the current owner, as determined by prior property law and ask whether non-owners are willing and able to offer enough to induce the owner to sell. Under current law, owners can be said to own the right to be free from substantial and unreasonable interference with their use or enjoyment of their property. If this standard applies to injunctions, as well as damages claims, then the homeowners own the right to stop the polluting activity. In this case, the factory must buy the right to commit the nuisance from the homeowners. Rather than comparing the offer price of the factory with the offer price of the homeowners (as done in the auction measure of efficiency), we compare the asking price of the homeowners with the offer price of the factory. Asking prices are likely to be higher than offer prices, and, in the case of the ideological plaintiff, may be infinite. In this kind of case, it is more likely the homeowners would refuse to sell their rights to be free from the nuisance and it would be efficient to grant the injunction.

(d) *Redistribution.* We might, instead, conclude that existing allocations of the entitlement are unfair or presumptively inefficient and alter them. In such a case, we might change the law to grant the company a right to operate without fear of nuisance liability. In this case, we ask whether the homeowners (who now do not own an entitlement to shut down the factory) would offer the factory enough to induce it to give up its privilege to operate. The answer is probably no, and if this measure of efficiency is adopted, the injunction should probably be denied.

(e) *Reverse auction.* Finally, we might ask which party would ask the most to give up the entitlement. If we grant the factory the right to operate, how much would the homeowners have to offer it before it would agree to give up its rights? In other words, what is its asking price? Conversely, we could look at the asking price of the homeowners. We could then compare the asking prices of the factory versus the homeowners and assign the entitlement to the party who would be least likely to sell it. This measure is perhaps the hardest to apply. On one hand, if the plant is profitable, the homeowners would have to offer it an awful lot to induce it to shut down. On the other hand, one ideological plaintiff would make the homeowners' asking price exceed the factory's asking price.

(f) *Social welfare.* Finally, we could de-couple efficiency analysis from reliance on market measures. After all, it is hard to place a dollar figure on what the community loses because children can no longer freely play outside because of polluted air or adults can no longer swim in the river running through the city. This does not mean that we do not need to compare costs and benefits of alternative solutions to land use conflicts. It does mean that another way to do this is to rely less heavily on numbers and more on a combination of dollar amounts and subjective consideration of the magnitude, the character, and the distribution of the benefits and burdens of different resolutions of the problem.

This review of different measures of efficiency shows that the baseline for our analysis matters a great deal. The use of fair market value as a measure of costs and benefits leads to different answers than if one focuses on offer and asking prices. Similarly, if we compare offer prices, we give greater importance to the distribution of wealth between the parties than if we compare values based on an initial allocation of the entitlement to a property owner. Shifting the entitlement from one party to the other similarly may affect determinations of relative value since asking prices are likely to be higher than offer prices. Granting a property entitlement often creates a sense of entitlement and has a profound psychological effect on the "owner" who is reluctant to part with her property. Moreover, as we have seen, considerations other than efficiency are central to nuisance law and substantially affect the assignment of entitlements and determinations about the reasonableness of particular interferences with use or enjoyment of land.

3. *The offer/asking problem and externalities.* The difference between offer and asking prices assumes added significance when we remember that in an entitlement decision we can use either measure to determine the costs and benefits to third parties. Suppose, for example, the Eden Roc Hotel was not a private concern but a municipally owned beach open to the public. The harm caused by the building of the addition to the Fontainebleau would be borne by all the residents who used the public beach or otherwise benefited from its availability. Transaction costs would certainly prevent all parties affected by the dispute from participating in a massive negotiation. Moreover, in estimating the value of keeping the public beach sunny to the third parties affected by the project, the decision maker could use either their offer prices or their asking prices. Their offer prices are likely to be much lower than their asking prices; they are likely to offer very little money to keep the Fontainebleau project from being built. If, however, we consider how much the Fontainebleau would have to bribe them to give up their right to have a sunny public beach, the number is likely to be considerably higher. Using the asking prices of all third parties affected by a land use decision may give a totally different answer from an analysis that uses their offer prices.

Consider also a dispute between a nuclear power plant and a citizens' group that opposes nuclear power as unreasonably dangerous. Is operation of the plant a nuisance? Using the offer prices of the members of the public that oppose operation of the facility, operation of the plant is efficient because the general public could not raise sufficient funds to compensate the plant for the substantial profits it would lose if it did not operate. Using the asking prices of the opponents, operation is almost certainly inefficient: One antinuclear fanatic could have an asking price that is infinite, and no amount of money could induce him to agree to allow the plant to go forward. Efficiency analysis cannot decide which procedure or method of measurement to adopt; other criteria, such as a theory of justice, are needed to answer this question.

4. *The difficulty of defining a "voluntary" exchange.* Voluntary exchanges increase social wealth by making both parties better off in their own terms. In contrast, involuntary or coerced exchanges do not make both parties better off; someone who is coerced may agree to an arrangement that leaves her worse off. To apply transaction cost analysis, it is necessary to define clearly what is and is not a voluntary exchange. But this is not easy to do; people with differing political views and theories of justice will disagree substantially on this question, particularly in their attitudes toward the problem of unequal bargaining power.

We must make judgments about which agreements are sufficiently voluntary to enforce and which are illegitimate impositions of power by one party over the other. We could define duress narrowly to include only physical duress (arm twisting) or physical threats (pressing a gun to the head); or we could define it more broadly to include economic duress caused by unequal bargaining power. There is no purely logical answer to this question.

Suppose you have fallen into a deep pit filled with poisonous snakes. I come along and observe you in the pit. I am not responsible for your predicament and have no legal duty to help you. I offer to sell you a ladder in exchange for half your future earnings. You agree to buy; I agree to sell. It is a Pareto superior exchange; you are happier with your life and half your future earnings than the alternative; I am happier as well with this outcome. Is the contract voluntary? There is no simple answer to this question. You obviously felt forced to agree; you paid an awful lot for the ladder. But you also benefited substantially by the deal. Is the contract fair? The terms are onerous for you, but so was the alternative. We could, consistent with a regime of freedom of contract, enforce this contract (because it was the result of voluntary choice and was mutually beneficial) or not enforce it (because it was the result of coerced choice and its terms are unconscionable).

5. *The difficulty of identifying transaction costs.* Deciding what is and is not a transaction cost is not always obvious. Imperfect information compounds the difficulty of distinguishing "transaction costs" from elements of wealth that are exchanged in the transaction. Posner includes "high information costs" as an example of a barrier to the free flow of resources and thus defines them as transaction costs. There is no reason why they must be so considered, however. Assume that one of the parties to an agreement is mistaken about important facts relevant to the agreement. For example, a union fails to bargain for prenotification of a plant closing because it is mistaken about both the likelihood of the plant closing and the benefits of prenotification in such circumstances. If the union had known these facts, it would have insisted on prenotification in its contract, perhaps in return for other concessions. If we treat information as a transaction cost, we should enforce the contract terms to which the parties would have agreed if they had perfect information; we can thus make both parties better off in their own terms. By giving the parties what they really wanted to bargain for, we are facilitating individual will. This is why treating imperfect information as a transaction cost maximizes social wealth; rather than redistributing a valuable resource and possibly making someone worse off, we merely perfect the process of free exchange, thereby benefiting both parties to the agreement.

Information does not have to be considered a transaction cost. It can be treated as a good that is traded in the market and that represents part and parcel of the subject matter of the transaction itself. After all, we do buy and sell information. If the union had wanted better information about the employment market and the likelihood of a plant closing, it could and should have purchased that information from the company. Why give the union the benefit of information it was not willing and able to pay for? Why should the court redistribute information from the company to the union, as it were, for free?

When we treat information as a mere cost of transacting, we enforce the result the parties would have reached in a hypothetical market in which information was redistributed. This approach socializes access to information. In contrast, when we treat information as a valuable resource in its own right, we conclude that the union received exactly what it was willing to pay for in its contract. We therefore maximize social wealth if we enforce the contract in accordance with its terms.

Logic alone cannot determine whether to treat a resource as a mere cost of transacting (creating a fair process) or as a constituent element of wealth, just as logic cannot define what is a free contract and what is a coerced contract. In both cases, the issue of how to define a fair bargaining process cannot be separated from a substantive judgment about which distributions of wealth and power are legitimate.

6. *Efficiency has a conservative bias.* Many critics of efficiency analysis have suggested that it has a conservative bias, partly because it gives greater weight to the interests of the wealthy and the large corporations that currently wield substantial economic power. Because value is defined by reference to willingness and ability to pay, and because of the offer/asking problem, the analysis tends to privilege the interests of property owners over the interests of non-owners. To the extent that property owners are content with the fact that they own property, the analysis is likely to lead unavoidably to outcomes that differ only in marginal ways from current arrangements.

A second indication of a conservative bias in the analysis is its requirement that the analyst hold everything constant but the particular entitlement in question. The *Fontainebleau* analysis, for example, assumed that both the existing distribution of wealth and *all other legal rules* remained the same. This assumption is necessary to simplify the analysis and produce an answer. If, instead of holding everything else constant, we were to put more than one rule up for grabs at a time — for example, by suggesting changes to the tax system, the antitrust laws, the bankruptcy laws, or the rules about what constitutes unfair competition — the analysis becomes indeterminate. This is because every choice depends on the background set of legal entitlements that define the market context in which the parties bargain. It is only when we pay attention to the market and institutional structures within which bargains take place that we can imagine alternative ways of operating a decentralized market system. In contrast, the method of holding everything constant but the one entitlement in question makes consideration of alternative market structures impossible. *See* Arthur Leff, *Economic Analysis of Law: Some Realism About Nominalism,* 60 Va. L. Rev. 451 (1974); Kennedy, *supra.*

7. *Commodification.* A final critique comes from Professor Margaret Jane Radin. Radin has argued that certain kinds of valued resources should not be traded in the market or otherwise treated as if they were commodities for sale; these interests are taken out of the market system (partly or totally) and effectively made inalienable. For example, we regulate safety conditions in the workplace to protect individual workers from being killed or maimed on the job, and we will not let people bargain away their right to a safe workplace. Protecting workers from unreasonably dangerous conditions may benefit the public by lowering costs, but it is also fundamentally designed to protect individual dignity. Margaret Jane Radin, *Market-Inalienability,* 100 Harv. L. Rev. 1849 (1987). Some issues are simply discussed more appropriately in nonmarket language, that is, in terms of justice and rights rather than wealth and efficiency. For example, Calabresi and Melamed argue that slavery may be inefficient because observing the plight of slaves makes "sensitive" people "unhappy." Guido Calabresi and A. Douglas Melamed, *Property Rules, Liability Rules, and Inalienability: One View of the Cathedral,* 85 Harv. L. Rev. 1089, 1111-1112 (1972). This is a pretty feeble way to condemn the institution of slavery. Do we really want to say that the reason slavery is bad is because it is inefficient, or would it be better to be able to say that it is evil and an affront to the values of liberty and equality? The language of efficiency simply cannot

capture much of what we mean when we talk about justice and fairness in social relationships. *See also* Margaret Jane Radin, *Residential Rent Control,* 15 Phil. & Pub. Aff. 350 (1986).

Professor Jane Cohen has criticized a proposal by Judge Posner to introduce more free market elements into the adoption process, effectively allowing people greater freedom to buy and sell children. Cohen imagines and describes the social context within which such market transactions would take place. Her description leaves substantial doubt about whether Posner's proposal would make our society better off than before. Jane Maslow Cohen, *Posnerism, Pluralism, Pessimism,* 67 B.U. L. Rev. 105 (1987). Professors Frances Miller and Tamar Frankel have similarly argued that market theory constitutes a wholly inappropriate model for public policy decisions about adoption. Frances Miller and Tamar Frankel, *The Inapplicability of Market Theory to Adoptions,* 67 B.U. L. Rev. 99 (1987).

§4.4.3.2   Nuisance Doctrine Applied to Light

PRAH v. MARETTI

321 N.W.2d 182 (Wis. 1982)

SHIRLEY S. ABRAHAMSON, Justice.

This appeal from a judgment of the circuit court for Waukesha county, Max Raskin, circuit judge, was certified to this court by the court of appeals, as presenting an issue of first impression, namely, whether an owner of a solar-heated residence states a claim upon which relief can be granted when he asserts that his neighbor's proposed construction of a residence (which conforms to existing deed restrictions and local ordinances) interferes with his access to an unobstructed path for sunlight across the neighbor's property. This case thus involves a conflict between one landowner (Glenn Prah, the plaintiff) interested in unobstructed access to sunlight across adjoining property as a natural source of energy and an adjoining landowner (Richard D. Maretti, the defendant) interested in the development of his land. . . .

According to the complaint, the plaintiff is the owner of a residence which was constructed during the years 1978-1979. The complaint alleges that the residence has a solar system which includes collectors on the roof to supply energy for heat and hot water and that after the plaintiff built his solar-heated house, the defendant purchased the lot adjacent to and immediately to the south of the plaintiff's lot and commenced planning construction of a home. The complaint further states that when the plaintiff learned of defendant's plans to build the house he advised the defendant that if the house were built at the proposed location, defendant's house would substantially and adversely affect the integrity of plaintiff's solar system and could cause plaintiff other damage. Nevertheless, the defendant began construction. The complaint further alleges that the plaintiff is entitled to "unrestricted use of the sun and its solar power" and demands judgment for injunctive relief and damages. . . .

. . . Plaintiff's home was the first residence built in the subdivision, and although plaintiff did not build his house in the center of the lot it was built in accordance with applicable restrictions. Plaintiff advised defendant that if the defendant's home were built at the proposed site it would cause a shadowing effect on the solar collectors which would reduce the efficiency of the system and possibly damage the system. To avoid these adverse effects, plaintiff requested defendant to locate his home an additional several feet away from the plaintiff's lot line, the exact number being disputed. Plaintiff and defendant failed to reach an agreement on the location of defendant's home before defendant started construction. . . .

We consider first whether the complaint states a claim for relief based on common law private nuisance. This state has long recognized that an owner of land does not have an absolute or unlimited right to use the land in a way which injures the rights of others. The rights of neighboring landowners are relative; the uses by one must not unreasonably impair the uses or enjoyment of the other. When one landowner's use of his or her property unreasonably interferes with another's enjoyment of his or her property, that use is said to be a private nuisance.

The private nuisance doctrine has traditionally been employed in this state to balance the rights of landowners, and this court has recently adopted the analysis of private nuisance set forth in the *Restatement (Second) of Torts*. The *Restatement* defines private nuisance as "a nontrespassory invasion of another's interest in the private use and enjoyment of land." *Restatement (Second) of Torts* sec. 821D (1977). The phrase "interest in the private use and enjoyment of land" as used in sec. 821D is broadly defined to include any disturbance of the enjoyment of property. . . .

Although the defendant's obstruction of the plaintiff's access to sunlight appears to fall within the *Restatement's* broad concept of a private nuisance as a nontrespassory invasion of another's interest in the private use and enjoyment of land, the defendant asserts that he has a right to develop his property in compliance with statutes, ordinances and private covenants without regard to the effect of such development upon the plaintiff's access to sunlight. In essence, the defendant is asking this court to hold that the private nuisance doctrine is not applicable in the instant case and that his right to develop his land is a right which is *per se* superior to his neighbor's interest in access to sunlight. This position is expressed in the maxim "cujus est solum, ejus est usque ad coelum et ad inferos," that is, the owner of land owns up to the sky and down to the center of the earth. The rights of the surface owner are, however, not unlimited.

The defendant is not completely correct in asserting that the common law did not protect a landowner's access to sunlight across adjoining property. At English common law a landowner could acquire a right to receive sunlight across adjoining land by both express agreement and under the judge-made doctrine of "ancient lights." Under the doctrine of ancient lights if the landowner had received sunlight across adjoining property for a specified period of time, the landowner was entitled to continue to receive unobstructed access to sunlight across the adjoining property. Under the doctrine the landowner acquired a negative prescriptive easement and could prevent the adjoining landowner from obstructing access to light.[8]

Although American courts have not been as receptive to protecting a landowner's access to sunlight as the English courts, American courts have afforded some protection to a landowner's interest in access to sunlight. American courts honor express easements to sunlight. American courts initially enforced the English common law doctrine of ancient lights, but later every state which considered the doctrine repudiated it as inconsistent with the needs of a developing country. Indeed, for just that reason this court concluded that an easement to light and air over adjacent property could not be created or acquired by prescription and has been unwilling to recognize such an easement by implication.

---

8. No American common law state recognizes a landowner's right to acquire an easement of light by prescription.

Many jurisdictions in this country have protected a landowner from malicious obstruction of access to light (the spite fence cases) under the common law private nuisance doctrine. If an activity is motivated by malice it lacks utility and the harm it causes others outweighs any social values. . . . Thus a landowner's interest in sunlight has been protected in this country by common law private nuisance law at least in the narrow context of the modern American rule invalidating spite fences.

This court's reluctance in the nineteenth and early part of the twentieth century to provide broader protection for a landowner's access to sunlight was premised on three policy considerations. First, the right of landowners to use their property as they wished, as long as they did not cause physical damage to a neighbor, was jealously guarded.

Second, sunlight was valued only for aesthetic enjoyment or as illumination. Since artificial light could be used for illumination, loss of sunlight was at most a personal annoyance which was given little, if any, weight by society.

Third, society had a significant interest in not restricting or impeding land development. This court repeatedly emphasized that in the growth period of the nineteenth and early twentieth centuries change is to be expected and is essential to property and that recognition of a right to sunlight would hinder property development. . . .

Considering these three policies, this court concluded that in the absence of an express agreement granting access to sunlight, a landowner's obstruction of another's access to sunlight was not actionable. These three policies are no longer fully accepted or applicable. They reflect factual circumstances and social priorities that are now obsolete.

First, society has increasingly regulated the use of land by the landowner for the general welfare.

Second, access to sunlight has taken on a new significance in recent years. In this case the plaintiff seeks to protect access to sunlight, not for aesthetic reasons or as a source of illumination but as a source of energy. Access to sunlight as an energy source is of significance both to the landowner who invests in solar collectors and to a society which has an interest in developing alternative sources of energy.

Third, the policy of favoring unhindered private development in an expanding economy is no longer in harmony with the realities of our society. The need for easy and rapid development is not as great today as it once was, while our perception of the value of sunlight as a source of energy has increased significantly.

Courts should not implement obsolete policies that have lost their vigor over the course of the years. The law of private nuisance is better suited to resolve landowners' disputes about property development in the 1980's than is a rigid rule which does not recognize a landowner's interest in access to sunlight. As we said in *Ballstadt v. Pagel,* 232 N.W. 862 (Wis. 1930), "What is regarded in law as constituting a nuisance in modern times would no doubt have been tolerated without question in former times." We read *State v. Deetz,* 224 N.W.2d 407 (Wis. 1974), as an endorsement of the application of common law nuisance to situations involving the conflicting interests of landowners and as rejecting per se exclusions to the nuisance law reasonable use doctrine.

In *Deetz* the court abandoned the rigid common law common enemy rule with respect to surface water and adopted the private nuisance reasonable use rule, namely that the landowner is subject to liability if his or her interference with the flow of surface waters unreasonably invades a neighbor's interest in the use and enjoyment of land. *Restatement (Second) of Torts,* sec. 822, 826, 829 (1977). This court concluded that the common enemy rule which served society "well in the days of burgeoning national expansion of the mid-nineteenth and early-twentieth centuries" should be abandoned because it was no longer "in harmony with the realities of our society." *Deetz, supra,* 224 N.W.2d 407. We recognized in *Deetz* that common law rules adapt to changing social values and conditions.

Yet the defendant would have us ignore the flexible private nuisance law as a means of resolving the dispute between the landowners in this case and would have us adopt an approach, already abandoned in *Deetz*, of favoring the unrestricted development of land and of applying a rigid and inflexible rule protecting his right to build on his land and disregarding any interest of the plaintiff in the use and enjoyment of his land. This we refuse to do.[13]

Private nuisance law, the law traditionally used to adjudicate conflicts between private landowners, has the flexibility to protect both a landowner's right of access to sunlight and another landowner's right to develop land. Private nuisance law is better suited to regulate access to sunlight in modern society and is more in harmony with legislative policy and the prior decisions of this court than is an inflexible doctrine of non-recognition of any interest in access to sunlight across adjoining land.

We therefore hold that private nuisance law, that is, the reasonable use doctrine as set forth in the *Restatement*, is applicable to the instant case. Recognition of a nuisance claim for unreasonable obstruction of access to sunlight will not prevent land development or unduly hinder the use of adjoining land. It will promote the reasonable use and enjoyment of land in a manner suitable to the 1980's. That obstruction of access to light might be found to constitute a nuisance in certain circumstances does not mean that it will be or must be found to constitute a nuisance under all circumstances. The result in each case depends on whether the conduct complained of is unreasonable.

Accordingly we hold that the plaintiff in this case has stated a claim under which relief can be granted. Nonetheless we do not determine whether the plaintiff in this case is entitled to relief. In order to be entitled to relief the plaintiff must prove the elements required to establish actionable nuisance, and the conduct of the defendant herein must be judged by the reasonable use doctrine. . . .

The circuit court concluded that because the defendant's proposed house was in conformity with zoning regulations, building codes and deed restrictions, the defendant's use of the land was reasonable. This court has concluded that a landowner's compliance with zoning laws does not automatically bar a nuisance claim. . . .

[O]ur examination of the record leads us to conclude that the record does not furnish an adequate basis for the circuit court to apply the proper legal principles on summary judgment. The application of the reasonable use standard in nuisance cases normally requires a full exposition of all underlying facts and circumstances. Too little

---

13. Defendant's position that a landowner's interest in access to sunlight across adjoining land is not "legally enforceable" and is therefore excluded *per se* from private nuisance law was adopted in *Fontainebleau Hotel Corp. v. Forty-five Twenty-five, Inc.*, 114 So. 2d 357 (Fla. App. 1959). . . .

We do not find the reasoning of *Fontainebleau* persuasive. . . . The court did not explain why an owner's interest in unobstructed light should not be protected or in what manner an owner's interest in unobstructed sunlight differs from an owner's interest in being free from obtrusive noises or smells or differs from an owner's interest in unobstructed use of water. The recognition of a *per se* exception to private nuisance law may invite unreasonable behavior.

is known in this case of such matters as the extent of the harm to the plaintiff, the suitability of solar heat in that neighborhood, the availability of remedies to the plaintiff, and the costs to the defendant of avoiding the harm. Summary judgment is not an appropriate procedural vehicle in this case when the circuit court must weigh evidence which has not been presented at trial.

Because the plaintiff has stated a claim of common law private nuisance upon which relief can be granted, the judgment of the circuit court must be reversed....

WILLIAM CALLOW, Justice, dissenting.

... The majority... concludes that this court's past reluctance to extend protection to a landowner's access to sunlight beyond the spite fence cases is based on obsolete policies which have lost their vigor over the course of the years. The three obsolete policies cited by the majority are: (1) Right of landowners to use their property as they desire as long as no physical damage is done to a neighbor; (2) In the past, sunlight was valued only for aesthetic value, not a source of energy; and (3) Society has a significant interest in not impeding land development.... The majority has failed to convince me that these policies are obsolete....

I firmly believe that a landowner's right to use his property within the limits of ordinances, statutes, and restrictions of record where such use is necessary to serve his legitimate needs is a fundamental precept of a free society which this court should strive to uphold....

... In the instant case, we are dealing with an action which seeks to restrict the defendant's private right to use his property, notwithstanding a complete lack of notice of restriction to the defendant and the defendant's compliance with applicable ordinances and statutes. The plaintiff who knew of the potential problem before the defendant acquired the land seeks to impose such use restriction to accommodate his personal, private benefit — a benefit which could have been accommodated by the plaintiff locating his home in a different place on his property or by acquiring the land in question when it was for sale prior to its acquisition by the defendant.

... The right of a property owner to lawful enjoyment of his property should be vigorously protected, particularly in those cases where the adjacent property owner could have insulated himself from the alleged problem by acquiring the land as a defense to the potential problem or by provident use of his own property.

The majority concludes that sunlight has not heretofore been accorded the status of a source of energy, and consequently it has taken on a new significance in recent years. Solar energy for home heating is at this time sparingly used and of questionable economic value because solar collectors are not mass produced, and consequently, they are very costly. Their limited efficiency may explain the lack of production.

Regarding the third policy the majority apparently believes is obsolete (that society has a significant interest in not restricting land development) ..., I concede the law may be tending to recognize the value of aesthetics over increased volume development and that an individual may not use his land in such a way as to harm the public. The instant case, however, deals with a private benefit. [At the same time, it] is clear that community planners are acutely aware of the present housing shortages, particularly among those two groups with limited financial resources, the young and the elderly.... While the majority's policy arguments may be directed to a cause of action for public nuisance, we are presented with a private nuisance case which I believe is distinguishable in this regard.

I would submit that any policy decisions in this area are best left for the legislature. "What is 'desirable' or 'advisable' or 'ought to be' is a question of policy, not a question of fact. What is 'necessary' or what is 'in the best interest' is not a fact and its determination by the judiciary is an exercise of legislative power when each involves political considerations." *In re City of Beloit,* 155 N.W.2d 633, 636 (Wis. 1968).... I would concur with these observations of the trial judge: "While temptation lingers for the court to declare by judicial fiat what is right and what should be done, under the facts in this case, such action under our form of constitutional government where the three branches each have their defined jurisdiction and power, would be an intrusion of judicial egoism over legislative passivity."....

In order for a nuisance to be actionable in the instant case, the defendant's conduct must be "intentional and unreasonable." It is impossible for me to accept the majority's conclusion that Mr. Maretti, in lawfully seeking to construct his home, may be intentionally and unreasonably interfering with the plaintiff's access to sunlight....

I conclude that plaintiff's solar heating system is an unusually sensitive use. In other words, the defendant's proposed construction of his home, under ordinary circumstances, would not interfere with the use and enjoyment of the usual person's property.... "The plaintiff cannot, by devoting his own land to an unusually sensitive use, such as a drive-in motion picture theater easily affected by light, make a nuisance out of conduct of the adjoining defendant which would otherwise be harmless."....

I further believe that the majority's conclusion that a cause of action exists in this case thwarts the very foundation of property law. Property law encompasses a system of filing and notice in a place for public records to provide prospective purchasers with any limitations on their use of the property. Such a notice is not alleged by the plaintiff. Only as a result of the majority's decision did Mr. Maretti discover that a legitimate action exists which would require him to defend the design and location of his home against a nuisance suit, notwithstanding the fact that he located and began to build his house within the applicable building, municipal, and deed restrictions....

I believe the facts of the instant controversy present the classic case of the owner of a solar collector who fails to take any action to protect his investment. There is nothing in the record to indicate that Mr. Prah disclosed his situation to Mr. Maretti prior to Maretti's purchase of the lot or attempted to secure protection for his solar collector prior to Maretti's submission of his building plans to the architectural committee. Such inaction should be considered a significant factor in determining whether a cause of action exists....

... I do not believe that an adjacent lot owner should be obliged to experience the substantial economic loss resulting from the lot being rendered unbuildable by the contour of the land as it relates to the location and design of the adjoining home using solar collectors....

NOTES AND QUESTIONS

1. *Light and air.* The vast majority of courts in the United States would hold that, in the absence of an agreement to the contrary, owners have absolute rights to develop

their property without liability for any interference with their neighbor's interests in light and air. This is often expressed by saying that no easement for light and air exists unless a contract creates it. One exception to this principle is that some courts will enjoin "spite fences"—structures that are erected for the *sole purpose* of maliciously harming the neighbor by interfering with her access to sunlight. *DeCecco v. Beach,* 381 A.2d 543 (Conn. 1977); Conn. Gen. Stat. §52-570. *But see Maioriello v. Arlotta,* 73 A.2d 374 (Pa. 1950) (holding that owners may build so as to obstruct light, air, and view of adjoining landowners, even though the structure serves no useful purpose and is erected solely to annoy the adjoining owner).

Another state that has adopted nuisance doctrine to adjudicate conflicts over light and air in some instances is New Hampshire. In *Tenn v. 889 Associates, Ltd.,* 500 A.2d 366 (N.H. 1985), for example, Justice David Souter applied nuisance law to a claim that construction of a building would interfere with light and air of the building next to it. Explicitly rejecting the rule in *Fontainebleau,* Justice Souter wrote:

> The present defendant urges us to adopt the *Fontainebleau* rule and thereby to refuse any common law recognition to interests in light and air, but we decline to do so. If we were so to limit the ability of the common law to grow, we would in effect be rejecting one of the wise assumptions underlying the traditional law of nuisance: that we cannot anticipate at any one time the variety of predicaments in which protection of property interests or redress for their violation will be justifiable. For it is just this recognition that has led the courts to avoid rigid formulations for determining when an interference with the use of property will be actionable, and to rest instead on the flexible rule that actionable, private nuisance consists of an unreasonable as well as a substantial interference with another person's use and enjoyment of his property. That is, because we have to anticipate that the uses of property will change over time, we have developed a law of nuisance that protects the use and enjoyment of property when a threatened harm to the plaintiff owner can be said to outweigh the utility of the defendant owner's conduct to himself and to the community.

Id. at 370. At the same time, the court upheld the lower court's determination that construction of the building would *not* constitute a nuisance since the plaintiff's building would continue to receive sufficient light characteristic of an urban area where buildings often buttress and block the sides of adjacent structures.

2. *The complex range of solutions for land use conflicts.* We have seen that some kinds of land use disputes between neighbors, such as conflicts over lateral and subjacent support, water rights, and light and air, are governed by specific sets of legal rules. Land use disputes not covered by these rules are governed by nuisance law.

The courts have adopted various approaches to settle land use disputes. At one extreme are the doctrines granting the victim absolute security from harm to certain property interests; when courts grant veto rights, they impose liability if the plaintiff can show that the defendant caused the harm. At another extreme are the doctrines granting the defendant an absolute privilege to engage in the activity without liability of any kind. In the middle are doctrines regulating the defendant's conduct only if it is deemed unreasonable; the standard of what conduct is reasonable or unreasonable may be defined by a general "reasonableness" requirement, negligence, and nuisance.

π veto rights (absolute security)	*reasonableness doctrines* (middle position: "it depends")	*Δ privilege* (*damnum absque injuria*)
• easement for lateral support of land • prior appropriation of water (veto rights in first user) • natural flow doctrine for diffuse surface water	• nuisance doctrine • negligence (lateral support of structures) • reasonable use doctrine for water • malice doctrine for spite fences	• common enemy rule for diffuse surface water • no easement for light and air • free use or absolute ownership of ground-water

Arguments and Counterarguments

The opinions in *Prah v. Maretti* address a rich source of policy arguments widely used by both lawyers and judges in adjudicating real property disputes. Lawyers appeal to these arguments to persuade the court to adopt a rule of law that favors their client's interests. It is essential for you to understand and master these arguments so that you can become an effective advocate for a client on either side of a dispute.

These arguments appeal to values that are widely shared. However, they also demonstrate that many values we hold may conflict. The fact that it is almost always possible to generate plausible, conventional legal arguments on both sides of a case in which both parties have intuitively attractive claims does not mean that it is impossible to resolve legal disputes. It simply means that decision makers must accommodate these conflicting moral impulses to make considered judgments about the relative strength of competing claims in particular social contexts.

This compilation of arguments is not meant to be exclusive. You will see both these arguments and others in legal analysis in both judicial opinions and legal scholarship. You will invent or construct new arguments yourself.

    I.   Rights Arguments
        a.   Justice and fairness in social relationships
            Rights arguments concern justice and fairness in social relationships. Many legal disputes can be described in terms of conflicting claims to freedom and security. Each side identifies an interest that is, or should be, protected by the legal system against interference by others. The plaintiff usually claims that the defendant's conduct has illegitimately deprived the plaintiff of the right to be secure from harm; the defendant has infringed on the plaintiff's legally protected interests in his property. The defendant usually claims, in response, that the interest claimed by the plaintiff does not merit legal protection, or at least the kind of protection sought by the plaintiff; at the same time, the defendant claims a legally protected interest in her own freedom of action. Protecting the plaintiff's right to security will illegitimately deprive the defendant of her autonomy and liberty in using her own property for her own purposes.

To make rights arguments persuasive, lawyers must attempt to describe the situation giving rise to the dispute in a way that will enable the decision maker to empathize with their client. This requires attention to the facts and an effort to characterize the fact situation in a way that supports the client's claim that she is entitled to prevail. The characterization of the fact situation, in combination with argument about the rights of the parties, appeals to values held by the decision maker that would prompt a decision one way or the other.

Rights arguments address the following questions:

What are the rights of the parties?

How should neighbors treat one another?

What limits on property rights are necessary to protect the legitimate interests of non-owners?

What is the fair result?

What constitutes justice in social relationships among neighbors and between property owners and the community?

   b. Categories of rights arguments

     1. Rights

Right to security

Sic utere tuo ut alienum non laedas (use your property so as not to harm the interests of others); property owners have the right to protect their property interests from harm by their neighbors' use of their property; the purpose of the rule of law is to protect each person's life and property from being harmed by others

Right to freedom of action

Damnum absque injuria (damage without legal redress); property owners have the right to use their property as they see fit; a property owner's use of her property should not make her neighbors' use of their property more difficult or expensive; the law should protect property owners' interests in freedom and liberty in controlling their property

     2. Morality

       (a) Individualism versus altruism

Altruism

Golden rule; look out for others; it is morally wrong for property owners to use their property in a way that wrongly inflicts harm on their neighbors' property interests

Individualism

Self-reliance; look out for oneself; each owner should foresee that others will develop their property and protect themselves from potential incompatible uses

       (b) Fault versus compensation

Compensation

As between two innocents, whoever caused the damage should pay

No liability without fault

Citizens should not be punished if they did nothing wrong; no liability if it was not foreseeable that use of one's property would harm one's neighbors' property

3. Reasonable expectations
   (a) Foreseeability
   Foresee consequences to others of your conduct
   Property owners and possessors should foresee the consequences to their neighbors of their land use and take precautions against harming neighboring owners
   Foresee development of neighboring land
   Property owners should foresee that others will develop their property and take precautions against incompatible land uses
   (b) Reliance on reasonable expectations
   Reasonable expectations
   Possessors reasonably expect their neighbors to adjust their land use to be compatible with neighborhood conditions and not to inflict unreasonable damage to neighboring property
   Reasonable expectations
   Property owners reasonably expect to be able to develop their own property; prior developers on neighboring land have no right to prevent later development on neighboring property each property owner reasonably expects to be able to develop her own property

4. Distribution: Who should fairly bear the loss?
   Developers should pay for the losses they impose on others
   Those who profit from an activity should bear its costs; those whose land development causes harm to others should have to bear the loss occasioned by their development rather than externalizing those costs onto their neighbors; all development should be consistent with prior vested property rights
   Developers should invest to protect their own property rather than externalizing those costs on others
   Those who profit from an activity should bear its costs; all developers should bear the costs of maintaining the safety of their own structures rather than externalizing those costs onto neighboring developers; those who develop property should foresee that neighbors will also develop and invest in protecting their own property

5. Equality
   Equal right to security
   All owners have an equal right to protect their property from injury by their neighbors
   Equal right to develop
   Later developers have the same rights to develop as earlier developers; the first builder should not be able to interfere with the equal freedom of others to develop their property by making later development more expensive

II. Social Utility Arguments
   a. Promoting the general welfare or maximizing social wealth
   Unlike rights arguments, social utility arguments are consequentialist in outlook. Rather than characterizing the inherent justice or injustice of acts or social relationships, utilitarian arguments judge legal rules by their consequences. Rules that have, on balance, good effects are to be

preferred over rules that cause more harm than good. Utilitarian analysis is based on comparison of costs and benefits of alternative legal
rules; costs and benefits are measured by the effects on behavior that
legal rules promote or discourage.

To make social utility arguments persuasive, lawyers must attempt
to persuade decision makers about the likely consequences of alternative
rules. They must then convince decision makers that the benefits of a
proposed legal rule outweigh its costs.

Social utility arguments address the following questions:

What are the social consequences of legal rules?

What kinds of behavior will different rules foster?

What incentives do the rules create?

Which rules maximize the general welfare or social utility?

   b. Categories of social utility arguments

      1. Behavior modification; investment in safety

        Encourage safe construction

Liability will encourage people to build safely and support existing
neighboring structures and preserve the neighborhood; it will encourage desirable investment in safety

Encourage self-protection

No liability means people will build better houses; they will support
their own houses

      2. Investment arguments

        Secure investment

Established investments should be protected; security of investment
will encourage people to build and develop their property because
they know the value of their investment will be protected by society;
people are more likely to invest in economic development of property
if they know the value of their investment is not vulnerable to complete destruction by incompatible neighboring uses

Competition

Freedom to use one's property as one sees fit without worrying about
effects on others will encourage desirable development; protecting
first uses establishes monopolies

      3. Cost internalization arguments

        Cost internalization

Those who engage in economic activities should compensate those
who are injured by their conduct; this will force them to internalize
the external costs of their conduct and will encourage results that are
more consistent with the general welfare; if people are not required to
internalize these external costs, their cost/benefit determinations are
skewed, as an activity may be profitable to the individual owner even
if it causes more social harm than good

Deregulation of economic activity

Incompatible land uses create joint costs because each owner inflicts
costs on the other; courts are not competent to judge very well the
costs and benefits of economic activity; it is better to let the market
determine which activities should prevail even if it is imperfect; those

who are harmed by economic activities can contract with offending parties to induce them to stop

4. Transaction cost/efficiency arguments
    Most valued user
    When transaction costs prevent bargaining, courts can increase social wealth by granting entitlements to those who value them most highly, *e.g.,* those who would purchase them in the absence of transaction costs
    Deference to the free market
    Although transaction costs may prevent bargains from going forward, private bargaining is more likely to approximate the socially desirable result than judicial fiat; courts should therefore hesitate to interfere in the market; courts should simply make the existing rules clear and enforce whatever private bargains are made; they should not attempt to mimic the result a competitive market would produce because this will invite too much uncertainty and government control

III. Judicial Role Arguments
  a. Defining the proper spheres of authority of legal institutions
      Judicial role or institutional role arguments are concerned with the proper relations among separate branches of government in the legal system. Arguments about the spheres of authority of different governmental actors revolve around the question of which government officials may appropriately modernize or change existing rules of law or patterns of social practice.
    Judicial role arguments address the following questions:
      What is the proper role of the courts as lawmakers?
      What is the proper division of lawmaking authority between the courts and the legislature?
      What is the proper way for courts to interpret and implement legislative enactments?
  b. Categories of judicial role arguments
    1. Precedential arguments
      (a) Broad versus narrow holding
           Broad holding
           Interpreting a prior case to establish a broad principle applicable to a large range of situations
           Narrow holding
           Interpreting a prior case to establish a holding suited to the specific, narrowly defined fact situation addressed in that case, and as not necessarily applying to a new situation involving arguably distinct features
      (b) Distinguish or reconcile apparently conflicting cases
           Distinguish a precedent
           Interpreting a prior case narrowly; explaining why the holding in that case is inapplicable to the present case and why there are good reasons of public policy to treat the current case differently from the prior case
           Reconcile apparently conflicting precedents

Explain why two apparently conflicting cases further a single underlying principle; or explain why they are distinguishable from each other

(c)   Enforce versus overrule precedent
Stare decisis
Promote stability of expectations and reliance on established rules of law by following precedent; promote evenhandedness and equality by treating like cases alike; allow people to rely on existing rules of law
Promote justice
Promote justice by modernizing legal rules to protect legitimate interests in accord with current social conditions and values

2.   Institutional role arguments
(a)   Common law
Judicial restraint
Judges should apply law, not make it; leave lawmaking to the legislature; judges are not elected, and even when they are elected, they are not accountable to the voters in the same way that legislatures are; citizens do not lobby judges to encourage them to make specific rulings in specific cases; because judges are removed from direct public accountability for their decisions, it is wrong for them to make policy in a democracy; any changes in law should be made by elected officials
Judicial activism
Judges have made law through the common law system for centuries; it is no more democratic to rely on the judgment of an earlier judge than for a current judge to use her own judgment; moreover if there is a gap, conflict, or ambiguity in the law then the court has no choice but to make law
Judges should change law when social values or social conditions change to act in ways that are fair and sensible; judges should not act mechanically; legislatures can always correct a judicial mistake by changing the law; and to the extent there are impediments to the legislature's doing this, there are impediments to adopting the best law in the first place; no way for judges to escape responsibility for the rules they enforce

(b)   Statutory interpretation
Remedial statutes broadly construed
Remedial statutes should be broadly construed to effectuate their purposes; any ambiguities should be resolved in favor of furthering the policies underlying the statute by an expansive interpretation of the statute; to interpret the statute narrowly would defeat the purposes the legislature sought to achieve and subvert legislative intent
Defer to clear statutory language
The courts should not go beyond the language of a statute; if the legislature had intended to go further than the clear language of the statute, it would have said so; courts have no right to rewrite statutes to include remedies and legal claims not explicitly pro-

vided by them; any common law rules not expressly changed by
the statute remain in effect; to add remedies or legal claims not
explicitly covered by the statute would subvert legislative intent

3. Institutional competence
Deference to the legislature
Judges are not competent to determine the social consequences of
new rules; legislatures can hold hearings and better assess the consequences of any changes in the law
Judicial responsibility
Judges have no choice but to make law, so they should do the best
they can; the parties' lawyers will have an incentive to bring forward
facts and arguments to advise the court; moreover, if judges are not
competent to determine the effects of new rules, they are also not
competent to determine the effects of existing rules; aside from
whether judges change the law, they have a responsibility to make
the best decisions they can; judges should acknowledge and shoulder
their responsibility for implementing the rule of law; the common
law system allows courts to adjust legal principles in light of changing
social values and in the context of specific cases; the legislature cannot
anticipate every problem

IV. Formal Realizability or Administrability
a. Predictability versus flexibility
Arguments about formal realizability or administrability concern the
proper form of legal rules. Rigid rules give clearer guidance about citizens' legal rights than vague standards. Yet rules lack flexibility and may
interfere with the ability to obtain justice in specific cases. Flexible
standards allow contextual judgments, fitting the law to the facts of
the case. Yet standards provide judges with discretion that they may
misuse.
Formal realizability arguments address the following questions:
Should legal rules be rigid or flexible?
When are bright-line distinctions better than case-by-case adjudication?
b. Categories of formal realizability arguments
1. Predictability versus justice in the specific case
(a) Predictability and uniformity
Rigid rules, mechanically applied, protect reasonable expectations based on existing law and allow citizens to plan with a
clear understanding of the rules governing their conduct; citizens have a right to know what conduct is prohibited and what
is allowed so that they can structure their conduct accordingly;
rigid application of rules also ensures that like cases will be
treated alike because mechanical application takes discretion
away from judges; rules therefore not only promote predictability but justice and equality
(b) Flexibility
Rigid rules are too strict, resulting in both under- and over-
inclusiveness; flexible standards allow justice in the individual
case

Standards may also be more predictable than rules; this is because rule systems can become complicated with many rules and specific exceptions, and it may be difficult to tell which specific rule applies to a fact situation; standards that appeal to the ultimate goals of the legal system, like fairness or social utility, may be easier to apply in practice

2. Relation between form and judicial role
    (1) Prevent arbitrary judicial discretion
         Rigid rules control judicial discretion and therefore protect individuals from arbitrary uses of government power
    (2) Promote justice
         Disabling judges from engaging in case-by-case adjudication to achieve justice in the individual case lessens faith in the legal system by leading to outcomes that are widely viewed as unjust

III. Relation between form and substance
    (a) Rules facilitate implementation of policy goals
         Rules promote investment because they allow planning; citizens know what conduct will result in liability and what conduct will be privileged; standards discourage investment because of uncertainty about whether economic development activities will result in liability to others
         Rules are easier to contract around than standards because it is clear who owns the entitlement; with standards, it is never clear what to bargain for; rules therefore promote desirable economic activity
    (b) Rules allow the bad person to walk the line
         Standards better discourage socially harmful conduct because owners know that they will be held responsible for socially harmful conduct; rules allow the bad person to walk the line — to find loopholes in the law — and therefore to violate the spirit of the law while following the letter; rules are rigid and underinclusive and do not prohibit all socially harmful conduct
         Standards encourage socially desirable investment because they give an owner the ability to argue that a use should be privileged because of its immense social value
         Standards better accord with ordinary expectations and customs in the trade, thereby increasing predictability; rules allow people to violate ordinary expectations, thereby increasing distrust in the marketplace and discouraging activity by raising the costs of collaborative activity.

5

Servitudes: Public Regulation of Private Agreements Restricting Land Use

§5.1 Servitudes

A *servitude* is a legal device that creates a right or an obligation that "runs with the land" or with an interest in land. *Restatement (Third) of Property (Servitudes)* §1.1 (2000). A right or obligation runs with the land if it "passes automatically to successive owners or occupiers of the land or the interest in land with which the right or obligation runs." *Id.* §1.1(a). For example, an owner may grant her neighbor a right to use a road or driveway crossing the owner's land. If the permission is informal and revocable at will by the owner of the land, it is called a *license.* When you invite friends over for dinner, you grant them a license to enter your house or apartment. When you enter a store, you do so on the basis of an implied license. When you go to your job, your employer has waived the right to exclude you from the premises and granted you privileged access to the property. Because licenses are generally revocable at will, they are not classified as servitudes. They are also not transferable (except for theater tickets, which are a special case) and cannot be inherited or devised by will.

If the permission is intended to be permanent or irrevocable, however, it is a type of servitude called an *easement.* This particular type of easement is also called a "right of way." Another example of an easement is a right granted to a utility company, such as an electric, telephone, cable television or sewer company to place poles, wires or pipes across or under one's land. A right of way places an obligation on the owner of the land on which the road sits to allow the neighbor to use the road for passage. If the obligation is intended to continue even if that owner sells the land on which the road sits, we say the "burden" of the servitude runs with the "burdened" or "servient" estate. This means that subsequent owners of that land have a continuing obligation to allow the road to be used by the easement owner — the beneficiary of the servitude. If the right to use the road is intended to pass to future owners of the neighboring land, we

317

say the right runs with the "benefited" or "dominant" estate. *Id.* §1.1(b). A right to do something on someone else's land is an *affirmative easement.*

Servitudes may be *negative* as well as affirmative. For example, one owner may promise another that she will restrict her property to residential uses. If the obligation is intended to be binding on all future owners of the land, the burden runs with the burdened land (the servient estate); if future owners of the neighbor's land are intended to be entitled to enforce the restriction, the benefit runs with the neighbor's benefited land (the dominant estate). Traditionally, restrictive servitudes could be created in three forms: *negative easements, restrictive covenants,* and *equitable servitudes.* Agreements restricting or regulating the use of land used for housing are common in both residential subdivisions and condominiums. Agreements restricting the use of real property held for commercial purposes are common among owners and tenants in shopping centers, office condominiums, and industrial parks. They are also used to restrict the use of commercial property such as gas stations or restaurants located in or near residential areas.

The law of easements developed first. The courts limited the number and kind of easements that could be created in order to prevent land from being burdened with obsolete or intrusive impediments to use or development. In response, landowners began to make contractual agreements by which they agreed to restrict the use of their own land for the benefit of either their landlord or neighboring owners. These agreements were called "covenants" and the courts developed a set of rules for covenants that differed from the rules that applied to easements. The law of covenants was initially created by the law courts in England and were called *real covenants.* They were traditionally enforced by damages, the remedy of the law courts. When technical and substantive rules limited the ability of owners to create or enforce such covenants, the equity courts extended enforcement of covenants by developing the law of *equitable servitudes,* relaxing some of those technical requirements and imposing land use restrictions when it seemed fair to do so even if those restrictions had not been formally created according to traditional legal requirements. Because the equity courts used injunctive relief rather than damages to enforce their judgments, the right to obtain an injunction was traditionally governed by equitable servitudes law rather than real covenants law.

The resulting law of servitudes is confusing. Professor Susan French, the Reporter for the American Law Institute's *Restatement (Third) of Property (Servitudes),* has observed that "[t]he concept of interests running with the land is elegantly simple, but the law governing servitude devices is a mess." Susan French, *Servitudes Reform and the New Restatement of Property: Creation Doctrines and Structural Simplification,* 73 Cornell L. Rev. 928 (1988). It is "the most complex and archaic body of American property law remaining in the twentieth century." *Id.* She notes that "[o]thers have described it more colorfully 'as an unspeakable quagmire,'[1] 'confounding intellectual experiences,'[2] and an area of the law full of 'rigid categories, silly distinctions, and unreconciled conflicts over basic values.'"[3] The law of servitudes encompasses a variety of doctrines developed at different periods by different court systems for different purposes. The doctrines sometimes contradict one another and often promote opposite policies;

---

1. Edward Rabin, *Fundamentals of Modern Real Property Law* 480 (2d ed. 1982).
2. Jan Z. Krasnowiecki, *Townhouses with Homes Associations: A New Perspective,* 123 U. Pa. L. Rev. 711, 717 (1975).
3. Charles Haar and Lance Liebman, *Property and Law* 909 (2d ed. 1985).

when they do, it is necessary to know which of the conflicting rules prevails. Don't be discouraged. The problem is not with you; it lies in the confused doctrines.

The *Restatement (Third) of Property (Servitudes)*[4] was adopted by the American Law Institute (ALI) in 1998 and published in final form in 2000. The ALI Restatements are not authoritative sources of law; however, they are often cited in court opinions as persuasive indications of the direction in which courts are or should be moving. The adoption of the *Restatement (Third)* is likely to affect the development of the law in this area for a generation or more.

The modern trend, adopted by the *Restatement (Third)*, is to unify various aspects of the law of easements, real covenants and equitable servitudes and to abolish various archaic distinctions. The *Restatement (Third)* proposes to abolish both the term "negative easement" and the term "equitable servitude." All obligations restricting what one can do with one's own land are to be called *negative* or *restrictive covenants*. Affirmative rights to do something on someone else's land are to be called *easements*. One particular type of easement has retained its traditional, special name: The right to remove materials (such as minerals or oil or gas or trees) from another's property is called a *profit* (traditionally a *profit à prendre*).

Covenants may be affirmative as well as negative. An *affirmative covenant* is an obligation to do something for the benefit of another owner or owners. An example would be a duty of a condominium owner to pay a fee to the condominium association to maintain the roof and other common areas of the building.

Four issues stand out in the law of servitudes. First, what are the *formal* requirements to create a right or obligation that will run with the land? When are *informally* created expectations enforceable by or against subsequent landowners? Second, when the meaning of a servitude is unclear, how should *ambiguities* be interpreted? Third, what are the *substantive* requirements for validity of servitudes? This question includes both (a) determining when land use restrictions are immediately void as against *public policy* and (b) determining when rights or obligations, although valid as contracts between the parties who agreed to them, will not be allowed to run with the land binding and/or benefiting future owners. Fourth, how can servitudes be modified or terminated?

§5.2 Licenses

Possessors of real property constantly grant non-owners permission to enter their property. This permission is normally intended to be temporary and is often limited to specific purposes. These rights, called *licenses*, are usually revocable at will by the grantor. No writing is required to create a license, and many licenses are implied by the circumstances. For example, a store open to the public conveys a clear message that members of the public are invited to enter the property for the purpose of browsing or shopping. Entering a store during business hours would not be deemed a trespass because entry onto the property is based on implied consent. The entry becomes a trespass only when the licensee refuses to leave after being asked to do so. Revocable licenses are not transferable, nor can they be inherited or left by will.[5]

---

4. I will subsequently refer simply to the *Restatement (Third)*.

5. Some terminology may be helpful. A transfer of a property interest during one's lifetime is called an inter vivos conveyance. When an owner leaves real property by will, we

Remember that the owner of property open to the public may not be free to exclude members of the public from that property if the exclusion is based on invidious discrimination. Public accommodations law limits the owner's right to exclude, effectively granting members of protected groups the same licenses proffered to members of groups who are not the victims of discrimination. Thus, although licenses are revocable at will, a store owner who revokes a license to a customer solely on the basis of that customer's race may well be violating a state civil rights law and perhaps the *Civil Rights Act of* 1866, 42 U.S.C. §1981.[6]

Licenses cannot be freely revoked in at least four circumstances. First, an owner who sells personal property to another that is located on her own land generally gives permission to the buyer to enter her land to remove the licensee's personal property. This creates a *license coupled with an interest*. The owner of the real property cannot exclude the licensee who reasonably exercises his license to recover personal property such as a car.

What happens if a property owner *promises* to grant a license? For example, when a person buys a ticket to see a movie, the theater owner agrees to let the ticket holder enter its property for the purpose of watching the movie. The license can be revoked by the theater owner after being issued; however, the ticket holder can sue the theater owner for breach of contract. The courts generally hold that theater tickets, unlike other licenses, are transferable; the ticket holder can give the tickets to her sister.

Subsections 5.3.1.1 (easements by estoppel) and 5.3.1.2 (constructive trusts) address two other circumstances in which courts have granted licensees immunity from revocation of their rights by the grantor. In these cases, the licenses are deemed irrevocable, at least for a certain period of time. These rules may also relax the rules that generally require a formal writing to create permanent interests in real property.

§5.3 Easements

§5.3.1 Creation by Implication

§5.3.1.1 Easements by Estoppel (Irrevocable Licenses)

Courts may prevent a real property owner from revoking a license if the owner grants the licensee the right to invest in improving property or otherwise induces the licensee to act in reasonable reliance on the license. We say the owner is *estopped* from denying continued access to his land for whatever period is deemed just under the circumstances. The doctrine of easement by estoppel effectively converts a revocable license into an irrevocable easement. Is this justified? If so, under what circumstances, and why?

---

say the testator (male) or testatrix (female) *devises* the real property to the *devisees*. Personal property is *bequeathed*, and the recipients are called *legatees*. An owner who dies without a will is *intestate*; her property will be distributed to her *heirs* as defined in the state *intestacy* statute.

6. *See supra* §2.2.1.1.

HOLBROOK v. TAYLOR
532 S.W.2d 763 (Ky. 1976)

MARVIN J. STERNBERG, Justice.

This is an action to establish a right to the use of a roadway, which is 10 to 12 feet wide and about 250 feet long, over the unenclosed, hilly woodlands of another. The claimed right to the use of the roadway is twofold: by prescription and by estoppel. . . .

In 1942 appellants purchased the subject property. In 1944 they gave permission for a haul road to be cut for the purpose of moving coal from a newly opened mine. The roadway was so used until 1949, when the mine closed. During that time the appellants were paid a royalty for the use of the road. In 1957 appellants built a tenant house on their property and the roadway was used by them and their tenant. The tenant house burned in 1961 and was not replaced. In 1964 the appellees bought their three-acre building site, which adjoins appellants, and the following year built their residence thereon. At all times prior to 1965, the use of the haul road was by permission of appellants. There is no evidence of any probative value which would indicate that the use of the haul road during that period of time was either adverse, continuous, or uninterrupted. The trial court was fully justified, therefore, in finding that the right to the use of this easement was not established by prescription.

As to the issue on estoppel, we have long recognized that a right to the use of a roadway over the lands of another may be established by estoppel. In *Lashley Telephone Co. v. Durbin*, 228 S.W. 423 (Ky. 1921), we said:

> Though many courts hold that a licensee is conclusively presumed as a matter of law to know that a license is revocable at the pleasure of the licensor, and if he expend money in connection with his entry upon the land of the latter, he does so at his peril . . . , yet it is the established rule in this state that where a license is not a bare, naked right of entry, but includes the right to erect structures and acquire an interest in the land in the nature of an easement by the construction of improvements thereon, the licensor may not revoke the license and restore his premises to their former condition after the licensee has exercised the privilege given by the license and erected the improvements at considerable expense. . . .

In *Gibbs v. Anderson*, 156 S.W.2d 876 (Ky. 1941), Gibbs claimed the right, by estoppel, to the use of a roadway over the lands of Anderson. The lower court denied the claim. We reversed. Anderson's immediate predecessor in title admitted that he had discussed the passway with Gibbs before it was constructed and had agreed that it might be built through his land. He stood by and saw Gibbs expend considerable money in this construction. We applied the rule announced in *Lashley Telephone Co. v. Durbin, supra*, and reversed with directions that a judgment be entered granting Gibbs the right to the use of the passway. . . .

In *Akers v. Moore*, 309 S.W.2d 758 (Ky. 1958), this court again considered the right to the use of a passway by estoppel. Akers and others had used the Moore branch as a public way of ingress and egress from their property. They sued Moore and others who owned property along the branch seeking to have the court recognize their right to the use of the roadway and to order the removal of obstructions which had been placed in the roadway. . . . Considering the right to the use of the strip of land between the right side of the creek bed and the highway, this court found that the evidence portrayed it very rough and apparently never improved, that it ran alongside the house in which one of the protestors lived, and that by acquiescence or by express consent of at least one of the protestors the right side of the roadway was opened up so as to change the roadway from its close proximity to the Moore residence. The relocated portion of the highway had only been used as a passway for about six years before the suit was filed. [We found an easement by estoppel.]

> We consider the fact that the appellees, Artie Moore . . . had stood by and acquiesced (if in fact they had not affirmatively consented) the change being made and permitted the appellants to spend money in fixing it up to make it passable and use it for six years without objecting. . . . [T]he law recognizes that one may acquire a license to use a passway or roadway where, with the knowledge of the licensor, he has in the exercise of the privilege spent money in improving the way or for other purposes connected with its use on the faith or strength of the license. Under such conditions the license becomes irrevocable and continues for so long a time as its nature calls for. This, in effect, becomes a grant through estoppel. . . . It would be unconscionable to permit the owners of this strip of land of trivial value to revoke the license by obstructing and preventing its use. 309 S.W.2d at 759.

In the present case the roadway had been used since 1944 by permission of the owners of the servient estate. The evidence is conflicting as to whether the use of the road subsequent to 1965 was by permission or by claim of right. Appellees contend that it had been used by them and others without the permission of appellants; on the other hand, it is contended by appellants that the use of the roadway at all times was by their permission. The evidence discloses that during the period of preparation for the construction of appellees' home and during the time the house was being built, appellees were permitted to use the roadway as ingress and egress for workmen, for hauling machinery and material to the building site, for construction of the dwelling, and for making improvements generally to the premises. Further, the evidence reflects that after construction of the residence, which cost $25,000, was completed, appellees continued to regularly use the roadway as they had been doing. Appellant J. S. Holbrook testified that in order for appellees to get up to their house he gave them permission to use and repair the roadway. They widened it, put in a culvert, and graveled part of it with "red dog," also known as cinders, at a cost of approximately $100. There is no other location over which a roadway could reasonably be built to provide an outlet for appellees.

No dispute had arisen between the parties at any time over the use of the roadway until the fall of 1970. Appellant J. S. Holbrook contends that he wanted to secure a writing from the appellees in order to relieve him from any responsibility for any damage that might happen to anyone on the subject road. On the other hand, Mrs. Holbrook testified that the writing was desired to avoid any claim which may be made by appellees of a right to the use of the roadway. Appellees testified that the writing was an effort to force them to purchase a small strip of land over which the roadway traversed, for the sum of $500. The dispute was not resolved and appellants erected a steel cable across the roadway to prevent its use and also constructed "no trespassing" signs. Shortly thereafter, the suit was filed to require the removal of the obstruction and to declare the right of appellees to the use of the roadway without interference.

The use of the roadway by appellees to get to their home from the public highway, the use of the roadway to take in heavy equipment and material and supplies for construction of the residence, the general improvement of the premises, the maintenance of the roadway, and the construction by appellees of a $25,000 residence, all with the actual consent of appellants or at least with their tacit approval, clearly demonstrates the rule laid down in *Lashley Telephone Co. v. Durbin, supra,* that the license to use the subject roadway may not be revoked. . . .

§5.3.1.2 *Constructive Trusts*

A *trust* is a property arrangement in which an owner, called the *settlor,* transfers property to another person, called the *trustee,* with instructions to manage the property for benefit of a third party, called the *beneficiary.* The trustee is said to have *legal title* to the property, while the beneficiary has *equitable* or *beneficial title.* For example, a parent may write a will providing that, if she dies while her children are minors, some portion of her property will be placed in a trust to be managed by her brother for the benefit of her children. Her brother (the trustee) will be obligated to use the income from the trust for the care of her children (the beneficiaries).

Most trusts are created expressly by a trust document or a will. However, the courts sometimes treat a property arrangement *as if* the grantor had created a trust arrangement, regardless of the grantor's intent. The courts call these arrangements *constructive trusts.* A constructive trust is

> one which is found to exist by operation of law or by "construction" of the court, regardless of any lack of express agreement between or intent on the part of the parties. When one party has been wrongfully deprived either by mistake, fraud, or some other breach of faith or confidence, of some right, benefit, or title to the property, a court may impose upon the present holder of legal title a constructive trust for the benefit of that party. Thus in order to prevent the unjust enrichment of the legal holder, such person is deemed to hold the property as a trustee for the beneficial use of that party which has been wrongfully deprived of its rights.

Steven Gifis, *Law Dictionary* 213 (1975). In recent years, courts have started to apply constructive trust doctrine in the context of real property. The following case is a good example.

RASE v. CASTLE MOUNTAIN RANCH, INC.
631 P.2d 680 (Mont. 1981)

JOHN C. SHEEHY, Justice.

Both sides appeal from a judgment entered by the Third Judicial District Court, Powell County, imposing a constructive trust for more than 40 cabin sites at Rock Creek Lake in Powell County, on real property now owned by Castle Mountain Ranch, Inc., successor to Ward Paper Box Company (Ward).

The cabin sites which surround Rock Creek Lake [about] 15 or 20 miles from Deer Lodge, Montana, were owned until 1972 by Rock Creek Irrigation, Inc., a subsidiary of Williams and Tavenner, Inc. (Tavenner), which operated the surrounding ranch. In 1972, Tavenner sold the ranch, including the lakeshore property, to Ward Paper Box Co. The ranch has since been transferred to Castle Mountain Ranch, Inc. Louis Ward is the principal shareholder or owner in both corporations and was the primary actor in the purchase of the ranch, including the cabin sites around Rock Creek Lake.

The respondents and cross-appellants here (plaintiffs in the District Court) are owners of summer homes and cabins around the lake. They and their predecessors, acting individually, at various times since 1922, built and improved summer homes, some quite substantial, on the Rock Creek Lake front, on real property owned by Tavenner, and with the consent and permission of Tavenner. The issue for us to decide, as in the District Court, is the nature and extent of any agreement between the cabin owners and Tavenner, individually or collectively, express or implied, for termination of the permission.

The cabins were built around the lake over a course of many years, by friends, neighbors and employees of the ranch owners, with their consent and possibly with their implied invitation. These were permanent structures, sometimes built with timber from the ranch and sometimes with the assistance of the ranch owners. The ranch owners owned one of the cabins. Reasons given for the ranch owners extending permission include the wish for companionship at the ranch, the help of the cabin owners in protecting the ranch properties, their availability for fire lookout and fire fighting, and their help in maintaining the roads, as well as their friendship and society.

For at least 50 years, relations between the cabin owners and the ranch owners were amicable. The cabins were inherited, bought and sold without interference from the ranch owners. Cabins were expanded and renovated, and the ranch owners were advised of sales or inheritance of the cabins, sometimes after the fact. Through the years, the cabins were modernized, expanded and improved. The ranch owners were aware of the continuing maintenance of the summer homes. County records, at the time of trial, indicated that the summer cabins had an assessed value of $300,000. The ranch owners did insist on permanent structures to be located on the cabin sites; no trailers or movable homes were permitted.

On some occasions, various cabin owners attempted to purchase the underlying cabin sites, but the ranch owners advised that the lake provided water for the ranch, and the ranch owners wanted to maintain control over the lake itself. The use of the lake for irrigation did not interfere with the owners' use of their cabins.

In the very earliest years, no documents were entered into between the ranch owners and cabin owners. After some period of time, some of the cabin owners entered into lease agreements with the ranch owners, but these agreements expired by their own terms. Starting in 1963, however, the cabin owners signed documents that were entitled "license agreements." These documents had been drafted by the lawyer for the ranch owners. All of the license agreements had the same general provisions, and essentially provided as follows:

1. A license from Rock Creek Irrigation, Inc. to the cabin owner for the use of the cabin site together with right of access thereto.

2. A term for the license, solely for a summer camp or cabin site, beginning January 1, 1963 and ending on termination.

3. A fee for $6.00 per year payable in advance or 50 cents per month for any part of a year on or before January 1 of each year.

4. A provision for the erection of structures on the cabin site by the licensee, to be approved in advance by the licensor, and providing that such structures should be removed by the licensee at termination, or the structures became the property of the licensor....

7. A termination provision which is the heart of this lawsuit and which provided: Either party may terminate this agreement at any time, without regard to payment periods, by written notice to the other specifying the date of termination, which notice shall be given not less than thirty (30) days prior to the termination date therein specified....

8. A provision that the relationship of landlord and tenant was not created between the parties, and that the license is personal to the licensee and not transferable to administrators, executors, successors or assigns of the licensee....

Tavenner did not ever serve a notice of termination upon any of the cabin owners. In the years from 1963 to 1972, the provisions of the license agreement were breached in many respects by various owners, without objection from Rock Creek Irrigation, Inc. Particularly, the cabins were bought and sold or transferred by inheritance without objection from the licensor.

Robert Tavenner testified, however, that the reason there were no terminations was "we had no thought of selling the ranch." He further said they had no reason to terminate the permissions, but "we wanted to be in a position to terminate if we had to."

It was probably assumed by all parties that the ownership of the ranch property would remain unchanged through the years. However, in 1969, on the death of one of the ranch owners, the position of the ranch owners changed, and the ranch property became available for sale. In 1972, Ward Paper Box Company entered the picture in the person of Louis Ward, its chief officer. He visited the ranch in the spring or early summer of 1972, and on July 21, 1972, his company (Ward) entered into a contract to purchase the ranch including the land surrounding Rock Creek Lake. The contract provided for a closing date of December 1, 1972. Attached to the contract for sale was a schedule of the license agreements which included the notation "consent of licensees to assignment not required."

Robert Tavenner, one of the ranch owners, testified that near the end of the negotiations, Louis Ward requested that Tavenner terminate the cabin owners. Tavenner refused. He testified:

Q. Now as a matter of fact if that had been made a condition of the sale you wouldn't have gone through with the sale?
A. We wouldn't have gone through, we told him that. If that had been we wouldn't have gone through.
Q. So, basically he took the sale and lake as it was, isn't that right?
A. After I told him that we had a family conference, he said let me have a little time to think about it. And a day or two went by and he said he would take the ranch as planned, the cabins and all.

On October 13, 1972, counsel for Ward mailed a letter to all cabin owners advising that the impending transfer of ranch property would be consummated on December 1, 1972, and which letter included the following paragraph:

We are writing on behalf of Ward Paper Box Company to advise you of this impending transfer and also to advise you that the purchaser has examined your license agreement and will construe it according to its literal terms. There have been no oral representations made to anyone with respect to the purchasers' intentions as to this property. You should therefore not assume that you have any rights or privileges other than those arising from your license agreement.

The transfer of the ranch property occurred according to schedule and on July 11, 1973, the new owners sent each of the cabin owners a notice of termination of their licenses. On December 20, 1973, the cabin owners filed their action in the District Court for interlocutory and permanent injunctive relief, and to quiet the title in their cabins and establish permanent easements thereto. . . .

[The District Court found] that Tavenner did not intend to cancel the cabin site arrangements while it owned the ranch; that although there were no express assurances, Robert Tavenner allowed cabin improvements, assuring the cabin owners from time to time that the license agreements were a "formality" and there was to be no change in the way the cabins were held by the cabin owners; that while the Tavenner corporation was involved in selling the ranch, it permitted Martin Olsen and James Blodgett to purchase homes from previous owners without informing the new purchasers of the impending sale, merely submitting the usual license agreement to the new owners for execution; that by allowing the cabin owners to make improvements and to assume a long-term occupancy, Tavenner misled the cabin owners into believing they did not have to fear the loss of their investment and so allowed them to act to their detriment; that Louis Ward was advised Tavenner would not sell the ranch if Ward insisted on the cancellation of the license agreements; that Ward agreed to take the property although he knew, or through the reasonable exercise of inquiry, should have known, that the cabin owners hoped for a long-term occupancy and had made substantial improvements based upon the implied assurances of Tavenner; and, that such conduct amounted to constructive fraud against the cabin owners.

To be sure, there were no express assurances from Tavenner that the cabin owners had any right of possession of the real property beyond the permission stated in the license agreements. It is equally clear that Tavenner engaged in a course of conduct, as we have set forth in our statement of the facts, that gave the cabin owners an implied assurance of a somewhat permanent tenure sufficient that they made substantial investments in erecting and maintaining the cabins openly recognized by Tavenner. From our review of the record, it is abundantly clear to us that while Tavenner, through the license agreements, wanted to be in position to terminate the permission for any cabin owner it might find undesirable, it was never the intention of Tavenner, in procuring the agreements or in permitting the improvements, to use the license agreements for a wholesale termination of every cabin owner's permission in one clatter. In fact, Tavenner refused to do just that. We determine from the record that it was the intention of Tavenner to have a degree of control over who possessed the cabins, though it never exercised that control; that it wanted to be in a position, if it felt the need, to terminate any undesirable possessors of the cabins; and perhaps that the execution of the license agreements and the requirement of a nominal sum per year eliminated any potential future claim of adverse possession or prescriptive right. . . .

In its conclusions of law, the District Court determined that the cabin owners had no right, title or interest in the lake property under the doctrine of adverse possession or prescriptive right, and their occupancy was based on permission from Ward's predecessors in interest. The District Court further concluded that the conduct of the predecessor landowners created a constructive trust in the improvements placed on the property by the cabin owners and that the trust was imposed upon Ward, as the landowners' successor in interest, as an equitable lien on the property in favor of the cabin owners. The court determined, as an exercise of equity, that the equitable lien could be satisfied by a continued use by the cabin owners for a reasonable period of time or by compensation and money for the value of the structures from Ward.

The evidence supports these conclusions sitting in equity, and we find the District Court properly so concluded. In its judgment and decree, the District Court provided that in lieu of cash payment from Ward, the cabin owners may continue to occupy their particular cabin sites with the right of ingress and egress until December 31, 1987, at which time the licenses to occupy should terminate and if the improvements were not removed as set forth in the license agreements, the improvements should become the property of Ward without payment. Additionally, the District Court provided that the cabin owners had the option (to be exercised by them before May 1, 1980), to receive payment from Ward for the cabin structures and fixtures. If any cabin owner and Ward could not agree on the purchase price, the court would reserve jurisdiction to hear evidence and to make a determination as to the amount Ward should pay for the improvements.

Ward contends that the judgment and decree violates the statute of frauds, the parol evidence rule, and disregards waiver by the cabin owners in signing the license agreements.

The statute of frauds, Mont. Code Ann. §70-20-101, provides in essence that no estate or interest in real property can be created except by an instrument in writing.

The parol evidence rule is found in two statutes, Mont. Code Ann. §§28-2-904 and 28-2-905, which provide in essence that the written agreement supersedes the oral negotiations or stipulations and that when the agreement is reduced to writing, it is to be considered as containing all the terms between the parties.

The written agreements relied upon by Ward are the purchase contract of July 21, 1972, the warranty deed from the seller to Ward, dated September 25, 1972, the further warranty deed, dated December 1, 1972, and a relevant commitment for title insurance, dated December 1, 1972. Attached to the contract for purchase was a schedule of the license agreements with the cabin owners, and, of course, the notation thereon, "consent of licensees to assignment not required."

There is an exception to the parol evidence rule when the validity of the agreement is the fact in dispute, Mont. Code Ann. §28-2-905(1)(b). Here the validity of the terms of the license agreements is the fact in dispute.

When the validity of the agreement is a fact in dispute, parol evidence is admissible, not to vary the terms of the instrument, but to show that what appears on its face as a valid, binding contract is in fact no such thing.

As to the statute of frauds set forth in Mont. Code Ann. §70-20-101, the next following statute, Mont. Code Ann. §70-20-102, provides an exception to the statute of frauds for "any trust . . . arising or being extinguished by implication or operation of law." This exception, of course, applies to a constructive trust.

Ward's contention on the waiver argument is again based on a 30-day clause in the license agreements, and the probable existence of a similar clause in the earlier lease agreements. The waiver argument is another way of saying that the provisions of the license agreements control absolutely, and thus is another string to Ward's bow in contending that the court should not look outside the license agreements to determine the intention of the parties. Waiver is a voluntary relinquishment of a known right and since the District Court concluded that the license agreements were not executed with the intention that the cabin owners abandoned their permissive rights in favor of a 30-day cancellation, a finding of waiver in the execution of the license agreements would be inconsistent with the court's conclusion that the license agreements did not reflect the true intention of the parties at the time.

. . . Following the judgment, the cabin owners moved the District Court to amend the judgment to provide for a possession of 50 years instead of the 13 years granted in the court's decree. The 50 years is contended to be the life expectancy of the cabins built on the lake properties.

. . . A court sitting in equity causes is empowered to determine the questions involved in the case and to do complete justice. The court has all of the power requisite to render justice between the parties, particularly if the intent and disposition of one of the parties is not to perform his contractual obligations. The court obviously framed its judgment and decree in this case so as to give the cabin owners an option to receive, from Ward, the value of the cabin improvements, or to enjoy their lakeside cabins for a term of years considerably shorter than the useful life of the cabins. Under either option, Ward will not be unjustly enriched, and recognition is given by the District Court to the long-term intentions of Tavenner and the cabin owners. Both parties won something from the District Court: the cabin owners, a recognition of their long-term rights and the value of their cabin improvements; and Ward, a method of obtaining eventually an unimpeded title to the lakeshore property. We find the result is equitable. . . .

[We] grant the cabin owners a period of six months from [the date this opinion is issued] in which the cabin owners shall have the option to be exercised by written notice to the defendant Ward, to receive payment for the cabin structures and fixtures. [Otherwise, they may continue to occupy the cabins until December 31, 1987.]

DAVID SHEA, Justice, specially concurring.

I concur in the opinion of the Court, with the exception that I would permit the plaintiffs to use the property for a substantially longer time than until December 31, 1987.

The only evidence in the record on the length of time the plaintiffs should be permitted to stay on the premises, was presented by the plaintiffs, and the evidence presented was 50 years. After the trial court made its decision, plaintiffs moved the trial court to amend its findings and conclusions to permit the 50 years, but the trial court refused to so amend the findings and conclusions.

I do not say that 50 years must be the figure, but there is no evidence in the record for the trial court's decision to permit the plaintiffs to stay on the land until only December 31, 1987. I do not, however, deem it proper for an appellate court to set the number of years; that is the function of the trial court.

I would affirm the trial court in all respects except that I would remand for a determination of the number of years the plaintiffs should be permitted to stay on the land, based on the evidence in the record. That evidence supports a decision far beyond December 31, 1987.

This case is a prime example of what Corporate America through its activities in the State of Montana is doing to the citizens. It demonstrates the difference between ownership of land owned by residents of Montana and ownership of land owned by outside corporations who use this state as an economic playground.

NOTES AND QUESTIONS

1. *Statute of frauds.* The statute of frauds, adopted in all jurisdictions, requires a writing to transfer most interests in real property. Easements are considered substantial property interests covered by the statute; the courts therefore hold that a writing is generally required to create an easement.[7] However, courts have adopted several ex-

---

7. This is not the case for easements (such as the easement for lateral support of land) that define the rights of neighbors toward each other in the absence of agreement to the contrary.

ceptions to the statute of frauds. Easements by estoppel are one exception; others, addressed later in this chapter, include easements by prescription, implication from prior use, and necessity.

2. *Oral easements and irrevocable licenses.* Easements by estoppel may be recognized in two quite different contexts.

a. *Oral easements.* The grantor may purport to convey an easement but fail to comply with the requisite formalities. This can occur (1) if an easement is granted orally; (2) in a writing that does not comply with the specific requirements of the local statute of frauds or (3) in the case of an ambiguous deed reference. *See, e.g., Bubis v. Kassin,* 733 A.2d 1232 (N.J. Super. Ct. App. Div. 1999) (rev'd on other grounds, 878 A.2d 815 (N.J. 2005). In these cases, recognition of an easement by estoppel enforces the presumed intent of the parties despite their failure to comply with formal requirements. Many courts will grant an easement despite the lack or inadequacy of a writing in these situations if the grantor intended to grant an easement and the grantee invests substantially in reasonable reliance on this representation. *See Prospect Development Co., Inc. v. Bershader,* 515 S.E.2d 291, 298-299 (Va. 1999) (fraudulent representations by seller that adjoining land would not be developed can entitle the buyer to a negative easement by estoppel preventing such development). An oral easement may also be granted (4) if the grantor committed fraud by deceiving the grantee. Some courts will *only* grant an easement by estoppel if it can be shown that the grantor committed fraud or misrepresentation. *See, e.g., Flaig v. Gramm,* 983 P.2d 396 (Mont. 1999).

b. *Irrevocable licenses.* Alternatively, the grantor may have intended to grant only a revocable license. In this case, recognition of an easement by estoppel is likely to *contradict* the original intent of the grantor, as in *Holbrook* and *Rase.* The use in both cases was permissive, and owners generally have the right to revoke licenses at will. Yet in both cases the courts refused to allow the license to be revoked by the grantor or his successor in interest. The *Holbrook* court granted a permanent easement even though the grantor clearly had intended to grant a revocable license. The *Rase* court granted the licensees a choice between a 13-year right of occupancy or the fair market value of their property interests. Rather than relaxing formalities, these cases involve protecting the interests of the licensee in relying on a relationship with the owner who granted continuing rights of access to the property. *See also Pinkston v. Hartley,* 511 So. 2d 168 (Ala. 1987) (license to lay sewer lines across defendant's property held irrevocable).

3. *Grantor's right to exclude versus grantee's reliance interest.* What justifies making a license irrevocable against the wishes of the grantor? Answering this question requires balancing the grantor's interest in controlling access to her property and the grantee's interest in reasonably relying on continued rights of access. In other words, courts must choose between *implementing the grantor's intent* and *protecting the grantee's interest in relying on continued access.* Courts may also need to choose between the formal arrangements set down in writing and the informal arrangements embodying the parties'

Such easements have historically been called "natural rights" since they implicitly accompany property ownership.

expectations and founded in social custom, the conduct of the parties, implicit understandings, or oral reassurances. When formal and informal arrangements diverge, courts must determine which best effectuates the intent of the parties. This becomes a problem if the licensor's actions have communicated conflicting messages to the licensee, simultaneously reserving the right to revoke the license and giving the licensee reason to believe that the license would not be revoked.

The law of adverse possession treats permission by the grantor as a defense to claims of rights of access by others. One who has entered property of another with the owner's permission cannot obtain title by adverse possession. This doctrine suggests that owners have full power to choose either to exclude others or to grant them permission to enter on their own terms. When the owner allows others to enter her property, she is exercising her power to control access to her property. Adverse possession doctrine is based on the premise that an owner should not lose her power to exclude others merely because she exercised her right to invite them in temporarily.

The law of irrevocable licenses, whether under a theory of easement by estoppel or constructive trust, is based on a contrary moral premise. When owners open up their property to others, they may, by their words and actions, create reasonable expectations of continued access to the property. When non-owners expend resources or labor in reasonable reliance on permitted access, the owner may be held to have waived the legal power to revoke that access. When owners grant rights of access to their property to others, they are not unconditionally free to revoke such access. Non-owners who have relied on a relationship with the owner that made such access possible in the past may be granted partial or total immunity from having such access revoked when this is necessary to achieve justice.

4. *Arguments for and against the doctrine.* Many courts will recognize an easement by estoppel if the grantee reasonably relies on the license and invests substantially on the basis of it even if the grantor never intended to grant permanent rights. They will do so because they believe the grantor should have known that a reasonable grantee would have understood the rights being granted to be more than temporary. Denying an easement would allow the grantor to commit a kind of fraud, whether intentional or negligent. In the leading case of *Stoner v. Zucker,* 83 P. 808 (Cal. 1906), for example, plaintiff granted defendant a revocable license to enter plaintiff's property to construct a ditch for carrying water. Defendant constructed the ditch at the substantial expense of $7,000. One year later, plaintiff revoked the license. Plaintiff argued, *id.* at 809:

> that a license in its very nature is a revocable permission, that whoever accepts that permission does it with knowledge that the permission may be revoked at any time; that the rule cannot be changed, therefore, because the licensee has foolishly or improvidently expended money in the hope of a continuance of a license, upon the permanent continuance of which he has no right in law or in equity to rely; that to convert such a parol license into a grant or easement under the doctrine of estoppel is destructive of the statute of frauds, which was meant to lay down an inflexible rule; and, finally, that there is no room or play for the operation of the doctrine of estoppel, since the licensor has in no way deceived the licensee by revocation, has put no fraud upon him, and has merely asserted a right which had been absolutely reserved to him by the very terms of his permission.

The court rejected this argument, holding instead, *id.* at 809-810, that

> it would be to countenance a fraud upon the part of the licensor if he were allowed, after expenditure of money by the licensees upon the faith of the license, to cut short by

revocation the natural term of its continuance and existence, and that under the doctrine of estoppel, the licensor would not be allowed to do this. The decision was that the licensor would be held to have conveyed an easement commensurate in its extent and duration with the right to be enjoyed. . . .

The recognized principle, therefore, is that where a licensee has entered under a parol license and has expended money, or its equivalent in labor, in the execution of the license, the license becomes irrevocable; the licensee will have a right of entry upon the lands of the licensor for the purpose of maintaining his structures or, in general, his rights under his license, and the license will continue for so long a time as the nature of it calls for.

Similarly, in *Shepard v. Purvine*, 248 P.2d 352 (Or. 1952), plaintiffs expended "substantial sums of money" in laying down pipes necessary to transport water from a spring on defendant's property. Defendants argued, *Id.* at 355, that if plaintiffs had wanted a permanent easement, they should have been

aware of the fact that such rights are normally granted by deed . . . and that if [they] had been acting with ordinary care in looking after their interests, . . . [they] would have asked for [a deed] and offered to pay the value of the water and the right of way in order to insure its permanency.

The court rejected this argument, *Id.* at 361-362, instead concluding:

Plaintiffs offer a satisfactory explanation for their failure to request and secure a transfer by deed of the rights granted them. They say that the gift to them was a friendly gesture on the part of C. M. Purvine, just as were the rights granted them by Barker and Mrs. Hiatt. These people were close friends and neighbors, and they were not dealing at arm's length. One's word was considered as good as his bond. Under the circumstances, for plaintiffs to have insisted upon a deed would have been embarrassing; in effect, it would have been expressing a doubt as to their friend's integrity. We do not believe the evidence warrants a conclusion that plaintiffs were negligent in not insisting upon a formal transfer of the rights accorded. An oral license promptly acted upon in the manner plaintiffs acted is just as valid, binding, and irrevocable as a deeded right of way.

See also Fast v. DeRaeve, 714 P.2d 1077 (Or. Ct. App. 1986) (reaffirming *Shepard v. Purvine*).

However, other courts will find an easement by estoppel only if the grantor intended to grant an easement rather than a license. For example, in *Henry v. Dalton*, 151 A.2d 362 (R.I. 1959), plaintiffs built a garage on their property in reliance on the defendant's grant of permission to use a driveway partially located on defendant's property to reach the garage. The court refused to recognize the doctrine of easement by estoppel, instead holding that licenses are revocable at the will of the grantor.

A parol license to do an act on the land of the licensor, while it justifies anything done by the licensee before revocation, is, nevertheless, revocable at the option of the licensor, and this, although the intention was to confer a continuing right and money had been expended by the licensee upon the faith of the license. This is plainly the rule of the statute [of frauds]. It is also, we believe, the rule required by public policy. It prevents the burdening of lands with restrictions founded upon oral agreements, easily misunderstood. It gives security and certainty to titles, which are most important to be preserved against defects and qualifications not founded upon solemn instruments. The jurisdiction of courts to enforce oral contracts for the sale of land, is clearly defined and well understood, and is indisputable; but to change what commenced in a license into an irrevocable right, on the ground of equitable estoppel, is another and quite different matter. It is far better, we think, that the law requiring interests in land to be evidenced by deed, should be observed, than to leave it to the chancellor to construe an executed license as a grant, depending upon what, in his view, may be equity in the special case.

Id. at 366. And in *Nelson v. American Telephone & Telegraph Co.*, 170 N.E. 416 (Mass. 1930), the Supreme Judicial Court of Massachusetts similarly required a writing to transfer an easement, holding that it was unreasonable to expend large sums of money installing telephone poles and lines on the basis of a mere license. The licensee "was . . . bound to know that the license was revocable." *Id.* at 420. *Accord, Kitchen v, Kitchen,* 641 N.W.2d 245 (Mich. 2002) (rejecting doctrine of easement by estoppel). *But see Silverleib v. Hebshie,* 596 N.E.2d 401, 403 (Mass. App. Ct. 1992) (holding that an easement may be recognized by estoppel when an ambiguous reference to the road was included in the deed and the licensee both understood the permission to be irrevocable and invested in reliance on what the grantee understood to be an easement).

5. *Constructive trust.* Some courts limit the constructive trust doctrine to relationships between family members or others having a so-called confidential relationship. *Sharper v. Harlem Teams for Self-Help, Inc.*, 696 N.Y.S.2d 109, 111 (App. Div. 1999). Others, like the Montana Supreme Court in *Rase*, do not so limit the doctrine. Other than this possible limitation, what is the difference between the doctrine of estoppel and the doctrine of constructive trust? Would *Holbrook* and *Rase* have been decided the same way under either doctrine?

PROBLEM

A college student lives in a dormitory room at a private college (the "College"). Before moving in, the student signed a document presented to her by the College, along with a pile of other forms signed at the time she paid her tuition. The document is entitled "License" and recites that the College grants her a license to occupy a room in a dormitory selected by the College for the academic year from September 1 through June 1. It provides that "this license is revocable for any reason by the College on forty-eight hours' notice."

In the middle of the school year, in February, the student writes a letter to the editor of the local newspaper criticizing the educational philosophy of the College. The College responds by notifying the student that she may continue as a student at the College but that she has two days to vacate her room at the dormitory. She comes to you for legal advice. What would you tell her?

§5.3.1.3 Prescriptive Easements

See supra §3.4, at 207-215.

§5.3.1.4 Easements Implied from Prior Use

Express easements are created by explicit agreement of the parties. Implied easements, in contrast, are recognized in particular kinds of relationships despite the absence of express contract to create an easement. Sometimes, implied easements effectuate the intent of the parties, as manifested in their conduct. Other times, implied easements may contradict the actual intent of the parties and be implied by law as a result of a public policy judgment about the fair or efficient allocation of property rights in the context of the relationship established by the parties. We have already seen easements created by estoppel and prescription and by constructive trust. Two other kinds of implied easements are easements implied from prior use, or *quasi-easements*, and easements by necessity.

GRANITE PROPERTIES LIMITED PARTNERSHIP v. MANNS
512 N.E.2d 1230 (Ill. 1987)

Justice HOWARD C. RYAN delivered the opinion of the court:

The plaintiff, Granite Properties Limited Partnership, brought this suit in the circuit court of Madison County, seeking to permanently enjoin the defendants, Larry and Ann Manns, from interfering with the plaintiff's use and enjoyment of two claimed easements over driveways which exist on the defendants' property. One driveway provides ingress to and egress from an apartment complex and the other to a shopping center. Both the apartment complex and the shopping center are situated on the plaintiff's property. . . .

As indicated [in the diagram on page 334] the parcels which are the subject of this appeal are adjoining tracts located to the south of Bethalto Drive and to the north of Rou des Chateaux Street in Bethalto, Illinois. The plaintiff and its predecessors in title owned all of the subject properties from 1963 or 1964 until 1982, at which time the parcel labeled "B" was conveyed by warranty deed to the defendants. The plaintiff currently owns the parcels labeled "A" and "E," which are on the opposite sides of parcel B. The shopping center situated on the parcel designated "A" extends from lot line to lot line across the east-west dimension of that property. To the north of the shopping center is an asphalt parking lot with approximately 191 feet of frontage on Bethalto Drive. To the east of the shopping center on the parcel labeled "D" is a separately owned health club. To the south of parcel A on the parcel denominated "C" are five four-family apartment buildings. The distance between the back of the shopping center and the property line of parcel C is 50 feet. The shopping center's underground utility facilities are located in this area. An apartment complex, known as the Chateau des Fleurs Apartments, is located on the parcel labeled "E." Both of the plaintiff's properties were developed prior to the time parcel B was sold to the defendants. Parcel B remains undeveloped.

The first claimed easement provides access to the rear of the shopping center which is located on parcel A. The center, which was built in 1967, contains several businesses, including a grocery store, a pharmacy, and doctors' offices. The rear of the center is used for deliveries, trash storage and removal, and utilities repair. To gain access to the rear of the shopping center for these purposes, trucks use a gravel driveway which runs along the lot line between parcel A and parcel B. A second driveway, located to the east of the shopping center on parcel D, enables the trucks to circle the shopping center without having to turn around in the limited space behind the stores.

Robert Mehann, the owner of the Save-A-Lot grocery store located in the shopping center, testified on direct examination that groceries, which are delivered to the

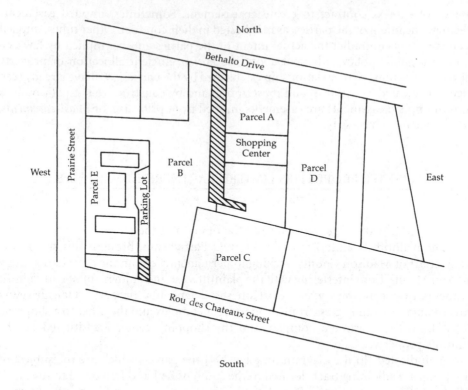

rear of the store, are loaded by forklift on a concrete pad poured for that purpose. Mehann indicated that there are large, double steel doors in the back of the store to accommodate items which will not fit through the front door. Mehann testified that semitrailer trucks make deliveries to the rear of the grocery store four days a week, with as many as two or three such trucks arriving daily. An average of 10 to 12 trucks a day, including semitrailer trucks, make deliveries to the grocery store. Mehann further explained on direct examination that because the area behind the Save-A-Lot building extends only 50 feet to the rear property line, it would be difficult, if not impossible, for a semitrailer truck to turn around in the back and exit the same way it came in. In response to a question as to whether it would be feasible to have trucks make front-door deliveries, Mehann suggested that such deliveries would be very disruptive; pallets that would not fit through the front door would have to be broken down into parts, requiring extra work, and there would not be adequate space in the front of the store to do such work during business hours. Mehann admitted on cross-examination that he had not investigated the cost of installing a front door which would be big enough for pallets of groceries to be brought in by forklift. Further cross-examination revealed that there would not be enough space to manipulate the forklift around the front of the store, although it could be run between the shelves of food to the back of the store.

Also called as a witness for Granite Properties Limited Partnership was Darrell Layman, a limited partner. Layman noted that the shopping center had been in continuous operation since 1967 and that the pattern for deliveries had always been to the rear of the individual stores. When asked whether he had "ever seen a semi back up in the rear of the shopping center and go out the way it came in," Layman responded, "That would be impossible." On cross-examination, however, Layman admitted that, although it was very difficult, he had seen semitrailer trucks exit the same way they came in. Layman also acknowledged on cross-examination that he had not investigated the cost of expanding the size of the front doors of the building. He also claimed that it "would seem impossible" to him to put in any kind of a hallway or passageway which would allow equipment to bring supplies into the stores from the front. On redirect examination, Layman explained that the delivery trucks follow no set schedule and, therefore, their presence may overlap at times. He stated that he had seen as many as four or five delivery trucks backed up. Layman opined that there was "no way" the trucks could back up and turn around when there were multiple trucks present.

The other claimed easement concerns ingress and egress over a driveway which leads into the parking area of the apartment complex situated on parcel E. The complex, which was erected in the 1960s prior to the conveyance of parcel B to the defendants, consists of three buildings containing 36 units. The parking lot, which is situated to the rear of the buildings, provides 72 parking spaces. The only access to the parking lot is by a driveway from Rou des Chateaux, a public street located to the south of the properties. The driveway, which cuts across a small panhandle on the southwestern corner of parcel B, has been in existence since the apartment complex was constructed. The terrain around the apartment complex is flat, including the area in front of the buildings along Prairie Street to the west.

Limited partner Darrell Layman testified at trial that if the area in front of the apartment complex, measuring 300 feet along Prairie Street and 30 feet deep, were to be converted into a parking lot, then there would be room for only 30 parking spaces. He admitted on direct examination that he had not investigated the cost of rocking or asphalting this area for that purpose. Although there was a distance of 20 feet between the apartment buildings, Layman opined that it would not be enough "usable space" to accommodate a driveway from Prairie Street to the existing parking lot because such driveway would interfere with stairways which lead to the basement apartments. Although he admitted that he did not investigate the cost of installing a driveway either between the buildings or adjacent to the end building on the north, Layman concluded that, based on his experience in the layout and design of apartment buildings, "it would be a dangerous situation" for the tenants of the apartments if a driveway were to be run between the buildings or next to their sides. Layman concluded his testimony by claiming that the plaintiff was unaware of any easement problems as to the driveways in question at the time parcel B was deeded to the defendants; otherwise, he asserted, "it would not have been deeded."

The defendant, Larry Manns, stated that he purchased parcel B from the plaintiff in the summer of 1982. Shortly afterwards, he had a survey made of the property. The survey indicated possible encroachments by the plaintiff as to the driveways in question. Finding no recorded easements following a title search, Manns stated that he notified the plaintiff to discontinue its use of the driveways. On cross-examination, Manns admitted that he saw the two driveways before he bought the subject property. . . .

The plaintiff contends in this court that it acquired, by implied reservation, easements over the driveways which provide access to the rear of the shopping center located on parcel A and to the parking lot of the apartment complex situated on parcel E. Plaintiff alleges that parcels A, B and E were held in common ownership by the plaintiff and its predecessors in title until 1982, at which time the defendants received a warranty deed to parcel B, that the driveways in question were apparent and obvious, permanent, and subject to continuous, uninterrupted, and actual use by the plaintiff and its predecessors in title until the time of severance of unity of ownership, and that the driveways are highly convenient and reasonably necessary for the beneficial use and enjoyment of the shopping center and the apartment complex. Therefore, the plaintiff maintains that, upon severance of unity of title, the defendants took parcel B subject to the servitudes then existing, as the parties are presumed to convey with reference to the existing conditions of the property. . . .

On the merits, the crucial issue is whether, in conveying that portion of its property now owned by the defendants (parcel B), the plaintiff retained easements by implication over the driveways in question. . . .

There are two types of implied easements — the easement by necessity and the easement implied from a preexisting use. The easement by necessity usually arises when an owner of land conveys to another an inner portion thereof, which is entirely surrounded by lands owned either by the grantor or the grantor plus strangers. Unless a contrary intent is manifested, the grantee is found to have a right-of-way across the retained land of the grantor for ingress to, and egress from, the land-locked parcel. Similarly, an easement is implied by way of necessity in the deed when the owner of lands retains the inner portion, conveying to another the balance.

The easement implied from a prior existing use, often characterized as a "quasi-easement," arises when an owner of an entire tract of land or of two or more adjoining parcels, after employing a part thereof so that one part of the tract or one parcel derives from another a benefit or advantage of an apparent, continuous, and permanent nature, conveys or transfers part of the property without mention being made of these incidental uses. In the absence of an expressed agreement to the contrary, the conveyance or transfer imparts a grant of property with all the benefits and burdens which existed at the time of the conveyance of the transfer, even though such grant is not reserved or specified in the deed. This court has stated on numerous occasions that an easement implied from a preexisting use is established by proof of three elements: first, common ownership of the claimed dominant and servient parcels and a subsequent conveyance or transfer separating that ownership; second, before the conveyance or transfer severing the unity of title, the common owner used part of the united parcel for the benefit of another part, and this use was apparent and obvious, continuous, and permanent; and third, the claimed easement is necessary and beneficial to the enjoyment of the parcel conveyed or retained by the grantor or transferor.

As the above discussion indicates, easements created by implication arise as an inference of the intention of the parties to a conveyance of land. This inference, which is drawn from the circumstances surrounding the conveyance alone, represents an attempt to ascribe an intention to parties who had not thought or had not bothered to put the intention into words, or to parties who actually had formed no intention conscious to themselves. To fill these common gaps resulting in incomplete thought, courts find particular facts suggestive of intent on the part of the parties to a conveyance. In the case of an easement implied from a preexisting use, proof of the prior use is evidence that the parties probably intended an easement, on the presumption that the grantor and the grantee would have intended to continue an important or necessary use of the land known to them that was apparently continuous and permanent in its nature. Where an easement by necessity is claimed, however, there is no requirement of proof of a known existing use from which to draw the inference of intention. This leaves proof of necessity alone to furnish the probable inference of intention, on the presumption that the grantor and the grantee do not intend to render the land unfit for occupancy.

This essentially is the position taken by . . . *Restatement of Property* §474 (1944). . . . The *Restatement* operates on the basis of eight "important circumstances" from which the inference of intention [to create or reserve an easement] may be drawn: whether the claimant is the conveyor or the conveyee; the terms of the conveyance; the consideration given for it; whether the claim is made against a simultaneous conveyee; the extent of necessity of the easement to the claimant; whether reciprocal benefits result to the conveyor and the conveyee; the manner in which the land was used prior to its conveyance; and the extent to which the manner of prior use was or might have been known to the parties. *Restatement of Property* §476 (1944). These eight factors vary in their importance and relevance according to whether the claimed easement originates out of necessity or for another reason.

In applying the *Restatement's* eight important circumstances to the present case, the fact that the driveways in question had been used by the plaintiff or its predecessors in title since the 1960s, when the respective properties were developed, that the driveways were permanent in character, being either rock or gravel covered, and that the defendants were aware of the driveways' prior uses before they purchased parcel B would tend to support an inference that the parties intended easements upon severance of the parcels in question. Although the prior uses which the plaintiff seeks to continue existed during the common ownership of the parcels in question, under circumstances where the defendants were fully informed by physical appearance of their existence, the defendants, nevertheless, argue that there are two factors which overwhelmingly detract from the implication of an easement: that the claimant is the conveyor and that the claimed easement can hardly be described as "necessary" to the beneficial use of the plaintiff's properties. Relying on the principle that a grantor should not be permitted to derogate from his own grant, the defendants urge this court to refuse to imply an easement in favor of a grantor unless the claimed easement is absolutely necessary to the beneficial use and enjoyment of the land retained by the grantor. The defendants further urge this court not to cast an unreasonable burden over their land through imposition of easements by implication where, as here, available alternatives affording reasonable means of ingress to and egress from the shopping center and the apartment complex allegedly exist.

While the degree of necessity required to reserve an easement by implication in favor of the conveyor is greater than that required in the case of the conveyee, even in the case of the conveyor, the implication from necessity will be aided by a previous use made apparent by the physical adaptation of the premises to it. Moreover, the necessity requirement will have a different meaning and significance in the case involving proof of prior use than it will in a case in which necessity alone supports the implication; otherwise, proof of prior use would be unnecessary. Thus, when circumstances such as an apparent prior use of the land support the inference of the parties' intention, the required extent of the claimed easement's necessity will be less than when necessity is the only circumstance from which the inference of intention will be drawn. While some showing of necessity for the continuance of the use must be shown where a prior use has been made, to the extent that the prior use strengthens the implication, the degree or extent of necessity requisite for implication is reduced. As one treatise concludes:

> If a previous use is continuous and apparent, an easement may be created by implication even though the need for the use to be made is not sufficiently great to meet the test of necessity as applied in the absence of such a previous use. Hence, the test is phrased in terms of *reasonable necessity* rather than in terms of unqualified necessity. A use is necessary, it is often said, when without it no effective use could be made of the land to be benefited by it. *Where, because of a continuous and apparent previous use, the test of necessity becomes that of reasonable necessity, it is said that a use is reasonably necessary when it is reasonably convenient to the use of the land benefited.* In fact, however, reasonable necessity too is a flexible test. *The more pronounced a continuous and apparent use is, the less the degree of convenience of use necessary to the creation of an easement by implication.* (Emphasis added.) 2 *American Law of Property* §8.43 (A. J. Casner ed. 1952)....

Professor Powell...suggests that in a case with proof of prior use, the word "necessity" should be replaced by the phrase "important to the enjoyment of the conveyed quasi-dominant [or quasi-servient] parcel." 3 R. Powell, *The Law of Real Property* §411[2] (P. Rohan ed. 1987)....

[T]he authorities agree that the degree or extent of necessity required to create an easement by implication differs in both meaning and significance depending on the existence of proof of prior use. Hence, given the strong evidence of the plaintiff's prior use of the driveways in question and the defendants' knowledge thereof, we must agree with the appellate court majority that the evidence in this case was sufficient to fulfill the elastic necessity requirement. We approve of the appellate court majority's application of the facts of this case to the law as we have described it herein. As the appellate majority thoroughly explained:

> While the trial court ruled that the driveway to the rear of the shopping center on the defendant's property was simply "more convenient...but not reasonably necessary" to the plaintiff's use of the property, this finding was premised on the assumption that the driveway on the other side of the shopping center provided adequate access for trucks making deliveries to the stores in the shopping center. The evidence was uncontradicted, however, that many of the deliveries were made by semitrailer trucks that would have to "jockey around quite a bit" in order to turn around behind the stores and that there may be as many as four or five trucks backed up at one time, making it impossible to turn around and go out the way they came in. For this reason, the pattern for deliveries to the stores had always been to circle around the shopping center, using the driveways on both sides. Use of the driveway on the defendant's property was thus quite beneficial to the fair enjoyment of the plaintiff's property, notwithstanding the driveway located on the other side of the shopping center. In view of these circumstances openly existing at the time of sale, it would be unreasonable to assume that the plaintiff intended to relinquish the use of this servitude on the defendant's property and assume the burden of trying to find alternate delivery routes to the stores in the shopping center. The evidence, moreover, regarding the difficulty of making deliveries to the front of the shopping center was sufficient to demonstrate the unreasonableness of such an alternative measure, despite the plaintiff's failure to establish the precise cost of reconstructing the shopping center for that purpose. We hold, therefore, that the

plaintiff sustained its burden of proof as to the implied easement for the shopping center and accordingly reverse the trial court's judgment denying injunctive relief as to this easement. Finally, with regard to the claimed easement over the defendant's property to the apartment complex parking lot, we find that the trial court's determination that such easement was "highly convenient and reasonably necessary" for the use and enjoyment of the complex was amply supported by the evidence at trial. The driveway in question had provided the only access to the parking lot behind the complex for over 15 years, and the evidence showed that the space between the buildings was inadequate to accommodate alternative driveways to the parking lot from Prairie Street, considering the plan of the buildings and the need to insure the safety of residents entering and leaving from basement apartments on the side of the buildings. The testimony indicated, moreover, that even if the plaintiff were required to construct a new parking lot in front of the buildings, there would not be adequate parking spaces for the tenants of the apartment building. We hold, therefore, that the trial court's ruling finding an implied easement for the plaintiff as to the apartment complex driveway should be affirmed. *Granite Properties Limited Partnership v. Manns*, 487 N.E.2d 1230, 1238 (Ill. App. Ct. 1986).

For the above reasons, the judgment of the appellate court is affirmed. . . .

§5.3.1.5   Easements by Necessity

FINN v. WILLIAMS

33 N.E.2d 226 (Ill. 1941)

Francis S. Wilson, Justice.

February 16, 1895, Charles H. Williams owned a tract of land in Salisburg township, in Sangamon county, consisting of approximately 140 acres. On the day named, Williams conveyed 39.47 acres to Thomas J. Bacon. In 1937, the plaintiffs, Eugene E. Finn and Curtis Estallar Finn, acquired the title to this tract. The defendant, Zilphia Jane Williams, inherited the remaining 100 acres. By their complaint filed in the circuit court of Sangamon county, plaintiffs charge that the nearest and only available means of egress from and ingress to their land to a highway and to any market for their livestock and crops is by means of a right of way over defendant's tract immediately to the north; that their tract is not located or situated on any public highway and is entirely surrounded by land of strangers and the defendant's tract; that prior to and during all the time the 40 acres and the 100 acres constituted one tract and were owned by defendant's husband, the only means of ingress and egress to and from the single tract to a highway was by right of way in a northerly direction through a third tract of land north and adjacent to the present tract of defendant, and that this open road is still used by defendant as her only means of egress and ingress from and to the highway. The relief sought was the declaration of a right of way easement of necessity from the north line of plaintiffs' tract through the defendant's tract, to the beginning of the right of way road through the third tract mentioned. Answering, the defendant admitted that plaintiffs' land is not located or situated on any public highway but averred that since its severance from her land it is and has been located on a private road leading to the south to a public highway. This averment, plaintiffs denied. . . .

Private permissive ways of ingress and egress over the land of strangers both to the east and to the south have been available to the successive owners, including plaintiffs, of the 40-acre tract since its severance from the 100-acre tract of the defendant in 1895, but each of the private ways over the lands of the adjoining strangers has been closed and, as defendant concedes, these permissive means of ingress and egress do not now exist. Two witnesses for defendant who had lived near the property in controversy for about sixty years testified to roads leading to the south and to the east from the 40-acre tract over the land of strangers. These roads were private roads over the property of strangers, and are now closed. Nathan Woodrum, defendant's son-in-law, testified that he had until recently lived on the 100-acre tract, and that a road through defendant's land connects with the road through the tract at the north, and that the road through this third tract is the only mode of access to the highway unless permission be obtained to go through the land of strangers. Since May, 1939, defendant has refused to permit plaintiff to travel further over the right of way through her tract. As a result of defendant's action, the plaintiffs have been unable to take their livestock and farm products to market, have had no means of egress from or ingress to their 40 acres on which they live, and have had to walk to the township highway, a distance of about three-quarters of a mile carrying such produce as they could.

The evidence does not sustain defendant's averment that plaintiffs have the use of a private road leading to the south to a public highway and defendant, by her concession that a present necessity exists, has apparently abandoned this claim. She maintains, however, that the necessity has arisen by reason of changed circumstances since the severance of the two tracts. Firmly established principles control. Where an owner of land conveys a parcel thereof which has no outlet to a highway except over the remaining lands of the grantor or over the land of strangers, a way by necessity exists over the remaining lands of the grantor. If, at one time, there has been unity of title, as here, the right to a way by necessity may lay dormant through several transfers of title and yet pass with each transfer as appurtenant to the dominant estate and be exercised at any time by the holder of the title thereto. Plaintiffs' land is entirely surrounded by property of strangers and the land of the defendant from which it was originally severed. A right of way easement of necessity was necessarily implied in the conveyance severing the two tracts in 1895, and passed by *mesne* conveyances to plaintiffs in 1937. The fact that the original grantee and his successors in interest have been permitted ingress to and egress from the 40 acres over the land owned by surrounding strangers is immaterial. When such permission is denied, as in the present case, the subsequent grantees may avail themselves of the dormant easement implied in the deed severing the dominant and servient estates. . . .

NOTES AND QUESTIONS

1. *Easements implied from prior use.* Easements by implication, also called "quasi-easements" or easements implied from prior use, may be recognized when an owner divides her property and sells one parcel, retaining the other for herself. If the grantor intends to retain an easement over the property conveyed to the buyer, the property burdened by the easement (the servient estate) is subject to an *easement by reservation* (because the seller reserved for herself an easement across the property being

conveyed). If, however, the grantor intends to grant the buyer an easement over the property retained by the grantor, then the property benefited by the easement (the dominant estate) is attached to an *easement by grant* (because the buyer has been granted an easement benefiting the land he has purchased).

Most easements by implication are rights of way for the passage of people or vehicles to get to the property, as in *Granite Properties*. Passage may be required for a variety of purposes, including obtaining access to a home, *Dubin v. Chesebrough Trust*, 116 Cal. Rptr.2d 872 (Ct. App. 2002); *Cheney v. Mueller*, 485 P.2d 1218 (Or. 1971), for continued access to sewer lines laid over the grantor's remaining property, *Bowers v. Andrews*, 557 A.2d 606 (Me. 1989), or to obtain access to a lake for recreational purposes, *Russakoff v. Scruggs*, 400 S.E.2d 529 (Va. 1991).

Easements implied from prior use are granted only if (a) two parcels were previously owned by a common grantor, (b) one parcel was previously used for the benefit of the other parcel in a manner that was visible and continuous, and (c) the use is "reasonably necessary" or "convenient" for enjoyment of the dominant estate. *Stansbury v. MDR Development, L.L.C.*, 871 A.2d 612 (Md. 2005).

The vast majority of litigation on easements by implication addresses the question of defining "reasonable necessity." The courts seem to agree that absolute necessity is not required for an easement implied from a preexisting use, while absolute necessity *is* required for an easement by necessity. *Bowers v. Andrews*, 557 A.2d 606 (Me. 1989). What does "reasonable necessity" mean?

In *Russakoff v. Scruggs*, 400 S.E.2d 529 (Va. 1991), a developer constructed a subdivision that included a human-made lake. Plaintiffs bought lots in the subdivision that were separated from the lake by a strip of the developer's land that had been reserved by the developer for flood plains and sewer and water lines. After the developer failed to pay taxes, the state sold the developer's property in a tax sale to defendant, who began to exclude plaintiffs from access to the lake. The element of preexisting ownership of the two parcels in a common grantor clearly existed. The questions in the case were whether the prior use was sufficiently visible and continuous to constitute an implied easement and whether recreational use of the lake was "reasonably necessary" for the enjoyment of plaintiffs' land. The court answered both questions in the affirmative on the grounds that the presence of the lake increased the value of the lots, that the buyers of the lots had presumed they would have access to the lake, and that those buyers in fact did use the lake for recreational purposes such as boating and ice skating and for obtaining water for sprinklers and gardening purposes.

Obviously, use of a lake, while highly desirable, is not "necessary." The court noted that absolute necessity was not required, as it would be if an easement by necessity were claimed, but that plaintiff had to establish "something more than simple convenience." *Id.* at 140. The court held, *Id.* at 140-141, that

> a purchaser of a lot would have a legitimate expectation of the right to access and use the lake where a visual inspection and reference to the plat incorporated in the deed of conveyance showed the existence of a lake within 20 feet of one's lot line, and where investigation would disclose that the 20-foot strip between the lake and the lot line was retained solely for certain utility and flood plain uses. The Canterbury East developers contemplated enjoyment of the lake, as a lake, by purchasers of the lots surrounding the lake. Under these circumstances, the easement at issue was reasonably necessary to the use and enjoyment of the lakeside lots.

Do you think this case was correctly decided?

2. *Statute of frauds.* Every state has a *statute of frauds* that requires certain kinds of contracts to be in writing for them to be enforceable. It is important to know that contracts to convey interests in real property are one of the most important types of legal rights regulated by the statute of frauds. The purpose of such statutes are to protect individuals from fraudulent claims that they made oral promises; requiring a writing protects us from such false claims — unless, of course, the "promisee" is willing to forge the promisor's signature. At the same time, when an oral promise has been made, the refusal to enforce it because it was not in writing effectively allows the one who made the promise to claim it was never made, and thus may allow fraud to be perpetrated by promisors.

Easements are interests in land and are generally required to be in writing before they will be enforceable under the statute of frauds. The doctrine of easement by implication is an equitable exception to the statute of frauds. Is this justified? Why not enforce the statute of frauds rigidly and require the parties to describe the easement in writing if it is part of their transaction? Which rule is more likely to effectuate the actual intent of the parties? Which rule is fair? How should the courts react when the parties make a mistake and fail to include in their written agreement all the terms on which they intended to agree?

3. *Easements by necessity.* An easement by necessity may be granted to the owner of a landlocked parcel over remaining lands of the grantor to obtain access to the parcel. *Tobias v. Dailey,* 998 P.2d 1091 (Ariz. Ct. App. 2000); *Stansbury v. MDR Development, L.L.C.,* 871 A.2d 612 (Md. 2005); *Fike v. Shelton,* 860 So.2d 1227 (Miss. Ct. App. 2003). The policies underlying the doctrine of easement by necessity are (a) to effectuate the intent of the parties and (b) to promote the efficient utilization of property. Sometimes these policies go together. Ordinarily, we can expect buyers not to agree to buy landlocked property unless they have guaranteed access to it by an easement over neighboring land. Thus, granting a right of access both promotes land utilization and the intent of the parties. As the court explains in *Hewitt v. Meaney,* 226 Cal. Rptr. 349, 351 (Ct. App. 1986), the "public policy is implemented by the law's presumption that a grantor implicitly conveys or reserves whatever is necessary to put property to beneficial use, despite the omission to make any such express provision." For this reason, "[t]he law thus presumes the common owner intended the easement."

Similarly, the Idaho Supreme Court held in *Burley Brick and Sand Company v. Cofer,* 629 P.2d 1166, 1168 (Idaho 1981), that

> [a] way of necessity is an easement arising from an implied grant or implied reservation; it is of common-law origin and is supported by the rule of sound public policy that lands should not be rendered unfit for occupancy or successful cultivation. Such a way is the result of the application of the presumption that whenever a party conveys property, he conveys whatever is necessary for the beneficial use of that property and retains whatever is necessary for the beneficial use of land he still possesses. Thus, the legal basis of a way of necessity is the presumption of a grant arising from the circumstances of the case.

Courts split, however, on what to do when these policies conflict. Many courts (perhaps most courts today) hold that the ultimate purpose of the rule is to effectuate the intent of the grantor. Thus, no easement of necessity will be recognized if it is clear that the grantor intended to sell, and the grantee knew she was buying, a landlocked parcel. This is the view taken by the *Restatement (Third). Restatement (Third) of Property (Servitudes)* §2.15 (2000). *See also Hewitt v. Meaney*, 226 Cal. Rptr. at 351 (holding that "an easement by necessity will not be imposed contrary to the actual intent of the parties"); *Shpak v. Oletsky*, 373 A.2d 1234 (Md. 1977) (holding that no law prohibits an owner from cutting herself off from all access to her land); *Vigeant v. Donel Realty Trust*, 540 A.2d 1243 (N.H. 1988) (no easement by necessity without implied intent).

In contrast, *Finn v. Williams* suggests that the ultimate goal is promoting the development of property by preventing property from becoming landlocked and taken out of the market. Similarly, in *Frederick v. Consolidated Waste Services, Inc.*, 573 A.2d 387, 389 (Me. 1990), the Maine Supreme Judicial Court held that

> an easement created by strict necessity [arises] when a grantor conveys a lot of land from a larger parcel, and that conveyed lot is "landlocked" by the grantor's surrounding land and cannot be accessed by a road or highway. Because of the strict necessity of having access to the landlocked parcel, an easement over the grantor's remaining land benefitting the landlocked lot is implied as a matter of law irrespective of the true intent of the common grantor.

573 A.2d at 389. The Vermont Supreme Court similarly held in *Traders, Inc. v. Bartholomew*, 459 A.2d 974, 978 (Vt. 1983), that

> [a] way of necessity rests on public policy often thwarting the intent of the original grantor or grantee, and arises "to meet a special emergency . . . in order that no land be left inaccessible for the purposes of cultivation." "Its philosophy is that the demands of our society prevent any man-made efforts to hold land in perpetual idleness as would result if it were cut off from all access by being completely surrounded by lands privately owned." 2 *Thompson on Real Property* §362, at 382 (1980).

Accord, Swan v. Hill, 855 So. 2d 459, 464 (Miss. Ct. App. 2003) ("The concern of the court is only whether alternative routes exist").

According to these courts, the policy underlying the doctrine of easement by necessity applies regardless of the parties' intent. Rather, the doctrine is a rule of law designed to regulate real estate transactions to prevent the parties from voluntarily locking out parcels of property from access to a public way. Which approach is better?

4. *Statutory regulation of landlocked parcels.* Some states have enacted statutes empowering the owner of a landlocked parcel to obtain an easement over neighboring land for access to a public road by application to a public official and payment of compensation to the landowner whose property is burdened by the easement. For example, Washington state has a statute, Wash. Rev. Code §8.24.010, that reads:

> An owner . . . of land which is so situate with respect to the land of another that it is necessary for its proper use and enjoyment to have and maintain a private way of necessity . . . across, over or through the land of such other, . . . may condemn and take lands of such other sufficient in area for the construction and maintenance of such private way of necessity. . . .

See also Ala. Code §18-3-20; Ark. Stat. §27-66-401; Mass. Gen. Laws ch. 82, §24; Or. Rev. Stat. §376.180.

PROBLEMS

1. Suppose the buyer in *Finn v. Williams* had talked with the grantor about the lack of access to public roads, and the parties had agreed that no easement was needed because the grantor had been using the roads over the neighboring lots without objection from those owners (but also without their explicit permission) and that the buyer would probably be able to continue to use those private roads. Then the neighbors close their roads, the buyer's land is landlocked, and the buyer claims an easement by necessity over the remaining lands of the grantor.

Should an easement by necessity be granted to the buyer to prevent the buyer's land from becoming landlocked when it is clear that the grantor did not intend to grant such an easement over the grantor's retained land? What arguments can you make on both sides of this question? What rule of law do you think should be adopted, and why?

2. The doctrine of easement by necessity applies when land has no access to a public road. Should it apply when property is physically located along to a public road but the cost of creating useable access to that road is prohibitively expensive? *Compare Schwab v. Timmons*, 589 N.W.2d 1 (Wis. 1999) (no easement by necessity granted merely because the cost of building a road over a bluff to a public road was $700,000; since access was physically available, the land was not landlocked, and necessity could not be established merely because obtaining access in that direction was prohibitively expensive) *with Mississippi Power Co. v. Fairchild*, 791 So.2d 262 (Miss. Ct. App. 2001) (power company entitled to easement by necessity if the only access to a public road was over a river because the cost of bridge construction would be prohibitive).

§5.3.2　CREATION BY EXPRESS AGREEMENT

§5.3.2.1　Historical Background

Easements arose out of the customary rights that were part of the communal system of agriculture in medieval England.[8] The lord of the manor would parcel out strips of land around the village to individual villagers to cultivate. The villagers were entitled to pasture their beasts and gather wood or turf on those lands after the harvest and on the nonarable lands near them. These rights on lands held in common are the historical antecedent of modern easements and profits.

A long historical process of enclosure of the common fields and pastures started in the sixteenth century and was completed by the early nineteenth century. Fencing common lands changed the old system to the modern form of private property, which is associated with the possessor's general right to exclude and to control the use of the property. Some negative easements, such as the right to lateral support of land, were characterized as *natural rights* and accompanied property ownership without the need

---

8. This historical material is based on A. W. B. Simpson, *A History of the Land Law* (2d ed. 1986).

for agreement with neighboring owners. Other easements — mostly affirmative easements such as rights of way — arose by *agreement* between the parties. Affirmative easements were usually recognized only if they vested in owners of neighboring land for the benefit of the use of that land; they were *appurtenant* to the benefited land.

§5.3.2.2   Formal Requirements to Create

(a)   Writing

Express easements are created by agreement of the parties; the owner of the burdened land grants to another an easement in the grantor's property. With the exceptions of prescriptive easements, easements by estoppel, implication, and necessity, and constructive trusts, easements must be in *writing* to be enforceable under the statute of frauds.[9] Easements are created by deed in which the named grantor recites that she grants an easement of a certain description to the named grantee. Deeds normally are signed only by the grantor. The transfer of an easement is analogous to the sale of a piece of property; it is treated as a grant of an interest in real property. Thus, we say that people buy and sell easements. Sometimes an easement is created by a deed that conveys the easement by itself; an owner, for example, may sell to his neighbor a right of way across the owner's own land. At other times, the easement is created at the same time a parcel of property burdened or benefited by the easement is sold; for example, the grantor may sell part of her land by a deed reciting that, in addition to granting ownership of the parcel to the grantee, the grantor also conveys to the grantee an easement of passage over the remaining land of the grantor.

(b)   Rule Against Reserving an Easement in a Third Party

Many states traditionally held that a grantor, *O*, may not sell a parcel of property to *A* while reserving an easement over *A*'s property in *B*. Some states may still retain this rule. *Estate of Thomson v. Wade*, 509 N.E.2d 309 (N.Y. 1987); *Beachside Bungalow Preservation Ass'n of Far Rockaway, Inc. v. Oceanview Assocs.*, 753 N.Y.S.2d 133 (App. Div. 2003); *Shirley v. Shirley*, 525 S.E.2d 274 (Va. 2000). Some courts have gotten around the rule by applying the doctrine of *estoppel* to prevent the grantee from interfering in the easement reserved to the third party. *Dalton v. Eller*, 284 S.W. 68 (Tenn. 1926). Many courts have now changed the traditional rule, allowing reservation of an easement in a third party. *Willard v. First Church of Christ, Scientist*, 498 P.2d 987 (Cal. 1972).

The traditional rule was created in feudal times and has no modern justification, especially since drafting around it is easy to do.[10] The grantor can simply convey

---

9. Other exceptions to the statute of frauds also exist, including fraud and part performance. *See* Chapter 9.

10. The traditional rule was based on the formalistic assertion that the grantor could only reserve a preexisting interest; since one can have no easement in one's own land, the grantor could not reserve an easement on retained land. To allow easements by reservation, English courts invented the fiction of a transfer of the property to the grantee and a *re-grant* of an easement by the grantee to the grantor in the conveyed land. This grant of an easement was allowed because the seller and buyer had entered a feudal, tenurial relationship of lord and

the property to the party who is intended to own the easement; that party then conveys the property to the ultimate grantee, reserving an easement over the property for herself. In the above example, *O* conveys the property to *B*, who then conveys it to *A*, reserving an easement for herself. The easement owner becomes the grantor, rather than a third-party grantee, and the easement will be recognized since the grantor may reserve an easement for herself. Failure to use this method may subject the lawyer to a malpractice claim by the client whose wishes were frustrated. At the same time, the ability to avoid the rule by using two pieces of paper rather than one makes it a pointless technicality that should be abandoned. *See Restatement (Third) of Property (Servitudes)* §2.6(c) (2000) (adopting this position and proposing to abolish the rule).

§5.3.2.3   Validity: Substantive Limitations on the Kinds of Easements That Can Be Created

(a)   Limits on Negative Easements

Courts traditionally limited the number of negative easements that could be created by contract to several kinds: (1) the right to lateral support of one's building, (2) rights to prevent both light and air from being blocked by construction on neighboring land, and (3) the right to prevent interference with the flow of an artificial stream such as an aqueduct. Judges were loath to recognize new easements partly because, until 1925, England lacked a working recording system to give notice of land use restrictions. Buyers could easily observe most affirmative easements, such as roads over the land, and thus were on *inquiry* notice of them; they had a duty to investigate to determine if any third parties had easements in the land. However, buyers would not be put on inquiry notice of negative easements since they were restrictions on use and therefore not observable; the mere fact that land had not previously been used in a particular way did not mean that it could not be used in that way. Without a recording system, buyers would be unfairly surprised by unusual negative easements and thus would hesitate to buy land. Limiting the number and type of negative easements that could be created thus served both to promote the alienability of land and to protect the interests of buyers in relying on their ability to use the land they were purchasing.

In addition, England allowed both negative and affirmative easements to be acquired by prescription. The doctrine of "ancient lights" allowed an owner of land who had long enjoyed unobstructed light and air to prevent construction on neighboring land that harmed those interests. If the category of negative easements was not strictly limited, then *any* new use of property could result in a complaint by the neighbor that such use interfered with the neighbor's rights, and the long-standing failure to engage in such a use meant that the right to introduce the use now had been lost by prescription. Taken to the extreme, the prescriptive easement doctrine could have prevented any new uses of property to which neighbors objected. Jesse Dukeminier and James E. Krier, *Property* 854-857 (4th ed. 1998).

---

tenant by their transfer of the property. This theory did not apply to a third party who was not a party to the transaction and therefore with whom no tenurial relationship had been established. The feudal system of land ownership is discussed later in this chapter.

Unlike England, the United States had recording systems from the beginning; the records in the Middlesex County Registry of Deeds in Cambridge, Massachusetts, for example, go back to 1690. Thus, the notice problem is of much less consequence here. Nor has the United States ever recognized a right to obtain a negative easement by prescription. Nonetheless, the courts in the United States originally adopted the view that no new negative easements could be created, partly because England recognized a different way to establish such restrictions by applying the law of covenants. Because new kinds of restrictions on land use can be created by using covenants rather than easements, it may be that limiting the number and kind of negative easements that can be created makes less sense. Courts and legislatures in this century have recognized new negative easements such as *conservation* easements (to prevent development of land held for environmental purposes), *historic preservation* easements (preventing destruction or alteration of buildings that have historical or architectural importance), and *solar easements* (to protect access to sunlight for solar energy). Most of these new easements have been created or recognized by statute. *See, e.g.,* Alaska Stat. §§34.17.010 to 060 (conservation easements).

Land use restrictions that do not fall within the traditional categories of allowable negative easements could always be created using the *covenant* form. For this reason, it seems unjustified to retain the traditional rule limiting the creation of negative easements. At the same time, the rule limiting the creation of new negative easements was justified to some extent because of differences between the law of easements and the law of covenants. Most important, covenants that become overly burdensome or of insubstantial benefit can be wiped out through the doctrines of changed conditions and undue hardship. These doctrines were not traditionally applied to easements.

The *Restatement (Third) of Property (Servitudes)* abolishes the distinction between negative easements and restrictive covenants, subjecting both to the changed conditions and undue hardship doctrines. *Id.* at §7.10. Instead of categorical rules about the types of easements that can be created, it would directly regulate land use restrictions by invalidating restrictions that serve no legitimate purpose or that contravene strong and articulable public policies. *Id.* at §§3.1 to 3.7.

(b) No Affirmative Easements to Act on One's Own Land

Easements were traditionally different from covenants in another way as well. The traditional law of easements did not allow creation of *an affirmative obligation to do something on someone's own land* for the benefit of other owners, such as a duty to build a structure or pay a monthly fee to a condominium association. Affirmative easements were rights to do something on someone else's land while negative easements and restrictive covenants were obligations not to do something on one's own land. The law of covenants developed to allow the creation of enforceable affirmative obligations that run with the land. The *Restatement (Third)* limits the term "easement" to affirmative easements, abolishing negative easements entirely. *Id.* at §1.2. It would treat all restrictions as "covenants" whether they are phrased as negative easements or restrictive covenants. It retains the classification of affirmative covenants.

§5.3.2.4   Running with the Land

(a)   Requirements for the Burden to Run with the Land

A central question about easements concerns the circumstances under which they *run with the land.* An easement that runs with the land is treated as if it were attached to that parcel so that any future owner of the parcel is benefited or burdened by the easement. In addressing this issue, one should look at it from both sides. The first question is whether the *burden* runs with the land. Is a future owner of the servient estate obligated to allow the easement owner continued access to or control over her land under the terms of the original easement? Easements created by implication, necessity, and estoppel generally are held to run with the land if they were intended to do so and are reasonably necessary for the enjoyment of the dominant estate. Easements that do not fit into one of these exceptions run with the land to burden future owners of the servient estate only if (1) the easement is in *writing,* (2) the original grantor who created the easement *intended* the easement to run with the land, and (3) subsequent owners of the servient estate had *notice* of the easement at the time of purchase of the servient estate.

Writing. The easement may be described in detail in the deed granting the property or the deed may refer to an earlier, recorded writing. For example, if a deed states that "this conveyance is subject to the easements and restrictions contained in the deed from *O* to *A*, recorded at Bk. 29837, page 214," the buyer can search the recording office to find the earlier deed and the writing requirement is satisfied. The writing requirement is satisfied even if the easement is not included in subsequent deeds to the servient estate; this is because future buyers are on notice of the writing in the earlier deed if it is in the "chain of title" and can be found by searching the deeds in the recording office. The required writing is the *original* writing creating the easement. *The easement does not have to be included in subsequent deeds.* It is good legal practice, however, to include a specific reference to existing easements when either the dominant or servient estate is transferred.

Intent. Easements bind future owners of the servient estate only if the grantor intends them to be bound. Intent may be clearly stated, as when the deed creating the easement states that the easement "is intended to run with the [benefited and/or burdened] land." If the conveyance is ambiguous as to the grantor's intent, intent may be implied. If the easement is one that is not likely to have been intended to be merely personal, such as a right given to a friend to swim in one's lake, but a permanent right, such as a right to lay utility lines across the servient estate, courts ordinarily will hold that it was intended to bind future owners of the burdened parcel.

Notice. Easements are binding on subsequent owners only if they have notice of them. Three kinds of notice exist. First, if the subsequent owners in fact know about the existence, they have *actual* notice. Second, if there are visible signs of use by non-owners, such as telephone poles, aboveground utility lines, or a path across the property, the owner may be put on *inquiry* notice. This means that a reasonable buyer would do further investigation to discover whether an easement exists. Third, if the deed conveying the easement is recorded in the proper registry of deeds in the proper place, and if the deed is in the chain of title — meaning that a title search of prior owners of the property would lead to discovery of the deed — then subsequent owners are deemed to be on *constructive* notice. This means that, whether they actually knew or did not know about the easement, they *should have known*. A reasonable buyer of property would conduct a title search and discover the existence of the easement. Owners are bound by easements they would have discovered had they performed the usual title search.

The recording system provides buyers of real property notice of prior encumbrances placed on the land they are buying and ensures that one selling land has the power to do so. Most jurisdictions have a registry of deeds where deeds, easements, mortgages, and long-term leases can be "recorded," or filed. These instruments are indexed under the name of the grantor and the grantee. Separate indexes are kept for grantors and grantees. In the *grantor index*, all instruments are listed both alphabetically and chronologically by the grantor's last name. In the *grantee index*, all instruments are listed both alphabetically and chronologically by the grantee's last name. A deed or easement granted by Johann Sebastian Bach to Wolfgang Mozart would be indexed under the name "Bach" in the grantor index and the name "Mozart" in the grantee index.

Assume Bach purchased a lot in 1960 and in 1965 granted his neighbor Mozart a deed conveying a right of way across Bach's property. Mozart promptly recorded the deed. Bach then sold his property to Béla Bartók in 1980, who promptly recorded the deed from Bach. Bartók now wants to sell the property to you. If the easement from Bach to Mozart was recorded, you will find it by researching the title to the property you are buying. You will look under Bartók's name in the grantee index and go backward until you find a deed granting the property to Bartók; you will find reference to a deed from Bach to Bartók. Then you will switch to the grantor index and look under the name of each prior grantor you have found (Bach and Bartók) during the time period when each owner owned the land to determine whether those owners granted any easements, mortgages, leases, or other interests in the property during their time of ownership. Thus, you will look under Bach's name in the grantor index starting at the date when Bach acquired his interest (the date of execution of the deed giving title to Bach) and stop on the date a deed transferring Bach's ownership rights was recorded by his buyer Bartók. Looking under Bach's name during his period of ownership (1960 to 1980) you will find reference in the grantor index to the easement granted from Bach to Mozart, and you would be on "record" or "constructive" notice of it and therefore bound by it. By looking up the actual deed referred to in the index, you can determine the location and scope of the easement.

(b) Requirements for the Benefit to Run with the Land
(Appurtenant versus In Gross)

The second question is whether the *benefit* runs with the land. Is the easement owned by the person to whom it was originally granted or by whoever happens to own the parcel of land it was intended to benefit? If the benefit runs with the land, it is treated as if it were attached to that particular parcel of land and is called an *appurtenant* easement. If it does not run with the land, it is not attached to a particular parcel of land and there is no dominant estate; such easements are called *easements in gross*. The test for distinguishing appurtenant easements from easements in gross is the intent of the grantor. A recitation in the deed that calls the easement "appurtenant" or states that it is intended to benefit future owners of the buyer's property will answer this question. But what happens when that intent is not unambiguously stated in the deed? The next case deals with this question.

GREEN v. LUPO

647 P.2d 51 (Wash. Ct. App. 1982)

JOHN A. PETRICH, Acting Chief Judge.

The plaintiffs, Don Green and his wife Florence, initiated this suit to specifically enforce an agreement to grant an easement. From a decree which determined that the contemplated easement was personal rather than appurtenant to their land as claimed, plaintiffs appeal. We reverse.

The issue raised on appeal is whether parol evidence is admissible to construe an easement as personal to the grantees where the easement is agreed in writing to be for ingress and egress for road and utilities purposes but the writing does not expressly characterize the easement as either personal or appurtenant. We believe that parol evidence was properly admitted here but the conclusion that the easement is personal to plaintiffs was erroneous.

The parties involved are adjoining landowners. The plaintiffs, once the owners of the entire tract, now retain several acres located south of the defendants' property. The defendants purchased their parcel (the north tract) from the plaintiffs by real estate contract. While they were still paying on that contract, the defendants requested a deed release to a small section of the north tract to allow financing for the construction of a home. The plaintiffs agreed in return for the promise of an easement along the southern 30 feet of the north tract when the defendants eventually obtained title. The express terms of the promised easement were contained in a written agreement which was executed in the form required for the conveyance of an interest in real property. Wash. Rev. Code §64.04.

The plaintiffs' development of their land for mobile home occupancy caused tension between the landowners. Apparently some of the occupants of plaintiffs' mobile home development used the easement as a practice runway for their motorcycles. When the defendants obtained title to the north tract they refused to formally grant the easement as promised. They also placed logs along the southern boundary of the easement to restrict access from the plaintiffs' property. The plaintiffs brought this action to obtain specific performance of the promise to grant an easement and to enjoin any interference with their use of the easement.

Evidence was admitted describing a single-family cabin or residence built by or for the plaintiffs in the northeast corner of the plaintiffs' tract. It was defendants' contention, and they so testified, that the purpose of the easement was to serve the plaintiffs in their personal use and occupancy of this cabin or home. They claimed the easement was not intended to serve the plaintiffs' entire tract, part of which had been developed as a mobile home site, and which had access by other existing roads.

The trial court concluded that an easement was granted for the use and benefit of the plaintiffs alone and could not be assigned or conveyed. The court ordered the plaintiffs' use to be limited to ingress and egress for their own home or cabin and prohibited the passage of motorcycles.

It was the duty of the court in construing the instrument which created the easement to ascertain and give effect to the intention of the parties. The intention of the parties is determined by a proper construction of the language of the instrument. Where the language is unambiguous other matters may not be considered; but where the language is ambiguous the court may consider the situation of the property and of the parties, and the surrounding circumstances at the time the instrument was executed, and the practical construction of the instrument given by the parties by their conduct or admissions. Simply stated parol evidence may always be used to explain ambiguities in written instruments and to ascertain the intent of the parties. . . .

The pivotal issue in deciding the propriety of admitting parol evidence is whether the written instrument is ambiguous. A written instrument is ambiguous when its terms are uncertain or capable of being understood as having more than one meaning.

The written instrument promised the easement specifically to the plaintiffs, to "Don Green and Florence B. Green," and described the easement as "for ingress and egress for road and utilities [purposes]." The designation of named individuals as dominant owners evidences an intent that the easement be personal to the named parties. The grant of an easement for ingress, egress and utilities to the owners of adjacent land is evidence of an intent that the easement benefit the grantees' adjacent land. We find that the instrument was ambiguous as to whether the easement granted was personal to the plaintiffs or appurtenant to their land. We therefore conclude that parol evidence was properly admitted.

The trial court's findings of fact are supported by competent evidence and are not assigned as error; they must be considered as verities on appeal. The court's findings do not, however, support the conclusion that the easement was personal. The court found that the easement was granted for ingress, egress, for road and utilities purposes. As we have noted, the grant of such an easement supports the conclusion that the easement was intended to be an easement appurtenant. In addition, the trial court found "the use of the easement by the plaintiff was *to obtain access to the land*, retained by plaintiff, for the construction and habitation by plaintiff in a cabin." (Italics ours.) This finding also supports the conclusion that the easement was intended to benefit plaintiffs' land.

The trial court's conclusion that the easement was personal to the plaintiffs was erroneous. There is a strong presumption in Washington that easements are appurtenant to some particular tract of land; personal easements, easements in gross, are not favored. . . . An easement is not in gross when there is anything in the deed or the situation of the property which indicates that it was intended to be appurtenant to land retained or conveyed by the grantor. Viewed in this light, the court's factual findings mandate the conclusion that the easement was intended to be appurtenant to plaintiffs' property.

Easements appurtenant become part of the realty which they benefit. Unless limited by the terms of creation or transfer, appurtenant easements follow possession of the dominant estate through successive transfers. The rule applies even when the dominant estate is subdivided into parcels, with each parcel continuing to enjoy the use of the servient tenement. . . . The terms of the easement promised do not limit its transfer. The easement promised the plaintiffs is appurtenant to their property and assignable to future owners of that property.

The defendants request that equitable limitations be imposed on any easement granted. A servient owner is entitled to impose reasonable restraints on a right of way to avoid a greater burden on the servient owner's estate than that originally contemplated in the easement grant, so long as such restraints do not unreasonably interfere with the dominant owner's use.

Testimony presented at trial showed that youngsters who now live on the dominant estate use their motorcycles on the easement in a fashion that constitutes a dangerous nuisance which was not considered when the easement was created. This evidence supports the imposition of equitable restrictions on the dominant owners' use, restrictions which will not unreasonably interfere with that use.

The trial court enjoined the use of motorcycles on the easement. There is insufficient evidence on the record to assess the impact of a complete ban on motorcycle use on the dominant estate's owners. Motorcycles are a common means of transportation. On its face, the ban appears to unreasonably interfere with the dominant owners' use of the easement. Although an equitable solution to the motorcycle problem is necessary, the trial court abused its discretion in imposing a ban on motorcycles without proper consideration of the ban's effect on the dominant owners' use of the easement.

Reversed and remanded with directions to modify the decree so as to declare the easement for ingress and egress for road and utility purposes to be appurtenant to plaintiffs' property and to devise reasonable restrictions to assure that the easement shall not be used in such a manner as to create a dangerous nuisance.

NOTES AND QUESTIONS

1. *Running of the benefit.* If an easement is intended to benefit whoever owns a particular parcel of land, the easement is said to be *appurtenant* to the dominant estate. The benefit will run with the land and be enforceable by future owners of the benefited land. If the benefit is not intended to run with ownership of a dominant parcel, it is an *easement in gross* enforceable by the beneficiary of the easement.[11] When an easement is *in gross*, it belongs personally to the grantee, not in connection with his ownership or use of any specific parcel of land. The most common modern kind of easement in gross is a right of way for utility lines over property. These easements are generally owned by utility companies that may own no property in the immediate vicinity of the easement.

2. *Test for distinguishing in gross from appurtenant easements.* How can you tell whether an easement is in gross or appurtenant? The primary criterion is the *intent of the grantor.* Clear language in the deed conveying the easement that describes it as appurtenant or in gross will ordinarily answer the question — unless surrounding circumstances show that the grantee was misled or otherwise treated unfairly. When the language in the deed is ambiguous, the court must look to surrounding circumstances and to policy considerations. If the easement is one that would be *useful* separate from ownership of neighboring land, such as a utility easement, the courts are likely to hold that it was intended to be in gross. Since utility easements, such as a right of way for telephone lines, would be useful to the utility company apart from ownership of neighboring property, they are likely to be deemed in gross. If the easement

---

11. They are also sometimes referred to as *personal* easements, as in *Green v. Lupo.* This terminology is somewhat confusing since some courts have further subdivided easements in gross into two categories: (1) *commercial* easements used for business purposes, such as a right of way for utility lines, and (2) *personal* easements used for individual convenience or pleasure, such as a right to swim in a private lake.

has little or no utility separate from ownership of neighboring land, and is useful to anyone who owns the parcel of land benefited by the easement — such as the right of way in *Green v. Lupo* — courts are likely to hold that the easement is appurtenant.

Courts often voice a constructional preference for appurtenant easements. They may say that there is a *presumption* that easements are appurtenant rather than in gross. *Lewitz v. Porath Family Trust,* 36 P.3d 120, 123 (Colo. Ct. App. 2001); *McLaughlin v. Board of Selectman of Amherst,* 646 N.E.2d 418, 423 (Mass. App. Ct. 1995). Courts have argued that appurtenant easements are preferable because they limit the number of persons with easements over the land to the number of neighboring parcels. They also argue that because appurtenant easements are limited to owners of neighboring or nearby property while easements in gross can be owned by anyone, easements in gross create more uncertainty about land use rights than appurtenant easements. One can check with the neighbors to see if any appurtenant rights exist, but it is harder to check with the general public to find owners of easements in gross. Can you think of a counterargument to this reasoning?

3. *Severability from the land.* The courts generally hold that an appurtenant easement *cannot* be *severed* from the land. An owner of the dominant estate who sells the land cannot retain the benefit of the servitude while giving up the land; nor can the beneficiary of the easement transfer the benefit of the easement to another while retaining ownership of the dominant estate. Appurtenant easements pass automatically to whoever owns the dominant estate and cannot be severed from ownership of that estate. *Cricklewood on the Bellamy Condominium Ass'n v. Cricklewood on the Bellamy Trust,* 805 A.2d 427 (N.H. 2002).

4. *Transferability of easements.* Appurtenant easements are transferable by definition; when the dominant estate is sold or given away, the new owner also owns the appurtenant easement attached to the land. Easements in gross were traditionally not transferable but are generally held to be transferable now, especially if they are commercial in nature, such as utility easements. *Restatement (Third) of Property (Servitudes)* §5.8 (2000). Profits (rights to enter land to remove material such as minerals or timber) were always presumed to be alienable. If an easement in gross is for personal convenience or enjoyment — for example, a right to swim in a private lake — courts may rule that the grantor did not intend the easement to be transferable to others. Some states retain the older rule holding that easements in gross are not transferable. *Gilder v. Mitchell,* 668 A.2d 879, 881 (Me. 1995); *Tupper v. Dorchester County,* 487 S.E.2d 187, 191 (S.C. 1997).

§5.3.3 INTERPRETATION OF AMBIGUOUS EASEMENTS: SCOPE AND APPORTIONMENT

§5.3.3.1 Appurtenant Easements

COX v. GLENBROOK COMPANY
371 P.2d 647 (Nev. 1962)

GORDON THOMPSON, Justice.

In this case Glenbrook Company, a family corporation, by complaint, and Cox and Detrick, copartners, by answer and counterclaim, each request a declaratory judgment as to the scope and extent of a certain right-of-way herein referred to as the "Quill Easement," granted Henry Quill by the Glenbrook Company in 1938. The conveying instrument reads:

> That said grantor, in consideration of the sum of ten dollars ($10.00), lawful money of the United States of America, to it in hand paid by the grantee, receipt whereof is hereby acknowledged, does by these presents grant, bargain, sell and convey to the said grantee an easement and right-of-way, with full right of use over the roads of the grantor as now located or as they may be located hereafter (but such relocation to be entirely at the expense of the grantor) from the State Highway known as U. S. Route 50 to the following described property: [description of Quill property] To have and to hold said right-of-way and easement unto the said grantee, his heirs and assigns forever.

1. The Facts

The relevant facts are not disputed. The Quill property contains 80 acres. Henry Quill died in 1943. In 1945 the administratrix of his estate sold the property, with appurtenances, to Kenneth F. Johnson for $8,600. In 1960 Johnson sold the property to Cox and Detrick for $250,000, $50,000 down, with the balance secured by trust deed and payable over an extended period.

    Cox and Detrick propose to subdivide their property into parcels of one acre or more, resulting in a minimum of 40 or a maximum of 60 separate parcels. The building on each parcel is to be limited to a residence and a guesthouse. Permanent, as distinguished from seasonal, homes are planned. A commercial development of the property is not contemplated. Zoning will permit the proposed development. . . . An advertising program to sell the individual parcels was commenced. Cox and Detrick anticipate a fully developed subdivision in ten years. The 80 acres are said to be surrounded on two sides by property owned by George Whittel, and on two sides by the property of Glenbrook Company. The Quill Easement is the only existing ingress to and egress from that tract.

    The property of Glenbrook Company fronts on Glenbrook Bay, Lake Tahoe. For more than 25 years it has operated a resort business. Its facilities consist of a beach, approximately 30 guest cottages, a tennis court, riding stables, foot paths for hiking, horse trails for riding, a golf course, a post office, a rodeo area, a service station, a bar, and a dining room and lounge at the Glenbrook Inn. The golf course may be used by nonguests upon paying a higher green fee. The bar is open to the public, as is the dining room when not completely reserved by guests. There is no gambling. Glenbrook is operated on a seasonal basis from mid-June through September and is widely known as a beautiful summer vacation resort for families, many of whom return year after year. The atmosphere sought to be maintained is that of peace, seclusion and quiet. The roads through the property are generally unpaved except for the main road from U.S. Highway 50 to the golf course. At the entrance to the main road is a sign stating that permission to pass over is revocable at any time. The main road is the only way in or out from the Glenbrook properties. In years past, from time to time, Glenbrook Company has sold small parcels of its property to individuals. In each instance it has granted the purchaser a right-of-way for ingress and egress.

The following rough sketch will, perhaps, be of some assistance.

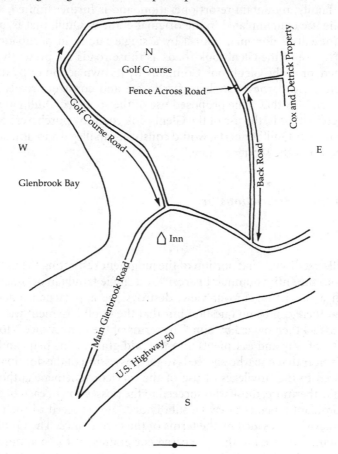

To get to the Cox and Detrick property one may take either the "golf course road" or the "back road." Before this action started, the "golf course road" was fenced off.... A portion of the "back road" was built in 1936 to provide a way to water tanks which supplied water for the golf course. In the late 1930s it was extended to the Quill (now Cox and Detrick) properties. Glenbrook Company, because of friendship with Quill, supplied the tractor and blade used in so extending the road. The road was, and is, narrow and unpaved. In most places it is wide enough for only one car. Trees, rocks and manzanita generally border it. There is an occasional "turn out." A worker, who extended the road to the Quill property in the late 1930s, stated that Quill just wanted "a rough road, so that he could go on up with a car." Cox frankly stated that he would like to use the "back road" if it "were passable," and that he definitely wanted to widen the road. That road has seldom been used by anyone except the four or five families having homes along its course, and their guests.

2. The Lower Court's Judgment

After trial before the court without a jury, judgment was entered declaring that the Quill Easement is limited in three respects: (a) "to such uses as are and will be reasonably consistent with the use to which the servient property is employed, that is, a conservative, family, mountain resort operation, and is further limited, as to reasonable use, to the use contemplated in the original grant to Quill, that is, access to and egress from the entire dominant parcel by a single family in occupancy, and their guests"; (b) "to use of the Glenbrook roads as those roads are presently constructed and maintained, or as the Glenbrook Company by its own action or by mutual agreement with interested parties, may hereafter locate and construct roads in the Glenbrook estate"; and (c) that "The proposed use of the so-called Quill Easement by the defendants herein, that is, the use of the Glenbrook roads by purchasers of subdivided parcels of the former Quill property, would constitute an illegal and unjustified burden and surcharge upon the servient estate." . . .

5.   Unwarranted Restrictions

(A)

We shall first discuss that portion of the judgment restricting the use to ingress to and egress from the entire dominant parcel "by a single family in occupancy and their guests." Such a restriction, in our view, destroys the appurtenant character of the easement. Yet, there can be no question but that the Quill Easement was appurtenant to the 80 acre tract then owned by him. The terms of the conveyance, "to have and to hold said right-of-way and easement unto the said grantee, his heirs and assigns forever," make it clear that one who succeeds to the possession of the dominant tenement, succeeds as well to the privileges of use of the servient tenement authorized by the conveyance. Furthermore, those who succeed to the possession of each of the parts into which the dominant tenement may be subdivided, also succeed to such privileges of use, unless otherwise provided by the terms of the conveyance. The Quill conveyance does not contain a restriction that the easement granted is to be appurtenant to the dominant estate only while such estate remains in single possession, and none may be imposed by judicial declaration.

(B)

The judgment further restricts the use of the easement to "use of the Glenbrook roads as those roads are presently constructed and maintained." We are uncertain as to the precise meaning of this restriction. If such language prohibits the owner of the dominant estate from making any improvements or repairs of the way, it is too restrictive. As a general rule, the owner of an easement may prepare, maintain, improve or repair the way in a manner and to an extent reasonably calculated to promote the purposes for which it was created. The owner may not, however, by such action, cause an undue burden upon the servient estate, nor an unwarranted interference with the independent rights of others who have a similar right of use. The action of Cox and Detrick in leveling or "rough grading" the "back road," to the extent that it was confined to the area within the exterior borders of the road as they existed when the easement was originally granted, was an improvement reasonably calculated to promote the purposes for which the easement was created. Such leveling or rough grading as so confined, would not, in itself, cause an undue burden upon the servient estate, nor constitute an unwarranted interference with the easement rights of other private property owners.

However, their conduct in attempting to widen the way is another matter. A careful study of the record makes it clear that the ultimate intention of the subdividers is to widen the "back road" in order that two cars going in opposite directions may pass comfortably at all points along its course. The conveying instrument does not specify the width of the way expressly; it does, however, refer to the "roads as now located." The "back road" as it existed at the time of the grant of easement, was described as a "small road," and wide enough for just one car. The record does not disclose that the predecessors of Cox and Detrick ever sought or attempted to widen the "back road." There is no evidence tending to indicate that either Glenbrook Company or Henry Quill contemplated or intended a wider road than existed when the grant was made. When the width is not specified, the conveying instrument must be construed in the light of the facts and circumstances existing at its date and affecting the property, the intention of the parties being the object of inquiry. Indeed, it is sometimes held, as a matter of law, that where the width of a right-of-way is not specified in the grant, it is limited to the width as it existed at the time of the grant. We need not go that far. We believe that the intention of the parties at the time of the grant, when there is evidence to indicate such intention, controls as to width.

As already stated, the only evidence in the record with reference to the "back road" indicates that Henry Quill desired a way wide enough for one car; that such was the character of the "back road" at that time, with occasional "turn outs." We must conclude, therefore, that such was the parties' intention in 1938 when the grant was made. If the width of the way is what the lower court had in mind when it restricted the easement to "use of the Glenbrook roads as those roads are presently constructed and maintained" (the record revealing no substantial change from 1938 to time of trial, except for the work of Cox and Detrick before mentioned), then we find ourselves in accord....

7. Area Wherein Judgment Is Premature

The judgment entered also declared that the proposed use of the Quill Easement would constitute an illegal burden and surcharge upon the servient estate.... The announced intention by the owners of the dominant estate as to their proposed future use of the easement does not, of itself, constitute an unreasonable burden upon the servient estate. When the facts concerning that use become known, an unreasonable burden upon the servient estate may, or may not result. That determination must await the presentation of evidence then in existence....

...In our judgment the lower court erred in declaring that the proposed use of the Quill Easement would constitute an unreasonable burden upon the servient estate, in the absence of existing evidence. It should have done no more than to announce, in general terms, the applicable legal principle within which a subsequent factual determination could be made if occasion therefore arises.

Conclusions

From the foregoing it is apparent that the parties seek a declaration of rights in the following respects:...

First: The privilege of use of the Glenbrook roads as located on January 7, 1938 (the date of the grant of easement) is not restricted by the terms of the grant, and is appurtenant to the dominant estate, and may be enjoyed by those who succeed to the possession of the dominant estate in its entirety or by those who succeed to the possession of the parts into which such estate may be subdivided.

Second: The owners of the easement may maintain, repair and improve the way in a manner reasonably calculated to promote the purposes for which the easement was created, provided, however, (a) such maintenance, repair or improvement is confined to the area within the exterior borders of the way as it existed on January 7, 1938 (the date of the grant of easement); (b) that such maintenance, repair, or improvement will not cause an undue burden upon the servient estate; (c) that such maintenance, repair or improvement will not cause an unwarranted interference with the independent rights of others who have a similar right of use.

Third: The owners of the easement may not widen the way, its width being limited, by reason of the evidence introduced, to the width of the way on January 7, 1938 (the date of the grant of easement); and, insofar as the portion of the way herein referred to as the "back road" is concerned, that width is sufficient only for one car with occasioned "turn outs."

Fourth: The owner of the servient estate has the right to relocate the way at its own expense, which right includes the right to barricade that portion of the existing way herein referred to as the "golf course road."

Fifth: The owners of the easement may not, by reason of their proposed subdivision development, or otherwise, cause an undue burden upon the servient estate, or an unwarranted interference with the independent rights of others who have a similar right of use. Whether such a burden or interference will occur cannot be conclusively declared upon existing evidence. In the event the owners of the easement proceed with their announced plan, their use of the way is limited to the extent herein noted. We believe it proper, however, at this time, to note that, should they proceed with their proposed plan, the trier of the facts in subsequent litigation, if it occurs, might or might not determine upon evidence then existing, that their use of the way causes an unreasonable burden upon the servient estate or an unwarranted interference with the independent rights of others who have a similar right of use; hence, any further action on their part to develop their property in the manner proposed is subject to such contingency....

§5.3.3.2 Easements in Gross

HENLEY v. CONTINENTAL
CABLEVISION OF ST. LOUIS COUNTY, INC.

692 S.W.2d 825 (Mo. Ct. App. 1985)

CARL R. GAERNTNER, Judge....

... Pursuant to an indenture recorded on April 8, 1922, plaintiffs' predecessors as trustees, were expressly granted the right to construct and maintain electric, telephone and telegraphic service on or over the rear five feet of all lots in the subdivision, and to grant easements to other parties for the purposes of creating and maintaining such systems. In July, 1922 and August, 1922, respectively, the trustees conveyed an easement to Southwestern Bell Telephone Company to "construct, reconstruct, repair, operate and maintain its lines for telephone and electric light purposes" and similarly to Union Electric to "keep, operate and maintain its lines consisting of cables, manholes, wires, fixtures and appurtenances thereto." Subsequently, in 1981 and 1982, defendant [Continental Cablevision of St. Louis County, Inc.] exercised licenses acquired from both utilities to enter upon these easements, and erected cables, wires and conduits for the purpose of transmitting television programs.

Plaintiffs [as trustees of University Park subdivision] filed an action for an injunction on December 29, 1983, seeking not only to enjoin a continuing trespass and compel the removal of defendant's wires and cables, but also seeking $300,000 in damages and the reasonable value of the use of plaintiffs' property for defendant's profit based upon *quantum meruit*. . . .

Both parties agree that the subject easements are easements in gross, *i.e.*, easements which belong to the owner independently of his ownership or possession of other land, and thus lacking a dominant tenement. The dispositive issue here is whether or not these easements are exclusive and therefore apportionable by the utilities to, in this case, defendant Continental Cablevision.

We believe the very nature of the 1922 easements obtained by both utilities indicates that they were intended to be exclusive and therefore apportionable. It is well settled that where the servient owner retains the privilege of sharing the benefit conferred by the easement, it is said to be "common" or non-exclusive and therefore not subject to apportionment by the easement owner. Conversely, if the rights granted are exclusive of the servient owners' participation therein, divided utilization of the rights granted are presumptively allowable. This principle stems from the concept that one who grants to another the right to use the grantor's land in a particular manner for a specified purpose but who retains no interest in exercising a similar right himself, sustains no loss if, within the specifications expressed in the grant, the use is shared by the grantee with others. On the other hand, if the grantor intends to participate in the use or privilege granted, then his retained right may be diminished if the grantee shares his right with others. Thus, insofar as it relates to the apportionability of an easement in gross, the term "exclusive" refers to the exclusion of the owner and possessor of the servient tenement from participation in the rights granted, not to the number of different easements in and over the same land.

Here, there is no claim that plaintiffs' predecessors had at the time the easements were granted, any intention to seek authority for, or any interest whatsoever in using the five foot strips for the construction and maintenance of either an electric power system or telephone and telegraphic service. Moreover, at no time during the ensuing sixty-three years have the trustees been authorized to furnish such services by any certificate of convenience and necessity issued by the Public Service Commission pursuant to Mo. Rev. Stat. §§392.260 and 393.170 (1978). Accordingly, the easements granted to Southwestern Bell and Union Electric were exclusive as to the grantors thereof and therefore apportionable.

Plaintiffs also argue defendant could acquire no rights from the utilities since their easements did not mention television cables, and that the cable attachments themselves constituted an extra burden on the property. We disagree. The owner of an easement may license or authorize third persons to use its right of way for purposes not inconsistent with the principal use granted. The 1922 easements granted to Union Electric expressly provided the right of ingress and egress by Union Electric, its successors and assigns, to "add to the number of and relocate all wires, cables, conduits, manholes, adding thereto from time-to-time. . . ." Similarly, the easement conveyed to

Southwestern Bell expressly contemplated the construction and maintenance of "all poles, cables, wires, conduits, lateral pipes, anchor guys and all other fixtures and appurtenances deemed necessary at anytime by [Southwestern Bell], its successors and assigns. . . ." It can hardly be said that the addition of a single coaxial cable to the existing poles for the purpose of transmitting television images and sound by electric impulse increases the burden on the servient tenement beyond the scope of the intended and authorized use. . . .

Although this is a case of first impression in Missouri, courts in other jurisdictions have addressed the legal effect of adding coaxial cables for television transmission to existing electric and telephone poles erected on easements without the consent of the owners of the fees. These courts have uniformly rejected arguments identical to those made by plaintiffs herein and have reached a conclusion similar to ours.

In *Jolliff v. Hardin Cable Television Co.*, 269 N.E.2d 588 (Ohio 1971), an easement granted to a power company for the transmission of electric power, including telegraph or telephone wires, was held to be an apportionable easement in gross by reason of the express language of the conveyance authorizing the grantee to lease some portion of its interest to third parties. In addressing the question of an additional burden on the servient tenements, the court noted that the attachment of a television coaxial cable to existing poles constituted no more of a burden than would installation of telephone wires, a burden clearly contemplated at the time of the grants.

In *Crowley v. New York Telephone Company*, 363 N.Y.S.2d 292 (Dist. Ct. 1975) it was held that the failure to make specific mention of cable television in a 1949 easement to locate telephone poles and wires on plaintiff's property could not be so narrowly interpreted as to prohibit the addition of television cables to the telephone poles. "Just as we must accept scientific advances, we must translate the rights of parties to an agreement in the light of such developments." 363 N.Y.S.2d at 294.

In *Hoffman v. Capitol Cablevision System, Inc.*, 383 N.Y.S.2d 674 (App. Div. 1976), the court concluded that the rights granted to two utilities were exclusive *vis-à-vis* the landowner, and were, therefore apportionable by the grantees. The addition of cable and equipment to already existing poles was held to constitute no additional burden since the defendant was doing only what the utilities were enabled to do. The court noted the general rule that easements in gross for commercial purposes are particularly alienable and transferable. For these reasons, the court held the failure to foresee and specifically refer to cable television in the grant was of no consequence.

The reasoning of the *Hoffman* court has recently been found persuasive by the California court in *Salvaty v. Falcon Cable Television*, 212 Cal. Rptr. 31 (Ct. App. 1985). The court stated:

> In the case at bench, the addition of cable television equipment on surplus space on the telephone pole was within the scope of the easement. Although the cable television industry did not exist at the time the easement was granted, it is part of the natural evolution of communications technology. Installation of the equipment was consistent with the primary goal of the easement, to provide for wire transmission of power and communication. We fail to see how the addition of cable equipment to a pre-existing utility pole materially increased the burden on appellant's property. 212 Cal. Rptr. at 34–35.

The unsurprising fact that the drafters of the 1922 easements did not envision cable television does not mandate the narrow interpretation of the purposes of the conveyance of rights and privileges urged by plaintiffs. The expressed intention of the predecessors of plaintiff trustees was to obtain for the homeowners in the subdivision the benefits of electric power and telephonic communications. Scientific and technological progress over the ensuing years have added an unforeseen dimension to such contemplated benefits, the transmission by electric impulse of visual and audio communication over coaxial cable. It is an inescapable conclusion that the intention of plaintiffs' predecessors was the acquisition and continued maintenance of available means of bringing electrical power and communication into the homes of the subdivision. Clearly, it is in the public interest to use the facilities already installed for the purpose of carrying out this intention to provide the most economically feasible and least environmentally damaging vehicle for installing cable systems....

NOTES AND QUESTIONS

1. *Scope.* Three issues arise in determining whether the owner of an easement is misusing it by going beyond the scope of activities contemplated by the grantor: (a) whether the use is of a *kind* contemplated by the grantor, (b) whether the use is so heavy that it constitutes an *unreasonable burden* on the servient estate not contemplated by the grantor, and (c) whether the easement can be *subdivided.*

2. *Kinds of uses encompassed by the easement.* The first issue is what kinds of activities are encompassed by the easement. For example, can a general right of way initially used for road purposes be used to place utility lines? Many courts hold that a general right of way may be used for any reasonable purpose. *Kelly v. Schmelz,* 439 S.W.2d 211 (Mo. Ct. App. 1969). Some courts disagree and hold that rights of way are limited to the specific purposes contemplated at the time they were created. For example, one court has held that a general right of way does not include a right to erect poles and maintain electric wires on or next to the roadway. *Ward v. McGlory,* 265 N.E.2d 78 (Mass. 1970). *Cf. Holmes v. Sprint United Telephone of Kansas,* 35 P.3d 928 (Kan. Ct. App. 2001) (digging a trench to bury telephone lines does not exceed scope of utility easement).

At issue in *Henley* was an easement for telephone and electric lines rather than a general right of way. Nonetheless, the court faced the analogous issue whether that limited easement included a right to place cable television lines. Most courts will agree with the result in *Henley* and interpret easements broadly. For example, in *Centel Cable Television Co. of Ohio v. Cook,* 567 N.E.2d 1010 (Ohio 1991), the court held that an easement for a "line for the transmission and/or distribution of electric energy thereover, for any and all purposes for which electric energy is now, or may hereafter be used" gave the grantee the right to lay cable television lines as well as electric lines. Is this result justified?

Grantors retain whatever rights they do not give away, but the question is *what* rights the grantor gave away when it granted the initial easement. Should easements be interpreted broadly or narrowly? Should the owner of a general right of way who acquired the easement initially for road purposes be allowed to use the road for other purposes such as phone or electric utility lines? What result is most likely to effectuate the intent of the parties? What result is more likely to promote the alienability of property? Should alienability of property be the preeminent goal? If not, what should be?

3. *Unreasonable additional burden.* The owner of an easement may be clearly engaged in the kind of activity contemplated by the easement but may still exceed

the scope of the easement. For example, the court in *Green v. Lupo*, although allowing motorcycle use over the road, stated that such use could be limited and regulated to protect the legitimate interests of the owner of the servient estate. Similarly, the court in *Cox* required the trial court to determine whether subdivision of the dominant estate would impose an unreasonable additional burden on the servient estate.

Defining whether an activity constitutes an unreasonable additional burden on the servient estate beyond that contemplated at the time the easement was created depends on the grantor's intent. When the grantor's intent is ambiguous, courts must balance the interests of the easement owner in freedom to develop his property against the interests of the servient estate owners in security from having their property overly burdened in a way they could not anticipate or should not have had to anticipate.

4. *Divisibility or apportionability.* The question of divisibility of appurtenant easements generally arises when the owner of the dominant estate subdivides the property and attempts to transfer to new owners rights to use the easement to obtain access to their property. Most courts agree with the *Cox* court in holding that an appurtenant easement "benefits the entire dominant estate and is apportionable among subsequent owners if the dominant estate is divided." Jon W. Bruce and James W. Ely, Jr., *The Law of Easements and Licenses in Land* 7.05[3], at 7-41 (1988); Gerald Korngold, *Private Land Use Arrangements: Easements, Real Covenants, and Equitable Servitudes* §5.05, at 186-193 (1990). *Accord, Krause v. Taylor,* 343 A.2d 767 (N.J. Super. Ct. App. Div. 1975) (holding that a dominant estate may be subdivided and use an easement for a right of way for access to each of parcels); *Restatement of Property* §488 (1944). Comment c to §488 notes:

> The burden upon a servient tenement frequently will not be greatly increased by permitting an easement appurtenant to attach to each of the parts into which the dominant tenement may be subdivided. Though some increase in burden may result from the fact that the number of users is increased by the subdivision, the extent of the use is still measured by the needs of the land which constituted the dominant tenement. Moreover, dominant tenements are ordinarily divisible and their division is so common that it is assumed that the possibility of their division is contemplated in their creation. Hence, unless forbidden by the manner or terms of its creation, the benefit of an easement appurtenant accrues upon a subdivision of a dominant tenement to the benefit of each of the parts into which it is subdivided.

When dealing with easements in gross, the question of divisibility of the easement is referred to as the issue of apportionability. When an easement in gross is *nonexclusive* — meaning the grantor, or owner of the servient estate, has reserved for herself the right to use the easement in conjunction with the grantee — the easement is generally held to be nonapportionable; the grantor herself could sell further rights to others so long as those new easements did not interfere with the use of the existing easement by the first grantee. The courts presume that under these circumstances, the grantor would want to retain the right to obtain the economic benefits of any future easements. When, however, the easement is *exclusive* — meaning the grantor has no right to use the easement in conjunction with the grantee — the easement is generally held to be apportionable. Since the grantor has no right to grant other easements, the grantee is not interfering with any rights the grantor might have to sell or lease use of the easement to others.

The *Restatement (Third)* provides, instead, that easements in gross can be divided unless this is contrary to the intent of the parties who created the easement or "unless the division unreasonably increases the burden on the servient estate." *Id.* §5.9. This appears to be consistent with the trend in the law, which is to answer the question by reference to the intent of the grantor. William B. Stoebuck & Dale A. Whitman, *The Law of Property* §8.11, at 465 (3d ed. 2000).

5. *Width of the road.* The court in *Cox* concludes that the grantor intended to allow the dominant estate to be subdivided but that the road was intended to be limited to a one-car width with existing "turn-abouts." Is this consistent? It is unlikely to be practicable to subdivide the dominant estate *unless* the easement is widened to at least two lanes. If the owner of the dominant estate has the right to subdivide his land, and each of his grantees will have a right to use the easement (so long as this collective use does not constitute an unreasonable additional burden on the servient estate), how can it be that the dominant estate owner has no right to a wider road? If the grantor could contemplate that the dominant estate would be subdivided, wouldn't the grantor also be able to foresee and contemplate the need for a wider road? How would Justice Thompson answer this question?

6. *Extension of the use.* In *Brown v. Voss,* 715 P.2d 514 (Wash. 1986), an owner of a road easement wanted to use the easement across the servient estate not only to obtain access to the dominant estate but to reach a subsequently acquired lot on the other side of the dominant estate. The traditional and probably still majority rule would prohibit this extension of the use of the easement. *Bateman v. Bd. of Appeals of Georgetown,* 775 N.E.2d 1276 (Mass. App. Ct. 2002). Although the Washington Supreme Court adopted this rule, allowing the owner of the servient estate to obtain damages, the damages awarded by the trial court were limited to one dollar. Moreover, the court denied injunctive relief that would have ordered cessation of the use. Allowing the use to continue, the court noted that the owner of the dominant estate intended to combine the two lots in order to build a single house on the border between them. Because the use would establish no additional burden on the servient estate, the court concluded that the "equities of the case" did not justify an injunction to stop the new use. In a dissenting opinion, Justice Dore argued any extension of the easement to nondominant property constitutes a "misuse" of the easement. If the newly acquired parcel was landlocked, the owner's remedy was either to negotiate with the owner of the servient estate or obtain an easement by necessity over the remaining land of the grantor of the landlocked parcel. How would you have ruled?

7. *Changing location of the easement.* Can the owner of the servient estate change the location of the easement? The traditional rule prevents this; the owner of the servient estate must obtain the consent of the easement holder to relocate it. *Herren v. Pettengill,* 538 S.E.2d 735 (Ga. 2000); *Koeppen v. Bolich,* 79 P3d 1100 (Mont. 2003). However, some recent cases and the *Restatement (Third) of Property (Servitudes)* §4.8(3) (2000), would allow the servient estate owner, at her own expense, to "make reasonable changes in the location or dimension of an easement, at the servient owner's expense, to permit normal use or development of the servient estate" if the changes do not "significantly lessen the utility of the servitude," §4.8(3)(a), "increase the burdens on the owner of the easement in its use and enjoyment," §4.8(3)(b), or "frustrate the purpose for which the easement was created," §4.8(3)(c). *M.P.M. Builders, LLC v. Dwyer,* 809 N.E.2d 1053 (Mass. 2004); *Huggins v. Wright,* 774 So.2d 408 (Miss. 2000); *Lewis v. Young,* 705 N.E.2d 649 (N.Y. 1998). One court has adopted a middle position, allowing the servient estate owner to relocate the easement so long as damages are paid to the dominant estate owner, *Umphres v. J.R. Mayer*

Enterprises, Inc., 889 S.W.2d 86 (Mo. Ct. App. 1994), while it allows relocation only after court proceedings, finding that relocation will not harm the easement owner, *Roaring Fork Club L.P. v. St. Jude's Co.*, 36 P.3d 1229 (Colo. 2001). As noted above, however, a fair number of recent courts have rejected the *Restatement (Third)'s* new rule. *See, e.g., MacMeekin v. Low Income Housing Institute, Inc.*, 45 P.3d 570 (Wash. Ct. App. 2002). Does the *Restatement (Third)'s* position represent a good change in the law?

PROBLEMS

1. Should the defendant owners of the dominant estate in *Cox* have the right to widen the road to accommodate a subdivision of 40 homes? Would this exceed the scope of the easement?

    a. What arguments could you make for the plaintiff that the width of the road should be set at the historical width existing at the time of the original conveyance?

    b. What arguments could you make for defendants that they have a right to widen the road to accommodate the subdivision of the dominant estate?

    c. How should the case be adjudicated, and why?

2. Assume now that the original easement was a two-lane road so there is no need to widen it. Would subdividing the dominant estate and building 40 homes constitute an unreasonable additional burden on the servient estate?

    a. What arguments could you make for the plaintiff that the subdivision would exceed the scope of the original easement and constitute an unreasonable additional burden on the servient estate?

    b. What arguments could you make for defendants that the subdivision would not constitute an unreasonable additional burden on the servient estate?

    c. How should the case be adjudicated, and why?

3. If plaintiff cannot obtain a court order to widen the road because such an improvement is outside the scope of the initial grant of the easement, but plaintiff does have a right to subdivide the dominant estate, can plaintiff obtain a right to widen the easement roads under the doctrine of easement by necessity, on the grounds that a single-lane road is inadequate for 40 houses?

§5.3.4 MODIFYING AND TERMINATING EASEMENTS

Easements last forever unless they are terminated (1) by agreement in writing (*release* of the easement by the holder); (2) by their own terms — for example, if the deed conveying the easement expressly states that it is to last for ten years; (3) by *merger*, when the holder of the servient estate becomes the owner of the dominant estate; (4) by *abandonment*, if it can be shown that the owner of the easement, by her conduct, indicated an intent to abandon the easement; or (5) by *adverse possession* or *prescription* by the owner of the servient estate or by a third party.

Sometimes courts terminate easements (6) because of *frustration of purpose*. "Traditional doctrine terminates obsolete easements either by a liberal application of the abandonment principle, or by finding that the purpose of the easement has become impossible to accomplish, or that the easement no longer serves its intended purpose, rather than by the changed conditions doctrine." *Restatement (Third) of Property (Servitudes)* §7.10 (2000). *See Glick v. Principal Mutual Life Ins. Co.*, 14 Mass. L. Rep. 261, 2002 Mass. Super, LEXIS 27 (Mass. Super. Ct. 2002) (parking easement terminated by frustration of purpose when dominant estate built a parking lot making the easement unnecessary). Covenants, unlike easements, were traditionally subject to termination in certain cases of *changed conditions*. The *Restatement (Third)* would substantially change the law by making easements, as well as covenants, subject to this doctrine. *Id.* §7.10 cmt. a. It also modifies this doctrine by making easements modifiable, as well as terminable. *Id.* §7.10. The *Restatement (Third)* provides that easements can be modified if changed conditions have made it "impossible as a practical matter to accomplish" the easement's purpose and may be terminated if modification is "not practicable." *Id.* For more on the changed conditions doctrine, *see infra* §5.4.4.1.

Many states have enacted "marketable title acts," which may require that easements, along with other encumbrances on property interests, be re-recorded periodically (generally every 30 to 50 years) to be binding on future purchasers. The purpose of these statutes is to limit how far back a buyer must look in the chain of title to determine the validity of the seller's title and the existence of encumbrances on the land. However, they also have the effect of making unenforceable those interests that were put in place a long time ago and were of insufficient importance to anyone to be re-recorded in compliance with the statute. Failure to comply with the marketable title act by re-recording the easement may leave the easement owner unprotected from a subsequent purchaser of the servient estate who, depending on the language in the statute, may be entitled to buy the property free of the burden of the easement.

§5.4 Covenants

§5.4.1 HISTORICAL BACKGROUND

Because the courts limited the number of negative easements that could be created, landowners began to enter contractual arrangements to get around these limitations.[12] However, contract law imposed additional problems. In the early nineteenth century, contract rights were generally not assignable to others. Promises were personal: A promise from *A* to *O* could not be enforced by anyone other than *O*; nor could *A* assign to anyone else the obligation to perform *A*'s contractual duties without the consent of *O*. However, the courts developed an exception to this principle of nonassignability in the context of real property; the benefits of contract rights were assignable if they were somehow conceived as being attached to an ownership interest in land created by two parties who had simultaneous rights in that land. This concept, called *privity of estate*, made it possible for both the benefit and the burden to run with the land.

---

12. This historical material is taken from A. W. B. Simpson, *A History of the Land Law* (2d ed. 1986).

The concept was originally articulated in *Spencer's Case,* 77 Eng. Rep. 72 (1583), the decision that created the law of *real covenants.* In that case, a couple conveyed a house and lot for a term of 21 years to a tenant who covenanted on behalf of himself and his assigns to build a brick wall on the lot. The tenant then assigned his interest in the land to another person who refused to build the wall. The court held that the affirmative covenant would be binding on the successor in interest (1) if it was in *writing,* (2) if it was *intended* to be binding on future tenants, (3) if it *touched and concerned* the land, and (4) if there was *privity of estate* between the covenanting parties. The concept of "privity of estate" was ambiguous; it probably meant that the parties had simultaneous interests in the same parcel of land (simultaneous privity), but it also could have meant that the restriction was imposed at the moment a property interest was transferred from one owner to another (instantaneous privity). Landlords and tenants clearly satisfied both these criteria, but what about buyers and sellers?

The law courts in England rejected the doctrine of instantaneous privity, holding that privity of estate did not apply to transfers of property from sellers to buyers; privity required simultaneous interests in the same parcel. If an owner wished to sell part of her land while ensuring that the property being sold would be restricted to a particular use, she could not do so under real covenants law. However, England had two court systems rather than one. Litigants who could not obtain relief in the law courts could approach the equity courts for relief from the harsh common law rule. The case of *Tulk v. Moxhay,* 41 Eng. Rep. 1143 (1848), created the law of *equitable servitudes.* In *Tulk,* the owner of several houses bordering Leicester Square sold the Square to a buyer with a covenant by the buyer and his heirs and assigns to maintain the Square and the garden within it and not to construct any buildings on it. The Square was sold several times, and a subsequent owner proposed to build on the Square. The original grantor sued the current owner of the Square, asking for an injunction ordering him to comply with the covenant. The chancellor held that the owner was bound by the covenant even though no privity of estate existed between the original covenanting parties because (1) the covenant was in *writing,* (2) it was *intended* to run with the land, (3) it *touched and concerned the land,* and (4) the current owner had purchased with *notice* of the restriction and thus was bound by good conscience to protect the expectations of the owner of the dominant estate. In effect, the court substituted the notice requirement for the privity requirement.

Courts in the United States adopted both real covenants and equitable servitudes law. The law of real covenants expanded the definition of privity. Some states did this by expanding the concept of simultaneous privity from the landlord-tenant relationship to situations in which one owner owns an easement in the property of the other and/or both owners have mutual easements in each other's property.[13] Most courts expanded the privity concept by adopting the instantaneous privity doctrine; they found privity to exist if a covenant was created in the context of a transfer of property through a grantor-grantee relationship. Thus, a covenant included in a deed of sale restricting use of the parcel might bind future owners of the property conveyed.[14] At the moment the deed passes from seller to buyer, the parties have a fleeting, instantaneous, simultaneous interest in the property, and the covenant was thought to attach itself to the property interest conveyed from seller to buyer.

---

13. This test was adopted in Massachusetts and is applied in the next principal case, *Whitinsville Plaza v. Kotseas.*

14. For a complete explanation of privity of estate, *see infra* §5.4.2.1.

Today the law of real covenants and equitable servitudes is being merged. The *Restatement (Third)* abolishes the distinction. The law of covenants was developed in the law courts in England and was enforced by the legal remedy of damages, while equitable servitudes were enforced by injunctions, the remedy of the equity courts that invented the doctrine. Until recently, privity was required to obtain damages for breach of a covenant. Today, covenants are likely to be enforceable either by damages or injunctive relief as long as they were in writing, intended to run with the land, the owner of the burdened estate was on notice of the restriction, and the covenant is one that is appropriate to impose on subsequent possessors of the servient estate for the benefit of future owners of the dominant estate (the traditional "touch and concern" requirement). Today the availability of damages and/or injunctive relief will be determined as they are in other contexts, based on their appropriateness to remedy the wrong at issue in the case.

Although the law of covenants is rapidly being modernized, many courts still adhere to some of the traditional technical requirements and distinctions between real covenants and equitable servitudes. Until the *Restatement (Third)* is widely adopted, it is still important to understand the traditional rules for real covenants. The next case explores some of them in the context of a widely used type of covenant—one that protects an owner from competition on nearby land.

§5.4.2 CREATION OF COVENANTS

§5.4.2.1 Express Agreement

DAVIDSON BROS., INC. v. D. KATZ & SONS, INC.
579 A.2d 288 (N.J. 1990)

MARIE GARIBALDI, J.

This case presents [the question of] whether a restrictive covenant in a deed, providing that the property shall not be used as a supermarket or grocery store, is enforceable against the original covenantor's successor, a subsequent purchaser with actual notice of the covenant....

...Prior to September 1980 plaintiff, Davidson Bros., Inc., along with Irisondra, Inc., a related corporation, owned certain premises located at 263-271 George Street and 30 Morris Street in New Brunswick (the "George Street" property). Plaintiff operated a supermarket on that property for approximately seven to eight months. The store operated at a loss allegedly because of competing business from plaintiff's other store, located two miles away (the "Elizabeth Street" property). Consequently, plaintiff and Irisondra conveyed, by separate deeds, the George Street property to defendant D. Katz & Sons, Inc., with a restrictive covenant not to operate a supermarket on the premises. Specifically, each deed contained the following covenant:

> The lands and premises described herein and conveyed hereby are conveyed subject to the restriction that said lands and premises shall not be used as and for a supermarket or grocery store of a supermarket type, however designated, for a period of forty (40) years from the date of this deed. This restriction shall be a covenant attached to and running with the lands.

The deeds were duly recorded in Middlesex County Clerk's office on September 10, 1980. According to plaintiff's complaint, its operation of both stores resulted in losses in both stores. Plaintiff alleges that after the closure of the George Street store, its Elizabeth Street store increased in sales by twenty percent and became profitable. Plaintiff held a leasehold interest in the Elizabeth Street property, which commenced in 1978 for a period of twenty years, plus two renewal terms of five years.

According to defendants New Brunswick Housing Authority (the "Authority") and City of New Brunswick (the "City"), the closure of the George Street store did not benefit the residents of downtown New Brunswick. Defendants allege that many of the residents who lived two blocks away from the George Street store in multi-family and senior-citizen housing units were forced to take public transportation and taxis to the Elizabeth Street store because there were no other markets in downtown New Brunswick, save for two high-priced convenience stores.

The residents requested the aid of the City and the Authority in attracting a new food retailer to this urban-renewal area. For six years, those efforts were unsuccessful. Finally, in 1986, an executive of C-Town, a division of a supermarket chain, approached representatives of New Brunswick about securing financial help from the City to build a supermarket.

Despite its actual notice of the covenant the Authority, on October 23, 1986, purchased the George Street property from Katz for $450,000, and agreed to lease from Katz at an annual net rent of $19,800.00, the adjacent land at 263-265 George Street for use as a parking lot. The Authority invited proposals for the lease of the property to use as a supermarket. C-Town was the only party to submit a proposal at a public auction. The proposal provided for an aggregate rent of one dollar per year during the five-year lease term with an agreement to make $10,000 in improvements to the exterior of the building and land. The Authority accepted the proposal in 1987. All the defendants in this case had actual notice of the restrictions contained in the deed and of plaintiff's intent to enforce the same. Not only were the deeds recorded but the contract of sale between Katz and the Housing Authority specifically referred to the restrictive covenant and the pending action.

Plaintiff filed this action in the Chancery Division against defendants D. Katz & Sons, Inc., the City of New Brunswick, and C-Town. They . . . requested a declaratory judgment that the noncompetition covenant was binding on all subsequent owners of the George Street property. . . .

II . . .

B. *New Jersey's treatment of noncompetitive covenants restraining the use of property*

Our inquiry of New Jersey law on restrictive property use covenants commences with a re-examination of the rule set forth in *Brewer v. Marshall & Cheeseman*, 19 N.J. Eq. 537 (E. & A. 1868), that a covenant will not run with the land unless it affects the physical use of the land. Hence, the burden side of a noncompetition covenant is personal to the covenantor and is, therefore, not enforceable against a purchaser. In *Brewer*, the court objected to all noncompetition covenants on the basis of public policy and refused to consider them in the context of the doctrine of equitable servitudes. . . . Because the burden of a noncompetition covenant is deemed to be personal in these cases, enforcement would be possible only against the original covenantor. As soon as the covenantor sold the property, the burden would cease to exist.

The *per se* prohibition that noncompetition covenants regarding the use of property do not run with the land is not supported by modern real-covenant law.... Commentators also consider the *Brewer* rule an anachronism and in need of change, as do we. Accordingly, to the extent that *Brewer* holds that a noncompetition covenant will not run with the land, it is overruled.

Plaintiff also argues that the "touch and concern" test likewise should be eliminated in determining the enforceability of fully negotiated contracts, in favor of a simpler "reasonableness" standard that has been adopted in most jurisdictions. That argument has some support from commentators, *see, e.g.*, Epstein, *Notice and Freedom of Contract in the Law of Servitudes*, 55 S.Cal.L.Rev. 1353, 1359-61 (1982) (contending that "touch and concern" complicates the basic analysis and limits the effectiveness of law of servitudes), including a reporter for the *Restatement (Third) of Property*, see French, *Servitudes Reform and the New Restatement of Property: Creation Doctrines and Structural Simplification*, 73 Cornell L.Rev. 928, 939 (1988) (arguing that "touch and concern" rule should be completely eliminated and that the law should instead directly tackle the "running" issue on public-policy grounds).

New Jersey courts, however, continue to focus on the "touch and concern" requirement as the pivotal inquiry in ascertaining whether a covenant runs with the land. Under New Jersey law, a covenant that "exercise[s] [a] direct influence on the occupation, use or enjoyment of the premises" satisfies the "touch and concern" rule. The covenant must touch and concern both the burdened and the benefitted property in order to run with the land. Because the law frowns on the placing of restrictions on the freedom of alienation of land, New Jersey courts will enforce a covenant only if it produces a countervailing benefit to justify the burden.

Unlike New Jersey, which has continued to rely on the "touch and concern" requirement, most other jurisdictions have omitted "touch and concern" from their analysis and have focused instead on whether the covenant is reasonable. *See, e.g., Doo v. Packwood*, 71 Cal.Rptr. 477 (Ct. App. 1968) (covenant not to sell groceries on property conveyed); *Sun Oil Co. v. Trent Auto Wash, Inc.*, 150 N.W.2d 818 (Mich. 1967) (covenant not to use retained land as gas station); *Hodge v. Sloan*, N Y 17 N.E. 335 (N.Y. 1887) (covenant not to sell sand on property conveyed). Even the majority of courts that have retained the "touch and concern" test have found that noncompetition covenants meet the test's requirements. *See, e.g., Singer v. Wong*, 404 A.2d 124 (Conn. Super. Ct. 1978) (restrictive covenant in deed providing that premises not be used as shopping center "touched and concerned" land because it materially affected value of land); *Whitinsville Plaza, Inc. v. Kotseas*, 390 N.E.2d 243 (Mass. 1979) (noncompetition covenant satisfied "touch and concern" rule within the ordinary sense and meaning of the phrase). *But see Savings Bank v. City of Blytheville*, 401 S.W.2d 26 (Ark 1966) (anticompetitive agreement increased value of land only indirectly therefore did not "touch and concern").

The "touch and concern" test has, thus, ceased to be, in most jurisdictions, intricate and confounding. Courts have decided as an initial matter that covenants not to compete do touch and concern the land. The courts then have examined explicitly the more important question of whether covenants are reasonable enough to warrant enforcement. The time has come to cut the gordian knot that binds this state's jurisprudence regarding covenants running with the land. Rigid adherence to the "touch and concern" test as a means of determining the enforceability of a restrictive covenant is not warranted. Reasonableness, not esoteric concepts of property law, should be the guiding inquiry into the validity of covenants at law. We do not abandon the "touch and concern" test, but rather hold that the test is but one of the factors a court should consider in determining the reasonableness of the covenant.

A "reasonableness" test allows a court to consider the enforceability of a covenant in view of the realities of today's commercial world and not in the light of outmoded theories developed in a vastly different commercial environment. Originally strict adherence to "touch and concern" rule in the old English common-law cases and in *Brewer*, was to effectuate the then pervasive public policy of restricting many, if not all, encumbrances of the land. Courts today recognize that it is not unreasonable for parties in commercial-property transactions to protect themselves from competition by executing noncompetition covenants. Businesspersons, either as lessees or purchasers may be hesitant to invest substantial sums if they have no minimal protection from a competitor starting a business in the near vicinity. Hence, rather than limiting trade, in some instances, restrictive covenants may increase business activity.

We recognize that "reasonableness" is necessarily a fact sensitive issue involving an inquiry into present business conditions and other factors specific to the covenant at issue. Nonetheless, as do most of the jurisdictions, we find that it is a better test for governing commercial transactions than are obscure anachronisms that have little meaning in today's commercial world. The pivotal inquiry, therefore, becomes what factors should a court consider in determining whether such a covenant is "reasonable" and hence enforceable. We conclude that the following factors should be considered:

1. The intention of the parties when the covenant was executed, and whether the parties had a viable purpose which did not at the time interfere with existing commercial laws, such as antitrust laws, or public policy.
2. Whether the covenant had an impact on the considerations exchanged when the covenant was originally executed. This may provide a measure of the value to the parties of the covenant at the time.
3. Whether the covenant clearly and expressly sets forth the restrictions.
4. Whether the covenant was in writing, recorded, and if so, whether the subsequent grantee had actual notice of the covenant.
5. Whether the covenant is reasonable concerning area, time or duration. Covenants that extend for perpetuity or beyond the terms of a lease may often be unreasonable.
6. Whether the covenant imposes an unreasonable restraint on trade or secures a monopoly for the covenantor. This may be the case in areas where there is limited space available to conduct certain business activities and a covenant not to compete burdens all or most available locales to prevent them from competing in such an activity.
7. Whether the covenant interferes with the public interest.
8. Whether, even if the covenant was reasonable at the time it was executed, "changed circumstances" now make the covenant unreasonable. . . .

In applying the "reasonableness" factors, trial courts may find useful the analogous standards we have adopted in determining the validity of employee covenants not to compete after termination of employment. Although enforcement of such a covenant is somewhat restricted because of countervailing policy considerations, we generally enforce an employee non-competition covenant as reasonable if it "simply protects the legitimate interests of the employer imposes no undue hardship on the employee, and is not injurious to the public." *Solari Indus. v. Malady*, 264 A.2d 53 (N.J. 1970). We also held in *Solari* that if such a covenant is found to be overbroad, it may be partially enforced to the extent reasonable under the circumstances. *Id. at* 585, 264 A.2d 53. That approach to the enforcement of restrictive covenants in deeds offers a mechanism for recognizing and balancing the legitimate concerns of the grantor, the successors in interest, and the public. . . .

There is insufficient evidence in this record to determine whether the covenant is reasonable. Nevertheless, we think it instructive to comment briefly on the application of the "reasonableness" factors to this covenant. We consider first the intent of the parties when the covenant was executed. It is undisputed that when plaintiff conveyed the property to Katz, it intended that the George Street store would not be used as a supermarket or grocery store for a period of forty years to protect his existing business at the Elizabeth Street store from competition. Plaintiff alleges that the purchase price negotiated between it and Katz took into account the value of the restrictive covenant and that Katz paid less for the property because of the restriction. There is no evidence, however, of the purchase price. It is also undisputed that the covenant was expressly set forth in a recorded deed, that the Authority took title to the premises with actual notice of the restrictive covenant, and, indeed, that all the defendants, including C-Town, had actual notice of the covenant.

The parties do not specifically contest the reasonableness of either the duration or area of the covenant. Aspects of the "touch and concern" test also remain useful in evaluating the reasonableness of a covenant, insofar as it aids the courts in differentiating between promises that were intended to bind only the individual parties to a land conveyance and promises affecting the use and value of the land that was intended to be passed on to subsequent parties. Covenants not to compete typically do touch and concern the land. In noncompetition cases, the "burden" factor of the "touch and concern" test is easily satisfied regardless of the definition chosen because the covenant restricts the actual use of the land. The Appellate Division properly concluded that the George Street store was burdened. However, we disagree with the Appellate Division's conclusion that in view of the covenant's speculative impact, the covenant did not provide a sufficient "benefit" to the Elizabeth Street property because it burdened only a small portion (George Street store) of the "market circle" (less than one-half acre in a market circle of 2000 acres).

The size of the burdened property relative to the market area is not a probative measure of whether the Elizabeth store was benefitted. Presumably, the use of the Elizabeth Street store as a supermarket would be enhanced if competition were lessened in its market area. If plaintiff's allegations that the profits of the Elizabeth Street store increased after the sale of the George Street store are true, this would be evidence that a benefit was "conveyed" on the Elizabeth Street store. Likewise, information that the area was so densely populated, that the George Street property was the only unique property available for a supermarket, would show that the Elizabeth Street store property was benefitted by the covenant. In this connection the C-Town executive in his deposition noted that the George Street store location "businesswise was promising because there's no other store in town." Such evidence, however, also should be considered in determining the "reasonableness" of the area covered by the covenant and whether the covenant unduly restrained trade.

Defendants' primary contention is that due to the circumstances of the neighborhood and more particularly the circumstances of the people of the neighborhood, plaintiff's covenant interferes with the public's interest. Whether that claim is essentially that the community has changed since the covenant was enacted or that the circumstances were such that when the covenant was enacted, it interfered with the public interest, we are unable to ascertain from the record. "Public interest" and "changed circumstances" arguments are extremely fact-sensitive. The only evidence that addresses those issues, the three affidavits of Mr. Keefe, Mr. Nero and Ms. Scott, are insufficient to support any finding with respect to those arguments.

The fact-sensitive nature of a "reasonableness" analysis make resolution of this dispute through summary judgment inappropriate. We therefore remand the case to the trial court for a thorough analysis of the "reasonableness" factors delineated herein.

The trial court must first determine whether the covenant was reasonable at the time it was enacted. If it was reasonable then, but now adversely affects commercial development and the public welfare of the people of New Brunswick, the trial court may consider whether allowing damages for breach of the covenant is an appropriate remedy. C-Town could then continue to operate but Davidson would get damages for the value of his covenant. On the limited record before us, however, it is impossible to make a determination concerning either reasonableness of the covenant or whether damages, injunctive relief, or any relief is appropriate....

STEWART POLLOCK, J., concurring....

My basic difference with the majority is that I believe the critical consideration in determining the validity of this covenant is whether it is reasonable as to scope and duration, a point that has never been at issue in this case. Nor has there ever been any question whether the original parties to the covenant, Davidson Bros., Inc. (Davidson), and D. Katz & Sons, Inc. (Katz) intended that the covenant should run with the land. Likewise, the New Brunswick Housing Authority (the Authority) and C-Town have never disputed that they did not have actual notice of the covenant or that there was privity between them and Katz. Finally, the defendants have not contended that the covenant constitutes an unreasonable restraint on trade or that it has an otherwise unlawful purpose, such as invidious discrimination. Davidson, moreover, makes the uncontradicted assertion that the covenant is a burden to the George Street property and benefits the Elizabeth Street property. Hence, the covenant satisfies the requirement that it touch and concern the benefitted and burdened properties.

The fundamental flaw in the majority's analysis is in positing that an otherwise-valid covenant can become invalid not because it results in an unreasonable restraint on trade, but because invalidation facilitates a goal that the majority deems worthy. Considerations such as "changed circumstances" and "the public interest," when they do not constitute such a restraint, should not affect the enforceability of a covenant. Instead, they should relate to whether the appropriate method of enforcement is an injunction or damages. A court should not declare a noncompetition covenant invalid merely because enforcement would lead to a result with which the court disagrees. This leads me to conclude that the only issue on remand should be whether the appropriate remedy is damages or an injunction.

Enforcement of the restriction by an injunction will deprive the downtown residents of the convenience of shopping at the George Street property. Refusal to enforce the covenant, on the other hand, will deprive Davidson of the benefit of its covenant. Thus, the case presents a tension between two worthy objectives: the continued operation of the supermarket for the benefit of needy citizens, and the enforcement of the covenant. An award of damages to Davidson rather than the grant of an injunction would permit the realization of both objectives....

I begin by questioning the majority's formulation and application of a reasonableness test for determining whether the covenant runs with the land. The law has long distinguished between the validity of a covenant between original-contracting parties from the enforceability of a covenant against the covenantor's successor-in-interest. Initial validity is a question of contract law; enforceability against subsequent parties is one of property law. That distinction need not foreclose a subsequent owner of the burdened property from challenging the validity of the contract between the original parties. The distinction, however, sharpens the analysis of the effect of the covenant.

In this case, the basic issue is enforceability of the covenant against the Authority and C-Town, successors in interest to Katz. Thus, the only relevant consideration is whether the covenant "touches and concerns" the benefitted and burdened properties....

The Court can decide the present case without introducing a new test. On the present record, no question exists about the running of the benefit of the covenant. First, the party seeking to enforce the covenant is Davidson, the original leaseholder, not a successor in interest, of the Elizabeth Street property. Second, as the language of the covenant indicates, the original contracting parties, Davidson and Katz, indicated that the covenant would run with the land. Third, Davidson makes the uncontradicted assertions that both stores were unprofitable before the sale, that the Elizabeth Street store after the sale of the George Street property enjoyed a twenty-per-cent sales increase, and that the reopening of the George Street property caused it to suffer a loss of income. Finally, as the majority recognizes, the lower courts erred in concluding that the covenant did not "touch and concern" the burdened and benefitted properties.

It is virtually inconceivable that the covenant does not benefit the Elizabeth Street property. New Jersey courts have declared variously that the benefit "must exercise direct influence upon the occupation, use or enjoyment of the premises," and that the covenant must confer "a direct benefit on the owner of land by reason of his ownership." Scholars have written that a covenant's benefit touches and concerns land if it renders the owner's interest in the land more valuable, or if "the parties as laymen and not as lawyers" would naturally view the covenant as one that aids "the promisee as landowner," C. Clark, *Real Covenants and Other Interests Which Run with the Land* 99 (2d ed. 1947) (Clark)....

The conclusion that this covenant "touches and concerns" the land should end the inquiry about enforceability against the Authority and C-Town. The majority, however, holds that the "touch and concern" test is "but one of the factors a court should consider in determining the reasonableness of the covenant." The majority's inquiry about reasonableness, however, confuses the issue of validity of the original contract between Davidson and Katz with enforceability against the subsequent owner, the Authority. This confusion of validity with enforceability threatens to add uncertainty to an already troubled area of the law....

The majority inaccurately asserts, that most jurisdictions "have focused on whether the covenant is reasonable enough to warrant enforcement." Not one case cited by the majority has concluded that a covenant that is reasonable against the original covenantor would be unreasonable against the covenantor's successor who takes with notice.... [T]he cited cases hold that a reasonable noncompetition cove-

nant binding on the original covenantor likewise result is that the majority's reasonableness test introduces unnecessary uncertainty in the analysis of covenants running with the land.

As troublesome as uncertainty is in other areas of the law, it is particularly
vexatious in the law of real property. The need for certainty in conveyancing, like
that in estate planning, is necessary for people to structure their affairs. Covenants
that run with the land can affect the value of real property not only at the time of sale,
but for many years thereafter. Consequently, vendors and purchasers, as well as their
successors, need to know whether a covenant will run with the land. The majority
acknowledges that noncompetition covenants play a positive role in commercial development. Notwithstanding that acknowledgement, the majority's reasonableness test
generates confusion that threatens the ability of commercial parties and their lawyers
to determine the validity of such covenants. This, in turn, impairs the utility of noncompetition covenants in real estate transactions.

As between the vendor and purchaser, a noncompetition covenant generally
should be treated as valid if it is reasonable in scope and duration, and neither an
unreasonable restraint on trade nor otherwise contrary to public policy. A covenant
would contravene public policy if, for example, its purpose were to secure a monopoly,
or to carry out an illegal object, such as invidious discrimination, *see, e.g.*, N.J. Stat.
§46:3-23 (declaring restrictive covenants in real estate transactions void if based on
race, creed, color, national origin, ancestry, marital status, or sex).

Applying those principles to the validity of the agreement between Davidson and
Katz, I find this covenant enforceable against defendants. The majority acknowledges
that "[t]he parties do not specifically contest the reasonableness of either the duration
or the area of the covenant." . . . Nothing in the record supports the conclusion that
when made or at present the subject covenant was an unreasonable restraint on trade
or otherwise contrary to public policy. . . .

For me the critical issue is whether the appropriate remedy for enforcing the
covenant is damages or an injunction. Ordinarily, as between competing land users,
the more efficient remedy for breach of a covenant is an injunction. R. Posner, *Economic Analysis of Law* 62 (1986); R. Epstein, *Notice and Freedom of Contract in the Law of
Servitudes*, 55 S.Cal. L. Rev. 1353-67 (1962); Calabresi and Melamed, *Property Rules,
Liability Rules, and Inalienability: One View of the Cathedral*, 85 Harv. L. Rev. 1089, 1118
(1972). *But see* Posner, *supra*, at 59; Calabresi and Melamed, *supra*, at 119 (discussing
situations in which damages are a more efficient remedy than an injunction). . . . Although an injunction might be the most efficient form of relief, it would
however deprive the residents of access to the George Street store.

The economic efficiency of an injunction, although persuasive, is not dispositive.
The right rule of law is not necessarily the one that is most efficient. In other cases, New
Jersey courts have allowed cost considerations other than efficiency to affect the award
of a remedy.

For example, in *Gilpin v. Jacob Ellis Realties, Inc.*, 135 A.2d 204 (N.J. Super. Ct.
App. Div. 1957), the court refused to approve an injunction, but upheld an award of
damages to the victim of a breach of a covenant. The property right at issue was a
covenant restricting the building of any structure more than fifteen feet tall within four
feet of one of the parties' common boundaries. Defendant, a builder, was the successor
to the land of the original covenantor. Plaintiff succeeded to ownership of the land
originally benefited by the covenant. Defendant and plaintiff were neighboring
landowners. Defendant breached the covenant. Remodeling the structure would

have cost defendant $11,500. The trial court had found that the breach harmed plaintiff to the extent of $1,000 in damages. Invoking the "doctrine of relative hardship," the Appellate Division held that the differences in these two figures were "so grossly disproportionate in amount as to justify the denial of the mandatory injunction." 135 A.2d at 209. At the same time, the Appellate Division upheld the $1,000-damages award to plaintiff. Thus, the court concluded that the appropriate remedy for enforcing the covenant was an award of damages, not an injunction.

Injunctions, moreover, are ordinarily issued in the discretion of the court. Hence, "[t]he court of equity has the power of devising its remedy and shaping it so as to fit the changing circumstances of every case and the complex relations of all the parties." *Sears, Roebuck & Co. v. Camp*, 1 A.2d 425 (N.J. E. & A. 1938) (*quoting* Pomeroy, *Equity Jurisprudence* §109 (5th ed. 1941)). In the exercise of its discretion, a court may deny injunctive relief when damages provide an available adequate remedy at law.

In the past, however, an injunction in cases involving real covenants and equitable servitudes "was granted almost as a matter of course upon a breach of the covenant. The amount of damages, and even the fact that the plaintiff has sustained *any* pecuniary damages [was] wholly immaterial." J.N. Pomeroy, *Equity Jurisprudence*, §1342 (5th ed. 1941). The roots of that tradition are buried deep in the English common law and are not suited for modern American commercial practices. In brief, the unswerving preference for injunctive relief over damages is an anachronism.

At English common law, as between grantors and grantees, covenants running with the land violated the public policy against encumbrances. The policy becomes understandable on realizing that England originally did not provide a system for recording encumbrances, such as restrictive covenants. Without a recording system, a subsequent grantee might not receive actual or constructive notice of such a covenant. . . .

For centuries, New Jersey has provided a means for recording restrictive covenants. Hence, the policy considerations that counseled against enforcement of restrictive covenants at English common law do not apply in this state. In the absence of an adequate remedy at law, moreover, the English equity courts filled the gap by providing equitable relief, such as an injunction. In this state, unlike in England, covenants between grantor and grantee are readily enforceable. Hence, the need for injunctive relief, as distinguished from damages, is less compelling in New Jersey than at English common law, where damages were not always available. I would rely on the rule that a court should not grant an equitable remedy when damages are adequate.

Here, moreover, the Authority holds a trump card not available to all other property owners burdened by restrictive covenants — the power to condemn. By recourse to that power, the Authority can vitiate the injunction by condemning the covenant and compensating Davidson for its lost benefit. That power does not alter the premise that an injunction is generally the most efficient form of relief. It merely emphasizes that the Authority through condemnation can effectively transform injunctive relief into a damages award. Arguably, the most efficient result is to enforce the covenant against the Authority and then remit it to its power of condemnation. This result would recognize the continuing validity of the covenant, compensate Davidson for its benefit, and permit the needy citizens of New Brunswick to enjoy convenient shopping.

Forcing the Authority to institute eminent-domain proceedings conceivably would waste judicial resources and impose undue costs on the parties. A more appropriate result is to award damages to Davidson for breach of the covenant. That would be true, I believe, even against a subsequent grantee that does not possess the power to condemn.

Money damages would compensate Davidson for the wrong done by the opening of the George Street supermarket. Davidson would be "given what plaintiffs are given in many types of cases — relief measured, so far as the court reasonably may do so, in damages." *Gilpin, supra*, 135 A.2d at 209. The award of money damages, rather than an injunction, might be the more appropriate form of relief for several reasons. First, a damages award is "particularly applicable to a case, such as this, wherein we are dealing with two commercial properties. . . ." *Id.* Second, the award of damages in a single proceeding would provide more efficient justice than an injunction in the present case, with a condemnation suit to follow. Davidson would be compensated for the loss of the covenant and the needy residents would enjoy more convenient shopping. That solution is both efficient and just.

I can appreciate why New Brunswick residents want a supermarket and why the Authority would come to their aid. Supermarkets may be essential for the salvation of inner cities and their residents. The Authority's motives, however noble, should not vitiate Davidson's right to compensation. The fair result, it seems to me, is for the Authority to compensate Davidson in damages for the breach of its otherwise valid and enforceable covenant.

Whitinsville Plaza v. Kotseas, 390 N.E.2d 243 (Mass. 1979). In 1968, Charles H. Kotseas and Paul Kotseas (Kotseas) owned land (Parcel A) that they sold to "122 Trust" (Trust) subject to a restrictive covenant by which Kotseas (the grantor) promised (a) not to use Kotseas's abutting retained land in competition with the discount store contemplated by the grantee and (b) to use the retained land only for enumerated business purposes. Among the permitted business uses of the land retained by Kotseas was a "drug store," defined in an appendix to the deed as a store selling prescribed types of merchandise. In addition, the deed recited that "[t]he foregoing restrictions shall be considered as covenants running with the land to which they are applicable and shall bind and inure to the benefit of the heirs and assigns of the respective parties to whom any part of the lands made subject to the above restrictions, covenants and conditions shall at any time become or belong during the period hereinbefore set forth."

In 1975, the Trust conveyed Parcel A to Whitinsville Plaza, Inc. (Plaza) and, thereafter, ceased operations. The deed to Plaza expressly made Plaza subject to, and gave it the benefit of, the restrictions and covenants in the 1968 deed from Kotseas to the Trust. At some later time, Kotseas leased a portion of its abutting land to Whitinsville CVS, Inc. (CVS) for use as a "discount department store and pharmacy." Plaza sued both Kotseas and CVS to enforce the covenant in the original deed granted by Kotseas to Trust, seeking both an injunction prohibiting the use of the retained land in violation of the restrictions and damages suffered because of the alleged violations.

The Massachusetts Supreme Judicial Court held that both the benefit of the covenant and the burden ran with the land, and remanded to determine whether the anticompetitive covenant was reasonable, and if so, the appropriate remedy. The Court found (1) that the covenant was in *writing* in the original deed from Kotseas to Trust; (2) that the language of the deed clearly stated that both the benefit of the covenant and the burden were *intended to run with the land;* (3) that CVS had *actual notice* of the covenant in the 1968 deed (because it had been told about it) and *constructive notice* (because the deed had been recorded and was in the chain of title so that

CVS should have been aware of it when it leased the neighboring land); and that (4) *privity of estate* existed between the original covenanting parties under the "mutual privity" because both parties had easements in the other's land. (5) The Court spent a great deal of time determining whether the covenant *touched and concerned the land*. Like the New Jersey Supreme Court, it overruled an earlier case to the contrary and held that anticompetitive covenants do touch and concern the burdened land because they limit land use and they touch and concern the benefited land because enhance its market value. The Court further noted:

> In what appears to have been an arm's-length transaction, Kotseas agreed in 1968 not to use retained land in competition with the Trust. We may assume (a) that Kotseas received compensation for thus giving up part of his ownership rights by limiting the uses he could make of the retained land, and (b) that freedom from destructive, next-door competition was part of the inducement for the Trust's purchase and of the price paid by the Trust. Plaza, a closely associated business entity, succeeded to the Trust's interest in 1975. One of these entities established a business, presumably at great cost to itself and in reliance on the contractually obtained limitation of competition in its own narrow market area. Notwithstanding the promise not to do so, Kotseas proceeded to lease land to CVS for the purpose of carrying on the business that it knew would, at least in part, compete with Plaza and divert customers from Plaza's premises. Acting with full knowledge of the 1968 arrangement, CVS participated in this inequitable conduct by Kotseas. If we assume for the moment that the 1968 covenants are reasonable in their application to the present facts, we cannot condone the conduct of Kotseas and CVS.
>
> . . . Prior decisions by this court establish what we believe is the proper direction. With respect to covenants in commercial leases, we have long held that reasonable anticompetitive covenants are enforceable by and against successors to the original parties. We have applied a similar rule with respect to covenants between fee owners when we could identify intelligible land-use planning goals. . . . In short, our decisions support what we hereby state to be the law: reasonable covenants against competition *may* be considered to run with the land when they serve a purpose of facilitating orderly and harmonious development for commercial use.

The Court noted, however, that, although such covenants could run with the land, they might be unenforceable if they result in an unreasonable restraint of trade under either the federal or state antitrust laws or under state common law. Justice Francis Quirico explained: "Our law is settled that a covenant restraining competition will be enforced if it is reasonably limited in time and space and consonant with the public interest."

NOTES AND QUESTIONS

1. *Defining the issue.* In the both *Davidson* and *Whitinsville Plaza*, the courts wrestled with three different issues. The first question was whether the covenant "ran with the land" to bind succeeding owners of the property that the original parties may have intended to restrict to certain uses and, in *Whitinsville Plaza*, whether the benefit could be enforced by a succeeding owner of the dominant estate intended to benefit from the restriction. The second issue was whether the covenant was unenforceable either because it violated public policy or because it was deemed "unreasonable." The third and final issue was what the remedy should be. The covenant could be

enforced by injunctive relief ordering the owner or possessor of the servient estate to comply with the covenant or by an award of damages for the harm caused by violation of the covenant or both. Note that one possibility was that the court refuse to issue an injunction, allowing the covenant to be ignored, but award damages, giving the beneficiary of the covenant compensation for the loss of property rights embodied in the covenant.

Let's start with the question of when covenants "run with the land" and use the *Whitinsville Plaza* case to illustrate operation of the law. Charles and Paul Kotseas (Kotseas)[15] sold land to 122 Trust (Trust) in 1968 with a grantor's promise not to use Kotseas's remaining land in competition with Trust. Trust conveyed the benefited parcel to Whitinsville Plaza. Grantor Kotseas then leased its remaining land to CVS. Four parties are present: the original covenanting parties (grantor Kotseas and grantee Trust) and the successor possessors (grantor's lessee CVS and grantee Trust's grantee Plaza).

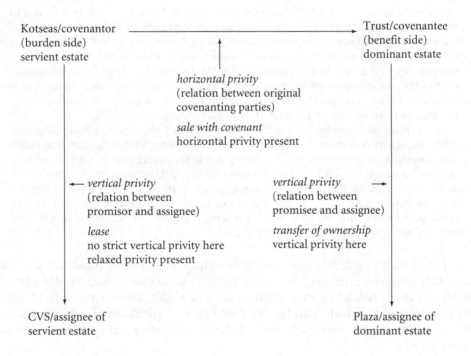

What would have happened if Kotseas had violated the covenant by operating a competing store on the retained land before the transfer from Trust to Plaza? The answer is simple. Kotseas is bound by normal contract law doctrine to Trust. However, both owners transferred their interests. Two issues appear: First, are the original covenanting parties still bound and benefited by the promise, and second, can the successor owner of the benefited parcel enforce the restriction against the successor lessee of the burdened parcel?

---

15. For simplicity, I will refer to the duo as "Kotseas" on the assumption that they formed a partnership and that the partnership entity is the contracting party.

2. *Rights and obligations of original covenanting parties.* The dominant estate was originally owned by Trust. Could Trust bring an action for damages or injunctive relief against CVS or Kotseas?

a. *Benefit of covenants held in gross.* Is Trust a proper plaintiff, that is, does it have the power to enforce the covenant once it sells the benefited parcel? The answer is almost certainly no for two reasons. First, the covenant is likely to be intended to benefit the current owner of the land and not prior possessors. Courts will generally allow enforcement by the original covenantee after transfer of the property only if the agreement contains explicit language to that effect. *Waikiki Malia Hotel, Inc. v. Kinkai Properties Ltd. Partnership,* 862 P.2d 1048, 1057-1059 (Haw. 1993). Second, courts have traditionally refused to impose the burden of a covenant on future owners of the servient estate if the benefit of the covenant is held in gross. Covenants that restrict land use interfere with both the right of free use of property and the marketability of the property. This cost is thought to be justified if there is a sufficient compensating benefit; when neighboring land is benefited, there is a presumption that the burden to the servient estate is more than offset by the benefit to the dominant estate. But when the benefit is held by someone who has no interest in land benefited by the restriction, the presumption falls away. Even though the promisee wishes to enforce the promise against the owner of the servient estate, most courts will not allow the promisee to do so, in most circumstances, even if the original covenanting parties intended this result. This policy protects the liberty and autonomy interests of current owners by limiting the power of the "dead hand" of prior owners to control the property once they are out of the picture and owns no land benefited by the restriction. *See Smith v. First Savings of Louisiana,* 575 So. 2d 1033 (Ala. 1991); *Garland v. Rosenshein,* 649 N.E.2d 756 (Mass. 1995).

Many courts make exceptions to the policy restricting enforcement of covenants whose benefit is held in gross when the covenant is held by a homeowners association on behalf of owners in the neighborhood, by a government entity, or by a charity. *Bennett v. Commissioner of Food and Agriculture,* 576 N.E.2d 1365 (Mass. 1991); *Inhabitants of Middlefield v. Church Mills Knitting Co.,* 35 N.E. 780 (Mass. 1894). *See also* Mass. Gen. Laws ch. 184, §§31, 32 (providing that a covenant restricting the price at which land is sold and limiting its use to low- or moderate-income residents is not invalid merely because the benefit is held in gross if the holder is a government entity or charitable corporation or trust).

The *Restatement (Third)* allows the benefit of a covenant to be enforced in gross but only if "the person seeking enforcement [can] demonstrate a legitimate interest in enforcing the servitude." *Id.* §2.6 cmt. d. Because the anticompetitive covenant was intended to benefit the owner of the dominant estate, it is unlikely the original covenantee can show a legitimate interest in enforcing the covenant, especially if the current owner of the dominant estate has no interest in enforcing it.

b. *Enforceability against original covenantor after the land is transferred.* Is Kotseas, the original promisor, bound by the covenant? If Kotseas had *sold* the property to CVS, instead of renting it to CVS, the answer would almost certainly be no. The purpose of the original covenant was to restrict the use of the servient estate; the current owner who breaches the covenant is liable for that breach. A prior owner is not legally responsible for the actions of the subsequent owners of the burdened land. However, because Kotseas *leased* the property to CVS, the answer is probably yes. Kotseas is almost certain to remain liable on the covenant to a proper plaintiff, subject to the possibility of damages and perhaps even injunctive relief. Leases are treated differently from sales because landlords retain substantial powers to control the use of the leased premises. A landlord who includes the covenant in the lease has the power to end the leasehold and evict the tenant if the tenant violates the lease. The landlord's failure to include such a covenant or to exercise the right to enforce such a covenant constitutes an independent breach of the covenant. In either case, the failure to control the actions of one's tenant can be attributed to the landlord because the landlord retains the power, and hence the duty, to ensure compliance with the covenant.

3. *Obligations of successors in interest.* Can Plaza, as successor owner of the dominant estate (the benefited parcel) obtain damages and/or injunctive relief against CVS, the subsequent possessor of the servient estate? First, it is important to analyze separately the benefit and the burden. Plaza can obtain a remedy against CVS only if both the benefit and the burden run with the land. It may be that the requirements are met for the benefit to run with the land, but the requirements are not met for the burden to run with the land (or vice versa); if so, then Plaza cannot obtain a remedy from CVS. Second, we must apply both the law of *real covenants* and the law of *equitable servitudes*. The major difference is that privity of estate was traditionally required for real covenants but not equitable servitudes. The distinction may matter because real covenants law traditionally determined whether damages were available, and equitable servitudes law determined whether injunctive relief was available. Some courts may still adhere to this distinction. Thus if privity of estate is missing, but the other requirements are met, some courts will allow Plaza to obtain injunctive relief but not damages against CVS.

Under the law of *real covenants*, land use restrictions run with the land when (1) the covenant is in *writing*; (2) the party to be bound (the owner of the burdened parcel) had *notice* of the restriction when she purchased the property;[16] (3) the grantor *intended* the restriction to run with the land on both sides, binding future owners of the servient estate and benefiting future owners of the dominant estate; (4) the restriction *touches and concerns* both the dominant and servient estates; and (5) *privity of estate* exists between the original covenanting parties (horizontal privity) and between those parties and succeeding owners (vertical privity). *Equitable servitudes law* contains the same elements with the exception of privity of estate. The *Restatement (Third)* unifies the law of real covenants and equitable servitudes by modifying but not entirely abolishing the doctrine of privity of estate.

Four of the five requirements are *formalities*, while only one (the touch and concern test) is *substantive*. Formal requirements regulate the manner in which a right or obligation is created; individuals who wish to create the right or obligation

---

16. Many authorities omit the notice requirement for real covenants, including it only in equitable servitudes law. However, recording statutes in every state protect buyers of land from servitudes of which they were not on notice when they purchased the land. Those who inherit property or obtain it by devise are similarly placed on constructive notice of any restrictions upon the land.

may do so as long as they adhere to the formalities. They are not designed to prevent or discourage particular behavior; rather, they are rules designed to ensure that actors communicate their intentions clearly, both to each other and to the judges who are empowered to enforce their agreements. Duncan Kennedy, *Form and Substance in Private Law Adjudication*, 89 Harv. L. Rev. 1685, 1691 (1976). Substantive requirements, on the other hand, limit the ability of individuals to create certain rights. They "prevent people from engaging in particular activities because those activities are morally wrong or otherwise flatly undesirable." *Id.* No amount of careful planning will enable an owner to avoid such a requirement. We will start with the formal requirements (writing, notice, intent, and privity) and then discuss the substantive touch and concern test.

   4. *Writing.* Covenants are ordinarily reduced to writing as part of a lease or deed transferring property rights. In *Whitinsville Plaza*, the covenant was clearly in writing in the deed by which Kotseas conveyed part of its property to Trust. This writing was sufficient for both the benefit side and burden side. It was not necessary to include the covenant in the deed transferring the servient estate from Trust to Plaza.

   Developers of residential subdivisions may similarly include covenants in the deed to each parcel of land they sell restricting the use of each parcel. Alternatively, they may record a *declaration* of restrictions applicable to the entire subdivision and/or a *plat* (a detailed map showing the restrictions) before any lot is sold. The deed or lease subsequently granted may or may not contain an explicit reference to the declaration or plat. Some states may require that the restriction be specifically mentioned in the deed or lease, even if only by reference to the earlier recorded declaration or plat. Most states, however, find that a covenant in a prior-recorded declaration or plat meets the writing requirement on the ground that the buyer is on notice of the prior recorded restriction and thus is bound by it in good conscience, making the restriction enforceable as an equitable servitude. *Citizens for Covenant Compliance v. Anderson*, 906 P.2d 1314 (Cal. 1995); *Arnold v. Chandler*, 428 A.2d 1235 (N.H. 1981).

   Representations made in sales literature do not count as writings; the requirement is that the restriction be in the document transferring the property interest or a prior recorded document in the chain of title. Some courts relax the strict writing requirement and apply the equitable doctrine of *estoppel* to enforce representations made in sales literature or orally when buyers rely on them. For example, in *PMZ Oil Co. v. Lucroy*, 449 So. 2d 201 (Miss. 1984), the developer told all lot purchasers that its 16-lot subdivision would be restricted to "one quality single-family dwelling per lot" and showed them an unrecorded plat noting the restrictions. Covenants restricting the lots to such uses were included in the deeds to all the lots sold. The buyers relied on the developer's oral representations by buying and building their homes. When the developer sought to build six townhouse condominiums on one of the lots it retained, the court enforced the oral promise by applying the equitable estoppel doctrine, accepting it as an exception to the statute of frauds. That doctrine "hold[s] a person to a representation made or a position assumed where otherwise inequitable consequences would result to another who, having the right to do so under all of the circumstances of the case, has in good faith relied thereon and been misled to his injury." *Id.* at 206. The court explained that the doctrine "has its roots in the morals and ethics of our society," as well as "[f]undamental notions of justice and fair dealings." *Id.* It applies "[w]henever in equity and good conscience persons ought to behave ethically toward one another...." *Id.* Although estoppel is applied to prevent fraud (intentional misrepresentation), the court found that it would apply even if the developer changed his mind after the representations were made. *Id.* at 207. Quoting from *Ute Park Summer Homes Association v. Maxwell Land Grant Co.*, 427 P.2d 249 (N.M. 1967), the court explained that a "grantor, who induces purchasers, by use of a plat, to believe that streets, squares, courts, parks, or other open areas shown on the plat will be kept open for their use and benefit, and the purchasers have acted upon such inducement, is required by common honesty to do that which he represented he would do." *Id.* at 251. *See also Warren v. Detlefson*, 663 S.W.2d 710, 712 (Ark. 1984) (oral representations that property would be restricted to single-family homes enforceable because of "parol representation[s] made in sales brochures, maps, advertising, or oral statements upon which the purchaser relied in making his decision to purchase").

Other courts, however, refuse to enforce oral representations or sales promises not included in prior-recorded documents. In *Bennett v. Charles Corp.*, 226 S.E.2d 559 (W. Va. 1976), the court allowed a developer to convert remaining unsold lots in a subdivided tract into a cemetery, in violation of the developer's oral promise to develop a tract as a residential subdivision. The court rigidly applied the statute of frauds, noting that no restrictive covenants were contained in either the deeds or a recorded plat. The court explained its holding as follows:

> The oral expression of intention made to the Bennetts at the time of sale constituted at most a promise to develop the tract in the future as a residential housing subdivision. When the defendant found it impossible to perform according to this promise, the use of the tract was changed. The basis of equitable estoppel is fraudulent or inequitable conduct. The acts of the defendant in the instant case do not rise to that level.

Id. at 564. *Accord, Kincheloe v. Milatzo*, 678 P.2d 855, 860 (Wyo. 1984) (oral representations enforceable only if developer engaged in intentional fraud, not if developer changed his mind because he could not sell the last lots or for some other reason).

5. *Notice.* The notice requirement is intended to protect the owner of the servient estate. It is formal because an owner wishing to create an enforceable covenant can ensure that appropriate notice is provided to future purchasers of the burdened parcels. The owner of the dominant estate who attempts to enforce the covenant is obviously on notice of it; the real question is whether the owner of the burdened estate knew or should have known the parcel was restricted when she purchased the land. Three kinds of notice are *actual, inquiry,* and *constructive.*

A buyer or lessee is on *actual* notice of the covenant if he was actually told about it or was otherwise made aware of it. In *Whitinsville Plaza*, it is unclear whether CVS was on actual notice of the restrictive covenant when it leased the servient estate from Kotseas.

The buyer or lessee is on *inquiry* notice if any condition of the premises indicated that the property was burdened by a covenant. Inquiry notice is likely to be important only in the context of affirmative easements, such as rights of way, which a buyer can observe and which suggest that another party may have interests in the land. The observable condition of the land is unlikely to put a reasonable buyer or lessee on notice of a restrictive or negative covenant.[17] One might argue that the lessee of land

---

17. Some courts may hold that buyers are on inquiry notice when a property is located in a neighborhood that has a uniform pattern of use (all single-family homes, for example). In such cases, the buyer may be obligated to search the deeds of surrounding lots to determine if they are restricted by covenants binding current owners (grantee's covenants). If enough of them are,

next to a shopping center owned by the same person should be on inquiry notice of possible anticompetitive covenants included in deeds or leases granted to occupants of the shopping center, given how common such covenants are. The inquiry in this case, however, is likely to be conducted by researching the registry of deeds to find any relevant recorded restrictions. That brings us to constructive notice.

A buyer or lessee is said to be on *constructive* notice if the covenant was recorded in the registry of deeds along with the deed or lease creating the covenant or if a declaration containing the restriction was recorded prior to sale. Such recording puts the purchaser on constructive notice of the covenant; a reasonable purchaser is expected to search the title to find out whether the property is burdened by any land use restrictions, and the buyer is deemed to know what she would have discovered had she performed a search of her chain of title. *See Schlup v. Bourdon,* 105 P.3d 720 (Kan. Ct. App. 2005) (unrecorded deed containing covenant to provide free gas to neighboring owner does not run with the land because it did not give notice to the succeeding owner of the servient estate).

Was CVS on constructive notice of the covenant in the Kotseas-Trust deed? The states disagree on this question. A notice problem arises when a restriction is placed in a deed of sale of a parcel binding the grantor's remaining land, and the grantor then sells or leases part of that remaining land, without any reference to the restriction in the deed. Suppose *O* owns Lots 1 and 2 and sells Lot 1 to *A* with an express covenant promising not to use *O*'s remaining Lot 2 for nonresidential purposes. *O* then sells Lot 2 to *B* without placing a restriction on the grantee *B* in the deed from *O* to *B*. Is *B* on constructive notice of the restriction in the *O-A* deed? Some courts hold that *B* is not on constructive notice of the restriction because it is outside the chain of title. These courts hold that the buyer of Lot 2 has only to look at prior deeds *to Lot* 2 granted by *O* and *O*'s predecessors in interest and need not look at all the deeds given out by *O* to all the property owned by *O* since *O* became the owner of Lot 2. Requiring the buyer of Lot 2 to examine deeds *O* has granted to land other than Lot 2 is a burden the buyer should not have to bear. *Puchalski v. Wedemeyer,* 586 N.Y.S.2d 387 (App. Div. 1991). Most courts, however, hold that *B* is on constructive notice of the restriction in the *O-A* deed. *Steagall v. Robinson,* 344 S.E.2d 803 (N.C. Ct. App. 1986); William B. Stoebuck & Dale A. Whitman, *The Law of Property* §8.28, at 500 (3d ed. 2000). They reason that the buyer is obligated to search all grants made by the seller during the time the seller owned the land being purchased (or at least all the deeds to contiguous land) to determine whether any of those written instruments includes reference to the land in question. If *O* has encumbered Lot 2 by a promise in prior deed to Lot 1, then *O* has no power to transfer ownership of Lot 2 free of the restriction and *B* is on notice of the restriction because *B* can find out about the purchase by researching the deeds granted by the owner of the land during the time of ownership.

6. *Intent to run with the land.* A deed or lease that includes a restrictive covenant will be deemed to show the grantor's intent for the covenant to be binding on future possessors if it recites (1) that the covenant is made to the grantor or grantee and "their heirs or assigns" and/or (2) that it "is intended to bind future owners" of the parcel described in the deed or explicitly states that the covenant is "intended to run with the land." What happens if the deed fails to include this language but merely states, for example, that the grantor agrees not to use his retained property for operation of a gas

---

some courts will hold that a "common plan" has been established, which burdens all lots within the borders of the area covered by the common plan. This topic is addressed *infra* at §5.4.3.

station? Should the courts presume that this covenant was intended to run with the land in the absence of language explicitly stating so? The courts generally hold that a covenant benefiting the owner of neighboring land is presumptively intended to run with the land so long as it touches and concerns the land. *See Sun Oil Co. v. Trent Auto Wash, Inc.,* 150 N.W.2d 818 (Mich. 1967) (holding that an anticompetitive covenant prohibiting use of land to operate a gas station was intended to run with the land despite a lack of language to that effect or reference to "heirs and assigns"); *Runyon v. Paley,* 416 S.E.2d 177, 185-187 (N.C. 1992) (presuming that the benefit was intended to run with the land if it is clear the burden was intended to run with the land). However, some courts require clear evidence of intent to run. *Charping v. J.P. Scurry & Co.,* 372 S.E.2d 120 (S.C. 1988); *Tennsco Corp. v. Attea,* 2002 WL 1298808 (Tenn. Ct. App. 2002).

The grantor in *Whitinsville Plaza* clearly intended both the benefit and the burden to run with the land. The covenantee, Trust, wanted to ensure that the seller Kotseas would not place a competing store on Kotseas's retained land next door. If Kotseas could simply sell or lease the retained land to another person the next day who did not know about the covenant and grant that person the right to operate a competing store, then the benefit of the covenant would be lost. Damages against Kotseas might not be sufficient to ensure that this did not happen; after all, if operation of a competing store were profitable, CVS might agree to indemnify Kotseas for the Kotseas's liability to Trust, thereby depriving Trust of the right to be free from unwanted competition. The only way to ensure that no competing store operated on Kotseas's retained land unless Trust consents would be to impose the requirement on future possessors of Kotseas's retained land. Because the benefit of the covenant could be obtained only by imposing it on future owners of the servient estate, the grantor probably intended the burden to run with the land even if the deed did not say so explicitly. Moreover, because the benefit increased the value of the dominant estate and because companies are sold or merged all the time, the parties probably intended any future owner of the dominant estate to be able to continue to enforce the covenant.

7. *Privity of estate.* The concept of privity of estate is confusing. On one hand, it contains the core principle of servitudes law; one piece of property is burdened for the benefit of another (so-called horizontal privity) and these benefits and burdens run to succeeding owners of both parcels (vertical privity). At the same time, the law of privity developed maddeningly complicated technical limitations that were unrelated to any legitimate policy concerns. Moreover, privity in its technical sense was never required under equitable servitudes law to obtain an injunction to enforce a servitude. For these reasons, the *Restatement (Third)* proposes formally abolishing the privity requirement. This seems sensible to most law professors because privity was never formally required to enforce a land use restriction as an equitable servitude and because the technicalities associated with privity did not make sense. On the other hand, a relaxed version of the privity requirement is central to what servitudes are all about because they impose obligations on future owners of the servient estate for the benefit of future owners of the dominant estate. Because some states retain the traditional strict privity requirements, *see Barner v. Chappell,* 585 S.E.2d 590 (Va. 2003), it is important to understand the traditional rules.

a. *Horizontal privity.* Horizontal privity regulates the relationship between the original covenanting parties. Because land use restrictions both limit the free use of land and may make it less alienable, they were traditionally thought to be unjustified unless the burden on land was outweighed by a compensating benefit to some other property owner. The horizontal privity requirement served to promote this purpose.

Two types of horizontal privity exist: (1) *mutual* privity and (2) *instantaneous* privity. Mutual privity exists when two owners have a simultaneous interest in the same parcel of land. The traditional example is the landlord-tenant relationship; the tenant has a present possessory interest in the land and the landlord has a future interest called a reversion — a right to recover possession at the end of the lease. Thus, a covenant will satisfy the horizontal privity requirement if it is contained in a lease of land. In England, this is the only way to satisfy the horizontal privity requirement. Massachusetts developed an alternative test for mutual privity; when an owner of one parcel has an appurtenant easement over another owner's parcel, the owners are in privity of estate and a covenant between them will be enforceable. This is the privity test applied by the court in *Whitinsville*, where privity was established because the court found that the parties had "mutual easements" in each other's property.

Mutual privity is missing when one owner sells land to another and the grantor retains no interests in the land being sold. However, courts in the United States adopted the *instantaneous privity* test, holding that a covenant intended to burden one parcel for the benefit of another can become attached to both parcels if it is created at the moment the owner of one parcel sells the other parcel. Thus, a covenant contained in a deed of sale transferring a property interest will satisfy the horizontal privity requirement. Similarly, a covenant in a lease (transferring a leasehold) or a mortgage (transferring a lien or right to foreclose) will satisfy the horizontal privity requirement. The anticompetitive covenant contained in the deed granted by Kotseas to Trust satisfies the horizontal privity requirement under the instantaneous privity test.

What kinds of relationships does horizontal privity exclude? The two most important situations that do not satisfy the traditional horizontal privity test are (1) agreements between neighbors that are not part of a simultaneous conveyance of another property right; (2) agreements between grantors and grantees that are not made at the same time as the conveyance of the property interest burdened or benefited by the covenant.[18] An example of the first problem is a contract among all the owners in a neighborhood to restrict the property to residential uses. Neighbors are not in privity of estate with each other merely because of their physical location near each other. An example of the second problem is a covenant made one week after the sale of a parcel; this does not satisfy the privity requirement because at that moment the grantor no longer owns the property of the grantee.

In both these cases, the parties can *create* privity of estate by selling all their parcels to a lawyer who sells them all back to the owners with the covenant contained in the new deeds. The ability to create horizontal privity by using a straw person is the reason why the privity requirement is a mere formality and the reason why it does not seem sensible to retain the requirement. Although horizontal privity was traditionally required for the *burden* to run with the land, some courts allowed the *benefit* to run to successor owners of the dominant estate even though horizontal privity was missing on the benefit side. *See Restatement of Property* §§534, 547, 548 (1944) (adopting this approach). Nor has horizontal privity ever been required to enforce a land use restriction by injunction as an equitable servitude. Because horizontal privity is a mere formality, and because it has never been required to enforce a covenant by injunction as an equitable servitude, the *Restatement (Third) of Property* §2.4 (2000) would abolish it entirely.

---

18. A third problem arises in the context of residential subdivisions when early buyers of lots try to enforce covenants entered into by later buyers. This topic is addressed *infra* at §5.4.3.

b. *Vertical privity.* Vertical privity refers to the relationship between the original covenanting parties and subsequent owners of each parcel. A *relaxed vertical privity* requirement would impose the burden on any future possessor of the burdened land and the benefit of the covenant on any future possessor of the benefited land. This is essentially the approach taken by equitable servitudes law and the *Restatement (Third)*. However, real covenants law adopted a *strict vertical privity* doctrine that included the technical requirement that the grantor not retain any future interests in the land. Thus vertical privity is present when an owner sells her property but not when she leases it. In *Whitinsville Plaza*, vertical privity is present on the benefit side because Trust transferred all its rights in the land to Plaza. However, on the burden side, Kotseas merely leased the land to CVS. Because Kotseas retained future powers to control the burdened land, there was no strict vertical privity on the burden side.

What relationships are excluded from the vertical privity idea? The three most important situations that do not satisfy the vertical privity test are (1) successors in interest who have an estate of lesser duration than the prior owner; (2) neighbors who are intended beneficiaries of the covenant but are not successor owners or possessors of the parcels owned by the covenanting parties; and (3) owners who derive their title from the grantor who imposed the restriction but who purchased their land before the sale of the parcel burdened by the covenant. As noted above, an example of the first situation is a landlord-tenant relationship. The *Restatement (Third)* drops the strict vertical privity requirement and allows the benefit and burden to pass to subsequent possessors of the dominant and servient estates whether or not the grantor retains a future interest. *Id.* §2.6.[19] However, under traditional real covenants law, because Kotseas retained a landlord's reversion in the parcel, strict vertical privity is absent and the burden of the covenant would not run with the land to CVS.[20] Under this traditional law, although horizontal privity existed between Kotseas and Trust, and vertical privity existed between Trust and Plaza (because Trust retained no future interest when it transferred the dominant estate to Plaza), Plaza could not sue CVS for damages because vertical privity is missing on the burden side between Kotseas and CVS. However, because privity is not required for enforcement of an equitable servitude, Plaza would be able to obtain an injunction stopping CVS from violating the covenant, so long as other requirements are met.

A much greater issue is involved in the second case where an owner who is not a successor in interest to either of the original covenanting parties seeks to enforce it. Most courts hold that an owner is entitled to enforce a land use restriction by injunction as an equitable servitude in the absence of horizontal or vertical privity if the covenantor intended to benefit the owner of that parcel despite the lack of strict or

---

19. However, the *Restatement (Third)* provides that most affirmative covenants are not enforceable in the absence of strict vertical privity on the burden side. §§5.2-5.3. The burdens of affirmative covenants are enforceable against lessees only if they can "more reasonably be performed by a person in possession than by the holder of a reversion in the burdened property." §5.3(3). Nonetheless, the *Third Restatement* does provide that the benefits of affirmative covenants can be enforced by a lessee if they are covenants to repair the property or if those benefits can be enjoyed by the lessee without diminishing their value to the lessor and without materially increasing the burden on the person obligated to perform the covenant. *Id.* at §5.3.

20. The requirement of horizontal privity is a formality, but the requirement of vertical privity is not. A landlord and tenant cannot establish strict vertical privity by a straw transaction unless the landlord gives up the reversion. This fact may have some implications for relations between landlords and subtenants. *See infra* §8.2. A relaxed version of vertical privity imposing the obligation on any subsequent possessor of the land would constitute a formality.

relaxed vertical privity. At the same time, most courts are reluctant to allow such an owner to enforce a covenant unless it is absolutely clear that she is an intended beneficiary. In *Runyon v. Paley,* 416 S.E.2d 177 (N.C. 1992), for example, Ruth Gaskins sold a parcel to Charles and Mary Robbins Runyon and then sold the parcel next to the Runyon lot to Donald and Jacqueline Brugh with a covenant restricting the Brugh lot to two single-family homes. After Gaskins died and her remaining land passed to her heir, the court allowed Gaskin's heir to enforce the covenant against the Brughs because she succeeded to the interest in the dominant estate. However, the court refused to allow the Runyons to enforce the covenant because the promise made by the Brughs was made for the benefit of the grantor's retained land, not lots previously sold by Gaskins. No vertical privity — strict or otherwise — could be shown even though both the Brughs and the Runyons obtained interests from Gaskins and the promise from the Brughs was probably intended to benefit both the Gaskin property and the Runyon property. *See also Brown v. Fuller,* 347 A.2d 127 (Me. 1975) (holding that public policy prevents creation of restrictions for the benefit of land not owned by the grantor except when there is a common plan or when landowners create mutual restrictions).

Most courts will allow any landowners in the vicinity who are "intended beneficiaries" of the restriction to enforce it whether or not they derive their titles from one of the covenanting parties. *See Allemong v. Frendzel,* 363 S.E.2d 487 (W. Va. 1987) (holding that adjacent owners who did not derive their title from the grantor could enforce a covenant by injunction because, as owners of neighboring land, they were intended beneficiaries of the covenant); *Muldawer v. Stribling,* 256 S.E.2d 357 (Ga. 1979); *Roehrs v. Lees,* 429 A.2d 388 (N.J. Super. Ct. 1981); *Restatement (Third) of Property (Servitudes)* §2.6 (2000). However, many (perhaps most) courts will not find neighbors outside the chain of title to be intended beneficiaries unless the document creating the covenant mentions their names (with the words "heirs and assigns") or otherwise clearly designates their parcels as dominant estates intended to benefit from the covenant.

The third case involves owners who do derive their title from the grantor of the property sold with a restrictive covenant but who purchased their lots before the sale of that property. Traditionally, the restriction is thought to benefit the grantor's remaining land and not land previously sold by the grantor, unless the conveyance expressly states that it is intended to benefit the owners of those previously sold lots. *Barner v. Chappell,* 585 S.E.2d 590 (Va. 2003).

8. *Substantive policy requirements: the "touch and concern" test.* Courts have traditionally allowed covenants to run with the land only if they "touch and concern" the land. This requirement is confusing and hard to define and the *Restatement (Third)* drops it, although as we shall see, it recreates the requirement in an altered form. In general, the test is intended to identify the kinds of obligations that should run with the burdened estate because they are intended to and legitimately will benefit current and future owners of the dominant estates.

In *Mercantile-Safe Deposit and Trust Co. v. Mayor and City Council of Baltimore,* 521 A.2d 734 (Md. 1987), the owner of a shopping center included a covenant in one of its leases requiring the lessee (the tenant) to restore the premises to certain conditions prior to the termination of the lease. In holding that the covenant to restore the condition of the premises ran with the land, the court found that it "touched and concerned" the land because "the thing required to be done . . . affect[ed] the quality, value, or mode of enjoying the [property interest conveyed]." *Accord,* 1515-1519 *Lakeview Blvd. Condominium Ass'n v. Apartment Sales Corp.,* 43 P.3d 1233, 1238 (Wash. 2002) (covenant must "concern the occupation or enjoyment of land"). Other courts state that the obligation and the right must affect the parties' interests "as landowners." *Regency Homes Association v. Egermayer,* 498 N.W.2d 783, 791 (Neb. 1993); *Runyon v. Paley,* 416 S.E.2d 177, 182-183 (N.C. 1992). "Where the burdens and benefits created by the covenant are of such a nature that they may exist independently from the parties' ownership interests in land, the covenant does not touch and concern the land and will not run with the land." *Runyon v. Paley, id.* at 183. *See also Thompson on Real Property, Thomas Edition* §61.04(d) (David A. Thomas ed. 1994); *Restatement of Property* §537 (1944).

On the burden side, an obligation touches and concerns the burdened estate if it relates to the use of the land and the obligation is intended to benefit current and future owners of the dominant estates. On the benefit side, an obligation touches and concerns the dominant estate if it improves enjoyment of that land or increases its market value. Restrictive covenants that limit land use, such as covenants limiting the land to residential purposes or prohibiting the sale of liquor on the land will almost certainly touch and concern both the dominant and servient estates. They touch and concern the servient estate because they restrict the use of the land; they touch and concern the dominant estate because the restriction is intended to benefit the owners of the dominant estates whoever they happen to be and because most purchasers of the dominant estates would consider the right to enforce the covenant as increasing the value or attractiveness of the benefited land.

The traditional refusal to enforce covenants when the benefit is held in gross (note 2(a), *supra*) is an application of the touch and concern test. As a policy matter, the beneficiary of a covenant who owns no land benefited by the covenant traditionally could not enforce the covenant in gross because the burden of the covenant to the servient estate was not offset by a compensating benefit to other land. The *Restatement (Third)* allows enforcement in gross if the beneficiary can "demonstrate a legitimate interest in enforcing the servitude." *Id.* §2.6 cmt. d. This approach retains a review for the substantive legitimacy of allowing enforcement by a beneficiary who wants to enforce the covenant for reasons other than their effect on improving the use or value of another parcel of land.

Affirmative obligations have often caused problems for the courts. It is now well accepted that obligations to pay dues to homeowners associations to maintain common areas of condominiums or residential neighbors touch and concern the land because they increase the value of the dominant estates and are associated with mutual obligations among owners that legitimately pass with ownership of the land. *Neponsit Property Owners' Association, Inc. v. Emigrant Industrial Savings Bank,* 15 N.E.2d 793 (N.Y. 1938). However, other kinds of affirmative obligations are more controversial.

For example, in *Nicholson v. 300 Broadway Corp.,* 164 N.E.2d 832, 835 (N.Y. 1959), the court held that a covenant to the effect that the owner of one parcel was to supply steam heat to the owner of the neighboring property "touched and concerned" the land because "it affected the legal relations of the parties to the covenant as owners of particular parcels of land." It did so because it gave the covenantee a "right, not possessed by other landowners, of having heat supplied to his building, as long as it stood, and it imposed upon the covenantor . . . , so long as the heat-producing facilities remained on its land, the burden, not cast upon other landowners, of furnishing heat to premises adjoining its own." *Id.* at 835. *Accord, E. J. Wimberly v. Lone Star Gas Co.,* 818 S.W.2d 868 (Tex. Ct. App. 1991) (holding that a contract between plaintiff gas company and the prior owner of defendant's land that granted the gas company the right to withdraw water from defendant's land touched and concerned the land). However, the court in *Eagle Enterprises v. Gross,* 349 N.E.2d 816 (N.Y. 1976), held that a promise by a subdivision developer to supply water from a well on its retained land to its grantee buyers did *not* touch and concern the land because "it [did] not substantially affect the ownership interest of landowners in the Orchard Hill subdivision" because water was to be supplied for only six months out of the year and the homeowners had other available sources of water.

Covenants to pay money (other than dues to homeowners associations) also raise problems for the courts. For example, in *Castlebrook, Ltd. v. Dayton Properties Ltd. Partnership,* 604 N.E.2d 808 (Ohio Ct. App. 1992), the court held that a covenant to return a tenant's security deposit did not touch and concern the land and hence was not binding on a successor landlord. In *Chesapeake Ranch Club, Inc. v. C.R.C. United Members, Inc.,* 483 A.2d 1334 (Md. Ct. Spec. App. 1984), the court held that a covenant to pay dues to belong to a recreational facility did not touch and concern the land. *But see Streams Sports Club, Ltd. v. Richmond,* 457 N.E.2d 1226 (Ill. 1983) (holding the opposite). Should a homeowner in a subdivision be bound by a restrictive covenant in the chain of title that requires the owner to pay dues to a health club? Would your answer change if the club admits anyone as a member (not just homeowners in the neighborhood), is profitable, and charges $1,000 a year while the owner is a nonathlete who has no interest in using the facilities?

Courts have also had trouble with affirmative covenants that require owners to continue particular uses, although some courts have enforced such covenants. *Compare Shalimar Association v. D.O.C. Enterprises, Inc.,* 688 P.2d 682 (Ariz. Ct. App. 1984) (requiring an owner to continue operating a golf course to comply with an affirmative covenant), *with Oceanside Community Associates v. Oceanside Land Co.,* 195 Cal. Rptr. 14 (Ct. App. 1983) (refusing to grant an injunction ordering an owner to renovate and operate a golf club but imposing a lien on the property for lost value to the dominant estates resulting from the failure to comply with the covenant).

The touch and concern test has sometimes been used to invalidate covenants that violate public policy. Susan French notes, "When a court invalidates a covenant obligation on the ground that it does not touch and concern the land, it makes a substantive judgment that the obligation should not be permitted to run with the land.... The real reasons for the invalidation are seldom, if ever, given." Susan French, *Servitudes Reform and the New Restatement of Property: Creation Doctrines and Structural Simplification,* 73 Cornell L. Rev. 928, 939–940 (1988). As *Whitinsville Plaza* shows, anticompetitive covenants were traditionally disfavored as contrary to public policy and were sometimes held not to touch and concern the land even though they regulated the use of land because the benefits to the dominant estate were merely economic. Courts also traditionally applied the touch and concern requirement to deny enforcement of covenants when the benefit of the covenant was held in gross; in such cases, the covenant did not touch or concern any dominant estate and thus the restriction was not balanced by any compensating benefit to other land.

Modern law tends to address public policy concerns more directly. As Justice Marie Garibaldi noted in *Davidson Bros.,* "Reasonableness, not esoteric concepts of property law, should be the guiding inquiry into the validity of covenants at law." The *Restatement (Third)* would abolish the touch and concern requirement and provide instead that covenants will run with the land unless they are unconscionable, without rational justification, or otherwise violate public policy. *Id.* §3.1. However, many courts still retain some version of the touch and concern requirement. *See, e.g., Fong v. Hashimoto,* 994 P.2d 500 (Haw. 2000) (benefit of covenant cannot be held in gross). Moreover, the *Restatement (Third)* seems to reintroduce the touch and concern element through the back door by providing that only "appurtenant" benefits and burdens, §5.2, should run with the land and then defining those as benefits and burdens "tied to ownership or occupancy of land" because they "obligate[ ] the owner or occupier of a particular unit or parcel in that person's capacity as owner or occupier" of land. §1.5(1). In addition, the *Restatement (Third)* notes that a servitude is appurtenant rather than in gross or personal only "if it serves a purpose that would be more useful to a successor to a property interest . . . than it would be to the original beneficiary. . . ." §4.5(1)(a). *Accord,* William B. Stoebuck & Dale A. Whitman, *The Law of Property* §8.15, at 480 (3d ed. 2000).

The *Restatement (Third)* also has adopted special rules to govern affirmative covenants. It recognizes that continued enforcement of affirmative obligations may become oppressive over time. "Covenants to pay for services or facilities are troublesome if there is no incentive for the service provider to control costs and there are no competitive pressures to keep prices reasonable. Covenants that require property owners to pay for services provided by the developer or another third party may present such problems, particularly where the obligation to pay is indefinite in duration or for a long term." *Id.* §7.12 cmt. a. Therefore it provides that affirmative covenants to pay money or provide services should terminate after a reasonable time if the document creating them has no definite termination point. *Id.* §7.12(1). In addition, "if the obligation becomes excessive in relation to the cost of providing the services or facilities or to the value received by the burdened estate," *Id.* §7.12(2), the changed conditions doctrine will apply.

9. *Summary.* Taking the example of *Whitinsville Plaza,* can the current owner of the dominant estate, Plaza, enforce the covenant not to compete against the current possessor of the servient estate, CVS? If not, can Plaza enforce the covenant against CVS's landlord, Kotseas (the original covenantor)? To determine whether the covenant ran with the land, we have to analyze *both* whether the benefit runs with the land to the succeeding owner of the dominant estate and whether the burden runs with the land to encumber the servient estate.

On the *benefit side,* we need to determine whether the current owner, Plaza, is entitled to enforce the covenant made with Plaza's predecessor Trust. We see that (a) the covenant was in *writing* in the original deed from Kotseas to Trust; (b) it was clearly *intended* to run with both the dominant estate because the conveyance states that the agreement shall be "considered as [a] covenant[ ] running with the land to which they are applicable and shall bind and inure to the benefit of the heirs and assigns of the respective parties to whom any part of the lands made subject to the above [covenant] shall at any time become or belong . . ."; and (c) under modern interpretations, an anticompetitive covenant satisfies both the *touch and concern test* and the *Restatement (Third)*'s view that servitudes should be allowed to run with the land if they are most useful if attached to land ownership. (d) *Notice* is not generally an issue on the benefit side since the notice requirement is intended to protect the servient owner. It thus appears that Plaza, the current possessor of the dominant estate, is a proper plaintiff entitled to sue to obtain injunctive relief to enforce the covenant.

However, before Plaza can obtain relief, we have to figure out if there is also a proper defendant; Plaza will only be able to obtain an injunction against the current possessor of the land, CVS, if the burden also runs with the land such that promise made by Kotseas to Trust is enforceable against CVS, the succeeding possessor of the servient estate.

On the *burden side,* we have already established (a) that the original covenant was in *writing;* (b) that it was *intended* to run with the servient estate (as well as the dominant estate) because the covenant states that the agreement shall be "considered as [a] covenant[ ] running with the land to which they are applicable and shall bind and inure to the benefit of the heirs and assigns of the respective parties to whom any part of the lands made subject to the above [covenant] shall at any time become or belong..." ; and (c) that it *touches and concerns* the land (because it limits land use to benefit the owner of neighboring land). However, it is not clear (d) whether CVS, the current possessor of the servient estate, was on either actual or constructive *notice* of the covenant. Most states would place CVS on constructive notice of the covenant in the deed from Kotseas to Trust on the neighboring land. Assuming CVS was on notice, the elements for enforcing the covenant as an *equitable servitude* are met on both the benefit and the burden side and Plaza is likely under *equitable servitudes law* to be able to seek injunctive relief ordering CVS to comply with the covenant. However, because injunctions are never granted automatically, it is up to the judge to determine whether injunctive relief is appropriate under the circumstances.

Can Plaza also obtain *damages* against CVS? Under modern law, the answer would probably be yes because both Plaza and CVS are successors in interest to the original covenanting parties and because this is a restrictive covenant. However, under traditional *real covenants law,* the answer is no because, although there is *horizontal privity* between the original covenanting parties (Kotseas and Trust) and Plaza is in *vertical privity* with Trust, CVS is *not* in strict vertical privity with Kotseas because CVS leased Kotseas' land and Kotseas retains a future interest.

Could Plaza obtain damages against Kotseas rather than CVS? The answer is probably yes because the act of leasing the servient estate to CVS without requiring CVS to abide by the restriction probably counts as an independent violation of the covenant made for the benefit of the owner of the dominant estate.

10. *Public policy.* A central question in both *Davidson* and *Whitinsville Plaza* was whether the anticompetitive covenants were reasonable. The question of whether such covenants violate federal or state antitrust laws is reviewed below at §5.5.5, and the question of when covenants are unenforceable because of public policy is covered below at §5.5.6, where the *Davidson* case on remand is included as a principal case.

11. *Remedies.* Should covenants normally be enforced by damages or injunctive relief? Traditional contract law holds that damages are the usual remedy for breach of contract while injunctions are awarded only when damages are inadequate. Property law, however, represents one of the most important areas in which damages are often thought inadequate because of the unique value attached to the *location* of land and the desire to use particular unique structures. The granting of an injunction, however, has always been discretionary.

Consider Judge Richard Posner's explanation for the predilection for injunctions in a case involving breach of an anticompetitive covenant. In *Walgreen Co. v. Sara Creek Property Co.,* 966 F.2d 273 (7th Cir. 1992), a shopping center landlord (Sara Creek) breached an anticompetitive covenant in a lease with a tenant pharmacy (Walgreen's) by arranging for a department store containing a pharmacy (Phar-Mor) to replace an anchor tenant whose business was doing badly. The issue was whether the covenant could be enforced by an injunction ordering the landlord not to allow a competitor to operate in the center or whether an injunction would be denied and the plaintiff relegated to damages. The Seventh Circuit upheld the trial court's decision to issue an injunction.

Judge Posner explained that damages are normally the remedy for breach of contract because the promisee receives damages to compensate for losing the benefit of the bargain, making the promisee indifferent as between performance and breach, while the promisor who is relieved from the promise can obtain the benefit of a more profitable bargain with another party, thereby shifting resources to a more valuable use without harming the promisee. If "the value of Phar-Mor's occupancy of the anchor premises may exceed the cost to Walgreen of facing increased competition[, . . .] society will be better off if Walgreen is paid its damages, equal to that cost, and Phar-Mor is allowed to move in rather than being kept out by an injunction." *Id.* at 274. However, Judge Posner concluded that in this case, an injunction was more likely to achieve the efficient result than damages. First, he noted that injunctive relief ordering compliance with the covenant would not necessarily end the matter; the parties could bargain for a contrary result. In contrast, damages are set by the court or by a jury rather than by the parties through private bargaining. Unless transaction costs block private bargaining, a number reached by the parties is more likely to represent the actual value of the entitlements in question than a number reached by a third party. If the parties can reach an agreement at an amount chosen by them, both will be better off. "A battle of experts is a less reliable method of determining the actual cost to Walgreen of facing new competition than negotiations between Walgreen and Sara Creek over the price at which Walgreen would feel adequately compensated for having to face that competition." *Id.* at 276.

At the same time, Judge Posner noted that transaction costs might block negotiation between the parties since they were in a situation of "bilateral monopoly" in which "two parties can deal only with each other: the situation that an injunction creates." *Id.* Walgreen can 'sell' its injunctive right only to Sara Creek, and Sara Creek can 'buy' Walgreen's surrender of its right to enjoin the leasing of the anchor tenant's space to Phar-Mor only from Walgreen." *Id.*

> The lack of alternatives in bilateral monopoly creates a bargaining range, and the costs of negotiating to a point within that range may be high. Suppose the cost to Walgreen of facing the competition of Phar-Mor at the Southgate Mall would be $1 million, and the benefit to Sara Creek of leasing to Phar-Mor would be $2 million. Then at any price between those figures for a waiver of Walgreen's injunctive right both parties would be better off, and we expect parties to bargain around a judicial assignment of legal rights if the assignment is inefficient. R. H. Coase, *The Problem of Social Cost*, 3 J.L. & Econ. 1 (1960). But each of the parties would like to engross as much of the bargaining range as possible — Walgreen to press the price toward $2 million, Sara Creek to depress it toward $1 million. With so much at stake, both parties will have an incentive to devote substantial resources of time and money to the negotiation process. The process may even break down, if one or both parties want to create for future use a reputation as a hard bargainer; and if it does break down, the injunction will have brought about an inefficient result. All these are in one form or another costs of the injunctive process that can be avoided by substituting damages.

Id. at 276. Thus, both damages and injunctions have both costs and benefits. The benefits of an injunction are that the parties get to bargain to determine who values the entitlement the most and to set the appropriate price; they also avoid the time and expense of litigation and the inaccuracy of damage awards set by a third party who is less knowledgeable about the benefits of anticompetitive covenants and their value to the parties than the parties themselves. The benefits of damages are that litigation can produce a result where transaction costs might prevent the parties from bargaining to a mutually beneficial result; indeed, the possibility that a jury would determine the appropriate level of damages might be an incentive to get the parties to agree to an appropriate resolution, thereby promoting rather than discouraging bargaining. In any event, Judge Posner concluded that the trial judge appropriately determined that "the costs (including forgone benefits) of the damages remedy would exceed the costs (including forgone benefits) of an injunction." *Id.* at 278.

Justice Stewart Pollock's concurring opinion in *Davidson* gives reasons to prefer damages over injunctive relief when enforcing covenants, at least in certain kinds of cases. In addition, Professor Ward Farnsworth criticizes the kind of reasoning presented by Judge Posner by noting that in nuisance cases he examined, the parties never bargained to rearrange the results reached by the court both because the winning party believed it deserved to win and because of hard feelings generated by the dispute, making the parties unwilling to compromise and transfer property rights even if this would otherwise have been in their mutual best interest. Ward Farnsworth, *Do Parties to Nuisance Cases Bargain After Judgment? A Glimpse Inside the Cathedral,* 66 U. Chi. L. Rev. 373 (1999). This may suggest that significant transaction costs may bar bargaining between the owners of the servient and dominant estates.

PROBLEM

A developer, *O*, creates a residential subdivision with 20 single-family homes and three apartment buildings. *O* conveys one lot located in the center of the subdivision to buyer *A*, with the following language:

> Grantee, *A*, covenants that a licensed day care center will operate on this lot for the benefit of other property owners in this subdivision who derive their title from Grantor, *O*.

A operates the day care center for five years and then transfers the property to *B*. *B* is concerned that the subdivision contains few residents who are nonwhite. Interested in creating a more diverse group of children, *B* advertises in the local newspaper for new applicants. Some parents of Asian American, African American, and Hispanic American or Latino children who live near the subdivision but not in it apply for spaces at the day care center, and *B* admits six children. Several parents who live in the subdivision complain that this new practice of serving children who do not live in the subdivision limits the number of spaces available for their children. Although no children in the subdivision have been turned away, the possibility exists that this may happen in the future. There is also evidence that some parents are motivated by racial prejudice in their desire to keep out children from other neighborhoods. Several parents have threatened to sue *B* to obtain an injunction enforcing the covenant.

B comes to see you at your law firm for legal advice.

1. *Interpretation of the covenant.* Does the covenant prohibit opening the day care center to children who do not live in the subdivision? What would you advise the client? How would you interpret the covenant if you were the judge?

2. *Touch and concern.* If the obligation limits use to children from the subdivision, does it touch and concern the land so as to be binding on future possessors? Does the touch and concern test cover *who* uses the land as well as *what* is done on it? Should the court use the touch and concern requirement as a proxy for a public policy judgment about the reasonableness of imposing the obligation and making it run with the land? What would you advise the client? How would you interpret the covenant if you were the judge?

3. *Public policy and remedies.* Should a covenant to operate a particular business run with the land, or is this an intolerable burden to impose on future owners? Should the obligation be enforceable by injunction or damages only? If an injunction is appropriate, what order can legitimately be issued: an order to operate the day care center, an order to convey the property to another owner who will operate it, an order to convey to the homeowners association for fair market value? If the remedy should be limited to damages, should they be calculated without limit or should they constitute a lien on the land, such that the plaintiffs can force the land to be sold to provide a fund to pay them? The lien remedy limits damages to the current fair market value of the land, while the ordinary damages remedy allows the plaintiffs to obtain any amount of damages they can prove even if this exceeds the fair market value of the land.

§5.4.2.2 Implied Reciprocal Negative Servitudes in Residential Subdivisions

An owner of a large tract of land wants to subdivide it and sell 100 lots. She wants to ensure that the lots are restricted to residential use and each lot to a single-family home. To accomplish this, she places covenants in each deed by which the purchaser agrees for herself, her heirs and assigns, to restrict the property to use as a single-family home. Does this accomplish her purpose under either the law of real covenants or equitable servitudes? For perhaps surprising reasons, the answer is no.

There is a serious privity problem here—even under equitable servitudes law, which does not require privity. Promises made by buyers to sellers restricting land use are generally interpreted to be intended to benefit the remaining land of the seller. When the seller later sells the remaining parcels, owners of those parcels are intended beneficiaries of the covenant and can sue earlier buyers if they breach the covenant. The early buyers were in horizontal privity with the seller, and the subsequent owners of the seller's remaining land are in vertical privity with her. However, suppose an early buyer wants to enforce a covenant entered into by a *later* buyer. We have to first interpret the promise made by the later buyer as being intended to benefit, not only remaining land of the grantor, but previously sold lots. But what is the warrant for assuming this? The developer could have sold many lots previously. Which ones are intended to be able to enforce a covenant made by a later buyer? How are later buyers on notice of the identity of the dominant estates? The developer may have owned property in several places. Which of the previously sold lots are intended to be dominant estates? We have a problem determining which lots are intended to be dominant estates, and we have a problem of notice to the servient owners of the exact number and identity of dominant estates entitled to enforce the covenant they made with the developer. The intent and notice problems exist because, at the time the later buyer purchases her lot, she has no relationship whatsoever with previous purchasers of land from the developer; there is no contract between them and no basis for finding them in privity of estate. The problem is even worse if the developer intentionally or negligently leaves the covenants out of the deeds to some of the lots located in the neighborhood. Are buyers of such lots burdened by covenants contained in the deeds to neighboring land?

The courts solved all these problems by inventing the doctrine of *implied reciprocal negative servitudes*. In the absence of both privity of contract and privity of estate, the courts turned to *third-party beneficiary* doctrine. Ordinarily, contracts are enforceable only by and against the contracting parties or their assignees. The courts determined that early buyers were *intended beneficiaries* of covenants made by later buyers if all their lots were part of a *common plan* or *scheme* of development, with all lots in the plan obligated to comply with the uniform plan of restrictions for the benefit of all other owners in the area. They went even further and imposed these obligations on owners who had no covenants in their chain of title whatsoever if the developer had created something that looked like a common plan, and it would be unjust to allow owners to violate the plan despite the lack of restrictions in their chain of title. These cases pose conflicts between the interests of owners in the free use of their land, especially when they have not agreed to restrict the use of their land, and the interests of other owners in relying on enforcement of a mutual plan of restrictions.

Statutes and subdivision regulations in many states now require developers to file a *declaration* prior to selling individual lots. The declaration will describe the area covered by the common plan and recite the covenants applicable to the lots. Buyers are on constructive notice of the restrictions in the declaration if it is recorded prior to their purchase and are deemed to impliedly agree to abide by the restrictions; these grantee covenants are deemed to be made for the benefit of all lots in the plan. The declaration also constitutes a promise by the developer to restrict the remaining lots when they are sold; this constitutes a *grantor covenant*. If a declaration is filed, an earlier buyer who sues a later buyer for violating a covenant can base her claim on both the grantor covenant and the grantee covenant. The later buyer is a subsequent possessor of property owned by the grantor, and the grantor's covenant to restrict her remaining land will run with the land to the later buyer. The later buyer also makes her own promise to that grantor (the grantee covenant), and the declaration clarifies that earlier buyers in the area are intended beneficiaries of the covenant.

EVANS v. POLLOCK
_____
796 S.W.2d 465 (Tex. 1990)

C. L. RAY, Justice . . . .
     . . . The doctrine of implied reciprocal negative easements applies when an owner of real property subdivides it into lots and sells a substantial number of those lots with

restrictive covenants designed to further the owner's general plan or scheme of development. The central issue is usually the existence of a general plan of development. The lots retained by the owner, or lots sold by the owner from the development without express restrictions to a grantee with notice of the restrictions in the other deeds, are burdened with what is variously called an implied reciprocal negative easement, or an implied equitable servitude, or negative implied restrictive covenant, that they may not be used in violation of the restrictive covenants burdening the lots sold with the express restrictions. A reasonably accurate general statement of the doctrine has been given as follows:

> [W]here a common grantor develops a tract of land for sale in lots and pursues a course of conduct which indicates that he intends to inaugurate a general scheme or plan of development for the benefit of himself and the purchasers of the various lots, and by numerous conveyances inserts in the deeds substantially uniform restrictions, conditions and covenants against the use of the property, the grantees acquire by implication an equitable right, variously referred to as an implied reciprocal negative easement or an equitable servitude, to enforce similar restrictions against that part of the tract retained by the grantor or subsequently sold without the restrictions to a purchaser with actual or constructive notice of the restrictions and covenants. *Minner v. City of Lynchburg*, 129 S.E.2d 673, 679 (Va. 1963). . . .

Facts

In September of 1947 Stanley and Sarah Agnes Hornsby (the Hornsbys), together with Charles and Bernice McCormick (McCormicks) platted a subdivision around Lake Travis from their commonly owned property in Travis County. They named the subdivision "Beby's Ranch Subdivision No. 1." The plat itself did not state any restrictions on land-use. The plat divided the property into seven blocks designated alphabetically "A" through "G." The plat did not further subdivide blocks C, D, E, and F, but blocks A, B, and G were divided into thirty-one lots. The subdivision is on a peninsula-like tract that extends into the lake, so that much of it has lake frontage. All of the platted lots are lakefront lots. Block G is located on the point of the peninsula. Block F is located on a hill and is surrounded by lakefront lots. . . .

Block F is also referred to as the "hilltop."

In October of 1947, before selling any lots other than two lots sold prior to the platting discussed below, the Hornsbys and McCormicks partitioned Beby's No. 1 between themselves. By partition deed the McCormicks received title to all of Blocks A, B, and C, and the Hornsbys got Blocks D, E, F, and G. Over the next several years, the Hornsbys and the McCormicks conveyed twenty-nine parcels of land from Beby's No. 1 to third parties or one another. Stanley Hornsby, a real estate attorney, and his law partner Louise Kirk, handled most of the legal work relating to the sale of lots, and the McCormicks made most of the sales. A real estate agent advertised some of the lakefront lots for sale in 1955, describing them as in "a restricted subdivision." Each deed from the Hornsbys and the McCormicks contained substantially the same restrictive covenants, including, among others, covenants: (1) prohibiting business or commercial use of the land conveyed; (2) restricting the land to residential use with only one dwelling per lot; and (3) providing that the restrictions could be changed by 3/4 of the property owners within the subdivision "voting according to front footage holdings on the 715 contour line" of the lake. In 1946 the McCormicks had conveyed two of the lakefront lots unburdened by any deed restrictions. When the original grantee conveyed the two lots to third parties in 1954, he had Hornsby draft the deeds. The deeds contained the restrictions that the property could not be used for any business or commercial purposes and that the restrictions could be altered by the "3/4 vote" along the 715 contour. Thus all lots conveyed ended up with substantially similar restrictions. All were lakefront lots, and voting rights under the restrictive covenants apparently were limited to lots with lake frontage.

The Hornsbys retained ownership of lots 4 through 8 in Block G and all of Block F. Both Hornsbys are now deceased, and the retained property passed to their devisees. The present dispute arose when the Hornsby devisees contracted to sell Thomas R. Pollock all of Block F and lots 4 and 5 in Block G for the purpose of building a marina, private club, and condominium development. Charles Evans and other owners whose deeds contained the restrictive covenants sued for equitable relief under the implied reciprocal negative easement doctrine. They sought declaration that the restrictive covenants enumerated above expressly imposed by deed upon their property were implied upon the Hornsby retained property. They further sought an injunction to prevent the Hornsby devisees from conveying the property without such deed restrictions. . . .

[The trial court held that the original subdividers, Stanley and Sarah Agnes Hornsby and Charles and Bernice McCormick, intended the restrictions to apply to all the lakefront lots but not to the hilltop. The court of appeals reversed, holding that none of the retained lots were restricted, on the ground that for the implied reciprocal negative easement doctrine to apply, the original grantors must have intended that the entire subdivision be similarly restricted.]

The Scope of a "Restricted District"

Provisions in restrictive covenants that the restrictions may be waived or modified by the consent of three-fourths of the lot owners constitute strong evidence that there is a general scheme or plan of development furthered by the restrictive covenants. The voting rights in the present case clearly attached only to lakefront lots. It was reasonable for the trial court to conclude that the restrictions were meant to apply only to the lakefront lots. The legal question is whether all the tracts in the development must be intended to be subject to the restrictions for the implied reciprocal negative easement doctrine to apply to any of the retained lots. We find it immaterial whether the question is phrased as whether the plan may be that some tracts are unrestricted while others are restricted, or whether the plan need only apply to certain similarly situated lots. We hold that the general plan or scheme may be that the restrictions only apply to certain well-defined similarly situated lots for the doctrine of implied reciprocal negative easements to apply as to such lots. Logical extensions of Texas decisions, as well as decisions from sister states, support our conclusion.

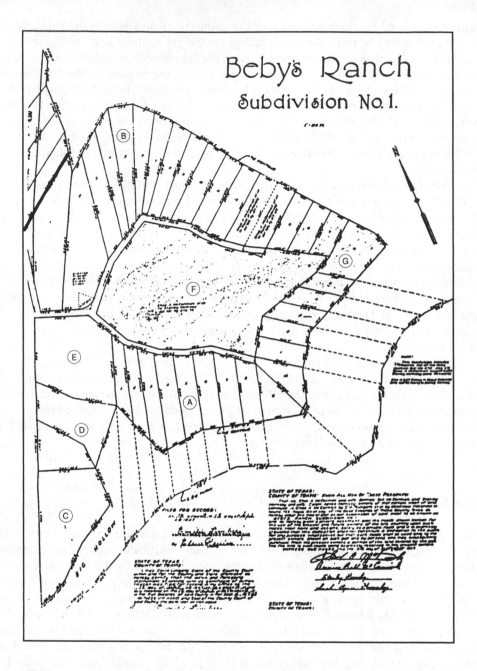

Texas cases support the conclusion that the restricted area need not be the whole subdivision. The facts in *Curlee v. Walker,* 244 S.W. 497 (Tex. 1922), were that after the creation of the Floral Heights Addition in the City of Wichita Falls, the developers set aside 18 blocks to be subject to restrictive covenants for ten years from date of purchase, that the land would be used for residential purposes only, that there would be one residence to two whole lots, and that the cost to construct the residence would be at least $3,000. This court in its opinion referred to the 18 blocks as the "restricted district" and referred to the plan as "[t]his general scheme or plan of creating a restricted residence district." 244 S.W. at 497. Thus a general scheme or plan need not apply to the whole tract or subdivision. . . . Similarly, in upholding the trial court's refusal to enforce restrictive covenants on other grounds, in *Canyon v. Ferguson*, 190 S.W.2d 831, 834 (Tex. Civ. App.-Fort Worth 1945, no writ), the appellate court wrote it was "not essential that there be a general scheme of restricting all of the lots in the additions. Valid restrictions could result from a scheme to restrict the lots in only one block, or those facing on only one street." . . .

The language from the Texas cases suggesting that the restricted district need not be the whole subdivision is in agreement with decisions from other states. . . .

. . . We have concluded that the weight of authority supports our conclusion that the restricted district need not be the whole subdivision nor include the whole retained tract. . . .

Sanborn v. McLean, 206 N.W. 496 (Mich. 1925). Defendant Christina McLean owned land on which she and her husband sought to build a gas station. It would be located behind their house in a "highgrade neighborhood" on Collingwood Avenue in Detroit, Michigan. All of the lots fronting on that portion of the road had once been owned by a single owner who imposed restrictive covenants on 53 of the 91 lots, limiting them to residential purposes. No restrictions appear in the chain of title to the McLean lot. The court held that the McLeans were on constructive notice of the restrictions in the deeds to neighboring properties and that the uniform residential character of the surrounding properties also put the McLeans on inquiry notice to determine whether there were restrictive covenants on neighboring lots that might be interpreted to create a plan to restrict the entire neighborhood to residential uses. Since a majority of the lots were restricted, the court inferred an intent to create a common plan even though a great number of the properties did not have restrictions in their line of title. Given evidence of an intent to create a common plan and constructive or inquiry notice on purchasers like the McLeans, the court imposed an implied reciprocal negative servitude restricting the McLean lot to residential purposes.

Riley v. Bear Creek Planning Committee, 551 P.2d 1213 (Cal. 1976). Ernest and Jewel Riley built a snow tunnel on their lot without first obtaining approval of the architectural control committee empowered by a recorded declaration to regulate land use in the area. The Rileys had purchased the first lot in the residential subdivision upon the representation of the seller that the properties would be subject to the recorded restrictions which they were given before buying the lot. However, the declaration containing the restrictions was not recorded until after they had purchased their lot; moreover, because of a mistake by the title company, their deed did not mention the restrictions. Allow it appeared clear that buyers who purchased lots after the declaration was recorded were subject to the restrictions, the California Supreme Court ruled that the Rileys were not subject to the restrictions because there was no writing in their deed limiting the use of their land and the intent of the owner to impose those restrictions was not binding on them. Evidence of their knowledge of the grantor's intent to impose restrictions was not admissible under the parol evidence rule (which excluded admission of oral evidence that contradicts a writing in certain cases) and the statute of frauds (which required interests in land to be in writing to be enforceable, *id.* at 1221-1222.

[There] is a practical consideration favoring the rule of *Werner v. Graham.* The grantee of property subject to mutually enforceable restrictions takes not just a servient tenement but, as owner of a dominant tenement, acquires a property interest in all other lots similarly burdened for the benefit of his property. That fact significantly affects the expectations of the parties and inevitably enters into the exchange of consideration between grantor and grantee. Even though the grantor omits to include the mutual restrictions in deeds to parcels thereafter severed from the servient tenement, those who take such property with notice, actual or constructive, of the restrictions are bound thereby. Thus, the recording statutes operate to protect the expectations of the grantee and secure to him the full benefit of the exchange for which he bargained. Where, however, mutually enforceable equitable servitudes are sought to be created outside the recording statutes, the vindication of the expectations of the original grantee, and for that matter succeeding grantees, is hostage not only to the good faith of the grantor, but, even assuming good faith, to the vagaries of proof by extrinsic evidence of actual notice on the part of grantees who thereafter take a part of the servient tenement either from the common grantor or as successors in interest to his grantees. The uncertainty thus introduced into subdivision development would in many cases circumvent any plan for the orderly and harmonious development of such properties and result in a crazy-quilt pattern of uses frustrating the bargained-for expectations of lot owners in the tract.

Justice Matthew Tobriner dissented, *id.* at 1222.

I cannot subscribe to the majority's conclusion that a buyer of a subdivision lot, who takes his deed with actual knowledge of a general plan of mutual restrictions applicable to the entire subdivision and who conducts himself for many years in a manner which demonstrates his belief that such restrictions apply to his property, may thereafter violate all such restrictions with impunity simply because the restrictions were inadvertently omitted from his individual deed. Contrary to the majority's suggestion, we need not decree this inequitable result in order to prevent fraud to maintain security in land titles; the very antithesis — a ruling that a buyer with *actual knowledge* of restrictions is thereby bound — ensures fairness and promotes security in land transactions; it implements the intention of both the buyer and the seller ....

The majority's holding will permit plaintiffs in this case to ignore restrictions designed to preserve natural beauty and property values in a carefully planned residential community. Although the use of all other lots in the community will continue to be restricted, plaintiffs will be free to subdivide their land into any number of small building sites, construct apartments or rent commercial space, ignore building lines and obstruct views from neighboring lots, raise livestock, and strip the land by removing trees and shrubs.

Common sense and substantive justice dictates that the plaintiffs should not be free to violate such restrictions. At the time of purchase plaintiffs had actual knowledge of those restrictions; the restrictions formed a part of the consideration exchanged by the parties. The restrictions continue to enhance the value of plaintiffs' individual lot because all other property owners in the subdivision are bound thereby ....

Accordingly, I would hold that the evidence offered by defendant committee is admissible to establish the existence of building restrictions binding upon plaintiffs.

NOTES AND QUESTIONS

1. *Implied reciprocal negative servitudes.* The doctrine of implied reciprocal negative servitudes, or reciprocal negative easements, was invented to deal with the intent, notice, and privity of estate issues that arise when a developer imposes grantee covenants on all lots in a residential subdivision and when the developer intentionally or

inadvertently leaves those restrictions off some of the lots. Covenants restricting land in a subdivision are mutually enforceable by and against all owners if the properties were all intended to be part of a *common scheme* or *general plan*. Today developers generally record a *declaration* prior to the sale of the first lot describing the common plan and providing buyers notice of the conditions, covenants, and restrictions (CC&Rs) applicable to the subdivision. *See Schovee v. Mikolasko,* 737 A.2d 578, 586-87 (Md. 1999) (lot not subject to covenants when it was excluded from them in the declaration; such lots are presumptively free of the restrictions, and there was insufficient contravening evidence in this case that developer intended to include that lot in the common plan). The common plan applies to each owner partly because this is the intent of the developer/grantor and partly because of reliance on it by buyers.

A common plan can be shown by various factors, such as the presence of restrictions in all or most deeds to property in the area, a recorded plat (map) showing the restrictions, the presence of restrictions in the last deed (since the grantor retains no land left to be benefited, the suggestion is that the intended beneficiaries of the promise are the other lots in the neighborhood), observance by owners of similar development of their land and conformity to the written restrictions, language stating that the covenants are intended to run with the land, and the recording of a declaration stating that the covenants are intended to be mutually enforceable. Gerald Korngold, *Private Land Use Arrangements: Easements, Real Covenants, and Equitable Servitudes* §9.09, at 301-302 (1990). Evidence tending to show the absence of a common plan is that some deeds are unrestricted and that the restrictions are nonuniform.

Some courts, however, reject the doctrine of implied reciprocal negative servitudes applied in *Evans v. Pollock,* holding instead that reciprocal covenants will be enforced only if the deeds themselves state that the property is part of a defined common plan or the developer records a declaration containing the restrictions prior to the sale of the properties sought to be burdened and benefited by them. *Citizens for Covenant Compliance v. Anderson,* 906 P.2d 1314, 1322-1323 (Cal. 1995) (approving the result in *Werner v. Graham,* 183 P.945 (Cal. 1919)).

2. *Developer's power to enforce the covenants.* Recall the rule restricting the enforceability of covenants when the benefit is held in gross. The declaration may give the developer the power to enforce the covenants by bringing a lawsuit to compel compliance. When the developer of a subdivision attempts to continue to enforce the covenant after the last parcel is sold, the courts may deny the developer standing to bring a suit to enforce the covenants because of the policies underlying the rule prohibiting the benefit of covenants to be held in gross. The developer's legitimate interest in retaining control over development in the subdivision is to increase the marketability of the lots; assuring prospective buyers that the subdivision is restricted to residential use, or even single-family homes, may increase the market value of the property and attract buyers. Once the developer leaves, however, she is an outsider whose legitimate interests have already been satisfied; continued control by the developer is seen as meddling. In addition, control by an absentee grantor resembles the powers exercised by feudal lords and is incompatible with the devolution of control over property to current owners. Freeing current owners from the "dead hand" of the past — and the continuing control of prior grantors in particular — promotes both the liberty of current owners and efficient use of land. There is therefore a strong, although not universal, presumption against continued enforcement by absentee developers who no longer own property in the neighborhood. *Garland v. Rosenshein,* 649 N.E.2d 756 (Mass. 1995) (benefit of covenant held in gross cannot be enforced);

Smith v. First Savings of Louisiana, 575 So. 2d 1033 (Ala. 1991) (refusing to allow the developer to retain control of the architectural review commission empowered to approve building changes in the subdivision once the last parcel was sold); *Armstrong v. Roberts,* 325 S.E.2d 769 (Ga. 1985) (developer cannot waive a covenant after all parcels are sold and it has no economic interest in the subdivision).

Some courts have allowed developers to continue to enforce covenants when the declaration allows this, at least where the owners have the power to amend the declaration and there is no showing that the developer "retained unreasonable or imperious control over artistic decisions of homeowners long after having completed the subdivision." *B.C.E. Development, Inc. v. Smith,* 264 Cal. Rptr. 55 (Ct. App. 1989) (allowing enforcement by the developer's successor in interest when the covenant provided for such enforcement and the declaration gave the homeowners association the power to amend the declaration and take control of the architectural commission by a two-thirds vote). In that case, "[e]quity might well decline to enforce such asserted control, especially if it were shown to be contrary to the then desires of the homeowners." *Id.* at 60. *Accord, Christiansen v. Casey,* 613 S.W.2d 906 (Mo. Ct. App. 1981).

Although the *Restatement (Third)* makes covenants enforceable when the benefit is held in gross, *id.* at §2.6(b), it still requires a legitimate interest in the party who seeks enforcement, *id.* at §2.6, cmt. d. What legitimate reasons, if any, could a developer have for retaining the power to enforce the covenants once the last unit is sold? Some states prohibit enforcement of covenants in gross by statute. Cal. Civ. Code §1462; Mont. Code §70-17-203.

3. *Enforcement by homeowners association.* It is well settled that, as agents of the property owners whose property is reciprocally benefited and burdened by servitudes, homeowners associations have standing to enforce those servitudes if the declaration gives them that power. The leading case is *Neponsit Property Owners' Association, Inc. v. Emigrant Industrial Savings Bank,* 15 N.E.2d 793 (N.Y. 1938). *Accord, Portola Hills Community Association v. James,* 5 Cal. Rptr. 2d 580 (Ct. App. 1992); *Raintree of Albemarle Homeowners Association v. Jones,* 413 S.E.2d 340 (Va. 1992). However, some courts will not allow the homeowners association to bring a suit to enforce the covenants if the declaration creating the association did not expressly grant it that power. *Palm Point Property Owners' Association of Charlotte County v. Pisarski,* 626 So. 2d 195 (Fla. 1993).

4. *The problem of unrestricted lots.* What happens if the developer fails to record a declaration or plat and imposes restrictive grantee covenants in most, but not all, of the deeds to property in the subdivision, and the grantor makes no promise to restrict the remaining lots? Can the owners of lots restricted by grantee covenants enforce them against buyers of the unrestricted lots? If the buyers of the remaining lots knew of the restriction and orally promised to comply with it, one might apply equitable estoppel doctrine in conjunction with third-party beneficiary doctrine to allow enforcement by prior and later buyers. But what if no oral statements are made by the buyers of the unrestricted lots promising to abide by the covenants?

Most courts hold that buyers of unrestricted lots are on constructive notice of covenants in other deeds in the vicinity sold by the same grantor. *Roper v. Camuso,* 829 A.2d 589, 595 (Md. 2003). *Sanborn v. McLean* went so far as to argue that a buyer in a residential neighborhood should be on inquiry notice if there is a uniform pattern of development that might suggest the existence of a common plan.

What evidence is sufficient to show a common plan? If too many of the lots in the subdivision are sold without restrictions, the court may find that no common scheme was in fact established, thus freeing all the unrestricted lots from the duty to comply with the covenants in their neighbors' deeds. *Petersen v. Beekmere, Inc.,* 283 A.2d 911 (N.J. Super. Ct. Ch. Div. 1971). *Sanborn v. McLean* imposed restrictive covenants on an entire neighborhood even though the covenants were included in only 53 of 91 deeds. Was this justified? *Compare Forster v. Hall,* 576 S.E.2d 746 (Va. 2003) (implied reciprocal negative servitude prohibiting mobile homes was enforced against unrestricted lots when 93 percent of lots were restricted).

What justifies limiting a property owner's right to develop his land when the deed he received from the seller neither had any restrictions in it nor referred to the restrictions in deeds previously granted to others in the subdivision? In *Riley,* the California Supreme Court rejected the ruling in *Sanborn* by holding a lot cannot be restricted unless those restrictions appear in the chain of title to that particular lot. Thus, the first buyers were not restricted because they purchased prior to the recordation of the declaration, even though they were on notice of the restrictions at the time they purchased. Do you agree with the court's ruling or with the dissenting opinion of Justice Tobriner?

In 1995, the California Supreme Court clarified *Riley* by holding that any buyer of a lot covered by a recorded declaration is bound by the restrictions in the declaration even if his deed nowhere mentions the declaration or the restrictions. *Citizens for Covenant Compliance v. Anderson,* 906 P.2d 1314 (Cal. 1995). The terms of a recorded declaration are impliedly included in the deeds to lots covered by the declaration. This leaves standing the ruling in *Riley* that exempts lots purchased before the declaration was recorded.

5. *Lots retained by the grantor.* Suppose all the covenants in the neighborhood contain grantee covenants restricting the property to single-family use. Moreover, the developer files a declaration to that effect describing all the property in the subdivision as restricted. The developer owns property across the street from this subdivision; the property is left undeveloped for several years after the subdivision is completed. The developer then seeks to build on this property in a manner inconsistent with the restrictions imposed on the subdivision. Can the developer do this? The question arises whether the neighboring tract should be treated as part of the common plan. If it was noted on the original plat, the courts are likely to hold that it was part of the common plan. But suppose it was never described on the plat or the declaration or orally as part of the development. May the developer sell to commercial users in a manner that does not constitute a common law nuisance but nonetheless interferes with the common residential scheme by substantially changing the environment? No promises of any kind were made to the buyers in the subdivision that the developer would not do this. Most courts hold that only parcels within the common scheme are restricted and that the grantor's intent to leave a tract or parcel out of the common scheme is determinative.

In *Duvall v. Ford Leasing Development Corp.,* 255 S.E.2d 470 (Va. 1979), a developer subdivided and built homes on a large tract in stages over a 25-year period. Each of the subdivisions was restricted to residential use. The developer then sold its remaining land, expressly providing in the deed that a portion of it would remain free of restrictions of any kind. The buyer of that land sold the unrestricted parcel to an owner who sought to establish a car sales and service business. Relying on the piecemeal development and the fact that it occurred over a long period of time, the court held that the development consisted of separate subdivisions and that the entire property was not subject to a single common plan. In contrast, the court in *Snow v. Van Dam,* 197 N.E.

224 (Mass. 1935), concluded that a lot across the street from the rest of a subdivision was intended to be in the same common plan, although it was sold more than 15 years after the first lot, because it was included in the description of the entire tract when it was registered and the delay in sale was caused by the inability to sell the property rather than an intent to exclude it from the restricted area.

When a developer that deliberately leaves some of its contiguous land out of the common scheme attempts to develop the retained land in a manner inconsistent with the common scheme, is there any argument for constraining the developer's ability to do this? Does it matter if the unrestricted lots are located outside but adjacent to the subdivision or inside it?

PROBLEMS

1. A famous architect develops a subdivision of 50 homes with an unusual design for the houses. The design is popular and the properties are sold for high prices. Before the first home was sold, the developer recorded a declaration that contained restrictive covenants preventing any external changes to the structures or landscaping without consent of the architectural review commission. The developer was identified by name in the declaration as the sole member of the architectural review commission. Every deed refers to the declaration.

   a. Five years after the last home was sold, a homeowner seeks to change the color of her house and to add a sunroom. The architect refuses to allow the changes, although none of the neighbors objects to them. The owner sues the architect, claiming that the covenant granting the architect continued control of the architectural review commission after the last unit was sold is unenforceable. The architect claims that the design of the houses is akin to a work of art, that she has a right to artistic control of the houses, and that the plaintiff voluntarily consented to this arrangement. Some of the neighbors support the architect's position in order to maintain the value of their homes. Who should win? Would your answer change if the problem arose 50 years after the last house was sold? Suppose the architect wrote a will leaving her right of enforcement to her daughter at her death. Could the daughter enforce the covenant?

   b. Now suppose the declaration grants the architect complete control of interior design, including furniture. A resident is paralyzed in an automobile accident and wants to change the furniture and the kitchen to make them wheelchair accessible. The architect refuses to agree to the change. No owner in the neighborhood objects to her proposed changes. The homeowner argues that the benefit of the covenant cannot be held in gross. Who should win? Is there another basis to invalidate the covenant? Should it be enforced?

2. A developer sells 50 lots in a subdivision with a grantee covenant in each deed by which each owner covenants not to use the property for nonresidential purposes and limits each lot to a single-family home. No grantor covenants are included, and no declaration is filed; however, the grantor/developer orally promises each owner that each lot will be restricted, and the sales literature characterizes the neighborhood as a "high-class restricted neighborhood." The buyer of the last lot sells the property to a

nonprofit organization that wishes to divide the house on the lot in two and turn it into a duplex that will be rented to two low-income families. Can it do so? Should it be able to do so?

3. A developer, *O*, orally promises to restrict all the land in a 40-lot subdivision to single-family homes. The deeds granted to the first 35 buyers include a grantee covenant restricting their use to single-family homes; the deeds further state, however, that the covenant "shall apply only to the property herein conveyed and shall not be construed as creating any requirement on the part of the grantor herein to restrict any of the remaining property located within the subdivision."[21] Many of the buyers note the limitation of the covenant and question *O* about it. *O* responds that of course she intends to put the restriction in all the deeds granted in the subdivision and that the limitation is a technicality meant to protect the developer from liability for damages. This will not affect the buyer's right to obtain injunctive relief against other lots in the subdivision. Buyer 36, *C*, purchases with notice of the restrictions in the earlier deeds and of the oral promise that *O* made to the first 35 buyers. However, *O* leaves the covenant out of *C*'s deed after *C* offers *O* a substantial amount of money to do so. The property purchased by *C* is worth $250,000 if restricted to a single-family home but is worth $1,500,000 if a four-story apartment building can be constructed. When *C* offered *O* this latter sum, *O* jumped at the chance and broke her oral promise to the prior purchasers. *O* has signed a purchase and sale agreement to convey the property to *C* for $1,500,000 and promised not to impose any restrictions on the use of the land. One of the neighbors finds out about this arrangement and brings a lawsuit against *C* and *O*, asking for a declaratory judgment that the land being sold to *C* will be limited for use as a single-family house. What should the court do?

4. A developer sells 45 of 50 lots in a subdivision, with grantee covenants restricting uses to single-family homes. The developer orally assures the buyers that all the lots will be restricted. The developer, however, has trouble selling the last five lots located on the edge of the development. A buyer offers to purchase three of the lots if they can be combined and an apartment building constructed with 25 apartments. The price is lower than the developer hoped to get for the three properties, but no other buyers seem ready to purchase the lots for use as single-family homes at prices that would allow the developer to make a profit. Then another buyer comes along who offers an extremely high price for the last two lots so long as no covenant is included in the deed; this buyer wants to build a gas station. Several of the owners of the restricted lots sue the owners of the lots that are to be developed as an apartment building and a gas station. Can they enforce the restrictions against these owners under current law? Should they be able to do so?

Now suppose the developer intended all along to sell the last five lots as unrestricted lots, and the buyers can prove that the developer intended to defraud them at the time of purchase, rather than merely changing her mind when the market went soft. Does this change your analysis?

5. A developer sells 45 of 50 lots in a subdivision, with grantee covenants restricting the properties to residential use. The developer makes no oral promises or representations of any kind to the buyers. No declaration is filed, and no grantor covenants are included in the deeds. The developer then sells the last five lots without restrictions. They are scattered through the subdivision rather than located on the edge or con-

---

21. This clause is adapted from Paul Goldstein, *Real Property* 740–741 (1984).

centrated in one place. One of the purchasers of the unrestricted lots wants to build a gas station. Can the owners enforce the restrictions against her?

6. A developer owns two large tracts located across the road from each other. The area is rural and undeveloped. The developer constructs a residential subdivision on one tract, with grantor and grantee covenants restricting the property to single-family homes. The developer also represents orally to the buyers that the area will be a pleasant residential neighborhood. All the lots contain the covenants, and uniform development occurs. Then the developer makes plans to turn the tract across the street into a shopping center. Can she do so?

§5.4.3 INTERPRETATION OF AMBIGUOUS COVENANTS

BLEVINS v. BARRY-LAWRENCE COUNTY
ASSOCIATION FOR RETARDED CITIZENS

707 S.W.2d 407 (Mo. 1986)

WARREN WELLIVER, Judge.

This is an appeal from a circuit court judgment enjoining appellant, Barry-Lawrence County Association for Retarded Citizens, from using its property as a group home for retarded individuals. Respondents, Jess and Nedra Blevins, brought this equitable action alleging that said use violates a restrictive covenant on the lot. . . . We reverse.

Appellant owns Lot 23 and the residence thereon in the Wildwood Estates Subdivision of Cassville, Missouri, and it plans on establishing a group home for eight unrelated mentally retarded persons. Respondents own Lot 24, which is across the street from appellant's property. The subdivision is protected by restrictive covenants, which provide in relevant part:

> 1. The aforesaid real property shall be used for residential purposes only. No buildings shall be erected, altered, placed or permitted to remain on said real property other than single or double family dwellings not to exceed two and one-half stories in height and private garages for not more than two cars. No detached structures shall be permitted.

Respondents argue that appellant's intended use of its property will contravene this covenant. Appellant responds by alleging (1) that its intended use does not violate the covenant; (2) that awarding an equitable injunction would violate public policy, as illustrated by the recently enacted Mo. Rev. Stat. §89.020 (Supp. 1985) which forbids either zoning ordinances or restrictive covenants from excluding group homes for mentally retarded individuals; and (3) that §89.020 must be given retroactive effect and, therefore, the provision of the restrictive covenant is void. . . .

It is a well-established rule that restrictive covenants are not favorites of the law, and when interpreting such covenants, courts should give effect to the intent of the parties as expressed in the plain language of the covenant; but, when there is any ambiguity or substantial doubt as to the meaning, restrictive covenants will be read narrowly in favor of the free use of property. . . .

The initial question is whether the group home for eight unrelated persons and two house parents violates the restriction against any use other than for "residential purposes only." In *Shepherd v. State*, 427 S.W.2d 382 (Mo. 1968), this Court interpreted the phrase "residential purposes" in a restrictive covenant. This Court quoted with approval the following definition of "residential purposes": "Giving the words their plain and ordinary meaning, we would say that . . . it is, one in which people reside or dwell, or which they make their homes, as distinguished from one which is used for commercial or business purposes." *Id.* at 388. Apartment buildings, therefore, were permitted under the covenant.

It is beyond doubt that the operation of the group home in question has all the characteristics of a residential as opposed to a commercial use. The home is owned and run by a non-profit organization, and the underlying theory behind establishing such a home is that it serves as a surrogate family arrangement. There is no commercial enterprise, and the home is neither a boarding house nor an institutional facility. The trial court found the following facts relative to the operation of the home:

> [Appellant] operates a number of "group homes" in which mentally retarded adults live in a residential setting with "house parents," often a husband and wife, who provide supervision and care for the retarded adults. . . . The group home as contemplated to be operated in Wildwood Estates by defendant is designed to allow the residents to develop their social, emotional and intellectual skills by living in a stable family-type environment. The house parents and residents function in an integrated family-style unit instead of as independent individuals who share only a place to sleep and eat. Residents are involved in performing simpl[e] household duties and participate in discussing, and if possible, resolving problems existing in the home and in making decisions as to the nature of group activities. Although ultimate decisions are left to house parents and/or the defendants [*sic*] board. The entire group often attends church, goes shopping and travels about the community in a body. . . . [F]ormal training for the retarded residents does not take place in the group home, but rather is conducted at an activity center or sheltered workshop during the workweek. Within the group home, the house parents encourage the development of social skills and simple homemaking skills by the individuals living there. The primary purpose of a residential group home is to provide a living situation as normal as possible for developmentally disabled residents of the community and is ordinarily not a temporary living arrangement but, depending upon the individual, a resident may remain in the group home months, years or for their entire lifetime. The trial court also found that prospective occupants of group homes are carefully screened and are admitted, at first, only on a trial basis. We believe that these findings of fact clearly indicate that appellant's intended use of Lot 23 as a group home is a residential purpose under the restrictive covenant.

Faced with a similar factual situation, a substantial number of courts have held that the operation of a group home is a residential purpose within the meaning of a covenant with such a restriction. [*See*] *Jackson v. Williams*, 714 P.2d 1017 (Okla. 1985). . . .

The remaining question is whether appellant's intended use of the property violates the second sentence of the restrictive covenant, which prohibits erecting, altering, placing or permitting any building "other than single or double family dwellings not to exceed two and one-half stories in height and private garages for not more than two cars." Respondents argue that this restriction is a restriction on the use of the property; and, if a restriction on use, appellant's group home is neither a single nor a double family dwelling.

By its plain terms, however, this restriction applies only to structures and not to the use of the property. The language, therefore, is substantially different than the covenant being construed in *London v. Handicapped Facilities Board of St. Charles County*, 637 S.W.2d 212, 214 (Mo. Ct. App. 1982), where the court enjoined a group home under a restriction prohibiting "[n]o more than one family shall live in any residence. . . ." The restriction more closely resembles the covenant in *Jackson v. Williams,* where the court held that the group home did not violate the second sentence of the restriction which permitted only single-family dwellings:

> The term "family" was, in fact, used without a definition and hence did not necessarily exclude from its meaning a group of unrelated persons living together in a home. This phrase was intended to describe the character of the structure rather than limit the use of the property to single-family residence[s]. When, as here, the restrictive covenant under consideration prohibits occupancy of more than one family unit but does not address itself to the composition of the family, a court is loath to restrict a family unit to that composed of persons who are related, one to another, by consanguinity or affinity. . . . [2]

Jackson, id. at 1023.

The record indicates that appellant does not intend to alter the structure of the residence on its lot. We hold, therefore, that appellant's intended use of its property does not violate the terms of the restrictive covenant. . . .

NOTES AND QUESTIONS

1. *Presumptions.* Courts traditionally interpreted ambiguous covenants in the manner that would be the "least burdensome to the free use of land." *Yogman v. Parrott,* 937 P.2d 1023 (Or. 1997). *Accord, Forster v. Hall,* 576 S.E.2d 746, 750 (Va. 2003)("restrictions of the free use of land . . . are disfavored by public policy and must be strictly construed"); *Country Club District Homes Ass'n v. Country Club Christian Church,* 118 S.W.3d 185 (Mo. Ct. App. 2003) ("restrictive covenants are regarded unfavorably and are strictly construed because the law favors the free and untrammeled use of real property"). Some courts state that covenants should be construed against the drafter; this usually means the grantor or developer. *Foods First, Inc. v. Gables Associates,* 418 S.E.2d 888, 889 (Va. 1992). The effect of such a presumption is generally to limit the effect of covenants in restricting land use. The policy basis of this traditional presumption is to promote the free use of land, the rights of owners to be free from control by others, and the free alienability of land. The effect of this presumption is to limit free contract by interpreting restrictions narrowly.

Today the touchstone for interpretation of covenants seems to be the *intent of the grantor. Riss v. Angel,* 934 P.2d 669, 675 (Wash. 1997). This intent must be shown by express language in the deed or a declaration but may be supplemented by extrinsic evidence where necessary to interpret an ambiguity. When the dispute involves subsequent purchasers, the interests of those who seek to use their property as they wish conflict with the reliance interests of those who believed that neighboring property would be restricted. Given the modern view that such reliance is reasonable and that reciprocal covenants often increase the value and attractiveness of property, the *Restatement (Third)* suggests that it is no longer generally acceptable that courts should

---

2. We need not reach the issue of whether the group home would satisfy a single or double family use restriction. However, it might be noted that a number of jurisdictions, whether interpreting a restrictive covenant or a zoning ordinance, hold that certain group homes may be a "family" unless an explicit definition contained in the covenant or ordinance dictates otherwise. . . .

err on the side of unburdening property from restrictions. §4.1 cmt. a. This new approach favors the security and reliance interests of those who bought property in reliance on covenants restricting neighboring land and promotes those interests over interests in the free use of land. The assumption is that limitations on land use may promote rather than impede alienability. At the same time, some courts do retain the traditional presumption. *Yogman v. Parrott, supra.*

2. *Residential versus commercial use.* Restrictive covenants limiting real property to "residential" use have caused much litigation recently over whether and under what circumstances a group home constitutes a "residential" or "commercial" use. *See, e.g., Country Club District Homes Ass'n v. Country Club Christian Church,* 118 S.W.3d 185 (Mo. Ct. App. 2003) (covenant restricting property to "residence lots" did not allow use for church purposes). What factors did the *Blevins* court consider in answering this question? Other cases holding that operation of a group home is a "residential" use within the meaning of a restrictive covenant include *Knudtson v. Trainor,* 345 N.W.2d 4 (Neb. 1984); *Berger v. State,* 364 A.2d 993 (N.J. 1976); *Hall v. Community of Damien of Molokai,* 911 P.2d 861 (N.M. 1996).

An appellate court in Washington state, however, found a group home for the elderly to be a commercial use in *Hagemann v. Worth,* 782 P.2d 1072 (Wash. Ct. App. 1989). In that case the covenant restricted land to "residential and recreational use," limited buildings to "single-family residences," and prohibited "business, industry, or commercial enterprise of any kind or nature." The court rejected the owner's argument that the group home was not a business since it had a charitable purpose. Rather, the court focused on the fact that the couple that owned and managed the home charged between $900 and $1,250 for room, board, and personal care to each elderly resident, obtained a boarding house license from the state, and derived their primary income from operation of the facility. The court noted that "[t]he term *business* is the antonym of *residential* and to provide residence to paying customers is not synonymous with a residential purpose." *Id.* at 1076. *Accord, Mains Farm Homeowners Association v. Worthington,* 824 P.2d 495 (Wash. Ct. App. 1992). Does this mean that an owner who rented a single-family house to a nuclear family for $1,500 a month was violating the covenant? If not, what is the difference?

3. *Restrictions to "single-family dwellings": Structure versus use.* Like *Blevins,* the court in *Knudtson v. Trainor, supra,* held that restricting property to "single family dwellings" was intended to regulate architectural style rather than the relationship among the persons occupying the structure. *Accord, Permian Basin Centers for Mental Health and Mental Retardation v. Alsobrook,* 723 S.W.2d 774, 777 (Tex. Ct. App. 1986). In contrast, the court in *Shaver v. Hunter,* 626 S.W.2d 574 (Tex. Ct. App. 1981), held that restriction limiting property to "residential uses" and defining a "residence" as "a single-family dwelling" expressed the "clear intent and the plain and unambiguous purpose" of the grantor to regulate the use of the dwelling as well as its structure, thereby excluding a group home. *Accord, Crane Neck Association, Inc. v. New York City/ Long Island County Services Group,* 460 N.E.2d 1336 (N.Y. 1984) (holding that a covenant restricting property to "single-family dwellings" was imposed to preserve the area as "a neighborhood of single-family dwellings, not only architecturally but also functionally"). Which meaning do you think is more likely to represent the grantor's actual intent? If a covenant restricting use to "single-family dwellings" is ambiguous, should the courts presumptively interpret the restriction as applying only to the kinds of structures that may be built or broadly as applying to the relationships among the

people living in the structure? What argument can you make on both sides of this question on the basis of rights and social utility considerations?

4. *Group homes as families.* The *Blevins* court never got to address the question whether a group home constituted a "family." In *Malcolm v. Shamie*, 290 N.W.2d 101 (Mich. Ct. App. 1980), the court held that "five mentally retarded women living with a foster parent in an environment therapeutically designed to emulate a more conventional family environment" constituted a "family" for purposes of a restrictive covenant precluding any building other than detached single-family dwellings. *Accord, Hall v. Community of Damien of Molokai, supra.* The court in *Malcolm* explained, 290 N.W.2d at 103:

> Five mentally retarded women living with a foster parent in an environment therapeutically designed to emulate a more conventional family environment should also be considered a family, and such use of the property, an appropriate family residential use. The residents are more than a group of unrelated individuals sharing a common roof. They do not have natural families on which to rely, and due to their unique circumstances, it is unlikely that these women will ever rejoin their parents or marry and form independent families. The substitute family provided by the group home allows the residents to lead more normal and meaningful lives within the community than would be feasible were they institutionalized.

Similarly, a concurring opinion in *Shaver v. Hunter, supra,* proposed the following definition of "family": "a stable housekeeping unit of two or more persons who are emotionally attached to each other and share a relationship that emulates traditional family values, promotes mutual protection, support, happiness, physical well-being and intellectual growth and is not in violation of the penal laws." 626 S.W.2d at 579 (Countiss, J., concurring).

In contrast, the majority opinion in *Shaver v. Hunter* held that the term "family" in the context of a covenant restricting occupancy to "single-family dwellings" meant "nuclear" or "extended" family. It found that a group home consisting of five unrelated women did not constitute a "family" since they were unrelated by blood, marriage, or adoption. *Accord, Crane Neck Association, supra* (holding that a group home of eight unrelated individuals did not constitute a family because they were unrelated by blood, marriage, or adoption and because of the presence of a significant number of rotating nonresident professional attendants); *Omega Corp. of Chesterfield v. Malloy,* 319 S.E.2d 728 (Va. 1984) (holding that a group home was not a family because of the type of supervision by counselors who were government employees). *Cf. Albert v. Zoning Hearing Bd. of North Abington Township,* 854 A.2d 401 (Pa. 2004) (halfway house for drug and alcohol rehabilitation not a "single-family detached dwelling" within the meaning of the local zoning law when inhabitants were transient, staying an average of two to six months).

5. *Public policy limits on restrictive covenants.* Several courts have held that although the operation of group homes violates covenants limiting property to "single-family dwellings," those covenants are unenforceable because they violate strong public policies prohibiting discrimination against persons with disabilities. In *Crane Neck Association, supra,* Justice Judith Kaye wrote an opinion holding that, although a group home did not constitute a single-family dwelling under a restrictive covenant, the covenant could not be equitably enforced because to do so would have contravened long-standing public policy favoring establishment of such residences for the mentally disabled. Similarly, in *Westwood Homeowners Association v. Tenhoff,* 745 P.2d 976 (Ariz. Ct. App. 1987), the court held that operation of a residential

facility for six developmentally disabled children and young adults violated a covenant prohibiting use of property for the care of persons with disabilities but that the covenant was contrary to public policy and unenforceable. Quoting Justice Thurgood Marshall, the court noted that "[e]xcluding group homes deprives the retarded of much of what makes for human freedom and fulfillment — the ability to form bonds and take part in the life of a community." *Id.* at 984 (quoting *Cleburne v. Cleburne Living Center,* 473 U.S. 432, 461 (1985)) (Marshall, J., concurring in the judgment in part and dissenting in part). *Accord, Craig v. Bossenbery,* 351 N.W.2d 596 (Mich. Ct. App. 1984) (covenant not enforceable as a matter of public policy).

In contrast, the court in *Shaver v. Hunter, supra,* held that a restrictive covenant limiting property to single-family dwellings that was intended to exclude a group home of unrelated individuals was neither unreasonable nor against public policy. The court in *Hagemann v. Worth, supra,* held that a restrictive covenant excluding a group home for the elderly did not violate public policy because it "does not impede furtherance of the public's interest in developing alternate residential care for the elderly; it does prohibit the location of that care facility when it violates the contractual rights of the parties." 782 P.2d at 1076. Is this argument convincing?

6. *Antidiscrimination statutes.* Restrictive covenants that discriminate against persons with disabilities may violate federal civil rights statutes, including the *Americans with Disabilities Act of* 1990 and the *Fair Housing Act of* 1968, as amended in 1988. *See, e.g., Hall v. Community of Damien of Molokai, supra.* The *Fair Housing Act* is covered in depth in Chapter 11. State antidiscrimination laws may also apply to exclusionary covenants.

PROBLEMS

1. A covenant restricts land to "residential purposes." An owner of a single-family home in the restricted area begins a home day care center, taking care of six children from 8:30 A.M. to 5:30 P.M. The center is licensed by the state. Has she violated the covenant? What are the arguments on both sides? *Compare Metzner v. Wojdyla,* 886 P.2d 154 (Wash. 1994) (holding that it is not a "residential" use) *with Berger v. State,* 364 A.2d 993 (N.J. 1976) (group home for preschool children with disabilities did not violate restrictive covenant limiting property to residential purposes).

2. In *Gabriel v. Cazier,* 938 P.2d 1209 (Idaho 1997), a covenant prohibited use of the property for a "business or trade." The homeowner's children gave swimming lessons to other children for profit during the summer months, giving about 18 lessons per week and earning $10,000 over the summer. The court held that covenant had not been violated. Do you agree?

§5.4.4 MODIFYING AND TERMINATING COVENANTS

§5.4.4.1 Changed Conditions

EL DI, INC. v. TOWN OF BETHANY BEACH

477 A.2d 1066 (Del. 1984)

DANIEL L. HERRMANN, Chief Justice for the majority.

This is an appeal from a permanent injunction granted by the Court of Chancery upon the petition of the plaintiffs, The Town of Bethany Beach, et al., prohibiting the defendant, El Di, Inc. ("El Di") from selling alcoholic beverages at Holiday House, a restaurant in Bethany Beach owned and operated by El Di. . . .

El Di purchased the Holiday House in 1969. In December 1981, El Di filed an application with the State Alcoholic Beverage Control Commission (the "Commission") for a license to sell alcoholic beverages at the Holiday House. On April 15, 1982, finding "public need and convenience," the Commission granted the Holiday House an on-premises license. The sale of alcoholic beverages at Holiday House began within 10 days of the Commission's approval. Plaintiffs subsequently filed suit to permanently enjoin the sale of alcoholic beverages under the license.

On appeal it is undisputed that the chain of title for the Holiday House lot included restrictive covenants prohibiting both the sale of alcoholic beverages on the property and nonresidential construction.[22] The same restriction was placed on property in Bethany Beach as early as 1900 and 1901 when the area was first under development.

As originally conceived, Bethany Beach was to be a quiet beach community. The site was selected at the end of the nineteenth-century by the Christian Missionary Society of Washington, D.C. In 1900, the Bethany Beach Improvement Company ("BBIC") was formed. The BBIC purchased lands, laid out a development and began selling lots. To insure the quiet character of the community, the BBIC placed restrictive covenants on many plots, prohibiting the sale of alcohol and restricting construction to residential cottages. Of the original 180 acre development, however, approximately 1/3 was unrestricted.

The Town of Bethany Beach was officially incorporated in 1909. The municipal limits consisted of 750 acres including the original BBIC land (hereafter the original or "old-Town"), but expanded far beyond the 180 acre BBIC development. The expanded acreage of the newly incorporated Town, combined with the unrestricted plots in the original Town, left only 15 percent of the new Town subject to the restrictive covenants.

Despite the restriction prohibiting commercial building ("no other than a dwelling or cottage shall be erected . . ."), commercial development began in the 1920's on property subject to the covenants. This development included numerous inns, restaurants, drug stores, a bank, motels, a town hall, shops selling various items including food, clothing, gifts and novelties and other commercial businesses. Of the 34 commercial buildings presently within the Town limits, 29 are located in the old-Town originally developed by BBIC. Today, Bethany Beach has a permanent population of some 330 residents. In the summer months the population increases to approximately 10,000 people within the corporate limits and to some 48,000 people within a 4 mile radius. In 1952, the Town enacted a zoning ordinance which established a central commercial district designated C-1 located in the old-Town section. Holiday House is located in this district.

---

22. The restrictive covenant stated:
This covenant is made expressly subject to and upon the following conditions: *viz.*, That no intoxicating liquors shall ever be sold on the said lot. . . .; a breach of which said condition [. . .] shall cause said lot to revert to and become again the property of the grantor, his heirs and assigns; and upon such breach of said conditions or restrictions, the same may be restrained or enjoined in equity by the grantor, his heirs or assigns, or by any co-lot owner in said plan or other party injured by such breach. — ED.

Since El Di purchased Holiday House in 1969, patrons have been permitted to carry their own alcoholic beverages with them into the restaurant to consume with their meals. This "brown-bagging" practice occurred at Holiday House prior to El Di's ownership and at other restaurants in the Town. El Di applied for a license to sell liquor at Holiday House in response to the increased number of customers who were engaging in "brown-bagging" and in the belief that the license would permit restaurant management to control excessive use of alcohol and use by minors. Prior to the time El Di sought a license, alcoholic beverages had been and continue to be readily available for sale at nearby licensed establishments including: one restaurant 1/2 mile outside the Town limits, 3 restaurants within a 4 mile radius of the Town, and a package store some 200-300 yards from the Holiday House. . . .

In granting plaintiffs' motion for a permanent injunction, the Court of Chancery rejected defendant's argument that changed conditions in Bethany Beach rendered the restrictive covenants unreasonable and therefore unenforceable. The Chancery Court found that although the evidence showed a considerable growth since 1900 in both population and the number of buildings in Bethany Beach, "the basic nature of Bethany Beach as a quiet, family oriented resort has not changed." The Court also found that there had been development of commercial activity since 1900, but that this "activity is limited to a small area of Bethany Beach and consists mainly of activities for the convenience and patronage of the residents of Bethany Beach."

The Trial Court also rejected defendant's contention that plaintiffs' acquiescence and abandonment rendered the covenants unenforceable. In this connection, the Court concluded that the practice of "brown-bagging" was not a sale of alcoholic beverages and that, therefore, any failure to enforce the restriction as against the practice did not constitute abandonment or waiver of the restriction.

We find that the Trial Court erred in holding that the change of conditions was insufficient to negate the restrictive covenant.

A court will not enforce a restrictive covenant where a fundamental change has occurred in the intended character of the neighborhood that renders the benefits underlying imposition of the restrictions incapable of enjoyment. Review of all the facts and circumstances convinces us that the change, since 1901, in the character of that area of the old-Town section now zoned C-1 is so substantial as to justify modification of the deed restriction. We need not determine a change in character of the entire restricted area in order to assess the continued applicability of the covenant to a portion thereof.

It is uncontradicted that one of the purposes underlying the covenant prohibiting the sale of intoxicating liquors was to maintain a quiet, residential atmosphere in the restricted area. Each of the additional covenants reinforces this objective, including the covenant restricting construction to residential dwellings. The covenants read as a whole evince an intention on the part of the grantor to maintain the residential, seaside character of the community.

But time has not left Bethany Beach the same community its grantors envisioned in 1901. The Town has changed from a church-affiliated residential community to a summer resort visited annually by thousands of tourists. Nowhere is the resultant change in character more evident than in the C-1 section of the old-Town. Plaintiffs argue that this is a relative change only and that there is sufficient evidence to support the Trial Court's findings that the residential character of the community has been maintained and that the covenants continue to benefit the other lot owners. We cannot agree.

In 1909, the 180 acre restricted old-Town section became part of a 750 acre incorporated municipality. Even prior to the Town's incorporation, the BBIC deeded out lots free of the restrictive covenants. After incorporation and partly due to the unrestricted lots deeded out by the BBIC, 85 percent of the land area within the Town was not subject to the restrictions. Significantly, nonresidential uses quickly appeared in the restricted area and today the old-Town section contains almost all of the commercial businesses within the entire Town. Moreover, these commercial uses have gone unchallenged for 82 years.

The change in conditions is also reflected in the Town's decision in 1952 to zone restricted property, including the lot on which the Holiday House is located, specifically for commercial use. Although a change in zoning is not dispositive as against a private covenant, it is additional evidence of changed community conditions.

Time has relaxed not only the strictly residential character of the area, but the pattern of alcohol use and consumption as well. The practice of "brown-bagging" has continued unchallenged for at least twenty years at commercial establishments located on restricted property in the Town. On appeal, plaintiffs rely on the Trial Court finding that the "brown-bagging" practice is irrelevant as evidence of waiver inasmuch as the practice does not involve the sale of intoxicating liquors prohibited by the covenant. We find the "brown-bagging" practice evidence of a significant change in conditions in the community since its inception at the turn of the century. Such consumption of alcohol in public places is now generally tolerated by owners of similarly restricted lots. The license issued to the Holiday House establishment permits the El Di management to better control the availability and consumption of intoxicating liquors on its premises. In view of both the ready availability of alcoholic beverages in the area surrounding the Holiday House and the long-tolerated and increasing use of "brown-bagging" enforcement of the restrictive covenant at this time would only serve to subvert the public interest in the control of the availability and consumption of alcoholic liquors. . . .

In view of the change in conditions in the C-1 district of Bethany Beach, we find it unreasonable and inequitable now to enforce the restrictive covenant. To permit unlimited "brown-bagging" but to prohibit licensed sales of alcoholic liquor, under the circumstances of this case, is inconsistent with any reasonable application of the restriction and contrary to public policy.

We emphasize that our judgment is confined to the area of the old-Town section zoned C-1. The restrictions in the neighboring residential area are unaffected by the conclusion we reach herein. . . .

ANDREW CHRISTIE, Justice, with whom MOORE, Justice, joins, dissenting.

I respectfully disagree with the majority.

I think the evidence supports the conclusion of the Chancellor, as finder of fact, that the basic nature of the community of Bethany Beach has not changed in such a way as to invalidate those restrictions which have continued to protect this community through the years as it has grown. Although some of the restrictions have been ignored and a portion of the community is now used for limited commercial purposes, the evidence shows that Bethany Beach remains a quiet, family-oriented resort where no liquor is sold. I think the conditions of the community are still consistent with the enforcement of a restrictive covenant forbidding the sale of intoxicating beverages.

In my opinion, the toleration of the practice of "brown bagging" does not constitute the abandonment of a longstanding restriction against the sale of alcoholic beverages. The restriction against sales has, in fact, remained intact for more than eighty years and any violations thereof have been short-lived. The fact that alcoholic beverages may be purchased right outside the town is not inconsistent with my view that the quiet-town atmosphere in this small area has not broken down, and that it can and should be preserved. Those who choose to buy land subject to the restrictions should be required to continue to abide by the restrictions.

I think the only real beneficiaries of the failure of the courts to enforce the restrictions would be those who plan to benefit commercially....

I think that restrictive covenants play a vital part in the preservation of neighborhood schemes all over the State, and that a much more complete breakdown of the neighborhood scheme should be required before a court declares that a restriction has become unenforceable....

NOTES AND QUESTIONS

1. *Changed conditions.* Covenants will not be enforced if *conditions have changed so drastically* inside the neighborhood restricted by the covenants that enforcement will be of *no substantial benefit* to the dominant estates, *Restatement of Property* §564 (1944). The change "must be so radical as to defeat the essential purpose of the covenant or render the covenant valueless to the parties." *Dierberg v. Wills,* 700 S.W.2d 461, 467 (Mo. Ct. App. 1985). The *Restatement (Third) of Property (Servitudes)* explains that very few cases result in application of the doctrine. "The test is stringent: Relief is granted only if the purpose of the servitude can no longer be accomplished." *Id.* at §7.10 cmt. a. Some state statutes also require covenants to be of "actual and substantial benefit" in order to be enforceable. Mass. Gen. Laws ch. 184 §30; N.Y. Real Prop. Acts Law §1951.

The changed conditions doctrine may also apply when substantial changes have occurred *outside* the restricted subdivision. Lots located on the fringe of the restricted area, however, may not invoke the changed conditions doctrine, even if the adjacent property is engaged in activity contrary to the covenant, if it is still possible for the restrictions to create benefit within the subdivision. If lots on the border of the restricted area could easily free themselves from the covenant, it would quickly lose its effect over time as succeeding blocks of fringe lots succumbed to external changes. The changed conditions doctrine is likely to apply to changes outside the restricted subdivision only when those changes have so adversely affected so many lots in the subdivision that enforcement is pointless. *River Heights Assocs. L.P. v. Batten,* 591 S.E.2d 683 (Va. 2004) (refusing to apply the changed conditions doctrine to allow lots on the edge of a restricted subdivision that had been rezoned for commercial use to develop commercially in violation of the covenant).

As *El Di* shows, determining when a covenant is no longer of substantial benefit is not a precise science. In *Allemong v. Frendzel,* 363 S.E.2d 487 (W. Va. 1987), the property was similarly subject to a restraint on the sale of liquor. The current owners of the servient estate, Donald and Lillian Frendzel, operated a grocery convenience store and began to sell liquor. Within a three-mile radius of the property were located numerous sales outlets for beer, including two establishments located within a quarter of a mile of the Frendzels' store. Because the area immediately surrounding the restricted parcel was predominantly residential and agricultural, however, the court held that there had not been "a radical change or changes in the neighborhood ... which would effectively destroy the objectives of the covenant and thus render it unenforceable." The court explained, *id.* at 492:

> We do not agree with the appellant that these commercial properties in the general vicinity of the restricted parcel significantly change the residential character of the immediate area. Even if we were to accept the appellant's contention, "every effort must be exerted to protect the unchanged portions of residential neighborhoods when businesses begin to encroach on the fringes." *Morris v. Nease,* 238 S.E.2d 844, 847 (W. Va. 1977).
>
> Based on the evidence, we believe that the nonresidential use of the property in the vicinity of the appellants' convenience store [has] not destroyed the essential objects and purposes of the restrictive covenant. We further believe that the benefits of the original plan envisioned by the grantor may be realized for that portion of the neighborhood which remains primarily residential and agricultural.

The *Restatement (Third)* alters the changed conditions doctrine in several crucial ways. First, it extends the doctrine to easements. Second, it uses termination rules to substitute for controls that had traditionally been applied through the touch and concern test. §7.10 cmt. a. Third, it suggests modification of the covenant in lieu of termination if modification will allow the covenant to serve its original purpose. Under this test, only if modification is not feasible is termination allowed. §7.10. Also, if the purpose of the servitude can be accomplished but "because of changed conditions the servient estate is no longer suitable for any use permitted by the servitude, a court may modify the servitude to permit other uses under conditions designed to preserve the benefits of the original servitude." *Id.* However, the *Restatement (Third)* cautions that a court should rarely intervene if a mechanism exists for terminating the covenant in a manner that does not require the unanimous consent of the beneficiaries, such as a supermajority vote of the members of a homeowners association. §7.10 cmt. a.

2. *Damages versus injunctive relief.* As noted above, damages were traditionally not awarded for breach of a covenant unless privity of estate was present under real covenants law, while injunctive relief was available even in the absence of privity. Because most owners want enforcement by injunctive relief and because it makes little sense to make it harder to obtain damages than injunctive relief (the reverse is usually the case), the courts appear now to be ready to award either an injunction or damages for violation of a covenant running with the land whether or not strict vertical privity is present. Remedies are chosen on the basis of their appropriateness under the circumstances.

When it comes to modifying or terminating a covenant, an alternative to complete nonenforcement is to allow the violation of the covenant to occur only upon the payment of damages to the owners of the dominant estates to compensate for the breach. *Restatement (Third) of Property (Servitudes)* §8.3 (2000); *Restatement of Property* §564 (1944). When might damages be an appropriate remedy in lieu of injunctive relief? Would they have been appropriate in *El Di?*

§5.4.4.2 Relative Hardship

Unlike the changed conditions doctrine, which focuses on whether the covenant remains of substantial benefit to the dominant estate, the *relative hardship* doctrine focuses on the servient estate. A covenant will not be enforced if the harm caused by enforcement, that is, the hardship to the owner of the servient estate, will be greater by a "considerable magnitude" than the benefit to the owner of the dominant estate, *Restatement of Property* §563 (1944). If the hardship is great and the benefit small, the courts may refuse to enforce the covenant. *Appel v. Presley Cos.,* 806 P.2d 1054 (N.M. 1991). If, however, the benefit of the covenant is substantial, the courts are unlikely to apply the doctrine even if the hardship to the servient estate is substantial.

For example, in *Lange v. Scofield,* 567 So. 2d 1299 (Ala. 1990), the court refused to enforce a covenant requiring that all owners of property adjoining or across the street from a parcel consent to the construction of a house on the parcel. One of the surrounding owners refused to give her consent, arguing that another house in the neighborhood would increase density and lower property values. The court found that construction would have no effect on property values and that any benefit received by the neighbor through enforcing the covenant would be negligible and far outweighed by the hardship that enforcement would cause the landowner who wished to construct the house.

The *Restatement (Third)* treats the relative hardship doctrine not as a basis for terminating or modifying servitudes, but, rather, as a factor to consider in determining the availability and selection of appropriate remedies. §8.3. If compliance with a covenant is unreasonable because the burden is great and the benefit small, the *Restatement (Third)* concludes that nonenforcement may be appropriate, but some amount of damages are probably appropriate to compensate the servitude beneficiary for the loss of the benefit of the covenant, small as it may be. §8.3, cmts. a, h.

In *Shalimar Association v. D.O.C. Enterprises, Inc.,* 688 P.2d 682 (Ariz. Ct. App. 1984), the court enforced an equitable servitude requiring an owner to continue operating a golf course against a complaint by the current owner that such a use was not profitable. It refused to apply either the changed conditions or relative hardship doctrines. "A mere change in economic conditions rendering it unprofitable to continue the restrictive use is not alone sufficient to justify abrogating the restrictive covenant." *Id.* at 691. What might justify this result? What is the argument on the other side?

§5.4.4.3   Other Equitable Defenses

In addition to the changed conditions and relative hardship doctrines, the courts have identified a number of general equitable doctrines that may result in nonenforcement of a servitude.

Acquiescence, abandonment, or unclean hands. The complaining party may be barred from enforcing the covenant if he has tolerated or failed to object to other violations of the covenant. Toleration may indicate an intent to abandon the covenant, and the defendant may reasonably rely on the failure to enforce the covenant in investing in her property. *See Morris v. Nease,* 238 S.E.2d 844 (W. Va. 1977). This may occur if the plaintiff:

(1)   has violated the covenant himself (*unclean hands*) or
(2)   has tolerated previous violations of the covenant by the owner of the servient estate (*acquiescence*) or

(3)   has tolerated violations of the covenants by owners of other restricted parcels in the neighborhood covered by the covenant (*abandonment*).

Estoppel. An owner of a dominant estate who orally represents to the owner of a servient estate that she will not enforce the covenant may be estopped from asserting her interests in enforcing the covenant if the owner of the servient estate changes his position in reliance on the oral statement

Laches. If the covenant has been ignored or breached for a substantial period of time — but less than the time necessary to establish prescriptive rights — the court may find that unexcused delay in enforcing the covenant prompted investment in reliance on the failure to object to the violation and that enforcement of the covenant would be unconscionable.

Marketable title acts. As with As with easements, many states have marketable title statutes that terminate restrictive convenants if they are not re-recorded after a specified period of time. *See, e.g.*, Mass. Gen. Laws ch. 184 §27.

Other ways to terminate covenants. Other ways to terminate covenants include:

1.   *Language in instrument.* Many subdivisions or condominium associations are subject to covenants that terminate within a stated number of years unless they are periodically renewed by the homeowners association or condominium owners association.

2.   *Merger.* As with easements, if the burdened and benefited estates come under the ownership of the same person, the covenants will terminate.

3.   *Release.* All parties affected by the covenant — both burdened and benefited estates — may agree in writing to terminate the covenant or release the property from it.

4.   *Prescription.* Open and notorious violation of the covenant without permission for the statutory period may terminate the covenant by operation of the statute of limitations.

PROBLEMS

1. A representative of a homeowners association (the "Association") in a residential subdivision comes to see you at your law office. She tells you the following story. A developer, O, created a residential subdivision, which includes 20 single-family homes, three apartment buildings, and a park. The deeds granted by the developer to the original buyers stated that the owners of each lot were to become members of the Association and to have votes in the Association proportional to the size of their lots. The by-laws of the Association were recorded at the recording office, and each of the deeds referred to the bylaws. The bylaws provided that the Association was to be managed by a board of directors elected by the owners and was to be in charge of maintaining the park for the benefit of the owners. The Association was also given the power to assess fees against the homeowners to pay for maintenance of the park.

In addition, the developer conveyed one lot located in the center of the subdivision near the park to buyer *A*, with the following language:

> Grantee, *A*, covenants that a licensed day care center will operate on this lot for the benefit of other property owners in this subdivision who derive their title from Grantor, *O*. Grantee, *A*, further covenants not to transfer ownership of the premises without first obtaining the consent in writing of the Homeowners Association. If, at any time within the next 30 years, the Homeowners Association disapproves of the way the day care center is being managed, it shall have the option to purchase the property for its fair market value, as determined by an independent appraiser.

A operates the day care center for five years and then, with the consent of the Association, transfers the property to *B*. Because of a rash of child abuse allegations at day care centers around the country, the cost of insuring day care centers skyrockets. Many insurers begin refusing to insure day care centers at all.

B notifies the Association that she has had a great deal of trouble obtaining liability insurance for injuries arising out of operation of the day care center. She may not be able to obtain insurance at all, and, if she finds a company willing to insure the center, the expected cost of the policy is so high that it may drive her out of business. Because of the difficulty in obtaining insurance, *B* would like to shut down the day care center and convert the premises to another commercial enterprise, such as a videotape rental store.

The Association is anxious for the day care center to continue operating. The representative of the Association asks for advice about the homeowners' legal rights. What questions would you ask her? What other information do you need to know? What advice would you give her?

2. Now assume that the day care center is unable to obtain insurance. The owner of the center claims that she should not be legally obligated to operate the center without insurance and that under the undue hardship doctrine she has a right to develop the property free of the covenant. She sues the Association for a declaratory judgment to that effect. As the judge deciding the case, how would you resolve it?

§5.4.4.4   Statutes

Some states have enacted statutes that regulate the enforceability of covenants and provide a variety of doctrines allowing those covenants to be removed over time. Massachusetts has a particularly wide-ranging statute. Read the statute carefully, word by word, phrase by phrase, to see how many ways you could defeat enforcement of a covenant.

MASSACHUSETTS GENERAL LAWS

Mass. Gen. Laws ch. 184, §30

No restriction shall in any proceeding be enforced or declared to be enforceable, . . . unless it is determined that the restriction is at the time of the proceeding of actual and substantial benefit to a person claiming rights of enforcement. There shall be a presumption that no restriction shall be of such actual and substantial benefit except in cases of gifts or devises for public, charitable or religious purposes, if any part of the subject land lies within a city or town having a population greater than one hundred thousand persons unless (1) such restriction at the time it was imposed is not more burdensome as to requirements for lot size, density, building height, set back, or other yard dimensions than such requirements established by restriction or restrictions applicable to the land of the persons for whose benefit rights of enforcement are claimed; or (2) such restriction is part of a common scheme applicable to four or more parcels contiguous except for any intervening streets or ways to land of the grantor or other premises purported to be benefited thereby; or (3) unless such restriction is in favor of contiguous land of the grantor. No restriction determined to be of such benefit shall be enforced or declared to be enforceable, except in appropriate cases by award of money damages, if (1) changes in the character of the properties affected or their neighborhood, in available construction materials or techniques, in access, services or facilities, in applicable public controls of land use or construction, or in any other conditions or circumstances, reduce materially the need for the restriction or the likelihood of the restriction accomplishing its original purposes or render it obsolete or inequitable to enforce except by award of money damages, or (2) conduct of persons from time to time entitled to enforce the restriction has rendered it inequitable to enforce except by award of money damages, or (3) in case of a common scheme the land of the person claiming rights of enforcement is for any reason no longer subject to the restriction or the parcel against which rights of enforcement are claimed is not in a group of parcels still subject to the restriction and appropriate for accomplishment of its purposes, or (4) continuation of the restriction on the parcel against which enforcement is claimed or on parcels remaining in a common scheme with it or subject to like restrictions would impede reasonable use of land for purposes for which it is most suitable, and would tend to impair the growth of the neighborhood or municipality in a manner inconsistent with the public interest or to contribute to deterioration of properties or to result in decadent or substandard areas or blighted open areas, or (5) enforcement, except by award of money damages, is for any other reason inequitable or not in the public interest.

BLAKELEY v. GORIN

313 N.E.2d 903 (Mass. 1974)

EDWARD F. HENNESSEY, J.

. . . The petitioners, owners of a parcel of land subject to certain restrictions known as the Commonwealth Restrictions, seek a determination and declaration that the restrictions are obsolete and unenforceable. . . .

The Commonwealth Restrictions date from the middle of the last century. By 1850 the condition of the tidal flats which composed the area now known as the Back Bay had become a nuisance, largely due to drainage problems. The Commonwealth determined to fill in the area and sell lots for dwellings, subject to restrictions in conformity with a comprehensive land use plan.

With some exceptions and minor variations the same stipulations and agreements were inserted into all the deeds to land in the Back Bay district, from the Commonwealth as grantor to various private grantees, beginning in 1857.

General Laws ch. 184, §30, on which the petitioners rely, provides that no restriction shall be enforced or declared to be enforceable unless it is determined that the restriction is, at the time of the proceeding, of actual and substantial benefit to a person claiming rights of enforcement. Further, even if a restriction is found to be of such benefit, it shall not be enforced except by award of money damages if any of several enumerated conditions are found to exist.

The facts are as follows. The petitioners are the owners of two parcels of land separated by Public Alley No. 437; the first is known as 2, 4, 6, 8, and 10 Commonwealth Avenue and the second as 13-15 Arlington Street and 1, 3, and 5 Newbury Street. The former is presently a vacant lot; the latter is the site of the Ritz-Carlton Hotel. Both are subject to various of the Commonwealth Restrictions. The petitioners plan to build on the former lot a 285 foot high hotel-apartment building, with a twelve-story structure as a bridge over the alley, connecting it with the Ritz-Carlton. Plans call for the new building to contain such restaurant and shopping facilities as are usually incidental to the running of a large hotel, and an underground garage for off-street parking as required by the Boston Zoning Code.

The respondents are the owners of 12-14 Commonwealth Avenue, a parcel which is adjacent to the petitioners' vacant lot and backs on the same alley. This property contains an eight-story building with eight apartments on each floor except the first, half facing Commonwealth Avenue and half the alley in back, half (the corner apartments) being of two rooms and half efficiency apartments. The thirty-two rear apartments derive their principal light and air from one window in each apartment on the alley.

Among the restrictions contained in the original deeds to the parcel numbered 4, 6, 8, and 10 Commonwealth Avenue are the following:

> (a) That a passageway, sixteen feet wide, is to be laid out in the rear of the premises, the same to be filled in by the Commonwealth, and to be kept open and maintained by the abutters in common. . . . (b) That any building erected on the premises . . . shall not in any event be used . . . for any . . . mercantile . . . purposes. . . . (c) That any building erected on the premises . . . shall not in any event be used for a stable. . . . (d) That no cellar or lower floor of any building shall be placed more than four feet below the level of the Mill Dam, as fixed by the top surface of the hammered stone at the Southeasterly corner of the emptying sluices. (e) That the front wall (of any building erected on the premises) . . . shall be set back twenty feet . . . provided that steps, windows, porticoes, and other usual projections appurtenant thereto, are to be allowed in said reserved space of twenty feet.

Among the restrictions contained in the original deed to the parcel numbered 2 Commonwealth Avenue are the same restrictions as those applicable to the parcel numbered 4, 6, 8, and 10 Commonwealth Avenue except that any building constructed thereon shall be set back from Commonwealth Avenue twenty-two feet, rather than twenty feet as stipulated for 4, 6, 8, and 10 Commonwealth Avenue. Among the restrictions contained in the original deeds to the parcels numbered 13-15 Arlington Street and 1, 3, and 5 Newbury Street is the following: "That a passageway, sixteen feet wide, is to be laid out in the rear of the premises," the same to be filled in by the Commonwealth, and to be kept open and maintained by the abutters in common. . . . "

We have found no error in the judge's decision that none of these restrictions shall be enforced, except in so far as he found that no damages shall be awarded. We note that the most difficult aspect of this case concerns the passageway. There will be no obstruction to the movements of persons or vehicles, since the bridge between the Ritz-Carlton building and the new building will start at a point thirteen feet above the ground. Nevertheless, the bridge will occupy most of the space between the two buildings for a height of twelve stories, with consequent effect on light and air. For this reason we have determined, as discussed later in this opinion, that damages are to be awarded for loss of light and air. . . .

Equity does not invariably and automatically grant specific enforcement of such restrictions on the use of land. While the usual grounds for denying such enforcement in a case involving real property is *laches*, or other inequitable conduct by the party seeking to enforce the restriction, this need not always be the case. The *Restatement of Property* §563 (1944) would deny enforcement, apparently without compensation, if the "harm done by granting the injunction will be disproportionate to the benefit secured thereby." The official comments . . . suggest[ ] that the standard be a "disproportion . . . of considerable magnitude." . . .

The . . . restriction . . . mandat[es] that the passageway behind the petitioners' lot, now Public Alley No. 437, shall "be kept open." The judge found, on evidence which clearly supports his findings, that the respondents have an actual and substantial benefit in the enforcement of this restriction and that the proposed building would violate it. However, his further findings that the restriction is obsolete and that the respondents are entitled to only nominal damages are plainly wrong. We nevertheless hold that, even though it is not obsolete, the restriction shall not be specifically enforced. . . . In lieu of specific enforcement, damages are to be awarded.

Considerable and conflicting evidence was adduced at trial as to the potential effect that bridging the alley would have on the light and air available to the apartments in the rear of the respondents' building. It appears that all parties are in agreement that the "bridge" would decrease the direct sunlight available to the apartments; the dispute is as to the magnitude of the decrease. The testimony on ambient light and on available air was conflicting as to whether there would be an increase or a decrease. Clearly there would be some effect on the property. There was testimony to support a finding that the effect would not be *de minimis* but would be substantial. . . .

There are several alternatives in [Mass. Gen. Laws] ch. 184, §30, which support the judge's decision to deny specific enforcement. On the evidence in this case, the petitioners have made a compelling case for such denial based on all of the following statutory grounds: "(1) changes in the character of the properties affected or their neighborhood . . . [and] in applicable public controls of land use or construction, or in any other conditions or circumstances, [which] reduce materially the need for the restriction or the likelihood of the restriction accomplishing its original purposes . . . or (4) continuation of the restriction on the parcel against which enforcement is claimed . . . would impede reasonable use of land for purposes for which it is most suitable, and would tend to impair the growth of the neighborhood or municipality in a manner inconsistent with the public interest . . . or (5) enforcement, except by award of money damages, is for any other reason inequitable or not in the public interest."

Applying these criteria, we observe that the evidence shows, *inter alia*, that the properties and the neighborhood have drastically changed. Single-family residences have been replaced by moderately high-rise buildings for apartments and institutional use. We have found that the passageway restriction is of an actual and substantial benefit in its effect on light and air, but the proposed bridge will have only a modest impact in view of the drastic changes which have already occurred. In particular, an occupant of the respondents' building, in looking out a rear window of that structure, would see to his immediate left and across the passageway the high-rise Ritz-Carlton building. As to the petitioners' unused land to that viewer's immediate left, on the same side of the passageway, it seems inevitable that, even if the bridge were not permitted, a building higher than the respondents' building would at some time be constructed on it. . . .

The record also clearly supports a conclusion that continued enforcement of the restriction would tend to impede reasonable use of the land for purposes for which it is most suitable. The uncontradicted evidence was that a free standing tower is economically unfeasible presumably because of the small size of the parcel, and that the plaintiffs' proposal for an apartment-hotel complex connected to the adjacent Ritz-Carlton is the most suitable use of the land.

The evidence supports a conclusion that the proposed bridge is not an arbitrary and unnecessarily large intrusion. The twelve stories of the bridge relate to twelve of the lower floors of the new building which are to be used as a hotel; above those floors there will be apartments. The hotel floors are feasible only if connected to the hotel services of the Ritz Carlton. Therefore, all considerations of equity, and the most suitable use of the property, support the planned bridge construction in size as well as purpose.

Weighing and comparing the interests of the parties and the public in accordance with the several provisions of §30 brings us almost inevitably to the conclusion that there should be no specific enforcement. In the words of provision (5) of the statute, which unquestionably confers the broadest discretion on the court, enforcement here would be inequitable and not in the public interest. The magnitude of the harm to the petitioners in specific enforcement of the restriction far exceeds that to the respondents in its denial. Moreover we are mandated by the statute to have due regard for the public interest in determining the manner of enforcement of a restriction. The land in question has been vacant for over a decade. We take judicial notice of the exceedingly high property tax rates current in the city of Boston and the beneficial effect on the tax base of the petitioners' plan to construct a multimillion dollar project of public usefulness on presently unutilized land. In the circumstances both the balance of equities between the parties and a consideration of the public interest require that the respondents accept money damages by way of enforcement of this restriction. . . .

The final decree is reversed and the case is remanded to the Superior Court, where damages are to be assessed for the loss of benefit in light and air. Such further evidence as the judge deems to be necessary shall be heard on the issue of damages. . . .

FRANCIS QUIRICO, Justice, dissenting, with whom REARDON, J., joins.

. . . I agree with today's holding by the court that the restriction with respect to the passageway "was designed to preserve light and air to the properties it benefited," and that "[a]s this urban area has grown and become ever more congested in the century since this restriction was first imposed, light and air have become more, not less, valuable. The restriction securing the respondents' rights to them is certainly not obsolete."

The question then becomes what remedy or relief is available to the parties. This court holds that notwithstanding its findings that the passageway restriction is of actual and substantial benefit to the respondents and that it has not become obsolete, the petitioners have the right, under the terms of Mass. Gen. Laws ch. 184, §30, to compel the respondents to receive money damages in lieu of their right to specific enforcement of the restriction. . . .

. . . I do not agree with the ultimate conclusion that under §30 the respondents' relief should be limited to money damages rather than specific enforcement of the restriction relating to the open passageway.

1. The court relies in part on its conclusion that "the properties and the neighborhood have drastically changed (since the restrictions were imposed). Single family residences have been replaced by moderately high-rise buildings for apartments and institutional use." I do not consider this change to be drastic. It seems clear to me from the record that Commonwealth Avenue in the block between Arlington and Berkeley streets, with its unique architectural and physical features, is one of the few remaining residential boulevards in the city, providing a welcome oasis amidst the skyward push of Boston's newer commercial buildings. Contrary to the court's conclusion, I believe that the erection of a twelve-story bridging structure at the very entrance of this block does constitute "an arbitrary and unnecessarily large intrusion" which is not justified by any change in the character of the area. . . .

NOTES AND QUESTIONS

1. As with easements, many states have marketable title statutes that terminate restrictive covenants if they are not re-recorded after a specified period of time. Mass. Gen. Laws ch. 184, §27; N.C. Gen. Stat. §§47B-2, 47B-4; Wis. Stat. §893.33(6). Other states place rigid time limits on the enforceability of covenants and do not let them be continued simply by re-recording them. Minn. Stat. §500.20. In those states, owners who wish to continue the covenants would have to enter a new agreement.

2. Was Blakeley v. Gorin correctly decided?

3. In Hess v. Gilson, 24 Mass. Law. Wkly. 1881 (May 20, 1996) (Land Ct.), defendants violated a restrictive covenant by building a house more than 20 feet above the height of local hilltops. However, because the plaintiff owners of the dominant estate failed to object while the construction was proceeding, and because the defendants' house obstructed the plaintiffs' view of only a "very small piece of sky," the Massachusetts Land Court applied the statute interpreted in Blakeley and held that it would be "inequitable to order specific enforcement of the restriction or to award the plaintiffs damages for its violation." Did the judge properly apply the statute?

PROBLEMS

1. Massachusetts has also adopted a statute providing that "[c]onditions or restrictions, unlimited as to time, by which the title or use of real property is affected, shall be limited to the term of thirty years after the date of the deed or other instrument or the date of the probate of the will creating them, except in cases of gifts or devises for public, charitable or religious purposes." Mass. Gen. Laws ch. 184, §23.

    a.   A developer creates a subdivision with covenants restricting each parcel to a single-family home. The declaration provides that the covenants are intended to last for 250 years. An owner challenges the covenant 100 years after its creation. Is the covenant enforceable?

    b.   Assume instead that the declaration provides that the covenants are intended to last "so long as an elementary school continues to exist on Elm Street." Is this covenant enforceable 35 years after its creation?

2. Georgia limits covenants to 20 years in municipalities with zoning laws. Ga. Code §44-5-60(b). A covenant provides that it will last for ten years and be renewed

automatically unless two thirds of the residents vote not to renew. Is such a covenant enforceable more than 20 years after its creation? *See Sweeney v. Landings Association, Inc.*, 595 S.E.2d 74 (Ga. 2004) (holding that it is).[23]

§5.5 Regulation of Covenants and Homeowners Associations

§5.5.1 COMMON INTEREST COMMUNITIES

§5.5.1.1 Homeowners Associations and Condominimus

Contractually created land use restrictions are normally enforced by owners of the dominant estates intended to benefit from the restrictions. It is increasingly common, however, for a developer of a subdivision to create a *homeowners association* (or, as the *Restatement (Third)* calls them, "common interest community associations," *Id.* at §6.2), that is empowered to enforce the covenants or restrictions, usually by bringing lawsuits to compel compliance. Residential and commercial condominium complexes similarly create condominium associations that usually have the power to enforce covenants. There has been an explosion of interest in this kind of housing arrangement in the last 30 years. As of 1990, 11 percent of all American housing was governed by a homeowners association. Evan McKenzie, Privatopia: Homeowners Associations and the Rise of Residential Private Governments 11 (1994). As much as 25 to 30 percent of the U.S. population may now be living in such housing. Jesse Dukeminier and James E. Krier, Property 919 (4th ed. 1998).

The homeowners association is created by a declaration filed by the developer prior to sale of the first lot. Each of the owners is a member of the association. Those owners are empowered to vote for the members of a board, called the board of trustees or board of managers, to manage the association's common interests. Not all residents of the neighborhood are entitled to vote; only owners have voting rights; tenants and other family members are not entitled to vote in board elections. Nor are voting rights allocated on the one person-one vote principle applicable to public elections; rather, they are allocated by reference to property interests. Just as shareholders of corporations generally have votes based on the number of shares they own, votes in homeowners associations may be unequal because they may be based on lot sizes.

In addition to enforcing covenants, homeowners associations may be empowered to collect dues and fees from the owners to maintain common areas such as roads and recreational facilities and rooftops and hallways of condominiums. They are also often empowered to promulgate bylaws or rules governing use of common areas and perhaps even the appearance and use of individual lots or units. In effect, these associations function somewhat like local governments, except that votes are not based on "one person-one vote" but are based on property ownership. This means that votes are limited to owners rather than tenants or other family members, and owners must

---

23. Although Ga. Code §44-5-60(d) allows automatic renewal of covenants in planned subdivisions with 15 or more units unless two thirds of owners agree to terminate them, the Georgia courts determined that statutes altering the length of covenants cannot be applied retroactively to covenants entered into before they was passed. *Appalachee Enters. v. Walker*, 463 S.E.2d 896 (Ga. 1995).

determine how they will vote when, for example, co-owners disagree about how to vote on a resolution.

Condominiums are a relatively recent form of common ownership of residential property, becoming widespread in the United States only in the 1960s.[24] Jesse Dukeminier and James E. Krier, Property 919-920 (4th ed. 1998). Each unit in a condominium is owned in fee simple by a particular person or entity. The common areas of the condominium — the exterior walls, the roof, the stairwells, hallways, and basement — are owned by all the unit owners collectively as tenants in common. Each owner finances the acquisition of his individual unit, ordinarily by getting a mortgage from a bank. If he defaults on his mortgage payments, the bank will foreclose on his individual unit; other units in the building will not be directly affected. In addition, each unit owner is responsible for property tax payments on his unit. Again, if he fails to make these payments, the city may foreclose on his individual unit to satisfy his tax obligations; other units are not affected by this.

Every owner in the condominium is a member of the condominium association. Ownership interests are generally proportional to the percentage of the building taken up by the individual unit. Thus, a larger apartment may have a larger ownership interest. Votes in the condominium association are generally determined by the ownership share; an owner of a 16 percent interest has 16 percent of the votes. (This is similar to the voting practices of shareholders in corporations.) As with homeowners associations, the condominium association generally picks a board of trustees to manage the common areas of the condominium, sign contracts on behalf of the condominium association for maintenance and rehabilitation, assess fees to maintain common areas, buy insurance for common areas, and enforce servitudes restricting use of individual units.

The condominium is normally set up by filing a *declaration* with the local recording office or registry of deeds. The deeds for each unit will refer to, and incorporate the terms of, the declaration. The declaration functions like a constitution for the condominium association; it defines the management structure of the condominium, explains how the board of trustees is to be chosen, and defines the powers of both the board of trustees and the condominium association itself. It normally enables the condominium association to pass *bylaws* or *rules* governing use of the units. The declaration may also include *covenants* restricting the use of the condominium as a whole and the use of individual units. The declaration also generally requires unit owners to pay monthly *fees* to the condominium association for purposes of maintaining common areas, obtaining insurance, and the like; owners are also required to contribute to periodic expenses that may not be covered by the basic fees, such as the cost of replacing the roof. Those fees, like the unit owners' votes, are proportional to their interests in the condominium.

State condominium statutes regulate condominiums by providing basic ground rules for the organization of the condominium. These statutes may define the basic structure of the condominium association, requiring a declaration, bylaws, and supermajority votes, such as 60 percent or 75 percent, for certain decisions of the association. The statutes ordinarily prohibit partition of common areas.

The *Restatement (Third)* refers to both homeowners associations and condominium associations as "common-interest communities." §§6.1, 6.2. The common interest element is based on the fact that owners are burdened (or benefited) by servitudes that

---

24. They are also used in commercial settings, such as office buildings.

require them to pay fees to maintain commonly owned property or to finance the operations of the association that provides services to both commonly owned and individually owned property and/or is empowered to enforce servitudes burdening the property in the neighborhood. §6.2. The California Supreme Court has now adopted the term "common interest development" and tangentially "community associations." *Nahrstedt v. Lakeside Village Condominium Association, Inc.*, 878 P.2d 1275 (Cal. 1994). Do these terms strike you as appropriate descriptions of homeowners and condominium associations?

Two kinds of conflicts are common in "common-interest communities." The first involves conflicts between unit owners and the developer of the condominium or subdivision, often over management contracts. The second involves conflicts among the unit owners themselves. This often takes the form of a lawsuit between an individual member and the association or board of trustees, with the plaintiff objecting to some policy judgment made by the association or some restriction placed on the use of the plaintiff's unit. Other times, the association may sue an individual member for violating the rules of the condominium or failing to pay her dues or assessed fees.

§5.5.1.2   Cooperatives

The condominium must be distinguished from the *cooperative*. In a cooperative arrangement, the entire building is owned by a single nonprofit cooperative corporation. Individual owners buy shares in the corporation and then lease their individual units from the corporation. Since ownership is vested in the corporation, the entire cooperative will be financed by a single mortgage loan obtained by the corporation itself. The monthly payment by each owner (in the form of rent) covers that owner's share of the mortgage payment, as well as fees for upkeep and management. If an individual owner fails to make her monthly payment to the corporation, other owners must make up the difference in order to prevent foreclosure. Defaulting tenants can be evicted by the corporation and lose their stock. The greater financial interdependence of cooperative owners makes this a more fragile structure than the condominium structure; it is therefore much less common. Because of the financial interdependence of cooperative owners, cooperatives often assume the power to approve or veto sales of particular units to protect other cooperative members' collective financial stake in the building.

§5.5.1.3   Community Land Trusts and Limited Equity Coops

In recent years, advocates for the poor have been creative in inventing new forms of landholding tailored to low-income persons. Two widely used forms are *limited equity cooperatives* and *community land trusts*. Although structured differently, the purpose of these ownership forms is "to remove land from the speculative market, create housing for low income people, and keep that housing affordable." Christopher Seeger, *The Fixed Price Preemptive Right in the Community Land Trust Lease: A Valid Response to the Housing Crisis or an Invalid Restraint on Alienation?*, 11 Cardozo L. Rev. 471 (1989). What follows is a brief introduction to these new forms of common ownership and a discussion of legal problems associated with them.

Community land trusts. A community land trust is a nonprofit corporation that generally has an elected board of directors (or board of trustees) and an open membership. The trust buys and holds title to property, ordinarily by acquiring inexpensive land located in a depressed area or land whose purchase is subsidized by government loans, loan guarantees, or subsidies. While retaining title to the land, the trust sells the building located on the land to a low-income purchaser or group of purchasers. Separating ownership of the land and the building requires a lease by the trust, as owner of the land, granting possessory rights to the owner of the building; this arrangement, called a *ground lease,* is common in commercial transactions involving large office buildings. The ground lease ordinarily lasts for a long time — often 99 years — and may be renewable. Because the trust retains title to the land and because, as a nonprofit organization, its purpose is to finance affordable housing for low-income persons, the trust sells the building and provides terms in the ground lease at rates that low-income persons can afford. The trust is willing and able to do so because (1) it retains title to the land and sells only the building; (2) as a nonprofit organization, its purpose is to provide affordable housing to low-income persons rather than to maximize profit or make a return on its investment; (3) it has purchased a structure in an area with low real estate values or one that needs repair; and (4) it ordinarily receives various forms of financial assistance, such as loan guarantees (low-interest government loans financed with tax-exempt bonds issued by a state housing finance agency), local property tax abatements, contributions from charitable organizations such as churches and synagogues, and direct government subsidies such as the federal Section 8 program, which gives qualified tenants the right to have a portion of their rent paid by the federal government.

A crucial aspect of the ground lease arrangement is the agreement between the owner and the lessee-purchaser that the building will be sold only to the community land trust, or to another low-income owner, at a price well below market value (not on the open market for its fair market value). This price ordinarily is fixed at an amount equal to the owner's initial investment (the purchase price) and future investment (mortgage principal payments plus costs of improvements made by the owner), with an adjustment for inflation. David Abramowitz, *Nuts and Bolts on Land Trusts, Housing Matters* 4-5 (Massachusetts Law Reform Inst., January/February 1989). Generally, the ground lease gives the community land trust a right of first refusal to purchase the building for the fixed price. This arrangement ensures that the property will remain low cost and therefore available to other low-income families and persons in the future.

Limited equity cooperatives. A limited equity cooperative has a purpose similar to a community land trust but is organized like a regular cooperative. The purchaser buys shares in the cooperative and obtains a lease to a particular unit. The contracts involved in this arrangement allow sale of the owner's shares at a fixed price, thus preventing the owner from benefiting from increases in the market value of the unit. Sometimes the owner is allowed to sell the shares to a third party at the fixed price; often the arrangement gives the cooperative a right of first refusal to purchase the shares, with their accompanying possessory rights, at the prearranged price. Judith Bernstein-Baker, *Cooperative Conversion: Is It Only for the Wealthy? Proposals That Promote Affordable Cooperative Housing in Philadelphia,* 61 Temple L. Rev. 393 (1988).

§5.5.1.4   Private Governments and Gated Communities

Homeowners associations raise numerous issues both about the legitimate scope of their powers over individual owners and their ability to engage in exclusionary conduct that may both discriminatorily deny access to the community and privatize previously public areas such as roads and recreational facilities. Some scholars laud the benefits of such associations, emphasizing the fact that the law grants owners the freedom to create forms of property ownership that are tailored to their individual interests. Purchase of property subject to covenants and governance by an association may be something that owners desire, increasing the attractiveness and value of the property. *See, e.g.,* Robert C. Ellickson, *Cities and Homeowners Associations,* 130 U. Pa. L. Rev. 1519 (1982). Others, however, criticize such associations because they often engage in exclusionary and sometimes discriminatory conduct. Homeowners associations also limit voting rights to owners, thereby disenfranchising renters. In addition, they may engage in oppressive micromanagement of individual units, thereby infringing on the liberty interests of owners to be free from control by their neighbors. Gerald E. Frug, Cities and Homeowners Associations: A Reply, 130 U. Pa. L. Rev. 1589 (1982); McKenzie, Privatopia, supra.

Some developers have completely privatized what had once been public facilities, such as roads, sidewalks, parks, and other recreational facilities. They may even post guards at the entrance to the neighborhood, creating a so-called gated community that limits entrance. Depending on one's viewpoint, such communities provide security to families and children by monitoring entrance, or they convert neighborhoods to private domains that are intended to protect residents from associating with persons different from themselves. By privatizing roads and recreational facilities and limiting voting rights to owners, they also create "private governments" that are either desirable results of free contract among like-minded individuals who have created the kind of housing and environment that suits their needs or are undesirable oligarchies that govern on the basis of property rights rather than norms of equal citizenship. What do you think? Consider the following materials.

§5.5.2   RELATIONS BETWEEN UNIT OWNERS AND DEVELOPERS

APPEL v. PRESLEY COMPANIES
806 P.2d 1054 (N.M. 1991)

GENE E. FRANCHINI, Justice.

Plaintiffs Daniel and Patricia Appel appeal from an order granting summary judgment to defendants The Presley Company of New Mexico (Presley) and Wolfe Company, Inc. (Wolfe). The Appels are homeowners in the Vista Del Sandia subdivision in Albuquerque, which is owned by Presley. Wolfe is a developer and the owner of a tract in the subdivision on which it intends to build four townhouses. In their complaint, the Appels asserted three claims: breach of restrictive covenants; negligent and fraudulent misrepresentation; and unfair trade practices. They requested a permanent injunction enjoining Wolfe from constructing any building on its lot unless it complied with the restrictive covenants applicable to the subdivision. The Appels also requested a permanent injunction enjoining Presley from constructing any building in the arroyo area of the subdivision. In addition, the Appels sought compensatory and punitive damages against Presley. We reverse and remand.

Facts

On January 3, 1979, Presley recorded with the Bernalillo County Clerk a replat for the Vista Del Sandia subdivision. On October 8, 1982, Presley recorded a set of restrictive covenants covering all the property shown on the replat, including a tract in the subdivision arroyo. The covenants regulated the land use, building type, quality, and size of the residential single-family dwellings that were to be placed on the subdivision property. In November 1982, the Appels met with Presley and its agents regarding the possible purchase of a lot in the subdivision. The Appels allege certain representations were made concerning lots in the subdivision and the purpose of the restrictive covenants. The Appels further allege that the restrictive covenants were used as a sales tool which they relied on in purchasing a lot and constructing their home. On April 25, 1984, the subdivision's Architectural Control Committee, consisting of three members who were all employees or officers of Presley, executed an amendment of the restrictive covenants. This amendment deleted nine lots from the effect of the restrictive covenants, including Lots 28-A and 30 which are involved in this appeal. Since the covenants were amended, some of the lots have been subdivided into smaller lots and townhouses have been constructed on them. Presley sold Lot 28-A to Wolfe in April 1988. Wolfe is replatting Lot 28-A into four lots for single family residences. No development plans exist for Lot 30, the arroyo lot.

I. Restrictive Covenants

... The Appels filed their complaint to enjoin Wolfe's proposed replatting and construction and to enjoin the construction of any buildings on Lot 30. The following provisions contained in the restrictive covenants were relied on by the trial court to authorize the amendments:

> 15. Architectural Control Committee: ... At any time, the then record owners of the majority of the lots shall have the power, through a duly recorded written instrument, to change the membership of the Committee or to withdraw from the Committee, or restore to it any of its powers and duties. ...
>
> 17. Terms of covenants: These covenants are to run with the land and shall be binding on all parties and all persons claiming under them for a period of thirty (30) years from the date these covenants are recorded, after which time said covenants shall be automatically extended for successive periods of ten (10) years, unless an instrument signed by a majority of the then lot owners of the lots have been recorded, agreeing to change said covenants in whole or in part. ...
>
> 20. Variance: A majority of the Architectural Control Committee, may from time to time, make amendments and/or exceptions to these restrictions, covenants and reservations without the consent of any of the owners of any of the other lots in said subdivision.

In particular, the trial court emphasized the "amendments and/or exceptions to these restrictions" language of paragraph 20 in the restrictive covenants. The trial court found that the language was unambiguous and that the covenant permitted the Architectural Control Committee to make exceptions and remove individual lots from the covenants. This court has recognized the importance of enforcing protective covenants where the clear language of the covenants, as well as the surrounding circumstances, indicates an intent to restrict use of land. In *Montoya v. Barreras,* 473 P.2d 363 (N.M. 1970), we refused to allow an individual lot to be removed from the effect of a restrictive covenant in spite of a provision in the covenant allowing change by majority approval. We held: "To permit individual lots within an area to be relieved of the burden of such covenants, in the absence of a clear expression in the instrument so providing, would destroy the right to rely on restrictive convenants which has traditionally been upheld by our law of real property." Id. at 365. Here, the trial court found the "amendments and/or exceptions to these restrictions" language to be the clear expression required by Montoya.

We agree that the language permitted the Architectural Control Committee to make amendments or exceptions to the restrictive covenant. However, courts have determined that provisions allowing amendment of subdivision restrictions are subject to a requirement of reasonableness. As stated in 7 G. Thompson, Real Property, §3171 (repl. 1962), "A court of equity will not enforce restrictions where there are circumstances that render their enforcement inequitable. . . ."

In *Flamingo Ranch Estates, Inc. v. Sunshine Ranches Homeowners, Inc.,* 303 So. 2d 665 (Fla. Dist. Ct. App. 1974), the court addressed a similar clause reserving to the land developer the right to alter, amend, repeal, or modify restrictions at any time in his sole discretion. The court noted the inherent inconsistency between an elaborate set of restrictive covenants, designed to provide for a general scheme or plan of development, and a clause reserving in the grantor the power to change or abandon any part of it. The court reconciled the inconsistency by reading into the restrictive clause a requirement of reasonableness. Thus, the clause allowing the owners the right to alter, amend, repeal, or modify these restrictions at any time in its sole discretion is a valid clause so long as it is exercised in a reasonable manner so as not to destroy the general scheme or plan of development.

The Supreme Court of Alabama also imposed a test of reasonableness when a developer exercised his reserved right to cancel or modify any of the restrictive covenants. *Moore v. Megginson,* 461 So. 2d 993 (Ala. 1982). The court affirmed the trial court's finding that the developer's "exercise of his right to cancel or modify the restrictive covenants 'must be reasonable, with due regard for the property rights and investments of the persons who relied upon the residential covenants which were in full force at the time of their purchase.'" *Id.*

A determination of whether the exceptions were reasonably exercised or whether they essentially destroyed the covenants requires resolution of a factual matter and, therefore, the summary judgment must be reversed and testimony should be taken accordingly. Additionally, if it is found that the exceptions were applied in an unreasonable manner, thereby breaching the covenants, the trial court should apply the doctrine of relative hardships.

As we stated in *Cunningham* [*v. Gross,* 699 P.2d 1075 (N.M. 1985)], any request for injunctive relief is directed to the sound discretion of the trial court. "In determining whether such relief should issue, the court may consider a number of factors and should balance equities and hardships where required." 699 P.2d at 1077. Factors for the trial court to consider include, *id.* at 1078:

(1) [T]he character of the interest to be protected, (2) the relative adequacy to the plaintiff of injunction in comparison with other remedies, (3) the delay, if any, in bringing suit, (4)

the misconduct of the plaintiff if any, (5) the interest of third persons, (6) the practicability of granting and enforcing the order or judgment, and (7) the relative hardship likely to result to the defendant if an injunction is granted and to the plaintiff if it is denied.

In view of the foregoing, we reverse and remand on the trial court's order granting summary judgment on Claim I....

II. Misrepresentation and Unfair Trade Practices Act

The trial court erred ... finding no material issue of fact regarding misrepresentation and violation of the *[Unfair] Trade Practices Act.* The trial court focused only on statements made by Presley representatives in 1982 about certain lots not being developable, ignoring other alleged misrepresentations concerning the effect of the covenants.... The Appels produced sufficient evidence to raise factual questions as to whether Presley misrepresented that Lot 30 would remain open space and that the covenants would maintain the intended character of the subdivision. Whether or not the statements made to the Appels about Lots 28-A and 30 were true or false at the time made are issues of fact to be determined at trial, not by the court on summary judgment.

The order granting summary judgment by the trial court is reversed on all three claims and the cause is remanded for reinstatement for trial upon the court's docket.

NOTES AND QUESTIONS

The developer of a condominium initially owns all the units and therefore controls the condominium association. Because the developer has more than 50 percent of the votes before the majority of the units are sold, the developer has substantial power to make policy for the condominium. Some developers in this situation arrange for management contracts in which the condominium hires the developer as manager of the condominium in exchange for management fees. Many problems have arisen with these contracts; owners often have found their terms unfair either because the fees charged by the developer-manager are exorbitant or because the contracts last for such long periods of time that the condominium owners cannot get out of them and hire someone else if they become dissatisfied with the way the place is being run.

A federal law passed in 1980, the Condominium and Cooperative Conversion Protection and Abuse Relief Act, 15 U.S.C. §§3601 to 3616, authorizes condominiums and cooperatives formed after 1980, by a two-thirds vote, to terminate without penalty management contracts of more than three years entered into between the association and the developer while the developer had majority control of the condominium or cooperative. §3607(a). The right to terminate lasts for only two years after the developer ceases to control the association or owns 25 percent or less of the units, whichever occurs first. §3607(b).

Many states have also passed statutes regulating these contracts, often providing that they can be rejected by a supermajority vote. For example, in *Tri-Properties, Inc. v. Moonspinner Condominium Association, Inc.,* 447 So. 2d 965 (Fla. Dist. Ct. App. 1984), the court applied a Florida statute that allowed 75 percent or more of the unit ownership rights to repudiate a management contract entered into between the developer and the condominium association when the developer controlled the association. In *Barclay v. DeVeau,* 429 N.E.2d 323 (Mass. 1981), the court held that the state condominium statute authorized condominium arrangements that granted substantial management power to developers. The court also held, however, that an implied time limit was contained in a provision in the condominium declaration allowing the developer to pick a majority of the members of the board of trustees so long as 12 units remained unsold. The developer could retain control of the board only during the "marketing phase," when it was making reasonable efforts to sell the units; after that, control would have to devolve to the other unit owners.

§5.5.3   RACIALLY DISCRIMINATORY COVENANTS

A racially restrictive covenant limits the sale, lease, or occupancy of real property to members of a particular race or excludes members of a particular race or races. Historically, most restrictive covenants were used to exclude African Americans from residential communities. Covenants were also widely used to exclude other groups, including American Indians, Jews, Asian Americans, and Hispanic Americans or Latinos. Now such covenants are unenforceable under constitutional, statutory, and common law and may even subject those who enter into them to monetary liability under civil rights statutes.

Until the 1948 decision of *Shelley v. Kraemer, infra,* the practice of including covenants in deeds restricting ownership, possession, and occupancy of the land to white persons was widespread. Moreover, in the vast majority of states, such covenants were valid and enforceable. A minority of states, by common law or statute, declared such covenants void and unenforceable as contrary to public policy. *See Erickson v. Sunset Memorial Park Association,* 108 N.W.2d 434 (Minn. 1961) (applying a state statute to compel a cemetery to sell plots to an American Indian woman and her husband contrary to a restrictive covenant); *In re George Washington Memorial Park Cemetery Association,* 145 A.2d 665 (N.J. Super. Ct. Ch. Div. 1958) (applying a state statute prohibiting racial discrimination by cemeteries and holding that a covenant restricting burial privileges to persons of the "white or caucasian race" was unenforceable under public policy).

SHELLEY v. KRAEMER
334 U.S. 1 (1948)

Mr. Chief Justice FRED VINSON delivered the opinion of the Court.

These cases present for our consideration questions relating to the validity of court enforcement of private agreements, generally described as restrictive covenants, which have as their purpose the exclusion of persons of designated race or color from the ownership or occupancy of real property. Basic constitutional issues of obvious importance have been raised.

The first of these cases comes to this Court on certiorari to the Supreme Court of Missouri. On February 16, 1911, thirty out of a total of thirty-nine owners of property fronting both sides of Labadie Avenue between Taylor Avenue and Cora Avenue in the city of St. Louis, signed an agreement, which was subsequently recorded, providing in part:

[T]he said property is hereby restricted to the use and occupancy for the term of Fifty (50) years from this date, so that it shall be a condition all the time and whether recited and referred to as [sic] not in subsequent conveyances and shall attach to the land, as a condition precedent to the sale of the same, that hereafter no part of said property or any portion thereof shall be, for said term of Fifty-years, occupied by any person not of the Caucasian race, it being intended hereby to restrict the use of said property for said period of time against the occupancy as owners or tenants of any portion of said property for resident or other purpose by people of the Negro or Mongolian Race.

The entire district described in the agreement included fifty-seven parcels of land. The thirty owners who signed the agreement held title to forty-seven parcels, including the particular parcel involved in this case. At the time the agreement was signed, five of the parcels in the district were owned by Negroes. One of those had been occupied by Negro families since 1882, nearly thirty years before the restrictive agreement was executed. The trial court found that owners of seven out of nine homes on the south side of Labadie Avenue, within the restricted district and "in the immediate vicinity" of the premises in question, had failed to sign the restrictive agreement in 1911. At the time this action was brought, four of the premises were occupied by Negroes, and had been so occupied for periods ranging from twenty-three to sixty-three years. A fifth parcel had been occupied by Negroes until a year before this suit was instituted.

On August 11, 1945, pursuant to a contract of sale, petitioners Shelley, who are Negroes, for valuable consideration received from one Fitzgerald a warranty deed to the parcel in question. The trial court found that petitioners had no actual knowledge of the restrictive agreement at the time of the purchase.

On October 9, 1945, respondents, as owners of other property subject to the terms

Photograph by George Harris. Reprinted by permission of Black Star Publishing.

of the restrictive covenant, brought suit in Circuit Court of the city of St. Louis praying that petitioners Shelley be restrained from taking possession of the property and that judgment be entered divesting title out of petitioners Shelley and revesting title in the immediate grantor or in such other person as the court should direct. The trial court denied the requested relief on the ground that the restrictive agreement, upon which respondents based their action, had never become final and complete because it was the intention of the parties to that agreement that it was not to become effective until signed by all property owners in the district, and signatures of all the owners had never been obtained.

The Supreme Court of Missouri sitting en banc reversed and directed the trial court to grant the relief for which respondents had prayed. That court held the agreement effective and concluded that enforcement of its provisions violated no rights guaranteed to petitioners by the Federal Constitution. At the time the court rendered its decision, petitioners were occupying the property in question.

The second of the cases under consideration comes to this Court from the Supreme Court of Michigan. The circumstances presented do not differ materially from the Missouri case. . . .

Petitioners have placed primary reliance on their contentions, first raised in the state courts, that judicial enforcement of the restrictive agreements in these cases has violated rights guaranteed to petitioners by the Fourteenth Amendment of the Federal Constitution and Acts of Congress passed pursuant to that Amendment.[4] Specifically, petitioners urge that they have been denied the equal protection of the laws, deprived of property without due process of law, and have been denied privileges and immunities of citizens of the United States. We pass to a consideration of those issues.

I

. . . It is well, at the outset, to scrutinize the terms of the restrictive agreements involved in these cases. In the Missouri case, the covenant declares that no part of the affected property shall be "occupied by any person not of the Caucasian race, it being intended hereby to restrict the use of said property . . . against the occupancy as owners or tenants of any portion of said property for resident or other purpose by people of the Negro or Mongolian Race." Not only does the restriction seek to proscribe use and occupancy of the affected properties by members of the excluded class, but as construed by the Missouri courts, the agreement requires that title of any person who uses his property in violation of the restriction shall be divested. The restriction of the covenant in the Michigan case seeks to bar occupancy by persons of the excluded class. It provides that "This property shall not be used or occupied by any person or persons except those of the Caucasian race."

---

4. The first section of the Fourteenth Amendment provides: "All persons born or naturalized in the United States, and subject to the jurisdiction thereof, are citizens of the United States and of the State wherein they reside. No State shall make or enforce any law which shall abridge the privileges or immunities of citizens of the United States; nor shall any State deprive any person of life, liberty, or property, without due process of law; nor deny to any person within its jurisdiction the equal protection of the laws."

It should be observed that these covenants do not seek to proscribe any particular use of the affected properties. Use of the properties for residential occupancy, as such, is not forbidden. The restrictions of these agreements, rather, are directed toward a designated class of persons and seek to determine who may and who may not own or make use of the properties for residential purposes. The excluded class is defined wholly in terms of race or color; "simply that and nothing more."

It cannot be doubted that among the civil rights intended to be protected from discriminatory state action by the Fourteenth Amendment are the rights to acquire, enjoy, own and dispose of property. Equality in the enjoyment of property rights was regarded by the framers of that Amendment as an essential pre-condition to the realization of other basic civil rights and liberties which the Amendment was intended to guarantee. Thus, §1978 of the Revised Statutes, derived from §1 of the Civil Rights Act of 1866 [now codified at 42 U.S.C. §1982] which was enacted by Congress while the Fourteenth Amendment was also under consideration, provides:

> All citizens of the United States shall have the same right, in every State and Territory, as is enjoyed by white citizens thereof to inherit, purchase, lease, sell, hold, and convey real and personal property.

. . . It is likewise clear that restrictions on the right of occupancy of the sort sought to be created by the private agreements in these cases could not be squared with the requirements of the Fourteenth Amendment if imposed by state statute or local ordinance. We do not understand respondents to urge the contrary. . . .

But the present cases, unlike those just discussed, do not involve action by state legislatures or city councils. Here the particular patterns of discrimination and the areas in which the restrictions are to operate, are determined, in the first instance, by the terms of agreements among private individuals. Participation of the State consists in the enforcement of the restrictions so defined. The crucial issue with which we are here confronted is whether this distinction removes these cases from the operation of the prohibitory provisions of the Fourteenth Amendment.

Since the decision of this Court in the *Civil Rights Cases*, 109 U.S. 3 (1883), the principle has become firmly embedded in our constitutional law that the action inhibited by the first section of the Fourteenth Amendment is only such action as may fairly be said to be that of the States. That Amendment erects no shield against merely private conduct, however discriminatory or wrongful.

We conclude, therefore, that the restrictive agreements standing alone cannot be regarded as a violation of any rights guaranteed to petitioners by the Fourteenth Amendment. So long as the purposes of those agreements are effectuated by voluntary adherence to their terms, it would appear clear that there has been no action by the State and the provisions of the Amendment have not been violated.

But here there was more. These are cases in which the purposes of the agreements were secured only by judicial enforcement by state courts of the restrictive terms of the agreements. The respondents urge that judicial enforcement of private agreements does not amount to state action; or, in any event, the participation of the State is so attenuated in character as not to amount to state action within the meaning of the Fourteenth Amendment. Finally, it is suggested, even if the States in these cases may be deemed to have acted in the constitutional sense, their action did not deprive petitioners of rights guaranteed by the Fourteenth Amendment. We move to a consideration of these matters.

II

That the action of state courts and of judicial officers in their official capacities is to be regarded as action of the State within the meaning of the Fourteenth Amendment, is a proposition which has long been established by decisions of this Court. . . .

One of the earliest applications of the prohibitions contained in the Fourteenth Amendment to action of state judicial officials occurred in cases in which Negroes had been excluded from jury service in criminal prosecutions by reason of their race or color. These cases demonstrate, also, the early recognition by this Court that state action in violation of the Amendment's provisions is equally repugnant to the constitutional commands whether directed by state statute or taken by a judicial official in the absence of statute. Thus, in *Strauder v. West Virginia,* 100 U.S. 303 (1880), this Court declared invalid a state statute restricting jury service to white persons as amounting to a denial of the equal protection of the laws to the colored defendant in that case. . . .

The action of state courts in imposing penalties or depriving parties of other substantive rights without providing adequate notice and opportunity to defend, has, of course, long been regarded as a denial of the due process of law guaranteed by the Fourteenth Amendment.

In numerous cases, this Court has reversed criminal convictions in state courts for failure of those courts to provide the essential ingredients of a fair hearing. . . .

But the examples of state judicial action which have been held by this Court to violate the Amendment's commands are not restricted to situations in which the judicial proceedings were found in some manner to be procedurally unfair. It has been recognized that the action of state courts in enforcing a substantive common-law rule formulated by those courts, may result in the denial of rights guaranteed by the Fourteenth Amendment, even though the judicial proceedings in such cases may have been in complete accord with the most rigorous conceptions of procedural due process. Thus, in *American Federation of Labor v. Swing,* 312 U.S. 321 (1941), enforcement by state courts of the common-law policy of the State, which resulted in the restraining of peaceful picketing, was held to be state action of the sort prohibited by the Amendment's guaranties of freedom of discussion. . . .

The short of the matter is that from the time of the adoption of the Fourteenth Amendment until the present, it has been the consistent ruling of this Court that the action of the States to which the Amendment has reference, includes action of state courts and state judicial officials. Although, in construing the terms of the Fourteenth Amendment, differences have from time to time been expressed as to whether particular types of state action may be said to offend the Amendment's prohibitory provisions, it has never been suggested that state court action is immunized from the operation of those provisions simply because the act is that of the judicial branch of the state government.

III

Against this background of judicial construction, extending over a period of some three-quarters of a century, we are called upon to consider whether enforcement by state courts of the restrictive agreements in these cases may be deemed to be the acts of those States; and, if so, whether that action has denied these petitioners the equal protection of the laws which the Amendment was intended to insure.

We have no doubt that there has been state action in these cases in the full and complete sense of the phrase. The undisputed facts disclose that petitioners were willing purchasers of properties upon which they desired to establish homes. The owners of the properties were willing sellers; and contracts of sale were accordingly consummated. It is clear that but for the active intervention of the state courts, supported by the full panoply of state power, petitioners would have been free to occupy the properties in question without restraint.

These are not cases, as has been suggested, in which the States have merely abstained from action, leaving private individuals free to impose such discriminations as they see fit. Rather, these are cases in which the States have made available to such individuals the full coercive power of government to deny to petitioners, on the grounds of race or color, the enjoyment of property rights in premises which petitioners are willing and financially able to acquire and which the grantors are willing to sell. The difference between judicial enforcement and nonenforcement of the restrictive covenants is the difference to petitioners between being denied rights of property available to other members of the community and being accorded full enjoyment of those rights on an equal footing.

The enforcement of the restrictive agreements by the state courts in these cases was directed pursuant to the common-law policy of the States as formulated by those courts in earlier decisions. In the Missouri case, enforcement of the covenant was directed in the first instance by the highest court of the State after the trial court had determined the agreement to be invalid for want of the requisite number of signatures. In the Michigan case, the order of enforcement by the trial court was affirmed by the highest state court. The judicial action in each case bears the clear and unmistakable imprimatur of the State. We have noted that previous decisions of this Court have established the proposition that judicial action is not immunized from the operation of the Fourteenth Amendment simply because it is taken pursuant to the state's common-law policy. Nor is the Amendment ineffective simply because the particular pattern of discrimination, which the State has enforced, was defined initially by the terms of a private agreement. State action, as that phrase is understood for the purposes of the Fourteenth Amendment, refers to exertions of state power in all forms. And when the effect of that action is to deny rights subject to the protection of the Fourteenth Amendment, it is the obligation of this Court to enforce the constitutional commands.

Respondents urge, however, that since the state courts stand ready to enforce restrictive covenants excluding white persons from the ownership or occupancy of property covered by such agreements, enforcement of covenants excluding colored persons may not be deemed a denial of equal protection of the laws to the colored persons who are thereby affected. This contention does not bear scrutiny. The parties have directed our attention to no case in which a court, state or federal, has been called upon to enforce a covenant excluding members of the white majority from ownership or occupancy of real property on grounds of race or color. But there are more fundamental considerations. The rights created by the first section of the Fourteenth Amendment are, by its terms, guaranteed to the individual. The rights established are personal rights. It is, therefore, no answer to these petitioners to say that the courts may also be induced to deny white persons rights of ownership and occupancy on grounds of race or color. Equal protection of the laws is not achieved through indiscriminate imposition of inequalities.

Nor do we find merit in the suggestion that property owners who are parties to these agreements are denied equal protection of the laws if denied access to the courts to enforce the terms of restrictive covenants and to assert property rights which the state courts have held to be created by such agreements. The Constitution confers upon no individual the right to demand action by the State which results in the denial of equal protection of the laws to other individuals. And it would appear beyond question that the power of the State to create and enforce property interests must be exercised within the boundaries defined by the Fourteenth Amendment. . . .

The historical context in which the Fourteenth Amendment became a part of the Constitution should not be forgotten. Whatever else the framers sought to achieve, it is clear that the matter of primary concern was the establishment of equality in the enjoyment of basic civil and political rights and the preservation of those rights from discriminatory action on the part of the States based on considerations of race or color. Seventy-five years ago this Court announced that the provisions of the Amendment are to be construed with this fundamental purpose in mind. Upon full consideration, we have concluded that in these cases the States have acted to deny petitioners the equal protection of the laws guaranteed by the Fourteenth Amendment. Having so decided, we find it unnecessary to consider whether petitioners have also been deprived of property without due process of law or denied privileges and immunities of citizens of the United States.

For the reasons stated, the judgment of the Supreme Court of Missouri and the judgment of the Supreme Court of Michigan must be reversed.

EVANS v. ABNEY
396 U.S. 435 (1970)

Mr. Justice HUGO BLACK delivered the opinion of the Court.

Once again this Court must consider the constitutional implications of the 1911 will of United States Senator A. O. Bacon of Georgia which conveyed property in trust to Senator Bacon's home city of Macon for the creation of a public park for the exclusive use of the white people of that city. As a result of our earlier decision in this case which held that the park, Baconsfield, could not continue to be operated on a racially discriminatory basis, *Evans v. Newton,* 382 U.S. 296 (1966), the Supreme Court of Georgia ruled that Senator Bacon's intention to provide a park for whites only had become impossible to fulfill and that accordingly the trust had failed and the parkland and other trust property had reverted by operation of Georgia law to the heirs of the Senator. Petitioners, the same Negro citizens of Macon who have sought in the courts to integrate the park, contend that this termination of the trust violates their rights to equal protection and due process under the Fourteenth Amendment. We granted certiorari because of the importance of the questions involved. For the reasons to be stated, we are of the opinion that the judgment of the Supreme Court of Georgia should be, and it is, affirmed.

The early background of this litigation was summarized by Mr. Justice Douglas in his opinion for the Court in *Evans v. Newton,* 382 U.S., at 297-298:

> In 1911 United States Senator Augustus O. Bacon executed a will that devised to the Mayor and Council of the City of Macon, Georgia, a tract of land which, after the death of the Senator's wife and daughters, was to be used as "a park and pleasure ground" for white

people only, the Senator stating in the will that while he had only the kindest feeling for the Negroes he was of the opinion that "in their social relations the two races (white and negro) should be forever separate." The will provided that the park should be under the control of a Board of Managers of seven persons, all of whom were to be white. The city kept the park segregated for some years but in time let Negroes use it, taking the position that the park was a public facility which it could not constitutionally manage and maintain on a segregated basis.

Thereupon, individual members of the Board of Managers of the park brought this suit in a state court against the City of Macon and the trustees of certain residuary beneficiaries of Senator Bacon's estate, asking that the city be removed as trustee and that the court appoint new trustees, to whom title to the park would be transferred. The city answered, alleging it could not legally enforce racial segregation in the park. The other defendants admitted the allegation and requested that the city be removed as trustee.

Several Negro citizens of Macon intervened, alleging that the racial limitation was contrary to the laws and public policy of the United States, and asking that the court refuse to appoint private trustees. Thereafter the city resigned as trustee and amended its answer accordingly. Moreover, other heirs of Senator Bacon intervened and they and the defendants other than the city asked for reversion of the trust property to the Bacon estate in the event that the prayer of the petition were denied.

The Georgia court accepted the resignation of the city as trustee and appointed three individuals as new trustees, finding it unnecessary to pass on the other claims of the heirs. On appeal by the Negro intervenors, the Supreme Court of Georgia affirmed, holding that Senator Bacon had the right to give and bequeath his property to a limited class, that charitable trusts are subject to supervision of a court of equity, and that the power to appoint new trustees so that the purpose of the trust would not fail was clear.

The Court in *Evans v. Newton, supra,* went on to reverse the judgment of the Georgia Supreme Court and to hold that the public character of Baconsfield "requires that it be treated as a public institution subject to the command of the Fourteenth Amendment, regardless of who now has title under state law." 382 U.S., at 302. Thereafter, the Georgia Supreme Court interpreted this Court's reversal of its decision as requiring that Baconsfield be henceforth operated on a nondiscriminatory basis. "Under these circumstances," the state high court held, "we are of the opinion that the sole purpose for which the trust was created has become impossible of accomplishment and has been terminated." *Evans v. Newton,* 148 S.E.2d 329, 330 (Ga. 1966). Without further elaboration of this holding, the case was remanded to the Georgia trial court to consider the motion of Guyton G. Abney and others, successor trustees of Senator Bacon's estate, for a ruling that the trust had become unenforceable and that accordingly the trust property had reverted to the Bacon estate and to certain named heirs of the Senator. The motion was opposed by petitioners and by the Attorney General of Georgia, both of whom argued that the trust should be saved by applying the cy pres doctrine to amend the terms of the will by striking the racial restrictions and opening Baconsfield to all the citizens of Macon without regard to race or color. The trial court, however, refused to apply cy pres. It held that the doctrine was inapplicable because the park's segregated, whites-only character was an essential and inseparable part of the testator's plan. Since the "sole purpose" of the trust was thus in irreconcilable conflict with the constitutional mandate expressed in our opinion in *Evans v. Newton,* the trial court ruled that the Baconsfield trust had failed and that the trust property had by operation of law reverted to the heirs of Senator Bacon. On appeal, the Supreme Court of Georgia affirmed.

We are of the opinion that in ruling as they did the Georgia courts did no more than apply well-settled general principles of Georgia law to determine the meaning and effect of a Georgia will. At the time Senator Bacon made his will Georgia cities and towns were, and they still are, authorized to accept devises of property for the establishment and preservation of "parks and pleasure grounds" and to hold the property thus received in charitable trust for the exclusive benefit of the class of persons named by the testator. Ga. Code Ann., ch. 69-5 (1967); Ga. Code Ann. §§108-203, 108-207 (1959). These provisions of the Georgia Code explicitly authorized the testator to include, if he should choose, racial restrictions such as those found in Senator Bacon's will. The city accepted the trust with these restrictions in it. When this Court in *Evans v. Newton, supra,* held that the continued operation of Baconsfield as a segregated park was unconstitutional, the particular purpose of the Baconsfield trust as stated in the will failed under Georgia law. The question then properly before the Georgia Supreme Court was whether as a matter of state law the doctrine of *cy pres* should be applied to prevent the trust itself from failing. Petitioners urged that the *cy pres* doctrine allowed the Georgia courts to strike the racially restrictive clauses in Bacon's will so that the terms of the trust could be fulfilled without violating the Constitution.

The Georgia *cy pres* statutes upon which petitioners relied provide:

> When a valid charitable bequest is incapable for some reason of execution in the exact manner provided by the testator, donor, or founder, a court of equity will carry it into effect in such a way as will as nearly as possible effectuate his intention. Ga. Code Ann. §108-202 (1959).

> A devise or bequest to a charitable use will be sustained and carried out in this State; and in all cases where there is a general intention manifested by the testator to effect a certain purpose, and the particular mode in which he directs it to be done shall fail from any cause, a court of chancery may, by approximation, effectuate the purpose in a manner most similar to that indicated by the testator. Ga. Code Ann. §113-815 (1959).

The Georgia courts have held that the fundamental purpose of these *cy pres* provisions is to allow the court to carry out the general charitable intent of the testator where this intent might otherwise be thwarted by the impossibility of the particular plan or scheme provided by the testator. But this underlying logic of the *cy pres* doctrine implies that there is a certain class of cases in which the doctrine cannot be applied. Professor Scott in his treatise on trusts states this limitation on the doctrine of *cy pres* which is common to many States as follows:

> It is not true that a charitable trust never fails where it is impossible to carry out the particular purpose of the testator. In some cases . . . it appears that the accomplishment of the particular purpose and only that purpose was desired by the testator and that he had no more general charitable intent and that he would presumably have preferred to have the whole trust fail if the particular purpose is impossible of accomplishment. In such a case the cy pres doctrine is not applicable. 4 A. Scott, The Law of Trusts §399, at 3085 (3d ed. 1967).

In this case, Senator Bacon provided an unusual amount of information in his will from which the Georgia courts could determine the limits of his charitable purpose. Immediately after specifying that the park should be for "the sole, perpetual and unending, use, benefit and enjoyment of the white women, white girls, white boys and white children of the City of Macon," the Senator stated that "the said property under no circumstances . . . [is] to be . . . at any time for any reason devoted to any other purpose or use excepting so far as herein specifically authorized." And the Senator continued:

> I take occasion to say that in limiting the use and enjoyment of this property perpetually to white people, I am not influenced by any unkindness of feeling or want of consideration for the Negroes, or colored people. On the contrary I have for them the kindest feeling, and for many of them esteem and regard, while for some of them I have sincere personal affection.
>
> I am, however, without hesitation in the opinion that in their social relations the two races . . . should be forever separate and that they should not have pleasure or recreation grounds to be used or enjoyed, together and in common.

The Georgia courts, construing Senator Bacon's will as a whole, concluded from this and other language in the will that the Senator's charitable intent was not "general" but extended only to the establishment of a segregated park for the benefit of white people. The Georgia trial court found that "Senator Bacon could not have used language more clearly indicating his intent that the benefits of Baconsfield should be extended to white persons only, or more clearly indicating that this limitation was an essential and indispensable part of his plan for Baconsfield." Since racial separation was found to be an inseparable part of the testator's intent, the Georgia courts held that the State's *cy pres* doctrine could not be used to alter the will to permit racial integration. The Baconsfield trust was therefore held to have failed, and, under Georgia law, "[w]here a trust is expressly created, but uses . . . fail from any cause, a resulting trust is implied for the benefit of the grantor, or testator, or his heirs." Ga. Code §108-106(4) (1959). The Georgia courts concluded, in effect, that Senator Bacon would have rather had the whole trust fail than have Baconsfield integrated.

When a city park is destroyed because the Constitution requires it to be integrated, there is reason for everyone to be disheartened. We agree with petitioners that in such a case it is not enough to find that the state court's result was reached through the application of established principles of state law. No state law or act can prevail in the face of contrary federal law, and the federal courts must search out the fact and truth of any proceeding or transaction to determine if the Constitution has been violated. Here, however, the action of the Georgia Supreme Court declaring the Baconsfield trust terminated presents no violation of constitutionally protected rights, and any harshness that may have resulted from the state court's decision can be attributed solely to its intention to effectuate as nearly as possible the explicit terms of Senator Bacon's will.

Petitioners first argue that the action of the Georgia court violates the United States Constitution in that it imposes a drastic "penalty," the "forfeiture" of the park, merely because of the city's compliance with the constitutional mandate expressed by this Court in *Evans v. Newton*. Of course, *Evans v. Newton* did not speak to the problem of whether Baconsfield should or could continue to operate as a park; it held only that its continued operation as a park had to be without racial discrimination. But petitioners now want to extend that holding to forbid the Georgia courts from closing Baconsfield on the ground that such a closing would penalize the city and its citizens for complying with the Constitution. We think, however, that the will of Senator Bacon and Georgia law provide all the justification necessary for imposing such a "penalty." The construction of wills is essentially a state-law question, and in this case the Georgia Supreme Court, as we read its opinion, interpreted Senator Bacon's will as embodying a preference for termination of the park rather than its integration. Given this, the Georgia court had no alternative under its relevant trust laws, which are long standing and neutral with regard to race, but to end the Baconsfield trust and return the property to the Senator's heirs.

A second argument for petitioners stresses the similarities between this case and the case in which a city holds an absolute fee simple title to a public park and then closes that park of its own accord solely to avoid the effect of a prior court order directing that the park be integrated as the Fourteenth Amendment commands. Yet, assuming *arguendo* that the closing of the park would in those circumstances violate the Equal Protection Clause, that case would be clearly distinguishable from the case at bar because there it is the State and not a private party which is injecting the racially discriminatory motivation. In the case at bar there is not the slightest indication that any of the Georgia judges involved were motivated by racial animus or discriminatory intent of any sort in construing and enforcing Senator Bacon's will. Nor is there any indication that Senator Bacon in drawing up his will was persuaded or induced to include racial restrictions by the fact that such restrictions were permitted by the Georgia trust statutes. On the contrary, the language of the Senator's will shows that the racial restrictions were solely the product of the testator's own full-blown social philosophy. Similarly, the situation presented in this case is also easily distinguishable from that presented in *Shelley v. Kraemer,* 334 U.S. 1 (1948), where we held unconstitutional state judicial action which had affirmatively enforced a private scheme of discrimination against Negroes. Here the effect of the Georgia decision eliminated all discrimination against Negroes in the park by eliminating the park itself, and the termination of the park was a loss shared equally by the white and Negro citizens of Macon since both races would have enjoyed a constitutional right of equal access to the park's facilities had it continued. . . .

Mr. Justice WILLIAM O. DOUGLAS, dissenting.

[P]utting the property in the hands of the heirs will not necessarily achieve the racial segregation that Bacon desired. We deal with city real estate. If a theatre is erected, Negroes cannot be excluded. If a restaurant is opened, Negroes must be served. If office or housing structures are erected, Negro tenants must be eligible. If a church is erected, mixed marriage ceremonies may be performed. If a court undertook to attach a racial-use condition to the property once it became "private," that would be an unconstitutional covenant or condition.

Bacon's basic desire can be realized only by the repeal of the Fourteenth Amendment. So the fact is that in the vicissitudes of time there is no constitutional way to assure that this property will not serve the needs of Negroes.

The Georgia decision, which we today approve, can only be a gesture toward a state-sanctioned segregated way of life, now passe. It therefore should fail as the imposition of a penalty for obedience to a principle of national supremacy.

Mr. Justice WILLIAM J. BRENNAN, JR., dissenting.

For almost half a century Baconsfield has been a public park. Senator Bacon's will provided that upon the death of the last survivor among his widow and two daughters title to Baconsfield would vest in the Mayor and Council of the City of Macon and their successors forever. Pursuant to the express provisions of the will, the Mayor and City Council appointed a Board of Managers to supervise the operation of the park, and from time to time these same public officials made appointments to fill vacancies on the Board. Senator Bacon also bequeathed to the city certain bonds which provided income used in the operation of the park.

The city acquired title to Baconsfield in 1920 by purchasing the interests of Senator Bacon's surviving daughter and another person who resided on the land. Some $46,000 of public money was spent over a number of years to pay the purchase price. From the outset and throughout the years the Mayor and City Council acted as trustees, Baconsfield was administered as a public park. T. Cleveland James, superintendent of city parks during this period, testified that when he first worked at Baconsfield it was a "wilderness . . . nothing there but just undergrowth everywhere, one road through there and that's all, one paved road." He said there were no park facilities at that time. In the 1930's Baconsfield was transformed into a modern recreational facility by employees of the Works Progress Administration, an agency of the Federal Government. WPA did so upon the city's representation that Baconsfield was a public park. WPA employed men daily for the better part of a year in the conversion of Baconsfield to a park. WPA and Mr. James and his staff cut underbrush, cleared paths, dug ponds, built bridges and benches, planted shrubbery, and, in Mr. James' words, "just made a general park out of it." Other capital improvements were made in later years with both federal and city money. The Board of Managers also spent funds to improve and maintain the park.

Although the Board of Managers supervised operations, general maintenance of Baconsfield was the responsibility of the city's superintendent of parks. Mr. James was asked whether he treated Baconsfield about the same as other city parks. He answered, "Yes, included in my appropriation. . . ." The extent of the city's services to Baconsfield is evident from the increase of several thousand dollars in the annual expenses incurred for maintenance by the Board of Managers after the Mayor and City Council withdrew as trustees in 1964.

The city officials withdrew after suit was brought in a Georgia court by individual members of the Board of Managers to compel the appointment of private trustees on the ground that the public officials could not enforce racial segregation of the park. The Georgia court appointed private trustees, apparently on the assumption that they would be free to enforce the racially restrictive provision in Senator Bacon's will. In *Evans v. Newton*, 382 U.S. 296 (1966), we held that the park had acquired such unalterable indicia of a public facility that for the purposes of the Equal Protection Clause it remained "public" even after the city officials were replaced as trustees by a board of private citizens. Consequently, Senator Bacon's discriminatory purpose could not be enforced by anyone. This Court accordingly reversed the Georgia court's acceptance of the city officials' resignations and its appointment of private trustees. On remand the Georgia courts held that since Senator Bacon's desire to restrict the park to the white race could not be carried out, the trust failed and the property must revert to his heirs. The Court today holds that that result and the process by which it was reached do not constitute a denial of equal protection. I respectfully dissent.

No record could present a clearer case of the closing of a public facility for the sole reason that the public authority that owns and maintains it cannot keep it segregated. . . . The reasoning of the Georgia Supreme Court is simply that Senator Bacon intended Baconsfield to be a segregated public park, and because it cannot be operated as a segregated public park any longer, the park must be closed down and Baconsfield must revert to Senator Bacon's heirs. This Court agrees that this "city park is [being] destroyed because the Constitution require[s] it to be integrated. . . ." No one has put forward any other reason why the park is reverting from the City of Macon to the heirs of Senator Bacon. It is therefore quite plain that but for the constitutional prohibition on the operation of segregated public parks, the City of Macon would continue to own and maintain Baconsfield.

I have no doubt that public park may constitutionally be closed down because it is too expensive to run or has become superfluous, or for some other reason, strong or weak, or for no reason at all. But under the Equal Protection Clause a State may not close down a public facility solely to avoid its duty to desegregate that facility. . . . When it is as starkly clear as it is in this case that a public facility would remain open but for the constitutional command that it be operated on a non-segregated basis, the closing of that facility conveys an unambiguous message of community involvement in racial discrimination. Its closing for the sole and unmistakable purpose of avoiding desegregation, like its operation as a segregated park, "generates [in Negroes] a feeling of inferiority as to their status in the community that may affect their hearts and minds in a way unlikely ever to be undone." *Brown v. Board of Education,* 347 U.S. 483, 494 (1954). It is no answer that continuing operation as a segregated facility is a constant reminder of a public policy that stigmatizes one race, whereas its closing occurs once and is over. That difference does not provide a constitutional distinction: state involvement in discrimination is unconstitutional, however short-lived.

The Court, however, affirms the judgment of the Georgia Supreme Court on the ground that the closing of Baconsfield did not involve state action. The Court concedes that the closing of the park by the city "solely to avoid the effect of a prior court order directing that the park be integrated" would be unconstitutional. However, the Court finds that in this case it is not the State or city but "a private party which is injecting the racially discriminatory motivation." The exculpation of the State and city from responsibility for the closing of the park is simply indefensible on this record. This discriminatory closing is permeated with state action: at the time Senator Bacon wrote his will Georgia statutes expressly authorized and supported the precise kind of discrimination provided for by him; in accepting title to the park, public officials of the City of Macon entered into an arrangement vesting in private persons the power to enforce a reversion if the city should ever incur a constitutional obligation to desegregate the park; it is a public park that is being closed for a discriminatory reason after having been operated for nearly half a century as a segregated public facility; and it is a state court that is enforcing the racial restriction that keeps apparently willing parties of different races from coming together in the park. That is state action in overwhelming abundance. I need emphasize only three elements of the state action present here.

First, there is state action whenever a State enters into an arrangement that creates a private right to compel or enforce the reversion of a public facility. Whether the right is a possibility of reverter, a right of entry, an executory interest, or a contractual right, it can be created only with the consent of a public body or official, for example the official action involved in Macon's acceptance of the gift of Baconsfield. The State's involvement in the creation of such a right is also involvement in its enforcement; the State's assent to the creation of the right necessarily contemplates that the State will enforce the right if called upon to do so. Where, as in this case, the State's enforcement role conflicts with its obligation to comply with the constitutional command against racial segregation the attempted enforcement must be declared repugnant to the Fourteenth Amendment. . . .

A finding of discriminatory state action is required here on a second ground. *Shelley v. Kraemer,* 334 U.S. 1 (1948), stands at least for the proposition that where parties of different races are willing to deal with one another a state court cannot keep them from doing so by enforcing a privately devised racial restriction. [S]o far as the record shows, this is a case of a state court's enforcement of a racial restriction to prevent willing parties from dealing with one another. The decision of the Georgia courts thus, under Shelley v. Kraemer, constitutes state action denying equal protection.

Finally, a finding of discriminatory state action is required on a third ground. In *Reitman v. Mulkey,* 387 U.S. 369 (1967), this Court announced the basic principle that a State acts in violation of the Equal Protection Clause when it singles out racial discrimination for particular encouragement, and thereby gives it a special preferred status in the law, even though the State does not itself impose or compel segregation. This approach to the analysis of state action was foreshadowed in Mr. Justice White's separate opinion in Evans v. Newton, supra. There Mr. Justice White comprehensively reviewed the law of trusts as that law stood in Georgia in 1905, prior to the enactment of §§69-504 and 69-505 of the Georgia Code. He concluded that prior to the enactment of those statutes "it would have been extremely doubtful" whether Georgia law authorized "a trust for park purposes when a portion of the public was to be excluded from the park." Sections 69-504 and 69-505 removed this doubt by expressly permitting dedication of land to the public for use as a park open to one race only. Thereby Georgia undertook to facilitate racial restrictions as distinguished from all other kinds of restriction on access to a public park. Reitman compels the conclusion that in doing so Georgia violated the Equal Protection Clause.

In 1911, only six years after the enactment of §§69-504 and 69-505, Senator Bacon, a lawyer, wrote his will. When he wrote the provision creating Baconsfield as a public park open only to the white race, he was not merely expressing his own testamentary intent, but was taking advantage of the special power Georgia had conferred by §§69-504 and 69-505 on testators seeking to establish racially segregated public parks. As Mr. Justice White concluded in Evans v. Newton, "the State through its regulations has become involved to such a significant extent" in bringing about the discriminatory provision in Senator Bacon's trust that the racial restriction "must be held to reflect . . . state policy and therefore to violate the Fourteenth Amendment." 382 U.S., at 311. This state-encouraged testamentary provision is the sole basis for the Georgia courts' holding that Baconsfield must revert to Senator Bacon's heirs. The Court's finding that it is not the State of Georgia but "a private party which is injecting the racially discriminatory motivation" inexcusably disregards the State's role in enacting the statute without which Senator Bacon could not have written the discriminatory provision.

This, then, is not a case of private discrimination. It is rather discrimination in which the State of Georgia is "significantly involved," and enforcement of the reverter is therefore unconstitutional. . . .

NOTES AND QUESTIONS

1. Covenants that prohibit sale or lease of dwellings to, or occupancy by, persons on the basis of race violate federal civil rights statutes, including the federal Fair Housing Act, 42 U.S.C. §§3601 et seq. (as amended in 1988), and the Civil Rights Act of 1866, 42 U.S.C. §§1981, 1982. These statutes were covered in Chapter 2 in connection with public accommodations and are further addressed in Chapter 10 below in connection with the transfer of interests in housing.

Today, it is likely that racially restrictive covenants would be held to violate public policy under the common law. Almost no litigation has been brought on this question, as most cases since 1948 simply cite *Shelley v. Kraemer* and do not address the common law question. Some states have passed statutes addressing the problem. For example, New Jersey law provides, at N.J. Stat. Ann. §46:3-23, that "[a]ny promise, covenant or restriction in a contract, mortgage, lease, deed or conveyance or in any other agreement affecting real property . . . which limits, restrains, prohibits or otherwise provides against the sale, grant, gift, transfer, assignment, conveyance, ownership, lease, rental, use or occupancy of real property to or by any person because of race, creed, color, national origin, ancestry, marital status or sex is hereby declared to be void as against public policy, wholly unenforceable. . . ." *See also* Cal. Civ. Code §53(a) (invalidating any provision in a "written instrument relating to real property" that purports to forbid or restrict the use by or the conveyance to "any person of a specified sex, race, color, religion, ancestry, national origin, or disability").[25]

2. Who was living in the house at the time the decision in *Shelley v. Kraemer* was announced? If the decision had gone the other way, and the decision of the Missouri Supreme Court had been upheld, what would have happened?

3. The fourteenth amendment provides: "[Nor] shall any State deprive any person of life, liberty, or property, without due process of law, nor deny to any person within its jurisdiction the equal protection of the laws." U.S. Const. amend. XIV. The Supreme Court held in the Civil Rights Cases, 109 U.S. 3 (1883), that the fourteenth amendment regulates the conduct of state government and state officials but not the conduct of private or nongovernmental actors. Since then, courts have attempted to draw the line between public and private conduct — between those states of affairs legitimately attributable to the state and those for which the state cannot legitimately be held legally responsible.[26]

The state action doctrine is based partly on the language of the fourteenth amendment, which expressly applics to the "States." Nonetheless, those who defend the doctrine argue that it acts as a vital protector of individual liberty and privacy by exempting private conduct from regulation by constitutional doctrine. By holding that court enforcement of discriminatory contracts constitutes state action, *Shelley v. Kraemer* promotes freedom by guaranteeing to all citizens the right to participate in the housing market on an equal basis. Those who oppose the doctrine argue that it raises the specter of government regulation of virtually all "private" conduct. For this reason, some legal scholars have severely criticized the opinion for failing to distinguish adequately a private sphere that is immune from control by the law.

Professor Lino Graglia has criticized the reasoning in *Shelley*, not because it held that state enforcement of a private contract constituted state action but because it gave no reason why the state action was unconstitutional. He intimates that contract

---

25. *See also* Cal. Civ. Code §1352.5 (authorizing the board of directors of a homeowners association to amend any declaration that contains a restriction on sale or occupancy based on race, color, religion, sex, familial status, marital status, disability, national origin, or ancestry); Cal. Gov't. Code §12956.1 (creating an administrative process to remove such restrictive covenants from deeds).

26. Note that this version of the public/private distinction is different from the version implicated in public accommodations statutes. *See supra* §2.2. There the question was whether private property had been sufficiently opened to the public to be considered in the business of serving the public in general in a nonselective manner, such that the owner would have no legitimate interest in discriminating against persons on an illegitimate basis.

enforcement is neutral; when the animus for discrimination comes from a private individual rather than a state actor, no public official has administered the law in an unequal manner. Thus, he concludes, the reasoning in *Shelley* makes no sense. Lino Graglia, *State Action: Constitutional Phoenix,* 67 Wash. U. L.Q. 777 (1989).

One can argue, however, that to the extent state property law empowered white homeowners to conspire to exclude African Americans and Asian Americans from the housing market, it was operating in an unequal manner. On these grounds, other scholars have strongly advocated the result in *Shelley.* Some have further argued that *Shelley* demonstrates the artificiality of the state action doctrine; any conduct the state does not prohibit may be understood as authorized by the state — the state has declared it lawful. By preventing other citizens from interfering with what the state has defined as lawful activities, the state necessarily imposes its coercive force — or threatens to do so — to protect particular liberties. For this reason, some legal scholars have argued that the state action doctrine should be scrapped.

Stephen Gardbaum, for example, argues that, even if the Constitution does not regulate private action, it does require "equal *protection of the law*" and common law rights regulating relations among individuals are part of the law to which constitutional equality norms must apply. Stephen Gardbaum, *The "Horizontal Effect" of Constitutional Rights,* 102 Mich. L. Rev. 387 (2003). This does not mean, however, that all conduct by private individuals should be governed by the Constitution's command of equality; people should be allowed to decide whom they would like to invite to their homes for dinner, even if their decision is based partly on race. Professor Louis Henkin explains that in appropriate cases, the constitutional right to equal protection of the law may be outweighed by a countervailing constitutional right to privacy and freedom of association — thereby exempting the private dinner party from constitutional scrutiny. Louis Henkin, Shelley v. Kraemer: Notes for a Revised Opinion, 110 U. Pa. L. Rev. 473 (1962). For other discussions of the state action doctrine, see Charles Black, "State Action," Equal Protection, and California's Proposition 14, 81 Harv. L. Rev. 69 (1967); Erwin Chemerinsky, Rethinking State Action, 80 Nw. U. L. Rev. 503 (1985); Louis Michael Seidman, Public Principle and Private Choice: The Uneasy Case for a Boundary Maintenance Theory of Constitutional Law, 96 Yale L.J. 106 (1987); Mark Tushnet, Shelley v. Kraemer and Theories of Equality, 33 N.Y.L. Sch. L. Rev. 383 (1988); Symposium on the State Action Doctrine of Shelley v. Kraemer, 67 Wash. U. L.Q. 673 (1989).

4. In *Rice v. Sioux City Memorial Park Cemetery,* 60 N.W.2d 110 (Iowa 1953), the court refused to impose damages against a cemetery that refused to bury plaintiff's deceased husband, who was killed in combat on active duty in Korea, because he was a person "of 11/16 Winnebago Indian blood and 5/16 white blood" and therefore not a "Caucasian" as required by a restrictive covenant in the contract of sale of the burial lot. The court refused to apply *Shelley* because, unlike the plaintiff in *Shelley,* the plaintiff in *Rice* had herself contractually agreed to the restriction. The court found that enforcement of the covenant in *Shelley* impinged on the interests of a noncontracting party and thus effectively "clothed the private acts with the character of state action," while enforcement of the covenant in *Rice* involves merely "indirect" state support for the discriminatory private agreement with "no active aid" being given to enforce the private agreement. *Id.* at 115. Is this distinction convincing? *See also Woytus v. Winkler,* 212 S.W.2d 411 (Mo. 1948) (holding a covenant prohibiting sale or rental to, or occupancy by, "a negro or negroes" not to violate public policy although the covenant could not be enforced because of the recent decision in *Shelley v. Kraemer*).

5. Why did the Georgia courts refuse to apply the cy pres doctrine in Evans v. Abney? Given the fact that civil rights laws prohibit discrimination in public accommodations, housing, and employment, would Senator Bacon's intent be furthered by transferring the property to his heirs or by desegregating the park?

6. Did the state of Georgia in *Evans v. Abney* promulgate and enforce state property law in a way that discriminated against African Americans? Did the Supreme Court do so? Do you agree with the majority opinion of Justice Black or the dissenting opinion of Justice Brennan? Or is neither opinion adequate?

7. The majority opinion in *Evans v. Abney* emphasizes that no evidence was presented showing that the public officials involved were motivated by discrimination. Those officials included the state legislature and the state courts. Contrast this with *Brown v. Board of Education*, 347 U.S. 483 (1954), where the Court, in striking down segregated school systems, focused not on the discriminatory intent of state officials but on the effects of segregation on black children. *See also Bush v. Gore*, 531 U.S. 98 (2000) (holding that a uniform standard for counting ballots that did not sufficiently constrain the discretion of vote counters resulted in "arbitrary and disparate treatment [of ballots], valu[ing] one person's vote over that of another" without regard to proof of intent by law makers to disenfranchise a particular class of voters). Is the Court's emphasis in *Evans v. Abney* on the motivations of state actors appropriate?

Conversely, when a city closed a public pool to prevent it from being integrated, the Supreme Court held, one year after deciding *Evans v. Abney,* that the city had not violated the equal protection clause despite its intent to discriminate on the basis of race because the pool closing treated persons of all races equally by denying everyone access to the pool. *Palmer v. Thompson*, 403 U.S. 217 (1971). Do you agree with this ruling? Is it possible to argue that the closing in *Evans v. Abney* violated the equal protection clause even if the closing in *Palmer v. Thompson* did not?

PROBLEMS

1. Suppose the owner of the house in *Shelley v. Kraemer* had complied with the covenant and refused to sell the house to the Shelleys. The seller and the other owners of property burdened by the covenant do not invoke the legal system by bringing a lawsuit. Rather, the Shelleys — the potential buyers — bring a lawsuit against the seller, asking for a declaratory judgment that the covenant is unenforceable and damages for mental distress caused by the seller's refusal to sell on the basis of plaintiffs' race. The state courts hold that sellers have a right to decide to whom to sell their property and are free to discriminate on the basis of race so long as they do not directly invoke the aid of the state courts to accomplish this. The Shelleys appeal the state court judgment to the United States Supreme Court, arguing that the state courts have acted to deprive them of equal protection of the laws. Would the Supreme Court reach the same result as in Shelley? How would you write the opinion if you were on the Supreme Court?

2. Is *Evans v. Abney* consistent with *Shelley v. Kraemer*? What are the arguments on both sides?

3. The equal protection clause of the Constitution prohibits operating a public park in a segregated fashion, as *Evans v. Abney* notes. After refusing to apply the cy pres doctrine to excise the racial restriction, the state court finds the trust to have failed and the property to revert to the heirs of the grantor. Section 1982 of the Civil Rights Act of 1866, 42 U.S.C. §1982, provides that

[a]ll citizens of the United States shall have the same right, in every State and Territory, as is enjoyed by white citizens thereof to inherit, purchase, lease, sell, hold, and convey real and personal property.

The statute clearly prohibits any state law that would prevent persons of a particular race from inheriting property. Does it also prevent the state from enforcing a racial restriction placed by a donor in a donative transfer? If it does, then the restriction would be stricken, the trust would not fail, and the park would remain open. Even if the equal protection clause of the Constitution does not prevent closure of the park to honor the donor's discriminatory intent, does §1982 prohibit enforcement of the racial restriction? *See* Florence Wagman Roisman, The Impact of the Civil Rights Act of 1866 on Racially Discriminatory Donative Transfers, 53 Ala. L. Rev. 463 (2002)(arguing that it does).

§5.5.4 RESTRAINTS ON ALIENATION

The common law has long contained a strong presumption that property owners should be able to transfer their interests. Attempts by owners to impose covenants restricting the ability of future owners to transfer property are strictly regulated and are often held to be invalid. The law traditionally determined the validity of restraints on alienation by reference to the type of property at issue. The greatest ownership interest one can have in land is called a "fee simple" or a "fee simple absolute."[27] Restraints on alienation of fee interests in land were traditionally held to be absolutely void on the formalistic ground that they were "repugnant to the fee." *See, e.g., Hankins v. Mathews,* 425 S.W.2d 608 (Tenn. 1968). Such restraints were viewed as incompatible with the very idea of ownership. However, restraints on alienation of lesser interests in land, such as leaseholds, were generally upheld; a covenant prohibiting a tenant from subletting is likely to be enforced even today. Rather than resting on formalistic arguments about whether a restraint on alienation is "repugnant" to a particular type of property interest, modern property law tends to view restraints on alienation as subject to a general test of reasonableness, upholding restraints deemed to be reasonable, while striking down those deemed unreasonable. At the same time, the traditional distinctions continue to matter; restraints on alienation of leaseholds are more likely to be upheld than restraints on alienation of fee interests.

Determining when restraints on alienation are and are not reasonable is a core task of property law. The rules promoting alienability serve a variety of policy goals. They promote efficiency by allowing property to shift easily to a more valued use. They promote liberty by freeing current owners from undue restrictions imposed by past owners. They promote equality both by promoting dispersal of ownership and preventing arbitrary or exclusionary interests, such as schemes to engage in wholesale racial discrimination in access to homes in a neighborhood. At the same time, restraints on alienations are sometimes held to be valid either to promote the interests of grantors in controlling future use or enhancing the value of units to be marketed or to promote the interests of neighbors in ensuring compliance with covenants.

The following materials cover five different types of restraints on alienation, including (1) direct restraints on transfer; (2) servitudes requiring the consent of either

---

27. On the meaning of "fee simple," *see infra* §6.3.1.

the grantor (the developer) or the association to transfer the property; (3) rights of first refusal (also called preemptive rights); (4) leasing restrictions and (5) restraints designed to keep housing affordable by low- and moderate-income families.

§5.5.4.1   Direct Restraints on Alienation

<u>HORSE POND FISH & GAME CLUB, INC. v. CORMIER</u>

581 A.2d 478 (N.H. 1990)

WILLIAM F. BATCHELDER, Justice.

The defendant, William A. Cormier, a member of the plaintiff Horse Pond Fish & Game Club, Inc., appeals a decision of the Superior Court (Murphy, J.) granting the plaintiff's motion for summary judgment. The result of the decision is to declare void the restraint against alienation contained in a deed conveying a certain parcel of land to the plaintiff. We reverse and remand to the trial court for further proceedings.

The plaintiff, Horse Pond Fish & Game Club, Inc., was organized and incorporated in 1945. In 1954 it obtained title to a parcel of land in Nashua (the Horse Pond property) by deed, free of restrictions. The Horse Pond property consists of the land surrounding Horse Pond adjacent to the United States Fish Hatchery and contains the Horse Pond Fish & Game clubhouse and shooting range. The members conduct the activities of a fish and game club on the property.

On December 9, 1958, the plaintiff deeded the Horse Pond property to two of its members, Caleb N. Bickford and Fred A. Parish, who conveyed it back to the plaintiff the same day, with the following restrictions written in the deed:

> That said parcel of land with the buildings thereon or any part thereof shall not be alienated from the Horse Pond Fish and Game Club, Inc. unless: 1. One hundred (100) percent vote of the Club at a special meeting called by written notice to all members and notifying all said members that the purpose of the meeting is to convey away the property or a part thereof. 2. The Club is officially dissolved.

The only reasonable interpretation of this action is that the members desired to encumber the title to the property by the restrictions against alienation as set forth in the deed. Since the plaintiff acquired the Horse Pond property, the neighborhood surrounding the property has become increasingly residential, with the result that the Horse Pond property is bordered on all sides by residential neighborhoods, except for the fish hatchery bounding the property to the east.

In 1987 the plaintiff registered with the charitable trust division of the attorney general's office as a charitable corporation. The plaintiff's articles of agreement, restated in its by-laws, which were revised as of September 29, 1981, recite its objectives.

> The purposes for which this club is organized are to conserve, restore, and manage the game, fish, and other wildlife and its habitat in Horse Pond and its environs; to seek to procure better fishing and hunting for sportsmen; to promote and maintain friendly relations with landowners and sportsmen, to cooperate in obtaining proper respect for and observation of the fish and game laws; and so far as possible to spread knowledge of

useful wildlife among the residents of Nashua and vicinity. The Association shall operate without profit, shall be non-political and non-sectarian.

Pursuant to the Horse Pond property deed restriction, and as a consequence of the increasingly residential character of the area surrounding the property, the plaintiff called a special meeting in July of 1988 to approve a land swap contemplated by a purchase and sale agreement between itself and Byfield Associates, a New Hampshire general partnership. Under the agreement, subject to approval by its membership, the plaintiff would retain its clubhouse and approximately seven contiguous acres of the Horse Pond property, and would swap the balance of the property for a certain parcel of land in Hollis (the Hollis property), plus $150,000 payable in three installments. The Hollis property is bounded by the Nashua River on one side and by property held by Lone Pine Hunters, an association similar to the plaintiff, on the other side. According to the plaintiff, the Hollis property is more suitable for its fishing and hunting purposes than the Horse Pond property.

At the special meeting, the defendant, William Cormier, who lives on land adjacent to the Horse Pond property and who is a member of the plaintiff, voted against the proposed land deal. Under the restriction contained in the deed, assuming it to be lawful, his vote was sufficient to block the intended transaction. After the meeting, the plaintiff filed a bill in equity in the superior court, seeking a declaration that the restriction in the deed was void as an unreasonable restraint against alienation. . . .

. . . Applying the rule of reasonable restraints, namely, that the validity of a restraint against alienation depends upon its reasonableness in regard to the justifiable interests of the parties, the court found the restraint in the deed invalid. Using the factors listed in *Restatement of Property* §406, comment i (1944) to determine reasonableness, the court held unreasonable the restriction requiring a one hundred percent vote of the plaintiff's members, because it was unlimited in duration, and found the restriction requiring the plaintiff to be dissolved before the Horse Pond property could be alienated to be unreasonable, in that it was "capricious and its enforcement would accomplish no worthwhile purpose." . . .

. . . For the reasons that follow, we find that the issue of whether the plaintiff is a charitable entity is material to the determination of the validity of the restrictions contained in the plaintiff's deed to the Horse Pond property.

"Much of modern property law operates on the assumption that freedom to alienate property interests which one may own is essential to the welfare of society." *Restatement (Second) of Property, Donative Transfers*, introductory note, at 143 (1983). Because all restraints against alienation are contrary to this policy of freedom of alienation, to be enforceable they must be reasonable in view of the justifiable interests of the parties. Correspondingly, unreasonable restraints will be held invalid.

The rule of "reasonable restraints," however, generally does not apply in the case of a gift to a charitable trust or charitable corporation. In other words, an express provision or condition against alienation contained in a gift made to a charitable trust or charitable corporation may constitute a valid restraint. This result is consistent with *Restatement of Property* §406, comment i at 2406-07 (1944), which states that one of the factors tending to show the reasonableness of the restraint is that "the one upon whom the restraint is imposed is a charity." . . . Yet a sale of land owned by a charitable entity may be permitted, despite a valid restraint against alienation, if a court of equity determines that, due to unforeseen circumstances, the sale is necessary and would be in the best interests of the charity.

Since the restraint against alienation contained in the plaintiff's deed to the Horse Pond property may be valid depending upon whether or not the plaintiff is a charitable entity, the issue as to the plaintiff's charitable status, which existed at the time the court ruled on the plaintiff's motion for summary judgment, is a material issue which precluded the court from granting a valid summary judgment in the present case. Accordingly, we reverse the court's decision and remand for further proceedings in accordance with this opinion. On remand, the court should determine whether the plaintiff is a charitable entity and, if so, whether the restraint against alienation contained in the deed is valid, or whether the plaintiff is a non-charitable entity, in which case the rule of reasonable restraints must be considered and the court's earlier determination that the restraint is unreasonable will stand. . . .

§5.5.4.2 Consent to Sell Provisions

(a) *Grantor Consent Clauses*

NORTHWEST REAL ESTATE CO. v. SERIO

144 A. 245 (Md. 1929)

HAMMOND URNER, J.

A deed in fee simple for a lot of ground contained, in addition to various building and use restrictions, a provision that the land should not be subsequently sold or rented, prior to a designated date, without the consent of the grantor. The decisive question in this case is whether the restraint thus sought to be imposed upon the alienation of the property is void as being repugnant to the granted estate.

[The covenant in the 1927 deed states:]

> And for the purposes of maintaining the property hereby conveyed and the surrounding property as a desirable high class residential section for themselves[,] their successors, heirs, executors, administrators and assigns that until January 1, 1932, no owner of the land hereby conveyed shall have the right to sell or rent the same without the written consent of the grantor herein which shall have the right to pass upon the character[,] desirability and other qualifications of the proposed purchaser or occupant of the property. . . .

On March 27, 1928, the grantees contracted in writing to sell the lot to Charles Serio and wife. . . . The Northwest Real Estate Company declined to give its consent to the sale and transfer for which the contract provided. The purchaser then brought this suit against the vendors and the company to compel the specific performance of the agreement without the consent of the company, on the theory that the quoted covenant is void, or with the judicially enforced consent of the company, if the covenant should be held to be valid, the averment being made in the bill of complaint that the company's refusal to consent was arbitrary and unreasonable. . . .

The restriction imposed by the deed of the Northwest Real Estate Company upon sales by its grantees and their successors was clearly repugnant to the fee-simple title which the deed conveyed. Its object was to deprive the grantees, until 1932, of the unrestrained power of alienation incident to the absolute ownership which the granting clause created.

CARROLL BOND, C.J., dissenting.

The restraint upon alienation included in the deed . . . seems clearly enough to be one intended merely to give the developer of a suburban area of land power to control the character of the development for a time long enough to secure a return of his capital outlay, and to give early purchasers of lots and buildings some security in their own outlay. In those objects there is nothing against the public interest. We can hardly hold that the modern method of developing city or suburban areas as single large enterprises is detrimental to the public. On the contrary, it seems to be often the only method by which such areas can be conveniently and economically opened, so that houses may be provided upon convenient terms, with all the neighborhood necessities of streets, sewers, and the like ready at the outset. The venture of capital for this purpose appears to be distinctly a public benefit rather than a detriment, one which it is to the public advantage to encourage and promote rather than to hinder. But we know that there are real, substantial dangers to be feared in such ventures, and that, under the modern conditions of rapid city growth and rapid shifts of city populations, one of the most important risks is probably that which comes from the chance of invasion into the new neighborhood of an element of the population which the people to whom the developer must look for the return of his outlay will regard as out of harmony with them. However fanciful may be the aversions which give rise to it, and however deplorable they may be, to the developer they and their consequences must be as real as destructive physical forces. And, if it is to the public interest that this method of development be encouraged rather than hindered, then practically there must be a public gain in removal or diminution of this deterring danger. And the temporary restraint on alienation which the parties here involved have adopted to that end must, I think, be viewed as in point of fact reasonable, and from the standpoint of the public interest actually desirable. And, if this is true, then I venture to think there is no substantial reason why the law should interfere with it, denying the parties the right to agree as they have agreed, or denying their agreement full validity.

RISTE v. EASTERN WASHINGTON BIBLE CAMP, INC.

605 P.2d 1294 (Wash. Ct. App. 1980)

WILLARD J. ROE, Judge.

Eastern Washington Bible Camp, Inc., owns land on Silver Lake in Spokane County. Part of the land was subdivided and lots sold only to people who agreed to subscribe to the tenets of the Assembly of God Church. In 1968, George Riste's parents contracted with Eastern Washington Bible Camp to purchase two lots. In 1974, when the contract was paid in full, at the request of plaintiff's surviving parent, defendant issued the deed to plaintiff Riste. Both the sales contract and the deed contained restrictions on occupancy and resale. Riste later attempted to sell the property contrary to the restrictions. Defendant Bible Camp refused to remove the restrictions and Riste sued for a declaration that the restrictions were invalid and for reformation of the deed. . . .

These restrictions state in part:

> 6. No residents or occupants of these premises shall conduct themselves in such a manner as to be in conflict with the general practises and principles of the General and District Council of the Assemblies of God. No building activities or work shall be permitted on these premises on any Sunday of the entire year. . . .
> 8. The property described herein shall not be resold to any person without written approval by the SELLER or its agent. Eastern Washington Bible Camp claims that a restriction limiting the sale of land to members of a church is reasonable and may be enforced by the courts.

Restriction No. 8 contains a direct restraint on alienation of land. The rule in Washington is that a clause in a deed prohibiting the grantee from conveying land to another without the approval of the grantor, when the grantor transferred a fee simple estate to the grantee, is void as repugnant to the nature of an estate in fee. As stated in Richardson v. Danson, 270 P.2d 802, 807 (Wash. 1954):

> The great weight of authority is that where the fee simple title to real estate passes under a deed or will, any restraint attempted to be imposed by the instrument upon the grantee or devisee is to be treated as void, and the grantee or devisee takes the property free of the void condition. An exception allows reasonable restraints that are justified by legitimate interests, such as "due on sale" clauses in real estate mortgages.

. . . This is a disabling restraint upon which there is a presumption of invalidity. It is upon public policy grounds that the restriction is invalidated. . . .

Restriction No. 6 in the deed is also invalid. Wash. Rev. Code §49.60.224, Law Against Discrimination, states:

> (1) Every provision in a written instrument relating to real property which purports to forbid or restrict the conveyance, encumbrance, occupancy, or lease thereof to individuals of a specified race, creed, color, national origin, or with any sensory, mental, or physical handicap, . . . which directly or indirectly limits the use or occupancy of real property on the basis of race, creed, color, national origin, or the presence of any sensory, mental, or physical handicap is void.
> (2) It is an unfair practice to . . . honor or attempt to honor such a provision in the chain of title. (Italics ours.) . . .

. . . Creed, as used in the statute and in its common dictionary meaning, refers to a system of religious beliefs. Restriction No. 6 in the deed concerns creed and is void under Wash. Rev. Code §49.60.224. . . .

Although we understand the desire of Eastern Washington Bible Camp to have an enclave at a quiet lake where there is no drinking or gambling, Sunday working, etc., and where people can enjoy themselves in their vacations in the warm environment of their church, the outright grant of the fee in this deed is fatal to their hopes. That is the extent of our holding. Even if these covenants were enforced, eventually, transfers by inheritance, dissolution actions, or foreclosures of judgments, etc., would tend to destroy the integrity of the plan.

Nothing in this opinion is to be construed as limiting the right of religious organizations to operate and maintain their own bible camps or church property, access to which is limited to those of the same persuasion. . . .

(b) Consent of the Association

AQUARIAN FOUNDATION, INC. v. SHOLOM HOUSE, INC.

448 So. 2d 1166 (Fla. Dist. Ct. App. 1984)

DANIEL S. PEARSON, Judge.

All is not peaceful at the Sholom House Condominium. In disregard of a provision of the declaration of condominium requiring the written consent of the condominium association's board of directors to any sale, lease, assignment or transfer of a unit owner's interest, Bertha Albares, a member of the board of directors, sold her condominium unit to the Aquarian Foundation, Inc. without obtaining such consent. Eschewing its right to ratify the sale, the association, expressly empowered by the declaration to "arbitrarily, capriciously, or unreasonably" withhold its consent, sued to set aside the conveyance, to dispossess Aquarian, and to recover damages under a clause in the declaration which provides that:

> In the event of a violation . . . by the unit owner of any of the covenants, restrictions and limitations, contained in this declaration, then in that event the fee simple title to the condominium parcel shall immediately revert to the association, subject to the association paying to said former unit owner, the fair appraised value thereof, at the time of reversion, to be determined as herein provided.

The trial court, after a non-jury trial, found that Albares had violated the declaration of condominium, thus triggering the reverter clause. Accordingly, it entered a judgment for the association, declaring the conveyance to Aquarian null and void, ejecting Aquarian, and retaining jurisdiction to award damages, attorneys' fees and costs after a determination of the fair appraised value of the property. Aquarian appeals. We reverse.

The issue presented by this appeal is whether the power vested in the association to arbitrarily, capriciously, or unreasonably withhold its consent to transfer constitutes an unreasonable restraint on alienation, notwithstanding the above-quoted reverter clause which mandates that the association compensate the unit owner in the event, in this case, of a transfer of the unit in violation of the consent requirement.

It is well settled that increased controls and limitations upon the rights of unit owners to transfer their property are necessary concomitants of condominium living. *See Hidden Harbour Estates, Inc. v. Norman*, 309 So. 2d 180 (Fla. Dist. Ct. App. 1975).

> [I]nherent in the condominium concept is the principle that to promote the health, happiness, and peace of mind of the majority of the unit owners since they are living in such close proximity and using facilities in common, each unit owner must give up a certain degree of freedom of choice which he might otherwise enjoy in separate, privately owned property. Condominium unit owners comprise a little democratic sub society of necessity more restrictive as it pertains to use of condominium property than may be existent outside the condominium organization. 309 So. 2d at 181-182.

Accordingly, restrictions on a unit owner's right to transfer his property are recognized as a valid means of insuring the association's ability to control the composition of the condominium as a whole. Indeed, it has been said of a restriction contained in a declaration of condominium that it "may have a certain degree of unreasonableness to it, and yet withstand attack in the courts. If it were otherwise, a unit owner could not rely on the restrictions found in the declaration of condominium, since such restrictions would be in a potential condition of continuous flux."[3]

---

3. On the other hand, post-formative actions of the association, such as rules promulgated by the board of directors, are subject to a test of reasonableness: that is, the board's actions must be reasonably related to the promotion of the health, happiness and peace of mind of the

Hidden Harbour Estates, Inc. v. Basso, 393 So. 2d 637, 640 (Fla. Dist. Ct. App. 1981). Thus, strict enforcement of the restrictions of an association's private constitution, that is, its declaration of condominium, protects the members' reliance interests in a document which they have knowingly accepted, and accomplishes the desirable goal of "allowing the establishment of, and subsequently protecting the integrity of, diverse types of private residential communities, [thus providing] genuine choice among a range of stable living arrangements." Robert Ellickson, Cities and Homeowners Associations, 130 U. Pa. L. Rev. 1519, 1527 (1982).

However, despite the law's recognition of the particular desirability of restrictions on the right to transfer in the context of condominium living, such restrictions will be invalidated when found to violate some external public policy or constitutional right of the individual. Merely because a declaration of condominium is in the nature of a private compact and a restriction contained therein is not subject to the same reasonableness requirement as a restriction contained in a public regulation, where the restriction constitutes a restraint on alienation, condominium associations are not immune from the requirement that the restraint be reasonable. Thus, while a condominium association's board of directors has considerable latitude in withholding its consent to a unit owner's transfer, the resulting restraint on alienation must be reasonable. In this manner the balance between the right of the association to maintain its homogeneity and the right of the individual to alienate his property is struck.

The basic premise of the public policy rule against unreasonable restraints on alienation, is that free alienability of property fosters economic growth and commercial development. Because "[t]he validity or invalidity of a restraint depends upon its long-term effect on the improvement and marketability of the property," *Iglehart v. Phillips,* 383 So. 2d 610, 614 (Fla. 1980), where the restraint, for whatever duration, does not impede the improvement of the property or its marketability, it is not illegal. Accordingly, where a restraint on alienation, no matter how absolute and encompassing, is conditioned upon the restrainer's obligation to purchase the property at the then fair market value, the restraint is valid.

The declaration of condominium in the present case permits the association to reject perpetually any unit owner's prospective purchaser for any or no reason. Such a provision, so obviously an absolute restraint on alienation, can be saved from invalidity only if the association has a corresponding obligation to purchase or procure a purchaser for the property from the unit owner at its fair market value. Otherwise stated, if, as here, the association is empowered to act arbitrarily, capriciously, and unreasonably in rejecting a unit owner's prospective purchaser, it must in turn be accountable to the unit owner by offering payment or a substitute market for the property. When this accountability exists, even an absolute and perpetual restraint on the unit owner's ability to select a purchaser is lawful.

The declaration of condominium involved in the instant case contains no language requiring the association to provide another purchaser, purchase the property from the unit owner, or, failing either of these, approve the proposed transfer. What it does contain is the reverter clause, which the association contends is the functional equivalent of a preemptive right and, as such, makes the restraint on alienation lawful.

---

unit owners. It has been noted that cases applying this same reasonableness test to a restriction contained in the declaration of condominium overlook the fact that a restriction appearing in a declaration of condominium owes its "very strong presumption of validity . . . [to] the fact that each individual unit owner purchases his unit knowing of and accepting the restrictions to be imposed." *Hidden Harbour Estates, Inc. v. Basso,* 393 So. 2d at 639.

In our view, the problem with the association's position is that the reverter clause imposes no obligation upon the association to compensate the unit owner within a reasonable time after the association withholds its consent to transfer, and the clause is not therefore the functional equivalent of a preemptive right. Instead, the clause and the association's obligation do not come into effect until a violation of the restriction on an unapproved transfer occurs. . . .

The association's accountability to the unit owner is illusory. There is no reasonable likelihood that a potential purchaser, apprised by the condominium documents that the consent of the association is required and that a purchase without consent vitiates the sale, would be willing to acquire the property without the association's consent.[5] Without a sale, there is no violation of the reverter clause. Without a violation of the reverter clause, the association has no obligation to pay the unit owner.

Effectively, then, the power of the association to arbitrarily, capriciously, and unreasonably withhold its consent to transfer prevents the activation of the reverter clause and eliminates the accountability of the association to the unit owner. Therefore, we conclude that the power of the association to arbitrarily, capriciously, and unreasonably withhold its consent to transfer is not saved by the reverter clause from being declared an invalid and unenforceable restraint on alienation. . . .

§5.5.4.3   Rights of First Refusal or Preemptive Rights

WOLINSKY v. KADISON

449 N.E.2d 151 (Ill. App. Ct. 1983)

DOM J. RIZZI, Justice:

In a three-count amended complaint, plaintiff, Debra Rae Wolinsky, sought damages from defendants, the Ambassador House Condominium Association, its Board of Directors individually and as the Board, Eugene Matanky & Associates, Inc., and Eugene Matanky & Associates Management Corporation, the companies employed to manage the condominium, and Andra Addis, an employee of the management companies. . . .

In count I of her amended complaint, plaintiff alleged that she owned unit 4D in the Ambassador House Condominium and that she was a member in good standing of the association. She further alleged that in late August 1978, she contracted to purchase unit 21F in the same condominium, and in early September she contracted to sell unit 4D. In late September, the board notified plaintiff that it was exercising its right of first refusal with regard to unit 21F,[26] and the seller of unit 21F then terminated its contract

---

5. We acknowledge, of course, that in this case a sale to Aquarian Foundation actually occurred. This does not, however, affect our view that such a sale would not ordinarily be expected to occur between parties dealing at arm's length. The record does not reflect the relationship between Albares and Aquarian that may have been responsible for Aquarian acquiring the property. . . .

26. Paragraph 19b of the declaration provides:

> During the period of twenty (20) days following receipt by the Board of such written notice, the Board, on behalf of all remaining Unit Owners, shall have the first right and option to purchase or lease such Unit (or to cause the same to be purchased or leased by the designee or designees, corporate or otherwise, of the Board) upon the same terms and conditions as stated in the aforesaid notice received by the Board.–ED.

with plaintiff. Plaintiff also alleged that the board had knowledge of the contents of the association's bylaws and that in exercising its right of first refusal, the board acted without the affirmative vote of two-thirds of the total ownership of the common elements as required under the bylaws.

Count II of plaintiff's complaint is predicated upon a violation of the Chicago condominium ordinance which provides, *inter alia*: "No person shall be denied the right to purchase or lease a unit because of race, religion, sex, sexual preference, marital status or national origin." Municipal Code of Chicago 1978, ch. 100.2, par. 100.2-4. Plaintiff alleged that defendants violated the ordinance because the board exercised the right of first refusal on the basis of the condominium management's report to the board that plaintiff is an unmarried female who would occupy unit 21F with her children. . . .

. . . Plaintiff argues that the dismissal of her complaint was improper because her complaint stated a cause of action for (1) unreasonable restraint on alienation; (2) violation of the bylaws of the condominium association, which she characterizes as a breach of fiduciary duty; (3) violation of the antidiscrimination section of the Chicago condominium ordinance; and (4) wilful and wanton misconduct. . . .

Defendants . . . argue that the right of first refusal exercised here is a reasonable restraint [on alienation]. Plaintiff contends that a right of first refusal is an unreasonable restraint on alienation when exercised, as it was here, to exclude current members of the association. In other words, plaintiff argues that the restraint here is unreasonable as applied. We believe that plaintiff adequately stated a cause of action under this theory.

A board must exercise a right of first refusal reasonably upon consideration of the prospective purchaser's qualifications in light of the economic and social reasons which justify the restraint itself. Thus, a requirement that the right of first refusal be exercised reasonably must be implied. The criteria for testing the reasonableness of an exercise of this power by a condominium association are (1) whether the reason for exercising the right of first refusal is rationally related to the protection, preservation or proper operation of the property and the purposes of the association as set forth in its governing instruments and (2) whether the power was exercised in a fair and nondiscriminatory manner . . . .

Next, plaintiff argues that her complaint was improperly dismissed since it stated a cause of action for violation of the bylaws of the association, which she characterizes as a breach of fiduciary duty. Plaintiff contends that defendants breached their fiduciary duty when they exercised a right of first refusal without first obtaining the requisite affirmative vote of the ownership. Article I, section 6 of the bylaws provides:

> The affirmative vote of not less than two-thirds (2/3) of the total ownership of the Common Elements is required in order to approve . . . (3) the purchase or sale of land or Units on behalf of all Unit Owners . . . .

[P]laintiff maintains that the declaration and the bylaws delineate the scope of the board's authority and that each board member "has a fiduciary duty to implement the will of the members of the association without exceeding its bounds." It is plaintiff's contention that by alleging her membership in the association and the board's failure to comply with the bylaws, she stated a cause of action based upon defendants' breach of a fiduciary duty owed to her as a member. We agree.

A fiduciary relationship exists where there is special confidence reposed in one who, in equity and good conscience, is bound to act in good faith with due regard to the interests of the other. We believe that all condominium association officers and board members become fiduciaries to some degree when they take office. Because the association officers and board members owe a fiduciary or quasi-fiduciary duty to the members of the association, they must act in a manner reasonably related to the exercise of that duty, and the failure to do so will result in liability not only for the association but also for the individuals themselves. We believe that a board's proper exercise of its fiduciary or quasi-fiduciary duty requires strict compliance with the condominium declaration and bylaws. Therefore, when the declaration or bylaws provide procedures to govern board action, those procedures should be followed. Here, by virtue of the declaration and bylaws, the board owed a duty to all members of the association to obtain a two-thirds affirmative vote of the ownership of the common elements before exercising a right of first refusal. Since plaintiff alleged that defendants exercised a right of first refusal without first obtaining the requisite affirmative vote of the ownership, we conclude that plaintiff stated a cause of action for breach of a fiduciary duty and that count I of her amended complaint was improperly dismissed.

We next address plaintiff's contention that count II of her amended complaint stated a cause of action for violation of the Chicago condominium ordinance, which prohibits discrimination with regard to the purchase and lease of condominium units. Municipal Code of Chicago 1978, ch. 100.2, par. 100.2-4. Plaintiff alleged that the board exercised its right of first refusal because plaintiff is an unmarried female who would occupy unit 21F with her children. Thus, plaintiff seeks damages for discrimination on the basis of her sex and her marital status. Discrimination on either ground is explicitly prohibited by the ordinance. We therefore believe that plaintiff's allegations bring her within the scope of the ordinance.

Defendants maintain that plaintiff failed to state a cause of action under the ordinance because defendants did not refuse to allow plaintiff to purchase unit 21F but merely prevented the seller from selling unit 21F to plaintiff by exercising the right of first refusal. We find no merit in defendants' contention. The antidiscrimination section of the ordinance provides: "No person shall be denied the right to purchase or lease a unit because of race, religion, sex, sexual preference, marital status or national origin." Municipal Code of Chicago 1978, ch. 100.2, par. 100.2-4. Plainly, by exercising a right of first refusal, a condominium association prevents a prospective purchaser from buying a unit. We therefore believe that if a right of first refusal is exercised so that a prospective purchaser is unable to purchase a unit because of his or her race, religion, sex, sexual preference, marital status or national origin, the ordinance has been violated....

NOTES AND QUESTIONS

1. *Total restraints on alienation of fee simple interests.* Restraints on alienation are covenants or conditions that restrict the ability of the owner of real property to sell or give away the property. The traditional rules distinguish three types of restraints.

    a. *Disabling restraints.* A disabling restraint directly forbids the owner from transferring her interest in the property. For example, "*O* conveys Blackacre to *A* and her heirs, but any transfer of Blackacre shall be null and void."

b. *Promissory restraints.* A promissory restraint is a covenant by which the grantee promises not to alienate his interest in the property. For example, "*O* conveys Blackacre to *A* in fee simple. *A* promises [or covenants] for himself, his heirs, and his assigns that Blackacre shall not be transferred."

c. *Forfeiture restraints.* A forfeiture restraint provides for a future interest that will vest if the owner attempts to transfer her interest in the property. For example, "*O* conveys Blackacre to *A*, but if *A* attempts to transfer the property, then to *B* and her heirs."

Total restraints on alienation of fee simple interests, whether in the form of disabling, promissory, or forfeiture restraints, are uniformly held void and unenforceable. *R.H. Macy & Co. v. May Department Stores Co.*, 653 A.2d 461 (Md. 1995); *Merritt v. McNabb*, 1995 WL 96808 (Tenn. Ct. App. 1995); *Loehr v. Kincannon*, 834 S.W.2d 445 (Tex. Ct. App. 1992). The policies underlying the rule against total restraints on alienation of fee simple interests include (1) promoting dispersal of ownership of property and preventing concentration of land in passive family dynasties, (2) encouraging individual autonomy by vesting control of resources in current owners, and (3) promoting social utility and efficiency by allowing property to be transferred to its most valued use.

Disabling restraints are far worse than promissory or forfeiture restraints because no one is entitled to waive the restraint. Forfeiture and promissory restraints, in contrast, do not necessarily take property out of the market; the owner burdened by the condition or covenant has the power to bargain with the future interest holder or the owner of the dominant estate to induce her to give up her rights. A covenant beneficiary can abandon the covenant and a forfeiture condition can be destroyed if the beneficiary of the future interest conveys the future interest to the present estate owner, thereby merging the two estates and destroying the condition. Is the ban on promissory and forfeiture restraints justified?

2. *Formalism; repugnant to the fee.* Courts traditionally have held that an absolute restraint on alienation is "repugnant" to the nature of a "fee simple" interest in real property. *Loehr v. Kincannon*, 834 S.W.2d at 447. The argument seems to be that a fee simple is a property interest that is by definition alienable so a restraint on alienation cannot attach to it. This argument is formalistic and circular; it gives no reason for refusing to allow the property to be inalienable. The argument is not wholly without content, however; it appeals to the idea that owners should presumptively have full control over the property they own, and one of the central powers that owners want and need is the power to transfer the property on terms chosen by them. Absolute prohibitions on alienation seem to contradict the very notion of ownership; hence, the traditional rule invalidating restraints on alienation of fee interests.

In contrast, the *Horse Pond* court holds that only *unreasonable* restraints on alienation are invalid. Reasonable restraints on alienation are valid, even if they attach to fee interests. The reasonableness formulation is the more modern one and is increasingly the rule articulated in the case law. It has been adopted by the *Restatement (Third) of Property (Servitudes)* §3.4 (2000). What would constitute a "reasonable" restraint on alienation? The Restatement (Third) provides that "[r]easonableness is determined by weighing the utility of the restraint against the injurious consequences of enforcing the restraint." *Id.*

3. *Partial restraints on alienation of fee simple interests.* Courts sometimes uphold partial restraints on alienation that last for a limited time or limit the transfer of

property to certain persons but do not constitute wholesale prohibitions on transfer. *Mardis v. Brantley*, 717 So. 2d 702, 709 (La. Ct. App. 1998). They may uphold such restraints either because they do not unduly limit the ability to transfer the property or because the restraint has a legitimate purpose that justifies the limit on alienability. Partial restraints on alienation may even increase alienability because grantors may be more likely to part with their property if they can control the future use or disposition of it. Nonetheless, restraints that totally prohibit alienation of fee interests for a period of time are generally held void. Those limiting transfer to particular persons are sometimes upheld. *Pritchett v. Turner*, 437 So. 2d 104 (Ala. 1983). However, other courts will strike them down on the ground that they are capricious or motivated by spite or malice. *See, e.g., Casey v. Casey*, 700 S.W.2d 46 (Ark. 1985) (striking down a restraint prohibiting land left in a will to the decedent's son ever to come into the possession of the decedent's daughter).

4. *Consent to sell clauses and preemptive rights.* As *Serio* and *Riste* show, covenants that require owners to obtain the consent of the grantor or developer of the subdivision or condominium are usually struck down by the courts as unreasonable restraints on alienation. *See Camino Gardens Association, Inc. v. McKim*, 612 So. 2d 636 (Fla. Dist. Ct. App. 1993); *Kenney v. Morgan*, 325 A.2d 419 (Md. 1974). Recall the traditional rule prohibiting the enforcement of a covenant when the benefit is held in gross; one reason for this rule is to ensure that control over the land devolves to a current owner rather than an absentee lord. For this reason, many courts will not allow a developer to exercise a consent to sale covenant once the last unit is sold. *See also* Cal. Civ. Code §1462 (prohibiting enforcement of covenants whose benefit is held in gross). The Restatement (Third) allows the benefit of covenants to be held in gross as long as the beneficiary can demonstrate a legitimate interest in enforcing the covenant, *Id.* at §2.6, cmt. d. How could the developer demonstrate such an interest? Assuming the developer could demonstrate such an interest, wouldn't the alienability problem be solved if the court read into the covenant an implied obligation to exercise the power to consent to sale reasonably? Or would that not solve the problem?

The dissenting opinion in *Serio* provides a policy argument in favor of enforcing covenants that give developers the power to consent to all future sales. The analysis in the majority opinion is based on the formalistic "repugnancy" thesis. Assume that the court would not imply a duty to act reasonably but would interpret the covenant to give the grantor full discretion to grant or withhold consent to any sale. Can you provide a better, policy-based justification for upholding such a provision than that given by the majority opinion in *Serio* of Justice Urner? How would the dissenting judge respond to these new arguments?

In contrast to covenants giving grantor/developers the continuing power to consent to sales, covenants that grant such powers to a homeowners or condominium association are ordinarily upheld either if they (a) require the association to act reasonably or (b) are in the form of *preemptive rights* that ensure that the owner can transfer the unit for its fair market value to the association or its members or that require the holder of the preemptive right to match any bona fide offers made by a third party. *Smith v. Mitchell*, 269 S.E.2d 608 (N.C. 1980). Rights of first refusal obviously limit the current owner's power to determine to whom the property will be transferred and may therefore inhibit the alienability of the property considerably. If they do not limit the discretion of the association in any way, they are likely to be struck down unless the court reads a reasonableness requirement into the covenant.

See Laguna Royale Owners Association v. Darger, 174 Cal. Rptr. 136 (Ct. App. 1981) (upholding such a covenant as long as consent was not unreasonably withheld). An alternative way to protect the interests of the unit owner is to ensure the payment of fair market value. Is this enough of a protection for the owner?

5. *Options.* An option to purchase is a right to buy property when one chooses to do so. It is a right to force an owner to sell. It is therefore the opposite of a preemptive right, which kicks in only when the current owner chooses to sell. Options are likely to be held to be unreasonable restraints on alienation if they are for a fixed price and have no termination date. *Sander v. Ball,* 781 So. 2d 527 (Fla. Dist. Ct. App. 2001) (purchase option for unlimited period with cap on purchase price is an unreasonable restraint on alienation). However, if they are for a limited time or ensure that the owner can receive fair market value, they are likely to be upheld.

6. Why shouldn't covenants that require the consent of the association or developer to sell property be enforced exactly as written? If an owner wants the right to sell a house or condominium unit at will, why shouldn't she look for a building whose declaration provides no limits on transfer of her interest? What social purposes are served by requiring that restraints on alienation in condominium complexes be exercised reasonably?

Sholom House appears to hold that condominium associations have an absolute right to exercise their contractual right to prevent a sale of a condominium unit if they pay the owner the fair market value of the property. *Wolinsky* appears to hold that a right of first refusal must be exercised in a way that is reasonably related to the association's legitimate interests. Can these cases be reconciled? When the declaration gives the association either a right of first refusal or a right to approve the sale, should the courts read into the declaration an implied reasonableness requirement, allowing the restraint to be exercised only if it is demonstrably related to the association's legitimate interests? Or should the court interpret the declaration as written to give the association an absolute right to decide whether to exercise its right of first refusal or its right to block the sale?

7. Would *Wolinsky* have come out the same way if the potential buyer were a third party rather than an owner of an existing condominium unit?

8. Would a preemptive right held by a condominium developer (the original owner of the units) constitute an unreasonable restraint on alienation?

9. *Cooperatives.* Discretionary powers over transfer are likely to be upheld in the special case of *cooperatives* because of the greater financial interdependence of the owners. At the same time, such powers may be utilized for purposes other than financial security; as with any such power, they may be used to exclude potential buyers thought to be undesirable and may be a cover for discrimination. Restraints on alienation of property held for use by low-income persons are likely to be upheld because the restraints serve the competing public purpose of preserving affordable housing that would not otherwise be created by ordinary market forces.

10. *Life estates.* Most courts uphold total restraints on alienation of life estates when they are in the form of forfeiture or promissory restraints. *Edwards v. Bradley,* 315 S.E.2d 196 (Va. 1984). Disabling restraints on life estates, however, are generally not enforced, again because a disabling restraint inflexibly refuses to identify anyone who has the power to waive enforcement of the restraint. *Deviney v. Nationsbank,* 993 . S.W.2d 443 (Tex. Ct. App. 1999); Restatement (Second) of Property (Donative

Transfers) §§4.1 to 4.2 (1983). One reason courts sometimes uphold restraints on alienation of life estates is that life estates are not alienable to a large degree anyway. Anyone who purchases a life estate has obtained a precarious interest that will terminate automatically the moment the grantor dies. In addition, most life estates are given to the grantor's children, with the remainder to go to some other members of the family — ordinarily, the grandchildren. This arrangement ensures that property will be available for two generations; since the property will be alienable by the grandchildren, it has not been taken out of the market permanently.

Some courts treat life estates as they do fee simple interests, holding that total restraints on alienation of life estates are void under all circumstances.

11. *Equitable interests.* Courts generally uphold restraints on alienation of beneficial or equitable interests in property. The settlor or trustor may direct, for example, that the beneficiary has no right to alienate her beneficial interest; this arrangement is sometimes called a *spendthrift trust* because it protects the beneficiary's right to a continuing stream of income from the trust by limiting the beneficiary's power to alienate the right to receive that income. Lawrence W. Waggoner, Richard V. Wellman, Gregory S. Alexander, and Mary Louise Fellows, *Family Property Law: Cases and Materials on Wills, Trusts, and Future Interests* 668-682 (1991). A settlor may also direct the trustee not to sell the trust assets, and such limitations will ordinarily be enforced. If those assets become unproductive, the trustee may go to court for approval of a sale of the assets to generate income for the beneficiary in line with the settlor's intent; such approval may be granted under the *cy pres* doctrine.

12. *Leaseholds: Limitations on subletting.* Courts ordinarily uphold limitations on the transfer of leaseholds. A lease stating that the tenant may not sublet or assign the leasehold, for example, is likely to be enforced. Complications arise, however, when the lease simply requires the consent of the landlord before the tenant sublets or assigns the leasehold. This issue is addressed in Chapter 8.

13. *Indirect restraints on alienation.* Some private controls on land use are so severe that they make the property very difficult to sell. Such restraints are sometimes struck down as "indirect" restraints on alienation, on the theory that the grantor should not be able to do indirectly what he could not do directly. If limitations on use of property are so extensive that the property cannot be used for any legitimate purposes, the property has no value and therefore is unalienable since no one would want to purchase it. In such cases, courts may find such limitations on use void as indirect restraints on alienation. Such claims, however, are difficult to win. The *Restatement (Third)* for example, invalidates indirect restraints only if they "lack[ ] a rational justification." *Id.* at §3.5(2). Obsolete restrictions are generally handled by the doctrines of changed conditions and relative hardship.

14. *Restraints on alienation as a cover for discrimination.* Are *Serio* and *Riste* cases about restraints on alienation or about antidiscrimination policy? Does the grantor have any legitimate interests in retaining the power to approve subsequent sales of property in the subdivision?

15. *Charities.* In *Horse Pond*, Justice Batchhelder notes that restraints on alienation are generally allowed when the holder of the property interest is a charity. Can you imagine what policies underlie this exception to the rule against unreasonable restraints on alienation? *Does the Horse Pond Fish* and *Game Club* have a charitable purpose? How should the trial judge answer this question?

Suppose the court concludes that the club is a charity. The question still remains whether sale of the land should be allowed, despite the restraint on alienation, because "due to unforeseen circumstances, the sale is necessary and would be in the best interests of the charity." Under the circumstances described in *Horse Pond*, should the court authorize the sale because of this equitable changed conditions doctrine?

16. *Low-income housing.* In recent years, charitable organizations called community development corporations (CDCs) have established housing for low-income families. To ensure that the housing remains available for such families, it is often subject to restraints on alienation that prohibit leasing the property or sale to a family that is not a low-income family. In *City of Oceanside v. McKenna*, 264 Cal. Rptr. 275 (Ct. App. 1990), Michael Shawn McKenna purchased a condominium in a development that had been sold by the city for less than its fair market value to a developer for the express purpose of creating housing affordable by low- and moderate-income persons. The units were subject to covenants that prohibited owners from renting their units out and from "failing to occupy the dwelling as the owner's principal place of residence for any period." McKenna got a new job in San Francisco and sought to rent his unit. The city sued him to enforce the covenant. The court noted that "[o]n determining whether a restraint on alienation is unreasonable, the court must balance the justification for the restriction against the quantum of the restraint. The greater the restraint, the stronger the justification must be to support it." *Id.* at 279. It held that the restriction on leasing was a reasonable restraint on alienation because "the provision of housing for low and moderate income persons is in keeping with the public policy of this state. . . . Thus, the restrictions support rather than offend the policies of this state." *Id.* at 1427-1428.

17. *Constructive trusts.* In *Alsup v. Montoya*, 488 S.W.2d 725 (Tenn. 1972), the testator, W. C. Alsup, left property to his daughters for life with a provision that the property not be sold. Some 50 years later, the daughters brought an action for a declaratory judgment that the property be sold because it could no longer be used profitably for agricultural purposes, the buildings had deteriorated, and the fertility of the land had declined. The court allowed both the life estates and the future interests to be sold, despite the restraint on alienation, on the equitable ground that this was what the grantor would have wanted under the circumstances and because a failure to allow the sale would have resulted in waste of the property. Accord, *Roper v. Edwards*, 373 S.E.2d 423 (N.C. 1988) (applying constructive trust doctrine to order a transfer of property subject to an unenforceable restraint on alienation when the owner of the restricted land had settled a lawsuit with the grantor with a promise to transfer the property to whomever the grantor appointed by will).

PROBLEM

A condominium declaration grants the association a right of first refusal at a price fixed by the condominium declaration. This price takes no account of inflation or increases in the market value of the land and is designed to maintain the unit's affordability for low-income persons. The price is set by a formula that allows recovery of the owner's purchase price plus additional principal payments and amounts paid for improvements in the unit. The owner of a unit attempts to sell his condominium unit at market value. Is the right of first refusal with a below-market fixed price an invalid restraint on alienation? What arguments could you make on both sides of this question? How should the courts resolve it?

§5.5.4.4   Restrictions on Leasing

WOODSIDE VILLAGE CONDOMINIUM
ASSOCIATION, INC. v. JAHREN

806 So.2d 452 (Fla. 2002)

HARRY LEE ANSTEAD, J. . . .

At issue is the validity of amendments to the Declaration of Condominium adopted by the condominium owners which restrict the leasing of units in Woodside Village. Woodside Village is a condominium development located in Clearwater, Florida, consisting of 288 units. It was established in 1979 pursuant to Florida's "Condominium Act," chapter 718, Florida Statutes. Petitioner, Woodside Village Condominium Association, Inc. ("Association"), is the condominium association that was formed pursuant to the Declaration of Condominium of Woodside Village ("Declaration"), recorded in the public records of Pinellas County. Respondents, Adolph S. Jahren and Gary M. McClernan, each own residential condominium units in Woodside Village.

[Section 10.3 of the] original Declaration of Condominium for Woodside Village [permitted leasing of condominium units but required Board of Directors approval for initial leases lasting more than one year.] In addition, §10.3 was amended in 1995 to require that all leases and renewals receive prior approval from the Board of Directors.

In 1997 some owners became concerned that units were increasingly becoming non-owner occupied, and that such a condition would have a negative impact on the quality of life in Woodside Village and on the market value of units. Accordingly, [while keeping the requirement of Board approval for leases,] §10.3 was amended in March of 1997 to limit the leasing of units to a term of no more than nine months in any twelve-month period. A provision was also added prohibiting owners from leasing their units during the first twelve months of ownership. [Another provision prohibited owners from renting more than three of their units at any one time.] These amendments were adopted by a vote of at least two-thirds of the unit owners as required by the Declaration. The following year the Association notified respondents in writing that two of their respective units were not in compliance with the nine-month lease restriction set out in §10.3 as amended.

When the respondents failed to come into compliance with the leasing restrictions, the Association filed complaints in circuit court seeking injunctions to enforce compliance with the provisions of the Declaration. Respondents [denied] that compliance could be mandated under Florida law. In addition, respondents filed counterclaims for declaratory and injunctive relief asserting that the lease restriction was unreasonable, arbitrary, and capricious, and had no purpose other than to effectively ban all leasing of units. Respondents also asserted the lease restriction was confiscatory and deprived them of lawful uses which were permissible at the time of purchase. Accordingly, respondents sought an injunction prohibiting the Association from enforcing the lease restriction or, alternatively, requiring the Association to compensate respondents for the fair market value of their units. . . .

Condominiums and the forms of ownership interests therein are strictly creatures of statute. *See* Flat. Stat. §§718.101–718.622. In Florida, Chapter 718, Florida Statutes, known as Florida's "Condominium Act," gives statutory recognition to the condominium form of ownership of real property and establishes a detailed scheme for the creation, sale, and operation of condominiums. Pursuant to §718.104(2), a condominium is created by recording a declaration of condominium in the public records of the county where the land is located.

The declaration, which some courts have referred to as the condominium's "constitution," strictly governs the relationships among the condominium unit owners and the condominium association. [B]ecause condominiums are a creature of statute courts must look to the statutory scheme as well as the condominium declaration and other documents to determine the legal rights of owners and the association.

From the outset, courts have recognized that condominium living is unique and involves a greater degree of restrictions upon the rights of the individual unit owners when compared to other property owners. For instance, in *White Egret Condominium, Inc. v. Franklin,* 379 So. 2d 346, 350 (Fla. 1979), we recognized that "reasonable restrictions concerning use, occupancy and transfer of condominium units are necessary for the operation and protection of the owners in the condominium concept." In *White Egret,* we quoted favorably from *Hidden Harbour Estates, Inc. v. Norman,* 309 So. 2d 180 (Fla. Dist. Ct. App. 1975), to further explain the restrictive nature of condominium ownership and living:

> Inherent in the condominium concept is the principle that to promote the health, happiness, and peace of mind of the majority of the unit owners since they are living in such close proximity and using facilities in common, each unit owner must give up a certain degree of freedom of choice which he might otherwise enjoy in separate, privately owned property. Condominium unit owners comprise a little democratic sub society of necessity more restrictive as it pertains to use of condominium property than may be existent outside the condominium organization.

Consistent with this analysis of condominium ownership, courts have acknowledged that "increased controls and limitations upon the rights of unit owners to transfer their property are necessary concomitants of condominium living." *Aquarian Foundation, Inc. v. Sholom House, Inc.,* 448 So. 2d 1166, 1167 (Fla. Dist. Ct. App. 1984). Indeed, section 718.104(5), Florida Statutes, expressly recognizes that a declaration of condominium may contain restrictions concerning the use, occupancy, and transfer of units. *See* §718.104(5).[*]

Courts have also consistently recognized that restrictions contained within a declaration of condominium should be clothed with a very strong presumption of validity when challenged. The logic behind this presumption was explained in *Hidden Harbour Estates, Inc. v. Basso,* 393 So. 2d 637, 639-40 (Fla. Dist. Ct. App. 1981), wherein the court reasoned:

> There are essentially two categories of cases in which a condominium association attempts to enforce rules of restrictive uses. The first category is that dealing with the validity of restrictions found in the declaration of condominium itself. The second category of cases involves the validity of rules promulgated by the association's board of

---

* Fla. Stat. §718.104(5) provides: "The declaration as originally recorded or as amended under the procedures provided therein may covenants and restrictions concerning the use, occupancy, and transfer of the units permitted by law with reference to real property. However, the rule against perpetuities shall not defeat a right given any person or entity by the declaration for the purpose of allowing unit owners to retain reasonable control over the use, occupancy, and transfer of units."

directors or the refusal of the board of directors to allow a particular use when the board is invested with the power to grant or deny a particular use.

In the first category, the restrictions are clothed with a very strong presumption of validity which arises from the fact that each individual unit owner purchases his unit knowing of and accepting the restrictions to be imposed. Such restrictions are very much in the nature of covenants running with the land and they will not be invalidated absent a showing that they are wholly arbitrary in their application, in violation of public policy, or that they abrogate some fundamental constitutional right. . . .

Significantly, Fla. Stat. §718.110 also provides broad authority for amending a declaration of condominium. In particular, section 718.110(1)(a) provides:

> If the declaration fails to provide a method of amendment, the declaration *may be amended as to all matters* except those listed in subsection (4) or subsection (8) if the amendment is approved by the owners of not less than two-thirds of the units. . . . (emphasis added)

Based upon this broad statutory authority and the provisions for amendment set out in the declaration of condominium, courts have recognized the authority of condominium unit owners to amend the declaration on a wide variety of issues, including restrictions on leasing. Of course, §718.110(1)(a) itself contains some restrictions on the amendment process. For example, pursuant to subsections (4) and (8), all unit owners must consent to amendments which materially alter or modify the size, configuration or appurtenances to the unit, change the percentage by which the unit owner shares the common expenses and owns the common surplus of the condominium, or permit timeshare estates to be created in any unit of the condominium, unless otherwise provided in the declaration as originally recorded. *See* Fla. Stat. §718.110(4), (8). These provisions are not at issue here.

In *Seagate Condominium Ass'n, Inc. v. Duffy,* 330 So. 2d 484 (Fla. Dist. Ct. App. 1976), the court upheld an amendment to the declaration of condominium prohibiting leasing of any units, except for limited periods in cases of hardship. The trial court held that the amendment was both an unreasonable restriction and an unlawful restraint on alienation and awarded damages for lost rents to the unit owners who challenged the amendment. On appeal, the Fourth District reversed, and explained, *id.* at 486-87:

> . . . The restriction . . . is reasonable. Given the unique problems of condominium living in general and the special problems endemic to a tourist oriented community in South Florida in particular, appellant's avowed objective — to inhibit transciency and to impart a certain degree of continuity of residence and a residential character to their community — is, we believe, a reasonable one, achieved in a not unreasonable manner by means of the restrictive provision in question. The attainment of this community goal outweighs the social value of retaining for the individual unit owner the absolutely unqualified right to dispose of his property in any way and for such duration or purpose as he alone so desires.

The district court upheld the amendment even as it was applied to unit owners who acquired their units prior to the amendments. . . .

We note that the majority of courts in other jurisdictions have held that a duly adopted amendment restricting either occupancy or leasing is binding upon unit owners who purchased their units before the amendment was effective. *See Ritchey v. Villa Nueva Condominium Ass'n,* 146 Cal.Rptr. 695, 700 (Cal. Ct. App. 1978); *Apple II Condominium Ass'n v. Worth Bank & Trust Co.,* 659 N.E.2d 93 (Ill. App. Ct. 1995); *Breezy Point Holiday Harbor Lodge-Beachside Apartment Owners' Ass'n v. B.P. P'ship,* 531 N.W.2d 917, 920 (Minn. Ct. App. 1995); *McElveen-Hunter v. Fountain Manor Ass'n, Inc.,* 399 S.E.2d 112 (N.C. 1991); *Shorewood West Condominium Ass'n v. Sadri,* 992 P.2d 1008, 1012 (Wash. 2000); *but see* 560 *Ocean Club, L.P. v. Ocean Club Condominium Ass'n (In re 560 Ocean Club, L.P.),* 133 B.R. 310, 320 (Bankr. D.N.J. 1991); *Breene v. Plaza Tower Ass'n,* 310 N.W.2d 730, 734 (N.D. 1981).

. . . In *Apple II Condominium Ass'n v. Worth Bank & Trust Co.,* the Illinois appellate court [upheld] the validity of a declaration amendment which restricted leasing of units to no more than once during ownership, with no lease exceeding twelve months. In enforcing the amendment, the court declared, 659 N.E.2d at 97:

> . . . In our view, neither the fact that there were no restrictions on the property when the Harmons purchased their unit nor the fact that the Harmons purchased the property for investment purposes is relevant to the proper resolution of the issues presented in this case. As purchasers of the condominium property, the Harmons are charged with knowledge of the Condominium Property Act and that the Declaration governing their unit was subject to amendment. Section 18.4(h) of the Act specifically recognizes that the Board may implement rules governing the "use of the property," so long as the restrictions do not impair those rights guaranteed by the First Amendment to the United States Constitution or the Free Speech provisions of the Illinois Constitution. In the absence of a provision either in the Amendment or in the original Declaration, condominium owners do not have vested rights in the status quo ante. . . .

The court further reasoned that the approval of the amendment by the association's membership made the leasing restriction a "category one" restriction under *Basso,* thereby elevating the level of deference given by the court. Accordingly, the court concluded that when an amendment has been passed by an association's membership it would presume the restriction was valid and uphold it unless it was shown that the restriction was arbitrary, against public policy, or in violation of some fundamental constitutional right.

We agree with this reasoning. To hold otherwise, we would have to conclude that the right to amend a declaration of condominium is substantially limited, well beyond those limitations imposed by the Legislature in section 718.110(4) and (8). We would also be faced with the difficult task of deciding what subjects could be addressed by the amendment process, a task much better suited for the Legislature, as can be seen by its imposition of restrictions in section 718.110. . . .

Respondents in this case purchased their units subject to the Declaration which expressly provides that it can be amended and sets forth the procedure for doing so. Section 14 of the Declaration generally provides that an amendment may be adopted by a supermajority of two-thirds of the owners.[5] Further, section 13 expressly states that each owner shall be governed by the Declaration as amended from time to time:

---

5. Section 14.5, however, provides in part that "no amendments shall discriminate against any apartment owner nor against any apartment or class or group of apartment owners unless the apartment owners so affected . . . consent; and no amendment shall change any apartment nor the share in the common elements, and other of its appurtenances nor increase

13. *Compliance and Default.* Each apartment owner shall be governed by and shall comply with the terms of this Declaration, the By-Laws and the Rules and Regulations adopted pursuant thereto, and Management Agreement, and said documents *as they may be amended from time to time.* Failure of the apartment owner to comply therewith shall entitle the Association or other apartment owners to the following relief in addition to other remedies provided in this Declaration and the Condominium Act....

(Emphasis added.) In addition, the legal description for each of respondents' units that were allegedly being used in violation of the lease restriction provides that the units are subject to the restrictions contained in the Declaration and subsequent amendments thereto.

Thus, we find that respondents were on notice that the unique form of ownership they acquired when they purchased their units in the Woodside Village Condominium was subject to change through the amendment process, and that they would be bound by properly adopted amendments....

We also conclude that the respondents have failed to demonstrate that the restriction, in and of itself, violates public policy or respondents' constitutional rights, at least as asserted herein.... As discussed above, most such restrictions simply come with the unique territory of condominium ownership. Indeed, it is restrictions such as these that distinguish condominium living from rental apartments or single-family residences. Hence, persons acquiring units in condominiums are on constructive notice of the extensive restrictions that go with this unique, and some would say, restrictive, form of residential property ownership and living. Accordingly, we conclude the amendment is valid and enforceable against respondents....

We recognize the concerns that owners, such as respondents, who purchased their individual condominium units for investments have regarding the imposition of lease restrictions through subsequent declaration amendments without the consent of all unit owners. The question is, of course, how far can two-thirds of the condominium owners go in restricting leasing rights in the condominium units. The answer will usually be found in the legislative scheme creating and governing condominiums. Although we believe such concerns are not without merit, we are constrained to the view that they are better addressed by the Legislature. If condominium owners are to be restrained in their enactment of such lease restrictions, it is appropriate that such restraint be set out in the legislative scheme that created and regulates condominiums and condominium living. As noted above, the Legislature has demonstrated its awareness of the need for limitations on the authority of unit owners to amend a declaration by its enactment of section 718.110(1)(a), (4), and (8). However, as noted, in this instance no provision in the Condominium Act prohibits the adoption of an amendment imposing a lease restriction, nor does any provision require the consent of all unit owners to adopt such an amendment. To the contrary, the Condominium Act provides broad authority for amending a declaration of condominium. *See* Fla. Stat. §718.110(1)(a)....

PEGGY A. QUINCE, J., specially concurring.

I concur in the majority's decision which quashes the decision by the Second District Court of Appeal. I write simply to urge the Legislature to seriously consider

---

the owner's share of the comman expences unless the owner of the apartments concerned ... joins in the execution of the amendment. "

placing some restrictions on present and/or future condominium owners' ability to alter the rights of existing condominium owners. At the time the units in question here were purchased, the owners had the right to lease their property with relatively few restrictions. One of the owners purchased his units in 1979 and had enjoyed this leasing right for eighteen years before the Declaration of Condominium was amended. The twelve-month lease which was permitted at the time these unit owners purchased their units is no longer valid. These owners can now only lease their property for nine months in any twelve month period. As the district court pointed out the amendment has deprived these owners of a valuable right that existed at the time of purchase. This valuable right may well have been the determinative factor for their decisions to buy these properties. As the district court suggested, there should at least be some type of "escape" provision for those "unit owners whose substantial property rights are altered by amendments to declarations adopted after they acquire their property."

NOTES AND QUESTIONS

1. As *Woodside Village* notes, most courts agree that leasing restrictions in condominium declarations can be retroactively imposed on owners who purchased units before those restrictions were adopted. However, the North Dakota Supreme Court disagreed with the reasoning of the Florida Supreme Court and held in *Breene v. Plaza Tower Ass'n*, 310 N.W.2d 730 (N.D. 1981), that restrictions on leasing of condominium units cannot be imposed retroactively on owners who purchased before the declaration was amended to impose such restrictions. The North Dakota statutes provided:

> The owner of a project shall, *prior to the conveyance of any condominiums therein,* record a declaration of restrictions relating to such project which restrictions shall be enforceable equitable servitudes where reasonable, and shall inure to and bind all owners of condominiums in the project. (emphasis added by N.D. Supreme Court)

The Court interpreted this language as follows, N.W.2d at 310:

> This language contemplates that notice of restrictions through the recording procedures must be given to prospective buyers prior to the conveyance of any condominium unit. Although the statute provides that the restrictions shall be enforceable equitable servitudes, the statute also provides that a prerequisite to the enforceability is that the restriction be recorded prior to the conveyance of any condominium unit. A necessary corollary of this is that a restriction adopted after the purchase of a condominium unit would not be enforceable against the purchaser except through the purchaser's acquiescence.

Is this argument convincing? Can you make a better argument against retroactive application of leasing restrictions on condominium owners? How could you interpret the statutory language to authorize retroactive leasing restrictions?

2. The *Restatement (Third)* requires unanimous consent for declaration amendments that "prohibit or materially restrict the use or occupancy or units," §6.10(2) or "that deprive owners of significant property or civil rights," §6.10 cmt. g. However, it makes this rule disclaimable; if the declaration provides otherwise, it is enforceable unless a statute prohibits retroactive enforcement. If the Florida Supreme Court had

adopted this interpretation of the common law, would it have changed the result in Woodside? Should the court adopt this approach?

§5.5.5 ANTICOMPETITIVE COVENANTS

Anticompetitive covenants are enforceable under the common law only if they are "reasonable." In *Whitinsville Plaza*, the Massachusetts Supreme Judicial Court defined reasonable anticompetitive covenants as ones that are "reasonably limited in time and space [and product line] and consonant with the public interest" and that "serve a purpose of facilitating orderly and harmonious development for commercial use." This approach has been adopted by other courts as well. *See Davidson Bros., Inc. v. D. Katz & Sons, Inc.*, 579 A.2d 288 (N.J. 1990); *Vermont National Bank v. Chittenden Trust Co.*, 465 A.2d 284 (Vt. 1983).

Most of the recent cases concerning anticompetitive covenants occur in the context of shopping center leases. Further, most claims proceed not on the basis of the common law reasonableness requirement but on the basis of federal antitrust policy contained in the *Sherman Antitrust Act*, 15 U.S.C. §§1 et seq. This act prohibits all contracts "in restraint of trade." However, as the court explains in *Optivision, Inc. v. Syracuse Shopping Center Associates*, 472 F. Supp. 665, 674, 676, 679 (N.D.N.Y. 1979):

> If this provision were to be read literally, all commercial contracts would be regarded as violative of the Act since every agreement binds the contracting parties to its terms, and, accordingly, restrains their commercial dealings to a certain extent. Recognizing that it was not Congress' intention to prohibit all contracts nor even all contracts that cause an insignificant or attenuated restraint of trade, the Supreme Court adopted the rule of reason as the standard of analysis for scrutinizing most business relations under the *Sherman Act*. Under this rule, all the circumstances presented by a particular case must be evaluated by the trier of fact to determine whether the complained of conduct imposes an unreasonable restraint on competition.
>
> In making this inquiry, consideration must be given to "the facts peculiar to the business in which the restraint is applied, the nature of the restraint and its effects, and the history of the restraint and the reasons for its adoption." The focus of the analysis must be upon the impact of the challenged activity on competitive conditions in the relevant market. Any benefits to competition are to be weighed against the competitive evils of the practice in question. . . .
>
> [T]he Court is unable to conclude that exclusivity clauses in shopping center leases are unreasonable in all possible circumstances. The competitive impact of such arrangements may vary considerably depending upon the availability of suitable alternate locations in the relevant market, and upon the strength of the remaining competition. In addition, there is a possible economic justification for a provision of this nature. In some situations, it may be necessary to include such a clause in a shopping center lease in order to attract to the center a certain type of store which might be unwilling to commit itself to a lease with high rentals if it knows that a competing store will be present in the center.
>
> . . . If an exclusivity provision is necessary to attract [a particular type of] store, such a clause has a beneficial impact on competition that will have to be considered along with any adverse competitive effects.

In *Dunafon v. Delaware McDonald's Corp.*, 691 F. Supp. 1232 (W.D. Mo. 1988), an owner promised lessee McDonald's that it would not grant a lease "to any persons to engage in a carry-out fast food restaurant in which food and beverages are dispensed that is in direct competition with lessee within the mall shopping center." An owner of a Taco Bell restaurant sued both the lessor and lessee for a declaratory judgment that the covenant violated the federal antitrust law, known as the Sherman Act. The court held that such covenants were not per se unlawful but would constitute unreasonable restraints on trade only if they violate the "rule of reason."

The rule of reason requires the court to examine the circumstances to determine whether the operation of the covenant actually effectuates an unreasonable restraint on competition. The court will first define the relevant product (or service) market and the effective geographic area in which competition is likely to be present. *See, Acme Markets, Inc. v. Wharton Hardware and Supply Corp.*, 890 F.Supp. 1230 (D.N.J. 1995). It will then compare the anticompetitive effect of the covenant with its pro-competitive effect. An anticompetitive covenant may increase competition because it provides security that induces a new competitor to enter the market, thereby generating new business and new competition. In Dunafon, the court determined that the covenant induced McDonald's to invest in creating a new restaurant and that the presence of this restaurant helped generate business for the shopping center. Because the area previously had little commercial property and few fast-service restaurants, the covenant may have had the effect of inducing new competition to emerge, rather than stifling it. Given the availability of nearby sites where competing fast food restaurants could locate, the court found that the pro-competitive effects of the covenant outweighed its anticompetitive effects and that it was therefore lawful and enforceable.

PROBLEM

An entrepreneur seeking to open a deli leases property on the first floor of a large downtown office building. Seeking to protect her business, the entrepreneur convinces the landlord to include the following language in the lease: "Landlord covenants not to permit any other property in the building to be used for operation of a deli." The entrepreneur opens and begins operating a profitable deli. Later, a second entrepreneur rents space in the building and opens a sit-down restaurant. The restaurant does not harm the deli's business because it caters to a different clientele. However, after a year, the restaurant begins subletting some of its space to a cart that sells convenient, deli-style sandwiches at lunchtime. The deli's business suffers as people start buying from the cart. The deli owner sues the landlord, the restaurant, and the cart owner seeking to enforce the covenant. She argues that the cart is effectively a "deli" because it sells deli-style sandwiches. She also argues that she never would have invested so much money, time, and labor in the deli if she had known that the landlord was going to allow another tenant to breach the covenant. The defendants respond that there is no breach, since a cart is simply not a deli. They argue in the alternative that even if the cart is effectively a deli, enforcing such an anticompetitive covenant is void as against public policy, because the labor force downtown needs convenient places to eat and competition is desirable. Which side should win?[28]

---

28. This problem is based on *Kobayashi v. Orion Ventures, Inc.*, 678 N.E.2d 180 (Mass. App. Ct. 1997).

§5.5.6 Public Policy Limitations and Review for Reasonableness

§5.5.6.1 Covenants

DAVIDSON BROTHERS, INC. v. D. KATZ & SONS, INC.[†]

643 A.2d 642 (Super. Ct. App. Div. 1994), *on remand from* 579 A.2d 288 (N.J. 1990)

The opinion of the court was delivered by WILLIAM M. D'ANNUNZIO, J.A.D.

Plaintiff Davidson Bros., Inc. (Davidson) appeals from a trial court judgment entered after a bench trial held on remand from the Supreme Court. *Davidson Bros., Inc. v. D. Katz & Sons, Inc.,* 579 A.2d 288 (N.J. 1990). Applying the reasonableness test formulated by the Supreme Court, the trial court determined that a covenant prohibiting the use as a supermarket of a property in downtown New Brunswick, New Jersey, was unenforceable. We now affirm.

Davidson operated a number of supermarkets in New Jersey. In 1952, it opened a supermarket of 10,000 square feet on George Street in downtown New Brunswick. In June 1978, Davidson took over an existing supermarket located at Elizabeth Street, also in New Brunswick but approximately two miles from the George Street store (hereinafter George Street), near the border with North Brunswick. Davidson paid $315,000 for the assets of the Elizabeth Street store (hereinafter Elizabeth Street), not including inventory, and made a substantial additional investment for improvements. Davidson leased the Elizabeth Street real property.

Davidson closed George Street in February 1979 because its volume had decreased after Davidson acquired Elizabeth Street. It sold George Street in September 1980 to defendant D. Katz & Sons, Inc. (Katz), a rug merchant. The deed to Katz contained the covenant in issue:

> The lands and premises described herein and conveyed hereby are conveyed subject to the restriction that said lands and premises shall not be used as and for a supermarket or grocery store of a supermarket type, however designated, for a period of forty (40) years from the date of this deed. This restriction shall be a covenant attached to and running with the lands.

The closing of George Street as a supermarket created a hardship for downtown residents, most of whom did not own or have ready access to motor vehicles. In response to their plight, the city government sought to attract another supermarket operator to the downtown area. The city's efforts culminated in the acquisition of George Street from Katz by the defendant New Brunswick Housing Authority, and the leasing of the property, for one dollar a year, to defendant C-Town, on condition that C-Town invest at least $10,000 for improvements and operate George Street as a supermarket.

Davidson commenced this action to enforce the covenant. Davidson appealed from an adverse summary judgment and we affirmed in an unreported opinion, utilizing traditional "touch and concern" analysis applicable to covenants alleged to run with the land.

Our Supreme Court granted Davidson's petition for certification and reversed and remanded for a trial. In doing so, the Court determined that "rigid adherence" to

---

[†] The New Jersey Supreme Court decision in this case is reproduced above at §5.4.2.1.

the "touch and concern" requirement was no longer warranted. It held that enforceability of a covenant would depend on its reasonableness, and that the principle of "touch and concern" is "but one of the factors." The Court then described eight factors to be considered in resolving the reasonableness issue:

1. The intention of the parties when the covenant was executed, and whether the parties had a viable purpose which did not at the time interfere with existing commercial laws, such as antitrust laws, or public policy.
2. Whether the covenant had an impact on the considerations exchanged when the covenant was originally executed. This may provide a measure of the value to the parties of the covenant at the time.
3. Whether the covenant clearly and expressly sets forth the restrictions.
4. Whether the covenant was in writing, recorded, and if so, whether the subsequent grantee had actual notice of the covenant.
5. Whether the covenant is reasonable concerning area, time or duration. Covenants that extend for perpetuity or beyond the terms of a lease may often be unreasonable.
6. Whether the covenant imposes an unreasonable restraint on trade or secures a monopoly for the covenantor. This may be the case in areas where there is limited space available to conduct certain business activities and a covenant not to compete burdens all or most available locales to prevent them from competing in such an activity.
7. Whether the covenant interferes with the public interest.
8. Whether, even if the covenant was reasonable at the time it was executed, "changed circumstances" now make the covenant unreasonable.

On remand, Davidson no longer sought injunctive relief. . . . [Davidson sold its] Elizabeth Street store to another supermarket operator in 1989 for $687,500. Davidson limited its claim to damages consisting of lost sales and profits during the two year period it competed with C-Town, and the reduced value of its Elizabeth Street store due to C-Town's competition.

Davidson's accountant testified that sales at Elizabeth Street for 1988 and 1989 were $1,452,000 less than they would have been had the George Street store not reopened. He calculated the lost profit on those sales to be $350,000. He also opined that due to the lower sales volume, Davidson sold the Elizabeth Street store for $567,000 less than it should have sold for.

Defendants' accountant disagreed. He testified that although Elizabeth Street may have lost sales due to C-Town's operation of George Street, those lost sales would not have been profitable. Defendants' accountant also testified that the Elizabeth Street store did not lose value as a result of C-Town's competition.

After a lengthy trial, the trial court rendered an oral opinion. Applying the eight factors announced by the Supreme Court, the court found that the 40 year term was unreasonably long (factor 5); that the covenant imposed an unreasonable restraint of trade (factor 6); and that it was contrary to the public interest (factor 7). Regarding factor seven, the court ruled that the covenant adversely impacted the public interest because "there is a substantial public need for the supermarket under the circumstances of this case."

The trial court deemed the damages issue to be moot because of its determination that the covenant was unreasonable and unenforceable. However, the court announced that it was unable to determine from the evidence that Davidson had sustained damages due to C-Town's competition.

We now affirm on the ground that the covenant was so contrary to public policy that it should not be recognized as a valid, enforceable obligation.

The proofs established that New Brunswick is a small city which continues to suffer from many of the maladies affecting the larger cities of New Jersey and the nation, especially in its core downtown area. This area, where George Street is located, has been the focus of a large scale redevelopment and revitalization effort measured in decades. Although this effort's emphasis has been on commercial projects primarily, the downtown area is also the site of many low to moderate income housing projects of the New Brunswick Housing Authority. These were federally funded projects, and many of their residents depended on George Street for their shopping requirements before Davidson closed the store. George Street is within two blocks of four of those housing projects with a total of 726 units.

The testimony of New Brunswick's Director of Policy, Planning and Economic Development, and his report which was introduced into evidence, provided a demographic profile of the city. There are a total of 3,148 households in the downtown area. Twenty-six percent of those households are below the poverty level, compared with seventeen percent in the balance of the city. Of the "family households" downtown, twenty-eight percent are female householders with children, compared with fourteen percent in the balance of the city. Of the female headed households, fifty-four percent are below the poverty level, which is consistent with the balance of the city. Thirty-seven percent of the downtown housing units have no vehicle, almost twice as many as the balance of the city. Seven hundred and forty-three downtown units are occupied by persons sixty-five years and older; twenty-one percent of those seniors are below the poverty level, almost double the proportion in the rest of the city. The downtown area, therefore, contains the city's greatest concentration of disadvantaged persons.

Davidson's closing of George Street further disadvantaged them. No other supermarket was within walking distance. For those who lacked access to motor vehicles, buses, taxis and dependence on others replaced a walk to the supermarket. The problem was especially difficult for female heads of household who used to send their children to the store or have their children accompany them. With the elimination of George Street, getting to the supermarket was a particularly difficult exercise in logistics and child care.

But inconvenience was not the only cost. Dr. James J. O'Connor testified for defendants as an expert in food marketing and distribution. Dr. O'Connor's experience involved hands-on management of his family's wholesale and retail food businesses, followed by academic and government experience in food distribution issues. Shortly before his testimony in this case, Dr. O'Connor had completed a study for the United States Department of Agriculture regarding supermarkets in United States cities. According to Dr. O'Connor, the absence of a supermarket in a low income city neighborhood makes food more expensive and has a negative impact on diet and, therefore, on the inner city population's health.

Dr. O'Connor also stated that the absence of a supermarket contributes to inner city decay, because a supermarket is a retail anchor that attracts other retail operations. Withdrawal of a supermarket tends to force other merchants to leave the same neighborhood. The resulting vacuum is filled by convenience stores or "ma and pa" groceries. They are more expensive and lack variety. They rarely have produce and, if they do have it, it is of poor quality. Moreover, selection of poultry and fish is very limited and very expensive. Dr. O'Connor opined that there is a general lack of inner city supermarkets in the nation, which poses a significant social policy problem.

Dr. O'Connor's uncontradicted testimony is consistent with the conclusions reached by a congressional committee. House Select Comm. on Hunger, 100th Cong., 1st Sess., Obtaining Food: Shopping Constraints on the Poor (Comm. Print 1987) (hereinafter Report). The committee concluded that "low-income consumers are unable to maximize their limited expendable resources for a basic need — food — because of the barriers of the [sic] location and transportation. Hence, the grip of hunger and poverty tightens around the low-income consumer." *Id.* at 1.

The committee recognized the exacerbating impact of "supermarket migration" on this problem, *Id.* at 4:

> Supermarket Migration
>
> During the late 1970's and early 1980's major supermarkets migrated away from the inner cities and low-income areas, toward the suburbs. Major reasons cited for the migration by the food industry include: high insurance rates, employment and security problems, and outmoded and understocked inner-city stores — conditions which keep profits low. The exodus to the suburbs provided cheaper land, better control over operational hazards and, in general, greater profits. According to the Food Marketing Institute, in 1981, 90 percent of the conventional grocery stores, located in low-income neighborhoods, [that] either closed voluntarily or went out of business, did so to relocate into the suburbs. These were the stores that had traditionally served low-income areas. During the same year, over one-half the new stores that opened were super stores locating in the suburbs and other higher-income areas.
>
> As these trends continue, low-income urban and rural consumers are faced with fewer food markets in the immediate vicinity of their homes and the greater expense in accessing reasonably priced foods. This migration has increased the economic drain on the urban and rural low-income consumer's already limited food budget, reducing, and in come cases, removing the opportunity for low-income households to shop competitively.hellip;

The committee also recognized the impact of the inner city consumers' limited shopping choices: "You have this perverse irony that the poorest have to pay more for a basic necessity of life." . . . *Id.* at 3. . . .

In its Report, the committee noted that experts and organizations addressing the problems of urban living recommended the provision of incentives to bring supermarkets back into the cities. The committee recommended, among other policy options, that "State and local governments should implement tax breaks and other incentives to . . . small- and medium-sized grocer[ies], and supermarket chains to encourage their expansion and/or relocation in low-income communities." *Id.* at 10.

New Brunswick's initial efforts to respond to the problem were unsuccessful. It attempted to provide and organize transportation, an option that proved to be ineffective. It also sought to find a downtown property easily adaptable to supermarket use and to attract another supermarket operator to run it. Other than the George street store, however, there was none available.

Senator John Lynch, the Mayor of New Brunswick during the relevant period, testified that initial approaches to supermarket operators were unsuccessful because too much capital was required to rehabilitate and convert other buildings to supermarket use. According to Senator Lynch the "problem was making the bottom line work because of assembling the property, providing relocation costs, dealing with [environmental] laws, all of those things that add cost to the bottom line." Moreover, many properties that had conversion potential were unavailable or had other problems.

On the other hand, George Street, the former supermarket, was capable of being easily reconverted to supermarket use.

New Jersey courts have refused to enforce contracts that violate public policy. See *Vasquez v. Glassboro Service Ass'n, Inc.,* 415 A.2d 1156 (N.J. 1980) (contract requiring migrant farmworker to leave barracks immediately upon discharge violates public policy). "No contract can be sustained if it is inconsistent with the public interest or detrimental to the common good." *Id.* at 98.

"The sources of public policy include federal and state legislation and judicial decisions." *Id.* The rehabilitation of our inner cities is a public policy of this State often expressed in relevant legislation.

The *New Jersey Economic Development Authority Act* (EDA), N.J.S.A. 34:1B-1 to -21, is intended to promote economic development generally throughout the State. As part of the EDA, the Legislature determined that the "provision of buildings, structures and other facilities to increase opportunity for employment in manufacturing, industrial, commercial, recreational, retail and service enterprises in the State is in the public interest." N.J.S.A. 34:1B-2b. The Legislature also specifically addressed the developmental problems of inner cities when it found:

> By virtue of their architectural and cultural heritage, their positions as principal centers of communication and transportation and their concentration of productive and energy efficient facilities, many municipalities are capable of ameliorating the conditions of deterioration which impede sound community growth and development; and *that building a proper balance of housing, industrial and commercial facilities and increasing the attractiveness of such municipalities to persons of all income levels is essential to restoring such municipalities as desirable places to live, work, shop and enjoy life's amenities.*

[N.J.S.A. 34:1B-2f (emphasis added).]

Similarly, in enacting the *New Jersey Urban Enterprise Zones Act,* N.J.S.A. 52:27H-60 to -89, the Legislature determined that "there persist in this State, particularly in its urban centers, areas of economic distress characterized by high unemployment, low investment of new capital, blighted conditions, obsolete or abandoned industrial or commercial structures, and deteriorating tax bases." N.J.S.A. 52:27H-61a. The Legislature also noted that revitalization of those areas required "application of the skills and entrepreneurial vigor of private enterprise; and it is the responsibility of government to provide a framework within which encouragement be given to private capital investment in these areas, disincentives to investment be removed or abated, and mechanisms be provided for the coordination and cooperation of private and public agencies in restoring the economic viability and prosperity of these areas." N.J.S.A. 52:27H-61 (emphasis added).

In support of these objectives, the Legislature offered a rich variety of subsidies and incentives to businesses operating in a designated enterprise zone. The City of New Brunswick currently is eligible for Open Competitive Urban Enterprise Zone Designation.

Other laws, too numerous to describe in detail, reveal how urban rehabilitation is imbedded in public policy and the public interest.*

Davidson's withdrawal from George Street caused difficulties and hardships of the nature mentioned earlier and made the downtown area a less hospitable and desirable place. Davidson had the right to terminate its George Street operation. In doing so, however, it imposed a restriction on the use of its former property designed to impede the relocation of another supermarket operation to the downtown area. The evidence supports the conclusion that the George Street store was peculiarly suited for supermarket use, and that there were no economically viable substitute locations. Consequently, the covenant, if enforced through injunctive relief or exposure to a judgment for damages, presented a formidable obstacle to remediation of the harm caused by Davidson's withdrawal. By harm, we mean the personal hardship caused by the withdrawal of a supermarket as well as the damage to the ongoing efforts of government and private enterprise to revitalize the city. We are persuaded, therefore, that, in the absence of any equivalent reciprocal benefit to the city, Davidson's scorched earth policy is so contrary to the public interest in these circumstances that the covenant is unreasonable and unenforceable. . . .

Affirmed.

NOTES AND QUESTIONS

1. *Reasonableness versus public policy.* Courts traditionally viewed covenants with suspicion because they interfered with the rights of owners to freely use their land and therefore inhibited alienability. The power of owners to contract to create covenants enforceable against successors was therefore limited to promote full ownership rights in current owners. Courts adopted rules of interpretation that narrowly construed covenants and applied the touch and concern test to invalidate covenants that infringed too greatly on the free use of land.

The traditional approach was problematic both because it was formalistic and because it limited too greatly the kinds of covenants that could be created. The touch and concern test was formalistic because it was unrelated to legitimate policy concerns. Instead of asking the metaphysical question of whether a covenant "touches and concerns land," the modern approach looks to see if there are policy reasons not to impose a covenant against a successor. It recognizes that covenants may increase the value of land and that they are valuable property rights in themselves. There is therefore a recognition of a need to balance the interests of the owners of servient estates in being free from obsolete or unduly restrictive servitudes and the interests of the owners of dominant estates in controlling the use of neighboring land.

The modern approach therefore replaced the touch and concern test with a reasonableness test. *Davidson* adopts this approach and engages in a broad consideration of the interests of both the dominant and servient estate owners, as well as the needs of the community. This represents a historical shift from a traditional suspicion of covenants as meddlesome interferences with the rights of owners that should be limited as much as possible to a more modern recognition of covenants as desirable property rights in themselves. It retains, however, the idea that such covenants *can* be meddlesome interferences with the free use of property and thus allows enforcement only where it can be shown to be reasonable to impose the obligation on the owner. Such obligations are reasonable if they benefit other owners in the community or if all owners are benefited by reciprocal obligations imposed on all owners in the community.

A third approach goes even further in the direction of protecting the interests of servitude beneficiaries. In 1985, California amended its statute to provide that covenants are enforceable "unless unreasonable." Cal. Civ. Code §1354. In contrast to the wide-ranging review for reasonableness evident in Davidson, a California court has interpreted this statute to mean that they are subject to a strong presumption of validity and will be struck down only if they violate public policy. In *Nahrstedt v. Lakeside Village Condominium Association*, 878 P.2d 1275 (Cal. Ct. App. 1994), the court upheld a covenant prohibiting pets in condominium units. The court explained that while rules adopted by the condominium association or board are subject to a general requirement of reasonableness, the same is not true for covenants contained in the declaration. Owners who purchase property subject to such existing covenants impliedly agree to be bound by them; they are therefore accorded a strong presumption of validity. *Hidden Harbour Estates v. Basso*, 393 So. 2d 637 (Fla. Dist. Ct. App. 1981). *Accord, Noble v. Murphy*, 612 N.E.2d 266 (Mass. 1993) (similarly upholding a ban on pets). A presumption of validity is justified because "a stable and predictable living environment is crucial to the success of condominiums and other common interest residential developments, and because recorded use restrictions are a primary means of ensuring this stability and predictability. . . ." 878 P.2d at 1278.

The *Restatement (Third)* adopts this approach, noting that servitudes are presumptively "valid." *Id.* §3.1. They are invalid only if they are "illegal or unconstitutional or violate[ ] public policy." Id. Comment a notes that this "applies the modern principle of freedom of contract to creation of servitudes." Parties are generally free to "contract as they wish, and courts will enforce their agreements without passing on their substance." Id. "The principle of freedom of contract is rooted in the notion that it is in the public interest to recognize that individuals have broad powers to order their own affairs." *Id.*

At the same time, the *Restatement (Third)* retains a substantial role for the courts in regulating and invalidating covenants. In addition to covenants that constitute unreasonable restraints on alienation and competition, the *Restatement (Third)* provides that "[s]ervitudes that are invalid because they violate public policy include, but are not limited to" those that are "arbitrary, spiteful, or capricious" or "that unreasonably burden[ ] a fundamental constitutional right" or are "unconscionable." *Id.* §3.1. Determining when a covenant violates public policy requires consideration of a host of values.

> h. Resolving public policy claims requires balancing interests. Resolving claims that a servitude violates public policy requires assessing the impact of the servitude, identifying the public interests that would be adversely affected by leaving the servitude in force, and weighing the predictable harm against the interests in enforcing the servitude. Only if the risks of social harm outweigh the benefits of enforcing the servitude is the servitude likely to be held invalid. The policies favoring freedom of contract, freedom to dispose of one's property, and protection of legitimate expectation interests nearly always weigh in favor of the validity of voluntarily created servitudes. A host of other policies, too numerous to catalog, may be adversely impacted by servitudes. Policies favoring privacy and liberty in choice of lifestyle, freedom of religion, freedom of speech and expression, access to the legal system, discouraging bad faith and unfair dealing, encouraging free competition, and socially productive uses of land have been implicated by servitudes. Other policies that become involved may include those protecting family relationships from coercive attempts to disrupt them, and protecting weaker groups in society from servitudes that exclude them from opportunities enjoyed by more fortunate groups to acquire desirable property for housing or access to necessary services.

Id. §3.1 cmt. h.

2. *Architectural review committees.* Some developers impose covenants requiring owners to obtain approval of an architectural review committee chosen by the homeowners association when they seek to make structural changes to their homes or even when they paint their shutters. In such cases, a recurrent issue is whether the architectural review committee, as an agent of the homeowners association, has a duty to act reasonably in administering the aesthetic controls imposed by the covenants, as well as whether the controls are reasonable in themselves.

Most courts hold such committees to a standard of reasonableness even if the covenants include no restrictions on the committee's discretion. For example, in *Westfield Homes, Inc. v. Herrick,* 593 N.E.2d 97 (Ill. App. Ct. 1992), the court held that an architectural review committee acted unreasonably when it refused to allow an owner to put in an above-ground swimming pool. The restrictive covenants explicitly prohibited certain types of construction, such as television antennas and clotheslines, but did not specifically prohibit swimming pools. The covenants required owners to obtain the approval of the architectural review committee before making any addition or change to existing structures; the covenants provided that the committee "shall, in its sole discretion, have the right to refuse to approve any such construction plans." The court noted that covenants should be "construed to give effect to the actual intention of the parties." *Id.* at 101. Despite the seemingly absolute grant of power to the committee, the court held that the "exercise of the power of review in a particular case must be reasonable and not arbitrary." *Id.* The committee could impose reasonable restrictions on the design and construction of the pool to minimize the auditory and visual impact on the neighboring properties but it could not absolutely prohibit construction of the pool. Accord, *Portola Hills Community Association v. James,* 5 Cal. Rptr. 2d 580 (Ct. App. 1992) (holding that it would be unreasonable for a homeowners association to ban a satellite dish when the dish would be located in the backyard and would not be visible to the neighbors); *Riss v. Angel,* 934 P.2d 669, 677-679 (Wash. 1997). *Cf. Nahrstedt v. Lakeside Village Condominium Association, Inc.,* 878 P.2d 1275 (Cal. 1994) ("In determining whether a restriction is 'unreasonable' under [Cal. Civ. Code] §1354, and thus not enforceable, the focus is on the restriction's effect on the project as a whole, not on the individual homeowner").

On the other hand, the Supreme Court of Oregon held that an architectural committee's decisions were unreviewable when the covenants gave it "discretion" to make such decisions and specifically provided that it be the "sole judge of the suitability" of the height of improvements. *Valenti v. Hopkins,* 926 P.2d 813 (Or. 1996). Justice Van Hoomissen noted that the plaintiffs had purchased property knowing that the committee had plenary discretion to make such decisions and that they therefore "approved the covenants." *Id.* at 817.

PROBLEMS

1. Suppose a homeowners association amends the covenants to provide that the homeowners intend to give the architectural review committee absolute power to approve or disapprove construction plans in the neighborhood. Should such a provision be enforceable or should it be held void as a matter of public policy?

2. In *Mulligan v. Panther Valley Property Owners Association,* 766 A.2d 1186 (N.J. Super. Ct. App. Div. 2001), a homeowners association in a gated residential community of more than 2,000 homes (including single-family homes, townhouses, and condo-

minium units) voted to amend applicable covenants to prohibit occupancy of any unit by a registered sex offender. Plaintiff unit owner challenged the amended covenant on the ground that it was unreasonable. Assume that the unit owner's 30-year-old son was convicted of a crime involving sexual activity with a 12-year-old. He moved back in with his mother after serving an eight-year sentence. The amendment to the declaration followed, requiring the mother either to move or not allow her son to remain in her house.

    a.   What is the association's argument that the amendment is reasonable and can be imposed retroactively?

    b.   What is the unit owner's argument that the amendment is unreasonable and/or cannot be applied retroactively?

    c.   What should the court do?

    3. The California Supreme Court upheld a "no pets" covenant in *Nahrstedt v. Lakeside Village Condominium Association, Inc.*, 878 P.2d 1275 (Cal. 1994) against a challenge that it was unreasonable. The California legislature overturned the result in Nahrstedt in 2000 by adopting a statute providing that "[n]o governing documents shall prohibit the owner of a separate interest within a common interest development from keeping at least one pet within the common interest development, subject to reasonable rules and regulations of the association." Cal. Civ. Code §1360.5. Then that same court interpreted the new law merely to prohibit an initial declaration banning pets but allowing condominium associations to amend such declarations to include a no pets rule. *Villa de las Palmas Homeowners Ass'n v. Terifaj*, 90 P.3d 1223 (Cal. 2004). Should courts uphold "no pets" covenants or strike them down as unreasonable or contrary to public policy? Did the California Supreme Court interpret §1360.5 correctly?

    4. When developers sell homes with rights to use commonly owned areas, such as a lake, recreational area, or road, there is normally a declaration creating a homeowners association with the power to impose assessments on owners to recover the costs of maintenance of those areas. If a developer fails to create such an association or the declaration does not initially give the association the power to tax owners to pay for maintenance of common areas or common easements, can the homeowners whose properties are appurtenant to the common areas or easements vote to create a homeowners association and/or impose assessments on owners who do not agree? *Compare Weatherby Lake Improvement Co. v. Sherman*, 611 S.W.2d 326 (Mo. Ct. App. 1980) (power to create a homeowners association to manage and maintain a commonly owned lake) and *Evergreen Highlands Ass'n v. West*, 73 P.3d 1 (Colo. 2003) (association has power to add new declaration provisions including provisions requiring membership in the homeowners association and authorizing, for the first time, mandatory assessments to maintain common areas) with *Wendover Road Property Owners Ass'n v. Kornicks*, 502 N.E.2d 226 (Ohio Ct. App. 1985) (owners cannot compel participation in the cost of improvements to commonly owned easements in the absence of a declaration creating a homeowners association with the power to impose such assessments).

    5. A covenant limiting property to residential use and barring any commercial use is interpreted to preclude operation of a family daycare center. Given the need for affordable, convenient daycare, does this covenant violate public policy? *See Terrien v. Zwit*, 648 N.W.2d 602 (Mich. 2002) (holding that it does not violate public policy, reversing lower court rulings to the contrary).

§5.5.6.2 Rules and Bylaws

O'BUCK v. COTTONWOOD VILLAGE
CONDOMINIUM ASSOCIATION, INC.
750 P.2d 813 (Alaska 1988)

JAY A. RABINOWITZ, Chief Justice....

John and Janie O'Buck, plaintiffs and appellants in this case, purchased a unit in the Cottonwood Village Condominiums in June 1981. At that time, the unit was pre-wired for a central television antenna and for Visions, an antenna-based cable system. It is impossible to watch television in the unit without an outdoor antenna or cable because of bad reception. The availability of an antenna was an important consideration for the O'Bucks in deciding to purchase their unit because they have four televisions and frequently watch different programs.

In 1984, the Board of Directors of the Cottonwood Village Association ("the Board" or "the Association") had to address a serious problem of roof leakage in the condominiums. Among the several causes of leakage were badly mounted antennae and foot traffic on the roof related to the antennae. The Association paid $155,000 to have the roofs repaired. In order to do the work, the contractors removed all the antennae from the roofs. Before any of the antennae were reinstalled, the Board adopted a rule prohibiting the mounting of television antennae anywhere on the buildings. The purposes of this rule were to protect the roof and to enhance the marketability of the condominium units. The Board further decided to make the MultiVisions cable system available as an alternative to antennae. The Board rejected other alternatives such as a satellite dish or antennae mounted on the sides of the buildings. The Board offered to pay the fifteen dollar hookup fee to MultiVisions and to pay for the depreciated value of the old antennae. The O'Bucks were paid $284.20 for their antenna, which had been damaged when contractors removed it from the roof. The O'Bucks now have one television hooked up to MultiVisions. Their other sets have no reception, and it would cost ten dollars per month per set to hook them up.

The O'Bucks subsequently filed a complaint against the Association seeking damages and an injunction against enforcement of the rule....

The O'Bucks challenge the Board's authority to adopt the rule. We conclude that the Board had authority to enact a rule banning television antennae from buildings under either of two provisions in the Declaration of Condominium, the "constitution" of the Association. *See* Alaska Stat. §34.07.010-.070.

First, article IX, section 4 of the Declaration authorizes the Board to adopt rules and regulations governing the use of the common areas, which include the roofs and walls of the buildings. That section provides:

> *Rules and Regulations.* Rules and regulations may be adopted by the Board of Directors concerning and governing the use of the general and limited common areas providing such rules and regulations shall be furnished to owners prior to the time they become effective and that such rules and regulations shall be uniform and nondiscriminatory.

Second, article XIX, section 1(d) of the Declaration authorizes the Board to require unit owners to take action to preserve a uniform exterior appearance to the buildings. That section provides:

In order to preserve a uniform exterior appearance to the building, the Board may require the painting of the building, decks and balconies, and prescribe the type and color of paint, and *may prohibit*, require, or regulate *any modification* or decoration of the building, decks and balconies undertaken or proposed by any owner. This power of the Board extends to screens, doors, awnings, rails *or other visible portions of each condominium unit and condominium building.* The Board may also require use of a uniform color of draperies or drapery lining for all units. (Emphasis supplied.) . . .

Given these two provisions, the Board had authority to ban antennae either on roof-protection grounds (under article IX, section 4) or on aesthetic grounds (under either section), both of which were given as reasons for the antennae rule. . . .

The O'Bucks also cite several provisions of the Declaration and Bylaws which explicitly prohibit or authorize the prohibition of other things, such as pets, modification of buildings, and posting of bills. They reason that since there is no explicit authorization to prohibit antennae, and since the Declaration and Bylaws contemplate the existence of antennae, a right to have an antenna is reasonably inferred and cannot be taken away without amending the Declaration or Bylaws. They rely on *Beachwood Villas Condominium v. Poor,* 448 So. 2d 1143, 1145 (Fla. Dist. Ct. App. 1984), which held: "provided that a board-enacted rule does not contravene either an express provision of the declaration or a right reasonably inferable therefrom, it will be found valid, within the scope of the board's authority." (Emphasis supplied.)

We do not find the O'Bucks' arguments persuasive. . . .

The absence of any provision explicitly authorizing the Board to ban antennae is not fatal to the Board's right to do so. As noted in *Beachwood Villas,* "[i]t would be impossible to list all restrictive uses in a declaration of condominium." 448 So. 2d at 1145. Thus, in that case the court upheld board-enacted rules regulating unit rentals and the occupancy of units by guests during the owner's absence. The court refused to find a reasonably inferable right and upheld the rules even in the absence of an express provision authorizing them. . . .

For these reasons, we hold that the Declaration and Bylaws granted the Board the authority to enact the subject rule banning television antennae on buildings.

Both parties agree that a condominium association rule will not withstand judicial scrutiny if it is not reasonable. This standard of review is supported by case law and legal commentary.

The superior court found that roof-mounted television antennae were one of a number of causes of leaking roofs. This finding has ample support in the record. The architect engaged by the Association to make recommendations as to what to do about the problem testified that television antennae caused problems on each of the twenty-two roofs in the condominium project. Other problems causing the leaking were age of the condominiums, their poor design, and problems of poor workmanship which went into the construction of the condominium buildings. He also testified that it was important to limit foot traffic on the roofs, as many owners were apparently causing damage to the roofs when walking there to adjust their antennae. The repairs to the roof cost the Association $155,000. These facts clearly justified the Board's action to limit or prohibit television antennae and foot traffic on the roofs.

If the roof problems were the only justification for the rule, the O'Bucks would have a stronger argument that the rule was unreasonable. This is because they hired an architect who designed a method of installing antennae on the sides of the buildings rather than the roofs. This method would involve only brief work on the roof to connect the coaxial cable, and the rest of the work could be done from a ladder or hydraulically operated bucket. The availability of this relatively inexpensive alternative would cast some doubt on the reasonableness of a blanket prohibition on antennae if the only purpose of the rule was to protect the roofs.

However, it is clear that other legitimate considerations also motivated the antenna ban. As discussed above, the Declaration specifically authorized the prohibition of modifications or decorations to preserve a uniform exterior appearance to the buildings. Numerous witnesses testified that the Board was influenced by the unsightliness of the antennae. It was estimated that each of the 104 units in the twenty-two buildings had an antenna protruding from the roof. Witnesses testified that the Board felt that the elimination of the forest of antennae combined with the availability of a state-of-the-art cable system would enhance the marketability of the units. This evidence is adequate to support the superior court's conclusion that aesthetics and improved marketability were grounds for the antenna ban.

It is clear that the O'Bucks do not agree that the antenna ban improved the exterior appearance of the buildings. They describe this goal as "[nothing] more than a sop to personal prejudice or unarticulated personal values." However, this is a facet of the freedom they sacrificed when they bought into a condominium association....

[C]ondominium owners consciously sacrifice some freedom of choice in their decision to live in this type of housing. Unit owners may not rely on the courts to strike down reasonable rules on the grounds of differences in aesthetic tastes.

In evaluating the reasonableness of a condominium association rule, it is necessary to balance the importance of the rule's objective against the importance of the interest infringed upon. In a case where a rule seriously curtails an important civil liberty — such as, for example, freedom of expression — we will look with suspicion on the rule and require a compelling justification. The antenna ban in the instant case curtails no significant interests. The only loss suffered is that the O'Bucks and the other owners must now pay a small monthly fee to receive television, and even this cost is offset to a degree by the savings from the lack of need to install and maintain an antenna. In some cases, we might consider a financial burden to be an important interest. However, the fee in this case is small in view of the wherewithal of the members of the Association.[6] For this reason, we find that the interests of the Association in improving the exterior appearance of the buildings and enhancing the marketability of the units more than adequately justify the small financial burden placed on the owners....

NEUMAN v. GRANDVIEW AT EMERALD HILLS, INC.

861 So. 2d 494 (Fla. Dist. Ct. App. 2003)

MARTHA C. WARNER, J.

We deny the motion for rehearing, withdraw our previously issued opinion, and substitute the following in its place.

---

6. The units were advertised at a cost of $97,000 in 1981.

The issue presented in this case is whether a condominium association rule banning the holding of religious services in the auditorium of the condominium constitutes a violation of Fla. Stat. §718.123, which precludes condominium rules from unreasonably restricting a unit owner's right to peaceably assemble. We hold that the rule does not violate the statute and affirm.

Appellee Grandview is a condominium association with 442 members, appellants being two of the members. Appellants reside at Grandview condominium during the winter months. The common elements of the condominium include an auditorium that members can reserve for social gatherings and meetings. Grandview enacted a rule governing the use of the auditorium in 1982, which provided that the auditorium could be used for meetings or functions of groups, including religious groups, when at least eighty percent of the members were residents of Grandview condominium. Generally, the only reservations made for the auditorium on Saturdays were by individual members for birthday or anniversary celebrations.

In January 2001, several unit owners reserved the auditorium between 8:30 and noon on Saturday mornings. While they indicated they were reserving it for a party, they actually conducted religious services. Approximately forty condominium members gathered for the services.

Upon discovering that religious services were being conducted on Saturdays in the auditorium, several other members complained to the Board of Directors ("Board"). The Board met in February to discuss restrictions on the use of the auditorium and common elements for religious services and activities. The meeting became very confrontational between those members supporting the use of the auditorium for religious services and those opposing such use. Based upon the controversial nature of the issue, the Board's desire not to have a common element tied up for the exclusive use of a minority of the members on a regular basis, and to avoid conflicts between different religious groups competing for the space, the Board first submitted the issue to a vote of the owners. Seventy percent of the owners voted in favor of prohibiting the holding of religious services in the auditorium. The Board then voted unanimously to amend the rule governing the use of the auditorium. The new rule provided that "no religious services or activities of any kind are allowed in the auditorium or any other common elements."

Appellants filed suit against Grandview seeking injunctive and declaratory relief to determine whether the rule violated their constitutional rights or was in violation of §718.123, and whether the rule was arbitrarily and capriciously enacted by the Board. Grandview answered, denying that the rule was arbitrary or violated appellants' statutory or constitutional rights. Appellants moved for a temporary injunction alleging that Grandview was not only preventing the owners from holding religious services, it was also prohibiting the use of the auditorium for holiday parties, including Christmas and Chanukah, based upon its prohibition against using the common elements "for religious activities of any kind." The court granted the motion as to the use of the auditorium for religious activities of any kind but denied it as it applied to the holding of religious services. Based upon the temporary injunction as to religious activities, Grandview amended its rule to limit the prohibition to the holding of religious services in the auditorium.

At a hearing on appellants' motion for a permanent injunction against the rule, the appellants relied primarily on §718.123, which prohibits condominium associations from unreasonably restricting the unit owners' rights to peaceable assembly. They argued that religious services fell into the category of a "peaceable assembly," and a categorical ban on the holding of religious services was per se unreasonable. Grandview maintained that it had the right to restrict the use of its common elements. Because the right of peaceable assembly did not mandate a right to conduct religious services, it had the right to poll its members and restrict the use based upon the majority's desires. As such, Grandview maintained the exercise of this right was reasonable.

In its final order denying the injunction, the court determined that because no state action was involved, the unit owners' constitutional rights of freedom of speech and religion were not implicated by Grandview's rule. The court determined that the rule did not violate §718.123, as the condominium association had the authority to enact this reasonable restriction on the use of the auditorium. Appellants challenge that ruling.

Chapter 718, Florida's "Condominium Act," recognizes the condominium form of property ownership and "establishes a detailed scheme for the creation, sale, and operation of condominiums." *Woodside Vill. Condo. Ass'n v. Jahren*, 806 So. 2d 452, 455 (Fla. 2002). Thus, condominiums are strictly creatures of statute. The declaration of condominium, which is the condominium's "constitution," creates the condominium and "strictly governs the relationships among the condominium units owners and the condominium association." *Id. at* 456. Under the declaration, the Board of the condominium association has broad authority to enact rules for the benefit of the community.

In *Hidden Harbour Estates, Inc. v. Norman*, 309 So. 2d 180, 181-82 (Fla. Dist. Ct. App. 1975), this court explained the unique character of condominium living which, for the good of the majority, restricts rights residents would otherwise have were they living in a private separate residence:

> It appears to us that inherent in the condominium concept is the principle that to promote the health, happiness, and peace of mind of the majority of the unit owners since they are living in such close proximity and using facilities in common, each unit owner must give up a certain degree of freedom of choice which he might otherwise enjoy in separate, privately owned property. Condominium unit owners comprise a little democratic sub society of necessity more restrictive as it pertains to use of condominium property than may be existent outside the condominium organization.

Section 718.123(1) recognizes the right of the condominium association to regulate the use of the common elements of the condominium (emphasis added):

> All common elements, common areas, and recreational facilities serving any condominium shall be available to unit owners in the condominium or condominiums served thereby and their invited guests for the use intended for such common elements, common areas, and recreational facilities, subject to the provisions of §718.106(4). The entity or entities responsible for the operation of the common elements, common areas, and recreational facilities may adopt reasonable rules and regulations pertaining to the use of such common elements, common areas, and recreational facilities. No entity or entities shall unreasonably restrict any unit owner's right to peaceably assemble or right to invite public officers or candidates for public office to appear and speak in common elements, common areas, and recreational facilities.

The statutory test for rules regarding the operation of the common elements of the condominium is reasonableness. The trial court found the rule preventing use of the auditorium for religious services was reasonable in light of the Board's concern for a serious potential for conflict of use which could arise among competing religious groups. Having polled the members and determined that a majority of the members approved the ban, the Board's rule assured that the auditorium was "available to unit owners in the condominium or condominiums served thereby and their invited guests for the use intended" in accordance with the statute. §718.123(1).

The appellants' main argument both at trial and on appeal suggests that because the statute mandates that the Board may not "unreasonably restrict any unit owner's right to peaceably assemble," §718.123(1), a categorical prohibition of all religious services exceeds the Board's powers, as the right to meet in religious worship would constitute the right to peaceably assemble. However, the right to peaceably assemble has traditionally been interpreted to apply to the right of the citizens to meet to discuss public or governmental affairs. *See United States v. Cruikshank*, 92 U.S. 542, 551-5 (1875). Assuming for purposes of this argument that the right to gather for religious worship is a form of peaceable assembly, the rule in question bans this particular form of assembly, but not all right to assemble. Certainly, a categorical ban on the right of members to use the auditorium for any gathering would be contrary to statute. However, the statute itself permits the reasonable regulation of that right. Prohibiting those types of assembly which will have a particularly divisive effect on the condominium community is a reasonable restriction. The Board found that permitting the holding of regular worship services and the competition among various religious groups for use of the auditorium would pose such conflict. Where the condominium association's regulations regarding common elements are reasonable and not violative of specific statutory limitations, the regulations should be upheld. The trial court found the restriction reasonable under the facts. No abuse of discretion has been shown.

The judgment of the trial court is affirmed.

NOTES AND QUESTIONS

Wolinsky v. Kadison, 449 N.E.2d 151 (Ill. App. Ct. 1983) (see supra §5.5.4.3), held that board members have fiduciary obligations to members of the association. The question then becomes what the standard should be for judging whether board members have met their obligations. Most courts hold boards to a standard of reasonableness. Decisions of architectural review committees, for example, will not be upheld if they are unreasonable.

The Court of Appeals of New York adopted a more lenient standard. *In Matter of Levandusky v. One Fifth Avenue Apartment Corp.*, 553 N.E.2d 1317 (N.Y. 1990), a dispute arose when a cooperative board refused to allow a unit owner to relocate a steam riser so that he could renovate his kitchen. The owner defied the board and relocated the riser anyway. The board sued, asking the court to order him to restore the riser to its original position. The trial court held that the board's refusal to allow the renovation to stay was unreasonable because relocation of the riser posed no danger to the building. The Appeals Court reversed, holding that board members are subject to a variation of the "business judgment rule" generally applicable to boards of directors of for-profit corporations. This rule immunizes officers and board members from liability if they act "in good faith and in the exercise of honest judgment in the lawful and legitimate furtherance of corporate purposes." *Id.* at 1321. "So long as the board acts for the purposes of the cooperative, within the scope of its authority and in good faith, courts will not substitute their judgment for the board's." *Id.*

The court acknowledged that "the broad powers of a cooperative board hold potential for abuse through arbitrary and malicious decision-making, favoritism, discrimination and the like." *Id.* at 1320. At the same time, the court noted that "the stability offered by community control, through a board, has its own economic and social benefits, and purchase of a cooperative apartment represents a voluntary choice to cede certain of the privileges of single ownership to a governing body . . . ." *Id.* at 1320-1321. However, allowing generalized review for reasonableness was viewed as inappropriate in this setting. Justice Kaye argued, *Id.* at 1323:

> Several related concerns persuade us that such a rule should apply here. As this case exemplifies, board decisions concerning what residents may or may not do with their living space may be highly charged and emotional. A cooperative or condominium is by nature a myriad of often competing views regarding personal living space, and decisions taken to benefit the collective interest may be unpalatable to one resident or another, creating the prospect that board decisions will be subjected to undue court involvement and judicial second-guessing. Allowing an owner who is simply dissatisfied with particular board action a second opportunity to reopen the matter completely before a court, which — generally without knowing the property — may or may not agree with the reasonableness of the board's determination, threatens the stability of the common living arrangement.
>
> Moreover, the prospect that each board decision may be subjected to full judicial review hampers the effectiveness of the board's managing authority. The business judgment rule protects the board's business decisions and managerial authority from indiscriminate attack. At the same time, it permits review of improper decisions, as when the challenger demonstrates that the board's action has no legitimate relationship to the welfare of the cooperative, deliberately singles out individuals for harmful treatment, is taken without notice or consideration of the relevant facts, or is beyond the scope of the board's authority.

Are you convinced by this argument?

PROBLEMS

1. Each unit in a five-story condominium complex has a porch. The condominium association passes a rule that provides that "no owner shall erect a structure on the porch." One owner builds a sukkah, a temporary structure used by Jews to celebrate the religious festival of Sukkot. The condominium association believes the ramshackle structure is unsightly and tells the owner to remove it and not to build any other structures like it in the future, even though it will be up for less than two weeks. The unit owner comes to you for advice. Is the restriction on use of the porch reasonable and enforceable?

2. A professional violinist purchases a condominium unit. Her neighbors complain that she disturbs them when she plays her violin. The violinist agrees not to play before 10 A.M. or after 7 P.M., but her neighbors are not satisfied. The condominium association passes a rule prohibiting all owners from playing musical instruments in their apartments. Is the rule reasonable and enforceable?

3. A homeowner installs a clothesline in her backyard to air dry her laundry. The bylaws of the association applicable to her property prohibit this, presumably for esthetic reasons and because hanging laundry outdoors is thought to lower property values. The owner argues that she is an environmentalist who is trying to save energy by not using her clothes dryer. She also feels an obligation to do so because of the rolling blackouts experienced by California in recent memory. Is the bylaw reasonable? Should a court enforce it?[29] *See* Dusty Horwitt, *The Right to Dry: Laundry on the Line,* Legal Aff. (Jan./Feb. 2004), http://legalaffairs.org/issues/January-February-2004/scene_horwitt_janfeb04.html.

4. Justice Clarence Thomas's father-in-law, Donald Lamp, hung an American flag outside the balcony of his condominium unit. The condominium association had passed a rule prohibiting any banners or flags outside units, including the American flag. It did so, it seems, for esthetic reasons and to preserve a uniform appearance of the units. Lamp was asked to abide by the rule, but he refused. After nationwide publicity, the association amended its policy to make an exception for the American flag. Tony Mauro, *An Unwelcome Mat for Free Speech,* USA Today, Aug. 18, 2004, at 13A. Most such disputes garner no such publicity. For example, a rule banning a flagpole (but not banning flags) was enforced in *Wyndham Foundation, Inc. v. Oulton,* 2001 Va. Cir. LEXIS 138 (Va. Cir. Ct. 2001) (ordering homeowners to comply with a rule of the homeowners association banning construction of "structures" on their property without approval of the association and ordering removal of a massive flagpole from their property). Is a rule banning all flags, including the American flag, outside a condominium unit reasonable and enforceable? What are the arguments on both sides? *See* Cal. Civ. Code §1353.6(a) (homeowners associations cannot prohibit the display of flags unless such a ban is needed to protect public health or safety or the flag would violate local, state, or federal law); Fla. Stat. §§720.304(2), 720.3075 (homeowners may display the flag regardless of any rule to the contrary); 765 Ill. Comp. Stat. 605/18.6, 805 Ill. Comp. Stat. 105/103.30 (prohibiting enforcement of a covenant that denies a homeowner the right to fly the American flag).

---

29. I owe this hypothetical to a Doonesbury cartoon by Garry Trudeau.

III

Common Ownership of Property

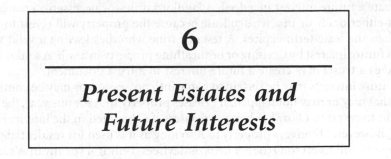

6

Present Estates and Future Interests

§6.1 Division of Ownership Over Time

Landowners may own property in common in two ways. They may own property *concurrently*. A husband and wife, for example, may own their home jointly; roommates may rent an apartment together. In these cases, they possess the property together and work out among themselves how it will be used. These types of concurrent interests are covered in Chapter 7, *infra*. A different way owners may share ownership is by divvying up ownership rights *over time*, with one owning the present right to possess the property and the other a future power to take possession from the present owner in specified circumstances. The legal system authorizes owners to divide present from future ownership. The *present estate* holder has the right to possess the property while her property rights last; the *future interest* holder will obtain the right to possess the property when and if the present interest terminates.

The grantor specifies the circumstances under which the property will shift in the future from the present interest holder to the future interest holder. Sometimes the circumstance is one over which the grantee has no control; for example, the grantor may convey property to *A* so long as she is alive and then provide that at *A*'s death, the property will transfer to *B*. The grantor in this case is not attempting to control directly what *A* does with the property; however, by deciding who will own the property at *A*'s death, the grantor often hopes to control *indirectly* what is done with the property — for example, by keeping the property in the family and making sure it is available for the grandchildren to inherit. Other times, the circumstance under which title shifts is one that the grantee can control; for example, the grantor may convey property to *A* so long as the property is used for residential purposes, but if it is ever used for nonresidential purposes, ownership will revert to the grantor. In this case, the loss of title to the property has the effect of acting as a sanction against the present owner for violating the conditions under which he obtained title. The creation of future interests may therefore constitute a direct or indirect attempt to control the future uses of real property.

Present and future interests may be created by sale, lease, will, or trust. A seller may create a future interest in a deed. A landlord or lessor necessarily creates a future interest either orally or in a written lease because the property will revert to the landlord when the lease term expires. A testator (one who dies leaving a valid will) may create a future interest by devising or bequeathing property in a will. A settlor (one who establishes a trust) may create a future interest in a trust document.[1]

Future interests may be certain to come into possession or may be contingent on events that may or may not happen. If O leases property to A for one year, the property is certain to revert to O (or her heirs or devisees if O has died in the interim) after one year. If, however, O conveys property to A so long as it is used for residential purposes, the property will revert to O (or her heirs or devisees) only if A (or any of A's successors in interest) violates the condition that the property be used only for residential purposes.

Future interests exist the moment they are created even though the future owner has no right to possess the property until the happening of the triggering event. Suppose O conveys property to A so long as it is used for residential purposes; if the property is ever used for nonresidential purposes within A's lifetime, the property shall go automatically to B or his heirs. The future interest in B comes into existence at the moment of the original conveyance to A; we say that B owns a future interest in the property, although B has no present right to occupy or use the property. B will have a right to possess, use, and control the property only if and when the condition is violated; the future interest will not "become possessory," as we say, unless and until the condition occurs.

The central legal questions here are whether the future interest is enforceable and, if so, whether the condition triggering the future interest has been violated or has occurred. If the interest is not enforceable by a particular person, it may nonetheless be enforceable by another person; for example, an interest that cannot be owned by a third party (other than the grantor or grantee) may be enforceable if owned by the grantor. If the future interest is unenforceable, we therefore face the question whether the current owner owns the property entirely free of the restriction or whether a reserved future interest remains in the grantor.

By delegating to property owners the power to create future interests, the legal system enables people to exercise some degree of control over who owns the property in the future and what the future owner is entitled to do with it. This is an awesome power. The law of future interests raises a host of complicated policy questions. The two most pressing are the problem of dead hand control and the problem of social hierarchy.

Problem of the dead hand. The *dead hand* problem arises because owners may seek to control who owns property long after they die. Allowing grantors or testators to do this may promote their interests and even enhance alienability; owners may be more

---

1. *Testator* (male) and *testatrix* (female) are the legal terms used to designate the person who writes a will controlling the disposition of property upon his or her death. The act of leaving real property by a will to a beneficiary is called *devising* the property; the act of leaving personal property is called *bequeathing* the property. The recipients of devised real property are called *devisees*. If someone dies without leaving a valid will, the property is divided up among the persons identified in the state *intestacy statute*. Those who inherit property under the state intestacy statute are called *heirs*. A trust is a property arrangement in which ownership rights are controlled by one person (the *trustee*) for the benefit of another identified individual (the *beneficiary*). The person establishing a trust, the *settlor,* does so in a written *trust document.*

willing to part with their property if they can control who owns it in the future. However, conditions may limit what owners may do with their property, thus interfering with freedom of future owners to control the property. This may both undermine the autonomy of future owners and the efficient use and transfer of property. The ability to create future interests, unless regulated by the legal system, could eventually clog up the market for real estate by attaching numerous and multiple conditions to property, restricting both what it can be used for and whether it can be bought and sold. Affected persons may be able to remove archaic restrictions by contract, in which the beneficiaries of the restraints on use or alienation agree to give up their rights. However, transaction costs may block such deals, especially if many persons are affected by the restraint; the costs of renegotiating the property arrangement may be so high that they interfere with efficient readjustment of property relations. Rigid enforcement of restrictions imposed long ago by grantors who could not anticipate current conditions would sometimes prevent property from being devoted to its best uses as social circumstances and needs change. The struggle for control between prior owners and current owners or between current owners and future owners requires a legal structure that balances their relative interests.

Hierarchy. A second problem associated with the ability to create future interests is the possibility that by imposing restraints on alienation and use, owners will have the wanted or unwanted effect of concentrating ownership in the hands of certain groups and excluding others. For example, if property ownership could be lawfully conditioned on the property's not being occupied by a person of a particular race, and if racial discrimination were a widespread social practice, the ability to own property would eventually be conditional on race, as more and more parcels of property were taken out of the general marketplace and limited to members of a particular race. Such a system would divide people into social classes based on race, with some persons, but not others, entitled to enter particular markets. We would have a racial caste system rather than a free market.

Similarly, if future interests were not regulated, owners would be able to prevent property from being transferred outside the family by restrictions on inheritability and transfer. While taking property out of the marketplace is sometimes a useful way to create secure expectations, it could also concentrate ownership in the hands of those who already own property and their descendants. As more property becomes tied up by restraints, more people would be excluded from the ability to participate in the real estate market. Access to property would therefore depend less on current needs and ability than on heredity.

To some extent, the marketplace is designed to decentralize power over social resources, dispersing it among citizens rather than concentrating it into the hands of government officials or a landed aristocracy. To maintain this decentralization of power, however, rules of law are necessary to prevent private owners from reconcentrating ownership by creating new monopolies or centers of power. For example, in *People ex rel. Moloney v. Pullman's Palace Car Co.*, 51 N.E. 664 (Ill. 1898), the Illinois Supreme Court required the corporate owner of a company town inhabited by 12,000 people to sell off most of the property. *Id.* at 674.

> [T]he existence of a town or city where the streets, alleys, school houses, business houses, sewerage system, hotels, churches, theaters, water-works, market places, dwellings and tenements are the exclusive property of a corporation is opposed to good public

policy and incompatible with the theory and spirit of our institutions. It is clearly the theory of our law, streets, alleys and public ways, and public school buildings, should be committed to the control of the proper public authorities, and that real estate should be kept as fully as possible in the channels of trade and commerce, and good public policy demands that the number of persons who should engage in the business of selling such articles as are necessary to the support, maintenance and comfort of the people of any community should not be restricted by the will of any person, natural or artificial, but should be left to be determined by the healthy, wholesome and natural operations of the rules of trade and business, free from all that which tends to stifle competition and foster monopolies.

Regulation of future interests may similarly help to maintain the dispersal of access to property so that a decentralized market system can function properly.

The relationship between future interests and the problems of dead hand control and social hierarchy can be better understood by considering the feudal origins of modern property law. To a large extent, the current legal rules grew out of, and responded to, the need to shift from the hierarchical social and economic structure of feudalism to the structure of the market, with its concomitant social structures of the state and the family. Modern rules of property law are significantly shaped by a reaction against the feudal structure and a commitment to wide dispersal of access to property.

§6.2 Historical Background: From Feudalism to the Market

§6.2.1 A MODERN ANALOGY

Feudalism died a long time ago, but remnants of feudal structures remain. Think of the relations between landlords and tenants: The tenant offers to pay the landlord periodic rental payments; in return for these rents, the landlord agrees to grant the tenant possession of a specified piece of property. The landlord also implicitly or explicitly agrees to provide certain services to the tenant in the form of maintenance of the property. Under this arrangement, the parties have divided the property interests between themselves. The tenant has the right to possess the property and to be protected through basic maintenance; the landlord has the right to receive the agreed-upon rents and to get the property back when the relationship terminates. Feudalism structured all of society into a pattern similar to this familiar one.

§6.2.2 THE FEUDAL HIERARCHY

Feudalism in England originated in 1066, when the Normans, under William the Conqueror, invaded and conquered England.[2] William created a form of social organization tied to land that linked almost everyone in the country in a huge social hierarchy. William rewarded the knights who had enabled him to prevail by seizing land from those who had resisted him and dividing it among his own men. In return for their lands, these *tenants-in-chief* would agree to pledge loyalty to the king and to

---

2. This discussion is based on A. W. B. Simpson, *A History of the Land Law* (2d ed. 1986).

provide certain services for the king—ordinarily by providing a certain number of knights for the king's army (called *knight-services*). By 1086 there were about 1,500 tenants-in-chief in England. The relationship between the king and these tenants-in-chief was a personal one between superior and inferior; rights in the land existed only during the tenant's life, and at first there was no right allowing heirs to inherit the land. Rights in the land were also contingent; failure to perform the services would cause the land to be forfeited to the monarch. The tenants did not own the land in any modern sense; they held the land of the king in return for periodic services to him.

The tenants-in-chief could provide knight-services directly by paying for knights to stay in their own households and be available as the king needed them. Most tenants-in-chief, however, made further deals with subtenants through the process of *subinfeudation*. In exchange for parcels of land they held "of the king," the tenants-in-chief would find subtenants who would agree to perform part of the services owed by the tenant-in-chief to the king. This subtenant could further subinfeudate by making an agreement with a subtenant of his own, and so on. At the bottom of the feudal ladder were the *tenants-in-demesne*, who actually worked the agricultural land. Everyone, except the king, was subordinate to some lord, and everyone, except the tenant-in-demesne, was lord of some tenant; those in the middle of the ladder, called *mesne lords*, were both tenant to some lord above them and lord of some tenant below them. At the *very* bottom of the feudal hierarchy were *villeins*—unfree men and women who did not even make it onto the feudal ladder.

The great lords ordinarily owned a manor house or castle and retained lands worked by villeins, or peasants. Their powers mixed what we would term property and sovereignty. The lord was both owner (proprietor of the land) and ruler (local political official). As the local ruler, the lord would hold court and decide disputes among tenants on the lord's manor. The distinction between *free* and *unfree tenure* was central since those possessed of free tenements had the right to bring lawsuits, called *real actions*, in the central royal courts where the common law developed. Until the sixteenth century, however, the villeins possessed of unfree tenure were relegated to the manorial courts of their lords and were subject to local custom—and the lord's whim.

§6.2.3   FREE TENURES

Lords and tenants were free to make whatever arrangements they wished. While no fixed rules governed the kinds of services that could be exacted, categories of tenurial relationships were quickly established, with two different kinds of obligations: *services* (the periodic obligations promised by the tenant-grantee to the lord-grantor) and *incidents* (infrequent liabilities, including inheritance taxes). It is of crucial importance that, over time, the services decreased in economic importance since their value was fixed, while the incidents increased in importance since their value kept pace with inflation.

§6.2.3.1   Tenures and Services

Military tenure. Most tenants-in-chief held their land in return for providing knights to help defend the land and engage in foreign wars. Within 100 years of its creation, the duty to provide knights was converted into the obligation to make a money payment called *scutage*. The tenants-in-chief would then exact scutage from their subtenants and so on down the ladder. By the mid-thirteenth century, the payment of scutage became the normal practice. It was regarded as a form of direct taxation and by the fourteenth century was controlled by Parliament.

Other military tenures included *castle-gard* (defense of the castle), *grand serjeanty* (service of a personal nature for the monarchy, such as carrying the king's sword at coronation), and *petit serjeanty* (providing an object for the king, such as a glove or sword, for court ceremonies).

Religious tenure. Lands granted to religious persons or institutions in return for religious services were held in *frankalmoin*. These grants were conditioned on spiritual services such as holding masses (*tenure by divine service*) or praying for the souls of the lord and his ancestors (*gift in free, pure, and perpetual alms*).

Economic tenure. All tenures other than knight-service or frankalmoin were eventually referred to as *socage tenure*. Services were of a fixed payment in either money, kind, or labor. By the mid-fifteenth century, socage tenants ordinarily owed money rents known as "quit rents" because by making the payment, the tenant was "quit" of other service.

§6.2.3.2　Feudal Incidents

Feudal services declined in importance as they were commuted to money payments and lost value since they were fixed and did not keep pace with inflation. Feudal incidents were infrequent liabilities that included a variety of occasions on which the lord would regain possession of the land or its profits — benefits that did keep pace with inflation.

Homage and fealty. Homage was the ceremony by which the tenant "became the lord's man," pledging fealty (faithful service) and cementing a personal relationship with reciprocal obligations. In return for homage, the lord would *warrant* or guarantee the tenant's title; the lord was bound to provide compensation if the lord's title to the land was found defective in litigation and the lord was barred from asserting any claim to the land.

Aids. Tenants were obliged to pay sums to help the lord through some financial crises. By 1215, the *Magna Carta* limited aids to ransoming the lord from captors, the knighting of the lord's eldest son, and the marriage of his eldest daughter.

Relief. In 1066, no principle of inheritability existed, especially for land held by military service since possession of the land depended on personal ability to serve as a knight. In 1100, however, King Henry I provided that the heir would have the automatic right to inherit the tenancy upon payment of a just *relief,* a sum often equal to a year's rent. Reliefs functioned like our modern inheritance taxes.

Wardship and marriage. If a tenant by knight-service or grand serjeanty died, leaving a minor heir under the age of 21, the lord would become the heir's guardian with the right to retain the profits of the land until the heir became 21. The lord was not accountable for the profits during the wardship. Wardships were viewed as investments since they were assignable and were the most lucrative of all the incidents of tenure. The lord would also have the right to sell the marriage of the ward by choosing a suitable spouse. The ward was not obligated to accept the marriage, but refusal was a serious matter since it might deprive the lord of a profitable transaction. In sharp contrast to tenure by knight-service, wardship of socage lands went to the nearest relative, who had a duty to render an account of his wardship in using the land for the benefit of the ward.

Escheat and forfeiture. If the tenant died without an heir, the land would *escheat* to the lord. If the tenant committed a *felony* (a breach of the tenant's oath of service to the lord), the land would similarly escheat to the lord. Lands were also *forfeit* to the crown in cases of high treason.

§6.2.4   UNFREE TENURES

Villeins were not included in the feudal ladder but were certainly part of the hierarchy, albeit at the bottom. Since they were not entitled to bring real actions in the royal courts to protect their interests in land, they had to rely on the local custom or the lord's will and present their cases in the manorial court. Their rights came to be recorded in manorial records with a copy given to the tenant. By the sixteenth century, the royal courts extended the protection of the common law to what was then known as *copyhold tenure*.

§6.2.5   GROWTH OF THE FEE SIMPLE

As a consequence of the tenurial system, a number of persons had interests in the same parcel of land. By subinfeudation, the lord's interest in the land was converted into the right to collect services from the tenants. Lawyers referred not to ownership of land but to the concept of *seisin*. The interests of mesne lords were considered property interests and were called *manors* or *seignories*. The lord who held a seignory in Black-acre (a traditional term for a parcel of land) was said to be *seised in service* of Blackacre. The tenant in occupation was *seised in demesne* of Blackacre. The holding of the tenant was called his *fee* or *fief* (feodum).

§6.2.5.1   Inheritability

As mentioned previously, fees were not inheritable immediately after the Conquest of 1066, since the tenurial relationship was personal and could be created only by actual acceptance of homage. After King Henry I's *Coronation Charter* of 1100, however, inheritance became a matter of course upon payment of relief and performance of homage by the heir.

§6.2.5.2   Alienability

It was always possible under early feudalism to transfer an interest in land by *subinfeudation*, accepting a subtenant in a tenurial relationship. It was not possible to simply transfer one's interest to another person and have him take one's place in the feudal ladder, becoming a tenant to one's lord. This second form of transfer, called transfer by *substitution,* could occur only with the lord's consent since the lord would need both to release the first tenant from the tenurial relationship and to accept the second. Because the tenurial relationship was personal, it was not possible simply to buy and sell the land.

When the tenurial relationship lost its personal quality, and services were both commuted to fixed money payments and began to lose their value, the lords' interests switched. Subinfeudation would not deprive the lord of the services due from the tenant; if the tenant did not provide the services, the lord would take the services from the proceeds of the land, regardless of whether the tenant had subinfeudated. By subinfeudating, however, the tenant was able to deprive the lord of the *incidents* of tenure since the lord had only the right to the value of the seignory of his tenant. If *O* had a tenant *A*, and *A* subinfeudated to his son *B* in return for a rose at midsummer, then *A* had a seignory worth one rose, and it is this seignory that determined the value of the incidents due to *O*. If *A* subinfeudated to a religious institution, it was even worse for the lord since a religious institution never dies, never commits a felony, and never leaves a minor heir who could become a ward; the lord thus was deprived of the most valuable incidents of tenure.

For this reason, the statute *Quia Emptores* was passed in 1290, allowing fees to be freely transferred but prohibiting further subinfeudation. The effect was to require all future transfers of interests in land to take place by substitution instead of subinfeudation. The statute shows the decline in importance of the personal relationship of lord and tenant and the corresponding increase in importance of feudal incidents. By the end of the thirteenth century, a transfer of a normal fee interest in land was granted by the language "*O* grants to *A* and his heirs." The fee interest in *A* thus became inheritable and alienable, meaning that *A*'s heir could inherit the property only if *A* had not sold it or given it away before *A*'s death.

In England, land was usually inherited by the first-born son (primogeniture); daughters would receive land only if no sons were alive to inherit. The rules of inheritance in other situations were complicated — and they were mandatory. It was not possible to devise real property by will until 1540.

§6.2.6　Avoiding Feudal Incidents

One of the driving forces in the history of land law was the desire to avoid feudal incidents. Today we would say that tenants were engaged in tax evasion — finding loopholes in the law. We have just seen how tenants could avoid feudal incidents by the process of subinfeudation. Each technique, however, brought a legal response. Abuse of subinfeudation led to *Quia Emptores* in 1290. Designed to shore up the feudal system, *Quia Emptores* wound up destroying it. Because the statute prohibited further subinfeudation, mesne lords eventually were all but eliminated through escheat and forfeiture. Remember that it was not possible to leave real property by will; thus, if a tenant died without any heirs, the land would revert to the lord. Eventually, most land in England was held directly from the crown.

After *Quia Emptores,* tenants renewed attempts to avoid feudal incidents by making transfers during their lifetime. For example, *O* would convey land to his son

A for life, and then to A's heir. By directly creating a future interest in A's heir, O ensured that the heir would take the property *by purchase* from O rather than *by descent* from A. Since A's heir would not inherit the property from A but would take it directly by a grant from O, A would not have to pay relief. The courts responded to this attempt at feudal tax evasion by prohibiting the arrangement. What became known as the *Rule in Shelley's Case* treated the interest in A's heir as an interest in A. A's heir would thus inherit from A and be liable for the feudal incident. Similarly, a conveyance from "O to A for life, then to O's heir," was treated as creating a future interest in O, thereby allowing O's heir to inherit the property from O rather than receiving it on the basis of a transfer from O. This practice, called the *doctrine of worthier title*, preserved the duty to pay the feudal incident. These rules lasted far beyond their original purposes and were transferred willy-nilly to United States law. Some of the property rules you will learn about are comprehensible *only* as holdovers from the feudal era and have no sensible modern justification. The Rule in Shelley's Case has been abolished almost everywhere in the United States, but the doctrine of worthier title retains significance.

§6.2.7   THE PERPETUAL CONFLICT BETWEEN THE GENERATIONS: DEAD HAND CONTROL AND ALIENABILITY

The desire to avoid feudal incidents by owners led to statutory and common law regulation of property interests designed to frustrate those attempts. The legal rules created in that process have legacies today in our property law. A second major force in the growth of the land law, besides the desire to avoid feudal incidents, was the wish to control the future use and ownership of land by keeping land in the family. This conflict between the generations was perpetual: Grantors wanted to control the future use of their property, while grantees wanted both to be freed of restrictions placed on them by their ancestors and to be free to impose their own restrictions on future generations. This conflict created a cycle of restrictions followed by legal mechanisms to avoid the restrictions. The courts wanted to protect both the grantor's right to control the future use and ownership of property and the grantee's right to be free of control by the dead hand of the past when circumstances changed.

The statute *Quia Emptores* created a deep paradox. Although intended to protect feudalism, it did so by enshrining at the core of the common law of property the key principle of *promoting the alienability of property*. Alienability is promoted by giving grantors the freedom to determine to whom and under what conditions they will part with their property. Grantors should therefore be able to impose restrictions on the future use of their property; their ability to do this encourages them to part with their property. At the same time, no one can use property that is burdened with restrictions; no one wants to purchase such property, and it is therefore not alienable. This dilemma creates a core tension in the rules governing property interests.

At first, a grant of land from "O to A and his heirs" gave A a life interest in the property, which would then be inherited by A's heir on his death. By applying the principle of alienability enshrined in *Quia Emptores*, however, the courts determined that a conveyance from O to A and his heirs gave A the right to convey the property during *A*'s life. But if *A* did this, *A*'s heir would have nothing left to inherit when *A* died. Thus, the heirs had the chance of inheriting only if *A* died before selling the land. This kind of property interest in *A* is called a *fee simple absolute.*

Parents tried to evade this rule with marriage settlements. Parents wanted to give property to sons on marriage — especially the second son, who had no right to inherit. However, parents also wanted the property to stay in the family. If they gave their son a fee simple absolute, he could sell it during his lifetime, disinherit his heir, and the property would leave the family. Parents would therefore convey property by a *fee simple conditional,* "to *A* and to the heirs of his body with his wife-to-be *X*." The idea was to make sure the land would be available to the heirs of *A* and *X*; if they died without leaving heirs, the property would revert to the grantor. The courts evaded this arrangement by providing that, once a child was born, *A* had the right to alienate the property in fee simple, thus disinheriting the heirs and defeating the grantor's attempt to keep the land in the family.

The law responded in 1285 with the statute *De Donis Conditionalibus,* which provided that the grantor's will be observed. A new estate was created, called the *fee tail,* by which the land would descend to the lineal heirs of the grantee until the line ran out, at which point it would revert to the grantor or his heirs. It was created by the language: "*O* to *A* and the heirs of his body." An owner of a fee tail could transfer his interest during his lifetime, but when he died the land would immediately pass to his heir. Such an arrangement interferes significantly with the alienability of the property since the grantee gets the property only for the life of the grantor. To promote alienability, the courts responded to fee tails by allowing a fictitious, collusive, and rather hilarious lawsuit known as the common recovery, to *bar the entail,* and change the interest into a fee simple that could then be sold free of any future interests in the present holder's heirs or in the grantor or his heirs.[3]

---

3. A. W. B. Simpson describes the common recovery in the following way:

> Suppose Smith to be tenant in tail in possession of Blackacre, which he wishes to sell for a fee simple to Jones. A collusive real action is brought by Jones against Smith on a feigned title, Jones having already paid or agreed to pay Smith for the land. In this action Jones claims a fee simple in the land. Smith appears in court and vouches one Brown to warranty. Brown does not dispute his obligation to warrant Smith's title, and the action then proceeds between Jones and Brown. Instead of putting up a defense Brown asks for "leave to imparl" — that is, he asks the court for an adjournment whilst he talks the matter over with Jones in the hope of reaching a settlement, and he and Jones leave court to have their imparlance. Brown promptly disappears. This is a contempt of court, and when Jones arrives back before the Justices and tells them that Brown has absconded, they at once give judgment in favor of Jones. The judgment is that Jones recovers the land, and that Brown is to convey to Smith lands of equal value to those recovered. Unfortunately Brown, who has been carefully selected for this reason (and paid for his trouble), has no land, so that the judgment can never [be] satisfied. If it ever was satisfied, then the land conveyed would be held on the same terms as that lost to Jones; it would be subject to the entail and to any interest in remainder or reversion after Smith's estate. Thus *if the judgment had been satisfied* neither the issue in tail nor the remaindermen or reversioner would suffer any loss, and although everybody knows that it never will be satisfied, the court's view is that it has done its best, and cannot be blamed if Brown is a man of straw. A blind eye is turned to the fact that the whole procedure is an obvious fraud, and neither the issue nor the remaindermen are allowed to do anything about it.

A. W. B. Simpson, *A History of the Land Law* 130 (2d ed. 1986).

§6.2.8   HISTORICAL CATEGORIES OF CURRENT SIGNIFICANCE

§6.2.8.1   Freehold and Nonfreehold Interests

The legal rules currently in force regulate the division of property into present and future interests in various ways. The most basic form of regulation limits the number of ways in which current and future interests may be divided. The particular ways of dividing interests over time are called *estates*. The most basic division in types of present interests is the distinction between *freehold* interests and *nonfreehold* interests. Nonfreehold interests are those associated with the landlord-tenant relationship; freehold interests are all other ownership interests. The distinction grows out of the medieval categorization of property interests between those whose owners had the right to bring real actions to protect their interests in royal courts and those who had no right to bring such actions and were relegated to manorial courts. The distinction retains modern significance in the sense that different legal rules apply to leaseholds than to other property interests. Landlord-tenant relations are covered in Chapter 8.

§6.2.8.2   Legal and Equitable Interests: Executory
Interests and the Development of Trusts

A trust is a property arrangement in which a grantor, called the *settlor* or *trustor*, conveys property to one person (the *trustee*) for the benefit of a third party, called the *beneficiary*. Both real and personal property can be used to create a trust. For example, a single parent, O, may write a will providing that in the event of her death, her house will go to her sister, A, as trustee, in trust for O's daughter, X. O may also provide that her bank account and the proceeds of a life insurance policy will go to A in trust for X. The document creating the trust arrangement, called the *declaration of trust* when the grantor appoints herself as trustee and a *deed of trust* when legal title is transferred to another as trustee, often has explicit instructions about how the property is to be used by the trustee and may be created in an *inter vivos* document (creating the trust during the settlor's life rather than at death) as well as in a will.

The trust arrangement originated in the equity courts of England. The trustee is said to hold *legal title* to the property since the law courts did not recognize trusts and would adjudicate the trustee to be the fee owner of the property. The beneficiary is said to hold *equitable* or *beneficial* title to the property since the chancery or equity courts would enforce the settlor's will by requiring the trustee to use the property for the benefit of the beneficiary.

Before 1536, the courts did not allow property owners to condition new freehold interests on events that could effectively cut off the interest before its natural termination date. For example, O could convey property to A and his heirs so long as the property is used for church purposes. The interest in A is called a *fee simple determinable* since the interest could end, or "determine," on violation of the condition, and the property revert to O or his heirs. Since the property might never revert to O, that is, the property could be used for church purposes permanently, O's interest is denominated a mere *possibility of reverter*.

It was not lawful, however, for the grantor, O, to create a contingent future interest in a third party that would divest or cut short an interest in either the grantor or a prior grantee; such interests are called *executory interests*. For example, *O* could not create a valid conveyance to *A*, so long as it is used for church purposes, then to *B*. Because *B*'s interest would cut short *A*'s prior freehold estate, it was therefore void. *B*'s interest is called a *shifting* executory interest since, if valid, it would allow the title to shift from *A* to *B*. It was said that the grantor had given a fee simple interest to *A* and could not derogate from his grant by providing a right of entry in a stranger.

Similarly, *O* could not convey the property to *B* in the future; for example, *O* could not lawfully grant property "to *B* when *B* graduates from law school." This interest would be a *springing* executory interest since it would "spring" from the grantor, divesting the grantor at some point in the future. This interest was void since, before the advent of recording statutes, freehold interests in land were conveyed by a ceremony known as *livery of seisin*, in which the parties would go to the land and the grantor would publicly hand the grantee a physical embodiment of the land, such as a twig or a clod of earth. The courts could not conceive how to create a springing executory interest since there was no one to whom the present interest could be given through livery of seisin.

The courts distinguished future interests that were to take effect at what was considered the natural termination of the prior estate, specifically, at the death of the first grantee. Thus, *O* could convey property to *A* for life, then to *B*. *A*'s *life estate* is a valid interest, as is *B*'s *remainder*.

The chancellor was the monarch's official who had custody of the great seal and was head of the monarch's clerks and a member of the monarch's council. Usually an ecclesiastical official, the chancellor began to hear claims by petitioners who had lost, or who were certain to lose, lawsuits in the royal common law courts but who nonetheless believed they were entitled to redress. The chancellor exercised his conscience to achieve a just result even if it went against the law. The common law courts used damages to enforce their judgments. The chancellor ordered people to act, thereby originating the modern injunction. Eventually, the chancery became a separate court system with a separate set of rules known as *equity*.

Property owners tried to get around the rules prohibiting shifting and springing executory interests by a device call the *use*. *O* would grant property "to *A* and his heirs to hold to the use of *B*." According to the law courts, the grantor had conveyed a fee simple interest to *A*; therefore, nothing remained to convey to *B*. The equity courts enforced the use by ruling that it would be unconscionable for *A* to use the property in a way that violated the grantor's intent. The equity courts called *B* the *cestui que use* (the one for whom the benefit of the grant was made) and would order *A* to manage the property for the benefit of *B*, for example, by paying to *B* the rents earned from the property.

Grantors began to employ uses to evade the rules of primogeniture, the prohibition on devising real property by will, and the prohibition on executory interests. For example, a grantor, *O*, could grant property to "*X* and his heirs to the use of *O* during *O*'s life, and then to such persons as *O* would appoint by will." This ingenious device not only evaded the inheritance laws but also enabled the grantor to avoid feudal incidents since the devisees would take by purchase from *O* rather than by descent or inheritance.

King Henry VIII abolished the use by the *Statute of Uses* in 1536 to restore his feudal revenues. The statute provided that uses should be "executed," meaning that they should be implemented in the sense that title should shift to the person for whom the property was held in use. Thus, a conveyance from "*O* to *A* and his heirs to the use of *B* and his heirs" would be interpreted under the *Statute of Uses* as creating a legal fee simple estate in *B*.

The effect of the statute was to authorize the creation of legal springing and shifting executory interests, which had been unrecognized by the law courts. A conveyance from "*O* to *A* and his heirs so long as used for church purposes, then to *B* to the use of *C*" became a fee simple subject to executory limitation in *A*, with a valid legal executory interest in *C*. However, the 1536 *Statute of Uses* also had the effect of making it again impossible to leave land by will, since the law courts would not recognize wills of real property and uses had been effectively abolished. Parliament responded by passing the *Statute of Wills* in 1540, authorizing property owners to devise real property by will.

Although the *Statute of Uses* intended to abolish the use, both the common law courts and the equity courts construed the statute narrowly. Eventually, they allowed grantors to circumvent the statute by the simple device of placing duties of *active management* on the trustee. A second device was to create a "use on a use" — "*O* grants to *X* and his heirs to the use of *A* and his heirs to the use of *B* and his heirs." The *Statute of Uses* was construed to execute the first use, giving *A* legal title to the property, but not the second use, giving *B* beneficial ownership of the property. These arrangements led to the modern law of trusts.

All freehold property interests can today be created in both a legal and equitable form. Thus, a grantor can create a legal life estate in *A* by granting property "to *A* for life, then to *B*." A grantor can create an equitable life estate in *A* by granting the property "to *X* in trust for *A* for life, then to *B*."

§6.3 The Estates System

§6.3.1 FEE SIMPLE INTERESTS

§6.3.1.1 Fee Simple Absolute

Property ownership without an associated future interest is called a *fee simple* or *fee simple absolute*. An owner of a fee simple interest in real property has the present right to possess and use the property, the right to sell it or give it away, and the right to devise it by will or leave it to her heirs. Because no one owns a future interest in the property, no other individual has any presently identifiable legal right to obtain ownership of the property in the future. Depending on what the fee simple owner chooses to do with the property, future owners include potential buyers, grantees by gift, beneficiaries of a trust, and devisees (if the owner leaves a will) or heirs (if the owner dies *intestate*, or without a will).

A conveyance[4] of a fee simple interest can be accomplished by the following language:

O to *A*
O to *A and her heirs*
O to *A in fee simple*

---

4. *Conveyance* is the technical word for a transfer of an interest in real property.

Under current law, owners are presumed to convey all the interests they own in property they convey unless the conveyance states otherwise. In other words, if the seller fails to indicate that he intends to create a future interest, the courts will presume that the grantee (buyer) receives all the ownership rights of the seller, that is, a fee simple interest in the property.

The language "*A* and her heirs" is technical in nature; it indicates a fee simple interest in *A*. The words "and her heirs" do not give *A*'s heirs any interests in the property. Of course, *A* may choose to leave the property to them in a will or, if *A* dies without a will, they may inherit the property. If, however, *A* chooses to write a will leaving the property to someone else or to sell the property during her lifetime, *A*'s potential heirs cannot complain; they have no ownership rights of their own. The language identifying the named owner *A* is referred to as "words of purchase" because it identifies who owns the property; the language "and her heirs" is referred to as "words of limitation" because it describes the kind of estate owned by *A* (a fee simple) rather than identifying who owns the property.

§6.3.1.2   Defeasible Fees

Present freehold interests are divided mainly into interests held for life and those held until the happening of some stated event (other than the present owner's death).

Present interests that terminate at the happening of a specified event, other than the death of the current owner, are called *defeasible fees*. The categories of defeasible fees relate to two crucial distinctions: (1) whether the future interest is in the grantor or in a third party, and (2) whether the future interest becomes possessory *automatically* when the stated event occurs or becomes possessory only if the future interest holder *chooses to assert* his property rights.

(a)   *When the future interest belongs to the grantor*

In this situation, two kinds of defeasible fees can be created.

1. *Automatic transfer.* When the future interest reverts automatically to the grantor on the happening of the stated event, the present interest is called a *fee simple determinable* and the future interest is called a *possibility of reverter.*

   > *O to A so long as used for residential purposes.*
   > *O to A while used for residential purposes.*
   > *O to A during residential use.*
   > *O to A unless used for nonresidential purposes.*
   > *O to A so long as used for residential purposes; if used for a nonresidential purpose, the property shall automatically revert to O.*

   Any of these conveyances creates a *fee simple determinable* in *A* with a possibility of reverter in *O* or his heirs or devisees. Any language denoting that the ownership is limited to a time period during which certain conditions are met will generally be interpreted as evidence of the grantor's intent to cut off ownership rights automatically when the condition is violated or met. When the condition is violated, ownership automatically shifts to *O* or her heirs or *O*'s devisees.

2. *Transfer upon grantor's assertion of property rights.* Instead of providing for automatic transfer of the property rights upon violation of the condition, the grantor may choose to retain for herself or her heirs the right to decide, at the time the condition is violated, whether to retake the property. If the future interest owner chooses to assert her rights when the condition is violated or the stated event occurs, the property ownership shifts to her; if she does not assert her rights, ownership stays with the current owner. The current interest is called a *fee simple subject to a condition subsequent* and the future interest is called a *right of entry* (sometimes also referred to as a *power of termination*).

> *O to A on condition that the property be used for residential purposes; in the event it is not so used, O shall have a right of entry.*
> *O to A, but if used for nonresidential purposes, O shall have a right of entry.*
> *O to A, provided that the property is used for residential purposes; if this condition is violated, O shall have a right of entry.*

Each of these conveyances creates a fee simple subject to condition subsequent with a right of entry in *O* or her heirs. If the property is used for nonresidential purposes, *A* retains ownership unless and until *O* asserts her right to regain possession of the property.

Possibilities of reverter and rights of entry were traditionally not transferable; they were deemed to be too insubstantial as property rights since they might never come into being. Some states may retain this traditional rule. However, the vast majority of states now hold that future interests are alienable as well as devisable and inheritable. *Concord Oil Co. v. Pennzoil Exploration & Production Co.,* 966 S.W.2d 451 (Tex. 1998).

Traditionally, a major difference between possibilities of reverter and rights of entry involves the statute of limitations for adverse possession. When a condition in a fee simple determinable is violated or occurs, the possibility of reverter kicks in automatically, giving the holder an immediate right of possession. The statute of limitations starts running immediately, and if the holder of the possibility of reverter does nothing for the statutory period, title will shift back to the current possessor. However, a right of entry does not become possessory until the holder asserts a right of possession; if the holder of the right of entry never asserts the right, the title will remain with the present estate owner. Theoretically, this means that violation of the condition in a fee simple subject to condition subsequent does not violate anyone's rights such that the statute of limitations is triggered only when the holder of the right of entry demands a right of possession from the present estate owner; continued possession under those circumstances arguably constitutes a trespass, but before that point, no trespass has occurred. Under this understanding, there is a huge difference between rights of entry and possibilities of reverter.

However, the modern approach is to treat the two types of future interest the same under one of two theories. First, the court may apply the doctrine of *laches* to prevent the holder of a right of entry from waiting too long to assert her right of entry; *laches* prevents recovery when an unreasonable delay in asserting legal rights unfairly prejudices another. Second, as a policy matter, it seems inappropriate for the one who violates a condition to face the perpetual possibility of a claim by the current holder of the right of entry. For this reason, the modern but not universal approach has been to start the running of the statute at the moment the condition is violated, making rights of entry effectively similar if not identical to possibilities of reverter. *Concord & Bay Point Land Co. v. City of Concord,* 280 Cal. Rptr. 623 (Ct. App. 1991).[5] One court has held that an owner of a right of entry has only a reasonable time to assert the right after the condition is violated and the owner waits too long, the interest is destroyed without regard to the statute of limitations for adverse possession. *Martin v. City of Seattle,* 765 P.2d 257 (Wash. 1988)("If a forfeiture is not declared within a reasonable time, the power of termination expires").

(b)   When the future interest belongs to a third party

When the future interest in a defeasible fee belongs to someone other than the grantor, the present interest is called a *fee simple subject to executory limitation,* and the future interest is called an *executory interest.* These interests are identical to the fee simple determinable, with ownership shifting automatically on the occurrence of the contingent event, except that ownership shifts to a third party rather than reverting to the grantor.

> *O to A so long as used for residential purposes, then to B.*

Any conveyance that transfers ownership to a third party on the happening of an event other than the current owner's death is a *fee simple subject to an executory limitation.* The executory interest in *B* automatically becomes possessory if the property is used for nonresidential purposes.[6]

§6.3.2   LIFE ESTATES

§6.3.2.1   Reversions and Remainders

Present ownership rights can be held during the life of a designated individual. A conveyance from *O to A for life* creates a *life estate* interest in *A.* This means that *A* owns the property during his lifetime. The future interest following a life estate can be either in the grantor or in a third party. If the property reverts to the grantor when *A* dies, the future interest is called a *reversion;* if the grantor designates a third party to obtain ownership when *A* dies, the future interest in the third party is called a *remainder.*

The difference between a life estate and a fee simple is that the owner of a fee simple can choose who will own the property after her death by either writing a will or availing herself of the state intestacy statute. In contrast, a life estate owner has no right to determine who owns the property on her death since ownership automatically shifts to the reversioner or remainder holder. If a life estate owner, *A,* sells her property to a

---

5. Two other crucial differences between automatic and nonautomatic contingent future interests occur in the context of invalid restrictions that either violate the rule against perpetuities, *see infra* §6.5.3, or are racially discriminatory, *see infra* §6.5.5. The remedies for violating these rules may differ substantially in some jurisdictions.

6. Executory interests are regulated by the rule against perpetuities and are deemed invalid under certain circumstances.

buyer, *B*, the buyer gets exactly what the seller had: an estate for the life of *A*. Thus, when *A* dies, the property will shift to the reversioner or remainder holder. *B*'s interest is called a *life estate for the life of another* or a *life estate per autre vie*.

> *O to A for life.*

This conveyance gives a life estate to *A* and automatically creates a reversion in *O*. When *A* dies, the property reverts to *O* or, if *O* is deceased, to his heirs or devisees. It is not necessary for the conveyance to mention the reversion; *O* retains whatever property rights are not given away. When *A* dies, his ownership rights terminate and ownership automatically shifts back to *O*.

> *O to A for life, then to B.*

This conveyance creates a life estate in *A*, with a remainder in *B*. Note that an executory interest divests a present estate while a reversion or remainder takes effect at the "natural" termination of the preceding estate, such as the death of a life tenant holder. A life estate may be subject to a divesting condition that would cause the interest to shift before the owner dies; the future interest would be an executory interest.

§6.3.2.2 Contingent and Vested Remainders

One final set of distinctions is important. We have seen that future interests following defeasible fees vest either in the grantor (*possibility of reverter* or *right of entry*) or in a third party (*executory interest*). Future interests following life estates also may vest either in the grantor (*reversion*) or in a third party (*remainder*). Remainders are further divided into two kinds: *contingent remainders* and *vested remainders*.

Contingent remainders. Remainders are contingent if one or both of two conditions are met: (1) if the remainder will take effect only upon the happening of an event that is not certain to happen, or (2) if the remainder will go to a person who cannot be ascertained at the time of the initial conveyance.

For example, a conveyance from "*O* to *A* for life, then to *B* if *B* has graduated from law school," creates a contingent remainder because at the time of the original conveyance from *O* to *A* it is not certain that *B* will graduate from law school. (If *B* does not graduate from law school, the property will revert to *O* on *A*'s death; if *B* later graduates from law school, the property will then spring to *B*.)[7]

Similarly, a conveyance from "*O* to *A* for life, then to the children of *B*," creates a contingent remainder in the children of *B* if *B* has no children upon the conveyance from *O* to *A*; this is the case because the children cannot be individually identified at the time of the conveyance from *O* to *A*. Another example of a contingent remainder is

---

7. This is the current law. Contingent remainders formerly were *destructible*: If they did not vest before the life estate terminated, they were destroyed. Thus, in the example, if *B* had not graduated from law school by the time *A* died, the property would revert to *O* in fee simple absolute. Under the current law in the vast majority of states, contingent remainders are not destructible. If *B* has not graduated from law school by the time *A* dies, the property will go to *O* as a fee simple subject to an executory limitation; if *B* graduates from law school later, the property will spring to *B* as an executory interest. *See infra* §6.3.2.3.

"*O* to *A* for life, then to the heirs of *B*." If *B* is alive at the time of the conveyance from *O* to *A*, it is impossible to tell who *B*'s heirs will be until *B* dies; only persons alive at the time of *B*'s death can inherit as "heirs" under the intestacy statute.

Vested remainders. Vested remainders include any remainders that are not contingent remainders. They are therefore remainders to persons who are identifiable at the time of the initial conveyance and for whom there are no conditions precedent (conditions that must occur before they will have the right to control the property) other than the natural termination of the prior life estate when the life estate owner dies. Vested remainders are of three kinds.

1. *Absolutely vested remainders.* This is a remainder that is not subject to change.
2. *Vested remainders subject to open.* This is a remainder that may be divided among persons who will be born in the future. For example, a conveyance from "*O* to *A* for life, then to the children of *B*," is a vested remainder if *B* has any living children at the time of the conveyance from *O* to *A*; it is *subject to open* because any children of *B* born after the conveyance from *O* to *A* may share in the property rights — they will own the property jointly. Under the *rule of convenience,* the courts will *close the class* when *A* dies so that the children can take possession at *A*'s death; they will not have to share the property with any after-born children.
3. *Vested remainders subject to divestment.* This is a vested remainder that may be destroyed by an event that occurs after the original conveyance. For example, a conveyance from "*O* to *A* for life, then to *B*, but if *B* has flunked out of law school, the property shall then revert to *O*," creates a vested remainder in *B* (since *B* is ascertained at the time of the conveyance to *A* and there are no conditions precedent to *B*'s taking the property) that is *subject to divestment* (because if the condition is met at any time — if *B* flunks out of law school — *B* will lose his right to obtain the property on the death of *A*).

Note that vested remainders subject to divestment may be functionally equivalent to some contingent remainders. Take the following two examples:

> *O to A for life, then to B if she survives A, otherwise to C.*
> *O to A for life, then to B, but if B does not survive A, then to C.*

These conveyances are functionally the same, but because of their wording the first probably[8] creates a contingent remainder in *B* (because *B*'s ownership rights are conditioned on her surviving *A*), while the second creates a vested remainder subject to divestment (because *B* will lose her interest if a subsequent event happens). Because of the functional equivalence, courts may use discretion in classifying the interest, depending on their views about the probable intent of the grantor and the legal consequences of the classification.

---

8. The result is open to interpretation by the courts; the surrounding circumstances, the sense of equity in the particular case, and general policy considerations may affect the judge's decision.

§6.3.2.3   Destructibility of Contingent Remainders

The law formerly provided that contingent remainders were "destroyed" in two circumstances. First, contingent remainders were destroyed if they did not vest before the preceding life estate ended. For example, in the conveyance "*O* to *A* for life, then to *B* if she has been elected president of the United States," the contingent remainder in *B* would be destroyed if *B* had not been elected president before the death of *A*.

Second, contingent remainders were destroyed by "merger." For example, in *Abo Petroleum Corp. v. Amstutz*, 600 P.2d 278 (N.M. 1979), James and Amanda Turknett conveyed property to each of their daughters, Ruby and Beulah Turknett. Each deed provided that the daughter would own the property "during her natural life" and that it would go to "her children if she have any at her death," but if she did not have children to "her heir or heirs." Since each of the alternative remainders was contingent, the parents retained a reversion. However, after the conveyance to the daughters, the parents conveyed new deeds to the daughters transferring their reversion to the daughters. Under traditional doctrine, since the prior estate (the reversion in the original grantor) had terminated by merger with contingent remainders before those contingent remainders became vested, they were destroyed.

The traditional rule effectively limited the ability of grantors to create contingent remainders that would vest far in the future. It effectively destroyed many future interests that could have vested after the death of the current life estate holder. Applying the rule therefore resulted in freeing land from archaic restrictions.[9]

Only a few states follow the traditional rule. The modern approach holds that contingent remainders are indestructible. Thus, in the first example, if *B* had not become president before *A* died, the property would revert to *O* as a fee simple subject to executory limitation with an executory interest in *B* that would vest and become possessory if *B* ever were elected president during her lifetime. Similarly, in *Abo Petroleum*, the contingent remainders were not destroyed when the parents conveyed their reversion to their daughters. Thus, the New Mexico Supreme Court held that when Beulah and Ruby Turknett conveyed their interests to the predecessors of Abo Petroleum Corp., the grantee received merely a life estate rather than a fee simple absolute, and at the death of each sister, her property would pass to her children as remainder holders. In addition, the rule providing for destruction of contingent remainders never applied to equitable estates. Thus, a contingent remainder in a trust would never have been destroyed by the termination of the preceding estate.

Contingent remainders likely to vest too far into the future are today regulated by the rule against perpetuities, discussed *infra* at §6.5.3.

§6.3.2.4   Doctrine of Worthier Title

Many states will interpret a conveyance from "*O* to *A* for life, remainder in the heirs of *O*" as "*O* to *A* for life, remainder in *O*." The remainder in *O*'s heirs is

---

9. It is important to note, however, that the rule did not apply to reversions since, as with all interests retained in the grantor, they were deemed already vested in the grantor.

converted into a reversion in the grantor. In the past this was an absolute rule; today, however, in many states it is simply a rule of construction that can be overcome by sufficiently clear language indicating that the grantor actually intends to give a remainder to his own heirs. As lawyer for the grantor, how would you draft the conveyance to ensure that the grantor's intent is followed? Many states have abrogated the doctrine by statute. *See* Cal. Civ. Code §1073. The rule retains force today even in such states because it applies to wills executed before the doctrine was abolished. *In re Estate of Grulke,* 546 N.W.2d 626 (Iowa Ct. App. 1996) (abrogating the doctrine but prospectively only, applying it to wills executed after the date of the decision). As lawyer for the grantor, how would you draft the conveyance to ensure that the grantor's intent is followed?

This rule originated in medieval tax avoidance schemes. If the property reverted to *O* on *A*'s death, it would be inherited by *O*'s heirs, who would have to pay inheritance taxes. If, however, the property shifted directly from *A* to *O*'s heirs as a future interest — specifically, as a remainder — then it would not be inherited on *O*'s death, having been transferred through creation of a future interest during *O*'s lifetime, thereby avoiding inheritance taxes.

The rule does have a current policy justification. *O*'s heirs cannot be determined until *O* dies. Thus, if for some reason it becomes necessary or appropriate to sell a fee simple interest in the property, it is not possible to do so until the death of *O*. Since we cannot tell who the heirs of *O* will be until *O* dies, it is not possible to buy the remainder from them to consolidate the life estate and remainder. The inability to create a fee simple interest by contract may very substantially interfere with the alienability of the property and thus may justify the rule. Note that restraints on alienation of life estates are usually enforced only when they are not disabling restraints, that is, when someone owns the right to enforce the restraint and may be induced to sell or waive that right. Can you imagine an alternative remedy for this problem that better respects the grantor's intent? Or is there no problem with a disabling restraint designed to last a lifetime?

§6.3.2.5   Rule in Shelley's Case

The Rule in *Shelley's Case* is similar to the doctrine of worthier title. It converts a remainder in the grantee's heirs into a remainder in the grantee. Thus, "*O* to *A* for life, remainder to *A*'s heirs" becomes "*O* to *A* for life, remainder to *A*." Since *A* owns both the life estate and the remainder, the two are merged into a fee simple. Thus, the rule converts "*O* to *A* for life, remainder to *A*'s heirs," into "*O* to *A* in fee simple absolute." The rule was similarly intended to respond to medieval tax evasion schemes, but it has been abolished in the vast majority of states. As with the doctrine of worthier title, it has a policy justification based on the impossibility of contracting with heirs during *A*'s lifetime. Again, is there an alternative remedy to this problem that better respects the grantor's intent? In states that have abolished the rule, what remedy would a present estate owner have if the owner wishes to create a fee simple interest by contract but was prevented from doing so by the inability to contract with unknown heirs?

The Rule can be avoided by careful drafting. The grantor can create a leasehold for a fixed term (a "term of years") rather than a life estate to avoid operation of the rule. For example, "*O* to *A* for 100 years if *A* lives so long, then to *A*'s heirs," avoids operation of the rule.

§6.3.3 FEE TAIL

The fee tail is an estate whose purpose is to keep the property in a family dynasty. The traditional words to create a fee tail are "*O* to *A* and the heirs of his body." This conveyance traditionally created a set of life estates in *A*. *A*'s lineal descendants, their descendants, and so on, until the blood line ran out, at which point the property would revert to *O* or *O*'s heirs; every fee tail is followed by either a reversion or a remainder to take effect when the blood line runs out. Because of its effect on marketability, the fee tail has been substantially abolished in the United States and is recognized in only four states (Delaware, Maine, Massachusetts, and Rhode Island).

The states have adopted a variety of ways to treat any fee tail interests that come up. Some states interpret a fee tail as a *fee simple absolute*, Cal. Civ. Code §763; *Restatement of Property* §104 (1936); others permit the fee tail but allow the fee tail owner to convert it to a fee simple by conveying the property in fee simple to another, Mass. Gen. Laws Ann. ch. 183, §45. Some states have interpreted fee tails as *life estates* in the present owner with a remainder in fee simple in her issue, Colo. Rev. Stat. §38-30-106 (changed to fee simple in 1983).[10]

§6.3.4 REGULATION OF FUTURE INTERESTS

We have seen that land use restrictions in the form of servitudes (easements, covenants, and equitable servitudes) generate conflicts between the interests of prior owners in controlling the future use of their real property and the interests of current owners in using their property as they see fit. Similarly, future interests generate conflicts between the interests of prior owners in controlling future use and disposition of their property and the interests of current owners in asserting control over the property.

Three kinds of legal rules regulate future interests. First, the rules give some guidance on how to interpret ambiguous conveyances; the most important doctrine of this kind is the *presumption against forfeitures*. Second, property law limits the ways in which owners divide property interests. To create an effective temporal division of property rights, ownership interests must be in the *form* of one of the established estates; a general rule prohibits the creation of new estates. Third, the legal rules regulate the *substance* of future interests by preventing owners from creating certain kinds of future interests. Some prohibitions, such as the rule against perpetuities and the rule against restraints on alienation, are intended to promote the relatively free transfer in the market place. Other doctrines are intended to protect interests in equality and liberty.

---

10. South Carolina has never recognized the English statute *De Donis Conditionalibus* and therefore continues to recognize the fee simple conditional; the owner cannot leave the property by will since it passes to her children, but after children are born, she can convey a fee simple absolute or mortgage the property. If the owner does not transfer the property before her death, the children inherit a fee simple conditional. William B. Stoebuck & Dale A. Whitman, *The Law of Property* §2.10, at 57-58 (3d ed. 2000).

§6.3.5 TRUSTS

The grantor (the "settlor") conveys property to a trustee to be managed for the benefit of the beneficiaries. The trustee, as holder of legal title, has the power to sell the property (the trust assets) and reinvest the proceeds in other assets if so doing is in the best interests of the beneficiaries, unless the settlor intended the property not to be sold. Unless the settlor instructs otherwise, the income of the trust assets is paid to the beneficiaries, and the principal assets are turned over to the beneficiaries when and if the trust terminates. The trustee has fiduciary obligations to act in the best interests of the beneficiary and is subject to liability to the beneficiary for mismanaging the trust assets.

Trusts are called equitable interests in property since they originated in the equity courts. They can be created in forms that correspond to all the legal estates described above, including life estates and defeasible fees. For example, a settlor could grant property to "*X* in trust for *A* for life, then to *A*'s children."

§6.3.6 SUMMARY

It may be useful to outline the previous discussion.

I.   No future interest: *fee simple absolute*
II. Defeasible fees
   A.   Future interest in grantor or her heirs
      1.   Automatic transfer
         (a)   Current interest: *fee simple determinable*
         (b)   Future interest: *possibility of reverter*
      2.   Transfer only if future interest owner asserts her interest
         (a)   Current interest: *fee simple subject to condition subsequent*
         (b)   Future interest: *right of entry*
   B.   Future interest in third party
      1.   Current interest: *fee simple subject to executory limitation*
      2.   Future interest: *executory interest*
III. Life estates
   A.   Current interest: *life estate*
   B.   Future interest
      1.   In grantor: *reversion*
      2.   In third party: *remainder*
         (a)   *vested remainders*
            (i)   *absolutely vested remainder*
            (ii)   *vested remainder subject to open*
            (iii) *vested remainder subject to divestment*
         (b)   *contingent remainders*
            (i)   condition precedent or
            (ii)   unascertained person

Estates System: Freehold Interests

Present Interest	Word Often Used to Create the Interest	Future I In Grantor	
Fee simple absolute	"to *A*" "and her heirs"	—	
Fee simple determinable	"so long as" "while" "during" "until" "unless"	Possibility of reverter	
Fee simple subject to condition subsequent	"provided that" "on condition" "but if"	Right of entry for condition broken (or power of termination)	—
Fee simple subject to executory limitation	"until (or unless) ..., then to ..., "but if ..., then to ...,"	—	Executory interest
Life estate	"for life"	Reversion	Remainder

§6.4 *Interpretation of Ambiguous Conveyances*

§6.4.1 PRESUMPTION AGAINST FORFEITURES AND THE GRANTOR'S INTENT

One important issue that frequently arises in real property cases is how to interpret an ambiguous conveyance. Grantors often use unclear, sometimes conflicting, language in describing the kind of estate conveyed. In interpreting ambiguous conveyances, two policies are important. Courts first seek to implement the *intent of the grantor*. When the grantor's intent is unclear, courts turn to public policy considerations; they attempt to further the free use and alienability of property by a presumption *against* finding a future interest. The presumption against forfeitures, however, is in tension with the principle of promoting the grantor's intent. Courts sometimes try to implement the contractual arrangement the parties most likely would have adopted had they anticipated the ambiguity; other times, courts ignore the presumed intent of parties and focus on the social goal of promoting free use and alienability of property. As you read the following material, consider how the courts should address this tension.

6.4.1.1   Fee Simple versus Defeasible Fee

WOOD v. BOARD OF COUNTY COMMISSIONERS OF FREMONT COUNTY
759 P.2d 1250 (Wyo. 1988)

C. STUART BROWN, Chief Justice.

Appellants Cecil and Edna Wood, husband and wife, appeal summary judgment favoring appellee, the Board of County Commissioners for Fremont County, Wyoming. By a 1948 warranty deed appellants conveyed land in Riverton, Wyoming, to Fremont County for the construction of a county hospital. They now contend that language in the deed created either a fee simple determinable or a fee simple subject to a condition subsequent with a right of reversion in them if the land ceased to be used for the hospital. [This case presents the question whether] cessation of appellee's hospital operation by sale of public hospital facilities to a private company constituted the occurrence of an event which divested appellee of its estate in property conditionally conveyed by appellants. The trial court found that appellants retained no interest in the land surrounding and under the old county hospital as a matter of law. We affirm.

On September 1, 1948, by warranty deed, appellants conveyed

[a] tract of land situated in the SE 1/4 SW 1/4, Sec. 26, Township 1, North Range 4 East, W.R.M., Fremont County, Wyoming, described . . . as follows: Beginning at the Southwest corner of said SE 1/4 SW 1/4, Sec. 26, aforesaid, thence east along the South line of said Section 310 feet, thence North at right angles to said South line 297 feet, thence West on a line parallel to said South line 310 feet, thence South 297 feet to the point of beginning, containing 2.1 acres. . . . Said tract is conveyed to Fremont County *for the purpose of constructing and maintaining thereon a County Hospital in memorial to the gallant men of the Armed Forces of the United States of America from Fremont County, Wyoming.* . . . (Emphasis added.)

This deed was recorded in the Fremont County Clerk's Office on December 14, 1948. Appellee constructed a hospital on the land and operated it there until November 18, 1983. At that time appellee sold the land and the original hospital facility to a private company. The buyer operated a hospital on the premises until September, 1984, at which time it moved the operation to a newly constructed facility. The private company then put the premises up for sale. . . .

. . . Appellants' argument boils down to whether or not the language ". . . for the purpose of constructing and maintaining thereon a County Hospital in memorial to the gallant men of the Armed Forces of the United States of America from Fremont County, Wyoming . . ." in the 1948 warranty deed is sufficient limiting language to create either 1) a fee simple determinable, or 2) a fee simple subject to a condition subsequent giving appellants title to the land. We review disputed language in a deed to determine the intent of the parties to it from the plain language in the deed considered as a whole. Also, Wyo. Stat. §34-2-101 (1977) provides, in pertinent part: "[E]very conveyance of real estate shall pass all the estate of the grantor . . . unless the intent to pass a less estate shall expressly appear or be necessarily implied in the terms of the grant."

A fee simple estate in land that automatically expires upon the happening of a stated event, not certain to occur, is a fee simple determinable. *Restatement of Property* §44, at 121 (1936). In *Williams v. Watt*, 668 P.2d 620, 627 (Wyo. 1983), we said:

The existence of an estate in fee simple determinable requires the presence of special limitations. The term "special limitation" denotes that part of the language of a conveyance which causes the created interest automatically to expire upon the occurrence of the stated event. An estate in fee simple determinable may be created so as to be defeasible upon the occurrence of an event which is not certain ever to occur. Words such as "so long as," "until," or "during" are commonly used in a conveyance to denote the presence of this type of special limitation. The critical requirement is that the language of special limitation must clearly state the particular circumstances under which the fee simple estate conveyed might expire. Language of conveyance that grants a fee simple estate in land for a special purpose, without stating the special circumstances that could trigger expiration of the estate, is not sufficient to create a fee simple determinable.

The plain language in the 1948 deed, stating that appellants conveyed the land to Fremont County for the purpose of constructing a county hospital, does not clearly state that the estate conveyed will expire automatically if the land is not used for the stated purpose. As such, it does not evidence an intent of the grantors to convey a fee simple determinable, and we hold that no fee simple determinable was created when the land was conveyed.

Use of the language conveying the land in "memorial" similarly fails to create a fee simple determinable. "Memorial" is defined in *Webster's Third New International Dictionary* 1409 (1971) as "[s]omething that serves to preserve memory or knowledge of an individual or event." The time for which the hospital should serve to "preserve" the memory or knowledge is not stated in the deed, just as the time for maintaining the hospital is not there stated. The language of conveyance fails to designate the time at which the hospital must be constructed as well as the time during which it must be maintained or during which the indicated memory must be preserved. The omission of such limiting language evidences an intent not to convey a fee simple determinable.

Similar reasoning applies to appellants' assertion that the language of conveyance created a fee simple subject to a condition subsequent. A fee simple subject to a condition subsequent is a fee simple estate in land that gives the grantor a discretionary power to terminate the grantee's estate after the happening of a stated event, not certain to occur. This type of interest is similar to the fee simple determinable in that the language of conveyance must clearly state the grantor's intent to create a discretionary power to terminate the estate he conveys. Words commonly used in a conveyance to denote the presence of a fee simple estate subject to a condition subsequent include "upon express condition that," "upon condition that," "provided that," or "if." In *J.M. Carey & Brother v. City of Casper*, 213 P.2d 263, 268 (Wyo. 1950), we quoted 19 *Am. Jur. Estates* §65 at 527 (1939), which said:

> It is a well-settled rule that conditions tending to destroy estates, such as conditions subsequent, are not favored in law. They are strictly construed. Accordingly, no provision will be interpreted to create such a condition if the language will bear any other reasonable interpretation, or unless the language, used unequivocally, indicates an intention upon the part of the grantor or devisor to that effect and plainly admits of such construction.

That rule has not lost its potency. Applying it to this case, we hold that the plain language of the 1948 warranty deed, while articulating that the land conveyed was to be used for a county hospital, does not clearly state an intent of the grantors to retain a discretionary power to reenter the land if the land ceased to be used for the stated purpose. Appellants did not convey a fee simple subject to a condition subsequent, and we will not create one by construction some forty years after the conveyance took place.

CATHEDRAL OF THE INCARNATION IN THE DIOCESE OF LONG ISLAND, INC. v. GARDEN CITY COMPANY

697 N.Y.S.2d 56 (App. Div. 1999)

Judges: CORNELIUS J. O'BRIEN, J.P., DANIEL W. JOY, WILLIAM D. FRIEDMANN and GLORIA GOLDSTEIN, JJ., concur.

By deed dated November 20, 1891, the heirs of Cornelia Stewart (hereinafter the Stewart heirs) sold to the Cathedral of the Incarnation in the Diocese of Long Island, Inc. (hereinafter the Cathedral), for the sum of $43,247.50, two parcels of real property in Garden City. Pursuant to a restriction contained in the deed, the premises were conveyed to the Cathedral "and its successors forever for the use of the Protestant Episcopal Church in the Diocese of Long Island but without any power, right, or authority to grant, convey, or mortgage the same or any part thereof in any way or manner whatsoever." The deed also contained the further restriction that the premises were not to be "used or occupied for any other use or purposes than as sites or grounds for buildings or institutions connected with said Cathedral and devoted to its religious uses or educational purposes."

In 1893 the Stewart heirs conveyed to the predecessor of the defendant Garden City Company (hereinafter the Company) certain other property in Garden City which Cornelia Stewart had also owned, inclusive of "[a]ll the right, title, property and interest of the [Stewart heirs], or any of them in and to any reversion or remainder in all or any of the lands conveyed to the said The Cathedral of the Incarnation in the Diocese of Long Island." The Cathedral continued to own and occupy the demised premises in accordance with the restrictions contained in the deed from the time of the conveyance in 1891 until the commencement of this action.

In 1993 the Cathedral, which was in severe financial distress, filed a voluntary petition in bankruptcy pursuant to Chapter 11. The United States Bankruptcy Court for the Eastern District of New York (Holland, J.), by stipulation and order dated October 28, 1993, directed that certain properties owned by the Cathedral be sold. In addition, the Cathedral entered into a contract to sell other portions of the property.

The Cathedral thereafter commenced this action pursuant to Real Prop. Acts. §1955 to modify or extinguish the restrictions and for authorization to dispose of the land pursuant to the contracts of sale.[11] In a verified answer with counterclaim, the Company asserted, *inter alia,* that it was the successor to all the rights, title, interest, and claims that belonged to the Stewart heirs, that the deed from the Stewart heirs to the Cathedral conveyed less than a full fee title so that the Company had the right

---

11. N.Y. Real Prop. Acts. §1955(1) provides:

1. Where land is held, whether or not in trust, for benevolent, charitable, educational, public or religious purposes and the use of such land is restricted to such purpose or to a particular application of or means of carrying out such purpose by a special limitation or condition subsequent created in the conveyance or devise under which the land is so held, or by an agreement to convey, reconvey or surrender the land or the estate so held upon a contingency relating to its use, an action may be brought in the supreme court to obtain relief from such restriction as provided in this section. . . . ED.

thereunder to assert ownership of the property upon its cessation of use for religious purposes by the Cathedral, that the restrictions in the deed created either a condition subsequent or a conditional limitation, and that Real Prop. Acts. §1955 as applied to extinguish the Company's interests was unconstitutional. The Cathedral subsequently moved for summary judgment.

By decision dated July 1, 1997, the Supreme Court, Nassau County, found that the Cathedral was entitled to summary judgment. The court observed that although a right of reentry (now known as a right of reacquisition) arose from the Cathedral's deed, the Company, as an assignee, could not enforce it since, when the deeds were made, the right of reacquisition was not assignable, devisable, or descendible. The court then noted that the circumstances of the case fell within the scope of Real Prop. Acts. §1955, and that the Cathedral's application to extinguish the restrictions should therefore be granted. The court found that "to require the [Cathedral] to hold the land in perpetuity is unconscionable." Moreover, the court stated that the Company had failed to establish its entitlement to any damages. . . . We affirm.

The insistence by the Company that, for the purposes of applying Real Prop. Acts. §1955, the court merely had to find that some kind of reversionary interest existed, without determining the specific reversionary interest created by the deed, is unpersuasive. Notably, the Company, in arguing that the court erred in finding that a possibility of reverter did not exist, appears to concede that the deed created either a possibility of reverter or a right of reentry. The Company, however, fails to cite any case law or language in the deed to support its claim that the deed created a possibility of reverter in the grantors rather than a mere right of reentry. Thus, contrary to the Company's position, absent any language in the deed itself providing for the automatic termination of the Cathedral's estate if the land were no longer used for church purposes, the court properly concluded that the deed created a right of reentry. Under the common law at the time the Stewart heirs made the deed to the Cathedral in 1891 and the deed to the Company in 1893, the right of reentry was not assignable or devisable. Therefore, any right of reentry would be rendered void by any attempt by the Stewart heirs to assign it to the Company. . . .

Moreover, with respect to the contention by the Company that in interpreting a deed, the intent of the grantors should prevail, there is nothing in the language of the deed nor in the record as a whole to support the conclusion that the Stewart heirs intended the Cathedral's estate to terminate automatically if the land were used for other than church purposes. . . .

The Company's challenge to the court's application of Real Prop. Acts. §1955 to extinguish the restrictions must also fail. Real Prop. Acts. §1955(3) provides that the Supreme Court, in determining whether to grant relief from certain restrictions upon the use of land held for charitable purposes, must consider and make findings with respect to various factors as set forth in the statute.[12]

---

12. N.Y. Real Prop. Acts. §1955(3) provides:

3. In determining whether relief shall be granted, and the nature of such relief, the court shall consider and shall make findings with respect to the following:
    (a) whether the primary purpose of the special limitation, condition subsequent or agreement to convey, reconvey or surrender was to restrict the use of the land;
    (b) whether the purpose of the restriction was to ensure that the substantial value of the land or of the estate subject to the special limitation, condition subsequent or agreement, rather than the land

... Under the statutory framework, the inquiry [is] whether the existence of the restriction substantially impedes the owner of the property in the furtherance of the purpose for which the land is held (Real Prop. Acts. §1955(3)(c)). [T]he Chancellor of the Cathedral, provided sufficient evidence that continued ownership of the properties is a burden and a drain on financial resources that could otherwise be used to provide programs and services to the community. The Company failed to present any evidence to the contrary. . . .

Moreover, the Company has not demonstrated its entitlement to damages under Real Prop. Acts. §1955(4)(e), which provides that the court, in its discretion, may award damages "for such injury as a party to the action may sustain by reason of extinguishment or modification of the restriction."[13] Notably, although Morton Kassover, a Vice President of the Company, testified at his deposition that construction of "smaller" homes could have a negative impact on the Company's commercial properties, there is nothing in the record to substantiate such speculation. Moreover, Kassover's conclusory assertions were insufficient to raise any factual issue as to how the Company would be damaged by the extinguishment of the restrictions.

Equally without merit is the Company's attack on the constitutionality of Real Prop. Acts. §1955 as applied to it. In the first place, the Company's discussion assumes that it does have a constitutionally-protected property interest arising from the 1891 deed. However, as the Supreme Court correctly held, that deed created a right of reentry in the grantors that was not assignable, and any such right is now therefore void and nonexistent. It is well settled that where there is no legitimate claim of entitlement to the property interest affected by a governmental decision, the requirements of procedural due process do not apply. . . .

---

itself, or such estate itself, be devoted to and employed for a benevolent, charitable, educational, public or religious purpose.

If the findings with respect to (a) and (b) are such as to make the following matters relevant or appropriate for consideration, the court shall also consider and make findings with respect to the following:

(c) whether the existence of the restriction is substantially impeding the owner of the land, or of the estate subject to the special limitation, condition subsequent or agreement, in the furtherance of the benevolent, charitable, educational, public or religious purposes for which the land is held;

(d) whether the person or persons who would have a right of entry, possessory estate resulting from the occurrence of a reverter, or right to conveyance, reconveyance or surrender of the land or estate in the event of breach of the restriction at the time of the action will suffer substantial damage by reason of extinguishment or modification of the restriction, and, in such event, whether damages or restitution of the land, or its value, in whole or in part, should be awarded to such person or persons. — ED.

13. N.Y. Real Prop. Acts. §1955(4) provides:

4. The judgment of the court may include, in the discretion of the court, an adjudication (a) that the restriction is discharged in whole or in part, or that its tenor is modified as provided in the judgment; (b) that the holder of the land or estate therein subject to the restriction be authorized or directed to convey, lease, mortgage or otherwise dispose of the land or estate therein free of the restriction and that the purchaser under such disposition shall take free of the restriction; (c) directing the use to which the avails of any such disposition shall be put; (d) declaring the interests that the owners of the possibility of reverter or right of entry, or persons having an interest pursuant to the agreement, shall have in any property paid for in whole or in part with the proceeds of the disposition; (e) awarding damages for such injury as a party to the action may sustain by reason of extinguishment or modification of the restriction. The judgment may include such other provisions as will in the opinion of the court further the benevolent, charitable, educational, public or religious purposes for which the land is held and such other provisions as equity may require. . . . — ED.

§6.4.1.2   Fee Simple versus Life Estate

EDWARDS v. BRADLEY

315 S.E.2d 196 (Va. 1984)

GEORGE M. COCHRAN, Justice.

In this appeal, the question presented to us is whether by certain provisions in her will a testatrix devised a fee simple estate or a life estate in real property therein described.

Viva Parker Lilliston died testate in 1969. Her will dated January 12, 1957, duly probated with a 1958 codicil irrelevant to this case, provided in part as follows:

> Item Twelve: I give and devise my farm situated on the Seaside from Locustville, in the County of Accomack, State of Virginia ... to my daughter, Margaret Lilliston Edwards, upon the conditions, set out in Item Fourteen. ...
>
> Item Fourteen: all gifts made to my daughter, Margaret L. Edwards, individually and personally, under Items Eleven and Twelve of this Will, whether personal estate or real estate, are conditioned upon the said Margaret L. Edwards keeping the gift or devise herein free from encumbrances of every description, and in the event the said Margaret L. Edwards shall attempt to encumber same or sell her interest, or in the event any creditor or creditors of said Margaret L. Edwards shall attempt to subject her interest in the gift or devise herein made to the payment of the debts of the said Margaret L. Edwards, then and in that event the interest of said Margaret L. Edwards therein shall immediately cease and determine, and the gift or devise shall at once become vested in her children, viz: Betty Belle Branch, Beverly Bradley, John R. Edwards, Bruce C. Edwards, Jill A. Edwards and Jackie L. Edwards, in equal shares in fee simple. ...

Margaret L. Jones, formerly Margaret L. Edwards, qualified as executrix under her mother's will. In 1979, Jones sought to have her children and their spouses execute an agreement to consent to her selling the farm devised to her. Only a daughter, Beverly Bradley, and the latter's husband declined to execute the agreement. In 1980, Jones died testate; in her will, executed in 1979, she left Bradley $1.00, and directed that the farm be sold and the proceeds distributed equally among her other children. The executors named in the will duly qualified. Bradley filed a bill of complaint in the trial court against these personal representatives and her five brothers and sisters, alleging that under the Lilliston will a life estate was devised to Jones with remainder to Jones's children. Bradley sought to enjoin the sale or encumbrance of the farm without her consent and asked that her interest therein be determined.

After hearing evidence presented by Bradley, the trial court determined that Jones had not violated any of the conditions specified in the Lilliston will. Edwards presented no evidence. The trial judge issued a letter opinion in which he stated his conclusion that under the Lilliston will a life estate in the farm was devised to Jones with remainder to her six named children in fee simple. A final decree, incorporating the opinion by reference, was entered March 25, 1981. On appeal, Edwards argued before us that Jones had fee simple title subject to valid ... conditional limitations and, having not violated the conditions, could freely dispose of the farm by will as she chose. Edwards argued in the alternative on brief that if the conditions were invalid Jones was vested with fee simple title without restrictions or conditions even though such unconditional vesting would have been contrary to her mother's intent to protect the farm from Jones's creditors.

There is no conflict in the evidence. Jones was in financial difficulties when the Lilliston will was executed. The will was prepared by an experienced attorney. One provision, referring specifically to the enabling statute, established a spendthrift trust for the benefit of another child of the testatrix.

The trial judge, in his opinion, noted that the "able and experienced" draftsman had used the words "fee simple" at least seven times in the will and codicil. Apparently, the judge reasoned that if a fee simple estate had been intended for Jones, the draftsman would have used that terminology in Item Twelve. Moreover, the judge stated that under Edwards's theory that Jones died vested with fee simple title, a creditor could then bring a creditor's suit to subject the land to the satisfaction of the debt contrary to the testamentary conditions and the intent of Lilliston. The judge further stated that the conditions set forth in Item Fourteen were repugnant to a fee simple estate but not to an estate for life. For these reasons, he ruled that a life estate was created under the Lilliston will.

As a general rule, a condition totally prohibiting the alienation of a vested fee simple estate or requiring a forfeiture upon alienation is void. As an exception to the rule, conditions prohibiting alienation of land granted to corporate entities for their special purposes are valid. A conditional limitation imposed upon a life estate, however, is valid. *See also Restatement on Property* §409 (1944), where such limitations, therein classified as forfeiture restraints, are said to be valid as to life estates.

It is apparent, therefore, that if Lilliston's will vested fee simple title to the farm in Jones, the unqualified restraint on alienation would be invalid and the property from the time of vesting would be subject to sale, encumbrance, or devise by her and subject to the claims of her creditors, results contrary to the express intent of the testatrix. On the other hand, if Lilliston's will vested a life estate in Jones, the unqualified restraint on alienation imposed by the testatrix would be valid. Jones could not acquire, as Edwards suggested, a life estate which, upon compliance with the testamentary conditions, became a fee simple estate at the time of her death. Jones acquired under the Lilliston will either a fee simple estate free of conditions and thus inconsistent with the testatrix's intent or a life estate subject to conditions and thus consistent with such intent.

The draftsman of the Lilliston will carefully avoided using in either Item Twelve or Item Fourteen the words "fee simple" which he had used elsewhere in the instrument. It is true, as Edwards observed, that he also did not use the words "life estate" in those clauses of the will. Under Va. Code §55-11 it is not necessary to use the words "in fee simple" to create a fee simple estate where real estate is devised without words of limitation unless a contrary intention shall appear by the will. In the present case, however, the real estate was devised with words of limitation and a contrary intention appears in the will. Moreover, unless there is a power of disposal in the first taker, Va. Code §55-7, a life estate may be created by implication as well as by explicit language, provided the will shows the requisite intent.

Since the testatrix established a spendthrift trust in another provision of her will, she was aware of the availability of that device but did not choose to use it for the benefit of Jones. Moreover, under Va. Code §55-7, the testatrix could have devised the land to Jones for life with a power of appointment under which Jones could have disposed of the property by will. She did not do so.

The intention of the testatrix is to be upheld if the will can be reasonably construed to effectuate such intent and if it is not inconsistent with an established rule of law. In addition, the language of the will is "to be understood in the sense in which the circumstances of the case show" that the testatrix intended. *Gray v. Francis,* 124 S.E. 446, 450 (Va. 1924). Here, the testatrix intended that Jones have the use and benefit of the real estate free of the claims of her creditors. The ultimate beneficiaries were Jones's children.

Although the will did not expressly designate the children as remaindermen, the conditional limitation to them indicated that they were intended to take the farm when their mother's interest terminated, whether by violation of the conditions or otherwise. Accordingly, we conclude that the trial court properly ruled that Jones acquired a life estate in the property with remainder at her death in fee simple to her six children.

We will affirm the decree of the trial court.

NOTES AND QUESTIONS

1. *Estates.* We could allow owners complete freedom to create future interests as they please. This approach would protect *freedom of contract* or *free disposition* of property. This is not the way the property law system developed. A variety of rules limits the ability of owners to create future interests both to protect the interests of current owners in using their property and having the power to transfer it and to protect social interests in efficient land use. These rules compromise between the interests of grantors and grantees. One regulatory rule is the *rule against creation of new estates,* discussed *infra* at §6.5.1. This rule prohibits owners from creating ownership packages that do not fit within one of the established estates; it helps ensure that sufficient rights are consolidated in owners so that they can act like owners. This means that the courts must interpret conveyances or wills to determine which estate the grantor intended to create. The court cannot simply ask what future interest the grantor intended to create; instead, the court must fit the future interest into an established category.

2. *Interpretation and the presumption against forfeitures.* Sometimes grantors do not use traditional language to create one of the estates. Other times, grantors use conflicting language, seeming to create one estate in one phrase and another estate in another phrase. In either case, courts must interpret the conveyance to determine what types of current and future interests were created and who owns the property. Two conflicting rules of interpretation dominate court discussions of this issue. On one hand, courts often proclaim their fealty to the goal of effectuating the *grantor's intent* to the extent it can be discerned from language in the deed or will or, possibly, from the surrounding circumstances. On the other hand, when the language is ambiguous, most courts also voice a preference for a construction of the language that will avoid recognition of a future interest. This is especially so if recognition of the future interest would mean that the present possessor lost her title to the future interest holder. As the Kansas Supreme Court stated in *Roberts v. Rhodes,* 643 P.2d 116, 118 (Kan. 1982): "Forfeitures are not favored in the law." This rule of interpretation creates a *presumption against forfeitures.* If it is possible to interpret the language to avoid loss of the property by the current owner, the courts will generally adopt this interpretation.

If the choice is between a future interest and mere precatory language (a statement of purpose not intended to be legally binding), the presumption is to recognize a fee simple absolute with no future interest. *Id.* at 118 ("[t]he general rule is well settled that the mere expression that property is to be used for a particular purpose will not in and of itself suffice to turn a fee simple into a determinable fee"). If the choice is either a covenant or a future interest, the presumption is against the future interest and in favor of the enforceable covenant because this will keep title with the current owner. If the choice is either a fee simple determinable or a fee simple subject to condition subsequent, the fee simple subject to condition subsequent is preferred because the current interest is not automatically forfeited when the condition is violated, thereby keeping ownership (at least for the time being) with the current owner. If the choice is between a life estate and a fee simple (defeasible or absolute), a fee simple interest is preferred. *Accord, Howson v. Crombie Street Congregational Church,* 590 N.E.2d 687 (Mass. 1992). *But see Edwards v. Bradley, supra* (finding a life estate rather than a fee simple when this will promote the grantor's intent to effectuate an enforceable restraint on alienation); *Cain v. Finnie,* 785 N.E.2d 1039 (Ill. App. Ct. 2003) (similarly interpreting a will leaving land to "Blanche Spurlock so long as she remains my widow" as a conditional life estate rather than as a fee simple determinable).

3. *Policies behind the presumption against forfeitures.* The choice of preferring either the interests of the current owner or the interests of the future interest holder involves a policy decision about the proper distribution of power over property between grantors and grantees. Enforcing the condition in the original conveyance by requiring a forfeiture promotes the interests of the grantor in controlling the future use and disposition of property; it also creates security for neighboring property owners who may benefit by the condition. In contrast, the presumption against forfeitures promotes the interests of current owners in controlling property in their possession, giving them greater freedom to change land uses as economic conditions and social values change; it also promotes social interests in deregulating economic activity to allow property owners the freedom to shift property to more valuable or desired uses. At the same time, the presumption against forfeitures may further the grantor's intent, on the theory that the grantor presumably intends to give away any interests she has and would be likely to make it very clear if she intended to retain a future interest.

4. *Purpose language.* When conveyances include language explaining the purpose of the transfer, such as in *Wood,* the vast majority of courts agree with *Wood* and will hold the language to be *precatory*—not intended to have any legal significance—and will interpret the conveyance to have transferred all the interests the grantor owned. If the grantors owned a fee simple, the courts presume that is what they intended to convey. This result follows from the presumption against forfeitures and protects the interests of the grantee, placing the burden on the grantors to be clear if they intend to retain a future interest in the property.

However, the courts are not unanimous on this score, as *Cathedral of the Incarnation* shows. The courts sometimes find a future interest in the absence of language clearly creating one. For example, in *Forsgren v. Sollie,* 659 P.2d 1068 (Utah 1983), a conveyance was interpreted to create a fee simple subject to condition subsequent when the deed stated both that the property was "conveyed on the condition that" the grantee construct a partition fence and, in a later sentence, that the property was "conveyed to be used as and for a church or residence purposes only." The court interpreted this language to create a right of entry in the grantor to retake the property if it were ever used for any purpose other than as a church or residence. The court interpreted the "condition" language to modify the later sentence, holding that this was sufficient to create a condition subsequent even though no words were included stating that the grantors retained a right of entry. *See also Restatement of Property* §45 cmt. *l* (1936) ("the phrase 'upon express condition that' usually indicates an intent to create an estate in fee simple subject to a condition subsequent, even when no express clause for re-entry, termination or reverter accompanies it"). As *Cathedral of the Incarnation* shows, the court could have adopted an alternative interpretation focusing only on the use limitation. If the property "is conveyed to be used as and for a church or residence purposes only," this might suggest that the conveyance (the transfer of title) was contingent on being restricted to these uses and that such title would end if the allowable uses ended. Like the court in *Forsgren*, the Appellate Division in *Cathedral of the Incarnation* interpreted words restricting the use of the property as creating a fee simple subject to condition subsequent.

Although most courts are reluctant to find a future interest in the absence of clear language creating one, some courts are eager to find a future interest when the property is donated for charitable purposes. In the absence of a future interest, the owner is entitled to shift the property to a non-charitable use, thereby possibly violating the intent of the grantor and harming the public interest by ending the charitable use. Property is often more valuable if sold on the open market than when reserved for charitable purposes. There are pressures therefore to sell such property. In order to help preserve charitable uses, courts sometimes interpret purpose language or use restrictions in ways that help preserve the charitable use of the property. They may apply the presumption against forfeitures to non-charitable property but not do so with respect to charitable property.

On the other hand, it is not clear that recognition of a future interest will promote charitable uses. After all, if the grantors had prevailed in *Wood* and reclaimed the property, they could have used the property for any purpose, including a non-charitable one. Moreover, the *Cathedral* court may have interpreted the restriction as a future interest simply for the purpose of killing it. After all, if the limitation on use had been interpreted as a covenant restricting use, the grantor might have attempted to enforce the covenant in gross. Interpreted as a right of entry, the court adopted an archaic rule that made such interests inalienable and went so far as to destroy the right of entry if the owner ever attempted to alienate it. The court could have reached the same result by applying the presumption against forfeitures, interpreting the conveyance as a fee simple subject to restrictive covenants, and then holding that the benefit of a covenant cannot be enforced in gross or that, if it is held in gross, the benefit cannot be conveyed to another. Alternatively, it could have applied the changed conditions doctrine on the ground that the grantee's inability to manage the property financially meant that the property would better serve the charitable purpose by being sold to discharge the owner's debts in bankruptcy.

When a deed states a charitable purpose for property or restricts its use to charitable purpose, courts have attempted to achieve the charitable purpose by adopting a number of different interpretations. Most hold the language to be precatory, applying the presumption against forfeitures. Under this approach, grantors who want to create enforceable restrictions on use should do so by creating a charitable trust. However, from time to time, courts have rejected this approach. Some courts grant substantial legal effect to language of purpose and may interpret it to create a future interest. William B. Stoebuck & Dale A. Whitman, *The Law of Property* §2.5, at 41 (3d ed. 2000). Some have found a future interest, as did the court in *Cathedral of the Incarnation* (either a possibility of reverter or a right of entry). Other courts have interpreted the purpose language or use restriction as an enforceable covenant, allowing the covenant to be enforced in gross at least in the context of charitable property. *Davis v. St. Joe School District*, 284 S.W.2d 635 (Ark. 1955). Still other courts have imposed a *constructive trust* on the property, obligating the current owner to use it for charitable purposes or transfer it to someone who will so use it. *United States v. Certain Land in Cape Girardeau*, 79 F. Supp. 558 (D. Mo. 1947).

5. *Restraints on alienation.* The Virginia Supreme Court in *Edwards v. Bradley* resolved what it saw as an ambiguity in the conveyance partly by reference to the fact that the property was subject to a restraint on alienation—a restraint that would be valid if attached to a life estate but void if attached to a fee simple. The presumption against forfeitures would suggest that the fee simple be chosen over the life estate, the restraint held void, and the property left with a fee simple absolute. The court refused to adopt this approach, instead focusing on the fact that the grantor intended to create a valid restraint on alienation and the only way to achieve that result was to interpret the conveyance as creating a life estate. Which of these interpretations is preferable and why?

6. *Changed conditions.* The changed conditions doctrine denying enforcement of covenants when circumstances are so drastically changed that they are no longer of benefit to the dominant estate has traditionally not applied to future interests. *Prieskorn v. Maloof,* 991 P.2d 511 (N.M. Ct. App. 1999). Some states, however, have statutes like the one at issue in *Cathedral of the Incarnation* that remove future interests in charitable properties. Should a court grant relief from such restrictions in the absence of a statute?

§6.4.2   TRUSTS AND THE *CY PRES* DOCTRINE

When a settlor establishes a charitable trust and has a *general intent* to contribute to some form of charity, and the particular charitable purpose identified by the settlor becomes impracticable or impossible to achieve, courts may apply the *cy pres* doctrine to carry out the settlor's charitable intent so far as possible by authorizing that the trust income be used for some other charity. This doctrine requires courts to determine whether the settlor's intent was general or particular; in other words, did the grantor intend to aid only the particular charity mentioned in the trust, or would the grantor have intended the trust income to benefit some other charity if the first beneficiary ended its existence? If the grantor's intent was general, the court may be called on to determine whether an alternate charity—ordinarily chosen by the trustee—is of a kind the settlor would have wished to benefit. If the trust fails because the settlor's charitable intent is no longer possible to accomplish, the court must then determine to whom the trust principal belongs.

In *In re Certain Scholarship Funds,* 575 A.2d 1325 (N.H. 1990), a testator established a charitable scholarship trust requiring that 80 percent of the annual income be used to provide a college education "for some Poor and worthy Keene boy who is a scholar in the Keene High School." A second settlor established a similar trust in his will, providing that the income be used "to provide tuition for one year for some worthy protestant boy" at Keene High School. The school board filed a petition asking the equity court to remove the religious and gender restrictions in these trusts under the *cy pres* doctrine to allow the school to award scholarships to students regardless of religion or sex. The New Hampshire Supreme Court held that the school board's participation in management of the trusts constituted state action and that the state constitution prohibited discrimination based on religion and gender. The court then noted:

> The trial court found, based upon the facts before it, that there was no indication that Mr. Wright or Mr. Alger would not have responded to the changes in attitudes experienced by society since the creation of these trusts. Furthermore, the court could not find, from language of the wills, any particular discriminatory intent. Thus, the trial court concluded that the primary intent of both testators was not to discriminate against women and non-Protestants, but to assist the students at Keene High School in their

pursuit of higher education. After finding a general intention to devote the property to a charitable purpose, and in the absence of a gift-over provision, the trial court invoked the doctrine of *cy pres* to reform the terms of the trusts.

Id. at 1328. The state supreme court rejected the state attorney general's recommendation that the public trustees be replaced by private trustees to effectuate the settlors' discriminatory intent. Instead, it upheld the trial court's ruling that the *cy pres* doctrine applied and that the income from the trusts could be paid to women and to non-Protestants.

> Our society permits discrimination in the private sector in recognizing that the nature of human beings is to associate with, and confer benefits upon, other human beings and institutions of their own choosing. Such private decision-making is a part of daily life in any society. However, when the decision-making mechanism, as here, is so entwined with public institutions and government, discrimination becomes the policy statement and product of society itself and cannot stand against the strong and enlightened language of our constitution.

Id. at 1329-1330. *See also In the Matter of Crichfield Trust,* 426 A.2d 88 (N.J. Super. Ct. Ch. Div. 1980) (applying the *cy pres* doctrine to reform a trust that established a college scholarship for male graduates of a public high school to permit award of scholarships to females as well); *Coffee v. William Marsh Rice University,* 408 S.W.2d 269, 271 (Tex. Ct. App. 1966)(using *cy pres* to excise racial restriction in endowment fund). *Cf. United States v. Hughes Memorial Home,* 396 F.Supp. 544 (D.W.Va. 1975)(*cy pres* doctrine applied to excise racial restriction on trust benefiting orphanage because racial exclusion from the orphanage would violate the federal Fair Housing Act).

In a similar case, however, the New York Court of Appeals substituted private trustees for the public trustees and allowed the trust to continue to be paid out only to men. Since the trust would, in the future, be administered privately, no state action was involved; nor did the use of the court's powers to replace the school district as trustee with a private trustee constitute "state action" in the eyes of the court since the discriminatory intent was purely on the part of the private donor. Rather, the trust constituted a private gift, which could be conditioned in a discriminatory manner without violating federal or state guarantees of equal protection of the laws. *Matter of Estate of Wilson,* 452 N.E.2d 1228 (N.Y. 1983).

Several states have passed statutes prohibiting racial discrimination in donative transfers as to real or personal property. Cal. Civ. Code §53(a) (invalidating any provision in a "written instrument relating to real property" which purports to forbid or restrict the use by or the conveyance to "any person of a specified sex, race, color, religion, ancestry, national origin, or disability"); N.J. Stat. §46:3-23 (invalidating all conditions and restrictions in *inter vivos* transactions limiting transfer to or use by "any person because of race, creed, color, national origin, ancestry, marital status or sex").

§6.5 *Regulatory Rules*

Future interests are regulated by both common law rules and statutes. The main structural rules include (1) the rule prohibiting the creation of new estates; (2) the rule against unreasonable restraints on alienation; (3) the rule against perpetuities; the (4) interpretive rule prohibiting "waste" of the present estate; (5) the prohibition on invalid racial conditions; and (6) the rule against unreasonable restraints on marriage.

§6.5.1   RULE AGAINST CREATION OF NEW ESTATES

The rules underlying the creation of future interests are intended to discourage the social hierarchy characteristic of feudalism and to promote a market system involving wide dispersal of property rights to prevent local monopolies. The commitment to these goals requires courts to decide which forms of property shall be recognized. We could just allow owners to create whatever future interests they want, but this is not how the law developed.

In light of this problem, courts follow a general *rule against the creation of new estates*. A conveyance that does not fit within any of the established categories (including fee simple absolute subject to covenants, defeasible fees, life estates, leaseholds, and in some states, fees tail) must be interpreted to create the most closely analogous estate.

This rule has both formal and substantive dimensions. *See* Thomas W. Merrill & Henry E. Smith, *Optimal Standardization in the Law of Property: The Numerus Clausus Principle*, 110 Yale L.J. 1 (2000). Formally, it means that grantors must put their conveyances in a recognizable form if they want courts to recognize the package of rights they intended to create. Substantively, it means that certain packages of rights will not be recognized. This limits the number of packages of ownership bundles that can be created, facilitating exchange both by making it easier to determine what one is buying and by ensuring that owners have certain basic rights when they acquire those standard bundles.

One important example is the *abolition of the fee tail*. A conveyance that purports to create a perpetual series of life estates will not be honored; it keeps the property in a single family and takes it out of the real estate market, thereby infringing on both the autonomy of future owners and social welfare. The few states that recognize the fee tail allow it to be converted to a fee simple or transmute it into a life estate, burdening the property for one or two generations but not permanently. The rule against creation of new estates helps consolidate property rights, either immediately or over time, in a single owner. It does this by limiting the power of grantors to create particular future interests. Consider how Justice Oliver Wendell Holmes, Jr., reacted to the following estate.

JOHNSON v. WHITON
34 N.E. 542 (Mass. 1893)

OLIVER WENDELL HOLMES, JR., J.

This is an action to recover a deposit paid under an agreement to purchase land. The land in question passed under the seventh clause of the will of Royal Whiton to his five grandchildren, and a deed executed by them was tendered to the plaintiff, but was refused, on the ground that one of the grandchildren, Sarah A. Whiton, could not convey a fee-simple absolute, and this action is brought to try the question. The clause of the will referred to is as follows: "After the decease of all my children, I give, devise, and bequeath to my granddaughter Sarah A. Whiton and her heirs on her father's side one-third part of all my estate, both real and personal, and to my other grandchildren and their heirs, respectively, the remainder, to be divided in equal parts between them."

We see no room for doubt that the legal title passed by the foregoing clause. We think it equally plain that the words "and her heirs on her father's side" are words of limitation, and not words of purchase. The only serious question is whether the effect of them was to give Sarah A. Whiton only a qualified fee, and whether, by reason of the

qualification, she is unable to convey a fee simple. . . . By the old la[...]
descent a man must be of the blood of the first purchaser, and descen[...]
purchaser. For instance, if the land had been acquired in fee simple b[...]
father, it could only have descended from her to her heirs on her fa[...]
great stretch to allow a limitation in the first instance to Sarah o[...]
descendible quality that it would have had in the case supposed. E[...]
as Mr. Challis argues, the grantee under such a limitation could convey a [...]
as he or she could have done if the estate actually had descended from the father. But ou[...]
statute of descent looks no further than the person himself who died seised of or entitled
to the estate. The analogy which lies at the foundation of the argument for the possibility
of such limitations is wanting. A man cannot create a new kind of inheritance. These and
other authorities show, too, that, except in the case of a grant by the king, if the words
"on her father's side" do not effect the purpose intended, they are to be rejected, leaving
the estate a fee simple. . . . Certainly, it would seem that in this commonwealth an estate
descending only to heirs on the father's side was a new kind of inheritance.

What we have to consider, however, is not the question of descent, but that of
alienability; and that question brings a further consideration into view. It would be most
unfortunate and unexpected if it should be discovered at this late day that it was possible
to impose such a qualification upon a fee, and to put it out of the power of the owners to
give a clear title for generations. In the more familiar case of an estate tail, the legislature
has acted, and the statute has been carried to the furthest verge by construction. It is not
too much to say that it would be plainly contrary to the policy of the law of Massachusetts to deny the power of Sarah A. Whiton to convey an unqualified fee.

Judgment for defendant.

§6.5.2   RULE AGAINST UNREASONABLE RESTRAINTS ON
ALIENATION

See supra §5.5.4, at pages 450-472.

§6.5.3   RULE AGAINST PERPETUITIES

§6.5.3.1   Traditional Rule

The *rule against perpetuities* invalidates future interests that may vest too far into
the future. Future interests are invalid unless they are certain to "vest" or fail to vest
within the lifetime of someone who is alive ("in being") at the creation of the interest or
no later than 21 years after her death. In John Chipman Gray's famous formulation:

> No interest is good unless it must vest, if at all, no later than 21 years after the death of some
> life in being at the creation of the interest.

John Chipman Gray, *The Rule Against Perpetuities* 1417 (4th ed. 1942).

The rule is technical, complicated and, in the minds of some, archaic. It has also
been substantially modified by statute in more than half the states. At the same time,
the policies underlying the rule still have substantial support among many judges,
legislators and scholars. The rule is "designed to prevent remoteness of vesting and
thereby leave control of the wealth of the world more in the hands of the living than in
the hands of the dead." *Thompson on Real Property, Thomas Edition* §28.01 (David A.

omas ed. 1994). Although modified by statute, it has been abolished entirely only in a ew states.

The rule against perpetuities is one of the most complex in the common law and has been the bane of law students for generations. The rule is difficult to apply to complicated conveyances. However, the rule is not difficult in the vast majority of cases. These materials will explain the rule in detail and show how to apply it to a series of representative problems. We first turn to the policy reasons behind the rule. Knowing why the rule matters may make it easier to understand why it is important to understand.

Limiting dead hand control: the policy behind the rule against perpetuities. Property owners may attempt to use future interests to control the use and disposition of property far into the future. The ability of property owners to create future interests therefore poses the danger of "dead hand control" of property, that is, control of current property use by persons who died many years ago. The rule against perpetuities is a partial response to this problem; it places some limits on the ability of current owners to create future interests. Just as the rule against restraints on alienation limits or prevents the owners from blocking the transfer of property after they have let go of it, the rule against perpetuities arguably promotes the free transfer of property in the marketplace by limiting the creation of future interests.

It is important to note, however, that the rule attempts to promote alienability by *limiting* the powers of present owners to control the future use of their property. The rule therefore represents a compromise between (1) the policy of allowing owners to determine who will own their property in the future and under what circumstances and (2) the policy of freeing owners from control by prior owners so that current owners can control both the use and disposition of their property. The rule against perpetuities is therefore analogous to rules extinguishing easements that have been abandoned and the rules freeing landowners from covenants under changed conditions.

How to apply the rule. The rule requires three steps. First, determine what future interests have been created. The rule against perpetuities applies only to *nonvested* interests. If it is a possibility of reverter, right of entry, reversion, or vested remainder (absolute or subject to divestment), the rule against perpetuities does not apply. If it is an executory interest, contingent remainder or vested remainder subject to open, the interest is "subject to" the rule against perpetuities and must be tested against the rule to see if the interest is valid. Second, if the rule applies, determine whether the future interest in question is valid or invalid under the rule. If there is any possibility the interest can vest more than 21 years after the death of everyone alive at the creation of the interest, it is invalid. If such a possibility exists, the interest violates the rule and is void. Third, if the future interest is invalid, determine what interests remain by striking out the invalid interest and seeing what is left. Whatever is left must comply with the rule as well. Let us consider these three steps in more depth.

(1) Identifying interests subject to the rule. *All future interests in the grantor are exempt* from the rule against perpetuities; these include *reversions* (following life estates and leaseholds) and *possibilities of reverter* and *rights of entry* (following defeasible fees). These future interests are "good" and will be enforced by the courts unless they are regulated by special statutory limitations other than the rule against perpetuities. The only interests in third parties that are similarly exempt from the rule against perpetuities are *vested remainders* (absolutely vested or vested subject to divestment).

Future interests subject to the rule against perpetuities are *executory interests, contingent remainders* and *vested remainders subject to open.* These interests must be tested to see whether they comply with the rule. Vested remainders subject to open are subject to the rule because some of the interests to the class members are vested and some are contingent (those belonging to persons who are not born at the creation of the interest). All future interests in third parties following defeasible fees (executory interests) are subject to the rule against perpetuities. Future interests in third parties following life estates (remainders) are subject to the rule only if they are contingent, that is, if there is a condition precedent to their vesting or if they are allocated to persons unascertained at the time of the original conveyance creating them. Vested remainders subject to open are partially contingent and therefore have traditionally been held subject to the rule.

A common example of a future interest traded in the marketplace is an *option to purchase,* which is the right to buy property for a stated price at some point in the future. Because options are rights to acquire property in the future, they are akin to executory interests and therefore are ordinarily subject to the rule against perpetuities. *Preemptive rights,* or *rights of first refusal,* similarly allow the holder to purchase property in the future whenever the current owner decides to sell. Some courts hold that preemptive rights are not subject to the rule against perpetuities because they allow the current owner either to obtain the fair market value or to have an offer by a third party matched by the owner of the preemptive right. Either way, the property is alienable. Other courts, however, hold that preemptive rights, like options to purchase, are subject to the rule against perpetuities.

Note that the name of an interest is fixed when it is created. Thus when an owner of a right of entry transfers the interest to another person, it remains a right of entry and does not change into an executory interest, even though it is held by someone other than the grantor or her heirs.

(2) Testing the interest to see if it may vest, if ever, too far into the future: seek a validating life. The rule invalidates interests that are not certain to "vest" within 21 years of the death of some "life in being" at the "creation of the interest." The goal is to determine whether there is any possibility at all that the executory interest or contingent remainder will "vest" more than 21 years after the death of any person alive at the creation of the interest. The *perpetuities period* is the time between the creation of the interest and 21 years after the death of the last person alive at the creation of the interest. The goal is to determine whether the interest may vest too far in the future after the perpetuities period has ended. The easiest way to do this is to look for a *validating life.* This is a person within whose lifetime (or no later than 21 years after that person's death),[15] the interest is certain to vest, if it ever does vest. It is helpful to define the terms of the rule.

---

15. The period is actually 21 years and nine months because the time of gestation is added onto the 21 years. For example, in a conveyance to *A* for life, then to the first child of *A* to reach 21, it is assumed that *A* can only have children during his lifetime (this is now factually incorrect given the existence of frozen sperm and frozen embryos and other new reproductive technologies) and that such children will reach 21 within 21 years of the death of *A.* This is assumed even though *A* might die after *A*'s spouse becomes pregnant but before the child is born, and such a child may not reach 21 until 21 years and nine months after the death of *A.*

(a) *"Creation of the interest."* A future interest is created by conveyance (sale) at the moment of the conveyance. It is created in a will at the moment the testator dies. It is created in a trust the moment the trust document is signed and the trust created if the trust is irrevocable, and if it is revocable, at the moment it becomes irrevocable.

(b) *"Vest."* The "vesting" moment is generally the moment when the contingency occurs that renders the interest certain to come into possession. The moment of vesting for an *executory interest* is the moment the contingency occurs. At exactly that moment, the future interest becomes possessory since the executory interest automatically takes effect when the contingency happens. Thus, in the conveyance "*O* to *A* so long as used for residential purposes, then to *B*," the executory interest in *B* will vest, if ever, at the moment the property is used for nonresidential purposes; at that moment *B* will gain the right to possess the property.

The moment of vesting for a *contingent remainder* is when the condition that makes it a contingent remainder disappears, regardless of whether the remainder becomes possessory at that moment. If, for example, the remainder is contingent because of a condition precedent, the remainder vests when the contingency happens. In the conveyance "*O* to *A* for life, then to *B* if *B* graduates from law school," the contingent remainder in *B* becomes vested when *B* graduates from law school, even if *A* is still alive; it will not become possessory in *B* until *A*'s death. In the conveyance "*O* to *A* for life, then to the first child of *B*," the contingent remainder in *B* becomes vested the moment *B* has a child; however, *B*'s child will gain possession only after *A* dies.

It is important to remember that interests in the grantor, such as possibilities of reverter, rights of entry, and reversions, were conceptualized as "vested" the moment they were created. This is because an owner of a fee simple absolute who conveys a fee simple determinable is carving out a present estate from a fee simple absolute which is clearly vested; the possibility of reverter is part of that vested interest that was not given away.

Thus, future interests in the grantor are thought to be vested at the moment of creation. Both contingent remainders and executory interests are vested at the moment the contingency disappears, but only executory interests necessarily become possessory at the same moment; a contingent remainder that has become vested may have to wait for the prior life estate or leasehold to terminate before it can become possessory.

Lives in being. The rule requires us to determine whether there is any chance the interest could vest more than 21 years after the deaths of everyone alive at the creation of the interest. The easiest way to apply the rule is to look for a "validating life." A validating life is someone within whose lifetime (or 21 years afterward) the future interest is certain to vest *if it ever vests*. If you cannot identify a validating life, the future interest is void. Corporations are not counted as "lives in being." In a conveyance "from *O* to *X Hospital* so long as used for hospital purposes, then to *B*," the only possible validating lives are those of *O* and *B*. The hospital is not counted as a life-in-being.

The "perpetuities period" is the time within which the interest must vest if it is to be upheld as good under the rule. That period begins at the creation of the interest and ends 21 years after the death of every person alive at the creation of the interest.

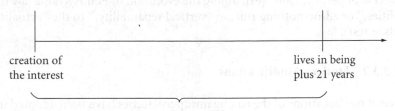

The question is whether there is any chance the interest will vest outside the perpetuities period.

(3) Remedy for violating the rule against perpetuities. The remedy for violating the rule is simply to strike, or cross out, the offending language. Thus, for example:

> *O to A for residential purposes, then to B.*

If the conveyance to *B* violates the rule against perpetuities (it does), strike out the words "then to *B*." We are left with "*O to A for residential purposes.*" This describes a fee simple determinable; since the possibility of reverter in *O* is not subject to the rule, the interest is valid.

> *O to A, but if the property is not used for residential purposes, then to B.*

If the conveyance to *B* violates the rule (it does), strike out the entire phrase "but if the property is not used for residential purposes, then to *B*," leaving "*O to A,*" creating a fee simple absolute in *A*. This is because merely striking out the words "then to *B*" leaves a conveyance that is not recognizable as a standard estate.

The different results in these two conveyances has been subject to criticism, especially because the possibility of reverter in *O* is just as pernicious a clog on title as an executory interest in *B* would be. Some courts therefore treat these conveyances alike and convert *A*'s interest to a fee simple in both cases.

Some "class gifts" are partially valid and partially invalid. For example, a conveyance from "*O to A* for life, then to the grandchildren of *A*" creates a vested remainder subject to open in the grandchildren if one grandchild is alive at the time of the conveyance to *A*. The interest in the living grandchild is vested while the interest in unborn grandchildren is contingent. If the class "closes" at the death of *A*, the grandchildren's interest will be valid because their interests will vest at the death of a life in being. However, if the class does not close at the death of *A*, then the interest in unborn grandchildren may violate the rule because *A* could have another child after the conveyance from *O* to *A* and that child could have a child more than 21 years after the death of *O*, *A*, and any children or grandchildren of *A* alive at the creation of the interest. Some states follow the "all or nothing rule," invalidating the entire class gift to the grandchildren of *A* because some of the interests may violate the rule. Other states split the difference and validate the vested interests in the grandchildren who are alive at the creation of the interest while striking down the contingent remainders ("vertical separability"). *See In re Estate of Weaver,* 572 A.2d 1249, 1253 (Pa. Super. Ct. 1990) (explaining the evolution of Pennsylvania law from the "possibilities," or all-or-nothing rule, to "vertical separability," to the "actualities," or wait-andsee test).

§6.5.3.2 Modern Modifications

Several modifications of the rule against perpetuities have been adopted in about half the states. Two of the most popular are the *wait and see* test and the *cy pres* doctrine.

(a) Wait and See, or Second Look

Some states modify the rule by using a "wait and see" or "second look" test. Under the traditional rule, a future interest is void if a *possibility* exists that it will vest outside the perpetuities period; this can be determined on the date of the conveyance. Under the wait and see test, the courts will not hold that a future interest violates the rule until the perpetuities period has passed and they are certain that the future interest has not vested within that period. For example, in the conveyance "*O* to *A* so long as used for residential purposes, then to *B*," the executory interest in *B* is void under the traditional rule because it is possible that the property will be used for residential purposes for 300 years, and then used for nonresidential purposes; obviously this would occur long after the deaths of *O, A,* and *B* plus 21 years. Under the traditional rule, therefore, the interest is void, and we are left with *O to A so long as used for residential purposes,* which is valid under the rule because the rule does not apply to possibilities of reverter.

In contrast, under the wait and see test, the courts will wait until the condition occurs or the perpetuities period ends, whichever comes first. In this case the perpetuities period ends 21 years after the death of the last of *O, A,* and *B*. If the property is used for nonresidential purposes before that period has lapsed, the executory interest is good and will be recognized; the property shifts to *B*. If, however, *O, A,* and *B* die and 21 years pass, and the property is still used for residential purposes, at that moment the future interest in *B* (actually *B*'s heirs or devisees since *B* is dead) is destroyed. We are left with a fee simple in the current owner of *A*'s interest.[16] The wait and see test in some form has been adopted in the majority of states — in some states in its traditional form and in others by a 90-year waiting period under the *Uniform Statutory Rule Against Perpetuities,* discussed below.

---

16. Note that this result differs from the result when an executory interest violates the traditional rule against perpetuities. Under the traditional rule, the offending language is stricken ("then to *B*"), and what is left is a fee simple determinable ("*O* to *A* so long as used for residential purposes"). In contrast, under the wait and see test, once the perpetuities period has lapsed, the future interest is normally stricken entirely, leaving a fee simple absolute in the present owner.

(b) Equitable Reformation or Cy Pres

A conveyance may violate the rule against perpetuities because it contains an age limit greater than 21. For example, "*O* to *A* for life, then to the first child of *B* to attain 25 years of age," creates a contingent remainder in the first child of *B* to reach 25 (assuming *B* has no children at the time of the initial conveyance), which violates the rule since a child could be born after the conveyance and reach 25 more than 21 years after the deaths of *O*, *A*, and *B*. Under the *cy pres* doctrine, a court may reduce the age contingency of 25 to 21 if this will validate the future interest. In this case it will because if any child of *B* is ever going to reach 21 years old, it will have to happen within 21 years of the death of *B*, who is a life in being at the creation of the interest.[17] Since the reduction in age in the conveyance from 25 to 21 saves the future interest, this test will reduce the age contingency to 21 and validate the future interest.

§6.5.3.3 Statutory Limits on Future Interests

Many states have passed statutes that codify the rule against perpetuities. Some states have passed other statutes that also affect future interests.

(a) Statutory Cut-offs for Possibilities of Reverter and Rights of Entry

The rule against perpetuities does not apply to rights of entry or possibilities of reverter. The common law courts in England treated these interests as vested from the very beginning since they defined interests in the grantor that were reserved when the present estate was created. Yet, as a matter of public policy, it makes no sense to worry about executory interests because of the problem of dead hand control while deferring to future interests in the heirs of the grantor that could similarly vest 300 years in the future.

This is especially true in light of the ability to evade the rule against perpetuities by careful drafting. For example, a grantor who wanted to convey property to *A* so long as used for residential purposes, then to *B*, could easily do so in a two-step transaction. The grantor could convey a fee simple determinable to *A*, retaining a possibility of reverter. The grantor would then convey her possibility of reverter to *B*. The transfer of the future interest to *B* does not convert it to an executory interest. Since it was a possibility of reverter, the rule against perpetuities does not apply and the policy of restricting dead hand control has been evaded. A second way to do this is for *O* to transfer a fee simple absolute to *B*, and then for *B* to convey a fee simple determinable to *A*; since *B*'s interest is a possibility of reverter rather than an executory interest, it is immune from the rule against perpetuities.

For these reasons, some states have passed statutes that cut off interests in the grantor following defeasible fees if the condition does not occur within a stated time

---

17. What do new reproductive technologies do to this traditional argument? Think about frozen, fertilized ova that may be implanted years after the death of the sperm donor and egg donor. *See* Les A. McCrimmon, *Gametes, Embryos and the Life in Being: The Impact of Reproductive Technology on the Rule Against Perpetuities*, 34 Real Prop. Prob. & Tr. J. 697 (2000).

period after the initial conveyance. These statutes correct the divergent treatment of interests in the grantor and interests in third parties. Massachusetts provides, for example, that possibilities of reverter and rights of entry are destroyed if they do not vest within 30 years of their creation. Mass. Gen Laws Ann. ch. 184A, §7.[18]

(b) Marketable Title Acts

Some states have marketable title statutes requiring that future interests be re-recorded periodically in the local registry of deeds (typically every 30 or 40 years) to remain valid and enforceable. *See, e.g.,* Iowa Code §614.24 (1985). Statutes that effectively nullify future interests have often been challenged on the grounds that they constitute a taking of property without just compensation. *Compare Trustees of Schools of Township No. 1 v. Batdorf,* 130 N.E.2d 111 (Ill. 1955) (upholding the validity of the Illinois statute) and *Presbytery of Southeast Iowa v. Harris,* 226 N.W.2d 232 (Iowa 1975) with *Board of Education v. Miles,* 207 N.E.2d 181 (N.Y. 1965) (holding invalid the New York statute). These laws are generally upheld today if they apply prospectively and give owners enough notice of the obligation to re-record their interests.

(c) Uniform Statutory Rule Against Perpetuities

A fairly recently drafted uniform law, the *Uniform Statutory Rule Against Perpetuities,* currently adopted in more than half the states, would validate future interests that otherwise violate the traditional rule against perpetuities if the interest vests at any time within 90 years of the date of its creation. Mary Louise Fellows, *Testing Perpetuity Reforms: A Study of Perpetuity Cases* 1984-1989, 25 Real Prop. Prob. & Tr. J. 597 (1991). This test applies the wait and see doctrine for interests that violate the traditional rule but limits the perpetuities period to 90 years rather than to "lives in being at the creation of the interest plus 21 years." The 90-year wait and see provision applies only to interests that would have been invalid under the traditional rule. About half the states have adopted some version of this statute. *See, e.g.,* Ga. Code §§44-6-200 to 44-6-206; Mass. Gen. Laws ch. 184A, §§1 to 11; Mich. Comp. Laws §§554.71 to 554.78; Or. Rev. Stat. §§105.950 to 105.975. If an interest violates the 90-year wait and see period, the statute authorizes the courts to reform the deed, will, or trust in the manner that most closely approximates the transferor's manifested plan of distribution and is within the allowable 90-year period.

The more radical reform implemented by the *Uniform Statutory Rule Against Perpetuities* is to exempt most commercial transactions from the rule entirely. Any transaction for value is exempt from the rule against perpetuities. Thus all property transferred by sale is exempt from the rule, including almost all options to purchase because they are generally granted only for a price. The statute applies the rule against perpetuities only to donative transfers (gifts or wills). Some donative transfers are exempt from the rule, including premarital or separation agreements and transfers to governmental or charitable entities when the future interest is held by another charitable entity. *Uniform Probate Code* §2-904.

---

18. Note that the Massachusetts statute does not apply to reversions or vested remainders, which remain exempt from both the rule against perpetuities and the statutory cut-off.

(d) Abolition of the Rule

One of the major applications of the rule against perpetuities has traditionally been to prevent the creation of perpetual family trusts. Wills creating trusts of income-generating personal property are generally written to conform to the dictates of the rule against perpetuities. However, at least fifteen states have abolished or substantially altered the rule against perpetuities. They have done so to allow the creation of so-called "dynasty trusts" of either real or personal property; such trusts generate income for the beneficiaries in perpetuity (or at any rate for a very long time) and take advantage of federal tax code provisions that make the gift tax-free. T.P. Gallanis, *The Future of Future Interests,* 60 Wash. & Lee L. Rev. 513, 516-520, 554-560 (2003); Garrett Moritz, *Dynasty Trusts and the Rule Against Perpetuities,* 116 Harv. L. Rev. 2588 (2003). Some states have abolished the rule against perpetuities either directly, as in states like Rhode Island, New Jersey, and South Dakota, R.I. Gen. Laws §34-11-38; N.J. Stat. §46:2F-9; S.D. Codified Laws §43-5-8, or indirectly by adopting a very long perpetuities period (Alaska Stat. §34.27.051 (1000 years); Fla. Stat. §689.225(2)(f) (360 years); Wash. Rev. Code §11.98.130 (150 years)). Others have abolished the rule for personal property but kept it in some form for real property, Del. Code tit. 25 §503. Still other states have reformed the rule by allowing trusts with unvested future interests to last forever but have limited the time period during which the power of alienation of the trust corpus (the principal giving rise to the income) can be suspended; this ensures that the property can become alienable after the perpetuities period, Alaska Stat. §34.27.100(a). Some states have abolished the rule as long as the trustee retains the power to alienate the trust corpus, Wis. Stat. §700.16(5). Finally, some states have abolished the rule but required the trust corpus to be distributed within a set time period, Del. Code tit. 25 §503(b).

§6.5.3.4 Examples and Explanations

To illustrate how the rule is applied, we will examine a series of problems, first identifying future interests and then applying the rule against perpetuities.

Caveat: It is important to note that the following examples will provide a false sense of precision and determinacy. The rules may be applied differently in different jurisdictions. Moreover, the law changes over time, and changes in perceptions of the relative interests of grantors, present owners, and owners of future interests may lead to changes in the way the rule is interpreted and applied.

For other explanations of the rule, *see* Carolyn Burgess Featheringill, *Understanding the Rule Against Perpetuities: A Step-by-Step Approach,* 13 Cumb. L. Rev. 161 (1982); Jesse Dukeminier, *A Modern Guide to Perpetuities,* 74 Cal. L. Rev. 1867, 1884 (1986); W. Barton Leach, *Perpetuities in a Nutshell,* 51 Harv. L. Rev. 638 (1938); W. Barton Leach, *Perpetuities: The Nutshell Revisited,* 78 Harv. L. Rev. 973 (1965).

Interests in the grantor. Future interests in the grantor or her heirs are exempt from the rule against perpetuities. For example:

1. *O to A as long as used for residential purposes.* The possibility of reverter in O is exempt from the rule against perpetuities and the interest is good. (Remember a statute may cut off possibilities of reverter if they do not vest within a certain number of years of the creation of the interest.)

2. *O to A for life.* The reversion in *O* is exempt from the rule against perpetuities and the interest is good.

Absolutely vested remainders. Remainders that are absolutely vested are immune from the rule.

3. *O to A for life, then to B.* The vested remainder in *B* is not subject to the rule. If *B* dies before *A*, then *B*'s heirs will get the property when *A* dies. If *A* dies before *B*, then *B* will get it when *A* dies.

Vested remainders subject to divestment. Remainders that are vested subject to divestment are immune from the rule.

4. *O to A for life, then to B, but if B marries C, then the property shall revert to O.* *B*'s remainder is *vested remainder subject to divestment* (or defeasance) and is valid.

Executory interests. Executory interests are subject to the rule against perpetuities. The main exception is that the rule does not apply if both the present estate owner and the future interest owner are *charities*. Because executory interests are subject to the rule, they are void unless they are certain to vest within 21 years of the death of some person alive at the creation of the interest. This means that executory interests are invalid unless they are limited in time. Moreover, the time limit must ensure that vesting, if it will ever occur, will happen within "lives-in-being plus 21 years." For example:

5. *O to A as long as used for residential purposes, then to B.* Because *A* owns a fee simple subject to executory limitation, the estate is inheritable and devisable and could last forever. It could also be used for residential purposes for a thousand years, long after *O, A, B* and everyone else alive at the creation of the interest has died and 21 years have passed. Because there is a possibility the executory interest in *B* may vest too far into the future, it is void. The traditional remedy is to strike out the words "then to *B*," leaving the words "*O to A as long as used for residential purposes.*" This is a recognizable estate (a fee simple determinable) and the possibility of reverter in *O* is immune from the rule and thus is good. Some courts, however, may strike out the whole condition, leaving *A* with a fee simple absolute.

6. *O to A, but if the property is ever used for nonresidential purposes, then to B.* *B*'s executory interest is invalid for the same reasons it was invalid in example #5 above. However, the remedy traditionally has been different. One cannot strike out only the words "then to *B*" because what is left is not a recognizable estate; it contains a "but if" clause but then does not say what happens if the condition is fulfilled. The wording of example #5 implied that the present estate would automatically terminate and revert to *O* as a possibility of reverter. Because this wording in example #6 cannot support that result, the courts traditionally struck out all the language after "*O to A*" and *A* would be left with a fee simple absolute rather than a fee simple determinable as in example #5. The difference is a formal one and does not have any real policy justification because the two conveyances are otherwise functionally identical. For this reason, some scholars and courts have suggested that the

two cases should be treated alike, one way or the other. If the policy behind the rule is to cut off future interests that may come into being too far into the future, it would seem sensible to treat possibilities of reverter like executory interests. If the executory interest is problematic because it may vest and become possessory a thousand years into the future, the same can be said of the possibility of reverter in O, even if it was traditionally considered already "vested." In that case, the appropriate remedy for both example #5 and #6 would be to strike the interest in B and leave A with a fee simple absolute.

7. *O to A, but if the property is used for nonresidential purposes within 21 years of this conveyance, then to B.* The executory interest in B is subject to the rule against perpetuities but does not violate it because it will vest, if ever, within 21 years of the conveyance and thus within 21 years of all lives in being at the creation of the interest. If vesting ever occurs, it will be within the perpetuities period even if everyone in the world died the day after the conveyance; the time limit prevents vesting later than 21 years after creation of the interest.

Contingent remainders. Contingent remainders are harder to analyze than executory interests. The trick is to search for a validating life. If the interest is certain to vest within the lifetime of one of the named individuals (or no later than 21 years after they have died), then it does not violate the rule and it will be good. For example:

8. *O to A for life, then to B if B marries C.* B's interest is a contingent remainder because there is a condition precedent that must take place before the interest could vest. The contingent remainder in B is good whether or not the jurisdiction has abrogated the rule of destructibility of contingent remainders.[19] In a state that allows contingent remainders to be destroyed, B's interest will be lost forever if B does not marry before A dies. Thus, it will vest, if at all, within A's lifetime and thus is good. If contingent remainders are not destructible, and B has not married before A dies, then the property reverts to O as a fee simple subject to executory limitation, and the property will spring to B if B marries C. The interest in B will vest, if ever, when B marries C; because this must happen during the lifetime of both B and C, both of whom were lives in being at the creation of the interest, then there is no chance the interest will vest more than 21 years after the death of some life in being at the creation of the interest.

9. *O to A for life, then to the children of B.* If B is alive at the time of the conveyance from O to A and B has children at that time, those children have a vested remainder subject to open. Their interest is subject to the rule against perpetuities but does not violate it because their interest will vest when A dies, the class will close, and there is no possibility the interest will vest more than 21 years after the death of A, a life in being at the creation of the interest.

If B has no children at the time of the conveyance, they have a contingent remainder because they are not ascertainable at that time. The remainder will vest when B has a child, and B must have a child, within

---

19. This rule provides that contingent remainders are "destroyed" if they do not vest immediately after the natural termination of the prior estate. This rule has been abolished almost everywhere. *See supra* §6.3.2.3.

B's lifetime (or nine months after *B*'s death if *B* is a man).[20] Of course, new reproductive technologies render this traditional assumption — that people can only have children during their lifetimes or shortly thereafter — more than problematic!

If *B* has a child before *A* dies, the remainder will vest and be "subject to open" because *B* could have more children.[21] If *A* dies before *B*, the class of children will close at that point, and title will shift to the children of *B*. Their interest is good because it vests right after *A*'s death. If *A* dies before *B* has had a child, and contingent remainders are destructible, the children's interest will fail, and *O* (or *O*'s heirs or devisees) will have a fee simple. If contingent remainders are indestructible, as they are in almost all states, the property will revert to *O* (or *O*'s heirs or devisees) as a reversion subject to the interest in the children of *B*. If *B* has a child, title will spring from *O* to *B*'s child. The interest in the "children of *B*" will vest, if at all, either right after *A* dies (if a child has been born before *A* died) or within the lifetime of *B* (if *A* dies before *B* and the property reverts to *O*, and *B* then has a child and the property springs to that child). If *B* dies childless before *A* dies, the property goes to *O* as a reversion at *A*'s death; if *B* dies childless after *A* dies, *O*'s reversion becomes a fee simple absolute.

10. *O to A for life, then to the first child of B to be elected President of the United States.* Whether or not *B* has children at the time of the conveyance, *B* could have a daughter who would be born after the conveyance, so she is not a life in being at the creation of the interest; she could become president more than 21 years after the death of *O*, *A*, *B* and any children of *B* (and anyone else in the world) alive at the creation of the interest, so the contingent remainder in *B*'s child violates the rule against perpetuities. There is no validating life here; there is no one alive at the creation of the interest within whose life (or 21 years later) it is certain that the interest will vest. Because the remainder is void, it is struck out, leaving "*O* to *A* for life"; *O* has a reversion that is not subject to the rule.

There are some well-known and rather humorous traps that have been studied by generations of law students.

Unborn widow. The first is the "unborn widow." A conveyance from "*O* to *A* for life, remainder to *A*'s widow for life, remainder to *A*'s surviving children" creates a contingent remainder in *A*'s surviving children that violates the traditional rule against perpetuities because *A* could marry someone who was born after the conveyance from *O* to *A*; such a person is not a life in being at the creation of the interest and cannot serve as a measuring life who could validate the interest in her children. Even though she may not be a life in being at the creation of the interest, her remainder is good because it will vest, if at all, when *A* dies. However, she may live longer than 21 years after the deaths of *A* and *O* (and everyone else alive at the creation of the interest) and thus her children's interests may vest outside the perpetuities period. This assumes that

---

20. The traditional rule actually should read "lives-in-being-plus-21-years *and nine months*" because the courts allowed for the time associated with gestation.

21. Under the *rule of convenience,* the class of children will close when *A* dies, and the children of *B* at that point will get the remainder even if *B* is still alive and could have more children.

"*A*'s surviving children" means "the children of *A* and *A*'s widow living at the time of *A*'s widow's death." The requirement that they "survive" means that there is a condition precedent to their interest vesting; they must survive the death of *A*'s widow. If the conveyance did not require them to survive *A*'s widow, their interests would vest when *A* died (even though they would not become possessory until the death of *A*'s widow). The requirement that they survive *A*'s widow delays their vesting because it creates a condition precedent to their being entitled to the interest; this requirement means that their interest may vest more than 21 years after the death of *A*.

Fertile octogenarian. If *O* grants property to "*A* for life, remainder to *A*'s grandchildren," the assumption has always been that *A* could have more children until she dies, even if she is 80 years old. This assumption used to be humorous but new reproductive technologies make it perfectly plausible today; imagine a frozen embryo of hers implanted in another woman who bears her child. The contingent remainder in the grandchildren (or vested remainder subject to open if there are grandchildren at the conveyance from *O* to *A*) violates the rule because *A* could have a child after the creation of the interest and that child could have a child more than 21 years after the death of *A* (and everyone else alive at the creation of the interest). *A*'s children alive at the time of the creation of the interest could all predecease *A*, with the property going back to *O* as a reversion. If the after-born child has a child more than 21 years later, the interest will have vested too remotely. Thus the remainder violates the rule and is invalid.

The endless will contest. *O* to *A* for life, then to *B*'s children after *A*'s will is probated. The will contest could last forever; there is no guarantee the lawsuit will ever end, making the contingent remainder in *B*'s children void. In addition, if *B* has no children at the time of the conveyance from *O* to *A*, then their interest is contingent because they are unascertained and the will could be probated more than 21 years after the deaths of *O*, *A*, and *B* and all other lives in being at the creation of the interest, giving a second reason to invalidate their contingent remainder.

Because interests retained by grantors are immune from the rule against perpetuities, a clever drafter can often avoid the rule in two ways. First, rather than convey an executory interest, the grantor should convey a fee simple determinable to the intended present estate holder, and then transfer (in a separate transaction) the grantor's retained possibility of reverter to the third party to whom the grantor had wished to create an executory interest. So, instead of "*O* to *A* as long as used for residential purposes, then to *B*," *O* should convey "to *A* as long as used for residential purposes," and in a separate transaction, *O* should convey her retained possibility of reverter to *B*. Alternatively, *O* could convey a fee simple absolute to *B*; *B* could then convey a fee simple determinable to *A*, keeping a possibility of reverter for herself.

§6.5.3.5   Options to Purchase

CENTRAL DELAWARE COUNTY AUTHORITY v.
GREYHOUND CORP.

588 A.2d 485 (Pa. 1991)

JOHN P. FLAHERTY, J.

In 1941 and 1950 the Baldwin Locomotive Works conveyed to the Central Delaware County Authority ("Authority") two parcels of land. The Authority paid $5,500 for the parcel conveyed in 1941 and $2,970 for the parcel conveyed in 1950. The deeds in both cases conveyed a fee simple interest subject to a restrictive covenant appearing in the encumbrance clause. The 1941 deed contains the following provision:

> It is specifically covenanted, stipulated, and agreed between the parties hereto that the said tract of land, while in the ownership and possession of the said Central Delaware County Authority and its successors, shall be kept available for and shall be used only for public purposes by the said Central Delaware County Authority and its successor or any other public instrumentality or other agency which may hereafter acquire title to the same. In the event that at any time hereafter said use shall be abandoned so that the said tract shall cease to be used for said public purposes, then and in such event the Baldwin Locomotive Works, its successors and assigns, shall have the right to repurchase, retake and reacquire the same upon the payment, either to the Central Delaware County Authority if owner thereof, or to any successor in right thereto, or to the municipalities for which the said vendee or its successors shall be acting, the sum of fifty-five hundred dollars ($5,500.00) above mentioned and herein provided to be paid therefor; or in the event of dispute, the said sum may be paid into Court in any appropriate proceeding for the benefit of any and all parties entitled to the same. In any such case, vendee shall have the right to remove all improvements.
>
> PROVIDED, HOWEVER, that if the Baldwin Locomotive Works does not pay the sum of fifty-five hundred dollars ($5,500.00) to the said Authority, or otherwise as above provided, within six months after the date when the authority or its successors in title abandons the said property for public purposes, or the date when notified by the Authority of its intention to abandon the property, then and in such event this covenant shall become void and of no effect.

The encumbrance clause of the 1950 deed is substantially the same as that of the 1941 deed, except that the phrase "by the said Central Delaware County Authority and its successors or any other public instrumentality which may hereafter acquire title to the same" does not appear, and repurchase is conditioned upon payment of $2,970 instead of $5,500.

The Authority operated a sewage treatment plant on this land for approximately twenty-six years. In 1980, the Authority ceased operation of the sewage treatment facility, but the Authority continues to maintain and possess the land. In 1983, it brought an action to quiet title in the land, alleging that the deed's public use, ownership and repurchase restrictions are void as violative of the rule against perpetuities.

... The trial court found that the restrictions of the deed do not violate the rule and that they are not an unreasonable restraint upon alienation. It concluded that the estates conveyed in the deeds are fee simple interests subject to a condition subsequent. Since a fee simple subject to a condition subsequent creates a present interest in the grantor, the conveyance did not, according to the trial court, violate the rule against perpetuities.

Superior Court, on appeal, held that the restriction in the deed was an option to purchase, not an interest subject to a condition subsequent. Since options to purchase are subject to the rule against perpetuities, and since this restriction allowed for the possibility that the option might vest later than twenty-one years after a life in being at the creation of the restriction, Superior Court held that the restrictions violated the rule. Superior Court determined that the restrictions were not invalid, however, on public policy grounds: "were we to find the rule against perpetuities applicable to this particular option contract, we would be creating a climate in which grantors would not freely give their properties for public use." The Authority petitioned for allowance of appeal and we granted allocatur. The principal issue on this appeal is whether Superior Court erred in determining that the rule against perpetuities did not invalidate the restrictive covenants.

The first question is whether Superior Court was correct in holding that the estate created was a repurchase option rather than an estate subject to a condition subsequent. A fee simple subject to a condition subsequent arises where the provision is that upon the happening of a certain event, the grantor has the right and power to terminate the conveyed estate. This estate is not subject to the rule against perpetuities because the right of reentry or power of termination which it creates is exempt from the rule. However, a repurchase option, as the restriction in the present case was held to be by Superior Court, is subject to the rule, for an option is not a vested estate.

The initial inquiry, then, is whether Superior Court was correct in deciding that the interest in this case was a repurchase option rather than a fee simple subject to a condition subsequent. We concur with Superior Court's analysis. While it is true that the deeds may be read to create a fee simple subject to a condition subsequent (the condition subsequent would be abandonment of public use followed by the payment of certain sums of money), the deeds can also be read to create a repurchase option conditioned upon the termination of public use. Like Superior Court, to resolve this ambiguity, we turn to the *Restatement of Property* for guidance:

> If the language and circumstances of a conveyance of an estate in fee simple are otherwise reasonably susceptible of two constructions, under one of which it creates either a possibility of reverter or power of termination, . . . and under the other of which it creates an option to repurchase, . . . the latter of the two constructions is preferred. The fact that the exercise of the reserved privilege requires the parting with money or other consideration, by the reserving conveyor is sufficiently indicative of the intent of the conveyor to create an option. . . . The finding of the option, under these facts, furthers the protective policy which underlies the rule against perpetuities, and is in accord with the general constructional preference for covenants rather than conditions. *Restatement of Property* §394, Comment c (1944).

We believe that section 394 accurately reflects the law of this Commonwealth in favoring interpretations of deed restrictions which bring the restriction within the ambit of the rule. Superior Court was not in error, therefore, in finding that the interest created was a repurchase option.

It remains to be considered, however, whether Superior Court was correct in also determining that the rule against perpetuities does not apply to the repurchase option on the grounds of public policy, *viz.*, that grantors would not freely give their properties for public use. In reaching this conclusion, Superior Court relied on this court's decision in *SEPTA v. Philadelphia Transportation Co.*, 233 A.2d 15 (Pa. 1967).

SEPTA involved the question whether the following language in a contract between the City of Philadelphia and the Philadelphia Transportation Company was valid:

> The City reserves the right to purchase all the property, leaseholds and franchises of the Company, subject to all indebtedness . . . upon July 1st, 1957, *or upon the first day of any July thereafter* by serving six months' notice . . . [for] an amount equal to par for its capital

stock then outstanding, to wit: the thirty million (30,000,000) dollars of capital stock now authorized plus any additional capital stock issued with the consent of the City hereunder. . . .

233 A.2d 15 (emphasis added). This court determined that the repurchase provisions of the contract did not violate the rule against perpetuities (1) because it was not an impress on land, but solely a contract right not within the rule; (2) because the interest, even if a violation of the common law rule, fell within the *Estates Act* of 1947, providing for a wait-and-see period; and (3) because public policy favors the city's right of repurchase.

As this court observed in *SEPTA*, the *Restatement of Property*, §401 provides, "A transaction which is exclusively contractual is not subject to the rule against perpetuities." Further, Comment b to §401 states: "A transaction is 'exclusively contractual,' within the meaning of that term as used in this Restatement, when, and only when, it concerns no specific land or thing other than land." The contract provision at issue in *SEPTA* did not fetter specific property, and thus was contractual within the meaning of §401. Since the provision was exclusively contractual, it did not fall within the rule against perpetuities. *SEPTA*, therefore, has no application to the present case, for here, the encumbrance clearly is an impress upon specific land and within the rule. Moreover, in *SEPTA* the majority determined that the agreement of 1957 acted as a conveyance to bring it within the *Estates Act* of 1947 and the wait-and-see rule incorporated therein. In the present case, however, the interest did not vest within twenty-one years, and, therefore, is subject to the rule. In short, *SEPTA* is significantly different from the present case on the facts and its holding is, therefore, inapplicable.

It remains only to consider whether for reasons independent of *SEPTA*, public policy requires that the rule not be given effect in this case. In *Barton v. Thaw*, 92 A. 312 (Pa. 1914), this court addressed the policy underlying the rule and the nature of the legal obligation which the rule imposes. In that case, this court voided a covenant in the deed which granted the option to purchase the surface in fee "at any future time whatsoever . . . at a price not exceeding one hundred dollars per acre." *Id.* The court held that the rule against perpetuities applied to this repurchase option which was unlimited in time, and the interest was, therefore, void. The rationale for this holding was that the rule against perpetuities is a "peremptory command of law," and thus is not subject to negation by a countervailing statement of public policy. The court described the policy underlying the rule as follows:

> Such an impress on land [one that violates the rule] ought not to be sustained, and it cannot be. It isolates the property. It takes it out of commerce. It removed [*sic*] it from the market. It halts improvements. It prevents the land from answering to the needs of growing communities. No homes can be built or towns laid out on land so encumbered, because the land always remains subject to be taken under the option. It is not a matter which affects the rights of individuals only. The entire community is interested. The welfare of the public is at stake. It is contrary to the well settled public policy of the state that such an option or right to purchase land should be held to be good. It was for the express purpose of destroying such serious hindrances to material and social prosperity and progress that the rule against perpetuities was brought forth. And the rule must be rigidly enforced. 92 A. at 316.

These considerations are as valid today as they were in 1914, when *Barton v. Thaw* was written. Now, as then, economic development and prosperity depends in important part upon the free alienability of land. It is for this reason that the rule against perpetuities is a "peremptory command of law" that "is to be remorselessly applied." The repurchase option is, therefore, void....

TEXACO REFINING AND MARKETING, INC. v. SAMOWITZ

570 A.2d 170 (Conn. 1990)

ELLEN PETERS, Chief Justice.

This appeal concerns the validity, under . . . the common law rule against perpetuities, of an option to purchase real property contained in a long-term commercial lease. The named plaintiff, Texaco Refining and Marketing, Inc., brought an action for specific performance of an option contract against the defendants, Jack Samowitz, Alex Klein, Sheila Klein, Gloria Walkoff and Marilyn Moss, as successors in interest to the lessor of a lease executed and recorded in 1964....

. . . On June 3, 1964, the named plaintiff and Kay Realty Corporation, the predecessor in interest of the defendants, executed a lease for property in Southington. The term of the leasehold was fifteen years, subject to renewal by the lessee, the plaintiff, for three additional five year periods. The plaintiff exercised two of these options for renewal.

The provision of the lease at issue in this appeal granted the plaintiff "the exclusive right, at lessee's option, to purchase the demised premises . . . at any time during the term of this lease or an extension or renewal thereof, from and after the 14th year of the initial term for the sum of $125,000." On August 14, 1987, during the second renewal period under the lease, the plaintiff gave notification, by certified mail, of its exercise of its option to purchase. When the defendants refused to transfer the property, the plaintiff brought this action, on December 30, 1987, for a judicial order of specific performance....

The defendants rely on the common law rule against perpetuities . . . for the unenforceability of the plaintiff's option to purchase their property. The rule against perpetuities states that "[n]o interest is good unless it must vest, if at all, not later than twenty-one years after some life in being at the creation of the interest." J. Gray, *The Rule Against Perpetuities* 191 (4th ed. 1942); *Connecticut Bank & Trust Co. v. Brody,* 392 A.2d 445, 449 (Conn. 1978). The defendants maintain that the option in this case did not vest within the time span mandated by the rule. We disagree.

The trial court determined that the option in the lease agreement did not violate the rule against perpetuities by construing the lease agreement as a series of discrete undertakings, first for an initial fourteen year term, and thereafter for each renewal term. Because the option could be exercised only within one of these discrete terms, none of which exceeded twenty-one years in length, the court held that the interest in the option would necessarily vest within the time period specified by the rule against perpetuities.

Whatever might be the merits of the trial court's construction of the lease agreement, we prefer to consider a more basic question: do options in long-term leases fall within the jurisdiction of the rule against perpetuities? Our precedents indicate that the rule applies to an unrestricted option to purchase real property; but not to an option to renew the term of a real property lease. We have not, however, previously considered the relationship between the rule against perpetuities and an option to purchase contained in a long-term commercial lease of real property.

The defendants have offered no reason of policy why we should extend the ambit of the rule against perpetuities to cover an option to purchase contained in a commercial lease. "The underlying and fundamental purpose of the rule is founded on the public policy in favor of free alienability of property and against restricting its marketability over long periods of time by restraints on its alienation." *Connecticut Bank & Trust Co. v. Brody, supra,* 392 A.2d at 449; 4 *Restatement, Property* pp. 2129-2133 (1944). An option coupled with a long-term commercial lease is consistent with these policy objectives because it stimulates improvement of the property and thus renders it more rather than less marketable. Any extension of the rule against perpetuities would, furthermore, be inconsistent with the legislative adoption of the "second look" doctrine, pursuant to which an interest subject to the rule may be validated, contrary to the common law, by the occurrence of events subsequent to the creation of the interest.

We therefore conclude that an option to purchase contained in a commercial lease, at least if the option must be exercised within the leasehold term, is valid without regard to the rule against perpetuities. This position is consistent with the weight of authority in the United States. The commentators have, for a long time, unanimously supported what has become the majority view. The plaintiff's option in this case was, therefore, enforceable.

§6.5.3.6 Preemptive Rights

CAMBRIDGE CO. v. EAST SLOPE INVESTMENT CORP.

700 P.2d 537 (Colo. 1985)

Jean E. Dubofsky, Justice. . . .

The Tenmile Creek Condominiums, located in Summit County, are operated by the Tenmile Creek Condominium Association (Association), a corporation composed of all condominium unit owners. Ownership of the sixty condominium units in the project is subject to the terms, covenants and conditions contained in the condominium declaration recorded in accordance with section 38-33-105, 16A Colo. Rev. Stat. (1982). Paragraph 29(i) of the declaration creates a "right of preemption" in the unit owners, defined as a first right to purchase, upon the same terms and conditions offered by a third party buyer, any other unit offered for sale:

> In the event an owner of a unit desires to sell such unit and receives bona fide offer for such sale, the unit shall be offered to the remaining owners who shall have a first right to purchase such offered unit for the same terms and conditions as the bona fide offer. Notice of such bona fide offer shall be given to the Tenmile Creek Condominium Association, which shall be responsible to notify the remaining unit owners of such offer by mailing notice to the remaining owners. The remaining unit owners shall have five days from the date of such mailing to accept such offer, and if not accepted, the sale may be made to such third party offeree.

All of the terms, covenants and conditions contained in the declaration are "deemed to run with the land" and are binding on all condominium unit owners and "their grantees, successors, heirs, executors, administrators, devisees or assigns."

East Slope Investment Corporation owned unit 211 of the Tenmile Creek Condominiums. On September 6, 1978, East Slope entered into a contract with Dolores and Donald Burgett for the sale of unit 211; when the contract was signed, the Burgetts gave

East Slope a $500 deposit. At the time the Burgetts entered into the contract, they were aware of the preemptive right set forth in paragraph 29(i) of the condominium declaration. Under the terms of the contract, the sale was to be closed on or before September 30, 1978.

On September 8, 1978, East Slope notified the Association of the terms of the proposed sale of unit 211. On September 11, 1978, the Association mailed a "notice of first right" to all condominium unit owners setting forth the terms of the proposed sale, and informing them that they could exercise their preemptive right within five days of the date the notice was mailed. Before the prescribed five day period had elapsed, the Cambridge Company, a condominium unit owner and general partnership formed to purchase and rent real estate, hand-delivered letters to the Association exercising its preemptive right and agreeing to be bound by the terms of sale set forth in the notice of first right. Cambridge Company tendered a $500 deposit with the letters.

On September 15, 1978, the Association informed East Slope and the Burgetts that the Cambridge Company had exercised its right of preemption. East Slope nonetheless conveyed unit 211 to the Burgetts, closing the sale on September 27, 1978.

The Cambridge Company instituted an action in the District Court of Summit County against East Slope and the Burgetts (the defendants), requesting that the conveyance of unit 211 to the Burgetts be set aside, that East Slope be ordered to convey the unit to the Cambridge Company, and that the defendants be ordered to pay $50,000 in damages. At trial to the court, the defendants contended that paragraph 29(i) violates the rule against perpetuities. . . .

The rule against perpetuities, incorporated into the Colorado common law, provides that "no interest in real property is valid unless it must vest, if at all, not later than 21 years after some life in being at the creation of the interest." *Crossroads Shopping Center v. Montgomery Ward and Co.*, 646 P.2d 330, 332 (Colo. 1981). The rule prevents the remote vesting of contingent interests in real property. A right of preemption, like the one in the present case, creates a specifically enforceable right to purchase real property whenever, in the future, the owner desires to sell; such a right traditionally has been viewed as a contingent equitable interest in real property subject to the rule against perpetuities. Therefore, we have held that the rule "applies" to preemptive rights.

A technical application of the rule against perpetuities in this case would void the preemptive right at issue. By the terms of the declaration, the preemptive right may be exercised by the current condominium unit owners or "their grantees, successors, heirs, executors, administrators, devisees or assigns." It is conceivable that a preemptive right could be exercised more than 21 years beyond the period of all lives in being relevant to the condominium declaration. Because any possibility, however remote, that an interest will vest beyond the period of the rule against perpetuities voids that interest under the rule, the interest created by the right of preemption in this case would be void under a mechanical application of the rule.

However, the rule against perpetuities is not merely a technical rule to be mechanically applied. The rule was created by judges to serve important considerations of public policy, and should be applied with those policies in mind. Courts generally have not favored remotely vesting contingent interests because of the likelihood that the interests will restrain alienation; where title is encumbered with remotely vesting contingent interests, buyers will be reluctant to purchase the property, inasmuch as the extent and duration of the title they are taking are uncertain. Indirect restraints on the alienability of property may lower its market value and deter the present owner from making valuable improvements. The rule against perpetuities prevents indirect restraints upon alienation from continuing indefinitely and enhances the alienability and beneficial use of property.

Courts have not applied the rule mechanically where its purposes will not be served. For example, an option in a lessee to purchase the leased premises within the term of the lease is exempt from the operation of the rule against perpetuities. The rationale for the exception is that an option to purchase contained in a lease encourages the lessee to improve the property; invalidation of such an option under the rule against perpetuities would defeat one of the purposes of the rule. In addition, courts may refuse to apply the rule against perpetuities where the presence of remotely vesting contingent interests serves public policies that outweigh the policies promoted by the rule. *E.g., Southeastern Pennsylvania Transportation Auth. v. Philadelphia Transportation Co.*, 233 A.2d 15 (Pa. 1967) (option in city to purchase transportation system promotes public welfare and will not be invalidated under the rule against perpetuities).

In the past we have considered the interrelationship between a preemptive right and the policies underlying the rule against perpetuities. In *Atchison* [*v. City of Englewood*, 463 P.2d 297, 301 (Colo. 1970)], the plaintiffs, their heirs and assigns possessed a first right to purchase a parcel of land upon the same terms and conditions as the owner was willing to accept from any third party. Noting first that the purpose of the rule against perpetuities is to keep property freely alienable, this court stated that an option to purchase for a fixed price normally would violate the rule because "with such an option outstanding the owner dare not place substantial improvements on the land, and the likelihood of anyone purchasing it is remote." 463 P.2d at 301. However, the court suggested, this reasoning does not apply to a preemption to purchase at an offer price received from a third party, and it is therefore "arguable" that the rule against perpetuities should not void such a preemption. The court did not reach a conclusion on this issue because it determined that a different aspect of the preemptive right created a sufficient restraint on the alienation of property to justify application of the rule against perpetuities: the right was

> in no manner connected with any land owned by [the plaintiffs]. . . . [T]here will be no land title interest of record to give any clue as to the identity of future successors in interest to the preemptive right. We feel that at some point in the infinite time at which [the defendant] might in the future conclude to sell the land, ascertaining and locating the owners of the preemptive right would be an unreasonable task. As a result, there would be a sufficiently unreasonable restraint upon the transferability of the property as to justify imposition of the rule against perpetuities. It may be said that we are stating a rule against alienation and giving it a label of the rule against perpetuities. Be that as it may, the result is the same. 463 P.2d at 303.

From *Atchison* we learn that the rule against perpetuities will be applied to preemptive rights only where the purposes of the rule, such as preventing a practical restraint upon alienation or encouraging improvement of the property, are served. In the present case, the preemptive right may be exercised only after the owner of a condominium unit formulates a desire to sell, and it must be exercised upon terms and conditions that the owner already has found acceptable. Therefore, unlike a fixed price option or preemption, the owner is assured of receiving market value for his property and will not be deterred from improving it or offering it for sale; nor will potential buyers, knowing that the market value of the property will remain intact, be deterred from purchasing the property. Moreover, unlike an option giving the holder the power to force a sale, the preemption here cannot be exercised unless the owner desires to sell; at that time, the only effect of the preemption is to change the identity of the buyer. In short, both the current and future owners of units subject to the preemptive right hold a title that is freely alienable at the full market price. For these reasons, the vast majority of courts have concluded that preemptions of the type involved here create no practical restraint on alienation.

The interference with alienation present in a requirement that a designated person be afforded a reasonable opportunity to meet any offer received from a third person by an owner desirous of selling is so slight that the major policies furthered by freedom of alienation are not infringed to a degree which requires invalidation. Under these circumstances, the owner has two potential buyers at the same price and is assured of a reasonably prompt culmination of the sale.

Moreover, the restraint on alienation identified in *Atchison*—the potential difficulty of locating the holder of the preemptive right—is not present here. Tenmile Creek Condominium's declaration requires all condominium unit owners to register their mailing addresses with the Tenmile Creek Condominium Association. The holders of the preemptive right in this case easily may be located and notified of their opportunity to exercise the preemptive right.

Because the preemptive right in this case poses no threat to the free alienability of the condominium units, we perceive no reason to invalidate the right under the rule against perpetuities. In so holding, we join a number of other jurisdictions that have reached the same conclusion.

NOTES AND QUESTIONS

1. *Options to purchase.* Options to purchase have traditionally been considered to be executory interests and subject to the rule against perpetuities. *Arundel Corp. v. Marie*, 860 A.2d 886 (Md. 2004). However, as noted above, at §6.5.3.3(c), the *Uniform Statutory Rule Against Perpetuities* (USRAP), now adopted in more than half the states, limits application of the rule against perpetuities to donative transfers. It thereby exempts options and preemptive rights from the rule against perpetuities as long as they were purchased for value, *see* USRAP §4(1). However, it is crucial to remember that options are still regulated by the common law rule against *unreasonable restraints on alienation*. Courts may refuse to enforce an option, especially if it is for a fixed price, if the option has no time limit and the option was not exercised within a reasonable period after its creation (unless the option is included in a lease). *Mr. Sign Sign Studios, Inc. v. Miguel*, 877 So.2d 47 (Fla. Dist. Ct. App. 2004).

The traditional rule against perpetuities invalidates options that have no time limit. However, courts sometimes interpret options to last for a shorter time period so that they will comply with the rule and be deemed valid. In *Broach v. City of Hampton*, 677 S.W.2d 851 (Ark. 1984), the Arkansas Supreme Court held that options to purchase would be interpreted not to extend beyond the life of the grantee where no explicit language in a deed mentioned heirs or assigns of the holder of the option, or did not otherwise indicate that the option extended beyond the life of the holder. Under this construction, the option would not violate the rule against perpetuities. This rule was extended in *Silvicraft, Inc. v. Southeast Timber Co.*, 805 S.W.2d 84 (Ark. Ct. App. 1991), to hold that the option cannot be transferred by the owner but is personal to him. It is not clear what the result would have been in *Silvicraft* had the owner of the option limited its time span to his own lifetime rather than leaving it without a time limit. *See Peterson v. Tremain*, 621 N.E.2d 385 (Mass. App. Ct. 1993) (holding that an option would be interpreted to require its exercise within reasonable time after expiration of ten-year grace period, to avoid a perpetuities problem); *Reynolds v. Gagen*, 739 N.Y.S.2d 704 (App, Div. 2002) (interpreting an option to last for the lives of the parties and thus not to violate the rule against perpetuities).

Chief Justice Ellen Peters argues in *Texaco* that options to purchase contained in leases promote, not inhibit, marketability of real property. The option limits the lessor's ability to transfer the property in the future but may induce the lessee to agree to the leasehold. The court's conclusion therefore rests on a judgment that the incentives created for the lessee outweigh the inhibition on the lessor and on third parties who might wish to purchase the property during the term of the option. If options to purchase have the potential both to inhibit and to stimulate investment in real property, how did the court determine which effect predominated? The court appears to have promulgated a general rule that all options to purchase in commercial real estate leases are valid per se under the rule against perpetuities. If the lessor could demonstrate by empirical evidence that the option was not a factor in inducing the leasehold and was therefore an overall inhibitor on marketability of the property, should the option be held void as against the policy underlying the rule against perpetuities?

2. *Contractual rights.* Note that the court in *Central Delaware* cites the *Restatement (First) of Property* §401 (1944) and *Southeastern Pennsylvania Transportation Authority v. Philadelphia Transportation Co.*, 233 A.2d 15 (Pa. 1967) (*SEPTA*), for the proposition that the rule against perpetuities does not apply to "exclusively contractual" transactions. What does this mean? *SEPTA* concerned an option to purchase "all the property" of a company that owned and operated the transit systems of the city of Philadelphia, including its train, bus and taxi facilities. The *SEPTA* court merely notes that the "purchase option is not an impress on land but is solely a contract right." *Id.* at 19. Comment b to *Restatement* §401 explains that a transaction is "exclusively contractual" when "it concerns no specific land." When an interest concerns a "specific parcel of land" the rule against perpetuities does apply. The majority in *SEPTA* justified exempting the option to purchase all of a company's property by arguing that the "historical purpose of the rule against perpetuities was to destroy serious hindrances to the beneficial and prosperous use of property." 233 A.2d at 19. Pennsylvania law does not recognize a "blanket condemnation of all remote options," but weighs the "interests of the community at large." *Id.* The court found that, under the circumstances of the case, "the danger of fettering the free use of property is outweighed by considerations of public concern and welfare." *Id.*

Chief Justice Bell issued a stinging dissent in *SEPTA*, arguing that an option to purchase all the property of a company, including its stock, its franchises and its real property, "does involve the fettering of property." *Id.* at 27. Bell argued that an option that can be exercised "at any time in the future without limit" clearly violates the rule. "Poetically expressed, the Option may be exercised at any time before the stars are old and the sun grows cold and the leaves of the judgment book unfold." *Id.* at 28. As for the majority's invocation of "public policy" and the "interests of the community at large," Justice Bell retorted, *id.* (emphasis in original):

> SEPTA, *if* ably managed (which, because of its multifarious functions and the
> varied and complicated problems which are certain to arise, is doubtful of accomplish-
> ment) is a desirable objective and a worthwhile public policy, but *that does not and cannot
> legalize the violation of any law or the destruction or abolition of the public policy of the
> Commonwealth, or the evasion of the many controlling decisions of this Court to the contrary.*
> The Majority cites no authority to support it and obviously proceeds on the recently
> adopted theory that a worthy objective validates and Constitutionalizes anything and
> everything, and every case is to be decided on a personal ad hoc basis. This substitutes
> uncertainty and confusion for certainty, clarity and stability, as well as for long-
> established and well-settled law, and borders on the ridiculous. I believe, although no
> one can be sure from the majority Opinion, that the practical result of that Opinion on
> this point is to judicially exterminate the Rule against Perpetuities, which it now writes off
> as "gone with the wind."

3. The *Restatement (Third) of Property (Servitudes)* §3.3 (2000) provides that the
rule against perpetuities "does not apply to servitudes or powers to create servitudes."
Comment b clarifies that the "rule stated in this section applies to options and rights of
first refusal with respect to the purchase of land. . . ." Illustration 1 further explains:

> *O* grants *A* an option to purchase Blackacre for $5,000. The option provides that it is
> binding on *O*'s heirs and assigns and is assignable by *A*. No time limit within which the
> option must be exercised is stated. The option is not invalid because it violates the rule
> against perpetuities. It may however, be invalid as an unreasonable restraint on
> alienation. . . .

Comment b justifies the proposed rule exempting options and preemptive rights
from the rule against perpetuities on three grounds. First, the goal of the rule against
perpetuities of curbing "excessive dead hand control of property retained in families
through intergenerational transfers" does not apply to options and preemptive rights,
which are generally used in commercial transactions or condominiums rather than
family inheritance situations. Second, the goal of the rule against perpetuities of
increasing the alienability of property by limiting the creation of contingent future
interests is better furthered by the rule against unreasonable restraints on alienation
because that rule allows case-by-case determinations of reasonableness while the traditional perpetuities period (lives in being plus 21 years) is too rigid and leads to arbitrary
results.

> [The] vice [of the rule against perpetuities is] that it operate[s] arbitrarily, applying a time
> limit totally unsuited to commercial transactions. Lives in being plus 21 years is too long
> for some servitude arrangements and irrational in others. For example, an option in gross
> should rarely, if ever be permitted to last as long as the rule would permit. As another
> example, the power of a property owners association to grant easements in common areas
> should be limited by the duration of the association, rather than by the lives of the
> developer's family and friends plus 21 years, or by a fixed period of 21 or 90 years.

Third, the comment argues that the "purpose of the restriction must be balanced
against the harm caused by the nature of the restraint, a process that is best carried out
under the rules against restraints on alienation, which permit a contextualized inquiry

into the utility of the arrangement. Accordingly, the rule stated in this section also applies to servitudes created in donative transfers." This clarifies that the proposed exemption of options and preemptive rights from the rule against perpetuities applies not only to commercial transactions but to family gifts as well.

The Reporter's note to §3.3 admits that it represents a minority position among the decided cases and that it is contrary to a few recent cases. In support of the proposed rule, the Reporter cites "leading commentators" (generally authors of law review articles), and a number of cases, including *Cambridge Co. v. East Slope Investment Corp.* and *SEPTA*, as well as the *lower court opinion* in *Central Delaware County Authority v. Greyhound Corp.,* which was overruled by the state supreme court opinion reprinted above. The Reporter candidly admits that the *Restatement* has chosen a minority position in an attempt to influence the future course of the law. Do you agree with the *Restatement* position?

4. *Interpretation and the rule against perpetuities. Central Delaware County Authority v. Greyhound Corp.* raises questions of both interpretation and the applicability of the rule against perpetuities. The first determination was whether the conveyance created a fee simple with a repurchase option or a fee simple subject to condition subsequent. This issue was important since, unlike options to purchase, rights of entry are not subject to the rule against perpetuities. The grantor could have avoided the result by more careful drafting of the conveyance. Does it make sense for future interests in the grantor to turn on such considerations?

5. *Charity to charity exception.* When a conveyance is made for charitable purposes, future interests following the present estate are generally held to be immune from the rule against perpetuities if the holder of the future interest is also a charity.

6. *Preemptive rights.* Most jurisdictions appear to retain the traditional rule that preemptive rights are subject to the rule against perpetuities. *See Kingston v. Robinson,* 596 A.2d 1378 (Del. 1991); *Ferrero Construction Co. v. Dennis Rourke Corp.,* 536 A.2d 1137 (Md. 1988); *Lake of the Woods Association, Inc. v. William M. McHugh,* 380 S.E.2d 872 (Va. 1989). As *Cambridge Co.* illustrates, however, some courts hold that preemptive rights providing for purchase at market valuation are not subject to the rule since they do not impede alienability of the land; thus, applying the rule would not serve its underlying purposes, either in general or in the context of specific types of transactions, such as commercial or charitable transactions. *Shiver v. Benton,* 304 S.E.2d 903 (Ga. 1983); *Wildenstein & Co. v. Wallis,* 595 N.E.2d 828 (N.Y. 1992); *Robroy Land Co. v. Prather,* 622 P.2d 367 (Wash. 1980); *Hartnett v. Jones,* 629 P.2d 1357 (Wyo. 1981). Courts adopting this approach often hold that preemptive rights must be exercised within a reasonable time in order to avoid invalidation as unreasonable restraints on alienation. *Shiver v. Benton, supra.* Moreover, as *Cambridge Co.* illustrates, most courts today will enforce reasonably exercised preemptive rights when they are held by condominium or homeowners associations, on the ground that such rights increase the market value and the alienability of the properties held by association members.

The majority of courts, however, apply the rule against perpetuities to freestanding preemptive rights not held by condominium or homeowners associations, on the ground that they *do* impede alienability.

> Some rights of first refusal permit the right's owner to purchase property at a fixed price if the property owner, his heirs, or assigns should ever desire to sell. Plainly a right of first refusal at a fixed price inhibits alienability. Often, with the passage of time, the fixed price will bear no relationship to the property's actual market value. . . .

A second type of right of first refusal permits the preemptioner to purchase the property at "market value" if the owner, his heirs or assigns should ever desire to sell. [A] right of first refusal to purchase at market value also effects a substantial restraint on alienability. A potential purchaser's offer might, in the preemptioner's opinion, exceed market value. The preemptioner could then contend that he need pay only some lesser amount. Fearing that a determination of the parties' rights would have to await the uncertain outcome of litigation, a prospective purchaser might be deterred from ever making an initial offer.

The third type of right of first refusal permits the preemptioner to purchase the property at a price equal to any bona fide offer that the owner, his heirs or assigns desire to accept. In this situation, however, many prospective purchasers, recognizing that a matching offer from the preemptioner will defeat their bids, simply will not bid on the property. This in turn will depress the property's value and discourage the owner from attempting to sell. . . . Similarly, if, as in this case, the right of first refusal is unrecorded, the task of ascertaining and locating the holder of the preemptive right at some remote point in the future might also become so difficult that the right of first refusal could constitute an unreasonable restraint on alienation.

Ferrero Construction Co. v. Dennis Rourke, supra, 536 A.2d at 1143. Which view do you find more convincing?

PROBLEM

Grantor, *O*, conveys property to *A* so long as used for residential purposes. *A* opens a law office on the premises, and *O* sues for a declaratory judgment that title has reverted to *O*. Possibilities of reverter are, of course, viewed as "vested" and thus exempt from the rule against perpetuities. *Alby v. Banc One Financial,* 82 P.3d 675 (Wash. Ct. App. 2003)(a possibility of reverter is "immediately vested in the grantor"). *A* responds that the policies underlying the common law rule against perpetuities apply to possibilities of reverter as well as to executory interests, and that it is nonsensical to continue to exempt possibilities of reverter from the rule on the grounds that they are "vested." *A* further argues that this proposed change in the law (applying the rule against perpetuities to possibilities of reverter) should be applied retroactively, on the ground that when the rule was first developed in the *Duke of Norfolk's Case,* 22 Eng. Rep. 931 (1681), it was applied retroactively to the conveyance in that case. What arguments could you make for the plaintiff? For the defendant? What should the court do?

§6.5.4 WASTE

MOORE v. PHILLIPS
627 P.2d 831 (Kan. Ct. App. 1981)

DAVID PRAGER, Justice Presiding:
This is a claim for waste asserted against the estate of a life tenant by remaindermen, seeking to recover damages for the deterioration of a farmhouse resulting from neglect by the life tenant. The life tenant was Ada C. Brannan. The defendant-appellant is her executrix, Ruby F. Phillips. The claimants-appellees are Dorothy Moore and Kent Reinhardt, the daughter and grandson of Ada C. Brannan.

The facts in the case are essentially as follows: Leslie Brannan died in 1962. By his will, he left his wife, Ada C. Brannan, a life estate in certain farmland containing a farmhouse, with remainder interests to Dorothy Moore and Kent Reinhardt. Ada C. Brannan resided in the farmhouse until 1964. She then rented the farmhouse until August 1, 1965, when it became unoccupied. From that point on, Ada C. Brannan rented all of the farmland but nobody lived in the house. It appears that from 1969 to 1971 it was leased to the remaindermen, but they did not live there. It is undisputed that the remaindermen inspected the premises from time to time down through the years. In 1973, Ada C. Brannan petitioned for a voluntary conservatorship because of physical infirmities. In 1976, Ada C. Brannan died testate, leaving her property to others. Dorothy Moore and Kent Reinhardt were not included in Ada's bounty. From the record, it is clear that Ada C. Brannan and her daughter, Dorothy Moore, were estranged from about 1964 on. This estrangement continued until Ada Brannan's death, although there was minimal contact between them from time to time.

After Ada Brannan's death, Dorothy Moore and Kent Reinhardt filed a demand against the estate of Ada Brannan on the theory of waste to recover damages for the deterioration of the farmhouse. The total damages alleged were in the amount of $16,159. Both the district magistrate and the district judge inspected the premises and found deterioration due to neglect by the life tenant. The district court found the actual damages to the house to be $10,433. The executrix of Ada's estate denied any neglect or breach of duty by Ada Brannan as life tenant. She asserted the defenses of laches or estoppel, the statute of limitation, and abandonment. These affirmative defenses were rejected by the district magistrate and the district judge, except the defense of laches or estoppel which the district magistrate sustained. On appeal, the district judge found that the defense of laches or estoppel was not applicable against the remaindermen in this case. Following entry of judgment in favor of the remaindermen, the executrix appealed.

It is important to note that the executrix does not contend, as points of error, that the life tenant was not responsible for deterioration of the farmhouse or that the action is barred by a statute of limitations. The amount of damages awarded is not contested. In her brief, the executrix-appellant asserts four points which essentially present a single issue: Whether the remaindermen, by waiting eleven years until the death of the life tenant before filing any claim or demand against the life tenant for neglect of the farmhouse, are barred by laches or estoppel?

The executrix contends, in substance, that laches and estoppel, although considered to be equitable defenses, are available in an action at law to recover damages. She points out that, under Kan. Stat. §58-2523, a remainderman may sue to prevent waste during the life of the tenant while the life tenancy is still in existence. She then notes that the remaindermen inspected the premises on numerous occasions during the eleven years the property was vacant; yet they made no demand that the farmhouse be kept in repair. They waited until the death of the life tenant to bring the action, because then they would not be faced with Ada's testimony which might defeat their claim.

The remaindermen, in their brief, dispute certain factual statements made by the executrix. They agree that the remaindermen had very limited contact with the life tenant after the estrangement. They contend that there is evidence to show the vast majority of the damage to the house occurred during the last two or three years of the life tenancy and that Dorothy Moore did, in fact, express concern to her mother about the deterioration of the house 15 to 20 times during the eleven-year period. They contend that mere passage of time does not constitute laches and that, in order to have laches or estoppel, the person claiming the same must show a detrimental change of position or prejudice of some kind. They argue that the executrix has failed to show any prejudice, since the fact of waste and deterioration is clear and undisputed and there is nothing the testimony of the life tenant could have added on that issue had she been at the trial. As to the failure of the remaindermen to file an action in the lifetime of the life tenant, the remaindermen argue that claimants had been advised to avoid contact with Ada Brannan unless it was absolutely necessary and that they did not want to make a claim during her lifetime since it would have only made a bad situation worse. They maintain that they had good reasons to wait until Ada's death to assert the claim. . . .

A life tenant is considered in law to be a trustee or quasi-trustee and occupies a fiduciary relation to the remaindermen. The life tenant is a trustee in the sense that he cannot injure or dispose of the property to the injury of the rights of the remaindermen, but he differs from a pure trustee in that he may use the property for his exclusive benefit and take all the income and profits.

It is the duty of a life tenant to keep the property subject to the life estate in repair so as to preserve the property and to prevent decay or waste. Stated in another way, the law imposes upon a tenant the obligation to return the premises to the landlord or remaindermen at the end of the term unimpaired by the negligence of the tenant.

The term "waste" implies neglect or misconduct resulting in material damages to or loss of property, but does not include ordinary depreciation of property due to age and normal use over a comparatively short period of time.

Waste may be either voluntary or permissive. Voluntary waste, sometimes spoken of as commissive waste, consists of the commission of some deliberate or voluntary destructive act. Permissive waste is the failure of the tenant to exercise the ordinary care of a prudent man for the preservation and protection of the estate.

The owner of a reversion or remainder in fee has a number of remedies available to him against a life tenant who commits waste. He may recover compensatory damages for the injuries sustained. He may have injunctive relief in equity, or, in a proper case, may obtain a receivership. The same basic remedies are available against either a tenant for years or a life tenant.

By statute in Kansas, Kan. Stat. Ann. §58-2523, "[a] person seized of an estate in remainder or reversion may maintain an action for waste or trespass for injury to the inheritance, notwithstanding an intervening estate for life or years." Thus a remainderman does not have to wait until the life tenant dies in order to bring an appropriate action for waste.

Where the right of action of the remainderman or landlord is based upon permissive waste, it is generally held that the injury is continuing in nature and that the statute of limitations does not commence to run in favor of the tenant until the expiration of the tenancy. Under certain state statutes, it has been held that the period of limitation commences at the time the waste is committed.

There is authority which holds that an action for waste may be lost by laches. Likewise, estoppel may be asserted as a defense in an action for waste. The doctrine of laches and estoppel are closely related, especially where there is complaint of delay which has placed another at a disadvantage. Laches is sometimes spoken of as a species of estoppel. Laches is a wholly negative thing, the result of a failure to act; estoppel on the other hand may involve an affirmative act on the part of some party of the lawsuit. The mere passage of time is not enough to invoke the doctrine of laches. Each case must be governed by its own facts, and what might be considered a lapse of sufficient time to defeat an action in one case might be insufficient in another. Laches, in legal significance, is not mere delay, but delay that works a disadvantage to another. . . .

The basic question for our determination is whether the district court erred in holding that the defense of laches or estoppel should not be applied in this case. We have concluded that the district court did not commit error in its rejection of the defense of laches or estoppel under the circumstances of this case. In reaching this conclusion, we have noted the following factors: The evidence is clear that the life tenant, Ada Brannan, failed to carry out her duty as life tenant and quasi-trustee to keep the property in reasonable repair. The claim of waste does not arise out of any act on the part of the remaindermen. Preservation of the property was the responsibility of the life tenant. There was evidence to show that the vast majority of the damage to the farmhouse occurred during the last two or three years of the life tenancy. The fact that permissive waste occurred was proved beyond question. If the life tenant had been alive, she could not very well have disputed the fact that the property has been allowed to deteriorate. Hence, any delay in filing the action until after Ada's death could not have resulted in prejudice to her executrix. There is no evidence in the record to support the defense of estoppel.

Furthermore, the evidence was undisputed that the life tenant was an elderly woman who died in August of 1976 at the age of 83. The position of Dorothy Moore was that she did not wish to file an action which would aggravate her mother and take funds which her mother might need during her lifetime. Even though Dorothy Moore was estranged from her mother, the law should not require her to sue her mother during her lifetime under these circumstances. As noted above, it was the tenant's obligation to see that the premises were turned over to the remaindermen in good repair at the termination of the life estate. Under all the circumstances in this case, we hold that the district court did not err in rejecting the defense of laches or estoppel. . . .

NOTES AND QUESTIONS

1. Judge Prager identifies two kinds of waste: voluntary and permissive. Voluntary waste is the result of "deliberate affirmative acts of the possessory tenant," while permissive waste is the result of "the failure of the possessory tenant to perform an affirmative duty imposed upon him for the benefit of the owners of future interests in the land." William B. Stoebuck & Dale A. Whitman, *The Law of Property* §4.1, at 147 (3d ed. 2000).

What happens if the life tenant's actions in changing the property *increase*, rather than decrease, the value or utility of the property? This is called *ameliorating waste* and is sometimes, but not always, condoned by the courts. For example, in *Melms v. Pabst Brewing Co.*, 79 N.W. 738 (Wis. 1899), the life tenant sold the property to the defendant Pabst Brewing Co., which thereby obtained a life estate *per autre vie*. The defendant demolished a large house on the lot and graded the land down to street level. Ordinarily, destruction of a dwelling would constitute waste; the court found, however, that the surrounding area in the city of Milwaukee had changed substantially since the original conveyance, leaving the house isolated and surrounded by factories and railroad tracks. Given the low value of the house as a residence and the fact that preparing the land for commercial development would greatly increase its market value, as well as allow it to be utilized, the court held that destruction of the house did not constitute waste. The court held that although the reversioner or remainder holder ordinarily is entitled to receive the property in substantially the same condition in which the life tenant received it, the life tenant is entitled to make fundamental changes to the property if "a complete and permanent change of surrounding conditions...has deprived the property of its value and usefulness as previously used." *Id.* at 741.

2. If property is no longer economically viable or personally useful in its prior form, can the life tenant sell it rather than develop it? There is no legal obstacle to selling the life estate, but who wants to buy a life estate? Property held under a life estate is likely to be marketable only if the life estate holder and remainder holders can agree to a sale of a fee simple interest in the property. Can a life tenant force the remainder holders to agree? In *Baker v. Weedon,* 262 So. 2d 641 (Miss. 1972), upon petition by the life tenant, the court held that a farm could be sold when its value as a farm had diminished to the point of being unproductive while its potential for commercial development remained sound, so long as the trial court found that this was in the best interest of all parties, including the remainder holders.

Suppose on remand the trial court had found that the remainder holders are wealthy and do not need income from either sale or lease of the land; they prefer to keep the land for a summer retreat, while the life estate owner is barely getting by because the farming income from the land is almost nil. Should the court order the sale on grounds of relative hardship? Whose rights should prevail?

3. The problem of changed circumstances just described could be better handled by creating a trust. For example, the grantor who wishes to provide for income to a child for her life, with the remainder going to the grandchildren on the child's death, could create a trust for the benefit of the child during her life and provide that the principal be handed over to the grandchildren on the death of the child. A trust arrangement vests legal title to the income-generating property in the trustee, allowing the trustee to sell the trust assets, if this is in the best interests of the beneficiary, without obtaining the consent of the remainder holders. Dukeminier and Krier argue that a legal life estate should "almost always be avoided." Jesse Dukeminier and James E. Krier, *Property* 227 (4th ed. 1998). They explain:

> It was a property arrangement suited to the great landed families of England in an age when land was the chief form of wealth, the basis of the family dynasty and the stately homes that passed from generation to generation, and when urban development proceeded slowly and land values remained relatively stable. A legal life estate is unsuited to a modern economy that regards land as just another form of income-producing wealth, which can swiftly appreciate in value under pressure for development and which must be managed effectively.

§6.5.5 RACIAL CONDITIONS

See supra at §5.5.3, at pages 433-450.

In *Charlotte Park and Recreation Commission v. Barringer,* 88 S.E.2d 114 (N.C. 1955), the court construed a deed by Osmond Barringer and his wife, who, along with several other persons and the City of Charlotte, conveyed land to a public agency, the Charlotte Park and Recreation Commission, to use as a public park "for use by the white race only." The deed provided that title was to revert automatically to the grantors or their heirs if the park should ever be used by nonwhite persons, on the condition that the grantors or their heirs pay $3,500 to the park commission. Racial segregation of the public park was later held unconstitutional; the park manager therefore no longer had the power to exclude nonwhites from the park. The question was whether the unconstitutional condition could be enforced by a court judgment affirming the possibility of reverter in the grantors' heirs.[22] The *Barringer* court held that the transfer of ownership occurred automatically at the moment the condition was violated and that no state action was therefore involved in transferring ownership from the park commission to the Barringers' heirs. The court explained:

> If negroes use the Bonnie Brae Golf Course, the determinable fee conveyed to plaintiff by Barringer, and his wife, automatically will cease and terminate by its own limitation expressed in the deed, and the estate granted automatically will revert to Barringer, by virtue of the limitation in the deed, provided he complies with the condition precedent by paying to plaintiff $3,500, as provided in the deed. The operation of this reversion provision is not by any judicial enforcement by the State Courts of North Carolina, and *Shelley v. Kraemer*, 334 U.S. 1, has no application. We do not see how any rights of appellants under the 14th Amendment to the U.S. Constitution, Section 1, or any rights secured to them by Title 42 U.S.C.A. §§1981, 1983, are violated.
>
> If negroes use Bonnie Brae Golf Course, to hold that the fee does not revert back to Barringer by virtue of the limitation in the deed would be to deprive him of his property without adequate compensation and due process in violation of the rights guaranteed to him by the 5th Amendment to the U.S. Constitution and by Art. 1, Sec. 17 of the N.C. Constitution, and to rewrite his deed by judicial fiat. . . .

Id. at 123. The court also held, however, that the conveyance from the city of Charlotte, which contained a similar condition and possibility of reverter, could not be enforced, on the ground that the unlawful condition had been made initially by a state governmental body and therefore constituted illegal state action.

In contrast, in *Capitol Federal Savings and Loan Association v. Smith*, 316 P.2d 252 (Colo. 1957), the court refused to enforce the future interest, instead vesting fee simple title in the purchaser. In that case, a group of property owners signed a covenant in 1942 agreeing for themselves, their heirs, and their assigns "not to sell or lease the said above described lots and parcels of land owned by them respectively . . . to any colored person or persons, and covenant and agree not to permit any colored person or persons to occupy said premises during the period from this date to January 1, 1990." It further provided that if any parcel were conveyed or leased in violation of the covenant, the interest of the African American owner "shall be forfeited to and rest in such of the then owners of all of said lots and parcels of land not included in such conveyance or lease who may assert title thereto by filing for record notice of their claim. . . ." The court held that regardless of whether the restriction was a covenant or

---

22. One oddity about the case is why the court interpreted the deed as a fee simple determinable rather than a fee simple subject to condition subsequent. The language in the deed contained contradictory language, stating *both* that the future interest would "revert" upon racial integration of the park *and* that it would do so only "on condition that" the grantors' heirs pay $3,500. Under the normal rules of construction, which include the presumption against forfeitures, the court could have determined that the conveyance was a fee simple subject to condition subsequent, thereby avoiding the automatic forfeiture. This result would have made the conclusion that no state action was needed to oust the present owner far more problematic.

an executory interest, the policies underlying *Shelley v. Kraemer* applied. The court explained:

> Counsel for defendants contend that the agreement in question entered into by the predecessors in interest of plaintiffs and defendants did not create a "private antiracial restrictive covenant." Instead they claim that it created a future interest in the land known as an executory interest. They assert "Such interest vested automatically in the defendants upon the happening of the events specified in the original instrument of grant, and the validity of the vesting did not in any way depend upon judicial action by the courts. The trial court's failure and refusal to recognize the vested interest of the defendants, and its ruling that the defendants have no title or interest in or to the property, deprived the defendants of their property without just compensation and without due process of law." We cannot agree. . . .
>
> No matter by what ariose terms the covenant under consideration may be classified by state counsel, it is still a racial restriction in violation of the Fourteenth Amendment to the Federal Constitution. That this is so has been definitely settled by the decisions of the Supreme Court of the United States. High sounding phrases or outmoded common law terms cannot alter the effect of the agreement embraced in the instant case. While the hands may seem to be the hands of Esau to a blind Isaac, the voice is definitely Jacob's. We cannot give our judicial approval or blessing to a contract such as is here involved. . . . Because the United States Supreme Court [in *Shelley v. Kraemer*] has extracted any teeth which such a covenant was supposed to have, no rights, duties or obligations can be based thereon.

Id. at 254-255. *Accord, Restatement (Second) of Property (Donative Transfers)* §4.2 cmt. t (1983) (forfeiture restraints on occupation or ownership of real property based on race, color, religion, or sex are unreasonable and unenforceable). Which approach do you find more persuasive?

PROBLEM

In *Hermitage Methodist Homes of Virginia, Inc. v. Dominion Trust Co.*, 387 S.E.2d 740 (Va. 1990), a testator named Jack Adams died, leaving a charitable trust providing income to the Prince Edward School, "so long as Prince Edward School Foundation admits to any school, operated or supported by it, only members of the White Race." His will further provided that if the school should ever "matriculate . . . any person who is not a member of the White Race, no further payment of income shall be made" to the school, but all income should go to the Miller School. Further gifts were provided to the Seven Hills School and then to Hampden-Sydney College if the prior recipient violated the "whites-only" provision of the trust. The final beneficiary of the successive gifts over was Hermitage Methodist Homes of Virginia; this final gift had no racial restriction built in.[23] At the time Adams wrote his will, Virginia Code §55-26 made it lawful to create a charitable trust for the education of white or "colored" persons but not of both. The statute was later repealed.

---

23. Note that the executory interest in Hermitage Methodist Homes did not violate the rule against perpetuities because of the charity to charity exception. Both the present estate owner (a school) and the owner of the ultimate executory interest (nursing home) were understood to be charities.

In 1987, the trustee sued the first beneficiary, Prince Edward School, because it had admitted African American students. The other legatees were brought in as defendants, with the trustee seeking guidance from the court as to who owned the right to receive income from the trust. Prince Edward argued that neither the trustee nor the court could divest it as beneficiary of the trust because such action would be unconstitutional by "giving continuing effect to the unconstitutional discriminatory requirements" of the repealed statute. Thus, Prince Edward asked the court to strike the discriminatory language from the will, give effect to the primary charitable intent of the testator to promote the education of children by the Prince Edward School Foundation, and order the trustee to pay it all trust income. The last beneficiary, Hermitage, argued that the trust was valid and that the language should be given its plain meaning to carry out the testator's intent. According to Hermitage, a "determinable event has occurred with regard to each" other income beneficiary, since they all admit nonwhite students; thus, the final beneficiary, Hermitage, is "entitled under the terms of the trust to receive all future trust income payments as they become due."

The trial court held that all "racially discriminatory conditions of the Trust are unconstitutional and void" and determined that Prince Edward School should continue receiving the income from the trust. The Virginia Supreme Court reversed, holding that even if it were unconstitutional to enforce a restrictive condition, depriving Prince Edward of the income from the trust effected no such enforcement. The condition in the trust did not take the form of a condition subsequent but was, rather, a "special limitation" that ended Prince Edward's beneficial ownership interest automatically as soon as the condition was violated. Thus, no court action was needed to alter ownership of the income from Prince Edward to Hermitage. Citing *Evans v. Abney*, the court noted that "we [do not] give effect to an invalid trust provision. Rather, we strike the entire gift to Prince Edward and the gifts to the other educational beneficiaries because the offending language cannot be stricken from the provision without changing the essential nature and quality of the estate." The court concluded:

> Because we find that the provision is a limitation, the same final result would be reached if we found that the trust's provisions were constitutional, as we have said earlier. By the natural operation of this limitation, if it were valid, upon the matriculation of a black student into Prince Edward, the school's interest terminated. And, because as counsel have represented, the educational institutions have all admitted black students, their respective interests in the trust proceeds can never vest into possession. Hermitage would be the ultimate beneficiary since no limitations are placed on its interest.

Id. at 746. *Compare* Cal. Civ. Code §53(a) (invalidating any provision in a "written instrument relating to real property" that purports to forbid or restrict the use by or the conveyance to "any person of a specified sex, race, color, religion, ancestry, national origin, or disability"); N.J. Stat. §46:3-23 (invalidating all conditions and restrictions in *inter vivos* transactions limiting transfer to or use by "any person because of race, creed, color, national origin, ancestry, marital status or sex").

Reargue *Hermitage Methodist Homes.* Use *Shelley v. Kraemer* and *Evans v. Abney* as precedent.

    a.   Make the argument for the present estate owner, the Prince Edward School, that it is entitled to retain the income from the trust, and that the court should apply the holding of *Shelley* and distinguish the holding of *Evans*.

b. Make the argument for the owner of the ultimate executory interest, Hermitage Homes, that it is entitled to the income from the trust, and that the court should apply the holding of *Evans* and distinguish the holding of *Shelley.*

Professor Jonathan Entin reports the history of the Prince Edward School:

The Prince Edward School Foundation was founded in June 1955 to establish private schools for white pupils in the event that the federal courts ordered the public schools of Prince Edward County to desegregate. Such an order seemed certain because the county school board was one of the defendants in *Brown v. Board of Education.* The order finally came in 1959. Local officials responded by shutting down the public schools. At the same time, the Foundation opened a private school known as Prince Edward Academy that enrolled almost every white student in the county. The Academy continued to enroll a large majority of the county's white pupils for some years after the Supreme Court ordered the public schools reopened on a desegregated basis in 1964.

Jonathan Entin, *Defeasible Fees, State Action, and the Legacy of Massive Resistance,* 34 Wm. & Mary L. Rev. 769 (1993). Does this knowledge change your analysis of the case?

§6.5.6 RULE AGAINST UNREASONABLE RESTRAINTS ON MARRIAGE

LEWIS v. SEARLES
452 S.W.2d 153 (Mo. 1970)

HENRY I. EAGER, Special Commissioner.

In this declaratory judgment suit plaintiff seeks to have the title to certain real estate quieted in her in fee and, in the process, to have a will construed. . . .

The will involved here was that of Letitia G. Lewis (the owner of the land) who died on Sept. 27, 1926; this will was probated shortly thereafter. At the time of her death the testatrix left surviving her two nieces, the plaintiff and Letitia L. LaForge, and a nephew, James R. Lewis. At the time of the institution of this suit Letitia LaForge had died leaving three children; one of these children had died, also leaving three children. The nephew had also died leaving two sons, both of whom have entered their appearance and have actively contested the suit. . . .

. . . The plaintiff was 95 years of age at the time of trial, and is presumably now about 96; she was thus approximately 53 years of age when the will was probated. We are told that the will was executed on May 31, 1911, when plaintiff was 38 years old. She has never been married. Since the death of the testatrix, plaintiff has been in continuous possession of the real estate.

Paragraph "Second" of the will was as follows: "Second, I devise to my niece, Hattie L. Lewis, all of my real and personal property of which I may die seized and possessed, so long as she remains single and unmarried. In the event that the said Hattie L. Lewis shall marry, then and in this event I desire that all of my property, both real and personal be divided equally between my nieces and nephews as follows, to the said Hattie L. Lewis, an undivided one third, to Letitia A. LaForge, wife of A. C. LaForge, an undivided one third, and to James R. Lewis an undivided one third." This is the only part in controversy.

In her petition plaintiff alleged the various relationships (including therein sundry unnecessary parties), described the real estate, attached a copy of the will, and prayed for an order of publication. She further alleged: that she had never been married; that she received an estate in fee under the will; that the restriction in the will against marriage was void; and that the other niece and the nephew of testatrix were deceased. The prayer was that a guardian *ad litem* be appointed for the minor defendants and others (which was done) and that title in fee to the land be quieted in her. The answer of J. R. (Dick) Lewis and Lilbourn Z. Lewis (children of the nephew) admitted plaintiff's possession and her right to possession, but denied that she was the owner of the fee. In a counterclaim they prayed that title in fee to an undivided one-third of the land be quieted in each of them under the terms of the will, subject to a life estate in plaintiff. In a reply to the counterclaim plaintiff reaffirmed her position that she was the owner in fee of all the land.

The trial court found (aside from formal and admitted facts) that it was the intention of the testatrix to give to plaintiff a life estate, and that "upon the death of said plaintiff that the fee title to said real estate vest in fee simple one-third to plaintiff, Hattie L. Lewis, one-third to Letitia L. LaForge and one-third to James R. Lewis, or to their descendants, hereinabove named."...

Plaintiff's counsel raise two points on this appeal, simply stated, but not so simply decided: (1) that all provisions of the will concerning the marriage of plaintiff are void as against public policy and should be stricken; (2) that in any event it was not testatrix's intention to devise to plaintiff a life estate with a one-third remainder in fee, but to devise to her a determinable fee in the whole of the property, to be reduced only in the event of her marriage. Respondents simply converse these points, and the issues are clearly drawn.

There is no doubt that the older cases in Missouri and elsewhere held that a provision in general restraint of marriage was void as against public policy. But, as stated by the author of the A.L.R. Annotation, 122 A.L.R. 7, 9, the courts have been reluctant to apply the rule and it has well-nigh been "eaten out with exceptions." One exception which has long been recognized is the right of a husband to terminate or decrease the extent of a devise to his wife upon her remarriage (subject, of course, to her statutory right to renounce the will). As said by Judge Lamm in *Knost* [*v. Knost*, 129 S.W. 665 (Mo. 1910)], it seems to be settled law that men "have a sort of mournful property right, so to speak, in the viduity of their wives. . . ." 129 S.W. at 667. The author of the A.L.R. Annotation says that "The preponderance of modern opinion seems to be that the right of a donor to attach such conditions as he pleases to his gift will outweigh the maxim that marriage should be free, except where such conditions are evidently attached through caprice rather than from a desire to carry out a reasonable purpose." The history of this most ancient rule is discussed in that Annotation. It is obvious that the cases on the subject are both conflicting and confusing, but that most, if not all, courts still give lip service to the doctrine. The tendency, however, is to consider whether, under the circumstances, the provision serves a legitimate purpose. And one reason which the author mentions as most commonly applied is the desire to furnish support to the devisee while single. . . .

Into this welter of conflict and confusion came the case of *Winget v. Gay*, 28 S.W.2d 999 (Mo. 1930). Plaintiff says that this case is not controlling because it was decided after the will in our case was probated. If that be the true rule, it would seem impossible ever to change the case law, since every such case is decided after the particular will involved has been probated. We follow *Winget* in part; in other respects it appears to be distinguishable. There the decedent had married a widow with three small children; the two born of his own marriage to her died, as did (later) the widow; two of her children were grown and living in their own homes. The other, the step-daughter involved in the case, was a semi-invalid but she remained with him until his death. She was forty-four when his will was executed. He devised to her all the residue of his property "as long as she remains single, and if she marry it is my will that she share equally with the other heirs." . . . The Court initially recognized the rule that provisions in general restraint of marriage are void . . . and then proceeded to impose its own exception. It held: that the testator's purpose, "when all the circumstances are considered," was merely to provide support for the stepdaughter while she was single and until such time as the obligation might be assumed by a husband; that, thus construed, his purpose and the provision did not "run counter" to public policy; and that he had the right to limit the duration of his bounty to the time of her probable dependency. . . .

[W]e find that the very wording of the will in our case expresses an intent of the testator to provide support for the plaintiff while she remained unmarried but, upon the happening of such a contingency, to require that she share with the other niece and the nephew. The provision did not constitute a penalty for marrying. This provision was obviously not inserted by whim or "caprice," for plaintiff was not to be cut off if she did marry. We conclude that the provision of the will concerning marriage was valid. . . .

The more difficult question remains: What estate did plaintiff take, a life estate or a determinable fee? The rule is very clear that each will must be construed as a whole to arrive at the intent of the testator, which, after all, is the ultimate guiding principle. We note: that testatrix said nothing about plaintiff's death; that there was no gift or limitation over upon plaintiff's death, and that this might result in total or partial intestacy if the will devised to her only a life estate; that plaintiff was to be given immediately one-third of the same property in fee, if she married; that it is not stated whether it was necessary for the nephew and the other niece to survive the plaintiff in order to receive one-third in fee upon plaintiff's marriage; that the devise to plaintiff was the only residuary clause in the will; that Mo. Rev. Stat. §474.480 (Vernon 1959) (effective in substantially similar form at that time) eliminates the necessity for the words "heirs and assigns," if no intention appears to convey only an estate for life and if no further devise is made to take effect after the death of the devisee. . . .

. . . As we read and reread paragraph "Second" of the present will, we are convinced that the testatrix was thinking only in terms of fee interests, *i.e.*, everything to plaintiff in fee conditioned upon her remaining single, and determinable (except for one-third) in the event of her marriage; and it was expressly provided that if she did marry, one-third (undoubtedly in fee, for there was no further limitation over) should go to each of the three (two nieces and a nephew). There is really no fairly expressed intent of any life estate in this will. . . . The will contains no devise of plaintiff's interest to anyone after her death. In the *Winget* case, . . . the courts have actually written into the wills the words "or upon her death" after the expressed contingency concerning marriage. Other authorities have done the same thing but to us it appears illogical. . . .

At this point we note again our Section 474.480. We quote it in full, as a matter of convenience. "In all devises of lands or other estate in this state, in which the words 'heirs and assigns,' or 'heirs and assigns forever,' are omitted, and no expressions are contained in the will whereby it appears that the devise was intended to convey an estate for life only, and no further devise is made of the devised premises, to take effect after the death of the devisee to whom the same is given, it shall be understood to be the intention of the testator thereby to devise an absolute estate in the same, and the devise conveys an estate in fee simple to the devisee, for all of the devised premises." In essence, this says that all devisees are in fee simple, if (1) no intent is expressed to create a life estate only, and (2) no further devise is made to take effect after the death of the devisee. . . . This statute evidences a policy of the state to liberalize the construction and effect of provisions in wills which are inartfully drawn, but in which there is no clear intent to devise less than a fee simple. We have concluded, after considerable difficulty, that there was no such intent here, either expressed or fairly to be inferred, and that plaintiff received a determinable fee in the real estate, subject to defeasance (of two-thirds) upon her marriage. . . .

We thus hold that plaintiff took a fee simple estate in all the real estate, subject to divestiture of an undivided two-thirds interest in the event of her marriage; in such event that two-thirds would vest equally, *per stirpes*, in the heirs at law of the other niece and nephew. . . .

RE-READING CONTRACTS: A FEMINIST ANALYSIS OF A CONTRACTS CASEBOOK
MARY JOE FRUG

34 Am. U. L. Rev. 1065, 1085-1087 (1985)

In *Jackson v. Seymour*,[24] Lucy Jackson, having sued her brother because he paid her considerably less for her land than it in fact was worth, manages to have the transaction set aside because of the parties' "confidential relationship." "The parties were brother and sister," the court explains. "He was a successful business man and she a widow in need of money." . . .

Connecting the language of the case with typical, gendered ideas about what women and men were generally like in the 1950s, and before, a reader might construe Mrs. Jackson's confidential relationship with her brother in the following manner. Most women need to depend on one man or another in order to get along, and the court's description of Mrs. Jackson as a "widow," along with indications of her poverty, and in contrast to her brother's economic success, suggest that Mrs. Jackson was shrouded with the entailments of emotional bereavement, vulnerability, and economic dependency. All of these characteristics, if they accurately described her situation, could have cast her into a relationship of dependence, trust, and confidence with her brother, in which she was weak and needy and he was strong and providing. This interpretation of Mrs. Jackson as victim simplifies the doctrinal issue in the case: a court will more closely scrutinize the terms of a contract on the grounds that it is based on a confidential relationship when one of the parties can be designated a weakling.

---

24. 71 S.E.2d 181 (Va. 1952).

In contrast, if one shuns or does not recognize the stereotypically gendered idea that poor widows have usually been victims, the doctrinal issue in the case is harder to resolve. Suppose, for example, that Mrs. Jackson was an emotionally vigorous woman whose widowhood was of so many years standing that she had long overcome the vulnerability she experienced when her husband died: or suppose that she was never so emotionally dependent on her husband that his death could affect her relationship with her brother. If neither party in *Jackson* is obviously a weakling, the standards the court used to intervene in the parties' contract are harder to understand. We can conceive of a confidential relationship based on deep intimacy and shifting dependencies, particularly between a brother and sister. We can imagine a relationship in which Mrs. Jackson sustained her brother through the trials and tribulations of his business affairs while he offered her economic assistance and emotional support when she needed help. However, overturning a contract based on this sort of confidential relationship would require more blatant judicial judgment calls than the objective theory of contract interpretation usually contemplates. It is not surprising, therefore, that the court in *Jackson* appears to depend on our not thinking of Mrs. Jackson as a vigorous widow and vigilant sister. Rather, the court and the casebook editors (through their silence) count on our complicity in the more typically gendered view of the widow as victim.

I do not mean to suggest that emotional dependency, poverty, or bereaved feelings are unnatural or odious; indeed I believe a court should intervene to protect men and women when their vulnerabilities prevent them from making contract judgments in their best interests. My point about the *Jackson* case is that the brevity of the court's reasoning and the words that the court uses to describe the parties encourage the readers to think of Mrs. Jackson in the gender stereotype of the pitiful widow. However innocently, the opinion reinforces a restrictive view that men are strong and women are weak, and it uses that limiting idea as an analytical shortcut to avoid a challenging doctrinal problem.

NOTES AND QUESTIONS

1. The *Restatement (Second) of Property (Donative Transfers)* provides:

§6.1 Restraints on Any First Marriage

(1) Except as stated in subsection (2), an otherwise effective restriction in a donative transfer which is designed to prevent the acquisition or retention of an interest in property by the transferee in the event of any first marriage of the transferee is invalid. If the restriction is invalid, the donative transfer takes effect as though the restriction had not been imposed.

(2) If the dominant motive of the transferor is to provide support until marriage, the restraint is normally valid.

§6.2 Restraints on Some First Marriages

An otherwise effective restriction in a donative transfer designed to prevent the acquisition or retention of an interest in the event of some, but not all, first marriages of the transferee is valid if, and only if, under the circumstances, the restraint does not unreasonably limit the transferee's opportunity to marry. If the restriction is invalid, the donative transfer takes effect as though the restriction had not been imposed.

§6.3   Restraints on Remarriage

An otherwise effective restriction in a donative transfer which is designed to prevent the acquisition or retention of an interest in property by the transferee in the event of remarriage of the transferee is valid only if:

(1)   The transferee was the spouse of the transferor, or
(2)   The restraint is reasonable under all the circumstances.

2. What insights does Professor Frug's argument shed on the rules concerning restraints on marriage?

3. Provisions in gifts of property encouraging separation or divorce are widely viewed with disfavor. They may be upheld if the "dominant motive of the transferor is to provide support in the event of separation or divorce, in which case the restraint is valid." *Restatement (Second) of Property* §7.1.

4. The *Restatement (Second) of Property (Donative Transfers)* §8.1 provides that "[a]n otherwise effective provision in a donative transfer which is designed to prevent the acquisition or retention of property on account of adherence to or rejection of certain religious beliefs or practice on the part of the transferee is valid." In *Shapira v. Union National Bank*, 315 N.E.2d 825 (Ohio Ct. Comm. Pleas 1974), the testator left a will with a bequest to his son on condition that he marry a Jewish woman. The will provided:

> My son Daniel Jacob Shapira should receive his share of the bequest only if he is married at the time of my death to a Jewish girl whose both parents were Jewish. In the event that at the time of my death he is not married to a Jewish girl whose both parents were Jewish, then his share of this bequest should be kept by my executor for a period of not longer than seven (7) years and if my said son Daniel Jacob gets married within the seven year period to a Jewish girl whose both parents were Jewish, my executor is hereby instructed to turn over his share of my bequest to him. In the event, however, that my said son Daniel Jacob is unmarried within the seven (7) years after my death to a Jewish girl whose both parents were Jewish, or if he is married to a non-Jewish girl, then his share of my estate . . . above should go to The State of Israel, absolutely.

The court upheld the condition against challenges by the son that the condition violated public policy under the common law and that enforcement by the court of the restriction would constitute state action under *Shelley v. Kraemer* interfering with the son's constitutional right to marry. The son cited *Loving v. Virginia*, 388 U.S. 1 (1967), a case striking down an antimiscegenation statute prohibiting white and black persons from marrying each other. In *Loving*, the Supreme Court held that the "freedom to marry has long been recognized as one of the vital personal rights essential to the orderly pursuit of happiness by free men." 388 U.S. at 12. The court rejected both the constitutional and the common law challenge. In rejecting the constitutional challenge, the court noted that it was using its power not to prevent the son from marrying but to prevent the son from inheriting property, although this admittedly enforced the father's attempt to limit the son's freedom in choosing a marriage partner.

The court also upheld the restraint on marriage under the common law, concluding that the restraint was partial rather than total. The court explained, *id.* at 829:

If the condition were that the beneficiary not marry anyone, the restraint would be general or total, and, at least in the case of a first marriage, would be held to be contrary to public policy and void. A partial restraint of marriage which imposes only reasonable restrictions is valid, and not contrary to public policy. The great weight of authority in the United States is that gifts conditioned upon the beneficiary's marrying within a particular religious class or faith are reasonable.

Since Jews represent a small minority of the population, the court considered but rejected the argument that the restraint placed an undue restriction on the son's right to marry. The court further found the requirement that the son marry within seven years of his father's death to be reasonable and "give the son ample opportunity for exhaustive reflection and fulfillment of the condition without constraint or oppression." *Id.* at 831-832. *Accord, Gordon v. Gordon*, 124 N.E.2d 228, 230 (Mass. 1955) (upholding condition in will that required beneficiaries to marry persons "born in the Hebrew faith"; court revokes gift to son when he married a Jew by choice (convert)). The *Restatement (Third) of Trusts* §29(c), cmt. j, illus. 3 (2001), takes the oppositie position. It provides that conditions limiting gifts if the recipient does not marry a person of a particular religion are void as against public policy because they interfere with the fundamental right to marry.

7

Concurrent Ownership and Family Property

§7.1 Varieties of Common Ownership

Property may be held by more than one person in many different ways. Property rights may be *divided* among several, or even many, persons, with specific sticks in the bundle of rights that make up property allocated to different persons or groups. Examples include landlord and tenant, present and future interests, and dominant and servient estates subject to servitudes. Property rights may be *shared* as well as divided. In other words, more than one person may have the right to control the same resource; both may have the right to the same stick in the bundle. For example, a wife and husband may together own a condominium apartment in an urban building as joint owners. In this arrangement *each* has a concurrent right to possess the entire condominium unit. They have to agree how the property will be used — whether they will live in the condominium or rent it out to others, how they will use each room, whom they will invite to dinner, and so on. They also share with other condominium owners the right to use common areas of the building. Disputes about the use and condition of common areas — such as whether to pay for a new roof — must be worked out in conjunction with the other condominium owners.

There are many different forms of common ownership. Some forms are relatively simple, granting common owners substantial freedom to manage the property as they see fit. Some common owners do this in consultation with one another; other owners formally or informally designate one or more persons to act as manager of their common property. These forms include common ownership of residential property, in the form of *tenancy in common* or *joint tenancy*, or *tenancy by the entirety*, and common ownership of businesses in the form of *partnerships*. In some states, spouses own all property acquired during the marriage jointly as *community property*. In these arrangements, the co-owners may manage the property informally by making decisions together from time to time, or they may enter formal contracts allocating their respective rights and responsibilities.

569

Other forms of common ownership allocate powers over the resource between owners and managers. In these forms, owners who retain ultimate power over the resource select a board of managers to take charge of the day-to-day operations of the property. In business corporations, for example, shareholder-owners elect a board of directors, which in turn chooses the managers of the company. Other examples include charitable trusts, such as private hospitals or universities, initially established by a state charter or by a private founder who endows the institution and sets up its management structure; this structure often consists of a board of trustees that chooses the president of the institution, who runs the institution in conjunction with subordinates hired to provide needed services.

Property is also owned in common by government entities. The federal government is one of the largest landowners in the United States. Significant chunks of property also are owned by state and local governments. Voters elect political leaders who pass laws delegating to administrative agencies the power to manage public lands such as schools, parks, highways, and government office buildings. Similarly, American Indian nations own substantial amounts of land on reservations. While some reservation land is owned individually in fee simple by members of each tribe, other land is held communally by the tribe as a whole; in turn, parcels of this communally held tribal land may be assigned by the tribal government to individual tribal members. Each tribal government and court system has its own method of overseeing the allocation and regulation of tribal land.

In the following sections, we will focus on two forms of common ownership of residential property: (1) co-ownership, including *tenancy in common, joint tenancy, and tenancy by the entirety;* and (2) family property, including the effects of marriage on property rights, the rights of unmarried couples (both male-female couples and same-sex couples), and child support. Finally, we will consider forfeiture laws that provide for loss of property used to commit a crime and the limits on forfeiture designed to protect innocent family members.

§7.2 Rights and Obligations of Co-owners

§7.2.1 TENANCY IN COMMON AND JOINT TENANCY

Tenancy in common. Each tenant in common, no matter how small her fractional interest, has the *right to possess* the entire parcel — unless all the cotenants agree otherwise by contract. Each cotenant has an "undivided interest," meaning that each owner has the right to possess the whole property; the fractional amount is important only for such questions as how the purchase price will be divided when the property is sold. In many situations, the cotenants may choose to possess the property together. For example, if family members own property as tenants in common, they may all live together on the property. Or the cotenants may agree, formally or informally, that only one of them will possess the property while the other cotenant(s) will live elsewhere.[1] When a tenant in common dies, his interest goes to his devisees under his will or to his heirs under the state intestacy statute if he has not left a will or otherwise disposed of the property.

---

1. If they cannot agree, their only remedy is *partition*, discussed below.

A tenancy in common may be transferred by the following language in a deed or will:

> *O conveys [or devises] Blackacre to A and B as tenants in common. O conveys [or devises] Blackacre to A, B, and C as tenants in common, with a 1/4 undivided interest in A, a 1/4 undivided interest in B, and a 1/2 undivided interest in C.*

Joint tenancy. Like tenants in common, each joint tenant has the right to possess the entire parcel. Unlike tenants in common, joint tenants have traditionally been required to possess equal fractional interests in the property.

1. *Right of survivorship.* The main difference between joint tenancy and tenancy in common is the *right of survivorship.* When a joint tenant dies, her property interest is immediately transferred to the remaining joint tenants in equal shares. Thus, in a joint tenancy owned by *A, B,* and *C,* each with a one-third undivided interest, *A*'s interest when she dies goes to *B* and *C* (that is, half to *B* and half to *C*). The result is that *B* and *C* own the property as joint tenants, each possessing a one-half undivided interest in the property. If *A* tries to devise her one-third interest, her will would have no effect; she has no right to devise her interest.[2]

2. *Formalities of creation.* Certain formalities were traditionally required to create a joint tenancy. These are often referred to as the *unity of time, title, interest and possession.* This means that (1) the interest of each joint tenant must be created at the same moment in *time;* (2) all joint tenants must acquire title by the same instrument or *title* (joint tenancy does not ordinarily arise by intestate succession); (3) all joint tenants must possess equal fractional undivided *interests* in the property and their interest must last the same amount of time; and (4) all joint tenants must have the right to *possess* the entire parcel. Some states have passed statutes that abolish one or more of these formalities. Other states have abolished joint tenancies entirely.

3. *Severance.* In a joint tenancy, the right of survivorship is a highly contingent one because a joint tenant who transfers her property interest can destroy the right of survivorship of her fellow owners. For example, if *A* and *B* own property as joint tenants, each owner has the right to obtain full ownership of the property when the other cotenant dies (the right of survivorship). If *A* sells her one-half undivided interest to *C,* however, the joint tenancy is *severed,* and *B*'s right of survivorship is destroyed. The result is that *B* and *C* will own the property as tenants in common.

    A joint tenant who wishes to destroy the right of survivorship while retaining her life interest can convey her interest to another who conveys it back. For example, if *A* and *B* own as joint tenants, *A* may convey her interest to a third party (a "straw" person), who reconveys the interest back to *A.* Because this destroys the unity of title and time, *A* and *B* will now own the property as tenants in common rather than as joint tenants.

---

2. However, *A* can easily obtain this result by *severing* the joint tenancy and creating a tenancy in common, in which case she would be able to devise her interest. Severance is explained below.

Can an owner achieve the same result by "conveying" her interest from herself as joint tenant to herself as tenant in common or otherwise designating an intent to destroy the right of survivorship? Traditionally, this could not be done, but the procedure was approved in *Riddle v. Harmon*, 162 Cal. Rptr. 530 (Ct. App. 1980). *Accord, Taylor v. Canterbury*, 92 P.3d 961 (Colo. 2004) Statutes in some states formally allow this procedure. Should this procedure be contingent on giving notice to the remaining joint tenant(s)? Consider a husband who secretly signs such a document and gives it to his daughter without telling his wife. When he dies, he attempts to leave his 50 percent interest to his daughter on the assumption that his wife's right of survivorship has been destroyed by severance. Should he be allowed to do this?

Severance occurs only between the selling owner and the remaining owners; it does not change the relations of the remaining owners among themselves. For example, if *A*, *B*, and *C* own property as joint tenants, and *A* conveys his interest to *D*, the result is that *D* owns a one-third interest as a tenant in common with *B* and *C*, who each own a one-third interest as joint tenants with each other. When *D* dies, her one-third interest will go to her heirs or devisees. However, when *B* dies, his interest goes to *C* as a surviving joint tenant, who will then own a two-thirds interest as a tenant in common with *D*.

Joint tenancies may be created by the following language in a deed or will:

> *O conveys [or devises] Blackacre to A and B as joint tenants. O conveys [or devises] Blackacre to A, B, and C as joint tenants.*

4. *Joint tenancy versus dual life estates with alternative contingent remainders.* It is possible to create an indestructible right of survivorship if one uses the form of life estates and remainders. For example:

> *O to A and B as life tenants, with a remainder in A if A survives B, and a remainder in B if B survives A.*

This conveyance creates alternative contingent remainders in *A* and *B*. Whoever dies second will obtain the remainder and, hence, the property in fee simple absolute. A conveyance of *A*'s life estate will *not* destroy the contingent remainder. *See Albro v. Allen*, 454 N.W.2d 85 (Mich. 1990) (interpreting a joint life estate with alternative contingent remainders). *But see Smith v. Rucker*, 593 S.E.2d 497 (S.C. Ct. App. 2004)(interpreting similar language to create a joint tenancy).

Interpretation problems and presumptions. What happens if the conveyance is ambiguous as to whether the grantor intended to create a tenancy in common or a joint tenancy? The current practice is to interpret the conveyance as a tenancy in common.[3] *Kipp v. Chips Estate*, 732 A.2d 127 (Vt. 1999). This presumption has been imposed in some states by statute, in others by common law. It replaces the traditional practice, which favored joint tenancies over tenancies in common. This presumption has influ-

---

3. However, jurisdictions that have the tenancy by the entirety, a form of joint tenancy only available to married couples, may presume that a conveyance to a married couple is held in a tenancy by the entirety. *Beal Bank v. Almand & Associates*, 780 So. 2d 45 (Fla. 2001). *See infra* §7.4.2.

enced the drafting practice in most states. If you want to clearly create a joint tenancy, you might say, "to *A* and *B* as joint tenants with right of survivorship."

   Transferability of cotenancy interests. Joint tenants and tenants in common are free to transfer their interests without the consent of their co-owners. Tenants in common may leave their interests to devisees by will; joint tenants cannot do this because their interests will automatically go to their surviving joint tenant(s) when they die. Remember, however, that when a joint tenant transfers his interest, the right of survivorship is destroyed and the grantee's interest is held as a tenancy in common with the other owners.

   Partition. Joint tenants or tenants in common have the power to file a lawsuit for *judicial partition* of commonly held property. In these proceedings, the court may order the property physically divided among the co-owners. If this is not feasible or appropriate, the court will order the property to be sold and the proceeds divided among the co-owners in proportion to their ownership shares. Co-owners may also agree among themselves to partition the property, either through physical division or by sale; this is called *voluntary partition.*

   Cotenants sometimes agree among themselves not to partition jointly held property; grantors also sometimes attempt to prevent partition by including restrictions against partition in a deed or will. Such agreements not to partition constitute restraints on alienation and were traditionally held to be void. William B. Stoebuck & Dale A. Whitman, *The Law of Property* §5.11, at 216 (3d ed. 2000). However, today courts are likely to uphold them if they are reasonably limited in time and have a reasonable purpose. *See Mansour Properties v. I-85/GA. 20 Ventures, Inc.*, 592 S.E.2d 836 (Ga. 2004) (upholding agreement not to partition when the contract gave plaintiff tenant in common a right of first refusal and the defendant co-owner failed to offer its interest to the plaintiff before seeking judicial partition); *Kopp v. Kopp*, 488 A.2d 636 (Pa. Super. Ct. 1985) (holding that a separation agreement restricting the husband's right to bring an action to compel partition of the family residence was not an unreasonable restraint on alienation when the restriction applied only so long as the wife was living in the house and would automatically end at her death). Note also that statutes prohibit partition of common areas of condominiums.

   Fiduciary obligations of cotenants or joint tenants to share the benefits and burdens of ownership. Concurrent owners are legally obligated to share certain benefits and burdens of ownership, although they are free to vary these arrangements by contract.

1. *Sharing the benefits of ownership.* Each co-owner has the right to possess the entire parcel. If one co-owner chooses to live in the commonly owned property and the other co-owner chooses not to live there, the general rule provides that the tenant in possession has *no duty to pay rent* to the nonpossessing tenant. This is the case because the possessory tenant is doing what she is legally entitled to do. However, some courts hold that there is a duty to pay rent and some states have imposed this obligation by statute. *See Byse v. Lewis*, 400 S.E.2d 618 (Ga. 1990).

      Joint tenants and tenants in common *do* have a duty to pay rent to their co-owners if they have *ousted* them. *Ouster* refers to an explicit act by which one co-owner wrongfully excludes others from the jointly owned property. Some courts also hold that co-owners in possession have a duty to pay rent if the property is too small to be physically occupied by all the co-owners; this situation is sometimes described as "constructive ouster" because the co-owners out of possession have been effectively excluded from the property. Note that the amount of rent owed is the fractional share of the rental value owned by the co-owners out of possession; a co-owner with a one-third interest in possession would have to pay only two-thirds of the fair rental value of the property to her co-owners out of possession.

In addition to sharing the right to possess the property, co-owners have the right to share any rents paid by third parties who are possessing the property. A cotenant also has the right to lease his interest *without* obtaining the consent of the other cotenants. In this case, the lessee obtains the lessor's rights, including the right to possess the entire parcel. The cotenants then have a right to share in the rents but only if they agree to be bound by the leasehold, thereby waiving their own rights to possess the property. The share of the rent belonging to each co-owner is based on that owner's fractional interest in the property. For example, suppose *A* and *B* own a condominium unit as tenants in common, with a one-quarter interest in *A* and a three-quarters interest in *B*. They rent the unit to *C*. *A* has a right to one-quarter of the rents paid by *C*, and *B* has a right to three-quarters of the rents paid by *C*, unless *A* and *B* agree otherwise.

2. *Sharing the burdens of ownership.* Co-owners generally have a duty to share basic expenses needed to keep the property, including *mortgage* payments, property *taxes* and other assessments, and property *insurance*, in accordance with their respective shares. Cotenants have no duty to share the costs of *major improvements*, such as adding a new room on a house, unless they agree to do so. Some courts will hold that co-owners also have a duty to share basic *maintenance* and *necessary repairs* of the premises so that it does not become dilapidated. *Baran v. Juskulski*, 689 A.2d 1283, 1287 (Md. Ct. Spec. App. 1997); William B. Stoebuck & Dale A. Whitman, *The Law of Property* §5.9, at 207-208 (3d ed. 2000). However, the authorities are mixed on this question, with some cases holding that there is no duty to pay for ordinary repairs unless they agree to do so. John G. Sprankling, *Understanding Property Law* §10.03[D], at 127-128 (2000). These courts seem reluctant to get into the business of determining what ordinary repairs are necessary. If such an obligation exists, a cotenant who has paid more than her fair share of such expenses may sue the other tenants for an accounting to obtain contribution for their fair share of those expenses. Co-owners do seem to be able to obtain a credit for repairs they have performed in calculating their monetary share of partition proceeds. The only issue is whether a co-owner can maintain a separate action for contribution from co-owners for their respective share of the expense of necessary repairs. Most courts hold that such an action can be maintained, at least where the one making the repairs notified the co-owners before incurring the expense.

In most states a co-owner who exclusively possesses the premises must bear the entire burden of expenses (including taxes, repairs, and mortgage payments) if the value of her occupation of the premises exceeds those payments. If the share of expenses that would ordinarily be borne by the tenants out of possession is less than the rental value belonging to the tenants out of possession, no action for contribution may be brought.*Barrow v. Barrow*, 527 So. 2d 1373 (Fla. 1988); William B. Stoebuck & Dale A. Whitman, *The Law of Property* §5.9, at 209 (3d ed. 2000). This principle substantially qualifies the rule that cotenants who are occupying the premises have no duty to pay rent to the co-owners who are not occupying the property. Although a co-tenant out of possession cannot sue a cotenant in possession for rent, a tenant in possession can sue her cotenants out of possession only for their share of expenses that exceeds the fair rental value to which they would be entitled if the property were leased out to a third party. *See Eteves v. Esteves*, 775 A.2d 163 (N.J. Super. Ct. App. Div. 2001)(in accounting after house was sold, parents who occupied the house for 18 years were entitled to be reimbursed by son for one-half of expenses of mortgage and maintenance but son was allowed a credit against that amount equal to the reasonable value of his parents' sole occupancy of the property).

3. *Accounting.* In many states, co-owners can bring a judicial proceeding for an *accounting* to require their co-owners to pay their portion of maintenance expenses or to force co-owners to hand over the requisite portion of rents earned from third parties who possessed the commonly held property.

Adverse possession and ouster. One cotenant cannot obtain adverse possession against another unless the possessing tenant makes clear to the nonpossessory tenant that he is asserting full ownership rights in the property to the exclusion of the other cotenants. Thus, in most states, one cotenant who lives in a house for 40 years or who collects rents for that period of time without sharing those rents with his co-owners will not acquire his cotenants' property interests by adverse possession. The courts generally require some affirmative act by which the nonpossessory tenant is put on notice that her co-owner is claiming adversely to the nonpossessory tenant's interests. *See, e.g., Parker v. Shecut*, 562 S.E.2d 620 (S.C. 2002) (ouster shown when brother made home his primary residence, changed the locks on the door, and refused to give his sister a key). The reason for this is that each cotenant has the legal right to possess the entire property; sole possession does not violate the property rights of the other owners and does not, therefore, constitute a trespass. Nonpossessory owners thus are not put on notice that the possessing owner is intending to claim his interest by adverse possession; moreover, the statute of limitations generally starts running only upon commission of an unlawful act such as a trespass. Because each owner has the right to possess the whole, no unlawful or tortious act has occurred by which the co-owner's property interests have been infringed. Courts strongly disagree about what acts are sufficient to constitute an ouster.

§7.2.2   TENANCY BY THE ENTIRETY

Tenancy by the entirety is a form of joint tenancy available only to married couples. It has been abolished in the majority of states, but is still available in about 20 states. Its current form is similar to joint tenancy, except that (1) the co-owners must be legally married; (2) the property cannot be partitioned except through a divorce proceeding; (3) in most states, the individual interest of each spouse cannot be sold, transferred, or encumbered by a mortgage without the consent of the other spouse, with the result that the right of survivorship cannot be destroyed by transfer of the interest of one party; and (4) in most states, creditors cannot attach property held through tenancy by the entirety to satisfy debts of one of the spouses. *Beal Bank, SSB v. Almand & Associates*, 780 So. 2d 45 (Fla. 2001). *See Bunker v. Peyton*, 312 F.3d 145 (4th Cir. 2002) (applying Va. law; tenancy by the entirety property not reachable by creditors in bankruptcy when both parties did not join in the debt); *In re Spears*, 313 B.R. 212 (W.D.Mich. 2004) (same, applying Mich. law). *But see United States v. Craft*, 535 U.S. 274 (2002)(an individual's interest in tenancy by the entirety property subject to federal tax lien for unpaid taxes). States that have the tenancy by the entirety may have a constructional preference for interpreting a conveyance to a married couple as intended to create a tenancy by the entirety. *See, e.g., Beal Bank, supra.*

Tenancy by the entirety was the traditional way for married couples to hold property. This form of joint ownership gave the husband the sole power to manage and control the disposition of the property. Similarly, states with community property systems, which provide that all property acquired during marriage is owned jointly by both spouses, traditionally gave management powers to the husband. These arrangements have been held to violate the equal protection clause by defining state property law in a way that discriminates on the basis of sex. *Kirchberg v. Feenstra*, 450 U.S. 455 (1981).

§7.3 *Conflicts over Rent and Possession*

OLIVAS v. OLIVAS
780 P.2d 640 (N.M. Ct. App. 1989)

Harris L. Hartz, Judge.

Respondent Sam Olivas (husband) appeals the property division in a divorce action. Petitioner Carolina Olivas (wife) and husband were divorced by a partial decree entered December 18, 1984. The district court did not enter its final order dividing property until August 31, 1987. The issues in this appeal arise, for the most part, as a consequence of the unusually lengthy delay between the divorce decree and the property division. . . . .

Husband and wife separated in June 1983, about two months before wife filed her petition for dissolution of marriage. The district court found that husband "chose to move out of the family home, and he then maintained another home where he also had his office for his business." Husband contends that the district court erred in failing to find that he had been constructively ousted from the family home. He requested findings and conclusions that the constructive ouster by his wife entitled him to half of the reasonable rental value of the home from the time of the initial separation.

Husband and wife held the family home as community property during the marriage and as tenants in common after dissolution. Although wife was the exclusive occupant of the house after the separation, ordinarily a cotenant incurs no obligation to fellow cotenants by being the exclusive occupant of the premises.

> [I]t is a well-settled principle of the common law that the mere occupation by a tenant of the entire estate does not render him liable to his co-tenant for the use and

occupation of any part of the common property. The reason is easily found. The right of each to occupy the premises is one of the incidents of a tenancy in common. Neither tenant can lawfully exclude the other. The occupation of one, so long as he does not exclude the other, is but the exercise of a legal right. If, for any reason, one does not choose to assert the right of common enjoyment, the other is not obliged to stay out; and if the sole occupation of one could render him liable therefor to the other, his legal right to the occupation would be dependent upon the caprice or indolence of his cotenant, and this the law would not tolerate. *Williams v. Sinclair Refining Co.*, 47 P.2d 910, 912 (N.M. 1935).

The result is otherwise, however, when the occupant has ousted the other cotenants. Although the term "ouster" suggests an affirmative physical act, even a reprehensible act, the obligation of the occupying cotenant to pay rent may arise in the absence of "actual" ouster when the realities of the situation, without there being any fault by either cotenant, prevent the cotenants from sharing occupancy. 4 G. Thompson, *Real Property* §1805, at 189 (J. Grimes Repl. 1979), states:

> [B]efore a tenant in common can be liable to his cotenants for rent for the use and occupation of the common property, his occupancy must be such as amounts to a denial of the right of his cotenants to occupy the premises jointly with him, or *the character of the property must be such as to make such joint occupancy impossible or impracticable.* [Emphasis added.]

We believe that it was this latter type of situation — an "ouster" in effect, without any physical act and perhaps without any fault — to which the New Mexico Supreme Court was referring when it recognized the doctrine of "constructive ouster" in the marital context in *Hertz v. Hertz*, 657 P.2d 1169 (N.M. 1983). The court wrote:

> [I]f one of the parties in a divorce case remains in possession of the community residence between the date of the divorce and the date of the final judgment dividing the community assets, then there *may* be a form of constructive ouster, exclusion, or an equivalent act which is created as to the right of common enjoyment by the divorced spouse not in possession. This exclusion may render the divorced spouse in possession of the community residence liable to the divorced spouse not in possession for the use and occupation of the residence between the date of the divorce and the date of the final judgment. To hold otherwise would mean that both divorced spouses should have continued to live with each other during the eighteen month interim or that both should have abandoned the property. 657 P.2d at 1179.

Applying the notion of constructive ouster in the marital context is simply another way of saying that when the emotions of a divorce make it impossible for spouses to continue to share the marital residence pending a property division, the spouse who — often through mutual agreement — therefore departs the residence may be entitled to rent from the remaining spouse. Although one can say that the departing spouse has been constructively "ousted," the term should not suggest physical misconduct, or any fault whatsoever, on the part of the remaining spouse.

Common law precedents support the proposition that the remaining spouse should pay rent to the cotenant when both cannot be expected to live together on the property. For example, when it is impractical for all cotenants to occupy the premises jointly, it is unnecessary that those claiming rent from the cotenant in possession first demand the right to move in and occupy the premises. *See Oechsner v. Courcier*, 155 S.W.2d 963 (Tex. Civ. App. 1941) (applying that principle when five heirs, with separate families totalling twenty-two members, were cotenants of a five-room cottage being occupied by one of the families). The impracticality of joint occupancy by the cotenants may result from the relations between the cotenants becoming "so strained and bitter that they could not continue to reside together in peace and concord." *Maxwell v. Eckert*, 109 A. 730, 731 (N.J. Eq. 1920). If, however, hostility flows only from the cotenant out of possession, ordinarily there would be no constructive ouster. *See O'Connell v. O'Connell*, 117 A. 634 (N.J. Eq. 1922) (wife left home and refused to return despite solicitation by husband). In that circumstance the departing spouse has "abandoned" his or her interest in possession, rather than being excluded.

One jurisdiction has gone so far as to create a rebuttable presumption of ouster of the spouse who moves out of the former marital residence upon divorce. *See Stylianopoulos v. Stylianopoulos*, 455 N.E.2d 477 (Mass. App. Ct. 1983) . . . .

Husband had the burden of proving constructive ouster in this case. Therefore, we must sustain the district court's ruling against husband unless the evidence at trial was such as to *compel* the district court to find ouster. Although the evidence of hostility between the spouses may have sustained a finding by the district court of constructive ouster, there was substantial evidence to support the inference that husband's purpose in leaving the community residence was to live with a girl friend and his departure was the reason wife filed for divorce; he was not pushed out but pulled. . . . Also, the delay of several years before husband demanded any rent from wife supports an inference of abandonment of his interest in occupancy. In short, the evidence was conflicting and did not compel a finding of constructive ouster.

We recognize the ambiguity in the district court's finding that defendant "chose to move out." Such language could be consistent with husband's departure being the result of marital friction, in which case there generally would be constructive ouster. On the other hand, the language could also be construed as referring to husband's abandoning the home to live with another woman. We choose the second construction of the finding, because "[i]n the case of uncertain, doubtful or ambiguous findings, an appellate court is bound to indulge every presumption to sustain the judgment." *Ledbetter v. Webb*, 711 P.2d 874, 879 (N.M. 1985). Moreover, it appeared from oral argument before this court that the issue of constructive ouster was framed in the district court in essentially the same manner as treated in this opinion. Therefore, we are comfortable in assuming that the district court applied the proper rule of law and in construing the district court's finding compatibly with its rejection of husband's proposed conclusion of law that there was a constructive ouster. . . .

NOTES AND QUESTIONS

Like the New Mexico courts, some courts adopt a version of the constructive ouster doctrine to require separated spouses to pay rent (equal to one-half the fair rental value) to the spouse who is no longer living at home. *In re Marriage of Watts*, 217 Cal. Rptr. 301 (Ct. App. 1985) (court may order husband to reimburse community for exclusive use of residence after separation); *Palmer v. Protrka*, 476 P.2d 185, 190 (Or. 1970) (when marital difficulties make co-occupancy impossible, requiring occupant to pay one-half of rental value seems closest to parties' intentions when they took title).

Other courts, however, refuse to make an exception for marital property and hold that cotenants in possession have no duty to pay rent unless they have affirmatively ousted their spouse by notifying them of an intent to exclude them from the joint property. *See Barrow v. Barrow*, 527 So. 2d 1373 (Fla. 1988) (ex-spouses who own residence as cotenants *after* final property distribution are treated like any other cotenants); *Kahnovsky v. Kahnovsky*, 21 A.2d 569 (R.I. 1941) (finding no ouster, although "separation was the result of marital difference").

Which approach is preferable? As the attorney for one of the parties in a divorce setting, how can you avoid this problem?

PROBLEMS

A woman lives with an abusive husband who has struck her several times.

1. The wife moves out after suffering battery at his hands. The husband asks her to return, but she refuses. They are separated for two years, then divorced. The wife sues the husband for one-half of the fair rental value of the house during the two-year period. Is the husband obligated to pay one-half the fair rental value of the house to the wife?

2. Now assume that, instead of the wife leaving, she throws the husband out of the house after the battery and tells him not to come back. They are separated for two years, then divorced. In the divorce proceedings, the wife is awarded ownership of the house. The husband argues that he is entitled to one-half of the fair rental value of the home for the period beginning with his ouster from the home until the divorce date. Is she obligated to pay rent to him? What are the arguments on both sides of this question? What do you think? Is this case the same as case #1 above or not? *See Cohen v. Cohen*, 746 N.Y.S.2d 22, 23 (App. Div. 2002) (ousted cotenant has no right to rent for period covered by court protective order excluding him from the property when tenant in possession had obtained that order because of cotenant's assaultive conduct).

§7.4   *Conflicts over Transfers by One Co-owner*

The basic rules of cotenancy provide that co-owners have the right to possess the entire property, the right to transfer their individual fractional interests, the right to share rents earned by the property in proportion to their ownership interests, and the duty to share maintenance and upkeep expenses. What happens when co-owners cannot agree among themselves about who will possess the property or how it should be used? The short answer is that they may resort to the legal procedures of requesting an *accounting* and, ultimately, *partition*. But an accounting is generally useful only as to financial matters — for example, if one co-owner has failed to pay her proportional share of the mortgage payments. And partition is a drastic remedy that may very well result in sale of the property; in that case, neither co-owner may wind up having the right to possess the property. Should some legal remedy short of partition be available to deal with conflicts about possession? Or should that be left to the parties themselves? The following cases address this question in the context of transfers of possession by one co-owner without the consent of the other.

§7.4.1   TENANCY IN COMMON AND JOINT TENANCY

§7.4.1.1   Family Conflicts over Use of Common Property

CARR v. DEKING
_____

765 P.2d 40 (Wash. Ct. App. 1988)

DALE M. GREEN, Judge . . . .

Joel Carr and his father, George Carr, now deceased, owned a parcel of land in Lincoln County as tenants in common. From 1974 through 1986 the Carrs leased the land to Richard Deking pursuant to a year-to-year oral agreement receiving one-third of the annual crop as rent. The Carrs paid for one-third of the fertilizer. In 1986, Joel Carr informed Mr. Deking he wanted cash rent beginning with the 1987 crop year. Mr. Deking was not receptive to this proposal.

In February 1987 Joel Carr wrote a letter to Mr. Deking to determine if he wanted to continue leasing the property. Mr. Deking did not respond. Instead he discussed the lease with George Carr. On February 18 Joel Carr went to his father's home and found Mr. Deking there discussing a possible 5-year lease. Joel Carr again indicated he wanted cash rent. Later that day, unbeknownst to Joel Carr, Mr. Deking and George Carr executed a written 10-year crop-share lease at the office of Mr. Deking's attorney. Under this lease, Mr. Deking agreed to pay all fertilizer costs. Joel Carr neither consented to nor ratified this lease and never authorized George Carr to act on his behalf.

In April Joel Carr gave notice to Mr. Deking that his tenancy would terminate at the end of the 1987 crop year. Mr. Deking responded that he would retain possession pursuant to the written lease with George Carr. In July Joel Carr commenced this action to declare that no valid lease existed, Mr. Deking had no right to farm the land and he should be required to vacate the land at the end of the 1987 crop year . . . .

. . . Joel Carr contends [that] the rights of Mr. Deking as lessee are subordinate to those of a nonjoining tenant in common. He argues public policy should prevent prospective lessees from going behind the back of one tenant in common to obtain a more favorable lease from the other.

On the other hand, it is Mr. Deking's position that George Carr could lawfully enter into a lease with respect to his own undivided one-half interest in the property, and Joel Carr was not entitled to bring an ejectment action to which George Carr did not agree. He asserts the proper remedy is partition, not ejectment.

It is well settled that each tenant in common of real property may use, benefit and possess the entire property subject only to the equal rights of cotenants. Thus, a cotenant may lawfully lease his own interest in the common property to another without the consent of the other tenant and without his joining in the lease. The nonjoining cotenant is not bound by this lease of the common property to third persons. The lessee "steps into the shoes" of the leasing cotenant and becomes a tenant in common with the other owners for the duration of the lease. A nonjoining tenant may not demand exclusive possession as against the lessee, but may only demand to be let into co-possession.

Applying these principles, we find Joel Carr is not entitled to eject Mr. Deking from the property. The proper remedy is partition and until that occurs, Mr. Deking is entitled to farm the land under the lease. There is no indication that this property is not amenable to physical partition. Joel Carr clearly has the right to that remedy. Joel Carr cites no authority and none has been found which would render the lease ineffective as between the estate of George Carr and Mr. Deking....

In view of our holding that the trial court properly denied Joel Carr's effort to eject Mr. Deking, Joel Carr is entitled to the benefit of the Deking-George Carr lease, at his election, until a partition of the property occurs. However, Joel Carr cannot claim the benefits contained in the Deking-George Carr lease without also accepting the other terms of that lease. Consequently, we remand to the trial court to determine Joel Carr's election choice [between] the prior oral lease with Mr. Deking [and] the Deking-George Carr lease....

§7.4.1.2 Death

TENHET v. BOSWELL
554 P.2d 330 (Cal. 1976)

STANLEY MOSK, Justice.

A joint tenant leases his interest in the joint tenancy property to a third person for a term of years, and dies during that term. We conclude that the lease does not sever the joint tenancy, but expires upon the death of the lessor joint tenant.

Raymond Johnson and plaintiff Hazel Tenhet owned a parcel of property as joint tenants. Assertedly without plaintiff's knowledge or consent, Johnson leased the property to defendant Boswell for a period of 10 years at a rental of $150 per year with a provision granting the lessee an "option to purchase."[2] Johnson died some three months after execution of the lease, and plaintiff sought to establish her sole right to possession of the property as the surviving joint tenant. After an unsuccessful demand upon defendant to vacate the premises, plaintiff brought this action to have the lease declared invalid....

II

An understanding of the nature of a joint interest in this state is fundamental to a determination of the question whether the present lease severed the joint tenancy. Civil Code section 683 provides in part: "A joint interest is one owned by two or more persons in equal shares, by a title created by a single will or transfer, when expressly declared in the will or transfer to be a joint tenancy...." This statute, requiring an express declaration for the creation of joint interests, does not abrogate the common law rule that four unities are essential to an estate in joint tenancy: unity of interest, unity of time, unity of title, and unity of possession.

---

2. The lease did not disclose that the lessor possessed only a joint interest in the property. To the contrary, the "option to purchase" granted to the lessee, which might more accurately be described as a right of first refusal, implied that the lessor possessed a fee simple. It provided in part: "Lessee is given a first exclusive right, privilege and option to purchase the house and lot covered by this lease.... If so purchased, Lessor will convey title by grant deed on the usual form subject only to easements or rights of way of record and liens or encumbrances specifically agreed to by and between Lessor and Lessee.[ ] Lessor shall furnish Lessee with a policy of title insurance at Lessor's cost...."

The requirement of four unities reflects the basic concept that there is but one estate which is taken jointly; if an essential unity is destroyed the joint tenancy is severed and a tenancy in common results. Accordingly, one of two joint tenants may unilaterally terminate the joint tenancy by conveying his interest to a third person. Severance of the joint tenancy, of course, extinguishes the principal feature of that estate — the *jus accrescendi* or right of survivorship. Thus, a joint tenant's right of survivorship is an expectancy that is not irrevocably fixed upon the creation of the estate; it arises only upon success in the ultimate gamble — survival — and then only if the unity of the estate has not theretofore been destroyed by voluntary conveyance, by involuntary alienation under an execution, or by any other action which operates to sever the joint tenancy.

Our initial inquiry is whether the partial alienation of Johnson's interest in the property effected a severance of the joint tenancy under these principles. It could be argued that a lease destroys the unities of interest and possession because the leasing joint tenant transfers to the lessee his present possessory interest and retains a mere reversion. Moreover, the possibility that the term of the lease may continue beyond the lifetime of the lessor is inconsistent with a complete right of survivorship.

On the other hand, if the lease entered into here by Johnson and defendant is valid only during Johnson's life, then the conveyance is more a variety of life estate *pur* [sic] *autre vie* than a term of years. Such a result is inconsistent with Johnson's freedom to alienate his interest during his lifetime.

We are mindful that the issue here presented is "an ancient controversy, going back to Coke and Littleton." Yet the problem is like a comet in our law: though its existence in theory has been frequently recognized, its observed passages are few. Some authorities support the view that a lease by a joint tenant to a third person effects a complete and final severance of the joint tenancy.

Others adopt a position that there is a temporary severance during the term of the lease. If the lessor dies while the lease is in force, under this view the existence of the lease at the moment when the right of survivorship would otherwise take effect operates as a severance, extinguishing the joint tenancy. If, however, the term of the lease expires before the lessor, it is reasoned that the joint tenancy is undisturbed because the joint tenants resume their original relation. The single conclusion that can be drawn from centuries of academic speculation on the question is that its resolution is unclear.

As we shall explain, it is our opinion that a lease is not so inherently inconsistent with joint tenancy as to create a severance, either temporary or permanent.

Under Civil Code sections 683 and 686 a joint tenancy must be expressly declared in the creating instrument, or a tenancy in common results. This is a statutory departure from the common law preference in favor of joint tenancy. Inasmuch as the estate arises only upon express intent, and in many cases such intent will be the intent of the joint tenants themselves, we decline to find a severance in circumstances which do not clearly and unambiguously establish that either of the joint tenants desired to terminate the estate.

If plaintiff and Johnson did not choose to continue the joint tenancy, they might have converted it into a tenancy in common by written mutual agreement. They might also have jointly conveyed the property to a third person and divided the proceeds. Even if they could not agree to act in concert, either plaintiff or Johnson might have severed the joint tenancy, with or without the consent of the other, by an act which was clearly indicative of an intent to terminate, such as a conveyance of her or his entire interest. Either might also have brought an action to partition the property, which, upon judgment, would have effected a severance. Because a joint tenancy may be created only by express intent, and because there are alternative and unambiguous means of altering the nature of that estate, we hold that the lease here in issue did not operate to sever the joint tenancy.

III

Having concluded that the joint tenancy was not severed by the lease and that sole ownership of the property therefore vested in plaintiff upon her joint tenant's death by operation of her right of survivorship, we turn next to the issue whether she takes the property unencumbered by the lease. . . .

By the very nature of joint tenancy, . . . the interest of the nonsurviving joint tenant extinguishes upon his death. And as the lease is valid only "in so far as the interest of the lessor in the joint property is concerned," it follows that the lease of the joint tenancy property also expires when the lessor dies.

This conclusion is borne out by decisions in this state involving liens on and mortgages of joint tenancy property. In *Zeigler v. Bonnell*, 126 P.2d 118 (Cal. Ct. App. 1942), the Court of Appeal ruled that a surviving joint tenant takes an estate free from a judgment lien on the interest of a deceased cotenant judgment debtor. The court reasoned that "The right of survivorship is the chief characteristic that distinguishes a joint tenancy from other interests in property. . . . The judgment lien of (the creditor) could attach only to the interest of his debtor. . . . That interest terminated upon [the debtor's] death." *Id.* at 119. After his death "the deceased joint tenant had no interest in the property, and his judgment creditor has no greater rights." *Id.* at 120.

A similar analysis was followed in *People v. Nogarr*, 330 P.2d 858 (Cal. Ct. App. 1958), which held that upon the death of a joint tenant who had executed a mortgage on the tenancy property, the surviving joint tenant took the property free of the mortgage. The court reasoned that "as the mortgage lien attached only to such interest as [the deceased joint tenant] had in the real property[,] when his interest ceased to exist the lien of the mortgage expired with it."

As these decisions demonstrate, a joint tenant may, during his lifetime, grant certain rights in the joint property without severing the tenancy. But when such a joint tenant dies his interest dies with him, and any encumbrances placed by him on the property become unenforceable against the surviving joint tenant. For the reasons stated a lease falls within this rule.

Any other result would defeat the justifiable expectations of the surviving joint tenant. Thus, if *A* agrees to create a joint tenancy with *B*, *A* can reasonably anticipate that when *B* dies *A* will take an unencumbered interest in fee simple. During his lifetime, of course, *B* may sever the tenancy or lease his interest to a third party. But to allow *B* to lease for a term continuing after his death would indirectly defeat the very purposes of the joint tenancy. For example, for personal reasons *B* might execute a 99-year lease on valuable property for a consideration of one dollar a year. *A* would then take a fee simple on *B*'s death, but would find his right to use the property — and its market value — substantially impaired. This circumstance would effectively nullify the benefits of the right of survivorship, the basic attribute of the joint tenancy.

On the other hand, we are not insensitive to the potential injury that may be sustained by a person in good faith who leases from one joint tenant. In some circumstances a lessee might be unaware that his lessor is not a fee simple owner but merely a joint tenant, and could find himself unexpectedly evicted when the lessor dies prior to expiration of the lease. This result would be avoided by a prudent lessee who conducts a title search prior to leasing, but we appreciate that such a course would often be economically burdensome to the lessee of a residential dwelling or a modest parcel of property. Nevertheless, it must also be recognized that every lessee may one day face the unhappy revelation that his lessor's estate in the leased property is less than a fee simple. For example, a lessee who innocently rents from the holder of a life estate is subject to risks comparable to those imposed upon a lessee of joint tenancy properly.

More significantly, we cannot allow extraneous factors to erode the functioning of joint tenancy. The estate of joint tenancy is firmly embedded in centuries of real property law and in the California statute books. Its crucial element is the right of survivorship, a right that would be more illusory than real if a joint tenant were permitted to lease for a term continuing after his death. Accordingly, we hold that under the facts alleged in the complaint the lease herein is no longer valid. . . .

§7.4.1.3 Divorce

KRESHA v. KRESHA
371 N.W.2d 280 (Neb. 1985)

D. Nick Caporale, Justice.

On August 30, 1979, Adolph Kresha and plaintiff-appellant, Rose M. Kresha, were husband and wife and the co-owners of two tracts of land. They are the parents of defendant-appellee, Joseph A. Kresha. On the aforesaid date the father, by written instrument and without the consent, knowledge, or authority of the mother, leased nonhomestead[4] lands to the son for a period of 6 years. The mother learned of the lease, at the latest, on March 12, 1980. Subsequently, on March 18, 1980, the mother filed an action for separate maintenance, which the father converted into a dissolution action. The dissolution decree awarded the subject lands to the mother. Following dismissal of the father's appeal of that decree to this court, a deed conveying the lands to the mother was recorded on August 16, 1982. On August 26, 1982, the mother wrote the son, advising that she was terminating his lease. The son, in turn, wrote the mother that he considered his lease to be valid, and remained on the lands. On March 2, 1983, the mother sent another notice directing the son to vacate the lands. Again, the son continued his occupancy. The mother then, on March 14, 1983, brought this forcible entry and detainer action in the county court to obtain possession of the lands. . . .

This jurisdiction has recognized that one of several tenants in common can lease his or her own interest to third persons. . . .

We conclude, therefore, that the father could and did encumber his own interest in the lands by the lease with his son, but did not encumber the mother's interest.

The next question is whether the mother, when the entire ownership of the lands was conveyed to her pursuant to the dissolution decree, took the lands subject to the

---

4. In some states, property used as a primary residence is statutorily protected against seizure by creditors (except for creditors who financed its acquisition). Surviving spouses may also have a right of survivorship to homestead property that cannot be eliminated by unilateral act of the deceased spouse. *See infra* §10.3.3.3.

son's leasehold interest in the father's former ownership interest. We conclude that she did.

In the final analysis the situation is not dissimilar to that presented in the acquisition of property from a fee owner which the purchaser knows to be encumbered by an existing lease. In such a situation the purchaser acquires the property subject to the lease.

In an attempt to avoid application of this general rule to the present case, the mother cites several cases from other jurisdictions in which a life tenant, mortgagor, or purchaser under a contract for deed executed a lease which the remainderman, mortgagee, or seller successfully refused to recognize once the life tenant died or the mortgagor or contract for deed purchaser defaulted. These cases, however, are not applicable. Here, the father owned, at the time of entering into the lease, a fee interest, whereas in the cases cited by the mother the lessors did not have fee title and simply undertook to encumber more than they owned....

Nor are we unmindful of *George & Teas v. George*, 267 Ark. 823, 591 S.W.2d 655 (1979), upon which the mother places substantial reliance. In *George* the Court of Appeals for the State of Arkansas set aside, upon motion of a purchaser without notice, the lease by the husband of real property owned jointly with his wife. The lease to the husband's mother was for a 99-year term and called for only a nominal rental. The mother knew her son was having marital difficulties, and the lease was entered into after the husband filed the last of two or three divorce actions. The wife did not learn of the lease until after it was ordered sold at judicial sale in satisfaction of the divorce decree. The *George* court stated the law permitted the husband in good faith and without fraud to convey his interest in nonhomestead property, subject to the wife's dower interest, but found that under the circumstances the lease constituted a fraudulent conveyance. It is sufficient to note the *George* facts are not the facts of the present case. There is nothing before us to indicate that the terms of the 6-year lease involved here are other than ordinary and customary. Moreover, the mother knew of the lease and its provisions throughout the dissolution proceedings and was free to develop all the facts surrounding it for the consideration of the dissolution court. Whether she did so is immaterial, particularly in view of the fact that the dissolution decree has become final....

NOTES AND QUESTIONS

1. *Leases by one co-owner.* Should common owners have the right to lease the premises without the consent of the cotenants? Is the rule promulgated in *Carr v. Deking* a good one?

2. *Remedies for leases by one cotenant.* The court in *Carr v. Deking* held that George Carr had the power to lease his one-half interest without Joel's consent. But in conclusion, it suggests that the son, Joel Carr, is "entitled to the benefit of the Deking-George Carr lease, at his election" until partition. Other courts have also held that a co-owner has a right to choose to participate in the lease and obtain his proportional share of the rent. *American Standard Life and Accident Insurance Co. v. Speros*, 494 N.W.2d 599 (N.D. 1993). Doesn't this assume that the agreed-upon rent is close to the fair rental value of the premises? Suppose Joel could show that the agreed-upon rent in the Deking-George Carr lease was only two-thirds of the fair rental value and had been discounted (reduced) because Deking knew he had the consent of only one of two joint

owners. Is either George or Joel entitled to an increase in the rent to make it reflect its fair rental value? Couldn't Joel force Deking to agree to such an increase by threatening to partition the property? If so, should Deking be required to pay fair rental value rather than the agreed-upon rent if he wishes to avoid partition?

3. *Leases by one joint tenant and the right of survivorship.* Courts are divided on the question of whether leases sever joint tenancies. Justice Mosk argues in *Tenhet v. Boswell* that "a lease is not so inherently inconsistent with joint tenancy as to create a severance." Isn't this circular reasoning? How does it help to ask whether a lease is consistent or inconsistent with something that the court is being asked to define? Compare the analysis in *Alexander v. Boyer*, 253 A.2d 359 (Md. 1969), in which the court held, contrary to *Tenhet v. Boswell*, that a lease by one joint tenant severs the joint tenancy. Judge Barnes explained that when the joint tenant "conveyed her possessory rights in the land" to a lessee for a term of years, she "thereby chang[ed] the nature of her 'interest' in the land from a present interest to a reversionary interest." In so doing, she parted with "all of her possessory rights for the term of the lease," thereby "destroy[ing] the unities of interest and possession in the joint tenancy" and terminating it. *Accord, Estate of Gulledge*, 673 A.2d 1278 (D.C. 1996). Is this explanation any less circular than that of Justice Mosk? What policies are relevant in answering the question whether a leasehold by one joint tenant destroys the right of survivorship of the other?

It might be argued that joint tenants have no justified expectations in their right of survivorship since it is so highly contingent on events that may not happen. After all, it can be lost if one dies first or if one's co-owner sells her interest in the property. On one hand, allowing severance may increase the alienability of property, especially if the court holds that leases given by one joint tenant do not survive the death of the lessor; few people will rent property if they know their possessory rights will end as soon as their landlord dies. On the other hand, the right of survivorship may increase the alienability of the property by decreasing the number of owners from two to one. This makes it easier for the property to be bought and sold since a potential lessee or buyer does not have to worry about obtaining the consent of more than one person. Which rule better promotes the reasonable use of property? How should the courts balance the right of each tenant to transfer her interest (a right of freedom of action) against the right of the co-owner to her right of survivorship (a right of security against loss of her property interest)?

4. *Mortgages and the right of survivorship.* Courts are also divided on the question of whether mortgages sever joint tenancies. In *Harms v. Sprague*, 473 N.E.2d 930 (Ill. 1984), two brothers, William and John Harms, owned real estates as joint tenants. John had granted a mortgage in his interest before his death. A mortgage is a security interest in the property, giving the holder of the mortgage (the mortgagee) the power to initiate a sale of the property to pay off a debt. Most states describe the borrower who grants the mortgage as the owner or title holder and the bank or lender who takes the mortgage as a "lienholder." A minority of states retain the older "title" theory, in which the lender takes title to the property, subject to an "equity of redemption" in the borrower who grants the mortgage. The trial court held that the mortgage severed the joint tenancy but the Illinois Supreme Court reversed, holding that a mortgage given by one joint tenant of his interest in the property did not sever the joint tenancy. Because the mortgage did not sever the joint tenant, John's interest automatically terminated when he died; thus, the court held, the mortgage did not survive as a lien on surviving joint tenant's property, and the surviving tenant, William, became

the sole owner of the estate. The court argued that Illinois had adopted the "lien" theory of mortgages rather than the "title" theory; thus, the mortgage did not constitute a "conveyance of title" and did not effectuate a severance.

States with the lien theory are likely to hold that mortgages do not sever joint tenancies, *see Brant v. Hargrove*, 632 P.2d 978 (Ariz. Ct. App. 1981), but some do provide that mortgages sever joint tenancies, *General Credit Co. v. Cleck*, 609 A.2d 553 (Pa. 1992). In states with the title theory, courts may consider a mortgage to be a transfer of ownership which has the effect of severing the joint tenancy. *Schaefer v. Peoples Heritage Savings Bank*, 669 A.2d 185 (Me. 1995). There is no substantive difference between "lien" theory states and "title" theory states; the difference today is merely verbal. Assuming that the question of severance should not depend on such a flimsy argument, how should the case have been decided, and why?

PROBLEM

In *Tenhet v. Boswell*, the court held that a lease by one joint tenant does not survive the death of the lessor. In *Kresha v. Kresha*, the court held that a lease by a spouse survives the divorce. Are the cases distinguishable? After all, while a joint tenant's interest terminates on death, a spouse's interest in property acquired during marriage is subject to equitable distribution on divorce. Are there good reasons to treat these cases differently? If not, which result is better?

§7.4.2   TENANCY BY THE ENTIRETY

SAWADA v. ENDO
561 P.2d 1291 (Haw. 1977)

BENJAMIN MENOR, Justice.

This is a civil action brought by the plaintiffs-appellants, Masako Sawada and Helen Sawada, in aid of execution of money judgments in their favor, seeking to set aside a conveyance of real property from judgment debtor Kokichi Endo to Samuel H. Endo and Toru Endo, defendants-appellees herein, on the ground that the conveyance as to the Sawadas was fraudulent.

On November 30, 1968, the Sawadas were injured when struck by a motor vehicle operated by Kokichi Endo. On June 17, 1969, Helen Sawada filed her complaint for damages against Kokichi Endo. Masako Sawada filed her suit against him on August 13, 1969. The complaint and summons in each case was served on Kokichi Endo on October 29, 1969.

On the date of the accident, Kokichi Endo was the owner, as a tenant by the entirety with his wife, Ume Endo, of a parcel of real property situate at Wahiawa, Oahu, Hawaii. By deed, dated July 26, 1969, Kokichi Endo and his wife conveyed the property to their sons, Samuel H. Endo and Toru Endo. This document was recorded in the Bureau of Conveyances on December 17, 1969. No consideration was paid by the grantees for the conveyance. Both were aware at the time of the conveyance that their father had been involved in an accident, and that he carried no liability insurance. Kokichi Endo and Ume Endo, while reserving no life interests therein, continued to reside on the premises.

On January 19, 1971, after a consolidated trial on the merits, judgment was entered in favor of Helen Sawada and against Kokichi Endo in the sum of $8,846.46. At the same time, Masako Sawada was awarded judgment on her complaint in the amount of $16,199.28. Ume Endo, wife of Kokichi Endo, died on January 29, 1971. She was survived by her husband, Kokichi. Subsequently, after being frustrated in their attempts to obtain satisfaction of judgment from the personal property of Kokichi Endo, the Sawadas brought suit to set aside the conveyance which is the subject matter of this controversy. The trial court refused to set aside the conveyance, and the Sawadas appeal.

I

The determinative question in this case is, whether the interest of one spouse in real property, held in tenancy by the entireties, is subject to levy and execution by his or her individual creditors. This issue is one of first impression in this jurisdiction.

A brief review of the present state of the tenancy by the entirety might be helpful. Dean Phipps, writing in 1951,[1] pointed out that only nineteen states and the District of Columbia continued to recognize it as a valid and subsisting institution in the field of property law. Phipps divided these jurisdictions into four groups. He made no mention of Alaska and Hawaii, both of which were then territories of the United States.

In the Group I states (Massachusetts, Michigan, and North Carolina) the estate is essentially the common law tenancy by the entireties, unaffected by the *Married Women's Property Acts*. As at common law, the possession and profits of the estate are subject to the husband's exclusive dominion and control. In all three states, as at common law, the husband may convey the entire estate subject only to the possibility that the wife may become entitled to the whole estate upon surviving him. As at common law, the obverse as to the wife does not hold true. Only in Massachusetts, however, is the estate in its entirety subject to levy by the husband's creditors. In both Michigan and North Carolina, the use and income from the estate is not subject to levy during the marriage for the separate debts of either spouse.

In the Group II states (Alaska, Arkansas, New Jersey, New York, and Oregon) the interest of the debtor spouse in the estate may be sold or levied upon for his or her separate debts, subject to the other spouse's contingent right of survivorship. Alaska, which has been added to this group, has provided by statute that the interest of a debtor spouse in any type of estate, except a homestead as defined and held in tenancy by the entirety, shall be subject to his or her separate debts.

In the Group III jurisdictions (Delaware, District of Columbia, Florida, Indiana, Maryland, Missouri, Pennsylvania, Rhode Island, Vermont, Virginia, and Wyoming) an attempted conveyance by either spouse is wholly void, and the estate may not be subjected to the separate debts of one spouse only.

In Group IV, the two states of Kentucky and Tennessee hold that the contingent right of survivorship appertaining to either spouse is separately alienable by him and attachable by his creditors during the marriage. The use and profits, however, may neither be alienated nor attached during coverture.

It appears, therefore, that Hawaii is the only jurisdiction still to be heard from on the question. Today we join that group of states and the District of Columbia

---

1. If they cannot agree, their only remedy is *partition*, discussed below.

which hold that under the *Married Women's Property Acts* the interest of a husband or a wife in an estate by the entireties is not subject to the claims of his or her individual creditors during the joint lives of the spouses. In so doing, we are placing our stamp of approval upon what is apparently the prevailing view of the lower courts of this jurisdiction.

Hawaii has long recognized and continues to recognize the tenancy in common, the joint tenancy, and the tenancy by the entirety, as separate and distinct estates. That the *Married Women's Property Act* of 1888 was not intended to abolish the tenancy by the entirety was made clear by the language of Act 19 of the Session Laws of Hawaii, 1903 (now Haw. Rev. Stat. §509-1). The tenancy by the entirety is predicated upon the legal unity of husband and wife, and the estate is held by them in single ownership. They do not take by moieties, but both and each are seized of the whole estate.

A joint tenant has a specific, albeit undivided, interest in the property, and if he survives his cotenant he becomes the owner of a larger interest than he had prior to the death of the other joint tenant. But tenants by the entirety are each deemed to be seized of the entirety from the time of the creation of the estate. At common law, this taking of the "whole estate" did not have the real significance that it does today, insofar as the rights of the wife in the property were concerned. For all practical purposes, the wife had no right during coverture to the use and enjoyment and exercise of ownership in the marital estate. All she possessed was her contingent right of survivorship.

The effect of the *Married Women's Property Acts* was to abrogate the husband's common law dominance over the marital estate and to place the wife on a level of equality with him as regards the exercise of ownership over the whole estate. The tenancy was and still is predicated upon the legal unity of husband and wife, but the Acts converted it into a unity of equals and not of unequals as at common law. No longer could the husband convey, lease, mortgage or otherwise encumber the property without her consent. The Acts confirmed her right to the use and enjoyment of the whole estate, and all the privileges that ownership of property confers, including the right to convey the property in its entirety, jointly with her husband, during the marriage relation. They also had the effect of insulating the wife's interest in the estate from the separate debts of her husband.

Neither husband nor wife has a separate divisible interest in the property held by the entirety that can be conveyed or reached by execution. A joint tenancy may be destroyed by voluntary alienation, or by levy and execution, or by compulsory partition, but a tenancy by the entirety may not. The indivisibility of the estate, except by joint action of the spouses, is an indispensable feature of the tenancy by the entirety. . . .

We are not persuaded by the argument that it would be unfair to the creditors of either spouse to hold that the estate by the entirety may not, without the consent of both spouses, be levied upon for the separate debts of either spouse. No unfairness to the creditor is involved here. We agree with the court in *Hurd v. Hughes*, 109 A. 418, 420 (Del. Ch. 1920): "But creditors are not entitled to special consideration. If the debt arose prior to the creation of the estate, the property was not a basis of credit, and if the debt arose subsequently the creditor presumably had notice of the characteristics of the estate which limited his right to reach the property."

We might also add that there is obviously nothing to prevent the creditor from insisting upon the subjection of property held in tenancy by the entirety as a condition precedent to the extension of credit. Further, the creation of a tenancy by the entirety may not be used as a device to defraud existing creditors.

Were we to view the matter strictly from the standpoint of public policy, we would still be constrained to hold as we have done here today. . . .

It is a matter of common knowledge that the demand for single-family residential lots has increased rapidly in recent years, and the magnitude of the problem is emphasized by the concentration of the bulk of fee simple land in the hands of a few. The shortage of single-family residential fee simple property is critical and government has seen fit to attempt to alleviate the problem through legislation. When a family can afford to own real property, it becomes their single most important asset. Encumbered as it usually is by a first mortgage, the fact remains that so long as it remains whole during the joint lives of the spouses, it is always available in its entirety for the benefit and use of the entire family. Loans for education and other emergency expenses, for example, may be obtained on the security of the marital estate. This would not be possible where a third party has become a tenant in common or a joint tenant with one of the spouses, or where the ownership of the contingent right of survivorship of one of the spouses in a third party has cast a cloud upon the title of the marital estate, making it virtually impossible to utilize the estate for these purposes.

If we were to select between a public policy favoring the creditors of one of the spouses and one favoring the interests of the family unit, we would not hesitate to choose the latter. But we need not make this choice for, as we pointed out earlier, by the very nature of the estate by the entirety as we view it, and as other courts of our sister jurisdictions have viewed it, "[a] unilaterally indestructible right of survivorship, an inability of one spouse to alienate his interest, and, importantly for this case, a broad immunity from claims of separate creditors remain among its vital incidents." *In re Estate of Wall*, 440 F.2d 215, 218 (D.C. Cir. 1971).

Having determined that an estate by the entirety is not subject to the claims of the creditors of one of the spouses during their joint lives, we now hold that the conveyance of the marital property by Kokichi Endo and Ume Endo, husband and wife, to their sons, Samuel H. Endo and Toru Endo, was not in fraud of Kokichi Endo's judgment creditors. . . .

H. Baird Kidwell, Justice, dissenting. . . .

The majority reaches its conclusion by holding that the effect of the *Married Women's Act* was to equalize the positions of the spouses by taking from the husband his common law right to transfer his interest, rather than by elevating the wife's right of alienation of her interest to place it on a position of equality with the husband's. I disagree. I believe that a better interpretation of the *Married Women's Acts* is that offered by the Supreme Court of New Jersey in *King v. Greene*, 153 A.2d 49, 60 (N.J. 1959):

> It is clear that the *Married Women's Act* created an equality between the spouses in New Jersey, insofar as tenancies by the entirety are concerned. If, as we have previously concluded, the husband could alienate his right of survivorship at common law, the wife, by virtue of the act, can alienate her right of survivorship. And it follows, that if the wife takes equal rights with the husband in the estate, she must take equal disabilities. Such are the dictates of common equality. Thus, the judgment creditors of either spouse may levy and execute upon their separate rights of survivorship.

One may speculate whether the courts which first chose the path to equality now followed by the majority might have felt an unexpressed aversion to entrusting a wife with as much control over her interest as had previously been granted to the husband with respect to his interest. Whatever may be the historical explanation for these decisions, I feel that the resultant restriction upon the freedom of the spouses to deal independently with their respective interests is both illogical and unnecessarily at odds with present policy trends. Accordingly, I would hold that the separate interest of the husband in entireties property, at least to the extent of his right of survivorship, is alienable by him and subject to attachment by his separate creditors, so that a voluntary conveyance of the husband's interest should be set aside where it is fraudulent as to such creditors, under applicable principles of the law of fraudulent conveyances.

NOTES AND QUESTIONS

1. *Marital property and male privileges.* In *Robinson v. Trousdale County*, 516 S.W.2d 626, 630-631 (Tenn. 1974), the court explained that the traditional rule granting control of tenancies by the entirety to the husband was based on "a judicially decreed recognition of the traditional pattern of married women being forced into a subservient and supportive role that is inherently unequal, patently unfair, and at variance with the concept of equality mandated by contemporary standards of justice."

In *Kirchberg v. Feenstra*, 450 U.S. 455, 456 (1981), the Supreme Court considered a Louisiana statute giving the "husband as 'head and master' of property jointly owned with his wife, the unilateral right to dispose of such property without his spouse's consent." The Court held that the statute violated the equal protection clause of the fourteenth amendment because the classification was not substantially related to achieving an important governmental interest.

2. *Married Women's Property Acts.* Many courts have interpreted their Married Women's Property statutes to abolish tenancy by the entirety. Others interpreted them to remove the husband's rights of control over the jointly owned property. A small number of states held — until recently — that their *Married Women's Property Acts* had no effect on tenancy by the entirety, thereby leaving the possession and profits of the property in the control of the husband as well as allowing future creation of new tenancies by the entirety. These states, including Massachusetts, Michigan, and North Carolina, have abolished the husband's prerogative by court decision or statute. Mass. Gen. Laws ch. 209, §1; Mich. Comp. Laws Ann. §557.71; N.C. Gen. Stat. §39-13.6.

3. *Creditors' rights to reach tenancy by the entirety property.* As *Sawada v. Endo* explains, some states have held that creditors cannot reach property held in the form of tenancy by the entirety to satisfy debts of one spouse without the consent of the other spouse; other states have held that creditors can attach the life interest of a tenant by the entirety, subject to a right of survivorship in that tenant's spouse. In the latter states, courts have discretion to deny a partition of the property while it is still being occupied by the other spouse. Which approach better protects the rights of women to gender equality?

4. *Tax liens.* In *United States v. Craft*, 535 U.S. 274 (2002), the wife of a delinquent taxpayer sued the United States to recover half the proceeds of the sale of tenancy by the entirety property. The United States had placed a lien on that portion of the proceeds to pay off her husband's delinquent federal taxes. She noted that under Michigan law, one tenant by the entirety has no interest separable from that of the spouse; state law did not allow her husbands' creditors to reach his interest to satisfy his unpaid debts

and he therefore had no individual interest in the property that could be reached by the federal government to pay his unpaid taxes. The Supreme Court disagreed, holding that his interest did constitute "property" or a "right to property" within the meaning of the federal tax lien legislation. Using the legal realist metaphor of property as a "bundle of sticks," Justice O'Connor explained that the husband had a number of "the most essential property rights: the right to use the property, to receive income produced, by it and to exclude others from it." *Id.* at 283. He also possessed the right to alienate the property with his wife's consent. "There is no reason to believe, however, that this one stick — the right of unilateral alienation — is essential to the category of 'property.'" *Id.* at 284. The Court noted it had previously decided that the government had the discretion to foreclose on an individual's interest in property even though he lacked the unilateral power of alienation. This would mean that the United States could force a sale of the property over the wife's objections to satisfy the husband's unpaid taxes. However, the Internal Revenue Service has recognized that this creates "adverse consequences for the non-liable spouse of the taxpayer" and thus the use of foreclosure in such cases will be "determined on a case-by-case basis." *See Collection Issues Related to Entireties Property,* Notice 2003-60, 2003-39 I.R.B. 643, 2003 WL 22100950 (Sept. 29, 2003). Once property is sold with the consent of both owners, as it was in *Craft,* the United States can take the husband's one-half share of the proceeds of the sale. This does not mean the delinquent taxpayer can *give* his property interest to his spouse and avoid paying the taxes. *Id.*

Justices Scalia, Thomas and Stevens dissented. Justice Scalia noted that the Court "nullifies (insofar as federal taxes are concerned, at least) a form of property ownership that was of particular benefit to the stay-at-home spouse or mother [who is] overwhelmingly unlikely to be the source of the individual indebtedness against which a tenancy by the entirety protects. Justice Thomas opined that state law defined the husband not to have any separate interest in the property; thus he had no individual "property" or "rights to property" to which the federal tax lien could attach.

5. *Presumptions.* Although ambiguous conveyances are normally interpreted as tenancies in common rather than joint tenancies, jurisdictions that have the tenancy by the entirety may presume that a conveyance to a married couple is held in a tenancy by the entirety. *Beal Bank v. Almand & Associates,* 780 So. 2d 45 (Fla. 2001).

6. *Homestead laws.* Homestead laws may protect the surviving spouse's ownership and occupancy rights in the family home free from demands of the decedent's creditors. Tex. Prob. Code §271. The effect of such laws may be to deprive the homeowner from transferring or encumbering her interests in the family home without the consent of both spousal owners.

PROBLEM

Can a couple create a tenancy by the entirety by contract? Couples who are not married may want to ensure that property is not sold or encumbered without the consent of either party. Unmarried male-female couples may wish to do this in the many states that have abolished tenancy by the entirety, and same-sex couples may wish to do this in the states (other than Massachusetts) that do not recognize same-sex marriages.

Agreements not to partition are generally held to be invalid restraints on alienation; however, such an agreement was enforced in *Kopp v. Kopp,* 488 A.2d 636

(Pa. Super. Ct. 1985). In that case a married male-female couple separated, retaining joint ownership of the house. The wife relinquished all rights to support from the husband; in exchange, he agreed that she would have sole rights to possess and use the house. Their separation agreement also prohibited partition of the house so long as the wife still lived there. The restraint would be removed if the wife died. The court held the restraint to be reasonable and not an invalid restraint on alienation because it was limited to a reasonable time.

Assume gay male couple buys a house together as joint tenants. The deed is recorded with a separate document containing a covenant between the two men in which each covenants not to bring an action for partition of the property so long as both live in the house. It also provides that partition should not be allowed before the parties have reached a comprehensive property settlement in the event they break up; that settlement can either be one they voluntarily agree to or one that is imposed by a court in the context of litigation. The covenant also states that neither party may encumber, mortgage, sell, or lease his undivided 50 percent shares without the consent of the other and that neither one owns a property interest that can be attached by creditors unless both owners agree to the transaction. The couple is attempting to create the incidents of a tenancy by the entirety through a contract even though they live in a state in which they cannot marry.

Are the covenants enforceable, including (a) the covenant limiting the right to partition, (b) the restraint on alienation, and (c) the attempt to limit the ability of creditors to reach the parties' individual interests? Or are they void, either because they constitute an attempt to create a new estate or because they constitute unreasonable restraints on alienation?

§7.5   Marital Property

§7.5.1   Historical Background

§7.5.1.1   Coverture, Dower, and Curtesy

Under the common law of England, single women (a *feme sole*) enjoyed the same rights to hold and manage property and to enter enforceable contracts as did men. Once married, however, the husband retained the sole power to possess and control the profits of all land owned by himself and his wife. The wife was called a *feme covert*, and her status was described by the institution of *coverture*. The husband and wife were treated as one person in the eyes of the law; that person was the husband. He had the power to convey his wife's property without her consent and to control all the profits of the land. In addition, his consent was required in order to sell her land.

In contrast to the rigidity of the law courts, the equity courts created a variety of mechanisms by which some married women could exercise property rights during marriage. First, they could enforce antenuptial agreements by which some husbands voluntarily gave control over property to their wives. Second, a trust could be created for the benefit of the wife, and she could enforce the trust as the beneficiary without her husband's consent. Fathers often took this route to keep property in their daughters' control rather than allowing it to pass to their prospective sons-in-law. William B. Stoebuck & Dale A. Whitman, *The Law of Property* §2.13, at 65-66 (3d ed. 2000).

The common law did give the wife certain important property interests to take effect at the death of her husband. The common law gave the surviving spouse a life estate in all or some of the land owned by the deceased spouse at the time of his death. The wife's *dower* interest consisted of a life estate in one-third of the freehold lands of which the husband was seised at any time during the marriage and that could be inherited by the couple's children. The wife's dower interest could not be alienated by her husband without her consent; nor could it be used to satisfy the husband's debts. The husband's equivalent *curtesy* interest consisted of a life estate in *all* the lands in which his wife owned a present freehold estate during the marriage and that was inheritable by issue of the couple. However, the husband's curtesy interest sprang into being *only* if the couple had a child capable of inheriting the property. William B. Stoebuck & Dale A. Whitman, *The Law of Property* §2.13, at 67-69 (3d ed. 2000).

Dower and curtesy remain in only a few states, and where they exist, the rights of husbands and wives have been equalized. The states that retain these institutions generally allow surviving spouses to choose between dower/curtesy and a statutorily defined share of marital assets owned by the decedent at the time of death.

§7.5.1.2 Married Women's Property Acts

In the second half of the nineteenth century (starting with Mississippi in 1839), all common law states passed *Married Women's Property Acts*. These statutes abolished coverture and removed the economic disabilities previously imposed on married women. After passage of the statutes, married women had the same rights as single women and married men to contract, to hold and manage property, and to sue and be sued. The wife's earnings were her separate property and could not be controlled or taken by her husband without her consent; nor could her separate property be seized by her husband's creditors. At the same time, these acts failed to achieve the aims of nineteenth-century women's rights advocates who "sought to emancipate wives' labor in the household as well as in the market, and to do so, advocated 'joint property' laws that would recognize wives' claims to marital assets to which husbands otherwise had title." Reva B. Siegel, *The Modernization of Marital Status Law: Adjudicating Wives' Rights to Earnings, 1860-1930*, 82 Geo. L.J. 2127 (1994). They argued that wives were "entitled to joint rights in marital property by reason of the labor they contributed to the family economy." Reva B. Siegel, *Home as Work: The First Woman's Rights Claims Concerning Wives' Household Labor, 1850-1880*, 103 Yale L.J. 1073, 1077 (1994). Many women worked inside the home for no wages; the *Married Women's Property Acts* failed to grant such women any rights in marital property, while family law doctrines preserved their duties to render services inside the home. Other women engaged in labor inside the home for which wages were earned, such as taking in laundry or sewing, keeping boarders, gardening and dairying, and selling the crops or milk products for cash. Although some states gave married women property rights in such earnings, most *Married Women's Property Acts* granted the husband control over such earnings or were interpreted by courts in this fashion on the ground that these acts were not intended to alter family law doctrines requiring women to provide services inside the home. *Id.* at 1181-1188. Since most men worked outside the home and most married women worked inside the home, gender equality in access to property was a long time in coming.

Most states also abolished dower and curtesy; at the same time, they amended intestacy laws to make surviving spouses heirs, allowing them to inherit the real and personal property owned by their deceased spouse at the time of death. Some states still retain dower and curtesy, but in those states the husband's and wife's interests have been equalized, and the surviving spouse is generally authorized to choose between the dower or curtesy interest in real estate owned during the marriage and the portion of the deceased spouse's property guaranteed to the surviving spouse by "statutory share" legislation. These statutes guarantee the survivor a specified portion of the deceased spouse's real and personal property, thereby overriding a will that leaves the spouse less than this minimum amount.

§7.5.2 COMMUNITY PROPERTY AND SEPARATE PROPERTY

Different rules define the property rights of spouses during marriage, on divorce or dissolution of the marriage, and on the death of one of the parties. Two basic systems govern marital property rights in the United States: the *separate property* system, in the majority of states, and the *community property system*, in effect in nine states.[5]

§7.5.2.1 Separate Property

During Marriage

In separate property states, spouses own their property separately, except to the extent they choose to share it or mingle it with their spouse's property. This means that each spouse owns whatever property he or she possessed before the marriage — such as a house, a car, stock, or a bank account — and is individually liable for prior debts. Creditors cannot go after a spouse's property to satisfy a debt individually undertaken by the other spouse. Property earned after the marriage, including wages and dividends, also is owned separately. A husband and wife may of course choose to share property with each other either informally, by sharing the costs of the household or giving part of individual earnings to the spouse, or formally, by having a joint bank account to which either spouse has access as a joint tenant.

It is important to note that spouses in separate property states are not perfectly free to keep all their property to themselves. Spouses have a legal duty to support each other, and this duty may require a sharing of property earned during the marriage. A spouse who fails to comply with this obligation may be forced to do so by a court order for maintenance, although this kind of lawsuit rarely happens outside of divorce or separation.

On Divorce

Most legal disputes about marital property involve divorce or the death of a spouse. All states regulate the distribution of property rights between the parties on divorce. Separate property states have statutes that provide for "*equitable distribution*"

---

5. Arizona, California, Idaho, Louisiana, Nevada, New Mexico, Texas, Washington, and Wisconsin.

of property owned by each of the parties on divorce, subject to a wide range of factors such as need (support for necessities, including child support), status (maintaining the lifestyle shared during the marriage), rehabilitation (support sufficient to allow one spouse to attain marketable skills such that support will no longer be needed), contribution (treating the marriage as a partnership and dividing the assets jointly earned from the enterprise), and, sometimes, fault. Judith Areen, *Cases and Materials on Family Law* 763-765 (4th ed. 1999). About one-fourth of the states allow marital fault to be considered and another fourth explicitly exclude "marital misconduct" as a factor. Leslie J. Harris, Lee E. Teitelbaum & Carol A. Weisbrod, *Family Law* 342 (1996). Specific factors that may be taken into account include age, health, occupation, income, vocational skills, contribution as a homemaker, dissipation of property during the marriage, income tax consequences, debts, obligations prior to marriage and contribution of one spouse to the education of the other. This system gives the trial judge great discretion in determining how the property should be shared or shifted between the parties. Often at issue are the standards to be used in dividing property, the weight to be given different factors, and the determination of the kinds of intangible resources that constitute "property" subject to equitable distribution on divorce.

Separate property states also have provision for "alimony," or periodic payments from one spouse to support the other. Until recently, alimony was routinely awarded to wives who were thought to be dependent on their husbands for income. However, with the huge recent increase in women in the workforce, as well as the advent of no-fault divorce, alimony has become exceptional and, when awarded, is often temporary. Current policy in most states aims at financial independence for the parties.

On Death

A spouse may dispose of her property by will. Notwithstanding her right to do so, separate property states may limit her ability to determine who gets her property on death. Many states provide for a *statutory forced share* of the decedent's estate, effectively allowing the widow or widower to override the will and receive a stated portion (usually one-third to one-half) of the estate. There is no obligation to leave separately owned property; spouses are generally free to give away their separate property during their lifetime. But the rules in force do protect the interests of a surviving spouse to the extent of defining an indefeasible right to receive a portion of the testator's *estate* (the property owned by the testator at the time of death). When no will is written, a spouse's separate property is inherited according to the state intestacy statute. While some states grant the surviving spouse the decedent's entire property, other states divide the property between the surviving spouse and the children.

§7.5.2.2 Community Property

During Marriage

In community property states, as in separate property states, property owned prior to the marriage, as well as property acquired after marriage by gift, devise, bequest, or inheritance, is separate property. The American Law Institute's *Principles of the Law of Family Dissolution*, adopted in 2002, favors the community property approach rather than the separate property approach. *See id.* §§4.01–4.12. All other property acquired during the marriage, including earnings, is community property and is owned equally by both spouses. In some community property states, earnings on separate property remain separate property. In several states, however, earnings from separate property, including interest, rents, and profits, become community property. Most states allow spouses to change, or "transmute," their property from separate to community property, and vice versa, by written agreement.

While community property is somewhat similar to joint tenancy since it is a form of common ownership, a better analogy can be drawn between community property and partnership. Since the 1960s, most states have granted spouses equal rights to manage community property; each spouse individually may deal with the community property without the consent of the other spouse. At the same time, managers of community property are fiduciaries; they have the duty to manage the property for the good of the community and to act in good faith to benefit the community. In addition, most states have statutes requiring *both* parties to agree to convey or mortgage interests in real property and in assets in a business in which both spouses participate. Community property states have widely divergent rules on whether community property can be reached by creditors of individual spouses. Some states protect such property from being reached by creditors of individual spouses unless both spouses consented to the transaction; others allow the community property to be used to satisfy debts incurred by one spouse; still others limit the portion of the community property reachable by such creditors.

On Divorce

A few community property states allocate property on divorce relatively mechanically by giving each spouse his or her separate property and half of the community property. Cal. Fam. Code §2550. Most community property states adopt the "equitable distribution" principle now existing in separate property states. Ariz. Rev. Stat. §25-318; Tex. Fam. Code §7.001; Wash. Rev. Code §26.09.080. The main issue arising in community property states is how to characterize specific items of property as separate or community property. As in separate property states, spouses may enter premarital agreements that alter the otherwise applicable rules. In particular, they may agree to treat community property as separate property and vice versa. On divorce, however, as in separate property states, such agreements may be reviewed to determine if they were voluntary and are fundamentally fair.

On Death

In community property states, a spouse may dispose of her separate property and one-half of the community property by will. Statutory forced share statutes do not generally exist in community property states, given the spouse's vested ownership of one-half of the community property.

§7.5.2.3 Premarital Agreements

Spouses may attempt to vary their respective property rights during marriage or at divorce by signing a premarital (antenuptial) agreement. Traditionally, such agreements were unenforceable on public policy grounds because they were thought to undermine stable marriages. *See Developments in the Law — The Law of Marriage and Family: Marriage as Contract and Marriage as Partnership: The Future of Antenuptial Agreement Law,* 116 Harv. L. Rev. 2075, 2078 (2003). Today however such agreements are generally enforceable. Although some courts hold that such agreements are enforceable whether or not they are reasonable, *Simeone v. Simeone,* 581 A.2d 162 (Pa. 1990), almost all states review them to see if they were voluntary, *In re Marriage of Bonds,* 5 P.3d 815 (Cal. 2000). *See In re Estate of Hollett,* 834 A.2d 348 (N.H. 2003) (premarital agreement involving $6 million estate entered into the night before the wedding was invalid because signed under duress and thus not voluntary). Some states go further and review premarital agreements for fairness, Wis. Stat. §767.255(*l*); *DeMatteo v. DeMatteo,* 762 N.E.2d 797 (Mass. 2002)(premarital agreement enforceable only if "fair and reasonable" at the time of enforcement); *Greenwald v. Greenwald,* 454 N.W.2d 34 (Wis. Ct. App. 1990), *overruled on other grounds by Meyer v. Meyer,* 620 N.W.2d 382 (Wis. 2000). Most states have a presumption in favor of such agreements, ignoring them only if they are "unconscionable," while some state subject such agreements to more searching review to determine if they are fair. *Compare In re Marriage of Bonds,* 83 Cal. Rptr. 2d 783 (Ct. App. 1999) (unconscionable standard) *with In re Marriage of Speigle,* 553 N.W.2d 309 (Iowa 1996) (reviewing the agreement for "fundamental fairness").

The *Uniform Premarital Agreement Act* (UPAA), adopted in about half the states, provides that premarital agreements are not enforceable against a party (1) if that party "did not execute the agreement voluntarily" and (2) the agreement is "unconscionable" and that party "was not provided a fair and reasonable disclosure of the property or financial obligations of the other party," did not voluntarily waive the right to disclosure in writing, and did not have (or reasonably could not have had) an adequate knowledge of the other party's financial assets. *Uniform Premarital Agreement Act §6. See* Conn. Gen. Stat. §§46b-36a to 46b-36j; N.J. Stat. §37:2-38; Va. Code §20-151. The UPAA has been passed in different forms in the states that adopted it. Many states determine unconscionability as of the date of execution of the agreement, as the UPAA suggests, Va. Code §20-151 ("unconscionable when it was executed"). However, others determine whether the agreement is "unconscionable at the time enforcement was sought", N.J. Stat. §37:2-38(b). *See also* Conn. Gen. Stat. §§46b-36a(a)(2) ("unconscionable when it was executed or when enforcement is sought").

The American Law Institute's *Principles of the Law of Family Dissolution,* adopted in 2002, recommends an approach very similar to that in the UPAA. However, it suggests enforcing the agreement unless enforcement "would work a substantial injustice"; this principle applies only if some years have passed since the marriage and the couple has either had a child or there has been a "change in circumstances" since the marriage that had a "substantial impact" on the parties or their children. *See id.* §7.05.

§7.5.2.4 Homestead Laws

Almost all states have homestead laws designed to protect the interests of a surviving spouse and children in the family home from the claims of creditors of the deceased spouse. They generally allow the spouse to live in the family home as long as she lives. Some states require the property to be registered as a homestead before the protections attach, while in others probate judges have the power to set aside homestead property as exempt from creditor's claims. Many states limit the value that can be exempted from execution to pay debts; if the property is worth more than this limit, the property (or a divisible portion of the land) may be sold to pay amounts that exceed the limitation. 3 *Thompson on Real Property, Second Thomas Edition* §21.04 (David A. Thomas ed. 2001). Some states go further and allow owners to devise homestead property free from the reach of creditors even if there is no surviving spouse or minor child. *Warburton v. McKean*, 877 So. 2d 50 (Fla. Dist. Ct. App. 2004).

§7.5.3   MARITAL BREAKUP

§7.5.3.1   Equitable Distribution of "Property" Acquired During Marriage

O'BRIEN v. O'BRIEN

489 N.E.2d 712 (N.Y. 1985)

RICHARD D. SIMONS, J.

In this divorce action, the parties' only asset of any consequence is the husband's newly acquired license to practice medicine. The principal issue presented is whether that license, acquired during their marriage, is marital property subject to equitable distribution under Domestic Relations Law §236(B)(5)....

I

Plaintiff and defendant married on April 3, 1971. At the time both were employed as teachers at the same private school. Defendant had a bachelor's degree and a temporary teaching certificate but required 18 months of postgraduate classes at an approximate cost of $3,000, excluding living expenses, to obtain permanent certification in New York. She claimed, and the trial court found, that she had relinquished the opportunity to obtain permanent certification while plaintiff pursued his education. At the time of the marriage, plaintiff had completed only three and one-half years of college but shortly afterward he returned to school at night to earn his bachelor's degree and to complete sufficient premedical courses to enter medical school. In September 1973 the parties moved to Guadalajara, Mexico, where plaintiff became a full-time medical student. While he pursued his studies defendant held several teaching and tutorial positions and contributed her earnings to their joint expenses. The parties returned to New York in December 1976 so that plaintiff could complete the last two semesters of medical school and internship training here. After they returned, defendant resumed her former teaching position and she remained in it at the time this action was commenced. Plaintiff was licensed to practice medicine in October 1980. He commenced this action for divorce two months later. At the time of trial, he was a resident in general surgery.

During the marriage both parties contributed to paying the living and educational expenses and they received additional help from both of their families. They disagreed on the amounts of their respective contributions but it is undisputed that in addition to performing household work and managing the family finances defendant was gainfully employed throughout the marriage, that she contributed all of her earnings to their living and educational expenses and that her financial contributions exceeded those of plaintiff. The trial court found that she had contributed 76% of the parties' income exclusive of a $10,000 student loan obtained by defendant. Finding that plaintiff's medical degree and license are marital property, the court received evidence of its value and ordered a distributive award to defendant.

Defendant presented expert testimony that the present value of plaintiff's medical license was $472,000. Her expert testified that he arrived at this figure by comparing the average income of a college graduate and that of a general surgeon between 1985, when plaintiff's residency would end, and 2012, when [plaintiff] would reach age 65. After considering Federal income taxes, an inflation rate of 10% and a real interest rate of 3% he capitalized the difference in average earnings and reduced the amount to present value. He also gave his opinion that the present value of defendant's contribution to plaintiff's medical education was $103,390. Plaintiff offered no expert testimony on the subject.

The court, after considering the life-style that plaintiff would enjoy from the enhanced earning potential his medical license would bring and defendant's contributions and efforts toward attainment of it, made a distributive award to her of $188,800, representing 40% of the value of the license, and ordered it paid in 11 annual installments of various amounts beginning November 1, 1982 and ending November 1, 1992. The court also directed plaintiff to maintain a life insurance policy on his life for defendant's benefit for the unpaid balance of the award and it ordered plaintiff to pay defendant's counsel fees of $7,000 and her expert witness fee of $1,000. It did not award defendant maintenance. . . .

II

The Equitable Distribution Law contemplates only two classes of property: marital property and separate property (Domestic Relations Law §236(B)(1)(c), (d)). The former, which is subject to equitable distribution, is defined broadly as "all property acquired by either or both spouses during the marriage and before the execution of a separation agreement or the commencement of a matrimonial action, *regardless of the form in which title is held*" (Domestic Relations Law §236(B)(1)(c) (emphasis added)). Plaintiff does not contend that his license is excluded from distribution because it is separate property; rather, he claims that it is not property at all but represents a personal attainment in acquiring knowledge. He rests his argument on decisions in similar cases from other jurisdictions and on his view that a license does not satisfy common-law concepts of property. Neither contention is controlling because decisions in other States rely principally on their own statutes, and the legislative history underlying them, and because the New York Legislature deliberately went beyond traditional property concepts when it formulated the Equitable Distribution Law. Instead, our statute recognizes that spouses have an equitable claim to things of value arising out of the marital relationship and classifies them as subject to distribution by focusing on the marital status of the parties at the time of acquisition. Those things acquired during marriage and subject to distribution have been classified as "marital property" although, as one commentator has observed, they hardly fall within the traditional property concepts because there is no common-law property interest remotely resembling marital property. "It is a statutory creature, is of no meaning whatsoever during the normal course of a marriage and arises full-grown, like Athena, upon the signing of a separation agreement or the commencement of a matrimonial action. It is hardly surprising, and not at all relevant, that traditional common law property concepts do not fit in parsing the meaning of 'marital property'" (Florescue, *"Market Value," Professional Licenses and Marital Property: A Dilemma in Search of a Horn,* 1982 N.Y. St. Bar Assn. Fam. L. Rev. 13 (Dec.)). Having classified the "property" subject to distribution, the Legislature did not attempt to go further and define it but left it to the courts to determine what interests come within the terms of section 236(B)(1)(c).

We made such a determination in *Majauskas v. Majauskas,* 463 N.E.2d 15 (N.Y. 1984), holding there that vested but unmatured pension rights are marital property subject to equitable distribution. Because pension benefits are not specifically identified as marital property in the statute, we looked to the express reference to pension rights contained in section 236(B)(5)(d)(4), which deals with equitable distribution of marital property, to other provisions of the equitable distribution statute and to the legislative intent behind its enactment to determine whether pension rights are marital property or separate property. A similar analysis is appropriate here and leads to the conclusion that marital property encompasses a license to practice medicine to the extent that the license is acquired during marriage.

Section 236 provides that in making an equitable distribution of marital property, "the court shall consider: . . . (6) any equitable claim to, interest in, or direct or indirect contribution made to the acquisition of such marital property by the party not having title, including joint efforts or expenditures and contributions and services as a spouse, parent, wage earner and homemaker, and *to the career or career potential* of the other party [and] . . . (9) the impossibility or difficulty of evaluating any component asset or any interest in a business, corporation or profession" (Domestic Relations Law §236(B)(5)(d)(6), (9) (emphasis added)). Where equitable distribution of marital property is appropriate but "the distribution of an interest in a business, corporation or *profession* would be contrary to law" the court shall make a distributive award in lieu of an actual distribution of the property (Domestic Relations Law §236(B)(5)(e) (emphasis added)). The words mean exactly what they say: that an interest in a profession or professional career potential is marital property which may be represented by direct or indirect contributions of the non-title-holding spouse, including financial contributions and nonfinancial contributions made by caring for the home and family.

The history which preceded enactment of the statute confirms this interpretation. Reform of section 236 was advocated because experience had proven that application of the traditional common-law title theory of property had caused inequities upon dissolution of a marriage. The Legislature replaced the existing system with equitable distribution of marital property, an entirely new theory which considered all the circumstances of the case and of the respective parties to the marriage. Equitable distribution was based on the premise that a marriage is, among other things, an economic partnership to which both parties contribute as spouse, parent, wage earner or homemaker. Consistent with this purpose, and implicit in the statutory scheme as a whole, is the view that upon dissolution of the marriage there should be a winding up of the parties' economic affairs and a severance of their economic ties by an equitable distribution of the marital assets. Thus, the concept of alimony, which often served as a means of lifetime support and dependence for one spouse upon the other long after the marriage was over, was replaced with the concept of maintenance which seeks to allow "the recipient spouse an opportunity to achieve [economic] independence."

The determination that a professional license is marital property is also consistent with the conceptual base upon which the statute rests. As this case demonstrates, few undertakings during a marriage better qualify as the type of joint effort that the statute's economic partnership theory is intended to address than contributions toward one spouse's acquisition of a professional license. Working spouses are often required to contribute substantial income as wage earners, sacrifice their own educational or career goals and opportunities for child rearing, perform the bulk of household duties and responsibilities and forego the acquisition of marital assets that could have been accumulated if the professional spouse had been employed rather than occupied with the study and training necessary to acquire a professional license. In this case, nearly all of the parties' nine-year marriage was devoted to the acquisition of plaintiff's medical license and defendant played a major role in that project. She worked continuously during the marriage and contributed all of her earnings to their joint effort, she sacrificed her own educational and career opportunities, and she traveled with plaintiff to Mexico for three and one-half years while he attended medical school there. The Legislature has decided, by its explicit reference in the statute to the contributions of one spouse to the other's profession or career (see Domestic Relations Law §236(B)(5)(d)(6), (9); (e)), that these contributions represent investments in the economic partnership of the marriage and that the product of the parties' joint efforts, the professional license, should be considered marital property. . . .

Plaintiff's principal argument . . . is that a professional license is not marital property because it does not fit within the traditional view of property as something which has an exchange value on the open market and is capable of sale, assignment or transfer. The position does not withstand analysis for at least two reasons. First, as we have observed, it ignores the fact that whether a professional license constitutes marital property is to be judged by the language of the statute which created this new species of property previously unknown at common law or under prior statutes. Thus, whether the license fits within traditional property concepts is of no consequence. Second, it is an overstatement to assert that a professional license could not be considered property even outside the context of section 236(B). A professional license is a valuable property right, reflected in the money, effort and lost opportunity for employment expended in its acquisition, and also in the enhanced earning capacity it affords its holder, which may not be revoked without due process of law. That a professional license has no market value is irrelevant. Obviously, a license may not be alienated as may other property and for that reason the working spouse's interest in it is limited. The Legislature has recognized that limitation, however, and has provided for an award in lieu of its actual distribution (see Domestic Relations Law §236(B)(5)(e)).

Plaintiff also contends that alternative remedies should be employed, such as an award of rehabilitative maintenance or reimbursement for direct financial contributions. The statute does not expressly authorize retrospective maintenance or rehabilitative awards and we have no occasion to decide in this case whether the authority to do so may ever be implied from its provisions. It is sufficient to observe that normally a working spouse should not be restricted to that relief because to do so frustrates the purposes underlying the Equitable Distribution Law. Limiting a working spouse to a maintenance award, either general or rehabilitative, not only is contrary to the economic partnership concept underlying the statute but also retains the uncertain and inequitable economic ties of dependence that the Legislature sought to extinguish by equitable distribution. Maintenance is subject to termination upon the recipient's remarriage and a working spouse may never receive adequate consideration for his or her contribution and may even be penalized for the decision to remarry if that is the only method of compensating the contribution. As one court said so well, "[t]he function of equitable distribution is to recognize that when a marriage ends, each of the spouses, based on the totality of the contributions made to it, has a stake in and right to a share of the marital assets accumulated while it endured, not because that share is needed, but because those assets represent the capital product of what was essentially a partnership entity" (*Wood v. Wood*, 465 N.Y.S.2d 475 (Sup. Ct. 1983)). The Legislature stated its intention to eliminate such inequities by providing that a supporting spouse's "direct or indirect contribution" be recognized, considered and rewarded (Domestic Relations Law §236(B)(5)(d)(6)).

Turning to the question of valuation, it has been suggested that even if a professional license is considered marital property, the working spouse is entitled only to reimbursement of his or her direct financial contributions.

By parity of reasoning, a spouse's down payment on real estate or contribution to the purchase of securities would be limited to the money contributed, without any remuneration for any incremental value in the asset because of price appreciation. Such a result is completely at odds with the statute's requirement that the court give full consideration to both direct and indirect contributions "made to the acquisition of such marital property by the party not having title, including joint *efforts* or expenditures and *contributions and services as a spouse, parent*, wage earner and *homemaker*" (Domestic Relations Law §236(B)(5)(d)(6) (emphasis added)). If the license is marital property, then the working spouse is entitled to an equitable portion of it, not a return of funds advanced. Its value is the enhanced earning capacity it affords the holder and although fixing the present value of that enhanced earning capacity may present problems, the problems are not insurmountable. Certainly they are no more difficult than computing tort damages for wrongful death or diminished earning capacity resulting from injury and they differ only in degree from the problems presented when valuing a professional practice for purposes of a distributive award, something the courts have not hesitated to do. The trial court retains the flexibility and discretion to structure the distributive award equitably, taking into consideration factors such as the working spouse's need for immediate payment, the licensed spouse's current ability to pay and the income tax consequences of prolonging the period of payment and, once it has received evidence of the present value of the license and the working spouse's contributions toward its acquisition and considered the remaining factors mandated by the statute, it may then make an appropriate distribution of the marital property including a distributive award for the professional license if such an award is warranted. When other marital assets are of sufficient value to provide for the supporting spouse's equitable portion of the marital property, including his or her contributions to the acquisition of the professional license, however, the court retains the discretion to distribute these other marital assets or to make a distributive award in lieu of an actual distribution of the value of the professional spouse's license....

BERNARD S. MEYER, Judge (concurring).

I concur in Judge Simons' opinion but write separately to point up for consideration by the Legislature the potential for unfairness involved in distributive awards based upon a license of a professional still in training.

An equity court normally has power to "'change its decrees where there has been a change of circumstances.'" The implication of Domestic Relations Law §236(B)(9)(b), which deals with modification of an order or decree as to maintenance or child support, is, however, that a distributive award pursuant to section 236(B)(5)(e), once made, is not subject to change. Yet a professional in training who is not finally committed to a career choice when the distributive award is made may be locked into a particular kind of practice simply because the monetary obligations imposed by the distributive award made on the basis of the trial judge's conclusion (prophecy may be a better word) as to what the career choice will be leaves him or her no alternative.

The present case points up the problem. A medical license is but a step toward the practice ultimately engaged in by its holder, which follows after internship, residency and, for particular specialties, board certification. Here it is undisputed that plaintiff was in a residency for general surgery at the time of the trial, but had the previous year done a residency in internal medicine. Defendant's expert based his opinion on the difference between the average income of a general surgeon and that of a college graduate of plaintiff's age and life expectancy, which the trial judge utilized, impliedly finding that plaintiff would engage in a surgical practice despite plaintiff's testimony that he was dissatisfied with the general surgery program he was in and was attempting to return to the internal medicine training he had been in the previous year. The trial judge had the right, of course, to discredit that testimony, but the point is that equitable distribution was not intended to permit a judge to make a career decision for a licensed spouse still in training. Yet the degree of speculation involved in the award made is emphasized by the testimony of the expert on which it was based. Asked whether his assumptions and calculations were in any way speculative, he replied: "Yes. They're speculative to the extent of, will Dr. O'Brien practice medicine? Will Dr. O'Brien earn more or less than the average surgeon earns? Will Dr. O'Brien live to age sixty-five? Will Dr. O'Brien have a heart attack or will he be injured in an automobile accident? Will he be disabled? I mean, there is a degree of speculation. That speculative aspect is no more to be taken into account, cannot be taken into account, and it's a question, again, Mr. Emanuelli, not for the expert but for the courts to decide. It's not my function nor could it be."

The equitable distribution provisions of the Domestic Relations Law were intended to provide flexibility so that equity could be done. But if the assumption as to career choice on which a distributive award payable over a number of years is based turns out not to be the fact (as, for example, should a general surgery trainee accidentally lose the use of his hand), it should be possible for the court to revise the distributive award to conform to the fact. And there will be no unfairness in so doing if either spouse can seek reconsideration, for the licensed spouse is more likely to seek reconsideration based on real, rather than imagined, cause if he or she knows that the nonlicensed spouse can seek not only reinstatement of the original award, but counsel fees in addition, should the purported circumstance on which a change is made turn out to have been feigned or to be illusory.

NOTES AND QUESTIONS

1. *"Property" divisible on divorce.* Almost all states reject New York's approach and hold that graduate degrees are *not* "property" whose value is divisible on divorce

under statutes providing for equitable distribution of "property" acquired during the marriage. Nonetheless, the *O'Brien* ruling has been repeatedly reaffirmed. *See Holterman v. Holterman*, 814 N.E.2d 765 (N.Y. 2004); *McSparron v. McSparron*, 662 N.E.2d 745 (N.Y. 1995). *See also Elkus v. Elkus*, 572 N.Y.S.2d 901 (App. Div. 1991) (holding that the value of the career and celebrity status of opera singer Frederica von Stade Elkus constituted property divisible on divorce to the extent her spouse contributed to and increased the value of her career). *Accord, Haugan v. Haugan*, 343 N.W.2d 796 (Wis. 1984). In *Mahoney v. Mahoney*, 453 A.2d 527 (N.J. 1982), the court rejected the idea that graduate degrees constitute property, on the grounds that (a) professional degrees do not resemble traditional property interests because they are not exchangeable or inheritable and, indeed, cannot be transferred in any way; (b) they are the cumulative product of many years of hard work and cannot be acquired by mere expenditure of money; (c) their value cannot be readily determined because "valuing a professional degree in the hands of any particular individual at the start of his or her career would involve a gamut of calculations that reduces to little more than guesswork," including what jobs the holder will have, what specialties she will practice, the location of practice, the length of interruptions in the career; and (d) because, unlike alimony, awards of property are final and unmodifiable, and courts therefore have no power to correct a mistake in the valuation of the license, no matter how gross the mistake. Justice Morris Pashman further argued that "[m]arriage is not a business arrangement in which the parties keep track of debits and credits, their accounts to be settled on divorce." *Id.* at 533. *See also Hoak v. Hoak*, 370 S.E.2d 473 (W. Va. 1988) (adopting this approach).

How does the New York Court of Appeals respond to these arguments? Note that it is generally accepted that the value of an interest in an ongoing medical practice or law partnership is "property" divisible on divorce. *Mace v. Mace*, 818 So. 2d 1130 (Miss. 2002).

2. *Reimbursement, rehabilitation, and distribution of enhanced earning potential.* Divorce cases involving graduate degrees raise several issues. First, does the supporting spouse have a right to be *reimbursed* for the payments made to support the degree-earning spouse or for the supporting spouse's opportunity costs (the earnings forgone by having to support the degree-earning spouse) or both? This remedy suggests a theory of restitution of benefits conferred on the degree-earning spouse. Although holding that graduate degrees are not property whose present value is divisible on divorce, the New Jersey Supreme Court did allow the trial court to order the degree-earning spouse to reimburse the supporting spouse for the financial contributions she made to her spouse's professional training. *Mahoney*, 453 A.2d at 534-535.

Second, should the supporting spouse be entitled to some form of *rehabilitation* payments enabling her to earn a similar degree or earning capacity? *See id.* at 535.

Third, should the supporting spouse share in the *future enhanced earning potential* of the spouse who earned the graduate degree? If so, how should that amount be measured? Should it be paid out immediately or over time, and, if over time, for how long? Should such an award be modifiable if changing circumstances make earlier predictions about the market value of the degree inaccurate?

In *Haugan v. Haugan*, 343 N.W.2d 796, 802-803 (Wis. 1984), Justice Shirley Abrahamson outlined a variety of approaches in answering these questions.

> One approach the trial court may consider is the cost value approach whereby it calculates the value of the supporting spouse's contributions, not only in terms of money

for education and living expenses but also in terms of services rendered during the marriage. In this case, for example, the wife worked full time outside the home and also performed the household duties, and the fair market value of those homemaking services might be considered along with her financial input. Furthermore, the trial court should consider adjusting the value of the supporting spouse's contributions by a fair rate of return or for inflation. Such an award is restitutionary in nature; it does not account for a return on the supporting spouse's investment in terms of a share in the future enhanced earnings of the student spouse. . . .

. . . In *DeLa Rosa* [*v. DeLa Rosa*, 309 N.W.2d 755, 759 (Minn. 1981)], the Minnesota court developed the following formula for awarding such compensation to the working wife:

> We subtract from . . . [the working spouse's] . . . earnings her own living expenses. This has the effect of imputing one-half of the living expenses and all the educational expenses to the student spouse. The formula subtracts from . . . [the working spouse's] . . . contributions one-half of the couple's living expenses, that amount being the contributions of the two parties which were not used for direct educational costs;
>
>> working spouse's financial contributions to joint living expenses and educational costs of student spouse
>> *less*
>> 1/2 (working spouse's financial contributions plus student spouse's financial contributions less cost of education)
>> *equals*
>> equitable award to working spouse. *DeLa Rosa, supra*, 309 N.W.2d at 759. . . .

A second approach is looking at opportunity costs. The trial court may in determining the award to the supporting spouse consider the income the family sacrificed because the student spouse attended school rather than accepting employment. In this case the wife introduced evidence that the husband's increased earnings during the seven-year marriage had he not pursued medical education and training would have been $45,700 after taxes, or $69,800 indexed for inflation.

A third approach enables the trial court to consider compensating the supporting spouse according to the present value of the student spouse's enhanced earning capacity. This approach recognizes the spouse's lost expectation of sharing in the enhanced earning capacity; it gives the supporting spouse a return on his or her "investment" in the student spouse measured by the student spouse's enhanced earning capacity. In this case an economist, called as a witness by the wife, estimated the value of the husband's enhanced earning capacity to be $266,000. The economist's figure was the product of multiplying the husband's after-tax annual enhanced earnings of $13,000 (the difference between the husband's annual salary as a physician and the 1979 mean salary for white college-educated males in his age group) by 32.3 (estimated years remaining in the husband's expected working life) discounted to its present value. Using this calculation the wife asserts she would be entitled to one half of the present value of the husband's enhanced earning capacity, or $133,000.

Because many unforeseen events may affect future earnings, this third approach has been subject to criticism. Calculations of the expected stream of income may not take into account such variables as market opportunities, individual career choices and abilities, and premature death. Other approaches are, however, subject to criticism for giving the student spouse a windfall and for failing to recognize the supporting spouse's lost expectations.

Another approach is a variation of the labor theory of value suggested by wife's counsel at oral argument. Under this approach the trial court considers the value of the supporting spouse's contribution to the marriage at one half of the student spouse's enhanced yearly earning power for as many years as the supporting spouse worked to support the student. Under this theory the wife's contribution might be valued at $45,500 (one half of $13,000 × 7), which perhaps should be discounted to present value.

As stated before, no mathematical formula or theory of valuation settles the case. Each case must be decided on its own facts. The guiding principles for the trial court are fairness and justice. . . .

Which is the best approach, and why?

3. *Modifiability of the property award.* Suppose the defendant in *O'Brien* takes a position in a clinic in which his earnings are substantially lower than estimated by the experts at trial. He petitions the court to modify the amount of the award based on his new, lower salary. The statute in question appears to allow modifications in alimony but not in property awards. Is there any way to characterize the ex-wife's property interest in the degree to allow the court to modify the award?

PROBLEM

California has addressed this problem by statute, creating a presumption that reimbursement is appropriate for contributions to a spouse's education that substantially enhance his earning potential. However, this award will be reduced or eliminated if the couple has already substantially benefited from the education (with a presumption that this has occurred after ten years of marriage), if the supporting spouse was similarly supported in receiving education, or the education enables the supported spouse to obtain employment that reduces support to which the supported spouse would otherwise be entitled. Cal. Fam. Code §2641. At the same time, the statute provides that contribution to education that increases a spouse's earning potential is a factor to be considered in determining whether alimony should be awarded. In determining whether one party will be required to provide support for the other, the courts are to consider a variety of additional factors, including the extent to which the earning capacity of each party is sufficient to maintain the standard of living established during the marriage, the length of the marriage, the needs of the parties, and the ability of each to support themselves and the other party. Cal. Fam. Code §§4320, 4330. The statutory language suggests that support is more likely to be awarded when the supported spouse is not able to use his or her own earning power in the marketplace to obtain the standard of living established during the marriage. *Cf. Schaefer v. Schaefer*, 642 N.W.2d 792 (Neb. 2002)(graduate degree is not property divisible on divorce but the fact that one spouse attained a degree with the aid of the other is a factor to be considered in dividing other marital assets as well as in determining whether to award alimony).

Assume a bill is introduced in the New York legislature to overrule the result in *O'Brien* and adopt the California approach, providing for reimbursement but not for distribution of enhanced earning potential and allowing contributions to a spouse's education to play a role in determining whether alimony should be paid. Would you favor passage of the bill?

§7.5.3.2   Rights in the Family Home

See supra §1.4.2, at pages 69-75.

§7.6   *Unmarried Partners*

§7.6.1   MALE-FEMALE COUPLES

WATTS v. WATTS
_____

405 N.W.2d 303 (Wis. 1987)

SHIRLEY S. ABRAHAMSON, Justice . . . .

The case involves a dispute between Sue Ann Evans Watts, the plaintiff, and James Watts, the defendant, over their respective interests in property accumulated during their nonmarital cohabitation relationship which spanned 12 years and produced two children. . . .

. . . The plaintiff and the defendant met in 1967, when she was 19 years old, was living with her parents and was working full time as a nurse's aide in preparation for a nursing career. Shortly after the parties met, the defendant persuaded the plaintiff to move into an apartment paid for by him and to quit her job. According to the amended complaint, the defendant "indicated" to the plaintiff that he would provide for her.

Early in 1969, the parties began living together in a "marriage-like" relationship, holding themselves out to the public as husband and wife. The plaintiff assumed the defendant's surname as her own. Subsequently, she gave birth to two children who were also given the defendant's surname. The parties filed joint income tax returns and maintained joint bank accounts asserting that they were husband and wife. The defendant insured the plaintiff as his wife on his medical insurance policy. He also took out a life insurance policy on her as his wife, naming himself as the beneficiary. The parties purchased real and personal property as husband and wife. The plaintiff executed documents and obligated herself on promissory notes to lending institutions as the defendant's wife.

During their relationship, the plaintiff contributed childcare and homemaking services, including cleaning, cooking, laundering, shopping, running errands, and maintaining the grounds surrounding the parties' home. Additionally, the plaintiff contributed personal property to the relationship which she owned at the beginning of the relationship or acquired through gifts or purchases during the relationship. She served as hostess for the defendant for social and business-related events. [P]eriodically, between 1969 and 1975, the plaintiff cooked and cleaned for the defendant and his employees while his business, a landscaping service, was building and landscaping a golf course.

From 1973 to 1976, the plaintiff worked 20-25 hours per week at the defendant's office, performing duties as a receptionist, typist, and assistant bookkeeper. From 1976 to 1981, the plaintiff worked 40-60 hours per week at a business she started with the defendant's sister-in-law, then continued and managed the business herself after the dissolution of that partnership. The plaintiff further alleges that in 1981 the defendant made their relationship so intolerable that she was forced to move from their home and their relationship was irretrievably broken. Subsequently, the defendant barred the plaintiff from returning to her business.

The plaintiff alleges that during the parties' relationship, and because of her domestic and business contributions, the business and personal wealth of the couple increased. Furthermore, the plaintiff alleges that she never received any compensation for these contributions to the relationship and that the defendant indicated to the plaintiff both orally and through his conduct that he considered her to be his wife and that she would share equally in the increased wealth.

The plaintiff asserts that since the breakdown of the relationship the defendant has refused to share equally with her the wealth accumulated through their joint efforts or to compensate her in any way for her contributions to the relationship. . . .

IV

[Plaintiff claims] that she and the defendant had a contract to share equally the property accumulated during their relationship. The essence of the complaint is that the parties had a contract, either an express or implied in fact contract, which the defendant breached.

Wisconsin courts have long recognized the importance of freedom of contract and have endeavored to protect the right to contract. A contract will not be enforced, however, if it violates public policy. . . .

[Defendant suggests that] any contract between the parties regarding property division contravenes public policy because the contract is based on immoral or illegal sexual activity. . . .

Courts have generally refused to enforce contracts for which the sole consideration is sexual relations, sometimes referred to as "meretricious" relationships. Courts distinguish, however, between contracts that are explicitly and inseparably founded on sexual services and those that are not. This court, and numerous other courts, have concluded that "a bargain between two people is not illegal merely because there is an illicit relationship between the two so long as the bargain is independent of the illicit relationship and the illicit relationship does not constitute any part of the consideration bargained for and is not a condition of the bargain." *In Matter of Estate of Steffes*, 290 N.W.2d 697, 709 (1980).

While not condoning the illicit sexual relationship of the parties, many courts have recognized that the result of a court's refusal to enforce contract and property rights between unmarried cohabitants is that one party keeps all or most of the assets accumulated during the relationship, while the other party, no more or less "guilty," is deprived of property which he or she has helped to accumulate.

[C]ourts recognize that their refusal to enforce what are in other contexts clearly lawful promises will not undo the parties' relationship and may not discourage others from entering into such relationships. A harsh, per se rule that the contract and property rights of unmarried cohabiting parties will not be recognized might actually encourage a partner with greater income potential to avoid marriage in order to retain all accumulated assets, leaving the other party with nothing. . . .

The plaintiff has alleged that she quit her job and abandoned her career training upon the defendant's promise to take care of her. A change in one party's circumstances in performance of the agreement may imply an agreement between the parties.

In addition, the plaintiff alleges that she performed housekeeping, childbearing, childrearing, and other services related to the maintenance of the parties' home, in addition to various services for the defendant's business and her own business, for which she received no compensation. Courts have recognized that money, property, or services (including housekeeping or childrearing) may constitute adequate consideration independent of the parties' sexual relationship to support an agreement to share or transfer property.

According to the plaintiff's complaint, the parties cohabited for more than twelve years, held joint bank accounts, made joint purchases, filed joint income tax returns, and were listed as husband and wife on other legal documents. Courts have held that such a relationship and "joint acts of a financial nature can give rise to an inference that the parties intended to share equally." *Beal v. Beal*, 577 P.2d 507, 510 (Or. 1978). The joint ownership of property and the filing of joint income tax returns strongly implies that the parties intended their relationship to be in the nature of a joint enterprise, financially as well as personally.

. . . We . . . conclude that public policy does not necessarily preclude an unmarried cohabitant from asserting a contract claim against the other party to the cohabitation so long as the claim exists independently of the sexual relationship and is supported by separate consideration. Accordingly, we conclude that the plaintiff in this case has pleaded the facts necessary to state a claim for damages resulting from the defendant's breach of an express or an implied in fact contract to share with the plaintiff the property accumulated through the efforts of both parties during their relationship. [W]e do not judge the merits of the plaintiff's claim; we merely hold that she be given her day in court to prove her claim.

V

The plaintiff's [next] theory of recovery involves unjust enrichment. Essentially, she alleges that the defendant accepted and retained the benefit of services she provided knowing that she expected to share equally in the wealth accumulated during their relationship. She argues that it is unfair for the defendant to retain all the assets they accumulated under these circumstances and that a constructive trust should be imposed on the property as a result of the defendant's unjust enrichment. . . .

Unlike claims for breach of an express or implied in fact contract, a claim of unjust enrichment does not arise out of an agreement entered into by the parties. Rather, an action for recovery based upon unjust enrichment is grounded on the moral principle that one who has received a benefit has a duty to make restitution where retaining such a benefit would be unjust.

Because no express or implied in fact agreement exists between the parties, recovery based upon unjust enrichment is sometimes referred to as "quasi contract," or contract "implied in law" rather than "implied in fact." Quasi contracts are obligations created by law to prevent injustice.

In Wisconsin, an action for unjust enrichment, or quasi contract, is based upon proof of three elements: (1) a benefit conferred on the defendant by the plaintiff, (2) appreciation or knowledge by the defendant of the benefit, and (3) acceptance or retention of the benefit by the defendant under circumstances making it inequitable for the defendant to retain the benefit. . . .

As part of his general argument, the defendant claims that the court should leave the parties to an illicit relationship such as the one in this case essentially as they are found, providing no relief at all to either party. . . .

As we have discussed previously, allowing no relief at all to one party in a so-called "illicit" relationship effectively provides total relief to the other, by leaving that party owner of all the assets acquired through the efforts of both. Yet it cannot seriously be argued that the party retaining all the assets is less "guilty" than the other. Such a result is contrary to the principles of equity. Many courts have held, and we now so hold, that unmarried cohabitants may raise claims based upon unjust enrichment following the termination of their relationships where one of the parties attempts to retain an unreasonable amount of the property acquired through the efforts of both.

In this case, the plaintiff alleges that she contributed both property and services to the parties' relationship. She claims that because of these contributions the parties' assets increased, but that she was never compensated for her contributions. She further alleges that the defendant, knowing that the plaintiff expected to share in the property accumulated, "accepted the services rendered to him by the plaintiff" and that it would be unfair under the circumstances to allow him to retain everything while she receives nothing. We conclude that the facts alleged are sufficient to state a claim for recovery based upon unjust enrichment.

As part of the plaintiff's unjust enrichment claim, she has asked that a constructive trust be imposed on the assets that the defendant acquired during their relationship. A constructive trust is an equitable device created by law to prevent unjust enrichment. To state a claim on the theory of constructive trust the complaint must state facts sufficient to show (1) unjust enrichment and (2) abuse of a confidential relationship or some other form of unconscionable conduct. The latter element can be inferred from allegations in the complaint which show, for example, a family relationship, a close personal relationship, or the parties' mutual trust. These facts are alleged in this complaint or may be inferred. Therefore, we hold that if the plaintiff can prove the elements of unjust enrichment to the satisfaction of the circuit court, she will be entitled to demonstrate further that a constructive trust should be imposed as a remedy.

VI

The plaintiff's last alternative legal theory on which her claim rests is the doctrine of partition. The plaintiff has asserted in her complaint a claim for partition of "all real and personal property accumulated by the couple during their relationship according to the plaintiff's interest therein and pursuant to Chapters 820 and 842, Wis. Stats."

In Wisconsin partition is a remedy under both the statutes and common law. Partition applies generally to all disputes over property held by more than one party. . . .

In this case, the plaintiff has alleged that she and the defendant were engaged in a joint venture or partnership, that they purchased real and personal property as husband and wife, and that they intended to share all the property acquired during their relationship. In our opinion, these allegations, together with other facts alleged in the plaintiff's complaint (*e.g.*, the plaintiff's contributions to the acquisition of their property) and reasonable inferences therefrom, are sufficient . . . to state a claim for an accounting of the property acquired during the parties' relationship and partition. We do not, of course, presume to judge the merits of the plaintiff's claim. Proof of her allegations must be made to the circuit court. We merely hold that the plaintiff has alleged sufficient facts in her complaint to state a claim for relief [for] statutory or common law partition.

AN ESSAY IN THE DECONSTRUCTION OF CONTRACT
DOCTRINE
CLARE DALTON

94 Yale L.J. 997, 1098-1101, 1104-1113 (1985)

... In [cohabitation] cases, ... there is a common presumption that agreements between intimates are not contractual. [E]xpress words are taken to be words of commitment but not of contract; conduct that in other circumstances would give rise to an implied-in-fact contract is instead attributed to the relationship. These cases also ... find no unjust enrichment where one party benefits the other.

One possible explanation for this presumption against finding contracts is that it accords with the parties' intentions. It can be argued that cohabitants generally neither want their agreements to have legal consequences, nor desire to be obligated to one another when they have stopped cohabiting. It can further be presented as a matter of fact that their services are freely given and taken within the context of an intimate relationship. If this is so, then a subsequent claim of unjust enrichment is simply unfounded.

This intention-based explanation, however, coexists in the opinions — indeed sometimes coexists within a single opinion — with two other, more overtly public, explanations that rest on diametrically opposed public policies. The first suggests that the arena of intimate relationships is too private for court intervention through contract enforcement to be appropriate. ...

While it has some intuitive appeal, the argument that intimate relationships are too private for court enforcement is at odds with the more general argument that all contractual relationships are private and that contract enforcement merely facilitates the private relationships described by contract. To overcome this apparent inconsistency, we must imagine a scale of privateness on which business arrangements, while mostly private, are still not as private as intimate arrangements. But then the rescue attempt runs headlong into the other prevailing policy argument, which separates out intimate arrangements because of their peculiarly public and regulated status. Under this view, it is the business relationship that by and large remains more quintessentially private.

According to this second argument, the area of non-marital agreements is too public for judicial intervention. The legislature is the appropriate body to regulate such arrangements; courts may not help create private alternatives to the public scheme. In *Hewitt* [*v. Hewitt*, 394 N.E.2d 1204 (Ill. 1979)], the supreme court directly follows its appeal to the intimate nature of the relationship with an acknowledgement of the regulated, and hence public, character of marriage-like relations. With respect to intimate relations conceived as public, the judiciary can then present itself as either passive or active. The argument for passivity is that judges should "stay out" of an arena already covered by public law. The argument for activity is that judges should reinforce public policy by deterring the formation of deviant relationships, either because they fall outside the legislative schemes organizing familial entitlement and property distribution, or because they offend public morality. ...

Two interpretive issues ... recur in the cases. The courts repeatedly consider how to evaluate the relationships out of which the agreements arise. They also repeatedly consider how to evaluate the role of sex in these relationships and in these agreements. ...

Courts frequently invoke the context of cohabitation relationships to avoid enforcing agreements arising out of them. The argument here is essentially that even if such agreements use language of promise, or commitment, or reciprocal obligation, that language must be understood, in the intimate context in which it is employed, as not involving any understanding that one party might use a court to enforce a duty forsaken, or a promise broken. . . .

A second common theme employing notions of manifestation and intent is the specific role of sex in the parties' arrangement. The boundaries of this debate are set both by the tradition that precludes enforcement of prostitution contracts for reasons of public policy, and by the acknowledgement that even cohabiting parties may form valid contracts about independent matters. In the case of cohabitation agreements, the question therefore becomes whether the sex contemplated by the parties contaminates the entire agreement to the point where it is seen to fall within the model of the prostitution contract, or whether other features of the agreement can be seen as independent and enforceable. . . .

The first use of consideration doctrine in this context shows up in the disinclination of courts to enforce contracts based on "meretricious" consideration. Courts frequently search beyond the express language of the agreement in order to "find" that sex is at the heart of the deal — specifically that the woman is providing sexual services in return for the economic security promised by the man. . . .

The second aspect of consideration doctrine of interest in this context is the traditional conclusion that the woman's domestic services cannot provide consideration for the promises made to her by the man. This is usually linked to the idea that the relationship itself is not one the parties see as having a legal aspect. The standard explanation is that the woman did not act in expectation of gain, but rather out of affection, or that she intended her action as a gift.

[Justice] Tobriner in the *Marvin* decision [*Marvin v. Marvin*, 557 P.2d 106 (Cal. 1976)] rejects this conclusion by recasting the issue as one properly belonging in the selfish world of business. Unless homemaking services are considered lawful and adequate consideration for a promise to pay wages, the entire domestic service industry will founder. . . .

There are several ways to begin a richer examination of the cohabitation cases. . . .

. . . What is the nature of this relationship, or what range of cohabitation arrangements precludes us from making general statements about the nature of the relationship? To what extent do these relationships need protection from authority, and to what extent do they require nurturing by authority? To what extent do they reflect the shared expectations of their participants, and to what extent the imposition of terms by one party on another? How can we harbor intimacy within institutions that offer the flexibility to accommodate individual need, while at the same time providing a measure of predictability and stability? What stake does the society have in limiting the forms of association it will recognize? Given our dependence on our social and cultural context, what freedom does any of us have to reimagine the terms of human association? . . .

. . . The dimension of these cohabitation cases that cries out for investigation is the images they contain of women, and of relationship. . . .

One powerful pair of contradictory images of woman paints the female cohabitant as either an angel or a whore. As angel, she ministers to her male partner out of noble emotions of love and self-sacrifice, with no thought of personal gain. It would demean both her services and the spirit in which they were offered to imagine that she expected a return — it would make her a servant. As whore, she lures the man into extravagant promises with the bait of her sexuality — and is appropriately punished for her immorality when the court declines to hold her partner to his agreement.

Although the image of the whore is of a woman who at one level is seeking to satiate her own lust, sex — in these cases — is traditionally presented as something women give to men. This is consistent both with the view of woman as angel, and with the different image of the whore as someone who trades sex for money. In either event, woman is a provider, not a partner in enjoyment. When a judge invokes this image, he supports the view that sex contaminates the entire agreement, and that the desire for sex is the only reason for the male partner's promises of economic support. If sex were viewed as a mutually satisfying element of the arrangement, it could be readily separated out from the rest of the agreement. In most cases, the woman's career sacrifices and childrearing and homemaking responsibilities would then provide the consideration for the economic support proffered by the man.

Marriage is often presented in the cases as the only way in which men and women can express a continuing commitment to one another. This suggests that when men do not marry women, they intend to avoid all responsibility for them. Women therefore bear the burden of protecting themselves by declining the irregular relationship. At the same time, the institution of marriage as an expression of caring is portrayed as so fragile that only the most unwavering support by the state will guarantee its survival. This could mean that other expressions of caring would entirely supplant marriage without vigilant enforcement of the socially endorsed forms of relationship, although that would be inconsistent with the portrayal of marriage as the only expression of commitment. Alternatively, it could mean that men and women would not choose to enter relationships of caring without pressure from the state.

These nightmarish images have much in common with what other disciplines tell us men think about women and relationship. The conception of women as either angels or whores is identified by Freud, and supported by feminist accounts. The evil power of female sexuality is a recurrent subject of myth and history. The contrast of men fearing relationship as entrapping, and women fearing isolation, is the subject of Carol Gilligan's work in the psychology of moral development; others have explored the origins of that difference in the context of psychoanalytic theory. Raising these images to the level of consciousness and inquiry therefore seems to me an important aspect to understanding this particular set of cases. It is also a way of stepping beyond the confines of current doctrine and beginning to think about other ways of handling the reciprocal claims cohabitants may make of one another.

NOTES AND QUESTIONS

1. *Meretricious relationship, contract and partnership.* States have adopted three quite different approaches to the problem of property rights between unmarried cohabitants upon dissolution of the relationship. The first approach, illustrated by the much-cited case *Hewitt v. Hewitt*, 394 N.E.2d 1204 (Ill. 1979), denies any remedy on the ground that a relationship between unmarried cohabitants is precluded by state statutes prohibiting common law marriage and abolishing claims for breach of promise to marry. The Illinois Supreme Court reasoned, *Id.* at 1207-1208:

The issue of unmarried cohabitants' mutual property rights . . . cannot appropriately be characterized solely in terms of contract law, nor is it limited to considerations of equity or fairness as between the parties to such relationships. There are major public policy questions involved in determining whether, under what circumstances, and to what extent it is desirable to accord some type of legal status to claims arising from such relationships. Of substantially greater importance than the rights of the immediate parties is the impact of such recognition upon our society and the institution of marriage. Will the fact that legal rights closely resembling those arising from conventional marriages can be acquired by those who deliberately choose to enter into what have heretofore been commonly referred to as "illicit" or "meretricious" relationships encourage formation of such relationships and weaken marriage as the foundation of our family-based society? In the event of death shall the survivor have the status of a surviving spouse for purposes of inheritance, wrongful death actions, workmen's compensation, etc.? And still more importantly: what of the children born of such relationships? What are their support and inheritance rights and by what standards are custody questions resolved? What of the sociological and psychological effects upon them of that type of environment? Does not the recognition of legally enforceable property and custody rights emanating from nonmarital cohabitation in practical effect equate with the legalization of common law marriage . . . ?

Similarly, in *Carnes v. Sheldon*, 311 N.W.2d 747 (Mich. Ct. App. 1981), Judge Dorothy Comstock Riley (now Chief Justice of the Michigan Supreme Court) further suggested that it should be presumed that household services are rendered gratuitously without expectation of a salary or other remuneration. She noted that "contracts made in consideration of meretricious relationships" are unenforceable, alluding to state laws criminalizing prostitution or payment for sexual services. After quoting the above passage from *Hewitt*, she concluded, "We are of the opinion that public policy questions of such magnitude are best left to the legislative process, which is better equipped to resolve the questions which inevitably will arise as unmarried cohabitation becomes an established feature of our society." *Id.* at 753.

The second approach, illustrated by the leading case of *Marvin v. Marvin*, 557 P.2d 106 (Cal. 1976), allows enforcement of a written or oral agreement between the parties to provide support in exchange for services. In these cases, a central question is how explicit the agreement needs to be and whether an agreement can be inferred from the conduct of the parties. *Marvin* held that in the absence of an express agreement, courts should attempt to determine whether the parties' conduct provides evidence of an agreement to pool their earnings and to hold all property acquired during their relationship as community property or to share resources otherwise. *Id.* at 122. Justice Matthew Tobriner noted that contracts between nonmarital partners should be enforced unless they are "expressly and inseparably based upon an illicit consideration of sexual services." *Id.* at 114. Finally, the court held that equitable remedies could also be employed, including constructive trust doctrine and restitution of the reasonable value of services rendered (*quantum meruit*). *Id.* at 122-123. *Accord, Carroll v. Lee*, 712 P.2d 923 (Ariz. 1986) (providing for partition of a house occupied by an unmarried couple when the couple split up).

The New York Court of Appeals rejected this approach in *Morone v. Morone*, 413 N.E.2d 1154 (N.Y. 1980). Like the California Supreme Court, the New York Court of Appeals would enforce an explicit oral agreement to share resources, but it would *not* allow an agreement to be implied from the conduct of the parties. Justice Bernard Meyer explained, *Id.* at 1157:

The major difficulty with implying a contract from the rendition of services for one another by persons living together is that it is not reasonable to infer an agreement to pay for the services rendered when the relationship of the parties makes it natural that the services were rendered gratuitously. As a matter of human experience personal services will frequently be rendered by two people living together because they value each other's company or because they find it a convenient or rewarding thing to do. For courts to attempt through hindsight to sort out the intentions of the parties and affix jural significance to conduct carried out within an essentially private and generally noncontractual relationship runs too great a risk of error. Absent an express agreement, there is no frame of reference against which to compare the testimony presented and the character of the evidence that can be presented becomes more evanescent. There is, therefore, substantially greater risk of emotion-laden afterthought, not to mention fraud, in attempting to ascertain by implication what services, if any, were rendered gratuitously and what compensation, if any, the parties intended to be paid. Some states require such contracts to be in writing to be enforceable. Minn. Stat. §513.075; Tex. Fam. Code §1.108.

The third approach provides for property distribution even though the parties were not legally married and did not enter any explicit agreement pertaining to support or property rights. Courts may adopt this approach based on the finding of an implicit agreement or by imposing a constructive trust to avoid unjust enrichment. *Pickens v. Pickens*, 490 So. 2d 872 (Miss. 1986); *Connell v. Francisco*, 898 P.2d 831 (Wash. 1995); *In re Marriage of Lindsey*, 678 P.2d 328 (Wash. 1984). In *Pickens*, the Mississippi Supreme Court found that the parties had created a relationship akin to a *partnership*. "Where parties such as these live together in what must at least be acknowledged to be a partnership and where, through their joint efforts, real property or personal property, or both, are accumulated, an equitable division of such property will be ordered upon the permanent breakup and separation." 490 So. 2d at 875-876. This approach rests on the assumption that the parties relied on each other and that both contributed to their ongoing relationship. Recovery is allowed based on the nature of the relationship rather than on a real or fictitious contract between the parties. Instead of finding a contract implied in fact from the conduct of the parties evidencing their actual intent to agree, the court imposed an agreement implied in law, which is binding on the parties regardless of their assent. This approach was recently proposed by the American Law Institute in the *ALI Principles of the Law of Family Dissolution* §§6.01–6.06, adopted in 2002. Some scholars have both defended this approach as protective of the justified expectations of the parties to the relationship (*see* Nancy D. Polikoff, *Making Marriage Matter Less: The ALI Domestic Partner Principles Are One Step in the Right Direction*, 2004 U. Chi. Legal F. 353), while others have criticized it for imposing obligations on individuals who did not voluntarily assume them and who may have deliberately chosen to eschew such obligations (*see* Marsha Garrison, *Is Consent Necessary? An Evaluation of the Emerging Law of Cohabitant Obligation*, 52 UCLA L. Rev. 815 (2005)).

While not calling it a partnership, the Wisconsin Supreme Court has similarly created a presumption that property acquired during a relationship is jointly owned and subject to a "just and equitable" distribution when the couple splits up. In *Connell*, the court applied the principles underlying the equitable distribution statute by analogy to an unmarried couple to obtain common law division of property when the couple broke up. The court distinguished such couples from married couples, however, by allowing division only of the property acquired during the relationship, not property acquired before the relationship began, as would be the case for married couples under the statute.

Which approach best promotes gender equality?

2. *Constructive trust.* In *Sullivan v. Rooney*, 533 N.E.2d 1372 (Mass. 1989), the court imposed a constructive trust on a house in which an unmarried couple with a long-term relationship had lived for several years.

> This case is another, in what appears likely to be an increasing number of cases, concerned with unraveling the property interests of two unmarried people who became disaffected after living together for a long time as if husband and wife. Here, we conclude that the defendant holds a one-half interest in residential premises in Reading in constructive trust for the plaintiff. We thus affirm the judgment entered in the Probate and Family Court directing the defendant to convey the premises to the plaintiff and himself as tenants in common.
>
> ... The parties had had a thirteen- or fourteen-year relationship, during seven of which they lived together and were engaged to be married at some indefinite future date. The plaintiff gave up her position as a flight attendant in order to maintain a home for the defendant. In 1977, while they were living in an apartment in Medford, they discussed buying a house, and, after some months of searching, they settled on purchasing the Reading home of the defendant's sister and her husband. Each thought of the transaction as a joint purchase of a home that would belong to both of them. On the way to the Registry of Deeds for the passing of papers, the defendant told the plaintiff that, in order to get 100% Veterans' Administration financing, he would have to take title in his name alone. The deed was so recorded.
>
> The parties lived together in the Reading house from January, 1978, to December, 1980, when the defendant, a career army officer who had been admitted to the bar of the Commonwealth, was transferred to Washington, D.C. While living in Reading, the defendant worked full-time during the day as an R.O.T.C. instructor and attended law school at night. He paid the mortgage obligations, taxes, utilities, and insurance on the house. The plaintiff, a waitress, put all her earnings and savings into the house, paying for the food and household supplies and for much of the furniture. She did all the housework, the decorating, and the entertaining of the defendant's colleagues. The defendant promised at various times to place the property in joint ownership, but he never did.
>
> In June, 1982, the plaintiff agreed, on the defendant's urging, to join the defendant in the Washington, D.C. area, where again she kept house while he paid their expenses. The defendant told the plaintiff that they should rent out the Reading house rather than sell it, so they would have a home to go back to in a few years and to which they could retire. After a year, the plaintiff, unhappy in Virginia, moved back to Massachusetts. The relationship deteriorated, and the two separated in late 1983. The plaintiff wished to move back into what she considered her home, the house in Reading, but the defendant told her she could not because it was rented.
>
> In 1984, the plaintiff brought this action to obtain title to the house as tenant in common with the defendant. The judge found that the defendant had promised to convey joint title at the time of the purchase, that he had reiterated that promise on several occasions up through early 1984 (when he told the plaintiff to send him a deed to sign), and that he admitted to having made these promises. The judge further found that, in reliance on these promises, the plaintiff was induced to stay in the relationship, to contribute her earnings and services, and to give up her home to move to Virginia. The judge also found that the plaintiff had made these contributions to her detriment, because she gave up her position as a flight attendant and lost career opportunities and job benefits. The judge ruled that the defendant would be unjustly enriched if he were allowed to keep sole title to the house. The judgment ordered the defendant to convey to the plaintiff a half-interest in the house. We transferred the defendant's appeal here. . . .

The plaintiff argues here that the defendant's oral promises to give her one-half the property are enforceable in the circumstances despite the defendant's reliance on the Statute of Frauds, and, alternatively, that the defendant holds one-half the property on a constructive trust in favor of the plaintiff.

We accept the plaintiff's argument that the evidence and the judge's findings demonstrate that the judgment should be upheld on the theory of a constructive trust.

The judge's unchallenged findings of fact demonstrate that there was a fiduciary relationship between the parties and that the defendant violated his fiduciary duty to the plaintiff. Equitable principles impose a constructive trust on property to avoid the unjust enrichment of a party who violates his fiduciary duty and acquires that property at the expense of the person to whom he owed that duty. Here the plaintiff was less educated (a high school graduate) and less experienced (she is a waitress) than the defendant (a career army officer attending law school at the time of the purchase of the house). She relied on him over a long period in important matters. That reliance was reasonable, and the defendant knew of and accepted the plaintiff's trust in him.

It would be unjust not to impose a constructive trust in this case. The plaintiff gave up her career as a flight attendant and undertook to maintain a home for the defendant while he advanced his career. She contributed her earnings and services to the home. The defendant's assurances to the plaintiff that they would own the property together (although title would be taken only in his name), his later promises to transfer title to joint ownership, and the plaintiff's reasonable reliance on those promises made by one in whom she reasonably placed special confidence call for the imposition of a constructive trust in the plaintiff's favor on one-half the Reading property.

Id. at 1373-1375. However, in *Collins v. Guggenheim*, 631 N.E.2d 1016 (Mass. 1994), the same court refused to impose a constructive trust on a farm jointly occupied and managed by an unmarried couple in the absence of "fraud, breach of fiduciary duty or other misconduct." The court did not cite its decision in *Sullivan.*

3. *Property rights on death.* The Mississippi Supreme Court has revisited the issue in *Pickens* in the context of the death of a long-time companion. In *Williams v. Mason*, 556 So. 2d 1045 (Miss. 1990), Roosevelt Adams promised Frances Mason in 1962 that if she would live in his home, take care of him, and "do his bidding," he would leave her all his property on his death. Mason lived with Adams for more than 20 years; when Adams died, he left a farm but, unfortunately, not a will or, indeed, any written memorandum of his promise to Mason. Adams never divorced his wife, who lived in Chicago, and he never promised to marry Mason. The court held that the promise to devise the property was unenforceable because it was not in writing, as required by the statute of frauds. Quoting Justice Oliver Wendell Holmes, the court explained:

> Holmes put the point well a century ago in *Bourke v. Callahan*, 35 N.E. 460 (Mass. 1893): We are aware that by our construction of Pub. Sts. C. 141, §1, the statute of frauds may be made an instrument of fraud. But this is always true, whenever the law prescribes a form for an obligation. The very meaning of such a requirement is that a man relies at his peril on what purports to be such an obligation without that form. . . .

Id. at 1048-1049. Although the court refused to enforce the promise, it created an equitable exception to the statute of frauds and allowed a limited remedy of restitution for the value of services rendered (*quantum meruit*), *id.* at 1049-1051:

> Notwithstanding these well settled principles, experience has taught that gross unfairness may result where one acts in good faith and lives up to an oral agreement

to provide services for another under circumstances such as today's. Our law has seen in such situations a potential for unjust enrichment, if not fraud. In recognition of these practical realities, the positive law of this state directs that a person, who provides services to another in good faith and in consequence of an oral agreement to devise property in exchange for the services, is not without enforceable rights. These rights arise not out of the agreement but the conduct of the parties. The promisee activates the rights the law affords by performing the services in good faith reliance on the promise.

When the parties have so acted with respect one to the other, that is, when one has provided services for the other in reasonable reliance upon a promise to give consideration therefor, our cases are legion that, upon the death of the promisor, the promisee may recover of and from the estate on a *quantum meruit* basis. In such cases the amount of recovery is limited to the monetary equivalent of the reasonable value of the services rendered to the decedent for which payment has not been received. Said sum becomes a charge against the assets of the estate.

Our law recognizes an additional basis upon which — assuming proper proof — a person such as Mason may recover. Where parties live together without benefit of marriage and where, through their joint efforts, [they] accumulate real property or personal property, or both, a party having no legal title nevertheless acquires rights to an equitable share enforceable at law. *Pickens v. Pickens*, 490 So. 2d 872, 875-876 (Miss. 1986)....

In so holding, we well realize that we hold enforceable rights predicated upon the conduct of the parties but unattended by any writing. Although neither the statute of frauds nor the statute of wills per se preclude *quantum meruit* recovery in such circumstances, we are not unaware that the policy considerations supporting the existence and enforcement of those statutes may be present nevertheless. Because the decedent is not available to provide his version of the matter, courts must view with a touch of skepticism claims for services rendered asserted only at death. We have in the past suggested that the party alleging such an agreement must prove its existence by [clear and convincing evidence].

We find that the Chancery Court was mindful of the heightened proof requirements as it proceeded to evaluate the evidence before it....

4. *Review of agreements for fairness.* When married couples seek to enforce premarital agreements, most states will review those agreements to see whether they are fair — or at least, not fundamentally unfair. Should the same review occur as to unmarried couples? The Massachusetts Supreme Judicial Court answered in the negative in the 1998 case of *Wilcox v. Trautz*, 693 N.E.2d 141 (Mass. 1998), explaining that "marriage gives each party substantial rights concerning the assets of the other which unmarried cohabitants do not have." *Id.* at 147. Agreements between unmarried partners are subject to ordinary contract law rather than the more searching inquiring into their "fairness and reasonableness" characteristic of antenuptial agreements. *Id.* Do you agree?

PROBLEM

On November 2, 2004, eleven states adopted laws or constitutional amendments banning same-sex marriage. The broad wording of the various amendments arguably goes even further than this. The Ohio constitutional amendment reads:

Only a union between one man and one woman may be a marriage valid in or recognized by this state and its political subdivisions. This state and its political subdivisions shall not create or recognize a legal status for relationships of unmarried individuals that intends to approximate the design, qualities, significance or effect of marriage.

The amendment to the Arkansas constitution reads:

> Marriage consists only of the union of one man and one woman. Legal status for unmarried persons which is identical or substantially similar to marital status shall not be valid or recognized in Arkansas, except that the legislature may recognize a common law marriage from another state between a man and a woman. . . .

Does the Ohio constitutional amendment prohibit Ohio courts from dividing the property of an unmarried male-female couple when they break up, as the Wisconsin court did in *Watts v. Watts?* Does the Arkansas amendment?

§7.6.2 SAME-SEX PARTNERS

§7.6.2.1 Marriage

Hawai'i came close to recognizing same-sex marriages in a 1993 decision called *Baehr v. Lewin*, 852 P.2d 44, 59 (Haw. 1993), in which the court held that denying individuals the freedom to marry others of the same sex presumptively constituted sex discrimination in violation of the equal protection clause of the Hawai'i Constitution. However, that route is now closed by a state constitutional amendment. Haw. Const. art. 1, §23. A similar decision in Alaska, *Brause v. Bureau of Vital Statistics*, 1998 WL 88743 (Alaska Super. Ct. 1998), was similarly preempted by constitutional amendment. S.J. Res. 42, 20th Leg., 2d Legis. Sess. (Alaska 1998) (passed Nov. 3, 1998).

The Supreme Court of Vermont held, in *Baker v. State of Vermont*, 744 A.2d 864 (Vt. 1999), that the "common benefits" provision of the Vermont Constitution requires the state to grant same-sex couples the legal incidents of marriage, whether or not the state chooses to call such relationships "marriages." Implementing this constitutional mandate, the Vermont legislature passed and the Governor signed a bill allowing "civil unions" but not "marriages" between same-sex partners. *See* Vt. Stat. tit. 15, §§1201-1206. Although there is no residency requirement to enter a civil union, there is a one-year residency requirement to bring a court action to dissolve a civil union. Connecticut has also passed legislation authorizing civil unions for same sex couples. Conn. Pub. Act 05-10 (Jan. 2005), 2005 Ct. S.B. 963, 2005 Conn. Legis. Serv. P.A. 05-10 (S.S.B. 963) (WEST). California and New Jersey have passed domestic partnership legislation that allow the creation of legal relationships that entail most but not all the rights and obligations associated with marriage. Cal. Fam. Code §§297–299.6; N.J. Stat. §26:8A–1 to –12.

Controversy exits over whether other jurisdictions will dissolve Vermont civil unions for couples domiciled outside Vermont. *Compare Salucco v. Alldredge*, 17 Mass. L. Rep. 498, 2004 Mass. Super. LEXIS 82 (Mass. Super. Ct. 2004) (dissolving a Vermont civil union for a couple domiciled in Massachusetts under the court's general equity jurisdiction) *with Rosengarten v. Downes*, 802 A.2d 170 (Conn. Ct. App. 2002) (refusing to grant a Connecticut couple dissolution of a Vermont civil union on the ground that the relationship was not a "marriage" under the law of either Vermont or Connecticut, that Connecticut statutes provided that same-sex marriage was against the public policy of Connecticut, and thus the court therefore had no subject matter jurisdiction over the relationship). If a court outside Vermont refuses to dissolve a Vermont civil union, an individual who wishes to dissolve the civil union would have to move back to Vermont for a year to bring a court action dissolving the civil union. Ordinarily, individuals are entitled to file for divorce where they are domiciled. A partner in a civil union who could not move back to Vermont for a year to end the civil union and who then married a third party in another state, such as New Jersey, would effectively have two spouses at the same time, one recognized under Vermont civil union law and another recognized under the marriage law of New Jersey. Given the obligations of marriage, which include duties to support one's spouse and children, does this make sense?

On November 18, 2003, the Massachusetts Supreme Judicial Court held in the case of *Goodridge v. Dept. of Public Health*, 798 N.E.2d 941 (Mass. 2004), that barring individuals from marrying each other solely because they were of the same sex violated the state constitutional guarantees of liberty and equality. Chief Justice Margaret Marshall wrote that the "Massachusetts Constitution affirms the dignity and equality of all individuals" and that "[i]t forbids the creation of second-class citizens." *Id.* at 948. *See also Opinion of the Justices to the Senate*, 802 N.E.2d 565 (Mass. 2004) (confirming that granting same-sex couples the right to civil unions but not civil marriage would violate the state constitution because it would confer a kind of second-class status to such couples). The Commonwealth of Massachusetts had defended limiting marriage to male-female couples on the grounds that marriage provided a favorable setting for procreation, that it ensured the optimal setting for child rearing, and that it preserved scarce state resources. The court found none of these goals constitutionally adequate, given the fact that child rearing often occurs outside traditional marriages and that the ability to procreate was never a prerequisite to marriage. It gave the legislature six months to alter the marriage laws in a manner consistent with its opinion. When that did not happen, same-sex couples began marrying in Massachusetts on May 17, 2004.

In *Loving v. Virginia*, 388 U.S. 1 (1967), the Supreme Court struck down an antimiscegenation statute prohibiting white and black persons from marrying each other, holding that the "freedom to marry has long been recognized as one of the vital personal rights essential to the orderly pursuit of happiness by free men." *Id.* at 12. The constitutional right to marry has not, however, yet been extended to same-sex couples because "marriage" has traditionally meant a relationship between a man and a woman. Should the constitutional right to marry be extended to same-sex couples?

§7.6.2.2 Property Division on Breaking Up or Death

Same-sex couples may enter into agreements just as male-female couples may to share property both during their relationship and at separation. *Posik v. Layton*, 695 So. 2d 759 (Fla. Dist. Ct. App. 1997); *Crooke v. Gilden*, 414 S.E.2d 645 (Ga. 1992). However, special problems may arise in enforceability that do not arise in the context of male-female arrangements. As of 1995, 22 states had "sodomy" statutes on the books, criminalizing certain types of sexual relationships between persons of the same sex. William

B. Rubenstein, *Cases and Materials on Sexual Orientation and the Law* 148 (2d ed. 1997). The Supreme Court rejected a constitutional challenge to a sodomy statute in *Bowers v. Hardwick*, 478 U.S. 186 (1986), but *Bowers* was overruled in 2002 in *Lawrence v. Texas*, which held that it is an unconstitutional deprivation of liberty to criminalize private consensual sexual relations between adults. However, most states have passed laws specifically prohibiting recognition of same-sex marriages, and some of those laws are worded so broadly that they arguably prohibit recognition of property or contract rights arising out of such relationships.

As with male-female couples, an alternative to enforcement of an express or implicit agreement is the application of constructive trust doctrine to prevent unjust enrichment. A same-sex couple that lives together for a significant period may create an interdependent financial and personal relationship that would justify distributing the property acquired during the relationship between the parties when they break up, especially if the parties agree to support each other and if failure to reallocate property rights would result in unjust enrichment of one of the parties. *See, e.g., Minieri v. Knittel*, No. 112233/00 (N.Y. Sup. Ct., 2001), 225 127 N.Y.S. 2d 872 (Sup Ct. 2001) 1 (June 5, 2001); *Doe v. Burkland*, 808 A.2d 1090 (R.I. 2002); *Gormley v. Robertson*, 83 P.3d 1042 (Wash. Ct. App. 2004).

In *Vásquez v. Hawthorne*, 33 P.3d 735 (Wash. 2001), a man involved in a "long-term, stable, cohabiting relationship" with another man died without leaving a will. If the men had been married, the survivor would have inherited the decedent's property as a surviving spouse under the state intestacy statute. A literal reading of the statute would preclude a remedy for the survivor. This result might be justified as well on the ground that disputes over the estates of decedents are minimized by the use of wills and the formal relationship of marriage or consanguinity that will grant property of the decedent to the decedent's surviving family members subject to the rights of decedent's creditors. Allowing unrelated parties to claim a share of the estate because of oral promises or relationships with the decedent will place ownership of the decedent's assets in doubt and open the way for fraudulent claims. Despite these dangers, the court in *Vasquez* allowed the decedent's partner to prove the existence of an implied partnership based on his relationship with the decedent and authorized the state courts to impose a constructive or equitable trust on the decedent's property that might allow the survivor to claim some or all of that property if such a partnership were found to exist.

PROBLEMS

1. Beginning on May 17, 2004, same-sex couples domiciled in Massachusetts began to marry there. Are other states obligated to recognize those marriages? Imagine a same-sex couple (Anne and Lily) married in Massachusetts that lives there for fifteen years. The couple divorces in a Massachusetts court, which awards the parties equitable distribution of the property acquired during the marriage and requires Anne to pay child support to the child that Lily bore with artificial insemination. Because Anne was married to Lily, she is a parent of the child under Massachusetts law and obligated to pay child support. Anne then moves to Michigan, taking her money and other personal property with her. Lily sues her in Michigan state court to enforce the Massachusetts equitable distribution and child support awards. Will those awards be enforced in

Michigan courts? On November 2, 2004, the voters in Michigan voted to amend the state constitution to provide:

> To secure and preserve the benefits of marriage for our society and for future generations of children, the union of one man and one woman in marriage shall be the only agreement recognized as a marriage or similar union for any purpose.

Presumably, under this constitutional provision, the Michigan courts would be obligated to refuse to recognize the Massachusetts court judgment because it is premised on a divorce decree, and such decrees are premised on recognizing the prior relationship between the two women as a "marriage."

Traditionally, marriages have been governed by the law of the place of celebration unless they violate a strong public policy of the jurisdiction asked to recognize the marriage. Most states have now passed laws like that amendment in Michigan that implicitly or expressly state that it violates public policy to recognize same-sex marriages validly celebrated elsewhere. *See, e.g.,* Alaska Stat. §25.05.013; Ariz. Rev. Stat. §25-101; Mo. Rev. Stat. §451.022; S.C. Code §20-1-10; Tenn. Code §36-3-113. Moreover, the federal *Defense of Marriage Act* (DOMA), 28 U.S.C. §1738C, gives states the power to pass such laws. DOMA provides:

> No State, territory, or possession of the United States, or Indian tribe, shall be required to give effect to any public act, record, or judicial proceeding of any other State, territory, possession, or tribe respecting a relationship between persons of the same sex that is treated as a marriage under the laws of such other State, territory, possession, or tribe, or a right or claim arising from such relationship.

Is DOMA constitutional? The full faith and credit clause of the U.S. constitution, U.S. Const., art. IV, §1, provides:

> Full Faith and Credit shall be given in each State to the public Acts, Records, and judicial Proceedings of every other State. And the Congress may by general Laws prescribe the Manner in which such Acts, Records and Proceedings shall be proved, and the Effect thereof.

Is DOMA consistent with the full faith and credit clause? Note that the second sentence of the clause gives Congress the power to "prescribe" the "effect" of foreign laws, records (such as marriage certificates?), and judicial proceedings. Does this clause allow Congress to pass a law denying full faith and credit to the court judgments of other states on a particular subject like same-sex marriage? Can Lily evade her child support and equitable distribution obligations by moving to Michigan?

2. In *Gormley v. Robertson*, 83 P.3d 1042 (Wash. Ct. App. 2004), the court ruled that unmarried same-sex couples, like unmarried male-female couples, may be entitled to court-ordered division of their property when the couple breaks up. Would such a result be banned in a state that adopted a constitutional amendment like that in Michigan, which provides that "the union of one man and one woman in marriage shall be the only agreement recognized as a marriage or similar union for any purpose"?

3. A gay male couple gets married in Massachusetts, where their marriage is valid, and lives there as a married couple for 30 years. The couple then moves to Michigan to

retire. Four years later, one of the men dies without leaving a will. The survivor claims a right to inherit the decedent's property as a surviving "spouse" under Michigan's intestacy statute. Can the survivor inherit?

§7.7   Children's Claims on Family Assets

§7.7.1   CHILD SUPPORT

BAYLISS v. BAYLISS
550 So. 2d 986 (Ala. 1989)

GORMAN HOUSTON, Justice.

We granted certiorari in this case to address the following issue: In Alabama, does a trial court have jurisdiction to require parents to provide post-minority support for college education to children of a marriage that has been terminated by divorce?

The trial court does have that jurisdiction. In a proceeding for dissolution of marriage or a modification of a divorce judgment, a trial court may award sums of money out of the property and income of either or both parents for the post-minority education of a child of that dissolved marriage, when application is made therefor, as in the case at issue, before the child attains the age of majority. In doing so, the trial court shall consider all relevant factors that shall appear reasonable and necessary, including primarily the financial resources of the parents and the child and the child's commitment to, and aptitude for, the requested education. The trial court may consider, also, the standard of living that the child would have enjoyed if the marriage had not been dissolved and the family unit had been preserved and the child's relationship with his parents and responsiveness to parental advice and guidance.

Patrick Bayliss was born of the marriage of Cherry R. Bayliss ("mother") and John Martin Bayliss III ("father"). This marriage was terminated by divorce when Patrick was 12 years old. When Patrick was 18, his mother filed a petition to modify the final judgment of divorce, [asking the court to order her ex-husband to help pay for college for Patrick. She alleged that Patrick was interested in going to college and had the aptitude for it, that his father was wealthy and refused to contribute to his college education, and that both she and her ex-husband had attended college.]

Alabama Code 1975, §30-3-1, provides, in pertinent part: "Upon granting a divorce, the court may give the custody and *education of the children of the marriage* to either father or mother, *as may seem right and proper....*" (Emphasis supplied.) ...

We have found no early Alabama appellate court cases that even discussed whether a college education was a "necessary" that a divorced parent had to provide a *minor child.* The earliest case that we have found involving the question of whether a college education is a necessary is *Middlebury College v. Chandler,* 16 Vt. 683 (1844). In that case, which involved a suit brought by Middlebury College against the father of a minor college student for the student's tuition and other college expenses, the Vermont Supreme Court refused to hold that a college education was a necessary, for the following reasons:

> The practical meaning of the term [necessaries] has always been in some measure relative, having reference as well to what may be called the conventional necessities of others in the same walks of life with the infant, as to his own pecuniary condition and

other circumstances. Hence a good common school education, at the least, is now fully recognized as one of the necessaries for an infant. Without it he would lack an acquisition which would be common among his associates, he would suffer in his subsequent influence and usefulness in society, and would ever be liable to suffer in his transactions of business. Such an education is moreover essential to the intelligent discharge of civil, political, and religious duties.

But it is obvious that the more extensive attainments in literature and science must be viewed in a light somewhat different. Though they tend greatly to elevate and adorn personal character, are a source of much private enjoyment, and may justly be expected to prove of public utility, yet in reference to men in general they are far from being necessary in a legal sense. The mass of our citizens pass through life without them. . . . *Id.* at 538-539.

Beginning with the landmark case of *Esteb v. Esteb*, 244 P. 264 (Wash. 1926), courts have increasingly recognized a college education as a legal necessary for minor children of divorced parents. Justice Askren wrote:

. . . The rule in *Middlebury College v. Chandler, supra*, was clearly based upon conditions which existed at that time. An opportunity at that early date for a common school education was small, for a high school education less, and for a college education was almost impossible to the average family, and was generally considered as being only within the reach of the most affluent citizens. While there is no reported case, it is hardly to be doubted that the courts at that time would have even held that a high school education was not necessary, inasmuch as very few were able to avail themselves of it. But conditions have changed greatly in almost a century that has elapsed since that time. Where the college graduate of that day was the exception, to-day such a person may almost be said to be the rule. The law in an attempt to keep up with the progress of society has gradually placed minimum standards for attendance upon public schools, and even provides punishment for those parents who fail to see that their children receive at least such minimum education. That it is the public policy of the state that a college education should be had, if possible, by all its citizens, is made manifest by the fact that the state of Washington maintains so many institutions of higher learning at public expense. It cannot be doubted that the minor who is unable to secure a college education is generally handicapped in pursuing most of the trades or professions of life, for most of those with whom he is required to compete will be possessed of that greater skill and ability which comes from such an education. 244 P. at 266-267. . . .

. . . Until *Ex parte Brewington*, 445 So. 2d 294 (Ala. 1983), our cases and the cases of the Court of Civil Appeals held that a trial court had no continuing equitable jurisdiction over the issues or parties to a divorce to require that a noncustodial parent provide support of any kind to any child that had reached the legislatively prescribed age of majority. In *Brewington*, we expanded our interpretation of the word "children" in the Alabama child support statute, to impose a duty on a divorced, noncustodial parent to support his children who continue to be disabled beyond the legislatively prescribed age of majority. We have previously interpreted the word "education" in the Alabama child support statute to include a college education as a necessary. We now expand the exception to the general rule — *i.e.*, the rule that a divorced, noncustodial parent has no duty to contribute to the support of his or her child after that child has reached the legislatively prescribed age of majority — beyond *Brewington, supra* (dealing with a physically or mentally disabled child) to include the college education exception. . . .

The appellate courts of Florida have held that the noncustodial, divorced parent of an adult child cannot be required to pay college education expenses, in the absence of a disability or agreement. *Grapin v. Grapin,* 450 So. 2d 853 (Fla. 1984). It appears that the Courts in Missouri, Alaska, and possibly Vermont, have also so held. The father also relies on cases from North Carolina, Colorado, Nebraska, New Mexico, Ohio, New York, and Kentucky; however, it appears that these cases are not applicable to a decision under Alabama law, because of the particular language of the jurisdictional child support statutes of those states.

In expanding the exception to the general rule (that a divorced, noncustodial parent has no duty to support his child after that child reaches majority) to include the college education exception, we are merely refusing to limit the word "children" to minor children, because of what we perceive to be just and reasonable in 1989. The Latin phrase *stare decisis et non quieta movere* (stare decisis) expresses the legal principle of certainty and predictability; for it is literally translated as "to adhere to precedents, and not to unsettle things which are established." *Black's Law Dictionary* (5th ed. *1979*). By this opinion, we are unsettling things that have been established by the appellate court of this State. . . . However, we are persuaded that the ground or reason of those prior decisions by the Court of Civil Appeals would not be consented to today by the conscience and the feeling of justice of all those whose obedience is required by the rule on which the ratio decidendi of those prior decisions was logically based.

Therefore, we overrule that portion of cases that are inconsistent with this opinion. . . .

Had the Bayliss family unit not been put asunder by divorce, would the father, who had attended college and was a man of significant means, have continued to provide a college education for Patrick (a young man who would be an Alpha Plus if this were Huxley's Brave New World) after Patrick reached 19 years of age? If so, the father's educational support obligations should not cease when Patrick reached 19 years of age. . . .

This Court in *Ogle v. Ogle,* 156 So. 2d at *349* (Ala. 1963), quoted the following from *Pass v. Pass,* 118 So. 2d 769, 773 (Miss. 1960), with approval:

> [W]e are living today in an age of keen competition, and if the children of today . . . are to take their rightful place in a complex order of society and government, and discharge the duties of citizenship as well as meet with success the responsibilities devolving upon them in their relations with their fellow man, the church, the state and nation, it must be recognized that their parents owe them the duty to the extent of their financial capacity to provide for them the training and education which will be of such benefit to them in the discharge of the responsibilities of citizenship. It is a duty which the parent not only owes to his child, but to the state as well, since the stability of our government must depend upon a well-equipped, a well-trained, and well-educated citizenship. We can see no good reason why this duty should not extend to a college education. Our statutes do not prohibit it, but they are rather susceptible of an interpretation to allow it. The fact is that the importance of a college education is being more and more recognized in matters of commerce, society, government, and all human relations, and the college graduate is being more and more preferred over those who are not so fortunate. No parent should subject his worthy child to this disadvantage if he has the financial capacity to avoid it.

This is the public policy of our State. Since the normal age for attending college extends beyond the age of 19 years, under §30-3-1 courts have the right to assure that the children of divorced parents, who are minors at the time of the divorce, are given the same right to a college education before and after they reach the age of 19 years that they probably would have had if their parents had not divorced....

NOTES AND QUESTIONS

1. Courts generally hold children of divorced parents are entitled "to be supported at least according to the standard of living to which they had grown accustomed prior to the separation of their parents." *Pascale v. Pascale*, 660 A.2d 485 (N.J. 1995). Does this include an obligation to pay for college? States seem to be evenly divided on the question of requiring noncustodial parents to pay for college education. *Milne v. Milne*, 556 A.2d 854 (Pa. Super. Ct. 1989) (19 jurisdictions require provision of higher education).

2. Some courts have interpreted legislation setting the age of majority — otherwise known as the age of "emancipation" — to liberate parents from duties of support at the same time the child is liberated from parental control. *Dowling v. Dowling*, 679 P.2d 480 (Alaska 1984); *In re Marriage of Plummer*, 735 P.2d 165 (Colo. 1987).

In holding that divorced parents have no legal duty to pay for their children's college education, the Florida Supreme Court explained, "[w]hile most parents willingly assist their adult children in obtaining a higher education that is increasingly necessary in today's fast-changing world, any duty to do so is a moral rather than a legal one." *Grapin v. Grapin*, 450 So. 2d 853, 854 (Fla. 1984). In Florida, the court noted, married parents have no legal obligation to pay for their children's college education; thus, the imposition of higher obligations on divorced parents would deny them equal protection under the law. But see *Dowling, supra* (Matthews, J., dissenting) ("[A] child should not suffer because his parents are divorced. The child of divorced parents should be in no worse position than a child from an unbroken home whose parents could be expected to supply a college education.... To terminate support when the parents are divorced creates a special disadvantage not shared by children whose parents remain together").

3. Professor John Langbein has argued that provision of a college education represents the major current mechanism — other than inheritance of a family home — by which wealth is transmitted between generations. John Langbein, *The Twentieth-Century Revolution in Family Wealth Transmission*, 86 Mich. L. Rev. 722, 732-734 (1988).

> My thesis is quite simple, and, I hope, quite intuitive. I believe that, in striking contrast to the patterns of last century and before, in modern times the business of educating children has become the main occasion for intergenerational wealth transfer. Of old, parents were mainly concerned to transmit the patrimony — prototypically the farm or the firm, but more generally, that "provision in life" that rescued children from the harsh fate of being a mere laborer. In today's economic order, it is education more than property, the new human capital rather than the old physical capital, that similarly advantages a child.
>
> We know that income levels correlate powerfully with education. In 1985 the median annual income of full-time male workers aged twenty-five and over who had completed some years of high school but had not graduated was under $20,000; for those who had completed four years of college the figure was above $30,000; and for those with more than four years of college, the figure approached $40,000. The comparable earnings figures for female workers were lower, but differences in educational attainment among women produced similar disparities in favor of the well educated.

Family wealth and its corollary, family income, are crucial determinants of access to education. A sociologist of education recently summed up the data in the following way: "The amount of schooling that individuals obtain and their school continuation decisions are strongly affected by characteristics of their families. Persons whose parents have more schooling, higher income, and better jobs; whose families are smaller; and who were raised in urban areas typically obtain more schooling than persons from less-advantaged backgrounds." . . .

A story in Newsweek in May of 1987 used figures on the annual cost of undergraduate education at Johns Hopkins. The $15,410 that Johns Hopkins charged in 1987 for tuition, room, and board constituted 31% of a family income of $50,000 per year. By contrast, the $2,000 that Johns Hopkins charged in 1960 represented only 15% of the inflation-adjusted equivalent family income for 1960, which was $13,505.

Now it is quite obvious that very few families can afford to pay 31% of family income, or anything near it, on what we would call — in an accounting sense — a current basis. That is especially true when the family has more than one child in the educational mill at the same time. For most families, therefore, these education expenses represent capital transfers in a quite literal sense: The money comes from savings, that is, from the family's capital; or debt is assumed, meaning that the money is borrowed from the family's future capital. . . .

Median household income in 1999 was $40,816; median household income for African American families was $27,910. Tuition, room, and board for Johns Hopkins in 2005-2006 amounts to $41,544, or roughly 102% of median annual household income and 149% of median income for African American households.

§7.7.2   The Family's Right to Live Together

See supra §1.2.4, at pages 30-32.

§7.7.3 Wills and Inheritance

See supra §1.4.1, at pages 63-69.

§7.8 *Forfeiture*

§7.8.1 Domestic Violence and Protective Orders

WISCONSIN DOMESTIC ABUSE
RESTRAINING ORDER STATUTE
Wis. Stat. Ann. §813.12

§813.12. *Domestic Abuse Restraining Orders and Injunctions*

(1)   *Definitions.* In this section:

    (a) "Domestic abuse" means any of the following engaged in by an adult family member or household member against another adult family member or household member:

1. Intentional infliction of physical pain, physical injury or illness.
2. Intentional impairment of physical condition....
3. A violation of §940.225(1), (2) or (3) [criminalizing sexual assault or rape].
4. A threat to engage in the conduct under subd. 1, 2 or 3.

(b) "Family member" means a spouse, a parent, a child or a person related by blood or adoption to another person.

(c) "Household member" means a person currently or formerly residing in a place of abode with another person....

(2) *Temporary restraining order.*

(a) A judge or family court commissioner shall issue a temporary restraining order ordering the respondent to refrain from committing acts of domestic abuse against the petitioner, to avoid the petitioner's residence, except as provided in par. (am), or any premises temporarily occupied by the petitioner or both, or to avoid contacting or causing any person other than a party's attorney to contact the petitioner unless the petitioner consents in writing, or any of these remedies requested in the petition, if all of the following occur:

1. The petitioner submits to the judge or family court commissioner a petition alleging the elements set forth under sub. (5)(a).
2. The judge or family court commissioner finds reasonable grounds to believe that the respondent has engaged in, or based on prior conduct of the petitioner and the respondent may engage in, domestic abuse of the petitioner....

(am) If the petitioner and the respondent are not married, the respondent owns the premises where the petitioner resides and the petitioner has no legal interest in the premises, in lieu of ordering the respondent to avoid the petitioner's residence under par. (a) the judge or family court commissioner may order the respondent to avoid the premises for a reasonable time until the petitioner relocates and shall order the respondent to avoid the new residence for the duration of the order.

(b) Notice need not be given to the respondent before issuing a temporary restraining order under this subsection....

(c) The temporary restraining order is in effect until a hearing is held on issuance of an injunction under sub. (4). The temporary restraining order is not voided if the respondent is admitted into a dwelling that the order directs him or her to avoid. A judge or family court commissioner shall hold a hearing on issuance of an injunction within 7 days after the temporary restraining order is issued, unless the time is extended upon the written consent of the parties or extended once for 14 days upon a finding that the respondent has not been served with a copy of the temporary restraining order although the petitioner has exercised due diligence....

(3) *Injunction.*

(a) A judge or family court commissioner may grant an injunction ordering the respondent to refrain from committing acts of domestic abuse against the petitioner, to avoid the petitioner's residence, except as provided in par. (am), or any premises temporarily occupied by the petitioner or both, or to avoid contacting or causing any person other than a party's attorney to contact the petitioner unless the petitioner consents to that contact in writing, or any combination of these remedies requested in the petition, if all of the following occur:

1. The petitioner files a petition alleging the elements set forth under sub. (5)(a).
2. The petitioner serves upon the respondent a copy of the petition and notice of the time for hearing on the issuance of the injunction, or the respondent serves upon the petitioner notice of the time for hearing on the issuance of the injunction.
3. After hearing, the judge or family court commissioner finds reasonable grounds to believe that the respondent has engaged in, or based upon prior conduct of the petitioner and the respondent may engage in, domestic abuse of the petitioner....

   (am) If the petitioner and the respondent are not married, the respondent owns the premises where the petitioner resides and the petitioner has no legal interest in the premises, in lieu of ordering the respondent to avoid the petitioner's residence under par. (a) the judge or family court commissioner may order the respondent to avoid the premises for a reasonable time until the petitioner relocates and shall order the respondent to avoid the new residence for the duration of the order....

(b) 1. An injunction under this subsection is effective according to its terms, for the period of time that the petitioner requests, but not more than 2 years....

(4) *Petition.*

(d) The petition shall allege facts sufficient to show the following:

1. The name of the petitioner and that the petitioner is the alleged victim.
2. The name of the respondent and that the respondent is an adult.
3. That the respondent engaged in, or based on prior conduct of the petitioner and the respondent may engage in, domestic abuse of the petitioner....

(b) The clerk of circuit court shall provide the simplified forms ... to help a person file a petition....

(5) *Enforcement assistance.* (a) If an order is issued under this section, upon request by the petitioner the court or family court commissioner shall order the sheriff to accompany the petitioner and assist in placing him or her in physical possession of his or her residence or to otherwise assist in executing or serving the temporary restraining order or injunction....

(6) *Arrest.* A law enforcement officer shall arrest and take a person into custody if all of the following occur:

(a) A petitioner under sub. (5) presents the law enforcement officer with a copy of a court order issued under sub. (3) or (4), or the law enforcement officer determines that such an order exists through communication with appropriate authorities.

(b) The law enforcement officer has probable cause to believe that the person has violated the court order issued under sub. (3) or (4) by any circuit court in this state.

(7)   *Penalty.*
>   (c)   Whoever knowingly violates a temporary restraining order or injunc-
>   tion issued under sub. (3) or (4) shall be fined not more than $1,000 or
>   imprisoned for not more than 9 months or both.
>   (d)   The petitioner does not violate the court order under sub. (3) or (4) if
>   he or she admits into his or her residence a person ordered under sub.
>   (3) or (4) to avoid that residence.

COTE v. COTE

599 A.2d 869 (Md. Ct. Spec. App. 1992)

ROSALYN B. BELL, Judge. . . .

Paula Cote and Charles Cote were married on November 8, 1966. The one child of the marriage is fully emancipated. On September 17, 1990, the parties had an altercation. While their versions differ, the trial judge implicitly found the actions at least to some extent were reciprocal. On September 20, Mr. Cote filed a complaint for a limited divorce against Ms. Cote in the Circuit Court for Prince George's County. On that same day, Ms. Cote filed a Petition for Protection from Domestic Violence, based on the events of September 17. [On October 1, the District Court issued an order barring Mr. Cote from entering the family home. When the order expired on October 31, Ms. Cote petitioned for an extension of the order which the court granted.]

Mr. Cote [argues that] the order barring him from his own real property was an unconstitutional taking of property without just compensation. We do not agree.

The Court of Appeals, in *Pitsenberger v. Pitsenberger*, 410 A.2d 1052 (Md. 1980), stated that three elements must be established in order to constitute a taking: (1) state action; (2) which affects a property interest in the constitutional sense; and (3) which deprives the owner of all beneficial use of his or her property. If all three of these elements are met, the State must pay compensation for the deprivation.

There is no question that the injunction here constituted state action. The trial court's order was issued under the authority of §1-203 of the Family Law Article enacted by the Legislature. . . .

The next question is whether there was a deprivation of a property interest. The trial court ruled that, because Mr. Cote did not lose title to the marital home, no unconstitutional taking occurred. This analysis by the trial judge was in error, as it ignores the Supreme Court's decision in *Fuentes v. Shevin*, 407 U.S. 67 (1972). In *Fuentes*, the Supreme Court held that a temporary, non-final deprivation of an individual's possessory interest in property may nonetheless constitute a taking for constitutional purposes. We hold that the trial judge's injunction did deprive Mr. Cote of a property interest, as that term has been defined for constitutional purposes.

Although the trial judge erred in holding that his injunction did not deprive Mr. Cote of some property interest, we hold that his ultimate conclusion, that Mr. Cote did not suffer an unconstitutional taking, was correct. . . . In *Pitsenberger*, the Court of Appeals stated: "Because his children have the use of the family home and family use personal property, [Mr. Pitsenberger] is in fact using his property to properly house his children. [Mr. Pitsenberger] therefore has not been deprived of all beneficial use of his property." *Pitsenberger*, 410 A.2d at 1060. In this case, Mr. Cote seeks to distinguish *Pitsenberger* on the grounds that no minor children are benefitting from the injunction entered by the trial court. Therefore, argues Mr. Cote, he retains no beneficial use of the marital property. While Mr. Cote correctly points out that there are no minor children in this case, we do not agree that he has been deprived of all beneficial use of the marital property.

We have held that the trial judge was authorized to issue an injunction to protect the parties from harm in this case. Under these circumstances, Mr. Cote obtained some tangible benefits from Ms. Cote remaining in the marital home. Specifically, he avoided the possibility of having to provide an alternative place for Ms. Cote to live during the pendency of the divorce. We therefore hold that the trial court's injunction barring Mr. Cote from the marital home did not constitute a taking of property without just compensation. . . .

PROBLEM

An unmarried heterosexual couple in Wisconsin have been living together for six years in a home owned by the man. They have a two-year-old child. After the man beats the woman, she obtains a temporary restraining order under Wis. Stat. Ann. §813.12(3)(am), and then an injunction under §813.12(4)(am), ordering the man to "to avoid the premises for a reasonable time until the petitioner relocates." She is unemployed and has trouble finding an affordable apartment for herself and the child. Jobs available to her do not enable her to pay for day care, and public assistance benefits are not sufficient to allow her to rent her own apartment. After six months, the man brings a lawsuit to evict her from the home, arguing that he has avoided the premises for a "reasonable" time and is entitled to recover possession of his house.

On what basis can plaintiff argue that he has avoided the premises "for a reasonable time" and that he is therefore entitled to evict his ex-partner? On what basis can defendant argue that plaintiff is not entitled to evict her and that she has a statutory right to remain while she makes reasonable efforts to find a new place to live? How should the court interpret what constitutes a "reasonable time until the petitioner relocates" under §813.12(4)(am)?

§7.8.2   FORFEITURE FOR A FAMILY MEMBER'S ILLEGAL CONDUCT

1. *Criminal and civil forfeiture.* Federal and state statutes provide for the forfeiture of property obtained through criminal activity or that is used to facilitate commission of those crimes. Criminal forfeiture laws allow courts to require such forfeiture in the course of imposing sentence on a person convicted of a crime, *see, e.g.,* 18 U.S.C. §982, while civil forfeiture statutes allow civil law suits by the government to recover such property, *see* 18 U.S.C. §§981–985. For example, someone who sells illegal drugs in her car may forfeit ownership of the car to the government; similarly, an owner may lose a home or business if illegal transactions take place there. *See also* 21 U.S.C. §881 (forfeiture of property related to drug crimes). These laws raise a number of complex issues.

2. *Burden of proof.* Until 2000, federal law authorized forfeiture of some types of property if there was "probable cause" to believe it was used to help commit a crime. This is an extremely low standard which requires only that there be reasonable grounds to suspect the property was used in connection with a crime; not only is it far below the "beyond a reasonable doubt" standard used for criminal convictions but it is even less

than the standard required in civil cases that require the fact finder to believe by a preponderance of the evidence that the claim has been proved. After protests by property owners, among others, Congress amended federal law in 2000 to require the government to prove by a preponderance of the evidence that the property is subject to forfeiture. *Civil Asset Forfeiture Reform Act of 2000* (CAFRA), Pub. L. No. 106-185, Apr. 25, 2000, 114 Stat. 202. 18 U.S.C. §983(c)(1), (2). If the reason for the forfeiture is that the property was used to facilitate a crime, the government must further show "that there was a substantial connection between the property and the offense." 18 U.S.C. §983(c)(3).

3. *Innocent owners.* Forfeiture laws have sometimes snared *innocent owners.* For example, in *United States v. Leasehold Interest in 121 Nostrand Avenue,* 760 F. Supp. 1015 (E.D.N.Y. 1991), the United States sought to evict a public housing tenant named Clara Smith who lived in the apartment with her two daughters, nine of her grandchildren (several of whom were in her legal custody), and two of her great-grandchildren. One of the granddaughters was arrested after selling crack cocaine to an undercover police officer in the apartment, and a search of the house pursuant to a valid search warrant found cocaine and drug paraphernalia there. Judge Jack Weinstein found that Clara Smith had made constant and vigilant efforts to stop her family members from using and selling drugs and that she could not have done more to prevent criminal activity by her granddaughter. Although both the drug forfeiture statute, 21 U.S.C. §881, and the *Anti-Drug Abuse Act of 1988,* Pub. L. No. 100-690, §5101, 102 Stat. 4181 (1988) (partially embodied at 42 U.S.C. §1437d(*l*)(6)), provided for forfeiture of a public housing tenancy if any drug-related activity occurred on the premises, whether or not it was committed by the tenant, the statutes in effect at the time, 18 U.S.C. §881(a)(7) (repealed), protected "innocent owners" who had no knowledge of the drug activity or, if they knew about it, had not consented to it and had taken reasonable steps to prevent it.

The 2000 amendments to federal forfeiture law contained in CAFRA enacted a single innocent owner defense applicable to most civil forfeitures. That law defines an innocent owner as one who "(i) did not know of the conduct giving rise to forfeiture; or (ii) upon learning of the conduct giving rise to the forfeiture, did all that reasonably could be expected under the circumstances to terminate such use of the property." 18 U.S.C. §983(d). The law specifically exempts innocent owners from being required to "take steps that [they] reasonably believe[ ] would be likely to subject [anyone other than the person whose conduct gives rise to the forfeiture] to physical danger." *Id.* §983(d)(2)(B)(ii).

In contrast, in *Department of Housing & Urban Development v. Rucker,* 535 U.S. 125 (2002), the Supreme Court interpreted a federal statute to allow eviction of innocent public housing tenants when members of their households have engaged in illegal drug use or sales on or off the housing site, 42 U.S.C. §1437d(*l*)(6) (requiring public housing authorities to use leases that provide that "any drug-related criminal activity on or off such premises, engaged in by a public housing tenant, any member of the tenant's household, or any guest or other person under the tenant's control, shall be cause for termination of [the] tenancy"). *See also* 24 C.F.R. §966.4(e)(12). The Court found no constitutional problem with forfeiture of property owned by an innocent party even if that tenant had done everything possible to prevent family members from using or selling drugs on the ground that the government was acting as an owner-landlord, placing conditions in the lease with which the tenants voluntarily concurred, and not as a sovereign regulating the lease terms or punishing an innocent party because of the criminal acts of another.

4. *State laws.* Many states have also passed statutes that either permit or require both private landlords and public housing authorities to evict tenants when the tenants or members of their families have sold or possessed illegal drugs in the apartment. *See, e.g.,* Mass. Gen. Laws ch. 139, §19 (authorizing a landlord to void a lease if a tenant or occupant uses the premises to keep, sell, or manufacture controlled substances); Mich. Comp. Laws §333.7521(1)(f). Like the federal statutes, these state laws attempt to balance competing interests in fairness to innocent family members and deterrence of drug activity. They balance the goal of protecting innocent tenants from eviction because of illegal conduct of their family members that the tenants could not reasonably have prevented, with the goal of protecting neighbors and others in the community from neighbors whose family members use or sell drugs. *Compare Lloyd Realty Corp. v. Albino,* 552 N.Y.S.2d 1008 (Civ. Ct. 1990) (refusing to allow eviction of a tenant who did not know about or acquiesce in drug transactions engaged in by her daughters and another occupant in the apartment) *with Spence v. O'Brien,* 446 N.E.2d 1070 (Mass. App. Ct. 1983) (authorizing eviction of a tenant even though the tenant had tried to stop her boyfriend from engaging in the illegal drug activity and repeatedly asked him to remove the drugs from the premises).

5. *Domestic violence.* In *United States v. Sixty Acres in Etowah County,* 930 F.2d 857 (11th Cir. 1991), the United States sought forfeiture of real property owned by Evelyn Charlene Ellis because her husband had used the property to engage in illegal drug sales. Although she knew about the sales, she claimed that she had not consented to them. She testified that she did not find out until after her marriage that her husband had been convicted of murdering his first wife, that he had choked her in a rage and threatened to kill her, that he owned guns and had intimidated her mother to give him a deed to some of her property. The trial court found that she had not consented to the use of the property for drug activity and that her husband's threats and violent conduct meant that she could not reasonably have been expected to control his conduct. The Eleventh Circuit reversed, finding that her justifiable fear of her husband "does not allow her to escape the consequences (in this case, forfeiture), for her consent to his illegal acts." *Id.* at 860. The court found that she was not under duress because she was not under an immediate threat of physical harm and that she "had ample opportunity to flee or to contact law enforcement agents regarding her husband's activities." *Id.* at 861. Do you agree?

6. *What property is subject to forfeiture?* In *In re Forfeiture of $5,264,* 439 N.W.2d 246 (Mich. 1989), the Michigan Supreme Court held that a store in which the owner had made two drug sales could be forfeited to the state under a state statute that provided for forfeiture of "[a]ny thing of value . . . used to facilitate" an illegal drug transaction. The court ruled that real property "facilitated" a sale only when it had a "substantial connection" with the underlying criminal activity. The recent amendments to the federal forfeiture laws similarly provide for forfeiture of property used to "facilitate" a crime only if the property has a "substantial connection" to the crime. 18 U.S.C. §983(c). What constitutes a substantial connection? When someone makes a single drug sale in her home, is this enough to result in forfeiture? Does it make a difference if the owner regularly makes sales in her home? Should places of business be treated differently from residences?

7. *Constitutional limits on forfeiture: takings clause and excessive fines.* In *Bennis v. Michigan,* 516 U.S. 442 (1996) (reprinted below at §12.2.3.2), a car jointly owned by a

husband and wife was seized by state authorities after the husband used the car to solicit and engage in sexual activity with a prostitute. Tina Bennis, the wife, claimed that forfeiture of her 50 percent ownership interest in the car was an unconstitutional, taking of property without just compensation. In a 5-4 vote, the Supreme Court disagreed, partly on the ground that property has long been subject to forfeiture when it is used to commit a crime even when this harms an innocent owner and partly because this practice was justified by the need to induce vigilance on the part of co-owners on how the property is used. Justice Ginsburg concurred on the ground that the value of the car was so low that it barely covered the costs of the proceedings that could be legitimately placed on the parties. In dissent, Justice Stevens argued that "we have regarded as axiomatic that persons cannot be punished when they have done no wrong. I would hold now what we have always assumed: that the principle is required by due process." *Id.* at 467. In contrast, in *Keshbro, Inc. v. City of Miami*, 801 So.2d 864 (Fla. 2001), the Florida Supreme Court held that the state had taken property without just compensation when the law required an apartment complex to be closed for one year after only two instances of illegal cocaine sales there. The court found the forfeiture unwarranted without compensation because the illegal activity was not so pervasive as to constitute either a private or public nuisance. *See also State ex rel. Pizza v. Rezcallah*, 702 N.E.2d 81 (Ohio 1998) (state law requiring one year closing of innocent owner's property who acted reasonably to prevent drug use on the premise constitutes an unconstitutional taking of property without just compensation).

In *Austin v. United States*, 509 U.S. 602 (1993), the United States brought forfeiture proceedings against the auto body shop and mobile home of a person convicted of bringing two ounces of cocaine from the shop to his home to facilitate a prearranged sale there. The Supreme Court held that the eighth amendment's prohibition of "excessive fines" applied to civil forfeiture proceedings and remanded for a determination of whether the forfeiture was constitutionally excessive. Since the *Austin* decision, lower courts have routinely found that forfeiture of real property is not unconstitutional when it was used to conduct criminal activity, *e.g., United States v. Collado*, 348 F.3d 323 (2d Cir. 2003)(civil forfeiture of property owner's building was not excessive or grossly disproportional to the gravity of the offense in violation of the eight amendment because it was used to facilitate distribution of controlled substances by the property owner's son).

Husband and wife was seized by state authorities after the husband used the car to
solicit and engage in sexual activity with a prostitute. The Bennis, the wife, claimed
that forfeiture of her co-ownership interest in the car was an unconstitutional
taking of property without just compensation. In a 5-4 vote, the Supreme Court disagreed. Forfeiture of co-owned that property has long been subject to forfeiture when
used to commit a crime even when this larger affirmation of lawyer and party, because
this practice was justified as the need to induce vigilance on the part of co-owners on
how the property is used. Justice Ginsburg concurred on the ground that the value of
the car was so low that it hardly covered the costs of the proceeding that could be
legitimately placed on the parties. In dissent, Justice Stevens argued that we have
regarded as innocent that person cannot be punished when they have done nothing.
I would hold now what we have always assumed, that the principle is required by due
process. Id. at 460. In contrast, in Koshita v. The City of Mexican, 601 So.2d 803, Fla.
2001, the Florida Supreme Court held that the state had taken property without just
compensation when the law required it apartment families to be taken for over
after only two instances of illegal cocaine sale there. The court found the forfeiture
disproportionate without compensation because the illegal activity was not so pervasive
to constitute criminal private or public nuisance. See also ter Jones v. Rosselini,
702 N.E.2d at (Ohio 2004) (state law requiring one-year closing of innocent owners'
property who acted reasonably to prevent drug use on the premises constitutes an
unconstitutional taking of property without just compensation).

In Sweet v. United States, 779 U.S. 602 (1993), the United States states brought forfeiture proceedings against the individual's shop and mobile home of a person convicted
of running two hundred cocaine from the shop to the house to facilitate premature
sale there. The Supreme Court found that the eighth amendment's prohibition of
excessive fines applied to civil forfeiture proceedings and remanded for a determination of whether the forfeiture was constitutionally excessive, since the court held,
was not excessive when it was used to conduct criminal activity. *e.g.* United States v.
Cullada, 548 F.3d 323, 2d Cir. 2005 (civil forfeiture of property owner's building was
not excessive grossly disproportional to the gravity of the owner's violation of the
eighth amendment because it was used to facilitate distribution of controlled substance
by the property owner's agent.

IV

Regulation of the Market for Shelter

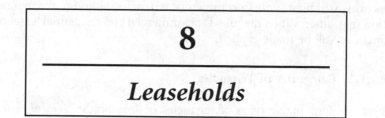

8

Leaseholds

§8.1 *Leasehold Estates*

§8.1.1 TYPES OF TENANCIES

Property interests known as leaseholds are familiar to most law students. The landlord agrees to transfer possession of the property for a specified period to the tenant in return for the tenant's promise to make a periodic rental payment. When the tenancy is over, possession ordinarily reverts to the landlord unless she has sold the property, conveying her interest to someone else. Landlord-tenant relationships therefore involve a division of property interests between the landlord and the tenant.

§8.1.1.1 Commercial and Residential Tenancies

Courts often divide tenancies into two categories: *residential* and *commercial.* Residential tenancies involve renting property for the purpose of establishing a home; commercial tenancies involve any nonresidential use, including operation of a business for profit or operation of a nonprofit institution such as a church, hospital, or university. The vast majority of the rules are the same for both types of tenancy, but there are some differences. Even when the rules are the same, courts analyze the two situations separately, on the assumption that the underlying policy considerations and the justified expectations of the parties may differ. In general, courts are more inclined to adopt common law rules regulating the terms of residential leases than of commercial leases, on the assumption that commercial tenants are more likely to have sufficient bargaining power and expertise to shape the contractual arrangement in their best interests, while residential tenants are less likely to bargain for appropriate terms in the contract that reflect their justified expectations. *See Wesson v. Leone Enterprises, Inc.,* 774 N.E.2d 611, 620 (Mass. 2002) ("we continue to recognize that there are significant differences between commercial and residential tenancies and the policy considerations appropriate to each").

Most of the materials in this chapter are devoted to residential tenancies. All the doctrines canvassed here apply to commercial tenancies, although the manner of their application may differ. When the rules for commercial and residential leaseholds differ, the distinctions will be made explicit.

§8.1.1.2   Categories of Tenancies

There are four major types of tenancies or leaseholds: *term of years, periodic tenancy, tenancy at will,* and *tenancy at sufferance.*

1. Term of years. A *term of years* lasts for a specified period of time determined by the parties. The period can be of any length. For example, a one-year lease is a term of years; so is a ten-year lease or a 60-day lease. A term of years ends automatically at the agreed-upon time, but it may be terminated before the end of the fixed period on the happening of some event or condition stated in the lease agreement.[1] The future interest retained by the landlord is called a *reversion.* If, at the time the lease is signed, the owner provides that the property will shift to a third party at the end of the leasehold, the future interest in the third party is called a *remainder.* The death of either party does not terminate the tenancy. The landlord is not entitled to evict the tenant before the end of the term; the only exception occurs when the tenant is breaching a material term of the lease, such as the covenant to pay rent.

2. Periodic tenancy. Periodic tenancies renew automatically at specified periods unless either the landlord or the tenant chooses to end the relationship. For example, many tenants have no written leases or specified end to their tenancy but pay monthly rent to the landlord. These arrangements create *month-to-month tenancies,* a form of periodic tenancy; they renew automatically each month if neither party notifies the other that he intends to end the relationship. By statute or common law, notice is required before either party can terminate the relationship and end the periodic tenancy. Many (but not all) states require a month's notice to end a month-to-month tenancy. The death of either the landlord or the tenant does not terminate the tenancy. Of course, the heirs or devisees of the deceased landlord or tenant may choose to end the tenancy, unless some statute or common law rule prevents this. Under this arrangement, the landlord can only evict the tenant by providing the requisite notice that the tenancy will not be renewed.

3. Tenancy at will. The *tenancy at will* is similar to a periodic tenancy except that it can be ended with no notice by either party. Many states have effectively abolished tenancies at will by requiring notice before a tenancy can be terminated; if the required notice is the same as that for a month-to-month tenancy, no real difference distinguishes the two. Of course, if statutes provide for different notice periods, the distinction remains significant. In addition, traditionally, the death of either the landlord or the tenant terminates the tenancy at will. This result differs from periodic tenancies or the term of years and may have important consequences. Although the landlord still needs to give the statutorily required notice to evict, the landlord may have an absolute

---

1. Legislation may require the landlord to use court proceedings to evict the holdover tenant and to provide a minimum amount of notice before the tenant can be evicted

right to do so since the tenancy is at an end. In contrast, the landlord under a periodic tenancy may not be able to terminate the tenancy if the tenant has a defense to eviction, such as violation of the implied warranty of habitability.

4. Tenancy at sufferance. A tenant rightfully in possession who wrongfully stays after the leasehold has terminated is called a *tenant at sufferance*, or a *holdover tenant*. The term is intended to distinguish between a tenant who wrongfully retains possession after the end of the lease term and a trespasser, who never had a right to possess the property. The legal procedures for ejecting trespassers often differ in significant ways from those for evicting holdover tenants. It may be lawful for an owner to physically eject a trespasser herself (this is called *self-help*) or to call on the police to do so, while an eviction proceeding and a court judgment are generally required to evict a tenant, including a tenant at sufferance. A landlord who accepts rent checks from a holdover tenant may be held to have agreed to a new tenancy calculated by the rental payment schedule (monthly checks creating a month-to-month tenancy).

§8.1.1.3 Statute of Frauds

Every state has a statute of frauds, which requires that interests in real property be in writing to be enforceable.[2] Most states require that leases of more than one year be in writing, while leases of one year or less are enforceable whether they are written or oral. Oral periodic tenancies are generally enforceable under the statute of frauds so long as the period is one year or less; month-to-month tenancies satisfy this condition because, although they could last more than one year in total, the relevant period — one month — is less than a year. Oral tenancies at will are valid as well.

§8.1.1.4 Regulation of Landlord-Tenant Relationships

In most states, landlord-tenant relationships are heavily regulated by both common law and state and federal statutes.

Procedural regulations impose formal requirements for *creating* the landlord-tenant relationship — for example, some require a writing for leases of more than one year. They also define the procedures required to *terminate* the relationship; these procedures ordinarily require *notice* and an *eviction proceeding* and court judgment to evict the tenant from the property. They may also provide for expedited court proceedings, often called *summary process*, to allow relatively quick evictions.

Substantive regulations define the parties' obligations to each other. For example, administrative agencies established by legislation may pass housing codes specifying the minimum requirements for conditions in an apartment, including heat, toilet and kitchen facilities, and pest control. Common law rules also govern the mutual obligations of the parties and impose implied terms in the contract. For example, all leaseholds include an implied covenant of quiet enjoyment by which the landlord promises not to disturb the tenant's use and enjoyment of the property.

Common law doctrines, and some statutes, define the circumstances under which a breach of the agreement by each of the parties entitles the other party to

---

2. Significant exceptions to this principle include adverse possession, prescriptive easements, easements by estoppel, and necessity.

end her performance of her contractual obligations. For example, the landlord's failure to comply with the housing code may relieve the tenant partially or totally of the obligation to pay rent.

Some implied terms are waivable by the parties, who may contract around them by agreeing to different arrangements. Other implied terms are compulsory or non-waivable; any contractual term purporting to waive or alter the implied term is void and unenforceable.

§8.1.2   IDENTIFYING LANDLORD-TENANT RELATIONSHIPS: SELF-HELP VERSUS JUDICIAL PROCESS

The following case deals with the question whether migrant farmworkers who reside in facilities provided by their employer are entitled to a court hearing before being evicted. Tenants are generally entitled to such legal process; others generally are not so entitled. Owners have the right to use *self-help* to eject a trespasser but must initiate eviction proceedings to dispossess a tenant. Some states, however, retain the traditional rule authorizing landlords to exercise self-help to displace tenants in at least some circumstances. *See Watson v. Brown*, 686 P.2d 12 (Haw. 1984) (commercial landlord may be able to use self-help to recover possession from tenant that failed to pay rent).

In addition to a right to retain possession in the absence of judicial eviction, tenants may have a right under certain circumstances to continued occupancy over the landlord's objections. The farmworkers' relationship with their employer has many of the elements of a landlord-tenant relationship: The employer transfers possession of a portion of the employer's property by allowing the farmworkers to live there in exchange for the farmworkers' promises to convey value back to the employer. Their relationship also appears different, in ways that may be significant, from that of most tenants. Many migrant farmworkers pay no rent; instead, they work for the employer in the fields. They are compensated for these services in the form of wages. This compensation *may* be reduced to account for the rental value of the employer's property they occupy. The exchange of land for services may make the relationship seem more like a feudal one than a modern contractual one.

Whether the employees are classified as tenants or otherwise, the common law may require employers to follow certain procedures to exclude an ex-employee from the employer's property. The important question therefore centers on the real procedures required to evict fired employees who, during their employment, were legally entitled to live on the employer's property. Can the employer-landlord eject them physically? Can he call the police and have them arrested? Or must the employer provide notice and obtain a court judgment?

NEW JERSEY ANTI-EVICTION ACT
N.J. Stat. Ann. §§2A:18-61.1 to 2A:18-61.12

§2A:18-61.1   *Removal of Residential Tenants; Grounds*

No lessee or tenant or the assigns, under-tenants or legal representatives of such lessee or tenant may be removed by the Superior Court from any house, building,

mobile home or land in a mobile home park or tenement leased for residential purposes, other than . . . owner-occupied premises with not more than two rental units or
a hotel, motel or other guest house or part thereof rented to a transient guest or
seasonal tenant . . . , except upon establishment of one of the following grounds as
good cause:

    a. The person fails to pay rent due and owing under the lease whether the same
be oral or written . . . ;

    b. The person has continued to be, after written notice to cease, so disorderly as
to destroy the peace and quiet of the occupants or other tenants living in said
house or neighborhood;

    c. The person has willfully or by reason of gross negligence caused or allowed
destruction, damage or injury to the premises;

    d. The person has continued, after written notice to cease, to substantially
violate or breach any of the landlord's rules and regulations governing
said premises, provided such rules and regulations are reasonable and
have been accepted in writing by the tenant or made a part of the lease at
the beginning of the lease term;

    e. . . . The person has continued, after written notice to cease, to substantially
violate or breach any of the covenants or agreements contained in the lease
for the premises where a right of reentry is reserved to the landlord in the
lease for a violation of such covenant or agreement, provided that such
covenant or agreement is reasonable and was contained in the lease at the
beginning of the lease term;

    f. The person has failed to pay rent after a valid notice to quit and notice of
increase of said rent, provided the increase in rent is not unconscionable and
complies with any and all other laws or municipal ordinances governing rent
increases . . . ;

    g. The landlord or owner (1) seeks to permanently board up or demolish the
premises because he has been cited by local or State housing inspectors for
substantial violations affecting the health and safety of tenants and it is
economically unfeasible for the owner to eliminate the violations; (2)
seeks to comply with local or State housing inspectors who have cited
him for substantial violations affecting the health and safety of tenants
and it is unfeasible to so comply without removing the tenant . . . ;
(3) seeks to correct an illegal occupancy because he has been cited by
local or State housing inspectors or zoning officers and it is unfeasible to
correct such illegal occupancy without removing the tenant; or (4) is a
governmental agency which seeks to permanently retire the premises from
the rental market pursuant to a redevelopment or land clearance plan in a
blighted area . . . ;

    h. The owner seeks to retire permanently the residential building or the mobile
home park from residential use or use as a mobile park, provided this paragraph shall not apply to circumstances covered under paragraph g. of this
section;

    i. The landlord or owner proposes, at the termination of a lease, reasonable
changes of substance in the terms and conditions of the lease, including
specifically any change in the term thereof, which the tenant, after written
notice, refuses to accept. . . .

j.   The person, after written notice to cease, has habitually and without legal justification failed to pay rent which is due and owing;

k.   The landlord or owner of the building or mobile home park is converting from the rental market to a condominium, cooperative or fee simple ownership of two or more dwelling units or park sites, except as hereinafter provided in subsection *l*. . . . No action for possession shall be brought pursuant to this subsection against a senior citizen tenant or disabled tenant with protected tenancy status pursuant to the "Senior Citizens and Disabled Protected Tenancy Act" [N.J. Stat. Ann. §§2A:18-61.22 *et seq.*[3]], as long as the agency has not terminated the protected tenancy status or the protected tenancy period has not expired;

l.   (1)   The owner of a building or mobile home park, which is constructed as or being converted to a condominium, cooperative or fee simple ownership, seeks to evict a tenant or sublessee whose initial tenancy began after the master deed, agreement establishing the cooperative or subdivision plat was recorded, because the owner has contracted to sell the unit to a buyer who seeks to personally occupy it and the contract for sale calls for the unit to be vacant at the time of closing . . . ;

     (2)   The owner of three or less condominium or cooperative units seeks to evict a tenant whose initial tenancy began by rental from an owner of three or less units after the master deed or agreement establishing the cooperative was recorded, because the owner seeks to personally occupy the unit, or has contracted to sell the unit to a buyer who seeks to personally occupy it and the contract for sale calls for the unit to be vacant at the time of closing;

     (3)   The owner of a building of three residential units or less seeks to personally occupy a unit, or has contracted to sell the residential unit to a buyer who wishes to personally occupy it and the contract for sale calls for the unit to be vacant at the time of closing;

m.   The landlord or owner conditioned the tenancy upon and in consideration for the tenant's employment by the landlord or owner as superintendent, janitor or in some other capacity and such employment is being terminated.

VÁSQUEZ v. GLASSBORO SERVICE ASSOCIATION, INC.
415 A.2d 1156 (N.J. 1980)

STEWART G. POLLOCK, J. . . .

. . . Glassboro [Service Association] is a non-profit corporation comprised of farmers who contracted with Glassboro for migrant farm labor. The farmers called Glassboro as they needed workers to pick crops, and Glassboro transported workers from its labor camp to the farms. The length of time that a worker stayed at a farm varied, depending primarily on the time needed to pick a crop. Glassboro paid the worker his wages, and the farmer paid Glassboro for those wages plus a commission for Glassboro's services.

---

3. This statute protects elderly persons and persons with disabilities from being evicted for up to 40 years if the reason for the eviction is to convert the unit to a condominium or cooperative. — ED

Only men were hired; the workers' families remained in Puerto Rico. Glassboro paid a farmworker $2.40 per hour and charged him $23 per week for meals. The worker agreed to work eight hours a day for six days a week, plus overtime as mutually agreed.

[In 1976, Glassboro negotiated a contract with the Puerto Rican Department of Labor.] The . . . contract stated that a worker was to pay for his transportation from Puerto Rico. If he completed his contract, he would be reimbursed for the cost of transportation from and provided return transportation to Puerto Rico. If the worker did not fulfill his contract, Glassboro was not obliged to reimburse him for the cost of transportation. Although the contract provided that Glassboro would furnish a non-negotiable airplane ticket to Puerto Rico for a worker who became physically unfit, there was no comparable provision for a worker who was fired. The contract period was for 28 weeks, or until December 1, whichever came first.

The contract provided that, if an employee was to be discharged, a hearing was to occur no later than five days after the employee was given notice of termination. The contract did not require a minimum amount of time to elapse between notice and termination of employment.

The contract provided further for administrative review within the Puerto Rican Department of Labor whenever a worker had a complaint "regarding the breach, application, interpretation or compliance" with the contract. If the Secretary of Labor determined that Glassboro had "not adequately remedied the complaint," the Secretary could represent the worker and sue Glassboro.

Pursuant to the contract, Glassboro supplied living quarters for workers at its labor camp in New Jersey. Those quarters consisted of barracks housing up to 30 men. Each worker received a mattress, bedding, and a locker. The barracks were equipped with common toilets, showers, and lavatories. Although some farmers charged the workers for housing while the workers were at the farms, Glassboro did not impose any extra charge for housing at its labor camp. The contract did not require a migrant farmworker to live at Glassboro's labor camp. Nonetheless, the parties contemplated that the farmworker would reside at the labor camp.

In 1976, [Natividad] Vásquez was recruited in Puerto Rico and came to New Jersey to work for Glassboro. According to Glassboro's foreman, Vásquez's work was not satisfactory. On July 19, 1976, the foreman told Vásquez that he was to be discharged. A few hours later Vásquez had his "hearing" with the foreman and a field representative of the Puerto Rican Department of Labor. Thereafter the foreman decided to complete the discharge, a decision Vásquez does not challenge in this action. Although there were vacant spaces at the Glassboro barracks, Vásquez was not permitted to remain overnight. The foreman told him to gather his belongings and leave.

Unable to speak English and without funds to return to Puerto Rico, Vásquez sought the assistance of the Farmworkers Corporation, a federally funded non-profit corporation dedicated to the needs of farmworkers. He also consulted with the Farmworkers Rights Project of the Civil Liberties Education and Action Fund of the American Civil Liberties Union of New Jersey. A Rutgers law student returned with Vásquez to the camp and requested that Vásquez be allowed to remain overnight. The request was refused. Vásquez stayed with a friend who was participating in a job training program conducted by the Farmworkers Corporation.

The Farmworkers Rights Project filed a complaint on July 22, 1976, seeking an order permitting Vásquez to reenter his living quarters and enjoining defendants from depriving him of the use of the quarters except through judicial process. . . .

Although Vásquez has since found housing, other workers have been evicted, one at 3:00 A.M. . . .

II

At common law, one who occupied premises as an employee of the owner and received the use of the premises as part compensation for his services or under a contract of employment was not considered a tenant.

The initial question is whether the Legislature intended to include migrant farm-workers in the phrase "in some other capacity" in N.J. Stat. Ann. §2a:18-61.1(m). . . . Where general words follow a specific enumeration, the principle of *ejusdem generis* requires that the general words are applicable only to the same class of things already mentioned. In N.J. Stat. Ann. §2a:18-61.1(m), the general words "in some other capacity" follow the specific enumeration of "superintendent" and "janitor." We determine that, within the meaning of the statute, a farmworker does not belong to the same class of employees as a janitor or superintendent. A farmworker who possesses a mattress and locker in an unpartitioned barracks while waiting to be sent to work on a farm is different from a superintendent or janitor residing with his or her family in an apartment house. The farmworkers are all men who come from Puerto Rico without their families. They live in large barracks with no privacy, sleeping in bunks in an unpartitioned room and sharing toilets and showers. Their occupancy of the barracks is intermittent, since it is a base camp for use while they are awaiting assignment to farms. . . .

Our analysis of the words of the statute, the absence of any illuminating legislative history, and the application of principles of statutory construction lead to the conclusion that a migrant farmworker is not a tenant within the meaning of N.J. Stat. Ann. §2a:18-61.1(m). The special characteristics of migrant workers' housing, the absence of a contractual provision for the payment of rent, the lack of privacy, the intermittent occupancy, and the interdependence of employment and housing support this conclusion. . . .

III

In ascertaining whether a farmworker is entitled to notice before dispossession, we turn next to the Glassboro contract. As stated above, the contract resulted from negotiations between the Puerto Rican Department of Labor and Glassboro. No migrant farmworker participated directly or through a labor union in the negotiations. The record does not demonstrate whether or not the Puerto Rican Department of Labor has the same interests as the migrant farmworkers. The Puerto Rican Department of Labor may have been concerned also about reducing unemployment in Puerto Rico by finding jobs for its residents on farms in New Jersey. Whatever the interests of the parties to the negotiations, a migrant farmworker was required to accept the contract as presented by Glassboro.

The contract in evidence is written in English. Although Vásquez spoke Spanish only, the record does not show that he received a Spanish translation of the contract. Nonetheless, he signed a copy of the contract.

Once a migrant farmworker came to Glassboro's labor camp in New Jersey, he depended on Glassboro for employment, transportation, food, and housing. He was separated by over 1300 miles from his home and family. Although an American citizen, he was isolated from most citizens in New Jersey by his inability to speak English. An invisible barrier separated a migrant farmworker from the rest of the State as he was shuttled from the labor camp to the farms. The lack of alternative housing emphasized the inequality between Glassboro and the migrant farmworkers. Once his employment ended, a farmworker lost not only his job but his shelter. The fear of discharge, and with it the loss of income, housing, and return passage to Puerto Rico permeated the contractual relationship. This is the setting in which we measure the contract against the public policy of the State.

Public policy eludes precise definition and may have diverse meanings in different contexts. The sources of public policy include federal and state legislation and judicial decisions.

In the past, courts in New Jersey have refused to enforce contracts that violate the public policy of the State. No contract can be sustained if it is inconsistent with the public interest or detrimental to the common good. Contracts have been declared invalid because they violate statutes, promote crime, interfere with the administration of justice, encourage divorce, violate public morality, or restrain trade. With respect to employment contracts that have an otherwise lawful purpose, courts have afforded judicial sanction to post-employment restrictive covenants only to the extent that the covenants are reasonable and comport with public policy.

The courts and Legislature of New Jersey have demonstrated a progressive attitude in providing legal protection for migrant farmworkers. [The State Legislature has passed legislation regulating housing conditions and sanitation for migrant farmworkers. In 1979, the federal government, pursuant to the *Occupational Safety and Health Act* of 1970, 29 U.S.C.A. §651 *et seq.*, assumed responsibility for inspection of many migrant labor camps.] The constant attention accorded by Congress and the State Legislature demonstrates a legislative concern for the well-being of migrant farmworkers.

In *State v. Shack*, 277 A.2d 369 (N.J. 1971), this Court reversed convictions for trespass of a fieldworker and an attorney for organizations providing services for migrant farmworkers. Declining to characterize the migrant farmworker as either tenant or employee, Chief Justice Weintraub wrote:

> We see no profit in trying to decide upon a conventional category and then forcing the present subject into it. That approach would be artificial and distorting. The quest is for a fair adjustment of the competing needs of the parties, in the light of the realities of the relationship between the migrant worker and the operator of the housing facility. 277 A.2d at 374.

The Court weighed the property rights of the farmer against the rights of the farmworkers to information and services and found that the balance tipped in favor of the farmworker. Underlying that conclusion was recognition of the fundamental right of the farmworker to live with dignity. As in *Shack*, the appropriate result in this case arises from the status and the relationship of the parties. . . .

The enlightened approach of the courts and the Legislature provides the context in which we assess the Glassboro contract and consider how a migrant farmworker should be dispossessed from his living quarters at a labor camp.

A basic tenet of the law of contracts is that courts should enforce contracts as made by the parties. However, application of that principle assumes that the parties are in positions of relative equality and that their consent is freely given. In recent years, courts have become increasingly sensitive to overreaching in contracts where there is an inequality in the status of the parties. . . .

In a variety of . . . situations, courts have revised contracts where there was an inequality in the bargaining power of the parties.

The principle has been applied also to leases. In *Kuzmiak v. Brookchester*, 111 A.2d 425 (N.J. Super. Ct. App. Div. 1955), the court invalidated a clause in an apartment lease exculpating a landlord from liability for negligence. . . . This Court took cognizance of the housing shortage and the inequality in bargaining power of landlords and tenants in *Marini v. Ireland*, 265 A.2d 526 (N.J. 1970). In *Marini*, this Court implied a covenant of habitability into a lease to permit a tenant to deduct the cost of repairing a toilet from rent due a landlord. More recently the inequality of bargaining power between landlord and tenant led this Court to comment that "lease agreements are frequently form contracts of adhesion. . . ." *Trentacost v. Brussel*, 412 A.2d 436, 442 (N.J. 1980). In *Trentacost*, the Court concluded that the implied covenant of habitability obliged a landlord to furnish reasonable safeguards, such as a lock on the front door of an apartment building, to protect tenants from foreseeable criminal activity on the premises.

A migrant farmworker has even less bargaining power than a residential tenant. Although the contract did not require a migrant farmworker to live at the labor camp, the realities of his employment forced him to stay at the camp. Residence at the labor camp benefited not only the farmworker, but also Glassboro and its member farmers. It was more convenient for them if the workers resided at the camp: the pool of labor was at hand, and the workers could be transported conveniently to the farms. The contract assured Glassboro that there would be a labor source available on its property.

Under the contract, once a worker's employment was ended, he had no right to stay at the camp. Glassboro's possible need for the bed of a discharged farmworker, particularly during the growing season, is relevant, but not persuasive. In this case, Glassboro had ample space for Vásquez, yet he was turned out of the barracks on the same day he was fired. The interest of neither the migrant farmworker nor the public is served by casting the worker adrift to fend for himself without reasonable time to find shelter.

The status of a worker seeking employment with Glassboro is analogous to that of a consumer who must accept a standardized form contract to purchase needed goods and services. Neither farmworkers nor consumers negotiate the terms of their contracts; both must accept the contracts as presented to them. In both instances, the contracts affect many people as well as the public interest.

With respect to a standardized form contract, the intention of the consumer has been described as "but a subjection more or less voluntary to terms dictated by the stronger party, terms whose consequences are often understood only in a vague way, if at all." Kessler, *Contracts of Adhesion — Some Thoughts About Freedom of Contract*, 43 Colum. L. Rev. 629, 632 (1943). . . . A contract where one party, as here, must accept or reject the contract does not result from the consent of that party. It is a contract of adhesion:

> There being no private consent to support a contract of adhesion, its legitimacy rests entirely on its compliance with standards in the public interest. The individual who is subject to the obligations imposed by a standard form thus gains the assurance that the rules to which he is subject have received his consent either directly or through their conforming to higher public laws and standards made and enforced by the public institu-

tions that legitimately govern him. Slawson, *Standard Form Contracts and Democratic Control of Lawmaking Power*, 84 Harv. L. Rev. 529, 566 (1971).

The absence of a provision in the contract for reasonable time to find housing after termination of his employment bespeaks Glassboro's superior bargaining position. Further, by failing to provide for a reasonable time to find alternative housing, the contract is inconsistent with the enlightened attitude of the Legislature and the courts towards migrant farmworkers.

The crux of this case thus becomes the unconscionability of the contract as it is sought to be enforced against the migrant workers. The unconscionability of the contract inheres not only in its failure to provide a worker with a reasonable opportunity to find alternative housing, but in its disregard for his welfare after termination of his employment. The inherent inequity of the contract arouses a sense of injustice and invokes the equitable powers of the courts. In the absence of any concern demonstrated for the worker in the contract, public policy requires the implication of a provision for a reasonable time to find alternative housing.

IV

At common law, on termination of employment, an employer could dispossess an employee who occupied premises incidental to his employment. Similarly, a landlord could dispossess peaceably a holdover tenant. To that extent, both an employer and landlord could use self-help to regain possession peaceably. The advantage to them was that they were assured of prompt restoration of the use of their property. However, an inherent vice in self-help is that it can lead to confrontations and breaches of the peace.

In the absence of self-help, a landlord or employer at common law was remitted to an action in ejectment. The problem with ejectment is that it was slow and expensive. . . .

With regard to real property occupied solely as a residence, the Legislature has resolved the dilemma by prohibiting entry without consent and by providing a summary dispossess proceeding. N.J. Stat. Ann. §2a:39-1 and N.J. Stat. Ann. §2a:18-53 *et seq.* Similarly, the Legislature has provided a summary dispossess proceeding for the removal of residential tenants. N.J. Stat. Ann. §2a:18-61.2. As explained above, migrant farmworkers are not tenants, and there is no comparable statute providing for their summary dispossession on termination of their employment. In fashioning a suitable remedy, we acknowledge that the realities of the relationship between the migrant worker and a farm labor service are unique and summon a judicial response unrestricted by conventional categories, such as employer-employee and landlord-tenant. . . .

In the absence of a contractual provision or legislation addressing the plight of a migrant farmworker on termination of his employment, the courts, exercising equitable jurisdiction, should devise a remedy to fit the circumstances of each case. Depending on the circumstances, an equitable adjustment of the rights of the parties may vary from one case to another. An appropriate remedy might include time in addition to that implied in the contract, assistance in obtaining alternative housing, return passage to Puerto Rico, or some other form of relief. By abolishing self-help and requiring dispossession through a judicial proceeding, we provide a forum for an equitable resolution of a controversy between a farm labor service and a migrant farmworker on termination of the latter's employment.

We are mindful of the special considerations pertaining to migrant farmworkers and of the need for a prompt resolution of disputes between farmworkers and a farm labor service. In general, a summary action under R. 4:67 should be a more appropriate proceeding than a plenary action. In fact, the present case was instituted on complaint and order to show cause returnable three days later, at which time the court heard testimony, reserved decision, and rendered a written opinion seven days later. We conclude that a dispute concerning the dispossession of a migrant farmworker on termination of his employment, whether instituted by a farm labor service or, as here, by a farmworker, should proceed in a summary manner under R. 4:67. . . .

JUSTICE AND THE LAW OF CONTRACTS: A CASE FOR THE TRADITIONAL APPROACH
ALAN SCHWARTZ

9 Harv. J.L. & Pub. Pol'y 107-110, 114-115 (1986)

By justice, I meant two things. One aspect . . . follows from utilitarian premises and basically holds that just outcomes arise when people are permitted to do the best they can, given their circumstances. This is because, the theory goes, people are the best judges of what maximizes their own utility; hence, allowing them to make unrestrained choices is most likely to maximize utility for the individual and for society as a whole. The second aspect of justice . . . is called justice as fair distribution. This principle holds that the state has an obligation to insure that the circumstances in which people are trying to do the best they can are not terribly unfair to them.

I want to begin this discussion of contract law by using the first concept of justice: that utilitarian and Kantian notion that says that just outcomes result when people are allowed to do the best they can. In the Nineteenth Century, contract law was thought to promote justice in this sense because contract law permitted the parties to make almost any agreement they wanted and would then enforce the result. This was seen as letting people do the best they could for themselves.

In the Twentieth Century, this traditional view is thought to be obsolete. It is commonly believed that contract law in the traditional sense is an obstacle to justice because it permits the strong to exploit the weak in the name of freedom of contract. Through such doctrines as unconscionability, contract law today is attempting to perform its traditional function of insuring justice in the marketplace, not by permitting people to do what they want to do, but by preventing them — in certain circumstances — from doing what they have agreed to do.

I argue that the traditional theory was — with some exceptions — basically correct for several reasons. The principal reason is that, while there are evils in markets, they are evils that judges, given the tools that are available to judges, can seldom rectify. They are evils best rectified by other social institutions. . . .

. . . My claim is that competition in markets prevents even very large firms from exploiting even very small consumers. . . .

The question regarding justice and contract law that ought to be asked is not one about how large firms are or how small consumers are, or about the vacuous concept of "unequal bargaining power," but about how well consumer markets work. If they do work well, there is little to worry about in terms of justice — that is, justice in the sense of allowing people to do the best they can for themselves under given circumstances. If markets do not work well, then there is room for improvement. . . .

. . . While it would be silly to deny that market imperfections often exist and cause markets to work badly, the best place to get help is through institutions other than the judiciary and through doctrines other than contract law. Even though markets are imperfect, judges should enforce the contracts they yield.

. . . It is said that market outcomes are unfair because while individuals may do the best they can in markets given their circumstances, the circumstances are unfair. Market outcomes can be analogized to political outcomes: In markets one votes with dollars, and people who have fewer dollars have fewer votes. I shall not discuss generally the question of wealth distribution in society. I do argue that contract law is the wrong vehicle for improving inequities in wealth. Why is that? Because not enforcing contract clauses, which is all judges can do, tends to make people poorer rather than richer.

To make a person poorer is meant here to shrink the number of options a person has available to improve his or her lot in life. Suppose a judge bans a contract clause. He has imposed a restriction on the choices available to persons who agree to it or would have agreed to it in preference to other contract clauses that firms could offer. Poor people tend to have fewer choices than rich people because they have less money. Poor people do have free will, however. If a judge bans a contract clause on the ostensible ground of protecting the poor, the judge actually is reducing the choices of poor people and is therefore preventing poor people from doing as well as they can, given their circumstances, in the realm of contractual choice.

BARGAINING, DURESS, AND ECONOMIC LIBERTY
ROBERT HALE
43 Colum. L. Rev. 603, 603-607, 625-628 (1943)

We live in what is known as a free economy. We did, at least, before it was subjected to the controls necessitated by the war, or, as some would say, before the advent of the New Deal. Government and law did not tell us what part each of us must play in the process of production, or assign to each of us our respective rations of coffee, gasoline or other materials. What work we should do and how much we might consume were determined by a process known as freedom of contract. Yet in that process there was more coercion, and government and law played a more significant part, than is generally realized.

That men may live, they must either be in a position each to produce the material necessities of life for his own use, or there must be some adequate incentive for production of the goods and services which people other than the producers may enjoy, and some means by which individual consumers can acquire some portion of them. In thinly settled lands it may be possible for each family to produce most of the things needed to satisfy its own wants. The law has only to recognize each family's property right in its farm and its products, and protect that property from interference. But in a land as thickly settled as ours, such individualistic methods of providing for wants would be wholly inadequate. We have to resort to the more efficient process of machine production, with its widespread division of labor. Almost every article or service that is produced is the fruit of the combined efforts of countless people, each working on a fractional part of the product. But the product is consumed only in small part, if at all, by its producers. Other people consume it, and the producers of this product consume the products of other people's labor. Goods are turned out collectively and consumed individually. Individuals could conceivably be conscripted to contribute their respective efforts to the collective process of production, and the products could be rationed out to each for his individual consumption. These are not the methods of our free economy. We rely instead, for the most part, on bargaining.

There are few, if any, who own enough of the collective output of goods ready for consumption to satisfy their needs for more than a brief period in the future. Some persons own more than enough of certain types of goods, but they must perforce acquire the use of other types as well. The owner of a shoe factory is in no danger of going ill-shod — he may wear his own shoes. But he cannot live on shoes alone. Like everyone else, he must *buy* food or starve. Even the producer and owner of food must as a rule buy other forms of food than those in which he has specialized. Any person, in order to live, must induce some of the owners of things which he needs, to permit him to use them. The owner has no legal obligation to grant the permission. But if offered enough money he will probably do so; for he, too, must obtain the permission of other owners to make use of *their* goods, and for this purpose he too needs money — more than he has at the outset. He needs it more than he needs his surplus of shoes. Indeed he values his right of ownership in the shoes solely for the power it gives him to obtain money with which to buy other things which he does not yet own.

The owner of the shoes or the food or any other product can insist on other people keeping their hands off his products. Should he so insist, the government will back him up with force. The owner of the money can likewise insist on other people keeping their hands off his money, and the government will likewise back *him* up with force. By *threatening* to maintain the legal barrier against the use of his shoes, their owner may be able to obtain a certain amount of money as the price of not carrying out his threat. And by threatening to maintain the legal barrier against the use of his money, the purchaser may be able to obtain a certain amount of shoes as the price of not withholding the money. A bargain is finally struck, each party consenting to its terms in order to avert the consequences with which the other threatens him.

This does not mean, of course, that in each purchase of a commodity, there is unfriendliness, or deliberation and haggling over terms. Market conditions may have standardized prices, so that each party knows that any haggling would be futile. Nevertheless the transaction is based on the bargaining power of the two parties. The seller would not part with the shoes, or produce them in the first place, if the law enabled him to get the buyer's money without doing so, nor would the buyer part with his money if the law enabled him to obtain the shoes without payment.

[W]ithout money, an individual has little chance of gaining access to any part of the goods produced. The law bars such access without the consent of some of those to whom it assigns the ownership of those goods.

How, then, does any purchaser obtain the money that will enable him to consume? We have already seen that the owner of products obtains it, by selling his products to buyers. But how did he come to be the owner of the products? The answer which first suggests itself is that he produced them. To the extent that this is true, it indicates that he made his contribution to the productive process, not by first making a bargain with consumers, but because he anticipated that his efforts would put him in a favorable position to make future bargains. But the answer is not wholly true. The owner did not produce the shoes by his own efforts alone. Other people have taken part in the production too — not only his employees, but those who have advanced the necessary capital, or taken any part in the production of the raw materials and fuel which he uses, or in transporting them to his factory.

Yet of all these innumerable producers of the shoes, only the owner of the factory acquires title to them. The others have all, at one time or another, waived their claims to any share in the ownership of the shoes. They have done so in a series of bargaining transactions, in which they received money, or promises to pay money. Through this series of bargains, the owner of the plant has acquired the full right of ownership in the shoes. This right enables him, if he is successful, to obtain from his customers more than enough to repay all the outlays he has made to the other participants — enough more to compensate him for his risk and labor in organizing and managing the plant, and perhaps even more than this.

As a result of these innumerable bargains, the owner and the other participants in the production obtain their respective money incomes, and these money incomes determine the share that each may obtain of the total goods and services turned out by the collective efforts of all the other members of society. And it is as a result of these bargains, or in anticipation of them, that each participant in these collective productive efforts makes his contribution. We rely on the bargaining process to serve the conflicting interests of individuals in securing a share of the collective output of society, and also to serve their common interest in the creation of that collective output.

Though these bargains lead to vast differences in the economic positions of different persons, whether as producers or as consumers, these differences have all resulted from transactions into which each has entered without any explicit requirement of law that he do so. But while there is no explicit legal requirement that one enter into any particular transaction, one's freedom to decline to do so is nevertheless circumscribed. One chooses to enter into any given transaction in order to avoid the threat of something worse — threats which impinge with unequal weight on different members of society. The fact that he exercised a choice does not indicate lack of compulsion. Even a slave makes a choice. The compulsion which drives him to work operates through his own will power. He makes the "voluntary" muscular movements which the work calls for, in order to escape some threat; and though he exercises will power and makes a choice, still, since he is making it under threat, his servitude is called "involuntary." And one who obeys some compulsory requirement of the law in order to avoid a penalty is likewise making a choice. If he has the physical power to disobey, his obedience is not a matter of physical necessity, but of choice. Yet no one would deny that the requirement of the law is a compulsory one. It restricts his liberty to act out of conformity to it.

Government has power to compel one to choose obedience, since it can threaten disobedience with death, imprisonment, or seizure of property. Private individuals are not permitted to make such threats to other individuals, save in exceptional circumstances such as self-defense. But there are other threats which may lawfully be made to induce a party to enter into a transaction. In the complex bargains made in the course of production, some parties who deal with the manufacturer surrender a portion of their property, others their liberty not to work for him, in order to avert his threat to withhold his money, while he, in turn, surrenders some part of the money he now owns, or some part of his right to keep from them money he may obtain in the future, to avert their threats of withholding from him their raw materials or their labor. And he may have surrendered property in the past, and the freedom to abstain from labor, in order to attain his position as owner of the plant and its products, and so to obtain the money with which to avert the threats of owners of the things he wishes to consume, to withhold those things from him. In consenting to enter into any bargain, each party yields to the threats of the other. In the absence of corrective legislation, each party, in order to induce the other to enter into a transaction, may generally threaten to exercise any of his legal rights and privileges, no matter how disadvantageous that exercise may be to the other party. As Justice Holmes said in 1896 in a well known dissenting opinion in *Vegelahn v. Guntner*, [167 Mass. 92, 107 (1896):]

> The word "threats" often is used as if, when it appeared that threats had been made, it appeared that unlawful conduct had begun. But it depends on what you threaten. As a general rule, even if subject to some exceptions, what you may do in a certain event you may threaten to do, that is, give warning of your intention to do in that event, and thus allow the other person the chance of avoiding the consequences. . . .

. . . The fact that transactions do not deviate from normal market values does not necessarily indicate that there is a fair relation between the respective bargaining powers of the parties. The market value of a property or a service is merely a measure of the strength of the bargaining power of the person who owns the one or renders the other, under the particular legal rights with which the law endows him, and the legal restrictions which it places on others. To hold unequal bargaining power economically justified, merely because each party obtains the market value of what he sells, no more and no less, is to beg the question.

As a result of governmental and private coercion under what is mistakenly called *laissez faire*, the economic liberty of some is curtailed to the advantage of others, while the economic liberty of all is curtailed to some degree. Absolute freedom in economic matters is of course out of the question. The most we can attain is a relative degree of freedom, with the restrictions on each person's liberty as tolerable as we can make them. It would be impossible for everyone to have unrestricted freedom to make use of any material goods of which there are not enough to go round. If some exercised a freedom to take all the goods they desired, the freedom of others to consume those goods would be gone. There can be no freedom to consume what does not exist, or what other consumers have already appropriated. To protect a consumer's liberty from annihilation at the hands of other consumers, the law curtails it in a more methodical and less drastic way, by forbidding the use of goods without the consent of the owner. In practice this means that the liberty to consume is conditioned on the payment of the market price. . . .

Liberty to consume would be restricted far more drastically than it is were there no restrictions on that other aspect of economic liberty, freedom to abstain from producing. We do not have slave labor, but there are nevertheless compulsions which force people to work. These compulsions affect different people in varying degree, and are usually far more tolerable than slavery, or than the famine which would doubtless ensue were there no compulsions to work at all. In our industrial society, an employee works in order to make a bargain with his employer and thus obtain the money with which to free himself from some of the restrictions which other people's property rights place on his freedom to consume. He induces the employer to pay him his wage by *threatening* not to work for him, and then not carrying out his threat. Not carrying it out involves temporary surrender of his liberty to be idle. He *must* surrender that liberty, under penalty of not having freedom to consume more than his present means would enable him to.

But the degree to which men surrender liberty in the sphere of production, in order to increase their freedom to consume, varies. One who is endowed by nature or by superior educational opportunities with the ability to render services which are relatively scarce and for which there is great demand, may be able to insist on a high salary as the price of not withholding that ability from the employer, and thus may attain a large measure of freedom to consume. Or he may organize a business of his own and with the profits buy his freedom to consume. At the same time the surrender of his liberty to be idle may involve little if any sacrifice, for the work is apt to be agreeable, or at least more so than idleness. And he may have a large measure of discretion (or liberty) in deciding just *how* he is to perform his work, whereas those who have to take inferior jobs may have to do just what they are told by superiors throughout the working day. The liberty of these people as producers is more closely restricted than is that of those who can bargain for supervisory positions, or who can become entrepreneurs, and for this greater sacrifice of liberty in the process of production, they generally gain less freedom as consumers, being able to bargain only for low wages. The market value of their labor may be low, reflecting the low degree of compulsion they can bring to the bargaining process, as compared to the compulsion brought to bear by the employer.

The employer's power to induce people to work for him depends largely on the fact that the law previously restricts the liberty of these people to consume, while he has the power, through the payment of wages, to release them to some extent from these restrictions. He has little power over those whose freedom to consume is relatively unrestricted, because they have large independent means, or who can secure freedom to consume from other employers, because of their ability to render services of a sort that is scarce and in great demand. Those who own enough property have sufficient liberty to consume, without yielding any of their liberty to be idle. Their property rights enable them to exert pressure of great effectiveness to induce people to enter into bargains to pay them money. The law endows them with the power to call on the governmental authorities to keep others from using what they own. For merely not exercising this power, they can obtain large money rewards, by leasing or selling it to someone who will utilize it. These rewards may in many instances amount only to postponed payments for services which the owners have rendered in the past in the process of production, but frequently they greatly exceed any such amount. In fact the owner may have rendered no services whatever himself, but may have acquired his property by government grant or by virtue of the fact that the law assigns property rights to those named in the will of the previous owner, or, if he makes no will, according to the intestacy laws. Bargaining power would be different were it not that the law endows some with rights that are more advantageous than those with which it endows others.

It is with these unequal rights that men bargain and exert pressure on one another. These rights give birth to the unequal fruits of bargaining. There may be sound reasons of economic policy to justify all the economic inequalities that flow from unequal rights. If so, these reasons must be more specific than a broad policy of private property and freedom of contract. With different rules as to the assignment of property rights, particularly by way of inheritance or government grant, we could have just as strict a protection of each person's property rights, and just as little governmental interference with freedom of contract, but a very different pattern of economic relationships. Moreover, by judicious legal limitation on the bargaining power of the economically and legally stronger, it is conceivable that the economically weak would acquire greater freedom of contract than they now have — freedom to resist more effectively the bargaining power of the strong, and to obtain better terms.

NOTES AND QUESTIONS

1. *Summary process versus self-help.* Owners are entitled to use self-help to remove licensees. If they refuse to leave, the owner may use reasonable force. Owners used to be entitled to use self-help to remove tenants as well, and the law in some states still allows this, particularly for commercial tenants. However, today almost all states outlaw self-help in removing tenants, instead obligating landlords to use court proceedings (eviction) to recover possession. Every state has a statute, often called *forced entry and detainer* or *summary process* laws, that enables landlords to recover possession in expeditious court proceedings. In most states, the landlord is statutorily obligated to use these procedures and not to engage in self-help to regain possession when the tenant has breached material lease terms or has wrongfully held over after the termination of the tenancy. The landlord is not entitled to simply place the tenant's belongings on the street and change the locks on the door.

2. *License versus lease.* The issue frequently arises whether an arrangement constitutes a license or a lease. This issue arises in the context of department store concessions, students living in college dormitories, apartment complex managers and migrant farmworkers, rights to place signs on billboards or monuments, and concessions at shopping malls. These cases are generally decided by asking whether the owner has transferred exclusive "possession" of a defined space; if so, a lease will be found. If control of a particular space is not granted, or such possession is not exclusive, a license is likely to be found. *H.E.Y. Trust v. Popcorn Express Co.*, 35 S.W.3d 55 (Tex. Ct. App. 2000). However, the cases are split, with some courts finding leases in all these cases and other courts finding mere licenses.

How should the courts distinguish between licenses and leases? If we focus on the extent to which the owner has retained control over the space in question, the result will depend on an evaluation of the import of the retained powers. Courts have reached differing results, for example, in the case of *students* in dormitories. *Compare Burch v. University of Kansas*, 756 P.2d 431 (Kan. 1988); *Green v. Dormitory Authority of the State of New York*, 577 N.Y.S.2d 675 (App. Div. 1991) (both holding that students in dormitories are "tenants") *with Houle v. Adams State College*, 547 P.2d 926 (Colo. 1976); *Cook v. University Plaza*, 427 N.E.2d 405 (Ill. App. Ct. 1981) (holding that they are not). In the case of *employees*, such as migrant farmworkers and apartment building managers, the cases focus on determining whether access to the apartment seems to be part of the employment relationship and intended to last only as long as the employee remains on the job. It also matters whether the employer/landlord has a particular space reserved for employees and if occupancy by a non-employee would interfere with the owner's ability to provide the services that employee renders. *Compare Chan v. Antepenko*, 250 Cal. Rptr. 851 (Ct. App. 1988) (building superintendent is not a tenant) *with Bigelow v. Bullard*, 901 P.2d 630 (Nev. 1995) (superintendent is a tenant). *Compare De Bruyn Produce Co. v. Romero*, 508 N.W.2d 150 (Mich. Ct. App. 1993) (migrant farmworkers are licensees, not tenants) *with State v. De Coster*, 653 A.2d 891 (Me. 1995) (migrant farmworkers are "tenants").

It is problematic to focus on the question of whether the owner of the land has granted "possession" over a defined space. Possession is a mixed factual/legal finding, and it may be circular to ask whether possession has been granted when the question we need to resolve is what constitutes possession. More important, we are asking whether possession was granted for the purpose of determining whether the summary process statutes apply — that is, to determine whether the owner is or is not entitled to engage in self-help in removing the tenant/licensee. The policies underlying summary process laws should be at center stage here: avoiding violent confrontation, giving owners quick procedures to recover possession, protecting the ability of tenants to be protected from wrongful eviction and to have enough time to be able to find another place to live and move there.

The Supreme Court of New Jersey avoided the metaphysical question of whether the farm owner had granted "possession" to the farmworkers or whether they had the status of "tenants." This allowed the court to invent its own procedures for eviction rather than using the statutory eviction procedures. In effect, the court ruled that the farmworkers were entitled to common law protection even if they were not tenants and even if the statutory procedures did not apply to them. Was this a good idea? Was it justified? Could the legislature have intended to allow owners to engage in self-help in cases not covered by the summary process law? *See, e.g., City of New York v. Utsey*, 714 N.Y.S.2d 410 (App. Div. 2000) (governmental owner may be obligated to use eviction proceedings against long-term squatters whose initial occupancy was nonpermissive if the owner acquiesced in their occupancy in a manner that demonstrates an intent to treat them as tenants at will).

3. *Contract language.* Could the issue be avoided if the parties had a written agreement? The answer depends on deciding whether the policy outlawing self-help is disclaimable. If it is disclaimable, then there should be no problem with the parties agreeing to call their arrangement a license, under which the licensee can be removed at will without court eviction proceedings. If it is nondisclaimable, then the language should not be determinative. The cases are not uniform. Courts have interpreted "lease" arrangements as licenses and "license" arrangements as leases. *Compare Halley v. Harden Oil Co.*, 357 S.E.2d 138 (Ga. Ct. App. 1987) (although contract stated that it was a "lease," owner retained possession, use and responsibility for maintenance of property and thus was merely a license); *Loren v. Marry*, 600 N.Y.S.2d 369 (App. Div. 1993) (same) *with American Jewish Theatre, Inc. v. Roundabout Theatre Co.*, 610 N.Y.S.2d 256 (App. Div. 1994) *and M & I First National Bank v. Episcopal Homes Management, Inc.*, 536 N.W.2d 175 (Wis. Ct. App. 1995) (both holding that "license" arrangements were leases).

4. *Easement versus lease.* The issue often arises whether an agreement to allow someone to place a sign on a billboard is a lease or an easement. In *Keller v. Southwood North Medical Pavilion, Inc.*, 959 P.2d 102 (Utah 1998), for example, a chiropractor leased space in a shopping center pursuant to a written agreement that contained a clause giving him the right to place a sign on a large monument located near the street. When the landlord sold the property, the new owner objected to the appearance of the tenant's sign and removed it, claiming that the agreement only gave the tenant a license to use the billboard. The tenant claimed that the landlord violated the state statute, which required landlords to use court eviction proceedings rather than self-help to recover possession of property from tenants and that the tenant was entitled to the statutorily prescribed treble damages. The court agreed with the landlord because the agreement did not identify any particular space on the sign that tenant had a right to occupy; the agreement was therefore to give a license and not a grant of "possessory" rights. *Compare Golden West Baseball Co. v. City of Anaheim*, 31 Cal. Rptr. 2d 378 (Ct. App. 1994) (right to use public sports stadium for professional baseball 80 days a year is an easement rather a lease despite contract language calling it a lease). Can you think of a better way to resolve these cases?

PROBLEMS

1. Two university students living in a college dormitory come to you with the following problem. Along with signing many other forms and documents, the students signed form dormitory contracts that stated "LICENSE" at the top of the first page. The contract granted the students a "license" to occupy a dormitory room in exchange for rent to be paid one semester at a time. The form stated that the university "reserved the right to cancel the license at any time for any reason with 24 hours' notice." It also stated: "This agreement is not a lease." One student placed a banner reading "SUPPORT THE LIVING WAGE CAMPAIGN" outside her window in an effort to persuade the university to raise the wages it pays to its lowest-paid employees to enable them to earn enough to live in the community without taking a second job. The other student placed a banner reading "ABORTION KILLS" outside her window. The university had a policy prohibiting students from placing any banners outside their windows. The students knew about the policy but decided to violate it on the ground that it interfered with their right to free speech. Because of their violations of the rules, they were given 24 hours to vacate their dormitory rooms. They were not suspended or otherwise punished for their conduct. A state statute provides that "tenants" cannot be evicted without one month's notice and a court eviction proceeding.

    a. What is the students' argument that they are "tenants" protected from eviction without judicial process?
    b. What is the school's argument that they are licensees, rather than tenants, and can be removed with self-help and no notice?
    c. How should the court rule?

2. A retail department store enters into a "license" agreement with an optometrist granting her the right to fit and sell prescription eyeglasses in the store. The agreement establishes a minimum floor space for the operation but leaves the location of the space to the store manager. It further provides for a "rental payment" equal to a percentage of sales proceeds. The optometrist operates the department for 20 years. The store then terminates the arrangement. The optometrist has trouble finding a suitable alternative location for her business and fails to leave. Must the store use eviction proceedings, or is it entitled to engage in self-help? Should eviction be required? *See Layton v. A. I. Namm & Sons*, 89 N.Y.S.2d 72 (App. Div. 1949) (no).

§8.2 Conflicts About Rent

§8.2.1 LANDLORD'S RIGHT TO RECEIVE RENT

The main rights reserved by the landlord in relation to the tenant are (1) the right to receive the agreed-upon *rent*; (2) the right to have the premises intact and not damaged, subject to normal wear and tear (tenant's duty not to commit *waste*); and (3) the landlord's *reversion*, or the right to regain possession at the end of the lease term (when the term of years ends or the landlord provides notice that a periodic tenancy or tenancy at will is to be terminated).

Most lawsuits brought by landlords against tenants are instituted because the tenant has failed to pay rent. In most of these cases, the landlord sues both for back rent owed and to regain possession (to evict the tenant). A smaller number of cases involve attempts to evict tenants for breaching other express or implied terms of the lease. These other terms may include a covenant not to damage the apartment, a covenant requiring the tenants not to interfere with the quiet enjoyment of neighboring tenants in the building, covenants not to keep pets in the apartment, and covenants not to sublet.

In some cases, the tenant breaches the lease by not paying the rent and refuses to leave. Here the landlord may seek to receive back rent and to evict the tenant. In other cases, the tenant breaches the lease by not paying rent and moves out before the end of the lease term. Here the landlord ordinarily attempts to re-rent the apartment and may sue the tenant for back rent; if the new "rental price" is less than the rent under the breached lease, the landlord may sue for the difference between the new rent and the old for the remaining period of the lease.

§8.2.1.1 Landlord's Remedies When Tenant Breaches and Refuses to Leave: Summary Process

Possession and back rent. If the tenant wrongfully stops paying rent or breaches other material terms in the lease and continues to occupy the premises, the landlord may sue the tenant for back rent (rent already due but not paid) and for possession (to evict the tenant and to be able to re-rent the apartment to someone else). Tenants may respond to such claims by asserting defenses, such as rights based on the implied warranty of habitability and retaliatory eviction.[4] The tenant may also argue that the landlord's attempt to evict the tenant constitutes unlawful discrimination based on family status, disability, race, or gender.[5]

The holdover tenant and the renewal of the tenancy. What happens if the tenant wrongfully holds over after the end of the lease term and *continues* to pay rent? The landlord may choose to accept a new tenancy relationship with the holdover tenant. Most states hold that the new tenancy is a periodic tenancy based on the rent payment; if the landlord accepts a rent check for one's month rent, a new month-to-month tenancy is established. A minority of states hold that a new term is created if the landlord accepts rent from a holdover tenant who was originally occupying under a term of years. In these states, the tenant is bound to another term of the same length as the original term. The tenant who holds over wrongfully is obligated to pay rent to the landlord for the time during which she occupies the premises.

The landlord is also free to take the opposite course of action, that is, to treat the tenant as a tenant at sufferance or a holdover tenant and sue for possession. If the landlord chooses the latter course, does the landlord have the right to collect rent from the holdover tenant before the eviction proceedings are completed? Some states hold that acceptance of the rent check proffered by the holdover tenant *necessarily* creates a new tenancy — regardless of whether the landlord intends to create a new tenancy. To evict the tenant, the landlord may have to go through the procedures to evict a

---

4. These doctrines are covered later in this chapter.
5. *See* Chapter 11.

month-to-month tenant, including providing the requisite notice. The landlord may attempt to avoid this result by suing immediately for possession and either (a) refusing to accept the tenant's proffered checks (or returning them to the tenant) or (b) cashing the checks while writing on the back of each check that the landlord is not agreeing to renew the tenancy but is merely using the check to cover the rental value of the property from the tenant at sufferance.

Self-help. A major issue when the tenant breaches the lease and refuses to leave is whether the landlord is entitled to engage in *self-help* to remove the tenant. Almost all states now hold that the landlord may *not* use self-help, at least in the residential context and often in the commercial context as well. The law today is generally that the landlord must evict the tenant through court proceedings. In *Berg v. Wiley*, 264 N.W.2d 145 (Minn. 1978), the tenant operated a restaurant pursuant to a written lease. The lease contained a covenant by the tenant not to make any changes in the building structure without the landlord's consent. After observing continued violations of this provision and having made several attempts to persuade the tenant to stop remodeling the building to no avail, the landlord changed the locks on the door of the tenant's restaurant, barring the tenant from the premises. The tenant sued the landlord for wrongful eviction. The court found for the tenant, holding that the only lawful means to dispossess a tenant who continues to occupy the premises and has not voluntarily surrendered her rights under the tenancy is to resort to judicial process. In so doing, the court rejected the traditional rule allowing landlords to use self-help to regain possession of leased premises if the landlord is legally entitled to possession and the landlord's means of reentry are "peaceable" rather than "forcible." The court argued that the legislature had provided a *summary procedure* to allow landlords a relatively quick judicial process for a court order allowing the landlord to recover possession. This procedure protected the landlord's rights adequately and prevented the landlord from taking the law into his own hands. Self-help, the court argued, is likely to become violent; moreover, the landlord may be mistaken about his right to possession, and he should not be "the judge of his own rights." The court noted that the landlord could also go to court for an immediate temporary restraining order to prevent the tenant from destroying the property.

Summary process. Most states have statutes providing for *summary process.* These proceedings allow relatively fast judicial determination of the landlord's claim of a right to regain possession of her property. The statutes are called by a variety of names, including *forcible entry and detainer, unlawful detainer, summary proceedings,* and *summary ejectment.* Summary process statutes often limit the issues that can be addressed in the lawsuit; for many years they were interpreted in ways that prevented tenants from raising defenses to the landlord's claim that she was entitled to possession of the premises.

These proceedings have become considerably less "summary" in recent years, as they have been interpreted by courts or amended by legislatures to allow tenants to raise an increasingly diverse number of defenses — chief among them the implied warranty of habitability. Some states, however, still prevent the tenant from raising defenses, such as the landlord's violation of the implied warranty of habitability, in summary proceedings. The United States Supreme Court has upheld this practice, holding that treating the "undertakings of the tenant and those of the landlord as independent rather than dependent covenants" is not a fundamentally unfair procedure that would violate the tenant's rights to due process of law under the fourteenth amendment. *See Lindsey v. Normet*, 405 U.S. 56, 68 (1972).

§8.2.1.2 Landlord's Remedies When Tenant Breaches and Leaves

(a) *Landlord's Duty to Mitigate Damages*

A different set of problems ensues if the tenant breaches the lease for a term of years by ceasing rent payments and moves out before the end of the lease term. The right to sue for possession is of no use since the tenant has already given up possession. In this situation, the landlord can choose among three remedies.

1. Accept the tenant's surrender. By moving out before the end of the lease term and ceasing rent payments, the tenant makes an implied offer to the landlord to end the term of years. The landlord may, if she chooses, "accept the tenant's surrender of the lease." This means that the landlord agrees that the tenant will not be legally obligated to pay the future rent.

It is important to note, however, that the landlord's acceptance of the tenant's surrender does *not* mean that the tenant is relieved of *all* financial liability. The landlord may still choose to sue the tenant for *back rent* owed but not paid for the time before the tenant abandoned the premises by moving out. In addition, the landlord may sue immediately (without waiting until the end of the lease term) for *damages* for breach of the lease — which is different from the amount of the *future rent*. As in other contractual settings you may have learned about, damages are likely to be measured by an estimate of the amount the landlord lost because of the tenant's failure to perform his obligations under the contract. This amount is *not* the remaining rent, but the *agreed-upon rental price minus the fair market price*. The theory is that, because the landlord can re-rent the apartment, all the landlord loses by the tenant's breach is the difference between the amount the tenant agreed to pay and the amount the landlord can get from a replacement tenant, plus the advertising and search costs of finding a replacement tenant and lost rent in the meantime. If the rental price is the same as or below the market price, damages are zero (plus the cost of locating the new tenant). The court is likely to add to the computation of damages the reasonable cost of finding a replacement — a cost the landlord would not have had to bear if the tenant had not breached.

2. Re-let on the tenant's account. The landlord may *refuse to accept the surrender*; instead, the landlord may, after notice to the tenant, actively look for a new tenant and *re-let the apartment on the tenant's account*. When a new tenant is found, the landlord may sue the former tenant for the difference between the old rental price and the new rent received from the new lessee, if the new rent is lower than the original rent. The new rent must be reasonable; the landlord cannot rent the apartment to her sister for $5 a month, and expect to recover the difference between the agreed-upon rent and the artificially low figure charged to her sister.

An issue that has often arisen in this context is how the landlord can make clear that she is refusing to accept the tenant's proffered surrender of the lease. In some states, the very act of re-letting the apartment will be taken as evidence that the landlord has accepted the surrender of the leasehold. In others, the act of re-letting does not preclude the landlord from asserting that she did not accept the surrender. In still others, the landlord must notify the tenant that she is re-letting on the tenant's account and that she refuses to accept the surrender in order to hold the tenant to the rent later.

Why does it matter whether the landlord is held to have accepted the surrender? Consider a situation in which the tenant under a one-year lease moves out after six months. The landlord finds a new tenant, who agrees to a month-to-month tenancy at the old rent. But this second tenant moves out after four months, with two months left on the year lease. The landlord looks for, but is unable to find, a new tenant. If the landlord has accepted the first tenant's surrender, then the landlord cannot sue the original tenant for the last two months' rent. If the landlord has *not* accepted the tenant's surrender, then the tenant will be obligated to reimburse the landlord for the last two months' rent.

3. Wait and sue for the rent at the end of the lease term versus mitigate damages. The traditional rule is that the landlord may do nothing, wait for the end of the lease term, and then sue the tenant for the remaining unpaid back rent. Rent comes due periodically; under a one-year lease with monthly rental payments, each rental payment is not due until that month arrives. Thus, the landlord could not immediately sue for the remaining rent in the middle of the lease term. To sue the tenant immediately for monetary compensation in the middle of the lease term, the landlord must ask for damages (rental price minus fair market price); to sue for the entire rent itself, the landlord must wait until the lease term ends.

Most states, however, now reject this option. Instead, they have started to apply the contract doctrine that requires the aggrieved party to *mitigate damages.* By sitting around and waiting for the unpaid rent to accumulate, the landlord arguably increases damages that could have been avoided by re-letting the apartment to another tenant. States that require the landlord to mitigate damages place an obligation on the landlord to act reasonably in seeking another tenant. If the landlord fails to mitigate damages by finding another tenant and waits until the end of the lease to sue for the accumulated back rent, the amount of the damages will be reduced by the amount that would have been avoided had the landlord mitigated damages by acting reasonably to find a replacement tenant. If the landlord does mitigate damages, he can still recover from the tenant the reasonable costs of finding a new tenant, the rent for the premises while the premises were vacant and the landlord was looking for a new tenant, and the difference between the rental price and the new rent paid by the replacement tenant if it is lower than the original rent.

Although under the traditional rule landlords had no duty to mitigate damages, the trend is clearly toward requiring mitigation, at least in the residential context. The policies behind the traditional rule, which imposes no duty to mitigate damages, seem flatly inconsistent with the traditional measure of damages that the landlord is entitled to receive if the landlord accepts the tenant's surrender and sues immediately. Recall that that measure is the difference between the rental price and the market price. In order to be made whole — to suffer no financial loss from the tenant's breach — the landlord *must* find a new tenant willing and able to pay the market rent. The following case addresses the question of the landlord's duty to mitigate damages.

SOMMER v. KRIDEL
378 A.2d 767 (N.J. 1977)

MORRIS PASHMAN, J. . . .

I

A. Sommer v. Kridel

. . . On March 10, 1972 the defendant, James Kridel, entered into a lease with the plaintiff, Abraham Sommer, owner of the "Pierre Apartments" in Hackensack, to rent apartment 6-L in that building. The term of the lease was from May 1, 1972 until April 30, 1974, with a rent concession for the first six weeks, so that the first month's rent was not due until June 15, 1972.

One week after signing the agreement, Kridel paid Sommer $690. Half of that sum was used to satisfy the first month's rent. The remainder was paid under the lease provision requiring a security deposit of $345. Although defendant had expected to begin occupancy around May 1, his plans were changed. He wrote to Sommer on May 19, 1972, explaining

> I was to be married on June 3, 1972. Unhappily the engagement was broken and the wedding plans cancelled. Both parents were to assume responsibility for the rent after our marriage. I was discharged from the U.S. Army in October 1971 and am now a student. I have no funds of my own, and am supported by my stepfather.
>
> In view of the above, I cannot take possession of the apartment and am surrendering all rights to it. Never having received a key, I cannot return same to you.
>
> I beg your understanding and compassion in releasing me from the lease, and will of course, in consideration thereof, forfeit the 2 months' rent already paid.
>
> Please notify me at your earliest convenience.

Plaintiff did not answer the letter.

Subsequently, a third party went to the apartment house and inquired about renting apartment 6-L. Although the parties agreed that she was ready, willing and able to rent the apartment, the person in charge told her that the apartment was not being shown since it was already rented to Kridel. In fact, the landlord did not re-enter the apartment or exhibit it to anyone until August 1, 1973. At that time it was rented to a new tenant for a term beginning on September 1, 1973. The new rental was for $345 per month with a six week concession similar to that granted Kridel.

Prior to re-letting the new premises, plaintiff sued Kridel in August 1972, demanding $7,000, the total amount due for the full two-year term of the lease. Following a mistrial, plaintiff filed an amended complaint asking for $5,000, the amount due between May 1, 1972 and September 1, 1973. The amended complaint included no reduction in the claim to reflect the six week concession provided for in the lease or the $690 payment made to plaintiff after signing the agreement. Defendant filed an amended answer to the complaint, alleging that plaintiff breached the contract, failed to mitigate damages and accepted defendant's surrender of the premises. He also counterclaimed to demand repayment of the $345 paid as a security deposit.

The trial judge ruled in favor of defendant. Despite his conclusion that the lease had been drawn to reflect "the 'settled law' of this state," he found that "justice and fair dealing" imposed upon the landlord the duty to attempt to re-let the premises and thereby mitigate damages. He also held that plaintiff's failure to make any response to defendant's unequivocal offer of surrender was tantamount to an acceptance, thereby terminating the tenancy and any obligation to pay rent. As a result, he dismissed both the complaint and the counterclaim. The Appellate Division reversed in a per curiam opinion, and we granted certification.

B. Riverview Realty Co. v. Perosio

This controversy arose in a similar manner. On December 27, 1972, Carlos Perosio entered into a written lease with plaintiff Riverview Realty Co. The agreement covered the rental of apartment 5-G in a building owned by the realty company at 2175 Hudson Terrace in Fort Lee. As in the companion case, the lease prohibited the tenant from subletting or assigning the apartment without the consent of the landlord. It was to run for a two-year term, from February 1, 1973 until January 31, 1975, and provided for a monthly rental of $450. The defendant took possession of the apartment and occupied it until February 1974. At that time he vacated the premises, after having paid the rent through January 31, 1974.

The landlord filed a complaint on October 31, 1974, demanding $4,000 in payment for the monthly rental from February 1, 1974 through October 31, 1974. Defendant answered the complaint by alleging that there had been a valid surrender of the premises and that plaintiff failed to mitigate damages. The trial court granted the landlord's motion for summary judgment against the defendant, fixing the damages at $4,000 plus $182.25 interest.

The Appellate Division affirmed the trial court, holding that it was bound by prior precedents, including *Joyce v. Bauman*, 174 A. 693 (N.J. 1934). Nevertheless, it freely criticized the rule which it found itself obliged to follow:

> There appears to be no reason in equity or justice to perpetuate such an unrealistic and uneconomic rule of law which encourages an owner to let valuable rented space lie fallow because he is assured of full recovery from a defaulting tenant. Since courts in New Jersey and elsewhere have abandoned ancient real property concepts and applied ordinary contract principles in other conflicts between landlord and tenant there is no sound reason for a continuation of a special real property rule to the issue of mitigation. . . .

We granted certification.

II

As the lower courts in both appeals found, the weight of authority in this State supports the rule that a landlord is under no duty to mitigate damages caused by a defaulting tenant.

This rule has been followed in a majority of states. . . .

Nevertheless, while there is still a split of authority over this question, the trend among recent cases appears to be in favor of a mitigation requirement.

The majority rule is based on principles of property law which equate a lease with a transfer of a property interest in the owner's estate. Under this rationale the lease conveys to a tenant an interest in the property which forecloses any control by the landlord; thus, it would be anomalous to require the landlord to concern himself with the tenant's abandonment of his own property.

For instance, in *Muller v. Beck,* 110 A. 831 (N.J. 1920), where essentially the same issue was posed, the court clearly treated the lease as governed by property, as opposed to contract, precepts.[3] . . .

Yet the distinction between a lease for ordinary residential purposes and an ordinary contract can no longer be considered viable. As Professor Powell observed, evolving "social factors have exerted increasing influence on the law of estates for years." 2 *Powell on Real Property* (1977 ed.), §221(1) at 180-181. The result has been that

> [t]he complexities of city life, and the proliferated problems of modern society in general, have created new problems for lessors and lessees and these have been commonly handled by specific clauses in leases. This growth in the number and detail of specific lease covenants has reintroduced into the law of estates for years a predominantly contractual ingredient. *Id.* at 181.

Thus in 6 *Williston on Contracts* §890A at 592 (3d ed. 1962), it is stated:

> There is a clearly discernible tendency on the part of courts to cast aside technicalities in the interpretation of leases and to concentrate their attention, as in the case of other contracts, on the intention of the parties. . . .

This Court has taken the lead in requiring that landlords provide housing services to tenants in accordance with implied duties which are hardly consistent with the property notions expressed in *Muller v. Beck, supra.* . . . *See Braitman v. Overlook Terrace Corp.,* 346 A.2d 76 (N.J. 1975) (liability for failure to repair defective apartment door lock); *Berzito v. Gambino,* 308 A.2d 17 (N.J. 1973) (construing implied warranty of habitability and covenant to pay rent as mutually dependent); *Marini v. Ireland,* 265 A.2d 526 (N.J. 1970) (implied covenant to repair); *Reste Realty Corp. v. Cooper,* 251 A.2d 268 (N.J. 1969) (implied warranty of fitness of premises for leased purpose). . . .

Application of the contract rule requiring mitigation of damages to a residential lease may be justified as a matter of basic fairness.[4] Professor McCormick first commented upon the inequity under the majority rule when he predicted in 1925 that eventually

> the logic, inescapable according to the standards of a "jurisprudence of conceptions" which permits the landlord to stand idly by the vacant, abandoned premises and treat them as the property of the tenant and recover full rent, will yield to the more realistic notions of social advantage which in other fields of the law have forbidden a recovery for damages which the plaintiff by reasonable efforts could have avoided. McCormick, *The Rights of the Landlord upon Abandonment of the Premises by the Tenant,* 23 Mich. L. Rev. 211, 221-22 (1925).

---

3. It is well settled that a party claiming damages for a breach of contract has a duty to mitigate his loss.

4. [W]e reserve for another day the question of whether a landlord must mitigate damages in a commercial setting.

Various courts have adopted this position.

The pre-existing rule cannot be predicated upon the possibility that a landlord may lose the opportunity to rent another empty apartment because he must first rent the apartment vacated by the defaulting tenant. Even where the breach occurs in a multi-dwelling building, each apartment may have unique qualities which make it attractive to certain individuals. Significantly, in *Sommer v. Kridel*, there was a specific request to rent the apartment vacated by the defendant; there is no reason to believe that absent this vacancy the landlord could have succeeded in renting a different apartment to this individual.

We therefore hold that antiquated real property concepts which served as the basis for the pre-existing rule, shall no longer be controlling where there is a claim for damages under a residential lease. Such claims must be governed by more modern notions of fairness and equity. A landlord has a duty to mitigate damages where he seeks to recover rents due from a defaulting tenant.

If the landlord has other vacant apartments besides the one which the tenant has abandoned, the landlord's duty to mitigate consists of making reasonable efforts to re-let the apartment. In such cases he must treat the apartment in question as if it was one of his vacant stock.

As part of his cause of action, the landlord shall be required to carry the burden of proving that he used reasonable diligence in attempting to re-let the premises. We note that there has been a divergence of opinion concerning the allocation of the burden of proof on this issue. While generally in contract actions the breaching party has the burden of proving that damages are capable of mitigation, here the landlord will be in a better position to demonstrate whether he exercised reasonable diligence in attempting to re-let the premises.

III

The *Sommer v. Kridel* case presents a classic example of the unfairness which occurs when a landlord has no responsibility to minimize damages. Sommer waited 15 months and allowed $4658.50 in damages to accrue before attempting to re-let the apartment. Despite the availability of a tenant who was ready, willing and able to rent the apartment, the landlord needlessly increased the damages by turning her away. While a tenant will not necessarily be excused from his obligations under a lease simply by finding another person who is willing to rent the vacated premises, here there has been no showing that the new tenant would not have been suitable. We therefore find that plaintiff could have avoided the damages which eventually accrued, and that the defendant was relieved of his duty to continue paying rent. Ordinarily we would require the tenant to bear the cost of any reasonable expenses incurred by a landlord in attempting to re-let the premises, but no such expenses were incurred in this case.

In *Riverview Realty Co. v. Perosio*, no factual determination was made regarding the landlord's efforts to mitigate damages, and defendant contends that plaintiff never answered his interrogatories. Consequently, the judgment is reversed and the case remanded for a new trial. Upon remand and after discovery has been completed, the trial court shall determine whether plaintiff attempted to mitigate damages with reasonable diligence, and if so, the extent of damages remaining and assessable to the tenant. As we have held above, the burden of proving that reasonable diligence was used to re-let the premises shall be upon the plaintiff.

In assessing whether the landlord has satisfactorily carried his burden, the trial court shall consider, among other factors, whether the landlord, either personally or through an agency, offered or showed the apartment to any prospective tenants, or advertised it in local newspapers. Additionally, the tenant may attempt to rebut such evidence by showing that he proffered suitable tenants who were rejected. However, there is no standard formula for measuring whether the landlord has utilized satisfactory efforts in attempting to mitigate damages, and each case must be judged upon its own facts. . . .

NOTES AND QUESTIONS

1. The traditional rule was that landlords have no duty to mitigate damages. Most states have followed the lead of New Jersey and changed their laws through statute or judicial decision to impose a duty to mitigate damages, at least in the context of residential leases. *E.g.*, Alaska Stat. §34.03.230; Cal. Civ. Code §1951.2; Ky. Rev. Stat. §383.670. The *Uniform Residential Landlord and Tenant Act*, §4.203(c) (1972), adopted in about half the states, rejects the traditional rule. Most states also now extend the duty to commercial leases. *See, e.g., Frenchtown Square Partn. v. Lemstone, Inc.*, 791 N.E.2d 417 (Ohio 2003)(commercial landlord has duty to mitigate damages); *Austin Hill Country Realty v. Palisades Plaza*, 948 S.W.2d 293 (Tex. 1997)(same).

Some states retain this rule of law. *Bowdoin Square, L.L.C. v. Winn-Dixie Montgomery, Inc.*, 873 So.2d 1091, 1100 (Ala. 2003); *Intl. Comm'n on English in the Liturgy v. Schwartz*, 573 A.2d 1303 (D.C. 1990); *Holy Properties, Ltd. v. Kenneth Cole Prods., Inc.*, 661 N.E.2d 694, 696 (N.Y. 1995) (commercial); *Stonehedge Square v. Movie Merchants*, 715 A.2d 1082 (Pa. 1998) (commercial). The *Restatement (Second) of Property* also adheres to the traditional rule. *Restatement (Second) of Property (Landlord and Tenant)* §12.1(3) & cmt. i (1977). Authority in New York on residential leases is conflicting. *Compare Whitehouse Estates, Inc. v. Post*, 662 N.Y.S.2d 982 (App. Div. 1997) *and Duda v. Thompson*, 647 N.Y.S.2d 401, 403-404 (N.Y. Sup. Ct. 1996) (no duty) *with 29 Holding Corp. v. Diaz*, 775 N.Y.S.2d 807 (Sup. Ct. 2004) *and Palumbo v. Donalds*, 754 N.Y.S.2d 856 (Civ. Ct. 2003)(duty to mitigate). However, New York statutes do give tenants the right to sublease or assign with the landlord's consent; they also entitle the tenant to get out of the lease if the landlords refuses consent unreasonably when the tenant finds a suitable subtenant. N.Y. Real Prop. L. §226-b.

2. The duty to mitigate damages is not an enforceable obligation in the sense that the landlord *must* attempt to re-let the premises. The landlord is perfectly free to leave the premises vacant. The rule simply means that, in a lawsuit against the tenant for back rent, the landlord can recover only the difference between the market rent and the contract rent provided for in the rental agreement with the original tenant, plus the costs of finding a replacement tenant. *But see Uniform Residential Landlord and Tenant Act* §4.203 (rental agreement terminates if landlord "fails to use reasonable efforts to rent the dwelling unit at a fair rental" and landlord can recover nothing).

Landlords who want to protect themselves are well advised to attempt to re-let the premises, even in jurisdictions that retain the traditional rule, given the possibility that the law may be changed at any time and be applied retroactively. If a landlord attempts to re-let and finds a new tenant who then fails to pay part or all of the rent, the landlord may want to go after the original tenant for the unpaid rent. If, however, the landlord has accepted the original tenant's surrender of the lease, he can only go after the new tenant. How can the landlord increase the likelihood that the courts will find that the landlord did not accept the tenant's surrender of the lease?

3. Some scholars argue that the duty to mitigate damages is efficient because it encourages landlords to rent the premises rather than leaving them vacant. Because the landlord can be compensated by the tenant for all the extra costs of re-letting the premises and still obtain the economic value of the leasehold, re-renting gives the landlord the benefit of the bargain; he is in the economic position he would have been in had the tenant performed. Moreover, the old tenant has been able to get out of an arrangement that was no longer in her interest; the new tenant has obtained an apartment, thus being made better off. Placing no duty on the landlord would allow him to leave the apartment vacant, thereby wasting a scarce resource. Alternatively, it would force the tenant to give up a job opportunity elsewhere, for example, and remain locked in to the apartment. Either result creates a loss of social wealth relative to re-letting the premises.

Others argue, however, that there is no such efficiency loss. The landlord bargained for the right not to have to look for another tenant before the end of the lease term. This right is a property right that the landlord owns; the tenant has no right to take this right from the landlord without offering adequate compensation. The only compensation that is adequate is the remainder of the bargained-for rent. If the tenant wanted a nine-month lease, she could have bargained for it. If the tenant wants to breach the 12-month lease by moving out early, she should have to compensate the landlord sufficiently to induce the landlord to agree to give up his right not to have to look for a new tenant. If the tenant is unwilling to compensate the landlord for the right to terminate the lease early, the cost to the landlord outweighs the benefit to the plaintiff.

Is either of these arguments convincing?

4. Does it matter whether the landlord specifically talked with the tenant about his desire not to have to look for new tenants? Should the courts distinguish between situations involving professional landlords who rent to many tenants and those who rent only a few units, perhaps in an owner-occupied building?

5. In a jurisdiction that imposes a duty on landlords to mitigate damages, what advice would you give a tenant who wanted to leave before the end of the lease term? Should she give the landlord notice before she leaves? Does the duty to mitigate damages protect her sufficiently so that she can leave in confidence that she will be relieved of rent obligations for the rest of the lease term? How can the tenant minimize her legal exposure?

6. *Acceleration clauses.* Some landlords attempt to contract around the duty to mitigate damages through an "acceleration clause," making the rest of the rent due immediately if the tenant abandons the premises or otherwise breaches the lease in a material way. This is a form of "liquidated damages," whereby the parties agree to the amount of damages due if one of them breaches. This remedy goes beyond waiting until the rent is due to sue to collect it; it allows the landlord to obtain the rest of the rent immediately upon breach and, if enforceable, would allow the landlord *also* to rent out the premises to another tenant. Some courts enforce such provisions on the ground that the parties voluntarily agreed to them; however, they generally also police the term and will not enforce the clause if it constitutes a "penalty" or if the amount owed is "unconscionable." As with other liquidated damages, they will be deemed to be an unenforceable penalty if they do not constitute a reasonable estimate of the actual damages the landlord is likely to suffer because of the breach. Most courts will not

allow such a clause to waive the duty to mitigate damages; while the remaining rent payments are what the landlord "could have expected to receive . . . over the term of the lease," the landlord is also expected to attempt to relet the premises and the accelerated rent payments will be reduced by the damages that would have been avoided by reletting. *HealthSouth Rehabilitation Corp. v. Falcon Management Co.,* 799 So. 2d 177, 185-186 (Ala. 2001); *Aurora Business Park Association v. Albert, Inc.,* 548 N.W.2d 153, 157-158 (Iowa 1996); *Restatement (Second) of Property, Landlord & Tenant* §12.1 cmt. k (1977).

7. *Burden of proof. Sommer* holds that the landlord has the burden to persuade the decision maker that he tried to mitigate damages and the amount lost because of the inability to do so. This appears to be the majority rule at leasrt in the case of residential tenancies. However, some states impose the burden on the tenant. *See, e.g., Cole Chemical Distributing, Inc. v. Gowing,* 2005 Tex. App. LEXIS 2109 (Tex. Ct. App. 2005). Which approach is better?

PROBLEM

A landlord who lives in a three-unit building rents two of the apartments. The building is located in an urban area with many universities and a shortage of rental housing; many prospective tenants look for housing much of the time. Most of the tenants are students, many of whom go elsewhere for the summer. Because the landlord lives in the building, she is concerned about finding tenants who will not be disruptive. She would also rather not have to look for tenants twice a year, in September and again in June. Because the state imposes a duty to mitigate damages, however, tenants have started leaving at the end of the school year and stopping rent payments. This constitutes a breach of the year-long lease; however, they know that the landlord will be able to find replacement tenants and that she has a "duty to mitigate damages." Because she can easily find new tenants, she is unlikely to come after them for the money.

The landlord comes to you for advice. She would rather not have to look for new tenants every June. Suppose she were to place in the lease a clause that states:

> If Tenant abandons or vacates the Leased Premises during the Term of this Lease, Landlord may elect to re-enter the premises and, at her option, relet the Leased Premises. If the Landlord elects not to relet the Leased Premises, Tenant shall be liable for the remainder of the rent due under the Lease until its expiration. Landlord has no duty to mitigate damages.

Would such a clause be enforceable? Should it be?

(b) *Regulation of Security Deposits*

Many landlords protect themselves from the possibility that tenants may fail to pay rent by requiring a security deposit, often in the amount of one or two months' rent at the beginning of the leasehold. Some states regulate security deposits by statutes that may (1) limit the amount that can be required as a security deposit; (2) require the landlord to place the deposit in a separate account; and (3) require the landlord to repay the security deposit to the tenant with interest at the termination of the leasehold, less any amounts deducted to pay for repairs necessitated by damage to the apartment caused by the tenant during the leasehold.

§8.2.2   RENT CONTROL

§8.2.2.1   Statutory Interpretation: Who Is Protected?

At the time of the lawsuit in the following case, §2204.6 of the New York City Rent and Eviction Regulations, which authorizes the issuance of a certificate for the eviction of persons occupying a rent-controlled apartment after the lease or other rental agreement of the tenant-of-record has expired or otherwise been terminated, provided in paragraph (d) that "[n]o occupant of housing accommodations shall be evicted under this section where the occupant is either the surviving spouse of the deceased tenant or some other member of the deceased tenant's family who has been living with the tenant." Who counts as a "member" of the deceased tenant's "family"?

<u>BRASCHI v. STAHL ASSOCIATES</u>
543 N.E.2d 49 (N.Y. 1989)

VITO J. TITONE, Judge.
Appellant, Miguel Braschi, was living with Leslie Blanchard in a rent-controlled apartment located at 405 East 54th Street from the summer of 1975 until Blanchard's death in September of 1986. In November of 1986, respondent, Stahl Associates Company, the owner of the apartment building, served a notice to cure on appellant contending that he was a mere licensee with no right to occupy the apartment since only Blanchard was the tenant of record. In December of 1986 respondent served appellant with a notice to terminate informing appellant that he had one month to vacate the apartment and that, if the apartment was not vacated, respondent would commence summary proceedings to evict him. . . .

It is fundamental that in construing the words of a statute "[t]he legislative intent is the great and controlling principle." Indeed, "the general purpose is a more important aid to the meaning than any rule which grammar or formal logic may lay down." Statutes are ordinarily interpreted so as to avoid objectionable consequences and to prevent hardship or injustice. Hence, where doubt exists as to the meaning of a term, and a choice between two constructions is afforded, the consequences that may result from the different interpretations should be considered. In addition, since rent-control laws are remedial in nature and designed to promote the public good, their provisions should be interpreted broadly to effectuate their purposes. Finally, where a problem as to the meaning of a given term arises, a court's role is not to delve into the minds of legislators, but rather to effectuate the statute by carrying out the purpose of the statute as it is embodied in the words chosen by the Legislature.

The present dispute arises because the term "family" is not defined in the rent-control code and the legislative history is devoid of any specific reference to the none-viction provision. All that is known is the legislative purpose underlying the enactment of the rent-control laws as a whole.

Rent control was enacted to address a "serious public emergency" created by "an acute shortage in dwellings," which resulted in "speculative, unwarranted and abnormal increases in rents." These measures were designed to regulate and control the housing market so as to "prevent exactions of unjust, unreasonable and oppressive rents and rental agreements and to forestall profiteering, speculation and other disruptive practices tending to produce threats to the public health . . . [and] to prevent uncertainty, hardship and dislocation." . . .

. . . The manifest intent of [the anti-eviction provision in the rent control law] is to restrict the landowners' ability to evict a narrow class of occupants other than the tenant of record. . . . Juxtaposed against this intent favoring the protection of tenants, is the over-all objective of a gradual "transition from regulation to a normal market of free bargaining between landlord and tenant." One way in which this goal is to be achieved is "vacancy decontrol," which automatically makes rent-control units subject to the less rigorous provisions of rent stabilization upon the termination of the rent-control tenancy.

Emphasizing the latter objective, respondent argues that the term "family member" as used in N.Y. Comp. Codes R. & Regs. tit. 9, §2204.6(d) should be construed, consistent with this State's intestacy laws, to mean relationships of blood, consanguinity and adoption in order to effectuate the over-all goal of orderly succession to real property. Under this interpretation, only those entitled to inherit under the laws of intestacy would be afforded noneviction protection. . . .

We . . . reject respondent's argument that the purpose of the noneviction provision of the rent-control laws is to control the orderly succession to real property in a manner similar to that which occurs under our State's intestacy laws. The noneviction provision does not concern succession to real property but rather is a means of protecting a certain class of occupants from the sudden loss of their homes. The regulation does not create an alienable property right that could be sold, assigned or otherwise disposed of and, hence, need not be construed as coextensive with the intestacy laws. . . .

[W]e conclude that the term family, as used in N.Y. Comp. Codes R. & Regs. tit. 9, §2204.6(d), should not be rigidly restricted to those people who have formalized their relationship by obtaining, for instance, a marriage certificate or an adoption order. The intended protection against sudden eviction should not rest on fictitious legal distinctions or genetic history, but instead should find its foundation in the reality of family life. In the context of eviction, a more realistic, and certainly equally valid, view of a family includes two adult lifetime partners whose relationship is long term and characterized by an emotional and financial commitment and interdependence. This view comports both with our society's traditional concept of "family" and with the expectations of individuals who live in such nuclear units. In fact, Webster's Dictionary defines "family" first as "a group of people united by certain convictions or common affiliation." Hence, it is reasonable to conclude that, in using the term "family," the Legislature intended to extend protection to those who reside in households having all of the normal familial characteristics. Appellant Braschi should therefore be afforded the opportunity to prove that he and Blanchard had such a household.

This definition of "family" is consistent with both of the competing purposes of the rent-control laws: the protection of individuals from sudden dislocation and the gradual transition to a free market system. Family members, whether or not related by blood, or law who have always treated the apartment as their family home will be protected against the hardship of eviction following the death of the named tenant, thereby furthering the Legislature's goals of preventing dislocation and preserving family units which might otherwise be broken apart upon eviction. This approach will foster the transition from rent control to rent stabilization by drawing a distinction between those individuals who are, in fact, genuine family members, and those who are mere roommates or newly discovered relatives hoping to inherit the rent-controlled apartment after the existing tenant's death.

The determination as to whether an individual is entitled to noneviction protection should be based upon an objective examination of the relationship of the parties. In making this assessment, the lower courts of this State have looked to a number of factors, including the exclusivity and longevity of the relationship, the level of emotional and financial commitment, the manner in which the parties have conducted their everyday lives and held themselves out to society, and the reliance placed upon one another for daily family services....

Appellant [Miguel Braschi] and [Leslie] Blanchard lived together as permanent life partners for more than 10 years. They regarded one another, and were regarded by friends and family, as spouses. The two men's families were aware of the nature of the relationship, and they regularly visited each other's families and attended family functions together, as a couple. Even today, appellant continues to maintain a relationship with Blanchard's niece, who considers him an uncle.

In addition to their interwoven social lives, appellant clearly considered the apartment his home. He lists the apartment as his address on his driver's license and passport, and receives all his mail at the apartment address. Moreover, appellant's tenancy was known to the building's superintendent and doormen, who viewed the two men as a couple.

Financially, the two men shared all obligations including a household budget. The two were authorized signatories of three safe-deposit boxes, they maintained joint checking and savings accounts, and joint credit cards. In fact, rent was often paid with a check from their joint checking account. Additionally, Blanchard executed a power of attorney in appellant's favor so that appellant could make necessary decisions — financial, medical and personal — for him during his illness. Finally, appellant was the named beneficiary of Blanchard's life insurance policy, as well as the primary legatee and coexecutor of Blanchard's estate. Hence, a court examining these facts could reasonably conclude that these men were much more than mere roommates....

RICHARD D. SIMONS, Judge, dissenting.

I would affirm. The plurality has adopted a definition of family which extends the language of the regulation well beyond the implication of the words used in it. In doing so, it has expanded the class indefinitely to include anyone who can satisfy an administrator that he or she had an emotional and financial "commitment" to the statutory tenant. Its interpretation is inconsistent with the legislative scheme underlying rent regulation, goes well beyond the intended purposes of N.Y. Comp. Codes R. & Regs. tit. 9, §2204.6(d), and produces an unworkable test that is subject to abuse....

Central to any interpretation of the regulatory language is a determination of its purpose. There can be little doubt that the purpose of section 2204.6(d) was to create succession rights to a possessory interest in real property where the tenant of record has died or vacated the apartment. It creates a new tenancy for every surviving family member living with decedent at the time of death who then becomes a new statutory tenant until death or until he or she vacates the apartment. The State concerns underlying this provision include the orderly and just succession of property interests (which includes protecting a deceased's spouse and family from loss of their longtime home) and the professed State objective that there be a gradual transition from government regulation to a normal market of free bargaining between landlord and tenant. Those objectives require a weighing of the interests of certain individuals living with the tenant of record at his or her death and the interests of the landlord in regaining possession of its property and rerenting it under the less onerous rent-stabilization laws. The interests are properly balanced if the regulation's exception is applied by using objectively verifiable relationships based on blood, marriage and adoption, as the State has historically done in the estate succession laws, family court acts and similar legislation. The distinction is warranted because members of families, so defined, assume certain legal obligations to each other and to third persons, such as creditors, which are not imposed on unrelated individuals and this legal inter-dependency is worthy of consideration in determining which individuals are entitled to succeed to the interest of the statutory tenant in rent-controlled premises. More-over, such an interpretation promotes certainty and consistency in the law and obviates the need for drawn out hearings and litigation focusing on such intangibles as the strength and duration of the relationship and the extent of the emotional and financial interdependency. So limited, the regulation may be viewed as a tempered response, balancing the rights of landlords with those of the tenant. To come within that protected class, individuals must comply with State laws relating to marriage or adoption. Plaintiff cannot avail himself of these institutions, of course, but that only points up the need for a legislative solution, not a judicial one. . . .

Rent control generally and section 2204.6, in particular, are in substantial dero-gation of property owners' rights. The court should not reach out and devise an expansive definition in this policy-laden area based upon limited experience and knowledge of the problems. The evidence available suggests that such a definition was not intended and that the ordinary and popular meaning of family in the tradi-tional sense should be applied. If that construction is not favored, the Legislature or the agency can alter it. . . .

NOTES AND QUESTIONS

1. What conception of "family" did the New York Court of Appeals use to interpret the statute? Did the purposes behind rent regulation aid the court in defining whom the lawmakers intended to protect by the "family member" provision?

2. In *East 10th Street Associates v. Estate of Goldstein*, 552 N.Y.S.2d 257 (App. Div. 1990), the court extended *Braschi* to cover rent-stabilized apartments, despite the fact that such apartments were subject to regulations that — unlike the rent-control reg-ulations at issue in *Braschi* — specifically defined "family member" to include "hus-band, wife, son, daughter, stepson, stepdaughter, father, mother, stepfather, stepmother, brother, sister, nephew, niece, uncle, aunt, grandfather, grandmother, grandson, granddaughter, father-in-law, mother-in-law, son-in-law, or daughter-in-law." The court explained:

> [W]e find that the decision in *Braschi* provides a controlling precedent herein since there is no significant distinction between the two regulatory schemes which would mandate a different definition of "family." Thus, in determining that "a more realistic, and certainly equally valid, view of a family includes two adult lifetime partners whose relationship is long-term and characterized by an emotional and financial commitment and interdependence," the Court of Appeals specifically placed this statement "[i]n the context of eviction," not "in the context of eviction from a rent controlled apartment." It

would be anomalous to hold that a life partner could be a valid family member for the purpose of protection from eviction from a rent-controlled apartment but not a valid family member insofar as eviction from a rent-stabilized apartment is concerned. . . .

Id. at 258-259.

Was this extension of the *Braschi* doctrine appropriate?

3. In *Athineos v. Thayer*, 545 N.Y.S.2d 337 (App. Div. 1989), the landlord attempted to evict a woman who had been reared as a daughter by a couple in a rent-controlled apartment but never formally adopted by them. Applying the rule of law in *Braschi*, the court ruled that the defendant could not be evicted since she was a family member.

> The evidence adduced here clearly established that all the parties involved, the Boutrosses, their children, and the respondent, considered themselves to be a family, and presented themselves as such. Thus the fact that their relationship had never been formalized by means of an adoption order should not result in their exclusion from the protections afforded by New York City's *Rent Control Law.*

Id. See also 2-4 Realty Associates v. Pittman, 547 N.Y.S.2d 515 (Sup. Ct. 1989) (holding that a son who had lived with his mother for many years could not be evicted when she died because they had lived as a "family," defined "to include those persons whose 'relationship is long-term and characterized by an emotional and financial commitment and interdependence' regardless of whether such persons share a jural or legally solemnized familial relationship").

4. In *Hudson v. Weiss*, 450 N.E.2d 234 (N.Y. 1983), the landlord sought to evict a tenant from a rent-controlled apartment on the ground that she had breached a term in her lease under which she covenanted not to allow anyone to occupy the premises with her who was not a member of her "immediate family." She lived with a man "with whom she [had] a loving relationship," but the court decided that because the couple was not married, the man was not a part of the tenant's immediate family. Is *Hudson* consistent with *Braschi*?

5. After the *Braschi* decision, the New York City rent regulations were amended to codify the holding of that case. N.Y. City Rent & Eviction Regs. §2204.6(d)(3) was amended to state:

> (3) For the purposes of this subdivision:
>
> (i) family member is defined as a husband, wife, son, daughter, stepson, stepdaughter, father, mother, stepfather, stepmother, brother, sister, nephew, niece, uncle, aunt, grandfather, grandmother, grandson, granddaughter, father-in-law, mother-in-law, son-in-law, or daughter-in-law of the tenant; or any other person residing with the tenant in the housing accommodation as a primary residence who can prove emotional and financial commitment, and interdependence between such person and the tenant. Although no single factor shall be solely determinative, evidence which is to be considered in determining whether such emotional and financial commitment and interdependence existed, may include, without limitation, such factors as listed below. In no event would evidence of a sexual relationship between such persons be required or considered.
>
> (a) longevity of the relationship;
>
> (b) sharing of or relying upon each other for payment of household or family expenses, and/or other common necessities of life;
>
> (c) intermingling of finances as evidenced by, among other things, joint ownership of bank accounts, personal and real property, credit cards, loan obligations, sharing a household budget for purposes of receiving government benefits, etc.;

(d) engaging in family-type activities by jointly attending family functions, holidays and celebrations, social and recreational activities, etc.;

(e) formalizing of legal obligations, intentions, and responsibilities to each other by such means as executing wills naming each other as executor and/or beneficiary, conferring upon each other a power of attorney and/or authority to make health care decisions each for the other, entering into a personal relationship contract, making a domestic partnership declaration, or serving as a representative payee for purposes of public benefits, etc.;

(f) holding themselves out as family members to other family members, friends, members of the community or religious institutions, or society in general, through their words or actions;

(g) regularly performing family functions, such as caring for each other or each other's extended family members, and/or relying upon each other for daily family services;

(h) engaging in any other pattern of behavior, agreement, or other action which evidences the intention of creating a long-term, emotionally committed relationship. . . .

These regulations were upheld by the New York Court of Appeals in *Rent Stabilization Association of New York City, Inc. v. Higgins*, 630 N.E.2d 626 (N.Y. 1993), against a claim that they constituted a taking of property without adequate compensation.

Was it inappropriate for the court in *Braschi* to define "family member" so broadly? Should the court have waited for the legislature to adopt a broader definition that might correspond to current social realities? Or does the fact that the regulations were amended to codify the court's decision demonstrate that the court's holding was not impermissibly activist? If we conclude that it was unlikely the legislature would have amended the regulations in the absence of the court opinion but that the court opinion, and the public reaction that followed it, changed the legislature's conception of the legitimate scope of the protective law, what should we conclude about the proper role of the court in a democratic society? Did the court act legitimately?

6. For discussion of legislation prohibiting discrimination in housing on the basis of sexual orientation, *see* Chapter 10.

PROBLEMS

1. Jane signs a one-year lease; she then marries Micah, and he moves in. What are Micah's rights under the lease? If Jane dies before the end of the term, can Micah stay on? Suppose a clause in the lease says "no subletting without permission of landlord. All new tenants (including roommates) must be approved by the landlord." Can the landlord disapprove of Micah as a tenant?

2. Can the landlord disapprove if Jane is a lesbian and her partner, Pam, moves in? Suppose the lease says "all new tenants other than spouses of the existing tenant must be approved." Can Jane rely on this contract provision to cover Pam? Can Jane rely on *Braschi* to argue that Pam is a "spouse"?

§8.2.2.2 The Economics of Rent Control

Some municipalities have passed laws restricting the amount by which landlords can raise the rent. Such laws are intended to allow landlords to obtain a reasonable return on their investment, while protecting the rights of tenants to continue living in their homes. Rent control has been repeatedly upheld against claims that it constitutes an unconstitutional taking of the landlord's property rights. *Pennell v. City of San Jose,* 485 U.S. 1 (1988).

The wisdom of rent control has long been debated. Rent control is a fixture in some cities, yet the vast majority of municipalities eschew it. Many economists argue that rent control both reduces social wealth overall and hurts the very people it is meant to help, therefore failing on both efficiency and distributive grounds. Other economists sharply dispute this account of its effects. The debate is complicated. Below is a brief introduction to some of the more widely rehearsed arguments.

The Argument Against Rent Control

The argument that rent control is inefficient is based on the familiar notion that in an "unregulated" market, both the price of housing services (rent) and the quantity of housing services provided will be determined by the interaction of supply and demand. Interfering with the market price of housing by setting it at an artificially low level will cause a housing shortage.

First, on the demand side, rent control will increase the quantity of rental housing demanded since more people will be willing and able to afford rental housing. Some people who could not afford housing at higher "market" prices will decide to seek apartments on their own rather than doubling up with others, living with family members, or being homeless.

Second, on the supply side, rent control will decrease the quantity of housing services supplied since a limit on rents will cause some landlords to leave the housing market either because the allowable rents do not cover their expenses or because alternative investments are more profitable. Some landlords will take apartments out of the rental housing market and convert them to other uses. Rent control is often coupled with restrictions on eviction or prohibitions on condominium conversion; in these cases, the disincentive to invest in rental housing is even greater. Less rental housing will be constructed than otherwise and fewer units of existing housing will be converted to rental housing stock if a limit is placed on allowable rents.

The upshot is that the supply of housing will go down and the demand for housing will rise, causing a shortage. This shortage is economically inefficient since it constitutes a misallocation of resources. Those who benefit from rent control (current tenants) are getting a resource for less than its "true cost"; they therefore have an incentive to overconsume housing since they are getting it partly for free. Rent control may induce an inefficiently high demand for housing because consumers do not have to pay the full cost of the housing. People who might otherwise have moved to smaller quarters when their children were grown, for example, may decide to stay in a place that is larger than they need. Others who would otherwise be unwilling or unable to afford to live on their own may decide to seek apartments because they do not have to pay the full cost. Inefficiency results if actors do not have to internalize the full costs of their conduct. Because rent control limits the profitability of rental housing, fewer units of housing will be provided as potential landlords will invest in other businesses, thus producing goods and services that are less valuable to consumers than rental housing. Rent control therefore decreases social wealth by redirecting investment away from its most highly valued uses while artificially raising demand for housing above the efficient level since consumers do not have to pay the full cost of housing.

Third, in addition to causing an overall decrease in social wealth by allocating resources inefficiently, rent control arguably has perverse distributive effects. By decreasing the supply of housing, it may *increase* the problem of homelessness. Since rent control helps only current tenants and does nothing to provide new housing for those without housing — and may even inhibit new construction — it hurts those without housing the most. The homeless poor will have an even harder time finding affordable housing than before rent control since the overall supply of housing will be artificially depressed and more people will be competing for the units that remain. Further, many of those who benefit from rent control are not low-income persons; relatively well-off people may happen to be occupying rent-controlled units while poor persons occupy market-rate apartments. Direct subsidies to poor families may be both less expensive and, perhaps, the only distributively fair way to help them.

Rent control will therefore (1) cause a shortage of rental housing; (2) reduce current and future investment in supplying rental housing below the socially optimal level, thereby exacerbating the shortage over the long run; (3) increase demand for rental housing above what it would be if consumers had to pay its true costs, resulting in overconsumption by existing tenants and those few new tenants who are able to find housing; and (4) provide a subsidy to existing tenants who may or may not be poor at the expense of landlords and those who are most vulnerable — the homeless poor.

For a detailed explanation of these and other arguments, *see* Richard Epstein, *Rent Control and the Theory of Efficient Regulation*, 54 Brook. L. Rev. 741 (1988); William Tucker, *The Excluded Americans* 152-166 (1990).

The Argument for Rent Control

Proponents of rent control, including some economists, have argued that the picture painted by critics is too simple. First, the economic argument against rent control presumes that in the absence of rent control, the supply and demand for housing would be determined by a competitive, unregulated market. This assumption may be unwarranted for a variety of reasons. The existing demand for home *ownership* is partly determined by federal tax and banking policy. For example, the interest paid on mortgage loans is deductible from federal income taxes. This tax expenditure represents a subsidy for homeowners that is not available to renters — although they may benefit by it in the form of lower rents. Federal banking policy provides insurance for home mortgages, which increases the availability of credit for home purchase and construction. Both of these subsidies to homeowners alter the allocation of resources that would exist in their absence. Similarly, exclusionary zoning laws both enhance the value of existing housing and prevent the construction of multifamily housing that would otherwise emerge. The absence of rent control would not leave an unregulated market governed only by supply and demand; both the supply of and demand for housing are affected by government subsidies in the form of tax, banking, and zoning laws. This does not mean that rent control necessarily improves social wealth overall. However, it does cast doubt on the idea that in the absence of rent control, the market could perform its magic allocative functions unhindered by government regulation. Further, it suggests that it is widely believed that a completely unregulated housing market is neither economically desirable nor politically feasible.

Second, rent control may have no effect on future investment in housing. Strict rent control *would* be very likely to inhibit new construction, but nearly all current rent control ordinances are "second generation," specifically *exempting* newly constructed housing from rent control. So long as new housing can be rented at uncontrolled market rents, there is no disincentive to provide new housing. No clear empirical evidence shows that second-generation rent control inhibits new construction. Michael J. Mandel, *Does Rent Control Hurt Tenants?: A Reply to Epstein*, 54 Brook. L. Rev. 1267, 1273 (1989). The price of new housing in a rent-controlled market may even be higher than in a non-rent-controlled market; if rent control causes a shortage, demand for housing will increase, and those who are willing and able to pay rents higher than the rent-controlled rents will be competing for a smaller supply of new housing, thereby bidding up the price. However, the resulting higher rent that new housing owners can obtain will increase profitability and may have the effect of inducing more new construction. The result might actually be *overproduction* of housing compared to a non-rent-controlled market, as the increased profitability of new housing induces new construction. (This assumes that new construction is not blocked by *other* government regulations, such as exclusionary zoning laws.)

Critics of rent control counter this argument by noting that the existence of rent control in a jurisdiction dampens investment in new housing, even if new housing is not covered, since investors *fear* that in the future rent controls may be retroactively extended to newly constructed housing. Defenders of rent control respond by noting that no city ever has done this and that it is unlikely to happen precisely because city governments agree that such a policy would be unwise. Because of this history, rational investors would properly discount any fears of retroactive controls on new housing.

Even if controls were imposed retroactively, they uniformly provide for reasonable return on investment, allowing owners to recoup the capital costs of construction, rehabilitation, and maintenance costs and to earn a rate of profit equal to comparably risky investments. The rate at which rents would be set therefore should not discourage new investment. Critics may respond by anecdotal evidence that rent control boards are incompetent and fail to allow rent increases mandated by law when owners invest in rehabilitation. Even if this is true, however, the proper response may be better administrative or judicial enforcement of landlords' rights under rent control laws rather than abolishing the system altogether.

Third, available evidence does not indicate that rent control leads to housing abandonment. Many cities with severe abandonment problems do not have rent control; something else may be the root cause of the problem of abandonment. Some studies about New York City, which does have rent control, suggest that the major causes of abandonment are the low incomes of renters who cannot afford even rent-controlled rents and high interest rates that make investment in rehabilitation and construction too expensive. There is also no empirical evidence that rent control leads systematically to reduced maintenance. This is not surprising, given the universal existence of building codes.

Fourth, even if rent control leads to a decrease in housing, its efficiency and distributive effects may be positive. The demand for housing is a function of both willingness and *ability* to purchase housing services. Low-income persons in many localities have insufficient resources to afford housing at all, even at rent-controlled rates. Leaving rents to the marketplace would not necessarily generate a supply of housing affordable to them — even if it increased the supply of housing. Many people, including those who work, simply do not earn enough to pay for housing, given its current costs. This fact may not only lead to a maldistribution of housing but be economically inefficient as well. Given the marginal utility of money, social wealth may be decreased, rather than increased, by allocating housing solely on the basis of ability to pay. Those at the bottom of the economic ladder may derive more utility out of new units of housing than do wealthier families, but they may not have the dollars to back up their demand in the market. If low-income families are too poor to afford housing even in an "unregulated" market, rent control may help to correct this market failure.

Finally, rent control benefits existing tenants by granting them security of tenure and discouraging would-be tenants from the market; such a result may be both economically and distributively appropriate. Because of a shortage of land, landlords may be earning "economic rents"; these are amounts of compensation greater than necessary to keep a particular unit in its current use. If rental housing is more profitable than comparably risky investments because of the existence of economic rents, imposition of rent control may merely decrease landlords' profits without affecting the supply of housing in any way; it will simply redistribute wealth between landlords and tenants. Landlords may, as a class, be wealthier than tenants as a class; given the tax advantages of ownership, most of those able to buy housing do so rather than rent it. Redistribution from landlords to existing tenants may be desirable from the dual standpoints of social justice and economic efficiency, given the decreasing marginal utility of money. Moreover, if a landlord's interest is simply in investing resources for profit while the tenant's interest is in establishing a stable home, it may be normatively desirable for the tenant's personal property interest to trump the landlord's investment interest. Other mechanisms, such as tax incentives, can be used to encourage the construction or rehabilitation of additional rental housing to satisfy new demand. Margaret Jane Radin, *Residential Rent Control*, 15 Phil. & Pub. Aff. 350 (1986).

Rent control may therefore (1) not reduce the supply of existing housing if economic rents are being earned; (2) not interfere with investment in new housing since it is exempted from rent control; (3) increase demand for housing to its appropriate level rather than decreasing it to an inappropriately low level caused by a maldistribution of wealth; and (4) properly protect existing tenants' abilities to remain secure in their homes, thereby protecting their personal interest in relying on continued stability in their home life and preventing the externalities associated with community dislocation. The poorest persons in the community will not be helped by the market anyway; they require alternative government policies either to enhance their ability to pay for housing or to make the provision of low-income housing more profitable through such techniques as inclusionary zoning.

For defenses of rent control, in addition to Mandel and Radin, *see* John I. Gilderbloom and Richard P. Appelbaum, *Rethinking Rental Housing* (1988); Kenneth K. Baar, *Would the Abolition of Rent Controls Restore a Free Market?*, 54 Brook. L. Rev. 1231 (1989); John Cirace, *Housing Market Instability and Rent Stabilization*, 54 Brook. L. Rev. 1275 (1989); and other articles in the symposium on rent control in that issue. *See also* Philip Weitzman, *Economics and Rent Regulation: A Call for a New Perspective*, 13 Rev. L. & Soc. Change 975 (1984-1985); Note, *Reassessing Rent Control: Its Economic Impact in a Gentrifying Housing Market*, 101 Harv. L. Rev. 1835 (1988).

§8.3   Conflicts About Occupancy

§8.3.1   LANDLORD'S DUTY TO DELIVER POSSESSION

Under the current majority rule, the landlord has the duty to deliver possession of the rented premises to the tenant at the beginning of the leasehold. *Restatement*

(Second) of Property (Landlord and Tenant) §6.2 (1977). If a prior tenant wrongfully holds over after his lease term expires, the landlord has an obligation in most jurisdictions to remove the prior tenant within a reasonable period of time by either instituting eviction proceedings or convincing the holdover tenant to leave. Failure to deliver actual possession of the premises to the new tenant constitutes a breach of the lease by the landlord. The tenant who has been shut out may either terminate the lease and recover damages as compensation for having to find another place to live or affirm the lease, withhold rent for the period during which she could not occupy the premises, and recover damages for the cost of temporarily renting alternative housing while the landlord undertakes eviction proceedings to remove the prior tenant.

A minority of jurisdictions follow the traditional rule, under which the landlord has only the duty to deliver the *right* to possession but no duty to deliver *actual* possession. In those states, it is the new tenant's responsibility to evict the holdover tenant by bringing ejectment or other appropriate proceedings. Since the landlord is not in default under the minority rule, the new tenant is legally obligated to pay the rent even though she is not in possession. The new tenant's remedy is to go after the holdover tenant for damages.

§8.3.2　Tenant's Right to Leave and Transfer the Leasehold versus Landlord's Right to Control Occupancy

§8.3.2.1　Transfer of the Landlord's Reversion

The landlord-tenant relationship divides property rights between the landlord and the tenant. The tenant's *leasehold* includes the right to possess the property in exchange for rent, subject to other terms of the agreement between the parties; the landlord's rights include the *reversion*—the right to obtain possession when the lease term ends—and the bargained-for right to collect rent from the tenant, again subject to other terms of the agreement between the parties.

Either party may transfer her property interest. What happens if the landlord sells the property? The new owner receives what the landlord was able to sell, that is, the landlord's reversion and the current right to collect rent and enforce the other terms of the lease. The new owner does not obtain an immediate right to possess the property; the tenant's leasehold interest survives. The new owner, of course, may end a month-to-month tenancy, for example, by giving one month's notice, just as the prior landlord could have done this. If the tenant has six months left on a one-year lease, however, the new owner takes the property subject to the remaining six-month possessory right in the tenant.

§8.3.2.2　Tenant's Right to Assign or Sublet

In defining the rights of tenants to transfer their possessory rights, we must distinguish three different situations. In some cases, the written lease or oral leasehold agreement is silent on the question whether the tenant has the right to assign or sublet her possessory rights. In other cases, the lease provides for assignment or subletting only with the landlord's consent. In still other cases, the lease prohibits assignment and subletting altogether. The legal issues in these situations are quite different, and it is important to remember this when dealing with a client.

(a) When the Lease Is Silent

Can the tenant transfer her leasehold? The answer is yes, unless the lease restricts the tenant's ability to transfer the leasehold. Although restraints on alienation of fee interests are generally void, restraints on alienation of other property interests are often upheld by the courts, including restraints attached to leaseholds and condominium units. If the lease agreement does not say anything about assignment or sublease, the general rule is that the tenant is entitled to transfer her possessory interests in the premises by either assignment or sublease. The courts justify this rule by reference to the policy of promoting alienability.

The transfer of the leasehold is called either an *assignment* or a *sublease.* An assignment conveys *all* the tenant's remaining property interests without retaining any future rights to enter the property; under a sublease or sublet the tenant retains some future interest or the right to control the property in the future. A sublease exists, for example, if a tenant has six months remaining on the lease and sublets the apartment to someone else for four months; since the tenant retains the right to regain possession for the last two months of the term of years, the transfer is a sublease rather than an assignment. A sublease may also exist if the tenant retains a right of entry that can be exercised if the subtenant violates one or more of the terms of the sublease agreement.

Why is it important to know whether the arrangement is a sublease or an assignment? Traditionally, under an assignment, the new tenant — the assignee — is responsible directly to the landlord for all the undertakings under the original lease. In other words, the tenant's covenants — including the covenant to pay rent and other covenants in the lease agreement — run with the land. Courts have traditionally used the concept of *privity of estate* to explain why the assignee is directly liable to the landlord for the covenants made by the original tenant to the landlord. The landlord and the assignee are not in *privity of contract* since they did not reach an agreement with each other. Since the original tenant has given up all interest in the property, however, the landlord and the assignee are thought to share interests in the property; they are therefore in privity of estate.

In contrast, under a sublease, the lease covenants do not run with the land as *real covenants.* The landlord has no right to sue the subtenant to enforce any of the covenants in the original lease, including the covenant to pay rent, if the requested relief is damages. The only exception is when the subtenant expressly promises the tenant to pay the rent to the landlord. In that case, the landlord may be able to sue the subtenant as a *third-party beneficiary* of the contract made between the tenant and subtenant; in other words, the landlord is the intended beneficiary of the subtenant's promise to the tenant. However, lease covenants probably *can* be enforced by injunction as equitable servitudes, so long as the subtenant has notice of them. Is the subtenant bound if she has not seen the original lease and that lease is not recorded? The courts are likely to find the subtenant on inquiry notice of the covenants in the original lease; the reasonable subtenant would inquire whether the tenant had made promises to the landlord restricting use of the premises.

The difficult question is whether the landlord can sue the subtenant for an injunction ordering the subtenant to comply with the covenant to pay rent. Some courts will not grant an injunction since the payment of rent is a money payment and resembles the payment of damages. Others grant an injunction because it constitutes enforcement of an affirmative covenant, even though that covenant requires the payment of money.

Suppose the tenant assigns his remaining six months on the lease to a new tenant (called the assignee). The assignee fails to pay the rent. The landlord may sue the original tenant for the unpaid rent because the original tenant remains in a contractual relationship with the landlord; the assignment does not relieve the tenant of the obligation to pay rent to the landlord. However, the landlord may instead choose to sue the assignee directly for the unpaid rent. Since the covenant to pay rent runs with the land, the assignee is directly liable to the landlord for the unpaid rent.

Suppose, in contrast, that the tenant *sublets* the apartment for four of the remaining six months, and the new tenant (called the subtenant) fails to pay the rent. Under this arrangement, the landlord can sue the original tenant (who remains contractually bound to pay the rent), but a court may hold that the landlord *cannot* sue the subtenant for the rent. Thus, if the landlord tries to sue the subtenant for the rent, the subtenant can get the complaint dismissed for failure to state a claim upon which relief can be granted. Note, however, that if neither the tenant nor the subtenant pays the rent, the landlord can evict the tenant (sue for possession from the tenant) and end the leasehold, thereby terminating the subtenant's right of possession since the subtenant can possess only what the tenant has a right to possess in the absence of a separate agreement with the landlord.

Note that, in either case, if the landlord chooses to sue the original tenant for the rent, the original tenant has a right to be reimbursed by the new tenant for the amount owed to the landlord. This is true whether the new tenant is an assignee or a subtenant. The tenant ordinarily will bring the subtenant into the lawsuit as a third-party defendant, claiming that, if the tenant is liable to the landlord, then the subtenant-assignee is liable to reimburse the tenant for this amount. This is true because the tenant and the subtenant-assignee have made a contract between themselves that the subtenant-assignee will pay the rent; this agreement is enforceable by the tenant against the subtenant-assignee.

The tenant may choose to sublet for a rental amount different from the amount owed to the landlord. Whether the new rent is less or more than the original rent, the tenant remains liable for the original amount only to the landlord. Thus if the subtenant is paying less than the rent owed to the landlord, the tenant must make up the difference. If the subtenant is paying more than the rent owed to the landlord, the tenant subtenant is allowed to keep the difference. (All this assumes that the rental agreement between the landlord and the original tenant does not limit the tenant's options in this regard.)

(b) When the Lease Requires the Landlord's Consent

Many leases provide for subletting or assignment only with the landlord's consent. These clauses may be phrased either in the negative or the affirmative, that is, "no subletting without the landlord's consent" or "subletting allowed subject to the landlord's consent."

These clauses sometimes use the general term "sublet" when what is really meant is "sublet or assign." Traditional doctrine held that, in order to promote the alienability of leaseholds, a lease that limits subletting but not assigning will be strictly construed to limit only subletting. However, the modern trend is to focus on the intent of the parties; since modern usage sometimes employs the term "subletting" to mean any transfers of the leasehold interest, a clause that provides for "no subletting without the landlord's consent" may very well be interpreted to prohibit subletting or assigning without the landlord's consent.

An issue that has occasioned much litigation recently is the question whether a criterion of "reasonableness" should be implied in the phrase "no subletting without the landlord's consent." This issue has arisen in both residential and commercial contexts. The law is currently unsettled in this area, as the following cases illustrate.

KENDALL v. ERNEST PESTANA, INC.
709 P.2d 837 (Cal. 1985)

ALLEN E. BROUSSARD, Justice.

This case concerns the effect of a provision in a commercial lease[1] that the lessee may not assign the lease or sublet the premises without the lessor's prior written consent. The question we address is whether, in the absence of a provision that such consent will not be unreasonably withheld, a lessor may unreasonably and arbitrarily withhold his or her consent to an assignment. This is a question of first impression in this court.

I

. . . The allegations of the complaint may be summarized as follows. The lease at issue is for 14,400 square feet of hangar space at the San Jose Municipal Airport. The City of San Jose, as owner of the property, leased it to Irving and Janice Perlitch, who in turn assigned their interest to respondent Ernest Pestana, Inc. Prior to assigning their interest to respondent, the Perlitches entered into a 25-year sublease with one Robert Bixler commencing on January 1, 1970. The sublease covered an original five year term plus four 5-year options to renew. The rental rate was to be increased every 10 years in the same proportion as rents increased on the master lease from the City of San Jose. The premises were to be used by Bixler for the purpose of conducting an airplane maintenance business.

Bixler conducted such a business under the name "Flight Services" until, in 1981, he agreed to sell the business to appellants Jack Kendall, Grady O'Hara and Vicki O'Hara. The proposed sale included the business and the equipment, inventory and improvements on the property, together with the existing lease. The proposed assignees had a stronger financial statement and greater net worth than the current lessee, Bixler, and they were willing to be bound by the terms of the lease.

The lease provided that written consent of the lessor was required before the lessee could assign his interest, and that failure to obtain such consent rendered the lease voidable at the option of the lessor. Accordingly, Bixler requested consent from the Perlitches' successor-in-interest, respondent Ernest Pestana, Inc. Respondent refused to consent to the assignment and maintained that it had an absolute right arbitrarily to refuse any such request. The complaint recites that respondent demanded "increased rent and other more onerous terms" as a condition of consenting to Bixler's transfer of interest.

---

1. We are presented only with a commercial lease and therefore do not address the question whether residential leases are controlled by the principles articulated in this opinion.

The proposed assignees brought suit for declaratory and injunctive relief and damages seeking, *inter alia*, a declaration "that the refusal of Ernest Pestana, Inc. to consent to the assignment of the lease is unreasonable and is an unlawful restraint on the freedom of alienation...."

II

The law generally favors free alienability of property, and California follows the common law rule that a leasehold interest is freely alienable. Contractual restrictions on the alienability of leasehold interests are, however, permitted. "Such restrictions are justified as reasonable protection of the interests of the lessor as to who shall possess and manage property in which he has a reversionary interest and from which he is deriving income." Schoshinski, *American Law of Landlord and Tenant* §815, at 578-79 (1980).

The common law's hostility toward restraints on alienation has caused such restraints on leasehold interests to be strictly construed against the lessor....[7] This is particularly true where the restraint in question is a "forfeiture restraint," under which the lessor has the option to terminate the lease if an assignment is made without his or her consent.

Nevertheless, a majority of jurisdictions have long adhered to the rule that where a lease contains an approval clause (a clause stating that the lease cannot be assigned without the prior consent of the lessor), the lessor may arbitrarily refuse to approve a proposed assignee no matter how suitable the assignee appears to be and no matter how unreasonable the lessor's objection. The harsh consequences of this rule have often been avoided through application of the doctrines of waiver and estoppel, under which the lessor may be found to have waived (or be estopped from asserting) the right to refuse consent to assignment.

The traditional majority rule has come under steady attack in recent years. A growing minority of jurisdictions now hold that where a lease provides for assignment only with the prior consent of the lessor, such consent may be withheld only where the lessor has a commercially reasonable objection to the assignment, even in the absence of a provision in the lease stating that consent to assignment will not be unreasonably withheld.

For the reasons discussed below, we conclude that the minority rule is the preferable position....

III

The impetus for change in the majority rule has come from two directions, reflecting the dual nature of a lease as a conveyance of a leasehold interest and a contract. The

---

7. There are many examples of the narrow effect given to lease terms purporting to restrict assignment. Covenants against assignment without the prior consent of the lessor have been held not to affect the lessee's right to sublease, to mortgage the leasehold, or to assign his or her interest to a cotenant. Such covenants also do not prevent transfer of a leasehold interest by will, by bankruptcy, by the personal representative of a deceased tenant, or by transfer among partners, or spouses. Covenants against assignment furthermore do not prohibit transfer of the stock of a corporate tenant, or assignment of a lease to a corporation wholly owned by the tenant.

policy against restraints on alienation pertains to leases in their nature as conveyances. Numerous courts and commentators have recognized that "[i]n recent times the necessity of permitting reasonable alienation of commercial space has become paramount in our increasingly urban society." *Schweiso v. Williams*, 198 Cal. Rptr. 238, 240 (Ct. App. 1984).

Civil Code section 711 provides: "Conditions restraining alienation, when repugnant to the interest created, are void." It is well settled that this rule is not absolute in its application, but forbids only unreasonable restraints on alienation. Reasonableness is determined by comparing the justification for a particular restraint on alienation with the quantum of restraint actually imposed by it. "[T]he greater the quantum of restraint that results from enforcement of a given clause, the greater must be the justification for that enforcement." *Wellenkamp v. Bank of America*, 148 Cal. Rptr. 379, 382 (Ct. App. 1978). . . .

The *Restatement Second of Property* adopts the minority rule on the validity of approval clauses in leases: "A restraint on alienation without the consent of the landlord of a tenant's interest in leased property is valid, *but the landlord's consent to an alienation by the tenant cannot be withheld unreasonably*, unless a freely negotiated provision in the lease gives the landlord an absolute right to withhold consent." (*Rest. 2d Property*, §15.2(2) (1977)) (italics added). A comment to the section explains: "The landlord may have an understandable concern about certain personal qualities of a tenant, particularly his reputation for meeting his financial obligations. The preservation of the values that go into the personal selection of the tenant justifies upholding a provision in the lease that curtails the right of the tenant to put anyone else in his place by transferring his interest, but this justification does not go to the point of allowing the landlord arbitrarily and without reason to refuse to allow the tenant to transfer an interest in leased property." (*Id.*, comment a.) Under the *Restatement* rule, the lessor's interest in the character of his or her tenant is protected by the lessor's right to object to a proposed assignee on reasonable commercial grounds. The lessor's interests are also protected by the fact that the original lessee remains liable to the lessor as a surety even if the lessor consents to the assignment and the assignee expressly assumes the obligations of the lease.

The second impetus for change in the majority rule comes from the nature of a lease as a contract. As the Court of Appeal observed in *Cohen v. Ratinoff*, 195 Cal. Rptr. 84, 88 (Ct. App. 1983), "[since the majority rule was adopted], there has been an increased recognition of and emphasis on the duty of good faith and fair dealing inherent in every contract." Thus, "[i]n every contract there is an implied covenant that neither party shall do anything which will have the effect of destroying or injuring the right of the other party to receive the fruits of the contract. . . ." *Universal Sales Corp. v. Cal. etc. Mfg. Co.*, 128 P.2d 665, 677 (Cal. 1942). "[W]here a contract confers on one party a discretionary power affecting the rights of the other, a duty is imposed to exercise that discretion in good faith and in accordance with fair dealing." *Cal. Lettuce Growers v. Union Sugar Co.*, 289 P.2d 785, 791 (Cal. 1955). Here the lessor retains the discretionary power to approve or disapprove an assignee proposed by the other party to the contract; this discretionary power should therefore be exercised in accordance with commercially reasonable standards. . . .

Under the minority rule, the determination whether a lessor's refusal to consent was reasonable is a question of fact. Some of the factors that the trier of fact may properly consider in applying the standards of good faith and commercial reasonableness are: financial responsibility of the proposed assignee; suitability of the use for the particular property; legality of the proposed use; need for alteration of the premises; and nature of the occupancy, *i.e.*, office, factory, clinic, etc.

Denying consent solely on the basis of personal taste, convenience or sensibility is not commercially reasonable. Nor is it reasonable to deny consent "in order that the landlord may charge a higher rent than originally contracted for." This is because the lessor's desire for a better bargain than contracted for has nothing to do with the permissible purposes of the restraint on alienation — to protect the lessor's interest in the preservation of the property and the performance of the lease covenants. . . .

In contrast to the policy reasons advanced in favor of the minority rule, the majority rule has traditionally been justified on three grounds. Respondent raises a fourth argument in its favor as well. None of these do we find compelling.

First, it is said that a lease is a conveyance of an interest in real property, and that the lessor, having exercised a personal choice in the selection of a tenant and provided that no substitute shall be acceptable without prior consent, is under no obligation to look to anyone but the lessee for the rent. This argument is based on traditional rules of conveyancing and on concepts of freedom of ownership and control over one's property.

A lessor's freedom at common law to look to no one but the lessee for the rent has, however, been undermined by the adoption in California of a rule that lessors — like all other contracting parties — have a duty to mitigate damages upon the lessee's abandonment of the property by seeking a substitute lessee. Furthermore, the values that go into the personal selection of a lessee are preserved under the minority rule in the lessor's right to refuse consent to assignment on any commercially reasonable grounds. Such grounds include not only the obvious objections to an assignee's financial stability or proposed use of the premises, but a variety of other commercially reasonable objections as well. The lessor's interests are further protected by the fact that the original lessee remains a guarantor of the performance of the assignee.

The second justification advanced in support of the majority rule is that an approval clause is an unambiguous reservation of absolute discretion in the lessor over assignments of the lease. The lessee could have bargained for the addition of a reasonableness clause to the lease (*i.e.*, "consent to assignment will not be unreasonably withheld"). The lessee having failed to do so, the law should not rewrite the parties' contract for them.

Numerous authorities have taken a different view of the meaning and effect of an approval clause in a lease, indicating that the clause is not "clear and unambiguous," as respondent suggests. As early as 1940, the court in *Granite Trust Bldg. Corp. v. Great Atlantic & Pacific Tea Co.*, 36 F. Supp. 77 (D. Mass. 1940), examined a standard approval clause and stated: "It would seem to be the better law that when a lease restricts a lessee's rights by requiring consent before these rights can be exercised, *it must have been in the contemplation of the parties that the lessor be required to give some reason for withholding consent.*" (*Id.*, at 78, italics added.) . . .

[T]he assertion that an approval clause "clearly and unambiguously" grants the lessor absolute discretion over assignments is untenable. It is not a rewriting of a contract, as respondent suggests, to recognize the obligations imposed by the duty of good faith and fair dealing, which duty is implied by law in every contract.

The third justification advanced in support of the majority rule is essentially based on the doctrine of *stare decisis*. It is argued that the courts should not depart from the common law majority rule because "many leases now in effect covering a substantial amount of real property and creating valuable property rights were carefully prepared by competent counsel in reliance upon the majority viewpoint." As pointed out above, however, the majority viewpoint has been far from universally held and has never been adopted by this court. Moreover, the trend in favor of the minority rule should come as no surprise to observers of the changing state of real property law in the 20th century. The minority rule is part of an increasing recognition of the contractual nature of leases and the implications in terms of contractual duties that flow therefrom. We would be remiss in our duty if we declined to question a view held by the majority of jurisdictions simply because it is held by a majority. As we stated in *Rodriguez v. Bethlehem Steel Corp.*, 525 P.2d 669, 676 (Cal. 1974), the "vitality [of the common law] can flourish only so long as the courts remain alert to their obligation and opportunity to change the common law when reason and equity demand it."

A final argument in favor of the majority rule is advanced by respondent and stated as follows: "Both tradition and sound public policy dictate that the lessor has a right, under circumstances such as these, to realize the increased value of his property." Respondent essentially argues that any increase in the market value of real property during the term of a lease properly belongs to the lessor, not the lessee. We reject this assertion. One California commentator has written:

> [W]hen the lessee executed the lease he acquired the contractual right for the exclusive use of the premises, and all of the benefits and detriment attendant to posses-sion, for the term of the contract. He took the downside risk that he would be paying too much rent if there should be a depression in the rental market.... Why should he be deprived of the contractual benefits of the lease because of the fortuitous inflation in the marketplace[?] By reaping the benefits he does not deprive the landlord of anything to which the landlord was otherwise entitled. The landlord agreed to dispose of possession for the limited term and he could not reasonably anticipate any more than what was given to him by the terms of the lease. His reversionary estate will benefit from the increased value from the inflation in any event, at least upon the expiration of the lease. Miller & Starr, *Current Law of Cal. Real Estate* §27:92 at 321 (1977 & 1984 Supp.).

Respondent here is trying to get more than it bargained for in the lease. A lessor is free to build periodic rent increases into a lease, as the lessor did here. Any increased value of the property beyond this "belongs" to the lessor only in the sense, as explained above, that the lessor's reversionary estate will benefit from it upon the expiration of the lease. We must therefore reject respondent's argument in this regard....

MALCOLM M. LUCAS, Justice, dissenting.

I respectfully dissent. In my view we should follow the weight of authority which, as acknowledged by the majority herein, allows the commercial lessor to withhold his consent to an assignment or sublease arbitrarily or without reasonable cause. The majority's contrary ruling, requiring a "commercially reasonable objection" to the assignment, can only result in a proliferation of unnecessary litigation.

The correct analysis is contained in the opinion of Justice Carl Anderson for the Court of Appeal in this case. I adopt the following portion of his opinion as my dissent: . . .

> The plain language of the lease provides that the lessee shall not assign the lease "without written consent of Lessor first had and obtained.... Any such assignment or subletting without this consent shall be void, and shall, at the option of Lessor, terminate this lease." The lease does not require that "consent may not unreasonably be withheld"; the lease does not provide that "the lessor may refuse consent only where he has a good faith reasonable objection to the assignment." Neither have the parties so contracted, nor

has the Legislature so required. Absent such legislative direction, the parties should be free to contract as they see fit.

Appellant urges this court to rewrite the contract by adding a limitation on the lessor's withholding of consent — that such consent may not be unreasonably withheld. He urges that such must be implied in the term "without written consent of lessor first had and obtained"; and he places the burden on the lessor to add language to negate that, if such be his intent — language such as "such consent may be arbitrarily, capriciously and/or unreasonably withheld."

However, it is obvious that the attorney for the lessor agreeing to such a term was entitled to rely upon the state of the law then existing in California. And at such time (Dec. 12, 1969), it is clear that California followed the "weight of authority" in these United States and allowed such consent to be arbitrarily or unreasonably withheld absent a provision to the contrary. . . .

To rewrite this contract (as appellant would have us do) for the benefit of one who was not an original party thereto, and to the detriment of one who stands in privity with one who was, and to hold that there is a triable issue of fact concerning whether respondents unreasonably withheld their consent when they had already contracted for that right, creates only mischief by breeding further uncertainty in the interpretation of otherwise unambiguously written contracts. To so hold only encourages needless future litigation.

We respectfully suggest that if California is to adopt the minority rule and reject the majority rule which recognizes the current proviso as valid, unambiguous and enforceable, that it do so by clear affirmative legislative action. To so defer to the legislative branch, protects not only this contract but those tens of thousands of landlords, tenants and lawyers who have relied on our unbroken line of judicial precedent. . . .

SLAVIN v. RENT CONTROL BOARD OF BROOKLINE

548 N.E.2d 1226 (Mass. 1990)

FRANCIS P. O'CONNOR, Justice.

Article XXXVIII of the Brookline rent control by-law provides in relevant part as follows:

> Section 9. *Evictions.* (a) No person shall bring any action to recover possession of a controlled rental unit unless: . . .
>
> (2) the tenant has violated an obligation or covenant of his tenancy other than the obligation to surrender possession upon proper notice and has failed to cure such violation after having received written notice thereof from the landlord; . . .
>
> (b) A landlord seeking to recover possession of a controlled rental unit shall apply to the board for a certificate of eviction. . . . If the board finds that the facts attested to in the landlord's petition are valid and in compliance with paragraph (a), the certificate of eviction shall be issued. . . .
>
> (c) A landlord who seeks to recover possession of a controlled rental unit without obtaining such certificate of eviction shall be deemed to have violated this By-law, and the Board may initiate a criminal prosecution for such violation.

The plaintiff landlord applied to the defendant rent control board of Brookline (board) for a certificate of eviction seeking to evict the defendant tenant Barry Myers on the ground that Myers had violated an obligation of his tenancy. The lease states:

> *Occupancy of Premises* — Tenant shall not assign nor underlet any part or the whole of the premises, nor shall permit the premises to be occupied for a period longer than a temporary visit by anyone except the individuals specifically named in the first paragraph

of this tenancy, their spouses, and any children born to them hereafter, without first obtaining on each occasion the assent in writing of Landlord.

After a hearing, the board found that the tenant had allowed an unauthorized person to occupy his apartment without first obtaining the landlord's written consent. Nonetheless, the board refused to issue the eviction certificate. The board based its refusal on its determination of law that, implicit in the lease provision requiring the landlord's consent prior to an assignment or a sublease or the permitting of other occupants, there is an "agreement on the part of the landlord to at least consider prospective tenants [and other permitted occupants] and not withhold consent unreasonably or unequivocally." The board found that the landlord had acted unreasonably because she had categorically refused to allow the tenant to bring in someone new after the original cotenant had moved out. Because of the landlord's unreasonable behavior, the board concluded that the tenant could not be said to have violated the lease. . . .

The issue whether a tenant's obligation, as specified in a residential lease, to obtain the written consent of a landlord before assigning the lease or subletting or permitting other occupants implies as a matter of law an obligation on the landlord's part to act reasonably in withholding consent has not been decided by this court. . . .

A majority of jurisdictions subscribe to the rule that a lease provision requiring the landlord's consent to an assignment or sublease permits the landlord to refuse arbitrarily or unreasonably. However, the board argues that the current trend is the other way, and cites numerous cases in support of that proposition. We note that every case cited by the board except two, which we discuss below, involved a commercial, not a residential, lease. Although the significance of the distinction between commercial and residential leases may be fairly debatable, we observe that in several of the cases cited by the board the court specifically states that its holding is limited to the commercial lease context. *See Kendall v. Ernest Pestana, Inc.*, 709 P.2d 837 (Cal. 1985).

Kruger v. Page Management Co., 432 N.Y.S.2d 295 (Sup. Ct. 1980), is the only purely residential lease case cited by the board. We get little help from that case because the reasonableness requirement in New York has been statutorily imposed. . . .

The board argues that we should be guided by the commercial lease cases because the reasons for implying a reasonableness requirement in a residential lease are at least as compelling as in a commercial lease. Our review of the commercial lease cases, however, and particularly of the rationale that appears to have motivated the courts in those cases to adopt a reasonableness requirement, does not persuade us that we should adopt such a rule in this case, which involves a residential lease in a municipality governed by a rent control law.

Two major concerns emerge from the commercial lease cases. First, courts have exhibited concern that commercial landlords may exercise their power to withhold consent for unfair financial gain. In several of the cases cited by the board, a commercial landlord refused to consent to a proposed subtenant and then attempted to enter into a new or revised lease for the same premises at a more favorable rental rate. However, in a rent control jurisdiction like Brookline there is little economic incentive to withhold consent in the residential lease context because the landlord has such limited control over the rent that can be charged.

The second concern that appears to have motivated the commercial lease decisions is a desire to limit restraints on alienation in light of the fact that "the necessity of reasonable alienation of commercial building space has become paramount in our ever-increasing urban society." *Homa-Goff Interiors, Inc. v. Cowden*, 350 So. 2d 1035,

1037 (Ala. 1977). However, this court has previously, albeit not recently, ruled that a commercial lease provision requiring a landlord's consent prior to an assignment, with no limitation on the landlord's ability to refuse, is not an unreasonable restraint on alienation. *68 Beacon St., Inc. v. Sohier*, 194 N.E. 303 (Mass. 1935). In light of our decision in *68 Beacon St., Inc.*, and in the absence of a demonstrable trend involving residential leases in other jurisdictions, we are not persuaded that there is such a "necessity of reasonable alienation of [residential] building space" that we ought to impose on residential landlords a reasonableness requirement to which they have not agreed. We are mindful that valid arguments in support of such a rule can be made, but there are also valid counter-arguments, not the least of which is that such a rule would be likely to engender a plethora of litigation about whether the landlord's withholding of consent was reasonable. The question is one of public policy which, of course, the Legislature is free to address. We note that the Legislature has spoken in at least four States: Alaska Stat. §34.03.060; Del. Code tit. 25, §5512(b); Haw. Rev. Stat. §516-63; N.Y. Real Prop. Law §226-b. . . .

NOTES AND QUESTIONS

1. In commercial leases, the trend appears to be toward adopting an implied reasonableness term in lease clauses that give the landlord the right to consent to sublet or assignment. *See Julian v. Christopher*, 575 A.2d 735, 736 n.1 (Md. 1990) (roughly 13 states have adopted the minority rule, which imposes a requirement that the lessor act reasonably). In *Warner v. Konover*, 553 A.2d 1138 (Conn. 1989), Chief Justice Ellen Peters rejected the majority rule, holding that the lessor could not refuse to allow an assignment of a commercial lease without reasonable justification, *id.* at 1140-1141:

> The precedent that we deem more persuasive [is] a case that neither party appears to have brought to the attention of the trial court. *Central New Haven Development Corporation v. La Crepe, Inc.*, 413 A.2d 840 (Conn. 1979), involved a landlord's action to recover damages from a commercial tenant for breach of a lease. The tenant defended against liability on the basis of a clause giving it unfettered discretion to cancel the lease because of the landlord's conceded failure, three years earlier, to obtain a nondisturbance agreement from the mortgagee. Although the tenant's option to cancel was in terms unlimited, and the lease contained a nonwaiver clause, we held that the tenant was in breach because it had unreasonably delayed its exercise of its option. We relied squarely on §205 (then §231) of the *Restatement (Second) of Contracts*, which provides: "Every contract imposes upon each party a duty of good faith and fair dealing in its performance and its enforcement."
>
> If a commercial lease imposes a duty of good faith and fair dealing upon a tenant, there is no reason not to impose a similar duty upon a landlord. The provisions of §205 of the Restatement are therefore as applicable in this case as they were in *La Crepe, Inc.* Accordingly, we hold that a landlord who contractually retains the discretion to withhold its consent to the assignment of a tenant's lease must exercise that discretion in a manner consistent with good faith and fair dealing. . . .

In contrast, in *First Federal Savings Bank of Indiana v. Key Markets*, 559 N.E.2d 600 (Ind. 1990), the court refused to imply a reasonableness requirement into a landlord consent clause. It explained the result this way, *id.* at 604:

> [C]ourts are bound to recognize and enforce contracts where the terms and the intentions of the parties can be readily determined from the language in the instrument. It

is not the province of courts to require a party acting pursuant to such a contract to be "reasonable," "fair," or show "good faith" cooperation. Such an assessment would go beyond the bounds of judicial duty and responsibility. It would be impossible for parties to rely on the written expressions of their duties and responsibilities. Further, it would place the court at the negotiation table with the parties. In the instant case, the court would decide what is "fair" or "reasonable" concerning the advantage or disadvantage of control of the leased property. The proper posture for the court is to find and enforce the contract as it is written and leave the parties where it finds them. It is only where the intentions of the parties cannot be readily ascertained because of ambiguity or inconsistency in the terms of a contract or in relation to extrinsic evidence that a court may have to presume the parties were acting reasonably and in good faith in entering into the contract.

In *Uno Restaurants, Inc. v. Boston Kenmore Realty Corp.*, 805 N.E.2d 957 (Mass. 2004), the Massachusetts Supreme Judicial court ruled that a covenant of good faith and fair dealing is implied in all leasehold agreements. Is this ruling consistent with the ruling in *Slavin?* How would Justice Peters answer this question? Justice O'Connor?

2. Suppose a commercial lease provides that the landlord has the "absolute right to approve or disapprove any sublease or assignment for any reason whatsoever." Should the courts enforce this or should they hold that it is an unreasonable restraint on alienation? *See Newman v. Hinky Dinky Omaha-Lincoln, Inc.*, 427 N.W.2d 50 (Neb. 1988) (holding that a landlord consent clause contains an implied reasonableness requirement but refusing to address the question whether explicit agreement to grant arbitrary discretion to the landlord to disapprove a sublet violates public policy). The California legislature responded to *Kendall* by adopting the implied reasonableness test for commercial leases, Cal. Civ. Code §§1995.020(b), 1995.260, but providing that it should apply prospectively only to new leases, Cal. Civ. Code §1995.270, and that the parties were substantially free to contract to the contrary, Cal. Civ. Code §1995.240 ("[a] restriction on transfer of a tenant's interest in a lease may provide that the transfer is subject to any express standard or condition, including, but not limited to, a provision that the landlord is entitled to some or all of any consideration the tenant receives from a transferee in excess of the rent under the lease").

Suppose the tenant of property on which a grocery store is operating arranges to sublease the property to a business owned by Japanese Americans. The landlord refuses to agree because of prejudice against the sublessees. What should the courts do if the landlord refuses to approve the sublease based on racially discriminatory motives? Should a lease provision granting the landlord the absolute right to approve or disapprove any subleases be enforceable under these circumstances?

3. Do the distinctions between commercial and residential leases relied on by the court in *Slavin* make sense to you? Do the reasons for implying a reasonableness requirement differ in the residential context? If the arguments applicable to commercial leases are inapplicable to residential leases, what other arguments could you make on behalf of the tenant? Note that Massachusetts extended the *Slavin* rule to commercial leases, refusing to adopt the *Kendall* approach. *21 Merchants Row Corp. v. Merchants Row, Inc.*, 587 N.E.2d 788 (Mass. 1992). Is there a difference between commercial and residential leases that justifies a different rule for each? Could you argue that residential leases, but not commercial leases, are subject to an implied duty of reasonableness?

4. The court in *Slavin* finds the laws in other states cited by the tenant to be inapposite since they are incorporated into the statutes rather than the common law of those states. *See, e.g.,* N.Y. Real Prop. Law §226-b(2)(a) (tenants can sublet with landlord's consent; such consent cannot be unreasonably withheld). What difference does

this make? On one hand, it can be argued that this question should be, and has been in other states, left to the legislature to address. On the other hand, since the theory underlying contract law is that the court should enforce the presumed intent of the parties, it might be argued that because these laws reflect changing values and expectations, the presumption underlying the common law rule no longer reflects the justified expectations of the parties. Would it have made a difference to the Massachusetts Supreme Judicial Court if the tenant could have identified another state that had modernized its law by common law ruling rather than statute? Should that make a difference? Doesn't some state have to be first?

PROBLEMS

1. Do you agree with the court's decision in *Slavin* not to read an implied reasonableness term into the phrase "no assigning or subletting without landlord's consent"?

(a) What arguments would you make on behalf of the landlord in *Slavin* against limiting the landlord's discretion to withhold consent to a sublease or assignment in the residential context?

(b) What arguments would you make on behalf of the residential tenant in *Slavin* in favor of interpreting the lease to read, "no assigning or subletting without landlord's consent, such consent not to be withheld unreasonably"?

2. Suppose a law student in the Commonwealth of Massachusetts has a one-year lease, running from September 1 through August 31, that states "no subletting or assignment without the landlord's consent." The law student wants to move out on June 1 and sublet the apartment for most of the summer so that she can move to Washington, D.C., for a summer job. Does it make any difference whether Massachusetts law requires landlords to mitigate damages? Is there anything the tenant can do to protect herself from being sued by the landlord?

§8.3.2.3 Tenant's Good Faith Duty to Operate

THE COLLEGE BLOCK v. ATLANTIC RICHFIELD CO.
254 Cal. Rptr. 179 (Ct. App. 1988)

HERBERT LOUIS ASHBY, Acting Presiding Justice. . . .

In 1965, respondent, The College Block (College Block) owned a parcel of undeveloped real property. College Block signed a 20-year lease with appellant Atlantic Richfield Company (ARCO) in which ARCO agreed to build and operate a gasoline service station on the property. Other provisions of the lease allowed ARCO to build, maintain and replace any buildings ARCO desired in operating a station, obligated ARCO to pay all applicable taxes, prohibited College Block from operating a gasoline station on other properties it owned or controlled, limited ARCO's use of the property to that of a service station, and allowed ARCO the right to cancel the lease if it could not obtain permits required in running a station. Pursuant to the lease, ARCO constructed and then operated for approximately 17 years a gasoline service station on the property.

The rent, pursuant to the lease, was determined by a percentage of the gasoline delivered, and irrespective of the gallons delivered, College Block was to receive a minimum of $1,000 per month.

On January 1, 1983, 39 months prior to the expiration of the lease, ARCO closed the station. When ARCO ceased operations, it paid College Block $1,000 per month for the months remaining on the lease. ARCO contended that it was responsible only for the minimum monthly rental because the lease did not contain an express covenant requiring it to operate the station. College Block brought suit alleging that ARCO was also responsible for additional sums College Block would have received had the station remained in business. College Block contended that it was entitled to damages because as a matter of law a covenant of continued operation was implied into the lease. . . .

The issue of whether there is an implied covenant of continued operation arises because the lease did not fix the rent, but guaranteed a minimum payment plus a percentage based upon the gasoline delivered. In having a percentage lease, the parties contemplated a lengthy association (20 years) during which rents would periodically be established by the market place.

A percentage lease provides a lessor with a hedge against inflation and automatically adjusts the rents if the location becomes more valuable. It is advantageous to the lessee if the "location proves undesirable or his enterprise proves unsuccessful." Thus, both parties share in the inherent business risk. Inherent within all percentage leases is the fundamental idea that the business must continually operate if it is to be successful. To make a commercial lease mutually profitable when the rent is a minimum plus a percentage, or is based totally on a percentage, a covenant to operate in good faith will be implied into the contract if the minimum rent is not substantial.

[C]ontracts are to be interpreted so as to make them reasonable without violating the intention of the parties. (Cal. Civ. Code, §1643.) To effectuate the intent of the parties, implied covenants will be found if after examining the contract as a whole it is so obvious that the parties had no reason to state the covenant, the implication arises from the language of the agreement, and there is a legal necessity. A covenant of continued operation can be implied into commercial leases containing percentage rental provisions in order for the lessor to receive that for which the lessor bargained.

We first examine the lease to determine that to which the parties bargained. The lease between ARCO and College Block required ARCO to build and operate a gasoline service station on the undeveloped property owned by College Block. Other provisions in the lease allowed ARCO to build and maintain any edifices ARCO desired in operating a service station, obligated ARCO to pay all applicable property and taxes and insurance, prohibited College Block from conducting a gasoline station on other properties College Block owned or controlled, gave ARCO the right of first refusal if College Block received an offer to sell the property, and limited ARCO's use of the property to that of the gasoline service station.

In addition, the rent was tied to the operation of the station. The rent provision, an essential part of the lease, did not set a minimum pay-ment irrespective of whether the property was utilized as a service station, but rather "irrespective of the number of gallons . . . delivered." "Without an on-going service station operation, no basis would exist to calculate the rent." *Continental Oil Co. v. Bradley*, 602 P.2d 1, 2 (Colo. 1979). The wording of this provision suggests that continued operation of the business was contemplated.

Further, it is incongruent to limit College Block's abilities to lease properties it owned or controlled for use as another gasoline station under the noncompetition clause, thus foreclosing College Block from securing another station if ARCO abandoned the premises, and to limit ARCO's ability to operate any other type of business on the property, yet to conclude that ARCO could cease operations when it desired. Contrary to ARCO's suggestion, the fact that ARCO and not College Block was obligated to build the gasoline service station is not controlling. Both parties were entitled to the expectations as bargained for in the lease. . . .

We now turn to whether the $1,000 rent minimum was "substantial." Contracts which determine rents by a percentage of sales inherently contain uncertainties. As discussed above, this type of contract is designed to adjust to the commercial realities of the day by reconciling the rent to the amount of sales. If a business is not profitable, courts are reluctant to force the lessee to continue to operate the business. However, as in all contracts, both parties are entitled to their reasonable expectations at the time the contract was entered into. If both parties contemplated continued operations of the business, a covenant of continued operation will be implied into the commercial lease containing a specified minimum plus a percentage when the guaranteed minimum is not substantial or adequate. In this way, the lessor will receive the benefit of the lessor's bargain.

"A substantial minimum" cannot be precisely defined and factual information on this issue must be examined before a covenant will be implied. By evaluating the facts surrounding the formulation of the contract, the courts determine if the specified sum provides the lessor with what was reasonably expected.

. . . The lease between ARCO and College Block was executed approximately 17 years prior to the cessation of operations. In the interim, great changes in property values, gasoline prices, and the amount of sales could have occurred. Before finding, as a matter of law, that a covenant of continued operation will be implied, the trier of fact must find that the $1,000, the guaranteed minimum, was not substantial and did not provide College Block with a fair return on its investment. The parties should be given an opportunity to submit evidence as to the facts and circumstances surrounding the contract to determine if, at the time the contract was entered into, the guaranteed rent was "substantial." We remand to the trial court so evidence may be heard on this issue. . . .

NOTES AND QUESTIONS

1. *Express covenants to operate.* Courts generally will enforce express covenants to operate. However, they will not force an unprofitable business to operate and are very likely to deny injunctive relief ordering the tenant to continue operating, relegating the landlord to damages on the ground that damages are an adequate remedy for the tenant's breach and because judges are not competent to manage the tenant's business operations to ensure compliance with the operating covenant. *Summit Town Centre, Inc. v. Shoe Show of Rocky Mount, Inc.*, 828 A.2d 995 (Pa. 2003) (enforcing an express covenant to operate by a damages remedy and denying injunctive relief).

2. *Implied covenants of continuous operation.* Most courts refuse to interpret percentage leases to find an implied covenant to operate a business continuously if the base rent is substantial. If the base rent is nominal or is much less than the fair rental value of the premises, however, most courts will find such an implied covenant. *See, e.g., Hornwood v. Smith's Food King No. 1*, 807 P.2d 208 (Nev. 1991) (determining the measure of damages for tenant's breach of implied duty to operate). Is an implied

duty to operate likely to be more consistent or less consistent with the actual intent of the parties at the time they contracted? Should commercial tenants be exempt from implied obligations on the grounds that commercial landlords are sufficiently sophisticated and can adequately protect themselves by including an explicit covenant to operate in their leases? Should the result depend on whether the tenant had a right to sublet or assign the lease? Does a negatively phrased duty not to use the premises for anything other than a restaurant include an affirmative duty to operate? What result best promotes the efficient use of property?

3. *Anchor stores.* Many shopping centers include large "anchor stores" that are intended to attract large numbers of patrons and to serve as a draw to the shopping center that would enable smaller stores there to attract customers. Does an anchor store have an implied obligation to continue operating?

In *Columbia East Associates v. Bi-Lo, Inc.,* 386 S.E.2d 259 (S.C. Ct. App. 1989), the court held that it did have such an obligation despite the absence of any affirmative obligation to that effect in the lease. Defendant Bi-Lo, a popular supermarket chain, leased space in the center of plaintiff's shopping center for a term of 20 years. The lease provided that the leased premises "shall be used only for the operation of a supermarket (for the sale of groceries, meats and/or other items generally sold by supermarkets)." When another supermarket in an adjacent shopping center closed, Bi-Lo took the opportunity to take over the space because it could thereby "eliminat[e] the competitor and [prevent another] competitor from taking over the [space]." *Id.* at 261. Although it had a right to sublet the original site, Bi-Lo failed to obtain a subtenant and made only minimal efforts to do so. Instead, it continued to pay the agreed-upon fixed rent, which did not include a percentage rent. Bi-Lo argued that, under the terms of the lease, it could vacate the premises and leave the store empty so long as it continued to pay rent. The landlord, Columbia East, argued that Bi-Lo was required either to operate a supermarket or to sublet to another for operation of a retail store. The court noted that Bi-Lo was an anchor tenant whose presence in the shopping center was intended by the landlord to bring customers to the smaller shops. Allowing Bi-Lo to leave without an adequate replacement would defeat the landlord's purpose in agreeing to the lease. The court held that the lease contained an implied obligation of good faith and that this encompassed a requirement of continuous operation on an anchor store even in the absence of a percentage rent agreement. Bi-Lo breached its lease by ceasing operations and by failing to make reasonable efforts to find a subtenant. Chief Judge Sanders concurred on the ground that Bi-Lo had breached the lease by using the premises not for operation of a supermarket but "for a purpose not allowed by the lease; namely, as part of a scheme to stifle competition." *Id.* at 263.

However, some other courts have disagreed with this result. For example, in *Oakwood Village LLC v. Albertsons, Inc.,* 104 P3d 1226, 2004 UT 101 (Utah 2004), the Utah Supreme Court refused to find an implied covenant of continuous operation in circumstances somewhat similar to those in *Bi-Lo.* Despite the fact that the landlord had leased the ground to the anchor tenant (which built its own store) for up to 65 years at a very low rent which did not rise over time did not impose any obligations on the tenant who closed the store after 21 years of operation and moved to another location nearby, leaving the other 25 stores in the center without the benefit of the anchor's business. The court refused to imply a covenant of operation either from the nominal rent or the potential 65-year duration. It focused on the fact that the lease did not have a percentage rent term and that the tenant had built its own store. It was not clear why the landlord gave a ground lease for such a low rent but the court concluded that, if this was a bad deal, the landlord had to live with it. Moreover, the tenant had the right to sublet or assign the premises without the landlord's consent. Nor did the implied covenant of good faith and fair dealing suggest imposing obligations that could not be inferred from the language of the lease. The court concluded, *id.* at 1241, ¶57:

> This lease is a complete and unambiguous agreement between competent commercial parties. Long-term commercial leases, by their nature, are risky. Neither side can foretell future market conditions with any certainty. We presume that both [landlord] and [tenant] bargained for the best terms and conditions each could get. Each party took the risk that unpredictable market forces would at some later day render the contractual terms unfavorable to themselves. Despite this risk, both parties willingly agreed to the terms in the lease. It is not our role to intervene now, construing the contract's unambiguous terms to mean something different from what the parties intended them to mean at the outset.

Accord, Daniel G. Kamin Kilgore Enterprises v. Brookshire Grocery Co., 81 Fed. Appx. 827, 2003 U.S. App. LEXIS 24299 (5th Cir. 2003) (lease clause providing that the tenant "shall use and occupy" the property "for the purpose of conduct[ing a] grocery" business does not imply a continuous operation obligation).

PROBLEM

In *Casa D'Angelo v. A & R Realty Co.*, 553 N.E.2d 515 (Ind. Ct. App. 1990), a restaurant, Casa D'Angelo, that leased its premises from plaintiff landlord, A & R Realty, decided to open a second restaurant within a mile of the first establishment. The tenant subsequently changed its operation from offering a full-service dinner menu to a limited offering of soup, salad, and sandwiches to walk-in customers only. Gross sales fell dramatically. The base rent was $825 per month, and the court assumed that this amount was substantial. However, the percentage rent (5 percent of gross sales) was also substantial, rising from $2,500 in 1978 to $18,752 in 1981 and a total of $36,230 for 1986. Eventually, the tenant closed the restaurant entirely but continued to pay the base rent of $825 per month for the remainder of the lease term.

The landlord sued for the amounts of percentage rent it would have earned had the tenant maintained its operation without interruption. The landlord based its claim on two separate theories.

(1) Plaintiff landlord argued that because the rent was calculated partly as a percentage of gross sales, the tenant had an implied covenant to act in good faith to generate those sales by remaining in operation for the remainder of the lease term. Plaintiff claimed that this result followed regardless of whether the lease called for a base rent and whether the base rent was substantial. The tenant restaurant argued that if the landlord had wanted a promise from the tenant to continue operating, the landlord should have bargained for it.

(2) Plaintiff argued that the tenant had expressly agreed to continue operating the restaurant because the lease stated that "Lessee shall use the premises for the operation of a restaurant facility and for no other purpose without first obtaining the written consent of Lessor...." The tenant, however, noted that most courts hold that a lease providing that the leased premises "are to be used for a certain prescribed purpose imports no obligation on the part of the lessee to use or continue to use the premises

for that purpose; such a provision is a covenant against a noncomplying use, not a covenant to use."

What arguments could you make on both sides of these questions? If you were the judge, how would you rule, and why?

§8.3.3 TENANT'S RIGHT TO STAY VERSUS LANDLORD'S RIGHT TO RECOVER POSSESSION

The landlord is entitled to evict the tenant if the tenant breaches material terms of the lease. The main reason for eviction is failure to pay rent or failure to pay rent on time. Is the landlord entitled to evict the tenant who has *not* breached any terms of the leasehold? A tenant with a term of years — a one-year lease, for example — cannot be evicted before the end of the term unless the tenant has breached the lease. The landlord has no obligation, however, to *renew* a leasehold. Thus, a landlord is entitled to refuse to renew a one-year lease for any reason. Landlords are also entitled to end periodic tenancies, such as month-to-month tenancies, by giving requisite notice.

There are some exceptions to the general principle that landlords may evict tenants at the end of the lease term. First, federal and state antidiscrimination statutes prohibit landlords from failing to renew leaseholds if the landlord's motivation is discriminatory. Second, tenants in units that are subject to statutory or local rent control ordinarily are protected from eviction unless the landlord can show just cause. Third, some states or localities also regulate eviction for the purpose of converting apartment units into condominiums. Fourth, federal law protects occupants of public housing from eviction without just cause. Fifth, tenants are protected from eviction if the landlord's motivation is to retaliate against them for asserting their right to habitable premises by calling the housing inspector, for example, to report housing code violations.

New Jersey has adopted a general statute allowing eviction in most private rental housing units only if the landlord can establish one of a number of stated just causes for eviction. (The statute is reprinted at *supra* §8.1.2, page 739.) Other states generally grant landlords freedom to choose whether to renew a term of years or to terminate a periodic tenancy, subject to the specific exceptions noted above. Would you favor passage of a general anti-eviction statute in your state? In the absence of legislation, should a good cause rule be adopted as a matter of common law?

§8.3.3.1 Just Cause Eviction

(a) Private Housing Market

New Jersey and the District of Columbia are the only jurisdictions that have adopted statutes granting tenants a right to continue in possession unless the landlord has just cause to end the tenancy or refuse to renew the leasehold. D.C. Code §45-2551. N.J. Stat. Ann. §§2A:18-61.1 to 2A:18-61.12 lists as good cause to evict tenant failures to pay rent or refrain from harming the premises as well as landlord decisions to move into the apartment or house, allow a close family member to do so, or change to a nonresidential rental use. Is this a good list? Is there anything you would add or subtract from it?

NEW JERSEY ANTI-EVICTION ACT

N.J. Stat. Ann. §§2A:18-61.1 to 2A:18-61.12
(1987 & Supp. 1992)

See statute reprinted *supra* at §8.1.2, at pages 642-644.

In *447 Associates v. Miranda*, 559 A.2d 1362 (N.J. 1989), a tenant, Carmen Miranda, shared an apartment with her child and paid the rent in cash after receiving and cashing her monthly public assistance check, which typically arrived on the third of the month or later. If Miranda had not yet received or cashed the check, the landlord's agent would return sometime later to receive payment. The building was then sold, and the new landlord increased the rent and insisted that the rent be paid on the first of the month by mail only, with a $25 penalty for payment after the fifth of the month. Miranda had trouble paying the rent on time and four out of six monthly rent payments were received by the landlord two to four days after the fifth of the month. Miranda failed to pay the late charges. The landlord sued to evict Miranda on the statutory grounds of nonpayment of rent, N.J. Stat. §2A:18-61.1(a), nonpayment of a rent increase (permissible so long as not "unconscionable"), §2A:18-61.1(f), and habitual late payment, §2A:18-61.1(j). The court found that the statute prohibited the landlord from making unreasonable "changes of substance in the terms and conditions of the lease," §2A:18-61.1(i), and that the landlord's insistence that the rent be paid by the fifth of the month by mail constituted an unreasonable change, *id.* at 534-535:

> In interpreting the reasonableness of a lease change, courts have properly looked to the circumstances of the case and to the interests of both the landlord and the tenant. . . .
>
> At oral argument defendant did not complain of the imposition of a rent deadline; rather, the difficulty here lay in the timing of that deadline. But for the landlord's insistence that the rent be paid by mail on the fifth of each month and not on some date shortly thereafter that defendant, making her best efforts, could have met, neither party would have had a problem.
>
> We do not mean to suggest that it is at all unreasonable for landlords to impose late fees. However, given that knowledge of their tenants' circumstances is assumed, landlords and owners must take the totality of those circumstances into account when making changes in the material terms or conditions of leases, and must avoid the imposition of changes that will cause undue hardship to tenants attempting in good faith to meet their rent obligations. Here, for example, defendant's payments were always mailed by the third of the month, but received sometimes as late as the ninth. The landlord could well have avoided difficulty with defendant by setting a deadline more realistically tailored to the needs of defendant, who was probably not plaintiff's only tenant receiving public assistance. By imposing a late fee on the fifth of the month, a deadline defendant was plainly incapable of meeting regularly without allowance for payment by hand, the landlord effectively increased defendant's rent by the amount of the penalty fee.
>
> It cannot be assumed that a lease change was reasonable or that an unreasonable change was consented to merely because it was included in a notice of rent increase ratified by continued possession of the leasehold estate. Thus in reviewing cases founded on challenges to lease changes, it will be important for trial courts both to examine the manner by which the lease changes were accomplished and to weigh the arguments supporting the lease changes as against tenants' claims of hardship. The trial court should make detailed factual findings and relate them to the applicable law. . . .

PROBLEM

1. Assume the facts of *447 Associates v. Miranda* occurred in a state without a just cause eviction statute.

    a. Defendant Miranda argues that the court should adopt a common law rule protecting the tenant's right to remain in possession absent good cause to evict. Make the arguments for the landlord and tenant on both sides of this question, and decide what the court should do.

    b. If a good cause rule is adopted as a matter of common law, has the landlord demonstrated sufficient cause to evict the tenant? Make the arguments on both sides and decide what you think the court should do.

2. A lease provides that the tenants in a condominium unit covenant will not cause "any nuisance; any offensive noise, odor or fumes; or any hazard to health." The two tenants each smoke one pack of cigarettes a day. In this older building, the smoke wafted upstairs to the neighboring condominium apartments, whose occupants complained of the secondhand smoke. After complaints by the neighbors, the landlord sues to evict the tenants for smoking in their own apartment and violating the lease terms. Before they took the apartment, the landlord had told the tenants that he had lived in and smoked in that apartment for years and received no complaints. Can the landlord evict them? *See* Ralph Ranalli & Jonathan Saltzman, *Jury Finds Heavy Smoking to Be Grounds for Eviction,* Boston Globe, June 16, 2005, at B1 (eviction allowed in *Gainsborough St. Realty Trust v. Haile,* No. 98-02279 (Mass. Housing Ct. 2005)); Stefanie Shaffer, *Lighting up in your condo? Think again.,* Natl. L.J., July 4, 2005, at 6.

(b) Publicly Subsidized Housing

The federal government subsidizes homeowners by allowing them to deduct the portion of their home mortgage payments attributable to interest from income subject to federal income taxation. A subsidy is provided to some low-income families through a program known as Section 8 housing, by which the federal government pays a significant portion of the tenants' rent owed to private landlords. The tenant finds the apartment and obtains the agreement of the landlord to participate in the program. In 1981, the statute was amended to prohibit eviction of tenants in Section 8 housing without "good cause." The statute now provides, at 42 U.S.C. §1437f(d)(1)(B):

> (d) Required provisions and duration of contracts for assistance payments. . . .
>
> (1) Contracts to make assistance payments entered into by a public housing agency with an owner of existing housing units shall provide (with respect to any unit) that — . . .
>
>   (B)(ii) during the term of the lease, the owner shall not terminate the tenancy except for serious or repeated violation of the terms and conditions of the lease, for violation of applicable Federal, State, or local law, or for other good cause;
>
>   (iii) during the term of the lease, any criminal activity that threatens the health, safety, or right to peaceful enjoyment of the premises by other tenant, any criminal activity that threatens the health, safety, or right to peaceful enjoyment of their residences by persons residing in the immediate vicinity of the premises, or any drug-

related criminal activity on or near such premises, engaged in by a tenant of any unit, any member of the tenant's household, or any guest or other person under the tenant's control, shall be cause for termination of tenancy;

(iv) any termination of tenancy shall be preceded by the owner's provision of written notice to the tenant specifying the grounds for such action . . .

Public housing owned and operated by public authorities or governmental agencies is similarly prohibited from evicting tenants in the absence of "serious or repeated violation of the terms or conditions of the lease or for other good cause." 42 U.S.C. §1437d(l)(4).

In *Templeton Arms v. Feins,* 531 A.2d 361 (N.J. Super. Ct. App. Div. 1987), the landlord sought to evict a Section 8 tenant on the ground that the landlord wanted to withdraw from the Section 8 program. The landlord argued that nothing in federal or state law required landlords to accept Section 8 tenants and thus the landlord argued that it should be free to withdraw from the program. It argued that the statute authorized eviction for "good cause," §1437f(d)(1)(B)(ii), and that a desire to end participation in the program constituted good cause. The tenant argued that the landlord's desire to withdraw from the Section 8 program did not constitute good cause; rather, good cause required a demonstration that the tenant had acted improperly, for example, by failing to pay rent. Alternatively, the landlord could show good cause by showing a demonstrable reason for the eviction, such as a desire to utilize the unit for personal or family use or for nonresidential purposes, and that the landlord's interest in terminating the tenancy outweighed the tenant's interest in remaining. The court held that the statute prohibited the landlord from withdrawing from the program and evicting the tenant without good cause. "A landlord's right to discontinue participation in the Section 8 program must be balanced against the tenant's right to be protected from arbitrary ouster."*Id.* at 370. Do you agree with this interpretation of the statute? What are the arguments on both sides?

§8.3.3.2 Regulation of Condominium Conversion

Many municipalities, and some states, regulate the conversion of rental housing to condominiums or cooperatives to protect tenants from eviction. Some local ordinances prohibit eviction of existing tenants when apartments are converted. *Kahn v. Brookline Rent Control Board,* 477 N.E.2d 390 (Mass. 1985) (local rent control ordinance). Some laws protect particular classes of tenants, such as the elderly or disabled. *See Senior Citizens and Disabled Protected Tenancy Act,* N.J. Stat. Ann. §2A:18-61.22 *et seq.* (granting elderly and disabled tenants protection from eviction for up to 40 years after conversion). Other statutes give tenants preference in purchasing either the building or their particular units within the building when it is converted by granting tenants preemptive rights or rights of first refusal; these rights entitle them to match any offers made by third parties and thus acquire the building or particular units within it. *See, e.g.,* D.C. Code §45-1631 *et seq.;* *Lealand Tenants Association, Inc. v. Johnson,* 572 A.2d 431 (D.C. 1990) (holding that a group of tenants was not entitled to exercise its right of first refusal to purchase a building since it had failed to match all the material terms of the offer made by a third party).

§8.4   Tenant's Rights to Habitable Premises

§8.4.1   THE COVENANT OF QUIET ENJOYMENT AND CONSTRUCTIVE EVICTION

MINJAK CO. v. RANDOLPH
528 N.Y.S.2d 554 (App. Div. 1988)

MEMORANDUM DECISION. . . .

In July of 1983 petitioner-landlord commenced the within summary non-payment proceeding against respondents Randolph and Kikuchi, tenants of a loft space on the fourth floor of petitioner's building on West 20th Street in Manhattan, alleging non-payment of rent since July 1981. The tenants' answer set forth as affirmative defenses that because they were unable to use two-thirds of the loft space due to the landlord's renovations and other conditions, they were entitled to an abatement of two-thirds of the rent, and that as to the remaining one-third space, they were entitled to a further rent abatement due to the landlord's failure to supply essential services. The tenants also counterclaimed for breach of warranty of habitability, seeking both actual and punitive damages and attorney's fees.

A trial was held in Civil Court before Justice Saxe in November of 1983. It was stipulated that rent was due and owing from October 1981 through November 1983 in the amount of $12,787 ($200 due for October 1981, $450 due each month from November 1981 through December 1982, and $567 per month since January 1983).

Respondents commenced residency of the loft space in 1976 pursuant to a commercial lease. Petitioner offered a commercial lease even though at the time of the signing of the lease the building was used predominantly for residential purposes and the respondents had informed petitioner that they would use the loft as their residence. The loft space measures 1700 square feet, approximately two-thirds of which is used as a music studio for Mr. Kikuchi, where he composes, rehearses and stores his very expensive electronic equipment and musical instruments. The remainder of the space is used as the tenants' residence.

Late in 1977, the fifth-floor tenant began to operate a health spa equipment business which included the display of fully working jacuzzis, bathtubs, and saunas. The jacuzzis and bathtubs were filled to capacity with water. From November 1977 through February 1982, respondents suffered at least 40 separate water leaks from the fifth floor. At times the water literally poured into the bedroom and bedroom closets of respondents' loft, ruining their clothes and other items. Water leaked as well into the kitchen, the bathroom and onto Mr. Kikuchi's grand piano and other musical instruments. Respondents' complaints to petitioner went unheeded.

In January of 1978 the fifth-floor tenant began to sandblast the walls, causing sand to seep through openings around pipes and cracks in the ceiling and into respondent's loft. The sand, which continued to fall into the loft even as the parties went to trial, got into respondent's clothes, bed, food and even their eyes.

In September of 1981 the landlord commenced construction work in the building to convert the building into a Class A multiple building. To convert the freight elevator into a passenger elevator, petitioner had the elevator shaft on respondent's side of the building removed. The workers threw debris down the elevator shaft, raising "huge clouds of dust" which came pouring into the loft and settled everywhere, on respondents' clothes, bed, food, toothbrushes and musical equipment. The musical equipment had to be covered at all times to protect it from the dust. Respondents began to suffer from eye and sinus problems, nausea, and soreness in their throats from the inhalation of the dust. Respondents attempted to shield themselves somewhat from the dust by putting up plastic sheets, only to have the workmen rip them down.

To demonstrate the hazardous nature of some of the construction work, respondents introduced evidence that as the landlord's workers were demolishing the stairs from the seventh floor down, no warning signs were posted, causing one visitor to come perilously close to falling through a hole in the stairs. The workers jackhammered a new entrance to the loft, permitting the debris to fall directly onto the floor of respondents' loft. The workmen would mix cement right on respondents' floor. A new entrance door to the loft was sloppily installed without a door sill, and loose bricks were left around the frame. A day later, brick fragments and concrete fell on tenant Randolph's head as she closed the door.

The record contains many more examples of dangerous construction and other conduct interfering with respondents' ability to use and enjoy possession of their loft. From 1981 until the time of trial, Kikuchi was completely unable to use the music studio portion of the loft. His musical instruments had been kept covered and protected against the sand and later the dust since 1978.

The jury rendered a verdict awarding respondents a rent abatement of 80% for July 1981 through November 1983, as compensatory damages on the theory of constructive eviction from the music studio portion of the loft; a 40% rent abatement for January 1981 through November 1983, on the remainder of the rent due for the residential portion of the premises, on a theory of breach of warranty of habitability; a 10% rent abatement on the rent attributable to the residential portion of the premises for all of 1979, on a breach of warranty of habitability theory; and punitive damages in the amount of $20,000. After trial the court granted respondents' motion made pursuant to Real Property Law Sec. 234 for reasonable attorney's fees, awarding respondents $5000. The court also granted petitioner's motion to set aside the verdict and for other relief, only to the extent of reducing the award for punitive damages to $5000. . . .

On appeal to the Appellate Term that court reversed the judgment. Holding that the doctrine of constructive eviction could not provide a defense to this non-payment proceeding, because tenants had not abandoned possession of the demised premises, the court reversed the jury's award as to the 80% rent abatement predicated on the constructive eviction theory. . . .

We agree with the holding and reasoning of *East Haven Associates v. Gurian*, 313 N.Y.S.2d 927 (Civ. Ct. 1970), that a tenant may assert as a defense to the nonpayment of rent the doctrine of constructive eviction, even if he or she has abandoned only a portion of the demised premises due to the landlord's acts in making that portion of the premises unusable by the tenant. . . . Indeed "compelling considerations of social policy and fairness" dictate such a result. . . .

. . . The evidence at trial fully supported a finding that respondents were compelled to abandon the music studio portion of the loft due to "the landlord's wrongful acts [which] substantially and materially deprive[d] the tenant[s] of the beneficial use and enjoyment" of that portion of the loft.

Petitioner does, however, correctly point out that as the constructive eviction claim was asserted as a defense to the nonpayment of rent and respondents did not request an abatement for any months other than those in which they did not pay rent, the jury's award of an 80% rent abatement as to the months July, August, September and half of October of 1981 must be stricken.

The award for punitive damages, as reduced by the Civil Court to $5000, should be reinstated as well. . . .

Although generally in breach of contract claims the damages to be awarded are compensatory, in certain instances punitive damages may be awarded when to do so would "deter morally culpable conduct." The determining factor is ". . . the moral culpability of the defendant," and whether the conduct implies a "criminal indifference to civil obligations."

[I]t has been recognized that punitive damages may be awarded in breach of warranty of habitability cases where the landlord's actions or inactions were intentional and malicious.

[W]e are satisfied that this record supports the jury's finding of morally culpable conduct in light of the dangerous and offensive manner in which the landlord permitted the construction work to be performed, the landlord's indifference to the health and safety of others, and its disregard for the rights of others, so as to imply even a criminal indifference to civil obligations. One particularly egregious example of the landlord's wanton disregard for the safety of others was the way in which the stair demolition was performed: steps were removed and no warning sign even posted. The landlord's indifference and lack of response to the tenants' repeated complaints of dust, sand and water leak problems demonstrated a complete indifference to their health and safety and a lack of concern for the damage these conditions could cause to the tenants' valuable personal property. Such indifference must be viewed as rising to the level of high moral culpability. Accordingly, the award of punitive damages is sustained. . . .

BLACKETT v. OLANOFF

358 N.E.2d 817 (Mass. 1976)

HERBERT P. WILKINS, Justice.

The defendant in each of these consolidated actions for rent successfully raised constructive eviction as a defense against the landlords' claim. The judge found that the tenants were "very substantially deprived" of quiet enjoyment of their leased premises "*for a substantial* time" (emphasis original). He ruled that the tenants' implied warranty of quiet enjoyment was violated by late evening and early morning music and disturbances coming from nearby premises which the landlords leased to others for use as a bar or cocktail lounge (lounge). The judge further found that, although the landlords did not intend to create the conditions, the landlords "had it within their control to correct the conditions which . . . amounted to a constructive eviction of each [tenant]." He also found that the landlords promised each tenant to correct the situation, that the landlords made some attempt to remedy the problem, but they were unsuccessful, and that each tenant vacated his apartment within a reasonable time. Judgment was entered for each tenant; the landlords appealed; and we transferred the appeals here. We affirm the judgments.

The landlords argue that they did not violate the tenants' implied covenant of quiet enjoyment because they are not chargeable with the noise from the lounge. The landlords do not challenge the judge's conclusion that the noise emanating from the lounge was sufficient to constitute a constructive eviction, if that noise could be attributed to the landlords.[3] Nor do the landlords seriously argue that a constructive eviction could not be found as [a] matter of law because the lounge was not on the same premises as the tenants' apartments. The landlords' principal contention, based on the denial of certain requests for rulings, is that they are not responsible for the conduct of the proprietors, employees, and patrons of the lounge.

Our opinions concerning a constructive eviction by an alleged breach of an implied covenant of quiet enjoyment sometimes have stated that the landlord must perform some act with the intent of depriving the tenant of the enjoyment and occupation of the whole or part of the leased premises. There are occasions, however, where a landlord has not intended to violate a tenant's rights, but there was nevertheless a breach of the landlord's covenant of quiet enjoyment which flowed as the natural and probable consequence of what the landlord did, what he failed to do, or what he permitted to be done. *Case v. Minot,* 33 N.E. 700 (Mass. 1893) (landlord authorizing another lessee to obstruct the tenant's light and air, necessary for the beneficial enjoyment of the demised premises). Although some of our opinions have spoken of particular action or inaction by a landlord as showing a presumed intention to evict, the landlord's conduct, and not his intentions, is controlling.

The judge was warranted in ruling that the landlords had it within their control to correct the condition which caused the tenants to vacate their apartments. The landlords introduced a commercial activity into an area where they leased premises for residential purposes. The lease for the lounge expressly provided that entertainment in the lounge had to be conducted so that it could not be heard outside the building and would not disturb the residents of the leased apartments. The potential threat to the occupants of the nearby apartments was apparent in the circumstances. The landlords complained to the tenants of the lounge after receiving numerous objections from residential tenants. From time to time, the pervading noise would abate in response to the landlord's complaints. We conclude that, as matter of law, the landlords had a right to control the objectionable noise coming from the lounge and that the judge was warranted in finding as a fact that the landlords could control the objectionable conditions.

This situation is different from the usual annoyance of one residential tenant by another where traditionally the landlord has not been chargeable with the annoyance.[4] Here we have a case more like *Case v. Minot,* 33 N.E. 700 (Mass. 1893), where the landlord entered into a lease with one tenant which the landlord knew permitted that tenant to engage in activity which would interfere with the rights of another tenant. There, to be sure, the clash of tenants' rights was inevitable, if each pressed those rights. Here, although the clash of tenants' interests was only a known potentiality initially,

---

3. There was evidence that the lounge had amplified music (electric musical instruments and singing, at various times) which started at 9:30 P.M. and continued until 1:30 A.M. or 2 A.M., generally on Tuesdays through Sundays. The music could be heard through the granite walls of the residential tenants' building, and was described variously as unbelievably loud, incessant, raucous, and penetrating. The noise interfered with conversation and prevented sleep. There was also evidence of noise from patrons' yelling and fighting.

4. The general, but not universal, rule, in this country is that a landlord is not chargeable because one tenant is causing annoyance to another....

The rule in New York appears to be that the landlord may not recover rent if he has had ample notice of the existence of conduct of one tenant which deprives another tenant of the beneficial enjoyment of his premises and the landlord does little or nothing to abate the nuisance....

experience demonstrated that a decibel level for the entertainment at the lounge, acoustically acceptable to its patrons and hence commercially desirable to its proprietors, was intolerable for the residential tenants.

Because the disturbing condition was the natural and probable consequence of the landlords' permitting the lounge to operate where it did and because the landlords could control the actions at the lounge, they should not be entitled to collect rent for residential premises which were not reasonably habitable. Tenants such as these should not be left only with a claim against the proprietors of the noisome lounge. To the extent that our opinions suggest a distinction between nonfeasance by the landlord, which has been said to create no liability . . . and malfeasance by the landlord, we decline to perpetuate that distinction where the landlord creates a situation and has the right to control the objectionable conditions.

NOTES AND QUESTIONS

1. *Express and implied terms in the landlord-tenant relationship.* The landlord-tenant relationship is governed partly by the *express terms* of any written lease. For example, the tenant may agree to perform required services, such as taking out the garbage, mowing the lawn, or replacing lightbulbs in common areas such as stairwells. The tenant may also covenant not to bring pets into the apartment or not to sublet or assign without the landlord's consent. The landlord may agree to pay for utilities such as heat and electricity.

The landlord-tenant relationship is also governed by *implied terms*. These terms need not be written down or even explicitly discussed to be legally binding. They may or may not be waivable by the parties. One important term implied in every landlord-tenant relationship by common law or statute is the *covenant of quiet enjoyment* by which the landlord impliedly promises not to disturb the tenant's quiet enjoyment of the property.

2. *The structure of landlord-tenant litigation.* It is important to understand the context in which landlord-tenant litigation arises. Remember that landlords and tenants are involved in an ongoing contractual relationship — the landlord has transferred to the tenant the right to possess the property in return for periodic rent payments. Most disputes arise because either the landlord has interfered with the tenant's possession or quiet enjoyment of the property or the tenant has breached his obligation to pay rent — or both.

Most lawsuits involve claims by the landlord against the tenant based on the tenant's failure to pay rent or on some claimed breach of the lease agreement. The landlord's complaint may seek either (a) payment of *back rent* owed to the landlord or (b) *possession* of the premises (otherwise known as *eviction*). The landlord may also make a claim for *damages* resulting from the tenant's breach of the lease — for example, the cost of repairing facilities damaged by the tenant. The tenant may answer each of these claims by denying that he has breached the lease (he has in fact paid the rent or he did not cause the damage). Or he may raise *defenses* to these claims, admitting that he stopped paying rent but asserting that he was entitled to do so because the landlord breached the agreement first.

It is important to separate the landlord's claim for *back rent* from the landlord's claim for *possession*. Some defenses are available to both claims; other defenses are available to only one. If the tenant can raise a successful defense to the landlord's claim for back rent, then the tenant may be relieved of the obligation to pay all or part of the rent otherwise owed for the period during which the tenant occupied the property without paying rent. If the tenant can raise a successful defense to the landlord's claim for possession, then the tenant may be allowed to continue living in the apartment despite the landlord's desire to evict the tenant.

In response to a lawsuit by the landlord, the tenant may also make *counterclaims* against the landlord if the rules of procedure allow this. Counterclaims may include claims for *damages* resulting from the landlord's breach of the lease. Some courts measure those damages by the reduced value of the leasehold caused by the breach of the implied warranty; they will order a rent *abatement* (a reduction in rent) owed for the period during the violation. Other courts measure damages in a manner independent of the rental value, allowing compensation for any significant harm that can be proven; such amounts may exceed the rental value. All courts will allow the tenant to recover damages if the landlord acted negligently and physical harm resulted to the tenant or an invitee on the premises; such damages also may exceed the rental value of the premises. The tenant may petition for *injunctive* relief, such as an order to the landlord to fix the apartment to comply with the local housing code. Rather than waiting for the landlord to sue the tenant, the tenant may sue the landlord initially with the tenant's claims. Such lawsuits ordinarily ask for either (a) damages resulting from the landlord's negligent maintenance or compensation for injuries resulting from the landlord's failure to comply with the housing code, or (b) an injunction ordering the landlord to fix the apartment to comply with the terms of the lease or the housing code.

3. *Actual eviction.* If the landlord breaches the lease by physically barring the tenant from the property, the tenant's obligation to pay rent ceases entirely. The placement of new locks on the door constitutes actual eviction. *Olin v. Goehler,* 694 P.2d 1129 (Wash. Ct. App. 1985). The tenant also may sue the landlord for damages for trespass and may seek an injunction ordering the landlord to reconvey possession of the premises to the tenant.

What happens if the landlord bars the tenant from only *part* of the leased property? A partial actual eviction constitutes a breach of the lease and provides the tenant with ample justification to move out before the end of the lease term; the tenant will not be liable for the rent after moving out. What happens if the tenant chooses to stay? The traditional rule relieves the tenant of the obligation to pay rent *completely* even though the tenant continues to occupy the rest of the premises. This rule may change, however; the trend seems to be to *abate* the rent (reduce it) to the fair market value of the property that remains. *Restatement (Second) of Property (Landlord and Tenant)* §6.1 (1977).

4. *Constructive eviction.* A constructive eviction occurs when the landlord substantially interferes with the tenant's quiet enjoyment of the premises. The defense of constructive eviction allows the tenant to stop rent payments and move out before the end of the lease term. The theory is that when the landlord allows the conditions in the apartment to deteriorate such that living in the apartment is either impossible or uncomfortable, her actions are functionally equivalent to physically barring the tenant from the premises.

What happens if the tenant stops paying rent and fails to move out? The traditional rule is that the tenant can raise a defense of constructive eviction only if he moves out within a reasonable period of time. To establish constructive eviction, the tenant must claim that the landlord's interference with the tenant's quiet enjoyment of the premises is so substantial that nobody in his right mind would stay there; the place is uninhabitable and, therefore, the landlord's actions are equivalent to barring the door. If, however, the tenant *stays*, then this can be used as evidence that the interference is not sufficiently serious to justify allowing the tenant to stop paying rent or ending the leasehold. *Barash v. Pennsylvania Terminal Real Estate Corp.*, 256 N.E.2d 707 (N.Y. 1970).

East Haven Associates, Inc. v. Gurian, 313 N.Y.S.2d 927 (Civ. Ct. 1970), on which the court in *Minjak* relies, held that tenants could establish a defense of *partial constructive eviction*. Under this doctrine, tenants can show that the landlord's actions have substantially deprived the tenant of the use and enjoyment of a portion of the property. The defense of partial constructive eviction may allow the tenant to continue living in the remaining part of the premises from which the tenant does not claim to have been constructively evicted. *Minjak* illustrates that the remedy for partial constructive eviction for the tenant who wants to stay is likely to be a partial, rather than complete, abatement of rent. The court in *East Haven* explained the basis for the doctrine, *id*. at 930-931:

> It cannot be seriously disputed that a major shortage in residential housing has prevailed in our metropolitan area for several decades. The clear effect has been to undermine so drastically the bargaining power of tenants in relation to landlords that grave questions as to the fairness and relevance of some traditional concepts of landlord-tenant law are presented.
>
> The very idea of requiring families to abandon their homes before they can defend against actions for rent is a baffling one in an era in which decent housing is so hard to get, particularly for those who are poor and without resources. It makes no sense at all to say that if part of an apartment has been rendered uninhabitable, a family must move from the entire dwelling before it can seek justice and fair dealing. *See Arbern Realty Co. v. Clay Craft Planters Co.*, 727 N.Y.S.2d 236 (App. Div. 2001) (applying the partial constructive eviction doctrine in the context of a commercial lease).

The *Restatement (Second) of Property (Landlord and Tenant)* §6.1 (1977) provides that "there is a breach of the landlord's obligations if, during the period the tenant is entitled to possession of the leased property, the landlord, or someone whose conduct is attributable to him, interferes with a permissible use of the leased property by the tenant." The *Second Restatement* departs from traditional law in several respects. First, it defines constructive eviction as interference that is "more than insignificant" rather than requiring the interference to be "substantial." Reporter's Note 1. Second, it adopts the *Blackett* doctrine, making the landlord liable for the acts of third parties "performed on property in which the landlord has an interest, which conduct could be legally controlled by him." Comment d. Third, it rejects the traditional requirement that the tenant abandon the premises before taking advantage of the constructive eviction doctrine, on the ground that "it makes the law completely unavailable to tenants who for one reason or another cannot move, *e.g.*, indigent urban apartment dwellers in many cities, and available only at great risk to others, who must first deprive themselves of such benefit as they are deriving from the premises before getting a ruling on whether they were justified in doing so." Reporter's Note 6.

5. *Landlord's liability for acts of other tenants.* The traditional rule, which appears to hold in most states, provides that constructive eviction may be shown only if the landlord has acted in a way that interfered with the tenant's interest in quiet enjoyment. Under the traditional rule, the landlord is not responsible for the acts of other tenants

unless the lease specifically includes an obligation to control the conduct of other tenants. The trend appears to be in the direction of the *Blackett* rule accepted by the *Second Restatement. Restatement (Second) of Property (Landlord and Tenant)* §6.1 (1977). *See also International Commission on English in the Liturgy v. Schwartz,* 573 A.2d 1303 (D.C. 1990) (adopting the *Blackett* rule).

The lease with the bar in *Blackett* contained a clause obligating the tenant not to disturb the quiet enjoyment of its neighbors. Would the case have come out the same way had that clause not been in the lease? Should a tenant have an implied duty not to disturb his neighbors such that violation of the duty would constitute a breach of the lease and entitle the landlord to evict the tenant? Should the landlord have not only the *right* but the *obligation* to evict a noisy tenant to protect the interests of neighboring tenants?

PROBLEM

A client comes into your office with the following story. She is a law student renting a third-floor apartment in a three-unit apartment house near the law school. She shares the apartment with two roommates; all three of them have signed the lease, which runs from September 1 to August 31. It is now November 10. Starting in October, the tenant occupying the second floor began making unwanted sexual comments to your client as she walked up to her apartment. He has never touched her and has not directly threatened to attack her. She is afraid of him because of these comments, which he now makes daily. She believes he waits for her to come home so that he can accost her on the stairway as she goes up to her apartment. If it were not for this neighbor, she would be very happy with the apartment, which is well maintained, reasonably priced, attractive, and close to both school and shopping. At the same time, she is considering moving out — something her roommates do not want her to do. She asks you for advice about her legal rights.

1. What questions would you ask her?
2. What options does she have?
3. What legal advice would you give her?

§8.4.2 IMPLIED WARRANTY OF HABITABILITY

§8.4.2.1 Doctrinal Development

Before the 1970s, most courts held that landlords had no implied duty to repair the rented premises and that leaseholds included no implied representations that the apartment was in habitable condition. The only exception to this principle was that landlords had a duty to fix latent defects known to them and not easily discoverable by the tenant. If the tenant wanted a warranty or a contractual obligation on the landlord to maintain the apartment, she had to bargain for it.

Courts also held that the contractual obligations of the landlord and tenant were *independent* rather than *dependent*. This meant that, contrary to other kinds of contracts, the parties' obligations to perform were not contingent on the other party's performance. Thus, the tenant's obligation to pay rent was enforceable by the landlord even if the landlord herself was violating a covenant to repair the premises. The tenant's only remedy was to sue the landlord for damages. To terminate the lease, the tenant needed to show constructive eviction; thus, any defects or failures to repair that did not rise to the level of constructive eviction prevented the tenant from lawfully getting out of the lease early, even if there was a covenant to repair and the landlord was breaching the agreement.

In recent years, most states have repudiated both the lack of a duty to repair or maintain and the independent covenants rule, at least in the context of residential housing. Starting around 1970, there was a virtual revolution in residential landlord-tenant law. Before 1970, courts viewed a leasehold solely as a transfer of a property interest; the landlord granted the tenant the right to possess the premises for a specified period of time, conditional on an agreed-upon rent. The landlord's obligations were limited to transferring possession; constructive eviction was seen as a failure to comply with this duty. The tenant had a duty to pay the rent and not to commit waste by damaging the property. No other obligations attended the relationship, which was governed by *caveat emptor* or *caveat lessee* — let the buyer beware.

This tradition rapidly unraveled after the decision in *Javins v. First National Realty Corp.*, one of the most famous property cases ever decided. As you read the opinion below, consider the reasons Judge J. Skelly Wright gives to change the law. Are they convincing?

JAVINS v. FIRST NATIONAL REALTY CORP.
428 F.2d 1071 (D.C. Cir. 1970)

J. SKELLY WRIGHT, Circuit Judge:
These cases present the question whether housing code violations which arise during the term of a lease have any effect upon the tenant's obligation to pay rent....
... We ... hold that a warranty of habitability, measured by the standards set out in the Housing Regulations for the District of Columbia, is implied by operation of law into leases of urban dwelling units covered by those Regulations and that breach of this warranty gives rise to the usual remedies for breach of contract.

I

... By separate written leases, each of the appellants rented an apartment in a three-building apartment complex in Northwest Washington known as Clifton Terrace. The landlord, First National Realty Corporation, filed separate actions in the Landlord and Tenant Branch of the Court of General Sessions on April 8, 1966, seeking possession on the ground that each of the appellants had defaulted in the payment of rent due for the month of April. The tenants, appellants here, admitted that they had not paid the landlord any rent for April. However, they alleged numerous [1500] violations of the Housing Regulations as "an equitable defense or (a) claim by way of recoupment or set-off in an amount equal to the rent claim," as provided in the rules of the Court of General Sessions.... Appellants conceded at trial, however, that this offer of proof reached only violations which had arisen since the term of the lease had commenced....

II

Since, in traditional analysis, a lease was the conveyance of an interest in land, courts have usually utilized the special rules governing real property transactions to resolve controversies involving leases. However, as the Supreme Court has noted in another context, "the body of private property law . . . more than almost any other branch of law, has been shaped by distinctions whose validity is largely historical." Courts have a duty to reappraise old doctrines in the light of the facts and values of contemporary life — particularly old common law doctrines which the courts themselves created and developed. As we have said before, "The continued vitality of the common law . . . depends upon its ability to reflect contemporary community values and ethics."

The assumption of landlord-tenant law, derived from feudal property law, that a lease primarily conveyed to the tenant an interest in land may have been reasonable in a rural, agrarian society; it may continue to be reasonable in some leases involving farming or commercial land. In these cases, the value of the lease to the tenant is the land itself. But in the case of the modern apartment dweller, the value of the lease is that it gives him a place to live. The city dweller who seeks to lease an apartment on the third floor of a tenement has little interest in the land 30 or 40 feet below, or even in the bare right to possession within the four walls of his apartment. When American city dwellers, both rich and poor, seek "shelter" today, they seek a well known package of goods and services — a package which includes not merely walls and ceilings, but also adequate heat, light and ventilation, serviceable plumbing facilities, secure windows and doors, proper sanitation, and proper maintenance. . . .

Some courts have realized that certain of the old rules of property law governing leases are inappropriate for today's transactions. In order to reach results more in accord with the legitimate expectations of the parties and the standards of the community, courts have been gradually introducing more modern precepts of contract law in interpreting leases. . . .

In our judgment the trend toward treating leases as contracts is wise and well considered. Our holding in this case reflects a belief that leases of urban dwelling units should be interpreted and construed like any other contract.

III

Modern contract law has recognized that the buyer of goods and services in an industrialized society must rely upon the skill and honesty of the supplier to assure that goods and services purchased are of adequate quality. In interpreting most contracts, courts have sought to protect the legitimate expectations of the buyer and have steadily widened the seller's responsibility for the quality of goods and services through implied warranties of fitness and merchantability. . . .

The rigid doctrines of real property law have tended to inhibit the application of implied warranties to transactions involving real estate. Now, however, courts have begun to hold sellers and developers of real property responsible for the quality of their product. For example, builders of new homes have recently been held liable to purchasers for improper construction on the ground that the builders had breached an implied warranty of fitness. In other cases courts have held builders of new homes liable for breach of an implied warranty that all local building regulations had been complied with. . . .

Despite this trend in the sale of real estate, many courts have been unwilling to imply warranties of quality, specifically a warranty of habitability, into leases of apartments. Recent decisions have offered no convincing explanation for their refusal; rather they have relied without discussion upon the old common law rule that the lessor is not obligated to repair unless he covenants to do so in the written lease contract. However, the Supreme Courts of at least two states, in recent and well reasoned opinions, have held landlords to implied warranties of quality in housing leases. *Lemle v. Breeden,* 462 P.2d 470 (Haw. 1969); *Reste Realty Corp. v. Cooper,* 251 A.2d 268 (N.J. 1969). In our judgment, the old no-repair rule cannot coexist with the obligations imposed on the landlord by a typical modern housing code, and must be abandoned in favor of an implied warranty of habitability. In the District of Columbia, the standards of this warranty are set out in the Housing Regulations.

IV

A

In our judgment the common law itself must recognize the landlord's obligation to keep his premises in a habitable condition. This conclusion is compelled by three separate considerations. First, we believe that the old rule was based on certain factual assumptions which are no longer true; on its own terms, it can no longer be justified. Second, we believe that the consumer protection cases discussed above require that the old rule be abandoned in order to bring residential landlord-tenant law into harmony with the principles on which those cases rest. Third, we think that the nature of today's urban housing market also dictates abandonment of the old rule.

The common law rule absolving the lessor of all obligation to repair originated in the early Middle Ages. Such a rule was perhaps well suited to an agrarian economy; the land was more important than whatever small living structure was included in the leasehold, and the tenant farmer was fully capable of making repairs himself. These historical facts were the basis on which the common law constructed its rule; they also provided the necessary prerequisites for its application.

Court decisions in the late 1800's began to recognize that the factual assumptions of the common law were no longer accurate in some cases. For example, the common law, since it assumed that the land was the most important part of the leasehold, required a tenant to pay rent even if any building on the land was destroyed. Faced with such a rule and the ludicrous results it produced, in 1863 the New York Court of Appeals declined to hold that an upper story tenant was obliged to continue paying rent after his apartment building burned down. The court simply pointed out that the urban tenant had no interest in the land, only in the attached building. . . .

These as well as other similar cases demonstrate that some courts began some time ago to question the common law's assumptions that the land was the most important feature of a leasehold and that the tenant could feasibly make any necessary repairs himself. Where those assumptions no longer reflect contemporary housing patterns, the courts have created exceptions to the general rule that landlords have no duty to keep their premises in repair.

It is overdue for courts to admit that these assumptions are no longer true with regard to all urban housing. Today's urban tenants, the vast majority of whom live in multiple dwelling houses, are interested, not in the land, but solely in "a house suitable for occupation." Furthermore, today's city dweller usually has a single, specialized skill unrelated to maintenance work; he is unable to make repairs like the "jack-of-all-trades" farmer who was the common law's model of the lessee. Further, unlike his agrarian predecessor who often remained on one piece of land for his entire life, urban tenants today are more mobile than ever before. A tenant's tenure in a specific apartment will often not be sufficient to justify efforts at repairs. In addition, the increasing complexity of today's dwellings renders them much more difficult to repair than the structures of earlier times. In a multiple dwelling repair may require access to equipment and areas in the control of the landlord. Low and middle income tenants, even if they were interested in making repairs, would be unable to obtain any financing for major repairs since they have no long-term interest in the property.

Our approach to the common law of landlord and tenant ought to be aided by principles derived from the consumer protection cases referred to above. In a lease contract, a tenant seeks to purchase from his landlord shelter for a specified period of time. The landlord sells housing as a commercial businessman and has much greater opportunity, incentive and capacity to inspect and maintain the condition of his building. Moreover, the tenant must rely upon the skill and bona fides of his landlord at least as much as a car buyer must rely upon the car manufacturer. In dealing with major problems, such as heating, plumbing, electrical or structural defects, the tenant's position corresponds precisely with "the ordinary consumer who cannot be expected to have the knowledge or capacity or even the opportunity to make adequate inspection of mechanical instrumentalities, like automobiles, and to decide for himself whether they are reasonably fit for the designed purpose." *Henningsen v. Bloomfield Motors, Inc.*, 161 A.2d 69, 78 (N.J. 1960).

Since a lease contract specifies a particular period of time during which the tenant has a right to use his apartment for shelter, he may legitimately expect that the apartment will be fit for habitation for the time period for which it is rented. We point out that in the present cases there is no allegation that appellants' apartments were in poor condition or in violation of the housing code at the commencement of the leases. Since the lessees continue to pay the same rent, they were entitled to expect that the landlord would continue to keep the premises in their beginning condition during the lease term. It is precisely such expectations that the law now recognizes as deserving of formal, legal protection.

Even beyond the rationale of traditional products liability law, the relationship of landlord and tenant suggests further compelling reasons for the law's protection of the tenants' legitimate expectations of quality. The inequality in bargaining power between landlord and tenant has been well documented. Tenants have very little leverage to enforce demands for better housing. Various impediments to competition in the rental housing market, such as racial and class discrimination and standardized form leases, mean that landlords place tenants in a take it or leave it situation. The increasingly severe shortage of adequate housing further increases the landlord's bargaining power and escalates the need for maintaining and improving the existing stock. Finally, the findings by various studies of the social impact of bad housing has led to the realization that poor housing is detrimental to the whole society, not merely to the unlucky ones who must suffer the daily indignity of living in a slum.

Thus we are led by our inspection of the relevant legal principles and precedents to the conclusion that the old common law rule imposing an obligation upon the lessee to repair during the lease term was really never intended to apply to residential urban leaseholds. Contract principles established in other areas of the law provide a more rational framework for the apportionment of landlord-tenant responsibilities; they strongly suggest that a warranty of habitability be implied into all contracts for urban dwellings.

B

We believe, in any event, that the District's housing code requires that a warranty of habitability be implied in the leases of all housing that it covers. The housing code — formally designated the Housing Regulations of the District of Columbia — was established and authorized by the Commissioners of the District of Columbia on August 11, 1955. Since that time, the code has been updated by numerous orders of the Commissioners. The 75 pages of the Regulations provide a comprehensive regulatory scheme setting forth in some detail: (a) the standards which housing in the District of Columbia must meet; (b) which party, the lessor or the lessee, must meet each standard; and (c) a system of inspections, notifications and criminal penalties. The Regulations themselves are silent on the question of private remedies.

Two previous decisions of this court, however, have held that the Housing Regulations create legal rights and duties enforceable in tort by private parties. . . .

The District of Columbia Court of Appeals gave further effect to the Housing Regulations in *Brown v. Southall Realty Co.*, 237 A.2d 834 (D.C. 1968). There the landlord knew at the time the lease was signed that housing code violations existed which rendered the apartment "unsafe and unsanitary." Viewing the lease as a contract, the District of Columbia Court of Appeals held that the premises were let in violation of Sections 2304 and 2501 of the Regulations and that the lease, therefore, was void as an illegal contract. In the light of *Brown*, it is clear not only that the housing code creates privately enforceable duties . . . , but that the basic validity of every housing contract depends upon substantial compliance with the housing code at the beginning of the lease term. The *Brown* court relied particularly upon Section 2501 of the Regulations which provides:

> Every premises accommodating one or more habitations shall be maintained and kept in repair so as to provide decent living accommodations for the occupants. This part of this Code contemplates more than mere basic repairs and maintenance to keep out the elements; its purpose is to include repairs and maintenance designed to make a premises or neighborhood healthy and safe.

By its terms, this section applies to maintenance and repair during the lease term. Under the *Brown* holding, serious failure to comply with this section before the lease term begins renders the contract void. We think it untenable to find that this section has no effect on the contract after it has been signed. To the contrary, by signing the lease the landlord has undertaken a continuing obligation to the tenant to maintain the premises in accordance with all applicable law.

This principle of implied warranty is well established. Courts often imply relevant law into contracts to provide a remedy for any damage caused by one party's illegal conduct. . . .[56]

---

56. As a general proposition, it is undoubtedly true that parties to a contract intend that applicable law will be complied with by both sides. We recognize, however, that reading statutory provisions into private contracts may have little factual support in the intentions of the particular parties now before us. But, for reasons of public policy, warranties are often implied into contracts by operation of law in order to meet generally prevailing standards of honesty and fair dealing. When the public policy has been enacted into law like the housing code, that policy will usually have deep roots in the expectations and intentions of most people. *See* Costigan, *Implied-in-Fact Contracts and Mutual Assent*, 33 Harv. L. Rev. 376, 383-385 (1920).

[T]hat the housing code must be read into housing contracts — a holding also required by the purposes and the structure of the code itself. The duties imposed by the Housing Regulations may not be waived or shifted by agreement if the Regulations specifically place the duty upon the lessor. Criminal penalties are provided if these duties are ignored. This regulatory structure was established by the Commissioners because, in their judgment, the grave conditions in the housing market required serious action. Yet official enforcement of the housing code has been far from uniformly effective. Innumerable studies have documented the desperate condition of rental housing in the District of Columbia and in the nation. . . .

We therefore hold that the Housing Regulations imply a warranty of habitability, measured by the standards which they set out, into leases of all housing that they cover.

V

In the present cases, the landlord sued for possession for nonpayment of rent. Under contract principles, however, the tenant's obligation to pay rent is dependent upon the landlord's performance of his obligations, including his warranty to maintain the premises in habitable condition. In order to determine whether any rent is owed to the landlord, the tenants must be given an opportunity to prove the housing code violations alleged as breach of the landlord's warranty.

At trial, the finder of fact must make two findings: (1) whether the alleged violations[63] existed during the period for which past due rent is claimed, and (2) what portion, if any or all, of the tenant's obligation to pay rent was suspended by the landlord's breach. If no part of the tenant's rental obligation is found to have been suspended, then a judgment for possession may issue forthwith. On the other hand, if the jury determines that the entire rental obligation has been extinguished by the landlord's total breach, then the action for possession on the ground of nonpayment must fail.[64]

The jury may find that part of the tenant's rental obligation has been suspended but that part of the unpaid back rent is indeed owed to the landlord. In these circumstances, no judgment for possession should issue if the tenant agrees to pay the partial rent found to be due. If the tenant refuses to pay the partial amount, a judgment for possession may then be entered. . . .

NOTES AND QUESTIONS

1. *Majority rule.* The implied warranty of habitability has been adopted in almost all states by statute or common law for residential tenancies. *Pugh v. Holmes,* 405 A.2d 897 (Pa. 1979). However, a few holdouts still refuse to apply the warranty to residential leases. *See, e.g., Harper v. Coleman,* 705 So. 2d 388 (Ala. 1996), *rev'd on other grounds by Ex parte Coleman,* 705 So. 2d 392 (Ala. 1997); *Bedell v. Los Zapatistas, Inc.,* 805 P.2d 1198

---

63. The jury should be instructed that one or two minor violations standing alone which do not affect habitability are de minimis and would not entitle the tenant to a reduction in rent.

64. As soon as the landlord made the necessary repairs rent would again become due. Our holding, of course, affects only eviction for nonpayment of rent. The landlord is free to seek eviction at the termination of the lease or on any other legal ground.

(Colo. Ct. App. 1991). *See also Ortega v. Flaim*, 902 P.2d 199 (Wyo. 1995) (no implied warranty), *superseded by statute*, Wyo. Stat. §1-21-1201 to -1211 (creating a duty to repair but denying the tenant a right to withhold rent; tenant entitled to bring court action to obtain damages or to be released from the leasehold).

Some states measure the landlord's obligations by reference to state or local housing codes, holding that the warranty is breached when the landlord fails to comply with applicable building code provisions so as to materially impair health and safety. Other courts, however, have measured the landlord's obligations independently of the applicable housing code, holding that landlords have an obligation to conform with "general community standards of suitability for occupancy." Robert S. Schoshinski, *American Law of Landlord and Tenant* §3:17, at 128 (1980). *See Detling v. Edelbrock*, 671 S.W.2d 265, 270 (Mo. 1984) (habitability to be judged by community standards, including but not limited to local housing codes). Examples of problems that are likely to violate the implied warranty include lack of heat or hot water, broken windows, pest infestation, and leaky roofs.

If a landlord fails to provide a necessary service, such as heat or hot water, does the tenant have an immediate right to a rent reduction when the problem occurs to compensate for the lowered rental value of the premises, or does the landlord have a grace period within which to fix the problem? Many courts hold that the implied warranty is not violated until the landlord has been notified of the problem and had a reasonable opportunity to fix it. *Chess v. Muhammad*, 430 A.2d 928, 929 (N.J. Super. Ct. 1981). However, some courts find a violation the moment the condition occurs, *Knight v. Hallsthammar*, 623 P.2d 268, 273 (Cal. 1981) (breach of warranty existed whether or not landlord had reasonable time to repair defects existing when he purchased the building), and others hold that the violation starts when the landlord is notified, *Berman & Sons, Inc. v. Jefferson*, 396 N.E.2d 981, 985-86 (Mass. 1979) (breach occurred when landlord received notice of lack of heat and hot water even though he promptly fixed the problem). Which approach is better?

2. *Judicial role.* Allowing the tenant to raise the landlord's violation of the housing code or analogous failures to provide habitable premises makes eviction proceedings considerably more complicated, drawn out, and expensive. Because of this, the defense seems to contradict the policy underlying summary process statutes, whose purpose was to provide the landlord with relatively expeditious proceedings for eviction of tenants who were violating the terms of the lease. Is the implied warranty of habitability compatible with the policies underlying summary process statutes? If so, how?

It may (or may not) be helpful to note that many states responded to the judicial creation of the implied warranty of habitability by incorporating it into their landlord-tenant legislation. To the extent the implied warranty violated the purpose or intent of the summary process statutes, these legislative enactments explicitly or implicitly amended the summary process procedure by allowing tenants to raise the warranty as a defense to a claim for possession.

Did Judge Wright engage in illegitimate judicial activism to create a new defense to the landlord's claim for possession? Or was Judge Wright's innovation in the law a legitimate implementation of the policies underlying the housing code?

3. *Remedies.* Various remedies are available to vindicate the tenant's rights under the implied warranty of habitability. In most states, the remedies available to tenants come from a combination of common law doctrines and specific statutory provisions, some of which may explicitly modify or limit common law remedies. The most important remedies are discussed below.

a. *Rescission, or the right to move out before the end of the lease term.* The landlord's violation of his contractual obligation to provide a habitable apartment entitles the tenant to stop performance of her contractual obligations. Thus, the tenant may repudiate the contract and move out before the end of the lease term without being liable for rent for the months remaining on the lease. This is the case when breach of the warranty of habitability results in a material change in housing conditions even when that change would not amount to constructive eviction. *Wesson v. Leone Enterprises, Inc.,* 774 N.E.2d 611 (Mass. 2002)(finding this result in the case of a commercial lease). Suppose the tenant moves out five months before the end of the lease term, and the landlord sues the tenant for the remaining five months' rent. If the tenant can show that the landlord violated the implied warranty of habitability, then the tenant has a defense to the landlord's claim for the remaining rent.

b. *Rent withholding.* If the landlord breaches the implied warranty of habitability, the tenant ordinarily has the right to stop paying rent and continue living in the premises. If the landlord sues the tenant for back rent owed, the tenant may raise the violation of the warranty as a defense to the claim for back rent. If the landlord has breached the implied warranty, then the tenant's failure to pay rent does not constitute a breach of the tenant's contractual obligations; rather, the tenant had a legal right to stop paying rent under the circumstances. (Note that this distinguishes the implied warranty of habitability from constructive eviction doctrine, which ordinarily requires the tenant to move out to become entitled to stop paying rent before the end of the lease term.) If the case goes to trial, the tenant may be required to repay a portion of the unpaid rent to the landlord.

If the landlord sues the tenant for possession on the grounds of non-payment of rent, the tenant can raise the violation of the warranty as a defense to the eviction proceedings. If the defense is established, the landlord will not be allowed to evict the tenant, who will be able to continue living in the apartment.

It is advisable for tenants who are contemplating rent withholding to determine whether any statutes regulate their ability to withhold rent. These statutes may, for example, require that the tenant give notice to the landlord of the defect in the premises before the tenant is entitled to withhold rent. They may also limit rent withholding to situations in which the tenant has verified the complaint by calling a local housing inspector to document the existence and seriousness of the housing code violation.

It is also advisable for tenants who stop paying rent to the landlord to deposit the usual rental amount in a separate account, called an *escrow* account. If it turns out that the tenant was not entitled to withhold rent, the court will order the tenant to pay back rent to the landlord. If the tenant is unable to pay this back rent within a reasonable period of time, the tenant can be evicted. It is therefore advisable for the tenant to save, rather than spend, the money that would otherwise be going to the landlord as the monthly rent. Some states may have statutes requiring tenants to make rental payments to an escrow account. In the alternative, these statutes may allow the landlord to go to court for an order requiring the tenant to pay the rent into an escrow account held by the court clerk pending adjudication.

Finally, tenants would be well advised to *notify* the landlord of the problem before withholding rent; courts are unlikely to find a violation of the implied warranty unless the landlord has been notified of the problem and then failed to correct it within a reasonable period of time. *Vanlandingham v. Ivanow*, 615 N.E.2d 1361, 1369 (Ill. App. Ct. 1993); *Hilder v. St. Peter*, 478 A.2d 202, 210 (Vt. 1984).

c. *Rent abatement.* When the landlord violates the implied warranty of habitability, the tenant ordinarily is entitled to a reduction in the rent, also known as *rent abatement.* The tenant can sue the landlord for a declaratory judgment that the landlord has violated the implied warranty of habitability and ask the court to order the landlord to reimburse the tenant for all or a portion of the rent previously paid to the landlord during the period of the violation.

Usually, however, the tenant withholds rent, waits to be sued by the landlord for back rent or possession, then argues that the rent should be abated for the period of the violation. When the case is adjudicated, the court ordinarily will determine what, if any, portion of the rent withheld should be paid back to the landlord. If the violation of the implied warranty is quite serious, the landlord may get nothing for the period of the violation. If the violation is less serious, the court may rule that the tenant is obligated to pay a portion of the rent, such as 25 or 50 percent.

The amount of the rent deduction depends on the test used in the jurisdiction. Some states apply a *fair market value* test. The amount of rent owed to the landlord during the period of the violation is based on the fair market value of the premises "as is" or with the defect. Most states simply *reduce* the rent by a percentage amount that reflects the seriousness of the violation and the amount of discomfort experienced by the tenant.

d. *Repair and deduct.* The tenant may be able to pay for needed repairs herself and then deduct the cost of the repairs from the rent paid to the landlord. Local statutes may regulate this practice by limiting the amount deducted or the kinds of repairs allowed.

e. *Injunctive relief, or specific performance.* Some states, by statute or common law, allow tenants to bring a lawsuit against the landlord for an injunction ordering the landlord to comply with the housing code by making needed repairs.

f. *Administrative remedies.* Finally, many states provide for administrative remedies. The local housing code may include procedures for enforcement by local housing inspectors. For example, the aggrieved tenant may be able to call the local housing inspector to ask for a rapid inspection of the apartment. If the inspector finds material violations of the housing code, the inspector may then contact the landlord herself and order repairs to be made. If the landlord fails to make repairs, the inspector may be empowered to bring a court action for injunctive relief, ordering the landlord to comply with the housing code. The inspector may also seek civil damages against the landlord as provided by statute; these damages are paid to the state rather than to the tenant. Finally, the local statute may provide that egregious violations of the housing code are punishable by criminal penalties such as fines and imprisonment.

g. *Criminal penalties.* As mentioned above, state building code statutes may provide for criminal penalties, including fines and imprisonment, for landlords who fail to fix dangerous and unlawful conditions in their apartment buildings. Judges have even ordered recalcitrant landlords to live for a period of time in one of their substandard buildings as punishment for continued and unconscionable violations of the law. Luz Delgado, *Landlord Forced to Live in His Decrepit Property*, Boston Globe, June 10, 1992, at 50.

h. *Compensatory damages.* In most cases, tenants raise the implied warranty of habitability as a defense to claims by landlords for back rent or possession. Sometimes, however, tenants bring claims for compensatory damages against landlords for violation of the implied warranty either as independent lawsuits or as counterclaims to landlord suits. A claim for damages may seek an amount of money that exceeds the rent rather than merely a reduction in the rent or reimbursement for some of the rent already paid. *See Hilder v. St. Peter, supra* (tenant claim for damages). Damages might exceed the amount of the rent if the violation harms valuable personal property of the tenant, such as the expensive musical equipment owned by the tenant in *Minjak* (*see supra* §8.4.1), or if the tenant seeks reimbursement for the costs of staying in a hotel while the premises were uninhabitable. Ordinarily, however, courts are likely to assume that a judgment for breach of the duty of habitability cannot exceed the agreed-upon rent on the ground that the rental amount constitutes the value of what was lost by the tenant.

Damages for personal injury may require a showing of negligence on the part of the landlord, which may or may not be present in the context of a violation of the implied warranty. This issue, as well as the question of damages for infliction of severe emotional distress, is discussed at below at §8.4.4.2.

4. *Commercial leases.* While most courts have adopted the modern view that the covenants in commercial leases are dependent rather than independent, some have retained the older view that they are independent. *Compare Wesson v. Leone Enterprises, Inc.,* 774 N.E.2d 611 (Mass. 2002) (covenants in commercial lease are dependent) *with Block Properties Co., Inc. v. American National Ins. Co.,* 998 S.W.2d 168 (Mo. Ct. App. 1999)(covenants in commercial lease independent unless lease terms state otherwise). On the other hand, while a few states find an implied warranty of suitability for intended purposes to commercial leases, *Wesson v. Leone Enterprises, Inc.,* 774 N.E.2d 611 (Mass. 2002)(landlord's failure to repair the roof did not amount to constructive eviction but was serious enough to be a breach of the implied warranty of suitability because it materially harmed the tenant's business, thereby allowing tenant to terminate the lease and recover relocation costs); *Davidow v. Inwood North Professional Group,* 747 S.W.2d 373 (Tex. 1988) (implied warranty of suitability for intended purpose applies to commercial lease), most still do not do so, holding that commercial leases have no implied warranties unless they state so explicitly. *Propst v. McNeill,* 932 S.W.2d 766 (Ark. 1996); *A.O. Smith Corp. v. Kaufman Grain Corp.,* 596 N.E.2d 1156 (Ill. Ct. App. 1992); *B.W.S. Investments v. Mid-Am Restaurants, Inc.,* 459 N.W.2d 759 (N.D. 1990).

PROBLEMS

Can a tenant waive the protections of the implied warranty of habitability? If it is waivable or disclaimable, then it is merely a *presumption* or *default* position that the courts will assume to be the agreement of the parties in the absence of language to the contrary. If the implied warranty is *nondisclaimable* or *nonwaivable*, it constitutes a *compulsory term* in the contract that the parties have no power to alter by agreement. *Javins* provided that "[a]ny private agreement to shift the duties would be illegal and unenforceable." 428 F.2d at 1082 n.58. This position is supported in most jurisdictions by statute or common law. *See, e.g., Hilder v. St. Peter, supra*; Mass. Gen. Laws Ann. ch. 186, §14.

1. Assume your state imposes a warranty of habitability on residential tenancies but imposes no implied warranty of habitability or suitability in commercial tenancies. Assume the same facts as in *Minjak*. The tenants rent a loft — a large open space — pursuant to a written agreement entitled "Commercial Lease," stating that the premises are leased for "commercial purposes." The landlord knows that the tenants will be using the space for work purposes, storing and using equipment to make electronic music, but the landlord knows also that the tenants intend to live in the space, treating it as their residence. The landlord fails to maintain the premises in a safe condition, allowing hazardous conditions — such as flooding in the tenants' apartment caused by the operation of a health club with jacuzzis upstairs, the presence of huge clouds of dust caused by the landlord's renovation work in common areas, and the formation of holes in the stairway — to develop unchecked. Two questions arise.

a. How would the courts interpret the lease — as a residential lease, a commercial lease, or a mixed residential/commercial lease?

b. If the courts interpret the lease as a commercial or a mixed residential/commercial lease, is it subject to the implied warranty of habitability, or does the "commercial" designation constitute an effective waiver by the tenant of the implied warranty?

2. Assume you are in a jurisdiction with a statute providing that the implied warranty of habitability is nondisclaimable in residential leaseholds. The legislature is considering a proposed amendment to the statute to allow tenants to waive the protections of the implied warranty. This does not mean that the landlord would be relieved of the obligation to comply with the relevant provisions of the housing code, which regulates the conditions in rental housing. Rather, the tenant would not be able to raise the landlord's failure to maintain the apartment in a habitable condition as a defense to a claim for possession or back rent. Thus, by waiving the protection of the implied warranty, the tenant agrees to pay rent regardless of any housing code violations; also, such violations do not entitle the tenant to move out before the end of the lease term and stop paying rent.

The local real estate board, an association of landlords, argues that landlords and tenants should be free to make whatever arrangements they wish. The board argues also that continued payment of the rent is essential to provide the landlord funds to pay for repairs to the apartment. The local tenants' association, on the other hand, argues that the tenant's right to withhold rent if the landlord fails to maintain the apartment in a habitable condition is the tenant's most powerful — and perhaps her only *effective* — way to induce recalcitrant landlords to comply with the housing code.

Suppose you are testifying before a legislative committee on the proposed amendment to the statute.

a. What arguments would you make on behalf of the real estate board to allow tenants to waive the protections of the implied warranty of habitability?

b. What arguments would you make on behalf of the tenants' association to make the protections of the implied warranty of habitability nondisclaimable?

§8.4.2.2 Arguments and Counterarguments on Compulsory Contract Terms

Compulsory contract terms are nonwaivable rights implied in certain kinds of contractual relationships. Important arguments and counterarguments recur in legal discussions of the advisability and legitimacy of making particular contract terms nondisclaimable. Scholarly debates about the wisdom of the implied warranty of habitability have spawned a rich variety of policy considerations relevant to this question. Many of these arguments have been identified and categorized by Professor Duncan Kennedy. Duncan Kennedy, *Distributive and Paternalist Motives in Contract and Tort Law, with Special Reference to Compulsory Terms and Unequal Bargaining Power*, 41 Md. L. Rev. 563 (1982).

The following summary should serve as a sort of tool kit for use in advocacy settings.

I. *Rights Arguments*

Rights arguments focus on the justice or fairness of alternative ways of regulating social relationships.

A. Freedom of Contract Arguments
  1. Enforce Voluntary Contracts: Freedom of Action
     a. People should be free to enter into whatever agreements they wish; making particular terms nonwaivable prevents tenants from agreeing to waive the right to withhold rent in return for lower rent, even if they wish to do so; compulsory terms interfere with contractual freedom by preventing individuals from doing the best they can, given their circumstances.
     b. Because of competition among landlords for tenants, landlords do not have the power to dictate terms to tenants; so long as a relatively competitive market for rental housing exists, landlords cannot as a class have disproportionate bargaining power over tenants as a class.[6]
  2. Unequal Bargaining Power: Coerced Contracts Entered Into Under Duress Are Not Voluntary
     a. Tenants and landlords have unequal bargaining power because housing is a *necessity* and because of *structural* disparities between landlords and tenants associated with the fact that landlords own real property and tenants do not; in addition, landlords often *collude* by using form leases drafted by real estate associations and including terms favorable to landlords.
     b. No one would voluntarily agree to rent an apartment that did not comply with minimum standards of habitability; the fact that people agree to do so is evidence not that they affirmatively wanted to agree

---

6. *See* Alan Schwartz, *Justice and the Law of Contracts: A Case for the Traditional Approach*, 9 Harv. J.L. & Pub. Pol'y 107 (1986).

but that they were forced to agree because they had no legally available alternatives.

    c.   Courts should enforce the agreement the parties would have made if they had relatively equal bargaining power; only such contracts can be rightfully deemed voluntary.

B.   Distributive Considerations

    1.   Unfair Burden

        a.   So long as a competitive market for rental property exists, the only source of unequal bargaining power between landlords and tenants is that landlords, as a class, may be richer than tenants as a class; tenants cannot afford to pay landlords enough to induce them to offer better housing; if tenants could do so, landlords would provide it because it would be profitable to do so.

        b.   Making the implied warranty of habitability nondisclaimable imposes new costs on the landlord since it exposes the landlord to the possibility that the tenant will stop paying rent; the landlord will therefore attempt to raise the rent to compensate for this new vulnerability. However, landlords will not be able to pass the entire cost on to tenants because if tenants were able to afford the true cost of the new duty, it would have been profitable for landlords to provide the term to begin with. Landlords will provide even luxury housing to tenants who can afford it; thus, when landlords try to raise the rent, some tenants will be unable or unwilling to pay a higher rent and will either double up with friends or family, move to a cheaper location, or become homeless. Because some tenants will exit the market when landlords try to raise the rent, landlords as a group will be unable to raise the rent sufficiently to pass on the entire cost of the new duty to the tenants; the result is that some wealth is redistributed between landlords as a class to tenants as a class.

        c.   This redistribution is unfair because it places the burden of dealing with poverty on a small subset of the population (that is, landlords) when the obligation to care for poor people should be shared by all taxpayers through rental subsidies or welfare programs; it amounts to a tax on landlords to help tenants. If tenants are too poor to be able to afford habitable housing, the proper remedy is to use the tax system to raise money to provide welfare payments for poor tenants, spreading the cost of providing essential housing services to all taxpayers rather than just the class of landlords. Landlords are not responsible for the poverty of tenants and should not unfairly have to bear the burden of rectifying it by themselves.

    2.   Justice in Ongoing Social Relationships

        a.   It is not unfair to require landlords to bear some of the costs of providing habitable housing; on the contrary, it would be unfair for landlords to make a living by providing substandard housing. Just as product manufacturers have obligations to provide safe products and employers have duties to provide safe workplaces, landlords have obligations to provide safe and habitable housing.

        b.   Landlords are engaged in the business of earning a living by renting property. In so doing, they create an ongoing relationship with their tenants. It is fair to require them to conduct those relationships in accordance with minimum standards of decency. No one has a right to earn a living from someone else's misery. Just as it is unlawful to enter a contract of slavery, it is unlawful to enter a contract by which one agrees to allow someone else to live in deplorable conditions. Tenants do not have economic incentives to invest in maintenance, since only the owner will recoup the value of the increased value of the property. It is therefore fair to place the burden on the landlord to provide premises consistent with contemporary standards and values.[7]

   c. The failure to comply with the implied warranty of habitability imposes costs on third parties who must deal with the social consequences of substandard housing; the community at large should not have to subsidize the landlord by protecting the landlord from liability for the social costs of substandard housing.

C. Paternalism
   1. Self-determination
      a. Individual citizens are the best judges of their own interests; the state should not prevent people from entering into voluntary agreements on the grounds that it is not in their best interest to enter into such agreements.
      b. If tenants are willing to waive rights in exchange for other contractual benefits, such as lower rent, they should be allowed to do so since they are entitled to self-determination; their choice should not be constrained by government on the ground that the choice is mistaken.
   2. Real Assent to Contract Terms and Limits to Assent
      a. Actual Intent of the Parties
         i. A contract by which tenants waive basic rights to habitability is unlikely to represent the actual intent of the parties; tenants may not read or understand what they are agreeing to when they sign form leases that may incorporate terms favorable to the landlord.
         ii. The only way to ascertain whether the tenant actually agreed to unfavorable terms is to have the landlord read a disclosure statement to the tenant—a sort of *Miranda* warning—explaining exactly what the tenant was giving up by waiving his rights, for example, that he was agreeing to continue to pay rent even though the landlord was violating her obligations under the contract and that the tenant had the legal right to withhold rent.
      b. Cognitive Distortion[8]
         i. Even if tenants understand what rights they are waiving, we should protect people from mistakes they are very likely to regret later; people often underestimate the possibility that bad things

---

7. *See* Bruce Ackerman, *Regulating Slum Housing Markets on Behalf of the Poor: Of Housing Codes, Housing Subsidies and Income Redistribution Policy*, 80 Yale L.J. 1093 (1971).
8. *See* Cass Sunstein, *Legal Interference with Private Preferences*, 52 U. Chi. L. Rev. 1129 (1986).

can happen (for example, that a landlord will fail to provide basic services in the apartment); they may also fail to understand the utility of withholding rent in inducing the landlord's compliance with the building code.

ii. Making particular claims compulsory protects people from the short-run temptation to give up entitlements that they know are in their long-term best interests, as forced saving in the form of Social Security payments, for example, protects people from failing to save for retirement or disability.

iii. Some preferences are the result of legal rules; people do not value what they feel they are not entitled to; making an entitlement nondisclaimable may cause people to value it more highly and therefore reflect their newly formed preferences; rather than preventing people from satisfying their wishes, compulsory terms may actually help people become conscious of what they really value.

c. Real Paternalism

i. *Minimum terms or unconscionability.* Some contractual agreements are so fundamentally unfair or unconscionable that they should not be enforced even if the parties have voluntarily agreed to them; it violates common decency and individual dignity for courts to enforce terms that are outrageously unfair.

ii. *Anti-paternalism.* So long as the parties voluntarily agree to the terms of an agreement, the state should not interfere, but rather should let the parties do the best they can for themselves, given their circumstances; it violates individual dignity for the courts to be policing the terms of voluntary agreements.

II. Economic Arguments

Economic arguments focus on the behavioral effects of, or incentives created by, alternative legal rules; the ultimate goal is to choose rules that promote social welfare.

A. Incentives to Invest in Safety and Maintenance

1. Available Income to Pay for Repairs

a. Requiring the tenant to pay rent ensures a steady source of income from which the landlord can pay for needed repairs; allowing the tenant to withhold rent means the landlord may have no resources to make needed repairs.

b. Enforcement of the housing code obligations is sufficiently ensured through administrative enforcement by the housing inspector.

2. Only Effective Sanction for Failing to Comply with the Housing Code

a. Rent withholding is not only an extremely effective way to prevent landlords from violating the housing code but may be the only effective remedy in an era of government cutbacks and a shortage of housing inspectors.

       b. Landlords can easily save some of their rental payments in a maintenance fund to prepare for any needed expenses.

  B. Effects on Allocative Efficiency in the Housing Market

     1. Pareto Optimality

Compulsory contract terms are necessarily inefficient because they interfere with the parties' ability to bargain for mutually beneficial terms. If the tenant is willing to live in a less well-maintained apartment, she should be able to enter into a contract for lower rent and then have money available to use for other things such as food and clothing. Moreover, the landlord is obligated to maintain the apartment under any existing housing code; all the implied warranty adds is the ability to get out of the lease or stop paying rent or obtain a rent reduction if the landlord fails to maintain the premises adequately. The tenant may well believe that the housing code constitutes a sufficient guarantee of performance and be willing to give up other enforcement mechanisms like the right to withhold rent. Preventing the tenant from making such an arrangement prevents both parties from maximizing their utility, thereby reducing social wealth. Third-party effects are minimal in this situation and are sufficiently addressed by zoning laws and the housing code.

     2. Market Imperfections

       a. *Externalities.* There are significant third-party effects of substandard housing. It is harmful to children and other inhabitants and produces medical problems that society ultimately must pay for; blighted areas have difficulty attracting new residents and business investment; even if the parties wish to agree to waive particular rights, others are negatively affected by housing contracts that do not give landlords sufficient incentives to comply with the housing code. Allowing waiver therefore decreases social welfare.

       b. *Imperfect information.* Tenants may not understand the significance of waiving the implied warranty of habitability; even when they do understand, they may incorrectly judge both the likelihood that a violation will occur and the utility of withholding rent if it does; if they had perfect information, they would refuse to waive the protections afforded by the warranty. Courts should enforce the results to which the parties would have agreed if they had possessed perfect information.

  C. Effects on Distribution

     1. Landlords Will Raise the Rent and Decrease the Supply of Housing

       a. Landlords will respond to the implied warranty by raising the rent. The tenant has the right to withhold rent or break the lease if problems arise; if the landlord is not able to fix the problems quickly, the landlord faces a greater possibility of loss of income than in a legal regime without the implied warranty. To compensate for this additional legal and economic exposure, the landlord will respond by raising the rent, hurting tenants—the very people the reformers intended to help.

       b. In a competitive market, any significant increase in rent will cause some tenants to leave the market. Because demand is sensitive to price (higher rents may reduce the quantity of housing demanded as some tenants double up or become homeless), landlords are unlikely to pass on to their tenants the full cost of the implied warranty. Marginal landlords who are barely making it will not be able to cover the full costs of the new regulation, and some of them will leave the rental housing market altogether. Thus, since the costs of doing business have gone up, the supply of housing will go down, as some landlords shift to more profitable investments. With a decreased supply of housing, even more competition for the housing remains, further raising the price and subjecting tenants to even higher rents, again hurting the very people the regulation was intended to benefit.

2. Effect of the Implied Warranty Will Depend on Existing Conditions in the Market

    a. It is impossible to predict, *a priori*, what effects the implied warranty will have on the market. The result depends on a host of factors affecting both demand and supply. For example, if demand is elastic, that is, extremely price-sensitive, and the price of housing services goes up even a little, quantity demanded falls precipitously. This may happen because tenants are already paying rents that are high relative to their incomes and simply cannot afford higher housing costs. Or it may be that tenants prefer not to pay any more and are willing to double up with roommates or family members or even move out of town to limit their housing expenses. If demand is highly elastic, landlords may simply be unable to pass the cost along to tenants. Any landlord who tries to do so will find no takers for her apartment and will be forced to lower the rent in order to stay in business.

    b. Imposition of the implied warranty may not decrease the supply of housing if landlords are earning economic rents, which exceed the minimum required to keep the investment in its current use. This could happen if land is scarce but demand is high because of both the necessity and the limited availability of housing. Landlords may be able to raise rents substantially, making housing far more profitable than equally risky investments. In a perfectly competitive market, more housing providers would enter the market, increasing the supply of housing and thereby lowering the price as tenants have more places available. If, however, the supply of housing cannot rise either because land is scarce or because zoning laws prohibit owners from increasing the size of their buildings or constructing rental housing in nonresidential areas, then rents will remain high for a long time. If landlords are earning economic rents with high profits, a reduction in those profits may allow them to stay in business and still earn more than they could in other businesses. The implied warranty would simply redistribute wealth between landlords and tenants but would not result in a decrease in the supply of housing.

    c. Even if one landlord cannot afford to stay in the rental housing business, another could still operate the building profitably. A landlord who cannot afford to repair an apartment and is prevented from evicting a particular tenant until the apartment is brought up to housing code standards may not be able to pay her monthly mortgage payments or property taxes if the tenant stops paying rent. If the landlord sells the building, or the bank forecloses on it for failure to pay the mortgage, or the city forecloses for failure to pay taxes, someone else may purchase the property at a much lower price than that paid by the original owner because of the repairs needed to continue operating the business. If the new owner's down payment and monthly mortgage payments are sufficiently low, she may be able to use rent receipts not only to make repairs but also to pay her mortgage, taxes, and insurance. Her initial costs are less; therefore the implied warranty is less burdensome since rental payments are sufficient to pay for current maintenance costs. If this happens, the property can still be used for rental housing purposes and will not be taken out of the rental housing market.

§8.4.3 RETALIATORY EVICTION

HILLVIEW ASSOCIATES v. BLOOMQUIST
440 N.W.2d 867 (Iowa 1989)

JAMES H. ANDREASEN, Justice....

Gracious Estates Mobile Home Park (Gracious Estates) is located in Des Moines. It is owned by Hillview Associates (Hillview), a partnership based in California. The general partner of Hillview is William Cavanaugh, a resident of California. Management of Gracious Estates has been delegated to a company known as Tandem Management Services, Inc. (Tandem), also owned by Cavanaugh and the other general partners of Hillview. Tandem employed Kathy Nitz as a regional manager, Gennie Smith as park manager and Doug Cavanaugh as property manager at Gracious Estates.

In January 1987 tenants at Gracious Estates began to meet informally to discuss their concerns over the physical condition of the trailer court and recent increases in rent. On January 28, 1987, the first meeting of a tenant's association was held in the clubhouse of Gracious Estates, and approximately 125 tenants came to the meeting. This meeting resulted in an agenda of specific concerns for the health, safety and quality of living in Gracious Estates. A volunteer leadership committee was established for the association, now known as the Gracious Estates Tenant's Association. In the course of organizing and articulating complaints, tenants contacted the Iowa Attorney General's office and their state representative.

On February 9, 1987, a meeting was held between approximately five members of the association, Ms. Nitz and the park maintenance supervisor. The tenants lodged several complaints at this meeting. This meeting lasted approximately one hour and was relatively calm. The relationship between the tenant's association and the management of Gracious Estates began to erode. The tenants were frustrated with the lack of action taken by the management of Gracious Estates.

A meeting with Ms. Nitz was scheduled for April 15, 1987. A meeting did occur on April 15 between representatives of the tenants association and Ms. Nitz. This "meeting" was held in Nitz's private office and lasted approximately five to ten minutes. The discussion quickly disintegrated into a shouting match which climaxed in a physical altercation between Nitz and one of the tenants, Kimber Davenport.

After this meeting, the management of the trailer court served ultimatums on all tenants requiring them to sign the park rules or be evicted. Management also sought out tenants not in the tenant's association in an attempt to start a rival tenants' association favorable to management. On April 22, 1987, Hillview served a thirty-day notice of termination on the following tenants: Tom and Sandra Bloomquist; Kimber and Reva Davenport; Richard and Nellie Swartz; and Donald and Judith Ray. At least one member of each of these married couples was present at the April 15 meeting. A former secretary of Ms. Nitz testified that "they'd [management] get these now, and then the rest later. That way it wouldn't look like they were doing it because they were members of an association."

Hillview later discovered that the thirty-day notice did not provide specific grounds for termination as required by statute. On June 4, 1987, Hillview again served each of these tenants with a notice of termination which provided a sixty-day period for them to leave. At the end of the sixty-day period, the tenants remained in possession. Hillview then served three-day notices to quit. The tenants remained in the park and Hillview filed a forcible entry and detainer action.

In this summary action for forcible entry and detainer, the tenants raised the defenses of retaliatory eviction and waiver....

III

The Iowa Legislature adopted remedial legislation for mobile home tenants in the *Mobile Home Parks Residential Landlord and Tenant Act.* Iowa Code §562B.32 (1987)....
[The Act] prohibits retaliatory conduct by landlords:

> 1. Except as provided in this section, a landlord shall not retaliate by increasing rent or decreasing services or by bringing or threatening to bring an action for possession or by failing to renew a rental agreement after any of the following:
> (a) The tenant has complained to a governmental agency charged with responsibility for enforcement of a building or housing code of a violation applicable to the mobile home park materially affecting health and safety. For this subsection to apply, a complaint filed with a governmental body must be in good faith.
> (b) The tenant has complained to the landlord of a violation under section 562B.16 [requiring landlords to maintain the premises in habitable condition].
> (c) The tenant has organized or become a member of a tenant's union or similar organization.
> (d) For exercising any of the rights and remedies pursuant to this chapter.
> 2. If the landlord acts in violation of subsection 1 of this section, the tenant . . . has a defense in an action for possession. In an action by or against the tenant, evidence of a complaint within six months prior to the alleged act of retaliation creates a presumption that the landlord's conduct was in retaliation. The presumption does not arise if the tenant made the complaint after notice of termination of the rental agreement. For the purpose of this subsection, "presumption" means that the trier of fact must find the existence of the fact presumed unless and until evidence is introduced which would support a finding of its nonexistence.
> 3. Notwithstanding subsections 1 and 2 of this section, a landlord may bring an action for possession if either of the following occurs:
> (a) The violation of the applicable building or housing code was caused primarily by lack of reasonable care by the tenant or other person in the household or upon the premises with the tenant's consent.

(b) The tenant is in default of rent three days after rent is due. . . .

Iowa Code §562B.32 (1987). . . .

IV

In 1968 the United States Court of Appeals for the District of Columbia held that a landlord was not free to evict a tenant in retaliation for the tenant's report of housing code violations. As a matter of statutory construction and for reasons of public policy, such an eviction would not be permitted. *Edwards v. Habib*, 397 F.2d 687, 699 (D.C. Cir. 1968). However, a tenant who proves a retaliatory purpose is not entitled to remain in possession in perpetuity. If the illegal purpose is dissipated, the landlord can, in the absence of legislation or a binding contract, evict the tenant for legitimate reasons or even for no reason at all. The question of permissible or impermissible purpose is one of fact for the court or jury.

In 1979 the Iowa Legislature adopted the *Uniform Residential Landlord and Tenant Act* and the *Mobile Home Parks Residential Landlord and Tenant Act*. Both acts prohibit retaliatory conduct. *See* Iowa Code §§562A.36 & 562B.32. In an action by or against the tenant, evidence of a complaint within six months prior to the alleged act of retaliation creates a presumption that the landlord's conduct was in retaliation. For the purpose of the statutory subsection "presumption" means the trier of fact must find the existence of the fact presumed unless and until evidence is introduced which could support a finding of its nonexistence.

As a matter of statutory construction, we hold this statutory presumption imposes a burden upon the landlord to produce evidence of legitimate nonretaliatory reasons to overcome the presumption. The tenant may then be afforded a full and fair opportunity to demonstrate pretext. The burden of proof of the affirmative defense of retaliatory termination of the lease remains upon the tenant. If the landlord does not meet the burden of producing evidence of a nonretaliatory reason for termination, the statutory presumption would compel a finding of retaliatory lease termination. If the landlord does produce evidence of a nonretaliatory purpose for terminating the lease, then the fact-finder must determine from all the evidence whether a retaliatory termination has been proven by a preponderance of the evidence. Although the burden of producing evidence shifts to the landlord once the tenant has offered evidence of a complaint within six months of the notice of termination, the burden of proof remains with the tenant to establish the affirmative defense.

In deciding whether a tenant has established a defense of retaliatory eviction, we consider the following factors, among others, tending to show the landlord's primary motivation was not retaliatory.

(a) The landlord's decision was a reasonable exercise of business judgment;

(b) The landlord in good faith desires to dispose of the entire leased property free of all tenants;

(c) The landlord in good faith desires to make a different use of the leased property;

(d) The landlord lacks the financial ability to repair the leased property and therefore, in good faith, wishes to have it free of any tenant;

(e) The landlord was unaware of the tenant's activities which were protected by statute;

   (f)   The landlord did not act at the first opportunity after he learned of the tenant's conduct;

   (g)   The landlord's act was not discriminatory. *Restatement (Second) of Property* §14.8 comment f (1977).

V

We find the tenants have offered substantial evidence of a retaliatory termination. They were active, vocal members of a newly-formed tenant's association. They made good faith complaints about the landlord's failure to maintain the mobile home park in a clean and safe condition. An employee of the landlord testified that certain leases were terminated because the tenants were active members of the tenants association. In response, the landlord has offered substantial evidence of a nonretaliatory reason for termination. The tenants who actively participated in the disturbance and physical abuse of Ms. Nitz during the April 15 meeting were notified of lease termination, other active members of the association were not.

    According to Ms. Nitz, the tenants surrounded her desk on April 15 and implored her to call California. One of the tenants, Kimber Davenport, placed both hands in the middle of Nitz's desk, leaned over the desk, shouted that Nitz had a "truck-driver's mentality" and that she wasn't a lady. Nitz asked the tenants to leave and all but Mr. and Mrs. Rathburn refused. Ms. Nitz then left her office and, after a cooling-off period, returned and demanded that the other tenants leave the office. She again demanded that they leave and threatened to call the police if they did not. The tenants began to leave. Mr. Davenport was the last to leave, and as he left he continued the verbal abuse of Ms. Nitz and gestured to her with his finger close to her face. According to Ms. Nitz, she pushed his finger away and Davenport struck her in the face, knocking her into a door-jamb. At that point, another tenant, Don Carlson, entered the room and physically removed Davenport.

    Davenport's testimony concerning the April 15 meeting was very different from Ms. Nitz's testimony. Davenport testified at the forcible entry and detainer trial that he was polite and reasonable during this meeting. Further, he claimed that he did not place his hands on Nitz's desk, shout at her, or strike her. Rather, he testified that he pushed her away with an open hand. Davenport's testimony loses credibility when it is compared with his prior testimony in a criminal case concerning this incident. In his prior testimony, Davenport admitted that he placed his hands in the middle of Ms. Nitz's desk, shouted insults at her, and struck her. Davenport's testimony concerning the April 15 meeting was very different from Ms. Nitz's testimony. Davenport testified at the forcible entry and detainer trial that he was polite and reasonable during this meeting. Further, he claimed that he did not place his hands on Nitz's desk, shout at her, or strike her. Rather, he testified that he pushed her away with an open hand. Davenport's testimony loses credibility when it is compared with his prior testimony in a criminal case concerning this incident. In his prior testimony, Davenport admitted that he placed his hands in the middle of Ms. Nitz's desk, shouted insults at her, and struck her.

    Several conclusions can fairly be drawn from the evidence. First, the April 15 meeting was initiated by members of a tenant's association in an attempt to address grievances with the management of the trailer court. This meeting disintegrated into a shouting match. The tenants were told to leave three times and they left only after a threat to call the police. We, like the trial court, conclude that Davenport did strike Ms.

Nitz in the face as he left the room. He was the principal agitator, quickly leaving the topic of improvements for the park and launching into a personal attack on Ms. Nitz.

Under Iowa law, tenants may organize and join a tenant's association free from fear of retaliation. The tenants may participate in activities designed to legitimately coerce a landlord into taking action to improve living conditions. The presumption of retaliatory eviction in Iowa Code §562B.32 protects legitimate activities of tenant unions or similar organizations.

The resolution of landlord-tenant grievances will normally involve some conflicts and friction between the parties. Arguments, even heated arguments with raised voices, cannot fairly be described as being in violation of proper conduct. There is, however, a limit to the type of conduct that will be tolerated. Kimber Davenport crossed beyond the line of legitimate behavior. Davenport has failed to establish by a preponderance of the evidence that the termination of his lease was retaliatory. The termination of the Davenports' lease was legitimate and thus cannot be said to be retaliation arising from his complaints or union activities.

Although the statutory presumption of retaliation has been neutralized by the evidence produced by Hillview, we find the evidence of retaliatory eviction concerning tenants Bloomquist, Swartz, and Ray, to be more convincing. Although they were present at the April 15 meeting and did participate in the arguments, they did not encourage or participate in the assault of Ms. Nitz. The landlord's response by an attempted termination of their leases can reasonably be attributed to their active membership in the tenant's organization and in response to legitimate complaints they had made.

We reject Hillview's argument that there must be specific intent to retaliate on the part of Hillview's general partner before the tenants can prevail on a defense of retaliatory eviction. The evidence reveals that the local and regional managers of Gracious Estates made the decision to evict these tenants. The general partner ratified this decision without direct participation in the decision-making process.

The acts of an agent are attributable to the principal. In this situation, to require specific intent by the general partner of a multi-state real estate business would frustrate the intention of Iowa Code §562B.32. Hillview's interpretation would allow mid-level managers to retaliate against tenant associations and seek refuge by keeping top-level directors uninformed of specific disputes with individual tenants. Tenants Bloomquist, Swartz, and Ray have established by a preponderance of the evidence their affirmative defense of retaliatory eviction. Tenants Davenport have not. . . .

IMPERIAL COLLIERY CO. v. FOUT
373 S.E.2d 489 (W. Va. 1988)

THOMAS B. MILLER, Justice:

Danny H. Fout, the defendant below, appeals a summary judgment dismissing his claim of retaliatory eviction based on the provisions of W. Va. Code §§55-3A-3(g), which is our summary eviction statute. Imperial Colliery had instituted an eviction proceeding and Fout sought to defend against it, claiming that his eviction was in retaliation for his participation in a labor strike.

This case presents two issues: (1) whether a residential tenant who is sued for possession of rental property under W. Va. Code §§55-3A-1, *et seq.*, may assert retaliation by the landlord as a defense, and (2) whether the retaliation motive must relate to the tenant's exercise of a right incidental to the tenancy.

Fout is presently employed by Milburn Colliery Company as a coal miner. For six years, he has leased a small house trailer lot in Burnwell, West Virginia, from Imperial Colliery Company. It is alleged that Milburn and Imperial are interrelated companies. A written lease was signed by Fout and an agent of Imperial in June, 1983. This lease was for a primary period of one month, and was terminable by either party upon one month's notice. An annual rental of $1.00 was payable in advance on January 1 of each year. No subsequent written leases were signed by the parties.

On February 14, 1986, Imperial advised Fout by certified letter that his lease would be terminated as of March 31, 1986. Fout's attorney corresponded with Imperial before the scheduled termination date. He advised that due to various family and monetary problems, Fout would be unable to timely vacate the property. Imperial voluntarily agreed to a two-month extension of the lease. A second letter from Fout's attorney, dated May 27, 1986, recited Fout's personal problems and requested that Imperial's attempts to oust Fout be held "in abeyance" until they were resolved. A check for $1.00 was enclosed to cover the proposed extension. Imperial did not reply.

On June 11, 1986, Imperial sued for possession of the property, pursuant to W. Va. Code §§55-3A-1, *et seq.*, in the Magistrate Court of Kanawha County. Fout answered and removed the suit to the circuit court on June 23, 1986. He asserted as a defense that Imperial's suit was brought in retaliation for his involvement in the United Mine Workers of America and, more particularly, in a selective strike against Milburn. Imperial's retaliatory motive was alleged to be in violation of the First Amendment rights of speech and assembly, and of the *National Labor Relations Act*, 29 U.S.C. §§151, *et seq.* Fout also counter-claimed, seeking an injunction against Imperial and damages for annoyance and inconvenience. . . .

Our initial inquiry is whether retaliation by the landlord may be asserted by the tenant as a defense in a suit under W. Va. Code §55-3A-3(g). . . .

It appears that the first case that recognized retaliatory eviction as a defense to a landlord's eviction proceeding was *Edwards v. Habib*, 397 F.2d 687 (D.C. Cir. 1968). . . .

[In that case,] the court reviewed at length the goals sought to be advanced by local sanitary and safety codes. It concluded that to allow retaliatory evictions by landlords would seriously jeopardize the efficacy of the codes. A prohibition against such retaliatory conduct was therefore to be implied, even though the regulations were silent on the matter.

Many states have protected tenant rights either on the *Edwards* theory or have implied such rights from the tenant's right of habitability. Others have utilized statutes analogous to section 5.101 of the *Uniform Residential Landlord and Tenant Act*, 7B U.L.A. 503 (1985),[6] which is now adopted in fifteen jurisdictions. Similar landlord

---

6. Section 5.101 of the *Uniform Act* provides, in part:

(a) Except as provided in this section, a landlord may not retaliate by increasing rent or decreasing services or by bringing or threatening to bring an action for possession after:

(1) the tenant has complained to a governmental agency charged with responsibility for enforcement of a building or housing code of a violation applicable to the premises materially affecting health and safety; or

(2) the tenant has complained to the landlord of a violation [of the requirement to maintain the premises] under Section 2.104; or

(3) the tenant has organized or become a member of a tenant's union or similar organization.

and tenant reform statutes in seventeen other states also provide protection for tenancy-related activities.

Under W. Va. Code §37-6-30, a tenant is, with respect to residential property, entitled to certain rights to a fit and habitable dwelling. In *Teller v. McCoy*, 253 S.E.2d 114 (W. Va. 1978), we spoke at some length of the common law right of habitability which a number of courts had developed to afford protection to the residential tenant. We concluded that these rights paralleled and were spelled out in more detail in W. Va. Code §37-6-30. . . .

The central theme underlying the retaliatory eviction defense is that a tenant should not be punished for claiming the benefits afforded by health and safety statutes passed for his protection. These statutory benefits become a part of his right of habitability. If the right to habitability is to have any meaning, it must enable the tenant to exercise that right by complaining about unfit conditions without fear of reprisal by his landlord.

After the seminal decision in *Edwards*, other categories of tenant activity were deemed to be protected. Such activity was protected against retaliation where it bore a relationship to some legitimate aspect of the tenancy. For example, some cases provided protection for attempts by tenants to organize to protect their rights as tenants. Others recognized the right to press complaints directly against the landlord via oral communications, petitions, and "repair and deduct" remedies.

A few courts recognize that even where a tenant's activity is only indirectly related to the tenancy relationship, it may be protected against retaliatory conduct if such conduct would undermine the tenancy relationship. Typical of these cases is *Windward Partners v. Delos Santos*, 577 P.2d 326 (Haw. 1978). There a group of month-to-month tenants gave testimony before a state land use commission in opposition to a proposal to redesignate their farm property from "agricultural" to "urban" uses. The proposal was sponsored by the landlord, a land developer. As a result of coordinated activity by the tenants, the proposal was defeated. Within six months, the landlord ordered the tenants to vacate the property and brought suit for possession.

The Hawaii Supreme Court noted that statutory law provided for public hearings on proposals to redesignate property, and specifically invited the views of the affected tenants. The court determined that the legislative policy encouraging such input would be jeopardized "if . . . [landlords] were permitted to retaliate against . . . tenants for opposing land use changes in a public forum." 577 P.2d at 333. . . .

The Legislature, in giving approval to the retaliation defense, must have intended to bring our State into line with the clear weight of case law and statutory authority outlined above. We accordingly hold that retaliation may be asserted as a defense to a summary eviction proceeding under W. Va. Code §§55-3A-1, *et seq.*, if the landlord's conduct is in retaliation for the tenant's exercise of a right incidental to the tenancy.

Fout seeks to bring this case within the *Windward* line of authority. He argues principally that Imperial's conduct violated a public policy which promotes the rights of association and free speech by tenants. We do not agree, simply because the activity that Fout points to as triggering his eviction was unrelated to the habitability of his premises.

From the foregoing survey of law, we are led to the conclusion that the retaliatory eviction defense must relate to activities of the tenant incidental to the tenancy. First Amendment rights of speech and association unrelated to the tenant's property interest are not protected under a retaliatory eviction defense in that they do not arise from the tenancy relationship. Such rights may, of course, be vindicated on other independent grounds. . . .

NOTES AND QUESTIONS

1. In the famous case of *Robinson v. Diamond Housing Corp.*, 463 F.2d 853 (D.C. Cir. 1972), the landlord, Diamond Housing, had brought an earlier lawsuit against the month-to-month tenant, Mrs. Robinson, for possession on the ground of nonpayment of rent. The landlord lost that lawsuit when the tenant successfully raised the defense of the landlord's violation of the warranty of habitability, *id.* at 858:

> Specifically, Mrs. Robinson introduced evidence showing that large pieces of plaster were missing throughout the house, that there was no step from the front walk to the front porch, that the front porch was shaky and unsafe, that there was a wall in the back bedroom which was not attached to the ceiling and which moved back and forth when pressed, that nails protruded along the side of the stairway, that there was a pane of glass missing from the living room window, and that the window frame in the kitchen was so far out of position that one could see into the back yard through the space between it and the wall.

The landlord brought a second lawsuit against the tenant, attempting to end the month-to-month tenancy by providing 30 days' notice. (Recall that periodic tenancies renew automatically unless one of the parties notifies the other that it intends to end the relationship.) The landlord hoped to evict Mrs. Robinson not because of nonpayment of rent but simply because the landlord wanted to end the periodic tenancy. The tenant argued that the landlord's attempt to end the periodic tenancy and evict her was in retaliation for her earlier assertion of her legal right to remain in the apartment because of the landlord's breach of the implied warranty of habitability. She argued that the landlord's retaliatory motivation constituted a defense to his claim for possession and that she had the right to continue to possess the property.

The landlord argued that he was unable or unwilling to make the legally required repairs on the premises necessary to put the housing in compliance with the housing code and that he intended to take the apartment off the rental market. If he were not entitled to end the month-to-month tenancy and evict the tenant under these circumstances, he would never be able to do so, and the court would have substantially transferred to the tenant the landlord's possessory rights in the property.

The court held that the tenant could successfully raise the defense of retaliatory eviction under these circumstances. Judge J. Skelly Wright argued, *id.* at 860-868:

> "In large measure, the scope and effectiveness of tenant remedies for substandard housing will be determined by the degree of protection given tenants against retaliatory actions by landlords. If a landlord is free to evict or otherwise harass a tenant who exercises his right to secure better housing conditions, few tenants will use the remedies for fear of being put out on the street." Daniels, *Judicial and Legislative Remedies for Substandard Housing: Landlord-Tenant Law Reform in the District of Columbia*, 59 Geo. L.J. 909, 943 (1971). . . .
> . . . The danger stems not from the possibility that landlords might take low-cost units off the market altogether, but rather from the possibility that they will do so selectively in order to "make an example" of a troublesome tenant who has the temerity to assert his legal rights in court. . . .
> . . . Diamond [the landlord] argues that [the retaliatory eviction doctrine] should not be applied to a case such as this where the landlord is prevented from collecting rent [because of a violation of the implied warranty of habitability], refuses to repair the premises, and wishes to take the housing off the market altogether. . . .

... Diamond Housing argues that permitting a retaliatory eviction defense here may mean that it will never be able to recover possession of its property. Nonreceipt of rent is a continuing injury, Diamond argues, and it will always want to remove the tenant so as to remove the source of injury. Yet ironically, so long as it is motivated by this goal, the *Edwards* [retaliatory eviction] defense will prevent achievement of it. Thus Diamond fears that its shotgun marriage to Mrs. Robinson may last till death do them part.

Moreover, Diamond points out, it is not trying to evict Mrs. Robinson so that it may rent the premises to someone else. It does not want a quickie divorce in order to permit a hasty remarriage. Rather, if freed from Mrs. Robinson, Diamond promises to beat a strategic retreat to a monastery where it will go and sin no more. Thus Diamond says that it intends to take the unit off the market altogether when Mrs. Robinson leaves — the very thing which this court has suggested a landlord do when he is unwilling or unable to repair the premises. There is nothing in the Housing Regulations which prevents it from going out of business, Diamond argues. Whatever limitations the law imposes on how it chooses its tenants, Diamond claims an absolute right to choose not to have any tenants. . . .

First, then, it should be noted that the *Edwards* defense deals with the landlord's subjective state of mind — that is, with his motive. If the landlord's actions are motivated by a desire to punish the tenant for exercising his rights or to chill the exercise of similar rights by other tenants, then they are impermissible.

It is commonplace, however, that a jury can judge a landlord's state of mind only by examining its objective manifestations. Thus when the landlord's conduct is "inherently destructive" of tenants' rights, or unavoidably chills their exercise, the jury may, under well recognized principles, presume that the landlord intended this result. An unexplained eviction following successful assertion of a defense [based on the landlord's breach of the implied warranty of habitability] falls within this inherently destructive category and hence gives rise to the presumption. Once the presumption is established, it is then up to the landlord to rebut it by demonstrating that he is motivated by some legitimate business purpose rather than by the illicit motive which would otherwise be presumed. We wish to emphasize, however, that the landlord's desire to remove a tenant who is not paying rent is not such a legitimate purpose. *Southall Realty* and the housing code guarantee the right of a tenant to remain in possession without paying rent when the premises are burdened with substantial housing code violations making them unsafe and unsanitary. The landlord of such premises who evicts his tenant because he will not pay rent is in effect evicting him for asserting his legal right to refuse to pay rent. . . .

Thus Diamond Housing is correct when it asserts it will never be able to evict Mrs. Robinson so long as it is motivated by a desire to rid itself of a tenant who is not paying rent. But it does not follow that Diamond will be burdened by its unwanted tenant forever. If Diamond comes forward with a legitimate business justification — other than the mere desire to get rid of a tenant exercising *Southall Realty* rights — it may be able to convince a jury that it is motivated by this proper concern. For example, if Diamond brought the premises up to housing code standards so that rent was again due and then evicted the tenant for some unrelated, lawful reason, the eviction would be permissible. Similarly, if Diamond were to make a convincing showing that it was for some reason impossible or unfeasible to make repairs, it would have a legitimate reason for evicting the tenant and taking the unit off the market.

It does not follow, however, that mere desire to take the unit off the market is by itself a legitimate business reason which will justify an eviction. Expression of such a desire begs the further question of why the landlord wishes to remove the unit. If he wishes to remove the unit for some sound business reason, then of course he is free to do so. But . . . a landlord who fails to come forward with a substantial business reason for removing a unit from the market — such as, for example, his financial inability to make the necessary repairs — may be presumed to have done so for an illicit reason. . . .

None of this is to say that the landlord may not go out of business entirely if he wishes to do so or that the jury is authorized to inspect his motives if he chooses to commit economic harakiri. There would be severe constitutional problems with a rule of law which required an entrepreneur to remain in business against his will. . . . Thus we hold that the landlord's right to discontinue rental of all his units in no way justifies a partial closing designed to intimidate the remaining tenants. . . .

Diamond argues that such a solution represents poor public policy and a poor reading of the applicable statutes. So long as the landlord is not receiving rent, the argument goes, he will certainly not be able to finance repairs. Yet so long as he cannot make repairs, he will not be able to collect rent. Unable to break out of this vicious circle, the landlord is likely to abandon the building altogether without even bothering with an attempted eviction. . . .

Although superficially persuasive, on closer analysis this argument turns out to be built on a series of non sequiturs. . . .

If . . . Diamond were unable to repair the premises — then, under the principles outlined above, an eviction would be permissible. But Diamond has failed to show that that situation is posed by this case. If the landlord is able to repair the premises, another method is available to him for complying with the requirements of Section 2301. Since a retaliatory eviction would be unlawful under *Edwards* and under the housing code, the landlord must choose the only lawful method of compliance — *i.e.*, he must repair the premises.

Judge Roger Robb wrote a blistering dissent, *id.* at 871-872:

I cannot accept the proposition espoused by the majority that when a landlord states under oath and without contradiction that he wishes to remove a housing unit from the market it will be presumed that his reasons are "illicit," unless he is able to prove to the satisfaction of a jury that he is financially unable to make necessary repairs or has some other "substantial business reason" for removing the unit from the market. I find no warrant in law for any such presumption or requirement of proof.

The theory of the majority seems to be that if not an outlaw a landlord is at least a public utility, subject to regulation by the court in conformity with its concept of public convenience and necessity. I reject that notion, which in practical application will commit to the discretion of a jury the management of a landlord's business and property.

The majority suggests that its decision will promote the development of more and better low-cost housing. This reasoning passes my understanding. In my judgment the majority's Draconian treatment of landlords will inevitably discourage investment in housing for rental purposes.

I dissent. I would affirm the judgment of the District of Columbia Court of Appeals.

Which position is more convincing?

2. *How long may the tenant stay?* How long may the tenant stay in the premises if the landlord is denied the right to evict the tenant? Most courts hold that the landlord may not evict the tenant until the landlord can show a legitimate, nonretaliatory business reason for the eviction. They may not refuse to renew a lease (or grant a periodic tenancy in place of a term of years) for a retaliatory reason. However, the Utah Supreme Court criticized this approach. Noting that "we cannot saddle the landlord with a perpetual tenant," and requiring the landlord to show that "his actions are not the result of retaliatory motives" will be a very difficult burden for a landlord to overcome, the court held that the tenant "should be permitted to remain until the

landlord has made the repairs required by law." *Building Monitoring Systems, Inc. v. Paxton*, 905 P.2d 1215, 1219 (Utah 1995). The court held that the tenant may be evicted anytime after repairs have been made as long as the tenant is also given "sufficient time, without the pressure normally exerted in a holdover eviction proceeding, to find other suitable housing."

A number of states have dealt with the issue by statute. Some states expressly apply the retaliatory eviction doctrine to the landlord's refusal to renew a tenancy, including a term of years. D.C. Code §45-2552(a); 765 Ill. Comp. Stat. §720/1; N.J. Stat. §2A:42-10.10(d). Some states have interpreted their statutes to apply to nonrenewal of a tenancy. *Van Buren Apartments v. Adams*, 701 P.2d 583 (Ariz. Ct. App. 1984) (interpreting Ariz. Rev. Stat. §33-1381). In contrast, some states have held that their statutes prohibit retaliatory eviction of month-to-month tenants but allow landlords to refuse to renew term-of-years or fixed term leases for retaliatory reasons. *Frenchtown Villa v. Meadors*, 324 N.W.2d 133 (Mich. Ct. App. 1982) (interpreting Mich. Comp. Laws §600.5720). Still other states adopt a middle position, prohibiting retaliatory eviction for a specified time. For example, California prohibits a landlord from retaliating against a tenant for exercising rights protected by the implied warranty for 180 days but allows landlords freedom to seek not to renew a periodic tenancy or to increase the rent or otherwise change the terms of the leasehold after that time. Cal. Civ. Code §1942.5. *Accord*, Conn. Gen. Stat. §47a-20 (prohibiting eviction for six months after a protected act by a tenant). New York has passed a statute that applies the retaliatory eviction doctrine to nonrenewal of a term of years but provides that "a landlord shall not be required ... to offer a new lease or a lease renewal for a term greater than one year and after such extension of a tenancy for one year shall not be required to further extend or continue such tenancy." N.Y. Real Prop.§223-b(2).

PROBLEMS

1. *See* Problem following *Rase v. Castle Mountain Ranch*, *supra* §5.3.1.2, at page 332.

2. A landlord owns five buildings. Two of the buildings, including Building 1, are in Cambridge, Massachusetts. The other buildings are in the nearby towns of Somerville, Arlington, and Brookline. The buildings have old furnaces that do not work well. All the tenants have month-to-month leases. Some of the tenants in each building meet to form a tenants association to complain to the landlord about inadequate heat and hot water. The landlord promises to fix the problem but does nothing about it. The members of the tenants association agree to stop paying rent. In Building 1, about half the tenants stop paying rent. In the other buildings, anywhere from 10 percent to 25 percent of the tenants similarly withhold rent.

The landlord responds by suing to evict all the tenants in Building 1 on the ground that the landlord intends to convert the building to nonresidential use as an office building. It is crucial to note that the landlord *does not* ask for possession on the ground that the tenants have breached their leases by not paying rent; they are legally entitled to stop paying rent. Rather, the landlord seeks only to end the periodic tenancies by providing the statutorily required one month's notice.

The tenants respond by raising the defense of retaliatory eviction. They appeal to *Hillview Associates v. Bloomquist* and to *Robinson v. Diamond Housing*, arguing that the landlord has no right to evict tenants if the landlord's *motive* is to retaliate against them for asserting rights guaranteed by the implied warranty of habitability. The landlord responds by arguing that there is an exception in both *Hillview* and *Robinson* for landlords who want to go out of business. The landlord claims that he has an absolute right to convert the building from rental housing to use as an office building, regardless of his motive. The tenants, however, argue that the landlord cannot take advantage of that exception unless the landlord goes out of the rental housing business entirely. Since the landlord is retaining four other buildings, the defense is not available. They argue that the landlord is using the eviction of these tenants as a way to intimidate the other tenants and prevent them from complaining to the authorities or withholding rent. If they can prove this in court, they argue that the landlord has no right to evict them.

What should the court do?

§8.4.4 LANDLORD'S LIABILITY TO TENANTS

§8.4.4.1 Consumer Protection Legislation

Most states have passed legislation specifically regulating landlord-tenant relations. Some states, for example, have enacted statutes codifying the implied warranty of habitability. In addition, many states have passed general consumer protection statutes. In recent years, many courts have held that tenants may bring claims against landlords as *consumers of housing services.*

Why do tenants bring claims under consumer protection acts when they have remedies under a statutory or common law implied warranty of habitability? They do so because some unfair trade practices or consumer protection statutes provide for multiple damages or reimbursement for attorney's fees or both. Multiple damages are awarded both to punish the wrongdoer and to deter wrongful conduct. Legislatures fear that compensatory damages may not be enough to deter fraudulent conduct since defendants may simply factor possible liability into their cost-benefit calculations, thus treating it as a cost of doing business. If the benefits of such conduct outweigh the costs, businesses may simply continue the unlawful conduct, thereby defeating the purpose of the legislation, which aims to protect consumers from such activity in the first place.

Various issues arise in these cases. First, courts must determine whether tenants are protected by general consumer protection statutes that prohibit "unfair" or "deceptive" trade practices in the sale of "goods" and "services" to consumers. Courts commonly hold that rental housing constitutes a "service" that is bought by tenants as consumers, thus enabling tenants to sue under these statutes. *Hernandez v. Stabach,* 193 Cal. Rptr. 350 (Ct. App. 1983); *Brown v. Veile,* 555 N.E.2d 1227 (Ill. App. Ct. 1990); *Love v. Amsler,* 441 N.W.2d 555 (Minn. Ct. App. 1989). Some courts, however, have held that the presence of specific landlord-tenant legislation, such as the *Uniform Residential Landlord and Tenant Act,* demonstrates a legislative intent to exclude tenants from coverage under other statutes and that tenants therefore cannot obtain additional remedies under general consumer protection legislation. *State v. Schwab,* 693 P.2d 108 (Wash. 1985).

Second, courts must define what kinds of conduct constitute "unfair" or "deceptive" practices. For example, the Massachusetts Supreme Judicial Court has held that including illegal and unenforceable clauses in residential leases constitutes an unfair and deceptive practice that "injures" tenants, even if the landlord never attempts to enforce the clause and the tenant admits never having read the clause. In the absence of reliance, however, damages are nominal. *Leardi v. Brown*, 474 N.E.2d 1094 (Mass. 1985). Other kinds of conduct held to constitute unfair or deceptive trade practices include retaliatory evictions, *Hernandez v. Stabach, supra*, and the failure to maintain rental housing in accordance with the housing code, *Dorgan v. Loukas*, 473 N.E.2d 1151 (Mass. App. Ct. 1985); *State v. Weller*, 327 N.W.2d 172 (Wis. 1982). Another central issue is addressed in the following problem.

PROBLEM

Consumer protection laws generally regulate those involved in "trade" or "business" or "commerce." If a landlord owns a two-unit building and rents out one unit, is she engaged in a trade or business? What arguments can be made on both sides? How should the court rule? *Compare Billings v. Wilson*, 493 N.E.2d 187 (Mass. 1986) (no) *with Stanley v. Moore*, 454 S.E.2d 225 (N.C. 1995) (yes).

§8.4.4.2   Landlord's Tort Liability to Tenants

Strict liability versus negligence. The ordinary remedies for the landlord's violation of the implied warranty of habitability are rescission (tenant moves out), rent withholding, or rent reduction; also available to the tenant are administrative remedies such as contacting the local housing inspector or bringing a court action for an injunction ordering the landlord to fix the premises. These remedies limit the amount of damages to the amount of the rent or less. Can the tenant sue the landlord for damages that *exceed* the amount of the rent during the period of the violation? This question is usually described as the extent of the landlord's tort liability to the tenant for injuries resulting from the landlord's violation of her duty to provide habitable premises. Are landlords liable for injuries to tenants caused by defects in the premises that may or may not result from the landlord's failure to take adequate care in maintaining the habitability of the premises?

Under the traditional rule, landlords were immune from liability to tenants for injuries arising out of the condition of the premises. *See Bowles v. Mahoney*, 202 F.2d 320 (D.C. Cir. 1952). Under the current practice, however, landlords *are* liable to tenants for injuries arising out of the landlord's negligence, including negligent failure to comply with housing codes or the implied warranty of habitability. *Whetzel v. Jess Fisher Management Co.*, 282 F.2d 943 (D.C. Cir. 1960) (overruling *Bowles v. Mahoney*). *Accord, New Haverford Partn. v. Stroot*, 772 A.2d 792 (Del. 2001) (landlord may be liable for negligently caused injury from toxic mold in building).

Should landlords be liable only when tenants can prove that the landlord acted negligently (acting so as to cause a foreseeable and unreasonable risk of harm), or should a strict liability standard apply, making the landlord liable if a defect in the premises caused the plaintiff's injuries, regardless of whether the landlord could have foreseen and prevented the harm by reasonable maintenance? A negligence claim is based on an allegation that the landlord is at fault or has acted unreasonably by not taking proper precautions or investing sufficiently in safety. A strict liability claim is based on the unreasonably dangerous condition of the building or the landlord's failure to comply with the housing code, regardless of whether a reasonable landlord would have known of and corrected the defect.

California adopted a strict liability standard in *Becker v. IRM*, 698 P.2d 116 (Cal. 1985), but overruled *Becker* in *Peterson v. Superior Court*, 899 P.2d 905 (Cal. 1995). In *Becker*, a tenant was injured when he slipped and fell against a shower door made of untempered glass that shattered. The court held that the landlord was strictly liable for damages arising out of a latent defect in the premises.

> Absent disclosure of defects, the landlord in renting the premises makes an implied representation that the premises are fit for use as a dwelling and the representation is ordinarily indispensable to the lease. The tenant purchasing housing for a limited period is in no position to inspect for latent defects in the increasingly complex modern apartment buildings or to bear the expense of repair whereas the landlord is in a much better position to inspect for and repair latent defects. The tenant's ability to inspect is ordinarily substantially less than that of a purchaser of the property.
>
> The tenant renting the dwelling is compelled to rely upon the implied assurance of safety made by the landlord. It is also apparent that the landlord by adjustment of price at the time he acquires the property, by rentals or by insurance is in a better position to bear the costs of injuries due to defects in the premises than the tenants.
>
> In these circumstances, strict liability in tort for latent defects existing at the time of renting must be applied to insure that the landlord who markets the product bears the costs of injuries resulting from the defects "rather than the injured persons who are powerless to protect themselves. . . ."
>
> The cost of protecting tenants is an appropriate cost of the enterprise. Within our marketplace economy, the cost of purchasing rental housing is obviously based on the anticipated risks and rewards of the purchase, and thus it may be expected that along with numerous other factors the price of used rental housing will depend in part on the quality of the building and reflect the anticipated costs of protecting tenants, including repairs, replacement of defects and insurance. Further, the landlord after purchase may be able to adjust rents to reflect such costs. The landlord will also often be able to seek equitable indemnity for losses.
>
> We conclude that the absence of a continuing business relationship between builder and landlord does not preclude application of strict liability in tort for latent defects existing at the time of the lease because landlords are an integral part of the enterprise and they should bear the cost of injuries resulting from such defects rather than the injured persons who are powerless to protect themselves.

698 P.2d at 122-124. However, in overruling *Becker*, the *Peterson* court explained, 899 P.2d at 912-913:

> The effect of imposing upon landlords liability without fault is to compel them to insure the safety of their tenants in situations in which injury is caused by a defect of which the landlord neither knew nor should have known. . . .
>
> . . . A landlord or hotel owner, unlike a retailer, often cannot exert pressure upon the manufacturer to make the product safe and cannot share with the manufacturer the costs of insuring the safety of the tenant, because a landlord or hotel owner generally has no "continuing business relationship" with the manufacturer of the defective product. As one commentator has observed: "If the objective of the application of the stream of commerce approach is to distribute the risk of providing a product to society by allowing an injured plaintiff to find a remedy for injury along the chain of distribution, it will probably fail in the landlord/tenant situation. The cost of insuring risk will not be distributed along the chain of commerce but will probably be absorbed by tenants who will pay increased rents. One could argue that this was not the effect sought by the court in earlier cases which anticipated that the cost of risk would be distributed vertically in the

stream of commerce." (Alice L. Perlman, Becker v. IRM Corporation: *Strict Liability in Tort for Residential Landlords*, 16 Golden Gate L. Rev. 349, 360 (1986).)

The prevailing rule is that the landlord is liable for harms to tenants only if she has acted negligently. This means that the landlord may be relieved of liability if the injury is caused by a latent defect of which the landlord could not reasonably have been aware. The South Carolina Supreme Court declined to adopt a strict liability standard in *Young v. Morrisey*, 329 S.E.2d 426, 428 (S.C. 1985), citing the "compelling reasons" of a trial court in New Jersey:

> (1) A landlord is not engaged in mass production whereby he places his product — the apartment — in a stream of commerce exposing it to a large number of customers; (2) he has not created the product with a defect which is preventable by greater care at the time of manufacture or assembly; (3) he does not have the expertise to know and correct the condition, so as to be saddled with responsibility for a defect regardless of negligence; (4) an apartment includes several rooms with many facilities constructed by many artisans with differing types of expertise, and subject to constant use and deterioration from many causes; (5) it is a commodity wholly unlike a product which is expected to leave a manufacturer's hands in a safe condition with an implied representation upon which the consumer relies; (6) the tenant may expect that at the time of letting there are no hidden dangerous defects known to the landlord of which the tenant has not been warned, but he does not expect that all will be perfect in his apartment for all the years of his occupancy; (7) to apply strict liability would impose an unjust burden on property owners; how can a property owner prevent a latent defect or repair when he has no way of detecting it? And if he can't prevent the defect, why should he be liable? [*Dwyer v. Skyline Apartments, Inc.*, 301 A.2d 463 (N.J. Super. Ct. App. Div. 1973), *aff'd mem.*, 311 A.2d 1 (1973).]

The choice between strict liability and negligence is a complicated one; it is considered a central subject in many torts courses. These notes are intended not to exhaust the subject but simply to flag the issue since it may well determine the outcome of certain kinds of landlord-tenant tort litigation.

Damages for emotional distress. A number of courts have allowed tenants to recover damages for intentional infliction of emotional distress resulting from a landlord's violation of statutory duties and the implied warranty of habitability. *Stoiber v. Honeychuck*, 162 Cal. Rptr. 194 (Ct. App. 1980); *Hilder v. St. Peter*, 478 A.2d 202 (Vt. 1984). *See also Thomas v. Goudreault*, 786 P.2d 1010 (Ariz. Ct. App. 1989) (interpreting the Arizona version of the *Uniform Residential Landlord and Tenant Act* to allow the tenant to recover damages for emotional distress). These cases ordinarily involve extreme and outrageous conduct such as the sexual harassment, persistent lack of heat, and severe pest infestation present in *Haddad v. Gonzalez*, 576 N.E.2d 658 (Mass. 1991). *See also Chryar v. Wolf*, 21 P.3d 428 (Colo. Ct. App. 2000) (landlord liable for damages for emotional distress when he wrongfully put the tenant's personal belongings on the street with a sign inviting people to take them); *Rodriguez v. Cambridge Housing Authority*, 823 N.E.2d 1249 (Mass. 2005)(landlord public housing authority liable for damages for severe emotional distress suffered by tenant and her son when she was violently attacked in her apartment by trespassers after the landlord negligently failed to change the locks on her apartment after it had been invaded and she had been attacked inside). *Accord, Simon v. Solomon,* 431 N.E.2d 556 (Mass. 1981).

PROBLEMS

1. *Intervening criminal conduct.* Courts have increasingly held landlords liable for negligently failing to provide sufficient security in the building, such as functioning locks on the front door to the building, when such failures have allowed intruders to enter the building and rape or otherwise attack a tenant. *See Kline v. 1500 Massachusetts Ave. Apt. Corp.,* 439 F.2d 477 (D.C. Cir. 1970); *Rodriguez v. Cambridge Housing Authority,* 823 N.E.2d 1249 (Mass. 2005); *Trentacost v. Brussel,* 412 A.2d 436 (N.J. 1980); *Smith v. Lagow Construction & Developing Co.,* 642 N.W.2d 187 (S.D. 2002).

A tenant notifies the landlord that another tenant in the building is selling drugs out of his apartment. The landlord does nothing. The tenant is held up at gunpoint and robbed in the hallway of the building by a customer of the drug dealer. The tenant sues the landlord for negligent infliction of emotional distress.

　　a.　What is the tenant's argument that she should be able to hold the landlord responsible for damages?
　　b.　What is the landlord's argument that he is not responsible for the harm?
　　c.　How should the court rule?

2. The problem of lead paint poisoning in children has resulted in substantial legislative activity. In 1992, Congress passed the *Residential Lead-Based Paint Hazard Reduction Act,* 42 U.S.C. §§4851-4856, which requires sellers and landlords to provide buyers or lessees of most property built before 1978 with a "lead hazard information pamphlet" and to disclose the presence of any known lead-based paint. §4852d. *See* 40 C.F.R. §§745.101 to 745.107.

States have also passed laws regulating lead paint in residential rental housing. Massachusetts, for example, requires landlords of families with children to remove or cover lead paint in the units. *See, e.g.,* Mass. Gen. Laws ch. 111, §197; *Ankiewicz v. Kinder,* 563 N.E.2d 684 (Mass. 1990) (applying the act). *But see Chapman v. Silber,* 760 N.E.2d 329, 335 (N.Y. 2001)("without notice of a specific dangerous condition, an out-of-possession landlord cannot be faulted for failing to repair it," so tenants whose children were injured by ingesting lead paint could not sue their landlord for damages for negligence when no N.Y. state law required landlords to test for lead paint).

Assume a state statute provides that "whenever a child under six years of age resides in any premises in which any paint, plaster or other accessible structural material contains dangerous levels of lead, the owner shall remove or contain said paint, plaster or other accessible structural materials." The statute also provides that a "landlord who fails to comply with the act shall be liable to any child injured because of that failure for damages."

A landlord fails to comply with the act and a four-year-old child becomes ill with lead poisoning after eating paint chips that fell from a window sill. The child's father sues the landlord for negligence, arguing that the landlord's failure to remove the lead paint in the apartment posed a foreseeable risk of harm to his child and caused his child's illness. The landlord seeks to reduce whatever liability may be found against her by arguing that the tenant was "contributorily negligent," *i.e.,* that if the father had been more vigilant, he would have prevented the child from ingesting the paint chips and the harm would not have occurred.

    a. What is the child's argument that the statute does not allow the landlord to raise a defense of contributory negligence?

    b. What is the landlord's argument that such a defense is consistent with the statute?

    c. How should the court rule?

9

Real Estate Transactions

---

§9.1 Structure of the Transaction

The sale of real property involves a host of complex issues, whether the transaction involves a single-family house, a condominium unit, a shopping center, an office building, or undeveloped land. At the same time, many aspects of these transactions have become routinized. In many jurisdictions, real estate sales are marked by the use of standardized forms and by the allocation of responsibility in relatively set ways among the parties. The purpose of this chapter is to introduce you to the basic structure of the real estate transaction and to highlight several issues that are likely to be of central importance in any transaction.

§9.1.1 ATTORNEY'S ROLE

Real estate transactions involve a host of legal issues and a variety of contracts. Attorneys may prepare these contracts, but in most states, brokers help the parties fill the blanks on form contracts. Michael Braunstein, *Structural Change and Inter-Professional Competitive Advantage: An Example Drawn from Residential Real Estate Conveyancing*, 62 Mo. L. Rev. 241, 262 (1997); Gary S. Moore, *Lawyers and the Residential Real Estate Transaction*, 26 Real Est. L.J. 351, 356-357 (1998). Although many attorneys believe that they should be involved, most land sale contracts are signed without the aid of an attorney on either side. It has been noted that attorneys appear to be involved in only about 40 percent of residential transactions. Braunstein, *supra*. In some cases, the contract will include an "attorney approval clause," giving the parties a specified time, such as three days, to consult with an attorney after signing the document and allowing the parties to withdraw if they wish. Alice N. Noble-Allgire, *Attorney Approval Clauses in Residential Real Estate Contracts — Is Half a Loaf Better than None?* 48 Kan. L. Rev. 339 (2000).

Although the increasing marginalization of lawyers in residential land sales in many areas may reduce the cost of such transactions to home buyers and sellers, it may also leave the parties subject to legal vulnerabilities of which they were not aware when they signed the agreement. It may be the case that the actual understanding of the parties of the meaning and effect of their deal may diverge from the provisions contained in form contracts. If this is the case, the courts will more and more have to deal with the question of what to do when the parties' actual expectations diverge from the formal terms of their agreement. On the other hand, it has been argued that litigation about these issues has clarified the rights of the parties (or will do so in the future) and that ordinary home purchasers do not need the participation of an attorney in the transaction to protect their rights. Braunstein, *supra* at 271-279.

On September 23, 2001, President Bush issued Executive Order No. 13224, directing the Office of Foreign Assets Control ("OFAC") of the Department of Treasury to block the transfer of property owned by foreign persons who "have committed, or who pose a significant risk of committing, acts of terrorism that threaten the security of U.S. nationals or the national security, foreign policy, or economy of the U.S." E.O. 13224. The Order further prohibits anyone in the U.S. from participating in transactions involving such "blocked" property. "This includes lawyers assisting clients with real estate transactions. Real estate lawyers must review OFAC's specially designated nationals and blocked persons list to assure that no payer/transferor or recipient/transferee is on the list, making that person's assets subject to freezing." Robert J. Pomerene, *Heads Up: Real Estate Attorneys: Orange Alert! You Have Been Enlisted in the Fight Against Terrorism,* 48 Boston B. J. 14 (Mar./Apr. 2004). Failure to comply could lead to substantial criminal and civil sanctions. The list is long and constantly being updated but is available on the Treasury Department website.

Title III of the USA Patriot Act passed shortly after September 11, 2001, amended the Bank Secrecy Act, 31 U.S.C. §§5311-5355, to require every "financial institution" to develop an internal anti-money laundering programs designed to prevent the financing of terrorism. The definition of "financial institution" includes reference to "persons involved in real estate closings and settlements," 31 U.S.C. §5312(U). The effect of this provision on real estate lawyers is uncertain. Kevin L. Shepherd, *The USA Patriot Act: Surprising Implications for Real Estate Lawyers* (A.B.A. 2004).

§9.1.2 BROKERS

Some sales are made directly by the owner with the buyer. In some cases, the owner sells the property directly to a friend, family member, business associate, or acquaintance. In other cases, the owner advertises the property in the newspaper and shows the place to prospective buyers individually or through an open house. In most cases, however, sellers hire real estate *brokers* (also called *agents* or *realtors*) to help sell the property. The seller normally signs a contract with the broker by which the broker agrees to look for prospective buyers and show the property to them, perhaps for a set period of time such as six months, in exchange for a commission, which is often 5 percent to 7 percent of the sale price. The agreement may also set the *asking price,* or the amount the seller would like to get for the property. The asking price may be higher than the amount the seller expects to get; the seller may reduce the price in response to a lower offer from a particular buyer.

There are three basic types of broker listing agreements.

1. *Exclusive right to sell.* This arrangement gives the broker the right to collect the commission if the property is sold to anyone during the period of the

contract, even if the sale is to a buyer that the owner found without the broker's help.

2. *Exclusive agency.* This entitles the broker to the commission, or a share of the commission, if the property is sold by her efforts or the efforts of any other broker, but not if the property is sold by the owner.

3. *Open, or nonexclusive.* The broker is entitled to a commission only if she is the first person to procure a buyer who is ready, willing, and able to buy. If anyone else, including the seller, finds a buyer first, the broker gets no commission.

Several types of listing agreements have either been outlawed by statute in some states or are discouraged by state regulators. Under the *net listing*, the broker takes her commission out of the purchase price to the extent it exceeds the seller's price. Many states prohibit this arrangement by statute, and others discourage it through regulations issued by the licensing commissions. D. Barlow Burke, Jr., *Law of Real Estate Brokers* §2.2.4, at 2:33-2:35 (2d ed. 1992); *Thompson on Real Property, Thomas Edition* §95.05(1) (David. A. Thomas ed. 1994). This arrangement is problematic because it creates a conflict of interest between the seller and the broker. Sellers often rely on the advice of brokers to help determine the price they should ask for their property. Under the net listing, the broker has an incentive to induce the seller to list the property for a price below its fair market value because the broker will pocket the excess. Conversely, if the property is sold at fair market value and is listed at that amount, the broker recovers nothing and therefore may have an incentive not to tell the seller about an offer that will earn the broker nothing.

Another practice discouraged by state regulators is the *option listing*, whereby the broker promises to buy the property at a set price, revealing the commission only when the option is exercised. Under this arrangement, the broker has an incentive to suggest to the seller that the property is worth less than it really is because the broker can resell the property for its fair market value, pocketing the difference.

Disputes sometimes break out between brokers and sellers when the broker finds a buyer who makes a down payment and signs a purchase and sale agreement but then, for whatever reason, the deal falls through. It is quite clear that the seller has a duty to pay the commission if the seller himself wrongfully backs out of the deal after the broker has found a ready, willing, and able buyer. But what happens if the buyer refuses to complete the transaction by paying the rest of the purchase price?

When the buyer backs out of the deal, brokers sometimes allege that they have the right to their sales commission because they fulfilled their contractual obligation to find a ready, willing, and able buyer. Until the middle of the twentieth century, the prevailing rule was that the broker's commission was indeed earned and due at the time the purchase and sale agreement was signed, regardless of whether the sale was actually completed. This result did not accord with the expectations of most sellers, who contemplated that the commission would be paid only if the deal went through since the commission is normally taken out of the purchase price paid by the buyer. This rule appears to still be the law in most states.

However, a substantial number of courts have changed the traditional rule, holding that the broker's commission is earned and due only if the sale is completed. *See Tristram's Landing, Inc. v. Wait,* 327 N.E.2d 727 (Mass. 1975); *Exotex Corp. v. Rinehart,* 3 P.3d 826 (Wyo. 2000). The seller has a duty to pay the commission if the seller defaults and backs out of the deal without a good reason, but the commission is not due if the buyer refuses to go forward. This emerging rule is based on the fact that the "owner hires the broker with the expectation of becoming liable for a commission only in the event a sale of the property is consummated, unless the title does not pass because of the owner's improper or frustrating conduct." *Ellsworth Dobbs, Inc. v. Johnson*, 236 A.2d 843, 853 (N.J. 1967). Although some courts find this rule to be nondisclaimable, *id.* at 856, others allow the parties to contract around it. *Cappezzuto v. John Hancock Mutual Life Insurance Co.*, 476 N.E.2d 188 (Mass. 1985).

In many communities, brokers use *multiple listing services* established by the local real estate board. Each broker who is a member of the listing service registers every exclusive listing she receives with the listing service. Other brokers will then have access to that information and can attempt to sell the property as well. If any sale goes through, the commission is shared by the listing service and the broker who arranged for the sale. Any broker who finds a buyer will share the commission with the broker hired by the seller.

Unauthorized practice of law. Every state requires lawyers to be licensed to practice law, and brokers who provide legal advice or draft complex legal documents for their clients may be subject to penalties for the unauthorized practice of law. *Toledo Bar Ass'n v. Chelsea Title Agency of Dayton, Inc.*, 2003 Ohio 6453, 800 N.E.2d 29 (Ohio 2003) (unauthorized practice of law for title agency to prepare deed for client when not written by licensed attorney). Brokers often provide standard land sale contracts for sellers and buyers to use. If they do no more than fill in the blanks on such forms, these activities are thought be an "incident to the business" of providing brokerage services, and courts are unlikely to find a violation of the laws prohibiting nonlawyers from "practicing law." However, if they draft deeds, mortgages, or other documents that transfer interests in real property, express opinions on the status of titles or zoning law and the like, or conduct closings, they may be found to have engaged in the unauthorized practice of law. These restrictions on the conduct of brokers are intended to "protect[] the public from the potentially severe economic and emotional consequences which may flow from erroneous advice given by persons untrained in the law." *State v. Buyers Service Co.*, 357 S.E.2d 15, 18 (S.C. 1987). *Accord, Doe v. McMaster*, 585 S.E.2d 773, 776-777 (S.C. 2003) (unauthorized practice of law to prepare closing documents in real estate transaction such as deeds and title opinions); *Ex Parte Watson*, 589 S.E.2d 760 (S.C. 2003) (nonlawyer title abstractors who examine public records and issue an opinion in a title search performed in connection with tax foreclosure sale are engaged in the unauthorized practice of law).

Some states have begun to loosen these regulations to allow brokers to perform functions that used to be performed by lawyers on the ground that this serves the public interest by lowering the costs of buying and selling real estate. The Supreme Court of New Jersey, for example, authorized brokers and title companies to conduct closings in an area of the state where it was typical for neither seller nor buyer to be represented by a lawyer at the closing. *In re Opinion No. 26 of the Committee on Unauthorized Practice of Law*, 654 A.2d 1344 (N.J. 1995). While holding that they were engaged in the practice of law, their activity was not "unauthorized" because it was in the public interest for them to help owners conduct real estate transactions, and there was not sufficient warrant to force every owner and every buyer to hire a lawyer in order to buy or sell real estate. *See also Countrywide Home Loans, Inc. v. Kentucky Bar Ass'n*, 113 S.W.3d 105 (Ky. 2003) (allowing laypersons to conduct real estate closings as long as they do not give legal advice); *Dressell v. Ameribank,* 664 N.W.2d 151 (Mich. 2003) (not unauthorized practice of law for title company to prepare leases, mortgages, and deeds).

Broker's duties to buyer. Although the broker is formally the agent of the seller, many buyers feel that the broker is also working for them. The buyer may deal exclusively with one broker, who shows her a range of places and helps her find a property that suits her needs. Although there is no formal contractual arrangement with the broker, the courts may impose on the broker certain fiduciary obligations toward the buyer. For example, if the broker fails to reveal relevant information to the buyer, the buyer may sue the broker for fraud. For example, in *Strawn v. Canuso,* 657 A.2d 420 (N.J. 1995), the court held that a broker had a duty to warn purchasers of homes in a residential subdivision that they were located next to a 56-acre landfill containing waste that had contaminated nearby lakes and groundwater and that the Environmental Protection Agency had advised against the use of the site for human habitation. Five months later, the legislative enacted a statute called the *New Residential Real Estate Off-Site Conditions Disclosure Act* that ratified this ruling but specified the types of conditions that must be disclosed to potential buyers. N.J. Stat. §46:3C-1 to -12. *See also Nobrega v. Edison Glen Associates,* 772 A.2d 368 (N.J. 2001) (holding that the new statute provides the sole remedies for nondisclosure of off-site conditions).

Buyer's duties to broker. What happens if the buyer attempts to arrange with the seller to buy the property independent of the broker to save the cost of the broker's commission? Ordinarily, the broker can sue the seller for breach of the listing agreement. But suppose the seller no longer has the money for some reason; can the broker sue the buyer as well? Some courts have held that "when a prospective buyer solicits a broker to find or to show him property which he might be interested in buying, and the broker finds property satisfactory to him which the owner agrees to sell at the price offered, and the buyer knows the broker will earn a commission for the sale from the owner, the law will imply a promise on the part of the buyer to complete the transaction with the owner." *Ellsworth Dobbs,* 236 A.2d at 859. This approach has been adopted in California, *Donnellan v. Rocks,* 99 Cal. Rptr. 692 (Ct. App. 1972), but rejected in Michigan and Virginia, *Rich v. Emerson-Dumont Distributing Corp.,* 222 N.W.2d 65 (Mich. Ct. App. 1974); *Professional Realty Corp. v. Bender,* 222 S.E.2d 810 (Va. 1976).

Buyer's brokers. In recent years, it has become increasingly common for some home buyers to hire their own brokers to advise them in purchasing a house. Such brokers work for the buyer, not the seller, and may perhaps be more trusted to tell the buyer whether the price being asked by the seller is reasonable. Buyer's brokers can be paid a percentage of the sale price, a fixed fee, or an hourly rate.

Dual agency. Conflicts may arise when a real estate agency provides broker's services to both buyers and sellers, since the buyer's broker will be attempting to minimize the sale price, while the seller's agent will try to get as much as possible for the property. Unless the law prohibits it, a single person may be in the business of representing both buyers and sellers, and it is possible that the seller will deal with a buyer who has engaged the same agent. While one might argue that such an agent would facilitate the deal, she also might fail to represent either side adequately. Many states have passed statutes that regulate such potential conflicts of interest, mainly by requiring disclosure that a broker is acting as a dual-agent. *See* Ga. Code Ann. §§10-6A-10 and 10-6A-12(a).

Many states now also allow a "designated agency," in which one broker in the agency represents the seller, while another represents the buyer in the transaction. Ann Morales Olazábal, *Redefining Realtor Relationships and Responsibilities: The Failure of State Regulatory Responses*, 40 Harv. J. Legis. 65, 75-76 (2003). Some states are now experimenting with allowing brokers to act as "transaction brokers," in which they do not represent either the seller or the buyer; instead, they act as professionals, giving independent advice on the transaction. *Id.* at 87-91. *See* Ga. Code §10-6A-3(14). But if brokers are not the agent of either the seller or the buyer, they cannot be liable for breach of fiduciary duty; while this may relieve the broker of worry about possible liability, it may also remove incentives to promote the interest of one or both parties to the transaction, and for this reason every state that has adopted this idea has imposed some statutory duties on such transaction brokers. *Id.* at 90-91. *See also Lombardo v. Albu,* 14 P.3d 288 (Ariz. 2000) (buyer's broker liable to seller for failing to disclose buyer's financial problems that were likely to — and that did — lead to the deal falling through).

§9.1.3   SALES CONTRACT

Prospective buyers will find out about property that is for sale by consulting listings in newspapers or going directly to real estate brokers. A broker may show many places to a prospective buyer. Unlike sellers, buyers are generally not limited to one broker; they may contact and deal with several brokers. There is usually no oral or written agreement between the buyer and the broker; the broker is officially working for the seller — although the broker may indeed want to be helpful to the buyer in order to consummate a sale. Some buyers may make arrangements for brokers to represent them; they may do this to make sure they get an independent opinion from someone whose job is to further their interests rather than the seller's interests. For example, buyers want to know whether the asking price of the property is out of line with the general market price, and the seller's broker has a financial interest in getting the highest price possible in order to maximize the commission.

When the buyer finds a place that she likes, she makes an offer to buy it. The offer may be oral or in writing. The buyer may offer to pay the entire sale price set by the seller. In most cases, however, the buyer will offer some lower amount. In some localities, the buyer may pay a nominal fee ($1,000 or so — nominal in relation to the price of the property) to show the seriousness of the offer. The seller may accept the offer or make a counteroffer above the buyer's suggestion but below the initial asking price. The buyer and seller may negotiate about other terms of the transaction as well, including when the seller would be able to move out and transfer possession, who will pay back taxes owed to the government, which side has the burden of repairing any known defects, and the like. When the parties agree on a price and on the general terms of the transaction, they proceed to the next formal step in the transaction: the purchase and sale agreement.

The purchase and sale agreement is a written contract, generally prepared by a lawyer who may work either for the buyer or the seller. Many transactions will involve lawyers on both sides, for the buyer and the seller (as well as lawyers for the banks lending the money for the transaction). At the same time, many transactions may involve a lawyer on only one side, with the other side unrepresented by counsel.

In the purchase and sale agreement, the seller agrees to convey title at a specific date in the future when the *closing* will take place. The buyer makes an immediate down payment or deposit (sometimes called an *earnest money deposit*) that often amounts to 10 percent of the purchase price; the buyer also promises to pay the rest of the purchase price at the closing. The date of the closing is negotiated by the parties, and is often one or two months after the purchase and sale agreement is signed. The buyer's obligations are normally made contingent on (1) the seller's ability to convey marketable title; (2) the buyer's ability to get adequate financing for the rest of the purchase price; and (3) inspections of the premises for structural defects, termites, and environmental hazards, such as radon and toxic waste generated by a leaking oil tank. The seller's performance is usually conditioned only on the buyer's paying the purchase price at the closing, but it may also be conditioned on the seller's finding a new place to live.

§9.1.4 EXECUTORY PERIOD

During the period between the signing of the purchase and sale agreement and the closing, many arrangements have to be made, including *inspecting* the property, arranging for *financing*, possibly arranging for the buyer to sell his old house, and researching the *title* of the premises to make sure the seller owns it free of encumbrances that might impede transfer of title or beneficial use of the property.

Inspections. First, the buyer will arrange for the various *inspections* of the premises. This is generally done by hiring professionals who will examine the property and provide opinions on the condition of the property.

Mortgage financing. Second, the buyer will also attempt to get *financing*, often by seeking a mortgage loan from a bank or lending institution. The buyer applies to the bank for a *loan* to pay the balance of the purchase price. If the buyer already owns a house that she intends to sell to raise the money to buy the new house, she may need only bridge financing for the period between the closing and the sale of her old house. If the old house is worth less than the new house she is buying, she may still need to borrow money in the long term to pay the balance of the purchase price. A buyer who does not already own real estate almost always needs to borrow money to pay some portion of the purchase price of the home. The bank and the buyer will negotiate about how large a down payment the buyer must make, the interest to be paid on the loan, and the time period over which the loan will be repaid.

The bank is also likely to insist on a *mortgage* to accompany the loan. A mortgage constitutes an agreement by the buyer that if the buyer defaults on the loan payments or other material terms of the mortgage agreement (such as maintaining insurance on the property and keeping it in good repair), the bank will be able to *foreclose* on the property by arranging for it to be sold, with the proceeds of the sale being used to satisfy the buyer's debt to the bank.

Thus, in addition to the purchase and sale agreement with the seller, the buyer will enter a second set of agreements with the bank that is financing the transaction. These agreements will include the *loan agreement*, which will set the amount and times at which payments are due by the borrower to the bank, and the *mortgage*, which will identify the circumstances under which defaults by the borrower (generally the failure to make the mortgage payments) will allow the lender to begin foreclosure proceedings.

The bank will be unwilling to lend the money to purchase the house without assuring itself that the buyer will be able to repay the loan and that the seller actually owns the house, meaning that no other property interests encumber the property (such as other mortgages) that would impair the value of the property as collateral for the loan. The bank will therefore ask the buyer for information about her credit history, job history, and current assets and salary. The bank will also make arrangements to assure itself that the seller has clear *title* to the house. It will do this by either (1) searching the title itself in the registry of deeds, (2) requiring the buyer to hire a lawyer to do this and provide evidence of a satisfactory result, or (3) requiring the buyer to buy *title insurance* from a title insurance company that will research the title and agree to guarantee the seller's title in return for a fee from the buyer. We will deal with title problems in greater depth later on in the chapter.

If the buyer cannot obtain financing, or the inspection reveals serious defects, or the seller's title is not "marketable," the buyer will be excused from the deal. If, however, all conditions are met, the parties proceed to the *closing*.

Many lawsuits arise because of disputes that occur during the executory period. The buyer may refuse to go forward with the deal, causing the seller to sue for the rest of the purchase price and for transfer of title to the buyer. The seller may refuse to sell, causing the buyer to sue for damages and/or for specific performance, that is, an order forcing the seller to transfer title to the property to the buyer in exchange for the agreed-upon purchase price.

§9.1.5 CLOSING

At the closing, the buyer will pay the rest of the purchase price to the seller in return for a deed to the property delivered by the seller to the buyer. The buyer or the lender may make a last-minute check of the records in the recording office to make sure that the property was not sold or encumbered between the time the title search was conducted and the time of the closing.

The seller will deliver the *deed* to the buyer. The deed will recite that the grantor (seller) conveys the property to the grantee (buyer). It will describe the property and be signed by the grantor. It may contain reference to easements and covenants restricting the use of the property. The deed may also contain various *warranties* by which the seller covenants that he has good title to the property.

In return, the buyer may pay over to the seller some portion of the purchase price beyond the deposit already paid when the purchase and sale agreement was signed. The lender will pay the rest of the purchase price, either directly to the seller or to the buyer for the buyer to endorse over to the seller. Simultaneously, the buyer will sign the loan agreement with the bank and the mortgage agreement. The bank, or the lawyer for the seller, will generally arrange immediately to record the deed. In fact, many closings take place at the registry of deeds.

A federal statute, the *Real Estate Settlement and Procedures Act (RESPA)*, 12 U.S.C. §§2601-2617, requires disclosure of all settlement costs and protects real estate buyers from having to pay kickbacks or other unearned and/or undisclosed fees by prohibiting acceptance of fees for rendering of real estate settlement services in connection with federally related mortgage loans "other than for services actually performed." *United States v. Gannon*, 684 F.2d 433 (7th Cir. 1982).

§9.1.6 AFTER THE CLOSING

Ordinarily, the deed replaces the purchase and sale agreement at the closing and is treated as the complete contractual arrangement between the parties. If the parties intend the promises in the purchase and sale agreement to be enforceable after the closing, the deed must normally provide explicitly that the purchase and sale agreement (or specific terms in it) will *survive the deed*. Otherwise, the buyer will be limited to remedies associated with or contained in the deed; specifically, the buyer may sue the seller for *breach of warranties* contained in the deed but not for breach of the purchase and sale agreement.

Some obligations survive the deed even though they are not explicitly mentioned in it. For example, if the seller lies to the buyer about the condition of the building, the buyer may be able to sue the seller for fraud even after the closing has taken place. Under these circumstances, the buyer may ask for damages or to rescind the deal by transferring title back to the seller and recovering the purchase price.

OFFER TO PURCHASE REAL ESTATE

TO _____ Date:_____
     (Seller and Spouse)
_____ From the Office of : _____
_____

The property herein referred to is identified as follows: _____
_____

Special provisions (if any) re fixtures, appliances, etc. _____
_____

hereby offer to buy said property, which has been offered to me by _____
_____ as the Broker(s) under the following terms and conditions:

CHECK ONE:

1. I will pay therefore $_____, of which   ❑   Check, subject to collection

   (a) $_____ is paid herewith as a deposit to bind this Offer   ❑   Cash

   (b) $_____ is to be paid as an additional deposit upon the execution of the Purchase and Sale Agreement provided for below.

   (c) $_____ is to be paid at the time of delivery of the Deed in cash, or by certified, cashier's, treasurer's or bank check(s).

   (d) $_____

   (e) $_____ Total Purchase Price

2. This Offer is good until _____ A.M. P.M. on _____, 20____ at or before which time a copy hereof shall be signed by you, the Seller and your (husband) (wife), signifying acceptance of this Offer, and returned to me forthwith, otherwise this Offer shall be considered as rejected and the money deposited herewith shall be returned to me forthwith.

3. The parties hereto shall, on or before _____ A.M. P.M. _____, 20____ execute the applicable Standard Form Purchase and Sale Agreement recommended by the Greater Boston Real Estate Board or any form substantially similar thereto, which, when executed, shall be the agreement between the parties hereto.

4. A good and sufficient Deed, conveying a good and clear record and marketable title shall be delivered at 12:00 Noon on _____, 20____ at the appropriate Registry of Deeds, unless some other time and place are mutually agreed upon in writing.

5. If I do not fulfill my obligations under this Offer, the above mentioned deposit shall forthwith become your property without recourse to either party. Said deposit shall be held by _____ as escrow agent subject to the terms hereof provided however that in the event of any disagreement between the parties, the escrow agent may retain said deposit pending instructions mutually given in writing by the parties. A similar provision shall be included in the Purchase and Sale Agreement with respect to any deposit held under its terms.

6. Time is of the essence hereof.

7. Disclosures: For one to four family residences, the Buyer hereby acknowledges receipt of the Home Inspectors: Facts for Consumers brochure produced by the Office of Consumer Affairs. For residential property constructed prior to 1978, Buyer must also sign Lead Paint "Property Transfer Notification."

8. The initialed riders, if any, attached hereto are incorporated herein by reference. Additional terms and conditions, if any: _____
_____
_____

NOTICE: This is a legal document that creates binding obligations. If not understood, consult an attorney.

WITNESS my hand and seal   Signed_____
                                Buyer   •
                                Buyer

_____ _____
Address/City/State/Zip   Phone Numbers (Work & Home)

This Offer is hereby accepted upon the foregoing terms and conditions at _____ A.M. / P.M. on _____, 20____
WITNESS my (our) hand(s) and seal(s)

_____ _____
Seller (or spouse)   Seller

RECEIPT FOR DEPOSIT

Date _____

Received from _____ Buyer the sum of $_____ as deposit under the terms

and conditions of above Offer, to be held by _____ as escrow agent.

Under regulations adopted pursuant to the Massachusetts license law:
All offers submitted to brokers or salespeople to purchase real property
that they have a right to sell shall be conveyed forthwith to the owner
of such real property.   _____
                                        Agent for Seller

This form has been made available through the courtesy of the Greater Boston Real Estate Board, and is protected by copyright laws.

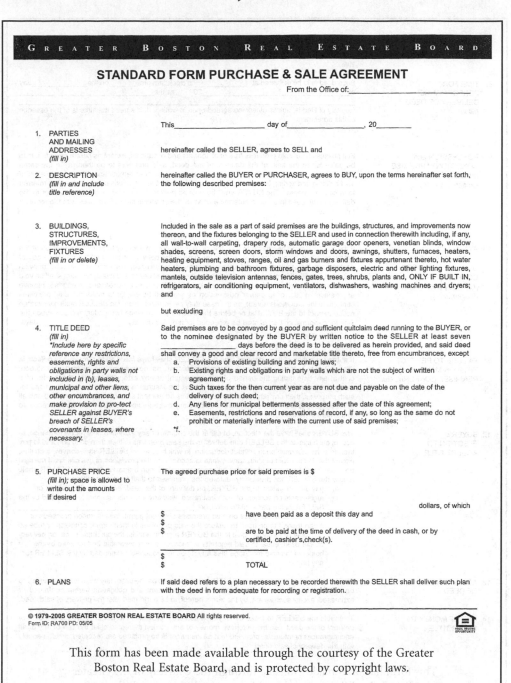

GREATER BOSTON REAL ESTATE BOARD

STANDARD FORM PURCHASE & SALE AGREEMENT

From the Office of:_____

This_____ day of_____, 20_____

1. PARTIES
   AND MAILING
   ADDRESSES
   (fill in)

   hereinafter called the SELLER, agrees to SELL and

2. DESCRIPTION
   *(fill in and include
   title reference)*

   hereinafter called the BUYER or PURCHASER, agrees to BUY, upon the terms hereinafter set forth,
   the following described premises:

3. BUILDINGS,
   STRUCTURES,
   IMPROVEMENTS,
   FIXTURES
   (fill in or delete)

   Included in the sale as a part of said premises are the buildings, structures, and improvements now
   thereon, and the fixtures belonging to the SELLER and used in connection therewith including, if any,
   all wall-to-wall carpeting, drapery rods, automatic garage door openers, venetian blinds, window
   shades, screens, screen doors, storm windows and doors, awnings, shutters, furnaces, heaters,
   heating equipment, stoves, ranges, oil and gas burners and fixtures appurtenant thereto, hot water
   heaters, plumbing and bathroom fixtures, garbage disposers, electric and other lighting fixtures,
   mantels, outside television antennas, fences, gates, trees, shrubs, plants and, ONLY IF BUILT IN,
   refrigerators, air conditioning equipment, ventilators, dishwashers, washing machines and dryers;
   and

   but excluding

4. TITLE DEED
   (fill in)
   *Include here by specific
   reference any restrictions,
   easements, rights and
   obligations in party walls not
   included in (b), leases,
   municipal and other liens,
   other encumbrances, and
   make provision to pro-tect
   SELLER against BUYER's
   breach of SELLER's
   covenants in leases, where
   necessary.*

   Said premises are to be conveyed by a good and sufficient quitclaim deed running to the BUYER, or
   to the nominee designated by the BUYER by written notice to the SELLER at least seven
   _____ days before the deed is to be delivered as herein provided, and said deed
   shall convey a good and clear record and marketable title thereto, free from encumbrances, except
   a. Provisions of existing building and zoning laws;
   b. Existing rights and obligations in party walls which are not the subject of written
      agreement;
   c. Such taxes for the then current year as are not due and payable on the date of the
      delivery of such deed;
   d. Any liens for municipal betterments assessed after the date of this agreement;
   e. Easements, restrictions and reservations of record, if any, so long as the same do not
      prohibit or materially interfere with the current use of said premises;
   *f.

5. PURCHASE PRICE
   *(fill in); space is allowed to
   write out the amounts
   if desired*

   The agreed purchase price for said premises is $

   dollars, of which

   $ _____ have been paid as a deposit this day and
   $ _____
   $ _____ are to be paid at the time of delivery of the deed in cash, or by
                      certified, cashier's,check(s).

   $ _____
   $ _____ TOTAL

6. PLANS

   If said deed refers to a plan necessary to be recorded therewith the SELLER shall deliver such plan
   with the deed in form adequate for recording or registration.

This form has been made available through the courtesy of the Greater
Boston Real Estate Board, and is protected by copyright laws.

7. REGISTERED TITLE

In addition to the foregoing, if the title to said premises is registered, said deed shall be in form sufficient to entitle the BUYER to a Certificate of Title of said premises, and the SELLER shall deliver with said deed all instruments, if any, necessary to enable the BUYER to obtain such Certificate of Title.

8. TIME FOR
    PERFORMANCE;
    DELIVERY OF DEED
    (fill in)

Such deed is to be delivered at_____o'clock (am/pm)_____on the_____day of_____20 , at the_____

Registry of Deeds, unless otherwise agreed upon in writing. It is agreed that time is of the essence of this agreement.

9. POSSESSION and
    CONDITION of PREMISE
    *(attach a list of
    exceptions, if any)*

Full possession of said premises free of all tenants and occupants, except as herein provided, is to be delivered at the time of the delivery of the deed, said premises to be then (a) in the same condition as they now are, reasonable use and wear thereof excepted, and (b) not in violation of said building and zoning laws, and (c) in compliance with the provisions of any instrument referred to in clause 4 hereof. The BUYER shall be entitled personally to enter said premises prior to the delivery of the deed in order to determine whether the condition thereof complies with the terms of this clause.

10. EXTENSION TO
    PERFECT TITLE
    OR MAKE PREMISES
    CONFORM
    *(Change period of time if
    desired).*

If the SELLER shall be unable to give title or to make conveyance, or to deliver possession of the premises, all as herein stipulated, or if at the time of the delivery of the deed the premises do not conform with the provisions hereof, then any payments made under this agreement shall be forthwith refunded and all other obligations of the parties hereto shall cease and this agreement shall be void without recourse to the parties hereto, unless the SELLER elects to use reasonable efforts to remove any defects in title, or to deliver possession as provided herein, or to make the said premises conform to the provisions hereof, as the case may be, in which event the SELLER shall give written notice thereof to the BUYER at or before the time for performance hereunder, and thereupon the time for performance hereof shall be extended for a period of thirty _____ days.

11. FAILURE TO PERFECT
    TITLE OR MAKE
    PERMISES CONFORM, etc.

If at the expiration of the extended time the SELLER shall have failed so to remove any defects in title, deliver possession, or make the premises conform, as the case may be, all as herein agreed, or if at any time during the period of this agreement or any extension thereof, the holder of a mortgage on said premises shall refuse to permit the insurance proceeds, if any, to be used for such purposes, then any payments made under this agreement shall be forthwith refunded and all other obligations of the parties hereto shall cease and this agreement shall be void without recourse to the parties hereto.

12. BUYER's
    ELECTION TO
    ACCEPT TITLE

The BUYER shall have the election, at either the original or any extended time for performance, to accept such title as the SELLER can deliver to the said premises in their then condition and to pay therefore the purchase price without deduction, in which case the SELLER shall convey such title, except that in the event of such conveyance in accord with the provisions of this clause, if the said premises shall have been damaged by fire or casualty insured against, then the SELLER shall, unless the SELLER has previously restored the premises to their former condition, either

    a. pay over or assign to the BUYER, on delivery of the deed, all amounts recovered or recoverable on account of such insurance, less any amounts reasonably expended by the SELLER for any partial restoration, or_____

    b. if a holder of a mortgage on said premises shall not permit the insurance proceeds or a part thereof to be used to restore the said premises to their former condition or tobe so paid over or assigned, give to the BUYER a credit against the purchase price, on delivery of the deed, equal to said amounts so recovered or recoverable and retained by the holder of the said mortgage less any amounts reasonably expended by the SELLER for any partial restoration.

13. ACCEPTANCE
    OF DEED

The acceptance of a deed by the BUYER or his nominee as the case may be, shall be deemed to be a full performance and discharge of every agreement and obligation herein contained or expressed, except such as are, by the terms hereof, to be performed after the delivery of said deed.

14. USE OF MONEY TO
    CLEAR TITLE

To enable the SELLER to make conveyance as herein provided, the SELLER may, at the time of delivery of the deed, use the purchase money or any portion thereof to clear the title of any or all encumbrances or interests, provided that all instruments so procured are recorded simultaneously with the delivery of said deed.

15. INSURANCE **Insert amount (list additional* *types of insurance and amounts* *as agreed)*	Until the delivery of the deed, the SELLER shall maintain insurance on said premises as follows: Type of Insurance Amount of Coverage a. Fire & Extended Coverage *$ b. *$ c. *$
16. ADJUSTMENTS *(list operating expenses, if* *any, or attach schedule)*	Collected rents, mortgage interest, water and sewer use charges, operating expenses (if any) according to the schedule attached hereto or set forth below, and taxes for the then current fiscal year, shall be apportioned and fuel value shall be adjusted, as of the day of performance of this agreement and the net amount thereof shall be added to or deducted from, as the case may be, the purchase price payable by the BUYER at the time of delivery of the deed. Uncollected rents for the current rental period shall be apportioned if and when collected by either party.
17. ADJUSTMENT OF UNASSESSED AND ABATED TAXES	If the amount of said taxes is not known at the time of the delivery of the deed, they shall be apportioned on the basis of the taxes assessed for the preceding fiscal year, with a reapportionment as soon as the new tax rate and valuation can be ascertained; and, if the taxes which are to be apportioned shall thereafter be reduced by abatement, the amount of such abatement, less the reasonable cost of obtaining the same, shall be apportioned between the parties, provided that neither party shall be obligated to institute or prosecute proceedings for an abatement unless herein otherwise agreed.
18. BROKER's FEE *(fill in fee with dollar amount or* *percentage;also name of* *Brokerage firm/s)*	A Broker's fee for professional services of_____ is due from the SELLER to_____ the Broker(s) herein, but if the SELLER pursuant to the terms of clause 21 hereof retains the deposits made hereunder by the BUYER, said Broker(s) shall be entitled to receive from the SELLER an amount equal to one-half the amount so retained or an amount equal to the Broker's fee for professional services according to this contract, whichever is the lesser.
19. BROKER(S) WARRANTY *(fill in name)*	The Broker(s) named herein_____ warrant(s) that the Broker(s) is (are) duly licensed as such by the Commonwealth of Massachusetts.
20. DEPOSIT *(fill in name)*	All deposits made hereunder shall be held in escrow by_____ as escrow agent subject to the terms of this agreement and shall be duly accounted for at the time for performance of this agreement. In the event of any disagreement between the parties, the escrow agent may retain all deposits made under this agreement pending instructions mutually given in writing by the SELLER and the BUYER.
21. BUYER's DEFAULT; DAMAGES	If the BUYER shall fail to fulfill the BUYER's agreements herein, all deposits made hereunder by the BUYER shall be retained by the SELLER as liquidated damages unless within thirty days after the time for performance of this agreement or any extension hereof, the SELLER otherwise notifies the BUYER in writing.
22. RELEASE BY HUSBAND OR WIFE	The SELLER's spouse hereby agrees to join in said deed and to release and convey all statutory and other rights and interests in said premises.
23. BROKER AS PARTY	The Broker(s) named herein join(s) in this agreement and become(s) a party hereto, insofar as any provisions of this agreement expressly apply to the Broker(s), and to any amendments or modifications of such provisions to which the Broker(s) agree(s) in writing.
24. LIABILITY OF TRUSTEE, SHAREHOLDER, BENEFICIARY, etc.	If the SELLER or BUYER executes this agreement in a representative or fiduciary capacity, only the principal or the estate represented shall be bound, and neither the SELLER or BUYER so executing, nor any shareholder or beneficiary of any trust, shall be personally liable for any obligation, express or implied, hereunder.
25. WARRANTIES AND REPRESENTATIONS *(fill in); if none, state "none"; if any* *listed, indicate by whom each* *warranty or representation was* *made*	The BUYER acknowledges that the BUYER has not been influenced to enter into this transaction nor has he relied upon any warranties or representations not set forth or incorporated in this agreement or previously made in writing, except for the following additional warranties and representations, if any, made by either the SELLER or the Broker(s):

26. CONTINGENCY CLAUSE
    (omit if not provided for in Offer to Purchase)

In order to help finance the acquisition of said premises, the BUYER shall apply for a conventional bank or other institutional mortgage loan of $_____ at prevailing rates, terms and conditions. If despite the BUYER's diligent efforts a commitment for such loan cannot be obtained on or before_____, 20_____ the BUYER may terminate this agreement by written notice to the SELLER and/or the Broker(s), as agent(s) for the SELLER, prior to the expiration of such time, whereupon any payments made under this agreement shall be forthwith refunded and all other obligations of the parties hereto shall cease and this agreement shall be void without recourse to the parties hereto. In no event will the BUYER be deemed to have used diligent efforts to obtain such commitment unless the BUYER submits a complete mortgage loan application conforming to the foregoing provisions on or before_____, 20_____.

27. CONSTRUCTION OF AGREEMENT

This instrument, executed in multiple counterparts, is to be construed as a Massachusetts contract, is to take effect as a sealed instrument, sets forth the entire contract between the parties, is binding upon and enures to the benefit of the parties hereto and their respective heirs, devisees, executors, administrators, successors and assigns, and may be cancelled, modified or amended only by a written instrument executed by both the SELLER and the BUYER. If two or more persons are named herein as BUYER their obligations hereunder shall be joint and several. The captions and marginal notes are used only as a matter of convenience and are not to be considered a part of this agreement or to be used in determining the intent of the parties to it.

28. LEAD PAINT LAW

The parties acknowledge that, under Massachusetts law, whenever a child or children under six years of age resides in any residential premises in which any paint, plaster or other accessible material contains dangerous levels of lead, the owner of said premises must remove or cover said paint, plaster or other material so as to make it inaccessible to children under six years of age.

29. SMOKE DETECTORS

The SELLER shall, at the time of the delivery of the deed, deliver a certificate from the fire department of the city or town in which said premises are located stating that said premises have been equipped with approved smoke detectors in conformity with applicable law.

30. ADDITIONAL PROVISIONS

The initialed riders, if any, attached hereto, are incorporated herein by reference.

FOR RESIDENTIAL PROPERTY CONSTRUCTED PRIOR TO 1978, BUYER MUST ALSO HAVE SIGNED LEAD PAINT "PROPERTY TRANSFER NOTIFICATION CERTIFICATION"

NOTICE: This is a legal document that creates binding obligations. If not understood, consult an attorney.

SELLER:_____ BUYER:_____
PRINT NAME:_____ PRINT NAME:_____
Taxpayer ID/Social Security No._____ Taxpayer ID/Social Security No._____
SELLER (or Spouse):_____ BUYER:_____
PRINT NAME:_____ PRINT NAME:_____
Taxpayer ID/Social Security No._____ Taxpayer ID/Social Security No._____

BROKER(S)

This form has been made available through the courtesy of the Greater Boston Real Estate Board, and is protected by copyright laws.

Sample Deed

Johann Sebastian Bach, Grantor, of 24 Main Street, Unit #6, Middletown, Middlesex County, Massachusetts, for consideration paid, and in full consideration of TWO HUNDRED EIGHTEEN THOUSAND FIVE HUNDRED DOLLARS ($218,500), grants to Clara and Robert Schumann, Grantees, wife and husband, of 75 Broad Street, Middletown, Massachusetts, as joint tenants with QUITCLAIM COVENANTS, Unit #6 in the 24 Main Street Condominium (a condominium subject to Massachusetts General Laws, chapter 183A) in Middletown, Middlesex County, Massachusetts, created by Master Deed dated August 23, 1992, recorded on August 25, 1992, at the Middlesex County Registry of Deeds, Book 14632, Page 75, together with an undivided 15.22 percent interest in said Unit and in the Common Areas of the buildings and land described in the Master Deed, being the lot marked "F" on the plan of land drawn by Wolfgang Amadeus Mozart, Civil Engineer, September 1932, which plan is filed with Middlesex Registry of Deeds, Book 10479, page 214 (being lot F on the plan filed with said Deed as filed plan No. 95) and said lot F is bounded and further described as follows: southwesterly by Main Street, by a slightly curved line, seventy-five feet; northwesterly by lot "E" on said plan one hundred twenty-six and 45/100 feet; northeasterly by land of owner unknown seventy-five feet; and southeasterly by the lot marked "G" on said plan, one hundred eighteen and 24/100 feet; containing, according to the plan, 9,315 square feet.

Being the same premises conveyed to Grantor by deed of Ludwig van Beethoven by deed dated July 31, 1990, and recorded at Book 12469, page 143.

Said premises are conveyed subject to the restrictions and conditions as set forth in paragraph 7 of said Master Deed, including:

(1)   no Unit shall be used other than for residential purposes by one (1) family;

(2)   the architectural integrity of the Building and the Units shall be preserved without modifications, including but not limited to the following restrictions: that no balcony, enclosure, awning, screen antenna, sign, banner or other device, and no exterior change, addition, structure, projection, decoration or other feature shall be erected or placed upon or attached to any Unit; no addition to or change or replacement (except, so far as practicable, with identical kind) of any exterior light, door knocker or other exterior hardware, exterior Unit door, or door frames shall be made and no painting or other decoration shall be done on any exterior part of surface of any Unit;

(3)   no Unit shall be leased without the consent of the Condominium Association.

The restrictions set forth in paragraphs (1), (2) & (3) above shall be for the benefit of all of the Unit Owners and the 24 Main Street Condominium Association, and:

(1)   shall be administered on behalf of said Owners by the Trustees of said 24 Main Street Condominium Association, duly chosen as provided for in the Master Deed;

(2)   shall be enforceable by the Trustees on behalf of the Condominium Association, insofar as permitted by law;

(3)   may be waived in specific cases by the Trustees; and

(4)   shall, as permitted by law be perpetual and run with the land, and may be extended from time to time in such manner as permitted or required by law for the continued enforceability thereof.

Said premises are also conveyed subject to easements, rights, conditions, and restrictions of record insofar as the same may be now in force and applicable.

WITNESS my hand and seal this 6th day of December 2005.

Johann Sebastian Bach

THE COMMONWEALTH OF MASSACHUSETTS

Middlesex, ss. December 6, 2005

Then personally appeared the above-named Johann Sebastian Bach and acknowledged the foregoing instrument to be his free act and deed before me.

Notary Public

Print Name:

My Commission Expires:

§9.2   Sales Contract

§9.2.1   FORMALITIES: STATUTE OF FRAUDS VERSUS PART PERFORMANCE AND ESTOPPEL

BURNS v. McCORMICK
_____

135 N.E. 273 (N.Y. 1922)

BENJAMIN N. CARDOZO, J.

In June, 1918, one James A. Halsey, an old man, and a widower, was living, without family or housekeeper, in his house in Hornell, New York. He told the plaintiffs, [who are husband and wife,] so it is said, that if they gave up their home and business in Andover, New York, and boarded and cared for him during his life, the house and lot, with its furniture and equipment, would be theirs upon his death. They did as he asked, selling out an interest in a little draying business in Andover, and boarding and tending him till he died, about five months after their coming. Neither deed nor will, nor memorandum subscribed by the promisor, exists to authenticate the promise. The plaintiffs asked specific performance. The defense is the statute of frauds (Real Property Law [Consol. Laws, ch. 50] §259).

We think the defense must be upheld. Not every act of part performance will move a court of equity, though legal remedies are inadequate, to enforce an oral agreement affecting rights in land. There must be performance "unequivocally referable" to the agreement, performance which alone and without the aid of words of promise is unintelligible or at least extraordinary unless as an incident of ownership, assured, if not existing.

"An act which admits of explanation without reference to the alleged oral contract or a contract of the same general nature and purpose is not, in general, admitted to constitute a part performance." *Woolley v. Stewart*, 118 N.E. 847, 848 (N.Y. 1918).

What is done must itself supply the key to what is promised. It is not enough that what is promised may give significance to what is done. The housekeeper who abandons other prospects of establishment in life and renders service without pay upon the oral promise of her employer to give her a life estate in land must find her remedy in an action to recover the value of the service. Her conduct, separated from the promise, is not significant of ownership, either present or prospective. On the other hand, the buyer who not only pays the price, but possesses and improves his acre, may have relief in equity without producing a conveyance. His conduct is itself the symptom of a promise that a conveyance will be made. Laxer tests may prevail in other jurisdictions. We have been consistent here.

Promise and performance fail when these standards are applied. The plaintiffs make no pretense that during the lifetime of Mr. Halsey they occupied the land as owners or under claim of present right. They did not even have possession. The possession was his; and those whom he invited to live with him were merely his servants or his guests. He might have shown them the door, and the law would not have helped them to return. Whatever rights they had were executory and future. The tokens of their title are not, then, to be discovered in acts of possession or dominion. The tokens must be found elsewhere if discoverable at all. The plaintiffs did, indeed, while occupants of the dwelling, pay the food bills for the owner as well as for themselves, and do the work of housekeepers. One who heard of such service might infer that it would be rewarded in some way. There could be no reasonable inference that it would be rewarded at some indefinite time thereafter by a conveyance of the land. The board might be given in return for lodging. The outlay might be merely an advance to be repaid in whole or part. "Time and care" might have been bestowed "From a vague anticipation that the affection and gratitude so created would, in the long run, insure some indefinite reward." *Maddison v. Alderson*, L. R. 8 App. Cas. [467,] 486. This was the more likely since there were ties of kinship between one of the plaintiffs and the owner. Even if there was to be a reward, not merely as of favor, but as of right, no one could infer, from knowledge of the service, without more, what its nature or extent would be. Mr. Halsey paid the taxes. He paid also for the upkeep of the land and building. At least, there is no suggestion that the plaintiffs had undertaken to relieve him of those burdens. He was the owner while he lived. Nothing that he had accepted from the plaintiffs evinces an agreement that they were to be the owners when he died.

We hold, then, that the acts of part performance are not solely and unequivocally referable to a contract for the sale of land. Since that is so, they do not become sufficient because part of the plaintiffs' loss is without a remedy at law. At law the value of board and services will not be difficult of proof. The loss of the draying business in Andover does not permit us to disregard the statute, though it may go without requital. We do not ignore decisions to the contrary in other jurisdictions. They are not law for us. Inadequacy of legal remedies, without more, does not dispense with the requirement that acts, and not words, shall supply the framework of the promise. That requirement has its origin in something more than an arbitrary preference of one form over others. It is "intended to prevent a recurrence of the mischief" which the statute would suppress. *Maddison v. Alderson, supra*, L. R. 8 App. Cas. at 478. The peril of perjury and error is latent in the spoken promise. Such, at least, is the warning of the statute, the estimate of policy that finds expression in its mandate. Equity, in assuming what is in substance a dispensing power, does not treat the statute as irrelevant, nor ignore the warning altogether. It declines to act on words, though the legal remedy is imperfect, unless the words are confirmed and illuminated by deeds. A power of dispensation, departing from the letter in supposed adherence to the spirit, involves an assumption of jurisdiction easily abused, and justified only within the limits imposed by history and precedent. The power is not exercised unless the policy of the law is saved.

In conclusion, we observe that this is not a case of fraud. No confidential relation has been abused. No inducement has been offered with the preconceived intention that it would later be ignored. The most that can be said against Mr. Halsey is that he made a promise which the law did not compel him to keep, and that afterwards he failed to keep it. We cannot even say of his failure that it was willful. He had made a will before the promise. Negligence or mere inertia may have postponed the making of another. The plaintiffs left the preservation of their agreement, if they had one, to the fallible memory of witnesses. The law exacts a writing. . . .

HICKEY v. GREEN
442 N.E.2d 37 (Mass. App. Ct. 1982)

R. AMMI CUTTER, Justice.

. . . Mrs. Gladys Green owns a lot (Lot S) in the Manomet section of Plymouth. In July, 1980, she advertised it for sale. On July 11 and 12, Hickey and his wife discussed with Mrs. Green purchasing Lot S and "orally agreed to a sale" for $15,000. Mrs. Green on July 12 accepted a deposit check of $500, marked by Hickey on the back, "Deposit on Lot . . . Massasoit Ave. Manomet . . . Subject to Variance from Town of Plymouth." Mrs. Green's brother and agent "was under the impression that a zoning variance was needed and [had] advised . . . Hickey to write" the quoted language on the deposit check. It turned out, however, by July 16 that no variance would be required. Hickey had left the payee line of the deposit check blank, because of uncertainty whether Mrs. Green or her brother was to receive the check and asked "Mrs. Green to fill in the appropriate name." Mrs. Green held the check, did not fill in the payee's name, and neither cashed nor endorsed it. Hickey "stated to Mrs. Green that his intention was to sell his home and build on Mrs. Green's lot."

"Relying upon the arrangements . . . with Mrs. Green," the Hickeys advertised their house on Sachem Road in newspapers on three days in July, 1980, and agreed with a purchaser for its sale and took from him a deposit check for $500 which they deposited in their own account. On July 24, Mrs. Green told Hickey that she "no longer intended to sell her property to him" but had decided to sell to another for $16,000. Hickey told Mrs. Green that he had already sold his house and offered her $16,000 for Lot S. Mrs. Green refused this offer.

The Hickeys filed this complaint seeking specific performance. Mrs. Green asserts that relief is barred by the Statute of Frauds contained in Mass. Gen. Laws ch. 259, §1. The trial judge granted specific performance. Mrs. Green has appealed.

The present rule applicable in most jurisdictions in the United States is succinctly set forth in *Restatement (Second) of Contracts*, §129 (1981). The section reads, "A contract for the transfer of an interest in land may be specifically enforced notwithstanding failure to comply with the Statute of Frauds if it is established that the party seeking enforcement, *in reasonable reliance on the contract* and on the continuing assent of the party against whom enforcement is sought, *has so changed his position that injustice can be avoided only by specific enforcement*" (emphasis supplied).[6] The earlier Massachusetts decisions laid down somewhat strict requirements for an estoppel precluding the assertion of the Statute of Frauds. Frequently there has been an actual change of possession and improvement of the transferred property, as well as full payment of the full purchase price, or one or more of these elements.

It is stated in Park, *Real Estate Law*, §883, at 334, that the "more recent decisions . . . indicate a trend on the part of the [Supreme Judicial] [C]ourt to find that the circumstances warrant specific performance." This appears to be a correct perception. . . .

The present facts reveal a simple case of a proposed purchase of a residential vacant lot, where the vendor, Mrs. Green, knew that the Hickeys were planning to sell their former home (possibly to obtain funds to pay her) and build on Lot S. The Hickeys, relying on Mrs. Green's oral promise, moved rapidly to make their sale without obtaining any adequate memorandum of the terms of what appears to have been intended to be a quick cash sale of Lot S. So rapid was action by the Hickeys that, by July 21, less than ten days after giving their deposit to Mrs. Green, they had accepted a deposit check for the sale of their house, endorsed the check, and placed it in their bank account. Above their signatures endorsing the check was a memorandum probably sufficient to satisfy the Statute of Frauds. . . . At the very least, the Hickeys had bound themselves in a manner in which, to avoid a transfer of their own house, they might have had to engage in expensive litigation. No attorney has been shown to have been used either in the transaction between Mrs. Green and the Hickeys or in that between the Hickeys and their purchaser.

There is no denial by Mrs. Green of the oral contract between her and the Hickeys. This, under §129 of the *Restatement*, is of some significance.[9] There can be no doubt (a) that Mrs. Green made the promise on which the Hickeys so promptly

---

6. Comments a and b to §129, read (in part):

a. . . . This section restates what is widely known as the "part performance doctrine." Part performance is not an accurate designation of such acts as taking possession and making improvements when the contract does not provide for such acts, but such acts regularly bring the doctrine into play. The doctrine is contrary to the words of the Statute of Frauds, but it was established by English courts of equity soon after the enactment of the Statute. Payment of purchase-money, without more, was once thought sufficient to justify specific enforcement, but a contrary view now prevails, since in such cases restitution is an adequate remedy. . . . Enforcement has . . . been justified on the ground that repudiation after "part performance" amounts to a "virtual fraud." A more accurate statement is that courts with equitable powers are vested by tradition with what in substance is a dispensing power based on the promisee's reliance, *a discretion to be exercised with caution* in the light of all the circumstances . . . [emphasis supplied].
b. . . . Two distinct elements enter into the application of the rule of this Section: first, the extent to which the evidentiary function of the statutory formalities is fulfilled by the conduct of the parties; second, the reliance of the promisee, providing a compelling substantive basis for relief in addition to the expectations created by the promise.

9. Comment d of *Restatement (Second) of Contracts*, §129, reads[:]

d. . . . Where specific enforcement is rested on a transfer of possession plus either part payment of the price or the making of improvements, it is commonly said that the action taken by the purchaser must be unequivocally referable to the oral agreement. But this requirement is not insisted on *if the making of the promise is admitted or is clearly proved*. The promisee *must act in reasonable reliance on the promise, before the promisor has repudiated* it, and the action must be such that the remedy of restitution is inadequate. If these requirements are met, *neither taking of possession nor payment of money nor the making of improvements is essential* . . . [emphasis supplied].

relied, and also (b) she, nearly as promptly, but not promptly enough, repudiated it because she had a better opportunity. The stipulated facts require the conclusion that in equity Mrs. Green's conduct cannot be condoned. This is not a case where either party is shown to have contemplated the negotiation of a purchase and sale agreement. If a written agreement had been expected, even by only one party, or would have been natural (because of the participation by lawyers or otherwise), a different situation might have existed. It is a permissible inference from the agreed facts that the rapid sale of the Hickeys' house was both appropriate and expected. These are not circumstances where negotiations fairly can be seen as inchoate.

. . . No public interest behind Mass. Gen. Laws ch. 259, §1 . . . in the simple circumstances before us, will be violated if Mrs. Green fairly is held to her precise bargain by principles of equitable estoppel. . . .

GARDNER v. GARDNER
454 N.W.2d 361 (Iowa 1990)

JERRY L. LARSON, Justice.

Mark and James Gardner (the brothers) conveyed their interest in Pottawattamie County farmland to their brother Harry to be used by him as security for a loan. The loan did not materialize, and the grantors requested that Harry reconvey their remainder interests. When Harry refused, the brothers filed this action to compel the reconveyance. . . .

In the settlement of their father's estate, Harry Gardner received a life estate in two-thirds of the real estate. One-third went directly to Harry's mother in fee simple. The remainder in the two-thirds of the real estate in which Harry received a life estate went to Harry's issue, and if he had none, to Harry's siblings. Harry has no issue.

In 1985, Harry was heavily indebted to the Citizens' State Bank of Oakland, Iowa. The bank refused to lend him any more money and called the loan due. Harry discussed the problems with his brothers and sister and solicited from them their remainder interest in the real estate. According to the brothers, Harry told them that he would attempt to refinance with the Federal Land Bank and, if he failed to do so, he would reconvey the remainder interest to them.

Harry's brothers, and his sister, conveyed their remainder interest in the real estate to Harry by a quitclaim deed. The deed did not mention any agreement to reconvey. According to the brothers, however, an oral agreement existed among the brothers to that effect.

Harry's application for a Federal Land Bank loan was denied, and the brothers requested the return of their remainder interests, and when Harry refused, they began this action. . . .

Under our statute of frauds, it is well established that a party who partially performs under the agreement may avoid the impact of the statute of frauds and introduce evidence of the oral contract. This is also in accordance with the general rule. The brothers in this case performed their part of the alleged oral agreement by conveying their remainder interests in the land. This was sufficient performance to take the alleged oral agreement from the operation of the statute of frauds.

The brothers also contend that Harry admitted the oral contract, and for that reason, it may be established notwithstanding the statute of frauds. Parol evidence establishing an agreement for the creation of an interest in real estate may be admitted where the agreement is established by oral evidence of the adverse party.

Although Harry disputed the fact at trial, there was some evidence in the record that he, at least partially, admitted an agreement to reconvey. The trial court erred in refusing to admit evidence of the alleged oral agreement. When the proffered evidence is considered, there is sufficient evidence to allow a fact finder to find an agreement to reconvey. . . .

NOTES AND QUESTIONS

1. *Gender roles and the construction of social reality.* In *Burns v. McCormick,* Justice Cardozo distinguished the acts of a "housekeeper who abandons other prospects of establishment in life and renders service without pay upon the oral promise of her employer to give her a life estate in land" from "the buyer who not only pays the price, but possesses and improves his acre." Cardozo explained that "[h]er conduct, separated from the promise, is not significant of ownership, either present or prospective," while "[h]is conduct is itself the symptom of a promise that a conveyance will be made." When discussing the housekeeper, Cardozo refers to "her" conduct; but when discussing a hypothetical buyer, he refers to "his" conduct. Why does he make this shift in gender? Plaintiffs were a married couple. Is there any evidence Cardozo considered the circumstances of the husband's conduct?

Why does Cardozo refer to the person providing personal services as a "housekeeper," while calling the one who improves the land a "buyer"? Doesn't the use of this language beg the question? Why is performing personal service less indicative of a contractual arrangement than payment of money? Does Cardozo assume that "housework" is normally performed by women for no compensation? Are housekeepers likely to engage in personal service in exchange for a chance of an indefinite reward, while those who work the land are unlikely to do so?

Cardozo suggests that the housekeeper's conduct is compatible with several explanations, while the "buyer's" conduct is susceptible of only one. According to Cardozo's understanding of social custom, a housekeeper might go to work for an employer, without wages, and pay for the food bills for both her employer and herself in exchange for lodging and the vague expectation of "some indefinite reward" that might be bestowed "in the long run." No "buyer," however, would pay a substantial sum of money and improve real property without having received a promise to convey the property to the buyer. Is it true that no other explanation might fit the set of facts, which includes (a) paying a large sum of money and (b) improving real property? Recall the cases about easements by estoppel and constructive trusts in Chapter 4.

2. *The family versus the market.* Consider the following descriptions of the relationship among gender roles, the family and the market.

In upholding the decision of the Illinois Supreme Court to deny Myra Bradwell admission to the Illinois bar because she was a woman, Justice Joseph P. Bradley wrote a famous concurring opinion for the United States Supreme Court, in which he wrote:

> [T]he civil law, as well as nature herself, has always recognized a wide difference in the respective spheres and destinies of man and woman. Man is, or should be, woman's protector and defender. The natural and proper timidity and delicacy which belongs to the female sex evidently unfits it for many of the occupations of civil life. The constitution

of the family organization, which is founded in the divine ordinance, as well as in the nature of things, indicates the domestic sphere as that which properly belongs to the domain and functions of womanhood.

Bradwell v. Illinois, 83 U.S. (16 Wall.) 130, 141 (1873) (Bradley, J., concurring).

Professor Frances Olsen explains the "images of the proper role of the state in the market and the family" underlying Justice Bradley's opinion:

> The maintenance of the private marketplace was believed to require the state to limit and direct its own action in order to maximize the opportunity of individuals to enter into whatever contracts they might wish to form. The expression of the will of the contracting parties was supposed to define the terms of the parties' relations; the state was not to tamper with these terms but was to treat each individual as an abstract equal. At the same time, the state was expected to enforce relations that were considered to be voluntarily defined by individuals through their contracts. In this sense, the arena of the marketplace was fully legalized, and the terms dictated by the will of the parties were enforceable by the power of the state through the courts....
>
> Within the family, however, privatization meant delegalization. The state refused to give legal effect to any effort by the parties to define the rights, duties, and liabilities of their own marriage. Once a man and a woman were married, they could no longer enter enforceable contracts with each other. Within the family, privatization created a limited "state of nature," in which the state refused to protect one family member from the harmful acts of any other family member. These refusals were an important part of what it meant for the family to be private and for the state not to intervene in the family relationship. It was generally not considered state intrusion, however, when the state undertook to define the marriage relation and to enforce the roles it decided each family member would fill. The notion that the family was private did not mean that the members should determine their own roles....

Frances Olsen, *The Family and the Market: A Study of Ideology and Legal Reform*, 96 Harv. L. Rev. 1497, 1521-1522 (1983).

In *Fitzpatrick v. Michael*, 9 A.2d 639 (Md. 1939), a case somewhat similar to *Burns v. McCormick*, the court refused specifically to enforce an employer's agreement to leave a substantial interest in his estate to a woman who worked as his nurse and remained with him until his death. The court held that specific performance is warranted only if the proffered services are sufficiently "rare and unusual." The court concluded that the claimant's work as "a nurse, chauffeur, companion, gardener, and housekeeper... involved no more than doing such things as a housewife often does as a part of the ordinary routine of life." Professor Mary Joe Frug notes that the court's dramatic devaluation of the kind of work Ms. Fitzpatrick performed for Mr. Michael ignored the social significance of the kind of work women have traditionally done, thereby indicating that "women's" work is inferior to "men's." In addition to nourishing this idea about gender, however, the court's distorted treatment of women's work functions as an analytical shortcut in the opinion: by analogizing Ms. Fitzpatrick's work to a "housewife's" work, the court avoids explaining why her services for Mr. Michael were not "rare and unusual." Mary Joe Frug, *Re-Reading Contracts: A Feminist Analysis of a Contracts Casebook*, 34 Am. U. L. Rev. 1065, 1081 (1985). *See also Borelli v. Brusseau*, 16 Cal. Rptr. 2d 16 (Ct. App. 1993) (when husband orally promised wife he would devise real property to her if she took care of him, and he left the property to his daughter instead, the court held the promise unenforceable because of lack of consideration since, as a spouse, she had a duty to support her husband, and a promise to pay her for doing what she was legally obligated to do was against public policy and void).

3. *Part performance.* The *part performance* doctrine allows an oral sales contract to be enforced if the buyer has taken substantial steps to complete the transaction. *Sharp v. Sumner,* 528 S.E.2d 791 (Ga. 2000); *Spears v. Warr,* 44 P.3d 742, 751-752, 2002 UT 24 ¶¶ 22-25 (Utah 2002). Justice Cardozo in *Burns* applied the traditional rule that the buyer must take steps that are "unequivocally referable" to a land sales contract. Today, courts do not require this degree of certainty, instead relying on three factors that ordinarily will suggest that a contract has been made: (1) payment of all or a substantial part of the *purchase price;* (2) taking *possession* of the property; and (3) making substantial *improvements* on the land. *Sullivan v. Porter,* 861 A.2d 625, 2004 ME 134 (Me. 2004). The states differ on whether all three are required or only one or two of the three. Payment of part of the purchase price is generally not enough to trigger the doctrine because the buyer can be made whole by having the money returned (with interest). However, payment of the purchase price in combination with one or both of the other factors is likely to be sufficient because they ordinarily would not occur without a promise to convey. Many cases rely on a combination of payment of part of the purchase price plus the taking of possession as sufficient to take the case out of the statute of frauds and allow enforcement.

4. *Estoppel.* An alternative basis for the part performance doctrine is *estoppel.* When the seller makes a promise on which the buyer relies substantially, it is not fair to allow the seller to claim that she did not make a promise if this would cause detriment to the buyer who reasonably relied on the promise to convey. *Roussalis v. Wyoming Medical Center,* 4 P.3d 209 (Wyo. 2000). The elements of promissory estoppel "demand evidence that establishes (1) the existence of a clear and definite promise which the promisor should reasonably expect to induce action by the promisee; (2) proof that the promisee acted to its detriment in reasonable reliance on the promise; and (3) a finding that injustice can be avoided only if the court enforces the promise." *Powell on Real Property* ¶ 880[2][ii] (Michael Allan Wolf ed. 2000). The buyer who has taken substantial steps to complete the transaction by taking possession or making improvements will ordinarily suffer hardship if the contract is not enforced. The seller may also seek specific enforcement of the contract if she has changed her position in reliance on the sale occurring, such as investing the proceeds in the purchase of another property.

How would *Burns v. McCormick* come out under the standard adopted in *Hickey v. Green?* Was the plaintiffs' reliance reasonable? Is the result unjust? How would *Hickey v. Green* have come out if Gladys Green had denied that she made the promise? How important was admission of the promise to the *Gardner* court? *See Brown v. Branch,* 758 N.E.2d 48, 53 (Ind. 2001) (oral promise to convey title to a house to his girlfriend not enforceable despite the fact that the girlfriend quit her job, dropped out of college and moved back to Indiana from Missouri; court holds that refusal to enforce the promise would not inflict "an unjust and unconscionable injury and loss").

5. *Constructive trust.* A third method of avoiding the statute of frauds is the *constructive trust* doctrine, which may be applied to prevent unjust enrichment when "property has been acquired in such circumstances that the holder of the legal title may not in good conscience retain the beneficial interest." *Davis v. Barnfield,* 833 So.2d 58, 64 (Ala. Ct. App. 2002). This doctrine may apply if the funds of one person are used to acquire property, but title is held in the name of another.

6. What constitutes a writing. Many cases deal with the question concerning what constitutes a writing sufficiently specific to satisfy the statute of frauds.

> What must the memorandum contain in order to satisfy the statute? In general, it must do the following with reasonable certainty: (1) identify the parties to the contract and show that a contract has been made by them or offered by the signatory to the other; (2) indicate the nature of the contract and its subject matter; (3) state the essential terms of the promises to be performed under the contract....
>
> [Further,] [t]he memorandum [must] be signed by the party against whom enforcement is sought or, as the original Statute put it, "the party to be charged."

2 E. Allan Farnsworth, *Contracts* §6.7, at 136 (1990). *See Durham v. Harbin*, 530 So. 2d 208 (Ala. 1988) (holding that a writing did not satisfy the statute of frauds when it was signed not by the party to be charged but only by his wife); *Clay v. Hanson*, 536 A.2d 1097 (D.C. 1988) (holding that a series of writings did not satisfy the statute of frauds because it did not contain an adequate description of the property and because the first writing did not identify the buyer and the second writing did not refer to the first writing to incorporate it by reference). When the parties sign a short contract called a *binder* that is intended to lead to negotiations for the terms of a longer sales contract, has the statute of frauds been satisfied? Some courts hold that the agreement is not enforceable because the parties intended further negotiation about its terms, *Behar v. Mawardi*, 702 N.Y.S.2d 326 (App. Div. 2000), while other courts hold that the binder is enforceable if the essential terms (such as the parties, the property, the price, and time for performance) are included, *McCarthy v. Tobin*, 706 N.E.2d 629 (Mass. 1999).

7. Formality versus informality. Would it be better to enforce the statute of frauds rigidly rather than creating equitable exceptions for part performance and estoppel? Do these exceptions enable the court to obtain justice in the individual case, or do they reward negligence and undermine predictability? Which rule is more likely to accord with the will of the parties? Which rule is more likely to reduce the costs of transactions? Which rule is more likely to prevent fraud?

In 1996, New Jersey amended its statute of frauds to eliminate the requirement that a contract for the sale of real of real property must be in writing. The statute only requires "a description of the real estate sufficient to identify it, the nature of the interest to be transferred, the existence of the agreement and the identity of the transferor and the transferee are proved by clear and convincing evidence." N.J. Stat. §25:1-13. A claimant may appeal to part performance or reliance to prove the existence of the agreement by clear and convincing evidence but the statute authorizes enforcement even without part performance or reliance by the buyer as long as the evidence of the existence and terms of the agreement is sufficiently strong. *See Barron v. Kipling Woods, LLC*, 838 A.2d 490 (N.J. Super. Ct. App. Div. 2004). Is this a good change in the law?

8. Judicial role. Is it compatible with the judicial role to read exceptions into general statutes such as the statute of frauds? Does it matter that judges have read exceptions into the statute of frauds for many years and that legislatures have generally not responded by amending the relevant statutes?

9. Family cases. Should an exception to the statute of frauds be made for agreements among family members? After all, doesn't the proposal to "put it in writing" suggest that one does not trust the other person? Would the world be a better place if family members asked one other to put everything in writing?

§9.2.2 What Constitutes a Breach of the Contract

§9.2.2.1 Misrepresentation and Fraudulent Nondisclosure

JOHNSON v. DAVIS

480 So. 2d 625 (Fla. 1985)

JAMES C. ADKINS, Justice.

. . . In May of 1982, the Davises entered into a contract to buy for $310,000 the Johnsons' home, which at the time was three years old. The contract required a $5,000 deposit payment, an additional $26,000 deposit payment within five days and a closing by June 21, 1982. . . .

Before the Davises made the additional $26,000 deposit payment, Mrs. Davis noticed some buckling and peeling plaster around the corner of a window frame in the family room and stains on the ceilings in the family room and kitchen of the home. Upon inquiring, Mrs. Davis was told by Mr. Johnson that the window had had a minor problem that had long since been corrected and that the stains were wallpaper glue and the result of ceiling beams being moved. There is disagreement among the parties as to whether Mr. Johnson also told Mrs. Davis at this time that there had never been any problems with the roof or ceilings. The Davises thereafter paid the remainder of their deposit and the Johnsons vacated the home. Several days later, following a heavy rain, Mrs. Davis entered the home and discovered water "gushing" in from around the window frame, the ceiling of the family room, the light fixtures, the glass doors, and the stove in the kitchen.

Two roofers hired by the Johnsons' broker concluded that for under $1,000 they could "fix" certain leaks in the roof and by doing so make the roof "watertight." Three roofers hired by the Davises found that the roof was inherently defective, that any repairs would be temporary because the roof was "slipping," and that only a new $15,000 roof could be "watertight."

The Davises filed a complaint alleging breach of contract, fraud and misrepresentation, and sought rescission of the contract and return of their deposit. The Johnsons counterclaimed seeking the deposit as liquidated damages. . . .

We . . . agree with the district court's conclusions under a theory of fraud and find that the Johnsons' statements to the Davises regarding the condition of the roof constituted a fraudulent misrepresentation entitling respondents to the return of their $26,000 deposit payment. In the state of Florida, relief for a fraudulent misrepresentation may be granted only when the following elements are present: (1) a false statement concerning a material fact; (2) the representor's knowledge that the representation is false; (3) an intention that the representation induce another to act on it; and (4) consequent injury by the party acting in reliance on the representation.

The evidence adduced at trial shows that after the buyer and the seller signed the purchase and sales agreement and after receiving the $5,000 initial deposit payment the Johnsons affirmatively repeated to the Davises that there were no problems with the roof. The Johnsons subsequently received the additional $26,000 deposit payment from the Davises. The record reflects that the statement made by the Johnsons was a false representation of material fact, made with knowledge of its falsity, upon which the Davises relied to their detriment as evidenced by the $26,000 paid to the Johnsons.

The doctrine of *caveat emptor* does not exempt a seller from responsibility for the statements and representations which he makes to induce the buyer to act, when under the circumstances these amount to fraud in the legal sense. To be grounds for relief, the false representations need not have been made at the time of the signing of the purchase and sales agreement in order for the element of reliance to be present. The fact that the false statements as to the quality of the roof were made after the signing of the purchase and sales agreement does not excuse the seller from liability when the misrepresentations were made prior to the execution of the contract by conveyance of the property. It would be contrary to all notions of fairness and justice for this Court to place its stamp of approval on an affirmative misrepresentation by a wrongdoer just because it was made after the signing of the executory contract when all of the necessary elements for actionable fraud are present. Furthermore, the Davises' reliance on the truth of the Johnsons' representation was justified and is supported by this Court's decision in *Besett v. Basnett*, 389 So. 2d 995 (1980), where we held "that a recipient may rely on the truth of a representation, even though its falsity could have been ascertained had he made an investigation, unless he knows the representation to be false or its falsity is obvious to him."

In determining whether a seller of a home has a duty to disclose latent material defects to a buyer, the established tort law distinction between misfeasance and nonfeasance, action and inaction must carefully be analyzed. The highly individualistic philosophy of the earlier common law consistently imposed liability upon the commission of affirmative acts of harm, but shrank from converting the courts into an institution for forcing men to help one another. This distinction is deeply rooted in our case law. Liability for nonfeasance has therefore been slow to receive recognition in the evolution of tort law.

In theory, the difference between misfeasance and nonfeasance, action and inaction is quite simple and obvious; however, in practice it is not always easy to draw the line and determine whether conduct is active or passive. That is, where failure to disclose a material fact is calculated to induce a false belief, the distinction between concealment and affirmative representations is tenuous. Both proceed from the same motives and are attended with the same consequences; both are violative of the principles of fair dealing and good faith; both are calculated to produce the same result; and, in fact, both essentially have the same effect.

Still there exists in much of our case law the old tort notion that there can be no liability for nonfeasance. The courts in some jurisdictions, including Florida, hold that where the parties are dealing at arms' length and the facts lie equally open to both parties, with equal opportunity of examination, mere nondisclosure does not constitute a fraudulent concealment. The Fourth District affirmed that rule of law in *Banks v. Salina*, 413 So. 2d 851 (Fla. Dist. Ct. App. 1982), and found that although the sellers had sold a home without disclosing the presence of a defective roof and swimming pool of which the sellers had knowledge, "[i]n Florida", there is no duty to disclose when parties are dealing at arms length." *Id.* at 852.

These unappetizing cases are not in tune with the times and do not conform with current notions of justice, equity and fair dealing. One should not be able to stand behind the impervious shield of *caveat emptor* and take advantage of another's ignorance. Our courts have taken great strides since the days when the judicial emphasis was on rigid rules and ancient precedents. Modern concepts of justice and fair dealing have given our courts the opportunity and latitude to change legal precepts in order to conform to society's needs. Thus, the tendency of the more recent cases has been to restrict rather than extend the doctrine of *caveat emptor*. The law appears to be working toward the ultimate conclusion that full disclosure of all material facts must be made whenever elementary fair conduct demands it.

The harness placed on the doctrine of *caveat emptor* in a number of other jurisdictions has resulted in the seller of a home being liable for failing to disclose material defects of which he is aware. This philosophy was succinctly expressed in *Lingsch v. Savage*, 29 Cal. Rptr. 201 (Ct. App. 1963):

> It is now settled in California that where the seller knows of facts materially affecting the value or desirability of the property which are known or accessible only to him and also knows that such facts are not known to or within the reach of the diligent attention and observation of the buyer, the seller is under a duty to disclose them to the buyer.

In *Posner v. Davis*, 395 N.E.2d 133 (Ill. 1979), buyers brought an action alleging that the sellers of a home fraudulently concealed certain defects in the home which included a leaking roof and basement flooding. Relying on *Lingsch*, the court concluded that the sellers knew of and failed to disclose latent material defects and thus were liable for fraudulent concealment. Numerous other jurisdictions have followed this view in formulating law involving the sale of homes. . . .

We are of the opinion, in view of the reasoning and results in *Lingsch*, *Posner* and the aforementioned cases decided in other jurisdictions, that the same philosophy regarding the sale of homes should also be the law in the state of Florida. Accordingly, we hold that where the seller of a home knows of facts materially affecting the value of the property which are not readily observable and are not known to the buyer, the seller is under a duty to disclose them to the buyer. This duty is equally applicable to all forms of real property, new and used.

In the case at bar, the evidence shows that the Johnsons knew of and failed to disclose that there had been problems with the roof of the house. Mr. Johnson admitted during his testimony that the Johnsons were aware of roof problems prior to entering into the contract of sale and receiving the $5,000 deposit payment. Thus, we agree with the district court and find that the Johnsons' fraudulent concealment also entitles the Davises to the return of the $5,000 deposit payment plus interest. . . .

JOSEPH A. BOYD, JR., Chief Justice, dissenting.

I respectfully but strongly dissent to the Court's expansion of the duties of sellers of real property. This ruling will give rise to a flood of litigation and will facilitate unjust outcomes in many cases. If, as a matter of public policy, the well settled law of this state on this question should be changed, the change should come from the legislature. . . .

Homeowners who attempt to sell their houses are typically in no better position to measure the quality, value, or desirability of their houses than are the prospective purchasers with whom such owners come into contact. Based on this and related considerations, the law of Florida has long been that a seller of real property with improvements is under no duty to disclose all material facts, in the absence of a fiduciary relationship, to a buyer who has an equal opportunity to learn all material information and is not prevented by the seller from doing so. This rule provides sufficient protection against overreaching by sellers. . . .

I do not agree with the Court's belief that the distinction between nondisclosure and affirmative statement is weak or nonexistent. It is a distinction that we should take special care to emphasize and preserve. Imposition of liability for seller's nondisclosure of the condition of improvements to real property is the first step toward making the seller a guarantor of the good condition of the property. . . .

Although as described in the majority opinion this change in the law sounds progressive, high-minded, and idealistic, it is in reality completely unnecessary. Prudent purchasers inspect property, with expert advice if necessary, before they agree to buy. Prudent lenders require inspections before agreeing to provide purchase money. Initial deposits of earnest money can be made with the agreement to purchase being conditional upon the favorable results of expert inspections. It is significant that in the present case the major portion of the purchase price was to be financed by the Johnsons who were to hold a mortgage on the property. If they had been knowingly trying to get rid of what they knew to be a defectively constructed house, it is unlikely that they would have been willing to lend $200,000 with the house in question as their only security.

NOTES AND QUESTIONS

1. *Misrepresentation.* Traditionally, the courts have differentiated misrepresentation, suppression, and nondisclosure as bases for claims of fraud in real estate transactions. An outright lie or *misrepresentation* of facts has always constituted fraud and may give rise to liability for damages as well as a right to rescind the sale. *Misrepresentation* consists of an affirmative statement by the seller or broker to the buyer of a fact (a) that is known to be false, (b) material to the transaction, (c) is reasonably relied on by the buyer in deciding to purchase, and (d) causes damage as a proximate result of the lie. If the misrepresentation is about a condition of the premises that is apparent to the buyer, a fraud claim may be denied on the ground that a reasonable buyer would have inspected the premises and discovered the evident defect, and thus any reliance on the seller's statement was unreasonable.

2. *Fact or opinion.* A recurring issue in misrepresentation cases is whether a statement constitutes a fact or an opinion. For example, the statement that "It's a great house" is often characterized as an opinion, which cannot subject the seller to liability for fraud. In *Ray v. Montgomery*, 399 So. 2d 230 (Ala. 1980), the court held that the statement that a house "was supported by hewn pine timbers, had good support, was 'a nice house,' was solid, and was in good condition" was an opinion and could not constitute fraud, even though the seller knew that the house was afflicted with termite damage. Do you agree?

3. *Suppression.* Courts traditionally held that sellers are under no obligations to disclose defects in the houses they are selling. Real estate sales were governed by the doctrine of *caveat emptor* — let the buyer beware. This doctrine still appears to be the majority rule in the case of *apparent defects.* As long as the seller does not affirmatively lie to the buyer about the condition of the premises (making a fraudulent misrepresentation), buyers are generally charged with notice of what an inspection of the premises would have revealed. *Puget Sound Service Corp. v. Dalarna Management Corp.*, 752 P.2d 1353 (Wash. Ct. App. 1988). However, some courts began to make exceptions to this principle if the buyer acted to *conceal* the defect or other otherwise *suppress knowledge* of it by a potential buyer. *Kracl v. Loseke*, 461 N.W.2d 67 (Neb. 1990); *Restatement (Second) of Torts* §550 (1977).

4. *Nondisclosure.* The traditional rule of *caveat emptor* is still followed in a number of states. *See, e.g., Urman v. South Boston Savings Bank*, 674 N.E.2d 1078 (Mass.

1997) (no common law duty to disclose latent defects; exception if duty is imposed by statute). In recent years, there has been a trend to require sellers and brokers of real estate to disclose information about *latent defects known to the seller* and not readily discoverable by a buyer. The failure to disclose such defects constitutes fraud and will entitle the buyer to rescind the sale and/or obtain damages caused by the fraud. *Shapiro v. Sutherland,* 76 Cal. Rptr.2d 101, 107 (Ct. App. 1998); *Alejandre v. Bull,* 98 P.3d 844, 848 (Wash. Ct. App. 2004). Some states limit this disclosure obligation to defects that pose a danger to the health or safety of persons who come on the land. *Blaylock v. Cary,* 709 So.2d 1128 (Ala. 1997); *Conahan v. Fisher,* 463 N.W.2d 118 (Mich. Ct. App. 1990); *Restatement (Second) of Torts* §353 (1977). Some states go further and require sellers to reveal material facts of which they are aware that materially affect the value or desirability of the property. *Assilzadeh v. Cal. Fed. Bank,* 98 Cal. Rptr.2d 176, 182 (Ct. App. 2000). Some states have imposed disclosure obligations by statute. Cal. Civ. Code §§1102 to 1102.17; N.J. Stat. §§46:3C-1 to -12 (*interpreted by Nobrega v. Edison Glen Assocs.,* 772 A.2d 368 (N.J. 2001)). They have not, however, generally extended this obligation to commercial property. *See, e.g., Futura Realty v. Lone Star Building Centers (Eastern) Inc.,* 578 So. 2d 363 (Fla. Dist. Ct. App. 1991).

5. *What information must be disclosed?* A claim that a defendant fraudulently failed to disclose certain information is premised on the assumption that the defendant had a duty to disclose that information to the plaintiff. This naturally raises the question concerning what information must be disclosed. In general, states that impose liability for nondisclosure require disclosure of nonobvious information that a reasonable buyer would want to know about and that might affect the terms of the transaction — especially the market value of the property — or induce the buyer to back out of the deal. *Chamberlaine & Flowers, Inc. v. McBee,* 356 S.E.2d 626 (W. Va. 1987) (holding that sellers have a duty to disclose "defects or conditions which substantially affect the value or habitability of the property and the existence of which are unknown to the purchaser and would not be disclosed by a reasonably diligent inspection").

Many cases imposing liability on sellers or brokers for fraudulent nondisclosure concern information about defective conditions that pose a risk of harm and that would not be apparent to a reasonable observer. For example, defendants have been found liable for fraudulent nondisclosure when they have failed to disclose that the building was infested by termites, *Obde v. Schlemeyer,* 353 P.2d 672 (Wash. Ct. App. 1960), that the roof leaked, *Chamberlaine & Flowers, Inc. v. McBee, supra,* and that the property was located next to a landfill contaminated with toxic waste and that federal environmental officials had written a report advising against use of the site for human habitation, *Strawn v. Canuso,* 657 A.2d 420 (N.J. 1995), *superseded by* N.J. Stat. §§46:3C-1 to 46:3C-12.

Failure to disclose defective conditions may give rise to liability even when they have not been proven to be dangerous but are nonetheless material to the transaction in the sense that most buyers would want to know about them. *See, e.g., Roberts v. Estate of Barbagallo,* 531 A.2d 1125 (Pa. Super. Ct. 1988) (imposing liability for fraudulent nondisclosure on both the seller and the real estate broker hired by the seller because they failed to reveal that the house was insulated with ureaformaldehyde foam insulation, a substance that had been banned in future house construction by the federal government).

Other kinds of information have also been deemed relevant. For example, in *Reed v. King,* 193 Cal. Rptr. 130 (Ct. App. 1983), the seller was held liable for failing to disclose that a woman and her four children were murdered in the house ten years prior to the sale. In holding that the disclosure of murder would be relevant to most buyers, the court argued, *id*. at 133:

> The murder of innocents is highly unusual in its potential for so disturbing buyers they may be unable to reside in a home where it has occurred. This fact may foreseeably deprive a buyer of the intended use of the purchase. Murder is not such a common occurrence that buyers should be charged with anticipating and discovering this disquieting possibility. Accordingly, the fact is not one for which a duty of inquiry and discovery can sensibly be imposed upon the buyer.

The court argued that one way to demonstrate that a fact is material is to show that knowledge of the fact would affect the market value of the property.

> Reputation and history can have a significant effect on the value of realty. "George Washington slept here" is worth something, however physically inconsequential that consideration may be. Ill-repute or "bad will" conversely may depress the value of property. Failure to disclose such a negative fact where it will have a foreseeably depressing effect on income expected to be generated by a business is tortious.

Id. See also Stambovsky v. Ackley, 572 N.Y.S.2d 672 (App. Div. 1991) (holding that seller had a duty to disclose that the house had a reputation as being haunted when the seller had spread those rumors herself, buyer was not local and had no way of knowing the house's reputation, and the reputation "impaired the value of the contract").

6. *The duty to disclose and the problem of trust.* If contracting parties have no duty to disclose information relevant to a transaction, then they must protect themselves by undertaking an independent investigation. The question whether there is a duty to disclose therefore poses a conflict between self-reliance and reliance on others with whom one enters market relationships. It also presents questions about the extent to which the law should encourage an atmosphere of trust or distrust in contractual relationships.

For example, *Bonnco Petrol, Inc. v. Epstein*, 560 A.2d 655 (N.J. 1989), concerned the sale of a home to a commercial entity. After extended negotiations, the "buyer" agreed to lease the property from the owner with an option to purchase that could be exercised at a specified date. The "seller" entrusted the buyer to amend the written contract drafts to accord with their oral agreement. The buyer, however, included a term in the contract that varied from the oral agreement. The seller skimmed the documents before signing them, relying on the buyer's claim that he amended the documents in accord with the parties' mutual understanding. The court found that the buyer misrepresented, by his silence, that the agreement signed by the seller conformed with earlier samples. The New Jersey Supreme Court concluded: "Silence in the face of an obligation to disclose amounts to equitable fraud." Justice Marie Garibaldi explained: "[I]t matters little that [the seller] failed to read the agreement carefully before signing. 'One who engages in fraud . . . may not urge that one's victim should have been more circumspect or astute.' . . . We find, therefore, that equitable fraud has occurred. There was an inaccurate assertion (in the form of a nondisclosure) as to a material element of the bargain, on which the [sellers] justifiably relied. Their reliance was justifiable because they entrusted the drafting of the documents to [buyer]." *Id.* at 661.

Would it be better to encourage everyone to read a contract carefully before signing? What rule would better reduce transaction costs? Which rule better discourages fraud? What arguments could you make on both sides of these questions?

7. *Legislation.* More than half the states have passed legislation requiring sellers to disclose defects in real property to prospective buyers. However, the obligations vary widely and some states allow sellers to avoid disclosure by getting the buyer to sign a contract disclaiming reliance on any information by the seller. *See* Craig W. Dallon, *Theories of Real Estate Broker Liability and the Effect of the "As Is" Clause,* 54 Fla. L. Rev. 395 (2002); James D. Lawlor, *Seller Beware,* A.B.A. J., August 1990, at 90. Would you favor passage of disclosure legislation in your state? Note that in 1992 Congress passed the *Residential Lead-Based Paint Hazard Reduction Act,* 42 U.S.C. §§4851-4856, requiring sellers and landlords of housing built before 1978 to provide buyers or lessees with a "lead hazard information pamphlet" and to disclose the presence of any known lead-based paint. §4852d. *See* 40 C.F.R. §§745.101 to 745.107.

8. *Waiver.* In *Danann Realty Corp. v. Harris,* 157 N.E.2d 597 (N.Y. 1959), plaintiff alleged that it was induced to lease a building held by defendants because of oral representations, falsely made by the defendants, as to the operating expenses of the building and as to the profits to be derived from the investment. The court quoted the following clause contained in the contract:

> The Purchaser has examined the premises agreed to be sold and is familiar with the physical condition thereof. The Seller has not made and does not make any representations as to the physical condition, rents, leases, *expenses, operation* or any other matter or thing affecting or related to the aforesaid premises, except as herein specifically set forth, and the Purchaser hereby *expressly acknowledges that no such representations have been made, and the Purchaser further acknowledges that it has inspected the premises and agrees to take the premises "as is."* . . . It is understood and agreed that all understandings and agreements heretofore had between the parties hereto are merged in this contract, which alone fully and completely expresses their agreement, *and that the same is entered into after full investigation, neither party relying upon any statement or representation,* not embodied in this contract, made by the other. The Purchaser has inspected the buildings standing on said premises and is thoroughly acquainted with their condition.

Id. at 598 (emphasis supplied by court).

The court held that generally a merger clause stating that the written agreement embodies the whole agreement does not protect the defendant from a claim of fraud. The court distinguished this case, however, noting that the contractual language was more specific, *id.* at 599-600:

> Here . . . plaintiff has in the plainest language announced and stipulated that it is not relying on any representations as to the very matter as to which it now claims it was defrauded. Such a specific disclaimer destroys the allegations in plaintiff's complaint that the agreement was executed in reliance upon these contrary oral representations. . . .
>
> [W]here a person has read and understood the disclaimer of representation clause, he is bound by it. [We have previously held,] as a matter of law, the allegation of plaintiffs "that they relied upon an oral statement made to them in direct contradiction of this provision of the contract." *Ernst Iron Works v. Duralith Corp.,* 200 N.E. 683, 685 (N.Y. 1936). The presence of such a disclaimer clause "is inconsistent with the contention that plaintiff relied upon the misrepresentation, and was led thereby to make the contract." *Kreshover v. Berger,* 119 N.Y.S. 737, 738 (App. Div. 1909). . . .
>
> [T]he plaintiff made a representation in the contract that it was not relying on specific representations not embodied in the contract, while, it now asserts, it was in fact relying on such oral representations. Plaintiff admits then that it is guilty of deliberately misrepresenting to the seller its true intention. To condone this fraud would place the

purchaser in a favored position. This is particularly so, where, as here, the purchaser confirms the contract, but seeks damages. If the plaintiff has made a bad bargain he cannot avoid it in this manner.

If the language here used is not sufficient to estop a party from claiming that he entered the contract because of fraudulent representations, then no language can accomplish that purpose. To hold otherwise would be to say that it is impossible for two businessmen dealing at arm's length to agree that the buyer is not buying in reliance on any representations of the seller as to a particular fact. . . .

Justice Stanley H. Fuld dissented, *id.* at 600, 602, 606:

If a party has actually induced another to enter into a contract by means of fraud. . . . I conceive that language may not be devised to shield him from the consequences of such fraud. The law does not temporize with trickery or duplicity, and this court, after having weighed the advantages of certainty in contractual relations against the harm and injustice which result from fraud, long ago unequivocally declared that "a party who has perpetrated a fraud upon his neighbor may [not] contract with him, in the very instrument by means of which it was perpetrated, for immunity against its consequences, close his mouth from complaining of it, and bind him never to seek redress. Public policy and morality are both ignored if such an agreement can be given effect in a court of justice. The maxim that fraud vitiates every transaction would no longer be the rule, but the exception." *Bridger v. Goldsmith*, 38 N.E. 458, 459 (N.Y. 1894). "In the realm of fact it is entirely possible for a party knowingly to agree that no representations have been made to him, while at the same time believing and relying upon representations which in fact have been made and in fact are false but for which he would not have made the agreement. To deny this possibility is to ignore the frequent instances in everyday experience where parties accept . . . and act upon agreements containing . . . exculpatory clauses in one form or another, but where they do so, nevertheless, in reliance upon the honesty of supposed friends, the plausible and disarming statements of salesmen, or the customary course of business. To refuse relief would result in opening the door to a multitude of frauds and in thwarting the general policy of the law." *Bates v. Southgate*, 31 N.E.2d 551, 558 (Mass. 1941). . . .

The guiding rule [is] that fraud vitiates every agreement which it touches. . . .

Contrary to the intimation in the court's opinion, the nonreliance clause cannot possibly operate as an estoppel against the plaintiff. Essentially equitable in nature, the principle of estoppel is to be invoked to prevent fraud and injustice, not to further them. The statement that the representations in question were not made was, according to the complaint, false to the defendant's knowledge. Surely, the perpetrator of a fraud cannot close the lips of his victim and deny him the right to state the facts as they actually exist. . . .

The *Danann* rule continues to be the law in many jurisdictions. *See Prudential Residential Services Ltd. Partn.*, 849 So.2d 914 (Ala. 2002); *Alires v. McGehee*, 85 P.3d 1191 (Kan. 2004); *Citibank, N.A. v. Plapinger*, 485 N.E.2d 974 (N.Y. 1985) (reaffirming the *Danann* rule). *Compare Janian v. Barnes*, 742 N.Y.S.2d 445 (App. Div. 2002)(specific integration clause stating that the parties are not relying on any oral statements not contained in the written contract bars a claim for fraudulent inducement) *with Dygert v. Leonard*, 525 N.Y.S.2d 436 (App. Div. 1988)("as is" clause does not protect seller from liability in cases of affirmative misrepresentation). *See also* Florrie Young Roberts, *Let the Seller Beware: Disclosures, Disclaimers, and "As Is" Clauses*, 31 Real Estate L.J. 303, 315 (2003).

Other courts, however, reject the *Danann* rule, holding instead that a fraud claim is still available despite an "as is" clause or a "non-reliance" clause when the seller affirmatively lies about the condition of the premises. The Supreme Court of New

Mexico held that a lessee was not precluded from claiming that the landlord fraudu-lently induced it to sign a lease by false statements about the amount of traffic and business at the shopping center, despite the presence of a clause stating that the tenant was not relying on any oral representations made by the lessor.

> Where one party to the contract has perpetrated a fraud upon the other, by means of which the latter was induced to enter into the contract, [one] cannot be precluded from seeking redress by a provision inserted in the contract by the party perpetrating the fraud, designed to shut the mouth of the adverse party as to such fraudulent representations which led up to the making of the contract.

Golden Cone Concepts, Inc. v. Villa Linda Mall, Ltd., 820 P.2d 1323, 1325 (N.M. 1991).

Similarly, in *Mulkey v. Waggoner*, 338 S.E.2d 755 (Ga. Ct. App. 1985), the seller failed to deliver to the purchaser a certificate, required by the contract, declaring the property to be free of termites and termite damage. At the closing, buyer Sheryl Waggoner refused to go ahead unless seller Z. A. Mulkey promised to give her such a certificate to complete the transaction. The seller's broker wrote into the sales con-tract the words: "The sale is as is condition." After the closing, when Waggoner dis-covered wood beetle damage and the fact that Mulkey had hired an exterminator two years earlier, she sued Mulkey for fraud. The court rejected defendant's argument that the "as is" clause in the contract absolutely precluded plaintiff from claiming that defendant had fraudulently induced her to sell. "[W]e are satisfied that an 'as is' clause concerns itself with obvious defects or at least those which are reasonably dis-cernable. . . . Had Mrs. Waggoner purchased the house unseen and accepted it with a patent defect easily exposed, the arguments of Mulkey may have had more validity." The clause could not be used to immunize the seller from liability for false oral state-ments upon which the buyer reasonably relied. *Accord, VSH Realty, Inc. v. Texaco, Inc.*, 757 F.2d 411 (1st Cir. 1985) (applying Massachusetts law) (despite "as is" clause, seller may be liable for fraud for partial disclosure that is misleading or false); *Ron Greenspan Volkswagen, Inc. v. Ford Motor Land Development Corp.*, 38 Cal. Rptr.2d 783, 787 (Ct. App. 1995); *Dito v. Orkin Exterminating Co., Inc*, 2005 Ohio 7, ¶13, 2005 Ohio App. LEXIS 2, **8 (Ohio 2005); *Snyder v. Lovercheck*, 992 P.2d 1079 (Wyo. 1999).

If sellers cannot enclose a clause in the contract of sale stating that the buyer agrees to buy the property "as is" or that the buyer is not relying on any oral statements made by the seller, how can sellers protect themselves from buyers who falsely allege that the seller made an oral statement on which the buyer relied?

9. *Implied warranty in the sale of new residential real estate.* In contrast to the traditional *caveat emptor* doctrine still applicable in some states to the sale of used residential housing, most states now protect buyers of new residential real estate by imposing an implied warranty of habitability. *Albrecht v. Clifford*, 767 N.E.2d 42 (Mass. 2002); *Berish v. Bornstein*, 770 N.E.2d 961 (Mass. 2002). Breach of this warranty may allow the buyer to rescind the sale or obtain damages.

PROBLEM

Sellers of a home seek to move because their ten-year-old son was sexually molested by an older minor boy living next door. The older boy was found guilty of the offense in juvenile court. The sellers feel torn about whether they should disclose this fact to potential buyers. They want to protect any families that might move into the home; at the same time, they know that revealing this information may make it much harder to sell their home. They are also aware that they cannot refuse to sell their home to a family with children because the federal *Fair Housing Act*, 42 U.S.C. §3601, prohibits discrimination against families with children. In addition, they know that juvenile records are supposed to be sealed to protect the identity of juvenile offenders, although they are not directly bound by that confidentiality provision and may lawfully reveal the information. Do they have an obligation to reveal the information? Should they? If they do not have such an obligation, does the broker have a duty to reveal the information?

§9.2.2.2   Seller's Failure to Provide Marketable Title

The purchase and sale agreement ordinarily requires the seller to be able to deliver "marketable title" at the date set for the closing. The seller's inability to do this will excuse the buyer from the deal. What kinds of defects in the title are sufficiently serious to justify allowing the buyer to get out of the deal? In *Conklin v. Davi*, 388 A.2d 598 (N.J. 1978), the validity of the title to a portion of the premises was based on the sellers' claim to have acquired the property by adverse possession. The buyers argued that they were justified in repudiating the agreement in the absence of record title, which the sellers could have acquired either by seeking a deed from the record owner or by bringing suit to quiet title to the property. The court rejected this argument, holding instead that a "marketable title" was one "free from reasonable doubt, but not from every doubt." Title based on adverse possession, the court concluded, is marketable if the adverse possession can be "clearly established." Some purchase and sale agreements require the title to be "valid of record" rather than merely "marketable" or "insurable." A requirement of "record validity" would not be met by an adverse possession claim. Given the possible uncertainties of adverse possession litigation and the fact that buyers may well hesitate to buy property so acquired, should a buyer be forced to conclude the transaction?

The main defects that make the title unmarketable are *encumbrances* and *chain of title defects*. Encumbrances are property interests in persons other than the grantor that seriously affect the value or usability of the property. These include possessory interests, such as conflicting titles and leases, and nonpossessory interests, such as easements, covenants, mortgages, and liens. *Chain of title defects* are mistakes or irregularities in the documents or procedures by which title has been transferred or encumbered over time. For example, a prior deed may turn out to have been forged, or the present deed may misdescribe the property.

§9.2.2.3   Seller's Breach of Warranty of Habitability

It is now well established that an implied warranty of habitability exists in the builder's initial sale of new homes but not in the sale of older homes. *Blagg v. Fred Hunt Co.*, 612 S.W.2d 321 (Ark. 1981); *Albrecht v. Clifford*, 767 N.E.2d 42 (Mass. 2002). *See also Berish v. Bornstein*, 770 N.E.2d 961 (Mass. 2002) (implied warranty of habitability in sale of new condominium unit). The implied warranty goes by many names, including "habitability," "fitness," "quality," or "good workmanship."

§9.2.2.4 Buyer's Failure to Make Good Faith Efforts to Obtain Financing

In *Bushmiller v. Schiller*, 368 A.2d 1044 (Md. Ct. Spec. App. 1977), the buyer changed her mind after signing the purchase and sale agreement and made no serious effort to obtain financing. The buyer argued that her obligations under the contract were contingent on her getting financing and that since she had not obtained financing she was free to back out of the deal and recover her $13,000 deposit. The seller claimed that the agreement contained an implied good faith term under which the buyer impliedly promised to make good faith efforts to obtain financing. Since the buyer failed to do this, the seller argued that he was entitled to keep the $13,000 deposit and to recover damages from the buyer of the difference between the contract price and the lower price at which the seller could sell the property to a third party. The court held that the buyer must undertake "reasonable efforts" to obtain financing and that the buyer was not contractually justified in simply changing her mind about the house.

§9.2.3 REMEDIES FOR BREACH OF THE PURCHASE AND SALE AGREEMENT

§9.2.3.1 Buyer's Remedies

A buyer whose seller has breached the purchase and sale agreement has four remedies.

1. *Specific performance.* The buyer can obtain an injunction ordering the seller to convey the property to the buyer by transferring title in exchange for the agreed-upon contract price. *Marioni v. 94 Broadway, Inc.*, 866 A.2d 208 (N.J. Super. Ct. App. Div. 2005).
2. *Damages.* The buyer may seek damages, measured in most states by the difference between the parcel's market value at the time of breach and contract price (expectation or benefit of the bargain damages), return of the deposit, and any additional expenses occasioned by the breach. A significant number of states, however, follow the English rule of *Flureau v. Thornhill*, 96 Eng. Rep. 638 (1776), and refuse to give the buyer expectation damages if the seller acted in good faith and believed he had good title at the time he entered the agreement; in these situations, the buyer may recover only the deposit, plus expenses. The buyer is entitled to expectation damages only if the seller did not in good faith believe he had good title, willfully or arbitrarily refused to complete the sale, or failed to perfect title when it was easy to do so. On one hand, the good faith rule has been severely criticized for treating real estate contracts differently from other types of contracts without justification. On the other hand, the different treatment has been justified by the difficulties with the recording system and the fact that reasonable sellers may be mistaken about the state of their title.
3. *Rescission.* The buyer may seek to rescind the deal and recover the down payment or deposit.
4. *Vendee's lien.* Rarely used, this remedy is based on the premise that the seller's breach of the purchase and sale agreement creates a debt owed by the seller to the buyer, that is, the amount of the deposit, which is secured by a lien on the

property. The property can therefore be sold to raise the funds to pay back the deposit. 2 Milton R. Friedman, *Contracts and Conveyances of Real Property* §12.2, at 1077-1118 (5th ed. 1991).

§9.2.3.2 Seller's Remedies

The seller whose buyer has breached the purchase and sale agreement also has four remedies.

1. *Specific performance.* The seller may be able to sue the buyer for the purchase price in exchange for the seller's handing over to the buyer the deed to the property, thus forcing the buyer to comply with the terms of the contract. This remedy may not be available everywhere. The theory behind specific performance for the buyer is that land is unique and that a money judgment will not put the buyer in the position she would have been in had the contract been performed. While this is true, money is *not* unique; the seller should not care whether the purchase price comes from the buyer or someone else. Nonetheless, the seller may be able to get specific performance either on the ground of mutuality (each side should have the same options as to remedies) or on the ground of the seller's inability to find another buyer. *But see Kesler v. Marshall,* 792 N.E.2d 893 (Ind. Ct. App. 2003)(denying specific performance to a seller who failed mitigate damages by attempting to find another buyer).

2. *Damages.* The seller may elect to sue for damages, measured by the contract price minus the market price of the parcel at the time of the breach, plus other expenses occasioned by the breach.

3. *Rescission and forfeiture of down payment.* The seller may simply attempt to rescind the deal, keeping the down payment or "earnest money" deposit paid by the buyer. Usually, the purchase and sale agreement explicitly provides the seller with the right to keep the down payment if the buyer breaches the contract. *See, e.g., Uzan v. 845 UN Ltd. P'ship,* 778 N.Y.S.2d 171 (App. Div. 2004) (seller could retain a deposit that amounted to 25 percent of the purchase price and exceeded $8 million when the buyer refused to go ahead with the deal).

4. *Vendor's lien.* Rarely used, this remedy presumes that the property belongs equitably to the buyer, who is obligated to purchase the property; it also presumes that the seller has a lien on the buyer's equitable title and that the property can be sold to satisfy the buyer's obligation to pay the rest of the purchase price to the seller. 2 Milton R. Friedman, *Contracts and Conveyances of Real Property* §12.1, at 1029-1077 (5th ed. 1991).

§9.2.4 RISK OF LOSS DURING THE EXECUTORY PERIOD: EQUITABLE CONVERSION

What happens if the house burns down during the executory period after the purchase and sale agreement has been signed but before the closing? Who bears the risk of loss — the seller or the buyer — if the contract does not answer this question? Must the buyer complete the transaction despite the loss, or may the buyer rescind and get her earnest money deposit back? Many courts hold that the risk of loss is on the buyer, under the doctrine of *equitable conversion*. Because the buyer has the equitable right to have the contract specifically enforced, for certain purposes it is appropriate to treat the buyer *as if* the transaction had already been completed. Thus, courts have often treated the buyer as the equitable owner during the executory period, despite the fact that the seller may retain the right to possess the property until the closing. *See, e.g., Continental Insurance Co. v. Brown*, 630 F. Supp. 302 (W.D. Va. 1986). This rule, however, has been subject to much criticism. "To say that equity will specifically enforce the contract certainly does not compel one to disregard reality and view the contract as already performed." William B. Stoebuck & Dale A. Whitman, *The Law of Property* §10.13 at 787 (3d ed. 2000). Moreover, this allocation of the risk rarely comports with the parties' expectations. In addition, the seller is much more likely to have insurance than the buyer. Finally, the seller is certainly in a better position to exercise care to avoid the loss. For these reasons, some courts have begun to reject the doctrine and place the risk of loss during the executory period on the seller, thereby allowing the buyer to get out of the deal. *Skelly Oil Co. v. Ashmore*, 365 S.W.2d 582 (Mo. 1963). This is also the approach taken by the *Uniform Vendor and Purchaser Risk Act*, which has been adopted in ten states. William B. Stoebuck & Dale A. Whitman, *The Law of Property* §10.13 at 795 (3d ed. 2000).

In practice, most purchase and sale agreements explicitly place the risk of loss on the vendor, and, in any event, most vendors have homeowner's insurance. In states that retain the equitable conversion principle, forcing the buyer to complete the contract at the agreed-upon price, is the seller entitled to keep the insurance proceeds for which he paid? Even if the risk of loss is not explicitly placed on the seller, most courts will not tolerate the seller's getting both the purchase price and the insurance proceeds, while the buyer pays full market value and gets a burned-out property. Instead, the courts are likely to impose a constructive trust on the insurance proceeds and require that the purchase price be reduced by the amount of those proceeds so that the seller does not receive a windfall.

§9.3 Deeds and Title Protection

§9.3.1 FORMALITIES

§9.3.1.1 Essential Terms

The deed must (1) identify the parties; (2) describe the property being conveyed; (3) state the grantor's intent to convey the property interest in question; and (4) contain the grantor's signature. The deed need not be recorded to transfer title; delivery of the deed to the grantee is sufficient. Most deeds are — and should be — recorded to protect the grantee's rights. To be recorded, most states require the deed to be acknowledged by a public notary or other official and some require one or more witnesses to the transaction. Thus, although *acknowledgments* are not necessary to transfer title (except in a few states), they usually accompany the transfer of the deed to enable the deed to be recorded.

The land being conveyed must be described in the deed. *See Firma, Inc. v. Twillman*, 126 S.W.3d 790 (Mo. Ct. App. 2004)(deed invalid when it failed to describe the property with reasonable certainty). The description must be sufficiently precise to locate the boundaries of the property. Those boundaries may be defined by reference to official surveys, "plats," or by "metes and bounds." Most of the land in the United States has been surveyed under the Government Survey System devised by Thomas Jefferson and first adopted by the Continental Congress in 1785. The system divides the land by a series of north-south and east-west lines and defines so-called townships, which are further subdivided into "sections."[1] These sections may be further divided into halves and quarters, or even smaller divisions. Property can be located within these quarter sections by reference to these official land parcels.

Property may also be described by a "plat" or subdivision map. A plat is a map produced by a private developer (not a government official) that describes the lots being created in a subdivision. These lots are generally the ones that actually will be bought and sold; their borders are often not straight. Often the subdivision is given a name and divided into "Blocks" with each Block being further subdivided into "lots." The plat is generally approved by a local agency before being filed in the recording office. Deeds may then describe the lot being sold by reference to the plat. So, for example, a lot being conveyed might be described as Block G, Lot 1 of Gerry's Landing Subdivision, recorded at Middletown County Registry of Deeds, Plat 46, in Plat Book 114, Page 75.

Property may also be described by "metes and bounds." This system starts at a defined point (usually described by a natural or artificial "monument" such as a fence or a street edge) and identifies the direction and distance of the first border, then the second border, and so on, until returning to the original point. In effect, it describes how one would walk around the borders of the property. Direction is notated in degrees (and minutes and seconds) east or west of due north or south. The convention is to state north or south first and then describe the east or west deviation. So a border that runs in a northwesterly direction would be notated as "North 45 degrees West 30 feet." Subsequent borders take a similar form until one returns to the starting place.

These approaches to land descriptions may be combined with the general location stated as the southwest quarter of a Township on the Government Survey and the particular lot described by a plat and/or a metes and bounds description. If a deed contains a mistaken description of the property, either party may sue to reform the deed.

§9.3.1.2 Delivery

A deed must be delivered to the grantee to effectuate a transfer of ownership. The purpose of the delivery requirement is to ensure that the grantor intends to part with the property and to clarify who owns it. When property is sold, this requirement usually raises no problems since few people will hand over such a large sum of money as the purchase price for real property without getting something in return. When, however, people give real property as a gift, ordinarily to family members, problems of delivery are common.

---

1. William B. Stoebuck & Dale A. Whitman, *The Law of Property* §11.2, at 821-822 (3d ed. 2000). The major north-south lines are called principal meridians, and the major east-west lines are called base lines. Parallel to the principal meridians at 6 mile intervals are north-south lines that divide the land into "ranges." Parallel to the base lines are east-west lines that divide the land into "townships." This system creates six-mile squares also referred to as "townships." Each township is divided in to 36 "sections." *Id.* at §11.2, at 774-775.

First, a person sometimes obtains physical possession of a deed, and may even record the deed, when the owner does not intend to transfer ownership. Possession of the deed or recording it, or both, may give rise to a *presumption* that the grantor intended to transfer ownership of the land. Most courts hold that this presumption can be overcome by extrinsic evidence that the original owner did not intend to transfer ownership, such as oral testimony that the owner intended to transfer ownership only at her death or evidence of an installment land contract, providing that the buyer would obtain title only after all payments are made to the seller. *Salter v. Hamiter*, 887 So. 2d 230 (Ala. 2004); *Blancett v. Blancett*, 102 P.3d 640 (N.M. 2004); *Sofsky v. Rosenberg*, 564 N.E.2d 662 (N.Y. 1990); *Jorgensen v. Crow*, 466 N.W.2d 120 (N.D. 1991). *See In re Estate of Hardy*, 805 So.2d 515 (Miss. 2002) (recording deed creates presumption of delivery but no delivery was found when grantor retained deeds until her death, they were found in her purse, and there was no other evidence of intent to transfer title). (Delivery of a deed is conclusive evidence of intent to transfer a current interest in the land; extrinsic evidence is admissible only to show fraudulent inducement.)

Second, someone may make out a deed in front of a notary public granting ownership of her home to her daughter, place the deed in a safety deposit box in her bank, and tell her daughter that she has given her the property on the condition that the daughter allow her to continue living in the house until her death. What happens if the woman then dies without having shown the deed to her daughter and leaving a will providing that her property be divided equally between her daughter and her son? The son claims a half interest in the house; her daughter claims that she owns it because her mother gave it to her before she died. Has the deed been "delivered"?

Some courts are reluctant to find delivery unless the deed has been physically handed over to the donee or to a third party who has instructions to deliver the deed. *Williams v. Cole*, 760 S.W.2d 944 (Mo. Ct. App. 1988). Most courts, oddly enough, find that "delivery" can occur even if the deed is not physically delivered to the donee. Rather, they adopt a doctrine of *constructive delivery* and hold that writing a deed and engaging in conduct that demonstrates an intent to transfer ownership is sufficient to constitute delivery. An intent to transfer ownership is more likely to be established if the deed is physically deposited in a safety deposit box or with a third party. *Kresser v. Peterson*, 675 P.2d 1193 (Utah 1984). Many courts hold that delivery of a deed to a third party, such as an attorney, with instructions to hand over the deed to the grantee at the grantor's death constitutes delivery of a vested remainder to the grantee, with a life estate retained by the grantor. *Pipes v. Sevier*, 694 S.W.2d 918 (Mo. Ct. App. 1985). Which rule strikes you as the better approach?

§9.3.2 TITLE COVENANTS

§9.3.2.1 Warranties of Title

Perhaps the most important elements of a real estate transaction are the seller's ability to convey title to the property to the buyer and the buyer's ability to rest assured that the buyer's ownership rights will be secure against other claimants. The buyer (or the mortgage lender's lawyer) will certainly want to search the seller's record title. But, as we will discover in the next section, the title search may not reveal some important defects in the chain of title. For this reason, the buyer may want additional assurances.

One form of additional assurance is the *title covenant* or *warranty of title* contained in the deed. Six standard covenants have developed and are explained below.

Present covenants. These covenants are breached, if at all, at the time of the conveyance (the closing). That is when the statute of limitations starts to run.

1. *Covenant of seisin.* This covenant is the grantor's promise that he owns the property interest (the estate) he is purporting to convey to the grantee. Thus, an owner of a leasehold would breach this covenant if he purported to convey a fee simple. Similarly, an owner of a one-half interest as a tenant in common would breach the covenant if he purported to convey full ownership of the property as a sole fee simple owner.

2. *Covenant of the right to convey.* This constitutes the grantor's promise that he has the power to transfer the interest purportedly conveyed to the grantee. Although in most cases the same as the covenant of seisin, it might differ in several instances. For example, a life estate burdened by an enforceable restraint on alienation would violate this covenant if the owner purported to convey it to the grantee. Similarly, if the property were adversely possessed by someone other than the seller, the seller would have record title (seisin) of the property but not the right to convey it.

3. *Covenant against encumbrances.* This is the grantor's promise that no mortgages, leases, liens, unpaid property taxes, or easements encumber the property other than those acknowledged in the deed itself.

Future covenants. These covenants are breached, if at all, after the closing, when the disturbance to the grantee's possession occurs. The statute of limitations starts to run when the grantee's possession is disturbed.

4. *Covenant of warranty.* By this covenant, the grantor promises to compensate the grantee for any monetary losses occasioned by the grantor's failure to convey the title promised in the deed.
    a. *General warranty deed.* A general warranty deed covenants against all defects in title.
    b. *Special warranty deed.* A special warranty deed limits the covenant to defects in title caused by the grantor's own acts but not by the acts of prior owners.
    c. *Quitclaim deed.* This is the name generally used for a deed that contains no warranty (or covenant) of title whatsoever. It purports to convey whatever interests in the property are owned by the grantor. It does not, however, promise that the grantor *in fact* owns the property interest that the grantor claims to own — or, indeed, any interest. It suffices to transfer whatever property interests the grantor has to the grantee, but does not provide the buyer with any real assurance that the grantor has the right to convey the interest the grantor purports to convey.

5. *Covenant of quiet enjoyment.* The grantor promises by this covenant that the grantee's possession will not be disturbed by any other claimant with a superior lawful title. This covenant is substantially the same as the covenant of warranty.

6. *Covenant for further assurances.* Rarely used, this covenant requires the seller to take further steps to cure defects in the grantor's title, such as paying an adverse possessor to leave the property or paying the owner of an encumbrance to release the encumbrance.

Some states have standardized the covenants by statute. These covenants may be contained in the deed by reference to the statute in which they are defined. They are thereby incorporated into the deed by reference.

§9.3.2.2   Remedies for Breach of Warranty of Title

The most widely used covenant is the covenant of warranty. If it turns out that the seller did not have the right to convey the property interest the deed purported to convey, the buyer can sue the seller for breach of the warranty of title. This covenant runs with the land and can be enforced by subsequent grantees as well. The damages for breach of the covenants of warranty, seisin, right to convey, and quiet enjoyment are generally measured by the *price* paid for the property that has been lost. This price is generally near the fair market value of the property *at the time of the closing.*

If the breach is discovered after the closing, the ousted buyer will not be able to recover the market value of the property at the time the buyer was ousted; moreover, the market value may be much higher than the original price. This result has often been criticized since it may very well not leave the buyer in the position the buyer would have been in had the original contract been performed; if the price of land has been rising since the closing, the buyer may not be able to purchase a similar piece of property for the same amount the buyer paid for the premises from which she was ousted. William B. Stoebuck & Dale A. Whitman, *The Law of Property* §11.13, at 913-914 (3d ed. 2000). At the same time, allowing the buyer to obtain from the seller more than the value paid places an uncertain and possibly onerous obligation on the seller for many years into the future. The availability of title insurance may suggest a better way to handle the problem.

The damages for breach of the covenant against encumbrances is either the cost of removing the encumbrance (that is, paying off the mortgage or buying out the covenant or easement) or the difference between the value of the property without the encumbrance and with it.

§9.3.3   RECORDING ACTS

§9.3.3.1   The Recording System

The recording system is intended to provide buyers of real property with the security of knowing that they will really own the property interests they are buying. They can use the system to find out whether the person purporting to own and sell the property indeed owns it and to ensure that neither the owner nor any of his predecessors in interest has conveyed to someone else all or part of the property interests that the seller has contracted to sell to the buyer.

Every state has passed a recording act, which provides for a central registry at each locality — often at the county level of government — where holders of real property interests can submit copies of deeds, mortgages, leases, easements, general plans, condominium declarations, judgment liens, and the like. Submitting a deed to the registry is called *recording the deed.*

The common law rule existing before the recording system was "first in time, first in right." This rule was based on the theory that the grantor could not convey what she did not own; once the property interest had been transferred to the first grantee, the grantor had nothing left to convey to the subsequent grantee.

Recording acts change the common law rule by defining the circumstances under which a buyer who has recorded his interest in the proper registry of deeds will prevail over a buyer who did not properly protect his interest by recording his deed. In general, a *subsequent purchaser who has no notice of a prior conveyance and who records his interest will prevail over any prior unrecorded interest.* Recording acts also define priorities when recorded deeds conflict. In general, a *purchaser who has no notice of a prior conveyance and records his deed is protected against any conflicting claimants who record their interests later.*

Recording acts define the property interests that may be recorded. Many statutes, for example, provide for recording only long-term leases. In cases of property interests not covered by the recording act, the common law rule of "first in time, first in right" applies.

It is important to recognize that recording acts do not *require* that a deed be recorded for a conveyance to be legally valid. The deed is valid against the grantor upon delivery with or without recording. When the seller delivers the deed to the buyer, the buyer becomes the lawful owner of the property — at least in the absence of conflicting claims by other grantees. The seller cannot dispossess the buyer on the ground that the seller's deed (received from the seller's grantor) was recorded but that the grantee had not yet recorded her deed. Similarly, a month-to-month tenant could not defend against an eviction proceeding brought by the new owner on the ground that the new owner had not recorded her deed and therefore did not own the property.

The function of recording ordinarily is to *adjudicate disputes* between multiple claimants to the same property by defining *priorities*. These priorities define whose interest will prevail in different kinds of disputes. Usually these disputes involve *multiple grantees* who have been granted the same interests by a common grantor. Sometimes, however, disputes arising between grantors and grantees do involve the recording system. For example, if the grantor purports to convey an interest that the grantor does not own and the grantor later obtains a deed to the property, the doctrine of *estoppel by deed* operates to vest the grantor's interest immediately in the grantee. This is generally true even if the grantor records her deed before the grantee records her deed.

The recording system will not protect the grantee against all risk. In many places, the buyer may have to check other parts of the court system to determine whether a lawsuit being brought affects ownership of the property, a will being probated affects the title, or a divorce proceeding being filed by the owners results in changes in property rights. Other points to check are whether the owner has declared bankruptcy and whether the tax authorities are planning to place a lien on the property to collect unpaid property taxes. Further, the recording system will not protect a buyer against a claim of adverse possession; for this reason, the buyer must investigate to determine whether any such claims may be in the wings. Finally, it is important to note that recording systems generally protect only buyers, not donees (the recipients of gifts).

Thus, if the donor gives the same property as a gift to two different people, the first donee wins under the common law rule.

§9.3.3.2 How to Conduct a Title Search

It is impossible for a buyer to find all the interests affecting a particular parcel of land without referring to some kind of index. It also is impossible for the system to work unless the buyer can limit his search to places where conflicting deeds are likely to be found; otherwise, a search of the hundreds of thousands of documents would be endless.

The simplest way to index and research the title is to file information by *tract*. Given the mathematical precision with which physical descriptions of the geographic bounds of each parcel of property can be made, it is possible to create a tract system whereby the buyer can find, in one place, all interests that purport to affect the title to that particular tract. The problem is that this is not how the recording system started, and converting to a tract system would be quite expensive. Most places do not have a tract index.

The typical recording office uses a *grantor-grantee index*. Separate files are kept for grantors and grantees. In the *grantor index*, all instruments are listed both alphabetically and chronologically by the grantor's last name. In the *grantee index*, all instruments are listed both alphabetically and chronologically by the grantee's last name. A deed from Johann Sebastian Bach to Wolfgang Mozart would be indexed under the name "Bach" in the grantor index and the name "Mozart" in the grantee index. The recording office ordinarily compiles volumes that cover particular time periods. For example, conveyances by grantors may be divided into one volume that includes conveyances made between 1900 and 1910, a second volume for the years 1910 to 1920, and so on. More recent conveyances may be grouped by year, and very recent conveyances by month and by day. The recent conveyances are later compiled in master volumes like those of the older conveyances to simplify the search process by limiting the number of places in which one must look.

The index describes the bare outlines of each transaction, including the grantor and grantee, a description of the land, the type of interest conveyed, the date recorded, and the book and page numbers where a copy of the document can be found. The title searcher must then look at each complete document.

Suppose you are planning to buy a house from J. S. Bach. You want to find out if and how Bach obtained title to the property. You would therefore *start in the grantee index* to find who his grantor was. You start in the present in the grantee index and go backward until you find a deed to Bach conveying the property in question. You find a reference to a deed in 1983 from Ludwig van Beethoven. To find out how Beethoven obtained his title, you look backward in the grantee index from 1983 until you find a conveyance to Beethoven. You continue this process until you have gone back far enough to assure yourself that the title will be good. The practice in each locality differs on how far back to go. It may be to look backward for 50 or 60 years, or until the beginning of the twentieth century, or until a title can be traced to some sovereign. In most places, the practice is not to go all the way back to the beginning of the recording system but some lesser number of years. Marketable title acts may describe a time period beyond which interests are lost if they are not re-recorded. When you are done, you have a list of grantors who are predecessors in interest of Bach.

Suppose you have gone back to 1900 to find a deed from Elizabeth Cady Stanton. You now switch to the *grantor index* and go forward in time under the name of *each grantor* you have found, starting on the date that grantor acquired her interest and going forward until you find an instrument conveying that interest to a subsequent grantee. The period for each search starts when the grantor *acquired* her interest (the date of *execution* of the first deed giving title to the grantor) and stops on the date a new conveyance of that interest is *recorded*. It is important to note that the search in the grantor index starts at the date of *execution* rather than at the date of *recording*. This is because the grantor may have mortgaged the property or encumbered it after acquiring it (after receiving the deed at the closing) but before recording her deed.

§9.3.3.3   Types of Recording Acts

As mentioned previously, each state has its own recording statute. The wording of the statute, as well as court interpretations of it, must be examined in detail to determine how it will apply to a particular dispute. Generally, recording acts are divided into three basic types: (1) race, (2) notice, and (3) race-notice.

Race statutes.   Under a race statute, as between successive purchasers of Blackacre, the person who records first prevails — she has won the race to the registry. This is true even if the person who records first *knows* about an earlier conveyance to someone else. These statutes exist only in a few states.

O conveys Blackacre to *A*, who does not record. *O* subsequently conveys Blackacre a second time to *B*. *B* knows of the earlier conveyance to *A*. *B* records the deed from *O* to *B*. In a lawsuit between *A* and *B*, *B* prevails.

An example of a race statute is N.C. Gen. Stat. §47-18(a):

> No (i) conveyance of land, or (ii) contract to convey, or (iii) option to convey, or (iv) lease of land for more than three years shall be valid to pass any property interest as against lien creditors or purchasers for a valuable consideration from the donor, bargainor or lessor but from the time of registration thereof in the county where the land lies, or if the land is located in more than one county, then in each county where any portion of the land lies to be effective as to the land in that county.

Notice statutes.   Under a notice statute, a subsequent purchaser prevails over an earlier purchaser only if the subsequent purchaser did not have notice of the earlier conveyance. Further, the notice statute protects any purchaser without notice against prior unrecorded interests even if the purchaser does not record first. For example:

O conveys Blackacre to *A*, who does not record. *O* then conveys Blackacre to *B*. *B* has no knowledge of the earlier conveyance from *O* to *A*. *B* prevails over *A* even though *B* does not record the deed from *O* to *B*. *B* also prevails over *A* even if *A* later records her deed from *O* to *A* before *B* records her deed from *O* to *B*.

An example of a notice statute is Iowa Code Ann. §558.41:

> An instrument affecting real estate is of no validity against subsequent purchasers for a valuable consideration, without notice,... unless the instrument is filed and recorded in the county in which the real estate is located, as provided in this chapter.

Race-notice statutes. Under a race-notice statute, a subsequent purchaser prevails over prior unrecorded interests only if she (1) had no notice of the prior conveyance at the time she acquired her interest and (2) records before the prior instrument is recorded. For example:

O conveys Blackacre to *A*, who does not record. *O* then conveys Blackacre to *B*. *B* has no knowledge of the earlier conveyance from *O* to *A*. *A* records; then *B* records. *A* prevails over *B* because, even though *B* did not have notice of *A*'s deed, *A* recorded before *B* did.

An example of a race-notice statute is Wash. Rev. Code §65.08.070:

> A conveyance of real property, when acknowledged by the person executing the same (the acknowledgment being certified as required by law), may be recorded in the office of the recording officer of the county where the property is situated. Every such conveyance not so recorded is void as against any subsequent purchaser or mortgagee in good faith and for a valuable consideration from the same vendor, his heirs or devisees, of the same real property or any portion thereof whose conveyance is first duly recorded. . . .

About half the states have notice statutes, and about half the states have race-notice statutes. *Thompson on Real Property, Thomas Edition* §92.13(b) (David A. Thomas ed. 1994).

§9.3.3.4   Chain of Title Problems

SABO v. HORVATH

559 P.2d 1038 (Alaska 1976)

ROBERT BOOCHEVER, Chief Justice. . . .

. . . Grover C. Lowery occupied land in the Chitna Recording District on October 10, 1964 for purposes of obtaining Federal patent. Lowery filed a location notice on February 24, 1965, and made his application to purchase on June 6, 1967 with the Bureau of Land Management (BLM). On March 7, 1968, the BLM field examiner's report was filed which recommended that patent issue to Lowery. On October 7, 1969, a request for survey was made by the United States Government. On January 3, 1970, Lowery issued a document entitled "Quitclaim Deed" to the Horvaths; Horvath recorded the deed on January 5, 1970 in the Chitna Recording District. Horvath testified that when he bought the land from Lowery, he knew patent and title were still in the United States Government, but he did not rerecord his interest after patent had passed to Lowery.

Following the sale to the Horvaths, further action was taken by Lowery and the BLM pertaining to the application for patent and culminating in issuance of the patent on August 10, 1973.

Almost immediately after the patent was issued, Lowery advertised the land for sale in a newspaper. He then executed a second document also entitled "quitclaim" to the Sabos on October 15, 1973. The Sabos duly recorded this document on December 13, 1973.

Luther Moss, a representative of the BLM, testified to procedures followed under the *Alaska Homesite Law* (43 U.S.C. §687a (1970)). After numerous steps, a plat is approved and the claimant notified that he should direct publication of his claim. In this case, Lowery executed his conveyance to the Horvaths after the BLM field report had recommended patent.

The first question this court must consider is whether Lowery had an interest to convey at the time of his transfer to the Horvaths. . . .

[W]e hold that at the time Lowery executed the deed to the Horvaths he had complied with the statute to a sufficient extent so as to have an interest in the land which was capable of conveyance.

Since the Horvaths received a valid interest from Lowery, we must now resolve the conflict between the Horvaths' first recorded interest and the Sabos' later recorded interest.

The Sabos, like the Horvaths, received their interest in the property by a quit-claim deed. They are asserting that their interest supersedes the Horvaths under Alaska's statutory recording system. Alaska Stat. §34.15.290 provides that:

> A conveyance of real property . . . is void as against a subsequent innocent purchaser . . . for a valuable consideration of the property . . . whose conveyance is first duly recorded. An unrecorded instrument is valid . . . as against one who has actual notice of it.

Initially, we must decide whether the Sabos, who received their interest by means of a quitclaim deed, can ever be "innocent purchaser[s]" within the meaning of Alaska Stat. §34.15.290. Since a "quitclaim" only transfers the interest of the grantor, the question is whether a "quitclaim" deed itself puts a purchaser on constructive notice. Although the authorities are in conflict over this issue, the clear weight of authority is that a quitclaim grantee can be protected by the recording system, assuming, of course, the grantee purchased for valuable consideration and did not otherwise have actual or constructive knowledge as defined by the recording laws. We choose to follow the majority rule and hold that a quitclaim grantee is not precluded from attaining the status of an "innocent purchaser."

In this case, the Horvaths recorded their interest from Lowery prior to the time the Sabos recorded their interest. Thus, the issue is whether the Sabos are charged with constructive knowledge because of the Horvaths' prior recordation. Horvath is correct in his assertion that in the usual case a prior recorded deed serves as constructive notice pursuant to Alaska Stat. §34.15.290, and thus precludes a subsequent recordation from taking precedence. Here, however, the Sabos argue that because Horvath recorded his deed prior to Lowery having obtained patent, they were not given constructive notice by the recording system. They contend that since Horvaths' recordation was outside the chain of title, the recording should be regarded as a "wild deed."

It is an axiom of hornbook law that a purchaser has notice only of recorded instruments that are within his "chain of title." If a grantor (Lowery) transfers prior to obtaining title, and the grantee (Horvath) records prior to title passing, a second grantee who diligently examines all conveyances under the grantor's name from the date that the grantor had secured title would not discover the prior conveyance. The rule in most jurisdictions which have adopted a grantor-grantee index system of recording is that a "wild deed" does not serve as constructive notice to a subsequent purchaser who duly records.

Alaska's recording system utilizes a "grantor-grantee" index. Had Sabo searched title under both grantor's and grantee's names but limited his search to the chain of title subsequent to patent, he would not be chargeable with discovery of the pre-patent transfer to Horvath.

On one hand, we could require Sabo to check beyond the chain of title to look for pretitle conveyances. While in this particular case the burden may not have been great, as a general rule, requiring title checks beyond the chain of title could add a significant burden as well as uncertainty to real estate purchases. To a certain extent, requiring title searches of records prior to the date of a grantor acquired title would thus defeat the purposes of the recording system. The records as to each grantor in the chain of title would theoretically have to be checked back to the later of the grantor's date of birth or the date when records were first retained.

On the other hand, we could require Horvath to rerecord his interest in the land once title passes, that is, after patent had issued to Lowery. As a general rule, rerecording an interest once title passes is less of a burden than requiring property purchasers to check indefinitely beyond the chain of title.

It is unfortunate that in this case due to Lowery's double conveyances, one or the other party to this suit must suffer an undeserved loss. We are cognizant that in this case, the equities are closely balanced between the parties to this appeal. Our decision, however, in addition to resolving the litigants' dispute, must delineate the requirements of Alaska's recording laws.

Because we want to promote simplicity and certainty in title transactions, we choose to follow the majority rule and hold that the Horvaths' deed, recorded outside the chain of title, does not give constructive notice to the Sabos and is not "duly recorded" under the *Alaskan Recording Act*, Alaska Stat. §34.15.290. Since the Sabos' interest is the first duly recorded interest and was recorded without actual or constructive knowledge of the prior deed, we hold that the Sabos' interest must prevail. . . .

NOTES AND QUESTIONS

1. *Notice.* In both notice and race-notice jurisdictions, only subsequent purchasers without notice of the earlier conveyance can prevail over the earlier grantee. Actual notice obviously violates this condition. But the import of the recording system is that *constructive notice* will also deprive a subsequent purchaser of protection. Constructive notice exists when the grantee, by conducting a reasonable title search, would have discovered the earlier conveyance. Problems may arise if a deed is recorded incorrectly; misspelling of a name or a clerical error in indexing the deed may result in a finding that a later purchaser was not on constructive notice of the prior conveyance. *Antonis v. Liberati*, 821 A.2d 666 (Pa. Commw. Ct. 2003). *But see First Citizens Nat'l Bank v. Sherwood*, 817 A.2d 501 (Pa. Super. Ct. 2003)(electronic indeces broaden search obligations so that a mortgage improperly recorded under the name of the beneficiary of a trust rather than the trustee was still found to provide constructive notice). *Inquiry notice* will be imputed if the subsequent purchaser would have discovered the conveyance had she acted reasonably to investigate facts at her disposal. If the property is being occupied by someone other than the grantor, for example, a purchaser is on inquiry notice that a prior claim may be hanging around. Inquiry notice will also exist if a recorded instrument refers to another property interest, such as a lease, condominium declaration, or general plan.

2. *Estoppel by deed. Sabo v. Horvath* concerns a dispute between two grantees. What would have happened if the grantor, Lowery, had claimed ownership of the

property as against the first grantees, the Horvaths, when the grantor finally received the patent from the government? The doctrine of *estoppel by deed* would enable the grantees to prevail. If a grantor purports to convey a property interest she does not own to a grantee, and the grantor subsequently comes to own the property interest by receiving the deed, ownership is automatically vested in the grantee. Thus, if *O* purports to convey property to *A*, but *O* does not own the property, *A* gets nothing; one can convey only what one owns. However, if *O* later obtains title to the property from *OO*, the doctrine of estoppel by deed vests title immediately in *A*. *O* is estopped from asserting ownership rights as against *A*.[2]

3. *Wild deeds. Sabo v. Horvath* deals with a peculiar version of the more general problem of deeds outside the "chain of title." This problem arises because it is impractical to require all buyers to search every one of the hundreds of thousands of deeds in the entire recording index. To make the search manageable, customary practice limits the search to the period between the date the grantor obtained his deed and the date a deed out from that grantor was recorded. Because it is sometimes possible that a predecessor in interest made a conveyance outside that period — either before or after — and because some buyers do not diligently record their interest, it is possible that some deeds relating to the property in question will not be found. Some deeds are recorded *too early* to appear in the chain of title (before a grantor obtained title to the property); others are recorded *too late* to be discovered (after a deed from that grantor was recorded).

   a. *Recorded too early. O* conveys property to *A* that *O* does not own. *A* records the deed. *OO*, the true owner, conveys the property to *O*. At this point, the property transfers automatically to *A* under the doctrine of estoppel by deed. However, unbeknownst to *A*, *O* then conveys title to *X*, a bona fide purchaser who has no knowledge of the conveyance from *O* to *A*. The majority of states will handle the situation just as the Alaska Supreme Court did. In these states, the first purchaser, *A*, would prevail in a contest between herself and the grantor, *O*. However, *X*, the second purchaser without notice of the earlier conveyance to *A*, would prevail in a contest with the first purchaser, *A*. This result obtains because *X* is required to search the records only so far back as the date when her grantor, *O*, acquired her interest; since *O* had purported to convey the interest to *A* *before O* obtained her title from *OO*, *X* would not be charged with notice of the conveyance to *A*. This result, of course, protects the interests of the second bona fide purchaser, *X*, at the expense of the earlier bona fide purchaser, *A*, perhaps on the ground that *A* acted negligently in purchasing property from someone who did not in fact possess the right to convey it.

   Some states require a more extended search on the part of the subsequent grantee; in these states, the doctrine of estoppel by deed is extended to apply to disputes not only between the grantor and the first grantee but between the first grantee and subsequent grantees. Under this theory, when the grantor gets the deed to the property already conveyed to the first grantee, title automatically passes to the first grantee, leaving the grantor nothing to convey to the subsequent purchaser.

---

2. This situation is analogous, but not identical, to the situation that obtained in *Sabo*. It is analogous only because the court concluded in *Sabo* that the grantor, Lowery, had undertaken sufficient acts under the federal statute to be considered the owner of the property conveyed to the first purchaser.

b. *Recorded too late.* O conveys to A, who does not record. A conveys to B, who records. O then conveys to Z, a bona fide purchaser without notice of the earlier conveyance from O to A. B then gets ahold of the deed from O to A and records it. In a contest between B and Z, Z would prevail because the deed from O to A was recorded too late. When Z bought the property, the deed from A to B had already been recorded, but since A had not yet recorded the deed from O to A, there is no way that Z could have found it. Neither A nor B was in O's chain of title at the time Z purchased, so Z had no way to learn of the conveyance to B.

Here is a second example. O conveys to A, who does not record. O then conveys to X, who has notice of the earlier conveyance to A. X records her deed; then A records her deed. X conveys to Z, who has no notice of the earlier conveyance to A. In a contest between A and Z, Z would prevail because the deed from O to A was recorded too late. Can you see why?

4. *Shelter doctrine.* The shelter doctrine allows a bona fide purchaser to convey property to a third party even if the third party is on notice of an earlier conveyance. For example, O conveys to A, who does not record. O then conveys to X, a bona fide purchaser without notice of the conveyance to A; X records. Because X had no notice of the earlier conveyance to A, and because X recorded first, X would prevail over A in either a notice jurisdiction or a race-notice jurisdiction. X then wants to convey to C, but C has notice of the earlier conveyance to from O to A. The *shelter doctrine* allows X to convey the property to C, despite C's knowledge of the earlier conveyance. This doctrine allows bona fide purchasers to convey title even if they subsequently find out, after they buy the property, of the earlier conveyance. The bona fide purchaser who records first obtains full rights in the property over the earlier buyer who did not record. Any other rule would restrict the bona fide purchaser's ability to transfer the property.

5. *Fraud.* Recording acts are intended to protect bona fide purchasers from fraud by assuring them that they will obtain good title to the property even if the seller has previously sold to someone else. To protect such buyers from fraud, however, these statutes authorize the seller to convey an interest they no longer own, thereby defrauding the first buyer. They therefore create a new property interest: a power in the grantor to transfer ownership from the first grantee, who did not record, to a second grantee. They fight fraud on the second buyer by affirmatively empowering the seller to commit a fraud on the first buyer, a power that was nonexistent before recording acts were in place. Is there any way to protect *both* the first buyer and the second buyer from the seller's double dealing without requiring a search of the entire recording office? Note that, although a grantee who is defrauded by a double-dealing grantor may lose title to the property to someone else, he may be able to sue the grantor for damages for fraud.

6. *Favored position of bona fide purchasers.* In *Matter of Edwards*, 962 F.2d 641 (7th Cir. 1992), the bona fide purchaser of property at a bankruptcy sale obtained title free and clear of a preexisting mortgage because the debtor who declared bankruptcy gave the court an old address for the mortgagee's lawyer; the mortgagee had listed its correct address, but the court clerk did not notice the discrepancy, so the mortgagee-lender was not notified of the bankruptcy sale of the property. Judge Richard Posner commented on the policies behind the protection of bona fide purchasers: "If purchasers at judicially approved sales of a bankrupt estate, and their lenders, cannot rely on the deed that they receive at the [bankruptcy] sale, it will be difficult to liquidate bankrupt

estates at positive prices." *Id.* at 643. Yet Posner noted the unfairness of this procedure to the innocent owner:

> To take away a person's property — and a lien is property — without compensation or even notice is pretty shocking, but we have property rights on both sides of the equation here, since [the mortgagee/lender] wants to take away property that [the buyer at the bankruptcy sale] purchased and [the buyer's lender] financed, without compensating them for their loss.

Id. at 645. Does the disappointed mortgagee have any claim against the debtor who listed the wrong address for the mortgagee?

7. *Statutory interpretation.* Why aren't buyers on constructive notice of any deeds recorded under the names of predecessors in interest? What justifies limiting the required search to time periods associated with the "chain of title"? Have the courts interpreted the meaning of "notice" in recording statutes, or have they rewritten them by creating an exception for situations not contemplated by the legislature? If you believe the courts have created an exception, are the courts justified on the grounds that the legislature could not have intended to require an unlimited search, or are the courts practicing illegitimate judicial activism and ignoring the plain language of the statute?

PROBLEMS

Determine how the following cases would be resolved in jurisdictions with (a) a race statute; (b) a notice statute; (c) a race-notice statute.

1. *O* to *A* (*A* does not record).
   O to *B* (*B* has notice of the earlier conveyance to *A*).
   B records. *A* records.
   B sues *A* for title.

2. *O* to *A* (*A* does not record).
   O to *B* (*B* has no actual notice of the earlier conveyance to *A*).
   B records.
   A records.
   B sues *A* for title.

3. *O* to *A* (*A* does not record).
   O to *B* (*B* has no actual notice of the earlier conveyance to *A*).
   A records.
   B records.
   B sues *A* for title.

4. *O* to *A* (*A* does not record).
   A to *B* (*B* records).
   O to *Z* (*Z* has no actual notice of deed from *O* to *A*; *Z* records).
   B records deed from *O* to *A*.

5. O to A (A does not record).
   O to X (X has notice of conveyance from O to A).
   X records.
   A records.
   X conveys to Z (Z has no actual notice of deed from O to A).

6. O to A (A does not record).
   O to X (X has notice of conveyance from O to A).
   A records.
   X records.
   X conveys to Z (Z has no actual notice of deed from O to A).

7. O to A (A does not record).
   O to X (X has no actual notice of conveyance from O to A).
   X records.
   A records.
   X conveys to C (C has notice of conveyance from O to A).

§9.3.3.5   Fraud and Forgery

ZURSTRASSEN v. STONIER

786 So.2d 65 (Fla. Dist. Ct. App. 2001)

MARTHA C. WARNER, C.J. . . .

Appellant, Klaus Zurstrassen, a citizen of Germany, and his brother, Rolf, a citizen of the United States, acquired title to two vacant lots in Indian River County in June 1997. The brothers intended to build on the lots and then sell them. On September 10, 1997, Klaus returned to Germany, leaving Rolf in charge of commencing construction. While construction commenced on one lot, a deed was recorded in the public records on September 25, 1997, purportedly conveying Klaus's ownership in the lots to his brother Rolf. Klaus claims that the deed was a forgery and that he had no knowledge of it.

Klaus returned from Germany in October, and construction on the one lot continued. Just before Klaus left again for Germany, the brothers agreed to sell the constructed home. Klaus met with a realtor to prepare a listing. The realtor researched the title and informed Klaus that his name did not appear on the last deed in the chain of title. He was not shown any deed and did not know that title was vested in his brother's name alone. Klaus asked Rolf about it, and Rolf told Klaus that he did not know why Klaus's name did not appear on the deed but that he should not be concerned with it. Because of the uncertainty created by the revelation of some title problems and the necessity of Klaus to return to Germany, the brothers signed a document between them recognizing Klaus's interest and the terms of the brothers' initial agreement regarding the properties. The agreement stated that title to the properties was in Rolf's name alone and it outlined the process of selling the properties and distributing the proceeds. Klaus then returned to Germany.

In June of 1998, Rolf transferred both lots to David Stonier by quitclaim deed. Stonier was unaware that Klaus made any claim to the property. Then in August of 1998, Stonier executed a warranty deed on one lot to the Wihlborgs. The deed to the Wihlborgs was mistakenly recorded in Brevard County and was not recorded in Indian River County until November 23, 1998.

While in Germany, Klaus was notified that the lots had been sold. However, when he returned to the United States, he immediately began investigating the title to the property and uncovered the forged deed and the subsequent deeds. He instituted suit to quiet title to the property and for rescission on November 9, 1998, and filed a notice of *lis pendens* on November 10, 1998, thirteen days before the Wihlborg deed was recorded in Indian River County. Both Stonier and the Wihlborgs answered the suit and claimed that Klaus was estopped from asserting any rights because he had acknowledged in the February 1998 agreement that title to the property was in his brother's name and he had delayed in objecting to any purported fraud. Stonier also alleged that he was a bona fide purchaser for value and filed a counterclaim for slander of title and damages.

Stonier and the Wihlborgs moved for summary judgment and conceded for purposes of the motion only that Klaus's deed to Rolf was a forgery. The trial court entered summary judgment in their favor on the quiet title and rescission claims, concluding that because Klaus was aware as of February 1998 that the property was titled solely in Rolf's name and failed to object, Klaus had waived or was estopped from asserting any right to object to any subsequent sale to Stonier. This appeal ensued.

Equitable Estoppel

We think Klaus is correct in his assertion that the forged deed is void and thus creates no legal title nor affords protection to those claiming under it. *See McCoy v. Love*, 382 So. 2d 647, 648 (Fla. 1979). In *Wright v. Blocker*, 198 So. 88, 91 (Fla. 1940), relied on in *McCoy*, the court said of the effect of such deeds, "[a] forged deed, in the sense defined above, is absolutely void and wholly ineffectual to pass title, even to a subsequent innocent purchaser from the grantee under such forged deed." . . .

Because the deed conveying title from Klaus to Rolf is void, it had no legal effect to transfer Klaus's ownership of the property to Rolf. Nevertheless, appellees still argue that Klaus should be estopped from asserting his claim that the deed was a forgery because of his subsequent knowledge of the forgery. The elements of estoppel are: (1) representation of a material fact by the party estopped to the party claiming the estoppel that is contrary to the fact later asserted by the estopped party; (2) reliance on that representation by the party claiming the estoppel; and (3) the party claiming the estoppel detrimentally changed their position due to such reliance. In the context of title to disputed land, estoppel prevents a party who by acts, words, or silence allows another to purchase title to property "under an erroneous opinion of title, without making known his claim," from afterwards exercising his or her legal right against such person. *Coram v. Palmer*, 63 Fla. 116, 58 So. 721, 722 (Fla. 1912). . . .

In the instant case, there were no representations by Klaus to either purchaser of the lots. Indeed, it does not appear that either Stonier or the Wihlborgs had any knowledge of the paper signed by both brothers which explained that title was in Rolf's name but both brothers would share in the profits.[2] Moreover, there is no

---

2. Stonier's claim that Rolf had good and valid title to the property is further belied to some extent by the fact that Rolf conveyed the property to Stonier by quitclaim deed. A quitclaim deed conveys whatever title the grantor has, if any. A quitclaim deed provides no warranties of the validity of title. Therefore, it is hard to say as a matter of law that Stonier could have relied on the validity of title conveyed through a quitclaim deed.

evidence of record that Klaus knew at the time he signed that paper that his signature had been forged onto a deed conveying his interest to his brother. *Cf. First S. Ins. Co. v. Ocean State Bank*, 562 So. 2d 798, 800 (Fla. Dist. Ct. App. 1990)(if owner knowingly cloaks another with indicia of ownership or authority, doctrine of estoppel precludes owner from complaining when a third party relies on representation to his detriment; but estoppel does not apply where indicia of ownership is not knowingly given by true owner, such as in case of forgery). All he knew as he was leaving for Germany was that the realtor reported that his name was not on the title, but he did not know the reason or the legal ramifications. In sum, there were material issues of fact regarding the defenses of equitable estoppel raised by both Stonier and the Wihlborgs.

Waiver

Likewise, there are issues of fact as to whether Klaus waived his right to contest the forged deed. "The elements of waiver are: (1) the existence at the time of the waiver of a right, privilege, advantage, or benefit which may be waived; (2) the actual or constructive knowledge of the right; and (3) the intention to relinquish the right." *Leonardo v. State Farm Fire & Cas. Co.*, 675 So. 2d 176, 178 (Fla. Dist. Ct. App. 1996). A waiving party must possess all of the material facts in order to constitute waiver. Waiver of fraud can occur where a party should have discovered the fraud through ordinary diligence.

Waiver may be implied by conduct, but that conduct must be clear. Thus, while forbearance for a reasonable time alone cannot constitute waiver, conduct leading one to believe that a right has been waived may imply such a waiver.

At the least, there is a question of fact as to whether Klaus acted diligently in discovering the forgery. Although he had been told the property was titled solely in Rolf's name, Rolf repeatedly assured him that he should not be concerned with title problems. Klaus had to leave for Germany immediately after learning that his name was not on the title. He began investigating the title immediately upon his return. Whether he should have started investigating earlier is a question of fact.

Ratification

Because Klaus did not know of the forgery, we also conclude that the court erred in granting summary judgment on the issue of ratification of the fraud. Ratification occurs where a party with full knowledge of all the material facts makes an affirmative showing of his or her express or implied intention to adopt an act or contract entered into without authority. The issue is one of fact. If a party knows of a fraud, does not reject it, and takes any material act inconsistent with an intent to avoid it or delays in asserting any remedial rights, then that party ratifies the fraud. However, in the instant case, there is no evidence that Klaus knew of the forgery so as to reject it. Even though he signed the paper acknowledging that title was in Rolf's name and authorizing Rolf to sell the property, Rolf led him to believe that the title problems were a mix up and not the true state of ownership of the property. On this record, material issues of fact remain as to the issue of ratification.

For the foregoing reasons, we reverse and remand for further proceedings.

McCOY v. LOVE
382 So. 2d 647 (Fla. 1980)

JOSEPH A. BOYD, JR., Justice. . . .

Mary V. Nowling Elliott, now deceased, brought an action seeking the cancellation of a deed. The trial court found that Mrs. Elliott, a simple, elderly woman who could neither read nor write, owned an undivided one-fifth interest in the minerals underlying a seventy-five acre tract of land. In January 1972 B. G. Russell offered to buy her entire interest, but she refused. She orally agreed to sell Mr. Russell two of the thirteen to fifteen mineral acres she owned for $3300.00. The trial court found further: Defendant Russell prepared the mineral deed, and instead of the two acres of minerals agreed upon, fraudulently substituted the clause: "one-fifth (1/5) interest in and to all the oil, gas, and other minerals" and then inserted the legal description of the 75 acres. Obviously, one-fifth of 75 acres is 15 acres, a deal that the Plaintiff had consistently refused to make.

Mrs. Elliott lived with her daughter, who could read, write, and understand simple things. The daughter looked over the instrument Russell had prepared. Although she did not understand the deed, she advised Mrs. Elliott that she guessed it was all right.

Several days later, Russell contacted Mrs. Elliott and told her that he had made a mistake in drawing up the deed. He offered to pay her $15,000 for the interest that had been conveyed. She refused and insisted on a reconveyance of that portion of the interest which she had not intended to sell. "[O]n February 16, 1972, Russell and his wife purported to reconvey to Plaintiff the thirteen seventy-fifths (13/75ths) interest of which she had been defrauded." On February 11, 1972, however, Russell conveyed a substantial portion of the same mineral rights to C. P. McClelland, who later conveyed to respondents Messrs. Love, Harris, and Carpenter. Mrs. Elliott remained ignorant of the Russell-McClelland and subsequent transactions until October 1973 when she wanted to sell more of her mineral rights and a title search revealed them. She sued for cancellation of the deed. . . .

A bona fide purchaser has the right to rely on the record title of his grantor, but this protection extends only to those purchasing a legal title. The recording of a void or forged deed is legally insufficient to create a legal title, and affords no protection to those claiming under it. . . .

. . . The trial court's findings of fact that the grantee committed fraud and that the grantor was not negligent do not compel the conclusion that there was such . . . an alteration of documents as to be the equivalent of a forgery. The grantor knew that she was executing and delivering a deed of mineral rights. The law charged her with the responsibility of informing herself as to the legal effect of the document she was signing.

Where all the essential legal requisites of a deed are present, it conveys legal title. Fraud in the inducement renders such a legally effective deed voidable in equity. We hold that the district court was correct in holding that the deed was merely voidable, and that it conveyed a legal title to the grantee.

Because of its holding that the deed was void, the trial court granted summary judgment in favor of the plaintiff. Therefore there were no findings of fact on the issue of the good faith of the purchasers from McClelland. While the district court was correct in holding the deed voidable rather than void, there was no basis for it to conclude from the record that the defendants were bona fide purchasers. The case should be remanded for trial of this factual issue. . . .

NOTES AND QUESTIONS

1. *Void or voidable?* When a deed has been obtained by fraud or forgery, it is classified as either *void* or *voidable*. If no further conveyances are made, a court will set aside the deed on the true owner's request. The difficult issue is determining what happens if the property has been conveyed to a bona fide purchaser, one who paid value and had no notice of the fraud or forgery. If the deed is *void*, then it conveys no title to the grantee and the grantee has no power to convey title to another; the bona fide purchaser is therefore not protected. If, however, the deed is merely *voidable* by the true owner, who was the victim of the foul play, then a subsequent bona fide purchaser will be able to obtain good title. In that case, the victim's sole remedy will be a suit for damages for fraud or conversion against the wrongdoer.

2. *Forgery.* Forged deeds are absolutely void and therefore transfer no interest to the grantee; nor can they be the basis of a transfer from the grantee to a subsequent bona fide purchaser even though that purchaser has no knowledge of the forgery. Thus, a bona fide purchaser who buys in reliance on the record title, which appears good, will obtain nothing. *Vanderwall v. Midkiff*, 421 N.W.2d 263 (Mich. Ct. App. 1988); *Nickels v. Cohn*, 764 S.W.2d 124, 135 (Mo. Ct. App. 1989); *First National Bank in Albuquerque v. Enriquez*, 634 P.2d 1266, 1268 (N.M. 1981). This universally recognized rule appears to conflict with the policies underlying the recording system, which is intended to give a bona fide purchaser assurance that she receives what she pays for and that the seller has a right to convey the property. Why do you suppose courts refuse to protect bona fide purchasers from forged deeds?

3. *Fraud.* In contrast to forged deeds, deeds obtained through fraud are generally voidable rather than void. They are voidable by the defrauded victim — the one who was fraudulently induced to transfer the property. Once the property passes to a bona fide purchaser without notice of the fraud, however, the conveyance can no longer be rescinded. *Fallon v. Triangle Management*, 215 Cal. Rptr. 748 (Ct. App. 1985). The reason for this distinction has been explained by a Maryland court as follows:

> A deed obtained through fraud, deceit or trickery is voidable as between the parties thereto, but not as to a bona fide purchaser. A forged deed, on the other hand, is void ab initio. . . .
>
> [A] forger can pass no better title than he has. . . . Consequently, there can be no bona fide holder of title under a forged deed. A forged deed, unlike one procured by fraud, deceit or trickery is void from its inception. The distinction between a deed obtained by fraud and one that has been forged is readily apparent. In a fraudulent deed an innocent purchaser is protected because the fraud practiced upon the signatory to such a deed is brought into play, at least in part, by some act or omission on the part of the person upon whom the fraud is perpetrated. He has helped in some degree to set into motion the very fraud about which he later complains. A forged deed, on the other hand, does not necessarily involve any action on the part of the person against whom the forgery is committed.

Harding v. Ja Laur, 315 A.2d 132 (Md. Ct. Spec. App. 1974). Courts seem to suggest that if the grantor has somehow participated in creating her own problem by negligence, she will be estopped from claiming a right to get the property back once it has passed into the hands of a bona fide purchaser.

Because of the fraud/forgery distinction, the courts have often had to contend with behavior that could be described as either forgery or fraud. For example, in

Harding v. Ja Laur, supra, plaintiff Lucille M. Harding claimed that defendant Ja Laur induced her to sign a blank page that she was told would be used merely to straighten out a boundary line but that was later affixed to a deed transferring a small portion of land that she owned. Defendant Ja Laur had wanted the land because it was contiguous to land it owned and was extremely valuable because it provided access to that land. On one hand, the court could have held that the case involved fraud rather than forgery because Ms. Harding had been induced to sign on the basis of a false impression of the document. On the other hand, the court could characterize the affixing of the signature to another legal document as a forgery since it involved an alteration of her signature, *id.* at 136:

> So that if a person has two deeds presented to him, and he thinks he is signing one but in actuality, because of fraud, deceit or trickery he signs the other, a bona fide purchaser, without notice, is protected. On the other hand, if a person is presented with a deed, and he signs that deed but the deed is thereafter altered, *e.g.* through a change in the description or affixing the signature page to another deed, that is forgery and a subsequent purchaser takes no title.

Given the possible difficulties in distinguishing fraud from forgery in some cases, does the distinction make sense?

§9.3.4 MARKETABLE TITLE ACTS

Marketable title acts attempt to solve the problem of defining how far back one must search in the grantor-grantee index by limiting searches to a reasonable period, often 30 to 40 years. When a person has a record title for the designated period of time, all prior claims or interests are extinguished. To preserve prior claims, owners must *re-record* their interest or file a *notice of claim* every 30 years or so after the recording of their initial deed.

§9.3.5 TITLE INSURANCE

Originally, lawyers conducted the title searches required to determine the validity of the seller's title. In some areas, this is still the case. In many places, however, lawyers for the mortgagee bank and for the buyer and seller no longer perform the work connected with a title search. Title insurance companies have emerged to fulfill this function. Some banks require the purchaser to buy title insurance as a condition for getting a mortgage loan from the bank. Even when insurance is not required, many purchasers will obtain it to protect their interests. In these cases, the title company will perform the title search. The insurance policy will explain that the company promises, in return for a premium, to insure the purchaser against losses occasioned by defects in title to the property. The policy ordinarily defines the kinds of defects it will cover. The insurance company may also promise to pay the costs of defending the title through litigation. Disputes may arise between title insurance companies and insureds over the interpretation of the insurance contract, especially as to what kinds of defects in title are covered by the contract. *See, e.g., Horn v. Lawyers Title Insurance Corp.,* 557 P.2d 206 (N.M. 1976); *Shotwell v. Transamerica Title Insurance Co.,* 588 P.2d 208 (Wash. 1978).

§9.3.6   TITLE REGISTRATION

Some jurisdictions have partially adopted a title registration system, or "Torrens system" (named after the person who came up with the idea). It is available in 19 states and Puerto Rico. Fred I. Feinstein, *Title Insurance: The Role of the Lawyer* 412 (Practising Law Institute, Real Estate Law and Practice Course Handbook Series 553, 556, Nov. 1995). An owner who wishes to register his land must file a petition for a judicial or quasi-judicial proceeding that is similar to an action to quiet title. Notice must be given to all persons having any interest in the land. The result of the adjudication is a certificate of registration or title. The official certificate of title states the identity of the property owner and includes descriptions of all encumbrances (easements, covenants, liens, mortgages, leases, and the like) affecting the title. The certificate is conclusive as to the title and is filed in the registrar's office. If an owner transfers his land, the deed must be brought to the registry and a new certificate issued. A title examiner for a purchaser need only examine the current certificate of title and the documents referred to in the list of encumbrances on the certificate.

Although this system simplifies title problems immensely, it is expensive to institute. Either the state would have to pay for a judicial proceeding to produce a certificate of title for every parcel in the state or the individual owner would have to bear the cost, which may amount to hundreds of dollars. Because the states that have adopted it have allowed owners to register their land on a voluntary basis, most land is still unregistered and governed by the old grantor-grantee record system.

In addition, some factors militate against the absolute conclusiveness that is supposed to attach to the title. What happens, for example, if it turns out that an earlier deed was forged? If the current certificate of title is absolutely conclusive — if it cannot be challenged — then an innocent person may lose the property because of the forgery. Note, however, that forgeries are rare because the "registry will not issue a new certificate in the ordinary course of business unless the old owner's duplicate is presented for cancellation. In addition, the registries in some states maintain files of signature cards against which purported conveyances are checked." William B. Stoebuck & Dale A. Whitman, *The Law of Property* §11.15, at 928 n.20 (3d ed. 2000).

§9.4   *Real Estate Finance*

§9.4.1   MORTGAGES

§9.4.1.1   Debtor Protection Legislation

Very few people can afford to buy land or a house without borrowing money. Both homeowners and businesses turn to lending institutions, such as banks, mortgage companies, and savings and loan associations, to borrow money to buy real estate. The lender will check out the credit history of the prospective borrower, his current employment, family assets, and other financial information to decide whether to lend money.

Borrowing money from a bank to finance a real estate purchase entails two separate contracts, although they are sometimes combined. The first is the *note*. This constitutes the borrower's promise to repay the principal amount of the loan with interest, in the amounts and at the times specified in the note. For example, if Béla

Bartók borrows $170,000 to buy a $200,000 house, the note might recite the obligation to repay $170,000 at 10 percent interest over 25 years. Generally, part of each installment payment represents interest and part represents repayment of the principal $170,000 amount. (In the beginning, most of the payment is allocated to interest.) The note creates a personal liability in Bartók to repay the money. The lender can sue Bartók for defaulting on Bartók's promises contained in the note.

The second contract is the *mortgage*. To obtain greater security for the repayment of the note, the lender will require Bartók to execute a mortgage on the property Bartók is buying. The mortgage will contain a series of promises by Bartók, including the promise to pay off the note in accordance with its terms, to maintain insurance on the property, to pay property taxes when due, and to maintain the property so that it does not become dilapidated and lose its market value, thereby impairing the lender's security. It will also contain Bartók's agreement to pledge the property as *collateral* to secure payment of the note. This means that if Bartók defaults on his loan payments or violates any other material terms of the mortgage, the lender has the ability to force the property to be sold and to use the proceeds of the sale to pay off the rest of the note. The sale may be conducted privately or under judicial supervision, depending on the rules in the jurisdiction in which the land is located. The forced sale of the property is called *foreclosure* or *foreclosing the mortgage*. The lender is the *mortgagee*; the buyer-homeowner is the *mortgagor*. The mortgagor-homeowner grants the mortgage (the *lien* or the *security interest*) to the mortgagee-bank.

The mortgagor's interest in the property is called the *equity of redemption* or *equity*. This name alludes to the origin of mortgages in the courts of equity in England. Originally, the owner-borrower would convey title to the property to the lender with a condition subsequent, allowing the borrower to pay off the debt on a certain day and thereby get the deed back. In the beginning, the lender would actually take possession of the property and "work" it (or hire others to do so) to make profits from the transaction. Later, the owner-borrower would keep possession of the property; the transfer of the deed was simply a security device to protect the lender's financial interest in repayment of the loan. If the borrower did not pay off the debt on the appointed day, she would lose the property forever. Since the land was usually worth more than the debt, the lender would often get a windfall. Borrowers began to ask the equity courts for relief from this result, and the chancellor responded by granting the borrower extra time to pay off the debt so that she could redeem the property (get it back). In so doing, the court effectively rewrote the contract, changing the terms of the condition. At first, this was subject to the equity court's discretion, but by the seventeenth century it was a matter of right. The borrower's interest came to be called the equity of redemption, while the mortgagee held title.[3]

---

3. Approximately ten jurisdictions retain this *title theory* of mortgages for some or all financing arrangements: Alabama, Connecticut, District of Columbia, Georgia, Maine, Massachusetts, New Hampshire, Pennsylvania, Rhode Island, Tennessee. *Restatement (Third) of Property (Mortgages)* §4.1, Note on Mortgage Theories Followed by American Jurisdictions (1997). The number is approximate because some states are less than clear about their approach. Most states subscribe to the *lien theory*, under which the borrower retains title to the property and the lender has merely a lien on the property. A few (like Maryland) adopt an *intermediate theory*, whereby the mortgagor has title until default occurs, at which point legal title passes to the mortgagee. With minor exceptions, no practical difference remains between the title theory and the lien theory in terms of the legal rights of the parties. *Restatement (Third) of Property (Mortgages)* §4.1 cmt. a.

Allowing the borrower some extra time to get the property back by paying off the debt protected the mortgagor's interest but left the mortgagee without any clear remedy. For this reason, the equity courts put a time limit on the mortgagor's right to redeem the property. The equity courts began a procedure called *foreclosure*, by which the lender could cut off the borrower's equity of redemption forever. At first, the court used a procedure called *strict foreclosure*, by which the court would give the borrower extra time to pay off the debt but provide that if the debt remained unpaid by a particular date, the mortgagor would automatically lose the property forever. If the property was worth less than the debt, the lender could then go after the mortgagor for a *deficiency judgment*. If the property was worth more than the debt, the mortgagee would have the right to keep the property without paying the excess value back to the mortgagor. This procedure has been substantially abolished in the United States and is available in only a couple of states where it is subject to judicial discretion. *See* Conn. Gen. Stat. §§49-15 and 49-24; Vt. Stat. tit. 12, §4528.

Because of the perceived unfairness of strict foreclosure, the courts began to order *foreclosure sales*. This is currently the practice in most states and is codified in legislation regulating the rights of mortgagors in foreclosure. After default by the mortgagor, the mortgagee brings a lawsuit to foreclose on the property. The mortgagor may prevent loss of his property by paying off the rest of the debt before foreclosure. If the mortgagee proves the existence of the mortgage and that the mortgagor defaulted on the mortgage, the court will order a foreclosure decree. The decree provides for public sale of the property by a court officer, payment of the outstanding balance of the debt to the mortgagee, and transfer of any excess proceeds to the mortgagor. Upon the foreclosure sale, the mortgagor's equity of redemption is cut off. If the sale does not bring in enough to pay off the debt, in many states the lender may bring an action for a *deficiency judgment* personally against the mortgagor for the rest of the debt. Some states prohibit deficiency judgments.

Some states add a *statutory right of redemption*. This should not be confused with the *equity of redemption*, which is the mortgagor's right to pay off the rest of the debt *before foreclosure* and redeem the property. The statutory right of redemption allows the mortgagor to buy back the property for the price bid at the foreclosure sale for a designated period (often a year) *after foreclosure*. These statutes generally allow the mortgagor to remain in possession of the property in the meanwhile.

Note that under current law, the mortgagor-borrower retains the right to possess the property during the term of the mortgage. The mortgage is a security device, not a transfer of possession.

A common problem arises with the price bid for the property at the foreclosure sale. Anyone can bid on the property at the foreclosure sale, including the mortgagor and the mortgagee. Often the mortgagee is the only entity or person bidding at the foreclosure sale. There is a danger that the mortgagee will make a low bid; the mortgagee will not only get the property and be able to sell it but may be able to go after the mortgagor for a deficiency judgment. If the mortgagee buys the property for a low price (below its fair market value), the mortgagee may (1) decrease the excess proceeds that must be paid over to the mortgagor, (2) resell the property and retain the proceeds over the amount paid at the foreclosure sale, and (3) be able to file a deficiency judgment against the mortgagor who has other assets.

States have developed a wide variety of mechanisms to ensure that the price bid at the foreclosure sale is near the fair market value. This will protect the interests of both the mortgagor and the mortgagee: The mortgagor is less likely to be subject to a deficiency judgment, and the mortgagee can use the proceeds of the sale to pay off the debt. First, the mortgagor has the right to bid at the foreclosure sale. This enables the mortgagor to go to another lender, which may be willing to lend the mortgagor the money so long as the property is worth more than the unpaid debt, and the property will constitute the security for *its* new loan. If the mortgagee bids too low, the mortgagor may be able to counter with a higher bid, forcing the mortgagee to bid more to get the property. Second, there must be public notice of the sale so that others can bid on the property. Third, some states prohibit deficiency judgments. This decreases the mortgagee's incentive to bid below the fair market value of the property. Fourth, many states allow a mortgagor to sue a mortgagee for unjust enrichment if the mortgagee buys the property at a low price and resells it within a short period of time for a much higher price. The mortgagee may be forced to disgorge the profits and turn them over to the mortgagor. This procedure protects the mortgagor's right to the excess proceeds and prevents the mortgagee from bidding low, reselling the property, and keeping those proceeds itself.

Fifth, many states require a *judicially supervised sale*. This means that the mortgagee must bring a lawsuit to foreclose on the property, with the sale overseen by the court. The court may ensure that the price bid at the sale is adequate. Moreover, judicial proceedings allow the mortgagor to prove that she did not default on the mortgage. Some states allow the mortgagor to waive the protection of a judicial sale by granting the mortgagee a *power of sale*. In this case, the mortgagee can conduct the public sale itself, after notice to all interested parties, without the need for judicial proceedings.

Another arrangement that bypasses the judicially supervised sale is the *deed of trust*, which is prevalent in some states. Under this arrangement, the borrower or *trustor* conveys title to a third party (called the *trustee*) as security for the trustor's payment of its debt obligation to the lender (called the *beneficiary*). If the trustor defaults, the trustee can arrange a public nonjudicial sale of the property to satisfy the debt.

Sixth, some states include a statutory right of redemption as a means to encourage market prices to be bid at the foreclosure sale. If the mortgagee bids below the fair market price, the mortgagor could go to another lender to obtain the money to buy back the property for the price paid at the foreclosure sale. A second bank might be willing to do this since the fair market value of the property securing its loan will be greater than the loan itself, giving it a greater amount of security. Many states, however, do not have a statutory right of redemption on the ground that the ability of the mortgagor to redeem the property for one year after foreclosure will actually decrease the market value of the property *at the time of the foreclosure sale* since the buyer cannot possess the property immediately and, in fact, has no assurance it will ever be able to possess the property.

In sum, the protections generally accorded to mortgagors, by common law or legislation, include the following:

1. *Equity of redemption.* This is the mortgagor's right to pay off the rest of the loan before foreclosure and avoid loss of the property.
2. *Notice of foreclosure proceedings.* The mortgagee must give the mortgagor notice of foreclosure proceedings it has commenced whether through judicially supervised sale or private sale by the mortgagee.
3. *Foreclosure proceedings.* Requiring a judicially supervised sale provides procedural protection for the mortgagor by requiring the mortgagee to prove the existence of the note and the mortgage and to prove that the mortgagor defaulted. The mortgagor may be able to prove that she did not default under the terms of the mortgage.

4. *Public notice of foreclosure sale.* The public nature of
possibility of having several potential buyers bid at
possibly raising the price and preventing a deficien

5. *Mortgagor's right to bid at the foreclosure sale.* The m
bid for the house at the foreclosure sale. This gives t
to buy back the property and increases the likelihoo
bid the fair market value of the property.

6. *Judicial supervision of the price.* If the buyer at the
low, the mortgagor may be empowered to bring a
gagee for breach of fiduciary duty. For example, if the mortgagee makes a low
bid and buys the property at foreclosure and then resells the property for a
much higher price shortly afterward, the mortgagor may be able to bring a
lawsuit forcing the mortgagee to disgorge the excess profits to the mortgagor.
See In re Krohn, 52 P.3d 774 (Ariz. 2002) (vacating the sale of property at a
trustee's sale for about $10,000 when its fair market value was $57,000).

7. *Reinstatement.* Some states allow the defaulting mortgagor to *reinstate* the
mortgage prior to foreclosure by curing all defaults through paying any unpaid
amounts due, along with the mortgagee's costs associated with the default. *See,
e.g.,* 735 Ill. Comp. Stat. 5/15-1602. This allows the mortgagor to keep the property by paying only the amounts then in default, not the entire remaining
amount of the loan.

In times of economic depression, legislatures have sometimes passed emergency
mortgage moratorium legislation. During the Great Depression, some states passed laws
protecting homeowners from foreclosure under certain circumstances. In *Home Building
& Loan Association v. Blaisdell,* 290 U.S. 398 (1934), the Supreme Court upheld the
constitutionality of the 1933 Minnesota *Mortgage Moratorium Act,* which temporarily
authorized courts to extend periods of redemption — the time during which the home-
owner-mortgagor could pay off the loan to the mortgagee — without being subject to a
foreclosure sale. More recently, a similar statute has been in effect in Iowa to protect
farmers from loss of their farms in times of economic emergency. Iowa Code §654.15.
Governor Terry Branstad declared an emergency on October 1, 1985, triggering application of the statute. *Bank of Craig v. Hughes,* 398 N.W.2d 216, 218 (Iowa Ct. App. 1986).

Finally, it is important to note that various federal and state laws currently
prohibit discrimination in the provision of real estate financing. In particular, the
Fair Housing Act of 1968, 42 U.S.C. §§3601 *et seq.,* reprinted in Chapter 10, makes it
unlawful for any person whose business includes financing residential real estate transactions to discriminate "against any person in making available such a transaction, or
in the terms or conditions of such a transaction, because of race, color, religion, sex,
handicap, familial status, or national origin." §3605.

§9.4.1.2   Regulating the Foreclosure Process

CENTRAL FINANCIAL SERVICES, INC. v. SPEARS
425 So. 2d 403 (Miss. 1983)

R.P. SUGG, Presiding Justice, for the Court:
The question in this case is whether a mortgagee, who purchases the mortgaged
property at a foreclosure sale must account to the mortgagor for the surplus arising

...ale of the property by the mortgagee within two weeks for two and one-half ... the amount bid by the mortgagee at the foreclosure sale.

Marshall Spears borrowed $1,250 from Central Financial Services, Inc. (CFS), and executed a promissory note and financial disclosure statement along with his wife, Ester Spears. They also executed a deed of trust covering certain real property described therein to secure the debt. The total amount secured was $1,797.30 which included principal, interest, insurance and fees.

Spears gave his son $625 or half the amount of the principal and expected him to assist in paying back the loan. They could not agree on an arrangement so payments on the promissory note fell into arrears. CFS advertised the property for sale under the terms of the deed of trust, but stopped the advertisement when Spears paid the amount in arrears including cost of the foreclosure proceedings. Spears and his son still could not agree upon how they could make payments on the note, so once again it became delinquent. On October 12, 1979, after advertising the sale in accord with section 89-1-55 Mississippi Code Annotated (1972), the sale was conducted and CFS bid $1,458.86, the amount of the indebtedness then due plus costs of foreclosure. There were no other bidders. Two days later, Spears was notified by an agent for CFS that he would have to vacate the premises. Spears claimed that this was the first time he was aware of the second sale and that he offered to pay the amount of the delinquency, but was told it was too late for that.

On October 24, 1979, CFS sold the property to Joe Stewart and Earl Aycock for $4,000. CFS then paid a $30 judgment lien on the property and realized a profit of $2,481.14. Aycock and Stewart sold the property to Roger C. Henderson on February 19, 1980 for $6,500. Henderson then made improvements to the property.

On March 11, 1980, Spears filed a bill of complaint in the Chancery Court of Lauderdale County which named CFS, Thomas B. Bourdeaux, Trustee, Joe Stewart, Earl Aycock and Roger Henderson as defendants. The bill prayed that the second foreclosure sale be set aside, alleging violation of Spears' constitutional rights, inadequate sale price and prayed for an injunction and other relief. The demurrer of the defendants was sustained and Spears appealed to this Court.

The appeal was submitted on March 3, 1981, and, in an unpublished opinion we held, "On the face of the complaint, taking as true Spears' allegation that the fair market value was $7,000, the consideration of $1,458.86 was so grossly inadequate as to shock the conscience of this Court." We reversed and remanded for a trial on the merits because of the gross inadequacy of consideration alleged on the face of the complaint.

The chancellor dismissed the case as against the trustee, Aycock, Stewart and Henderson, but found that the sale price at the second foreclosure sale was so inadequate that it shocked the conscience of the court. He determined from the evidence presented that the property had a fair market value of $6,000 at the time of the sale and ordered CFS to respond in damages based on the difference between fair market value and the price paid at the foreclosure sale. CFS appealed. Spears did not cross-appeal so the dismissal of the action against the trustee, Aycock, Stewart and Henderson is not at issue.

We have reviewed our cases involving adequacy of consideration as a ground for setting aside a foreclosure sale. These cases do not address the issue involved in this case but do lay down the general rule that mere inadequacy of price is not sufficient to set aside a foreclosure sale unless the price is so inadequate as to shock the conscience of the court. . . .

In this case, the chancellor found that the sale price was so inadequate it shocked his conscience. This finding is amply supported by the evidence because CFS bid only $1,458.86 at the foreclosure sale and twelve days later sold the property for $4,000. We hold that a sale of mortgaged property within twelve days of the foreclosure sale at a price two and one-half times the bid of the mortgage is so inadequate, it would be "impossible to state it to a man of common sense without producing an exclamation at the inequality of it." The chancellor did not set the sale aside; instead, he fashioned a remedy with which we agree in principle.

CFS was in compliance with the statutory law pertaining to the advertisement and sale of real property under deeds of trust. However, the sale of the property by CFS twelve days later resulted in a windfall to it of approximately $2,500. We deem this windfall to be unjust. If CFS had bid $4,000 at the foreclosure sale it would have been entitled to recover the amount of its indebtedness plus the expense of the sale, with the surplus being payable to Spears. Certainly a sale twelve days later for $4,000 enabled CFS to recover $2,500 more than it risked in the transaction it made when it advanced $1,250 to Spears.

We agree with the chancellor that the sale price was so inadequate that it shocks the conscience of this Court. However, we are of the opinion that the decree should be modified to reduce the amount of recovery against CFS.

The chancellor ordered the difference between the fair market value, which he fixed at $6,000, and the amount bid by CFS be returned to Spears. CFS should not be required to suffer any pecuniary loss, which it would do under the decree of the chancellor. There is no evidence of any conspiracy between appellant and its vendees to defraud appellee by fixing the sales price below market value; rather, the sale was an arms length transaction. We are of the opinion, and hold, that the difference between the amount bid and the $4,000 received by CFS at the private sale twelve days later should be used in computing the amount due Spears.

The record shows that the total amount of the indebtedness due at the time of the foreclosure sale was $1,458.86. Interest on this amount at the rate fixed in the note for twelve days amounts to $13.51. CFS also paid off a $30 judgment lien against the property and is entitled to credit for the judgment lien. We therefore, reduce the chancellor's award to $2,497.63. . . .

PROBLEMS

1. A husband and wife own a house as joint tenants. The husband generally pays the bills. He suffers from alcoholism, and, as his condition worsens, he stops paying attention to household matters and fails to pay the bills, including the mortgage. The couple receive notice of foreclosure through the mail, but the husband hides the notice from his wife. The bank forecloses on the house. Only then does the wife learn about both her husband's failure to pay the bills and the foreclosure proceedings. The state in which they live has no statutory right of redemption. She brings a lawsuit against the bank, which purchased the property at the foreclosure sale, and asks the court to allow her to reclaim the property by paying the unpaid bills. She has enough money to do so. Although there is no statutory right of redemption, she appeals to a civil procedure rule stating that "the court may relieve a party from a final judgment for the following reasons: (1) mistake, inadvertence, surprise, or excusable neglect . . . ; or (6) any other reason justifying relief from the operation of the judgment." *See* Mass. R. Civ. P. 60(b). What arguments can you make on both sides? What should the court do?

2. A law student lives in an apartment with a one-year lease that runs from September 1 to August 31. The apartment is in a great location near the school, and the lessor orally promises that she will renew the lease to allow the lessee to stay there during her three years at law school. The lease allows the lessee to sublet or assign the leasehold with the lessor's consent; the lessor orally promises to grant consent if the lessee finds subtenants or assignees for the summer. On December 25, the student receives a notice from a bank with a heading stating "Notice to Quit," informing her that her lessor has defaulted on her mortgage payments, that the bank has foreclosed on the property, purchased the building at the foreclosure sale, and is now the owner. The purchase price at the foreclosure sale was sufficient to pay off the unpaid debt to the bank. The letter further states: "Your lease is no longer valid. You are hereby given notice that as of February 1, your leasehold is terminated, and you must move out by that date." The tenant would like to stay in the apartment. Does she have any rights under existing law? If not, should the court interpret the common law in light of the policies underlying the foreclosure statute to allow the tenant to remain in the apartment? How long should she be allowed to stay there?

§9.4.2   INSTALLMENT LAND CONTRACTS

An installment land contract is an alternative financing arrangement for purchasing real property. Under an installment land contract, the buyer makes a down payment to the seller and signs a single contract with the seller, in which the buyer promises to pay the rest of the purchase price to the seller at the times and in the amounts specified in the contract. At the end of the contract, the seller will convey title to the property to the buyer. The contract normally allows the seller to regain possession of the property on the buyer's default. It also ordinarily allows the seller to keep the payments already made by the buyer as *liquidated damages* for the buyer's breach of the agreement. Liquidated damages are damages for breach of contract set in advance by the parties themselves as part of their agreement.

This arrangement poses the same problems for the buyer as the mortgage does, but states often provide such buyer-borrowers fewer procedural protections than are granted to mortgagors. Some states implicitly or explicitly prohibit installment land contracts by making the protections of the mortgage foreclosure statute nonwaivable. Other states treat some installment land contracts like mortgages. States that allow installment land contracts may permit the seller to regain possession of the property but will examine the amounts paid by the buyer to determine whether they are grossly disproportionate to the damages suffered by the seller. Damages that are too high are considered a *penalty* or a *forfeiture*, and the court will order the seller to disgorge part of that amount back to the buyer.

§9.4.2.1   Forfeiture

STONEBRAKER v. ZINN
286 S.E.2d 911 (W. Va. 1982)

THOMAS B. MILLER, Chief Justice: . . .

. . . On October 2, 1978, Richard and Mildred Zinn (vendors) agreed to sell to Samuel and Diana Stonebraker (purchasers) a house and land located in Preston

County for the sum of $25,000. The contract entered into by the parties acknowledged receipt of a $1,500 down payment and established a financing arrangement whereby the vendors agreed to accept the balance of the purchase price, $23,500, in monthly installments of $189.09 at an annual interest rate of 9 percent. A deed of trust lien in favor of the First Federal Savings and Loan of Waynesburg, Pennsylvania, previously given by the vendors, was acknowledged. The vendors were obligated, upon payment in full by the purchasers, to convey marketable title to the property by deed. The vendors agreed to make payments on the note secured by the deed of trust.

Purchasers took possession of the property and assumed all other responsibilities normally associated with homeownership, including payment of property insurance and taxes, maintenance and repairs. The contract provided for liquidated damages in the event the purchasers abandoned the property. The amount of the liquidated damages was the amount the purchasers had paid on the purchase price at the time of abandonment.[1]

The purchasers occupied the premises from November 1978 to November 1979 and made monthly payments. In November 1979, the purchasers notified the vendors that they could not afford both the cost of the necessary repairs to the property and the monthly house payments, and that they intended to vacate the premises. Prior to December 1, 1979, the purchasers vacated the property....

The purchasers claim that the forfeiture clause in the contract is a penalty because the damages retained by the vendors are grossly disproportional to their actual damages and, therefore, it is unenforceable. The vendors argue that the clause is a valid liquidated damage clause.

Considerable recognition is given to the premise that parties entering into an agreement may avoid all future questions of damages which may result from a violation thereof by agreeing to a definite sum to be paid upon such a violation....

[In] *Charleston Lumber Company v. Friedman*, 61 S.E. 815 (W. Va. 1908), [we outlined] the circumstances when parties may properly contract for liquidated damages:

> Where the damages are uncertain and not readily capable of ascertainment in amount by any known or safe rule, whether such uncertainty lies in the nature of the subject, or in the particular circumstances of the case; or ... where from the nature of the case and tenor of the agreement, it is apparent that the damages have already been the subject of actual fair estimate and adjustment between the parties.

This Court has also held that a clause for damages in a contract is a penalty rather than a liquidated damage provision when the amount is grossly disproportional in comparison to the damages actually incurred....

---

1. The pertinent portion of the contract in regard to liquidated damages is:

If the Purchasers fail to make any of the monthly payments above called for, when due, ..., and said default continues for a period of sixty (60) days, or if the Purchasers shall *abandon* said property, the Vendors shall have the right, at their option, to rescind and cancel the present sale and declare this contract as null and void thereafter, and the amount of the purchase price paid by the Purchasers hereunder shall be considered and treated as rent and liquidated damages due to the Vendors for the use of the said premises during the time this contract was in effect and for failure to perform or comply with the terms of the contract, and the Vendors shall have the right to take possession of said real estate without further demand or notice. (Emphasis added.)

In determining whether the amount forfeited by a purchaser through liquidated damages under an installment land contract is so grossly disproportional to the damages actually incurred, courts take into account not only the loss of fair rental value to the vendor, but also costs involved in the sale of the property, depreciation, attorney fees and other directly related expenses arising by virtue of the purchaser's abandonment of the property. In *Valdez v. Christensen*, 404 P.2d 343 (Idaho 1965), there was a $90,000 contract with $25,000 paid on the purchase price which permitted the vendors to keep all payments made if the purchasers defaulted. The trial court found that the loss of rental, depreciation and other items totalled $21,450 and left a $3,550 balance against the $25,000 down payment. The trial court additionally charged against the down payment attorney's fees in the amount of $850 and ordered repayment of $2,700 by the vendors to the purchasers. On appeal, the trial court was reversed for ordering the repayment: "As the record now stands it does not appear that a forfeiture of $2,700 as additional damages for the breach of a contract of the magnitude of that here involved would be unconscionable or sufficient to amount to a penalty." *Valdez*, 404 P.2d at 346....

In the present case, the vendors retained $3,850. The parties appear to agree that the $189.09 payment was a fair monthly rental for the property. The vendors point out that in addition to the rental payments, they incurred expenses for the original sale and conveyance of the property and expenses in selling the property a second time. They also allege that the purchasers damaged the property during their possession.

Based upon our previous discussion, we do not believe that the retention by the vendors of approximately $3,850 ($1,500 down payment plus monthly payments of $189.09 for approximately twelve months) was excessive. The monthly payments of $189.09 are reasonable as a rental value for a home valued at $25,000. The total monthly payments were approximately $2,350 up to the time of the default. The $1,500 representing the initial down payment does not represent an excessive retention when the various expenses the vendors incurred in conjunction with regaining the property are taken into account.

Obviously, each case will turn on its own facts since the higher the deposit and monthly rental the more the vendor retains on a default. It is also apparent that the longer the contract is in effect the greater the sum will be on default. Another factor that has a bearing, which is not present in this case, is whether the purchaser has placed permanent improvements on the premises which substantially increase its value....

§9.4.2.2 Making Mortgage Protection Nondisclaimable

SEBASTIAN v. FLOYD

585 S.W.2d 381 (Ky. 1979)

J. CALVIN AKER, Justice.

This case presents the question whether a clause in an installment land sale contract providing for forfeiture of the buyer's payments upon the buyer's default may be enforced by the seller.

The movant, Jean Sebastian, contracted on November 8, 1974, to buy a house and lot situated in Covington, Kentucky, from Perl and Zona Floyd, respondents in this motion for review. Sebastian paid $3,800.00 down and was to pay the balance of the $10,900.00 purchase price, plus taxes, insurance, and interest at the rate of 8 1/2% per annum, in monthly installments of $120.00. A forfeiture clause in the contract provided that if Sebastian failed to make any monthly payment and remained in default for 60 days, the Floyds could terminate the contract and retain all payments previously made as rent and liquidated damages.

During the next 21 months, Sebastian missed seven installments. Including her down payment, she paid the Floyds a total of $5,480.00, rather than the $6,320.00 which was called for by the terms of the contract. Of this amount, $4,300.00, or nearly 40% of the contract price, had been applied against the principal.

The Floyds brought suit in the Kenton Circuit Court against Sebastian in August, 1976, seeking a judgment of $700.00 plus compensation for payments for taxes and insurance, and seeking enforcement of the forfeiture clause. Sebastian admitted by her answer that she was in default but asked the court not to enforce the forfeiture clause. . . .

When a typical installment land contract is used as the means of financing the purchase of property, legal title to the property remains in the seller until the buyer has paid the entire contract price or some agreed-upon portion thereof, at which time the seller tenders a deed to the buyer. However, equitable title passes to the buyer when the contract is entered. The seller holds nothing but the bare legal title, as security for the payment of the purchase price.

There is no practical distinction between the land sale contract and a purchase money mortgage, in which the seller conveys legal title to the buyer but retains a lien on the property to secure payment. The significant feature of each device is the seller's financing the buyer's purchase of the property, using the property as collateral for the loan.

Where the purchaser of property has given a mortgage and subsequently defaults on his payments, his entire interest in the property is not forfeited. The mortgagor has the right to redeem the property by paying the full debt plus interest and expenses incurred by the creditor due to default. In order to cut off the mortgagor's right to redeem, the mortgagee must request a court to sell the property at public auction. From the proceeds of the sale, the mortgagee recovers the amount owed him on the mortgage, as well as the expenses of bringing suit; the mortgagor is entitled to the balance, if any. . . .

We are of the opinion that a rule treating the seller's interest as a lien will best protect the interests of both buyer and seller. Ordinarily, the seller will receive the balance due on the contract, plus expenses, thus fulfilling the expectations he had when he agreed to sell his land. In addition, the buyer's equity in the property will be protected. . . .

NOTES AND QUESTIONS

When a buyer defaults under an installment land contract or other real estate financing arrangement, two separate legal issues arise. The first is the *forfeiture* question. Does the seller have the right not only to regain possession of the property but to retain all payments made by the buyer? The second issue concerns whether the buyer has a *right of redemption*. Does the buyer have the right after default to continue in possession of the property by paying off all or some of the rest of the purchase price?

1. *Universal mortgage foreclosure protection.* In answering these questions, courts have developed a variety of approaches. The first approach handles these questions in

one fell swoop by holding that installment land contracts are equivalent to mortgages and therefore must be governed by the same rules. This gives buyers under installment land contracts the full range of protections available to mortgagors, including an equity of redemption (the right to retain the property by paying the rest of the purchase price at or before the foreclosure sale), the procedural protections of the foreclosure statutes (including notice of intent to foreclose and perhaps a judicially supervised public sale), and the right to recover any proceeds of the foreclosure sale in excess of the unpaid debt.[4] This approach, adopted by the Kentucky court in *Sebastian v. Floyd*, effectively makes the protections of mortgage foreclosure statutes nondisclaimable.

2. *Treating some installment land contracts as mortgages.* A second approach extends mortgage protections only to *some* installment land contracts. Colorado, for example, has developed a test to distinguish installment land contracts that must be treated like mortgages from those that may be enforced according to their own terms. In *Grombone v. Krekel*, 754 P.2d 777 (Colo. Ct. App. 1988), the court held that trial courts have the discretion to make this determination based on a range of factors, including "the amount of the vendee's equity in the property, the length of the default period, the willfulness of the default, whether the vendee has made improvements, and whether the property has been adequately maintained." *Id.* at 779. If the buyer has made a large down payment, occupied the property for a long time, and paid a substantial portion of the purchase price, the court is likely to provide the buyer with all the protections accorded a mortgagee, including a right to redeem, a right to notice and a foreclosure sale, and a right to recover proceeds from the foreclosure sale exceeding the unpaid debt. *See also Petersen v. Hartell*, 707 P.2d 232 (Cal. 1985); *Skendzel v. Marshall*, 301 N.E.2d 641 (Ind. 1973); *Bean v. Walker*, 464 N.Y.S.2d 895 (App. Div. 1983).

3. *Forfeiture.* Finally, some states hold that the buyer has no right of redemption under installment land contracts; thus, the seller has the right to get the property back on the buyer's default and to eject the buyer from the property. The only question in these states is whether the amount of payments already made by the buyer so exceeds the seller's damages as to constitute an unconscionable *forfeiture* or *penalty*. If it does, the buyer may have a right to be reimbursed for part of the down payment. This is the approach taken by the West Virginia Supreme Court of Appeals in *Stonebraker v. Zinn*.

4. *Comparing the interests of lenders and borrowers.* Chief Justice Rose Bird, of the California Supreme Court, has argued that all installment land contracts should be given the same protections granted to mortgages.

> The predominant use of installment land sale contracts has been to finance the purchase of housing by low-income families and individuals unable to qualify for conventional mortgage financing or government loan guarantee programs.
>
> Providing installment contract vendees the same protections that are afforded to mortgagors would eliminate some abusive practices of vendors, who have exploited the lack of legal sophistication and limited capacity to litigate of their low-income clients. Most important, defaulting vendees would be able to avoid the loss of their homes by paying only the delinquent amounts. Under the majority's holding, a wilfully defaulting vendee may avoid this fate only by paying the outstanding balance in full. This is an

---

4. It is often unclear whether the courts are interpreting the mortgage foreclosure statute to apply to all land financing arrangements (thus holding that the legislature *intended* to regulate installment land contracts by its passage of the mortgage foreclosure statute) or whether the courts are changing the common law rules governing installment land contracts to make them cohere with the policy judgments underlying the legislation addressed to mortgages.

unjustifiably harsh burden to place on the low-income and middle-income families and individuals who will be most affected.

Petersen v. Hartell, 707 P.2d at 245-246.

In the same case, Justice Stanley Mosk advocated granting the trial court discretion to "weigh the equities of the case to determine the just result":

> As the majority readily admit, the equities in the case at bar weigh heavily against the vendees. "The Petersens' monthly payments were erratic and delinquent almost from the beginning even though the seller made clear her need of the payments for her support. By April 1973 the Petersens had made only 58 out of the 65 payments then due, and their first attempt to reinstate the contract was not until 29 months later, when they tendered $250 out of the $1,800 that was by then overdue and unpaid."
>
> As between the deliberately defaulting vendees and the elderly vendor who desperately needed the modest payments on the contract for her very survival, the equities clearly favor the latter. . . .

Id. at 248. Similarly, the Indiana Supreme Court held in *Skendzel v. Marshall* that the question whether an installment land contract should be treated like a mortgage should depend on case-by-case determinations of whether "forfeiture" of the buyer's accumulated equity in the property would be consistent with "generally accepted principles of fairness and equity." 301 N.E.2d at 646. The buyer who has paid most of the purchase price "has acquired a substantial interest in the property, which, if forfeited, would result in substantial injustice." *Id.* Is this argument circular? If the seller is entitled to keep the proceeds and evict the buyer, then the buyer will not have "acquired a substantial interest in the property." The buyer will have "acquired" such an interest only if the courts strike down the forfeiture provision in the contract. What then makes the forfeiture unjust? Justice Hunter argues, *id.* at 645-650:

> Under a typical conditional land contract, the vendor retains legal title until the total contract price is paid by the vendee. Payments are generally made in periodic installments. Legal title does not vest in the vendee until the contract terms are satisfied, but equitable title vests in the vendee at the time the contract is consummated. When the parties enter into the contract, all incidents of ownership accrue to the vendee. The vendee assumes the risk of loss and is the recipient of all appreciation in value. The vendee, as equitable owner, is responsible for taxes. The vendee has a sufficient interest in land so that upon sale of that interest, he holds a vendor's lien.
>
> This Court has held, consistent with the above notions of equitable ownership, that a land contract, once consummated constitutes a present sale and purchase. . . . The Court, in effect, views a conditional land contract as a sale with a security interest in the form of legal title reserved by the vendor. Conceptually, therefore, the retention of the title by the vendor is the same as reserving a lien or mortgage. Realistically, vendor-vendee should be viewed as mortgagee-mortgagor. To conceive of the relationship in different terms is to pay homage to form over substance. . . .
>
> Forfeiture is closely akin to strict foreclosure — a remedy developed by the English courts which did not contemplate the equity of redemption. . . . A forfeiture — like a strict foreclosure at common law — is often offensive to our concepts of justice and inimical to the principles of equity. This is not to suggest that a forfeiture is an inappropriate remedy for the breach of all land contracts. In the case of an abandoning, absconding vendee, forfeiture is a logical and equitable remedy. Forfeiture would also be appropriate where the vendee has paid a minimal amount on the contract at the time of default and seeks to

retain possession while the vendor is paying taxes, insurance, and other upkeep in order to preserve the premises. Of course, in this latter situation, the vendee will have acquired very little, if any, equity in the property. However, a court of equity must always approach forfeitures with great caution, being forever aware of the possibility of inequitable dispossession of property and exorbitant monetary loss. We are persuaded that forfeiture may only be appropriate under circumstances in which it is found to be consonant with notions of fairness and justice under the law. . . .

Consider what the situation would look like if the buyer were treated like a renter or tenant. If the monthly payment to the lender is near the fair rental value of the property, isn't the only difference between a renter and a buyer the amount of the down payment? Or is there also a distinction in the sense that the buyer is entitled to treat the property as her own, renovating the property and making structural changes as she sees fit, and thus develops expectations based on considering the property as her own? Does the buyer have no right to develop a personal attachment to the property given the seller's right to end the agreement if the buyer defaults?

5. *Low-income buyers.* Will regulation of installment land contracts make things better or worse for low-income families who do not qualify for conventional mortgages?

§9.4.3 EQUITABLE MORTGAGES

KOENIG v. VAN REKEN
279 N.W.2d 590 (Mich. Ct. App. 1979)

VINCENT J. BRENNAN, Presiding Judge.

In 1970, plaintiff [Helen Koenig] owned a home in Oakland County with a market value of $60,000 that was encumbered by three mortgages totaling $25,933.26. The real estate taxes on plaintiff's home had become delinquent and foreclosure proceedings had begun on one of the mortgages. Plaintiff was then approached by defendant, Stanley Van Reken, who proposed that for a fee of 10 percent he would "service" the mortgages and pay the delinquent taxes. Subsequently, on June 16, 1970, plaintiff and defendant Stanley Van Reken executed three documents that form the basis of this action.

The first of these documents, entitled "AGREEMENT," stated that plaintiff desired to prevent the loss of her home and provided that defendant Stanley Van Reken purchase the property, redeem it from tax sale and mortgage foreclosure, and give plaintiff an exclusive right to repurchase according to the terms of a lease-option agreement that was also executed between the parties.

The second document was a warranty deed which conveyed the property from plaintiff to defendants for a stated consideration of $28,600. Plaintiff alleges that the deed was silent as to consideration when she signed it, that the figure of $28,600 was added subsequently, and that she never received any such consideration.

The third document provided that Stanley Van Reken was to lease the premises to plaintiff for a 3-year period at a fixed monthly rent of $300. Plaintiff was also to receive an exclusive option to repurchase the premises during the term of the lease for a price of $32,318.79, with a downpayment of $3,500 and monthly payments of $300 which were to include taxes, insurance, principal and interest.

At no time during the negotiations that led to the execution of these documents was plaintiff represented by an attorney, and all three documents were prepared by Stanley Van Reken.

The parties operated under the lease from June 16, 1970, to February, 1972, and during this time plaintiff made total payments of $5,800. In February, 1972, plaintiff defaulted in a monthly rental payment. Plaintiff was thereupon evicted from the home.

[Plaintiff sued to have the deed executed by her to be declared an equitable mortgage.]

. . . The court of equity protects the necessitous by looking through form to the substance of the transaction. Although no set criterion has been established, the controlling factor in determining whether a deed absolute on its face should be deemed a mortgage is the intention of the parties. Such intention may be gathered from the circumstances attending the transaction including the conduct and relative economic positions of the parties and the value of the property in relation to the price fixed in the alleged sale. Under Michigan law, it is well settled that the adverse financial condition of the grantor, coupled with the inadequacy of the purchase price for the property, is sufficient to establish a deed absolute on its face to be a mortgage. *Ellis v. Wayne Real Estate Co.*, 97 N.W.2d 758 (Mich. 1959).

In *Ellis, supra,* plaintiffs initially sought a loan from defendant to save their home from forfeiture. After hurried negotiations, the plaintiffs executed a quitclaim deed to defendant and simultaneously entered into a land contract under which the plaintiffs were to repurchase the property. The defendant then satisfied a default and paid the delinquent taxes. In noting the discrepancy between the price paid by the defendant and the value of the property, the Court held that the transaction constituted a loan by defendant secured by a mortgage on the property.

In taking the plaintiff's well-pleaded facts in the present case as true, there is a close parallel with *Ellis, supra.* Here the plaintiff, while in financial distress, sought help from the defendants in saving her home from foreclosure. Although plaintiff was not desirous of selling her home, she entered into a transaction which conveyed her equity worth over $30,000 for less than $4,000. While financial embarrassment of the grantor and inadequacy of consideration do not provide an infallible test, they are an indication that the parties did not consider the conveyance to be absolute. We note that the lease-back arrangement entered into by the parties effectively circumvented the right to redeem, which is designed to protect purchasers such as plaintiff in times of financial crisis. In applying these facts to the aforementioned case law, it could be found without difficulty that the subject transaction constituted a mortgage to secure a loan in the amount of defendants' initial expenditure. . . .

NOTES AND QUESTIONS

An equitable mortgage is declared when a transfer of a deed was intended merely to provide security for a loan rather than a sale of the property. Equitable mortgages effectively circumvent the statute of frauds. What conduct is necessary to turn what looks like a conveyance into a security arrangement? In *Flack v. McClure*, 565 N.E.2d 131 (Ill. App. Ct. 1990), the court identified factors to consider in determining whether an equitable mortgage should be recognized.

Six factors [should] be considered by the trial judge to determine whether an equitable mortgage exists. Those factors include whether a debt exists, the relationship of the parties, whether legal assistance was available, the sophistication and circumstances of each party, the adequacy of the consideration and who retained possession of the property.

Id. at 136. *Cf. Hudson v. Vandiver,* 810 So.2d 617 (Miss. Ct. App. 2002) (transfer of title interpreted as intent to provide security for a promise to pay contractors for services to be rendered). The court in *Koenig v. Van Reken* also relied on various factors in assessing whether to recognize an equitable mortgage. But what, exactly, is the ultimate standard to which the factors are relevant? Does the court in *Koenig* find that the parties *intended* to create a security arrangement rather than a sale, or is the intent of the parties irrelevant? What is the rule of law promulgated by the court in *Koenig?*

In *Johnson v. Cherry,* 726 S.W.2d 4 (Tex. 1987), plaintiff Richard Johnson purchased property for $125,000, with his grantor reserving a vendor's lien on the property. When Johnson and his wife were later divorced, Johnson purchased his ex-wife's community interest in the property with a note promising to pay over time. Johnson encountered difficulty paying all his debts, which totaled $120,000. He entered into a series of transactions with defendants F. G. Cherry and the Texas State Bank of Tatum whereby he gave a deed to the property to defendants, and they gave him a one-year lease on the land with an option to repurchase it. In return for the general warranty deed, Johnson received $120,000 from Cherry, who assumed the $38,000 remaining balance on the note to Johnson's ex-wife. The lease provided for two semiannual payments of $12,510 each; also, Johnson could exercise his option for $132,000 and reassume the note to his ex-wife. When Johnson defaulted on his lease payments, Johnson sued defendants to cancel the deed on the grounds that it was a mortgage on his homestead prohibited by the Texas constitution.

In granting Johnson's request, the Texas Supreme Court held that a transfer of a deed will be treated as a mortgage when "the parties actually intended the instrument as a mortgage." *Id.* at 5. Concluding that the evidence supported the jury's finding that the parties intended the deed as a mortgage, the court explained, *id.* at 7:

> In addition to Johnson's testimony regarding his intentions, the evidence was that the repurchase price was exactly 10% more than the original price; the land was worth almost twice as much as the original "sale" price; the lease price equaled exactly 9% interest on the balance of the note to Johnson's ex-wife assumed by Cherry and 18% interest on the alleged purchase price; Johnson was indebted to other creditors for approximately $119,000 of the $120,000 he received from Cherry; Johnson was within one week of losing the land entirely; and Johnson had told a real estate agent he was not interested in listing his property for sale.

If the parties had signed a contract stating that the "transfer of this deed is intended to be a sale and not a mortgage," would the case have come out any differently? Should it?

PROBLEM

A bank acquires title to a house at a foreclosure sale. It wants to get around all rules about mortgages, installment land contracts, and equitable mortgages, so it

adopts the simple device of asking mortgagors to waive the ⌐
statute. The bank sells the property to a buyer for a purchase
to a financing arrangement with the bank. The buyer makes
with the bank, which lends the rest of the purchase price to th
a mortgage to the bank. The mortgage contract has a waive

> Mortgagor agrees to waive the benefits of the mortgage statute. I
> any payments due under this mortgage, Mortgagee has the right
> the property without a foreclosure sale and to keep any paymen

The state mortgage statute merely recites that "all mortgages shall be subject to the provisions of this act." It has no language specifically stating whether the protections afforded by the statute are disclaimable or waivable by the mortgagor. Should the mortgagor have the right to waive the protections of the mortgage statute?

10

Fair Housing Law

§10.1 Intentional Discrimination or Discriminatory Treatment

§10.1.1 Race Discrimination

§10.1.1.1 Fair Housing Act

FAIR HOUSING ACT
42 U.S.C. §§3601-3631

§3601. Declaration of Policy

It is the policy of the United States to provide, within constitutional limitations, for fair housing throughout the United States.

§3602. Definitions . . .

(b) "Dwelling" means any building, structure, or portion thereof which is occupied as, or designed or intended for occupancy as, a residence by one or more families, and any vacant land which is offered for sale or lease for the construction or location thereon of any such building, structure, or portion thereof.

(c) "Family" includes a single individual. . . .

(e) "To rent" includes to lease, to sublease, to let and otherwise to grant for a consideration the right to occupy premises not owned by the occupant. . . .

(h) "Handicap" means, with respect to a person —

(1) a physical or mental impairment which substantially limits one or more of such person's major life activities,

(2) a record of having such an impairment, or

(3) being regarded as having such an impairment, but such term does not include current, illegal use of or addiction to a controlled substance as defined in section 802 of Title 21. . . .

(i) "Aggrieved person" includes any person who —

(1) claims to have been injured by a discriminatory housing practice; or

(2) believes that such person will be injured by a discriminatory housing practice that is about to occur.

(k) "Familial status" means one or more individuals (who have not attained the age of 18 years) being domiciled with —

(1) a parent or another person having legal custody of such individual or individuals; or

(2) the designee of such parent or other person having such custody, with the written permission of such parent or other person.

The protections against discrimination on the basis of familial status shall apply to any person who is pregnant or is in the process of securing legal custody of any individual who has not attained the age of 18 years. . . .

§3603. *Declaration of Policy . . .*

Exemptions

(b) Nothing in section 3604 of this title (other than subsection (c)) shall apply to —

(1) any single-family house sold or rented by an owner: *Provided,* That such private individual owner does not own more than three such single-family houses at any one time: . . . *Provided further,* That after December 31, 1969, the sale or rental of any such single-family house shall be excepted from the application of this subchapter only if such house is sold or rented (A) without the use in any manner of the sales or rental facilities or the sales or rental services of any real estate broker, agent, or salesman, or of such facilities or services of any person in the business of selling or renting dwellings, or of any employee or agent of any such broker, agent, salesman, or person and (B) without the publication, posting or mailing, after notice, of any advertisement or written notice in violation of section 3604(c) of this title . . . , or

(2) rooms or units in dwellings containing living quarters occupied or intended to be occupied by no more than four families living independently of each other, if the owner actually maintains and occupies one of such living quarters as his residence. . . .

§3604. *Discrimination in Sale or Rental of Housing and Other Prohibited Practices*

As made applicable by section 3603 of this title and except as exempted by sections 3603(b) and 3607 of this title, it shall be unlawful —

(a) To refuse to sell or rent after the making of a bona fide offer, or to refuse to negotiate for the sale or rental of, or otherwise make unavailable or deny, a dwelling to any person because of race, color, religion, sex, familial status, or national origin.

(b) To discriminate against any person in the terms, conditions, or privileges of sale or rental of a dwelling, or in the provision of services or facilities in connection therewith, because of race, color, religion, sex, familial status, or national origin.

(c) To make, print, or publish, or cause to be made, printed, or published any notice, statement, or advertisement, with respect to the sale or rental of a dwelling that indicates any preference, limitation, or discrimination based on race, color, religion, sex, handicap, familial status, or national origin, or an intention to make any such preference, limitation, or discrimination.

(d) To represent to any person because of race, color, religion, sex, handicap, familial status, or national origin that any dwelling is not available for inspection, sale, or rental when such dwelling is in fact so available.

(e) For profit, to induce, or attempt to induce any person to sell or rent any dwelling by representations regarding the entry or prospective entry into the neighborhood of a person or persons of a particular race, color, religion, sex, handicap, familial status, or national origin.

(f)(1) To discriminate in the sale or rental, or to otherwise make unavailable or deny, a dwelling to any buyer or renter because of a handicap of—

(A) that buyer or renter;

(B) a person residing in or intending to reside in that dwelling after it is so sold, rented, or made available; or

(C) any person associated with that buyer or renter.

(2) To discriminate against any person in the terms, conditions, or privileges of sale or rental of a dwelling, or in the provision of services or facilities in connection with such dwelling, because of a handicap of—

(A) that buyer or renter;

(B) a person residing in or intending to reside in that dwelling after it is so sold, rented, or made available; or

(C) any person associated with that person.

(3) For purposes of this subsection, discrimination includes—

(A) a refusal to permit, at the expense of the handicapped person, reasonable modifications of existing premises occupied or to be occupied by such person if such modifications may be necessary to afford such person full enjoyment of the premises except that, in the case of a rental, the landlord may where it is reasonable to do so condition permission for a modification on the renter agreeing to restore the interior of the premises to the condition that existed before the modification, reasonable wear and tear excepted;

(B) a refusal to make reasonable accommodations in rules, policies, practices, or services, when such accommodations may be necessary to afford such person equal opportunity to use and enjoy a dwelling; or

(C) in connection with the design and construction of covered multifamily dwellings for first occupancy after the date that is 30 months after September 13, 1988, a failure to design and construct those dwellings in such a manner that—

(i) the public use and common use portions of such dwellings are readily accessible to and usable by handicapped persons;

(ii) all the doors designed to allow passage into and within all premises within such dwellings are sufficiently wide to allow passage by handicapped persons in wheelchairs; and

(iii) all premises within such dwellings contain the following features of adaptive design:

(I) an accessible route into and through the dwelling;

(II) light switches, electrical outlets, thermostats, and other environmental controls in accessible locations;

(III) reinforcements in bathroom walls to allow later installation of grab bars; and

(IV) usable kitchens and bathrooms such that an individual in a wheelchair can maneuver about the space. . . .

(7) As used in this subsection, the term "covered multifamily dwellings" means—

(A) buildings consisting of 4 or more units if such buildings have one or more elevators; and

(B) ground floor units in other buildings consisting of 4 or more units. . . .

§3605. *Discrimination in Residential Real Estate-Related Transactions*

(a) *In general.* It shall be unlawful for any person or other entity whose business includes engaging in residential real estate-related transactions to discriminate against any person in making available such a transaction, or in the terms or conditions of such a transaction, because of race, color, religion, sex, handicap, familial status, or national origin.

(b) *Definition.* As used in this section, the term "residential real estate-related transaction" means any of the following:

(1) The making or purchasing of loans or providing other financial assistance—

(A) for purchasing, constructing, improving, repairing, or maintaining a dwelling; or

(B) secured by residential real estate.

(2) The selling, brokering, or appraising of residential real property. . . .

§3607. *Exemption*

(a) Religious Organizations and Private Clubs

Nothing in this title shall prohibit a religious organization, association, or society, or any nonprofit institution or organization operated, supervised or controlled by or in conjunction with a religious organization, association, or society, from limiting the sale, rental or occupancy of dwellings which it owns or operates for other than a commercial purpose to persons of the same religion, or from giving preference to such persons, unless membership in such religion is restricted on account of race, color, or national origin. Nor shall anything in this subchapter prohibit a private club not in fact open to the public, which as an incident to its primary purpose or purposes provides lodgings which it owns or operates for other than a commercial purpose, from limiting the rental or occupancy of such lodgings to its members or from giving preference to its members.

(b) Numbers of Occupants; Housing for Older Persons; Persons Convicted of Making or Distributing Controlled Substances

(1) Nothing in this subchapter limits the applicability of any reasonable local, State, or Federal restrictions regarding the maximum number of occupants permitted

to occupy a dwelling. Nor does any provision in this title regarding familial status apply with respect to housing for older persons.

(2) As used in this section, "housing for older persons" means housing—

(A) provided under any State or Federal program that the Secretary determines is specifically designed and operated to assist elderly persons (as defined in the State or Federal program); or

(B) intended for, and solely occupied by, persons 62 years of age or older; or

(C) intended and operated for occupancy by persons 55 years of age or older, and—

(i) at least 80 percent of the occupied units are occupied by at least one person who is 55 years of age or older;

(ii) the housing facility or community publishes and adheres to policies and procedures that demonstrate the intent required under this subparagraph; and

(iii) the housing facility or community complies with rules issued by the Secretary for verification of occupancy, which shall—

(I) provide for verification by reliable surveys and affidavits; and

(II) include examples of the types of policies and procedures relevant to a determination of compliance with the requirement of clause (ii). Such surveys and affidavits shall be admissible in administrative and judicial proceedings for the purposes of such verification.

(3) Housing shall not fail to meet the requirements for housing for older persons by reason of:

(A) persons residing in such housing as of the date of enactment of this Act who do not meet the age requirements of subsections (2)(B) or (C): *provided,* That new occupants of such housing meet the age requirements of subsections (2)(B) or (C); or

(B) unoccupied units: *provided,* That such units are reserved for occupancy by persons who meet the age requirements of subsections (2)(B) or (C).

(4) Nothing in this subchapter prohibits conduct against a person because such person has been convicted by any court of competent jurisdiction of the illegal manufacture or distribution of a controlled substance as defined in section 102 of the *Controlled Substances Act* (21 U.S.C. 802).

(5)(A) A person shall not be held personally liable for monetary damages for a violation of this title if such person reasonably relied, in good faith, on the application of the exemption under this subsection relating to housing for older persons.

(B) For the purposes of this paragraph, a person may only show good faith reliance on the application of the exemption by showing that—

(i) such person has no actual knowledge that the facility or community is not, or will not be, eligible for such exemption; and

(ii) the facility or community has stated formally, in writing, that the facility or community complies with the requirements for such exemption.

§3613.   *Enforcement by Private Persons*

(a) Civil Action

(1)(A) An aggrieved person may commence a civil action in an appropriate United States district court or State court not later than 2 years after the occurrence or the termination of an alleged discriminatory housing practice . . . to obtain appropriate relief with respect to such discriminatory housing practice or breach. . . .

(b) Appointment of Attorney by Court

Upon application by a person alleging a discriminatory housing practice or a person against whom such a practice is alleged, the court may—

(1) appoint an attorney for such person; or

(2) authorize the commencement or continuation of a civil action under subsection (a) of this section without the payment of fees, costs, or security, if in the opinion of the court such person is financially unable to bear the costs of such action.

(c) Relief Which May Be Granted

(1) In a civil action under subsection (a) of this section, if the court finds that a discriminatory housing practice has occurred or is about to occur, the court may award to the plaintiff actual and punitive damages, and . . . may grant as relief, as the court deems appropriate, any permanent or temporary injunction, temporary restraining order, or other order (including an order enjoining the defendant from engaging in such practice or ordering such affirmative action as may be appropriate).

(2) In a civil action under subsection (a) of this section, the court, in its discretion, may allow the prevailing party, other than the United States, a reasonable attorney's fee and costs. . . .

§3617. *Interference, Coercion, or Intimidation; Enforcement by Civil Action*

It shall be unlawful to coerce, intimidate, threaten, or interfere with any person in the exercise or enjoyment of, or on account of his having exercised or enjoyed, or on account of his having aided or encouraged any other person in the exercise or enjoyment of, any right granted or protected by section 3603, 3604, 3605, or 3606 of this title.

§10.1.1.2 Discrimination by Housing Providers

ASBURY v. BROUGHAM
866 F.2d 1276 (10th Cir. 1989)

JAMES A. PARKER, District Judge.

Plaintiff Rosalyn Asbury brought suit under 42 U.S.C. §1982[1] and the *Fair Housing Act*, 42 U.S.C. §§3601 *et seq.* (FHA), claiming that the defendants refused to rent or to allow her to inspect or negotiate for the rental of an apartment or townhouse at Brougham Estates in Kansas City. Defendants Leo Brougham, individually and doing business as Brougham Estates and Brougham Management Company, and Wanda Chauvin, his employee, appeal a jury verdict awarding Asbury compensatory damages of $7,500 against them upon a finding that the defendants discriminated against her on

---

1. Section 1982 provides: "All citizens of the United States shall have the same right, in every State and Territory, as is enjoyed by white citizens thereof to inherit, purchase, lease, sell, hold, and convey real and personal property." — ED.

the basis of race and/or sex. Leo Brougham appeals from the jury verdict awarding punitive damages in the amount of $50,000 solely against him. . . .

I. *Sufficiency of Evidence Supporting a Finding of Racial Discrimination in Violation of §1982 and FHA*

42 U.S.C. §1982 and the FHA both prohibit discrimination on the basis of race. In order to prevail on a claim made under these statutes, plaintiff must prove a discriminatory intent. A violation occurs when race is a factor in a decision to deny a minority applicant the opportunity to rent or negotiate for a rental, but race need not be the only factor in the decision. In addition, §3604(d) of the FHA specifically prohibits dissemination of false information about the availability of housing because of a person's race. Accordingly, failure to provide a minority applicant with the same information about availability of a rental unit or the terms and conditions for rental as is provided to white "testers," results in false information being provided and is cognizable as an injury under the FHA.

A. Asbury's Prima Facie Case Under §1982 and FHA

The three-part burden of proof analysis established in *McDonnell Douglas Corp. v. Green*, 411 U.S. 792 (1973), a Title VII employment discrimination case, has been widely applied to FHA and §1982 claims. Under the *McDonnell Douglas* analysis, plaintiff first must come forward with proof of a *prima facie* case of discrimination. Second, if plaintiff proves a *prima facie* case, the burden shifts to defendants to produce evidence that the refusal to rent or negotiate for a rental was motivated by legitimate, non-racial considerations. Third, once defendants by evidence articulate non-discriminatory reasons, the burden shifts back to plaintiff to show that the proffered reasons were pretextual.

The proof necessary to establish a *prima facie* case under the FHA also establishes a *prima facie* case of racial discrimination under §1982. In order to establish her *prima facie* case, plaintiff had to prove that:

(1) she is a member of a racial minority;
(2) she applied for and was qualified to rent an apartment or townhouse in Brougham Estates;
(3) she was denied the opportunity to rent or to inspect or negotiate for the rental of a townhouse or apartment; and
(4) the housing opportunity remained available.

A review of the evidence in this case shows that plaintiff established her *prima facie* case. Defendants stipulated that Asbury is black. Plaintiff testified that on February 23, 1984, she went to Brougham Estates with her daughter to obtain rental housing. At the rental office at Brougham Estates, Asbury encountered Wanda Chauvin, the manager, and explained to Chauvin that she was being transferred to Kansas City and needed to rent housing. Asbury told Chauvin that she needed to secure housing by the middle of March or the beginning of April. In response, Chauvin said there were no vacancies, but told Asbury she could call back at a later time to check on availability. Chauvin provided no information concerning availability of rental units that would assist Asbury in her efforts to rent an apartment or townhouse at Brougham Estates. Asbury asked for the opportunity to fill out an application, but Chauvin did not give her an application, again stating that there were no vacancies and that she kept no waiting list. Asbury also requested floor plans or the opportunity to view a model unit, and Chauvin refused. Instead, Chauvin suggested Asbury inquire at the Westminister Apartments, an apartment complex housing mostly black families. Although Chauvin did not ask Asbury about her qualifications, plaintiff was employed with the Federal Aviation Authority at a salary of $37,599. Based on her salary, defendants concede that Asbury would likely be qualified to rent an apartment or townhouse at Brougham Estates....

Although there was a conflict in the evidence as to the availability of housing at the time Asbury attempted to inspect and negotiate for rental, there was abundant evidence from which the jury could find that housing was available. Defendants testified that families with a child are housed exclusively in the townhouses at Brougham Estates, and that there were no townhouses available on the date Asbury inquired. Asbury introduced evidence suggesting that both apartments and townhouses were available and, in addition, that exceptions previously had been created to allow children to reside in the apartments.

On February 24, 1984, the day after Asbury inquired about renting, Asbury's sister-in-law, Linda Robinson, who is white, called to inquire about the availability of two-bedroom apartments. The woman who answered the telephone identified herself as "Wanda" and invited Robinson to come to Brougham Estates to view the apartments. The following day, February 25, 1984, Robinson went to the rental office at Brougham Estates and met with Wanda Chauvin. Chauvin provided Robinson with floor plans of available one- and two-bedroom apartments at Brougham Estates. Robinson specifically asked Chauvin about rental to families with children, and Chauvin did not tell Robinson that children were restricted to the townhouse units. Robinson accompanied Chauvin to inspect a model unit and several available two-bedroom apartments. Upon inquiry by Robinson, Chauvin indicated that the apartments were available immediately and offered to hold an apartment for her until the next week.

Asbury also provided evidence indicating that townhouses were available for rent. On February 1, 1984, Daniel McMenay, a white male, notified Brougham Estates that he intended to vacate his townhouse. On April 4, 1984, Brougham Estates rented the townhouse vacated by McMenay to John Shuminski, a white male. On March 10, 1984, Randall Hockett, a white male, also rented a townhouse at Brougham Estates. In addition, Asbury provided computer data sheets generated by Brougham Estates which indicated that a third townhouse was unoccupied at the time of her inquiry on February 23, 1984 and remained vacant as of April 10, 1984. There was also evidence that a building which included townhouse units had been closed for the winter but would be available for rent beginning in the spring. On February 22, 1984, one day prior to Asbury's inquiry into vacancies, James Vance, a white male, paid a deposit for a townhouse which he occupied when the building opened on April 10, 1984. Since Asbury testified that she told Chauvin she did not need to occupy a rental unit until the beginning of April, the jury could have concluded that at least one of the townhouses which was subsequently rented to the white males was available at the time Asbury inquired. Although defendants took the position at trial that the townhouses were closed or out of order for repair and therefore not available to rent, the jury was free to accept the evidence of availability presented by the plaintiff.

Since Asbury met her burden of proving a *prima facie* case of racial discrimination, the burden shifted to defendants to prove a legitimate, non-discriminatory reason for denial of housing.

B. Failure of Proof of Legitimate, Non-discriminatory Reason for Rejection

Defendants claimed their legitimate, non-discriminatory reasons for rejecting Asbury arose out of the policies at Brougham Estates that families with one child could rent townhouses but not apartments, and that families with more than one child were not permitted to move into Brougham Estates. Defendants further argued that they made no exceptions to these rules. Defendants contended that in accordance with these rental policies, no appropriate housing was available for Asbury when she inquired. However, plaintiff introduced evidence indicating that exceptions to these rules had been made on several occasions; families with children had rented apartments, and families with more than one child had been permitted to move into Brougham Estates. Asbury was not provided information about the terms and conditions that gave rise to an exception to the policy concerning children being restricted to the townhouses. The jury could therefore find that defendants' reasons for denying Asbury the opportunity to negotiate for rental were not legitimate and non-discriminatory.

Defendants also argue that evidence of a high percentage of minority occupancy in Brougham Estates conclusively rebuts the claim of intentional racial discrimination. Although such statistical data is relevant to rebutting a claim of discrimination, statistical data is not dispositive of a claim of intentional discrimination. Moreover, there was other evidence from which the jury could have determined that race was a motivating factor in defendants' decision to refuse to negotiate with Asbury for a rental unit.

II. Sufficiency of Evidence Supporting Punitive Damages Award

Defendant Brougham contends that there was insufficient evidence supporting the jury's award of punitive damages against him because he never met or dealt with the plaintiff, the actions of Chauvin should not be attributed to him, and he did not promulgate any discriminatory policies or procedures.

Punitive damages may be awarded against a defendant "when the defendant's conduct is shown to be motivated by evil motive or intent, or when it involves reckless or callous indifference to the federally protected rights of others." *Smith v. Wade*, 461 U.S. 30, 56 (1983). The jury has discretion to award punitive damages to punish outrageous conduct on the part of a defendant and to deter similar conduct in the future.

Plaintiff advanced two theories supporting Brougham's liability for punitive damages: (1) Brougham's own discriminatory conduct in establishing rental policies, procedures and rules; and (2) his authorization or ratification of discriminatory conduct by Chauvin, his employee. We find sufficient evidence to establish liability under either theory.

In this case, Asbury presented evidence that Leo Brougham was the managing partner of Brougham Estates and Brougham Management Company. Brougham established all policies, rules and rental procedures for Brougham Estates. Chauvin worked for Brougham who instructed her about the rental policies and procedures. Among the policies and procedures implemented by Brougham were the requirements that Chauvin routinely and untruthfully tell people over the phone that there were no vacancies, whether or not vacancies existed, but that Chauvin then encourage the individuals to come in, inspect the premises and discuss upcoming vacancies. Brougham established the requirement of visual observation of a prospective tenant. Although a policy that prospective tenants must be visually scrutinized is not necessarily improper, under the circumstances of this case, the jury could have inferred that the policy operated to screen prospective tenants on the basis of race and that, at a minimum, Brougham was callously indifferent to this result of his policy. Indeed, this policy had given rise to several administrative complaints by single black females prior to Asbury's inquiry about a vacancy. Brougham was aware of previous claims of discriminatory practices in the rental of units at Brougham Estates.

Another policy established by Brougham was that a family with a child could occupy only a townhouse. Chauvin was advised of this policy. Brougham testified that he made no exceptions to the policy, and he testified specifically that no tenant or prospective tenant with a child could obtain permission to be excepted from the rule. Plaintiff, however, produced evidence that exceptions had been created on occasion. Those exceptions had been authorized by Brougham and had been made on an individual basis. . . . From the evidence presented, the jury could have determined that the policies established and implemented by defendant Brougham directly fostered the discrimination which Asbury experienced, that Brougham should have been aware that this might occur, and that Brougham was recklessly or callously indifferent to it happening.

Plaintiff also offered evidence tending to prove that Brougham ratified Chauvin's actions. [After investigating, Brougham] determined [that] Asbury had only one child and therefore fit within the residential policies of Brougham Estates. . . . Furthermore, the jury could have drawn the inference that Brougham's failure to apologize or otherwise remedy the situation, after personally investigating Asbury's claim of discrimination at Brougham Estates, was an acceptance and ratification of Chauvin's treatment of Asbury.

Having reviewed the record in this case, we find that there was substantial evidence supporting and a reasonable basis for the jury's verdict awarding both compensatory and punitive damages, and we affirm the district court's decision to deny defendants' motion for a new trial. . . .

UNITED STATES v. STARRETT CITY ASSOCIATES

840 F.2d 1096 (2d Cir. 1988)

ROGER J. MINER, J. . . .

Appellants [Starrett City Associates, Starrett City, Inc. and Delmar Management Company (collectively "Starrett")] constructed, own and operate "Starrett City," the largest housing development in the nation, consisting of 46 high-rise buildings containing 5,881 apartments in Brooklyn, New York. . . .

Starrett has sought to maintain a racial distribution by apartment of 64% white, 22% black and 8% hispanic at Starrett City. Starrett claims that these racial quotas are necessary to prevent the loss of white tenants, which would transform Starrett City into a predominantly minority complex. Starrett points to the difficulty it has had in attracting an integrated applicant pool from the time Starrett City opened, despite extensive advertising and promotional efforts. Because of these purported difficulties, Starrett adopted a tenanting procedure to promote and maintain the desired racial balance. This procedure has resulted in relatively stable percentages of whites and minorities living at Starrett City between 1975 and the present.

The tenanting procedure requires completion of a preliminary information card stating, *inter alia*, the applicant's race or national origin, family composition, income and employment. The rental office at Starrett City receives and reviews these applications. Those that are found preliminarily eligible, based on family composition, income, employment and size of apartment sought, are placed in "the active file," in which separate records by race are maintained for apartment sizes and income levels. Applicants are told in an acknowledgement letter that no apartments are presently available, but that their applications have been placed in the active file and that they will be notified when a unit becomes available for them. When an apartment becomes available, applicants are selected from the active file for final processing, creating a processed applicant pool. As vacancies arise, applicants of a race or national origin similar to that of the departing tenants are selected from the pool and offered apartments.

In December 1979, a group of black applicants brought an action against Starrett in the United States District Court for the Eastern District of New York. . . . Plaintiffs alleged that Starrett's tenanting procedures violated federal and state law by discriminating against them on the basis of race. The parties stipulated to a settlement in May 1984, and a consent decree was entered subsequently. The decree provided that Starrett would, depending on apartment availability, make an additional 35 units available each year for a five-year period to black and minority applicants.

The government commenced the present action against Starrett in June 1984, "to place before the [c]ourt the issue joined but left expressly unresolved" in the . . . consent decree: the "legality of defendants' policy and practice of limiting the number of apartments available to minorities in order to maintain a prescribed degree of racial balance." The complaint alleged that Starrett, through its tenanting policies, discriminated in violation of the *Fair Housing Act*. . . .

Starrett maintained that the tenanting procedures [were intended to] "achieve and maintain integration and were not motivated by racial animus." To support their position, appellants submitted the written testimony of three housing experts. They described the "white flight" and "tipping" phenomena, in which white residents migrate out of a community as the community becomes poor and the minority population increases, resulting in the transition to a predominantly minority community. Acknowledging that "the tipping point for a particular housing development, depending as it does on numerous factors and the uncertainties of human behavior, is difficult to predict with precision," one expert stated that the point at which tipping occurs has been estimated at from 1% to 60% minority population, but that the consensus ranged between 10% and 20%. . . .

Title VIII of the *Civil Rights Act of 1968* (*"Fair Housing Act"* or "the Act"), 42 U.S.C. §§3601-3631 (1982), was enacted pursuant to Congress' thirteenth amendment powers, "to provide, within constitutional limitations, for fair housing throughout the United States." 42 U.S.C. §3601. Section 3604 of the statute prohibits discrimination because of race, color or national origin in the sale or rental of housing by, *inter alia*: (1) refusing to rent or make available any dwelling, *id.* §3604(a); (2) offering discriminatory "terms, conditions or privileges" of rental, *id.* §3604(b); (3) making, printing or publishing "any notice, statement, or advertisement . . . that indicates any preference, limitation, or discrimination based on race, color . . . or national origin," *id.* §3604(c); and (4) representing to any person "that any dwelling is not available for . . . rental when such dwelling is in fact so available," *id.* §3604(d).

Housing practices unlawful under Title VIII include not only those motivated by a racially discriminatory purpose, but also those that disproportionately affect minorities. Section 3604 "is designed to ensure that no one is denied the right to live where they choose for discriminatory reasons." Although "not every denial, especially a temporary denial, of low-income public housing has discriminatory impact on racial minorities" in violation of Title VIII, an action leading to discriminatory effects on the availability of housing violates the Act.

Starrett's allocation of public housing facilities on the basis of racial quotas, by denying an applicant access to a unit otherwise available solely because of race, produces a "discriminatory effect . . . [that] could hardly be clearer," *Burney v. Housing Auth.*, 551 F. Supp. 746, 770 (W.D. Pa. 1982). . . .

Both Starrett and the government cite to the legislative history of the *Fair Housing Act* in support of their positions. This history consists solely of statements from the floor of Congress. These statements reveal "that at the time that Title VIII was enacted, Congress believed that strict adherence to the anti-discrimination provisions of the [A]ct" would eliminate "racially discriminatory housing practices [and] ultimately would result in residential integration." *Burney*, 551 F. Supp. at 769. Thus, Congress saw the antidiscrimination policy as the means to effect the antisegregation-integration policy. While quotas promote Title VIII's integration policy, they contravene its antidiscrimination policy, bringing the dual goals of the Act into conflict. The legislative history provides no further guidance for resolving this conflict.

We therefore look to analogous provisions of federal law enacted to prohibit segregation and discrimination as guides in determining to what extent racial criteria may be used to maintain integration. . . .

Although any racial classification is presumptively discriminatory, a race-conscious affirmative action plan does not necessarily violate federal constitutional or statutory provisions. However, a race-conscious plan cannot be "ageless in reach into the past, and timeless in ability to affect the future." *Wygant v. Jackson Bd. of Educ.*, 476 U.S. 267 (1986) (plurality opinion). A plan employing racial distinctions must be temporary in nature with a defined goal as its termination point. Moreover, we observe that societal discrimination alone seems "insufficient and over expansive" as the basis for adopting so-called "benign" practices with discriminatory effects "that work against innocent people," *Wygant*, 476 U.S. at 276, in the drastic and burdensome way that rigid racial quotas do. Furthermore, the use of quotas generally should be based on some history of racial discrimination or imbalance within the entity seeking to employ them. Finally, measures designed to increase or ensure minority participation, such as "access" quotas, have generally been upheld. However, programs designed to maintain integration by limiting minority participation, such as ceiling quotas, are of doubtful validity, because they "single[ ] out those least well represented in the political process to bear the brunt of a benign program," *Fullilove* [*v. Klutznick*, 448 U.S. 448, 519 (1980)] (Marshall, J., concurring).

Starrett's use of ceiling quotas to maintain integration at Starrett City lacks each of these characteristics. First, Starrett City's practices have only the goal of integration maintenance. The quotas already have been in effect for ten years. Appellants predict that their race-conscious tenanting practices must continue for at least fifteen more years, but fail to explain adequately how that approximation was reached. In any event, these practices are far from temporary. Since the goal of integration maintenance is purportedly threatened by the potential for "white flight" on a continuing basis, no definite termination date for Starrett's quotas is perceivable. Second, appellants do not assert, and there is no evidence to show, the existence of prior racial discrimination or discriminatory imbalance adversely affecting whites within Starrett City or appellants' other complexes. On the contrary, Starrett City was initiated as an integrated complex, and Starrett's avowed purpose for employing race-based tenanting practices is to maintain that initial integration. Finally, Starrett's quotas do not provide minorities with access to Starrett City, but rather act as a ceiling to their access. Thus, the impact of appellants' practices falls squarely on minorities, for whom Title VIII was intended to open up housing opportunities. Starrett claims that its use of quotas serves to keep the numbers of minorities entering Starrett City low enough to avoid setting off a wave of "white flight." Although the "white flight" phenomenon may be a factor "take[n] into account in the integration equation," it cannot serve to justify attempts to maintain integration at Starrett City through inflexible racial quotas that are neither temporary in nature nor used to remedy past racial discrimination or imbalance within the complex. . . .

We do not intend to imply that race is always an inappropriate consideration under Title VIII in efforts to promote integrated housing. We hold only that Title VIII does not allow appellants to use rigid racial quotas of indefinite duration to maintain a fixed level of integration at Starrett City by restricting minority access to scarce and desirable rental accommodations otherwise available to them. We therefore affirm the judgment of the district court.

JON O. NEWMAN, J., dissenting. . . .

. . . Though the terms of the statute literally encompass the defendants' actions, the statute was never intended to apply to such actions. This statute was intended to bar perpetuation of segregation. To apply it to bar maintenance of integration is precisely contrary to the congressional policy "to provide, within constitutional limitations, for fair housing throughout the United States." 42 U.S.C. §3601.

We have been wisely cautioned by Learned Hand that "[t]here is no surer way to misread a document than to read it literally." That aphorism is not always true with respect to statutes, whose text is always the starting point for analysis and sometimes the ending point. But literalism is not always the appropriate approach even with statutes, as the Supreme Court long ago recognized: "It is a familiar rule, that a thing may be within the letter of the statute and yet not within the statute, because not within its spirit, nor within the intent of its makers."

Title VIII bars discriminatory housing practices in order to end segregated housing. Starrett City is not promoting segregated housing. On the contrary, it is maintaining integrated housing. It is surely not within the spirit of the *Fair Housing Act* to enlist the Act to bar integrated housing. . . . A law enacted to enhance the opportunity for people of all races to live next to each other should not be interpreted to prevent a landlord from maintaining one of the most successful integrated housing projects in America. . . .

. . . Respected civil rights advocates like the noted psychologist, Dr. Kenneth Clark [support Starrett City's policy]. In the words of Dr. Clark: "[I]t would be a tragedy of the highest magnitude if this litigation were to lead to the destruction of one of the model integrated communities in the United States."

Because the *Fair Housing Act* does not require this tragedy to occur, I respectfully dissent.

<h2 style="text-align:center">NOTES AND QUESTIONS</h2>

1. *Remedies.* The *Fair Housing Amendments Act of 1988* (FHAA) amended the *Fair Housing Act of 1968* (FHA) significantly by prohibiting discrimination against families with children (familial status) and against persons with disabilities (handicap). It also beefed up the 1968 act by extending the statute of limitations from six months to two years and by eliminating a $1,000 limit on punitive damages. *See United States v. Big D Enters.*, 184 F.3d 924 (8th Cir. 1999) (sustaining an award of $1000 in compensatory damages and $100,000 in punitive damages in case involving intentional racial discrimination in rental housing). The act also granted the Department of Housing and Urban Development (HUD) the power to enforce the statute; under prior law, HUD was limited to attempting to resolve disputes by persuading housing providers to comply with the statute.

Under the current act, aggrieved persons may file a lawsuit in federal court for injunctive relief and for compensatory and punitive damages, 42 U.S.C. §3613. They may choose instead to file a complaint with HUD, which has the power to investigate and mediate the dispute, as well as to hear and adjudicate the complaint. If HUD has certified a state agency as competent to adjudicate fair housing disputes, HUD will refer the complaint to that state agency rather than handle the complaint itself. §3610(f). If HUD itself investigates the complaint and finds reasonable cause to believe a violation of the law has been committed, it must issue a "charge" on behalf of the aggrieved person, explaining the "the facts upon which the Secretary has found reasonable cause to believe that a discriminatory housing practice has occurred." §3610. When a charge is filed, either the complainant or the respondent may elect to have the complaint heard in federal court rather than in an administrative proceeding held by HUD through an administrative law judge (ALJ). §3612(a). If this option is chosen, HUD will authorize the United States Attorney General to file the lawsuit in federal district court, which is entitled to grant both compensatory and punitive damages, as well as injunctive relief. §3612(o). If no party elects to go to federal court, HUD will conduct a hearing if the complainant so desires. §3612(b). The ALJ is empowered to issue injunctive relief as well as assessing damages, which are limited to $10,000 for first offenses, §3610(g)(3)(A), $25,000 if the defendant has been adjudged to have committed one other offense within five years before the filing of the charge, §3610(g)(3)(B), and $50,000 if defendant committed two or more offenses within seven years, §3610(g)(3)(C), except that the penalties in (B) and (C) may be imposed without reference to the time limits if the same "natural person" committed them. Either plaintiff or defendant may appeal the ALJ's finding to federal court. §3610(i). In addition to enforcement by HUD or a state agency under §§3610 and 3612 and civil actions in federal court brought by the aggrieved party under §3613, the Attorney General is empowered to bring lawsuits against persons who have engaged in a "pattern or practice of resistance to the full enjoyment of any rights" granted by the act under §3614.

2. *Who is liable and standard of liability.* Claims under the FHA can be based either on a showing of discriminatory treatment (intent) or disparate impact. Discriminatory treatment claims involve intentionally treating members of the protected

class differently from others so as to deny particular persons housing opportunities. Disparate impact claims allege that defendant's actions have a disproportionate, exclusionary impact on members of a protected group and that the impact is not justified by legitimate government or business objectives.

As *Asbury* demonstrates, employers are generally vicariously liable for the acts of their employees; thus landlords or real estate brokerage firms may be liable if their agents engage in discriminatory conduct. *See Holley v. Crank*, 400 F.3d 667 (9th Cir. 2004). However, officers of corporations are not generally personally liable unless they acted as an employee or agent of the corporation to direct or approve those discriminatory practices. *Meyer v. Holley*, 537 U.S. 280 (2003).

3. *Prima facie case for discriminatory treatment claims. Asbury v. Brougham* describes the traditional elements of a *prima facie* case under the *Fair Housing Act* for a claim based on discriminatory treatment. Note that this test, articulated in *Asbury*, applies only to claims based on the defendant's "refusal to sell" or "refusal to lease" to plaintiff. A landlord who selectively takes a particular apartment off the market, refusing to rent it to anyone so as to avoid renting it to a member of a protected class, may be violating the statute on the ground that such conduct constitutes a "refusal to deal" or "otherwise make[s] unavailable or den[ies]" housing because of race. 42 U.S.C. §3604(a).

4. *Defendant's justification.* If the plaintiff can produce evidence of the various elements of the *prima facie* case, the burden shifts to the defendant to show a nondiscriminatory reason for the differential treatment. If the defendant fails to assert any such justification and the factfinder is persuaded that the plaintiff has proved the *prima facie* case, the plaintiff will prevail. If the defendant articulates and produces evidence of nondiscriminatory reasons for its actions, plaintiff must show that those reasons are pretextual. If the plaintiff shows that the defendant's justification was pretextual, the jury may conclude (but is not required to conclude) that the real reason for the denial was discriminatory. *Reeves v. Sanderson Plumbing Products, Inc.*, 530 U.S. 133 (2000) (describing the plaintiff's burden in an employment discrimination case). What reasons did defendant articulate in *Asbury*? Are they legitimate under the current statute as amended in 1988? How did the plaintiff attempt to show that the proffered reasons were pretextual?

5. *Racial steering.* Many cases brought under the *Fair Housing Act* concern claims against realtors who have engaged in "racial steering." This practice involves showing African American customers housing in certain areas and white customers housing in other areas. It also involves not telling African American customers about the availability of housing in certain areas. Such practices violate the act by "otherwise mak[-ing] unavailable" housing because of race, *United States v. Mitchell*, 580 F.2d 789 (5th Cir. 1978), and violating the express prohibition against discrimination in "real estate-related transactions" in 42 U.S.C. §3605, which prohibits discrimination by real estate brokers. Racial steering is a form of *redlining*, a practice of marking territory within a municipality in which brokers and lenders (and possibly sellers) will refuse to help individuals obtain housing for discriminatory reasons.

Proving that a realtor has engaged in racial steering often involves the use of "testers." Testers are "individuals who, without an intent to rent or purchase a home or apartment, pose as renters or purchasers for the purpose of collecting evidence of unlawful . . . practices." *Havens Realty Corp. v. Coleman*, 455 U.S. 363 (1982). Testing is done, for example, by using one or more persons to pose as a potential buyer in seeking assistance from a realtor. The plaintiff in *Asbury* used a form of testing when her sister-in-law approached the defendant landlord and asked for housing in the same complex in which the plaintiff had been denied housing. Testers may approach a realtor who has told an African American customer that no housing is available in a certain area; if the realtor shows houses in that area to the white buyer that were not shown to the African American buyer, it may be possible to draw an inference that the realtor was discriminating against the initial buyer on account of her race. Similarly, a white tester may approach a seller to see whether the seller offers different terms than were offered to a prior potential African American purchaser.

6. *Standing.* Who is entitled to bring a lawsuit under the *Fair Housing Act*? Two categories of persons have *standing* to sue to enforce the statute: those who are directly injured by discriminatory acts, and those who have sufficient incentive to litigate the case. Those who are denied housing opportunities in violation of the act clearly have standing to sue. It is also clear that the statute protects whites who are denied housing because of their association with African Americans. *Littlefield v. Mack*, 750 F. Supp. 1395 (N.D. Ill. 1990) (white plaintiff was evicted from her apartment and harassed by defendant landlord because her boyfriend was African American and because they had a child). White persons are also entitled to bring an action against a realtor who engaged in racial steering on the ground that they have been denied the "right to the important social, professional, business and economic, political and aesthetic benefits of interracial associations that arise from living in integrated communities free from discriminatory housing practices." *Havens Realty Corp. v. Coleman*, 455 U.S. at 376. The Supreme Court also held in *Havens* that testers have standing to bring claims in federal court under the *Fair Housing Act* against realtors and sellers who have engaged in racial discrimination. Finally, the Court held that an organization devoted to promoting equal access to housing could bring a lawsuit against a realtor who engaged in steering if it could demonstrate that the defendant's steering practices caused it to devote extra resources to identify available housing and counteract the defendant's steering practices.

7. *Advertising.* Advertisements that limit housing to whites clearly violate the provision of the *Fair Housing Act* that makes it unlawful to "make, print, or publish-... any notice, statement, or advertisement, with respect to the sale or rental of a dwelling that indicates any preference, limitation, or discrimination based on race, color, religion, sex, handicap, familial status, or national origin, or an intention to make any such preference, limitation, or discrimination." 42 U.S.C. §3604(c). Can the housing provider *indirectly* demonstrate an interest in customers of a certain race?

In *Ragin v. The New York Times Co.*, 923 F.2d 995 (2d Cir. 1991), the court held that a newspaper's practice of publishing real estate advertisements almost always showing white models in a city with a significant population of African Americans and other minorities might violate the *Fair Housing Act* by showing a discriminatory preference. The district court held that the ultimate issue for the factfinder was whether "[t]o an ordinary reader the natural interpretation of the advertisements published [in the newspaper] is that they indicate a racial preference in the acceptance of tenants." In affirming the lower court's opinion, the Second Circuit explained, in an opinion by Judge Ralph Winter:

> Section 3604 (c) states in pertinent part that it is unlawful: "To ... publish ... any ... advertisement, with respect to the sale or rental of a dwelling that indicates any preference ... based on race." ... Beginning our analysis with the statutory language, the first critical word is the verb "indicates." Giving that word its common meaning, we read

the statute to be violated if an ad for housing suggests to an ordinary reader that a particular race is preferred or dispreferred for the housing in question....

Moreover, the statute prohibits all ads that indicate a racial preference to an ordinary reader whatever the advertiser's intent....

The next question is whether and in what circumstances the use of models may convey an illegal racial message....

...Advertising is a make-up-your-own world in which one builds an image from scratch, selecting those portrayals that will attract targeted consumers and discarding those that will put them off. Locale, setting, actions portrayed, weather, height, weight, gender, hair color, dress, race and numerous other factors are varied as needed to convey the message intended. A soft-drink manufacturer seeking to envelop its product in an aura of good will and harmony may portray a group of persons of widely varying nationalities and races singing a cheerful tune on a mountaintop. A chain of fast-food retailers may use models of the principal races found in urban areas where its stores are located. Similarly, a housing complex may decide that the use of models of one race alone will maximize the number of potential consumers who respond, even though it may also discourage consumers of other races.

In advertising, a conscious racial decision regarding models thus seems almost inevitable. All the statute requires is that in this make-up-your-own world the creator of an ad not make choices among models that create a suggestion of a racial preference. The deliberate inclusion of a black model where necessary to avoid such a message seems to us a far cry from the alleged practices that are at the core of the debate over quotas. If race-conscious decisions are inevitable in the make-up-your-own world of advertising, a statutory interpretation that may lead to some race-conscious decisionmaking to avoid indicating a racial preference is hardly a danger to be averted at all costs.

Id. at 999-1001. *See also Spann v. Colonial Village, Inc.*, 899 F.2d 24 (D.C. Cir. 1990); *Saunders v. General Services Corp.*, 659 F. Supp. 1042 (E.D. Va. 1986) (holding that exclusive use of white models in advertising literature might operate as a steering method to indicate a racial preference). The *Spann* case was settled in 1995 for $841,000. Ann Mariano, *Mobil Land to Settle Bias Case; Firm's Condo Ads Failed Test on Racial Makeup*, Wash. Post, June 10, 1995, at E01.

8. *Tipping. Starrett City* presents the possible conflict between integration and nondiscrimination. The dissenting opinion in *Starrett City* cites Dr. Kenneth Clark in support of the idea of allowing the use of racial quotas to prevent "tipping" and thereby to promote the development of integrated communities. Dr. Clark's testimony provided the factual basis for the ruling in *Brown v. Board of Education*, 347 U.S. 483 (1954), which focused on the psychological harm that segregated schools inflicted on African American children. Another noted scholar, Professor Derrick Bell, has criticized the use of such quotas. Bell notes that it is wrong for African American citizens to be denied housing they would otherwise get simply because of white prejudice. In effect, when an exclusionary quota is used to prevent tipping, the number of housing units available to African Americans is measured by the extent of white prejudice in the housing complex; the more prejudice, the lower the tipping level and the fewer the units available to African American purchasers or renters. Bell argues that "[a] so-called benign housing quota seems invidious to the blacks excluded by its operation. They are no less victims of housing bias than are those excluded from neighborhoods by restrictive covenants." Derrick Bell, *And We Are Not Saved: The Elusive Quest for Racial Justice* 153 (1989). *See also United States v. Charlottesville Redevelopment & Housing Authority*, 718 F. Supp. 461 (W.D. Va. 1989) (agreeing with the holding of *Starrett City*).

Can a landlord in an area dominated by African Americans actively seek white tenants to move into the complex as a means of promoting integration? *See South Suburban Housing Center v. Greater South Suburban Board of Realtors*, 935 F.2d 868 (7th Cir. 1991) (yes).

9. *State laws.* Almost every state has some kind of fair housing law. Such laws may regulate more types of discrimination than covered by the federal Fair Housing Act. For example, many state laws prohibit discrimination on the basis of marital status or age while some laws prohibit discrimination because of sexual orientation. In addition, these state laws may apply to housing that is exempt from the Fair Housing Act, such as owner-occupied three-unit buildings or claims that are barred by the federal statute of limitations but timely under state law. When state law mimicks federal law, discrimination victims may bring claims under both federal and state statutes.

PROBLEMS

1. An owner places an advertisement in the newspaper stating: "Shopping center in white community looking for tenants." Has the owner violated the *Fair Housing Act*?

2. You are the lawyer for a newspaper that runs housing advertisements, some of which include pictures. Your client is worried about the recent cases holding publishers liable for publishing advertisements with only white models. Does every advertisement have to include models of different races? Formulate a general policy for the newspaper on how to handle this issue to avoid violating the *Fair Housing Act*.

3. Two apartments are available in an apartment building. An African American woman applies for either of the apartments and is rejected. The landlord rents one apartment to a white woman and the other apartment to an African American man. The African American woman's income, job stability, and so on, were equivalent to, or better than, that of the tenants who were accepted. The landlord has never rented an apartment to a single African American woman. She comes to you for legal advice. Does she have a claim for either race or sex discrimination under the *Fair Housing Act*? What factual research would you need to conduct to answer this question?

4. The following advertisement appears in a newspaper: "Two men seek roommate; white males only." Does this violate §3604(c)? Specifically, does the statute apply to decisions about who will live with a person in his own home or apartment, or does it apply only to sales or to rental decisions by landlords?

5. Would it violate the statute for three women to seek a female roommate by limiting their invitation in a newspaper advertisement to "women only"?

6. Suppose *Starrett City* had discriminated against African American tenants in the past. The owner adopts a preference for African American applicants as a way to make up for its past violations of the law. It will accept two African American tenants for every white tenant until the percentage of African American tenants equals the percentage of African Americans in New York City. Does this violate the *Fair Housing Act*?

7. Your client is a real estate broker with the following questions.

    a. Although she has no illegitimate racial animus, her customers do. If she shows potential buyers houses that she knows sellers will refuse to sell to them because of the buyer's race or ethnicity, she is wasting her time. Her competitors do not do this, and it simply costs too much to pursue sales that are not going to happen. If the owners who engage her services ask her not to show their houses to members of a particular race, and she complies with this request, has she violated the *Fair Housing Act*?

b. A buyer expresses a preference for living in an area that is predominantly white and asks the broker to explain the local racial balance in different neighborhoods. Can the broker answer this question?

c. A buyer wants to live in an "integrated" community. Can the broker give the buyer information about which neighborhoods are "integrated"? *See Hannah v. Sibcy Cline Realtors*, 769 N.E.2d 876, 2001 Ohio 3912 (Ohio Ct. App. 2001)(broker has no duty to answer questions about the racial makeup of a community when a mother wanted to live in a racially integrated community so that her children would not be the only African American children in the school, noting that some courts have held that a broker who answers such a question may be liable for unlawful racial steering, while other courts have held that a broker has not engaged in steering when the racial information is provided in response to a buyer's question).

8. *Harassment.* Section 3617 of the *Fair Housing Act* makes it "unlawful to coerce, intimidate, threaten, or interfere with any person in the exercise or enjoyment of" any "right granted or protected" by the Act. Do the rights granted by the Act include the right to be free from harassment or intimidation by neighbors? In *Halprin v. Prairie Single Family Homes of Dearborn Park Ass'n*, 388 F.3d 327 (7th Cir. 2004), plaintiffs claimed, not that they were prevented from acquiring housing, but that both their neighbors and the homeowners association itself ganged up on them and subjected them to continuing harassment, because they were Jewish. Those acts allegedly included writing anti-Semitic graffiti on their wall, damaging their trees, destroying minutes of board meetings at which the president had threatened to "make an example" of them. Judge Posner noted that the statutory language in §3617 clearly covers activities such as redlining that prevent people from acquiring property; nor was the complaint that the terms and conditions under which they had acquired the property were discriminatory. Rather, the complaint here was about post-acquisition harassment—activity arguably not covered by §3604. The court held that such harassment is a violation of §3617 because a HUD regulation, 34 C.F.R. §100.400(c)(2), interprets §3617 as prohibiting conduct that interferes with the "enjoyment of a dwelling." However, the court did not reach the question of whether the regulation was a valid interpretation of §3617. What do you think?

§10.1.1.3 Civil Rights Act of 1866

Section 1 of the *Civil Rights Act of 1866*, passed pursuant to the thirteenth amendment and reenacted in 1870 after passage of the fourteenth amendment, provides that "[a]ll citizens of the United States shall have the same right, in every State and Territory, as is enjoyed by white citizens thereof to inherit, purchase, lease, sell, hold, and convey real and personal property." 42 U.S.C. §1982. For more than a century, §1982 was interpreted as prohibiting states from passing statutes that deprived African Americans of the capacity to buy or lease real property. The act was interpreted, however, not to encompass discrimination by private housing providers unless mandated by state legislation. This situation changed in 1968 with *Jones v. Alfred Mayer Co.*, 392 U.S. 409 (1968).

Decided the same year Congress passed the *Fair Housing Act, Jones* held that §1982 applied to private acts of discrimination as well as to discriminatory legislation. Today almost all cases brought under the *Fair Housing Act* also allege a violation of §1982.

<u>CITY OF MEMPHIS v. GREENE</u>

451 U.S. 100 (1981)

Justice JOHN PAUL STEVENS delivered the opinion of the Court.

[The City of Memphis, Tennessee, closed the north end of West Drive, a street that crosses a white residential community, thus preventing traffic from a predominantly black community to the north from obtaining access to the street. Black residents challenged the street closing as a violation of §1982. Finding no proof that defendant acted with discriminatory intent, the Supreme Court found no violation of §1982.]

[T]he threshold inquiry under §1982 must focus on the relationship between the street closing and the property interests of the respondents. [T]he statute would support a challenge to municipal action benefiting white property owners that would be refused to similarly situated black property owners. For official action of that kind would prevent blacks from exercising the same property rights as whites. But respondents' evidence failed to support this legal theory. Alternatively, . . . the statute might be violated by official action that depreciated the value of property owned by black citizens. But this record discloses no effect on the value of property owned by any member of the respondent class. Finally, the statute might be violated if the street closing severely restricted access to black homes, because blacks would then be hampered in the use of their property. Again, the record discloses no such restriction.

The injury to respondents established by the record is the requirement that one public street rather than another must be used for certain trips within the city. We need not assess the magnitude of that injury to conclude that it does not involve any impairment to the kind of property interests that we have identified as being within the reach of §1982. . . .

Justice THURGOOD MARSHALL, with whom Justice BRENNAN and Justice BLACKMUN join, dissenting.

[The majority's] analysis ignores the plain and powerful symbolic message of the "inconvenience." Many places to which residents of the area north of Hein Park would logically drive lie to the south of the subdivision. Until the closing of West Drive, the most direct route for those who lived on or near Springdale St. was straight down West Drive. Now the Negro drivers are being told in essence: "You must take the long way around because you don't live in this 'protected' white neighborhood." Negro residents of the area north of Hein Park testified at trial that this is what they thought the city was telling them by closing West Drive. . . . In my judgment, this message constitutes a far greater adverse impact on respondents than the majority would prefer to believe.

The psychological effect of this barrier is likely to be significant. In his unchallenged expert testimony in the trial court, Dr. Marvin Feit, a professor of psychiatry at the University of Tennessee, predicted that the barrier between West Drive and Springdale St. will reinforce feelings about the city's "favoritism" toward whites and will "serve as a monument to racial hostility." The testimony of Negro residents and of a real estate agent familiar with the area provides powerful support for this prediction. . . . I cannot subscribe to the majority's apparent view that the city's erection of this "monument to racial hostility" amounts to nothing more than a "slight inconvenience." . . .

. . . It is simply unrealistic to suggest, as does the Court, that the harm suffered by respondents has no more than "symbolic significance," and it defies the lessons of history and law to assert that if the harm is only symbolic, then the federal courts cannot recognize it. *Compare Plessy v. Ferguson,* 163 U.S. 537, 551 (1896) ("We consider the underlying fallacy of the plaintiff's argument to consist in the assumption that the enforced separation of the two races stamps the colored race with a badge of inferiority. If this be so, it is not by reason of anything found in the act, but solely because the colored race chooses to put that construction upon it"), *with Brown v. Board of Education,* 347 U.S. 483, 494 (1954) ("To separate them from others . . . solely because of their race generates a feeling of inferiority as to their status in the community that may affect their hearts and minds in a way unlikely ever to be undone. . . . Whatever may have been the extent of psychological knowledge at the time of *Plessy v. Ferguson,* this finding is amply supported by modern authority"). The message the city is sending to Negro residents north of Hein Park is clear, and I am at a loss to understand why the majority feels so free to ignore it. . . .

PROBLEM

The *Fair Housing Act* exempts owner-occupied buildings with four or fewer units. A landlord who owns and lives in a two-story house rents the second floor as a separate apartment. She refuses to rent to an African American family. Does the family have a claim against the landlord under §1982, or is the landlord entitled to discriminate under §3603(b)(2)? What arguments can you make on both sides of this question? *See Bills v. Hodges,* 628 F.2d 844, 845 n.1 (4th Cir. 1980); *Morris v. Cizek,* 503 F.2d 1303 (7th Cir. 1974); *Johnson v. Zaremba,* 381 F. Supp. 165 (N.D. Ill. 1973) (§1982 claim available).

§10.1.2   Sex Discrimination: Sexual Harassment

EDOUARD v. KOZUBAL
2002 Mass. Comm. Discrim. LEXIS 154 (Mass.
Comm'n Against Discrimination, 2002)

BETTY E. WAXMAN, Hearing Officer

On March 27, 1998, Elizabeth Edouard ("Complainant"), filed a complaint of discrimination with the Massachusetts Commission Against Discrimination ("Commission"), charging Antoni Kozubal with sexual harassment in violation of Mass. Gen. Laws ch. 151B, §4, 18. The charge is based on incidents spanning July 28, 1997 to October 13, 1997 in which the Respondent, who was Complainant's landlord, sought to have Complainant accompany him on a "date" in exchange for a reduction in Complainant's rental deposit, slapped Complainant on the buttocks, squeezed Complainant's breasts and nipples, and attempted to rape her. . . .

II. Findings of Fact

1. The Complainant, Elizabeth Edouard, is a certified nursing assistant and a former school bus driver, with two sons ages thirteen (13) and five (5) as of the public hearing date. At the time of the public hearing, the Complainant was married but separated from her husband. . . .

3. On the day that Complainant signed the lease, Respondent invited her to accompany him to Plymouth, MA. When Complainant declined, Respondent told her that he was going to invite her another time for a weekend visit to Plymouth.

4. On Saturday, July 26, 1997 [and on Sunday, July 27, 1997,] Respondent repeatedly called Complainant. . . .

6. On July 28, 1997, Complainant went to Respondent's office to pick up a key for the apartment. She saw his car, but Respondent did not answer the doorbell. Complainant called Respondent from a shopping mall. He answered the phone and told her, "If you can't help me, I can't help you." These words and their implication made Complainant angry. She drove back to Respondent's office and again rang the doorbell. Respondent answered the doorbell but refused to give Complainant a key unless she gave him three months rent in advance. Complainant objected to paying three months rent in advance on the basis that they had agreed to a prepayment of two months rent, consisting of the first months rent and a security deposit. When she questioned why the payment had increased, the Respondent said, "Because I invited you to go to Plymouth and you didn't go. If you can't help me, I can't help you either. Everybody pays three months rent, so now you pay three months." Complainant was shocked by Respondent's words but paid the three months rent and was given a key. Complainant moved into the apartment a couple of weeks later.

7. Several weeks after Complainant moved into the apartment, she was in the lobby or hallway of her building with her two children. Respondent appeared and said, "You're being mean to me, what happened?" Complainant replied by saying, "Tony, I can't talk to you." Respondent proceeded to slap Complainant on her buttocks in a half-joking manner. Her eldest son reacted to the incident by telling his mother that "it's not nice to let people do that to you."

8. Some time in August, 1997, Respondent used his key to try to enter Complainant's apartment but a double lock barred his entrance. Respondent spoke through the door, asking Complainant's oldest son where his mother was. The son told Respondent that his mother was in the shower. Respondent told the son to convey the message that he wanted to go take Complainant to Plymouth for the weekend.

9. Some time before October, 1997, Respondent called Complainant and told her he was going to move her to the first floor of her apartment building because her kids were jumping too much on the second floor. Complainant said that before she moved, she would have to inspect the new apartment. Complainant testified that they met at the new apartment on October 13, 1997. At one point during the inspection she was looking inside the kitchen cabinets for roaches. Her arms were raised to the cabinets, and she had her back to Respondent. She felt Respondents arms encircling her breasts and his

hands squeezing her nipples. Complainant tried to turn around and push Respondent away, but was not successful. Respondent pushed Complainant so that she fell to the floor on her stomach. He then tried to grab her legs and put his fingers in her pants. Complainant resisted by trying to crawl away from him and push him away with her feet. After several minutes, Complainant was able to get out of the apartment. According to Complainant, Respondent was trying to touch her "private parts."...

10. Complainant went upstairs to her apartment and called 911. Police officers responded to her call and Complainant explained what happened. Respondent was arrested that day. A court record indicates that a criminal complaint against Respondent was issued on November 17, 1997. It specifies that a charge of Assault with Intent to Rape was disposed of by entry of a *Nolle Prosequi* on July 21, 1998, and that charges of Indecent Assault and Battery on a Person Fourteen (14) or over were disposed of on May 12, 1999 with Findings of Sufficient Facts on two counts. The charges were continued without guilty findings until May 10, 2001, with supervised probation for six months. Respondent was ordered to stay away from Complainant.

11. Several weeks after the assault, Complainant left her apartment early one morning when it was still dark to go to her job as a school bus driver. She was startled to see Respondent standing in the shadows. Respondent told Complainant not to be afraid and that if she would "drop the case," he would let her stay in the apartment for the remaining term of the lease without paying any more rent. Complainant got into her car, went to work, and called the police to report that Respondent had violated the restraining order. Respondent was arrested a second time....

13. Following the incidents with Respondent, Complainant was scared, depressed, and experienced diminished self-esteem. Complainant testified that she felt like Respondent treated her like a prostitute. She took a month's sick leave from work immediately after the assault incident and stayed out of work until after Thanksgiving, 1997. Following the assault, Complainant started to see a licensed clinical social worker for therapy at the South Bay Mental Health Center. She testified that she began therapy about three weeks after the assault... The therapeutic notes indicate... that she began treatment on December 24, 1997 and that the therapy continued until May 1998. Complainant's husband, who was working in Florida at the time, blamed Complainant for the incidents. Although Complainant and her sons moved to Florida in August 1998, they moved back to Massachusetts in August 2000....

III. Conclusions of Law

Sexual harassment is defined in Mass. Gen. Laws ch. 151B §1(18) as "sexual advances, requests for sexual favors, and other verbal or physical conduct of a sexual nature when (a) submission to or rejection of such advances, requests or conduct is made explicitly or implicitly a term or condition of employment or as a basis for employment decisions; (b) such advances, requests or conduct have the purpose or effect of unreasonably interfering with an individual's work performance by creating an intimidating, hostile, humiliating or sexually offensive work environment. Discrimination on the basis of sex shall include, but not be limited to, sexual harassment." The form of harassment defined in subpart (a) in the statute is known as *quid pro quo* harassment. The form of harassment defined in subpart (b) in the statute is known as hostile environment harassment. In this case, Complainant alleges both types of sexual harassment.

To establish a *prima facie* case of discrimination by *quid pro quo* harassment, Complainant must demonstrate that (a) she is a member of a protected class; (b) she was subject to unwelcome sexual conduct; (c) the tangible terms or conditions of her situation adversely changed; and (d) the change was causally connected to her rejection of the sexual advances.

Complainant is a member of a protected class on the basis of her sex. She was subject to unwelcome sexual conduct in July 1997 when Respondent insisted that she go on a "date" with him to Plymouth, MA. Complainant was shocked and angry at Respondent's attempt to coerce her into a relationship with him. She communicated that Respondent's conduct was unwelcome by refusing his solicitation. As a direct result of her refusal, Complainant was forced to pre-pay an additional month's rent as a deposit. Based on the foregoing, I conclude that the terms and conditions of Complainant's rental situation were adversely affected and that the change was causally connected to Complainant's rejection of Respondent's sexual advances. These factors establish a *prima facie* case of *quid pro quo* sexual harassment.

Complainant has also established a case of hostile environment sexual harassment as a result of her unrebutted claims that in August 1997, Respondent slapped her on the buttocks and that in October 1997 he grabbed her breasts, squeezed her nipples, and attempted to rape her. Such conduct qualifies as the type of sexually charged behavior which is unwelcome and has the effect of creating a hostile, humiliating or offensive environment.

In arriving at the conclusion that Complainant has proven *quid pro quo* sexual discrimination and hostile environment sexual harassment in a landlord-tenant context, I note that Respondent failed to appear at the hearing and introduce evidence to rebut the claims against him. Thus, Complainant has established an unrebutted *prima facie* case in support of her allegations. Although Complainant would be entitled to prevail on this ground alone, she exceeded this threshold obligation by testifying in a sincere and credible manner.

. . . The unrebutted evidence establishes convincingly that Complainant was propositioned, penalized for rejecting the proposition, and assaulted twice in a blatantly sexual manner. Court records reinforce the claims by establishing that Respondent pled guilty to or admitted to sufficient facts in regard to charges of Indecent Assault and Battery, that a restraining order was imposed against him, and that Respondent was arrested a second time for violating the restraining order. Accordingly, Complainant has made out a case of sexual harassment by her landlord under Mass. Gen. Laws ch. 151B §4(18). . . .

An award of monetary damages is appropriate to compensate Complainant for the emotional distress she suffered as a victim of the Respondents' unlawful discrimination. . . .

Complainant testified convincingly that following the incidents with Respondent, she was scared, depressed, and experienced diminished self-esteem. She felt as though she had been treated like a prostitute. Complainant's distress was compounded by the fact that her husband, who was working in Florida at the time, blamed her for the incidents. She attributes ongoing marital problems, in part, to the incidents with Respondent.

No proof of physical injury or psychiatric consultation is necessary to sustain an award for emotional distress. *See Labonte* v. *Hutchins & Wheeler*, 678 N.E.2d 853, 860

(Mass. 1997) (a finding of discrimination, by itself, permits an inference of emotional distress as a normal adjunct of such discrimination). In this case, however, the claim of emotional distress is enhanced by the fact that Complainant did seek counseling with a licensed clinical social worker at the South Bay Mental Health Center in order to cope with symptoms of post traumatic stress disorder resulting from the sexual assault. Complainant's diagnostic formulation by the Center confirms that she was experiencing symptoms of the disorder consisting of flashbacks, sleep disturbance, fears, and avoidance. Complainant participated in approximately twenty counseling sessions offered by the Center. She also took a month's sick leave from work immediately after the incident, staying out of work until after Thanksgiving, 1997. These arrangements attest to the detrimental impact that Respondent's harassment had on Complainant's life.

I conclude that Complainant is entitled to $50,000.00 in emotional distress damages based on the foregoing evidence....

NOTES AND QUESTIONS

1. The Massachusetts fair housing statute expressly defines sexual harassment as a form of sex discrimination. In contrast, the federal Fair Housing Act has no such provision. Nonetheless, the Supreme Court has held that sexual harassment does constitute sex discrimination in the employment context, at least when the perpetrator is a male supervisor and the victim is a female employee. *Meritor Savings Bank, FSB v. Vinson*, 477 U.S. 57 (1986)(interpreting Title VII of the *Civil Rights Act of 1964*). In such cases, it appears that the courts presume the employer would not have engaged in the conduct had the employee been a man. Several courts have held that sexual harassment of a female tenant by a male landlord or real estate broker similarly constitutes sex discrimination. *Krueger v. Cuomo*, 115 F.3d 487 (7th Cir. 1997); *People of the State of New York v. Merlino*, 694 F. Supp. 1101 (S.D.N.Y. 1988); *Grieger v. Sheets*, 689 F.Supp. 835 (N.D. Ill. 1988). *See also Williams v. Poretsky Management, Inc.*, 955 F.Supp. 490 (D. Md. 1996) (sexual harassment of tenant by superintendant violates Fair Housing Act); *Beliveau v. Caras*, 873 F.Supp. 1393 (C.D.Cal. 1995)(same).

2. *How severe must the harassment be?* In *DiCenso v. Cisneros*, 96 F.3d 1004 (7th Cir. 1996), when the landlord came to the tenant's apartment to collect the rent he caressed her arm and back, and said that if she could not pay the rent, she could "take care of it in other ways"; when she slammed the door in his face, he called her a "bitch" and a "whore." The Seventh Circuit noted that employment discrimination cases had recognized sex discrimination in the context of a "hostile environment" and that those cases required the employer's conduct must be "sufficiently severe or pervasive to alter the condition's of the victim's employment," *id.* at 1008 (*quoting Harris v. Forklift Sytems, Inc.*, 510 U.S. 16, 21 (1993)), and that this one incident did not rise to that level. Do you agree? *See* Michele Adams, *Knowing Your Place: Theorizing Sexual Harassment at Home*, 40 Ariz. L. Rev. 17 (1998)(arguing that housing discrimination should be subject to different standards than employment discrimination because of the importance of the home as a safe place).

Would the plaintiff in *DiCenso* have a remedy under §3604(c)? *See* Robert G. Schwemm & Rigel C. Oliveri, *A New Look at Sexual Harassment under the Fair Housing Act: The Forgotten Role of §3604(c)*, 2002 Wis. L. Rev. 771 (arguing in the affirmative).

3. *Same-sex harassment.* A male landlord makes sexually suggestive comments to a male tenant. Is this sex discrimination? The Supreme Court has held in an employment discrimination case that same-sex sexual harassment *may* constitute discrimination, but only if the harassment is "because of" sex. *Oncale v. Sundowner Offshore Services, Inc.*, 523 U.S. 75 (1998). What does this mean? "The critical issue . . . is whether members of one sex are exposed to disadvantageous terms or conditions of employment to which members of the other sex are not exposed." *Id.* at 80. Justice Ginsburg explained, *id.* at 80-81 (emphasis in original):

Courts and juries have found the inference of discrimination easy to draw in most male-female sexual harassment situations, because the challenged conduct typically involves explicit or implicit proposals of sexual activity; it is reasonable to assume those proposals would not have been made to someone of the same sex. The same chain of inference would be available to a plaintiff alleging same-sex harassment, if there were credible evidence that the harasser was homosexual. But harassing conduct need not be motivated by sexual desire to support an inference of discrimination on the basis of sex. A trier of fact might reasonably find such discrimination, for example, if a female victim is harassed in such sex-specific and derogatory terms by another woman as to make it clear that the harasser is motivated by general hostility to the presence of women in the workplace. A same-sex harassment plaintiff may also, of course, offer direct comparative evidence about how the alleged harasser treated members of both sexes in a mixed-sex workplace. Whatever evidentiary route the plaintiff chooses to follow, he or she must always prove that the conduct at issue was not merely tinged with offensive sexual connotations, but actually constituted "*discrimina[-tion]* . . . because of . . . sex.*"

Is it fair for the courts to presume that a male landlord who sexually harasses a female tenant is discriminating "because of sex" but not to make the same assumption when a male landlord sexually harasses a male tenant? Is a finding of sex discrimination justified when a gay male landlord sexually harasses a male tenant but not justified when the landlord is not gay? What does it mean to discriminate "because of sex"? *Cf. Campbell v. Garden City Plumbing & Heating, Inc.*, 2004 MT 231, 97 P.3d 546 (Mont. 2004)(4-3 decision holding that a male employee did not meet burden of showing sex discrimination in employment when his male supervisors and co-workers sexually harassed him; plaintiff lost because he did not prove that he was treated differently because of his sex, either because of hostility to men (as opposed to women) or because he was treated differently than he would have been treated had he been a woman).

4. *Sexual orientation.* It is quite clear that a landlord commits race discrimination if she refuses to rent to a white female tenant because that tenant's boyfriend is African American. By analogy, it appears clear that a refusal to rent to someone who is gay commits sex discrimination because the denial is based on the sex of the persons to whom the prospective tenant is attracted or has a relationship. In addition, such a landlord is engaged in a form of sex stereotyping by assuming that tenants should only have sexual partners of the opposite sex. *See Price Waterhouse v. Hopkins*, 490 U.S. 228 (1989) (sex discrimination in employment when employer engaged in sex stereotyping by not giving partnership to a woman who was deemed "too masculine"). However, no court has held that discrimination in the housing market on the basis of sexual orientation constitutes sex discrimination, partly because only about a dozen states have statutes expressly prohibiting discrimination in public accommodations or housing on the basis of sexual orientation (*see* §10.1.4, below), and the courts have interpreted

the antidiscrimination laws not to show evidence of a legislative intent to prohibit discrimination based on sexual orientation. *But see Baehr v. Lewin*, 852 P.2d 44 (Hawai'i 1993)(holding that refusal to allow same-sex couples to marry is unlawful sex discrimination under state constitution).

PROBLEMS

1. An owner of a house lives in the first-floor apartment and rents the top floor as a separate apartment. The owner sexually harasses the tenant, engaging in the same kind of outrageous conduct as the landlord in *Edouard v. Kozubal*. What legal rights does the tenant have?

2. A gay male couple wish to rent an apartment, and the landlord refuses because of their sexual orientation. The landlord rents other apartments to unmarried heterosexual couples. One of the two men sues the landlord under the *Fair Housing Act*, claiming that the landlord discriminated against him "because of . . . sex," arguing that if he had been a woman, the landlord would have rented the apartment to the couple. Does the landlord's conduct constitute sex discrimination?

3. A male landlord sexually harasses both a male tenant and a female tenant. Other tenants in the building are not harassed. Has the landlord engaged in discrimination "because of sex"? *Compare Holman v. Indiana*, 211 F.3d 399 (7th Cir. 2000) ("Title VII does not cover the 'equal opportunity' or 'bisexual' harasser . . . because such a person is not *discriminating* on the basis of sex. He is not treating one sex better (or worse) than the other; he is treating both sexes the same (albeit badly)") *with Steiner v. Showboat Operating Co.*, 25 F.3d 1459 (9th Cir. 1994) ("even if [the employer] used sexual epithets equal in intensity and in an equally degrading manner against male employees, he cannot thereby 'cure' his conduct toward women"). Does it matter whether the landlord harasses them in different ways? *See Kopp v. Samaritan Health System, Inc.*, 13 F.3d 264 (8th Cir. 1993) (discrimination present when harassment of women was more severe than harassment of men); *Chiapuzio v. BLT Operating Corp.*, 826 F.Supp. 1334 (D. Wyo. 1993) (employer committed sex discrimination by sexually harassing both a husband and wife who worked for him when the harassment took different forms, *i.e.*, asking the wife to have sex with him, while telling her husband he could make love to her better than the husband could).

4. If a landlord excludes single males while renting to single females and married couples, has he engaged in sex discrimination?

5. One tenant in an apartment building sexually harasses another tenant in the hallways. The victim asks the landlord to evict the harasser. The landlord takes no action. Has the landlord violated the Fair Housing Act? Does it matter whether the lease contains an express covenant by the tenant not to disturb the quiet enjoyment of other tenants? *See Neudecker v. Boisclair Corp.*, 351 F.3d 361 (11th Cir. 2003) (tenant harassed because of his disability by other tenants had a Fair Housing Act claim against the landlord, who revealed the disability to the other tenants and failed to act to stop the harassment); *Reeves v. Carrollsburg Condominium Unit Owners Ass'n*, 1997 U.S. Dist. LEXIS 21762 (D.D.C. 1997) (homeowners association may be liable for sex discrimination when it failed to intervene to protect a homeowner from sexual harassment by another unit owner in common areas when condominium regulations prohibited owners from interfering with the use of common areas).

§10.1.3 DISCRIMINATION BASED ON FAMILY STATUS

§10.1.3.1 Familial Status: Families with Children

HUMAN RIGHTS COMMISSION v. LABRIE, INC.
668 A.2d 659 (Vt. 1995)

FREDERIC W. ALLEN, C.J.

Defendants LaBrie, Inc., Linda LaBrie and Ernest LaBrie appeal from superior court orders, which held that defendants committed unfair housing practices by discriminating against persons with minor children in violation of Vt. Stat. tit. 9 §4503(a). Defendants claim that (1) the court's findings on disparate-treatment discrimination are clearly erroneous because the evidence did not show any intent to discriminate, . . . (5) the court committed plain error by holding Ernest LaBrie personally liable for unfair housing practices. . . . We affirm.

On May 1, 1981, Linda and Ernest LaBrie purchased Limehurst Mobile Home Park. The Park consists of thirty-three mobile home lots. Most of the residents own their own mobile homes and rent only the lot. LaBrie, Inc. purchased the Park from Ernest and Linda LaBrie on October 30, 1987. Ernest and Linda LaBrie are the sole corporate officers and shareholders of LaBrie, Inc. Ernest LaBrie is the president, and Linda LaBrie is the vice-president and treasurer. The office of LaBrie, Inc. is in their home. The Park is managed primarily by Linda, who is responsible for renting units, collecting rent, and making all general management decisions. She also sets policies, rules, and lease terms, and approves residents for tenancy. Ernest is primarily responsible for maintenance under the direction of Linda but is aware of the decisions made by Linda.

When the LaBries purchased the Park, the lease term on occupancy stated "that only one family shall occupy a mobile home on a permanent basis." In 1982, the LaBries changed the occupancy provision to:

> Lessees, who have entered into a lease agreement after April 1, 1982, shall *not* be permitted to have *children under the age of 18 years* reside in their mobile home unit. Lessee hereby agrees that lessee shall terminate this lease and vacate the premises prior to having said children reside in their mobile home. (Emphasis added.)

In July 1988, the occupancy provision was essentially the same but stated in addition, "This age restriction applies to all lots at Limehurst Mobile Home Park based on VSA 9-4508(b)."

In April 1989, the occupancy provision was revised to state:

> Lessees who have entered into a lease agreement after July 1, 1988 shall *not* be permitted to have *more than two permanent occupants* per lease premises. . . . Lessees prior to July 1, 1988, who have more than two permanent occupants shall be grandfathered, but the number of occupants cannot expand beyond what existed as of July 1, 1988. (Emphasis added.)

Currently, only one mobile home in the Park houses a family with a minor child. This family moved into the Park prior to 1982. No persons with minor children moved into the Park after the LaBries purchased it, even after the occupancy provision was changed from adults-only to a two-occupant maximum. The population of the Park declined from May 1981 to May 1990, from ninety-five residents to sixty residents. The

LaBries also own two other mobile home parks, four homes leased as residential units, and twelve mobile homes throughout Vermont. There are minor children living in many of these homes.

Scott and Luanne McCarthy purchased a mobile home in the Park for $7,000 in August 1986. Linda LaBrie sent them a letter on August 1, 1986, accepting their application, and stating: "We remind you that Limehurst Mobile Home Park is an adult park and if you should have children in the future you will be required to vacate Limehurst Mobile Home Park prior to the arrival of said child." In July 1989, the McCarthys contacted a broker to sell their mobile home because Luanne was pregnant. The broker determined that the McCarthys should ask $18,000 for their home.

The McCarthys' son was born September 18, 1989. When they returned home from the hospital, they found a letter from Linda LaBrie informing them that they must vacate the premises "upon arrival of your third occupant." Following the letter, the McCarthys received telephone calls, visits, and additional letters from Linda LaBrie telling them to vacate the Park. On December 28, 1989, the McCarthys were served with a summons and complaint for eviction brought by the LaBries in the name of LaBrie, Inc. d/b/a Limehurst Mobile Home Park.

When the McCarthys informed the LaBries that they had accepted a deposit for the sale of their home, the LaBries delayed the sale, indicating that they would not act on the purchasers' application until the eviction action was resolved. The purchasers' application was approved February 25, 1990, and the McCarthys sold their mobile home on March 2, 1990, for $13,000. At trial, the broker testified that one-half of potential purchasers were ineligible because a minor child in the family put them over the occupancy limit. There was conflicting evidence regarding the value of the home, but the court determined that the fair market value of the home at the time of the sale was $13,000.

From September 1989 through March 1990, while living at the Park, Luanne McCarthy felt humiliated by Linda LaBrie's demands to vacate the premises. Consequently, she did not leave her home often. She was unable to sleep and had chest pains. The McCarthys moved from the Park to the home of Scott McCarthy's parents, where they had to share a family room in the basement with their newborn child. Luanne McCarthy worried about their inability to find their own housing; her chest pains increased and she was given two medications to relieve stress.

The McCarthys filed a complaint with the Human Rights Commission, which commenced this action in Washington Superior Court in October 1990, alleging that defendants LaBrie, Inc., Linda LaBrie, and Ernest LaBrie violated the *Fair Housing and Public Accommodations Act*, Vt. Stat. tit. 9 §4503(a)(1)-(3), by discriminating against persons intending to occupy a dwelling with one or more minor children. The Commission contended that the restrictive occupancy limit for the Park (1) was adopted for the purpose of discriminating against persons with minor children by either limiting or eliminating them from occupancy in the Park, and (2) although facially neutral, has an unlawful discriminatory impact because it excluded persons with minor children in significant numbers. Defendants maintained that the occupancy limit was necessary due to limited water and septic capacity.

At trial, both parties presented expert testimony on the capacity of the septic system and water supply at the Park. Defendants' expert testified that the septic system at the Park was adequate to serve a maximum of sixty-six people. The court found that the expert had not performed the tests necessary to properly assess the potential capacity of the septic system, and concluded that there was no credible evidence that the system could not support an increase in population in the Park. Similarly, the court found that there was no credible evidence that water supply or water pressure was inadequate to serve more than sixty-six people. Although the court acknowledged the LaBries' fear that problems — which had existed prior to installation of a new well and replacement of their leachfields — would reoccur, it concluded that the LaBries have less restrictive alternatives available to them than the two-person occupancy limit.

The court concluded that plaintiff had established that the McCarthys were evicted due to the presence of a minor child, and that persons with minor children were constructively denied access to housing in the Park by the two-person occupancy limit. Further, the court concluded that defendants had not established the occupancy limit as a legitimate business necessity arising from septic and water capacities of the Park. Accordingly, the court held that defendants had violated Vt. Stat. tit. 9 §4503(a) and awarded the McCarthys $2,700 in attorney's fees for the eviction proceeding, $1,500 for the emotional distress and humiliation suffered as a result of defendants' actions, $3,000 for loss of civil rights caused by the eviction and by restricting potential purchasers, and $3,000 in punitive damages. The court also awarded the Human Rights Commission civil penalties of $6,000. In subsequent orders, the court permanently enjoined defendants from adopting or enforcing a two-person-per-lot occupancy limit at the Limehurst Mobile Home Park, and awarded plaintiff $51,072 in attorney's fees, $2,194.39 for expenses and $240 for discovery costs. Defendants appeal....

The *Vermont Fair Housing and Public Accommodations Act* (FHPA), Vt. Stat. tit. 9 §§4500-4507, prohibits discrimination in renting "a dwelling or other real estate to any person because of the race, sex, sexual orientation, age, marital status, religious creed, color, national origin or handicap of a person, or because a person intends to occupy a dwelling with one or more minor children, or because a person is a recipient of public assistance." Vt. Stat. tit. 9 §4503(a)(1). Discrimination on the basis of age, or because a person intends to occupy a dwelling with one or more minor children, has been prohibited in the rental of dwelling units in Vermont since 1986....

Mobile home lot rentals were, however, covered by a separate provision enacted in 1988, which did not strictly prohibit discrimination on the basis of age or because a person intended to occupy a dwelling with one or more minor children. The mobile-home-lot-rental provision was repealed in 1989, when the Legislature revised Vermont's housing discrimination laws to comply with the federal *Fair Housing Act* Amendments of 1988. Thus, Vermont's general housing-discrimination provision has been applicable to the rental of mobile home lots since 1989.

FHPA is patterned on Title VIII of the *Civil Rights Act of 1968 (Fair Housing Act)*, 42 U.S.C. §§3601-3631, and therefore, in construing FHPA, we consider cases construing the federal statute. Courts analyzing Title VIII, the federal housing-discrimination statute, often rely on cases analyzing Title VII, the federal employment-discrimination statute.... Accordingly, we also consider Vermont and federal employment-discrimination law in analyzing the instant case.

Plaintiff alleged violations of FHPA under two theories of discrimination law: (1) disparate treatment — defendants intentionally discriminated against members of a statutorily protected category because of their membership in that group, and (2) disparate impact — defendants' facially neutral policy has a disproportionate effect on a statutorily protected category. The trial court found defendants liable for housing discrimination under both theories. We do not address defendants' challenges to the trial court's finding of disparate impact because we uphold the trial court's decision on the theory of disparate treatment.

Defendants first claim that the court erred in finding disparate treatment or intent to discriminate in the absence of any direct evidence of discrimination against persons with minor children. Intentional discrimination may be shown by circumstantial or direct evidence. Thus, the short answer to defendants' challenge is that no direct evidence is necessary to prove a disparate-treatment discrimination claim. Indeed, direct evidence of unlawful discrimination is often difficult to obtain.

In this case, however, plaintiff presented direct evidence of discrimination. . . . [E]vidence of a discriminatory practice prior to civil rights legislation, coupled with a post-legislation pattern of maintaining the status quo, may be sufficient to establish the intent to continue the discrimination through a neutral policy. In this case, the trial court found that defendants clearly excluded minor children from the Park prior to 1989. That year, Vermont's mobile-home-lot-rental provision was repealed, and defendants changed the occupancy provision in their leases from adults-only to a two-person maximum. Although the new occupancy provision appears neutral on its face, defendants have maintained the status quo at the Park—no minor children have moved into the Park since defendants purchased it. This evidence is sufficient to infer that the two-person occupancy limit was adopted for the purpose of eliminating or limiting persons with minor children from the Park. Based on defendants' actions against the McCarthys and defendants' pattern and practice of excluding minor children from the Park, we conclude that there was no clear error in the trial court finding an intent to discriminate against persons intending to occupy a dwelling with one or more minor children.

Pursuant to Vt. Stat. tit. 9 §4504(4), defendants assert as an affirmative defense that their actions against the McCarthys were based on a legitimate, nondiscriminatory occupancy limit. Section 4504(4) provides that the unfair-housing-practices provisions do not apply "to limit a landlord's right to establish and enforce legitimate business practices necessary to protect and manage the rental property, such as the use of references. However, this subdivision shall not be used as a pretext for discrimination in violation of this section." FHPA is a remedial statute; thus, we construe it generously and read exemptions narrowly. . . .

At trial, defendants maintained that their occupancy limit is based on legitimate septic and water capacity considerations. They presented evidence that the septic system at the Park was capable of handling a maximum of sixty-six people—or two persons per lot. They also presented evidence on the limits of the Park's water supply. The trial court rejected this defense, finding that defendants had failed to present credible evidence that an increase in the number of occupants per living unit would adversely affect the septic or water systems. It also found that there are less restrictive alternatives available to defendants. The court, therefore, concluded that the business necessity advanced by defendants was not legitimate, but rather, a mere pretext for discriminating against persons with minor children. . . .

The federal *Fair Housing Act* has . . . an occupancy restriction provision, which allows only reasonable local, state or federal restriction on the maximum number of occupants per dwelling. *See* 42 U.S.C.A. §3607(b)(1). Courts have found privately imposed occupancy limits, such as the limit imposed by defendants in this case, to unreasonably limit or exclude persons with minor children, and therefore, violate the *Fair Housing Act. See, e.g., United States v. Lepore*, 816 F. Supp. 1011, 1023 (M.D. Pa. 1991) (court cannot conclude two-person-per-mobile-home lot limitation is reasonable when defendants have never attempted any water-saving or septic-system alternatives). We agree that a privately enforced occupancy limit must be at minimum reasonable.

Defendants failed to show that their actions against the McCarthys were reasonable or that the sixty-six-person limit was reasonable. . . .

PROBLEMS

1. A landlord refused to rent to a childless married couple when they refused to sign a document stating that they would not have children while living in the apartment and would move if the wife became pregnant. *Wasserman v. Three Seasons Association No. 1, Inc.*, 998 F. Supp. 1445 (S.D. Fla. 1998). They sued the landlord under the *Fair Housing Act*, claiming discrimination because of familial status. The landlord contended that the couple is not covered by 42 U.S.C. §3602(k) because they were not yet living with a child, and the woman was not pregnant. The prospective tenants contended, however, that they were "aggrieved persons" entitled to bring a lawsuit. The *Fair Housing Act* defines "aggrieved person" to include "any person who — (1) claims to have been injured by a discriminatory housing practice; or (2) believes that such person will be injured by a discriminatory housing practice that is about to occur." §3602(i). Judge James Lawrence King ruled in favor of the landlord, ruling that plaintiffs were not "aggrieved persons" within the meaning of the FHA because their claimed injury did not bear a sufficient nexus to actual discrimination against members of protected class. What is the plaintiffs' argument that the landlord did violate the FHA? What is the defendant's response? How should the court have ruled?

2. A lesbian couple applies for a foster parents license. Before they are licensed by the state, they notify their landlord of their intention to act as foster parents. The landlord objects and sues to evict them. The tenants argue that they are protected by the "familial status" provisions of the *Fair Housing Act* because, as foster parents, they would be the "designee" of the children's legal guardian (the state agency in charge of the child). *See* §3602(k)(2). The landlord contends that they are not protected by the statute since they have not yet been designated as foster parents and are not yet living with a foster child. Moreover, the landlord points to the qualification in the definition of "familial status" in §3602(k), which states that "[t]he protections against discrimination on the basis of familial status shall apply to any person who is pregnant or is in the process of securing legal custody of any individual who has not attained the age of 18 years." The landlord notes that prospective foster parents are not "pregnant"; moreover, they are not in the process of "securing legal custody" since the state is the legal guardian of foster children, and foster parents are mere "designees" of the state. Are prospective foster parents protected by the *Fair Housing Act*? For one view, *see Gorski v. Troy*, 929 F.2d 1183 (7th Cir. 1991) (holding that they are protected by the FHA).

3. A landlord rents apartments to married couples with children and to single persons without children. The landlord refuses to rent to a single mother who has never been married. The landlord argues that she has religious objections to sex outside of marriage and wishes not to rent to mothers who have children out of wedlock. The excluded tenant sues the landlord, claiming that she was excluded because of familial status. Is she protected under the *Fair Housing Act*?

4. A landlord converts an apartment building to housing for older persons, evicting current tenants who have children. Are those tenants protected under the *Fair Housing Act*?

§10.1.3.2 Marital Status: Unmarried Couples

McCREADY v. HOFFIUS

586 N.W.2d 723 (Mich. 1998), *vacated and remanded,*
593 N.W.2d 545 (1999)

MARILYN KELLY, J.

We granted leave in this case to determine whether the defendants violated the *Civil Rights Act*, Mich. Comp. Laws §37.2502(1), when they refused to rent to the unmarried plaintiffs. We conclude that the defendants discriminated against the plaintiffs on the basis of their marital status in violation of the *Civil Rights Act*. Defendants' constitutional freedom of religion rights do not supersede the plaintiffs' civil rights under the act....

I. Factual and Procedural Background

Defendants John and Terry Hoffius, a married couple, own residential property in Jackson, Michigan, which they rent. In June 1993, plaintiffs Kristal McCready and Keith Kerr answered defendants' advertisement about the property. Defendants refused to rent it to these plaintiffs when they learned that McCready and Kerr were single, but intended to live together. Similarly, plaintiff Rose Baiz telephoned defendants about the property a month later. Defendants refused to rent to Baiz, also, when they learned that she was not married to plaintiff Peter Perusse, yet planned to live with him. Defendant John Hoffius told these plaintiffs that unmarried cohabitation violated his religious beliefs.

Plaintiffs filed two separate complaints with the Jackson Fair Housing Commission. Testers from the commission posed as potential renters and contacted defendants. Defendants did not ask the marital status of all the testers. However, they refused to permit unmarried couples to inspect the apartments, claiming that the units were available only to married couples. They stated that usually they did not rent to unmarried couples.

Plaintiffs filed two separate actions in circuit court. Defendants moved for summary disposition, arguing in part that plaintiffs failed to state a claim upon which relief could be granted, because the *Civil Rights Act* does not protect unmarried cohabitation. Defendants argued alternatively that, if the act protects unmarried cohabitation, it is unconstitutional, because it would force defendants to violate their sincerely held religious beliefs against unmarried cohabitation....

II. Analysis ...

B. Marital Status

The *Civil Rights Act* prohibits discrimination based on marital status. The question before us is whether the state's interest in providing equal access to housing to all regardless of their membership in prescribed categories supersedes defendants' religious rights. It is complicated by the existence of an antiquated and rarely enforced statute prohibiting lewd and lascivious behavior.[5]

First, we examine the language of the *Civil Rights Act* itself. It provides, in pertinent part, Mich. Comp. Laws §37.2502:

> (1) A person engaging in a real estate transaction, or a real estate broker or salesman, shall not on the basis of religion, race, color, national origin, age, sex, familial status, or marital status of a person or a person residing with that person:
> (a) Refuse to engage in a real estate transaction with a person.

Being that the act is remedial, we construe it liberally. We strive to give effect to the Legislature's intent in drafting it.

The Court of Appeals noted correctly that the purpose of the act was to prevent discrimination based on membership in certain classes. It was intended to eliminate the effects of offensive or demeaning stereotypes, prejudices, and biases. However, we cannot agree with the Court of Appeals determination that the act does not protect the plaintiffs in this case.

The sole factor that defendants employed in determining that plaintiffs were unworthy of renting their available apartments was plaintiffs' marital status. The Legislature's intent to prohibit discrimination based on this factor is made clear by the inclusion of "marital status" in the act. "The language is simple, and its meaning is not difficult to comprehend." It seeks to prohibit discrimination "based on *whether* a person is married." *Miller v. C. A. Muer Corp.*, 362 N.W.2d 650 (Mich. 1984). Nothing in the legislative history of the *Civil Rights Act* limits the term "marital status" to protecting married couples only.

When faced with a similar argument, that "marital status" does not include unmarried couples, the California Supreme Court recently determined that "the statutory language banning discrimination based on 'marital status' naturally carries both meanings [married and unmarried]." *Smith v. Fair Employment and Housing Comm'n*, 913 P.2d 909 (Cal. 1996). We agree. Where the language of a statute is clear and unambiguous, the courts must apply the statute as written.

In this case, the defendants refused to rent to plaintiffs because their marital status is "single" and, therefore, unmarried. We will not read the act to shield such a discriminatory act.

1. STATUS VERSUS CONDUCT

The defendants argue that they did not discriminate against plaintiffs because of their marital status; rather, they refused to rent to plaintiffs on the basis of their perception of plaintiffs' conduct.

In *Swanner v. Anchorage Equal Rights Comm'n*, 874 P.2d 274 (Alaska 1994), the Alaska Supreme Court interpreted the definition of marital status as used in its statute, one similar to Michigan's, which prohibits discrimination in real estate transactions. In

---

5. Mich. Comp. Laws §750.335 provides: Any man or woman, not being married to each other, who shall lewdly and lasciviously associate and cohabit together, and any man or woman, married or unmarried, who shall be guilty of open and gross lewdness and lascivious behavior, shall be guilty of a misdemeanor....

Swanner, the court affirmed an Anchorage Equal Rights Commission order that the landlord's policy against renting to unmarried couples constituted unlawful discrimination based on marital status. The landlord would have rented his properties to certain couples had they been married, and refused to rent to them after learning they were single. The court concluded that the landlord had unlawfully discriminated on the basis of marital status.

When the Alaska Supreme Court decided *Swanner*, the Alaska Legislature had already struck down its statute prohibiting cohabitation. That court's analysis of "marital status" is still instructive to this Court. The landlord in *Swanner* argued, as the landlords argue here, that he did not discriminate against anyone on the basis of marital status. Rather, he asserted, he discriminated because of the applicant's conduct, and such discrimination is not prohibited by the statute.

The court in *Swanner* found that the landlord "cannot reasonably claim that he does not rent or show property to cohabiting couples based on their conduct (living together outside of marriage) and not their marital status when their marital status (unmarried) is what makes their conduct immoral in [the landlord's] opinion." 874 P.2d at 278, n.4. We agree with this analysis.

Here, the defendants contend that their refusal to rent to plaintiffs was based on plaintiffs' conduct, not on their status, and that this discrimination is legally acceptable. We find that defendants' reasoning defies "legal examination and legislative resolve alike." *Dane Co. v. Norman*, 497 N.W.2d 714 (Wis. 1993) (Heffernan, C.J., dissenting). By rejecting this argument, we join the high courts of Alaska, Massachusetts, and California that recently rejected similar arguments.[9]

In *Attorney General v. Desilets*, 636 N.E.2d 233 (Mass. 1994), the Massachusetts Supreme Judicial Court found that an analysis of the [defendant landlords'] concerns shows that it is marital status and not sexual intercourse that lies at the heart of the defendants' objection. If married couple A wanted to cohabit in an apartment owned by the defendants, they would have no objection. If unmarried couple B wanted to cohabit in an apartment owned by the defendants, they would have great objection. The controlling and discriminating difference between the two situations is the difference in the marital status of the two couples.

Plaintiffs' marital status, and not their conduct in living together, is the root of the defendants' objection to renting apartments to the plaintiffs.

The Court of Appeals accurately noted that the public policy of this state favors the institution of marriage. Acknowledging that, we agree with the court in *Smith*, *supra*, that "one can recognize marriage as laudable, or even as favored, while still extending protection against housing discrimination to persons who do not enjoy that status."

2. LEWD AND LASCIVIOUS CONDUCT

The Court of Appeals panel decided that the Legislature would not have intended the *Civil Rights Act* to insulate conduct made criminal by the statute prohibiting lewd and lascivious behavior by unmarried couples. Mich. Comp. Laws §750.335. Conse-

---

9. *Swanner v. Anchorage Equal Rights Comm'n*, 874 P.2d 274 (Alaska 1994); *Attorney General v. Desilets*, 636 N.E.2d 233 (Mass. 1994); and *Smith v. Fair Employment and Housing Comm'n*, 913 P.2d 909 (Cal. 1996).

quently, according to the panel, cohabitation must not be protected conduct under the *Civil Rights Act*. The panel "declined to recognize the *Civil Rights Act* as preventing housing discrimination against unmarried couples and at the same time legitimizing criminal conduct." We find the Court of Appeals reasoning unpersuasive.

By protecting plaintiffs' right to equal access to housing, the Court cannot be said to legitimize criminal conduct. The lewd and lascivious behavior statute has not been used to successfully prosecute unmarried couples who were cohabitating for nearly sixty years.

In 1940, two married couples that had essentially swapped spouses were convicted of violating the statute. *People v. Davis*, 293 N.W. 734 (Mich. 1940), and *People v. June*, 293 N.W. 906 (Mich. 1940). This Court unanimously reversed the convictions. We found that the lewd and lascivious nature of the relationships had not been shown, although the prosecutor had provided proof that the men were cohabitating with each other's wives.

Recently, in the employment context, a federal district court reviewed the living arrangement of a police officer to determine whether he had violated Michigan's statute. At the time, the officer was living with a woman who was not his wife. The judge found that "cohabitating with one who is not one's wife is not, without more, lewd and lascivious conduct." *Briggs v. North Muskegon Police Dep't*, 563 F. Supp. 585, 591 (W.D. Mich. 1983).

The statute does not prohibit cohabitation per se. To be found guilty under it, the couple must "lewdly and lasciviously associate." In this case, there is insufficient evidence that the plaintiffs intended to engage in lewd and lascivious behavior.[12]

Finally, the issue before this Court is not whether plaintiffs violated, or might in the future violate, the lewd and lascivious behavior statute. It is whether the defendants violated plaintiffs' civil rights. We find that they did.

III. Religious Defenses

The defendants assert that the *Civil Rights Act* violates their religious freedom rights under art. 1, §4 of the Michigan Constitution and under the First Amendment of the United States Constitution.

The United States Constitution forbids restrictions to the free exercise of religion. The United States Supreme Court recently ruled that the *Religious Freedom Restoration Act* is unconstitutional.[13] The method to test the constitutionality of alleged restrictions on religious freedom is found in *Employment Div., Oregon Human Resources Dep't v. Smith*, 494 U.S. 872 (1990). It holds that a law burdening a religious practice must be neutral and of general applicability.

The defendants concede that the *Civil Rights Act* is neutral. However, they contend that the act fails the general applicability prong of the test, because it creates nonreligious exemptions. They point to the exemptions concerning owner-occupied leased residences, Mich. Comp. Laws §37.2503(1)(a), (b), and the exclusion of "marital status" from the forms of discrimination applicable to housing accommodations at state institutions of higher learning. Defendants conclude that, because the Legislature

---

12. The parties have not directly attacked the constitutional validity of the statute. Thus, we will not undertake such an analysis.

13. *City of Boerne v. Flores*, 521 U.S. 507 (1997).

provided these exemptions but no exemptions for religiously motivated landlords, the *Civil Rights Act* fails the general applicability prong.

We cannot agree. The law is generally applicable because it prohibits all discrimination and has no religious motivation. The statute contains no language singling out any religious group or practice. It "applies to all people involved in renting or selling property, and does not specify or imply applicability to a particular religious group." *See Swanner*, 874 P.2d at 280.

We agree with the California Supreme Court, which addressed this claim when made by the landlord in *Smith, supra* at 1161.

[The landlord's] religion may not permit her to rent to unmarried cohabitants, but "the right of free exercise does not relieve an individual of the obligation to comply with a valid and neutral law of general applicability on the ground that the law proscribes (or prescribes) conduct that his religion prescribes (or proscribes)."

Thus, we conclude that the *Civil Rights Act* does not violate the Free Exercise Clause of the First Amendment of the United States Constitution.

Next, we turn to defendants' claim that the act violates their religious freedom under art. 1, §4 of the Michigan Constitution of 1963. We analyze the *Civil Rights Act* under the compelling state interest test developed by the United States Supreme Court in *Wisconsin v. Yoder*, 406 U.S. 205 (1972), and *Sherbert v. Verner*, 374 U.S. 398 (1963).

The test has five elements: (1) whether a defendant's belief, or conduct motivated by belief, is sincerely held; (2) whether a defendant's belief, or conduct motivated by belief, is religious in nature; (3) whether a state regulation imposes a burden on the exercise of such belief or conduct; (4) whether a compelling state interest justifies the burden imposed upon a defendant's belief or conduct; and (5) whether there is a less obtrusive form of regulation available to the state. *Yoder*, 406 U.S. at 214-230....

[D]efendants could not prevail on the legal questions. For purposes of analysis, we concede to the defendants' benefit the first three prongs of the test.

The fourth prong requires an examination of whether a compelling state interest in providing equal access to housing justifies the burden on defendants' beliefs. The Michigan Legislature has determined that the need for housing is so fundamental as to necessitate the passing of the *Civil Rights Act*. Its objective was to ensure that no one be denied equal access to housing on the basis of, among other things, their marital status. The state's need to provide equal access to such a fundamental need as housing outweighs defendants' religious beliefs that they should not rent to an unmarried couple.

The state does not require that the defendants violate their sincerely held religious beliefs. It requires only that, if they wish to participate in the real estate market by offering housing for rent, they must comply with the *Civil Rights Act*. The burden placed on the defendants' religious beliefs affects their commercial activities sooner than their beliefs. In *United States v. Lee*, 455 U.S. 252 (1982), the Supreme Court stated: "When followers of a particular sect enter into commercial activity as a matter of choice, the limits they accept on their own conduct as a matter of conscience and faith are not to be superimposed on the statutory schemes which are binding on others in that activity."

Finally, defendants have provided no argument to convince us that the state could have accomplished its goal of equal access to housing by less obtrusive means. We have not identified a less obtrusive alternative to eradicate discrimination in real estate transactions.

The defendants' freedom to exercise their religion under the Michigan and federal constitutions is not violated by requiring their compliance with the *Civil Rights Act* under the facts of this case....

The defendants readily admit that they would have rented their housing accommodations to plaintiffs had plaintiffs been married to one another. Marital status is defined in the context of the presence or absence of marriage. Thus, the defendants' refusal to rent their apartments to plaintiffs solely because they are unmarried constituted marital status discrimination in violation of the *Civil Rights Act*. The act protects unmarried cohabitants against this housing discrimination. . . .

The United States Supreme Court, in *Trafficante v. Metropolitan Life Ins. Co.*, 409 U.S. 205, 211 (1972), stated that eradicating discrimination in housing is of the highest priority. Our holding is consistent with that laudable goal.

Even assuming that the defendants' beliefs are sincerely held and religiously based and that the *Civil Rights Act* imposes a burden on those beliefs, defendants' religious freedom rights have not been violated. A compelling state interest in eradicating discrimination in real estate transactions justifies the burden on their beliefs. In addition, a less obtrusive form of regulation has not been shown to be available to the state. . . .

PATRICIA J. BOYLE, J., dissenting. . . .

"[M]arital status," which is not otherwise defined in the pertinent portion of the statute, refers to the status of being married. It follows logically that the term marital status . . . does not encompass the "status" of being an unmarried cohabitating[1] couple.

The majority correctly notes that California, Alaska, and Massachusetts have found that marital status carries the meaning of both married and unmarried. In my view, the language of Michigan's statute, which is the best evidence of the Legislature's intent, does not support this conclusion. However, even if the term were deemed ambiguous, the public policy embodied in statutes criminalizing cohabitation, Mich. Comp. Laws §750.335, and renouncing common-law marriage, Mich. Comp. Laws §551.2, refute the claim that the Michigan Legislature intends to guarantee access to housing to individuals who choose to cohabit with persons of the opposite sex. Other courts addressing the issue have concluded that retention of "fornication statute," or the repeal by statute of common-law marriages,[2] evidence a public policy inconsistent with defining marital status to encompass cohabitation. *State v. French*, 460 N.W.2d 2 (Minn. 1990); *Mister v. ARK Partnership*, 553 N.E.2d 1152 (Ill. Ct. App. 1990). *See also Jasniowski v. Rushing*, 678 N.E.2d 743 (Ill. Ct. App. 1997) (*Mister* was held to be no longer controlling in light of the decriminalization of cohabitation by Illinois Public Act 86-490, effective January 1, 1990).

The Legislature has not repealed the prohibition against cohabitation. Contrary to the majority's implication, the fact that a criminal statute has not been successfully prosecuted does not somehow render the prohibited conduct legal or the criminal statute void. . . .

This is a paradigm of an issue of magnitude requiring legislative evaluation and resolution of competing factors, such as the legal status of unmarried cohabitation, the need for access to housing, and the free exercise of religion. The Legislature can define

---

1. Cohabitation is defined in Black's Dictionary, as "to live together as husband and wife." In *Dane Co. v. Norman*, 497 N.W.2d 714 (Wis. 1993), the Wisconsin Supreme Court held that living together is conduct, not status.

2. The public policy of this state disfavors the grant of mutually enforceable property rights to knowingly unmarried cohabitants. *Carnes v. Sheldon*, 311 N.W.2d 747 (1981); *Featherston v. Steinhoff*, 575 N.W.2d 6 (Mich. Ct. App. 1997).

marital status to include cohabitants. The Legislature has not done so, and we should not do so by judicial fiat. To ascribe to the Legislature an intention to burden a religious belief in the interest of protecting the conduct at issue[5] requires a suspension of disbelief that is beyond me. . . .

NOTES AND QUESTIONS

1. *Uncertainty in the law.* After the decision reported above, the Michigan Supreme Court vacated the decision and remanded the case to determine whether the statute violated the landlords' free exercise rights by requiring them to rent to a cohabiting unmarried couple, 593 N.W.2d 545 (Mich. 1999). In precisely the opposite direction, a Ninth Circuit decision holding that an Alaska marital status law could not be constitutionally applied to landlords having religious objections to renting to an unmarried couple was vacated on the ground that the case was not ripe for decision. *Thomas v. Anchorage Equal Rights Commission,* 165 F.3d 692 (9th Cir. 1999), *opinion withdrawn and remanded to dismiss the complaint on ground that the case was not ripe for decision,* 220 F.3d 1134 (9th Cir. 2000). *But see Thomas v. Anchorage Equal Rights Comm'n,* 102 P.3d 937 (Alaska 2004) (upholding the constitutionality of applying the prohibition against marital status discrimination against a landlord who had religious objections to renting property to an unmarried couple).

Courts generally agree with the conclusion that prohibitions against discrimination because of "marital status" protects both those who are married and those who are unmarried. Two other issues, however, are quite contentious: First, is the refusal to rent to an unmarried couple prohibited discrimination because of marital *status* or allowable exclusion on the basis of the *conduct* of cohabitation? Second, if state statutes prohibiting marital status discrimination in housing require landlords to rent to cohabiting unmarried couples, do such statutes violate the constitutional rights of the landlords to the free exercise of religion under either the First Amendment or the relevant state constitution?

2. *Marital status or the conduct of cohabitation.* Several courts have held that state statutes that prohibit discrimination in housing on the basis of marital status do not prevent landlords from refusing to rent to unmarried couples. They reason that the discrimination is based on the *conduct of cohabitation* outside of marriage, rather than the mere *status* of being unmarried. *Mister v. A.R.K. Partnership,* 553 N.E.2d 1152 (Ill. 1990); *State by Cooper v. French,* 460 N.W.2d 2 (Minn. 1990); *North Dakota Fair Housing Council, Inc. v. Peterson,* 625 N.W.2d 551 (S.D. 2001); *McFadden v. Elma Country Club,* 613 P.2d 146, 150 (Wash. Ct. App. 1980); *County of Dane v. Norman,* 497 N.W.2d 714 (Wis. 1993).

Other courts that have addressed the issue agree with *McCready* that refusal to deal with an unmarried couple constitutes discrimination on the basis of marital status. *See Swanner v. Anchorage Equal Rights Commission,* 874 P.2d 274 (Alaska 1994); *Smith v. Fair Employment and Housing Commission,* 913 P.2d 909 (Cal. 1996); *Markham v. Colonial Mortgage Service Co.,* 605 F.2d 566 (D.C. Cir. 1979); *Attorney General v. Desilets,* 636 N.E.2d 233 (Mass. 1994). *See also Jasniowski v. Rushing,* 678 N.E.2d 743 (Ill. Ct. App. 1997) (overruling *Mister* after decriminalization of fornication

---

5. The majority does not acknowledge the heavy presumption against repeal by implication.

and holding that it does constitute marital status discrimination to refuse to rent to an unmarried couple).

The Supreme Court's recent decision in *Lawrence v. Texas*, 539 U.S. 558 (2003) has changed the legal landscape in this area by holding that it is an unconstitutional deprivation of due process of law to criminalize consensual sexual conduct between adults in the privacy of the home. Although that decision overturned sodomy laws that had generally been applied only to homosexuals, the decision also effectively wiped out various state statutes that had prohibited sexual conduct outside of marriage between adults. Thus, landlords can no longer argue that they are justified in refusing to rent to unmarried male-female couples because those couples are engaged in criminal behavior by having a sexual relationship outside of marriage.

3. *Religious freedom.* Courts have generally agreed with *McCready* in rejecting claims that fair housing laws violate the religious rights of landlords if they require them to rent to unmarried couples. *Swanner v. Anchorage Equal Rights Commission*, 874 P.2d 274, 278 (Alaska 1994); *Jasniowski v. Rushing*, 678 N.E.2d 743 (Ill. Ct. App. 1997). However, several courts have held that laws requiring landlords to rent property to unmarried couples would violate their constitutional rights to free exercise of religion under either the federal or state constitution. *State by Cooper v. French*, 460 N.W.2d 2, 5-6 (Minn. 1990). *See also Thomas v. Anchorage Equal Rights Commission*, 165 F.3d 692 (9th Cir. 1999) (holding that a fair housing law could not be constitutionally applied to force landlords to rent to unmarried couples), *opinion withdrawn and remanded to dismiss the complaint on ground that the case was not ripe for decision*, 220 F.3d 1134 (9th Cir. 2000). *Cf. Attorney General v. Desilets*, 636 N.E.2d 233, 235 (Mass. 1994) (holding that the state constitution protected a landlord's right not to rent to a cohabiting, unmarried couple unless the plaintiff could demonstrate a compelling state interest in applying the marital status discrimination rules to such landlords).

In *State by Cooper v. French, supra* at 11, the court explained:

> There are certain moral values and institutions that have served western civilization well for eons. *See Maynard v. Hill*, 125 U.S. 190 (1888) (characterizing marriage as "the foundation of family and society, without which there would be neither civilization nor progress"). This generation does not have a monopoly on either knowledge or wisdom. Before abandoning fundamental values and institutions, we must pause and take stock of our present social order: millions of drug abusers; rampant child abuse; a rising underclass without marketable job skills; children roaming the streets; children with only one parent or no parent at all; and children growing up with no one to guide them in developing any set of values. How can we expect anything else when the state itself contributes, by arguments of this kind, to further erosion of fundamental institutions that have formed the foundation of our civilization for centuries?

Chief Justice Peter Popovich, joined by Justices Rosalie Wahl and Alexander Keith, dissented, arguing that defendant's conduct constituted discrimination on the basis of marital status and that the constitutional protection of defendant's religious beliefs did not include a constitutional right to enter the marketplace and engage in discrimination, *id.* at 15-16.

> [B]y entering the public marketplace one is subjecting oneself to laws concerning public behavior, including anti-discrimination laws, that must be balanced against first amendment interests. There is no first amendment right to yell "fire" in a crowded theater. Upon entering the public marketplace appellant could no longer consider just his rights and

beliefs, but became subject to certain state laws and the rights of potential tenants. The legislature has not exempted an isolated sale or rental of property other than the property where the landlord resides. As respondent states, "the First Amendment does not bestow upon the individual an absolute right to require others in the marketplace to adopt those values as a precondition to doing business with him or her." Appellant is free, in his private life, to not associate with anyone whom he feels has the "appearance of evil," but when someone voluntarily enters the public marketplace he may encounter laws that are inconsistent with his religious beliefs. While the Act imposes a burden on French's sincerely held religious belief that living together is sinful, such a burden is greatly lessened because it occurred only when French voluntarily entered into the rental marketplace — by crossing over the line drawn by the legislature — and thus subjecting himself to potentially burdensome regulations such as the Act's prohibition of marital status discrimination. . . .

If the state shows it has a compelling or overriding interest for the burdensome regulation it can prevent a religious-based exemption from that regulation. If the state interest is compelling, it will overbalance any burden on religious beliefs. The question thus is whether the State of Minnesota has a compelling or overriding interest in enforcing the *Human Rights Act*'s prohibition of marital status discrimination in rental housing. . . .

Courts have repeatedly recognized there is a compelling state interest in eradicating invidious discrimination. . . .

4. *Religious Freedom Restoration Acts.* The first and fourteenth amendments to the U.S. Constitution protect the "free exercise" of religion. In *Employment Division v. Smith*, 494 U.S. 872 (1990), the Supreme Court held that no violation of the free exercise clause occurs when a neutral and generally applicable regulatory law places a burden on an individual's religion. With several very narrow exceptions, only laws that prohibit specific religious practices or coerce individuals to engage in religious practices raise constitutional issues of free exercise. Under this formulation, it would be unlikely that the Court would find that an antidiscrimination law violated the free exercise clause if it required a landlord to rent to an unmarried cohabiting couple. Such a law does not require anyone to do anything; it merely regulates the housing market and conditions the job of being a landlord on complying with the antidiscrimination regulations.

In response to *Smith*, Congress passed the *Religious Freedom Restoration Act* (RFRA)[2] in 1993, granting exemptions from government regulations that substantially burden the free exercise of religion unless the government could show a compelling governmental interest for the regulation and that the interest cannot be achieved in a manner less restrictive of religious practice. In 1997, the Supreme Court held RFRA unconstitutional at least as applied to state governments because Congress's power under the fourteenth amendment to regulate the states to protect religious "liberty" could not go beyond the protections afforded by the first amendment. *City of Boerne v. Flores*, 521 U.S. 507 (1997). Because Congress was, in effect, trying to expand federal protection for religious freedom beyond what the Court believed was encompassed by the first amendment, and because Congress was attempting to regulate the states, it exceeded its powers. The meaning and scope of the decision are hotly contested because it involves emerging issues of both federalism and separation of powers.

---

2. 42 U.S.C. §§2000bb-1 to 2000bb-3. The act was later amended by the *Religious Land Use and Institutionalized Persons Act of 2000*, Pub. L. No. 106-274, 115 Stat. 803 (Sept. 22, 2000).

In response to *City of Boerne*, a number of states have passed state statutory versions of RFRA. Alabama amended its constitution to include a version of RFRA. Ala. Const. amend. 622, §V. Other states that passed such laws by statute include Arizona, Ariz. Stat. §41-1493.01; Connecticut, Conn. Gen. Stat. §52-571b; Florida, Fla. Stat. §§761.01-761.05; Idaho, Idaho Code §73-402; Illinois, 775 Ill. Comp. Stat. §35/1-99; New Mexico, N.M. Stat. §§28-22-1 to 28-22-5; Oklahoma, Okla. Stat. tit. 51 §§251-258; Rhode Island, R.I. Gen. Laws §§42-80.1-1 to 42-80.1-4; South Carolina, S.C. Code §§1-32-10 to 1-32-60; and Texas, Tex. Civ. Prac. & Rem. Code §§110.001-110.012. A landlord could argue that these laws implicitly limit the reach of the state antidiscrimination laws. If this is true, and if these state RFRAs are constitutional, then landlords could argue that they cannot be required to rent apartments to unmarried couples, whether of the same or opposite sex, if this imposes a burden on their religious beliefs or practice. They would further argue that no compelling government interest justifies the intrusion on their free exercise of religion and/or that those interests can be achieved without burdening religious freedom.

PROBLEMS

1. In *Hudson v. Weiss*, 450 N.E.2d 234 (N.Y. 1983), a landlord sought to evict a tenant from a rent-controlled apartment on the ground that she had breached a term in her lease under which she covenanted not to allow anyone to occupy the premises with her who was not a member of her "immediate family." She lived with a man "with whom she [had] a loving relationship," but the landlord claimed that, because the couple was not married, the man was not a part of the tenant's immediate family. The tenant argued that the lease term discriminated against her on the basis of marital status. The court found that the man was not a member of the tenant's "immediate family" and that it would not constitute marital status discrimination to enforce the covenant. Do you agree?

2. A state prohibits discrimination in rental housing because of marital status. After passage of the state fair housing law, it passes a state version of RFRA, prohibiting the enforcement of any governmental regulation that "substantially burdens" the "free exercise of religion" unless the state can demonstrate a "compelling governmental interest" and that objective cannot be obtained in a manner "less restrictive of religious freedom." A landlord claims that the state RFRA entitles her to refuse to rent to a cohabiting unmarried heterosexual couple. What is her argument? What is the couple's argument? How should the court rule?

§10.1.4   DISCRIMINATION BASED ON SEXUAL ORIENTATION

STATE EX REL. SPRAGUE v. CITY OF MADISON
555 N.W.2d 409 (Wis. Ct. App. 1996)

ROBERT D. SUNDBY, J. Ann Hacklander-Ready and Maureen Rowe appeal from a decision affirming the Madison Equal Opportunity Commission's (MEOC) Decision and Order which found that they refused to rent housing to Carol Sprague as their housemate because of her sexual orientation, in violation of §3.23(4)(a) of the *Madison General Ordinances* (MGO). . . . We conclude that the trial court correctly found that §3.23, MGO, unambiguously applied to housemates at the time this action arose. . . .

At all times relevant to this action Hacklander-Ready leased a four-bedroom house. She had the owner's permission to allow others to live with her and share in the payment of rent. In the fall of 1988, Maureen Rowe began living with Hacklander-Ready and paying rent. In April 1989 they advertised for housemates to replace two women who were moving out. They chose Sprague from among numerous applicants. They knew her sexual orientation when they extended their offer to her. Sprague accepted their offer and made a rent deposit on May 4, 1989. However, the following day Hacklander-Ready informed Sprague that they were withdrawing their offer because they were not comfortable living with a person of her sexual orientation.

Sprague filed a complaint with MEOC alleging that appellants discriminated against her on the basis of sexual orientation, contrary to §3.23(4)(a), MGO. . . .

At the time of the events in issue, §3.23, MGO, provided:

(1) Declaration of Policy. The practice of providing equal opportunities in housing . . . without regard to . . . sexual orientation . . . is a desirable goal of the City of Madison and a matter of legitimate concern to its government. . . . In order that the peace, freedom, safety and general welfare of all inhabitants of the City may be protected and ensured, it is hereby declared to be the public policy of the City of Madison to foster and enforce to the fullest extent the protection by law of the rights of all its inhabitants to equal opportunity to . . . housing. . . .

(2)(b) "Housing" shall mean any building, structure, or part thereof which is used or occupied, or is intended, arranged or designed to be used or occupied, as a residence, home or place of habitation of one or more human beings. . . .

(4) It shall be an unfair discrimination practice and unlawful and hereby prohibited:

(a) For any person having the right of ownership or possession or the right of transfer, sale, rental or lease of any housing, or the agent of any such person, to refuse to transfer, sell, rent or lease, or otherwise to deny or withhold from any person such housing because of . . . sexual orientation. . . .

(b) Nothing in this ordinance shall prevent any person from renting or leasing housing, or any part thereof, to solely male or female persons if such housing or part thereof is rented with the understanding that toilet and bath facilities must be shared with the landlord or with other tenants.

Sprague claims that §3.23, MGO, was intended to apply to housemate arrangements.[1] . . . Section 3.23(4), MGO, unambiguously prohibits any person having right of rental to refuse to rent to any person because of the person's sexual orientation. Hacklander-Ready concedes that she held the lease to the house and that she had the right to rent the property to others. Further, she and Rowe admit that the sole reason they withdrew their offer was Sprague's sexual orientation. Finally, the room that appellants sought to rent falls within the definition of housing under §3.23(2)(b), MGO, as a part of a building intended as a place of habitation for one or more human beings.

While appellants correctly argue that a statute is ambiguous if it may be construed in different ways by reasonably well-informed persons, we fail to see any reasonable interpretation that would make §3.23, MGO, inapplicable in this case. Appellants also correctly note that a court may resort to construction if the literal meaning of a

---

1. In September 1989, subsequent to the commencement of this action, the Madison City Council amended the Equal Opportunities Ordinance by adding §3.23(c), MGO, which states, "Nothing in this ordinance shall affect any person's decision to share occupancy of a lodging room, apartment or dwelling unit with another person or persons."

statute produces an absurd or unreasonable result. However, applying §3.23(4) to the rental of a room within a house with shared common areas is not unreasonable or absurd. Because we find that the ordinance clearly and unambiguously applies to the subleasing of housing by a person having the right of rental, our inquiry in this respect is at an end.

Appellants argue that to apply the ordinance to the lease of housing by a tenant to a housemate makes §3.24(4)(a), MGO, unconstitutional in its application.... Appellants cite many cases which they argue support their constitutional challenge: *NAACP v. Alabama,* 357 U.S. 449 (1958); *Griswold v. Connecticut,* 381 U.S. 479 (1965); *Moore v. City of East Cleveland,* 431 U.S. 494 (1977).... However, those cases deal either with the right to privacy in the home or family or the right to engage in first amendment activity free of unwarranted governmental intrusion. Appellants gave up their unqualified right to such constitutional protection when they rented housing for profit. The restrictions placed by the Madison City Council on persons who rent housing for profit are not unreasonable and do not encroach upon appellant's constitutional protections. We therefore reject appellants' challenge to the constitutionality of §3.24, MGO, as applied....

NOTES AND QUESTIONS

1. At least 17 jurisdictions have passed statutes that specifically or by judicial interpretation prohibit housing discrimination based on sexual orientation. For example, the *Wisconsin Equal Rights Law,* Wis. Stat. §101.22, provides that "all persons shall have an equal opportunity for housing regardless of . . . sexual orientation." Sexual orientation is defined as "having a preference for heterosexuality, homosexuality, bisexuality, having a history of such a preference or being identified with such a preference." Wis. Stat. §111.32(13m). The statute provides that it is unlawful to discriminate "[b]y refusing to sell [or] rent . . . housing," §106.50(2)(a), and "[by] engaging in the harassment of a tenant," §106.50(2)(f).

Other jurisdictions that prohibit housing discrimination on the basis of sexual orientation include Connecticut, Conn. Gen. Stat. §§46a-81a & 46a-81e; the District of Columbia, D.C. Code §§1-2515; Hawai'i, Haw. Stat. §§368-1, 378-1 *et seq.*; Illinois, 775 Ill. Comp. Stat. 5/3-101 to 5/3-106; Maine, Me. Rev. Stat. tit. 5, §§4552, 4582, *see* LEXSEE 2005 Me. ALS 10; Md. Code art. 49B §19; Massachusetts, Mass. Gen. Laws Ann. ch. 151B, §§1 *et seq.*; Minnesota, Minn. Stat. Ann. §363.03, subd. 2; New Hampshire, N.H. Rev. Stat. §§354-A:8 to 354-A:10; New Jersey, N.J. Stat. Ann. §§10:5-1 *et seq.*; N.M. Stat. §28-1-7; New York, N.Y. Exec. Law §291; Rhode Island, R.I. Gen. Laws §§34-37-1 to 34-37-5.4; and Vermont, Vt. Stat. Ann. tit. 9, §§4502, 4503 Wash. Rev. Code §§49.60.010 to .040. In addition, the *California Unruh Civil Rights Act,* Cal. Civ. Code §51 (Deering 1990), has been interpreted to prohibit discrimination in housing on the basis of sexual orientation. *See Hubert v. Williams,* 184 Cal. Rptr. 161 (App. Dept. Super. Ct. 1982). More than 100 cities also have passed local ordinances prohibiting discrimination in the real estate market based on sexual orientation. *See* Boston Code tit. 12, ch. 40; Chicago Mun. Code, ch. 199; Philadelphia Fair Prac. Ordinance, ch. 9-1100; New York City, Admin. Code §8-102(20); Los Angeles Mun. Code, ch. IV; and San Francisco Code, art. 33, §3301. For a review of the law on discrimination based on sexual orientation, *see* William B. Rubenstein, *Cases and Materials on Sexual Orientation and the Law* (2d ed. 1997).

2. The *Sprague* court found that the ordinance unambiguously applied to choices of roommates. Do you agree? What is the argument on the other side?

3. In *170 West 85 Street HDFC v. Jones*, 673 N.Y.S.2d 830 (Civ. Ct. 1998), the court held that a cooperative corporation may have engaged in unlawful discrimination because of sexual orientation when it refused to allow Vance Jones, the gay life partner of Richard Watts, an owner of a cooperative apartment who had died of AIDS, to purchase the unit and remain living there. The proprietary lease provided that the corporation could not "unreasonably withhold consent to assignment of the lease and a transfer of the Shares to a financially responsible member of the Shareholder's *family* (other than the Shareholder's spouse, as to whom no consent is required) who shall have accepted all the terms and conditions of this lease." *Id.* at 834 (emphasis in original). Both a New York City ordinance and the lease itself prohibited the corporation from discriminating on the basis of sexual orientation. Citing an earlier rent control case that defined a gay life partner to be a "family" member for the purpose of succeeding to rights in a rent-controlled apartment, *Braschi v. Stahl Associates*, 543 N.E.2d 49 (N.Y. 1989),[3] the court noted that Jones fit within a "more comprehensive definition of family member." 673 N.Y.S.2d at 834. This would thus negate the corporation's assertion that Jones was "a licensee whose license had expired, thereby vitiating any independent non-discriminatory grounds which [it] could have asserted to obtain possession of the subject apartment." *Id.*

4. *Damages.* In *In re Application of 119-121 East 97th Street Corp. v. New York City Commission on Human Rights*, 642 N.Y.S.2d 638 (App. Div. 1996), the court upheld a damages award of $100,000 for mental anguish and imposed a civil penalty of $25,000 against landlords who had engaged in highly abusive conduct of a gay tenant with AIDS. The defendants had burglarized the tenant's apartment, disabled his door locks, turned off his electricity, refused to accept his timely rent checks, refused to renew his lease, and commenced eviction proceedings against him. They had also verbally and physically accosted him in public, calling him a "faggot punk," "male whore," and "sicko." They knew he had AIDS and told him they hoped he died. They left threatening messages on his answering machine, distributed a notice to tenants in his building informing them of his Human Rights complaint and HIV status and warned the tenants not to cooperate with him. The court upheld the damages award on the ground that the abuse was both "horrendous" and malicious, *id.* at 644:

> In any event, decency and justice call out for redress to this respondent. The award herein will not only compensate complainant for the mental distress he suffered but will also serve as a deterrent to others who might emulate petitioners' actions. An agenda of spite, malice and bias, acted upon over an extended period of time, resulting in the severe emotional and mental abuse of a tenant, seriously ill with AIDS, will not be met with half-hearted sanctions or "slaps on the wrist," and we concur in the award for mental anguish.

PROBLEMS

1. A lesbian couple living in a 25-unit apartment building is often taunted by teenagers living across the street whenever the couple leaves or enters the building.

   a. Does the couple have a claim against the teenagers under the Wisconsin statute?

---

3. This case is included *supra* at §8.2.2.1.

    b.   Suppose the teenagers live in the same building on another floor. The couple asks the landlord to stop the abusive conduct; the landlord does nothing. Does the couple have a claim against the landlord for violating the Wisconsin statute?

2. Two gay men argue that a landlord's refusal to rent to them constitutes sex discrimination. They argue that it would clearly constitute race discrimination to refuse to rent to two roommates because they were not of the same race and that the same argument applies in the context of sex. They further argue that the landlord rents to unmarried heterosexual couples and that the only reason they have been denied housing is that they are of the same sex. How will the landlord respond to this argument? How will the prospective tenants answer the landlord's arguments?

3. An owner of a three-unit building lives on the first floor with her six-year-old son and rents out the apartments on the second and third floors. Her city prohibits housing discrimination on the basis of both marital status and sexual orientation.

    a.   She refuses to rent to unmarried couples because she believes that her religion would count it to be a sin for her to facilitate sexual relations outside of marriage. She has therefore refused to rent the apartments either to same-sex couples or to male-female couples who are not married. She has, however, rented the second floor apartment to a gay man under a lease that prohibits him from having long-term visitors. When a lesbian couple seeks to rent the third-floor apartment, she refuses. Her city has an ordinance prohibiting discrimination "because of" marital status and sexual orientation. Has she violated the law?

    b.   Now assume she rents the second-floor apartment to an unmarried male-female couple and offers the third-floor apartment for rent. She is willing to rent to individuals regardless of their sexual orientation and to male-female couples whether or not they are married. However, she will not rent to a gay or lesbian couple and insists on a lease that would prohibit subletting and having long-term visitors. Although her religion is opposed to cohabitation outside of marriage, she does not feel it is a sin to rent to an unmarried straight couple. However, her religion strongly condemns same-sex sexual relationships, and it would violate her sincerely held religious beliefs to rent to a cohabiting same-sex couple. She is sued by a gay male couple when she refuses to rent them the open apartment. Has she violated the law?

4. A state court rules that a state statute entitles landlords to refuse to rent apartments to gay, lesbian, and bisexual persons because such rentals would substantially burden their exercise of their religion and that eradication of discrimination because of sexual orientation was not a "compelling state interest" within the meaning of the state religious freedom statute. Another landlord refuses to rent to heterosexual couples on the ground that landlords are entitled to use religious reasons to refuse to rent to gay couples. She claims that her religious beliefs support the choice to engage in a same-sex relationship and that she wants to make housing available to gay and lesbian couples who may have trouble finding housing elsewhere. Has she violated the state statute prohibiting discrimination on the basis of sexual orientation?

§10.1.5   DISCRIMINATION AGAINST PERSONS WITH DISABILITIES

§10.1.5.1   Persons with AIDS

POFF v. CARO

549 A.2d 900 (N.J. Super. Ct. Law Div. 1987)

BURRELL IVES HUMPHREYS, A.J.S.C. . . .

The major and novel issue before this Court is whether a property owner violates the New Jersey *Law Against Discrimination* by refusing to rent to homosexuals because the owner fears that the homosexuals may later acquire the disease known as AIDS. . . .

The *Law Against Discrimination* protects the physically handicapped against discrimination based on that handicap. N.J. Stat. Ann. §10:5-4.1. The defendant questions whether a person suffering from AIDS is a handicapped person within the meaning of the *Law Against Discrimination.* An examination of the disease shows that such a person is clearly handicapped.

AIDS is a terrifying disease which has no known cure. It is transmitted primarily through the blood. Sexual intercourse, whether by homosexuals or heterosexuals, can result in an interchange of blood, and thereby infect another with the disease. . . .

AIDS attacks and eliminates the body's defense system against disease. Once those systems are eliminated, germs otherwise harmless can and do produce devastating and ultimately lethal diseases.

The AIDS disease is sweeping the country and indeed the world. Many public health experts view AIDS as an epidemic. Some compare it to the Black Plague.

Thus, unless medical science can find a cure, a sufferer from AIDS is faced with the grim prospect of a debilitating disease and early death. In such a setting, a person suffering from AIDS clearly has a severe handicap within the meaning of the *Law Against Discrimination.* . . .

The complainants here do not have AIDS and therefore do not have a "handicap." However, discrimination based on a perception of a handicap is within the protection of the *Law Against Discrimination.* . . .

The facts presented here by the Division show a strong prima facie case of discrimination, to wit, that the landlord refused to rent because he believed that the three males would likely get AIDS because they were homosexuals. At the present time AIDS is more prevalent in the homosexual community. That may be changing. In any event the fact that a homosexual is more likely to get AIDS does not afford a valid basis for a belief that these three homosexual men will become infected with AIDS. That would be akin to a belief that if a race or an ethnic group is more likely to contract a particular contagious disease, a member of that race or ethnic group will contract that disease.

The Division's position is further fortified by its persuasive argument that the landlord's conduct would constitute a violation of the laws prohibiting discrimination by reason of sex or marital status. *See* N.J. Stat. §10:5-4.

The conduct of the landlord here, if ultimately proven, is proscribed by the provisions of the law prohibiting discrimination against persons with perceived handicaps. . . .

NOTES AND QUESTIONS

1. *Computing damages.* In *Barton v. New York City Commission on Human Rights*, 531 N.Y.S.2d 979 (Sup. Ct. 1988), *aff'd as modified,* 542 N.Y.S.2d 176 (App. Div. 1989), a dentist terminated a rental agreement with another dentist to whom he had sublet part of his medical offices because the latter treated patients with AIDS referred to him by the Gay Men's Health Crisis (GMHC), a social service agency listing the names of physicians willing to treat AIDS patients. The subtenant, Dr. John W. Wolf, filed a complaint with the New York City Human Rights Commission, claiming that defendant had violated New York City Administrative Code §§8-105(4), 8-107(5)(b), 8-108, and 8-109(1) by discriminating on the basis of physical handicap. The Human Rights Commission held that persons with AIDS are "physically handicapped" within the meaning of the antidiscrimination ordinance and that defendant had terminated plaintiff's sublease because plaintiff treated AIDS patients. Defendant's explanation that he was concerned that proper sterilization procedures would not be followed was pretextual, the commission concluded. Moreover, defendant's fear that he would lose patients and staff if the office were filled with AIDS patients was not a legitimate defense: "It is well settled that customer preference can never be the basis for discrimination." The commission awarded Dr. Wolf $15,000 in damages for mental anguish. On appeal to the trial court, Judge Helen E. Freedman upheld the damages award, quoting Dr. Wolf's testimony:

> Well, I'm a gay man. I have many friends . . . who either had AIDS or ARC [AIDS-related complex]. . . . The dentist[s] that I used to work for as a dental assistant, Dr. Iott and Dr. Zac, both treated persons with AIDS and I knew that they were being inundated. There were relatively few who were willing to do so. The need was becoming greater and greater, and I wanted to do a service to my community.

531 N.Y.S.2d at 986. Judge Freedman continued:

> [Dr. Wolf] further testified that when he removed his name from the GMHC referral list he felt that he "was abandoning a good deal of friends and community."
>
> His lover Paul Barile testified that Dr. Wolf sustained "a loss of professional morality," meaning that he was "a dedicated person to his profession and also to the gay community. His inability to practice . . . to service the needs [of] the community manifested itself in that he felt a loss of professionalism." Barile testified that during the period that the practice was restricted Wolf suffered severe mental anguish and depression, causing him to smoke excessively, overeat, [and] be "very irritable" and "very short fused." As a result the two had less sexual contact with each other.

Id. On appeal, the Appellate Division reduced the damage award to $5,000 on the ground that $15,000 was "grossly excessive" and "shocking to one's sense of fairness." What do you think? How should the court determine an appropriate level of damages?

2. *Federal Rehabilitation Act of 1973.* In addition to the *Fair Housing Act,* the *Federal Rehabilitation Act of 1973,* 29 U.S.C. §794, prohibits discrimination on the basis of handicap in federally funded programs. That act provides, in part:

> No otherwise qualified individual with a disability . . . shall, solely by reason of her or his disability, be excluded from the participation in, be denied the benefits of, or be subjected to discrimination under any program or activity receiving Federal financial assistance.

Although disagreements and uncertainties may arise about what constitutes "federal financial assistance," it clearly includes any direct transfer payments made by the government, such as those made to public housing programs and to individual tenants for use in paying for private housing (Section 8 housing). *See Housing Authority of Lake Charles v. Pappion*, 540 So. 2d 567 (La. Ct. App. 1989) (Section 8 housing); *Whittier Terrace Associates v. Hampshire*, 532 N.E.2d 712 (Mass. App. Ct. 1989) (private housing subsidized by HUD).

Many cases address the issue of identifying which persons with handicaps are "otherwise qualified" for the program financed by federal funds under the *Federal Rehabilitation Act*. A spate of recent cases has addressed the question whether handicapped tenants are "otherwise qualified" to remain in publicly subsidized housing. In *Pappion, supra*, the court held that a paranoid schizophrenic tenant was not "otherwise qualified" to remain in a subsidized housing project because he interfered with the quiet enjoyment of other tenants by making loud noises, threatening other residents, and engaging in "bizarre" behavior. In *City Wide Associates v. Penfield*, 564 N.E.2d 1003 (Mass. 1991), however, the court found that a tenant in subsidized Section 8 housing who suffered from a mental disability manifested by her hearing voices was "otherwise qualified" despite the fact that she had responded to the auditory hallucinations by striking the walls of the apartment, causing superficial damage amounting to less than one month's rent. The court justified its holding on the ground that the tenant had not disturbed the quiet enjoyment of neighboring tenants and had promised to obtain counseling.

§10.1.5.2   Reasonable Accommodation of Persons with Disabilities

In *Schuett Investment Co. v. Anderson*, 386 N.W.2d 249 (Minn. Ct. App. 1986), a physically handicapped tenant with a back problem faced eviction after failing to remove boxes that constituted a fire hazard. The court disallowed the eviction, noting that the tenant had made arrangements to have the boxes removed before the time of the court hearing and that the *Federal Rehabilitation Act* placed an obligation on the landlord to make reasonable accommodations for the tenant's handicap. In *Whittier Terrace Associates v. Hampshire*, 532 N.E.2d 712 (Mass. App. Ct. 1989), the court held that a landlord could not evict a tenant who violated the rules of the project by keeping a cat in the apartment. The tenant had a psychiatric disability and had an emotional attachment to, and perhaps even a psychological dependence on, the cat; moreover, the cat did not bother any of the neighbors. In an analogous case based on state law in California, the court held that a deaf tenant's roommate had a claim for refusal to rent because of the deaf person's signal dog, even though the plaintiff roommate was not deaf. *Schwab v. Rondel Homes, Inc.*, 262 Cal. Rptr. 138 (Ct. App. 1989).

The *Fair Housing Act*, as amended by the *Fair Housing Amendments Act of 1988*, provides that it constitutes illegal discriminatory conduct to

> refus[e] to permit, at the expense of the handicapped person, reasonable modifications of existing premises occupied or to be occupied by such person if such modifications may be necessary to afford such person full enjoyment of the premises except that, in the case of a rental, the landlord may where it is reasonable to do so condition permission for a modification on the renter agreeing to restore the interior of the premises to the condition that existed before the modification, reasonable wear and tear excepted....

42 U.S.C. §3604(f)(3)(A). The statute further provides that the landlord may not "refus[e] to make reasonable accommodations in rules, policies, practices, or services, when such accommodations may be necessary to afford such person equal opportunity to use and enjoy a dwelling." 42 U.S.C. §3604(f)(3)(B).

The Department of Housing and Urban Development has promulgated regulations to implement the *Fair Housing Act*. The section relevant to the landlord's obligations to permit reasonable modifications, 24 C.F.R. §100.203(c), contains several examples:

> Example (1): A tenant with a handicap asks his or her landlord for permission to install grab bars in the bathroom at his or her own expense. It is necessary to reinforce the walls with blocking between studs in order to affix the grab bars. It is unlawful for the landlord to refuse to permit the tenant, at the tenant's own expense, from making the modifications necessary to add the grab bars. However, the landlord may condition permission for the modification on the tenant agreeing to restore the bathroom to the condition that existed before the modification, reasonable wear and tear excepted. It would be reasonable for the landlord to require the tenant to remove the grab bars at the end of the tenancy. The landlord may also reasonably require that the wall to which the grab bars are to be attached be repaired and restored to its original condition, reasonable wear and tear excepted. However, it would be unreasonable for the landlord to require the tenant to remove the blocking, since the reinforced walls will not interfere in any way with the landlord's or the next tenant's use and enjoyment of the premises and may be needed by some future tenant.
>
> Example (2): An applicant for rental housing has a child who uses a wheelchair. The bathroom door in the dwelling unit is too narrow to permit the wheelchair to pass. The applicant asks the landlord for permission to widen the doorway at the applicant's own expense. It is unlawful for the landlord to refuse to permit the applicant to make the modification. Further, the landlord may not, in usual circumstances, condition permission for the modification on the applicant paying for the doorway to be narrowed at the end of the lease because a wider doorway will not interfere with the landlord's or the next tenant's use and enjoyment of the premises.

The regulation pertinent to the landlord's duty to make reasonable accommodations in rules and practices, 24 C.F.R. §100.204, contains the following examples:

> Example (1): A blind applicant for rental housing wants to live in a dwelling unit with a seeing eye dog. The building has a "no pets" policy. It is a violation of §100.204 for the owner or manager of the apartment complex to refuse to permit the applicant to live in the apartment with a seeing eye dog because, without the seeing eye dog, the blind person will not have an equal opportunity to use and enjoy a dwelling.
>
> Example (2): Progress Gardens is a 300 unit apartment complex with 450 parking spaces which are available to tenants and guests of Progress Gardens on a "first come first served" basis. John applies for housing in Progress Gardens. John is mobility impaired and is unable to walk more than a short distance and therefore requests that a parking space near his unit be reserved for him so he will not have to walk very far to get to his apartment. It is a violation of §100.204 for the owner or manager of Progress Gardens to refuse to make this accommodation. Without a reserved space, John might be unable to live in Progress Gardens at all or, when he has to park in a space far from his unit, might have great difficulty getting from his car to his apartment unit. The accommodation therefore is necessary to afford John an equal opportunity to use and enjoy a dwelling. The accommodation is reasonable because it is feasible and practical under the circumstances.

PROBLEMS

1. A mobile home park charges its residents a fee of $1.50 a day for the presence of long-term guests and $25 per month for guest parking. A tenant whose daughter's health condition requires a full-time attendant argues that the owner violated the *Fair Housing Act*'s reasonable accommodation provisions by refusing to waive the charges for her attendant. The Ninth Circuit has held that the regulation would violate §3604(f)(3)(B) if it had an "unequal impact" on persons with disabilities and resulted in an "exclusionary effect" so long as the financial impact on the landlord was not "unduly burdensome." *United States v. California Mobile Home Park Management Co.*, 29 F.3d 1413 (9th Cir. 1994). Do you agree with this formulation of what §3604(f)(3)(B) requires? Assume that the financial burden to the landlord is minimal and that enforcement of the policy will not cause the tenants to move. Should accommodation be required under the terms of the statute?

2. A tenant living on the first floor of a three-unit building of three stories is in a car accident and is paralyzed from the waist down. He wants, at his own expense, to install a ramp to enable him to enter the front door without assistance since his wheelchair could not negotiate the steps to the front porch. Without such a ramp, he cannot return home. The small front yard will be largely taken up by the ramp if the ramp is installed. The landlord objects to the installation of the ramp on esthetic and economic grounds. She can demonstrate that the market value of the property will decline from $200,000 to $180,000 if the ramp is installed. The tenant argues that he will pay to have the ramp removed if he moves out of the apartment. Is the landlord required to allow the tenant to install the ramp? *See Rodriguez v. Montalvo*, 337 F.Supp.2d 212 (D.Mass. 2004) (presumptive Fair Housing Act duty to allow tenant to affix permanent ramp to back entrance of building when landlord gave no proof this would cause him any financial harm).

§10.1.6 ECONOMIC DISCRIMINATION

§10.1.6.1 Welfare Recipients

ATTORNEY GENERAL v. BROWN

511 N.E.2d 1103 (Mass. 1987)

NEIL L. LYNCH, Justice.

... In October, 1983, the Attorney General filed suit against Harold Brown, alleging violations of Mass. Gen. Laws ch. 151B, §4(6) and (10), and seeking declaratory and injunctive relief and damages for "Section 8 certificate holders." The Attorney General claimed that Brown violated Mass. Gen. Laws ch. 151B, §4(10), which prohibits landlords from discriminating against recipients of public assistance or housing subsidies including rental assistance "solely because the individual is such a recipient." It was further alleged that, because most of such recipients are members of minorities, Brown violated Mass. Gen. Laws ch. 151B, §4(6), which prohibits certain persons, including landlords of multiple dwelling or contiguously located housing accommodations from refusing to rent or to lease to, and from discriminating against, individuals "because of the race, religious creed, color, national origin, sex, age, ancestry or marital status" of such persons. On April 1, 1986, the judge granted the plaintiff's motion for summary judgment and ruled that Brown was in violation of Mass. Gen. Laws ch. 151B, §4(6) and (10). Brown appealed and we granted direct appellate review. We reverse. . . .

. . . In his order of April 1, 1986, the Housing Court judge found that the Boston Housing Authority (BHA) and the Executive Office of Communities and Development (EOCD), which issue Section 8 certificates in the Boston area [pursuant to 42 U.S.C. §1437f], currently provide Section 8 assistance payments on behalf of 3,670 and 2,826 eligible families, respectively. Approximately 50% of the families who received Section 8 certificates through BHA and EOCD are unable to secure housing for which they can use their certificates, "principally because of discrimination against Section 8 certificate holders." He also found that Section 8 certificate holders are "overwhelmingly blacks and other minorities."

The judge further found that Harold Brown, who owns or has a general partnership interest in 8,000 residential units of which 3,000 are in the Allston-Brighton area of Boston, refused to process rental applications from holders of Section 8 certificates. Between July, 1982, and May, 1984, Brown had approximately 800 apartments in the one-bedroom to three-bedroom category that were within the fair market rentals allowed under Section 8. The reasons given by Brown for his practice of refusing to rent to Section 8 certificate holders were as follows: He would not rent to anyone who did not make an advance payment of the last month's rent and sign the lease form used by Brown's own realty company; Section 8 leases are materially less advantageous to him; it is more costly to deal with the administrative bureaucracy of the Section 8 program, and he loses money from a tenant from whom he cannot collect the last month's rent. . . .

The judge granted summary judgment for the Attorney General and held that Brown's practice of refusing to process rental applications from Section 8 certificate holders was a violation of Mass. Gen. Laws ch. 151B, §4(10). He found that Brown's reasons were directed at the regulatory and administrative requirements of the program and, therefore, constituted discrimination against a Section 8 certificate holder "solely because the individual is such a recipient." He also granted summary judgment for the Attorney General on the alleged violation of Mass. Gen. Laws ch. 151B, §4(6), stating that Brown's practice of refusing to process applications from Section 8 certificate holders had a disproportionate impact on members of minorities. . . .

In his opposition to the plaintiff's motion for summary judgment, Brown claimed that he had legitimate business reasons for refusing to accept Section 8 tenants. He stated in his affidavit that he wished to use his own lease form because the Section 8 lease was less advantageous to him and that, in some instances, housing authorities have allowed variations. He further claimed that it was important for him to be able to collect the last month's rent and, in some cases, one month's rent as a security deposit, because he could earn more money in interest than the amount which he must return to the tenant.

In his appeal Brown claims that he did not violate Mass. Gen. Laws ch. 151B, §4(10), since he did not discriminate against Section 8 certificate holders "solely" because they were recipients of such assistance. He claims that summary judgment was inappropriate due to disputed issues of fact material to his claims.

It is clear that local housing authorities cannot make accommodations which conflict with the provisions of the Section 8 program. The regulations do not allow for advance payment of the last month's rent. *See* 24 C.F.R. §§882.105(b) and 882.112(b)[4] (1986). Advance payment is limited to a security deposit of $50 or one month's total tenant payment, whichever is greater. 24 C.F.R. §882.112(a) (1986). The regulations

---

4. This section was redesignated 24 C.F.R. §882.414 in 1995. — ED.

provide for remedies in the event that the tenant vacates the premises owing rent. 24 C.F.R. §882.112(b).

A local housing authority could not approve Brown's standard lease since it contains provisions which are clearly contrary to the provisions of the Section 8 program. Under the regulations, the lease must comply with requirements of the program and cannot contain certain prohibited lease provisions. 24 C.F.R. §882.209(k) & Appendix I (1986). Brown's lease contained provisions such as those requiring advance payment of the last month's rent and a security deposit over and above that allowed under the regulations.

. . . Brown claims that legitimate business reasons kept him from renting to Section 8 certificate holders, primarily his loss of the cash flow engendered from his collecting, in advance, the last month's rent and a security deposit equal to one month's rent. That these reasons are related to the requirements of the Section 8 program does not necessarily equate with discrimination "solely" on the basis of the individual's status as a Section 8 certificate holder. Brown should have an opportunity to litigate the issue whether his reasons are legitimate business reasons which are not satisfied by the protections afforded by the regulations of the Section 8 program.

The Attorney General claims that the protections gained from the collection of the last month's rent in advance are provided by 24 C.F.R. §882.105(b), which provides that, when a tenant leaves in violation of the lease, a landlord may collect from the housing authority the total rent payment for that month plus 80% of the total rent payment for an additional month, provided the apartment remains vacant. It is unclear whether, in the present case, these protections are enough to dispel the negative effects, if any, that would inure to Brown in his not being able to collect from Section 8 certificate holders an advance of the last month's rent and a security deposit greater than that allowed by Section 8 regulations. Furthermore, Brown contends that not only is he forced to forgo the security afforded by the advance payments that he normally collects, but also that he is being deprived of the benefits of a positive cash flow for various of his projects as well.

The Attorney General claims that any loss due to the inability of Brown to collect the last month's rent is "de minimis" since under Mass. Gen. Laws ch. 186, §15B, a landlord must place a tenant's security deposit in a separate account and pay the tenant 5% annual interest. While the amount of interest over 5% that a landlord may be able to obtain on an advance of the last month's rent on an individual apartment may be "de minimis," that is not necessarily the case here. As stated above, Brown owns or has interest in 3,000 residential units in the Allston-Brighton area of Boston and between July, 1982, and May, 1984, had approximately 800 units that fell within Section 8 guidelines. An interest spread of 1% in Brown's favor would be a substantial economic benefit and it does not necessarily follow that his attempt to maintain that benefit constitutes discrimination "solely" because the individuals seeking tenancy were recipients of assistance under the Section 8 program. Thus, since issues of fact must be resolved, the plaintiff is not entitled to summary judgment. . . .

Judgment reversed.

§10.1.6.2   Discrimination Based on Income

In *Harris v. Capital Growth Investors XIV*, 805 P.2d 873 (Cal. 1991), a landlord refused to rent to two women, Tamela Harris and Muriel Jordan, who were "female heads of low income families whose income consists solely of public assistance benefits" because the landlord had a policy of renting only to tenants who have gross monthly incomes of at least three times the rent to be charged. Plaintiffs sued, claiming that the income requirement was not necessary to protect the landlord's legitimate business interests and that under the California *Unruh Civil Rights Act* (Civ. Code §§51, 52), the income requirement constituted discriminatory treatment on the basis of income and created an unjustified disparate impact on women. The court rejected both claims.

In an earlier case, *In re Cox*, 474 P.2d 992 (Cal. 1970), the California Supreme Court had liberally interpreted the *Unruh Civil Rights Act*, applying it to an exclusion of a patron of a business establishment for reasons not involving the specific categories listed in the act, such as race and color. The court held that a shopping center did not have the right to exclude the customer based only on his association with a young man "who wore long hair and dressed in an unconventional manner." Despite the listing of specific types of discrimination in the statute, the court concluded "that the *Unruh Act* prohibited all 'arbitrary discrimination by a business enterprise' and that the listing was 'illustrative rather than restrictive' of the kinds of discrimination prohibited by the Act." In *Marina Point, Ltd. v. Wolfson*, 640 P.2d 115 (Cal. 1982), the court applied *Cox* to hold that the owner of an apartment complex violated the act by refusing to rent to families with minor children.

In *Harris*, Justice Malcolm Lucas distinguished *Cox* and *Marina Point*, noting that the listed categories, as well as the decisions in those cases, involved "personal as opposed to economic characteristics — a person's geographical origin, physical attributes, and personal beliefs" and that the list did not include any reference to "financial or economic status." The court noted that "[b]usiness establishments have an obvious and important interest in obtaining full and timely payment for the goods and services they provide," 805 P.2d at 873, and that the minimum income policy merely pursues "the objective of securing payment" in a reasonable manner. *Id.* at 875. If this policy were illegal, the landlord would respond by raising rents to compensate for the added vulnerability to nonpayment. The court noted that "plaintiffs' view of the Act would involve the courts of this state in a multitude of microeconomic decisions we are ill equipped to make." *Id.* at 887.

In a dissenting opinion, Justice Allen Broussard stated that the "effect of the majority's holding today is that the poor no longer have standing to challenge arbitrary and invidious discrimination against them as a class under the *Unruh Act*. We know that the poor are discriminated against." *Id.* at 897. While "[i]t is obvious that a minimum income policy might be invoked legitimately by a business to ensure payments for goods sold on credit, it should be equally obvious that minimum income policies might be abused, motivated solely by a discriminatory animus." *Id.* at 898. Moreover, Justice Broussard argued, "poverty is [no] less a 'personal characteristic' than long hair or unconventional dress. Neither is immutable; both personal appearance and poverty are likely to inspire in us certain stereotypical views that will likely color our perceptions. Indeed, the person with long hair or unconventional dress is far more able to escape from discrimination based on these characteristics than the person suffering the ills of poverty. . . ." *Id.*

The majority also rejected the disparate impact claim. Plaintiffs had argued that a "disproportionate number of families receiving public assistance are headed by women," that "[w]omen generally have lower average incomes than men," and that defendant's minimum-income policy "excludes a disproportionate number of female-

headed households from the pool of applicants to whom defendants will rent units."
Id. at 889-890. The court narrowly interpreted the *Unruh Act*, finding that it prohibited
intentional discriminatory treatment alone and that a disparate impact claim could not
be made out under the act. What would have happened if plaintiffs had based their
claim on the federal *Fair Housing Act* instead?

§10.2   Disparate Impact Claims

§10.2.1   RACIALLY DISCRIMINATORY ZONING PRACTICES

HUNTINGTON BRANCH, NAACP v.
TOWN OF HUNTINGTON

844 F.2d 926 (2d Cir.), *review declined in part and judgment
aff'd sub nom. Town of Huntington v. Huntington Branch,
NAACP,* 488 U.S. 15 (1988)

IRVING R. KAUFMAN, Circuit Judge:

Twenty years ago, widespread racial segregation threatened to rip civil society
asunder. In response, Congress adopted broad remedial provisions to promote integration. One such statute, Title VIII of the *Civil Rights Act of 1968,* 42 U.S.C. §§3601-3631
(1982 & Supp. III 1985) ("*Fair Housing Act*"), was enacted "to provide, within constitutional limitations, for fair housing throughout the United States." 42 U.S.C. §3601.
Today, we are called upon to decide whether an overwhelmingly white suburb's zoning
regulation, which restricts private multi-family housing projects to a largely minority
"urban renewal area," and the Town Board's refusal to amend that ordinance to allow
construction of subsidized housing in a white neighborhood violates the *Fair Housing
Act.*

The Huntington Branch of the National Association for the Advancement of
Colored People (NAACP), Housing Help, Inc. (HHI), and two black, low-income
residents of Huntington appeal from an adverse judgment of the United States District
Court for the Eastern District of New York (Glasser, J.), following a bench trial, in their
suit against the Town of Huntington (the Town) and members of its Town Board.
Appellants allege that the Town violated Title VIII by restricting private construction
of multi-family housing to a narrow urban renewal area and by refusing to rezone the
parcel outside this area where appellants wished to build multi-family housing. Specifically, appellants sought to construct an integrated, multi-family subsidized apartment complex in Greenlawn/East Northport, a virtually all-white neighborhood. The
Town's zoning ordinance, however, prohibited private construction of multi-family
housing outside a small urban renewal zone in the Huntington Station neighborhood,
which is 52% minority. Thus, appellants petitioned the Town to revise its code to
accommodate the project. When the Town refused, appellants brought this class-
action to compel the change under Title VIII. . . .

Huntington is a town of approximately 200,000 people located in the northwest
corner of Suffolk County, New York. In 1980, 95% of its residents were white. Blacks
comprised only 3.35% of the Town's population and were concentrated in areas known
as Huntington Station and South Greenlawn. Specifically, 43% of the total black
population lived in four census tracts in Huntington Station and 27% in two census
tracts in the South Greenlawn area. Outside these two neighborhoods, the Town's

population was overwhelmingly white. Of the 48 census tracts in the Town in 1980, 30 contained black populations of less than 1%.

The district court found that the Town has a shortage of affordable rental housing for low and moderate-income households. The Town's Housing Assistance Plan (HAP), which is adopted by the Town Board and filed with HUD as part of Huntington's application for federal community development funds, reveals that the impact of this shortage is three times greater on blacks than on the overall population. Under the 1982-1985 HAP, for example, 7% of all Huntington families required subsidized housing, while 24% of black families needed such housing.

In addition, a disproportionately large percentage of families in existing subsidized projects are minority. In Gateway Gardens, a public housing project built in 1967, 38 of 40 units were occupied by blacks and Hispanics in 1984. Seventy-four percent of those on the project's waiting list were minority. In Whitman Village, a 260-unit HUD subsidized development built in 1971, 56% of the families were minority in 1984. Lincoln Manor, which was built in 1980, is a 30-unit HUD Section 8 project. Thirty percent of the households and 45% of those on the waiting list were minority in 1984. Under a HUD Section 8 program, lower income families can obtain certificates to supplement their rent. Each family, however, must locate its own apartment. In January 1984, 68% of families holding certificates and 61% of those on the waiting list were minority....

Under the Town's zoning ordinance, multi-family housing is permitted only in an "R-3M Apartment District." The relevant portion of section 198-20(A)...limits private construction of multi-family housing to the Town's urban renewal area, where 52% of the residents are minority....

The Town's zoning ordinance also includes a special category for multi-family housing for senior citizens called "R-RM Retirement Community District." Only one such development — Paumanack Village — has been built in Huntington. It is the only multi-family housing for low income people which is situated in an overwhelmingly white neighborhood. The development itself is largely white, having a black occupancy of 3%. Only one vacant parcel of land in Huntington currently is zoned R-3M and thus would be eligible for the appellants' proposed development: the MIA site, which is at the northeast corner of Broadway and New York Avenue, is partially zoned C-6 and partially zoned R-3M....

In response to the great need for subsidized housing in the Town, HHI decided to sponsor an integrated housing project for low-income families. HHI determined that the project could foster racial integration only if it were located in a white neighborhood outside the Huntington Station and South Greenlawn areas. This decision eliminated consideration of the MIA site, the only vacant R-3M property located in the urban renewal area....

After a lengthy search, HHI determined that a 14.8 acre parcel located at the corner of Elwood and Pulaski Roads in the Town was well suited for a 162-unit housing project. This flat, largely cleared and well-drained property was near public transportation, shopping and other services, and immediately adjacent to schools.

Ninety-eight percent of the population within a one-mile radius of the site is white. HHI set a goal of 25% minority occupants. The district court found that "a significant percentage of the tenants [at Matinecock Court] would have belonged to minority groups." HHI officials determined that the property was economically feasible and offered a lengthy option period....

HHI obtained its option to purchase the Elwood-Pulaski parcel on January 23, 1980....

Throughout 1980, HHI sought to advance its project by gaining the approval of the Town Board to rezone the property to R-3M from its R-40 designation. . . . Robert Ralph, a director of HHI, addressed the Town Board on February 26, 1980, at a public hearing. The district court found that he filed a document requesting "a commitment by the Town to amend the zoning ordinance to allow multi-family rental construction by a private developer." In August 1980, HHI and National Housing Partnership, an owner-manager of federally subsidized housing, filed a joint application with HUD for Section 8 funding for the project.

At the time HHI applied for the Section 8 funding, Huntington had a Housing Assistance Plan, which had been approved by HUD. Pursuant to the provisions of the *Housing and Community Development Act of 1974*, 42 U.S.C. §§5301-20 (1982 & Supp. III 1985), when a town has such a plan, HUD must refer a Section 8 application to the Town for comment. In an October 14, 1980, letter to Alan H. Weiner, HUD Area Manager, Town Supervisor Ken-neth C. Butterfield set forth seven reasons why Huntington opposed the project. It reads, in pertinent part, as follows:

> The Town's professional staff in the Planning, Legal and Community Development Departments have reviewed the proposal and have submitted the following comments:
>
> 1　The HUD-approved Housing Assistance Plan (both the three-year goal submitted with the Community Development Block Grant 1979-80 application and the annual goal submitted with the 1980-1981 Community Development Block Grant) contains no "new construction" units as a program goal.
> 2　The plan for development cannot be carried out within the existing single family R-40 (1 acre) zoning.
> 3　The development is located at the intersection of two heavily trafficked streets.
> 4　The site plan presents a poor parking plan in terms of location with respect to the units, substandard in size and the lack of streets results in very poor fire protection access.
> 5　The development is located adjacent to both the Long Island Railroad as well as a LILCO substation. This is in addition to the heavy traffic conditions.
> 6　The site plan shows recreation and/or play areas very inadequate for the number and type of dwelling units being proposed.
> 7　The three and four-bedroom units are quite undersized; have poor layout; bedrooms are much too small; living space is unrealistic; no storage; one full and two half-baths for a family of 6 to 8 is not realistic.

In conclusion, I do not recommend HUD approval of this proposal based on the material reviewed and the comments presented above.

When the proposal became public, substantial community opposition developed. A group called the Concerned Citizens Association was formed, and a petition containing 4,100 signatures against the proposal was submitted to the Town Board. A protest meeting in November drew about 2,000 persons. Supervisor Butterfield was the principal speaker and assured the audience of his opposition to the project. Matinecock Court came before the Town Board at a meeting on January 6, 1981. The Board rejected the proposed zoning change [on the ground that the location was inappropriate due to "lack of transportation, traffic hazard and disruption of the existing residential patterns."]

[T]his case requires what has been called "disparate impact" or "disparate effects" analysis, not "disparate treatment" analysis. A disparate impact analysis examines a facially-neutral policy or practice, such as a hiring test or zoning law, for its differential impact or effect on a particular group. Disparate treatment analysis, on the other hand, involves differential treatment of similarly situated persons or groups. The line is not always a bright one, but does adequately delineate two very different kinds of discrimination claims. . . .

The *prima facie* standard for Title VIII disparate impact cases involving public defendants is a question of first impression in this circuit. . . .

Under disparate impact analysis, as other circuits have recognized, a *prima facie* case is established by showing that the challenged practice of the defendant "actually or predictably results in racial discrimination; in other words that it has a discriminatory effect." The plaintiff need not show that the decision complained of was made with discriminatory intent. . . .

The Act's stated purpose to end discrimination requires a discriminatory effect standard; an intent requirement would strip the statute of all impact on *de facto* segregation. . . .

Practical concerns . . . militate against inclusion of intent in any disparate impact analysis. [A]s this court noted in *Robinson v. 12 Lofts Realty, Inc.*, 610 F.2d 1032, 1043 (2d Cir. 1979), "clever men may easily conceal their motivations." This is especially persuasive in disparate impact cases where a facially neutral rule is being challenged. Often, such rules bear no relation to discrimination upon passage, but develop into powerful discriminatory mechanisms when applied. . . .

Once a *prima facie* case of adverse impact is presented, as occurred here, the inquiry turns to the standard to be applied in determining whether the defendant can nonetheless avoid liability under Title VIII. The Third Circuit in *Resident Advisory Board v. Rizzo*, 564 F.2d 126 (3d Cir. 1977), and the Seventh Circuit in *Metropolitan Housing Development Corp. v. Village of Arlington Heights*, 558 F.2d 1283 (7th Cir. 1977) (*Arlington Heights II*), have both made useful contributions to this inquiry. Both circuits essentially recognize that in the end there must be a weighing of the adverse impact against the defendant's justification. As phrased by the Third Circuit, the defendant must prove that its actions furthered, in theory and in practice, a legitimate, bona fide governmental interest and that no alternative would serve that interest with less discriminatory effect. *Rizzo*, 564 F.2d at 148-149. We agree with that formulation. . . . The Seventh Circuit adds two other factors that can affect the ultimate determination on the merits. One factor is whether there is any evidence of discriminatory intent on the part of the defendant. Though we have ruled that such intent is not a requirement of the plaintiff's *prima facie* case, there can be little doubt that if evidence of such intent is presented, that evidence would weigh heavily on the plaintiff's side of the ultimate balance. The other factor is whether the plaintiff is suing to compel a governmental defendant to build housing or only to require a governmental defendant to eliminate some obstacle to housing that the plaintiff itself will build. In the latter circumstance, a defendant would normally have to establish a somewhat more substantial justification for its adverse action than would be required if the defendant were defending its decision not to build. . . .

The discriminatory effect of a rule arises in two contexts: adverse impact on a particular minority group and harm to the community generally by the perpetuation of segregation. In analyzing Huntington's restrictive zoning, however, the lower court concentrated on the harm to blacks as a group, and failed to consider the segregative effect of maintaining a zoning ordinance that restricts private multi-family housing to an area with a high minority concentration. . . .

Seventy percent of Huntington's black population reside in Huntington Station and South Greenlawn. Matinecock Court, with its goal of 25% minorities, would begin desegregating a neighborhood which is currently 98% white. Indeed, the district court found that a "significant percentage of the tenants" at Matinecock Court would belong to minority groups. The court, however, failed to take the logical next step and find that the refusal to permit projects outside the urban renewal area with its high concentration of minorities reinforced racial segregation in housing. This was erroneous. Similarly, the district court found that the Town has a shortage of rental housing affordable for low and moderate-income households, that a "disproportionately" large percentage of the households using subsidized rental units are minority citizens, and that a disproportionately large number of minorities are on the waiting lists for subsidized housing and existing Section 8 certificates. But it failed to recognize that Huntington's zoning ordinance, which restricts private construction of multi-family housing to the largely minority urban renewal area, impedes integration by restricting low-income housing needed by minorities to an area already 52% minority. We thus find that Huntington's refusal to amend the restrictive zoning ordinance to permit privately-built multi-family housing outside the urban renewal area significantly perpetuated segregation in the Town.

On the question of harm to blacks as a group, the district court emphasized that 22,160 whites and 3,671 minorities had incomes below 200% of the poverty line, a cutoff close to the Huntington Housing Authority's qualification standards. Thus, the district court focused on the greater absolute number of poor whites compared with indigent minorities in Huntington. . . . By relying on absolute numbers rather than on proportional statistics, the district court significantly underestimated the disproportionate impact of the Town's policy. . . .

The parties have stipulated that 28% of minorities in Huntington and 11% of whites have incomes below 200% of the poverty line. What they dispute is the meaning of these statistics. Judge Glasser found that, as the Town contends, there is no showing of discriminatory effect because a majority of the victims are white. We disagree. . . . Under the Huntington HAP for 1982-1985, 7% of all Huntington families needed subsidized housing, while 24% of the black families needed such housing. In addition, minorities constitute a far greater percentage of those currently occupying subsidized rental projects compared to their percentage in the Town's population. Similarly, a disproportionately high percentage (60%) of families holding Section 8 certificates from the Housing Authority to supplement their rents are minorities, and an equally disproportionate percentage (61%) of those on the waiting list for such certificates are minorities. Therefore, we conclude that the failure to rezone the Matinecock Court site had a substantial adverse impact on minorities.

In sum, we find that the disproportionate harm to blacks and the segregative impact on the entire community resulting from the refusal to rezone create a strong *prima facie* showing of discriminatory effect. . . . Thus, we must consider the Town's asserted justifications.

Once a plaintiff has made a *prima facie* showing of discriminatory effect, a defendant [1] must present bona fide and legitimate justifications for its action [2] [and demonstrate that no less discriminatory alternative can serve those ends]. For analytical ease, the second prong should be considered first. Concerns can usually be divided between "plan-specific" justifications and those which are "site-specific."

"Plan-specific" problems can be resolved by the less discriminatory alternative of requiring reasonable design modifications. "Site-specific" justifications, however, would usually survive this prong of the test. Those remaining reasons are then scrutinized to determine if they are legitimate and bona fide. By that, we do not intend to devise a search for pretext. Rather, the inquiry is whether the proffered justification is of substantial concern such that it would justify a reasonable official in making this determination. Of course, a concern may be non-frivolous, but may not be sufficient because it is not reflected in the record.

Appellants challenge both the ordinance which restricts privately-built multi-family housing to the urban renewal area and the Town Board's decision to refuse to rezone the Elwood-Pulaski site.... On appeal, appellees... contend that the ordinance is designed to encourage private developers to build in the deteriorated area of Huntington Station.... The Town asserts that limiting multi-family development to the urban renewal area will encourage restoration of the neighborhood because, otherwise, developers will choose to build in the outlying areas and will bypass the zone. The Town's goal, however, can be achieved by less discriminatory means, by encouraging development in the urban renewal area with tax incentives or abatements....

We turn next to the Town's reasons rejecting the Elwood-Pulaski site. The 1980 letter written by Town Supervisor Butterfield detailed seven justifications for the Town's refusal to rezone: (1) inconsistency with the Town's Housing Assistance Plan; (2) inconsistency with zoning; (3) traffic considerations; (4) parking and fire protection problems; (5) proximity to the railroad and Long Island Lighting Company substation; (6) inadequate recreation and play areas; and (7) undersized and unrealistic units. As the judge below noted, the first two beg the question because appellants are challenging the Town's zoning ordinance. More significantly, as we have already indicated, the Town simply relied on the existence of the Housing Assistance Plan and the zoning ordinance and failed to present any substantial evidence indicating why precluding plaintiff from building a multi-family housing project outside the urban renewal area would impair significant interests sought to be advanced by the HAP and the ordinance. The fourth, sixth and seventh problems are "plan-specific" issues which could presumably have been solved with reasonable design modifications at the time appellants applied for rezoning of the parcel. The fifth concern also is largely plan-specific because proper landscaping could shield the project from the railroad and substation.

Thus, only the traffic issue and health hazard from the substation are site-specific. At trial, however, none of Huntington's officials supported these objections.... Accordingly, we find the reasons asserted are entirely insubstantial.

The sewage problem was first raised at trial by appellees' expert Portman. Appellees now advance it as an additional concern. The district court, however, chose not to consider it. We agree. Post hoc rationalizations by administrative agencies should be afforded "little deference" by the courts, and therefore cannot be a bona fide reason for the Town's action. Moreover, the sewage concern could hardly have been significant if municipal officials only thought of it after the litigation began. If it did not impress itself on the Town Board at the time of rejection, it was obviously not a legitimate problem. In sum, the only factor in the Town's favor was that it was acting within the scope of its zoning authority, and thus we conclude that the Town's justifications were weak and inadequate.

In balancing the showing of discriminatory effect against the import of the Town's justifications, we note our agreement with the Seventh Circuit that the balance should be more readily struck in favor of the plaintiff when it is seeking only to enjoin a municipal defendant from interfering with its own plans rather than attempting to compel the defendant itself to build housing. As the *Arlington Heights II* court explained, "courts are far more willing to prohibit even nonintentional action by the state which interferes with an individual's plan to use his own land to provide integrated housing." 558 F.2d at 1293. Bearing in mind that the plaintiffs in this case seek only the freedom to build their own project, we conclude that the strong showing of discriminatory effect resulting from the Town's adherence to its R-3M zoning category and its refusal to rezone the Matinecock Court site far outweigh the Town's weak justifications. Accordingly, to recapitulate, we find that the Town violated Title VIII by refusing to amend the zoning ordinance to permit private developers to build multi-family dwellings outside the urban renewal area. We also find that the Town violated Title VIII by refusing to rezone the Matinecock Court site. We thus reverse the district court and direct entry of judgment in appellants' favor. . . .

 Ordinarily, HHI would not be automatically entitled to construct its project at its preferred site. The Town might well have legitimate reasons for preferring some alternative site to the one preferred by HHI. . . .

 This case, however, is not ordinary. First, we recognize the protracted nature of this litigation, which has spanned over seven years. Further delay might well prove fatal to this private developer's plans. Second, other than its decision in December 1987 to build 50 units of low-income housing in the Melville section, the Town has demonstrated little good faith in assisting the development of low-income housing. After the Town began receiving federal community development funds, HUD found it necessary to pressure the Town continually to include commitments for construction of subsidized family housing in the Town's HAPs. Because of the Town's lack of progress in constructing such housing, HUD imposed special conditions on the Town's community development grants for the 1978 fiscal allocation. Thereafter, HUD continued to express its dissatisfaction with the Town's performance. This history, while it does not rise to a showing of discriminatory intent, clearly demonstrates a pattern of stalling efforts to build low-income housing.

 . . . We therefore refuse to remand this case to the district court to determine the suitability of the 63 sites outside the urban renewal area. Rather, we find that site-specific relief is appropriate in this case.

 Accordingly, we direct the district court to include in its judgment provision ordering the Town to rezone the 14.8 acre Matinecock Court site located at the corner of Elwood and Pulaski Roads in Huntington Township to R-3M status. The judgment should also order the Town to strike from its R-3M zoning ordinance that portion which limits private multi-family housing projects to the urban renewal area.

NOTES AND QUESTIONS

 1. *Equal protection and the intent requirement.* In *Village of Arlington Heights v. Metropolitan Housing Development Corp.*, 429 U.S. 252 (1977), a developer applied for a rezoning of a 15-acre parcel from single-family to multiple-family use, intending to build 190 clustered townhouses for low- and moderate-income tenants. The town refused to rezone and the developer sued, claiming that the failure to rezone had a discriminatory effect on African Americans because they were less likely than white persons to be able to afford single-family homes in the town and that this effect violated

the equal protection clause. Only 27 of the town's 64,000 residents were African American. Applying its ruling in *Washington v. Davis*, 426 U.S. 229 (1976), the Supreme Court held that the equal protection clause of the fourteenth amendment was violated only if a state actor engaged in intentional or purposeful discrimination and that racially disproportionate impacts of neutral governmental policies did not violate the state's obligation to provide equal protection of the laws. Plaintiff had to prove that a discriminatory purpose was a "motivating factor" in the governmental decision in order to establish a constitutional violation. *Accord, City of Cuyahoga Falls v. Buckeye Community Hope Foundation*, 538 U.S. 188 (2003).

2. *Disparate impact claims.* Although the Supreme Court has never ruled on the issue, it now appears settled that disparate impact claims are available under the *Fair Housing Act*, as they are in employment discrimination cases under Title VII of the 1964 *Civil Rights Act*, although several courts have held that such claims are available only against government, not private, defendants. *Village of Bellwood v. Dwivedi*, 895 F.2d 1521, 1533-1534 (7th Cir. 1990); *Brown v. Artery Organization, Inc.*, 654 F. Supp. 1106 (D.D.C. 1987). Facially neutral policies that have a discriminatory impact on protected groups will violate the *Fair Housing Act* unless they further "a legitimate, bona fide governmental interest" and "no alternative course of action could be adopted that would enable that interest to be served with less discriminatory impact." *See Dews v. Town of Sunnyvale*, 109 F. Supp. 2d 526 (N.D. Tex. 2000) (city's one-acre minimum lot size and ban on apartments imposed a disparate impact on racial minorities, by excluding many minority families from the city, that was not justified by sufficiently strong governmental interests).

The plaintiff may create a rebuttable presumption that a defendant's policies or practices create an unlawful disparate impact either (1) by showing statistical evidence that the defendant's policy or practice has a significantly greater impact on a class of persons protected by the *Fair Housing Act* than it does on others; or (2) that the policy or practice tends to perpetuate segregation. In establishing a disproportionate effect, plaintiffs ordinarily should rely on local statistics, but national statistics may be deemed relevant as well. Those statistics should focus on the relative *percentages* of people in each group affected by the policy rather than their absolute numbers. Moreover, the challenged discriminatory effects must be "significant." *Pfaff v. HUD*, 88 F.3d 739, 745 (9th Cir. 1996); *Simms v. First Gibraltar Bank*, 83 F.3d 1546, 1555 (5th Cir. 1996).

If plaintiff can establish a disparate impact, then defendant is obligated "to proffer a valid justification" for its policy in order to overcome the plaintiff's *prima facie* case. The nature of the defendant's burden has been defined somewhat differently among the Circuit Courts. The Second Circuit, for example, held in *Huntington* that the defendant "must present bona fide and legitimate justifications for its action with no less discriminatory alternatives available." 844 F.2d at 939. The "bona fide" element requires defendant to demonstrate that the asserted policy is the real reason for the defendant's actions and not merely a post hoc rationalization designed to serve as a cover for intentional discrimination. In addition to requiring defendant to provide a valid and substantial justification for its policy, some courts have also required defendant to show that its policy cannot be achieved by a less discriminatory alternative. Other courts, such as the Seventh Circuit, have not adopted the two-step analysis where plaintiff shows a disparate impact and defendant then responds by demonstrating justification for its policy. Instead, they consider the impact and the justification as two of four factors relevant to determining whether an unlawful disparate impact has been shown. The other two factors are whether some evidence of discriminatory intent exists; and whether the defendant was being asked affirmatively to provide housing or simply to refrain from interfering in a developer's project. *Metropolitan Housing Development Corp. v. Village of Arlington Heights*, 558 F.2d 1283 (7th Cir. 1977) (*Arlington Heights II*).

Once defendant provides a justification for its policy, some courts have held that this ends the matter. The First Circuit decision in *Langlois v. Abington Housing Authority*, 207 F.3d 43 (1st Cir. 2000), for example, holds that if the defendant has a "valid justification" for its policy that amounts to a "legitimate and substantial goal," then the defendant should win the case. As Judge Boudin explained, "we do not think that the courts' job is to 'balance' objectives, with individual judges deciding which seem to them more worthy." *Id.* at 51. Most courts have agreed with *Huntington* that the court must balance the justification for the policy against the disparate impact, adding another step to the analysis. Once plaintiff has shown a disproportionate or segregatory effect, and defendant has provided a valid justification for its policy, the court must weigh the adverse impact against the defendant's justification.

3. *Disparate impact cases against private defendants.* Disparate impact cases are usually brought against public defendants (such as municipalities or HUD) that act in ways that promote segregation or otherwise deny housing opportunities in a discriminatory manner. Some disparate impact cases also have been brought against private defendants. For example, in *Betsey v. Turtle Creek Associates*, 736 F.2d 983 (4th Cir. 1984), the landlord converted an apartment complex to "adults-only" housing.[5] This change in policy necessitated evictions of many of the current residents. The court held that plaintiffs had demonstrated a *prima facie* case of disparate impact because 54 percent of nonwhite households faced eviction, compared to only 14 percent of white households. *See also Congdon v. Strine*, 854 F. Supp. 355 (E.D. Pa. 1994); *Bronson v. Crestwood Lake Section 1 Holding Corp.*, 724 F. Supp. 148 (S.D.N.Y. 1989) (both applying disparate impact analysis to a private landlord).

In *Brown v. Artery Organization, Inc.*, 654 F. Supp. 1106 (D.D.C. 1987), however, the court held that disparate impact claims were available only against government entities. To prevail against a private defendant, the claimant must prove discriminatory intent. Most of the plaintiffs were African American and Latino tenants of a low-rent apartment complex who had sought to challenge the landlord's decision to convert the building to high-rent units, a change that would have resulted in evicting almost all of the 2,000 residents. The court rejected the plaintiff's attempt to claim that the conversion and subsequent evictions would create a disproportionate impact based on race and that it would have a segregative effect. Although strong evidence of a disparate impact was present, the court held that plaintiffs could prevail only if they could prove that the conversion was motivated by a discriminatory intent, *id.* at 1116:

> While it makes perfect sense to charge a governmental entity with violations of the statute if its actions — by way of regulations, ordinances, zoning decisions, or the like — have the effect of fostering or perpetuating racial segregation, there is no indication that the Congress had in mind the far-reaching consequences of the application of such a rule on private landlords or developers.

---

5. Note that today, this would violate the *Fair Housing Act*'s prohibition against discrimination against children ("familial status") unless the complex satisfied the definition of an elderly-housing complex.

A rule which imposed the burden of responsibility on such individuals or entities for the racial effects of their housing conversions irrespective of their purpose or intent would not only render them responsible for consequences over which they have no control (e.g., the racial mix in the community as a whole); but for the reasons cited below, it would also be likely to halt in their tracks most, if not all, private efforts to upgrade deteriorated housing stock in many of the large cities of this nation. The perpetuation and the spread of the resulting blight is not in the public interest, and plaintiffs have cited no evidence that it represents an objective of the *Fair Housing Act*.

It is an unfortunate fact, for which individual private landowners have no more responsibility than any other member of the community, that the income of a disproportionate number of blacks and members of other minority groups is such that, although they are able to afford low income housing, many cannot afford the rentals being charged for upgraded or luxury housing. As a consequence, if a disproportionate effect or impact on minorities were alone sufficient to call for injunctive relief under the statute, the inhabitants of low-rent private housing largely populated by minorities would be entitled on this basis to judicial orders halting the upgrading or conversion of such housing in all or almost all circumstances. That, as indicated, is not what Congress intended.

Similarly, in *Boyd v. LeFrak Organization*, 509 F.2d 1110 (2d Cir. 1975), the court held that a "private landlord in choosing his tenants is free to use any grounds he likes so long as no discriminatory purpose is shown." *Id.* at 1114. Plaintiffs were a class of African American recipients of public assistance who were rejected by defendants when they applied to rent apartments because defendants required their tenants to have a weekly net income equal to at least 90 percent of the monthly rent, or, alternatively, a co-signer of the lease whose weekly net income was equal to 110 percent of a month's rent. This requirement excluded all public assistance recipients, except for the very small number who could find an acceptable co-signer, and a large majority of such recipients in New York were either African American or Puerto Rican. The court rejected the plaintiff's claim that the defendants' tenant selection criteria set unnecessarily high financial standards and had a disparate impact on African American applicants, excluding them from the opportunity to rent.

Do you agree that disparate impact claims should be available only against public defendants, such as municipalities and public housing authorities? Does any support for this distinction exist in the language or policies underlying the *Fair Housing Act*? Does it matter that a developer can rebut such a claim by a legitimate business justification?

4. *Defendant's justification.* Should the defendant have the burden of showing *both* that its actions are justified by legitimate government objectives *and* that these objectives cannot be achieved in a less discriminatory fashion? Or should the burden of coming up with less discriminatory alternatives rest on the plaintiff? How heavy is the burden? Which party is better situated to bear it?

PROBLEM

An African American woman with two children is denied an apartment in a landlord's building. She is a welfare recipient. The landlord has historically refused to rent to welfare recipients. The woman brings a lawsuit claiming that the landlord's policy of not renting to welfare recipients has an impermissible disparate impact on three protected groups: African Americans, women (of all races), and children. Does she have a chance of winning? Should such a claim prevail? *See Bronson v. Crestwood Lake Section 1 Holding Corp.*, 724 F. Supp. 148 (S.D.N.Y. 1989) (holding that plaintiff demonstrated a *prima facie* unlawful disparate racial impact from a landlord's refusal to rent to Section 8 voucher holders).

§10.2.2   SEX DISCRIMINATION: SHELTERS FOR BATTERED WOMEN

DOE v. CITY OF BUTLER

892 F.2d 315 (3d Cir. 1989)

DOLORES KORMAN SLOVITER, Circuit Judge....

Plaintiffs are three battered women using fictitious names who filed suit in district court in the Western District of Pennsylvania after the defendants, the City of Butler, acting through the City Council, and the Mayor, refused to approve the application by the Volunteers Against Abuse Center of Butler County, Inc. (VAAC) seeking to use a building at 404 N. Washington Street, which it had contracted to buy, as a temporary shelter for abused women and children....

... The City Council ... denied VAAC's application [for a special permit] on the ground that VAAC "has not established that the proposed use is within the provisions of the Zoning Ordinance" limiting transitional dwellings to six residents, excluding staff or supervisory personnel.... The Council identified as additional reasons for its disapproval of VAAC's application the adverse impact of the shelter on density, parking, property values, and on the neighborhood's character as single-family residential....

[The City of Butler zoning ordinance defines a transitional dwelling as "a building occupied for residential purposes by not more than six individuals being provided temporary special care plus a supervisory family or individual. Such transitional dwellings may be operated for the benefit of foster-placed individuals, for those recovering from drug, alcoholic or other diseases or those unable because of mental or physical handicaps to care for themselves." It further allows such housing only with the approval of the City Council after a finding that it is in harmony with the appearance of orderly development of the district, and limits such housing to no more than six unrelated persons.]

[Plaintiffs contend] that the Butler Zoning ordinance is invalid ... because it violates the *Fair Housing Act* (Title VIII), 42 U.S.C. §§3601-3631 (1982), which prohibits certain specified discrimination in housing. To make out a *prima facie* case under Title VIII, a plaintiff can show either discriminatory treatment, or discriminatory effect alone, without proof of discriminatory intent. In this case, plaintiffs allege that the zoning ordinance has a discriminatory effect on protected groups.

At the time the district court ruled, the relevant provision of Title VIII prohibited "mak[ing] unavailable ... a dwelling to any person because of ... sex," 42 U.S.C. §3604(A) (1982), and the district court limited its discussion to gender discrimination. The court held that plaintiffs had not demonstrated a violation of the Act because the ordinance is facially neutral and applies to all transitional dwellings, regardless of whether their intended occupants are male or female. The court also held that plaintiffs had not proven their disparate impact claim, because they failed to show that its application has fallen more harshly on women than on men.

We agree that the fact that the ordinance will have an impact on group homes established for abused women does not alone establish discriminatory effect, because the resident limitation would have a comparable effect on males if the transitional dwelling was established for a different group, such as, for example, recovering male alcoholics. On the basis of the record established, we cannot conclude that the district court erred in rejecting the Title VIII challenge made on the basis of sex discrimination.

The 1988 amendments to Title VIII added a provision making Title VIII applicable to "familial status" as well as race, color, religion, sex or national origin. 42 U.S.C.A. §3604(A) (West Supp. 1989). Familial status is defined under the Act to include "one or more individuals (who have not attained the age of 18 years) being domiciled with — (1) a parent or another person having legal custody of such individual or individuals. . . ." 42 U.S.C.A. §3602(k) (West. Supp. 1989). . . .

Plaintiffs argue that the across-the-board restriction on the number of residents who may occupy a transitional dwelling operates to limit or exclude women with children in violation of the familial status provision of Title VIII. [They argue] that it is not economically feasible to have a transitional dwelling for abused women limited to six residents. If children are counted for that purpose, it will, plaintiffs claim, violate amended Title VIII by adversely affecting the ability of abused mothers to bring their children with them when seeking refuge. We cannot discount the possibility that the six-person limit may in fact have a general dampening effect on the ability of women with children to take advantage of transitional dwellings.

We do not have a full record before us on this question, and are reluctant to decide this issue on this record. The parties have not cited any case on point nor have we found one. However, further inquiry into the legislative history, which the parties have not fully addressed on appeal, may offer some insight into the congressional view of the scope of the familial status provisions in the context presented here. The district court may wish to invite HUD, which is the administrative agency responsible for enforcement of Title VIII, to present its views as an amicus. We will therefore remand to the district court so that it can decide, in the first instance, whether the across-the-board limit on the number of residents in a transitional dwelling violates Title VIII as amended.

JANE R. ROTH, District Judge, dissenting. . . .

. . . When Congress referred to "familial status," it was concerned with the plight of single families, not with the plight of families who desired to live communally. . . .

There is nothing in the language of the *Fair Housing Act* or the legislative history, to support the proposition that the Act is intended to extend protection to families who wish to live in groups. I find no need for the court below to explore this issue more fully. . . .

PROBLEMS

1. The court in *Doe v. Butler* concludes that the exclusion of group homes is neutral with respect to sex because it excludes both shelters for battered women and group homes that might be occupied by men, such as a house for recovering alcoholics. Can you think of a counterargument? How might the exclusion of shelters for battered women impose a disparate impact on women as compared to men?

2. A landlord refuses to rent to welfare recipients. As plaintiff's attorney, how would you persuade the court that the "no welfare recipients" policy has a disparate

impact on the basis of either race or sex, or both, that is unjustified by any legitimate interest of the landlord? What would you argue as defendant's attorney to persuade the court that the policy is consistent with the *Fair Housing Act*? What rule of law should the court promulgate to implement the statutory language and policies?

§10.2.3 NONTRADITIONAL FAMILIES

§10.2.3.1 Restrictive Covenants

See supra §5.4.3, at pages 406-411.

§10.2.3.2 Exclusionary Zoning

(a) Federal Constitution

VILLAGE OF BELLE TERRE v. BORAAS
416 U.S. 1 (1974)

Mr. Justice WILLIAM O. DOUGLAS delivered the opinion of the Court.

Belle Terre is a village on Long Island's north shore of about 220 homes inhabited by 700 people. Its total land area is less than one square mile. It has restricted land use to one-family dwellings excluding lodging houses, boarding houses, fraternity houses, or multiple-dwelling houses. The word "family" as used in the ordinance means, "[o]ne or more persons related by blood, adoption, or marriage, living and cooking together as a single housekeeping unit, exclusive of household servants. A number of persons but not exceeding two (2) living and cooking together as a single housekeeping unit though not related by blood, adoption, or marriage shall be deemed to constitute a family."

Appellees, the Dickmans, are owners of a house in the village and leased it in December 1971 for a term of 18 months to Michael Truman. Later Bruce Boraas became a colessee. Then Anne Parish moved into the house along with three others. These six are students at nearby State University at Stony Brook and none is related to the other by blood, adoption, or marriage. When the village served the Dickmans with an "Order to Remedy Violations" of the ordinance, the owners plus three tenants thereupon brought this action under 42 U.S.C. §1983 for an injunction and a judgment declaring the ordinance unconstitutional. . . .

This case brings to this Court a different phase of local zoning regulations from those we have previously reviewed. *Euclid v. Ambler Realty Co.*, 272 U.S. 365 (1926), involved a zoning ordinance classifying land use in a given area into six categories. . . .

The main thrust of *Euclid* in the mind of the Court was in the exclusion of industries and apartments, and as respects that it commented on the desire to keep residential areas free of "disturbing noises"; "increased traffic"; the hazard of "moving and parked automobiles"; the "depriving children of the privilege of quiet and open spaces for play, enjoyed by those in more favored localities." The ordinance was sanctioned because the validity of the legislative classification was "fairly debatable" and therefore could not be said to be wholly arbitrary. . . .

If the ordinance segregated one area only for one race, it would immediately be suspect under the reasoning of *Buchanan v. Warley*, 245 U.S. 60 (1917), where the Court invalidated a city ordinance barring a black from acquiring real property in a white residential area by reason of an 1866 Act of Congress, 42 U.S.C. §1982, and an 1870 Act, §17, now 42 U.S.C. §1981, both enforcing the Fourteenth Amendment. . . .

The present ordinance is challenged on several grounds: that it interferes with a person's right to travel; that it interferes with the right to migrate to and settle within a State; that it bars people who are uncongenial to the present residents; that it expresses the social preferences of the residents for groups that will be congenial to them; that social homogeneity is not a legitimate interest of government; that the restriction of those whom the neighbors do not like trenches on the newcomers' rights of privacy; that it is of no rightful concern to villagers whether the residents are married or unmarried; that the ordinance is antithetical to the Nation's experience, ideology, and self-perception as an open, egalitarian, and integrated society.

We find none of these reasons in the record before us. It is not aimed at transients. . . . It involves no "fundamental" right guaranteed by the Constitution, such as voting, the right of association, the right of access to the courts, or any rights of privacy. We deal with economic and social legislation where legislatures have historically drawn lines which we respect against the charge of violation of the Equal Protection Clause if the law be "reasonable, not arbitrary" and bears "a rational relationship to a [permissible] state objective."

It is said, however, that if two unmarried people can constitute a "family," there is no reason why three or four may not. But every line drawn by a legislature leaves some out that might well have been included. That exercise of discretion, however, is a legislative, not a judicial, function.

It is said that the Belle Terre ordinance reeks with an animosity to unmarried couples who live together. There is no evidence to support it; and the provision of the ordinance bringing within the definition of a "family" two unmarried people belies the charge.

The ordinance places no ban on other forms of association, for a "family" may, so far as the ordinance is concerned, entertain whomever it likes.

The regimes of boarding houses, fraternity houses, and the like present urban problems. More people occupy a given space; more cars rather continuously pass by; more cars are parked; noise travels with crowds.

A quiet place where yards are wide, people few, and motor vehicles restricted are legitimate guidelines in a land-use project addressed to family needs. This goal is a permissible one. . . . The police power is not confined to elimination of filth, stench, and unhealthy places. It is ample to lay out zones where family values, youth values, and the blessings of quiet seclusion and clean air make the area a sanctuary for people. . . .

Mr. Justice THURGOOD MARSHALL, dissenting. . . .

My disagreement with the Court today is based upon my view that the ordinance in this case unnecessarily burdens appellees' First Amendment freedom of association and their constitutionally guaranteed right to privacy. . . .

The freedom of association is often inextricably entwined with the constitutionally guaranteed right of privacy. The right to "establish a home" is an essential part of the liberty guaranteed by the Fourteenth Amendment. And the Constitution secures to an individual a freedom "to satisfy his intellectual and emotional needs in the privacy of his own home."*Stanley v. Georgia,* 394 U.S. 557, 565 (1969). Constitutionally protected privacy is, in Mr. Justice Brandeis' words, "as against the Government, the right to be let alone . . . the right most valued by civilized man."*Olmstead v. United States,* 277 U.S. 438, 478 (1928) (dissenting opinion). The choice of household companions — of whether a person's "intellectual and emotional needs" are best met by living with family, friends, professional associates, or others — involves deeply personal considerations as to the kind and quality of intimate relationships within the home. That decision surely falls within the ambit of the right to privacy protected by the Constitution. . . .

The instant ordinance discriminates on the basis of just such a personal lifestyle choice as to household companions. It permits any number of persons related by blood or marriage, be it two or twenty, to live in a single household, but it limits to two the number of unrelated persons bound by profession, love, friendship, religious or political affiliation, or mere economics who can occupy a single home. Belle Terre imposes upon those who deviate from the community norm in their choice of living companions significantly greater restrictions than are applied to residential groups who are related by blood or marriage, and compose the established order within the community. The village has, in effect, acted to fence out those individuals whose choice of lifestyle differs from that of its current residents. . . .

Because I believe that this zoning ordinance creates a classification which impinges upon fundamental personal rights, it can withstand constitutional scrutiny only upon a clear showing that the burden imposed is necessary to protect a compelling and substantial governmental interest. . . .

A variety of justifications have been proffered in support of the village's ordinance. It is claimed that the ordinance controls population density, prevents noise, traffic and parking problems, and preserves the rent structure of the community and its attractiveness to families. [T]hese are all legitimate and substantial interests of government. But I think it clear that the means chosen to accomplish these purposes are both overinclusive and underinclusive, and that the asserted goals could be as effectively achieved by means of an ordinance that did not discriminate on the basis of constitutionally protected choices of lifestyle. The ordinance imposes no restriction whatsoever on the number of persons who may live in a house, as long as they are related by marital or sanguinary bonds — presumably no matter how distant their relationship. Nor does the ordinance restrict the number of income earners who may contribute to rent in such a household, or the number of automobiles that may be maintained by its occupants. In that sense the ordinance is underinclusive. On the other hand, the statute restricts the number of unrelated persons who may live in a home to no more than two. It would therefore prevent three unrelated people from occupying a dwelling even if among them they had but one income and no vehicles. While an extended family of a dozen or more might live in a small bungalow, three elderly and retired persons could not occupy the large manor house next door. Thus the statute is also grossly overinclusive to accomplish its intended purposes.

There are some 220 residences in Belle Terre occupied by about 700 persons. The density is therefore just above three per household. The village is justifiably concerned with density of population and the related problems of noise, traffic, and the like. It could deal with those problems by limiting each household to a specified number of adults, two or three perhaps, without limitation on the number of dependent children. The burden of such an ordinance would fall equally upon all segments of the community. It would surely be better tailored to the goals asserted by the village than the ordinance before us today, for it would more realistically restrict population density and growth and their attendant environmental costs. Various other statutory mechanisms also suggest themselves as solutions to Belle Terre's problems—rent control, limits on the number of vehicles per household, and so forth, but, of course, such schemes are matters of legislative judgment and not for this Court. Appellants also refer to the necessity of maintaining the family character of the village. There is not a shred of evidence in the record indicating that if Belle Terre permitted a limited number of unrelated persons to live together, the residential, familial character of the community would be fundamentally affected.

By limiting unrelated households to two persons while placing no limitation on households of related individuals, the village has embarked upon its commendable course in a constitutionally faulty vessel. I would find the challenged ordinance unconstitutional. But I would not ask the village to abandon its goal of providing quiet streets, little traffic, and a pleasant and reasonably priced environment in which families might raise their children. Rather, I would commend the village to continue to pursue those purposes but by means of more carefully drawn and even-handed legislation. . . .

(b) State Constitutions

CHARTER TOWNSHIP OF DELTA v. DINOLFO
351 N.W.2d 831 (Mich. 1984)

JAMES H. BRICKLEY, J. . . .

In July and September of 1977, the Sierawski and Dinolfo "families" moved into homes in plaintiff township. The defendants' homes are located in an R 3, Moderate Density Residential District, which allows for single-family dwellings, duplexes, and quadruplexes. The defendants' homes qualify only as single-family dwellings. Each household consists of a husband and wife, that couple's several children, and six unrelated single adults. All members of these households are members of The Work of Christ Community, a nonprofit and federally tax-exempt organization chartered by the State of Michigan. Each of these households functions as a family in a single housekeeping unit and members intend to reside in their respective households permanently. All of the members of these "families" have adopted their lifestyle as a means of living out the Christian commitment that they stress is an important part of their lives.

Over a year after defendants occupied these residences with their "families," plaintiff's planning department sent violation notices citing them for having more than one unrelated individual residing in their homes in violation of the plaintiff's zoning ordinance. Plaintiff's zoning ordinance limits those groups which can live in single-family dwellings to an individual, or a group of two or more persons related by blood, adoption, or marriage, and not more than one unrelated person, excluding servants. It is undisputed that the space requirements of the township building ordinance were not violated by the number of persons in each of the defendant's households. Indeed, that ordinance would allow for three more persons to live in homes the size of those owned by defendants.

Defendants jointly filed an application for a variance from the family definition section of the plaintiff's zoning ordinance, which was denied by the Zoning Board of Appeals. . . .

Defendants . . . argue that the net effect of plaintiff's enforcement of this ordinance is to totally exclude them from the township in violation of their constitutional rights. . . . [They] argue that the ordinance, by interfering with their chosen lifestyle and religious needs, is an impairment of their fundamental rights of privacy, association, and free exercise of religion in violation of the United States and Michigan Constitutions. . . .

[I]n *Village of Belle Terre v. Boraas,* 416 U.S. 1 (1974), the Supreme Court [affirmed] the constitutionality of a local zoning ordinance that is in all significant respects identical to the ordinance in question here. . . .

. . . We must then accept the defendants' challenge that we examine the Delta Township ordinance in light of Michigan's Constitution. . . .

Plaintiff lists the objectives of this ordinance: preservation of traditional family values, maintenance of property values and population and density control. We cannot disagree that those are not only rational but laudable goals. Where the difficulty arises, however, is when plaintiff attempts to convince us that the classification at hand — limiting to two the number of unrelated persons who may occupy a residential dwelling together or with a biological family — is reasonably related to the achievement of those goals. It is precisely this rational relationship between the means used to achieve the legislative goals that must exist in order for this deprivation of the defendants' use of their property to pass the due process test.

Running through plaintiff's arguments is the assumption that unrelated persons will manifest a behavior pattern different from the biological family. They see "the potential for occupancy by one 'nuclear family' together with any number of unrelated and unruly individuals who view regular late night parties as a common bond and a proper function of child rearing."

If defendants succeed here, plaintiff fears that the next group taking advantage of the opportunity might not be of defendants' character. Plaintiff suggests that the "common bond of the group . . . [might be] not the Work of Christ, but the Work of Satan."

Amicus curiae, Michigan Townships Association, is even more direct in its perception of the evils that will result if non-related persons are allowed to live as a functional family.

> The purpose of such regulations is to prohibit the influx of informal residential groups of people whose primary inclination is toward the enjoyment of a licentious style of living.
>
> While it seems apparent that defendants are not of this character, it would seem equally apparent that allowing in excess of six unrelated individuals to occupy a single-family dwelling unit would allow college fraternities, "hippie" communes, motorcycle clubs, and assorted loosely structured groups of people associating for the purpose of enjoying a purely licentious style of living to locate at will in settled, low density residential neighborhoods and, perhaps even worse in duplexes, quadruplexes, and even in high-density apartment buildings. No somber recitations of anthropologists and sociologists are required to make one visualize the problems of noise, nuisance, vehicular traffic, and general disruption of orderly and peaceful living that could be brought about by permitting such arrangements.

We agree with *amicus* to the extent that the residential nature of a neighborhood is a proper subject for legislative protection. . . .

But we fail to see how plaintiff's ordinance furthers these goals. We, therefore, must part company with the United States Supreme Court. . . .

Here, plaintiff attempts to have us accept its assumption that different and undesirable behavior can be expected from a functional family. Yet, we have been given not a single argument in support of such an assumption, only the assumption. Defendants, on the other hand, relying on decisions from other jurisdictions construing their own state constitutions, present a compelling argument that the means are not rationally related to the end sought.

Those states that have rejected *Belle Terre* have stressed that a line drawn near the limit of the traditional family is both over- and under-inclusive. Unrelated persons are artificially limited to as few as two, while related families may expand without limit. Under the instant ordinance, twenty male cousins could live together, motorcycles, noise, and all, while three unrelated clerics could not. A greater example of over- and under-inclusiveness we cannot imagine. The ordinance indiscriminately regulates where no regulation is needed and fails to regulate where regulation is most needed. . . .

We know from common experience that, while the motorcycle gang argument is a threatening one, it is more a symbol, one that is not by any stretch of the imagination representative of the lifestyle of the countless people who seek residential living in something other than the biological family setting. As to the specter of a "Work of Satan" group that could slip in if defendants succeed here, we note that if this ordinance were upheld it would not keep out Ma Barker and her sons. . . .

There has been no evidence presented nor do we know of any that unrelated persons, as such, have any less a need for the advantages of residential living or that they have as a group behavior patterns that are more opprobrious than the population at large. In the absence of such demonstration to justify this kind of classification, the ordinance can only be termed arbitrary and capricious under the Due Process Clause of the Michigan Constitution. The plight of the defendants in this case — who certainly defy the plaintiff's stereotype of the unrelated family — represents the best evidence of the perniciousness of allowing unexamined assumptions to become the basis of regulatory classification. . . .

The plaintiff is not, as a result of anything we say here today, without authority to regulate the behavior it finds inimical to its concept of a residential neighborhood, including a rational limitation on the numbers of persons that may occupy a dwelling. Plaintiff need not open its residential borders to transients and others whose lifestyle is not the functional equivalent of "family" life. Nor are the plaintiffs precluded from distinguishing between the biological family and a functional family when it is rational to do so, such as in limiting the number of persons who may occupy a dwelling for such valid reasons as health, fire safety, or density control.

We find that plaintiff's ordinance is capricious, arbitrary, and in violation of the Due Process Clause of the Michigan Constitution in that it limits the composition of groups in a manner that is not rationally related to the stated goals of the zoning ordinance. . . .

NOTES AND QUESTIONS

1. *Protection of the traditional family.* In *Moore v. City of East Cleveland*, 431 U.S. 494 (1977), the Supreme Court limited the holding in *Belle Terre* to nontraditional families, finding that the Constitution protects the right of traditional family members to live together. The ordinance in *Moore*, like many in the country, limited occupancy of dwelling units in the city to members of a single family. However, the ordinance contained an unusual definition of "family" that recognized only a few categories of

related individuals. Inez Moore violated the ordinance by living with her son and her two grandsons, the latter being *cousins* rather than brothers. Because she refused to remove the grandchild who was not the child of the son living with her, Moore was convicted of a criminal offense, fined $25, and *sentenced to five days in jail*. The Court held that the ordinance violated her constitutional right to privacy, distinguishing *Belle Terre* on the ground that Belle Terre's ordinance applied only to unrelated individuals.

But one overriding factor sets this case apart from *Belle Terre*. The ordinance there affected only unrelated individuals. It expressly allowed all who were related by "blood, adoption, or marriage" to live together, and in sustaining the ordinance we were careful to note that it promoted "family needs" and "family values." East Cleveland, in contrast, has chosen to regulate the occupancy of its housing by slicing deeply into the family itself. This is no mere incidental result of the ordinance. On its face it selects certain categories of relatives who may live together and declares that others may not. In particular, it makes a crime of a grandmother's choice to live with her grandson in circumstances like those presented here.

When a city undertakes such intrusive regulation of the family, neither *Belle Terre* nor *Euclid* governs; the usual judicial deference to the legislature is inappropriate....

... The city seeks to justify [the ordinance] as a means of preventing overcrowding, minimizing traffic and parking congestion, and avoiding an undue financial burden on East Cleveland's school system. Although these are legitimate goals, the ordinance before us serves them marginally, at best. For example, the ordinance permits any family consisting only of husband, wife, and unmarried children to live together, even if the family contains a half dozen licensed drivers, each with his or her own car. At the same time it forbids an adult brother and sister to share a household, even if both faithfully use public transportation. The ordinance would permit a grandmother to live with a single dependent son and children, even if his school-age children number a dozen, yet it forces Mrs. Moore to find another dwelling for her grandson John, simply because of the presence of his uncle and cousin in the same household. We need not labor the point. Section 1341.08 has but a tenuous relation to alleviation of the conditions mentioned by the city....

... Our decisions establish that the Constitution protects the sanctity of the family precisely because the institution of the family is deeply rooted in this Nation's history and tradition. It is through the family that we inculcate and pass down many of our most cherished values, moral and cultural.

Ours is by no means a tradition limited to respect for the bonds uniting the members of the nuclear family. The tradition of uncles, aunts, cousins, and especially grandparents sharing a household along with parents and children has roots equally venerable and equally deserving of constitutional recognition. Over the years millions of our citizens have grown up in just such an environment, and most, surely, have profited from it. Even if conditions of modern society have brought about a decline in extended family households, they have not erased the accumulated wisdom of civilization, gained over the centuries and honored throughout our history, that supports a larger conception of the family. Out of choice, necessity, or a sense of family responsibility, it has been common for close relatives to draw together and participate in the duties and the satisfactions of a common home.... Especially in times of adversity, such as the death of a spouse or economic need, the broader family has tended to come together for mutual sustenance and to maintain or rebuild a secure home life. This is apparently what happened here....

Id. at 498-499, 503-505. Does the Supreme Court's distinction between *Belle Terre* and *Moore* make sense to you?

2. *State constitutional protection of nontraditional families.* The majority of state courts accept the reasoning of *Belle Terre* and interpret their constitutions as lacking protection for nontraditional families. *See, e.g., Ladue v. Horn,* 720 S.W.2d 745 (Mo. Ct. App. 1986). A minority of state courts, such as the Michigan Supreme Court, have held that their state constitutions provide *greater* protection for nontraditional family access to real property than the federal constitution, as construed by the Supreme Court in *Belle Terre.* Cases similar to *Dinolfo* include *City of Santa Barbara v. Adamson,* 610 P.2d 436 (Cal. 1980) (invalidating restrictive ordinance); *Borough of Glassboro v. Vallorosi,* 568 A.2d 888 (N.J. 1990) (same); *McMinn v. Town of Oyster Bay,* 488 N.E.2d 1240 (N.Y. 1985) (invalidating an ordinance that limited occupancy to persons related by blood, marriage, or adoption, or two unrelated persons over the age of 62).

(c) Fair Housing Act

PROBLEM

On remand in *Doe v. City of Butler,* how could you argue that the ordinance discriminates on the basis of familial status as defined in the *Fair Housing Act*? What is the counterargument? How should the court rule? *See, e.g., Gilligan v. Jamco Development Corp.,* 108 F.3d 246 (9th Cir. 1997) (refusal to accept welfare recipients *may* impose a disparate impact on families with children).

§10.2.4 GROUP HOMES FOR PERSONS WITH DISABILITIES

§10.2.4.1 AIDS Hospices

ASSOCIATION OF RELATIVES AND FRIENDS OF AIDS PATIENTS (AFAPS) v. REGULATIONS AND PERMITS ADMINISTRATION, OR ADMINISTRACIÓN DE REGLAMENTOS Y PERMISOS (ARPE)
740 F. Supp. 95 (D.P.R. 1990)

JOSÉ ANTONIO FUSTE, J.

[Plaintiff AFAPS challenged a governmental agency's refusal to grant a special permit for operation of an AIDS hospice by an evangelical religious organization on the ground that it violated the *Fair Housing Act*'s prohibition on discrimination on the basis of handicap. The agency, ARPE, had justified the refusal to grant the special permit because the area was limited to agricultural use, under a zoning designation of "A-1." The court found that plaintiff had proved both a discriminatory treatment claim and a disparate impact claim.]

From the outset, A.F.A.P.S.'s attempt to establish an AIDS hospice at the Sabana Ward site was met with organized and vocal opposition from a group of Luquillo residents calling themselves the "Residents' Committee" ("Consejo de Residentes")....The Residents' Committee has expressed its opposition to the hospice through petitions, picket lines, graffiti, an administrative complaint, letters to various public bodies, a local court action, and appearances on local television programs. Ms. Figueroa and the Serranos testified to receiving threats from Residents' Committee members due to their support of the hospice. Their efforts to dialogue with community residents failed. Among the reasons expressed by Residents' Committee members for opposing the hospice are the possibility that mosquitoes might transmit the AIDS virus to the community; the undesirability of having former drug users and homosexuals living in Sabana Ward; the belief that the hospice site is flood prone, thus giving rise to a risk of contamination through inundation; the risk of transmitting AIDS-related infections such as pneumonia; the risk that the hospice might decrease the value of surrounding property; the risk that hospice residents might pose a danger to students attending a nearby school. . . .

Defendants [claim] that here the expressions of "irrational fear" were made by community members and cannot be attributed to A.R.P.E. . . .

We agree with defendants to the extent that in the ordinary course of affairs a decisionmaker is not to be saddled with every prejudice and misapprehension of the people he or she serves and represents. On the other hand, a decisionmaker has a duty not to allow illegal prejudices of the majority to influence the decisionmaking process. A racially discriminatory act would be no less illegal simply because it enjoys broad political support. Likewise, if an official act is performed simply in order to appease the discriminatory viewpoints of private parties, that act itself becomes tainted with discriminatory intent even if the decisionmaker personally has no strong views on the matter. . . .

After considering the evidence in its totality, the court cannot avoid the conclusion that A.R.P.E. acted in furtherance of the misguided and discriminatory notions held by many Luquillo residents concerning AIDS patients or at least bowed to political pressure exerted by these residents. By the same token, the court finds A.R.P.E.'s stated reason for denying the permit to be a pretext. . . .

First, that A.R.P.E. was pressured and lobbied by opponents of the hospice to deny the A.F.A.P.S. permit is undeniable. Opposition to the hospice was repeatedly expressed in a manner demonstrating an intent to discriminate against AIDS patients and a misunderstanding of the way in which the AIDS virus is transmitted. In short, the residents did not want AIDS patients living among them "because they make non-handicapped people uncomfortable." . . .

Second, prior to the denial of the use permit there is no evidence that the A-1 zoning classification was a factor in A.R.P.E.'s decisionmaking. Jorge Serrano testified that during his three meetings with Regional Director García agricultural zoning was never raised as a possible barrier to the application. . . . The total absence of any pre-denial discussion of the A-1 classification, coupled with A.R.P.E.'s public discussion of other factors, in particular the importance of public opinion, persuades the court that A.R.P.E.'s late blooming concern over agricultural zoning was less than genuine.

Third, and contrary to the testimony of Regional Director García, A.R.P.E. clearly had authority to grant the special use permit if it wished to. Although the land in question was zoned for agriculture, Topic 4, Section 17.01 of the El Yunque Regulations allows A.R.P.E. to grant a variation when to do so would be "in the best interest of the community." . . .

Finally, the evidence tends to show that the El Yunque Regulations were selectively enforced against plaintiffs. While we acknowledge that A.R.P.E. is entitled a certain degree of selectivity in enforcement, the circumstances of this case indicate that its strict application of the El Yunque Regulations was unusual. A.R.P.E. did not cite a single instance other than the hospice where a use permit has been denied as inconsistent with the El Yunque Regulations. Plaintiffs, however, presented uncontradicted evidence that A.R.P.E. at the very least has acquiesced to numerous zoning violations in the Luquillo area since the El Yunque Regulations took effect. . . .

Given the foregoing, we conclude that [ARPE intended] to prevent AIDS patients from residing in the Luquillo area and thereby ward off public opposition from the area residents. . . .

[The court also found that the denial of the special permit had a disparate impact against persons with disabilities. Applying the four-prong test articulated in *Metropolitan Housing Development Corp. v. Village of Arlington Heights*, 558 F.2d 1283 (7th Cir. 1977), the court found that (1) denial of the permit had an adverse impact on handicapped individuals; (2) evidence of discriminatory intent was present; (3) the state interest was weak since it had granted exceptions in the past and had presented no evidence to justify the denial; and (4) plaintiff's case was strengthened by the fact that it was merely asking to be allowed to go ahead with a privately financed project.]

§10.2.4.2 Group Homes for Persons with Mental Illness

FAMILYSTYLE OF ST. PAUL, INC. v. CITY OF ST. PAUL
923 F.2d 91 (8th Cir. 1991)

ROGER L. WOLLMAN, Circuit Judge. . . .

Familystyle [of St. Paul, Inc.] provides rehabilitative services to mentally ill persons and operates residential group homes for them in St. Paul, Minnesota. Familystyle sought special use permits for the addition of three houses to its existing campus of group homes, intending to expand its capacity from 119 to 130 mentally ill persons. Twenty-one of Familystyle's houses, including the three proposed additions, are clustered in a one and one-half block area. On the condition that Familystyle would work to disperse its facilities, the St. Paul City Council issued temporary permits for the three additional houses. Familystyle failed to meet the conditions of the special use permits, and the permits expired. After St. Paul denied renewal of the permits, Familystyle exchanged its license for one excluding the three additional houses.

Relying upon the provisions of the *Fair Housing Amendment Act of 1988*, Familystyle challenges the city ordinance and state laws that bar the addition of these three houses to its campus. . . .

Minnesota requires facilities that provide residential services for people with mental illness and retardation to be licensed. Minnesota seeks through the licensing of group homes to place the mentally ill in the least restrictive environment possible and to allow them "the benefits of normal residential surroundings." Minn. Stat. §245A.11, subd. 1. "Care, treatment, and deinstitutionalization of mentally ill adults [is] a matter of special state concern" in Minnesota. *Northwest Residence, Inc. v. City of Brooklyn Center*, 352 N.W.2d 764, 772 (Minn. Ct. App. 1984).

An integral part of the licensing process guarantees that residential programs are geographically situated, to the extent possible, in locations where residential services are needed, where they would be a part of the community at large, and where access to other necessary services is available. Minn. Stat. §245A.11, subd. 4. This licensing requirement reflects the goal of deinstitutionalization — a philosophy of creating a full range of community-based services and reducing the population of state institutions. . . .

Deinstitutionalization of the mentally ill is advanced in Minnesota by requiring a new group home to be located at least a quarter mile from an existing residential program unless the local zoning authority grants a conditional use or special use permit. Minn. Stat. §245A.11, subd. 4. The St. Paul zoning code similarly requires community residential facilities for the mentally impaired to be located at least a quarter of a mile apart. . . .

Familystyle argues that the Minnesota and St. Paul dispersal requirements are invalid because they limit housing choices of the mentally handicapped and therefore conflict with the language and purpose of the 1988 Amendments to the *Fair Housing Act.* We disagree. We perceive the goals of non-discrimination and deinstitutionalization to be compatible. Congress did not intend to abrogate a state's power to determine how facilities for the mentally ill must meet licensing standards. Minnesota's dispersal requirements address the need of providing residential services in mainstream community settings. The quarter-mile spacing requirement guarantees that residential treatment facilities will, in fact, be "in the community," rather than in neighborhoods completely made up of group homes that re-create an institutional environment — a setting for which Familystyle argues. We cannot agree that Congress intended the *Fair Housing Amendment Act of 1988* to contribute to the segregation of the mentally ill from the mainstream of our society. The challenged state laws and city ordinance do not affect or prohibit a retarded or mentally ill person from purchasing, renting, or occupying a private residence or dwelling.

The state plays a legitimate and necessary role in licensing services for the mentally impaired. We agree with the district court that the dispersal requirement as part of the licensure process is a legitimate means to achieve the state's goals in the process of deinstitutionalization of the mentally ill. Accordingly, we conclude that the *Minnesota Human Services Licensing Act* and the St. Paul zoning code do not violate the *Fair Housing Amendment Act of 1988.* . . .

NOTES AND QUESTIONS

1. *Spacing requirements for group homes.* In *Horizon House Developmental Services, Inc. v. Town of Upper Southampton,* 804 F. Supp. 683 (E.D. Pa. 1992), *aff'd,* 995 F.2d 217 (3d Cir. 1993), a case similar to *Familystyle,* the court invalidated a municipal spacing requirement for group homes. A nonprofit organization leased two single-family homes, each housing three or four people with mental retardation. The township then enacted an ordinance that (a) prohibited group homes providing permanent care or professional supervision within 3,000 feet of one another or within 3,000 feet of any educational, religious, recreational, or institutional entity; (b) required a six-foot-high fence surrounding group homes; and (c) required a conditional use permit. The ordinance also defined "single-family homes" to exclude group homes for purposes of the zoning ordinance. The ordinance was later amended, reducing the spacing requirement from 3,000 to 1,000 feet. Judge Lowell A. Reed, Jr. held that the ordinance violated the *Fair Housing Act,* rejecting the town's claim that the ordinance was rationally tailored to promote integration of persons with mental retardation into the community. Citing *Starrett City,* Judge Reed noted that "integration is not an adequate justification under the FHAA" for a zoning requirement that "disadvantages a class of people protected by the FHAA by indefinitely limiting access of that class to housing, by setting an upper limit or cap or quota on the number of persons with handicap who may live in the Township." 804 F. Supp. at 695. *Accord, Association for Advancement of the Mentally Handicapped, Inc. v. City of Elizabeth,* 876 F. Supp. 614

(D.N.J. 1994) (invalidating a local ordinance that prohibited group homes for persons with developmental disabilities within 1,500 feet of another such group home, shelter for victims of domestic violence, school or day care center, or if "existing community residences or community shelters within the township exceed 50 persons or 0.5% of the township population, whichever is greater"); *Larkin v. State of Michigan*, 89 F.3d 285 (6th Cir. 1996) (applying disparate impact analysis and holding that the goal of "preventing the 'clustering' of people with disabilities to promote their 'integration' into the community was not an adequate justification under the FHAA" to prevent licensing an adult foster care residential facility within 1,500 feet of another facility).

Familystyle justifies the spacing requirement, not as an effort to achieve integration, but as necessary to promote the mental health of group home residents. Is this sufficient to distinguish it from *Horizon House*? Is *Familystyle* consistent with *Starrett City*? If not, which case is correctly decided?

2. *Limits on the number of unrelated persons who can live together.* In *Edmonds v. Oxford House, Inc.*, 514 U.S. 725 (1995), a nonprofit organization, Oxford House-Edmonds, attempted to open a group home for 10 to 12 adults recovering from drug addiction and alcoholism. Although the town zoning law allowed any number of "family" members related by "genetics, adoption, or marriage" to live together, it limited to five the number of unrelated persons who could live together. Oxford House challenged the zoning restriction as discriminatory against persons with disabilities, both because it made a dwelling "unavailable . . . because of a handicap," §3604(f)(1)(A), and because the town failed to make "reasonable accommodations" in its "rules, policies [and] practices, §3604(f)(3)(B)." The town defended by pointing to the *Fair Housing Act*'s exemption for "any reasonable local, State, or Federal restrictions regarding the maximum number of occupants permitted to occupy a dwelling." 42 U.S.C. §3607(b)(1). The Supreme Court found the exemption unavailable on the ground that the town's law did not prescribe "the maximum number of occupants" a dwelling unit could house because it did not limit the number of traditional family members who could live together. Justice Ginsburg wrote: "We hold that §3607(b)(1) does not exempt prescriptions of the family-defining kind, *i.e.*, provisions designed to foster the family character of a neighborhood. Instead, §3607(b)(1)'s absolute exemption removes from the FHA's scope only total occupancy limits, *i.e.*, numerical ceilings that serve to prevent overcrowding in living quarters." 514 U.S. at 728. The opinion is significant because it suggests, although it does not hold, that the *Fair Housing Act* is intended to regulate local zoning laws that have a disparate impact on a protected group. It does not address the substantive question whether the ordinance had a disparate impact on persons with disabilities that was not justified by an overriding governmental interest. Many other federal cases have held that local zoning ordinances and permitting decisions are subject to both discriminatory treatment and disparate impact analysis under the FHA. *See, e.g.*, *Bangerter v. Orem City Corp.*, 46 F.3d 1491 (10th Cir. 1995) (local zoning ordinances subject to both discriminatory treatment and disparate impact analysis under the FHA); *Potomac Group Home Corp. v. Montgomery County, Maryland*, 823 F. Supp. 1285 (D. Md. 1993) (applying both kinds of analysis to a local zoning ordinance that imposed special permitting requirements for group homes for persons with disabilities).

3. *Disparate impact analysis, reasonable accommodation and restrictions to single-family use.* Courts have generally held that land use restrictions having the effect of excluding group homes for people with disabilities violate the FHA both because they impose an unjustified disparate impact — making housing "unavailable" under §3604(f)(1) — and because they fail to accord with the requirement to make reasonable

accommodations for persons with disabilities, as required by §3604(f)(3)(B). For example, *Oxford House, Inc. v. Town of Babylon*, 819 F. Supp. 1179 (E.D.N.Y. 1993), held that a zoning law restricting occupancy to traditional families had a disparate impact on persons with disabilities because "[r]ecovering alcoholics or drug addicts require a group living arrangement in a residential neighborhood for psychological and emotional support during the recovery process. As a result, residents of an Oxford House are more likely than those without handicaps to live with unrelated individuals." *Id.* at 1183. The court further held that the disparate impact imposed by the zoning law was not justified by a sufficiently strong governmental interest; "the house is well maintained and does not in any way burden the Town or alter the residential character of the neighborhood." *Id.* The court also noted indications of discriminatory intent on the part of the town council, including statements made at a public meeting strongly suggesting that the neighbors were "hostile" to residents of Oxford House and expressed fears for the safety of their children. In addition to finding a disparate impact, the court held that the town had failed to make reasonable accommodations in its zoning code to prevent exclusion of the group home's residents from the community. *Accord, Tsombanidis v. City of West Haven*, 129 F. Supp. 2d 136 (D. Conn. 2001). *See also Hall v. Community of Damien of Molokai*, 911 P.2d 861 (N.M. 1996) (interpreting restrictive covenant limiting property to single-family use not to prohibit group home for four persons with disabilities and holding that, if the covenant did prevent establishment of the group home, it would create an unlawful disparate impact on persons with disabilities).

The courts have come to a similar result applying reasonable accommodation analysis. *See, e.g., Smith & Lee Associates, Inc. v. City of Taylor, Michigan*, 102 F.3d 781 (6th Cir. 1996) (city failed to make reasonable accommodation for an adult foster care facility by allowing it to locate in an area limited to "single-family homes"); *Judy B. v. Borough of Tioga*, 889 F. Supp. 792 (M.D. Pa. 1995) (applying reasonable accommodation analysis to invalidate a borough decision denying a variance to turn a motel into a single room occupancy residence for homeless persons, many of whom were recovering alcoholics, drug addicts, or who suffered from a mental or physical disability that hindered their ability to live independently).

In *Brandt v. Chebanse*, 82 F.3d 172 (7th Cir. 1996), the court held that a city did not violate the *Fair Housing Act* when it refused to grant a variance that would have allowed a property owner to establish a four-unit residence for persons with disabilities in an area restricted to single-family homes. The proposed occupants would not have been living together as a group but would have had four separate units. According to Judge Frank Easterbrook, no disparate impact claim could be brought because the city agreed to allow the plaintiff to establish her multi-unit residence in another part of town and the city was not required, as a reasonable accommodation, to relax its restrictions on multi-family occupancy in the single-family home neighborhood, *id..* at 175:

> The variance is not necessary to allow handicapped persons to live in Chebanse, for those capable of independent living (the only ones who could use the proposed structure) could live as easily, if somewhat more expensively, in new or remodeled single-family houses. Brandt does not argue that the *Fair Housing Act* requires municipalities to eliminate rules that increase the expense of housing for all persons equally. Is the proposed accommodation "reasonable" in the sense that it is cost-justified? Again, not on this record. The costs include an increased potential for flooding and the loss of whatever tranquility single-family zoning offers to a neighborhood with little corresponding benefit — for

the proposed multi-unit building could be built as easily in the many tracts of suburbia or rural America already open to multi-family buildings.... Unless the *Fair Housing Act* has turned the entire United States into a multi-family dwelling zone, Brandt must lose. It doesn't, so she does.

Similarly, in *Hemisphere Building Co. v. Village of Richton Park*, 171 F.3d 437 (7th Cir. 1999), the court held that the FHA does not require a town to issue a special permit to a developer of housing for wheelchair users by increasing the number of allowable units to make those units more affordable for persons with disabilities. Do you agree with the results in *Brandt* and *Hemisphere*? What would the argument be on the other side?

4. *Equal protection.* In *City of Cleburne v. Cleburne Living Center*, 473 U.S. 432 (1985), the city zoning ordinance required operators of "hospitals for the feeble-minded" to obtain special use permits to operate. When the city denied a permit for a group home for mentally retarded persons, the owner sued, claiming that the permit requirement violated the rights of mentally retarded citizens to equal protection of the laws under the fourteenth amendment. The Supreme Court agreed, noting that the city did not require a special use permit for other multiple-resident dwellings, including apartment buildings, dormitories, hotels, nursing homes, or fraternities. The Court concluded that the city could articulate no rational basis for differential treatment of persons with mental retardation, *id.* at 446-450:

> To withstand equal protection review, legislation that distinguishes between the mentally retarded and others must be rationally related to a legitimate governmental purpose.... The State may not rely on a classification whose relationship to an asserted goal is so attenuated as to render the distinction arbitrary or irrational....
>
> The District Court found that the City Council's insistence on the permit rested on several factors. First, the Council was concerned with the negative attitude of the majority of property owners located within 200 feet of the Featherston facility, as well as with the fears of elderly residents of the neighborhood. But mere negative attitudes, or fear, unsubstantiated by factors which are properly cognizable in a zoning proceeding, are not permissible bases for treating a home for the mentally retarded differently from apartment houses, multiple dwellings, and the like....
>
> Second, the Council... was concerned that the facility was across the street from a junior high school, and it feared that the students might harass the occupants of the Featherston home. But the school itself is attended by about 30 mentally retarded students, and denying a permit based on such vague, undifferentiated fears is again permitting some portion of the community to validate what would otherwise be an equal protection violation....
>
> Fourth, the Council was concerned with the size of the home and the number of people that would occupy it....
>
> In the courts below the city also urged that the ordinance is aimed at avoiding concentration of population and at lessening congestion of the streets. These concerns obviously fail to explain why apartment houses, fraternity and sorority houses, hospitals and the like, may freely locate in the area without a permit. So, too, the expressed worry about fire hazards, the serenity of the neighborhood, and the avoidance of danger to other residents fail rationally to justify singling out a home such as 201 Featherston for the special use permit, yet imposing no such restrictions on the many other uses freely permitted in the neighborhood.
>
> The short of it is that requiring the permit in this case appears to us to rest on an irrational prejudice against the mentally retarded, including those who would occupy the Featherston facility and who would live under the closely supervised and highly regulated conditions expressly provided for by state and federal law.

PROBLEMS

1. Suppose the City of St. Paul experiences a sudden influx of immigrants, such as Soviet Jews or persons from Southeast Asia. To integrate these immigrants into the community more effectively, the city council passes an ordinance prohibiting all immigrants from buying or renting homes or apartments on the same block as another immigrant family. Under the reasoning of *Familystyle*, would such an ordinance be enforceable under the *Fair Housing Act*? Suppose the ordinance prohibits all African American families from living next door to another African American family as a means to combat racial segregation. Does this violate the *Fair Housing Act*?

2. An organization buys a house to set up a group home for mentally retarded persons. Opposition to the group home develops in the neighborhood. In response to community pressure, the city amends its zoning ordinance to require that all facilities housing more than four unrelated persons together have one parking space off the street for every two residents. The city council justifies the ordinance by noting that unrelated persons are more likely to have more cars than family members who may share a vehicle and that residents in group homes need more parking for supervisors, visitors, and doctors. Moreover, the city is relatively built up and most houses do not have off-street parking. Streets are quite congested, and parking spaces are hard to find. The effect of the ordinance, however, is to make it financially impossible to set up the group home in the city. The organization sues the city, arguing that the new ordinance violates the *Fair Housing Act*. What arguments could you make on behalf of plaintiffs? On behalf of defendant city? What should the court do?

§10.2.5 SEXUAL ORIENTATION

PROBLEM

A university provides housing for married couples. A gay couple sues the university, claiming that the exclusion of gay couples violates a local law that prohibits discrimination because of sexual orientation. The plaintiffs claim that the university policy has a disparate impact on gay and lesbian couples because they, unlike heterosexual couples, cannot get married even if they want to do so. What are the arguments on both sides? How should the court rule? *See Levin v. Yeshiva University*, 2001 WL 735762 (N.Y. 2001) (holding that such a policy imposed a disparate impact on gay and lesbian couples under the New York City law prohibiting sexual orientation discrimination and remanding to determine whether the disparate impact bore a "significant relationship to a significant business objective").

§10.2.6 RELIGION

In 1997, in *Flores v. City of Boerne*, 521 U.S. 507 (1997), the Supreme Court held unconstitutional a federal statute called the *Religious Freedom Restoration Act* (RFRA) that had prohibited states from enforcing laws that had imposed a substantial burden on religious freedom unless the law was justified by a compelling state interest.[6] On

---

6. RFRA may still be constitutional as applied to federal statutes and administrative actions.

September 22, 2000, President Clinton signed the *Religious Land Use and Institutio-nalized Persons Act of 2000 (RLU-IPA)*, 42 U.S.C. §§2000cc to 2000cc-5 (Pub. L. No. 106-274, 114 Stat. 803, Sept. 22, 2000 (S. 2869)). This statute attempts to revise certain aspects of RFRA by curing the constitutional impediments identified in *City of Boerne*. It protects the religious exercise rights of prisoners and also prohibits governments from "impos[ing] or implement[ing] a land use regulation in a manner that imposes a substantial burden on the religious exercise of a person, including a religious assem-bly or institution" unless the regulation furthers "a compelling governmental inter-est" and "is the least restrictive means of furthering that compelling governmental interest." 42 U.S.C. §2000cc. To meet the constitutional requirements set out in *City of Boerne*, the statute applies only (a) if the affected activity receives federal funds, or (b) if either the substantial burden or the removal of the burden would affect "interstate commerce," or (c) if the burden is imposed in the course of govern-mental procedures that involve "individualized assessments of the proposed uses for the property involved." *Id.* at §2000cc(a)(2). The statute further provides that no government "shall impose or implement a land use regulation that (A) totally excludes religious assemblies from a jurisdiction; or (B) unreasonably limits religious assemblies, institutions, or structures within a jurisdiction."*Id.* at §2000cc(b)(3). *See Cottonwood Christian Center v. Cypress Redevelopment Agency*, 218 F.Supp.2d 1203 (C.D. Cal. 2002)(enforcing Religious Land Use Act against a municipality that denied a conditional use permit and sought to take property by eminent domain when owner wished to build a church on the property). The constitutionality of the RLU-IPA was in doubt but the prisoner provisions have been unanimously upheld by the Supreme Court in an opinion that suggests that it may be upheld in the land use context as well. *Cutter v. Wilkinson*, 2005 U.S. LEXIS 4346 (2005). *Cf. Midrash Sephardi, Inc. v. Town of Surfside*, 366 F.3d 1214 (11th Cir. 2004) (sustaining the act as an effort to accommodate the nondiscriminatory free exercise of religion at least where religious land uses were treated differently from other private clubs).

PROBLEMS

1. A group of Orthodox Jewish students sued Yale University to challenge its policy of requiring all students (other than married students or students over 21) in their first and second years to live in coeducational residence halls. They claimed that their "religious beliefs and obligations regarding sexual modesty forbid them to reside in the coeducational housing provided and mandated by Yale." They sought and were denied exemptions from the policy. The District Court rejected their claim that Yale had violated the *Fair Housing Act*, noting that Yale had reserved rooms for each of the plaintiffs and had in no way denied them housing. Plaintiffs claimed that the housing offered was not of a type that they could accept because of their religious beliefs. *Hack v. President and Fellows of Yale College*, 16 F. Supp. 2d 183 (D. Conn. 1998), *aff'd*, 237 F.3d 81 (2d Cir. 2000).

How could the plaintiffs argue that the university policy had a disparate impact on them because of their religion in violation of the *Fair Housing Act*? What is Yale's defense to this argument? How should the court have ruled?

2. A city zoning law prohibits structures more than two stories tall in a residential subdivision otherwise composed entirely of single-family homes. A church seeks to renovate its facility to obtain more space. It plans to construct a seven-story tower to

accommodate both its religious services and other activities, including a soup kitchen and a homeless shelter that will accommodate thirty people. Assuming the *Religious Land Use and Institutionalized Persons Act of 2000* is upheld as constitutional, is the church entitled to do this under the terms of the act?

3. A church allows homeless persons to sleep on its landing and front steps. The city seeks to prevent this on the ground that it provides shelters for the homeless where they will be safer than sleeping outside. Some homeless persons refuse to go to the shelters either because they are dangerous or they value the freedom of being outside a facility. The church claims that it has a first amendment right to the free exercise of religion that allows it to grant sanctuary to the poor. The city argues that its policy prohibiting sleeping outdoors is a neutral law of general application. *See Employment Division v. Smith*, 494 U.S. 872 (1990) (holding that no violation of the free exercise clause occurs when a neutral and generally applicable regulatory law places a burden on an individual's religion). However, this policy is not embodied in any particular statute or ordinance. Should the first amendment's protection for the "free exercise of religion" protect the church's right to allow homeless persons to sleep on its front steps? *See Fifth Avenue Presbyterian Church v. City of New York*, 293 F.3d 570 (2d Cir. 2002)(yes).

§10.2.7 NATIONAL ORIGIN DISCRIMINATION

PROBLEM

A landlord refuses to rent to tenants who do not speak English. A tenant claims that this policy constitutes national origin discrimination because it has an unjustified disparate impact on persons born outside the United States.

1. Does the policy impose a disparate impact based on national origin?
2. If so, is it justified by a legitimate business interest?

§10.2.8 LAND USE REGULATION AND LOW-INCOME FAMILIES

§10.2.8.1 Exclusionary Zoning

SOUTHERN BURLINGTON COUNTY, NAACP v.
TOWNSHIP OF MOUNT LAUREL
336 A.2d 713 (N.J. 1975)

FREDERICK W. HALL, J.

This case attacks the system of land use regulation by defendant Township of Mount Laurel on the ground that low and moderate income families are thereby unlawfully excluded from the municipality. . . .

There is not the slightest doubt that New Jersey has been, and continues to be, faced with a desperate need for housing, especially of decent liv-ing accommodations economically suitable for low and moderate income families. . . .

Plaintiffs represent the minority group poor (black and Hispanic) seeking such quarters. But they are not the only category of persons barred from so many municipalities by reason of restrictive land use regulations. We have reference to young and elderly couples, single persons and large, growing families not in the poverty class, but who still cannot afford the only kinds of housing realistically permitted in most places — relatively high-priced, single-family detached dwellings on sizeable lots and, in some municipalities, expensive apartments. We will, therefore, consider the case from the wider viewpoint that the effect of Mount Laurel's land use regulation has been to prevent various categories of persons from living in the township because of the limited extent of their income and resources. In this connection, we accept the representation of the municipality's counsel at oral argument that the regulatory scheme was not adopted with any desire or intent to exclude prospective residents on the obviously illegal bases of race, origin or believed social incompatibility. . . .

I. *The Facts*

Mount Laurel is a flat, sprawling township, 22 square miles, or about 14,000 acres, in area, on the west central edge of Burlington County. . . .

Under the present ordinance, 29.2% of all the land in the township, or 4,121 acres, is zoned for industry. . . . At the time of trial no more than 100 acres . . . were actually occupied by industrial uses. They had been constructed in recent years, mostly in several industrial parks, and involved tax ratables of about 16 million dollars. The rest of the land so zoned has remained undeveloped. [As] happens in the case of so many municipalities, much more land has been so zoned than the reasonable potential for industrial movement or expansion warrants. At the same time, however, the land cannot be used for residential development under the general ordinance.

The amount of land zoned for retail business use under the general ordinance is relatively small — 169 acres, or 1.2% of the total. . . .

The balance of the land area, almost 10,000 acres, has been developed until recently in the conventional form of major subdivisions. The general ordinance provides for four residential zones, designated R-1, R-1D, R-2 and R-3. All permit only single-family, detached dwellings, one house per lot — the usual form of grid development. Attached townhouses, apartments (except on farms for agricultural workers) and mobile homes are not allowed anywhere in the township under the general ordinance. . . . The dwellings are substantial; the average value in 1971 was $32,500 and is undoubtedly much higher today.

The general ordinance requirements, while not as restrictive as those in many similar municipalities, nonetheless realistically allow only homes within the financial reach of persons of at least middle income. The R-1 zone requires a minimum lot area of 9,375 square feet, a minimum lot width of 75 feet at the building line, and a minimum dwelling floor area of 1,100 square feet if a one-story building and 1,300 square feet if one and one-half stories or higher. . . . The R-2 zone, comprising a single district of 141 acres in the northeasterly corner, has been completely developed. While it only required a minimum floor area of 900 square feet for a one-story dwelling, the minimum lot size was 11,000 square feet; otherwise the requisites were the same as in the R-1 zone.

The general ordinance places the remainder of the township, outside of the industrial and commercial zones and the R-1D district (to be mentioned shortly), in the R-3 zone. This zone comprises over 7,000 acres — slightly more than half of the total municipal area [and requires a minimum lot size of about one-half acre (20,000 square feet), and the lot width at the building line must be 100 feet].

The R-1D district [reduces] the minimum lot area from 20,000 square feet required in the R-3 zone to 10,000 square feet (12,000 square feet for corner lots) but with the proviso that one-family houses — the single permitted dwelling use — "shall not be erected in excess of an allowable development density of 2.25 dwelling units per gross acre." The minimum lot width at the building line must be 80 feet and the minimum dwelling floor area is the same as in the R-3 zone....

A variation from conventional development has recently occurred in some parts of Mount Laurel, as in a number of other similar municipalities, by use of the land use regulation device known as "planned unit development" (PUD). This scheme differs from the traditional in that the type, density and placement of land uses and buildings, instead of being detailed and confined to specified districts by local legislation in advance, is determined by contract, or "deal," as to each development between the developer and the municipal administrative authority, under broad guidelines laid down by state enabling legislation and an implementing local ordinance. The stress is on regulation of density and permitted mixture of uses within the same area, including various kinds of living accommodations with or without commercial and industrial enterprises....

[Mt. Laurel approved four PUD projects before the state enabling legislation was repealed in 1977.] While multi-family housing in the form of rental garden, medium rise and high rise apartments and attached townhouses is for the first time provided for, as well as single-family detached dwellings for sale, it is not designed to accommodate and is beyond the financial reach of low and moderate income families, especially those with young children. The aim is quite the contrary; as with the single-family homes in the older conventional subdivisions, only persons of medium and upper income are sought as residents....

Still another restrictive land use regulation was adopted by the township through a supplement to the general zoning ordinance enacted in September 1972 creating a new zone, R-4, Planned Adult Retirement Community (PARC).... The enactment recited a critical shortage of adequate housing in the township suitable "for the needs and desires of senior citizens and certain other adults over the age of 52." The permission was essentially for single ownership development of the zone for multi-family housing (townhouses and apartments), thereafter to be either rented or sold as cooperatives or condominiums. The extensive development requirements detailed in the ordinance make it apparent that the scheme was not designed for, and would be beyond the means of, low and moderate income retirees....

All this affirmative action for the benefit of certain segments of the population is in sharp contrast to the lack of action, and indeed hostility, with respect to affording any opportunity for decent housing for the township's own poor living in substandard accommodations, found largely in the section known as Springville (R-3 zone). The 1969 Master Plan Report recognized it and recommended positive action. The continuous official reaction has been rather a negative policy of waiting for dilapidated premises to be vacated and then forbidding further occupancy. An earlier non-governmental effort to improve conditions had been effectively thwarted. In 1968 a private non-profit association sought to build subsidized, multi-family housing in the Springville section with funds to be granted by a higher level governmental agency. Advance municipal approval of the project was required. The Township Committee responded with a purportedly approving resolution, which found a need for "moderate" income housing in the area, but went on to specify that such housing must be constructed subject to all zoning, planning, building and other applicable ordinances and codes.

This meant single-family detached dwellings on 20,000 square foot lots. (Fear was also expressed that such housing would attract low income families from outside the township.) Needless to say, such requirements killed realistic housing for this group of low and moderate income families.[8]

The record thoroughly substantiates the findings of the trial court that over the years Mount Laurel "has acted affirmatively to control development and to attract a selective type of growth" and that "through its zoning ordinances has exhibited economic discrimination in that the poor have been deprived of adequate housing and the opportunity to secure the construction of subsidized housing, and has used federal, state, county and local finances and resources solely for the betterment of middle and upper-income persons."

There cannot be the slightest doubt that the reason for this course of conduct has been to keep down local taxes on *property* (Mount Laurel is not a high tax municipality) and that the policy was carried out without regard for non-fiscal considerations with respect to *people*, either within or without its boundaries. This conclusion is demonstrated not only by what was done and what happened, as we have related, but also by innumerable direct statements of municipal officials at public meetings over the years which are found in the exhibits. . . .

This policy of land use regulation for a fiscal end derives from New Jersey's tax structure, which has imposed on local real estate most of the cost of municipal and county government and of the primary and secondary education of the municipality's children. The latter expense is much the largest, so, basically, the fewer the school children, the lower the tax rate. Sizeable industrial and commercial ratables are eagerly sought and homes and the lots on which they are situated are required to be large enough, through minimum lot sizes and minimum floor areas, to have substantial value in order to produce greater tax revenues to meet school costs. Large families who cannot afford to buy large houses and must live in cheaper rental accommodations are definitely not wanted, so we find drastic bedroom restrictions for, or complete prohibition of, multi-family or other feasible housing for those of lesser income.

This pattern of land use regulation has been adopted for the same purpose in developing municipality after developing municipality. Almost every one acts solely in its own selfish and parochial interest and in effect builds a wall around itself to keep out those people or entities not adding favorably to the tax base, despite the location of the municipality or the demand for varied kinds of housing. There has been no effective intermunicipal or area planning or land use regulation. All of this is amply demonstrated by the evidence in this case as to Camden, Burlington and Gloucester counties. . . . One incongruous result is the picture of developing municipalities rendering it impossible for lower paid employees of industries they have eagerly sought and welcomed with open arms (and, in Mount Laurel's case, even some of its own lower paid municipal employees) to live in the community where they work.

---

8. The record is replete with uncontradicted evidence that, factually, low and moderate income housing cannot be built without some form of contribution, concession or incentive by some level of government. Such, under various state and federal methods, may take the form of public construction or some sort of governmental assistance or encouragement to private building. Multi-family rental units, at a high density, or, at most, low cost single-family units on very small lots, are economically necessary and in turn require appropriate local land use regulations.

The other end of the spectrum should also be mentioned because it shows the source of some of the demand for cheaper housing than the developing municipalities have permitted. Core cities were originally the location of most commerce and industry. Many of those facilities furnished employment for the unskilled and semiskilled. These employees lived relatively near their work, so sections of cities always have housed the majority of people of low and moderate income, generally in old and deteriorating housing. Despite the municipally confined tax structure, commercial and industrial ratables generally used to supply enough revenue to provide and maintain municipal services equal or superior to those furnished in most suburban and rural areas.

The situation has become exactly the opposite since the end of World War II. Much industry and retail business, and even the professions, have left the cities. Camden is a typical example. The testimonial and documentary evidence in this case as to what has happened to that city is depressing indeed. For various reasons, it lost thousands of jobs between 1950 and 1970, including more than half of its manufacturing jobs (a reduction from 43,267 to 20,671, while all jobs in the entire area labor market increased from 94,507 to 197,037). A large segment of retail business faded away with the erection of large suburban shopping centers. The economically better situated city residents helped fill up the miles of sprawling new housing developments, not fully served by public transit. In a society which came to depend more and more on expensive individual motor vehicle transportation for all purposes, low income employees very frequently could not afford to reach outlying places of suitable employment and they certainly could not afford the permissible housing near such locations. These people have great difficulty in obtaining work and have been forced to remain in housing which is overcrowded, and has become more and more substandard and less and less tax productive. There has been a consequent critical erosion of the city tax base and inability to provide the amount and quality of those governmental services — education, health, police, fire, housing and the like — so necessary to the very existence of safe and decent city life. This category of city dwellers desperately needs much better housing and living conditions than is available to them now, both in a rehabilitated city and in outlying municipalities. They make up, along with the other classes of persons earlier mentioned who also cannot afford the only generally permitted housing in the developing municipalities, the acknowledged great demand for low and moderate income housing.

II. The Legal Issue

The legal question before us, as earlier indicated, is whether a developing municipality like Mount Laurel may validly, by a system of land use regulation, make it physically and economically impossible to provide low and moderate income housing in the municipality for the various categories of persons who need and want it and thereby, as Mount Laurel has, exclude such people from living within its confines because of the limited extent of their income and resources. . . .

We conclude that every such municipality must, by its land use regulations, presumptively make realistically possible an appropriate variety and choice of housing. More specifically, presumptively it cannot foreclose the opportunity of the classes of people mentioned for low and moderate income housing and in its regulations must affirmatively afford that opportunity, at least to the extent of the municipality's fair share of the present and prospective regional need therefor. These obligations must be met unless the particular municipality can sustain the heavy burden of demonstrating peculiar circumstances which dictate that it should not be required so to do.[10]

We reach this conclusion under state law and so do not find it necessary to consider federal constitutional grounds urged by plaintiffs. We begin with some fundamental principles as applied to the scene before us.

Land use regulation is encompassed within the state's police power. . . .

It is elementary theory that all police power enactments, no matter at what level of government, must conform to the basic state constitutional requirements of substantive due process and equal protection of the laws. . . . It is required that, affirmatively, a zoning regulation, like any police power enactment, must promote public health, safety, morals or the general welfare. . . .

[A central issue is] *whose* general welfare must be served or not violated in the field of land use regulation. Frequently the decisions in this state . . . have spoken only in terms of the interest of the enacting municipality, so that it has been thought, at least in some quarters, that such was the only welfare requiring consideration. It is, of course, true that many cases have dealt only with regulations having little, if any, outside impact where the local decision is ordinarily entitled to prevail. However, it is fundamental and not to be forgotten that the zoning power is a police power of the state and the local authority is acting only as a delegate of that power and is restricted in the same manner as is the state. So, when regulation does have a substantial external impact, the welfare of the state's citizens beyond the borders of the particular municipality cannot be disregarded and must be recognized and served. . . .

This brings us to the relation of housing to the concept of general welfare just discussed and the result in terms of land use regulation which that relationship mandates. There cannot be the slightest doubt that shelter, along with food, are the most basic human needs. . . .

It is plain beyond dispute that proper provision for adequate housing of all categories of people is certainly an absolute essential in promotion of the general welfare required in all local land use regulation. Further, the universal and constant need for such housing is so important and of such broad public interest that the general welfare which developing municipalities like Mount Laurel must consider extends beyond their boundaries and cannot be parochially confined to the claimed good of the particular municipality. It has to follow that, broadly speaking, the presumptive obligation arises for each such municipality affirmatively to plan and provide, by its land use regulations, the reasonable opportunity for an appropriate variety and choice of housing, including, of course, low and moderate cost housing, to meet the needs, desires and resources of all categories of people who may desire to live within its boundaries. Negatively, it may not adopt regulations or policies which thwart or preclude that opportunity.

It is also entirely clear, as we pointed out earlier, that most developing municipalities, including Mount Laurel, have not met their affirmative or negative obligations, primarily for local fiscal reasons. . . .

In sum, we are satisfied beyond any doubt that, by reason of the basic importance of appropriate housing and the longstanding pressing need for it, especially in the low

---

10. While, as the trial court found, Mount Laurel's actions were deliberate, we are of the view that the identical conclusion follows even when municipal conduct is not shown to be intentional, but the effect is substantially the same as if it were.

and moderate cost category, and of the exclusionary zoning practices of so many municipalities, conditions have changed, and . . . judicial attitudes must be altered . . . to require, as we have just said, a broader view of the general welfare and the presumptive obligation on the part of developing municipalities at least to afford the opportunity by land use regulations for appropriate housing for all. . . .

We turn to application of these principles in appraisal of Mount Laurel's zoning ordinance, useful as well, we think, as guidelines for future application in other municipalities.

The township's general zoning ordinance (including the cluster zone provision) permits, as we have said, only one type of housing — single-family detached dwellings. This means that all other types — multi-family including garden apartments and other kinds housing more than one family, town (row) houses, mobile home parks — are prohibited. Concededly, low and moderate income housing has been intentionally excluded. While a large percentage of the population living outside of cities prefers a one-family house on its own sizeable lot, a substantial proportion do not for various reasons. Moreover, single-family dwellings are the most expensive type of quarters and a great number of families cannot afford them. Certainly they are not pecuniarily feasible for low and moderate income families, most young people and many elderly and retired persons, except for some of moderate income by the use of low cost construction on small lots.

As previously indicated, Mount Laurel has allowed some multi-family housing by agreement in planned unit developments, but only for the relatively affluent and of no benefit to low and moderate income families. And even here, the contractual agreements between municipality and developer sharply limit the number of apartments having more than one bedroom. . . . The design of such limitations is obviously to restrict the number of families in the municipality having school age children and thereby keep down local education costs. Such restrictions are so clearly contrary to the general welfare as not to require further discussion.

Mount Laurel's zoning ordinance is also so restrictive in its minimum lot area, lot frontage and building size requirements, earlier detailed, as to preclude single-family housing for even moderate income families. Required lot area of at least 9,375 square feet in one remaining regular residential zone and 20,000 square feet (almost half an acre) in the other, with required frontage of 75 and 100 feet, respectively, cannot be called small lots and amounts to low density zoning, very definitely increasing the cost of purchasing and improving land and so affecting the cost of housing. As to building size, the township's general requirements of a minimum dwelling floor area of 1,100 square feet for all one-story houses and 1,300 square feet for all of one and one-half stories or higher is without regard to required minimum lot size or frontage or the number of occupants. . . . Again it is evident these requirements increase the size and so the cost of housing. The conclusion is irresistible that Mount Laurel permits only such middle and upper income housing as it believes will have sufficient taxable value to come close to paying its own governmental way.

Akin to large lot, single-family zoning restricting the population is the zoning of very large amounts of land for industrial and related uses. Mount Laurel has set aside almost 30% of its area, over 4,100 acres, for that purpose; the only residential use allowed is for farm dwellings. In almost a decade only about 100 acres have been developed industrially. Despite the township's strategic location for motor transportation purposes, as intimated earlier, it seems plain that the likelihood of anywhere near the whole of the zoned area being used for the intended purpose in the foreseeable future is remote indeed and that an unreasonable amount of land has thereby been removed from possible residential development, again seemingly for local fiscal reasons.

Without further elaboration at this point, our opinion is that Mount Laurel's zoning ordinance is presumptively contrary to the general welfare and outside the intended scope of the zoning power in the particulars mentioned. A facial showing of invalidity is thus established, shifting to the municipality the burden of establishing valid superseding reasons for its action and non-action. We now examine the reasons it advances.

The township's principal reason in support of its zoning plan and ordinance housing provisions, advanced especially strongly at oral argument, is the fiscal one previously adverted to, *i.e.*, that by reason of New Jersey's tax structure which substantially finances municipal governmental and educational costs from taxes on local real property, every municipality may, by the exercise of the zoning power, allow only such uses and to such extent as will be beneficial to the local tax rate. In other words, the position is that any municipality may zone extensively to seek and encourage the "good" tax ratables of industry and commerce and limit the permissible types of housing to those having the fewest school children or to those providing sufficient value to attain or approach paying their own way taxwise.

We have previously held that a developing municipality may properly zone for and seek industrial ratables to create a better economic balance for the community *vis-à-vis* educational and governmental costs engendered by residential development, provided that such was ". . . done reasonably as part of and in furtherance of a legitimate comprehensive plan for the zoning of the entire municipality." *Gruber v. Mayor and Township Committee of Raritan Township*, 186 A.2d 489, 493 (N.J. 1962). We adhere to that view today. But we were not there concerned with, and did not pass upon, the validity of municipal exclusion by zoning of types of housing and kinds of people for the same local financial end. We have no hesitancy in now saying, and do so emphatically, that, considering the basic importance of the opportunity for appropriate housing for all classes of our citizenry, no municipality may exclude or limit categories of housing for that reason or purpose. While we fully recognize the increasingly heavy burden of local taxes for municipal governmental and school costs on homeowners, relief from the consequences of this tax system will have to be furnished by other branches of government. It cannot legitimately be accomplished by restricting types of housing through the zoning process in developing municipalities. . . .

By way of summary, what we have said comes down to this. As a developing municipality, Mount Laurel must, by its land use regulations, make realistically possible the opportunity for an appropriate variety and choice of housing for all categories of people who may desire to live there, of course including those of low and moderate income. It must permit multifamily housing, without bedroom or similar restrictions, as well as small dwellings on very small lots, low cost housing of other types and, in general, high density zoning, without artificial and unjustifiable minimum requirements as to lot size, building size and the like, to meet the full panoply of these needs. Certainly when a municipality zones for industry and commerce for local tax benefit purposes, it without question must zone to permit adequate housing within the means of the employees involved in such uses. (If planned unit developments are authorized, one would assume that each must include a reasonable amount of low and moderate income housing in its residential "mix," unless opportunity for such housing has already been realistically provided for elsewhere in the municipality.) The amount of land removed from residential use by allocation to industrial and commercial purposes must be reasonably related to the present and future potential for such purposes. In other words, such municipalities must zone primarily for the living welfare of people and not for the benefit of the local tax rate. . . .

III. The Remedy . . .

. . . The township is granted 90 days from the date hereof, or such additional time as the trial court may find it reasonable and necessary to allow, to adopt amendments to correct the deficiencies herein specified. It is the local function and responsibility, in the first instance at least, rather than the court's, to decide on the details of the same within the guidelines we have laid down. If plaintiffs desire to attack such amendments, they may do so by supplemental complaint filed in this cause within 30 days of the final adoption of the amendments. . . .

. . . The municipality should first have full opportunity to itself act without judicial supervision. We trust it will do so in the spirit we have suggested, both by appropriate zoning ordinance amendments and whatever additional action encouraging the fulfillment of its fair share of the regional need for low and moderate income housing may be indicated as necessary and advisable. (We have in mind that there is at least a moral obligation in a municipality to establish a local housing agency pursuant to state law to provide housing for its resident poor now living in dilapidated, unhealthy quarters.) . . . Should Mount Laurel not perform as we expect, further judicial action may be sought by supplemental pleading in this cause. . . .

NOTES AND QUESTIONS

1. *Minority rule.* Although much heralded, the *Mount Laurel* doctrine is a minority rule. Only a few states have explicitly interpreted their state constitutions to limit exclusionary zoning.

2. *Property and regulation.* Does the limitation on exclusionary zoning imposed by the court in *Mount Laurel* infringe on property rights, or does it protect them? Does it regulate the market for real property, or does it constitute a form of deregulation?

3. *Mount Laurel II.* In *Mount Laurel I*, the Supreme Court of New Jersey ordered the township of Mount Laurel to amend its zoning law to remove unconstitutional restrictions on the development of low- and moderate-income housing. This remedy depended, to some extent, on trusting the presumed good faith of municipal officials. That trust turned out to be unwarranted. Many municipalities, including Mount Laurel, evaded or ignored the constitutional mandate in *Mount Laurel I*. Mount Laurel, for example, responded by rezoning 20 acres of land for low-income housing — less than one-quarter of 1 percent of the town's entire area — on which, for various reasons, it was exceedingly unlikely that low-income housing would ever be built. Other communities similarly failed to comply with the constitutional mandate.

New challenges were brought against the zoning ordinances of many municipalities, including a second case against Mount Laurel itself. Six of these cases were consolidated in a single appeal to the New Jersey Supreme Court, which issued a second *Mount Laurel* opinion in 1983. *Southern Burlington County NAACP v. Township of Mount Laurel,* 456 A.2d 390 (N.J. 1983) (*Mount Laurel II*). Chief Justice Robert

Wilentz's 120-page opinion in *Mount Laurel II* took more than two years to produce. Under *Mount Laurel II*, the obligation to provide a realistic opportunity for decent housing for a municipality's *resident* poor was extended to cover every municipality in the state rather than being limited to "developing" communities, as under *Mount Laurel I*. Moreover, all communities identified as "growth" areas in the State Development Guide Plan, issued independently by the Division of State and Regional Planning in the Department of Community Affairs, were obligated to provide for a municipality's fair share of the *regional* housing need for low- and moderate-income persons.

In addition, the court in *Mount Laurel II* imposed a series of affirmative remedies to encourage the construction of low- and moderate-income housing. Those remedies included:

a. *Procedural innovations.* The court provided for the appointment of three "regional" trial judges to handle all cases involving challenges to exclusionary zoning ordinances in the northern, central, and southern regions of New Jersey. This arrangement was intended to generate consistent definitions of "regions," and the housing needs of each region, to determine in an orderly way each community's fair share of the regional housing need. Further, when possible, each case was to be limited to one trial and one set of appeals; this was meant to avoid the pattern of municipal amendments of zoning ordinances in the middle of litigation, which often had required remands to judge the validity of the newly amended zoning ordinance—an endless process that effectively prevented final determination of the case.

b. *Affirmative remedies.* The court required municipalities to use affirmative remedies to encourage the development of housing for low- and moderate-income persons if the *Mount Laurel* obligations could not be met in any other way. If municipalities failed to comply with the constitutional mandate, the courts in charge of these cases were empowered to order affirmative remedies. Those remedies included:

   i. *Government subsidies*—encouraging or requiring the use of available state or federal housing subsidies

   ii. *Incentive zoning*—providing incentives to private developers to set aside a portion of their developments for low- and moderate-income housing, for example, by relaxing various restrictions in a zoning ordinance (typically density limits) in exchange for the construction of certain numbers of low- and moderate-income housing units

   iii. *Mandatory set-asides*—requiring that developers include a minimum amount of lower-income housing in their projects to get a permit to build

   iv. *Builder's remedy*—ordering a municipality to allow a developer to construct a particular project that includes a substantial amount of lower-income housing unless the "municipality establishes that because of environmental or other substantial planning concerns, the plaintiff's proposed project is clearly contrary to sound land use planning"

   v. *Appointment of a master to revise the zoning ordinance*—in extreme cases of municipal disregard of the law, appointing a master to rewrite the zoning ordinance to comply with the constitutional obligation to provide for the municipality's resident poor or its fair share of the regional low-income housing need.

4. *Legislation.* The *Mount Laurel II* opinion openly invited the New Jersey legislature to enact legislation implementing the constitutional obligation to prevent exclusionary zoning practices. In fact, the rather drastic nature of the remedies in *Mount Laurel II* — made necessary, in the court's opinion, by the municipalities' collective violation of the law — produced the desired result. The legislature enacted the *Fair Housing Act of 1985*, N.J. Stat. Ann. §§52:27D-301 to 52:27D-329 (1986), which transferred authority over *Mount Laurel* cases to a state administrative agency called the Council on Affordable Housing. The act also placed a temporary moratorium on the controversial builder's remedy; it also allowed municipalities to buy their way out of the *Mount Laurel* obligation by paying neighboring communities to absorb up to half of their fair-share obligation. The *Fair Housing Act* was upheld by the New Jersey Supreme Court in *Hills Development Co. v. Bernards Township*, 510 A.2d 621 (N.J. 1986) (often called *Mount Laurel III*). The builder's remedy survives, however, and is available when the municipality fails to comply fully with its statutory obligations. *Toll Brothers, Inc. v. Township of West Windsor*, 803 A.2d 53 (N.J. 2002).

California, Massachusetts, and Oregon also have adopted legislation to limit exclusionary zoning. Cal. Gov't Code §§65580 to 65589.8; Mass. Gen. Laws ch. 40B, §§20 to 23; Or. Rev. Stat. §§197.005 to 197.850. California's statute, which resembles the *New Jersey Fair Housing Act*, mandates comprehensive planning by a state agency to ensure that local zoning laws take into account each municipality's fair share of the regional low-income housing need. Both New Jersey and California employ inclusionary zoning techniques such as set-asides and density bonuses. In contrast, Massachusetts enacted a statute known as the "*Anti-Snob Zoning Act*," empowering developers to challenge local permit denials by appealing unfavorable local zoning board decisions to a state review board, which is authorized to overturn local board decisions that exclude low-income housing needed in the municipality. Oregon, like Massachusetts, prevents local governments from excluding low-cost housing. *See* Harold McDougall, *From Litigation to Legislation in Exclusionary Zoning*, 22 Harv. C.R.-C.L. L. Rev. 623 (1987). *See also Britton v. Town of Chester*, 595 A.2d 492 (N.H. 1991) (adopting the *Mount Laurel* doctrine as an interpretation of the state zoning enabling act).

In recent years, many municipalities have adopted linkage ordinances that condition real estate development on either providing low-income housing or paying a tax to a municipal fund for this purpose.[7]

5. *Efficiency.* Do inclusionary zoning techniques that require developers to provide a certain percentage of housing units for low-income persons have positive or negative effects on social welfare? Some scholars have argued that government-mandated inclusionary zoning likely will be inefficient. Professor Robert Ellickson has argued that such zoning effectively imposes a tax on new construction because some units that would not otherwise be profitable must be included in the development, thereby raising the costs of providing new housing. When the cost of new housing is artificially raised by government regulation, less will be provided, thereby exacerbating the already existing shortage of low-income housing and interfering with the filtering mechanism by which wealthy homeowners move to better housing and

---

7. The constitutionality of this practice is addressed in *infra* §12.2.6.

leave their prior residences for less wealthy consumers. Robert C. Ellickson, *The Irony of "Inclusionary Zoning,"* 54 S. Cal. L. Rev. 1167 (1981). Other scholars, however, have contended that such techniques are likely to *restore* the efficient use of land by *removing* inefficient restrictions on development contained in existing exclusionary zoning laws. Laws that exclude low-income housing from the community arguably decrease social welfare by attempting to create protected subdivisions without accounting for the externalities of limiting low-income housing to urban areas. They may also artificially increase the cost of low-income housing by excluding it from areas in which developers could otherwise profitably build it. Andrew G. Dietderich, *An Egalitarian's Market: The Economics of Inclusionary Zoning Reclaimed,* 24 Fordham Urb. L.J. 23 (1996)(arguing that inclusionary zoning is efficient).

6. *Has inclusionary zoning worked?* Recent evidence indicates that inclusionary zoning programs have stimulated a significant amount of low-income housing construction. Those who have benefited, however, are more likely to be elderly people (rather than families with children) who have greater resources than the very poorest persons. Because inclusionary zoning also is more likely to occur in suburban areas, the benefits are more likely to go to white persons than to African American and Latino families. Sharon Perlman Krefetz, Margaret Guzman, and Michael Brown, *Suburban Exclusion in the 1990s: High Walls, Small Toeholds* (1990) (manuscript in possession of the author). For criticism of the effectiveness of *Mount Laurel* in helping the urban poor, *see* John O. Calmore, *Fair Housing v. Fair Housing: The Problems of Providing Increased Housing Opportunities Through Spacial Deconcentration,* 14 Clearinghouse Rev. 7 (1980).

7. *Growth controls.* In *Zuckerman v. Town of Hadley,* 813 N.ED.2d 843, 849 (Mass. 2004), the Massachusetts Supreme Judicial Court held that a town's permanent limit on the number of building permits that can be issued annually for single-family homes designed to limit the number of children in public school "is inherently and unavoidably detrimental to the public welfare, and therefore not a legitimate zoning purpose" and thus unconstitutional. Justice Cordy explained: "Despite the perceived benefits that enforced isolation may bring to a town facing a new wave of permanent home seekers, it does not serve the general welfare of the Commonwealth to permit one particular town to deflect that wave onto its neighbors." *Id.* at 850.

§10.2.8.2 Homelessness

See supra §2.5, at pages 173-176.

11

Zoning: Governmental Land Use Planning

§11.1 The Planning Process

§11.1.1 Legislative Process: Enacting the Zoning Ordinance

§11.1.1.1 Zoning Enabling Acts

State governments are the ultimate repositories of the "police power," the authority to enforce regulations promoting health, welfare, and safety. One of the major ways states regulate property is by delegating power to municipalities to regulate land use. States delegate zoning power to individual municipalities through general legislation, often called *zoning enabling acts*. This legislation delegates power to municipalities to promulgate zoning laws regulating the type and level of use in different districts within the municipality. The acts define both the scope of the powers delegated to municipalities and the procedures by which the zoning process operates.

The enabling acts generally authorize municipalities to engage in two kinds of regulation: use and area zoning. *Use* zoning is accomplished by dividing the municipality into districts and regulating the kinds of uses allowed within each district. For example, some areas may allow only agricultural uses; others may allow residential uses; still others may allow commercial uses (stores and restaurants); and, finally, others permit industrial uses. Zoning is usually cumulative; the uses form a pyramidal structure, with the most intensive uses at the top. Residential housing is ordinarily allowed in industrial districts — if anyone is willing to place housing there — but not the reverse; industry is excluded from residential areas. *Area* zoning regulates the size of lots, the height of buildings, and requirements to set back structures a certain distance from the property borders. The requirements may differ from district to district; some residential districts may allow multi-family housing while others allow only single-family dwellings.

§11.1.1.2 The Comprehensive Plan and Zoning Ordinance

The zoning enabling act generally requires the municipal government to establish a *comprehensive plan* for the municipality as a whole. Today most jurisdictions require the adoption of a plan that is separate from the zoning ordinance itself, showing the general divisions of the municipality into residential, agricultural, commercial and industrial uses and describing the objectives of the plan and the policies and standards that are to guide real estate development within the jurisdiction. Use and area districts are established in accordance with a rational scheme for promoting development in a way that separates incompatible uses. The idea is to avoid nuisances *before* they arise. The zoning process is also intended to allow flexibility; amendments to the zoning law or exceptions to it may be arranged more easily and economically than bargaining among all the owners bound by a set of private covenants or restrictions.

Voters in the municipality elect the local governing body, such as the city council.[1] The governing body is the legislative branch of government and has the power to adopt a local law governing land use in the municipality, called the *zoning ordinance* or *by-law*. The zoning ordinance is the equivalent of a local statute and is enforceable until it is changed by the governing body.

Both the comprehensive plan and the zoning ordinance itself are generally prepared by a *planning commission* before adoption by the *city council* or other legislative body. Planning commissions are composed of community members appointed by the local legislative body. The planning commission holds public hearings, investigates and obtains relevant information, develops the comprehensive plan, and often the zoning law as well, and recommends changes over time in the local zoning law or in standards for applying or administering it. The commission is often aided by a *planning department* composed of professional city planners. If the municipality is too small to have a planning department, it may hire a private planning firm to aid it in drafting a comprehensive plan and/or the zoning law itself.

The planning commission also receives petitions from particular landowners who are seeking amendments to the zoning law as it applies to their particular parcels. Such petitions are called *rezoning* petitions. Although the planning commission has no power to pass a zoning law itself, it does hold public hearings on such petitions and makes recommendations to the city council or other legislative body to accept or reject such petitions, and its recommendations are often accepted by the lawmaking body.

Because the city council enacted the zoning ordinance and has the power to change it, one course of action for a property owner who would like to develop her property in ways prohibited by the zoning ordinance is to seek a rezoning from the city council. Rezoning may be done for particular parcels or for whole districts or portions of districts when conditions warrant changing the ordinance.

---

1. Cities and towns are organized in a wide variety of ways. Cities ordinarily have a popularly elected legislative body, called the *city council*, which has the power to pass local laws, called *ordinances*. Cities may or may not have an executive branch, usually called the *mayor*, whose powers vary widely among different cities. Towns are generally smaller than cities and may have different forms of government. The *town meeting* form of government is still used in numerous New England towns; all voters are entitled to attend regularly scheduled town meetings to vote on local laws, called *by-laws*. The town may have an executive board, called the *board of selectmen*, and a separate body to resolve zoning disputes, called the *zoning board* or *board of adjustment*.

Most state zoning enabling acts require any changes in the zoning ordinance to accord with the general plan. This does not mean the plan cannot be changed over time. It does mean, however, that zoning decisions are intended to be made with a large, long-range view of how uses harmonize in the city as a whole. Some courts will hold city councils strictly to the requirement that zoning proceed in accord with a general plan, striking down any zoning amendments that are not sufficiently justified as part of a comprehensive plan. *Love v. Board of County Commissioners of Bingham County*, 671 P.2d 471 (Idaho 1983). Other courts grant greater discretion to the governing body. In either case, one strategy for a property owner aggrieved by a zoning amendment is to argue that the change is not in accord with the existing comprehensive plan or that it is not consistent with any rational plan.

§11.1.1.3 Planned Unit Developments

Most zoning ordinances establish specific use districts. Sometimes, however, even more flexibility is desired than can be obtained by the legislative process of zoning amendment or the administrative process of variances and exceptions. In some cases, municipalities have established *planned unit developments* in which the zoning board or its planning staff work to establish overall density requirements and then work directly with developers of a particular area to construct a rational scheme that mixes uses (such as commercial and residential) in a desirable way. The plan is then approved by the zoning board, usually after public hearings with public participation.

§11.1.1.4 Conditional or Contract Zoning

Developers who want to construct projects that are inconsistent with zoning requirements may approach the planning board or the city council with a proposal to *rezone* the parcel in a manner that will authorize the project. When this happens the governing bodies often wish to affect the appearance or uses of the property to protect the neighborhood from negative externalities or to improve neighborhood amenities. They sometimes do so by negotiating with the owner over the zoning change and then allowing the rezoning subject to specified conditions designed to ensure that the development is not harmful to the neighbors or the community. These conditions may involve anything from special limitations on uses, to specially tailored height or bulk restrictions, to requiring dedication of land to the city to widen abutting public streets. This process is called *contract* or *conditional zoning*.

Contract zoning has often been challenged in court as (1) unauthorized by the zoning enabling act; (2) inconsistent with the comprehensive plan; or (3) illegal preferential "spot zoning."[2] It has also been challenged as an unconstitutional form of lawmaking on the ground that laws should not be negotiated with a private party but should be adopted through open procedures that can be monitored by the public. While some cases strike down contract zoning, others approve it, and some state statutes now expressly authorize it. Ariz. Rev. Stat. §§9-462.01(E), 11-832; Daniel R. Mandelker, *Land Use Law* §6.64, at 276 (4th ed. 1997).

---

2. *See infra* §11.2.3.2.

Some courts distinguish between so-called bilateral and unilateral arrangements. Bilateral agreements involve promises on both sides, by the owner and by the city. For example, the city may promise to rezone the lot in return for a promise by the owner to restrict the otherwise allowable development on her lot and perhaps to record the restrictions as covenants. Such bilateral contracts are often struck down partly because they may bypass statutory procedures that require public hearings to amend the zoning law. *Old Canton Hills Homeowners Association v. City of Jackson*, 749 So. 2d 54 (Miss. 1999) (noting that contract zoning is unlawful because it binds the municipality before it has had the statutorily required public hearing and unlawfully circumvents the public decision making process). Unilateral promises are commitments by the owner to agree to certain conditions (again, often recorded) in order to induce the municipality to rezone the land. Such arrangements protect the rights of the public to attend a public hearing on the rezoning proposal but still raise issues about whether such ad hoc decision making is desirable or promotes corruption and unfair deviations from the comprehensive plan.

Municipalities began to engage in contract or conditional zoning because traditional Euclidean zoning laws proved to be too inflexible. At the same time, it flies in the face of the requirement that the zoning law be consistent with a "comprehensive plan." Rather than rational planning that looks at the overall pattern of land use and development, parcel by parcel decisions may result in unanticipated consequences and slow erosion of governing principles over time. Moreover, this raises the possibility of special deals with politically connected citizens, resulting in zoning changes that are not in the public interest.

Contract zoning is more likely to be struck down if it is bilateral than if it is unilateral. Bilateral zoning is especially problematic because the governing body is attempting either to bind itself contractually to pass a particular zoning law or to deprive a later governing body of the power to pass whatever law it wants or to amend the existing zoning law. *Hale v. Osborn Coal Enterprises, Inc.*, 729 So. 2d 853 (Ala. Civ. App. 1997); *Buckhorn Ventures, LLC v. Forsyth County*, 585 S.E.2d 229 (Ga. Ct. App. 2003); *Dacy v. Village of Ruidoso*, 845 P.2d 793 (N.M. 1992); William B. Stoebuck & Dale A. Whitman, *The Law of Property* §9.25, at 626 (3d ed. 2000). Cf. *Durand v. IDC Bellingham, LLC*, 793 N.E.2d 359 (Mass. 2003) (not illegal contract zoning to rezone land after the owner volunteered to donate $8 million to the town to build a new school).

Some courts hold unilateral conditional zoning to be just as illegal as bilateral conditional zoning. *Dacy, supra*. However, when the restrictions on the rezoned property are agreed to voluntarily by the landowner as part of the rezoning process, courts are increasingly likely to uphold the arrangement. *Rando v. Town of North Attleboro*, 692 N.E.2d 544 (Mass. App. Ct. 1998). These unilateral restrictions are often called *conditional* (rather than contract) zoning because no promise is made by the governing body that effects a bargaining away of the police power.

§11.1.2   Administrative Procedures: The Zoning Board of Adjustment

In addition to authorizing the municipal government to create a comprehensive plan and to enact a zoning ordinance, the zoning enabling act authorizes the municipality to delegate power to a local agency, often called the *zoning board* or *board of adjustment*, to administer the zoning law. The zoning ordinance ordinarily gives the zoning board the power to grant variances or special exceptions from the restrictions imposed by the zoning ordinance. A *variance* is a permit to develop a parcel in a way that otherwise violates the zoning ordinance; variances are granted in cases of special hardship. *Special exceptions* are permits to develop in ways that are conditionally authorized by the zoning ordinance. For example, an ordinance may allow a particular use only if certain circumstances are established; showing those circumstances gives the property owner a right to the special permit.

Property owners who are aggrieved by zoning board decisions may appeal to the courts. If the owner can find relief neither in the zoning board nor in the courts, it is always possible to attempt to persuade the municipality to amend its zoning ordinance.

Public opinion and citizens associations are quite powerful in zoning law and practice. Organized citizen groups may affect both the general shape of the zoning law and individual zoning board decisions on particular development proposals. Property developers must contend with neighborhood opposition to particular projects and may well need to negotiate with citizens organizations to obtain their consent or acquiescence. Zoning boards and city councils may block particular developments until changes are made so as to address the concerns of neighbors and community activists.

§11.2   Zoning: Police Power and Property Rights

§11.2.1   Historical Background

Mugler v. Kansas, 23 U.S. 623 (1887). In the nineteenth century, the courts generally upheld regulatory laws that limited the uses to which land could be put. For example, in the 1887 case of *Mugler v. Kansas*, 123 U.S. 623 (1887), the Supreme Court held that a state statute that prohibited the manufacture and sale of alcoholic beverages did not constitute a "taking" of plaintiff's property. It reached this result even though the brewery had been constructed solely for the purpose of manufacturing such beverages, the property had "little value" for any other purpose, and that purpose had been lawful at the time plaintiff invested in building the factory and its business. The Court declared that "A prohibition simply upon the use of property for purposes that are declared, by valid legislation, to be injurious to the health, morals, or safety of the community, cannot, in any just sense, be deemed a taking or an appropriation of property." 123 U.S. at 668–669. A central component of the *police power* reserved to the states by the Constitution is the power to protect the public. The police power, noted the Court, "is not . . . burdened with the condition that the State must compensate such individual owners for pecuniary losses they may sustain, by reason of their not being permitted, by a noxious use of their property, to inflict injury upon the community." *Mugler v. Kansas* held that laws cannot constitute unconstitutional takings of property as long as they are intended, in good faith, to protect the public from harm of any kind, as long as they do not amount to an actual "taking" of title to the property or deprive the owner of possessory rights.

Powell v. Pennyslvania, 27 U.S. 678 (1888). The Supreme Court clarified *Mugler* a year later in the 1888 case of *Powell v. Pennsylvania*, 127 U.S. 678 (1888). That case held that it was permissible to outlaw completely the manufacture of oleomargarine, as long as the legislature passed the law for the purpose of protecting public health and preventing fraud. The legislation would not be struck down merely because it was "unwise" or because the court disagreed with the legislature about its necessity, even if "the value of [the owner's] property employed therein would be entirely lost and he be deprived of the means of livelihood." *Id.* at 686, 682.

Hadacheck v. Sebastian, 239 U.S. 394 (1915). In the 1915 case of *Hadacheck v. Sebastian*, 239 U.S. 394 (1915), the Court upheld an ordinance prohibiting operation of a brickyard, although the owner had made excavations on the land that prevented it from being utilized for any other purpose. The brickyard had been established outside the borders of Los Angeles and had been perfectly lawful at the time it was established. Subsequently, the area was incorporated into the city of Los Angeles, homes were built around it, and the operation of the brickyard constituted a common law nuisance despite the fact that the neighbors had come to the nuisance. Even though the owner had invested in reliance on existing law, which authorized operation of the facility, the legislation was upheld on the ground that no one could have a vested right to commit a nuisance and an operation that was not a nuisance initially might become so when circumstances changed. As long as the prohibition was designed to protect the community from a nuisance or a "noxious use," it would not constitute a taking of property. *Accord, Goldblatt v. Hempstead,* 369 U.S. 590 (1962) (upholding a town regulation that barred continued operation of an existing sand and gravel operation in order to protect public safety).

Buchanan v. Warley, 245 U.S. 60 (1917). Twenty-one years after the Supreme Court approved "separate but equal" public accommodations, thereby approving state-mandated racial segregation in *Plessy v. Ferguson*, it struck down a local zoning law that promoted racial segregation in housing. The Louisville city ordinance in *Buchanan* prohibited both white persons and African Americans from purchasing homes on a street that included a majority of owners of the opposite race. Justice Day explained: "Property is more than the mere thing which a person owns. It is elementary that it includes the right to acquire, use, and dispose of it. The Constitution protects these essential attributes of property." *Id.* at 74. The Court acknowledged that "dominion over property springing from ownership is not absolute and unqualified." *Id.* While reaffirming state-mandated racial segregation in public accommodations, *Id.* at 81, the Court found zoning laws that prohibit the sale of real property on the basis of race deny "property rights . . . by due process of law" and therefore "not a legitimate exercise of the police power" because they "annul[ ] . . . the civil right of a white to dispose of his property if he saw fit to do so to a person of color and of a colored person to make such disposition to a white person," *id.* at 81-82. Thus, although the Court mentioned the "right to acquire" property, its focus in striking down the ordinance was denial of the "right to sell."

Pennsylvania Coal Co. v. Mahon, 260 U.S. 393 (1922). However, all this changed in 1922 when the Supreme Court first struck down a land use regulation as an unconstitutional "taking" of property. In *Pennsylvania Coal Co. v. Mahon,* 260 U.S. 393 (1922), plaintiff homeowners sued to prevent the Pennsylvania Coal Company from mining under their property in such a way as to remove subjacent support and cause a subsidence of the surface and of their house. Although the plaintiffs had previously contracted to allow the company to dig under their land and to undermine the support for that land, a subsequent state regulatory statute required all mining companies to conduct operations in a manner that did not undermine support for surface structures. The Supreme Court, in an opinion by Justice Oliver Wendell Holmes, noted that the case presented a conflict between public powers and private property rights. Balancing those interests, the Court held that the statute exceeded the legitimate scope of the police power by wrongfully infringing on constitutionally protected property rights, *Id.* at 412-416:

> Government hardly could go on if to some extent values incident to property could not be diminished without paying for every such change in the general law. As long recognized some values are enjoyed under an implied limitation and must yield to the police power. But obviously the implied limitation must have its limits or the contract and due process clauses are gone. One fact for consideration in determining such limits is the extent of the diminution. When it reaches a certain magnitude, in most if not in all cases there must be an exercise of eminent domain and compensation to sustain the act. So the question depends upon the particular facts. The greatest weight is given to the judgment of the legislature but it always is open to interested parties to contend that the legislature has gone beyond its constitutional power.
>
> This is the case of a single private house. No doubt there is a public interest even in this, as there is in every purchase and sale and in all that happens within the commonwealth. Some existing rights may be modified even in such a case. But usually in ordinary private affairs the public interest does not warrant much of this kind of interference. A source of damage to such a house is not a public nuisance even if similar damage is inflicted on others in different places. The damage is not common or public. The extent of the public interest is shown by the statute to be limited, since the statute ordinarily does not apply to land when the surface is owned by the owner of the coal. Furthermore, it is not justified as a protection of personal safety. That could be provided for by notice. Indeed the very foundation of this bill is that the defendant gave timely notice of its intent to mine under the house. On the other hand the extent of the taking is great. It purports to abolish what is recognized in Pennsylvania as an estate in land — a very valuable estate — and what is declared by the Court below to be a contract hitherto binding the plaintiffs. If we were called upon to deal with the plaintiffs' position alone we should think it clear that the statute does not disclose a public interest sufficient to warrant so extensive a destruction of the defendant's constitutionally protected rights. . . .
>
> It is our opinion that the act cannot be sustained as an exercise of the police power, so far as it affects the mining of coal under streets or cities in places where the right to mine such coal has been reserved. As said in a Pennsylvania case, "For practical purposes, the right to coal consists in the right to mine it." *Commonwealth v. Clearview Coal Co.*, 100 A. 820 (Pa. 1917). What makes the right to mine coal valuable is that it can be exercised with profit. To make it commercially impracticable to mine certain coal has very nearly the same effect for constitutional purposes as appropriating or destroying it. This we think that we are warranted in assuming that the statute does. . . .
>
> The general rule at least is that while property may be regulated to a certain extent, if regulation goes too far it will be recognized as a taking. It may be doubted how far exceptional cases, like the blowing up of a house to stop a conflagration, go — and if they go beyond the general rule, whether they do not stand as much upon tradition as upon principle. In general it is not plain that a man's misfortunes or necessities will justify his shifting the damages to his neighbor's shoulders. We are in danger of forgetting that a strong public desire to improve the public condition is not enough to warrant achieving the desire by a shorter cut than the constitutional way of paying for the change. As we already have said this is a question of degree — and therefore cannot be disposed of by general propositions. . . .

We assume, of course, that the statute was passed upon the conviction that an exigency existed that would warrant it, and we assume that an exigency exists that would warrant the exercise of eminent domain. But the question at bottom is upon whom the loss of the changes desired should fall. So far as private persons or communities have seen fit to take the risk of acquiring only surface rights, we cannot see that the fact that their risk has become a danger warrants the giving to them greater rights than they bought.

Justice Louis Brandeis dissented, *Id.* at 417-422:

Coal in place is land, and the right of the owner to use his land is not absolute. He may not so use it as to create a public nuisance, and uses, once harmless, may, owing to changed conditions, seriously threaten the public welfare. Whenever they do, the Legislature has power to prohibit such uses without paying compensation. . . .

Every restriction upon the use of property imposed in the exercise of the police power deprives the owner of some right theretofore enjoyed, and is, in that sense, an abridgment by the state of rights in property without making compensation. But restriction imposed to protect the public health, safety or morals from dangers threatened is not a taking. The restriction here in question is merely the prohibition of a noxious use. The property so restricted remains in the possession of its owner. The state does not appropriate it or make any use of it. The state merely prevents the owner from making a use which interferes with paramount rights of the public. Whenever the use prohibited ceases to be noxious — as it may because of further change in local or social conditions — the restriction will have to be removed and the owner will again be free to enjoy his property as heretofore.

The restriction upon the use of this property cannot, of course, be lawfully imposed, unless its purpose is to protect the public. But the purpose of a restriction does not cease to be public, because incidentally some private persons may thereby receive gratuitously valuable special benefits. Thus, owners of low buildings may obtain, through statutory restrictions upon the height of neighboring structures, benefits equivalent to an easement of light and air. . . .

It is said that one fact for consideration in determining whether the limits of the police power have been exceeded is the extent of the resulting diminution in value, and that here the restriction destroys existing rights of property and contract. But values are relative. If we are to consider the value of the coal kept in place by the restriction, we should compare it with the value of all other parts of the land. That is, with the value not of the coal alone, but with the value of the whole property. The rights of an owner as against the public are not increased by dividing the interests in his property into surface and subsoil. The sum of the rights in the parts can not be greater than the rights in the whole. The estate of an owner in land is grandiloquently described as extending *ab orco usque ad coe lum.* But I suppose no one would contend that by selling his interest above 100 feet from the surface he could prevent the state from limiting, by the police power, the height of structures in a city. And why should a sale of underground rights bar the state's power? For aught that appears the value of the coal kept in place by the restriction may be negligible as compared with the value of the whole property, or even as compared with that part of it which is represented by the coal remaining in place and which may be extracted despite the statute. . . .

The [majority seems to assume that in] order to justify [an] exercise of the police power [which upsets expectations based on existing contracts] there must be "an average reciprocity of advantage" as between the owner of the property restricted and the rest of the community; and that here such reciprocity is absent. Reciprocity of advantage is an important consideration, and may even be an essential [one], where the state's power is exercised for the purpose of conferring benefits upon the property of a neighborhood, as in drainage projects. But where the police power is exercised, not to confer benefits upon property owners but to protect the public from detriment and danger, there is in my opinion, no room for considering reciprocity of advantage. There was no reciprocal advantage to the owner prohibited from using his oil tanks in 248 U.S. 498; his brickyard, in 239 U.S. 394; his livery stable, in 237 U.S. 171; his billiard hall, in 225 U.S. 623; his oleomargarine factory, in 127 U.S. 678; his brewery, in 123 U.S. 623; unless it be the advantage of living and doing business in a civilized community. That reciprocal advantage is given by the act to the coal operators.

Although the result in *Pennsylvania Coal* was effectively repudiated in *Keystone Bituminous Coal Association v. DeBenedictis*, 480 U.S. 470 (1987), which upheld the constitutionality of a similar law, regulations that "go too far" may still be deemed unconstitutional takings of property.

Village of Euclid v. Ambler Realty Co., 272 U.S. 365 (1926). Four years after *Pennsylvania Coal*, in *Village of Euclid v. Ambler Realty Co.*, 272 U.S. 365 (1926), a developer who had purchased a 68-acre parcel for industrial purposes challenged a zoning law that prohibited industrial uses on most of the parcel and caused a 75 percent reduction in the market value of the land. The Supreme Court found that the ordinance served a legitimate public interest and thus did not unconstitutionally deprive the plaintiff of protected property rights under the fourteenth amendment even though the decrease in market value of the land was very substantial, *Id.* at 387-397:

> The ordinance now under review, and all similar laws and regulations, must find their justification in some aspect of the police power, asserted for the public welfare. The line which in this field separates the legitimate from the illegitimate assumption of power is not capable of precise delimitation. It varies with circumstances and conditions. A regulatory zoning ordinance, which would be clearly valid as applied to the great cities, might be clearly invalid as applied to rural communities. In solving doubts, the maxim *sic utere tuo ut alienum non lae das*, which lies at the foundation of so much of the common law of nuisances, ordinarily will furnish a fairly helpful clew. And the law of nuisances, likewise, may be consulted, not for the purpose of controlling, but for the helpful aid of its analogies in the process of ascertaining the scope of, the power. Thus the question whether the power exists to forbid the erection of a building of a particular kind or for a particular use, like the question whether a particular thing is a nuisance, is to be determined, not by an abstract consideration of the building or of the thing considered apart, but by considering it in connection with the circumstances and the locality. A nuisance may be merely a right thing in the wrong place, like a pig in the parlor instead of the barnyard. If the validity of the legislative classification for zoning purposes be fairly debatable, the legislative judgment must be allowed to control.
>
> There is no serious difference of opinion in respect of the validity of laws and regulations fixing the height of buildings within reasonable limits, the character of materials and methods of construction, and the adjoining area which must be left open, in order to minimize the danger of fire or collapse, the evils of overcrowding and the like, and excluding from residential sections offensive trades, industries and structures likely to create nuisances.
>
> Here, however, the exclusion is in general terms of all industrial establishments, and it may thereby happen that not only offensive or dangerous industries will be excluded, but those which are neither offensive nor dangerous will share the same fate. But this is no more than happens in respect of many practice-forbidding laws which this court has upheld, although drawn in general terms so as to include individual

cases that may turn out to be innocuous in themselves. The inclusion of a reasonable margin, to insure effective enforcement, will not put upon a law, otherwise valid, the stamp of invalidity. Such laws may also find their justification in the fact that, in some fields, the bad fades into the good by such insensible degrees that the two are not capable of being readily distinguished and separated in terms of legislation. In the light of these considerations, we are not prepared to say that the end in view was not sufficient to justify the general rule of the ordinance, although some industries of an innocent character might fall within the proscribed class. It cannot be said that the ordinance in this respect "passes the bounds of reason and assumes the character of a merely arbitrary fiat." ...

The matter of zoning has received much attention at the hands of commissions and experts, and the results of their investigations have been set forth in comprehensive reports. These reports which bear every evidence of painstaking consideration, concur in the view that the segregation of residential, business and industrial buildings will make it easier to provide fire apparatus suitable for the character and intensity of the development in each section; that it will increase the safety and security of home life, greatly tend to prevent street accidents, especially to children, by reducing the traffic and resulting confusion in residential sections, decrease noise and other conditions which produce or intensify nervous disorders, preserve a more favorable environment in which to rear children, etc. With particular reference to apartment houses, it is pointed out that the development of detached house sections is greatly retarded by the coming of apartment houses, which has sometimes resulted in destroying the entire section for private house purposes; that in such sections very often the apartment house is a mere parasite, constructed in order to take advantage of the open spaces and attractive surroundings created by the residential character of the district. Moreover, the coming of one apartment house is followed by others, interfering by their height and bulk with the free circulation of air and monopolizing the rays of the sun which otherwise would fall upon the smaller homes, and bringing, as their necessary accompaniments, the disturbing noises incident to increased traffic and business, and the occupation, by means of moving and parked automobiles, of larger portions of the streets, thus detracting from their safety and depriving children of the privilege of quiet and open spaces for play, enjoyed by those in more favored localities — until, finally, the residential character of the neighborhood and its desirability as a place of detached residences are utterly destroyed. Under these circumstances, apartment houses, which in a different environment would be not only entirely unobjectionable but highly desirable, come very near to being nuisances.

If these reasons, thus summarized, do not demonstrate the wisdom or sound policy in all respects of those restrictions which we have indicated as pertinent to the inquiry, at least, the reasons are sufficiently cogent to preclude us from saying, as it must be said before the ordinance can be declared unconstitutional, that such provisions are clearly arbitrary and unreasonable, having no substantial relation to the public health, safety, morals, or general welfare. ...

It is true that when, if ever, the provisions set forth in the ordinance in tedious and minute detail, come to be concretely applied to particular premises, including those of the appellee, or to particular conditions, or to be considered in connection with specific complaints, some of them, or even many of them, may be found to be clearly arbitrary and unreasonable. ... Under these circumstances, therefore, it is enough for us to determine, as we do, that the ordinance in its general scope and dominant features, so far as its provisions are here involved, is a valid exercise of authority, leaving other provisions to be dealt with as cases arise directly involving them.

Nectow v. City of Cambridge, 277 U.S. 183 (1928). Two years later, in *Nectow v. City of Cambridge*, 277 U.S. 183 (1928), a vacant lot was bisected by a newly enacted zoning ordinance. The bulk of the parcel was zoned for industrial uses, but one vacant part of the parcel was limited to residential use. Although the vacant part was 100 feet wide, the master who heard the case found that the city might widen the street in such a manner as to reduce the depth of that lot to 65 feet and that as a result, "no practical use can be made of the land in question for residential purposes, because . . . there would not be adequate return on the amount of any investment for the development of the property." The Supreme Court held that the statute, as applied to this portion of the land, impermissibly infringed on constitutionally protected property rights. Is this finding consistent with the ruling in *Euclid*, which appeared to find constitutional a 75 percent reduction in market value without regard to the owner's investment in the land? The Court explained its result, *Id.* at 187-189:

> The last finding of the master is: "I am satisfied that the districting of the plaintiff's land in a residence district would not promote the health, safety, convenience, and general welfare of the inhabitants of that part of the defendant city, taking into account the natural development thereof and the character of the district and the resulting benefit to accrue to the whole city and I so find."
>
> It is made pretty clear that because of the industrial and railroad purposes to which the immediately adjoining lands to the south and east have been devoted and for which they are zoned, the locus is of comparatively little value for the limited uses permitted by the ordinance.
>
> We quite agree with the opinion expressed below that a court should not set aside the determination of public officers in such a matter unless it is clear that their action "has no foundation in reason and is a mere arbitrary or irrational exercise of power having no substantial relation to the public health, the public morals, the public safety or the public welfare in its proper sense." *Euclid v. Ambler Co.*, [272 U.S.] at 395.
>
> An inspection of a plat of the city upon which the zoning districts are outlined, taken in connection with the master's findings, shows with reasonable certainty that the inclusion of the locus in question is not indispensable to the general plan. The boundary line of the residential district before reaching the locus runs for some distance along the streets, and to exclude the locus from the residential district requires only that such line shall be continued 100 feet further along Henry street and thence south along Brookline street. There does not appear to be any reason why this should not be done. Nevertheless, if that were all, we should not be warranted in substituting our judgment for that of the zoning authorities primarily charged with the duty and responsibility of determining the question. But that is not all. The governmental power to interfere by zoning regulations with the general rights of the land owner by restricting the character of his use, is not unlimited, and, other questions aside, such restriction cannot be imposed if it does not bear a substantial relation to the public health, safety, morals, or general welfare. Here, the express finding of the master, already quoted, confirmed by the court below, is that the health, safety, convenience, and general welfare of the inhabitants of the part of the city affected will not be promoted by the disposition made by the ordinance of the locus in question. This finding of the master, after a hearing and an inspection of the entire area affected, supported, as we think it is, by other findings of fact, is determinative of the case. That the invasion of the property of plaintiff in error was serious and highly injurious is clearly established; and, since a necessary basis for the support of that invasion is wanting, the action of the zoning authorities comes within the ban of the Fourteenth Amendment and cannot be sustained.

Thus, while the Court in *Euclid* appeared to uphold the constitutionality of a zoning ordinance because it was reasonably related to legitimate public purposes, even though it imposed a 75 percent reduction in the land's market value, the Court in *Nectow* judged the application of the zoning law to be impermissible because the public purposes underlying the law were not thought to justify its imposition. *Euclid* and *Nectow* therefore illustrate different sides of the dilemma outlined by Justice Holmes in *Pennsylvania Coal.* How should the conflict between public powers and private property rights be resolved?

§11.2.2 Limits to Zoning Laws Designed to Protect Preexisting Property Rights

The three doctrines in this section all involve legal protections for property owners from retroactive application of zoning laws when those laws unfairly surprise owners who invested in reliance on preexisting laws by denying them the ability to use the property in a manner that was permitted before the zoning law was instituted or changed. The source and status of these doctrines (prior nonconforming uses, variances, and vested rights) is unclear. They may constitute applications of the federal or state constitutional rules prohibiting uncompensated "takings" of property. However, the cases applying these rules tend to treat them as nonconstitutional doctrines, suggesting that they are based on an interpretation of the state's zoning enabling act or its administrative law code. Consider in each case the appropriate limits to retroactive land use restrictions. These cases represent current applications of the dilemmas described in *Pennsylvania Coal, Euclid,* and *Nectow.*

§11.2.2.1 Prior Nonconforming Uses

TOWN OF BELLEVILLE v. PARRILLO'S, INC.
416 A.2d 388 (N.J. 1980)

ROBERT L. CLIFFORD, J. . . .
[S]ometime prior to 1955 Parrillo's operated as a restaurant and catering service on Harrison Street, Belleville. On January 1, 1955 the Town enacted a new zoning ordinance of which all provisions pertinent here are still in effect. The system created under that ordinance provided for zoning under which specific permitted uses for each zone were itemized. Uses not set forth for a particular zone were deemed prohibited. Parrillo's was situated in a "B" residence zone, which did not allow restaurants. However, because it had been in existence prior to the effective date of the zoning ordinance, defendant's establishment qualified as a preexisting nonconforming use[3] and, under the terms of the ordinance, was allowed to remain in operation.

In 1978 defendant's owners made certain renovations in the premises. Upon their completion Parrillo's opened as a discotheque. We readily acknowledge that included among those for whom the term "discotheque" has not, at least until this case, found its way into their common parlance are some members of this Court; and on the assumption that there may be others whose experience has denied them an intimate familiarity with the term and the milieu to which it applies, we pause to extend the

---

3. N.J. Stat. Ann. §40:55d-5 defines a "nonconforming use" as "a use or activity which was lawful prior to the adoption, revision or amendment of a zoning ordinance, but which fails to conform to the requirements of the zoning district in which it is located by reason of such adoption, revision, or amendment." — ED.

benefit of definition. Webster's Third New International Dictionary 63a (1976) informs us that a discotheque is a "small intimate nightclub for dancing to recorded music; broadly: a nightclub often featuring psychedelic and mixed-media attractions (as slides, movies, and special lighting effects)." "Disco" appears to be an accepted abbreviation. Defendant's operation is closer to the broad definition above than it is to a small or intimate cabaret.

Shortly after they had opened under the new format, Parrillo's owners applied for a discotheque license as required by the Town's ordinance regulating dancehalls. Although the application was denied, defendant continued business as usual. Thereupon the municipal construction code official filed the charges culminating in the conviction under review. The municipal court imposed a fine of $250.00.

On a trial *de novo* after defendant's appeal to the Superior Court, Law Division, the defendant was again found guilty. . . .

The Appellate Division reversed. . . .

Superior Court Judge Joseph Walsh . . . made extensive and specific findings of fact. They are amply supported by the record and are as follows:

The business was formerly advertised as a restaurant; it is now advertised as a "disco." It was formerly operated every day and now it is open but one day and three evenings. The primary use of the dance hall was incidental to dining; now it is the primary use. The music was formerly provided by live bands and now it is recorded and operated by a so-called "disc-jockey." An admission charge of $3.00 on the Wednesday opening and $5.00 on the Friday and Saturday openings is now mandatory as opposed to any prior entry charge. There is no charge for Sunday. Formerly there was but one bar; now there are several.

During the course of the testimony it was admitted that the business is operated as a "disco." Normal lighting in the premises was altered to psychedelic lighting, colored and/or revolving, together with mirrored lighting. The premises were crowded and there were long lines waiting to enter. There are now fewer tables than the prior use required and on one occasion there were no tables. The music was extremely loud and the premises can accommodate 431 persons legally. There have been numerous complaints from residents adjacent to the area. During the course of the testimony "disco" dancing was described by the owners as dancing by "kids" who "don't hold each other close." The bulk of the prior business was food catering; now there is none. The foods primarily served at the present time are "hamburgers" and "cheeseburgers," although there are other selections available to people who might come in earlier than the "disco" starting time.

On the basis of these findings Judge Walsh concluded that there had been a prohibited change in the use of the premises. He found to be dispositive the straightforward proposition that "a 'disco' is a place wherein you dance and a restaurant a place wherein you eat. It is as simple as that" — an unvarnished exercise in reductionism, perhaps, but one fully justified in this case. He concluded that the defendant had "abandoned all the pretenses of the continued existence of a restaurant as it was before." We agree with that conclusion. . . .

Historically, a nonconforming use has been looked upon as "a use of land, buildings or premises that lawfully existed prior to the enactment of a zoning ordinance and which is maintained after the effective date of such ordinance even though it does not comply with the use restrictions applicable to the area in which it is situated." 6 R. Powell, *The Law of Real Property*, ¶871 (Perm. ed. 1979). Under the Municipal Land Use Act, N.J. Stat. Ann. §§40:55D-1 *et seq.*, such property is deemed to have acquired a vested right to continue in such form, irrespective of the restrictive zoning provisions:

Any nonconforming use or structure existing at the time of the passage of an ordinance may be continued upon the lot or in the structure so occupied and any such structure may be restored or repaired in the event of partial destruction thereof. (N.J. Stat. Ann. §40:55d-68.)

This statutory guarantee against compulsory termination, however, is not without limit. Because nonconforming uses are inconsistent with the objectives of uniform zoning, the courts have required that consistent with the property rights of those affected and with substantial justice, they should be reduced to conformity as quickly as is compatible with justice. In that regard the courts have permitted municipalities to impose limitations upon nonconforming uses. Such restrictions typically relate to the change of use; the enlargement or extension of the repair or replacement of nonconforming structures; and limits on the duration of nonconforming uses through abandonment or discontinuance.

The method generally used to limit nonconforming uses is to prevent any increase or change in the nonconformity. Under that restrictive view our courts have held that an existing nonconforming use will be permitted to continue only if it is a continuance of substantially the same kind of use as that to which the premises were devoted at the time of the passage of the zoning ordinance. In that regard nonconforming uses may not be enlarged as of right except where the change is so negligible or insubstantial that it does not warrant judicial or administrative interference. Where there is doubt as to whether an enlargement or change is substantial rather than insubstantial, the courts have consistently declared that it is to be resolved against the enlargement or change.

In the instant case it is acknowledged by all parties that the former restaurant had constituted a proper preexisting nonconforming use. The issue then becomes whether the conversion from a restaurant to a discotheque represented a substantial change, and was thus improper. Fundamental to that inquiry is an appraisal of the basic character of the use, before and after the change.

Courts that have engaged in that appraisal have proceeded with a caution approaching suspicion.... *Hantman v. Randolph Twp.*, 155 A.2d 554 (N.J. Super. Ct. App. Div. 1959), well illustrates the proper analysis for examining changes in nonconforming uses. In *Hantman*, the plaintiffs owned a commercial bungalow colony which was primarily dedicated to seasonal use. When the area in which the colony was situated was zoned for residential use, the plaintiffs' property was afforded preexisting nonconforming use status by the Township. In 1957 the plaintiffs attempted to convert the bungalows into dwellings suitable for year-round occupancy. That effort was challenged by the Township on the ground that the change would constitute an unlawful extension of the nonconforming use....

... Reviewing the facts the court established that the plaintiffs' bungalows were in fact nonconforming uses. It then proceeded to address the question of whether permitting full-time occupancy would effect a substantial change in the premises. Answering in the affirmative, the court declared, "an increase in the time period during which a nonconforming use is operated may justifiably be the basis for finding an unlawful extension thereof, just as changes in the functional use of the land or increases in the area of use have been." Recognizing that nonconforming uses are disfavored, the Appellate Division emphasized the deleterious effect that year-round operation of the bungalows might have upon the general welfare of the municipality.... Noting that where there is doubt as to the substantiality of the extension, it should be disapproved, the court found the proposed conversion represented a substantial, and therefore unlawful, change in the nonconforming property. We fully approve of and adopt the approach and analytical framework of the *Hantman* court. . . .

We have already expressed our agreement with the municipal court and with Judge Walsh, presiding at the trial *de novo*, that defendant's conversion of the premises from a restaurant to a discotheque resulted in a substantial, and therefore impermissible, change. The entire character of the business has been altered. What was once a restaurant is now a dancehall. Measured by the zoning ordinance the general welfare of the neighborhood has been demonstrably affected adversely by the conversion of defendant's business. Our strong public policy restricting nonconforming uses requires reversal of the judgment below. . . .

Reversed. The cause is remanded to the Superior Court, Law Division, for entry there of a judgment of conviction.

§11.2.2.2   Variances

COCHRAN v. FAIRFAX COUNTY BOARD OF ZONING APPEALS

594 S.E.2d 571 (Va. 2004)

CHARLES S. RUSSELL, J.

These three cases involve decisions by local boards of zoning appeals (collectively and individually, BZA) upon applications for variances from the local zoning ordinances. Although the facts and proceedings differ in each case, and will be discussed separately, the governing principles of law are the same. We therefore consider and decide the cases in a single opinion.

The Fairfax Case

Michael R. Bratti was the owner of a tract of land containing approximately 20,470 square feet, in the McLean area of Fairfax County. The property was zoned R-2, a residential classification permitting two dwelling units per acre, and was improved by a home in which Bratti had resided for eight years. The zoning ordinance required side yard setbacks of at least 15 feet from the property lines. Bratti's existing home fit well within the setbacks.

Bratti filed an application with the BZA for four variances. He proposed to demolish his existing home and erect a much larger house on the site. The proposed structure would come within 13 feet of the northerly property line, rather than the 15 feet required by the ordinance, and would be further extended into the setback area by three exterior chimneys which would extend beyond the northerly wall of the house. The proposed house would be 71 feet wide and 76 feet from front to back. The proposed encroachment into the side yard setback would extend the entire 76 foot depth of the house.

It was undisputed that Bratti's proposed house could be built upon the existing lot without any need for a variance by simply moving it two feet to the south, plus the additional distance required by the chimneys. Bratti explained to the Board, however, that he desired to have a "side-load" garage on the south side of his house and that a reduction of two feet of open space on the south side would make it inconvenient for vehicles to turn into the garage. The present house had a "front-load" garage which opened directly toward the street. When it was pointed out to Bratti that he could avoid this problem by reconfiguring his proposed house to contain a "front-load" garage, he responded that such a house would have less "curb appeal" than the design he proposed.

If the house were built in its proposed location, but reduced in size by two feet to comply with the zoning ordinance, there would be a resulting loss of 152 square feet of living space. The topography of the lot was such that it rose 42 feet vertically throughout its 198-foot depth from the street to the rear property line. However, there were two relatively level areas shown on the plans for the proposed dwelling, one in front of the house and one in the rear. It was conceded that an additional 152 square feet of living space could have been constructed in either of these areas, but Bratti explained that he wanted to use the level area in front of the house as a play area for children and for additional parking, and that he was unwilling to encroach upon the level area in the rear because he desired to use it as a large outdoor courtyard which he said was "the central idea in the house."

The proposed dwelling had two stories. A third story could have been added as a matter of right, without variances. Bratti conceded that this could easily be done and would more than accommodate the 152 square feet lost by compliance with the zoning ordinance, but that it would be aesthetically undesirable, causing the house to appear to be a "towering structure" as seen from the street.

Over the opposition of a number of neighbors, the BZA granted all four variances. The BZA made findings of fact, including the following: "3. The lot suffers from severe topographical conditions which the applicant has worked hard to accommodate. . . . 5. The requests are modest." This was followed by a conclusion of law: "That the applicant has satisfied the Board that physical conditions as listed above exist which under a strict interpretation of the Zoning Ordinance would result in practical difficulty or unnecessary hardship that would deprive the user of all reasonable use of the land and/or buildings involved."

The objecting neighbors petitioned the circuit court for certiorari. The Board of Supervisors of Fairfax County obtained leave of court to enter the case as an additional petitioner, opposing the variances. The court, after a hearing, affirmed the decision of the BZA and entered an order dismissing the petition for writ of certiorari. The objecting neighbors and the Board of Supervisors brought this appeal.

The Pulaski Case

Jack D. Nunley and Diana M. Nunley owned a corner lot in the Town of Pulaski that contained .6248 acre. The lot was bounded by public streets on three sides. A street 40 feet wide ran along the front of the property and the intersection of that street with a street approximately 30 feet wide formed the southeastern corner of the lot. The 30-foot street ran northward from the intersection, forming the eastern boundary of the lot, and then curved to the west to form the lot's northern boundary. The curvature was gradual, having a radius of 34.53 feet. This curve formed the northeasterly corner of the lot.

The property was zoned R-1, a residential classification which contained a special provision relating to corner lots: "The sideyard on the side facing the side street shall be at least 15 feet from both main and accessory structures." Town of Pulaski, Va., Zoning Ordinance, art. IV §2.6.2 (2002).

The Nunleys petitioned the BZA for a variance from the required 15-foot set back to zero feet, in order to construct a garage at the northeast corner of the lot, the northeast corner of which would be placed tangent to the curving property line. There was no existing garage on the property, and the Nunleys explained that placing a garage in this location would provide the easiest access to the street. The topography of the lot was difficult, the curve along the 30-foot street lying at a considerable elevation above the floor level of the existing house. The garage could be constructed closer to the house without the need for a variance, but this would require construction of a ramp that would add considerably to the expense of the project. Also, the Nunleys explained, there was a stone retaining wall, five feet in height, behind the house that would be weakened or destroyed if the garage were to be built closer to the house.

Neighbors objected, pointing out to the BZA that the construction of the garage so close to the corner would create a blind area that would be dangerous for traffic coming around the curve on the 30-foot street. They also complained that it would be an "eyesore" and would destroy existing vegetation.

The BZA had some difficulty with the question whether the Nunleys' request involved a "hardship" as required by law. The BZA held four meetings to discuss the question and obtained an opinion from the town attorney. The BZA eventually granted the Nunleys a modified variance, permitting an accessory structure no closer than five feet from the northern projected boundary and no closer than 15 feet from the eastern projected boundary of the property. The modified variance also provided that construction should not "alter or destroy the aesthetic looks of existing vegetation bordering the northern projected boundary" of the property.

Virginia C. MacNeal, a neighbor who had objected to the variance before the BZA, filed a petition for certiorari in the circuit court. The court, in a letter opinion, affirmed the decision of the BZA and denied the petition for certiorari. Virginia C. MacNeal brought this appeal.

The Virginia Beach Case

Jack and Rebecca Pennington owned a 1.25-acre parcel of land in a subdivision known as Avalon Terrace, in the City of Virginia Beach. The property was improved by their home, in which they had lived for many years, and a detached garage containing 528 square feet which they had built in 1972. The property was zoned R-10, a single-family residential classification permitting four dwelling units per acre. The ordinance contained a limitation on "accessory structures" by requiring that they "do not exceed five hundred (500) square feet of floor area or twenty (20) percent of the floor area of the principal structure, whichever is greater." The size of the Penningtons' home was such that the 500 square-foot limitation applied to their property.

The Penningtons applied to the BZA for a variance permitting accessory structures containing a total of 816 square feet, in lieu of the 500-square foot limitation. They explained that the purpose of the request was to permit the construction of a storage shed, 12 by 24 feet, adjacent to the garage, and also to bring into conformity the 28 square feet by which the existing garage exceeded the limitation imposed by the zoning ordinance.

The Penningtons could have built the storage shed as an appendage or as an addition to the existing house without the need for any variance, but their representative explained to the BZA that their lot was so large that the shed would be nearly invisible from the street and would have no impact upon neighboring properties. He contended that the obvious purpose of the size limitation on accessory structures, as contained in the ordinance, was to inhibit the erection of large, unsightly outbuildings on small lots. He pointed out that the Penningtons' lot was so large that four dwelling sites could be carved out of it, and that therefore the impact of a small additional outbuilding would be minimal and would not contravene the spirit of the zoning ordinance. He also pointed out that a number of the neighbors were related to the Penningtons and that no neighbors had any objection to their request.

The zoning administrator of the City of Virginia Beach opposed the request, pointing out that there was no need for a variance because the desired storage shed could be built as an appurtenance to the existing house. The zoning administrator had no objection to a variance to the extent of the 28 square feet needed to bring the existing garage into conformity with the zoning ordinance. The BZA granted the variance to bring the garage into conformity, but denied the remainder of the Penningtons' request on the ground that no "hardship" existed.

The Penningtons filed a petition for certiorari in the circuit court. At a hearing on the petition, counsel for the Penningtons asserted a claim of hardship that had not been presented to the BZA: Mr. Pennington was seriously ill and disabled. His wife had full-time employment, was the "bread-winner" of the family and was therefore unable to care for him during the day. The Penningtons' daughter, who had recently graduated from college, had returned to live with the Penningtons and assist in the care of her father. The storage shed was needed as a place to store her belongings. The court ruled that a hardship existed, overruled the decision of the BZA and granted the Penningtons' requested variance. The BZA brought this appeal.

Analysis

Zoning is a valid exercise of the police power of the Commonwealth. Zoning ordinances, of necessity, regulate land use uniformly within large districts. It is impracticable to tailor such ordinances to meet the condition of each individual parcel within the district. The size, shape, topography or other conditions affecting such a parcel may, if the zoning ordinance is applied to it as written, render it relatively useless. Thus, a zoning ordinance, valid on its face, might be unconstitutional as applied to an individual parcel, in violation of Article 1, §11 of the Constitution of Virginia.

Therefore, the BZA has authority to grant variances only to avoid an unconstitutional result. We said in *Commonwealth v. County Utilities*, 290 S.E. 2d 867, 872 (Va. 1982)(emphasis added):

> All citizens hold property subject to the proper exercise of police power for the common good. Even where such an exercise results in substantial diminution of property values, an owner has no right to compensation therefor. *Miller v. Schoene*, 276 U.S. 272 (1928), *Hadacheck v. Sebastian*, 239 U.S. 394 (1915). In *Penn Central Transportation Co. v. City of New York*, 438 U.S. 104 (1978), the Supreme Court held that no taking occurs in the circumstances unless the regulation interferes with *all reasonable beneficial uses of the property, taken as a whole.*

The BZA, when considering an application for a variance, acts only in an administrative capacity. Under fundamental constitutional principles, administrative officials and agencies are empowered to act only in accordance with standards prescribed by the legislative branch of government. To hold otherwise would be to substitute the will of individuals for the rule of law. The General Assembly has prescribed such standards regulating the authority of the BZA to grant variances by enacting Va. Code §15.2-2309(2) which provides, in pertinent part:

> Boards of zoning appeals shall have the following powers and duties:
> . . . (2) To authorize . . . such variance as defined in §15.2-2201 from the terms of the ordinance as will not be contrary to the public interest, when, owing to special conditions a literal enforcement of the provisions will result in unnecessary hardship; . . . as follows: . . . where by reason of exceptional topographic conditions or other extraordinary situation or condition of the piece of property . . . the strict application of the terms of the ordinance would effectively prohibit or unreasonably restrict the utilization of the property or where the board is satisfied, upon the evidence heard by it, that the granting of the variance will alleviate a clearly demonstrable hardship approaching confiscation, as distinguished from a special privilege or convenience sought by the applicant . . .

No such variance shall be authorized by the board unless it finds, *Comm. of Virginia v. County Utilities Corp.*, 290 S.E. 2d 867, 872 (Va. 1982):

> "(a) That the strict application of the ordinance would produce undue hardship" . . . [W]e construe the statutory terms "effectively prohibit or unreasonably restrict the utilization of the property," "unnecessary hardship" and "undue hardship" in that light and hold that the BZA has no authority to grant a variance unless the effect of the zoning ordinance, as applied to the piece of property under consideration, would, in the absence of a variance, "interfere with all reasonable beneficial uses of the property, taken as a whole."

Conclusion

Notwithstanding the presumption of correctness to which the decision of the BZA is entitled, Va. Code §15.2-2314, each of the present cases fails to meet the foregoing standard. The proposed house in *Fairfax* could have been reconfigured or moved two feet to the south, avoiding the need for a variance. Indeed, the project could simply have been abandoned and the existing use continued in effect. The proposed garage in *Pulaski* could have been moved to another location on the lot, or the project abandoned. The shed in *Virginia Beach* could have been built as an addition to the existing house, or the project abandoned. Without any variances, each of the properties retained substantial beneficial uses and substantial value. The effect of the respective zoning ordinances upon them in no sense "interfered with all reasonable beneficial uses of the property, taken as a whole."

Compelling reasons were presented in favor of each of the applications for variances: The desires of the owners, supported by careful planning to minimize harmful effects to neighboring properties; probable aesthetic improvements to the neighborhood as a whole, together with a probable increase in the local tax base; greatly increased expense to the owners if the plans were reconfigured to meet the requirements of the zoning ordinances; lack of opposition, or even support of the application by neighbors; and serious personal need, by the owners, for the proposed modification.

When the impact of the zoning ordinance is so severe as to meet the foregoing standard, the BZA becomes vested with wide discretion in tailoring a variance that will alleviate the "hardship" while remaining "in harmony with the intended spirit and purpose of the ordinance." Va. Code §15.2-2309(2). Factors such as those advanced in support of the variances in these cases are appropriate for consideration by the BZA in a case that falls within that discretionary power, but they are immaterial in a case in which the BZA has no authority to act. The threshold question for the BZA in considering an application for a variance as well as for a court reviewing its decision, is whether the effect of the zoning ordinance upon the property under consideration, as it stands, interferes with "all reasonable beneficial uses of the property, taken as a whole." If the answer is in the negative, the BZA has no authority to go further.

For these reasons, we will reverse the judgments of the circuit courts in each of the cases, vacate the resolutions of the Boards of Zoning Appeals of the County of Fairfax and the Town of Pulaski, respectively, reinstate the resolution of the Board of Zoning Appeals of the City of Virginia Beach, and enter final judgments here.

NOTES AND QUESTIONS

Most states allow zoning boards to grant variances only when application of the zoning ordinance to a particular owner results in "exceptional and undue hardship" *see, e.g.*, N.J. Stat. §40:55D-70(c), and the test for "undue hardship" is quite strict. A variance will not be granted where the hardship is self-imposed, and some courts hold that the owner's refusal to sell the property for fair market value to a neighbor who is willing and able to buy constitutes a self-imposed hardship. *Perez v. Bd. of Appeals of Norwood*, 765 N.E.2d 768 (Mass. App. Ct. 2002) (no variance when hardship was self-imposed because of owner's acts in separating the property into different parcels that caused the problem). In addition, hardship will generally not be found unless there is no economically viable use of the property (or no reasonable return on the owner's investment) if the zoning law is enforced. *See Commons v. Westwood Zoning Bd. Of Adjustment*, 410 A.2d 1138, 1142 (N.J. 1980) (variance only granted when "no effective use can be made of the property in the event the variance is denied").

Determining what is an economically viable use can be a tricky understaking. *See, e.g., Janssen v. Holland Charter Twp. Zoning Bd. of Appeals*, 651 N.W.2d 464 (Mich. Ct. App. 2002)(granting a variance when the income derived from the property was $19,000 per year while the property taxes were $7900 on the ground that this did not give the owner a "reasonable economic return"). Many states add the requirement that the property must be different in some unique way from surrounding property, such as having an unduly narrow frontage or an odd shape or elevation, and that the hardship arise out of this unique condition of the land.

Some states allow variances to be granted on a lesser showing of *practical difficulties*. Ind. Code §36-7-4-918.5, *applied in Metropolitan Board of Zoning v. McDonald's Corp.*, 481 N.E.2d 141 (Ind. Ct. App. 1985); Daniel P. Selmi & James A. Kushner, *Land Use Regulation: Cases and Materials* 87 (1999). To show practical difficulties, the owner must prove significant economic injury from enforcement of the zoning ordinance. Some states interpret the "practical difficulties" test to mean the same thing as the unnecessary hardship test. The zoning enabling acts in some states require a showing *both* of unnecessary hardship and practical difficulties; others allow a variance if *either* of these tests is met. Some states go further and allow variances to be issued in unusual circumstances if this will provide a significant public benefit and the variance can be granted "without substantial detriment to the public good and will not substantially impair the intent and purpose" of the zoning ordinance. N.J. Stat. §40:55D-70(d), *interpreted in Cell South of New Jersey, Inc. v. Zoning Bd. of Adjustment of West Windsor Township,* 796 A.2d 247 (N.J. 2002).

Variances are generally granted to relax lot and building restrictions, not use restrictions. Some states expressly prohibit use variances entirely. Cal. Gov't Code §65906. Others prohibit them from being granted by zoning boards on the ground that they are effectively rezonings that should be voted on by the city council (or other lawmaking body) and not granted by an administrative agency such as the zoning board. Some states allow use variances to be granted upon a showing of unnecessary hardship while allowing area variances to be granted on the lower standard of demonstration of practical difficulties. Daniel P. Selmi & James A. Kushner, *Land Use Regulation: Cases and Materials* 87 (1999).

It is important to note that, although the formal test for obtaining a variance should make it difficult to obtain one, in many locales, zoning boards routinely grant variances if the requested variance is not a dramatic change in the structure and if no one (especially abutting neighbors) objects to the granting of the variance. In effect, zoning boards often ignore the law and grant variances when there is no showing that the owner has been deprived of economically viable use. Michael D. Donovan, Note, *Zoning Variation Administration in Vermont,* 8 Vt. L. Rev. 371 (1983); Jesse Dukeminier, Jr. & Clyde L. Stapleton, *The Zoning Board of Adjustment: A Case Study in Misrule,* 50 Ky. L.J. 273 (1962); Julian Conrad Juergensmeyer & Thomas E. Roberts, *Land Use Planning and Control Law* §5.15, at 207 (1998). In such cases, there is little chance the grant of the variance will be challenged in court because neither the owner who wants the variance nor the zoning board that grants it nor the neighbors who are not adverse to the variance has objections that would prompt any of them to bring an appeal. On the other hand, if a board grants a variance when hardship is absent, there is every likelihood that neighbors who are aggrieved by the variance will challenge the grant. If the statute or the zoning ordinance gives these neighbors standing to challenge the grant of the variance, and if the zoning board granted the variance when the standard was not met, the appellate court is likely to reverse the board's decision.

§11.2.2.3   Vested Rights

STONE v. CITY OF WILTON
331 N.W.2d 398 (Iowa 1983)

Arthur McGiverin, Justice.

Plaintiffs Alex and Martha Stone appeal from the dismissal of their petition for declaratory judgment, injunctive relief and damages in an action regarding defendant City of Wilton's rezoning from multi-family to single-family residential of certain real estate owned by plaintiffs. The issues raised by plaintiffs focus on the validity of the rezoning ordinance. . . . We find no error in trial court's rulings and affirm its decision.

This appeal is a zoning dispute involving approximately six acres of land in the city of Wilton, Iowa. Plaintiffs purchased the undeveloped land in June 1979 with the intent of developing a low income, federally subsidized housing project. The project was to consist of several multi-family units; therefore, feasibility of the project depended upon multi-family zoning of the tract. At the time of purchase approximately one-fourth of plaintiffs' land was zoned R-1, single-family residential, and the remainder was zoned R-2, multi-family residential.

After the land was purchased, plaintiffs incurred expenses for architectural fees and engineering services in the preparation of plans and plats to be submitted to the city council and its planning and zoning commission. In addition, plaintiffs secured a Farmers' Home Administration (FHA) loan commitment for construction of the project. . . .

In December 1979 plaintiffs filed a preliminary plat for the project with the city clerk. In March 1980, following a public meeting, the planning and zoning commission recommended to the city council that land in the northern part of the city be rezoned to single-family residential due to alleged inadequacies of sewer, water and electrical services. The rezoning recommendation affected all of plaintiffs' property plus tracts owned by two other developers. Plaintiffs' application on May 21, 1980, for a building permit to construct multi-family dwellings was denied due to the pending rezoning recommendation.

In May 1980, plaintiffs filed a petition against the city seeking a declaratory judgment invalidating any rezoning of their property, temporary and permanent injunctions to prohibit passage of any rezoning ordinance, and in the event of rezoning, $570,000 damages for monies expended on the project, anticipated lost profits and alleged reduction in the value of plaintiffs' land. . . .

In accordance with the recommendation of the planning and zoning commission, the city council passed an ordinance rezoning the land from R-2 to R-1 in June 1980. Following the council's rezoning decision, the planning and zoning commission approved plaintiffs' preliminary plat. . . .

Validity of the Rezoning Ordinance

Plaintiffs raise several constitutional and statutory challenges to the validity of the rezoning ordinance. . . .

Land use restrictions (such as at issue here) reasonably related to the promotion of the health, safety, morals, or general welfare repeatedly have been upheld even though the challenged regulations destroyed or adversely affected recognized real property interests or flatly prohibited the most beneficial use of the property. Hence, such laws, when justifiable under the police power, validly enacted and not arbitrary or unreasonable, generally are held not to be invalid as taking of property for public use without compensation. However, some instances of government regulation are "so onerous as to constitute a taking which constitutionally requires compensation." *Goldblatt v. Town of Hempstead*, 369 U.S. 590, 594 (1962).

A

We focus initially on the general claims which plaintiffs make concerning the validity of the rezoning. Controlling our review of the enactment's validity is the principle that the validity of a police power enactment, such as zoning, depends on its reasonableness; however, "[the Supreme Court] has often said that 'debatable questions as to reasonableness are not for the courts but for the legislature. . . .'" *Goldblatt*, 369 U.S. at 595.

The zoning ordinance at issue was passed as a general welfare measure. It affected not only Stones' proposed housing project, but also land owned by Land, Ltd. and Wilton Sunset Housing Corporation, which intended to erect multi-family housing for the elderly. The city council's stated reasons for rezoning this section of the city from R-2 to R-1 were as follows: (1) The existing zoning was no longer appropriate to the current and anticipated growth and development of the area; (2) the existing zoning would create a greater density than now appropriate; (3) the existing zoning would create a traffic and pedestrian flow too great for the existing street and sidewalk systems in the area; and (4) the city's electrical, water and sewer systems were inadequate for a concentration of multi-family dwellings in that area of town.

Plaintiffs, however, claim the above were mere pretext. They contend that the council disregarded its comprehensive plan. They further argue that the council was prompted by a desire to advance the private economic interests of a member of the planning and zoning commission and by racial discrimination against the "type" of persons who might live in plaintiffs' housing project. The trial court disagreed and so do we. "If the [city council] gave full consideration to the problem presented, including the needs of the public, changing conditions, and the similarity of other land in the same area, then it has zoned in accordance with a comprehensive plan." *Montgomery v. Bremer County Board of Supervisors*, 299 N.W.2d 687, 695 (Iowa 1980). On the record in this case, we cannot conclude that the council's stated reasons, which are recognized as valid reasons for zoning, Iowa Code §§414.2, 3 (1981), were mere pretext....

Plaintiffs also suggested that questions concerning the "types" of tenants in the housing project were racially motivated and affected the council's decision to rezone. The evidence is clear that the Wilton city council was faced with a number of competing concerns in regard to the proper zoning of the area of the city in which plaintiffs' land was situated. It is precisely because legislative bodies, like this city council, are faced with balancing numerous competing considerations that courts refrain from reviewing the merits of their decisions if at least a debatable question exists as to the reasonableness of their action.

"But racial discrimination is not just another competing consideration. When there is a proof that a discriminatory purpose has been a motivating factor in the decision, this judicial deference is no longer justified." *Village of Arlington Heights v. Metropolitan Housing Development Corp.*, 429 U.S. 252, 265-266 (1977). We are unable to find sufficient evidence in the record to conclude that plaintiffs carried their burden of proof. We find that discriminatory purpose was not a motivating factor in the council's decision to rezone.

In sum, zoning is not static. A city's comprehensive plan is always subject to reasonable revisions designed to meet the ever-changing needs and conditions of a community. We conclude that the council rationally decided to rezone this section of the city to further the public welfare in accordance with a comprehensive plan....

B

As stated earlier, the inevitable restrictions on individual uses of property which accompany zoning normally do not constitute a taking. Plaintiffs, however, claim to have had a vested right in developing their property as subsidized, multi-family housing and, therefore, the rezoning allegedly amounted to a taking of this right. Consequently, they contend the zoning ordinance should be inapplicable to their project. We disagree.

The record shows that a factor in the Stones' choice of property was zoning which permitted multi-family residences. Immediately after purchasing the property in Wilton, plaintiffs made certain expenditures in preparation for obtaining the necessary government financing and in order to comply with city ordinances for platting and building permits. These expenditures totaled approximately $7,900, plus the time and effort expended personally by the plaintiffs.

The standard for determining if a property owner has vested rights in a zoning classification was set forth in *Board of Supervisors of Scott County v. Paaske*, 98 N.W.2d 827, 831 (Iowa 1959):

> It is impossible to fix a definite percentage of the total cost which establishes vested rights and applies to all cases. It depends on the type of the project, its location, ultimate cost, and *principally the amount accomplished under conformity*. Each case must be decided on its own merits, taking these elements into consideration. (Emphasis added.)

Prior to rezoning, Paaske purchased a parcel of land onto which he planned to move five houses. The county granted him a permit to move the houses. Paaske excavated the basements for four houses; placed a septic tank underground for the fifth house; laid concrete footings for the basement of two houses; entered into a contract for the building of the foundations under all five houses, and placed a substantial amount of building materials on the property before the land was rezoned. We concluded that Paaske's endeavors prior to rezoning were so substantial that he had a vested right in completing his project.

In the present case, one of the factors leading to the purchase of this land in Wilton was the fact that it was zoned for multi-family residences. Plaintiffs secured funding from the FHA and engaged the services of an architect and engineer who drew up plans and plats. But these were only the most preliminary steps towards construction. The architect's plans were not the working blueprints of a contractor. The trial court stated they were "the kind [of plans] that one could find in *Better Homes and Gardens* [magazine]." No construction bids were sought and no construction contracts were let. No materials were placed on the site and no construction or earth work was started. We agree with the trial court that plaintiffs' efforts and expenditures prior to rezoning were not so substantial as to create vested rights in the completion of the housing project on that particular tract of land in Wilton.

Under the facts of this case, plaintiffs had to prove they had a vested right to complete their intended project in order to argue that the rezoning constituted a taking. All that the rezoning did was to deprive plaintiffs of what they considered to be the land's most beneficial use. If, as we have found, the ordinance is a valid exercise of police power, the fact that it deprives the property of its most beneficial use does not render it an unconstitutional taking.

"In determining where a zoning regulation ends and a taking of property begins, the test is essentially one of reasonableness." C. Rhyne, *The Law of Local Government Operations*, §26.16 at 745 (1980). We do not believe that rezoning a portion of plaintiffs' property from R-2 to R-1 exceeded the bounds of reasonableness. The city council clearly could have reasonably believed that the general welfare interests of the community outweighed the Stones' investment interest in constructing subsidized, multi-family housing.

Even if the testimony of Stones' expert is accepted, the change in zoning resulted in, at most, a 42% decrease in value of their property. Such economic impact does not constitute a taking in light of the council's reasonable belief that the public welfare required a change in zoning. *See Euclid v. Ambler Realty Co.*, 272 U.S. 365 (1926) (75% diminution in value caused by zoning law did not constitute a taking). Other evidence, however, showed the rezoning to R-1 only slightly affected the fair market value of plaintiffs' land.

Plaintiffs' claim to a right to realize their investment expectations overlooks the fact that "rights granted by legislative action under police power can be taken away when in the valid exercise of its discretion the legislative body sees fit." [*Keller v. City of Council Bluffs*, 66 N.W.2d 113, 119 (Iowa 1954).] At most, the decision of the council "took" from plaintiffs a sizeable tax shelter. Because the reasonableness of the council's decision to rezone plaintiffs' property clearly is at least a fairly debatable question, we cannot substitute our view of reasonableness for that of the council.

We hold that the ordinance which rezoned an area of the city of Wilton that included a portion of plaintiffs' land is valid and applicable to plaintiffs' land and proposed project. . . .

NOTES AND QUESTIONS

Most states agree with the standard in *Stone v. City of Wilton:* owners have vested rights to existing zoning regulations if they have invested substantially in reliance on those regulations. Many states require the granting of a building permit before they will find a vested right while some do not. *Compare Prince George's County v. Sunrise Development Ltd. Partn.*, 623 A.2d 1296, 1304 (Md. 1993)(building permit required) *with* Va. Code §15.2-2307 (no building permit required). On the other hand, the granting of a building permit — without more — is generally not enough. The owner must make substantial expenditures in good faith reliance on existing law. Julian Conrad Juergensmeyer & Thomas E. Roberts, *Land Use Planning and Control Law* §5.28, at 228 (1998).

A minority of states grants developers vested rights if they have obtained site-specific approval for development, such as a preliminary subdivision plan. Such protections mean that a vested right is created even before a building permit is issued; New Jersey provides such protection without any need to demonstrate substantial expenditures. *See, e.g.*, N.J. Stat. §§40:55D-49 to 40:55D-052. *Cf.* Va. Code §15.2-2307 (also requires substantial expenditures). Some states go so far as to grant developers vested rights to use their land in accordance with the zoning law in place at the time they *apply for* a site-specific permit. Colo. Rev. Stat. §§24-68-101 to -106; Mass. Gen. Laws ch. 40A, §6; Tex. Loc. Gov't Code §245.002 to -006; Wash. Rev. Code §§19.27.095, 58.17.033.

PROBLEMS

1. In *Cumberland Farms v. Town of Groton*, 719 A.2d 465 (Conn. 1998), land use as a gas stations was rezoned for residential use. The gas station was allowed to continue operation as a prior nonconforming use. However, when the owner was required by federal environmental statutes to clean up pollution causing by leaking underground storage tanks on the property, the owner sought to open a little convenience store on the property along with the gas station to raise enough money to pay for the cleanup. Assume that the income from operation of the gas station is not sufficient to pay for the environmental cleanup but that the owner could sell the property at as very low price to

someone who could clean up the property, demolish the gas station and construct condominiums on the land. Such a sale would end the prior nonconforming use and clean up the property but the current owner would have lost his business and received very little in selling the land. The current owner cannot convert the property to condominiums himself because no bank would loan him the money for the project. The property has a viable economic use for another owner but the only economically viable use for the current owner is to open the convenience store and keep operating the gas station.

> a. Is the current owner entitled to open a small convenience store on the gas station property under the prior nonconforming use doctrine?
> b. If not, is the owner entitled to a variance allowing him to do this?

2. A licensed day care center operates on a parcel of property that is rezoned for residential use. The day care use is allowed to continue as a prior nonconforming use. The cost of insurance rises so dramatically that it may no longer be profitable to operate the day care center. The site is suitable for a single-family dwelling, but the structure is not; the cost of renovating the day care center to convert it to a single-family home is roughly equivalent to the cost of tearing it down and building an entirely new structure. The owner of the day care center wishes to convert the property for use as classroom facilities for deaf high school students, who would take some classes at the center and other classes with hearing students at the high school. The building is suited to such a use.

> a. *Prior nonconforming use.* Would this constitute an unlawful extension of a prior nonconforming use under the standards articulated in *Belleville v. Parrillo's?*
> b. *Variance.* If it would constitute an unlawful extension, is the owner of the day care center likely to obtain a variance under the standards articulated in *Commons v. Westwood Zoning Board of Adjustment?*
> c. *Vested rights.* The owner gets the property rezoned for school purposes, begins plans to convert the building, hires and pays fees to an architect and signs a contract with a building contractor to renovate the day care center and a contract with the school board to provide classes in sign language for the deaf high school students in the school district. Both contracts are contingent on obtaining a building permit as required by the local zoning law. The owner applies for, but has not yet been granted, a building permit and has spent a total of $20,000. The neighbors organize opposition to the location of the project and successfully induce the city council to rescind its rezoning of the parcel, effectively returning the parcel to residential use. The owner of the parcel sues the city, claiming that the second rezoning interferes with her vested rights in the prior zoning classification. She argues that owners have vested rights to use property in accordance with existing zoning classifications if they invest substantial amounts of money (in addition to the purchase price of the parcel) in plans to build on the parcel in reasonable reliance on the existing classification. The city argues that no vested rights can arise until a building permit has actually issued, regardless of the sum the owner has spent in preparatory plans. Which rule should the court adopt?

§11.2.3　Limits on Preferential Zoning

§11.2.3.1　Special Exceptions

Unlike a variance, which grants the property owner the right to something ordinarily prohibited by the zoning law to avoid undue hardship, a special exception describes a conditional use permitted by the zoning law. Special exceptions are zoning uses permitted when legislatively established conditions are met. Unlike variances, there is a presumption that the owner can engage in the permitted use so long as the established conditions are met. For example, in *North Shore Steak House, Inc. v. Board of Appeals of the Incorporated Village of Thomaston,* 282 N.E.2d 606 (N.Y. 1972), the local zoning law gave the zoning board the discretion, when a zoning boundary line divided a lot owned by a single person or entity, to permit a use authorized on either portion of the lot to extend to the entire lot for a distance of no more than 25 feet beyond the boundary line of the "greater restricted zone." The zoning board had discretion to authorize such a special exception "in appropriate cases, after public notice and hearing, and subject to appropriate conditions and safeguards, and in harmony with the general purpose of this ordinance." Plaintiff restaurant owned a lot whose back portion was zoned for single family use and sought a special exception to extend its parking lot 25 feet into the single-family zone. After the zoning board denied the request, the owner sued the board and obtained a court judgment overturning the board's decision. The court noted that the conditions described in the zoning law had been met because the owner had a bifurcated lot; extension of the parking lot would be beneficial to the community by solving the problem of congestion in the parking lot, which had caused cars to back up into the street. At the same time, the court noted that the board could issue the permit subject to reasonable conditions.

Special exceptions generally require sufficient direction to the zoning board. Vague conditions that grant the zoning board too much power may be struck down as improper delegations of legislative power from the municipal governing body that passed the zoning code to the administrative zoning board. In *Cope v. Inhabitants of the Town of Brunswick,* 464 A.2d 223 (Me. 1983), a zoning law gave the zoning board the power to grant an exception to allow multi-unit apartment buildings in a certain area, so long as this would "not adversely affect the health, safety, or general welfare of the public." After the zoning board denied the owner's request for the special exception, the owner challenged the board's action in court, which struck down the condition relating to public welfare on the ground that it did not give sufficient guidance to the board and effectively delegated legislative power to an unelected administrative agency. As a remedy, the court ordered the town to grant the permit since, by establishing the exception, the enacting legislative body had already determined that the use would ordinarily not be detrimental to the community. In contrast, the Colorado Supreme Court upheld a zoning law that provided that certain uses were "permitted" within an identified district but which retained in the zoning agency the right to review each proposed use on the basis of "neighborhood compatibility." *City of Colorado Springs v. SecurCare Self Storage, Inc.,* 10 P.3d 1244 (Colo. 2000).

§11.2.3.2　Spot Zoning

Spot zoning refers to selective rezoning by the municipal legislative body of a single parcel or small group of parcels of land. Such zoning gives the owner(s) a discriminatory benefit that is inconsistent with the zoning of the surrounding area, is detrimental to the community, and is not justified as a police power measure designed to promote the public welfare. It is very difficult to win a spot zoning challenge; municipalities generally are entitled to rezone land when this is deemed to be in the public interest. *See, e.g., Durand v. IDC Bellingham,* 793 N.E.2d 359 (Mass. 2003) (rezoning of land to allow previously prohibited development not arbitrary or unreasonable when done after developer offered to pay municipality $8 million to allow a new high school to be built); *Save Our Rural Environment v. Snohomish County,* 662 P.2d 816 (Wash. 1983) (denying a spot zoning challenge to a municipal decision changing the zoning law to allow construction of an industrial park near a residential neighborhood). Spot zoning originated in state constitutional proscriptions on "special legislation," that is, government grants or benefits given to individual citizens that are not justified as measures intended to promote the general welfare.

§11.2.4 Exclusionary Zoning

See supra, §10.2.8.1, at pages 899-910.

§11.2.5 Equal Protection, Substantive Due Process, & Free Speech

VILLAGE OF WILLOWBROOK v. OLECH
528 U.S. 562 (2000)

PER CURIAM.
Respondent Grace Olech and her late husband Thaddeus asked petitioner Village of Willowbrook to connect their property to the municipal water supply. The Village at first conditioned the connection on the Olechs granting the Village a 33-foot easement. The Olechs objected, claiming that the Village only required a 15-foot easement from other property owners seeking access to the water supply. After a 3-month delay, the Village relented and agreed to provide water service with only a 15-foot easement.

Olech sued the Village claiming that the Village's demand of an additional 18-foot easement violated the Equal Protection Clause of the Fourteenth Amendment. Olech asserted that the 33-foot easement demand was "irrational and wholly arbitrary"; that the Village's demand was actually motivated by ill will resulting from the Olechs' previous filing of an unrelated, successful lawsuit against the Village; and that the Village acted either with the intent to deprive Olech of her rights or in reckless disregard of her rights.

The District Court dismissed the lawsuit pursuant to Federal Rule of Civil Procedure 12(b)(6) for failure to state a cognizable claim under the Equal Protection Clause. Relying on Circuit precedent, the Court of Appeals for the Seventh Circuit reversed, holding that a plaintiff can allege an equal protection violation by asserting that state action was motivated solely by a "spiteful effort to 'get' him for reasons wholly unrelated to any legitimate state objective." It determined that Olech's complaint sufficiently alleged such a claim. We granted certiorari to determine whether the Equal Protection Clause gives rise to a cause of action on behalf of a "class of one" where the plaintiff did not allege membership in a class or group.

Our cases have recognized successful equal protection claims brought by a "class of one," where the plaintiff alleges that she has been intentionally treated differently from others similarly situated and that there is no rational basis for the difference in treatment. In so doing, we have explained that "the purpose of the equal protection clause of the Fourteenth Amendment is to secure every person within the State's jurisdiction against intentional and arbitrary discrimination, whether occasioned by express terms of a statute or by its improper execution through duly constituted agents." *Sioux City Bridge Co.* v. *Dakota County*, 260 U.S. 441, 445 (1923).

That reasoning is applicable to this case. Olech's complaint can fairly be construed as alleging that the Village intentionally demanded a 33-foot easement as a condition of connecting her property to the municipal water supply where the Village required only a 15-foot easement from other similarly situated property owners. The complaint also alleged that the Village's demand was "irrational and wholly arbitrary" and that the Village ultimately connected her property after receiving a clearly adequate 15-foot easement. These allegations, quite apart from the Village's subjective motivation, are sufficient to state a claim for relief under traditional equal protection analysis. We therefore affirm the judgment of the Court of Appeals, but do not reach the alternative theory of "subjective ill will" relied on by that court. . . .

Justice STEPHEN BREYER, concurring in the result.

The Solicitor General and the village of Willowbrook have expressed concern lest we interpret the Equal Protection Clause in this case in a way that would transform many ordinary violations of city or state law into violations of the Constitution. It might be thought that a rule that looks only to an intentional difference in treatment and a lack of a rational basis for that different treatment would work such a transformation. Zoning decisions, for example, will often, perhaps almost always, treat one landowner differently from another, and one might claim that, when a city's zoning authority takes an action that fails to conform to a city zoning regulation, it lacks a "rational basis" for its action (at least if the regulation in question is reasonably clear).

This case, however, does not directly raise the question whether the simple and common instance of a faulty zoning decision would violate the Equal Protection Clause. That is because the Court of Appeals found that in this case respondent had alleged an extra factor as well — a factor that the Court of Appeals called "vindictive action," "illegitimate animus," or "ill will." . . .

In my view, the presence of that added factor in this case is sufficient to minimize any concern about transforming run-of-the-mill zoning cases into cases of constitutional right. For this reason, along with the others mentioned by the Court, I concur in the result.

NOTES AND QUESTIONS

1. *Equal protection.* The fourteenth amendment provides: "Nor shall any state deprive any person of life, liberty, or property, without due process of law; nor deny to any person within its jurisdiction the equal protection of the laws." Certain classifications, such as racial distinctions, are deemed inherently suspect and therefore presumptively unconstitutional. They will be upheld only if they are necessary to achieve a compelling governmental interest. Other classifications, such as those based on sex, are subject to an intermediate level of scrutiny; they must bear a substantial relationship to an important government objective. Most socioeconomic legislation, however, is subject to a rational basis test; differential treatment of two classes of persons will

be upheld if the classification is arguably rationally related to a legitimate government purpose. This latter test will almost always be satisfied. Erwin Chemerinsky, *Constitutional Law* §9.1 (2002). However, as *Willowbrook v. Olech* attests, it may sometimes be possible to challenge government actions such as applications of zoning or building regulations as violations of the equal protection clause when the municipality treats similarly situated properties differently and cannot present a legitimate defense of this differential treatment. *See City of Cleburne v. Cleburne Living Center*, 473 U.S. 432 (1985) (city violates equal protection clause when it requires group homes for persons with mental retardation to seek special permits to operate but does not impose this requirement on other group homes such as fraternities or nursing homes, and city can present no legitimate government justification for the differential treatment but is based solely on an "irrational prejudice against the mentally retarded").

2. *Substantive due process.* The fourteenth amendment also prohibits states from depriving persons of "property, without due process of law." Although this provision appears to be merely procedural (requiring notice and a hearing, for example, before the deprivation), courts have interpreted it to provide some substantive protection for property owners. In *Willowbrook v. Olech*, the due process claim focused, not on the fact that Grace Olech was treated differently from other property owners, but on the claim that the town had no legitimate government purpose whatsoever in demanding an easement that was 18-feet wider than what appeared to be reasonably necessary for the provision of water service.

At a minimum, the due process clause protects owners from deprivation of "property" rights by "arbitrary and capricious" government actions. *Nectow v. City of Cambridge*, 277 U.S. 183, 187-88 (1928). *Accord, Pennell v. City of San Jose*, 485 U.S. 1, 12 (1988) (due process is violated if regulatory law is "arbitrary, discriminatory, or demonstrably irrelevant to the policy the legislature is free to adopt"); *Village of Arlington Heights v. Metropolitan Housing Development Corp.*, 429 U.S. 252, 263 (1977) (owners have a "right to be free from arbitrary or irrational zoning actions"); *C & M Developers, Inc. v. Bedminster Township Zoning Hearing Bd.*, 820 A.2d 143, 154 (Pa. 2002) (zoning ordinance presumed valid unless "unreasonable, arbitrary, or not substantially related to ... police power interests"). For example, in *Marks v. City of Chesapeake*, 883 F.2d 308 (4th Cir. 1989), the court reversed the city's refusal to issue a special permit for a palmistry studio on the ground that the denial was based on irrational neighborhood objections. This claim is easier to prove when a governmental authority denies a permit or zoning classification to an owner who is similarly situated to another owner who had previously been granted a similar permit. *See, e.g., Board of Commissioners of Roane County v. Parker*, 88 S.W.3d 916 (Tenn. Ct. App. 2002). *See also City of Seattle v. McCoy*, 4 P.3d 159, 172-174 (Wash. Ct. App. 2000)(application of forfeiture law closing property for one year because of illegal drug activity on the premises is a violation of due process of law because it is "unduly oppressive" when the owner took all reasonable steps to prevent the activity).

3. *Free speech.* In *City of Erie v. Pap's A.M.*, 529 U.S. 277 (2000), the Supreme Court upheld the constitutionality of a zoning ordinance that effectively banned nude dancing in the city against a claim that it violated the constitutionally protected free speech rights of the owner. The Court found that the law was a valid content-neutral regulation of conduct rather than expression, and it was geared to protecting the people from the secondary effects of adult entertainment establishments. *Accord, Barnes v. Glen Theatre, Inc.*, 501 U.S. 560, 570 (1991)(government has legitimate interest in preventing public nudity that is "unrelated to the suppression of free expression").

However, in *Mendoza v. Licensing Bd. of Fall River* 827 N.E.2d 180 (Mass. 2005), the state supreme court interpreted its state constitutional free speech guarantee more broadly and found that, while the city could regulate the time, place, and manner of the practice, the city could not completely ban nude dancing from anywhere in the city.

PROBLEM

A town's zoning ordinance requires setbacks of ten feet in a particular area of the town. The zoning board routinely grants variances from this restriction as long as construction is kept five feet away from the boundary, as long as none of the abutting neighbors objects. This practice violates the express terms of the zoning ordinance itself, as well as the state's zoning enabling act, both of which allow variances to be granted only if the owner can demonstrate extreme hardship.

An owner applies for a variance to add a dining room onto her single family home, seeking to build it so that it will be five feet from the boundary of her property. One of the four abutting neighbors objects and the zoning board denies the variance. The owner sues the town, claiming that this deprives her of equal protection of the laws, citing *Willowbrook v. Olech*. The owner points out that two of her neighbors in the immediate neighborhood were granted variances to build structures that extended to five feet from the border of their properties. The zoning board defends the denial on the ground that it is rational to allow neighbors veto power over variances because such variances will affect their property more than that of anyone else. The owner contends that this effective delegation of discretion to the neighbors denies her equal protection of the laws. Who is right?

§11.3 *Ethical Issues in Real Estate Development: SLAPP Suits*

In recent years, developers have faced increasing opposition from community groups over commercial development near their homes or from environmental groups who fear the adverse environmental effects of particular projects. When developers require government permits to proceed, these groups may effectively block development by intervening in public proceedings to voice opposition to the project; sometimes they succeed in persuading government officials to deny issuance of the needed permits. Some developers have struck back by bringing lawsuits against such community groups to intimidate them into dropping their opposition. The most common action brought is a claim of defamation, in which the developer alleges that defendants have made false statements intended to harm the developer's reputation. Most courts have dismissed these lawsuits, on the grounds that (1) defendants have free speech rights to petition the government, or (2) the statements alleged to have been made by defendants constitute opinions, not statements of fact, and thus cannot be true or false.

For example, in *Westfield Partners, Ltd. v. Hogan*, 740 F. Supp. 523 (N.D. Ill. 1990), a developer purchased three parcels of land at the end of a public street for the purpose of developing single-family homes. The owners of houses along the street petitioned the town government to decommission or vacate the street as a public way and turn it into a private way; by so doing, they hoped to block the project and thereby prevent increased traffic along their road and new construction near their neighborhood. After the town granted the homeowners' request, the developer sued the homeowners for interfering in the developer's prospective business advantage and for conspiring with state officials to deprive the developer of its property without due process of law in violation of the federal civil rights statute, 42 U.S.C. §1983.

The court characterized the case as a "SLAPP" suit ("strategic lawsuits against public participation"), a term invented by Penelope Canan and George W. Pring. *See* Penelope Canan and George W. Pring, *SLAPPs: Getting Sued for Speaking Out* (1996). "A SLAPP suit is one filed by developers, unhappy with public protest over a proposed development, filed against leading critics in order to silence criticism of the proposed development." *Westfield Partners*, 740 F. Supp. at 525. The court dismissed the lawsuit on the ground that defendants had a first amendment right to petition public officials.

In 1994, Massachusetts passed a statute to deal with the problem, Mass. Gen. Laws. ch. 231, §59H. The statute provides:

> In any case in which a party asserts that the civil claims, counterclaims, or cross claims against said party are based on said party's exercise of its right of petition under the constitution of the United States or of the commonwealth, said party may bring a special motion to dismiss. The court shall advance any such special motion so that it may be heard and determined as expeditiously as possible. The court shall grant such special motion, unless the party against whom such special motion is made shows that: (1) the moving party's exercise of its right to petition was devoid of any reasonable factual support or any arguable basis in law and (2) the moving party's acts caused actual injury to the responding party....
>
> As used in this section, the words "a party's exercise of its right of petition" shall mean any written or oral statement made before or submitted to a legislative, executive, or judicial body, or any other governmental proceeding; any written or oral statement made in connection with an issue under consideration or review by a legislative, executive, or judicial body, or any other governmental proceeding; any statement reasonably likely to encourage consideration or review of an issue by a legislative, executive, or judicial body or any other governmental proceeding; any statement reasonably likely to enlist public participation in an effort to effect such consideration; or any other statement falling within constitutional protection of the right to petition government.

See Office One, Inc. v. Lopez, 769 N.E.2d 749 (Mass. 2000)(applying the statute and dismissing a lawsuit based on complaints about defendants' attempts to oppose sale of property held by the Federal Deposit Insurance Corp. (FDIC)). *See also* Cal. Civ. Proc. §425.16; N.Y. Civ. Rights L. §§70-a & 76-a; N.Y. C.P.L.R. §§3211(g) & 3212(h).

In *Wigwam Associates, Inc. v. McBride*, 24 Mass. Law. Wkly. 364 (Oct. 30, 1995) (Mass. Super. Ct. 1995), Massachusetts Superior Court Judge Diane Kottmyer held that defendants who unsuccessfully petitioned the government in an effort to force the plaintiff subdivision developer to convert a private common drive into a public street are not entitled to have a subsequent lawsuit by the plaintiff dismissed as a SLAPP suit under Mass. Gen. Laws ch. 231, §59H. Plaintiff claimed that defendants "badmouthed" the plaintiff to prospective home buyers. The court held that this conduct occurred outside the context of petitioning the government.

Retaliation by SLAPP suit defendants. Defendants in SLAPP suits have several avenues of recourse. They may bring a countersuit (called a "SLAPP-back") for the tort of malicious prosecution, claiming that the lawsuit against them is frivolous, without substantial basis, and motivated by malice. They may seek sanctions against the plaintiff's attorney through the state board of bar overseers, on the grounds that the plaintiff's attorney has violated state ethical guidelines against bringing litigation for the sole purpose of harassment. If the suit was brought in federal court, they may ask for Rule 11 sanctions, on the grounds that the claim lacks any basis in law.

Professional responsibility. The *Model Rules of Professional Conduct* provide that a "lawyer shall not bring or defend a proceeding, or assert or controvert an issue therein, unless there is a basis for doing so that is not frivolous, which includes a good faith argument for an extension, modification, or reversal of the existing law." Rule 3.1. The comment to Rule 3.1 states that "[t]he advocate has a duty to use legal procedure for the fullest benefit of the client's cause, but also a duty not to abuse legal procedure."

PROBLEM

You represent a real estate developer who is interested in constructing a shopping center in an area of a city near residential housing. The center is to include a movie theater and various stores. Some homeowners and tenants in the area form a neighborhood organization to oppose some aspects of the plan, on the grounds that the area is already overcrowded, that it is difficult for residents to find parking on the street, and that the influx of customers would overburden the local roads. The organization publishes and distributes a leaflet stating that the "developer does not have the best interests of the ommunity in mind" and that the "developer has ruined other neighborhoods."

Your client believes his project would bring jobs and needed economic development to the city and that it is appropriate to the surrounding area. He knows that local opposition may effectively block the development if he cannot get the required approvals and permits from the zoning board. He also believes the accusations against him in the leaflet are false and insulting. The developer speaks to a senior partner in your firm and asks her to draft a complaint of defamation against the members of the neighborhood association who distributed the leaflet, charging that they made false statements of fact that injured the developer's reputation by lowering him in the estimation of the community and deterring third parties from associating or dealing with him. *Prosser and Keeton on Torts* §111, at 774. His sole purpose for bringing the lawsuit is to intimidate the opponents of his project to prevent them from opposing it before the zoning board and the city council. The partner asks you to draft the complaint.

You know that people cannot be liable for defamation if what they say is an opinion rather than a statement of fact. *Id.* §113A, at 813-815. You also know that both the rules of court and the rules of professional responsibility in your jurisdiction require you, as an attorney and officer of the court, not to file a claim unless you have a reasonable basis for doing so; filing a lawsuit for the sole purpose of harassing the defendant violates your professional obligations to the system of justice. If you violate the ethical code, your law firm — and you personally — could be liable to sanctions by the board of bar overseers and ultimately the state supreme court. You also realize that the developer likely could find some lawyer willing to file the lawsuit as a way of intimidating those who are opposed to the development project.

How would you approach this problem? Is the case "close enough" to justify filing the lawsuit? If you know that the client has a plausible libel claim but that his sole purpose is to intimidate people in the community to derail their opposition to the project, is it appropriate to file the lawsuit? Should you discuss with your client the question of the misuse of the legal system? Should you discuss the issue with other lawyers in your firm? Does filing the lawsuit improve your client's chances of getting what he wants? What advice would you give him?

§11.4 Environmental Regulations: Liability of Property Owners for Cleanup of Hazardous Waste

Land use regulations are imposed not only by local zoning laws but by state and federal environmental protection laws. In 1980, Congress passed the *Comprehensive Environmental Response, Compensation and Liability Act* (CERCLA), and in 1986 followed with the *Superfund Amendments and Reauthorization Act* (SARA), 42 U.S.C. §§9601-9675 (1988). This statute authorizes the Environmental Protection Agency (EPA) to respond or to require others to respond to imminent and substantial danger to the public health or welfare or the environment caused by release of a hazardous substance from a facility. CERCLA imposes liability on persons who formerly either owned or operated a facility when hazardous substances were released and on some present owners and operators of such facilities. This liability is strict, joint, and several, meaning that a single company may be required to pay the entire cost of the cleanup even if 100 companies contributed to and are liable for the damage. Each person found liable may go after other potential defendants to share the cost of the cleanup, but if other responsible parties cannot be found, or their companies have dissolved or are insolvent, any responsible party may be saddled with the entire cost.

Defenses under CERCLA are minimal. Parties are not responsible for (1) acts of God; (2) acts of war; and (3) acts or omissions of third parties with whom the defendant had no contractual relationship, if the defendant shows that it exercised due care and took all reasonable precautions against foreseeable acts of the third party. In 1986, the passage of SARA added a defense for "innocent owners" who made good faith efforts to determine whether the land was polluted but did not discover any preexisting pollution damage before purchasing the property. If the owner later discovers that the property is contaminated, the owner may not transfer the property without disclosing this fact to the purchaser. Failure to disclose causes the seller to be liable for the cleanup even if the seller did not cause the contamination.

Most states have adopted legislation designed to encourage or compel property owners to clean up toxic waste sites. Some states require that the presence of hazardous waste be made known to buyers, allowing the sale to be rescinded if notice is not provided. Ind. Code §13-25-3-2; Anne Slaughter Andrew and Elizabeth L. Dusold, *Seller Beware: The Indiana Responsible Property Transfer Law*, 24 Ind. L. Rev. 761 (1991). Other states impose strict liability on property owners to clean up their property or to reimburse the state for cleanup costs; to ensure payment for the cleanup, these states impose a "superlien" on the property, which takes priority over all or most other debts. *See* Jeffrey T. Cox, *Industrial Property Transactions and Hazardous Waste Cleanup in America: An Analysis of State Innovations*, 15 U. Dayton L. Rev. 471 (1990). New Jersey's *Industrial Site Recovery Act*, the most stringent in the country, prohibits certain owners from transferring their property until they either *certify* that no hazardous substances remain on the property or execute an approved cleanup plan. N.J. Stat. §§13:1k-6 *et seq.*

Real property lawyers must become experts in both state and federal environmental law. While it is impossible to cover this complicated subject in an overview on property law, the following case is included to introduce you to the ways in which environmental regulations may impinge on real estate transactions. Consider the statutory interpretation and policy arguments recited by Justice Ruth Abrams. Do you agree or disagree with the court's interpretation of the statute?

ACME LAUNDRY CO. v. SECRETARY OF ENVIRONMENTAL AFFAIRS
575 N.E.2d 1086 (Mass. 1991)

RUTH I. ABRAMS, Justice.

Acme Laundry Company and Acme Laundry Company, Inc., filed suit alleging that the Department of Environmental Quality Engineering (DEQE) acted wrongfully by placing a lien on their property pursuant to the Massachusetts *Oil and Hazardous Material Release Prevention Act.* Mass. Gen. Laws ch. 21E, §13 (1990 ed.). Both sides moved for summary judgment. The judge allowed the defendants' motion for summary judgment, and the plaintiffs appealed. We transferred the case on our own motion. We affirm.

. . . Acme Laundry Company, Inc. (Acme I), was organized in 1916 by the Eldredge family. Acme I acquired a parcel of land in Chatham, and operated a laundry business at that site from 1916 to 1985. In February, 1986, Acme I contracted to sell the property where it had conducted the laundry business. In December, 1986, Acme I adopted a plan of liquidation and dissolution. At that time, Acme I conveyed twelve parcels of land, including the site of the Chatham laundry business, to Acme Laundry Company (Acme II), a partnership. Acme II succeeded to the rights of Acme I in the contract for sale. In December, 1986, Kenneth Eldredge was the president of Acme I and Leo Eldredge was the treasurer. The Eldredges also were general partners of Acme II.

The prospective purchasers of the laundry site engaged an environmental engineering firm to examine the site. As part of that examination, two No. 6 fuel oil storage tanks were removed from underground. One tank had a hole in it, and the surrounding soil was discovered to be saturated with No. 6 fuel oil. The chief of the Chatham fire department notified the DEQE of the contamination. Harold Bolster, a DEQE employee, inspected the site in January, 1987. He spoke to Kenneth Eldredge, who stated that Acme II would clean up the contaminated site. In February, 1987, the DEQE sent Acme II a notice of responsibility confirming Kenneth Eldredge's acceptance of responsibility, on behalf of Acme II, for the release of oil. The letter notified Acme II that DEQE had reason to believe that Acme II was a responsible party with liability under Mass. Gen. Laws ch. 21E, §5(a)(1), that this liability might include up to triple the cost of "all response costs incurred by the Department, including all contract, administrative, and personnel costs" and "all damages for injury, destruction, or loss of natural resources due to the release." Tracking the language of the statute, the DEQE warned Acme II that any such liability constitutes a debt to the Commonwealth and creates a lien on all Acme II's property. The letter noted that Kenneth Eldredge had informed the DEQE that Acme II intended to take the necessary response actions and had hired Goldberg Zoino Associates (GZA) to determine the extent of the contamination and necessary remedial action. The letter advised Acme II that a site assessment and recommendations for remedial action, along with all data generated by the assessment, must be submitted for review and approval by the DEQE.

The report prepared by GZA indicates significant oil contamination on the site. The thickest part of soil saturation extends more than twenty feet below the water table, and oil floating on the groundwater and dissolved in it extends beyond the area of oil-saturated soil. The groundwater flows toward Ryders Cove, fifty feet from the site, and Frost Fish Creek, two hundred feet from the site. Ryders Cove and Frost Fish Creek have been designated as areas of critical environmental concern by the Executive Office of Environmental Affairs.

In April, 1987, Acme Laundry Company, Inc. (Acme III) was incorporated. Leo Eldredge is the president, Kenneth Eldredge is the treasurer, and both are directors of Acme III. Acme III is not engaged in the laundry business....

On October 22, 1987, Acme II divided the property containing the contaminated soil into four parcels. One parcel includes all of the contaminated soil; the other three are free of contamination. Acme II conveyed the contaminated lot to Acme III. The only business of Acme III is holding property....

In November, 1987, [after a number of studies were conducted at the site,] the DEQE recorded a Statement of Claim and Notice of Lien, pursuant to Mass. Gen. Laws ch. 21E, §13, against the property owned by Acme III. The property described included all four parcels of land. In November, 1988, the DEQE filed a discharge of the earlier lien and substituted two Statements of Claim, placing a lien on all properties owned by Acme II and Acme III in Barnstable county.

On January 24, 1989, Acme II and Acme III filed this action requesting a declaration that the lien is invalid and that the three parcels of property unaffected by the release cannot in the future be subjected to a ch. 21E lien. The complaint also requested an injunction requiring the DEQE to discharge the current lien and preventing the DEQE from imposing a future lien under ch. 21E on the three parcels of uncontaminated land. A second amended complaint was filed in June, 1989, which added requests for damages and for a declaration that Acme II is not a liable party under Mass. Gen. Laws ch. 21E.

The plaintiffs state that the gravamen of their claim is that the DEQE could not place a lien on their property pursuant to the Massachusetts *Oil and Hazardous Material Release Prevention Act*, Mass. Gen. Laws ch. 21E, "because the DEQE has incurred no costs for the 'assessment, containment, and removal'" of hazardous materials. Therefore, we look to the statute to determine how the Legislature defined "assessment" costs and when such costs can be the basis for a lien.

Chapter 21E "is drafted in a comprehensive fashion to compel the prompt and efficient cleanup of hazardous material." The statute provides that the costs of cleanup are to be borne by those who are responsible for the release because they own or owned the land or because they caused the spill. The Legislature provided the DEQE with a number of different means of prodding a responsible party into undertaking cleanup actions, of ensuring that such actions are both timely and appropriate, and of recovering costs from the responsible party.[4] The lien provision used by the DEQE in this case is one of the tools provided by the statute to aid the Commonwealth in ensuring that cleanup is prompt and efficient. Section 13 provides that "[a]ny liability to the com-

---

4. ... A violator is subject to civil penalty, a fine, or imprisonment. Mass. Gen. Laws ch. 21E, §11 (1990 ed.). A responsible party may be liable to the Commonwealth for up to three times the costs incurred by the Commonwealth for response costs. Mass. Gen. Laws. ch. 21E, §5.

monwealth under this chapter shall constitute a debt to the commonwealth. Any such debt . . . shall constitute a lien on all property owned by persons liable under this chapter when a statement of claim naming such persons is recorded or filed." Mass. Gen. Laws ch. 21E, §13 (1990 ed.). To determine which persons are liable under the chapter and the extent of liability, we refer to §5. Section 5 imposes liability without fault for releases of hazardous materials on various parties, including persons who currently own a contaminated site, or did own such a site at the time hazardous material was stored or disposed of at the site, and "any person who otherwise caused or is legally responsible for a release" of oil or hazardous material. This liability is imposed "(i) to the commonwealth for all costs of assessment, containment and removal incurred pursuant to [§§4 and 8] relative to such release . . . [and] (ii) to the commonwealth for all damages for injury to and for destruction or loss of natural resources, including the costs of assessing and evaluating such injury, destruction or loss, incurred or suffered as a result of such release. . . ." Mass. Gen. Laws ch. 21E, §5(a) (1990 ed.).

We therefore must examine §§4 and 8 to determine what "costs of assessment, containment, and removal" create liability. Section 4 authorizes the department "to take or arrange for such response actions as it reasonably deems necessary." Mass. Gen. Laws ch. 21E, §4 (1990 ed.). Section 8 authorizes the department to enter any site in order to "undertake such actions relative to the assessment, containment, and removal" of releases. The section specifies that the department may enter a site to "investigate, sample, and inspect" records, conditions, or property. Mass. Gen. Laws ch. 21E, §8 (1990 ed.). The "response actions" authorized by §4 and "assessment" authorized under §8 are defined in the act. "Response action" means "assess, assessment, contain, containment, remove, and removal." Mass. Gen. Laws ch. 21E, §2 (1990 ed.). "Assessment" means "such investigations, monitoring, surveys, testing, and other information gathering activities to identify: (1) the existence, source, nature, and extent of a release . . . (2) the extent of danger . . . and (3) those persons liable. . . . The term shall also include, without limitation, studies, services and investigations to plan, manage and direct assessment, containment, and removal actions, to determine and recover the costs thereof, and to otherwise accomplish the purpose of this chapter." Mass. Gen. Laws ch. 21E, §2 (1990 ed.). In sum, ch. 21E provides that liability under §5(a)(i), and thus a debt to the Commonwealth under §13, is created where the Commonwealth engages in "investigations, monitoring . . . and other information gathering activities . . . [including], without limitation, studies, services, and investigations to plan, manage, and direct assessment . . . actions. . . ." If the DEQE incurs costs for any of those activities, then it has the authority and discretion to place a lien on all property of a responsible person by filing or recording a statement of claim. A statement of claim is defined by the statute as an instrument "declaring a lien upon the property . . . for the payment of amounts due or to become due from such person . . . to the commonwealth under this chapter." Mass. Gen. Laws ch. 21E, §2 (1990 ed.). Thus, once the Commonwealth has incurred assessment costs, it may place a lien securing both the costs already incurred and those costs which will be incurred and become due in the course of ongoing monitoring and supervision. . . .

The plaintiffs maintain that the Commonwealth cannot be considered to have incurred "assessment" costs because Kenneth Eldredge, acting on behalf of Acme II, agreed to accept responsibility for the release and to perform necessary cleanup operations. The plaintiffs argue that ch. 21E should be interpreted as providing that no liability to the Commonwealth can accrue if a responsible party agrees to perform the cleanup. The words of the statute are to the contrary. . . .

The plaintiffs suggest that we look beyond the statute to Federal law for guidance in interpreting ch. 21E. They note the relationship between ch. 21E and the *Comprehensive Environmental Response, Compensation, and Liability Act of* 1980 (CERCLA), 42 U.S.C. §§9601 *et seq.*, which is in many ways analogous to the Massachusetts statute. They point in particular to a provision of CERCLA which authorized the Environmental Protection Agency (EPA) to take response actions "*unless* the [EPA] determines that such removal and remedial action will be properly done by the owner." (Emphasis added.) 42 U.S.C. §9604(a)(1) (1983 ed.) (amended 1986). The applicable Federal regulation repeated this explicit limitation on EPA action when the EPA is convinced that the owner will clean up properly. 40 C.F.R. §300.61 (1989 ed.). The plaintiffs urge us to infer from the Federal provisions that the Massachusetts Legislature intended a similar result when it drafted ch. 21E, and ask us to import the Federal limitation on agency action into Massachusetts law. The use of such an inference of legislative intent to interpret ch. 21E in this case is inappropriate for three reasons. First, the Legislature provided definitions of the essential terms as used in the chapter, so that the meaning of the provisions has been set forth by the Legislature. Because the language of the statute is the principal source of insight into the legislative intent, we decline to alter the meaning of the State statute by reference to a "legislative intent" derived from a Federal statute. . . . Second, the Massachusetts provision is significantly different from the Federal provision in that the Federal provision contained an extra phrase which was omitted from the Massachusetts provision. The DEQE is authorized "to take or arrange for such response actions as it reasonably deems necessary." Mass. Gen. Laws ch. 21E, §4 (1990 ed.). Unlike §9604 of CERCLA, section 4 contains no language limiting the authority of the agency to act. The Legislature chose to structure the DEQE's authorization to take response actions free from the limitation expressed in CERCLA. . . . Third, Congress has eliminated the limitation on EPA action which formerly existed. CERCLA currently authorizes the EPA to take any response measures which the EPA "deems necessary to protect the public health or welfare of the environment. When the [EPA] determines that such action will be done properly and promptly by the . . . responsible party, the [EPA] *may* allow such person to carry out the action . . ." (emphasis added). 42 U.S.C.A. §9604(a)(1), as amended, Pub. L. 99-499, tit. I, §104(a) (West Supp. 1991). The applicable Federal regulation also has been rescinded. *See* 40 C.F.R. §300 (1990). Thus, Congress has found it preferable to eliminate the limitation on agency action, with the result that §9604 of CERCLA now resembles ch. 21E, §4, more closely. We decline to mold our interpretation of ch. 21E on a Federal provision which was significantly different from the Massachusetts law at the outset, and which now has been eliminated from Federal law.

Finally, the plaintiffs argue that the purposes of ch. 21E are undercut when the DEQE places a lien on property of a responsible party who has expressed an intention to perform cleanup operations. They argue that the funds gained from selling the unaffected parcels of land could be used to help finance cleanup operations. While it is possible that funds generated by the sale of the uncontaminated lots might be used to finance a cleanup, there is no guarantee that the proceeds would be so used. If, in fact, the plaintiffs need to sell the uncontaminated parcels in order to finance the cleanup, the regulations allow them to provide alternative security in the form of a trust fund, standby trust fund, letter of credit, escrow deposit, or surety bond. 310 Mass. Regs. Code §40.170(2) and (3). The DEQE states that, before summary judgment entered, it offered to release the lien if the plaintiffs provided such alternative security, and the plaintiffs refused. The DEQE asserts that, had the plaintiffs agreed to provide alternative security at any time during the litigation, the DEQE would have released the lien. In these circumstances, we consider that the lien has functioned effectively to secure the Commonwealth's recovery of its costs without interfering with the plaintiffs' ability to finance cleanup operations.

The plaintiffs also argue that the lien provision functions as a disincentive for responsible parties to perform cleanup operations themselves. This argument is not convincing. We believe that the Commonwealth's ability to place a lien to secure recovery of costs incurred for planning, monitoring, and supervising ongoing cleanup operations provides a powerful incentive to a responsible party to conclude the cleanup process as quickly and efficiently as possible. If a responsible party's unsupported expression of willingness to clean up, in the face of transfer of properties, is enough to prevent the Commonwealth from employing the §13 lien provision or recovering monitoring costs, then the party's incentive will be simply to delay, because delay would entail no extra costs and would postpone expenditures for cleanup. Such a result would not "compel prompt and efficient cleanup."

Judgment affirmed.

FRANCIS P. O'CONNOR, Justice (dissenting, with whom NOLAN and LYNCH, JJ., join). . . .

The court's construction of ch. 21E as authorizing the imposition of a lien on all of the plaintiffs' real estate impairs, and perhaps destroys, the plaintiffs' — responsible parties' — capacity to complete the response action they agreed to undertake. In addition, the result reached by the court . . . removes the primary motive that a responsible party would otherwise have to undertake response action rather than leave it to the department, namely, cost control. Control would reside with the responsible party only if he could undertake the cleanup under §9 and not simultaneously be liable for costs incurred by the department over which he would have no control. It is not to be expected that an informed owner of a contaminated site would agree to undertake a cleanup project at his expense when he will also be liable for open-ended duplicate "monitoring" costs incurred and passed on by department employees over whom he has no control. The history of this case, including its present posture, convincingly supports the conclusion that the court's holding will defeat the legislative objective in enacting ch. 21E, which is to encourage responsible parties to clean up their own mess. Therefore, and also because the court's holding is unfaithful to the statutory language, I dissent. I would reverse the summary judgment for the defendants and I would remand this case to the Superior Court for the entry of a judgment declaring the asserted liens to be invalid and of no effect and ordering the defendants to file and record in the registry of deeds for Barnstable County a written release of all liens claimed.

V
Property and Sovereignty

12

Regulatory Takings Law

§12.1 *Property as a Mediator Between Citizens and the State*

§12.1.1 DEFINING VERSUS DEFENDING PROPERTY RIGHTS

Property rights serve "twin roles — as protector of individual rights against other citizens, and as safeguard against excessive government interference." Jeremy Paul, *The Hidden Structure of Takings Law*, 64 S. Cal. L. Rev. 1393, 1402 (1991). Property rights mediate disputes by defining legal relations among people regarding control of valued resources. Property rights are not absolute because owners do not live alone; their rights are limited to protect the legitimate interests of other owners and of non-owners who may be affected by the exercise of those property rights. Because property rights must be limited to protect the property and personal rights of others, the state must have the power to *define* the scope of property rights so as to establish the basic framework of legal relationships in the market and to ensure that property rights are not exercised in ways that infringe on the legitimate interests of other owners or the public at large. Thus, the state must have the power to pass laws regulating and limiting the use of property to protect public health, safety and welfare.

At the same time, granting the state the power to define property rights leaves individuals vulnerable to state infringement of those rights. The state may misuse its power to define property rights and go too far, thereby taking property rights away from owners to which they should be entitled. Property rights not only protect people against other persons but serve as a bulwark against state power. By delegating power to individuals and groups to control specific resources, the state attempts to decentralize power relationships. Individuals, rather than officials in a centralized state bureaucracy, have control of many of society's most valued resources. To maintain this decentralization, owners must be protected from having their property rights seized or unduly infringed by the state. Property rights must be *defended* from illegitimate encroachment by the state.

This dual role of property law creates an awful dilemma. How can the state both *define* property rights and be *limited* by them? If the state can simply redefine the incidents of property to readjust relations among private persons, then property rights cannot serve as a limit to state power. Some limit must be imposed on the state's ability to redefine property rights in order to *defend* property owners from illegitimate governmental power. But if the definition of property rights is frozen while circumstances change, the state is deprived of the ability to regulate the use of property to promote the general welfare. Professor Paul notes that "[t]o reconcile American law's double-edged reliance on property concepts, [we] must successfully distinguish between the courts' role as definers and defenders of property rights." *Id.* at 1415.

The fifth amendment to the U.S. Constitution attempts to fulfill this dual function by prohibiting the federal government from "taking" private property "for public use without just compensation." This limitation on governmental power has been held to apply to the state governments through the fourteenth amendment, which prohibits the states from "depriving" citizens of property "without due process of law." The fourteenth amendment does not include a takings clause in its text; however, this segment of the due process clause has been interpreted to include a substantive component that prevents the states from taking private property without just compensation. *Chicago, B. & Q. R. Co. v. Chicago*, 166 U.S. 226 (1897).

The *police power* of the states encompasses the original power of the state governments to pass legislation regulating private conduct to protect the public health, welfare and safety. For example, the state exercises its police power when it passes a law limiting the speed on public highways or environmental protection legislation prohibiting activities that cause air pollution. *Every* exercise of the police power by the states affects existing property interests in some way. For example, when the states reduced highway speeds to 55 miles per hour, some truckers went out of business and others found that their businesses became less profitable. Environmental protection legislation similarly altered the profitability of many businesses. Yet these harms to private property interests need not be compensated by the state. When the state acts within the legitimate sphere of the police power, the infringement on private property interests is *damnum absque injuria* — damage without legal redress.

In contrast to the police power, the *eminent domain* power of the states is the power to take or "condemn" private property, expropriating it, paying just compensation to the owner, and transferring the property to some use designed to further the public welfare. A typical exercise of the eminent domain power occurs when the state takes private property in order to build a highway. When this happens, the state may use eminent domain proceedings to obtain a court judgment transferring ownership of the property from the private owner to the state in return for just compensation.

The problem of *regulatory takings* arises because state actions intended to regulate private conduct to promote the public welfare sometimes have disproportionately negative effects on some property holders. For example, a law intended to protect the environment by regulating air pollution may unintentionally render a particular factory obsolete and unlawful to operate. From a property owner's standpoint, a law that deprives the owner of *all* use of her property takes that property just as surely as outright seizure by the government. Must compensation be provided when the value of property is directly or indirectly affected by legislation? How great must the impact be on the owner before it is deemed equivalent to a public expropriation of the property? When are such disparate impacts justified? How do we identify which limits on property rights constitute legitimate sacrifices for the good of the community and which are unfair burdens that individual property holders should not have to bear in the absence of compensation? Are there some limitations on property rights that owners should not have to suffer at all, even if compensation is paid?

The takings clause mediates between the police power and the eminent domain power. It does this by defining when a purported exercise of the police power has gone "too far" in infringing on private property rights without adequate public justification, thus constituting an exercise of the eminent domain power that can be accomplished only by compensating the owner for the loss of her property rights.

The takings clause has three separate elements: (a) a taking (b) for public use (c) without just compensation. The government may take property only for a "public use"; the Supreme Court has interpreted this to require the taking to effectuate a legitimate *public purpose*. If the taking does not further a public purpose, the government may not effectuate it; the taking can be enjoined by court order. If the taking does further a public purpose, the government may proceed *so long as it provides just compensation to the owner*. Thus, if the public use test is met, the takings clause does *not* prevent the government from taking property. It is "designed not to limit the governmental interference with property rights *per se*, but rather to secure *compensation* in the event of otherwise proper interference amounting to a taking." *Lingle v. Chevron U.S.A. Inc.*, 2005 U.S. LEXIS 4342, *16 (U.S. 2005). All private property is held subject to the possibility that it may be taken by the government, with compensation for the fair market value of the property that was taken, when needed for legitimate public purposes. Regulatory takings law therefore involves determining the circumstances under which government acts or regulations require compensation to property holders whose interests are negatively affected by government regulation.

§12.1.2   HISTORICAL BACKGROUND

See supra §11.2.1, at pages 915-922.

§12.1.3   *PER SE* TAKINGS AND THE *AD HOC* TEST

The Supreme Court has often said that it "has been unable to develop any 'set formula' for determining when 'justice and fairness' require that economic injuries caused by public action be compensated by the government, rather than remain disproportionately concentrated on a few persons." *Penn Central Transp. Co. v. New York City*, 438 U.S. 104, 124 (1978). Rather, the Court generally looks at the "particular circumstances" of each case, "engaging in . . . essentially *ad hoc*, factual inquiries," focusing on three major factors: (1) the "character of the government action"; (2) the protection of "reasonable, investment-backed expectations"; and (3) the "economic impact" of the regulation on the particular owner. *Id.* This "question necessarily requires a weighing of private and public interests." *Agins v. Tiburon*, 447 U.S. 255, 261 (1980). *Accord, Tahoe-Sierra Preservation Council, Inc. v. Tahoe Regional Planning Agency*, 535 U.S. 302, 326 (2002) ("we have 'generally eschewed' any set formula for determining" when a regulation goes "too far" and becomes a taking).

In evaluating these three factors, the Court's goal is to apply the ultimate test of "fairness and justice." The takings clause serves "to bar Government from forcing some people alone to bear public burdens which, in all fairness and justice, should be borne by the public as a whole."*Armstrong v. United States*, 364 U.S. 40, 49 (1960) (*quoted in Lingle v. Chevron U.S.A. Inc.*, 2005 U.S. LEXIS 4342, *16 (2005)). It is of more than passing interest that the standard the Supreme Court has adopted to determine whether a regulation is an unconstitutional "taking" of property is whether the burden it imposes on the owner is just or fair. This *ad hoc* test places the concepts of fairness and justice at the heart of both the takings clause and property law itself. It also assumes that owners have obligations as well as rights. Owners must live with substantial regulation designed to protect the interests of others affected by the exercise of their property rights, including both other owners and non-owners, as well as the community at large. Nevertheless, fairness and justice place limits on the obligations individual owners can be forced to bear for the good of the community.

While the Court normally applies this *ad hoc*, multifactor test to determine when a regulation becomes a taking, it has flirted with the attempt to develop a number of *per se* tests to identify types of regulations that constitute *categorical takings* for which compensation is required regardless of how important the public interest is in the regulation. The number of situations that represent *per se* takings has fluctuated over time. For a while the Court appeared to be intent on identifying more *per se* takings. However, it signaled a retreat from this effort in important cases decided in 2001 and 2002, in which it emphasized the wisdom of avoiding *per se* rules and, instead required lower courts to undertake a "careful examination and weighing of all the relevant circumstances," *Tahoe-Sierra Preservation Council, Inc. v. Tahoe Regional Planning Agency*, 535 U.S. 302, 327 (2002) (*quoting Palazzolo v. Rhode Island*, 533 U.S. 606, 636 (2001) (O'Connor, J., concurring)). The Supreme Court recently clarified that there are only "two categories of regulatory action that generally will be deemed *per se* takings." *Lingle v. Chevron U.S.A. Inc.*, 2005 U.S. LEXIS 4342, *16 (2005). Those include:

1. Government-mandated "permanent physical invasions of property," *Id.* at *18; *see Loretto v. Teleprompter Manhattan CATV Corp.*, 458 U.S. 419 (1982); and

2. Regulations that "completely deprive an owner of *all* economically viable use of her property [unless] background principles of nuisance and property law independently restrict the owner's intended use of the property," *Lingle, supra* at *19 (emphasis in original); *see Lucas v. South Carolina Coastal Council*, 505 U.S. 1003 (1992).

It is important to note that these cases will only "generally" will be deemed *per se* takings. They apply in "relatively narrow" circumstances, *Lingle, supra* at *18. Thus even these two classes of cases are not always deemed takings of property.

The vast majority of cases will be analyzed under the *ad hoc* test identified in *Penn Central Transp. Co. v. New York City*, 438 U.S. 104 (1978). Most regulations will be upheld under this test as legitimate exercises of the police power despite their impact on property use or value. However, there are three categories of cases that have significantly more chance to be deemed unconstitutional takings of property under this test. They include:

3. Deprivation of certain core property rights or estates in land, *Babbitt v. Youpee*, 519 U.S. 234 (1997); *Hodel v. Irving*, 481 U.S. 704 (1987);

4. Retroactive deprivation of vested rights belonging to owners who invested in reasonable reliance on a prior regulatory authorization, *Kaiser Aetna v. United States*, 444 U.S. 164, 179-180 (1979);

5. Required dedications of property imposed as conditions on land use development permits when those "exactions [do not] substantially advance[ ] the *same* interests that land-use authorities asserted would allow them to deny

the permit altogether," *Lingle, supra* at *35-*36; *see Dolan v. City of Tigard*, 512 U.S. 374 (1994); *Nollan v. California Coastal Comm'n*, 483 U.S. 825 (1987).

For about 25 years, the Court suggested that a regulatory taking would be found if a law "does not substantially advance legitimate state interests," *Agins v. City of Tiburon*, 447 U.S. 255 (1980). However, the Supreme Court unanimously ruled in 2005 that a regulation cannot be ruled to be an unconstitutional taking on this basis, *Lingle v. Chevron U.S.A. Inc., supra*. A regulation *can* be struck down as a violation of substantive due process of law if it is "arbitrary, discriminatory, or demonstrably irrelevant to the policy the legislature is free to adopt," *Pennell v. City of San Jose*, 485 U.S. 1, 12 (1988); *see also Lingle v. Chevron, supra*, at **25 ("a regulation that fails to serve any legitimate governmental objective may be so arbitrary or irrational that it runs afoul of the [substantive protections] of the Due Process Clause."). This standard has generally required great deference to legislative discretion (*see supra* §11.2.4), but we can expect to see more litigation making due process claims in the future, and such claims can prevail if the decision maker is convinced that the regulation is not reasonably related to legitimate government interests. *Cf. City of Monterey v. Del Monte Dunes at Monterey, Ltd.*, 526 U.S. 687 (1999) (sustaining a jury verdict under 42 U.S.C. §1983 that a city's denial of a permit to develop beachfront property was not reasonably related to the city's proffered justifications and thus not related to a legitimate public purpose).

The *per* se categories are an application of the general rule; they merely identify particular circumstances that are almost certain to be classified as regulatory takings. For that reason, we will begin by examining the *ad hoc* test to learn the factors that determine whether a regulation will be deemed an unconstitutional taking of property and how those factors relate to the basic test of "fairness and justice." We will then examine the two categories that have sometimes been deemed *per se* takings of property as well as the latter three categories of cases that, although governed by the *ad hoc* test, are more likely than other kinds of cases to require compensation under the takings clause.

§12.2   *Ad Hoc Test: Fairness and Justice*

MILLER v. SCHOENE
276 U.S. 272 (1928)

Mr. Justice HARLAN FISKE STONE delivered the opinion of the Court.

Acting under the *Cedar Rust Act of Virginia*, Va. Code §§885-893 (1924), defendant in error, the state entomologist, ordered the plaintiffs in error to cut down a large number of ornamental red cedar trees growing on their property, as a means of preventing the communication of a rust or plant disease with which they were infected to the apple orchards in the vicinity....

The Virginia statute presents a comprehensive scheme for the condemnation and destruction of red cedar trees infected by cedar rust. By section 1 it is declared to be unlawful for any person to "own, plant or keep alive and standing" on his premises any red cedar tree which is or may be the source or "host plant" of the communicable plant disease known as cedar rust, and any such tree growing within a certain radius of any apple orchard is declared to be a public nuisance, subject to destruction. Section 2 makes it the duty of the state entomologist, "upon the request in writing of ten or more reputable freeholders of any county or magisterial district, to make a preliminary investigation of the locality . . . to ascertain if any cedar tree or trees . . . are the source of, harbor or constitute the host plant for the said disease . . . and constitute a menace to the health of any apple orchard in said locality, and that said cedar tree or trees exist within a radius of two miles of any apple orchard in said locality." If affirmative findings are so made, he is required to direct the owner in writing to destroy the trees and, in his notice, to furnish a statement of the "fact found to exist whereby it is deemed necessary or proper to destroy" the trees and to call attention to the law under which it is proposed to destroy them. Section 5 authorizes the state entomologist to destroy the trees if the owner, after being notified, fails to do so. . . .

As shown by the evidence and as recognized in other cases involving the validity of this statute, cedar rust is an infectious plant disease in the form of a fungoid organism which is destructive of the fruit and foliage of the apple, but without effect on the value of the cedar. Its life cycle has two phases which are passed alternately as a growth on red cedar and on apple trees. It is communicated by spores from one to the other over a radius of at least two miles. It appears not to be communicable between trees of the same species, but only from one species to the other, and other plants seem not to be appreciably affected by it. The only practicable method of controlling the disease and protecting apple trees from its ravages is the destruction of all red cedar trees, subject to the infection, located within two miles of apple orchards.

The red cedar, aside from its ornamental use, has occasional use and value as lumber. It is indigenous to Virginia, is not cultivated or dealt in commercially on any substantial scale, and its value throughout the state is shown to be small as compared with that of the apple orchards of the state. Apple growing is one of the principal agricultural pursuits in Virginia. The apple is used there and exported in large quantities. Many millions of dollars are invested in the orchards, which furnish employment for a large portion of the population, and have induced the development of attendant railroad and cold storage facilities.

On the evidence we may accept the conclusion of the Supreme Court of Appeals that the state was under the necessity of making a choice between the preservation of one class of property and that of the other wherever both existed in dangerous proximity. It would have been none the less a choice if, instead of enacting the present statute, the state, by doing nothing, had permitted serious injury to the apple orchards within its borders to go on unchecked. When forced to such a choice the state does not exceed its constitutional powers by deciding upon the destruction of one class of property in order to save another which, in the judgment of the legislature, is of greater value to the public. It will not do to say that the case is merely one of a conflict of two private interests and that the misfortune of apple growers may not be shifted to cedar owners by ordering the destruction of their property; for it is obvious that there may be, and that here there is, a preponderant public concern in the preservation of the one interest over the other. And where the public interest is involved preferment of that interest over the property interest of the individual, to the extent even of its destruction, is one of the distinguishing characteristics of every exercise of the police power which affects property. . . .

We need not weigh with nicety the question whether the infected cedars constitute a nuisance according to the common law; or whether they may be so declared by statute. For where, as here, the choice is unavoidable, we cannot say that its exercise, controlled by considerations of social policy which are not unreasonable, involves any denial of due process. . . .

PENN CENTRAL
TRANSPORTATION CO. v. NEW YORK CITY
438 U.S. 104 (1978)

Mr. Justice William J. BRENNAN delivered the opinion of the court, in which STEWART, WHITE, MARSHALL, BLACKMUN, and POWELL, JJ., joined.

The question presented is whether a city may, as part of a comprehensive program to preserve historic landmarks and historic districts, place restrictions on the development of individual historic landmarks—in addition to those imposed by applicable zoning ordinances—without effecting a "taking" requiring the payment of "just compensation." Specifically, we must decide whether the application of New York City's Landmarks Preservation Law to the parcel of land occupied by Grand Central Terminal has "taken" its owners' property in violation of the Fifth and Fourteenth Amendments.

I. . . .

Over the past 50 years, all 50 States and over 500 municipalities have enacted laws to encourage or require the preservation of buildings and areas with historic or aesthetic importance. These nationwide legislative efforts have been [based on] a widely shared belief that structures with special historic, cultural, or architectural significance enhance the quality of life for all. . . .

Under the New York City *Landmarks Preservation Law*, . . . the Landmarks Preservation Commission (Commission) [may] designate a building to be a "landmark," situated on a particular "landmark site," or will designate an area to be a "historic district." After the Commission makes a designation, New York City's Board of Estimate . . . may modify or disapprove the designation, and the owner may seek judicial review of the final designation decision. . . . Final designation as a landmark . . . imposes a duty upon the owner to keep the exterior features of the building "in good repair" [and requires] Commission [approval of] any proposal to alter the exterior architectural features of the landmark or to construct any exterior improvement on the landmark site. . . . Under New York City's zoning laws, owners of real property who have not developed their property to the full extent permitted by the applicable zoning laws are allowed to transfer development rights to [nearby] parcels.

This case involves the application of New York City's Landmarks Preservation Law to Grand Central Terminal (Terminal). The Terminal, which is owned by the Penn Central Transportation Co. and its affiliates (Penn Central), is one of New York City's most famous buildings. Opened in 1913, it is regarded not only as providing an ingenious engineering solution to the problems presented by urban railroad stations, but also as a magnificent example of the French beaux-arts style. . . .

[T]he Commission designated the Terminal a "landmark" and designated the "city tax block" it occupies a "landmark site" [and the] Board of Estimate confirmed this action on September 21, 1967. Although appellant Penn Central had opposed the designation before the Commission, it did not seek judicial review of the final designation decision.

[Four months later,] appellant Penn Central . . . entered into a [lease] with appellant UGP Properties, Inc., [under which] UGP was to construct a [50 story-high] office building above the Terminal. . . .

The Commission rejected two different plans for the building on the ground that "balanc[ing] a 55-story office tower above a flamboyant Beaux-Arts facade seems nothing more than an aesthetic joke. Quite simply, the tower would overwhelm the Terminal by its sheer mass. . . ."

Appellants did not seek judicial review of the denial of either certificate. . . . Instead, appellants filed suit in New York Supreme Court, Trial Term, claiming . . . that the application of the Landmarks Preservation Law had "taken" their property without just compensation in violation of the Fifth and Fourteenth Amendments and arbitrarily deprived them of their property without due process of law in violation of the Fourteenth Amendment. . . .

II . . .

A

. . . The question of what constitutes a "taking" for purposes of the Fifth Amendment has proved to be a problem of considerable difficulty. While this Court has recognized that the "Fifth Amendment's guarantee . . . [is] designed to bar Government from forcing some people alone to bear public burdens which, in all fairness and justice, should be borne by the public as a whole," *Armstrong* v. *United States*, 364 U.S. 40, 49 (1960), this Court, quite simply, has been unable to develop any "set formula" for determining when "justice and fairness" require that economic injuries caused by public action be compensated by the government, rather than remain disproportionately concentrated on a few persons. *See Goldblatt* v. *Hempstead*, 369 U.S. 590, 594 (1962). Indeed, we have frequently observed that whether a particular restriction will be rendered invalid by the government's failure to pay for any losses proximately caused by it depends largely "upon the particular circumstances [in that] case." *United States* v. *Central Eureka Mining Co.*, 357 U.S. 155, 168 (1958); *see United States* v. *Caltex, Inc.*, 344 U.S. 149, 156 (1952).

In engaging in these essentially ad hoc, factual inquiries, the Court's decisions have identified several factors that have particular significance. The economic impact of the regulation on the claimant and, particularly, the extent to which the regulation has interfered with distinct investment-backed expectations are, of course, relevant considerations. So, too, is the character of the governmental action. A "taking" may more readily be found when the interference with property can be characterized as a physical invasion by government, *see, e. g., United States* v. *Causby*, 328 U.S. 256 (1946), than when interference arises from some public program adjusting the benefits and burdens of economic life to promote the common good.

"Government hardly could go on if to some extent values incident to property could not be diminished without paying for every such change in the general law," *Pennsylvania Coal Co.* v. *Mahon*, 260 U.S. 393, 413 (1922), and this Court has accordingly recognized, in a wide variety of contexts, that government may execute laws or programs that adversely affect recognized economic value. . . .

More importantly for the present case, in instances in which a state tribunal reasonably concluded that "the health, safety, morals, or general welfare" would be promoted by prohibiting particular contemplated uses of land, this Court has upheld land-use regulations that destroyed or adversely affected recognized real property interests. Zoning laws are, of course, the classic example, *see Euclid* v. *Ambler Realty*

Co., 272 U.S. 365 (1926) (prohibition of industrial use); *Gorieb* v. *Fox*, 274 U.S. 603, 608 (1927) (requirement that portions of parcels be left unbuilt); *Welch* v. *Swasey*, 214 U.S. 91 (1909) (height restriction), which have been viewed as permissible governmental action even when prohibiting the most beneficial use of the property. . . .

Zoning laws generally do not affect existing uses of real property, but "taking" challenges have also been held to be without merit in a wide variety of situations when the challenged governmental actions prohibited a beneficial use to which individual parcels had previously been devoted and thus caused substantial individualized harm. *Miller* v. *Schoene*, 276 U.S. 272 (1928), is illustrative. In that case, . . . [a] unanimous Court [found no taking when the state ordered the destruction of many ornamental red cedar trees to prevent the transmission of cedar rust fatal to apple trees cultivated nearby.] The Court held that the State might properly make "a choice between the preservation of one class of property and that of the other" and since the apple industry was important in the State involved, concluded that the State had not exceeded "its constitutional powers by deciding upon the destruction of one class of property [without compensation] in order to save another which, in the judgment of the legislature, is of greater value to the public." *Id.* at 279.

Again, *Hadacheck* v. *Sebastian*, 239 U.S. 394 (1915), upheld a law prohibiting the claimant from continuing his otherwise lawful business of operating a brickyard in a particular physical community on the ground that the legislature had reasonably concluded that the presence of the brickyard was inconsistent with neighboring uses. *See also Walls* v. *Midland Carbon Co.*, 254 U.S. 300 (1920) (law prohibiting manufacture of carbon black upheld); *Reinman* v. *Little Rock*, 237 U.S. 171 (1915) (law prohibiting livery stable upheld); *Mugler* v. *Kansas*, 123 U.S. 623 (1887) (law prohibiting liquor business upheld).

Goldblatt v. *Hempstead, supra*, [upheld a 1958 city safety ordinance that] effectively prohibited the claimant from continuing a sand and gravel mining business that had been operated on the particular parcel since 1927. The Court upheld the ordinance against a "taking" challenge, although the ordinance prohibited the present and presumably most beneficial use of the property and had, like the regulations in *Miller* and *Hadacheck*, severely affected a particular owner. The Court assumed that the ordinance did not prevent the owner's reasonable use of the property since the owner made no showing of an adverse effect on the value of the land. Because the restriction served a substantial public purpose, the Court thus held no taking had occurred. . . .

Pennsylvania Coal Co. v. *Mahon*, 260 U.S. 393 (1922) [found a taking when a law] forbade any mining of coal that caused the subsidence of any house, unless the house was the property of the owner of the underlying coal and was more than 150 feet from the improved property of another. Because the statute made it commercially impracticable to mine the coal, and thus had nearly the same effect as the complete destruction of rights claimant had reserved from the owners of the surface land, the Court held that the statute was invalid as effecting a "taking" without just compensation. *See generally* Michelman, *Property, Utility, and Fairness: Comments on the Ethical Foundations of "Just Compensation" Law*, 80 Harv. L. Rev. 1165, 1229-1234 (1967).

Finally, government actions that may be characterized as acquisitions of resources to permit or facilitate uniquely public functions have often been held to constitute "takings." *United States* v. *Causby*, 328 U.S. 256 (1946), is illustrative. In holding that direct overflights above the claimant's land that destroyed the present use of the land as a chicken farm, constituted a "taking," *Causby* emphasized that Government had not "merely destroyed property [but was] using a part of it for the flight of its planes." *Id.*, at 262-263, n.7. . . .

B

. . . Appellants urge that the Landmarks Law has deprived them of any gainful use of their "air rights" above the Terminal and that, irrespective of the value of the remainder of their parcel, the city has "taken" their right to this superjacent airspace, thus entitling them to "just compensation" measured by the fair market value of these air rights.

[T]he submission that appellants may establish a "taking" simply by showing that they have been denied the ability to exploit a property interest that they heretofore had believed was available for development is quite simply untenable. Were this the rule, this Court would have erred not only in upholding laws restricting the development of air rights, but also in approving those prohibiting both the subjacent, and the lateral development of particular parcels. "Taking" jurisprudence does not divide a single parcel into discrete segments and attempt to determine whether rights in a particular segment have been entirely abrogated. In deciding whether a particular governmental action has effected a taking, this Court focuses rather both on the character of the action and on the nature and extent of the interference with rights in the parcel as a whole — here, the city tax block designated as the "landmark site."

Secondly, appellants, focusing on the character and impact of the New York City law, argue that it effects a "taking" because its operation has significantly diminished the value of the Terminal site. Appellants concede that the decisions sustaining other land-use regulations, which, like the New York City law, are reasonably related to the promotion of the general welfare, uniformly reject the proposition that diminution in property value, standing alone, can establish a "taking," *see Euclid* v. *Ambler Realty Co.*, 272 U.S. 365 (1926) (75% diminution in value caused by zoning law); *Hadacheck* v. *Sebastian*, 239 U.S. 394 (1915) (87 1/2% diminution in value); and that the "taking" issue in these contexts is resolved by focusing on the uses the regulations permit. Appellants, moreover, also do not dispute that a showing of diminution in property value would not establish a "taking" if the restriction had been imposed as a result of historic-district legislation, but appellants argue that New York City's regulation of individual landmarks is fundamentally different from zoning or from historic-district legislation because the controls imposed by New York City's law apply only to individuals who own selected properties.

Stated baldly, appellants' position appears to be that the only means of ensuring that selected owners are not singled out to endure financial hardship for no reason is to hold that any restriction imposed on individual landmarks pursuant to the New York City scheme is a "taking" requiring the payment of "just compensation." Agreement with this argument would, of course, invalidate not just New York City's law, but all comparable landmark legislation in the Nation. We find no merit in it.

It is true, as appellants emphasize, that both historic-district legislation and zoning laws regulate all properties within given physical communities whereas landmark laws apply only to selected parcels. But, contrary to appellants' suggestions, landmark laws are not like discriminatory, or "reverse spot," zoning: that is, a land-use decision which arbitrarily singles out a particular parcel for different, less favorable treatment than the neighboring ones. In contrast to discriminatory zoning, which is the antithesis of land-use control as part of some comprehensive plan, the New York City law embodies a comprehensive plan to preserve structures of historic or aesthetic interest wherever they might be found in the city, and as noted, over 400 landmarks and 31 historic districts have been designated pursuant to this plan....

... It is, of course, true that the Landmarks Law has a more severe impact on some landowners than on others, but that in itself does not mean that the law effects a "taking." Legislation designed to promote the general welfare commonly burdens some more than others. The owners of the brickyard in *Hadacheck*, of the cedar trees in *Miller* v. *Schoene*, and of the gravel and sand mine in *Goldblatt* v. *Hempstead*, were uniquely burdened by the legislation sustained in those cases.[30] Similarly, zoning laws often affect some property owners more severely than others but have not been held to be invalid on that account. For example, the property owner in *Euclid* who wished to use its property for industrial purposes was affected far more severely by the ordinance than its neighbors who wished to use their land for residences.

In any event, appellants' repeated suggestions that they are solely burdened and unbenefited is factually inaccurate. This contention overlooks the fact that the New York City law applies to vast numbers of structures in the city in addition to the Terminal — all the structures contained in the 31 historic districts and over 400 individual landmarks, many of which are close to the Terminal. Unless we are to reject the judgment of the New York City Council that the preservation of landmarks benefits all New York citizens and all structures, both economically and by improving the quality of life in the city as a whole — which we are unwilling to do — we cannot conclude that the owners of the Terminal have in no sense been benefited by the Landmarks Law. Doubtless appellants believe they are more burdened than benefited by the law, but that must have been true, too, of the property owners in *Miller*, *Hadacheck*, *Euclid*, and *Goldblatt*....

C

... We now must consider whether the interference with appellants' property is of such a magnitude that "there must be an exercise of eminent domain and compensation to sustain [it]." *Pennsylvania Coal Co.* v. *Mahon*, 260 U.S., at 413. That inquiry may be narrowed to the question of the severity of the impact of the law on appellants' parcel,

---

30. Appellants attempt to distinguish these cases on the ground that, in each, government was prohibiting a "noxious" use of land and that in the present case, in contrast, appellants' proposed construction above the Terminal would be beneficial. We observe that the uses in issue in *Hadacheck, Miller,* and *Goldblatt* were perfectly lawful in themselves. They involved no "blameworthiness, ... moral wrongdoing or conscious act of dangerous risk-taking which [induced society] to shift the cost to a [particular] individual." Sax, Takings and the Police Power, 74 Yale L. J. 36, 50 (1964). These cases are better understood as resting not on any supposed "noxious" quality of the prohibited uses but rather on the ground that the restrictions were reasonably related to the implementation of a policy-not unlike historic preservation-expected to produce a widespread public benefit and applicable to all similarly situated property.

Nor, correlatively, can it be asserted that the destruction or fundamental alteration of a historic landmark is not harmful. The suggestion that the beneficial quality of appellants' proposed construction is established by the fact that the construction would have been consistent with applicable zoning laws ignores the development in sensibilities and ideals reflected in landmark legislation like New York City's.

and its resolution in turn requires a careful assessment of the impact of the regulation on the Terminal site.

[T]he New York City law does not interfere in any way with the present uses of the Terminal. Its designation as a landmark not only permits but contemplates that appellants may continue to use the property precisely as it has been used for the past 65 years: as a railroad terminal containing office space and concessions. So the law does not interfere with what must be regarded as Penn Central's primary expectation concerning the use of the parcel. More importantly, on this record, we must regard the New York City law as permitting Penn Central not only to profit from the Terminal but also to obtain a "reasonable return" on its investment.

Appellants, moreover, exaggerate the effect of the law on their ability to make use of the air rights above the Terminal in two respects. First, it simply cannot be maintained, on this record, that appellants have been prohibited from occupying *any* portion of the airspace above the Terminal. While the Commission's actions in denying applications to construct an office building in excess of 50 stories above the Terminal may indicate that it will refuse to issue a certificate of appropriateness for any comparably sized structure, nothing the Commission has said or done suggests an intention to prohibit *any* construction above the Terminal. The Commission's report emphasized that whether any construction would be allowed depended upon whether the proposed addition "would harmonize in scale, material, and character with [the Terminal]." Since appellants have not sought approval for the construction of a smaller structure, we do not know that appellants will be denied any use of any portion of the airspace above the Terminal.

Second, to the extent appellants have been denied the right to build above the Terminal, it is not literally accurate to say that they have been denied *all* use of even those pre-existing air rights. Their ability to use these rights has not been abrogated; they are made transferable to at least eight parcels in the vicinity of the Terminal, one or two of which have been found suitable for the construction of new office buildings. Although appellants and others have argued that New York City's transferable development-rights program is far from ideal, the New York courts here supportably found that, at least in the case of the Terminal, the rights afforded are valuable. While these rights may well not have constituted "just compensation" if a "taking" had occurred, the rights nevertheless undoubtedly mitigate whatever financial burdens the law has imposed on appellants and, for that reason, are to be taken into account in considering the impact of regulation.

On this record, we conclude that the application of New York City's Landmarks Law has not effected a "taking" of appellants' property. The restrictions imposed are substantially related to the promotion of the general welfare and not only permit reasonable beneficial use of the landmark site but also afford appellants opportunities further to enhance not only the Terminal site proper but also other properties.

Affirmed.

Mr. Justice REHNQUIST, with whom The Chief Justice BURGER and Mr. Justice STEVENS join, dissenting.

Of the over one million buildings and structures in the city of New York, appellees have singled out 400 for designation as official landmarks. . . . The question in this case is whether the cost associated with the city of New York's desire to preserve a limited number of "landmarks" within its borders must be borne by all of its taxpayers or whether it can instead be imposed entirely on the owners of the individual properties. . . .

. . . Typical zoning restrictions may, it is true, so limit the prospective uses of a piece of property as to diminish the value of that property in the abstract because it may not be used for the forbidden purposes. But any such abstract decrease in value will more than likely be at least partially offset by an increase in value which flows from similar restrictions as to use on neighboring properties. All property owners in a designated area are placed under the same restrictions, not only for the benefit of the municipality as a whole but also for the common benefit of one another. In the words of Mr. Justice Holmes, speaking for the Court in *Pennsylvania Coal Co. v. Mahon*, 260 U.S. 393, 415 (1922), there is "an average reciprocity of advantage."

Where a relatively few individual buildings, all separated from one another, are singled out and treated differently from surrounding buildings, no such reciprocity exists. The cost to the property owner which results from the imposition of restrictions applicable only to his property and not that of his neighbors may be substantial — in this case, several million dollars — with no comparable reciprocal benefits. And the cost associated with landmark legislation is likely to be of a completely different order of magnitude than that which results from the imposition of normal zoning restrictions. . . . Under the historic-landmark preservation scheme adopted by New York, the property owner is under an affirmative duty to *preserve* his property *as a landmark* at his own expense. . . . The property has been thus subjected to a nonconsensual servitude not borne by any neighboring or similar properties. . . .

Appellees are not prohibiting a nuisance. The record is clear that the proposed addition to the Grand Central Terminal would be in full compliance with zoning, height limitations, and other health and safety requirements. Instead, appellees are seeking to preserve what they believe to be an outstanding example of beaux arts architecture. Penn Central is prevented from further developing its property basically because *too good* a job was done in designing and building it. The city of New York, because of its unadorned admiration for the design, has decided that the owners of the building must preserve it unchanged for the benefit of sightseeing New Yorkers and tourists. . . .

[A] multimillion dollar loss has been imposed on appellants; it is uniquely felt and is not offset by any benefits flowing from the preservation of some 400 other "landmarks" in New York City. Appellees have imposed a substantial cost on less than one one-tenth of one percent of the buildings in New York City for the general benefit of all its people. It is exactly this imposition of general costs on a few individuals at which the "taking" protection is directed. . . .

Keystone Bituminous Coal Association v. DeBenedictis, 480 U.S. 470 (1987).
To prevent subsidence of surface land, a Pennsylvania statute required coal mining companies to leave undisturbed 50 percent of the coal beneath the surface of land supporting public buildings, noncommercial buildings used by the public, dwellings, and cemeteries. In addition, Pennsylvania had a peculiar estate in land, called the *support estate*, consisting of either the right to support of the surface or the right to undermine the surface. This right would ordinarily be owned by either the owner of the surface or the owner of the subsurface mineral rights. The Supreme Court held, in a 5-4 decision, that the statute did not constitute a taking of property even though it required the coal mining companies in the case to leave about 27 million tons of coal in place and deprived them of all value of the support estate that they had previously purchased from the owners of the surface estates.

In an opinion joined by Justices Brennan, Marshall, Blackmun and White, Justice John Paul Stevens argued that the "character of the governmental action involved here leans heavily against finding a taking" because the law was designed to conserve surface land areas, enhance public safety by preventing the collapse of land occupied by owners, preserve water drainage and prevent harm to the water supply; in all these ways, the law protected the public from "a significant threat to the common welfare." *Id.* at 485. Moreover, the property as a whole retained significant economic value; only 2 percent of the coal was required to be kept in place. The fact that the parties had contracted to divide up the rights in the surface and the subsurface did not impede the ability of the state to regulate the property use to protect the public welfare. Nor could the state's choice to identify the right to keep or undermine surface support as a separate "estate in land" prevent the state from later passing a regulatory law designed to protect the public welfare. Such a law is similar to an amendment to a city zoning law decreasing allowable heights of buildings; such laws are constitutional even though owner routinely buy and sell the "air rights" over existing buildings.

Keystone was very similar to *Pennsylvania Coal Co. v. Mahon*, 260 U.S. 393, 415 (1922), the 1922 decision that invented the modern doctrine that regulations of property use might constitute unconstitutional takings of property when regulation goes "too far." However, unlike the owner in *Keystone*, the owner in *Pennsylvania Coal* had won. Stevens distinguished the earlier case by noting that the Court had viewed the earlier statute as serving a private rather than a public purpose because the law did not apply when the surface and the subsurface were both owned by the same party.

Chief Justice Rehnquist dissented along with Justices Powell, O'Connor and Scalia, on the ground that the case was indistinguishable from *Pennsylvania Coal Co.* and that the statute had the effect of expropriating the 27 million tons of coal required to be kept in place as well as the support estate itself. The statute therefore interfered with the coal company's investment-backed expectations that it would be able to mine that coal. Rehnquist argued that compensation is required "where the government has physically taken an identifiable segment of property," as well as a recognized estate in land, *Id.* at 517-519 (Rehnquist, C.J., dissenting).

NOTES AND QUESTIONS

1. *Central principle of the takings clause.* The takings clause serves "to bar Government from forcing some people alone to bear public burdens which, in all fairness and justice, should be borne by the public as a whole." *Armstrong v. United States*, 364 U.S. 40, 49 (1960). A regulation of property will therefore be deemed an unconstitutional taking if "fairness and justice" require us to conclude that "the public at large, rather than a single owner, must bear the burden of an exercise of state power in the public interest." *Agins v. Tiburon*, 447 U.S. 255, 260 (1980). Regulations are not unconstitutional takings if they are "properly treated as part of the burden of common citizenship," *Kimball Laundry Co. v. United States*, 338 U.S. 1 (1949).

2. *Relevant factors.* How do the courts determine whether "fairness and justice" require the cost of a regulatory law to be shared among taxpayers rather than being borne by the individual property owners whose interests are negatively affected by the regulation? The Supreme Court has stated that this "question necessarily requires a weighing of private and public interests," *Agins v. Tiburon*, 447 U.S. 255, 261 (1980). *Penn Central* identified three factors central to this determination: "the economic impact

of the regulation, its interference with reasonable investment backed expectations, and the character of the government action." *Kaiser Aetna v. United States*, 444 U.S. 164, 175 (1979).

3. *Character of the government action.* The state is generally empowered to legislate to protect the public without compensating those whose property interests suffer a resultant economic impact. "Government hardly could go on if to some extent values incident to property could not be diminished without paying for every such change in the general law," *Pennsylvania Coal Co.* v. *Mahon*, 260 U.S. 393, 413 (1922). However, if "protecting the public welfare" is sufficient to characterize a government action as a legitimate regulation rather than an unconstitutional taking, then the government will be able to destroy property interests at will without compensation by using the form of a regulatory law rather than outright exercise of the eminent domain power and the takings clause will be meaningless. On the other hand, by defining "nuisance" or "public welfare" narrowly, courts will interfere in the legislatures' ability to protect people from harm and to promote the general welfare; moreover, activist judges would be substituting their own judgment for that of democratically elected representatives.

In *Keystone*, the majority characterized coal mining that caused subsidence of surface land and the destruction of structures as a nuisance; the law therefore legitimately prevented some property owners from causing harm to other property owners and the public at large. As in *Miller v. Schoene*, the legislature had to choose one property interest over the other when they came into conflict. The dissent, however, characterized the regulations as a physical taking of the 27 million tons of coal required to be left in place. The dissent further argued that the regulations constituted an expropriation of the support estate owned by the coal company; conversely, the majority argued that because the support estate was normally owned by either the surface owner or the owner of the mineral rights, it did not constitute a separate property interest for the purpose of the takings clause. *Cf. Machipongo Land & Coal Co. v. Commw. of Pennsylvania*, 799 A.2d 751, 760, 767 (Pa. 2002) (holding that for the purpose of applying the takings clause, the division of estates under Pa. law into surface, mineral, and support estates is "without significance"; the relevant property is the "parcel as a whole").

This raises the question how to determine whether a regulatory law is legitimately preventing an owner from *harming* others by imposing negative externalities on neighbors or the community or is illegitimately requiring the owner to contribute a *benefit* to the community. The disputes between the majority and minority opinions in both *Penn Central* and *Keystone* revolve around this issue. They also concern the issue of whether the law illegitimately imposes a *disparate impact* on a few owners or constitutes a *legitimate general regulatory law* affecting a class of property that is appropriately subject to heightened restrictions. It is clear that owners have no vested right to destroy the environment and pollute neighboring property; the common law of nuisance has always limited an owner's property rights in this regard. In contrast, if the city government needs new office space and wants to take a private home to be used for that purpose, there is no question it must compensate the owner for the taking. But drawing the line between harm-preventing and benefit-conferring legislation is, of course, not an exact science. The apple tree owners in *Miller v. Schoene* could argue that the cedar tree owners were committing a nuisance by maintaining trees on their property that were causing great destruction on neighboring property. The cedar tree owners could respond that they were not at fault and had done nothing wrong and therefore could not be made to pay for the costs of protecting the apple industry in the state. Indeed, in a case very similar to *Miller v. Schoene*, the Florida Supreme Court required compensation to be paid. *Department of Agriculture and Consumer Services v. Mid-Florida Growers, Inc.*, 521 So. 2d 101, 103 (Fla. 1988) (holding that the state had to pay just compensation when it destroyed healthy orange trees to prevent the spread of citrus canker because "destruction of the healthy trees benefited the entire citrus industry and, in turn, Florida's economy, thereby conferring a public benefit rather than preventing a public harm").

In considering the "character of the government action," the goal is to "identify those regulations whose effects are functionally comparable to government appropriation or invasion of private property," *Lingle v. Chevron U.S.A., supra* at *4-*5. Regulations that have been found to be takings under this test include construction of a dam that results in flooding of property, *Pumpelly v. Green Bay Co.*, 80 U.S. 166 (1872), government-mandated permanent physical invasion of property by the wires and boxes of a cable television company, *Loretto v. Teleprompter Manhattan CATV Corp.*, 458 U.S. 419 (1982), low-flying military planes that made the property uninhabitable and destroyed the owner's business, *United States v. Causby*, 328 U.S. 256 (1946), and conversion of inheritable property into a life estate effectively transferring part of a recognized estate in land from one person to another, *Babbitt v. Youpee*, 519 U.S. 234 (1997); *Hodel v. Irving*, 481 U.S. 704 (1987). Regulations that have been upheld under this test include laws that prevent owners from causing harm to their neighbors or the public as a whole, such as laws prohibiting the commission of a private or public nuisance or conduct that has similar negative externalities, *Goldblatt v. Hempstead*, 369 U.S. 590 (1962)(prohibiting operation of a quarry in a residential area); *Hadacheck v. Sebastian*, 239 U.S. 394 (1915)(prohibiting operation of a brick mill in a residential area), *Mugler v. Kansas*, 123 U.S. 623 (1887) (prohibiting manufacture of alcoholic beverages). Regulations have also been upheld if they limit land use in a manner that benefits society and creates an "average reciprocity of advantage," *Pennsylvania Coal Co. v. Mahon*, 260 U.S. 393, 415 (1922), such as zoning laws, *Euclid v. Ambler Realty Co.*, 272 U.S. 365 (1926)(upholding a zoning law restricting property to residential use even though it reduced the fair market value of the property by 75%), public accommodation statutes, *Heart of Atlanta Motel, Inc. v. United States*, 379 U.S. 241 (1964), and historic preservation statutes, *Penn Central Transp. Co. v. New York City*, 438 U.S. 104 (1978).

4. *Economic impact.* The greater the diminution in value, the more likely the regulation will be characterized as a taking. Complete deprivation of any "economically viable use" is likely to be a taking unless the regulation denies property rights that never existed in the first place, such as the right to commit a nuisance, *Lucas v. South Carolina Coastal Council*, 505 U.S. 1003 (1992). On the other hand, no owner is guaranteed the most beneficial use of the property. Moreover, regulatory laws can be passed and applied to economic conduct even if this has the effect of depriving the parties of bargained-for contractual rights. For example, the Supreme Court has repeatedly upheld the constitutionality of rent control laws as long as they guarantee the landlord a reasonable return on her investment. *Yee v. City of Escondido*, 503 U.S. 519 (1992); *Pennell v. City of San Jose*, 485 U.S. 1 (1988); *Block v. Hirsch*, 256 U.S. 135 (1921).

The extent of the diminution in value depends on how the courts define property interests. Consider a zoning law that prohibits construction above four stories. The owner may identify the "right to build above four stories" as a separate property right. This is plausible because "air rights" can be bought and sold and are valuable property interests. Thus, if this is a separate property right, the ordinance takes 100 percent of its value by prohibiting any construction in this airspace. If, however, the property right is defined more broadly as "the right to build on one's parcel," then the ordinance will take a much lesser percentage of the total property value since it allows construction up to four stories. The diminution in value of the "right to build" may be only 30 percent of the market value of the property without any height restriction. The question is how to identify the "denominator" against which the deprivation will be compared. The majority in *Keystone* noted that the regulations required owners of property without structures to leave only 2 percent of the coal in place; further, the support estate was not considered a separate property interest for purposes of determining the extent of diminution in value. The dissent, in contrast, noted that the 27 million tons of coal that the regulations required to be kept in place, as well as the support estate, constituted separate property interests whose value the regulations diminished by 100 percent.

5. *Interference with reasonable investment-backed expectations.* A regulation is more likely to be held a taking if a citizen has already invested substantially in reasonable reliance on an existing statutory or regulatory scheme. *See Stone v. City of Wilton,* 331 N.W.2d 398 (Iowa 1983) (a change in zoning cannot be imposed retroactively on a developer who has received a building permit and already spent substantial amounts of money on architectural and construction work for a particular project in reliance on existing zoning regulations and the permit itself). It is less likely to be ruled a taking if the regulation prevents the owner from realizing an expected benefit in the future, imposing a mere opportunity cost, as was the case in *Penn Central. Compare Kaiser Aetna v. United States,* 444 U.S. 164, 179-180 (1979) (taking found when a private marina invested in connecting a private lagoon with navigable waters and was required to allow free public access to the lagoon) *with Euclid v. Ambler Realty Co.,* 272 U.S. 365 (1926) (no taking when owner purchased undeveloped property for industrial development purposes and the city subsequently enacted a zoning ordinance restricting future development of the land to residential uses, reducing its market value by 75 percent).

The dilemma here is that people must have some right to rely on existing law at the time they invest; otherwise, the state could pass a general law subjecting all property in the state to being taken for public use without just compensation, thereby rendering the constitutional protection meaningless. At the same time, the legislature must have the power to change the law to impose greater restrictions on land use when circumstances change or new scientific discoveries arise concerning the importance of wetlands, navigable waters, and fragile coastland to the environment.

6. *Theories to identify regulatory takings.* Several theories have been proposed to distinguish regulatory takings from legitimate regulations, including (a) tradition, (b) efficiency, and (c) distributive justice.

a.   *Tradition.* One answer looks to traditional definitions of property interests to determine which government actions constitute "takings" of "property" that must be compensated. Traditional doctrine may identify both the type of activity that constitutes a nuisance (thereby helping to distinguish harm prevention from benefit extraction) and the strands of rights that constitute core

Summary of Takings Factors

	More likely to be held to be a taking requiring compensation	More likely to be held to be a legitimate application of the police power not requiring compensation
Character of government action	• a forced *permanent physical invasion* of property (*Loretto; Causby*) • *extraction of a benefit* for the good of the community or a forced transfer of property rights from *A* to *B* (*Babbitt; Hodel*)	• *regulation of property use* in a manner that achieves an *average reciprocity of advantage* (*Euclid*) • a limitation on property use designed to *protect the community from harm* or to respond to negative externalities (*Keystone, Hadacheck, Goldblatt, Mugler*) • a choice between incompatible property interests (*Miller v. Schoene; Keystone*)
Economic impact	• the regulation denies the owner any economically viable use of the land (*Lucas*) • the regulation destroys almost all the value of the property in a manner unjustified by a sufficient public interest	• the regulation leaves the owner with an economically viable use of the land or a "reasonable return on the owner's investment" (*Keystone, Penn Central, Pennell*) • the diminution in value, even if great, is justified by a sufficiently strong public interest in protecting the public from harm (*Keystone, Hadacheck, Goldblatt, Mugler*)
Interference with reasonable investment-backed expectations	• it interferes with *vested rights,* such as investments based on reasonable reliance on prior regulatory approvals or laws unless those regulations can be justified as preventing a nuisance or other harm caused by the property use (*Kaiser Aetna*) • it interferes with an existing *present use* of the property (*Stone v. Wilton*)	• it imposes an *opportunity loss*—preventing the owner from realizing the benefits of a contemplated future use (*Penn Central*) • the change in the law is one that could or should have been anticipated such that the owner's *reliance* on the continuation of prior law was *unreasonable* • the regulation of a contractual relationship rather than a forced transfer of property interests from one person to another (*Yee; Pennell; Block*)

property rights. But how does one identify what property rights are traditional? Should the courts look just to the common law, or should they consider long-standing legislative alterations to common law rights? Recognizing that property law has changed over time (sometimes dramatically), one must identify both a particular time — and a particular jurisdiction — to identify the property interests to which "tradition" will refer. How should this be done? Should changes over time be recognized as evolution of the tradition or departure from it? *See* Margaret Jane Radin, *Government Interests and Takings: Cultural Commitments of Property and the Role of Political Theory* in Reinterpreting Property 166, 172-77 (1993) (noting that sudden large changes in property law are more likely to be held to be takings while the same changes occurring gradually over a long period of time are less likely to be seen as takings because gradual evolution alters expectations of what rights go along with ownership).

Even when the rules appear to be clear, determining their scope involves discretion and judgment; prior cases can, after all, be distinguished. Moreover, property rights have always been subject to restrictions incorporated in various equitable doctrines, such as *laches*, estoppel and the *sic utere* doctrine (use your rights so as not to injure the legitimate rights of others). Should the source of traditional property law be the relatively clear *rules* that developed over time (and at what time?) or the background *principles* that modify and condition otherwise applicable rights? *See* Frank Michelman, *Property, Federalism, and Jurisprudence: A Comment on* Lucas *and Judicial Conservatism*, 35 Wm. & Mary L. Rev. 301 (1993). A final problem is that the common law definition of property was developed by unelected judges; why should their definition of "property" have greater legitimacy than the definition embodied in statutes promulgated by elected legislators who are responding to public needs and contemporary social values? *See* Louise A. Halper, *Untangling the Nuisance Knot*, 26 B.C. Envtl. Aff. L. Rev. 89 (1998); Louise A. Halper, *Why the Nuisance Knot Can't Undo the Takings Muddle*, 28 Ind. L. Rev. 329 (1995).

b. *Efficiency.* In an important article, Frank Michelman argued that compensation should be required when it will help to promote efficient (that is, wealth maximizing) legislation. Frank Michelman, *Property, Utility, and Fairness: Comments on the Ethical Foundations of "Just Compensation" Law*, 80 Harv. L. Rev. 1165, 1184 (1967). Michelman explained that a utilitarian should be concerned about weighing the gains from public projects against three kinds of costs: (1) the harms to uncompensated victims resulting from the project, (2) the settlement or administrative costs of arranging for compensation for those victims, and (3) the demoralization costs that would accrue if the victims were not compensated and believed that this lack of compensation was unfair. He argued that from a utilitarian perspective, compensation should be awarded when the demoralization costs of failing to compensate are greater than the settlement costs of arranging for compensation. Other scholars have similarly used efficiency analysis to argue for and against compensation for the effects of particular changes in regulatory laws. *See, e.g.,* Daniel Farber, *Economic Analysis and Just Compensation*, 12 Int'l Rev. L. & Econ. 125 (1992); William A. Fischel, *Introduction: Utilitarian Balancing and Formalism in Takings*, 88 Colum. L. Rev. 1581 (1988); Louis Kaplow, *An Economic Analysis of Legal Transitions*, 99 Harv. L. Rev. 509 (1986).

The efficiency argument that would justify requiring compensation when regulatory laws impinge on property rights rests on the proposition that legislation is wealth maximizing if its benefits outweigh its costs. Sometimes, however, legislatures pass statutes that cause more harm than good because the legislature is responding to special interest groups. Requiring compensation for those whose property interests are harmed by legislation *tests* the proposition that the legislation benefits the public welfare by requiring those who benefit from the policy to compensate those who lose. If the winners win more than the losers lose, the winners should be willing to raise taxes to pay for the program since they will gain more from the legislation than it costs them in taxes; if winners are not willing to pay for the program by compensating those who lose, we have evidence that the program benefits them less than it harms the property owners adversely affected by it. In this case the legislation is not efficient and should not have been passed in the first place; requiring compensation will prevent legislators from passing an inefficient law.

There are a number of efficiency arguments that would justify not compensating owners when regulatory laws impinge on their property rights. First, the administrative costs of compensating everyone injured by any regulation are enormous and may outweigh any benefit derived from the regulation. Second, requiring compensation may mean that efficient legislation, which benefits the public by preventing activities whose social costs outweigh their benefits, will not be passed; this may happen when people irrationally underestimate the risks of current conduct (for example, people seek the short-run benefits of industrial development and fail to take into account the long-run harm to the environment). If government fails to adopt wealth-maximizing policies because of irrational desires to refuse to adopt cost-justified tax expenditures, government policy will lower social wealth and welfare by adopting an inefficiently low level of regulation. Third, compensation removes incentives for economic actors to foresee both the effects of their conduct on others and the likelihood that their conduct will be regulated in the future; providing compensation for changes in regulatory law creates insurance against adverse changes in land use regulation, causing developers to over invest in socially harmful activities. In contrast, if no compensation is provided, developers will discount the profitability of activity that is likely to be regulated in the future, decreasing the likelihood that they will engage in socially destructive conduct. *See* Kaplow, *supra*.

c.   *Distributive arguments.* Takings doctrine in fact rest on distributive concerns. The central question is whether the regulation causes a loss that the individual property owner should, in all fairness and justice, bear as a member of society for the good of the community as a whole.

The distributive argument for requiring compensation is that this ensures that the costs of public programs benefiting the community are borne by taxpayers as a group rather than unfairly imposed on individual property owners. When particular owners suffer unique burdens from regulation, there is no average reciprocity of advantage; therefore, they should be compensated unless their use of the property is morally wrongful.

The distributive argument against requiring compensation is that regulations prevent owners from engaging in activities that harm the public welfare. Because individuals have no right to commit a nuisance or to engage in activities that cause substantial negative externalities, they have no right to be compensated when those regulations impinge on their property interests; they have not lost anything to which they were entitled in the first place. Regulations generally create an "average reciprocity of advantage"; those harmed by the regulation are also benefited by it because it regulates not only their activities but their neighbors' as well. The distributive effect is therefore fair because the burdens of the regulation are balanced by a compensating benefit.

7. *Judicial takings.* Almost all claims that property has been unlawfully "taken" without compensation involve challenges to legislative or administrative actions. Can a judicial interpretation of the common law or a change in a common law rule constitute a taking of property? *See* Barton H. Thompson, Jr., *Judicial Takings*, 76 Va. L. Rev. 1449 (1990) (arguing that property owners should be able to challenge common law rulings as takings of property). Such a finding would be problematic. On one hand, the courts generally define the rights that go along with property ownership through the common law process; if changes in common law rules represented takings of property, the courts could never modernize the law. They might even be disempowered from holding that a prior case was distinguishable from the current case. On the other hand, a state supreme court's interpretation of common law could unfairly divest owners of rights they had assumed belonged to them, thereby unjustly interfering with investment-backed expectations.

In *McBryde Sugar Co. v. Robinson*, 504 P.2d 1330, 517 P.2d 26 (Haw. 1973), the Hawai'i Supreme Court overruled a Territorial Court decision holding that two sugar plantation owners possessed certain water rights in their land. *Territory v. Gay*, 31 Haw. 376, 387-388, *aff'd*, 52 F.2d 356 (9th Cir. 1930). The Hawai'i Supreme Court held that this pre-statehood decision had unlawfully divested native Hawaiians of their traditional customary rights of access to water and that the state had the exclusive right to control the flow of the river in question. The property owners whose water rights were divested by the *McBryde* decision brought a federal civil rights suit against state officials, claiming that the court's decision in *McBryde* effectuated a taking of their property rights. The state defended on the grounds that the *McBryde* court overruled a prior decision in an effort to correct an error, that the overruled decision had itself effectuated a taking of native Hawaiians' property, and that the sugar companies never had rights to the land free of preexisting water easements. The Ninth Circuit ruled, in *Robinson v. Ariyoshi*, 753 F.2d 1468 (9th Cir. 1984), *aff'g* 441 F. Supp. 559 (D. Haw. 1977), that the *McBryde* decision unconstitutionally took the "vested" property rights of the plantation owners without compensation. After *Ariyoshi*, could the holders of the water rights easements who prevailed in *McBryde* have brought an action against the state, claiming that the original Territorial Court decision divesting them of their water rights constituted a taking of property without just compensation?

In *State ex rel. Thornton v. Hay*, 462 P.2d 671 (Or. 1969), the Oregon Supreme Court applied the common law doctrine of custom in ruling that the public had a right of access to dry sand areas of beaches for recreational purposes. Although the court narrowed this ruling in *McDonald v. Halvorson*, 780 P.2d 714 (Or. 1989), holding that the doctrine of custom applied only to beaches for which proof could be shown of actual public use, it reaffirmed that the ruling applied to beaches for which customary use could be shown. In *Stevens v. City of Cannon Beach*, 854 P.2d 449 (Or. 1993), Oregon beachfront owners charged that the doctrine of custom had been newly announced in *Thornton* in 1969 and that it effectuated a taking of the property of beachfront owners without compensation. The U.S. Supreme Court denied *certiorari*, in *Stevens v. City of Cannon Beach*, 510 U.S. 1207 (1994), but Justices Scalia and O'Connor dissented from that decision, Justice Scalia writing that although "the Constitution leaves the law of real property to the States," a state may not "deny" property rights "by invoking nonexistent rules of state substantive law." Justice Scalia argued that the Oregon Supreme Court had misapplied the English doctrine of custom. "It is by no means clear that the facts — either as to the entire Oregon coast, or as to the small segment at issue here — meet the requirements for the English doctrine of custom." He explained that a state cannot get around the constitutional obligation to compensate owners for a taking "by the simple device of asserting retroactively that the property it has taken never existed at all," *id.* (*quoting Hughes v. Washington*, 389 U.S. 290, 296-297 (1967) (Stewart, J., concurring)). "No more by judicial decree than by legislative fiat may a State transform private property into public property without compensation." *Id.*

What does it mean to say that the Oregon Supreme Court misapplied the English doctrine of custom? Isn't the issue the definition of the *Oregon* doctrine of custom? How could the Oregon Supreme Court get that wrong, if it is the final arbiter of what Oregon law is? Is Justice Scalia suggesting that the Oregon Supreme Court acted in bad faith by changing property rights while purporting to interpret existing law? Does it matter that the Oregon Supreme Court viewed the case as one of first impression?

8. *Takings statutes.* A few states have passed statutes that go beyond the takings clause in protecting owners from uncompensated deprivation of property rights. Both the federal government[1] and many states have passed *assessment* laws that require government entities to consider the impact of regulations on private property owners before promulgating them to avoid unconstitutional takings of property and to review regulations if they are challenged as regulatory takings or if they are likely reduce property values by a set amount. *See, e.g.*, Del. Code tit. 29, §605; Fla. Stat. §70.001.

A few states have passed laws that allow either injunctive relief or just compensation when regulatory laws reduce the value of property, even if that reduction would not constitute an unconstitutional taking of property. Some states require compensation if an owner's property values are reduced by a particular percentage unless the regulation fits into an established exemption. *See* Tex. Gov't Code §§2007.001 to 2007.045 (*Private Real Property Rights Preservation Act*) (both injunctive relief and damages available for state agency regulations that reduce property value by 25 percent or more unless the regulation fits within a list of exemptions). Other states provide relief if a regulation imposes an unfair or inordinate burden on a property owner, even if that burden would not amount to an unconstitutional taking, effectively leaving it to the courts to determine what constitutes an unfair burden. *See* Fla. Stat. §70.001(a) (*Bert J. Harris, Jr. Private Property Rights Protection Act of 1995*) (granting relief when a "new" law or regulation "unfairly affects real property" by imposing an "inordinate burden" on an existing use of real property by impairing the owner's "reasonable, investment-backed expectation for the existing use of the real property" or by leaving the owner "with existing or vested uses that are unreasonable such that the property owner bears permanently a disproportionate share of a burden imposed for the good of the public, which in fairness should be borne by the public at large").

---

1. In 1988, President Reagan issued an Executive Order that is still in effect that requires all federal agencies to conduct a "takings impact analysis" of all regulations that may affect the use of private property to avoid government actions that might result in an unconstitutional taking of property. Exec. Order No. 12,630, 3 C.F.R. §554 (1988), *reprinted in* 5 U.S.C. §601.

Oregon has adopted the most radical law. On Nov. 2, 2004, the voters adopted a state law known as *Measure 37* that requires compensation when any regulation "that restricts the use of real property" and is enacted after an owner or a family member acquires title to land if the regulation "has the effect of reducing the fair market value of property" unless the regulation restricts activities "commonly and historically recognized as public nuisances under common law" or protects "public health and safety, such as fire and building codes, health and sanitation regulations, solid or hazardous waste regulations, and pollution control regulations." The measure applies both to statutes and to zoning ordinances. *See http://www.oregon.gov/LCD/measure37.shtml.* As written, the law would apparently both preserve existing zoning and environmental laws but, in the absence of compensation, prohibit, any future changes in those laws that would reduce the value of property, such as downzoning laws that reduce the allowable heights of buildings or stricter environmental regulations.

PROBLEMS

1. A scientific research company builds a facility to test chemical weapons in the middle of a busy city. The company has a contract with the U.S. Department of Defense to undertake the research. Word of the purpose of the facility leaks out to the general public. A referendum is placed on the ballot to amend the zoning ordinance to prohibit the testing of chemical weapons anywhere in the city. The company explains that the facility is perfectly safe; scientific experts agree that operation of the plant poses little, if any, danger of causing public health problems. Nonetheless, the public is frightened by the prospect of the facility and votes for the referendum. The company sues the city, claiming that enforcement of the amended zoning law would interfere with its vested rights and constitute a taking of property without just compensation. The multimillion-dollar facility is not structured for other kinds of scientific research and would have to be substantially rebuilt in order to convert to other research purposes; application of the ordinance therefore would destroy millions of dollars of the company's investment. The city responds that the amendment regulates a public nuisance and protects the community from any possible contagion from the facility. Does the regulation take the company's property rights? How should the case be resolved?

2. In 1991, the Pennsylvania Supreme Court ruled that a historic preservation law similar to the one at issue in *Penn Central* effected an unconstitutional taking of property under the Pennsylvania Constitution because the statute required the owner to preserve the building in its current form and to bear all the costs of preserving the property. "A man's home and property used to be his castle," the court noted. "Because one's property was built in a certain architectural style or designed by a particular architect does not make it any less his castle." *United Artists Theater Circuit, Inc. v. City of Philadelphia*, 595 A.2d 6, 13 (Pa. 1991), *rev'd*, 635 A.2d 612 (Pa. 1993). "When a specific piece of property is targeted and treated differently from neighboring properties, no . . . reciprocity [of advantage] exists." *Id.* at 14 n.10. However, two years later, the court changed its mind and reversed its decision. *United Artists Theater Circuit, Inc. v. City of Philadelphia*, 635 A.2d 612 (Pa. 1993). The court now agreed with the result in *Penn Central*, finding historic preservation laws to serve the general public and that it would inefficient and infeasible for governments to buy and operate all historic properties; such laws were therefore necessary to effectuate the public purpose of preserving historic properties. It held that a regulation would nevertheless

effect a taking within the meaning of the state constitution if its impact on the owner were "unduly oppressive." *Id.* at 618. Because the statute allowed exceptions in cases of undue hardship and because the law allowed the owner economically viable use of the land, no taking had occurred. *Id.*

Do you agree with the ruling in *Penn Central* or with the dissenting opinion? What are the arguments on both sides, and who should win? Consider the following fact situation.

A law school owns a student center and dormitories designed by a famous architect. Although designated as a historic monument, the student is too small for the current study body center, and its internal spaces are cramped and unsuited to current university architectural standards. Moreover, the school has expanded both its student body and its faculty by about 50 percent, making the facilities inadequate for its current purposes. It wants to expand its physical facilities and would like to demolish all these buildings to create a modern student and dormitory center. However, designation of the buildings as historic monuments prevents the change and requires the school to maintain the properties as is. What is the school's argument that the historic preservation law effects an unconstitutional taking of property? What is the state's response? If you were on the Supreme Court, how would you rule and what would you say in the opinion?

3. *Wetlands.* Wetlands are important to the environment in myriad ways. They prevent flooding, release vegetative matter into other waters to feed fish, help cleanse rivers by recycling nutrients, and serve as habitats for animals. *See http://mbgnet.mobot.org/fresh/wetlands/why.htm* (Missouri Botanical Garden 2002). In *Friedenburg v. N.Y. State Dept. of Envtl. Conservation,* 767 N.Y.S.2d 451 (App. Div. 2003), the court found a taking under the *Penn Central* test when a wetlands law denied a waterfront owner the right to build anything on the land, thereby lowering the property value by 95 percent. The court acknowledged enormously important public interests in avoiding destruction of wetlands but held that such a severe impact on the owner meant that the regulation did not result in an "average reciprocity of advantage." Was the case correctly decided? *Accord, Woodland Manor, III Assocs. v. Reisma,* 2003 R.I. Super. LEXIS 35 (2003)(finding a taking under the *Penn Central* test when wetlands regulations prevented development of 20 of the owner's 89 acres).

§12.3 Per Se Takings

§12.3.1 Physical Invasions

PRUNEYARD SHOPPING CENTER v. ROBINS
447 U.S. 74 (1980)

Mr. Justice WILLIAM H. REHNQUIST delivered the opinion of the Court....

Appellant PruneYard is a privately owned shopping center in the city of Campbell, Cal. It covers approximately 21 acres — 5 devoted to parking and 16 occupied by walkways, plazas, sidewalks, and buildings that contain more than 65 specialty shops, 10 restaurants, and a movie theater. The PruneYard is open to the public for the purpose of encouraging the patronizing of its commercial establishments. It has a policy not to permit any visitor or tenant to engage in any publicly expressive activity, including the circulation of petitions, that is not directly related to its commercial purposes. This policy has been strictly enforced in a nondiscriminatory fashion. The PruneYard is owned by appellant Fred Sahadi.

Appellees are high school students who sought to solicit support for their opposition to a United Nations resolution against "Zionism." On a Saturday afternoon they set up a card table in a corner of PruneYard's central courtyard. They distributed pamphlets and asked passersby to sign petitions, which were to be sent to the President and Members of Congress. Their activity was peaceful and orderly and so far as the record indicates was not objected to by PruneYard's patrons.

Soon after appellees had begun soliciting signatures, a security guard informed them that they would have to leave because their activity violated PruneYard regulations. The guard suggested that they move to the public sidewalk at the PruneYard's perimeter. Appellees immediately left the premises and later filed this lawsuit in the California Superior Court of Santa Clara County. They sought to enjoin appellants from denying them access to the PruneYard for the purpose of circulating their petitions. . . .

The California Supreme Court [held] that the California Constitution protects "speech and petitioning, reasonably exercised, in shopping centers even when the centers are privately owned." It concluded that appellees were entitled to conduct their activity on PruneYard property. . . .

Before this Court, appellants contend that their constitutionally established rights under the Fourteenth Amendment to exclude appellees from adverse use of appellants' private property cannot be denied by invocation of a state constitutional provision or by judicial reconstruction of a State's laws of private property. . . .

Appellants . . . contend that a right to exclude others underlies the Fifth Amendment guarantee against the taking of property without just compensation and the Fourteenth Amendment guarantee against the deprivation of property without due process of law.

It is true that one of the essential sticks in the bundle of property rights is the right to exclude others. *Kaiser Aetna v. United States*, 444 U.S. 164, 179-180 (1979). And here there has literally been a "taking" of that right to the extent that the California Supreme Court has interpreted the State Constitution to entitle its citizens to exercise free expression and petition rights on shopping center property. But it is well established that "not every destruction or injury to property by governmental action has been held to be a 'taking' in the constitutional sense." *Armstrong v. United States*, 364 U.S. 40, 48 (1960). Rather, the determination whether a state law unlawfully infringes a landowner's property in violation of the Taking Clause requires an examination of whether the restriction on private property "forc[es] some people alone to bear public burdens which, in all fairness and justice, should be borne by the public as a whole." *Id.*, at 49. This examination entails inquiry into such factors as the character of the governmental action, its economic impact, and its interference with reasonable investment-backed expectations. When "regulation goes too far it will be recognized as a taking." *Pennsylvania Coal Co. v. Mahon*, 260 U.S. 393, 415 (1922).

Here the requirement that appellants permit appellees to exercise state-protected rights of free expression and petition on shopping center property clearly does not amount to an unconstitutional infringement of appellants' property rights under the Taking Clause. There is nothing to suggest that preventing appellants from prohibiting this sort of activity will unreasonably impair the value or use of their property as a shopping center. The PruneYard is a large commercial complex that covers several city blocks, contains numerous separate business establishments, and is open to the public at large. The decision of the California Supreme Court makes it clear that the Prune-Yard may restrict expressive activity by adopting time, place, and manner regulations that will minimize any interference with its commercial functions. Appellees were orderly, and they limited their activity to the common areas of the shopping center. In these circumstances, the fact that they may have "physically invaded" appellants' property cannot be viewed as determinative.

This case is quite different from *Kaiser Aetna v. United States, supra. Kaiser Aetna* was a case in which the owners of a private pond had invested substantial amounts of money in dredging the pond, developing it into an exclusive marina, and building a surrounding marina community. The marina was open only to fee-paying members, and the fees were paid in part to "maintain the privacy and security of the pond." *Id.*, at 168. The Federal Government sought to compel free public use of the private marina on the ground that the marina became subject to the federal navigational servitude because the owners had dredged a channel connecting it to "navigable water."

The Government's attempt to create a public right of access to the improved pond interfered with Kaiser Aetna's "reasonable investment backed expectations." We held that it went "so far beyond ordinary regulation or improvement for navigation as to amount to a taking. . . ." *Id.*, at 178. Nor as a general proposition is the United States, as opposed to the several States, possessed of residual authority that enables it to define "property" in the first instance. A State is, of course, bound by the Just Compensation Clause of the Fifth Amendment, but here appellants have failed to demonstrate that the "right to exclude others" is so essential to the use or economic value of their property that the state-authorized limitation of it amounted to a "taking." . . .

Mr. Justice HARRY A. BLACKMUN joins the opinion of the Court except that sentence thereof, which reads: "Nor as a general proposition is the United States, as opposed to the several States, possessed of residual authority that enables it to define 'property' in the first instance."

Mr. Justice THURGOOD MARSHALL, concurring. . . .

Appellants' claim in this case amounts to no less than a suggestion that the common law of trespass is not subject to revision by the State, notwithstanding the California Supreme Court's finding that state-created rights of expressive activity would be severely hindered if shopping centers were closed to expressive activities by members of the public. If accepted, that claim would represent a return to the era of *Lochner v. New York*, 198 U.S. 45 (1905), when common-law rights were also found immune from revision by State or Federal Government. Such an approach would freeze the common law as it has been constructed by the courts, perhaps at its 19th-century state of development. It would allow no room for change in response to changes in circumstance. The Due Process Clause does not require such a result.

On the other hand, I do not understand the Court to suggest that rights of property are to be defined solely by state law, or that there is no federal constitutional barrier to the abrogation of common-law rights by Congress or a state government. The constitutional terms "life, liberty, and property" do not derive their meaning solely from the provisions of positive law. They have a normative dimension as well, establishing a sphere of private autonomy which government is bound to respect. Quite serious constitutional questions might be raised if a legislature attempted to abolish certain categories of common-law rights in some general way. Indeed, our cases demonstrate that there are limits on governmental authority to abolish "core" common-law rights, including rights against trespass, at least without a compelling showing of necessity or a provision for a reasonable alternative remedy.

That "core" has not been approached in this case. . . .

Mr. Justice LEWIS F. POWELL, JR., with whom Mr. Justice WHITE joins, concurring in part and in the judgment.

The State may not compel a person to affirm a belief he does not hold. . . .

A property owner . . . may be faced with speakers who wish to use his premises as a platform for views that he finds morally repugnant. Numerous examples come to mind. A minority-owned business confronted with distributors from the American Nazi Party or the Ku Klux Klan, a church-operated enterprise asked to host demonstrations in favor of abortion, or a union compelled to supply a forum to right-to-work advocates could be placed in an intolerable position if state law requires it to make its private property available to anyone who wishes to speak. The strong emotions evoked by speech in such situations may virtually compel the proprietor to respond. . . .

On the record before us, I cannot say that customers of this vast center would be likely to assume that appellees' limited speech activity expressed the views of the PruneYard or of its owner. . . .

LORETTO v. TELEPROMPTER MANHATTAN CATV CORP.
458 U.S. 419 (1982)

Justice THURGOOD MARSHALL delivered the opinion of the Court.

This case presents the question whether a minor but permanent physical occupation of an owner's property authorized by government constitutes a "taking" of property for which just compensation is due under the Fifth and Fourteenth Amendments of the Constitution. New York law provides that a landlord must permit a cable television company to install its cable facilities upon his property. N. Y. Exec. Law §828(1). In this case, the cable installation occupied portions of appellant's roof and the side of her building. The New York Court of Appeals ruled that this appropriation does not amount to a taking. Because we conclude that such a physical occupation of property is a taking, we reverse. . . .

[Appellant Jean Loretto purchased a five-story rental apartment building located at 303 West 105th Street, New York City in 1971. The previous owner had granted appellees Teleprompter Corp. and Teleprompter Manhattan CATV (collectively Teleprompter) permission to install a crossover cable on the building (serving other property but not the Loretto property) and the exclusive privilege of furnishing cable television (CATV) services to the tenants at some point in the future. The cable measured slightly less than one-half inch in diameter and ran approximately 36 feet in length along the side of the building; Teleprompter also installed two directional taps measuring 4 inches by 4 inches by 4 inches and two cable boxes measuring 18 inches by 12 inches by 6 inches for a total displaced volume of about one and a half cubic feet. On January 1, 1973, New York state adopted a law that required residential landlords to allow cable television companies to install cable boxes and cables on their property to enable tenants to get access to cable television, N.Y. Exec. Law §828. The state commission established by that law later ruled that landlords were entitled to a nominal fee of $1 when such cables are installed.]

Appellant [Loretto] did not discover the existence of the cable until after she had purchased the building. She brought a class action against Teleprompter in 1976 on behalf of all owners of real property in the State on which Teleprompter has placed CATV components, alleging that Teleprompter's installation was a trespass and, insofar as it relied on §828, a taking without just compensation.... [The Supreme Court and the Court of Appeals both upheld the constitutionality of the statute. We reverse.] We conclude that a permanent physical occupation authorized by government is a taking without regard to the public interests that it may serve....

[T]he Court has often upheld substantial regulation of an owner's use of his own property where deemed necessary to promote the public interest. At the same time, we have long considered a physical intrusion by government to be a property restriction of an unusually serious character for purposes of the Takings Clause. Our cases further establish that when the physical intrusion reaches the extreme form of a permanent physical occupation, a taking has occurred. In such a case, "the character of the government action" not only is an important factor in resolving whether the action works a taking but also is determinative.

When faced with a constitutional challenge to a permanent physical occupation of real property, this Court has invariably found a taking. As early as 1872, in *Pumpelly* v. *Green Bay Co.*, 13 Wall. 166, this Court held that the defendant's construction, pursuant to state authority, of a dam which permanently flooded plaintiff's property constituted a taking....

In *Kaiser Aetna* v. *United States*, 444 U.S. 164 (1979), the Court held that the Government's imposition of a navigational servitude requiring public access to a pond was a taking where the landowner had reasonably relied on Government consent in connecting the pond to navigable water. The Court emphasized that the servitude took the land-owner's right to exclude, "one of the most essential sticks in the bundle of rights that are commonly characterized as property." *Id.*, at 176. The Court explained [that] "the imposition of the navigational servitude in this context will result in an *actual physical invasion* of the privately owned marina..." *Id.... Kaiser Aetna* reemphasizes that a physical invasion is a government intrusion of an unusually serious character.

Another recent case underscores the constitutional distinction between a permanent occupation and a temporary physical invasion. In *PruneYard Shopping Center* v. *Robins*, 447 U.S. 74 (1980), the Court upheld a state constitutional requirement that shopping center owners permit individuals to exercise free speech and petition rights on their property, to which they had already invited the general public. The Court emphasized that the State Constitution does not prevent the owner from restricting expressive activities by imposing reasonable time, place, and manner restrictions to minimize interference with the owner's commercial functions. Since the invasion was temporary and limited in nature, and since the owner had not exhibited an interest in excluding all persons from his property, "the fact that [the solicitors] may have 'physically invaded' [the owners'] property cannot be viewed as determinative." *Id.*, at 84.

In short, when the "character of the governmental action" is a permanent physical occupation of property, our cases uniformly have found a taking to the extent of the occupation, without regard to whether the action achieves an important public benefit or has only minimal economic impact on the owner....

The historical rule that a permanent physical occupation of another's property is a taking has more than tradition to commend it. Such an appropriation is perhaps the most serious form of invasion of an owner's property interests. To borrow a metaphor, *cf. Andrus* v. *Allard,* 444 U.S. 51, 65-66 (1979), the government does not simply take a single "strand" from the "bundle" of property rights: it chops through the bundle, taking a slice of every strand.

Property rights in a physical thing have been described as the rights "to possess, use and dispose of it." *United States* v. *General Motors Corp.,* 323 U.S. 373, 378 (1945). To the extent that the government permanently occupies physical property, it effectively destroys *each* of these rights. First, the owner has no right to possess the occupied space himself, and also has no power to exclude the occupier from possession and use of the space. The power to exclude has traditionally been considered one of the most treasured strands in an owner's bundle of property rights. Second, the permanent physical occupation of property forever denies the owner any power to control the use of the property; he not only cannot exclude others, but can make no nonpossessory use of the property. Although deprivation of the right to use and obtain a profit from property is not, in every case, independently sufficient to establish a taking, it is clearly relevant. Finally, even though the owner may retain the bare legal right to dispose of the occupied space by transfer or sale, the permanent occupation of that space by a stranger will ordinarily empty the right of any value, since the purchaser will also be unable to make any use of the property.

Moreover, an owner suffers a special kind of injury when a *stranger* directly invades and occupies the owner's property. [P]roperty law has long protected an owner's expectation that he will be relatively undisturbed at least in the possession of his property. To require, as well, that the owner permit another to exercise complete dominion literally adds insult to injury. *See* Michelman, *Property, Utility, and Fairness: Comments on the Ethical Foundations of "Just Compensation" Law,* 80 Harv. L. Rev. 1165, 1228, and n. 110 (1967). Furthermore, such an occupation is qualitatively more severe than a regulation of the *use* of property, even a regulation that imposes affirmative duties on the owner, since the owner may have no control over the timing, extent, or nature of the invasion.

The traditional rule also avoids otherwise difficult line-drawing problems. Few would disagree that if the State required landlords to permit third parties to install swimming pools on the landlords' rooftops for the convenience of the tenants, the requirement would be a taking. If the cable installation here occupied as much space, again, few would disagree that the occupation would be a taking. But constitutional protection for the rights of private property cannot be made to depend on the size of the area permanently occupied. . . .

Teleprompter's cable installation on appellant's building constitutes a taking under the traditional test. The installation involved a direct physical attachment of plates, boxes, wires, bolts, and screws to the building, completely occupying space immediately above and upon the roof and along the building's exterior wall. . . .

. . . Teleprompter notes that the law applies only to buildings used as rental property, and draws the conclusion that the law is simply a permissible regulation of the use of real property. We fail to see, however, why a physical occupation of one type of property but not another type is any less a physical occupation. Insofar as Teleprompter means to suggest that this is not a permanent physical invasion, we must differ. So long as the property remains residential and a CATV company wishes to retain the installation, the landlord must permit it.[17]

---

17. It is true that the landlord could avoid the requirements of §828 by ceasing to rent the building to tenants. But a landlord's ability to rent his property may not be conditioned on his

Finally, we do not agree with appellees that application of the physical occupation rule will have dire consequences for the government's power to adjust landlord-tenant relationships. This Court has consistently affirmed that States have broad power to regulate housing conditions in general and the landlord-tenant relationship in particular without paying compensation for all economic injuries that such regulation entails. *See, e. g., Heart of Atlanta Motel, Inc.* v. *United States,* 379 U.S. 241 (1964) (discrimination in places of public accommodation); *Home Building & Loan Assn.* v. *Blaisdell,* 290 U.S. 398 (1934) (mortgage moratorium); *Block* v. *Hirsh,* 256 U.S. 135 (1921) (rent control). In none of these cases, however, did the government authorize the permanent occupation of the landlord's property by a third party. Consequently, our holding today in no way alters the analysis governing the State's power to require landlords to comply with building codes and provide utility connections, mailboxes, smoke detectors, fire extinguishers, and the like in the common area of a building. So long as these regulations do not require the landlord to suffer the physical occupation of a portion of his building by a third party, they will be analyzed under the multifactor inquiry generally applicable to nonpossessory governmental activity. *See Penn Central Transportation Co.* v. *New York City,* 438 U.S. 104 (1978).

Our holding today is very narrow. We affirm the traditional rule that a permanent physical occupation of property is a taking. In such a case, the property owner entertains a historically rooted expectation of compensation, and the character of the invasion is qualitatively more intrusive than perhaps any other category of property regulation. We do not, however, question the equally substantial authority upholding a State's broad power to impose appropriate restrictions upon an owner's *use* of his property. . . . The issue of the amount of compensation that is due, on which we express no opinion, is a matter for the state courts to consider on remand.

Justice HARRY BLACKMUN, with whom Justice BRENNAN and Justice WHITE, join, dissenting. . . .

The Court of Appeals found, first, that §828 represented a reasoned legislative effort to arbitrate between the interests of tenants and landlords and to encourage development of an important educational and communications medium. . . . Second, the court concluded that the statute's economic impact on appellant was *de minimis* because §828 did not affect the fair return on her property. Third, the statute did not interfere with appellant's reasonable investment-backed expectations. When appellant purchased the building, she was unaware of the existence of the cable. Thus, she could not have invested in the building with any reasonable expectation that the one-eighth cubic foot of space occupied by the cable television installment would become income-productive. . . .

The Court's recent Takings Clause decisions teach that *nonphysical* government intrusions on private property, such as zoning ordinances and other land-use restrictions . . . may diminish the value of private property far more than minor physical touchings. Nevertheless, as the Court recognizes, it has "often upheld substantial

---

forfeiting the right to compensation for a physical occupation. Teleprompter's broad "use-dependency" argument proves too much. For example, it would allow the government to require a landlord to devote a substantial portion of his building to vending and washing machines, with all profits to be retained by the owners of these services and with no compensation for the deprivation of space. It would even allow the government to requisition a certain number of apartments as permanent government offices. The right of a property owner to exclude a stranger's physical occupation of his land cannot be so easily manipulated.

regulation of an owner's use of his own property where deemed necessary to promote the public interest." . . .

Surprisingly, the Court draws an even finer distinction today — between "temporary physical invasions" and "permanent [physical occupations." When the government authorizes the latter type of intrusion, the Court would find "a taking without regard to the public interests" the regulation may serve. Yet . . . the newly created distinction is even less substantial than the distinction between physical and nonphysical intrusions that the Court already has rejected.

First, what does the Court mean by "permanent"? [A]s the Court itself concedes, §828 does not require appellant to permit the cable installation forever, but only "[so] long as the property remains residential and a CATV company wishes to retain the installation." This is far from "permanent."

The Court reaffirms that "States have broad power to regulate housing conditions in general and the landlord-tenant relationship in particular without paying compensation for all economic injuries that such regulation entails." Thus, §828 merely defines one of the many statutory responsibilities that a New Yorker accepts when she enters the rental business. If appellant occupies her own building, or converts it into a commercial property, she becomes perfectly free to exclude Teleprompter from her one-eighth cubic foot of roof space. But once appellant chooses to use her property for rental purposes, she must comply with all reasonable government statutes regulating the landlord-tenant relationship. . . .

[T]he Court's talismanic distinction between a continuous "occupation" and a transient "invasion" finds no basis in either economic logic or Takings Clause precedent. In the landlord-tenant context, the Court has upheld against takings challenges rent control statutes permitting "temporary" physical invasions of considerable economic magnitude. *See, e.g., Block v. Hirsh*, 256 U.S. 135 (1921) (statute permitting tenants to remain in physical possession of their apartments for two years after the termination of their leases). Moreover, precedents record numerous other "temporary" officially authorized invasions by third parties that have intruded into an owner's enjoyment of property far more deeply than did Teleprompter's long-unnoticed cable. *See, e.g., PruneYard Shopping Center v. Robins*, 447 U.S. 74 (1980) (leafletting and demonstrating in busy shopping center) . . .

Setting aside history, the Court also states that the permanent physical occupation authorized by §828 is a *per se* taking because it uniquely impairs appellant's powers to dispose of, use, and exclude others from, her property. In fact, the Court's discussion nowhere demonstrates how §828 impairs these private rights in a manner *qualitatively* different from other garden-variety landlord-tenant legislation.

[I]f someone buys appellant's apartment building, but does not use it for rental purposes, that person can have the cable removed, and use the space as he wishes. . . . Even if another landlord buys appellant's building for rental purposes, §828 does not render the cable-occupied space valueless. As a practical matter, the regulation ensures that tenants living in the building will have access to cable television for as long as that building is used for rental purposes, and thereby likely increases both the building's resale value and its attractiveness on the rental market.

In any event, §828 differs little from the numerous other New York statutory provisions that require landlords to install physical facilities "permanently occupying" common spaces in or on their buildings. As the Court acknowledges, the States traditionally — and constitutionally — have exercised their police power "to require landlords to . . . provide utility connections, mailboxes, smoke detectors, fire extinguishers, and the like in the common area of a building." Like §828, these provisions merely ensure tenants access to services the legislature deems important, such as water, electricity, natural light, telephones, intercommunication systems, and mail service. . . .

The Court also suggests that §828 unconstitutionally alters appellant's right to control the *use* of her one-eighth cubic foot of roof space. But other New York multiple dwelling statutes not only oblige landlords to surrender significantly larger portions of common space for their tenants' use, but also compel the *landlord*—rather than the tenants or the private installers—to pay for and to maintain the equipment. For example, New York landlords are required by law to provide and pay for mailboxes that occupy more than five times the volume that Teleprompter's cable occupies on appellant's building. If the State constitutionally can insist that appellant make this sacrifice so that her tenants may receive mail, it is hard to understand why the State may not require her to surrender less space, *filled at another's expense,* so that those same tenants can receive television signals. . . .

NOTES AND QUESTIONS

1. *The physical invasion "rule."* The Supreme Court often repeats that a *per se* taking occurs when a law authorizes a permanent physical invasion of property. *See Lingle v. Chevron U.S.A. Inc.,* 2005 U.S. LEXIS 4342, *18 (2005)(compensation required "where government requires an owner to suffer a permanent physical invasion of her property"); *Palazzolo v. Rhode Island,* 533 U.S. 606, 617 (2002) ("even a minimal 'permanent physical occupation of real property' requires compensation"). Although *Loretto* tries to establish a clear rule, it is important to recall that not all physical invasions of property by the state are takings of property and that the rule announced in *Loretto* "is very narrow." 458 U.S. at 441. Besides outright seizures of property and the circumstances in *Loretto*, the Court has found a taking of property because of a forced physical invasion in only a few other cases. Moreover, it has often found forced physical invasions of property to be constitutional, even when done by strangers, as evidenced by *PruneYard. See also Heart of Atlanta Motel, Inc. v. United States,* 379 U.S. 241 (1964) (public accommodations law mandating access to places of public accommodation does not violate the takings clause). *But see Glosemeyer v. United States,* 45 Fed. Cl. 771 (2000) (federal Rails-to-Trails statute effectuates an unconstitutional taking of property by forcing a servient land owner to grant a public recreational easement when a railroad easement ends by abandonment under state property law).

The *Loretto* opinion attempts to distinguish *PruneYard.* Consider the cases described below in these notes. Is the Court successful in distinguishing the two cases? If not, which one is correct?

2. *Cases finding a taking on the basis of a permanent physical invasion by a stranger.* Besides *Loretto*, a few other cases are routinely cited for the proposition that forced physical invasion or occupation of property by a stranger constitutes a *per se* taking. Here are the most widely cited cases.

Pumpelly v. Green Bay Co., 80 U.S. 166 (1872). When a statute authorized a canal company to build a dam and flood the plaintiff's land, the Supreme Court had no trouble in finding that this constitutes a *per se* taking of plaintiff's property. The court found that it would be "a very curious and unsatisfactory result" if the state could "destroy [the] value [of property] entirely," or "inflict irreparable and permanent injury" to it or even cause its "total destruction" and avoid paying compensation merely because the government did not formally "take" title to the land. *Id.* at 177-178. "Such a construction would pervert the constitutional provision[]." *Id.* at 178.

United States v. Causby, 328 U.S. 256 (1946). Military aircraft flew so close to the ground and caused such extreme noise over plaintiffs' property near an airport that it both rendered plaintiffs' home uninhabitable and made it impossible for them to operate their chicken farm because the noise frightened the chickens and caused them to fly into the walls, killing many of them. Although owners own the airspace over their land, and the passage of planes overhead is technically a trespass, all land ownership is subject to an airspace servitude that allows this. But because the planes were flying so low to the ground, the Court found that this exceeded the scope of the public servitude and thus the entry and passage of the planes constituted a forced taking of a public easement over the plaintiffs' land. Although the "airspace is a public highway, . . . it is obvious that if the landowner is to have full enjoyment of land, he must have exclusive control of the immediate reaches of the enveloping atmosphere. Otherwise buildings could not be erected, trees could not be planted, and even fences could not be run." *Id.* at 264.

Kaiser Aetna v. United States, 444 U.S. 164 (1979). As *PruneYard* and *Loretto* explain, in *Kaiser Aetna*, the owner and lessee of a shallow, private lagoon invested substantial amounts of money in developing the property, connecting it to navigable waters in the ocean, and creating a marina that was to be open only to fee-paying members. Navigable waters are subject to a servitude that allows public access for navigation purposes. The federal government tried to force the owners to grant public access to the lagoon once it had been converted into navigable waters. Although upholding the navigational servitude doctrine, the Supreme Court noted that the owners had invested in developing the marina and connecting the lagoon to the ocean in the expectation that they would continue to be able to control access to the lagoon and charge its members fees to pay for maintenance of the lagoon; the property became included in the navigable waters of the United States only because of the owner's investment. A public access requirement would have converted at least some of the property from land controlled by a private fee-paying club into land freely open to the public. The owners would therefore have lost "one of the most essential sticks in the bundle of rights that are commonly characterized as property — the right to exclude others." *Id.* at 176. This distinguished the case from *Heart of Atlanta Motel, supra,* which had held that it was not a taking of property to require places of public accommodation that extend a general invitation to the public to serve the public without invidious discrimination. Although Congress could exercise its power under the commerce clause to require the owner to allow free public access to its lagoon, *Kaiser Aetna* holds that it cannot do so under the circumstances of this case without compensating the owner.

Nollan v. California Coastal Comm'n, 483 U.S. 825 (1987), held that a taking occurred when a regulatory commission required a beach front owner to grant a public easement of passage along the beach as a condition of obtaining a variance to expand the house. Note that this case presents special analytical problems because the law did not require the owner to admit the public or grant a public easement of passage. Nor did the owner have a constitutional right to expand the house; it would not have constituted a taking of property to prohibit the owner making the house bigger because the owner retained the right to renovate the house at the same size, and the property clearly had economically viable use at that size. The constitutional question was whether the state could condition the granting of a special permit to enlarge the house on obtaining the owner's agreement to dedicate a public easement of passage. The case is discussed extensively in *Dolan v. City of Tigard*, reprinted below at §12.4.3.

3. *Cases finding no taking despite a forced physical invasion by a stranger.* Besides *PruneYard*, the most important cases authorizing permanent physical invasion of land are those upholding the constitutionality of antidiscrimination laws, including public accommodation, fair housing, and employment discrimination laws. No takings claims have ever reached the Supreme Court to challenge either the employment discrimination laws or the fair housing laws. Both require owners to suffer the physical invasion of property by strangers they would rather exclude. In the case of the *Fair Housing Act*, 42 U.S.C. §§3601–3631, owners covered by the act can be compelled by injunction to transfer their property to a prospective buyer when the only reason for refusing to sell to that buyer is the buyer's race, sex, disability or religion. Similarly, a landlord may be required to rent property to a tenant without regard to that person's race or sex, disability, or religion.

Heart of Atlanta Motel, Inc. v. United States, 379 U.S. 241 (1964). Title II of the *Civil Rights Act of 1964*, 42 U.S.C. §2000a, requires, among other things, that hotels and motels accept customers regardless of race. Since the statute provides for injunctive relief alone, it authorizes courts to issue injunctions mandating that owners allow strangers to stay in their premises that those owners would rather exclude. Besides finding the statute to be properly enacted pursuant to Congress's power to regulate interstate commerce, the Supreme Court held, with no analysis whatsoever, that it did not "find any merit in the claim that the Act is a taking of property without just compensation." *Id.* at 261.

4. *Physical invasions by those in contractual relationships with the owner.* The Supreme Court has repeatedly upheld anti-eviction laws that grant tenants the right to continue renting their apartments as long as they pay the agreed-upon rent and do not damage the property or violate other material terms of the lease, even if these laws authorize occupation beyond the end of the lease term.

Block v. Hirsh, 256 U.S. 135 (1921). In *Block v. Hirsh*, the Court upheld against a takings challenge a statute that permitted tenants to remain in physical possession of their apartments after the termination of their leases at rents set by a rent control commission. The owner could evict the tenant only if the tenant were in breach of the lease or if the owner sought to regain possession for occupancy by herself or her family. Justice Holmes noted that the statute guaranteed the owner a "reasonable rent" and that the statutory eviction controls were justified by the emergency conditions of a housing shortage in Washington, D.C., brought on by an influx of people during World War I. *Accord, Edgar A. Levy Leasing Co. v. Siegel*, 258 U.S. 242 (1922) (upholding a similar New York law).

Yee v. City of Escondido, 503 U.S. 519 (1992). The Supreme Court reaffirmed *Block v. Hirsh* in *Yee*, holding that an anti-eviction law that allowed mobile home owners to continue renting the land in the mobile home park on which their homes sat, even after the end of the lease term, did not amount to a forced physical invasion of the park owner's property. The statute allowed the park owner to give six months' notice and then go out of business, evict the mobile home tenants, and convert the property to other uses. It did not matter to the Court that the effect of the anti-eviction law, when combined with the applicable rent control statute, allowed the mobile home owner to sell the home in place and transfer the tenancy to the new owner of the mobile home (at the rent-controlled rent) without the consent of the park owner. The buyer of the mobile home who would become the new tenant would of course be a stranger to the park owner. In effect, this law gave the tenants an absolute right to assign their leasehold even if assignment was prohibited by the lease. Such a buyer/assignee would pay more to buy such mobile homes because they were located in a rent-controlled environment; the mobile home owner, rather than the landlord, would reap the economic benefit of this one time premium. None of this was relevant to the question of whether the law constituted a taking even though it imposed a forced physical occupation by a stranger. Rather, the Court concluded that what mattered was the initial "invitation" to occupy the land. *Id.* at 532. "Because they voluntarily open their property to occupation by others, petitioners cannot assert a *per se* right to compensation based on their inability to exclude particular individuals." *Id.* at 531. The statutes here did "not authorize an unwanted physical occupation" of the park owners' land; rather, they were "a regulation of [the park owners'] use of their property, and thus [did] not amount to a *per se* taking." *Id.* at 532. However, the court did note that the ordinance allowed the owner to go out of business and that "[a] different case would be presented were the statute, on its face or as applied, to compel a landowner over objection to rent his property or to refrain in perpetuity from terminating a tenancy." *Id.* at 528.

5. *Does the landlord have a right to occupy her own land?* State courts have generally upheld anti-eviction laws against takings challenges even when those laws prevent the landlord from converting the property to another use. But some courts have struck down such statutes as unconstitutional takings of property when they prevent the landlord from evicting a tenant so the landlord can move into the property herself. *Cwynar v. City and County of San Francisco*, 109 Cal. Rptr.2d 233 (Ct. App. 2001); *Sabato v. Sabato*, 342 A.2d 886 (N.J. Super. Ct. Law Div. 1975). Other courts, however, have upheld such statutes. *See Puttrich v. Smith*, 407 A.2d 842, 843 (N.J. Super. Ct. App. Div. 1979)(overruling *Sabato* on the ground that "the legislature could constitutionally decide . . . that an owner's right to utilize his property must yield to a tenant's interest in keeping his home").

In *Flynn v. City of Cambridge*, 418 N.E.2d 335 (Mass. 1981), the court upheld a condominium conversion law that prohibited the landlords from evicting a tenant so they could convert the building into condominiums and move into the property themselves. The court found that owners who bought property after law was put into effect had no reasonable expectation they would be able to convert the apartment building into condominiums. Those who owned the property prior to the condominium conversion law did have a legitimate complaint, but the law did not effect an unconstitutional taking because they retained their "primary expectation concerning the use of the property" and they were still able to "obtain a reasonable return on [their] investment." *Id.* at 339-340.

Over a vigorous dissent by Justice Rehnquist, the Supreme Court granted a summary dismissal for want of a substantial federal question in *Fresh Pond Shopping Center, Inc. v. Callahan*, 464 U.S. 875 (1983). In that case, the local ordinance required the landlord to obtain a permit from the local rent control board to take an apartment off the rental housing market and develop the land by building a parking lot and movie theater. The city refused to grant the corporate owner a permit to demolish a six-unit apartment building to build a parking lot. The rent control law allowed owners to evict tenants if they intended to occupy the property themselves as their home. Because the owner was a corporation rather than a person, it could not claim that it was interested in occupying the apartment itself; thus it had no power under the ordinance to obtain possession. The current tenant had the right to stay in the apartment as long as she liked, subject to the lease obligations to pay rent and take care not to injure the property. Rehnquist argued that this amounted to a "permanent physical invasion, like that involved in *Loretto*" and that it further constituted "a transfer of control over the reversionary interest" in the property from the landlord to the tenant. *Id.* at 876-878. The eight other Justices must have disagreed with this assessment when they voted to dismiss the appeal. How would you have voted?

6. *Does the landlord have a right to go out of business?* Most anti-eviction laws have exceptions that allow the landlord to go out of business and devote the property to uses other than residential rental uses. But some laws do not allow eviction for this purpose. In *Nash v. City of Santa Monica*, 688 P.2d 894 (Cal. 1984), *appeal dismissed*, 470 U.S. 1046 (1985), the California Supreme Court upheld a rent control ordinance prohibiting removal of rental units from the housing market by conversion or demolition without a removal permit.[2] Citing *Fresh Pond*, the court sustained the ordinance against a takings challenge by an owner who was prevented from evicting his tenants and tearing the building down. Although he was earning a fair return on his investment, the landlord claimed a right to "go out of business" as a landlord, demolish the building, and wait for the value of the property to appreciate before selling or developing it. The California Supreme Court rejected this argument, noting that the property had no "personal or sentimental value to him," that he did not plan to live there, and that "adverse economic effects of land use regulation do not give rise to a constitutional claim so long as the property retains value." *Id.* at 900 n.6.

In contrast, the New York Court of Appeals struck down an antiwarehousing law that prohibited owners of single room occupancy hotels from shutting down and going out of business. In *Seawall Associates v. City of New York*, 542 N.E.2d 1059 (N.Y. 1989), the City of New York imposed a moratorium on conversion of structures containing single-room occupancy hotels (SRO properties) and passed an ordinance requiring owners of SRO properties to rehabilitate all vacant units and offer them for rent. The ordinance imposed heavy penalties for violations, but allowed owners to purchase exemptions if they were able either (a) to pay roughly $45,000 per vacant unit, or (b) to replace the units taken off the market with other units, or (c) to demonstrate hardship, or (d) to show that there was no reasonable possibility that the owner could make a reasonable rate of return (defined as a net annual return of 8 ½ percent of the assessed value of the property as an SRO multiple dwelling). The Court of Appeals of New York struck down the ordinance as a taking of property under both the federal and state constitutions, *Id.* at 1063-1065, partly on the ground that it required owners to rent their rooms to strangers. Unlike anti-eviction laws that require owners to keep renting to existing tenants, this law compelled the owners "to admit persons as tenants" and "to surrender the most basic attributes of private property, the rights of possession and exclusion." *Id.* This constituted a forced physical invasion by third parties, akin to the takings found in *Loretto* and *Causby*. "Where, as here, owners are forced to accept the

---

2. California has since passed a law allowing landlords to go out of business. *Ellis Act*, Cal. Gov't Code §7060.

occupation of their properties by persons not already in residence, the resulting deprivation of rights in those properties is sufficient to constitute a physical taking for which compensation is required." *Id.* Can this ruling be reconciled with *Heart of Atlanta Motel?* With *Yee?*

7. *IOLTAs.* Many challenges have been brought to state programs using interest on lawyers' trust accounts (IOLTAs) to pay for legal services for the poor. The Supreme Court recently resolved this issue at least for purposes of the federal takings clause.

Phillips v. Washington Legal Foundation, 524 U.S. 156 (1998). A public interest organization challenged a Texas practice, used by almost every state, that requires lawyers to place client funds held by lawyers into a common pool managed by the state in order to generate interest on those funds so that the interest (so-called "Interest on Lawyers' Trust Accounts" or "IOLTAs") could be used to help fund legal services for the poor. Texas had argued that the interest earned on the pooled account was not the client's "property" because it was only earned because the state mandated pooling of funds and thus the client lost nothing that she would ever have earned. The Supreme Court held that interest earned on such accounts was "property" belonging to the client whose funds generated the interest even if the client's account was so small and held for so short a time that it would not have generated any interest unless it were pooled with other such accounts. Rather than looking to state law to determine whether the interest was the client's property, Justice Rehnquist observed that states generally hold that "interest follows the principal" and ruled as a matter of federal constitutional law that whoever owns the principal also owns the interest, unless the contract provides otherwise. *Id.* at 165 (*citing Webb's Fabulous Pharmacies, Inc. v. Beckwith*, 449 U.S. 155, 162 (1980) for the proposition that "any interest follows the principal"). This federal principle apparently overrides any state law to the contrary.

Brown v. Legal Foundation of Washington, 538 U.S. 216 (2003). In a follow-up case several years later, the Supreme Court addressed the issue of whether IOLTA programs constitute unconstitutional takings of property. On remand in the *Phillips* case, the trial court had held that, even though the interest was *property* of the client, the IOLTA program did not constitute a *taking* of property because the program applied only to client funds that would not have earned interest absent the program and that the clients therefore "lost nothing of economically realizable value." *Washington Legal Foundation v. Texas Equal Access to Justice*, 86 F. Supp. 2d 624, 643 (D. Tex. 2000). The Supreme Court affirmed but on a different theory. It held by a 5-4 vote in *Brown v. Legal Foundation of Washington*, 538 U.S. 216 (2003), that the IOLTA program had indeed "taken property" belonging to the clients; on the other hand, the Court ruled that it had not done so "without just compensation." Justice Stevens explained that no compensation was due because the clients would not have earned any interest on their funds absent the IOLTA program; thus their loss of this interest caused them no economic loss and just compensation is measured "by the property owner's loss rather than the government's gain," *Id.* at 235-236. Further, no compensation is due for the "nonpecuniary consequences" of using the interest for purposes other than those that might have been chosen by the owner. *Id.* at 236-237. Justice Scalia argued in dissent that the "just compensation owed to former owners of confiscated property is the fair market value of the property taken," 538 U.S. at 243. Although owners of the interest would not have earned it but for the IOLTA program, Justice Scalia argued that it is a fact is that they earned the interest, that *Phillips* held that the interest is the client's "property" within the meaning of the fourteenth amendment, and that this property has value that can be measured by the amount actually earned and taken by the government.

Does the *Brown* decision place the *Loretto* holding in doubt? *Brown* held that no compensation is constitutionally required if the owner of the property loses nothing of economic value because of the regulation. On remand in *Loretto*, the state court approved allowing the cable commission to determine just compensation for the cable attachment — an amount it set at a nominal damages payment of $1 on the ground that adding a cable television connection to residential rental property either does not decrease the value of the owner's land or increases it. Richard Siegler, *Cable Television Service*, N.Y. L.J. (July 3, 1996), at 3. The majority decision in *Brown* reaffirmed the *Loretto* ruling that "when the government appropriates part of a rooftop in order to provide cable TV access for apartment tenants . . . it is required to pay for that share no matter how small." 538 U.S. at 233-234. Is this principle consistent with the result in *Brown*? If not, which case is correct?

PROBLEMS

1. A New Jersey statute grants low-income elderly persons and persons with disabilities a protected tenancy of up to 40 years after an apartment building is converted to a condominium. *Senior Citizens and Disabled Protected Tenancy Act*, N.J. Stat. Ann. §§2A:18-61.22 to 2A:18-61.39. This means that the landlord cannot evict such a tenant even if the landlord intends to occupy the unit herself or make it available to a member of her family. This statute was upheld against a takings challenge in *Troy v. Renna*, 727 F.2d 287 (3d Cir. 1984). *See also Edgewater Investment Associates v. Borough of Edgewater*, 510 A.2d 1178 (N.J. 1986) (upholding retroactive application of the statute). Assume a takings challenge to the law reaches the Supreme Court. A landlord wishes to evict a tenant so the landlord can move into the apartment herself. The tenant has a disability and therefore the statutory right to remain for up to 40 years. Does the New Jersey statute take the landlord's property without just compensation?

2. Most states now have restraining order statutes that allow victims of domestic violence to obtain emergency injunctions on an *ex parte* basis (meaning without prior notice to the other party) to exclude from the home a household member who has allegedly beaten or otherwise assaulted them. Assume an unmarried heterosexual couple has lived together in the man's house for five years. He begins to beat her and she obtains a restraining order excluding him from the house. The order stays in effect for three months while she looks for a new place to live. He brings a lawsuit claiming that, because the title to the house is in his name and the couple is not married, she has no property interest in the house; to exclude him from his own home, even for a short period of time, without a criminal conviction, therefore constitutes a taking of property without just compensation. Is he right? What arguments could you make on both sides? How would you resolve the issue?

3. In *Loretto*, Justice Marshall distinguishes the cases that allow substantial regulation of landlord-tenant relationships. "In none of these cases," he explains, "did the government authorize the permanent occupation of the landlord's property by a third party." The federal *Fair Housing Act* (*see* above §10.1) prohibits racial discrimination in the sale of real property and provides for injunctive relief. Consider

an owner who is subject to this law who refuses to sell her house to an African American family; the family sues the owner, seeking a court order requiring sale of the property to them, and the court agrees, ordering the owner to sell the property for its fair market value to the prospective buyers. The court order effects a permanent physical occupation of the property by strangers. Is this case distinguishable from *Loretto*?

§12.3.2 DEPRIVATION OF ECONOMICALLY VIABLE USE

LUCAS v. SOUTH CAROLINA COASTAL COUNCIL
505 U.S. 1003 (1992)

Justice ANTONIN SCALIA delivered the opinion of the Court.

In 1986, petitioner David H. Lucas paid $975,000 for two residential lots on the Isle of Palms in Charleston County, South Carolina, on which he intended to build single family homes. In 1988, however, the South Carolina Legislature enacted the *Beachfront Management Act*, S.C. Code §§48-39-250 *et seq.* (Act), which had the direct effect of barring petitioner from erecting any permanent habitable structures on his two parcels. A state trial court found that this prohibition rendered Lucas's parcels "valueless." This case requires us to decide whether the Act's dramatic effect on the economic value of Lucas's lots accomplished a taking of private property under the Fifth and Fourteenth Amendments requiring the payment of "just compensation." U.S. Const., Amdt. 5.

I

A

South Carolina's expressed interest in intensively managing development activities in the so-called "coastal zone" dates from 1977 when, in the aftermath of Congress's passage of the federal *Coastal Zone Management Act of 1972*, 86 Stat. 1280, as amended, 16 U.S.C. §§1451 *et seq.*, the legislature enacted a *Coastal Zone Management Act* of its own. *See* S.C. Code §§48-39-10 *et seq.* (1987). In its original form, the South Carolina Act required owners of coastal zone land that qualified as a "critical area" (defined in the legislation to include beaches and immediately adjacent sand dunes) to obtain a permit from the newly created South Carolina Coastal Council (respondent here) prior to committing the land to a "use other than the use the critical area was devoted to on [September 28, 1977]."

In the late 1970's, Lucas and others began extensive residential development of the Isle of Palms, a barrier island situated eastward of the City of Charleston. Toward the close of the development cycle for one residential subdivision known as "Beachwood East," Lucas in 1986 purchased the two lots at issue in this litigation for his own account. No portion of the lots, which were located approximately 300 feet from the beach, qualified as a "critical area" under the 1977 Act; accordingly, at the time Lucas acquired these parcels, he was not legally obliged to obtain a permit from the Council in advance of any development activity. His intention with respect to the lots was to do what the owners of the immediately adjacent parcels had already done: erect single-family residences. He commissioned architectural drawings for this purpose.

The *Beachfront Management Act* brought Lucas's plans to an abrupt end. Under that 1988 legislation, the Council was directed to establish a "baseline" connecting the landward-most "point[s] of erosion . . . during the past forty years" in the region of the Isle of Palms that includes Lucas's lots. In action not challenged here, the Council fixed this baseline landward of Lucas's parcels. That was significant, for under the Act construction of occupable improvements was flatly prohibited seaward of a line drawn 20 feet landward of, and parallel to, the baseline. The Act provided no exceptions.

B

Lucas promptly filed suit in the South Carolina Court of Common Pleas, contending that the *Beachfront Management Act*'s construction bar effected a taking of his property without just compensation. Lucas did not take issue with the validity of the Act as a lawful exercise of South Carolina's police power, but contended that the Act's complete extinguishment of his property's value entitled him to compensation regardless of whether the legislature had acted in furtherance of legitimate police power objectives. Following a bench trial, the court agreed. . . .

The Supreme Court of South Carolina reversed. . . . The Court ruled that when a regulation respecting the use of property is designed "to prevent serious public harm," no compensation is owing under the Takings Clause regardless of the regulation's effect on the property's value. . . .

We granted certiorari.

III

A

Prior to Justice Holmes' exposition in *Pennsylvania Coal Co. v. Mahon*, 260 U.S. 393 (1922), it was generally thought that the Takings Clause reached only a "direct appropriation" of property, *Legal Tender Cases*, 12 Wall. 457, 551 (1871), or the functional equivalent of a "practical ouster of [the owner's] possession." *Transportation Co. v. Chicago*, 99 U.S. 635, 642 (1879). Justice Holmes recognized in *Mahon*, however, that if the protection against physical appropriations of private property was to be meaningfully enforced, the government's power to redefine the range of interests included in the ownership of property was necessarily constrained by constitutional limits. If, instead, the uses of private property were subject to unbridled, uncompensated qualification under the police power, "the natural tendency of human nature [would be] to extend the qualification more and more until at last private property disappear[ed]." *Id.*, at 415. These considerations gave birth in that case to the oft-cited maxim that, "while property may be regulated to a certain extent, if regulation goes too far it will be recognized as a taking." *Id.*

Nevertheless, our decision in *Mahon* offered little insight into when, and under what circumstances, a given regulation would be seen as going "too far" for purposes of the Fifth Amendment. In 70-odd years of succeeding "regulatory takings" jurisprudence, we have generally eschewed any "set formula" for determining how far is too far, preferring to "engag[e] in . . . essentially ad hoc, factual inquiries," *Penn Central Transportation Co. v. New York City*, 438 U.S. 104, 124 (1978). We have, however, described at least two discrete categories of regulatory action as compensable without case-specific inquiry into the public interest advanced in support of the restraint. The first encompasses regulations that compel the property owner to suffer a physical "invasion" of his property. In general (at least with regard to permanent invasions), no matter how minute the intrusion, and no matter how weighty the public purpose behind it, we have required compensation. For example, in *Loretto v. Teleprompter Manhattan CATV Corp.*, 458 U.S. 419 (1982), we determined that New York's law requiring landlords to allow television cable companies to emplace cable facilities in their apartment buildings constituted a taking, even though the facilities occupied at most only 1 1/2 cubic feet of the landlords' property.

The second situation in which we have found categorical treatment appropriate is where regulation denies all economically beneficial or productive use of land. *See Agins v. Tiburon*, 447 U.S. 255, 260 (1980). As we have said on numerous occasions, the Fifth Amendment is violated when land-use regulation "does not substantially advance legitimate state interests *or denies an owner economically viable use of his land.*" *Id.* (emphasis added).[7]

We have never set forth the justification for this rule. Perhaps it is simply, as Justice Brennan suggested, that total deprivation of beneficial use is, from the landowner's point of view, the equivalent of a physical appropriation. Surely, at least, in the extraordinary circumstance when no productive or economically beneficial use of land is permitted, it is less realistic to indulge our usual assumption that the legislature is simply "adjusting the benefits and burdens of economic life," *Penn Central Transportation Co.*, 438 U.S., at 124, in a manner that secures an "average reciprocity of advantage" to everyone concerned. *Pennsylvania Coal Co. v. Mahon*, 260 U.S., at 415. And the functional basis for permitting the government, by regulation, to affect property values without compensation — that "Government hardly could go on if to some extent values incident to property could not be diminished without paying for every such change in the general law," *id.*, at 413 — does not apply to the relatively rare situations where the government has deprived a landowner of all economically beneficial uses.

On the other side of the balance, affirmatively supporting a compensation requirement, is the fact that regulations that leave the owner of land without economically beneficial or productive options for its use — typically, as here, by requiring land to be left substantially in its natural state — carry with them a heightened risk that private property is being pressed into some form of public service under the guise of

---

7. Regrettably, the rhetorical force of our "deprivation of all economically feasible use" rule is greater than its precision, since the rule does not make clear the "property interest" against which the loss of value is to be measured. When, for example, a regulation requires a developer to leave 90% of a rural tract in its natural state, it is unclear whether we would analyze the situation as one in which the owner has been deprived of all economically beneficial use of the burdened portion of the tract, or as one in which the owner has suffered a mere diminution in value of the tract as a whole. . . . The answer to this difficult question may lie in how the owner's reasonable expectations have been shaped by the State's law of property — *i.e.*, whether and to what degree the State's law has accorded legal recognition and protection to the particular interest in land with respect to which the takings claimant alleges a diminution in (or elimination of) value. In any event, we avoid this difficulty in the present case, since the "interest in land" that Lucas has pleaded (a fee simple interest) is an estate with a rich tradition of protection at common law, and since the South Carolina Court of Common Pleas found that the *Beachfront Management Act* left each of Lucas's beachfront lots without economic value.

mitigating serious public harm. . . . The many statutes on the books, both state and federal, that provide for the use of eminent domain to impose servitudes on private scenic lands preventing developmental uses, or to acquire such lands altogether, suggest the practical equivalence in this setting of negative regulation and appropriation.

We think, in short, that there are good reasons for our frequently expressed belief that when the owner of real property has been called upon to sacrifice all economically beneficial uses in the name of the common good, that is, to leave his property economically idle, he has suffered a taking.

B

The trial court found Lucas's two beachfront lots to have been rendered valueless by respondent's enforcement of the coastal-zone construction ban. Under Lucas's theory of the case, which rested upon our "no economically viable use" statements, that finding entitled him to compensation. Lucas believed it unnecessary to take issue with either the purposes behind the *Beachfront Management Act*, or the means chosen by the South Carolina Legislature to effectuate those purposes. The South Carolina Supreme Court, however, thought otherwise. In its view, the *Beachfront Management Act* was no ordinary enactment, but involved an exercise of South Carolina's "police powers" to mitigate the harm to the public interest that petitioner's use of his land might occasion. By neglecting to dispute the findings enumerated in the Act or otherwise to challenge the legislature's purposes, petitioner "concede[d] that the beach/dune area of South Carolina's shores is an extremely valuable public resource; and that discouraging new construction in close proximity to the beach/dune area is necessary to prevent a great public harm." In the court's view, these concessions brought petitioner's challenge within a long line of this Court's cases sustaining against Due Process and Takings Clause challenges the State's use of its "police powers" to enjoin a property owner from activities akin to public nuisances. *See Mugler v. Kansas*, 123 U.S. 623 (1887) (law prohibiting manufacture of alcoholic beverages); *Hadacheck v. Sebastian*, 239 U.S. 394 (1915) (law barring operation of brick mill in residential area); *Miller v. Schoene*, 276 U.S. 272 (1928) (order to destroy diseased cedar trees to prevent infection of nearby orchards); *Goldblatt v. Hempstead*, 369 U.S. 590 (1962) (law effectively preventing continued operation of quarry in residential area).

It is correct that many of our prior opinions have suggested that "harmful or noxious uses" of property may be proscribed by government regulation without the requirement of compensation. For a number of reasons, however, we think the South Carolina Supreme Court was too quick to conclude that that principle decides the present case. The "harmful or noxious uses" principle was the Court's early attempt to describe in theoretical terms why government may, consistent with the Takings Clause, affect property values by regulation without incurring an obligation to compensate — a reality we nowadays acknowledge explicitly with respect to the full scope of the State's police power. We made this very point in *Penn Central Transportation Co.*, where, in the course of sustaining New York City's landmarks preservation program against a takings challenge, we rejected the petitioner's suggestion that *Mugler* and the cases following it were premised on, and thus limited by, some objective conception of "noxiousness":

> [T]he uses in issue in *Hadacheck, Miller,* and *Goldblatt* were perfectly lawful in themselves. They involved no "blameworthiness,... moral wrongdoing or conscious act of dangerous risk-taking which induce[d society] to shift the cost to a pa[rt]icular individual." Sax, *Takings and the Police Power,* 74 Yale L.J. 36, 50 (1964). These cases are better understood as resting not on any supposed "noxious" quality of the prohibited uses but rather on the ground that the restrictions were reasonably related to the implementation of a policy—not unlike historic preservation—expected to produce a widespread public benefit and applicable to all similarly situated property. 438 U.S., at 133-134, n.30.

"Harmful or noxious use" analysis was, in other words, simply the progenitor of our more contemporary statements that "land-use regulation does not effect a taking if it 'substantially advance[s] legitimate state interests.'..." *Nollan, supra,* at 834.

The transition from our early focus on control of "noxious" uses to our contemporary understanding of the broad realm within which government may regulate without compensation was an easy one, since the distinction between "harm-preventing" and "benefit-conferring" regulation is often in the eye of the beholder. It is quite possible, for example, to describe in either fashion the ecological, economic, and aesthetic concerns that inspired the South Carolina legislature in the present case. One could say that imposing a servitude on Lucas's land is necessary in order to prevent his use of it from "harming" South Carolina's ecological resources; or, instead, in order to achieve the "benefits" of an ecological preserve. *Compare, e.g., Claridge v. New Hampshire Wetlands Board,* 485 A.2d 287, 292 (N.H. 1984) (owner may, without compensation, be barred from filling wetlands because landfilling would deprive adjacent coastal habitats and marine fisheries of ecological support), *with, e.g., Bartlett v. Zoning Comm'n of Old Lyme,* 282 A.2d 907, 910 (Conn. 1971) (owner barred from filling tidal marshland must be compensated, despite municipality's "laudable" goal of "preserv[ing] marshlands from encroachment or destruction"). Whether one or the other of the competing characterizations will come to one's lips in a particular case depends primarily upon one's evaluation of the worth of competing uses of real estate. A given restraint will be seen as mitigating "harm" to the adjacent parcels or securing a "benefit" for them, depending upon the observer's evaluation of the relative importance of the use that the restraint favors. Whether Lucas's construction of single-family residences on his parcels should be described as bringing "harm" to South Carolina's adjacent ecological resources thus depends principally upon whether the describer believes that the State's use interest in nurturing those resources is so important that any competing adjacent use must yield.[12]

When it is understood that "prevention of harmful use" was merely our early formulation of the police power justification necessary to sustain (without compensation) any regulatory diminution in value; and that the distinction between regulation that "prevents harmful use" and that which "confers benefits" is difficult, if not impossible, to discern on an objective, value-free basis; it becomes self-evident that noxious-use logic cannot serve as a touchstone to distinguish regulatory "takings"—which require compensation—from regulatory deprivations that do not require com-

---

12. In Justice Blackmun's view, even with respect to regulations that deprive an owner of all developmental or economically beneficial land uses, the test for required compensation is whether the legislature has recited a harm-preventing justification for its action. Since such a justification can be formulated in practically every case, this amounts to a test of whether the legislature has a stupid staff. We think the Takings Clause requires courts to do more than insist upon artful harm-preventing characterizations.

pensation. A fortiori the legislature's recitation of a noxious-use justification cannot be the basis for departing from our categorical rule that total regulatory takings must be compensated. If it were, departure would virtually always be allowed. The South Carolina Supreme Court's approach would essentially nullify *Mahon*'s affirmation of limits to the noncompensable exercise of the police power. Our cases provide no support for this: None of them that employed the logic of "harmful use" prevention to sustain a regulation involved an allegation that the regulation wholly eliminated the value of the claimant's land.

Where the State seeks to sustain regulation that deprives land of all economically beneficial use, we think it may resist compensation only if the logically antecedent inquiry into the nature of the owner's estate shows that the proscribed use interests were not part of his title to begin with. This accords, we think, with our "takings" jurisprudence, which has traditionally been guided by the understandings of our citizens regarding the content of, and the State's power over, the "bundle of rights" that they acquire when they obtain title to property. It seems to us that the property owner necessarily expects the uses of his property to be restricted, from time to time, by various measures newly enacted by the State in legitimate exercise of its police powers; "[a]s long recognized, some values are enjoyed under an implied limitation and must yield to the police power." *Pennsylvania Coal Co. v. Mahon*, 260 U.S., at 413. And in the case of personal property, by reason of the State's traditionally high degree of control over commercial dealings, he ought to be aware of the possibility that new regulation might even render his property economically worthless (at least if the property's only economically productive use is sale or manufacture for sale), *see Andrus v. Allard*, 444 U.S. 51, 66-67 (1979) (prohibition on sale of eagle feathers). In the case of land, however, we think the notion pressed by the Council that title is somehow held subject to the "implied limitation" that the State may subsequently eliminate all economically valuable use is inconsistent with the historical compact recorded in the Takings Clause that has become part of our constitutional culture.[15]

Where "permanent physical occupation" of land is concerned, we have refused to allow the government to decree it anew (without compensation), no matter how weighty the asserted "public interests" involved — though we assuredly would permit the government to assert a permanent easement that was a pre-existing limitation upon the landowner's title. *Compare Scranton v. Wheeler*, 179 U.S. 141, 163 (1900) (interests of "riparian owner in the submerged lands... bordering on a public navigable water" held subject to Government's navigational servitude), *with Kaiser Aetna v. United*

---

15. After accusing us of "launch[ing] a missile to kill a mouse," Justice Blackmun expends a good deal of throw-weight of his own upon a noncombatant, arguing that our description of the "understanding" of land ownership that informs the Takings Clause is not supported by early American experience. That is largely true, but entirely irrelevant. The practices of the States prior to incorporation of the Takings and Just Compensation Clauses, *see Chicago, B. & Q. R. Co. v. Chicago*, 166 U.S. 226 (1897) — which, as Justice Blackmun acknowledges, occasionally included outright physical appropriation of land without compensation — were out of accord with any plausible interpretation of those provisions. Justice Blackmun is correct that early constitutional theorists did not believe the Takings Clause embraced regulations of property at all, but even he does not suggest (explicitly, at least) that we renounce the Court's contrary conclusion in *Mahon*. Since the text of the Clause can be read to encompass regulatory as well as physical deprivations (in contrast to the text originally proposed by Madison) ("No person shall be... obliged to relinquish his property, where it may be necessary for public use, without a just compensation"), we decline to do so as well.

States, 444 U.S., at 178-180 (imposition of navigational servitude on marina created and rendered navigable at private expense held to constitute a taking). We believe similar treatment must be accorded confiscatory regulations, *i.e.*, regulations that prohibit all economically beneficial use of land: Any limitation so severe cannot be newly legislated or decreed (without compensation), but must inhere in the title itself, in the restrictions that background principles of the State's law of property and nuisance already place upon land ownership. A law or decree with such an effect must, in other words, do no more than duplicate the result that could have been achieved in the courts — by adjacent landowners (or other uniquely affected persons) under the State's law of private nuisance, or by the State under its complementary power to abate nuisances that affect the public generally, or otherwise.[16]

On this analysis, the owner of a lake bed, for example, would not be entitled to compensation when he is denied the requisite permit to engage in a landfilling operation that would have the effect of flooding others' land. Nor the corporate owner of a nuclear generating plant, when it is directed to remove all improvements from its land upon discovery that the plant sits astride an earthquake fault. Such regulatory action may well have the effect of eliminating the land's only economically productive use, but it does not proscribe a productive use that was previously permissible under relevant property and nuisance principles. The use of these properties for what are now expressly prohibited purposes was always unlawful, and (subject to other constitutional limitations) it was open to the State at any point to make the implication of those background principles of nuisance and property law explicit. In light of our traditional resort to "existing rules or understandings that stem from an independent source such as state law" to define the range of interests that qualify for protection as "property" under the Fifth (and Fourteenth) amendments, this recognition that the Takings Clause does not require compensation when an owner is barred from putting land to a use that is proscribed by those "existing rules or understandings" is surely unexceptional. When, however, a regulation that declares "off-limits" all economically productive or beneficial uses of land goes beyond what the relevant background principles would dictate, compensation must be paid to sustain it.[17]

The "total taking" inquiry we require today will ordinarily entail (as the application of state nuisance law ordinarily entails) analysis of, among other things, the degree of harm to public lands and resources, or adjacent private property, posed by the claimant's proposed activities, the social value of the claimant's activities and their suitability to the locality in question, and the relative ease with which the alleged harm can be avoided through measures taken by the claimant and the government (or adjacent private landowners) alike. The fact that a particular use has long been engaged in by similarly situated owners ordinarily imports a lack of any common-law prohibition (though changed circumstances or new knowledge may make what was previously

---

16. The principal "otherwise" that we have in mind is litigation absolving the State (or private parties) of liability for the destruction of "real and personal property, in cases of actual necessity, to prevent the spreading of a fire" or to forestall other grave threats to the lives and property of others. *Bowditch v. Boston*, 101 U.S. 16, 18-19 (1880).

17. Of course, the State may elect to rescind its regulation and thereby avoid having to pay compensation for a permanent deprivation. *See First English Evangelical Lutheran Church of Glendale v. County of Los Angeles*, 482 U.S. 304, 321 (1987). But "where the [regulation has] already worked a taking of all use of property, no subsequent action by the government can relieve it of the duty to provide compensation for the period during which the taking was effective." *Id.*

permissible no longer so). So also does the fact that other landowners, similarly situated, are permitted to continue the use denied to the claimant.

It seems unlikely that common-law principles would have prevented the erection of any habitable or productive improvements on petitioner's land; they rarely support prohibition of the "essential use" of land. The question, however, is one of state law to be dealt with on remand. We emphasize that to win its case South Carolina must do more than proffer the legislature's declaration that the uses Lucas desires are inconsistent with the public interest, or the conclusory assertion that they violate a common-law maxim such as *sic utere tuo ut alienum non lae das*. As we have said, a "State, by *ipse dixit*, may not transform private property into public property without compensation...." *Webb's Fabulous Pharmacies, Inc. v. Beckwith*, 449 U.S. 155, 164 (1980). Instead, as it would be required to do if it sought to restrain Lucas in a common-law action for public nuisance, South Carolina must identify background principles of nuisance and property law that prohibit the uses he now intends in the circumstances in which the property is presently found. Only on this showing can the State fairly claim that, in proscribing all such beneficial uses, the *Beachfront Management Act* is taking nothing.[18]

The judgment is reversed and the cause remanded for proceedings not inconsistent with this opinion....

Justice ANTHONY M. KENNEDY, concurring in the judgment....

The South Carolina Court of Common Pleas found that petitioner's real property has been rendered valueless by the State's regulation. The finding appears to presume that the property has no significant market value or resale potential. This is a curious finding, and I share the reservations of some of my colleagues about a finding that a beach front lot loses all value because of a development restriction. While the Supreme Court of South Carolina on remand need not consider the case subject to this constraint, we must accept the finding as entered below. Accepting the finding as entered, it follows that petitioner is entitled to invoke the line of cases discussing regulations that deprive real property of all economic value.

The finding of no value must be considered under the Takings Clause by reference to the owner's reasonable, investment-backed expectations. The Takings Clause, while conferring substantial protection on property owners, does not eliminate the police power of the State to enact limitations on the use of their property. The rights conferred by the Takings Clause and the police power of the State may coexist without conflict. Property is bought and sold, investments are made, subject to the State's power to regulate. Where a taking is alleged from regulations which deprive the property of all value, the test must be whether the deprivation is contrary to reasonable, investment-backed expectations.

There is an inherent tendency towards circularity in this synthesis, of course; for if the owner's reasonable expectations are shaped by what courts allow as a proper exercise of governmental authority, property tends to become what courts say it is.

---

18. Justice Blackmun decries our reliance on background nuisance principles at least in part because he believes those principles to be as manipulable as we find the "harm prevention benefit"/"conferral" dichotomy. There is no doubt some leeway in a court's interpretation of what existing state law permits — but not remotely as much, we think, as in a legislative crafting of the reasons for its confiscatory regulation. We stress that an affirmative decree eliminating all economically beneficial uses may be defended only if an objectively reasonable application of relevant precedents would exclude those beneficial uses in the circumstances in which the land is presently found.

Some circularity must be tolerated in these matters, however, as it is in other spheres. The definition, moreover, is not circular in its entirety. The expectations protected by the Constitution are based on objective rules and customs that can be understood as reasonable by all parties involved.

In my view, reasonable expectations must be understood in light of the whole of our legal tradition. The common law of nuisance is too narrow a confine for the exercise of regulatory power in a complex and interdependent society. The State should not be prevented from enacting new regulatory initiatives in response to changing conditions, and courts must consider all reasonable expectations whatever their source. The Takings Clause does not require a static body of state property law; it protects private expectations to ensure private investment. I agree with the Court that nuisance prevention accords with the most common expectations of property owners who face regulation, but I do not believe this can be the sole source of state authority to impose severe restrictions. Coastal property may present such unique concerns for a fragile land system that the State can go further in regulating its development and use than the common law of nuisance might otherwise permit.

The Supreme Court of South Carolina erred, in my view, by reciting the general purposes for which the state regulations were enacted without a determination that they were in accord with the owner's reasonable expectations and therefore sufficient to support a severe restriction on specific parcels of property. The promotion of tourism, for instance, ought not to suffice to deprive specific property of all value without a corresponding duty to compensate. Furthermore, the means as well as the ends of regulation must accord with the owner's reasonable expectations. Here, the State did not act until after the property had been zoned for individual lot development and most other parcels had been improved, throwing the whole burden of the regulation on the remaining lots. This too must be measured in the balance. . . .

Justice HARRY A. BLACKMUN, dissenting.

Today the Court launches a missile to kill a mouse. . . .

. . . The Court creates its new taking jurisprudence based on the trial court's finding that the property had lost all economic value. This finding is almost certainly erroneous. Petitioner still can enjoy other attributes of ownership, such as the right to exclude others, "one of the most essential sticks in the bundle of rights that are commonly characterized as property." *Kaiser Aetna v. United States*, 444 U.S. 164, 176 (1979). Petitioner can picnic, swim, camp in a tent, or live on the property in a movable trailer. State courts frequently have recognized that land has economic value where the only residual economic uses are recreation and camping. Petitioner also retains the right to alienate the land, which would have value for neighbors and for those prepared to enjoy proximity to the ocean without a house.

. . . I find no evidence in the record supporting the trial court's conclusion that the damage to the lots by virtue of the restrictions was "total." . . .

The Court [has] create[d] a new scheme for regulations that eliminate all economic value. From now on, there is a categorical rule finding these regulations to be a taking unless the use they prohibit is a background common-law nuisance or property principle.

This Court repeatedly has recognized the ability of government, in certain circumstances, to regulate property without compensation no matter how adverse the financial effect on the owner may be. More than a century ago, the Court explicitly upheld the right of States to prohibit uses of property injurious to public health, safety, or welfare without paying compensation: "A prohibition simply upon the use of property for purposes that are declared, by valid legislation, to be injurious to the health, morals, or safety of the community, cannot, in any just sense, be deemed a taking or an appropriation of property." *Mugler v. Kansas*, 123 U.S. 623, 668-669 (1887). On this basis, the Court upheld an ordinance effectively prohibiting operation of a previously lawful brewery, although the "establishments will become of no value as property." *Id.*, at 664.

Mugler was only the beginning in a long line of cases. In *Powell v. Pennsylvania*, 127 U.S. 678 (1888), the Court upheld legislation prohibiting the manufacture of oleomargarine, despite the owner's allegation that "if prevented from continuing it, the value of his property employed therein would be entirely lost and he be deprived of the means of livelihood." *Id.*, at 682. In *Hadacheck v. Sebastian*, 239 U.S. 394 (1915), the Court upheld an ordinance prohibiting a brickyard, although the owner had made excavations on the land that prevented it from being utilized for any purpose but a brickyard. In *Miller v. Schoene*, 276 U.S. 272 (1928), the Court held that the Fifth Amendment did not require Virginia to pay compensation to the owner of cedar trees ordered destroyed to prevent a disease from spreading to nearby apple orchards. The "preferment of [the public interest] over the property interest of the individual, to the extent even of its destruction, is one of the distinguishing characteristics of every exercise of the police power which affects property." *Id.*, at 280. . . .

More recently, in *Goldblatt v. Hempstead*, 369 U.S. 590 (1962), the Court upheld a town regulation that barred continued operation of an existing sand and gravel operation in order to protect public safety. "Although a comparison of values before and after is relevant," the Court stated, "it is by no means conclusive." *Id.*, at 594. In 1978, the Court declared that "in instances in which a state tribunal reasonably concluded that 'the health, safety, morals, or general welfare' would be promoted by prohibiting particular contemplated uses of land, this Court has upheld land-use regulation that destroyed . . . recognized real property interests." *Penn Central Transp. Co.*, 438 U.S., at 125. In *First Lutheran Church v. Los Angeles County*, 482 U.S. 304 (1987), the owner alleged that a floodplain ordinance had deprived it of "all use" of the property. The Court remanded the case for consideration whether, even if the ordinance denied the owner all use, it could be justified as a safety measure.[10] And in *Keystone Bituminous Coal* [*Association v. DeBenedictis*, 480 U.S. 470 (1970)], the Court summarized over 100 years of precedent: "the Court has repeatedly upheld regulations that destroy or adversely affect real property interests." 480 U.S. at 489, n.18. . . .

These cases rest on the principle that the State has full power to prohibit an owner's use of property if it is harmful to the public. "[S]ince no individual has a right to use his property so as to create a nuisance or otherwise harm others, the State has not 'taken' anything when it asserts its power to enjoin the nuisance-like activity." *Keystone Bituminous Coal*, 480 U.S., at 491, n.20. It would make no sense under this theory to suggest that an owner has a constitutionally protected right to harm others, if only he makes the proper showing of economic loss.

Ultimately even the Court cannot embrace the full implications of its per se rule: it eventually agrees that there cannot be a categorical rule for a taking based on economic value that wholly disregards the public need asserted. Instead, the Court

---

10. On remand, the California court found no taking in part because the zoning regulation "involves this highest of public interests — the prevention of death and injury." *First Lutheran Church v. Los Angeles*, 258 Cal. Rptr. 893 (Ct. App. 1989), *cert. denied*, 493 U.S. 1056 (1990).

decides that it will permit a State to regulate all economic value only if the State prohibits uses that would not be permitted under "background principles of nuisance and property law."

Until today, the Court explicitly had rejected the contention that the government's power to act without paying compensation turns on whether the prohibited activity is a common-law nuisance. The brewery closed in *Mugler* itself was not a common-law nuisance, and the Court specifically stated that it was the role of the legislature to determine what measures would be appropriate for the protection of public health and safety. In upholding the state action in *Miller*, the Court found it unnecessary to "weigh with nicety the question whether the infected cedars constitute a nuisance according to common law; or whether they may be so declared by statute." 276 U.S., at 280. Instead the Court has relied in the past, as the South Carolina Court has done here, on legislative judgments of what constitutes a harm.

The Court rejects the notion that the State always can prohibit uses it deems a harm to the public without granting compensation because "the distinction between 'harm-preventing' and 'benefit-conferring' regulation is often in the eye of the beholder." Since the characterization will depend "primarily upon one's evaluation of the worth of competing uses of real estate," the Court decides a legislative judgment of this kind no longer can provide the desired "objective, value-free basis" for upholding a regulation. The Court, however, fails to explain how its proposed common law alternative escapes the same trap.

The threshold inquiry for imposition of the Court's new rule, "deprivation of all economically valuable use," itself cannot be determined objectively. As the Court admits, whether the owner has been deprived of all economic value of his property will depend on how "property" is defined. The "composition of the denominator in our 'deprivation' fraction," is the dispositive inquiry. Yet there is no "objective" way to define what that denominator should be. "We have long understood that any land-use regulation can be characterized as the 'total' deprivation of an aptly defined entitlement. . . . Alternatively, the same regulation can always be characterized as a mere 'partial' withdrawal from full, unencumbered ownership of the landholding affected by the regulation. . . ." Michelman, *Takings, 1987*, 88 Colum. L. Rev. 1600, 1614 (1988). . . .

Even more perplexing, however, is the Court's reliance on common-law principles of nuisance in its quest for a value-free taking jurisprudence. In determining what is a nuisance at common law, state courts make exactly the decision that the Court finds so troubling when made by the South Carolina General Assembly today: they determine whether the use is harmful.

Common-law public and private nuisance law is simply a determination whether a particular use causes harm. There is nothing magical in the reasoning of judges long dead. They determined a harm in the same way as state judges and legislatures do today. If judges in the 18th and 19th centuries can distinguish a harm from a benefit, why not judges in the 20th century, and if judges can, why not legislators? There simply is no reason to believe that new interpretations of the hoary common law nuisance doctrine will be particularly "objective" or "value-free." Once one abandons the level of generality of *sic utere tuo ut alienum non lae das*, one searches in vain, I think, for anything resembling a principle in the common law of nuisance.

Finally, the Court justifies its new rule that the legislature may not deprive a property owner of the only economically valuable use of his land, even if the legislature finds it to be a harmful use, because such action is not part of the "long recognized" "understandings of our citizens." These "understandings" permit such regulation only if the use is a nuisance under the common law. Any other course is "inconsistent with the historical compact recorded in the Takings Clause." It is not clear from the Court's opinion where our "historical compact" or "citizens' understanding" comes from, but it does not appear to be history.

The principle that the State should compensate individuals for property taken for public use was not widely established in America at the time of the Revolution. "The colonists . . . inherited . . . a concept of property which permitted extensive regulation of the use of that property for the public benefit — regulation that could even go so far as to deny all productive use of the property to the owner if, as Coke himself stated, the regulation 'extends to the public benefit . . . for this is for the public, and every one hath benefit by it.'" F. Bosselman, D. Callies & J. Banta, *The Taking Issue* 80-81 (1973), quoting *The Case of the King's Prerogative in Saltpetre*, 12 Co. Rep. 12-13 (1606) (hereinafter Bosselman).

Even into the 19th century, state governments often felt free to take property for roads and other public projects without paying compensation to the owners. . . .

Although, prior to the adoption of the Bill of Rights, America was replete with land use regulations describing which activities were considered noxious and forbidden, the Fifth Amendment's Taking Clause originally did not extend to regulations of property, whatever the effect. Most state courts agreed with this narrow interpretation of a taking. . . .

Even when courts began to consider that regulation in some situations could constitute a taking, they continued to uphold bans on particular uses without paying compensation, notwithstanding the economic impact, under the rationale that no one can obtain a vested right to injure or endanger the public. . . .

Nor does history indicate any common-law limit on the State's power to regulate harmful uses even to the point of destroying all economic value. Nothing in the discussions in Congress concerning the Taking Clause indicates that the Clause was limited by the common-law nuisance doctrine. Common law courts themselves rejected such an understanding. . . . *Commonwealth v. Parks*, 30 N.E. 174 (1892) (Holmes, J.) ("[T]he legislature may change the common law as to nuisances, and may move the line either way, so as to make things nuisances which were not so, or to make things lawful which were nuisances.").

In short, I find no clear and accepted "historical compact" or "understanding of our citizens" justifying the Court's new taking doctrine. . . .[26]

Justice JOHN PAUL STEVENS, dissenting. . . .

[T]he Court's new [categorical] rule [requiring compensation when an owner is denied economically viable use of his land] is wholly arbitrary. A landowner whose property is diminished in value 95% recovers nothing, while an owner whose property is diminished 100% recovers the land's full value. . . .

---

26. The Court asserts that all early American experience, prior to and after passage of the Bill of Rights, and any case law prior to 1897 are "entirely irrelevant" in determining what is "the historical compact recorded in the Takings Clause." Nor apparently are we to find this compact in the early federal taking cases, which clearly permitted prohibition of harmful uses despite the alleged loss of all value, whether or not the prohibition was a common-law nuisance, and whether or not the prohibition occurred subsequent to the purchase. I cannot imagine where the Court finds its "historical compact," if not in history.

Moreover, because of the elastic nature of property rights, the Court's new rule will also prove unsound in practice. In response to the rule, courts may define "property" broadly and only rarely find regulations to effect total takings....

On the other hand, developers and investors may market specialized estates to take advantage of the Court's new rule. The smaller the estate, the more likely that a regulatory change will effect a total taking. Thus, an investor may, for example, purchase the right to build a multi-family home on a specific lot, with the result that a zoning regulation that allows only single-family homes would render the investor's property interest "valueless." In short, the categorical rule will likely have one of two effects: Either courts will alter the definition of the "denominator" in the takings "fraction," rendering the Court's categorical rule meaningless, or investors will manipulate the relevant property interests, giving the Court's rule sweeping effect. To my mind, neither of these results is desirable or appropriate, and both are distortions of our takings jurisprudence....

Like many bright-line rules, the categorical rule established in this case is only "categorical" for a page or two in the U.S. Reports. No sooner does the Court state that "total regulatory takings must be compensated," than it quickly establishes an exception to that rule.

The exception provides that a regulation that renders property valueless is not a taking if it prohibits uses of property that were not "previously permissible under relevant property and nuisance principles." The Court thus rejects the basic holding in *Mugler v. Kansas*, 123 U.S. 623 (1887). There we held that a state-wide statute that prohibited the owner of a brewery from making alcoholic beverages did not effect a taking, even though the use of the property had been perfectly lawful and caused no public harm before the statute was enacted. We squarely rejected the rule the Court adopts today.... Under our reasoning in *Mugler*, a state's decision to prohibit or to regulate certain uses of property is not a compensable taking just because the particular uses were previously lawful. Under the Court's opinion today, however, if a state should decide to prohibit the manufacture of asbestos, cigarettes, or concealable firearms, for example, it must be prepared to pay for the adverse economic consequences of its decision. One must wonder if Government will be able to "go on" effectively if it must risk compensation "for every such change in the general law." *Mahon*, 260 U.S., at 413.

The Court's holding today effectively freezes the State's common law, denying the legislature much of its traditional power to revise the law governing the rights and uses of property....

Arresting the development of the common law is not only a departure from our prior decisions; it is also profoundly unwise. The human condition is one of constant learning and evolution — both moral and practical. Legislatures imfplement that new learning; in doing so they must often revise the definition of property and the rights of property owners. Thus, when the Nation came to understand that slavery was morally wrong and mandated the emancipation of all slaves, it, in effect, redefined "property." On a lesser scale, our ongoing self-education produces similar changes in the rights of property owners: New appreciation of the significance of endangered species, the importance of wetlands, and the vulnerability of coastal lands, shapes our evolving understandings of property rights.

Of course, some legislative redefinitions of property will effect a taking and must be compensated — but it certainly cannot be the case that every movement away from common law does so. There is no reason, and less sense, in such an absolute rule. We live in a world in which changes in the economy and the environment occur with increasing frequency and importance. If it was wise a century ago to allow Government "the largest legislative discretion" to deal with "the special exigencies of the moment," *Mugler*, 123 U.S., at 669, it is imperative to do so today. The rule that should govern a decision in a case of this kind should focus on the future, not the past.[5] . . .

[Justice DAVID H. SOUTER stated that he would have dismissed the writ of certiorari as improvidently granted. The factual conclusion of the trial court — that Lucas had been deprived of any economically viable use of his property — was "questionable" but was not reviewed by the state supreme court; thus it could not be reviewed by the Supreme Court. Without fully airing this issue, the Court could not adequately clarify what constitutes a total taking requiring compensation or the exceptions to the compensation requirement that the Court proceeds to recognize.]

Palazzolo v. Rhode Island, 533 U.S. 606 (2001). Anthony Palazzolo was denied permits to develop his waterfront property in Rhode Island by a state agency charged with enforcing laws regulating construction on the coast. After several unsuccessful attempts to obtain approval to fill in his coastal marshlands and develop 74 homes there, Palazzolo sued the State of Rhode Island, seeking $3,150,000 in compensation for a taking of his property. He argued, on the authority of *Lucas*, that he had been denied all economically viable use of his property because it appeared that the Rhode Island Coastal Resources Management Council would not allow him to build anything on the waterfront property. It did appear that the agency would allow him to develop the upland part of the property away from the water; that development was worth $200,000.

The Rhode Island Supreme Court rejected his takings claim for three reasons. First, the court held that his claim was not ripe for decision; the state agency had merely rejected several development proposals and had not issued a final ruling that clearly denied any right to develop the marshland area. Second, the court held that Palazzolo had not been deprived of all economic value because he could develop the upland property away from the water. Third, the court noted that at the time Palazzolo acquired title to the property from the prior owner (a corporation in which he had held shares and eventually became the sole shareholder), the law regulating coastal development was already in place. The court held that Palazzolo could have no "reasonable" investment-backed expectations at the time he acquired title if existing laws at the time he acquired title made his intended use of the property illegal. In effect, the state court created a safe haven rule that would have protected the state from any takings claim by an owner who obtained title after a regulatory law restricting the use of that property came into effect.

The Supreme Court reversed the first and third findings and reserved judgment on the second. Over the objections of three dissenters, the Court found, first, that the evidence was sufficiently clear that the coastal agency would not allow any of the marshland to be filled in; thus the scope of the permitted development was clear

---

5. Even measured in terms of efficiency, the Court's rule is unsound. The Court today effectively establishes a form of insurance against certain changes in land-use regulations. Like other forms of insurance, the Court's rule creates a "moral hazard" and inefficiencies: In the face of uncertainty about changes in the law, developers will overinvest, safe in the knowledge that if the law changes adversely, they will be entitled to compensation. *See generally* Farber, *Economic Analysis and Just Compensation*, 12 Int'l Rev. of Law & Econ. 125 (1992).

and the takings claim was ripe for decision. *See MacDonald, Sommer & Frates v. Yolo County*, 477 U.S. 340, 351 (1986); *Williamson County Regional Planning Comm'n v. Hamilton Bank of Johnson City*, 473 U.S. 172 (1985)(both holding that a takings claim is not ripe for decision unless the state has made a final decision on the scope of the permitted development).

Second, the Supreme Court refused to define the constitutional standard for determining whether Palazzolo had been denied all economically viable use of his land. Because it appeared that he could develop some of his land, but not all of it, the Court was confronted with the "denominator" question reserved in *Lucas*. Was the development ban a 100 percent taking of the portion of his land that could not be developed or only a partial taking of his whole parcel (the upland land that could be developed combined with the marshland that could not be developed)? Palazzolo had argued that it was irrelevant that he was allowed to develop 18 acres in the upland part of his property; because the wetlands law prevented him from building on his substantial waterfront property, that law had effectively converted a substantial portion of his property into a "nature reserve," denying him 100 percent of the value of that land. In deciding whether this was a partial taking or a total taking, he argued that the relevant denominator was the developable tract or some subset of his whole property. The fact that he was allowed to develop part of his property did not alter the fact that he was denied the right to develop most of his land; the land he could not develop had been deprived of all economically viable use. The Supreme Court found that Palazzolo had effectively waived this argument below. However, Justice Kennedy observed that "[s]ome of our cases indicate that the extent of deprivation effected by a regulatory action is measured against the value of the parcel as a whole, but we have at times expressed discomfort with the logic of this rule . . ." 533 U.S. at 631.

Third, the Supreme Court reversed the ruling that states are insulated from taking claims merely because an owner has acquired title after a regulatory law went into effect. The fact that the owner took title with notice of the regulation did not, by itself, immunize the state from facing a challenge to the regulation as a taking of property. Justice Kennedy explained, *id.* at 627–630:

> The right to improve property, of course, is subject to the reasonable exercise of state authority, including the enforcement of valid zoning and land-use restrictions. The Takings Clause, however, in certain circumstances allows a landowner to assert that a particular exercise of the State's regulatory power is so unreasonable or onerous as to compel compensation. Just as a prospective enactment, such as a new zoning ordinance, can limit the value of land without effecting a taking because it can be understood as reasonable by all concerned, other enactments are unreasonable and do not become less so through passage of time or title. Were we to accept the State's rule, the postenactment transfer of title would absolve the State of its obligation to defend any action restricting land use, no matter how extreme or unreasonable. A State would be allowed, in effect, to put an expiration date on the Takings Clause. This ought not to be the rule. Future generations, too, have a right to challenge unreasonable limitations on the use and value of land.
>
> Nor does the justification of notice take into account the effect on owners at the time of enactment, who are prejudiced as well. Should an owner attempt to challenge a new regulation, but not survive the process of ripening his or her claim (which, as this case demonstrates, will often take years), under the proposed rule the right to compensation may not be asserted by an heir or successor, and so may not be asserted at all. The State's rule would work a critical alteration to the nature of property, as the newly regulated

landowner is stripped of the ability to transfer the interest which was possessed prior to the regulation. The State may not by this means secure a windfall for itself....

We have no occasion to consider the precise circumstances when a legislative enactment can be deemed a background principle of state law or whether those circumstances are present here. It suffices to say that a regulation that otherwise would be unconstitutional absent compensation is not transformed into a background principle of the State's law by mere virtue of the passage of title.

Because the lower court had found that this was not a 100 percent taking of the property's value, the *Lucas* rule did not apply. However, the general multifactor *Penn Central* test did apply and the Supreme Court remanded the case to be addressed under that standard.

Justice O'Connor concurred, agreeing that the acquisition of title after a regulatory law was passed did not protect the state from a takings claim. She explained, *Id.* at 632-633 (O'Connor, J., concurring):

> The more difficult question is what role the temporal relationship between regulatory enactment and title acquisition plays in a proper *Penn Central* analysis. Today's holding does not mean that the timing of the regulation's enactment relative to the acquisition of title is immaterial to the *Penn Central* analysis. Indeed, it would be just as much error to expunge this consideration from the takings inquiry as it would be to accord it exclusive significance. Our polestar instead remains the principles set forth in *Penn Central* itself and our other cases that govern partial regulatory takings. Under these cases, interference with investment-backed expectations is one of a number of factors that a court must examine. Further, the regulatory regime in place at the time the claimant acquires the property at issue helps to shape the reasonableness of those expectations....
>
> If investment-backed expectations are given exclusive significance in the *Penn Central* analysis and existing regulations dictate the reasonableness of those expectations in every instance, then the State wields far too much power to redefine property rights upon passage of title. On the other hand, if existing regulations do nothing to inform the analysis, then some property owners may reap windfalls and an important indicium of fairness is lost. As I understand it, our decision today does not remove the regulatory backdrop against which an owner takes title to property from the purview of the *Penn Central* inquiry. It simply restores balance to that inquiry. Courts properly consider the effect of existing regulations under the rubric of investment-backed expectations in determining whether a compensable taking has occurred. As before, the salience of these facts cannot be reduced to any "set formula." The temptation to adopt what amount to *per se* rules in either direction must be resisted. The Takings Clause requires careful examination and weighing of all the relevant circumstances in this context....

Justice Scalia concurred but disagreed strongly with Justice O'Connor on this point, *id.* at 636 (Scalia, J., concurring):

> In my view, the fact that a restriction existed at the time the purchaser took title (other than a restriction forming part of the "background principles of the State's law of property and nuisance") should have no bearing upon the determination of whether the restriction is so substantial as to constitute a taking. The "investment-backed expectations" that the law will take into account do not include the assumed validity of a restriction that in fact deprives property of so much of its value as to be unconstitutional.

Justices Ginsburg, Souter, and Breyer dissented, disagreeing with the majority's conclusion that the state agency had come to a final ruling with regard to the extent of development permitted on the property.

Tahoe-Sierra Preservation Council, Inc. v. Tahoe Regional Planning Agency, 535 U.S. 302 (2002). A regional planning agency placed a temporary moratorium on construction around Lake Tahoe. The moratorium officially lasted for 32 months, but a court injunction effectively extended the ban on construction for as much as 6 years. The construction ban was intended to allow the agency time to develop a plan to limit construction around the lake to prevent the loss of Lake Tahoe's "exceptional clarity." Unlike most lakes, Lake Tahoe lacked algae that obscures the water clarity; the district court found that undue development could change runoff patterns in a manner that would not only destroy this clarity, but that it would be impossible to fix for 700 years, if at all. Petitioners were owners of land around the lake who claimed that the temporary building moratorium took all economically viable use of their property for the period in which it was in effect and that this amounted to a categorical (although temporary) taking of their property for which they were entitled to compensation under the rule in *Lucas*.

The Court disagreed, refusing to find that a temporary building moratorium was a *per se* taking of property. Justice Stevens explained that, despite the attempts in *Loretto* and *Lucas* to develop some rules that could identify categorical takings, the Court has "'generally eschewed' any set formula" for identifying regulatory takings, instead engaging in "essentially *ad hoc*, factual inquiries." *Id.* at 326. "Indeed," wrote Justice Stevens, "we still resist the temptation to adopt *per se* rules in our cases involving partial regulatory takings, preferring to examine 'a number of factors' rather than a simple 'mathematically precise' formula." *Id.* The majority opinion went on to quote Justice O'Connor's concurring opinion in *Palazzolo* at some length, agreeing with her inclination to "resist[ ] the temptation to adopt what amount to *per se* rules in either direction." *Id.* at 321 (*quoting Palazzolo, supra*, 533 U.S. at 636 (O'Connor, J., concurring)).

The Court acknowledged that a prior case, *First English Evangelical Lutheran Church of Glendale v. County of Los Angeles*, 482 U.S. 304 (1987), had held that owners are entitled to sue for compensation for temporary takings of their property. When a regulation is determined to be a taking, the government may either enforce the regulation and pay compensation for the loss of property rights or decide to forego enforcing the regulation and pay compensation for the temporary loss of property rights during the time the regulation limited the use of the property. However, Justice Stevens explained that *First English* merely held that compensation should be paid when a taking is found; it did not hold that a temporary limit on construction necessarily constituted a taking.

The Court clarified that it meant what it said in *Lucas*: only a 100% diminution in value of the property—a "complete elimination of value"—triggered the *Lucas* rule. *Id.* at 330. Any lesser deprivation of value is governed by the multifactor *Penn Central* test. *See also Lingle v. Chevron U.S.A.*, 2005 U.S. LEXIS 4342, *19 (U.S. 2005) (*Lucas* applies to regulations that "completely deprive an owner of *all* economically viable use of her property"). Because ownership extends over time as well as space, a temporary moratorium, by definition, does not result in a complete elimination of value, *id.* at 334-335:

[T]he extreme categorical rule that any deprivation of all economic use, no matter how brief, constitutes a compensable taking surely cannot be sustained. [Such a rule] would apply to numerous "normal delays in obtaining building permits, changes in zoning ordinances, variances, and the like," as well as to orders temporarily prohibiting access to crime scenes, businesses that violate health codes, fire-damaged buildings, or other areas that we cannot now foresee. Such a rule would undoubtedly require changes in numerous practices that have long been considered permissible exercises of the police power. As Justice Holmes warned in *Mahon*, "government hardly could go on if to some extent values incident to property could not be diminished without paying for every such change in the general law." 260 U.S. at 413. A rule that required compensation for every delay in the use of property would render routine government processes prohibitively expensive or encourage hasty decisionmaking. Such an important change in the law should be the product of legislative rulemaking rather than adjudication.

Chief Justice Rehnquist dissented, along with Justices Scalia and Thomas. They argued that the development ban, as extended by court injunction, had actually lasted for 6 years and that such a long moratorium was not reasonably related to legitimate land use planning needs. The functional effect of the moratorium was to temporarily deny the owners all economically viable use of their land, *Id.* at 348 (Rehnquist, C.J., dissenting):

> The regulation in *Lucas* was the "practical equivalence" of a long-term physical appropriation, *i.e.*, a condemnation, so the Fifth Amendment required compensation. The "practical equivalence," from the landowner's point of view, of a "temporary" ban on all economic use is a forced leasehold. For example, assume the following situation: Respondent is contemplating the creation of a National Park around Lake Tahoe to preserve its scenic beauty. Respondent decides to take a 6-year leasehold over petitioners' property, during which any human activity on the land would be prohibited, in order to prevent any further destruction to the area while it was deciding whether to request that the area be designated a National Park.
>
> Surely that leasehold would require compensation.

NOTES AND QUESTIONS

1. *Facial versus "as applied" challenges to regulations.* A facial challenge to a regulation is a claim that enforcement of the regulation would *necessarily* constitute a taking of private property *in every case*; thus, under *no* circumstances would the application of the statute be constitutional. In contrast, a challenge to a regulation "as applied" argues that the *effect* of the regulation on a *particular* parcel or parcels of property owned by the plaintiff constitutes a taking of the plaintiff's property. Facial challenges are likely to succeed only in where a law imposes a permanent physical invasion of property, *Loretto v. Teleprompter Manhattan CATV Corp.*, 458 U.S. 419 (1982), or completely extinguishes a core property right, such as the right to pass on fee simple property at death, *Babbitt v. Youpee*, 519 U.S. 234 (1997). Otherwise, the owner must demonstrate the economic impact on the value of a particular parcel of property to show that a law effects a taking as applied to that property.

2. *Ripeness.* As *Palazzolo* explains, the Supreme Court has held that a claim that one's property has been unconstitutionally taken without just compensation is premature (not "ripe") if the agency empowered to regulate the land use has not made a final decision on the scope of the permitted development. In general, this means that an owner must apply for a permit to develop the land and be denied that right in a manner that suggests that further applications will be fruitless. *MacDonald, Sommer & Frates v. Yolo County*, 477 U.S. 340 (1986); *Williamson County Regional Planning Com-*

mission v. Hamilton Bank of Johnson City, 473 U.S. 172 (1985). Moreover, the owner must exhaust all appeals and administrative remedies available under state law before challenging the state's development limitation as a taking. *Suitum v. Tahoe Regional Planning Agency*, 520 U.S. 725 (1997). *Accord, City of Monterey v. Del Monte Dunes at Monterey, Ltd.*, 526 U.S. 687, 721 (1999) (a takings claim is not ripe until the owner has "been denied an adequate postdeprivation remedy").

An owner who wishes to make a facial challenge to a regulatory law may do so by choosing to sue in federal court; however, owners may not bring "as-applied" takings claims in federal court before exhausting all state remedies, and those remedies include bringing suit in state court to argue that the regulation constitutes a taking of property. Moreover, once an owner goes to state court to argue that a regulatory law constitutes a taking of property as applied to that owner's property, and the state courts rule on the owner's takings claim, the only way to attain federal court review is by appealing through the state court system and then seeking a writ of *certiorari* from the Supreme Court. The owner is not entitled to bring an action in federal district to challenge the ruling of a state supreme court as effecting an unconstitutional taking because the federal full faith and credit statute, 28 U.S.C. §1738, requires federal courts to give preclusive effect to final state court judgments. *San Remo Hotel L.P. v. City and County of San Francisco*, 2005 U.S. LEXIS 4848 (2005).

In *City of Monterey, supra*, the Supreme Court found that a city could not avoid a takings challenge by repetitive and unfair procedures that never seem to result in a final determination of the scope of the permitted land use. *Palazzolo* reaffirmed the conclusion that, when a city has repeatedly denied development permits, a court may conclude that further applications would have been fruitless and that the scope of the permitted development is known with sufficient finality and certainty to entertain the takings challenge.

3. *Civil rights.* Section 1983 authorizes a party who has been deprived of a federal right under the color of state law to seek relief through "an action at law, suit in equity, or other proper proceeding for redress." 42 U.S.C. §1983. *City of Monterey, supra*, held in 1999 that an owner may sue the city under §1983 for violating its civil rights by taking its property through repeatedly rejecting development proposals over a five-year period, thus arguably denying the owner economically viable use of the property. The Supreme Court affirmed the trial court finding for the plaintiff that the city had both taken the owner's property and denied plaintiff equal protection of the laws by treating the owner differently from other similarly situated owners without adequate reason.

City of Monterey approved the use of §1983 as a remedy for a takings claim even though the effect of the ruling was to allow a jury rather than the judge to decide whether a taking had occurred. The Supreme Court held that this was permissible in that the jury's discretion was constrained by proper instructions limiting them to determining whether the "the city's particular decision to deny Del Monte Dunes' final development proposal was reasonably related to the city's proffered justifications." *Id.* at 706. The decision did not "attempt a precise demarcation of the respective provinces of judge and jury in determining whether a zoning decision substantially advances legitimate governmental interests." *Id.* at 722. However, it did reject the idea that allowing juries a role would "undermine the uniformity of the law and eviscerate state and local zoning authority by subjecting all land-use decisions to plenary, and potentially inconsistent, jury review." *Id.*

4. *Inverse condemnation.* Inverse condemnation refers to a lawsuit for damages by a property owner against a public body whose regulations are alleged to have taken the

owner's property without just compensation. In the usual eminent domain case, the public body brings condemnation proceedings against the property and the court sets the amount of just compensation required. Lawsuits by property owners for damages are the "inverse" of this procedure. The Supreme Court approved the right to obtain damages, as well as injunctive relief, in *First English Evangelical Lutheran Church v. County of Los Angeles*, 482 U.S. 304 (1987).

5. *Temporary takings.* As *Palazzolo* notes, *First English* held that owners could obtain damages for a *temporary taking* if they were prevented from using their property for any period. A court judgment that a regulation constitutes a taking of property leaves the regulatory body with the choice of enforcing the regulation (in which case compensation must be paid for a permanent taking) or rescinding the regulation (in which case the owner may have a claim for damages for a temporary taking for the period when the regulation was enforced against him). However, *Palazzolo* explained that a building ban does not necessarily constitute a taking, especially if it is temporary. And even the permanent ban on construction in *First English* was later found not to be a taking because the property was located on a floodplain and the authorities had determined that it was dangerous to build there. *First Lutheran Church v. Los Angeles*, 258 Cal. Rptr. 893 (Ct. App. 1989), *cert. denied*, 493 U.S. 1056 (1990).

6. *Environmental protection laws.* Many owners have brought inverse condemnation cases challenging the application of environmental protection statutes to their property. Many statutes designed to protect the environment also severely restrict the development of particular types of land, such as wetlands and habitats for endangered species. The courts have traditionally upheld these regulations, even when they have severely limit land development, by analogy to nuisance laws, which prevent owners from using their land in a way that will injure the community. *See, e.g., Gardner v. New Jersey Pinelands Commission*, 593 A.2d 251 (N.J. 1991); *Presbytery of Seattle v. King County*, 787 P.2d 907 (Wash. 1990); *Just v. Marinette County*, 201 N.W.2d 761 (Wis. 1972). Recently, however, some courts (especially the Federal Circuit and the Court of Federal Claims) have suggested or ruled that compensation is required when wetlands or endangered species act regulations have prevented all development of land. *Tulare Lake Basin Water Storage District v. United States*, 49 Fed. Cl. 313 (Fed. Cl. 2001)(Endangered Species Act); *Palm Beach Isles Associates v. United States*, 231 F.3d 1354 (Fed. Cir. 2000)(wetlands); *Laguna Gatuna, Inc. v. United States*, 50 Fed. Cl. 336 (2001)(Clean Water Act regulations); *Florida Rock Industries, Inc. v. United States*, 45 Fed. Cl. 21 (1999)(wetlands). These cases present a number of difficult issues.

    a.   *The "denominator" problem.* The *Lucas* rule applies when an owner has been deprived of "economically viable use." To determine how great the diminution in value has been, we need to determine the denominator of the fraction. Consider a developer who seeks to develop 50 acres. Does a regulation prohibiting development of five acres constitute a 100 percent taking of the five acres or only a 10 percent taking of the 50 acres? Is the denominator 5 or 50? In *Loveladies Harbor, Inc. v. United States*, 28 F.3d 1171 (Fed. Cir. 1999), the Federal Circuit held that the courts must use a "flexible approach, designed to account for factual nuances" to determine the appropriate "denominator" for calculating the economic impact of a regulation. One possibility is the "whole property" owned by the developer — in this case, the entire 50 acres. The other possibility is the "developable tract" or the area that could have been developed under reasonable zoning laws — in this case the five acres.

When air rights are at issue, the courts have consistently held that a height limit does not constitute a 100 percent taking of air rights over that limit; the denominator is the tract as a whole. However, the Federal Circuit has recently held that, in the context of wetlands regulations, the denominator is the developable tract. *Palm Beach Isles Associates v. United States*, 208 F.3d 1374 (Fed. Cir. 2000) (relevant parcel was a 50.7-acre tract out of an original 311.7-acre purchase); *Loveladies Harbor, Inc. v. United States* (relevant parcel was a 12.5-acre tract out of an original 51-acre purchase).

Both *Palazzolo* and *Tahoe-Sierra* suggest that the relevant property is the "parcel as a whole"—both spacially and over time. However, they do not definitively resolve the issue. Did the Rhode Island Supreme Court correctly conclude that Palazzolo's coastal property had not suffered a 100 percent deprivation of economically viable use when he was able to develop the upland area?

b. *Background principles of property law.* If wetlands laws deprive owners of "economically viable use," are they constitutional because they fit within the "nuisance" exception to *Lucas* or otherwise are based on "background principles of property law" that regulate conduct that never was part of the owner's title in the first place? On remand in *Lucas*, the South Carolina Supreme Court held that construction of housing on the coast would not have constituted a public or private nuisance under the common law existing before the regulatory laws limited such development. *Lucas v. South Carolina Coastal Council*, 424 S.E.2d 484 (S.C. 1992). A central question, however, is the relevance of the *cumulative impact* of development. What happens if the development of a particular lot would not, by itself, constitute a nuisance, but the development of *all* the lots in a sensitive area would have a cumulative effect of destroying scarce ecological resources, such as a coastline or wetlands, and therefore constitute both a public and a private nuisance? In *Florida Rock Industries, Inc. v. United States*, 45 Fed. Cl. 21 (1999), the Federal Circuit ruled that destruction of wetlands would not have constituted a nuisance under prior law that existed at the time the owner purchased the property and thus a regulation that prohibited dredging was a taking when it deprived the owner of all economically viable use of the land. *Accord, Bowles v. United States*, 31 Fed. Cl. 37 (1994). What is the argument on the other side? *Cf. First Lutheran Church v. Los Angeles*, 258 Cal. Rptr. 893 (Ct. App. 1989) (not a taking to prohibit reconstruction of a buildings at a Bible camp destroyed by a flood because floods could reoccur in the area and public safety concerns justified a prohibition on occupancy to protect human life).

PROBLEMS

1. Was *Miller v. Schoene* correctly decided (*see above* at §12.2)? Is it consistent with *Lucas*? Does it matter whether the cedar trees constituted a "nuisance" or not? Consider that the Florida Supreme Court, in a similar case, required compensation to be paid. *See, Department of Agriculture and Consumer Services v. Mid-Florida Growers, Inc.*, 521 So. 2d 101, 103 (Fla. 1988) (holding that the state had to pay just compensation when it destroyed healthy orange trees to prevent the spread of citrus canker because "destruction of the healthy trees benefited the entire citrus industry and, in turn, Florida's economy, thereby conferring a public benefit rather than preventing a public harm").

2. A developer who owns a 50 acres of property subdivides it and sells 45 single-family homes one-acre lots. One five-acre parcel remains but is designated as wetlands; under state law, the owner is prohibited from building anything on it. The developer sues the state, arguing that the wetlands regulation deprives her of any economically viable use for the 5 acres of wetlands; the diminution in value for this parcel is 100 percent. The state claims that the parcel represents 10 percent of the total area that the developer had owned and that since the developer had sold 45 homes, she was not deprived of economically viable use for her property. How should the court analyze this question? Is this a 100 percent taking of the 5 acres or a 10 percent taking of the 50 acres? Should the owner be entitled to compensation for her inability to develop the five-acre parcel?

3. On remand in *Lucas*, the South Carolina Supreme Court held that Lucas's conduct would not constitute a nuisance under the state's common law and that he was therefore entitled to compensation for the temporary taking of his property and permanent damages if the regulation were prospectively enforced. 424 S.E.2d 484 (S.C. 1992). Suppose the decision had come out the other way — that the extensive damage caused by construction on wetlands cumulatively would constitute a public nuisance under state common law — and Lucas again appealed to the Supreme Court. How would the Court rule? How should it rule?

4. In *Hunziker v. State*, 519 N.W.2d 367 (Iowa 1994), a lot owner was prevented from building a house on his lot when excavators discovered an American Indian burial mound made between 1,000 and 2,500 years ago in the middle of his property. A state statute in effect at the time the developer purchased the land authorized the state archeologist to prohibit owners from disinterring human remains found on private land if they had historic significance. The archeologist so found and required a buffer zone around the mound to protect its continued existence. The original developers of the subdivision refunded the purchase price and took back title and then sued the state, claiming that their inability to develop the lot deprived them of all economically viable use and that the statute, as applied to the lot, constituted a taking of property. The court held that the *Lucas* rule did not apply because the restriction on developing property where human beings are buried was part of the law of Iowa at the time the owner purchased the land and thus "inhered in the title." Because state law did not allow development in these circumstances, the owner could not have had a legitimate expectation of being able to so develop the property. The case is appealed to the Supreme Court. Should it affirm or reverse? It should be noted that state laws have traditionally regulated and required the preservation of marked cemeteries but that only recently have states passed laws protected older unmarked graves of American Indians (*see* below §15.6). Does this historical fact matter?

5. Property is often damaged pursuant to police activities. A car may be hit in a chase; a building may be damaged in pursuit of a criminal. Most courts hold that no compensation is required when such injuries occur. In *Eggleston v. Pierce County*, 64 P.3d 618 (Wash. 2003), the court found no taking when a home was rendered uninhabitable because of damage that occurred when police executed a search of the house pursuant to a valid search warrant. The police came to the house to arrest the owner's son for drug-dealing; he engaged in an exchange of fire with the police and killed a police officer. The search warrant authorized the police to take evidence from the home; that evidence included two walls, one of which was load-bearing. Its removal made the house unstable and uninhabitable. The court held that the seizure of evidence for a criminal trial can never be a taking; nor did the damage to the home pursuant to

the police efforts to apprehend a criminal. *Accord, Customer Co. v. City of Sacramento*, 895 P.2d 900 (Cal. 1995). In contrast, in *Steele v. City of Houston*, 603 S.W.2d 786 (Tex. 1980), the court found a taking when police had burned down an innocent person's home to eject suspects. *Accord, Wegner v. Milwaukee Mut. Ins. Co.*, 479 N.W.2d 38 (Minn. 1991). Which approach is correct?

§12.4 Special Cases

§12.4.1 DEPRIVATION OF CORE PROPERTY RIGHTS

Professor Margaret Jane Radin coined the term "conceptual severance" to describe the practice of identifying particular strands or sets of strands in the bundle of rights that may characterize property holding as severable and identifiable property interests for the purpose of takings analysis. Conceptual severance, Radin says,

> consists of delineating a property interest consisting of just what the government action has removed from the owner, and then asserting that that particular whole thing has been permanently taken. Thus this strategy hypothetically or conceptually "severs" from the whole bundle of rights just those strands that are interfered with by the regulation, and then hypothetically or conceptually construes those strands in the aggregate as a separate whole thing.

Margaret Jane Radin, *The Liberal Conception of Property: Cross Currents in the Jurisprudence of Takings*, 88 Colum. L. Rev. 1667, 1676 (1988). For example, a zoning ordinance that prohibits construction above five stories may be said to have taken the owner's "air rights" above that level because the owner would otherwise be able to sell the air rights to another developer.

Changes in legal rules that retroactively destroy or reallocate particular strands in the bundle of property rights may be viewed as "takings" of property that must be compensated. The problem, however, is that *every* regulation may be viewed as taking particular strands in the bundle of property rights. Consider the following case.

BABBITT v. YOUPEE
519 U.S. 234 (1997)

See supra §1.4.1, at pages 63-69.

NOTES AND QUESTIONS

1. *Was allotment a taking of property?* As Justice Ginsburg notes, the *General Allotment Act of 1887* provided for the breakup of communally held tribal property into allotments held by individual tribal members. Congress took property owned by Indian nations and transferred title over that land to individual tribal members, who then owned bits of what had been tribal land. The act was intended to destroy tribal culture, and eventually tribal sovereignty, and to speed the assimilation and Christianization of American Indians by giving them individual property rights. When the

General Allotment Act was passed, Congress negotiated with individual tribes to obtain their agreement to allotment. Even prior to the act, treaties with certain tribes provided for allotment, but the United States generally proceeded with allotment only with the tribe's consent.

In *Lone Wolf v. Hitchcock,* 187 U.S. 553 (1903), however, the Supreme Court upheld forced allotment, over the objections of the affected tribe, even when this violated the explicit terms of prior treaties. The Court held that Congress had exercised "plenary authority" over American Indian nations "from the beginning, and the power has always been deemed a political one, not subject to be controlled by the judicial department of the government." *Id.* at 565. The Court interpreted this plenary power as immunizing Congress from any express constitutional provisions — including the takings clause. Under this ruling, the government could take Indian property without paying just compensation even if the Indians' property rights were recognized by treaty. The Court held that Congress "possessed ... full administrative power ... over Indian tribal property." *Id.* at 568. Justice White explained, *id:*

> In effect, the action of Congress now complained of was but an exercise of such power, a mere change in the form of investment of Indian tribal property, the property of those who, as we have held, were in substantial effect the wards of the government. We must presume that Congress acted in perfect good faith in the dealings with the Indians of which complaint is made, and that the legislative branch of the government exercised its best judgment in the premises. In any event, as Congress possessed full power in the matter, the judiciary cannot question or inquire into the motives which prompted the enactment of this legislation. If injury was occasioned, which we do not wish to be understood as implying, by the use made by Congress of its power, relief must be sought by an appeal to that body for redress and not to the courts.

The Supreme Court has since held that the federal government is generally (but not always) obligated to pay just compensation when it takes tribal property "recognized" by treaty or statute. *United States v. Sioux Nation of Indians,* reprinted at §13.3.2, *infra.*

Did forced allotment constitute a taking of property without just compensation? Suppose Congress passed a law providing that a factory owned by General Motors be divided among General Motors' shareholders. Instead of owning stock in an ongoing business corporation, each shareholder would own in fee simple a room or a floor in the factory. Would this constitute a taking of the corporation's property without just compensation? Would it constitute a taking of the shareholders' property interests in their stock?

Was it fair for the Supreme Court to uphold the legislation that created the problem of fractionated shares (the *General Allotment Act*) but to strike down the legislation passed to correct the problems created by the act? If the original allotment policy effected an unconstitutional taking of tribal property, should this have affected the result in *Babbitt?*

2. *Right to alienate property.* Can the law prohibit an owner from alienating her property?

Andrus v. Allard, 444 U.S. 51 (1979). The *Eagle Protection Act* and the *Migratory Bird Treaty Act* were designed to protect various species of birds from extinction. The statutes prohibited the sale of eagle feathers, including those acquired before the act was passed. In the Court held that the statute did not effect a taking of property without just compensation despite the total ban on sale, *Id.* at 65-66:

> The regulations challenged here do not compel the surrender of the artifacts, and there is no physical invasion or restraint upon them. Rather, a significant restriction has been imposed on one means of disposing of the artifacts. But the denial of one traditional property right does not always amount to a taking. At least where an owner possesses a full "bundle" of property rights, the destruction of one "strand" of the bundle is not a taking, because the aggregate must be viewed in its entirety.
>
> Regulations that bar trade in certain goods have been upheld against claims of unconstitutional taking. For example, the Court has sustained regulations prohibiting the sale of alcoholic beverages despite the fact that individuals were left with previously acquired stocks. *Everard's Breweries v. Day*, 265 U.S. 545, 563 (1924), involved a federal statute that forbade the sale of liquors manufactured and bought before passage of the statute. The claim by beer dealers that were prevented from selling their stock of beer that the law took their property in violation of the fifth amendment was tersely rejected. *Cf. Mugler v. Kansas*, 123 U.S. 623 (1887) (state constitutional amendment prohibiting the manufacture and sale of alcoholic beverages promoted the public health, welfare, safety, and morals by outlawing a public nuisance and thus did not unconstitutionally take the property of a brewery owner).

Is *Andrus v. Allard* consistent with *Babbitt*?

3. *Future interests and covenants.* Courts and legislatures have often changed the rules regulating the estates system. Some of these changes have allowed individuals to create future interests that had previously been illegal. For example, the *Uniform Statutory Rule Against Perpetuities*, adopted in more than half the states validates some future interests that violate the traditional rule against perpetuities. Other changes have invalidated future interests that had previously been lawful. For example, some states limit possibilities of reverter and options to purchase property to a set period, such as 30 years. Other states require future interests to be re-recorded every 30 or 40 years to remain viable. Can these changes in law be applied retroactively to property interests created before they were passed?

Some courts allow time limits to be placed on contingent future interests created before passage of the statute on the ground that the owner had "no more than an expectation, a possibility" that an interest might accrue in the future. *Trustees of Schools of Township No. 1 v. Batdorf*, 130 N.E.2d 111 (Ill. 1955) (upholding a marketable title act that retroactively limited possibilities of reverter and rights of entry created before passage of the act to 50 years). However, they usually do not allow previously created future interests to be completely wiped out unless the owner is given an opportunity to re-register the interest. *See id.* (upholding application of the act to interests created more than 50 years before the effective date of the statute if those interests were not re-recorded within one year after the statute was passed). *Accord, Cline v. Johnson County Board of Education*, 548 S.W.2d 507 (Ky. 1977); *Town of Brookline v. Carey*, 245 N.E.2d 446 (Mass. 1969). One court has upheld the retroactive application of a statute that converted an automatic possibility of reverter into a right of entry against a takings challenge. *Walton v. City of Red Bluff*, 3 Cal. Rptr. 2d 275 (Ct. App. 1991). However, some courts have held that some statutory changes in the rule against perpetuities effect unconstitutional takings of property if retroactively applied to property interests created before passage of the statute. *Lake of the Woods Association, Inc. v. William M. McHugh*, 380 S.E.2d 872 (Va. 1989) (holding that retroactive application of the wait and see test would unconstitutionally take present estates that would have prevailed over future estates invalid under the traditional rule against perpetuities).

Most of the cases abolishing male privileges associated with tenancy by the entirety apply the statutes retroactively to tenancies created before the effective date of the statute. Retroactive application is arguably legitimate here because the unequal property rights associated with tenancies by the entirety probably violate the equal protection clause. *Kirchberg v. Feenstra*, 450 U.S. 455 (1981). *But see West v. First Agricultural Bank*, 419 N.E.2d 262 (Mass. 1981) (refusing to apply retroactively a change in tenancy by the entirety law granting women equal management powers over property).

Courts ordinarily do not find a taking when statutes retroactively alter the enforceability of covenants by modifying the changed conditions or relative hardship doctrines. *Blakeley v. Gorin*, 313 N.E.2d 903 (Mass. 1974). However, some courts have found takings when a statute retroactively increases or decreases the time period during which a covenant will be enforceable. *Appalachee Enters. v. Walker*, 463 S.E.2d 896 (Ga. 1995)(unconstitutional to apply a statute allowing covenants to last for 30 years when the developer purchased the property in reliance on a prior statute that limited covenants to 20 years).

4. *Taxation and the takings clause.* All taxation by its very nature "takes" property by requiring payments of money to the government but if every tax were a taking of property then the taxing power would be meaningless. Taxes must comply with other constitutional requirements, however. In *Magoun v. Illinois Trust and Savings Bank*, 170 U.S. 283 (1898), the Supreme Court upheld progressive taxation of estates, ruling that it did not violate equal protection of the laws to impose higher rates of taxation on larger estates. Justice William McKenna explained that inheritance taxes are imposed, not on the property itself but on the succession. Moreover, the "right to take property by devise or descent is the creature of the law, and not a natural right — a privilege, and therefore the authority which confers it may impose conditions upon it." *Id.* at 289. Is this observation consistent with the ruling in *Babbitt?*

PROBLEMS

1. A state adopts a statute extending the rule against perpetuities to possibilities of reverter and rights of entry on the ground it never made any sense to strike down an executory interest in a third party under the rule against perpetuities while enforcing an identical possibility of reverter held by a descendant of the grantor. If the statute applies to conveyances made prior to the effective date of the statute, would this constitute a taking of property without just compensation?

2. Does the state have to compensate an owner if it acquires the owner's property by adverse possession? What are the arguments on both sides of this question? *Compare Pascoag Reservoir & Dam, LLC v. State of Rhode Island*, 217 F.Supp.2d 206 (D.R.I. 2002), *aff'd on other grounds*, 337 F.3d 87 (1st Cir. 2003) (holding that compensation is constitutionally required) *with Weidner v. State*, 860 P.2d 1205 (Alaska 1993); *Stickney v. City of Saco*, 770 A.2d 592, 2001 ME 69 (Me. 2001)(both holding that no compensation is due).

3. The first two versions of the *Indian Land Consolidation Act (ILCA)*, were held unconstitutional in *Hodel v. Irving* and *Babbitt v. Youpee*. Congress tried again, passing a third version of the law in 2000, which it then amended in 2004. The new version is complicated. *See* 25 U.S.C. §2206. It authorizes the Indian nations to pass their own

probate laws governing inheritance and devise, rather than using state probate laws to determine descent and devise. If the tribe does not pass such a code, the new ILCA prescribes a federal probate code to determine devise and descent. In general, the property of an allottee who dies intestate will go to the decedent's surviving spouse, with the remainder in the decedent's lineal descendants (children, grandchildren, or great-grandchildren), or the decedent's parents or siblings, and if the decedent leaves no such relatives, the interest will go to the tribe as the last heir (unless a co-owner buys the interest for its fair market value). If the interest is less than 5 percent of the total undivided ownership of the property, the remainder can go only to one person — the oldest eligible child, grandchild, great-grandchild, parent or sibling, with the tribe as heir of last resort. The allottee can get around these restrictions by writing a valid will. If there is no tribal probate code regulating devise, the allottee may devise the interest to lineal descendants, any co-owner of the allotment, the tribe, or any Indian. The owner may also give a life estate to any person (such as a non-Indian spouse or child), with the remainder interest to be held by the tribe. The statute also gives the Secretary of the Interior the power to partition highly-fractionated allotments (with more than 100 owners or 50 to 99 owners if none owns more than a 10 percent interest). At such a partition sale, the only eligible buyers would be the tribe, the tribe's members, descendants of the original allottee, or co-owners of the interest if they are members of another tribe. Is this version of the law likely to be upheld by the Supreme Court?

4. In *Bormann v. Board of Supervisors in and for Kossuth County*, 584 N.W.2d 309 (Iowa 1998), a state law authorized the creation of "agricultural areas" in which particular owners were entitled to immunity from certain nuisance claims by neighbors. Similar "right-to-farm" statutes have been enacted in many states. Neighbors challenged the statute because it deprived them of rights they had under prior law to be protected against nuisances committed on neighboring property. The Iowa Supreme Court held the statute unconstitutionally took the right to be free from nuisances from owners in the affected areas and granted farmers a kind of easement — a right to commit a nuisance affecting neighboring property. Because property law traditionally gave owners the right to be free from unreasonable and substantial interferences with their use or enjoyment of their property, the Iowa Supreme Court concluded that the statute authorizing farmers to commit nuisances effectuated an unconstitutional taking of the property rights of those affected by what would otherwise have constituted an actionable nuisance. Assume the Supreme Court agrees to hear the case on appeal. Should the court's ruling be affirmed or reversed?

5. *Rights of first refusal.*

    a. Massachusetts has a statute that gives the municipality where is located a right of first refusal to purchase land of five acres or more used and zoned for agricultural purposes. The municipality has the right to match a bona fide third party offer and take title to the land for that price. It also has the option to purchase the land for its fair market value if the owner discontinues the agricultural use. The act only applies if the owner has applied to the municipality and been granted the right to have the land assessed as agricultural land for property tax purposes, resulting in much lower than normal property taxes on the land. Mass. Gen. Laws ch. 61A, §14. Does the statute violate the takings clause?

    b. A local condominium conversion ordinance gives tenants a right of first refusal to purchase their units if the landlord chooses to convert the apartment building to condominiums. Does the ordinance violate the takings clause?

§12.4.2 VESTED RIGHTS

§12.4.2.1 Established Investments

A lot is zoned for institutional use and, in reliance on that zoning designation, a university obtains a building permit, complying with all applicable construction regulations, and builds a classroom building. Two years after the building is completed, the city completes a "downzoning" project and rezones much of the land in the city to limit the placement and development of institutional and commercial uses and increase areas zoned for housing. The land on which the classroom building sits is now placed in a district limited to residential uses. Is the university obligated to tear down the building and construct an apartment building in its place? The answer is no, partly because it is likely the state zoning enabling act and the city zoning ordinance itself have provisions to grandfather prior nonconforming uses and partly because any such requirement would almost certainly constitute a taking of property without just compensation.

Once an owner invests substantially in reliance on applicable zoning and building requirements, the owner acquires a "vested right" to the existing use which cannot be changed retroactively unless the regulatory law is designed to prevent the owner from committing a nuisance or otherwise harming individuals or the public. In *Dobbins v. Los Angeles*, 195 U.S. 223 (1904), the Supreme Court held that a zoning law prohibiting the use of a parcel of land for a gasworks could not be retroactively applied to an owner unless just compensation was paid when the use was lawful at the time the owner bought the property, the owner had already invested substantially in the project and had begun construction. However, it also held that retroactive regulations are lawful without compensation when the legislating body could have rationally believed that the regulation was needed to prevent the owner from committing a public or private nuisance or otherwise causing harm to individuals or to property. In *Dobbins*, however, the Court found that, because the property was located in an industrial district, there was no indication that the law had been changed to prevent a nuisance or other harm to neighboring owners or the public.

In contrast, *Mugler v. Kansas*, 123 U.S. 623 (1887) upheld a state constitutional amendment prohibiting the manufacture and sale of alcoholic beverages on the ground that it promoted the public health, welfare, safety, and morals by outlawing a public nuisance and thus did not unconstitutionally take the property of a brewery owner. *See also Keystone Bituminous Coal Association v. DeBenedictis*, 480 U.S. 470 (1970) (upholding a regulatory law requiring substantial amounts of coal to be left in place under the ground to support the surface and prevent subsidence of surface structures); *Goldblatt v. Hempstead*, 369 U.S. 590 (1962) (upholding a law that prevents continued operation of a quarry in residential area); *Miller v. Schoene*, 276 U.S. 272 (1928) (upholding an order to destroy diseased cedar trees to prevent infection of nearby orchards); *Hadacheck v. Sebastian*, 239 U.S. 394 (1915) (upholding a law barring operation of brick mill in a residential area).

The vested rights principle was applied in *Kaiser Aetna v. United States*, 444 U.S. 164 (1979), when the Supreme Court found that a private, fee-paying marina club could not be forced to provide free public access to its lagoon when it invested in an expensive construction project to connect the lagoon to public navigable waters. The Supreme Court held that requiring the club to allow access to its property by non-paying members of the public would interfere with its "reasonable investment backed expectations" as well as imposing a forced physical invasion by strangers to its land. *Id.* at 175, 179-180.[3]

Laws that adjust the burdens of economic life, such as consumer protection laws, workplace regulations, and changes in tort laws that require compensation when one causes harm to others, have almost never been ruled to be unconstitutional takings of property. However, some such changes so alter established expectations that they have been challenged as unconstitutional takings of property; although such claims generally fail, the courts do take them seriously. For example, in the 1960s, the federal government promoted the construction of low-income housing by private developers by providing mortgage insurance that allowed the developers to obtain funds from private lenders for 40-year low-interest mortgages. In return, the developers consented to have the constructed properties be subject to extensive government regulation, though the terms of the mortgages provided that they could be pre-paid without government approval after 20 years and that doing so would lift the restrictions arising from the regulations. To stop a mass withdrawal of properties from the low-income housing program through prepayment after 20 years, Congress enacted statutes that effectively nullified the right to prepayment after 20 years sans government approval. However, in *Cienega Gardens v. United States,* 331 F.3d 1319 (Fed. Cir. 2003), the Federal Circuit held that the developers had a vested property right to "buy out" of the low-income housing program and that the legislation denying this right constituted a taking as a matter of law under the *Penn Central* test.

Such laws are also subject to due process analysis. The Supreme Court has interpreted the Constitution's prohibition on the "deprivation of property without due process of law" to contain a substantive dimension. U.S. Const., amend. XIV §1. The due process clause not only requires that adequate procedures be implemented to deprive owners of property (*procedural due process*), such as notice and a hearing, but prohibits certain types of deprivations from occurring at all (*substantive due process*). Among the substantive protections for property are prohibitions on retroactive legislation.

In *Eastern Enterprises v. Apfel,* 524 U.S. 498 (1998), the Supreme Court held in a split decision that a 1992 congressional statute (the *Coal Act*) effected an unconstitutional deprivation of property when it imposed retroactive liability on a coal company to pay health benefits for retired coal miners. That company had signed earlier labor agreements obligating it to contribute certain amounts to trust funds established for this purpose. The 1992 statute required Eastern Enterprises to contribute new funds for health benefits for retired coal miners who had worked for it before 1966 even though it left the coal business in 1966.

A four-judge plurality would have held that economic regulation such as the 1992 *Coal Act* may effectuate an unconstitutional taking of property.[4] "Congress has considerable leeway to fashion economic legislation, including the power to affect con-

---

3. This topic is further explored in chapter 11 in the sections dealing with prior nonconforming uses (§11.2.2.1) and vested rights under zoning law (§11.2.2.3).

4. Previous cases considering whether economic regulations effect takings include: *Concrete Pipe & Products of California, Inc. v. Construction Laborers Pension Trust for Southern California,* 508 U.S. 602 (1993); *Connolly v. Pension Benefits Guaranty Corp.,* 475 U.S. 211 (1986); *Usery v. Turner Elkhorn Mining Co.,* 428 U.S. 1 (1976).

tractual commitments between private parties." 524 U.S. at 528. It may even "impose retroactive liability to some degree, particularly where it is 'confined to short and limited periods required by the practicalities of producing national legislation.'" *Id.* (*quoting Pension Benefit Guaranty Corp. v. R.A. Gray & Co.*, 467 U.S. 717, 731 (1986)). However, such legislation will be unconstitutional "if it imposes severe retroactive liability on a limited class of parties that could not have anticipated the liability, and the extent of that liability is substantially disproportionate to the parties' experience." 524 U.S. at 528-529. In this case, the Court found this standard met because plaintiff's new liability of $50 to $100 million was not proportional to its experience with the plan and substantially interfered with Eastern's investment-backed expectations by imposing retroactive obligations based on events that happened 30 years earlier. In addition, no pattern of regulation would have placed Eastern on notice that such large, disproportionate, retroactive obligations might be forthcoming.

However, a five-judge majority agreed that the takings clause was inapposite. Justice Kennedy voted with the four-judge plurality to hold the *Coal Act* unconstitutional as applied to Eastern. However, he did not believe the takings clause applies to this kind of case. A majority of the Court appears to have agreed with his conclusion that the takings clause applies only to takings of specific property interests, such as interests in real property or interests in a particular identifiable fund of money; it does not apply to general obligations to pay money from whatever funds one possesses. Nonetheless, Justice Kennedy voted with the four-judge plurality to strike down the law under the due process clause, arguing that the problem with the law was not that it "took" property but its unfair retroactive nature. "If retroactive laws [of great severity] change the legal consequences of transactions long closed, the change can destroy the reasonable certainty and security which are the very objects of property ownership." *Id.* at 548-549. (Kennedy, J., concurring in the judgment and dissenting in part).

The four other dissenting judges believed that the *Coal Act* was not unfair retroactive legislation. Justice Stevens noted that, at the time Eastern was in business, there "was an implicit understanding on both sides of the bargaining table that the operators would provide the miners with lifetime health benefits," *Id.* at 551 (Stevens, J., dissenting). Subsequent legislation requiring an employer to honor this understanding would not result in any fundamental unfairness. Justice Breyer, joined by four Justices, argued that the *Coal Act* did not violate due process both because Eastern had led its employees to expect that it would take care of them and because it was not unfair to require Eastern to compensate its own workers for medical problems caused by their exposure to coal dust on the job. "Insofar as working conditions created a risk of future health problems for those miners, Eastern created those conditions." *Id.* at 560 (Breyer, J., dissenting).

§12.4.2.2 Forfeiture and the Innocent Owner

BENNIS v. MICHIGAN
516 U.S. 442 (1996)

Chief Justice WILLIAM REHNQUIST delivered the opinion of the Court.

Petitioner was a joint owner, with her husband, of an automobile in which her husband engaged in sexual activity with a prostitute. A Michigan court ordered the automobile forfeited as a public nuisance, with no offset for her interest, notwithstanding her lack of knowledge of her husband's activity. We hold that the Michigan court order did not offend the Due Process Clause of the Fourteenth Amendment or the Takings Clause of the Fifth Amendment.

Detroit police arrested John Bennis after observing him engaged in a sexual act with a prostitute in the automobile while it was parked on a Detroit city street. Bennis was convicted of gross indecency. The State then sued both Bennis and his wife, petitioner Tina B. Bennis, to have the car declared a public nuisance and abated as such under §§600.3801 and 600.3825 of Michigan's Compiled Laws.

Petitioner defended against the abatement of her interest in the car on the ground that, when she entrusted her husband to use the car, she did not know that he would use it to violate Michigan's indecency law. The Wayne County Circuit Court rejected this argument, declared the car a public nuisance, and ordered the car's abatement. In reaching this disposition, the trial court judge recognized the remedial discretion he had under Michigan's case law. He took into account the couple's ownership of "another automobile," so they would not be left "without transportation." He also mentioned his authority to order the payment of one-half of the sale proceeds, after the deduction of costs, to "the innocent co-title holder." He declined to order such a division of sale proceeds in this case because of the age and value of the car (an 11-year-old Pontiac sedan recently purchased by John and Tina Bennis for $600); he commented in this regard: "[T]here's practically nothing left minus costs in a situation such as this." . . .

The gravamen of petitioner's due process claim is . . . [that she] was entitled to contest the abatement by showing she did not know her husband would use it to violate Michigan's indecency law. But a long and unbroken line of cases holds that an owner's interest in property may be forfeited by reason of the use to which the property is put even though the owner did not know that it was to be put to such use.

Our earliest opinion to this effect is Justice Story's opinion for the Court in *The Palmyra*, 12 Wheat. 1, 6 L. Ed. 531 (1827). The Palmyra, which had been commissioned as a privateer by the King of Spain and had attacked a United States vessel, was captured by a United States war ship and brought into Charleston, South Carolina, for adjudication. On the Government's appeal from the Circuit Court's acquittal of the vessel, it was contended by the owner that the vessel could not be forfeited until he was convicted for the privateering. The Court rejected this contention, explaining: "The thing is here primarily considered as the offender, or rather the offence is attached primarily to the thing." *Id.*, at 14. . . .

In *Van Oster v. Kansas*, 272 U.S. 465 (1926), this Court upheld the forfeiture of a purchaser's interest in a car misused by the seller. Van Oster purchased an automobile from a dealer but agreed that the dealer might retain possession for use in its business. The dealer allowed an associate to use the automobile, and the associate used it for the illegal transportation of intoxicating liquor. The State brought a forfeiture action pursuant to a Kansas statute, and Van Oster defended on the ground that the transportation of the liquor in the car was without her knowledge or authority. This Court rejected Van Oster's claim:

> It is not unknown or indeed uncommon for the law to visit upon the owner of property the unpleasant consequences of the unauthorized action of one to whom he has entrusted it. . . . [C]ertain uses of property may be regarded as so undesirable that the owner surrenders his control at his peril. . . .

Id., at 467-468. . . .

Notwithstanding this well-established authority rejecting the innocent-owner defense, petitioner argues that we should in effect overrule it by importing a culpability requirement from cases having at best a tangential relation to the "innocent owner" doctrine in forfeiture cases. She cites *Foucha v. Louisiana*, 504 U.S. 71 (1992), for the proposition that a criminal defendant may not be punished for a crime if he is found to be not guilty. She also argues that our holding in *Austin v. United States*, 509 U.S. 602 (1993), that the Excessive Fines Clause limits the scope of civil forfeiture judgments, "would be difficult to reconcile with any rule allowing truly innocent persons to be punished by civil forfeiture."

In *Austin*, the Court held that because "forfeiture serves, at least in part, to punish the owner," forfeiture proceedings are subject to the limitations of the Eighth Amendment's prohibition against excessive fines. 509 U.S. at 618. In this case, . . . Michigan's Supreme Court emphasized with respect to the forfeiture proceeding at issue: "It is not contested that this is an equitable action," in which the trial judge has discretion to consider "alternatives [to] abating the entire interest in the vehicle." 527 N.W.2d, at 495.

In any event, . . . forfeiture also serves a deterrent purpose distinct from any punitive purpose. Forfeiture of property prevents illegal uses "both by preventing further illicit use of the [property] and by imposing an economic penalty, thereby rendering illegal behavior unprofitable." *Calero-Toledo v. Pearson Yacht Leasing Co.*, 416 U.S. 663, 687 (1974). This deterrent mechanism is hardly unique to forfeiture. For instance, because Michigan also deters dangerous driving by making a motor vehicle owner liable for the negligent operation of the vehicle by a driver who had the owner's consent to use it, petitioner was also potentially liable for her husband's use of the car in violation of Michigan negligence law. Mich. Comp. Laws Ann. §257.401 (1990). "The law thus builds a secondary defense against a forbidden use and precludes evasions by dispensing with the necessity of judicial inquiry as to collusion between the wrongdoer and the alleged innocent owner." *Van Oster*, 272 U.S., at 467-468.

Petitioner also claims that the forfeiture in this case was a taking of private property for public use in violation of the Takings Clause of the Fifth Amendment, made applicable to the States by the Fourteenth Amendment. But if the forfeiture proceeding here in question did not violate the Fourteenth Amendment, the property in the automobile was transferred by virtue of that proceeding from petitioner to the State. The government may not be required to compensate an owner for property which it has already lawfully acquired under the exercise of governmental authority other than the power of eminent domain. *United States v. Fuller*, 409 U.S. 488, 492 (1973). . . .

At bottom, petitioner's claims depend on an argument that the Michigan forfeiture statute is unfair because it relieves prosecutors from the burden of separating co-owners who are complicit in the wrongful use of property from innocent co-owners. This argument, in the abstract, has considerable appeal. . . . Its force is reduced in the instant case, however, by the Michigan Supreme Court's confirmation of the trial court's remedial discretion, and petitioner's recognition that Michigan may forfeit her and her husband's car whether or not she is entitled to an offset for her interest in it.

We conclude today, as we concluded 75 years ago, that the cases authorizing actions of the kind at issue are "too firmly fixed in the punitive and remedial jurisprudence of the country to be now displaced." The State here sought to deter illegal activity that contributes to neighborhood deterioration and unsafe streets. The Bennis automobile, it is conceded, facilitated and was used in criminal activity. Both the trial court and the Michigan Supreme Court followed our longstanding practice, and the judgment of the Supreme Court of Michigan is therefore affirmed.

Justice CLARENCE THOMAS, concurring....

As the Court notes, evasion of the normal requirement of proof before punishment might well seem "unfair." One unaware of the history of forfeiture laws and 200 years of this Court's precedent regarding such laws might well assume that such a scheme is lawless — a violation of due process....

This case is ultimately a reminder that the Federal Constitution does not prohibit everything that is intensely undesirable. As detailed in the Court's opinion and the cases cited therein, forfeiture of property without proof of the owner's wrongdoing, merely because it was "used" in or was an "instrumentality" of crime has been permitted in England and this country, both before and after the adoption of the Fifth and Fourteenth Amendments....

Improperly used, forfeiture could become more like a roulette wheel employed to raise revenue from innocent but hapless owners whose property is unforeseeably misused, or a tool wielded to punish those who associate with criminals, than a component of a system of justice. When the property sought to be forfeited has been entrusted by its owner to one who uses it for crime, however, the Constitution apparently assigns to the States and to the political branches of the Federal Government the primary responsibility for avoiding that result.

Justice RUTH BADER GINSBURG, concurring....

First, it bears emphasis that the car in question belonged to John Bennis as much as it did to Tina Bennis. At all times he had her consent to use the car, just as she had his. And it is uncontested that Michigan may forfeit the vehicle itself. The sole question, then, is whether Tina Bennis is entitled not to the car, but to a portion of the proceeds (if any there be after deduction of police, prosecutorial, and court costs) as a matter of constitutional right.

Second, it was "critical" to the judgment of the Michigan Supreme Court that the nuisance abatement proceeding is an "equitable action." That means the State's Supreme Court stands ready to police exorbitant applications of the statute. It shows no respect for Michigan's high court to attribute to its members tolerance of, or insensitivity to, inequitable administration of an "equitable action."

Nor is it fair to charge the trial court with "blatant unfairness" in the case at hand. That court declined to order a division of sale proceeds, as the trial judge took pains to explain, for two practical reasons: the Bennises have "another automobile," and the age and value of the forfeited car (an 11-year-old Pontiac purchased by John and Tina Bennis for $600) left "practically nothing" to divide after subtraction of costs.

Michigan, in short, has not embarked on an experiment to punish innocent third parties. Nor do we condone any such experiment. Michigan has decided to deter Johns from using cars they own (or co-own) to contribute to neighborhood blight, and that abatement endeavor hardly warrants this Court's disapprobation.

Justice JOHN PAUL STEVENS, with whom Justice SOUTER and Justice BREYER join, dissenting....

...I would reverse because petitioner is entirely without responsibility for [her husband's] act. Fundamental fairness prohibits the punishment of innocent people.

. . . In other contexts, we have regarded as axiomatic that persons cannot be punished when they have done no wrong. I would hold now what we have always assumed: that the principle is required by due process.

The unique facts of this case demonstrate that petitioner is entitled to the protection of that rule. . . . Without knowledge that he would commit such an act in the family car, or that he had ever done so previously, surely petitioner cannot be accused of failing to take "reasonable steps" to prevent the illicit behavior. She is just as blameless as if a thief, rather than her husband, had used the car in a criminal episode.

Forfeiture of an innocent owner's property that plays a central role in a criminal enterprise may be justified on reasoning comparable to the basis for imposing liability on a principal for an agent's torts. Just as the risk of *respondeat superior* liability encourages employers to supervise more closely their employees' conduct, so the risk of forfeiture encourages owners to exercise care in entrusting their property to others. But the law of agency recognizes limits on the imposition of vicarious liability in situations where no deterrent function is likely to be served; for example, it exonerates the employer when the agent strays from his intended mission and embarks on a "frolic of his own." In this case, petitioner did not "entrust" the car to her husband on the night in question; he was entitled to use it by virtue of their joint ownership. There is no reason to think that the threat of forfeiture will deter an individual from buying a car with her husband — or from marrying him in the first place — if she neither knows nor has reason to know that he plans to use it wrongfully. . . .

The absence of any deterrent value reinforces the punitive nature of this forfeiture law. But petitioner has done nothing that warrants punishment. She cannot be accused of negligence or of any other dereliction in allowing her husband to use the car for the wholly legitimate purpose of transporting himself to and from his job. She affirmatively alleged and proved that she is not in any way responsible for the conduct that gave rise to the seizure. If anything, she was a victim of that conduct. In my opinion, these facts establish that the seizure constituted an arbitrary deprivation of property without due process of law. . . .

Justice ANTHONY KENNEDY, dissenting.

The forfeiture of vessels pursuant to the admiralty and maritime law has a long, well-recognized tradition, evolving as it did from the necessity of finding some source of compensation for injuries done by a vessel whose responsible owners were often half a world away and beyond the practical reach of the law and its processes. The prospect of deriving prompt compensation from *in rem* forfeiture, and the impracticality of adjudicating the innocence of the owners or their good-faith efforts in finding a diligent and trustworthy master, combined to eliminate the owner's lack of culpability as a defense. . . .

This forfeiture cannot meet the requirements of due process. Nothing in the rationale of the Michigan Supreme Court indicates that the forfeiture turned on the negligence or complicity of petitioner, or a presumption thereof, and nothing supports the suggestion that the value of her co-ownership is so insignificant as to be beneath the law's protection.

For these reasons, and with all respect, I dissent.

NOTES AND QUESTIONS

Justice Ginsburg, who furnished the crucial fifth vote for the majority in *Bennis*, relied on the fact that the trial court had declined to order a division of sale proceeds because the Bennises have "another automobile" and because the low value of the car meant that there would be "practically nothing" to divide after subtraction of costs. Is this reasoning consistent with *Babbitt v. Youpee*? Can you reconcile the two cases? Note Justice Stevens's comment in *Bennis* that "the blatant unfairness of using petitioner's property to compensate for her husband's offense is not diminished by its modest value." If the cases are not consistent, which holding is preferable?

PROBLEMS

1. In *Keshbro, Inc. v. City of Miami*, 801 So.2d 864 (Fla. 2001), the Florida Supreme Court upheld the temporary closure of a motel that had been the site of numerous drug and prostitution offenses but overturned an order closing an apartment complex for one year when it had been the site of only two illegal drug sales. The court held that the city had taken the property of the apartment complex owner without just compensation because the illegal activity was not so pervasive as to constitute either a private or public nuisance. Did the court rule correctly? Is this result consistent with Bennis?

2. In *City of Seattle v. McCoy*, 4 P.3d 159 (Wash. Ct. App. 2000), the court found a regulatory taking when restaurant was temporarily closed as a drug nuisance when the owner had acted reasonably and done as much as possible to prevent the drug use. The court found a total taking under *Lucas* and that the nuisance exception to *Lucas* did not apply because it interpreted state law not to impose absolute liability for nuisance on an owner who took all reasonable steps to prevent illegal activity on the property. The court held that abatement of a business could not be based on illegal acts of business patrons when the owners were not aware of or involved in the illegal activity. Is this result consistent with *Bennis*? See also *State ex rel. Pizza v. Rezcallah*, 702 N.E.2d 81 (Ohio 1998) (state law requiring one year closing of innocent owner's property who acted reasonably to prevent drug use on the premise constitutes an unconstitutional taking of property without just compensation).

3. In *Department of Housing & Urban Development v. Rucker*, 535 U.S. 125 (2002), the Supreme Court interpreted a federal statute to allow eviction of innocent public housing tenants when members of their households have engaged in illegal drug use or sales on or off the housing site. *See* 42 U.S.C. §1437d(*l*)(6) (requiring public housing authorities to use leases that provide that "any drug-related criminal activity on or off such premises, engaged in by a public housing tenant, any member of the tenant's household, or any guest or other person under the tenant's control, shall be cause for termination of [the] tenancy"). *See also* 24 C.F.R. §966.4(e)(12). The Court found no constitutional problem with forfeiture of property owned by an innocent party even if that tenant had done everything possible to prevent family members from using or selling drugs on the ground that the government was acting as an owner-landlord placing conditions in the lease with which the tenants voluntarily concurred and not as a sovereign regulating the lease terms or punishing an innocent party because of the criminal acts of another. Is this holding consistent with the holdings in *Keshbro* and *McCoy*? Do you agree?

4. *Japanese American internment.* In World War II, the United States government forced some 120,000 Japanese American citizens into internment camps for up to four years. Although the Supreme Court upheld internment against constitutional claims as

mandated by military necessity, *see Korematsu v. United States*, 323 U.S. 214 (1944), Congress later found internment unwarranted and passed a statute in 1988 that provided for reparations for those affected. When a suit was brought against the United States for damages arising out of internment, one of the claims was that internment resulted in a taking of property without just compensation because individuals were excluded from their homes and businesses. Although the District Court for the District of Columbia originally found the claims timely, that ruling was later reversed by the Federal Circuit. *Hohri v. United States*, 847 F.2d 779 (Fed. Cir. 1988), *rev'g, Hohri v. United States*, 782 F.2d 227 (D.D.C. 1986).

Suppose the claim were timely and could be litigated today. The Supreme Court has held that there is no compensable taking when the government impinges on property rights during a military emergency. *United States v. Caltex*, 344 U.S. 149 (1952)(oil companies whose facilities were ordered destroyed by the army during wartime had no right to compensation). However, Congress determined that there was no legitimate military justification for the internment of Japanese American citizens in World War II. Moreover, the plaintiffs in *Hohri* argued that they had evidence that government wrongfully concealed information that would have demonstrated that internment was not warranted. Supposing these claims could be proven and the statute of limitations on suit had not run, do the internees have a takings claim against the United States?

§12.4.3 EXACTIONS AND LINKAGE REQUIREMENTS

DOLAN v. CITY OF TIGARD
512 U.S. 374 (1994)

Chief Justice WILLIAM REHNQUIST delivered the opinion of the Court. . . .

The State of Oregon enacted a comprehensive land use management program in 1973. Or. Rev. Stat. §§197.005-197.860 (1991). The program required all Oregon cities and counties to adopt new comprehensive land use plans that were consistent with the statewide planning goals. The plans are implemented by land use regulations which are part of an integrated hierarchy of legally binding goals, plans, and regulations. Pursuant to the State's requirements, the city of Tigard, a community of some 30,000 residents on the southwest edge of Portland, developed a comprehensive plan and codified it in its Community Development Code (CDC). The CDC requires property owners in the area zoned Central Business District to comply with a 15% open space and landscaping requirement, which limits total site coverage, including all structures and paved parking, to 85% of the parcel. After the completion of a transportation study that identified congestion in the Central Business District as a particular problem, the city adopted a plan for a pedestrian/bicycle pathway intended to encourage alternatives to automobile transportation for short trips. The CDC requires that new development facilitate this plan by dedicating land for pedestrian pathways where provided for in the pedestrian/bicycle pathway plan.

The city also adopted a Master Drainage Plan (Drainage Plan). The Drainage Plan noted that flooding occurred in several areas along Fanno Creek, including areas near petitioner's property. The Drainage Plan also established that the increase in impervious surfaces associated with continued urbanization would exacerbate these flooding problems. To combat these risks, the Drainage Plan suggested a series of improvements to the Fanno Creek Basin, including channel excavation in the area next to petitioner's property. Other recommendations included ensuring that the flood-plain remains free of structures and that it be preserved as greenways to minimize flood damage to structures. The Drainage Plan concluded that the cost of these improve-ments should be shared based on both direct and indirect benefits, with property owners along the waterways paying more due to the direct benefit that they would receive. . . .

Petitioner Florence Dolan owns a plumbing and electric supply store located on Main Street in the Central Business District of the city. The store covers approximately 9,700 square feet on the eastern side of a 1.67-acre parcel, which includes a gravel parking lot. Fanno Creek flows through the southwestern corner of the lot and along its western boundary. The year-round flow of the creek renders the area within the creek's 100-year floodplain virtually unusable for commercial development. The city's comprehensive plan includes the Fanno Creek floodplain as part of the city's greenway system.

Petitioner applied to the city for a permit to redevelop the site. Her proposed plans called for nearly doubling the size of the store to 17,000 square feet, and paving a 39-space parking lot. The existing store, located on the opposite side of the parcel, would be razed in sections as construction progressed on the new building. In the second phase of the project, petitioner proposed to build an additional structure on the northeast side of the site for complementary businesses, and to provide more parking. The proposed expansion and intensified use are consistent with the city's zoning scheme in the Central Business District.

The City Planning Commission granted petitioner's permit application subject to conditions imposed by the city's CDC. The CDC establishes the following standard for site development review approval: "Where landfill and/or development is allowed within and adjacent to the 100-year floodplain, the city shall require the dedication of sufficient open land area for greenway adjoining and within the floodplain. This area shall include portions at a suitable elevation for the construction of a pedestrian/bicycle pathway within the floodplain in accordance with the adopted pedestrian/bicycle plan." Thus, the Commission required that petitioner dedicate the portion of her property lying within the 100-year floodplain for improvement of a storm drainage system along Fanno Creek and that she dedicate an additional 15-foot strip of land adjacent to the floodplain as a pedestrian/bicycle pathway.

The dedication required by that condition encompasses approximately 7,000 square feet, or roughly 10% of the property. In accordance with city practice, petitioner could rely on the dedicated property to meet the 15% open space and landscaping requirement mandated by the city's zoning scheme. The city would bear the cost of maintaining a landscaped buffer between the dedicated area and the new store. . . .

The Commission made a series of findings concerning the relationship between the dedicated conditions and the projected impacts of petitioner's project. First, the Commission noted that "[i]t is reasonable to assume that customers and employees of the future uses of this site could utilize a pedestrian/bicycle pathway adjacent to this development for their transportation and recreational needs." The Commission noted that the site plan has provided for bicycle parking in a rack in front of the proposed building and "[i]t is reasonable to expect that some of the users of the bicycle parking provided for by the site plan will use the pathway adjacent to Fanno Creek if it is constructed." In addition, the Commission found that creation of a convenient, safe pedestrian/bicycle pathway system as an alternative means of transportation "could offset some of the traffic demand on [nearby] streets and lessen the increase in traffic congestion."

The Commission went on to note that the required floodplain dedication would be reasonably related to petitioner's request to intensify the use of the site given the increase in the impervious surface. The Commission stated that the "anticipated increased storm water flow from the subject property to an already strained creek and drainage basin can only add to the public need to manage the stream channel and floodplain for drainage purposes." Based on this anticipated increased storm water flow, the Commission concluded that "the requirement of dedication of the floodplain area on the site is related to the applicant's plan to intensify development on the site." The Tigard City Council approved the Commission's final order....

Petitioner appealed to the Land Use Board of Appeals (LUBA) on the ground that the city's dedication requirements were not related to the proposed development, and, therefore, those requirements constituted an uncompensated taking of their property under the Fifth Amendment. In evaluating the federal taking claim, LUBA assumed that the city's findings about the impacts of the proposed development were supported by substantial evidence. Given the undisputed fact that the proposed larger building and paved parking area would increase the amount of impervious surfaces and the runoff into Fanno Creek, LUBA concluded that "there is a 'reasonable relationship' between the proposed development and the requirement to dedicate land along Fanno Creek for a greenway." With respect to the pedestrian/bicycle pathway, LUBA noted the Commission's finding that a significantly larger retail sales building and parking lot would attract larger numbers of customers and employees and their vehicles. It again found a "reasonable relationship" between alleviating the impacts of increased traffic from the development and facilitating the provision of a pedestrian/bicycle pathway as an alternative means of transportation.

The Oregon Court of Appeals affirmed, ejecting petitioner's contention that in *Nollan v. California Coastal Comm'n*, 483 U.S. 825 (1987), we had abandoned the "reasonable relationship" test in favor of a stricter "essential nexus" test. The Oregon Supreme Court affirmed. The court also disagreed with petitioner's contention that the *Nollan* Court abandoned the "reasonably related" test. Instead, the court read *Nollan* to mean that an "exaction is reasonably related to an impact if the exaction serves the same purpose that a denial of the permit would serve." The court decided that both the pedestrian/bicycle pathway condition and the storm drainage dedication had an essential nexus to the development of the proposed site. Therefore, the court found the conditions to be reasonably related to the impact of the expansion of petitioner's business. We granted certiorari because of an alleged conflict between the Oregon Supreme Court's decision and our decision in *Nollan, supra*.

II

The Takings Clause of the Fifth Amendment of the United States Constitution, made applicable to the States through the Fourteenth Amendment, *Chicago, B. & Q. R. Co. v. Chicago*, 166 U.S. 226, 239 (1897), provides: "[N]or shall private property be taken for public use, without just compensation." One of the principal purposes of the Takings Clause is "to bar Government from forcing some people alone to bear public burdens which, in all fairness and justice, should be borne by the public as a whole." *Armstrong v. United States*, 364 U.S. 40, 49 (1960). Without question, had the city simply required petitioner to dedicate a strip of land along Fanno Creek for public use, rather than conditioning the grant of her permit to redevelop her property on such a dedication, a taking would have occurred. Such public access would deprive petitioner of the right to exclude others, "one of the most essential sticks in the bundle of rights that are commonly characterized as property." *Kaiser Aetna v. United States*, 444 U.S. 164, 176 (1979).

On the other side of the ledger, the authority of state and local governments to engage in land use planning has been sustained against constitutional challenge as long ago as our decision in *Euclid v. Ambler Realty Co.*, 272 U.S. 365 (1926). "Government hardly could go on if to some extent values incident to property could not be diminished without paying for every such change in the general law." *Pennsylvania Coal Co. v. Mahon*, 260 U.S. 393, 413 (1922). A land use regulation does not effect a taking if it "substantially advance[s] legitimate state interests" and does not "den[y] an owner economically viable use of his land." *Agins v. Tiburon*, 447 U.S. 255, 260 (1980).

The sort of land use regulations discussed in the cases just cited, however, differ in two relevant particulars from the present case. First, they involved essentially legislative determinations classifying entire areas of the city, whereas here the city made an adjudicative decision to condition petitioner's application for a building permit on an individual parcel. Second, the conditions imposed were not simply a limitation on the use petitioner might make of her own parcel, but a requirement that she deed portions of the property to the city. In *Nollan, supra*, we held that governmental authority to exact such a condition was circumscribed by the Fifth and Fourteenth Amendments. Under the well-settled doctrine of "unconstitutional conditions," the government may not require a person to give up a constitutional right — here the right to receive just compensation when property is taken for a public use — in exchange for a discretionary benefit conferred by the government where the property sought has little or no relationship to the benefit.

Petitioner contends that the city has forced her to choose between the building permit and her right under the Fifth Amendment to just compensation for the public easements. Petitioner does not quarrel with the city's authority to exact some forms of dedication as a condition for the grant of a building permit, but challenges the showing made by the city to justify these exactions. She argues that the city has identified "no special benefits" conferred on her, and has not identified any "special quantifiable burdens" created by her new store that would justify the particular dedications required from her which are not required from the public at large.

III

In evaluating petitioner's claim, we must first determine whether the "essential nexus" exists between the "legitimate state interest" and the permit condition exacted by the city. *Nollan*, 483 U.S. at 837. If we find that a nexus exists, we must then decide the required degree of connection between the exactions and the projected impact of the proposed development. We were not required to reach this question in *Nollan*, because we concluded that the connection did not meet even the loosest standard. Here, however, we must decide this question.

A

We addressed the essential nexus question in *Nollan*. The California Coastal Commission demanded a lateral public easement across the Nollans' beachfront lot in exchange for a permit to demolish an existing bungalow and replace it with a three-bedroom house. The public easement was designed to connect two public beaches that were separated by the Nollans' property. The Coastal Commission had asserted that the public easement condition was imposed to promote the legitimate state interest of diminishing the "blockage of the view of the ocean" caused by construction of the larger house.

We agreed that the Coastal Commission's concern with protecting visual access to the ocean constituted a legitimate public interest. We also agreed that the permit condition would have been constitutional "even if it consisted of the requirement that the Nollans provide a viewing spot on their property for passersby with whose sighting of the ocean their new house would interfere." 483 U.S. at 836. We resolved, however, that the Coastal Commission's regulatory authority was set completely adrift from its constitutional moorings when it claimed that a nexus existed between visual access to the ocean and a permit condition requiring lateral public access along the Nollans' beachfront lot. How enhancing the public's ability to "traverse to and along the shorefront" served the same governmental purpose of "visual access to the ocean" from the roadway was beyond our ability to countenance. The absence of a nexus left the Coastal Commission in the position of simply trying to obtain an easement through gimmickry, which converted a valid regulation of land use into "an out-and-out plan of extortion." *Id.*

No such gimmicks are associated with the permit conditions imposed by the city in this case. Undoubtedly, the prevention of flooding along Fanno Creek and the reduction of traffic congestion in the Central Business District qualify as the type of legitimate public purposes we have upheld. It seems equally obvious that a nexus exists between preventing flooding along Fanno Creek and limiting development within the creek's 100-year floodplain. Petitioner proposes to double the size of her retail store and to pave her now-gravel parking lot, thereby expanding the impervious surface on the property and increasing the amount of stormwater runoff into Fanno Creek.

The same may be said for the city's attempt to reduce traffic congestion by providing for alternative means of transportation. In theory, a pedestrian/bicycle pathway provides a useful alternative means of transportation for workers and shoppers. . . .

B. . .

The second part of our analysis requires us to determine whether the degree of the exactions demanded by the city's permit conditions bear the required relationship to the projected impact of petitioner's proposed development. *Nollan, supra,* 483 U.S., at 834, quoting *Penn Central,* 438 U.S. 104, 127 (1978) ("'[A] use restriction may constitute a taking if not reasonably necessary to the effectuation of a substantial government purpose'"). Here the Oregon Supreme Court deferred to what it termed the "city's unchallenged factual findings" supporting the dedication conditions and found them to be reasonably related to the impact of the expansion of petitioner's business.

The city required that petitioner dedicate "to the city as Greenway all portions of the site that fall within the existing 100-year floodplain [of Fanno Creek] . . . and all property 15 feet above [the floodplain] boundary." In addition, the city demanded that the retail store be designed so as not to intrude into the greenway area. The city relies on the Commission's rather tentative findings that increased stormwater flow from petitioner's property "can only add to the public need to manage the [floodplain] for drainage purposes" to support its conclusion that the "requirement of dedication of the floodplain area on the site is related to the applicant's plan to intensify development on the site."

The city made the following specific findings relevant to the pedestrian/bicycle pathway: "In addition, the proposed expanded use of this site is anticipated to generate additional vehicular traffic thereby increasing congestion on nearby collector and arterial streets. Creation of a convenient, safe pedestrian/bicycle pathway system as an alternative means of transportation could offset some of the traffic demand on these nearby streets and lessen the increase in traffic congestion."

The question for us is whether these findings are constitutionally sufficient to justify the conditions imposed by the city on petitioner's building permit. Since state courts have been dealing with this question a good deal longer than we have, we turn to representative decisions made by them.

In some States, very generalized statements as to the necessary connection between the required dedication and the proposed development seem to suffice. *See, e.g., Billings Properties, Inc. v. Yellowstone County,* 394 P.2d 182 (Mont. 1964); *Jenad, Inc. v. Scarsdale,* 218 N.E.2d 673 (N.Y. 1966). We think this standard is too lax to adequately protect petitioner's right to just compensation if her property is taken for a public purpose.

Other state courts require a very exacting correspondence, described as the "specifi[c] and uniquely attributable" test. The Supreme Court of Illinois first developed this test in *Pioneer Trust & Savings Bank v. Mount Prospect,* 176 N.E.2d 799, 802 (Ill. 1961). Under this standard, if the local government cannot demonstrate that its exaction is directly proportional to the specifically created need, the exaction becomes "a veiled exercise of the power of eminent domain and a confiscation of private property behind the defense of police regulations." 176 N.E.2d at 802. We do not think the Federal Constitution requires such exacting scrutiny, given the nature of the interests involved.

A number of state courts have taken an intermediate position, requiring the municipality to show a "reasonable relationship" between the required dedication and the impact of the proposed development. Typical is the Supreme Court of Nebraska's opinion in *Simpson v. North Platte,* 292 N.W.2d 297, 301 (Neb. 1980), where that court stated: "The distinction, therefore, which must be made between an appropriate exercise of the police power and an improper exercise of eminent domain is whether the requirement has some reasonable relationship or nexus to the use to which the property is being made or is merely being used as an excuse for taking property simply because at that particular moment the landowner is asking the city for some license or permit." Thus, the court held that a city may not require a property owner to dedicate private property for some future public use as a condition of obtaining a building permit when such future use is not "occasioned by the construction sought to be permitted." 292 N.W.2d at 302.

Some form of the reasonable relationship test has been adopted in many other jurisdictions. . . .

We think the "reasonable relationship" test adopted by a majority of the state courts is closer to the federal constitutional norm than either of those previously discussed. But we do not adopt it as such, partly because the term "reasonable relationship" seems confusingly similar to the term "rational basis" which describes the minimal level of scrutiny under the Equal Protection Clause of the Fourteenth Amendment. We think a term such as "rough proportionality" best encapsulates what we hold to be the requirement of the Fifth Amendment. No precise mathematical calculation is required, but the city must make some sort of individualized determination that the required dedication is related both in nature and extent to the impact of the proposed development.

. . . We turn now to analysis of whether the findings relied upon by the city here, first with respect to the floodplain easement, and second with respect to the pedestrian/ bicycle path, satisfied these requirements.

It is axiomatic that increasing the amount of impervious surface will increase the quantity and rate of storm-water flow from petitioner's property. Therefore, keeping the floodplain open and free from development would likely confine the pressures on Fanno Creek created by petitioner's development. In fact, because petitioner's property lies within the Central Business District, the Community Development Code already required that petitioner leave 15% of it as open space and the undeveloped floodplain would have nearly satisfied that requirement. But the city demanded more — it not only wanted petitioner not to build in the floodplain, but it also wanted petitioner's property along Fanno Creek for its Greenway system. The city has never said why a public greenway, as opposed to a private one, was required in the interest of flood control.

The difference to petitioner, of course, is the loss of her ability to exclude others. As we have noted, this right to exclude others is "one of the most essential sticks in the bundle of rights that are commonly characterized as property." *Kaiser Aetna*, 444 U.S., at 176. It is difficult to see why recreational visitors trampling along petitioner's floodplain easement are sufficiently related to the city's legitimate interest in reducing flooding problems along Fanno Creek, and the city has not attempted to make any individualized determination to support this part of its request.

The city contends that recreational easement along the Greenway is only ancillary to the city's chief purpose in controlling flood hazards. It further asserts that unlike the residential property at issue in *Nollan*, petitioner's property is commercial in character and therefore, her right to exclude others is compromised. The city maintains that "[t]here is nothing to suggest that preventing [petitioner] from prohibiting [the easements] will unreasonably impair the value of [her] property as a [retail store]." *Prune-Yard Shopping Center v. Robins*, 447 U.S. 74, 83 (1980).

Admittedly, petitioner wants to build a bigger store to attract members of the public to her property. She also wants, however, to be able to control the time and manner in which they enter. The recreational easement on the Greenway is different in character from the exercise of state-protected rights of free expression and petition that we permitted in *PruneYard*. In *PruneYard*, we held that a major private shopping center that attracted more than 25,000 daily patrons had to provide access to persons exercising their state constitutional rights to distribute pamphlets and ask passersby to sign their petitions. We based our decision, in part, on the fact that the shopping center "may restrict expressive activity by adopting time, place, and manner regulations that will minimize any interference with its commercial functions." *Id.*, at 83. By contrast, the city wants to impose a permanent recreational easement upon petitioner's property that borders Fanno Creek. Petitioner would lose all rights to regulate the time in which the public entered onto the Greenway, regardless of any interference it might pose with her retail store. Her right to exclude would not be regulated, it would be eviscerated.

If petitioner's proposed development had somehow encroached on existing greenway space in the city, it would have been reasonable to require petitioner to provide some alternative greenway space for the public either on her property or elsewhere. But that is not the case here. We conclude that the findings upon which the city relies do not show the required reasonable relationship between the floodplain easement and the petitioner's proposed new building.

With respect to the pedestrian/bicycle pathway, we have no doubt that the city was correct in finding that the larger retail sales facility proposed by petitioner will increase traffic on the streets of the Central Business District. The city estimates that the proposed development would generate roughly 435 additional trips per day. Dedications for streets, sidewalks, and other public ways are generally reasonable exactions to avoid excessive congestion from a proposed property use. But on the record before us, the city has not met its burden of demonstrating that the additional number of vehicle and bicycle trips generated by the petitioner's development reasonably relate to the city's requirement for a dedication of the pedestrian/bicycle pathway easement. The city simply found that the creation of the pathway "could offset some of the traffic demand . . . and lessen the increase in traffic congestion."

As Justice Peterson of the Supreme Court of Oregon explained in his dissenting opinion, however, "[t]he findings of fact that the bicycle pathway system '*could* offset some of the traffic demand' is a far cry from a finding that the bicycle pathway system *will*, or is *likely to*, offset some of the traffic demand." 854 P.2d, at 447 (emphasis in original). No precise mathematical calculation is required, but the city must make some effort to quantify its findings in support of the dedication for the pedestrian/bicycle pathway beyond the conclusory statement that it could offset some of the traffic demand generated. . . .

The judgment of the Supreme Court of Oregon is reversed, and the case is remanded for further proceedings consistent with this opinion.

Justice JOHN PAUL STEVENS, with whom Justice BLACKMUN and Justice GINSBURG join, dissenting. . . .

The Court is correct in concluding that the city may not attach arbitrary conditions to a building permit or to a variance even when it can rightfully deny the application outright. I also agree that state court decisions dealing with ordinances that govern municipal development plans provide useful guidance in a case of this kind. Yet the Court's description of the doctrinal underpinnings of its decision, the phrasing of its fledgling test of "rough proportionality," and the application of that test to this case run contrary to the traditional treatment of these cases and break considerable and unpropitious new ground. . . .

Candidly acknowledging the lack of federal precedent for its exercise in rulemaking, the Court purports to find guidance in 12 "representative" state court decisions. To do so is certainly appropriate. The state cases the Court consults, however, either fail to support or decidedly undermine the Court's conclusions in key respects. . . .

Not one of the state cases cited by the Court announces anything akin to a "rough proportionality" requirement. . . . Thus, although these state cases do lend support to the Court's reaffirmance of *Nollan*'s reasonable nexus requirement, the role the Court accords them in the announcement of its newly minted second phase of the constitutional inquiry is remarkably inventive.

In addition, the Court ignores the state courts' willingness to consider what the property owner gains from the exchange in question. The Supreme Court of Wisconsin, for example, found it significant that the village's approval of a proposed subdivision plat "enables the subdivider to profit financially by selling the subdivision lots as home-building sites and thus realizing a greater price than could have been obtained if he had sold his property as unplatted lands." *Jordan v. Village of Menomonee Falls*, 137 N.W.2d 442, 448 (Wis. 1965). The required dedication as a condition of that approval was permissible "[i]n return for this benefit." *Id.* In this case, moreover, Dolan's acceptance of the permit, with its attached conditions, would provide her with benefits that may well go beyond any advantage she gets from expanding her business. As the United States pointed out at oral argument, the improvement that the city's drainage plan contemplates would widen the channel and reinforce the slopes to increase the carrying capacity during serious floods, "confer[ring] considerable benefits on the property owners immediately adjacent to the creek." . . .

It is not merely state cases, but our own cases as well, that require the analysis to focus on the impact of the city's action on the entire parcel of private property. In *Penn Central Transportation Co. v. New York City*, 438 U.S. 104 (1978), we stated that takings jurisprudence "does not divide a single parcel into discrete segments and attempt to determine whether rights in a particular segment have been entirely abrogated." *Id.*, at 130-131. Instead, this Court focuses "both on the character of the action and on the nature and extent of the interference with rights in the parcel as a whole." *Id.* . . .

The Court's assurances that its "rough proportionality" test leaves ample room for cities to pursue the "commendable task of land use planning," even twice avowing that "[n]o precise mathematical calculation is required," are wanting given the result that test compels here. Under the Court's approach, a city must not only "quantify its findings," and make "individualized determination[s]" with respect to the nature and the extent of the relationship between the conditions and the impact, but also demonstrate "proportionality." The correct inquiry should instead concentrate on whether the required nexus is present and venture beyond considerations of a condition's nature or germaneness only if the developer establishes that a concededly germane condition is so grossly disproportionate to the proposed development's adverse effects that it manifests motives other than land use regulation on the part of the city. . . .

Applying its new standard, the Court finds two defects in the city's case. First, while the record would adequately support a requirement that Dolan maintain the portion of the floodplain on her property as undeveloped open space, it does not support the additional requirement that the floodplain be dedicated to the city. Second, while the city adequately established the traffic increase that the proposed development would generate, it failed to quantify the offsetting decrease in automobile traffic that the bike path will produce. Even under the Court's new rule, both defects are, at most, nothing more than harmless error.

In her objections to the floodplain condition, Dolan made no effort to demonstrate that the dedication of that portion of her property would be any more onerous than a simple prohibition against any development on that portion of her property. Given the commercial character of both the existing and the proposed use of the property as a retail store, it seems likely that potential customers "trampling along petitioner's floodplain," are more valuable than a useless parcel of vacant land. Moreover, the duty to pay taxes and the responsibility for potential tort liability may well make ownership of the fee interest in useless land a liability rather than an asset. That may explain why Dolan never conceded that she could be prevented from building on the floodplain. The City Attorney also pointed out that absent a dedication, property owners would be required to "build on their own land" and "with their own money" a storage facility for the water runoff. Dolan apparently "did have that option," but chose not to seek it. If Dolan might have been entitled to a variance confining the city's condition in a manner this Court would accept, her failure to seek that narrower form of relief at any stage of the state administrative and judicial proceedings clearly should preclude that relief in this Court now.

The Court's rejection of the bike path condition amounts to nothing more than a play on words. Everyone agrees that the bike path "could" offset some of the increased traffic flow that the larger store will generate, but the findings do not unequivocally state that it will do so, or tell us just how many cyclists will replace motorists. Predictions on such matters are inherently nothing more than estimates. Certainly the assumption that there will be an offsetting benefit here is entirely reasonable and should suffice whether it amounts to 100 percent, 35 percent, or only 5 percent of the increase in automobile traffic that would otherwise occur. If the Court proposes to have the federal judiciary micro-manage state decisions of this kind, it is indeed extending its welcome mat to a significant new class of litigants. Although there is no reason to believe that state courts have failed to rise to the task, property owners have surely found a new friend today. . . .

Justice DAVID SOUTER, dissenting.

This case, like *Nollan v. California Coastal Comm'n*, 483 U.S. 825 (1987), invites the Court to examine the relationship between conditions imposed by development permits, requiring landowners to dedicate portions of their land for use by the public, and governmental interests in mitigating the adverse effects of such development. *Nollan* declared the need for a nexus between the nature of an exaction of an interest in land (a beach easement) and the nature of governmental interests. The Court treats this case as raising a further question, not about the nature, but about the degree, of connection required between such an exaction and the adverse effects of development. The Court's opinion announces a test to address this question, but as I read the opinion, the Court does not apply that test to these facts, which do not raise the question the Court addresses.

First, as to the floodplain and Greenway, the Court acknowledges that an easement of this land for open space (and presumably including the five feet required for needed creek channel improvements) is reasonably related to flood control, but argues that the "permanent recreational easement" for the public on the Greenway is not so related. If that is so, it is not because of any lack of proportionality between permit condition and adverse effect, but because of a lack of any rational connection at all between exaction of a public recreational area and the governmental interest in providing for the effect of increased water runoff. That is merely an application of *Nollan*'s nexus analysis. As the Court notes, "[i]f petitioner's proposed development had somehow encroached on existing greenway space in the city, it would have been reasonable to require petitioner to provide some alternative greenway space for the public." But that, of course, was not the fact, and the city of Tigard never sought to justify the public access portion of the dedication as related to flood control. It merely argued that whatever recreational uses were made of the bicycle path and the one foot edge on either side, were incidental to the permit condition requiring dedication of the 15-foot easement for an 8-foot-wide bicycle path and for flood control, including open space requirements and relocation of the bank of the river by some five feet. It seems to me such incidental recreational use can stand or fall with the bicycle path, which the city justified by reference to traffic congestion. As to the relationship the Court examines, between the recreational easement and a purpose never put forth as a justification by the city, the Court unsurprisingly finds a recreation area to be unrelated to flood control.

Second, as to the bicycle path, the Court again acknowledges the "theor [etically]" reasonable relationship between "the city's attempt to reduce traffic congestion by providing [a bicycle path] for alternative means of transportation," and the "correct" finding of the city that "the larger retail sales facility proposed by petitioner will increase traffic on the streets of the Central Business District." The Court only faults the city for saying that the bicycle path "could" rather than "would" offset the increased traffic from the store. That again, as far as I can tell, is an application of *Nollan*, for the Court holds that the stated connection ("could offset") between traffic congestion and bicycle paths is too tenuous; only if the bicycle path "would" offset the increased traffic by some amount, could the bicycle path be said to be related to the city's legitimate interest in reducing traffic congestion.

I cannot agree that the application of *Nollan* is a sound one here, since it appears that the Court has placed the burden of producing evidence of relationship on the city, despite the usual rule in cases involving the police power that the government is presumed to have acted constitutionally. Having thus assigned the burden, the Court concludes that the City loses based on one word ("could" instead of "would"), and despite the fact that this record shows the connection the Court looks for. Dolan has put forward no evidence that the burden of granting a dedication for the bicycle path is unrelated in kind to the anticipated increase in traffic congestion, nor, if there exists a requirement that the relationship be related in degree, has Dolan shown that the exaction fails any such test. The city, by contrast, calculated the increased traffic flow that would result from Dolan's proposed development to be 435 trips per day, and its Comprehensive Plan, applied here, relied on studies showing the link between alternative modes of transportation, including bicycle paths, and reduced street traffic congestion. *Nollan*, therefore, is satisfied, and on that assumption the city's conditions should not be held to fail a further rough proportionality test or any other that might be devised to give meaning to the constitutional limits. As Members of this Court have said before, "the common zoning regulations requiring subdividers to . . . dedicate certain areas to public streets, are in accord with our constitutional traditions because the proposed property use would otherwise be the cause of excessive congestion." *Pennell v. San Jose*, 485 U.S. 1, 20 (1988) (Scalia, J., concurring in part and dissenting in part). The bicycle path permit condition is fundamentally no different from these. . . .

NOTES AND QUESTIONS

1. *Linkage ordinances.* In recent years, many municipalities have enacted amendments to their zoning ordinances requiring certain developers of commercial property and/or residential housing either to directly provide low-income housing or child care facilities or to pay a fee that is devoted to a fund for these purposes. The theory behind low-income housing linkage is that new construction exacerbates local shortages in low-income housing by increasing employment, and therefore the demand for housing, in the locality. Since the increased demand is not entirely met by new construction, competition for existing housing both raises rents and pushes out lower-income tenants. It is not profitable to build low-income housing in the absence of governmental subsidies since poor persons cannot afford to pay even the minimum costs for housing; for this reason, the market does not respond to housing shortages by constructing new low-income housing. New development is therefore thought to increase

homelessness or to push low-income persons out of the city or into undesirable neighborhoods.

Child care linkage packages are intended to address the market's inadequate response to the increase in women in the work force and the shortage of affordable child care. Increased development puts pressure on existing child care facilities, again by increasing demand and raising prices. Lower-income persons may not earn enough to afford child care when placed in competition with new workers.

In both cases, development is thought to create externalities — exacerbating the shortages in both low-income housing and affordable child care services. Linkage programs are intended to internalize these costs by requiring developers to account to the community for those externalities by helping to alleviate the pressure on housing and child care caused by their development programs. Will these programs survive *Nollan* and *Dolan*?

2. *Impact fees.* Some courts have held that the holdings in *Nollan* and *Dolan* do not apply to impact fees at all because both cases involved required dedications of land. *Garneau v. City of Seattle*, 147 F.3d 802 (9th Cir. 1998); *Blue Jeans Equities West v. City & County of San Francisco*, 4 Cal. Rptr. 2d 114 (Ct. App. 1992). This approach finds strong support in dicta in recent decisions in *Lingle v. Chevron U.S.A. Inc.*, 2005 U.S. LEXIS 4342, *16 (U.S. 2005) and *City of Monterey v. Del Monte Dunes at Monterey, Ltd.*, 526 U.S. 687 (1999), both of which characterize the rulings in *Nollan* and *Dolan* as applying to "land-use decisions conditioning approval of development on the dedication of property to public use," *City of Monterey*, 526 U.S. at 702-703. *Accord, Lingle, supra* at *35- 36. This interpretation of *Nollan* and *Dolan* would mean that the nexus test applies only when the government action being demanded of the property owner is independently an unconstitutional taking of property; forcing an owner to dedicate land to the public or to grant the public an easement over the owner's land is a *per se* taking of property rights (unless it fits in an exception to this rule) and the Supreme Court has strongly suggested that this is what triggering the nexus test in *Nollan* and the "rough proportionality" test in *Dolan*. However, most lower courts have applied the *Nollan-Dolan* test to monetary exactions. *Erlich v. Culver City*, 911 P.2d 429 (Cal. 1996); *Benchmark Land Co. v. City of Battle Ground*, 14 P.3d 172 (Wash. Ct. App. 2000).

3. *Legislation or adjudication.* If the *Nollan-Dolan* test applies to monetary linkage requirements, a further question is whether the *Nollan-Dolan* test applies only to individualized decisions rather than general legislative judgments. In both *Nollan* and *Dolan*, a government agency made an individualized determination that a particular owner had an obligation to dedicate a particular amount of land to the city. There was no regulatory law requiring all owners to engage in similar dedications; rather, both cases involved individualized determinations more akin to adjudications. A linkage law differs from the particularized determinations at issue in *Nollan* and *Dolan* because it represents a general regulatory law affecting many or all parcels of land in an area. It may therefore create an "average reciprocity of advantage" like a general zoning law rather than an expropriation of property from an individual owner that is out of proportion to any harms caused by that owner.

Some courts have held that it is sufficient for a city to a general determination that particular types of development have particular impacts and impose fees reasonably related to those impacts. For example, a city might commission a study that demonstrates that new commercial development increases the need for housing and this need increases demand on the existing housing supply, bidding up prices and pushing out low-income families who cannot find affordable housing because the market does not find it profitable to build low-income housing. *Commercial Builders of Northern California v. City of Sacramento,* 941 F.2d 872 (9th Cir. 1991) (upholding a linkage fee for construction of low-income housing); *San Remo Hotel L.P. v. City and County of San Francisco,* 41 P.3d 87, 102-103 (Cal. 2002), *aff'd on other grounds,* 2005 U.S. LEXIS 4848 (June 20, 2005) (*Nollan-Dolan* test applies to a housing replacement fee that is determined on an ad hoc or individualized or "adjudicative" basis but not to general legislatively determined fees); *Home Builders Ass'n of Dayton & Miami Valley v. City of Beaver Creek,* 729 N.E.2d 349, 2000 Ohio 115 (Ohio 2000) (upholding legislatively determined impact fee under *Nollan/Dolan* test); *Holmdel Builders Association v. Holmdel,* 583 A.2d 277 (N.J. 1990) (upholding inclusionary zoning requirements on the ground that "[w]e find a sound basis to support a legislative judgment that there is a reasonable relationship between unrestrained nonresidential development and the need for affordable residential development").

Other courts have disagreed, noting that, because *Dolan* requires individualized determinations that impact fees bear a "rough proportionality" to the externalities of the development, this might not be sufficient and studies might have to be conducted for each parcel subjected to the exaction. They have struck down impact fees that could not be shown to be related to the particular impacts of the development of particular parcels of land. *See Volusia County v. Aberdeen at Ormond Beach, L.P.,* 760 So.2d 126 (Fla. 2000) (uniform impact fee to fund schools was unconstitutional as applied to mobile home park only open to persons over 55); *San Telmo Associates v. City of Seattle,* 735 P.2d 673 (Wash. 1987) (striking down an ordinance that prohibited owners from demolishing low-income housing and converting it to nonresidential use unless they made relocation assistance payments to tenants and replaced a specified percentage of the low-income housing lost with other suitable housing). *Cf. San Remo Hotel, supra* (finding the ordinance to be constitutional on its face because the housing replacement fee bore a reasonable relationship to the loss of housing in the great majority of cases but also entertaining a claim that the fee as applied to the property in the case did not bear a reasonable relationship to the housing lost from the conversion).

4. *Government benefits.* In *Ruckelshaus v. Monsanto Co.,* 467 U.S. 986 (1984), the Supreme Court held that the takings clause was not violated by a federal law requiring that businesses applying for government permission to use an insecticide disclose trade secrets to the government and consent to government use and disclosure of those trade secrets. *But see Philip Morris, Inc. v. Reilly,* 312 F.3d 24 (1st Cir. 2002) (state law requirement company disclosure of ingredients used in tobacco products is an unconstitutional taking of the company's property in its trade secrets). In a footnote in *Nollan,* Justice Scalia distinguished *Monsanto* by arguing that a right to register and sell an insecticide was a "valuable government benefit" and not an established property right, whereas the "right to build on one's own property — even though its exercise can be subjected to legitimate permitting requirements — cannot remotely be described as a 'government benefit.'" *Nollan,* 483 U.S. at 833 n.2. Thus, Justice Scalia concluded, the "announcement that the application for (or granting of) the permit will entail the yielding of a property interest cannot be regarded as establishing the voluntary 'exchange,' that we found to have occurred in *Monsanto.*" *Id.* Justice Brennan disagreed, arguing that *Nollan* was indistinguishable from *Monsanto,* 483 U.S. at 860 n.10:

> Both Monsanto and the Nollans hold property whose use is subject to regulation; Monsanto may not sell its property without obtaining government approval and the

Nollans may not build new development on their property without government approval. Obtaining such approval is as much a "government benefit" for the Nollans as it is for Monsanto. If the Court is somehow suggesting that "the right to build on one's own property" has some privileged natural rights status, the argument is a curious one. By any traditional labor theory of value justification for property rights, . . . *See, e.g.*, J. Locke, *The Second Treatise of Civil Government* 15-26 (1947 ed.), Monsanto would have a superior claim, for the chemical formulae which constitute its property only came into being by virtue of Monsanto's efforts.

In *Wyman v. James*, 400 U.S. 309 (1971), the Supreme Court held that the fourth amendment's prohibition against unreasonable searches and seizures was not violated by a New York law requiring that welfare recipients agree, as a condition of receiving benefits, to home inspections. The Court concluded that the home visits were not coerced because the family could avoid them by declining to agree to accept welfare benefits. Compare this conclusion with Justice Scalia's suggestion in *Nollan* that the state law conditioning the building permit on the owner's granting an easement to the public was coercive and an "out-and-out plan of extortion." Suppose Barbara James, the public assistance recipient in *Wyman*, had characterized the home visits as a taking of her property rights rather than a violation of the fourth amendment. Is *Wyman* covered by *Monsanto* or by the *Nollan/Dolan* line of cases? Note that while Justices Scalia and Rehnquist would certainly view welfare as a "government benefit" rather than a vested property right, the condition in *Wyman* is a physical invasion of property (the home visit), although not a permanent easement of access. Consider further than the "permanent" invasion of the cable box in *Loretto* was required by law only so long as the property was held for residential rental purposes. Is greater coercion involved in *Wyman* or in *Dolan*? Is the intrusion greater in *Wyman* or in *Loretto*? Can you reconcile all these cases?

PROBLEMS

1. In *Town of Flower Mound v. Stafford Estates Ltd. Partn.*, 135 S.W.3d 620 (Tex. 2004), the town conditioned its approval of a subdivision development on the developer's paying to rebuild an abutting road. The developer built the subdivision and the rebuilt the road and then sued the town to recover the cost of the road construction. When the court found that the improvements were "not necessary to accommodate the impact of the subdivision," *id.* at 622, it held the condition to violate the takings clause. The case differed from *Nollan* and *Dolan* because it did not require a dedication of land or an easement to the public; it did require a private developer to rebuild a public road. The Supreme Court has recently described the holdings in *Nollan* and *Dolan* as applying to "land-use decisions conditioning approval of development on the dedication of property to public use," *City of Monterey*, 526 U.S. at 702-703. *Accord, Lingle, supra* at *33 ("*Nollan* and *Dolan* involved . . . government demands that a landowner dedicate an easement allowing public access to her property as a condition of obtaining a development permit"). The Texas Supreme Court explained, *id.* at 639-640, that "[f]or purposes of determining whether an exaction as a condition of government approval of development is a compensable taking, we see no important distinction between a dedication of property to the public and a requirement that

property already owned by the public be improved. The *Dolan* standard should apply to both." Was *Flower Mound* correctly decided?

2. In *Home Builders Ass'n of Northern California v. City of Napa*, 108 Cal. Rptr. 2d 60 (Ct. App. 2001), the court upheld a city's inclusionary zoning law against the claim that it violated the takings clause when it required 10 percent of all newly constructed residential units to be "affordable." What are the arguments on both sides of this question and who should have won the case?

3. In *San Remo Hotel L.P. v. City and County of San Francisco*, 41 P.3d 87, 102-103 (Cal. 2002), *aff'd on other grounds*, 2005 U.S. LEXIS 4848 (June 20, 2005), the California Supreme Court upheld against a takings challenge the application of an ordinance that required the San Remo Hotel in San Francisco to pay a $567,000 fee for converting rooms that had been rented to longer term residents to rooms for tourists (with stays of seven days or less) and daily renters. The ordinance prohibited the conversion of residential hotels to tourist hotels without replacing the lost units on a one-for-one basis or paying a fee to the city to allow it to replace the lost units. The ordinance was intended to "benefit the general public by minimizing adverse impact on the housing supply and on displaced low income, elderly, and disabled persons resulting form the loss of residential hotel units through their conversion and demolition." It was accompanied by findings that the city had recently lost thousands of such units, that many low income, elderly and disabled persons reside in such units, and these conversions had created a low-income housing "emergency" in San Francisco.

Upholding the law against a takings claim, Justice Kathryn Mickle Werdegar wrote for the court that the ordinance was not subject to *Nollan-Dolan* analysis because it constituted generally applicable legislation with set terms that gave owners the choice of one-to-one replacement of converted units or payment of a legislatively determined fee to offset the costs of the lost units. *Id.* at 102-103. She further noted that the taking of money is always treated differently under the takings clause because all taxes constitute takings of money and the courts defer to legislative determinations of appropriate taxes. *Id.* at 106. She finally noted that the majority found that, even if the *Nollan-Dolan* test applied, the law would be constitutional because "the housing replacement fees bear a reasonable relationship to loss of housing." *Id.* at 107.

Justice Janice Rogers Brown wrote a blistering dissent, *id.* at 120-128.

> Americans are a diverse group of hard-working, confident, and creative people molded into a nation not by common ethnic identity, cultural legacy, or history; rather, Americans have been united by a dream — a dream of freedom, a vision of how free people might live. The dream has a history. The idea that property ownership is the essential prerequisite of liberty has long been "a fundamental tenet of Anglo-American constitutional thought." (Ely, *The Guardian of Every Other Right* (1998) p. 43.) "Indeed, the framers saw property ownership as a buffer protecting individuals from government coercion. Arbitrary redistribution of property destroyed liberty, and thus the framers hoped to restrain attacks on property rights." (*Ibid.*) "Property must be secured, or liberty cannot exist" (Adams, *A Balanced Government* (1790) *in Discourses on Davila* (1805), *reprinted in* 6 *The Works of John Adams* (1851 ed.) p. 280), because property and liberty are, upon examination, one and the same thing.
>
> Private property is in essence a cluster of rights inuring to the benefit of the owner, freely exchangeable in accordance with the terms of private agreements, and recognized and protected by common consent. In the case of real property, this cluster of rights includes the right to exclude persons from certain physical space. In the case of intellectual property, it may include the right to employ a valuable method or process to the exclusion

of others. In other words, private property represents zones of individual sovereignty — regions of autonomy within which we make our own choices.

But private property, already an endangered species in California, is now entirely extinct in San Francisco. The City and County of San Francisco has implemented a neo-feudal regime where the nominal owner of property must use that property according to the preferences of the majorities that prevail in the political process or, worse, the political powerbrokers who often control the government independently of majoritarian preferences. Thus, "the lamb [has been] committed to the custody of the wolf." (6 *The Works of John Adams, supra,* at p. 280.) San Francisco has redefined the American dream. Where once government was closely constrained to increase the freedom of individuals, now property ownership is closely constrained to increase the power of government. Where once government was a necessary evil because it protected private property, now private property is a necessary evil because it funds government programs. . . .

. . . The [ordinance] places the burden of providing low-income housing disproportionately on a relatively small group of hotel owners. These hotel owners certainly did not cause poverty in San Francisco; indeed, for a long time they voluntarily helped relieve the problem by leasing some or all of their rooms on a long-term basis to low-income residents. But as the economy of the City shifted, this residential use of their hotel rooms became increasingly unprofitable, and hotel owners began to abandon the residential rental business. It was then that the City, facing constitutional constraints on taxation and other sources of revenue, began to see the hotel owners as the most convenient — if not the most equitable — off-budget solution to its housing problems. If the City were devising a tax that would subsidize low-cost housing, I strongly doubt it would limit its tax to the owners of a few hundred residence hotels, but in the often surreal world of political expedience, these ill-fated business people were ordered to use their property for the benefit of the poor, thereby greatly depressing the market value of that property. . . .

The express purpose of the [ordinance] was to preserve the City's stock of low-income residential housing by requiring hotel owners to continue leasing their rooms as residences, or to replace those residential units if they chose to convert the rooms to tourist use. Obviously, the [ordinance] is facially unconstitutional. If a person took my car and asked a ransom for its return, he or she would be guilty of theft. But what if the City, seeking to provide transportation to the poor, orders me to operate an informal carpool, or if I prefer, to buy the City a replacement car? When presented with a similar hypothetical at oral argument, the San Francisco City Attorney declared such a rule a mere "regulation of use." I disagree. The essence of private property is the right to use that property as one sees fit and for one's own advantage. The police power permits the government to regulate that use so as to promote health, safety, and the general welfare, but it does not permit the government to achieve its social agenda by ordering a political minority to dedicate its property to the benefit of a group the government wishes to favor. [S]uch a regulation amounts, in practical effect, to a transfer of title and requires the government to pay its way. . . .

. . . This is *not* a tough case. Here, property unquestionably has been taken. No matter the analysis, the facts of this case come down to one thing — the City and County of San Francisco has expropriated the property and resources of a few hundred hotel owners in order to ameliorate — off budget and out of sight of the taxpayer — its housing shortage. In short, this ordinance is not a matter of efficiently organizing the uses of private property for the common advantage; instead, it is expressly designed to shift wealth from one group to another by the raw exercise of political power, and as such, it is a per se taking requiring compensation.

The majority rejects the legal theories on which the property owners have proceeded, but it fails to confront the more basic issue that prefigures all others: the City has replaced taxation and the provision of public services with a regulation that orders certain people to use their private property to do the government's work. . . .

... [P]roperty owners, given a choice, will prefer to own property in a community having appropriate and mutually beneficial regulations, because such property has greater value by reason of the regulation. Accordingly, regulatory authority is not inherently confiscatory in all cases.

But the corollary of this rule — one I think is implicit in the takings clause of the state Constitution — is that a regulation *is* a taking if, rather than promoting "an average reciprocity of advantage," it is merely designed to benefit one class of citizens at the expense of another; that is, if it simply shifts wealth by a raw act of government power. The government, in that case, has deprived the property owner of a right associated with his property, shifting that right to another party, but it has in no sense compensated the owner by enhancing, in some real way, the value of the rights the owner has retained.

In short, it might be perfectly legitimate for the City to help the low-income residents of San Francisco, but it may not do so at the expense of some small class of persons simply by legislating a transfer of property rights....

Nor can the HCO be justified under the theory that the City is merely requiring property owners to continue the existing use of their property. Such a rule would punish a property holder for using property in a way that proved popular. Moreover, it fails to recognize the effect of shifting economic conditions and therefore locks property into unproductive uses. But most important, such a rule represents a dedication of property rights to the public, and in all fairness the public should have to pay for these rights, just as a private party would....

Here, the City has essentially said to 500 unlucky hotel owners: We lack the public funds to fill the need for affordable housing in San Francisco, so you should solve the problem for us by using your hotels to house poor people. The City might as well have ordered the owners of small grocery stores to give away food at cost. The federal takings clause "bar[s] Government from forcing some people alone to bear public burdens which, in all fairness and justice, should be borne by the public as a whole." *Armstrong v. United States*, 364 U.S. 40, 49 (1960). I believe the same principle underlies our state takings clause. Accordingly, I would find the HCO facially unconstitutional....

Once again a majority of this court has proved that "If enough people get together and act in concert, they can take something and not pay for it." *Landgate, Inc. v. California Coastal Com.*, 953 P.2d 1188, 1207 n.1 (Cal. 1998) (dis. opn. of Brown, J.), *quoting* O'Rourke, Parliament of Whores 232 (1991). But theft is still theft. Theft is theft even when the government approves of the thievery. Turning a democracy into a kleptocracy does not enhance the stature of the thieves; it only diminishes the legitimacy of the government. Like Justice Rehnquist, I "see no reason why [constitutional protections of property rights] should be relegated to the status of a poor relation." The right to express one's individuality and essential human dignity through the free use of property is just as important as the right to do so through speech, the press, or the free exercise of religion. Nevertheless, the property right is now — in California, at least — a hollow one....

What do you think? Does the San Francisco ordinance violate the takings clause?

§12.5 *Just Compensation*

ALMOTA FARMERS ELEVATOR & WAREHOUSE v. UNITED STATES
409 U.S. 470 (1972)

Mr. Justice POTTER STEWART delivered the opinion of the Court.

Since 1919 the petitioner, Almota Farmers Elevator & Warehouse Co., has conducted grain elevator operations on land adjacent to the tracks of the Oregon-Washington Railroad and Navigation Company in the State of Washington. It has occupied the land under a series of successive leases from the railroad. In 1967, the Government instituted this eminent domain proceeding to acquire the petitioner's property interest by condemnation. At that time there were extensive buildings and other improvements that had been erected on the land by the petitioner, and the then current lease had 7½ years to run.

In the District Court the Government contended that just compensation for the leasehold interest, including the structures, should be "the fair market value of the legal rights possessed by the defendant by virtue of the lease as of the date of taking," and that no consideration should be given to any additional value based on the expectation that the lease might be renewed. The petitioner urged that, rather than this technical "legal rights theory," just compensation should be measured by what a willing buyer would pay in an open market for the petitioner's leasehold.

As a practical matter, the controversy centered upon the valuation to be placed upon the structures and their appurtenances. The parties stipulated that the Government had no need for these improvements and that the petitioner had a right to remove them. But that stipulation afforded the petitioner only what scant salvage value the buildings might bring. The Government offered compensation for the loss of the use and occupancy of the buildings only over the remaining term of the lease. The petitioner contended that this limitation upon compensation for the use of the structures would fail to award what a willing buyer would have paid for the lease with the improvements, since such a buyer would expect to have the lease renewed and to continue to use the improvements in place. The value of the buildings, machinery, and equipment in place would be substantially greater than their salvage value at the end of the lease term, and a purchaser in an open market would pay for the anticipated use of the buildings and for the savings he would realize from not having to construct new improvements himself. In sum, the dispute concerned whether Almota would have to be satisfied with its right to remove the structures with their consequent salvage value or whether it was entitled to an award reflecting the value of the improvements in place beyond the lease term. . . .

The Fifth Amendment provides that private property shall not be taken for public use without "just compensation." "And 'just compensation' means the full monetary equivalent of the property taken. The owner is to be put in the same position monetarily as he would have occupied if his property had not been taken." *United States v. Reynolds*, 397 U.S. 14, 16 (1970). To determine such monetary equivalence, the Court early established the concept of "market value": the owner is entitled to the fair market value of his property at the time of the taking. And this value is normally to be ascertained from "what a willing buyer would pay in cash to a willing seller."

By failing to value the improvements in place over their useful life — taking into account the possibility that the lease might be renewed as well as the possibility that it might not — the Court of Appeals in this case failed to recognize what a willing buyer would have paid for the improvements. If there had been no condemnation, Almota would have continued to use the improvements during a renewed lease term, or if it sold the improvements to the fee owner or to a new lessee at the end of the lease term, it would have been compensated for the buyer's ability to use the improvements in place over their useful life. As Judge Friendly wrote for the Court of Appeals for the Second Circuit:

Lessors do desire, after all, to keep their properties leased, and an existing tenant usually has the inside track to a renewal for all kinds of reasons — avoidance of costly alterations, saving of brokerage commissions, perhaps even ordinary decency on the part of landlords. Thus, even when the lease has expired, the condemnation will often force the tenant to remove or abandon the fixtures long before he would otherwise have had to, as well as deprive him of the opportunity to deal with the landlord or a new tenant — the only two people for whom the fixtures would have a value unaffected by the heavy costs of disassembly and reassembly. The condemnor is not entitled to the benefit of assumptions, contrary to common experience, that the fixtures would be removed at the expiration of the stated term. *United States v. Certain Property, Borough of Manhattan,* 388 F.2d 596, 601-602 (2d Cir. 1967).

It seems particularly likely in this case that Almota could have sold the leasehold at a price that would have reflected the continued ability of the buyer to use the improvements over their useful life. Almota had an unbroken succession of leases since 1919, and it was in the interest of the railroad, as fee owner, to continue leasing the property, with its grain elevator facilities, in order to promote grain shipments over its lines. In a free market, Almota would hardly have sold the leasehold to a purchaser who paid only for the use of the facilities over the remainder of the lease term, with Almota retaining the right thereafter to remove the facilities — in effect, the right of salvage. . . .

United States v. Petty Motor Co., 327 U.S. 372 (1946), upon which the Government primarily relies, does not lead to a contrary result. The Court did indicate that the measure of damages for the condemnation of a leasehold is to be measured in terms of the value of its use and occupancy for the remainder of the lease term, and the Court refused to elevate an expectation of renewal into a compensable legal interest. But the Court was not dealing there with the fair market value of improvements. Unlike *Petty Motor,* there is no question here of creating a legally cognizable value where none existed, or of compensating a mere incorporeal expectation. The petitioner here has constructed the improvements and seeks only their fair market value. *Petty Motor* should not be read to allow the Government to escape paying what a willing buyer would pay for the same property.

The Government argues that it would be unreasonable to compensate Almota for the value of the improvements measured over their useful life, since the Government could purchase the fee and wait until the expiration of the lease term to take possession of the land. Once it has purchased the fee, the argument goes, there is no further expectancy that the improvements will be used during their useful life since the Government will assuredly require their removal at the end of the term. . . . [But the government] may not take advantage of any depreciation in the property taken that is attributable to the project itself. At the time of the taking in this case, there was an expectancy that the improvements would be used beyond the lease term. But the Government has sought to pay compensation on the theory that at that time there was no possibility that the lease would be renewed and the improvements used beyond the lease term. It has asked that the improvements be valued as though there were no possibility of continued use. That is not how the market would have valued such improvements; it is not what a private buyer would have paid Almota.

"The constitutional requirement of just compensation derives as much content from the basic equitable principles of fairness, as it does from technical concepts of property law." *United States v. Fuller,* 409 U.S. 488, 490 (1973). It is, of course, true that

Almota should be in no better position than if it had sold its leasehold to a private buyer. But its position should surely be no worse. . . .

Mr. Justice WILLIAM H. REHNQUIST, with whom THE CHIEF JUSTICE, Mr. Justice WHITE, and Mr. Justice BLACKMUN join, dissenting.

Petitioner is entitled to compensation for so much of its private "property" as was taken for public use. The parties concede that petitioner's property interest here taken was the unexpired portion of a 20-year lease on land owned by the Oregon-Washington Railroad & Navigation Co. near Colfax, Washington. The Court recognizes the limited nature of petitioner's interest in the real property taken, but concludes that it was entitled to have its leasehold and improvements valued in such a way as to include the probability that petitioner's 20-year lease would have been renewed by the railroad at its expiration.

There is a plausibility about the Court's resounding endorsement of the concept of "fair market value" as the touchstone for valuation, but the result reached by the Court seems to me to be quite at odds with our prior cases. Even in its sharply limited reading of *United States v. Petty Motor Co.*, 327 U.S. 372 (1946), the Court concedes that the petitioner's expectation of having its lease renewed upon expiration is not itself an interest in property for which it may be compensated. But the Court permits the same practical result to be reached by saying that, at least in the case of improvements, the fair market value may be computed in terms of a willing buyer's expectation that the lease would be renewed.

In *United States v. Petty Motor Co.*, *supra*, the Government acquired by condemnation the use of a structure occupied by tenants in possession under leases for various unexpired terms. The Court held that the measure of damages for condemnation of a leasehold is the value of the tenant's use of the leasehold for the remainder of the agreed term, less the agreed rent. The Court considered the argument, essentially the same raised by petitioner here, that a history of past renewal of the leases to existing tenants creates a compensable expectancy, but held that the right to compensation should be measured solely on the basis of the remainder of the tenant's term under the lease itself. In so deciding, the Court stated: "The fact that some tenants had occupied their leaseholds by mutual consent for long periods of years does not add to their rights." . . .

While the inquiry as to what property interest is taken by the condemnor and the inquiry as to how that property interest shall be valued are not identical ones, they cannot be divorced without seriously undermining a number of rules dealing with the law of eminent domain that this Court has evolved in a series of decisions through the years. The landowner, after all, is interested, not in the legal terminology used to describe the property taken from him by the condemnor, but in the amount of money he is to be paid for that property. It will cause him little remorse to learn that his hope for a renewal of a lease for a term of years is not a property interest for which the Government must pay, if in the same breath he is told that the lesser legal interest which he owns may be valued to include the hoped-for renewal. . . .

It is quite apparent that the property on which the owner operates a prosperous retail establishment would command more in an open market sale than the fair value of so much of the enterprise as was "private property" within the meaning of the Fifth Amendment. Yet *Mitchell v. United States*, 267 U.S. 341 (1925), stands squarely for the proposition that the value added to the property taken by the existence of a going business is no part of the just compensation for which the Government must pay for taking the property: "No recovery therefor can be had now as for a taking of the business. There is no finding as a fact that the government took the business, or that what it did was intended as a taking. If the business was destroyed, the destruction was an unintended incident of the taking of land." *Id.*, at 345. . . .

If permissible methods of valuation are to be . . . totally set free from the property interest that they purport to value, it is difficult to see why the same standards should not be applied to a going business. Although the Government does not take the going business, and although the business is not itself a "property" interest within the Fifth Amendment, since purchasers on the open market would have paid an added increment of value for the property because a business was located on it, it may well be that such increment of value is properly included in a condemnation award under the Court's holding today. And it will assuredly make no difference to the property owner to learn that destruction of a going business is not compensable, if he be assured that the property concededly taken upon which the business was located may be valued in such a way as to include the amount a purchaser would have paid for the business. . . .

In at least partially cutting loose the notion of "just compensation" from the notion of "private property" that has developed under the Fifth Amendment, the Court departs from the settled doctrine of numerous prior cases that have quite rigorously adhered to the principle that destruction of value by itself affords no occasion for compensation. While the Court purports to follow this well-established principle by requiring the compensation paid to be determined on the basis of private property actually taken, its endorsement of valuation computed in part on an expectancy that is no part of the property taken represents a departure from this settled doctrine. I therefore dissent.

UNITED STATES v. 564.54 ACRES OF LAND, MORE OR LESS
441 U.S. 506 (1979)

Mr. Justice THURGOOD MARSHALL delivered the opinion of the Court.

At issue in this case is the proper measure of compensation when the Government condemns property owned by a private nonprofit organization and operated for a public purpose. In particular, we must decide whether the Just Compensation Clause of the Fifth Amendment requires payment of replacement cost rather than fair market value of the property taken. . . .

Respondent, the Southeastern Pennsylvania Synod of the Lutheran Church in America, operates three nonprofit, summer camps along the Delaware River. In June 1970, the United States initiated a condemnation proceeding to acquire respondent's land for a public recreational project. Before trial, the Government offered to pay respondent $485,400 as the fair market value of its property. Respondent rejected the offer and demanded approximately $5.8 million, the asserted cost of developing functionally equivalent substitute facilities at a new site. This substantial award was necessary, respondent contended, because the new facilities would be subject to financially burdensome regulations from which existing facilities were exempt under grandfather provisions. . . .

II

A

In giving content to the just compensation requirement of the Fifth Amendment, this Court has sought to put the owner of condemned property "in as good a position pecuniarily as if his property had not been taken." *Olson v. United States*, 292 U.S. 246, 255 (1934). However, this principle of indemnity has not been given its full and literal force. Because of serious practical difficulties in assessing the worth an individual places on particular property at a given time, we have recognized the need for a relatively objective working rule. The Court therefore has employed the concept of fair market value to determine the condemnee's loss. Under this standard, the owner is entitled to receive "what a willing buyer would pay in cash to a willing seller" at the time of the taking.

Although the market-value standard is a useful and generally sufficient tool for ascertaining the compensation required to make the owner whole, the Court has acknowledged that such an award does not necessarily compensate for all values an owner may derive from his property. Thus, we have held that fair market value does not include the special value of property to the owner arising from its adaptability to his particular use. As Mr. Justice Frankfurter wrote for the Court in *Kimball Laundry Co. v. United States*, 338 U.S. 1, 5 (1949):

> The value of property springs from subjective needs and attitudes; its value to the owner may therefore differ widely from its value to the taker. Most things, however, have a general demand which gives them a value transferable from one owner to another. As opposed to such personal and variant standards as value to the particular owner whose property has been taken, this transferable value has an external validity which makes it a fair measure of public obligation to compensate the loss incurred by an owner as a result of the taking of his property for public use. In view, however, of the liability of all property to condemnation for the common good, loss to the owner of nontransferable values deriving from his unique need for property or idiosyncratic attachment to it, like loss due to an exercise of the police power, is properly treated as part of the burden of common citizenship.

In short, the concept of fair market value has been chosen to strike a fair "balance between the public's need and the claimant's loss" upon condemnation of property for a public purpose.

But while the indemnity principle must yield to some extent before the need for a practical general rule, this Court has refused to designate market value as the sole measure of just compensation. For there are situations where this standard is inappropriate. As we held in *United States v. Commodities Trading Corp.*, 339 U.S. 121, 123 (1950):

> [W]hen market value has been too difficult to find, or when its application would result in manifest injustice to owner or public, courts have fashioned and applied other standards. . . . Whatever the circumstances under which such constitutional questions arise, the dominant consideration always remains the same: What compensation is "just" both to an owner whose property is taken and to the public that must pay the bill?

Hence, we must determine whether application of the fair-market-value standard here would be impracticable or whether an award of market value would diverge so substantially from the indemnity principle as to violate the Fifth Amendment.

B

The instances in which market value is too difficult to ascertain generally involve property of a type so infrequently traded that we cannot predict whether the prices previously paid, assuming there have been prior sales, would be repeated in a sale of the condemned property. This might be the case, for example, with respect to public facilities such as roads or sewers. But respondent's property does not fall in this category. There was a market for camps, albeit not an extremely active one. The Government's expert witness presented evidence concerning 11 recent sales of comparable facilities in the vicinity, and estimated that respondent's camps could have been sold within six months to a year after they were offered for sale. . . . Thus, it seems clear that respondent's property had a readily discernible market value. The only remaining inquiry is whether such an award would impermissibly deviate from the indemnity principle.

Emphasizing that the primary value of the condemned property lies in the use to which it is put, respondent argues that compensating only for market value would be unjust in the present context. Because new facilities would bear financial burdens imposed by regulations to which the existing camps were not subject, an award of market value would preclude continuation of respondent's use. Respondent therefore concludes that such a recovery would be insufficient to indemnify for its loss.

However, it is not at all unusual that property uniquely adapted to the owner's use has a market value on condemnation which falls far short of enabling the owner to preserve that use. Such a situation may often arise, for example, where a family home has been built to the owner's tastes, but is old and deteriorated, or where property, like respondent's camps, is exempt from regulations applicable to new facilities. Yet the Court has previously determined that nontransferable values arising from the owner's unique need for the property are not compensable, and has found that this divergence from full indemnification does not violate the Fifth Amendment.

We are unable to discern why a different result should obtain here. . . .

Finally, that the camps may have benefited the community does not warrant compensating respondent differently from other private owners. The community benefit which the camps conferred might provide an indication of the public's loss upon condemnation of the property. But we cannot accept the Court of Appeals' conclusion that this loss is relevant to assessing the compensation due a private entity. . . . [M]any condemnees use their property in a manner that confers a benefit on the community, and there is no sound basis for considering this factor only in condemnations of property owned by nonprofit organizations. And to make the measure of compensation depend on a jury's subjective estimation of whether a particular use "benefits" the community would conflict with this Court's efforts to develop relatively objective valuation standards.

In sum, we find no circumstances here that require suspension of the normal rules for determining just compensation. Respondent, like other private owners, is not entitled to recover for nontransferable values arising from its unique need for the property. To the extent denial of such an award departs from the indemnity principle, it is justified by the necessity for a workable measure of valuation. Allowing respondent the fair market value of its property is thus consistent with the "basic equitable principles of fairness," *United States v. Fuller*, 409 U.S. 488, 490 (1973), underlying the Just Compensation Clause. . . .

NOTES AND QUESTIONS

1. In *United States v. 50 Acres of Land*, 469 U.S. 24 (1984), the United States condemned land owned by the city of Duncanville, Texas, for use as part of a flood control project. The city was legally obligated to replace the facilities taken since they were used as a sanitary landfill. The Supreme Court addressed a question left unresolved in *564.54 Acres of Land*: whether a public entity whose land is taken by the government has a right to replacement cost rather than merely fair market value when it has a legal obligation to replace the facilities lost by the taking. The fair market value of the property taken in *50 Acres* was $199,950; the cost of acquiring a substitute site and developing it as a landfill amounted to more than $1,276,000. The court held that the public condemnee has no right to more than the fair market value of the property taken unless that value is not ascertainable.

Justice Stevens argued, first, that there was no reason to give public entities greater rights than private persons. Second, the use of fair market value is the appropriate measure because it "achieves a fair 'balance between the public's need and the claimant's loss.'" *Id.* at 33. Third, if "the replacement facility is more costly that the condemned facility, it is presumably more valuable," *Id.* at 34, and the condemnee has no right to be subsidized by the government in obtaining this increased value. Fourth, the replacement cost approach would add great "uncertainty and complexity" to the valuation determination. *Id.* at 35. Finally, this approach would diverge "from the principle that just compensation must be measured by an objective standard that disregards subjective values which are only of significance to an individual owner." *Id.*

2. An elderly man has been living in his home for 63 years. His daughter has lived with him for the past 10 years and intends to stay in the house after he dies. The state plans to condemn his house as part of a plan to change the path of a highway. State officials attempt to negotiate with him to obtain a mutually agreeable price for his house. He insists that he does not want to sell. "I was born here, and my mother was born here, and I want to die here and pass this house on to my daughter. I would not sell this house if you offered me ten million dollars." The state condemns the house anyway. How should just compensation be measured? On one hand, the fair market value of the house — the amount an abstract buyer and seller would agree upon — is clearly much less than the owner's asking price. Market value cannot compensate the owner for what he lost. On the other hand, owners can always inflate the value of their property by claiming personal interests in it. Should owners be given extra compensation if the property being taken is personal, such as a home, rather than merely commercial? If so, how should the amount be measured? If not, why is the market measure of damages "just" as an approximation of what the owner lost? If you were writing a statute to provide extra compensation for this kind of property, what would the statute provide?

3. Takings of property are allowed only if "just compensation" is paid. If it is not *possible* to pay just compensation — if money damages will not adequately replace what the owner lost, can there be a taking at all? If the property being taken is of a type in which the owner has justly developed a personal investment, should scrutiny of the project's necessity at least be heightened?

4. One of the parcels of property through which a highway will run is a church. How should the court determine just compensation?

5. When a business is located at a site taken by eminent domain, the owner often loses not only the land and buildings but the goodwill associated with operating the

business at that location. For example, the owner of a pharmacy not only could sell the land and buildings in which the business operates, or assign the leasehold, but could sell the pharmacy business as well. When the government takes the land, the business must move to another location if it is to continue to operate at all. Yet it is often not possible for a business to move and retain its full value. Some customers may not want to shop in a different location; land prices or rents may be higher elsewhere, and the business may have to pay for advertising to let customers know the change in location. "Goodwill" refers to the "value which inheres in the fixed and favorable consideration of customers, arising from an established and well-known and well-conducted business." *Los Angeles Gas & Electric Corp. v. Railroad Commission*, 289 U.S. 287, 313 (1933). "Going-concern value" refers to "the many advantages inherent in acquiring an operating business as compared to starting a new business with only land, buildings and equipment in place." *Gray Line Bus Co. v. Greater Bridgeport Transit District*, 449 A.2d 1036, 1039 (Conn. 1982). These advantages include operating efficiencies and avoidance of start-up costs.

The Supreme Court has refused to grant compensation for either goodwill or going-concern value on the ground that only the land and buildings are taken; the business is free to relocate elsewhere. Any costs associated with the move and any inability to move elsewhere are merely incidental results of the taking of the land and are uncompensable. *Mitchell v. United States*, 267 U.S. 341 (1925). Similarly, when a house is taken, the owner is compensated for the fair market value of the house, not the costs of moving to a new location. *See* Lynda J. Oswald, *Goodwill and Going-Concern Value: Emerging Factors in the Just Compensation Equation*, 32 B.C. L. Rev. 283, 310 (1991). One exception to this principle is applied in temporary takings, which may entitle the business owner to compensation for loss of goodwill. In *Kimball Laundry Co. v. United States*, 338 U.S. 1 (1949), the government temporarily took over a factory from 1942 to 1946, retaining most of the employees and using the laundry for military purposes. The Court accepted the owner's argument that because the taking was temporary, the owner was unable to re-establish its business elsewhere during the takeover. Thus, the loss of going-concern value was compensable.

Some states have passed legislation providing for compensation for goodwill when a business is inextricably tied to a particular location and the loss cannot be avoided by relocation of the business after the land and structures are taken. Cal. Civ. Proc. Code §1263.510; Wyo. Stat. §1-26-713. Some state courts have also allowed compensation for business losses in narrow instances if the business is not easily movable because of the unique character of the property. *See, e.g., State v. Hammer*, 550 P.2d 820 (Alaska 1976); *Housing Authority v. Southern Railway*, 264 S.E.2d 174 (Ga. 1980); *Housing & Redevelopment Authority v. Naegele Outdoor Advertising Co.*, 282 N.W.2d 537 (Minn. 1979).

6. Was the result in *Almota* consistent with the holding of *United States v. Petty Motor Co.*, 327 U.S. 372 (1946)? Was it consistent with the rule in *Kimball Laundry* and *Mitchell* that compensation is generally not required for loss of business goodwill proximately caused by a taking of land and buildings?

7. *Partial takings.* If the state takes 40 acres from an owner of a 100-acre tract, it must compensate the owner not only for the fair market value of the 40 acres but for any reduction in value to the remaining 60 acres caused by the taking of the 40. *State v. Weiswasser*, 693 A.2d 864 (N.J. 1997) (owner is entitled to compensation for diminution of value of remaining property that is specifically attributable to visibility lost as direct result of removal of portions of property through partial-taking condemnation); *State*

Department of Transportation & Development v. Regard, 567 So. 2d 1174 (La. Ct. App. 1990). This reduction in the value of the remaining 60 acres is called *severance damages*. *Portland Natural Gas Transp. System v. 19.2 Acres of Land*, 318 F.3d 279 (1st Cir. 2003). However, if the taking *increases* the value of the remaining 60 acres by providing them a *special benefit* that will not accrue to the public at large (for example, by placing the land along a major road in a way that will increase its attractiveness to retail business), courts will generally offset the severance damages by the amount of the special benefit to the owner of the remaining 60 acres. *Department of Transportation v. Rowe*, 531 S.E.2d 836, 841 (N.C. Ct. App. 2000); *State of Oregon v. Fullerton*, 34 P.3d 1180 (Or. Ct. App. 2001); John G. Sprankling, *Understanding Property Law* §39.07, at 649 (2000).

However, some courts allow an offset for both the special *and* the general benefits accruing to the remaining property. *Los Angeles County v. Continental Development Corp.*, 941 P.2d 809 (Cal. 1997). Moreover, courts are divided on the question of whether the government may offset the special benefit accruing to the retained land against the amount owed the owner for the land that actually was taken. For example, assume the 40 acres taken by the government are worth $100,000 but that the taking increases the value of the remaining 60 acres by $50,000. The Supreme Court *has* allowed the increase in value to the remaining 60 acres to be offset against the amount due the owner for the taking of the 40 acres (as long as it is a special benefit rather than a general benefit); thus, the owner would receive only $50,000. *Bauman v. Ross*, 167 U.S. 548 (1897); *United States v. 930.65 Acres of Land*, 299 F. Supp. 673, 678 (D. Kan. 1968). Some states agree. *Acierno v. State of Delaware*, 643 A.2d 1328 (Del. 1994). However, most states do not allow such an offset. For example, a court recently struck down a North Carolina statute that allowed the increased value of retained land due to special benefits to offset a just compensation award that would otherwise be paid to the owner to compensate for the value of the taken land, although it would have allowed the special benefits to the retained land to be used to offset the amount of any severance damages. *Department of Transportation v. Rowe*, 531 S.E.2d 836 (N.C. Ct. App. 2000). This accords with the rule in most states that would award the owner the full $100,000 (the value of the taken land), not reduce that award by the increase in the value of the retained land that will result from the taking. *Williams Natural Gas Co. v. Perkins*, 952 P.2d 483 (Okla. 1997).

§12.6   Public Use

§12.6.1   FEDERAL CONSTITUTION

KELO v. CITY OF NEW LONDON

2005 U.S. LEXIS 5011 (June 23, 2005)

Justice JOHN PAUL STEVENS delivered the opinion of the Court, in which KENNEDY, SOUTER, GINSBURG, and BREYER, JJ., joined.

In 2000, the city of New London approved a development plan that, in the words of the Supreme Court of Connecticut, was "projected to create in excess of 1,000 jobs, to increase tax and other revenues, and to revitalize an economically distressed city, including its downtown and waterfront areas." In assembling the land needed for this project, the city's development agent has purchased property from willing sellers and proposes to use the power of eminent domain to acquire the remainder of the property from unwilling owners in exchange for just compensation. The question presented is whether the city's proposed disposition of this property qualifies as a "public use" within the meaning of the Takings Clause of the Fifth Amendment to the Constitution.[1]

I

The city of New London (hereinafter City) sits at the junction of the Thames River and the Long Island Sound in southeastern Connecticut. Decades of economic decline led a state agency in 1990 to designate the City a "distressed municipality." In 1996, the Federal Government closed the Naval Undersea Warfare Center, which had been located in the Fort Trumbull area of the City and had employed over 1,500 people. In 1998, the City's unemployment rate was nearly double that of the State, and its population of just under 24,000 residents was at its lowest since 1920.

These conditions prompted state and local officials to target New London, and particularly its Fort Trumbull area, for economic revitalization. To this end, respondent New London Development Corporation (NLDC), a private nonprofit entity established some years earlier to assist the City in planning economic development, was reactivated. In January 1998, the State authorized a $5.35 million bond issue to support the NLDC's planning activities and a $10 million bond issue toward the creation of a Fort Trumbull State Park. In February, the pharmaceutical company Pfizer Inc. announced that it would build a $ 300 million research facility on a site immediately adjacent to Fort Trumbull; local planners hoped that Pfizer would draw new business to the area, thereby serving as a catalyst to the area's rejuvenation. After receiving initial approval from the city council, the NLDC continued its planning activities and held a series of neighborhood meetings to educate the public about the process. In May, the city council authorized the NLDC to formally submit its plans to the relevant state agencies for review. Upon obtaining state-level approval, the NLDC finalized an integrated development plan focused on 90 acres of the Fort Trumbull area.

The Fort Trumbull area is situated on a peninsula that juts into the Thames River. The area comprises approximately 115 privately owned properties, as well as the 32 acres of land formerly occupied by the naval facility (Trumbull State Park now occupies 18 of those 32 acres). The development plan encompasses seven parcels. Parcel 1 is designated for a waterfront conference hotel at the center of a "small urban village" that will include restaurants and shopping. This parcel will also have marinas for both recreational and commercial uses. A pedestrian "riverwalk" will originate here and continue down the coast, connecting the waterfront areas of the development. Parcel 2 will be the site of approximately 80 new residences organized into an urban neighborhood and linked by public walkway to the remainder of the development, including the state park. This parcel also includes space reserved for a new U.S. Coast Guard Museum. Parcel 3, which is located immediately north of the Pfizer facility, will contain at least 90,000 square feet of research and development office space. Parcel 4A is a 2.4-acre site that will be used either to support the adjacent state park, by providing parking or retail services for visitors, or to support the nearby marina. Parcel 4B will include a renovated marina, as well as the final

---

1. "Nor shall private property be taken for public use, without just compensation." U.S. Const., Amdt. 5. That Clause is made applicable to the States by the Fourteenth Amendment. *See* Chicago, B. & Q. R. Co. v. Chicago, 166 U.S. 226 (1897).

stretch of the riverwalk. Parcels 5, 6, and 7 will provide land for office and retail space, parking, and water-dependent commercial uses.

The NLDC intended the development plan to capitalize on the arrival of the Pfizer facility and the new commerce it was expected to attract. In addition to creating jobs, generating tax revenue, and helping to "build momentum for the revitalization of downtown New London," the plan was also designed to make the City more attractive and to create leisure and recreational opportunities on the waterfront and in the park.

The city council approved the plan in January 2000, and designated the NLDC as its development agent in charge of implementation. *See* Conn. Gen. Stat. §8-188. The city council also authorized the NLDC to purchase property or to acquire property by exercising eminent domain in the City's name. *Id.* at §8-193. The NLDC successfully negotiated the purchase of most of the real estate in the 90-acre area, but its negotiations with petitioners failed. As a consequence, in November 2000, the NLDC initiated the condemnation proceedings that gave rise to this case.

II

Petitioner Susette Kelo has lived in the Fort Trumbull area since 1997. She has made extensive improvements to her house, which she prizes for its water view. Petitioner Wilhelmina Dery was born in her Fort Trumbull house in 1918 and has lived there her entire life. Her husband Charles (also a petitioner) has lived in the house since they married some 60 years ago. In all, the nine petitioners own 15 properties in Fort Trumbull—4 in parcel 3 of the development plan and 11 in parcel 4A. Ten of the parcels are occupied by the owner or a family member; the other five are held as investment properties. There is no allegation that any of these properties is blighted or otherwise in poor condition; rather, they were condemned only because they happen to be located in the development area.

In December 2000, petitioners brought this action in the New London Superior Court. They claimed, among other things, that the taking of their properties would violate the "public use" restriction in the Fifth Amendment. After a 7-day bench trial, the Superior Court granted a permanent restraining order prohibiting the taking of the properties located in parcel 4A (park or marina support). It, however, denied petitioners relief as to the properties located in parcel 3 (office space).[4]

After the Superior Court ruled, both sides took appeals to the Supreme Court of Connecticut. That court held, over a dissent, that all of the City's proposed takings were valid. [R]elying on cases such as *Hawaii Housing Authority v. Midkiff*, 467 U.S. 229 (1984), and *Berman v. Parker*, 348 U.S. 26 (1954), the court held that such economic development qualified as a valid public use under both the Federal and State Constitutions. . . .

---

4. While this litigation was pending before the Superior Court, the NLDC announced that it would lease some of the parcels to private developers in exchange for their agreement to develop the land according to the terms of the development plan. Specifically, the NLDC was negotiating a 99-year ground lease with Corcoran Jennison, a developer selected from a group of applicants. The negotiations contemplated a nominal rent of $ 1 per year, but no agreement had yet been signed.

The three dissenting justices would have imposed a "heightened" standard of judicial review for takings justified by economic development. Although they agreed that the plan was intended to serve a valid public use, they would have found all the takings unconstitutional because the City had failed to adduce "clear and convincing evidence" that the economic benefits of the plan would in fact come to pass.

We granted certiorari to determine whether a city's decision to take property for the purpose of economic development satisfies the "public use" requirement of the Fifth Amendment.

III

Two polar propositions are perfectly clear. On the one hand, it has long been accepted that the sovereign may not take the property of *A* for the sole purpose of transferring it to another private party *B*, even though *A* is paid just compensation. On the other hand, it is equally clear that a State may transfer property from one private party to another if future "use by the public" is the purpose of the taking; the condemnation of land for a railroad with common-carrier duties is a familiar example. Neither of these propositions, however, determines the disposition of this case.

As for the first proposition, the City would no doubt be forbidden from taking petitioners' land for the purpose of conferring a private benefit on a particular private party. Nor would the City be allowed to take property under the mere pretext of a public purpose, when its actual purpose was to bestow a private benefit. The takings before us, however, would be executed pursuant to a "carefully considered" development plan. The trial judge and all the members of the Supreme Court of Connecticut agreed that there was no evidence of an illegitimate purpose in this case. Therefore, as was true of the statute challenged in *Midkiff*, 467 U.S., at 245, the City's development plan was not adopted "to benefit a particular class of identifiable individuals."

On the other hand, this is not a case in which the City is planning to open the condemned land — at least not in its entirety — to use by the general public. Nor will the private lessees of the land in any sense be required to operate like common carriers, making their services available to all comers. But although such a projected use would be sufficient to satisfy the public use requirement, this "Court long ago rejected any literal requirement that condemned property be put into use for the general public." *Id.*, at 244. Indeed, while many state courts in the mid-19th century endorsed "use by the public" as the proper definition of public use, that narrow view steadily eroded over time. Not only was the "use by the public" test difficult to administer (*e.g.*, what proportion of the public need have access to the property? at what price?), but it proved to be impractical given the diverse and always evolving needs of society.[8] Accordingly, when this Court began applying the Fifth Amendment to the States at the close of the 19th century, it embraced the broader and more natural interpretation of public use as "public purpose." Thus, in a case upholding a mining company's use of

---

8. From upholding the Mill Acts (which authorized manufacturers dependent on power-producing dams to flood upstream lands in exchange for just compensation), to approving takings necessary for the economic development of the West through mining and irrigation, many state courts either circumvented the "use by the public" test when necessary or abandoned it completely. *See Nichols*, The Meaning of Public Use in the Law of Eminent Domain, 20 B. U. L. Rev. 615, 619-624 (1940) (tracing this development and collecting cases)....

an aerial bucket line to transport ore over property it did not own, Justice Holmes' opinion for the Court stressed "the inadequacy of use by the general public as a universal test." *Strickley v. Highland Boy Gold Mining Co.*, 200 U.S. 527, 531 (1906).[9] We have repeatedly and consistently rejected that narrow test ever since.

The disposition of this case therefore turns on the question whether the City's development plan serves a "public purpose." Without exception, our cases have defined that concept broadly, reflecting our longstanding policy of deference to legislative judgments in this field.

In *Berman v. Parker*, 348 U.S. 26 (1954), this Court upheld a redevelopment plan targeting a blighted area of Washington, D. C., in which most of the housing for the area's 5,000 inhabitants was beyond repair. Under the plan, the area would be condemned and part of it utilized for the construction of streets, schools, and other public facilities. The remainder of the land would be leased or sold to private parties for the purpose of redevelopment, including the construction of low-cost housing.

The owner of a department store located in the area challenged the condemnation, pointing out that his store was not itself blighted and arguing that the creation of a "better balanced, more attractive community" was not a valid public use. Writing for a unanimous Court, Justice Douglas refused to evaluate this claim in isolation, deferring instead to the legislative and agency judgment that the area "must be planned as a whole" for the plan to be successful. The Court explained that "community redevelopment programs need not, by force of the Constitution, be on a piecemeal basis—lot by lot, building by building." The public use underlying the taking was unequivocally affirmed, *Id.* at 33:

> We do not sit to determine whether a particular housing project is or is not desirable. The concept of the public welfare is broad and inclusive.... The values it represents are spiritual as well as physical, aesthetic as well as monetary. It is within the power of the legislature to determine that the community should be beautiful as well as healthy, spacious as well as clean, well-balanced as well as carefully patrolled. In the present case, the Congress and its authorized agencies have made determinations that take into account a wide variety of values. It is not for us to reappraise them. If those who govern the District of Columbia decide that the Nation's Capital should be beautiful as well as sanitary, there is nothing in the Fifth Amendment that stands in the way.

In *Hawaii Housing Authority v. Midkiff*, 467 U.S. 229 (1984), the Court considered a Hawaii statute whereby fee title was taken from lessors and transferred to lessees (for just compensation) in order to reduce the concentration of land ownership. We unanimously upheld the statute and rejected the Ninth Circuit's view that it was "a naked attempt on the part of the state of Hawaii to take the property of A and transfer it to B solely for B's private use and benefit." Reaffirming *Berman*'s deferential approach to legislative judgments in this field, we concluded that the State's purpose of eliminating the "social and economic evils of a land oligopoly" qualified as a valid public use. Our opinion also rejected the contention that the mere fact that the State immediately transferred the properties to private individuals upon condemnation somehow diminished the public character of the taking. "It is only the taking's purpose, and not its mechanics," we explained, that matters in determining public use. *Id.*, at 244.

---

9. *See also Clark v. Nash*, 198 U.S. 361 (1905) (upholding a statute that authorized the owner of arid land to widen a ditch on his neighbor's property so as to permit a nearby stream to irrigate his land).

In that same Term we decided another public use case that arose in a purely economic context. In *Ruckelshaus v. Monsanto Co.*, 467 U.S. 986 (1984), the Court dealt with provisions of the Federal Insecticide, Fungicide, and Rodenticide Act under which the Environmental Protection Agency could consider the data (including trade secrets) submitted by a prior pesticide applicant in evaluating a subsequent application, so long as the second applicant paid just compensation for the data. We acknowledged that the "most direct beneficiaries" of these provisions were the subsequent applicants, but we nevertheless upheld the statute under *Berman* and *Midkiff*. We found sufficient Congress' belief that sparing applicants the cost of time-consuming research eliminated a significant barrier to entry in the pesticide market and thereby enhanced competition.

Viewed as a whole, our jurisprudence has recognized that the needs of society have varied between different parts of the Nation, just as they have evolved over time in response to changed circumstances. Our earliest cases in particular embodied a strong theme of federalism, emphasizing the "great respect" that we owe to state legislatures and state courts in discerning local public needs. For more than a century, our public use jurisprudence has wisely eschewed rigid formulas and intrusive scrutiny in favor of affording legislatures broad latitude in determining what public needs justify the use of the takings power.

IV

Those who govern the City were not confronted with the need to remove blight in the Fort Trumbull area, but their determination that the area was sufficiently distressed to justify a program of economic rejuvenation is entitled to our deference. The City has carefully formulated an economic development plan that it believes will provide appreciable benefits to the community, including — but by no means limited to — new jobs and increased tax revenue. As with other exercises in urban planning and development,[12] the City is endeavoring to coordinate a variety of commercial, residential, and recreational uses of land, with the hope that they will form a whole greater than the sum of its parts. To effectuate this plan, the City has invoked a state statute that specifically authorizes the use of eminent domain to promote economic development. Given the comprehensive character of the plan, the thorough deliberation that preceded its adoption, and the limited scope of our review, it is appropriate for us, as it was in *Berman*, to resolve the challenges of the individual owners, not on a piecemeal basis, but rather in light of the entire plan. Because that plan unquestionably serves a public purpose, the takings challenged here satisfy the public use requirement of the Fifth Amendment.

To avoid this result, petitioners urge us to adopt a new bright-line rule that economic development does not qualify as a public use. Putting aside the unpersuasive suggestion that the City's plan will provide only purely economic benefits, neither precedent nor logic supports petitioners' proposal. Promoting economic development is a traditional and long accepted function of government. There is, moreover, no principled way of distinguishing economic development from the other public purposes that we have recognized. In our cases upholding takings that facilitated agriculture and mining, for example, we emphasized the importance of those industries to the welfare of the States in question in *Berman*, we endorsed the purpose of transforming a blighted area

---

12. *Cf. Village of Euclid v. Ambler Realty Co.*, 272 U.S. 365 (1926).

into a "well-balanced" community through redevelopment;[13] in *Midkiff*, we upheld the interest in breaking up a land oligopoly that "created artificial deterrents to the normal functioning of the State's residential land market"; and in *Monsanto*, we accepted Congress' purpose of eliminating a "significant barrier to entry in the pesticide market." It would be incongruous to hold that the City's interest in the economic benefits to be derived from the development of the Fort Trumbull area has less of a public character than any of those other interests. Clearly, there is no basis for exempting economic development from our traditionally broad understanding of public purpose.

Petitioners contend that using eminent domain for economic development impermissibly blurs the boundary between public and private takings. Again, our cases foreclose this objection. Quite simply, the government's pursuit of a public purpose will often benefit individual private parties. For example, in *Midkiff*, the forced transfer of property conferred a direct and significant benefit on those lessees who were previously unable to purchase their homes. In *Monsanto*, we recognized that the "most direct beneficiaries" of the data-sharing provisions were the subsequent pesticide applicants, but benefiting them in this way was necessary to promoting competition in the pesticide market. The owner of the department store in *Berman* objected to "taking from one businessman for the benefit of another businessman," referring to the fact that under the redevelopment plan land would be leased or sold to private developers for redevelopment.[15] Our rejection of that contention has particular relevance to the instant case: "The public end may be as well or better served through an agency of private enterprise than through a department of government — or so the Congress might conclude. We cannot say that public ownership is the sole method of promoting the public purposes of community redevelopment projects." *Id.* at 34.[16]

---

13. It is a misreading of *Berman* to suggest that the only public use upheld in that case was the initial removal of blight. The public use described in Berman extended beyond that to encompass the purpose of developing that area to create conditions that would prevent a reversion to blight in the future. *See* 348 U.S., at 34-35 ("It was not enough, [the experts] believed, to remove existing buildings that were insanitary or unsightly. It was important to redesign the whole area so as to eliminate the conditions that cause slums. . . . The entire area needed redesigning so that a balanced, integrated plan could be developed for the region, including not only new homes, but also schools, churches, parks, streets, and shopping centers. In this way it was hoped that the cycle of decay of the area could be controlled and the birth of future slums prevented"). Had the public use in Berman been defined more narrowly, it would have been difficult to justify the taking of the plaintiff's nonblighted department store.

15. Notably, as in the instant case, the private developers in Berman were required by contract to use the property to carry out the redevelopment plan.

16. Nor do our cases support Justice O'Connor's novel theory that the government may only take property and transfer it to private parties when the initial taking eliminates some "harmful property use." There was nothing "harmful" about the nonblighted department store at issue in Berman; nothing "harmful" about the lands at issue in the mining and agriculture cases, *see, e.g., Strickley;* and certainly nothing "harmful" about the trade secrets owned by the pesticide manufacturers in Monsanto. In each case, the public purpose we upheld depended on a private party's future use of the concededly nonharmful property that was taken. By focusing on a property's future use, as opposed to its past use, our cases are faithful to the text of the Takings Clause. See U.S. Const., Amdt. 5. ("Nor shall private property be taken for public use, without just compensation"). Justice O'Connor's intimation that a "public purpose" may not be achieved by the action of private parties, confuses the purpose of a taking with its mechanics, a mistake we warned of in *Midkiff*, 467 U.S., at 244. *See also Berman*, 348 U.S., at 33-34 ("The public end may be as well or better served through an agency of private enterprise than through a department of government").

It is further argued that without a bright-line rule nothing would stop a city from transferring citizen *A*'s property to citizen *B* for the sole reason that citizen *B* will put the property to a more productive use and thus pay more taxes. Such a one-to-one transfer of property, executed outside the confines of an integrated development plan, is not presented in this case. While such an unusual exercise of government power would certainly raise a suspicion that a private purpose was afoot,[17] the hypothetical cases posited by petitioners can be confronted if and when they arise. They do not warrant the crafting of an artificial restriction on the concept of public use.[19]

Alternatively, petitioners maintain that for takings of this kind we should require a "reasonable certainty" that the expected public benefits will actually accrue. Such a rule, however, would represent an even greater departure from our precedent. "When the legislature's purpose is legitimate and its means are not irrational, our cases make clear that empirical debates over the wisdom of takings — no less than debates over the wisdom of other kinds of socioeconomic legislation — are not to be carried out in the federal courts." *Midkiff*, 467 U.S., at 242. Indeed, earlier this Term we explained why similar practical concerns (among others) undermined the use of the "substantially advances" formula in our regulatory takings doctrine. *See Lingle* v. *Chevron U.S.A. Inc.*, 2005 U.S. LEXIS 4342 (2005) (noting that this formula "would empower — and might often require — courts to substitute their predictive judgments for those of elected legislatures and expert agencies"). The disadvantages of a heightened form of review are especially pronounced in this type of case. Orderly implementation of a comprehensive redevelopment plan obviously requires that the legal rights of all interested parties be established before new construction can be commenced. A constitutional rule that required postponement of the judicial approval of every condemnation until the likelihood of success of the plan had been assured would unquestionably impose a significant impediment to the successful consummation of many such plans.

Just as we decline to second-guess the City's considered judgments about the efficacy of its development plan, we also decline to second-guess the City's determinations as to what lands it needs to acquire in order to effectuate the project. "It is not for the courts to oversee the choice of the boundary line nor to sit in review on the size of a particular project area. Once the question of the public purpose has been decided, the amount and character of land to be taken for the project and the need for a particular

---

17. Courts have viewed such aberrations with a skeptical eye. *See, e.g., 99 Cents Only Stores v. Lancaster Redevelopment Agency*, 237 F. Supp. 2d 1123 (C.D. Cal. 2001); cf. *Cincinnati v. Vester*, 281 U.S. 439, 448 (1930) (taking invalid under state eminent domain statute for lack of a reasoned explanation). These types of takings may also implicate other constitutional guarantees. *See Village of Willowbrook v. Olech*, 528 U.S. 562 (2000) (per curiam).

19. A parade of horribles is especially unpersuasive in this context, since the Takings Clause largely operates as a conditional limitation, permitting the government to do what it wants so long as it pays the charge." *Eastern Enterprises v. Apfel*, 524 U.S. 498, 545 (1998) (KENNEDY, J., concurring in judgment and dissenting in part). Speaking of the takings power, Justice Iredell observed that "it is not sufficient to urge, that the power may be abused, for, such is the nature of all power-such is the tendency of every human institution: and, it might as fairly be said, that the power of taxation, which is only circumscribed by the discretion of the Body, in which it is vested, ought not to be granted, because the Legislature, disregarding its true objects, might, for visionary and useless projects, impose a tax to the amount of nineteen shillings in the pound. We must be content to limit power where we can, and where we cannot, consistently with its use, we must be content to repose a salutory confidence." *Calder v. Bull*, 3 U.S. 386, 400 (1798)(opinion concurring in result).

tract to complete the integrated plan rests in the discretion of the legislative branch." *Berman*, 348 U.S., at 35-36.

In affirming the City's authority to take petitioners' properties, we do not minimize the hardship that condemnations may entail, notwithstanding the payment of just compensation. We emphasize that nothing in our opinion precludes any State from placing further restrictions on its exercise of the takings power. Indeed, many States already impose "public use" requirements that are stricter than the federal baseline. Some of these requirements have been established as a matter of state constitutional law,[22] while others are expressed in state eminent domain statutes that carefully limit the grounds upon which takings may be exercised.[23] As the submissions of the parties and their *amici* make clear, the necessity and wisdom of using eminent domain to promote economic development are certainly matters of legitimate public debate.[24] This Court's authority, however, extends only to determining whether the City's proposed condemnations are for a "public use" within the meaning of the Fifth Amendment to the Federal Constitution. Because over a century of our case law interpreting that provision dictates an affirmative answer to that question, we may not grant petitioners the relief that they seek.

The judgment of the Supreme Court of Connecticut is affirmed.

It is so ordered.

Justice ANTHONY M. KENNEDY, concurring....

This Court has declared that a taking should be upheld as consistent with the Public Use Clause, U.S. Const., Amdt. 5., as long as it is "rationally related to a conceivable public purpose." *Hawaii Housing Authority v. Midkiff*, 467 U.S. 229, 241 (1984). This deferential standard of review echoes the rational-basis test used to review economic regulation under the Due Process and Equal Protection Clauses, *see, e.g., FCC v. Beach Communications, Inc.*, 508 U.S. 307, 313-314 (1993); *Williamson v. Lee Optical of Okla., Inc.*, 348 U.S. 483 (1955). The determination that a rational-basis standard of review is appropriate does not, however, alter the fact that transfers intended to confer benefits on particular, favored private entities, and with only incidental or pretextual public benefits, are forbidden by the Public Use Clause.

A court applying rational-basis review under the Public Use Clause should strike down a taking that, by a clear showing, is intended to favor a particular private party, with only incidental or pretextual public benefits, just as a court applying rational-basis review under the Equal Protection Clause must strike down a government classification that is clearly intended to injure a particular class of private parties, with only incidental or pretextual public justifications. *See Cleburne v. Cleburne Living Center*,

---

22. *See, e.g., County of Wayne v. Hathcock*, 684 N.W.2d 765 (Mich. 2004).

23. Under California law, for instance, a city may only take land for economic development purposes in blighted areas. Cal. Health & Safety Code Ann. §§33030-33037. *See, e.g., Redevelopment Agency of Chula Vista v. Rados Bros.*, 115 Cal. Rptr. 2d 234 (Ct. App. 2002).

24. For example, some argue that the need for eminent domain has been greatly exaggerated because private developers can use numerous techniques, including secret negotiations or precommitment strategies, to overcome holdout problems and assemble lands for genuinely profitable projects. Others argue to the contrary, urging that the need for eminent domain is especially great with regard to older, small cities like New London, where centuries of development have created an extreme overdivision of land and thus a real market impediment to land assembly.

Inc., 473 U.S. 432, 446-447, 450 (1985); *Department of Agriculture v. Moreno*, 413 U.S. 528, 533-536 (1973)....

A court confronted with a plausible accusation of impermissible favoritism to private parties should treat the objection as a serious one and review the record to see if it has merit, though with the presumption that the government's actions were reasonable and intended to serve a public purpose. Here, the trial court conducted a careful and extensive inquiry into "whether, in fact, the development plan is of primary benefit to . . . the developer [*i.e.*, Corcoran Jennison], and private businesses which may eventually locate in the plan area [*e.g.*, Pfizer], and in that regard, only of incidental benefit to the city." The trial court considered . . . respondents' awareness of New London's depressed economic condition and evidence corroborating the validity of this concern; the substantial commitment of public funds by the State to the development project before most of the private beneficiaries were known; evidence that respondents reviewed a variety of development plans and chose a private developer from a group of applicants rather than picking out a particular transferee beforehand; and the fact that the other private beneficiaries of the project are still unknown because the office space proposed to be built has not yet been rented.

The trial court concluded, based on these findings, that benefiting Pfizer was not "the primary motivation or effect of this development plan"; instead, "the primary motivation for [respondents] was to take advantage of Pfizer's presence." Likewise, the trial court concluded that "there is nothing in the record to indicate that . . . [respon-[respondents] were motivated by a desire to aid [other] particular private entities." . . . This case, then, survives the meaningful rational basis review that in my view is required under the Public Use Clause.

Petitioners and their *amici* argue that any taking justified by the promotion of economic development must be treated by the courts as *per se* invalid, or at least presumptively invalid. Petitioners overstate the need for such a rule, however, by making the incorrect assumption that review under *Berman* and *Midkiff* imposes no meaningful judicial limits on the government's power to condemn any property it likes. A broad *per se* rule or a strong presumption of invalidity, furthermore, would prohibit a large number of government takings that have the purpose and expected effect of conferring substantial benefits on the public at large and so do not offend the Public Use Clause.

My agreement with the Court that a presumption of invalidity is not warranted for economic development takings in general, or for the particular takings at issue in this case, does not foreclose the possibility that a more stringent standard of review than that announced in *Berman* and *Midkiff* might be appropriate for a more narrowly drawn category of takings. There may be private transfers in which the risk of undetected impermissible favoritism of private parties is so acute that a presumption (rebuttable or otherwise) of invalidity is warranted under the Public Use Clause. This demanding level of scrutiny, however, is not required simply because the purpose of the taking is economic development.

This is not the occasion for conjecture as to what sort of cases might justify a more demanding standard, but it is appropriate to underscore aspects of the instant case that convince me no departure from *Berman* and *Midkiff* is appropriate here. This taking occurred in the context of a comprehensive development plan meant to address a serious city-wide depression, and the projected economic benefits of the project cannot be characterized as *de minimus*. The identity of most of the private beneficiaries were unknown at the time the city formulated its plans. The city complied with elaborate procedural requirements that facilitate review of the record and inquiry into the city's purposes. In sum, while there may be categories of cases in which the transfers are so suspicious, or the procedures employed so prone to abuse, or the purported benefits are so trivial or implausible, that courts should presume an impermissible private purpose, no such circumstances are present in this case.

For the foregoing reasons, I join in the Court's opinion.

Justice SANDRA DAY O'CONNOR, with whom The Chief Justice, Justice SCALIA, and Justice THOMAS join, dissenting.

Over two centuries ago, just after the Bill of Rights was ratified, Justice Chase wrote:

> An ACT of the Legislature (for I cannot call it a law) contrary to the great first principles of the social compact, cannot be considered a rightful exercise of legislative authority.... A few instances will suffice to explain what I mean.... [A] law that takes property from A. and gives it to B: It is against all reason and justice, for a people to entrust a Legislature with SUCH powers; and, therefore, it cannot be presumed that they have done it.*Calder v. Bull*, 3 U.S. 386, 388 (1798) (emphasis deleted).

Today the Court abandons this long-held, basic limitation on government power. Under the banner of economic development, all private property is now vulnerable to being taken and transferred to another private owner, so long as it might be upgraded — *i.e.*, given to an owner who will use it in a way that the legislature deems more beneficial to the public — in the process. To reason, as the Court does, that the incidental public benefits resulting from the subsequent ordinary use of private property render economic development takings "for public use" is to wash out any distinction between private and public use of property — and thereby effectively to delete the words "for public use" from the Takings Clause of the Fifth Amendment. Accordingly I respectfully dissent....

Where is the line between "public" and "private" property use? We give considerable deference to legislatures' determinations about what governmental activities will advantage the public. But were the political branches the sole arbiters of the public-private distinction, the Public Use Clause would amount to little more than hortatory fluff. An external, judicial check on how the public use requirement is interpreted, however limited, is necessary if this constraint on government power is to retain any meaning....

This case . . . presents an issue of first impression: Are economic development takings constitutional? I would hold that they are not. We are guided by two precedents about the taking of real property by eminent domain. In *Berman*, we upheld takings within a blighted neighborhood of Washington, D.C. The neighborhood had so deteriorated that, for example, 64.3% of its dwellings were beyond repair. It had become burdened with "overcrowding of dwellings," "lack of adequate streets and alleys," and "lack of light and air." Congress had determined that the neighborhood had become "injurious to the public health, safety, morals, and welfare" and that it was necessary to "eliminate all such injurious conditions by employing all means necessary and appropriate for the purpose," including eminent domain. Mr. Berman's department store was not itself blighted. Having approved of Congress' decision to eliminate the harm to the public emanating from the blighted neighborhood, however, we did not second-guess its decision to treat the neighborhood as a whole rather than lot-by-lot. *See*

Midkiff, 467 U.S., at 244 ("it is only the taking's purpose, and not its mechanics, that must pass scrutiny").

In *Midkiff*, we upheld a land condemnation scheme in Hawaii whereby title in real property was taken from lessors and transferred to lessees. At that time, the State and Federal Governments owned nearly 49% of the State's land, and another 47% was in the hands of only 72 private landowners. Concentration of land ownership was so dramatic that on the State's most urbanized island, Oahu, 22 landowners owned 72.5% of the fee simple titles. The Hawaii Legislature had concluded that the oligopoly in land ownership was "skewing the State's residential fee simple market, inflating land prices, and injuring the public tranquility and welfare," and therefore enacted a condemnation scheme for redistributing title.

In those decisions, we emphasized the importance of deferring to legislative judgments about public purpose. Because courts are ill-equipped to evaluate the efficacy of proposed legislative initiatives, we rejected as unworkable the idea of courts' "'deciding on what is and is not a governmental function and . . . invalidating legislation on the basis of their view on that question at the moment of decision, a practice which has proved impracticable in other fields.'" *Id.*, at 240-241. . . .

The Court's holdings in *Berman* and *Midkiff* were true to the principle underlying the Public Use Clause. In both those cases, the extraordinary, precondemnation use of the targeted property inflicted affirmative harm on society — in *Berman* through blight resulting from extreme poverty and in *Midkiff* through oligopoly resulting from extreme wealth. And in both cases, the relevant legislative body had found that eliminating the existing property use was necessary to remedy the harm. Thus a public purpose was realized when the harmful use was eliminated. Because each taking *directly* achieved a public benefit, it did not matter that the property was turned over to private use. Here, in contrast, New London does not claim that Susette Kelo's and Wilhelmina Dery's well-maintained homes are the source of any social harm. Indeed, it could not so claim without adopting the absurd argument that any single-family home that might be razed to make way for an apartment building, or any church that might be replaced with a retail store, or any small business that might be more lucrative if it were instead part of a national franchise, is inherently harmful to society and thus within the government's power to condemn.

In moving away from our decisions sanctioning the condemnation of harmful property use, the Court today significantly expands the meaning of public use. It holds that the sovereign may take private property currently put to ordinary private use, and give it over for new, ordinary private use, so long as the new use is predicted to generate some secondary benefit for the public — such as increased tax revenue, more jobs, maybe even aesthetic pleasure. But nearly any lawful use of real private property can be said to generate some incidental benefit to the public. Thus, if predicted (or even guaranteed) positive side-effects are enough to render transfer from one private party to another constitutional, then the words "for public use" do not realistically exclude *any* takings, and thus do not exert any constraint on the eminent domain power. . . .

It was possible after *Berman* and *Midkiff* to imagine unconstitutional transfers from A to B. Those decisions endorsed government intervention when private property use had veered to such an extreme that the public was suffering as a consequence. Today nearly all real property is susceptible to condemnation on the Court's] theory. . . .

Any property may now be taken for the benefit of another private party, but the fallout from this decision will not be random. The beneficiaries are likely to be those citizens with disproportionate influence and power in the political process, including large corporations and development firms. As for the victims, the government now has license to transfer property from those with fewer resources to those with more. The Founders cannot have intended this perverse result. "That alone is a *just* government," wrote James Madison, "which *impartially* secures to every man, whatever is his *own.*" For the National Gazette, Property, (Mar. 29, 1792), *reprinted in* 14 Papers of James Madison 266 (R. Rutland et al. eds. 1983).

I would hold that the takings in both Parcel 3 and Parcel 4A are unconstitutional, reverse the judgment of the Supreme Court of Connecticut, and remand for further proceedings.

Justice CLARENCE THOMAS, dissenting.

Long ago, William Blackstone wrote that "the law of the land ... postpones even public necessity to the sacred and inviolable rights of private property." 1 *Commentaries on the Laws of England* 134-135 (1765). The Framers embodied that principle in the Constitution, allowing the government to take property not for "public necessity," but instead for "public use." Amdt. 5. Defying this understanding, the Court replaces the Public Use Clause with a "'Public Purpose'" Clause (or perhaps the "Diverse and Always Evolving Needs of Society" Clause (capitalization added)), a restriction that is satisfied, the Court instructs, so long as the purpose is "legitimate" and the means "not irrational". This deferential shift in phraseology enables the Court to hold, against all common sense, that a costly urban-renewal project whose stated purpose is a vague promise of new jobs and increased tax revenue, but which is also suspiciously agreeable to the Pfizer Corporation, is for a "public use."

I cannot agree. If such "economic development" takings are for a "public use," any taking is, and the Court has erased the Public Use Clause from our Constitution, as Justice O'Connor powerfully argues in dissent. I do not believe that this Court can eliminate liberties expressly enumerated in the Constitution and therefore join her dissenting opinion. ...

The most natural reading of the [Public Use] Clause is that it allows the government to take property only if the government owns, or the public has a legal right to use, the property, as opposed to taking it for any public purpose or necessity whatsoever. At the time of the founding, dictionaries primarily defined the noun "use" as "the act of employing any thing to any purpose." 2 S. Johnson, *A Dictionary of the English Language* 2194 (4th ed. 1773). The term "use," moreover, "is from the Latin *utor*, which means 'to use, make use of, avail one's self of, employ, apply, enjoy, etc." J. Lewis, *Law of Eminent Domain* §165, p. 224, n. 4 (1888). When the government takes property and gives it to a private individual, and the public has no right to use the property, it strains language to say that the public is "employing" the property, regardless of the incidental benefits that might accrue to the public from the private use. The term "public use," then, means that either the government or its citizens as a whole must actually "employ" the taken property.

Granted, another sense of the word "use" was broader in meaning, extending to "convenience" or "help," or "qualities that make a thing proper for any purpose." 2 Johnson 2194. Nevertheless, read in context, the term "public use" possesses the narrower meaning. Elsewhere, the Constitution twice employs the word "use," both times in its narrower sense. Claeys, *Public-Use Limitations and Natural Property Rights*, 2004 Mich. St. L. Rev. 877, 897. Article 1, §10 provides that "the net Produce of all Duties and Imposts, laid by any State on Imports or Exports, shall be for the Use of the Treasury of the United States," meaning the Treasury itself will control the taxes, not use it to any beneficial end. And Article I, §8 grants Congress power "to raise and support Armies, but no Appropriation of Money to that Use shall be for a longer Term than two Years." Here again, "use" means "employed to raise and support Armies," not anything directed to achieving any military end. The same word in the Public Use Clause should be interpreted to have the same meaning.... The Constitution's text, in short, suggests that the Takings Clause authorizes the taking of property only if the public has a right to employ it, not if the public realizes any conceivable benefit from the taking.

The Constitution's common-law background reinforces this understanding. The common law provided an express method of eliminating uses of land that adversely impacted the public welfare: nuisance law. Blackstone and Kent, for instance, both carefully distinguished the law of nuisance from the power of eminent domain. Blackstone rejected the idea that private property could be taken solely for purposes of any public benefit. "So great ... is the regard of the law for private property," he explained, "that it will not authorize the least violation of it; no, not even for the general good of the whole community." 1 Blackstone 135. He continued: "If a new road ... were to be made through the grounds of a private person, it might perhaps be extensively beneficial to the public; but the law permits no man, or set of men, to do this without the consent of the owner of the land." *Id.* Only "by giving [the landowner] full indemnification" could the government take property, and even then "the public [was] now considered as an individual, treating with an individual for an exchange." *Id.* When the public took property, in other words, it took it as an individual buying property from another typically would: for one's own use. The Public Use Clause, in short, embodied the Framers' understanding that property is a natural, fundamental right, prohibiting the government from "taking *property* from A. and giving it to B." *Calder v. Bull*, 3 U.S. 386, 388 (1798)....

Early American eminent domain practice largely bears out this understanding of the Public Use Clause....

States employed the eminent domain power to provide quintessentially public goods, such as public roads, toll roads, ferries, canals, railroads, and public parks. Though use of the eminent domain power was sparse at the time of the founding, many States did have so-called Mill Acts, which authorized the owners of grist mills operated by water power to flood upstream lands with the payment of compensation to the upstream landowner. Those early grist mills "were regulated by law and compelled to serve the public for a stipulated toll and in regular order," and therefore were actually used by the public. J. Lewis, *Law of Eminent Domain* §178, at 246, & n.3 (1888). They were common carriers—quasi-public entities. These were "public uses" in the fullest sense of the word, because the public could legally use and benefit from them equally....

To be sure, some early state legislatures tested the limits of their state-law eminent domain power. Some States enacted statutes allowing the taking of property for the purpose of building private roads. These statutes were mixed; some required the private landowner to keep the road open to the public, and others did not. Later in the 19th century, moreover, the Mill Acts were employed to grant rights to private manufacturing plants, in addition to grist mills that had common-carrier duties. *See, e.g.,* M. Horwitz, *The Transformation of American Law 1780-1860*, at 51-52 (1977).

These early uses of the eminent domain power are often cited as evidence for the broad "public purpose" interpretation of the Public Use Clause, but in fact the constitutionality of these exercises of eminent domain power under state public use restrictions was a hotly contested question in state courts throughout the 19th and into the 20th century.... The disagreement among state courts, and state legislatures' attempts to circumvent public use limits on their eminent domain power, cannot obscure that the Public Use Clause is most naturally read to authorize takings for public use only if the government or the public actually uses the taken property....

Our current Public Use Clause jurisprudence, as the Court notes, has rejected this natural reading of the Clause. The Court adopted its modern reading blindly, with little discussion of the Clause's history and original meaning.... Today's questionable application of these cases is further proof that the "public purpose" standard is not susceptible of principled application. This Court's reliance by rote on this standard is ill advised and should be reconsidered....

...I would revisit our Public Use Clause cases and consider returning to the original meaning of the Public Use Clause: that the government may take property only if it actually uses or gives the public a legal right to use the property....

The consequences of today's decision are not difficult to predict, and promise to be harmful. So-called "urban renewal" programs provide some compensation for the properties they take, but no compensation is possible for the subjective value of these lands to the individuals displaced and the indignity inflicted by uprooting them from their homes. Allowing the government to take property solely for public purposes is bad enough, but extending the concept of public purpose to encompass any economically beneficial goal guarantees that these losses will fall disproportionately on poor communities. Those communities are not only systematically less likely to put their lands to the highest and best social use, but are also the least politically powerful. If ever there were justification for intrusive judicial review of constitutional provisions that protect "discrete and insular minorities," *United States v. Carolene Products Co.*, 304 U.S. 144, 152 n. 4 (1938), surely that principle would apply with great force to the powerless groups and individuals the Public Use Clause protects. The deferential standard this Court has adopted for the Public Use Clause is therefore deeply perverse. It encourages "those citizens with disproportionate influence and power in the political process, including large corporations and development firms" to victimize the weak (*see ante*, O'CONNOR, J., dissenting).

Those incentives have made the legacy of this Court's "public purpose" test an unhappy one. In the 1950's, no doubt emboldened in part by the expansive understanding of "public use" this Court adopted in *Berman*, cities "rushed to draw plans" for downtown development. B. Frieden & L. Sagalayn, Downtown, Inc. How America Rebuilds Cities 17 (1989). "Of all the families displaced by urban renewal from 1949 through 1963, 63 percent of those whose race was known were nonwhite, and of these families, 56 percent of nonwhites and 38 percent of whites had incomes low enough to qualify for public housing, which, however, was seldom available to them." *Id.*, at 28. Public works projects in the 1950's and 1960's destroyed predominantly minority communities in St. Paul, Minnesota, and Baltimore, Maryland. *Id.*, at 28-29. In 1981, urban planners in Detroit, Michigan, uprooted the largely "lower-income and elderly" Poletown neighborhood for the benefit of the General Motors Corporation. J. Wylie, *Poletown: Community Betrayed* 58 (1989). Urban renewal projects have long been associated with the displacement of blacks; "in cities across the country urban renewal came to be known as 'Negro removal.'" Pritchett, *The "Public Menace" of Blight: Urban Renewal and the Private Uses of Eminent Domain*, 21 Yale L. & Pol'y Rev. 1, 47 (2003). Over 97 percent of the individuals forcibly removed from their homes by the "slum-clearance" project upheld by this Court in *Berman* were black. 348 U.S. at 30. Regrettably, the predictable consequence of the Court's decision will be to exacerbate these effects.

§12.6.2   STATE CONSTITUTIONS

Most state supreme courts have interpreted their state constitutions in a manner consistent with the federal interpretation. *See, e.g., City of Oakland v. Oakland Raiders,* 646 P.2d 835 (Cal. 1982); *Township of West Orange v. 769 Assocs.,* 800 A.2d 86 (N.J. 2002). However, some state supreme courts have adopted a different path, interpreting their state constitutional "public use" requirements more stringently than has the U.S. Supreme Court.

First, some courts have adopted a version of the test proposed by Justice Kennedy and held that the public use test is not met unless "the public benefits and characteristics of the intended use substantially predominate over the private nature of that use." *See Bailey v. Myers,* 76 P.3d 898 (Ariz. Ct. App. 2003) (city could not take private property on which automobile service station was located for transfer to private developers to construct a retail shopping and office center); *Tolksdorf v. Griffith,* 626 N.W.2d 163 (Mich. 2001) (private roads act unconstitutional taking of property for a "predominantly private purpose" when it allowed owner to get access to landlocked parcel by buying easement over neighboring land); *City of Bozeman v. Vaniman,* 898 P.2d 1208 (Mont. 1995)(not a public purpose to take property for space in visitor's center to be occupied by private Chamber of Commerce); *Casino Reinvestment Development Authority v. Banin,* 727 A.2d 102 (N.J. Super. Ct. 1998) (a taking from a homeowner for transfer to a casino owned by Donald Trump did not serve a public taking when the purpose of the taking was to facilitate construction of a parking lot for the casino but the conveyance did not limit use of the property for this purpose through an enforceable covenant or otherwise and thus the new private owner would be empowered to use the property for other, possibly private, purposes).

Second, some courts have adopted a version of the test proposed by Justice O'Connor and held that property cannot be taken and transferred from one owner to another unless the nature of the property itself justifies the taking. For example, property may be taken and transferred to another owner if its condition is dangerous to occupants or neighbors and in need in demolition or if it is "blighted" and in need of redevelopment to counteract slum conditions. *See Arvada Urban Renewal Auth. v. Columbine Professional Plaza Ass'n,* 85 P.3d 1066 (Colo. 2004)(not a public purpose to take a private lake for a new Wal-Mart unless there was a recent finding that the property was blighted). *Accord, Karesh v. City Council of Charleston,* 247 S.E.2d 342 (S.C. 1978).

Third, some courts have held that the taking must be justified in the sense that the public purpose could not be achieved in any other way than through a taking of one owner's property and transfer to another. *Southwestern Illinois Dev. Auth. v. Nat'l City Envtl.,* 768 N.E.2d 1, 263 Ill. Dec. 241 (Ill. 2002) (not a public purpose to take a factory's property to expand a parking lot for a race track next door). *Accord, Wayne County v. Hathcock,* 684 N.W.2d 765 (Mich. 2004).

Finally, some courts have adopted a version of the approach proposed by Justice Thomas and held that "public use" means either "public ownership" or "use by the public," thereby denying the power to take property from any private person if it is to be transferred to another and used privately rather than by the public at large. *Manufactured Housing Communities of Washington v. Washington,* 13 P.3d 183 (Wash. 2000).

In a dramatic recent development, the Michigan Supreme Court unanimously overruled its famous 1981 decision in *Poletown Neighborhood Council v. City of Detroit,* 304 N.W.2d 455 (Mich. 1981), *overruled by Wayne County v. Hathcock,* 684 N.W.2d 765 (Mich. 2004), which had held that the public use requirement was met when a city took private homes and other properties in a residential area and transferred those lots to General Motors Corp. to construct an automobile manufacturing plant. *Poletown* had held that the goal of economic development was a sufficient public purpose to justify the use of the eminent domain power despite the transfer of the parcels to private ownership. However, on July 30, 2004, the Michigan Supreme Court issued its ruling in *Wayne County v. Hathcock, supra*, agreeing with the South Carolina Supreme Court that economic development was not a sufficient purpose to justify the condemnation of private lands for transfer to another private owner. Rather, the court held that use of the eminent domain power to transfer property from one private owner to another satisfies the public use test only when (1) "public necessity of the extreme sort" requires collective action; (2) the property will be "subject to public oversight after transfer to a private entity"; and the property is selected because of "facts of independent public significance" about the property being taken, rather than advantage to the private entity to whom the property is transferred, such as a conclusion that the area is blighted and in need of redevelopment that is unlikely to occur without public action of this sort. *Id.* at 781-783.

PROBLEM

The Washington Supreme Court struck down a state law granting existing mobile home tenants a right of first refusal if the landlord ever sought to sell the property on which their mobile homes sat. *Manufactured Housing Communities of Washington v. Washington*, 13 P.3d 183 (Wash. 2000). The court defined "public use" as Justice Thomas would have us read the U.S. Constitution to mean "use by the public." The court explained, *Id.*at 196:

> Although preserving dwindling housing stocks for a particularly vulnerable segment of society provides a "public benefit," this public benefit does not constitute a public use. . . . If it is something in which he has the actual right of property there is no rule of law nor principle of equity which would warrant a court in taking it from him against his will for the benefit of another. No amount of hardship in a given case would justify the establishment of such a precedent. The next step in the invasion of the right of property would be to invite the courts to measure the comparative needs of private parties, and compel a transfer to the one most needing and who might best utilize the property. If a man may be required to surrender what is his own, because he does not need it and cannot use it, and because another does need it and can use it, then there is no reason why he may not be required to surrender what he needs but little because another needs it much. A doctrine so insidiously dangerous should never find lodgment in the body of the law through judicial declaration.

Do you agree with this ruling? What are the arguments on both sides? *See also* Mass. Gen. Laws ch. 40L, §5 (granting the state a right of first refusal in certain agricultural lands in the state to prevent conversion of agricultural lands to residential or commercial use).

13

American Indian Nations

§13.1 History of Federal Indian Law

It is impossible to understand tribal sovereignty and property without knowing the basic history of federal law governing the relations between American Indian nations and the United States. Federal policy has continually reversed itself, swinging between efforts to assimilate and absorb Indians into United States culture and efforts to respect Indian nations as separate sovereigns. Current policy is an amalgam of this complicated history.

The subject is amazingly complex. A very good general history is Francis Paul Prucha, *The Great Father* (1984). The following discussion outlines the twists and turns of federal Indian law and is based on Robert N. Clinton, Nell Jessup Newton, and Monroe Price, *American Indian Law: Cases and Materials* 137-164 (3d ed. 1991).

The Trade and Intercourse Act Era (1789-1835). The Constitution attempted to centralize power over relations between American Indian nations and the United States in the federal government. The Indian commerce clause authorized Congress to regulate "Commerce . . . with the Indian Tribes." U.S. Const. art. 1, §8, cl. 3. Pursuant to this power, Congress passed the first of many *Trade and Intercourse Acts* in 1790, ch. 33, 1 Stat. 137 (codified at 25 U.S.C. §177). These acts were intended to allow the frontier to advance while preventing wars with Indian nations. These goals often conflicted; nonetheless, federal statutes attempted to achieve these goals by adopting several general policies. First, the acts attempted to prevent incursion on Indian lands by providing that no sale of Indian lands would be recognized under United States law unless the land was first acquired by the federal government or the sale was specifically approved by the federal government after acquiring the land in a treaty with the relevant Indian nation. For example, the *Trade and Intercourse Act of 1790* provided:

> That no sale of lands made by any Indians, or any nation or tribe of Indians within the United States, shall be valid to any person or persons, or to any state, whether having the right of preemption to such lands or not, unless the same shall be made and duly executed as some public treaty, held under the authority of the United States.

1069

Second, the acts regulated trade with Indians and Indian nations to prevent fraudulent trading practices and incursion on Indian hunting grounds, each of which exacerbated tensions and sometimes led to war. The Act of 1790 was superseded by later acts in 1793, 1796, 1802, and 1834. Third, the acts provided for punishment of individuals who committed crimes both inside the United States and inside "Indian country." Fourth, federal policy was implemented in specific cases by negotiating treaties with individual Indian nations. This policy continued until 1871.

Court decisions in this period established that Indian nations had a property right to the lands they occupied, described by Chief Justice Marshall as "Indian title" or "title of occupancy." This property right gave each Indian nation full power to use its property and to exercise sovereign powers within its borders. Marshall also established, however, that the ultimate "fee title" to tribal lands rested in the United States government, which held those lands in trust for the relevant Indian nation, subject to that nation's title of occupancy. *Johnson v. M'Intosh*, 21 U.S. (8 Wheat.) 543 (1823).

The Removal Period (1835-1861). The eastern states were interested in removing Indian nations that remained within their borders. At first, the United States encouraged tribes and tribal members to move west of the Mississippi River. By the 1830s, the federal government abandoned this policy and forced the tribes in the South and in the Northwest Territory to move to Indian Territory, part of which later became the state of Oklahoma. This process entailed coercing various tribes, including the Cherokees, Creeks, Choctaws, and Chickasaws in the south, and other tribes in the north, to sign treaties by which they gave up all or most of their lands in exchange for lands in Indian Territory. These treaties generally promised that the United States would not disturb the tribes further and would allow each Indian nation to exercise sovereign power within its territory.

The Reservation Policy (1861-1887). As the westward expansion continued, the United States forced numerous tribes in the West to sign treaties by which they ceded to the United States vast areas of land — in most cases, the overwhelming percentage of their lands. In return, the United States would generally agree to respect tribal sovereignty within the reserved lands and to provide monetary payments, enumerated supplies (such as food, medicine, and horses), and services (such as health or education). Many of the Indian wars of this period revolved around efforts by the United States government to force Indians to live on reservations and abandon the lands where they had lived for thousands of years.

The Allotment Period and Forced Assimilation (1871-1934). In 1871, Congress ended formal treaty-making with Indian nations. Treaties had required the consent of both the president and the Senate and the relevant Indian nation. With the end of treaty-making, Congress could pass laws regulating Indian nations; this meant that the House of Representatives would also have to pass the legislation, but the laws could be passed and enforced without obtaining the consent of the affected Indian nation. In practice, not much changed. The United States had often forced Indian nations to agree to treaties, so their consent was often illusory. Moreover, after 1871 the United States continued the process of attempting to get at least formal consent of the Indian nation affected by legislation. However, the United States also passed and enforced legislation over the objections of Indian nations.

The *General Allotment Act of 1887*, also known as the *Dawes Act*, was an attempt to force American Indians to assimilate into United States culture by breaking up the tribal land mass into individual parcels of private property owned by individual tribal members. The eventual goal was to terminate tribal status, end tribal sovereignty, and obliterate tribal culture. Congress hoped to encourage Indians to adopt an agricultural lifestyle and to give up hunting and fishing. The *Dawes Act*, as passed in 1887, provided for dividing reservations into individual allotments of 160 acres to each family head, 80 acres to each single person over 18 and to each orphan under 18, and 40 acres to other single persons under 18. Individual allotments were to be held in trust for 25 years by the federal government and to be inalienable during that period. This was to prevent Indians who had no understanding of what it meant to treat land as a commodity from selling the land immediately. It was hoped that Indians would learn to farm and develop a western, sedentary agricultural life in place of the nomadic hunting life of many tribes in the West. This policy was supported by other legislation providing for punishment of individual Indians who engaged in traditional religious practices. Later legislation allowed leasing of restricted trust allotment land and authorized removal of restraints on alienation for Indians deemed "competent."

Lands not allotted were called "surplus lands" and were available to be sold to the federal government and then offered for sale to non-Indians. Thus, reservations were opened to settlement by non-Indians for the first time. In almost all cases, this forced opening of Indian country violated the explicit promises made in treaties by the United States government.

Through both removal of restraints on alienation and sale of surplus lands, roughly two-thirds of all lands of Indian nations were transferred to non-Indian ownership between 1887 and 1934, decreasing tribal ownership from 138 million acres to 48 million acres.

The Indian Reorganization Act Period (1934-1940). For various reasons, the allotment policy was a terrible failure. In 1934, Congress reversed the allotment policy by enacting the *Indian Reorganization Act of 1934* (IRA), ch. 576, 48 Stat. 984 (codified at 25 U.S.C. §§461-479). The act ended allotment, provided mechanisms for the tribes to repurchase land to reconsolidate the tribal land base, encouraged the reorganization of tribal governments and court systems under constitutions adopted by the tribes and approved by the Bureau of Indian Affairs, and extended the period of restraints on alienation of restricted trust allotments.

Many tribes refused to adopt constitutions under the act because of the required approval by the Bureau of Indian Affairs and because many of the constitutions adopted under the statute closely resembled non-Indian models of government, which differ in significant ways from traditional tribal political, economic, and religious organization. Nonetheless, within 12 years of the adoption of the act, 161 tribal constitutions had been adopted under the IRA provisions.

The Termination Era (1940-1962). After the New Deal era, the tide again turned away from tribal sovereignty and culture and toward assimilation. Congress passed a series of statutes terminating tribal status for 109 tribes. Any existing reservations of these tribes were disbanded, ending both federal trust supervision and tribal government. Congress also passed Public Law No. 280, transferring civil and criminal jurisdiction previously exercised by federal courts to state authorities in some states. Act of August 15, 1953, ch. 505, 67 Stat. 588 (codified in part at 18 U.S.C. §1162 and 28 U.S.C. §1360). The Bureau of Indian Affairs also set up a relocation program to encourage Indians to move to urban areas.

     The Self-Determination Era (1962-Present). Since the 1960s, both Democratic and Republican administrations have adopted general policies encouraging tribal government and economic organization and development in the form of corporations. At the same time, the *Indian Civil Rights Act of 1968,* 25 U.S.C. §§1301 *et seq.,* imposed most of the provisions of the Bill of Rights on tribal governments. Although the statute arguably protected the rights of tribal members and others in Indian country against tribal governments, the statute may have imposed court procedures and legal arrangements at odds with many tribal cultures and traditional governing processes.

     Increased activity of tribal governments included exercising long dormant treaty rights, such as rights to hunt and fish on public lands that had been ceded to the federal government, and asserting rights to water resources in the western part of the United States. Lawsuits were brought claiming relief for violations of the *Trade and Intercourse Acts.*

§13.2   *Original Indian Title*

§13.2.1   "Title of Occupancy"

See supra §1.1.1, at pages 3–14.

§13.2.2   Takings Doctrine

See supra §1.1.2, at 14–20.

§13.3   *Recognized Title*

§13.3.1   Treaty Abrogation

TREATY WITH THE CHEROKEES FEBRUARY 14, 1883
quoted in Felix S. Cohen's Handbook of Federal
Indian Law 80 (1982 ed.)

     [The Government of the United States affirms its] anxious desire . . . to secure to the Cherokee nation of Indians . . . *a permanent* home, and which shall, under the most solemn guarantee of the United States be, and remain, theirs forever — a home that shall never, in all future time, be embarrassed by having extended around it the lines, or placed over it the jurisdiction of a Territory or State, nor be pressed upon by the extension, in any way, of any of the limits of any existing Territory or State. . . .

STATEMENT TO THE LAKE MOHONK CONFERENCE
SUPPORTING THE DAWES ACT (1885)
LYMAN ABBOTT

quoted in Francis Paul Prucha, The Great Father 2:624 (1984)

Three hundred thousand people have no right to hold a continent and keep at bay a race able to people it and provide the happy homes of civilization. We do owe the Indians sacred rights and obligations, but one of those duties is not the right to let them hold forever the land they did not occupy, and which they were not making fruitful for themselves or others.

THE GREAT FATHER: THE UNITED STATES GOVERNMENT
AND THE AMERICAN INDIANS
FRANCIS PAUL PRUCHA

2:743-744 (1984)

White agitation for changes in the Indian Territory [what became the state of Oklahoma] intensified in the 1880s as new elements came to the fore. Westerners' desire for land, played upon by railroad interests, caused a decade of increasing pressure to open parts of the Territory to homesteaders, and federal officials supported by the humanitarian reformers found new arguments for dividing the Indians' land and absorbing the Indians as citizens of the United States.

The business interests were tireless advocates. Aided by Elias Cornelius Boudinot, of the prominent Ridge faction of the Cherokees, they fostered a group of professional promoters called "boomers," who by propaganda and direct action determined to force open the lands in the territory.... Such activities, together with a tremendous flood of boomer literature, led to organized Oklahoma colonies on the borders of the Indian Territory in Kansas and Texas that claimed the right to homestead in the territory and that, led by such organizers as C. C. Carpenter, David L. Payne, and William L. Couch, made forays into the territory and established incipient communities before they were driven out by federal troops.

The illegal invasions of the Indian Territory stirred new support for the Indians among humanitarians concerned with Indian rights, but the pressure was too great to withstand....

The vacant lands of the Oklahoma District were a powerful magnet for land-hungry westerners, and the reformers, too, could not abide continuing failure to make full use of the lands. When Commissioner [of Indian Affairs] J. D. C. Atkins proposed to move various Indian groups into the district in an attempt to end the agitation for white settlement of the region, Charles C. Painter of the Indian Rights Association replied vigorously, "The purpose to fill up Oklahoma [District] with settlers will never sleep, and ought never to sleep, until it is accomplished," he wrote. "Such an anomaly as is there presented can never be sanctioned and made permanent — that of an immense territory, valuable for its vast resources, and needed to meet the demand for homes by our increasing population, kept empty by the use of the army. It must, it will be opened in some way; it will be occupied and used by somebody."

Little by little, the government gave way. Congressional friends of the boomers regularly introduced bills for opening lands in the territory for homesteading, and in 1889 they succeeded. On March 2, 1889, Congress authorized homesteading in the

Oklahoma District, and President Benjamin Harrison proclaimed the lands open to settlement at noon on April 22, 1889. Fifty thousand homeseekers lined the area waiting for the signal to advance, and when the blast of the bugle sounded, the first of the dramatic Oklahoma "runs" was under way. . . .

§13.3.2 Takings Doctrine

UNITED STATES v. SIOUX NATION OF INDIANS
448 U.S. 371 (1980)

Mr. Justice HARRY A. BLACKMUN delivered the opinion of the Court. . . .

For over a century now the Sioux Nation has claimed that the United States unlawfully abrogated the *Fort Laramie Treaty* of April 29, 1868, 15 Stat. 635, in Art. II of which the United States pledged that the Great Sioux Reservation, including the Black Hills, would be "set apart for the absolute and undisturbed use and occupation of the Indians herein named." The *Fort Laramie Treaty* was concluded at the culmination of the Powder River War of 1866-1867, a series of military engagements in which the Sioux tribes, led by their great chief, Red Cloud, fought to protect the integrity of earlier-recognized treaty lands from the incursion of white settlers.

The *Fort Laramie Treaty* included several agreements central to the issues presented in this case. First, it established the Great Sioux Reservation, a tract of land bounded on the east by the Missouri River, on the south by the northern border of the State of Nebraska, on the north by the forty-sixth parallel of north latitude, and on the west by the one hundred and fourth meridian of west longitude, in addition to certain reservations already existing east of the Missouri. The United States "solemnly agree[d]" that no unauthorized persons "shall ever be permitted to pass over, settle upon, or reside in [this] territory."

Second, the United States permitted members of the Sioux tribes to select lands within the reservation for cultivation. In order to assist the Sioux in becoming civilized farmers, the Government promised to provide them with the necessary services and materials, and with subsistence rations for four years.

Third, in exchange for the benefits conferred by the treaty, the Sioux agreed to relinquish their rights under the Treaty of September 17, 1851, to occupy territories outside the reservation, while reserving their "right to hunt on any lands north of North Platte, and on the Republican Fork of the Smoky Hill river, so long as the buffalo may range thereon in such numbers as to justify the chase." The Indians also expressly agreed to withdraw all opposition to the building of railroads that did not pass over their reservation lands, not to engage in attacks on settlers, and to withdraw their opposition to the military posts and roads that had been established south of the North Platte River.

Fourth, Art. XII of the treaty provided:

> No treaty for the cession of any portion or part of the reservation herein described which may be held in common shall be of any validity or force as against the said Indians, unless executed and signed by at least three fourths of all the adult male Indians, occupying or interested in the same.

The years following the treaty brought relative peace to the Dakotas, an era of tranquility that was disturbed, however, by renewed speculation that the Black Hills, which were included in the Great Sioux Reservation, contained vast quantities of gold

The Black Hills of South Dakota
Photograph by Richard Erdoes.

and silver. In 1874 the Army planned and undertook an exploratory expedition into the Hills, both for the purpose of establishing a military outpost from which to control those Sioux who had not accepted the terms of the *Fort Laramie Treaty*, and for the purpose of investigating "the country about which dreamy stories have been told." Lieutenant Colonel George Armstrong Custer led the expedition of close to 1,000 soldiers and teamsters, and a substantial number of military and civilian aides. Custer's journey began at Fort Abraham Lincoln on the Missouri River on July 2, 1874. By the end of that month they had reached the Black Hills, and by mid-August had confirmed the presence of gold fields in that region. The discovery of gold was widely reported in newspapers across the country. Custer's florid descriptions of the mineral and timber resources of the Black Hills, and the land's suitability for grazing and cultivation, also received wide circulation, and had the effect of creating an intense popular demand for the "opening" of the Hills for settlement. The only obstacle to "progress" was the *Fort Laramie Treaty* that reserved occupancy of the Hills to the Sioux.

Having promised the Sioux that the Black Hills were reserved to them, the United States Army was placed in the position of having to threaten military force, and occasionally to use it, to prevent prospectors and settlers from trespassing on lands reserved to the Indians. For example, in September 1874, General Sheridan sent instructions to Brigadier General Alfred H. Terry, Commander of the Department of Dakota, at Saint Paul, directing him to use force to prevent companies of prospectors from trespassing on the Sioux Reservation. . . .

Eventually, however, the Executive Branch of the Government decided to abandon the Nation's treaty obligation to preserve the integrity of the Sioux territory. In a letter dated November 9, 1875, to Terry, Sheridan reported that he had met with President Grant, the Secretary of the Interior, and the Secretary of War, and that the President had decided that the military should make no further resistance to the occupation of the Black Hills by miners, "it being his belief that such resistance only increased their desire and complicated the troubles." These orders were to be enforced "quietly," and the President's decision was to remain "confidential."

With the Army's withdrawal from its role as enforcer of the *Fort Laramie Treaty*, the influx of settlers into the Black Hills increased. The Government concluded that the only practical course was to secure to the citizens of the United States the right to mine the Black Hills for gold. Toward that end, the Secretary of the Interior, in the spring of 1875, appointed a commission to negotiate with the Sioux. The commission was headed by William B. Allison. The tribal leaders of the Sioux were aware of the mineral value of the Black Hills and refused to sell the land for a price less than $70 million. The commission offered the Indians an annual rental of $400,000, or payment of $6 million for absolute relinquishment of the Black Hills. The negotiations broke down.

In the winter of 1875-1876, many of the Sioux were hunting in the unceded territory north of the North Platte River, reserved to them for that purpose in the *Fort Laramie Treaty*. On December 6, 1875, for reasons that are not entirely clear, the Commissioner of Indian Affairs sent instructions to the Indian agents on the reservation to notify those hunters that if they did not return to the reservation agencies by January 31, 1876, they would be treated as "hostiles." Given the severity of the winter, compliance with these instructions was impossible. On February 1, the Secretary of the Interior nonetheless relinquished jurisdiction over all hostile Sioux, including those Indians exercising their treaty-protected hunting rights, to the War Department. The Army's campaign against the "hostiles" led to Sitting Bull's notable victory over Custer's forces at the battle of the Little Big Horn on June 25. That victory, of course, was short-lived, and those Indians who surrendered to the Army were returned to the reservation, and deprived of their weapons and horses, leaving them completely dependent for survival on rations provided them by the Government.

In the meantime, Congress was becoming increasingly dissatisfied with the failure of the Sioux living on the reservation to become self-sufficient. The Sioux' entitlement to subsistence rations under the terms of the *Fort Laramie Treaty* had expired in 1872. Nonetheless, in each of the two following years, over $1 million was appropriated for feeding the Sioux. In August 1876, Congress enacted an appropriations bill providing that "hereafter there shall be no appropriation made for the subsistence" of the

Sioux, unless they first relinquished their rights to the hunting grounds outside the reservation, ceded the Black Hills to the United States, and reached some accommodation with the Government that would be calculated to enable them to become self-supporting. Toward this end, Congress requested the President to appoint another commission to negotiate with the Sioux for the cession of the Black Hills.

This commission, headed by George Manypenny, arrived in the Sioux country in early September and commenced meetings with the head men of the various tribes. The members of the commission impressed upon the Indians that the United States no longer had any obligation to provide them with subsistence rations. The commissioners brought with them the text of a treaty that had been prepared in advance. The principal provisions of this treaty were that the Sioux would relinquish their rights to the Black Hills and other lands west of the one hundred and third meridian, and their rights to hunt in the unceded territories to the north, in exchange for subsistence rations for as long as they would be needed to ensure the Sioux's survival. In setting out to obtain the tribes' agreement to this treaty, the commission ignored the stipulation of the *Fort Laramie Treaty* that any cession of the lands contained within the Great Sioux Reservation would have to be joined in by three-fourths of the adult males. Instead, the treaty was presented just to Sioux chiefs and their leading men. It was signed by only 10% of the adult male Sioux population.

Congress resolved the impasse by enacting the 1876 "agreement" into law as the Act of Feb. 28, 1877 (*1877 Act*), 19 Stat. 254. The Act had the effect of abrogating the earlier *Fort Laramie Treaty*, and of implementing the terms of the Manypenny Commission's "agreement" with the Sioux leaders.

The passage of the *1877 Act* legitimized the settlers' invasion of the Black Hills, but throughout the years it has been regarded by the Sioux as a breach of this Nation's solemn obligation to reserve the Hills in perpetuity for occupation by the Indians....

II

[This case has a tortured procedural history. In 1946, Congress passed the *Indian Claims Commission Act*, 60 Stat. 1049, 25 U.S.C. §§70 *et seq.*, creating a new forum to hear and adjudicate tribal grievances that had previously arisen. The commission found that Congress, in 1877, had made no effort to give the Sioux full value for the ceded reservation lands. The only new obligation assumed by the government in exchange for the Black Hills was its promise to provide the Sioux with subsistence rations, an obligation that had no relationship to the value of the property acquired. The Court of Claims affirmed the commission's holding that the *1877 Act* effected a taking of the Black Hills and of rights-of-way across the reservation, but reversed the commission's determination that the Sioux Nation was also entitled to compensation for the gold that had been taken.]

IV

A

In reaching its conclusion that the *1877 Act* effected a taking of the Black Hills for which just compensation was due the Sioux under the Fifth Amendment, the Court of Claims relied upon the "good faith effort" test developed in its earlier decision in *Three*

Tribes of Fort Berthold Reservation v. United States, 390 F.2d 686 (Ct. Cl. 1968). The *Fort Berthold* test had been designed to reconcile two lines of cases decided by this Court that seemingly were in conflict. The first line, exemplified by *Lone Wolf v. Hitchcock*, 187 U.S. 553 (1903), recognizes "that Congress possesse[s] a paramount power over the property of the Indians, by reason of its exercise of guardianship over their interests, and that such authority might be implied, even though opposed to the strict letter of a treaty with the Indians." *Id.*, at 565. The second line, exemplified by the more recent decision in *Shoshone Tribe v. United States*, 299 U.S. 476 (1937), concedes Congress' paramount power over Indian property, but holds, nonetheless, that "[t]he power does not extend so far as to enable the Government 'to give the tribal lands to others, or to appropriate them to its own purposes, without rendering, or assuming an obligation to render, just compensation.'" *Id.*, at 497 (quoting *United States v. Creek Nation*, 295 U.S. 103 (1935)). In *Shoshone Tribe*, Mr. Justice Cardozo, in speaking for the Court, expressed the distinction between the conflicting principles in a characteristically pithy phrase: "Spoliation is not management." 299 U.S., at 498.

The *Fort Berthold* test distinguishes between cases in which one or the other principle is applicable:

> It is obvious that Congress cannot simultaneously (1) act as trustee for the benefit of the Indians, exercising its plenary powers over the Indians and their property, as it thinks is in their best interests, and (2) exercise its sovereign power of eminent domain, taking the Indians' property within the meaning of the Fifth Amendment to the Constitution. In any given situation in which Congress has acted with regard to Indian people, it must have acted either in one capacity or the other. Congress can own two hats, but it cannot wear them both at the same time.
>
> Some guideline must be established so that a court can identify in which capacity Congress is acting. The following guideline would best give recognition to the basic distinction between the two types of congressional action: Where Congress makes a good faith effort to give the Indians the full value of the land and thus merely transmutes the property from land to money, there is no taking.
>
> This is a mere substitution of assets or change of form and is a traditional function of a trustee. 390 F.2d, at 691.

Applying the *Fort Berthold* test to the facts of this case, the Court of Claims concluded that, in passing the *1877 Act*, Congress had not made a good-faith effort to give the Sioux the full value of the Black Hills. The principal issue presented by this case is whether the legal standard applied by the Court of Claims was erroneous.

B

The Government contends that the Court of Claims erred insofar as its holding that the *1877 Act* effected a taking of the Black Hills was based on Congress' failure to indicate affirmatively that the consideration given the Sioux was of equivalent value to the property rights ceded to the Government. It argues that "the true rule is that Congress must be assumed to be acting within its plenary power to manage tribal assets if it reasonably can be concluded that the legislation was intended to promote the welfare of the tribe." The Government derives support for this rule principally from this Court's decision in *Lone Wolf v. Hitchcock*.

[In *Lone Wolf*, representatives of the Kiowa, Comanche, and Apache Tribes claimed that the United States had taken their property in violation of an earlier treaty, which, like the *Fort Laramie Treaty of 1868*, required agreement by three-fourths of the adult male tribal members. The Court's principal holding in *Lone Wolf* was that "it was never doubted" that Congress had the power to abrogate treaties with American Indian nations.]

In the penultimate paragraph of the opinion, however, the Court in *Lone Wolf* went on to make some observations seemingly directed to the question whether the Act at issue might constitute a taking of Indian property without just compensation. The Court there stated:

> The act of June 6, 1900, which is complained of in the bill, . . . purported to give an adequate consideration for the surplus lands not allotted among the Indians or reserved for their benefit. . . . [T]he action of Congress now complained of was but an exercise of [Congress' administrative power over Indian land], a mere change in the form of investment of Indian tribal property, the property of those who, as we have held, were in substantial effect the wards of the government. *We must presume that Congress acted in perfect good faith in the dealings with the Indians of which complaint is made, and that the legislative branch of the government exercised its best judgment in the premises.* In any event, as Congress possessed full power in the matter, the judiciary cannot question or inquire into the motives which prompted the enactment of this legislation. If injury was occasioned, which we do not wish to be understood as implying, by the use made by Congress of its power, relief must be sought by an appeal to that body for redress and not to the courts. The legislation in question was constitutional. *Id.* (Emphasis supplied.)

The Government relies on the italicized sentence in the quotation above to support its view "that Congress must be assumed to be acting within its plenary power to manage tribal assets if it reasonably can be concluded that the legislation was intended to promote the welfare of the tribe." Several adjoining passages in the paragraph, however, lead us to doubt whether the *Lone Wolf* Court meant to state a general rule applicable to cases such as the one before us.

First, *Lone Wolf* presented a situation in which Congress "purported to give an adequate consideration" for the treaty lands taken from the Indians. In fact, the Act at issue set aside for the Indians a sum certain of $2 million for surplus reservation lands surrendered to the United States. In contrast, the background of the *1877 Act* "reveals a situation where Congress did not 'purport' to provide 'adequate consideration,' nor was there any meaningful negotiation or arm's-length bargaining, nor did Congress consider it was paying a fair price."

Second, given the provisions of the Act at issue in *Lone Wolf*, the Court reasonably was able to conclude that "the action of Congress now complained of was but . . . a mere change in the form of investment of Indian tribal property." Under the Act of June 6, 1900, each head of a family was to be allotted a tract of land within the reservation of not less than 320 acres, an additional 480,000 acres of grazing land were set aside for the use of the tribes in common, and $2 million was paid to the Indians for the remaining surplus. In contrast, the historical background to the opening of the Black Hills for settlement, and the terms of the *1877 Act* itself, would not lead one to conclude that the Act effected "a mere change in the form of investment of Indian tribal property."

Third, it seems... that the Court's conclusive presumption of congressional good faith was based in large measure on the idea that relations between this Nation and the Indian tribes are a political matter, not amenable to judicial review. That view, of course, has long since been discredited in taking cases, and was expressly laid to rest in *Delaware Tribal Business Comm. v. Weeks*, 430 U.S. 73, 84 (1977)....

The foregoing considerations support our conclusion that the passage from *Lone Wolf* here relied upon by the Government has limited relevance to this case. More significantly, *Lone Wolf*'s presumption of congressional good faith has little to commend it as an enduring principle for deciding questions of the kind presented here....[29]

C

We turn to the question whether the Court of Claims' inquiry in this case was guided by an appropriate legal standard. We conclude that it was....

The "good faith effort" and "transmutation of property" concepts referred to in *Fort Berthold* are opposite sides of the same coin. They reflect the traditional rule that a trustee may change the form of trust assets as long as he fairly (or in good faith) attempts to provide his ward with property of equivalent value. If he does that, he cannot be faulted if hindsight should demonstrate a lack of precise equivalence. On the other hand, if a trustee (or the government in its dealings with the Indians) does not attempt to give the ward the fair equivalent of what he acquires from him, the trustee to that extent has taken rather than transmuted the property of the ward. In other words, an essential element of the inquiry under the *Fort Berthold* guideline is determining the adequacy of the consideration the government gave for the Indian lands it acquired. That inquiry cannot be avoided by the government's simple assertion that it acted in good faith in its dealings with the Indians. 601 F.2d, at 1162.

D

We next examine the factual findings made by the Court of Claims, which led it to the conclusion that the *1877 Act* effected a taking. First, the Court found that "[t]he only item of 'consideration' that possibly could be viewed as showing an attempt by Congress to give the Sioux the 'full value' of the land the government took from them was the requirement to furnish them with rations until they became self-sufficient."...

Second, the court found, after engaging in an exhaustive review of the historical record, that neither the Manypenny Commission, nor the congressional Committees that approved the *1877 Act*, nor the individual legislators who spoke on its behalf on the floor of Congress, ever indicated a belief that the Government's obligation to provide

---

29. Of course, it has long been held that the taking by the United States of "unrecognized" or "aboriginal" Indian title is not compensable under the Fifth Amendment. *Tee-Hit-Ton Indians v. United States*, 348 U.S. 272 (1955). The principles we set forth today are applicable only to instances in which "Congress by treaty or other agreement has declared that thereafter Indians were to hold the lands permanently." *Id.*, at 277. In such instances, "compensation must be paid for subsequent taking." *Id.*, at 277-278.

the Sioux with rations constituted a fair equivalent for the value of the Black Hills and the additional property rights the Indians were forced to surrender....

A third finding lending some weight to the Court's legal conclusion was that the conditions placed by the Government on the Sioux's entitlement to rations "further show that the government's undertaking to furnish rations to the Indians until they could support themselves did not reflect a congressional decision that the value of the rations was the equivalent of the land the Indians were giving up, but instead was an attempt to coerce the Sioux into capitulating to congressional demands."...

Finally, the Court of Claims rejected the Government's contention that the fact that it subsequently had spent at least $43 million on rations for the Sioux (over the course of three-quarters of a century) established that the *1877 Act* was an act of guardianship taken in the Sioux' best interest. The court concluded: "The critical inquiry is what Congress did — and how it viewed the obligation it was assuming — at the time it acquired the land, and not how much it ultimately cost the United States to fulfill the obligation." It found no basis for believing that Congress, in 1877, anticipated that it would take the Sioux such a lengthy period of time to become self-sufficient, or that the fulfillment of the Government's obligation to feed the Sioux would entail the large expenditures ultimately made on their behalf. We find no basis on which to question the legal standard applied by the Court of Claims, or the findings it reached, concerning Congress' decision to provide the Sioux with rations....

V

In sum, we conclude that the legal analysis and factual findings of the Court of Claims fully support its conclusion that the terms of the *1877 Act* did not effect "a mere change in the form of investment of Indian tribal property." *Lone Wolf v. Hitchcock*, 187 U.S., at 568. Rather, the *1877 Act* effected a taking of tribal property, property which had been set aside for the exclusive occupation of the Sioux by the *Fort Laramie Treaty of 1868*. That taking implied an obligation on the part of the Government to make just compensation to the Sioux Nation, and that obligation, including an award of interest, must now, at last, be paid....

Mr. Justice WILLIAM H. REHNQUIST, dissenting....

[T]he dissenting judges in the Court of Claims opinion under review pointedly stated: "The majority's view that the rations were not consideration for the Black Hills is untenable. What else was the money for?"

I think the Court today rejects that conclusion largely on the basis of a view of the settlement of the American West which is not universally shared. There were undoubtedly greed, cupidity, and other less-than-admirable tactics employed by the Government during the Black Hills episode in the settlement of the West, but the Indians did not lack their share of villainy either. It seems to me quite unfair to judge by the light of "revisionist" historians or the mores of another era actions that were taken under pressure of time more than a century ago.

Different historians, not writing for the purpose of having their conclusions or observations inserted in the reports of congressional committees, have taken different positions than those expressed in some of the materials referred to in the Court's opinion. This is not unnatural, since history, no more than law, is not an exact (or for that matter an inexact) science....

Another history highlights the cultural differences which made conflict and brutal warfare inevitable:

> The Plains Indians seldom practiced agriculture or other primitive arts, but they were fine physical specimens; and in warfare, once they had learned the use of the rifle, [were] much more formidable than the Eastern tribes who had slowly yielded to the white man. Tribe warred with tribe, and a highly developed sign language was the only means of inter-tribal communication. The effective unit was the band or village of a few hundred souls, which might be seen in the course of its wanderings encamped by a water-course with tipis erected; or pouring over the plain, women and children leading dogs and packhorses with their trailing travois, while gaily dressed braves loped ahead on horseback. They lived only for the day, recognized no rights of property, robbed or killed anyone if they thought they could get away with it, inflicted cruelty without a qualm, and endured torture without flinching. S. Morison, *The Oxford History of the American People* 539-540 (1965).

That there was tragedy, deception, barbarity, and virtually every other vice known to man in the 300-year history of the expansion of the original 13 Colonies into a Nation which now embraces more than three million square miles and 50 States cannot be denied. But in a court opinion, as a historical and not a legal matter, both settler and Indian are entitled to the benefit of the Biblical adjuration: "Judge not, that ye be not judged."

NOTES AND QUESTIONS

1. What justifies allowing the federal government to take the recognized property of American Indian nations so long as it does so in "good faith" and attempts to grant "equivalent value"? Outside the Indian context, when the government takes property without paying just compensation its good faith or bad faith is irrelevant; it is obligated to pay just compensation, and this duty is enforceable in the courts. Does the Supreme Court believe the United States government can be trusted when it deals with Indian lands but not when it deals with non-Indian lands? Is there any basis for such a conclusion?

2. Why was the Sioux Nation denied the value of the gold taken by the miners? The commission had ruled that the federal government was responsible for the loss of the gold, worth $450,000, because the 1868 treaty contained a promise by the United States that unauthorized persons would not be permitted to enter the reservation, and the removal of the gold was the "direct and natural consequence of President Grant's order that the Army withdraw from the Black Hills and stop interfering with the miners attempting to enter there." The Court of Claims overturned the commission's ruling that the Sioux Nation was entitled to such compensation. 601 F.2d 1157 (Ct. Cl. 1979). Chief Judge Daniel M. Friedman explained that "the government neither brought the miners onto the Black Hills land nor encouraged them to settle there. On the contrary, the government originally attempted to exclude them, and Congress repeatedly criticized the miners' trespassing onto the land." *Id.* at 1172.

While it is true that the government is not ordinarily responsible for the actions of trespassers, the state's failure to enforce the trespass laws may constitute state action that unconstitutionally takes property without just compensation. Suppose, for example, a group of homeless people move into an apartment that has recently become vacant. The owner, who has been looking for a new tenant, calls the police to remove the trespassers. After hearing about the problem, the mayor calls the chief of police and orders her not to remove the tenants. The landlord goes to court to obtain an eviction order; although he is clearly entitled to relief under prior state law, the court fails to enforce that law. There is no general change in property law; other landlords are routinely granted evictions under these circumstances. The owner brings an action in federal court, arguing that the city's failure to enforce the trespass laws in this case constitutes a taking of its property without just compensation. How would Chief Judge Friedman rule on this case? Is this situation distinguishable from *Sioux Nation*? If not, does this mean *Sioux Nation* was incorrectly decided?

3. Of what relevance is Justice Rehnquist's observation that in the history of the expansion of the United States into Indian country, savagery was practiced by both sides? Does this advance the determination whether the amount of compensation given to the Sioux Nation was adequate? What does Justice Rehnquist's description of the "Plains Indians" add to the analysis? Does the view he expresses justify taking Indian lands without just compensation? If not, why is it there?

4. In 1946, Congress passed the *Indian Claims Commission Act*, creating a special commission (which lasted until 1978) to hear claims based on pre-1946 takings of Indian lands. In 1978, remaining cases were transferred to the Court of Claims, which was empowered to hear claims based on post-1946 takings. The commission interpreted its mandate as limited to providing compensation; it never undertook to purchase or obtain the return of state or federal lands wrongfully taken from Indian nations. Compensation was granted for takings of both original Indian title land and recognized title land; the amount of compensation due was measured by the value of the land at the time of the taking — in many cases, low, nineteenth century values. Interest was due on the payment only in takings of recognized title land since such takings arguably violated the fifth amendment. No interest was payable for takings of original Indian title lands since, under the reasoning of *Tee-Hit-Ton Indians v. United States* (reprinted at *supra* §1.1.2), these lands did not constitute "property" within the meaning of the fifth amendment.

§13.3.3   Current Indian Land Claims

See supra §1.1.3, at 20–24.

§13.4   *Restricted Trust Allotments*

See supra §1.4.1, at 63–69.

VI

Beyond Real Property

14

Intellectual Property

§14.1 Intangible Property

Traditionally, the most important property rights concerned tangible objects—most notably, land. Wealth is increasingly embodied in less tangible resources, such as financial assets. The least tangible thing imaginable is an idea. Can one own an idea? Most ideas are free for public use, but they—as well as other intangible assets—are sometimes granted the status of property. Intellectual property law regulates control over the products of intellectual effort. It is one of the fastest growing areas of property law and of legal practice.

The core subjects of intellectual property law—trademarks, copyrights, and patents—are all governed by federal statutes. The U.S. Constitution authorizes Congress to "promote the progress of science and useful arts, by securing for limited times to authors and inventors the exclusive right to their respective writings and discoveries." U.S. Const. art. I, §8, cl. 8. Pursuant to this clause, Congress has passed legislation protecting both copyrights and patents. Copyright law grants exclusive rights in literary and artistic works, including books, poetry, song, dance, dramatic works, computer programs, movies, sculpture, and paintings. Patent law grants exclusive rights in inventions, including processes, machines, and compositions of matter. Robert P. Merges, Peter S. Menell, & Mark A. Lemley, *Intellectual Property in the New Technological Age* 23-24 (2000).

A third major area of intellectual property law is trademark law. Trademark law grants exclusive rights in symbols that indicate the source of goods or services. Unlike copyright and patent law, trademark and unfair competition law originated in state common law; federal legislation generally supplements, but does not displace, the common law in these areas. Trademark law grew out of the law of unfair competition and misappropriation, which prohibits companies from using information obtained from competitors in ways that unfairly appropriate the products of their competitors' efforts.

State common law has recently developed "publicity rights" to protect the ability of individuals to control the commercial use of their names or images. Limited protection has also emerged for "moral rights" that give artists the ability to prevent their works from being mutilated or misrepresented by subsequent owners.

Intellectual property law is beset by internal tensions. Ideas are generally not subject to ownership. We must be free to use ideas generated by both ourselves and others in order to engage in all human activity. Too much private property in ideas would limit our autonomy and block desirable economic activity by creating insuperable transaction costs. At the same time, exclusive control over certain intellectual products is necessary both to protect the ability of authors and inventors to get credit for their works and to create economic incentives to spur intellectual inquiry. Determining when the products of human effort should be subject to the creator's control and when they should become the common property of humankind is the core problem of intellectual property law.

§14.2 Unfair Competition and Misappropriation

See supra §1.3.1, at pages 32-45.

§14.3 Trademark Law

A trademark is a name, symbol, or type of packaging that identifies the producer of a good or service. Unlike copyright and patent law, trademark law is primarily based on state common law, not federal statute. The patent and copyright clause of the U.S. Constitution authorizes Congress to provide protection for original works of authorship and inventions. U.S. Const. art. I, §8, cl. 8. The first trademark laws, passed by Congress in 1870 and 1876, were struck down as unconstitutional in 1879 by the Supreme Court because they applied without regard to originality or novelty, crucial requirements for copyrights and patents. *United States v. Steffens* (*The Trade-Mark Cases*), 100 U.S. 82 (1879). Congress did, however, have the power to regulate interstate commerce. U.S. Const. art. I, §8, cl. 3. Because the Court considered trademarks to be a form of property within the purview of state regulation, Congress responded by passing statutes in 1881 and 1905 that addressed the interstate use of trademarks. The current federal trademark act, called the *Lanham Act*, 15 U.S.C. §§1051-1127, provides for the registration of trademarks created by state law, along with some rights that may supplement or displace state law.

Trademark law gives the owner of the "mark" the exclusive right to use it in connection with the sale of a particular good or service in a particular area. This protects consumers from the *confusion* resulting from different companies using the same or similar names. *See Jordache Enterprises, Inc. v. Levi Strauss & Co.*, 841 F. Supp. 506 (S.D.N.Y. 1993) (holding that "Jordache Basics 101" may be confusingly similar to "Levi's 501 jeans"). However, trademark law does not give consumers a legal claim; rather, only a company that is using the mark may sue to prevent competitors from appropriating the goodwill associated with its mark. Trademark law grows out of state unfair competition law that prohibits "palming off" one's products as those of another. It therefore protects the goodwill associated with a particular company or product line from unfair competition.

Unlike copyright and patents, trademarks only garner protection if they are *used in commerce* to sell goods or services. Failure to use a mark for a long time may constitute *abandonment* of it. The first to use the mark in connection with a business establishes the mark and will prevail over a later user. The trademark's value, of course, is much more than just ease of identification. Once customers develop loyalty to a brand name, the trademark itself has substantial value. A name can become associated with quality, and this goodwill is a substantial property interest. For this reason, a trademark infringement will be found if confusion may result from a competitor's later use of a mark.

Words that describe goods generally (*generic names*) cannot be trademarked both because they are unlikely to signal a particular maker and because competitors are likely to need to use those words to sell their goods. Names that began by representing particular companies may become generic over time if people start using the trade name to mean the product itself, such as Scotch tape or Kleenex. *See America Online v. AT&T Corp.*, 243 F.3d 812 (4th Cir. 2001) ("instant messaging" and "you have mail" cannot be trademarked because they are generic terms; however, "Buddy List" may not be generic in the eyes of the public).

The *Lanham Act*, 15 U.S.C. §§1051-1127, provides notice of trademarks by allowing them to be registered with the federal Patent and Trademark Office. 15 U.S.C. §1072. Those wishing to register a mark must assert that they are currently using the mark in connection with a business or that they intend to do so shortly. Use must commence within 24 months at the latest. Like the recording system for deeds, registration places the whole world on actual or constructive notice of existing trademarks. Later users of a mark cannot claim to have used it in good faith or without knowledge of its prior use. A trademark may not be registered if it was in prior use by another (unless that use has been abandoned) or if there is a likelihood of confusion.

QUALITEX CO. v. JACOBSON PRODUCTS CO.
514 U.S. 159 (1995)

Justice STEPHEN BREYER delivered the opinion of the Court.

The question in this case is whether the *Trademark Act of 1946* (*Lanham Act*), 15 U.S.C. §§1051-1127, permits the registration of a trademark that consists, purely and simply, of a color. We conclude that, sometimes, a color will meet ordinary legal trademark requirements. And, when it does so, no special legal rule prevents color alone from serving as a trademark.

The case before us grows out of petitioner Qualitex Company's use (since the 1950's) of a special shade of green-gold color on the pads that it makes and sells to dry cleaning firms for use on dry cleaning presses. In 1989, respondent Jacobson Products (a Qualitex rival) began to sell its own press pads to dry cleaning firms; and it colored those pads a similar green-gold. In 1991, Qualitex registered the special green-gold color on press pads with the Patent and Trademark Office as a trademark. Qualitex subsequently added a trademark infringement count, 15 U.S.C. §1114(1), to an unfair competition claim, §1125(a), in a lawsuit it had already filed challenging Jacobson's use of the green-gold color. . . .

The *Lanham Act* gives a seller or producer the exclusive right to "register" a trademark, 15 U.S.C. §1052, and to prevent his or her competitors from using that trademark, §1114(1). Both the language of the Act and the basic underlying principles of trademark law would seem to include color within the universe of things that can qualify as a trademark. The language of the *Lanham Act* describes that universe in the broadest of terms. It says that trademarks "include any word, name, symbol, or device, or any combination thereof." §1127. Since human beings might use as a "symbol" or "device" almost anything at all that is capable of carrying meaning, this language, read literally, is not restrictive. The courts and the Patent and Trademark Office have authorized for use as a mark a particular shape (of a Coca-Cola bottle), a particular sound (of NBC's three chimes), and even a particular scent (of plumeria blossoms on sewing thread). If a shape, a sound, and a fragrance can act as symbols why, one might ask, can a color not do the same?

A color is also capable of satisfying the more important part of the statutory definition of a trademark, which requires that a person "use" or "intend to use" the mark "to identify and distinguish his or her goods, including a unique product, from those manufactured or sold by others and to indicate the source of the goods, even if that source is unknown." 15 U.S.C. §1127.

True, a product's color is unlike "fanciful," "arbitrary," or "suggestive" words or designs, which almost *automatically* tell a customer that they refer to a brand. The imaginary word "Suntost," or the words "Suntost Marmalade," on a jar of orange jam immediately would signal a brand or a product "source"; the jam's orange color does not do so. But, over time, customers may come to treat a particular color on a product or its packaging (say, a color that in context seems unusual, such as pink on a firm's insulating material or red on the head of a large industrial bolt) as signifying a brand. And, if so, that color would have come to identify and distinguish the goods — *i.e.*, "to indicate" their "source" — much in the way that descriptive words on a product (say, "Trim" on nail clippers or "Car-Freshner" on deodorizer) can come to indicate a product's origin. In this circumstance, trademark law says that the word (*e.g.*, "Trim"), although not inherently distinctive, has developed "secondary meaning." *See Inwood Laboratories, Inc. v. Ives Laboratories, Inc.*, 456 U.S. 844, 851, n.11 (1982) ("Secondary meaning" is acquired when "in the minds of the public, the primary significance of a product feature . . . is to identify the source of the product rather than the product itself"). . . .

We cannot find in the basic objectives of trademark law any obvious theoretical objection to the use of color alone as a trademark, where that color has attained "secondary meaning" and therefore identifies and distinguishes a particular brand (and thus indicates its "source"). In principle, trademark law, by preventing others from copying a source-identifying mark, "reduce[s] the customer's costs of shopping and making purchasing decisions," 1 J. McCarthy, *McCarthy on Trademarks and Unfair Competition* §2.01[2], pp. 2-3 (3d ed. 1994), for it quickly and easily assures a potential customer that *this* item — the item with this mark — is made by the same producer as other similarly marked items that he or she liked (or disliked) in the past. At the same time, the law helps assure a producer that it (and not an imitating competitor) will reap the financial, reputation-related rewards associated with a desirable product. The law thereby "encourage[s] the production of quality products," and simultaneously discourages those who hope to sell inferior products by capitalizing on a consumer's inability quickly to evaluate the quality of an item offered for sale. It is the source-distinguishing ability of a mark — not its ontological status as color, shape, fragrance, word, or sign — that permits it to serve these basic purposes. And, for that reason, it is difficult to find, in basic trademark objectives, a reason to disqualify absolutely the use of a color as a mark.

Neither can we find a principled objection to the use of color as a mark in the important "functionality" doctrine of trademark law. The functionality doctrine prevents trademark law, which seeks to promote competition by protecting a firm's reputation, from instead inhibiting legitimate competition by allowing a producer to control a useful product feature. It is the province of patent law, not trademark law, to encourage invention by granting inventors a monopoly over new product designs or functions for a limited time, 35 U.S.C. §§154, 173, after which competitors are free to use the innovation. If a product's functional features could be used as trademarks, however, a monopoly over such features could be obtained without regard to whether they qualify as patents and could be extended forever (because trademarks may be renewed in perpetuity).... This Court consequently has explained that, "in general terms, a product feature is functional," and cannot serve as a trademark, "if it is essential to the use or purpose of the article or if it affects the cost or quality of the article," that is, if exclusive use of the feature would put competitors at a significant non-reputation-related disadvantage. *Inwood Laboratories, Inc., supra,* at 850, n.10. Although sometimes color plays an important role (unrelated to source identification) in making a product more desirable, sometimes it does not. And, this latter fact — the fact that sometimes color is not essential to a product's use or purpose and does not affect cost or quality — indicates that the doctrine of "functionality" does not create an absolute bar to the use of color alone as a mark.

It would seem, then, that color alone, at least sometimes, can meet the basic legal requirements for use as a trademark. It can act as a symbol that distinguishes a firm's goods and identifies their source, without serving any other significant function.... Indeed, the District Court, in this case, entered findings... that show Qualitex's green-gold press pad color has met these requirements. The green-gold color acts as a symbol. Having developed secondary meaning (for customers identified the green-gold color as Qualitex's), it identifies the press pads' source. And, the green-gold color serves no other function.... Accordingly, unless there is some special reason that convincingly militates against the use of color alone as a trademark, trademark law would protect Qualitex's use of the green-gold color on its press pads....

Respondent Jacobson Products says that there are ... special reasons why the law should forbid the use of color alone as a trademark. We shall explain, in turn, why we, ultimately, find them unpersuasive.

First, Jacobson says that, if the law permits the use of color as a trademark, it will produce uncertainty and unresolvable court disputes about what shades of a color a competitor may lawfully use. Because lighting (morning sun, twilight mist) will affect perceptions of protected color, competitors and courts will suffer from "shade confusion" as they try to decide whether use of a similar color on a similar product does, or does not, confuse customers and thereby infringe a trademark. Jacobson adds that the "shade confusion" problem is "more difficult" and "far different from" the "determination of the similarity of words or symbols."

We do not believe, however, that color, in this respect, is special. Courts traditionally decide quite difficult questions about whether two words or phrases or symbols are sufficiently similar, in context, to confuse buyers. They have had to compare, for example, such words as "Bonamine" and "Dramamine" (motion-sickness remedies); "Huggies" and "Dougies" (diapers); "Cheracol" and "Syrocol" (cough syrup); "Cyclone" and "Tornado" (wire fences); and "Mattres" and "1-800-Mattres" (mattress franchisor telephone numbers)....

Second, Jacobson argues, as have others, that colors are in limited supply. Jacobson claims that, if one of many competitors can appropriate a particular color for use as a trademark, and each competitor then tries to do the same, the supply of colors will soon be depleted.... [I]n the context of a particular product, only some colors are usable. By the time one discards colors that, say, for reasons of customer appeal, are not usable, and adds the shades that competitors cannot use lest they risk infringing a similar, registered shade, then one is left with only a handful of possible colors. And, under these circumstances, to permit one, or a few, producers to use colors as trademarks will "deplete" the supply of usable colors to the point where a competitor's inability to find a suitable color will put that competitor at a significant disadvantage.

This argument is unpersuasive, however, largely because it relies on an occasional problem to justify a blanket prohibition. When a color serves as a mark, normally alternative colors will likely be available for similar use by others. Moreover, if that is not so — if a "color depletion" or "color scarcity" problem does arise — the trademark doctrine of "functionality" normally would seem available to prevent the anticompetitive consequences that Jacobson's argument posits, thereby minimizing that argument's practical force.

The functionality doctrine...forbids the use of a product's feature as a trademark where doing so will put a competitor at a significant disadvantage because the feature is "essential to the use or purpose of the article" or "affects [its] cost or quality." The functionality doctrine thus protects competitors against a disadvantage (unrelated to recognition or reputation) that trademark protection might otherwise impose, namely their inability reasonably to replicate important non-reputation-related product features....

NOTES AND QUESTIONS

1. *Dilution.* In 1996, the *Lanham Act* was amended to protect owners of "famous marks" against "dilution of the distinctive quality of the mark" by giving them the right to obtain injunctive relief against competing uses even in the absence of consumer confusion. 15 U.S.C. §1125(c) (codifying the *Federal Trademark Dilution Act of 1995*, Pub. L. No. 104-374, §3 (1996)). The statute explicitly allows use of a mark in "comparative commercial advertising." *Id.* at §1125(c)(4)(A). State anti-dilution laws continue to apply to "non-famous" marks.

A mark may be diluted either because of *tarnishment* or *blurring*. Tarnishment occurs if a company sells inferior quality products. For example, the Singer name is commercially associated with sewing machines. If a business starts selling Singer vacuum cleaners, and they are of inferior quality, the Singer name might come to be associated with shoddy products and the value of the Singer name associated with sewing machines might decrease.[1] Blurring occurs when a distinctive mark begins to lose its association with a particular company. For example, Pepperidge Farm obtained an injunction ordering Nabisco to stop selling goldfish-shaped cheddar cheese-flavored crackers because this particular product was strongly associated with Pepperidge Farm, and sale of similar products by Nabisco would dilute the distinctive quality of Pepperidge Farm's mark. *Nabisco, Inc. v. PF Brands, Inc.*, 191 F.3d 208 (2d Cir. 1999) (partially overruled on other grounds by *Moseley v. V Secret Catalogue*, 537 U.S. 418 (2003) requiring proof of actual dilution rather than mere likelihood of dilution).

At issue is whether injunctive relief should be granted in the absence of proof of actual economic harm. Some courts allow relief based solely on the possibility of blurring. *Nabisco, Inc., supra.* Other courts have held that dilution can be established only by showing actual economic harm resulting from the competing product.

---

1. In case anyone is wondering, the author is not related to the original owners of the Singer Sewing Machine Company.

Ringling Brothers-Barnum & Bailey Combined Shows, Inc. v. Utah Division of Travel Development, 170 F.3d 449 (4th Cir. 1999) (denying a dilution claim when defendant used a phrase associated with plaintiff—"THE GREATEST SHOW ON EARTH"—because plaintiff failed to show economic harm). Which approach makes more sense?

2. *Cybersquatting & gripe websites.* Some people obtained domain names for web sites for the sole purpose of selling them to copyright holders. Often no confusion resulted from this because anyone accessing the website would know immediately that it was not owned by the company in question. However, in the spirit of the federal *Anti-Dilution Act*, Congress passed the *Anticybersquatting Consumer Protection Act* (ACPA), 15 U.S.C. §1125(d) in 1999. This law prohibits anyone from registering or using a domain name "with bad faith intent to profit from another's trademark." Anyone who obtains a domain name with the intent of selling it to the relevant company would almost certainly be in violation of the act. *See, e.g., Virtual Works, Inc. v. Volkswagen of America, Inc.*, 238 F.3d 264 (4th Cir. 2001) (*www.vw.net* domain name violates ACPA when registered by Virtual Works, Inc. because the company intended to profit from the name recognition attached to the common abbreviation for Volkswagen).

Disagreements have arisen among courts however, about gripe websites that intend to criticize a company by using its name or its name plus a disparaging word such as "sucks." Although it has been argued that this is a noncommercial use outside the scope of the ACPA and that the first amendment protects such usages, one court has granted relief against such a site when the owner sought to "get even" with the trademark owner. *Morrison & Foerster v. Wick*, 94 F. Supp. 2d 1125 (D. Colo. 2000). Most courts, however, have held that use of a company's trademarked name in a website address is neither a trademark violation nor a violation of the *Lanham Act* when the name was not used for commercial purposes in a manner that would confuse potential customers. *See Bosley Medical Institute, Inc. v. Kremer*, 403 F.3d 672 (9th Cir. 2005). However, such uses may still violate the ACPA if they are done "with bad faith intent to profit" from the trademarked name.

PROBLEM

See §2.2.1.2, Problem 3, at page 144. How should the case have been adjudicated? Is the term "Redskins" "immoral, deceptive, or scandalous" within the meaning of the *Lanham Act*, 15 U.S.C. §1052(a)? Does the first amendment's protection for free speech protect the trademark owner's right to use the name?

§14.4   *Copyright Law*

§14.4.1   Original Works of Authorship

Copyright law is regulated by a federal statute that substantially preempts state law on the subject. 17 U.S.C. §§101 *et seq.* The *Copyright Act* grants owners of "original works of authorship" that are fixed in a "tangible medium of expression," §102, exclusive rights to copy, distribute, perform or display those works publicly and to make derivative works from them, §106. Ideas and facts cannot be copyrighted; only original *expressions* of ideas can be protected by copyright law. Authors own what they create unless they performed "work for hire"; such works are owned by the author's employer. §201(b). Copyright protection lasts for the life of the author plus 70 years, after which time the work becomes part of the public domain. With respect to works for hire, the copyright lasts for 95 years from the date of first publication or 120 years from the date of creation, whichever expires first. §302(c).

Only "original" works of "authorship" are protected. The following case considers what this means.

COPYRIGHT ACT OF 1976

17 U.S.C. §§101 *et seq.*

§102. Subject matter of copyright: In general

(a) Copyright protection subsists, in accordance with this title, in original works of authorship fixed in any tangible medium of expression, now known or later developed, from which they can be perceived, reproduced, or otherwise communicated, either directly or with the aid of a machine or device. Works of authorship include the following categories:

(1)   literary works;
(2)   musical works, including any accompanying words;
(3)   dramatic works, including any accompanying music;
(4)   pantomimes and choreographic works;
(5)   pictorial, graphic, and sculptural works;
(6)   motion pictures and other audiovisual works;
(7)   sound recordings; and
(8)   architectural works.

(b) In no case does copyright protection for an original work of authorship extend to any idea, procedure, process, system, method of operation, concept, principle, or discovery, regardless of the form in which it is described, explained, illustrated, or embodied in such work.

§106. Exclusive rights in copyrighted works

Subject to sections 107 through 122, the owner of copyright under this title has the exclusive rights to do and to authorize any of the following:

(1)   to reproduce the copyrighted work in copies or phonorecords;
(2)   to prepare derivative works based upon the copyrighted work;
(3)   to distribute copies or phonorecords of the copyrighted work to the public by sale or other transfer of ownership, or by rental, lease, or lending;
(4)   in the case of literary, musical, dramatic, and choreographic works, pantomimes, and motion pictures and other audiovisual works, to perform the copyrighted work publicly;
(5)   in the case of literary, musical, dramatic, and choreographic works, pantomimes, and pictorial, graphic, or sculptural works, including the indi-

vidual images of a motion picture or other audiovisual work, to display the copyrighted work publicly; and

(6) in the case of sound recordings, to perform the copyrighted work publicly by means of a digital audio transmission.

§107. Limitations on exclusive rights: Fair use

Notwithstanding the provisions of sections 106 . . . , the fair use of a copyrighted work, including such use by reproduction in copies or phonorecords or by any other means specified by that section, for purposes such as criticism, comment, news reporting, teaching (including multiple copies for classroom use), scholarship, or research, is not an infringement of copyright. In determining whether the use made of a work in any particular case is a fair use the factors to be considered shall include—

(1) the purpose and character of the use, including whether such use is of a commercial nature or is for nonprofit educational purposes;

(2) the nature of the copyrighted work;

(3) the amount and substantiality of the portion used in relation to the copyrighted work as a whole; and

(4) the effect of the use upon the potential market for or value of the copyrighted work.

The fact that a work is unpublished shall not itself bar a finding of fair use if such finding is made upon consideration of all the above factors.

FEIST PUBLICATIONS, INC. v.
RURAL TELEPHONE SERVICE CO., INC.

499 U.S. 340 (1991)

Justice Sandra Day O'Connor, J., delivered the opinion of the Court.

This case requires us to clarify the extent of copyright protection available to telephone directory white pages.

Rural Telephone Service Company, Inc., is a certified public utility that provides telephone service to several communities in northwest Kansas. It is subject to a state regulation that requires all telephone companies operating in Kansas to issue annually an updated telephone directory. Accordingly, as a condition of its monopoly franchise, Rural publishes a typical telephone directory, consisting of white pages and yellow pages. The white pages list in alphabetical order the names of Rural's subscribers, together with their towns and telephone numbers. The yellow pages list Rural's business subscribers alphabetically by category and feature classified advertisements of various sizes. Rural distributes its directory free of charge to its subscribers, but earns revenue by selling yellow pages advertisements.

Feist Publications, Inc., is a publishing company that specializes in area-wide telephone directories. Unlike a typical directory, which covers only a particular calling area, Feist's area-wide directories cover a much larger geographical range, reducing the need to call directory assistance or consult multiple directories. The Feist directory that is the subject of this litigation covers 11 different telephone service areas in 15 counties and contains 46,878 white pages listings — compared to Rural's approximately 7,700 listings. Like Rural's directory, Feist's is distributed free of charge and includes both white pages and yellow pages. Feist and Rural compete vigorously for yellow pages advertising.

As the sole provider of telephone service in its service area, Rural obtains subscriber information quite easily. Persons desiring telephone service must apply to Rural and provide their names and addresses; Rural then assigns them a telephone number. Feist is not a telephone company, let alone one with monopoly status, and therefore lacks independent access to any subscriber information. To obtain white pages listings for its area-wide directory, Feist approached each of the 11 telephone companies operating in northwest Kansas and offered to pay for the right to use its white pages listings.

Of the 11 telephone companies, only Rural refused to license its listings to Feist. Rural's refusal created a problem for Feist, as omitting these listings would have left a gaping hole in its area-wide directory, rendering it less attractive to potential yellow pages advertisers. . . .

Unable to license Rural's white pages listings, Feist used them without Rural's consent. Feist began by removing several thousand listings that fell outside the geographic range of its area-wide directory, then hired personnel to investigate the 4,935 that remained. These employees verified the data reported by Rural and sought to obtain additional information. As a result, a typical Feist listing includes the individual's street address; most of Rural's listings do not. Notwithstanding these additions, however, 1,309 of the 46,878 listings in Feist's 1983 directory were identical to listings in Rural's 1982-1983 white pages. Four of these were fictitious listings that Rural had inserted into its directory to detect copying.

Rural sued for copyright infringement in the District Court for the District of Kansas taking the position that Feist, in compiling its own directory, could not use the information contained in Rural's white pages. Rural asserted that Feist's employees were obliged to travel door-to-door or conduct a telephone survey to discover the same information for themselves. Feist responded that such efforts were economically impractical and, in any event, unnecessary because the information copied was beyond the scope of copyright protection. . . .

This case concerns the interaction of two well-established propositions. The first is that facts are not copyrightable; the other, that compilations of facts generally are. . . .

There is an undeniable tension between these two propositions. Many compilations consist of nothing but raw data — *i.e.*, wholly factual information not accompanied by any original written expression. . . . The key to resolving the tension lies in understanding why facts are not copyrightable. The *sine qua non* of copyright is originality. To qualify for copyright protection, a work must be original to the author. Original, as the term is used in copyright, means only that the work was independently created by the author (as opposed to copied from other works), and that it possesses at least some minimal degree of creativity. . . . Originality does not signify novelty; a work may be original even though it closely resembles other works so long as the similarity is fortuitous, not the result of copying. To illustrate, assume that two poets, each ignorant of the other, compose identical poems. Neither work is novel, yet both are original and, hence, copyrightable.

Originality is a constitutional requirement. The source of Congress' power to enact copyright laws is Article I, §8, cl. 8, of the Constitution, which authorizes Congress to "secure for limited Times to Authors . . . the exclusive Right to their respective Writings." In two decisions from the late 19th century — *The Trade-Mark Cases*, 100 U.S. 82 (1879); and *Burrow-Giles Lithographic Co. v. Sarony*, 111 U.S. 53 (1884) — this Court defined the crucial terms "authors" and "writings." In so doing, the Court made it unmistakably clear that these terms presuppose a degree of originality. . . .

It is this bedrock principle of copyright that mandates the law's seemingly disparate treatment of facts and factual compilations. "No one may claim originality as to facts." This is because facts do not owe their origin to an act of authorship. The distinction is one between creation and discovery: The first person to find and report a particular fact has not created the fact; he or she has merely discovered its existence. . . .

Factual compilations, on the other hand, may possess the requisite originality. The compilation author typically chooses which facts to include, in what order to place them, and how to arrange the collected data so that they may be used effectively by readers. These choices as to selection and arrangement, so long as they are made independently by the compiler and entail a minimal degree of creativity, are sufficiently original that Congress may protect such compilations through the copyright laws. Thus, even a directory that contains absolutely no protectible written expression, only facts, meets the constitutional minimum for copyright protection if it features an original selection or arrangement.

This protection is subject to an important limitation. The mere fact that a work is copyrighted does not mean that every element of the work may be protected. Originality remains the *sine qua non* of copyright; accordingly, copyright protection may extend only to those components of a work that are original to the author. Thus, if the compilation author clothes facts with an original collocation of words, he or she may be able to claim a copyright in this written expression. Others may copy the underlying facts from the publication, but not the precise words used to present them. Where the compilation author adds no written expression but rather lets the facts speak for themselves, the expressive element is more elusive. The only conceivable expression is the manner in which the compiler has selected and arranged the facts. Thus, if the selection and arrangement are original, these elements of the work are eligible for copyright protection. No matter how original the format, however, the facts themselves do not become original through association.

This inevitably means that the copyright in a factual compilation is thin. Notwithstanding a valid copyright, a subsequent compiler remains free to use the facts contained in another's publication to aid in preparing a competing work, so long as the competing work does not feature the same selection and arrangement. . . .

It may seem unfair that much of the fruit of the compiler's labor may be used by others without compensation. As Justice Brennan has correctly observed, however, this is not "some unforeseen byproduct of a statutory scheme." *Harper & Row, Publishers, Inc. v. Nation Enterprises*, 471 U.S. 539, 589 (1985) (dissenting opinion). It is, rather, "the essence of copyright," and a constitutional requirement. The primary objective of copyright is not to reward the labor of authors, but "to promote the Progress of Science and useful Arts." Art. I, §8, cl. 8. To this end, copyright assures authors the right to their original expression, but encourages others to build freely upon the ideas and information conveyed by a work. This principle, known as the idea/expression or fact/expression dichotomy, applies to all works of authorship. As applied to a factual compilation, assuming the absence of original written expression, only the compiler's selection and arrangement may be protected; the raw facts may be copied at will. This result is neither unfair nor unfortunate. It is the means by which copyright advances the progress of science and art.

... In enacting the *Copyright Act of 1976*, 17 U.S.C. §§101 *et seq.*, Congress [reaffirmed the view that copyright law protects only original works rather than the "sweat of the brow" by dropping] reference to "all the writings of an author" and replac[ing] it with the phrase "original works of authorship." 17 U.S.C. §102(a). . . . [The 1976 *Copyright Act* made clear] that compilations [are] not copyrightable *per se.* . . . The definition of "compilation" is found in §101 of the 1976 Act. It defines a "compilation" in the copyright sense as "a work formed by the collection and assembling of preexisting materials or of data *that* are selected, coordinated, or arranged *in such a way that* the resulting work as a whole constitutes an original work of authorship" (emphasis added).

The purpose of the statutory definition is to emphasize that collections of facts are not copyrightable *per se.* [A] compilation, like any other work, is copyrightable only if it satisfies the originality requirement ("an *original* work of authorship"). Although §102 states plainly that the originality requirement applies to all works, the point was emphasized with regard to compilations to ensure that courts would not repeat the mistake of the [courts that had protected the "sweat of the brow" in the absence of originality]. . . .

In summary, the 1976 revisions to the *Copyright Act* leave no doubt that originality, not "sweat of the brow," is the touchstone of copyright protection in directories and other fact-based works. . . . The revisions explain with painstaking clarity that copyright requires originality, §102(a); that facts are never original, §102(b); that the copyright in a compilation does not extend to the facts it contains, §103(b); and that a compilation is copyrightable only to the extent that it features an original selection, coordination, or arrangement, §101.

The question is whether . . . Feist, by taking 1,309 names, towns, and telephone numbers from Rural's white pages, cop[ied] anything that was "original" to Rural[.] Certainly, the raw data does not satisfy the originality requirement. . . . Rather, these bits of information are uncopyrightable facts. . . .

The question that remains is whether Rural selected, coordinated, or arranged these uncopyrightable facts in an original way. . . . The selection, coordination, and arrangement of Rural's white pages do not satisfy the minimum constitutional standards for copyright protection. . . . In preparing its white pages, Rural simply takes the data provided by its subscribers and lists it alphabetically by surname. The end product is a garden-variety white pages directory, devoid of even the slightest trace of creativity.

Rural's selection of listings could not be more obvious: It publishes the most basic information — name, town, and telephone number — about each person who applies to it for telephone service. This is "selection" of a sort, but it lacks the modicum of creativity necessary to transform mere selection into copyrightable expression. Rural expended sufficient effort to make the white pages directory useful, but insufficient creativity to make it original.

Nor can Rural claim originality in its coordination and arrangement of facts. The white pages do nothing more than list Rural's subscribers in alphabetical order. This arrangement may, technically speaking, owe its origin to Rural [b]ut there is nothing remotely creative about arranging names alphabetically in a white pages directory . . . . It is not only unoriginal, it is practically inevitable. This time-honored tradition does not possess the minimal creative spark required by the *Copyright Act* and the Constitution.

We conclude that the names, towns, and telephone numbers copied by Feist were not original to Rural and therefore were not protected by the copyright in Rural's combined white and yellow pages directory.... Because Rural's white pages lack the requisite originality, Feist's use of the listings cannot constitute infringement. This decision should not be construed as demeaning Rural's efforts in compiling its directory, but rather as making clear that copyright rewards originality, not effort. As this Court noted more than a century ago, "'great praise may be due to the plaintiffs for their industry and enterprise in publishing this paper, yet the law does not contemplate their being rewarded in this way.'" *Baker v. Selden*, 101 U.S. 99, 105 (1880).

§14.4.2 CONTRIBUTORY INFRINGEMENT

In 5-4 decision, the Supreme Court held in *Sony Corp. v. Universal City Studios*, 464 U.S. 417 (1984), that a video cassette recorder (VCR) manufacturer (Sony) and retailers were not liable for contributing to copyright infringement merely because VCRs could be used to copy works protected by the copyright law. Although VCR purchasers could use them to violate the copyright laws, the Supreme Court found that Sony's Betamax VCR machines were capable of substantial non-infringing uses; in particular, they allowed viewers to "time-shift," recording a television show as it aired and then viewing it at a later time. Because this practice "enlarges the television viewing audience..., a significant amount of television programming may be used in this manner without objection from the owners of the copyrights on the programs." *Id.* at 421. Indeed, it appeared that consumers used the VCRs primarily for time-shifting. Moreover, the plaintiffs in this case who did object to time-shifting (Universal City Studios, Inc. and Walt Disney Productions) were unable to show that the practice impaired the commercial value of their copyrights. "The purpose of copyright is to create incentives for creative effort.... [A] use that has no demonstrable effect upon the potential market for, or the value of, the copyrighted work need not be prohibited in order to protect the author's incentive to create. The prohibition of such noncommercial uses would merely inhibit access to ideas without any countervailing benefit." *Id.* at 450-451. Because the Court concluded that VCRs were "capable of commercially significant noninfringing uses," *Id.* at 442, it held that their mere manufacture or sale were not sufficient to constitute "contributory infringement" even if the VCRs were used by their owners for infringing uses.

Justices Blackmun, Marshall, Powell, and Rehnquist dissented. Justice Blackmun's opinion noted that the fair use exception for scholarship, education or news reporting generally promoted "*productive* use[s] that result[ ] in some added benefit to the public beyond that produced by the first author's work." 464 U.S. at 478 (Blackmun, J., dissenting). Adopting a different test than the majority, they would have held that "at least where the proposed use is an unproductive one, a copyright owner need prove only a potential for harm to the market for or the value of the copyrighted work. Infringement thus would be found if the copyright owner demonstrates a reasonable possibility that harm will result from the proposed use." *Id.* at 482. They noted the VCR sales could harm copyright owners in a variety of ways, such as reducing attendance at movie theaters and videotape rentals.

The issues arose in a related but new context when the hugely popular Napster program that allowed individuals to log onto its system and share their digital music files with others who were similarly logged on. In *A & M Records, Inc. v. Napster, Inc.*,

114 F. Supp. 2d 896 (N.D. Cal. 2000), *aff'd in part and rev'd in part,* 239 F.3d 1004 (9th Cir. 2001), *on remand,* 2001 WL 227083 (N.D. Cal. 2001), Judge Marilyn Hall Patel granted a preliminary injunction against Napster on the ground that it had probably engaged in both direct and contributory infringement of copyright when it knowingly helped users to download and thus copy music, most but not all of which was copyrighted. The Ninth Circuit agreed but ordered the trial court to narrow the injunction to apply only to copyrighted works. Napster had argued that it did not contribute to copyright violations because music sharing constituted a fair use. Although the recording industry strongly believes that programs like Napster hurt CD sales, at least one 2004 study by Felix Oberholzer-Gee & Koleman Strumpf suggested that music downloads may not necessarily decrease record sales. *See http://www.unc.edu/~cigar/ papers/FileSharing_March2004.pdf. See also* Raymond Shih Ray Ku, *The Creative Destruction of Copyright: Napster and the New Economics of Digital Technology,* 69 U.Chi. L. Rev. 263 (2002)(criticizing the result in *Napster* and arguing that digital copies should not receive copyright protection). *Cf. Gucci America, Inc. v. Hall & Associates,* 135 F. Supp. 2d 409 (S.D.N.Y. 2001) (on-line service provider not liable for postings they have no reason to know are infringing but may be liable if they allow the posting to stay on-line after learning of the infringement).

When Napster was shut down, it was replaced by software programs, such as Grokster and Gnutella, that allowed individuals to communicate directly with other individuals without the need to copy their music files to a central computer ("peer-to-peer transfers"). Improvements in technology also made it possible to share and download movies as well as music. The recording and movie industries sued the companies who offered these services for contributory infringement and the case eventually reached the Supreme Court.

METRO-GOLDWYN-MAYER STUDIOS INC. v. GROKSTER, LTD.

2005 U.S. LEXIS 5212 (June 27, 2005)

Justice DAVID SOUTER delivered the opinion of the Court.

The question is under what circumstances the distributor of a product capable of both lawful and unlawful use is liable for acts of copyright infringement by third parties using the product. We hold that one who distributes a device with the object of promoting its use to infringe copyright, as shown by clear expression or other affirmative steps taken to foster infringement, is liable for the resulting acts of infringement by third parties.

I . . .

Respondents, Grokster, Ltd., and StreamCast Networks, Inc., defendants in the trial court, distribute free software products that allow computer users to share electronic files through peer-to-peer networks, so called because users' computers communicate directly with each other, not through central servers. The advantage of peer-to-peer networks over information networks of other types shows up in their substantial and growing popularity. Because they need no central computer server to mediate the exchange of information or files among users, the high-bandwidth communications capacity for a server may be dispensed with, and the need for costly server storage space is eliminated. Since copies of a file (particularly a popular one) are available on many users' computers, file requests and retrievals may be faster than on other types of networks, and since file exchanges do not travel through a server, communications can take place between any computers that remain connected to the network without risk that a glitch in the server will disable the network in its entirety. Given these benefits in security, cost, and efficiency, peer-to-peer networks are employed to store and distribute electronic files by universities, government agencies, corporations, and libraries, among others.

Other users of peer-to-peer networks include individual recipients of Grokster's and StreamCast's software, and although the networks that they enjoy through using the software can be used to share any type of digital file, they have prominently employed those networks in sharing copyrighted music and video files without authorization. A group of copyright holders (MGM for short, but including motion picture studios, recording companies, songwriters, and music publishers) sued Grokster and StreamCast for their users' copyright infringements, alleging that they knowingly and intentionally distributed their software to enable users to reproduce and distribute the copyrighted works in violation of the Copyright Act, 17 U.S.C. §101 *et seq.* MGM sought damages and an injunction. . . .

Discovery during the litigation revealed the way the software worked, the business aims of each defendant company, and the predilections of the users. Grokster's eponymous software employs what is known as FastTrack technology, a protocol developed by others and licensed to Grokster. StreamCast distributes a very similar product except that its software, called Morpheus, relies on what is known as Gnutella technology. A user who downloads and installs either software possesses the protocol to send requests for files directly to the computers of others using software compatible with FastTrack or Gnutella. . . .

. . . Grokster and StreamCast use no servers to intercept the content of the search requests or to mediate the file transfers conducted by users of the software, there being no central point through which the substance of the communications passes in either direction.

Although Grokster and StreamCast do not therefore know when particular files are copied, a few searches using their software would show what is available on the networks the software reaches. MGM commissioned a statistician to conduct a systematic search, and his study showed that nearly 90% of the files available for download on the FastTrack system were copyrighted works.[5] Grokster and StreamCast dispute this figure, raising methodological problems and arguing that free copying even of copyrighted works may be authorized by the rightholders. They also argue that potential noninfringing uses of their software are significant in kind, even if infrequent in practice. Some musical performers, for example, have gained new audiences by distributing their copyrighted works for free across peer-to-peer networks, and some distributors of unprotected content have used peer-to-peer networks to disseminate files, Shakespeare being an example. . . .

. . . MGM's evidence gives reason to think that the vast majority of users' downloads are acts of infringement, and because well over 100 million copies of the software

---

5. By comparison, evidence introduced by the plaintiffs in *A & M Records, Inc. v. Napster, Inc.,* 239 F.3d 1004 (9th Cir. 2001), showed that 87% of files available on the Napster filesharing network were copyrighted, id., at 1013.

in question are known to have been downloaded, and billions of files are shared across the FastTrack and Gnutella networks each month, the probable scope of copyright infringement is staggering.

Grokster and StreamCast concede the infringement in most downloads, and it is uncontested that they are aware that users employ their software primarily to download copyrighted files . . .

Grokster and StreamCast are not, however, merely passive recipients of information about infringing use. The record is replete with evidence that from the moment Grokster and StreamCast began to distribute their free software, each one clearly voiced the objective that recipients use it to download copyrighted works, and each took active steps to encourage infringement.

After the notorious file-sharing service, Napster, was sued by copyright holders for facilitation of copyright infringement, *A & M Records, Inc. v. Napster, Inc.*, 114 F. Supp. 2d 896 (N.D. Cal. 2000), *aff'd in part, rev'd in part*, 239 F.3d 1004 (9th Cir. 2001), StreamCast gave away a software program of a kind known as OpenNap, designed as compatible with the Napster program and open to Napster users for downloading files from other Napster and OpenNap users' computers. Evidence indicates that "it was always [StreamCast's] intent to use [its OpenNap network] to be able to capture email addresses of [its] initial target market so that [it] could promote [its] StreamCast Morpheus interface to them"; indeed, the OpenNap program was engineered "to leverage Napster's 50 million user base." . . .

. . . StreamCast developed promotional materials to market its service as the best Napster alternative. . . .

The evidence that Grokster sought to capture the market of former Napster users is sparser but revealing, for Grokster launched its own OpenNap system called Swaptor and inserted digital codes into its Web site so that computer users using Web search engines to look for "Napster" or "free filesharing" would be directed to the Grokster Web site, where they could download the Grokster software. And Grokster's name is an apparent derivative of Napster.

. . . Morpheus in fact allowed users to search specifically for "Top 40" songs, which were inevitably copyrighted. Similarly, Grokster sent users a newsletter promoting its ability to provide particular, popular copyrighted materials.

In addition to this evidence of express promotion, marketing, and intent to promote further, the business models employed by Grokster and StreamCast confirm that their principal object was use of their software to download copyrighted works. Grokster and StreamCast receive no revenue from users, who obtain the software itself for nothing. Instead, both companies generate income by selling advertising space, and they stream the advertising to Grokster and Morpheus users while they are employing the programs. As the number of users of each program increases, advertising opportunities become worth more. While there is doubtless some demand for free Shakespeare, the evidence shows that substantive volume is a function of free access to copyrighted work. Users seeking Top 40 songs, for example, or the latest release by Modest Mouse, are certain to be far more numerous than those seeking a free Decameron, and Grokster and StreamCast translated that demand into dollars.

Finally, there is no evidence that either company made an effort to filter copyrighted material from users' downloads or otherwise impede the sharing of copyrighted files. Although Grokster appears to have sent e-mails warning users about infringing content when it received threatening notice from the copyright holders, it never blocked anyone from continuing to use its software to share copyrighted files.

StreamCast not only rejected another company's offer of help to monitor infringement, but blocked the Internet Protocol addresses of entities it believed were trying to engage in such monitoring on its networks....

...The District Court held that those who used the Grokster and Morpheus software to download copyrighted media files directly infringed MGM's copyrights, a conclusion not contested on appeal, but the court nonetheless granted summary judgment in favor of Grokster and StreamCast as to any liability arising from distribution of the then current versions of their software. Distributing that software gave rise to no liability in the court's view, because its use did not provide the distributors with actual knowledge of specific acts of infringement.

The Court of Appeals affirmed. In the court's analysis, a defendant was liable as a contributory infringer when it had knowledge of direct infringement and materially contributed to the infringement. But the court read *Sony Corp. of America v. Universal City Studios, Inc.*, 464 U.S. 417 (1984), as holding that distribution of a commercial product capable of substantial noninfringing uses could not give rise to contributory liability for infringement unless the distributor had actual knowledge of specific instances of infringement and failed to act on that knowledge. The fact that the software was capable of substantial noninfringing uses in the Ninth Circuit's view meant that Grokster and StreamCast were not liable, because they had no such actual knowledge, owing to the decentralized architecture of their software. The court also held that Grokster and StreamCast did not materially contribute to their users' infringement because it was the users themselves who searched for, retrieved, and stored the infringing files, with no involvement by the defendants beyond providing the software in the first place.

The Ninth Circuit also considered whether Grokster and StreamCast could be liable under a theory of vicarious infringement. The court held against liability because the defendants did not monitor or control the use of the software, had no agreed-upon right or current ability to supervise its use, and had no independent duty to police infringement. We granted certiorari.

II

A

MGM and many of the *amici* fault the Court of Appeals's holding for upsetting a sound balance between the respective values of supporting creative pursuits through copyright protection and promoting innovation in new communication technologies by limiting the incidence of liability for copyright infringement. The more artistic protection is favored, the more technological innovation may be discouraged; the administration of copyright law is an exercise in managing the trade-off.

The tension between the two values is the subject of this case, with its claim that digital distribution of copyrighted material threatens copyright holders as never before, because every copy is identical to the original, copying is easy, and many people (especially the young) use file-sharing software to download copyrighted works. This very breadth of the software's use may well draw the public directly into the debate over copyright policy, and the indications are that the ease of copying songs or movies using software like Grokster's and Napster's is fostering disdain for copyright protection. As the case has been presented to us, these fears are said to be offset by the different concern that imposing liability, not only on infringers but on distributors of software based on its potential for unlawful use, could limit further development of beneficial technologies.[8]

The argument for imposing indirect liability in this case is, however, a powerful one, given the number of infringing downloads that occur every day using Stream-Cast's and Grokster's software. When a widely shared service or product is used to commit infringement, it may be impossible to enforce rights in the protected work effectively against all direct infringers, the only practical alternative being to go against the distributor of the copying device for secondary liability on a theory of contributory or vicarious infringement.

One infringes contributorily by intentionally inducing or encouraging direct infringement, and infringes vicariously by profiting from direct infringement while declining to exercise a right to stop or limit it. Although "the Copyright Act does not expressly render anyone liable for infringement committed by another," *Sony Corp. v. Universal City Studios*, 464 U.S. at 434, these doctrines of secondary liability emerged from common law principles and are well established in the law.

B

Despite the currency of these principles of secondary liability, this Court has dealt with secondary copyright infringement in only one recent case, and because MGM has tailored its principal claim to our opinion there, a look at our earlier holding is in order. In *Sony Corp. v. Universal City Studios, supra*, this Court addressed a claim that secondary liability for infringement can arise from the very distribution of a commercial product. There, the product, novel at the time, was what we know today as the videocassette recorder or VCR. Copyright holders sued Sony as the manufacturer, claiming it was contributorily liable for infringement that occurred when VCR owners taped copyrighted programs because it supplied the means used to infringe, and it had constructive knowledge that infringement would occur. At the trial on the merits, the evidence showed that the principal use of the VCR was for "'time-shifting,'" or taping a program for later viewing at a more convenient time, which the Court found to be a fair, not an infringing, use. There was no evidence that Sony had expressed an object of bringing about taping in violation of copyright or had taken active steps to increase its profits from unlawful taping. Although Sony's advertisements urged consumers to buy the VCR to "'record favorite shows'" or "'build a library'" of recorded programs, neither of these uses was necessarily infringing.

On those facts, with no evidence of stated or indicated intent to promote infringing uses, the only conceivable basis for imposing liability was on a theory of contributory infringement arising from its sale of VCRs to consumers with knowledge that some would use them to infringe. But because the VCR was "capable of commercially significant noninfringing uses," we held the manufacturer could not be faulted solely on the basis of its distribution. *Id.*, at 442. . . .

---

8. The mutual exclusivity of these values should not be overstated, however. On the one hand technological innovators, including those writing filesharing computer programs, may wish for effective copyright protections for their work. On the other hand the widespread distribution of creative works through improved technologies may enable the synthesis of new works or generate audiences for emerging artists.

This analysis reflected patent law's traditional staple article of commerce doctrine, now codified, that distribution of a component of a patented device will not violate the patent if it is suitable for use in other ways. 35 U.S.C. §271(c); *Aro Mfg. Co. v. Convertible Top Replacement Co.*, 377 U.S. 476, 485 (1964). The doctrine was devised to identify instances in which it may be presumed from distribution of an article in commerce that the distributor intended the article to be used to infringe another's patent, and so may justly be held liable for that infringement. . . .

In sum, where an article is "good for nothing else" but infringement, there is no legitimate public interest in its unlicensed availability, and there is no injustice in presuming or imputing an intent to infringe. Conversely, the doctrine absolves the equivocal conduct of selling an item with substantial lawful as well as unlawful uses, and limits liability to instances of more acute fault than the mere understanding that some of one's products will be misused. It leaves breathing room for innovation and a vigorous commerce.

The parties and many of the *amici* in this case think the key to resolving it is the *Sony* rule and, in particular, what it means for a product to be "capable of commercially significant noninfringing uses." MGM advances the argument that granting summary judgment to Grokster and StreamCast as to their current activities gave too much weight to the value of innovative technology, and too little to the copyrights infringed by users of their software, given that 90% of works available on one of the networks was shown to be copyrighted. Assuming the remaining 10% to be its noninfringing use, MGM says this should not qualify as "substantial," and the Court should quantify *Sony* to the extent of holding that a product used "principally" for infringement does not qualify. . . . Grokster and StreamCast reply by citing evidence that their software can be used to reproduce public domain works, and they point to copyright holders who actually encourage copying. Even if infringement is the principal practice with their software today, they argue, the noninfringing uses are significant and will grow.

We agree with MGM that the Court of Appeals misapplied *Sony*, which it read as limiting secondary liability quite beyond the circumstances to which the case applied. *Sony* barred secondary liability based on presuming or imputing intent to cause infringement solely from the design or distribution of a product capable of substantial lawful use, which the distributor knows is in fact used for infringement. The Ninth Circuit has read *Sony's* limitation to mean that whenever a product is capable of substantial lawful use, the producer can never be held contributorily liable for third parties' infringing use of it; it read the rule as being this broad, even when an actual purpose to cause infringing use is shown by evidence independent of design and distribution of the product, unless the distributors had "specific knowledge of infringement at a time at which they contributed to the infringement, and failed to act upon that information." Because the Circuit found the StreamCast and Grokster software capable of substantial lawful use, it concluded on the basis of its reading of *Sony* that neither company could be held liable, since there was no showing that their software, being without any central server, afforded them knowledge of specific unlawful uses.

This view of *Sony*, however, was error, converting the case from one about liability resting on imputed intent to one about liability on any theory. Because *Sony* did not displace other theories of secondary liability, and because we find below that it was error to grant summary judgment to the companies on MGM's inducement claim, we do not revisit *Sony* further, as MGM requests, to add a more quantified description of the point of balance between protection and commerce when liability rests solely on distribution with knowledge that unlawful use will occur. It is enough to note that the Ninth Circuit's judgment rested on an erroneous understanding of *Sony* and to leave further consideration of the *Sony* rule for a day when that may be required.

C

Sony's rule limits imputing culpable intent as a matter of law from the characteristics or uses of a distributed product. But nothing in *Sony* requires courts to ignore evidence of intent if there is such evidence, and the case was never meant to foreclose rules of fault-based liability derived from the common law. Thus, where evidence goes beyond a product's characteristics or the knowledge that it may be put to infringing uses, and shows statements or actions directed to promoting infringement, *Sony*'s staple-article rule will not preclude liability.

The classic case of direct evidence of unlawful purpose occurs when one induces commission of infringement by another, or "entices or persuades another" to infringe, B*lack's Law Dictionary* 790 (8th ed. 2004), as by advertising. . . .

The rule on inducement of infringement as developed in the early cases is no different today. Evidence of "active steps . . . taken to encourage direct infringement," *Oak Industries, Inc. v. Zenith Electronics Corp.*, 697 F. Supp. 988, 992 (ND Ill. 1988), such as advertising an infringing use or instructing how to engage in an infringing use, show an affirmative intent that the product be used to infringe, and a showing that infringement was encouraged overcomes the law's reluctance to find liability when a defendant merely sells a commercial product suitable for some lawful use.

For the same reasons that *Sony* took the staple-article doctrine of patent law as a model for its copyright safe-harbor rule, the inducement rule, too, is a sensible one for copyright. We adopt it here, holding that one who distributes a device with the object of promoting its use to infringe copyright, as shown by clear expression or other affirmative steps taken to foster infringement, is liable for the resulting acts of infringement by third parties. We are, of course, mindful of the need to keep from trenching on regular commerce or discouraging the development of technologies with lawful and unlawful potential. Accordingly, just as *Sony* did not find intentional inducement despite the knowledge of the VCR manufacturer that its device could be used to infringe, mere knowledge of infringing potential or of actual infringing uses would not be enough here to subject a distributor to liability. Nor would ordinary acts incident to product distribution, such as offering customers technical support or product updates, support liability in themselves. The inducement rule, instead, premises liability on purposeful, culpable expression and conduct, and thus does nothing to compromise legitimate commerce or discourage innovation having a lawful promise.

III

A

The only apparent question about treating MGM's evidence as sufficient to withstand summary judgment under the theory of inducement goes to the need on MGM's part to adduce evidence that StreamCast and Grokster communicated an inducing message to their software users. The classic instance of inducement is by advertisement or solicitation that broadcasts a message designed to stimulate others to commit violations. MGM claims that such a message is shown here. It is undisputed that StreamCast beamed onto the computer screens of users of Napster-compatible programs ads urging the adoption of its OpenNap program, which was designed, as its name implied, to invite the custom of patrons of Napster, then under attack in the courts for facilitating massive infringement. Those who accepted StreamCast's Open-Nap program were offered software to perform the same services, which a factfinder could conclude would readily have been understood in the Napster market as the ability to download copyrighted music files. Grokster distributed an electronic news-letter containing links to articles promoting its software's ability to access popular copyrighted music. And anyone whose Napster or free file-sharing searches turned up a link to Grokster would have understood Grokster to be offering the same file-sharing ability as Napster, and to the same people who probably used Napster for infringing downloads; that would also have been the understanding of anyone offered Grokster's suggestively named Swaptor software, its version of OpenNap. And both companies communicated a clear message by responding affirmatively to requests for help in locating and playing copyrighted materials.

In StreamCast's case, of course, the evidence just described was supplemented by other unequivocal indications of unlawful purpose in the internal communications and advertising designs aimed at Napster users ("When the lights went off at Nap-ster . . . where did the users go?") Whether the messages were communicated is not to the point on this record. The function of the message in the theory of inducement is to prove by a defendant's own statements that his unlawful purpose disqualifies him from claiming protection (and incidentally to point to actual violators likely to be found among those who hear or read the message). Proving that a message was sent out, then, is the preeminent but not exclusive way of showing that active steps were taken with the purpose of bringing about infringing acts, and of showing that infringing acts took place by using the device distributed. Here, the summary judgment record is replete with other evidence that Grokster and StreamCast, unlike the manufacturer and dis-tributor in *Sony*, acted with a purpose to cause copyright violations by use of software suitable for illegal use.

Three features of this evidence of intent are particularly notable. First, each com-pany showed itself to be aiming to satisfy a known source of demand for copyright infringement, the market comprising former Napster users. StreamCast's internal docu-ments made constant reference to Napster, it initially distributed its Morpheus software through an OpenNap program compatible with Napster, it advertised its OpenNap program to Napster users, and its Morpheus software functions as Napster did except that it could be used to distribute more kinds of files, including copyrighted movies and software programs. Grokster's name is apparently derived from Napster, it too initially offered an OpenNap program, its software's function is likewise comparable to Nap-ster's, and it attempted to divert queries for Napster onto its own Web site. Grokster and StreamCast's efforts to supply services to former Napster users, deprived of a mechanism to copy and distribute what were overwhelmingly infringing files, indicate a principal, if not exclusive, intent on the part of each to bring about infringement.

Second, this evidence of unlawful objective is given added significance by MGM's showing that neither company attempted to develop filtering tools or other mecha-nisms to diminish the infringing activity using their software. While the Ninth Circuit treated the defendants' failure to develop such tools as irrelevant because they lacked an independent duty to monitor their users' activity, we think this evidence underscores Grokster's and StreamCast's intentional facilitation of their users' infringement.[12]

Third, there is a further complement to the direct evidence of unlawful objective. It is useful to recall that StreamCast and Grokster make money by selling advertising space, by directing ads to the screens of computers employing their software. As the record shows, the more the software is used, the more ads are sent out and the greater the advertising revenue becomes. Since the extent of the software's use determines the gain to the distributors, the commercial sense of their enterprise turns on high-volume use, which the record shows is infringing. This evidence alone would not justify an inference of unlawful intent, but viewed in the context of the entire record its import is clear. . . .

The unlawful objective is unmistakable.

B

In addition to intent to bring about infringement and distribution of a device suitable for infringing use, the inducement theory of course requires evidence of actual infringement by recipients of the device, the software in this case. As the account of the facts indicates, there is evidence of infringement on a gigantic scale, and there is no serious issue of the adequacy of MGM's showing on this point in order to survive the companies' summary judgment requests. Although an exact calculation of infringing use, as a basis for a claim of damages, is subject to dispute, there is no question that the summary judgment evidence is at least adequate to entitle MGM to go forward with claims for damages and equitable relief. . . .

In sum, this case is significantly different from *Sony* and reliance on that case to rule in favor of StreamCast and Grokster was error. *Sony* dealt with a claim of liability based solely on distributing a product with alternative lawful and unlawful uses, with knowledge that some users would follow the unlawful course. The case struck a balance between the interests of protection and innovation by holding that the product's capability of substantial lawful employment should bar the imputation of fault and consequent secondary liability for the unlawful acts of others.

MGM's evidence in this case most obviously addresses a different basis of liability for distributing a product open to alternative uses. Here, evidence of the distributors' words and deeds going beyond distribution as such shows a purpose to cause and profit from third-party acts of copyright infringement. If liability for inducing infringement is ultimately found, it will not be on the basis of presuming or imputing fault, but from inferring a patently illegal objective from statements and actions showing what that objective was.

There is substantial evidence in MGM's favor on all elements of inducement, and summary judgment in favor of Grokster and StreamCast was error. On remand, reconsideration of MGM's motion for summary judgment will be in order.

The judgment of the Court of Appeals is vacated, and the case is remanded for further proceedings consistent with this opinion.

It is so ordered.

---

12. Of course, in the absence of other evidence of intent, a court would be unable to find contributory infringement liability merely based on a failure to take affirmative steps to prevent infringement, if the device otherwise was capable of substantial noninfringing uses. Such a holding would tread too close to the Sony safe harbor.

Justice RUTH BADER GINSBURG, with whom THE CHIEF JUSTICE and Justice KENNEDY join, concurring. . . .

[T]he question in this case is whether Grokster and StreamCast are liable for the direct infringing acts of others. Liability under our jurisprudence may be predicated on actively encouraging (or inducing) infringement through specific acts (as the Court's opinion develops) or on distributing a product distributees use to infringe copyrights, if the product is not capable of "substantial" or "commercially significant" noninfringing uses. While the two categories overlap, they capture different culpable behavior. Long coexisting, both are now codified in patent law. *Compare* 35 U.S.C. §271(b) (active inducement liability), with §271(c) (contributory liability for distribution of a product not "suitable for substantial noninfringing use").

In *Sony*, 464 U.S. 417, the Court considered Sony's liability for selling the Betamax video cassette recorder. It did so enlightened by a full trial record. Drawing an analogy to the staple article of commerce doctrine from patent law, the *Sony* Court observed that the "sale of an article . . . adapted to [a patent] infringing use" does not suffice "to make the seller a contributory infringer" if the article "is also adapted to other and lawful uses." *Id.* at 441.

"The staple article of commerce doctrine" applied to copyright, the Court stated, "must strike a balance between a copyright holder's legitimate demand for effective — not merely symbolic — protection of the statutory monopoly, and the rights of others freely to engage in substantially unrelated areas of commerce." *Sony*, 464 U.S. at 442. "Accordingly," the Court held, "the sale of copying equipment, like the sale of other articles of commerce, does not constitute contributory infringement if the product is widely used for legitimate, unobjectionable purposes. Indeed, it need merely be capable of substantial noninfringing uses." *Ibid.* Thus, to resolve the *Sony* case, the Court explained, it had to determine "whether the Betamax is capable of commercially significant noninfringing uses." *Ibid.*

To answer that question, the Court considered whether "a significant number of [potential uses of the Betamax were] noninfringing." *Ibid.* The Court homed in on one potential use — private, noncommercial time-shifting of television programs in the home (*i.e.*, recording a broadcast TV program for later personal viewing). Time-shifting was noninfringing, the Court concluded, because in some cases trial testimony showed it was authorized by the copyright holder, and in others it qualified as legitimate fair use. Most purchasers used the Betamax principally to engage in time-shifting, a use that "plainly satisfied" the Court's standard. Thus, there was no need in *Sony* to "give precise content to the question of how much [actual or potential] use is commercially significant." *Id.* Further development was left for later days and cases.

The Ninth Circuit went astray . . . when that court granted summary judgment to Grokster and StreamCast on the charge of contributory liability based on distribution of their software products. Relying on its earlier opinion in *A&M Records, Inc. v. Napster, Inc.*, 239 F.3d 1004 (9th Cir. 2001), the Court of Appeals held that "if substantial noninfringing use was shown, the copyright owner would be required to show that the defendant had reasonable knowledge of specific infringing files." "A careful examination of the record," the court concluded, "indicates that there is no genuine issue of material fact as to noninfringing use." The appeals court pointed to the band Wilco, which made one of its albums available for free downloading, to other recording artists who may have authorized free distribution of their music through the Internet, and to public domain literary works and films available through Grokster's and StreamCast's software. Although it acknowledged MGM's assertion that "the vast majority of the software use is for copyright infringement," the court concluded that Grokster's and StreamCast's proffered evidence met *Sony's* requirement that "a product need only be *capable* of substantial noninfringing uses."

This case differs markedly from *Sony*. Here, there has been no finding of any fair use and little beyond anecdotal evidence of noninfringing uses. In finding the Grokster and StreamCast software products capable of substantial noninfringing uses, the District Court and the Court of Appeals appear to have relied largely on declarations submitted by the defendants. These declarations include assertions (some of them hearsay) that a number of copyright owners authorize distribution of their works on the Internet and that some public domain material is available through peer-to-peer networks including those accessed through Grokster's and StreamCast's software. . . .

Even if the absolute number of noninfringing files copied using the Grokster and StreamCast software is large, it does not follow that the products are therefore put to substantial noninfringing uses and are thus immune from liability. The number of noninfringing copies may be reflective of, and dwarfed by, the huge total volume of files shared. . . .

In sum, when the record in this case was developed, there was evidence that Grokster's and StreamCast's products were, and had been for some time, overwhelmingly used to infringe, and that this infringement was the overwhelming source of revenue from the products. Fairly appraised, the evidence was insufficient to demonstrate, beyond genuine debate, a reasonable prospect that substantial or commercially significant noninfringing uses were likely to develop over time. On this record, the District Court should not have ruled dispositively on the contributory infringement charge by granting summary judgment to Grokster and StreamCast.

If, on remand, the case is not resolved on summary judgment in favor of MGM based on Grokster and StreamCast actively inducing infringement, the Court of Appeals, I would emphasize, should reconsider, on a fuller record, its interpretation of *Sony's* product distribution holding.

Justice STEPHEN J. BREYER, with whom Justice STEVENS and Justice O'CONNOR join, concurring.

I agree with the Court that the distributor of a dual-use technology may be liable for the infringing activities of third parties where he or she actively seeks to advance the infringement. I further agree that, in light of our holding today, we need not now "revisit" *Sony Corp. of America v. Universal City Studios, Inc.*, 464 U.S. 417 (1984). Other Members of the Court, however, take up the *Sony* question: whether Grokster's product is "capable of 'substantial' or 'commercially significant' noninfringing uses." (GINSBURG J., concurring) (quoting *Sony, supra*, at 442). And they answer that question by stating that the Court of Appeals was wrong when it granted summary judgment on the issue in Grokster's favor. I write to explain why I disagree with them on this matter.

I

The Court's opinion in *Sony* and the record evidence (as described and analyzed in the many briefs before us) together convince me that the Court of Appeals' conclusion has adequate legal support.

A

I begin with *Sony's* standard. In *Sony*, the Court considered the potential copyright liability of a company that did not itself illegally copy protected material, but rather sold a machine — a Video Cassette Recorder (VCR) — that could be used to do so. A buyer could use that machine for *non*infringing purposes, such as recording for later viewing (sometimes called "time-shifting") uncopyrighted television programs or copyrighted programs with a copyright holder's permission. The buyer could use the machine for infringing purposes as well, such as building libraries of taped copyrighted programs. Or, the buyer might use the machine to record copyrighted programs under circumstances in which the legal status of the act of recording was uncertain (*i.e.*, where the copying may, or may not, have constituted a "fair use"). Sony knew many customers would use its VCRs to engage in unauthorized copying and "library-building." But that fact, said the Court, was insufficient to make Sony itself an infringer. And the Court ultimately held that Sony was not liable for its customers' acts of infringement.

In reaching this conclusion, the Court recognized the need for the law, in fixing *secondary* copyright liability, to "strike a balance between a copyright holder's legitimate demand for effective — not merely symbolic — protection of the statutory monopoly, and the rights of others freely to engage in substantially unrelated areas of commerce." . . . The Court wrote that the sale of copying equipment, "like the sale of other articles of commerce, does not constitute contributory infringement if the product is widely used for legitimate, unobjectionable purposes. *Indeed, it need merely be capable of substantial noninfringing uses.*" Sony, 464 U.S., at 442, 78 L. Ed. 2d 574, 104 S. Ct. 774 (emphasis added). The Court ultimately characterized the legal "question" in the particular case as "whether [Sony's VCR] is *capable of commercially significant noninfringing uses*" (while declining to give "precise content" to these terms). *Id.* (emphasis added).

It then applied this standard. The Court had before it a survey (commissioned by the District Court and then prepared by the respondents) showing that roughly 9% of all VCR recordings were of the type — namely, religious, educational, and sports programming — owned by producers and distributors testifying on Sony's behalf who did not object to time-shifting. A much higher percentage of VCR *users* had at one point taped an authorized program, in addition to taping unauthorized programs. And the plaintiffs — not a large class of content providers as in this case — owned only a small percentage of the total available unauthorized programming. But of all the taping actually done by Sony's customers, only around 9% was of the sort the Court referred to as authorized.

The Court found that the magnitude of authorized programming was "significant," and it also noted the "significant potential for future authorized copying." 464 U.S. at 444. The Court supported this conclusion by referencing the trial testimony of professional sports league officials and a religious broadcasting representative. It also discussed (1) a Los Angeles educational station affiliated with the Public Broadcasting Service that made many of its programs available for home taping, and (2) Mr. Rogers' Neighborhood, a widely watched children's program. On the basis of this testimony and other similar evidence, the Court determined that producers of this kind had authorized duplication of their copyrighted programs "in significant enough numbers to create a *substantial* market for a noninfringing use of the" VCR. *Id.* at 447 (emphasis added).

The Court, in using the key word "substantial," indicated that these circumstances alone constituted a sufficient basis for rejecting the imposition of secondary liability. *See id.*, at 456 ("Sony demonstrated a significant likelihood that *substantial* numbers of copyright holders" would not object to time-shifting (emphasis added)). Nonetheless, the Court buttressed its conclusion by finding separately that, in any event, unauthorized time-shifting often constituted not infringement, but "fair use." *Id.* at 447-456.

B

When measured against *Sony*'s underlying evidence and analysis, the evidence now before us shows that Grokster passes *Sony*'s test — that is, whether the company's product is capable of substantial or commercially significant noninfringing uses. For one thing, petitioners' (hereinafter MGM) own expert declared that 75% of current files available on Grokster are infringing and 15% are "likely infringing." That leaves some number of files near 10% that apparently are noninfringing, a figure very similar to the 9% or so of authorized time-shifting uses of the VCR that the Court faced in *Sony*.

As in *Sony*, witnesses here explained the nature of the noninfringing files on Grokster's network without detailed quantification. Those files include:

— Authorized copies of music by artists such as Wilco, Janis Ian, Pearl Jam, Dave Matthews, John Mayer, and others.
— Free electronic books and other works from various online publishers, including Project Gutenberg.
— Public domain and authorized software, such as WinZip 8.1.
— Licensed music videos and television and [movie segments distributed via digital video packaging with the permission of the copyright holder.

The nature of these and other lawfully swapped files is such that it is reasonable to infer quantities of current lawful use roughly approximate to those at issue in *Sony*. At least, MGM has offered no evidence sufficient to survive summary judgment that could plausibly demonstrate a significant quantitative difference. To be sure, in quantitative terms these uses account for only a small percentage of the total number of uses of Grokster's product. But the same was true in *Sony*, which characterized the relatively limited authorized copying market as "substantial." . . .

Importantly, *Sony* also used the word "capable," asking whether the product is "*capable of*" substantial noninfringing uses. Its language and analysis suggest that a figure like 10%, if fixed for all time, might well prove insufficient, but that such a figure serves as an adequate foundation where there is a reasonable prospect of expanded legitimate uses over time And its language also indicates the appropriateness of looking to potential future uses of the product to determine its "capability."

Here the record reveals a significant future market for noninfringing uses of Grokster-type peer-to-peer software. Such software permits the exchange of *any* sort of digital file — whether that file does, or does not, contain copyrighted material. As more and more uncopyrighted information is stored in swappable form, it seems a likely inference that lawful peer-to-peer sharing will become increasingly prevalent.

And that is just what is happening. Such legitimate noninfringing uses are coming to include the swapping of: *research information* (the initial purpose of many peer-to-peer networks); *public domain films* (*e.g.*, those owned by the Prelinger Archive);

historical recordings and digital educational materials (*e.g.*, those stored on the Internet Archive); *digital photos* (OurPictures, for example, is starting a P2P photo-swapping service); *"shareware"* and *"freeware"* (*e.g.*, Linux and certain Windows software); *secure licensed music and movie files* (Intent MediaWorks, for example, protects licensed content sent across P2P networks); *news broadcasts past and present* (the BBC Creative Archive lets users "rip, mix and share the BBC"); *user-created audio and video files* (including "podcasts" that may be distributed through P2P software); *and all manner of free "open content" works collected by Creative Commons* (one can search for Creative Commons material on StreamCast). I can find nothing in the record that suggests that this course of events will *not* continue to flow naturally as a consequence of the character of the software taken together with the foreseeable development of the Internet and of information technology.

There may be other now-unforeseen noninfringing uses that develop for peer-to-peer software, just as the home-video rental industry (unmentioned in *Sony*) developed for the VCR. But the foreseeable development of such uses, when taken together with an estimated 10% noninfringing material, is sufficient to meet *Sony*'s standard. And while *Sony* considered the record following a trial, there are no facts asserted by MGM in its summary judgment filings that lead me to believe the outcome after a trial here could be any different. The lower courts reached the same conclusion.

Of course, Grokster itself may not want to develop these other noninfringing uses. But *Sony*'s standard seeks to protect not the Groksters of this world (which in any event may well be liable under today's holding), but the development of technology more generally. And Grokster's desires in this respect are beside the point.

II

The real question here, I believe, is not whether the record evidence satisfies *Sony*. As I have interpreted the standard set forth in that case, it does. . . .

Instead, the real question is whether we should modify the *Sony* standard, as MGM requests, or interpret *Sony* more strictly, as I believe Justice Ginsburg's approach would do in practice. . . .

As I have said, *Sony* itself sought to "strike a balance between a copyright holder's legitimate demand for effective — not merely symbolic — protection of the statutory monopoly, and the rights of others freely to engage in substantially unrelated areas of commerce." Thus, to determine whether modification, or a strict interpretation, of *Sony* is needed, I would ask whether MGM has shown that *Sony* incorrectly balanced copyright and new-technology interests. In particular: (1) Has *Sony* (as I interpret it) worked to protect new technology? (2) If so, would modification or strict interpretation significantly weaken that protection? (3) If so, would new or necessary copyright-related benefits outweigh any such weakening?

A

The first question is the easiest to answer. *Sony*'s rule, as I interpret it, has provided entrepreneurs with needed assurance that they will be shielded from copyright liability as they bring valuable new technologies to market.

Sony's rule is clear. That clarity allows those who develop new products that are capable of substantial noninfringing uses to know, *ex ante*, that distribution of their product will not yield massive monetary liability. At the same time, it helps deter them from distributing products that have no other real function than — or that are specifically intended for — copyright infringement, deterrence that the Court's holding today reinforces (by adding a weapon to the copyright holder's legal arsenal).

Sony's rule is strongly technology protecting. The rule deliberately makes it difficult for courts to find secondary liability where new technology is at issue. It establishes that the law will not impose copyright liability upon the distributors of dual-use technologies (who do not themselves engage in unauthorized copying) unless the product in question will be used *almost exclusively* to infringe copyrights (or unless they actively induce infringements as we today describe). *Sony* thereby recognizes that the copyright laws are not intended to discourage or to control the emergence of new technologies, including (perhaps especially) those that help disseminate information and ideas more broadly or more efficiently. Thus *Sony*'s rule shelters VCRs, typewriters, tape recorders, photocopiers, computers, cassette players, compact disc burners, digital video recorders, MP3 players, Internet search engines, and peer-to-peer software. But *Sony*'s rule does not shelter descramblers, even if one could *theoretically* use a descrambler in a noninfringing way.

Sony's rule is forward looking. It does not confine its scope to a static snapshot of a product's current uses (thereby threatening technologies that have undeveloped future markets). Rather, as the VCR example makes clear, a product's market can evolve dramatically over time. And *Sony* — by referring to a *capacity* for substantial noninfringing uses — recognizes that fact. *Sony*'s word "capable" refers to a plausible, not simply a theoretical, likelihood that such uses will come to pass, and that fact anchors *Sony* in practical reality.

Sony's rule is mindful of the limitations facing judges where matters of technology are concerned. Judges have no specialized technical ability to answer questions about present or future technological feasibility or commercial viability where technology professionals, engineers, and venture capitalists themselves may radically disagree and where answers may differ depending upon whether one focuses upon the time of product development or the time of distribution. Consider, for example, the question whether devices can be added to Grokster's software that will filter out infringing files. MGM tells us this is easy enough to do, as do several *amici* that produce and sell the filtering technology. Grokster says it is not at all easy to do, and not an efficient solution in any event, and several apparently disinterested computer science professors agree Which account should a judge credit? *Sony* says that the judge will not necessarily have to decide.

Given the nature of the *Sony* rule, it is not surprising that in the last 20 years, there have been relatively few contributory infringement suits — based on a product distribution theory — brought against technology providers (a small handful of federal appellate court cases and perhaps fewer than two dozen District Court cases in the last 20 years). I have found nothing in the briefs or the record that shows that *Sony* has failed to achieve its innovation-protecting objective.

B

The second, more difficult, question is whether a modified *Sony* rule (or a strict interpretation) would significantly weaken the law's ability to protect new technology.

Justice Ginsburg's approach would require defendants to produce considerably more concrete evidence—more than was presented here—to earn *Sony*'s shelter. That heavier evidentiary demand, and especially the more dramatic (case-by-case balancing) modifications that MGM and the Government seek, would, I believe, undercut the protection that *Sony* now offers.

To require defendants to provide, for example, detailed evidence—say business plans, profitability estimates, projected technological modifications, and so forth—would doubtless make life easier for copyrightholder plaintiffs. But it would simultaneously increase the legal uncertainty that surrounds the creation or development of a new technology capable of being put to infringing uses. Inventors and entrepreneurs (in the garage, the dorm room, the corporate lab, or the boardroom) would have to fear (and in many cases endure) costly and extensive trials when they create, produce, or distribute the sort of information technology that can be used for copyright infringement. They would often be left guessing as to how a court, upon later review of the product and its uses, would decide when necessarily rough estimates amounted to sufficient evidence. They would have no way to predict how courts would weigh the respective values of infringing and noninfringing uses; determine the efficiency and advisability of technological changes; or assess a product's potential future markets. The price of a wrong guess—even if it involves a good-faith effort to assess technical and commercial viability—could be large statutory damages (not less than $ 750 and up to $ 30,000 *per infringed work.* 17 U.S.C. §504(c)(1). The additional risk and uncertainty would mean a consequent additional chill of technological development.

C

The third question—whether a positive copyright impact would outweigh any technology-related loss—I find the most difficult of the three. I do not doubt that a more intrusive *Sony* test would generally provide greater revenue security for copyright holders. But it is harder to conclude that the gains on the copyright swings would exceed the losses on the technology roundabouts.

For one thing, the law disfavors equating the two different kinds of gain and loss; rather, it leans in favor of protecting technology. As *Sony* itself makes clear, the producer of a technology which *permits* unlawful copying does not himself *engage* in unlawful copying—a fact that makes the attachment of copyright liability to the creation, production, or distribution of the technology an exceptional thing. Moreover, *Sony* has been the law for some time. And that fact imposes a serious burden upon copyright holders like MGM to show a need for change in the current rules of the game, including a more strict interpretation of the test.

In any event, the evidence now available does not, in my view, make out a sufficiently strong case for change. . . .

Will an unmodified *Sony* lead to a significant diminution in the amount or quality of creative work produced? Since copyright's basic objective is creation and its revenue objectives but a means to that end, this is the underlying copyright question. And its answer is far from clear.

Unauthorized copying likely diminishes industry revenue, though it is not clear by how much. *Compare* S. Liebowitz, Will MP3 Downloads Annihilate the Record Industry? The Evidence So Far, p. 2 (June 2003), http://www.utdallas.edu/liebowit/intprop/records.pdf (file sharing has caused a decline in music sales), and Press Release, Informa Media Group Report (citing Music on the Internet (5th ed. 2004)) (estimating total lost sales to the music industry in the range of $2 billion annually), at http://www.informatm.com, *with* F. Oberholzer & K. Strumpf, The Effect of File Sharing on Record Sales: An Empirical Analysis, p. 24 (Mar. 2004), www.unc.edu/cigar/papers/FileSharing_March2004.pdf (academic study concluding that "file sharing has no statistically significant effect on purchases of the average album"), *and* McGuire, Study: File-Sharing No Threat to Music Sales (Mar. 29, 2004), http://www.washingtonpost.com/ac2/wp-dyn/A34300-2004 Mar29?language=printer (discussing mixed evidence).

The extent to which related production has actually and resultingly declined remains uncertain, though there is good reason to believe that the decline, if any, is not substantial. *See, e.g.,* M. Madden, Pew Internet & American Life Project, Artists, Musicians, and the Internet, p. 21, http://www.pewinternet.org/pdfs/PIP_Artists.Musicians_Report.pdf (nearly 70% of musicians believe that file sharing is a minor threat or no threat at all to creative industries); Benkler, *Sharing Nicely: On Shareable Goods and the Emergence of Sharing as a Modality of Economic Production,* 114 Yale L. J. 273, 351-352 (2004) ("Much of the actual flow of revenue to artists — from performances and other sources — is stable even assuming a complete displacement of the CD market by peer-to-peer distribution. . . . It would be silly to think that music, a cultural form without which no human society has existed, will cease to be in our world [because of illegal file swapping]").

More importantly, copyright holders at least potentially have other tools available to reduce piracy and to abate whatever threat it poses to creative production. As today's opinion makes clear, a copyright holder may proceed against a technology provider where a provable specific intent to infringe (of the kind the Court describes) is present. Services like Grokster may well be liable under an inducement theory.

In addition, a copyright holder has always had the legal authority to bring a traditional infringement suit against one who wrongfully copies. Indeed, since September 2003, the Recording Industry Association of America (RIAA) has filed "thousands of suits against people for sharing copyrighted material." Walker, New*Movement Hits Universities: Get Legal Music,* Washington Post, Mar. 17, 2005, p. E1. These suits have provided copyright holders with damages; have served as a teaching tool, making clear that much file sharing, if done without permission, is unlawful; and apparently have had a real and significant deterrent effect.

Further, copyright holders may develop new technological devices that will help curb unlawful infringement. Some new technology, called "digital watermarking" and "digital fingerprinting," can encode within the file information about the author and the copyright scope and date, which "fingerprints" can help to expose infringers. Other technology can, through encryption, potentially restrict users' ability to make a digital copy.

At the same time, advances in technology have discouraged unlawful copying by making *lawful* copying (*e.g.,* downloading music with the copyright holder's permission) cheaper and easier to achieve. Several services now sell music for less than $1 per song. (Walmart.com, for example, charges $0.88 each). Consequently, many consumers initially attracted to the convenience and flexibility of services like Grokster are now migrating to lawful paid services (services with copying permission) where they can enjoy at little cost even greater convenience and flexibility without engaging in unlawful swapping.

Thus, lawful music downloading services — those that charge the customer for downloading music and pay royalties to the copyright holder — have continued to grow and to produce substantial revenue. And more advanced types of *non*-music-oriented P2P networks have also started to develop, drawing in part on the lessons of Grokster.

Finally, as *Sony* recognized, the legislative option remains available. Courts are less well suited than Congress to the task of "accommodating fully the varied permutations of competing interests that are inevitably implicated by such new technology." *Sony*, 464 U.S. at 431.

I do not know whether these developments and similar alternatives will prove sufficient, but I am reasonably certain that, given their existence, a strong demonstrated need for modifying *Sony* (or for interpreting *Sony*'s standard more strictly) has not yet been shown. That fact, along with the added risks that modification (or strict interpretation) would impose upon technological innovation, leads me to the conclusion that we should maintain *Sony*, reading its standard as I have read it. As so read, it requires affirmance of the Ninth Circuit's determination of the relevant aspects of the *Sony* question.

For these reasons, I disagree with Justice Ginsburg, but I agree with the Court and join its opinion.

§14.4.3 FAIR USE

SUNTRUST BANK v. HOUGHTON MIFFLIN CO.
268 F.3d 1257 (11th Cir. 2001)

STANLEY F. BIRCH, JR., Circuit Judge:

In this opinion, we decide whether publication of The Wind Done Gone ("TWDG"), a fictional work admittedly based on Margaret Mitchell's Gone With the Wind ("GWTW"), should be enjoined from publication based on alleged copyright violations. The district court granted a preliminary injunction against publication of TWDG. . . . We vacate the injunction and remand for consideration of the remaining claims.

I. Background . . .

SunTrust is the trustee of the Mitchell Trust, which holds the copyright in GWTW. Since its publication in 1936, GWTW has become one of the best-selling books in the world, second in sales only to the Bible. The Mitchell Trust has actively managed the copyright, authorizing derivative works and a variety of commercial items. It has entered into a contract authorizing, under specified conditions, a second sequel to GWTW to be published by St. Martin's Press. The Mitchell Trust maintains the copyright in all of the derivative works as well.

Alice Randall, the author of TWDG, persuasively claims that her novel is a critique of GWTW's depiction of slavery and the Civil-War era American South. To this end, she appropriated the characters, plot and major scenes from GWTW into the first half of TWDG. . . .

After discovering the similarities between the books, SunTrust asked Houghton Mifflin to refrain from publication or distribution of TWDG, but Houghton Mifflin refused the request. Subsequently, SunTrust filed an action alleging copyright infringement, violation of the Lanham Act, and deceptive trade practices, and immediately filed a motion for a temporary restraining order and a preliminary injunction. . . .

II. Discussion

Our primary focus at this stage of the case is on the appropriateness of the injunctive relief granted by the district court. In our analysis, we must evaluate the merits of SunTrust's copyright infringement claim, including Houghton Mifflin's affirmative defense of fair use. As we assess the fair-use defense, we examine to what extent a critic may use a work to communicate her criticism of the work without infringing the copyright in that work. To approach these issues in the proper framework, we should initially review the history of the Constitution's Copyright Clause and understand its relationship to the First Amendment.

A. HISTORY AND DEVELOPMENT OF THE COPYRIGHT CLAUSE

The Copyright Clause finds its roots in England, where, in 1710, the Statute of Anne "was designed to destroy the booksellers' monopoly of the booktrade and to prevent its recurrence." L. Ray Patterson, *Understanding the Copyright Clause*, 47 J. Copyright Soc'y USA USA 365, 379 (2000). This Parliamentary statute assigned copyright in books to authors, added a requirement that only a new work could be copyrighted, and limited the duration, which had been perpetual, to two fourteen-year terms. It is clear that the goal of the Statute of Anne was to encourage creativity and ensure that the public would have free access to information by putting an end to "the continued use of copyright as a device of censorship." Patterson at 379. The Framers of the U.S. Constitution relied on this statute when drafting the Copyright Clause of our Constitution, which reads, "The Congress shall have Power . . . to promote the Progress of Science . . . by securing for limited Times to Authors . . . the exclusive Right to their respective Writings . . . ." U.S. Const. art. 1, §8, cl. 8. Congress directly transferred the principles from the Statute of Anne into the copyright law of the United States in 1783, first through a recommendation to the states to enact similar copyright laws, and then in 1790, with the passage of the first American federal copyright statute.

The Copyright Clause was intended "to be the engine of free expression." *Harper & Row Publishers, Inc. v. Nation Enters.*, 471 U.S. 539, 558 (1985). To that end, copyright laws have been enacted achieve the three main goals: the promotion of learning, the protection of the public domain, and the granting of an exclusive right to the author.

1. Promotion of Learning

In the United States, copyright has always been used to promote learning by guarding against censorship. Throughout the nineteenth century, the copyright in literature was limited to the right "to publish and vend books." Patterson, at 383. The term "copy" was interpreted literally; an author had the right only to prevent others from copying and selling her particular literary work. This limited right ensured that a maximum number of new works would be created and published. It was not until the 1909 Act, which codified the concept of a derivative work, that an author's right to protect his original work against imitation was established. . . .

As a further protection of the public interest, until 1976, statutory copyright law required that a work be published before an author was entitled to a copyright in that work. Therefore, in order to have the sole right of publication for the statutory period, the author was first required to make the work available to the public. In 1976, copyright was extended to include any work "fixed in any tangible medium of expression" in order to adapt the law to technological advances. *Copyright Act of 1976*, 17 U.S.C. §102(a). Thus, the publication requirement was removed, but the fair use right was codified to maintain the constitutionally mandated balance to ensure that the public has access to knowledge.

The Copyright Act promotes public access to knowledge because it provides an economic incentive for authors to publish books and disseminate ideas to the public. Without the limited monopoly, authors would have little economic incentive to create and publish their work. Therefore, by providing this incentive, the copyright law promotes the public access to new ideas and concepts.

2. Protection of the Public Domain

The second goal of the Copyright Clause is to ensure that works enter the public domain after an author's rights, exclusive, but limited, have expired. Parallel to the patent regime, the limited time period of the copyright serves the dual purpose of ensuring that the work will enter the public domain and ensuring that the author has received "a fair return for [her] labors." *Harper & Row*, 471 U.S. at 5463. This limited grant "is intended to motivate the creative activity of authors . . . by the provision of a special reward, and to allow the public access to the products of their genius after the limited period of exclusive control has expired." *Sony Corp. of America v. Univ. City Studios, Inc.*, 464 U.S. 417, 429 (1984). The public is protected in two ways: the grant of a copyright encourages authors to create new works, . . . and the limitation ensures that the works will eventually enter the public domain, which protects the public's right of access and use.

3. Exclusive Rights of the Author

Finally, the Copyright Clause grants the author limited exclusive rights in order to encourage the creation of original works. Before our copyright jurisprudence developed, there were two separate theories of copyright in England — the natural law copyright, which was the right of first publication, and the statutory copyright, which was the right of continued publication. The natural law copyright, which is not a part of our system, implied an ownership in the work itself, and thus was preferred by the booksellers and publishers striving to maintain their monopoly over literature as well as by the Crown to silence "seditious" writings. Even after passage of the Statute of Anne, the publishers and booksellers resisted the loss of their monopoly in the courts for more than sixty years. Finally, in 1774, the House of Lords ruled that the natural law copyright, that is, the ownership of the work itself, expires upon publication of the book, when the statutory copyright attaches.

This bifurcated system was carried over into our copyright law. As of the 1909 Act, an author had "state common law protection [that] persisted until the moment of general publication." *Estate of Martin Luther King, Jr. v. CBS, Inc.*, 194 F.3d 1211, 1214 (11th Cir. 1999). After the work was published, the author was entitled to federal statutory copyright protection if she had complied with certain federal requirements (i.e. publication with notice). If not, the work was released into the public domain. The system illustrates that the author's ownership is in the copyright, and not in the work itself, for if the author had an ownership interest in the work itself, she would not lose that right if she published the book without complying with federal statutory copyright requirements. Compliance with the copyright law results in the guarantee of copyright to the author for a limited time, but the author never owns the work itself....

This has an important impact on modern interpretation of copyright, as it emphasizes the distinction between ownership of the work, which an author does not possess, and ownership of the copyright, which an author enjoys for a limited time. In a society oriented toward property ownership, it is not surprising to find many that erroneously equate the work with the copyright in the work and conclude that if one owns the copyright, they must also own the work....

B. THE UNION OF COPYRIGHT AND THE FIRST AMENDMENT

The Copyright Clause and the First Amendment,[11] while intuitively in conflict, were drafted to work together to prevent censorship; copyright laws were enacted in part to prevent private censorship and the First Amendment was enacted to prevent public censorship. There are "conflicting interests that must be accommodated in drawing a definitional balance" between the Copyright Clause and the First Amendment. 1 Melville B. Nimmer & David Nimmer, *Nimmer on Copyright* §1.10[B][1] (2001). In establishing this balance "on the copyright side, economic encouragement for creators must be preserved and the privacy of unpublished works recognized. Freedom of speech[, on the other hand,] requires the preservation of a meaningful public or democratic dialogue, as well as the uses of speech as a safety valve against violent acts, and as an end in itself." *Id.*

In copyright law, the balance between the First Amendment and copyright is preserved, in part, by the idea/expression dichotomy and the doctrine of fair use.

1. The Idea/Expression Dichotomy

Copyright cannot protect an idea, only the expression of that idea. The result is that "copyright assures authors the right to their original expression, but encourages others to build freely upon the ideas and information conveyed by the work." *Feist Publications, Inc. v. Rural Tel. Serv. Co.*, 499 U.S. 340, 349-350 (1991). It is partly through this idea/expression dichotomy that copyright law embodies the First Amendment's underlying goal of encouraging open debate and the free exchange of ideas. Holding an

---

11. "Congress shall make no law...abridging the freedom of speech..." U.S. Const. amend. I.

infringer liable in copyright for copying the expression of another author's ideas does not impede First Amendment goals because the public purpose has been served — the public already has access to the idea or the concepts. A new author may use or discuss the idea, but must do so using her own original expression.

2. Fair Use

First Amendment privileges are also preserved through the doctrine of fair use.[15] Until codification of the fair-use doctrine in the 1976 Act, fair use was a judge-made right developed to preserve the constitutionality of copyright legislation by protecting First Amendment values. Had fair use not been recognized as a right under the 1976 Act, the statutory abandonment of publication as a condition of copyright that had existed for over 200 years would have jeopardized the constitutionality of the new Act because there would be no statutory guarantee that new ideas, or new expressions of old ideas, would be accessible to the public. Included in the definition of fair use are "purposes such as criticism, comment, news reporting, teaching..., scholarship, or research." §107. The exceptions carved out for these purposes are at the heart of fair use's protection of the First Amendment, as they allow later authors to use a previous author's copyright to introduce new ideas or concepts to the public. Therefore, within the limits of the fair-use test, any use of a copyright is permitted to fulfill one of the important purposes listed in the statute.

Because of the First Amendment principles built into copyright law through the idea/expression dichotomy and the doctrine of fair use, courts often need not entertain related First Amendment arguments in a copyright case.

The case before us calls for an analysis of whether a preliminary injunction was properly granted against an alleged infringer who, relying largely on the doctrine of fair use, made use of another's copyright for comment and criticism. As discussed herein, *copyright does not immunize a work from comment and criticism*. Therefore, the narrower question in this case is to what extent a critic may use the protected elements of an original work of authorship to communicate her criticism without infringing the copyright in that work. As will be discussed below, this becomes essentially an analysis of the fair use factors. As we turn to the analysis required in this case, we must remain cognizant of the First Amendment protections interwoven into copyright law....

C. APPROPRIATENESS OF INJUNCTIVE RELIEF

... SunTrust is not entitled to relief in the form of a preliminary injunction unless it has proved each of the following four elements: "(1) a substantial likelihood of success on the merits, (2) a substantial threat of irreparable injury if the injunction were not granted, (3) that the threatened injury to the plaintiff outweighs the harm an injunction may cause the defendant, and (4) that granting the injunction would not disserve the public interest." *Am. Red Cross v. Palm Beach Blood Bank, Inc.*, 143 F.3d 1407, 1410 (11th Cir. 1998).

---

15. §107 ("Fair use of a copyrighted work...for purposes such as criticism [or] comment...is not an infringement of copyright.").

1. Substantial Likelihood of Success on the Merits

a. Prima Facie Copyright Infringement   The first step in evaluating the likelihood that SunTrust will succeed on merits is to determine whether it has established the prima facie elements of a copyright infringement claim: (1) that SunTrust owns a valid copyright in GWTW and (2) that Randall copied *original* elements of GWTW in TWDG. . . .

The first element, SunTrust's ownership of a valid copyright in GWTW, is not disputed. Houghton Mifflin does assert, however, that SunTrust did not establish the second element of infringement, that TWDG appropriates copyright-protected expression from GWTW. In order to prove copying, SunTrust was required to show a "substantial similarity" between the two works such that "an average lay observer would recognize the alleged copy as having been appropriated from the copyrighted work." Not all copying of a work is actionable, however, for, . . . "no author may copyright facts or ideas. The copyright is limited to those aspects of the work-termed 'expression' that display the stamp of the author's originality." *Harper & Row*, 471 U.S. at 547. Thus, we are concerned with substantial similarities between TWDG and GWTW only to the extent that they involve the copying of original, protected expression.

There is no bright line that separates the protectable expression from the non-protectable idea in a work of fiction. . . . At one end of the spectrum, *scenes a faire* — the stock scenes and hackneyed character types that "naturally flow from a common theme" — are considered "ideas," and therefore are not copyrightable. But as plots become more intricately detailed and characters become more idiosyncratic, they at some point cross the line into "expression" and are protected by copyright. . . .

Our own review of the two works reveals substantial use of GWTW. TWDG appropriates numerous characters, settings, and plot twists from GWTW. For example, Scarlett O'Hara, Rhett Butler, Bonnie Butler, Melanie Wilkes, Ashley Wilkes, Gerald O'Hara, Ellen O'Hara, Mammy, Pork, Dilcey, Prissy, Belle Watling, Carreen O'Hara, Stuart and Brenton Tarleton, Jeems, Philippe, and Aunt Pittypat, all characters in GWTW, appear in TWDG. Many of these characters are renamed in TWDG: Scarlett becomes "Other," Rhett Butler becomes "R.B.," Pork becomes "Garlic," Prissy becomes "Miss Priss," Philippe becomes "Feleepe," Aunt Pittypat becomes "Aunt Pattypit," etc. In several instances, Randall renamed characters using Mitchell's descriptions of those characters in GWTW: Ashley becomes "Dreamy Gentleman," Melanie becomes "Mealy Mouth," Gerald becomes "Planter." The fictional settings from GWTW receive a similarly transparent renaming in TWDG: Tara becomes "Tata," Twelve Oaks Plantation becomes "Twelve Slaves Strong as Trees." TWDG copies, often in wholesale fashion, the descriptions and histories of these fictional characters and places from GWTW, as well as their relationships and interactions with one another. TWDG appropriates or otherwise explicitly references many aspects of GWTW's plot as well, such as the scenes in which Scarlett kills a Union soldier and the scene in which Rhett stays in the room with his dead daughter Bonnie, burning candles. After carefully comparing the two works, we agree with the district court that, particularly in its first half, TWDG is largely "an encapsulation of [GWTW] [that] exploits its copyrighted characters, story lines, and settings as the palette for the new story." . . .

b. Fair Use   Randall's appropriation of elements of GWTW in TWDG may nevertheless not constitute infringement of SunTrust's copyright if the taking is protected as a "fair use." The codification of the fair-use doctrine in the Copyright Act provides:

> Notwithstanding the provisions of sections 106 and 106A, the fair use of a copy-righted work . . . for purposes such as criticism, comment, news reporting, teaching (including multiple copies for classroom use), scholarship, or research, is not an infringement of copyright. In determining whether the use made of a work in any particular case is a fair use the factors to be considered shall include —
>
> (1) the purpose and character of the use, including whether such use is of a commercial nature or is for nonprofit educational purposes;
>
> (2) the nature of the copyrighted work;
>
> (3) the amount and substantiality of the portion used in relation to the copyrighted work as a whole; and
>
> (4) the effect of the use upon the potential market for or value of the copyrighted work.

§107. In assessing whether a use of a copyright is a fair use under the statute, we bear in mind that the examples of possible fair uses given are illustrative rather than exclusive, and that "all [of the four factors] are to be explored, and the results weighed together in light of the purposes of copyright." *Campbell v. Acuff-Rose Music, Inc.*, 510 U.S. 569, 557-78 (1994). [O]ne of the most important purposes to consider is the free flow of ideas — particularly criticism and commentary.

Houghton Mifflin argues that TWDG is entitled to fair-use protection as a parody of GWTW. In *Campbell*, the Supreme Court held that parody, although not specifically listed in §107, is a form of comment and criticism that may constitute a fair use of the copyrighted work being parodied. Parody, which is directed toward a particular literary or artistic work, is distinguishable from satire, which more broadly addresses the institutions and mores of a slice of society. Thus, "parody needs to mimic an original to make its point, and so has some claim to use the creation of its victim's . . . imagination, whereas satire can stand on its own two feet and so requires justification for the very act of borrowing."

Before considering a claimed fair-use defense based on parody, however, the Supreme Court has required that we ensure that "a parodic character may reasonably be perceived" in the allegedly infringing work. The Supreme Court's definition of parody in *Campbell*, however, is somewhat vague. On the one hand, the Court suggests that the aim of parody is "comic effect or ridicule," but it then proceeds to discuss parody more expansively in terms of its "commentary" on the original. In light of the admonition in *Campbell* that courts should not judge the quality of the work or the success of the attempted humor in discerning its parodic character, we choose to take the broader view. For purposes of our fair-use analysis, we will treat a work as a parody if its aim is to comment upon or criticize a prior work by appropriating elements of the original in creating a new artistic, as opposed to scholarly or journalistic, work. Under this definition, the parodic character of TWDG is clear. TWDG is not a general commentary upon the Civil-War-era American South, but a specific criticism of and rejoinder to the depiction of slavery and the relationships between blacks and whites in GWTW. The fact that Randall chose to convey her criticisms of GWTW through a work of fiction, which she contends is a more powerful vehicle for her message than a scholarly article, does not, in and of itself, deprive TWDG of fair-use protection. We therefore proceed to an analysis of the four fair-use factors.

i. Purpose and Character of the Work

The first factor in the fair-use analysis, the purpose and character of the allegedly infringing work, has several facets. The first is whether TWDG serves a commercial purpose or nonprofit educational purpose. §107(1). Despite whatever educational function TWDG may be able to lay claim to, it is undoubtedly a commercial product.... The fact that TWDG was published for profit is the first factor weighing against a finding of fair use.

However, TWDG's for-profit status is strongly overshadowed and outweighed in view of its highly transformative use of GWTC's copyrighted elements. "The more transformative the new work, the less will be the significance of other factors, like commercialism, that may weigh against a finding of fair use." *Campbell*, 510 U.S. at 579. "The goal of copyright, to promote science and the arts, is generally furthered by the creation of transformative works." *Id.* A work's transformative value is of special import in the realm of parody, since a parody's aim is, by nature, to transform an earlier work.

The second factor in the "purpose and character" analysis relevant to this case is to what extent TWDG's use of copyrighted elements of GWTW can be said to be "transformative." The inquiry is "whether the new work merely supersedes the objects of the original creation, or instead adds something new, with a further purpose or different character, altering the first with new expression, meaning, or message." *Campbell*, 510 U.S. at 579. The issue of transformation is a double-edged sword in this case. On the one hand, the story of Cynara and her perception of the events in TWDG certainly adds new "expression, meaning, [and] message" to GWTW. From another perspective, however, TWDG's success as a pure work of fiction depends heavily on copyrighted elements appropriated from GWTW to carry its own plot forward.

However, as noted above, TWDG is more than an abstract, pure fictional work. It is principally and purposefully a critical statement that seeks to rebut and destroy the perspective, judgments, and mythology of GWTW. Randall's literary goal is to explode the romantic, idealized portrait of the antebellum South during and after the Civil War. In the world of GWTW, the white characters comprise a noble aristocracy whose idyllic existence is upset only by the intrusion of Yankee soldiers, and, eventually, by the liberation of the black slaves. Through her characters as well as through direct narration, Mitchell describes how both blacks and whites were purportedly better off in the days of slavery: "The more I see of emancipation the more criminal I think it is. It's just ruined the darkies," says Scarlett O'Hara. Free blacks are described as "creatures of small intelligence . . . like monkeys or small children turned loose among treasured objects whose value is beyond their comprehension, they ran wild - either from perverse pleasure in destruction or simply because of their ignorance." Blacks elected to the legislature are described as spending "most of their time eating goobers and easing their unaccustomed feet into and out of new shoes."

As the district court noted: "The earlier work is a third-person epic, whereas the new work is told in the first-person as an intimate diary of the life of Cynara. Thematically, the new work provides a different viewpoint of the antebellum world." While told from a different perspective, more critically, the story is transformed into a very different tale, albeit much more abbreviated. Cynara's very language is a departure from Mitchell's original prose; she acts as the voice of Randall's inversion of GWTW. She is the vehicle of parody; she is its means — not its end. It is clear within the first fifty pages of Cynara's fictional diary that Randall's work flips GWTW's traditional race roles, portrays powerful whites as stupid or feckless, and generally sets out to demystify GWTW and strip the romanticism from Mitchell's specific account of this period of our history. Approximately the last half of TWDG tells a completely new story that, although involving characters based on GWTW characters, features plot elements found nowhere within the covers of GWTW.

Where Randall refers directly to Mitchell's plot and characters, she does so in service of her general attack on GWTW. In GWTW, Scarlett O'Hara often expresses disgust with and condescension towards blacks; in TWDG, Other, Scarlett's counterpart, is herself of mixed descent. In GWTW, Ashley Wilkes is the initial object of Scarlett's affection; in TWDG, he is homosexual. In GWTW, Rhett Butler does not consort with black female characters and is portrayed as the captain of his own destiny. In TWDG, Cynara ends her affair with Rhett's counterpart, R., to begin a relationship with a black Congressman; R. ends up a washed out former cad. In TWDG, nearly every black character is given some redeeming quality — whether depth, wit, cunning, beauty, strength, or courage — that their GWTW analogues lacked.

In light of this, we find it difficult to conclude that Randall simply tried to "avoid the drudgery in working up something fresh." *Campbell*, 510 U.S. at 580. It is hard to imagine how Randall could have specifically criticized GWTW without depending heavily upon copyrighted elements of that book. A parody is a work that seeks to comment upon or criticize another work by appropriating elements of the original. "Parody needs to mimic an original to make its point, and so has some claim to use the creation of its victim's (or collective victims') imagination." *Campbell*, 510 U.S. at 580-81. Thus, Randall has fully employed those conscripted elements from GWTW to make war against it. Her work, TWDG, reflects transformative value because it "can provide social benefit, by shedding light on an earlier work, and, in the process, creating a new one." *Campbell*, 510 U.S. at 579.

While "transformative use is not absolutely necessary for a finding of fair use, . . . the more transformative the new work, the less will be the significance of other factors." *Id.* In the case of TWDG, consideration of this factor certainly militates in favor of a finding of fair use, and, informs our analysis of the other factors, particularly the fourth, as discussed below.

ii.   Nature of the Copyrighted Work

The second factor, the nature of the copyrighted work, recognizes that there is a hierarchy of copyright protection in which original, creative works are afforded greater protection than derivative works or factual compilations. GWTW is undoubtedly entitled to the greatest degree of protection as an original work of fiction. This factor is given little weight in parody cases, however, "since parodies almost invariably copy publicly known, expressive works." *Campbell*, 510 U.S. at 586.

iii.   Amount and Substantiality of the Portion Used

The third fair-use factor is "the amount and substantiality of the portion used in relation to the copyrighted work as a whole." §107(3). It is at this point that parody presents uniquely difficult problems for courts in the fair-use context, for "parody's humor, or in any event its comment, necessarily springs from recognizable allusion to its object through distorted imitation. . . . When parody takes aim at a particular original work, the parody must be able to 'conjure up' at least enough of that original to make the object of its critical wit recognizable." *Campbell*, 510 U.S. at 588 Once enough has been taken to "conjure up" the original in the minds of the readership, any further taking must specifically serve the new work's parodic aims.

GWTW is one of the most famous, popular, and enduring American novels ever written. Given the fame of the work and its primary characters, SunTrust argues that very little reference is required to conjure up GWTW. As we have already indicated in our discussion of substantial similarity, TWDG appropriates a substantial portion of the protected elements of GWTW. Houghton Mifflin argues that TWDG takes nothing from GWTW that does not serve a parodic purpose, the crux of the argument being that a large number of characters had to be taken from GWTW because each represents a different ideal or stereotype that requires commentary, and that the work as a whole could not be adequately commented upon without revisiting substantial portions of the plot, including its most famous scenes. . . .

There are numerous instances in which TWDG appropriates elements of GWTW and then transforms them for the purpose of commentary. TWDG uses several of GWTW's most famous lines, but vests them with a completely new significance. For example, the final lines of GWTW, "Tomorrow, I'll think of some way to get him back. After all, tomorrow is another day," are transformed in TWDG into "For all those we love for whom tomorrow will not be another day, we send the sweet prayer of resting in peace." . . .

On the other hand, however, we are told that not all of TWDG's takings from GWTW are clearly justified as commentary. We have already determined that TWDG is a parody, but not every parody is a fair use. SunTrust contends that TWDG, at least at the margins, takes more of the protected elements of GWTW than was necessary to serve a parodic function.

For example, in a sworn declaration to the district court, Randall stated that she needed to reference the scene from GWTW in which Jeems is given to the Tarleton twins as a birthday present because she considers it "perhaps the single most repellent paragraph in Margaret Mitchell's novel: a black child given to two white children as a birthday present . . . as if the buying and selling of children thus had no moral significance." Clearly, such a scene is fair game for criticism. However, in this instance, SunTrust argues that TWDG goes beyond commentary on the occurrence itself, appropriating such nonrelevant details as the fact that the twins had red hair and were killed at Gettysburg. There are several other scenes from GWTW, such as the incident in which Scarlett threw a vase at Ashley while Rhett was hidden on the couch, that are retold or alluded to without serving any apparent parodic purpose. Similar taking of the descriptions of characters and the minor details of their histories and interactions that arguably are not essential to the parodic purpose of the work recur throughout . . . But we must determine whether the use is fair. In doing so, we are reminded that literary relevance is a highly subjective analysis ill- suited for judicial inquiry. Thus we are presented with conflicting and opposing arguments relative to the amount taken and whether it was too much or a necessary amount.

The Supreme Court in *Campbell* did not require that parodists take the bare minimum amount of copyright material necessary to conjure up the original work. Parody "must be able to conjure up *at least* enough of [the] original to make the object of its critical wit recognizable." *Campbell*, 510 U.S. at 588. . . .

A use does not necessarily become infringing the moment it does more than simply conjure up another work. Rather, "once enough has been taken to assure identification, how much more is reasonable will depend, say [1] on the extent to which the [work's] *overriding purpose and character is to parody* the original or, in contrast [2] the likelihood that the parody may serve as *a market substitute* for the original." *Campbell*, 510 U.S. at 588. As to the first point, it is manifest that TWDG's *raison d'etre* is to parody GWTW. The second point indicates that any material we suspect is "extraneous" to the parody is unlawful only if it negatively effects the potential market for or value of the original copyright. Based upon this record at this juncture, we cannot determine in any conclusive way whether "'the quantity and value of the materials used'" are reasonable in relation to the purpose of the copying.'" *Id.* at 586.

iv. Effect on the Market Value of the Original

The final fair-use factor requires us to consider the effect that the publication of TWDG will have on the market for or value of SunTrust's copyright in GWTW, including the potential harm it may cause to the market for derivative works based on GWTW.... "The only harm to derivatives that need concern us . . . is the harm of market substitution. The fact that a parody may impair the market for derivative uses by the very effectiveness of its critical commentary is no more relevant under copyright that the like threat to the original market." *Campbell*, 510 U.S. at 593.

As for the potential market, SunTrust proffered evidence in the district court of the value of its copyright in GWTW. Several derivative works of GWTW have been authorized, including the famous movie of the same name and a book titled Scarlett: The Sequel. GWTW and the derivative works based upon it have generated millions of dollars for the copyright holders. SunTrust has negotiated an agreement with St. Martin's Press permitting it to produce another derivative work based on GWTW, a privilege for which St. Martin's paid "well into seven figures." Part of this agreement was that SunTrust would not authorize any other derivative works prior to the publication of St. Martin's book.

An examination of the record, with its limited development as to relevant market harm due to the preliminary injunction status of the case, discloses that SunTrust focuses on the value of GWTW and its derivatives, but fails to address and offers little evidence or argument to demonstrate that TWDG would supplant demand for SunTrust's licensed derivatives. However, the Supreme Court and other appeals courts have made clear that, particularly in cases of parody, evidence of harm to the potential market for or value of the original copyright is crucial to a fair use determination....

In contrast, the evidence proffered in support of the fair use defense specifically and correctly focused on market substitution and demonstrates why Randall's book is unlikely to displace sales of GWTW. Thus, we conclude, based on the current record, that SunTrust's evidence falls far short of establishing that TWDG or others like it will act as market substitutes for GWTW or will significantly harm its derivatives. Accordingly, the fourth fair use factor weighs in favor of TWDG.

c. Summary of the Merits

We reject the district court's conclusion that SunTrust has established its likelihood of success on the merits. To the contrary, based upon our analysis of the fair use factors we find, at this juncture, TWDG is entitled to a fair-use defense....

PROBLEMS

1. *Research articles.* In *American Geophysical Union v. Texaco Inc.*, 60 F.3d 913 (2d Cir. 1994), the Second Circuit found that Texaco had not engaged in a fair use when it photocopied articles in scientific journals for use by its 400 to 500 research scientists. The scientists would review copies of journals and arrange to photocopy whole articles to be placed in file drawers until needed. The court determined that although scholars generally are not paid for the articles they produce in scholarly journals, the journals themselves lost income they would have garnered had Texaco negotiated licensing fees with the journal publishers or purchased enough copies for use by its scientists who wanted to archive copies. Although the court considered Texaco's for-profit nature to be relevant, it did not view this fact alone to be determinative of the outcome of the case. Universities and law schools routinely arrange to photocopy scholarly articles for both archival and current use by faculty members. Does this constitute a fair use?

2. *Fan fiction.* Many fans of particular books, movies, or television shows like to write stories involving the characters and/or the worlds created by the authors of those works. Some of these works are parodies but many are more a form of homage to the original work. This work is sometimes published on the Internet and shared among amateurs. A major center of this work is www.fanfiction.net, a website that publishes this fiction and, as so many websites, contains advertisements for products. Copyrights extends to "derivative works," 17 U.S.C. §§103, 106, which are defined as "work based upon one or more preexisting works, such as a translation, musical arrangement, dramatization, fictionalization, motion picture version, sound recording, art reproduction, abridgment, condensation, or any other form in which a work may be recast, transformed, or adapted," *id.* at §101. Fan fiction seems clearly to be a derivative work and may well violate the *Copyright Act.* Some authors vigilantly police such uses while other authors are happy to have their fans imagine new stories involving the worlds and characters they created. When these derivative works are published on a website like *fanfiction.net*, do they constitute a fair use of the copyrighted work? *Compare* Rebecca Tushnet, *Using Law and Identity to Script Cultural Production: Legal Fictions: Copyright, Fan Fiction, and a New Common Law*, 17 Loy. L.A. Ent. L.J. 651 (1997) (arguing that fan fiction should be legally protected as a fair use).

§14.5 Patent Law

Patent law grants inventors of processes, machines, and compositions of matter a monopoly over their inventions for up to 20 years. 35 U.S.C. §§101 *et seq.* Unlike copyrights, which exist from the moment a work is first fixed into a tangible form, patents are granted by a government agency, the Patent and Trademark Office, after application by the inventor. The patent will be granted only if four requirements are met: (1) the subject matter of the invention must be patentable, *i.e.*, a "machine," method of "manufacture" or "composition of matter," 35 U.S.C. §101; (2) the invention must be novel; (3) non-obvious; and (4) useful.

§14.5.1   PROPERTY IN GENETIC INFORMATION

See supra §1.3.2, at pages 45-53.

§14.5.2 Business Methods

Until recently, it was not possible to patent a "business method" because most business and financial innovations were either considered not to be "novel" or to be unpatentable because they did not involve physical processes. However, after the Federal Circuit decided that business methods are patentable, *State Street Bank & Trust Co. v. Signature Financial Group*, 149 F.3d 1368 (Fed. Cir. 1998), the Patent Office has issued hundreds of patents covering methods of doing business.

What constitutes a "novel" and "non-obvious" business method is hard to sort out. For example, in *Amazon.com, Inc. v. Barnesandnoble.com, Inc.*, 73 F. Supp. 2d 1228 (W.D. Wash. 1999), *rev'd*, 239 F.3d 1343 (Fed. Cir. 2001), plaintiff Amazon.com, an on-line retailer, sued a competitor, Barnesandnoble.com, alleging infringement of Amazon.com's patent for a "one-click" method for placing purchase orders over the Internet. This method allowed users to place personal information with the company that it could access on later visits to allow the buyer to complete a purchase by one computer mouse click on a "buy" button. Defendant argued that the patent was invalid because the invention of this method was neither novel nor non-obvious. The trial court granted plaintiff a preliminary injunction ordering defendant to cease using a similar one-click method on its web site without plaintiff's consent.

Trial Judge Pechman held that the one-click method was a substantial advance over the "prior art," which used the prior multiple step "shopping cart" model. The shopping cart model would allow purchasers to place items they wished to purchase in a "shopping cart" and later revisit that shopping cart to give personal information and purchase the selected items. Many buyers would abort the purchase process after selecting an item either because they changed their minds or found the buying process confusing or tiresome. The one-click method ensured that the sale would go through more expeditiously. This method was both novel and non-obvious because "there [was] insufficient evidence in the record regarding a teaching, suggestion, or motivation in the prior art that would lead one of ordinary skill in the art of e-commerce to combine the references" in prior patents and practices in a way that would obviously suggest the one-click method. 73 F. Supp. 2d at 1235. The new method was obviously useful because it helped ensure that buyers would complete their purchases once they decided to buy. After invention of the one-click method, other e-commerce retailers followed suit, suggesting both that the method was not obvious and that it was useful. The Ninth Circuit reversed, finding that several prior methods of internet purchasing *did* anticipate the one-click method, making it neither novel nor non-obvious.

§14.6 *Publicity Rights*

MARTIN LUTHER KING, JR. CENTER FOR SOCIAL CHANGE v. AMERICAN HERITAGE PRODUCTS

296 S.E.2d 697 (Ga. 1982)

HAROLD N. HILL, JR., Presiding Justice:

The plaintiffs are the Martin Luther King, Jr. Center for Social Change (the Center),[2] Coretta Scott King, as administratrix of Dr. King's estate, and Motown

---

2. The Center is a nonprofit corporation that seeks to promote the ideals of Dr. King.

Record Corporation, the assignee of the rights to several of Dr. King's copyrighted speeches. Defendant James F. Bolen is the sole proprietor of a business known as B & S Sales, which manufactures and sells various plastic products as funeral accessories. Defendant James E. Bolen, the son of James F. Bolen, developed the concept of marketing a plastic bust of Dr. Martin Luther King, Jr., and formed a company, B & S Enterprises, to sell the busts, which would be manufactured by B & S Sales. B & S Enterprises was later incorporated under the name of American Heritage Products, Inc.

Although Bolen sought the endorsement and participation of the Martin Luther King, Jr. Center for Social Change, Inc., in the marketing of the bust, the Center refused Bolen's offer. Bolen pursued the idea, nevertheless, hiring an artist to prepare a mold and an agent to handle the promotion of the product. Defendant took out two half-page advertisements in the November and December 1980 issues of Ebony magazine, which purported to offer the bust as "an exclusive memorial" and "an opportunity to support the Martin Luther King, Jr., Center for Social Change." The advertisement stated that "a contribution from your order goes to the King Center for Social Change." Out of the $29.95 purchase price, defendant Bolen testified he set aside 3% or $.90, as a contribution to the Center. The advertisement also offered "free" with the purchase of the bust a booklet about the life of Dr. King entitled "A Tribute to Dr. Martin Luther King, Jr."

In addition to the two advertisements in Ebony, defendant published a brochure or pamphlet which was inserted in 80,000 copies of newspapers across the country. The brochure reiterated what was stated in the magazine advertisements, and also contained photographs of Dr. King and excerpts from his copyrighted speeches. The brochure promised that each "memorial" (bust) is accompanied by a Certificate of Appreciation "testifying that a contribution has been made to the Martin Luther King, Jr., Center for Social Change."

Defendant James E. Bolen testified that he created a trust fund for that portion of the earnings which was to be contributed to the Center. The trust fund agreement, however, was never executed, and James E. Bolen testified that this was due to the plaintiffs' attorneys' request to cease and desist from all activities in issue. Testimony in the district court disclosed that money had been tendered to the Center, but was not accepted by its governing board. Also, the district court found that, as of the date of the preliminary injunction, the defendants had sold approximately 200 busts and had outstanding orders for 23 more.

On November 21, 1980, and December 19, 1980, the plaintiffs demanded that the Bolens cease and desist from further advertisements and sales of the bust, and on December 31, 1980, the plaintiffs filed a complaint in the United States District Court for the Northern District of Georgia. . . . The motion for an injunction sought (1) an end to the use of the Center's name in advertising and marketing the busts, (2) restraint of any further copyright infringement and (3) an end to the manufacture and sale of the plastic busts. The defendants agreed to discontinue the use of the Center's name in further promotion. Therefore, the court granted this part of the injunction. The district court found that the defendants had infringed the King copyrights and enjoined all further use of the copyrighted material.

In ruling on the third request for injunction, the court confronted the plaintiffs' claim that the manufacture and sale of the busts violated Dr. King's right of publicity which had passed to his heirs upon Dr. King's death. The defendants contended that no such right existed, and hence, an injunction should not issue. . . .

[T]he Eleventh Circuit Court of Appeals has certified the following questions:

(1) Is the "right of publicity" recognized in Georgia as a right distinct from the right of privacy?

(2) If the answer to question (1) is affirmative, does the "right to publicity" survive the death of its owner? Specifically, is the right inheritable and devisable?

(3) If the answer to question (2) is also affirmative, must the owner have commercially exploited the right before it can survive his death?

(4) Assuming the affirmative answers to questions (1), (2) and (3), what is the guideline to be followed in defining commercial exploitation and what are the evidentiary prerequisites to a showing of commercial exploitation? . . .

The right of publicity may be defined as a celebrity's right to the exclusive use of his or her name and likeness. The right is most often asserted by or on behalf of professional athletes, comedians, actors and actresses, and other entertainers. This case involves none of those occupations. As is known to all, from 1955 until he was assassinated on April 4, 1968, Dr. King, a Baptist minister by profession, was the foremost leader of the civil rights movement in the United States. He was awarded the Nobel Prize for Peace in 1964. Although not a public official, Dr. King was a public figure, and we deal in this opinion with public figures who are neither public officials nor entertainers. Within this framework, we turn to the questions posed.

1. Is the "right of publicity" recognized in Georgia as a right distinct from the right of privacy?

Georgia has long recognized the right of privacy. . . . In *Pavesich v. New England Life Ins. Co.*, 50 S.E. 68 (Ga. 1905), the picture of an artist was used without his consent in a newspaper advertisement of the insurance company. Analyzing the right of privacy, this court held: "The publication of a picture of a person, without his consent, as a part of an advertisement, for the purpose of exploiting the publisher's business, is a violation of the right of privacy of the person whose picture is reproduced, and entitles him to recover without proof of special damage." If the right to privacy had not been recognized, advertisers could use photographs of private citizens to promote sales and the professional modeling business would not be what it is today.

In the course of its opinion the *Pavesich* court said several things pertinent here. It noted that the commentators on ancient law recognized the right of personal liberty, including the right to exhibit oneself before the public at proper times and places and in a proper manner. As a corollary, the court recognized that the right of personal liberty included the right of a person not to be exhibited before the public, saying: "The right to withdraw from the public gaze at such times as a person may see fit, when his presence in public is not demanded by any rule of law is also embraced within the right of personal liberty. Publicity in one instance and privacy in the other is each guaranteed. If personal liberty embraces the *right of publicity*, it no less embraces the correlative right of privacy; and this is no new idea in Georgia law." (Emphasis supplied.)

Recognizing the possibility of a conflict between the right of privacy and the freedoms of speech and press, this court said: "There is in the publication of one's picture for advertising purposes not the slightest semblance of an expression of an idea, a thought, or an opinion, within the meaning of the constitutional provision which guarantees to a person the right to publish his sentiments on any subject." The defendants in the case now before us make no claim under these freedoms and we find no violation thereof.

Observing in dicta that the right of privacy in general does not survive the death of the person whose privacy is invaded, the *Pavesich* court said: "While the right of privacy is personal, and may die with the person, we do not desire to be understood as assenting to the proposition that the relatives of the deceased can not, in a proper case, protect the memory of their kinsman, not only from defamation, but also from an invasion into the affairs of his private life after his death. This question is not now involved, but we do not wish anything said to be understood as committing us in any way to the doctrine that against the consent of relatives the private affairs of a deceased person may be published and his picture or statue exhibited." 50 S.E. at 76.

Finding that Pavesich, although an artist, was not recognized as a public figure, the court said: "It is not necessary in this case to hold, nor are we prepared to do so, that the mere fact that a man has become what is called a public character, either by aspiring to public office, or by holding public office, or by exercising a profession which places him before the public, or by engaging in a business which has necessarily a public nature, gives to everyone the right to print and circulate his picture." 50 S.E. at 79-80. Thus, although recognizing the right of privacy, the *Pavesich* court left open the question facing us involving the likeness of a public figure.

On the other hand, in *Waters v. Fleetwood*, 91 S.E.2d 344 (Ga. 1956), it was held that the mother of a 14-year-old murder victim could not recover for invasion of the mother's privacy from a newspaper that published and sold separately photographs of her daughter's body taken after it was removed from a river. There the court found that publication and reproduction for sale of a photograph incident to a matter of public interest or to a public investigation could not be a violation of anyone's right of privacy.

The "right of publicity" was first recognized in *Haelan Laboratories v. Topps Chewing Gum*, 202 F.2d 866 (2d Cir. 1953). There plaintiff had acquired by contract the exclusive right to use certain ball players' photographs in connection with the sales of plaintiff's chewing gum. An independent publishing company acquired similar rights from some of the same ball players. Defendant, a chewing gum manufacturer competing with plaintiff and knowing of plaintiff's contracts, acquired the contracts from the publishing company. As to these contracts the court found that the defendant had violated the ball players' "right of publicity" acquired by the plaintiff, saying: We think that, in addition to and independent of that right of privacy (which in New York derives from statute), a man has a right in the publicity value of his photograph, *i.e.*, the right to grant the exclusive privilege of publishing his picture, and that such a grant may validly be made 'in gross,' *i.e.*, without an accompanying transfer of a business or of anything else. Whether it be labelled a 'property' right is immaterial; for here, as often elsewhere, the tag 'property' simply symbolizes the fact that courts enforce a claim which has pecuniary worth.

"This right might be called a 'right of publicity.' For it is common knowledge that many prominent persons (especially actors and ball-players), far from having their feelings bruised through public exposure of their likenesses, would feel sorely deprived if they no longer received money for authorizing advertisements, popularizing their countenances, displayed in newspapers, magazines, busses, trains and subways. This right of publicity would usually yield them no money unless it could be made the subject of an exclusive grant which barred any other advertiser from using their pictures." ...

In *Palmer v. Schonhorn Enterprises*, 232 A.2d 458 (N.J. Super. Ct. 1967), Arnold Palmer, Gary Player, Doug Sanders and Jack Nicklaus obtained summary judgment against the manufacturer of a golf game which used the golfers' names and short biographies without their consent. Although written as a right of privacy case, much of what was said is applicable to the right of publicity. In its opinion the court said: . . . "The names of plaintiffs have become internationally famous, undoubtedly by reason of talent as well as hard work in perfecting it. This is probably true in the cases of most so-called celebrities, who have attained national or international recognition in a particular field of art, science, business or other extraordinary ability. They may not all desire to capitalize upon their names in the commercial field, beyond or apart from that in which they have reached their known excellence. However, because they presently do not should not be justification for others to do so because of the void. They may desire to do it later. . . . It is unfair that one should be permitted to commercialize or exploit or capitalize upon another's name, reputation or accomplishments merely because the owner's accomplishments have been highly publicized."

In *Haelan Laboratories, supra*, the court was concerned with whether a celebrity has the right to the exclusive use of his or her name and likeness. In *Palmer, supra*, the court was concerned with whether a person using the celebrity's name for the user's commercial benefit has the right to do so without authorization. At this point it should be emphasized that we deal here with the unauthorized use of a person's name and likeness for the commercial benefit of the user, not with a city's use of a celebrity's name to denominate a street or school.

The right to publicity is not absolute. In *Hicks v. Casablanca Records*, 464 F. Supp. 426 (S.D.N.Y. 1978), the court held that a fictional novel and movie concerning an unexplained eleven-day disappearance by Agatha Christie, author of numerous mystery novels, were permissible under the first amendment. On the other hand, in *Zacchini v. Scripps-Howard Broadcasting Co.*, 433 U.S. 562 (1977), a television station broadcast on its news program plaintiff's 15-second "human cannonball" flight filmed at a local fair. The Supreme Court held that freedom of the press does not authorize the media to broadcast a performer's entire act without his consent, just as the media could not televise a stage play, prize fight or baseball game without consent. Quoting from Kalven, *Privacy in Tort Law — Were Warren and Brandeis Wrong?*, 31 Law & Contemp. Prob. 326, 332 (1966), the Court said: "The rationale for [protecting the right of publicity] is the straight-forward one of preventing unjust enrichment by the theft of good will. No social purpose is served by having the defendant get free some aspect of the plaintiff that would have market value and for which he would normally pay." . . .

[T]he courts in Georgia have recognized the rights of private citizens, as well as entertainers, not to have their names and photographs used for the financial gain of the user without their consent, where such use is not authorized as an exercise of freedom of the press. We know of no reason why a public figure prominent in religion and civil rights should be entitled to less protection than an exotic dancer or a movie actress. Therefore, we hold that the appropriation of another's name and likeness, whether such likeness be a photograph or sculpture, without consent and for the financial gain of the appropriator is a tort in Georgia, whether the person whose name and likeness is used is a private citizen, entertainer, or as here a public figure who is not a public official. . . .

. . . We conclude that while private citizens have the right of privacy, public figures have a similar right of publicity, and that the measure of damages to a public figure for violation of his or her right of publicity is the value of the appropriation to the user. As thus understood the first certified question is answered in the affirmative.

2. Does the "right of publicity" survive the death of its owner (*i.e.*, is the right inheritable and devisable)? . . .

The right of publicity is assignable during the life of the celebrity, for without this characteristic, full commercial exploitation of one's name and likeness is practically impossible. That is, without assignability the right of publicity could hardly be called a "right." . . .

The courts that have considered the problem are not . . . unanimous. . . . In *Factors Etc., Inc. v. Pro Arts, Inc.*, 579 F.2d 215 (2d Cir. 1978),[3] Elvis Presley had assigned his right of publicity to Boxcar Enterprises, which assigned that right to Factors after Presley's death. Defendant Pro Arts published a poster of Presley entitled "In Memory." In affirming the grant of injunction against Pro Arts, the Second Circuit Court of Appeals said: "The identification of this exclusive right belonging to Boxcar as a transferable property right compels the conclusion that the right survives Presley's death. The death of Presley, who was merely the beneficiary of an income interest in Boxcar's exclusive right, should not in itself extinguish Boxcar's property right. Instead, the income interest, continually produced from Boxcar's exclusive right of commercial exploitation, should inure to Presley's estate at death like any other intangible property right. To hold that the right did not survive Presley's death, would be to grant competitors of Factors, such as Pro Arts, a windfall in the form of profits from the use of Presley's name and likeness. At the same time, the exclusive right purchased by Factors and the financial benefits accruing to the celebrity's heirs would be rendered virtually worthless."

In *Lugosi v. Universal Pictures*, 603 P.2d 425 (Cal. 1979),[4] the Supreme Court of California, in a 4 to 3 decision, declared that the right of publicity expires upon the death of the celebrity and is not descendible. Bela Lugosi appeared as Dracula in Universal Picture's movie by that name. Universal had acquired the movie rights to the novel by Bram Stoker. Lugosi's contract with Universal gave it the right to exploit Lugosi's name and likeness in connection with the movie. The majority of the court held that Lugosi's heirs could not prevent Universal's continued exploitation of Lugosi's portrayal of Count Dracula after his death. The court did not decide whether Universal could prevent unauthorized third parties from exploitation of Lugosi's appearance as Dracula after Lugosi's death.

In *Memphis Development Foundation v. Factors Etc., Inc.*, 616 F.2d 956 (6th Cir. 1980), Factors, which had won its case against Pro Arts in New York (see above), lost against the Memphis Development Foundation under the Court of Appeals for the Sixth Circuit's interpretation of Tennessee law. There, the Foundation, a non-profit corporation, planned to erect a statue of Elvis Presley in Memphis and solicited contributions to do so. Donors of $25 or more received a small replica of the proposed statue. The Sixth Circuit reversed the grant of an injunction favoring Factors, holding that a celebrity's right of publicity was not inheritable even where that right had been exploited during the celebrity's life.[5] The court reasoned that although recognition of the right of publicity during life serves to encourage effort and inspire creative endeavors, making the right inheritable would not. . . .

---

3. *But see Pirone v. MacMillan*, 894 F.2d 579 (2d Cir. 1990) (holding that publicity rights are solely based on statutory law in New York and that the right of publicity was not descendible). — ED.

4. *See* Cal. Civ. Code §3344.1 (overruling *Lugosi* and holding that publicity rights are descendible and transferable after the celebrity's death). — ED.

5. The Second Circuit has now accepted the Sixth Circuit's interpretation of Tennessee law. *Factors Etc., Inc. v. Pro Arts, Inc.*, 652 F.2d 278 (2d Cir. 1981).

For the reasons which follow we hold that the right of publicity survives the death of its owner and is inheritable and devisable. Recognition of the right of publicity rewards and thereby encourages effort and creativity. If the right of publicity dies with the celebrity, the economic value of the right of publicity during life would be diminished because the celebrity's untimely death would seriously impair, if not destroy, the value of the right of continued commercial use. Conversely, those who would profit from the fame of a celebrity after his or her death for their own benefit and without authorization have failed to establish their claim that they should be the beneficiaries of the celebrity's death. Finally, the trend since the early common law has been to recognize survivability, notwithstanding the legal problems which may thereby arise. We therefore answer question 2 in the affirmative.

3. Must the owner of the right of publicity have commercially exploited that right before it can survive?

Exploitation is understood to mean commercial use by the celebrity other than the activity which made him or her famous, *e.g.*, an inter vivos transfer of the right to the use of one's name and likeness. The cases which have considered this issue . . . involved entertainers. The net result of following them would be to say that celebrities and public figures have the right of publicity during their lifetimes (as others have the right of privacy), but only those who contract for bubble gum cards, posters and tee shirts have a descendible right of publicity upon their deaths. That we should single out for protection after death those entertainers and athletes who exploit their personae during life, and deny protection after death to those who enjoy public acclamation but did not exploit themselves during life, puts a premium on exploitation. Having found that there are valid reasons for recognizing the right of publicity during life, we find no reason to protect after death only those who took commercial advantage of their fame.

Perhaps this case more than others brings the point into focus. A well known minister may avoid exploiting his prominence during life because to do otherwise would impair his ministry. Should his election not to take commercial advantage of his position during life *ipso facto* result in permitting others to exploit his name and likeness after his death? In our view, a person who avoids exploitation during life is entitled to have his image protected against exploitation after death just as much if not more than a person who exploited his image during life.

Without doubt, Dr. King could have exploited his name and likeness during his lifetime. That this opportunity was not appealing to him does not mean that others have the right to use his name and likeness in ways he himself chose not to do. Nor does it strip his family and estate of the right to control, preserve and extend his status and memory and to prevent unauthorized exploitation thereof by others. Here, they seek to prevent the exploitation of his likeness in a manner they consider unflattering and unfitting. We cannot deny them this right merely because Dr. King chose not to exploit or commercialize himself during his lifetime.

Question 3 is answered in the negative, and therefore we need not answer question 4.

CHARLES L. WELTNER, Justice, concurring specially.

[I]n proclaiming this new "right of publicity," we have created an open-ended and ill-defined force which jeopardizes a right of unquestioned authenticity—free speech. It should be noted that our own constitutional provision, Art. I, Sec. I, Par. IV, Constitution of Georgia, traces its lineage to the first Constitution of our State, in 1777, antedating the First Amendment by fourteen years. Its language is plain and all-encompassing: "No law shall ever be passed to curtail, or restrain the liberty of speech, or of the press; any person may speak, write and publish his sentiments, on all subjects, being responsible for the abuse of that liberty."

But the majority says that the fabrication and commercial distribution of a likeness of Dr. King is not "speech," thereby removing the inquiry from the ambit of First Amendment or Free Speech inquiries.

To this conclusion I most vigorously dissent. When our Constitution declares that anyone may "speak, write and publish his sentiments, on all subjects" it does not confine that freedom exclusively to verbal expression. Art. I, Sec. I, Par. IV, Constitution of Georgia. Human intercourse is such that ofttimes the most powerful of expressions involve no words at all, *e.g.*, Jesus before Pilate; Thoreau in the Concord jail; King on the bridge at Selma.

Do not the statues of the Confederate soldiers which inhabit so many of our courthouse squares express the sentiments of those who raised them?

Are not the busts of former chief justices, stationed within the rotunda of this very courthouse, expressions of sentiments of gratitude and approval?

Is not the portrait of Dr. King which hangs in our Capitol an expression of sentiment?

Manifestly so.

If, then, a two-dimensional likeness in oil and canvas is an expression of sentiment, how can it be said that a three-dimensional likeness in plastic is *not*?

But, says the majority, our new right to publicity is violated only in cases involving financial gain.

Did the sculptors of our Confederate soldiers, and of our chief justices, labor without gain? Was Dr. King's portraitist unpaid for his work?

If "financial gain" is to be the watershed of violation *vel non* of this new-found right, it cannot withstand scrutiny. It is rare, indeed, that any expression of sentiment beyond casual conversation is not somehow connected, directly or indirectly, to "financial gain." For example, a school child wins a $25 prize for the best essay on Dr. King's life. Is this "financial gain?" Must the child then account for the winnings?

The essay, because of its worth, is reprinted in a commercial publication. Must the publisher account?

The publication is sold on the newsstand. Must the vendor account?

The majority will say "free speech." Very well. The same child wins a $25 prize in the school art fair. His creation — a bust of Dr. King.

Must he account?

The local newspaper prints a photograph of the child and of his creation. Must it account?

The school commissions replicas of the bust to raise money for its library. Must it account?

UNICEF reproduces the bust on its Christmas cards. Must it account?

Finally, a purely commercial venture undertakes to market replicas of the bust under circumstances similar to those of this case. Must it account?

Obviously, the answers to the above questions will vary, and properly so, because the circumstances posited are vastly different. The dividing line, however, cannot be fixed upon the presence or absence of "financial gain." Rather, it must be grounded in the community's judgment of what, *ex aequo et bono*, is unconscionable.

Were it otherwise, this "right of publicity," fully extended, would eliminate scholarly research, historical analysis, and public comment, because food and shelter, and the financial gain it takes to provide them, are still essentials of human existence.

Were it otherwise, no newspaper might identify any person or any incident of his life without accounting to him for violation of his "right to publicity."

Were it otherwise, no author might refer to any event in history wherein his reference is identifiable to any individual (or his heirs!) without accounting for his royalties. . . .

Each lawful restraint [on speech] finds its legitimacy, then, *not* because it is laid against some immutable rule (like the weights and measures of the Bureau of Standards) but because it is perceived that it would be irresponsible to the interest of the community — to the extent of being *unconscionable* — that such conduct go unrestrained.

The doctrine of unjust enrichment finds its genesis in such a reckoning. It can be applied to just such a matter as that before us. Were we to do so, we could avoid entering the quagmire of combining considerations of "right of privacy," "right of publicity," and considerations of *inter vivos* exploitation. We would also retain our constitutional right of free speech uncluttered and uncompromised by these new impediments of indeterminate application.

And we could sanction relief *in this case* — where relief is plainly appropriate.

NOTES AND QUESTIONS

1. *Imitators.* A recent version of the right of publicity has been used to challenge advertisements that *imitate* artists as a way to appropriate their image. The singer and actress Bette Midler brought a lawsuit against Young & Rubicam, an advertising agency that had hired one of her former backup singers to imitate Midler's rendition of her 1973 hit "Do You Want to Dance?" to promote Ford Motor Co.'s Mercury Sable car. Midler claimed that the agency had stolen her voice. The U.S. Court of Appeals for the Ninth Circuit agreed, holding that "when a distinctive voice of a professional singer is widely known and deliberately imitated in order to sell a product, the sellers have appropriated what is not theirs and have committed a tort in California." *Midler v. Ford Motor Co.*, 849 F.2d 460, 463 (9th Cir. 1988). *Accord, Waits v. Frito-Lay, Inc.*, 978 F.2d 1093 (9th Cir. 1992) (singer Tom Waits obtains $375,000 in compensatory damages and $2 million in punitive damages against company that imitated his distinctive voice and singing style in a radio commercial).

Does prohibition of imitation go too far? In *White v. Samsung Electronics America, Inc.*, 971 F.2d 1395 (9th Cir. 1992), the court held that a copyright violation might well be established when a company used a robot in advertising that was intended to evoke images of Vanna White and the game show in which she became famous. Samsung was clearly using her image to sell its products without her consent in a way that might have created confusion as to whether White had agreed to allow her image to be used by the company. However, in a dissent to a decision denying a petition for rehearing, 989 F.2d 1512, 1512-1513 (9th Cir. 1993), Judge Kozinski criticized the ruling.

Saddam Hussein wants to keep advertisers from using his picture in unflattering contexts. Clint Eastwood doesn't want tabloids to write about him. Rudolf Valentino's heirs want to control his film biography. The Girl Scouts don't want their image soiled by association with certain activities. George Lucas wants to keep Strategic Defense Initiative fans from calling it "Star Wars." Pepsico doesn't want singers to use the word "Pepsi" in their songs. Guy Lombardo wants an exclusive property right to ads that show big bands playing on New Year's Eve. Uri Geller thinks he should be paid for ads showing psychics bending metal through telekinesis. Paul Prudhomme, that household name, thinks the same about ads featuring corpulent bearded chefs. And scads of copyright holders see purple when their creations are made fun of.

Something very dangerous is going on here. Private property, including intellectual property, is essential to our way of life. It provides an incentive for investment and innovation; it stimulates the flourishing of our culture; it protects the moral entitlements of people to the fruits of their labors. But reducing too much to private property can be bad medicine. Private land, for instance, is far more useful if separated from other private land by public streets, roads and highways. Public parks, utility rights-of-way and sewers reduce the amount of land in private hands, but vastly enhance the value of the property that remains.

So too it is with intellectual property. Overprotecting intellectual property is as harmful as underprotecting it. Creativity is impossible without a rich public domain. Nothing today, likely nothing since we tamed fire, is genuinely new: Culture, like science and technology, grows by accretion, each new creator building on the works of those who came before. Overprotection stifles the very creative forces it's supposed to nurture.

The panel's opinion is a classic case of overprotection. Concerned about what it sees as a wrong done to Vanna White, the panel majority erects a property right of remarkable and dangerous breadth: Under the majority's opinion, it's now a tort for advertisers to *remind* the public of a celebrity. Not to use a celebrity's name, voice, signature or likeness; not to imply the celebrity endorses a product; but simply to evoke the celebrity's image in the public's mind. This Orwellian notion withdraws far more from the public domain than prudence and common sense allow. It conflicts with the *Copyright Act* and the Copyright Clause. It raises serious First Amendment problems. It's bad law, and it deserves a long, hard second look.

The Ninth Circuit found a likely violation of publicity rights when licensed airport Cheers bars used animatronic robots that resembled two characters from the Cheers television show. Although the actors had no right to prevent dissemination of the show itself, they had the right to prevent use of their images to sell products related to the show. *Wendt v. Host International,* 125 F.3d 806 (9th Cir. 1997) (applying California law). Does this distinction make sense?

2. *Free speech.* Does the right of publicity interfere with the right of free speech? *See Parks v. La Face Records, supra* (grappling with the conflict between free speech rights and property rights in one's name). After playwright Susan Ross wrote a play based on the life of the singer Janis Joplin, she was sued by Joplin's family and Manny Fox, a New York producer who owns the rights to make a film and play based on Joplin's life, on the ground that Ross had wrongly appropriated the plaintiffs' right of publicity in Joplin's image without obtaining the consent of Joplin's estate. The family claimed "the exclusive right to exploit stage productions, theatrical films and television productions based on the life and times of Janis Joplin." Judge Coughenour held that the play was a protected form of expression under the first amendment and that Joplin's family could not control artistic expressions based on her life. *Joplin Enterprises v. Allen,* 795 F. Supp. 349 (W.D. Wash. 1992). *See also ETW Corp. v. Jireh Publishing, Inc.,* 332 F.3d 915 (6th Cir. 2003) (first amendment prevents assertion of publicity right against an artist who painted Tiger Woods's victory at 1997 Master Tournament); *Matthews v. Wozencraft,* 15 F.3d 432 (5th Cir. 1994) (despite publicity right, defendant

is entitled to produce a fictionalized biography without plaintiff's consent). Do you agree with the majority or dissenting opinions in the *Martin Luther King* case?

3. *Lanham Act.* Section 43(a) of the federal *Lanham Act*, 15 U.S.C. §1125, may support a publicity rights claim because it creates a civil claim against any person who identifies his product so to deceive consumers as to the association of the producer of the product with another person or to cause consumers to falsely believe that other person has sponsored or approved of the product. *See Parks v. La Face Records*, 329 F.3d 437 (6th Cir. 2003)(civil rights leader Rosa Parks may have a Lanham Act claim against OutKast and record producer LaFace Records for using her name as the title for a song). In contrast, to show infringement of the common law right of publicity, the claimant need not show a possibility of confusion; all that is required is unauthorized use. *Cf. Tyne v. Time Warner Entertainment Co.*, 2005 Fla. LEXIS 728 (Fla. 2005)(state statute prohibiting use of a person's name or likeness for "commercial purposes" does not apply to a movie like *The Perfect Storm* that dramatizes real events and persons and does not directly promote a good or service).

4. *Cultural icons.* The images of famous people become part of popular culture — a common asset of the community. Absolute protection of someone's image would prevent others from commenting on or referring to the image without permission from the owner. At the same time, commercial exploitation of someone's image may harm an individual by associating him with a product with which he does not want to be associated. Such exploitation could also limit a celebrity's ability to derive commercial benefit from his own popularity. Should it make a difference if someone is simply trying to make money from a person's image — for example, using him to sell a product — or using his image in an artistic or literary fashion? Compare *Groucho Marx Productions, Inc. v. Day and Night Co.*, 689 F.2d 317 (2d Cir. 1982) (right of publicity does not survive the death of the owner; producers of a play mimicking the Marx Brothers could not be held liable to his heirs) with *John W. Carson v. Here's Johnny Portable Toilets, Inc.*, 698 F.2d 831 (6th Cir. 1983) (holding that defendant could not imitate Ed McMahon's introduction of Johnny Carson — "Here's Johnny!" — to sell its portable toilets). *See also* Cal. Civ. Code §§3344, 3344.1; Fla. Stat. §540.08; Tenn. Code Ann. §§47-25-1101 to 47-25-1108 (protecting the right of publicity).

5. *Titles.* In *Rogers v. Grimaldi*, 875 F.2d 994 (2d Cir. 1989), dancer and film star Ginger Rogers sued film maker Federico Fellini for using her name in a movie called *Ginger and Fred.* That movie was about two cabaret dancers who became known to their fans as Fred and Ginger because they imitated Fred Astaire and Ginger Rogers in their act. The court held that the use of a title is protected by the first amendment unless it has "no artistic relevance" to the underlying work, or if there is artistic relevance, that the title "explicitly misleads as to the source of the content of the work." *Id.* at 999. Applying this test, the court concluded that use of Ginger Rogers's name in the title was protected by the first amendment and thus barred claims based on either publicity rights or the Lanham Act. In contrast, the court in *Parks v. La Face Records*, 329 F.3d 437 (6th Cir. 2003), granted civil rights leader Rosa Parks the right to go forward with publicity rights and Lanham Act claims against the band OutKast and record producer LaFace Records for using her name as the title for a song. The district court had concluded that the title was artistically relevant to the song lyrics because the lyrcs contain the phrase "Everybody move to the back of the bus" — a phrase obviously related to Parks. The Sixth Circuit reversed, holding that a jury could conclude that the song was not about Rosa Parks in any way. The "back of the bus" phrase was used to suggest that competitors to OutKast should get back and let OutKast get out front. This

use starkly contrast, for example, with the song "Rosa, Rosa" by blues artist Otis Taylor, which is clearly a tribute to Rosa Parks. Were the *Rogers* and *Parks* cases correctly decided?

PROBLEMS

Do companies have a free speech right to the commercial use of the name of a famous person who has been dead more than 100 years? A surviving relative of Tasunke Witko (known in English as Crazy Horse) sought to prevent a beer company from selling "Crazy Horse Malt Liquor" on the ground that the law of the Rosebud Sioux Nation recognized a form of publicity right that was descendible and still in existence more than a century after the death of Crazy Horse. Crazy Horse was a spiritual leader of the Sioux people and opposed the use of liquor in any form. The Rosebud Sioux Trial Court strongly suggested that tribal law would recognize such a right but found no jurisdiction in tribal court because the beer was not sold on the reservation. Although the Rosebud Sioux Supreme Court reversed on the jurisdictional finding, a subsequent ruling by a federal judge held that the trial court had no jurisdiction over the claim. *In the Matter of the Estate of Tasunke Witko v. G. Heileman Brewing Co.* (Civ. No. 93-204) (Rosebud Sioux Tr. Ct., Oct. 25, 1994), *rev'd* (Rosebud Sioux Sup. Ct. May 1, 1996), *judgment vacated by Hornell Brewing Co. v. Rosebud Sioux Tribal Court*, 133 F.3d 1087 (8th Cir. 1998).

1. Suppose a suit is brought in state court in a state where the beer is sold seeking an injunction against the use of Crazy Horse's name in connection with the sale of liquor. Assume that the state in which suit is brought recognizes publicity rights but does not allow them to be inherited, at least where the individual did not take advantage of commercial use of the name during his lifetime. Plaintiff claims that publicity rights are a form of personal property and that the law of the domicile of a person at the time of death ordinarily applies to determine who inherits such property at death. Because Crazy Horse was domiciled on the Rosebud Sioux Reservation at his death, Rosebud law should apply to govern the case. Defendant beer company argues that such cases concern the regulation of business enterprises, and the law of the place where goods are sold should control the case. Which law should apply?

2. Assume now that the court has decided to apply its own law (the law of the place of sale) and is asked by plaintiff to allow publicity rights to be inherited whether or not they were exploited during life, citing *Martin Luther King, Jr.* Defendant argues that publicity rights should not be inherited. Alternatively, if they are inherited, they should lapse at some point after death — certainly after 100 years have passed. How should this issue be resolved?

3. Defendant now argues that it has a first amendment free speech right to use the name of a deceased public figure to sell its product. Argue both sides of this legal issue. How should it be resolved?

§14.7 Moral Rights

In many European countries, artists have the right to prevent the mutilation or alteration of their artworks after the works have been sold. This legally protected interest is called "moral right," or *droit moral*. Artworks protected by moral rights are effectively encumbered by a covenant, which "runs with" the artwork when it is sold, containing an implied promise not to mutilate the artwork so as to destroy the artist's vision. Such rights are generally inalienable; they interpret the interest in preserving the artist's vision as a collective good that benefits the community and that cannot be traded away.

Until recently, moral rights were not recognized in the United States. *See, e.g., Vargas v. Esquire,* 164 F.2d 522 (7th Cir. 1947); *Crimi v. Rutger's Presbyterian Church,* 89 N.Y.S.2d 813 (Sup. Ct. 1949). In 1979, however, California passed the *California Art Preservation Act,* Cal. Civ. Code §§987-989, which permits injunctive relief, damages, and attorney's fees for intentional or threatened mutilation or alteration of an artist's work. A bill was passed in New York in 1983 prohibiting alterations that would harm the artist's reputation. *New York Artists' Authorship Rights Act,* N.Y. Arts & Cult. Aff. Law §14.03(1). Moral rights legislation has been passed in at least nine jurisdictions in the United States. *See, e.g.,* Conn. Gen. Stat. §42-116; Mass. Gen. Laws ch. 231, §85S; Pa. Stat. tit. 73, §§2101-2110; R.I. Gen. Laws §5-62-2(e); M. Nimmer and D. Nimmer, *Nimmer on Copyright: A Treatise on the Law of Literary, Musical and Artistic Property, and the Protection of Ideas* §8.21[A], at 8-247 (1987).

In 1990, Congress passed the *Visual Artists Rights Act* (VARA), 17 U.S.C. §§101, 106a, and 113, granting living artists rights to protect "works of visual art" unless the works are "made for hire," §101(B), or are "applied art," meaning "ornamentation or decoration that is affixed to otherwise utilitarian objects," *Carter v. Helmsley-Spear, Inc.,* 71 F.3d 77, 84-85 (2d Cir. 1995). The statute grants the artist the right to prevent "any intentional distortion, mutilation, or other modification of [the] work which would be prejudicial to his or her honor or reputation," §106a(a)(3)(A), and to prevent any intentional or grossly negligent destruction of a work of "recognized stature," §106a(a) (3)(B). Owners of buildings can remove works of art, such as murals, floor mosaics, or architectural components, if they can do so without destroying or mutilating them, so long as they make a good faith effort to notify the artist. §113(d)(2). The artist's right to prevent mutilation of the work that is part of a building is lost if the artist fails to remove the work or pay for its removal. If the artwork cannot be removed without destroying it, the artist who has not waived her right to do so may have the power to prevent destruction of the work and therefore may have the extraordinary power to control whether the building is renovated, destroyed or redeveloped. The act allows the artist to waive this right, §106a(e), and the owner who wishes to change the building may have to purchase the right from the artist. Building developers ordinarily require artists to waive their rights to prevent destruction of the work when they are embedded in a building such that they cannot be removed without destroying them. Note that only works of "recognized stature" are protected from destruction. *Cf. Phillips v. Pembroke Real Estate, Inc.,* 288 F.Supp.2d 89 (D. Mass. 2003) (VARA does not prevent removal of sculptures from a public park, even though they were specifically designed for that terrain, and location and the artist thought separation from the setting would destroy the artistic integrity of the sculptures); *Phillips v. Pembroke Real Estate, Inc.,* 819 N.E.2d 579 (Mass. 2004)(same result under *Massachusetts Art Preservation Act,* Mass. Gen. Laws ch. 231, §85S).

15

Property in People

§15.1 *Property Rights in Human Beings*

What limits should the legal system impose on the conversion of human interests into exchangeable property rights? Does it make sense to use the vocabulary of property and market exchange to describe interests in human bodies and in people themselves? Is anything lost by using the imagery of property to evaluate these kinds of issues? Should there be a presumption that all interests are exchangeable? In recent years, law and economics scholars have used market and property images to analyze almost every imaginable legal problem. *See* Richard Posner, *Economic Analysis of Law* (3d ed. 1986). Professor Margaret Jane Radin has argued that the use of market rhetoric to analyze all legal issues has the effect of wrongfully "commodifying" human experience by conceptualizing all human relationships in terms of market exchange. She argues that certain types of property interests are so crucial to individual dignity, self-fulfillment, the ability to form essential human relationships, and the ability to participate as a member of political society that they should be treated as personal rights rather than as exchangeable interests in a market. Margaret Jane Radin, *Market-Inalienability*, 100 Harv. L. Rev. 1849 (1987).

Market rhetoric is extremely useful, but it may be inappropriate in some cases. The materials in this chapter explore this issue by addressing a variety of interests in controlling people and human bodies, including the issues of slavery, children, body parts and human genes, frozen embryos, and human remains.

§15.2 *Slavery*

DRED SCOTT v. SANDFORD[1]

60 U.S. (19 How.) 393 (1857)

Mr. Chief Justice ROGER B. TANEY delivered the opinion of the court.

---

1. The case report misspells Sanford's name as Sandford. — ED.

[Dred Scott, once a slave but now claiming to be a citizen of the state of Missouri, sued John Sanford, a citizen of New York, to obtain his freedom. Scott based federal jurisdiction on diversity of citizenship between the parties, raising the question in the court's mind whether Scott was in fact a citizen of Missouri. In 1834, Scott's former owner had taken him from Missouri, a slave state, to Illinois, a free state, where they lived for two years before moving to Minnesota, then part of the Louisiana Territory, before returning to Missouri in 1838. Scott was then sold to Sanford. Slavery was illegal in Illinois under state law and in Minnesota under the federal statute called the *Missouri Compromise*, Act of March 6, 1820, 3 Stat. 545. Sanford argued that Scott was not a citizen of Missouri and hence could not bring a lawsuit in federal court based on diversity of citizenship. Scott claimed to be both a Missouri citizen and a free man, based on his having obtained freedom by domicile for a long period in a state and a territory that did not recognize the status of slavery for its domiciliaries. Sanford claimed that neither Illinois nor the *Missouri Compromise* could constitutionally act to deprive him of his property interest in Scott when they returned to a state that recognized property interests in slaves.]

I

. . . The plaintiff in error, who was also the plaintiff in the court below, was, with his wife and children, held as slaves by the defendant, in the State of Missouri; and he brought this action in the Circuit Court of the United States for that district, to assert the title of himself and his family to freedom. . . .

[The first question concerned whether the court had jurisdiction to hear the case. Such jurisdiction existed in federal court over suits between "Citizens of different States," U.S. Const. art III, §2, cl. 1. Plaintiff Dred Scott claimed that he was a citizen of Missouri and defendant Sanford a citizen of New York. The issue that had to be decided was whether the plaintiff was a "citizen" as defined in the Constitution.]

The question simply is this: Can a negro, whose ancestors were imported into this country, and sold as slaves, become a member of the political community formed and brought into existence by the Constitution of the United States, and as such become entitled to all the rights, and privileges, and immunities, guarantied by that instrument to the citizen? One of which rights is the privilege of suing in a court of the United States in the cases specified in the Constitution.

It will be observed, that the plea applies to that class of persons only whose ancestors were negroes of the African race, and imported into this country, and sold and held as slaves. The only matter in issue . . . is, whether the descendants of such slaves, when they shall be emancipated, or who are born of parents who had become free before their birth, are citizens of a State, in the sense in which the word citizen is used in the Constitution of the United States. . . .

The words "people of the United States" and "citizens" are synonymous terms, and mean the same thing. They both describe the political body who, according to our republican institutions, form the sovereignty, and who hold the power and conduct the Government through their representatives. They are what we familiarly call the "sovereign people," and every citizen is one of this people, and a constituent member of this sovereignty. The question before us is, whether the class of persons described in the plea in abatement compose a portion of this people, and are constituent members of this sovereignty? We think they are not, and that they are not included, and were not intended to be included, under the word "citizens" in the Constitution, and can therefore claim none of the rights and privileges which that instrument provides for and secures to citizens of the United States. On the contrary, they were at that time considered as a subordinate and inferior class of beings, who had been subjugated by the dominant race, and, whether emancipated or not, yet remained subject to their authority, and had no rights or privileges but such as those who held the power and the Government might choose to grant them. . . .

[W]e must not confound the rights of citizenship which a State may confer within its own limits, and the rights of citizenship as a member of the Union. . . . [P]re-P]revious to the adoption of the Constitution of the United States, every State had the undoubted right to confer on whomsoever it pleased the character of citizen, and to endow him with all its rights. But this character of course was confined to the boundaries of the State, and gave him no rights or privileges in other States beyond those secured to him by the laws of nations and the comity of States. . . .

It is very clear, therefore, that no State can, by any act or law of its own, passed since the adoption of the Constitution, introduce a new member into the political community created by the Constitution of the United States. It cannot make him a member of this community by making him a member of its own. And for the same reason it cannot introduce any person, or description of persons, who were not intended to be embraced in this new political family, which the Constitution brought into existence, but were intended to be excluded from it.

The question then arises, whether the provisions of the Constitution, in relation to the personal rights and privileges to which the citizen of a State should be entitled, embraced the negro African race, at that time in this country, or who might afterwards be imported, who had then or should afterwards be made free in any State; and to put it in the power of a single State to make him a citizen of the United States, and endue him with the full rights of citizenship in every other State without their consent? Does the Constitution of the United States act upon him whenever he shall be made free under the laws of a State, and raised there to the rank of a citizen, and immediately clothe him with all the privileges of a citizen in every other State, and in its own courts?

The court thinks the affirmative of these propositions cannot be maintained. . . .

In the opinion of the court, the legislation and histories of the times, and the language used in the Declaration of Independence, show, that neither the class of persons who had been imported as slaves, nor their descendants, whether they had become free or not, were then acknowledged as a part of the people, nor intended to be included in the general words used in that memorable instrument. . . .

[African Americans] had for more than a century before been regarded as beings of an inferior order, and altogether unfit to associate with the white race, either in social or political relations; and so far inferior, that they had no rights which the white man was bound to respect; and that the negro might justly and lawfully be reduced to slavery for his benefit. He was bought and sold, and treated as an ordinary article of merchandise and traffic, whenever a profit could be made by it. This opinion was at that time fixed and universal in the civilized portion of the white race. It was regarded as an axiom in morals as well as in politics, which no one thought of disputing, or supposed to be open to dispute; and men in every grade and position in society daily and habitually acted upon it in their private pursuits, as well as in matters of public concern, without doubting for a moment the correctness of this opinion. . . .

The language of the Declaration of Independence . . . would seem to embrace the whole human family, and if they were used in a similar instrument at this day would be so understood. But it is too clear for dispute, that the enslaved African race were not intended to be included, and formed no part of the people who framed and adopted this declaration; for if the language, as understood in that day, would embrace them, the conduct of the distinguished men who framed the Declaration of Independence would have been utterly and flagrantly inconsistent with the principles they asserted; and instead of the sympathy of mankind, to which they so confidently appealed, they would have deserved and received universal rebuke and reprobation.

Yet the men who framed this declaration were great men — high in literary acquirements — high in their sense of honor, and incapable of asserting principles inconsistent with those on which they were acting. They perfectly understood the meaning of the language they used, and how it would be understood by others; and they knew that it would not in any part of the civilized world be supposed to embrace the negro race, which, by common consent, had been excluded from civilized Governments and the family of nations, and doomed to slavery. They spoke and acted according to the then established doctrines and principles, and in the ordinary language of the day, and no one misunderstood them. The unhappy black race were separated from the white by indelible marks, and laws long before established, and were never thought of or spoken of except as property, and when the claims of the owner or the profit of the trader were supposed to need protection.

This state of public opinion had undergone no change when the Constitution was adopted. . . .

[T]here are two clauses in the Constitution which point directly and specifically to the negro race as a separate class of persons, and show clearly that they were not regarded as a portion of the people or citizens of the Government then formed.

One of these clauses reserves to each of the thirteen States the right to import slaves until the year 1808, if it thinks proper. And the importation which it thus sanctions was unquestionably of persons of the race of which we are speaking, as the traffic in slaves in the United States had always been confined to them. And by the other provision the States pledge themselves to each other to maintain the right of property of the master, by delivering up to him any slave who may have escaped from his service, and be found within their respective territories. By the first above-mentioned clause, therefore, the right to purchase and hold this property is directly sanctioned and authorized for twenty years by the people who framed the Constitution. And by the second, they pledge themselves to maintain and uphold the right of the master in the manner specified, as long as the Government they then formed should endure. And these two provisions show, conclusively, that neither the description of persons therein referred to, nor their descendants, were embraced in any of the other provisions of the Constitution; for certainly these two clauses were not intended to confer on them or their posterity the blessings of liberty, or any of the personal rights so carefully provided for the citizen. . . .

And upon a full and careful consideration of the subject, the court is of opinion, that, upon the facts stated in the plea in abatement, Dred Scott was not a citizen of Missouri within the meaning of the Constitution of the United States, and not entitled to sue in its courts. . . .

II

The act of Congress, upon which the plaintiff relies, declares that slavery and involuntary servitude, except as a punishment for crime, shall be forever prohibited in all that part of the territory ceded by France, under the name of Louisiana, which lies north of thirty-six degrees thirty minutes north latitude, and not included within the limits of Missouri. And the difficulty which meets us at the threshold of this part of the inquiry is, whether Congress was authorized to pass this law under any of the powers granted to it by the Constitution; for if the authority is not given by that instrument, it is the duty of this court to declare it void and inoperative, and incapable of conferring freedom upon any one who is held as a slave under the laws of any one of the States. . . .

[The] power of Congress over the person or property of a citizen can never be a mere discretionary power under our Constitution and form of Government. The powers of the Government and the rights and privileges of the citizen are regulated and plainly defined by the Constitution itself. . . .

[An] act of Congress which deprives a citizen of the United States of his liberty or property, merely because he came himself or brought his property into a particular Territory of the United States, and who had committed no offence against the laws, could hardly be dignified with the name of due process of law. . . .

[The] right of property in a slave is distinctly and expressly affirmed in the Constitution. The right to traffic in it, like an ordinary article of merchandise and property, was guarantied to the citizens of the United States, in every State that might desire it, for twenty years. And the Government in express terms is pledged to protect it in all future time, if the slave escapes from his owner. This is done in plain words — too plain to be misunderstood. And no word can be found in the Constitution which gives Congress a greater power over slave property, or which entitles property of that kind to less protection than property of any other description. The only power conferred is the power coupled with the duty of guarding and protecting the owner in his rights.

Upon these considerations, it is the opinion of the court that the act of Congress which prohibited a citizen from holding and owning property of this kind in the territory of the United States north of the line therein mentioned, is not warranted by the Constitution, and is therefore void; and that neither Dred Scott himself, nor any of his family, were made free by being carried into this territory; even if they had been carried there by the owner, with the intention of becoming a permanent resident.

[The Court then answered Scott's contention that his sojourn in Illinois and Minnesota had rendered him free by holding that his status was to be determined by Missouri law, his current domicile, and that under Missouri law, he remained a slave.]

RACE AND HISTORY: SELECTED
ESSAYS 1938-1988
JOHN HOPE FRANKLIN
155-156, 159-160 (1989)

. . . The colonists argued in the Declaration of Independence that they were oppressed; and they wanted their freedom. Thomas Jefferson, in an early draft, went so far as to accuse the king of England of imposing slavery on them; but more "practical" heads prevailed, and that provision was stricken from the Declaration.

Even so, the Declaration said "all men are created equal." "Black men as well as white men?" some wondered. Every man had an inalienable right to "life, liberty, and the pursuit of happiness." "Every black man as well as every white man?" some could well have asked.

How could the colonists make distinctions in their revolutionary philosophy? They either meant that *all* men were created equal or they did not mean it at all. They either meant that *every* man was entitled to life, liberty, and the pursuit of happiness, or they did not mean it at all. . . .

[At the Constitutional Convention,] Northerners, who regarded slaves as property, insisted that for the purpose of representation they could not be counted as people. Southern slaveholders, while cheerfully admitting that slaves were property, insisted that they were also people and should be counted as such. It is one of the remarkable ironies of the early history of this democracy that the very men who had shouted so loudly that all men were created equal could not now agree on whether or not persons of African descent were men at all.

The irony was compounded when, in the so-called major compromise of the Constitution, the delegates agreed that a slave was three-fifths of a man, meaning that five slaves were to be counted as three persons. The magic of racism can work magic with the human mind. . . .

If slaveholders feared possible insurrections by their slaves, they were no less apprehensive about the day-to-day attrition of the institution caused by slaves running away. They wanted to be certain that the Constitution recognized slaves as property and that it offered protection to that property, especially runaways. Significantly, there was virtually no opposition to the proposal that states give up fugitive slaves to their owners. The slaveowners had already won such sweeping constitutional recognition of slavery that the fugitive slave provision may be regarded as something of an anticlimax. . . .

And the Constitution required that slaves who ran away were not to enjoy the freedom that they had won in their own private war for independence, but were to be returned to those who claimed title to them. Consequently, there was a remarkable distinction between fighting for one's political independence, which the patriots expected to win, and fighting for one's freedom from slavery, which these same patriots made certain that the slaves would not win.

SURROGACY, SLAVERY, AND THE OWNERSHIP OF LIFE
ANITA L. ALLEN
13 Harv. J.L. & Pub. Pol'y 139, 142-144 (1990)

In the early 1800s, a happy little girl by the name of Polly Crocket was living in Illinois. One dismal autumn night, Polly was kidnapped and sold into slavery in Missouri. Her first owner was a poor farmer; the second, a wealthy gentleman named Taylor Berry whose wife trained Polly as a seamstress. Polly grew up and was permitted to marry another of Berry's slaves. Polly managed to have two children, Lucy and Nancy, before her husband was sold to a distant owner "way down South."

The years passed. With deaths and marriages, the ownership of Polly and her daughter was passed in and out of the Berry family. Encouraged by Polly, daughter Nancy escaped to freedom in Canada. Desperate to join her, Polly attempted to escape and made it all the way to Chicago. Because the Fugitive Slave Laws were in effect, however, "negro-catchers" were permitted to arrest her and return her to her owner in Missouri.

Upon return to Missouri, Polly took the bold step of finding a good lawyer. She successfully sued for her freedom on the theory that she was not a slave, but legally a free woman who had been wrongfully sold into slavery.

Now a free woman and anxious to have her family together again, Polly decided to buy her daughter Lucy out of slavery. But Lucy was not for sale. Lucy was "legitimately" owned by a Mr. Mitchell, who wanted to keep Lucy to please his wife. Polly filed a lawsuit against Mr. Mitchell on September 8, 1842, for the possession of her daughter, Lucy. During the seventeen-month pendency of her mother's civil suit, poor Lucy was locked away in jail.

Polly's suit finally ended in victory, and she was awarded possession of Lucy. On the final day of the trial, Polly's lawyer, the slave-holding jurist Edward Bates, summed up his case to the jury:

> Gentleman of the jury, I am a slave-holder myself, but thanks to Almighty God I am above the base principle of holding anybody a slave that has a right to her freedom as this girl has been proven to have; she was free before she was born; her mother was free but kidnapped in her youth, and sacrificed to the greed of negro-traders, and no free woman can give birth to a slave child, as it is in direct violation of the laws of God and man.

This poignant story vividly illustrates the sense in which the legal concept of ownership completely lacks inherent moral content. It can work like a two-edged sword. Polly legally owned herself, yet she lived most of her life as a slave. Once she proved in court that the master who possessed her did not lawfully own her, she gained standing to sue for the recovery of her own daughter, Lucy. But Lucy was also the precious putative property of another owner, who had acquired her through a "legitimate" commercial transaction and was not willing to sell her to Polly. Extant property law favored Mr. Mitchell; it certainly could not compel him to sell. Thus, Polly resorted to slave law to prove unlawful possession. By proving that she was not in fact a slave at the time of her daughter's birth, Polly was able to persuade the court that she was the rightful owner of her daughter. In the end, mother and daughter owned themselves. But the institution of slavery remained intact, and Mr. Mitchell was out the price of a housemaid.

STATUS, CONTRACT, AND
PROMISES UNKEPT
AVIAM SOIFER

90 Yale L.J. 1916 (1987)

When the war ended, . . . Congress tried to transform slaves and Southern society, and, in effect, to recapitulate Maine's progressive evolution rapidly through constitutional amendments and statutes. The notorious failure of that effort and the rise of the sharecropping system, which sometimes imposed even more virulent forms of servitude on former slaves such as the convict leasing system, demonstrates anew that there is a chasm between the moment of liberation and the attainment of freedom. . . .

. . . "[N]ecessitous men are not, truly speaking, free men." A problem in any consideration of the morass of contracts and disputes about them, of course, is the determination of how necessitous or unfree someone has to be before relief from an apparent contractual obligation becomes appropriate. . . .

...From the southern perspective, the Thirteenth Amendment expropriated property worth billions of dollars, without compensation....

We cannot know how Lincoln would have directed the federal government to protect former slaves. He may have intended to provide forty-acre plots, to be purchased by freedmen with profits they made by farming confiscated southern land. We do know that the promise of forty acres (with or without the mule) was more than a mere pipe dream. General Banks took some preliminary steps towards land redistribution in Louisiana during the war. General William T. Sherman's famous Field Order No. 15 specifically allocated forty-acre plots to freed slaves. We also know something of Lincoln's hopes, suggested, for example, in his instruction to General Banks, to create "some practical system by which the two races could gradually live themselves out of their old relation to each other, and both come out better prepared for the new." ...

Even more than nineteenth century Americans' aversion to redistribution of property by government — at least when the redistribution was visible — the ideology of formalistic contract law was, I believe, directly implicated in the emergence of a practical peonage system after the war....

...After the war, the most private and individualistic legal categories seemed quickly and convincingly to overcome all others. Contract law triumphed in the legal imagination and permeated popular belief....

Paradoxically, when many former masters and slaves declined to enter into voluntary contracts with one another, the Freedmen's Bureau forced them into "contractual" relationships. General Banks had imposed a mandatory year-long contract scheme in occupied Louisiana during the war. The Bureau officials developed variations on the theme, stressing order rather than consent....

After Appomattox, the former slaves had been *given* their freedom in the eyes of most Americans; they were *freedmen* and not free men. Under the tutelage of overburdened and often unsympathetic army officers, blacks soon learned firsthand of the formal, binding nature of contracts. They had precious little autonomy and soon found their responsibility under the year-long contracts they were required to sign, contracts binding them to the land until they paid off the credit advanced for seed and supplies, to be remarkably reminiscent of slavery. Freedmen's Bureau officials, anxious to get the South back to work, often functioned as replacements and functional equivalents for the overseers whose job description had been formally eliminated by emancipation.

Unrealistic presumptions of equal bargaining power prevailed in both private and public legal realms. When we cast aside the doctrinal baggage of those presumptions, however, we begin to see that the hegemony of these presumptions may not have been inevitable. The contemporary law of labor contracts remained distinct from the main body of contract law; its special rules for special cases — for sailors and women, for example — belied appeals to a universal legal science of contracts. The dominant rubric in these areas remained master-servant law, replete with a host of accompanying paternalistic assumptions and exceptions....

Many Americans decried governmental intrusion as they hastened to put the war behind them and to resume the economic race of life. President Andrew Johnson's controversial February 1866 veto message concerning the Freedmen's Bureau Bill illustrated a new emphasis on avoiding paternalism at almost all costs, and certainly at the cost of protecting the freedmen. Johnson claimed that the bill would discriminate against "millions of the white race, who are honestly toiling from day to day for their subsistence." Indeed, although the President purported to support the freedmen in "their entire independence and equality in making contracts for their labor," he adamantly rejected any role for the federal government in guaranteeing these rights. The freedmen, according to Johnson, had to establish and support "their own asylums and schools." To Johnson, the race of life for former slaves was underway; the national government had done enough already.

. . . For a brief historical moment, however, Johnson's views did not prevail. . . . In [the *Civil Rights Act of 1866*, passed over Johnson's veto], Congress emphasized both its sense that the Thirteenth Amendment empowered the federal government to enforce a long list of civil rights and its willingness to use the machinery of the federal government, including but not limited to the federal courts, to guarantee "full and equal benefit of all laws and proceedings." . . .

But daily life soon triumphed over legal promises promulgated hundreds of miles away. The chaos of war and the political and legal battles of early Reconstruction gave way to renewed faith in the purported symmetries of private law as the infrastructure of social order. In particular, the legal faith of the Gilded Age rested primarily on contract law and its formal assumptions about free will.umptions about fr

. . . Faith in perceived principles of contract law was . . . evident in 1875, when Justice Swayne, writing for a unanimous Court, tried to "roll back the tide of time, and to imagine [him]self back in Mississippi before abolition." Having accomplished this feat, Swayne defeated a black man's contractual claim to a share in the cotton crop produced on the plantation where he toiled. Even accepting the truth of the former slave's account, Justice Swayne reasoned, slaves could not contract in Mississippi at that time as a matter of law. Accordingly, the Court held that the former slave clearly had no legal claim. . . .

. . . Judges emphasized that choices between liberty and paternalism were either/ or matters of principle. The reality of the sharecropper's bargaining position, whether he was black or white, had no place in the legal categories through which appellate judges enforced their own views about government regulation of the natural struggle of life . . . .

The Thirteenth Amendment was soon irrelevant to everything but the most overt physical constraint . . . . Admittedly, gang labor was generally eliminated and, at least for a time, many black women could choose not to work in the fields. But the postbellum status and working conditions of the black sharecropper or field hand often were no better, and sometimes were worse, than his place within the peculiar institution. He was a free man contracting for his services, but only within a web of legal doctrines that forbade plantation owners to "entice" someone else's laborer, and criminal fraud statutes that promised prison and a chain gang, or the convict-lease system, if he tried to escape his contract. Moreover, the constant threat of extralegal enforcement assured that the former slave remained both on and in his place.

By 1883, the Supreme Court had determined in the *Civil Rights Cases* that:

> When a man has emerged from slavery, and by the aid of beneficent legislation has shaken off the inseparable concomitants of that state, there must be some stage in the progress of his elevation when he takes the rank of a mere citizen, and ceases to be the special favorite of the laws. . . .

Following the conservative redemption of the South and accompanying the rise of virulent racism in the Jim Crow era, the Supreme Court retreated to a position of almost complete deference to whatever results politics or the market might yield. . . .

The Antelope, 23 U.S. 66 (1825). When a pirate ship captured three vessels (one each from the U.S., Spain and Portugal) off the coast of Africa and took Africans from each ship, and one of those vessels was later captured off the coast of the United States with many of the captured Africans aboard, the Supreme Court had to determine whether to treat the captured Africans as slaves and return them to their "owners" or to treat them as free persons. Because the United States had outlawed the slave trade (but not slavery) in 1808, the Court ruled that the persons taken from the American ship should be freed. No owner claimed the Africans aboard the Portuguese ship so they were freed as well. But the Court ordered the persons aboard to Spanish ship to be returned to their owners if they could prove their claims of title.

Chief Justice John Marshall explained that this was a case "in which the sacred rights of liberty and of property come in conflict with each other." *Id.* at 114. Quoting John Locke, Marshall easily concluded that slavery violated natural law. "That it is contrary to the law of nature will scarcely be denied. That every man has a natural right to the fruits of his own labour, is generally admitted; and that no other person can rightfully deprive him of those fruits, and appropriate them against his will, seems to be the necessary result of this admission." *Id.* at 120. However, the slave trade had been long been engaged in by the "Christian and civilized nations of world" and "claimed all the sanction which could be derived from long usage, and general acquiescence." *Id.* at 115. The Court thus concluded that the slave trade was not contrary to the law of nations. Given a conflict between natural law and the positive law adopted by the nations of the world, the Court held that the positive law must prevail. "Slavery, then, has its origin in force; but as the world has agreed that it is a legitimate result of force, the state of things which is thus produced by general consent, cannot be pronounced unlawful." *Id.* at 121. Marshall explained, *id.* at 121-122:

> Whatever might be the answer of a moralist to this question, a jurist must search for its legal solution, in those principles of action which are sanctioned by the usages, the national acts, and the general assent, of that portion of the world of which he considers himself as a part, and to whose law the appeal is made. If we resort to this standard as the test of international law, the question, as has already been observed, is decided in favour of the legality of the trade. Both Europe and America embarked in it; and for nearly two centuries, it was carried on without opposition, and without censure. A jurist could not say, that a practice thus supported was illegal, and that those engaged in it might be punished, either personally, or by deprivation of property.

Recall that Marshall had similarly concluded in 1823 in reference to colonial claims of title over Indian lands that "[c]onquest gives a title which the Courts of the conqueror cannot deny, whatever the private and speculative opinions of individuals may be, respecting the original justice of the claim which has been successfully asserted." *Johnson v. M'Intosh*, 21 U.S. 543 (1823).

NOTES AND QUESTIONS

1. *The* Dred Scott *decision. Dred Scott* was only the second decision in United States history (the first being *Marbury v. Madison*, 5 U.S. 137 (1803)) in which the Supreme Court had held an act of Congress unconstitutional. *Dred Scott* is known for invalidating the *Missouri Compromise*, which had outlawed slavery in the territo-

ries, and for Chief Justice Taney's conclusion that African Americans were not "citizens" as defined in the federal Constitution.

What were Chief Justice Taney's reasons for concluding that African Americans were not citizens of the United States as defined in the Constitution? Did these arguments apply to free African Americans, who were not descended from slaves? Was citizenship tied to free status or merely to race? Chief Justice Taney argues that the language of equality and freedom in the Declaration of Independence could not have been intended to include African Americans, because then "the conduct of the distinguished men who framed the Declaration of Independence would have been utterly and flagrantly inconsistent with the principles they asserted." What follows from this inconsistency?

Chief Justice Taney emphasizes the constitutional clauses that explicitly recognize and protect slavery: the right to import slaves until 1808 and the fugitive slave clause, requiring all states to return slaves to their masters. Those clauses state:

> The Migration or Importation of Such Persons as any of the States now existing shall think proper to admit, shall not be prohibited by the Congress prior to the Year one thousand eight hundred and eight, but a Tax or duty may be imposed on such Importation, not exceeding ten dollars for each Person. [U.S. Const. art. I, §9, cl. 1.]

> No Person held to Service of Labour in one State, under the Laws thereof, escaping into another, shall, in Consequence of any Law or Regulation therein, be discharged from such Service or Labour, but shall be delivered up on Claim of the Party to whom such Service or Labour may be due. [U.S. Const. art. IV, §2, cl. 3.]

What arguments could Chief Justice Taney have made to interpret the Constitution — despite these clauses — to conclude that African Americans were in fact "citizens" as defined in the Constitution?

2. *Slavery, sharecropping, and private property.* Professor Soifer describes the policy decisions (a) not to distribute land to freed slaves, (b) to confirm land titles in preexisting plantation owners who had rebelled against the United States and appropriated the labor of others, and (c) not to exact compensation from masters for past wages and damages for deprivation of liberty for freed slaves. He further describes the effects of contract law on agreements made between freed slaves and landowners whose land they worked. It was thought to be "paternalistic" to regulate contractual relationships — this would amount to a denial of respect for individual autonomy.

The combination of these facts meant that the bargaining power between the freed slaves and existing landowners after the Civil War was woefully unequal. The result was a sharecropping system that tied persons to the land and expropriated the value of their labor in ways reminiscent of slavery

What conception of freedom of contract would identify sharecropping arrangements as voluntary agreements? What conception of the origin and justification of property rights would vest title to land worked by slaves in their former masters and fail to distribute land or damages to freed slaves? What alternative conceptions can you imagine?

3. Did the Supreme Court do the right thing in *The Antelope*? What is the judge's appropriate role if a judge believes that the law violates fundamental norms of justice? *See* Robert M. Cover, *Justice Accused: Antislavery and the Judicial Process* (1975) (criticizing antislavery judges who felt bound by "the law" to return slaves to their purported masters).

§15.3 *Children*

IN THE MATTER OF BABY M
537 A.2d 1227 (N.J. 1988)

ROBERT N. WILENTZ, C.J....

I. Facts

In February 1985, William Stern and Mary Beth Whitehead entered into a surrogacy contract. It recited that Stern's wife, Elizabeth, was infertile, that they wanted a child, and that Mrs. Whitehead was willing to provide that child as the mother with Mr. Stern as the father.

The contract provided that through artificial insemination using Mr. Stern's sperm, Mrs. Whitehead would become pregnant, carry the child to term, bear it, deliver it to the Sterns, and thereafter do whatever was necessary to terminate her maternal rights so that Mrs. Stern could thereafter adopt the child. Mrs. Whitehead's husband, Richard, was also a party to the contract; Mrs. Stern was not.... Although Mrs. Stern was not a party to the surrogacy agreement, the contract gave her sole custody of the child in the event of Mr. Stern's death. Mrs. Stern's status as a nonparty to the surrogate parenting agreement presumably was to avoid the application of the baby-selling statute to this arrangement. N.J. Stat. Ann. 9:3-54.[2]

Mr. Stern, on his part, agreed to attempt the artificial insemination and to pay Mrs. Whitehead $10,000 after the child's birth, on its delivery to him. In a separate contract, Mr. Stern agreed to pay $7,500 to the Infertility Center of New York ("ICNY")....

[The Sterns entered the arrangement because Mrs. Stern learned that she might have multiple sclerosis and feared that pregnancy] might precipitate blindness, paraplegia, or other forms of debilitation. Based on the perceived risk, the Sterns decided to forego having their own children. The decision had special significance for Mr. Stern. Most of his family had been destroyed in the Holocaust. As the family's only survivor, he very much wanted to continue his bloodline.

Initially the Sterns considered adoption, but were discouraged by the substantial delay apparently involved and by the potential problem they saw arising from their age and their differing religious backgrounds. They were most eager for some other means to start a family.

...Mrs. Whitehead's [willingness to act as a "surrogate mother"] apparently resulted from her sympathy with family members and others who could have no children (she stated that she wanted to give another couple the "gift of life"); she also wanted the $10,000 to help her family....

Mrs. Whitehead realized, almost from the moment of birth, that she could not part with this child. She had felt a bond with it even during pregnancy. Some indication of the attachment was conveyed to the Sterns at the hospital when they told Mrs. Whitehead what they were going to name the baby. She apparently broke into tears and indicated that she did not know if she could give up the child. She talked about

---

2. This statute has been repealed, 1993 N.J. Laws ch. 345, §20. *See* Lisa J. Trembly, *Untangling the Adoption Web: New Jersey's Move to Legitimize Independent Adoptions*, 18 Seton Hall Legis. J. 371 (1993).—ED.

how the baby looked like her other daughter, and made it clear that she was experiencing great difficulty with the decision.

Nonetheless, Mrs. Whitehead was, for the moment, true to her word. Despite powerful inclinations to the contrary, she turned her child over to the Sterns on March 30 at the Whiteheads' home. . . .

Later in the evening of March 30, Mrs. Whitehead became deeply disturbed, disconsolate, stricken with unbearable sadness. She had to have her child. She could not eat, sleep, or concentrate on anything other than her need for her baby. The next day she went to the Sterns' home and told them how much she was suffering.

The depth of Mrs. Whitehead's despair surprised and frightened the Sterns. She told them that she could not live without her baby, that she must have her, even if only for one week, that thereafter she would surrender her child. The Sterns, concerned that Mrs. Whitehead might indeed commit suicide, not wanting under any circumstances to risk that, and in any event believing that Mrs. Whitehead would keep her word, turned the child over to her. It was not until four months later, after a series of attempts to regain possession of the child, that Melissa was returned to the Sterns, having been forcibly removed from the home where she was then living with Mr. and Mrs. Whitehead, the home in Florida owned by Mary Beth Whitehead's parents. . . .

The struggle over Baby M began when it became apparent that Mrs. Whitehead could not return the child to Mr. Stern. Due to Mrs. Whitehead's refusal to relinquish the baby, Mr. Stern filed a complaint seeking enforcement of the surrogacy contract. . . . [The court issued an *ex parte* order to Mrs. Whitehead to hand the child over to the Sterns. When the Sterns appeared at the Whitehead's house with the process server and the police to enforce the order,] Mr. Whitehead fled with the child, who had been handed to him through a window while those who came to enforce the order were thrown off balance by a dispute over the child's current name. . . .

Eventually the Sterns discovered where the Whiteheads were staying, commenced supplementary proceedings in Florida, and obtained an order requiring the Whiteheads to turn over the child. Police in Florida enforced the order, forcibly removing the child from her grandparents' home. She was soon thereafter brought to New Jersey and turned over to the Sterns. . . .

[Trial Court Judge Sorkow] held that the surrogacy contract was valid; ordered that Mrs. Whitehead's parental rights be terminated and that sole custody of the child be granted to Mr. Stern; and, after hearing brief testimony from Mrs. Stern, immediately entered an order allowing the adoption of Melissa by Mrs. Stern, all in accordance with the surrogacy contract. . . .

II. Invalidity and Unenforceability of Surrogacy Contract

We have concluded that this surrogacy contract is invalid. Our conclusion has two bases: direct conflict with existing statutes and conflict with the public policies of this State, as expressed in its statutory and decisional law. . . .

A. CONFLICT WITH STATUTORY PROVISIONS

The surrogacy contract conflicts with: (1) laws prohibiting the use of money in connection with adoptions; (2) laws requiring proof of parental unfitness or abandonment before termination of parental rights is ordered or an adoption is granted; and (3) laws that make surrender of custody and consent to adoption revocable in private placement adoptions.

(1)   Our law prohibits paying or accepting money in connection with any placement of a child for adoption. N.J. Stat. Ann. §9:3-54a. Violation is a high misdemeanor. N.J. Stat. Ann. §9:3-54c. Excepted are fees of an approved agency (which must be a non-profit entity, N.J. Stat. Ann. §9:3-38a) and certain expenses in connection with childbirth. N.J. Stat. Ann. §9:3-54b.7 . . .

Mr. Stern knew he was paying for the adoption of a child; Mrs. Whitehead knew she was accepting money so that a child might be adopted; the Infertility Center knew that it was being paid for assisting in the adoption of a child. The actions of all three worked to frustrate the goals of the statute. . . .

. . . The evils inherent in baby-bartering are loathsome for a myriad of reasons. The child is sold without regard for whether the purchasers will be suitable parents. The natural mother does not receive the benefit of counseling and guidance to assist her in making a decision that may affect her for a lifetime. In fact, the monetary incentive to sell her child may, depending on her financial circumstances, make her decision less voluntary. . . .

Baby-selling potentially results in the exploitation of all parties involved. Conversely, adoption statutes seek to further humanitarian goals, foremost among them the best interests of the child. The negative consequences of baby-buying are potentially present in the surrogacy context, especially the potential for placing and adopting a child without regard to the interest of the child or the natural mother.

(2)   The termination of Mrs. Whitehead's parental rights, called for by the surrogacy contract and actually ordered by the court, fails to comply with the stringent requirements of New Jersey law. Our law, recognizing the finality of any termination of parental rights, provides for such termination only where there has been a voluntary surrender of a child to an approved agency or to the Division of Youth and Family Services ("DYFS"), accompanied by a formal document acknowledging termination of parental rights, N.J. Stat. Ann. §§9:2-16, -17; N.J. Stat. Ann. §9:3-41; N.J. Stat. Ann. §30:4C-23, or where there has been a showing of parental abandonment or unfitness. . . .

In this case a termination of parental rights was obtained not by proving the statutory prerequisites but by claiming the benefit of contractual provisions. [A] contractual agreement to abandon one's parental rights, or not to contest a termination action, will not be enforced in our courts. The Legislature would not have so carefully, so consistently, and so substantially restricted termination of parental rights if it had intended to allow termination to be achieved by one short sentence in a contract.

Since the termination was invalid, it follows, as noted above, that adoption of Melissa by Mrs. Stern could not properly be granted.

(3)   The provision in the surrogacy contract stating that Mary Beth Whitehead agrees to "surrender custody . . . and terminate all parental rights" contains no clause giving her a right to rescind. It is intended to be an irrevocable

consent to surrender the child for adoption — in other words, an irrevocable commitment by Mrs. Whitehead to turn Baby M over to the Sterns and thereafter to allow termination of her parental rights. . . .

[New Jersey statutes provide that no surrender of the custody of a child shall be valid unless the surrender is made to a state agency, is in writing and conforms to particular requirements, declares the person's desire to relinquish custody, acknowledges termination of parental rights to the state agency, and acknowledges full understanding of the effect of the surrender. N.J. Stat. Ann. §§9:2-14, 9:2-16, 9:2-17.]

It is clear that the Legislature so carefully circumscribed all aspects of a consent to surrender custody — its form and substance, its manner of execution, and the agency or agencies to which it may be made — in order to provide the basis for irrevocability. It seems most unlikely that the Legislature intended that a consent not complying with these requirements would also be irrevocable, especially where, as here, that consent falls radically short of compliance. . . .

These strict prerequisites to irrevocability constitute a recognition of the most serious consequences that flow from such consents: termination of parental rights, the permanent separation of parent from child, and the ultimate adoption of the child. Because of those consequences, the Legislature severely limited the circumstances under which such consent would be irrevocable. The legislative goal is furthered by regulations requiring approved agencies, prior to accepting irrevocable consents, to provide advice and counseling to women, making it more likely that they fully understand and appreciate the consequences of their acts. N.J. Admin. Code tit. 10 §121A-5.4(c). . . .

. . . The provision in the surrogacy contract, agreed to before conception, requiring the natural mother to surrender custody of the child without any right of revocation is one more indication of the essential nature of this transaction: the creation of a contractual system of termination and adoption designed to circumvent our statutes.

B. PUBLIC POLICY CONSIDERATIONS

The surrogacy contract's invalidity, resulting from its direct conflict with the above statutory provisions, is further underlined when its goals and means are measured against New Jersey's public policy. The contract's basic premise, that the natural parents can decide in advance of birth which one is to have custody of the child, bears no relationship to the settled law that the child's best interests shall determine custody. . . .

The surrogacy contract violates the policy of this State that the rights of natural parents are equal concerning their child, the father's right no greater than the mother's. "The parent and child relationship extends equally to every child and to every parent, regardless of the marital status of the parents." N.J. Stat. Ann. §9:17-40. . . . The whole purpose and effect of the surrogacy contract was to give the father the exclusive right to the child by destroying the rights of the mother. . . .

The only legal advice Mary Beth Whitehead received regarding the surrogacy contract was provided in connection with the contract that she previously entered into with another couple. Mrs. Whitehead's lawyer was referred to her by the Infertility Center, with which he had an agreement to act as counsel for surrogate candidates. His services consisted of spending one hour going through the contract with the Whiteheads, section by section, and answering their questions. Mrs. Whitehead received no further legal advice prior to signing the contract with the Sterns. . . .

Under the contract, the natural mother is irrevocably committed before she knows the strength of her bond with her child. She never makes a totally voluntary, informed decision, for quite clearly any decision prior to the baby's birth is, in the most important sense, uninformed, and any decision after that, compelled by a preexisting contractual commitment, the threat of a lawsuit, and the inducement of a $10,000 payment, is less than totally voluntary. Her interests are of little concern to those who controlled this transaction. . . .

Worst of all, however, is the contract's total disregard of the best interests of the child. There is not the slightest suggestion that any inquiry will be made at any time to determine the fitness of the Sterns as custodial parents, of Mrs. Stern as an adoptive parent, their superiority to Mrs. Whitehead, or the effect on the child of not living with her natural mother.

This is the sale of a child, or, at the very least, the sale of a mother's right to her child, the only mitigating factor being that one of the purchasers is the father. Almost every evil that prompted the prohibition on the payment of money in connection with adoptions exists here.

The differences between an adoption and a surrogacy contract should be noted, since it is asserted that the use of money in connection with surrogacy does not pose the risks found where money buys an adoption.

First, and perhaps most important, all parties concede that it is unlikely that surrogacy will survive without money. Despite the alleged selfless motivation of surrogate mothers, if there is no payment, there will be no surrogates, or very few. That conclusion contrasts with adoption; for obvious reasons, there remains a steady supply, albeit insufficient, despite the prohibitions against payment. The adoption itself, relieving the natural mother of the financial burden of supporting an infant, is in some sense the equivalent of payment.

Second, the use of money in adoptions does not produce the problem — conception occurs, and usually the birth itself, before illicit funds are offered. With surrogacy, the "problem," if one views it as such, consisting of the purchase of a woman's procreative capacity, at the risk of her life, is caused by and originates with the offer of money.

Third, with the law prohibiting the use of money in connection with adoptions, the built-in financial pressure of the unwanted pregnancy and the consequent support obligation do not lead the mother to the highest paying, ill-suited, adoptive parents. She is just as well-off surrendering the child to an approved agency. In surrogacy, the highest bidders will presumably become the adoptive parents regardless of suitability, so long as payment of money is permitted.

Fourth, the mother's consent to surrender her child in adoptions is revocable, even after surrender of the child, unless it be to an approved agency, where by regulation there are protections against an ill-advised surrender. In surrogacy, consent occurs so early that no amount of advice would satisfy the potential mother's need, yet the consent is irrevocable. . . .

In the scheme contemplated by the surrogacy contract in this case, a middle man, propelled by profit, promotes the sale. Whatever idealism may have motivated any of the participants, the profit motive predominates, permeates, and ultimately governs the transaction. The demand for children is great and the supply small. The availability of contraception, abortion, and the greater willingness of single mothers to bring up their children has led to a shortage of babies offered for adoption. The situation is ripe for the entry of the middleman who will bring some equilibrium into the market by increasing the supply through the use of money.

Intimated, but disputed, is the assertion that surrogacy will be used for the benefit of the rich at the expense of the poor. *See, e.g.,* Margaret Jane Radin, *Market-Inalienability,* 100 Harv. L. Rev. 1849, 1930 (1987). In response it is noted that the Sterns are not rich and the Whiteheads not poor. Nevertheless, it is clear to us that it is unlikely that surrogate mothers will be as proportionately numerous among those women in the top twenty percent income bracket as among those in the bottom twenty percent. Put differently, we doubt that infertile couples in the low-income bracket will find upper income surrogates. . . .

The point is made that Mrs. Whitehead agreed to the surrogacy arrangement, supposedly fully understanding the consequences. Putting aside the issue of how compelling her need for money may have been, and how significant her understanding of the consequences, we suggest that her consent is irrelevant. There are, in a civilized society, some things that money cannot buy. In America, we decided long ago that merely because conduct purchased by money was "voluntary" did not mean that it was good or beyond regulation and prohibition. Employers can no longer buy labor at the lowest price they can bargain for, even though that labor is "voluntary," 29 U.S.C. §206 (1982), or buy women's labor for less money than paid to men for the same job, 29 U.S.C. §206(d), or purchase the agreement of children to perform oppressive labor, 29 U.S.C. §212, or purchase the agreement of workers to subject themselves to unsafe or unhealthful working conditions, 29 U.S.C. §§651 to 678 (*Occupational Safety and Health Act of 1970*). There are, in short, values that society deems more important than granting to wealth whatever it can buy, be it labor, love, or life. Whether this principle recommends prohibition of surrogacy, which presumably sometimes results in great satisfaction to all of the parties, is not for us to say. We note here only that, under existing law, the fact that Mrs. Whitehead "agreed" to the arrangement is not dispositive. . . .

The surrogacy contract is based on principles that are directly contrary to the objectives of our laws. It guarantees the separation of a child from its mother; it looks to adoption regardless of suitability; it totally ignores the child; it takes the child from the mother regardless of her wishes and her maternal fitness; and it does all of this, it accomplishes all of its goals, through the use of money.

Beyond that is the potential degradation of some women that may result from this arrangement. In many cases, of course, surrogacy may bring satisfaction, not only to the infertile couple, but to the surrogate mother herself. The fact, however, that many women may not perceive surrogacy negatively but rather see it as an opportunity does not diminish its potential for devastation to other women.

In sum, the harmful consequences of this surrogacy arrangement appear to us all too palpable. In New Jersey the surrogate mother's agreement to sell her child is void. Its irrevocability infects the entire contract, as does the money that purports to buy it. . . .

NOTES AND QUESTIONS

1. *Baby-selling.* The contract in *Baby M* raises a host of legal questions. It is important to distinguish several issues. One question is whether the arrangement

constitutes a criminal act in violation of state law prohibiting baby-selling. If it does, the mere fact of entering the contractual arrangement may subject the parties to criminal penalties. A second, and quite different, question is whether the contract is enforceable. It may very well be that the legislature did not intend to impose criminal penalties for surrogacy arrangements — such as those imposed on persons who buy and sell drugs or controlled substances — but that these agreements were unenforceable as a matter of contract law. As the law currently stands, the states do not seem to be treating surrogacy as a crime that would subject the parties to punishment by fine or imprisonment.

  2. *Enforcement of surrogacy agreements.* The enforceability of surrogacy contracts raises a series of issues.

  a. *Void or voidable?* One possibility is that the courts could hold the contract *void as against public policy.* This is what the Supreme Court of New Jersey did in *Baby M.* Under this approach, the court approaches the case as if there were no agreement; the standard rule for settling a custody dispute is "the best interests of the child." A second possibility is to hold the contract *voidable* by the birth mother rather than absolutely void. Under this approach, the birth mother — but not the biological father — has the right to reject the contract. If she rejects the contract, custody is determined by the best interests of the child. A mother who was willing to hand over her child pursuant to the surrogacy agreement would be able to do so and would be able to obtain a court judgment ordering the contract parents to pay her the money owed on the agreement.

  b. *Damages or specific performance?* If the contract is enforceable, then the appropriate remedy for breach must be determined. One possibility is *specific performance* through an injunction ordering the mother to hand over the child in accordance with the contract terms. Such a result might comport with traditional law in that specific performance is often ordered when an item being sold is unique, such as land or artwork. Children are obviously unique, but should they be considered items for sale? If specific performance is denied, courts may enforce the contract by damages only.

  3. *Disagreement in the courts.* Like the Supreme Court of New Jersey, Michigan courts have refused to enforce surrogacy arrangements. *See Doe v. Kelley,* 307 N.W.2d 438 (Mich. Ct. App. 1981) (interpreting the Michigan Adoption Law to prohibit the exchange of money for surrogacy); *Yates v. Keane,* Nos. 9758, 9772, slip op. (Mich. Cir. Ct. Jan. 21, 1988) (holding that surrogacy contracts are void as contrary to public policy and therefore are unenforceable).

  Other courts have held that surrogacy contracts are voidable rather than void per se. The Supreme Court of Kentucky has held that the birth mother in a surrogacy arrangement has the right to void the contract if she changes her mind during pregnancy or immediately after birth. *Surrogate Parenting Associates v. Commonwealth ex rel. Armstrong,* 704 S.W.2d 209 (Ky. 1986). *See also Matter of Adoption of Baby Girl, L.J.,* 505 N.Y.S.2d 813 (Surr. Ct. 1986) (holding that surrogate parenting agreements are not void but are voidable if they do not conform with state adoption statutes).

  The Supreme Court of California has held, in contrast, that surrogate mother contracts are specifically enforceable, at least where both the egg and sperm are donated by individuals other than the surrogate mother who bears the child. *Johnson v. Calvert,*

851 P.2d 776 (Cal. 1993). More broadly, however, the court held that "she who intended to procreate the child — that is, she who intended to bring about the birth of a child that she intended to raise as her own — is the natural mother under California law," suggesting that such contracts might be enforceable even if the egg were that of the surrogate mother. *Id.* at 782.

4. *Policy considerations.* In *Johnson v. Calvert*, the majority opinion stated:

> Anna [Johnson] and some commentators have expressed concern that surrogacy contracts tend to exploit or dehumanize women, especially women of lower economic status. Anna's objections center around the psychological harm she asserts may result from the gestator's relinquishing the child to whom she has given birth. Some have also cautioned that the practice of surrogacy may encourage society to view children as commodities, subject to trade at their parents' will. . . .
>
> We are unpersuaded that gestational surrogacy arrangements are so likely to cause the untoward results Anna cites as to demand their invalidation on public policy grounds. Although common sense suggests that women of lesser means serve as surrogate mothers more often than do wealthy women, there has been no proof that surrogacy contracts exploit poor women to any greater degree than economic necessity in general exploits them by inducing them to accept lower-paid or otherwise undesirable employment. We are likewise unpersuaded by the claim that surrogacy will foster the attitude that children are mere commodities; no evidence is offered to support it. The limited data available seem to reflect an absence of significant adverse effects of surrogacy on all participants.
>
> The argument that a woman cannot knowingly and intelligently agree to gestate and deliver a baby for intending parents carries overtones of the reasoning that for centuries prevented women from attaining equal economic rights and professional status under the law. To resurrect this view is both to foreclose a personal and economic choice on the part of the surrogate mother, and to deny intending parents what may be their only means of procreating a child of their own genetic stock. Certainly in the present case it cannot seriously be argued that Anna, a licensed vocational nurse who had done well in school and who had previously borne a child, lacked the intellectual wherewithal or life experience necessary to make an informed decision to enter into the surrogacy contract.

Id. at 785. However, Justice Joyce Kennard, the lone dissenting judge and the only woman on the court at the time, argued that a pregnant woman is "more than a mere container or breeding animal; she is a conscious agent of creation no less than the genetic mother." *Id.* at 797-798. Justice Kennard would have granted custody based on the best interests of the child.

Some analysts have supported the decision in *Baby M.* Martha A. Field, *Surrogate Motherhood: The Legal and Human Issues* 151 (1990) (arguing that either surrogate mother contracts should not be enforceable at all or the surrogate mother should have a right to change her mind for some time after the child is born); Patricia J. Williams, *The Alchemy of Race and Rights* 217-219, 224-226 (1991) (arguing that enforcing a contract signed at a discrete point of time may wind up "enslav[ing]" the one who signed it by depriving a surrogate mother of the power to exit an arrangement she comes to understand as extraordinarily harmful to her).

Others have argued that such contracts should be presumptively enforceable. For example, Professor Marjorie Shultz has argued:

> I see medical progress as expanding the potential for expression and effectuation of personal intentions. Accordingly, I propose that legal rules governing modern procreative arrangements and parental status should recognize the importance and the legitimacy of

individual efforts to project intentions and decisions into the future. Where such intentions are deliberate, explicit and bargained for, where they are the catalyst for reliance and expectations, as is the case in technologically-assisted reproductive arrangements, they should be honored.

Marjorie Maguire Shultz, *Reproductive Technology and Intent-Based Parenthood: An Opportunity for Gender Neutrality*, 1990 Wis. L. Rev. 297, 302-303. *Accord*, Carmel Shalev, *Birth Power: The Case for Surrogacy* (1989). Judge Richard Posner has argued that surrogacy contracts should be specifically enforced because (a) they are mutually beneficial to the parties; (b) they benefit the child because without them the child would not have been born; (c) there is no evidence that women, in general, misunderstand the distress they will feel at having to give up the baby; (d) poor women are better off if they have the choice to enter such agreements to make money; (e) women are competent to make voluntary and informed choices and it is paternalistic to assume that they are not competent to do so; and (f) commodification of the surrogacy relation is unlikely to affect social norms or attitudes toward the sanctity of human life. Richard Posner, *The Ethics and Economics of Enforcing Contracts of Surrogate Motherhood*, 5 J. Contemp. Health L. & Pol'y 21 (1989).

Should surrogacy arrangements be enforced? If so, by specific performance or by damages? If they should not be enforced, should they be void or voidable?

§15.4 Frozen Embryos

In vitro fertilization techniques can enable couples with fertility problems to have children. Because the failure rate of the procedure is very high, the practice is to attempt to fertilize a number of eggs, allow them to begin dividing, and to implant some of the fertilized ova. Those that are not used initially are preserved for later use if the current implantation fails to result in a pregnancy. Disputes over the disposition of these fertilized ova[3] have generated a host of difficult legal issues.

Are preembryos persons or property? In *Davis v. Davis*, 842 S.W.2d 588 (Tenn. 1992), Mary Sue Davis and Junior Davis disagreed over the use of seven of Mary Sue's preserved ova, fertilized by Junior's sperm. After the couple divorced, Mary Sue sought to have some of these frozen embryos implanted so that she could have a child. Junior objected. In an opinion by Judge W. Dale Young, the trial court held that "life begins at conception," that "human embryos are not property" but children, that it was in the best interests of those children to be available for implantation, and that "custody" of the children should be awarded to Mary Sue. *Id.* at 594. If this is correct, could Mary Sue Davis be vulnerable to a charge of child neglect or reckless abandonment if she chose *not* to implant the fertilized embryos?

The court of appeals reversed, noting that fetuses are not "persons" for a variety of purposes under Tennessee law. For example, the state's wrongful death statute does not allow a wrongful death for a viable fetus that is not first born alive; moreover, abortions were lawful in the state under a scheme that granted fetuses more protection

---

3. Courts variously characterize the fertilized ova as embryos, frozen embryos, preembryos, and prezygotes. In this context, the terms are interchangeable, although they may have different connotations and rhetorical effects.

as they developed. Consequently, the court held that the parties "share an interest in the seven fertilized ova" and therefore have the right to joint control with equal voice over their disposition.

The Tennessee Supreme Court agreed with the court of appeals that frozen embryos were not "persons" under Tennessee law, but did not categorize them as "property" either:

> [P]reembryos are not, strictly speaking, either "persons" or "property," but occupy an interim category that entitles them to special respect because of their potential for human life. It follows that any interest that Mary Sue Davis and Junior Davis have in the pre-embryos in this case is not a true property interest. However, they do have an interest in the nature of ownership, to the extent that they have decision-making authority concerning disposition of the preembryos, within the scope of policy set by law. . . .

Id. at 597.

In contrast, in *Kass v. Kass*, 1995 WL 110368 (N.Y. Sup. Ct. 1995), a New York trial judge held that preembryos were "in the nature of a property interest." *Id.* at *1. However, the appellate division reversed on contractual grounds, sidestepping the issue of whether embryos are persons or property under New York law. 663 N.Y.S.2d 581, 585 (N.Y.A.D. 2 Dept. 1997), *aff'd*, 696 N.E.2d 174 (N.Y. 1998). Should preembryos be categorized as persons, property, or something in between? Does attempting this categorization even make sense?

Competing rights. Courts that have ruled on the matter usually characterize disputes over preembryos as conflicts between the right of one party to procreate and the right of the other party not to be forced to become a parent against their will. The latter right usually trumps. However, in dicta, some courts have expressed willingness to carve out an exception when the party seeking to implant the preembryos could not procreate any other way.

In *Davis*, the court of appeals reversed on rights grounds. "It would be repugnant and offensive to constitutional principles to order Mary Sue to implant these fertilized ova against her will. It would be equally repugnant to order Junior to bear the psychological, if not the legal, consequences of paternity against his will." 1990 WL 130807, at *3 (Tenn. Ct. App. 1990). Do you agree that it would be *equally* repugnant?

By the time *Davis* reached the Tennessee Supreme Court, Mary Sue Davis (now Mary Sue Stowe) had remarried and no longer wanted to use the preembryos herself but sought authority to donate them to a childless couple. Her ex-husband, also now remarried, vehemently opposed such a donation and preferred to see the preembryos destroyed. Agreeing with the appeals court's resolution of the conflict between the right to procreate and the right to avoid procreation, the court held that Junior Davis's interest in avoiding unwanted parenthood should prevail over Mary Sue Stowe's interest in donating the preembryos to avoid the burden of knowing that the lengthy and invasive procedures she had undergone were futile. The court further noted that the case would be closer if she were seeking to use the preembryos herself, "but only if she could not achieve parenthood by any other reasonable means." The court concluded, 842 S.W.2d at 604:

> Ordinarily, the party wishing to avoid procreation should prevail, assuming that the other party has a reasonable possibility of achieving parenthood by means other than use of the

preembryos in question. If no other reasonable alternatives exist, then the argument in favor of using the preembryos to achieve pregnancy should be considered. However, if the party seeking control of the preembryos intends merely to donate them to another couple, the objecting party obviously has the greater interest and should prevail. . . .

In *J.B. v. M.B.*, 751 A.2d 613 (N.J. Super. Ct. App. Div. 2000), the ex-husband in a divorce proceeding sought control of preembryos for the purpose of impregnating a woman if he later developed a new relationship or for donation to an infertile couple. The ex-wife objected and wanted the preembryos destroyed. In ruling for the ex-wife, the court relied on a rights analysis mirroring that in *Davis. Id.* at 618-619:

> In the present case, the wife's right not to become a parent seemingly conflicts with the husband's right to procreate. The conflict, however, is more apparent than real. Recognition and enforcement of the wife's right would not seriously impair the husband's right to procreate. Though his right to procreate using the wife's egg would be terminated, he retains the capacity to father children.
> On the other hand, enforcing the husband's right to procreate using the embryos at issue in this case could result in the birth of the wife's biological child. Even if the wife were relieved of the financial and custodial responsibility for her child, the fact that her biological child would exist in an environment controlled by strangers is understandably unacceptable to the wife.

On review, 2001 WL 909294 (N.J. 2001), the New Jersey Supreme Court affirmed the lower court's rights analysis. *Id.* at *9:

> M.B.'s right to procreate is not lost if he is denied an opportunity to use or donate the preembryos. M.B. is already a father and is able to become a father to additional children, whether through natural procreation or further in vitro fertilization. In contrast, J.B.'s right not to procreate may be lost through attempted use or through donation of the preembryos. Implantation, if successful, would result in the birth of her biological child and could have life-long emotional and psychological repercussions.

Unlike the courts in *Davis* and *J.B.*, the trial court in *Kass* expressed a different conception of the rights involved. Under this analysis, the woman would always have control of the preembryos in a divorce proceeding despite her husband's objection, on the ground that once the eggs were fertilized, the husband had no right to force the wife to stop the pregnancy, *id.* at *3:

> Just as an in vivo husband's "right to avoid procreation" is waived and ceases to exist after intercourse in a coital reproduction, such right should be deemed waived and non-existent after his participation in an in vitro program. Upon entering he knows, or should have known, that technology is such that the possibility and probability of a delayed implantation are very real. Absent some indication of a contrary intent, the agreement to participate, if it does not expressly provide for such an eventuality, must be deemed an agreement to permit a delayed implantation.

In reversing, the appellate division stated that the trial court "committed a fundamental error in equating a prospective mother's decision whether to undergo implantation of pre-zygotes which are the product of her participation in an [in vitro fertilization] procedure with a pregnant woman's right to exercise exclusive control over the fate of her []fetus." 663 N.Y.S.2d 581, 585 (N.Y.A.D. 2 Dept. 1997), *aff'd*, 696 N.E.2d 174 (N.Y. 1998). Which rights analysis do you agree with? Can you think of an alternative way to frame the issue?

Biological parenthood is central to the prevailing rights analysis described above. For instance, in *Litowitz v. Litowitz*, 10 P.3d 1086 (Wash. Ct. App. 2000), *rev'd*, 48 P.3d 261 (Wash. 2000), Becky Litowitz could not provide the eggs herself because of a hysterectomy. The couple hired a third party to donate eggs, subsequently fertilized by David Litowitz's sperm. After a divorce, Becky sought to have the eggs implanted in a surrogate to produce a child she would raise. However, the court awarded control to David, who wanted to donate the eggs to an infertile couple in another state. Because Becky's own eggs had not been used to produce the preembryos, the court reasoned that David's disposing of the preembryos as he wished would not infringe on her right not to procreate. Conversely, the court ruled that Becky's desired implantation of the preembryos in a surrogate to produce a child Becky would raise *would* infringe on David's right not to procreate. Do you agree with this result? Is it fair to allow one party to invoke their right not to procreate to prevent the other party from using the pre-embryos to beget a child, and then donate the preembryos to a couple in another state? Should the right not to procreate only govern when the party invoking it actually seeks *not* to procreate, rather than to procreate elsewhere? What rights should the woman who donated the eggs have if she chooses to assert them? Note that the trial court's decision was reversed on appeal because the parties' contract with the agency provided for destruction of the preembryos if they were not implanted within five years.

Contracts regarding preembryos. If the parties sign an agreement regarding disposition of the preembryos in the event of a dispute, should the agreement be enforced? Court have generally held that the wishes of the parties should be honored if ascertainable. *See, e.g., Kass*, 663 N.Y.W.2d at 590 ("where the parties have indicated their mutual intent regarding the disposition of the pre-zygotes in the event of the occurrence of a contingency that decision must be scrupulously honored"); *Litowitz v. Litowitz*, 48 P.3d 261 (Wash. 2002)(enforcing contract between husband and wife that fertilized embryos would be thawed out and destroyed if they were not implanted within 5 years).

Does it make sense to "scrupulously honor" the intent of the parties in this context? Is the court truly refraining from interfering with the parties' expressed wishes? Isn't the court interfering with one party's wishes no matter how it decides? Would the court have ruled the same way if the agreement gave one party a right to procreate over the other's objection?

In *A.Z. v. B.Z.*, 725 N.E.2d 1051 (Mass. 2000), the Supreme Judicial Court of Massachusetts held an agreement granting ultimate control of fertilized ova to the wife unenforceable because it violated a public policy against forcing a person to become a parent against his or her will. *Accord, J.B. v. M.B.*, 751 A.2d 613 (N.J. Super. Ct. App. Div. 2000). Should all contracts regarding the disposition of preembryos be invalid? Or should they be enforced when they do not result in one party becoming a parent against their will?

Although a lower New Jersey court agreed with this rule, *J.B. v. M.B.*, 751 A.2d 613 (N.J. Super. Ct. App. Div. 2000), the Supreme Court of New Jersey modified, announcing that the "better rule, and the one we adopt, is to enforce agreements entered into at the time in vitro fertilization is begun, subject to the right of either party to change his or her mind about disposition up to the point of use or destruction of any stored preembryos." 2001 WL 909294 at *11. How is this rule different from the one promulgated in

A.Z. v. B.Z.? Is the "right of either party to change his or her mind" tantamount to a blanket invalidation of all contracts regarding the disposition of preembryos?

Differing approaches or underlying unity? Since only a handful of courts have spoken on the issue of in vitro fertilization disputes, the law in most states remains uncertain. The few courts that have approached the issue have done so in several different ways. In what ways do these approaches conflict? Is the law in this area simply an unsettled mess? Consider that fact that the *result* in all the cases is the same: none of the courts have allowed preembryos to be implanted over the objection of a party who wants the preembryos discarded. Are the courts using different arguments to achieve the same result? Is there some underlying or hidden reason for this uniform result? Or is the uniformity of result a coincidence?

§15.5   Body Parts and Human Genes

See supra §1.3.2, at pages 45-53.

§15.6   American Indian Human Remains

WANA THE BEAR v. COMMUNITY CONSTRUCTION, INC
180 Cal. Rptr. 423 (Ct. App. 1982)

COLEMAN BLEASE, Associate Justice.

Plaintiff Wana the Bear, a direct descendant of the Bear People Lodge of the Miwok Indians, seeks reversal of a judgment that the Native American burial ground under development by defendant Community Construction, Inc., is not a cemetery entitled to protection under the California cemetery law.

This case comes to us shrouded in the history of an ancient Indian people whose remains, bulldozed from their resting place, stir the anguish of their descendants. But there is no succor for these profound sensitivities in the law to which plaintiff appeals, the sepulchral confines of the California cemetery law. . . .

On August 6, 1979, a final subdivision map was approved by the Stockton City Council and defendant went about excavating the subject property in the course of developing a residential tract. In the fall of 1979, defendant uncovered human remains on the property. Defendant continued developing the property, disinterring the remains of over 200 human beings. The burial ground had been used by the Miwok Indians until they were driven out of the area between 1850 and 1870. The site is known to be a burial ground and has been the subject of numerous archeological studies. The site still contains the remains of six or more persons. Plaintiff, a descendant of the Bear People Lodge of the Miwok Indians and related to some or all of the persons whose remains lie there, brought suit to enjoin further excavation and other "desecration" of the property on July 1, 1980. . . .

The central issue in this case is whether the burial ground achieved a protectable status as a public cemetery under the 1872 cemetery law by virtue of its prior status as a public grave yard. We hold that it did not.

Plaintiff seeks enforcement by injunction of Health and Safety Code section 7052, which makes criminal the disinterment of human remains without authority of law. He argues that the section protects a cemetery, as defined by Health and Safety Code section 8100: "Six or more human bodies being buried at one place constitute the place a cemetery." He alleges, and we take it as true, that six or more human bodies are buried on the burial site. In order to escape the problem that the burial site does not comply with either of the two methods of creating a public cemetery, dedication or prescriptive use, plaintiff argues that section 8100, by virtue of its derivation from the 1854 cemetery law, applies to burial sites created prior to 1873 which, he claims, became public cemeteries, by the law of 1854, without dedication or prescriptive use.

The 1854 law made punishable the mutilation of any public grave yard and the disinterment of any deceased person in any grave yard. It defined a public grave yard as follows: "Where the bodies of six or more persons are buried, it is . . . a public grave yard." In 1872, this statute was replaced by chapter V of the new Political Code. It enacted the two means for creating a public cemetery, dedication and prescriptive use. Section 3106 of the Political Code read essentially as Health and Safety Code section 8100 does now: "Six or more human bodies being buried at one place constitutes the place a cemetery." Section 3105 vested title to lands "used as a public cemetery or graveyard, situated in or near to any city, town, or village, and used by the inhabitants thereof continuously, without interruption, as a burial-ground for five years" in the inhabitants and prohibited use of the lands "for any other purpose than a public cemetery." Section 3107 delineated the manner of dedicating public lands to "cemetery" or burial purposes. When the Health and Safety Code was created in 1939, these provisions were carried over into the present law.

Plaintiff claims that the presence of six or more bodies at the burial site in the period between 1854 and the time when the Miwoks were driven out (sometime between 1850 and 1870) rendered the burial ground a "public grave yard," indelibly impressing it with such character. But the 1854 law was not incorporated into the 1872 and subsequent law as claimed by plaintiff. The 1872 law did not simply reenact section 4 of the 1854 act (making a place where six bodies were buried a "public grave yard"). It added a prescriptive use condition, vesting title of the grave yard in the city or village using it only when the land was "used as a public cemetery . . . continuously, without interruption, as a burial-ground for five years." It further declared that "[n]o part of (the code was) retroactive unless expressly so declared." . . . The Miwoks were no longer using the burial ground in 1873, when chapter V of the Political Code replaced the 1854 law; therefore, the burial ground was not made a cemetery by the operation of new section 3106.

Plaintiff finally makes a claim that public policy protects places where the dead are buried. There is indeed such a policy, but it is codified in the statutes governing the disposition of human remains. But they also establish the limits of the policy chosen by the Legislature. The legislative judgment is binding on us in the absence of a supervening constitutional right and none has been claimed. . . .

The judgment is affirmed.

TALKING GOD
TONY HILLERMAN
1-6 (1989)

Through the doorway which led from her receptionist-secretary's office into her own, Catherine Morris Perry instantly noticed the box on her desk. It was bulky — perhaps three feet long and almost as high. . . .

"Where'd that come from?" Catherine said, indicating the box.

"Federal Express," Markie said. "I signed for it."

"Am I expecting anything?"

"Not that you told me about . . ." . . .

With her free hand Catherine Perry was slicing the tape away with the letter opener. She thought that this box was probably a result of that story in the Washington Post. Any time the museum got into the news, it reminded a thousand old ladies of things in the attic that should be saved for posterity. Since she was quoted, one of them had sent this trash to her by name. What would it be? A dusty old butter churn? A set of family albums?

"[You got a message from] somebody in the anthropology division. I put her name on the slip. Wants you to call. Said it was about the Indians wanting their skeletons back."

"Right," Catherine said. She pulled open the top flaps. Under them was a copy of the Washington Post, folded to expose the story that had quoted her. Part of it was circled in black.

MUSEUM OFFERS COMPROMISE IN OLD BONE CONTROVERSY

The title irritated Catherine. There had been no compromise. She had simply stated the museum's policy. If an Indian tribe wanted ancestral bones returned, it had only to ask for them and provide some acceptable proof that the bones in question had indeed been taken from a burial ground of the tribe. The entire argument was ridiculous and demeaning. . . . She glanced at the circled paragraph.

Mrs. Catherine Perry, an attorney for the museum and its spokesperson on this issue, said the demand by the Paho Society for the reburial of the museum's entire collection of more than 18,000 Native American skeletons was 'simply not possible in light of the museum's purpose.'

"She said the museum is a research institution as well as a gallery for public display, and that the museum's collection of ancient human bones is a potentially important source of anthropological information. She said that Mr. Highhawk's suggestion that the museum make plaster casts of the skeletons and rebury the originals was not practical 'both because of research needs and because the public has the right to expect authenticity and not to be shown mere reproductions.'"

The clause "the right to expect authenticity" was underlined. Catherine Morris Perry frowned at it, sensing criticism. She picked up the newspaper. Under it, atop a sheet of brown wrapping paper, lay an envelope. Her name had been written neatly on it. She opened it and pulled out a single sheet of typing paper. While she read, her idle hand was pulling away the layer of wrapping paper which had separated the envelope from the contents of the box.

Dear Mrs. Perry:

You won't bury the bones of our ancestors because you say the public has the right to expect authenticity in the museum when it comes to look at skeletons. Therefore I am sending you a couple of authentic skeletons of ancestors. I went to the cemetery in the woods behind the Episcopal Church of Saint Luke. I used authentic anthropological methods to locate the burials of authentic white Anglo types . . . and to make sure they would be perfectly authentic, I chose two whose identities you can personally confirm yourself. I ask that you accept these two skeletons for authentic display to your clients and release the bones of two of my ancestors so that they may be returned to their rightful place in Mother Earth. The names of these two authentic—

Mrs. Bailey was standing beside her now. "Honey," she said. "What's wrong?" Mrs. Bailey paused. "There's bones in that box," she said. "All dirty, too."

Mrs. Morris Perry put the letter on the desk and looked into the box. From underneath a clutter of what seemed to be arm and leg bones a single empty eye socket stared back at her. She noticed that Mrs. Bailey had picked up the letter. She noticed dirt. Damp ugly little clods had scattered on the polished desk top.

"My God," Mrs. Bailey said. "John Neldine Burgoyne. Jane Burgoyne. Weren't those—Aren't these your grandparents?"

NOTES AND QUESTIONS

1. *Reburial of American Indian human remains found on private property. Wana the Bear* was partly overturned by California legislation expressly protecting American Indian burial sites. Cal. Gov't Code §6254(r); Cal. Health & Safety Code §7050.5; Cal. Pub. Res. Code §§5097.94, 5097.98, 5097.99. The legislation requires property owners who discover American Indian human remains on their property to notify public officials and to negotiate with representatives of the affected tribe for reburial of the remains and associated objects. *See People v. Van Horn*, 267 Cal. Rptr. 804 (Ct. App. 1990) (upholding the constitutionality of the statute and requiring an archaeologist to return two objects found in a site he excavated on private land while making a survey for the city of Vista, California, which was in the process of determining whether to buy the land); Thomas Boyd, *Disputes Regarding the Possession of Native American Religious and Cultural Objects and Human Remains: A Discussion of the Applicable Law and Proposed Legislation*, 55 Mo. L. Rev. 883 (1990); Walter Echo-Hawk, *Museum Rights vs. Indian Rights: Guidelines for Assessing Competing Legal Interests in Native Cultural Resources*, 14 N.Y.U. Rev. L. & Soc. Change 437 (1986).

At least 13 states have passed legislation to protect all unmarked graves, including American Indian burial sites on private land owned by non-Indians. *See, e.g.*, Ala. Code §§41-3-1 to 41-3-6; Idaho Code §§27-501 to 27-504; Ill. Ann. Stat. ch. 20, §§3440/1 to 3440/16; Neb. Stat. §§12-1202 to 12-1212; Okla. Stat. Ann. tit. 21, §§1168-1168.6, tit. 53, §361; Wash. Rev. Code Ann. §§27.44.020 to 27.44.901, 27.53.060, 68.60.040*et seq.*

It is well-settled that the descendants of persons who are buried in a recognized cemetery may acquire an implied easement of access to the land where their ancestors are buried. They also may be entitled to an injunction preventing the owner of the land from defacing the graves or interfering with the "reverential character" of the graves. *Bogner v. Villiger*, 796 N.E.2d 679 (Ill. App. Ct. 2003). *Accord, Mallock v. Southern Memorial Park, Inc.*, 561 So.2d 330 (Fla. Dist. Ct. App. 1990)(discussing a Florida statute that creates such rights); *Sanford v. Vinal*, 552 N.E.2d 579 (Mass. App. Ct. 1990)(discussing abandonment of such an easement).

2. *Reburial of American Indian human remains and funerary objects found on federal and tribal land.* The *Native American Graves Protection and Repatriation Act*, 25 U.S.C. §§3001-3013, 18 U.S.C. §1170, passed by Congress on November 16, 1990, provides that American Indian and Native Hawaiian human remains and funerary objects placed with the body upon burial that are found on tribal or federal lands after

the effective date of the statute belong to the lineal descendants of the person buried with the items. If such descendants cannot be found, the items belong to the tribe on whose tribal land they were found or to the tribe having the closest cultural affiliation with them. 25 U.S.C. §3002(a). Sacred objects "needed by traditional Native American religious leaders for the practice of traditional Native American religions by their present day adherents" (25 U.S.C. §3001(3)(C)) and "objects of cultural patrimony" that have "ongoing historical, traditional or cultural importance central to the Native American group or culture" similarly belong to the tribe on whose land they are found or to the tribe having the closest affiliation with the objects. 25 U.S.C. §3002(a).

3. *Return of human remains held by museums.* As of 1991, the Smithsonian Institution and other institutions in the United States held approximately 300,000 human remains of Americans Indians. Robert Clinton, Nell Jessup Newton, and Monroe Price, *American Indian Law* 771 (3d ed. 1991). The *Native American Graves Protection and Repatriation Act* provides that human remains and cultural items held by federal agencies and museums receiving federal funds shall be turned over to lineal descendants or to the appropriate American Indian tribe or Native Hawaiian organization. 25 U.S.C. §3005(a). The only exception to this rule occurs when "the items are indispensable for completion of a specific scientific study, the outcome of which would be of major benefit to the United States." 25 U.S.C. §3005(b). Such items shall be returned within 90 days of the completion of the scientific study. Although the Smithsonian Institution is expressly excluded from coverage by the statute, 25 U.S.C. §3001(4) and (8), it is required to return those remains by the *National Museum of the Indian Act,* 20 U.S.C. §§80q to 80q-15 (Supp. 1990), passed November 28, 1989. This statute requires the Smithsonian to return "any Indian human remains . . . identified by a preponderance of the evidence as those of a particular individual or as those of an individual culturally affiliated with a particular Indian tribe, . . . upon the request of the descendants of such individual or of the Indian tribe." 20 U.S.C. §80q-9(c). It therefore allows the museum to retain any human remains for study that cannot be proven to have a connection to an identifiable tribe. As between the museum and American Indian nations, who has a stronger claim to the unidentified human remains held by the Smithsonian? For an analysis of "cultural property," *see* Patty Gerstenblith, *Identity and Cultural Property: The Protection of Cultural Property in the United States,* 73 B.U. L. Rev. 559 (1995).

PROBLEMS

1. A museum subject to the *Native American Graves Protection and Repatriation Act* has been asked to return its human remains. The museum argues that the remains are needed for a scientific study to extract DNA material from the bones for the purpose of genetically tracing which tribes evolved from other tribes and where their ancestors originated. It is hoped that the study will teach a great deal about migration patterns and the prehistory of America.

    a. Is this study "specific," as required by §3005(b)?

    b. Is it "of major benefit to the United States," as required by §3005(b)? Is other information needed to answer this question?

2. In a famous case, human remains more than 9,000 years old were found on federal land in Washington State. When the Army Corps of Engineers sought to return the remains of the "Kennewick man" to a group of Columbia River tribes, a group of

scientists objected on the ground that the physiological features of the Kennewick man meant that he was Caucasian rather than Indian, that he could not be a lineal ancestor of the tribes in the area, and that examination of the remains was essential for scientific purposes. They are very eager to study the remains for scientific purposes because the presence of a Caucasian in the area at that time would change anthropologists' views of human biological and social history. The tribes contended that his genetic makeup was irrelevant and that if he had died in that spot 9,000 years ago, then he was on tribal land and within the jurisdiction of the tribe, and it would violate their religious beliefs not to rebury his remains. They also claimed a right to rebury him and a religious claim to prevent him from being prodded by scientists. The Ninth Circuit sided with the scientists on the ground that the Kennewick man was not a Native American and that the tribes could not prove they were related to him. The statute defines "Native American'" as "relating to, a tribe, people, or culture *that is* indigenous to the United States," 25 U.S.C. §3001(9) (emphasis added), and the court determined that the use of the present tense implied that to take control of the remains, the tribe must prove they are related to a currently existing tribe or culture rather than asserting a relation between a past tribe or culture. Given his age, it was impossible to do that and the tribes lost because they could not meet that burden. *Bonnichsen v. United States Dep't of Army*, 367 F.3d 864 (9th Cir. 2004). *See* Rebecca Tsosie, *Privileging Claims to the Past: Ancient Human Remains and Contemporary Cultural Values*, 31 Ariz. St. L. J. 583 (1999). Did the court interpret the statute correctly? Did it do the right thing?

3. The California legislation adopted after *Wana the Bear* required reburial of human remains on other land. Suppose the Miwok Indians had argued before the California legislature that the bodies of their ancestors had to remain where they were found because moving the bodies would disturb their souls. The Miwoks further argued that the ground where the ancestors were found was holy land. They therefore sought legislation that would prohibit removal and reburial of human remains from ground deemed to be holy by the tribe most closely affiliated with the persons whose remains were found.

    a.   What arguments could you make in favor of the legislation?
    b.   What arguments could you make against it?
    c.   What is the right thing to do?

TABLE OF CASES

Principal cases and their page numbers appear in italics.

2-4 Realty Assocs. v. Pittman, 374

21 Merchants Row Corp. v. Merchants Row, Inc., 691

29 Holding Corp. v. Diaz, 667

50 Acres of Land, United States v., 1046, 1048

119-121 East 97th St Corp. v. New York City Comm'n on Human Rights, 861

170 West 85 Street HDFC v. Jones, 861

447 Assocs. v. Miranda, 698, 699

564.54 Acres of Land, More or Less, United States v., 1046

930.65 Acres of Land, United States v., 1051

1515-1519 Lakeview Blvd. Condominium Ass'n v. Apartment Sales Corp., 387

A & M Records v. Napster, 1099

A.Z. v. B.Z., 1165–1166

Abbott v. Bragdon, 150–151

Abo Petroleum Corp. v. Amstutz, 511

Ackaa v. Tommy Hilfiger, 128

Ackerman v. Food-4-Less, 128

Acierno v. State of Delaware, 1051

Acme Laundry Co. v. Secretary of Envtl. Affairs, 945

Acme Markets, Inc. v. Wharton Hardware and Supply Corp., 473

Acton v. Blundell, 90, 253, 261

Adams v. Cleveland-Cliffs Iron Co., 272

Adams v. Star Enter., 283

Adoption of Baby Girl, L.J., In the Matter of, 1160

Adoption of Greta, In re, 55

Agins v. Tiburon, 955, 957, 966, 933, 1028

Akau v. Olohana Corp., 172

Albert v. Zoning Hearing Bd. Of North Abington Township, 410

Albinger v. Harris, 75

Albrecht v. Clifford, 775, 776

Albro v. Allen, 572

Alby v. Banc One Financial, 553

Alderwood Associates v. Washington Environmental Council, 161

Alejandre v. Bull, 771

Alexander v. Boyer, 586

Algermissen v. Sutin, 212

Alires v. McGehee, 774

Allemong v. Frendzel, 387, 415

Almota Farmers Elevator & Warehouse v. United States, 1042, 1050

Alsup v. Montoya, 465

Amalgamated Food Employees Union v. Logan Valley Plaza, 105, 153, 154

Amazon.com, Inc. v. Barnesandnoble.com, Inc., 1129

American Geophysical Union v. Texaco, Inc., 1128

American Jewish Theatre, Inc. v. Roundabout Theatre Co., 657

American Standard Life & Accident Ins. Co. v. Speros, 585

American Trading Real Estate Properties, Inc. v. Town of Trumbull, 198

American Transmission, Inc. v. Channel 7 of Detroit, Inc., 114

America Online v. AT&T Corp., 1089

Andrus v. Allard, 980

Ankiewicz v. Kinder, 741

The Antelope, 1152, 1153

Antonis v. Liberati, 789

A.O. Smith Corp. v. Kaufman Grain Corp., 718

Appalachee Enters. v. Walker, 425, 1015

Appel v. Presley Cos., 417, 429

Aquarian Found., Inc. v. Sholom House, Inc., 455, 467

Arguello v. Conoco, Inc., 128

Arlington Heights, Village of v. Metropolitan Hous. Dev. Corp., 874, 877

Armory v. Delamirie, 96

Armstrong v. Francis Corp., 232, 237, 238, 242, 260, 289

Armstrong v. Roberts, 402

Armstrong v. United States, 955, 960, 966, 977, 1028, 1042

Arnold v. Chandler, 381

Aronow v. Silver, 76

Arundel Corp. v. Marie, 549

Arvada Urban Renewal Auth. v. Columbine Professional Plaza Ass'n, 1066

Asbury v. Brougham, 822, 831

Assilzadeh v. Cal. Fed. Bank, 771
Association for Advancement of the Mentally
    Handicapped, Inc. v. City of Elizabeth,
    893
*Association of Relatives & Friends of AIDS
    Patients (AFAPS) v. Regulations & Permits
    Administration, or Administración de
    Reglamentos y Permisos (ARPE)*, 890
Athineos v. Thayer, 674
Attorney General v. Brown, 867
Attorney General v. Desilets, 851, 855, 856
Aurora Business Park Association v. Albert,
    Inc., 669
Austin v. United States, 635, 1021
Austin Hill Country Realty v. Palisades Plaza,
    667
Autocephalous Greek-Orthodox Church of
    Cyprus v. Goldberg & Feldman Fine Arts,
    Inc., 101, 226

Babbitt v. Youpee, 64, 68, 69, 956, 968, 969,
    1008, 1013, 1014, 1015, 1016, 1024
Baby M, In the Matter of, 1154, 1159
Baehr v. Lewin, 620, 843
Bailey v. Bailey, 72
Bailey v. Myers, 1065
Baker v. Selden, 1099
Baker v. State of Vermont, 620
Baker v. Weedon, 557
Bangerter v. Orem City Corp., 894
Bank of Craig v. Hughes, 803
Banner v. United States, 22, 218, 222
In re Banning, 172
Baran v. Juskulski, 574
Barash v. Pennsylvania Terminal Real Estate
    Corp., 707
Barchowsky v. Silver Farms, Inc., 211
Barclay v. DeVeau, 433
Bargmann v. Soll Oil Co., 271
Barner v. Chappell, 384, 387
Barnes v. Glen Theatre, Inc., 940
Barron v. Kipling Woods, LLC,
Barrow v. Barrow, 575, 579
Barton v. New York City Commn. on Human
    Rights, 864
Barton v. Thaw, 544
Batchelder v. Allied Stores International, Inc.,
    161
Bateman v. Bd. of Appeals of Georgetown, 363
Bates v. Quality Ready Mix Co., 276
Bates v. Southgate, 774
Bayliss v. Bayliss, 624
Bauman v. Ross, 1051
B.C.E. Development, Inc. v. Smith, 405
Beachside Bungalow Preservation Ass'n of Far
    Rockaway, Inc. v. Oceanview Assocs., 345
Beal Bank v. Almand & Associates, 572, 576,
    592

Beal v. Beal, 610
Bean v. Walker, 810
Becker v. IRM, 739
Bedell v. Los Zapatistas, Inc., 714
Beecher v. Wetherby, 16
Behar v. Mawardi, 766
Behrens v. Behrens, 73
Beliveau v. Caras, 841
Bell v. Town of Wells, 201
Belle Terre, Village of, v. Boraas, 883, 887, 888,
    889, 890
Belleville v. Parrillo's, Inc., 922, 936
Bellwood, Village of, v. Dwivendi, 878
Benchmark Land Co. v. City of Battle Ground,
    1037
Bennett v. Charles Corp., 382
Bennett v. Commissioner of Food & Agric.,
    379
Bennis v. Michigan, 634, 1020,
    1024, 1025
Berg v. Wiley, 660
Berger v. State, 409, 411
Berish v. Bornstein, 775, 776
Berman v. Parker, 1053, 1054, 1056, 1057,
    1058, 1065
Berman & Sons, Inc. v. Jefferson, 715
Betsey v. Turtle Creek Assocs., 879
Big D Enters., United States v., 830
Bigelow v. Bullard, 656
Billings Properties, Inc. v. Yellowstone
    County, 1031
Billings v. Wilson, 738
Bills v. Hodges, 837
Bishop v. Reinhold, 216
Blackett v. Olanoff, 703, 707, 708
Blagg v. Fred Hunt Co., 776
Blakeley v. Gorin, 420, 424, 1015
Blancett v. Blancett, 781
Blatchford v. Native Village of Noatak, 22
Blaylock v. Cary, 771
*Blevins v. Barry-Lawrence County Assn. for
    Retarded Citizens, 406*
Blue Jeans Equities West v. City &
    County of San Francisco, 1037
Block v. Hirsh, 982, 983, 986
Block Properties Co., Inc. v. American
    National Ins. Co., 718
Board of Commissioners of Roane
    County v. Parker, 940
Board of Directors of Rotary International v.
    Rotary Club of Duarte, 141
Board of Educ. v. Miles, 536
Boerne, City of v. Flores, 852, 857, 897
Bogner v. Villiger, 1169
Bonds, In re Marriage of, 598
Bonnco Petrol, Inc. v. Epstein, 772
Bonnichsen v. United States Dep't of Army,
    1171

Boomer v. Atlantic Cement Co., 280, 286, 288, 295

Borelli v. Brusseau, 764

Bormann v. Board of Supervisors in and for Kossuth County, 277, 1017

Borough of. *See name of borough*

Bosarge v. State ex rel. Price, 282

Bosley Medical Institute, Inc. v. Kremer, 1093

Bourke v. Callahan, 618

Bowdoin Square, L.L.C. v. Winn-Dixie Montgomery, Inc., 667

Bowers v. Andrew, 341

Bowers v. Elida Road Video & Books, Inc., 282

Bowers v. Hardwick, 622

Bowles v. Mahoney, 738

Bowles v. United States, 1011

Boyd v. LeFrak Organization, 880

Boy Scouts of America v. Dale, *133*, 140, 143

Bozeman v. Vaniman, 1065

Bradley v. American Smelting & Ref. Co., 271, 272

Bradwell v. Illinois, 764

Bragdon v. Abbott, 150

Brandt v. Chebanse, 895

Brant v. Hargrove, 587

Braschi v. Stahl Assocs., *670*, 673, 674, 675, 861

Brause v. Bureau of Vital Statistics, 620

Breene v. Plaza Towers Assn., 469

Bridger v. Goldsmith, 774

Britton v. Town of Chester, 909

Broach v. City of Hampton, 549

Bronson v. Crestwood Lake Section 1 Holding Corp., 879, 881

Brookline v. Carey, 1015

Brooks v. Chicago Downs Assn., Inc., 121

Brotherton v. Cleveland, 52

Brown v. Artery Organization, Inc., 878, 879

Brown v. Board of Educ., 445, 449, 561, 833, 837

Brown v. Branch, 765

Brown v. Fuller, 387

Brown v. Gobble, *179*, 193, 207

Brown v. Humble Oil Refining Co., 85

Brown v. Legal Foundation of Washington, 989

Brown v. Southall Realty Co., 713

Brown v. Veile, 737

Brown v. Voss, 363

Browning Oil Co., Inc. v. Luecke, 89

Bubis v. Kassin, 329

Buchanan v. Warley, 884, 916

Buckhorn Ventures, LLC v. Forsyth County, 914

Building Monitoring Systems v. Paxton, 736

Bunker v. Peyton, 576

Burch v. University of Kansas, 656

Burley Brick & Sand Co. v. Cofer, 342

Burns v. McCormick, *758*, 763, 764, 765

Bushmiller v. Schiller, 777

Bush v. Gore, 449

Buyers Service Co., State v., 746

B.W.S. Invs. v. Mid-Am Restaurants, Inc., 718

Byse v. Lewis, 573

C & M Developers, Inc. v. Bedminster Township Zoning Hearing Bd., 940

Cain v. Finnie, 524

California Mobile Home Park Mgmt. Co., United States v., 867

Caltex, United States v., 960, 1025

Cambridge Co. v. East Slope Inv. Corp., *546*, 552

Camino Gardens Association, Inc. v. McKim, 462

Campbell v. Acuff-Rose Music Inc., 1123

Campbell v. Garden City Plumbing & Heating, Inc., 842

Candela v. Port Motors, Inc., 102

Capitol Fed. Sav. & Loan Assn. v. Smith, 558

Cappezzuto v. John Hancock Mutual Life Insurance Co., 746

Carlsen v. Rivera, 102

Carnes v. Sheldon, 615, 854

Carparts Distribution Center, Inc. v. Automotive Wholesalers Ass'n of New England, 152

Carpenter v. Ruperto, 196

Carr v. Deking, *580*, 585

Carroll v. Lee, 615

Carson v. Here's Johnny Portable Toilets, Inc., 1139

Carter v. Helmsley-Spear, 1141

Casa D'Angelo v. A & R Realty Co., 696

Casey v. Casey, 462

Casino Reinvestment Dev. Auth. v. Banin, 1065

Castlebrook, Ltd. v. Dayton Properties Ltd. Partnership, 389

Cathedral of the Incarnation in the Diocese of Long Island, Inc. v. Garden City Company, *518*, 524, 525

Causby, United States v., 960, 961, 968, 984, 988

Causey v. Sewell Cadillac-Chevrolet, Inc., 128

Cayuga Indian Nation of New York v. Cuomo, 22

Cayuga Indian Nation of New York v. Pataki, 23

Cell South of New Jersey, Inc. v. Zoning Bd. of Adjustment of West Windsor Township, 931

Centel Cable Television Co. v. Cook, 361

Central Delaware County Auth. v. Greyhound Corp., *541*, 550, 552

Central Fin. Servs., Inc. v. Spears, *803*

Certain Land in Cape Girardeau, United
    States v., 525
Certain Scholarship Funds, In re, 526
Chamberlaine & Flowers, Inc. v. McBee, 771
Chan v. Antepenko, 656
Chaplin v. Saunders, 193, 197
Chapman v. Higbee, 128
Chapman v. Silber, 741
Charash v. Oberlin College, 225
Charlotte Park & Recreation Commn. v.
    Barringer, 357
Charlottesville Redevelopment & Hous. Auth.,
    United States v., 833
Charping v. J.P. Scurry & Co., 384
Charrier v. Bell, 92
Charter Township of Delta v. Dinolfo, 886, 890
Cheek v. Wainwright, 193
Cheney Bros. v. Doris Silk Corp., 43
Cheney v. Mueller, 341
Chesapeake Ranch Club, Inc. v. C.R.C. United
    Members, Inc., 389, 940
Chess v. Muhammad, 715
Chiapuzio v. BLT Operating Corp., 843
Chicago, B. & Q. R. Co. v. Chicago, 954
Chicago, City of, v. Beretta U.S.A. Corp.,
    283
Chicago Flood Litigation, In re, 271
Christian v. Wal-Mart Stores, Inc., 128
Christiansen v. Casey, 402
Chryar v. Wolf, 740
Cienega Gardens v. United States, 1019
Cincinnati, City of, v. Beretta U.S.A. Corp.,
    283
Citibank, N.A. v. Plapinger, 774
Citizens for Covenant Compliance v.
    Anderson, 381, 401, 403
City of. *See name of city*
City Wide Assocs. v. Penfield, 865
Civil Rights Cases, 127, 436, 447, 1151
Clay v. Hanson, 766
Clearview Coal Co., Commonwealth v., 917
Cleburne v. Cleburne Living Ctr., 411, 896,
    940, 1059
Cline v. Johnson County Bd. of Educ., 1015
*Cochran v. Fairfax County Board of Zoning
    Appeals, 925*
Coffee v. William Marsh Rice University, 527
Cohen v. Cohen, 579
Cole Chemical Distributing, Inc. v. Gowing,
    669
Coleman, Ex parte, 714
Collado, United States v., 635
College Block v. Atlantic Richfield Co., 692
Collins v. Guggenheim, 618
Cologne v. Westfarms Assocs., 160
Colorado Springs, City of, v. SecurCare Self
    Storage, Inc., 937
Columbia East Assocs. v. Bi-Lo, Inc., 695

Commercial Builders v. City of Sacramento,
    1037
Commonwealth v. *See name of party*
Commons v. Westwood Zoning Bd. of
    Adjustment, 930, 936
*Community Feed Store, Inc. v. Northeastern
    Culvert Corp., 207, 211, 214*
CompuServe v. Cyber Promotions, Inc., 115
Conahan v. Fisher, 771
Concerned Citizens of Brunswick County
    Taxpayers Assn. v. Rhodes, 172
Concord & Bay Point Land Co. v. City of
    Concord, 508
Concord Oil Co. v. Pennzoil Exploration &
    Production Co., 507
Congdon v. Strine, 879
Conklin v. Davi, 776
Connecticut Bank & Trust Co. v. Brody, 545
Connell v. Francisco, 616
Continental Ins. Co. v. Brown, 779
Cook v. University Plaza, 656
Cooper v. Smith, 76
Cope v. Inhabitants of Brunswick, 937
Cornelius v. Benevolent Protective Order of
    the Elks, 129
Cote v. Cote, 631
Cottonwood Christian Center v. Cypress
    Redevelopment Agency, 898
County of . *See name of county*
Country Club District Homes Ass'n v.
    Country Club Christian Church, 408, 409
Countrywide Home Loans, Inc. v, Kentucky
    Bar Ass'n, 746
Cox, In re, 870
Cox v. Glenbrook Company, 353
Craft, U.S. v., 576, 591, 592
Craig v. Bossenbery, 411
Crane Neck Assn., Inc. v. New York City/
    Long Island County Servs. Group, 409, 410
Crichfield Trust, In the Matter of, 527
Cricklewood on the Bellamy Condominium
    Ass'n v. Cricklewood on the Bellamy Trust,
    353,
Crimi v. Rutger's Presbyterian Church, 1141
Crooke v. Gilden, 621
Cumberland Farms v. Town of Groton, 935
Curtis v. Anderson, 76
Customer Co. v. City of Sacramento, 1012
Cutter v. Wilkinson, 898
Cuyahoga Falls, City of, v. Buckeye
    Community Hope Foundation, 878
Cwynar v. City and County of San Francisco,
    987

Dacy v. Village of Ruidoso, 914
Dale v. Boy Scouts of America, 133
Dalton v. Eller, 345
Danann Realty Corp. v. Harris, 773, 774

Dane, County of, v. Norman, 851
Davidow v. Inwood N. Professional Group, 718
Davidson Bros., Inc. v. D. Katz & Sons, Inc., 367, 377, 389, 391, 393, 472, 474, 480
Davison v. City of Tucson, 176
Daniel G. Kamin Kilgore Enterprises v. Brookshire Grocery Co., 696
Davis v. Davis, 1162, 1164
Davis v. Barnfield, 765
Davis v. St. Joe School Distict, 525
Daytona Beach, City of v. Tona-Rama, Inc., 168, 172, 214
D.B. v. Bloom, 150
DeCecco v. Beach, 277, 308
De Bruyn Produce Co. v. Romero, 656
De Coster, State v., 656
DeLa Rosa v. DeLa Rosa, 606
DeMatteo v. DeMatteo, 598
Department of Agric. & Consumer Servs. v. Mid-Florida Growers, Inc., 968, 1011
Department of Housing & Urban Development v. Rucker, 633, 1025
Department of Transportation v. Rowe, 1050, 1051
DeSario v. Industrial Excess Land Fill, Inc., 283
Desnick v. American Broadcasting Companies, Inc., 108, 114, 116
Detling v. Edelbrock, 715
Deviney v. Nationsbank, 463
Devins v. Borough of Bogota, 198
DiCenso v. Cisneros, 841
Dierberg v. Wills, 415
Dews v. Town of Sunnyvale, 878
District of Columbia v. Beretta, U.S.A., Corp., 283
Dito v. Orkin Exterminating Co., Inc, 775
Dobbins v. Los Angeles, 1018
Doe v. Burkland, 622
Doe v. City of Butler, 881, 882, 890
Doe v. Kelley, 1160
Doe v. McMaster, 746
Dolan v. City of Tigard, 957, 985, 1026, 1036, 1037, 1039, 1040
Donnellan v. Rocks, 747
Dorgan v. Loukas, 738
Dowling v. Dowling, 627
Dred Scott v. Sandford, 1143, 1152
Dressell v. Ameribank, 747
Dubin v. Chesebrough Trust, 341
Duda v. Thompson, 776
Duke of Norfolk's Case, 553
Dunafon v. Delaware McDonald's Corp., 472
Durand v. IDC Bellingham, 914, 938
Durham v. Harbin, 766
Durham v. Red Lake Fishing and Hunting Club, Inc., 129

Duvall v. Ford Leasing Dev. Co., 403
Dwyer v. Skyline Apartments, Inc., 740
Dygert v. Leonard, 774

Eagle Enters. v. Gross, 389
Eastern Enters. v. Apfel, 1019
East Haven Assocs., Inc. v. Gurian, 702
East 10th St. Assocs. v. Estate of Goldstein, 673
Ebay, Inc. v. Bidder's Edge, Inc., 44, 115
Edgar A. Levy Leasing Co. v. Siegel, 986
Edgewater Inv. Assocs. v. Borough of Edgewater, 990
Edmonds v. Oxford House, Inc., 894
Edouard v. Kozubal, 837, 843
Edwards, Matter of, 791
Edwards v. Bradley, 463, 521, 524, 526
Edwards v. Habib. 728, 731
Eggleston v. Pierce County, 1012
E. J. Wimberly v. Lone Star Gas Co., 388
Erie, City of, v. Pap's A.M., 940
El Di, Inc. v. Town of Bethany Beach, 411, 416
Elkus v. Elkus, 605
Elliff v. Texon Drilling Co., 83
Ellis v. Jansing, 196
Ellsworth Dobbs, Inc. v. Johnson, 746, 747
Emery v. Caravan of Dreams, Inc., 150
Emery v. Dreams Spirits, Inc., 150
Employment Div., Oregon Human Resources Dept. v. Smith, 852, 857, 899
Erickson v. Sunset Mem. Park Assn., 433
Ernst Iron Works v. Duralith Corp., 773
Erlich v. Culver City, 1037
Estate of . *See name of party*
Eteves v. Esteves, 575
ETW Corp. v. Jireh Publishing, Inc., 1138
Euclid, Village of, v. Ambler Realty Co., 277, 883, 919, 921, 922, 935, 960
Evans v. Abney, 439, 449, 560, 561
Evans v. Merriweather, 91
Evans v. Newton, 439, 440, 441, 442, 444, 446
Evans v. Pollock, 395, 401
Everard's Breweries v. Day, 1014
Evergreen Highlands Ass'n v. West, 482
Exotex Corp. v. Rhinehart, 745
Eyerman v. Mercantile Trust Co., 69

Fallon v. Triangle Mgmt., 797
Familystyle of St. Paul, Inc. v. City of St. Paul, 892
Fast v. DeRaeve, 331
Fears v. Y.J. Land Corp., 214
Featherston v. Steinhoff, 854
Feist Publications, Inc. v. Rural Telephone Service Co., 44, 1095
Ferrero Constr. Co. v. Dennis Rourke Corp., 552, 553

Fifth Avenue Presbyterian Church v. City of New York, 899
Fike v. Shelton, 342
Finley v. Teeter Stone, Inc., 259
Finn v. Williams, 339, 343, 344
Firma, Inc. v. Twillman, 779
First Citizens Nat'l Bank v. Sherwood, 789
First English Evangelical Lutheran Church v. County of Los Angeles, 997, 1007, 1009
First Fed. Sav. Bank v. Key Mkts., 690
First Lady, LLC. V. JMF Properties, LLC, 237
First Natl. Bank v. Enriquez, 797
Fitzpatrick v. Michael, 764
Flack v. McClure, 813
Flaig v. Gramm, 329
Flores v. City of Boerne, 897
Florida Rock Indus., Inc. v. United States, 1010, 1011
Flower Mound, Town of, v. Stafford Estates Ltd. Partn., 1039
Flowers v. TJX Cos., 128
Flureau v. Thornhill, 777
Flynn v. City of Cambridge, 987
Fogerty v. State, 223
Fong v. Hashimoto, 390
Fontainebleau Hotel Corp. v. Forty-Five Twenty-Five, Inc., 213, *284*, 290, 305
Food Lion, Inc. v. Capital Cities/ABC Inc., 114, 115, 116
Foods First, Inc. v. Gables Assoc., 408
Ford v. Schering-Plough Corp., 152
Forest Hills Garden Corp. v. Baroth, 213
Forfeiture of $5,264, In re, 634
Forsgren v. Sollie, 524
Forster v. Hall, 403, 408
Fortyune v. American Multi-Cinema, Inc., 151
Foster v. Back Bay Spas, 144
Frederick v. Consolidated Waste Servs., Inc., 343
French, State by Cooper v., 854, 855
Frenchtown Square Partn. v. Lemstone, Inc., 667
Frenchtown Villa v. Meadors, 736
Fresh Pond Shopping Ctr., Inc. v. Callahan, 987, 988
Friedenburg v. N.Y. State Dept. of Envtl. Conservation, 976
Friendswood Dev. Co. v. Smith-Southwest Indus., Inc., 251, 259, 260
Fullilove v. Klutznick, 828
Funk v. Haldeman, 87
Futura Realty v. Lone Star Building Centers (Eastern) Inc., 771

Gabriel v. Cazier, 411
Gainsborough St. Realty Trust v. Haile, 611
Gannon, United States v., 750
Garafine v. Monmouth Park Jockey Club, 121

Garcia v. Garcia, 186
Garcia v. Sanchez, 215
Gardner v. Gardner, 762, 765
Gardner v. New Jersey Pinelands Commn., 1010
Garland v. Rosenshein, 379, 401
Garneau v. City of Seattle, 1037
Garrett v. Tandy Corp., 128
Gary, City of, v. Smith & Wesson Corp., 283
Generalow v. Steinberger, 217
General Auto Service Station v. Maniatis, 224
General Credit Co. v. Cleck, 587
General Motors, United States v., 15
George Washington Mem. Park Cemetery Assn., In re, 433
Geragosian v. Union Realty Co., 216
Gilder v. Mitchell, 353
Gill v. LDI, 272
Gilligan v. Jamco Development Corp., 890
Gilmore v. Driscoll, 248
Gilpin v. Jacob Ellis Realties, 217
Gion v. City of Santa Cruz, 168, 169, 171, 224
Glass v. Goeckel, 170
Glaser v. Bayliff, 197
Glassboro, Borough of, v. Vallorosi, 890
Glick v. Principal Mutual Life Ins. Co., 365
Glosemeyer v. United States, 984
Goldblatt v. Hempstead, 916, 932, 960
Golden Cone Concepts, Inc. v. Villa Linda Mall, Ltd., 775
Golden West Baseball Co v. City of Anaheim, 657
Goodridge v. Dept. of Public Health, 621
Gordon v. Gordon, 567
Gormley v. Robertson, 622, 623
Gorski v. Troy, 848
Goulding v. Cook, 217, 222
Granite Properties Ltd. Partnership v. Manns, 333, 339
Grapin v. Grapin, 626, 627
Grappo v. Blanks, 193, 195
Gray Line Bus Co. v. Greater Bridgeport Transit Dist., 1049
Gray v. Francis, 522
Greater Providence Chamber of Commerce v. State of Rhode Island, 170
Green v. Dixon, 197
Green v. Dormitory Auth., 656
Green v. Lupo, 350, 352, 353, 362
Green Party of New Jersey v. Hartz Mountain Industries, Inc., 159
Greenwald v. Greenwald, 598
Greta, In re Adoption of, 55
Griswold v. Connecticut, 860
Grombone v. Krekel, 810
Groucho Marx Prods., Inc. v. Day & Night Co., 1139
Gruen v. Gruen, 75

Grulke, In re Estate of, 512
Gucci American v. Hall & Assocs., 1100
Gulledge, Estate of, 586

Hack v. President and Fellows of Yale College, 898
Hadacheck v. Sebastian, 916, 928, 961, 962, 963, 968, 970, 994, 1000, 1018
Haddad v. Gonzalez, 740
Hagemann v. Worth, 409, 411
Hail v. Reed, 87
Haith v. Atchison County, 236
Hale v. Osborn Coal Enters., Inc., 914
Halley v. Harden Oil Co., 657
Hall v. Community of Damien of Molokai, 409, 410, 411, 895
Hall v. Phillips, 281
Halpern v. Lacy Inv. Corp., 196
Halprin v. Prairie Single Family Homes of Dearborn Park Ass'n, 835
Halverson v. Skagit Country, 236
Hammer, State v., 1050
Hampton v. Dillard Dept. Stores, Inc., 128
Han Farms, Inc. v. Molitor, 211
Hanes v. Continental Grain Co., 271
Hankins v. Mathews, 450
Hannah v. Sibcy Cline Realtors, 835
Harambasic v. Owens, 212
Harding v. Ja Laur, 797
Hardy, In re Estate of, 781
Harjo v. Pro-Football, Inc., 144
Harms v. Sprague, 586
Harper v. Coleman, 714
Harris v. Capital Growth Investors XIV, 869
Harris v. Forklift Sytems, Inc., 841
Harris v. Lynch, 192
Hartnett v. Jones, 552
Haugan v. Haugan, 605
Havens Realty Corp. v. Coleman, 831
HealthSouth Rehabilitation Corp. v. Falcon Management Co., 669
Heart of Atlanta Motel, Inc. v. United States, 127, 968, 982, 984, 985, 986, 988
Hecht v. Superior Court, 53
Heiman v. Parish, 76
Heins Implement Co. v. Missouri Highway & Transportation Commn., 237
Hemisphere Building Co. v. Village of Richton Park, 896
Hendle v. Stevens, 97
Henley v. Continental Cablevision, 358
Henry v. Dalton, 331
Hermitage Methodist Homes v. Dominion Trust Co., 559
Hernandez v. Stabach, 737, 738
Herren v. Pettengill, 363
Hewitt v. Hewitt, 612, 614, 615
Hewitt v. Meaney, 342, 343

H.E.Y. Trust v. Popcorn Express Co., 656
Hickey v. Green, 760
Hidden Harbour Estates, Inc. v. Basso, 456
Hilder v. St. Peter, 717, 718, 719, 740
Hills Dev. Co. v. Bernards Twp., 909
Hillview Assocs. v. Bloomquist, 726, 736
Hoak v. Hoak, 605
Hodel v. Irving, 64, 65, 67, 68, 956, 968, 1016
Hodge v. Ginsberg, 31
Hodge v. Sloan, 369
Hodgins v. Sales, 212
Hoery v. United States, 272
Hoffman v. Capitol Cablevision System, Inc., 360
Hoffman v. United Iron and Metal Co., 211
Hohri v. United States, 1025
Holbrook v. Taylor, 321, 329, 332
Hollett, In re Estate of, 598
Holley v. Crank, 831
Holman v. Indiana, 843
Holmdel Builders Assn. v. Holmdel, 1037
Holmes v. Sprint United Telephone of Kansas, 361
Holterman v. Holterman, 605
Holy Properties Ltd. v. Kenneth Cole Products, Inc., 667
Home Builders Ass'n of Dayton & Miami Valley v. City of Beaver Creek, 1037
Home Builders Ass'n of Northern California v. City of Napa, 1039
Home Building & Loan Assn. v. Blaisdell, 803, 982
Horizon House v. Town of Upper Southampton, 893
Hornell Brewing Co. v. Rosebud Sioux Tribal Court, 1140
Horn v. Lawyers Title Ins. Corp., 798
Hornwood v. Smith's Food King No. 1, 694
Horse Pond Fish & Game Club, Inc. v. Cormier, 451, 461, 464, 465
Houle v. Adams State College, 656
Housing Auth. v. Pappion, 865
Housing Auth. v. Southern Railway, 1050
Housing & Redevelopment Auth. v. Naegele Outdoor Adver. Co., 1050
Houston & T.C. Ry. Co. v. East, 252, 261
Hovendick v. Ruby, 192
Howard v. Kunto, 194
Howard Opera House Ass'n v. Urban Outfitters, Inc., 271
Howson v. Crombie Street Congregational Church, 524
Hoyts Cinemas Corp., United States v., 151
Hubert v. Williams, 860
Hudgens v. National Labor Relations Bd., 105, 158, 161, 162, 163
Hudson v. Vandiver, 814
Hudson v. Weiss, 674, 858

Huggins v. Wright, 363
Hughes Memorial Home, United States v., 527
Hughes v. Washington, 974
Human Rights Commn. v. Labrie, Inc., 844
Huntington Branch, NAACP v. Town of Huntington, 871
Hunziker v. State, 1012
Hurd v. Hughes, 589

Ileto v. Glock, Inc., 283
Illinois Cent. R.R. Co. v. Illinois, 166
Illinois Dev. Auth. V. Nat'l City Envtl., 1066
Imperial Colliery Co. v. Fout, 730
Inhabitants of Middlefield v. Church Mills Knitting Co., 10
In re. *See name of party or matter*
Intel Corp. v. Hamidi, 115
International Commn. on English in the Liturgy v. Schwartz, 667, 708
International News Serv. v. Associated Press, 32
In the Matter of. *See name of party*

Jackson v. Seymour, 564, 565
Jackson v. Williams, 407, 408
James v. Arms Technology, Inc., 283
Janian v. Barnes, 774
Janssen v. Holland Charter Twp. Zoning Bd. of Appeals, 930
Jacque v. Steenberg Homes, Inc., 116
Jarvis v. Gillespie, 192
Jasniowski v. Rushing, 854
Javins v. First Natl. Realty Corp., 709, 719
J.B. v. M.B., 1164, 1165
Jedlicka v. Clemmer, 224
Jenkins v. CSX Transportation, Inc., 277
Jiggetts v. Grinker, 31
Johnson v. Calvert, 1160, 1161
Johnson v. Cherry, 814
Johnson v. City of Dallas, 174
Johnson v. Coshatt, 212
Johnson v. Davis, 767
Johnson v. M'Intosh, 4, 14, 16, 19, 29, 76, 1070, 1152
Johnson v. Stanley, 212
Johnson v. Whiton, 528
Johnson v. Zaremba, 837
Jones v. Alfred Mayer Co., 127, 129, 835
Jones v. Cullen, 212
Jones v. Wagner, 215
Joplin Enters. v. Allen, 1138
Jordache Enters., Inc. v. Levi Strauss & Co., 1088
Jorgensen v. Crow, 781
Judy B. v. Borough of Tioga, 895
Julian v. Christopher, 690
Just v. Marinette County, 1010

Kahn v. Brookline Rent Control Bd., 700
Kahnovsky v. Kahnovsky, 579
Kaiser Aetna v. United States, 956, 967, 969, 970, 977, 978, 980, 985, 996, 999, 1018, 1028, 1032
Ka Pa'akai O Ka'aina v. Land Use Commn., State of Hawaii, 172
Karesh v. City Council of Charleston, 1066
Kass v. Kass, 1163, 1164
Katzenbach v. McClung, 127
Keller v. Southwood North Medical Pavilion, Inc., 657
Kellner v. Capelini, 281
Kelo v. City of New London, 1051
Kelly v. Schmelz, 361
Kendall v. Ernest Pestana, Inc., 683, 689
Kenney v. Morgan, 462
Keshbro, Inc. v. City of Miami, 635, 1024
Kesler v. Marshall, 778
Keystone Bituminous Coal Assn. v. DeBenedictis, 280, 919, 965, 966, 967, 969, 1000, 1018
Kimball Laundry Co. v. United States, 966, 1046, 1050
Kincheloe v. Milatzo, 382
King, In re Marriage of, 71
Kingston v. Lawrence, 552
Kipp v. Chips Estate, 572
Kirchberg v. Feenstra, 576, 591, 1015
Kitchen v. Kitchen, 332
Klebs v. Yim, 248, 249
Kline v. 1500 Massachusetts Ave. Apt. Corp., 741
Knight v. Hallsthammar, 715
Knitwaves, Inc. v. Lollytogs, Ltd., 43
Knost v. Knost, 562
Knudtson v. Trainor, 409
Knuth v. Vogels, 217
Koenig v. Van Reken, 812, 814
Koeppen v. Bolich, 409
Kopp v. Kopp, 573, 592
Kopp v. Samaritan Health System, Inc., 843
Korematsu v. United States, 1025
Koresko v. Farley, 215
Kracl v. Loseke, 770
Krause v. Taylor, 362
Kresha v. Kresha, 584, 587
Kreshover v. Berger, 773
Kresser v. Peterson, 781
Krohn, In re, 803
Krosmico v. Pettit, 192
Krueger v. Cuomo, 841

Ladue v. Horn, 890
Laguna Gatuna, Inc. v. United States, 1010
Laguna Royale Owners Assn. v. Darger, 463
Lake of the Woods Assn., Inc. v. McHugh, 552, 1015

Landgate, Inc. v. California Coastal Commn., 1042

Lane v. W.J. Curry & Sons, 215, 283

Lange v. Scofield, 417

Langlois v. Abington Hous. Auth., 879

Lara v. Cinemark USA, Inc., 151

Large v. Clinchfield Coal Co., 259

Larkin v. State of Michigan, 894

Lawrence v. Texas, 622, 856

Lawrence v. Town of Concord, 193

Layton v. A.I. Namm & Sons, 658

Lealand Tenants Assn., Inc. v. Johnson, 700

Leardi v. Brown, 738

Leasehold Interest in Nostrand Ave., United States v., 633

Lechmere v. NLRB, 163

Leffingwell v. Glendenning, 217

Lepore, United States v., 847

Levandusky v. One Fifth Avenue Apartment Corp, Matter of, 488

Levin v. Yeshiva University, 897

Lew v. Superior Court, 273, 282

Lewis v. Searles, 561

Lewis v. Young, 363

Lewitz v. Porath Family Trust, 353

Leydon v. Town of Greenwich, 171

Limestone Dev. Corp. v. Village of Lemont, 214

Lindh v. Surman, 76

Lindsey v. Normet, 661

Lindsey, In re Marriage of, 718

Lingle v. Chevron U.S.A. Inc., 955, 956, 957, 968, 984, 1007, 1037, 1039, 1058

Lingvall v. Bartmess, 212

Lipton v. Lipton, 76

Litowitz v. Litowitz, 1165

Littlefield v. Mack, 832

Livingwell (North) Inc. v. Pennsylvania Human Relations Commn., 143

Lloyd Corp., Ltd. v. Tanner, 105, *153*, 159, 161, 162

Lloyd Realty Corp. v. Albino, 634

Local 1330, United Steel Workers v. United States Steel Corp., 55

Locklin v. City of Lafayette, 237

Loehr v. Kincannon, 461

Lombardo v. Albu, 748

Lone Wolf v. Hitchcock, 1031, 1078

Long v. Dilling Mechanical Contractors, Inc., 97

Long Branch, City of, v. Liu, 225

Loren v. Marry, 657

Loretto v. Teleprompter Manhattan CATV Corp., 956, 968, *979*, 984, 984, 985, 988, 989, 990, 992, 1007, 1008, 1039

Los Angeles County 1207 v. Continental Development Corp., 1050

Los Angeles Gas & Elec. Corp. v. Railroad Commn., 1049

Los Osos Valley Assocs. v. City of San Luis Obispo, 259

Love v. Amsler, 737

Love v. Bd. of Cty. Commrs. of Bingham Cty., 913

Loveladies Harbor, Inc. v. United States, 1010

Loving v. Virginia, 566, 621

Lucas v. Rawl Family Ltd. Partn., 236

Lucas v. South Carolina Coastal Council, 956, 968, 970, *991*, 1007, 1008, 1010, 1011, 1012, 1025

M & I First Natl. Bank v. Episcopal Homes Mgmt., Inc., 657

M.P.M. Builders, LLC v. Dwyer, 363

MacDonald, Sommer & Frates v. Yolo County, 1004, 1008

Mace v. Mace, 605

Machipongo Land & Coal Co. v. Commw. of Pennsylvania, 967

MacMeekin v. Low Income Housing Institute, Inc., 364

MacNeil v. Time Ins. Co., 152

Madden v. Queens County Jockey Club, Inc., 121

Magoun v. Illinois Trust and Savings Bank, 1016

Mahoney v. Mahoney, 605

Mains Farm Homeowners Assn. v. Worthington, 409

Maioriello v. Arlotta, 277, 308

Malcolm v. Shamie, 410

Mallock v. Southern Memorial Park, Inc., 1169

Mansour Properties v. I-85/GA. 20 Ventures, Inc., 573

Manufactured Housing Communities of Washington v. State of Washington, 573

Manufacturers Gas & Oil Co. v. Indiana Natural Gas & Oil Co., 88

Marbury v. Madison, 1152

Mardis v. Brantley, 462

Marina Point, Ltd. v. Wolfson, 870

Marioni v. 94 Broadway, Inc., 777

Markham v. Colonial Mortgage Serv. Co., 855

Marks v. City of Chesapeake, 940

Marriage of . *See name of party*

Marsh v. Alabama, 105, 153, 154, 156, 157, 158, 159, 161

Martin A. v. Gross, 31

Martin Luther King, Jr. Ctr. for Social Change v. American Heritage Prods., 1129

Martin v. City of Seattle, 508

Marvin v. Marvin, 613, 615

Marzocca v. Ferone, 122

Mason v. Loveless, 224

Massachusetts Coalition for the Homeless v.
  Secretary of Human Services, 31
Matcha v. Mattox, 172
Matthews v. Bay Head Improvement Assn., 164,
  173
Matthews v. Wozencraft, 1138
Maxwell v. Eckert, 578
Maynard v. Hill, 856
McBryde Sugar Co. v. Robinson, 973
McCabe v. City of Parkersburg, 244
McCaleb v. Pizza Hut of America, Inc., 128
McCarthy v. Tobin, 766
McCoy v. Love, 794
McCready v. Hoffius, 849, 855
McDonald v. Halvorson, 172, 973
McDonald v. Harris, 211
McDonnell Douglas Corp. v. Green, 823
McFadden v. Elma Country Club, 855
McGill v. Wahl, 212
McLaughlin v. Board of Selectmen of
  Amherst, 353
McMinn v. Town of Oyster Bay, 890
McQueen v. Black, 196
McSparron v. McSparron, 605
Medical Laboratory Management Consultants v.
  ABC, 114
Melms v. Pabst Brewing Co., 556
Melnick v. CSX Corp., 284
Memphis, City of v. Greene, 836
Mendoza v. Licensing Bd. of Fall River, 941
Mercantile-Safe Deposit & Trust Co. v. Mayor
  of Baltimore, 387
Meritor Sav. Bank, FSB v. Vinson, 841
Merritt v. McNabb, 461
Metro-Goldwyn-Mayer Studios Inc. v. Grokster,
  Ltd., 1100
Metropolitan Board of Zoning v. McDonald's
  Corp., 930
Metropolitan Hous. Dev. Corp. v. Village of
  Arlington Heights, 874
Metzner v. Wojdyla, 411
Meyer v. Holley, 831
Meyer v. Meyer, 598
Miami, City of, v. Keshbro, Inc., 282
Midler v. Ford Motor Co., 1137
Midrash Sephardi, Inc. v. Town of Surfside,
  898
Mid-Valley Resources, Inc. v. Engelson, 196
Mihalczo v. Borough of Woodmont, 213
Miller v. Schoene, 928, *957,* 961, 963, 967, 968,
  994, 1000, 1011, 1018
Milne v. Milne, 627
Minieri v. Knittel, 622
Minjak Co. v. Randolph, 701, 707, 718, 719
Mississippi Power Co. v. Fairchild, 344
Mister v. A.R.K. Partnership, 854
Mitchel v. United States, 13, 19
Mitchell, United States v., 831, 1045, 1050

Monterey v. Del Monte Dunes at Monterey,
  Ltd., 957, 1008, 1009, 1037, 1039
Moore v. City of E. Cleveland, 999, 1033
Moore v. Phillips, 553
Moore v. Regents of the Univ. of California, 45,
  53
Morone v. Morone, 615
Morris v. Cizek, 837
Morris v. Nease, 416, 417
Morris v. Office Max, Inc., 128
Morrison & Foerster v. Wicke, 1093
Morrissey v. Haley, 223
Morvant, United States v., 150
Mr. Sign Sign Studios, Inc. v. Miguel, 549
Mugler v. Kansas, 915, 961, 968, 970, 994, 999,
  1000, 1003, 1015, 1018
Muldawer v. Stribling, 387
Mulkey v. Waggoner, 775
Mulligan v. Panther Valley Property Owners
  Assn., 481
Muskatell v. City of Seattle, 259

NAACP v. Alabama, 860
Nabisco, Inc. v. PF Brands, Inc., 1092
Nahrstedt v. Lakeside Village Condominium
  Assn., 427, 480, 481, 482
Nash v. City of Santa Monica, 988
Nation v. Apache Greyhound Park, Inc.,
  121
National Basketball Assn. v. Motorola, Inc.,
  43, 44, 45
Nectow v. City of Cambridge, 920, 922, 940
Nelson v. American Tel. & Tel. Co., 332
Neponsit Property Owners' Assn., Inc. v.
  Emigrant Indus. Sav. Bank, 388, 402
Neptune City, Borough of, v. Borough of
  Avon-by-the-Sea, 164
Neudecker v. Boisclair Corp., 843
New Haverford Partn. v. Stroot, 738
New Jersey Coalition Against War in the
  Middle East v. J.M.B. Realty Corp., 158
Neuman v. Grandview at Emerald Hills, Inc.
  485
Newman v. Hinky Dinky Omaha-Lincoln,
  Inc., 691
Newman v. Sathyavaglswaran, 52
New York, State of v. Fermenta ASC Corp.,
  272, 281
New York v. Merlino, 841
New York, City of, v. Utsey, 657
New York State Club Assn., Inc. v. City of
  New York, 141
Nicholson v. Broadway Corp., 388
Nickels v. Cohn, 797
Noah v. AOL Time Warner Inc., 143
Noble v. Murphy, 480
Nobrega v. Edison Glen Associates, 747,
  771

Nollan v. California Coastal Commn., 957, 985, 994, 1028, 1029, 1035, 1036, 1037, 1038, 1039, 1040

Nome 2000 v. Fagerstrom, 187, 198, 207

Noone v. Price, 243, 248

North Dakota Fair Housing Council, Inc. v. Peterson, 855

North Shore Steak House, Inc. v. Board of Appeals, 937

Northwest Real Estate Co. v. Serio, 453, 462, 464

Nwakpuda v. Falley's, Inc., 128

Oakland, City of, v. Oakland Raiders, 1065

Oakwood Village LLC v. Albertsons, Inc., 695

Obde v. Schlemeyer, 771

O'Brien v. O'Brien, 599, 607

O'Buck v. Cottonwood Village Condominium Assn., Inc., 483

Oceanside, City of, v. McKenna, 465

Oceanside Community Assocs. v. Oceanside Land Co., 389

Office One, Inc. v. Lopez, 942

Old Canton Hills Homeowners Assn. v. City of Jackson, 914

Olds v. Appleby, 116

Olin v. Goehler, 706

Olivas v. Olivas, 576

O'Keeffe v. Snyder, 225

Omega Corp. of Chesterfield v. Malloy, 410

Oncale v. Sundowner Offshore Servs., Inc., 842

Oneida, County of, v. Oneida Indian Nation, 21

Oneida Indian Nation v. County of Oneida, 21

Opinion No. 26, In re, 746

Opinion of the Justices, 171

Optivision, Inc. v. Syracuse Shopping Ctr. Assocs., 472

Oregon, State of, v. Fullerton, 1050

Oregon Paralyzed Veterans of America v. Regal Cinemas, Inc., 151

Ortega v. Flaim, 715

Osborne v. Power, 273

Oxford House, Inc. v. Town of Babylon, 895

Oyama v. California, 20

Padilla v. Lawrence, 271

Page County Appliance Ctr., Inc. v. Honeywell, Inc., 273

Palazzolo v. Rhode Island, 956, 984, 1004, 1007, 1009, 1010

Palm Beach Isles Assocs. v. United States, 1010

Palm Point Property Owners' Assn. v. Pisarski, 402

Palmer v. Protrka, 578

Palmer v. Thompson, 449

Palumbo v. Donalds, 667

Parker v. Metropolitan Life Ins. Co., 152

Parker v. Shecut, 575

Parks Hiway Enterprises, LLC v. CEM Leasing, Inc., 281

Parks v. La Face Records, 1138, 1139

Pascale v. Pascale, 74, 627

Pascoag Reservoir & Dam, LLC v. State of Rhode Island, 1061

Patterson v. McLean Credit Union, 127

Penn Central Transp. Co. v. City of New York, 928, 955, 956, *959,* 966, 967, 968, 969, 970, 975, 976, 982, 992, 993, 994, 1000, 1005, 1007, 1019, 1030, 1033

Pennell v. City of San Jose, 676, 785, 940, 957, 968, 970, 1036

Pennsylvania Coal Co. v. Mahon, 916, 919, 922, 960, 961, 963, 965, 966, 967, 968, 977, 992, 993, 996, 1028

Pension Benefit Guaranty Corp. v. R.A. Gray & Co., 1019

People of. *See name of state*

People ex rel. Moloney v. Pullman's Palace Car Co., 495

Percheman, United States v., 14

Perez v. Bd. of Appeals of Norwood, 930

Perkins v. Perkins, 72

Permian Basin Centers for Mental Health and Mental Retardation v. Alsobrook, 409

Perry v. Command Performance, 127

Perry v. Heirs at Law and Distributees of Gadsden, 196

Petersen v. Hartell, 810, 811

Peterson v. Beekmere, Inc., 403

Peterson v. Superior Court, 739

Peterson v. Tremain, 550

Petitions for Rulemaking, In re, 31

Petsch v. Widger, 196, 207

Petty Motor Co., United States v., 1044

Pfaff v. HUD, 878

PGA Tour, Inc. v. Martin, 152

Philip Morris, Inc. v. Reilly, 1038

Phillip v. University of Rochester, 128

Phillips v. Pembroke Real Estate, Inc., 1141

Phillips v. Washington Legal Foundation, 989

Pickens v. Pickens, 616, 619

Pierce v. Casady, 215

Pierson v. Post, 76, 77, 78, *83*

Pinkston v. Hartley, 329

Pipes v. Sevier, 781

Pizza, State ex rel., v. Rezcallah, 635, 1025

Platts v. Sacramento N. Ry., 259

Plummer, In re Marriage of, 627

PMZ Oil Co. v. Lucroy, 381

Poff v. Caro, 863

Poletown Neighborhood Council v. City of Detroit, 1065

Popov v. Hayashi, 79, 83

Portland Natural Gas Transp. System v. 19.2
    Acres of Land, 1050
Portola Hills Community Assn. v. James, 402,
    481
Posik v. Layton, 621
Potomac Group Home Corp. v. Montgomery
    County, Maryland, 894
Pottinger v. City of Miami, 173, 175
Powell v. Pennsylvania, 915
Powers v. Judd, 236
Prah v. Maretti, 238, *302*, 309
Presbytery of Seattle v. King County, 1010
Presbytery of Southeast Iowa v. Harris, 536
Price ex rel. Estate of Price v. City of Seattle,
    249
Price Waterhouse v. Hopkins, 842
Prieskorn v. Maloof, 526
Prince George's County v. Sunrise
    Development Ltd. Partn., 935
Pritchett v. Turner, 462
Propst v. McNeill, 718
Professional Realty Corp. v. Bender, 747
Pro-Football, Inc. v. Harjo, 144
Prospect Development Co., Inc. v. Bershader,
    329
Prudential Residential Services Ltd. Partn.,
    774
PruneYard Shopping Ctr. v. Robins, 158, 161,
    162, *976*, 980, 983, 984, 985, 1032
Public Access Shoreline Hawaii (PASH) v.
    Hawaii County Planning Commn., 172
Public Service Co. of Colo. v. Van Wyck, 272
Puchalski v. Wedemeyer, 383
Puget Sound Serv. Corp. v. Dalarna Mgmt.
    Corp., 770
Pugh v. Holmes, 714
Pumpelly v. Green Bay Co., 968, 980, 984
Puttrich v. Smith, 987

Qualitex Co. v. Jacobson Products Co., 1089
Quarles v. Arcega, 197
Quinnipiac Council, Boy Scouts of Am., Inc.
    v. Commn. on Human Rights &
    Opportunities, 129, 142

Ragin v. New York Times Co., 832
Raintree of Albemarle Homeowners Assn. v.
    Jones, 402
Raleigh Avenue Beach Ass'n. v. Atlantis Beach
    Club, Inc., 170, 172
Ramsey v. Ramsey, 73
Rando v. Town of North Attleboro, 914
Rase v. Castle Mountain Ranch, Inc., 323, 329,
    332, 736
Ray v. Montgomery, 770
Reed v. King, 771
Reeves v. Carrollsburg Condominium Unit
    Owners Ass'n, 843

Reeves v. Sanderson Plumbing Products, Inc.,
    831
Regency Homes Assn. v. Egermayer, 388
Rent Stabilization Assocs. v. Higgins, 675
Reynolds v. Gagen, 550
R.H. Macy & Co. v. May Department Stores
    Co., 461
RHN Corp. v. Veibell, 224
Rhodes v. Cahill, 193
Rhone v. Loomis, 127
Rice v. Sioux City Mem. Park Cemetery, 448
Rich v. Emerson-Dumont Distrib. Corp., 747
Riddle v. Harmon, 572
Riley v. Bear Creek Planning Comm., 399
Ringling Bros.–Barnum & Bailey Combined
    Shows, Inc. v. Utah Div. of Travel Dev.,
    1093
Riss v. Angel, 408
Riste v. Eastern Washington Bible Camp, Inc.,
    454, 462, 464
River Heights Assocs. L.P. v. Batten, 415
Riverview Realty Co. v. Perosio, 664
Roaring Fork Club L.P. v. St. Jude's Co., 364
Robarge v. Willett, 195
Roberts v. Estate of Barbagallo, 771
Roberts v. Rhodes, 523
Roberts v. United States Jaycees, 141, 142
Robins v. PruneYard Shopping Center, 161
Robinson v. Ariyoshi, 973
Robinson v. Diamond Hous. Corp., 733, 736
Robinson v. Trousdale County, 591
Robroy Land Co. Inc. v. Prather, 552
Rodrigue v. Copeland, 273
Rodirguez v. Bethlehem Steel Corp., 687
Rodriguez v. Cambridge Housing Authority,
    740, 741
Rodriguez v. Montalvo, 867
Roehrs v. Lees, 387
Rogers v. Grimaldi, 1139
Rogers v. Marlin, 211
Romero v. Garcia, *185*, 197
Ron Greenspan Volkswagen, Inc. v. Ford
    Motor Land Development Corp., 775
Roper v. Camuso, 402
Roper v. Edwards, 465
Rosengarten v. Downes, 620
Roussalis v. Wyoming Medical Center, 765
Ruckelshaus v. Monsanto, 1038, 1055
Runyon v. McCrary, 127
Runyon v. Paley, 384, 387, 388
Russakoff v. Scruggs, 341

Sabato v. Sabato, 987
Sabo v. Horvath, *787*, 789, 790
Sambo's Restaurant, Inc. v. City of Ann
    Arbor, 144
Salmon v. Peterson, 249
Salter v. Hamiter, 781

Salucco v. Alldredge, 620
Sanborn v. McLean, 399, 402, 403
San Diego Gas & Elec. Co. v. Superior Court, 227, 271
Sander v. Ball, 463
Sanford v. Vinal, 1169
San Remo Hotel L.P. v. City and County of San Francisco, 1009, 1037, 1038, 1039
Santa Barbara v. Adamson, 890
San Telmo Assoc. v. City of Seattle, 1038
Saunders v. General Serv. Corp., 833
Save Our Rural Environment v. Snohomish County, 938
Sawada v. Endo, 587, 591
Schaefer v. Peoples Heritage Savings Bank, 587
Schaefer v. Schaefer, 607
Scheg v. Agway, Inc., 283
Schlup v. Bourdon, 383
Schmid, State v., 118, 158
Schneider Natl. Carriers, Inc. v. Bates, 271, 273
Schovee v. Mikolasko, 401
Schuett Inv. Co. v. Anderson, 865
Schwab v. Rondel Homes, Inc., 865
Schwab, State v., 737
Schwab v. Timmons, 344
Scott Hudgens, 105
Seattle, City of, v. McCoy, 282, 940, 1025
Seattle-First Natl. Bank v. NLRB, 163
Seawall Assocs. v. City of New York, 988
Sebastian v. Floyd, 808, 810
Sellers v. Philip's Barber Shop, 127
SEPTA v. Philadelphia Transp. Co., 543, 544, 551, 552
Shack, State v., 104, 115, 118, 171, 647
Shalimar Assn. v. D.O.C. Enters., Inc., 389, 417
Shapira v. Union Natl. Bank, 566
Shapiro v. Sutherland, 771
Sharp v. Sumner, 765
Sharper v. Harlem Teams for Self-Help, 332
Shaver v. Hunter, 409, 410, 411
Shelley v. Kraemer, 433, 443, 445, 446, 447, 448, 449, 558, 559, 560, 561, 566
Shelley's Case, 512
Shelton v. Strickland, 194
Shepard v. Purvine, 331
Sherrill v. Oneida Indian Nation of New York, 22
Shiffman v. Empire Blue Cross and Blue Shield, 114, 115
Shirley v. Shirley, 345
Shiver v. Benton, 552
Shoshone Tribe v. United States, 1078
Shotwell v. Transamerica Title Ins. Co., 798
Shpak v. Oletsky, 343
Shultz v. Johnson, 223

Shutes v. Platte Chem. Co., 271
Silverleib v. Hebshie, 332
Silvester v. Spring Valley Country Club, 271
Silvicraft, Inc. v. Southeast Timber Co., 550
Simeone v. Simeone, 598
Simms v. First Gilbraltar Bank, 878
Simon v. Solomon, 741
Sioux Nation of Indians, United States v., 634
Sipriano v. Great Springs Waters of America, Inc., 90
Sixty Acres in Etowah County, United States v., 634
Skelly Oil Co. v. Ashmore, 779
Skendzel v. Marshall, 810, 811
Slavin v. Rent Control Bd. of Brookline, 688, 691
Smith v. Fair Employment and Housing Commission, 850
Smith v. First Sav. of Louisiana, 379, 402
Smith v. Hayden, 192, 193
Smith v, Krebs, 189
Smith v. Lagow Construction & Developing Co., 741
Smith v. Mitchell, 462
Smith v. Rucker, 572
Smith v. Tippett, 193, 194, 196
Smith v. Wade, 825
Smith & Lee Associates, Inc. v. City of Taylor, 895
Snow v. Van Dam, 403
Snyder v. Lovercheck, 775
Sofsky v. Rosenberg, 781
Solomon R. Guggenheim Found. v. Lubell, 226
Somerville v. Jacobs, 218, 222
Sommer v. Kridel, 770, 666
Songbyrd, Inc. v. Estate of Albert B. Grossman, 225
Sony Corp. v. Universal City Studios, Inc., 1099
South Suburban Hous. Ctr. v. Greater S. Suburban Bd. of Realtors, 834
Southeastern Pennsylvania Transp. Authority v. Philadelphia Transp. Co., 548, 550
Southern Burlington County NAACP v. Township of Mount Laurel (Mount Laurel I), 899, 907
Southwestern Illinois Dev. Auth. v. Nat'l City Envtl. , 1066
Spall v. Janota, 248
Spann v. Colonial Village, Inc., 833
Sparling v. Fon du Lac Township, 212
Spears, In re, 576
Spears v. Warr, 765
Spence v. O'Brien, 634
Spencer's Case, 366
Speigle, In re Marriage of, 598
Spinnell v. Quigley, 88

Sprague, State ex rel., v. Madison, 858, 860
Sprecher v. Adamson, 249
Spur Indus. v. Webb, 277
Stallworth v. Stallworth, 73
Stambovsky v. Ackley, 772
Stanley v. Moore, 738
Stansbury v. MDR Development, L.L.C., 341, 342
Staron v. McDonald's Corp., 150
Starrett City Assocs., United States v., 826, 833, 834, 893, 894
State Dept. of Transportation v. Regard, 1050
State ex rel. . *See name of party*
State v. . *See name of party*
State Street Bank & Trust Co. v. Signature Financial Group, 1129
Steagall v. Robinson, 383
Steele v. City of Houston, 1021
Steffens, United States v., 1088
Steiner v. Showboat Operating Co., 843
Stevens v. City of Cannon Beach, 973
Stevenson v. E.F. Dupont de Nemours, 272
Stickney v. City of Saco, 198, 1016
Stiefel v. Lindemann, 211
Stoiber v. Honeychuck, 740
Stolow v. Stolow, 74
Stone v. City of Wilton, 931, 935, 969, 970
Stonebraker v. Zinn, 806, 810
Stonehedge Square v. Movie Merchants, 667
Stoner v. Zucker, 330
Storey v. Patterson, 217
Strawn v. Canuso, 747, 771
Streams Sports Club, Ltd. v. Richmond, 389
Suitum v. Tahoe Regional Planning Agency, 1008
Sullivan v. Porter, 765
Sullivan v. Rooney, 617, 618
Summit Town Centre, Inc. v. Shoe Show of Rocky Mount, Inc., 694
Sun Oil Co. v. Trent Auto Wash, Inc., 369
Suntrust Bank v. Houghton Mifflin Co., 1117
Surrogate Parenting Assocs. v. Commonwealth ex rel. Armstrong, 1160
Swan v. Hill, 343
Swanner v. Anchorage Equal Rights Commn., 850
Sweeney v. Landings Association, Inc., 425

Tahoe-Sierra Preservation Council, Inc. v. Tahoe Regional Planning Agency, 955, 956, 1006
Tapscott v. Lessee of Cobbs, 97, 201
Tasunke Witko v. G. Heileman Brewing Co., 1140
Taylor v. Canterbury, 572
Tee-Hit-Ton Indians v. United States, 14, 19, 1080, 1083
T & E Indus. v. Safety Light Corp., 273

Templeton Arms v. Feins, 700
Tenhet v. Boswell, 581, 586, 587
Tenn v. 889 Assocs., Ltd., 308
Tennsco Corp. v. Attea, 384
Terrien v. Zwit, 482
Territory v. Gay, 973
Terry v. Lock Hospitality, Inc., 96
Texaco Ref. & Mktg., Inc. v. Samowitz, 545, 550
Thomas v. Anchorage Equal Rights Commn., 850, 851, 855, 856
Thomas v. Goudreault, 740
Thomson, Estate of, v. Wade, 345
Thornton, State ex rel., v. Hay, 168, 172, 973
Thurston v. Hancock, 248
Tilden v. Hayward, 31
Tioga Coal Co. v. Supermarkets Gen. Corp., 203
Tobe v. City of Santa Ana, 175
Tobias v. Dailey, 342
Toledo Bar Ass'n v. Chelsea Title Agency of Dayton, Inc., 746
Tolksdorf v. Griffith, 1065
Toll Brothers, Inc. v. Township of West Windsor, 909
Totman v. Malloy, 207
Town of . *See name of town*
Traders, Inc. v. Bartholomew, 343
Trentacost v. Brussel, 648
Tresemer v. Albuquerque Pub. Sch. Dist., 224
Tri-Properties, Inc. v. Moonspinner Condominium Assn., Inc., 432
Tristram's Landing, Inc. v. Wait, 745
Troy v. Renna, 990
Trustees of Schools of Township No. 1 v. Batdorf, 536, 1015
Tsombanidis v. City of West Haven, 895
Tucker v. Toia, 31
Tulare Lake Basin Water Storage District v. United States, 1010
Tulk v. Moxhay, 366
Tupper v. Dorchester County, 353
Turner v. Wong, 128
Twitchell, Commonwealth v., 55
Tyne v. Time Warner Entertainment Co., 1139

Umphres v. J.R. Mayer Enters., Inc., 363
United Food and Commercial Workers Union, Local 919, AFL-CIO v. Crystal Mall Associates, L.P., 160
United Artists Theater Circuit, Inc. v. City of Philadelphia, 975
United States v. . *See name of party*
United States Jaycees v. Bloomfield, 137
United States Jaycees v. Iowa Civil Rights Commn., 137

United States Jaycees v. Massachusetts Commn. Against Discrimination, 143
United States Jaycees v. McClure, 137, 142
United States v. Percheman, 14
Uno Restaurants, Inc. v. Boston Kenmore Realty Corp., 691
Upton v. JWP Businessland, 53, 55
Urban League of Rhode Island v. Sambo's of Rhode Island, 144
Urban Site Venture II Limited Partnership v. Levering Associates, L.P., 216
Urman v. South Boston Savings Bank, 770
Uston v. Airport Casino, Inc., 120
Uston v. Resorts Intl. Hotel, Inc., 116, 120, 123, 171
Ute Park Summer Homes Assn. v. Maxwell Land Grant Co., 382
Uzan v. 845 UN Ltd. P'ship, 778

Valenti v. Hopkins, 481
Van Buren Apartments v. Adams, 736
Vanderwall v. Midkiff, 797
Van Horn, People v., 1169
Vanlandingham v. Ivanow, 717
Vargas v. Esquire, 1141
Vásquez v. Glassboro Serv. Assn., Inc., 478
Vásquez v. Hawthorne, 622
Vegelahn v. Guntner, 654
Ventron Corp., State v., 273
Vermont Natl. Bank v. Chittenden Trust Co., 472
Vigeant v. Donel Realty Trust, 343
Vigil v. Haber, 76
Vigilant Ins. Co. of America v. Housing Authority of the City of El Paso, 225
Villa de las Palmas Homeowners Ass'n v. Terifaj, 482
Villa Nova Resort, Inc. v. State, 214
Village of . *See name of village*
Virtual Works, Inc. v. Volkswagen of America, Inc., 1093
Volusia County v. Aberdeen at Ormond Beach, L.P., 1038
VSH Realty, Inc. v. Texaco, Inc., 775

Waikiki Malia Hotel, Inc. v. Kinkai Properties Ltd. Partnership, 379
Waits v. Frito-Lay, Inc., 1137
Walgreen Co. v. Sara Creek Property Co., 391
Walker Drug Co., Inc. v. La Sal Oil Co., 112
Wall, In re Estate of, 590
Wal-Mart Stores, Inc. v. Samara Bros., Inc., 43
Walton v. City of Red Bluff, 1015
Wana the Bear v. Community Constr., Inc., 1166, 1169, 1171
Warburton v. McKean, 599
Ward v. McGlory, 361
Warnack v. Coneen Family Trust, 211, 212

Warner v. Konover, 690
Warren v. Detlefson, 382
Warsaw v. Chicago Metallic Ceilings, Inc., 209, 212, 217
Washington v. Davis, 878
Washington v. Duty Free Shoppers, Ltd., 127
Washington Legal Foundation v. Texas Equal Access to Justice, 989
Wasserman v. Three Seasons Assn. No. 1, Inc., 848
Watson, Ex Parte, 746
Watson v. Brown, 642
Watson v. Fraternal Order of Eagles, 127, 128
Watts, In re Marriage of, 578
Watts v. Watts, 608, 620
Wayne County v. Hathcock, 1066
Weatherby Lake Improvement Co. v. Sherman, 482
Weaver, In re Estate of, 534
Webb's Fabulous Pharmacies, Inc. v. Beckwith, 989
Wegner v. Milwaukee Mut. Ins. Co., 1012
Weidner v. State, 249, 1016
Weiswasser, State v., 1050
Weller, State v., 738
Welsh v. Boy Scouts of Am., 137
Wendover Road Property Owners Ass'n v. Kornicks, 482
Wendt v. Host International, 1138
Werner v. Graham, 400, 401
Wesley v. Don Stein Buick, Inc., 128
Wesson v. Leone Enterprises, Inc., 639, 716, 718
West v. First Agric. Bank, 1015
West Des Moines, City of, v. Engler, *161*
West Orange, Township of, v. 769 Assocs., 1065
Westfield Homes, Inc. v. Herrick, 481
Westfield Partners, Ltd. v. Hogan, 941
Westland Skating Center v. Gus Machado Buick, Inc., 237
Westleigh v. Conger, 75
Westmoreland & Cambria Natural Gas Co. v. Dewitt, 88
Westwood Homeowners Assn. v. Tenhoff, 410
Whaley v. County of Tuscola, 52
Whetzel v. Jess Fisher Mgmt. Co., 738
White v. Samsung Electronics America, Inc., 1137
Whitehouse Estates, Inc. v. Post, 667
Whitinsville Plaza v. Kotseas, 366, 369, 376, 377, 378, 381, 382, 385, 386, 389, 390, 391, 472
Whittier Terrace Assocs. v. Hampshire, 865
Wigwam Assocs., Inc. v. McBride, 942
Wilcox v. Trautz, 619
Wildenstein & Co. v. Wallis, 552

Willard v. First Church of Christ, Scientist,
     345
Williams v. Cole, 781
Williams v. Mason, 618
Williams v. Poretsky Management, Inc., 841
Williams v. South & South Rentals, 216
Williams Natural Gas Co. v. Perkins, 1051
Williamson County Regional Planning
     Commn. v. Hamilton Bank of Johnson
     City, 1004, 1008
Willowbrook, Village of, v. Olech, 938, 940, 941
Wilson, Matter of Estate of, 527
Wilson v. Handley, 277
Winget v. Gay, 563
Wolinsky v. Kadison, 458, 463, 488
Wood v. Board of County Commrs. Of Fremont
     County, 516, 524
Wood v. Hoglund, 211
Wood v. Leadbitter, 117

Wood v. State, 161
Woodland Manor, III Assocs. v. Reisma, 976
Woodside Village Condominium Association,
     Inc. V. Jahren, 466, 487
Woytus v. Winkler, 448
Wyman v. James, 1038
Wyndham Foundation, Inc. v. Oulton, 490

Yates v. Keane, 1160
Yeakel v. Driscoll, 217
Yee v. City of Escondido, 968, 970, 986, 988
Yogman v. Parrott, 408, 409
Young v. Bryco Arms, 283
Young v. Morrisey, 740

Zuckerman v. Town of Hadley, 910
Zuni Tribe of N.M., United States ex rel., v.
     Platt, 211
Zurstrassen v. Stonier, 793

United States Code of Federal Regulations

24 C.F.R. §966.4(e)(12)   633
40 C.F.R. §§745.101 to 745.107)   741, 773

United States Code

5 U.S.C. §601   974
11 U.S.C. §548(a)   50
12 U.S.C. §§2601-2617 (Real Estate Settlement and Procedures Act)   750
15 U.S.C. §1 et seq.(Sherman Antitrust Act)   472
15 U.S.C. §§1051-1127 (Lanham Act)   1088, 1089,1092
15 U.S.C. §1052   144, 1093
15 U.S.C. §1064   144
15 U.S.C. §1125(c) (Federal Trademark Dilution Act of 1995)   1139
15 U.S.C. §1125(d) (Anticybersquatting Consumer Protection Act)   1093
15 U.S.C. §§3601-3616 (Condominium and Cooperative Conversion Protection and Abuse Relief Act)   432
16 U.S.C. §§470 et seq. (National Historic Preservation Act)   152
17 U.S.C. §§101 et seq. (Copyright Act)   43, 1093, 1094, 1098, 1101
17 U.S.C. §§101, 106A, 113 (Visual Artists Rights Act of 1990)   1141
17 U.S.C. §504(c)(1)   1115
18 U.S.C. §881   633
18 U.S.C. §881(a)(7) (repealed)   633
18 U.S.C. §§981-985   632
18 U.S.C. §983(c)   634
18 U.S.C. §983(c)(1), (2)   633
18 U.S.C. §983(c)(3)   634
18 U.S.C. §983(d)   633
18 U.S.C. §1162   1072
20 U.S.C. §§80q to 80q-15 (National Museum of the Indian Act)   1170

21 U.S.C. §881   632
21 U.S.C. §881(a)(7) (Civil Asset Forfeiture Reform Act)   632
25 U.S.C. §§70 et seq. (Indian Claims Commission Act)   20, 1077
25 U.S.C. §177 (Trade and Intercourse Act)   20, 1069
25 U.S.C. §§461-479 (Indian Reorganization Act)   65, 1071
25 U.S.C. §1301 (Indian Civil Rights Act of 1968)   1072
25 U.S.C. §§1721 et seq. (Maine Indian Claims Settlement Act)   23
25 U.S.C. §2206 (Indian Land Consolidation Act)   64, 66, 1016
25 U.S.C. §§3001-3013   1169, 1170
18 U.S.C. §1170 (Native American Graves Protection and Repatriation Act)   96, 1169
28 U.S.C. §1360   1072
28 U.S.C. §1362   22
28 U.S.C. §1505   14
28 U.S.C. §1738 (Full Faith and Credit Statute)   1009
28 U.S.C. §1738C (Defense of Marriage Act)   623
29 U.S.C. §§151 et seq. (National Labor Relations Act)   105, 731
29 U.S.C. §§157, 158 (National Labor Relations Act)   162
29 U.S.C. §206   1159
29 U.S.C. §§651 et seq. (Occupation Safety and Health Act of 1970)   647, 1159
29 U.S.C. §794 (Federal Rehabilitation Act of 1973)   864, 865
29 U.S.C. §§2101-2102 (Worker Adjustment and Retraining Notification Act)   62
31 U.S.C. §§5311-5355 (Bank Secrecy Act)   744
31 U.S.C. §5312 (U)   744
33 U.S.C. §§1251-1376 (Clean Water Act)   282
35. U.S.C. §§et seq.   1128
35 U.S.C. §§154, 173   1091

35 U.S.C. §271(b), (c)	1105
36 U.S.C. §30901	133, 138
42 U.S.C. §§601-619 (Personal Responsibility and Work Opportunity Act of 1996)	31, 55
42 U.S.C. §1437d(*l*)	633, 700, 1025
42 U.S.C. §1437f	868
42 U.S.C. §1437f(d)(1)(4)	700
42 U.S.C. §1437f(d)(1)(B)	699, 700
42 U.S.C. §§1981-1982 (*Civil Rights Act of 1866*)	125, 126, 320, 436, 446, 558, 884
42 U.S.C. §1982 (Civil Rights Act of 1866)	125, 126, 436, 446, 450, 450, 823, 835, 884
42 U.S.C. §1983	558, 883, 942, 957
42 U.S.C. §§2000a to 2000a-6 (*Civil Rights Act of 1964, Title II*)	124, 126, 128, 144, 149, 986
42 U.S.C. §§2000bb to 2000bb-4 (Religious Freedom Restoration Act)	857
42 U.S.C. §§2000cc to 20000cc-5 (Religious Land Use and Constitutional Persons Act of 2000)	898
42 U.S.C. §§2701 et seq. (Economic Opportunity Act of 1964)	106
42 U.S.C. §2809	104
42 U.S.C. §§2861-2864	104
42 U.S.C. §§3601-3619, 3631 (*Fair Housing Act*)	145, 446, 776, 803, 817, 822, 827, 829, 830, 847, 848, 866, 871, 881, 882, 894 (at 964, *Fair Housing Amendments Act of 1988*)
42 U.S.C. §§4851-4856 (Residential Lead-Based Paint Hazard Reduction Act)	741, 773
42 U.S.C. §§5301-20 (Housing and Community Development Act of 1974)	873
42 U.S.C. §§6901-6957 (Comprehensive Environmental Response and Liability Act–the"Superfund Act" or CERCLA)	282, 948
42 U.S.C. §§7401-7642 (Clean Air Act)	282
42 U.S.C. §§9601-9675 (Superfund Amendments and Reauthorization, or SARA)	282, 944
42 U.S.C. §§12101-12213 (*Americans with Disabilities Act of 1990, Title III*)	144, 145, 151, 152
43 U.S.C. §687a (Alaska Homesite Law)	787
43 U.S.C. §1068	193
43 U.S.C. §1601 et seq.	19
49 U.S.C. §§10741, 11101 (Interstate Commerce Act)	126

Public Laws

Pub. L. No. 95-568, §8(a)(2)	104
Pub. L. 99-499, 100 Stat. 1613 (Superfund Amendments and Reauthorization Act of 1986 (SARA))	282
Pub. L. 102-166, 105 Stat. 1071 (Civil Rights Act of 1991)	127
Pub. L. 105-304, 112 Stat. 2860 (Digital Millennium Copyright Act)	1070
Pub. L. 106-274, 115 Stat. 803 (Religious Land Use and Institutional Persons Act of 2000)	857, 898

Alabama

Code

§18-3-20	344
§30-3-1	624, 626
§§41-3-1 to 41-3-6	1169

Alaska

Statutes

§09.10.030	189
§09.25.050	189
§25.05.013	623
§34.03.060	690
§34.03.230	667
§34.70.010-.070	483
§34.15.290 (Alaskan Recording Act)	788, 789
§§34.17.010 to .060	347
§34.27.051	537
§34.27.100(a)	537
§§34.07.010 to 34.07.070	483

Arkansas

Code

§18-60-213	222

Statutes

Annotated

§27-66-401 (1987)	344

Kansas
Statutes Annotated

§58-2523	554, 555

Kentucky
Revised Statutes Annotated

§383.670	667
§413.150	198

Louisiana
Civil Code

§3412	93
§3414	93
§3418	94
§3421	93, 94
§3423	93
§3473	196
§3475	196
§3486	196

Maine
Revised Statutes

tit. 5, §§4552, 4582	860
tit. 5 §4553	847

Maryland
Code

art. 49B § 19	860

Family Law

art. 1-203	631

Massachusetts
Massachusetts Regulations

§40.170(2), (3)	948
§§101.4, 3308.1, 3309.1, 3310.2 (*State Building Code*)	250

General Laws Annotated

ch. 18, §2	31
ch. 21E, §§4-13	945-949
ch. 21G, §§1-19 (Massachusetts Water Management Act)	236
ch. 40A, §6	935
ch. 40B, §§20-23	909
ch. 40L, §5	1067
ch. 61A, §14	1017
ch. 82, §24	344
ch. 111, §197	741
ch. 139, §19	634
ch. 141, §1	720

ch. 143, §3	250
ch. 143, §3A	250
ch. 143, §57	250
ch. 143, §59	250
ch. 143, §93	250
ch. 143, §94	250
ch. 151B, §1	839, 860
ch. 151B, §4	837, 840, 867, 868
ch. 183A	757
ch. 183, §45	513
ch. 184, §23	424
ch. 184, §27	418, 424
ch. 184, §30	415, 419, 420, 422, 423
ch. 184, §§31, 32	379
ch. 184A, §§1-11	625
ch. 184A, §7	536
ch. 186, §14	719
ch. 209, §1	591
ch. 231, §59H	942
ch.231, §85S (*Massachusetts Art Preservation Act*)	1141
ch. 259, §1	760, 762

Michigan
Compiled Laws Annotated

§37.2502 (Civil Rights Act)	849-855
§37.2503	852
§§125.1601 et seq. (Economic Development Corporations Act)	1014
§333.7521(1)(f)	634
§551.2	854
§§554.71 to 554.78	536
§557.71	591
§§600.3801 to 600.3825	722, 1020
§600.5720	736
§750.335	850

Minnesota
Statutes

§245A.11	892
§363.03(2)	860
§500.20	424
§513.075	616

Missouri
Annotated Statutes

§89.020	406
§§392.260, 397.170	359
§451.022	622

Missouri
Revised Statutes

§474.480	583

Mississippi
Code Annotated

89-1-55	804

Montana
Code Annotated

§§28-2-904 to	
28-2-905	327
§40-4-202 (*Montana Equitable*	
Distribution Statute)	70, 72
§§70-20-101 to 70-20-102	327
§70-17-203	402

Nebraska
Statutes

§§12-1202	
to 12-1212	1169

New Hampshire
Statutes Annotated

§§354-A:8 to 354;A10	860

New Jersey
Admin. Code

tit. 10 §121A-5.4(C)	1157

Statutes Annotated

§§2A:18-53 et seq.	649
§§2A:18-61.1 to 2A:18-61.12	
(*New Jersey Anti-Eviction*	
Act)	642, 646,
	697, 698
§2A:18-61.22 (Senior Citizens	
and Disabled Protected	
Tenancy Act)	644, 649,
	700, 990
§2A:39-1	649
§2A:42-10.10	736
§2A:170-31	104, 113
§2C:18-3	104, 113
§§9:2-14, -16, -17	1157
§9:3-38a	1156
§9:3-41	1156
§9:3-54 (repealed)	1154, 1156
§9:17-40	1157
§§10:5-1 to 10:5-49 (*New*	
Jersey Law Against	
Discrimination)	132, 133, 860
§13:1K-6 (Industrial Site	
Recovery Act)	944

§25:1-13	766
§26:8A–1 to –12 (*Domestic Partnerships*)	620
§30:4C-23	1156
§§34:1B-1 to 34:1B-21 (Economic	
Development Authority Act)	478
§37:2-38	598
§40:55D-2(i)	
§40:55D-5	922
§§40:55D-49 to 40:55D-052	935
§40:55D-68	924
§40:55D-70(c)	930
§40:55D-70(d)	931
§46:2F-9	537
§46:3-23	374
§§46:36C-1 to 46:36C-12	745, 771
§§47B-2, 47B-4	424
§§56:10-1 et seq. (Franchise	
Practices Act)	1042
§§52:27D-301 to 52:27D-329	
(Fair Housing Act of 1985)	909
§§52:27H-60 to 52:27H-89	
(Urban Enterprise Zones Act)	478

New Mexico
Statutes

§28-1-7	860
§§28-22-1 to 28-22-5	858

Statutes Annotated

§23-1-22	187
§37-1-22	196

New York

Arts & Cultural Affairs Law	
214.03(1) (New York Artists'	
Authorship Rights Act)	1140

Civil Rights Law

§70-a	942
§76-a	942

C.P.L.R.

§3211(g)	942
§3212(h)	942

Domestic Relations Law

§236(B)	599, 600, 601,
	602, 603, 604

Executive Law

§291	860
§828(1)	979, 980-983

Real Property Law

§223-b(2)	736
§226-b	667, 690, 691
§234	702
§259	758
§522	192
§715 (Bawdy House Law)	617
§1951	415
§1955	518, 519

Rent & Eviction Regulations

§2204.6	670, 671, 672, 673

North Carolina

General Statutes

§1-35	198
§§1-340 to 1-351	222
§39-13.6	591
§47-18(a)	786
§47a-10	457
§47a-28	457
§47b-2	424
§47b-4	424

North Dakota

Century Code

§28-01-01	198
§§47-04.1-02 to 47-04.1-07	454

Ohio

Revised Code Annotated

§1701.59	62
§2108.02(B)	52

Oklahoma

Statutes Annotated

tit. 21, §§1168 to 1168.6	1169
tit. 51, §§251 to 258	858
tit. 53, §361	1169

Oregon

Revised Statutes

§§105.950 to 105.975	539
§§197.005 to 197.850	909, 1026
§376.180	344

Pennsylvania

Statutes

tit. 73, §§2101-10	1141
Estates Act of 1947	544

Rhode Island

General Laws

§5-62-2(e)	1141
§34-11-38	537
§§34-37-1 to 34-37-5.4	860
§§42-80.1-1 to 42-80.1-4	858

South Carolina

Code

§§1-32-10 to 1-32-60	858
§20-1-10	623
§§48-39-250 et seq. (Beachfront Management Act)	94, 991

South Dakota

Codified Laws

§43-5-8	537
§46A-10A-70	236

Tennessee

Code Annotated

§47-25-1139	
§36-3-113	623

Texas

Civ. Proc. & Rem. Code

§§110.001 to 110.012	858
§16.024	197
§16.025	197
§16.026	197

Family Code

§1.108	616
§7.001	597

Local Government Code

§245.002 to -006	935

Government Code

§§2007.001 to 2007.045 (Private Real Property Rights Preservation Act)	974

Penal Code

§21.06	603

Probate Code

§271	592
§52.117	254

Vermont

Statutes Annotated

tit. 9 §§4502, 4503	844
tit. 9 §§4500 to 4507 (Vermont Fair Housing and Public Accommodations Act)	846, 847, 860
tit. 9 §4503	845, 846
tit. 9 §4508	844
tit. 12 §501	210
tit. 12 §4528	801
tit. 15 §§1201-1206 (*Civil Unions*)	620

Virginia

Code

§15.2-2307	935
§15.2-2309(2)	929, 930
§15.2-2314	929
§20-151	598
§55-7	522
§55-11	522
§55-26	559
§§885 to 893 (1924) (Cedar Rust Act)	957

Washington

Revised Code

§8.24.010	343
§11.98.130	537
§§19.27.095, 58.17.033	935
§26.09.080	597
§§26.16.010 to 26.16.020, 26.16.200	588
§§27.44.020 to 27.44.901	1169
§27.53.060	1169
§49.60.010 to .040	860
§49.60.224	455
§64.04	350
§65.08.070	787
§§68.60.040 et seq.	1169

West Virginia

Code

§37-6-30	732
§55-3A-1	730, 731, 732
§55-3A-3(g)	730, 731

Wisconsin

Statutes Annotated

§49.141(2)(b)	31
§101.22	860
§106.50	860
§111.32(13m)	860
§135.02(4)(a)	1044
§135.03	1044
§700.16(5)	537
§767.255(*l*)	598
§813.12 (Wisconsin Domestic Abuse Restraining Order Statute)	628, 632
§§820, 842	611
§893.29	198
§893.33(6)	424

Wyoming

Statutes

§1-21-1201 to -1211	715
§1-26-713	1050
§34-2-101	516

Model Codes

Model Rules of Professional Conduct	943

Uniform Acts

Uniform Commercial Code	102, 225
Uniform Partnership Act	1039
Uniform Premarital Agreement Act	598
Uniform Probate Code	536
Uniform Residential Landlord and Tenant Act	667, 728, 731, 737, 740
Uniform Statutory Rule Against Perpetuities	534, 536, 549, 1015
Uniform Vendor and Purchaser Risk Act	779

Abandoned property. See Lost property
Access, right of reasonable, 103-176
Accretion, 225
Adverse possession
   generally, 179-226
   actual, 191-194
   adverse or hostile, 194
   border disputes, 179-184
   claim of right, 195
   claims against government, 197
   color of title, 185-187, 197
   continuous, 194
   elements of, 191-196
   exclusive, 194
   good faith, 196-197
   justifications for, 193-207
   open and notorious, 193-194
   personal property, 225-226
   squatters, 187-191
   statutory period, 197
   tacking, 194
   vacant land, 187-191
AIDS, 863-865, 890-892
Alienation, restraints on
   generally, 450-472
   anticompetitive covenants, 472-473
   condominiums, 458-460
   leaseholds, 466-472
   marriage, restraints on, 561-567
   racial restrictions, 433-449
   trusts, 439-446
American Indian nations
   conquest, 3-24
   cultural objects, 92-100
   current Indian land claims, 20-24
   history of American Indian law, 1069-1071
   human remains, 1166-1171
   original Indian title, 3-20, 1072
   recognized title, 1072-1083
   restricted trust allotments, 63-69
   takings clause, 1074-1083
   treaty abrogation, 1072-1074
   Trade and Intercourse Acts, 1069-1070
Americans with Disabilities Act of 1990,
   145-149
Animals, wild, 76-83
Antitrust law
   anticompetitive covenants, 472-473

Arguments, 237-242, 309-316, 720-726
   compulsory contract terms, 720-726
   economic analysis, 286-302
   formal realizability, 240-242, 315-316
   judicial role, 313-315
   paternalism, 722-723
   precedent, 261-265
   rights and fairness, 238, 309-311, 723-726
   social utility, 239-240, 311-313, 723-726
   statutory interpretation, 129-130
Avulsion, 225

Battered women
   domestic violence restraining order
      statutes, 628-631
   drug forfeiture statutes, 632-635
   takings clause and restraining order
      statutes, 990
Beaches, rights of access, 164-172
Body parts, ownership of, 45-53
Brokers, 744-748
Building codes, 249-251
Business property
   antitrust, 472-473
   commercial leases, 690-692
   genetic information, 45-53
   news, 32-45
   publicity rights, 1129-1140
   unfair competition, 32-45

Child support, 624-628
Children
   discrimination against, 844-849
   welfare benefits, 867-869
Civil rights legislation
   Americans with Disabilities Act of 1990,
      144-149
Civil Rights Act of 1866, 835-837
Civil Rights Act of 1964, Tide II (public
      accommodations), 124-125
Civil Rights Act of 1968,
   Title VIII (Fair-Housing Act), 817-835
   public accommodations laws, 124-153
Commercial leases
   assignment and sublease, 682-688
   good-faith duty to operate, 692-696
   options to purchase in, 541-546
Common ownership. Cooperatives

joint tenancy, 571-576, 580-587
leases, conflicts over, 576-580
marriage and, 576-579, 584-585
tenancy by the entirety, 575-576, 587-592
tenancy in common, 570-571, 572-575, 579-587
See also Condominiums
Community property. *See* Marital property rights
Condominiums
generally, 425-428
condominium associations, 425-427
condominium rules, 483-488
consent to sell, 453-458
first refusal, rights of, 458-466
leasing restrictions, 466-472
restraints on alienation, 458-474
rule against perpetuities, 546-553
Conquest, 3-24
Constructive trusts, 323-332
Contingent remainders
generally, 508-511
destructibility, 511
Cooperatives
generally, 427
low-income housing, 427-428
Copyright, 1093-1128
Covenants. *See* Servitudes
Cy pres doctrine
perpetuities, 534-535
trusts, 526-527

Dedication of property, 223-225
Deeds, 874, 880-881
Disability rights
AIDS, 863-865, 890-892
housing, 830-865, 890-897
mental illness, 892-897
mental retardation, 892-896
physical disabilities, 144-149, 844-849, 863-867
public accommodations, 144-149
zoning, exclusionary, 899-910
Discrimination
AIDS, 150-151, 863-865, 890-892
Civil Rights Act of 1866, 835-837
Civil Rights Act of 1964, 124-125
children, 844-849
disability, 144-149, 844-849, 863-867
domestic violence, 628-632
economic, 867-871
family status, 844-858, 883-890
Fair Housing Act, 817-910
generally, 949-1059
homelessness, 173-176
housing, 817-910
marital status, 849-858
mental illness, 892-897

national origin, 899
public accommodations, 116-153
race, 124-133, 817-837, 871-881
sex, 132-133, 837-843, 881-882
sexual harassment, 817-837
sexual orientation, 858-862, 897
slavery, 1143-1153
welfare recipients, 867-869
zoning, 871-910
Distribution of property, 4-8
Divorce. *See* Marital property
Due process
substantive, 938-941

Easements
generally, 320-365
affirmative, 347
apportionment, 353-364
appurtenant, 352-358
constructive trusts, 323-332
divisibility, 353-364
estoppel, 320-323
express, 344-353
historical background, 344
implied from prior use, 332-339
in gross, 358-364
interpretation, 353-364
light and air, 284-316
necessity, 339-344
negative, 346-347
prescriptive, 207-215
running with the land, 347-353
scope, 353-364
support, 242-271
termination, 364-365
transferability, 353
Economic analysis, 286-302
Environmental regulation, 944-949
Equal protection of the laws,
zoning, 938-941
Equitable distribution. *See* Marital property
Equitable servitudes. *See* Servitudes
Estates system
generally, 505-515
defeasible fees, 506-508
equitable interests, 503-504, 513
executory interests, 508
fee simple, 499, 505-508
fee tail, 513
feudal incidents, 498-501
feudal services, 497-498
freehold interests, 503
future interests, 505-515
leaseholds, 639-742
life estates, 508-513
new estates, rule against creating, 528-529
presumption against forfeitures, 515-525
racial conditions, 557-561

remainders, 508-511
restraints on alienation, 450-473
restraints on marriage, 561-567
reversions, 508
rule against perpetuities, 529-553
tenures, 497-499
trusts, 514, 526-527
waste, 553-557
Estoppel, 224, 320-323

Familial status discrimination.
    families with children, 844-849
    marital status, 849-858
    nontraditional, 883-890
    sexual orientation, 858-862, 897
    See also Discrimination
Family property
    general, 569-635
    child support, 624-628
    community property, 595, 596-597
    divorce, 69-75, 584-587, 599-607
    domestic violence, 628-632
    forfeiture for illegal conduct, 632-635
    gifts, 75
    house, ownership on divorce, 69-75
    marital property, 593-608
    nontraditional families, 608-624
    separate property, 595-596
    unmarried couples, 608-624
    wills & inheritance, 63-69
    zoning, 883-890
Fee simple
    absolute, 505
    determinable, 506-508
    history of, 499-501
    interpretation of ambiguous conveyances,
        515-526
    subject to condition subsequent, 506
    subject to executory limitation, 508
Feudalism, 496-505
Finance, real estate
    generally, 799-815
    equitable mortgages, 812-815
    foreclosure, 798-806
    installment land contracts, 806
    mortgages, 799-806
Finders, 92-95
First refusal, rights of, 546-553
Formal realizability, 240-242
Frauds, statute of, 758-765
Freehold estates. *See* Estates system
Free speech
    state constitutions, 158-164
    U.S. Constitution, 153-158
Future interests.
    definitions, 506-514
    historical background, 496-505
    perpetuities, 529-553

statutory cut-offs, 535 *See also* Estates
    system

Gay and lesbian persons. *See* Sexual
    orientation
Gender equality.
    child support, 624-628
    frozen embryos, 1162-1166
    housing, 837-843, 593-608
    public accommodations, 132
    real estate transactions, 837-844
    restraints on marriage, 561-567
    sexual harassment, 837-844
    surrogate motherhood, 1154-1162
    tenancy by the entirety, 587-593
    unmarried couples, 608-624
    welfare benefits, 867-869
    See also Discrimination
Genetic information. *See* Business property
Gifts, 75
Government benefits
    AFDC (Aid to Families with Dependent
        Children), 31
    discrimination against recipients, 867-869
    housing benefits, 30-32
    public land distribution, 24-26
Government Grant
    generally, 24-32
    basic needs, 30-32
    freed slaves, 26-30
    homestead acts, 24-25, 607
    land grants, 24-26
    squatters, 25-26
Group homes
    equal protection clause, 881-890
    exclusionary zoning, 899-910
    Fair Housing Act, 890-897
    as families, 881-897
    restrictive covenants, 406-411

Habitability. *See* Warranty of habitability
Hohfeldian analysis, 198-202
Homelessness, 173-176
Homestead laws. *See* Marital property

Informal transfers of title
    acquiescence, 223
    adverse possession, 179-226
    dedication, 224
    estoppel, 224
    oral agreement, 223
Installment land contracts. *See* Finance, real
    estate
Intellectual Property
    generally, 1087-1088
    business methods, 1129
    copyright, 1093-1129
    genetic information, 45-53

moral rights, 1140-1141
patent, 1128-1129
publicity rights, 1129-1140
trademark, 1088-1093
unfair competition, 32-45

Joint tenancy. *See* Common ownership
Judicial role arguments, 310-311

Labor & Investment, 32-63
    patents in human genes, 45-53
    unfair competition, 32-45
    work & family, 53-55
Land use
    flooding, 2532-237
    light and air, 284-285, 302-309
    nuisance, 227-232, 271-309
    support, 242-261
    water rights, 232-242
    zoning, 911-949
Landlord-tenant law
    generally, 639-742
    assignment, 680-692
    commercial leases, 609-692
    condominium conversion, 700
    constructive eviction, 701-708
    consumer protection legislation, 737-738
    covenant of quiet enjoyment, 701-708
    duty to mitigate damages, 661-669
    emotional distress, intentional infliction of, 740-741
    eviction, 641-65, 656-657, 657-669, 697-742
    good-faith duty to operate, 692-697
    implied warranty of habitability, 699-740
    landlord's liability, 727-730
    landlord's remedies, 659-669
    leaseholds, 639-641
    occupancy conflicts, 679-699
    possession, landlord's duty to deliver, 679-680
    rent, disputes about, 658-679
    rent control, 669-679
    residential leases, 639-640
    retaliatory eviction, 726-737
    security deposits, 669
    sublease, 680-692
    tenant's remedies, 699-742
    tort liability of landlord, 738-742
    warranty of habitability, 708-726
Leases. *See* Landlord-tenant law; Commercial leases
Licenses
    generally, 319-320
    constructive trusts, 323-332
    easements by estoppel, 320-323
Life estates. *See* Estates system
Light and air, 284-285, 302-309
Limited equity cooperatives, 432-433

Lost property, 92-96
Low-income housing cooperatives, 427-428

Marital property
    generally, 593-607
    community property, 595, 596-597
    curtesy, 593-594
    divorce, 584-587, 599-607
    domestic violence, 628-632
    dower, 593-594
    equitable distribution, 599-607
    homestead laws, 598-599
    Married Women's Property Acts, 594-595
    premarital agreements, 597-598
    restraints on marriage, 561-567
    separate property, 595-596
    tenancy by the entirety, 572-593
Marketable title, 776
Marriage, restraints on, 561-567
Married Women's Property Acts. *See* Marital property
Mislaid property. *See* Lost property
Mortgages. *See* Finance, real estate

Neighbors, conflicts between
    nuisance, 271-316
    servitudes, 317-490
    zoning, 938-949
News, property in, 32-45
Nontraditional families
    group homes, 406-411, 890-897
    lesbian and gay couples, 592-593, 619-624
    unmarried couples, 608-624
Nuisance, 227-232, 271-309

Oil and gas, 83-89

Patents, 1128-1129
Perpetuities, rule against
    generally, 529-541
    cy pres, 535
    examples, 537-541
    options to purchase, 541-546
    rights of first refusal (preemptive rights), 546-553
    traditional rule, 529-534
    wait and see, 534
Possession
    adverse, 179-226
    finders, 92-95
    human genes, 45-53
    improving trespasser, 215-223
    oil and gas, 83-89
    relativity of title, 97-102
    water, 89-91
    wild animals, 76-79
Precedent, 261-265
Preemptive rights. *See* First refusal, rights of

Prescriptive easements, 207-215
Private rights of action, 249-250
Privity of estate. *See* Servitudes
Professional responsibility
    SLAPP suits, 941-944
Property
    derivation from competing sovereigns, 3-14
Property in people
    generally, 1143-1171
    children, 1154-1162
    frozen embryos, 1162-1166
    human genes, 45-53
    Indian human remains, 1166-1171
    slavery, 1143-1153
Public accommodations statutes
    generally, 124-153
    federal laws, 124-131
    private clubs. 128-129
    state laws, 132-144
Publicity, right of, 1129-1140
Public trust doctrine, 164-173
Purchase and sale agreements. *See also* Real
            estate transactions
    generally, 752-758
    fraud, 767-776
    remedies for breach of, 777-778
    risk of loss, 778-779
    statute of frauds, 758-767

Race discrimination
    housing, 817-837, 871-881
    public accommodations, 124-144
    restrictive covenants, 433-449
    trusts, 439-449
    zoning, 871-881
Real covenants. *See* Servitude
Real estate finance. *See* Finance, real estate
Real estate transactions
    generally, 743-815
    attorneys, 743-744
    brokers, 744-748
    closing, 750
    deeds, 750
    equitable conversion, 778-779
    equitable mortgages, 812-815
    executory period, 749-750
    financing, 777, 779-815
    forfeiture, 803-808
    installment land contracts, 806-812
    fraudulent nondisclosure, 767-775
    marketable title, 776
    misrepresentation (fraud), 767-775
    mortgages, 799-806
    nondisclaimable, 808-812
    purchase and sale agreements, 752-758
    recording acts, 783-799
    sales contract, 748-749
    statute of frauds, 758-767
    title, 779-799

warranty of habitability, 776
Realtors. *See* Brokers
Recording acts
    generally, 783-799
    chain of title, 787-793
    forgery, 793-798
    fraud, 793-798
    marketable title, 776-798
Regulatory takings. *See* Takings clause
Remainders
    contingent, 508-509, 511
    vested, 509-510
    See also Estates system
Rent control, 670-679
Restraints on alienation. *See* Alienation
Rights arguments, 237, 309-311, 720-723
Rights of access. *See* Free speech

Servitudes
    abandonment, 417
    acquiescence, 417
    anticompetitive, 472-473
    changed conditions, 411-416 easements,
            320-365
    equitable defenses, 417-419
    express agreement, 367-394
    generally, 317-490
    historical background, 365-367
    implied reciprocal negative servitudes , 394-
            406
    interpretation, 406-411
    privity of estate, 384-387
    public policy limitations, 474-490
    racial restrictions, 433-450
    relative hardship, 416-417
    restraints on alienation, 450-472
    restrictions on leasing, 466-472
    review for reasonableness, 474-490
    running with the land, 377-394
    statutory regulation, 419-424
    termination, 411-419
    See also Easements
Sex discrimination. *See* Discrimination;
            Gender equality
Sexual harassment. *See* Battered women;
            Discrimination
Sexual orientation
    AIDS and, 150-151, 863-865, 890,
    Americans with Disabilities Act, 145-149
    discrimination, 858-863, 897
    family property, 670-675
    unmarried couples, 608-624
Shelley's Case, Rule in, 512-513
SLAPP suits (strategic lawsuits against public
            participation), 941-944
Slavery, 1143-1153
Social utility arguments, 239-240, 311-313,
            723-726
Solar energy, 302-309

Statute of frauds
  generally, 758-766
  estoppel, 758-766
  part performance, 758-766
Statutory interpretation, 129-131
Support rights
  lateral, 243-251
  subjacent, 251-261
Surrogate motherhood, 1154-1162

Tacking. *See* Adverse possession
Takings clause
  generally, 953-1067
  American Indian nations, 14-20, 1069-1083
  conceptual severance, 1012-1013
  just compensation, 1042-1051
  linkage, 1026-1042
  physical invasions, 976-990
  public use, 1051-1067
  vested rights, 931-936
Tenancy by the entirety. See Marital property
Tenancy in common. *See* Common
        ownership
Title
  generally, 781-799
  insurance, 798
  protection, 781-799
  recording acts, 783-799
  registration, 798-799
  relativity of, 97-102
  warranties of title, 781-783
Trademark, 1088-1093
Trespass
  beaches, 164-173
  encroaching structures, 215-217
  free-speech access rights, 153-164
  improving trespasser, 215-223
  public accommodations, 124-153
  public-policy limits on right to exclude,
        103-116
  right of reasonable access, 116-124
Trusts
  charitable, 526-527
  constructive, 323-332

cy pres doctrine, 526-527
  equitable interests, 503-505
  racial discrimination, 439-450

Unfair competition, 32-45

Vested remainders. *See* Remainders
Vested rights. *See* Zoning

Warranty of habitability
  leases, 708-726
  sale of new property, 776
  See also Landlord-tenant law
Waste, 553-557
Water rights
  generally, 232-242
  commercial resource, 89-91
  surface water, 232-242
  flooding, 232-242
  groundwater, or percolating water, 90
  streams, 91
Welfare benefits. *See* Government
        benefits
Wills & inheritance, 63-69
Worthier title, doctrine of, 511-512

Zoning.
  administration, 914-915
  discriminatory, 871-910
  enabling acts, 911
  exclusionary, 871-910
  generally, 911-949
  planned unit developments, 913
  planning, 911-915
  prior nonconforming uses, 922-925
  rezoning, 937-938
  SLAPP suits, 941-944
  special exceptions, 937
  spot zoning, 937-938
  variances, 925-931
  vested rights, 931-936. *See also* Takings
        clause